The Pocket Oxford-Duden
German Dictionary

# The Pocket
# Oxford-Duden
# German
# Dictionary

English—German
German—English

Edited by the Dudenredaktion
and the German Section of the
Oxford University Press
Dictionary Department

**Chief Editors**

M. CLARK

O. THYEN

OXFORD UNIVERSITY PRESS
1997

# OXFORD

UNIVERSITY PRESS

Great Clarendon Street, Oxford OX2 6DP

Oxford University Press is a department of the University of Oxford.
It furthers the University's objective of excellence in research, scholarship,
and education by publishing worldwide in

Oxford  New York

Athens  Auckland  Bangkok  Bogotá  Buenos Aires  Calcutta
Cape Town  Chennai  Dar es Salaam  Delhi  Florence  Hong Kong  Istanbul
Karachi  Kuala Lumpur  Madrid  Melbourne  Mexico City  Mumbai
Nairobi  Paris  São Paulo  Singapore  Taipei  Tokyo  Toronto  Warsaw

with associated companies in  Berlin  Ibadan

Published in the United States
by Oxford University Press Inc., New York

© Oxford University Press and
Bibliographisches Institut & F. A. Brockhaus AG 1992

First published 1992
Paperback first published 1995
Revised edition 1997

British Library Cataloguing in Publication Data

Data available

Library of Congress Cataloging in Publication Data

Data available

ISBN 0-19-860136-0
ISBN 0-19-860131-X (pbk)

5  7  9  10  8  6  4

Printed and bound in Great Britain by
Caledonian International Book Manufacturing Ltd, Glasgow

# Foreword

The *Pocket Oxford–Duden German Dictionary* has been designed to meet the needs of students, tourists, and all those who require quick and reliable answers to their translation questions. It provides clear guidance on selecting the most appropriate translation, numerous illustrative examples to help with problems of construction and usage, and precise information on grammar, style, and pronunciation.

Based on the much acclaimed *Oxford–Duden German Dictionary*, this easy-to-use pocket dictionary carries the authority of two of the world's foremost dictionary publishers, Oxford University Press and the Dudenverlag, making use of the unparalleled databases maintained and continually expanded by the two publishers for their celebrated native-speaker dictionaries. Its reliability and clarity make it an invaluable aid to understanding, speaking, and writing everyday idiomatic German in the nineteen nineties.

MICHAEL CLARK
*Oxford University Press*

## Editors and Contributors

*in Oxford*

Michael Clark
Bernadette Mohan
Maurice Waite
Ursula Lang
Trish Stableford
Tim Connell
Neil Morris
Ting Morris

*in Mannheim*

Olaf Thyen
Werner Scholze-Stubenrecht
Brigitte Alsleben
Ulrike Röhrenbeck
Magdalena Seubel
Eva Vennebusch

# Key to entries

- pronunciation given in IPA
  *Aussprache in internationaler Lautschrift*

- indication of approximate equivalence
  *Angabe ungefährer Entsprechungen*

**bailiff** ['beɪlɪf] *n.* ≈ Gerichtsvollzieher, *der*

- cross-reference to a synonymous headword
  *Verweis auf synonymes Stichwort*

**barrow** ['bærəʊ] *n.* **a)** Karre, *die;* Karren, *der;* **b)** *see* **wheelbarrow**

- stress mark
  *Betonungszeichen*

- irregular plural
  *unregelmäßige Pluralform*

**basis** ['beɪsɪs] *n., pl.* **bases** ['beɪsiːz] Basis, *die;* Grundlage, *die*

- regional/national label
  *räumliche Zuordnung*

- gloss where no translation is possible
  *Umschreibung, wenn eine Übersetzung nicht möglich ist*

**Belisha beacon** [bəliːʃə 'biːkn] *n.* *(Brit.)* gelbes Blinklicht an Zebrastreifen

- compound block with a swung dash representing the first element of each compound
  *Kompositablock mit Tilde für den ersten Teil jeder Zusammensetzung*

**black:** ~**berry** ['blækbərɪ] *n.* Brombeere, *die;* ~**bird** *n.* Amsel, *die;* ~**board** *n.* Wand]tafel, *die;* ~**currant** *n.* schwarze Johannisbeere

- idiomatic phrase
  *feste Wendung*

- swung dash representing the headword
  *die Tilde vertritt das Stichwort*

- style labels
  (also given for translations)
  *Stilschichtangaben*
  *(auch für Übersetzungen)*

**boot** [buːt] **1.** *n.* **a)** Stiefel, *der;* **give sb. the** ~ *(fig. coll.)* jmdn. rausschmeißen *(ugs.);* **b)** *(Brit.: of car)* Kofferraum, *der.* **2.** *v. t.* *(coll.: kick)* kicken *(ugs.)*

- irregular past tenses
  *unregelmäßige Verbformen*

**break** [breɪk] **1.** *v.t.*, **broke** [brəʊk], **broken** ['brəʊkn] **a)** brechen

- grammatical categories
  *Gliederung nach grammatischen Gesichtspunkten*

- phrasal verbs listed under main verb
  *Verben in festen Verbindungen mit Präpositionen oder Adverbien (Phrasal verbs) im Anschluß an das jeweilige einfache Verb*

- semantic categories
  *Gliederung nach Bedeutungsunterschieden*

- collocators
  *Kollokatoren*

- sense indicator
  *Indikator*

**break 'down 1.** *v.i.* zusammenbrechen; ⟨*Verhandlungen:*⟩ scheitern; ⟨*Auto:*⟩ eine Panne haben. **2.** *v.t.* **a)** aufbrechen ⟨*Tür*⟩; brechen ⟨*Widerstand*⟩; niederreißen ⟨*Barriere, Schranke*⟩; **b)** *(analyse)* aufgliedern. **break 'in 1.** *v.i. (into building etc.)* einbrechen. **2.** *v.t.* **a)** zureiten ⟨*Pferd*⟩; **b)** einlaufen ⟨*Schuhe*⟩: **c)** ~ the door in die Tür aufbrechen. **break into** *see* ~ 2 b. **break 'off 1.** *v.t.* abbrechen; abreißen ⟨*Faden*⟩; auflösen ⟨*Verlobung*⟩. **2.** *v.i.* **a)** abbrechen; **b)** *(cease)* aufhören. **break 'out** *v.i.* ausbrechen; ~ out in spots/a rash Pickel/ einen Ausschlag bekommen

- information on syntax
  *syntaktische Angabe*

- usage example
  *Anwendungsbeispiel*

- subject labels
  *Bereichsangaben*

**feature** ['fiːtʃə(r)] **1.** *n.* **a)** *usu. in pl. (part of face)* Gesichtszug, *der*; **b)** *(characteristic)* [charakteristisches] Merkmal; be a ~ of sth. charakteristisch für etw. sein; **c)** *(Journ. etc.)* Feature, *das*; **d)** *(Cinemat.)* ~ [film] Hauptfilm, *der*

- cross-references for additional information
  *Verweise auf zusätzliche Informationen*

**fifty** ['fɪftɪ] **1.** *adj.* fünfzig. **2.** *n.* Fünfzig, *die.* See also eight; eighty 2

# Erläuterungen zum Text

- grammatische Angaben
  *grammatical information*

- Bereichsangaben
  *subject labels*

- Verweise auf das Grundwort
  (bei einer Ableitung)
  *references to root word
  (from a derivative)*

- Betonung und Quantität
  *stress and vowel length*

**beschneiden** *unr. tr. V.* **a)** cut ⟨*hedge*⟩; prune ⟨*bush*⟩; cut back ⟨*tree*⟩; **einem Vogel die Flügel ~:** clip a bird's wings; **b)** *(Med., Rel.)* circumcise; **Beschneidung die; ~, ~en a)** *s.* **beschneiden a:** cutting; pruning; cutting back; **b)** *(Med., Rel.)* circumcision

**beschummeln** *tr. V.* *(ugs.)* cheat; diddle *(Brit. coll.)*

- Aussprache in internationaler Lautschrift
  *pronunciation given in IPA*

**Balkon** [bal'kɔn, bal'koːn] **der; ~s, ~s** [bal'kɔns] *od.* **~e** [bal'koːnə] **a)** balcony; **b)** *(im Theater, Kino)* circle

- Kollokatoren
  *collocators*

- Indikatoren
  *sense indicators*

**beschreiben** *unr. tr. V.* **a)** write on; *(vollschreiben)* write ⟨*page, side, etc.*⟩; *(darstellen)* describe

- die Tilde vertritt das Stichwort
  *swung dash representing the headword*

**bestanden** *Adj.* **von** *od.* **mit etw. ~ sein** have sth. growing on it; **mit Tannen ~e Hügel** fir-covered hills

- Verweis auf ein Synonym
  *cross-reference to a synonymous headword*

**berappen** *tr., itr. V.* *(ugs.)* *s.* **blechen**

- Anwendungsbeispiel
  *usage example*

**Beruf der; ~[e]s, ~e** occupation; *(akademischer)* profession; *(handwerklicher)* trade; **was sind Sie von ~?** what do you do for a living?

- Redensart
  *idiomatic phrase*

- Sprichwort
  *proverb*

**Besen der; ~s, ~** broom; **ich fress' einen ~, wenn das stimmt** *(salopp)* I'll eat my hat if that's right *(coll.)*; **neue ~ kehren gut** *(Spr.)* a new broom sweeps clean *(prov.)*

| | |
|---|---|
| • Kompositablock<br>*compound block* | **blut-, Blut-:** ~**unterlaufen** *Adj.* suffused with blood *postpos.*; bloodshot *(eyes)*; ~**vergießen** das; ~s bloodshed; ~**vergiftung** die blood-poisoning *no indef. art., no pl.*; ~**wurst** die black pudding |
| • Angaben zur Syntax<br>*information on syntax* | |
| • Gliederung nach grammatischen Gesichtspunkten<br>*grammatical categories* | **beschweren 1.** *refl. V.* complain *(über + Akk., wegen about)*; **2.** *tr. V.* weight down |
| • Gliederung nach Bedeutungsunterschieden<br>*semantic categories* | **beschränkt 1.** *Adj.* **a)** *(dumm)* dull-witted; **b)** *(engstirnig)* narrow-minded; **2.** *adv.* narrow-mindedly |
| • Kompositionsfuge<br>*dot between elements of a compound* | **Bei·name** der epithet |
| • räumliche Zuordnung des Stichworts/der Übersetzung<br>*regional labels for the head-words/translations* | **Beis[e]l** das; ~s, *od.* ~n *(österr.)* pub *(Brit. coll.)*; bar *(Amer.)*<br><br>**Benzin** das; ~s petrol *(Brit.)*; gasoline *(Amer.)*; gas *(Amer. coll.)*; *(Wasch~)* benzine |
| • zusätzliche Glosse zur Bedeutung des Stichworts<br>*additional gloss specifying the sense of the headword* | **Bütten·papier** das handmade paper *(with deckle-edge)* |
| • Angaben zur Stilschicht<br>*style labels* | **bestatten** *tr. V. (geh.)* inter *(formal)*; bury; **Bestattung** die; ~, ~en *(geh.)* |

# Contents

## Proprietary Names

This dictionary includes some words which are, or are asserted to be, proprietary names or trade marks. The presence or absence of such assertions should not be regarded as affecting the legal status of any proprietary name or trade mark.

# Die für das Englische verwendeten Zeichen der Lautschrift

| | | | | | | | |
|---|---|---|---|---|---|---|---|
| ɑː | barb | bɑːb | | m | mat | mæt |
| ã | séance | 'seɪãs | | n | not | nɒt |
| æ | fat | fæt | | ŋ | sing | sɪŋ |
| æ̃ | lingerie | 'læ̃ʒərɪ | | ɒ | got | gɒt |
| aɪ | fine | faɪn | | ɔː | paw | pɔː |
| aʊ | now | naʊ | | ɔɪ | boil | bɔɪl |
| b | bat | bæt | | p | pet | pet |
| d | dog | dɒg | | r | rat | ræt |
| dʒ | jam | dʒæm | | s | sip | sɪp |
| e | met | met | | ʃ | ship | ʃɪp |
| eɪ | fate | feɪt | | t | tip | tɪp |
| eə | fairy | 'feərɪ | | tʃ | chin | tʃɪn |
| əʊ | goat | gəʊt | | θ | thin | θɪn |
| ə | ago | ə'gəʊ | | ð | the | ðə |
| ɜː | fur | fɜː(r) | | uː | boot | buːt |
| f | fat | fæt | | ʊ | book | bʊk |
| g | good | gʊd | | ʊə | tourist | 'tʊərɪst |
| h | hat | hæt | | ʌ | dug | dʌg |
| ɪ | bit, lately | bɪt, 'leɪtlɪ | | v | van | væn |
| ɪə | nearly | 'nɪəlɪ | | w | win | wɪn |
| iː | meet | miːt | | x | loch | lɒx |
| j | yet | jet | | z | zip | zɪp |
| k | kit | kɪt | | ʒ | vision | 'vɪʒn |
| l | lot | lɒt | | | | |

:    Längezeichen, bezeichnet Länge des unmittelbar davor stehenden Vokals, z. B. boot [buːt].

'    Betonung, steht unmittelbar vor einer betonten Silbe, z. B. ago [ə'gəʊ].

(r)    Ein „r" in runden Klammern wird nur gesprochen, wenn im Textzusammenhang ein Vokal unmittelbar folgt, z. B. pare [peə(r)]; pare away [peər ə'weɪ].

# Phonetic information given in the German-English section

The pronunciation of German is largely regular, and phonetic transcriptions have only been given where additional help is needed. In all other cases only the position of the stressed syllable and the length of the vowel in that syllable are shown: a long vowel is indicated by an underline, e.g. Maß, a short vowel by a dot placed underneath, e.g. Masse.

# Phonetic symbols used in transcriptions of German words

| | | | | | | |
|---|---|---|---|---|---|---|
| a | hat | hat | ŋ | lang | laŋ |
| a: | Bahn | ba:n | o | Moral | mo'ra:l |
| ɐ | Ober | 'o:bɐ | o: | Boot | bo:t |
| ɐ̯ | Uhr | u:ɐ̯ | o̜ | loyal | lo̜a'ja:l |
| ã | Ensemble | ã'sã:bl̩ | õ | Fondue | fõ'dy: |
| ã: | Abonnement | abɔnə'mã: | õ: | Fond | fõ: |
| ai | weit | vait | ɔ | Post | pɔst |
| au | Haut | haut | ø | Ökonom | øko'no:m |
| b | Ball | bal | ø: | Öl | ø:l |
| ç | ich | ıç | œ | göttlich | 'gœtlıç |
| d | dann | dan | œ̃: | Parfum | par'fœ̃: |
| dʒ | Gin | dʒın | ɔy | Heu | hɔy |
| e | egal | e'ga:l | p | Pakt | pakt |
| e: | Beet | be:t | pf | Pfahl | pfa:l |
| ɛ | mästen | 'mɛstn̩ | r | Rast | rast |
| ɛ: | wählen | 'vɛ:lən | s | Hast | hast |
| ɛ̃ | Mannequin | 'manəkɛ̃ | ʃ | schal | ʃa:l |
| ɛ̃: | Cousin | ku'zɛ̃: | t | Tal | ta:l |
| ə | Nase | 'na:zə | ts | Zahl | tsa:l |
| f | Faß | fas | tʃ | Matsch | matʃ |
| g | Gast | gast | u | kulant | ku'lant |
| h | hat | hat | u: | Hut | hu:t |
| i | vital | vi'ta:l | u̯ | aktuell | ak'tu̯ɛl |
| i: | viel | fi:l | ʊ | Pult | pʊlt |
| i̯ | Studie | 'ʃtu:di̯ə | v | was | vas |
| ı | Birke | 'bırkə | x | Bach | bax |
| j | ja | ja: | y | Physik | fy'zi:k |
| k | kalt | kalt | y: | Rübe | 'ry:bə |
| l | Last | last | ỹ | Nuance | 'nỹã:sə |
| l̩ | Nabel | 'na:bl̩ | ʏ | Fülle | 'fʏlə |
| m | Mast | mast | z | Hase | 'ha:zə |
| n | Naht | na:t | ʒ | Genie | ʒe'ni: |
| n̩ | baden | 'ba:dn̩ | | | |

' Glottal stop, e.g. beachten [bə'|axtn̩].

: Length sign, indicating that the preceding vowel is long, e.g. Chrom [kro:m].

˜ Indicates a nasal vowel, e.g. Fond [fõ:].

' Stress mark, immediately preceding a stressed syllable, e.g. Ballon [ba'lɔŋ].

# English abbreviations used in the Dictionary/ Im Wörterverzeichnis verwendete englische Abkürzungen

| | | | |
|---|---|---|---|
| abbr(s). | abbreviation(s) | Footb. | Football |
| abs. | absolute | Gastr. | Gastronomy |
| adj(s). | adjective(s) | Geog. | Geography |
| Admin. | Administration, Administrative | Geol. | Geology |
| adv. | adverb | Geom. | Geometry |
| Aeronaut. | Aeronautics | Her. | Heraldry |
| Agric. | Agriculture | Hist. | History, Historical |
| Amer. | American, America | Hort. | Horticulture |
| Anat. | Anatomy | imper. | imperative |
| arch. | archaic | impers. | impersonal |
| Archaeol. | Archaeology | incl. | including |
| Archit. | Architecture | indef. | indefinite |
| art. | article | Information Sci. | Information Science |
| Astrol. | Astrology | int. | interjection |
| Astron. | Astronomy | interrog. | interrogative |
| Astronaut. | Astronautics | Ir. | Irish, Ireland |
| attrib. | attributive | iron. | ironical |
| Austral. | Australian, Australia | joc. | jocular |
| Biol. | Biology | Journ. | Journalism |
| Bookk. | Bookkeeping | lang. | language |
| Bot. | Botany | Ling. | Linguistics |
| Brit. | British, Britain | Lit. | Literature |
| Chem. | Chemistry | lit. | literal |
| Cinemat. | Cinematography | masc. | masculine |
| coll. | colloquial | Math. | Mathematics |
| collect. | collective | Mech. | Mechanics |
| comb. | combination | Mech. Engin. | Mechanical Engineering |
| Commerc. | Commerce, Commercial | Med. | Medicine |
| compar. | comparative | Metalw. | Metalwork |
| condit. | conditional | Meteorol. | Meteorology |
| conj. | conjunction | Mil. | Military |
| def. | definite | Min. | Mineralogy |
| Dent. | Dentistry | Motor Veh. | Motor Vehicles |
| derog. | derogatory | Mus. | Music |
| dial. | dialect | Mythol. | Mythology |
| Diplom. | Diplomacy | n. | noun |
| Dressm. | Dressmaking | Naut. | Nautical |
| Eccl. | Ecclesiastical | neg. | negative |
| Ecol. | Ecology | N. Engl. | Northern English |
| Econ. | Economics | ns. | nouns |
| Educ. | Education | Nucl. Phys. | Nuclear Physics |
| Electr. | Electricity | obj. | object |
| ellipt. | elliptical | Ornith. | Ornithology |
| emphat. | emphatic | P | Proprietary name |
| esp. | especially | Parl. | Parliament |
| euphem. | euphemistic | pass. | passive |
| excl. | exclamation, exclamatory | Pharm. | Pharmacy |
| expr. | expressing | Philos. | Philosophy |
| fem. | feminine | Photog. | Photography |
| fig. | figurative | phr(s). | phrase(s) |
| | | Phys. | Physics |

| | | | |
|---|---|---|---|
| Physiol. | Physiology | Scot. | Scottish, Scotland |
| pl. | plural | sing. | singular |
| poet. | poetical | sl. | slang |
| Polit. | Politics | Sociol. | Sociology |
| poss. | possessive | St. Exch. | Stock Exchange |
| postpos. | postpositive | sth. | something |
| p.p. | past participle | subord. | subordinate |
| pred. | predicative | suf. | suffix |
| pref. | prefix | superl. | superlative |
| prep. | preposition | Surv. | Surveying |
| pres. | present | symb. | symbol |
| pres. p. | present participle | tech. | technical |
| pr. n. | proper noun | Teleph. | Telephony |
| pron. | pronoun | Telev. | Television |
| prov. | proverbial | Theol. | Theology |
| Psych. | Psychology | Univ. | University |
| p.t. | past tense | usu. | usually |
| Railw. | Railways | v. aux. | auxiliary verb |
| RC Ch. | Roman Catholic Church | Vet. Med. | Veterinary Medicine |
| | | v. i. | intransitive verb |
| refl. | reflexive | v. refl. | reflexive verb |
| rel. | relative | v. t. | transitive verb |
| Relig. | Religion | v. t. & i. | transitive and |
| rhet. | rhetorical | | intransitive verb |
| sb. | somebody | Woodw. | Woodwork |
| Sch. | School | Zool. | Zoology |
| Sci. | Science | | |

# German abbreviations used in the Dictionary/ Im Wörterverzeichnis verwendete deutsche Abkürzungen

| | | | |
|---|---|---|---|
| a. | anderes; andere | berlin. | berlinisch |
| ä. | ähnliches; ähnliche | bes. | besonders |
| Abk. | Abkürzung | Bez. | Bezeichnung |
| adj. | adjektivisch | bibl. | biblisch |
| Adj. | Adjektiv | bild. Kunst | bildende Kunst |
| adv. | adverbial | Biol. | Biologie |
| Adv. | Adverb | Börsenw. | Börsenwesen |
| Akk. | Akkusativ | Bot. | Botanik |
| amerik. | amerikanisch | BRD | Bundesrepublik Deutschland |
| Amtsspr. | Amtssprache | | |
| Anat. | Anatomie | brit. | britisch |
| Anthrop. | Anthropologie | Bruchz. | Bruchzahl |
| Archäol. | Archäologie | Buchf. | Buchführung |
| Archit. | Architektur | Buchw. | Buchwesen |
| Art. | Artikel | Bürow. | Bürowesen |
| Astrol. | Astrologie | chem. | chemisch |
| Astron. | Astronomie | christl. | christlich |
| A. T. | Altes Testament | Dat. | Dativ |
| attr. | attributiv | DDR | Deutsche Demokratische Republik |
| Bauw. | Bauwesen | | |
| Bergmannsspr. | Bergmannssprache | | |

| | | | |
|---|---|---|---|
| Dekl. | Deklination | jur. | juristisch |
| Demonstrativ- | Demonstrativ- | Kardinalz. | Kardinalzahl |
| pron. | pronomen | kath. | katholisch |
| d. h. | das heißt | Kaufmannsspr. | Kaufmannssprache |
| dichter. | dichterisch | Kfz-W. | Kraftfahrzeugwesen |
| Druckerspr. | Druckersprache | Kinderspr. | Kindersprache |
| Druckw. | Druckwesen | Kochk. | Kochkunst |
| dt. | deutsch | Konj. | Konjunktion |
| DV | Datenverarbeitung | Kunstwiss. | Kunstwissenschaft |
| ehem. | ehemals, ehemalig | landsch. | landschaftlich |
| Eisenb. | Eisenbahn | Landw. | Landwirtschaft |
| elektr. | elektrisch | Literaturw. | Literaturwissenschaft |
| Elektrot. | Elektrotechnik | Luftf. | Luftfahrt |
| engl. | englisch | ma. | mittelalterlich |
| etw. | etwas | MA. | Mittelalter |
| ev. | evangelisch | marx. | marxistisch |
| fachspr. | fachsprachlich | Math. | Mathematik |
| fam. | familiär | Med. | Medizin |
| Ferns. | Fernsehen | Meeresk. | Meereskunde |
| Fernspr. | Fernsprechwesen | Met. | Meteorologie |
| fig. | figurativ | Metall. | Metallurgie |
| Finanzw. | Finanzwesen | Metallbearb. | Metallbearbeitung |
| Flugw. | Flugwesen | Milit. | Militär |
| Forstw. | Forstwesen | Mineral. | Mineralogie |
| Fot. | Fotografie | mod. | modifizierend |
| Frachtw. | Frachtwesen | Modalv. | Modalverb |
| Funkw. | Funkwesen | Münzk. | Münzkunde |
| Gastr. | Gastronomie | Mus. | Musik |
| Gattungsz. | Gattungszahl | Mythol. | Mythologie |
| Gaunerspr. | Gaunersprache | Naturw. | Naturwissenschaft |
| geh. | gehoben | Neutr. | Neutrum |
| Gen. | Genitiv | niederdt. | niederdeutsch |
| Geneal. | Genealogie | Nom. | Nominativ |
| Geogr. | Geographie | nordamerik. | nordamerikanisch |
| Geol. | Geologie | nordd. | norddeutsch |
| Geom. | Geometrie | nordostd. | nordostdeutsch |
| Handarb. | Handarbeit | nordwestd. | nordwestdeutsch |
| Handw. | Handwerk | ns. | nationalsozialistisch |
| Her. | Heraldik | N. T. | Neues Testament |
| hess. | hessisch | o. | ohne; oben |
| Hilfsv. | Hilfsverb | o. ä. | oder ähnliches; |
| hist. | historisch | | oder ähnliche |
| Hochschulw. | Hochschulwesen | od. | oder |
| Holzverarb. | Holzverarbeitung | Ordinalz. | Ordinalzahl |
| Indefinitpron. | Indefinitpronomen | ostd. | ostdeutsch |
| indekl. | indeklinabel | österr. | österreichisch |
| Indik. | Indikativ | Päd. | Pädagogik |
| Inf. | Infinitiv | Papierdt. | Papierdeutsch |
| Informationst. | Informationstechnik | Parapsych. | Parapsychologie |
| Interj. | Interjektion | Parl. | Parlament |
| iron. | ironisch | Part. | Partizip |
| intr. | intransitiv | Perf. | Perfekt |
| Jagdw. | Jagdwesen | Pers. | Person |
| Jägerspr. | Jägersprache | pfälz. | pfälzisch |
| jmd. | jemand | Pharm. | Pharmazie |
| jmdm. | jemandem | Philos. | Philosophie |
| jmdn. | jemanden | Physiol. | Physiologie |
| jmds. | jemandes | Pl. | Plural |
| Jugendspr. | Jugendsprache | Plusq. | Plusquamperfekt |

| | | | |
|---|---|---|---|
| Postw. | Postwesen | Sup. | Superlativ |
| präd. | prädikativ | Textilw. | Textilwesen |
| Präp. | Präposition | Theol. | Theologie |
| Präs. | Präsens | thüring. | thüringisch |
| Prät. | Präteritum | Tiermed. | Tiermedizin |
| Pron. | Pronomen | tr. | transitiv |
| Psych. | Psychologie | Trenn. | Trennung |
| Raumf. | Raumfahrt | u. | und |
| Rechtsspr. | Rechtssprache | u. a. | und andere[s] |
| Rechtsw. | Rechtswesen | u. ä. | und ähnliches |
| refl. | reflexiv | ugs. | umgangssprachlich |
| regelm. | regelmäßig | unbest. | unbestimmt |
| Rel. | Religion | unpers. | unpersönlich |
| Relativpron. | Relativpronomen | unr. | unregelmäßig |
| rhein. | rheinisch | usw. | und so weiter |
| Rhet. | Rhetorik | v. | von |
| röm. | römisch | V. | Verb |
| röm.-kath. | römisch-katholisch | verächtl. | verächtlich |
| Rundf. | Rundfunk | veralt. | veraltet; veraltend |
| s. | siehe | Verhaltensf. | Verhaltensforschung |
| S. | Seite | verhüll. | verhüllend |
| scherzh. | scherzhaft | Verkehrsw. | Verkehrswesen |
| schles. | schlesisch | Versiche- | Versicherungswesen |
| schott. | schottisch | rungsw. | |
| Schülerspr. | Schülersprache | vgl. | vergleiche |
| Schulw. | Schulwesen | Vkl. | Verkleinerungsform |
| schwäb. | schwäbisch | Völkerk. | Völkerkunde |
| schweiz. | schweizerisch | Völkerr. | Völkerrecht |
| Seemannsspr. | Seemannssprache | Volksk. | Volkskunde |
| Seew. | Seewesen | volkst. | volkstümlich |
| Sexualk. | Sexualkunde | vulg. | vulgär |
| Sg. | Singular | Werbespr. | Werbesprache |
| s. o. | siehe oben | westd. | westdeutsch |
| Soldatenspr. | Soldatensprache | westfäl. | westfälisch |
| Sozialvers. | Sozialversicherung | Wieder- | Wiederholungs- |
| Soziol. | Soziologie | holungsz. | zahlwort |
| spött. | spöttisch | wiener. | wienerisch |
| Spr. | Sprichwort | Winzerspr. | Winzersprache |
| Sprachw. | Sprachwissenschaft | Wirtsch. | Wirtschaft |
| Steuerw. | Steuerwesen | Wissensch. | Wissenschaft |
| Stilk. | Stilkunde | Wz. | Warenzeichen |
| Studentenspr. | Studentensprache | Zahnmed. | Zahnmedizin |
| s. u. | siehe unten | z. B. | zum Beispiel |
| Subj. | Subjekt | Zeitungsw. | Zeitungswesen |
| subst. | substantivisch; | Zollw. | Zollwesen |
| | substantiviert | Zool. | Zoologie |
| Subst. | Substantiv | Zus. | Zusammensetzung |
| südd. | süddeutsch | Zusschr. | Zusammenschreibung |
| südwestd. | südwestdeutsch | | |

# A

**A, ¹a** [eɪ] *n.* A, a, *das*

**²a** [ə, *stressed* eɪ] *indef. art.* ein/eine/ein; **he is a gardener/a Frenchman** er ist Gärtner/Franzose; **she did not say a word** sie sagte kein Wort

**AA** *abbr. (Brit.)* Automobile Association *britischer Automobilklub*

**aback** [ə'bæk] *adv.* **be taken ~:** erstaunt sein

**abandon** [ə'bændən] *v. t.* verlassen ⟨*Ort, Person*⟩; aufgeben ⟨*Prinzip*⟩

**abase** [ə'beɪs] *v. t.* erniedrigen

**abashed** [ə'bæʃt] *adj.* beschämt

**abate** [ə'beɪt] *v. i.* nachlassen

**abattoir** ['æbətwɑː(r)] *n.* Schlachthof, *der*

**abbey** ['æbɪ] *n.* Abtei, *die*

**abbot** ['æbət] *n.* Abt, *der*

**abbreviate** [ə'briːvɪeɪt] *v. t.* abkürzen. **abbreviation** [əbriːvɪ'eɪʃn] *n.* Abkürzung, *die*

**abdicate** ['æbdɪkeɪt] *v. t.* abdanken. **abdication** [æbdɪ'keɪʃn] *n.* Abdankung, *die*

**abdomen** ['æbdəmɪn] *n.* Bauch, *der*. **abdominal** [æb'dɒmɪnl] *adj.* Bauch-

**abduct** [əb'dʌkt] *v. t.* entführen. **abduction** [əb'dʌkʃn] *n.* Entführung, *die*

**aberration** [æbə'reɪʃn] *n.* Abweichung, *die*

**abet** [ə'bet] *v. t.,* -tt- helfen (+ *Dat.*); **aid and ~:** Beihilfe leisten (+ *Dat.*)

**abhor** [əb'hɔː(r)] *v. t.,* -rr- verabscheuen. **abhorrent** [əb'hɒrənt] *adj.* abscheulich

**abide** [ə'baɪd] **1.** *v. i.* **~ by** befolgen ⟨*Gesetz, Vorschrift*⟩; [ein]halten ⟨*Versprechen*⟩. **2.** *v. t.* ertragen; **I can't ~ dogs** ich kann Hunde nicht ausstehen

**ability** [ə'bɪlɪtɪ] *n.* **a)** *(capacity)* Fähigkeit, *die*; **have the ~ to do sth.** etw. können; **b)** *(cleverness)* Intelligenz, *die*; **c)** *(talent)* Begabung, *die*

**abject** ['æbdʒekt] *adj.* elend; bitter ⟨*Armut*⟩; demütig ⟨*Entschuldigung*⟩

**ablaze** [ə'bleɪz] *adj.* **be ~:** in Flammen stehen

**able** ['eɪbl] *adj.* **a) be ~ to do sth.** etw. können; **b)** *(competent)* fähig. **able-bodied** ['eɪblbɒdɪd] *adj.* kräftig; tauglich ⟨*Soldat, Matrose*⟩. **ably** ['eɪblɪ] *adv.* geschickt; gekonnt

**abnormal** [æb'nɔːml] *adj.* abnorm; a[b]normal ⟨*Interesse, Verhalten*⟩. **abnormality** [æbnɔː'mælɪtɪ] *n.* Abnormität, *die*

**aboard** [ə'bɔːd] **1.** *adv.* an Bord. **2.** *prep.* an Bord (+ *Gen.*); **~ the bus** im Bus; **~ ship** an Bord

**abode** [ə'bəʊd] *n.* **of no fixed ~:** ohne festen Wohnsitz

**abolish** [ə'bɒlɪʃ] *v. t.* abschaffen. **abolition** [æbə'lɪʃn] *n.* Abschaffung, *die*

**abominable** [ə'bɒmɪnəbl] *adj.* abscheulich; scheußlich

**aborigine** [æbə'rɪdʒɪnɪ] *n.* Ureinwohner, *der*

**abort** [ə'bɔːt] *v. t.* abtreiben ⟨*Baby*⟩. **abortion** [ə'bɔːʃn] *n.* Abtreibung, *die*. **abortive** [ə'bɔːtɪv] *adj.* mißlungen ⟨*Plan*⟩; fehlgeschlagen ⟨*Versuch*⟩

**abound** [ə'baʊnd] *v. i.* **~ in sth.** an etw. *(Dat.)* reich sein

**about** [ə'baʊt] **1.** *adv.* **a)** *(all around)* rings[her]um; *(here and there)* überall; **all ~:** ringsumher; **b)** *(near)* **be ~:** dasein; hiersein; **c) be ~ to do sth.** gerade etw. tun wollen; **d) be out and ~:** aktiv sein; **e)** *(approximately)* ungefähr. **2.** *prep.* **a)** *(all round)* um [... herum]; **b)** *(concerning)* über (+ *Akk.*); **know ~ sth.** von etw. wissen; **a question ~ sth.** eine Frage zu etw.; **what was it ~?** worum ging es?

**above** [ə'bʌv] **1.** *adv.* **a)** *(position)* oben; *(higher up)* darüber; **b)** *(direction)* nach oben. **2.** *prep. (position)* über (+ *Dat.*); *(direction, more than)* über (+ *Akk.*); **~ all** vor allem. **a'bove-mentioned** *adj.* oben genannt

**abrasion** [ə'breɪʒn] *n. (graze)* Hautab-
schürfung, *die*
**abrasive** [ə'breɪsɪv] **1.** *adj.* **a)** scheu-
ernd; Scheuer-; **b)** *(fig.: harsh)* aggressiv. **2.** *n.* Scheuermittel, *das*
**abreast** [ə'brest] *adv.* **a)** nebeneinander; **b)** *(fig.)* **keep ~ of sth.** sich über
etw. *(Akk.)* auf dem laufenden halten
**abroad** [ə'brɔːd] *adv.* im Ausland;
*(direction)* ins Ausland
**abrupt** [ə'brʌpt] *adj.*, **a'bruptly** *adv.*
**a)** *(sudden[ly])* abrupt; plötzlich; **b)**
*(brusque[ly])* schroff
**abscess** ['æbsɪs] *n.* Abszeß, *der*
**abscond** [əb'skɒnd] *v. t.* sich entfernen
**absence** ['æbsəns] *n.* Abwesenheit,
*die;* **the ~ of sth.** der Mangel an etw.
*(Dat.)*
**absent** ['æbsənt] *adj.* abwesend; **be ~
from school/work** in der Schule/am
Arbeitsplatz fehlen. **absentee** [æb-
sən'tiː] *n.* Fehlende, *der/die;* Abwe-
sende, *der/die.* **absent-minded** [æb-
sənt'maɪndɪd] *adj.* geistesabwesend;
*(habitually)* zerstreut
**absolute** ['æbsəluːt] *adj.* absolut; ausgemacht *(Lüge, Skandal).* **abso-
'lutely** *adv.* absolut; völlig *(verrückt);* **you're ~ right!** du hast völlig
recht; **~ not!** auf keinen Fall!
**absolve** [əb'zɒlv] *v. t.* **~ from** entbinden von *(Pflichten);* lossprechen von
*(Schuld)*
**absorb** [əb'sɔːb] *v. t.* **a)** aufsaugen
*(Flüssigkeit);* **b)** abfangen *(Schlag,
Stoß);* **c)** *(fig.: engross)* ausfüllen. **ab-
sorbent** [əb'sɔːbənt] *adj.* saugfähig.
**ab'sorbing** *adj.* faszinierend
**abstain** [əb'steɪn] *v. i.* **~ from sth.** sich
einer Sache *(Gen.)* enthalten; **~ |from
voting|** sich der Stimme enthalten
**abstemious** [əb'stiːmɪəs] *adj.* enthaltsam
**abstention** [əb'stenʃn] *n. (from voting)* Stimmenthaltung, *die*
**abstinence** ['æbstɪnəns] *n.* Abstinenz,
*die*
**abstract** ['æbstrækt] **1.** *adj.* abstrakt.
**2.** *n.* Zusammenfassung, *die*
**absurd** [əb'sɜːd] *adj.* absurd; *(ridiculous)* lächerlich. **absurdity** [əb'sɜːdɪ-
tɪ] *n.* Absurdität, *die.* **ab'surdly** *adv.*
lächerlich
**abundance** [ə'bʌndəns] *n.* **|an| ~ of
sth.** eine Fülle von etw.
**abundant** [ə'bʌndənt] *adj.* reich **(in an
+ Dat.)**
**abuse 1.** [ə'bjuːz] *v. t.* beschimpfen. **2.**

[ə'bjuːs] *n.* Beschimpfungen *Pl.* **ab-
usive** [ə'bjuːsɪv] *adj.* beleidigend;
**become ~:** ausfallend werden
**abysmal** [ə'bɪzml] *adj. (coll.: bad)* katastrophal *(ugs.)*
**abyss** [ə'bɪs] *n.* Abgrund, *der*
**AC** *abbr.* alternating current Ws
**academic** [ækə'demɪk] *adj.* akademisch
**academy** [ə'kædəmɪ] *n.* Akademie,
*die*
**accede** [æk'siːd] *v. i.* **a)** zustimmen **(to
Dat.);** **b) ~ |to the throne|** den Thron
besteigen
**accelerate** [ək'seləreɪt] **1.** *v. t.* beschleunigen. **2.** *v. i.* sich beschleunigen; *(Auto, Fahrer:)* beschleunigen.
**acceleration** [əkselə'reɪʃn] *n.* Beschleunigung, *die.* **accelerator** [ək-
'seləreɪtə(r)] *n.* **~ |pedal|** Gas[pedal],
*das*
**accent** ['æksənt] *n.* Akzent, *der.* **ac-
centuate** [ək'sentjʊeɪt] *v. t.* betonen
**accept** [ək'sept] *v. t.* **a)** annehmen;
entgegennehmen *(Dank, Spende);*
übernehmen *(Verantwortung);* **b)** *(acknowledge)* akzeptieren. **acceptable**
[ək'septəbl] *adj.* akzeptabel; annehmbar *(Preis, Gehalt).* **acceptance** [ək-
'septəns] *n.* **a)** Annahme, *die;* **b)** *(acknowledgement)* Anerkennung, *die*
**access** ['ækses] *n.* **a)** *(admission)* **gain
~:** Einlaß finden; **b)** *(opportunity to
use or approach)* Zugang, *der* **(to zu).**
**accessible** [ək'sesɪbl] *adj.* **a)** *(reach-
able)* erreichbar; **b)** *(available, understandable)* zugänglich **(to für)**
**accession** [ək'seʃn] *n.* Amtsantritt,
*der;* **~ |to the throne|** Thronbestei-
gung, *die*
**accessory** [ək'sesərɪ] *n.* **a) accessories**
*pl.* Zubehör, *das;* **b)** *(dress article)* Ac-
cessoire, *das*
**accident** ['æksɪdənt] *n.* **a)** Unfall, *der;*
**b)** *(chance)* Zufall, *der;* **by ~:** zufällig;
**c)** *(mistake)* Versehen, *das;* **by ~:** versehentlich. **accidental** [æksɪ'dentl]
*adj. (chance)* zufällig; *(unintended)*
unbeabsichtigt. **acci'dentally** *adv.
(by chance)* zufällig; *(by mistake)* versehentlich
**acclaim** [ə'kleɪm] *v. t.* feiern
**acclimatize** [ə'klaɪmətaɪz] *v. t.* **get or
become ~d** sich akklimatisieren
**accolade** ['ækəleɪd] *n. (praise)* **~|s|**
Lob, *das*
**accommodate** [ə'kɒmədeɪt] *v. t.* **a)**
unterbringen; *(hold)* Platz bieten
**(+ Dat.);** **b)** *(oblige)* gefällig sein

(+ *Dat.*). **accommodating** [ə'kɒmədeɪtɪŋ] *adj.* zuvorkommend. **accommodation** [əkɒmə'deɪʃn] *n.* Unterkunft, *die*

**accompaniment** [ə'kʌmpənɪmənt] *n.* Begleitung, *die*

**accompanist** [ə'kʌmpənɪst] *n.* Begleiter, *der*/Begleiterin, *die*

**accompany** [ə'kʌmpənɪ] *v. t.* begleiten

**accomplice** [ə'kʌmplɪs] *n.* Komplize, *der*/Komplizin, *die*

**accomplish** [ə'kʌmplɪʃ] *v. t.* vollbringen ⟨*Tat*⟩; erfüllen ⟨*Aufgabe*⟩. **accomplished** [ə'kʌmplɪʃt] *adj.* fähig; **he is an ~ speaker/dancer** er ist ein erfahrener Redner/vollendeter Tänzer. **ac·complishment** *n.* a) *(completion)* Vollendung, *die;* b) *(achievement)* Leistung, *die; (skill)* Fähigkeit, *die*

**accord** [ə'kɔːd] **1.** *n.* Übereinstimmung, *die;* **of one's own ~:** aus eigenem Antrieb; **with one ~:** geschlossen. **2.** *v. t.* ~ **sb. sth.** jmdm. etw. gewähren. **accordance** [ə'kɔːdəns] *n.* **in ~ with** in Übereinstimmung mit. **ac·cording** *adv.* ~ **to** nach; ~ **to him** nach seiner Aussage. **ac·cordingly** *adv. (as appropriate)* entsprechend; *(therefore)* folglich

**accordion** [ə'kɔːdɪən] *n.* Akkordeon, *das*

**accost** [ə'kɒst] *v. t.* ansprechen

**account** [ə'kaʊnt] *n.* a) *(Finance)* Rechnung, *die; (at bank, shop)* Konto, *das;* b) *(consideration)* **take ~ of sth., take sth. into ~:** etw. berücksichtigen; **take no ~ of sth./sb.** etw./jmdn. unberücksichtigt lassen; **don't change your plans on my ~:** ändert nicht meinetwegen eure Pläne; **on ~ of** wegen; **on no ~:** auf [gar] keinen Fall; c) *(report)* Bericht, *der;* d) **call sb. to ~:** jmdn. zur Rechenschaft ziehen. **ac·count for** *v. t.* Rechenschaft ablegen über (+*Akk.*); *(explain)* erklären

**accountable** [ə'kaʊntəbl] *adj.* verantwortlich

**accountancy** [ə'kaʊntənsɪ] *n.* Buchhaltung, *die*

**accountant** [ə'kaʊntənt] *n.* [Bilanz]buchhalter, *der*/-halterin, *die*

**ac·count number** *n.* Kontonummer, *die*

**accrue** [ə'kruː] *v. i.* ⟨*Zinsen:*⟩ auflaufen; ~ **to sb.** ⟨*Reichtümer, Einnahmen:*⟩ jmdm. zufließen

**accumulate** [ə'kjuːmjʊleɪt] **1.** *v. t.*

sammeln. **2.** *v. i.* ⟨*Menge, Staub:*⟩ sich ansammeln; ⟨*Geld:*⟩ sich anhäufen. **accumulation** [əkjuːmjʊ'leɪʃn] *n.* [An]sammeln, *das; (being accumulated)* Anhäufung, *die*

**accuracy** ['ækjʊrəsɪ] *n.* Genauigkeit, *die*

**accurate** ['ækjʊrət] *adj.,* '**accurately** *adv.* genau; *(correct[ly])* richtig

**accusation** [ækjuː'zeɪʃn] *n.* Anschuldigung, *die; (Law)* Anklage, *die*

**accusative** [ə'kjuːzətɪv] *adj. & n.* ~ |**case**| Akkusativ, *der*

**accuse** [ə'kjuːz] *v. t.* beschuldigen; *(Law)* anklagen (**of** wegen + *Gen.*)

**accustom** [ə'kʌstəm] *v. t.* gewöhnen (**to an** + *Akk.*); **grow/be ~ed to sth.** sich an etw. *(Akk.)* gewöhnen/an etw. *(Akk.)* gewöhnt sein. **accustomed** [ə'kʌstəmd] *attrib. adj.* gewohnt; üblich

**ace** [eɪs] *n.* As, *das*

**ache** [eɪk] **1.** *v. i.* schmerzen; weh tun. **2.** *n.* Schmerz, *der*

**achieve** [ə'tʃiːv] *v. t.* zustande bringen; erreichen ⟨*Ziel, Standard*⟩. **a·chievement** *n.* a) *see* **achieve:** Zustandebringen, *das;* Erreichen, *das;* b) *(thing accomplished)* Leistung, *die*

**acid** ['æsɪd] **1.** *adj.* sauer. **2.** *n.* Säure, *die.* **acidic** [ə'sɪdɪk] *adj.* säuerlich. **acidity** [ə'sɪdɪtɪ] *n.* Säure, *die*

**acid:** ~ '**rain** *n.* saurer Regen; ~ **test** *n. (fig.)* Feuerprobe, *die*

**acknowledge** [ək'nɒlɪdʒ] *v. t.* a) zugeben ⟨*Tatsache, Fehler, Schuld*⟩; b) sich erkenntlich zeigen für ⟨*Dienste, Bemühungen*⟩; erwidern ⟨*Gruß*⟩; c) bestätigen ⟨*Empfang, Bewerbung*⟩; ~ **a letter** den Empfang eines Briefes bestätigen. **acknowledg[e]ment** [ək'nɒlɪdʒmənt] *n.* a) *(admission)* Eingeständnis, *das;* b) *(thanks)* Dank, *der* (**of** für); c) *(of letter)* Bestätigung [des Empfangs]

**acne** ['æknɪ] *n.* Akne, *die*

**acorn** ['eɪkɔːn] *n.* Eichel, *die*

**acoustic** [ə'kuːstɪk] *adj.* akustisch. **a·coustics** *n. pl.* Akustik, *die*

**acquaint** [ə'kweɪnt] *v. t.* **be ~ed with sb.** mit jmdm. bekannt sein. **acquaintance** [ə'kweɪntəns] *n.* a) ~ **with sb.** Bekanntschaft mit jmdm.; **make sb.'s ~:** jmds. Bekanntschaft machen; b) *(person)* Bekannte, *der/die*

**acquiesce** [ækwɪ'es] *v. i.* einwilligen (**in** in + *Akk.*)

**acquire** [ə'kwaɪə(r)] *v. t.* sich *(Dat.)* anschaffen ⟨*Gegenstände*⟩; erwerben

⟨*Besitz, Kenntnisse*⟩. **acquisition** [ækwɪ'zɪʃn] *n.* Erwerb, *der;* *(thing)* Anschaffung, *die.* **acquisitive** [ə'kwɪzɪtɪv] *adj.* raffsüchtig

**acquit** [ə'kwɪt] *v.t.,* -tt- freisprechen. **acquittal** [ə'kwɪtl] *n.* Freispruch, *der*

**acre** ['eɪkə(r)] *n.* Acre, *der*

**acrid** ['ækrɪd] *adj.* beißend ⟨*Geruch, Rauch*⟩; bitter ⟨*Geschmack*⟩

**acrimonious** [ækrɪ'məʊnɪəs] *adj.* bitter; erbittert ⟨*Streit*⟩

**acrobat** ['ækrəbæt] *n.* Akrobat, *der/*Akrobatin, *die.* **acrobatic** [ækrə-'bætɪk] *adj.* akrobatisch. **acrobatics** [ækrə'bætɪks] *n.* Akrobatik, *die*

**acronym** ['ækrənɪm] *n.* Akronym, *das*

**across** [ə'krɒs] **1.** *adv. (from one side to the other)* darüber; *(from here to there)* hinüber; **be 9 miles** ~: 9 Meilen breit sein. **2.** *prep.* über (+ *Akk.*); *(on the other side of)* auf der anderen Seite (+ *Gen.*)

**act** [ækt] **1.** *n.* **a)** *(deed)* Tat, *die;* **b)** *(Theatre)* Akt, *der;* **c)** *(pretence)* Theater, *das;* **put on an** ~: Theater spielen; **d)** *(Law)* Gesetz, *das.* **2.** *v.t.* spielen ⟨*Stück*⟩. **3.** *v.i.* **a)** *(perform actions)* handeln; **b)** *(behave)* sich verhalten; ~ **as** fungieren als; **c)** *(perform play)* spielen; **d)** *(have effect)* ~ **on sth.** auf etw. *(Akk.)* wirken. **'acting 1.** *n.* *(Theatre etc.)* die Schauspielerei. **2.** *adj. (temporary)* stellvertretend

**action** ['ækʃn] *n.* **a)** *(doing sth.)* Handeln, *das;* **take** ~: Schritte *od.* etwas unternehmen; **put a plan into** ~: einen Plan in die Tat umsetzen; **put sth. out of** ~: etw. außer Betrieb setzen; **b)** *(act)* Tat, *die;* **c)** *(legal process)* [Gerichts]verfahren, *das;* **d) die in** ~: im Kampf fallen. **action 'replay** *n.* Wiederholung [in Zeitlupe]

**activate** ['æktɪveɪt] *v.t.* **a)** in Gang setzen; **b)** *(Chem., Phys.)* aktivieren

**active** ['æktɪv] *adj.,* **'actively** *adv.* aktiv

**activist** ['æktɪvɪst] *n.* Aktivist, *der/*Aktivistin, *die*

**activity** [æk'tɪvɪtɪ] *n.* Aktivität, *die*

**actor** ['æktə(r)] *n.* Schauspieler, *der*

**actress** ['æktrɪs] *n.* Schauspielerin, *die*

**actual** ['æktʃʊəl] *adj.* eigentlich; wirklich ⟨*Name*⟩. **'actually** *adv. (in fact)* eigentlich; *(by the way)* übrigens; *(believe it or not)* sogar

**acumen** ['ækjʊmen] Scharfsinn, *der;* **business** ~: Geschäftssinn, *der*

**acupuncture** ['ækjʊpʌnktʃə(r)] *n.* Akupunktur, *die*

**acute** [ə'kju:t] *adj.* **a)** spitz ⟨*Winkel*⟩; **b)** *(critical; Med.)* akut

**AD** *abbr.* **Anno Domini** n. Chr.

**ad** [æd] *n. (coll.)* Annonce, *die*

**adamant** ['ædəmənt] *adj.* unnachgiebig; **be** ~ **that** ...: darauf bestehen, daß ...

**adapt** [ə'dæpt] *v.t.* **a)** anpassen (to *Dat.*); ~ **oneself to sth.** sich an etw. *(Akk.)* gewöhnen; **b)** bearbeiten ⟨*Text, Theaterstück*⟩. **adaptable** [ə'dæptəbl] *adj.* anpassungsfähig. **adaptation** [ædəp'teɪʃn] *n.* **a)** Anpassung, *die;* **b)** *(version)* Adap[ta]tion, *die;* *(of story, text)* Bearbeitung, *die.* **adapter, adaptor** [ə'dæptə(r)] *n.* Adapter, *der*

**add** [æd] **1.** *v.t.* hinzufügen (to *Dat.*); ~ **two and two** zwei und zwei zusammenzählen. **2.** *v.i.* ~ **to** vergrößern ⟨*Schwierigkeiten, Einkommen*⟩. **add 'up 1.** *v.i.* ~ **up to sth.** *(fig.)* auf etw. *(Akk.)* hinauslaufen. **2.** *v.t.* zusammenzählen

**adder** ['ædə(r)] *n.* Viper, *die*

**addict 1.** [ə'dɪkt] *v.t.* **be** ~**ed** süchtig sein (to nach). **2.** ['ædɪkt] *n.* Süchtige, *der/die.* **addiction** [ə'dɪkʃn] *n.* Sucht, *die* (to nach). **addictive** [ə'dɪktɪv] *adj.* **be** ~: süchtig machen

**addition** [ə'dɪʃn] *n.* **a)** Hinzufügen, *das;* *(adding up)* Addieren, *das;* *(process)* Addition, *die;* **in** ~: außerdem; **in** ~ **to** zusätzlich zu; **b)** *(thing added)* Ergänzung, *die* (to zu). **additional** [ə'dɪʃənl] *adj.* zusätzlich

**additive** ['ædɪtɪv] *n.* Zusatz, *der*

**address** [ə'dres] **1.** *v.t.* **a)** *(mark with* ~*)* adressieren (to an + *Akk.*); **b)** *(speak to)* anreden; sprechen zu ⟨*Zuhörern*⟩. **2.** *n.* **a)** *(on letter)* Adresse, *die;* **b)** *(speech)* Ansprache, *die.* **addressee** [ædre'si:] *n.* Adressat, *der/*Adressatin, *die*

**adept** ['ædept] *adj.* geschickt (**in, at** in + *Dat.*)

**adequate** ['ædɪkwət] *adj.* **a)** angemessen (to *Dat.*); *(suitable)* passend; **b)** *(sufficient)* ausreichend. **'adequately** *adv.* **a)** *(sufficiently)* ausreichend; **b)** *(suitably)* angemessen ⟨*gekleidet, qualifiziert usw.*⟩

**adhere** [əd'hɪə(r)] *v.i.* haften, *(by glue)* kleben (**to** an + *Dat.*). **adhesion** [əd-'hi:ʒn] *n.* Haften, *das.* **adhesive** [əd-'hi:sɪv] **1.** *adj.* gummiert ⟨*Briefmarke*⟩; Klebe⟨*band*⟩. **2.** *n.* Klebstoff, *der*

**adjacent** [ə'dʒeɪsənt] *adj.* angrenzend; ~ **to** neben *(position:* + *Dat.; direction:* + *Akk.*).

**adjective** ['ædʒɪktɪv] *n.* Adjektiv, *das*

**adjoin** [ə'dʒɔɪn] *v. t.* grenzen an (+ *Akk.*)

**adjourn** [ə'dʒɜ:n] **1.** *v. t. (break off)* unterbrechen; *(put off)* aufschieben. **2.** *v. i.* sich vertagen; ~ **for lunch/half an hour** eine Mittagspause/halbstündige Pause einlegen. **a'djournment** *n. (of court)* Vertagung, *die; (of meeting)* Unterbrechung, *die*

**adjudicate** [ə'dʒu:dıkeıt] *v. i. (in court, tribunal)* das Urteil fällen; *(in contest)* entscheiden

**adjust** [ə'dʒʌst] **1.** *v. t.* einstellen; ~ **sth. [to sth.]** etw. [an etw. *(Akk.)*] anpassen. **2.** *v. i.* ⟨*Person:*⟩ sich anpassen (to an + *Akk.*). **adjustable** [ə'dʒʌstəbl] *adj.* einstellbar; verstellbar ⟨*Gerät*⟩. **a'djustment** *n.* Einstellung, *die; (to situation etc.)* Anpassung, *die*

**ad-lib** [æd'lıb] **1.** *adj.* improvisiert. **2.** *v. i.,* -bb- improvisieren

**administer** [æd'mınıstə(r)] **a)** *(manage)* verwalten; **b)** leisten ⟨*Hilfe*⟩; verabreichen ⟨*Medikamente*⟩. **administration** [ədmını'streıʃn] *n.* Verwaltung, *die.* **administrative** [əd'mınıstrətıv] *adj.* Verwaltungs-. **administrator** [əd'mınıstreıtə(r)] *n.* Administrator, *der;* Verwalter, *der*

**admirable** ['ædmərəbl] *adj.* bewundernswert

**admiral** ['ædmərəl] *n.* Admiral, *der*

**admiration** [ædmə'reıʃn] *n.* Bewunderung, *die* (of, for für)

**admire** [əd'maıə(r)] *v. t.* bewundern.

**admirer** [əd'maıərə(r)] *n.* Bewunderer, *der*/Bewunderin, *die*

**admission** [əd'mıʃn] *n.* **a)** *(entry)* Zutritt, *der;* **b)** *(charge)* Eintritt, *der;* **c)** *(confession)* Eingeständnis, *das*

**admit** [əd'mıt] *v. t.,* -tt-: **a)** *(let in)* hinein-/hereinlassen; **b)** *(acknowledge)* zugeben. **admittance** [əd'mıtəns] *n.* Zutritt, *der.* **admittedly** [əd'mıtıdlı] *adv.* zugegeben[ermaßen]

**admonish** [əd'mɒnıʃ] *v. t.* ermahnen

**ado** [ə'du:] *n.* **without more** ~: ohne weiteres Aufhebens

**adolescence** [ædə'lesns] *n.* die Zeit des Erwachsenenwerdens. **adolescent** [ædə'lesnt] **1.** *n.* Heranwachsende, *der/die.* **2.** *adj.* heranwachsend

**adopt** [ə'dɒpt] *v. t.* **a)** adoptieren; **b)** *(take over)* annehmen ⟨*Glaube, Kultur*⟩; **c)** *(take up)* übernehmen ⟨*Methode*⟩; einnehmen ⟨*Standpunkt, Haltung*⟩. **adoption** [ə'dɒpʃn] *n.* **a)** Adoption, *die;* **b)** *(taking over)* Annahme,

*die;* **c)** *(taking up)* Übernahme, *die; (of point of view)* Einnahme, *die*

**adorable** [ə'dɔ:rəbl] *adj.* bezaubernd

**adoration** [ædə'reıʃn] *n.* Verehrung, *die*

**adore** [ə'dɔ:(r)] *v. t.* verehren

**adorn** [ə'dɔ:n] *v. t.* schmücken. **a'dornment** *n.* Verzierung, *die;* ~**s** Schmuck, *der*

**adrenalin** [ə'drenəlın] *n.* Adrenalin, *das*

**Adriatic** [eıdrı'ætık] *pr. n.* ~ [Sea] Adriatisches Meer

**adrift** [ə'drıft] *adj.* **be** ~: treiben

**adroit** [ə'drɔıt] *adj.* geschickt

**adulation** [ædjʊ'leıʃn] *n.* Vergötterung, *die*

**adult** ['ædʌlt, ə'dʌlt] **1.** *adj.* erwachsen. **2.** *n.* Erwachsene, *der/die*

**adulterate** [ə'dʌltəreıt] *v. t.* verunreinigen

**adultery** [ə'dʌltərı] *n.* Ehebruch, *der*

**advance** [əd'vɑ:ns] **1.** *v. t.* **a)** *(also Mil.)* vorrücken lassen; **b)** *(put forward)* vorbringen ⟨*Plan, Meinung*⟩; **c)** *(further)* fördern; **d)** *(pay before due date)* vorschießen; ⟨*Bank:*⟩ leihen. **2.** *v. i.* **a)** *(also Mil.)* vorrücken; ⟨*Prozession:*⟩ sich vorwärts bewegen; **b)** *(fig.: make progress)* vorankommen. **3.** *n.* **a)** Vorrücken, *das; (fig.: progress)* Fortschritt, *der;* **b)** *usu. in pl. (personal approach)* Annäherungsversuch, *der;* **c)** *(on salary)* Vorschuß, *der;* **d)** **in** ~: im voraus. **advanced** [əd'vɑ:nst] *adj.* fortgeschritten

**advantage** [əd'vɑ:ntıdʒ] *n.* Vorteil, *der;* **take** ~ **of sb.** jmdn. ausnutzen; **be to one's** ~: für jmdn. von Vorteil sein; **turn sth. to [one's]** ~: etw. ausnutzen. **advantageous** [ædvən'teıdʒəs] *adj.* vorteilhaft

**advent** ['ædvent] *n.* Beginn, *der;* **A**~: Advent, *der*

**adventure** [əd'ventʃə(r)] *n.* Abenteuer, *das.* **adventurous** [əd'ventʃərəs] *adj.* abenteuerlustig

**adverb** ['ædvɜ:b] *n.* Adverb, *das*

**adversary** ['ædvəsərı] *n. (enemy)* Widersacher, *der*/Widersacherin, *die; (opponent)* Kontrahent, *der*/Kontrahentin, *die*

**adverse** ['ædvɜ:s] *adj.* **a)** *(unfavourable)* ungünstig; **b)** *(contrary)* widrig ⟨*Wind, Umstände*⟩. **adversity** [əd'vɜ:sıtı] *n.* **a)** *no pl.* Not, *die;* **b)** *usu. in pl.* Widrigkeit, *die*

**advert** ['ædvɜ:t] *n. (Brit. coll.) see* **advertisement**

**advertise** ['ædvətaız] 1. *v. t.* werben für; *(by small ad)* inserieren; ausschreiben ⟨Stelle⟩. 2. *v. i.* werben; *(in newspaper)* inserieren; annoncieren.
**advertisement** [əd'vɜːtɪsmənt] *n.* Anzeige, *die;* TV ~: Fernsehspot, *der.*
**advertiser** ['ædvətaızə(r)] *n. (in newspaper)* Inserent, *der/*Inserentin, *die.* **advertising** ['ædvətaızıŋ] *n.* Werbung, *die; attrib.* Werbe-
**advice** [əd'vaıs] *n.* Rat, *der;* take sb.'s ~: jmds. Rat *(Dat.)* folgen
**advisable** [əd'vaızəbl] *adj.* ratsam
**advise** [əd'vaız] *v. t.* beraten; ~ sth. zu etw. raten; *(inform)* unterrichten (of über + *Akk.).* **adviser, advisor** [əd'vaızə(r)] *n.* Berater, *der/*Beraterin, *die.* **advisory** [əd'vaızərı] *adj.* beratend
**advocate** 1. ['ædvəkət] *n. (of a cause)* Befürworter, *der/*Befürworterin, *die; (Law)* [Rechts]anwalt, *der/*-anwältin, *die.* 2. ['ædvəkeıt] *v. t.* befürworten
**aerial** ['eərıəl] 1. *adj.* Luft-. 2. *n.* Antenne, *die*
**aero-** [eərəʊ] *in comb.* Aero-
**aerodynamic** *adj.* aerodynamisch
**aeronautics** [eərə'nɔːtıks] *n.* Aeronautik, *die*
**aeroplane** ['eərəpleın] *n. (Brit.)* Flugzeug, *das*
**aerosol** ['eərəsɒl] *n. (spray)* Spray, *der od. das; (container)* ~ [spray] Spraydose, *die*
**aesthetic** [iːs'θetık] *adj.* ästhetisch
**afar** [ə'fɑː] *adv.* from ~: aus der Ferne
**affable** ['æfəbl] *adj.* freundlich
**affair** [ə'feə(r)] *n.* a) *(concern)* Angelegenheit, *die;* b) *in pl. (business)* Geschäfte *Pl.;* c) *(love ~)* Affäre, *die*
**affect** [ə'fekt] *v. t.* a) *(act on)* sich auswirken auf (+ *Akk.);* b) *(emotionally)* betroffen machen
**affectation** [æfek'teıʃn] *n. (studied display)* Verstellung, *die; (artificiality)* Affektiertheit, *die*
**affected** [ə'fektıd] *adj.* affektiert; gekünstelt ⟨Sprache, Stil⟩
**affection** [ə'fekʃn] *n.* Zuneigung, *die.* **affectionate** [ə'fekʃənət] *adj.* anhänglich; liebevoll ⟨Umarmung⟩. **af-'fectionately** *adv.* liebevoll
**affiliate** [ə'fılıeıt] *v. t.* be ~d to sth. an etw. *(Akk.)* angegliedert sein
**affinity** [ə'fınıtı] *n.* a) *(relationship)* Verwandtschaft, *die* (to mit); b) *(liking)* Neigung, *die* (for zu); feel an ~ to or for sb./sth. sich zu jmdm./etw. hingezogen fühlen

**affirm** [ə'fɜːm] *v. t. (assert)* bekräftigen ⟨Absicht⟩; beteuern ⟨Unschuld⟩; *(state as a fact)* bestätigen. **affirmation** [æfə'meıʃn] *n. (of intention)* Bekräftigung, *die; (of fact)* Bestätigung, *die.*
**affirmative** [ə'fɜːmətıv] 1. *adj.* affirmativ; bejahend ⟨Antwort⟩. 2. *n.* answer in the ~: bejahend antworten
**afflict** [ə'flıkt] *v. t. (physically)* plagen; *(mentally)* quälen; peinigen; be ~ed with sth. von etw. befallen sein. **affliction** [ə'flıkʃn] *n.* Leiden, *das*
**affluence** ['æfluəns] *n.* Reichtum, *der.* **affluent** ['æfluənt] *adj.* reich
**afford** [ə'fɔːd] *v. t.* a) sich *(Dat.)* leisten; b) *(provide)* bieten; gewähren ⟨Schutz⟩
**affray** [ə'freı] *n.* Schlägerei, *die*
**affront** [ə'frʌnt] 1. *v. t.* beleidigen. 2. *n.* Beleidigung, *die*
**afield** [ə'fiːld] *adv.* far ~ *(direction)* weit hinaus; *(place)* weit draußen
**afloat** [ə'fləʊt] *pred. adj.* a) *(floating)* über Wasser; flott ⟨Schiff⟩; b) *(at sea)* auf See; be ~: auf dem Meer treiben
**afoot** [ə'fʊt] *pred. adj.* im Gange
**aforementioned** [ə'fɔːmenʃnd], **aforesaid** [ə'fɔːsed] *adjs.* obenerwähnt *od.* -genannt
**afraid** [ə'freıd] *adj.* be ~ |of sb./sth.| [vor jmdm./etw.] Angst haben; be ~ to do sth. Angst davor haben, etw. zu tun; I'm ~ so/not ich fürchte ja/nein
**afresh** [ə'freʃ] *adv.* von neuem
**Africa** ['æfrıkə] *pr. n.* Afrika *(das).* **African** ['æfrıkən] 1. *adj.* afrikanisch. 2. *n.* Afrikaner, *der/*Afrikanerin, *die*
**after** ['ɑːftə(r)] 1. *adv.* a) *(later)* danach; b) *(behind)* hinterher. 2. *prep.* a) *(in time)* nach; two days ~: zwei Tage danach; b) *(behind)* hinter (+ *Dat.);* c) ask ~ sb./sth. nach jmdm./etw. fragen; d) ~ all schließlich. 3. *conj.* nachdem. **'after-care** *n. (Med.)* Nachbehandlung, *die.* **'after-effect** *n.* Nachwirkung, *die*
**aftermath** ['ɑːftəmæθ, 'ɑːftəmɑːθ] *n.* Nachwirkungen *Pl.*
**after:** ~'noon *n.* Nachmittag, *der;* this/tomorrow ~: heute/morgen nachmittag; in the ~: am Nachmittag; *(regularly)* nachmittags; ~shave *n.* After-shave, *das;* ~thought *n.* nachträglicher Einfall
**afterwards** ['ɑːftəwədz] *adv.* danach
**again** [ə'gen, ə'geın] *adv.* wieder; *(one more time)* noch einmal; ~ and ~, time and |time| ~: immer wieder; back ~: wieder zurück

**against** [ə'genst, ə'geɪnst] *prep.* gegen
**age** [eɪdʒ] **1.** *n.* **a)** Alter, *das;* **what ~ are you?** wie alt bist du?; **at the ~ of** im Alter von; **come of ~:** volljährig werden; **be under ~:** zu jung sein; **b)** *(great period)* Zeitalter, *das;* **~s** *(coll.: a long time)* eine Ewigkeit. **2.** *v. t.* altern lassen. **3.** *v. i.* altern. **aged** *adj.* **a)** [eɪdʒd] **be ~ five** fünf Jahre alt sein; **a boy ~ five** ein fünfjähriger Junge; **b)** ['eɪdʒɪd] *(elderly)* bejahrt
**age: ~-group** *n.* Altersgruppe, *die;* **~ limit** *n.* Altersgrenze, *die*
**agency** ['eɪdʒənsɪ] *n.* *(business establishment)* Geschäftsstelle, *die; (news/ advertising ~)* Agentur, *die*
**agenda** [ə'dʒendə] *n.* Tagesordnung, *die*
**agent** ['eɪdʒənt] *n.* Vertreter, *der/*Vertreterin, *die; (spy)* Agent, *der/*Agentin, *die*
**aggravate** ['ægrəveɪt] *v. t.* **a)** *(make worse)* verschlimmern; **b)** *(annoy)* aufregen; ärgern. **aggravating** ['ægrəveɪtɪŋ] *adj.* ärgerlich. **aggravation** [ægrə'veɪʃn] *n.* **a)** Verschlimmerung, *die;* **b)** *(annoyance)* Ärger, *der*
**aggregate** ['ægrɪgət] **1.** *n.* Gesamtmenge, *die.* **2.** *adj.* gesamt
**aggression** [ə'greʃn] *n.* Aggression, *die*
**aggressive** [ə'gresɪv] *adj.,* **ag'gressively** *adv.* aggressiv. **ag'gressiveness** *n.* Aggressivität, *die*
**aggressor** [ə'gresə(r)] *n.* Aggressor, *der*
**aggrieved** [ə'griːvd] *v. t.* *(resentful)* verärgert; *(offended)* gekränkt
**aghast** [ə'gɑːst] *pred. adj.* bestürzt
**agile** ['ædʒaɪl] *adj.* beweglich; flink ⟨*Bewegung*⟩. **agility** [ə'dʒɪlɪtɪ] *n.* Beweglichkeit, *die; (of movement)* Flinkheit, *die*
**agitate** ['ædʒɪteɪt] **1.** *v. t.* **a)** *(shake)* schütteln; **b)** *(disturb)* erregen. **2.** *v. i.* agitieren. **agitation** [ædʒɪ'teɪʃn] *n.* **a)** *(shaking)* Schütteln, *das;* **b)** *(emotional)* Erregung, *die.* **agitator** ['ædʒɪteɪtə(r)] *n.* Agitator, *der*
**agnostic** [æg'nɒstɪk] *n.* Agnostiker, *der/*Agnostikerin, *die*
**ago** [ə'gəʊ] *adv.* **ten years ~:** vor zehn Jahren; **[not] long ~:** vor [nicht] langer Zeit
**agog** [ə'gɒg] *pred. adj.* gespannt
**agonize** ['ægənaɪz] *v. i.* **~ over sth.** sich *(Dat.)* den Kopf über etw. *(Akk.)* zermartern
**agony** ['ægənɪ] *n.* Todesqualen *Pl.*

**agree** [ə'griː] **1.** *v. i.* **a)** *(consent)* einverstanden sein (**to, with** mit); **b)** *(hold similar opinion)* einer Meinung sein; **they ~d [with me]** sie waren derselben Meinung [wie ich]; **c)** *(reach similar opinion)* **~ on sth.** sich über etw. *(Akk.)* einigen; **d)** *(harmonize)* übereinstimmen; **e) ~ with sb.** *(suit)* jmdm. bekommen. **2.** *v. t.* vereinbaren.
**agreeable** [ə'griːəbl] *adj.* **a)** *(pleasing)* angenehm; **b) be ~ [to sth.]** [mit etw.] einverstanden sein. **agreeably** [ə'griːəblɪ] *adv.* angenehm. **agreed** [ə'griːd] *adj.* einig; vereinbart ⟨*Summe, Zeit*⟩. **a'greement** *n.* Übereinstimmung, *die;* **be in ~ [about sth.]** sich *(Dat.)* [über etw. *(Akk.)*] einig sein
**agricultural** [ægrɪ'kʌltʃərl] *adj.* landwirtschaftlich
**agriculture** ['ægrɪkʌltʃə(r)] *n.* Landwirtschaft, *die*
**aground** [ə'graʊnd] *adj.* **go** *or* **run ~:** auf Grund laufen
**ahead** [ə'hed] *adv.* voraus; **~ of** vor (+ *Dat.*); **be ~ of the others** *(fig.)* den anderen voraus sein
**aid** [eɪd] **1.** *v. t.* **a) ~ sb. [to do sth.]** jmdm. helfen[, etw. zu tun]; **~ed by** unterstützt von; **b)** *(promote)* fördern. **2.** *n.* **a)** *(help)* Hilfe, *die;* **with the ~ of sth./sb.** mit Hilfe einer Sache *(Gen.)/*mit jmds. Hilfe; **in ~ of sb./sth.** zugunsten von jmdm./etw.; **b)** *(source of help)* Hilfsmittel, *das* (**to** für)
**aide** [eɪd] *n.* Berater, *der/*Beraterin, *die*
**Aids** [eɪdz] *n.* Aids *(das)*
**ailment** ['eɪlmənt] *n.* Gebrechen, *das*
**aim** [eɪm] **1.** *v. t.* ausrichten ⟨*Schußwaffe, Rakete*⟩; **~ sth. at sb./sth.** etw. auf jmdn./etw. richten. **2.** *v. i.* **a)** zielen (**at** auf + *Akk.*); **b) ~ to do sth.** beabsichtigen, etw. zu tun; **~ at** *or* **for sth.** *(fig.)* etwas anstreben. **3.** *n.* Ziel, *das;* **take ~ [at sth./sb.]** [auf etw./jmdn.] zielen. **'aimless** *adj.,* **'aimlessly** *adv.* ziellos
**air** [eə(r)] **1.** *n.* **a)** Luft, *die;* **be/go on the ~:** senden; ⟨*Programm:*⟩ gesendet werden; **by ~:** mit dem Flugzeug; *(by ~ mail)* mit Luftpost; **b)** *(facial expression)* Miene, *die;* **c)** **put on ~s** sich aufspielen. **2.** *v. t.* *(ventilate)* lüften; *(make public)* [öffentlich] darlegen
**air: ~-bed** *n.* Luftmatratze, *die;* **~borne** *adj.* **be ~borne** sich in der Luft befinden; **~-conditioned** *adj.* klimatisiert; **~-conditioning** *n.* Klimaanlage, *die;* **~craft** *n., pl. same*

Flugzeug, *das;* ~**craft-carrier** *n.* Flugzeugträger, *der;* ~ **fare** *n.* Flugpreis, *der;* ~**field** *n.* Flugplatz, *der;* ~ **force** *n.* Luftwaffe, *die;* ~**gun** *n.* Luftgewehr, *das;* ~ **hostess** *n.* Stewardeß, *die;* ~ **letter** *n.* Aerogramm, *das;* ~**line** *n.* Fluggesellschaft, *die;* ~ **mail** *n.* Luftpost, *die;* by ~ **mail** mit Luftpost; ~**man** ['eəmən] *n., pl.* ~**men** [~mən] Flieger, *der;* ~**plane** *n.* *(Amer.)* Flugzeug, *das;* ~**port** *n.* Flughafen, *der;* ~ **raid** *n.* Luftangriff, *der;* ~-**raid shelter** *n.* Luftschutzraum, *der;* ~**ship** *n.* Luftschiff, *das;* ~**sick** *adj.* luftkrank; ~**tight** *adj.* luftdicht; ~-**traffic controller** *n.* Fluglotse, *der*

**airy** *adj.* luftig ⟨*Büro, Zimmer*⟩

**aisle** [aıl] *n.* Gang, *der;* (*of church*) Seitenschiff, *das*

**ajar** [ə'dʒɑ:(r)] *adj.* be ~: einen Spaltbreit offenstehen

**akin** [ə'kın] *adj.* be ~ to sth. einer Sache *(Dat.)* ähnlich sein

**alarm** [ə'lɑ:m] **1.** *n.* **a)** Alarm, *der;* give *or* raise the ~: Alarm schlagen; **b)** *(fear)* Angst, *die.* **2.** *v. t.* aufschrecken. **a'larm clock** *n.* Wecker, *der*

**alas** [ə'læs] *int.* ach

**albatross** ['ælbətrɒs] *n.* Albatros, *der*

**album** ['ælbəm] *n.* Album, *das*

**alcohol** ['ælkəhɒl] *n.* Alkohol, *der.* **alcoholic** [ælkə'hɒlık] **1.** *adj.* alkoholisch. **2.** *n.* Alkoholiker, *der*/Alkoholikerin, *die.* **alcoholism** ['ælkəhɒlızm] *n.* Alkoholismus, *der*

**alcove** ['ælkəʊv] *n.* Alkoven, *der*

**ale** [eıl] *n.* Ale, *das*

**alert** [ə'lɜ:t] **1.** *adj.* wachsam. **2.** *n.* Alarmbereitschaft, *die;* on the ~: auf der Hut. **3.** *v. t.* alarmieren; ~ sb. [to sth.] jmdn. [vor etw. *(Dat.)*] warnen

**'A level** *n.* *(Brit. Sch.)* ≈ Abitur, *das*

**algebra** ['ældʒıbrə] *n.* Algebra, *die*

**Algeria** [æl'dʒıərıə] *pr. n.* Algerien *(das)*

**alias** ['eılıəs] **1.** *adv.* alias. **2.** *n.* angenommener Name

**alibi** ['ælıbaı] *n.* Alibi, *das*

**alien** ['eılıən] **1.** *adj.* **a)** *(strange)* fremd; **b)** *(foreign)* ausländisch. **2.** *n.* **a)** *(from another world)* Außerirdische, *der/die;* **b)** *(Admin.: foreigner)* Ausländer, *der*/Ausländerin, *die.* **alienate** ['eılıəneıt] *v. t.* befremden. **alienation** [eılıə'neıʃn] *n.* Entfremdung, *die*

**'alight** [ə'laıt] *v. i.* **a)** aussteigen (**from** aus); **b)** ⟨*Vogel:*⟩ sich niedersetzen

**'alight** *adj.* be/catch ~: brennen; set sth. ~: etw. in Brand setzen

**align** [ə'laın] *v. t.* **a)** *(place in a line)* ausrichten; **b)** *(bring into line)* in eine Linie bringen. **a'lignment** *n.* Ausrichtung, *die;* out of ~: nicht richtig ausgerichtet

**alike** [ə'laık] *pred. adj.* ähnlich; *(indistinguishable)* gleich

**alimony** ['ælımənı] *n.* Unterhaltszahlung, *die*

**alive** [ə'laıv] *pred. adj.* **a)** lebendig; **b)** *(aware)* be ~ to sth. sich *(Dat.)* einer Sache *(Gen.)* bewußt sein; **c)** *(swarming)* be ~ with wimmeln von

**alkali** ['ælkəlaı] *n., pl.* ~s *or* ~es Alkali, *das*

**all** [ɔ:l] **1.** *attrib. adj.* **a)** *(entire extent or quantity of)* ganz; ~ **day** den ganzen Tag; ~ **my money** all mein Geld; mein ganzes Geld; **b)** *(entire number of)* alle; ~ **the books** alle Bücher; ~ **my books** all[e] meine Bücher; ~ **the others** alle anderen; **c)** *(any whatever)* jeglicher/jegliche/jegliches; **d)** *(greatest possible)* **in** ~ **innocence** in aller Unschuld. **2.** *n.* **a)** *(~ persons)* alle; ~ **of us we** **are alle; the happiest of** ~: der/ die Glücklichste unter *od.* von allen; **b)** *(every bit)* ~ **of it** alles; ~ **of the money** das ganze Geld; **c)** ~ **of** *(coll.: as much as)* **be** ~ **of seven feet tall** gut sieben Fuß groß sein; **d)** *(~ things)* alles; ~ **I need is the money** ich brauche nur das Geld; **that is** ~: das ist alles; **the most beautiful of** ~: der/die/das Schönste von allen; **most of** ~: am meisten; **it was** ~ **but impossible** es war fast unmöglich; **it's** ~ **the same to me** es ist mir ganz egal; **can I help you at** ~? kann ich Ihnen irgendwie behilflich sein?; **she has no talent at** ~: sie hat überhaupt kein Talent; **nothing at** ~: gar nichts; **not at** ~ **happy/well** überhaupt nicht glücklich/gesund; **not at** ~! überhaupt nicht!; *(acknowledging thanks)* gern geschehen!; **if at** ~: wenn überhaupt; **in** ~: insgesamt; **e)** *(Sport)* **two [goals]** ~: zwei zu zwei; *(Tennis)* **thirty** ~: dreißig beide. **3.** *adv.* ganz; ~ **but fast;** ~ **the better/ worse [for that]** um so besser/schlimmer; ~ **at once** *(suddenly)* plötzlich; **be** ~ '**in** *(exhausted)* total erledigt sein *(ugs.);* **sth. is** ~ **right** etw. ist in Ordnung; *(tolerable)* etw. ist ganz gut; **I'm** ~ **right** mir geht es ganz gut; **yes,** ~ **right** ja, gut; **it's** ~ **right by me** das ist mir recht

**allay** [ə'leɪ] v. t. zerstreuen ⟨Besorgnis, Befürchtungen⟩

**all-'clear** n. Entwarnung, die

**allegation** [ælɪ'geɪʃn] n. Behauptung, die

**allege** [ə'ledʒ] v. t. behaupten. **alleged** [ə'ledʒd] adj., **allegedly** [ə'ledʒɪdlɪ] adv. angeblich

**allegiance** [ə'li:dʒəns] n. Loyalität, die (to gegenüber)

**allegory** ['ælɪgərɪ] n. Allegorie, die

**allergic** [ə'lɜ:dʒɪk] adj. allergisch (to gegen)

**allergy** ['ælədʒɪ] n. Allergie, die

**alleviate** [ə'li:vɪeɪt] v. t. abschwächen

**alley** ['ælɪ] n. [schmale] Gasse

**alliance** [ə'laɪəns] n. Bündnis, das; (league) Allianz, die

**allied** ['ælaɪd] adj. be ~ to or with sb./ sth. mit jmdm./etw. verbündet sein

**alligator** ['ælɪgeɪtə(r)] n. Alligator, der

**'all-in** adj. Pauschal-

**allocate** ['æləkeɪt] v. t. zuweisen, zuteilen (to Dat.). **allocation** [ælə-'keɪʃn] n. Zuweisung, die; (ration) Zuteilung, die

**allot** [ə'lɒt] v. t., -tt-: ~ sth. to sb. jmdm. etw. zuteilen. **al'lotment** n. (Brit.: plot of land) ≈ Schrebergarten, der

**allow** [ə'laʊ] 1. v. t. erlauben; zulassen; ~ sb. to do sth. jmdm. erlauben, etw. zu tun; be ~ed to do sth. etw. tun dürfen. 2. v. i. ~ for sth. etw. berücksichtigen. **allowance** [ə'laʊəns] n. a) Zuteilung, die; (for special expenses) Zuschuß, der; b) make ~s for sth./sb. etw./jmdn. berücksichtigen

**alloy** ['ælɔɪ] n. Legierung, die

**all:** ~**-round** adj. Allround-; ~**-'rounder** n. Allroundtalent, das; ~**-time** adj. ~**-time record** absoluter Rekord

**allude** [ə'lu:d] v. i. ~ to sich beziehen auf (+ Akk.); (indirectly) anspielen auf (+ Akk.). **allusion** [ə'lu:ʒn] n. Hinweis, der; (indirect) Anspielung, die

**ally** ['ælaɪ] n. Verbündete, der/die; **the Allies** die Alliierten

**almighty** [ɔ:l'maɪtɪ] adj. allmächtig; **the A~:** der Allmächtige

**almond** ['ɑ:mənd] n. Mandel, die

**almost** ['ɔ:lməʊst] adv. fast; beinahe

**alms** [ɑ:mz] n. Almosen, das

**alone** [ə'ləʊn] 1. pred. adj. allein; alleine (ugs.). 2. adv. allein

**along** [ə'lɒŋ] 1. prep. entlang (position: + Dat.; direction: + Akk.). 2. adv.

weiter; **I'll be ~ shortly** ich komme gleich; **all ~:** die ganze Zeit [über]. **along'side 1.** adv. daneben. **2.** prep. neben (position: + Dat.; direction: + Akk.)

**aloof** [ə'lu:f] **1.** adv. abseits; **hold ~ from sb.** sich von jmdm. fernhalten. **2.** adj. distanziert

**aloud** [ə'laʊd] adv. laut; **read [sth.] ~:** [etw.] vorlesen

**alphabet** ['ælfəbet] n. Alphabet, das. **alphabetical** [ælfə'betɪkl] adj., **alpha'betically** adv. alphabetisch

**alpine** ['ælpaɪn] adj. alpin

**Alps** [ælps] pr. n. pl. **the ~:** die Alpen

**already** [ɔ:l'redɪ] adv. schon

**Alsation** [æl'seɪʃn] n. [deutscher] Schäferhund

**also** ['ɔ:lsəʊ] adv. auch; (moreover) außerdem

**altar** ['ɔ:ltə(r), 'ɒltə(r)] n. Altar, der

**alter** ['ɔ:ltə(r), 'ɒltə(r)] **1.** v. t. ändern. **2.** v. i. sich verändern. **alteration** [ɔ:ltə-'reɪʃn, ɒltə'reɪʃn] n. Änderung, die

**alternate 1.** [ɔ:l'tɜ:nət] adj. sich abwechselnd. **2.** ['ɔ:ltəneɪt] v. t. abwechseln lassen. **3.** ['ɔ:ltəneɪt] v. i. sich abwechseln. **al'ternately** adv. abwechselnd

**alternative** [ɔ:l'tɜ:nətɪv] **1.** adj. alternativ; Alternativ-. **2.** n. **a)** (choice) Alternative, die; **b)** (possibility) Möglichkeit, die. **al'ternatively** adv. oder aber; **or ~:** oder aber auch

**although** [ɔ:l'ðəʊ] conj. obwohl

**altitude** ['æltɪtju:d] n. Höhe, die

**altogether** [ɔ:ltə'geðə(r)] adv. völlig; (on the whole) im großen und ganzen; (in total) insgesamt; **not ~ [true/convincing]** nicht ganz [wahr/überzeugend]

**altruistic** [æltrʊ'ɪstɪk] adj. altruistisch

**aluminium** [æljʊ'mɪnɪəm] (Brit.), **aluminum** [ə'lu:mɪnəm] (Amer.) ns. Aluminium, das

**always** ['ɔ:lweɪz] adv. immer; (repeatedly) ständig

**AM** abbr. **amplitude modulation** AM

**am** see **be**

**a.m.** [eɪ'em] adv. vormittags; **[at] one/four ~:** [um] ein/vier Uhr früh

**amalgamate** [ə'mælgəmeɪt] **1.** v. t. vereinigen. **2.** v. i. sich vereinigen. ⟨Firmen:⟩ fusionieren. **amalgamation** [əmælgə'meɪʃn] n. Vereinigung, die; (of firms) Fusion, die

**amass** [ə'mæs] v. t. anhäufen

**amateur** ['æmətə(r)] n. Amateur, der; attrib. Amateur-; Laien-. **amateur-**

**ish** ['æmətərıʃ] *adj.* laienhaft; amateurhaft

**amaze** [ə'meɪz] *v.t.* verblüffen; verwundern. **a'mazement** *n.* Verblüffung, *die;* Verwunderung, *die.* **amazing** [ə'meɪzɪŋ] *adj. (remarkable)* erstaunlich; *(astonishing)* verblüffend

**Amazon** ['æməzən] *pr. n.* the ~: der Amazonas

**ambassador** [æm'bæsədə(r)] *n.* Botschafter, *der/*Botschafterin, *die*

**amber** ['æmbə(r)] 1. *n.* a) Bernstein, *der;* b) *(traffic light)* Gelb, *das.* 2. *adj.* Bernstein-; *(colour)* bernsteinfarben; gelb ⟨*Verkehrslicht*⟩

**ambiguity** [æmbɪ'gjuːɪtɪ] *n.* Zweideutigkeit, *die*

**ambiguous** [æm'bɪgjʊəs] *adj.* zweideutig

**ambition** [æm'bɪʃn] *n.* Ehrgeiz, *der; (aspiration)* Ambition, *die.* **ambitious** [æm'bɪʃəs] *adj.* ehrgeizig

**ambivalent** [æm'bɪvələnt] *adj.* ambivalent

**amble** ['æmbl] *v.i.* schlendern

**ambulance** ['æmbjʊləns] *n.* Krankenwagen, *der;* Ambulanz, *die*

**ambush** ['æmbʊʃ] 1. *n.* Hinterhalt, *der;* lie in ~: im Hinterhalt liegen. 2. *v.t.* [aus dem Hinterhalt] überfallen

**amen** [ɑː'men, eɪ'men] 1. *int.* amen. 2. *n.* Amen, *das*

**amenable** [ə'miːnəbl] *adj.* zugänglich, aufgeschlossen (to *Dat.*)

**amend** [ə'mend] *v.t.* berichtigen; abändern ⟨*Gesetzentwurf, Antrag*⟩. **a'mendment** *n. (to motion)* Abänderungsantrag, *der; (to bill)* Änderungsantrag, *der*

**amends** [ə'mendz] *n. pl.* make ~ [to sb.] es [bei jmdm.] wiedergutmachen; make ~ for sth. etw. wiedergutmachen

**amenity** [ə'miːnɪtɪ] *n., usu. in pl.* amenities *(of town)* kulturelle und Freizeiteinrichtungen

**America** [ə'merɪkə] *pr. n.* Amerika *(das).* **American** [ə'merɪkən] 1. *adj.* amerikanisch; **sb. is ~:** jmd. ist Amerikaner/Amerikanerin. 2. *n. (person)* Amerikaner, *der/*Amerikanerin, *die.* **Americanize** [ə'merɪkənaɪz] *v.t.* amerikanisieren

**amiable** ['eɪmɪəbl] *adj.* umgänglich

**amicable** ['æmɪkəbl] *adj.* freundschaftlich; gütlich ⟨*Einigung*⟩. **amicably** ['æmɪkəblɪ] *adv.* in [aller] Freundschaft

**amid[st]** [ə'mɪd(st)] *prep.* inmitten; *(fig.: during)* bei

**amiss** [ə'mɪs] 1. *pred. adj.* verkehrt; **is anything ~?** stimmt irgend etwas nicht? 2. *adv.* **take sth. ~:** etw. übelnehmen

**ammonia** [ə'məʊnɪə] *n.* Ammoniak, *das*

**ammunition** [æmjʊ'nɪʃn] *n.* Munition, *die*

**amnesia** [æm'niːzɪə] Amnesie, *die*

**amnesty** ['æmnɪstɪ] *n.* Amnestie, *die*

**amok** [ə'mɒk] *adv.* **run ~:** Amok laufen

**among[st]** [ə'mʌŋ(st)] *prep.* unter (+ *Dat.*); ~ **other things** unter anderem; **they often quarrel ~ themselves** sie streiten oft miteinander

**amoral** [eɪ'mɒrl] *adj.* amoralisch

**amorphous** [ə'mɔːfəs] *adj.* formlos; amorph ⟨*Masse*⟩

**amount** [ə'maʊnt] 1. *v.i.* ~ **to sth.** sich auf etw. *(Akk.)* belaufen; *(fig.)* etw. bedeuten. 2. *n.* a) *(total)* Betrag, *der;* Summe, *die;* b) *(quantity)* Menge, *die*

**amp** [æmp] *n.* Ampere, *das*

**amphibian** [æm'fɪbɪən] 1. *adj.* amphibisch. 2. *n.* Amphibie, *die.* **amphibious** [æm'fɪbɪəs] *adj.* amphibisch

**amphitheatre** ['æmfɪθɪətə(r)] *n.* Amphitheater, *das*

**ample** ['æmpl] *adj.* a) *(spacious)* weitläufig ⟨*Garten, Räume*⟩; reichhaltig ⟨*Mahl*⟩; b) *(enough)* ~ **room/food** reichlich Platz/zu essen

**amplifier** ['æmplɪfaɪə(r)] *n.* Verstärker, *der*

**amplify** ['æmplɪfaɪ] *v.t.* verstärken; *(enlarge on)* weiter ausführen

**amputate** ['æmpjʊteɪt] *v.t.* amputieren. **amputation** [æmpjʊ'teɪʃn] *n.* Amputation, *die*

**amuse** [ə'mjuːz] *v.t.* a) *(interest)* unterhalten; ~ **oneself by doing sth.** sich *(Dat.)* die Zeit damit vertreiben, etw. zu tun; b) *(make laugh or smile)* amüsieren. **a'musement** *n.* Belustigung, *die;* ~ **arcade** Spielhalle, *die.* **amusing** [ə'mjuːzɪŋ] *adj.* amüsant

**an** [ən, *stressed* æn] *indef. art. see also* ²**a:** ein/eine/ein

**anaemia** [ə'niːmɪə] *n.* Blutarmut, *die;* Anämie, *die.* **anaemic** [ə'niːmɪk] *adj.* blutarm; anämisch

**anaesthetic** [ænɪs'θetɪk] *n.* Anästhetikum, *das;* **general ~:** Narkosemittel, *das;* **local ~:** Lokalanästhetikum, *das*

**anagram** ['ænəgræm] *n.* Anagramm, *das*

**analogy** [ə'nælədʒɪ] *n.* Analogie, *die*

**analyse** ['ænəlaɪz] *v.t.* analysieren.

**analysis** [ə'nælɪsɪs] *n., pl.* **analyses**
[ə'nælɪsiːz] Analyse, *die.* **analyst**
['ænəlɪst] *n.* **a)** *(Psych.)* Analytiker,
*der/*Analytikerin, *die;* **b)** *(Econ.,
Polit., etc.)* Experte, *der.* **analytic**
[ænə'lɪtɪk], **analytical** [ænə'lɪtɪkl] *adj.*
analytisch. **analyze** *(Amer.) see* **analyse**
**anarchist** ['ænəkɪst] *n.* Anarchist,
*der/*Anarchistin, *die*
**anarchy** ['ænəkɪ] *n.* Anarchie, *die*
**anatomical** [ænə'tɒmɪkl] *adj.* anatomisch
**anatomy** [ə'nætəmɪ] *n.* Anatomie, *die*
**ancestor** ['ænsestə(r)] *n.* Vorfahr, *der.*
**ancestry** ['ænsestrɪ] *n.* Abstammung, *die*
**anchor** ['æŋkə(r)] **1.** *n.* Anker, *der.* **2.**
*v. t.* verankern. **3.** *v. i.* ankern. **an-
chorage** ['æŋkərɪdʒ] *n.* Ankerplatz,
*der*
**anchovy** ['æntʃəvɪ] *n.* Sardelle, *die*
**ancient** ['eɪnʃənt] *adj.* alt; historisch
⟨*Gebäude usw.*⟩; *(of antiquity)* antik
**and** [ənd, *stressed* ænd] *conj.* und; **for
weeks ~ weeks** wochenlang; **better ~
better** immer besser
**anecdote** ['ænɪkdəʊt] *n.* Anekdote,
*die*
**anemia, anemic** *(Amer.) see* **anaem-**
**angel** ['eɪndʒl] *n.* Engel, *der.* **angelic**
[æn'dʒelɪk] *adj.* engelhaft
**anger** ['æŋgə(r)] **1.** *n.* Zorn, *der* **(at**
über + *Akk.*); *(fury)* Wut, *die* **(at** über
+ *Akk.*). **2.** *v. t.* verärgern; *(infuriate)*
wütend machen
**¹angle** ['æŋgl] *n.* **a)** *(Geom.)* Winkel,
*der;* **at an ~ of 60°** im Winkel von 60°;
**at an ~:** schief; **b)** *(fig.)* Gesichtspunkt, *der*
**²angle** *v. i.* angeln; *(fig.)* **~ for sth.** sich
um etw. bemühen. **angler** ['æŋglə(r)]
*n.* Angler, *der/*Anglerin, *die*
**Anglican** ['æŋglɪkən] **1.** *adj.* anglikanisch. **2.** *n.* Anglikaner, *der/*Anglika-
nerin, *die*
**Anglo-** [æŋgləʊ] *in comb.* anglo-/
Anglo-. **Anglo-Saxon** [~'sæksn] **1.**
*n.* Angelsachse, *der/*Angelsächsin,
*die; (language)* Angelsächsisch, *das.*
**2.** *adj.* angelsächsisch
**angrily** ['æŋgrɪlɪ] *adv.* verärgert;
*(stronger)* zornig
**angry** ['æŋgrɪ] *adj.* böse; verärgert
⟨*Person, Stimme, Geste*⟩; *(stronger)*
zornig; wütend; **be ~ at** *or* **about sth.**
wegen etw. böse sein; **be ~ with** *or* **at
sb.** mit jmdm. *od.* auf jmdn. böse sein;
**get ~:** böse werden

**anguish** ['æŋgwɪʃ] *n.* Qualen *Pl.*
**angular** ['æŋgjʊlə(r)] *adj.* eckig ⟨*Gebäude, Struktur*⟩; kantig ⟨*Gesicht*⟩
**animal** ['ænɪməl] **1.** *n.* Tier, *das.* **2.**
*adj.* tierisch
**animate 1.** ['ænɪmeɪt] *v. t.* beleben. **2.**
['ænɪmət] *adj.* beseelt ⟨*Leben, Körper*⟩; belebt ⟨*Objekt, Welt*⟩. **ani-
mated** ['ænɪmeɪtɪd] *adj.* lebhaft ⟨*Diskussion, Gebärde*⟩; **~ cartoon** Zeichentrickfilm, *der.* **animation** [ænɪ-
'meɪʃn] *n.* **a)** Lebhaftigkeit, *die;* **b)**
*(Cinemat.)* Animation, *die*
**animosity** [ænɪ'mɒsɪtɪ] *n.* Feindseligkeit, *die*
**aniseed** ['ænɪsiːd] *n.* Anis[samen], *der*
**ankle** ['æŋkl] *n.* Fußgelenk, *das*
**annex 1.** [ə'neks] *v. t.* annektieren
⟨*Land, Territorium*⟩. **2.** ['æneks] *n.* Anbau, *der.* **annexe** *see* **annex 2**
**annihilate** [ə'naɪɪleɪt] *v. t.* vernichten.
**annihilation** [ənaɪɪ'leɪʃn] *n.* Vernichtung, *die*
**anniversary** [ænɪ'vɜːsərɪ] *n.* Jahres-
tag, *der;* **wedding ~:** Hochzeitstag, *der*
**annotate** ['ænəteɪt] *v. t.* kommentie-
ren
**announce** [ə'naʊns] *v. t.* bekanntgeben; ansagen ⟨*Programm*⟩; *(over
Tannoy etc.)* durchsagen; *(in newspaper)* anzeigen ⟨*Heirat usw.*⟩. **announcement** *n.* Bekanntgabe, *die;
(over Tannoy etc.)* Durchsage, *die; (in
newspaper)* Anzeige, *die.* **an'nouncer**
*n.* Ansager, *der/*Ansagerin, *die*
**annoy** [ə'nɔɪ] *v. t.* **a)** ärgern; **b)** *(harass)*
schikanieren. **annoyance** [ə'nɔɪəns]
*n.* Verärgerung, *die; (nuisance)* Plage,
*die.* **annoyed** [ə'nɔɪd] *adj.* **be ~ [at** *or*
**with sb./sth.]** ärgerlich [auf *od.* über
jmdn./über etw.] sein; **he got very ~:**
er hat sich darüber sehr geärgert. **an-
'noying** *adj.* ärgerlich; lästig ⟨*Gewohnheit, Person*⟩
**annual** ['ænjʊəl] **1.** *adj.* **a)** *(reckoned by
the year)* Jahres-; **~ rainfall** jährliche
Regenmenge; **b)** *(recurring yearly)*
[all]jährlich ⟨*Ereignis, Feier*⟩; Jahres-
⟨*bericht, -hauptversammlung*⟩. **2.** *n.* **a)**
Jahrbuch, *das; (of comic etc.)* Jahres-
album, *das;* **b)** *(plant)* einjährige
Pflanze. **'annually** *adv.* jährlich
**annul** [ə'nʌl] *v. t.,* **-ll-** annullieren; auflösen ⟨*Vertrag*⟩
**anonymous** [ə'nɒnɪməs] *adj.* anonym
**anorak** ['ænəræk] *n.* Anorak, *der*
**anorexia** [ænə'reksɪə] *n.* Anorexie, *die*
*(Med.);* Magersucht, *die (volkst.)*
**another** [ə'nʌðə(r)] **1.** *pron.* **a)** *(an*

*additional one)* noch einer/eine/eins; ein weiterer/eine weitere/ein weiteres; **b)** *(counterpart)* wieder einer/eine/eins; **c)** *(a different one)* ein anderer/eine andere/ein anderes. **2.** *adj.* **a)** *(additional)* noch ein/eine; ein weiterer/eine weitere/ein weiteres; **after** ~ **six weeks** nach weiteren sechs Wochen; **b)** *(different)* ein anderer/eine andere/ein anderes

**answer** ['ɑːnsə(r)] **1.** *n.* **a)** *(reply)* Antwort, *die* (to auf + *Akk.*); **b)** *(to problem)* Lösung, *die* ·(to *Gen.*); *(to calculation)* Ergebnis, *das*. **2.** *v. t.* **a)** beantworten ⟨*Brief, Frage*⟩; antworten auf (+ *Akk.*) ⟨*Frage, Hilferuf, Einladung, Inserat*⟩; eingehen auf (+ *Akk.*) ⟨*Angebot, Vorschlag*⟩; sich stellen zu ⟨*Beschuldigung*⟩; erhören ⟨*Gebet*⟩; erfüllen ⟨*Bitte, Wunsch*⟩; ~ **sb.** jmdm. antworten; **b)** ~ **the door/bell** an die Tür gehen. **3.** *v. i.* **a)** *(reply)* antworten; ~ **to sth.** sich zu etw. äußern; **b)** *(be responsible)* ~ **for sth.** für etw. die Verantwortung übernehmen; **c)** ~ **to a description** einer Beschreibung *(Dat.)* entsprechen. **answerable** ['ɑːnsərəbl] *adj.* verantwortlich (for für; to *Dat.*). **'answering machine** *n.* Anrufbeantworter, *der*

**ant** [ænt] *n.* Ameise, *die*

**antagonism** [æn'tægənɪzm] *n.* Feindseligkeit, *die* (towards, against gegenüber). **antagonist** [æn'tægənɪst] *n.* Gegner, *der*/Gegnerin, *die*. **antagonistic** [æntægə'nɪstɪk] *adj.* feindlich. **antagonize** [æn'tægənaɪz] *v. t.* ~ **sb.** sich *(Dat.)* jmdn. zum Feind machen

**antarctic** [ænt'ɑːktɪk] **1.** *adj.* antarktisch. **2.** *n.* **the A~**: die Antarktis

**antelope** ['æntɪləʊp] *n.* Antilope, *die*

**antenna** [æn'tenə] *n.* **a)** *pl.* ~**e** [æn'teniː] *(Zool.)* Fühler, *der*; **b)** *pl.* ~**s** *(Amer.: aerial)* Antenne, *die*

**anthem** ['ænθəm] *n.* Chorgesang, *der*

**anthology** [æn'θɒlədʒɪ] *n.* Anthologie, *die*

**anthropology** [ænθrə'pɒlədʒɪ] *n.* Anthropologie, *die*

**anti-** [æntɪ] *pref.* anti-/Anti-

**anti-'aircraft** *adj.* *(Mil.)* Flugabwehr-; ~ **gun** Flak, *die*

**antibiotic** [æntɪbaɪ'ɒtɪk] *n.* Antibiotikum, *das*

**antic** ['æntɪk] *n.* *(trick)* Mätzchen, *das* *(ugs.)*; *(of clown)* Possen, *der*

**anticipate** [æn'tɪsɪpeɪt] *v. t.* **a)** *(expect)* erwarten; *(foresee)* voraussehen; ~

*trouble* mit Ärger rechnen; **b)** *(consider before due time)* vorwegnehmen. **anticipation** [æntɪsɪ'peɪʃn] *n.* Erwartung, *die*

**anti'climax** *n.* Abstieg, *der*

**anti'clockwise** *adv., adj.* gegen den Uhrzeigersinn

**anti'cyclone** *n.* Hochdruckgebiet, *das*

**antidote** ['æntɪdəʊt] *n.* Gegenmittel, *das* (for, against, to gegen)

**'antifreeze** *n.* Frostschutzmittel, *das*

**antiquated** ['æntɪkweɪtɪd] *adj.* antiquiert; veraltet

**antique** [æn'tiːk] **1.** *adj.* antik ⟨*Möbel, Schmuck usw.*⟩. **2.** *n.* Antiquität, *die*; ~ **shop** Antiquitätenladen, *der*

**antiquity** [æn'tɪkwɪtɪ] *n.* Altertum, *das*; Antike, *die*

**anti'septic 1.** *adj.* antiseptisch. **2.** *n.* Antiseptikum, *das*

**anti'social** *adj.* asozial

**antithesis** [æn'tɪθəsɪs] *n., pl.* **antitheses** [æn'tɪθəsiːz] Gegenstück, *das* (of, to zu)

**antler** ['æntlə(r)] *n.* Geweihsprosse, *die*; [pair of] ~**s** Geweih, *das*

**anvil** ['ænvɪl] *n.* Amboß, *der*

**anxiety** [æŋ'zaɪətɪ] *n.* Angst, *die*; *(concern about future)* Sorge, *die* (about wegen)

**anxious** ['æŋkʃəs] *adj.* **a)** *(troubled)* besorgt (about um); **b)** *(eager)* sehnlich; **be** ~ **for sth.** sich nach etw. sehnen. **'anxiously** *adv.* **a)** besorgt; **b)** *(eagerly)* sehnsüchtig

**any** ['enɪ] **1.** *adj.* **a)** *(some)* [irgend]ein/eine; **not** ~: kein/keine; **have you** ~ **wool/wine?** haben Sie Wolle/Wein?; **b)** *(one)* ein/eine; **c)** *(all, every)* jeder/jede/jedes; [at] ~ **time** jederzeit; **d)** *(whichever)* jeder/jede/jedes [beliebige]; **choose** ~ |**one**| **book/**~ **books you like** suchen Sie sich *(Dat.)* irgendein Buch/irgendwelche Bücher aus. **2.** *pron.* **a)** *(some)* in condit., interrog., or neg. sentence *(replacing sing. n.)* einer/eine/ein[e]s; *(replacing collect. n.)* welcher/welche/welches; *(replacing pl. n.)* welche; **not** ~: keiner/keine/kein[e]s/*Pl.* keine; **without** ~: ohne; **b)** *(no matter which)* irgendeiner/irgendeine/irgendein[e]s/irgendwelche *Pl.* **3.** *adv.* **do you feel** ~ **better today?** fühlen Sie sich heute [etwas] besser?; **if it gets** ~ **colder** wenn es noch kälter wird; **I can't wait** ~ **longer** ich kann nicht [mehr] länger warten

**'anybody** *n. & pron.* **a)** *(whoever)* jeder; **b)** *(somebody)* [irgend]jemand; *after neg.* niemand

**'anyhow** *adv.* **a)** *see* **anyway; b)** *(haphazardly)* irgendwie

**'anyone** *see* **anybody**

**'anything 1.** *n. & pron.* **a)** *(whatever thing)* was [immer]; alles, was; **b)** *(something)* irgend etwas; *after neg.* nichts; **c)** *(a thing of any kind)* alles. **2.** *adv.* **not ~ like as ... as** keineswegs so ... wie

**'anyway** *adv.* **a)** *(in any case, besides)* sowieso; **b)** *(at any rate)* jedenfalls

**'anywhere** *adv.* **a)** *(in any place) (wherever)* überall, wo; wo [immer]; *(somewhere)* irgendwo; **not ~ near as ... as** *(coll.)* nicht annähernd so ... wie; **b)** *(to any place) (wherever)* wohin [auch immer]; *(somewhere)* irgendwohin

**apart** [ə'pɑːt] *adv.* **a)** *(separately)* getrennt; **~ from ...:** außer ...; **b)** *(into pieces)* auseinander

**apartheid** [ə'pɑːteɪt] *n.* Apartheid, *die*

**apartment** [ə'pɑːtmənt] *n.* **a)** *(room)* Apartment, *das;* **b)** *(Amer.: flat)* Wohnung, *die*

**apathetic** [æpə'θetɪk] *adj.* apathisch **(about** gegenüber)

**apathy** ['æpəθɪ] *n.* Apathie, *die* **(about** gegenüber)

**ape** [eɪp] **1.** *n.* [Menschen]affe, *der.* **2.** *v. t.* nachahmen

**aperitif** [əperɪ'tiːf] *n.* Aperitif, *der*

**aperture** ['æpətʃə(r)] *n.* Öffnung, *die*

**apex** ['eɪpeks] *n.* Spitze, *die*

**aphrodisiac** [æfrə'dɪzɪæk] *n.* Aphrodisiakum, *das*

**apiece** [ə'piːs] *adv.* je; **they cost a penny ~:** sie kosten einen Penny das Stück

**apologetic** [əpɒlə'dʒetɪk] *adj.* entschuldigend; **be ~:** sich entschuldigen **apologize** [ə'pɒlədʒaɪz] *v. i.* sich entschuldigen **(to** bei)

**apology** [ə'pɒlədʒɪ] *n.* Entschuldigung, *die;* **make an ~:** sich entschuldigen **(to** bei)

**apoplectic** [æpə'plektɪk] *adj.* apoplektisch; **~ fit** Schlaganfall, *der*

**apostle** [ə'pɒsl] *n.* Apostel, *der*

**apostrophe** [ə'pɒstrəfɪ] *n.* Apostroph, *der;* Auslassungszeichen, *das*

**appal** *(Amer.:* **appall)** [ə'pɔːl] *v. t.,* **-ll-** entsetzen. **ap'palling** *adj.* entsetzlich

**apparatus** [æpə'reɪtəs] *n.* *(equipment)* Gerät, *das;* *(gymnastic)* Geräte *Pl.;* *(machinery, lit. or fig.)* Apparat, *der;* **a piece of ~:** ein Gerät

**apparent** [ə'pærənt] *adj.* **a)** *(clear)* offensichtlich; offenbar ⟨*Bedeutung, Wahrheit*⟩; **b)** *(seeming)* scheinbar. **ap'parently** *adv.* **a)** *(clearly)* offensichtlich; **b)** *(seemingly)* scheinbar

**apparition** [æpə'rɪʃn] *n.* [Geister]erscheinung, *die*

**appeal** [ə'piːl] **1.** *v. i.* **a)** *(Law etc.)* Einspruch einlegen; **b)** *(make earnest request)* **~ to sb. for sth./to do sth.** jmdn. um etw. ersuchen/jmdn. ersuchen, etw. zu tun; **c)** *(address oneself)* **~ to sb./sth.** an jmdn./etw. appellieren; **d)** *(be attractive)* **~ to sb.** jmdm. zusagen. **2.** *n.* **a)** *(Law etc.)* Einspruch, *der* **(to** bei); *(to higher court)* Berufung, *die* **(to** bei); **b)** *(request)* Appell, *der;* **an ~ to sb. for sth.** eine Bitte an jmdn. um etw.; **c)** *(attraction)* Reiz, *der.* **ap'pealing** *adj.* **a)** *(imploring)* flehend; **b)** *(attractive)* ansprechend; verlockend ⟨*Idee*⟩

**appear** [ə'pɪə(r)] *v. i.* **a)** *(become visible, arrive)* erscheinen; ⟨*Licht, Mond:*⟩ auftauchen; *(present oneself)* auftreten; **b)** *(occur)* vorkommen; **c)** *(seem)* **~ [to be] ...:** scheinen ... [zu sein]. **ap'pearance** [ə'pɪərəns] *n.* **a)** *(becoming visible)* Auftauchen, *das;* *(arrival)* Erscheinen, *das;* *(of performer etc.)* Auftritt, *der;* **b)** *(look)* Äußere, *das;* **to all ~s** allem Anschein nach; **c)** *(semblance)* Anschein, *der;* **d)** *(occurrence)* Vorkommen, *das*

**appease** [ə'piːz] *v. t.* besänftigen; *(Polit.)* beschwichtigen

**append** [ə'pend] *v. t.* anhängen **(to an** + *Akk.*); *(add)* anfügen **(+** *Dat.*). **appendage** [ə'pendɪdʒ] *n.* Anhängsel, *das;* *(addition)* Anhang, *der*

**appendicitis** [əpendɪ'saɪtɪs] *n.* Blinddarmentzündung, *die*

**appendix** [ə'pendɪks] *n., pl.* **appendices** [ə'pendɪsiːz] *or* **~es a)** Anhang, *der* **(to** zu); **b)** *(Anat.)* Blinddarm, *der*

**appetite** ['æpɪtaɪt] *n.* **a)** Appetit, *der* **(for auf** + *Akk.*); **b)** *(fig.)* Verlangen, *das* **(for** nach). **appetizer** ['æpɪtaɪzə(r)] *n.* Appetitanreger, *der.* **appetizing** ['æpɪtaɪzɪŋ] *adj.* appetitlich

**applaud** [ə'plɔːd] **1.** *v. i.* applaudieren; [Beifall] klatschen. **2.** *v. t.* applaudieren **(+** *Dat.*). **applause** [ə'plɔːz] *n.* Beifall, *der;* Applaus, *der*

**apple** ['æpl] *n.* Apfel, *der*

**appliance** [ə'plaɪəns] *n.* Gerät, *das*

**applicable** [ə'plɪkəbl] *adj.* **a)** anwendbar **(to auf** + *Akk.*); **b)** *(appropriate)* geeignet; zutreffend ⟨*Fragebogenteil*⟩

**applicant** ['æplɪkənt] *n.* Bewerber, *der*/Bewerberin, *die* (for um); *(claimant)* Antragsteller, *der*/-stellerin, *die*

**application** [æplɪ'keɪʃn] *n.* **a)** *(request)* Bewerbung, *die* (for um); *(for passport, licence, etc.)* Antrag, *der* (for auf + *Akk.*); ~ **form** Antragsformular, *das;* **b)** *(putting)* Auftragen, *das* (to auf + *Akk.*); **c)** *(use)* Anwendung, *die*

**apply** [ə'plaɪ] **1.** *v.t.* **a)** auftragen ⟨*Creme, Farbe*⟩ (to auf + *Akk.*); **b)** *(make use of)* anwenden. **2.** *v.i.* **a)** *(have relevance)* zutreffen (to auf + *Akk.*); **b)** ~ |to sb.| for sth. [jmdn.] um etw. bitten; *(for passport etc.)* [bei jmdm.] etw. beantragen; *(for job)* sich [bei jmdm.] um etw. bewerben

**appoint** [ə'pɔɪnt] *v.t.* **a)** *(fix)* bestimmen; festlegen ⟨*Zeitpunkt, Ort*⟩; **b)** *(to job)* einstellen; *(to office)* ernennen.

**ap'pointment** *n.* **a)** *(to job)* Einstellung, *die; (to office)* Ernennung, *die* (as zum/zur); **b)** *(job)* Stelle, *die;* **c)** *(arrangement)* Termin, *der;* **make an ~ with sb.** sich *(Dat.)* von jmdm. einen Termin geben lassen; **by ~:** nach Anmeldung

**appreciable** [ə'priːʃəbl] *adj.* **a)** *(perceptible)* nennenswert ⟨*Unterschied, Einfluß*⟩; spürbar ⟨*Veränderung, Wirkung*⟩; merklich ⟨*Verringerung, Anstieg*⟩; **b)** *(considerable)* beträchtlich.

**appreciably** [ə'priːʃəblɪ] *adv.* **a)** *(perceptibly)* spürbar ⟨*verändern*⟩; merklich ⟨*sich unterscheiden*⟩; **b)** *(considerably)* beträchtlich

**appreciate** [ə'priːʃɪeɪt] **1.** *v.t.* **a)** *([correctly] estimate)* [richtig] einschätzen; *(understand)* verstehen; *(be aware of)* sich *(Dat.)* bewußt sein (+ *Gen.*); **b)** *(be grateful for)* schätzen; *(enjoy)* genießen. **2.** *v.i.* im Wert steigen. **appreciation** [əpriːʃɪ'eɪʃn] *n.* **a)** *([correct] estimation)* [richtige] Einschätzung; *(understanding)* Verständnis, *das* (of für); *(awareness)* Bewußtsein, *das;* **b)** *(gratefulness)* Dankbarkeit, *die; (enjoyment)* Gefallen, *das* (of an + *Dat.*). **appreciative** [ə'priːʃətɪv] *adj. (grateful)* dankbar (of für); *(approving)* anerkennend

**apprehend** [æprɪ'hend] *v.t.* **a)** *(arrest)* festnehmen; **b)** *(understand)* erfassen. **apprehension** [æprɪ'henʃn] *n.* Besorgnis, *die.* **apprehensive** [æprɪ'hensɪv] *adj.* besorgt

**apprentice** [ə'prentɪs] *n.* Lehrling, *der* (to bei). **ap'prenticeship** *n.*

*(training)* Lehre, *die; (learning period)* Lehrzeit, *die*

**approach** [ə'prəʊtʃ] **1.** *v.i.* sich nähern; *(in time)* nahen. **2.** *v.t.* **a)** *(come near to)* sich nähern (+ *Dat.*); **b)** *(approximate to)* nahekommen (+ *Dat.*); **c)** *(appeal to)* sich wenden an (+ *Akk.*). **3.** *n.* **a)** [Heran]nahen, *das;* **b)** *(approximation)* Annäherung, *die* (to an + *Akk.*); **c)** *(appeal)* Herantreten, *das* (to an + *Akk.*); **d)** *(access)* Zugang, *der; (road)* Zufahrtsstraße, *die.* **approachable** [ə'prəʊtʃəbl] *adj.* **a)** *(friendly)* umgänglich; **b)** *(accessible)* zugänglich

**appropriate** [ə'prəʊprɪət] *adj.* geeignet (to, for für). **2.** [ə'prəʊprɪeɪt] *v.t.* sich *(Dat.)* aneignen. **appropriately** [ə'prəʊprɪətlɪ] *adv.* gebührend; passend ⟨*gekleidet, genannt*⟩

**approval** [ə'pruːvl] *n.* **a)** *(sanctioning)* Genehmigung, *die; (of proposal)* Billigung, *die; (agreement)* Zustimmung, *die;* **b)** **on ~** *(Commerc.)* zur Probe

**approve** [ə'pruːv] **1.** *v.t.* **a)** *(sanction)* genehmigen ⟨*Plan, Projekt*⟩; billigen ⟨*Vorschlag*⟩; **b)** *(find good)* gutheißen. **2.** *v.i.* ~ **of** billigen; zustimmen (+ *Dat.*) ⟨*Plan*⟩. **approving** [ə'pruːvɪŋ] *adj.* zustimmend ⟨*Worte*⟩; anerkennend ⟨*Blicke*⟩

**approximate** [ə'prɒksɪmət] *adj.* ungefähr *attr.* **ap'proximately** *adv.* ungefähr. **approximation** [əprɒksɪ'meɪʃn] *n.* **a)** Annäherung, *die* (to an + *Dat.*); **b)** *(estimate)* Annäherungswert, *der*

**Apr.** *abbr.* April Apr.

**apricot** ['eɪprɪkɒt] *n.* Aprikose, *die*

**April** ['eɪprəl] *n.* April, *der;* ~ **fool** April[s]narr, *der; see also* **August**

**apron** ['eɪprən] *n.* Schürze, *die*

**apt** [æpt] *adj.* **a)** *(suitable)* passend; treffend ⟨*Bemerkung*⟩; **b)** **be ~ to do sth.** dazu neigen, etw. zu tun

**aptitude** ['æptɪtjuːd] *n.* Begabung, *die* **'aptly** *adv.* passend

**aqualung** ['ækwəlʌŋ] *n.* Tauchgerät, *das*

**aquarium** [ə'kweərɪəm] *n., pl.* ~**s** or **aquaria** [ə'kweərɪə] Aquarium, *das*

**Aquarius** [ə'kweərɪəs] *n.* der Wassermann

**aquatic** [ə'kwætɪk] *adj.* aquatisch; Wasser-; ~ **plant** Wasserpflanze, *die*

**aqueduct** ['ækwɪdʌkt] *n.* Aquädukt, *der od. das*

**Arab** ['ærəb] **1.** *adj.* arabisch. **2.** *n.* Araber, *der*/Araberin, *die*

**Arabian** [ə'reɪbɪən] 1. *adj.* arabisch. 2. *n.* Araber, *der*/Araberin, *die*

**Arabic** ['ærəbɪk] 1. *adj.* arabisch. 2. *n.* Arabisch, *das; see also* **English 2 a**

**arbitrary** ['ɑ:bɪtrərɪ] *adj.* willkürlich

**arbitrate** ['ɑ:bɪtreɪt] 1. *v. t.* schlichten ⟨*Streit*⟩. 2. *v. i.* ~ [upon sth.] [in einer Sache] vermitteln. **arbitration** [ɑ:bɪ'treɪʃn] *n.* Vermittlung, *die; (in industry)* Schlichtung, *die;* **arbitrator** ['ɑ:bɪtreɪtə(r)] *n.* Vermittler, *der; (in industry)* Schlichter, *der*

**arc** [ɑ:k] *n.* [Kreis]bogen, *der*

**arcade** [ɑ:'keɪd] *n.* Arkade, *die*

**arch** [ɑ:tʃ] 1. *n.* Bogen, *der; (of foot)* Wölbung, *die.* 2. *v. t.* beugen ⟨*Rücken*⟩; ~ its back ⟨*Katze:*⟩ einen Buckel machen

**arch-** *pref.* Erz-

**archaeological** [ɑ:kɪə'lɒdʒɪkl] *adj.* archäologisch

**archaeologist** [ɑ:kɪ'ɒlədʒɪst] *n.* Archäologe, *der*/Archäologin, *die*

**archaeology** [ɑ:kɪ'ɒlədʒɪ] *n.* Archäologie, *die*

**archaic** [ɑ:'keɪɪk] *adj.* veraltet

**arch'bishop** *n.* Erzbischof, *der*

**archeology** etc. *(Amer.) see* **archaeology** *etc.*

**archery** ['ɑ:tʃərɪ] *n.* Bogenschießen, *das*

**archetype** ['ɑ:kɪtaɪp] *n. (original)* Urfassung, *die; (typical specimen)* Prototyp, *der*

**architect** ['ɑ:kɪtekt] *n.* Architekt, *der*/Architektin, *die*

**architectural** [ɑ:kɪ'tektʃərl] *adj.* architektonisch

**architecture** ['ɑ:kɪtektʃə(r)] *n.* Architektur, *die*

**archive** ['ɑ:kaɪv] 1. *n.,* usu. in pl. Archiv, *das.* 2. *v. t.* archivieren

**arctic** ['ɑ:ktɪk] 1. *adj.* arktisch; A~ Circle nördlicher Polarkreis; A~ Ocean Nordpolarmeer, *das.* 2. *n.* the A~: die Arktis

**ardent** ['ɑ:dənt] *adj.* leidenschaftlich; brennend ⟨*Wunsch*⟩; *(eager)* begeistert

**ardor** *(Amer.),* **ardour** *(Brit.)* ['ɑ:də(r)] *n.* Leidenschaft, *die*

**arduous** ['ɑ:djʊəs] *adj.* anstrengend

**are** *see* **be**

**area** ['eərɪə] *n.* a) *(surface measure)* Fläche, *die;* Flächeninhalt, *der;* b) *(region)* Gelände, *das; (of wood, marsh, desert)* Gebiet, *das; (of city, country)* Gegend, *die;* parking/picnic ~: Park-/Picknickplatz, *der;* c) *(subject field)* Gebiet, *das*

**arena** [ə'ri:nə] *n.* Arena, *die*

**aren't** [ɑ:nt] *(coll.)* = are not; *see* **be**

**Argentina** [ɑ:dʒən'ti:nə] *pr. n.* Argentinien *(das).* **Argentinian** [ɑ:dʒən'tɪnɪən] 1. *adj.* argentinisch. 2. *n.* Argentinier, *der*/Argentinierin, *die*

**arguable** ['ɑ:gjʊəbl] *adj. (questionable)* fragwürdig. **arguably** ['ɑ:gjʊəblɪ] *adv.* möglicherweise

**argue** ['ɑ:gju:] 1. *v. t.* a) *(maintain)* ~ that ...: die Ansicht vertreten, daß ...; b) *(with reasoning)* darlegen ⟨*Grund, Standpunkt*⟩. 2. *v. i.* ~ with sb. sich mit jmdm. streiten; ~ for/against sth. für/gegen etw. eintreten; ~ about sth. sich über/um etw. *(Akk.)* streiten. **argument** ['ɑ:gjʊmənt] *n.* a) *(reason)* Begründung, *die;* ~s for/against sth. Argumente für/gegen etw.; b) *(reasoning process)* Argumentieren, *das;* c) *(disagreement, quarrel)* Auseinandersetzung, *die.* **argumentative** [ɑ:gju'mentətɪv] *adj.* widerspruchsfreudig

**arid** ['ærɪd] *adj.* trocken

**Aries** ['eəri:z] *n.* der Widder

**arise** [ə'raɪz] *v. i.,* **arose** [ə'rəʊz], **arisen** [ə'rɪzn] a) *(originate)* entstehen; b) *(present itself)* auftreten; ⟨*Gelegenheit:*⟩ sich bieten; c) *(result)* ~ from or out of sth. von etw. herrühren

**aristocracy** [ærɪ'stɒkrəsɪ] *n.* Aristokratie, *die*

**aristocrat** ['ærɪstəkræt] *n.* Aristokrat, *der*/Aristokratin, *die.* **aristocratic** [ærɪstə'krætɪk] *adj.* aristokratisch

**arithmetic** [ə'rɪθmətɪk] *n.* Arithmetik, *die*

**¹arm** [ɑ:m] *n.* Arm, *der*

**²arm** 1. *n.* a) usu. in pl. *(weapon)* Waffe, *die;* up in ~s *(fig.)* in Harnisch (about wegen); b) in pl. *(heraldic device)* Wappen, *das.* 2. *v. t.* bewaffnen

**armada** [ɑ:'mɑ:də] *n.* Armada, *die*

**arm:** ~band *n.* Armbinde, *die;* ~chair *n.* Sessel, *der*

**armed** [ɑ:md] *adj.* bewaffnet; ~ forces Streitkräfte *Pl.*

**armistice** ['ɑ:mɪstɪs] *n.* Waffenstillstand, *der*

**armor** *(Amer.),* **armour** *(Brit.)* ['ɑ:mə(r)] *n.* a) *(Hist.)* Rüstung, *die;* b) *(steel plates)* Panzerung, *die*

**'armpit** *n.* Achselhöhle, *die*

**army** ['ɑ:mɪ] *n.* Heer, *das;* join the ~: zum Militär gehen

**aroma** [ə'rəʊmə] *n.* Duft, *der.* **aromatic** [ærə'mætɪk] *adj.* aromatisch

**arose** *see* **arise**

**around** [ə'raʊnd] 1. *adv.* a) *(on every*

*side)* |**all**| ~: überall; **b)** *(round)* herum; **c)** *(in various places)* **ask/look ~:** herumfragen/sich umsehen. **2.** *prep.* **a)** um [... herum]; **b)** *(approximately)* ~ **3 o'clock** gegen 3 Uhr; **sth.** |**costing**| ~ **£2** etw. für ungefähr 2 Pfund

**arouse** [ə'raʊz] *v. t.* **a)** *(awake)* |auf|wecken; **b)** *(excite)* erregen; erwecken ⟨*Interesse, Begeisterung*⟩; ~ **suspicion** Verdacht erregen

**arrange** [ə'reɪndʒ] **1.** *v. t.* **a)** *(order)* anordnen; **b)** *(settle, agree)* ausmachen, vereinbaren ⟨*Termin*⟩; planen ⟨*Urlaub*⟩; **they ~d to meet the following day** sie verabredeten sich für den nächsten Tag. **2.** *v. i.* *(plan)* sorgen (for für). **ar'rangement** *n.* **a)** *(ordering, order)* Anordnung, *die;* **b)** *(settling, agreement)* Vereinbarung, *die;* **c)** *in pl. (plans)* Vorkehrungen; **make ~s** Vorkehrungen treffen

**arrears** [ə'rɪəz] *n. pl.* Schulden *Pl.;* **be in ~ with sth.** mit etw. im Rückstand sein

**arrest** [ə'rest] **1.** *v. t.* **a)** verhaften, *(temporarily)* festnehmen ⟨*Person*⟩; **b)** *(stop)* aufhalten. **2.** *n.* Verhaftung, *die;* **under ~:** festgenommen

**arrival** [ə'raɪvl] *n.* Ankunft, *die;* **new ~s** Neuankömmlinge

**arrive** [ə'raɪv] *v. i.* **a)** ankommen; ~ **at a conclusion/an agreement** zu einem Schluß/einer Einigung kommen; **b)** ⟨*Stunde, Tag, Augenblick:*⟩ kommen

**arrogance** ['ærəgəns] *n.* Arroganz, *die*

**arrogant** ['ærəgənt] *adj.* arrogant

**arrow** ['ærəʊ] *n.* Pfeil, *der*

**arse** [ɑːs] *n. (coarse)* Arsch, *der (derb)*

**arsenal** ['ɑːsənl] *n.* Waffenlager, *das*

**arsenic** ['ɑːsənɪk] *n.* **a)** Arsenik, *das;* **b)** *(element)* Arsen, *das*

**arson** ['ɑːsn] *n.* Brandstiftung, *die.* **arsonist** ['ɑːsənɪst] *n.* Brandstifter, *der/* Brandstifterin, *die*

**art** [ɑːt] *n.* **a)** Kunst, *die;* **works of ~:** Kunstwerke *Pl.;* ~ **college or school** Kunsthochschule, *die;* ~**s and crafts** Kunsthandwerk, *das;* **b)** *in pl. (branch of study)* Geisteswissenschaften

**artery** ['ɑːtərɪ] *n. (Anat.)* Schlagader, *die;* Arterie, *die (bes. fachspr.)*

**artful** ['ɑːtfl] *adj.* schlau

**'art gallery** *n.* Kunstgalerie, *die*

**arthritic** [ɑː'θrɪtɪk] *adj.* arthritisch.

**arthritis** [ɑː'θraɪtɪs] *n.* Arthritis, *die (fachspr.);* Gelenkentzündung, *die*

**artichoke** ['ɑːtɪtʃəʊk] *n.* |**globe**| ~: Artischocke, *die*

**article** ['ɑːtɪkl] *n.* **a)** *(in magazine,*

*newspaper; Ling.)* Artikel, *der;* **b) an ~ of furniture/clothing** ein Möbel-/Kleidungsstück; **an ~ of value** ein Wertgegenstand

**articulate** [ɑː'tɪkjʊlət] *adj.* redegewandt; **be ~/not very ~:** sich gut/nicht sehr gut ausdrücken |können|

**articulated** [ɑː'tɪkjʊleɪtɪd] *adj.* ~ **'lorry** Sattelzug, *der*

**artificial** [ɑːtɪ'fɪʃl] *adj.* **a)** künstlich; Kunst-; *(not real)* unecht; ~ **limb** Prothese, *die;* **b)** *(affected)* gekünstelt

**artificial:** ~ **insemi'nation** *n.* künstliche Besamung; ~ **in'telligence** *n.* künstliche Intelligenz; ~ **respi'ration** *n.* künstliche Beatmung

**artillery** [ɑː'tɪlərɪ] *n.* Artillerie, *die*

**artisan** ['ɑːtɪzn, ɑːtɪ'zæn] *n.* |Kunst|handwerker, *der*

**artist** ['ɑːtɪst] *n.* Künstler, *der/*Künstlerin, *die*

**artiste** [ɑː'tiːst] *n.* Artist, *der/*Artistin, *die*

**artistic** [ɑː'tɪstɪk] *adj.* **a)** *(of art)* Kunst-; künstlerisch; **b)** *(naturally skilled in art)* künstlerisch veranlagt

**'artless** *adj.* arglos

**as** [əz, *stressed* æz] **1.** *adv., conj.* **a)** he is **as tall as I am** er ist so groß wie ich; **as quickly as you can/as possible** so schnell du kannst/wie möglich; **b)** *(though)* **small as he was** obwohl er klein war; **c)** *(however much)* **try as he might/would, he could not concentrate** sosehr er sich auch bemühte, er konnte sich nicht konzentrieren; **d)** *expr. manner* wie; **as you may already have heard, ...:** wie Sie vielleicht schon gehört haben, ...; **as it were** sozusagen; **e)** *expr. time* als; während; **as we climbed the stairs** als wir die Treppe hinaufgingen; **as we were talking** während wir uns unterhielten; **f)** *expr. reason* da. **2.** *prep.* **a)** *(in the function of)* als; **as an artist** als Künstler; **speaking as a mother ...:** als Mutter ...; **b)** *(like)* wie; **c) the same as ...:** der-/die-/dasselbe wie ...; **such as** wie zum Beispiel. **3.** **as for ...:** was ... angeht *od.* betrifft; **as** |**it**| **is** wie die Dinge liegen; **the place is untidy enough as it is** es ist hier |so| schon unordentlich genug; **as of ...** *(Amer.)* von ... an; **as to** hinsichtlich (+ *Gen.*); **as yet** bis jetzt; noch

**asbestos** [æz'bestɒs] *n.* Asbest, *der*

**ascend** [ə'send] **1.** *v. i.* **a)** *(go up)* hinaufsteigen; *(climb up)* hinaufklettern; *(by vehicle)* hinauffahren; **b)** *(rise)* aufsteigen; ⟨*Hubschrauber:*⟩ höhersteigen; c) *(slope upwards)* ⟨*Hügel, Straße:*⟩ ansteigen. **2.** *v. t.* **a)** *(go up)* hinaufsteigen ⟨*Treppe, Leiter, Berg*⟩; **b)** ~ **the throne** den Thron besteigen **A'scension Day** *n.* Himmelfahrtstag, *der*

**ascent** [ə'sent] *n.* Aufstieg, *der*
**ascertain** [æsə'teɪn] *v. t.* feststellen; ermitteln ⟨*Fakten, Daten*⟩
**ascribe** [ə'skraɪb] *v. t.* zuschreiben (to *Dat.*)
**¹ash** [æʃ] *n. (tree)* Esche, *die*
**²ash** *n. (from fire etc.)* Asche, *die*
**ashamed** [ə'ʃeɪmd] *adj.* beschämt; **be** ~: sich schämen (of wegen)
**ashen** ['æʃn] *adj.* aschfahl ⟨*Gesicht*⟩
**ashore** [ə'ʃɔː(r)] *adv.* an Land
**'ash-tray** *n.* Aschenbecher, *der*
**Ash 'Wednesday** *n.* Aschermittwoch, *der*
**Asia** ['eɪʃə] *pr. n.* Asien *(das)*. **Asian** ['eɪʃən] **1.** *adj.* asiatisch. **2.** *n.* Asiat, *der*/Asiatin, *die*
**aside** [ə'saɪd] *adv.* beiseite; zur Seite
**ask** [ɑːsk] **1.** *v. t.* **a)** fragen; ~ **sb.** |**sth.**| jmdn. [nach etw.] fragen; **b)** *(seek to obtain)* ~ **sth.** um etw. bitten; **how much are you ~ing for that car?** wieviel verlangen Sie für das Auto?; ~ **sb. to do sth.** jmdn. [darum] bitten, etw. zu tun; **c)** *(invite)* einladen. **2.** *v. i.* ~ **after sb./sth.** nach jmdm./etw. fragen; ~ **for sth./sb.** etw./jmdn. verlangen
**askance** [ə'skæns, ə'skɑːns] *adv.* **look** ~ **at sb.** jmdn. befremdet ansehen
**askew** [ə'skjuː] *adv., pred. adj.* schief
**asleep** [ə'sliːp] *pred. adj.* schlafend; **be/lie** ~: schlafen; **fall** ~: einschlafen
**asparagus** [ə'spærəgəs] *n.* Spargel, *der*
**aspect** ['æspekt] *n.* Aspekt, *der*
**aspersion** [ə'spɜːʃn] *n.* **cast** ~**s on sb./ sth.** jmdn./etw in den Schmutz ziehen
**asphalt** ['æsfælt] *n.* Asphalt, *der*
**asphyxiate** [æs'fɪksɪeɪt] *v. t. & i.* ersticken
**aspiration** [æspə'reɪʃn] *n.* Streben, *das*
**aspire** [ə'spaɪə(r)] *v. i.* ~ **to** *or* **after sth.** nach etw. streben
**aspirin** ['æspərɪn] *n.* Aspirin ⓌⒹ, *das;* Kopfschmerztablette, *die*
**ass** [æs] *n.* Esel, *der*
**assailant** [ə'seɪlənt] *n.* Angreifer, *der*/ Angreiferin, *die*
**assassin** [ə'sæsɪn] *n.* Mörder, *der*/ Mörderin, *die*. **assassinate** [ə'sæsɪneɪt] *v. t.* ermorden; **be** ~**d** einem Attentat zum Opfer fallen. **assassina-**

**tion** [əsæsɪ'neɪʃn] *n.* Mord, *der* **(of an** + *Dat.*); ~ **attempt** Attentat, *das* **(on** auf + *Akk.*)
**assault** [ə'sɔːlt] **1.** *n.* Angriff, *der; (fig.)* Anschlag, *der*. **2.** *v. t.* angreifen
**assemble** [ə'sembl] **1.** *v. t.* **a)** zusammentragen; zusammenrufen ⟨*Menschen*⟩; **b)** *(fit together)* zusammenbauen. **2.** *v. i.* sich versammeln. **assembly** [ə'semblɪ] *n.* **a)** *(meeting)* Versammlung, *die; (in school)* Morgenandacht, *die;* **b)** *(fitting together)* Zusammenbau, *der.* **as'sembly line** *n.* Fließband, *das*
**assent** [ə'sent] **1.** *v. i.* zustimmen (to *Dat.*). **2.** *n.* Zustimmung, *die*
**assert** [ə'sɜːt] *v. t.* **a)** geltend machen; ~ **oneself** sich durchsetzen; **b)** *(declare)* behaupten; beteuern ⟨*Unschuld*⟩. **assertion** [ə'sɜːʃn] *n.* **a)** Geltendmachen, *das;* **b)** *(declaration)* Behauptung, *die.* **assertive** [ə'sɜːtɪv] *adj.* energisch ⟨*Person*⟩; bestimmt ⟨*Ton, Verhalten*⟩
**assess** [ə'ses] *v. t.* einschätzen; festsetzen ⟨*Steuer*⟩ **(at** auf + *Akk.*). **as'sessment** *n.* **a)** Einschätzung, *die;* **b)** *(tax to be paid)* Steuerbescheid, *der*
**asset** ['æset] *n.* **a)** Vermögenswert, *der;* **b)** *(useful quality)* Vorzug, *der* **(to** für); *(person)* Stütze, *die; (thing)* Hilfe, *die*
**assiduous** [ə'sɪdjʊəs] *adj.* **a)** *(diligent)* eifrig; **b)** *(conscientious)* gewissenhaft
**assign** [ə'saɪn] *v. t.* **a)** *(allot)* zuweisen (to *Dat.*); **b)** *(appoint)* zuteilen; ~ **sb. to do sth.** jmdn. damit betrauen, etw. zu tun. **as'signment** *n.* **a)** *(allotment)* Zuweisung, *die; (appointment)* Zuteilung, *die;* **b)** *(task)* Aufgabe, *die*
**assimilate** [ə'sɪmɪleɪt] *v. t.* angleichen (to, with an + *Akk.*). **assimilation** [əsɪmɪ'leɪʃn] *n.* Angleichung, *die* (to, with an + *Akk.*)
**assist** [ə'sɪst] **1.** *v. t.* helfen (+ *Dat.*). **2.** *v. i.* helfen; ~ **with sth./in doing sth.** bei etw. helfen/helfen, etw. zu tun. **assistance** [ə'sɪstəns] *n.* Hilfe, *die.* **assistant** [ə'sɪstənt] *n. (helper)* Helfer, *der*/Helferin, *die; (subordinate)* Mitarbeiter, *der*/Mitarbeiterin, *die; (of professor, artist)* Assistent, *der*/Assistentin, *die; (in shop)* Verkäufer, *der*/Verkäuferin, *die*
**associate 1.** [ə'səʊʃɪət, ə'səʊsɪət] *n. (partner)* Partner, *der*/Partnerin, *die; (colleague)* Kollege, *der*/Kollegin, *die.* **2.** [ə'səʊʃɪeɪt, ə'səʊsɪeɪt] *v. t.* in Verbindung bringen; **be** ~**d in** Verbin-

dung stehen. **3.** [əˈsəʊʃɪeɪt, əˈsəʊsɪeɪt] *v. i.* ~ **with sb.** mit jmdm. Umgang haben. **association** [əsəʊsɪˈeɪʃn] *n.* **a)** *(organization)* Vereinigung, *die;* **b)** *(mental connection)* Assoziation, *die;* **c)** *(connection)* Verbindung, *die*

**assorted** [əˈsɔːtɪd] *adj.* gemischt

**assortment** [əˈsɔːtmənt] *n.* Sortiment, *das;* **a good ~ of hats |to choose from|** eine gute Auswahl an Hüten

**assume** [əˈsjuːm] *v. t.* **a)** voraussetzen; **assuming that ...:** vorausgesetzt, daß ...; **b)** *(undertake)* übernehmen ⟨*Amt, Pflichten*⟩; **c)** *(take on)* annehmen ⟨*Namen, Rolle*⟩. **assumption** [əˈsʌmpʃn] *n.* Annahme, *die;* **going on the ~ that ...:** vorausgesetzt, daß ...

**assurance** [əˈʃʊərəns] *n.* **a)** Zusicherung, *die;* **b)** *(self-confidence)* Selbstsicherheit, *die*

**assure** [əˈʃʊə(r)] *v. t.* **a)** versichern (+ *Dat.*); **b)** *(convince)* ~ **sb./oneself** jmdn./sich überzeugen; **c)** *(make certain or safe)* gewährleisten. **assured** [əˈʃʊəd] *adj.* gewährleistet ⟨*Erfolg*⟩; **be ~ of sth.** sich *(Dat.)* einer Sache *(Gen.)* sicher sein

**asterisk** [ˈæstərɪsk] *n.* Sternchen, *das*

**astern** [əˈstɜːn] *adv.* *(Naut., Aeronaut.)* achtern; *(towards the rear)* achteraus

**asteroid** [ˈæstərɔɪd] *n.* Asteroid, *der*

**asthma** [ˈæsmə] *n.* Asthma, *das.* **asthmatic** [æsˈmætɪk] **1.** *adj.* asthmatisch. **2.** *n.* Asthmatiker, *der*/Asthmatikerin, *die*

**astonish** [əˈstɒnɪʃ] *v. t.* erstaunen. **a'stonishing** *adj.* erstaunlich. **a'stonishment** *n.* Erstaunen, *das*

**astound** [əˈstaʊnd] *v. t.* verblüffen. **a'stounding** *adj.* erstaunlich

**astray** [əˈstreɪ] *adv.* **sth. goes ~** *(is mislaid)* etw. wird verlegt; *(is lost)* etw. geht verloren; **go/lead ~** *(fig.)* in die Irre gehen/führen

**astride** [əˈstraɪd] **1.** *adv.* rittlings ⟨*sitzen*⟩. **2.** *prep.* rittlings auf (+ *Dat.*)

**astringent** [əˈstrɪndʒənt] *adj.* scharf

**astrologer** [əˈstrɒlədʒə(r)] *n.* Astrologe, *der*/Astrologin, *die*

**astrological** [æstrəˈlɒdʒɪkl] *adj.* astrologisch

**astrology** [əˈstrɒlədʒɪ] *n.* Astrologie, *die*

**astronaut** [ˈæstrənɔːt] *n.* Astronaut, *der*/Astronautin, *die*

**astronomer** [əˈstrɒnəmə(r)] *n.* Astronom, *der*/Astronomin, *die*

**astronomical** [æstrəˈnɒmɪkl] *adj.* astronomisch

**astronomy** [əˈstrɒnəmɪ] *n.* Astronomie, *die*

**astute** [əˈstjuːt] *adj.* scharfsinnig

**asylum** [əˈsaɪləm] *n.* Asyl, *das*

**at** [ət, *stressed* æt] *prep.* **a)** *expr. place* an (+ *Dat.*); **at the station** am Bahnhof; **at the baker's/butcher's/grocer's** beim Bäcker/Fleischer/Kaufmann; **at the chemist's** in der Apotheke/Drogerie; **at the supermarket** im Supermarkt; **at the party** auf der Party; **at the office/hotel** im Büro/Hotel; **at Dover** in Dover; **b)** *expr. time* **at Christmas** [zu *od.* an] Weihnachten; **at six o'clock** um sechs Uhr; **at midnight** um Mitternacht; **at midday** am Mittag; **at |the age of|** 40 mit 40; im Alter von 40; **at this/the moment** in diesem/im Augenblick *od.* Moment; **c)** *expr. price* **at £2.50 |each|** zu *od.* für [je] 2,50 Pfund; **d)** *expr. speed* **at 30 m. p. h.** *etc.* mit dreißig Meilen pro Stunde *usw.;* **e)** **at that** *(at that point)* dabei; *(at that provocation)* daraufhin; *(moreover)* noch dazu.

**ate** *see* **eat**

**atheism** [ˈeɪθɪɪzm] *n.* Atheismus, *der.* **atheist** [ˈeɪθɪɪst] *n.* Atheist, *der*/Atheistin, *die*

**Athens** [ˈæθɪnz] *pr. n.* Athen *(das)*

**athlete** [ˈæθliːt] *n.* Athlet, *der*/Athletin, *die;* *(runner, jumper)* Leichtathlet, *der*/Leichtathletin, *die.* **athletic** [æθˈletɪk] *adj.* sportlich. **ath'letics** *n.* Leichtathletik, *die*

**Atlantic** [ətˈlæntɪk] **1.** *adj.* atlantisch; **~ Ocean** Atlantischer Ozean. **2.** *pr. n.* Atlantik, *der*

**atlas** [ˈætləs] *n.* Atlas, *der*

**atmosphere** [ˈætməsfɪə(r)] *n.* Atmosphäre, *die.* **atmospheric** [ætməsˈferɪk] *adj.* atmosphärisch

**atom** [ˈætəm] *n.* Atom, *das.* '**atom bomb** *n.* Atombombe, *die*

**atomic** [əˈtɒmɪk] *adj.* Atom-

**atomizer** [ˈætəmaɪzə(r)] *n.* Zerstäuber, *der*

**atone** [əˈtəʊn] *v. i.* es wiedergutmachen; **~ for sth.** etw. wiedergutmachen. **a'tonement** *n.* Buße, *die*

**atrocious** [əˈtrəʊʃəs] *adj.* grauenhaft; scheußlich ⟨*Wetter, Benehmen*⟩. **a'trociously** *adv.* grauenhaft; scheußlich ⟨*sich benehmen*⟩. **atrocity** [əˈtrɒsɪtɪ] *n.* **a)** *(wickedness)* Grauenhaftigkeit, *die;* **b)** *(deed)* Greueltat, *die*

**attach** [əˈtætʃ] *v. t.* **a)** *(fasten)* befestigen (to an + *Dat.*); **please find ~ed a copy of the letter** beigeheftet ist eine

Kopie des Briefes; b) *(fig.)* ~ **import-ance to sth.** einer Sache *(Dat.)* Gewicht beimessen

**attaché** [ə'tæʃeɪ] *n.* Attaché, *der.* **at-'taché case** *n.* Diplomatenkoffer, *der*

**attached** [ə'tætʃt] *adj. (emotionally)* be ~ **to sb./sth.** an jmdm./etw. hängen

**at'tachment** *n.* **a)** *(act or means of fastening)* Befestigung, *die;* **b)** *(affection)* Anhänglichkeit, *die* **(to an +** *Akk.);* **c)** *(accessory)* Zusatzgerät, *das*

**attack** [ə'tæk] **1.** *v. t.* **a)** angreifen; *(ambush, raid)* überfallen; *(fig.: criticize)* attackieren; **b)** *(affect)* ⟨*Krankheit:*⟩ befallen. **2.** *v. i.* angreifen. **3.** *n.* Angriff, *der; (ambush)* Überfall, *der; (fig.: criticism)* Attacke, *die; (of illness)* Anfall, *der.* **at'tacker** *n.* Angreifer, *der/*Angreiferin, *die*

**attain** [ə'teɪn] *v. t.* erreichen. **at'tain-ment** *n.* Verwirklichung, *die*

**attempt** [ə'tempt] **1.** *v. t.* versuchen. **2.** *n.* Versuch, *der*

**attend** [ə'tend] **1.** *v. i.* **a)** *(give care and thought)* aufpassen; *(apply oneself)* ~ **to sth.** *(deal with sth.)* sich um etw. kümmern; **b)** *(be present)* anwesend sein **(at** bei**). 2.** *v. t.* **a)** *(be present at)* teilnehmen an **(+** *Dat.); (go regularly to)* besuchen; **b)** *(wait on)* bedienen **(+** *Dat.);* **c)** ⟨*Arzt:*⟩ behandeln. **at-'tendance** [ə'tendəns] *n.* Anwesenheit, *die; (number of people)* Teilnehmerzahl, *die.* **attendant** [ə'tendənt] *n.* **a)** |*lavatory*| ~: Toilettenmann, *der/-*frau, *die;* |*cloakroom*| ~: Garderobenmann, *der/-*frau, *die;* **museum** ~: Museumswärter, *der/-*wärterin, *die;* **b)** *(member of entourage)* Begleiter, *der/*Begleiterin, *die*

**attention** [ə'tenʃn] **1.** *n.* **a)** Aufmerksamkeit, *die;* **attract** |*sb.'s*| ~: |jmdn.| auf sich *(Akk.)* aufmerksam machen; **pay** ~ **to sb./sth.** jmdn./etw. beachten; **pay** ~! gib acht!; paß auf!; **hold sb.'s** ~: jmds. Interesse wachhalten; ~ **Miss Jones** *(on letter)* zu Händen [von] Miss Jones; **b)** *(Mil.)* **stand to** ~: stillstehen. **2.** *int.* **a)** Achtung; **b)** *(Mil.)* stillgestanden

**attentive** [ə'tentɪv] *adj.* aufmerksam

**attic** ['ætɪk] *n. (room)* Dachboden, *der; (habitable)* Dachkammer, *die*

**attire** [ə'taɪə(r)] *n.* Kleidung, *die*

**attitude** ['ætɪtjuːd] *n.* **a)** Haltung, *die;* **b)** *(mental* ~*)* Einstellung, *die*

**attorney** [ə'tɜːnɪ] *n.* **a)** Bevollmächtig-te, *der/die;* **power of** ~: Vollmacht,

*die;* **b)** *(Amer.: lawyer)* [Rechts]anwalt, *der/-*anwältin, *die*

**attract** [ə'trækt] *v. t.* **a)** *(draw)* anziehen; **auf sich** *(Akk.)* ziehen ⟨*Interesse, Blick, Kritik*⟩; **b)** *(arouse pleasure in)* anziehend wirken auf **(+** *Akk.);* **c)** *(arouse interest in)* reizen **(about an +** *Dat.).* **attraction** [ə'trækʃn] *n.* **a)** Anziehung, *die; (force, lit. or fig.)* Anziehung[skraft], *die;* **b)** *(fig.: thing that attracts)* Attraktion, *die; (charm)* Verlockung, *die;* Reiz, *der.* **attractive** [ə'træktɪv] *adj.* **a)** anziehend; **b)** *(fig.)* attraktiv; reizvoll ⟨*Vorschlag, Möglichkeit, Idee*⟩

**attribute 1.** ['ætrɪbjuːt] *n.* Eigenschaft, *die.* **2.** [ə'trɪbjuːt] *v. t.* zuschreiben **(to** *Dat.).* **attributive** [ə'trɪbjʊtɪv] *adj. (Ling.)* attributiv

**aubergine** ['əʊbəʒiːn] *n.* Aubergine, *die*

**auburn** ['ɔːbən] *adj.* rötlichbraun

**auction** ['ɔːkʃn] **1.** *n.* Versteigerung, *die.* **2.** *v. t.* versteigern. **auctioneer** [ˌɔːkʃə'nɪə(r)] *n.* Auktionator, *der/* Auktionatorin, *die*

**audacious** [ɔː'deɪʃəs] *adj.* **a)** *(daring)* kühn; verwegen; **b)** *(impudent)* dreist. **audacity** [ɔː'dæsɪtɪ] *n.* **a)** *(daringness)* Kühnheit, *die;* Verwegenheit, *die;* **b)** *(impudence)* Dreistigkeit, *die*

**audible** ['ɔːdɪbl] *adj.* hörbar

**audience** ['ɔːdɪəns] *n.* **a)** Publikum, *das;* **b)** *(formal interview)* Audienz, *die* **(with** bei**)**

**audio** ['ɔːdɪəʊ] *adj.* Ton-. **'audio typ-ist** *n.* Phonotypist, *der/-*typistin, *die.* **audio'visual** *adj.* audiovisuell

**audit** ['ɔːdɪt] **1.** *n.* ~ |*of the accounts*| Rechnungsprüfung, *die.* **2.** *v. t.* prüfen

**audition** [ɔː'dɪʃn] **1.** *n. (singing)* Vorsingen, *das; (dancing)* Vortanzen, *das; (acting)* Vorsprechen, *das.* **2.** *v. i. (sing)* vorsingen; *(dance)* vortanzen; *(act)* vorsprechen. **3.** *v. t.* vorsingen/ vortanzen/vorsprechen lassen

**auditor** ['ɔːdɪtə(r)] *n.* Buchprüfer, *der/-*prüferin, *die*

**auditorium** [ɔːdɪ'tɔːrɪəm] *n.* Zuschauerraum, *der*

**Aug.** *abbr.* August Aug.

**augment** [ɔːg'ment] *v. t.* verbessern ⟨*Einkommen*⟩; aufstocken ⟨*Fonds*⟩

**augur** ['ɔːgə(r)] **1.** *v. t.* bedeuten; versprechen ⟨*Erfolg*⟩. **2.** *v. i.* ~ **well/ill for sth./sb.** ein gutes/schlechtes Zeichen für etw./jmdn. sein

**August** ['ɔːgəst] *n.* August, *der;* **in** ~: im August; **last/next** ~: letzten/nächsten August; **the first of/on the first of** ~: der erste/am ersten August

**aunt** [ɑ:nt] n. Tante, die

**auntie, aunty** ['ɑ:ntɪ] n. (coll.) Täntchen, das; (with name) Tante, die

**au pair** [əʊ 'peə(r)] n. Au-pair-Mädchen, das

**aura** ['ɔ:rə] n. Aura, die

**auspices** ['ɔ:spɪsɪs] n. pl. **under the ~ of sb./sth.** unter jmds./einer Sache Schirmherrschaft

**auspicious** [ɔ:'spɪʃəs] adj. günstig; vielversprechend ⟨Anfang⟩

**austere** [ɒ'stɪə(r)] adj. a) (strict, stern) streng; b) (severely simple) karg. **austerity** [ɒ'sterɪtɪ] n. a) (strictness) Strenge, die; b) (severe simplicity) Kargheit, die; c) (lack of luxuries) wirtschaftliche Einschränkung

**Australia** [ɒ'streɪlɪə] pr. n. Australien (das). **Australian** [ɒ'streɪlɪən] 1. adj. australisch. 2. n. Australier, der/Australierin, die

**Austria** ['ɒstrɪə] pr. n. Österreich (das). **Austrian** ['ɒstrɪən] 1. adj. österreichisch. 2. n. Österreicher, der/Österreicherin, die

**authentic** [ɔ:'θentɪk] adj. authentisch. **authenticity** [ɔ:θen'tɪsɪtɪ] n. Authentizität, die

**author** ['ɔ:θə(r)] n. Autor, der/Autorin, die; (profession) Schriftsteller, der/Schriftstellerin, die

**authoritarian** [ɔ:θɒrɪ'teərɪən] 1. adj. autoritär. 2. n. autoritäre Person

**authoritative** [ɔ:'θɒrɪtətɪv] adj. maßgebend; zuverlässig ⟨Bericht, Information⟩

**authority** [ɔ:'θɒrɪtɪ] n. a) Autorität, die; **in ~:** verantwortlich; b) **the authorities** die Behörde[n]

**authorization** [ɔ:θəraɪ'zeɪʃn] n. Genehmigung, die

**authorize** ['ɔ:θəraɪz] v. t. a) ermächtigen; bevollmächtigen; b) (sanction) genehmigen

**auto** ['ɔ:təʊ] n., pl. ~s (Amer. coll.) Auto, das

**auto-** [ɔ:təʊ] in comb. auto-/Auto-

**autobio'graphical** adj. autobiographisch

**autobi'ography** n. Autobiographie, die

**autocratic** [ɔ:tə'krætɪk] adj. autokratisch

**autograph** ['ɔ:təgrɑ:f] 1. n. Autogramm, das. 2. v. t. signieren

**automate** ['ɔ:təmeɪt] v. t. automatisieren

**automatic** [ɔ:tə'mætɪk] 1. adj. automatisch. 2. n. (weapon) automatische Waffe; (vehicle) Fahrzeug mit Automatikgetriebe. **automatically** [ɔ:tə'mætɪkəlɪ] adv. automatisch

**automation** [ɔ:tə'meɪʃn] n. Automation, die

**automobile** ['ɔ:təməbi:l] n. (Amer.) Auto, das

**autonomous** [ɔ:'tɒnəməs] adj. autonom. **autonomy** [ɔ:'tɒnəmɪ] n. Autonomie, die

**autopsy** ['ɔ:tɒpsɪ] n. Autopsie, die

**autumn** ['ɔ:təm] n. Herbst, der; **in [the] ~:** im Herbst. **autumnal** [ɔ:'tʌmnl] adj. herbstlich

**auxiliary** [ɔ:g'zɪljərɪ] 1. adj. Hilfs-. 2. n. a) Hilfskraft, die; b) (Ling.) Hilfsverb, das

**avail** [ə'veɪl] 1. n. **be of no ~:** nichts nützen; **to no ~:** vergebens. 2. v. refl. **~ oneself of sth.** von etw. Gebrauch machen

**available** [ə'veɪləbl] adj. a) (at one's disposal) verfügbar; b) (obtainable) erhältlich; lieferbar ⟨Waren⟩

**avalanche** ['ævəlɑ:nʃ] n. Lawine, die

**avarice** ['ævərɪs] n. Geldgier, die; Habsucht, die. **avaricious** [ævə'rɪʃəs] adj. geldgierig; habsüchtig

**avenge** [ə'vendʒ] v. t. rächen

**avenue** ['ævənju:] n. Allee, die; (fig.) Weg, der (to zu)

**average** ['ævərɪdʒ] 1. n. Durchschnitt, der; **on ~:** im Durchschnitt; durchschnittlich. 2. adj. durchschnittlich. 3. v. t. a) (find the ~ of) den Durchschnitt ermitteln von; b) (amount on to) durchschnittlich betragen. 4. v. i. **~ out at** im Durchschnitt betragen

**averse** [ə'vɜ:s] adj. **be ~ to sth.** einer Sache (Dat.) abgeneigt sein. **aversion** [ə'vɜ:ʃn] n. Abneigung, die (to gegen)

**avert** [ə'vɜ:t] v. t. abwenden; verhüten ⟨Unfall⟩

**aviary** ['eɪvɪərɪ] n. Vogelhaus, das

**aviation** [eɪvɪ'eɪʃn] n. Luftfahrt, die

**avid** ['ævɪd] adj. (enthusiastic) begeistert; **be ~ for sth.** (eager, greedy) begierig auf etw. (Akk.) sein

**avocado** [ævə'kɑ:dəʊ] n., pl. ~s: ~ [pear] Avocado[birne], die

**avoid** [ə'vɔɪd] v. t. a) meiden ⟨Ort⟩; **~ a cyclist** einem Radfahrer ausweichen; **~ the boss when he's in a temper** geh dem Chef aus dem Weg, wenn er schlechte Laune hat; b) (refrain from, escape) vermeiden. **avoidable** [ə'vɔɪdəbl] *adj.* vermeidbar. **avoidance** [ə'vɔɪdəns] *n.* Vermeidung, *die*

**await** [ə'weɪt] *v. t.* erwarten

**awake** [ə'weɪk] **1.** *v. i.,* awoke [ə'wəʊk], awoken [ə'wəʊkn] erwachen. **2.** *v. t.,* awoke, awoken wecken. **3.** *pred. adj.* wach; **wide** ~: hellwach

**awaken** [ə'weɪkn] *v. t. & i. (esp. fig.) see* **awake** 1, 2

**award** [ə'wɔːd] **1.** *v. t.* verleihen ‹*Preis, Auszeichnung*›; zusprechen ‹*Sorgerecht, Entschädigung*›; gewähren ‹*Zahlung, Gehaltserhöhung*›. **2.** *n. (prize)* Auszeichnung, *die*

**aware** [ə'weə(r)] *adj.* **be** ~ **of sth.** sich (*Dat.*) einer Sache (*Gen.*) bewußt sein; **be** ~ **that** ...: sich (*Dat.*) [dessen] bewußt sein, daß ... **a'wareness** *n.* Bewußtsein, *das*

**awash** [ə'wɒʃ] *adj.* **be** ~ *(flooded)* unter Wasser stehen

**away** [ə'weɪ] **1.** *adv.* **a)** *(at a distance)* entfernt; **play** ~ *(Sport)* auswärts spielen; **b)** *(to a distance)* weg; fort; **c)** *(absent)* nicht da. **2.** *adj. (Sport)* auswärts präd.; Auswärts-

**awe** [ɔː] *n.* Ehrfurcht, *die* (of vor + *Dat.*)

**awful** ['ɔːfl] *adj.,* '**awfully** *adv.* furchtbar

**awkward** ['ɔːkwəd] *adj.* **a)** *(difficult to use)* ungünstig; **be** ~ **to use** unhandlich sein; **b)** *(clumsy)* unbeholfen; **c)** *(embarrassing)* peinlich; **d)** *(difficult)* schwierig; ungünstig ‹*Zeitpunkt*›

**awning** ['ɔːnɪŋ] *n. (on house)* Markise, *die; (of tent)* Vordach, *das*

**awoke, awoken** *see* **awake**

**awry** [ə'raɪ] *adv.* schief; **go** ~ *(fig.)* schiefgehen *(ugs.);* ‹*Plan:*› fehlschlagen

**axe** [æks] *n.* Axt, *die;* Beil, *das*

**axis** ['æksɪs] *n., pl.* **axes** ['æksiːz] Achse, *die*

**axle** ['æksl] *n.* Achse, *die*

# B

**B, b** [biː] *n.* B, b, *das*
**BA** *abbr.* **Bachelor of Arts**
**babble** ['bæbl] *v. i.* **a)** *(talk incoherently)* stammeln; **b)** *(talk foolishly)*

[dumm] schwatzen; **c)** ‹*Bach:*› plätschern

**baboon** [bə'buːn] *n.* Pavian, *der*

**baby** ['beɪbɪ] *n.* **a)** Baby, *das;* **have a ~/be going to have a ~:** ein Kind bekommen; **b)** *(childish person)* **be a ~:** sich wie ein kleines Kind benehmen. '**baby-carriage** *n. (Amer.)* Kinderwagen, *der*

'**babyish** *adj.* kindlich ‹*Aussehen*›; kindisch ‹*Benehmen, Person*›

**baby:** ~-**minder** *n.* Tagesmutter, *die;* ~-**sit** *v. i.,* forms as **sit** 1 babysitten *(ugs.);* auf das Kind/die Kinder aufpassen; ~-**sitter** *n.* Babysitter, *der*

**bachelor** ['bætʃələ(r)] *n.* **a)** Junggeselle, *der;* **b)** *(Univ.)* **B~ of Arts/Science** Bakkalaureus der philosophischen Fakultät/der Naturwissenschaften

**back** [bæk] **1.** *n.* **a)** *(of person, animal)* Rücken, *der; (of house, cheque)* Rückseite, *die; (of vehicle)* Heck, *das; (inside car)* Rücksitz, *der;* **stand ~ to ~:** Rücken an Rücken stehen; ~ **to front** verkehrt rum; **turn one's ~ on sb.** jmdm. den Rücken zuwenden; *(fig.)* jmdn. im Stich lassen; **turn one's ~ on sth.** *(fig.)* sich um etw. nicht kümmern; **get** *or* **put sb.'s ~ up** *(fig.)* jmdn. wütend machen; **be glad to see the ~ of sb./sth.** *(fig.)* froh sein, jmdn./etw. nicht mehr sehen zu müssen; **have one's ~ to the wall** *(fig.)* mit dem Rücken zur Wand stehen; **put one's ~ into sth.** *(fig.)* sich für etw. mit allen Kräften einsetzen; **with the ~ of one's hand** mit dem Handrücken; **at the ~ [of the book]** hinten [im Buch]; **b)** *(Sport: player)* Verteidiger, *der.* **2.** *adj.* hinter... **3.** *adv.* zurück; **two miles ~:** vor zwei Meilen; ~ **and forth** hin und her; **there and ~:** hin und zurück; **a week/month ~:** vor einer Woche/vor einem Monat. **4.** *v. t.* **a)** *(assist)* unterstützen; **b)** *(bet on)* wetten od. setzen auf (+ *Akk.*); **c)** zurücksetzen [mit] ‹*Fahrzeug*›. **5.** *v. i.* zurücksetzen; ~ **into/out of sth.** rückwärts in etw. *(Akk.)*/aus etw. fahren; ~ **on to sth.** hinten an etw. *(Akk.)* grenzen. **back 'down** *v. i.* nachgeben. **back 'out** *v. i.* rückwärts herausfahren; ~ **out of sth.** *(fig.)* von etw. zurücktreten. **back 'up** *v. t.* unterstützen; untermauern ‹*Anspruch, These*›

**back:** ~-**ache** *n.* Rückenschmerzen *Pl.;* ~-**bencher** [bæk'bentʃə(r)] *n. (Brit. Parl.)* [einfacher] Abgeordneter/[einfache] Abgeordnete; ~-**bone** *n.*

Rückgrat, *das;* ~**chat** *n. (coll.)* [freche] Widerrede; ~**date** *v. t.* zurückdatieren (to auf + *Akk.*); ~ '**door** *n.* Hintertür, *die*

'**backer** *n.* Geldgeber, *der*

**back:** ~-'**fire** *v. i.* knallen; *(fig.)* fehlschlagen; **it** ~**fired on me/him** *etc.* der Schuß ging nach hinten los *(ugs.);* ~**ground** *n.* Hintergrund, *der; (social status)* Herkunft, *die;* ~**hand** *(Tennis etc.)* **1.** *adj.* Rückhand-; **2.** *n.* Rückhand, *die;* ~-'**handed** *adj.* **a)** *(Tennis etc.)* Rückhand-; **b)** *(fig.)* indirekt; zweifelhaft ⟨*Kompliment*⟩; ~'**hander** *n. (sl.: bribe)* Schmiergeld, *das*

'**backing** *n. (support)* Unterstützung, *die*

**back:** ~**lash** *n. (fig.)* Gegenreaktion, *die;* ~**log** *n.* Rückstand, *der;* ~ **number** *n.* alte Nummer; ~-**pedal** *v. i.* die Pedale rückwärts treten; ~ '**seat** *n.* Rücksitz, *der;* ~**side** *n.* Hinterteil, *das (ugs.);* ~**stage** *adv.* go ~**stage** hinter die Bühne gehen; ~ **street** *n.* kleine Seitenstraße; ~**stroke** *n.* Rückenschwimmen, *das*

**backward** ['bækwəd] **1.** *adj.* **a)** rückwärts gerichtet; Rückwärts-; **b)** *(reluctant, shy)* zurückhaltend; **c)** *(underdeveloped)* rückständig ⟨*Land, Region*⟩. **2.** *adv. see* **backwards**

**backwards** ['bækwədz] *adv.* **a)** nach hinten; **the child fell** [over] ~ **into the water** das Kind fiel rückwärts ins Wasser; **bend** *or* **lean over** ~ **to do sth.** *(fig. coll.)* sich zerreißen, um etw. zu tun *(ugs.);* **b)** *(oppositely to normal direction)* rückwärts; ~ **and forwards** hin und her

**back:** ~**water** *n. (fig.)* Kaff, *das (ugs.);* ~ '**yard** *n.* Hinterhof, *der*

**bacon** ['beɪkn] *n.* [Frühstücks]speck, *der*

**bacterium** [bæk'tɪərɪəm] *n., pl.* **bacteria** [bæk'tɪərɪə] Bakterie, *die*

**bad** [bæd] *adj.,* **worse** [wɜːs], **worst** [wɜːst] **a)** schlecht; *(rotten)* schlecht, verdorben ⟨*Fleisch, Fisch, Essen*⟩; faul ⟨*Ei, Apfel*⟩; **not** ~ *(coll.)* nicht schlecht; nicht übel; **b)** *(naughty)* ungezogen, böse ⟨*Kind, Hund*⟩; **c)** *(offensive)* [use] ~ **language** Kraftausdrücke [benutzen]; **d)** *(regretful)* **feel** ~ **about sth.** etw. bedauern; **I feel** ~ **about him** ich habe seinetwegen ein schlechtes Gewissen; **e)** *(serious)* schlimm ⟨*Sturz, Krise*⟩; schwer ⟨*Fehler, Krankheit, Unfall*⟩; **f)** *(Commerc.)* **a** ~ **debt** eine uneinbringliche Schuld

**bade** *see* **bid 1 b**

**badge** [bædʒ] *n.* Abzeichen, *das*

**badger** ['bædʒə(r)] *n.* Dachs, *der*

'**badly** *adv.,* **worse** [wɜːs], **worst** [wɜːst] **a)** schlecht; **b)** schwer ⟨*verletzt, beschädigt*⟩; **c)** *(urgently)* dringend

**bad-mannered** [bæd'mænəd] *adj.* **be** ~: schlechte Manieren haben

**badminton** ['bædmɪntən] *n.* Federball, *der; (als Sport)* Badminton, *das*

**bad-tempered** [bæd'tempəd] *adj.* griesgrämig

**baffle** ['bæfl] *v. t.* ~ **sb.** jmdm. unverständlich sein. **baffling** ['bæflɪŋ] *adj.* rätselhaft

**bag** [bæg] **1.** *n.* Tasche, *die; (sack)* Sack, *der; (hand~)* Handtasche, *die; (plastic* ~*)* Beutel, *der; (small paper* ~*)* Tüte, *die;* ~**s of** *(sl.: large amount)* jede Menge. **2.** *v. t.,* -**gg-:** **a)** in Säcke/Beutel/Tüten füllen; **b)** *(claim possession of)* sich *(Dat.)* schnappen *(ugs.)*

**baggage** ['bægɪdʒ] *n.* Gepäck, *das.* '**baggage reclaim** *n.* Gepäckausgabe, *die*

**baggy** ['bægɪ] *adj.* weit [geschnitten] ⟨*Kleid, Hose*⟩; *(through long use)* ausgebeult ⟨*Hose*⟩

'**bagpipe**[s] *n.* Dudelsack, *der*

**Bahamas** [bə'hɑːməz] *pr. n. pl.* **the** ~: die Bahamas

¹**bail** [beɪl] **1.** *n.* Kaution, *die;* **be** [out] **on** ~: gegen Kaution auf freiem Fuß sein. **2.** *v. t.* ~ **sb.** out jmdn. gegen Kaution freibekommen; *(fig.)* jmdm. aus der Klemme helfen *(ugs.)*

²**bail** *v. t. (scoop)* ~ [out] ausschöpfen. '**bail out** *v. i.* ⟨*Pilot:*⟩ abspringen

**bailiff** ['beɪlɪf] *n.* ≈ Gerichtsvollzieher, *der*

**bait** [beɪt] **1.** *v. t.* mit einem Köder versehen. **2.** *n.* Köder, *der*

**bake** [beɪk] *v. t. & i.* backen. '**baker** *n.* Bäcker, *der.* **bakery** ['beɪkərɪ] *n.* Bäckerei, *die*

**baking:** ~-**powder** *n.* Backpulver, *das;* ~-**tin** *n.* Backform, *die;* ~-**tray** *n.* Kuchenblech, *das*

**balance** ['bæləns] **1.** *n.* **a)** *(instrument)* Waage, *die;* **b)** *(fig.)* **be** *or* **hang in the** ~: in der Schwebe sein; **c)** *(steady position)* Gleichgewicht, *das;* **keep/lose one's** ~: das Gleichgewicht halten/verlieren; *(fig.)* sein Gleichgewicht bewahren/verlieren; **strike a** ~ **between** *(fig.)* den Mittelweg finden zwischen (+ *Dat.*); **d)** *(Bookk.: difference)* Bilanz, *die; (state of bank account)* Kontostand, *der;* **on** ~ *(fig.)* al-

les in allem; ~ **sheet** Bilanz, *die;* e)
*(Econ.)* ~ **of payments** Zahlungsbilanz, *die;* f) *(remainder)* Rest, *der.* 2.
*v. t.* **a)** *(weigh up)* abwägen; **b)** *(bring
into or keep in* ~*)* balancieren; auswuchten ⟨*Rad*⟩; **c)** *(equal, neutralize)*
ausgleichen; ~ **each other, be** ~**d** sich
*(Dat.)* die Waage halten. '**balanced**
*adj.* ausgewogen; ausgeglichen ⟨*Person, Team, Gemüt*⟩
**balcony** ['bælkənɪ] *n.* Balkon, *der*
**bald** [bɔːld] *adj.* kahl ⟨*Kopf*⟩; kahlköpfig, glatzköpfig ⟨*Person*⟩
**bale** [beɪl] *n.* Ballen, *der*
**balk** [bɔːlk] **1.** *v. t.* **they were ~ed in
their plan** ihr Plan wurde blockiert. **2.**
*v. i.* sich sträuben **(at** gegen)
**Balkan** ['bɔːlkən] **1.** *adj.* Balkan-. **2.** *n.
pl.* **the ~s** der Balkan
¹**ball** [bɔːl] *n.* **a)** Ball, *der; (Billiards etc.,
Croquet)* Kugel, *die;* **be on the ~** *(coll.:
be alert)* auf Zack sein *(ugs.);* **b)** *(of
wool, string, fluff, etc.)* Knäuel, *das*
²**ball** *n. (dance)* Ball, *der*
**ballad** ['bæləd] *n.* Ballade, *die*
**ballast** ['bæləst] *n.* Ballast, *der*
**ball-bearing** *n.* Kugellager, *das*
**ballerina** [bælə'riːnə] *n.* Ballerina, *die*
**ballet** ['bæleɪ] *n.* Ballett, *das;* ~ **dancer**
Ballettänzer, *der*/Ballettänzerin, *die*
**balloon** [bə'luːn] *n.* **a)** Ballon, *der;*
**hot-air** ~: Heißluftballon, *der;* **b)**
*(toy)* Luftballon, *der*
**ballot** ['bælət] *n.* Abstimmung, *die;*
|secret] ~: geheime Wahl
**ball:** ~**-pen,** ~**-point** '**pen** *ns.* Kugelschreiber, *der;* ~**room** *n.* Tanzsaal,
*der*
**balm** [bɑːm] *n.* Balsam, *der*
**balmy** ['bɑːmɪ] *adj. (mild)* mild
**Baltic** ['bɔːltɪk] **1.** *pr. n.* Ostsee, *die.* **2.**
*adj.* ~ **Sea** Ostsee, *die*
**balustrade** [bælə'streɪd] *n.* Balustrade, *die*
**bamboo** [bæm'buː] *n.* Bambus, *der*
**ban** [bæn] **1.** *v. t.,* -nn- verbieten; ~ **sb.
from doing sth.** jmdm. verbieten, etw.
zu tun. **2.** *n.* Verbot, *das*
**banal** [bə'nɑːl] *adj.* banal
**banana** [bə'nɑːnə] *n.* Banane, *die*
**band** [bænd] **1.** *n.* **a)** Band, *das;* **a ~ of
light/colour** ein Streifen Licht/Farbe;
**b)** *(range of values)* Bandbreite, *die;* **c)**
*(organized group)* Gruppe, *die; (of robbers, outlaws, etc.)* Bande, *die;* **d)**
*(Mus.)* [Musik]kapelle, *die; (pop
group, jazz* ~*)* Band, *die.* **2.** *v. i.* ~
**together |with sb.|** sich [mit jmdm.] zusammenschließen

**bandage** ['bændɪdʒ] **1.** *n.* Verband,
*der; (as support)* Bandage, *die.* **2.** *v. t.*
verbinden; bandagieren ⟨*verstauchtes] Gelenk usw.*⟩
**bandit** ['bændɪt] *n.* Bandit, *der*
**band:** ~**stand** *n.* Musiktribüne, *die;*
~**wagon** *n.* climb *or* jump on |to] the
~**wagon** *(fig.)* auf den fahrenden Zug
aufspringen *(fig.)*
¹**bandy** ['bændɪ] *v. t.* **they were ~ing
words/insults** sie stritten sich/beschimpften sich gegenseitig
²**bandy** *adj.* krumm; **he is ~-legged** er
hat O-Beine *(ugs.)*
**bang** [bæŋ] **1.** *v. t.* knallen *(ugs.);*
schlagen; zuknallen *(ugs.)* ⟨*Tür, Fenster, Deckel*⟩; ~ **one's head on sth.** mit
dem Kopf an etw. *(Akk.)* knallen
*(ugs.).* **2.** *v. i. (strike)* ~ |**against sth.|**
[gegen etw.] knallen *(ugs.);* ~ **shut**
⟨*Tür:*⟩ zuknallen *(ugs.).* **3.** *n.* **a)** *(blow)*
Schlag, *der;* **b)** *(noise)* Knall, *der.* **4.**
*adv.* go ~ ⟨*Gewehr, Feuerwerkskörper:*⟩ krachen
'**banger** *n. (sl.)* **a)** *(sausage)* Würstchen, *das;* **b)** *(firework)* Kracher, *der*
*(ugs.);* **c)** *(car)* Klapperkiste, *die (ugs.)*
**bangle** ['bæŋgl] *n.* Armreif, *der*
**banish** ['bænɪʃ] *v. t.* verbannen **(from**
aus)
**banister** ['bænɪstə(r)] *n.* [Treppen]geländer, *das*
**banjo** ['bændʒəʊ] *n., pl.* ~**s** *or* ~**es**
Banjo, *das*
¹**bank** [bæŋk] *n.* **a)** *(slope)* Böschung,
*die;* **b)** *(of river)* Ufer, *das*
²**bank** **1.** *n. (Finance)* Bank, *die.* **2.** *v. i.*
~ **at/with ...:** ein Konto haben bei ...;
~ **on sth.** *(fig.)* auf etw. *(Akk.)* zählen.
**3.** *v. t.* zur Bank bringen
**bank:** ~ **account** *n.* Bankkonto, *das;*
~ **card** *n.* Scheckkarte, *die;* ~ **clerk**
*n.* Bankangestellte, *der/die*
'**banker** *n.* Bankier, *der*
**bank 'holiday** *n. (Brit.)* Feiertag, *der*
'**banking** *n.* Bankwesen, *das*
**bank:** ~ **manager** *n.* Zweigstellenleiter/-leiterin [einer/der Bank]; ~**note**
*n.* Banknote, *die*
**bankrupt** ['bæŋkrʌpt] **1.** *n.* Bankrotteur, *der.* **2.** *adj.* go ~: Bankrott machen. **3.** *v. t.* bankrott machen. **bankruptcy** ['bæŋkrʌptsɪ] *n.* Konkurs,
*der;* Bankrott, *der*
**banner** ['bænə(r)] *n.* Banner, *das; (on
two poles)* Spruchband, *das*
**banns** [bænz] *n. pl.* Aufgebot, *das*
**banquet** ['bæŋkwɪt] *n.* Bankett, *das*
**baptism** ['bæptɪzm] *n.* Taufe, *die*

**Baptist** ['bæptɪst] *n.* Baptist, *der*/Baptistin, *die*
**baptize** [bæp'taɪz] *v. t.* taufen
**bar** [bɑː(r)] **1.** *n.* **a)** Stange, *die; (shorter, thinner also)* Stab, *der; (of cage, prison)* Gitterstab, *der;* **a ~ of soap** ein Stück Seife; **a ~ of chocolate** eine Tafel Schokolade; **b)** *(for refreshment)* Bar, *die; (counter)* Theke, *die.* **2.** *v. t.,* **-rr-: a)** *(fasten)* verriegeln; **b)** **~ sb.'s way** jmdm. den Weg versperren; **c)** *(prohibit, hinder)* verbieten; **~ sb. from doing sth.** jmdn. daran hindern, etw. zu tun. **3.** *prep.* abgesehen von; **~ none** ohne Einschränkung
**barb** [bɑːb] *n.* Widerhaken, *der*
**barbarian** [bɑː'beərɪən] *n.* Barbar, *der*
**barbaric** [bɑː'bærɪk] *adj.* barbarisch
**barbarity** [bɑː'bærɪtɪ] *n.* Grausamkeit, *die*
**barbecue** ['bɑːbɪkjuː] **1.** *n.* **a)** *(party)* Grillparty, *die;* **b)** *(food)* Grillgericht, *das.* **2.** *v. t.* grillen
**barbed wire** [bɑːbd 'waɪə(r)] *n.* Stacheldraht, *der*
**barber** ['bɑːbə(r)] *n.* [Herren]friseur, *der*
**'bar code** *n.* Strichcode, *der*
**bare** [beə(r)] **1.** *adj.* nackt; *(leafless, unfurnished)* kahl; *(empty)* leer; äußerst ⟨*Notwendige*⟩; **do sth. with one's ~ hands** etw. mit den bloßen Händen tun. **2.** *v. t.* entblößen ⟨*Kopf, Arm, Bein*⟩; blecken ⟨*Zähne*⟩. **'barefaced** *adj. (fig.)* unverhüllt. **'barefoot 1.** *adj.* barfüßig. **2.** *adv.* barfuß
**barely** ['beəlɪ] *adv.* kaum; knapp ⟨*vermeiden, entkommen*⟩
**bargain** ['bɑːgɪn] **1.** *n.* **a)** *(agreement)* Abmachung, *die;* **into the ~:** darüber hinaus; **b)** *(thing offered cheap)* günstiges Angebot; *(thing acquired cheaply)* guter Kauf. **2.** *v. i.* **a)** *(discuss)* handeln; **b)** **~ for** *or* **on sth.** *(expect sth.)* mit etw. rechnen
**barge** [bɑːdʒ] **1.** *n.* Kahn, *der.* **2.** *v. i.* **~ into sb.** jmdn. anrempeln; **~ in** *(intrude)* hineinplatzen/hereinplatzen *(ugs.)*
**baritone** ['bærɪtəʊn] **1.** *n.* Bariton, *der.* **2.** *adj.* Bariton-
**'bark** [bɑːk] *n. (of tree)* Rinde, *die*
**²bark 1.** *n. (of dog)* Bellen, *das.* **2.** *v. i.* bellen; **be ~ing up the wrong tree** auf dem Holzweg sein
**barley** ['bɑːlɪ] *n.* Gerste, *die*
**bar: ~maid** *n. (Brit.)* Bardame, *die;* **~man** ['bɑːmən] *n., pl.* **~men** ['bɑːmən] Barmann, *der*

**barmy** ['bɑːmɪ] *adj. (sl.: crazy)* bescheuert *(salopp)*
**barn** [bɑːn] *n. (Brit.: for grain etc.)* Scheune, *die; (Amer.: for animals)* Stall, *der*
**barnacle** ['bɑːnəkl] *n.* Rankenfüßer, *der*
**barometer** [bə'rɒmɪtə(r)] *n.* Barometer, *das*
**baron** ['bærn] *n.* Baron, *der;* Freiherr, *der;* **baroness** ['bærənɪs] *n.* Baronin, *die;* Freifrau, *die*
**baroque** [bə'rɒk, bə'rəʊk] **1.** *n.* Barock, *das.* **2.** *adj.* barock
**barracks** ['bærəks] *n. pl.* Kaserne, *die*
**barrage** ['bærɑːʒ] *n. (Mil.)* Sperrfeuer, *das;* **a ~ of questions** ein Bombardement von Fragen
**barrel** ['bærl] *n.* **a)** Faß, *das;* **b)** *(of gun)* Lauf, *der*
**barren** ['bærn] *adj.* unfruchtbar
**barricade** [bærɪ'keɪd] **1.** *n.* Barrikade, *die.* **2.** *v. t.* verbarrikadieren
**barrier** ['bærɪə(r)] *n.* Barriere, *die; (at level crossing etc.)* Schranke, *die*
**barring** ['bɑːrɪŋ] *prep.* außer im Falle (+ *Gen.*)
**barrister** ['bærɪstə(r)] *n. (Brit.)* **~[-at-law]** Barrister, *der;* ≈ [Rechts]anwalt/-anwältin vor höheren Gerichten
**barrow** ['bærəʊ] *n.* **a)** Karre, *die;* Karren, *der;* **b)** *see* **wheelbarrow**
**barter** ['bɑːtə(r)] **1.** *v. t.* [ein]tauschen; **~ sth. for** [*else*] etw. für *od.* gegen etw. [anderes] [ein]tauschen. **2.** *v. i.* Tauschhandel treiben. **3.** *n.* Tauschhandel, *der*
**base** [beɪs] **1.** *n.* **a)** *(of lamp, mountain)* Fuß, *der; (of cupboard, statue)* Sockel, *der; (fig.: support)* Basis, *die;* **b)** *(Mil.)* Basis, *der;* Stützpunkt, *der.* **2.** *v. t.* **a)** **be ~d on sth.** sich auf etw. *(Akk.)* gründen; **~ sth. on sth.** etw. auf etw. *(Dat.)* aufbauen; **b)** *in pass.* **be ~d in Paris** *(permanently)* in Paris sitzen; *(temporarily)* in Paris sein
**'baseball** *n.* Baseball, *der*
**basement** ['beɪsmənt] *n.* Untergeschoß, *das;* **a ~ flat** eine Kellerwohnung
**bash** [bæʃ] *v. t.* [heftig] schlagen
**bashful** ['bæʃfl] *adj.* schüchtern
**basic** ['beɪsɪk] *adj.* grundlegend; Grund⟨*prinzip, -bestandteil, -lohn, -gehalt usw.*⟩; Haupt⟨*problem, -grund, -sache*⟩; **be ~ to sth.** wesentlich für etw. sein. **basically** ['beɪsɪkəlɪ] *adv.* im Grunde; grundsätzlich ⟨*übereinstimmen*⟩; *(mainly)* hauptsächlich
**basil** ['bæzɪl] *n.* Basilikum, *das*

**basin** ['beɪsn] *n.* **a)** Becken, *das; (wash-~)* Waschbecken, *das; (bowl)* Schüssel, *die;* **b)** *(of river)* Becken, *das*

**basis** ['beɪsɪs] *n., pl.* **bases** ['beɪsi:z] Basis, *die;* Grundlage, *die*

**bask** [bɑ:sk] *v. i.* sich [wohlig] wärmen

**basket** ['bɑ:skɪt] *n.* Korb, *der.* '**basketball** *n.* Basketball, *der*

**Basle** [bɑ:l] *pr. n.* Basel *(das)*

**bass** [beɪs] **1.** *n.* **a)** Baß, *der;* **b)** *(coll.) (double-~)* [Kontra]baß, *der; (~ guitar)* Baß, *der.* **2.** *adj.* Baß-. **bass guitar** *n.* Baßgitarre, *die*

**bassoon** [bə'su:n] *n.* Fagott, *das*

**bastard** ['bɑ:stəd] **1.** *adj.* unehelich. **2.** *n.* **a)** uneheliches Kind; **b)** *(coll. derog.: person)* Schweinehund, *der (derb)*

**baste** ['beɪst] *v. t.* [mit Fett] begießen

**bastion** ['bæstɪən] *n.* Bastei, *die*

¹**bat** [bæt] *n. (Zool.)* Fledermaus, *die*

²**bat 1.** *n. (Sport)* Schlagholz, *das; (for table-tennis)* Schläger, *der;* **do sth. off one's own ~** *(fig.)* etw. auf eigene Faust tun. **2.** *v. t.,* -tt- schlagen

³**bat** *v. t.* **not ~ an eyelid** nicht mit der Wimper zucken

**batch** [bætʃ] *n.* **a)** *(of loaves)* Schub, *der;* **b)** *(of people)* Gruppe, *die; (of books, papers)* Stapel, *der*

**bated** ['beɪtɪd] *v. t.* **with ~ breath** mit angehaltenem Atem

**bath** [bɑ:θ] **1.** *n., pl.* **~s** [bɑ:ðz] **a)** Bad, *das;* **have** *or* **take a ~:** ein Bad nehmen; **b)** *(tub)* Badewanne, *die;* **room with ~:** Zimmer mit Bad; **c)** *usu. in pl. (building)* Bad, *das.* **2.** *v. t. & i.* baden.

'**bath cubes** *n. pl.* Badesalz, *das*

**bathe** [beɪð] *v. t. & i.* baden. **bather** ['beɪðə(r)] *n.* Badende, *der/die.* '**bathing** ['beɪðɪŋ] *n.* Baden, *das.* '**bathing-costume**, '**bathing-suit** *ns.* Badeanzug, *der*

**bath:** **~-mat** *n.* Bademate, *die;* **~room** *n.* Badezimmer, *das; ~* **salts** *n. pl.* Badesalz, *das; ~* **towel** *n.* Badetuch, *das; ~* **tub** *see* **bath 1 b**

**baton** ['bætn] *n.* **a)** *(truncheon)* Schlagstock, *der;* **b)** *(Mus.)* Taktstock, *der*

**batsman** ['bætsmən] *n., pl.* **batsmen** ['bætsmən] Schlagmann, *der*

**battalion** [bə'tæljən] *n.* Bataillon, *das*

¹**batter** ['bætə(r)] *v. t. (strike)* einschlagen auf (+ *Akk.*)

²**batter** *n. (Cookery)* [Back]teig, *der*

**battery** ['bætərɪ] *n.* Batterie, *die*

**battery:** **~ charger** *n.* Batterieladegerät, *das; ~* '**farming** *n.* Batteriehaltung, *die; ~* '**hen** *n.* Batteriehuhn, *das*

**battle** ['bætl] **1.** *n.* Schlacht, *die; (fig.)* Kampf, *der.* **2.** *v. i.* kämpfen

**battle:** **~axe** *n. (coll.: woman)* Schreckschraube, *die (ugs.); ~* **field,** **~ground** *ns.* Schlachtfeld, *das*

**battlements** ['bætlmənts] *n. pl.* Zinnen *Pl.*

'**battleship** *n.* Schlachtschiff, *das*

**batty** ['bætɪ] *adj. (sl.)* bekloppt *(salopp)*

**bauble** ['bɔ:bl] *n.* Flitter, *der*

**baulk** *see* **balk**

**Bavaria** [bə'veərɪə] *pr. n.* Bayern *(das).* **Bavarian** [bə'veərɪən] **1.** *adj.* bay[e]-risch. **2.** *n.* Bayer, *der/*Bayerin, *die*

**bawdy** ['bɔ:dɪ] *adj.* zweideutig; *(stronger)* obszön

¹**bay** [beɪ] *n. (of sea)* Bucht, *die*

²**bay** *n.* **a)** *(space in room)* Erker, *der;* **b)** |parking-|~: Stellplatz, *der*

³**bay** *n.* **hold** *or* **keep sb./sth. at ~:** sich *(Dat.)* jmdn./etw. vom Leib halten

**bayonet** ['beɪənɪt] *n.* Bajonett, *das*

**bay** '**window** *n.* Erkerfenster, *das*

**bazaar** [bə'zɑ:(r)] *n.* Basar, *der*

**BBC** *abbr.* **British Broadcasting Corporation** BBC, *die*

**BC** *abbr.* **before Christ** v. Chr.

**be** [bi:] *v., pres. t.* **I am** [əm, *stressed* æm], **he is** [ɪz], **we are** [ə(r), *stressed* ɑ:(r)]; *p. t.* **I was** [wəz, *stressed* wɒz], **we were** [wə(r), *stressed* wɜ:(r)]; *pres. p.* **being** ['bi:ɪŋ]; *p. p.* **been** [bɪn, *stressed* bi:n] **1.** *copula* **a)** sein; **she is a mother/ an Italian/a teacher** sie ist Mutter/Italienerin/Lehrerin; **be sensible!** sei vernünftig!; **be ill/unwell** krank sein/sich nicht wohl fühlen; **I am well** es geht mir gut; **I am hot** mir ist heiß; **I am freezing** mich friert es; **how are you/is she?** wie geht's *(ugs.)/*geht es ihr?; **it is the 5th today** heute haben wir den Fünften; **who's that?** wer ist das?; **if I were you** an deiner Stelle; **it's hers** es ist ihrs; **b)** *(cost)* kosten; **how much are the eggs?** was kosten die Eier?; **two times three is six, two threes are six** zweimal drei ist *od.* sind sechs; **c)** *(constitute)* bilden. **2.** *v. i.* **a)** *(exist)* [vorhanden] sein; **there is/are ...:** es gibt ...; **for the time being** vorläufig; **be that as it may** wie dem auch sei; **b)** *(remain)* bleiben; **I shan't be a moment** ich komme sofort; **let it be** laß es sein; **let him/her be** laß ihn/sie in Ruhe; **c)** *(happen)* stattfinden; sein; **d)** *(go, come)* **be off with you!** geh/geht!; **I'm off home** ich gehe jetzt nach Hause; **she's from Australia** sie stammt *od.* ist aus Australien; **e)** *(go or come* on visit) sein; **have you [ever] been to London?** bist du schon einmal in London gewesen?; **has anyone been?** ist jemand dagewesen? 3. v. aux. **a)** forming passive werden; **the child was found** das Kind wurde gefunden; **German is spoken here** hier wird Deutsch gesprochen; **b)** forming continuous tenses, active **he is reading** er liest [gerade]; **I am leaving tomorrow** ich reise morgen [ab]; **the train was departing when I got there** der Zug fuhr gerade ab, als ich ankam; **c)** forming continuous tenses, passive **the house is/was being built** das Haus wird/wurde [gerade] gebaut; **d)** expr. arrangement, obligation **be to** sollen; **I am to go/to inform you** ich soll gehen/Sie unterrichten; **e)** expr. destiny **they were never to meet again** sie sollten sich nie wieder treffen; **f)** expr. condition **if I were to tell you that …:** wenn ich dir sagen würde, daß … 4. **bride-/husband-to-be** zukünftige Braut/zukünftiger Ehemann

**beach** [biːtʃ] n. Strand, der; **on the ~:** am Strand. **'beach wear** n. Strandkleidung, die

**beacon** ['biːkn] n. Leuchtfeuer, das; (Naut.) Leuchtbake, die

**bead** [biːd] n. Perle, die; **~s** Perlen Pl.; Perlenkette, die; **~s of dew/sweat** Tau-/Schweißtropfen

**beak** [biːk] n. Schnabel, der

**beaker** ['biːkə(r)] n. Becher, der

**beam** [biːm] n. 1. **a)** (timber etc.) Balken, der; **b)** (ray etc.) [Licht]strahl, der. 2. v. i. **a)** (shine) strahlen; glänzen; **b)** (smile) strahlen; **~ at sb.** jmdn. anstrahlen

**bean** [biːn] n. Bohne, die; **full of ~s** (fig. coll.) putzmunter (ugs.)

**¹bear** [beə(r)] n. Bär, der

**²bear** [beə(r)] 1. v. t., **bore** [bɔː(r)], **borne** [bɔːn] **a)** tragen; aufweisen (Spuren, Ähnlichkeit); tragen, führen (Namen, Titel); **~ some/little relation to sth.** einen gewissen/wenig Bezug zu etw. haben; **b)** (endure, tolerate) ertragen (Schmerz, Kummer); with neg. ertragen, aushalten (Schmerz); ausstehen (Geruch, Lärm); **c)** (be fit for) vertragen; **it will not ~ scrutiny** es hält einer Überprüfung nicht stand; **it does not ~ thinking about** daran darf man gar nicht denken; **d)** (give birth to) gebären (Kind, Junges). 2. v. i., **bore**, **borne: ~ left** (Person:) sich links halten; **the path ~s to the left** der Weg führt nach

links. **bear 'out** v. t. (fig.) bestätigen (Bericht, Erklärung); **~ sb. out** jmdm. recht geben. **'bear with** v. t. Nachsicht haben mit

**bearable** ['beərəbl] adj. erträglich

**beard** [bɪəd] n. Bart, der. **'bearded** adj. bärtig. **be ~:** einen Bart haben

**'bearer** n. (carrier) Träger, der/Trägerin, die; (of message, cheque) Überbringer, der/Überbringerin, die

**'bearing** n. **a)** (behaviour) Verhalten, das; **b)** (relation) Bezug, der; **have some/no ~ on sth.** relevant/irrelevant für etw. sein; **c)** (Mech. Engin.) Lager, das; **d)** (compass ~) Position, die; **take a compass ~:** den Kompaßkurs feststellen; **get one's ~s** sich orientieren; (fig.) sich zurechtfinden

**beast** [biːst] n. Tier, das; (fig.: brutal person) Bestie, die. **'beastly** adj., adv. (coll.) scheußlich

**beat** [biːt] 1. v. t., **beat**, **beaten** ['biːtn] schlagen; klopfen (Teppich); (surpass) brechen (Rekord); **hard to ~:** schwer zu schlagen; **it ~s me how/why …:** es ist mir ein Rätsel wie/warum …; **~ time** den Takt schlagen; **~ it!** (sl.) hau ab! (ugs.); see also **beaten** 2. 2. v. i., **beat**, **beaten** schlagen (on auf + Akk.); (Regen, Hagel:) prasseln (against gegen). 3. n. **a)** (stroke, throbbing) Schlagen, das; (Mus.) (rhythm) Takt, der; (single ~) Schlag, der; **b)** (of policeman) Runde, die. **beat 'off** v. t. abwehren (Angriff). **beat 'up** v. t. zusammenschlagen (Person)

**beaten** ['biːtn] 1. see **beat** 1, 2. 2. adj. **a)** off the **~ track** weit abgelegen; **b)** gehämmert (Silber, Gold)

**'beating** n. **a)** (punishment) **a ~:** Schläge Pl.; Prügel Pl.; **b)** (defeat) Niederlage, die; **c)** **take some/a lot of ~:** nicht leicht zu übertreffen sein

**'beat-up** adj. (sl.) ramponiert (ugs.)

**beautiful** ['bjuːtɪfl] adj. schön; wunderschön (Augen, Aussicht, Morgen)

**beautify** ['bjuːtɪfaɪ] v. t. verschönen

**beauty** ['bjuːtɪ] n. Schönheit, die; (beautiful feature) Schöne, das; **the ~ of it** das Schöne daran

**beauty: ~ parlour** see **~ salon; ~ queen** n. Schönheitskönigin, die; **~ salon** n. Kosmetiksalon, der; **~ spot** n. Schönheitsfleck, der; (place) schönes Fleckchen [Erde]

**beaver** ['biːvə(r)] n. Biber, der

**became** see **become**

**because** [bɪ'kɒz] 1. conj. weil. 2. adv. **~ of** wegen (+ Gen.)

**beckon** ['bekn] *v. t. & i.* winken (to sb. jmdm.); *(fig.)* locken

**become** [bɪ'kʌm] **1.** *copula,* **became** [bɪ'keɪm], **become** werden; ~ **a politician** Politiker werden; ~ **a nuisance/ rule** zu einer Plage/zur Regel werden. **2.** *v. i.,* **became, become** werden; **what has** ~ **of him?** was ist aus ihm geworden? **3.** *v. t.,* **became, become** *(suit)* ~ **sb.** jmdm. stehen

**becoming** [bɪ'kʌmɪŋ] *adj.* **a)** *(fitting)* schicklich *(geh.);* **b)** *(flattering)* vorteilhaft ⟨*Hut, Kleid, Frisur*⟩

**bed** [bed] *n.* **a)** Bett, *das; (without bedstead)* Lager, *das;* in ~: im Bett; ~ **and breakfast** Zimmer mit Frühstück; **get out of/into** ~: aufstehen/ins Bett gehen; **go to** ~: ins Bett gehen; **put sb. to** ~: jmdn. ins Bett bringen; **b)** *(flat base)* Unterlage, *die; (of machine)* Bett, *das;* **c)** *(in garden)* Beet, *das;* **d)** *(of sea, lake)* Grund, *der; (of river)* Bett, *das.* **'bedclothes** *n. pl.* Bettzeug, *das.* **bedding** ['bedɪŋ] *n.* Matratze und Bettzeug

**bedlam** ['bedləm] *n., no indef. art.* Tumult, *der*

**'bedpan** *n.* Bettpfanne, *die*

**bedraggled** [bɪ'dræɡld] *adj. (soaked)* durchnäßt; *(with mud)* verdreckt

**bed:** ~**ridden** *adj.* bettlägerig; ~**room** *n.* Schlafzimmer, *das;* ~**side** *n.* Seite des Bettes, *die;* ~**side table/ lamp** Nachttisch, *der*/Nachttischlampe, *die;* ~**-sit,** ~**-'sitter** *ns. (coll.)* Wohnschlafzimmer, *das;* ~**spread** *n.* Tagesdecke, *die;* ~**stead** *n.* Bettgestell, *das;* ~**time** *n.* Schlafenszeit, *die;* **at** ~**time** vor dem Zubettgehen; **a** ~**time story** eine Gutenachtgeschichte

**bee** [biː] *n.* Biene, *die*

**beech** [biːtʃ] *n.* Buche, *die*

**beef** [biːf] **1.** *n.* **a)** Rindfleisch, *das;* **b)** *(coll.: muscles)* Muskeln. **2.** *v. t.* ~ **up** stärken. **beefburger** ['biːfbɜːɡə(r)] *n.* Beefburger, *der*

**bee:** ~**hive** *n.* Bienenstock, *der;* ~**keeper** *n.* Imker, *der*/Imkerin, *die;* ~**keeping** *n.* Imkerei, *die;* ~**line** *n.* **make a** ~**line for sth./sb.** schnurstracks auf etw./jmdn. zustürzen

**been** *see* **be**

**beer** [bɪə(r)] *n.* Bier, *das*

**beet** [biːt] *n.* Rübe, *die*

**beetle** ['biːtl] *n.* Käfer, *der*

**'beetroot** *n.* rote Beete *od.* Rübe

**before** [bɪ'fɔː(r)] **1.** *adv.* **a)** *(of time)* vorher; *(already)* schon; **the day** ~: am Tag zuvor; **never** ~: noch nie; **b)** *(ahead in position)* vor[aus]. **2.** *prep. (of time; position)* vor (+ *Dat.*); *(direction)* vor (+ *Akk.*); **the day** ~ **yesterday** vorgestern; ~ **now/then** früher/vorher; ~ **Christ** vor Christus; ~ **leaving, he phoned** bevor er wegging, rief er an. **3.** *conj.* bevor. **be'forehand** *adv.* vorher; *(in anticipation)* im voraus

**beg** [beg] **1.** *v. t.,* **-gg-: a)** betteln um; **b)** *(ask earnestly for)* ~ **sth.** um etw. bitten. **2.** *v. i.,* **-gg-** betteln (**for** um)

**began** *see* **begin**

**beggar** ['beɡə(r)] *n.* **a)** Bettler, *der*/Bettlerin, *die;* **b)** *(coll.)* **poor** ~: armer Teufel

**begin** [bɪ'ɡɪn] **1.** *v. t.,* **-nn-, began** [bɪ'ɡæn], **begun** [bɪ'ɡʌn] ~ **sth.** [mit] etw. beginnen; ~ **doing** *or* **to do sth.** anfangen *od.* beginnen, etw. zu tun. **2.** *v. i.,* **-nn-, began, begun** anfangen; ~ [**up**]**on sth.** etw. anfangen. **be'ginner** *n.* Anfänger, *der*/Anfängerin, *die.* **be'ginning** *n.* Anfang, *der;* **at** *or* **in the** ~: am Anfang; **at the** ~ **of February/the month** Anfang Februar/des Monats; **from the** ~: von Anfang an

**begrudge** [bɪ'ɡrʌdʒ] *v. t.* ~ **sb. sth.** jmdm. etw. mißgönnen; ~ **doing sth.** etw. ungern tun

**begun** *see* **begin**

**behalf** [bɪ'hɑːf] *n.* **on** *or* *(Amer.)* **in** ~ **of sb./sth.** für jmdn./etw.; *(more formally)* im Namen von jmdm./etw.

**behave** [bɪ'heɪv] **1.** *v. i.* sich verhalten; sich benehmen; **well-/ill-** *or* **badly** ~**d** brav/ungezogen. **2.** *v. refl.* ~ **oneself** sich benehmen. **behaviour** [bɪ'heɪvjə(r)] *n.* Verhalten, *das*

**behead** [bɪ'hed] *v. t.* enthaupten

**behind** [bɪ'haɪnd] **1.** *adv.* hinten; *(further back)* **be miles** ~: kilometerweit zurückliegen; **stay** ~: dableiben; **leave sb./sth.** ~: jmdn./etw. zurücklassen; **fall** ~: zurückbleiben; *(fig.)* in Rückstand geraten; **be/get** ~ **with one's payments/rent** mit seinen Zahlungen/der Miete im Rückstand sein/in Rückstand geraten. **2.** *prep.* **a)** hinter (+ *Dat.*); **one** ~ **the other** hintereinander; **b)** *(towards rear of)* hinter (+ *Akk.*)

**being** ['biːɪŋ] *n.* **a)** *(existence)* Dasein, *das;* **in** ~: bestehend; **come into** ~: entstehen; **b)** *(person etc.)* Wesen, *das*

**belated** [bɪ'leɪtɪd] *adj.,* **be'latedly** *adv.* verspätet

**belch** [beltʃ] **1.** *v. i.* heftig aufstoßen; rülpsen *(ugs.).* **2.** *n.* Rülpser, *der (ugs.)*

**belfry** ['belfrɪ] *n.* Glockenturm, *der*
**Belgian** ['beldʒən] **1.** *n.* Belgier, *der*/Belgierin, *die.* **2.** *adj.* belgisch
**Belgium** ['beldʒəm] *pr. n.* Belgien *(das)*
**belie** [bɪ'laɪ] *v. t.,* **belying** [bɪ'laɪɪŋ] hinwegtäuschen über ‹*Tatsachen, wahren Zustand*›; nicht erfüllen ‹*Versprechen*›; nicht entsprechen ‹*Vorstellung (Dat.)*›
**belief** [bɪ'li:f] *n.* **a)** Glaube, *der* (**in an** + *Akk.*); **in the ~ that …**: in der Überzeugung, daß …; **b)** *(Relig.)* Glaube[n], *der*
**believable** [bɪ'li:vəbl] *adj.* glaubhaft
**believe** [bɪ'li:v] **1.** *v. i.* glauben (**in an** + *Dat.*); *(have faith)* glauben (**in an** + *Akk.*) ‹*Gott, Himmel usw.*›; **I ~ so/not** ich glaube schon/nicht. **2.** *v. t.* glauben; **~ sb.** jmdm. glauben; **I don't ~ you** das glaube ich dir nicht; **make ~ that …**: so tun, als ob …
**Belisha beacon** [bəli:ʃə 'bi:kn] *n. (Brit.)* gelbes Blinklicht an Zebrastreifen
**belittle** [bɪ'lɪtl] *v. t.* herabsetzen
**bell** [bel] *n.* Glocke, *die;* (*door~*) Klingel, *die*
**belligerent** [bɪ'lɪdʒərənt] *adj.* kriegführend ‹*Nation*›; streitlustig ‹*Person*›
**bellow** ['beləʊ] **1.** *v. i.* brüllen. **2.** *v. t.* ~ |out| brüllen ‹*Befehl*›
**bellows** ['beləʊz] *n. pl.* Blasebalg, *der*
**belly** ['belɪ] *n.* Bauch, *der.* **'bellyache** *n.* Bauchschmerzen *Pl.*
**belong** [bɪ'lɒŋ] *v. i.* ~ **to sb./sth.** jmdm./zu etw. gehören; ~ **to a club** einem Verein angehören; **where does this ~?** wo gehört das hin? **be'longings** *n. pl.* Habe, *die;* Sachen *Pl.*
**beloved** [bɪ'lʌvɪd] **1.** *adj.* geliebt. **2.** *n.* Geliebte, *der/die*
**below** [bɪ'ləʊ] **1.** *adv.* **a)** *(position)* unten; *(lower down)* darunter; **from ~:** von unten [herauf]; **b)** *(direction)* nach unten; hinunter. **2.** *prep.* unter *(position:* + *Dat.; direction:* + *Akk.)*
**belt** [belt] *n.* Gürtel, *der;* (*for tools, weapons, ammunition*) Gurt, *der;* (*of trees*) Streifen, *der.* **belt 'up** *v. i. (Brit. sl.)* die Klappe halten *(salopp)*
**bemused** [bɪ'mju:zd] *adj.* verwirrt
**bench** [bentʃ] *n.* Bank, *die;* (*worktable*) Werkbank, *die*
**bend** [bend] **1.** *n.* Beuge, *die;* (*in road*) Kurve, *die.* **2.** *v. t.,* **bent** [bent] biegen; beugen ‹*Arm, Knie*›; anwinkeln ‹*Bein*›. **3.** *v. i.,* **bent** sich biegen; *(bow)* sich bücken. **bend 'down** *v. i.* sich

bücken. **bend 'over** *v. i.* sich nach vorn beugen
**beneath** [bɪ'ni:θ] *prep.* **a)** *(unworthy of)* ~ **sb.,** ~ **sb.'s dignity** unter jmds. Würde *(Dat.);* **b)** *(arch./literary: under)* unter *(+ Dat.)*
**benefactor** ['benɪfæktə(r)] *n.* Wohltäter, *der;* (*patron*) Gönner, *der*
**beneficial** [benɪ'fɪʃl] *adj.* nützlich; vorteilhaft ‹*Einfluß*›
**benefit** ['benɪfɪt] **1.** *n.* **a)** Vorteil, *der;* **be of ~ to sb./sth.** jmdm./einer Sache von Nutzen sein; **have the ~ of** den Vorteil *(+ Gen.)* haben; **with the ~ of** mit Hilfe *(+ Gen.);* **for sb.'s ~:** in jmds. Interesse *(Dat.);* **b)** *(allowance)* Beihilfe, *die;* **unemployment ~:** Arbeitslosenunterstützung, *die.* **2.** *v. t.* nützen *(+ Dat.).* **3.** *v. i.* ~ **by/from sth.** von etw. profitieren
**benevolent** [bɪ'nevələnt] *adj.* **a)** gütig; **b)** wohltätig ‹*Institution, Verein*›
**benign** [bɪ'naɪn] *adj.* gütig; *(Med.)* gutartig
**bent** [bent] **1.** *see* **bend** 2, 3. **2.** *n. (liking)* Neigung, *die* (**for** zu). **3. a)** *adj.* krumm; **b)** *(Brit. sl.: corrupt)* link *(salopp)*
**bequeath** [bɪ'kwi:ð] *v. t.* ~ **sth. to sb.** jmdm. etw. hinterlassen. **bequest** [bɪ'kwest] *n.* Legat, *das* (**to an** + *Akk.*)
**bereaved** [bɪ'ri:vd] *n.* **the ~:** der/die Hinterbliebene/die Hinterbliebenen
**beret** ['bereɪ] *n.* Baskenmütze, *die*
**Berlin** [bɜ:'lɪn] *pr. n.* Berlin *(das)*
**Berne** [bɜ:n] *pr. n.* Bern *(das)*
**berry** ['berɪ] *n.* Beere, *die*
**berserk** [bə'sɜ:k] *adj.* rasend; **go ~:** durchdrehen *(ugs.)*
**berth** [bɜ:θ] *n. (for ship)* Liegeplatz, *der;* (*sleeping-place*) (*in ship*) Koje, *die;* (*in train*) Schlafwagenbett, *das*
**beside** [bɪ'saɪd] *prep.* **a)** neben *(+ Dat.);* ~ **the sea/lake** am Meer/ See; **b) be ~ the point** nichts damit zu tun haben; **c)** ~ **oneself** außer sich
**besides** [bɪ'saɪdz] **1.** *adv.* außerdem. **2.** *prep.* außer
**besiege** [bɪ'si:dʒ] *v. t.* belagern
**best** [best] **1.** *adj.* best…; **the ~ part of an hour** fast eine ganze Stunde. **2.** *adv.* am besten. **3.** *n.* **the ~:** der/die/das Beste; **do one's ~:** sein bestes tun; **make the ~ of it** das Beste daraus machen; **at ~:** bestenfalls. **best 'man** *n.* Trauzeuge, *der* (*des Bräutigams*). **best 'seller** *n.* Bestseller, *der*
**bet** [bet] **1.** *v. t. & i.,* **-tt-,** ~ *or* ~**ted** wetten; **I ~ him £10** ich habe mit ihm um

10 Pfund gewettet; ~ **on** sth. auf etw. *(Akk.)* setzen. **2.** *n.* Wette, *die; (fig. coll.)* Tip, *der*

**betray** [bɪˈtreɪ] *v. t.* verraten (**to an** + *Akk.*). **betrayal** [bɪˈtreɪəl] *n.* Verrat, *der*

**better** [ˈbetə(r)] **1.** *adj.* besser; ~ **and** ~: immer besser; **be much** ~ *(recovered)* sich viel besser fühlen; **get** ~ *(recover)* gesund werden; **the** ~ **part of** sth. der größte Teil einer Sache *(Gen.)*. **2.** *adv.* besser; ~ **'off** *(financially)* besser gestellt; **be** ~ **off without** sb./sth. ohne jmdn./etw. besser dran sein; **I'd** ~ **be off now** ich gehe jetzt besser. **3.** *n.* **get the** ~ **of** sb./sth. jmdn./etw. unterkriegen *(ugs.);* **a change for the** ~: eine vorteilhafte Veränderung. **4.** *v. t.* übertreffen

**'betting shop** *n.* Wettbüro, *das*

**between** [bɪˈtwiːn] **1.** *prep.* **a)** |in| ~: zwischen *(position:* + *Dat.; direction:* + *Akk.);* **b)** *(amongst)* unter (+ *Dat.);* ~ **ourselves,** ~ **you and me** unter uns *(Dat.)* gesagt; **c)** ~ **them/us** *(by joint action of)* gemeinsam; ~ **us we had 40p** wir hatten zusammen 40 Pence. **2.** *adv.* |in| ~: dazwischen; *(in time)* zwischendurch

**beverage** [ˈbevərɪdʒ] *n.* Getränk, *das*

**beware** [bɪˈweə(r)] *v. t. & i.; only in imper. and inf.* ~ |**of**| sb./sth. sich vor jmdm./etw. in acht nehmen; ~ **of doing** sth. sich davor hüten, etw. zu tun; '~ **of the dog'** „Vorsicht, bissiger Hund!"

**bewilder** [bɪˈwɪldə(r)] *v. t.* verwirren. **be'wilderment** *n.* Verwirrung, *die*

**bewitch** [bɪˈwɪtʃ] *v. t.* verzaubern; *(fig.)* bezaubern

**beyond** [bɪˈjɒnd] **1.** *adv.* **a)** *(in space)* jenseits; *(on other side of wall, mountain range, etc.)* dahinter; **b)** *(in time)* darüber hinaus; **c)** *(in addition)* außerdem. **2.** *prep.* **a)** *(at far side of)* jenseits (+ *Gen.);* **b)** *(later than)* nach; **c)** *(out of reach or comprehension or range)* über ... (+ *Akk.*) hinaus

**bias** [ˈbaɪəs] **1.** *n.* Voreingenommenheit, *die.* **2.** *v. t.,* -s- *or* -ss- beeinflussen; **be ~ed in favour of/against** sth./ sb. für etw./jmdn. eingestellt sein/gegen etw./jmdn. voreingenommen sein

**bib** [bɪb] *n.* Lätzchen, *das*

**Bible** [ˈbaɪbl] *n.* Bibel, *die.* **biblical** [ˈbɪblɪkl] *adj.* biblisch

**bibliography** [bɪblɪˈɒɡrəfɪ] *n.* Bibliographie, *die*

**biceps** [ˈbaɪseps] *n.* Bizeps, *der*

**bicker** [ˈbɪkə(r)] *v. i.* sich zanken

**bicycle** [ˈbaɪsɪkl] **1.** *n.* Fahrrad, *das; attrib.* Fahrrad-; ~ **clip** Hosenklammer, *die.* **2.** *v. i.* radfahren

**bid** [bɪd] **1.** *v. t.* **a)** -dd-, bid *(at auction)* bieten; **b)** -dd-, bade [bæd, beɪd] *or* bid, bidden [ˈbɪdn] *or* bid: ~ sb. **welcome/goodbye** jmdn. willkommen heißen/sich von jmdm. verabschieden. **2.** *v. i.,* -dd-, bid **a)** werben (**for** um); **b)** *(at auction)* bieten. **3.** *n.* **a)** *(at auction)* Gebot, *das;* **b)** *(attempt)* Versuch, *der*

**bidden** *see* bid 1

**'bidder** *n.* Bieter, *der*/Bieterin, *die*

**bide** [ˈbaɪd] *v. t.* ~ **one's time** den richtigen Augenblick abwarten

**bifocal** [baɪˈfəʊkl] **1.** *adj.* Bifokal-. **2.** *n. in pl.* Bifokalgläser *Pl.*

**big** [bɪɡ] *adj.* groß

**bigamy** [ˈbɪɡəmɪ] *n.* Bigamie, *die*

**big-'headed** *adj. (coll.)* eingebildet

**bigoted** [ˈbɪɡətɪd] *adj.* eifernd

**big:** ~ **'toe** *n.* große Zehe; ~ **'top** *n.* Zirkuszelt, *das;* ~ **'wheel** *n. (at fair)* Riesenrad, *das*

**bike** [baɪk] *(coll.)* **1.** *n. (bicycle)* Rad, *das; (motor cycle)* Maschine, *die.* **2.** *v. i.* radfahren/[mit dem] Motorrad fahren

**bikini** [bɪˈkiːnɪ] *n.* Bikini, *der*

**bilingual** [baɪˈlɪŋɡwəl] *adj.* zweisprachig

**bilious** [ˈbɪljəs] *adj. (Med.)* Gallen-; ~ **attack** Gallenanfall, *der*

**¹bill** [bɪl] *n. (of bird)* Schnabel, *der*

**²bill** *n.* **a)** *(Parl.)* Gesetzentwurf, *der;* **b)** *(note of charges)* Rechnung, *die; could we have the* ~ *please?* wir möchten zahlen; **c)** *(poster)* |**stick**| **no ~s** „|Plakate| ankleben verboten"

**'billboard** *n.* Reklametafel, *die*

**billet** [ˈbɪlɪt] **1.** *n.* Quartier, *das.* **2.** *v. t.* einquartieren (**with, on** bei)

**'billfold** *n. (Amer.)* Brieftasche, *die*

**billiards** [ˈbɪljədz] *n.* Billard[spiel], *das*

**billion** [ˈbɪljən] *n.* **a)** *(thousand million)* Milliarde, *die;* **b)** *(Brit.: million million)* Billion, *die*

**billy-goat** [ˈbɪlɪɡəʊt] *n.* Ziegenbock, *der*

**bin** [bɪn] *n.* Behälter, *der; (for bread)* Brotkasten, *der; (for rubbish)* Mülleimer, *der*

**binary** [ˈbaɪnərɪ] *adj.* binär

**bind** [baɪnd] *v. t.,* bound [baʊnd] **a)** fesseln ⟨*Person, Tier*⟩; *(bandage)* wickeln ⟨*Glied, Baum*⟩; verbinden ⟨*Wunde*⟩ (**with** mit); **b)** *(fasten together)* zusammenbinden; **c)** binden ⟨*Buch*⟩; **d)** be

**bound up with sth.** *(fig.)* eng mit etw. verbunden sein; **e) be bound to do sth.** *(required)* verpflichtet sein, etw. zu tun; *(certain)* etw. ganz bestimmt tun; **it is bound to rain** es wird bestimmt regnen. '**binder** *n. (for papers)* Hefter, *der; (for magazines)* Mappe, *die.* '**binding 1.** *adj.* bindend ⟨*Vertrag, Abkommen*⟩ **(on** für). **2.** *n. (of book)* Einband, *der*

**bingo** ['bɪŋgəʊ] *n.* Bingo, *das*

**binoculars** [bɪ'nɒkjʊləz] *n. pl.* [a pair of] ~: Fernglas, *das*

**biodegradable** [baɪəʊdɪ'greɪdəbl] *adj.* biologisch abbaubar

**biographer** [baɪ'ɒgrəfə(r)] *n.* Biograph, *der*/Biographin, *die*

**biographical** [baɪə'græfɪkl] *adj.* biographisch

**biography** [baɪ'ɒgrəfɪ] *n.* Biographie, *die*

**biological** [baɪə'lɒdʒɪkl] *adj.* biologisch

**biologist** [baɪ'ɒlədʒɪst] *n.* Biologe, *der*/Biologin, *die*

**biology** [baɪ'ɒlədʒɪ] *n.* Biologie, *die*

**biotechnology** [baɪəʊtek'nɒlədʒɪ] *n.* Biotechnologie, *die*

**birch** [bɜːtʃ] *n.* Birke, *die*

**bird** [bɜːd] *n.* Vogel, *der*

**bird: ~ cage** *n.* Vogelkäfig, *der;* **~'s-eye 'view** *n.* Vogelperspektive, *die;* **~'s nest** *n.* Vogelnest, *das*

**Biro,** (P) ['baɪrəʊ] *n., pl.* **~s** Kugelschreiber, *der;* Kuli, *der (ugs.)*

**birth** [bɜːθ] *n.* **a)** Geburt, *die;* **give ~** ⟨*Frau:*⟩ entbinden; ⟨*Tier:*⟩ jungen; werfen; **give ~ to a child** ein Kind zur Welt bringen; **b)** *(of movement, fashion, etc.)* Aufkommen, *das*

**birth: ~ certificate** *n.* Geburtsurkunde, *die;* **~ control** *n.* Geburtenkontrolle, *die;* **~day** *n.* Geburtstag, *der; attrib.* Geburtstags-; **~place** *n.* Geburtsort, *der*

**biscuit** ['bɪskɪt] *n. (Brit.)* Keks, *der*

**bisect** [baɪ'sekt] *v. t.* halbieren

**bishop** ['bɪʃəp] *n.* **a)** *(Eccl.)* Bischof, *der;* **b)** *(Chess)* Läufer, *der*

**¹bit** [bɪt] *n.* **a)** *(for horse)* Gebiß, *das;* **b)** *(of drill)* [Bohr]einsatz, *der*

**²bit** *n. (piece)* Stück, *das;* **not a** *or* **one ~** *(not at all)* überhaupt nicht; **a ~ tired/ too early** ein bißchen müde/zu früh; **be a ~ of a coward/bully** ein ziemlicher Feigling sein/den starken Mann markieren *(ugs.)*

**³bit** *n. (Computing)* Bit, *das*

**⁴bit** *see* **bite 1, 2**

**bitch** [bɪtʃ] *n.* **a)** *(dog)* Hündin, *die;* **b)** *(sl. derog.: woman)* Miststück, *das (derb)*

**bite** [baɪt] **1.** *v. t.,* bit [bɪt], bitten ['bɪtn] beißen; ⟨*Moskito usw.:*⟩ stechen. **2.** *v. i.,* bit, bitten beißen/stechen; *(take bait)* anbeißen. **3.** *n.* Biß, *der; (piece)* Bissen, *der; (wound)* Bißwunde, *die; (by mosquito etc.)* Stich, *der.* **bite 'off** *v. t.* abbeißen

**biting** ['baɪtɪŋ] *adj.* beißend

**bitten** *see* **bite 1, 2**

**bitter** ['bɪtə(r)] *adj.* bitter. '**bitterly** *adv.* bitterlich ⟨*weinen, sich beschweren*⟩; **~ cold** bitterkalt. '**bitterness** *n.* Bitterkeit, *die*

**bizarre** [bɪ'zɑː(r)] *adj.* bizarr

**black** [blæk] **1.** *adj.* **a)** schwarz; **~ and blue** *(fig.)* grün und blau; **in ~ and white** *(fig.)* schwarz auf weiß; **in the ~** *(in credit)* in den schwarzen Zahlen; **b)** **B~** *(dark-skinned)* schwarz. **2.** *n.* **a)** Schwarz, *das;* **b)** **B~** *(person)* Schwarze, *der/die.* **3.** *v. t.* bestreiken ⟨*Betrieb*⟩; boykottieren ⟨*Arbeit*⟩. **black 'out 1.** *v. t.* verdunkeln. **2.** *v. i.* das Bewußtsein verlieren

**black: ~berry** ['blækbərɪ] *n.* Brombeere, *die;* **~bird** *n.* Amsel, *die;* **~board** *n.* [Wand]tafel, *die;* **~currant** *n.* schwarze Johannisbeere

**blacken** ['blækn] *v. t.* schwärzen; verfinstern ⟨*Himmel*⟩

**black: ~ 'eye** *n.* blaues Auge; **B~ 'Forest** *pr. n.* Schwarzwald, *der;* **~ 'ice** *n.* Glatteis, *das;* **~leg** *n. (Brit.)* Streikbrecher, *der*/-brecherin, *die;* **~list** *n.* schwarze Liste; **~list** *v. t.* auf die schwarze Liste setzen; **~mail** *v. t.* erpressen; **2.** *n.* Erpressung, *die;* **~ market** *n.* schwarzer Markt

'**blackness** *n.* Schwärze, *die; (darkness)* Finsternis, *die*

**black: ~-out** *n.* **a)** Verdunkelung, *die, (Theatre, Radio)* Blackout, *der;* **b)** *(Med.)* **have a ~-out** das Bewußtsein verlieren; **B~ 'Sea** *pr. n.* Schwarze Meer, *das;* **~smith** ['blæksmɪθ] *n.* Schmied, *der;* **~ spot** *n.* Gefahrenstelle, *die*

**bladder** ['blædə(r)] *n.* Blase, *die*

**blade** [bleɪd] *n.* **a)** *(of sword, knife, razor, etc.)* Klinge, *die; (of saw, oar, propeller)* Blatt, *das;* **b)** *(of grass)* Spreite, *die*

**blame** [bleɪm] **1.** *v. t.* **~ sb.** [for sth.] jmdm. die Schuld [an etw. *(Dat.)*] geben; **be to ~** [for sth.] an etw. *(Dat.)* schuld sein; **~ sth.** [for sth.] etw. [für

etw.] verantwortlich machen. **2.** *n.*
Schuld, *die.* '**blameless** *adj.* untadelig

**blancmange** [blə'mɒnʒ] *n.* Flammeri, *der*

**bland** [blænd] *adj.* mild; *(suave)* verbindlich

**blank** [blæŋk] **1.** *adj.* **a)** leer; kahl
⟨*Wand, Fläche*⟩; **b)** *(empty)* frei. **2.** *n.*
**a)** *(space)* Lücke, *die;* **b)** *(cartridge)*
Platzpatrone, *die;* **c) draw a ~:** kein
Glück haben. **blank 'cheque** *n.*
Blankoscheck, *der; (fig.)* Blankovollmacht, *die*

**blanket** ['blæŋkɪt] *n.* Decke, *die;* **wet
'~ ~** *(fig.)* Trauerkloß, *der (ugs.)*

**blare** ['bleə(r)] **1.** *v.i.* ⟨*Lautsprecher:*⟩
plärren; ⟨*Trompete:*⟩ schmettern. **2.**
*v.t.* **~ [out]** [hinaus]plärren ⟨*Worte*⟩;
[hinaus]schmettern ⟨*Melodie*⟩

**blasé** ['blɑːzeɪ] *adj.* blasiert

**blasphemous** ['blæsfəməs] *adj.* lästerlich

**blasphemy** ['blæsfəmɪ] *n.* Blasphemie, *die*

**blast** [blɑːst] **1.** *n.* **a) a ~ [of wind]** ein
Windstoß; **b)** *(of horn)* Tuten, *das.* **2.**
*v.t. (blow up)* sprengen. **blast 'off** *v.i.*
abheben

'**blasted** *adj. (damned)* verdammt *(salopp)*

'**blast-off** *n.* Abheben, *das*

**blatant** ['bleɪtənt] *adj.* **a)** *(flagrant)*
eklatant; **b)** *(unashamed)* unverhohlen; unverfroren ⟨*Lüge*⟩

**blaze** [bleɪz] **1.** *n.* Feuer, *das.* **2.** *v.i.*
brennen; lodern *(geh.)*

**blazer** ['bleɪzə(r)] *n.* Blazer, *der*

**bleach** [bliːtʃ] **1.** *v.t.* bleichen. **2.** *n.*
Bleichmittel, *das*

**bleak** ['bliːk] *adj.* **a)** öde ⟨*Landschaft
usw.*⟩; **b)** *(unpromising)* düster

**bleat** [bliːt] *v.i.* ⟨*Schaf:*⟩ blöken;
⟨*Ziege:*⟩ meckern

**bled** *see* **bleed**

**bleed** [bliːd] *v.i., bled* [bled] bluten

**bleeper** ['bliːpə(r)] *n.* Kleinempfänger, *der*

**blemish** ['blemɪʃ] *n.* Fleck, *der*

**blend** [blend] **1.** *v.t.* mischen. **2.** *v.i.*
sich mischen lassen. **3.** *n.* Mischung,
*die.* '**blender** *n.* Mixer, *der*

**bless** [bles] *v.t.* segnen; **~ you!** *(after
sb.' sneezes)* Gesundheit! **blessed**
['blesɪd] *adj.* **a)** *(revered)* heilig; **b)**
*(cursed)* verdammt *(salopp).* '**blessing** *n.* Segen, *der*

**blew** *see* ¹**blow**

**blight** [blaɪt] *n. (fig.)* Fluch, *der*

**blind** [blaɪnd] **1.** *adj.* blind; **~ in one
eye** auf einem Auge blind. **2.** *adv.*
blindlings. **3.** *n.* Jalousie, *die; (made of
cloth)* Rouleau, *das; (of shop)* Markise, *die.* **4.** *v.t.* blenden. '**blindfold 1.**
*v.t.* die Augen verbinden (+ *Dat.*). **2.**
*adj.* mit verbundenen Augen *nachgestellt.* '**blinding** *adj.* blendend.
'**blindly** *adv.* [wie] blind; *(fig.)* blindlings. '**blindness** *n.* Blindheit, *die*

**blink** [blɪŋk] *v.i.* **a)** blinzeln; **b)** *(shine
intermittently)* blinken

'**blinkers** *n. pl.* Scheuklappen *Pl.*

**bliss** [blɪs] *n.* [Glück]seligkeit, *die.*
**blissful** ['blɪsfl] *adj.* [glück]selig

**blister** ['blɪstə(r)] **1.** *n.* Blase, *die.* **2.**
*v.i.* ⟨*Haut:*⟩ Blasen bekommen; ⟨*Anstrich:*⟩ Blasen werfen

**blizzard** ['blɪzəd] *n.* Schneesturm, *der*

**blob** [blɒb] *n. (drop)* Tropfen, *der;
(small mass)* Klacks, *der (ugs.)*

**block** [blɒk] **1.** *n.* **a)** Klotz, *der; (for
chopping on)* Hackklotz, *der; (of concrete or stone, building-stone)* Block,
*der;* **b)** *(building)* [Häuser]block, *der;*
**~ of flats/offices** Wohnblock, *der/*Bürohaus, *das.* **2.** *v.t.* versperren ⟨*Tür,
Straße, Durchgang, Sicht*⟩; verstopfen
⟨*Pfeife, Abfluß*⟩; verhindern ⟨*Fortschritt*⟩. **block 'up** *v.t.* verstopfen;
versperren ⟨*Eingang*⟩

**blockade** [blɒ'keɪd] **1.** *n.* Blockade,
*die.* **2.** *v.t.* blockieren

**blockage** ['blɒkɪdʒ] *n.* Block, *der; (of
pipe, gutter)* Verstopfung, *die*

**block: ~ 'booking** *n.* Gruppenbuchung, *die; ~* '**capital** *n.* Blockbuchstabe, *der; ~***head** *n.* Dummkopf,
*der; ~* '**letters** *n. pl.* Blockschrift, *die*

**bloke** [bləʊk] *n. (Brit. coll.)* Typ, *der
(ugs.)*

**blonde** [blɒnd] **1.** *adj.* blond. **2.** *n.*
Blondine, *die*

**blood** [blʌd] *n.* Blut, *das*

**blood: ~ donor** *n.* Blutspender, *der/*
-spenderin, *die; ~* **group** *n.* Blutgruppe, *die; ~***hound** *n.* Bluthund,
*der; ~* **pressure** *n.* Blutdruck, *der;
~***shed** *n.* Blutvergießen, *das; ~***shot**
*adj.* blutunterlaufen; **~-stained** *adj.*
blutbefleckt; **~stream** *n.* Blutstrom,
*der; ~* **test** *n.* Blutprobe, *die;
~***thirsty** *adj.* blutrünstig; **~ transfusion** *n.* Bluttransfusion, *die;
~-***vessel** *n.* Blutgefäß, *das*

'**bloody 1.** *adj.* **a)** blutig; *(running with
blood)* blutend; **b)** *(sl.: damned)* verdammt *(salopp).* **2.** *adv. (sl.: damned)*
verdammt *(salopp)*

**bloom** [blu:m] **1.** *n.* Blüte, *die;* **be in ~:** in Blüte stehen. **2.** *v. i.* blühen

**blossom** ['blɒsəm] **1.** *n. (flower)* Blüte, *die; (mass)* Blütenmeer, *das (geh.).* **2.** *v. i.* blühen; ⟨*Mensch:*⟩ aufblühen

**blot** [blɒt] **1.** *n. (of ink)* Tintenklecks, *der; (stain)* Fleck, *der.* **2.** *v. t.,* **-tt-** ablöschen ⟨*Tinte, Papier*⟩. **blot 'out** *v. t.. (fig.)* auslöschen

**blotchy** ['blɒtʃɪ] *adj.* fleckig

'**blotting-paper** *n.* Löschpapier, *das*

**blouse** [blaʊz] *n.* Bluse, *die*

¹**blow** [bləʊ] **1.** *v. i.,* blew [blu:], blown [bləʊn] ⟨*Wind:*⟩ wehen; ⟨*Sturm:*⟩ blasen. **2.** *v. t.,* blew, blown: **a)** blasen; ⟨*Wind:*⟩ wehen; machen ⟨*Seifenblase*⟩; ~ **sb. a kiss** jmdm. eine Kußhand zuwerfen; **b)** ~ **one's nose** sich *(Dat.)* die Nase putzen; **c)** ~ **sth. to pieces** etw. in die Luft sprengen. **blow 'out 1.** *v. t.* ausblasen. **2.** *v. i.* ausgeblasen werden. **blow 'over 1.** *v. i.* umgeblasen werden; ⟨*Streit, Sturm:*⟩ sich legen. **2.** *v. t.* umblasen. **blow 'up 1.** *v. t.* **a)** *(shatter)* [in die Luft] sprengen; **b)** aufblasen ⟨*Ballon*⟩; aufpumpen ⟨*Reifen*⟩; **c)** *(coll.: exaggerate)* hochspielen. **2.** *v. i. (explode)* explodieren

²**blow** *n.* **a)** Schlag, *der; (with axe)* Hieb, *der;* **come to ~s** handgreiflich werden; **b)** *(disaster)* [schwerer] Schlag. '**blow-dry** *v. t.* fönen. '**blowlamp** *n.* Lötlampe, *die*

**blown** *see* ¹**blow**

**blubber** ['blʌbə(r)] *n.* Walspeck, *der*

**blue** [blu:] **1.** *adj.* blau. **2.** *n.* **a)** Blau, *das;* **b)** have the ~s deprimiert sein; **c)** *(Mus.)* the ~s der Blues; **d)** out of the ~: aus heiterem Himmel

**blue:** ~**bell** *n.* Glockenblume, *die;* ~**bottle** *n.* Schmeißfliege, *die;* ~**-collar** *adj.* ~**-collar worker** Arbeiter, *der/*Arbeiterin, *die;* ~ '**jeans** *pl.* Blue jeans *Pl.;* ~**print** *n. (fig.)* Entwurf, *der*

**bluff** [blʌf] **1.** *n.* Bluff, *der (ugs.);* **call sb.'s ~:** es darauf ankommen lassen *(ugs.).* **2.** *v. i. & t.* bluffen *(ugs.)*

**blunder** ['blʌndə(r)] **1.** *n.* [schwerer] Fehler. **2.** *v. i.* **a)** *(make mistake)* einen [schweren] Fehler machen; **b)** *(move blindly)* tappen

**blunt** [blʌnt] **1.** *adj.* **a)** stumpf; **b)** *(outspoken)* direkt; glatt *(ugs.)* ⟨*Ablehnung*⟩. **2.** *v. t.* ~ [the edge of] stumpf machen. '**bluntly** *adv.* direkt; glatt ⟨*ablehnen*⟩

**blur** [blɜ:(r)] **1.** *v. t.,* **-rr-:** **a)** verwischen;

**b)** *(become indistinct)* verschwimmen; **his vision was ~red** er sah alles verschwommen. **2.** *n. (smear)* Fleck, *der; (dim image)* verschwommener Fleck

**blurt** [blɜ:t] *v. t.* ~ **out** herausplatzen mit *(ugs.)*

**blush** [blʌʃ] **1.** *v. i.* rot werden. **2.** *n.* Rotwerden, *das*

**bluster** ['blʌstə(r)] *v. i.* sich aufplustern *(ugs.)*

**blustery** ['blʌstərɪ] *adj.* stürmisch

**boar** [bɔ:(r)] *n.* |wild| ~: Keiler, *der*

**board** [bɔ:d] **1.** *n.* **a)** Brett, *das; (black~)* Tafel, *die; (notice-~)* Schwarzes Brett; **above** ~ *(fig.)* korrekt; **b)** *(Commerc.)* ~ |of directors| Vorstand, *der; (supervisory ~)* Aufsichtsrat, *der;* **c)** *(Naut., Aeronaut.)* **on** ~: an Bord; **d)** ~ **and lodging** Unterkunft und Verpflegung; **full** ~: Vollpension, *die.* **2.** *v. t.* ~ **the ship/plane** an Bord des Schiffes/Flugzeuges gehen; ~ **the train/bus** in den Zug/Bus einsteigen

'**boarder** *n. (Sch.)* Internatsschüler, *der/*-schülerin, *die*

'**board game** *n.* Brettspiel, *das*

**boarding:** ~**-house** *n.* Pension, *die;* ~ **pass** *n.* Bordkarte, *die;* ~**-school** *n.* Internat, *das*

**board:** ~ **meeting** *n.* Vorstandssitzung, *die;* ~**-room** *n.* Sitzungssaal, *der*

**boast** [bəʊst] *v. i.* prahlen. **boastful** ['bəʊstfl] *adj.* prahlerisch

**boat** [bəʊt] *n.* Boot, *das*

¹**bob** [bɒb] *v. i.,* **-bb-:** ~ |up and down| sich auf und nieder bewegen

²**bob** *n.* (~**-sied**) Bob, *der*

**bobbin** ['bɒbɪn] *n.* Spule, *die*

**bob:** ~**-sled,** ~**-sleigh** *ns.* Bobschlitten, *der*

**bodice** ['bɒdɪs] *n.* Mieder, *das; (part of dress)* Oberteil, *das*

**bodily** ['bɒdɪlɪ] *adj.* körperlich; ~ **needs** leibliche Bedürfnisse

**body** ['bɒdɪ] *n.* **a)** Körper, *der;* **b)** *(corpse)* Leiche, *die;* **c)** *(group)* Gruppe, *die; (with particular function)* Organ, *das.* '**bodyguard** *n. (single)* Leibwächter, *der; (group)* Leibwache, *die.* '**bodywork** *n.* Karosserie, *die*

**bog** [bɒg] **1.** *n.* Moor, *das; (marsh, swamp)* Sumpf, *der.* **2.** *v. t.,* **-gg-:** **be/ get ~ged down** *(fig.)* sich verzettelt haben/sich verzetteln

**boggle** ['bɒgl] *v. i. (coll.)* **the mind ~s** da kann man nur [noch] staunen

**bogus** ['bəʊgəs] *adj.* falsch

¹**boil** [bɔɪl] **1.** *v. i. & t.* kochen. **2.** *n.*

come to/go off the ~: zu kochen anfangen/aufhören; **bring to the ~:** zum Kochen bringen. **boil 'down** v. i. ~ **down to sth.** (fig.) auf etw. hinauslaufen. **boil 'over** v. i. überkochen

**²boil** n. (Med.) Furunkel, der

**'boiler** n. Kessel, der

**'boiling-point** n. Siedepunkt, der

**boisterous** ['bɔɪstərəs] adj. ausgelassen

**bold** [bəʊld] adj. **a)** (courageous) mutig; (daring) kühn; **b)** auffallend ⟨Farbe, Muster⟩. **'boldly** adv. (courageously) mutig; (daringly) kühn

**Bolivia** [bə'lɪvɪə] pr. n. Bolivien (das)

**bollard** ['bɒlɑːd] n. (Brit.) Poller, der

**bolster** ['bəʊlstə(r)] **1.** n. (pillow) Nackenrolle, die. **2.** v. t. (fig.) stärken

**bolt** [bəʊlt] **1.** n. **a)** (on door or window) Riegel, der; (on gun) Kammerverschluß, der; **b)** (metal pin) Schraube, die; (without thread) Bolzen, der. **2.** v. i. davonlaufen; ⟨Pferd:⟩ durchgehen; ⟨Fuchs, Kaninchen:⟩ flüchten. **3.** v. t. **a)** verriegeln ⟨Tür, Fenster⟩; **b)** (fasten with ~s) verschrauben/mit Bolzen verbinden; **c)** ~ [down] hinunterschlingen ⟨Essen⟩. **4.** adv. ~ upright kerzengerade

**bomb** [bɒm] **1.** n. Bombe, die. **2.** v. t. bombardieren

**bombard** [bɒm'bɑːd] v. t. beschießen. **bom'bardment** n. Beschuß, der

**bombastic** [bɒm'bæstɪk] adj. bombastisch

**bomber** ['bɒmə(r)] n. (Air Force) Bomber, der (ugs.)

**'bomb-shell** n. Bombe, die; (fig.) Sensation, die

**bond** [bɒnd] n. **a)** Band, das; in pl. (shackles) Fesseln; **b)** (adhesion) Verbindung, die; **c)** (Commerc.) Anleihe, die

**bone** [bəʊn] **1.** n. Knochen, der; (of fish) Gräte, die. **2.** v. t. den/die Knochen herauslösen aus; entgräten ⟨Fisch⟩. **bone 'dry** adj. knochentrocken (ugs.). **bone 'idle** adj. stinkfaul (salopp)

**bonfire** ['bɒnfaɪə(r)] n. Freudenfeuer, das; (for rubbish) Feuer, das

**bonnet** ['bɒnɪt] n. **a)** (woman's) Haube, die; (child's) Häubchen, das; **b)** (Brit. Motor Veh.) Motorhaube, die

**bonus** ['bəʊnəs] n. zusätzliche Leistung; (to shareholders) Bonus, der; **Christmas ~:** Weihnachtsgratifikation, die

**bony** ['bəʊnɪ] adj. **a)** Knochen-; (like

bone) knochenartig; **b)** (skinny) knochendürr (ugs.); spindeldürr

**boo** [buː] **1.** int. to surprise sb. huh; expr. disapproval, contempt buh. **2.** n. Buh, das (ugs.). **3.** v. t. ausbuhen (ugs.). **4.** v. i. buhen (ugs.)

**booby** ['buːbɪ] n. Trottel, der (ugs.). **'booby prize** n. Preis für den schlechtesten Teilnehmer an einem Wettbewerb. **'booby trap** n. **a)** Falle, mit der man jmdm. einen Streich spielen will; **b)** (Mil.) versteckte Sprengladung

**book** [bʊk] **1.** n. Buch, das; (for accounts) Rechnungsbuch, das; (for exercises) [Schreib]heft, das. **2.** v. t. buchen ⟨Reise, Flug, Platz [im Flugzeug]⟩; [vor]bestellen ⟨Eintrittskarte, Tisch, Zimmer, Platz [im Theater]⟩. **3.** v. i. buchen. **book 'in 1.** v. i. sich eintragen. **2.** v. t. eintragen. **book 'up** v. i. & t. buchen; **be ~ed up** ⟨Hotel usw.:⟩ ausgebucht sein

**book:** ~**case** n. Bücherschrank, der; ~**ends** n. pl. Buchstützen

**'booking office** n. [Fahrkarten]schalter, der

**book:** ~**keeper** n. Buchhalter, der/-halterin, die; ~**keeping** n. Buchführung, die; Buchhaltung, die

**booklet** ['bʊklɪt] n. Broschüre, die

**book:** ~**maker** n. (in betting) Buchmacher, der; ~**mark** n. Lesezeichen, das; ~**seller** n. Buchhändler, der/-händlerin, die; ~**shelf** n. Bücherbord, das; ~**shop** n. Buchhandlung, die; ~**stall** n. Bücherstand, der; ~**store** n. (Amer.) Buchhandlung, die; ~ **token** n. Büchergutschein, der; ~**worm** n. Bücherwurm, der

**¹boom** [buːm] n. **a)** (for camera or microphone) Ausleger, der; **b)** (Naut.) Baum, der

**²boom** [buːm] **1.** v. i. **a)** dröhnen; **b)** ⟨Geschäft, Verkauf, Gebiet:⟩ sich sprunghaft entwickeln. **2.** n. **a)** Dröhnen, das; **b)** (in business or economy) Boom, der

**boomerang** ['buːməræŋ] n. Bumerang, der

**boon** [buːn] n. Segen, der (to für)

**boorish** ['bʊərɪʃ] adj. rüpelhaft

**boost** [buːst] **1.** v. t. in die Höhe treiben ⟨Preis, Wert⟩; stärken ⟨Selbstvertrauen, Moral⟩. **2.** n. Auftrieb, der

**boot** [buːt] **1.** n. **a)** Stiefel, der; **give sb. the ~** (fig. coll.) jmdn. rausschmeißen (ugs.); **b)** (Brit.: of car) Kofferraum, der. **2.** v. t. (coll.: kick) kicken (ugs.)

**booth** [buːð] n. **a)** Bude, die; **b)** (telephone ~) Zelle, die

**'bootleg** *adj.* schwarz verkauft/gebrannt

**booze** [bu:z] *(coll.)* 1. *v. i.* saufen *(derb).* 2. *n.* Alkohol, *der*

**border** ['bɔːdə(r)] 1. *n.* a) Rand, *der; (of table-cloth, handkerchief)* Bordüre, *die;* b) *(of country)* Grenze, *die;* c) *(flower-bed)* Rabatte, *die.* 2. *attrib. adj.* Grenz⟨*stadt, -streit*⟩. 3. *v. t.* a) *(adjoin)* [an]grenzen an (+ *Akk.*); b) *(put a ~ to, act as ~ to)* umranden; einfassen. 4. *v. i.* ~ **on** a) *see* 3 a; b) *(resemble)* grenzen an (+ *Akk.*). **'borderline** 1. *n.* Grenzlinie, *die.* 2. *adj.* be ~: auf der Grenze liegen; **a ~ case/ candidate** ein Grenzfall

**¹bore** [bɔː(r)] 1. *v. t.* bohren. 2. *n. (of firearm)* Kaliber, *das*

**²bore** 1. *n.* a) it's a real ~: es ist wirklich ärgerlich; **what a ~!** wie ärgerlich!; b) *(person)* Langweiler, *der (ugs.).* 2. *v. t.* langweilen; be ~d sich langweilen

**³bore** *see* **²bear**

**boredom** ['bɔːdəm] *n.* Langeweile, *die*

**'borehole** *n.* Bohrloch, *das*

**boring** ['bɔːrɪŋ] *adj.* langweilig

**born** [bɔːn] 1. be ~: geboren werden. 2. *adj.* geboren; **be a ~ orator** der geborene Redner sein

**borne** *see* **²bear**

**borough** ['bʌrə] *n. (town)* Stadt, *die; (village)* Gemeinde, *die*

**borrow** ['bɒrəʊ] *v. t.* leihen (**from** von, bei); *(from library)* entleihen. **'borrower** *n. (from bank)* Kreditnehmer, *der; (from library)* Entleiher, *der*

**bosom** ['bʊzəm] *n.* Brust, *die*

**boss** [bɒs] 1. *n. (coll.)* Boß, *der (ugs.);* Chef, *der.* 2. *v. t.* ~ |about *or* around| herumkommandieren *(ugs.).* **'bossy** *adj. (coll.)* herrisch

**botanical** [bə'tænɪkl] *adj.* botanisch

**botanist** ['bɒtənɪst] *n.* Botaniker, *der*/Botanikerin, *die*

**botany** ['bɒtənɪ] *n.* Botanik, *die*

**botch** [bɒtʃ] 1. *v. t.* pfuschen bei *(ugs.).* 2. *v. i.* pfuschen *(ugs.).* **botch 'up** *v. t. (bungle)* verpfuschen *(ugs.)*

**both** [bəʊθ] 1. *adj.* beide; ~ |the| **brothers** beide Brüder. 2. *pron.* beide; ~ |of them| **are dead** beide sind tot; ~ **of you/them are** ...: ihr seid/sie sind beide ... 3. *adv.* ~ **A and B** sowohl A als [auch] B; **he and I were ~ there** er und ich waren beide da

**bother** ['bɒðə(r)] 1. *v. t.* a) I **can't ~ed** ich habe keine Lust; b) *(annoy)* lästig sein (+ *Dat.*); ⟨*Lärm, Licht:*⟩

stören; ⟨*Schmerz, Zahn:*⟩ zu schaffen machen (+ *Dat.*); **I'm sorry to ~ you, but ...:** es tut mir leid, wenn ich Sie störe, aber ...; c) *(worry)* Sorgen machen (+ *Dat.*); ⟨*Problem, Frage:*⟩ beschäftigen. 2. *v. i.* **don't ~ to do it** Sie brauchen es nicht zu tun; **you needn't/shouldn't have ~ed** das wäre nicht nötig gewesen; **don't ~!** nicht nötig! 3. *n.* a) *(trouble)* Ärger, *der;* b) *(effort)* Mühe, *die.* 4. *int. (coll.)* wie ärgerlich!

**bottle** ['bɒtl] 1. *n.* Flasche, *die;* **a ~ of beer** eine Flasche Bier. 2. *v. t.* a) *(put into ~s)* in Flaschen [ab]füllen; b) *(preserve in jars)* einmachen. **bottle 'up** *v. t.* a) *(conceal)* in sich *(Dat.)* aufstauen; b) *(trap)* einschließen

**bottle:** ~ **bank** *n.* Altglasbehälter, *der;* ~-**neck** *n. (fig.)* Flaschenhals, *der (ugs.);* ~-**opener** *n.* Flaschenöffner, *der;* ~-**top** *n.* Flaschenverschluß, *der*

**bottom** ['bɒtəm] 1. *n.* a) unteres Ende; *(of cup, glass, box)* Boden, *der; (of valley, well, shaft)* Sohle, *die; (of hill, cliff, stairs)* Fuß, *der;* b) *(buttocks)* Hinterteil, *das (ugs.);* c) *(of sea, lake)* Grund, *der;* d) *(farthest point)* **at the ~ of the garden/street** hinten im Garten/ am Ende der Straße; e) *(underside)* Unterseite, *die;* f) *(fig.)* **start at the ~:** ganz unten anfangen; **be ~ of the class** der/die Letzte in der Klasse sein. 2. *adj.* a) *(lowest)* unterst...; *(lower)* unter...; b) *(fig.: last)* letzt... **'bottomless** *adj.* bodenlos; unendlich tief ⟨*Meer, Ozean*⟩

**bough** [baʊ] *n.* Ast, *der*

**bought** *see* **buy** 1

**boulder** ['bəʊldə(r)] *n.* Felsbrocken, *der*

**boulevard** ['buːləvɑːd] *n.* Boulevard, *der*

**bounce** [baʊns] 1. *v. i.* a) springen; b) *(coll.)* ⟨*Scheck:*⟩ platzen *(ugs.).* 2. *v. t.* aufspringen lassen ⟨*Ball*⟩. 3. *n.* Aufprall, *der.* **'bouncer** *n. (coll.)* Rausschmeißer, *der (ugs.).* **bouncing** ['baʊnsɪŋ] *adj.* stramm ⟨*Baby*⟩. **bouncy** ['baʊnsɪ] *adj.* gut springend ⟨*Ball*⟩; *(fig.: lively)* munter

**¹bound** [baʊnd] 1. *n., usu. in pl. (limit)* Grenze, *die;* **within the ~s of possibility** im Bereich des Möglichen; **sth. is out of ~s to sb.** der Zutritt zu etw. ist [für jmdn.] verboten. 2. *v. t.* be ~ed by **sth.** durch etw. begrenzt werden

**²bound** 1. *v. i.* hüpfen. 2. *n.* Satz, *der*

**³bound** *pred. adj.* **be ~ for home/**
Frankfurt auf dem Heimweg/nach
Frankfurt unterwegs sein; **homeward**
**~:** auf dem Weg nach Hause

**⁴bound** *see* **bind**

**boundary** ['baʊndərɪ] *n.* Grenze, *die*

**'boundless** *adj.* grenzenlos

**bounty** ['baʊntɪ] *n.* Kopfgeld, *das*

**bouquet** [bʊ'keɪ] *n.* [Blumen]strauß,
*der*

**bourgeois** ['bʊəʒwɑ:] **1.** *n., pl. same*
Bürger, *der*/Bürgerin, *die.* **2.** *adj.* bürgerlich

**bout** [baʊt] *n.* **a)** *(contest)* Wettkampf,
*der;* **b)** *(fit)* Anfall, *der*

**boutique** [bu:'ti:k] *n.* Boutique, *die*

**'bow** [bəʊ] **a)** *(curve, weapon, Mus.)*
Bogen, *der;* **b)** *(knot, ribbon)* Schleife,
*die*

**²bow** [baʊ] **1.** *v. i.* **a)** **~ [to sb.]** sich [vor
jmdm.] verbeugen; **b)** *(submit)* sich
beugen **(to** *Dat.).* **2.** *n.* Verbeugung,
*die*

**³bow** [baʊ] *n. (Naut.)* Bug, *der*

**bowel** ['baʊəl] *n. (Anat.)* **~s** *pl., (Med.)*
**~:** Darm, *der*

**'bowl** [bəʊl] *n. (basin)* Schüssel, *die;*
*(shallower)* Schale, *die; (of spoon)*
Schöpfteil, *der; (of pipe)* Kopf, *der*

**²bowl 1.** *n.* **a)** *(ball)* Kugel, *die;* **b)** *in pl.*
*(game)* Bowls, *das.* **2.** *v. i.* **a)** *(play* **~s)**
Bowls spielen; **b)** *(Cricket)* werfen

**bow-legged** ['bəʊlegɪd] O-beinig
*(ugs.)*

**'bowler** ['bəʊlə(r)] *n. (Cricket)* Werfer,
*der*

**²bowler** *n.* **~ [hat]** Bowler, *der*

**'bowling** *n.* **[ten-pin] ~:** Bowling, *das;*
**go ~:** bowlen gehen. **'bowling-alley**
*n.* Bowlingbahn, *die.* **'bowling-**
**green** *n. Rasenfläche für Bowls*

**bow** [bəʊ]: **~-'tie** *n.* Fliege, *die;*
**~-window** *n.* Erkerfenster, *das*

**'box** [bɒks] *n.* Kasten, *der; (bigger)* Kiste, *die; (of cardboard)* Schachtel, *die*

**²box 1.** *n.* **he gave him a ~ on the ear[s]**
er gab ihm eine Ohrfeige. **2.** *v. t.* **a)** **he**
**~ed his ears** *or* **him round the ears** er
ohrfeigte ihn; **b)** *(Sport)* **~ sb.** gegen
jmdn. boxen. **3.** *v. i.* boxen. **'boxer** *n.*
Boxer, *der.* **'boxing** *n.* Boxen, *das*

**boxing: B~ Day** *n.* zweiter Weihnachtsfeiertag; **~-glove** *n.* Boxhand-
schuh, *der;* **~-match** *n.* Boxkampf,
*der;* **~-ring** *n.* Boxring, *der*

**box: ~ number** *n. (at newspaper of-*
*fice)* Chiffre, *die; (at post office)* Postfach, *das;* **~-office** *n.* Kasse, *die;*
**~-room** *n. (Brit.)* Abstellraum, *der*

**boy** [bɔɪ] *n.* Junge, *der*

**boycott** ['bɔɪkɒt] **1.** *v. t.* boykottieren.
**2.** *n.* Boykott, *der*

**'boy-friend** *n.* Freund, *der*

**'boyish** *adj.* jungenhaft

**bra** [brɑ:] *n.* BH, *der (ugs.)*

**brace** [breɪs] **1.** *n.* **a)** *(connecting piece)*
Klammer, *die; (strut)* Strebe, *die;*
*(Dent.)* [Zahn]spange, *die;* **b)** *in pl.*
*(trouser-straps)* Hosenträger. **2.** *v. refl.*
**~ oneself for sth.** sich auf etw. *(Akk.)*
vorbereiten

**bracelet** ['breɪslɪt] *n.* Armband, *das*

**bracing** ['breɪsɪŋ] *adj.* belebend

**bracken** ['brækn] *n.* [Adler]farn, *der*

**bracket** ['brækɪt] **1.** *n.* **a)** *(support)*
Konsole, *die;* **b)** *(mark)* Klammer,
*die.* **2.** *v. t.* einklammern

**brag** [bræg] *v. i. & t.,* **-gg-** prahlen
**(about** mit)

**braid** [breɪd] **1.** *n.* **a)** *(plait)* Flechte, *die*
*(geh.);* Zopf, *der;* **b)** *(woven band)*
Borte, *die; (on uniform)* Litze, *die.* **2.**
*v. t.* flechten

**Braille** [breɪl] *n.* Blindenschrift, *die*

**brain** [breɪn] *n.* Gehirn, *das*

**brain: ~-child** *n. (coll.)* Geistespro-
dukt, *das;* **~less** *adj.* hirnlos;
**~wash** *v. t.* einer Gehirnwäsche unterziehen; **~wave** *n. (coll.: inspira-*
*tion)* genialer Einfall

**'brainy** *adj.* intelligent

**brake** [breɪk] **1.** *n.* Bremse, *die.* **2.** *v. t.*
**& i.** bremsen; **braking distance** Brems-
weg, *der.* **'brake light** *n.* Bremslicht,
*das*

**bramble** ['bræmbl] *n.* Dornenstrauch,
*der*

**bran** [bræn] *n.* Kleie, *die*

**branch** [brɑ:ntʃ] **1.** *n.* **a)** *(bough)* Ast,
*der; (twig)* Zweig, *der;* **b)** *(of artery,*
*antlers)* Ast, *der;* **c)** *(office)* Zweigstelle, *die; (shop)* Filiale, *die.* **2.** *v. i.* sich
verzweigen. **branch 'off** *v. i.* abzwei-
gen. **branch 'out** *v. i. (fig.)* **~ out into**
**sth.** sich auch mit etw. befassen

**'branch line** *n.* Nebenstrecke, *die*

**brand** [brænd] *n.* **a)** *(trade mark)* Mar-
kenzeichen, *das; (goods of particular*
*make)* Marke, *die;* **b)** *(mark)* Brand-
mal, *das*

**brandish** ['brændɪʃ] *v. t.* schwenken;
schwingen ‹*Waffe*›

**brand: ~ name** *n.* Markenname, *der;*
**~-new** *adj.* nagelneu *(ugs.)*

**brandy** ['brændɪ] *n.* Weinbrand, *der*

**brash** [bræʃ] *adj.* dreist

**brass** [brɑ:s] *n.* Messing, *das; attrib.*
Messing-; **the ~** *(Mus.)* das Blech; **~**

**player** *(Mus.)* Blechbläser, *der;* **get down to ~ tacks** zur Sache kommen.
**brass 'band** *n.* Blaskapelle, *die*
**brassière** ['bræzjə(r)] *n.* Büstenhalter, *der*
**brat** [bræt] *n.* Balg, *das od. der (ugs.)*
**bravado** [brə'vɑːdəʊ] *n.* **do sth. out of ~:** so waghalsig sein, etw. zu tun
**brave** [breɪv] **1.** *adj.* tapfer. **2.** *n.* [indianischer] Krieger. **3.** *v. t.* trotzen *(+ Dat.).* **'bravely** *adv.* tapfer.
**bravery** ['breɪvərɪ] *n.* Tapferkeit, *die*
**bravo** [brɑː'vəʊ] *int.* bravo
**brawl** [brɔːl] **1.** *v. i.* sich schlagen. **2.** *n.* Schlägerei, *die*
**brawny** ['brɔːnɪ] *adj.* muskulös
**bray** [breɪ] **1.** Iah, *das.* **2.** *v. i. ⟨Esel:⟩* iahen
**brazen** ['breɪzn] **1.** *adj.* dreist; *(shameless)* schamlos. **2.** *v. t.* **~ |out|** trotzen *(+ Dat.);* **~ it out** *(deny guilt)* es abstreiten; *(not admit guilt)* es nicht zugeben
**brazier** ['breɪzɪə(r)] *n.* Kohlenbecken, *das*
**Brazil** [brə'zɪl] *pr. n.* Brasilien *(das).*
**Bra'zil nut** *n.* Paranuß, *die*
**breach** [briːtʃ] **1.** *n.* **a)** *(violation)* Verstoß, *der* (of gegen); **~ of faith/duty** Vertrauensbruch, *der*/Pflichtverletzung, *die;* **b)** *(of relations)* Bruch, *der;* **c)** *(gap)* Bresche, *die; (fig.)* Riß, *der.* **2.** *v. t.* durchbrechen
**bread** [bred] *n.* Brot, *das;* **a piece of ~ and butter** ein Butterbrot
**bread:** **~-bin** *n.* Brotkasten, *der;* **~-board** *n.* [Brot]brett, *das;* **~crumb** *n.* Brotkrume, *die;* **~crumbs** *(coating)* Paniermehl, *das;* **~-knife** *n.* Brotmesser, *das;* **~line** *n.* **be or live on/below the ~line** gerade noch/nicht einmal mehr das Notwendigste zum Leben haben
**breadth** [bredθ] *n.* Breite, *die*
**'bread-winner** *n.* Ernährer, *der*/Ernährerin, *die*
**break** [breɪk] **1.** *v. t.,* **broke** [brəʊk], **broken** ['brəʊkn] **a)** brechen; *(so as to damage)* zerbrechen; kaputtmachen *(ugs.);* zerreißen *⟨Seil⟩; (fig.: interrupt)* unterbrechen; brechen *⟨Bann, Zauber, Schweigen⟩;* **the TV/my watch is broken** der Fernseher/meine Uhr ist kaputt *(ugs.);* **~ the habit** es sich *(Dat.)* abgewöhnen; **b)** *(fracture)* brechen *⟨Arm, Bein usw.⟩;* **c)** brechen *⟨Vertrag, Versprechen⟩;* verstoßen gegen *⟨Regel, Gesetz⟩;* **d)** *(surpass)* brechen *⟨Rekord⟩;* **e)** *(cushion)*

auffangen *⟨Schlag, jmds. Fall⟩.* **2.** *v. i.,* **broke, broken a)** kaputtgehen *(ugs.); ⟨Faden, Seil:⟩* [zer]reißen *⟨Glas, Tasse, Teller:⟩* zerbrechen; *⟨Eis:⟩* brechen; **~ in two/in pieces** durchbrechen/zerbrechen; **b) ~ into** einbrechen in *(+ Akk.) ⟨Haus⟩;* aufbrechen *⟨Auto, Safe⟩;* **~ into laughter/tears** in Gelächter/Tränen ausbrechen; **~ into a trot/run** zu traben/laufen anfangen; **c)** *(escape)* **~ out of prison** aus dem Gefängnis ausbrechen; **~ free** *or* **loose** sich losreißen; **d)** *⟨Welle:⟩* sich brechen **(on/against** an *+ Dat.);* **e)** *⟨Tag:⟩* anbrechen; *⟨Sturm:⟩* losbrechen; **f) sb's voice is ~ing** jmd. kommt in den Stimmbruch. **3.** *n.* **a)** Bruch, *der; (of rope)* Reißen, *das;* **a ~ with sb./sth.** ein Bruch mit jmdm./etw.; **b)** *(gap)* Lücke, *die; (broken place)* Sprung, *der;* **c)** *(dash)* **they made a sudden ~:** sie stürmten plötzlich davon; **d)** *(interruption)* Unterbrechung, *die; (pause, holiday)* Pause, *die;* **take or have a ~:** Pause machen; **e)** *(coll.: chance)* Chance, *die.* **break 'down 1.** *v. i.* zusammenbrechen; *⟨Verhandlungen:⟩* scheitern; *⟨Auto:⟩* eine Panne haben. **2.** *v. t.* **a)** aufbrechen *⟨Tür⟩;* brechen *⟨Widerstand⟩;* niederreißen *⟨Barriere, Schranke⟩;* **b)** *(analyse)* aufgliedern. **break 'in 1.** *v. i. (into building etc.)* einbrechen. **2.** *v. t.* **a)** zureiten *⟨Pferd⟩;* **b)** einlaufen *⟨Schuhe⟩;* **c) ~ the door in** die Tür aufbrechen. **'break into** *see* **~ 2 b. break 'off 1.** *v. t.* abbrechen; abreißen *⟨Faden⟩;* auflösen *⟨Verlobung⟩.* **2.** *v. i.* **a)** abbrechen; **b)** *(cease)* aufhören. **break 'out** *v. i.* ausbrechen; **~ out in spots/a rash** Pickel/einen Ausschlag bekommen. **break 'up 1.** *v. t.* **a)** *(~ into pieces)* zerkleinern; ausschlachten *⟨Auto⟩;* aufbrechen *⟨Erde⟩;* **b)** *(disband)* auflösen. **2.** *v. i.* **a)** *(~ into pieces, lit. or fig.)* zerbrechen; **b)** *(disband)* sich auflösen; *⟨Schule:⟩* schließen; *⟨Schüler, Lehrer:⟩* in die Ferien gehen; **c) ~ up |with sb.|** sich [von jmdm.] trennen
**breakable** ['breɪkəbl] **1.** *adj.* zerbrechlich. **2.** *n.* **~s** zerbrechliche Dinge
**breakage** ['breɪkɪdʒ] *n.* Zerbrechen, *das;* **~s must be paid for** zerbrochene Ware muß bezahlt werden
**'breakdown** *n.* **a)** *(of vehicle)* Panne, *die; (in machine)* Störung, *die;* **~ truck/van** Abschleppwagen, *der;* **b)** *(Med.)* Zusammenbruch, *der;* **c)** *(analysis)* Aufschlüsselung, *die*

'**breaker** n. a) (wave) Brecher, der; b) ~'s [yard] Autoverwertung, die
**breakfast** ['brekfəst] 1. n. Frühstück, das; for ~: zum Frühstück. 2. v.i. frühstücken. '**breakfast cereal** n. ≈ Frühstücksflocken Pl. **breakfast** '**television** n. Frühstücksfernsehen, das
'**break-in** n. Einbruch, der
'**breaking** n. ~ **and entering** (Law) Einbruch, der
**break:** ~**neck** adj. halsbrecherisch; ~**through** n. Durchbruch, der; ~-**up** n. Auflösung, die; (of relationship) Bruch, der; ~**water** n. Wellenbrecher, der
**breast** [brest] n. Brust, die
**breast:** ~**bone** n. Brustbein, das; ~-**feed** v.t. & i. stillen; ~-**stroke** n. Brustschwimmen, das
**breath** [breθ] n. a) Atem, der; get one's ~ back wieder zu Atem kommen; hold one's ~: den Atem anhalten; be out of ~: außer Atem sein; say sth. under one's ~: etw. vor sich (Akk.) hin murmeln; b) (one respiration) Atemzug, der. **Breathalyser** (Brit.), **Breathalyzer** (P) ['breθəlaizə(r)] n. Alcotest-Röhrchen Ⓦ, das; ~ **test** Alcotest Ⓦ, der
**breathe** [briːð] 1. v.i. atmen; ~ **in** einatmen; ~ **out** ausatmen. 2. v.t. a) ~ [in/out] ein-/ausatmen; b) (utter) hauchen. '**breather** ['briːðə(r)] n. Verschnaufpause, die
'**breathless** adj. atemlos (with vor + Dat.)
'**breath-taking** adj. atemberaubend
**bred** see **breed** 1, 2
**breeches** ['brɪtʃɪz] n. pl. [pair of] ~: [Knie]bundhose, die; [riding-]~: Reithose, die
**breed** [briːd] 1. v.t., **bred** [bred] a) (cause) erzeugen; b) züchten 〈Tiere, Pflanzen〉. 2. v.i., **bred** sich vermehren. 3. n. (of animals) Rasse, die. '**breeding** n. [good] ~: gute Erziehung
**breeze** [briːz] n. Brise, die. **breezy** ['briːzɪ] adj. windig
**brevity** ['brevɪtɪ] n. Kürze, die
**brew** [bruː] 1. v.t. brauen 〈Bier〉; ~ [up] kochen 〈Kaffee, Tee usw.〉. 2. v.i. a) 〈Bier:〉 gären; 〈Kaffee, Tee:〉 ziehen; b) 〈Unwetter:〉 sich zusammenbrauen. 3. n. (brewed beer/tea) Bier, das/Tee, der. '**brewer** n. Brauer, der; (firm) Brauerei, die. **brewery** ['bruːərɪ] n. Brauerei, die

**bribe** [braib] 1. n. Bestechung, die. 2. v.t. bestechen; ~ sb. to do/into doing sth. jmdn. bestechen, damit er etw. tut. **bribery** ['braibərɪ] n. Bestechung, die
**brick** [brɪk] 1. n. Ziegelstein, der; (toy) Bauklötzchen, das. 2. adj. Ziegelstein-. '**bricklayer** n. Maurer, der. '**bricklaying** n. Mauern, das
**bridal** ['braidl] adj. Braut-
**bride** [braid] n. Braut, die. '**bridegroom** n. Bräutigam, der. **bridesmaid** ['braidzmeid] n. Brautjungfer, die
¹**bridge** [brɪdʒ] 1. n. a) Brücke, die; b) (Naut.) [Kommando]brücke, die; c) (of nose) Nasenbein, das; d) (of spectacles) Steg, der. 2. v.t. eine Brücke bauen über (+ Akk.)
²**bridge** n. (Cards) Bridge, das
**bridle** ['braidl] n. Zaum, der. '**bridle path** n. Reitweg, der
¹**brief** [briːf] adj. a) kurz; gering 〈Verspätung〉; b) (concise) knapp; in ~, to be ~: kurz gesagt
²**brief** 1. n. (instructions) Instruktionen Pl.; (Law: case) Mandat, das. 2. v.t. Instruktionen geben (+ Dat.); (inform) unterrichten. '**briefcase** n. Aktentasche, die. '**briefing** n. Briefing, das; (of reporters) Unterrichtung, die
'**briefly** adv. a) kurz; b) (concisely) knapp; kurz
**briefs** [briːfs] n. pl. [pair of] ~: Slip, der
**brigade** [brɪ'geɪd] n. (Mil.) Brigade, die. **brigadier** [brɪgə'dɪə(r)] n. Brigadegeneral, der
**bright** [braɪt] adj. a) hell; grell 〈Scheinwerfer[licht]〉, Sonnenlicht〉; strahlend 〈Sonnenschein, Augen, Tag〉; leuchtend 〈Farbe, Blume〉; ~ **intervals/periods** Aufheiterungen; b) (cheerful) fröhlich; c) (clever) intelligent. **brighten** ['braɪtn] 1. v.t. ~ [up] aufhellen. 2. v.i. the weather or it is ~ing [up] es klärt sich auf. '**brightly** adv. a) hell; b) (cheerfully) fröhlich. '**brightness** n. see **bright:** a) Helligkeit, die; Grelle, die; Strahlen, das; Leuchtkraft, die; b) Fröhlichkeit, die; c) Intelligenz, die
**brilliance** ['brɪliəns] n. see **brilliant:** a) Helligkeit, die; Leuchten, das; b) Genialität, die; Glanz, der
**brilliant** ['brɪliənt] adj. a) hell 〈Licht〉; leuchtend 〈Farbe〉; b) genial 〈Mensch, Gedanke, Leistung〉; glänzend 〈Verstand, Aufführung, Idee〉
**brim** [brɪm] 1. n. Rand, der; (of hat) [Hut]krempe, die. 2. v.i., -mm-: be

**~ming with sth.** randvoll mit etw. sein.
**brim-'full** *pred. adj.* randvoll **(with mit)**

**brine** [braɪn] *n.* Salzwasser, *das*

**bring** [brɪŋ] *v. t.*, **brought** [brɔːt] a) bringen; *(as a present or favour)* mitbringen; **~ sth. with one** etw. mitbringen; b) **~ sb. to do sth.** jmdn. dazu bringen, etw. zu tun; **I could not ~ myself to do it** ich konnte es nicht über mich bringen, es zu tun. **bring a'bout** *v. t.* verursachen. **bring 'back** *v. t.* a) *(return)* zurückbringen; *(from a journey)* mitbringen; b) *(recall)* in Erinnerung bringen; c) *(restore, reintroduce)* wieder einführen. **bring 'down** *v. t.* a) herunterbringen; b) *(kill, wound)* zur Strecke bringen; c) senken ⟨*Preise, Inflationsrate, Fieber*⟩. **bring 'forward** *v. t.* a) nach vorne bringen; b) vorbringen ⟨*Argument*⟩; zur Sprache bringen ⟨*Fall, Angelegenheit*⟩; c) vorverlegen ⟨*Termin*⟩ (to auf + *Akk.*). **bring 'in** *v. t.* hereinbringen; einbringen ⟨*Gesetzesvorlage, Verdienst, Summe*⟩. **bring 'off** *v. t. (conduct successfully)* zustande bringen. **bring 'on** *v. t.* a) *(cause)* verursachen; b) *(Sport)* einsetzen. **bring 'out** *v. t.* a) herausbringen; b) hervorheben ⟨*Unterschied*⟩; c) einführen ⟨*Produkt*⟩; herausbringen ⟨*Buch, Zeitschrift*⟩. **bring 'up** *v. t.* a) heraufbringen; b) *(educate)* erziehen; *(rear)* aufziehen; c) zur Sprache bringen ⟨*Angelegenheit, Thema, Problem*⟩

**brink** [brɪŋk] *n.* Rand, *der;* **be on the ~ of doing sth.** nahe daran sein, etw. zu tun

**brisk** [brɪsk] *adj.* flott ⟨*Gang*⟩; forsch ⟨*Person, Art*⟩; frisch ⟨*Wind*⟩; *(fig.)* rege ⟨*Handel, Nachfrage*⟩; lebhaft ⟨*Geschäft*⟩. **'briskly** *adv.* flott

**bristle** ['brɪsl] 1. *n.* Borste, *die.* 2. *v. i.* a) **~ [up]** ⟨*Haare:*⟩ sich sträuben; b) **~ with** *(fig.)* starren vor (+ *Dat.*). **bristly** ['brɪslɪ] *adj.* borstig

**Britain** ['brɪtn] *pr. n.* Großbritannien *(das)*

**British** ['brɪtɪʃ] 1. *adj.* britisch; **he/she is ~:** er ist Brite/sie ist Britin. 2. *n. pl.* **the ~:** die Briten. **British 'Isles** *pr. n. pl.* Britische Inseln

**Briton** ['brɪtn] *n.* Brite, *der*/Britin, *die*

**Brittany** ['brɪtənɪ] *pr. n.* Bretagne, *die*

**brittle** ['brɪtl] *adj.* spröde ⟨*Material*⟩

**broach** [brəʊtʃ] *v. t.* anschneiden ⟨*Thema*⟩

**broad** [brɔːd] *adj.* a) breit; *(extensive)* weit ⟨*Ebene, Land*⟩; ausgedehnt ⟨*Fläche*⟩; b) *(explicit)* klar ⟨*Hinweis*⟩; breit ⟨*Lächeln*⟩; c) *(main)* grob; *(generalized)* allgemein; d) stark ⟨*Akzent*⟩.

**broad 'bean** *n.* Saubohne, *die*

**broadcast** ['brɔːdkɑːst] 1. *n.* Sendung, *die;* *(live)* Übertragung, *die.* 2. *v. t.*, **broadcast** senden; übertragen ⟨*Livesendung*⟩. 3. *v. i.*, **broadcast** senden. **'broadcasting** *n.* Senden, *das;* *(live)* Übertragen, *das;* **work in ~:** beim Funk arbeiten

**broaden** ['brɔːdn] 1. *v. t.* a) verbreitern; b) ausweiten ⟨*Diskussion*⟩. 2. *v. i.* sich verbreitern; *(fig.)* sich erweitern

**'broadly** *adv.* a) deutlich ⟨*hinweisen*⟩; breit ⟨*grinsen, lächeln*⟩; b) *(in general)* allgemein ⟨*beschreiben*⟩; **~ speaking** allgemein gesagt

**broad: ~-'minded** *adj.* tolerant; **~side** *n.* Breitseite, *die*

**brocade** [brə'keɪd] *n.* Brokat, *der*

**broccoli** ['brɒkəlɪ] *n.* Brokkoli, *der*

**brochure** ['brəʊʃə(r)] *n.* Broschüre, *die;* Prospekt, *der*

**broil** ['brɔɪl] *v. t. (esp. Amer.)* grillen

**broke** [brəʊk] 1. *see* **break** 1, 2. 2. *pred. adj. (coll.)* pleite *(ugs.)*

**broken** ['brəʊkn] 1. *see* **break** 1, 2. 2. *adj.* a) zerbrochen; gebrochen ⟨*Bein, Hals*⟩; verletzt ⟨*Haut*⟩; abgebrochen ⟨*Zahn*⟩; gerissen ⟨*Seil*⟩; kaputt *(ugs.)* ⟨*Uhr, Fernsehen, Fenster*⟩; **~ glass** Glasscherben; b) *(imperfect)* gebrochen; **in ~ English** in gebrochenem Englisch; c) *(fig.)* ruiniert ⟨*Ehe*⟩; gebrochen ⟨*Mensch, Herz*⟩. **'broken-down** *adj.* baufällig ⟨*Gebäude*⟩; kaputt *(ugs.)* ⟨*Wagen*⟩. **broken-'hearted** *adj.* untröstlich

**broker** ['brəʊkə(r)] *n.* Makler, *der*

**brolly** ['brɒlɪ] *n. (Brit. coll.)* [Regen]schirm, *der*

**bronchitis** [brɒŋ'kaɪtɪs] *n.* Bronchitis, *die*

**bronze** [brɒnz] 1. *n.* Bronze, *die.* 2. *attrib. adj.* Bronze-; *(coloured like ~)* bronzefarben

**brooch** [brəʊtʃ] *n.* Brosche, *die*

**brood** [bruːd] 1. *n.* Brut, *die.* 2. *v. i.* [vor sich *(Akk.)* hin] brüten

**brook** [brʊk] *n.* Bach, *der*

**broom** [bruːm] *n.* a) Besen, *der;* b) *(Bot.)* Ginster, *der.* **'broom-cupboard** *n.* Besenschrank, *der.* **'broomstick** *n.* Besenstiel, *der*

**broth** [brɒθ] *n.* Brühe, *die*

**brothel** ['brɒθl] *n.* Bordell, *das*

**brother** ['brʌðə(r)] *n.* Bruder, *der;* **my ~s and sisters** meine Geschwister.

**'brotherhood** *n.* *(organization)* Bruderschaft, *die.* **'brother-in-law** *n.,* *pl.* **brothers-in-law** Schwager, *der*
**brought** *see* **bring**
**brow** [braʊ] *n.* **a)** *(eye~)* Braue, *die;* **b)** *(forehead)* Stirn, *die;* **c)** *(of hill)* Kuppe, *die*
**'browbeat** *v. t., forms as* **beat 1** einschüchtern
**brown** [braʊn] **1.** *adj.* braun. **2.** *n.* Braun, *das.* **brown 'bread** *n.* ≈ Mischbrot, *das*
**Brownie** ['braʊnɪ] *n.* Wichtel, *die*
**brown 'paper** *n.* Packpapier, *das*
**browse** [braʊz] *v. i. (in shop)* sich umsehen; *(read)* blättern (**through** in + *Dat.*)
**bruise** [bruːz] **1.** *n.* **a)** *(Med.)* blauer Fleck; **b)** *(on fruit)* Druckstelle, *die.* **2.** *v. t.* quetschen ⟨*Obst, Pflanzen*⟩; ~ **oneself/one's leg** sich stoßen/sich am Bein stoßen
**brunette** [bruːˈnet] **1.** *n.* Brünette, *die.* **2.** *adj.* brünett
**brunt** [brʌnt] *n.* **bear the ~ of the attack/financial cuts** von dem Angriff/ von den Einsparungen am meisten betroffen sein
**brush** [brʌʃ] **1.** *n.* **a)** Bürste, *die;* *(for sweeping)* Besen, *der;* *(with short handle)* Handfeger, *der;* *(for painting or writing)* Pinsel, *der;* **b)** *(skirmish)* Zusammenstoß, *der;* **c)** *(light touch)* flüchtige Berührung. **2.** *v. t.* **a)** kehren; fegen; abbürsten ⟨*Kleidung*⟩; ~ **one's teeth/hair** sich *(Dat.)* die Zähne putzen/die Haare bürsten; **b)** *(touch in passing)* streifen. **3.** *v. i.* ~ **past sb./sth.** jmdn./etw. streifen. **brush 'up** *v. t. & i.* ~ **up [on]** auffrischen ⟨*Kenntnisse usw.*⟩
**brusque** [brʌsk] *adj.,* **'brusquely** *adv.* schroff
**Brussels** ['brʌslz] *pr. n.* Brüssel *(das).* **Brussels 'sprouts** *n. pl.* Rosenkohl, *der*
**brutal** ['bruːtl] *adj.* brutal. **brutality** [bruːˈtælɪtɪ] *n.* Brutalität, *die.* **brutally** ['bruːtəlɪ] *adv.* brutal
**brute** [bruːt] **1.** *n.* **a)** *(animal)* Bestie, *die;* **b)** *(person)* Rohling, *der.* **2.** *attrib. adj.* **by ~ force** mit roher Gewalt
**B.Sc.** *abbr.* **Bachelor of Science**
**BST** *abbr.* **British Summer Time** Britische Sommerzeit
**bubble** ['bʌbl] **1.** *n.* Blase, *die;* *(small)* Perle, *die.* **2.** *v. i.* ⟨*Wasser, Schlamm, Lava:*⟩ Blasen bilden. **'bubble bath** *n.* Schaumbad, *das*

**'buck** [bʌk] *n.* *(deer, chamois)* Bock, *der;* *(rabbit, hare)* Rammler, *der*
**'buck** *n.* **pass the ~ to sb.** jmdm. die Verantwortung aufhalsen
**'buck** *(coll.)* **1.** *v. i.* ~ **'up a)** *(make haste)* sich ranhalten *(ugs.);* **b)** *(cheer up)* ~ **up!** Kopf hoch! **2.** *v. t.* ~ **one's ideas up** *(coll.)* sich zusammenreißen
**'buck** *n.* *(Amer. sl.)* Dollar, *der*
**bucket** ['bʌkɪt] *n.* Eimer, *der*
**buckle** ['bʌkl] **1.** *n.* Schnalle, *die.* **2.** *v. t.* **a)** zuschnallen; ~ **sth. on/up** etw. anschnallen/festschnallen; **b)** verbiegen ⟨*Stoßstange, Rad*⟩. **3.** *v. i.* ⟨*Rad, Metallplatte:*⟩ [sich] verbiegen
**bud** [bʌd] **1.** *n.* Knospe, *die;* **come into ~/be in ~:** Knospen treiben. **2.** *v. i.,* -dd- Knospen treiben
**Buddhism** ['bʊdɪzm] *n.* Buddhismus, *der.* **Buddhist** ['bʊdɪst] **1.** *n.* Buddhist, *der*/Buddhistin, *die.* **2.** *adj.* buddhistisch
**budge** [bʌdʒ] **1.** *v. i.* sich rühren; ⟨*Gegenstand:*⟩ sich bewegen. **2.** *v. t.* bewegen
**budgerigar** ['bʌdʒərɪɡɑː(r)] *n.* Wellensittich, *der*
**budget** ['bʌdʒɪt] **1.** *n.* Etat, *der;* Haushalt[splan], *der.* **2.** *v. i.* ~ **for sth.** etw. [im Etat] einplanen
**budgie** ['bʌdʒɪ] *n. (coll.)* Wellensittich, *der*
**buff** [bʌf] **1.** *adj.* gelbbraun. **2.** *n. (coll.: enthusiast)* Fan, *der (ugs.)*
**buffalo** ['bʌfələʊ] *n., pl.* ~**es** *or same* Büffel, *der*
**buffer** ['bʌfə(r)] *n.* Prellbock, *der;* *(on vehicle; also fig.)* Puffer, *der*
**buffet** ['bʊfeɪ] *n.* Büfett, *das.* **'buffet car** *n.* Büfettwagen, *der*
**bug** [bʌɡ] *n. (also coll.: microphone)* Wanze, *die*
**buggy** ['bʌɡɪ] *n. (pushchair)* Sportwagen, *der*
**bugle** ['bjuːɡl] *n.* Bügelhorn, *das*
**build** [bɪld] **1.** *v. t.,* **built** [bɪlt] bauen; *(fig.)* aufbauen ⟨*System, Gesellschaft, Zukunft*⟩. **2.** *v. i.,* **built** bauen. **3.** *n.* Körperbau, *der.* **build 'in** *v. t.* einbauen. **build 'on** aufbauen auf (+ *Dat.*); bebauen ⟨*Gebiet*⟩. **build 'up 1.** *v. t.* aufhäufen ⟨*Reserven, Mittel*⟩; kräftigen ⟨*Personen, Körper*⟩; steigern ⟨*Produktion, Kapazität*⟩; stärken ⟨[*Selbst*]*vertrauen*⟩; aufbauen ⟨*Firma, Geschäft*⟩. **2.** *v. i.* ⟨*Spannung, Druck:*⟩ zunehmen; ⟨*Schlange, Rückstau:*⟩ sich bilden; ⟨*Verkehr:*⟩ sich verdichten
**'builder** *n.* Bauunternehmer, *der*

'**building** *n.* a) Bau, *der;* b) *(structure)* Gebäude, *das.* '**building-site** *n.* Baustelle, *die.* '**building society** *n.* *(Brit.)* Bausparkasse, *die*

**built** *see* **build 1, 2**

**built:** ~-**in** *adj.* a) eingebaut; Einbau-⟨*schrank, küche usw.*⟩; b) *(fig.: instinctive)* angeboren; ~-**up** *adj.* bebaut; ~-**up area** Wohngebiet, *das;* *(Motor Veh.)* geschlossene Ortschaft

**bulb** [bʌlb] *n.* a) *(Bot., Hort.)* Zwiebel, *die;* b) *(of lamp)* [Glüh]birne, *die*

**Bulgaria** [bʌl'geərɪə] *pr. n.* Bulgarien *(das).* **Bulgarian** [bʌl'geərɪən] **1.** *adj.* bulgarisch. **2.** *n.* a) *(person)* Bulgare, *der*/Bulgarin, *die;* b) *(language)* Bulgarisch, *das; see also* **English 2 a**

**bulge** [bʌldʒ] **1.** *n.* Ausbeulung, *die;* ausgebeulte Stelle. **2.** *v. i.* sich wölben

**bulk** [bʌlk] *n.* a) *(large quantity)* **in** ~: in großen Mengen; b) *(large shape)* massige Gestalt; c) *(size)* Größe, *die;* d) *(greater part)* der größte Teil; *(of population, votes)* Mehrheit, *die.* '**bulky** *adj.* sperrig ⟨*Gegenstand*⟩; massig ⟨*Gestalt, Körper*⟩

**bull** [bʊl] *n.* Bulle, *der;* *(esp. for bullfight)* Stier, *der*

'**bulldog** *n.* Bulldogge, *die*

**bulldozer** ['bʊldəʊzə(r)] *n.* Planierraupe, *die*

**bullet** ['bʊlɪt] *n.* Kugel, *die*

**bulletin** ['bʊlɪtɪn] *n.* Bulletin, *das*

'**bulletproof** *adj.* kugelsicher

'**bullfight** *n.* Stierkampf, *der*

**bullion** ['bʊljən] *n.* **gold** ~: Goldbarren *Pl.*

**bullock** ['bʊlək] *n.* Ochse, *der*

**bull:** ~-**ring** *n.* Stierkampfarena, *die;* ~'**s-eye** *n.* *(of target)* Schwarze, *das*

**bully** ['bʊlɪ] **1.** *n.* *(schoolboy etc.)* ≈ Rabauke, *der;* *(boss)* Tyrann, *der.* **2.** *v. t.* schikanieren; *(frighten)* einschüchtern

¹**bum** [bʌm] *n.* *(Brit. sl.)* Hintern, *der* *(ugs.)*

²**bum** *n.* *(Amer. sl.: tramp)* Penner, *der* *(salopp)*

**bumble-bee** ['bʌmblbi:] *n.* Hummel, *die*

**bump** [bʌmp] **1.** *n.* a) *(sound)* Bums, *der;* *(impact)* Stoß, *der;* b) *(swelling)* Beule, *die;* c) *(hump)* Buckel, *der* *(ugs.).* **2.** *adv.* bums. **3.** *v. t.* anstoßen. '**bump into** *v. t.* a) stoßen an (+ *Akk.*); b) *(meet by chance)* zufällig [wieder]treffen

'**bumper 1.** *n.* Stoßstange, *die.* **2.** *attrib. adj.* Rekord⟨*ernte, -jahr*⟩

'**bumpy** *adj.* holp[e]rig ⟨*Straße, Fahrt, Fahrzeug*⟩; uneben ⟨*Fläche*⟩; unruhig ⟨*Flug*⟩

**bun** [bʌn] *n.* süßes Brötchen; *(currant* ~) Korinthenbrötchen, *das*

**bunch** [bʌntʃ] *n.* a) *(of flowers)* Strauß, *der;* *(of grapes, bananas)* Traube, *die;* *(of parsley, radishes)* Bund, *das;* ~ **flowers/grapes** Blumenstrauß, *der*/ Traube, *die;* **a** ~ **of keys** ein Schlüsselbund; b) *(lot)* Anzahl, *die;* **the best** *or* **pick of the** ~: der/die/das Beste [von allen]; c) *(of people)* Haufen, *der (ugs.)*

**bundle** ['bʌndl] *n.* Bündel, *das;* *(of papers)* Packen, *der*

**bung** [bʌŋ] **1.** *n.* Spund, *der.* **2.** *v. t. (sl.)* schmeißen *(ugs.).* **bung 'up** *v. i.* be/ get ~**ed up** verstopft sein/verstopfen

**bungalow** ['bʌŋgələʊ] *n.* Bungalow, *der*

**bungle** ['bʌŋgl] *v. t.* stümpern bei

**bunk** [bʌŋk] *n.* *(in ship, lorry)* Koje, *die;* *(in sleeping-car)* Bett, *das;* *(*~-**bed)** Etagenbett, *das*

**bunker** ['bʌŋkə(r)] *n.* Bunker, *der*

**bunny** ['bʌnɪ] *n.* Häschen, *das*

**buoy** [bɔɪ] *n.* Boje, *die*

**buoyancy** ['bɔɪənsɪ] *n.* Auftrieb, *der*

**buoyant** ['bɔɪənt] *adj.* schwimmend; **be** ~: schwimmen

**burden** ['bɜ:dn] **1.** *n.* Last, *die;* **become a** ~ *(fig.)* zur Last werden. **2.** *v. t.* belasten **(with** mit)

**bureau** ['bjʊərəʊ, bjʊə'rəʊ] *n.* a) *(Brit.: writing-desk)* Sekretär, *der;* b) *(office)* Büro, *das*

**bureaucracy** [bjʊə'rɒkrəsɪ] *n.* Bürokratie, *die.* **bureaucrat** ['bjʊərəkræt] *n.* Bürokrat, *der*/Bürokratin, *die.* **bureaucratic** [bjʊərə'krætɪk] *adj.* bürokratisch

**burglar** ['bɜ:glə(r)] *n.* Einbrecher, *der.* '**burglar alarm** *n.* Alarmanlage, *die* **burglary** ['bɜ:glərɪ] *n.* Einbruch, *der.* **burgle** ['bɜ:gl] *v. t.* einbrechen in (+ *Akk.*); **the shop/he was** ~**d** in dem Laden/bei ihm wurde eingebrochen

**burial** ['berɪəl] *n.* Begräbnis, *das*

**burly** ['bɜ:lɪ] *adj.* stämmig

**Burma** ['bɜ:mə] *pr. n.* Birma *(das)*

**burn** [bɜ:n] **1.** *n.* *(on the skin)* Verbrennung, *die;* *(on material)* Brandfleck, *der.* **2.** *v. t.,* ~**t** [bɜ:nt] *or* ~**ed** a) verbrennen; ~ **oneself/one's hand** sich verbrennen/sich ⟨*Dat.*⟩ die Hand verbrennen; ~ **a hole in sth.** ein Loch in etw. *(Akk.)* brennen; b) als Brennstoff verwenden ⟨*Gas, Öl usw.*⟩; heizen mit ⟨*Kohle, Holz, Torf*⟩; c) *(spoil)* anbrennen lassen ⟨*Fleisch, Kuchen*⟩; be ~t angebrannt sein. **3.** *v. i.*, ~t *or* ~ed brennen; ~ **to death** verbrennen; she ~s easily sie bekommt leicht einen Sonnenbrand. **burn 'down** *v. t. & i.* niederbrennen

'**burner** *n.* Brenner, *der*

'**burning** *adj.* glühend ⟨*Leidenschaft, Haß, Wunsch*⟩; brennend ⟨*Wunsch, Frage, Problem*⟩

**burnt** *see* burn 2, 3

**burp** [bɜ:p] (*coll.*) **1.** *n.* Rülpser, *der* (*ugs.*). **2.** *v. i.* rülpsen (*ugs.*)

**burrow** ['bʌrəʊ] **1.** *n.* Bau, *der*. **2.** *v. i.* [sich (*Dat.*)] einen Gang graben

**burst** [bɜ:st] **1.** *n.* a) (*split*) Bruch, *der*; b) (*of firing*) Salve, *die*; c) (*fig.*) **a ~ of applause/cheering** ein Beifallsausbruch/Beifallsrufe *Pl.* **2.** *v. t.*, burst zum Platzen bringen; platzen lassen ⟨*Luftballon*⟩; ~ **pipe** Rohrbruch, *der*. **3.** *v. i.*, burst a) platzen; ⟨*Bombe:*⟩ explodieren; ⟨*Damm:*⟩ brechen; ⟨*Flußufer:*⟩ überschwemmt werden; ⟨*Furunkel, Geschwür:*⟩ aufgehen; b) be ~ing with sth. zum Bersten voll sein mit etw.; be ~ing with pride/impatience/excitement vor Stolz/Ungeduld platzen/vor Aufregung außer sich sein. '**burst into** *v. t.* a) eindringen in; b) ~ **into tears/laughter** in Tränen/Gelächter ausbrechen; ~ **into flames** in Brand geraten. **burst 'out** *v. i.* a) herausstürzen; b) (*exclaim*) losplatzen; c) ~ **out laughing/crying** in Lachen/Tränen ausbrechen

**bury** ['berɪ] *v. t.* a) begraben; b) (*hide*) vergraben; ~ **one's face in one's hands** das Gesicht in den Händen vergraben; c) ~ **one's teeth in sth.** seine Zähne in etw. (*Akk.*) graben

**bus** [bʌs] *n.* Bus, *der*

**bus:** ~-**conductor** *n.* Busschaffner, *der;* ~-**driver** *n.* Busfahrer, *der;* ~ **fare** *n.* [Bus]fahrpreis, *der*

**bush** [bʊʃ] *n.* a) Busch, *der;* b) (*shrubs*) Gebüsch, *das.* '**bushy** *adj.* buschig

**busily** ['bɪzɪlɪ] *adj.* eifrig

**business** ['bɪznɪs] *n.* a) (*trading operation*) Geschäft, *das; (company, firm*) Betrieb, *der; (large*) Unternehmen, *das;* b) (*buying and selling*) Geschäfte *Pl.;* c) (*task, province*) Aufgabe, *die;* **mind your own ~!** kümmere dich um deine [eigenen] Angelegenheiten!; d) (*difficult matter*) Problem, *das*

**business:** ~ **letter** *n.* Geschäftsbrief, *der;* ~-**like** *adj.* geschäftsmäßig ⟨*Art*⟩; geschäftstüchtig ⟨*Person*⟩;

~-**man** *n.* Geschäftsmann, *der;* ~ **school** *n.* kaufmännische Fachschule; ~-**woman** *n.* Geschäftsfrau, *die*

**busker** ['bʌskə(r)] *n.* Straßenmusikant, *der*

**bus:** ~-**route** *n.* Buslinie, *die;* ~ **shelter** *n.* Wartehäuschen, *das;* ~-**station** *n.* Omnibusbahnhof, *der;* ~-**stop** *n.* Bushaltestelle, *die*

¹**bust** [bʌst] *n.* a) (*sculpture*) Büste, *die;* b) ~ [*measurement*] Oberweite, *die*

²**bust** (*coll.*) **1.** *adj.* kaputt (*ugs.*). **2.** *v. t.*, ~ed *or* bust (*break*) kaputtmachen (*ugs.*); ~ **sth. open** etw. aufbrechen. **3.** *v. i.*, ~ed *or* bust kaputtgehen (*ugs.*)

'**bus-ticket** *n.* Busfahrkarte, *die*

**bustle** ['bʌsl] **1.** *v. i.* ~ **about** geschäftig hin und her eilen. **2.** *n.* Betrieb, *der*

**bustling** ['bʌslɪŋ] *adj.* belebt ⟨*Straße, Stadt, Markt usw.*⟩; rege ⟨*Tätigkeit*⟩

**busy** ['bɪzɪ] **1.** *adj.* a) beschäftigt (**at,** **with** mit); arbeitsreich ⟨*Leben*⟩; ziemlich hektisch ⟨*Zeit*⟩; **I'm ~ now** ich habe jetzt zu tun; **he was ~ packing** er war mit Packen beschäftigt; b) (*Amer. Teleph.*) besetzt. **2.** *v. refl.* ~ **oneself** sich beschäftigen (**with** mit). '**busybody** *n.* G[e]schäfthuber, *der*

**but 1.** [bət, *stressed* bʌt] *conj.* aber; *correcting after a negative* sondern; **not that book ~ this one** nicht das Buch, sondern dieses. **2.** [bət] *prep.* außer (+ *Dat.*); **the next/last ~ one** der/die/ das übernächste/vorletzte

**butcher** ['bʊtʃə(r)] **1.** *n.* Fleischer, *der.* **2.** *v. t.* (*murder*) niedermetzeln

**butler** ['bʌtlə(r)] *n.* Butler, *der*

¹**butt** [bʌt] *n.* a) (*of rifle*) Kolben, *der;* b) (*of cigarette, cigar*) Stummel, *der*

²**butt** *n.* (*object of teasing or ridicule*) Zielscheibe, *die*

³**butt 1.** *n.* (*push*) (*by person*) [Kopf]stoß, *der; (by animal*) Stoß [mit den Hörnern]. **2.** *v. t. & i.* mit dem Kopf/den Hörnern stoßen. **butt 'in** *v. i.* dazwischenreden

**butter** ['bʌtə(r)] **1.** *n.* Butter, *die.* **2.** *v. t.* buttern

**butter:** ~-**bean** *n.* Mondbohne, *die;* ~**cup** *n.* Butterblume, *die;* ~**fly** *n.* a) Schmetterling, *der;* b) ~ [*stroke*] Delphinstil, *der*

**buttock** ['bʌtək] *n.* Hinterbacke, *die;* Gesäßhälfte, *die;* ~s Gesäß, *das*

**button** ['bʌtn] **1.** *n.* Knopf, *der.* **2.** *v. t.* ~ [*up*] zuknöpfen. '**buttonhole 1.** *n.* a) Knopfloch, *das;* b) (*flower*) Knopflochblume, *die.* **2.** *v. t.* zu fassen kriegen (*ugs.*)

**buttress** ['bʌtrɪs] *n. (Archit.)* Mauerstütze, *die*
**buxom** ['bʌksəm] *adj.* drall
**buy** [baɪ] **1.** *v. t.*, **bought** [bɔːt] kaufen; ~ **sb./oneself sth.** jmdm./sich etw. kaufen. **2.** *n.* [Ein]kauf, *der;* **be a good** ~: preiswert sein. **buy 'up** *v. t.* aufkaufen
'**buyer** *n.* Käufer, *der*/Käuferin, *die*
**buzz** [bʌz] **1.** *n.* Summen, *das.* **2.** *v. i.* summen. **buzz 'off** *v. i. (sl.)* abhauen *(salopp)*
'**buzzer** *n.* Summer, *der*
**by** [baɪ] **1.** *prep.* **a)** *(near, beside)* an (+ *Dat.*); bei; *(next to)* neben; ~ **the window/river** am Fenster/Fluß; **b)** *(to position beside)* zu; **c)** *(about, in the possession of)* bei; **d)** **[all] by herself/himself** *etc.* [ganz] allein[e]; **e)** *(along)* entlang; *(via)* über (+ *Akk.*); **f)** *(passing)* vorbei an (+ *Dat.*); **g)** *(during)* bei; **by day/night** bei Tag/Nacht; **h)** *(through the agency of)* von; **written by** ...: geschrieben von ...; **i)** *(through the means of)* durch; **by bus/ship** *etc.* mit dem Bus/Schiff *usw.;* **by air/sea** mit dem Flugzeug/Schiff; **j)** *(not later than)* bis; **by now/this time** inzwischen; **k)** *indicating unit* pro; **by the minute/hour** pro Minute/Stunde; **by day/month by month** Tag für Tag/ Monat für Monat; **10 ft. by 20 ft.** 10 [Fuß] mal 20 Fuß; **l)** *indicating amount* one by one einzeln; **two by two/three by three** zu zweit/dritt; **m)** *indicating factor* durch; **8 divided by 2 is 4** 8 geteilt durch 2 ist 4; **n)** *indicating extent* um; **wider by a foot** um einen Fuß breiter; **o)** *(according to)* nach. **2.** *adv.* **a)** *(past)* vorbei; **b)** *(near)* close/ near by in der Nähe; **c) by and large** im großen und ganzen
**bye[-bye]** ['baɪ(baɪ)] *int. (coll.)* tschüs *(ugs.)*
**bye-law** *see* **by-law**
'**by-election** *n.* Nachwahl, *die*
**bygone** ['baɪgɒn] *adj.* vergangen
'**by-law** *n. (esp. Brit.)* Verordnung, *die*
'**bypass** **1.** *n.* Umgehungsstraße, *die.* **2.** *v. t.* **a) the road ~es the town** die Straße führt um die Stadt herum; **b)** *(fig.)* übergehen
'**by-product** *n.* Nebenprodukt, *das*
'**by-road** *n.* Nebenstraße, *die*
**bystander** ['baɪstændə(r)] *n.* Zuschauer, *der*/Zuschauerin, *die*
**byte** ['baɪt] *n. (Computing)* Byte, *das*
'**byway** *n.* Seitenweg, *der*
'**byword** *n.* Inbegriff, *der* (for *Gen.*)

# C

**C, c** [siː] *n.* C, c, *das*
**C.** *abbr.* **a)** Celsius C; **b) Centigrade** C
**cab** [kæb] *n.* **a)** *(taxi)* Taxi, *das;* **b)** *(of lorry, truck)* Fahrerhaus, *das; (of train)* Führerstand, *der*
**cabaret** ['kæbəreɪ] *n.* Varieté, *das; (satirical)* Kabarett, *das*
**cabbage** ['kæbɪdʒ] *n.* Kohl, *der;* **red/ white** ~: Rot-/Weißkohl, *der*
**cabin** ['kæbɪn] *n. (in ship) (for passengers)* Kabine, *die; (for crew)* Kajüte, *die; (in aircraft)* Kabine, *die*
**cabinet** ['kæbɪnɪt] *n.* **a)** Schrank, *der; (in bathroom, for medicines)* Schränkchen, *das;* |display| ~: Vitrine, *die;* **b) the C~** *(Polit.)* das Kabinett; **C~ Minister** Minister, *der*
**cable** ['keɪbl] **1.** *n.* **a)** *(rope)* Kabel, *das; (of ~-car etc.)* Seil, *das;* **b)** *(Electr., Teleph.)* Kabel, *das;* **c)** *(message)* Kabel, *das.* **2.** *v. t.* kabeln ⟨Mitteilung, Nachricht⟩. '**cable-car** *n.* Drahtseilbahn, *die.* **cable 'television** *n.* Kabelfernsehen, *das*
**cache** [kæʃ] *n.* geheimes [Waffen-/ Proviant-]lager
**cackle** ['kækl] **1.** *n.* **a)** *(of hen)* Gackern, *das;* **b)** *(laughter)* [meckerndes] Gelächter. **2.** *v. i.* **a)** ⟨Henne:⟩ gackern; **b)** *(laugh)* meckernd lachen
**cactus** ['kæktəs] *n., pl.* **cacti** ['kæktaɪ] *or* ~**es** Kaktus, *der*
**caddie** ['kædɪ] *n. (Golf)* Caddie, *der*
**caddy** ['kædɪ] *n.* Dose, *die*
**cadet** [kə'det] *n.* Offiziersschüler, *der;* **naval/police** ~: Marinekadett/Anwärter für den Polizeidienst
**cadge** [kædʒ] *v. t.* [sich *(Dat.)*] erbetteln
**café, cafe** ['kæfeɪ] *n.* Lokal, *das; (tearoom)* Café, *das*
**cafeteria** [kæfɪ'tɪərɪə] *n.* Cafeteria, *die*
**caffeine** ['kæfiːn] *n.* Koffein, *das*
**cage** [keɪdʒ] **1.** *n.* **a)** Käfig, *der;* **b)** *(of lift)* Fahrkabine, *die.* **2.** *v. t.* einsperren
**cagey** ['keɪdʒɪ] *adj. (coll.)* zugeknöpft

*(ugs.);* be ~ **about sth.** mit etw. hinterm Berg halten *(ugs.)*

**Cairo** ['kaɪərəʊ] *pr. n.* Kairo *(das)*

**cajole** [kə'dʒəʊl] *v. t.* ~ **sb. into sth.**/ **doing sth.** jmdm. etw. einreden/jmdm. einreden, etw. zu tun

**cake** [keɪk] **1.** *n.* Kuchen, *der;* **a** ~ **of soap** ein Riegel *od.* Stück Seife. **2.** *v. t.* verkrusten; **~d with dirt/blood** schmutz-/blutverkrustet

**calamity** [kə'læmɪtɪ] *n.* Unheil, *das*

**calcium** ['kælsɪəm] *n.* Kalzium, *das*

**calculate** ['kælkjʊleɪt] **1.** *v. t.* **a)** berechnen; *(by estimating)* ausrechnen; **b)** be **~d to do sth.** darauf abzielen, etw. zu tun. **2.** *v. i.* ~ **on doing sth.** damit rechnen, etw. zu tun. '**calculated** *adj.* kalkuliert ⟨*Risiko*⟩; vorsätzlich ⟨*Handlung*⟩. **calculation** [kælkjʊ-'leɪʃn] *n.* **a)** *(result)* Rechnung, *die;* **he is out in his ~s** er hat sich verrechnet; **b)** *(calculating)* Berechnung, *die.* **calculator** ['kælkjʊleɪtə(r)] *n.* Rechner, *der*

**calculus** ['kælkjʊləs] *n.* **differential/ integral ~:** Differential-/Integralrechnung, *die*

**calendar** ['kælɪndə(r)] *n.* Kalender, *der;* *attrib.* Kalender-

**¹calf** [kɑːf] *n., pl.* **calves** Kalb, *das*

**²calf** *n., pl.* **calves** *(Anat.)* Wade, *die*

**calibre** *(Brit.; Amer.:* **caliber***)* ['kælɪbə(r)] *n.* Kaliber, *das*

**calico** ['kælɪkəʊ] *n.* Kattun, *der*

**California** [kælɪ'fɔːnɪə] *pr. n.* Kalifornien *(das)*

**caliper** *see* **calliper**

**call** [kɔːl] **1.** *v. i.* **a)** rufen; ~ **to sb.** jmdm. etwas zurufen; ~ |**out**| **for help** um Hilfe rufen; **b)** *(pay brief visit)* [kurz] besuchen **(at** *Akk.***);** ~ **on sb.** jmdn. besuchen; ~ **round** vorbeikommen *(ugs.);* ~ **at a port/station** einen Hafen anlaufen/an einem Bahnhof halten; **c)** *(Teleph.)* **who is ~ing, please?** wer spricht da, bitte?; **thank you for ~ing** vielen Dank für Ihren Anruf! **2.** *v. t.* **a)** rufen; aufrufen ⟨*Namen, Nummer*⟩; **b)** *(cry to, summon)* rufen; *(to a duty, to do sth.)* aufrufen; **c)** *(by radio/telephone)* rufen/ anrufen; *(initially)* Kontakt aufnehmen mit; **d)** *(rouse)* wecken; **e)** einberufen ⟨*Konferenz*⟩; ausrufen ⟨*Streik*⟩; **f)** *(name)* nennen; **he is ~ed Bob** er heißt Bob; **what is it ~ed in English?** wie heißt das auf englisch? **3.** *n.* **a)** Ruf, *der;* **a ~ for help** ein Hilferuf; **be on ~:** Bereitschaftsdienst haben; **b)**

*(visit)* Besuch, *der;* **make** *or* **pay a ~ on sb.,** **make** *or* **pay sb. a ~:** jmdn. besuchen; **c)** *(telephone ~)* Anruf, *der;* **give sb. a ~:** jmdn. anrufen; **make a ~:** telefonieren; **d)** *(invitation, summons)* Aufruf, *der;* **e)** *(need, occasion)* Anlaß, *der.* **call 'back 1.** *v. t.* zurückrufen. **2.** *v. i.* zurückrufen; *(come back)* zurückkommen. '**call for 1.** *v. t.* **a)** *(send for, order)* bestellen; **b)** *(collect)* abholen; **c)** *(require, demand)* erfordern; **this ~s for a celebration** das muß gefeiert werden. **call 'in 1.** *v. i.* vorbeikommen *(ugs.)* **(on** bei). **2.** *v. t.* zu Rate ziehen ⟨*Fachmann usw.*⟩. **call 'off** *v. t.* absagen ⟨*Treffen, Verabredung*⟩; rückgängig machen ⟨*Geschäft*⟩; lösen ⟨*Verlobung*⟩; *(end)* abbrechen ⟨*Streik*⟩. '**call on** *v. t.* **a)** *see* ~ **1b; b)** *see* ~ |**up**|**on.** **call 'out 1.** *v. t.* alarmieren ⟨*Truppen*⟩; zum Streik aufrufen ⟨*Arbeitnehmer*⟩. **2.** *v. i. see* ~ **1a. call 'up** *v. t.* **a)** *(by telephone)* anrufen; **b)** *(Mil.)* einberufen. '**call [up]on** *v. t.* ~ **upon sb.'s generosity** an jmds. Großzügigkeit *(Akk.)* appellieren; ~ |**up**|**on sb. to do sth.** jmdn. auffordern, etw. zu tun

'**call-box** *n.* Telefonzelle, *die*

'**caller** *n.* *(visitor)* Besucher, *der*/Besucherin, *die; (on telephone)* Anrufer, *der*/Anruferin, *die*

'**call-girl** *n.* Callgirl, *das*

'**calling** *n.* Beruf, *der*

**calliper** ['kælɪpə(r)] *n.* **a)** |**a pair of**| **~s** Tasterzirkel, *der;* **b)** *(Med.)* Beinschiene, *die*

**callous** ['kæləs] *adj.* gefühllos; herzlos ⟨*Handlung, Verhalten*⟩

'**call-up** *n.* *(Mil.)* Einberufung, *die*

**calm** [kɑːm] **1.** *n.* *(stillness)* Stille, *die; (serenity)* Ruhe, *die.* **2.** *adj.* ruhig. **3.** *v. t.* ~ **sb.** |**down**| jmdn. beruhigen. **4.** *v. i.* ~ |**down**| sich beruhigen. '**calmly** *adv.* ruhig; gelassen. '**calmness** *n.* Ruhe, *die; (of water)* Stille, *die*

**Calor gas, (P)** ['kælə gæs] *n.* Butangas, *das*

**calorie** ['kælərɪ] *n.* Kalorie, *die*

**calves** *pl. of* **¹,²calf**

**camber** ['kæmbə(r)] *n.* Wölbung, *die*

**came** *see* **come**

**camel** ['kæml] *n.* Kamel, *das*

**camera** ['kæmərə] *n.* Kamera, *die.* '**cameraman** *n.* Kameramann, *der*

**camouflage** ['kæməflɑːʒ] **1.** *n.* Tarnung, *die.* **2.** *v. t.* tarnen

**camp** [kæmp] **1.** *n.* Lager, *das.* **2.** *v. i.* ~ |**out**| campen; *(in tent)* zelten; **go ~ing** Campen/Zelten fahren/gehen

**campaign** [kæm'peɪn] **1.** *n.* **a)** *(Mil.)* Feldzug, *der;* **b)** *(organized action)* Kampagne, *die;* **publicity** ~: Werbekampagne, *die.* **2.** *v. i.* ~ **for/against sth.** sich für etw. einsetzen/gegen etw. etwas unternehmen; **be** ~**ing** ⟨*Politiker:*⟩ im Wahlkampf stehen

'**camp-bed** *n.* Campingliege, *die*

'**camper** *n.* *(person)* Camper, *der/* Camperin, *die*

'**camping** *n.* Camping, *das; (in tent)* Zelten, *das.* '**camping-ground** *(Amer.),* '**camping site** *ns.* Campingplatz, *der*

'**campsite** *n.* Campingplatz, *der*

**campus** ['kæmpəs] *n.* Campus, *der*

¹**can** [kæn] **1.** *n.* **a)** *(milk* ~, *watering-*~) Kanne, *die; (for oil, petrol)* Kanister, *der; (Amer.: for refuse)* Eimer, *der;* **b)** *(for preserving)* [Konserven]dose, *die;* **a** ~ **of tomatoes/beer** eine Dose Tomaten/Bier. **2.** *v. t.,* **-nn-** konservieren

²**can** [kən, *stressed* kæn] *v. aux., only in pres.* can, *neg.* cannot ['kænət], *(coll.)* can't [kɑːnt], *past* could [kʊd], *neg. (coll.)* couldn't ['kʊdnt] können; *(have right, be permitted)* dürfen; können; **I can't do that** das kann ich nicht; *(it would be wrong)* das kann ich nicht tun; **you can't smoke here** hier dürfen Sie nicht rauchen; **could you ring me tomorrow?** könnten Sie mich morgen anrufen?; **I could have killed him** ich hätte ihn umbringen können; [**that**] **could be** [**so**] das könnte *od.* kann sein

**Canada** ['kænədə] *pr. n.* Kanada *(das).* **Canadian** [kə'neɪdɪən] **1.** *adj.* kanadisch. **2.** *n.* Kanadier, *der/*Kanadierin, *die*

**canal** [kə'næl] *n.* Kanal, *der*

**canary** [kə'neərɪ] *n.* Kanarienvogel, *der*

**Ca'nary Islands** *pr. n. pl.* Kanarische Inseln *Pl.*

**cancel** ['kænsl] **1.** *v. t., (Brit.)* -**ll**- absagen ⟨*Besuch, Urlaub, Reise, Sportveranstaltung*⟩; ausfallen lassen ⟨*Veranstaltung, Vorlesung, Zug, Bus*⟩; fallenlassen ⟨*Pläne*⟩; rückgängig machen ⟨*Einladung, Vertrag*⟩; zurücknehmen ⟨*Bestellung, Auftrag*⟩; kündigen ⟨*Abonnement*⟩; abbestellen ⟨*Zeitung*⟩. **2.** *v. i., (Brit.)* -**ll**-: ~ [**out**] sich [gegenseitig] aufheben. **cancellation** [kænsə'leɪʃn] *n. see* **cancel 1**: Absage, *die;* Ausfall, *der;* Fallenlassen, *das;* Rückgängigmachen, *das;* Zurücknahme, *die;* Stornierung, *die;* Kündigung, *die;* Abbestellung, *die*

**cancer** ['kænsə(r)] *n.* **a)** *(Med.)* Krebs, *der;* **b)** **C**~ *(Astrol., Astron.)* der Krebs

**candelabra** [kændɪ'lɑːbrə] *n.* Leuchter, *der*

**candid** ['kændɪd] *adj.* offen; ehrlich ⟨*Ansicht, Bericht*⟩

**candidate** ['kændɪdət, 'kændɪdeɪt] *n.* Kandidat, *der/*Kandidatin, *die*

**candle** ['kændl] *n.* Kerze, *die*

**candle:** ~**light** *n.* Kerzenlicht, *das;* ~**stick** *n.* Kerzenhalter, *der; (elaborate)* Leuchter, *der;* ~**wick** *n. (material)* Frottierplüsch, *der*

**candour** *(Brit., Amer.:* **candor)** ['kændə(r)] *n. see* **candid**: Offenheit, *die;* Ehrlichkeit, *die*

**candy** ['kændɪ] *n. (Amer.) (sweets)* Süßigkeiten *Pl.; (sweet)* Bonbon, *das od. der.* '**candyfloss** ['kændɪflɒs] *n.* Zuckerwatte, *die*

**cane** [keɪn] **1.** *n.* **a)** *(stem)* Rohr, *das; (of raspberry, blackberry)* Sproß, *der;* **b)** *(material)* Rohr, *das;* **c)** *(stick)* [Rohr]stock, *der.* **2.** *v. t.* [mit dem Stock] schlagen

**canine** ['keɪnaɪn] *adj.* **a)** *(of dog[s])* Hunde-; **b)** ~ **tooth** Eckzahn, *der*

**canister** ['kænɪstə(r)] *n.* Büchse, *die; (for petrol, oil, etc.)* Kanister, *der*

**cannabis** ['kænəbɪs] *n. (hashish)* Haschisch, *das; (marijuana)* Marihuana, *das*

**canned** [kænd] *adj.* Dosen-; in Dosen *nachgestellt;* ~ **meat/fruit** Fleisch-/Obstkonserven *Pl.;* ~ **beer** Dosenbier; ~ **food** [Lebensmittel]konserven *Pl.;* ~ **music** Musikkonserve, *die*

**cannibal** ['kænɪbl] *n.* Kannibale, *der/*Kannibalin, *die.* **cannibalism** ['kænɪbəlɪzm] *n.* Kannibalismus, *der*

**cannon** ['kænən] **1.** *n.* Kanone, *die.* **2.** *v. i. (Brit.)* ~ **into sb./sth.** mit etw./ jmdm. zusammenprallen. '**cannonball** *n.* Kanonenkugel, *die*

**cannot** *see* ²**can**

**canny** ['kænɪ] *adj. (shrewd)* schlau

**canoe** [kə'nuː] *n.* Paddelboot, *das; (Indian* ~, *Sport)* Kanu, *das.* **canoeist** [kə'nuːɪst] *n.* Paddelbootfahrer, *der/* -fahrerin, *die*

**canon** ['kænən] *n.* **a)** *(general law, criterion)* Grundregel, *die;* **b)** *(Eccl.: person)* Kanoniker, *der*

**canonize** ['kænənaɪz] *v. t.* kanonisieren ⟨*Heiligen*⟩; heiligsprechen ⟨*Märtyrer*⟩

'**can-opener** *n.* Dosenöffner, *der*

**canopy** ['kænəpɪ] *n.* Baldachin, *der; (over entrance)* Vordach, *das*

**can't** [kɑːnt] *(coll.)* = **cannot**; *see* ²**can**

**cantankerous** [kæn'tæŋkərəs] *adj.* streitsüchtig

**canteen** [kæn'tiːn] *n.* Kantine, *die*

**canter** ['kæntə(r)] **1.** *n.* Handgalopp, *der.* **2.** *v. i.* leicht galoppieren

**canvas** ['kænvəs] *n.* Leinwand, *die*

**canvass** ['kænvəs] **1.** *v. t.* Wahlwerbung treiben in ‹*einem Wahlkreis, Gebiet*›; Wahlwerbung treiben bei ‹*Wählern, Bürgern*›. **2.** *v. i.* werben (**on behalf of** für); ~ **for votes** um Stimmen werben. '**canvasser** *n.* *(for votes)* Wahlhelfer, *der*/-helferin, *die*

**canyon** ['kænjən] *n.* Cañon, *der*

**cap** [kæp] **1.** *n.* **a)** Mütze, *die*; *(nurse's, servant's)* Haube, *die*; *(with peak)* Schirmmütze, *die*; *(skull-~)* Kappe, *die*; **b)** *(of bottle, jar)* [Verschluß]kappe, *die*; *(petrol ~, radiator-~)* Deckel, *der.* **2.** *v. t.*, **-pp-**: **a)** verschließen ‹*Flasche*›; zudecken ‹*Bohrloch*›; mit einer Schutzkappe versehen ‹*Zahn*›; **b)** *(fig.)* überbieten; **to ~ it all** obendrein

**capability** [keɪpə'bɪlɪtɪ] *n.* Fähigkeit, *die*

**capable** ['keɪpəbl] *adj.* **a) be ~ of sth.** ‹*Person:*› zu etw. imstande sein; **b)** *(gifted, able)* fähig

**capacity** [kə'pæsɪtɪ] *n.* **a)** Fassungsvermögen, *das*; **the machine is working to ~:** die Maschine ist voll ausgelastet; **a seating ~ of 300** 300 Sitzplätze; **b)** *(measure)* Rauminhalt, *der*; Volumen, *das*; **measure of ~:** Hohlmaß, *das*; **c)** *(position)* Eigenschaft, *die*; **in his ~ as ...:** in seiner Eigenschaft als ...

¹**cape** [keɪp] *n.* *(garment)* Umhang, *der*; Cape, *das*

²**cape** *n. (Geog.)* Kap, *das*; **the C~** [**of Good Hope**] das Kap der guten Hoffnung; **C~ Town** Kapstadt *(das)*

**caper** ['keɪpə(r)] *v. i.* ~ [**about**] [herum]tollen

**capital** ['kæpɪtl] **1.** *attrib. adj.* **a)** Todes‹*strafe, -urteil*›; Kapital‹*verbrechen*›; **b)** groß, Groß‹*buchstabe*›; **c)** *(principal)* Haupt‹*stadt*›. **2.** *n.* **a)** *(letter)* Großbuchstabe, *der*; **b)** *(city, town)* Hauptstadt, *die*; **c)** *(stock, wealth)* Kapital, *das*

**capitalism** ['kæpɪtəlɪzm] *n.* Kapitalismus, *der.* **capitalist** ['kæpɪtəlɪst] **1.** *n.* Kapitalist, *der*/Kapitalistin, *die*. **2.** *adj.* kapitalistisch

**capitalize** ['kæpɪtəlaɪz] **1.** *v. t.* groß schreiben ‹*Buchstaben, Wort*›. **2.** *v. i.* ~ **on sth.** aus etw. Kapital schlagen *(ugs.)*

**capital 'punishment** *n.* Todesstrafe, *die*

**capitulate** [kə'pɪtjʊleɪt] *v. i.* kapitulieren. **capitulation** [kəpɪtjʊ'leɪʃn] *n.* Kapitulation, *die*

**capricious** [kə'prɪʃəs] *adj.* launisch

**Capricorn** ['kæprɪkɔːn] *n.* der Steinbock

**capsize** [kæp'saɪz] **1.** *v. t.* zum Kentern bringen. **2.** *v. i.* kentern

**capsule** ['kæpsjuːl] *n.* Kapsel, *die*

**captain** ['kæptɪn] **1.** *n.* Kapitän, *der*; *(Army)* Hauptmann, *der.* **2.** *v. t.* ~ **a team** Kapitän einer Mannschaft sein

**caption** ['kæpʃn] *n.* *(heading)* Überschrift, *die*; *(under photograph, drawing)* Bildunterschrift, *die*; *(Cinemat., Telev.)* Untertitel, *der*

**captivate** ['kæptɪveɪt] *v. t.* fesseln. **captivating** ['kæptɪveɪtɪŋ] *adj.* bezaubernd; einnehmend ‹*Lächeln*›

**captive** ['kæptɪv] **1.** *adj.* gefangen; **be taken ~:** gefangengenommen werden. **2.** *n.* Gefangener, *der*/Gefangene, *die*. **captivity** [kæp'tɪvɪtɪ] *n.* Gefangenschaft, *die*; **be held in ~:** gefangengehalten werden

**captor** ['kæptə(r)] *n.* **his ~:** der, der/die, die ihn gefangennahm

**capture** ['kæptʃə(r)] **1.** *n.* **a)** *(of thief etc.)* Festnahme, *die*; *(of town)* Einnahme, *die*; **b)** *(thing, person)* Fang, *der.* **2.** *v. t.* festnehmen ‹*Person*›; [ein]fangen ‹*Tier*›; einnehmen ‹*Stadt*›; gefangennehmen ‹*Phantasie*›

**car** [kɑː(r)] *n.* Auto, *das*; Wagen, *der*; **by ~:** mit dem Auto

**carafe** [kə'ræf] *n.* Karaffe, *die*

**caramel** ['kærəmel] *n.* Karamel, *der*; *(toffee)* Karamelbonbon, *das*

**carat** ['kærət] *n.* Karat, *das*; **a 22-~ gold ring** ein 22karätiger Goldring

**caravan** ['kærəvæn] *n.* *(Brit.)* Wohnwagen, *der.* '**caravan site** *n.* Campingplatz für Wohnwagen

**carbohydrate** [kɑːbəʊ'haɪdreɪt] *n.* Kohlenhydrat, *das*

**carbon** ['kɑːbən] *n.* Kohlenstoff, *der*

**carbon:** ~ '**copy** *n.* Durchschlag, *der*; ~ **dioxide** [~ daɪ'ɒksaɪd] *n.* Kohlendioxid, *das*; ~ **paper** *n.* Kohlepapier, *das*

**carburettor** *(Amer.:* **carburetor**) [kɑːbə'retə(r)] *n.* Vergaser, *der*

**carcass** *(Brit. also:* **carcase**) ['kɑːkəs] *n.* Kadaver, *der*

'**car crash** *n.* Autounfall, *der*

**card** [kɑːd] *n.* Karte, *die*; **play ~s** Karten spielen

**card:** ~**board** *n.* Pappe, *die;* ~**board 'box** *n.* [Papp]karton, *der; (smaller)* [Papp]schachtel, *die;* ~ **game** *n.* Kartenspiel, *das*

**cardigan** ['kɑːdɪgən] *n.* Strickjacke, *die*

**cardinal** ['kɑːdɪnl] **1.** *adj.* grundlegend ⟨*Frage, Doktrin, Pflicht*⟩; Kardinal- ⟨*fehler, -problem*⟩; Haupt⟨*punkt, -merkmal*⟩. **2.** *n. (Eccl.)* Kardinal, *der.* **cardinal 'number** *n.* Kardinalzahl, *die.* **cardinal 'sin** *n.* Todsünde, *die*

**care** [keə(r)] **1.** *n.* **a)** *(anxiety)* Sorge, *die;* **b)** *(pains)* Sorgfalt, *die;* **c)** *(caution)* Vorsicht, *die;* **take** ~: aufpassen; **d) medical** ~: ärztliche Betreuung; **e)** *(charge)* Obhut, *die (geh.);* **put sb. in** ~/**take sb. into** ~: jmdn. in Pflege geben/nehmen; ~ **of** *(on letter)* bei; **take** ~ **of sb./sth.** *(ensure safety of)* auf jmdn./etw. aufpassen; *(attend to)* sich um jmdn./etw. kümmern. **2.** *v. i.* ~ **for sb./sth.** *(look after)* sich um jmdn./ etw. kümmern; *(like)* jmdn./etw. mögen; ~ **to do sth.** etw. tun mögen; I don't ~ **[whether/how/what** *etc.*] es ist mir gleich[, ob/wie/was *usw.*]

**career** [kə'rɪə(r)] **1.** *n.* Beruf, *der.* **2.** *v. i.* rasen; ⟨*Pferd, Reiter:*⟩ galoppieren

**carefree** *adj.* sorgenfrei

**careful** ['keəfl] *adj. (thorough)* sorgfältig; *(cautious)* vorsichtig; **[be]** ~! Vorsicht!; **be** ~ **of sb./sth.** *(be cautious of)* sich vor jmdm./etw. in acht nehmen; **be** ~ **with sb./sth.** vorsichtig mit jmdm./etw. umgehen. **'carefully** *adv. (thoroughly)* sorgfältig; *(attentively)* aufmerksam; *(cautiously)* vorsichtig

**careless** ['keəlɪs] *adj.* **a)** *(inattentive)* unaufmerksam; *(thoughtless)* gedankenlos; leichtsinnig ⟨*Fahrer*⟩; nachlässig ⟨*Arbeiter, Arbeit*⟩; gedankenlos ⟨*Bemerkung, Handlung*⟩; unachtsam ⟨*Fahren*⟩; **b)** *(nonchalant)* ungezwungen. **'carelessly** *adv. (without care)* nachlässig; *(thoughtlessly)* gedankenlos. **'carelessness** *n. (lack of care)* Nachlässigkeit, *die; (thoughtlessness)* Gedankenlosigkeit, *die*

**caress** [kə'res] **1.** *n.* Liebkosung, *die.* **2.** *v. t.* liebkosen

**'caretaker** *n.* Hausmeister, *der*/-meisterin, *die*

**'car ferry** *n.* Autofähre, *die*

**cargo** ['kɑːgəʊ] *n.* Fracht, *die.* **'cargo boat, 'cargo ship** *ns.* Frachter, *der*

**Caribbean** [kærɪ'biːən] **1.** *n.* the ~: die Karibik. **2.** *adj.* karibisch

**caricature** ['kærɪkətjʊə(r)] **1.** *n.* Karikatur, *die.* **2.** *v. t.* karikieren

**carnage** ['kɑːnɪdʒ] *n.* Gemetzel, *das*

**carnal** ['kɑːnl] *adj.* sinnlich

**carnation** [kɑː'neɪʃn] *n.* [Garten]nelke, *die*

**carnet** ['kɑːneɪ] *n. (of motorist)* Triptyk, *das;* **|camping|** ~: Ausweis für Camper

**carnival** ['kɑːnɪvl] *n.* Volksfest, *das*

**carnivorous** [kɑː'nɪvərəs] *adj.* fleischfressend

**carol** ['kærl] *n.* **|Christmas|** ~: Weihnachtslied, *das*

**carp** [kɑːp] *n., pl. same* Karpfen, *der*

**'car-park** *n.* Parkplatz, *der; (building)* Parkhaus, *das*

**carpenter** ['kɑːpɪntə(r)] *n.* Zimmermann, *der; (for furniture)* Tischler, *der*/Tischlerin, *die.* **carpentry** ['kɑːpɪntrɪ] *n.* Zimmerhandwerk, *das; (in furniture)* Tischlerhandwerk, *das*

**carpet** ['kɑːpɪt] *n.* Teppich, *der.* **'carpet-slipper** *n.* Hausschuh, *der.* **'carpet-sweeper** *n.* Teppichkehrer, *der*

**'car-port** *n.* Einstellplatz, *der*

**carriage** ['kærɪdʒ] *n.* **a)** *(horse-drawn)* Kutsche, *die;* **b)** *(Railw.)* Wagen, *der.* **'carriageway** *n.* Fahrbahn, *die*

**carrier** ['kærɪə(r)] *n.* **a)** *(bearer)* Träger, *der;* **b)** *(firm)* Transportunternehmen, *das.* **'carrier-bag** *n.* Tragetasche, *die.* **'carrier pigeon** *n.* Brieftaube, *die*

**carrot** ['kærət] *n.* Möhre, *die*

**carry** ['kærɪ] *v. t.* **a)** tragen; *(emphasizing destination)* bringen; **b)** *(possess)* besitzen ⟨*Autorität, Gewicht*⟩. **carry a'way** *v. t.* forttragen; **be** *or* **get carried away** sich hinreißen lassen. **carry 'on 1.** *v. t.* fortführen; ~ **on |doing sth.|** weiterhin etw. tun. **2.** *v. i.* weitermachen. **carry 'out** *v. t.* durchführen; ausführen ⟨*Anweisung, Auftrag*⟩; vornehmen ⟨*Verbesserungen*⟩

**'carry-cot** *n.* Babytragetasche, *die*

**cart** [kɑːt] **1.** *n.* Wagen, *der.* **2.** *v. t. (sl.)* schleppen

**cartilage** ['kɑːtɪlɪdʒ] *n.* Knorpel, *der*

**carton** ['kɑːtn] *n.* [Papp]karton, *der; (of drink)* Tüte, *die; (of cream, yoghurt)* Becher, *der*

**cartoon** [kɑː'tuːn] *n.* humoristische Zeichnung; *(satirical)* Karikatur, *die; (film)* Zeichentrickfilm, *der*

**cartridge** ['kɑːtrɪdʒ] *n.* **a)** *(for gun)* Patrone, *die;* **b)** *(of film; cassette)* Kassette, *die*

'**cart-wheel** n. (Gymnastics) Rad, das; turn or do ~s radschlagen
**carve** [kɑ:v] 1. v.t. a) tranchieren ⟨Fleisch, Braten, Hähnchen⟩; b) (from wood) schnitzen; (from stone) meißeln. 2. v.i. ~ in wood/stone in Holz schnitzen/in Stein meißeln. **carving** ['kɑ:vɪŋ] n. (in or from wood) Schnitzerei, die; (in or from stone) Skulptur, die. '**carving-knife** n. Tranchiermesser, das
'**car wash** n. Waschanlage, die
**cascade** [kæs'keɪd] n. Kaskade, die
¹**case** [keɪs] n. a) (instance, matter, set of arguments) Fall, der; it is [not] the ~ that ...: es trifft [nicht] zu, daß ...; in ~ ...: falls ...; [just] in ~: für alle Fälle; in ~ of emergency im Notfall; in any ~: jedenfalls; in that ~: in diesem Fall; b) (Med., Police, Soc. Serv., etc.) Fall, der; c) (Law) Fall, der; (action) Verfahren, das; d) (Ling.) Fall, der; Kasus, der (fachspr.)
²**case** n. a) Koffer, der; (brief-~) [Akten]tasche, die; b) (for spectacles, cigarettes) Etui, das; c) (crate) Kiste, die; d) [display-]~: Schaukasten, der
**cash** [kæʃ] 1. n. Bargeld, das; pay [in] ~, pay ~ down bar zahlen. 2. v.t. einlösen ⟨Scheck⟩
**cash:** ~ and 'carry n. cash and carry; (store) Cash-and-carry-Laden, der; ~card n. Geldautomatenkarte, die; ~ desk n. (Brit.) Kasse, die; ~ dispenser n. Geldautomat, der
**cashier** [kæ'ʃɪə(r)] n. Kassierer, der/Kassiererin, die
**cash:** ~point n. Geldautomat, der; ~ register n. [Registrier]kasse, die
**casino** [kə'si:nəʊ] n. Kasino, das
**cask** [kɑ:sk] n. Faß, das
**casket** ['kɑ:skɪt] n. a) Kästchen, das; b) (Amer.: coffin) Sarg, der
**casserole** ['kæsərəʊl] n. Schmortopf, der
**cassette** [kə'set, kæ'set] n. Kassette, die. **cas'sette-deck** n. Kassettendeck, das. **cas'sette recorder** n. Kassettenrecorder, der
**cast** [kɑ:st] 1. v.t., cast a) werfen; b) (shape, form) gießen; c) abgeben ⟨Stimme⟩. 2. n. a) (Med.) Gipsverband, der; b) (actors) Besetzung, die. **cast a'side** v.t. beiseite schieben ⟨Vorschlag⟩; vergessen ⟨Sorgen⟩; fallenlassen ⟨Hemmungen⟩. **cast 'off** v.i. & t. (Naut.) losmachen
**castanets** [kæstə'nets] n. pl. Kastagnetten Pl.

'**castaway** n. Schiffbrüchige, der/die
**caste** [kɑ:st] n. Kaste, die
**cast 'iron** n. Gußeisen, das
**castle** ['kɑ:sl] n. Burg, die; (mansion) Schloß, das
'**cast-offs** n. pl. abgelegte Sachen
**castor** ['kɑ:stə(r)] n. (wheel) Rolle, die
**castor:** ~ 'oil n. Rizinusöl, das; ~ sugar n. Raffinade, die
**castrate** [kæ'streɪt] v.t. kastrieren. **castration** [kæ'streɪʃn] n. Kastration, die
**casual** ['kæʒjʊəl] adj. ungezwungen; leger ⟨Kleidung⟩; beiläufig ⟨Bemerkung⟩; flüchtig ⟨Bekannter, Bekanntschaft, Blick⟩; unbekümmert ⟨Haltung, Einstellung⟩. '**casually** adv. ungezwungen; beiläufig ⟨bemerken⟩; flüchtig ⟨anschauen⟩; leger ⟨sich kleiden⟩
**casualty** ['kæʒjʊəltɪ] n. a) (injured person) Verletzte, der/die; (in battle) Verwundete, der/die; (dead person) Tote, der/die; b) (hospital department) Unfallstation, die
**cat** [kæt] n. Katze, die
**catalogue** (Amer.: **catalog**) ['kætələg] 1. n. Katalog, der. 2. v.t. katalogisieren
**catalyst** ['kætəlɪst] n. Katalysator, der. **catalytic** [kætə'lɪtɪk] adj. ~ converter Katalysator, der
**catapult** ['kætəpʌlt] 1. n. Katapult, das. 2. v.t. katapultieren
**cataract** ['kætərækt] n. a) Katarakt, der; b) (Med.) grauer Star
**catarrh** [kə'tɑ:(r)] n. Katarrh, der
**catastrophe** [kə'tæstrəfɪ] n. Katastrophe, die. **catastrophic** [kætə'strɒfɪk] adj. katastrophal
**catch** [kætʃ] 1. v.t., caught [kɔ:t] a) fangen; ~ hold of sb./sth. jmdn./etw. festhalten; (to stop oneself falling) sich an jmdm./etw. festhalten; get sth. caught or ~ sth. on/in sth. mit etw. an/in etw. (Dat.) hängenbleiben; ~ one's finger in the door sich (Dat.) den Finger in der Tür einklemmen; b) (travel by) nehmen; (be in time for) [noch] erreichen; c) (surprise) ~ sb. doing sth. jmdn. [dabei] erwischen, wie er etw. tut (ugs.); d) (become infected with) sich (Dat.) zuziehen; ~ sth. from sb. sich bei jmdm. mit etw. anstecken; ~ a cold sich erkälten; ~ it (fig. coll.) etwas kriegen (ugs.); e) ~ sb.'s attention/interest jmds. Aufmerksamkeit erregen/jmds. Interesse wecken. 2. v.i., caught a) (begin to burn) [anfangen zu]

brennen; **b)** *(become hooked up)* hängenbleiben; ⟨*Haar, Faden:*⟩ sich verfangen. **3.** *n.* **a)** *(of ball)* make a ~: fangen; **b)** *(amount caught, lit. or fig.)* Fang, *der;* **c)** *(difficulty)* Haken, *der* (in an + *Dat.*); **d)** *(of door)* Schnapper, *der.* **catch 'on** *v.i. (coll.)* **a)** *(become popular)* [gut] ankommen *(ugs.);* **b)** *(understand)* kapieren *(ugs.).* **catch 'up 1.** *v.t.* ~ sb. up jmdn. einholen. **2.** *v.i.* ~ up gleichziehen; ~ up on sth. etw. nachholen
'**catching** *adj.* ansteckend
'**catchy** *adj.* eingängig
**categorical** [kætɪ'gɒrɪkl] *adj.* kategorisch
**category** ['kætɪgərɪ] *n.* Kategorie, *die*
**cater** ['keɪtə(r)] *v.i.* ~ for sb./sth. für jmdn./etw. [die] Speisen und Getränke liefern; *(fig.)* auf jmdn./etw. eingestellt sein. '**caterer** *n.* Lieferant von Speisen und Getränken. '**catering** *n.* **a)** *(trade)* Gastronomie, *die;* **b)** *(service)* Lieferung von Speisen und Getränken
**caterpillar** ['kætəpɪlə(r)] *n.* Raupe, *die*
**cathedral** [kə'θi:drl] *n.* Dom, *der*
**Catherine wheel** ['kæθrɪn wi:l] *n.* Feuerrad, *das*
**Catholic** ['kæθəlɪk] **1.** *adj.* katholisch. **2.** *n.* Katholik, *der*/Katholikin, *die.* **Catholicism** [kə'θɒlɪsɪzm] *n.* Katholizismus, *der*
**catkin** ['kætkɪn] *n. (Bot.)* Kätzchen, *das*
'**Cat's-eye, (P)** *n. (Brit.: on road)* Bodenrückstrahler, *der*
**cattle** ['kætl] *n. pl.* Rinder *Pl.*
**caught** *see* **catch 1, 2**
**cauldron** ['kɔ:ldrən] *n.* Kessel, *der*
**cauliflower** ['kɒlɪflaʊə(r)] *n.* Blumenkohl, *der*
**cause** [kɔ:z] **1.** *n.* **a)** Ursache, *die* (of für *od. Gen.*); *(person)* Verursacher, *der*/Verursacherin, *die;* **be the** ~ **of sth.** etw. vérursachen; **b)** *(reason)* Grund, *der;* ~ **for sth.** Grund zu etw.; **c)** *(object of support)* Sache, *die;* |in] **a good** ~: [für] eine gute Sache. **2.** *v.t.* verursachen; erregen ⟨*Aufsehen, Ärgernis*⟩*;* hervorrufen ⟨*Unruhe, Verwirrung*⟩*;* ~ **sb. worry/pain** jmdm. Sorge/Schmerzen bereiten; ~ **sb. to do sth.** jmdn. veranlassen, etw. zu tun
**causeway** ['kɔ:zweɪ] *n.* Damm, *der*
**caustic** ['kɔ:stɪk] *adj.* ätzend; *(fig.)* bissig; beißend ⟨*Spott*⟩
**caution** ['kɔ:ʃn] **1.** *n.* **a)** Vorsicht, *die;* **b)** *(warning)* Warnung, *die.* **2.** *v.t.*

*(warn)* warnen; *(warn and reprove)* verwarnen **(for wegen)**
**cautious** ['kɔ:ʃəs] *adj.,* '**cautiously** *adv.* vorsichtig
**cavalry** ['kævəlrɪ] *n.* Kavallerie, *die*
**cave** [keɪv] *n.* Höhle, *die.* **cave 'in** *v.i.* einbrechen
'**caveman** *n.* Höhlenbewohner, der
**cavern** ['kævən] *n.* Höhle, *die.* **cavernous** ['kævənəs] *adj.* höhlenartig
**caviar[e]** ['kævɪɑ:(r)] *n.* Kaviar, *der*
**cavity** ['kævɪtɪ] *n.* Hohlraum, *der; (in tooth)* Loch, *das*
**CB** *abbr.* **citizen's band** CB
**cc** [si:'si:] *abbr.* **cubic centimetre(s)** $cm^3$
**CD** *abbr.* **compact disc** CD
**cease** [si:s] **1.** *v.i.* aufhören. **2.** *v.t.* **a)** *(stop)* aufhören; **b)** *(end)* aufhören mit; einstellen ⟨*Bemühungen*⟩*.* '**cease-fire** *n.* Waffenruhe, *die*
**cedar** ['si:də(r)] *n.* Zeder, *die*
**ceiling** ['si:lɪŋ] *n.* **a)** Decke, *die;* **b)** *(upper limit)* Maximum, *das*
**celebrate** ['selɪbreɪt] *v.t. & i.* feiern. '**celebrated** *adj.* berühmt. **celebration** [selɪ'breɪʃn] *n.* Feier, *die.* **celebrity** [sɪ'lebrɪtɪ] *n.* Berühmtheit, *die*
**celery** ['selərɪ] *n.* Sellerie, *der od. die*
**celibate** ['selɪbət] *adj.* zölibatär *(Rel.);* ehelos
**cell** [sel] *n.* Zelle, *die*
**cellar** ['selə(r)] *n.* Keller, *der*
**cellist** ['tʃelɪst] *n.* Cellist, *der*/Cellistin, *die*
**cello** ['tʃeləʊ] *n., pl.* ~s Cello, *das*
**Cellophane, (P)** ['seləfeɪn] *n.* Cellophan ⓦ, *das*
**Celsius** ['selsɪəs] *adj.* Celsius
**cement** [sɪ'ment] **1.** *n.* Zement, *der.* **2.** *v.t.* zementieren; *(stick together)* zusammenkleben. **ce'ment-mixer** *n.* Betonmischmaschine, *die*
**cemetery** ['semɪtərɪ] *n.* Friedhof, *der*
**censor** ['sensə(r)] **1.** *n.* Zensor, *der.* **2.** *v.t.* zensieren. '**censorship** *n.* Zensur, *die*
**censure** ['senʃə(r)] *v.t.* tadeln
**census** ['sensəs] *n.* Volkszählung, *die*
**cent** [sent] *n.* Cent, *der*
**centenary** [sen'ti:nərɪ] *adj. & n.* ~ |**celebrations**| Hundertjahrfeier, *die*
**center** *(Amer.) see* **centre**
**centigrade** ['sentɪgreɪd] *see* **Celsius**
**centimetre** *(Brit.; Amer.:* **centimeter)** ['sentɪmi:tə(r)] *n.* Zentimeter, *der*
**centipede** ['sentɪpi:d] *n.* Tausendfüßler, *der*
**central** ['sentrl] *adj.* zentral

**Central:** ~ **A'merica** *pr. n.* Mittel-amerika *(das);* ~ **'Europe** *pr. n.* Mit-teleuropa *(das);* ~ **Euro'pean** *adj.* mitteleuropäisch; **c~ 'heating** *n.* Zentralheizung, *die*

**centralize** ['sentrəlaɪz] *v. t.* zentrali-sieren

**central reser'vation** *n. (Brit.)* Mit-telstreifen, *der*

**centre** ['sentə(r)] *(Brit.)* **1.** *n.* **a)** Mitte, *die; (of circle)* Mittelpunkt, *der;* **b)** *(of area, city)* Zentrum, *das.* **2.** *adj.* mitt-ler... **3.** *v. i.* ~ **on sth.** sich auf etw. *(Akk.)* konzentrieren; ~ **|a|round sth.** sich um etw. drehen. **4.** *v. t.* **a)** in der Mitte anbringen; **b)** *(concentrate)* be ~d **|a|round sth.** etw. zum Mittelpunkt haben; ~ **sth. on sth.** etw. auf etw. *(Akk.)* konzentrieren. **centre-'for-ward** *n.* Mittelstürmer, *der*

**centrifugal** [sentrɪ'fju:gl] *adj.* ~ **force** Zentrifugalkraft, *die;* Fliehkraft, *die*

**century** ['sentʃərɪ] *n. (hundred-year period from a year ..00)* Jahrhundert, *das; (hundred years)* hundert Jahre

**ceramic** [sɪ'ræmɪk] *adj.* keramisch

**cereal** ['sɪərɪəl] *n.* Getreide, *das; (breakfast dish)* Getreideflocken *Pl.*

**ceremonial** [serɪ'məʊnɪəl] **1.** *adj.* fei-erlich; *(prescribed for ceremony)* zere-moniell. **2.** *n.* Zeremoniell, *das*

**ceremony** ['serɪmənɪ] *n.* Feier, *die; (formal act)* Zeremonie, *die*

**certain** ['sɜ:tn, 'sɜ:tɪn] *adj.* **a)** *(settled, definite)* bestimmt; **b) be ~ to do sth.** etw. bestimmt tun; **c)** *(confident, sure to happen)* sicher; **d)** *(indisputable)* un-bestreitbar; **e) a ~ Mr Smith** ein ge-wisser Herr Smith; **to a ~ extent** in ge-wisser Weise. **'certainly** *adv.* **a)** *(ad-mittedly)* sicher|lich|; *(definitely)* be-stimmt; **b)** *(in answer)* |aber| sicher; |most| ~ **'not!** auf |gar| keinen Fall!

**certainty** ['sɜ:tntɪ, 'sɜ:tɪntɪ] *n.* **a) be a ~:** sicher sein; **b)** *(absolute conviction)* Gewißheit, *die*

**certificate** [sə'tɪfɪkət] *n.* Urkunde, *die; (of action performed)* Schein, *der*

**certify** ['sɜ:tɪfaɪ] *v. t.* bescheinigen; be-stätigen; **this is to ~ that ...:** hiermit wird bescheinigt *od.* bestätigt, daß ...

**cf.** *abbr.* **compare** vgl.

**chafe** [tʃeɪf] *v. t.* wund scheuern

**chaff** [tʃɑ:f] *n.* Spreu, *die*

**chaffinch** ['tʃæfɪntʃ] *n.* Buchfink, *der*

**chagrin** ['ʃægrɪn] *n.* Kummer, *der*

**chain** [tʃeɪn] **1.** *n.* Kette, *die;* ~ **of shops/hotels** Laden-/Hotelkette, *die.* **2.** *v. t.* |an|ketten (**to** an + *Akk.*)

**chain:** ~ **re'action** *n.* Kettenreakti-on, *die;* ~**-saw** *n.* Kettensäge, *die;* ~**-smoker** *n.* Kettenraucher, *der/* -raucherin, *die;* ~ **store** Kettenladen, *der*

**chair** [tʃeə(r)] **1.** *n.* **a)** Stuhl, *der; (arm~, easy ~)* Sessel, *der;* **b)** *(profes-sorship)* Lehrstuhl, *der;* **c)** *(at meeting)* Vorsitz, *der.* **2.** *v. t.* den Vorsitz haben bei

**chair:** ~**-back** *n.* Rückenlehne, *die;* ~**-lift** *n.* Sessellift, *der;* ~**-man** ['tʃeə-mən] *n., pl.* ~**-men** ['tʃeəmən] Vorsit-zende, *der/die*

**chalet** ['ʃæleɪ] *n.* Chalet, *das*

**chalk** [tʃɔ:k] **1.** *n.* Kreide, *die.* **2.** *v. t.* mit Kreide schreiben/malen *usw.*

**challenge** ['tʃælɪndʒ] **1.** *n.* Herausfor-derung, *die.* **2.** *v. t.* **a)** *(to contest etc.)* herausfordern; **b)** *(fig.)* auffordern; *(question)* in Frage stellen. **'chal-lenger** *n.* Herausforderer, *der/*Her-ausforderin, *die.* **'challenging** ['tʃæ-lɪndʒɪŋ] *adj.* herausfordernd; fesselnd ⟨*Problem*⟩; anspruchsvoll ⟨*Arbeit*⟩

**chamber** ['tʃeɪmbə(r)] *n.* Kammer, *die*

**chamber:** ~**-maid** *n.* Zimmermäd-chen, *das;* ~ **music** *n.* Kammermu-sik, *die;* ~**-pot** *n.* Nachttopf, *der*

**chameleon** [kə'mi:lɪən] *n.* Chamäle-on

**chamois** ['ʃæmwɑ:] *n.* **a)** Gemse, *die;* **b)** ['ʃæmɪ] ~**-leather|** Chamois|leder|, *das*

**champagne** [ʃæm'peɪn] *n.* Sekt, *der; (from Champagne)* Champagner, *der*

**champion** ['tʃæmpɪən] **1.** *n.* **a)** *(de-fender)* Verfechter, *der/*Verfechterin, *die;* **b)** *(Sport)* Meister, *der/*Meisterin, *die.* **2.** *v. t.* verfechten ⟨*Sache*⟩; sich einsetzen für ⟨*Person*⟩. **'champion-ship** *n.* Meisterschaft, *die*

**chance** [tʃɑ:ns] **1.** *n.* **a)** *(fortune, trick of fate)* Zufall, *der; attrib.* zufällig; ~ **encounter** Zufallsbegegnung, *die;* **game of ~:** Glücksspiel, *das;* **by ~:** zu-fällig; **take a ~:** es riskieren; **the ~s are that ...:** es ist wahrscheinlich, daß ...; **by |any| ~, by some ~ or other** zufällig; **b)** *(opportunity, possibility)* Chance, *die;* **get a/the ~ to do sth.** ei-ne/die Gelegenheit haben, etw. zu tun. **2.** *v. t.* riskieren

**chancellor** ['tʃɑ:nsələ(r)] *n.* Kanzler, *der;* **C~ of the Exchequer** *(Brit.)* Schatzkanzler, *der*

**chandelier** [ʃændə'lɪə(r)] *n.* Kron-leuchter, *der*

**change** [tʃeɪndʒ] **1.** *n.* **a)** Veränderung, *die;* Änderung, *die; (of job, sur-roundings, government, etc.)* Wechsel, *der;* b) *(for the sake of variety)* Abwechslung, *die;* for a ~: zur Abwechslung; c) *(money)* Wechselgeld, *das;* [loose *or* small] ~: Kleingeld, *das;* [here is] 15 marks ~: 15 Mark zurück; keep the ~: [es] stimmt so. 2. *v. t.* a) *(switch)* wechseln; auswechseln ‹Glühbirne, Batterie›; ~ one's clothes sich umziehen; ~ one's address/name seine Anschrift/seinen Namen ändern; ~ trains/buses umsteigen; b) *(transform)* verwandeln (into in + Akk.); *(alter)* ändern; c) *(exchange)* eintauschen (for für); wechseln ‹Geld›. 3. *v. i.* a) *(alter)* sich ändern; ‹Person, Land:› sich verändern; b) *(into something else)* sich verwandeln; c) *(put on other clothes)* sich umziehen.

**change 'over** *v. i.* ~ over from sth. to sth. von etw. zu etw. übergehen

**changeable** ['tʃeɪndʒəbl] *adj.* veränderlich

'**changing room** *n.* *(Brit.)* Umkleideraum, *der*

**channel** ['tʃænl] 1. *n. (also Telev., Radio)* Kanal, *der;* the C~ *(Brit.)* der [Ärmel]kanal. 2. *v. t. (fig.)* lenken. '**Channel Islands** *pr. n. pl.* Kanalinseln *Pl.*

**chant** [tʃɑːnt] 1. *v. t.* skandieren; *(Eccl.)* singen. 2. *v. i.* Sprechchöre anstimmen; *(Eccl.)* singen. 3. *n.* Sprechchor, *der; (Eccl.)* Gesang, *der*

**chaos** ['keɪɒs] *n.* Chaos, *das.* **chaotic** [keɪ'ɒtɪk] *adj.* chaotisch

¹**chap** [tʃæp] *n. (Brit. coll.)* Bursche, *der;* Kerl, *der*

²**chap** *v. t.,* -pp- aufplatzen lassen

**chapel** ['tʃæpl] *n.* Kapelle, *die*

**chaperon** ['ʃæpərəʊn] 1. *n.* Anstandsdame, *die.* 2. *v. t.* beaufsichtigen

**chaplain** ['tʃæplɪn] *n.* Kaplan, *der*

**chapter** ['tʃæptə(r)] *n.* Kapitel, *das*

**char** [tʃɑː(r)] *v. t. & i.,* -rr- verkohlen

**character** ['kærɪktə(r)] *n.* a) Charakter, *der;* b) *(in novel etc.)* Figur, *die;* c) *(coll.: extraordinary person)* Original, *das;* d) *(symbol)* Zeichen, *das.* **characteristic** [kærɪktə'rɪstɪk] 1. *adj.* charakteristisch (of für). 2. *n.* charakteristisches Merkmal. **characterize** ['kærɪktəraɪz] *v. t.* charakterisieren

**charade** [ʃə'rɑːd] *n.* Scharade, *die; (fig.)* Farce, *die*

**charcoal** ['tʃɑːkəʊl] *n.* Holzkohle, *die*

**charge** [tʃɑːdʒ] 1. *n.* a) *(price)* Preis, *der; (for services)* Gebühr, *die;* b) be in

~ of sth. für etw. die Verantwortung haben; take ~: die Verantwortung übernehmen; c) *(Law: accusation)* Anklage, *die;* d) *(attack)* Angriff, *der;* e) *(of explosives, electricity)* Ladung, *die.* 2. *v. t.* a) ~ sb. sth., ~ sth. to sb. jmdm. etw. berechnen; b) *(Law: accuse)* anklagen (with wegen); c) *(Electr.)* [auf]laden ‹Batterie›; d) *(rush at)* angreifen. 3. *v. i.* a) *(attack)* angreifen; b) *(coll.: hurry)* sausen

**charitable** ['tʃærɪtəbl] *adj.* a) wohltätig; b) *(lenient)* großzügig

**charity** ['tʃærɪtɪ] *n.* a) Wohltätigkeit, *die;* b) *(organization)* wohltätige Organisation

**charlady** ['tʃɑːleɪdɪ] *n. (Brit.)* Putzfrau, *die*

**charlatan** ['ʃɑːlətən] *n.* Scharlatan, *der*

**charm** [tʃɑːm] 1. *n.* a) *(act)* Zauber, *der;* b) *(talisman)* Talisman, *der;* c) *(attractiveness)* Reiz, *der; (of person)* Charme, *der.* 2. *v. t.* bezaubern. '**charming** *adj.* bezaubernd

**chart** [tʃɑːt] 1. *n.* a) *(map)* Karte, *die;* b) *(graph etc.)* Schaubild, *das;* c) the ~s die Hitliste. 2. *v. t. (fig.: describe)* schildern

**charter** ['tʃɑːtə(r)] 1. *n.* a) Charta, *die;* b) on ~ gechartert. 2. *v. t.* chartern ‹Schiff, Flugzeug›. **chartered accountant** *n. (Brit.)* Wirtschaftsprüfer, *der/*-prüferin, *die*

'**charter flight** *n.* Charterflug, *der*

**charwoman** ['tʃɑːwʊmən] *n.* Putzfrau, *die*

**chase** [tʃeɪs] 1. *n.* Verfolgungsjagd, *die.* 2. *v. t. (pursue)* jagen; ~ sth. *(fig.)* einer Sache *(Dat.)* nachjagen. 3. *v. i.* ~ after sb./sth. hinter jmdm./etw. herjagen. **chase 'up** *v. t. (coll.)* ausfindig machen

**chasm** ['kæzm] *n.* Kluft, *die*

**chassis** ['ʃæsɪ] *n., pl. same* ['ʃæsɪz] Chassis, *das;* Fahrgestell, *das*

**chaste** [tʃeɪst] *adj.* keusch

**chastening** ['tʃeɪsənɪŋ] *adj.* ernüchternd

**chastise** [tʃæ'staɪz] *v. t.* züchtigen

**chastity** ['tʃæstɪtɪ] *n.* Keuschheit, *die*

**chat** [tʃæt] 1. *n.* Schwätzchen, *das.* 2. *v. i.,* -tt- plaudern; ~ with *or* to sb. about sth. mit jmdm. von etw. plaudern. **chat 'up** *v. t. (Brit. coll.)* anmachen *(ugs.)*

'**chat show** *n.* Talk-Show, *die*

**chattels** ['tʃætəlz] *n. pl.* bewegliche Habe *(geh.)*

**chatter** ['tʃætə(r)] **1.** *v. i.* **a)** schwatzen; **b)** ⟨*Zähne:*⟩ klappern. **2.** *n.* Schwatzen, *das.* '**chatterbox** *n.* Quasselstrippe, *die (ugs.)*
**chatty** ['tʃætɪ] *adj.* gesprächig
**chauffeur** ['ʃəʊfə(r)] **1.** *n.* Fahrer, *der;* Chauffeur, *der.* **2.** *v. t.* fahren
**chauvinist** ['ʃəʊvɪnɪst] *n.* Chauvinist, *der/*Chauvinistin, *die.* **chauvinistic** [ʃəʊvɪ'nɪstɪk] *adj.* chauvinistisch
**cheap** [tʃiːp] *adj.* billig. **cheapen** ['tʃiːpn] *v. t. (fig.)* herabsetzen. '**cheaply** *adv.* billig
**cheat** [tʃiːt] **1.** *n.* Schwindler, *der/* Schwindlerin, *die.* **2.** *v. t. & i.* betrügen
¹**check** [tʃek] **1.** *n.* **a)** Kontrolle, *die;* **make/keep a ~ on** kontrollieren; **b)** *(Amer.: bill)* Rechnung, *die.* **2.** *v. t.* **a)** *(restrain)* unter Kontrolle halten; **b)** *(examine)* nachprüfen; kontrollieren ⟨*Fahrkarte*⟩; **c)** *(stop)* aufhalten. **3.** *v. i.* **~ on sth.** etw. überprüfen; **~ with sb.** bei jmdm. nachfragen. **check 'in** *v. t. & i. (at airport)* einchecken. **check 'out 1.** *v. t.* überprüfen. **2.** *v. i.* abreisen. **check 'up** *v. i.* **~ up [on]** überprüfen
²**check** *n. (pattern)* Karo, *das*
**checkers** ['tʃekəz] *(Amer.) see* **draughts**
**check: ~-in** *n.* Abfertigung, *die;* **~-list** *n.* Checkliste, *die;* **~mate 1.** *n.* [Schach]matt, *das;* **2.** *int.* [schach]matt; **~-out [desk]** *n.* Kasse, *die;* **~-point** *n.* Kontrollpunkt, *der;* **~-up** *n. (Med.)* Untersuchung, *die*
**cheek** [tʃiːk] *n.* **a)** Backe, *die;* Wange, *die (geh.);* **b)** *(impertinence)* Frechheit, *die.* **cheekily** *adv.,* '**cheeky** *adj.* frech
**cheep** [tʃiːp] **1.** *v. i.* piep[s]en. **2.** *n.* Piep[s]en, *das*
**cheer** [tʃɪə(r)] **1.** *n.* **a)** *(applause)* Beifallsruf, *der;* **b)** in *pl. (Brit. coll.)* prost! **2.** *v. t.* **a)** *(applaud)* **~ sth./sb.** etw. bejubeln/jmdm. zujubeln; **b)** *(gladden)* aufmuntern. **3.** *v. i.* jubeln. **cheer 'on** *v. t.* anfeuern ⟨*Sportler*⟩. **cheer 'up 1.** *v. t.* aufheitern. **2.** *v. i.* bessere Laune bekommen; **~ up!** Kopf hoch!
**cheerful** [[tʃɪəfl] *adj. (in good spirits)* fröhlich; *(bright, pleasant)* heiter. '**cheerfully** *adv.* vergnügt
'**cheering 1.** *adj.* fröhlich stimmend. **2.** *n.* Jubeln, *das*
**cheerio** [tʃɪərɪ'əʊ] *int. (Brit. coll.)* tschüs *(ugs.)*
'**cheery** *adj.* fröhlich

**cheese** [tʃiːz] *n.* Käse, *der.* '**cheese-board** *n.* Käseplatte, *die.* '**cheese-cake** *n.* Käsetorte, *die*
**cheetah** ['tʃiːtə] *n.* Gepard, *der*
**chef** [ʃef] *n.* Küchenchef, *der; (as profession)* Koch, *der*
**chemical** ['kemɪkl] **1.** *adj.* chemisch. **2.** *n.* Chemikalie, *die*
**chemist** ['kemɪst] *n.* **a)** *(scientist)* Chemiker, *der/*Chemikerin, *die;* **b)** *(Brit.: pharmacist)* Drogist, *der/*Drogistin, *die;* **~'s [shop]**Drogerie, *die.* **chemistry** ['kemɪstrɪ] *n.* Chemie, *die*
**cheque** [tʃek] *n.* Scheck, *der;* **pay by ~:** mit [einem] Scheck bezahlen. '**cheque-book** *n.* Scheckbuch, *das.* '**cheque card** *n.* Scheckkarte, *die*
**cherish** ['tʃerɪʃ] *v. t.* hegen ⟨*Hoffnung, Gefühl*⟩; in Ehren halten ⟨*[Erinnerungs]gegenstand*⟩
**cherry** ['tʃerɪ] *n.* Kirsche, *die*
**chess** [tʃes] *n., no art.* das Schach[spiel]
**chess: ~-board** *n.* Schachbrett, *das;* **~-man** *n.* Schachfigur, *die;* **~-player** *n.* Schachspieler, *der/*-spielerin, *die*
**chest** [tʃest] *n.* **a)** Kiste, *die;* **b)** *(Anat.)* Brust, *die;* **get sth. off one's ~** *(fig. coll.)* sich *(Dat.)* etw. von der Seele reden; **c)** **~ [measurement]** Brustumfang, *der*
**chestnut** ['tʃesnʌt] **1.** *n.* **a)** Kastanie, *die;* **b)** *(colour)* Kastanienbraun, *das.* **2.** *adj. (colour)* **~[-brown]** kastanienbraun. '**chestnut-tree** *n.* Kastanie, *die*
**chest of 'drawers** *n.* Kommode, *die*
**chew** [tʃuː] *v. t. & i.* kauen. '**chewing-gum** *n.* Kaugummi, *der od. das*
**chic** [ʃiːk] *adj.* schick; elegant
**chick** [tʃɪk] *n.* **a)** Küken, *das;* **b)** *(sl.: young woman)* Biene, *die (ugs.)*
**chicken** ['tʃɪkɪn] **1.** *n.* **a)** Huhn, *das;* *(grilled, roasted)* Hähnchen, *das;* **b)** *(coll.: coward)* Angsthase, *der.* **2.** *adj. (coll.)* feig[e]. **3.** *v. i.* **~ out** *(sl.)* kneifen
'**chicken-pox** [~pɒks] *n.* Windpocken *Pl.*
**chicory** ['tʃɪkərɪ] *n. (plant)* Chicorée, *der od. die; (for coffee)* Zichorie, *die*
**chief** [tʃiːf] **1.** *n.* **a)** Oberhaupt, *das; (of tribe)* Häuptling, *der;* **b)** *(of department)* Leiter, *der;* **~ of police** Polizeipräsident, *der.* **2.** *adj., usu. attrib.* **a)** Haupt-; **b)** *(leading)* führend. '**chiefly** *adv.* hauptsächlich
**chieftain** ['tʃiːftən] *n.* Stammesführer, *der*

**chilblain** ['tʃɪlbleɪn] n. Frostbeule, die
**child** [tʃaɪld] n., pl. ~**ren** ['tʃɪldrən]
Kind, das. '**childbirth** n. Geburt,
die. '**childhood** n. Kindheit, die
**childish** ['tʃaɪldɪʃ] adj., '**childishly**
adv. kindisch. '**childishness** n. (behaviour) kindisches Benehmen
**child:** ~**less** adj. kinderlos; ~**like**
adj. kindlich; ~-**minder** ['~maɪn-
də(r)] n. (Brit.) Tagesmutter, die
**children** pl. of **child**
'**child's play** n. (fig.) ein Kinderspiel
**Chile** ['tʃɪlɪ] n. Chile (das)
**chill** [tʃɪl] 1. n. Kühle, die; (illness) Erkältung, die. 2. v. t. kühlen
**chilli** ['tʃɪlɪ] n., pl. ~**es** Chili, der
'**chilly** adj. kühl; **I am rather** ~: mir ist
ziemlich kühl ·
**chime** [tʃaɪm] 1. n. Geläute, das. 2.
v. i. läuten; ⟨Turmuhr:⟩ schlagen
**chimney** ['tʃɪmnɪ] n. Schornstein, der.
'**chimney-sweep** n. Schornsteinfeger, der
**chimpanzee** [tʃɪmpən'zi:] n. Schimpanse, der
**chin** [tʃɪn] n. Kinn, das
**China** ['tʃaɪnə] pr. n. China (das)
**china** n. Porzellan, das; (crockery) Geschirr, das
**Chinese** [tʃaɪ'ni:z] 1. adj. chinesisch.
2. n. a) pl. same (person) Chinese,
der/Chinesin, die; b) (language) Chinesisch, das; see also **English 2 a**
**chink** n. (gap) Spalt, der
**chip** [tʃɪp] 1. n. a) Splitter, der; b) in pl.
(Brit.: potato~s) Pommes frites Pl.; c)
(Gambling) Chip, der. 2. v. t., -**pp**- anschlagen. **chip 'in** (coll.) 1. v. i. a) (interrupt) sich einmischen; b) (contribute money) etwas beisteuern. 2. v. t.
(contribute) beisteuern
'**chipboard** n. Spanplatte, die
**chipmunk** ['tʃɪpmʌŋk] n. Chipmunk,
das
**chiropodist** [kɪ'rɒpədɪst] n. Fußpfle-
ger, der/-pflegerin, die
**chiropody** [kɪ'rɒpədɪ] n. Fußpflege,
die
**chirp** [tʃɜ:p] 1. v. i. zwitschern;
⟨Grille:⟩ zirpen. 2. n. Zwitschern, das;
Zirpen, das
**chisel** ['tʃɪzl] 1. n. Meißel, der; (for
wood) Stemmeisen, das. 2. v. t., (Brit.)
-**ll**- meißeln; (in wood) hauen
**chit** [tʃɪt] n. Notiz, die
**chit-chat** ['tʃɪttʃæt] n. Plauderei, die
**chivalrous** ['ʃɪvlrəs] adj. ritterlich.
**chivalry** ['ʃɪvlrɪ] n. Ritterlichkeit, die
**chives** [tʃaɪvz] n. Schnittlauch, der

**chloride** ['klɔ:raɪd] n. Chlorid, das
**chlorine** ['klɔ:ri:n] n. Chlor, das
**chock** [tʃɒk] n. Bremsklotz, der.
'**chock-a-block** pred adj. vollge-
pfropft
**chocolate** ['tʃɒklət] n. Schokolade,
die
**choice** [tʃɔɪs] 1. n. a) Wahl, die; from
~: freiwillig; b) (variety) Auswahl,
die. 2. adj. ausgewählt
**choir** [kwaɪə(r)] n. Chor, der. '**choir-
boy** n. Chorknabe, der
**choke** [tʃəʊk] 1. v. t. a) ersticken; b)
(block up) verstopfen. 2. v. i. (temporarily) keine Luft [mehr] bekommen;
(permanently) ersticken (**on** an +
Dat.). 3. n. (Motor Veh.) Choke, der
**cholera** ['kɒlərə] n. Cholera, die
**cholesterol** [kə'lestərɒl] n. Cholesterin, das
**choose** [tʃu:z] 1. v. t., **chose** [tʃəʊz],
**chosen** ['tʃəʊzn] a) wählen; b) (decide)
~/~ **not to do sth.** sich dafür/dagegen
entscheiden, etw. zu tun. 2. v. i., **chose**,
**chosen** wählen (**between** zwischen); ~
**from sth.** aus etw./(from several) unter
etw. (Dat.) [aus]wählen. **choos[e]y**
['tʃu:zɪ] adj. wählerisch
**chop** [tʃɒp] 1. n. a) Hieb, der; b) (of
meat) Kotelett, das; c) **get the** ~ (coll.:
be dismissed) rausgeworfen werden
(ugs.). 2. v. t., -**pp**- hacken ⟨Holz⟩;
kleinschneiden ⟨Fleisch, Gemüse⟩.
'**chopper** n. (axe) Beil, das; (cleaver)
Hackbeil, das
'**choppy** adj. bewegt
**choral** ['kɔ:rl] adj. Chor-
**chord** [kɔ:d] n. (Mus.) Akkord, der
**chore** [tʃɔ:(r)] n. [lästige] Routine-
arbeit
**chortle** ['tʃɔ:tl] 1. v. i. vor Lachen
glucksen. 2. n. Glucksen, das
**chorus** ['kɔ:rəs] n. a) Chor, der; b) (of
song) Chorus, der
**chose, chosen** see **choose**
**chow** [tʃaʊ] n. (Amer. sl.: food) Futter,
das (salopp)
**Christ** [kraɪst] n. Christus (der)
**christen** ['krɪsn] v. t. taufen. '**christening** n. Taufe, die
**Christian** ['krɪstjən] 1. adj. christlich.
2. n. Christ, der/Christin, die. **Chris-
tianity** [krɪstɪ'ænɪtɪ] n. das Christentum
'**Christian name** n. Vorname, der
**Christmas** ['krɪsməs] n. Weihnachten,
das od. Pl.; **merry** or **happy** ~: frohe
od. fröhliche Weihnachten; **at** ~: [zu]
Weihnachten

**Christmas:** ~ **'Day** *n*. erster Weihnachtsfeiertag; ~ **'Eve** *n*. Heiligabend, *der;* ~ **tree** *n*. Weihnachtsbaum, *der*

**chrome** [krəʊm], **chromium** ['krəʊmɪəm] *ns.* Chrom, *das.* '**chromiumplated** *adj*. verchromt

**chronic** ['krɒnɪk] *adj*. chronisch

**chronicle** ['krɒnɪkl] *n*. Chronik, *die*

**chronological** [krɒnə'lɒdʒɪkl] *adj*. chronologisch

**chrysalis** ['krɪsəlɪs] *n., pl.* ~es Puppe, *die*

**chrysanthemum** [krɪ'sænθɪməm] *n*. Chrysantheme, *die*

**chubby** ['tʃʌbɪ] *adj*. pummelig

**chuck** [tʃʌk] *v. t.* (coll.) schmeißen (ugs.). **chuck 'away, chuck 'out** *v. t.* (coll.) wegschmeißen (ugs.)

**chuckle** ['tʃʌkl] **1.** *v. i.* leise [vor sich hin] lachen (**at** über + *Akk.*). **2.** *n*. leises, glucksendes Lachen

**chug** [tʃʌg] *v. i.,* -gg- tuckern

**chum** [tʃʌm] *n*. (coll.) Kumpel, *der* (salopp)

**chunk** [tʃʌŋk] *n*. dickes Stück. '**chunky** *adj*. **a)** (small and sturdy) stämmig; **b)** dick ⟨Pullover⟩

**church** [tʃɜːtʃ] *n*. Kirche, *die;* **go to** ~: in die Kirche gehen; **the C~ of England** die Kirche von England. '**churchyard** *n*. Friedhof, *der* (bei einer Kirche)

**churlish** ['tʃɜːlɪʃ] *adj*. (ill-bred) ungehobelt; (surly) griesgrämig

**churn** [tʃɜːn] *n*. (Brit.) Butterfaß, *das.* **churn 'out** *v. t.* massenweise produzieren (ugs.)

**chute** [ʃuːt] *n*. Schütte, *die; (for persons)* Rutsche, *die*

**CIA** *abbr.* (Amer.) **Central Intelligence Agency** CIA, *der od. die*

**CID** *abbr.* (Brit.) **Criminal Investigation Department** C.I.D.; **the** ~: die Kripo

**cider** ['saɪdə(r)] *n*. ≈ Apfelwein, *der*

**cigar** [sɪ'gɑː(r)] *n*. Zigarre, *die*

**cigarette** [sɪgə'ret] *n*. Zigarette, *die*

**cigarette:** ~-**end** *n*. Zigarettenstummel, *der;* ~-**lighter** *n*. Feuerzeug, *das;* ~-**packet** *n*. Zigarettenschachtel, *die*

**cinders** ['sɪndəz] *n. pl.* Asche, *die*

**cine** ['sɪnɪ]: ~ **camera** *n*. Filmkamera, *die;* ~ **film** *n*. Schmalfilm, *der*

**cinema** ['sɪnɪmə] *n*. Kino, *das;* **go to the** ~: ins Kino gehen

**cinnamon** ['sɪnəmən] *n*. Zimt, *der*

**cipher** ['saɪfə(r)] *n*. Geheimschrift, *die;* **in** ~: chiffriert

**circle** ['sɜːkl] **1.** *n*. Kreis, *der.* **2.** *v. i.* kreisen. **3.** *v. t.* umkreisen

**circuit** ['sɜːkɪt] *n*. **a)** (Electr.) Schaltung, *die;* **b)** (Motor-racing) Rundkurs, *der*

**circular** ['sɜːkjʊlə(r)] **1.** *adj*. (round) kreisförmig. **2.** *n*. Rundschreiben, *das*

**circulate** ['sɜːkjʊleɪt] **1.** *v. i.* zirkulieren; ⟨Personen, Wein usw.:⟩ herumgehen (ugs.). **2.** *v. t.* in Umlauf setzen; herumgehen lassen ⟨Buch, Bericht⟩ (**around** in + *Dat.*). **circulation** [sɜːkjʊ'leɪʃn] *n*. **a)** (Physiol.) Kreislauf, *der;* **poor** ~: Kreislaufstörungen *Pl.;* **b)** (copies sold) verkaufte Auflage

**circumcise** ['sɜːkəmsaɪz] *v. t.* beschneiden

**circumference** [sə'kʌmfərəns] *n*. Umfang, *der*

**circumstances** ['sɜːkəmstənsɪz] *n. pl.* Umstände; **in** *or* **under the** ~: unter diesen·Umständen; **under no** ~: unter keinen Umständen

**circus** ['sɜːkəs] *n*. Zirkus, *der*

**CIS** *abbr.* **Commonwealth of Independent States** GUS

**cissy** ['sɪsɪ] *see* sissy

**cistern** ['sɪstən] *n*. Wasserkasten, *der; (in roof)* Wasserbehälter, *der*

**citation** [saɪ'teɪʃn] *n*. Zitat, *das*

**cite** [saɪt] *v. t.* (quote) zitieren; anführen ⟨Beispiel⟩

**citizen** ['sɪtɪzən] *n*. **a)** (of town, city) Bürger, *der*/Bürgerin, *die;* **b)** (of state) [Staats]bürger, *der*/-bürgerin, *die.* '**citizenship** *n*. Staatsbürgerschaft, *die*

**citrus** ['sɪtrəs] *n*. ~ [**fruit**] Zitrusfrucht, *die*

**city** ['sɪtɪ] *n*. [Groß]stadt, *die.* **city 'centre** *n*. Stadtzentrum, *das*

**civic** ['sɪvɪk] *adj*. [staats]bürgerlich; ~ **centre** Verwaltungszentrum der Stadt

**civil** ['sɪvl] *adj*. **a)** (not military) zivil; **b)** (polite, obliging) höflich; **c)** (Law) Zivil-. **civil engi'neer** *n*. Bauingenieur, *der*/-ingenieurin, *die.* **civil engi-'neering** *n*. Hoch- und Tiefbau, *der*

**civilian** [sɪ'vɪljən] **1.** *n*. Zivilist, *der.* **2.** *adj*. Zivil-

**civility** [sɪ'vɪlɪtɪ] *n*. Höflichkeit, *die*

**civilization** [sɪvɪlaɪ'zeɪʃn] *n*. Zivilisation, *die*

**civilized** ['sɪvɪlaɪzd] *adj*. zivilisiert

**civil:** ~ '**law** *n*. Zivilrecht, *das;* ~ '**rights** *n. pl.* Bürgerrechte; ~ '**servant** *n*. ≈ Staatsbeamte, *der*/-beamtin, *die;* **C~ 'Service** *n*. öffentlicher Dienst; ~ '**war** *n*. Bürgerkrieg, *der*

**clad** [klæd] *adj. (arch./literary)* gekleidet (**in** in + *Akk.*)
**claim** [kleɪm] **1.** *v. t.* **a)** beanspruchen
⟨*Thron, Gebiete*⟩; fordern ⟨*Lohnerhöhung, Schadenersatz*⟩; beantragen
⟨*Sozialhilfe usw.*⟩; **b)** *(assert)* behaupten. **2.** *v. i. (Insurance)* Ansprüche geltend machen. **3.** *n.* Anspruch, *der* (**to**
auf + *Akk.*); **lay ~ to** sth. auf etw.
*(Akk.)* Anspruch erheben. **claimant**
['kleɪmənt] *n.* Antragsteller, *der/*-stel-
lerin, *die*
**clairvoyant** [kleə'vɔɪənt] **1.** *n.* Hellse-
her, *der/*Hellseherin, *die*. **2.** *adj.* hell-
seherisch
**clam** [klæm] **1.** *n.* Klaffmuschel, *die*.
**2.** *v. i.*, **-mm-:** **~ up** *(coll.)* den Mund
nicht [mehr] aufmachen
**clamber** ['klæmbə(r)] *v. i.* klettern
**clammy** ['klæmɪ] *adj.* feucht; kalt und
schweißig ⟨*Haut*⟩; klamm ⟨*Kleidung*⟩
**clamour** *(Brit.; Amer.:* **clamor**⟩ ['klæ-
mə(r)] **1.** *n. (noise, shouting)* Lärm,
*der;* lautes Geschrei. **2.** *v. i.* **~ for** sth.
nach etw. schreien
**clamp** [klæmp] **1.** *n.* Klammer, *die;*
*(Woodw.)* Schraubzwinge, *die*. **2.**
*v. t.* klemmen; einspannen ⟨*Werk-
stück*⟩. **3.** *v. i. (fig.)* **~ down on** sb./sth.
gegen jmdn./etw. rigoros vorgehen
**clan** [klæn] *n.* Sippe, *die;* ⟨*of Scottish
Highlanders)* Clan, *der*
**clandestine** [klæn'destɪn] *adj.* heimlich
**clang** [klæŋ] **1.** *n. (of bell)* Läuten, *das;*
*(of hammer)* Klingen, *das*. **2.** *v. i.*
⟨*Glocke:*⟩ läuten; ⟨*Hammer:*⟩ klingen
**clap** [klæp] **1.** *n.* **a)** Klatschen, *das;* **b)**
**~ of thunder** Donnerschlag, *der*. **2.**
*v. i.*, **-pp-** klatschen. **3.** *v. t.*, **-pp-: ~
one's hands** in die Hände klatschen; **~**
sth. etw. beklatschen; **~ sb.** jmdm.
Beifall klatschen. **'clapping** *n.* Applaus, *der*
**claret** ['klærət] **1.** *n.* roter Bordeaux-
wein. **2.** *adj.* weinrot
**clarification** [klærɪfɪ'keɪʃn] *n.* Klar-
stellung, *die*
**clarify** ['klærɪfaɪ] *v. t.* klären ⟨*Situation
usw.*⟩; *(by explanation)* klarstellen; erläutern ⟨*Bedeutung, Aussage*⟩
**clarinet** [klærɪ'net] *n.* Klarinette, *die*
**clarity** ['klærɪtɪ] *n.* Klarheit, *die*
**clash** [klæʃ] **1.** *v. i.* **a)** scheppern
*(ugs.);* **b)** *(meet in conflict)* zusammenstoßen; **c)** *(disagree)* sich streiten; **d)**
⟨*Interesse, Ereignis:*⟩ kollidieren,
⟨*Farbe:*⟩ sich beißen *(ugs.)* (**with** mit).
**2.** *v. t.* gegeneinanderschlagen. **3.** *n.* **a)**

*(of cymbals)* Dröhnen, *das;* **b)** *(meeting in conflict)* Zusammenstoß, *der;* **c)**
*(disagreement)* Auseinandersetzung,
*die;* **d)** *(of personalities, colours)* Un-
verträglichkeit, *die; (of events)* Überschneiden, *das*
**clasp** [klɑːsp] **1.** *n.* Verschluß, *der*. **2.**
*v. t.* umklammern
**class** [klɑːs] **1.** *n.* Klasse, *die; (in society)* Gesellschaftsschicht, *die; (Sch.:
lesson)* Stunde, *die*. **2.** *v. t.* einstufen
(**as** als). **'class-conscious** *adj.* klas-
senbewußt
**classic** ['klæsɪk] **1.** *adj.* klassisch. **2.** *n.*
Klassiker, *der;* **~s** Altphilologie, *die*
**classical** ['klæsɪkl] *adj.* klassisch
**classification** [klæsɪfɪ'keɪʃn] *n.* Klas-
sifikation, *die*
**classified** ['klæsɪfaɪd] *adj.* **a)** *(secret)*
geheim; **b)** **~ advertisement** Kleinanzeige, *die*
**classify** ['klæsɪfaɪ] *v. t.* klassifizieren
**class: ~-mate** *n.* Klassenkamerad,
*der/*-kameradin, *die;* **~-room** *n.*
Klassenzimmer, *das*
**'classy** *adj. (coll.)* klasse
**clatter** ['klætə(r)] **1.** *n.* Klappern, *das*.
**2.** *v. i.* **a)** klappern; **b)** *(move or fall
with a ~)* poltern
**clause** [klɔːz] *n.* **a)** Klausel, *die;* **b)**
*(Ling.)* Teilsatz, *der;* **subordinate** ~:
Nebensatz, *der*
**claustrophobia** [klɒstrə'fəʊbɪə] *n.*
Klaustrophobie, *die*. **claustro-
phobic** [klɒstrə'fəʊbɪk] *adj.* beeng-
end ⟨*Ort*⟩
**claw** [klɔː] **1.** *n.* Kralle, *die; (of crab
etc.)* Schere, *die*. **2.** *v. t.* kratzen
**clay** [kleɪ] *n.* Lehm, *der; (for pottery)*
Ton, *der*
**clean** [kliːn] **1.** *adj.* sauber; frisch ⟨*Wäsche, Hemd*⟩. **2.** *adv.* glatt. **3.** *v. t.* saubermachen; putzen ⟨*Zimmer, Schuh*⟩;
reinigen ⟨*Teppich, Kleidung, Wunde*⟩;
**~ one's teeth** sich *(Dat.)* die Zähne
putzen. **4.** *n.* **give** sth. **a ~:** etw. putzen.
**clean 'out** *v. t.* **a)** saubermachen; **b)**
*(sl.)* **~ sb. out** *(take all sb.'s money)*
jmdn. [total] schröpfen *(ugs.)*. **clean
'up 1.** *v. t.* **a)** aufräumen; **b)** *(fig.)* säubern. **2.** *v. i.* aufräumen
**'cleaner** *n.* **a)** Raumpfleger, *der/*-pfle-
gerin, *die; (woman also)* Putzfrau, *die;*
**b)** *usu. in pl. (dry-~)* Reinigung, *die;*
**take** sth. **to the ~'s** etw. in die Reinigung bringen
**cleanliness** ['klenlɪnɪs] *n.* Reinlichkeit, *die*
**cleanly** ['kliːnlɪ] *adv.* sauber

**cleanse** [klenz] *v. t.* [gründlich] reinigen. '**cleanser** *n.* Reinigungsmittel, *das*

'**clean-shaven** *adj.* glattrasiert

**clear** [klɪə(r)] **1.** *adj.* **a)** klar; scharf ⟨*Bild*⟩; **make oneself ~:** sich deutlich [genug] ausdrücken; **make it ~** [**to sb.**] **that ...:** [jmdm.] klar und deutlich sagen, daß ...; **b)** *(complete)* **three ~ days** volle drei Tage; **c)** *(unobstructed)* frei; **keep sth. ~** *(not block)* etw. frei halten. **2.** *adv.* **keep ~ of sth./sb.** etw./jmdn. meiden; **please stand** *or* **keep ~ of the door** bitte von der Tür zurücktreten. **3.** *v. t.* **a)** räumen ⟨*Straße*⟩; abräumen ⟨*Schreibtisch*⟩; freimachen ⟨*Abfluß, Kanal*⟩; **~ a space for sb./sth.** für jmdn./etw. Platz machen; **b)** *(empty)* räumen ⟨*Briefkasten*⟩; **c)** *(remove)* wegräumen; beheben ⟨*Verstopfung*⟩; **d)** *(show to be innocent)* freisprechen; **e)** *(get permission for)* ~ **sth. with sb.** etw. von jmdm. genehmigen lassen. **4.** *v. i.* **a)** ⟨*Wetter, Himmel:*⟩ sich aufheitern; **b)** *(disperse)* sich verziehen. **5.** *n.* **we're in the ~** *(free of suspicion)* auf uns fällt kein Verdacht; *(free of trouble)* wir haben es geschafft. **clear 'off** *v. i.* abhauen *(salopp)*. **clear 'out 1.** *v. t.* ausräumen. **2.** *v. i.* *(coll.)* verschwinden. **clear 'up 1.** *v. t.* **a)** wegräumen ⟨*Abfall*⟩; aufräumen ⟨*Platz, Sachen*⟩; **b)** *(explain)* klären. **2.** *v. i.* **a)** aufräumen; **b)** ⟨*Wetter:*⟩ sich aufhellen

**clearance** [klɪərəns] *n.* **a)** *(of obstruction)* Beseitigung, *die;* **b)** *(clear space)* Spielraum, *der*

'**clear cut** *adj.* klar umrissen; klar ⟨*Abgrenzung, Ergebnis*⟩

'**clearing** *n.* Lichtung, *die*

'**clearly** *adv.* **a)** *(distinctly)* klar; deutlich ⟨*sprechen*⟩; **b)** *(manifestly, unambiguously)* eindeutig; klar ⟨*denken*⟩

'**clearway** *n.* *(Brit.)* Straße mit Halteverbot

**cleaver** [kli:və(r)] *n.* Hackbeil, *das*

**clef** [klef] *n.* Notenschlüssel, *der*

**cleft** [kleft] *n.* Spalte, *die*

**clench** [klentʃ] *v. t.* zusammenpressen; **~ one's fist** *or* **fingers** die Faust ballen; **~ one's teeth** die Zähne zusammenbeißen

**clergy** [klɜ:dʒɪ] *n. pl.* Geistlichkeit, *die;* Klerus, *der.* **clergyman** [klɜ:dʒɪmən] *n., pl.* ~**men** [klɜ:dʒɪmən] Geistliche, *der*

**clerical** [klerɪkl] *adj.* Büro⟨*arbeit, -personal*⟩; ~ **error** Schreibfehler, *der*

**clerk** [klɑ:k] *n.* *(in bank)* Bankangestellte, *der/die;* *(in office)* Büroangestellte, *der/die*

**clever** [klevə(r)] *adj.* **a)** klug; **b)** *(skilful)* geschickt; **c)** *(ingenious)* geistreich ⟨*Idee, Argument*⟩; **d)** *(smart, cunning)* clever. '**cleverly** *adv.* **a)** klug; **b)** *(skilfully)* geschickt

**cliché** [kli:ʃeɪ] *n.* Klischee, *das*

**click** [klɪk] **1.** *n.* Klicken, *das.* **2.** *v. i.* klicken

**client** [klaɪənt] *n.* **a)** Klient, *der/* Klientin, *die;* **b)** *(customer)* Kunde, *der/* Kundin, *die*

**clientele** [kli:ɒntel] *n.* *(of shop)* Kundschaft, *die*

**cliff** [klɪf] *n.* Kliff, *das.* '**cliff-hanger** *n.* Thriller, *der*

**climate** [klaɪmət] *n.* Klima, *das*

**climax** [klaɪmæks] *n.* Höhepunkt, *der*

**climb** [klaɪm] **1.** *v. t.* hinaufsteigen; klettern auf ⟨*Baum*⟩; ⟨*Auto:*⟩ hinaufkommen ⟨*Hügel*⟩. **2.** *v. i.* **a)** klettern (**up auf** + *Akk.*); **b)** ⟨*Flugzeug, Sonne:*⟩ aufsteigen. **3.** *n.* Aufstieg, *der.* **climb 'down** *v. i.* **a)** hinunterklettern; **b)** *(fig.)* nachgeben

'**climb-down** *n.* Rückzieher, *der (ugs.)*

**climber** [klaɪmə(r)] *n.* Bergsteiger, *der*

**clinch** [klɪntʃ] **1.** *v. t.* zum Abschluß bringen; perfekt machen *(ugs.)* ⟨*Geschäft*⟩. **2.** *n.* *(Boxing)* Clinch, *der*

**cling** [klɪŋ] *v. i.,* **clung** [klʌŋ] sich klammern (**to an** + *Akk.*). '**cling film** *n.* Klarsichtfolie, *die*

**clinic** [klɪnɪk] *n.* Klinik, *die.* **clinical** [klɪnɪkl] *adj.* **a)** *(Med.)* klinisch; **b)** *(dispassionate)* nüchtern

**clink** [klɪŋk] **1.** *n.* *(of glasses)* Klirren, *das;* *(of coins)* Klimpern, *das.* **2.** *v. i.* ⟨*Flaschen:*⟩ klirren; ⟨*Münzen:*⟩ klimpern. **3.** *v. t.* klirren mit ⟨*Glas*⟩; klimpern mit ⟨*Kleingeld*⟩

'**clip** [klɪp] **1.** *n.* Klammer, *die;* *(for paper)* Büroklammer, *die.* **2.** *v. t.,* -**pp**- klammern (**[on] to an** + *Akk.*)

²**clip** *v. t.,* -**pp**- *(cut)* schneiden ⟨*Fingernägel, Haar, Hecke*⟩; stutzen ⟨*Flügel*⟩

**clique** [kli:k] *n.* Clique, *die*

**cloak** [kləʊk] **1.** *n.* Umhang, *der.* **2.** *v. t.* [ein]hüllen. '**cloakroom** *n.* Garderobe, *die;* *(Brit. euphem.: lavatory)* Toilette, *die*

**clock** [klɒk] **1.** *n.* **a)** Uhr, *die;* [**work**] **against the ~:** gegen die Zeit [arbeiten]; **round the ~:** rund um die Uhr; **b)** *(coll.)* *(speedometer)* Tacho, *der (ugs.);* *(milometer)* ≈ Kilometerzähler, *der.* **2.** *v. t.* ~ [**up**] zu verzeichnen haben

⟨*Erfolg*⟩; erreichen ⟨*Geschwindigkeit*⟩.
**clock** 'in, **clock** 'on *v. i.* [bei Arbeitsantritt] stechen. **clock** 'off, **clock** 'out *v. i.* [bei Arbeitsschluß] stechen
'**clockwise** *adv., adj.* im Uhrzeigersinn
'**clockwork** *n.* Uhrwerk, *das;* **a ~ car.** ein Aufziehauto; **as regular as ~** *(fig.)* absolut regelmäßig
**clog** [klɒg] **1.** *n.* Clog, *der; (traditional)* Holzschuh, *der.* **2.** *v. t.,* **-gg-:** ~ |up| verstopfen
**cloister** ['klɔɪstə(r)] *n.* Kreuzgang, *der*
**clone** [kləʊn] **1.** *n.* Klon, *der.* **2.** *v. t.* klonen
**close 1.** [kləʊs] *adj.* **a)** *(in space)* dicht; nahe; **be ~ to** sth. nahe bei *od.* an etw. *(Dat.)* sein; **at ~ quarters** aus der Nähe betrachtet; **b)** *(in time)* nahe (**to an** + *Dat.*); **c)** eng ⟨*Freund, Zusammenarbeit*⟩; nahe ⟨*Verwandte, Bekanntschaft*⟩; **d)** eingehend ⟨*Untersuchung, Prüfung usw.*⟩; **e)** hart ⟨*Wett[kampf], Spiel*⟩; knapp ⟨*Ergebnis*⟩; **that was a ~ call** *or* **shave** *(coll.)* das war knapp! **2.** [kləʊs] *adv.* nah[e]; ~ **by** in der Nähe; ~ **to** sb./sth. nahe bei jmdm./etw. **3.** [kləʊz] *v. t.* **a)** *(shut)* schließen; zuziehen ⟨*Vorhang*⟩; schließen ⟨*Laden, Fabrik*⟩; sperren ⟨*Straße*⟩; **b)** *(conclude)* schließen ⟨*Diskussion, Versammlung*⟩. **4.** [kləʊz] *v. i.* **a)** *(shut)* sich schließen; **b)** ⟨*Laden, Fabrik:*⟩ schließen, *(ugs.)* zumachen. **5.** [kləʊz] *n.* Ende, *das;* Schluß, *der;* **come** *or* **draw to a ~:** zu Ende gehen; **bring** *or* **draw** sth. **to a ~:** etw. zu Ende bringen.
**close** [kləʊz] '**down 1.** *v. t.* schließen; stillegen ⟨*Werk*⟩. **2.** *v. i.* geschlossen werden; ⟨*Werk:*⟩ stillgelegt werden. **close** 'in *v. i.* ⟨*Nacht, Dunkelheit:*⟩ hereinbrechen; ⟨*Tage:*⟩ kürzer werden; ~ **in on** umzingeln. **close** 'off *v. t.* [ab]sperren
**closed** [kləʊzd] *adj.* geschlossen; **we're ~:** wir haben geschlossen.
'**closed-circuit** *adj.* ~ **television** interne Fernsehanlage
**close-down** ['kləʊzdaʊn] *n. (Radio, Telev.)* Sendeschluß, *der*
**closed** '**shop** *n.* Closed Shop, *der*
**closely** ['kləʊslɪ] *adv.* **a)** dicht; **b)** *(intimately)* eng; **c)** genau ⟨*befragen, prüfen*⟩; streng ⟨*bewachen*⟩
**closet** ['klɒzɪt] *n. (Amer.: cupboard)* Schrank, *der*
**close-up** ['kləʊsʌp] *n.* ~ |**picture/shot**| Nahaufnahme, *die*

**closing** ['kləʊzɪŋ]: ~ **date** *n. (for competition)* Einsendeschluß, *der; (to take part)* Meldefrist, *die;* ~-**time** *n. (of pub)* Polizeistunde, *die*
**closure** ['kləʊʒə(r)] *n.* Schließung, *die; (of road)* Sperrung, *die*
**clot** [klɒt] **1.** *n.* **a)** *(blood)* Gerinnsel, *das;* **b)** *(Brit. sl.: stupid person)* Trottel, *der.* **2.** *v. i.,* **-tt-** ⟨*Blut:*⟩ gerinnen
**cloth** [klɒθ] *n., pl.* ~**s** [klɒθs] **a)** Stoff, *der;* Tuch, *das;* **b)** *(dish-~)* Spültuch, *das; (table-~)* [Tisch]decke, *die*
**clothe** [kləʊð] *v. t.* kleiden
**clothes** [kləʊðz] *n. pl.* Kleider *Pl.;* **put one's ~ on** sich anziehen; **take one's ~ off** sich ausziehen
'**clothes:** ~-**brush** *n.* Kleiderbürste, *die;* ~-**line** *n.* Wäscheleine, *die;* ~-**peg** *(Brit.),* ~-**pin** *(Amer.)* ns. Wäscheklammer, *die*
**clothing** ['kləʊðɪŋ] *n.* Kleidung, *die*
**clotted cream** [klɒtɪd 'kri:m] *n.* sehr fetter Rahm
**cloud** [klaʊd] *n.* **a)** Wolke, *die;* **every ~ has a silver lining** *(prov.)* es hat alles sein Gutes; **b)** ~ **of dust/smoke** Staub-/Rauchwolke, *die.* **cloud** 'over *v. i.* sich bewölken
'**cloudburst** *n.* Wolkenbruch, *der*
'**cloudless** *adj.* wolkenlos
'**cloudy** *adj.* bewölkt ⟨*Himmel*⟩; trübe ⟨*Wetter, Flüssigkeit, Glas*⟩
**clout** [klaʊt] *(coll.)* **1.** *n.* Schlag, *der.* **2.** *v. t.* hauen *(ugs.)*
¹**clove** [kləʊv] *n.* ~ |**of garlic**| [Knoblauch]zehe, *die*
²**clove** *n. (spice)* [Gewürz]nelke, *die*
**clover** ['kləʊvə(r)] *n.* Klee, *der.*
'**cloverleaf** *n.* Kleeblatt, *das*
**clown** [klaʊn] **1.** *n.* Clown, *der.* **2.** *v. i.* ~ |**about** *or* **around**| den Clown spielen
**cloying** ['klɔɪɪŋ] *adj.* süßlich
**club** [klʌb] **1.** *n.* **a)** *(weapon)* Keule, *die; (golf-~)* Schläger, *der;* **b)** *(association)* Klub, *der;* Verein, *der; (Cards)* Kreuz, *das;* ~**s are trumps** Kreuz ist Trumpf; **the ace/seven of** ~**s** das Kreuzas/die Kreuzsieben. **2.** *v. t.,* **-bb-** *(beat)* prügeln; *(with ~)* knüppeln. **3.** *v. i.,* **-bb-:** ~ **together** *(to buy something)* zusammenlegen
**cluck** [klʌk] **1.** *n.* Gackern, *das.* **2.** *v. i.* gackern
**clue** [klu:] *n.* Anhaltspunkt, *der; (in criminal investigation)* Spur, *die;* **not have a ~:** keine Ahnung haben. '**clueless** *adj. (coll.)* unbedarft *(ugs.)*
**clump** [klʌmp] *n.* Gruppe, *die; (of grass)* Büschel, *das*

**clumsy** ['klʌmzɪ] *adj.* schwerfällig, unbeholfen ‹*Person, Bewegung*›; plump ‹*Form, Figur, Nachahmung*›

**clung** *see* **cling**

**cluster** ['klʌstə(r)] **1.** *n. (of grapes, berries)* Traube, *die; (of fruit, flowers)* Büschel, *das; (of stars, huts)* Haufen, *der.* **2.** *v. i.* ~ **[a]round sb./sth.** sich um jmdn./etw. scharen *od.* drängen

**clutch** [klʌtʃ] **1.** *v. t.* umklammern. **2.** *v. i.* ~ **at sth.** nach etw. greifen; *(fig.)* sich an etw. *(Akk.)* klammern. **3.** *n.* **a)** *in pl. (fig.: control)* Klauen; **b)** *(Motor Veh.)* Kupplung, *die*

**clutter** ['klʌtə(r)] **1.** *n.* Durcheinander, *das.* **2.** *v. t.* ~ **[up] the table/room** überall auf dem Tisch/im Zimmer herumliegen

**cm.** *abbr.* **centimetre[s]** cm.

**Co.** *abbr.* **a) company** Co.; **b) county**

**c/o** *abbr.* **care of** bei; c/o

**coach** [kəʊtʃ] **1.** *n.* **a)** *(horse-drawn)* Kutsche, *die;* **b)** *(Railw.)* Wagen, *der;* **c)** *(bus)* [Reise]bus, *der;* **by** ~ : mit dem Bus; **d)** *(Sport)* Trainer, *der*/Trainerin, *die.* **2.** *v. t.* trainieren. '**coach station** *n.* Busbahnhof, *der.* '**coach tour** *n.* Rundreise [im Omnibus]

**coagulate** [kəʊˈægjʊleɪt] **1.** *v. t.* gerinnen lassen. **2.** *v. i.* gerinnen

**coal** [kəʊl] *n.* Kohle, *die.* '**coalfield** *n.* Kohlenrevier, *das*

**coalition** [kəʊəˈlɪʃn] *n. (Polit.)* Koalition, *die*

**coal:** ~-**mine** *n.* [Kohlen]bergwerk, *das;* ~-**miner** *n.* [im Kohlenbergbau tätiger] Grubenarbeiter; ~-**mining** *n.* Kohlenbergbau, *der*

**coarse** [kɔːs] *adj.* **a)** *(in texture)* grob; **b)** *(unrefined, obscene)* derb

**coast** [kəʊst] **1.** *n.* Küste, *die.* **2.** *v. i.* im Freilauf fahren. **coastal** ['kəʊstl] *adj.* Küsten-. '**coaster** *n.* **a)** *(mat)* Untersetzer, *der;* **b)** *(ship)* Küstenmotorschiff, *das*

**coast:** ~**guard** *n.* Küstenwache, -wacht, *die;* ~**line** *n.* Küste, *die*

**coat** [kəʊt] **1.** *n.* **a)** Mantel, *der;* **b)** *(layer)* Schicht, *die; (of paint)* Anstrich, *der;* **c)** *(animal's hair, fur, etc.)* Fell, *das.* **2.** *v. t.* überziehen; *(with paint)* streichen

'**coat-hanger** *n.* Kleiderbügel, *der*

'**coating** *n.* Schicht, *die*

**coat of 'arms** *n.* Wappen, *das*

**coax** [kəʊks] *v. t.* überreden

**cobble** ['kɒbl] *n.* Pflasterstein, *der*

**cobbler** ['kɒblə(r)] *n.* Schuster, *der*

'**cobble-stone** *see* **cobble**

**cobra** ['kɒbrə] *n.* Kobra, *die*

**cobweb** ['kɒbweb] *n.* Spinnengewebe, *das;* Spinnennetz, *das*

**cocaine** [kəˈkeɪn] *n.* Kokain, *das*

**cock** [kɒk] **1.** *n.* Hahn, *der.* **2.** *v. t.* spitzen ‹*Ohren*›; ~ **a/the gun** den Hahn spannen. **cock-a-hoop** [kɒkəˈhuːp] *adj.* überschwenglich

**cockatoo** [kɒkəˈtuː] *n.* Kakadu, *der*

**cockerel** ['kɒkərəl] *n.* junger Hahn

**cock-eyed** ['kɒkaɪd] *adj.* **a)** *(crooked)* schief; **b)** *(absurd)* verrückt

**cockle** ['kɒkl] *n.* Herzmuschel, *die*

**cockney** ['kɒknɪ] **1.** *adj.* Cockney-. **2.** *n.* Cockney, *der*

'**cockpit** *n.* Cockpit, *das*

**cockroach** ['kɒkrəʊtʃ] *n.* [Küchen-, Haus-]schabe, *die*

**cocktail** ['kɒkteɪl] *n.* Cocktail, *der.* '**cocktail cabinet** *n.* Hausbar, *die.* '**cocktail party** *n.* Cocktailparty, *die*

**cocoa** ['kəʊkəʊ] *n.* Kakao, *der*

**coconut** ['kəʊkənʌt] *n.* Kokosnuß, *die*

**cocoon** [kəˈkuːn] *(Zool.)* Kokon, *der*

**cod** [kɒd] *n., pl. same* Kabeljau, *der*

**COD** *abbr.* **cash on delivery,** *(Amer.)* **collect on delivery** p. Nachn.

**code** [kəʊd] **1.** *n.* **a)** *(statutes etc.)* Gesetzbuch, *das;* ~**s of behaviour** Verhaltensnormen; **b)** *(system of signals)* Code, *der;* **be in** ~ : verschlüsselt sein. **2.** *v. t.* chiffrieren; verschlüsseln. '**code-name** *n.* Deckname, *der.* '**code-word** *n.* Kennwort, *das*

**cod-liver 'oil** *n.* Lebertran, *der*

**co-driver** ['kəʊdraɪvə(r)] *n.* Beifahrer, *der*/-fahrerin, *die*

**coed** ['kəʊed] *(esp. Amer. coll.)* **1.** *n.* Studentin, *die.* **2.** *adj.* ~ **school** gemischte Schule

**coeducational** [kəʊedjʊˈkeɪʃənl] *adj.* koedukativ; Koedukations-

**coerce** [kəʊˈɜːs] *v. t.* zwingen; ~ **sb. into sth.** jmdn. zu etw. zwingen. **coercion** [kəʊˈɜːʃn] *n.* Zwang, *der*

**coexist** [kəʊɪgˈzɪst] *v. i.* koexistieren. **coexistence** [kəʊɪgˈzɪstəns] *n.* Koexistenz, *die*

**C. of E.** [siːəʊˈviː] *abbr.* **Church of England**

**coffee** ['kɒfɪ] *n.* Kaffee, *der;* **three black/white** ~**s** drei [Tassen] Kaffee ohne/mit Milch

**coffee:** ~ **bar** *n.* Café, *das;* ~-**bean** *n.* Kaffeebohne, *die;* ~-**break** *n.* Kaffeepause, *die;* ~-**cup** *n.* Kaffeetasse, *die;* ~-**pot** *n.* Kaffeekanne, *die;* ~ **shop** *n.* Kaffeestube, *die;* ~-**table** *n.* Couchtisch, *der*

**coffin** ['kɒfɪn] *n.* Sarg, *der*

**cog** [kɒg] *n. (Mech.)* Zahn, *der*

**cogent** ['kəʊdʒənt] *adj.* überzeugend ⟨*Argument*⟩; zwingend ⟨*Grund*⟩

**cognac** ['kɒnjæk] *n.* Cognac, *der* ⓦ

**cog:** ~-**railway** *n.* Zahnradbahn, *die;* ~-**wheel** *n.* Zahnrad, *das*

**cohere** [kəʊ'hɪə(r)] *v. i.* zusammenhalten. **coherent** [kəʊ'hɪərənt] *adj.* zusammenhängend

**coil** [kɔɪl] **1.** *v. t.* aufwickeln; *(twist)* aufdrehen. **2.** *v. i.* ~ **round sth.** etw. umschlingen. **3.** *n.* **a)** ~s of rope/wire aufgerollte Seile *Pl.*/aufgerollter Draht; **b)** *(single turn)* Windung, *die;* **c)** *(Electr.)* Spule, *die*

**coin** [kɔɪn] **1.** *n.* Münze, *die.* **2.** *v. t.* prägen ⟨*Wort, Redewendung*⟩

**coincide** [kəʊɪn'saɪd] *v. i.* **a)** *(in time)* zusammenfallen; **b)** *(agree)* übereinstimmen (**with** mit). **coincidence** [kəʊ'ɪnsɪdəns] *n.* Zufall, *der.* **coincidental** [kəʊɪnsɪ'dentl] *adj.* zufällig

**coke** [kəʊk] *n.* Koks, *der*

**colander** ['kʌləndə(r)] *n.* Sieb, *das*

**cold** [kəʊld] **1.** *adj.* **a)** kalt; **I feel** ~**:** mir ist kalt; **b)** *(fig.)* [betont] kühl ⟨*Person, Aufnahme, Begrüßung*⟩. **2.** *adv.* kalt. **3.** *n.* **a)** Kälte, *die;* **b)** *(illness)* Erkältung, *die;* ~ **[in the head]** Schnupfen, *der.* **cold-blooded** ['kəʊldblʌdɪd] *adj.* **a)** wechselwarm ⟨*Tier*⟩; **b)** kaltblütig ⟨*Person, Mord*⟩

'**coldly** *adv.* [betont] kühl

**coleslaw** ['kəʊlslɔ:] *n.* Krautsalat, *der*

**collaborate** [kə'læbəreɪt] *v. i.* **a)** zusammenarbeiten; ~ **[with sb.] on sth.** zusammen [mit jmdm.] an etw. *(Dat.)* arbeiten; **b)** *(with enemy)* kollaborieren. **collaboration** [kəlæbə'reɪʃn] *n.* Zusammenarbeit, *die;* (*with enemy*) Kollaboration, *die.* **collaborator** [kə'læbəreɪtə(r)] *n.* Mitarbeiter, *der*/-arbeiterin, *die;* (*with enemy*) Kollaborateur, *der*/Kollaborateurin, *die*

**collage** ['kɒlɑ:ʒ] *n.* Collage, *die*

**collapse** [kə'læps] **1.** *n.* **a)** *(of person)* Zusammenbruch, *der;* **b)** *(of structure)* Einsturz, *der;* **c)** *(of negotiations)* Scheitern, *das;* (*of company*) Zusammenbruch, *der.* **2.** *v. i.* **a)** *(Person:)* zusammenbrechen; **b)** *(Stuhl:)* zusammenbrechen; ⟨*Gebäude:*⟩ einstürzen; **c)** ⟨*Verhandlungen:*⟩ scheitern; ⟨*Unternehmen:*⟩ zusammenbrechen; **d)** *(fold down)* ⟨*Regenschirm, Fahrrad, Tisch:*⟩ sich zusammenklappen lassen. **collapsible** [kə'læpsɪbl] *adj.* Klapp- ⟨*stuhl, -tisch, -fahrrad*⟩

**collar** ['kɒlə(r)] **1.** *n.* **a)** Kragen, *der;* **b)** *(for dog)* [Hunde]halsband, *das.* **2.** *v. t.* schnappen *(ugs.).* '**collar-bone** *n.* Schlüsselbein, *das*

**colleague** ['kɒli:g] *n.* Kollege, *der*/Kollegin, *die*

**collect** [kə'lekt] **1.** *v. i.* sich versammeln; ⟨*Staub, Müll usw.:*⟩ sich ansammeln. **2.** *v. t.* sammeln; aufsammeln ⟨*Müll, leere Flaschen usw.*⟩; *(coll.: fetch)* abholen ⟨*Menschen, Dinge*⟩; ~ **one's wits/thoughts** seine Gedanken sammeln. **col'lected** *adj.* **a)** *(gathered)* gesammelt; **b)** *(calm)* gesammelt; gelassen. **collection** [kə'lekʃn] *n.* **a)** *(collecting)* Sammeln, *das;* (*coll.: of goods, persons*) Abholen, *das;* **b)** *(amount of money collected)* Sammlung, *die;* (*in church*) Kollekte, *die;* (*from post-box*) Leerung, *die;* **d)** *(of stamps etc.)* Sammlung, *die.* **collective** [kə'lektɪv] *adj.* kollektiv *nicht präd.* **collective 'bargaining** *n.* Tarifverhandlungen *Pl.*

**collector** [kə'lektə(r)] *n.* **a)** *(of stamps etc.)* Sammler, *der*/Sammlerin, *die;* **b)** *(of taxes)* Einnehmer, *der*/Einnehmerin, *die.* **col'lector's item, col'lector's piece** *ns.* Sammlerstück, *das*

**college** ['kɒlɪdʒ] *n.* **a)** *(esp. Brit. Univ.)* College, *das;* **b)** *(place of further education)* Fach[hoch]schule, *die;* **go to** ~ *(esp. Amer.)* studieren

**collide** [kə'laɪd] *v. i.* zusammenstoßen (**with** mit)

**collie** ['kɒlɪ] *n.* Collie, *der*

**colliery** ['kɒljərɪ] *n.* Kohlengrube, *die*

**collision** [kə'lɪʒn] *n.* Zusammenstoß, *der;* **on a** ~ **course** *(lit. or fig.)* auf Kollisionskurs

**colloquial** [kə'ləʊkwɪəl] *adj.* umgangssprachlich

**collusion** [kə'lu:ʒn] *n.* geheime Absprache

**Cologne** [kə'ləʊn] **1.** *pr. n.* Köln *(das).* **2.** *attrib. adj.* Kölner

**cologne** *see* **eau-de-Cologne**

**Colombia** [kə'lɒmbɪə] *pr. n.* Kolumbien *(das)*

**colon** ['kəʊlən] *n.* Doppelpunkt, *der*

**colonel** [kɜ:nl] *n.* Oberst, *der*

**colonial** [kə'ləʊnɪəl] *adj.* Kolonial-; kolonial

**colonize** ['kɒlənaɪz] *v. t.* kolonisieren

**colony** ['kɒlənɪ] *n.* Kolonie, *die*

**color** *etc. (Amer.) see* **colour** *etc.*

**colossal** [kə'lɒsl] *adj.* ungeheuer; gewaltig ⟨*Bauwerk*⟩

**colour** ['kʌlə(r)] *(Brit.)* **1.** *n.* Farbe,

*die;* **what ~ is it?** welche Farbe hat es?; **change ~:** die Farbe ändern; **he is off ~:** ihm ist nicht gut. **2.** *v. t.* **a)** *(give ~ to)* Farbe geben (+ *Dat.*); **b)** *(paint)* malen; **c)** *(stain, dye)* färben. **3.** *v. i.* **~ |up|** erröten. '**colour-blind** *adj.* farbenblind

**coloured** ['kʌləd] *(Brit.)* **1.** *adj.* **a)** farbig; **b)** *(of non-white descent)* farbig; **~ people** Farbige *Pl.* **2.** *n.* Farbige, *der/die*

'**colour film** *n.* Farbfilm, *der*

**colourful** ['kʌləfl] *adj. (Brit.)* bunt; anschaulich 〈*Sprache, Stil, Bericht*〉

'**colouring** *(Brit.)* **a)** *(colours)* Farben *Pl.;* **b)** **~ |matter|** *(in food etc.)* Farbstoff, *der*

'**colourless** *adj. (Brit.)* farblos

**colour: ~ photograph** *n.* Farbaufnahme, *die;* **~ scheme** *n.* Farb[en]zusammenstellung, *die;* **~ supplement** *n.* Farbbeilage, *die;* **~ television** *n.* Farbfernsehen, *das; (set)* Farbfernsehgerät, *das;* **~ transparency** *n.* Farbdia, *das*

**colt** [kəʊlt] *n.* [Hengst]fohlen, *das*

**column** ['kɒləm] *n.* **a)** Säule, *die;* **b)** *(of page)* Spalte, *die;* **sports ~:** Sportteil, *der.* **columnist** ['kɒləmɪst] *n.* Kolumnist, *der/*Kolumnistin, *die*

**coma** ['kəʊmə] *n.* Koma, *das;* **in a ~:** im Koma

**comb** [kəʊm] **1.** *n.* Kamm, *der.* **2.** *v. t.* **a)** kämmen; **~ sb.'s/one's hair** jmdm./sich die Haare kämmen; **b)** *(search)* durchkämmen

**combat** ['kɒmbæt] **1.** *n.* Kampf, *der.* **2.** *v. t.* bekämpfen. **combatant** ['kɒmbətənt] *n.* Kombattant, *der*

**combination** [kɒmbɪ'neɪʃn] *n.* Kombination, *die.* **combi'nation lock** *n.* Kombinationsschloß, *das*

**combine 1.** [kəm'baɪn] *v. t.* zusammenfügen (**into** zu); verbinden 〈*Substanzen*〉. **2.** *v. i. (join together)* 〈*Stoffe:*〉 sich verbinden. **3.** ['kɒmbaɪn] *n.* **~ |harvester|** Mähdrescher, *der*

**combustion** [kəm'bʌstʃn] *n.* Verbrennung, *die*

**come** [kʌm] *v. i.,* **came** [keɪm], **come** [kʌm] kommen; **~ here!** komm [mal] her!; **|I'm| coming!** [ich] komme schon!; **the train came into the station** der Zug fuhr in den Bahnhof ein; **Christmas is coming** bald ist Weihnachten; **the handle has ~ loose** der Griff ist lose; **nothing came of it** es ist nichts daraus geworden. **come a'bout** *v. i.* passieren. **come across**

**1.** [--'-] *v. i. (be understood)* verstanden werden. **2.** ['---] *v. t.* begegnen (+ *Dat.*). **come a'long** *v. i. (coll.)* **a)** *(hurry up)* **~ along!** komm/kommt!; **b)** *(make progress)* **~ along nicely** gute Fortschritte machen; **c)** *(to place)* mitkommen (**with** mit). **come 'back** *v. i.* zurückkommen. **come by 1.** ['--] *v. t. (obtain)* bekommen. **2.** [-'-] *v. i.* vorbeikommen. **come 'down** *v. i.* **a)** *(fall)* 〈*Schnee, Regen, Preis:*〉 fallen; **b)** *(~ lower)* herunterkommen; **c)** *(land)* [not]landen; *(crash)* abstürzen. **come 'in** *v. i. (enter)* hereinkommen; **~ in!** herein! '**come into** *v. t.* **a)** *(enter)* hereinkommen in (+ *Akk.*); **b)** *(inherit)* erben. **come off 1.** [-'-] *v. i.* **a)** 〈*Griff, Knopf:*〉 abgehen; *(be removable)* sich abnehmen lassen; **b)** *(succeed)* 〈*Pläne, Versuche:*〉 Erfolg haben; **c)** *(take place)* stattfinden. **2.** ['--] *v. t.* **~ off a horse/bike** vom Pferd/Fahrrad fallen; **~ 'off it!** *(coll.)* nun mach mal halblang! *(ugs.).* **come on 1.** [-'-] *v. i.* **a)** *(continue coming, follow)* kommen; **~ on!** komm, komm/kommt, kommt!; *(encouraging)* na, komm; **b)** *(make progress)* **~ on very well** gute Fortschritte machen. **2.** ['--] *v. t.* **see ~ upon. come 'out** *v. i.* **a)** herauskommen; **b)** *(fig.)* 〈*Sonne, Wahrheit, Buch:*〉 herauskommen; **c)** **~ out with** herausrücken mit *(ugs.).* **come 'over 1.** *v. i.* herüberkommen. **2.** *v. t. (coll.)* kommen über (+ *Akk.*). **come 'round** *v. i.* **a)** *(visit)* vorbeischauen; **b)** *(recover)* wieder zu sich kommen. **come 'through 1.** *v. i.* durchkommen. **2.** *v. t. (survive)* überleben. **come to 1.** ['--] *v. t. (amount to)* 〈*Rechnung, Kosten:*〉 sich belaufen auf (+ *Akk.*). **2.** [-'-] *v. i.* wieder zu sich kommen. '**come under** *v. t.* **a)** *(be classed as or among)* kommen unter (+ *Akk.*); **b)** *(be subject to)* kommen unter (+ *Akk.*). **come 'up** *v. i.* **a)** *(~ higher)* hochkommen; **b)** **~ up to sb.** *(approach for talk)* auf jmdn. zukommen; **c)** *(present itself)* sich ergeben; **d)** **~ up to** *(reach)* reichen bis an (+ *Akk.*); entsprechen (+ *Dat.*) 〈*Erwartungen*〉; **e)** **~ up against sth.** *(fig.)* auf etw. *(Akk.)* stoßen; **f)** **~ up with** vorbringen 〈*Vorschlag*〉; wissen 〈*Lösung, Antwort*〉. '**come upon** *v. t. (meet by chance)* begegnen (+ *Dat.*)

'**come-back** *n. (to profession etc.)* Comeback, *das*

**comedian** [kə'miːdɪən] *n.* Komiker,

*der.* **comedienne** [kəmi:dɪ'en] *n.* Komikerin, *die*

'**come-down** *n.* Abstieg, *der*

**comedy** ['kɒmɪdɪ] **a)** *n.* Lustspiel, *das;* Komödie, *die;* **b)** *(humour)* Witz, *der;* Witzigkeit, *die*

**comet** ['kɒmɪt] *n.* Komet, *der*

**comeuppance** [kʌm'ʌpəns] *n.* get one's ~: die Quittung kriegen *(fig.)*

**comfort** ['kʌmfət] **1.** *n.* **a)** *(consolation)* Trost, *der;* **b)** *(physical wellbeing)* Behaglichkeit, *die;* **c)** *in pl.* Komfort, *der.* **2.** *v.t.* trösten. **comfortable** ['kʌmfətəbl] *adj.* **a)** bequem ⟨*Bett, Schuhe*⟩; komfortabel ⟨*Haus, Zimmer*⟩; **a ~ victory** ein leichter Sieg; **b)** *(at ease)* **be/feel ~:** sich wohl fühlen. **comfortably** ['kʌmfətəblɪ] *adv.* bequem; leicht ⟨*gewinnen*⟩

'**comfort station** *n. (Amer.)* öffentliche Toilette

**comfy** ['kʌmfɪ] *adj. (coll.)* bequem; gemütlich ⟨*Haus, Zimmer*⟩

**comic** ['kɒmɪk] **1.** *adj.* komisch. **2.** *n.* **a)** *(comedian)* Komiker, *der*/Komikerin, *die;* **b)** *(periodical)* Comic-Heft, *das.* **comical** ['kɒmɪkl] *adj.* komisch

**coming** ['kʌmɪŋ] **1.** *adj.* **in the ~ week** kommende Woche. **2.** *n.* **~s and goings** das Kommen und Gehen

**comma** ['kɒmə] *n.* Komma, *das*

**command** [kə'mɑ:nd] **1.** *v.t.* **a)** *(order)* befehlen **(sb.** jmdm.**);** **b)** *(be in ~ of)* befehligen ⟨*Schiff, Armee*⟩; **c)** verfügen über (+ *Akk.*) ⟨*Gelder, Wortschatz*⟩. **2.** *n.* **a)** Kommando, *das; (in writing)* Befehl, *der;* **have/take ~ of** das Kommando über (+ *Akk.*) ... haben/übernehmen; **b)** *(mastery, possession)* Beherrschung, *die*

**commandeer** [kɒmən'dɪə(r)] *v.t.* requirieren

**com'mander** *n.* Führer, *der*

**com'manding** *adj.* **a)** gebieterisch ⟨*Erscheinung, Stimme*⟩; imposant ⟨*Gestalt*⟩; **b)** beherrschend ⟨*Ausblick, Lage*⟩. **commanding 'officer** *n.* Befehlshaber, *der*/Befehlshaberin, *die*

**com'mandment** *n.* Gebot, *das*

**commemorate** [kə'meməreɪt] *v.t.* gedenken (+ *Gen.*). **commemoration** [kəmemə'reɪʃn] *n.* Gedenken, *das;* **in ~ of** zum Gedenken an (+ *Akk.*)

**commence** [kə'mens] *v.t. & i.* beginnen. **com'mencement** *n.* Beginn, *der*

**commend** [kə'mend] *v.t. (praise)* loben. **commendable** [kə'mendəbl] *adj.* lobenswert; löblich. **commen-**

**dation** [kɒmen'deɪʃn] *n. (praise)* Lob, *das; (official)* Belobigung, *die; (award)* Auszeichnung, *die*

**comment** ['kɒment] **1.** *n.* Bemerkung, *die* **(on** über + *Akk.*); *(note)* Anmerkung, *die* **(on** über + *Akk.*); **no ~!** *(coll.)* kein Kommentar! **2.** *v.i.* **~ on sth.** über etw. *(Akk.)* Bemerkungen machen; **he ~ed that ...:** er bemerkte, daß ... **commentary** ['kɒməntərɪ] *n.* **a)** Kommentar, *der* **(on** zu); **b)** *(Radio, Telev.)* **[live** *or* **running] ~:** Live-Reportage, *die.* **commentator** ['kɒmənteɪtə(r)] *n.* Kommentator, *der*/Kommentatorin, *die; (Sport)* Reporter, *der*/Reporterin, *die*

**commerce** ['kɒmɜ:s] *n.* Handel, *der*

**commercial** [kə'mɜ:ʃl] **1.** *adj.* Handels-; kaufmännisch ⟨*Ausbildung*⟩. **2.** *n.* Werbespot, *der.* **commercialism** [kə'mɜ:ʃəlɪzm] *n.* Kommerzialismus, *der.* **commercialize** [kə'mɜ:ʃəlaɪz] *v.t.* kommerzialisieren

**commercial: ~ 'television** *n.* Werbefernsehen, *das; ~* '**vehicle** *n.* Nutzfahrzeug, *das*

**commiserate** [kə'mɪzəreɪt] *v.i.* **~ with sb.** jmdm. sein Mitgefühl aussprechen **(on** zu)

**commission** [kə'mɪʃn] **1.** *n.* **a)** *(official body)* Kommission, *die;* **b)** *(instruction, piece of work)* Auftrag, *der;* **c)** *(Mil.)* Ernennungsurkunde, *die;* **d)** *(pay of agent)* Provision, *die;* **e) in/out of ~** ⟨*Auto, Maschine*⟩ in/außer Betrieb. **2.** *v.t.* beauftragen ⟨*Künstler*⟩; **in Auftrag geben** ⟨*Gemälde usw.*⟩

**commissionaire** [kəmɪʃə'neə(r)] *n. (esp. Brit.)* Portier, *der*

**commissioner** [kə'mɪʃənə(r)] *n. (of police)* Präsident, *der*

**commit** [kə'mɪt] *v.t.,* **-tt-: a)** begehen ⟨*Verbrechen, Fehler, Ehebruch*⟩; **b)** *(pledge, bind)* **~ oneself/sb. to doing sth.** sich/jmdn. verpflichten, etw. zu tun; **c)** *(entrust)* anvertrauen **(to** *Dat.*); **d) ~ sb. for trial** jmdm. dem Gericht überstellen. **com'mitment** *n.* Verpflichtung **(to** gegenüber). **com'mitted** *adj.* engagiert

**committee** [kə'mɪtɪ] *n.* Ausschuß, *der*

**commodity** [kə'mɒdɪtɪ] *n.* **a)** **household ~:** Haushaltsartikel, *der;* **b)** *(St. Exch.)* [vertretbare] Ware; *(raw material)* Rohstoff, *der*

**common** ['kɒmən] **1.** *adj.* **a)** *(belonging to all)* gemeinsam; **b)** *(public)* öffentlich; **c)** *(usual)* gewöhnlich; *(frequent)* häufig; allgemein verbreitet

⟨*Sitte, Redensart*⟩; **d)** *(vulgar)* ordinär.
**2.** *n.* **a)** *(land)* Gemeindeland, *das;* **b)**
**have sth./nothing/a lot in ~** |**with sb.**|
etw./nichts/viel [mit jmdm.] ge-
mein[sam] haben. **'commoner** *n.*
Bürgerliche *der/die*
**'common-law** *adj.* **she's his ~ wife** sie
lebt mit ihm in eheähnlicher Gemeinschaft
**'commonly** *adv.* im allgemeinen
**common: C~ 'Market** *n.* gemeinsa-
mer Markt; **~place 1.** *n.* Gemeinplatz, *der;* **2.** *adj.* alltäglich
**Commons** ['kɒmənz] *n. pl.* **the** |**House
of**| **~:** das Unterhaus
**common: ~ 'sense** *n.* gesunder
Menschenverstand; **~wealth** *n.* **the**
|**British**| **C~wealth** das Common-
wealth
**commotion** [kə'məʊʃn] *n.* Tumult,
*der*
**communal** ['kɒmjʊnl] *adj.* **a)** *(of or for
the community)* gemeindlich; **b)** *(for
common use)* gemeinsam
**commune** ['kɒmju:n] *n.* Kommune,
*die*
**communicate** [kə'mju:nɪkeɪt] **1.** *v.t.*
übertragen ⟨*Krankheit*⟩; übermitteln
⟨*Informationen*⟩; vermitteln ⟨*Gefühle,
Ideen*⟩. **2.** *v.i.* **~ with sb.** mit jmdm.
kommunizieren. **communication**
[kəmju:nɪ'keɪʃn] *n.* **a)** *(of information)*
Übermittlung, *die;* **b)** *(message)* Mitteilung, *die* (**to an** + *Akk.*). **communi'cation-cord** *n.* Notbremse.
*die.* **communi'cations satellite** *n.*
Nachrichtensatellit, *der*
**communicative** [kə'mju:nɪkətɪv] *adj.*
gesprächig
**Communion** [kə'mju:nɪən] *n.* |**Holy**| **~**
*(Protestant Ch.)* das [heilige] Abend-
mahl; *(RC Ch.)* die [heilige] Kommunion
**communiqué** [kə'mju:nɪkeɪ] *n.* Kom-
muniqué, *das*
**communism** ['kɒmjʊnɪzm] *n.* Kommunismus, *der;* **C~:** der Kommunismus. **Communist, communist**
['kɒmjʊnɪst] **1.** *n.* Kommunist,
*der/*Kommunistin, *die.* **2.** *adj.* kommunistisch
**community** [kə'mju:nɪtɪ] *n.* **a)** *(organized body)* Gemeinwesen, *das;* **the
Jewish ~:** die jüdische Gemeinde; **b)**
*no pl. (public)* Öffentlichkeit, *die.*
**com'munity centre** *n.* Gemeinde-
zentrum, *das*
**commute** [kə'mju:t] **1.** *v.t.* umwan-
deln ⟨*Strafe*⟩ (**to in** + *Akk.*). **2.** *v.i.*

pendeln. **com'muter** *n.* Pendler,
*der/*Pendlerin, *die*
**¹compact** [kəm'pækt] *adj.* kompakt
**²compact** ['kɒmpækt] *n.* Puderdose
[mit Puder(stein)]
**compact 'disc** *n.* Compact Disc, *die*
**companion** [kəm'pænjən] *n.* Begleiter, *der/*Begleiterin, *die.* **com'pan-
ionship** *n.* Gesellschaft, *die*
**company** ['kʌmpənɪ] *n.* **a)** *(persons as-
sembled, companionship)* Gesell-
schaft, *die;* **expect ~:** Besuch *od.* Gäste erwarten; **keep sb. ~:** jmdm. Gesellschaft leisten; **b)** *(firm)* Gesellschaft, *die;* **~ car** Firmenwagen, *der;*
**c)** *(of actors)* Truppe, *die;* Ensemble,
*das;* **d)** *(Mil.)* Kompanie, *die*
**comparable** ['kɒmpərəbl] *adj.* ver-
gleichbar (**to, with** mit)
**comparative** [kəm'pærətɪv] **1.** *adj.* **a)**
*(relative)* relativ; **in ~ comfort** relativ
komfortabel; **b)** *(Ling.)* komparativ
*(fachspr.);* **a ~ adjective/adverb** ein
Adjektiv/Adverb im Komparativ. **2.**
*n. (Ling.)* Komparativ, *der.* **com-
'paratively** *adv.* verhältnismäßig
**compare** [kəm'peə(r)] **1.** *v.t.* vergleichen (**to, with** mit); **~d with** *or* **to sb./
sth.** verglichen mit *od.* im Vergleich
zu jmdm./etw. **2.** *v.i.* sich vergleichen
lassen. **comparison** [kəm'pærɪsn] *n.*
Vergleich, *der;* **in** *or* **by ~** |**with sb./
sth.**| im Vergleich [zu jmdm./etw.]
**compartment** [kəm'pɑ:tmənt] *n. (in
drawer, desk, etc.)* Fach, *das; (of railway carriage)* Abteil, *das*
**compass** ['kʌmpəs] *n.* **a)** *in pl.* |**a pair
of**| **~es** ein Zirkel; **b)** *(for navigating)*
Kompaß, *der*
**compassion** [kəm'pæʃn] *n.* Mitgefühl, *das* (**for** mit). **compassionate**
[kəm'pæʃənət] *adj.* mitfühlend; **on ~
grounds** aus persönlichen Gründen;
*(for family reasons)* aus familiären
Gründen
**compatible** [kəm'pætɪbl] *adj.* vereinbar; zueinander passend ⟨*Personen*⟩;
*(Computing)* kompatibel
**compel** [kəm'pel] *v.t.,* **-ll-** zwingen
**compendium** [kəm'pendɪəm] *n.*
Kompendium, *das*
**compensate** ['kɒmpenseɪt] **1.** *v.i.* **~
for sth.** etw. ersetzen. **2.** *v.t.* **~ sb. for
sth.** jmdn. für etw. entschädigen.
**compensation** [kɒmpen'seɪʃn] *n.*
Ersatz, *der; (for damages, injuries,
etc.)* Schaden[s]ersatz, *der*
**compère** ['kɒmpeə(r)] *n. (Brit.)* Con-
férencier, *der*

**compete** [kəm'pi:t] *v. i.* konkurrieren (for um); *(Sport)* kämpfen

**competence** ['kɒmpɪtəns] *n.* Fähigkeiten *Pl.*

**competent** ['kɒmpɪtənt] *adj.* fähig; **not ~ to do sth.** nicht kompetent, etw. zu tun. '**competently** *adv.* kompetent

**competition** [kɒmpɪ'tɪʃn] *n.* **a)** *(contest)* Wettbewerb, *der; (in magazine etc.)* Preisausschreiben, *das;* **b)** *(those competing)* Konkurrenz, *die*

**competitive** [kəm'petɪtɪv] *adj.* wettbewerbsfähig ⟨*Preis, Unternehmen*⟩; **~ sports** Leistungssport, *der*

**competitor** [kəm'petɪtə(r)] *n.* Konkurrent, *der/*Konkurrentin, *die; (in contest, race)* Teilnehmer, *der/*-nehmerin, *die*

**compile** [kəm'paɪl] *v. t.* zusammenstellen

**complacency** [kəm'pleɪsənsɪ] *n.* Selbstzufriedenheit, *die*

**complacent** [kəm'pleɪsənt] *adj.* selbstzufrieden

**complain** [kəm'pleɪn] *v. i.* sich beklagen (**about, at** über + *Akk.*); **~ of sth.** über etw. *(Akk.)* klagen. **complaint** [kəm'pleɪnt] *n.* **a)** Beschwerde, *die;* **b)** *(ailment)* Leiden, *das*

**complement** 1. ['kɒmplɪmənt] *n.* **a)** *(what completes)* Vervollständigung, *die;* **b)** *(full number)* **a |full| ~** : die volle Zahl; *(of people)* die volle Stärke. 2. ['kɒmplɪment] *v. t.* ergänzen. **complementary** [kɒmplɪ'mentərɪ] *adj.* **a)** *(completing)* ergänzend; **b)** *(completing each other)* einander ergänzend

**complete** [kəm'pli:t] 1. *adj.* **a)** vollständig; *(in number)* vollzählig; **b)** *(finished)* fertig; **c)** *(absolute)* völlig ⟨*Idiot*⟩; absolut ⟨*Katastrophe*⟩; total, *(ugs.)* blutig ⟨*Anfänger*⟩. 2. *v. t.* **a)** *(finish)* beenden; fertigstellen ⟨*Gebäude, Arbeit*⟩; **b)** ausfüllen ⟨*Formular*⟩. **com'pletely** *adv.* völlig; absolut ⟨*erfolgreich*⟩. **completion** [kəm'pli:ʃn] *n.* Beendigung, *die; (of building, work)* Fertigstellung, *die*

**complex** ['kɒmpleks] 1. *adj.* kompliziert. 2. *n.* Komplex, *der*

**complexion** [kəm'plekʃn] *n.* Gesichtsfarbe, *die; (fig.)* Gesicht, *das*

**complexity** [kəm'pleksɪtɪ] *n.* Kompliziertheit, *die*

**complicate** ['kɒmplɪkeɪt] *v. t.* komplizieren. '**complicated** *adj.* kompliziert. **complication** [kɒmplɪ'keɪʃn] *n.* Komplikation, *die*

**complicity** [kəm'plɪsɪtɪ] *n.* Mittäterschaft, *die* (**in** bei)

**compliment** 1. ['kɒmplɪmənt] *n.* Kompliment, *das; in pl. (formal greetings)* Grüße *Pl.;* **pay sb. a ~** : jmdm. ein Kompliment machen. 2. ['kɒmplɪment] *v. t.* **~ sb. on sth.** jmdm. Komplimente wegen etw. machen. **complimentary** [kɒmplɪ'mentərɪ] *adj.* **a)** schmeichelhaft; **b)** *(free)* Frei-

**comply** [kəm'plaɪ] *v. i.* **~ with sth.** nach etw. richten; **he refused to ~** : er wollte sich nicht danach richten

**component** [kəm'pəʊnənt] 1. *n.* Bestandteil, *der.* 2. *adj.* **a ~ part** ein Bestandteil

**compose** [kəm'pəʊz] *v. t.* **a)** bilden; **be ~d of** sich zusammensetzen aus; **b)** verfassen ⟨*Rede, Gedicht*⟩; abfassen ⟨*Brief*⟩; **c)** *(Mus.)* komponieren. **com'poser** *n.* Komponist, *der/*Komponistin, *die.* **composition** [kɒmpə'zɪʃn] *n.* **a)** *(constitution) (of soil etc.)* Zusammensetzung, *die; (of picture)* Aufbau, *der;* **b)** *(essay)* Aufsatz, *der; (Mus.)* Komposition, *die*

**compost** ['kɒmpɒst] *n.* Kompost, *der.* '**compost heap** *n.* Komposthaufen, *der*

**composure** [kəm'pəʊʒə(r)] *n.* Gleichmut, *der*

**¹compound** 1. ['kɒmpaʊnd] *adj.* **a)** zusammengesetzt; **b)** *(Med.)* **~ fracture** komplizierter Bruch. 2. ['kɒmpaʊnd] *n.* **a)** *(mixture)* Mischung, *die;* **b)** *(Ling.)* Kompositum, *das;* **c)** *(Chem.)* Verbindung, *die.* 3. ['kəm'paʊnd] *v. t.* verschlimmern ⟨*Schwierigkeiten, Verletzung usw.*⟩

**²compound** ['kɒmpaʊnd] *n.* umzäuntes Gelände

**compound 'interest** *n.* Zinseszinsen *Pl.*

**comprehend** [kɒmprɪ'hend] *v. t.* verstehen. **comprehensible** [kɒmprɪ'hensɪbl] *adj.* verständlich. **comprehension** [kɒmprɪ'henʃn] *n.* Verständnis, *das*

**comprehensive** [kɒmprɪ'hensɪv] 1. *adj.* **a)** umfassend; **b)** **~ school** Gesamtschule, *die;* **c)** *(insurance)* Vollkasko-. 2. *n.* Gesamtschule, *die*

**compress** 1. [kəm'pres] *v. t.* **a)** *(squeeze)* zusammenpressen (**into** zu); **b)** komprimieren ⟨*Luft, Gas, Bericht*⟩. 2. ['kɒmpres] *n.* Kompresse, *die.* **compression** [kəm'preʃn] *n.* Kompression, *die.* **compressor** [kəm'presə(r)] *n.* Kompressor, *der*

**comprise** [kəm'praɪz] *v. t. (include)* umfassen; *(consist of)* bestehen aus
**compromise** ['kɒmprəmaɪz] **1.** *n.* Kompromiß, *der.* **2.** *v. i.* Kompromisse/einen Kompromiß schließen. **3.** *v. t.* kompromittieren
**compulsion** [kəm'pʌlʃn] *n.* Zwang, *der;* be under no ~ to do sth. keineswegs etw. tun müssen. **compulsive** [kəm'pʌlsɪv] *adj.* **a)** zwanghaft; **he is a ~ gambler** er ist dem Spiel verfallen; **b) this book is ~ reading** von diesem Buch kann man sich nicht losreißen. **compulsory** [kəm'pʌlsərɪ] *adj.* obligatorisch
**compunction** [kəm'pʌŋkʃn] *n.* Schuldgefühle
**computer** [kəm'pju:tə(r)] *n.* Computer, *der*
**computer: ~-aided, ~-assisted** *adjs.* computergestützt; **~ program** *n.* Programm, *das;* **~ programmer** *n.* Programmierer, *der/* Programmiererin, *die;* **~ programming** *n.* Programmieren, *das;* **~ terminal** *n.* Terminal, *das*
**computing** [kəm'pju:tɪŋ] *n.* EDV, *die;* elektronische Datenverarbeitung
**comrade** ['kɒmreɪd, 'kɒmrɪd] *n.* Kamerad, *der/* Kameradin, *die.* '**comradeship** *n.* Kameradschaft, *die*
**con** [kɒn] *(coll.)* **1.** *n.* Schwindel, *der.* **2.** *v. t.,* -nn- reinlegen *(ugs.);* **~ sb. into sth.** jmdm. etw. aufschwatzen *(ugs.)*
**concave** ['kɒnkeɪv] *adj.* konkav
**conceal** [kən'si:l] *v. t.* verbergen *(from* vor + *Dat.).* **con'cealment** *n.* Verbergen, *das*
**concede** [kən'si:d] *v. t.* zugeben
**conceit** [kən'si:t] *n.* Einbildung, *die.* **con'ceited** *adj.* eingebildet
**conceivable** [kən'si:vəbl] *adj.* vorstellbar; **it is scarcely ~ that ...:** man kann sich *(Dat.)* kaum vorstellen, daß ... **conceivably** [kən'si:vəblɪ] *adj.* möglicherweise; **he cannot ~ have done it** er kann es unmöglich getan haben
**conceive** [kən'si:v] **1.** *v. t.* **a)** empfangen ⟨*Kind*⟩; **b)** *(form in mind)* sich *(Dat.)* vorstellen; haben ⟨*Idee, Plan*⟩. **2.** *v. i.* **a)** *(become pregnant)* empfangen; **b) ~ of sth.** sich *(Dat.)* etw. vorstellen
**concentrate** ['kɒnsəntreɪt] **1.** *v. t.* konzentrieren. **2.** *v. i.* sich konzentrieren *(on auf + Akk.).* '**concentrated** *adj.* konzentriert. **concentration** [kɒnsən'treɪʃn] *n.* Konzentration, *die*

**concentric** [kən'sentrɪk] *adj.* konzentrisch
**concept** ['kɒnsept] *n.* Begriff, *der;* *(idea)* Vorstellung, *die.* **conception** [kən'sepʃn] **a)** Vorstellung, *die (of* von); **b)** *(of child)* Empfängnis, *die*
**concern** [kən'sɜ:n] **1.** *v. t.* **a)** *(affect)* betreffen; **so far as ... is ~ed** was ... betrifft; **'to whom it may ~'** ≈ „Bestätigung"; *(on certificate, testimonial)* ≈ „Zeugnis"; **b)** *(interest)* **~ oneself with** *or* **about sth.** sich mit etw. befassen; **c)** *(trouble)* beunruhigen. **2.** *n.* **a)** *(anxiety)* Besorgnis, *die; (interest)* Interesse, *das;* **b)** *(matter)* Angelegenheit, *die;* **d)** *(firm)* Unternehmen, *das.* **con'cerned** [kən'sɜ:nd] *adj.* **a)** *(involved)* betroffen; *(interested)* interessiert; **as** *or* **so far as I'm ~:** was mich betrifft; **b)** *(troubled)* besorgt. **con'cerning** *prep.* bezüglich
**concert** ['kɒnsət] *n.* Konzert, *das*
**concerted** [kən'sɜ:tɪd] *adj.* vereint
**concert: ~-goer** *n.* Konzertbesucher, *der/* -besucherin, *die;* **~-hall** *n.* Konzertsaal, *der*
**concertina** [kɒnsə'ti:nə] *n.* Konzertina, *die*
**concerto** [kən'tʃeətəʊ] *n.* Konzert, *das*
**concession** [kən'seʃn] *n.* Konzession, *die.* **concessionary** [kən'seʃənərɪ] *adj.* Konzessions-; **~ rate/fare** ermäßigter Tarif
**conciliatory** [kən'sɪljətərɪ] *adj.* versöhnlich
**concise** [kən'saɪs] *adj.* kurz und prägnant; knapp, konzis ⟨*Stil*⟩
**conclude** [kən'klu:d] **1.** *v. t.* **a)** *(end)* beschließen; **b)** *(infer)* schließen **(from** aus); **c)** *(reach decision)* beschließen. **2.** *v. i. (end)* schließen. **concluding** [kən'klu:dɪŋ] *adj.* abschließend. **conclusion** [kən'klu:ʒn] *n.* **a)** *(end)* Abschluß, *der;* **in ~:** zum Abschluß; **b)** *(result)* Ausgang, *der;* **c)** *(inference)* Schluß, *der;* **draw** *or* **reach a ~:** zu einem Schluß kommen. **conclusive** [kən'klu:sɪv] *adj.,* **con'clusively** *adv.* schlüssig
**concoct** [kən'kɒkt] *v. t.* zubereiten; zusammenbrauen ⟨*Trank*⟩. **concoction** [kən'kɒkʃn] *n.* Gebräu, *das*
**concourse** ['kɒnkɔ:s] *n.* Halle, *die;* **station ~:** Bahnhofshalle, *die*
**concrete** ['kɒnkri:t] **1.** *adj.* konkret. **2.** *n.* Beton, *der; attrib.* Beton-; **aus Beton** *präd.* '**concrete-mixer** *n.* Betonmischer, *der*

**concur** [kən'kɜː(r)] *v. i.*, **-rr-:** ~ |with sb.| |in sth.| [jmdm.] [in etw. *(Dat.)*] zustimmen. **concurrent** [kən'kʌrənt] *adj.*, **con'currently** *adv.* gleichzeitig

**concussion** [kən'kʌʃn] *n.* Gehirnerschütterung, *die*

**condemn** [kən'dem] *v. t.* a) *(censure)* verdammen; b) *(Law: sentence)* verurteilen (to zu); c) für unbewohnbar erklären ⟨*Gebäude*⟩. **condemnation** [kɒndem'neɪʃn] *n.* Verdammung, *die*

**condensation** [kɒnden'seɪʃn] *n.* a) *(condensing)* Kondensation, *die;* b) *(water)* Kondenswasser, *das*

**condense** [kən'dens] **1.** *v. t.* a) komprimieren; **~d milk** Kondensmilch, *die;* b) *(Phys., Chem.)* kondensieren. **2.** *v. i.* kondensieren

**condescend** [kɒndɪ'send] *v. i.* ~ **to do sth.** sich dazu herablassen, etw. zu tun. **conde'scending** *adj.* herablassend

**condition** [kən'dɪʃn] *n.* a) *(stipulation)* [Vor]bedingung, *die;* on |the| ~ that ...: unter der Voraussetzung, daß ...; b) *in pl. (circumstances)* Umstände *Pl.;* **weather/living ~s** Witterungs-/Wohnverhältnisse; **working ~s** Arbeitsbedingungen; c) *(of athlete etc.)* Form, *die; (of thing)* Zustand, *der; (of patient)* Verfassung, *die;* d) *Med.)* Leiden, *das.* **conditional** [kən'dɪʃənl] *adj.* a) bedingt; **be ~ |up|on sth.** von etw. abhängen; b) *(Ling.)* Konditional-

**con'ditioner** *n.* Frisiermittel, *das*

**condolence** [kən'dəʊləns] *n.* Anteilnahme, *die;* **letter of ~:** Beileidsbrief, *der*

**condom** ['kɒndɒm] *n.* Kondom, *das od. der*

**condominium** ['kɒndə'mɪnɪəm] *n. (Amer.)* Appartementhaus [mit Eigentumswohnungen]

**condone** [kən'dəʊn] *v. t.* hinwegsehen über (+ *Akk.*); *(approve)* billigen

**conducive** [kən'djuːsɪv] *adj.* **be ~ to sth.** einer Sache *(Dat.)* förderlich sein

**conduct 1.** ['kɒndʌkt] *n.* a) *(behaviour)* Verhalten, *das;* b) *(way of ~ing)* Führung, *die.* **2.** [kən'dʌkt] *v. t.* a) führen; b) *(Mus.)* dirigieren; c) *(Phys.)* leiten; d) **~ed tour** Führung, *die.* **conduction** [kən'dʌkʃn] *n. (Phys.)* Leitung, *die.* **conductor** [kən'dʌktə(r)] *n.* a) *(Mus.)* Dirigent, *der/*Dirigentin, *die;* b) *(of bus, tram)* Schaffner, *der.* **conductress** [kən'dʌktrɪs] *n.* Schaffnerin, *die*

**cone** [kəʊn] *n.* a) Kegel, *der; (traffic ~)* Leitkegel, *der;* b) *(Bot.)* Zapfen, *der;* c) **ice-cream ~:** Eistüte, *die*

**confectioner** [kən'fekʃənə(r)] *n.* **~'s** |shop| Süßwarengeschäft, *das.* **con'fectionery** *n.* Süßwaren *Pl.*

**confederation** [kən'fedə'reɪʃn] *n.* [Staaten]bund, *der*

**confer** [kən'fɜː(r)] **1.** *v. t.*, **-rr-:** ~ **sth.** |up|on sb. jmdm. etw. verleihen. **2.** *v. i.*, **-rr-:** ~ **with sb.** sich mit jmdm. beraten

**conference** ['kɒnfərəns] *n.* a) Konferenz, *die;* b) **be in ~:** in einer Besprechung sein. '**conference-room** *n.* Konferenzraum, *der*

**confess** [kən'fes] **1.** *v. t.* a) gestehen; b) *(Eccl.)* beichten. **2.** *v. i.* a) ~ **to sth.** etw. gestehen; b) *(Eccl.)* beichten (to sb. jmdm.). **confession** [kən'feʃn] *n.* a) Geständnis, *das;* b) *(Eccl.: of sins etc.)* Beichte, *die*

**confetti** [kən'fetɪ] *n.* Konfetti, *das*

**confide** [kən'faɪd] **1.** *v. i.* ~ **in sb.** sich jmdm. anvertrauen. **2.** *v. t.* ~ **sth. to sb.** jmdm. etw. anvertrauen

**confidence** ['kɒnfɪdəns] *n.* a) *(firm trust)* Vertrauen, *das;* **have ~ in sb./sth.** Vertrauen zu jmdm./etw. haben; **have |absolute| ~ that ...:** |absolut| sicher sein, daß ...; b) *(assured expectation)* Gewißheit, *die;* c) *(self-reliance)* Selbstvertrauen, *das;* d) **in ~:** im Vertrauen; **this is in |strict| ~:** das ist [streng] vertraulich. '**confidence trick** *n. (Brit.)* Trickbetrug, *der*

**confident** ['kɒnfɪdənt] *adj.* a) zuversichtlich (**about** in bezug auf + *Akk.*); **be ~ that ...:** sicher sein, daß ... ; b) *(self-assured)* selbstbewußt

**confidential** [kɒnfɪ'denʃl] *adj.* vertraulich. **confidentiality** [kɒnfɪdenʃɪ'ælɪtɪ] *n.* Vertraulichkeit, *die.* **confi'dentially** *adv.* vertraulich

'**confidently** *adv.* zuversichtlich

**confine** [kən'faɪn] *v. t.* a) einsperren; **be ~d to bed/the house** ans Bett/Haus gefesselt sein; b) *(fig.)* ~ **oneself to doing sth.** sich darauf beschränken, etw. zu tun. **con'fined** *adj.* begrenzt. **con'finement** *n. (imprisonment)* Einsperrung, *die.* **confines** ['kɒnfaɪnz] *n. pl.* Grenzen

**confirm** [kən'fɜːm] *v. t.* bestätigen. **confirmation** [kɒnfə'meɪʃn] *n.* a) Bestätigung, *die;* b) *(Protestant Ch.)* Konfirmation, *die; (RC Ch.)* Firmung, *die.* **con'firmed** *adj.* eingefleischt ⟨*Junggeselle*⟩; überzeugt ⟨*Vegetarier*⟩

**confiscate** ['kɒnfɪskeɪt] *v. t.* beschlag-

nahmen. **confiscation** [kɒnfɪs'keɪʃn]
*n.* Beschlagnahme, *die*
**conflict 1.** ['kɒnflɪkt] *n.* **a)** *(fight)*
Kampf, *der;* **b)** *(clashing)* Konflikt,
*der.* **2.** [kən'flɪkt] *v. i. (be incompatible)*
sich *(Dat.)* widersprechen; ~ **with sth.**
einer Sache *(Dat.)* widersprechen.
**con'flicting** *adj.* widersprüchlich
**conform** [kən'fɔːm] *v. i.* **a)** entsprechen (**to** *Dat.*); **b)** *(comply)* sich einfügen; ~ **to** *or* **with sth./with sb.** sich
nach etw./jmdm. richten. **conform-**
**ist** [kən'fɔːmɪst] *n.* Konformist,
*der/*Konformistin, *die.* **conformity**
[kən'fɔːmɪtɪ] *n.* Übereinstimmung, *die*
(**with, to** mit)
**confound** [kən'faʊnd] *v. t.* **a)** *(defeat)*
vereiteln; **b)** *(confuse)* verwirren.
**con'founded** *adj. (coll. derog.)* verdammt
**confront** [kən'frʌnt] *v. t.* **a)** gegenüberstellen; ~ **sb. with sth./sb.** jmdn.
mit etw./[mit] jmdm. konfrontieren;
**b)** *(stand facing)* gegenüberstehen
(+ *Dat.*). **confrontation** [kɒnfrən-
'teɪʃn] *n.* Konfrontation, *die*
**confuse** [kən'fjuːz] *v. t.* **a)** *(disorder)*
durcheinanderbringen; **b)** *(mix up*
*mentally)* verwechseln; **c)** *(perplex)*
verwirren. **con'fused** *adj.* konfus;
wirr ⟨*Gedanken, Gerüchte*⟩; verworren
⟨*Lage, Situation*⟩. **confusing** [kən-
'fjuːzɪŋ] *adj.* verwirrend. **confusion**
[kən'fjuːʒn] *n.* **a)** Verwirrung, *die;*
*(mixing up)* Verwechslung, *die;* **b)**
*(embarrassment)* Verlegenheit, *die*
**congeal** [kən'dʒiːl] *v. i.* gerinnen
**conger** ['kɒŋgə(r)] *n.* ~ [eel] Seeaal, *der*
**congested** [kən'dʒestɪd] *adj.* verstopft ⟨*Straße, Nase*⟩. **congestion**
[kən'dʒestʃn] *n. (of traffic)* Stauung,
*die;* **nasal** ~: verstopfte Nase
**conglomerate** [kən'lɒmərət] *n. (Com-*
*merc.)* Großkonzern, *der.* **con-**
**glomeration** [kənglɒmə'reɪʃn] *n.*
Anhäufung, *die*
**congratulate** [kən'grætjʊleɪt] *v. t.*
gratulieren (+ *Dat.*); ~ **sb./oneself on**
**sth.** jmdm./sich zu etw. gratulieren.
**congratulations** [kəngrætjʊ'leɪʃnz]
**1.** *int.* ~! herzlichen Glückwunsch!
(**on** zu). **2.** *n. pl.* Glückwünsche *Pl.*
**congregate** ['kɒŋgrɪgeɪt] *v. i.* sich versammeln. **congregation** [kɒŋgrɪ-
'geɪʃn] *n. (Eccl.)* Gemeinde, *die*
**congress** ['kɒŋgres] *n.* Kongreß, *der;*
C~ *(Amer.)* der Kongreß. **congres-**
**sional** [kən'greʃənl] *adj.* Kongreß-
**conical** ['kɒnɪkl] *adj.* kegelförmig

**conifer** ['kɒnɪfə(r)] *n.* Nadelbaum, *der*
**conjecture** [kən'dʒektʃə(r)] **1.** *n.* Vermutung, *die.* **2.** *v. t.* vermuten. **3.** *v. i.*
Vermutungen anstellen
**conjugate** ['kɒndʒʊgeɪt] *v. t. (Ling.)*
konjugieren. **conjugation** [kɒndʒʊ-
'geɪʃn] *n. (Ling.)* Konjugation, *die*
**conjunction** [kən'dʒʌŋkʃn] *n.* **a)** Verbindung, *die;* **in** ~ **with** in Verbindung
mit; **b)** *(Ling.)* Konjunktion, *die*
**conjure** ['kʌndʒə(r)] *v. i.* zaubern; **con-**
**juring trick** Zaubertrick, *der.* **con-**
**jure 'up** *v. t.* heraufbeschwören
**conjurer, conjuror** ['kʌndʒərə(r)] *n.*
Zauberkünstler, *der/*-künstlerin, *die*
**connect** [kə'nekt] **1.** *v. t.* verbinden
(**to, with** mit). **2.** *v. i.* ~ **with sth.** mit
etw. zusammenhängen. **con'nected**
*adj.* zusammenhängend. **connec-**
**tion,** *(Brit.)* **connexion** [kə'nekʃn]
*n.* **a)** *(act, state)* Verbindung, *die;* **b)**
*(fig.: of ideas)* Zusammenhang, *der;* **in**
~ **with** im Zusammenhang mit; **c)**
*(train, bus, etc.)* Anschluß, *der*
**connoisseur** [kɒnə'sɜː(r)] *n.* Kenner,
*der*
**connotation** [kɒnə'teɪʃn] *n.* Assoziation, *die*
**conquer** ['kɒŋkə(r)] *v. t.* besiegen; erobern ⟨*Land*⟩. **conqueror** ['kɒŋkə-
rə(r)] *n. (of a country)* Eroberer, *der*
**conquest** ['kɒŋkwest] *n.* Eroberung,
*die*
**conscience** ['kɒnʃəns] *n.* Gewissen,
*das;* **have a clear/guilty** ~: ein gutes/
schlechtes Gewissen haben
**conscientious** [kɒnʃɪ'enʃəs] *adj.*
pflichtbewußt; *(meticulous)* gewissenhaft; ~ **objector** Wehrdienstverweige-
rer [aus Gewissensgründen]. **consci-**
**'entiously** *adv.* pflichtbewußt; *(me-*
*ticulously)* gewissenhaft
**conscious** ['kɒnʃəs] *adj.* **a)** **he is not** ~
**of it** es ist ihm nicht bewußt; **b)** *pred.*
*(awake)* bei Bewußtsein *präd.;* **c)**
*(realized by doer)* bewußt ⟨*Versuch,*
*Bemühung*⟩. **consciousness** ['kɒn-
ʃəsnɪs] *n.* Bewußtsein, *das*
**conscript 1.** [kən'skrɪpt] *v. t.* einberufen. **2.** ['kɒnskrɪpt] *n.* Einberufene,
*der/die.* **conscription** [kən'skrɪpʃn]
*n.* Wehrpflicht, *die*
**consecrate** ['kɒnsɪkreɪt] *v. t.* weihen
**consecutive** [kən'sekjʊtɪv] *adj.* aufeinanderfolgend ⟨*Monate, Jahre*⟩;
fortlaufend ⟨*Zahlen*⟩. **con'secut-**
**ively** *adj.* hintereinander
**consensus** [kən'sensəs] *n.* Einigkeit,
*die*

**consent** [kən'sent] 1. v. i. zustimmen.
2. n. (agreement) Zustimmung, die (to
zu); by common or general ~: nach
allgemeiner Auffassung
**consequence** ['kɒnsɪkwəns] n. a)
(result) Folge, die; in ~: folglich; as a
~: infolgedessen; b) (importance) Bedeutung, die. **consequent** ['kɒnsɪ-
kwənt] adj. daraus folgend. 'consequently adv. infolgedessen
**conservation** [kɒnsə'veɪʃn] n. Erhaltung, die; wildlife ~: Schutz wildle-
bender Tierarten. **conservationist**
[kɒnsə'veɪʃənɪst] n. Naturschützer,
der/-schützerin, die
**conservative** [kən'sɜːvətɪv] 1. adj. a)
konservativ; b) vorsichtig (Schätzung); c) C~ (Brit. Polit.) konservativ;
the C~ Party die Konservative Partei.
2. n. C~ (Brit. Polit.) Konservative,
der/die. **con'servatively** adv. vorsichtig (geschätzt)
**conservatory** [kən'sɜːvətərɪ] n. Win-
tergarten, der
**conserve** [kən'sɜːv] v. t. erhalten;
schonen (Kräfte)
**consider** [kən'sɪdə(r)] v. t. a) (think
about) ~ sth. an etw. (Akk.) denken;
he's ~ing emigrating er denkt daran,
auszuwandern; b) (reflect on) sich
(Dat.) überlegen; c) (regard as) halten
für; all things ~ed alles in allem. **considerable** [kən'sɪdərəbl] adj., con-
'siderably adv. erheblich. **considerate** [kən'sɪdərət] adj. rücksichtsvoll; (thoughtfully kind) entgegenkommend. **consideration** [kən-
sɪdə'reɪʃn] n. a) Überlegung, die; take
sth. into ~: etw. berücksichtigen; the
matter is under ~: die Angelegenheit
wird geprüft; b) (thoughtfulness)
Rücksichtnahme, die. **con'sidering**
prep. ~ sth. wenn man etw. bedenkt;
~ [that] ...: wenn man bedenkt, daß ...
**consign** [kən'saɪn] v. t. anvertrauen
(to Dat.). **con'signment** n. (Commerc.) Sendung, die; (large) Ladung,
die
**consist** [kən'sɪst] v. i. ~ of bestehen
aus. **consistency** [kən'sɪstənsɪ] n. a)
(density) Konsistenz, die; b) (being
consistent) Konsequenz, die
**consistent** [kən'sɪstənt] adj. a) (compatible [miteinander] vereinbar; b)
(uniform) gleichbleibend (Qualität);
c) (unchanging) konsequent
**consolation** [kɒnsə'leɪʃn] n. Trost,
der. **conso'lation prize** n. Trost-
preis, der

**console** [kən'səʊl] v. t. trösten
**consolidate** [kən'sɒlɪdeɪt] v. t. festi-
gen
**consonant** ['kɒnsənənt] n. Konsonant, der
**consort** [kən'sɔːt] v. i. verkehren (with
mit)
**consortium** [kən'sɔːtɪəm] n., pl. con-
sortia [kən'sɔːtɪə] Konsortium, das
**conspicuous** [kən'spɪkjʊəs] adj. a)
(visible) unübersehbar; b) (obvious)
auffallend
**conspiracy** [kən'spɪrəsɪ] n. (con-
spiring) Verschwörung, die; (plot)
Komplott, das
**conspire** [kən'spaɪə(r)] v. i. sich verschwören
**constable** ['kʌnstəbl, 'kɒnstəbl] n.
(Brit.) Polizist, der/Polizistin, die.
**constabulary** [kən'stæbjʊlərɪ] n. Polizei, die
**constant** ['kɒnstənt] adj. a) (unceasing) ständig; b) (unchanging) gleichbleibend. 'constantly adv. a) (un-
ceasingly) ständig; b) (unchangingly)
konstant
**constellation** [kɒnstə'leɪʃn] n. Stern-
bild, das
**consternation** [kɒnstə'neɪʃn] n. Bestürzung, die
**constipated** ['kɒnstɪpeɪtɪd] adj. be ~:
an Verstopfung leiden. **constipation** [kɒnstɪ'peɪʃn] n. Verstopfung,
die
**constituency** [kən'stɪtjʊənsɪ] n.
Wahlkreis, der
**constituent** [kən'stɪtjʊənt] n. a) (part)
Bestandteil, der; b) (Polit.) Wähler,
der/Wählerin, die
**constitute** ['kɒnstɪtjuːt] v. t. a) (form,
be) sein; ~ a threat to eine Gefahr sein
für; b) (make up) bilden. **constitution** [kɒnstɪ'tjuːʃn] n. a) (of person)
Konstitution, die; b) (of state) Verfassung, die. **constitutional** [kɒnstɪ-
'tjuːʃənl] adj. (of constitution) der Verfassung nachgestellt; (in harmony with
constitution) verfassungsmäßig
**constrain** [kən'streɪn] v. t. zwingen.
**constraint** [kən'streɪnt] n. (limitation) Einschränkung, die
**constrict** [kən'strɪkt] v. t. verengen.
**constriction** [kən'strɪkʃn] n. Veren-
gung, die
**construct** [kən'strʌkt] v. t. bauen;
(fig.) erstellen (Plan). **construction**
[kən'strʌkʃn] n. a) (constructing) Bau,
der; be under ~: im Bau sein; b) (thing
constructed) Bauwerk, das. **con-**

**structive** [kən'strʌktɪv] *adj.* konstruktiv

**consul** ['kɒnsl] *n.* Konsul, *der.* **consulate** ['kɒnsjʊlət] *n.* Konsulat, *das*

**consult** [kən'sʌlt] *v.t.* konsultieren ⟨*Arzt, Fachmann*⟩; ~ **a book** in einem Buch nachsehen. **consultant** [kən'sʌltənt] *n.* Berater, *der*/Beraterin, *die;* (*Med.*) Chefarzt, *der*/-ärztin, *die.* **consultation** [kɒnsəl'teɪʃn] *n.* Beratung, *die*

**consume** [kən'sju:m] *v.t.* verbrauchen; (*eat, drink*) konsumieren. **consumer** *n.* Verbraucher, *der*/Verbraucherin, *die.* **consumer goods** *n. pl.* Konsumgüter

**consumption** [kən'sʌmpʃn] *n.* Verbrauch, *der* (of an + *Dat.*); (*eating or drinking*) Verzehr, *der* (of von)

**cont.** *abbr.* **continued** Forts.

**contact** 1. ['kɒntækt] *n.* Berührung, *die;* (*fig.*) Kontakt, *der;* **be in ~ with sth.** etw. berühren; **be in ~ with sb.** (*fig.*) mit jmdm. Kontakt haben. 2. ['kɒntækt, kən'tækt] *v.t.* sich in Verbindung setzen mit. **contact lens** *n.* Kontaktlinse, *die*

**contagious** [kən'teɪdʒəs] *adj.* ansteckend

**contain** [kən'teɪn] *v.t.* **a)** (*hold, include*) enthalten; **b)** (*prevent from spreading*) aufhalten. **container** *n.* Behälter, *der;* (*cargo ~*) Container, *der;* **cardboard/wooden ~:** Pappkarton, *der*/Holzkiste, *die*

**contaminate** [kən'tæmɪneɪt] *v.t.* verunreinigen; (*with radioactivity*) verseuchen. **contamination** [kəntæmɪ'neɪʃn] *n.* Verunreinigung, *die;* (*with radioactivity*) Verseuchung, *die*

**contemplate** ['kɒntəmpleɪt] *v.t.* **a)** betrachten; (*mentally*) nachdenken über (+ *Akk.*); **b)** (*expect*) rechnen mit; (*consider*) ~ **sth./doing sth.** an etw. (*Akk.*) denken/daran denken, etw. zu tun. **contemplation** [kɒntəm'pleɪʃn] *n.* Betrachtung, *die;* (*mental*) Nachdenken, *das* (of über + *Akk.*)

**contemporary** [kən'tempərərɪ] 1. *adj.* zeitgenössisch. 2. *n.* Zeitgenosse, *der*/-genossin, *die*

**contempt** [kən'tempt] *n.* Verachtung, *die* (of, for für). **contemptible** [kən'temptɪbl] *adj.* verachtenswert. **contemptuous** [kən'temptjʊəs] *adj.* verächtlich

**contend** [kən'tend] *v.i.* **be able/have to ~ with** fertigwerden können/müssen mit. **con'tender** *n.* Bewerber, *der*/Bewerberin, *die*

¹**content** ['kɒntent] *n.* **a)** *in pl.* Inhalt, *der;* |**table of**| ~s Inhaltsverzeichnis, *das;* **b)** (*amount contained*) Gehalt, *der* (of an + *Dat.*)

²**content** [kən'tent] 1. *pred. adj.* zufrieden. 2. *v.t.* zufriedenstellen; ~ **oneself with sth./sb.** sich mit etw./jmdm. zufriedengeben. **con'tented** *adj.,* **con'tentedly** *adv.* zufrieden

**contention** [kən'tenʃn] *n.* **a)** Streit, *der;* **b)** (*point asserted*) Behauptung, *die.* **contentious** [kən'tenʃəs] *adj.* strittig ⟨*Punkt, Thema*⟩

**con'tentment** *n.* Zufriedenheit, *die*

**contest** 1. ['kɒntest] *n.* Wettbewerb, *der.* 2. [kən'test] *v.t.* **a)** bestreiten; in Frage stellen ⟨*Behauptung*⟩; **b)** (*Brit.: compete for*) kandidieren für. **contestant** [kən'testənt] *n.* (*competitor*) Teilnehmer, *der*/Teilnehmerin, *die*

**context** ['kɒntekst] *n.* Kontext, *der;* **in/out of ~:** im/ohne Kontext; **in this ~:** in diesem Zusammenhang

**continent** ['kɒntɪnənt] *n.* Kontinent, *der;* **the C~:** das europäische Festland. **continental** [kɒntɪ'nentl] *adj.* **a)** kontinental; **b)** **C~** (*mainland European*) kontinental[europäisch]. **continental 'breakfast** *n.* kontinentales Frühstück. **continental 'quilt** *n.* (*Brit.*) [Stepp]federbett, *das*

**contingent** [kən'tɪndʒənt] *n.* Kontingent, *das*

**continual** [kən'tɪnjʊəl] *adj.,* **con'tinually** *adv.* (*frequent[ly]*) ständig; (*without stopping*) unaufhörlich

**continuation** [kəntɪnjʊ'eɪʃn] *n.* Fortsetzung, *die*

**continue** [kən'tɪnju:] 1. *v.t.* fortsetzen; ~**d on page 2** „Fortsetzung auf S. 2"; ~ **doing** *or* **to do sth.** etw. weiter tun; **it ~d to rain** es regnete weiter. 2. *v.i.* (*persist*) ⟨*Wetter, Zustand, Krise usw.:*⟩ andauern; (*persist in doing sth.*) nicht aufhören; ~ **with sth.** mit etw. fortfahren. **continuity** [kɒntɪ'nju:ɪtɪ] *n.* Kontinuität, *die.* **continuous** [kən'tɪnjʊəs] *adj.* **a)** ununterbrochen; anhaltend ⟨*Regen, Sonnenschein*⟩; ständig ⟨*Kritik, Streit*⟩; durchgezogen ⟨*Linie*⟩; **b)** (*Ling.*) ~ |**form**| Verlaufsform, *die.* **con'tinuously** *adv.* ununterbrochen; ständig ⟨*sich ändern*⟩

**contort** [kən'tɔ:t] *v.t.* verdrehen. **contortion** [kən'tɔ:ʃn] *n.* Verdrehung, *die*

**contour** ['kɒntʊə(r)] Kontur, *die;* ~ **map** Höhenlinienkarte, *die*

**contraband** ['kɒntrəbænd] n.
Schmuggelware, die
**contraception** [kɒntrə'sepʃn] n.
Empfängnisverhütung, die. **contraceptive** [kɒntrə'septɪv] 1. adj. empfängnisverhütend. 2. n. Verhütungsmittel, das
**contract** 1. ['kɒntrækt] n. Vertrag, der; ~ of employment Arbeitsvertrag, der; be under ~ to do sth. vertraglich verpflichtet sein, etw. zu tun. 2. [kən'trækt] v.t. (Med.) sich (Dat.) zuziehen. 3. v.i. a) ~ to do sth. sich vertraglich verpflichten, etw. zu tun; b) (become smaller, be drawn together) sich zusammenziehen. **contraction** [kən'trækʃn] n. Kontraktion, die. **contractor** [kən'træktə(r)] n. Auftragnehmer, der/-nehmerin, die
**contradict** [kɒntrə'dɪkt] v.t. widersprechen (+ Dat.). **contradiction** [kɒntrə'dɪkʃn] n. Widerspruch, der; in ~ to sb./sth. im Widerspruch zu jmdm./etw. **contradictory** [kɒntrə'dɪktərɪ] adj. widersprüchlich
**contralto** [kən'træltəʊ] n., pl. ~s Alt, der
**contraption** [kən'træpʃn] n. (coll.) [komisches] Gerät
**contrary** ['kɒntrərɪ] 1. adj. a) entgegengesetzt; be ~ to sth. im Gegensatz zu etw. stehen; b) [kən'treərɪ] (coll.: perverse) widerspenstig. 2. n. the ~: das Gegenteil; on the ~: im Gegenteil. 3. adv. ~ to sth. entgegen einer Sache
**contrast** 1. [kən'trɑːst] v.t. gegenüberstellen. 2. ['kɒntrɑːst] n. Kontrast, der (with zu); in ~, ...: im Gegensatz dazu, ...; [be] in ~ with sth. im Gegensatz zu etw. [stehen]. **con'trasting** adj. gegensätzlich
**contravene** [kɒntrə'viːn] v.t. verstoßen gegen. **contravention** [kɒntrə'venʃn] n. Verstoß, der (of gegen)
**contribute** [kən'trɪbjuːt] 1. v.t. ~ sth. [to or towards sth.] etw. [zu etw.] beitragen. 2. v.i. ~ to charity für karitative Zwecke spenden; ~ to the success of sth. zum Erfolg einer Sache (Gen.) beitragen. **contribution** [kɒntrɪ'bjuːʃn] n. Beitrag, der; (for charity) Spende, die (to für); make a ~: einen Beitrag leisten; (to charity) etwas spenden. **contributor** [kən'trɪbjʊtə(r)] n. (to encyclopaedia etc.) Mitarbeiter, der/Mitarbeiterin, die
**contrite** ['kɒntraɪt] adj. zerknirscht
**contrive** [kən'traɪv] v.t. ~ to do sth. es fertigbringen, etw. zu tun

**control** [kən'trəʊl] 1. n. a) Kontrolle, die (of über + Akk.); keep ~ of sth. etw. unter Kontrolle halten; be in ~ [of sth.] die Kontrolle [über etw. (Akk.)] haben; [go or get] out of ~: außer Kontrolle [geraten]; [get sth.] under ~: [etw.] unter Kontrolle [bringen]; b) (device) Regler, der; ~s Schalttafel, die. 2. v.t., -ll- kontrollieren; lenken (Auto); zügeln (Zorn); regeln (Verkehr). **con'trol centre** n. Kontrollzentrum, das. **con'trol desk** n. Schaltpult, das
**con'troller** n. (director) Leiter, der/Leiterin, die
**control: ~ panel** n. Schalttafel, die; **~ room** n. Kontrollraum, der; **~ tower** n. Kontrollturm, der
**controversial** [kɒntrə'vɜːʃl] adj. umstritten
**controversy** ['kɒntrəvɜːsɪ, kən'trɒvəsɪ] n. Auseinandersetzung, die
**convalesce** [kɒnvə'les] v.i. genesen. **convalescence** [kɒnvə'lesəns] n. Genesung, die
**convection** [kən'vekʃn] n. (Phys., Meteorol.) Konvektion, die
**convector** [kən'vektə(r)] n. Konvektor, der
**convene** [kən'viːn] 1. v.t. einberufen. 2. v.i. zusammenkommen
**convenience** [kən'viːnɪəns] n. a) for sb.'s ~ zu jmds. Bequemlichkeit; at your ~: wann es Ihnen paßt; b) (toilet) [public] ~: [öffentliche] Toilette. **convenience food** n. Fertignahrung, die
**convenient** [kən'viːnɪənt] adj. günstig; (useful) praktisch; would it be ~ to or for you? würde es Ihnen passen? **con'veniently** adv. a) günstig (gelegen, angebracht); b) (opportunely) angenehmerweise
**convent** ['kɒnvənt] n. Kloster, das
**convention** [kən'venʃn] n. a) Brauch, der; b) (assembly) Konferenz, die; c) (agreement) Konvention, die. **conventional** [kən'venʃənl] adj. konventionell
**converge** [kən'vɜːdʒ] v.i. ~ [on each other] aufeinander zulaufen
**conversant** [kən'vɜːsənt] pred. adj. vertraut (with mit)
**conversation** [kɒnvə'seɪʃn] n. Unterhaltung, die; have a ~: ein Gespräch führen. **conversational** [kɒnvə'seɪʃnl] adj. ~ English gesprochenes Englisch
**¹converse** [kən'vɜːs] v.i. (formal) ~

|with sb.| |about *or* on sth.| sich |mit jmdm.| |über etw. *(Akk.)*| unterhalten
²**converse** ['kɒnvɜːs] 1. *adj.* entgegengesetzt; umgekehrt ⟨Fall, Situation⟩. 2. *n.* Gegenteil, *das.* **conversely** [kən'vɜːslı] *adj.* umgekehrt
**conversion** [kən'vɜːʃn] *n.* a) Umwandlung, *die* (into in + *Akk.*); b) *(adaptation)* Umbau, *der;* c) *(of person)* Bekehrung, *die* (to zu)
**convert** [kən'vɜːt] 1. *v.t.* umwandeln (into in + *Akk.*); ~ sb. |to sth.| jmdn. |zu etw.| bekehren. 2. [kən'vɜːt] *v.i.* ~ into sth. sich in etw. *(Akk.)* umwandeln lassen. 3. ['kɒnvɜːt] *n.* Konvertit, *der*/Konvertitin, *die.* **convertible** [kən'vɜːtıbl] 1. *adj.* be ~ into sth. sich in etw. *(Akk.)* umwandeln lassen. 2. *n.* Kabrio|lett|, *das*
**convex** ['kɒnveks] *adj.* konvex
**convey** [kən'veı] *v.t.* befördern. **conveyance** [kən'veıəns] *n.* a) *(transportation)* Beförderung, *die;* b) *(formal: vehicle)* Beförderungsmittel, *das.* **con'veyancing** *n.* *(Law)* ~ |of property| |Eigentums|übertragung, *die.* **con'veyor** [kən'veıə(r)] *n.* ~ |belt| Fließband, *das*
**convict** 1. ['kɒnvıkt] *n.* Strafgefangene, *der/die.* 2. [kən'vıkt] *v.t.* verurteilen. **conviction** [kən'vıkʃn] *n.* a) *(Law)* Verurteilung, *die* (for wegen); b) *(belief)* Überzeugung, *die*
**convince** [kən'vıns] *v.t.* überzeugen; ~ sb. that ...: jmdn. davon überzeugen, daß ...; be ~d that ...: davon überzeugt sein, daß ... **convincing** [kən'vınsıŋ] *adj.,* **con'vincingly** *adv.* überzeugend
**convivial** [kən'vıvıəl] *adj.* fröhlich
**convoluted** ['kɒnvəluːtıd] *adj.* *(complex)* kompliziert
**convoy** ['kɒnvɔı] *n.* Konvoi, *der;* in ~: im Konvoi
**convulse** [kən'vʌls] *v.t.* be ~d with sich krümmen vor (+ *Dat.*). **convulsions** [kən'vʌlʃnz] *n. pl.* Krämpfe
**coo** [kuː] *v.i.* gurren
**cook** [kʊk] 1. *n.* Koch, *der*/Köchin, *die.* 2. *v.t.* kochen ⟨Mahlzeit⟩; *(fry, roast)* braten; *(boil)* kochen. 3. *v.i.* kochen. **cook 'up** *v.t.* erfinden ⟨Geschichte⟩
'**cookbook** *n.* *(Amer.)* Kochbuch, *das*
'**cooker** *n.* *(Brit.)* Herd, *der*
**cookery** ['kʊkərı] *n.* Kochen, *das.* '**cookery book** *n.* *(Brit.)* Kochbuch, *das*
**cookie** ['kʊkı] *n.* *(Amer.)* Keks, *der*

'**cooking** *n.* Kochen, *das.* '**cooking apple** *n.* Kochapfel, *der.* '**cooking utensil** *n.* Küchengerät, *das*
**cool** [kuːl] 1. *adj.* a) kühl; store in a ~ place kühl aufbewahren; b) *(unemotional, unfriendly)* kühl; *(calm)* ruhig. 2. *n.* Kühle, *die.* 3. *v.i.* abkühlen. 4. *v.t.* kühlen; *(from high temperature)* abkühlen. **cool 'down, cool 'off** *v.i. & t.* abkühlen
**coolly** ['kuːllı] *adv.* *(calmly)* ruhig; *(unemotionally)* kühl
**coop** [kuːp] 1. *n.* *(for poultry)* Hühnerstall, *der.* 2. *v.t.* ~ up einpferchen
**co-operate** [kəʊ'ɒpəreıt] *v.i.* mitarbeiten (in bei); *(with each other)* zusammenarbeiten (in bei). **co-operation** [kəʊɒpə'reıʃn] *n.* Zusammenarbeit, *die.* **co-operative** [kəʊ'ɒpərətıv] 1. *adj.* kooperativ; *(helpful)* hilfsbereit. 2. *n.* Genossenschaft, *die*
**co-ordinate** [kəʊ'ɔːdıneıt] *v.t.* koordinieren. **co-ordination** [kəʊɔː'neıʃn] *n.* Koordination, *die*
**cop** [kɒp] *n.* *(sl.: police officer)* Bulle, *der (salopp)*
**cope** [kəʊp] *v.i.* ~ with sb./sth. mit jmdm./etw. fertig werden
**Copenhagen** [kəʊpn'heıgn] *pr. n.* Kopenhagen *(das)*
**copier** ['kɒpıə(r)] *n.* *(machine)* Kopiergerät, *das*
**co-pilot** ['kəʊpaılət] *n.* Kopilot, *der*/Kopilotin, *die*
**copious** ['kəʊpıəs] *adj.* reichhaltig
¹**copper** ['kɒpə(r)] *n.* Kupfer, *das*
²**copper** *(Brit. sl.)* see **cop**
**coppice** ['kɒpıs], **copse** [kɒps] *ns.* Wäldchen, *das*
**copulate** ['kɒpjʊleıt] *v.i.* kopulieren
**copy** ['kɒpı] 1. *n.* a) *(reproduction)* Kopie, *die;* b) *(specimen)* Exemplar, *das.* 2. *v.t. & i.* kopieren; *(transcribe)* abschreiben. '**copyright** *n.* Urheberrecht, *das*
**coral** ['kɒrl] *n.* Koralle, *die*
**cord** [kɔːd] *n.* a) Kordel, *die;* b) *(cloth)* Cord, *der;* c) in pl. *(trousers)* |pair of| ~s Cordhose, *die*
**cordial** ['kɔːdıəl] 1. *adj.* herzlich. 2. *n.* *(drink)* Sirup, *der.* '**cordially** *adv.* herzlich
**cordon** ['kɔːdn] 1. *n.* Kordon, *der.* 2. *v.t.* ~ |off| absperren
**corduroy** ['kɔːdərɔı, 'kɔːdjʊrɔı] *n.* Cordsamt, *der*
**core** [kɔː(r)] 1. *n.* *(of fruit)* Kerngehäuse, *das.* 2. *v.t.* entkernen
**cork** [kɔːk] 1. *n.* a) *(bark)* Kork, *der;* b)

*(bottle-stopper)* Korken, *der.* 2. *v.t.* zukorken. '**corkscrew** *n.* Korkenzieher, *der*

¹**corn** [kɔ:n] *n.* Getreide, *das*

²**corn** *n.* *(on foot)* Hühnerauge, *das*

**corned beef** [kɔ:nd 'bi:f] *n.* Corned beef, *das*

**corner** ['kɔ:nə(r)] 1. *n.* **a)** Ecke, *die;* *(curve)* Kurve, *die;* **on the ~:** an der Ecke/in der Kurve; **b)** *(of mouth, eye)* Winkel, *der.* 2. *v.t.* *(fig.)* in die Enge treiben. 3. *v.i.* die Kurve nehmen. '**corner kick** *n.* *(Footb.)* Eckball, *der.* '**cornerstone** *n.* *(fig.)* Eckpfeiler, *der*

**cornet** ['kɔ:nɪt] *n.* **a)** *(Brit.: for icecream)* [Eis]tüte, *die;* **b)** *(Mus.)* Kornett, *das*

**corn:** ~**flakes** *n. pl.* Corn-flakes *Pl.;* ~**flour** *(Brit.),* ~**starch** *(Amer.) ns.* Maismehl, *das*

'**corny** *adj.* *(coll.: trite)* abgedroschen

**coronation** [kɒrə'neɪʃn] *n.* Krönung, *die*

**coroner** ['kɒrənə(r)] *n.* Coroner, *der;* *Beamter, der gewaltsame od. unnatürliche Todesfälle untersucht*

**coronet** ['kɒrənet] *n.* Krone, *die*

¹**corporal** ['kɔ:pərl] *adj.* körperlich

²**corporal** *n.* ≈ Hauptgefreite, *der*

**corporation** [kɔ:pə'reɪʃn] *n.* Stadtverwaltung, *die*

**corps** [kɔ:(r)] *n., pl. same* [kɔ:z] Korps, *das*

**corpse** [kɔ:ps] *n.* Leiche, *die*

**corpulent** ['kɔ:pjʊlənt] *adj.* korpulent

**correct** [kə'rekt] 1. *v.t.* korrigieren. 2. *adj.* korrekt; **that is ~:** das stimmt. **correction** [kə'rekʃn] *n.* Korrektur, *die.* **cor'rectly** *adv.* korrekt

**correspond** [kɒrɪ'spɒnd] *v.i.* **a)** ~ |to each other| einander entsprechen; ~ **to sth.** einer Sache *(Dat.)* entsprechen; **b)** *(communicate)* ~ **with sb.** mit jmdm. korrespondieren. **correspondence** [kɒrɪ'spɒndəns] *n.* **a)** Übereinstimmung, *die* **(with,** to mit); **b)** *(communication)* Briefwechsel, *der.* **correspondent** [kɒrɪ'spɒndənt] *n.* *(reporter)* Korrespondent, *der/*Korrespondentin, *die.* **corre'sponding** *adj.* entsprechend **(to** *Dat.).* **corre'spondingly** *adv.* entsprechend

**corridor** ['kɒrɪdɔ:(r)] *n.* **a)** Flur, *der;* **b)** *(Railw.)* [Seiten]gang, *der*

**corroborate** [kə'rɒbəreɪt] *v.t.* bestätigen

**corrode** [kə'rəʊd] 1. *v.t.* zerfressen. 2. *v.i.* zerfressen werden. **corrosion** [kə'rəʊʒn] *n.* Korrosion, *die*

**corrugated** ['kɒrəgeɪtɪd] *adj.* ~ **cardboard** Wellpappe, *die;* ~ **iron** Wellblech, *das*

**corrupt** [kə'rʌpt] 1. *adj.* *(depraved)* verdorben *(geh.);* *(influenced by bribery)* korrupt. 2. *v.t.* *(deprave)* korrumpieren; *(bribe)* bestechen. **corruption** [kə'rʌpʃn] *n.* *(moral deterioration)* Verdorbenheit, *die (geh.);* *(corrupt practices)* Korruption, *die*

**corset** ['kɔ:sɪt] *n.* Korsett, *das*

**Corsica** ['kɔ:sɪkə] *pr. n.* Korsika *(das)*

**cortège** [kɔ:'teɪʒ] *n.* Trauerzug, *der*

**cosh** [kɒʃ] *(Brit. coll.)* 1. *n.* Totschläger, *der.* 2. *v.t.* niederknüppeln

**cosmetic** [kɒz'metɪk] 1. *adj.* kosmetisch. 2. *n.* Kosmetikum, *das*

**cosmic** ['kɒzmɪk] *adj.* kosmisch

**cosmonaut** ['kɒzmənɔ:t] *n.* Kosmonaut, *der/*Kosmonautin, *die*

**cosmopolitan** [kɒzmə'pɒlɪtən] *adj.* kosmopolitisch

**cosmos** ['kɒzmɒs] *n.* Kosmos, *der*

**cosset** ['kɒsɪt] *v.t.* [ver]hätscheln

**cost** [kɒst] 1. *n.* **a)** Kosten *Pl.;* **b)** *(fig.)* Preis, *der;* **at all ~s, at any ~:** um jeden Preis. 2. *v.t.* **a)** *p.t., p.p.* cost *(lit. or fig.)* kosten; **how much does it ~?** was kostet es?; **b)** *p.t., p.p.* **costed** *(Commerc.: fix price of)* ~ **sth.** den Preis für etw. kalkulieren. '**cost-effective** *adj.* rentabel

'**costly** *adj.* teuer

**cost:** ~ **of 'living** *n.* Lebenshaltungskosten *Pl.;* ~ **price** *n.* Selbstkostenpreis, *der*

**costume** ['kɒstju:m] *n.* Kleidermode, *die;* *(theatrical ~)* Kostüm, *das*

**cosy** ['kəʊzɪ] *adj.* gemütlich

**cot** [kɒt] *n.* Kinderbett, *das*

**cottage** ['kɒtɪdʒ] *n.* Cottage, *das*

**cottage:** ~ **'cheese** *n.* Hüttenkäse, *der;* ~ **industry** *n.* Heimarbeit, *die;* ~ '**pie** *n.* mit Kartoffelbrei überbackenes Hackfleisch

**cotton** ['kɒtn] 1. *n.* Baumwolle, *die;* *(thread)* Baumwollgarn, *das.* 2. *attrib. adj.* Baumwoll-. 3. *v.i.* ~ '**on** *(coll.)* kapieren *(ugs.).* **cotton 'wool** *n.* Watte, *die*

**couch** [kaʊtʃ] *n.* Couch, *die*

**couchette** [ku:'ʃet] *n.* *(Railw.)* Liegesitz, *der*

**cough** [kɒf] 1. *n.* Husten, *der.* 2. *v.i.* husten. '**cough mixture** *n.* Hustensaft, *der*

**could** *see* ²**can**

**couldn't** ['kʊdnt] *(coll.)* = **could not;** *see* ²**can**

**council** ['kaʊnsl] *n*. Rat, *der;* **local ~:** Landschaft, *die;* **in the ~:** auf dem Land. **countryman** ['kʌntrɪmən] *n.,* *pl*. **countrymen** ['kʌntrɪmən] Lands-mann, *der.* '**countryside** *n*. **a)** *(rural areas)* Land, *das;* **b)** *(rural scenery)* Landschaft, *die*

**councillor** ['kaʊnsələ(r)] *n*. Ratsmit-glied, *das*

'**council tax** *n*. *(Brit.)* Gemeindesteu-er, *die*

**county** ['kaʊntɪ] *n*. *(Brit.)* Grafschaft, *die*

**counsel** ['kaʊnsl] **1.** *n*. **a)** Rat[schlag], *der;* **b)** *pl. same (Law)* ·Rechtsanwalt, *der/*-anwältin, *die.* **2.** *v. t., (Brit.)* **-ll**-beraten. **counsellor,** *(Amer.)* **coun-selor** ['kaʊnsələ(r)] *n*. Berater, *der/*Beraterin, *die*

**coup** [ku:] *n*. **a)** Coup, *der;* **b)** *see* **coup d'état. coup d'état** [ku: deɪ'ta:] *n*. Staatsstreich, *der*

**coupé** ['ku:peɪ] *n*. Coupé, *das*

¹**count** [kaʊnt] **1.** *n*. Zählen, *das;* **keep ~ |of sth.|** [etw.] zählen; **lose ~:** sich verzählen. **2.** *v. t.* **a)** zählen; **b)** *(in-clude)* mitzählen; **not ~-ing** abgesehen von; **c)** *(consider)* halten für; **~ oneself lucky** sich glücklich schätzen können. **3.** *v. i.* **a)** zählen; **~ |up| to ten** bis zehn zählen; **b)** *(be included)* zählen. '**count on** *v. t.* **~ on sb./sth.** sich auf jmdn./etw. verlassen. **count 'up** *v. t.* zusammenzählen

**couple** [kʌpl] *n*. **1.** **a)** *(pair)* Paar, *das;* *(married)* [Ehe]paar, *das;* **b) a ~ |of|** *(a few)* ein paar; *(two)* zwei. **2.** *v. t.* kop-peln

**coupon** ['ku:pɒn] *n*. **a)** *(for rations)* Marke, *die;* **b)** *(in advertisement)* Cou-pon, *der*

**courage** ['kʌrɪdʒ] *n*. Mut, *der.* **cour-ageous** [kə'reɪdʒəs] *adj.,* **cou'rage-ously** *adv.* mutig

**courgette** [kʊə'ʒet] *n*. *(Brit.)* Zucchi-no, *der*

²**count** *n*. *(nobleman)* Graf, *der*

'**countdown** *n*. Countdown, *der od. das*

**courier** ['kʊrɪə(r)] *n*. **a)** *(Tourism)* Rei-seleiter, *der/*-leiterin, *die;* **b)** *(mess-enger)* Kurier, *der*

**countenance** ['kaʊntɪnəns] **1.** *n*. *(literary: face)* Antlitz, *das.* **2.** *v. t.* *(for-mal: approve)* gutheißen

**course** [kɔ:s] *n*. **a)** *(of ship, plane)* Kurs, *der;* **~ |of action|** Vorgehenswei-se, *die;* **b) of ~:** natürlich; **c) in due ~:** zu gegebener Zeit; **in the ~ of the day/his life** im Lauf[e] des Tages/seines Lebens; **d)** *(of meal)* Gang, *der;* **e)** *(Sport)* Kurs, *der;* **|golf-|~:** [Golf]platz, *der;* **f)** *(Educ.)* Kurs[us], *der;* **g)** *(Med.)* **a ~ of treatment** eine Kur

¹**counter** ['kaʊntə(r)] *n*. **a)** *(in shop)* Ladentisch, *der;* *(in cafeteria)* Büfett, *das;* *(in bank)* Schalter, *der;* **b)** *(for games)* Spielmarke, *die*

²**counter** **1.** *adj*. Gegen-. **2.** *v. t.* **a)** *(op-pose)* begegnen (+ *Dat.*); **b)** *(act against)* kontern. **3.** *adv*. **go ~ to** zuwi-derlaufen (+ *Dat.*)

**court** [kɔ:t] **1.** *n*. **a)** Hof, *der;* **b)** *(Ten-nis, Squash)* Platz, *der;* **c)** *(Law)* Ge-richt, *das.* **2.** *v. t.* **~ sb.** jmdn. umwer-ben

**counter: ~'act** *v. t.* entgegenwirken (+ *Dat.*); **~-attack** *n*. Gegenangriff, *der;* **~balance** *v. t.* *(fig.)* ausglei-chen; **~-'espionage** *n*. Spionageab-wehr, *die*

**courteous** ['kɜ:tɪəs] *adj.* höflich. **courtesy** ['kɜ:təsɪ] *n*. Höflichkeit, *die* **court: ~-house** *n*. *(Law)* Gerichtsge-bäude, *das;* **~ 'martial** *n., pl.* **~s mar-tial** *(Mil.)* Kriegsgericht, *das;* **~yard** *n*. Hof, *der*

**counterfeit** ['kaʊntəfɪt] **1.** *adj*. ge-fälscht; **~ money** Falschgeld, *das.* **2.** *v. t.* fälschen. '**counterfeiter** *n*. Fäl-scher, *der/*Fälscherin, *die*

**cousin** ['kʌzn] *n*. **|first| ~:** Cousin, *der/*Cousine, *die*

**cove** [kəʊv] *n*. *(Geog.)* [kleine] Bucht **covenant** ['kʌvənənt] *n*. formelle Übereinkunft

**counter: ~foil** *n*. Kontrollabschnitt, *der;* **~part** *n*. Gegenstück, *das* *(of* zu); **~-pro'ductive** *adj.* **sth. is ~-productive** etw. bewirkt das Gegen-teil des Gewünschten; **~sign** *v. t.* ge-genzeichnen

**countess** ['kaʊntɪs] *n*. Gräfin, *die* '**countless** *adj.* zahllos **country** ['kʌntrɪ] *n*. **a)** Land, *das;* **sb's |home| ~:** jmds. Heimat; **b)** *(~ side)*

**cover** ['kʌvə(r)] **1.** *n*. **a)** *(piece of cloth)* Decke, *die;* *(of cushion, bed)* Bezug, *der;* *(lid)* Deckel, *der;* *(of hole, engine, typewriter, etc.)* Abdeckung, *die;* **b)** *(of book)* Einband, *der;* *(of magazine)* Umschlag, *der;* **c) |send sth.| under sep-arate ~:** [etw.] mit getrennter Post [schicken]; **d) take ~ |from sth.|** Schutz [vor etw. *(Dat.)*] suchen; **under** ~ *(from rain)* überdacht. **2.** *v.t.* **a)** bedecken; beziehen ‹*Sessel, Kisses*›; zudecken ‹*Pfanne*›; **the roses are ~ed with greenfly** die Rosen sind voller Blattläuse; **b)** *(include)* abdecken; **c)** *(Journ.)* berichten über ( + *Akk.*); **d)** decken ‹*Kosten*›. **cover 'up** *v.t.* **1.** zudecken; *(fig.)* vertuschen. **2.** *v.i.* ~ **up for sb.** jmdn. decken

**coverage** ['kʌvərɪdʒ] *n. (Journ.)* Berichterstattung, *die*

'**cover charge** *n.* [Preis für das] Gedeck

'**covering** *n.* Decke, *die;(of chair, bed)* Bezug, *der.* '**covering letter** *n.* Begleitbrief, *der*

**covert** ['kʌvət] *adj.* versteckt

'**cover-up** *n.* Verschleierung, *die*

**covet** ['kʌvɪt] *v.t.* begehren *(geh.).* **covetous** ['kʌvɪtəs] *adj.* begehrlich *(geh.)*

**cow** [kaʊ] *n.* Kuh, *die*

**coward** ['kaʊəd] *n.* Feigling, *der.* **cowardice** ['kaʊədɪs] *n.* Feigheit, *die.* '**cowardly** *adj.* feig[e]

'**cowboy** *n.* Cowboy, *der*

**cower** ['kaʊə(r)] *v.i.* sich ducken

**cow:** ~**-shed** *n.* Kuhstall, *der;* ~**slip** *n.* Schlüsselblume, *die*

**coy** [kɔɪ] *adj.* gespielt schüchtern

**cozy** *(Amer.) see* **cosy**

**crab** [kræb] *n.* Krabbe, *die.* '**crabapple** *n.* Holzapfel, *der*

**crack** [kræk] **1.** *n.* **a)** *(noise)* Krachen, *das;* **b)** *(in china etc.)* Sprung, *der; (in rock)* Spalte, *die;(chink)* Spalt, *der;* **c)** *(coll.: try)* **have a** ~ **at sth./doing sth.** versuchen, etw. zu tun. **2.** *attrib. adj. (coll.)* erstklassig. **3.** *v.t.* **a)** knacken ‹*Nuß, Problem, Kode*›; **b)** *(make a* ~ *in)* anschlagen ‹*Porzellan usw.*›; **c)** ~ **a joke** einen Witz machen; **d)** ~ **a whip** mit einer Peitsche knallen. **4.** *v.i.* ‹*Porzellan usw.*:› einen Sprung/Sprünge bekommen. **crack 'down** *v.i. (coll.)* ~ **down** [**on sb./sth.**] [gegen jmdn./etw.] [hart] vorgehen. **crack 'up** *v.i. (coll.)* ‹*Person*:› zusammenbrechen

**cracked** [krækt] *adj.* gesprungen ‹*Porzellan usw.*›; rissig ‹*Verputz*›

**cracker** ['krækə(r)] *n.* **a)** [Christmas] ~ ≈ Knallbonbon, *der od. das;* **b)** *(biscuit)* Cracker, *der.* '**crackers** *pred. adj. (Brit. coll.)* übergeschnappt *(ugs.)*

**crackle** ['krækl] **1.** *v.i.* knistern; ‹*Feuer*:› prasseln. **2.** *n.* Knistern, *das*

**cradle** ['kreɪdl] **1.** *n.* Wiege, *die.* **2.** *v.t.* wiegen

**craft** [krɑːft] *n.* **a)** *(trade)* Handwerk, *das; (art)* Kunsthandwerk, *das;* **b)** *pl. same (boat)* Boot, *das.* **craftsman** ['krɑːftsmən] *n., pl.* **craftsmen** ['krɑːftsmən] Handwerker, *der.* '**crafty** *adj.* listig

**crag** [kræg] *n.* Felsspitze, *die.* '**craggy** *adj.* **a)** felsig; **b)** zerfurcht ‹*Gesicht*›

**cram** [kræm] **1.** *v.t.,* -**mm**- *(overfill)* vollstopfen *(ugs.); (force)* stopfen. **2.** *v.i.,* -**mm**- *(for exam)* büffeln *(ugs.)*

**cramp** [kræmp] **1.** *n. (Med.)* Krampf, *der.* **2.** *v.t.* einengen

**cranberry** ['krænbəri] *n.* Preiselbeere, *die*

**crane** [kreɪn] **1.** *n.* Kran, *der.* **2.** *v.t.* ~ **one's neck** den Hals recken

¹**crank** [kræŋk] *n. (Mech. Engin.)* [Hand]kurbel, *die*

²**crank** *n.* Irre, *der/die (salopp)*

'**crankshaft** *n. (Mech. Engin.)* Kurbelwelle, *die*

'**cranky** *adj. (eccentric)* schrullig

**cranny** ['kræni] *n.* Ritze, *die*

**crash** [kræʃ] **1.** *n.* **a)** *(noise)* Krachen, *das;* **b)** *(collision)* Zusammenstoß, *der;* **have a** ~: einen Unfall haben. **2.** *v.i.* **a)** *(make a noise, go noisily)* krachen; **b)** *(have a collision)* einen Unfall haben; ‹*Flugzeug, Flieger*:› abstürzen; ~ **into sth.** gegen etw. krachen. **3.** *v.t.* **a)** *(smash)* schmettern; **b)** *(cause to have collision)* einen Unfall haben mit

**crash:** ~ **barrier** *n.* Leitplanke, *die;* ~ **course** *n.* Intensivkurs, *der;* ~**-helmet** *n.* Sturzhelm, *der*

**crass** [kræs] *adj.* kraß

**crate** [kreɪt] *n.* Kiste, *die*

**crater** ['kreɪtə(r)] *n.* Krater, *der*

**cravat** [krə'væt] *n.* Krawatte, *die*

**crave** [kreɪv] *v.t.* **a)** *(beg)* erbitten; **b)** *(long for)* sich sehnen nach. '**craving** *n.* Verlangen, *das (for nach)*

**crawl** [krɔːl] **1.** *v.i.* **a)** kriechen; ‹*Baby, Insekt*:› krabbeln; **b)** *(coll.)* ~ **to sb.** vor jmdm. kriechen. **2.** *n.* **a)** **go at a** ~: im Schneckentempo fahren; **b)** *(swimming-stroke)* Kraulen, *das.* '**crawler lane** *n.* Kriechspur, *die*

**crayfish** ['kreɪfɪʃ] *n., pl. same* Flußkrebs, *der*

**crayon** ['kreɪən] *n.* [coloured] ~: Buntstift, *der; (wax)* Wachsmalstift, *der*

**craze** [kreɪz] *n.* Begeisterung, *die*

**crazy** ['kreɪzi] *adj.* verrückt; **be ~ about sb./sth.** *(coll.)* nach jmdm./etw. verrückt sein *(ugs.)*

**creak** [kriːk] **1.** *n.* Knarren, *das.* **2.** *v.i.* knarren

**cream** [kri:m] **1.** *n.* **a)** Sahne, *die;* **b)** *(dessert, cosmetic)* Creme, *die.* **2.** *adj.* ~-[-coloured] creme[farben]. **cream 'cheese** *n.* ≈ Frischkäse, *der*

**'creamy** *adj. (with cream)* sahnig; *(like cream)* cremig

**crease** [kri:s] **1.** *n. (pressed)* Bügelfalte, *die; (accidental)* Falte, *die.* **2.** *v. t. (press)* eine Falte bügeln in (+ *Akk.*); *(accidentally)* zerknittern. **3.** *v. i.* Falten bekommen; knittern. **'crease-resistant** *adj.* knitterfrei

**create** [kri:'eɪt] *v. t.* schaffen; verursachen 〈*Verwirrung*〉; machen 〈*Eindruck*〉. **creation** [kri:'eɪʃn] *n.* Schaffung, *die; (of the world)* Schöpfung, *die (geh.).* **creative** [kri:'eɪtɪv] *adj.* kreativ. **creator** [kri:'eɪtə(r)] *n.* Schöpfer, *der/*Schöpferin, *die*

**creature** ['kri:tʃə(r)] *n.* Geschöpf, *das*

**crèche** [kreʃ] *n.* [Kinder]krippe, *die*

**credentials** [krɪ'denʃlz] *n. pl.* Zeugnis, *das*

**credibility** [kredɪ'bɪlɪtɪ] *n.* Glaubwürdigkeit, *die*

**credible** ['kredɪbl] *adj.* glaubwürdig

**credit** ['kredɪt] **1.** *n.* **a)** *(honour)* Ehre, *die;* **take the ~ for sth.** die Anerkennung für etw. einstecken; **b)** *(Commerc.)* Kredit, *der.* **2.** *v. t.* **a)** glauben; **b)** *(Finance)* gutschreiben. **creditable** ['kredɪtəbl] *adj.* anerkennenswert

**'credit card** *n.* Kreditkarte, *die*

**creditor** ['kredɪtə(r)] *n.* Gläubiger, *der/*Gläubigerin, *die*

**creed** [kri:d] *n.* Glaubensbekenntnis, *das*

**creek** [kri:k] *n.* **a)** *(Brit.: of coast)* [kleine] Bucht; **b)** *(of river)* [kurzer] Flußarm

**creep** [kri:p] **1.** *v. i., crept* [krept] kriechen; *(move timidly, slowly, stealthily)* schleichen. **2.** *n.* **a)** *(sl.: person)* Fiesling, *der (salopp);* **b)** *(coll.)* **give sb. the ~s** jmdn. nicht [ganz] geheuer sein. **'creeper** *n.* Kletterpflanze, *die.* **'creepy** *adj.* unheimlich

**cremate** [krɪ'meɪt] *v. t.* einäschern. **cremation** [krɪ'meɪʃn] *n.* Einäscherung, *die.* **crematorium** [kremə-'tɔ:rɪəm] *n.* Krematorium, *das*

**creosote** ['kri:əsəʊt] *n.* Kreosot, *das*

**crept** *see* **creep 1**

**crescent** ['kresənt] *n.* Mondsichel, *die*

**cress** [kres] *n.* Kresse, *die*

**crest** [krest] *n.* Kamm, *der.* **'crestfallen** *adj.* niedergeschlagen

**Crete** [kri:t] *pr. n.* Kreta *(das)*

**cretin** ['kretɪn] *n. (coll.)* Trottel, *der*

**crevasse** [krɪ'væs] *n.* Gletscherspalte, *die*

**crevice** ['krevɪs] *n.* Spalt, *der*

**crew** [kru:] *n.* Besatzung, *die.* **'crew-cut** *n.* Bürstenschnitt, *der*

**crib** [krɪb] **1.** *n.* Krippe, *die.* **2.** *v. t., -bb- (coll.)* abkupfern *(salopp)*

**crick** [krɪk] *n.* **a** ~ **[in one's neck/back]** ein steifer Hals/Rücken

**¹cricket** ['krɪkɪt] *n.* Kricket, *das*

**²cricket** *n. (Zool.)* Grille, *die*

**'cricket bat** *n.* Schlagholz, *das*

**'cricketer** *n.* Kricketspieler, *der/* -spielerin, *die*

**cried** *see* **cry**

**crime** [kraɪm] *n.* **a)** Verbrechen, *das;* **b)** *collect.* **a wave of ~:** eine Welle von Straftaten; **~ doesn't pay** Verbrechen lohnen sich nicht

**criminal** ['krɪmɪnl] **1.** *adj.* kriminell; strafbar; **act** *or* **deed/offence** Straftat, *die.* **2.** *n.* Kriminelle, *der/die*

**crimson** ['krɪmzn] **1.** *adj.* purpurrot. **2.** *n.* Purpurrot, *das*

**cringe** [krɪndʒ] *v. i.* zusammenzucken

**crinkle** ['krɪŋkl] **1.** *n.* Knitterfalte, *die.* **2.** *v. t.* zerknittern. **3.** *v. i.* knittern

**cripple** ['krɪpl] **1.** *n.* Krüppel, *der.* **2.** *v. t.* zum Krüppel machen; *(fig.)* lähmen. **crippled** ['krɪpld] *adj.* verkrüppelt

**crisis** ['kraɪsɪs] *n., pl.* **crises** ['kraɪsi:z] Krise, *die*

**crisp** [krɪsp] **1.** *adj.* knusprig. **2.** **a)** *n. usu. in pl. (Brit.: potato ~)* [Kartoffel]chip, *der;* **b)** **be burned to a ~:** verbrannt sein. **'crispbread** *n.* Knäckebrot, *das*

**'crispy** *adj.* knusprig

**criss-cross** ['krɪskrɒs] **1.** *adj.* ~ **pattern** Muster aus gekreuzten Linien. **2.** *adv.* kreuz und quer. **3.** *v. t.* wiederholt schneiden

**criterion** [kraɪ'tɪərɪən] *n., pl.* **criteria** [kraɪ'tɪərɪə] Kriterium, *das*

**critic** ['krɪtɪk] *n.* Kritiker, *der/*Kritikerin, *die.* **critical** ['krɪtɪkl] *adj.* kritisch; **be ~ of sb./sth.** jmdn./etw. kritisieren. **critically** ['krɪtɪkəlɪ] *adv.* kritisch; **~ ill** ernstlich krank

**criticism** ['krɪtɪsɪzm] *n.* Kritik, *die* (**of** an + *Dat.*)

**criticize** ['krɪtɪsaɪz] *v. t.* kritisieren (**for** wegen)

**croak** [krəʊk] **1.** *n. (of frog)* Quaken, *das; (of person)* Krächzen, *das.* **2.** *v. i.* 〈*Frosch:*〉 quaken; 〈*Person:*〉 krächzen. **3.** *v. t.* krächzen

**crochet** ['krəʊʃeı] **1.** *n.* Häkelarbeit, *die;* ~ **hook** Häkelhaken, *der.* **2.** *v.t.* häkeln

**crock** [krɒk] *n. (coll.)* |old| ~ *(person)* altes Wrack, *das (fig.); (vehicle)* [alte] Klapperkiste *(ugs.)*

**crockery** ['krɒkərı] *n.* Geschirr, *das*

**crocodile** ['krɒkədaıl] *n.* Krokodil, *das*

**crocus** ['krəʊkəs] *n.* Krokus, *der*

**crony** ['krəʊnı] *n.* Kumpel, *der (ugs.)*

**crook** [krʊk] *n.* **a)** *(coll.: rogue)* Gauner, *der;* **b)** *(shepherd's)* Hirtenstab, *der*

**crooked** ['krʊkıd] *adj.* krumm; *(fig.: dishonest)* betrügerisch

**crop** [krɒp] *n.* **1.** [Feld]frucht, *die; (season's yield)* Ernte, *die.* **2.** *v.t.* stutzen ⟨*Haare usw.*⟩. **crop 'up** *v.i.* auftauchen

**'cropper** *n. (coll.)* **come a ~:** einen Sturz bauen *(ugs.)*

**croquet** ['krəʊkeı] *n.* Krocket[spiel], *das*

**croquette** [krə'ket] *n.* Krokette, *die*

**cross** [krɒs] **1.** *n.* **a)** Kreuz, *das;* **b)** *(mixture)* Mischung, *die* (**between** aus). **2.** *v.t.* **a)** [über]kreuzen; ~ **one's arms/legs** die Arme verschränken/die Beine übereinanderschlagen; **keep one's fingers ~ed |for sb.|** *(fig.)* [jmdm.] die *od.* den Daumen drücken; **b)** *(go across)* kreuzen; überqueren ⟨*Straße, Gebirge*⟩; durchqueren ⟨*Land, Zimmer*⟩; ~ **sb.'s mind** *(fig.)* jmdm. einfallen; **c)** *(Brit.)* **a ~ed cheque** ein Verrechnungsscheck; **d)** ~ **oneself** sich bekreuzigen. **3.** *v.i.* aneinander vorbeigehen; ~ **|in the post|** ⟨*Briefe:*⟩ sich kreuzen. **4.** *adj.* verärgert; **sb. will be ~:** jmd. wird ärgerlich *od.* böse werden; **be ~ with sb.** böse auf jmdn. sein. **cross 'out** *v.t.* ausstreichen. **cross 'over** *v.t.* überqueren; *abs.* hinübergehen

**cross:** ~**bar** *n.* **a)** [Fahrrad]stange, *die;* **b)** *(Sport)* Querlatte, *die;* ~-**check 1.** *n.* Gegenprobe, *die;* **2.** *v.t.* [nochmals] nachprüfen; nachkontrollieren; ~-**country 1.** *adj.* Querfeldein-; **2.** *adv.* querfeldein; ~-**examination** *n.* Kreuzverhör, *das;* ~-**examine** *v.t.* ins Kreuzverhör nehmen; ~-**eyed** ['krɒsaıd] *adj.* [nach innen] schielend; **be ~-eyed** schielen; ~-**fire** *n.* Kreuzfeuer, *das*

**'crossing** *n.* **a)** *(act)* Überquerung, *die;* **b)** *(pedestrian ~)* Überweg, *der*

**'crossly** *adv.* verärgert

**cross:** ~ **'purposes** *n. pl.* **talk at ~**

**purposes** aneinander vorbeireden; ~-**reference** *n.* Querverweis, *der;* ~**roads** *n. sing.* Kreuzung, *die; (fig.)* Wendepunkt, *der;* ~-**section** *n.* Querschnitt, *der;* ~**word** *n.* ~**word |puzzle|** Kreuzworträtsel, *das*

**crotchet** ['krɒtʃıt] *n. (Brit. Mus.)* Viertelnote, *die*

**crouch** [kraʊtʃ] *v.i.* [sich zusammen]kauern

**crow** [krəʊ] *n.* Krähe, *die;* **as the ~ flies** Luftlinie

**'crowbar** *n.* Brechstange, *die*

**crowd** [kraʊd] **1.** *n.* [Menschen]menge, *die.* **2.** *vt.* füllen. **3.** *v.i.* sich sammeln. **'crowded** *adj.* überfüllt

**crown** [kraʊn] **1.** *n.* Krone, *die.* **2.** *v.t.* **a)** krönen; **b)** überkronen ⟨*Zahn*⟩

**crucial** ['kru:ʃl] *adj.* entscheidend (**to** für)

**crucifix** ['kru:sıfıks] *n.* Kruzifix, *das.* **crucifixion** [kru:sı'fıkʃn] *n.* Kreuzigung, *die*

**crucify** ['kru:sıfaı] *v.t.* kreuzigen

**crude** [kru:d] *adj.* **a)** roh; ~ **oil** Rohöl, *das;* **b)** *(fig.)* grob ⟨*Entwurf, Worte*⟩

**cruel** ['kru:əl] *adj.* grausam. **cruelty** ['kru:əltı] *n.* Grausamkeit, *die*

**cruise** [kru:z] **1.** *v.i. (at random)* ⟨*Fahrzeug, Fahrer:*⟩ herumfahren. **2.** *n.* Kreuzfahrt, *die.* **'cruise missile** *n.* Marschflugkörper, *der.* **'cruiser** *n.* Kreuzer, *der*

**crumb** [krʌm] *n.* Krümel, *der*

**crumble** ['krʌmbl] **1.** *v.t.* zerkrümeln ⟨*Keks, Kuchen*⟩. **2.** *v.i.* ⟨*Mauer:*⟩ zusammenfallen. **crumbly** ['krʌmblı] *adj.* krümelig ⟨*Keks, Kuchen*⟩; bröckelig ⟨*Gestein*⟩

**crumpet** ['krʌmpıt] *n. weiches Hefeküchlein zum Toasten*

**crumple** ['krʌmpl] **1.** *v.t.* **a)** *(crush)* zerdrücken; **b)** *(wrinkle)* zerknittern. **2.** *v.i.* knittern

**crunch** [krʌntʃ] **1.** *v.t.* [geräuschvoll] knabbern ⟨*Keks*⟩. **2.** *v.i.* ⟨*Schnee, Kies:*⟩ knirschen. **3.** *n.* Knirschen, *das;* **when it comes to the ~:** wenn es hart auf hart geht. **'crunchy** *adj.* knusprig

**crusade** [kru:'seıd] **1.** *n. (Hist.; also fig.)* Kreuzzug, *der.* **2.** *v.i. (fig.)* zu Felde gehen. **cru'sader** *n. (Hist.)* Kreuzfahrer, *der*

**crush** [krʌʃ] **1.** *v.t.* **a)** quetschen; **b)** *(powder)* zerstampfen; **c)** *(fig.)* niederschlagen. **2.** *n. (crowd)* Gedränge, *das*

**crust** [krʌst] *n.* Kruste, *die.* **'crusty** *adj.* knusprig

**crutch** [krʌtʃ] *n.* Krücke, *die;* **go about on ~es** an Krücken gehen

**crux** [krʌks] *n.* **the ~ of the matter** der springende Punkt bei der Sache

**cry** [kraɪ] **1.** *n. (of grief)* Schrei, *der; (of words)* Schreien, *das;* **a far ~ from ...** *(fig.)* etwas ganz anderes als ... **2.** *v. i.* **a)** rufen; *(loudly)* schreien; **b)** *(weep)* weinen (**over** wegen). **cry 'off** *v. i.* absagen. **cry 'out** *v. i.* aufschreien

**'crying** *adj.* **it's a ~ shame** es ist eine wahre Schande

**crypt** [krɪpt] *n.* Krypta, *die*

**cryptic** ['krɪptɪk] *adj.* geheimnisvoll

**crystal** ['krɪstl] **1.** *n.* **a)** Kristall, *der;* **b)** *(glass)* Bleikristall, *das.* **2.** *adj. (made of ~ glass)* kristallen. **crystallize** ['krɪstəlaɪz] *v. i.* kristallisieren; *(fig.)* feste Form annehmen

**cub** [kʌb] *n.* **a)** Junge, *das; (of wolf, fox, dog)* Welpe, *der;* **b)** **Cub** *see* **Cub Scout**

**Cuba** ['kjuːbə] *n.* Kuba *(das)*

**cubby[-hole]** ['kʌbɪ(həʊl)] *n.* Kämmerchen, *das*

**cube** [kjuːb] *n.* Würfel, *der.* **cubic** ['kjuːbɪk] *adj.* **a)** würfelförmig; **b)** Kubik*(meter usw.)*

**cubicle** ['kjuːbɪkl] *n.* Kabine, *die*

**'Cub Scout** *n.* Wölfling, *der*

**cuckoo** ['kʊkuː] *n.* Kuckuck, *der.* **'cuckoo clock** *n.* Kuckucksuhr, *die*

**cucumber** ['kjuːkʌmbə(r)] *n.* [Salat]gurke, *die*

**cuddle** ['kʌdl] **1.** *n.* enge Umarmung. **2.** *v. t.* schmusen mit; hätscheln ⟨*kleines Kind*⟩. **3.** *v. i.* schmusen

**cuddly** ['kʌdlɪ] *adj.* zum Schmusen nachgestellt. **cuddly 'toy** *n.* Plüschtier, *das*

**cudgel** ['kʌdʒl] *n.* Knüppel, *der*

**¹cue** [kjuː] *n. (Billiards etc.)* Queue, *das*

**²cue** *n. (Theatre)* Stichwort, *das*

**¹cuff** [kʌf] *n.* **a)** Manschette, *die;* **off the ~** *(fig.)* aus dem Stegreif; **b)** *(Amer.: trouser turn-up)* [Hosen]aufschlag, *der*

**²cuff** **1.** *v. t.* **~ sb.** jmdm. einen Klaps geben. **2.** *n.* Klaps, *der*

**'cuff-link** *n.* Manschettenknopf, *der*

**cul-de-sac** ['kʌldəsæk] *n.* Sackgasse, *die*

**culinary** ['kʌlɪnərɪ] *adj.* kulinarisch

**culminate** ['kʌlmɪneɪt] *v. i.* gipfeln; **~ in sth.** in etw. *(Dat.)* seinen Höchststand erreichen. **culmination** [kʌlmɪ'neɪʃn] *n.* Höhepunkt, *der*

**culottes** [kjuː'lɒts] *n. pl.* Hosenrock, *der*

**culprit** ['kʌlprɪt] *n.* Täter, *der*/Täterin, *die*

**cult** [kʌlt] *n.* Kult, *der*

**cultivate** ['kʌltɪveɪt] *v. t.* kultivieren *(auch fig.);* bestellen ⟨*Acker, Land*⟩; anbauen ⟨*Pflanzen*⟩. **cultivation** [kʌltɪ'veɪʃn] *n. see* **cultivate:** Kultivierung, *die;* Bestellen *das;* Anbau, *der*

**culture** ['kʌltʃə(r)] *n.* Kultur, *die.* **'cultured** *adj.* kultiviert

**cumbersome** ['kʌmbəsəm] *adj.* hinderlich ⟨*Kleider*⟩; sperrig ⟨*Pakete*⟩; schwerfällig ⟨*Arbeitsweise*⟩

**cunning** ['kʌnɪŋ] **1.** *n.* Schläue, *die.* **2.** *adj.* schlau

**cup** [kʌp] *n.* **a)** Tasse, *die;* **b)** *(prize, competition)* Pokal, *der;* **c)** *(~ful)* Tasse, *die;* **a ~ of coffee/tea** eine Tasse Kaffee/Tee

**cupboard** ['kʌbəd] *n.* Schrank, *der*

**'Cup Final** *n.* Pokalendspiel, *das*

**cupful** ['kʌpfl] *n.* Tasse, *die;* **a ~ of water** eine Tasse Wasser

**curable** ['kjʊərəbl] *adj.* heilbar

**curate** ['kjʊərət] *n.* Kurat, *der*

**curator** [kjʊə'reɪtə(r)] *n. (of museum)* Direktor, *der*/Direktorin, *die*

**curb** [kɜːb] *v. t.* zügeln

**curdle** ['kɜːdl] *v. i.* gerinnen

**cure** [kjʊə(r)] **1.** *n.* [Heil]mittel, *das* (**for** gegen); *(fig.)* Mittel, *das.* **2.** *v. t.* **a)** heilen; **b)** [ein]pökeln ⟨*Fleisch*⟩

**curfew** ['kɜːfjuː] *n.* Ausgangssperre, *die*

**curiosity** [kjʊərɪ'ɒsɪtɪ] *n.* **a)** Neugier[de], *die;* **b)** *(object)* Wunderding, *das*

**curious** ['kjʊərɪəs] *adj.* **a)** *(inquisitive)* neugierig; **b)** *(strange, odd)* seltsam

**curl** [kɜːl] **1.** *n.* Locke, *die.* **2.** *v. t.* locken. **3.** *v. i.* **a)** sich locken; **b)** ⟨*Straße, Fluß:*⟩ sich winden. **'curler** *n.* Lockenwickler, *der.* **'curly** *adj.* lockig

**currant** ['kʌrənt] *n.* Korinthe, *die*

**currency** ['kʌrənsɪ] *n. (money)* Währung, *die;* **foreign currencies** Devisen

**current** ['kʌrənt] **1.** *adj.* **a)** verbreitet ⟨*Meinung*⟩; gebräuchlich ⟨*Wort*⟩; **b)** laufend ⟨*Jahr, Monat*⟩; **c)** *(the present)* aktuell ⟨*Ereignis, Mode*⟩; Tages-⟨*politik, -preis*⟩; **~ affairs** Tagespolitik, *die.* **2.** *n.* **a)** *(of water, air)* Strömung, *die;* **b)** *(Electr.)* Strom, *der.* **'current account** *n.* Girokonto, *das*

**'currently** *adv.* zur Zeit

**curriculum** [kə'rɪkjʊləm] *n.* Lehrplan, *der.* **curriculum vitae** [~ 'viːtaɪ] *n.* Lebenslauf, *der*

**¹curry** ['kʌrɪ] *n.* Curry[gericht], *das*
**²curry** *v.t.* ~ **favour [with sb.]** sich [bei jmdm.] einschmeicheln
**curse** [kɜ:s] **1.** *n.* Fluch, *der.* **2.** *v.t.* verfluchen. **3.** *v.i.* fluchen
**cursory** ['kɜ:sərɪ] *adj.* flüchtig
**curt** [kɜ:t] *adj.* kurz angebunden; kurz und schroff ⟨*Brief*⟩
**curtain** ['kɜ:tən] *n.* Vorhang, *der;* **draw** *or* **pull the** ~**s** *(open)* die Vorhänge aufziehen; *(close)* die Vorhänge zuziehen
**curtsy** ['kɜ:tsɪ] **1.** *n.* Knicks, *der.* **2.** *v.i.* einen Knicks machen (**to** vor + *Dat.*)
**curve** [kɜ:v] **1.** *v.t.* krümmen. **2.** *v.i.* ⟨*Straße, Fluß:*⟩ eine Biegung machen. **3.** *n.* Kurve, *die*
**cushion** ['kʊʃn] **1.** *n.* Kissen, *das.* **2.** *v.t.* dämpfen ⟨*Aufprall, Stoß*⟩
**cushy** ['kʊʃɪ] *adj. (coll.)* bequem
**custard** ['kʌstəd] *n.* ≈ Vanillesoße, *die*
**custodian** [kʌs'təʊdɪən] *n. (of museum)* Wächter, *der*/Wächterin, *die; (of valuables)* Hüter, *der*/Hüterin, *die*
**custody** ['kʌstədɪ] *n.* **a)** *(care)* Obhut, *die;* **b)** *(imprisonment)* **[be] in** ~: in Haft [sein]
**custom** ['kʌstəm] *n.* **a)** Brauch, *der;* **b)** *in pl. (duty on imports)* Zoll, *der.* '**customs officer** *n.* Zollbeamter, *der*/-beamtin, *die.* **customary** ['kʌstəmərɪ] *adj.* üblich
**customer** ['kʌstəmə(r)] *n.* Kunde, *der*/Kundin, *die*
**cut** [kʌt] **1.** *v.t.,* **-tt-, cut a)** schneiden; durchschneiden ⟨*Seil*⟩; ~ **one's leg** sich *(Dat. od. Akk.)* ins Bein schneiden; **b)** abschneiden ⟨*Scheibe*⟩; schneiden ⟨*Hecke*⟩; mähen ⟨*Getreide, Gras*⟩; ~ **one's nails** sich *(Dat.)* die Nägel schneiden; **c)** *(reduce)* senken ⟨*Preise*⟩; kürzen ⟨*Lohn*⟩; **d)** ~ **sth. short** *(interrupt)* etw. abbrechen. **2.** *v.i.,* **-tt-, cut a)** ⟨*Messer:*⟩ schneiden; **b)** ~ **through** *or* **across the field/park** [quer] über das Feld/durch den Park gehen. **3.** *n.* **a)** *(act of cutting)* Schnitt, *der;* **b)** *(stroke, blow) (with knife)* Schnitt, *der; (with sword, whip)* Hieb, *der;* **c)** *(reduction)* Kürzung, *die; (in prices)* Senkung, *die; (in services)* Verringerung, *die;* **d)** *(of meat)* Stück, *das.* **cut a'way** *v.t.* abschneiden. **cut 'back** *v.t.* **a)** *(reduce)* einschränken; **b)** *(prune)* stutzen. **cut 'down 1.** *v.t.* **a)** fällen ⟨*Baum*⟩; **b)** *(reduce)* einschränken. **2.** *v.i.* ~ **down on sth.** etw. einschränken. **cut 'off** *v.t.* abschnei-

den; unterbrechen ⟨*Telefongespräch, Sprecher*⟩. **cut 'out 1.** *v.t.* **a)** ausschneiden (of aus); **b) be** ~ **out for** geeignet sein zu. **2.** *v.i.* ⟨*Motor:*⟩ aussetzen. **cut 'up** *v.t.* zerschneiden
**cutlery** ['kʌtlərɪ] *n.* Besteck, *das*
**cutlet** ['kʌtlɪt] *n.* Kotelett, *das*
'**cut-price** *adj.* herabgesetzt
'**cutting 1.** *adj.* beißend ⟨*Bemerkung, Antwort*⟩. **2.** *n. (from newspaper)* Ausschnitt, *der*
**c. v.** *abbr.* **curriculum vitae**
**cycle** ['saɪkl] **1.** *n.* **a)** *(recurrent period)* Zyklus, *der;* **b)** *(bicycle)* Rad, *das.* **2.** *v.i.* radfahren. **cyclist** ['saɪklɪst] *n.* Radfahrer, *der*/-fahrerin, *die*
**cylinder** ['sɪlɪndə(r)] *n.* Zylinder, *der.* **cylindrical** [sɪ'lɪndrɪkl] *adj.* zylindrisch
**cymbals** ['sɪmblz] *n. pl.* Becken *Pl.*
**cynic** ['sɪnɪk] *n.* Zyniker, *der.* **cynical** ['sɪnɪkl] *adj.* zynisch; bissig ⟨*Bemerkung, Worte*⟩. **cynicism** ['sɪnɪsɪzm] *n.* Zynismus, *der*
**Cyprus** ['saɪprəs] *pr. n.* Zypern *(das)*
**Czech** [tʃek] **1.** *adj.* tschechisch. **2.** *n.* **a)** *(language)* Tschechisch, *das;* **b)** *(person)* Tscheche, *der*/Tschechin, *die*
**Czechoslovakia** [tʃekəʊsləˈvækɪə] *pr.n. (Hist.)* die Tschechoslowakei.
**Czechoslovakian** [tʃekəʊsləˈvækɪən] *(Hist.)* **1.** *adj.* tschechoslowakisch. **2.** *n.* Tschechoslowake, *der*/Tschechoslowakin, *die*
**Czech Republic** *pr. n.* Tschechische Republik; Tschechien *(das)*

# D

**D, d** [di:] *n.* D, d, *das*
**dab** [dæb] **1.** *n.* Tupfer, *der.* **2.** *v.t.,* **-bb-** abtupfen; ~ **sth. on** *or* **against sth.** etw. auf etw. *(Akk.)* tupfen
**dabble** ['dæbl] *v.i.* ~ **in sth.** sich in etw. *(Dat.)* versuchen
**dachshund** ['dækshʊnd] *n.* Dackel, *der*
**dad** [dæd] *n. (coll.)* Vater, *der*
**daddy** ['dædɪ] *n. (coll.)* Vati, *der (fam.)*
**daddy-'long-legs** *n.* Schnake, *die*
**daffodil** ['dæfədɪl] *n.* Osterglocke, *die*

**daft** [dɑːft] *adj.* doof *(ugs.)*

**dagger** ['dægə(r)] *n.* Dolch, *der*

**daily** ['deɪlɪ] 1. *adj.* täglich; ~ |news|-**paper** Tageszeitung, *die.* 2. *adv.* täglich. 3. *n.* Tageszeitung, *die*

**dainty** ['deɪntɪ] *adj.* zierlich; anmutig ⟨*Bewegung, Person*⟩; zart ⟨*Gesichts-züge*⟩

**dairy** ['deərɪ] *n.* a) Molkerei, *die*; b) *(shop)* Milchladen, *der*

**dais** ['deɪs] *n.* Podium, *das*

**daisy** ['deɪzɪ] *n.* Gänseblümchen, *das*

**dam** [dæm] 1. *n.* [Stau]damm, *der.* 2. *v.t.*, **-mm-:** a) ~ |up| sth. etw. ab-blocken; b) aufstauen ⟨*Fluß*⟩

**damage** ['dæmɪdʒ] 1. *n.* Schaden, *der.* 2. *v.t.* beschädigen. **damaging** ['dæmɪdʒɪŋ] *adj.* schädlich (**to** für)

**damn** [dæm] 1. *v.t.* verdammen. 2. *adj., adv., int. (coll.)* verdammt *(ugs.).* 3. *n.* **he doesn't give** *or* **care a ~:** ihm ist es völlig wurscht *(ugs.)*

**damp** [dæmp] 1. *adj.* feucht. 2. *v.t. see* **dampen.** 3. *n.* Feuchtigkeit, *die*

**dampen** ['dæmpn] *v.t.* befeuchten; *(fig.)* dämpfen ⟨*Begeisterung, Eifer*⟩

**dampness** *n.* Feuchtigkeit, *die*

**dance** [dɑːns] 1. *v.i. & t.* tanzen. 2. *n.* a) Tanz, *der*; b) *(party)* Tanzveranstal-tung, *die*; *(private)* Tanzparty, *die*. **dance-hall** *n.* Tanzsaal, *der*

**dancer** *n.* Tänzer, *der*/Tänzerin, *die*

**dandelion** ['dændɪlaɪən] *n.* Löwen-zahn, *der*

**dandruff** ['dændrʌf] *n.* [Kopf]schup-pen *Pl.*

**Dane** [deɪn] *n.* Däne, *der*/Dänin, *die*

**danger** ['deɪndʒə(r)] *n.* Gefahr, *die*; **in/out of ~:** in/außer Gefahr. **dan-gerous** ['deɪndʒərəs] *adj.*, '**danger-ously** *adv.* gefährlich

**dangle** ['dæŋgl] 1. *v.i.* baumeln (**from** an + *Dat.*). 2. *v.t.* baumeln lassen

**Danish** ['deɪnɪʃ] 1. *adj.* dänisch; **sb. is ~:** jmd. ist Däne/Dänin. 2. *n.* Dä-nisch, *das; see also* **English 2 a**

**dank** [dæŋk] *adj.* feucht

**Danube** ['dænjuːb] *pr. n.* Donau, *die*

**dare** [deə(r)] 1. *v.t.* a) |es| wagen; ~ **to do sth.** |es| wagen, etw. zu tun; b) *(challenge)* ~ **sb. to do sth.** jmdn. auf-stacheln, etw. zu tun; **I ~ you!** trau dich! 2. *n.* Mutprobe, *die.* **daring** ['deərɪŋ] *adj.* kühn

**dark** [dɑːk] 1. *adj.* dunkel; *(dark-haired)* dunkelhaarig; ~**-blue/-brown** dunkelblau/-braun; ~ **glasses** dunkle Brille. 2. *n.* a) Dunkel, *das*; **in the ~:** im Dunkeln; **keep sb. in the ~** *(fig.)*

jmdn. im dunkeln lassen; b) *no art. (nightfall)* Einbruch der Dunkelheit.

**darken** ['dɑːkn] *v.t.* verdunkeln.

**darkness** *n.* Dunkelheit, *die*

**dark-room** *n.* Dunkelkammer, *die*

**darling** ['dɑːlɪŋ] *n.* Liebling, *der*

**darn** [dɑːn] *v.t.* stopfen

**dart** [dɑːt] 1. *n.* a) *(missile)* Pfeil, *der*; b) *(Sport)* Wurfpfeil, *der*; ~**s** *sing. (game)* Darts, *das.* 2. *v.i.* sausen.

**dartboard** *n.* Dartscheibe, *die*

**dash** [dæʃ] 1. *v.i.* sausen. 2. *v.t. (fling)* schleudern. 3. *n.* a) **make a ~:** rasen *(ugs.)* (**for** zu); b) *(horizontal stroke)* Gedankenstrich, *der*; c) *(small amount)* Schuß, *der*

**dashboard** *n.* Armaturenbrett, *das*

**data** ['deɪtə, 'dɑːtə] *n.* Daten *Pl.* **data 'processing** *n.* Datenverarbeitung, *die*

¹**date** [deɪt] *n. (Bot.)* Dattel, *die*

²**date** 1: *n.* a) Datum, *das*; *(on coin etc.)* Jahreszahl, *die*; ~ **of birth** Geburtsda-tum, *das*; **be out of ~:** altmodisch sein; **to ~:** bis heute; b) *(coll.: appoint-ment)* Verabredung, *die*; **have/make a ~ with sb.** mit jmdm. verabredet sein/ sich mit jmdm. verabreden. 2. *v.t.* a) datieren; b) *(coll.: make seem old)* alt machen. 3. *v.i.* ~ **back to/~ from** stammen aus. **dated** ['deɪtɪd] *adj.* alt-modisch. **date-line** *n.* Datumsgren-ze, *die*

**dative** ['deɪtɪv] *adj. & n.* ~ |case| Dativ, *der*

**daub** [dɔːb] *v.t. (smear)* beschmieren; *(put crudely)* schmieren

**daughter** ['dɔːtə(r)] *n.* Tochter, *die*. **daughter-in-law** *n., pl.* **daughters-in-law** Schwiegertochter, *die*

**daunt** [dɔːnt] *v.t.* entmutigen

**dawdle** ['dɔːdl] *v.i.* bummeln *(ugs.)*

**dawn** [dɔːn] 1. *v.i.* dämmern; **sth. ~s |up|on sb.** etw. dämmert jmdm. 2. *n.* [Morgen]dämmerung, *die*; **at ~:** im Morgengrauen

**day** [deɪ] *n.* Tag, *der*; **all ~ |long|** den ganzen Tag [lang]; **for two ~s** zwei Ta-ge [lang]; **the ~ before yesterday/after tomorrow** vorgestern/übermorgen; ~ **after ~:** Tag für Tag; ~ **in** ~ **out** tag-aus, tagein; **in the ~s when ...:** zu der Zeit, als ...; **these ~s** heutzutage; **in those ~s** damals

**day:** ~**break** *n.* Tagesanbruch, *der*; ~**-dream** 1. *n.* Tagtraum, *der*; 2. *v.i.* träumen; ~**light** *n.* Tageslicht, *das*; **in broad ~light** am hellichten Tag[e]; ~**-re'turn** *n.* Tagesrückfahrkarte, die; ~-**time** n. Tag, der; ~-**to-~** adj. [tag]täglich; ~ **trip** n. Tagesausflug, der

**daze** ['deɪz] v. t. benommen machen. **dazed** ['deɪzd] adj. benommen

**dazzle** ['dæzl] v. t. blenden

**DC** abbr. **direct current** GS

**dead** [ded] 1. adj. a) tot; b) plötzlich ⟨Halt⟩; genau ⟨Mitte⟩; c) (numb) taub. 2. adv. völlig; ~ **straight** schnurgerade; ~ **easy/slow** kinderleicht/ganz langsam; ~ **on time** auf die Minute; ~ **tired** todmüde

**deaden** ['dedn] v. t. dämpfen; betäuben ⟨Schmerz⟩

**dead:** ~ **'end** n. Sackgasse, die; ~ **'heat** n. totes Rennen; ~**line** n. [letzter] Termin; ~**lock** n. völliger Stillstand

**deadly** ['dedlɪ] adj. tödlich; (fig. coll.: boring) todlangweilig

**Dead 'Sea** pr. n. Tote Meer, das

**deaf** [def] adj. taub; ~ **and dumb** taubstumm. **deafen** ['defn] v. t. ~ **sb.** bei jmdm. zur Taubheit führen; **I was ~ed by the noise** (fig.) ich war von dem Lärm wie betäubt. **'deafening** adj. ohrenbetäubend. **'deafness** n. Taubheit, die

**¹deal** [diːl] 1. v. t., **dealt** [delt] a) (Cards) austeilen; b) ~ **sb. a blow** jmdm. einen Schlag versetzen. 2. v. i., **dealt** a) (do business) ~ **in sth.** mit etw. handeln; b) ~ **with sth.** (occupy oneself) sich mit etw. befassen; (manage) mit etw. fertig werden; (be about) von etw. handeln; ~ **with sb.** mit jmdm. fertig werden. 3. n. (coll.: arrangement) Geschäft, das. **deal 'out** v. t. verteilen

**²deal** n. **a great** or **good ~ :** viel; (often) ziemlich viel; **a great** or **good ~ of** viel

**'dealer** n. a) Händler, der; b) (Cards) Geber, der; **he's the ~ :** er gibt

**'dealings** n. pl. **have ~ with sb.** mit jmdm. zu tun haben

**dealt** see ¹**deal** 1, 2

**dean** [diːn] n. (Eccl.) Dechant, der

**dear** [dɪə(r)] 1. adj. a) lieb; **sb./sth. is ~ to sb.['s heart]** jmd. liebt jmdn./etw.; (beginning letter) **D~ Sir/Madam** Sehr geehrter Herr/Sehr verehrte gnädige Frau; **D~ Mr Jones/Mrs Jones** Sehr geehrter Herr Jones/Sehr verehrte Frau Jones; **D~ Malcolm/Emily** Lieber Malcolm/Liebe Emily; b) (expensive) teuer. 2. int. ~, ~!, ~ **me!**, **oh** ~! [ach] du liebe od. meine Güte! **'dearly** adv. a) von ganzem Herzen; b) (at high price) teuer

**dearth** [dɜːθ] n. Mangel, der (of an + Dat.)

**death** [deθ] n. a) Tod, der; ... **to ~ :** zu Tode ...; **bleed to ~ :** verbluten; b) (instance) Todesfall, der

**death:** ~ **penalty** n. Todesstrafe, die; ~ **sentence** n. Todesurteil, das; ~**-trap** n. lebensgefährliche Sache

**debatable** [dɪ'beɪtəbl] adj. (questionable) fraglich

**debate** [dɪ'beɪt] n. Debatte, die

**debit** ['debɪt] 1. n. Soll, das. 2. v. t. belasten ⟨Konto⟩

**debris** ['debriː] n. Trümmer Pl.

**debt** [det] n. Schuld, die; **be in ~ :** Schulden haben; **get into ~ :** in Schulden geraten. **debtor** ['detə(r)] n. Schuldner, der/Schuldnerin, die

**début** (Amer.: **debut**) ['deɪbuː, 'deɪbjuː] n. Debüt, das

**Dec.** abbr. **December** Dez.

**decade** ['dekeɪd] n. Jahrzehnt, das

**decadent** ['dekədənt] adj. dekadent

**decanter** [dɪ'kæntə(r)] n. Karaffe, die

**decay** [dɪ'keɪ] 1. v. i. verrotten; ⟨Gebäude:⟩ zerfallen; ⟨Zahn:⟩ faul werden. 2. n. Verrotten, das; (of building) Zerfall, der; (of tooth) Fäule, die

**deceased** [dɪ'siːst] 1. adj verstorben. 2. n. Verstorbene, der/die

**deceit** [dɪ'siːt] n. Täuschung, die. **deceitful** [dɪ'siːtfl] adj. falsch ⟨Person, Art⟩; hinterlistig ⟨Trick⟩

**deceive** [dɪ'siːv] v. t. täuschen; (be unfaithful to) betrügen

**December** [dɪ'sembə(r)] n. Dezember, der; see also **August**

**decency** ['diːsənsɪ] n. Anstand, der

**decent** ['diːsənt] adj. anständig

**deception** [dɪ'sepʃn] n. Betrug, der; (being deceived) Täuschung, die. **deceptive** [dɪ'septɪv] adj. trügerisch

**decibel** ['desɪbel] n. Dezibel, das

**decide** [dɪ'saɪd] 1. v. t. a) (settle, judge) entscheiden über (+ Akk.); b) (resolve) ~ **that** ...: beschließen, daß ...; ~ **to do sth.** sich entschließen, etw. zu tun. 2. v. i. sich entscheiden (**in favour of** zugunsten von, **against** gegen). **de'cided** adj., **de'cidedly** adv. entschieden

**deciduous** [dɪ'sɪdjʊəs] adj. ~ **tree** ≈ Laubbaum, der

**decimal** ['desɪml] 1. n. Dezimalbruch, der. 2. adj. Dezimal-; ~ **'point** Komma, das

**decimate** ['desɪmeɪt] v. t. dezimieren

**decipher** [dɪ'saɪfə(r)] v. t. entziffern

**decision** [dɪ'sɪʒn] n. Entscheidung,

*die.* **decisive** [dɪ'saɪsɪv] *adj.* entscheidend

**deck** [dek] *n.* Deck, *das;* on ~: an Deck; **below** ~|s| unter Deck. '**deckchair** *n.* Liegestuhl, *der*

**declaration** [deklə'reɪʃn] *n.* Erklärung, *die*

**declare** [dɪ'kleə(r)] *v. t.* erklären; kundtun *(geh.)* ⟨*Wunsch, Absicht*⟩; ~ **sth./sb.** |to be| sth. etw./jmdn. für etw. erklären

**declension** [dɪ'klenʃn] *n.* Deklination, *die*

**decline** [dɪ'klaɪn] **1.** *v. i.* nachlassen; ⟨*Anzahl:*⟩ sinken. **2.** *v. t.* **a)** ablehnen; **b)** *(Ling.)* deklinieren. **3.** *n. see* 1: Nachlassen, *das*/Sinken, *das* (in *Gen.*); **be on the** ~: nachlassen/sinken

**decode** [di:'kəʊd] *v. t.* entziffern

**decompose** [di:kəm'pəʊz] *v. i.* sich zersetzen

**décor** ['deɪkɔ:(r)] *n.* Ausstattung, *die*

**decorate** ['dekəreɪt] *v. t.* **a)** schmücken ⟨*Raum, Straße, Baum*⟩; verzieren ⟨*Kuchen, Kleid*⟩; *(paint)* streichen; *(wallpaper)* tapezieren; **b)** *(award medal etc. to)* auszeichnen.

**decoration** [dekə'reɪʃn] *n.* **a)** Schmücken, *das; (with paint)* Streichen, *das; (with wallpaper)* Tapezieren, *das; (adornment)* Schmuck, *der;* **c)** *(medal etc.)* Auszeichnung, *die.* **decorative** ['dekərətɪv] *adj.* dekorativ.

**decorator** ['dekəreɪtə(r)] *n.* Maler, *der; (paper-hanger)* Tapezierer, *der*

**decorum** [dɪ'kɔ:rəm] *n.* Schicklichkeit, *die (geh.)*

**decoy** ['di:kɔɪ] *n.* Lockvogel, *der*

**decrease** **1.** [dɪ'kri:s] *v. i.* abnehmen; ⟨*Stärke:*⟩ nachlassen. **2.** [dɪ'kri:s] *v. t.* [ver]mindern ⟨*Wert, Lärm*⟩; schmälern ⟨*Popularität, Macht*⟩. **3.** ['di:kri:s] *n.* Rückgang, *der; (in weight)* Abnahme, *die; (in strength)* Nachlassen, *das; (in value, noise)* Minderung, *die*

**decree** [dɪ'kri:] **1.** *n.* Dekret, *das;* Erlaß, *der.* **2.** *v. t.* verfügen

**decrepit** [dɪ'krepɪt] *adj.* altersschwach; *(dilapidated)* heruntergekommen

**dedicate** ['dedɪkeɪt] *v. t.* ~ **sth. to sb.** jmdm. etw. widmen. '**dedicated** *adj.* **a)** *(devoted)* be ~ to sth./sb. nur für etw./jmdn. leben; **b)** *(to vocation)* hingebungsvoll; **a** ~ **teacher** ein Lehrer mit Leib und Seele. **dedication** [dedɪ'keɪʃn] *n.* **a)** Widmung, *die* (to *Dat.*); **b)** *(devotion)* Hingabe, *die*

**deduce** [dɪ'dju:s] *v. t.* ~ **sth.** |from sth.| etw. [aus etw.] schließen

**deduct** [dɪ'dʌkt] *v. t.* ~ **sth.** |from sth.| etw. [von etw.] abziehen. **deduction** [dɪ'dʌkʃn] *n.* **a)** *(deducting)* Abzug, *der;* **b)** *(deducing, thing deduced)* Ableitung, *die;* **c)** *(amount)* Abzüge *Pl.*

**deed** [di:d] *n.* **a)** Tat, *die;* **b)** *(Law)* Urkunde, *die*

**deem** [di:m] *v. t.* erachten für

**deep** [di:p] **1.** *adj. (lit. or fig.)* tief; tiefgründig ⟨*Bemerkung*⟩; **water ten feet** ~: drei Meter tiefes Wasser; **take a** ~ **breath** tief Atem holen; **be** ~ **in thought** in Gedanken versunken sein. **2.** *adv.* tief. '**deepen 1.** *v. t.* vertiefen. **2.** *v. i.* sich vertiefen. **deep-'freeze** *v. t.* tiefgefrieren. '**deeply** *adv. (lit. or fig.)* tief; äußerst ⟨*interessiert, dankbar*⟩

**deer** [dɪə(r)] *n., pl. same* Hirsch, *der; (roe*~*)* Reh, *das*

**deface** [dɪ'feɪs] *v. t.* verunstalten

**defamation** [defə'meɪʃn] *n.* Diffamierung, *die.* **defamatory** [dɪ'fæmətərɪ] *adj.* diffamierend

**default** [dɪ'fɔ:lt, dɪ'fɒlt] **1.** *n.* **lose/go by** ~: durch Abwesenheit verlieren/nicht zur Geltung kommen; **win by** ~: durch Nichterscheinen des Gegners gewinnen. **2.** *v. i.* ~ **on one's payments/ debts** seinen Zahlungsverpflichtungen nicht nachkommen

**defeat** [dɪ'fi:t] **1.** *v. t.* besiegen. **2.** *n. (being* ~*ed)* Niederlage, *die; (*~*ing)* Sieg, *der (of* über + *Akk.*). **de'featist** *adj.* defätistisch

**defect 1.** ['di:fekt] *n.* **a)** *(lack)* Mangel, *der;* **b)** *(shortcoming)* Fehler, *der.* **2.** [dɪ'fekt] *v. i.* überlaufen (to zu). **defection** [dɪ'fekʃn] *n.* Flucht, *die.* **defective** [dɪ'fektɪv] *adj.* defekt ⟨*Maschine*⟩; fehlerhaft ⟨*Material, Arbeiten, Methode*⟩. **defector** [dɪ'fektə(r)] *n.* Überläufer, *der/*-läuferin, *die*

**defence** [dɪ'fens] *n. (Brit.)* Verteidigung, *die; (means of* ~*)* Schutz, *der.* **de'fenceless** *adj.* wehrlos

**defend** [dɪ'fend] *v. t.* verteidigen. **defendant** [dɪ'fendənt] *n. (Law) (accused)* Angeklagte, *der/die; (sued)* Beklagte, *der/die.* **de'fender** *n.* Verteidiger, *der*

**defense** etc. *(Amer.) see* **defence** etc.

**defensive** [dɪ'fensɪv] **1.** *adj.* defensiv. **2.** *n.* be on the ~: in der Defensive sein

¹**defer** [dɪ'fɜ:(r)] *v. t.,* -rr- aufschieben

²**defer** *v. i.,* -rr-: ~ |to sb.| sich |jmdm.| beugen. **deference** ['defərəns] *n.* Re-

spekt, *der;* **in** ~ **to sb./sth.** aus Achtung vor jmdm./etw. **deferential** [defə'renʃl] *adj.* respektvoll

**defiance** [dɪ'faɪəns] *n.* Trotz, *der;* **in** ~ **of sb./sth.** jmdm./einer Sache zum Trotz

**defiant** [dɪ'faɪənt] *adj.,* **de'fiantly** *adv.* trotzig

**deficiency** [dɪ'fɪʃənsɪ] *n.* Mangel, *der*

**deficient** [dɪ'fɪʃənt] *adj.* unzulänglich; **sb./sth. is** ~ **in sth.** jmdm./einer Sache mangelt es an etw. *(Dat.)*

**deficit** ['defɪsɪt] *n.* Defizit, *das* (**of** an + *Dat.*)

**defile** [dɪ'faɪl] *v.t.* verpesten ⟨*Luft*⟩; beflecken ⟨*Reinheit, Unschuld*⟩

**define** [dɪ'faɪn] *v.t.* definieren

**definite** ['defɪnɪt] *adj.* bestimmt; eindeutig ⟨*Antwort, Entscheidung, Beschluß, Verbesserung*⟩; klar umrissen ⟨*Ziel, Plan*⟩; klar ⟨*Vorstellung*⟩; genau ⟨*Zeitpunkt*⟩. **'definitely 1.** *adv.* bestimmt; eindeutig ⟨*festgelegt, größer sein, verbessert*⟩; endgültig ⟨*entscheiden*⟩. **2.** *int.* *(coll.)* na, klar *(ugs.)*

**definition** [defɪ'nɪʃn] *n.* Definition, *die;* *(Telev., Phot.)* Schärfe, *die*

**definitive** [dɪ'fɪnɪtɪv] *adj.* endgültig ⟨*Beschluß, Antwort, Urteil*⟩; *(authoritative)* maßgeblich

**deflate** [dɪ'fleɪt] *v.t.* die Luft ablassen aus; *(fig.)* ernüchtern. **deflation** [dɪ'fleɪʃn] *n.* *(Econ.)* Deflation, *die*

**deflect** [dɪ'flekt] *v.t.* brechen ⟨*Licht*⟩; ~ **sb./sth. [from sb./sth.]** jmdn./etw. [von jmdm./einer Sache] ablenken

**deform** [dɪ'fɔ:m] *v.t.* deformieren. **deformed** [dɪ'fɔ:md] *adj.* entstellt ⟨*Gesicht*⟩; verunstaltet ⟨*Person, Körperteil*⟩. **deformity** [dɪ'fɔ:mɪtɪ] *n.* *(malformation)* Verunstaltung, *die*

**defraud** [dɪ'frɔ:d] *v.t.* ~ **sb. [of sth.]** jmdn. [um etw.] betrügen

**defray** [dɪ'freɪ] *v.t.* bestreiten

**defrost** [di:'frɒst] *v.t.* auftauen ⟨*Speisen*⟩; abtauen ⟨*Kühlschrank*⟩

**deft** [deft] *adj.,* **'deftly** *adv.* sicher und geschickt

**defunct** [dɪ'fʌŋkt] *adj.* defekt ⟨*Maschine*⟩; veraltet ⟨*Gesetz*⟩

**defuse** [di:'fju:z] *v.t.* entschärfen

**defy** [dɪ'faɪ] *v.t.* **a)** *(resist openly)* ~ **sb.** jmdm. trotzen; **b)** *(refuse to obey)* ~ **sb./sth.** sich jmdm./einer Sache widersetzen

**degenerate** [dɪ'dʒenəreɪt] *v.i.* ~ **[into sth.]** [zu etw.] verkommen

**degradation** [degrə'deɪʃn] *n.* Erniedrigung, *die*

**degrade** [dɪ'greɪd] *v.t.* erniedrigen

**degree** [dɪ'gri:] *n.* **a)** Grad, *der;* **20** ~**s** 20 Grad; **b)** *(academic rank)* [akademischer] Grad

**de-ice** [di:'aɪs] *v.t.* enteisen

**deign** [deɪn] *v.t.* ~ **to do sth.** sich [dazu] herablassen, etw. zu tun

**deity** ['di:ɪtɪ] *n.* Gottheit, *die*

**dejected** [dɪ'dʒektɪd] *adj.* niedergeschlagen. **dejection** [dɪ'dʒekʃn] *n.* Niedergeschlagenheit, *die*

**delay** [dɪ'leɪ] **1.** *v.t. (make late)* aufhalten; verzögern ⟨*Ankunft, Abfahrt*⟩; **the train has been** ~**ed** der Zug hat Verspätung. **2.** *v.i.* warten. **3.** *n.* **a)** Verzögerung, *die* (**to** bei); **b)** *(Transport)* Verspätung, *die*

**delectable** [dɪ'lektəbl] *adj.* köstlich

**delegate 1.** ['delɪgət] *n.* Delegierte, *der/die.* **2.** ['delɪgeɪt] *v.t.* delegieren (**to** an + *Akk.*). **delegation** [delɪ'geɪʃn] *n.* Delegation, *die*

**delete** [dɪ'li:t] *v.t.* streichen (**from** in + *Dat.*); *(Computing)* löschen. **deletion** [dɪ'li:ʃn] *n.* Streichung, *die;* *(Computing)* Löschung, *die*

**deliberate** [dɪ'lɪbərət] *adj.* **a)** *(intentional)* absichtlich; bewußt ⟨*Lüge, Irreführung*⟩; **b)** *(fully considered)* wohlüberlegt. **de'liberately** *adv.* absichtlich. **deliberation** [dɪlɪbə'reɪʃn] *n.* Überlegung, *die;* *(discussion)* Beratung, *die*

**delicacy** ['delɪkəsɪ] *n.* **a)** *(tactfulness and care)* Feingefühl, *das;* **b)** *(food)* Delikatesse, *die*

**delicate** ['delɪkət] *adj.* zart; *(requiring careful handling)* empfindlich; delikat ⟨*Frage, Angelegenheit*⟩

**delicatessen** [delɪkə'tesən] *n.* Feinkostgeschäft, *das*

**delicious** [dɪ'lɪʃəs] *adj.* köstlich

**delight** [dɪ'laɪt] **1.** *v.t.* erfreuen. **2.** *v.i.* **sb.** ~**s in doing sth.** es macht jmdm. Freude, etw. zu tun. **3.** *n.* Freude, *die* (**at** über + *Akk.*; **in** an + *Dat.*). **de'lighted** *adj.* **be** ~ ⟨*Person:*⟩ hocherfreut sein; **be** ~ **by** *or* **with sth.** sich über etw. *(Akk.)* freuen. **delightful** [dɪ'laɪtfl] *adj.* wunderbar; köstlich ⟨*Geschmack*⟩; reizend ⟨*Person, Landschaft*⟩. **de'lightfully** *adv.* wunderbar

**delinquent** [dɪ'lɪŋkwənt] **1.** *n.* Randalierer, *der.* **2.** *adj.* kriminell

**delirious** [dɪ'lɪrɪəs] *adj.* **be** ~: im Delirium sein; **be** ~ **[with sth.]** *(fig.)* außer sich [vor etw. *(Dat.)*] sein

**delirium** [dɪ'lɪrɪəm] *n.* Delirium, *das*

**deliver** [dɪ'lɪvə(r)] *v. t.* **a)** bringen; liefern ⟨*Ware*⟩; zustellen ⟨*Post, Telegramm*⟩; überbringen ⟨*Botschaft*⟩; **b)** halten ⟨*Rede*⟩. **delivery** [dɪ'lɪvərɪ] *n.* Lieferung, *die; (of letters, parcels)* Zustellung, *die.* **de'livery van** *n.* Lieferwagen, *der*

**delta** ['deltə] *n.* Delta, *das*

**delude** [dɪ'lju:d] *v. t.* täuschen

**deluge** ['delju:dʒ] **1.** *n.* sintflutartiger Regen. **2.** *v. t.* überschwemmen

**delusion** [dɪ'lju:ʒn] *n.* Illusion, *die*

**de luxe** [də'lʌks] *adj.* Luxus-

**demand** [dɪ'mɑ:nd] **1.** *n.* Forderung, *die (for nach); (for commodity)* Nachfrage, *die; sth./sb. is in ~*: etw. ist gefragt/jmd. ist begehrt. **2.** *v. t.* verlangen (**of, from** von); fordern ⟨*Recht*⟩. **de'manding** *adj.* anspruchsvoll

**demented** [dɪ'mentɪd] *adj.* wahnsinnig

**de'mobilize** *v. t.* demobilisieren ⟨*Armee, Kriegsschiff*⟩; aus dem Kriegsdienst entlassen ⟨*Soldat*⟩

**democracy** [dɪ'mɒkrəsɪ] *n.* Demokratie, *die.* **Democrat** ['deməkræt] *n. (Amer. Polit.)* Demokrat, *der/*Demokratin, *die.* **democratic** [demə'krætɪk] *adj.,* **democratically** [demə'krætɪkəlɪ] *adv.* demokratisch

**demolish** [dɪ'mɒlɪʃ] *v. t.* abreißen. **demolition** [demə'lɪʃn] *n.* Abriß, *der; ~* **work** Abbruchsarbeit, *die*

**demon** ['di:mən] *n.* Dämon, *der*

**demonstrate** ['demənstreɪt] **1.** *v. t.* zeigen; *(be proof of)* zeigen; beweisen. **2.** *v. i.* demonstrieren. **demonstration** [demən'streɪʃn] *n. (also Pol. etc.)* Demonstration, *die; (proof)* Beweis, *der.* **demonstrative** [də'mɒnstrətɪv] *adj.* **a)** offen ⟨*Person*⟩; **b)** *(Ling.)* Demonstrativ-. **demonstrator** ['demənstreɪtə(r)] *n. (Pol. etc.)* Demonstrant, *der/*Demonstrantin, *die*

**demoralize** [dɪ'mɒrəlaɪz] *v. t.* demoralisieren

**demote** [di:'məʊt] *v. t.* degradieren (**to** zu). **demotion** [di:'məʊʃn] *n.* Degradierung, *die* (**to** zu)

**demur** [dɪ'mɜ:(r)] *v. i.,* **-rr-** Einwände erheben

**demure** [dɪ'mjʊə(r)] *adj.* betont zurückhaltend

**den** [den] *n.* Höhle, *die*

**denial** [dɪ'naɪəl] *n. (refusal)* Verweigerung, *die; (of request)* Ablehnung, *die*

**denim** ['denɪm] *n.* Denim ⓦ, *der;* Jeansstoff, *der; ~* **jacket** Jeansjacke, *die; ~s* Bluejeans *Pl.*

**Denmark** ['denmɑ:k] *pr. n.* Dänemark *(das)*

**denomination** [dɪnɒmɪ'neɪʃn] *n. (Relig.)* Konfession, *die*

**denote** [dɪ'nəʊt] *v. t.* bezeichnen

**denounce** [dɪ'naʊns] *v. t.* denunzieren; *(accuse publicly)* beschuldigen

**dense** [dens] *adj.* **a)** dicht; massiv ⟨*Körper*⟩; **b)** *(stupid)* dumm. **'densely** *adv.* dicht; *~* **packed** dichtgedrängt. **density** ['densɪtɪ] *n.* Dichte, *die*

**dent** [dent] **1.** *n.* Beule, *die.* **2.** *v. t.* einbeulen

**dental** ['dentl] *adj.* Zahn-. **dental floss** ['dentl flɒs] *n.* Zahnseide, *die*

**dentist** ['dentɪst] *n.* Zahnarzt, *der/*-ärztin, *die.* **dentistry** ['dentɪstrɪ] *n.* Zahnheilkunde, *die*

**denture** ['dentʃə(r)] *n. ~[s]* Zahnprothese, *die*

**denunciation** [dɪnʌnsɪ'eɪʃn] *n.* Denunziation, *die; (public accusation)* Beschuldigung, *die*

**deny** [dɪ'naɪ] *v. t. (declare untrue)* bestreiten; *(refuse) ~* **sb. sth.** jmdm. etw. verweigern; *~* **sb.'s request** jmdm. seine Bitte abschlagen

**deodorant** [di:'əʊdərənt] **1.** *adj.* deodorierend. **2.** *n.* Deodorant, *das*

**depart** [dɪ'pɑ:t] *v. i.* **a)** *(go away)* weggehen; **b)** *(set out, leave)* abfahren; *(on one's journey)* abreisen; **c)** *(fig.: deviate)* abweichen (**from** von)

**department** [dɪ'pɑ:tmənt] *n.* Abteilung, *die; (government ~)* Ministerium, *das; (of university)* Seminar, *das.* **de'partment store** *n.* Kaufhaus, *das*

**departure** [dɪ'pɑ:tʃə(r)] *n.* **a)** Abreise, *die; (of train, bus, ship)* Abfahrt, *die; (of aircraft)* Abflug, *der;* **b)** *(deviation) ~* **from sth.** Abweichen von etw. **de'parture lounge** *n.* Abflughalle, *die*

**depend** [dɪ'pend] *v. i.* **a)** *~* [**up**]**on** abhängen von; **it/that** *~***s** es kommt drauf an; **b)** *(rely, trust) ~* [**up**]**on** sich verlassen auf (+ *Akk.*); *(have to rely on)* angewiesen sein auf (+ *Akk.*). **dependable** [dɪ'pendəbl] *adj.* zuverlässig. **dependant** [dɪ'pendənt] *n.* Abhängige, *der/die.* **dependence** [dɪ'pendəns] *n.* Abhängigkeit, *die.* **dependent** [dɪ'pendənt] **1.** *n. see* **dependant. 2.** *adj.* abhängig

**depict** [dɪ'pɪkt] *v. t.* darstellen

**deplete** [dɪ'pli:t] *v. t.* erheblich verringern

**deplorable** [dɪ'plɔ:rəbl] *adj.* beklagenswert

**deplore** [dɪ'plɔː(r)] *v. t.* **a)** *(disapprove of)* verurteilen; **b)** *(regret)* beklagen

**deploy** [dɪ'plɔɪ] *v. t.* einsetzen

**deport** [dɪ'pɔːt] *v. t.* ausweisen. **deportation** [diːpɔː'teɪʃn] *n.* Ausweisung, *die*

**depose** [dɪ'pəʊz] *v. t.* absetzen

**deposit** [dɪ'pɒzɪt] **1.** *n.* **a)** *(in bank)* Depot, *das; (credit)* Guthaben, *das; (Brit.: at interest)* Sparguthaben, *das;* **b)** *(first instalment)* Anzahlung, *die;* **put down a ~ on sth.** eine Anzahlung für etw. leisten; **c)** *(on bottle)* Pfand, *das.* **2.** *v. t.* **a)** *(lay down)* ablegen; abstellen ⟨*etw. Senkrechtes*⟩; **b)** *(in bank)* deponieren. **de'posit account** *n.* *(Brit.)* Sparkonto, *das*

**depot** ['depəʊ] *n.* Depot, *das*

**depraved** [dɪ'preɪvd] *adj.* verdorben. **depravity** [dɪ'prævɪtɪ] *n.* Verdorbenheit, *die*

**depreciate** [dɪ'priːʃɪeɪt] *v. i.* an Wert verlieren. **depreciation** [dɪpriːʃɪ'eɪʃn] *n.* Wertverlust, *der*

**depress** [dɪ'pres] *v. t.* **a)** *(deject)* deprimieren; **b)** *(push down)* herunterdrücken. **depressed** [dɪ'prest] *adj.* deprimiert. **de'pressing** *adj.,* **de'pressingly** *adv.* deprimierend. **depression** [dɪ'preʃn] *n.* **a)** Depression, *die;* **b)** *(sunk place)* Vertiefung, *die;* **c)** *(Meteorol.)* Tief[druckgebiet], *das;* **d)** *(Econ.)* Wirtschaftskrise, *die*

**deprivation** [deprɪ'veɪʃn] *n.* Entbehrung, *die*

**deprive** [dɪ'praɪv] *v. t.* **~ sb. of sth.** jmdm. etw. nehmen; *(prevent from having)* jmdm. etw. vorenthalten. **deprived** [dɪ'praɪvd] *adj.* benachteiligt ⟨*Kind, Familie usw.*⟩

**depth** [depθ] *n.* **a)** Tiefe, *die;* **in ~:** gründlich; **in the ~s of winter** im tiefsten Winter. **'depth-charge** *n.* Wasserbombe, *die*

**deputation** [depjʊ'teɪʃn] *n.* Abordnung, *die*

**deputize** ['depjʊtaɪz] *v. i.* **~ for sb.** jmdn. vertreten

**deputy** ['depjʊtɪ] *n.* [Stell]vertreter, *der/*-vertreterin, *die; attrib.* stellvertretend

**derail** [dɪ'reɪl] *v. t.* **be ~ed** entgleisen. **de'railment** *n.* Entgleisung, *die*

**deranged** [dɪ'reɪndʒd] *adj.* [mentally] **~:** geistesgestört

**derelict** ['derɪlɪkt] **1.** *adj.* verlassen und verfallen. **2.** *n.* Ausgestoßene, *der/die*

**deride** [dɪ'raɪd] *v. t.* sich lustig machen

über ( + *Akk.*). **derision** [dɪ'rɪʒn] *n.* Spott, *der.* **derisive** [dɪ'raɪsɪv] *adj. (ironical)* spöttisch; *(scoffing)* verächtlich. **derisory** [dɪ'raɪzərɪ] *adj. (ridiculously inadequate)* lächerlich

**derivation** [derɪ'veɪʃn] *n.* Ableitung, *die*

**derivative** [dɪ'rɪvətɪv] **1.** *adj.* abgeleitet; *(lacking originality)* nachahmend. **2.** *n.* Ableitung, *die*

**derive** [dɪ'raɪv] **1.** *v. t.* **~ sth. from sth.** etw. aus etw. gewinnen; **~ pleasure from sth.** Freude an etw. *(Dat.)* haben. **2.** *v. i.* **~ from** beruhen auf ( + *Dat.*)

**derogatory** [dɪ'rɒgətərɪ] *adj.* abfällig

**derrick** ['derɪk] *n.* [Derrick]kran, *der*

**derv** [dɜːv] *n.* Diesel[kraftstoff], *der*

**descend** [dɪ'send] **1.** *v. i.* **a)** *(go down)* hinuntergehen / -steigen / -klettern / -fahren; *(come down)* herunterkommen; ⟨*Fallschirm, Flugzeug:*⟩ niedergehen; **b)** *(slope downwards)* abfallen; **c)** **~ on sb.** jmdn. überfallen. **2.** *v. t. (go/come down)* hinunter- / heruntergehen / -steigen / -klettern / -fahren. **descendant** [dɪ'sendənt] *n.* Nachkomme, *der.* **de'scended** *adj.* **be ~ from sb.** von jmdm. abstammen. **descent** [dɪ'sent] *n.* **a)** Abstieg, *der; (of parachute, plane)* Niedergehen, *das;* **b)** *(lineage)* Herkunft, *die*

**describe** [dɪ'skraɪb] *v. t.* beschreiben. **description** [dɪ'skrɪpʃn] *n.* **a)** Beschreibung, *die;* **b)** *(sort, class)* Art, *die.* **descriptive** [dɪ'skrɪptɪv] *adj.* beschreibend; *(vivid)* anschaulich; **a purely ~ report** ein reiner Tatsachenbericht

**desecrate** ['desɪkreɪt] *v. t.* entweihen

**¹desert** ['dezət] *n.* Wüste, *die*

**²desert** [dɪ'zɜːt] **1.** *v. t.* verlassen. **2.** *v. i.* ⟨*Soldat:*⟩ desertieren. **de'serted** *adj.* verlassen. **de'serter** *n.* Deserteur, *der.* **desertion** [dɪ'zɜːʃn] *n.* Desertion, *die*

**desert 'island** [dezət 'aɪlənd] *n.* einsame Insel

**deserts** [dɪ'zɜːts] *n. pl.* **get one's [just] ~:** das bekommen, was man verdient hat

**deserve** [dɪ'zɜːv] *v. t.* verdienen. **deserving** [dɪ'zɜːvɪŋ] *adj.* verdienstvoll; **a ~ cause** ein guter Zweck

**design** [dɪ'zaɪn] **1.** *n.* Entwurf, *der; (pattern)* Muster, *das; (established form of machine, engine, etc.)* Bauweise, *die; (general idea, construction)* Konstruktion, *die.* **2.** *v. t.* entwerfen; **be ~ed to do sth.** etw. tun sollen

**designate** ['dezɪgneɪt] v.t. a) bezeichnen; b) (appoint) designieren (geh.). **designation** [dezɪg'neɪʃn] n. Bezeichnung, die

'**designer** n. Designer, der/ Designerin, die; (of machines) Konstrukteur, der/Konstrukteurin, die; attrib. Modell‹-kleidung, -jeans›

**desirability** [dɪzaɪərə'bɪlɪtɪ] n. Wunschbarkeit, die

**desirable** [dɪ'zaɪərəbl] adj. wünschenswert

**desire** [dɪ'zaɪə(r)] 1. n. Wunsch, der (for nach); (longing) Sehnsucht, die (for nach). 2. v.t. sich (Dat.) wünschen; (long for) sich sehnen nach

**desist** [dɪ'zɪst] v.i. (literary) einhalten (geh.); ~ from sth. von etw. ablassen (geh.)

**desk** [desk] n. a) Schreibtisch, der; (in school) Tisch, der; b) (cash ~) Kasse, die; (reception ~) Rezeption, die

**desolate** ['desələt] adj. trostlos. **desolation** [desə'leɪʃn] n. Trostlosigkeit, die

**despair** [dɪ'speə(r)] 1. n. Verzweiflung, die; be the ~ of sb. jmdn. zur Verzweiflung bringen. 2. v.i. verzweifeln. **desperate** ['despərət] adj. verzweifelt; extrem ‹Maßnahmen›; be ~ for sth. etw. dringend brauchen. **desperation** [despə'reɪʃn] n. Verzweiflung, die

**despicable** [dɪ'spɪkəbl] adj. verabscheuungswürdig

**despise** [dɪ'spaɪz] v.t. verachten

**despite** [dɪ'spaɪt] prep. trotz

**despondent** [dɪ'spɒndənt] adj. bedrückt

**despot** ['despɒt] n. Despot, der

**dessert** [dɪ'zɜ:t] n. Nachtisch, der. **des'sert spoon** n. Dessertlöffel, der

**destination** [destɪ'neɪʃn] n. Reiseziel, das; (of goods) Bestimmungsort, der; (of train, bus) Zielort, der

**destine** ['destɪn] v.t. bestimmen; be ~d to do sth. dazu bestimmt sein, etw. zu tun

**destiny** ['destɪnɪ] n. Schicksal, das

**destitute** ['destɪtjuːt] adj. mittellos

**destroy** [dɪ'strɔɪ] v.t. zerstören. **de'stroyer** n. (also Naut.) Zerstörer, der. **destruction** [dɪ'strʌkʃn] n. Zerstörung, die. **destructive** [dɪ'strʌktɪv] adj. zerstörerisch; verheerend ‹Sturm, Feuer›

**detach** [dɪ'tætʃ] v.t. entfernen; abnehmen ‹wieder zu Befestigendes›; herausnehmen ‹innen Befindliches›.

**detachable** [dɪ'tætʃəbl] adj. abnehmbar. **detached** [dɪ'tætʃt] adj. a) (impartial) unvoreingenommen; (unemotional) unbeteiligt; b) a ~ house ein Einzelhaus. **de'tachment** n. a) see detach: Entfernen, das; Abnehmen, das; Herausnehmen, das; b) (Mil.) Abteilung, die

**detail** ['diːteɪl] 1. n. Einzelheit, die; Detail, das; in ~: Punkt für Punkt; go into ~[s] ins Detail gehen. 2. v.t. a) einzeln ausführen; b) (Mil.) abkommandieren. **detailed** ['diːteɪld] adj. detailliert; eingehend ‹Studie›

**detain** [dɪ'teɪn] v.t. a) festhalten; (take into confinement) verhaften; b) (delay) aufhalten. **detainee** [diːteɪ'niː] n. Verhaftete, der/die

**detect** [dɪ'tekt] v.t. entdecken; wahrnehmen ‹Bewegung›; aufdecken ‹Irrtum, Verbrechen›. **detection** [dɪ'tekʃn] n. Entdeckung, die; (of error, crime) Aufdeckung, die. **detective** [dɪ'tektɪv] n. Detektiv, der; private ~: Privatdetektiv, der; ~ work Ermittlungsarbeit, die; ~ story Detektivgeschichte, die. **detector** [dɪ'tektə(r)] n. Detektor, der

**detention** [dɪ'tenʃn] n. a) Festnahme, die; (confinement) Haft, die; b) (Sch.) Nachsitzen, das

**deter** [dɪ'tɜː(r)] v.t., -rr- abschrecken

**detergent** [dɪ'tɜːdʒənt] n. Waschmittel, das

**deteriorate** [dɪ'tɪərɪəreɪt] v.i. sich verschlechtern; ‹Haus:› verfallen. **deterioration** [dɪtɪərɪə'reɪʃn] n. see deteriorate: Verschlechterung, die; Verfall, der

**determination** [dɪtɜːmɪ'neɪʃn] n. Entschlossenheit, die

**determine** [dɪ'tɜːmɪn] v.t. a) (decide) beschließen; b) (be a decisive factor for) bestimmen; c) (ascertain) feststellen. **determined** [dɪ'tɜːmɪnd] adj. a) be ~ to do sth. etw. unbedingt tun wollen; b) (resolute) entschlossen

**deterrent** [dɪ'terənt] n. Abschreckungsmittel, das (to für)

**detest** [dɪ'test] v.t. verabscheuen. **detestable** [dɪ'testəbl] adj. verabscheuenswert

**detonate** ['detəneɪt] 1. v.t. zünden. 2. v.i. detonieren. **detonation** [detə'neɪʃn] n. Detonation, die. **detonator** ['detəneɪtə(r)] n. Sprengkapsel, die

**detour** ['diːtʊə(r)] n. Umweg, der; (diversion) Umleitung, die

**detract** [dɪ'trækt] *v. i.* ~ **from sth.** etw. beeinträchtigen

**detriment** ['detrɪmənt] *n.* **to the ~ of sth.** zum Nachteil einer Sache *(Gen.)*. **detrimental** [detrɪ'mentl] *adj.* schädlich; **be ~ to sth.** einer Sache *(Dat.)* schaden

**deuce** [dju:s] *n. (Tennis)* Einstand, *der*

**devaluation** [di:vælju:'eɪʃn] *n.* Abwertung, *die*

**devalue** [di:'vælju:] *v. t.* abwerten

**devastate** ['devəsteɪt] *v. t.* verwüsten; *(fig.)* niederschmettern. **devastating** ['devəsteɪtɪŋ] *adj.* verheerend; *(fig.)* niederschmetternd. **devastation** [devə'steɪʃn] *n.* Verwüstung, *die*

**develop** [dɪ'veləp] **1.** *v. t.* entwickeln; erschließen ⟨*natürliche Ressourcen*⟩; bekommen ⟨*Krankheit, Fieber, Lust*⟩; ~ **a taste for sth.** Geschmack an etw. *(Akk.)* finden. **2.** *v. i.* sich entwickeln **(from** aus; **into** zu). **de'veloper** *n.* **a)** *(Photog.)* Entwickler, *der;* **b)** *(of land)* Bauunternehmer, *der*

**de'veloping country** *n.* Entwicklungsland, *das*

**de'velopment** *n.* Entwicklung, *die* **(from** aus; **into** zu); *(of natural resources etc.)* Erschließung, *die*

**deviant** ['di:vɪənt] *adj.* abweichend

**deviate** ['di:vɪeɪt] *v. i.* abweichen. **deviation** [di:vɪ'eɪʃn] *n.* Abweichung, *die*

**device** [dɪ'vaɪs] *n.* Gerät, *das; (as part of sth.)* Vorrichtung, *die;* **leave sb. to his own ~s** jmdn. sich *(Dat.)* selbst überlassen

**devil** ['devl] *n.* Teufel, *der;* **the D~:** der Teufel. **'devilish** *adj.* teuflisch

**devious** ['di:vɪəs] *adj.* **a)** *(winding)* verschlungen; ~ **route** Umweg, *der;* **b)** *(unscrupulous, insincere)* hinterhältig

**devise** [dɪ'vaɪz] *v. t.* entwerfen; schmieden ⟨*Pläne*⟩

**devoid** [dɪ'vɔɪd] *adj.* ~ **of sth.** *(lacking)* ohne etw.; *(free from)* frei von etw.

**devolution** [di:və'lu:ʃn] *n. (Polit.)* Dezentralisierung, *die*

**devote** [dɪ'vəʊt] *v. t.* widmen **(to** *Dat.*). **de'voted** *adj.* treu; aufrichtig ⟨*Freundschaft, Liebe, Verehrung*⟩; **be ~ to sb.** jmdn. innig lieben. **devotion** [dɪ'vəʊʃn] *n.* ~ **to sb./sth.** Hingabe an jmdn./etw.

**devour** [dɪ'vaʊə(r)] *v. t.* verschlingen

**devout** [dɪ'vaʊt] *adj.* fromm

**dew** [dju:] *n.* Tau, *der*

**dexterity** [dek'sterɪtɪ] *n.* Geschicklichkeit, *die*

**dextrous** ['dekstrəs] *adj.* geschickt

**diabetes** [daɪə'bi:ti:z] *n.* Zuckerkrankheit, *die.* **diabetic** [daɪə'betɪk] **1.** *adj.* zuckerkrank ⟨*Person*⟩. **2.** *n.* Diabetiker, *der*/Diabetikerin, *die*

**diabolical** [daɪə'bɒlɪkl] *adj.* teuflisch

**diagnose** ['daɪəgnəʊz] *v. t.* diagnostizieren; feststellen ⟨*Fehler*⟩. **diagnosis** [daɪəg'nəʊsɪs] *n., pl.* **diagnoses** [daɪəg'nəʊsi:z] Diagnose, *die;* **make a ~:** eine Diagnose stellen

**diagonal** [daɪ'ægənl] **1.** *adj.* diagonal. **2.** *n.* Diagonale, *die.* **di'agonally** *adv.* diagonal

**diagram** ['daɪəgræm] *n.* Diagramm, *das*

**dial** ['daɪəl] **1.** *n. (of clock or watch)* Zifferblatt, *das; (of gauge, meter, etc.)* Skala, *die; (Teleph.)* Wählscheibe, *die.* **2.** *v. t. & i., (Brit.)* **-ll-** *(Teleph.)* wählen; ~ **direct** selbst wählen; *(dial extension)* durchwählen

**dialect** ['daɪəlekt] *n.* Dialekt, *der*

**dialling** *(Amer.:* **dialing):** ~ **code** *n.* Vorwahl, *die;* ~ **tone** Wählton, *der*

**dialogue** ['daɪəlɒg] *n.* Dialog, *der*

**'dial tone** *n. (Amer.)* Wählton, *der*

**diameter** [daɪ'æmɪtə(r)] *n.* Durchmesser, *der.* **diametrical** [daɪə'metrɪkl] *adj.,* **dia'metrically** *adv.* diametral

**diamond** ['daɪəmənd] *n.* **a)** Diamant, *der;* **b)** *(figure)* Raute, *die;* **c)** *(Cards)* Karo, *das; see also* **club I c**

**diaper** ['daɪəpə(r)] *n. (Amer.)* Windel, *die*

**diaphragm** ['daɪəfræm] *n.* Diaphragma, *das*

**diarrhoea** *(Amer.:* **diarrhea)** [daɪə'rɪə] *n.* Durchfall, *der*

**diary** ['daɪərɪ] *n.* **a)** Tagebuch, *das;* **b)** *(for appointments)* Terminkalender, *der*

**dice** [daɪs] **1.** *n.* Würfel, *der.* **2.** *v. t. (Cooking)* würfeln

**dicey** ['daɪsɪ] *adj. (sl.)* riskant

**dictate** [dɪk'teɪt] *v. t. & i.* diktieren; *(prescribe)* vorschreiben; ~ **to** Vorschriften machen (+ *Dat.*). **dictation** [dɪk'teɪʃn] *n.* Diktat, *das.* **dictator** [dɪk'teɪtə(r)] *n.* Diktator, *der.* **dictatorial** [dɪktə'tɔ:rɪəl] *adj.* diktatorisch. **dic'tatorship** *n.* Diktatur, *die*

**dictionary** ['dɪkʃənərɪ] *n.* Wörterbuch, *das*

**did** *see* **do**

**diddle** ['dɪdl] *v. t. (sl.)* übers Ohr hauen *(ugs.)*

**didn't** ['dɪdnt] *(coll.)* **= did not;** *see* **do**

**die** [daɪ] *v. i.,* **dying** ['daɪɪŋ] sterben **(of,**

from an + *Dat.*); ⟨*Tier, Pflanze:*⟩ eingehen; **be dying to do sth.** darauf brennen, etw. zu tun; **be dying for sth.** etw. unbedingt brauchen. **die 'down** *v. i.* ⟨*Sturm, Wind, Protest:*⟩ sich legen; ⟨*Flammen:*⟩ kleiner werden; ⟨*Feuer:*⟩ herunterbrennen; ⟨*Lärm:*⟩ leiser werden. **die 'out** *v. i.* aussterben

**'die-hard** *n.* Ewiggestrige, *der/die*

**diesel** ['di:zl] *n.* ~ |**engine**| Diesel[motor], *der;* ~ |**fuel**| Diesel[kraftstoff], *der*

**diet** ['daɪət] **1.** *n.* Diät, *die;* **be/go on a** ~: eine Schlankheitskur machen. **2.** *v. i.* eine Schlankheitskur machen

**differ** ['dɪfə(r)] *v. i. (be different)* sich unterscheiden

**difference** ['dɪfərəns] *n.* **a)** Unterschied, *der;* **make no** ~ |**to sb.**| |jmdm.| nichts ausmachen; **it makes a** ~: es ist ein *od. (ugs.)* macht einen Unterschied; **b)** *(disagreement)* Meinungsverschiedenheit, *die*

**different** ['dɪfərənt] *adj.* verschieden; *(pred. also)* anders; *(attrib. also)* ander...; **be** ~ **from** or *(esp. Brit.)* **to** or *(Amer.)* **than** ...: anders sein als ...

**differentiate** [dɪfə'renʃɪeɪt] *v. t. & i.* unterscheiden (**between** zwischen + *Dat.*)

**'differently** *adv.* anders (**from,** *esp. Brit.* **to** als)

**difficult** ['dɪfɪkəlt] *adj.* schwierig. **'difficulty** *n.* Schwierigkeit, *die;* **with** |**great**| ~: |sehr| mühsam; **get into difficulties** in Schwierigkeiten kommen

**diffident** ['dɪfɪdənt] *adj.* zaghaft; *(modest)* zurückhaltend

**diffuse 1.** [dɪ'fju:z] *v. t.* verbreiten. **2.** *v. i.* sich ausbreiten (**through** in + *Dat.*). **3.** [dɪ'fju:s] *adj.* diffus

**dig** [dɪg] **1.** *v. i.,* -gg-, dug [dʌg] graben (**for** nach). **2.** *v. t.,* -gg-, dug graben; umgraben ⟨*Erde, Garten*⟩. **dig 'out** *v. t.* ausgraben. **dig 'up** *v. t.* ausgraben; umgraben ⟨*Garten*⟩; aufreißen ⟨*Straße*⟩

**digest** [dɪ'dʒest, daɪ'dʒest] *v. t.* verdauen. **digestion** [dɪ'dʒestʃn, daɪ'dʒestʃn] *n.* Verdauung, *die*

**'digger** *n.* Bagger, *der*

**digit** ['dɪdʒɪt] *n.* Ziffer, *die*

**digital** ['dɪdʒɪtl] *adj.* Digital-

**dignified** ['dɪgnɪfaɪd] *adj.* würdig; *(stately)* würdevoll

**dignify** ['dɪgnɪfaɪ] *v. t.* Würde verleihen (+ *Dat.*)

**dignitary** ['dɪgnɪtərɪ] *n.* Würdenträger, *der;* **dignitaries** *(prominent people)* Honoratioren

**dignity** ['dɪgnɪtɪ] *n.* Würde, *die*

**digress** [daɪ'gres] *v. i.* abschweifen. **digression** [daɪ'greʃn] *n.* Abschweifung, *die*

**dike** [daɪk] *n.* Deich, *der*

**dilapidated** [dɪ'læpɪdeɪtɪd] *adj.* verfallen ⟨*Gebäude*⟩; verwahrlost ⟨*Erscheinung*⟩

**dilate** [daɪ'leɪt] **1.** *v. i.* sich weiten. **2.** *v. t.* ausdehnen

**dilemma** [dɪ'lemə, daɪ'lemə] *n.* Dilemma, *das*

**diligence** ['dɪlɪdʒəns] *n.* Fleiß, *der*

**diligent** ['dɪlɪdʒənt] *adj.,* **'diligently** *adv.* fleißig

**dilute 1.** [daɪ'lju:t, 'daɪlju:t] *adj.* verdünnt. **2.** [daɪ'lju:t] *v. t.* verdünnen

**dim** [dɪm] **1.** *adj.* **a)** schwach ⟨*Licht, Flackern*⟩; dunkel ⟨*Zimmer*⟩; verschwommen ⟨*Gestalt*⟩; **b)** *(vague)* verschwommen; **c)** *(coll.: stupid)* beschränkt. **2.** *v. i.* schwächer werden

**dime** [daɪm] *n. (Amer. coll.)* Zehncentstück, *das*

**dimension** [dɪ'menʃn, daɪ'menʃn] *n.* Dimension, *die;* ~**s** *(measurements)* Abmessungen; Maße

**diminish** [dɪ'mɪnɪʃ] **1.** *v. i.* nachlassen; ⟨*Vorräte, Einfluß:*⟩ abnehmen; ⟨*Wert, Ansehen:*⟩ geringer werden. **2.** *v. t.* verringern; schmälern ⟨*Ansehen, Ruf*⟩

**dimple** ['dɪmpl] *n.* Grübchen, *das*

**dim:** ~**wit** *n. (coll.)* Dummkopf, *der (ugs.);* ~**-witted** ['dɪmwɪtɪd] *adj. (coll.)* dusselig *(salopp)*

**din** [dɪn] *n.* Lärm, *der*

**dine** [daɪn] *v. i.* [zu Mittag/zu Abend] essen. **'diner** *n.* Gast, *der*

**dinghy** ['dɪŋɡɪ, 'dɪŋ] *n.* Ding[h]i, *das; (inflatable)* Schlauchboot, *das*

**dingy** ['dɪndʒɪ] *adj.* schmuddelig

**dining** ['daɪnɪŋ]: ~**car** *n.* Speisewagen, *der;* ~**-room** *n.* Eßzimmer, *das; (in hotel etc.)* Speisesaal, *der*

**dinner** ['dɪnə(r)] *n. (at midday)* Mittagessen, *das; (in the evening)* Abendessen, *das; (formal)* Diner, *das.* **'dinner-table** *n.* Eßtisch, *der.* **'dinnertime** *n.* Essenszeit, *die;* **at** ~**-time** zur Essenszeit; *(12–2 p. m.)* mittags

**dinosaur** ['daɪnəsɔ:(r)] *n.* Dinosaurier, *der*

**dint** [dɪnt] *n.* **by** ~ **of** durch; **by** ~ **of doing sth.** indem jmd. etw. tut

**dip** [dɪp] **1.** *v. t.,* -pp-: **a)** [ein]tauchen (**in** in + *Akk.*); **b)** ~ **one's headlights** abblenden. **2.** *v. i.* sinken; *(incline)* abfallen. **3.** *n.* **a)** *(in road)* Senke, *die;* **b)** *(coll.: bathe)* [kurzes] Bad

**diphtheria** [dɪf'θɪərɪə] *n.* Diphtherie, *die*

**diphthong** ['dɪfθɒŋ] *n.* Diphthong, *der*

**diploma** [dɪ'pləʊmə] *n.* Diplom, *das*

**diplomacy** [dɪ'pləʊməsɪ] *n.* Diplomatie, *die*

**diplomat** ['dɪpləmæt] *n.* Diplomat, *der*/Diplomatin, *die*

**diplomatic** [dɪplə'mætɪk] *adj.,* **diplo'matically** *adv.* diplomatisch

**dire** ['daɪə(r)] *adj.* furchtbar

**direct** [dɪ'rekt, daɪ'rekt] **1.** *v. t.* **a)** *(turn)* richten (to[wards] auf + *Akk.*); ~ **sb. to a place** jmdn. den Weg zu einem Ort weisen; **b)** *(control)* leiten; regeln ⟨*Verkehr*⟩; **c)** *(order)* anweisen; **d)** *(Theatre, Cinemat., etc.)* Regie führen bei. **2.** *adj.* direkt; durchgehend ⟨*Zug*⟩; unmittelbar ⟨*Ursache, Auswirkung, Erfahrung, Verantwortung*⟩; genau ⟨*Gegenteil*⟩; direkt ⟨*Widerspruch*⟩; diametral ⟨*Gegensatz*⟩; ~ **speech** direkte Rede. **3.** *adv.* direkt.

**direct 'current** *n.* Gleichstrom, *der.*

**direct 'hit** *n.* Volltreffer, *der*

**direction** [daɪ'rekʃn] *n.* **a)** Richtung, *die;* **in the ~ of London** in Richtung London; **b)** *(guidance)* Führung, *die;* **c)** *usu. in pl. (order)* Anordnung, *die;* ~**s** [for use] Gebrauchsanweisung, *die*

**directly** *adv.* **a)** direkt; unmittelbar ⟨*folgen, verantwortlich sein*⟩; **b)** *(exactly)* genau; **c)** *(at once)* umgehend; **d)** *(shortly)* gleich

**di'rect object** *n.* direktes Objekt

**director** [daɪ'rektə(r)] *n.* **a)** *(Commerc.)* Direktor, *der*/Direktorin, *die;* **board of ~s** Aufsichtsrat, *der;* **b)** *(Theatre, Cinemat., etc.)* Regisseur, *der*/Regisseurin, *die*

**directory** [daɪ'rektərɪ] *n. (telephone ~)* Telefonbuch, *das; (of tradesmen etc.)* Branchenverzeichnis, *das;* ~ **enquiries** *(Brit.),* ~ **information** *(Amer.)* [Fernsprech]auskunft, *die*

**dirt** [dɜːt] *n.* Schmutz, *der;* ~ **cheap** spottbillig. '**dirty 1.** *adj.* schmutzig; **get sth. ~:** etw. schmutzig machen. **2.** *v. t.* schmutzig machen

**disa'bility** *n.* Behinderung, *die*

**disabled** [dɪs'eɪbld] *adj.* behindert

**disad'vantage** *n.* Nachteil, *der;* **at a ~:** im Nachteil

**disa'gree** *v. i.* anderer Meinung sein; ~ **with sb./sth.** mit jmdm./etw. nicht übereinstimmen; ~ **[with sb.] about** *or* **over sth.** sich [mit jmdm.] über etw. *(Akk.)* nicht einig sein. **dis-**

**a'greeable** *adj.* unangenehm. **disa'greement** *n.* **a)** *(difference of opinion)* Uneinigkeit, *die;* **be in ~ with sb./sth.** mit jmdm./etw. nicht übereinstimmen; **b)** *(quarrel)* Meinungsverschiedenheit, *die;* **c)** *(discrepancy)* Diskrepanz, *die*

**disal'low** *v. t.* verbieten; *(Sport)* nicht geben ⟨*Tor*⟩

**disap'pear** *v. i.* verschwinden; ⟨*Brauch, Tierart:*⟩ aussterben. **disap'pearance** *n.* Verschwinden, *das*

**disap'point** *v. t.* enttäuschen. **disap'pointed** *adj.* enttäuscht. **disap'pointing** *adj.* enttäuschend. **disap'pointment** *n.* Enttäuschung, *die*

**disap'proval** *n.* Mißbilligung, *die*

**disap'prove** *v. i.* dagegen sein; ~ **of sb./sth.** jmdn. ablehnen/etw. mißbilligen

**dis'arm** *v. t.* entwaffnen. **disarmament** [dɪs'ɑːməmənt] *n.* Abrüstung, *die*

**disarray** [dɪsə'reɪ] *n.* Unordnung, *die;* **in ~:** in Unordnung

**disaster** [dɪ'zɑːstə(r)] *n.* Katastrophe, *die;* ~ **area** Katastrophengebiet, *das.* **disastrous** [dɪ'zɑːstrəs] *adj.* katastrophal; verhängnisvoll ⟨*Irrtum, Entscheidung, Politik*⟩

**dis'band 1.** *v. t.* auflösen. **2.** *v. i.* sich auflösen

**disbe'lief** *n.* Unglaube, *der;* **in ~:** ungläubig

**disbe'lieve** *v. t.* ~ **sb./sth.** jmdm./etw. nicht glauben

**disc** [dɪsk] *n.* Scheibe, *die; (record)* Platte, *die;* **floppy ~:** Floppy disk, *die;* **hard ~** *(fixed)* Festplatte, *die*

**discard** [dɪs'kɑːd] *v. t.* wegwerfen; fallenlassen ⟨*Vorschlag, Idee*⟩

**discern** [dɪ'sɜːn] *v. t.* wahrnehmen. **discernible** [dɪ'sɜːnɪbl] *adj.* erkennbar. **di'scerning** *adj.* kritisch

**discharge 1.** [dɪs'tʃɑːdʒ] *v. t.* **a)** entlassen **(from** aus); freisprechen ⟨*Angeklagte*⟩; **b)** ablassen ⟨*Flüssigkeit, Gas*⟩. **2.** ['dɪstʃɑːdʒ] *n.* **a)** Entlassung, *die* **(from** aus); *(of defendant)* Freispruch, *der;* **b)** *(emission)* Ausfluß, *der*

**disciple** [dɪ'saɪpl] *n.* **a)** *(Relig.)* Jünger, *der;* **b)** *(follower)* Anhänger, *der*/Anhängerin, *die*

**disciplinary** [dɪsɪ'plɪnərɪ] *adj.* disziplinarisch; ~ **action** Disziplinarmaßnahmen

**discipline** ['dɪsɪplɪn] **1.** *n.* Disziplin, *die.* **2.** *v. t.* disziplinieren; *(punish)* bestrafen

**'disc jockey** *n.* Diskjockey, *der*
**dis'claim** *v. t.* abstreiten
**disclose** [dɪs'kləʊz] *v. t.* enthüllen; bekanntgeben ⟨*Information, Nachricht*⟩.
**dis'closure** *n.* Enthüllung, *die; (of information, news)* Bekanntgabe, *die*
**disco** ['dɪskəʊ] *n., pl.* ~s *(coll.)* Disko, *die*
**dis'colour** *(Brit.; Amer.:* **discolor**) *v. t.* verfärben
**dis'comfort** *n.* **a)** *no pl. (slight pain)* Beschwerden *Pl.;* **b)** *(hardship)* Unannehmlichkeit, *die*
**disconcert** [dɪskən'sɜːt] *v. t.* irritieren
**discon'nect** *v. t.* abtrennen; abstellen ⟨*Telefon*⟩
**disconsolate** [dɪs'kɒnsələt] *adj.* **a)** *(unhappy)* unglücklich; **b)** *(inconsolable)* untröstlich
**discon'tent** *n.* Unzufriedenheit, *die.* **discon'tented** *adj.* unzufrieden
**discon'tinue** *v. t.* einstellen
**discord** ['dɪskɔːd] *n.* **a)** Zwietracht, *die;* **b)** *(Mus.)* Dissonanz, *die.* **discordant** [dɪs'kɔːdənt] *adj.* **a)** *(conflicting)* gegensätzlich; **b)** **a** ~ **note** ein Mißton
**discothèque** ['dɪskətek] *n.* Diskothek, *die*
**discount** **1.** ['dɪskaʊnt] *n. (Commerc.)* Rabatt, *der* **(on** auf + *Akk.).* **2.** [dɪ'skaʊnt] *v. t. (disbelieve)* unberücksichtigt lassen
**discourage** [dɪ'skʌrɪdʒ] *v. t.* **a)** entmutigen; **b)** *(advise against)* abraten. **di'scouragement** *n.* **a)** Entmutigung, *die;* **b)** *(depression)* Mutlosigkeit, *die.* **discouraging** [dɪ'skʌrɪdʒɪŋ] *adj.* entmutigend
**dis'courteous** *adj.* unhöflich. **dis'courtesy** *n.* Unhöflichkeit, *die*
**discover** [dɪ'skʌvə(r)] *v. t.* **a)** entdecken; **b)** *(by search)* herausfinden. **di'scovery** *n.* Entdeckung, *die*
**dis'credit** **1.** *n.* Mißkredit, *der;* **bring** ~ **on sb./sth.,** **bring sb./sth. into** ~: jmdn./etw. in Mißkredit bringen. **2.** *v. t.* in Mißkredit bringen
**discreet** [dɪ'skriːt] *adj.,* **di'screetly** *adv.* diskret
**discrepancy** [dɪ'skrepənsɪ] *n.* Diskrepanz, *die*
**discretion** [dɪ'skreʃn] *n. (prudence)* Umsicht, *die*
**discriminate** [dɪ'skrɪmɪneɪt] *v. i.* **a)** unterscheiden; **b)** ~ **against/in favour of sb.** jmdn. diskriminieren/bevorzugen. **discrimination** [dɪskrɪmɪ'neɪʃn] *n.* **a)** Unterscheidung, *die;* **b)** Diskri-

minierung, *die* **(against** *Gen.);* ~ **in favour of** Bevorzugung ( + *Gen.*)
**discus** ['dɪskəs] *n.* Diskus, *der*
**discuss** [dɪ'skʌs] *v. t.* besprechen; *(debate)* diskutieren über ( + *Akk.*). **discussion** [dɪ'skʌʃn] *n.* Gespräch, *das; (debate)* Diskussion, *die*
**disdain** [dɪs'deɪn] **1.** *n.* Verachtung, *die.* **2.** *v. t.* verachten; ~ **to do sth.** zu stolz sein, etw. zu tun. **disdainful** [dɪs'deɪnfl] *adj.* verächtlich
**disease** [dɪ'ziːz] *n.* Krankheit, *die.* **diseased** [dɪ'ziːzd] *adj.* krank
**disem'bark** *v. i.* von Bord gehen
**disen'chant** *v. t.* ernüchtern; **he became** ~**ed with her/it** sie/es hat ihn desillusioniert
**disen'gage** *v. t.* lösen **(from** aus, von); ~ **the clutch** auskuppeln
**disen'tangle** *v. t.* entwirren; *(extricate)* befreien **(from** aus)
**dis'figure** *v. t.* entstellen
**disgrace** [dɪs'greɪs] *n.* **1.** Schande, *die* **(to** für). **2.** *v. t.* Schande machen ( + *Dat.*); ~ **oneself** sich blamieren. **di'sgraceful** [dɪs'greɪsfl] *adj.* skandalös; **it's** ~: es ist ein Skandal
**disgruntled** [dɪs'grʌntld] *adj.* verstimmt
**disguise** [dɪs'gaɪz] **1.** *v. t.* verkleiden ⟨*Person*⟩; verstellen ⟨*Stimme*⟩; tarnen ⟨*Gegenstand*⟩. **2.** *n.* Verkleidung, *die*
**disgust** [dɪs'gʌst] **1.** *n. (nausea)* Ekel, *der* **(at** vor + *Dat.*); *(revulsion)* Abscheu, *der* **(at** vor + *Dat.*); *(indignation)* Empörung, *die* **(at** über + *Akk.*). **2.** *v. t.* anwidern; *(fill with nausea)* ekeln; *(fill with indignation)* empören. **dis'gusted** *adj.* angewidert; *(nauseated)* angeekelt; *(indignant)* empört. **dis'gusting** *adj.* widerlich
**dish** [dɪʃ] *n.* **a)** Schale, *die; (deeper)* Schüssel, *die;* ~**es** *(crockery)* Geschirr, *das;* **wash** or *(coll.)* **do the** ~**es** Geschirr spülen; **b)** *(type of food)* Gericht, *das.* **dish 'out** *v. t.* **a)** austeilen ⟨*Essen*⟩; **b)** *(coll.: distribute)* verteilen. **dish 'up** *v. t.* auftragen
**'dishcloth** *n.* Spültuch, *das*
**dis'hearten** *v. t.* entmutigen
**dishevelled** *(Amer.:* **disheveled)** [dɪ'ʃevld] *adj.* zerzaust ⟨*Haar*⟩; ungepflegt ⟨*Erscheinung*⟩
**dis'honest** *adj.,* **dis'honestly** *adv.* unehrlich. **dis'honesty** *n.* Unehrlichkeit, *die*
**dis'honour** **1.** *n.* Unehre, *die.* **2.** *v. t.* beleidigen. **dishonourable** [dɪs'ɒnərəbl] *adj.* unehrenhaft

'**dishwasher** *n.* Geschirrspülmaschine, *die*

**disil'lusion** 1. *v.t.* ernüchtern. 2. *n.* Desillusion, *die* (with über + *Akk.*). **disil'lusionment** *n.* Desillusionierung, *die*

**disin'fect** *v.t.* desinfizieren. **disinfectant** [dɪsɪn'fektənt] 1. *adj.* desinfizierend. 2. *n.* Desinfektionsmittel, *das*

**dis'integrate** *v.i.* zerfallen. **disintegration** [dɪsɪntɪ'greɪʃn] *n.* Zerfall, *der*

**dis'interested** *adj.* a) *(impartial)* unvoreingenommen; b) *(coll.: uninterested)* desinteressiert

**disjointed** [dɪs'dʒɔɪntɪd] *adj.* unzusammenhängend

**disk** *see* disc

**diskette** [dɪ'sket] *n.* Diskette, *die*

**dis'like** 1. *v.t.* nicht mögen; ~ doing sth. etw. ungern tun. 2. *n.* Abneigung, *die* (of, for gegen); take a ~ to sb./sth. eine Abneigung gegen jmdn./etw. empfinden

**dislocate** ['dɪsləkeɪt] *v.t.* ausrenken; auskugeln ⟨*Schulter, Hüfte*⟩

**dis'lodge** *v.t.* entfernen (from aus)

**dis'loyal** *adj.* illoyal (to gegenüber). **dis'loyalty** *n.* Illoyalität, *die* (to gegenüber)

**dismal** ['dɪzməl] *adj.* trist

**dismantle** [dɪs'mæntl] *v.t.* demontieren; abbauen ⟨*Schuppen, Gerüst*⟩

**dismay** [dɪs'meɪ] 1. *v.t.* bestürzen. 2. *n.* Bestürzung, *die* (at über + *Akk.*)

**dismiss** [dɪs'mɪs] *v.t.* entlassen; *(reject)* ablehnen. **dismissal** [dɪs'mɪsl] *n.* Entlassung, *die*

**dis'mount** *v.i.* absteigen

**diso'bedience** *n.* Ungehorsam, *der*

**diso'bedient** *adj.* ungehorsam

**diso'bey** *v.t.* nicht gehorchen (+ *Dat.*); nicht befolgen ⟨*Befehl*⟩

**dis'order** *n.* a) Durcheinander, *das*; b) *(Med.)* Störung, *die*. **dis'orderly** *adj. (untidy)* unordentlich; ~ conduct ungebührliches Benehmen

**dis'organized** *adj.* chaotisch

**dis'orientated, dis'oriented** *adj.* desorientiert

**dis'own** *v.t.* verleugnen

**disparage** [dɪ'spærɪdʒ] *v.t.* herabsetzen. **disparaging** [dɪ'spærɪdʒɪŋ] *adj.* abschätzig

**disparity** [dɪ'spærɪtɪ] *n.* Ungleichheit, *die*

**dispatch** [dɪ'spætʃ] 1. *v.t.* a) schicken; b) *(kill)* töten. 2. *n.* Bericht, *der*

**dispel** [dɪ'spel] *v.t.,* -ll- vertreiben; zerstreuen ⟨*Besorgnis, Befürchtung*⟩

**dispensable** [dɪ'spensəbl] *adj.* entbehrlich

**dispensary** [dɪ'spensərɪ] *n.* Apotheke, *die*

**dispense** [dɪ'spens] *v.i.* ~ with verzichten auf (+ *Akk.*)

**dispersal** [dɪ'spɜːsl] *n.* Zerstreuung, *die*

**disperse** [dɪ'spɜːs] 1. *v.t.* zerstreuen. 2. *v.i.* sich zerstreuen

**dispirited** [dɪ'spɪrɪtɪd] *adj.* entmutigt

**dis'place** *v.t.* verschieben; *(supplant)* ersetzen

**display** [dɪ'spleɪ] 1. *v.t.* zeigen; ausstellen ⟨*Waren*⟩. 2. *n.* Ausstellung, *die; (of goods)* Auslage, *die; (ostentatious show)* Zurschaustellung, *die*

**dis'please** *v.t.* ~ sb. jmds. Mißfallen erregen. **dis'pleasure** *n.* Mißfallen, *das*

**disposable** [dɪ'spəʊzəbl] *adj.* Wegwerf-

**disposal** [dɪ'spəʊzl] *n.* Beseitigung, *die;* have sth./sb. at one's ~: etw./ jmdn. zur Verfügung haben; be at sb.'s ~: jmdm. zur Verfügung stehen

**dispose** [dɪ'spəʊz] *v.t.* ~ sb. to sth. jmdn. zu etw. veranlassen; ~ sb. to do sth. jmdn. dazu veranlassen, etw. zu tun. **di'spose of** *v.t.* beseitigen; *(settle)* erledigen

**disposed** [dɪ'spəʊzd] *adj.* be ~ to do sth. dazu neigen, etw. zu tun; be well ~ towards sb./sth. jmdm. wohl gesinnt sein/einer Sache *(Dat.)* positiv gegenüberstehen. **disposition** [dɪspə'zɪʃn] *n.* Veranlagung, *die; (nature)* Art, *die*

**dis'prove** *v.t.* widerlegen

**dispute** [dɪ'spjuːt] 1. *n.* Streit, *der* (over um). 2. *v.t.* a) *(discuss)* sich streiten über (+ *Akk.*); b) *(oppose)* bestreiten

**disqualifi'cation** *n.* Ausschluß, *der; (Sport)* Disqualifikation, *die*

**dis'qualify** *v.t.* ausschließen (from von); *(Sport)* disqualifizieren

**disre'gard** 1. *v.t.* ignorieren. 2. *n.* Mißachtung, *die* (of, for *Gen.*); *(of wishes, feelings)* Gleichgültigkeit, *die* (for, of gegenüber)

**dis'reputable** *adj.* verrufen

**disrepute** [dɪsrɪ'pjuːt] *n.* Verruf, *der;* bring sb./sth. into ~: jmdn./etw. in Verruf bringen

**disre'spect** *n.* Mißachtung, *die;* show ~ for sb./sth. keine Achtung vor jmdm./etw. haben. **disre'spectful** *adj.* respektlos

**disrupt** [dɪs'rʌpt] *v. t.* stören. **disruption** [dɪs'rʌpʃn] *n.* Störung, *die.* **disruptive** [dɪs'rʌptɪv] *adj.* störend

**dissatis'faction** *n.* Unzufriedenheit, *die*

**dis'satisfied** *adj.* unzufrieden

**dissect** [dɪ'sekt] *v. t.* sezieren

**dissent** [dɪ'sent] **1.** *v. i.* **a)** *(refuse to assent)* nicht zustimmen; ~ **from sth.** mit etw. nicht übereinstimmen; **b)** *(disagree)* ~ **from sth.** von etw. abweichen. **2.** *n.* Ablehnung, *die; (from majority)* Abweichung, *die*

**dissertation** [dɪsə'teɪʃn] *n.* Dissertation, *die*

**dis'service** *n.* **do sb. a** ~: jmdm. einen schlechten Dienst erweisen

**dissident** ['dɪsɪdənt] *n.* Dissident, *der*/Dissidentin, *die*

**dis'similar** *adj.* unähnlich (**to** *Dat.*)

**dissociate** [dɪ'səʊʃɪeɪt] *v. t.* trennen; ~ **oneself** sich distanzieren (**from** von)

**dissolve** [dɪ'zɒlv] **1.** *v. t.* auflösen. **2.** *v. i.* sich auflösen

**dissuade** [dɪ'sweɪd] *v. t.* abbringen (**from** von)

**distance** ['dɪstəns] *n.* **a)** Entfernung, *die* (**from** zu); **b)** *(way to cover)* Strecke, *die;* **from a** ~: von weitem; **in/into the** ~: in der/die Ferne

**distant** ['dɪstənt] *adj.* **a)** fern; entfernt ⟨*Ähnlichkeit, Verwandtschaft, Verwandte*⟩; **b)** *(reserved)* distanziert

**dis'taste** *n.* Abneigung, *die* (**for** gegen). **dis'tasteful** *adj.* unangenehm

**distend** [dɪ'stend] *v. t.* erweitern

**distil,** *(Amer.)* **distill** [dɪ'stɪl] *v. t.* destillieren; brennen ⟨*Branntwein*⟩. **distillation** [dɪstɪ'leɪʃn] *n.* Destillation, *die.* **distillery** [dɪ'stɪlərɪ] *n.* Brennerei, *die*

**distinct** [dɪ'stɪŋkt] *adj.* deutlich; *(different)* verschieden. **distinction** [dɪ'stɪŋkʃn] *n.* Unterschied, *der.* **distinctive** [dɪ'stɪŋktɪv] *adj.* unverwechselbar. **dis'tinctly** *adv.* deutlich

**distinguish** [dɪ'stɪŋgwɪʃ] **1.** *v. t.* **a)** *(make out)* erkennen; **b)** *(differentiate)* unterscheiden; **c)** *(characterize)* kennzeichnen; **d)** ~ **oneself** [**by sth.**] sich [durch etw.] hervortun. **2.** *v. i.* unterscheiden; ~ **between** auseinanderhalten. **distinguished** [dɪ'stɪŋgwɪʃt] *adj.* angesehen; glänzend ⟨*Laufbahn*⟩; vornehm ⟨*Aussehen*⟩

**distort** [dɪ'stɔːt] *v. t.* verzerren; *(fig.)* verdrehen. **distortion** [dɪ'stɔːʃn] *n.* Verzerrung, *die; (fig.)* Verdrehung, *die*

**distract** [dɪ'strækt] *v. t.* ablenken; ~ sb.['s attention from sth.] jmdn. [von etw.] ablenken. **di'stracted** *adj.* von Sinnen *nachgestellt; (mentally far away)* abwesend. **distraction** [dɪ'strækʃn] *n.* **a)** *(diversion)* Ablenkung, *die; (interruption)* Störung, *die;* **b)** **drive sb. to** ~: jmdn. zum Wahnsinn treiben

**distraught** [dɪ'strɔːt] *adj.* aufgelöst (**with** vor + *Dat.*); verstört ⟨*Blick*⟩

**distress** [dɪ'stres] **1.** *n.* **a)** Kummer, *der* (**at** über + *Akk.*); **b)** *(pain)* Qualen *Pl.;* **c) an aircraft/ship in** ~: ein Flugzeug in Not/ein Schiff in Seenot. **2.** *v. t.* nahegehen (+ *Dat.*). **di'stressing** *adj.* erschütternd. **di'stress signal** *n.* Notsignal, *das*

**distribute** [dɪ'strɪbjuːt] *v. t.* verteilen (**to** an + *Akk.;* **among** unter + *Akk.*); *(Commerc.)* vertreiben. **distribution** [dɪstrɪ'bjuːʃn] *n.* Verteilung, *die; (Commerc.)* Vertrieb, *der.* **distributor** [dɪ'strɪbjʊtə(r)] *n.* Verteiler, *der*/Verteilerin, *die; (Commerc.)* Vertreiber, *der*

**district** ['dɪstrɪkt] *n.* Gegend, *die; (Admin.)* Bezirk, *der.* **district 'nurse** *n.* *(Brit.)* Gemeindeschwester, *die*

**dis'trust** [dɪs'trʌst] **1.** *n.* Mißtrauen, *das* (**of** gegen). **2.** *v. t.* mißtrauen (+ *Dat.*)

**disturb** [dɪ'stɜːb] *v. t.* **a)** stören; '**do not** ~!' „bitte nicht stören!"; **b)** *(worry)* beunruhigen. **disturbance** [dɪ'stɜːbəns] *n.* Störung, *die;* **political** ~s politische Unruhen. **disturbed** [dɪ'stɜːbd] *adj.* besorgt; [**mentally**] ~: geistig gestört

**disuse** [dɪs'juːs] *n.* **fall into** ~: außer Gebrauch kommen

**disused** [dɪs'juːzd] *adj.* stillgelegt; leerstehend ⟨*Gebäude*⟩

**ditch** [dɪtʃ] **1.** *n.* Graben, *der.* **2.** *v. t.* *(sl.)* sausenlassen ⟨*Plan*⟩; sitzenlassen ⟨*Familie, Freund*⟩

**dither** ['dɪðə(r)] *v. i.* schwanken

**ditto** ['dɪtəʊ] *n., pl.* ~s ebenso; ditto; ~ **marks** Unterführungszeichen, *das*

**divan** [dɪ'væn] *n.* [Polster]liege, *die*

**dive** [daɪv] **1.** *v. i., dived or (Amer.)* **dove** [dəʊv] **a)** einen Kopfsprung machen; *(when already in water)* tauchen; **b)** ⟨*Vogel, Flugzeug usw.:*⟩ einen Sturzflug machen. **2.** *n.* **a)** Kopfsprung, *der; (of bird, aircraft, etc.)* Sturzflug, *der;* **b)** *(coll.: place)* Spelunke, *die.* **'diver** *n.* **a)** *(Sport)* Kunstspringer, *der*/-springerin, *die;* **b)** *(as profession)* Taucher, *der*/Taucherin, *die*

**diverge** [daɪ'vɜːdʒ] v. i. auseinandergehen. **divergent** [daɪ'vɜːdʒənt] adj. auseinandergehend

**diverse** [daɪ'vɜːs] adj. verschieden

**diversion** [daɪ'vɜːʃn] n. a) Ablenkung, die; create a ~: ein Ablenkungsmanöver durchführen; b) (Brit.: alternative route) Umleitung, die

**diversity** [daɪ'vɜːsɪtɪ] n. Vielfalt, die

**divert** [daɪ'vɜːt] v. t. umleiten ⟨Verkehr, Fluß⟩; ablenken ⟨Aufmerksamkeit⟩

**divide** [dɪ'vaɪd] 1. v. t. a) teilen; ~ sth. in two etw. [in zwei Teile] zerteilen; b) (distribute) aufteilen (among/between unter + Akk. od. Dat.); c) (Math.) dividieren (fachspr.), teilen (by durch). 2. v. i. sich teilen; ~ |from sth.| von etw. abzweigen. **divide 'out** v. t. aufteilen (among/between unter + Akk. od. Dat.); (distribute) verteilen an (+ Akk.). **divide 'up** v. t. aufteilen

**dividend** ['dɪvɪdend] n. Dividende, die

**dividers** [dɪ'vaɪdəz] n. pl. Stechzirkel, der

**divine** [dɪ'vaɪn] adj. göttlich

**diving** ['daɪvɪŋ] n. Kunstspringen, das. **'diving-board** n. Sprungbrett, das. **'diving-suit** n. Taucheranzug, der

**divinity** [dɪ'vɪnɪtɪ] n. a) Göttlichkeit, die; b) (god) Gottheit, die

**divisible** [dɪ'vɪzɪbl] adj. teilbar (by durch)

**division** [dɪ'vɪʒn] n. a) Teilung, die; b) (Math.) Dividieren, das; c) (section, part) Abteilung, die; d) (group) Gruppe, die; e) (Mil. etc.) Division, die; f) (Footb. etc.) Liga, die; Spielklasse, die; (in British football) Division, die

**divorce** [dɪ'vɔːs] 1. n. [Ehe]scheidung, die. 2. v. t. ~ one's husband/wife sich von seinem Mann/seiner Frau scheiden lassen. **divorced** [dɪ'vɔːst] adj. geschieden; get ~: sich scheiden lassen

**divulge** [daɪ'vʌldʒ] v. t. preisgeben

**DIY** abbr. do-it-yourself

**dizzy** ['dɪzɪ] adj. schwind[e]lig; I feel ~: mir ist schwindlig

**do** [də, stressed duː] 1. v. t., neg. coll. don't [dəʊnt], pres. t. he does [dʌz], neg. (coll.) doesn't ['dʌznt], p. t. did [dɪd], neg. (coll.) didn't ['dɪdnt], pres. p. doing ['duːɪŋ], p.p. done [dʌn] a) machen ⟨Hausaufgaben, Hausarbeit, Examen, Handstand⟩; erfüllen ⟨Pflicht⟩; verrichten ⟨Arbeit⟩; vorführen ⟨Trick, Nummer, Tanz⟩; durchführen ⟨Test⟩; machen ⟨Übersetzung, Kopie, Bett⟩; schaffen ⟨Pensum⟩; (clean) putzen;

(arrange) [zurecht]machen ⟨Haare⟩; schminken ⟨Lippen, Augen, Gesicht⟩; machen (ugs.) ⟨Nägel⟩; (cut) schneiden ⟨Nägel⟩; (paint) machen (ugs.) ⟨Zimmer⟩; streichen ⟨Haus, Möbel⟩; (repair) in Ordnung bringen; do the shopping / washing-up / cleaning einkaufen [gehen]/abwaschen/saubermachen; what can I do for you? (in shop) was darf's sein?; do sth. about sth./sb. etw. gegen etw./jmdn. unternehmen; b) (cook) braten; well done durch[gebraten]; c) (solve) lösen ⟨Problem, Rätsel⟩; machen ⟨Puzzle, Kreuzworträtsel⟩; d) (sl.: swindle) reinlegen (ugs.); do sb. out of sth. jmdn. um etw. bringen; e) (satisfy) zusagen (+ Dat.). 2. v. i., forms as 1: a) (act) tun; do as they do mach es wie sie; b) (fare) how are you doing? wie geht's dir?; c) (get on) vorankommen; (in exams) abschneiden; do well/badly at school gut/schlecht in der Schule sein; d) how do you do? (formal) guten Tag/Morgen/Abend!; e) (serve purpose) tun; (suffice) [aus]reichen; (be suitable) gehen; that won't do das geht nicht; that will do! jetzt aber genug! 3. v. substitute, forms as 1: you mustn't act as he does du darfst nicht so wie er handeln; You went to Paris, didn't you? – Yes, I did Du warst doch in Paris, nicht wahr? – Ja[, stimmt]; come in, do! komm doch herein! 4. v. aux. forms as 1: I do love Greece Griechenland gefällt mir wirklich gut; little did he know that …: er hatte keine Ahnung, daß …; do you know him? kennst du ihn?; what does he want? was will er?; I don't or do not wish to take part ich möchte nicht teilnehmen; don't be so noisy! seid [doch] nicht so laut! 5. n. [duː], pl. do's or dos [duːz] (Brit. coll.) Feier, die; Fete, die (ugs.). do a'way with v. t. abschaffen. 'do for v. t. (coll.) do for sb. jmdn. fertigmachen (ugs.); be done for erledigt sein. do 'in v. t. (sl.) kaltmachen (salopp). do 'up v. t. a) (fasten) zumachen; binden ⟨Schnürsenkel, Fliege⟩; b) (wrap) einpacken. 'do with v. t. I could do with …: ich brauche … 'do without v. t. do without sth. auf etw. (Akk.) verzichten

**docile** ['dəʊsaɪl] adj. sanft; (submissive) unterwürfig

**'dock** [dɒk] 1. n. a) Dock, das; b) usu. in pl. (area) Hafen, der. 2. v. t. [ein]docken. 3. v. i. anlegen

²**dock** n. (in lawcourt) Anklagebank, die; **stand/be in the ~:** ≈ auf der Anklagebank sitzen

¹**docker** n. Hafenarbeiter, der

¹**dockyard** n. Schiffswerft, die

**doctor** ['dɒktə(r)] 1. n. **a)** Arzt, der/Ärztin, die; as address Herr/Frau Doktor; **b)** (holder of degree) Doktor, der. 2. v.t. (coll.) verfälschen

**doctrine** ['dɒktrɪn] n. Lehre, die

**document** ['dɒkjʊmənt] n. Dokument, das; Urkunde, die

**documentary** [dɒkjʊ'mentərɪ] 1. adj. dokumentarisch. 2. n. (film) Dokumentarfilm, der

**dodge** [dɒdʒ] 1. v.i. ausweichen. 2. v.t. ausweichen (+ Dat.) ⟨Schlag, Hindernis usw.⟩; entkommen (+ Dat.) ⟨Polizei, Verfolger⟩. 3. n. (trick) Trick, der

**dodgems** ['dɒdʒəmz] n. pl. [Auto]skooterbahn, die; **have a ride/go on the ~:** Autoskooter fahren

**dodgy** ['dɒdʒɪ] adj. (Brit. coll.) (unreliable) unsicher; (risky) gewagt

**doe** [dəʊ] n. (deer) Damtier, das; (rabbit) [Kaninchen]weibchen, das

**does** [dʌz] see do

**doesn't** ['dʌznt] (coll.) = does not; see do

**dog** [dɒg] 1. n. Hund, der. 2. v.t., -gg- verfolgen; (fig.) heimsuchen

**dog:** ~**-biscuit** n. Hundekuchen, der; ~**-collar** n. [Hunde]halsband, das; (joc.: clerical collar) Kollar, das; ~**-eared** adj. **a ~-eared book** ein Buch mit Eselsohren

**dogged** ['dɒgɪd] adj. hartnäckig ⟨Weigerung, Verurteilung⟩; zäh ⟨Durchhaltevermögen, Ausdauer⟩

**dogma** ['dɒgmə] n. Dogma, das. **dogmatic** [dɒg'mætɪk] adj. dogmatisch

**doing** ['duːɪŋ] n. Tun, das

**do-it-yourself** [duːɪtjə'self] 1. adj. Do-it-yourself-. 2. n. Heimwerken, das

**doldrums** ['dɒldrəmz] n. pl. **in the ~** (in low spirits) niedergeschlagen; (Econ.) in einer Flaute

**dole** [dəʊl] 1. n. (coll.) **the ~:** Stempelgeld, das (ugs.); **be/go on the ~:** stempeln gehen (ugs.). 2. v.t. ~ **out** [in kleinen Mengen] verteilen

**doll** [dɒl] n. Puppe, die

**dollar** ['dɒlə(r)] n. Dollar, der

**dollop** ['dɒləp] n. (coll.) Klacks, der (ugs.)

¹**doll's house** n. Puppenhaus, das

**dolphin** ['dɒlfɪn] n. Delphin, der

**domain** [də'meɪn] n. Gebiet, das

**dome** [dəʊm] n. Kuppel, die

**domestic** [də'mestɪk] adj. **a)** (household) häuslich; (family) familiär ⟨Angelegenheit, Reibereien⟩; **b)** (Econ.) inländisch; Binnen-; **c)** ~ **animal/cat** Haustier, das/-katze, die

**domesticated** [də'mestɪkeɪtɪd] adj. gezähmt ⟨Tier⟩; (fig.) häuslich

**dominant** ['dɒmɪnənt] adj. vorherrschend

**dominate** ['dɒmɪneɪt] v.t. beherrschen. **domination** [dɒmɪ'neɪʃn] n. [Vor]herrschaft, die (over über + Akk.)

**domineering** [dɒmɪ'nɪərɪŋ] adj. herrisch

**domino** ['dɒmɪnəʊ] n. Domino[stein], der; ~es sing. (game) Domino[spiel], das; **play ~es** Domino spielen

¹**don** [dɒn] v.t. (Liter.) anlegen (geh.)

²**don** n. (Univ.) Dozent, der

**donate** [dəʊ'neɪt] v.t. spenden; (on large scale) stiften. **donation** [də'neɪʃn] n. Spende, die (to für); (large-scale) Stiftung, die

**done** [dʌn] see do

**donkey** ['dɒŋkɪ] n. Esel, der

**donor** ['dəʊnə(r)] n. Spender, der/Spenderin, die

**don't** [dəʊnt] (coll.) = do not; see do

**doodle** ['duːdl] v.i. [herum]kritzeln

**doom** [duːm] 1. n. Verhängnis, das. 2. v.t. verurteilen; **be ~ed** verloren sein; **be ~ed to fail** or **failure** zum Scheitern verurteilt sein

**door** [dɔː(r)] n. Tür, die; (of castle, barn) Tor, das; **out of ~s** im Freien; **go out of ~s** nach draußen gehen

**door:** ~**bell** n. Türklingel, die; ~**-handle** n. Türklinke, die; ~**mat** n. Fußmatte, die; ~**step** n. Türstufe, die; **on one's/the ~step** (fig.) vor jmds. Tür; ~**way** n. Eingang, der

**dope** [dəʊp] 1. n. **a)** (sl.: narcotic) Stoff, der (salopp); **b)** (coll.: fool) Dussel, der (ugs.). 2. v.t. dopen ⟨Pferd, Athleten⟩

**dormant** ['dɔːmənt] adj. ruhend ⟨Tier, Pflanze⟩; untätig ⟨Vulkan⟩

**dormitory** ['dɔːmɪtərɪ] n. Schlafsaal, der

**dormouse** ['dɔːmaʊs] n., pl. **dormice** ['dɔːmaɪs] Haselmaus, die

**dose** [dəʊs] 1. n. Dosis, die. 2. v.t. ~ **sb. with sth.** jmdm. etw. geben

**dot** [dɒt] n. Punkt, der; **on the ~:** auf den Punkt genau

**dote** [dəʊt] v.i. ~ **on sb./sth.** jmdn./etw. abgöttisch lieben

**dotted** ['dɒtɪd] *adj.* gepunktet

**dotty** ['dɒtɪ] *adj. (coll.) (silly)* dümm-lich; *(feeble-minded)* vertrottelt *(ugs.);* *(absurd)* blödsinnig *(ugs.)*

**double** ['dʌbl] 1. *adj.* doppelt; ~ **bed/room** Doppelbett, *das/*-zimmer, *das;* be ~ **the height/width/length** doppelt so hoch/breit/lang sein. 2. *adv.* dop-pelt. 3. *n.* **a)** Doppelte, *das;* **b)** *(twice as much)* doppelt soviel; *(twice as many)* doppelt so viele; **c)** *(person)* Doppelgänger, *der/*-gängerin, *die;* **d)** *in pl. (Tennis etc.)* Doppel, *das;* **e)** at the ~ *(Mil.)* im Laufschritt; *(fig.)* ganz schnell. 4. *v. t.* verdoppeln. 5. *v. i.* sich verdoppeln. **double 'back** *v. i.* kehrt-machen *(ugs.).* **double 'up** krümmen (with vor + *Dat.*)

**double:** ~-**'bass** *n.* Kontrabaß, *der;* ~-**'check** *v. t. (verify twice)* zweimal kontrollieren; *(verify in two ways)* zweifach überprüfen; ~ **'chin** *n.* Doppelkinn, *das;* ~-**'cross** *v. t.* ein Doppelspiel treiben mit; ~-**decker** *n.* [dʌbl'dekə(r)] *n.* Doppeldeckerbus, *der;* ~ **'glazing** *n.* Doppelverglasung, *die;* ~-**'jointed** *adj.* sehr gelenkig

**doubly** ['dʌblɪ] *adv.* doppelt

**doubt** [daʊt] 1. *n.* Zweifel, *der* (about, as to, of an + *Dat.*); ~[s] [about *or* as to sth./as to whether ...] *(as to future)* Ungewißheit, *(as to fact)* Unsicherheit [über etw. *(Akk.)*/darüber, ob ...]; **there's no ~ that ...:** es besteht kein Zweifel daran, daß ...; ~[s] *(hesitations)* Bedenken *Pl.* (about gegen); no ~ *(certainly)* gewiß; *(probably)* sicher-lich. 2. *v. i.* zweifeln. 3. *v. t.* zweifeln an (+ *Dat.*); **I don't** ~ **it** or **it** ich be-zweifle das nicht; **I** ~ **whether** *or* **if** *or* **that ...:** ich bezweifle, daß ... **doubt-ful** ['daʊtfl] *adj.* skeptisch *(Wesen);* ungläubig *(Blick)*

**dough** [dəʊ] *n.* **a)** Teig, *der;* **b)** *(sl.: money)* Knete, *die (salopp).* **'dough-nut** *n.* [Berliner] Pfannkuchen, *der*

**douse** [daʊs] *v. t.* übergießen; *(extin-guish)* ausmachen

**'dove** [dʌv] *n.* Taube, *die*

**'dove** [dəʊv] *see* **dive 1**

**dowdy** ['daʊdɪ] *adj.* unansehnlich; *(shabby)* schäbig

**'down** [daʊn] *n. (feathers)* Daunen *Pl.*

**'down** 1. *adv.* **a)** *(to lower place)* her-unter/hinunter; *(in lift)* abwärts; **b)** *(in lower place, downstairs)* unten; ~ **there/here** da/hier unten; **the next floor** ~: ein Stockwerk tiefer; **be** ~ **with an illness** eine Krankheit haben;

**be three points/games** ~: mit drei Punkten/Spielen zurückliegen. 2. *prep.* herunter/hinunter; **lower** ~ **the river** weiter unten am Fluß; **walk** ~ **the hill/road** den Berg/die Straße herun-tergehen; **fall** ~ **the stairs/steps** die Treppe/Stufen herunterstürzen; **fall** ~ **a hole/ditch** in ein Loch/ einen Gra-ben fallen; **go** ~ **the pub** in die Kneipe gehen; **live just** ~ **the road** ein Stück weiter unten in der Straße wohnen; **be** ~ **the pub/town** in der Kneipe/Stadt sein; **I've got coffee [all]** ~ **my skirt** mein ganzer Rock ist voll Kaffee. 3. *v. t. (coll.)* schlucken *(ugs.) (Getränk);* ~ **tools** die Arbeit niederlegen

**down:** ~-**and-'out** *n.* Stadtstreicher, *der/*-streicherin, *die;* ~**cast** *adj.* nie-dergeschlagen; ~**fall** *n.* Untergang, *der;* ~-**'hearted** *adj.* niedergeschla-gen; ~**'hill** *adv.* bergab; ~ **payment** *n.* Anzahlung, *die;* ~**pour** *n.* Regen-guß, *der;* ~**'right** *adj.* ausgemacht; glatt *(Lüge);* ~**stairs** 1. [-'-] *adv.* die Treppe hinunter *(gehen, fallen, kom-men);* unten *(wohnen, sein);* 2. ['--] *adj.* im Erdgeschoß *nachgestellt;* ~**'stream** *adv.* flußabwärts; ~-**to-'earth** *adj.* sachlich; ~**town** *adv.* im/ *(direction)* ins Stadtzentrum; ~-**trod-den** *adj.* unterdrückt; ~ **'under** *adv. (coll.)* in/*(to)* nach Australien/ Neu-seeland

**downward** ['daʊnwəd] 1. *adj.* nach unten gerichtet. 2. *adv.* abwärts *(sich bewegen);* nach unten *(sehen, gehen).* **downwards** ['daʊnwədz] *see* **down-ward 2**

**dowry** ['daʊrɪ] *n.* Aussteuer, *die*

**doze** [dəʊz] 1. *v. i.* dösen *(ugs.).* 2. *n.* Nickerchen, *das (ugs.).* **doze 'off** *v. i.* eindösen *(ugs.)*

**dozen** ['dʌzn] *n.* **a)** Dutzend, *das;* **half a** ~: sechs; **b)** *in pl. (coll.: many)* Dut-zende *Pl.*

**Dr** *abbr.* **doctor** Dr.

**drab** [dræb] *adj.* langweilig; trostlos *(Landschaft);* eintönig *(Leben)*

**draft** [drɑːft] 1. *n.* **a)** *(of speech)* Kon-zept, *das; (of treaty, bill)* Entwurf, *der;* **b)** *(Amer.) see* **draught. 2.** *v. t.* entwer-fen. **drafty** *(Amer.) see* **draughty**

**drag** [dræg] 1. *v. t.,* -gg- schleppen. 2. *v. i.,* -gg- schleifen; *(fig.: pass slowly)* sich [hin]schleppen. 3. *n. (sl.)* **in** ~: in Frauenkleidung. **drag 'on** *v. i.* sich [da]hin schleppen

**dragon** ['drægn] *n.* Drache, *der.* **'dra-gonfly** *n.* Libelle, *die*

**drain** [dreɪn] **1.** *n.* Abflußrohr, *das; (underground)* Kanalisationsrohr, *das; (grating at roadside)* Gully, *der;* **go down the ~** *(fig. coll.)* für die Katz sein *(ugs.).* **2.** *v. t.* **a)** trockenlegen ⟨*Teich*⟩; entwässern ⟨*Land*⟩; ableiten ⟨*Wasser*⟩; **b)** *(Cookery)* abgießen ⟨*Wasser, Gemüse*⟩; **c)** austrinken ⟨*Glas*⟩. **3.** *v. i.* ⟨*Flüssigkeit:*⟩ ablaufen; ⟨*Geschirr, Gemüse:*⟩ abtropfen. **drainage** ['dreɪnɪdʒ] *n.* Kanalisation, *die.* **'draining-board** *(Brit.; Amer.:* **'drainboard)** *n.* Abtropfbrett, *das.* **'drainpipe.** *n.* Regen[abfall]rohr, *das*

**drake** [dreɪk] *n.* Enterich, *der*

**drama** ['drɑːmə] *n.* Drama, *das.* **dramatic** [drəˈmætɪk] *adj.* dramatisch. **dramatist** ['dræmətɪst] *n.* Dramatiker, *der*/Dramatikerin, *die.* **dramatize** ['dræmətaɪz] *v. t.* dramatisieren

**drank** *see* **drink 2**

**drape** [dreɪp] **1.** *v. t.* drapieren. **2.** *n.* *(Amer.:* curtain) Vorhang, *der.* **'draper** *n. (Brit.)* Textilkaufmann, *der;* **~'s [shop]** Textilgeschäft, *das*

**drastic** ['dræstɪk] *adj.* drastisch

**draught** [drɑːft] *n.* [Luft]zug, *der;* **there's a ~:** es zieht

**'draughtboard** *n. (Brit.)* Damebrett, *das*

**'draughts** *n. (Brit.)* Damespiel, *das*

**'draughtsman** [~men] *n., pl.* **draughtsmen** [~mən] Zeichner, *der*/Zeichnerin, *die*

**'draughty** *adj.* zugig

**draw** [drɔː] **1.** *v. t.,* **drew** [druː], **drawn** [drɔːn] **a)** *(pull)* ziehen; **~ the curtains/blinds** *(close)* die Vorhänge zuziehen/ die Jalousien herunterlassen; **~ sth. towards one** etw. zu sich heranziehen; **b)** *(attract)* anlocken; **be ~n to sb.** von jmdm. angezogen werden; **c)** *(take out)* herausziehen; schöpfen ⟨*Wasser*⟩; **~ money from the bank** Geld bei der Bank holen/abheben; **d)** beziehen ⟨*Gehalt, Rente, Arbeitslosenunterstützung*⟩; **e)** ziehen ⟨*Strich*⟩; zeichnen ⟨*geometrische Figur, Bild*⟩; **f)** ziehen ⟨*Parallele, Vergleich*⟩; herausstellen ⟨*Unterschied*⟩. **2.** *v. i.* **drew, drawn: ~ to an end** zu Ende gehen. **3.** *n.* **a)** *(raffle)* Tombola, *die;* **b)** *[result of]* drawn game) Unentschieden, *das.* **draw 'back 1.** *v. t.* zurückziehen. **2.** *v. i.* zurückweichen. **draw 'in** *v. i.* einfahren; ⟨*Tage:*⟩ kürzer werden. **draw 'out** *v. i.* abfahren; ⟨*Tage:*⟩ länger werden. **draw 'up 1.** *v. t.* **a)** aufsetzen

⟨*Vertrag*⟩; aufstellen ⟨*Liste*⟩; **b)** *(pull closer)* heranziehen. **2.** *v. i.* [an]halten

**draw:** **~back** *n.* Nachteil, *der;* **~bridge** *n.* Zugbrücke, *die*

**drawer** [drɔː(r), 'drɔːə(r)] *n.* Schublade, *die*

**'drawing** *n. (sketch)* Zeichnung, *die*

**drawing:** **~board** *n.* Zeichenbrett, *das;* **~pin** *n. (Brit.)* Reißzwecke, *die;* **~room** *n.* Salon, *der*

**drawl** [drɔːl] **1.** *v. i.* gedehnt sprechen. **2.** *n.* gedehntes Sprechen

**drawn** *see* **draw 1, 2**

**dread** [dred] **1.** *v. t.* sich sehr fürchten vor ( + *Dat.*); **the ~ed day/moment** der gefürchtete Tag/Augenblick. **2.** *n.* Angst, *die.* **dreadful** ['dredfl] *adj.* schrecklich; *(coll.: very bad)* fürchterlich; **I feel ~** *(unwell)* ich fühle mich scheußlich *(ugs.).* **'dreadfully** *adv.* schrecklich; *(coll.: very badly)* fürchterlich

**dream** [driːm] **1.** *n.* Traum, *der;* **have a ~ about sb./sth.** von jmdm./etw. träumen. **2.** *v. i. & t.* **dreamt** [dremt] *or* **dreamed** träumen

**dreary** ['drɪərɪ] *adj.* trostlos

**dredge** [dredʒ] *v. t.* ausbaggern. **'dredger** *n.* Bagger, *der*

**dregs** [dregz] *n. pl.* [Boden]satz, *der*

**drench** [drentʃ] *v. t.* durchnässen

**dress** [dres] **1.** *n.* Kleid, *das; (clothing)* Kleidung, *die.* **2.** *v. t.* **a)** anziehen; **be well ~ed** gut gekleidet sein; **get ~ed** sich anziehen; **b)** verbinden ⟨*Wunde*⟩. **3.** *v. i.* sich anziehen. **dress 'up** *v. i.* sich feinmachen

**'dresser** *n.* **a)** Anrichte, *die;* **b)** *(Amer.)* see **dressing-table**

**'dressing** *n.* **a)** *no pl.* Anziehen, *das;* **b)** *(Cookery)* Dressing, *das;* **c)** *(Med.)* Verband, *der*

**dressing:** **~gown** *n.* Bademantel, *der;* **~room** *n. (Sport)* Umkleideraum, *der; (for actor)* Garderobe, *die;* **~table** *n.* Frisierkommode, *die*

**dress:** **~maker** *n.* Damenschneider, *der*/-schneiderin, *die;* **~making** *n.* Damenschneiderei, *die;* **~ rehearsal** *n.* Generalprobe, *die*

**drew** *see* **draw 1, 2**

**dribble** ['drɪbl] *v. i.* **a)** *(slobber)* sabbern; **b)** *(Sport)* dribbeln

**dried** [draɪd] *adj.* getrocknet; **~ fruit[s]** Dörrobst, *das;* **~ milk** Trockenmilch, *die*

**drier** ['draɪə(r)] *n. (for hair)* Trockenhaube, *die; (hand-held)* Fön ⓦ, *der; (for laundry)* [Wäsche]trockner, *der*

**drift** [drɪft] 1. *n.* **a)** *(of snow or sand)* Verwehung, *die;* **b)** *(gist)* **get** *or* **catch the ~ of sth.** etw im wesentlichen verstehen. 2. *v. i.* **a)** treiben; ⟨*Wolke:*⟩ ziehen; **b)** ⟨*Sand, Schnee:*⟩ zusammengeweht werden. '**driftwood** *n.* Treibholz, *das*

**drill** [drɪl] 1. *n.* **a)** *(tool)* Bohrer, *der;* **b)** *(Mil.: training)* Drill, *der.* 2. *v. t. & i.* bohren (**for** nach)

**drink** [drɪŋk] 1. *n.* Getränk, *das; (alcoholic)* Glas, *das; (not with food)* Drink, *der;* **have a ~:** [etwas] trinken; *(alcoholic)* ein Glas trinken. 2. *v. t. & i.* **drank** [dræŋk], **drunk** [drʌŋk] trinken. **drinkable** ['drɪŋkəbl] *adj.* trinkbar. '**drinking-water** *n.* Trinkwasser, *das*

**drip** [drɪp] 1. *n.* **a)** Tropfen, *das;* **b)** *(coll.: feeble person)* Schlappschwanz, *der (salopp).* 2. *v. i.* -**pp**- tropfen; **be ~ping with water/moisture** triefend naß sein. '**drip-dry** *adj.* bügelfrei '**dripping** *n. (Cookery)* Schmalz, *das*

**drive** [draɪv] 1. *n.* **a)** Fahrt, *die;* **b)** *(private road)* Zufahrt, *die; (entrance) (to small building)* Einfahrt, *die; (to large building)* Auffahrt, *die;* **c)** *(energy)* Tatkraft, *die;* **d)** *(Psych.)* Trieb, *der;* **e)** *(Motor Veh.)* **left-hand/right-hand ~:** Links-/Rechtssteuerung, *die.* 2. *v. t.,* **drove** [drəʊv], **driven** ['drɪvn] **a)** fahren; **b)** treiben ⟨*Tier*⟩; **c)** *(compel to move)* vertreiben (**out of, from** aus); **d)** *(fig.)* **~ sb. to sth.** jmdn. zu etw. treiben; **~ sb. to do sth.** *or* **into doing sth.** jmdn. dazu treiben, etw. zu tun; **e)** *(power)* antreiben. 3. *v. i.,* **drove, driven a)** fahren; **can you ~?** kannst du Auto fahren?; **b)** *(go by car)* mit dem [eigenen] Auto fahren. '**drive at** *v. t. (fig.)* hinauswollen auf ( + *Akk.*); **what are you driving at?** worauf wollen Sie hinaus? **drive a'way** 1. *v. i.* wegfahren. 2. *v. t.* **a)** wegfahren; **b)** *(chase away)* vertreiben. **drive 'off** *see* drive away. **drive 'on** *v. i.* weiterfahren. **drive 'up** *v. i.* vorfahren (**to** vor + *Dat.*) '**drive-in** *adj.* Drive-in-; **~ cinema** *or* *(Amer.)* **movie |theater|** Autokino, *das*

**drivel** ['drɪvl] *n.* Gefasel, *das (ugs.);* **talk ~:** faseln *(ugs.)*

**driven** *see* drive 2, 3

**driver** ['draɪvə(r)] *n.* Fahrer, *der/*Fahrerin, *die; (of locomotive)* Führer, *der/*Führerin, *die;* **~s license** *(Amer.)* Führerschein, *der*

**driving** ['draɪvɪŋ] 1. *n.* Fahren, *das.* 2. *adj.* peitschend ⟨*Regen*⟩

**driving: ~-instructor** *n.* Fahrlehrer, *der/*-lehrerin, *die;* **~-lesson** *n.* Fahrstunde, *die;* **~-licence** *n.* Führerschein, *der;* **~-school** *n.* Fahrschule, *die;* **~-test** *n.* Fahrprüfung, *die*

**drizzle** ['drɪzl] 1. *n.* Nieseln, *das.* 2. *v. i.* **it's drizzling** es nieselt

**drone** [drəʊn] 1. *v. i.* **a)** ⟨*Biene:*⟩ summen; ⟨*Maschine:*⟩ brummen; **b)** ⟨*Rezitator:*⟩ leiern. 2. *n. see* 1: Summen, *das;* Brummen, *das;* Geleier, *das*

**drool** [druːl] *v. i.* **~ over** eine kindische Freude haben an ( + *Dat.*)

**droop** [druːp] *v. i.* herunterhängen; ⟨*Blume:*⟩ den Kopf hängen lassen

**drop** [drɒp] 1. *n.* **a)** Tropfen, *der;* **in ~s** tropfenweise; **b)** *(decrease)* Rückgang, *der.* 2. *v. i.,* -**pp**-: **a)** *(fall) (accidentally)* [herunter]fallen; *(deliberately)* sich [hinunter]fallen lassen; **b)** *(in amount etc.)* sinken; ⟨*Preis, Wert:*⟩ sinken, fallen; ⟨*Wind:*⟩ sich legen; ⟨*Stimme:*⟩ sich senken. 3. *v. t.,* -**pp**-: **a)** fallen lassen; abwerfen ⟨*Bomben, Nachschub*⟩; **b)** *(discontinue, abandon)* fallenlassen; **c)** *(omit)* auslassen. **drop 'by, drop 'in** *v. i.* vorbeikommen. **drop 'off** 1. *v. i.* **a)** *(fall off)* abfallen; **b)** *(fall asleep)* einnicken. 2. *v. t.* absetzen ⟨*Fahrgast*⟩. **drop 'out** *v. i.* **a)** herausfallen (**of** aus); **b)** *(withdraw)* aussteigen *(ugs.)* (**of** aus); *(beforehand)* seine Teilnahme absagen '**drop-out** *n.* Aussteiger, *der/*Aussteigerin, *die*

**drought** [draʊt] *n.* Dürre, *die*

**drove** *see* drive 2, 3

**drown** [draʊn] 1. *v. i.* ertrinken. 2. *v. t.* ertränken; **be ~ed** ertrinken

**drowsy** ['draʊzɪ] *adj.* schläfrig; *(on just waking)* verschlafen

**drudgery** ['drʌdʒərɪ] *n.* Schufterei, *die*

**drug** [drʌg] 1. *n.* **a)** *(Med.)* [Arznei]mittel, *das;* **b)** *(narcotic)* Droge, *die;* **be on ~s** Rauschgift nehmen. 2. *v. t.,* -**gg**- betäuben ⟨*Person*⟩; **~ sb.'s food/drink** jmds. Essen/Getränk *(Dat.)* ein Betäubungsmittel beimischen

**drug: ~ addict** *n.* Drogensüchtige, *der/die;* **~ addiction** *n.* Drogensucht, *die;* **~-store** *n. (Amer.)* Drugstore, *der*

**drum** [drʌm] 1. *n.* **a)** Trommel, *die;* **b)** *in pl. (in jazz or pop)* Schlagzeug, *das;* **c)** *(container)* Faß, *das.* 2. *v. i.* trommeln. **drum 'up** *v. i.* auftreiben '**drummer** *n.* Schlagzeuger, *der* '**drumstick** *n.* **a)** Trommelschlegel, *der;* **b)** *(Cookery)* Keule, *die*

**drunk** [drʌŋk] **1.** *adj.* be ~: betrunken sein; get ~: betrunken werden (on von); *(intentionally)* sich betrinken ⟨on mit⟩. **2.** *n.* Betrunkene, *der/die*

**drunkard** ['drʌŋkəd] *n.* Trinker, *der/* Trinkerin, *die*

**drunken** ['drʌŋkn] *attrib. adj.* betrunken; *(habitually)* ständig betrunken; ~ **driving** Trunkenheit am Steuer.

'**drunkenness** *n.* Betrunkenheit, *die;* *(habitual)* Trunksucht, *die*

**dry** [draɪ] **1.** *adj.* trocken; trocken, *(very ~)* herb ⟨Wein⟩; ausgetrocknet ⟨Flußbett⟩; get *or* become ~: trocknen. **2.** *v. t.* **a)** trocknen ⟨Haare, Wäsche⟩; abtrocknen ⟨Geschirr, Baby⟩; ~ **oneself** sich abtrocknen; ~ **one's eyes** *or* **tears/hands** sich *(Dat.)* die Tränen abwischen/die Hände abtrocknen; **b)** *(preserve)* trocknen; dörren ⟨Obst, Fleisch⟩. **3.** *v. i.* trocknen. **dry 'out** *v. t. & i.* trocknen. **dry 'up 1.** *v. t.* abtrocknen. **2.** *v. i.* **a)** *(~ the dishes)* abtrocknen; **b)** ⟨Brunnen, Quelle:⟩ versiegen; ⟨Fluß, Teich:⟩ austrocknen

**dry:** ~-'**clean** *v. t.* chemisch reinigen; ~-'**cleaner's** *n.* chemische Reinigung; ~-'**cleaning** *n.* chemische Reinigung

'**dryer** *see* drier

'**dryness** *n.* Trockenheit, *die*

**dual** ['dju:əl] *adj.* doppelt. **dual 'carriageway** *n. (Brit.)* Straße mit Mittelstreifen. **dual-'purpose** *adj.* zweifach verwendbar

**dubious** ['dju:bɪəs] *adj. (doubting)* unschlüssig; *(suspicious)* zweifelhaft

**duchess** ['dʌtʃɪs] *n.* Herzogin, *die*

**duck** [dʌk] **1.** *n.* Ente, *die.* **2.** *v. i.* sich [schnell] ducken. **3.** *v. t.* ~ **one's head** den Kopf einziehen

**duckling** ['dʌklɪŋ] *n.* Entenküken, *das*

**duct** [dʌkt] *n.* Rohr, *das; (for air)* Ventil, *das*

**dud** [dʌd] **1.** *n. (useless thing)* Niete, *die (ugs.); (counterfeit)* Fälschung, *die.* **2.** *adj.* mies *(ugs.);* schlecht; *(fake)* gefälscht; geplatzt ⟨Scheck⟩

**due** [dju:] **1.** *adj.* **a)** *(owed)* geschuldet; zustehend ⟨Eigentum, Recht usw.⟩; **there's sth. ~ to me, I've got sth. ~:** mir steht etw. zu; **b)** *(immediately payable)* fällig; **c)** *(that it is proper to give or use)* gebührend; angemessen ⟨Belohnung⟩; **be ~ to sb.** jmdm. gebühren; **with all ~ respect** bei allem gebotenen Respekt; **d)** *(attributable)* **the mistake was ~ to negligence** der Fehler war durch Nachlässigkeit verursacht; **it's ~ to**

---

**her that we missed the train** ihretwegen verpaßten wir den Zug; **e)** *(scheduled, expected);* **be ~ to do sth.** etw. tun sollen; **be ~ ⟨to arrive⟩** ankommen sollen; **f)** *(likely to get, deserving)* **be ~ for sth.** etw. verdienen. **2.** *adv.* **a)** ~ **north** genau nach Norden; **b)** ~ **to** auf Grund (+ *Gen.*); aufgrund (+ *Gen.*). **3.** *n.* **a)** **give sb. his** ~: jmdm. Gerechtigkeit widerfahren lassen; **b)** ~**s** *(fees)* Gebühren *Pl.*

**duel** ['dju:əl] *n.* Duell, *das*

**duet** [dju:'et] *n. (for voices)* Duett, *das; (instrumental)* Duo, *das*

**duffle** ['dʌfl]: ~ **bag** *n.* Matchbeutel, *der;* ~ **coat** *n.* Dufflecoat, *der*

**dug** *see* **dig**

**duke** [dju:k] *n.* Herzog, *der*

**dull** [dʌl] **1.** *adj.* **a)** *(stupid)* beschränkt; *(slow to understand)* begriffsstutzig; **b)** *(boring)* langweilig; **c)** *(gloomy)* trübe ⟨Wetter, Tag⟩. **2.** *v. t.* abstumpfen ⟨Geist, Sinne, Verstand⟩

**duly** ['dju:lɪ] *adv.* ordnungsgemäß

**dumb** [dʌm] *adj.* **a)** stumm; **b)** *(coll.: stupid)* doof *(ugs.)*

**dumbfounded** [dʌm'faʊndɪd] *adj.* sprachlos

**dummy** ['dʌmɪ] *n.* **a)** *(of tailor)* Schneiderpuppe, *die; (in shop)* Schaufensterpuppe, *die; (of ventriloquist)* Puppe, *die; (stupid person)* Dummkopf, *der (ugs.);* **like a stuffed ~:** wie ein Ölgötze *(ugs.);* **b)** *(imitation)* Attrappe, *die;* **c)** *(esp. Brit.: for baby)* Schnuller, *der*

**dump** [dʌmp] **1.** *n.* **a)** *(place)* Müllkippe, *die; (heap)* Müllhaufen, *der; (permanent)* Müllhalde, *die;* **b)** *(Mil.)* Depot, *das;* **c)** *(coll.: town)* Kaff, *das (ugs.).* **2.** *v. t. (dispose of)* werfen; *(deposit)* abladen ⟨Sand, Müll usw.⟩; *(leave)* lassen; *(place)* abstellen

**dumpling** ['dʌmplɪŋ] *n.* Kloß, *der*

**dumps** *n. pl.* **be** *or* **feel down in the ~:** ganz down sein *(ugs.)*

**dunce** [dʌns] *n.* Null, *die (ugs.)*

**dune** [dju:n] *n.* Düne, *die*

**dung** [dʌŋ] *n.* Dung, *der*

**dungarees** [dʌŋgə'ri:z] *n. pl.* Latzhose, *die*

**dungeon** ['dʌndʒən] *n.* Kerker, *der*

**dunk** [dʌŋk] *v. t.* tunken

**dupe** [dju:p] **1.** *v. t.* übertölpeln. **2.** *n.* Dumme, *der/die*

**duplex** ['dju:pleks] *adj. (esp. Amer.) (two-storey)* zweistöckig ⟨Wohnung⟩; *(two-family)* Zweifamilien⟨haus⟩

**duplicate 1.** ['dju:plɪkət] *adj.* **a)** *(identical)* Zweit-; **b)** *(twofold)* doppelt. **2.** *n.*

Kopie, *die; (second copy of letter/document/key)* Duplikat, *das;* in ~: in doppelter Ausfertigung. 3. ['dju:plɪkeɪt] *v. t.* **a)** *(make a copy of, make in ~)* ~ **sth.** eine zweite Anfertigung von etw. machen; **b)** *(on machine)* vervielfältigen; **c)** *(do twice)* noch einmal tun

**durable** ['djʊərəbl] *adj.* haltbar; dauerhaft ‹*Friede, Freundschaft usw.*›

**duration** [djʊə'reɪʃn] *n.* Daùer, *die*

**duress** [djʊə'res] *n.* Zwang, *der*

**during** ['djʊərɪŋ] *·prep.* während; *(at a point in)* in (+ *Dat.*)

**dusk** [dʌsk] *n.* Einbruch der Dunkelheit

**dust** [dʌst] **1.** *n.* Staub, *der.* **2.** *v. t.* abstauben ‹*Möbel*›; ~ **a room/ house** in einem Zimmer/Haus Staub wischen. **3.** *v. i.* Staub wischen. **'dustbin** *n. (Brit.)* Mülltonne, *die.* **'dustcart** *(Brit.)* Müllwagen, *der*

**'duster** *n.* Staubtuch, *das*

**dust:** ~**jacket** *n.* Schutzumschlag, *der;* ~**man** [~mən] *n., pl.* ~**men** [~mən] *(Brit.)* Müllmann, *der;* ~**pan** *n.* Kehrschaufel, *die*

**'dusty** *adj.* staubig; verstaubt ‹*Bücher, Möbel*›

**Dutch** [dʌtʃ] **1.** *adj.* holländisch; **sb. is** ~: jmd. ist Holländer/Holländerin. **2.** *n.* **a)** *(language)* Holländisch, *das; see also* **English 2 a;** **b) the** ~ *pl.* die Holländer

**Dutch:** ~ **'courage** *n.* angetrunkener Mut; ~**man** [~mən] *n., pl.* ~**men** [~mən] Holländer, *der;* ~**woman** *n.* Holländerin, *die*

**dutiful** ['dju:tɪfl] *adj.* pflichtbewußt

**duty** ['dju:tɪ] *n.* **a)** Pflicht, *die; (task)* Aufgabe, *die;* **be on** ~: Dienst haben; **off** ~: nicht im Dienst; **be off** ~: keinen Dienst haben; ‹*ab ... Uhr*› dienstfrei sein; **b)** *(tax)* Zoll, *der;* **pay** ~ **on sth.** Zoll für etw. bezahlen. **'dutyfree** *adj.* zollfrei

**duvet** ['du:veɪ] *n.* Federbett, *das*

**dwarf** [dwɔːf] *n., pl.* ~**s** *or* **dwarves** ['dwɔːvz] Zwerg, *der/*Zwergin, *die*

**dwell** [dwel] *v. i.,* **dwelt** [dwelt] *(literary)* wohnen. **'dwell [up]on** *v. t. (in discussion)* sich ausführlich befassen mit; *(in thought)* in Gedanken verweilen bei

**'dwelling** *n.* Wohnung, *die*

**dwelt** *see* **dwell**

**dwindle** ['dwɪndl] *v. i.* ~ **[away]** abnehmen; ‹*Unterstützung, Interesse:*› nachlassen; ‹*Vorräte:*› schrumpfen

**dye** [daɪ] **1.** *n.* Färbemittel, *das.* **2.** *v. t.,* ~**ing** ['daɪɪŋ] färben

**dying** ['daɪɪŋ] *adj.* sterbend; absterbend ‹*Baum*›

**dyke** *see* **dike**

**dynamic** [daɪ'næmɪk] *adj.* dynamisch.
**dynamism** ['daɪnəmɪzm] *n.* Dynamik, *die*

**dynamite** ['daɪnəmaɪt] *n.* Dynamit, *das*

**dynamo** ['daɪnəməʊ] *n.* Dynamo, *der; (in car)* Lichtmaschine, *die*

**dynasty** ['dɪnəstɪ] *n.* Dynastie, *die*

**dysentry** ['dɪsəntrɪ] *n.* Ruhr, *die*

# E

**E, e** [iː] *n.* E, e, *das*

**E.** *abbr.* **a) east** O; **b) eastern** ö.

**each** [iːtʃ] **1.** *adj.* jeder/jede/jedes; **they cost** *or* **are a pound** ~: sie kosten ein Pfund pro Stück. **2.** *pron.* **a)** jeder/jede/jedes; **b)** ~ **other** sich

**eager** ['iːgə(r)] *adj.* eifrig; **be** ~ **to do sth.** etw. unbedingt tun wollen. **'eagerly** *adv.* eifrig; gespannt ‹*warten*›

**eagle** ['iːgl] *n.* Adler, *der*

**¹ear** [ɪə(r)] *n.* Ohr, *das*

**²ear** *n. (Bot.)* Ähre, *die*

**ear:** ~**ache** *n.* Ohrenschmerzen *Pl.;* ~**drum** *n.* Trommelfell, *das*

**earl** [ɜːl] *n.* Graf, *der*

**'ear lobe** *n.* Ohrläppchen, *das*

**early** ['ɜːlɪ] **1.** *adj.* früh. **2.** *adv.* früh; **I am a bit** ~: ich bin etwas zu früh gekommen; ~ **next week** Anfang der nächsten Woche; ~ **in June** Anfang Juni; **from** ~ **in the morning till late at night** von früh [morgens] bis spät [nachts]; ~ **on** schon früh

**ear:** ~**mark** *v. t.* vorsehen; ~**muffs** *n. pl.* Ohrenschützer, *Pl.*

**earn** [ɜːn] *v. t.* verdienen; *(bring in as income or interest)* einbringen

**earnest** ['ɜːnɪst] **1.** *adj.* ernsthaft. **2.** *n.* **in** ~: mit vollem Ernst

**earnings** ['ɜːnɪŋz] *n. pl.* Verdienst, *der; (of business etc.)* Ertrag, *der*

**ear:** ~**phones** *n. pl.* Kopfhörer, *der;*

~**-plug** *n*. Ohropax, *das* Ⓦ; ~**-ring** *n*. Ohrring, *der;* ~**shot** *n*. out of/ within ~ shot außer/in Hörweite

**earth** [ɜːθ] **1.** *n. (also Brit. Electr.)* Erde, *die;* how/what *etc.* on ~ ...? wie/ was *usw.* in aller Welt ...? **2.** *v. t. (Brit. Electr.)* erden

**earthenware** ['ɜːθnweə(r)] **1.** *n*. Tonwaren *Pl.* **2.** *adj.* Ton~

**earth:** ~**quake** *n*. Erdbeben, *das;* ~**worm** *n*. Regenwurm, *der*

'**earthy** *adj.* **a)** erdig; **b)** *(coarse)* derb

**earwig** ['ɪəwɪg] *n*. Ohrwurm, *der*

**ease** [iːz] **1.** *n*. **a)** set sb. at ~: jmdn. beruhigen; at |one's| ~: entspannt; be *or* feel at |one's| ~: sich wohl fühlen; |stand| at ~! *(Mil.)* rührt euch!; **b)** with ~ *(without difficulty)* mit Leichtigkeit. **2.** *v. t.* lindern ⟨Schmerz, Kummer⟩; entspannen ⟨Lage⟩; verringern ⟨Belastung, Druck, Spannung⟩. **3.** *v. i.* nachlassen

**easel** ['iːzl] *n*. Staffelei, *die*

**easily** ['iːzɪlɪ] *adv.* leicht

**easiness** ['iːzɪnɪs] *n*. Leichtigkeit, *die*

**east** [iːst] **1.** *n*. **a)** Osten, *der;* in/to|wards|/from the ~: im/nach/von Osten; to the ~ of östlich von; **b)** *usu.* E~ *(Geog., Polit.)* Osten, *der*. **2.** *adj.* östlich; Ost⟨küste, -wind, -grenze⟩. **3.** *adv.* nach Osten; ~ of östlich von. '**East Ber'lin** *pr. n. (Hist.)* Ostberlin, *das*. '**eastbound** *adj.* ⟨Zug, Verkehr *usw.*⟩ in Richtung Osten

**Easter** ['iːstə(r)] *n*. Ostern, *das od. Pl.* '**Easter egg** *n*. Osterei, *das*

**easterly** ['iːstəlɪ] *adj.* östlich; ⟨Wind⟩ aus östlichen Richtungen

**eastern** ['iːstən] *adj.* östlich; Ost⟨grenze, -hälfte, -seite⟩; ~ Germany Ostdeutschland, *das*. **Eastern 'Europe** *pr. n.* Osteuropa, *das*

**Easter 'Sunday** *n*. Ostersonntag, *der*

**East:** ~ **'German** *(Hist.)* **1.** *adj.* ostdeutsch; **2.** *n.* Ostdeutsche, *der/die;* ~ '**Germany** *pr. n. (Hist.)* Ostdeutschland *(das)*

**eastward(s)** [iːstwəd(z)] *adv.* ostwärts

**easy** ['iːzɪ] **1.** *adj.* **a)** leicht; on ~ terms auf Raten ⟨kaufen⟩; **b)** sorglos ⟨Leben, Zeit⟩; **c)** *(free from constraint)* ungezwungen. **2.** *adv.* leicht; **easier said than done** leichter gesagt als getan; **take it ~!** *(calm down!)* beruhige dich! '**easy chair** *n*. Sessel, *der*. **easy-'going** *adj.* entspannt; *(lax)* nachlässig

**eat** [iːt] *v. t. & i.*, **ate** [et, eɪt], **eaten** ['iːtn] essen; ⟨Tier:⟩ fressen. **eat a'way** *v. t.*

⟨Rost, Säure:⟩ zerfressen. **eat 'out** *v. i.* essen gehen. **eat 'up** *v. t.* aufessen; ⟨Tier:⟩ auffressen

**eaten** *see* **eat**

**eau-de-Cologne** [əʊdəkə'ləʊn] *n*. Kölnisch Wasser, *das*

**eaves** [iːvz] *n. pl.* Dachgesims, *das*. '**eavesdrop** *v. i.* lauschen; ~ on belauschen. '**eavesdropper** *n*. Lauscher, *der/*Lauscherin, *die*

**ebb** [eb] **1.** *n*. Ebbe, *die;* **be at a low** ~ *(fig.)* ⟨Person, Stimmung, Moral:⟩ auf dem Nullpunkt sein. **2.** *v. i.* zurückgehen; ~ **away** *(fig.)* dahinschwinden. '**ebb-tide** *n*. Ebbe, *die*

**ebony** ['ebənɪ] *n*. Ebenholz, *das*

**EC** *abbr.* European Community EG

**eccentric** [ik'sentrɪk] **1.** *adj.* exzentrisch. **2.** *n.* Exzentriker, *der/*Exzentrikerin, *die*. **eccentricity** [eksen'trɪsɪtɪ] *n*. Exzentrizität, *die*

**ecclesiastical** [ɪkliːzɪ'æstɪkl] *adj.* kirchlich; geistlich ⟨Musik⟩

**echo** ['ekəʊ] **1.** *n*. Echo, *das*. **2.** *v. t.* zurückwerfen; *(fig.: repeat)* wiederholen

**éclair** [eɪ'kleə(r)] *n*. Eclair, *das*

**eclipse** [ɪ'klɪps] *n. (Astron.)* Finsternis, *die;* ~ **of the sun** Sonnenfinsternis, *die*

**ecological** [ɪkə'lɒdʒɪkl] *adj.* ökologisch

**ecology** [ɪ'kɒlədʒɪ] *n*. Ökologie, *die*

**economic** [iːkə'nɒmɪk] *adj.* **a)** Wirtschafts⟨politik, -abkommen, -system⟩; wirtschaftlich ⟨Entwicklung, Zusammenbruch⟩; **b)** *(giving adequate return)* wirtschaftlich

**economical** [iːkə'nɒmɪkl] *adj.* wirtschaftlich; sparsam ⟨Person⟩; **be** ~ **with sth.** mit etw. haushalten. **eco'nomically** *adv.* wirtschaftlich; *(not wastefully)* sparsam

**economics** [iːkə'nɒmɪks] *n*. Wirtschaftswissenschaft, *die (meist Pl.)*

**economist** [ɪ'kɒnəmɪst] *n*. Wirtschaftswissenschaftler, *der/*-wissenschaftlerin, *die*

**economize** [ɪ'kɒnəmaɪz] *v. i.* sparen; ~ **on sth.** etw. sparen

**economy** [ɪ'kɒnəmɪ] *n*. **a)** *(frugality)* Sparsamkeit, *die;* **b)** *(instance)* Einsparung, *die;* **make economies** zu Sparmaßnahmen greifen; **c)** *(of country etc.)* Wirtschaft, *die*. **e'conomy size** *n*. Haushaltspackung, *die*

**ecstasy** ['ekstəsɪ] *n*. Ekstase, *die*. **ecstatic** [ɪk'stætɪk] *adj.* ekstatisch

**ECU, ecu** ['eɪkjuː] *abbr.* European currency unit Ecu, *der od. die*

**eddy** ['edɪ] *n*. Strudel, *der*

**edge** [edʒ] 1. *n.* a) *(of knife, razor, weapon)* Schneide, *die;* **on ~** *(fig.)* nervös *od.* gereizt **(about** wegen); b) *(of solid, bed, table)* Kante, *die; (of sheet of paper, road, forest, cliff)* Rand, *der.* 2. *v. i.* sich schieben

**edgy** ['edʒɪ] *adj.* nervös

**edible** ['edɪbl] *adj.* eßbar

**edict** ['i:dɪkt] *n.* Erlaß, *der*

**edit** ['edɪt] *v. t.* herausgeben ⟨*Zeitung*⟩; redigieren ⟨*Buch, Artikel, Manuskript*⟩. **edition** [ɪ'dɪʃn] *n.* Ausgabe, *die.* **editor** ['edɪtə(r)] *n.* Redakteur, *der/*Redakteurin, *die; (of particular work)* Bearbeiter, *der/*Bearbeiterin, *die; (of newspaper)* Herausgeber, *der/*-geberin, *die.* **editorial** [edɪ'tɔ:rɪəl] 1. *n.* Leitartikel, *der.* 2. *adj.* redaktionell

**educate** ['edjʊkeɪt] *v. t.* a) *(bring up)* erziehen; *(train mind and character of)* bilden; b) *(provide schooling for)* **he was ~d at ...:** er hat seine Ausbildung in ... erhalten. **educated** ['edjʊkeɪtɪd] *adj.* gebildet. **education** [edjʊ'keɪʃn] *n.* Erziehung, *die; (system)* Erziehungswesen, *das.* **educational** [edjʊ'keɪʃənl] *adj.* pädagogisch; Lehr-⟨*film, -spiele, -anstalt*⟩; Erziehungs-⟨*methoden, -arbeit*⟩

**EEC** *abbr.* European Economic Community EWG

**eerie** ['ɪərɪ] *adj.* unheimlich

**eel** [i:l] *n.* Aal, *der*

**effect** [ɪ'fekt] *n.* a) Wirkung, *die* (**on** auf + *Akk.*); **the ~s of sth. on sth.** die Auswirkungen einer Sache *(Gen.)* auf etw. *(Akk.);* **take ~:** die erwünschte Wirkung erzielen; **in ~:** in Wirklichkeit; b) **come into ~:** gültig werden; ⟨*Gesetz:*⟩ in Kraft treten; **put into ~:** in Kraft setzen ⟨*Gesetz*⟩; verwirklichen ⟨*Plan*⟩; **with ~ from 2 November/Monday** mit Wirkung vom 2. November/ von Montag

**effective** [ɪ'fektɪv] *adj.* a) wirksam ⟨*Mittel, Maßnahmen*⟩; **be ~** ⟨*Arzneimittel:*⟩ wirken; b) *(in operation)* gültig; **~ from/as of** mit Wirkung vom. **effectively** *adv. (in fact)* effektiv; *(with effect)* wirkungsvoll

**effectual** [ɪ'fektjʊəl] *adj.* wirksam

**effeminate** [ɪ'femɪnət] *adj.* unmännlich

**effervescent** [efə'vesənt] *adj.* sprudelnd; *(fig.)* übersprudelnd

**efficiency** [ɪ'fɪʃənsɪ] *n. (of person)* Fähigkeit, *die;* Tüchtigkeit, *die; (of machine, factory, engine)* Leistungsfähig-

keit, *die; (of organization, method)* gutes Funktionieren

**efficient** [ɪ'fɪʃənt] *adj.* fähig ⟨*Person*⟩; tüchtig ⟨*Arbeiter, Sekretärin*⟩; leistungsfähig ⟨*Maschine, Motor, Fabrik*⟩; gut funktionierend ⟨*Methode, Organisation*⟩. **efficiently** *adj.* gut

**effigy** ['efɪdʒɪ] *n.* Bildnis, *das*

**effluent** ['efluənt] Abwässer *Pl.*

**effort** ['efət] *n.* a) Anstrengung, *die;* Mühe, *die;* **make an/every ~** *(physically)* sich anstrengen; *(mentally)* sich bemühen; b) *(attempt)* Versuch, *der.* **effortless** *adj.* mühelos

**effrontery** [ɪ'frʌntərɪ] *n.* Dreistigkeit, *die;* **have the ~ to do sth.** die Stirn besitzen, etw. zu tun

**effusive** [ɪ'fju:sɪv] *adj.* überschwenglich; exaltiert *(geh.)* ⟨*Person*⟩

**e. g.** [i:'dʒi:] *abbr.* for example z. B.

**egg** [eg] *n.* Ei, *das.* **egg 'on** *v. t.* anstacheln

**egg: ~-cup** *n.* Eierbecher, *der;* **~-shell** *n.* Eierschale, *die;* **~-timer** *n.* Eieruhr, *die;* **~-white** *n.* Eiweiß, *das;* **~ yolk** *n.* Eigelb, *das*

**ego** ['egəʊ, 'i:gəʊ] *n., pl.* **~s** a) *(Psych.)* Ego, *das;* b) *(self-esteem)* Selbstbewußtsein, *das*

**Egypt** ['i:dʒɪpt] *pr. n.* Ägypten *(das).* **Egyptian** [ɪ'dʒɪpʃn] 1. *adj.* ägyptisch. 2. *n. (person)* Ägypter, *der/*Ägypterin, *die*

**eiderdown** ['aɪdədaʊn] *n.* Federbett, *das*

**eight** [eɪt] 1. *adj.* acht; **at ~:** um acht; **half past ~:** halb neun; **~ thirty** acht Uhr dreißig; **~ ten/fifty** zehn nach acht/vor neun; *(esp. in timetable)* acht Uhr zehn/fünfzig; **~-year-old boy** achtjähriger Junge; **an ~-year-old** ein Achtjähriger/eine Achtjährige; **at [the age of] ~, aged ~:** mit acht Jahren; **~ times** achtmal. 2. *n.* Acht, *die;* **the first/last ~:** die ersten/letzten acht; **there were ~ of us present** wir waren [zu] acht

**eighteen** [eɪ'ti:n] 1. *adj.* achtzehn. 2. *n.* Achtzehn, *die; See also* **eight.** **eighteenth** [eɪ'ti:nθ] 1. *adj.* achtzehnt... 2. *n. (fraction)* Achtzehntel, *das. See also* **eight.**

**eighth** [eɪtθ] 1. *adj.* acht...; **be/come ~:** achter sein/als achter ankommen; **~-largest** achtgrößt... 2. *n. (in sequence)* achte, *der/die/das; (in rank)* Achte, *der/die/das; (fraction)* Achtel, *das;* **the ~ of May** der achte Mai

**eightieth** ['eɪtɪɪθ] *adj.* achtzigst...

**eighty** ['eɪtɪ] 1. *adj.* achtzig. 2. *n.* Achtzig, *die;* **the eighties** *(years)* die achtziger Jahre; **be in one's eighties** in den Achtzigern sein. *See also* **eight**
**Eire** ['eərə] *pr. n.* Irland, *das;* Eire, *das*
**either** ['aɪðə(r), 'iː:ðə(r)] 1. *adj.* **a)** *(each)* **at ~ end of the table** an beiden Enden des Tisches; **b)** *(one or other)* [irgend]ein … [von beiden]; **take ~ one** nimm einen/eine/eins von [den] beiden. 2. *pron.* **a)** *(each)* beide *Pl.;* **I can't cope with ~:** ich kann mit keinem von beiden fertig werden; **b)** *(one or other)* einer/eine/ein[e]s [von beiden]. 3. *adv.* auch [nicht]; **'I don't like that ~:** ich mag es auch nicht. 4. *conj.* **~ … or …:** entweder … oder …; *(after negation)* weder … noch …
**eject** ['ɪdʒekt] 1. *v. t.* **a)** *(from hall, meeting)* hinauswerfen **(from** aus); **b)** ⟨*Gerät:*⟩ auswerfen; ⟨*Person:*⟩ herausholen ⟨*Kassette*⟩. 2. *v. i.* sich hinauskatapultieren. **ejector seat** ['ɪdʒektə siːt] *n.* Schleudersitz, *der*
**eke out** [iːk 'aʊt] *v. t.* strecken
**elaborate** 1. ['ɪ'læbərət] *adj.* kompliziert; kunstvoll [gearbeitet] ⟨*Arrangement, Verzierung*⟩. 2. ['ɪ'læbəreɪt] *v. i.* mehr ins Detail gehen; **~ on** näher ausführen
**elapse** ['ɪ'læps] *v. i.* ⟨*Zeit:*⟩ vergehen
**elastic** ['ɪ'læstɪk] 1. *adj.* elastisch. 2. *n.* **(~ band)** Gummiband, *das.* **elastic 'band** *n.* Gummiband, *das*
**elated** ['ɪ'leɪtɪd] *adj.* freudig erregt; **be or feel ~:** in Hochstimmung sein. **elation** ['ɪ'leɪʃn] *n.* freudige Erregung
**elbow** ['elbəʊ] 1. *n.* Ell[en]bogen, *der.* 2. *v. t.* **~ sb. aside** jmdn. mit dem Ellenbogen zur Seite stoßen. **'elbow room** *n.* Ell[en]bogenfreiheit, *die*
**¹elder** ['eldə(r)] 1. *attrib. adj.* älter… 2. *n.* **a)** *(senior)* Ältere, *der/die;* **b)** *(village ~, church ~)* Älteste, *der/die*
**²elder** *n.* *(Bot.)* Holunder, *der.* **'elderberry** *n.* Holunderbeere, *die*
**elderly** ['eldəlɪ] 1. *adj.* älter. 2. *n. pl.* **the ~:** ältere Menschen
**eldest** ['eldɪst] *adj.* ältest…
**elect** ['ɪ'lekt] 1. *adj. postpos.* gewählt; **the President ~:** der designierte Präsident. 2. *v. t.* wählen; **~ sb. chairman** jmdn. zum Vorsitzenden wählen. **election** ['ɪ'lekʃn] *n.* Wahl, *die;* **general ~:** allgemeine Wahlen. **e'lection campaign** *n.* Wahlkampagne, *die*
**electioneer** [ɪlekʃə'nɪə(r)] *v. i.* **be/go ~ing** Wahlkampf machen

**elector** [ɪ'lektə(r)] *n.* Wähler, *der/* Wählerin, *die.* **electoral** [ɪ'lektərl] *adj.* Wahl-. **electorate** [ɪ'lektərət] *n.* Wähler *Pl.*
**electric** [ɪ'lektrɪk] *adj.* elektrisch; Elektro⟨*kabel, -motor, -herd, -kessel*⟩; Strom⟨*versorgung*⟩; *(fig.)* spannungsgeladen ⟨*Atmosphäre*⟩. **electrical** [ɪ'lektrɪkl] *adj.* elektrisch; Elektro⟨*abteilung, -handel, -geräte*⟩
**electric:** **~ 'blanket** *n.* Heizdecke, *die;* **~ 'fire** *n.* [elektrischer] Heizofen
**electrician** [ɪlek'trɪʃn] *n.* Elektriker, *der/*Elektrikerin, *die*
**electricity** [ɪlek'trɪsɪtɪ] *n.* Elektrizität, *die*
**electric 'shock** *n.* Stromschlag, *der*
**electrify** [ɪ'lektrɪfaɪ] *v. t.* elektrifizieren; *(fig.)* elektrisieren
**electrocute** [ɪ'lektrəkjuːt] *v. t.* durch Stromschlag töten
**electrode** [ɪ'lektrəʊd] *n.* Elektrode, *die*
**electron** [ɪ'lektrɒn] *n.* Elektron, *das*
**electronic** [ɪlek'trɒnɪk] *adj.* elektronisch. **electronics** [ɪlek'trɒnɪks] *n.* Elektronik, *die*
**elegance** ['elɪgəns] *n.* Eleganz, *die*
**elegant** ['elɪgənt] *adj.* elegant
**element** ['elɪmənt] *n.* **a)** Element, *das;* **b)** *(Electr.)* Heizelement, *das;* **c)** **~s** *(rudiments)* Grundlagen *Pl.* **elementary** [elɪ'mentərɪ] *adj.* elementar; grundlegend ⟨*Fakten, Wissen*⟩; Grundschul⟨*bildung*⟩; Grund⟨*kurs, -ausbildung, -kenntnisse*⟩
**elephant** ['elɪfənt] *n.* Elefant, *der*
**elevate** ['elɪveɪt] *v. t.* [empor]heben. **elevation** [elɪ'veɪʃn] *n.* **a)** *(height)* Höhe, *die;* **b)** *(Archit.)* Aufriß, *der*
**elevator** ['elɪveɪtə(r)] *n.* *(Amer.)* Aufzug, *der;* Fahrstuhl, *der*
**eleven** [ɪ'levn] 1. *adj.* elf. 2. *n.* *(also Sport)* Elf, *die. See also* **eight**
**elevenses** [ɪ'levnzɪz] *n. sing. or pl.* *(Brit. coll.)* ≈ zweites Frühstück [gegen elf Uhr]
**eleventh** [ɪ'levnθ] 1. *adj.* elft…; **at the ~ hour** in letzter Minute. 2. *n.* *(fraction)* Elftel, *das. See also* **eighth**
**elf** [elf] *n., pl.* **elves** [elvz] Elf, *der/* Elfe, *die*
**elicit** [ɪ'lɪsɪt] *v. t.* entlocken **(from** Dat.); gewinnen ⟨*Unterstützung*⟩
**eligible** ['elɪdʒɪbl] *adj.* **be ~ for sth.** *(fit)* für etw. geeignet sein; *(entitled)* zu etw. berechtigt sein
**eliminate** [ɪ'lɪmɪneɪt] *v. t.* **a)** *(remove)* beseitigen; ausschließen ⟨*Möglich-*

*keit*⟩; b) *(exclude)* ausschließen; **be ~d** *(Sport)* ausscheiden. **elimination** [ɪlɪmɪ'neɪʃn] *n.* **a)** *(removal)* Beseitigung, *die;* **process of ~:** Ausleseverfahren, *das;* b) *(exclusion)* Ausschluß, *der; (Sport)* Ausscheiden, *das*

**élite** [eɪ'li:t] *n.* Elite, *die*

**ellipse** [ɪ'lɪps] *n.* Ellipse, *die.* **elliptical** [ɪ'lɪptɪkl] *adj.* elliptisch

**elm** [elm] *n.* Ulme, *die*

**elongated** ['i:lɒŋgeɪtɪd] *adj.* langgestreckt

**elope** [ɪ'ləʊp] *v. i.* durchbrennen *(ugs.)*

**eloquence** ['eləkwəns] *n.* Beredtheit, *die.* **eloquent** ['eləkwənt] *adj.* beredt ⟨*Person*⟩; gewandt ⟨*Stil, Redner*⟩

**else** [els] *adv.* **a)** *(besides)* sonst [noch]; **somebody/something ~:** [noch] jemand anders/noch etwas; **everybody/ everything ~:** alle anderen/alles andere; **who/what/when/how ~?** wer/was/ wann/wie sonst noch?; **why ~?** warum sonst?; b) *(instead)* ander...; **sb. ~'s hat** der Hut von jmd. anders; **anybody/anything ~?** [irgend] jemand anders/etwas anderes?; **somebody/something ~:** jemand anders/etwas anderes; **everybody/everything ~:** alle anderen/alles andere; **c)** *(otherwise)* sonst; **or ~:** oder aber; **do it or ~ ...!** tun Sie es, sonst ...! '**elsewhere** *adv.* woanders

**elude** [ɪ'lu:d] *v. t.* *(avoid)* ausweichen (+ *Dat.*); *(escape from)* entkommen (+*Dat.*). **elusive** [ɪ'lu:sɪv] *adj.* schwer zu erreichen ⟨*Person*⟩; schwer zu fassen ⟨*Straftäter*⟩; schwer definierbar ⟨*Begriff, Sinn*⟩

**elves** *pl. of* elf

**emaciated** [ɪ'meɪsɪeɪtɪd] *adj.* abgezehrt

**emancipated** [ɪ'mænsɪpeɪtɪd] *adj.* emanzipiert: **become ~:** sich emanzipieren

**emancipation** [ɪmænsɪ'peɪʃn] *n.* Emanzipation, *die*

**embalm** [ɪm'bɑ:m] *v. t.* einbalsamieren

**embankment** [ɪm'bæŋkmənt] *n.* Damm, *der*

**embargo** [ɪm'bɑ:gəʊ] *n., pl.* ~es Embargo, *das*

**embark** [ɪm'bɑ:k] *v. i.* **a)** sich einschiffen **(for** nach); **b) ~ |up|on sth.** etw. in Angriff nehmen. **embarkation** [embɑ:'keɪʃn] *n.* Einschiffung, *die*

**embarrass** [ɪm'bærəs] *v. t.* in Verlegenheit bringen. **embarrassed** [ɪm'bærəst] *adj.* verlegen; **feel ~:** verlegen

sein. **em'barrassing** *adj.* peinlich. **em'barrassment** *n.* Verlegenheit, *die*

**embassy** ['embəsɪ] *n.* Botschaft, *die*

**embellish** [em'belɪʃ] *v. t.* beschönigen ⟨*Wahrheit*⟩; ausschmücken ⟨*Geschichte, Bericht*⟩

**embers** ['embəz] *n. pl.* Glut, *die*

**embezzle** ['ɪmbezl] *v. t.* unterschlagen

**embitter** [ɪm'bɪtə(r)] *v. t.* verbittern

**emblem** ['embləm] *n.* Emblem, *das*

**embody** [ɪm'bɒdɪ] *v. t.* verkörpern

**embrace** [ɪm'breɪs] **1.** *v. t.* umarmen; *(fig.: accept, adopt)* annehmen. **2.** *v. i.* sich umarmen. **3.** *n.* Umarmung, *die*

**embroider** [ɪm'brɔɪdə(r)] *v. t.* sticken ⟨*Muster*⟩; besticken ⟨*Tuch, Kleid*⟩; *(fig.)* ausschmücken. **embroidery** [ɪm'brɔɪdərɪ] *n.* Stickerei, *die*

**embroil** [ɪm'brɔɪl] *v. t.* **become/be ~ed in sth.** in etw. (*Akk.*) verwickelt werden/sein

**embryo** ['embrɪəʊ] *n.* Embryo, *der*

**emerald** ['emərəld] **1.** *n.* Smaragd, *der.* **2.** *adj.* smaragdgrün

**emerge** [ɪ'mɜ:dʒ] *v. i.* auftauchen **(from aus, from behind** hinter + *Dat.*); ⟨*Wahrheit:*⟩ an den Tag kommen; **it ~s that ...:** es stellt sich heraus, daß ...

**emergency** [ɪ'mɜ:dʒənsɪ] **1.** *n.* Notfall, *der;* **in an** *or* **in case of ~:** im Notfall. **2.** *adj.* Not-

**emigrant** ['emɪgrənt] *n.* Auswanderer, *der*/Auswanderin, *die*

**emigrate** ['emɪgreɪt] *v. i.* auswandern **(to** nach, **from** aus). **emigration** [emɪ'greɪʃn] *n.* Auswanderung **(to** nach, **from** aus)

**eminence** ['emɪnəns] *n.* hohes Ansehen

**eminent** ['emɪnənt] *adj.* bedeutend; herausragend

**emission** [ɪ'mɪʃn] *n.* Emission, *die (fachspr.); (process also)* Abgabe, *die*

**emit** [ɪ'mɪt] *v. t.,* -tt- abgeben, emittieren *(fachspr.)* ⟨*Wärme, Strahlung usw.*⟩; ausstoßen ⟨*Rauch*⟩

**emotion** [ɪ'məʊʃn] *n.* Gefühl, *das.* **emotional** [ɪ'məʊʃənl] *adj.* emotional; Gemüts⟨*zustand, -störung*⟩; gefühlvoll ⟨*Stimme*⟩. **e'motionally** *adv.* emotional; gefühlvoll ⟨*sprechen*⟩; **~ disturbed** seelisch gestört

**emotive** [ɪ'məʊtɪv] *adj.* emotional

**emperor** ['empərə(r)] *n.* Kaiser, *der*

**emphasis** ['emfəsɪs] *n., pl.* **emphases** ['emfəsi:z] Betonung, *die;* **lay** *or* **place** *or* **put ~ on sth.** etw. betonen

**emphasize** ['emfəsaɪz] v. t. betonen
**emphatic** [ɪm'fætɪk] adj. nachdrücklich; demonstrativ ⟨Ablehnung⟩; **be ~
that …:** darauf bestehen, daß … **em-
'phatically** adv. nachdrücklich
**empire** ['empaɪə(r)] n. Reich, das
**employ** [ɪm'plɔɪ] v. t. **a)** (take on) einstellen; (have working for one) beschäftigen; **be ~ed by a company** bei
einer Firma arbeiten; **b)** (use) einsetzen (for, in, on für); anwenden ⟨Me-
thode, List⟩ (for, in, on bei). **employee** (Amer.: **employe**) [emplɔɪ-
'i:, em'plɔɪi:] n. Angestellte, der/die.
**employer** [ɪm'plɔɪə(r)] n. Arbeitge-
ber, der/-geberin, die. **employment**
[ɪm'plɔɪmənt] n. **a)** (work) Arbeit, die;
**b)** (regular trade or profession) Beschäftigung, die. **em'ployment
agency** n. Stellenvermittlung, die
**empower** [ɪm'paʊə(r)] v. t. (authorize)
ermächtigen; (enable) befähigen
**empress** ['emprɪs] n. Kaiserin, die
**emptiness** ['emptɪnɪs] n. Leere, die
**empty** ['emptɪ] **1.** adj. leer; frei ⟨Sitz,
Parkplatz⟩. **2.** v. t. leeren; (pour)
schütten (over über + Akk.). **3.** v. i.
sich leeren. **'empty-handed** adj. mit
leeren Händen
**EMS** abbr. **European Monetary System**
EWS
**emulate** ['emjʊleɪt] v. t. nacheifern
(+ Dat.)
**emulsion** [ɪ'mʌlʃn] n. Emulsion, die
**enable** [ɪ'neɪbl] v. t. **~ sb. to do sth.** es
jmdm. ermöglichen, etw. zu tun
**enamel** [ɪ'næml] **1.** n. Email, das. **2.**
v. t., (Brit.) -ll- emaillieren
**enchant** [ɪn'tʃɑːnt] v. t. verzaubern;
(delight) entzücken. **en'chanted** adj.
verzaubert. **en'chanting** adj. ent-
zückend. **en'chantment** n. Verzau-
berung, die; (fig.) Zauber, der
**encircle** [ɪn'sɜːkl] v. t. umgeben
**encl.** abbr. **enclosed, enclosure[s]** Anl.
**enclave** ['enkleɪv] n. Enklave, die
**enclose** [ɪn'kləʊz] v. t. **a)** (surround)
umgeben; (shut up or in) einschließen; **b)** (with letter) beilegen (with, in
Dat.); **please find ~d** anbei erhalten
Sie. **enclosure** [ɪn'kləʊʒə(r)] n. **a)** (in
zoo) Gehege, das; **b)** (with letter) Anlage, die
**encore** ['ɒŋkɔː(r)] **1.** int. Zugabe. **2.** n.
Zugabe, die
**encounter** [ɪn'kaʊntə(r)] **1.** v. t. (as adversary) treffen auf (+ Akk.); (by
chance) begegnen (+ Dat.); stoßen
auf (+ Akk.) ⟨Problem, Widerstand

usw.⟩. **2.** n. (chance meeting) Begegnung, die
**encourage** [ɪn'kʌrɪdʒ] v. t. ermutigen;
(promote) fördern. **encouragement**
n. Ermutigung, die (from durch)
**encroach** [ɪn'krəʊtʃ] v. i. **~ on** eindringen in (+ Akk.); in Anspruch nehmen
⟨Zeit⟩
**encumber** [ɪn'kʌmbə(r)] v. t. belasten.
**encumbrance** [ɪn'kʌmbrəns] n. Belastung, die
**encyclopaedia** [ɪnsaɪklə'piːdɪə] n.
Lexikon, das; Enzyklopädie, die. **en-
cyclopaedic** [ɪnsaɪklə'piːdɪk] adj.
enzyklopädisch
**end** [end] **1.** n. **a)** Ende, das; (of nose,
hair, finger) Spitze, die; **from ~ to ~:**
von einem Ende zum anderen; **at the
~ of 1987/March** Ende 1987/März; **in
the ~:** schließlich; **come to an ~:** ein
Ende nehmen; **be at an ~:** zu Ende
sein; **b)** (of box, packet, etc.) Schmal-
seite, die; (top/bottom surface) Ober-/
Unterseite, die; **on ~:** hochkant; **make
~s meet** (fig.) zurechtkommen; **no ~
of** (coll.) unendlich viel/viele; **c)** (remnant) Rest, der; (of cigarette) Stummel, der; **d)** (purpose, object) Ziel, das;
**~ in itself** Selbstzweck, der. **2.** v. t. beenden. **3.** v. i. enden. **end 'up** v. i. enden; **~ up in** (coll.) landen in
(+ Dat.); **~ up [as] a teacher** (coll.)
schließlich Lehrer werden
**endanger** [ɪn'deɪndʒə(r)] v. t. gefährden
**endear** [ɪn'dɪə(r)] v. t. **~ sb./sth./one-
self to sb.** jmdn./etw./sich bei jmdm.
beliebt machen. **en'dearing** adj. reizend; gewinnend ⟨Lächeln, Art⟩
**endeavour** (Brit.; Amer.: **endeavor**)
[ɪn'devə(r)] **1.** v. i. **~ to do sth.** sich bemühen, etw. zu tun. **2.** n. Bemühung,
die; (attempt) Versuch, der
**'ending** n. Schluß, der; (of word) Endung, die
**endive** ['endaɪv] n. Endivie, die
**'endless** adj. endlos. **'endlessly** adv.
unaufhörlich ⟨streiten, schwatzen⟩
**endorse** [ɪn'dɔːs] v. t. **a)** indossieren
⟨Scheck⟩; **b)** beipflichten (+ Dat.)
⟨Meinung⟩; billigen ⟨Entscheidung,
Handlung⟩; unterstützen ⟨Vorschlag⟩;
**c)** (Brit. Law) einen Strafvermerk
machen auf (+ Akk. od. Dat.). **en-
'dorsement** n. **a)** (of cheque) Indos-
sament, das; **b)** (support) Billigung,
die; (of proposal) Unterstützung, die;
**c)** (Brit. Law) Strafvermerk, der
**endow** [ɪn'daʊ] v. t. [über Stiftungen/

eine Stiftung] finanzieren; stiften ⟨*Preis, Lehrstuhl*⟩; be ~ed with charm/a talent for music Charme/musikalisches Talent besitzen

**endurable** [ɪn'djʊərəbl] *adj.* erträglich

**endurance** [ɪn'djʊərəns] *n.* Ausdauer, *die*

**endure** [ɪn'djʊə(r)] *v.t.* ertragen

**enema** ['enəmə] *n.* Einlauf, *der*

**enemy** ['enəmɪ] **1.** *n.* Feind, *der* (of, to *Gen.*). **2.** *adj.* feindlich

**energetic** [enə'dʒetɪk] *adj.* energiegeladen; *(active)* tatkräftig

**energy** ['enədʒɪ] *n.* Energie, *die*

**enforce** [ɪn'fɔːs] *v.t.* durchsetzen; sorgen für ⟨*Disziplin*⟩; ~d erzwungen ⟨*Schweigen*⟩; unfreiwillig ⟨*Untätigkeit*⟩

**engage** [ɪn'geɪdʒ] **1.** *v.t.* **a)** *(hire)* einstellen ⟨*Arbeiter*⟩; engagieren ⟨*Sänger*⟩; **b)** wecken ⟨*Interesse*⟩; auf sich *(Akk.)* ziehen ⟨*Aufmerksamkeit*⟩; **c)** ~ the clutch/first gear einkuppeln/ den ersten Gang einlegen. **2.** *v.i.* ~ in sth. sich in etw. *(Dat.)* beteiligen; ~ in politics sich politisch engagieren. **engaged** [ɪn'geɪdʒd] *adj.* **a)** be ~ |to be married| [mit jmdm.] verlobt sein; get ~ |to be married| |to sb.| sich [mit jmdm.] verloben; **b)** be ~ in sth./ in doing sth. mit etw. beschäftigt sein/ damit beschäftigt sein, etw. zu tun; be otherwise ~: etwas anderes vorhaben; **c)** besetzt ⟨*Toilette, [Telefon]anschluß, Nummer*⟩; ~ signal or tone *(Brit.)* Besetztzeichen, *das*. **en'gagement** *n.* **a)** *(to be married)* Verlobung, *die* (to mit); **b)** *(appointment)* Verabredung, *die*. **en'gagement ring** *n.* Verlobungsring, *der*

**engaging** [ɪn'geɪdʒɪŋ] *adj.* bezaubernd; einnehmend ⟨*Persönlichkeit, Art*⟩

**engine** ['endʒɪn] *n.* **a)** Motor, *der*; *(rocket/jet* ~*)* Triebwerk, *das*; **b)** *(locomotive)* Lok[omotive], *die*. **'engine driver** *n.* Lok[omotiv]führer, *der*

**engineer** [endʒɪ'nɪə(r)] **1.** *n.* **a)** Ingenieur, *der*/Ingenieurin, *die*; *(service* ~, *installation* ~*)* Techniker, *der*/Technikerin, *die*; **b)** *(Amer.: engine-driver)* Lok[omotiv]führer, *der*. **2.** *v.t.* arrangieren. **engi'neering** *n.* Technik, *die*

**England** ['ɪŋglənd] *pr. n.* England *(das)*

**English** ['ɪŋglɪʃ] **1.** *adj.* englisch; he/ she is ~: er ist Engländer/sie ist Engländerin. **2.** *n.* **a)** Englisch, *das*; say sth. in ~: etw. auf englisch sagen; I cannot *or* do not speak ~: ich spreche kein Englisch; translate into/from |the| ~: ins Englische/aus dem Englischen übersetzen; **b)** *pl.* the ~: die Engländer

**English:** ~ 'Channel *pr. n.* the ~ Channel der [Ärmel]kanal; ~man [~mən] *n., pl.* ~men [~mən] Engländer, *der*; ~woman *n.* Engländerin, *die*

**engrave** [ɪn'greɪv] *v.t.* gravieren; eingravieren ⟨*Namen, Figur usw.*⟩. **engraving** [ɪn'greɪvɪŋ] *n.* Stich, *der*; *(from wood)* Holzschnitt, *der*

**engross** [ɪn'grəʊs] *v.t.* fesseln; be ~ed in sth. in etw. *(Akk.)* vertieft sein; become *or* get ~ed in sth. sich in etw. *(Akk.)* vertiefen

**engulf** [ɪn'gʌlf] *v.t.* verschlingen

**enhance** [ɪn'hɑːns] *v.t.* erhöhen ⟨*Wert, Aussichten, Schönheit*⟩; verstärken ⟨*Wirkung*⟩; heben ⟨*Aussehen*⟩

**enigma** [ɪ'nɪgmə] *n.* Rätsel, *das*. **enigmatic** [enɪg'mætɪk] *adj.* rätselhaft

**enjoy** [ɪn'dʒɔɪ] **1.** *v.t.* **a)** I ~ed the book/work das Buch/die Arbeit hat mir gefallen; he ~s reading/travelling er liest/reist gern; **b)** genießen ⟨*Rechte, Privilegien, Vorteile*⟩. **2.** *v. refl.* sich amüsieren. **enjoyable** [ɪn-'dʒɔɪəbl] *adj.* schön; angenehm ⟨*Empfindung, Arbeit*⟩; unterhaltsam ⟨*Buch, Film, Stück*⟩. **en'joyment** *n.* Vergnügen, *das* (of an + *Dat.*)

**enlarge** [ɪn'lɑːdʒ] **1.** *v.t.* vergrößern; verbreitern ⟨*Straße, Durchgang*⟩. **2.** *v.i.* ~ |up|on sth. etw. weiter ausführen. **en'largement** *n.* Vergrößerung, *die*; *(making wider)* Verbreiterung, *die*

**enlighten** [ɪn'laɪtn] *v.t.* aufklären (on, as to über + *Akk.*). **en'lightenment** *n.* Aufklärung, *die*

**enlist** [ɪn'lɪst] **1.** *v.t.* *(obtain)* gewinnen. **2.** *v.i.* ~ |for the army/navy| in die Armee/Marine eintreten; ~ |as a soldier| Soldat werden

**enliven** [ɪn'laɪvn] *v.t.* beleben

**enmity** ['enmɪtɪ] *n.* Feindschaft, *die*

**enormous** [ɪ'nɔːməs] *adj.* enorm; riesig, gewaltig ⟨*Figur, Tier, Menge*⟩. **e'normously** *adv.* enorm

**enough** [ɪ'nʌf] **1.** *adj.* genug; there's ~ room es ist Platz genug. **2.** *n.* genug; be ~ to do sth. genügen, etw. zu tun; have had ~ |of sb./sth.| genug [von jmdm./etw.] haben; I've had ~! jetzt reicht's mir aber! **3.** *adv.* genug; oddly/funnily ~: merkwürdiger-/ *(ugs.)* komischerweise

**enquire, enquiry** *see* **inquir-**

**enrage** [in'reidʒ] *v. t.* wütend machen; **be ~d by sth.** über etw. *(Akk.)* wütend werden

**enrich** [in'ritʃ] *v. t.* reich machen; *(fig.)* bereichern

**enrol** *(Amer.: enroll)* [in'rəul] 1. *v. i.*, -ll- sich einschreiben; ~ **for a course** sich zu einem Kurs anmelden. 2. *v. t.* einschreiben. **en'rolment** *(Amer.: en'rollment)* *n.* Einschreibung, *die*

**en route** [ã̃ 'ruːt] *adv.* unterwegs; ~ **to Scotland/for Edinburgh** auf dem Weg nach Schottland/Edinburgh

**ensign** ['ensain, 'ensn] *n.* Hoheitszeichen, *das*

**enslave** [in'sleiv] *v. t.* versklaven

**ensue** [in'sjuː] *v. i.* folgen **(from, on** aus); **the discussion which ~d** die anschließende Diskussion

**ensure** [in'ʃuə(r)] *v. t.* ~ **that ...** *(see to it that)* gewährleisten, daß ...; ~ **sth.** etw. gewährleisten

**entail** [in'teil] *v. t.* mit sich bringen; **sth. ~s doing sth.** etw. bedeutet, daß man etw. tun muß

**entangle** [in'tæŋgl] *v. t.* sich verfangen lassen; **get** *or* **become ~d in** *or* **with sth.** sich in etw. *(Dat.)* verfangen

**enter** ['entə(r)] 1. *v. i.* a) hineingehen; ⟨*Fahrzeug:*⟩ hineinfahren; *(come in)* hereinkommen; *(into room)* eintreten; b) *(register as competitor)* sich zur Teilnahme anmelden **(for an** + *Dat.*). 2. *v. t.* a) [hinein]gehen in (+ *Akk.*); ⟨*Fahrzeug:*⟩ [hinein]fahren in (+ *Akk.*); betreten ⟨*Gebäude, Zimmer*⟩; einlaufen in (+ *Akk.*) ⟨*Hafen*⟩; einreisen in (+ *Akk.*) ⟨*Land*⟩; *(come into)* [herein]kommen in (+ *Akk.*); b) teilnehmen an (+ *Dat.*) ⟨*Rennen, Wettbewerb*⟩; c) *(in book etc.)* eintragen **(in in** + *Akk.*). **'enter into** *v. t.* aufnehmen ⟨*Verhandlungen*⟩; eingehen ⟨*Verpflichtung*⟩; schließen ⟨*Vertrag*⟩. **'enter [up]on** *v. t.* beginnen

**enterprise** ['entəpraiz] *n.* a) *(undertaking)* Unternehmen, *das;* **free/private ~:** freies/privates Unternehmertum; b) *(enterprising spirit)* Unternehmungsgeist, *der.* **enterprising** ['entəpraiziŋ] *adj.* unternehmungslustig

**entertain** [entə'tein] *v. t.* a) *(amuse)* unterhalten; b) *(receive as guest)* bewirten; c) haben ⟨*Vorstellung*⟩; hegen *(geh.)* ⟨*Gefühl, Verdacht, Zweifel*⟩; *(consider)* in Erwägung ziehen. **enter'tainer** *n.* Unterhalter, *der*/Unterhalterin, *die.* **enter'taining** *adj.*

unterhaltsam. **enter'tainment** *n.* a) *(amusement)* Unterhaltung, *die;* b) *(performance, show)* Veranstaltung, *die*

**enthral** *(Amer.: enthrall)* [in'θrɔːl] *v. t.,* -ll- gefangennehmen *(fig.)*

**enthuse** [in'θjuːz] *(coll.)* 1. *v. i.* in Begeisterung ausbrechen **(about** über + *Akk.*). 2. *v. t.* begeistern

**enthusiasm** [in'θjuːziæzm] *n.* Begeisterung, *die.* **enthusiast** [in'θjuːziæst] *n.* Enthusiast, *der;* *(for sports)* Fan, *der;* **a DIY ~:** ein begeisterter Heimwerker. **enthusiastic** [inθjuː- zi'æstik] *adj.* begeistert; **not be very ~ about doing sth.** keine große Lust haben, etw. zu tun

**entice** [in'tais] *v. t.* locken **(into in** + *Akk.*); ~ **sb. into doing** *or* **to do sth.** jmdn. dazu verleiten, etw. zu tun

**entire** [in'taiə(r)] *adj.* a) *(whole)* ganz; b) *(intact)* vollständig. **en'tirely** *adv.* a) *(wholly)* völlig; b) *(solely)* ganz ⟨*für sich behalten*⟩; voll ⟨*verantwortlich sein*⟩; **it's up to you ~:** es liegt ganz bei dir. **entirety** [in'taiərəti] *n.* **in its ~:** in seiner/ihrer Gesamtheit

**entitle** [in'tait] *v. t.* berechtigen **(to** zu); ~ **sb. to do sth.** jmdm. das Recht geben, etw. zu tun; **be ~d to [claim] sth.** Anspruch auf etw. *(Akk.)* haben; **be ~d to do sth.** das Recht haben, etw. zu tun

**entourage** [ɒntʊ'rɑːʒ] *n.* Gefolge, *das*

**entrails** ['entreilz] *n. pl.* Eingeweide *Pl.*

**¹entrance** [in'trɑːns] *v. t.* hinreißen

**²entrance** ['entrəns] *n.* *(way in)* Eingang, *der* **(to** *Gen. od.* zu); *(for vehicles)* Einfahrt, *die.* **'entrance fee** *n.* Eintrittsgeld, *das*

**entrant** ['entrənt] *n.* *(for competition, race, etc.)* Teilnehmer, *der*/Teilnehmerin, *die* **(for** *Gen.,* **an** + *Dat.*)

**entreat** [in'triːt] *v. t.* anflehen. **en'treaty** *n.* flehentliche Bitte

**entrepreneur** [ɒntrəprə'nɜː(r)] *n.* Unternehmer, *der*/Unternehmerin, *die*

**entrust** [in'trʌst] *v. t.* ~ **sb. with sth.** jmdm. etw. anvertrauen; ~ **sb./sth. to sb./sth.** jmdn./etw. jmdm./einer Sache anvertrauen; ~ **a task to sb.** jmdn. mit einer Aufgabe betrauen

**entry** ['entri] *n.* a) Eintritt, *der* **(into in** + *Akk.*); *(into country)* Einreise, *die;* **'no ~'** *(for people)* „Zutritt verboten"; *(for vehicles)* „Einfahrt verboten"; b) *(way in)* Eingang, *der;* *(for vehicle)* Einfahrt, *die;* c) *(registration, item)*

Eintragung, *die* (**in**, **into** in + *Akk. od. Dat.*); *(in dictionary, encyclopaedia)* Eintrag, *der*

**entry:** ~ **fee** *n.* Eintrittsgeld, *das;* ~ **form** *n.* Anmeldeformular, *das;* ~ **visa** *n.* Einreisevisum, *das*

**envelop** [ɪnˈveləp] *v. t.* [ein]hüllen (**in** in + *Akk.*); **be** ~**ed in flames** ganz von Flammen umgeben sein

**envelope** [ˈenvələup, ˈɒnvələup] *n.* [Brief]umschlag, *der*

**enviable** [ˈenvɪəbl] *adj.* beneidenswert

**envious** [ˈenvɪəs] *adj.* neidisch (**of** auf + *Akk.*)

**environment** [ɪnˈvaɪərənmənt] *n.* Umwelt, *die; (surrounding objects, region)* Umgebung, *die.* **environmental** [ɪnvaɪərənˈmentl] *adj.* Umwelt-. **environˈmentalist** *n.* Umweltschützer, *der*/-schützerin, *die.* **environˈmentally** *adv.* ~ **friendly** umweltfreundlich

**envisage** [ɪnˈvɪzɪdʒ] *v. t.* sich *(Dat.)* vorstellen

**envoy** [ˈenvɔɪ] *n.* Gesandte, *der*/Gesandtin, *die*

**envy** [ˈenvɪ] **1.** *n.* Neid, *der;* **you'll be the** ~ **of all your friends** sie werden die Freunde werden dich beneiden. **2.** *v. t.* beneiden; ~ **sb. sth.** jmdn. um etw. beneiden

**enzyme** [ˈenzaɪm] *n.* Enzym, *das*

**ephemeral** [ɪˈfemərl] *adj.* kurzlebig

**epic** [ˈepɪk] **1.** *adj.* episch. **2.** *n.* Epos, *das*

**epidemic** [epɪˈdemɪk] **1.** *adj.* epidemisch. **2.** *n.* Epidemie, *die*

**epilepsy** [ˈepɪlepsɪ] *n.* Epilepsie, *die.* **epileptic** [epɪˈleptɪk] **1.** *adj.* epileptisch; epileptischer Anfall. **2.** *n.* Epileptiker, *der*/Epileptikerin, *die*

**episode** [ˈepɪsəud] *n.* **a)** Episode, *die;* **b)** *(of serial)* Folge, *die*

**epitaph** [ˈepɪtɑːf] *n.* Grab[in]schrift, *die*

**epitome** [ɪˈpɪtəmɪ] *n.* Inbegriff, *der.* **epitomize** [ɪˈpɪtəmaɪz] *v. t.* ~ **sth.** der Inbegriff einer Sache *(Gen.)* sein

**epoch** [ˈiːpɒk] *n.* Epoche, *die.* **ˈepoch-making** *adj.* epochemachend

**equal** [ˈiːkwl] **1.** *adj.* **a)** gleich; ~ **in** *or* **of** ~ **height/size/importance** *etc.* gleich hoch/groß/wichtig *usw.;* **b)** **be** ~ **to sth./sb.** *(strong, clever, etc. enough)* einer Sache/jmdm. gewachsen sein. **2.** *n.* Gleichgestellte, *der/die;* **have no** ~: nicht seines-/ihresgleichen haben. **3.** *v. t., (Brit.)* **-ll-:** ~ **sb.** es

jmdm. gleich tun; **three times four** ~**s twelve** drei mal vier ist [gleich] zwölf.

**equality** [ɪˈkwɒlɪtɪ] *n.* Gleichheit, *die; (equal rights)* Gleichberechtigung, *die.* **equalize** [ˈiːkwəlaɪz] *v. i. (Sport)* den Ausgleich[streffer] erzielen. **ˈequalizer** *n. (Sport)* Ausgleich[streffer], *der.* **ˈequally** *adv.* gleich; *(just as)* ebenso; **in gleiche Teile** *⟨aufteilen⟩;* gleichmäßig *⟨verteilen⟩.* **equal opporˈtunity** *n.* Chancengleichheit, *die.* **ˈequals sign** *n. (Math.)* Gleichheitszeichen, *das*

**equanimity** [ekwəˈnɪmɪtɪ] *n.* Gelassenheit, *die*

**equate** [ɪˈkweɪt] *v. t.* gleichsetzen (**with** mit). **equation** [ɪˈkweɪʒn] *n. (Math.)* Gleichung, *die*

**equator** [ɪˈkweɪtə(r)] *n.* Äquator, *der*

**equilibrium** [iːkwɪˈlɪbrɪəm] *n., pl.* **equilibria** [iːkwɪˈlɪbrɪə] *or* ~**s** Gleichgewicht, *das*

**equinox** [ˈekwɪnɒks] *n.* Tagundnachtgleiche, *die*

**equip** [ɪˈkwɪp] *v. t.,* **-pp-** ausrüsten *⟨Fahrzeug, Armee⟩;* ausstatten *⟨Küche⟩;* **fully** ~**ped** komplett ausgerüstet/ausgestattet; ~ **sb./oneself [with sth.]** jmdn./sich [mit etw.] ausrüsten. **eˈquipment** *n.* Ausrüstung, *die; (of kitchen, laboratory)* Ausstattung, *die; (needed for activity)* Geräte

**equivalent** [ɪˈkwɪvələnt] **1.** *adj.* gleichwertig; **be** ~ **to sth.** einer Sache *(Dat.)* entsprechen. **2.** *n.* **a)** *(thing, person)* Pendant, *das;* Gegenstück, *das* (of zu); **b) be the** ~ **of sth.** *(have same result)* einer Sache *(Dat.)* entsprechen

**equivocal** [ɪˈkwɪvəkl] *adj.* zweideutig

**era** [ˈɪərə] *n.* Ära, *die*

**eradicate** [ɪˈrædɪkeɪt] *v. t.* ausrotten

**erase** [ɪˈreɪz] *v. t.* auslöschen; *(with rubber, knife)* ausradieren; *(from tape, also Computing)* löschen. **eˈraser** *n.* [pencil] ~: Radiergummi, *der*

**erect** [ɪˈrekt] **1.** *adj.* aufrecht. **2.** *v. t.* errichten; aufstellen *⟨Standbild, Mast, Verkehrsschild, Gerüst, Zelt⟩.* **erection** [ɪˈrekʃn] *n.* **a)** *see* erect 2: Errichtung, *die;* Aufstellen, *das;* **b)** *(Physiol.)* Erektion, *die*

**ermine** [ˈɜːmɪn] *n.* Hermelin, *der*

**erode** [ɪˈrəud] *v. t.* **a)** *⟨Säure, Rost:⟩* angreifen; *⟨Wasser:⟩* auswaschen; *⟨Wind:⟩* verwittern lassen; **b)** *(fig.)* unterminieren. **erosion** [ɪˈrəuʒn] *n.* **a)** *see* erode a: Angreifen, *das;* Auswaschung, *die;* Verwitterung, *die;* **b)** *(fig.)* Unterminierung, *die*

**erotic** [ɪ'rɒtɪk] *adj.* erotisch

**err** [ɜː(r)] *v. i.* sich irren

**errand** ['erənd] *n.* Botengang, *der;* *(shopping)* Besorgung, *die;* **go on** *or* **run an ~:** einen Botengang/eine Besorgung machen. **'errand boy** *n.* Laufbursche, *der*

**erratic** [ɪ'rætɪk] *adj.* unregelmäßig; sprunghaft ⟨*Wesen, Person, Art*⟩; launenhaft ⟨*Verhalten*⟩

**erroneous** [ɪ'rəʊnɪəs] *adj.* falsch; irrig ⟨*Schlußfolgerung, Annahme*⟩

**error** ['erə(r)] *n. (mistake)* Fehler, *der;* *(wrong opinion)* Irrtum, *der;* **in ~:** irrtümlich[erweise]

**erudite** ['eruːdaɪt] *adj.* gelehrt

**erupt** [ɪ'rʌpt] *v. i.* ausbrechen. **eruption** [ɪ'rʌpʃn] *n.* Ausbruch, *der*

**escalate** ['eskəleɪt] *v. i.* sich ausweiten *(into* zu); ⟨*Preise, Kosten:*⟩ [ständig] steigen. **escalator** ['eskəleɪtə(r)] *n.* Rolltreppe, *die*

**escapade** [eskə'peɪd] *n.* Eskapade, *die (geh.)*

**escape** [ɪ'skeɪp] **1.** *n.* Flucht, *die* **(from** aus); **have a narrow ~:** gerade noch einmal davonkommen. **2.** *v. i.* **a)** fliehen **(from** aus); *(successfully)* entkommen *(from Dat.);* **b)** ⟨*Gas:*⟩ ausströmen; ⟨*Flüssigkeit:*⟩ auslaufen. **3.** *v. t.* **a)** entkommen *(+ Dat.)* ⟨*Verfolger, Feind*⟩; entgehen *(+ Dat.)* ⟨*Bestrafung, Gefangennahme, Tod*⟩; verschont bleiben von ⟨*Zerstörung, Auswirkungen*⟩; **b)** *(not be remembered by)* entfallen sein *(+ Dat.).* **e'scape route** *n.* Fluchtweg, *der*

**escapism** [ɪ'skeɪpɪzm] *n.* Realitätsflucht, *die*

**escort** **1.** ['eskɔːt] *n.* **a)** Begleitung, *die;* *(Mil.)* Eskorte, *die;* **b)** *(hired companion)* Begleiter, *der*/Begleiterin, *die.* **2.** [ɪ'skɔːt] *v. t.* begleiten; *(lead)* führen; *(Mil.)* eskortieren

**Eskimo** ['eskɪməʊ] **1.** *adj.* Eskimo-. **2.** *n., pl.* **~s** *or same* Eskimo, *der*/Eskimofrau, *die;* **the ~[s]** die Eskimos

**esoteric** [esəʊ'terɪk] *adj.* esoterisch

**especial** [ɪ'speʃl] *attrib. adj.* [ganz] besonder... **especially** [ɪ'speʃəlɪ] *adv.* besonders

**espionage** ['espɪɒnɑːʒ] *n.* Spionage, *die*

**espresso** [e'spresəʊ] *n., pl.* **~s** *(coffee)* Espresso, *der.* **e'spresso bar** *n.* Espressobar, *die*

**Esq.** [ɪ'skwaɪə(r)] *abbr.* Esquire ≈ Hr.; *(on letter)* ≈ Hrn.; **Jim Smith, ~:** Hr./Hrn. Jim Smith

**essay** ['eseɪ] *n.* Essay, *der;* Aufsatz, *der (bes. Schulw.)*

**essence** ['esəns] *n.* **a)** Wesen, *das;* *(gist)* Wesentliche, *das;* **in ~:** im Wesentlichen; **b)** *(Cookery)* Essenz, *die*

**essential** [ɪ'senʃl] **1.** *adj.* **a)** *(fundamental)* wesentlich; **b)** *(indispensable)* unentbehrlich; lebensnotwendig ⟨*Versorgungseinrichtungen, Güter*⟩; unabdingbar ⟨*Qualifikation, Voraussetzung*⟩; **it is ~ that ...:** es ist unbedingt notwendig, daß ... **2.** *n. pl.* **the ~s** *(fundamentals)* das Wesentliche; *(items)* das Notwendigste. **es'sentially** *adv.* im Grunde

**establish** [ɪ'stæblɪʃ] *v. t.* **a)** schaffen ⟨*Einrichtung, Präzedenzfall*⟩; gründen ⟨*Organisation, Institut*⟩; errichten ⟨*Geschäft, System*⟩; **b)** *(secure acceptance for)* etablieren; **become ~ed** sich einbürgern; **c)** *(prove)* beweisen; **d)** *(discover)* feststellen. **established** [ɪ'stæblɪʃt] *adj.* bestehend ⟨*Ordnung*⟩; etabliert ⟨*Schriftsteller*⟩; *(accepted)* üblich; fest ⟨*Brauch*⟩; feststehend ⟨*Tatsache*⟩; **become ~:** sich durchsetzen. **e'stablishment** *n.* **a)** *(setting up, foundation)* Gründung, *die;* **b)** |**business|** **~:** Unternehmen, *das*

**estate** [ɪ'steɪt] *n.* **a)** *(landed property)* Gut, *das;* **b)** *(Brit.: housing ~)* [Wohn]siedlung, *die;* **c)** *(of deceased person)* Erbmasse, *die.* **e'state agent** *n. (Brit.)* Grundstücksmakler, *der;* **e'state car** *n. (Brit.)* Kombiwagen, *der*

**esteem** [ɪ'stiːm] **1.** *n.* Wertschätzung, *die (geh.) (for Gen.,* für). **2.** *v. t.* schätzen; **highly ~ed** hochgeschätzt

**estimate** **1.** ['estɪmət] *n.* **a)** Schätzung, *die;* **at a rough ~:** grob geschätzt; **b)** *(Commerc.)* Kostenvoranschlag, *der.* **2.** ['estɪmeɪt] *v. t.* schätzen *(at* auf + *Akk.).* **estimation** [estɪ'meɪʃn] *n.* Schätzung, *die;* **in sb.'s ~:** nach jmds. Schätzung

**estuary** ['estjʊərɪ] *n.* [Trichter]mündung, *die*

**etc.** *abbr.* et cetera usw.

**etch** [etʃ] *v. t.* ätzen *(on* auf + *Akk.);* *(on metal also)* ⟨*bes. Künstler:*⟩ radieren; *(fig.)* einprägen **(in, on** *Dat.).* **'etching** *n. (Art)* Radierung, *die*

**eternal** [ɪ'tɜːnl] *adj.,* **e'ternally** *adv.* ewig

**eternity** [ɪ'tɜːnɪtɪ] *n.* Ewigkeit, *die*

**ether** ['iːθə(r)] *n.* Äther, *der.* **ethereal** [ɪ'θɪərɪəl] *adj.* ätherisch

**ethical** ['eθɪkl] *adj.* ethisch

**ethics** ['eθɪks] *n.* **a)** Moral, *die; (moral philosophy)* Ethik, *die;* **b)** *usu. constr. as pl. (moral code)* Ethik, *die (geh.)*

**Ethiopia** [i:θɪ'əʊpɪə] *pr. n.* Äthiopien *(das)*

**ethnic** ['eθnɪk] *adj.* ethnisch

**etiquette** ['etɪket] *n.* Etikette, *die*

**etymology** [etɪ'mɒlədʒɪ] *n.* Etymologie, *die*

**eulogy** ['ju:lədʒɪ] *n.* Lobrede, *die*

**euphemism** ['ju:fəmɪzm] *n.* Euphemismus, *der.* **euphemistic** [ju:fə'mɪstɪk] *adj.* verhüllend

**euphoria** [ju:'fɔ:rɪə] *n.* Euphorie, *die (geh.)*

**Euro-** ['jʊərəʊ] *in comb.* euro-/Euro-. **'Eurocheque** *n.* Euroscheck, *der*

**Europe** ['jʊərəp] *pr. n.* Europa *(das)*. **European** [jʊərə'pi:ən] **1.** *adj.* europäisch; ~ |Economic| Community Europäische [Wirtschafts]gemeinschaft. **2.** *n.* Europäer, *der*/Europäerin, *die*

**euthanasia** [ju:θə'neɪzɪə] *n.* Euthanasie, *die*

**evacuate** [ɪ'vækjʊeɪt] *v. t.* evakuieren (**from** aus). **evacuation** [ɪvækjʊ'eɪʃn] *n.* Evakuierung, *die* (**from** aus)

**evade** [ɪ'veɪd] *v. t.* ausweichen (+ *Dat.*) ⟨*Angriff, Angreifer, Schlag, Problem, Frage*⟩; sich entziehen (+ *Dat.*) ⟨*Verhaftung, Verantwortung*⟩; entkommen (+ *Dat.*) ⟨*Verfolger, Verfolgung*⟩; hinterziehen ⟨*Steuern*⟩; ~ **doing** sth. vermeiden, etw. zu tun

**evaluate** [ɪ'væljʊeɪt] *v. t.* einschätzen; bewerten ⟨*Daten*⟩

**evangelical** [i:væn'dʒelɪkl] *adj.* missionarisch *(fig.); (Protestant)* evangelikal. **evangelist** [ɪ'vændʒəlɪst] *n.* Evangelist, *der*

**evaporate** [ɪ'væpəreɪt] **1.** *v. i.* verdunsten. **2.** *v. t.* verdunsten lassen. **evaporated 'milk** *n.* Kondensmilch, *die* **evaporation** [ɪvæpə'reɪʃn] *n.* Verdunstung, *die*

**evasion** [ɪ'veɪʒn] *n.* Umgehung, *die; (of responsibility, question)* Ausweichen, *das* (**of** vor + *Dat.*); **tax** ~: Steuerhinterziehung, *die.* **evasive** [ɪ'veɪsɪv] *adj.* **a)** **be/become** ~: ausweichen; **b)** ausweichend ⟨*Antwort*⟩

**eve** [i:v] *n.* Vorabend, *der* (**of** *Gen.*); *(day)* Vortag, *der* (**of** *Gen.*)

**even** ['i:vn] **1.** *adj.* **a)** eben ⟨*Boden, Fläche*⟩; gleich hoch ⟨*Stapel, Stuhl-, Tischbein*⟩; **be of ~ height/length** gleich hoch/lang sein; **b)** gerade ⟨*Zahl, Seite, Hausnummer*⟩; **c)** **be** *or*

**get** ~ **with sb.** *(quits)* es jmdm. heimzahlen; **break** ~: die Kosten decken. **2.** *adv.* sogar; selbst; sogar noch ⟨*weniger, schlimmer usw.*⟩; ~ **if** selbst wenn; ~ **so** [aber] trotzdem; **not** *or* **never** ~ ...: [noch] nicht einmal ... **even 'up** *v. t.* ausgleichen

**evening** ['i:vnɪŋ] *n.* Abend, *der; this/ tomorrow* ~: heute/morgen abend; **in the** ~: am Abend; *(regularly)* abends. **'evening class** *n.* Abendkurs, *der.* **'evening dress** *n.* Abendkleidung, *die*

**'evenly** *adv.* gleichmäßig

**'even-numbered** *adj.* gerade

**event** [ɪ'vent] *n.* **a)** **in the** ~ **of his dying** *or* **death** im Falle seines Todes; **in the** ~: letzten Endes; **in the** ~ **of rain** bei Regenwetter; **b)** *(occurrence)* Ereignis, *das.* **e'ventful** *adj.* ereignisreich

**eventual** [ɪ'ventjʊəl] *adj.* **predict sb.'s** ~ **downfall** vorhersagen, daß jmd. schließlich zu Fall kommen wird; **the career of Napoleon and his** ~ **defeat** der Aufstieg Napoleons und schließlich seine Niederlage. **eventuality** [ɪventjʊ'ælɪtɪ] *n.* Eventualität, *die.* **e'ventually** *adv.* schließlich

**ever** ['evə(r)] *adv.* **a)** *(always)* immer; **for** ~: für immer; ewig ⟨*lieben, dasein, leben*⟩; ~ **since** |then| seit [dieser Zeit]; **b)** *(at any time)* je[mals]; **hardly** ~: so gut wie nie; **c)** *in comb. with compar. adj. or adv.* noch; ~-**increasing** ständig zunehmend; **d)** *(coll.)* **what** ~ **does he want?** was will er nur?; **why** ~ **not?** warum denn nicht? **'evergreen 1.** *adj.* immergrün. **2.** *n.* immergrüne Pflanze. **ever'lasting** *adj.* **a)** *(eternal)* immerwährend; ewig ⟨*Leben*⟩; unvergänglich ⟨*Ruhm, Ehre*⟩; **b)** *(incessant)* endlos

**every** ['evrɪ] *adj.* **a)** jeder/jede/jedes; ~ **one** jeder/jede/jedes [einzelne]; **your** ~ **wish** all[e] deine Wünsche; **she comes** ~ **day** sie kommt jeden Tag; ~ **three/few days** alle drei/paar Tage; ~ **other** (~ **second, almost** ~) jeder/jede/ jedes zweite; **b)** *(the greatest possible)* all ⟨*Respekt, Aussicht*⟩

**every:** ~**body** *n. & pron.* jeder; ~**body else** alle anderen; ~**day** *attrib. adj.* alltäglich; Alltags⟨*kleidung, -sprache*⟩; **in** ~**day life** im Alltag; ~**one** *see* ~**body;** ~**place** *(Amer.) see* ~**where;** ~**thing** *n. & pron.* alles; ~**where** *adv.* überall; ~**where you go/look** wohin man auch geht/sieht

**evict** [ɪ'vɪkt] *v. t.* ~ **sb.** |**from his home**|

jmdn. zur Räumung [seiner Wohnung] zwingen. **eviction** [ɪ'vɪkʃn] n. Zwangsräumung, die; the ~ of the tenant die zwangsweise Vertreibung des Mieters

**evidence** ['evɪdəns] n. a) Beweis, der; (indication) Anzeichen, das; be ~ of sth. etw. beweisen; b) (Law) Beweismaterial, das; give ~: aussagen

**evident** ['evɪdənt] adj. offensichtlich; be ~ to sb. jmdm. klar sein; it soon became ~ that ...: es stellte sich bald heraus, daß ... **'evidently** adv. offensichtlich

**evil** ['i:vl, 'i:vɪl] 1. adj. böse; schlecht ⟨Charakter, Einfluß, System⟩. 2. n. a) Böse, das; b) (bad thing) Übel, das

**evocative** [ɪ'vɒkətɪv] adj. be ~ of sth. etw. heraufbeschwören

**evoke** [ɪ'vəʊk] v. t. heraufbeschwören; hervorrufen ⟨Bewunderung, Überraschung⟩; erregen ⟨Interesse⟩

**evolution** [i:və'lu:ʃn] n. Entwicklung, die; (Biol.) Evolution, die

**evolve** [ɪ'vɒlv] 1. v. i. sich entwickeln (from aus, into zu). 2. v. t. entwickeln

**ewe** [ju:] n. Mutterschaf, das

**ex-** pref. Ex-⟨Freundin, Präsident, Champion⟩; Alt-⟨[bundes]kanzler⟩

**exacerbate** [ek'sæsəbeɪt] v. t. verschärfen ⟨Lage⟩; verschlechtern ⟨Zustand⟩

**exact** [ɪg'zækt] 1. adj. genau. 2. v. t. fordern; erheben ⟨Gebühr⟩. **exacting** [ɪg'zæktɪŋ] n. anspruchsvoll; hoch ⟨Anforderung⟩. **exactitude** [ɪg'zæktɪtju:d] Genauigkeit, die. **exactly** [ɪg'zæktlɪ] adv. genau; not ~ (coll. iron.) nicht gerade. **exactness** [ɪg'zæktnɪs] n. Genauigkeit, die

**exaggerate** [ɪg'zædʒəreɪt] v. t. übertreiben. **exaggeration** [ɪgzædʒə'reɪʃn] n. Übertreibung, die

**exam** [ɪg'zæm] (coll.) see **examination** b

**examination** [ɪgzæmɪ'neɪʃn] n. a) (inspection; Med.) Untersuchung, die; b) (Sch. etc.) Prüfung, die; (final ~ at university) Examen, das

**examine** [ɪg'zæmɪn] v. t. a) (inspect; Med.) untersuchen (for auf + Akk.); prüfen ⟨Dokument, Gewissen⟩; kontrollieren ⟨Ausweis, Gepäck⟩; b) (Sch. etc.) prüfen (in in + Dat.); c) (Law) verhören. **examiner** [ɪg'zæmɪnə(r)] n. Prüfer, der/Prüferin, die

**example** [ɪg'zɑ:mpl] n. Beispiel, das; for ~: zum Beispiel; **make an ~ of sb.** ein Exempel an jmdm. statuieren

**exasperate** [ɪg'zæspəreɪt] v. t. (irrit-

ate) verärgern; (infuriate) zur Verzweiflung bringen. **exasperation** [ɪg'zæspəreɪʃn] n. see **exasperate**: Ärger, der/Verzweiflung, die (with über + Akk.); in ~: verärgert/verzweifelt

**excavate** ['ekskəveɪt] v. t. a) ausschachten; (with machine) ausbaggern; b) (Archaeol.) ausgraben. **excavation** [ekskə'veɪʃn] n. a) Ausschachtung, die; (with machine) Ausbaggerung, die; b) (Archaeol.) Ausgrabung, die. **excavator** ['ekskəveɪtə(r)] n. Bagger, der

**exceed** [ɪk'si:d] v. t. a) (be greater than) übertreffen (in + Dat.) ⟨Kosten, Summe, Anzahl:⟩ übersteigen (by um); b) (go beyond) überschreiten; hinausgehen über (+ Akk.) ⟨Auftrag, Befehl⟩. **ex'ceedingly** adv. äußerst; ausgesprochen ⟨häßlich, dumm⟩

**excel** [ɪk'sel] 1. v. t., -ll- übertreffen; ~ oneself (lit. or iron.) sich selbst übertreffen. 2. v. i., -ll- sich hervortun (at, in in + Dat.)

**excellence** ['eksələns] n. hervorragende Qualität. **excellent** ['eksələnt] adj. hervorragend

**except** [ɪk'sept] 1. prep. ~ [(coll.) for] außer (+ Dat.); ~ for (in all respects other than) abgesehen von. 2. v. t. ausnehmen (from bei); ~ed ausgenommen. **ex'cepting** prep. außer (+ Dat.). **exception** [ɪk'sepʃn] n. Ausnahme, die; **take ~ to** Anstoß nehmen an (+ Dat.). **exceptional** [ɪk'sepʃənl] adj. außergewöhnlich. **ex'ceptionally** adv. a) (as an exception) ausnahmsweise; b) (remarkably) ungewöhnlich

**excerpt** ['eksɜ:pt] n. Auszug, der (from aus)

**excess** [ɪk'ses] n. a) Übermaß, das (of an + Dat.); **eat/drink to ~:** übermäßig essen/trinken; b) esp. in pl. (over-indulgence) Exzeß, der; c) be in ~ of sth. etw. übersteigen; d) (surplus) Überschuß, der

**excess** ['ekses]: ~ 'baggage n. Mehrgepäck, das; ~ 'fare n. Mehrpreis, der; **pay the ~ fare** nachlösen

**excessive** [ɪk'sesɪv] adj. übermäßig; übertrieben ⟨Forderung, Lob, Ansprüche⟩; unmäßig ⟨Esser, Trinker⟩. **ex'cessively** adv. übertrieben; unmäßig ⟨essen, trinken⟩

**exchange** [ɪks'tʃeɪndʒ] 1. v. t. a) tauschen ⟨Plätze, Ringe, Küsse⟩; umtauschen ⟨Geld⟩; wechseln ⟨Blicke, Worte⟩; ~ insults sich beleidigen; b) *(give in place of another)* eintauschen (for für, gegen); umtauschen ⟨*[ge-kaufte] Ware*⟩ (for gegen). 2. *n.* **a)** Tausch, *der;* **in ~:** dafür; **in ~ for sth.** für etw.; **b)** *(of money)* Umtausch, *der;* **~ rate, rate of ~:** Wechselkurs, *der;* **c)** *(Teleph.)* Fernmeldeamt, *das*

**exchequer** [ɪks'tʃekə(r)] *n. (Brit.)* Schatzamt, *das*

**excise** ['eksaɪz] *n.* Verbrauchsteuer, *die;* **Customs and E~** *(Brit.)* Amt für Zölle und Verbrauchsteuer

**excitable** [ek'saɪtəbl] *adj.* leicht erregbar

**excite** [ɪk'saɪt] *v. t.* **a)** *(thrill)* begeistern; **b)** *(agitate)* aufregen. **ex'cited** *adj.* aufgeregt (**at** über + *Akk.*); **get ~:** sich aufregen. **ex'citement** *n.* Aufregung, *die; (enthusiasm)* Begeisterung, *die.* **exciting** [ɪk'saɪtɪŋ] *adj.* aufregend; *(full of suspense)* spannend

**exclaim** [ɪk'skleɪm] **1.** *v. t.* ausrufen. **2.** *v. i.* aufschreien. **exclamation** [eksklə'meɪʃn] *n.* Ausruf, *der.* **excla'mation mark,** *(Amer.)* **excla'mation point** *ns.* Ausrufezeichen, *das*

**exclude** [ɪk'sklu:d] *v. t.* ausschließen. **excluding** [ɪk'sklu:dɪŋ] *prep.* **~ drinks/VAT** Getränke ausgenommen/ ohne Mehrwertsteuer. **exclusion** [ɪk-'sklu:ʒn] *n.* Ausschluß, *der.* **exclusive** [ɪk'sklu:sɪv] *adj.* **a)** alleinig ⟨*Besitzer, Kontrolle*⟩; Allein⟨*eigentum*⟩; *(Journ.)* Exklusiv⟨*bericht, -interview*⟩; **b)** *(select)* exklusiv; **c)** **~ of** ohne. **ex-'clusively** *adv.* ausschließlich

**excrement** ['ekskrɪmənt] *n.* Kot, *der (geh.)*

**excrete** [ɪk'skri:t] *v. t.* ausscheiden

**excruciating** [ɪk'skru:'ʃɪeɪtɪŋ] *adj.* unerträglich

**excursion** [ɪk'skɜ:ʃn] *n.* Ausflug, *der*

**excusable** [ɪk'skju:zəbl] *adj.* entschuldbar; verzeihlich

**excuse 1.** [ɪk'skju:z] *v. t.* **a)** entschuldigen; **~ oneself** sich entschuldigen; **~ me** Entschuldigung; **b)** *(release, exempt)* befreien **(from** von). **2.** [ɪk-'skju:s] *n.* Entschuldigung, *die*

**ex-di'rectory** *adj. (Brit. Teleph.)* Geheim⟨*nummer, -anschluß*⟩; **be ~:** nicht im Telefonbuch stehen

**execute** ['eksɪkju:t] *v. t.* **a)** hinrichten; **b)** *(put into effect)* ausführen. **execution** [eksɪ'kju:ʃn] *n.* **a)** Hinrichtung, *die;* **b)** *(putting into effect)* Ausführung, *die.* **exe'cutioner** *n.* Scharfrichter, *der*

**executive** [ɪg'zekjʊtɪv] **1.** *n.* leitender Angestellter/leitende Angestellte. **2.** *adj.* leitend ⟨*Stellung, Funktion*⟩

**executor** [ɪg'zekjʊtə(r)] *n. (Law)* Testamentsvollstrecker, *der*

**exemplary** [ɪg'zemplərɪ] *adj.* **a)** *(model)* vorbildlich; **b)** *(deterrent)* exemplarisch

**exemplify** [ɪg'zemplɪfaɪ] *v. t.* veranschaulichen

**exempt** [ɪg'zempt] **1.** *adj.* |be| **~** |from sth.| |von etw.| befreit |sein|. **2.** *v. t.* befreien. **exemption** [ɪg'zempʃn] *n.* Befreiung, *die*

**exercise** ['eksəsaɪz] **1.** *n.* **a)** Übung, *die;* **b)** *no pl. (physical exertion)* Bewegung, *die;* **take ~:** sich *(Dat.)* Bewegung schaffen. **2.** *v. t.* ausüben ⟨*Recht, Macht, Einfluß*⟩; walten lassen ⟨*Vorsicht*⟩. **3.** *v. i.* sich *(Dat.)* Bewegung schaffen. **'exercise book** *n.* [Schul]heft, *das*

**exert** [ɪg'zɜ:t] **1.** *v. t.* aufbieten ⟨*Kraft*⟩; ausüben ⟨*Einfluß, Druck*⟩. **2.** *v. refl.* sich anstrengen. **exertion** [ɪg'zɜ:ʃn] *n.* **a)** *(of strength, force)* Aufwendung, *die; (of influence, pressure)* Ausübung, *die;* **b)** *(effort)* Anstrengung, *die*

**exhale** [eks'heɪl] *v. t. & i.* ausatmen

**exhaust** [ɪg'zɔ:st] **1.** *v. t.* erschöpfen; erschöpfend behandeln ⟨*Thema*⟩. **2.** *n.* *(Motor Veh.)* Auspuff, *der; (gases)* Auspuffgase *Pl.* **ex'hausted** *adj.* erschöpft. **ex'hausting** *adj.* anstrengend. **exhaustion** [ɪg'zɔ:stʃn] *n.* Erschöpfung, *die.* **exhaustive** [ɪg-'zɔ:stɪv] *adj.* umfassend. **ex'haustpipe** *n.* Auspuffrohr, *das*

**exhibit** [ɪg'zɪbɪt] **1.** *v. t.* ausstellen; zeigen ⟨*Mut, Symptome, Angst usw.*⟩. **2.** *n.* Ausstellungsstück, *das.* **exhibition** [eksɪ'bɪʃn] *n.* Ausstellung, *die;* **make an ~ of oneself** sich unmöglich aufführen. **exhibitor** [ɪg'zɪbɪtə(r)] *n.* Aussteller, *der*/Ausstellerin, *die*

**exhilarated** [ɪg'zɪləreɪtɪd] *adj.* belebt. **exhilarating** [ɪg'zɪləreɪtɪŋ] *adj.* belebend. **exhilaration** [ɪgzɪlə'reɪʃn] *n.* |feeling of| **~:** Hochgefühl, *das*

**exhort** [ɪg'zɔ:t] *v. t.* ermahnen

**exile** ['eksaɪl] **1.** *n.* **a)** Exil, *das;* **in/into ~:** im/ins Exil; **b)** *(person)* Verbannte, *der/die.* **2.** *v. t.* verbannen

**exist** [ɪg'zɪst] *v. i.* existieren; ⟨*Zweifel, Gefahr, Problem, Einrichtung:*⟩ bestehen; **~ on sth.** von etw. leben. **existence** [ɪg'zɪstəns] *n.* Existenz, *die, (mode of living)* Dasein, *das;* **be in/come into ~:** existieren/entstehen

**exit** ['eksɪt] *n. (way out)* Ausgang, *der* (from aus); *(for vehicle)* Ausfahrt, *die.* '**exit visa** *n.* Ausreisevisum, *das*
**exonerate** [ɪg'zɒnəreɪt] *v. t.* entlasten
**exorbitant** [ɪg'zɔːbɪtənt] *adj.* [maßlos] überhöht
**exorcize** ['eksɔːsaɪz] *v. t.* austreiben
**exotic** [ɪg'zɒtɪk] *adj.* exotisch
**expand** [ɪk'spænd] 1. *v. i.* **a)** sich ausdehnen; *(Commerc.)* expandieren; **b)** ~ on weiter ausführen. 2. *v. t.* ausdehnen; *(Commerc.)* erweitern
**expanse** [ɪk'spæns] *n.* [weite] Fläche
**expansion** [ɪk'spænʃn] *n.* Ausdehnung, *die; (Commerc.)* Expansion, *die*
**expect** [ɪk'spekt] *v. t.* **a)** erwarten; ~ to do sth. damit rechnen, etw. zu tun; ~ sb. to do sth. damit rechnen, daß jmd. etw. tut; *(require)* von jmdm. erwarten, daß er etw. tut; **b)** *(coll.: think, suppose)* glauben; **I** ~ **so** ich glaube schon. **expectancy** [ɪk'spektənsɪ] *n.* Erwartung, *die.* **expectant** [ɪk'spektənt] *adj.* erwartungsvoll; ~ **mother** werdende Mutter. **ex'pectantly** *adv.* erwartungsvoll; gespannt ⟨*warten*⟩.
**expectation** [ekspek'teɪʃn] *n.* Erwartung, *die*
**expedient** [ɪk'spiːdɪənt] 1. *adj.* angebracht. 2. *n.* Mittel, *das*
**expedition** [ekspɪ'dɪʃn] *n.* Expedition, *die*
**expel** [ɪk'spel] *v. t.,* **-ll-** ausweisen (from aus); ~ **sb. from school** jmdn. von der Schule verweisen
**expend** [ɪk'spend] *v. t.* **a)** aufwenden (lup|on für); **b)** *(use up)* aufbrauchen (lup|on für). **expendable** [ɪk'spendəbl] *adj.* entbehrlich; **be** ~: geopfert werden können
**expenditure** [ɪk'spendɪtʃə(r)] *n.* **a)** *(amount spent)* Ausgaben *Pl.* (on für); **b)** *(spending)* Ausgabe, *die*
**expense** [ɪk'spens] *n.* **a)** Kosten *Pl.;* at sb.'s ~: auf jmds. Kosten *(Akk.);* at one's own ~: auf eigene Kosten; **b)** *usu. in pl. (Commerc. etc.: amount spent [and repaid])* Spesen *Pl.;* **c)** *(fig.)* [be] at the ~ of sth. auf Kosten von etw. [gehen]. **ex'pense account** *n.* Spesenabrechnung, *die;* put sth. on one's ~: etw. als Spesen abrechnen. **expensive** [ɪk'spensɪv] *adj.,* **ex'pensively** *adv.* teuer
**experience** [ɪk'spɪərɪəns] 1. *n.* Erfahrung, *die; (event)* Erlebnis, *das.* 2. *v. t.* erleben; haben ⟨*Schwierigkeiten*⟩· verspüren ⟨*Kälte, Schmerz, Gefühl*⟩. **ex'perienced** *adj.* erfahren

**experiment** 1. [ɪk'sperɪmənt] *n.* **a)** Experiment, *das,* Versuch, *der* (on an + *Dat.*); **b)** *(fig.)* Experiment, *das.* 2. [ɪk'sperɪment] *v. i.* Versuche anstellen (on an + *Dat.*). **experimental** [ɪksperɪ'mentl] *adj.* experimentell; Experimentier⟨*theater, -kino*⟩
**expert** ['ekspɜːt] 1. *adj.* ausgezeichnet; **be** ~ **in** *or* **at sth.** Fachmann *od.* Experte für etw. sein; **be** ~ **in** *or* **at doing sth.** etw. ausgezeichnet können. 2. *n.* Fachmann, *der;* Experte, *der*/Expertin, *die;* **be an** ~ **in** *or* **at/on sth.** Fachmann *od.* Experte in etw. *(Dat.)*/für etw. sein. **expertise** [ekspɜː'tiːz] *n.* Fachkenntnisse; *(skill)* Können, *das*
**expire** [ɪk'spaɪə(r)] *v. i.* ablaufen. **expiry** [ɪk'spaɪərɪ] *n.* Ablauf, *der*
**explain** [ɪk'spleɪn] 1. *v. t., also abs.* erklären. 2. *v. refl., often abs.* please ~ [yourself] bitte erklären Sie mir das. **explain a'way** *v. t.* eine [plausible] Erklärung finden für
**explanation** [eksplə'neɪʃn] *n.* Erklärung, *die;* need ~: einer Erklärung *(Gen.)* bedürfen
**explanatory** [ɪk'splænətərɪ] *adj.* erklärend; erläuternd ⟨*Bemerkung*⟩
**explicable** [ɪk'splɪkəbl] *adj.* erklärbar
**explicit** [ɪk'splɪsɪt] *adj.* klar; ausdrücklich ⟨*Zustimmung, Erwähnung*⟩. **ex'plicitly** *adv.* ausdrücklich; deutlich ⟨*beschreiben, ausdrücken*⟩
**explode** [ɪk'spləʊd] 1. *v. i.* explodieren. 2. *v. t.* zur Explosion bringen
**exploit** 1. ['eksplɔɪt] *n.* Heldentat, *die.* 2. [ɪk'splɔɪt] *v. t.* ausbeuten ⟨*Arbeiter usw.*⟩; ausnutzen ⟨*Gutmütigkeit, Freund, Unwissenheit*⟩. **exploitation** [eksplɔɪ'teɪʃn] *n. see* exploit 2: Ausbeutung, *die;* Ausnutzung, *die*
**exploration** [eksplə'reɪʃn] *n.* Erforschung, *die; (fig.)* Untersuchung, *die*
**exploratory** [ɪk'splɒrətərɪ] *adj.* Forschungs-
**explore** [ɪk'splɔː(r)] *v. t.* erforschen; *(fig.)* untersuchen. **ex'plorer** *n.* Entdeckungsreisende, *der/die*
**explosion** [ɪk'spləʊʒn] *n.* Explosion, *die.* **explosive** [ɪk'spləʊzɪv] 1. *adj.* explosiv. 2. *n.* Sprengstoff, *der*
**export** 1. [ɪk'spɔːt, 'ekspɔːt] *v. t.* exportieren; ausführen. 2. ['ekspɔːt] *n.* Export, *der.* **ex'porter** *n.* Exporteur, *der*
**expose** [ɪk'spəʊz] *v. t.* **a)** *(uncover)* freilegen; entblößen ⟨*Haut, Körper*⟩; **b)** offenbaren ⟨*Schwäche*⟩; aufdecken ⟨*Mißstände, Verbrechen*⟩; entlarven ⟨*Täter, Spion*⟩; **c)** *(subject)* ~ **to sth.** ei-

ner Sache *(Dat.)* aussetzen; **d)** *(Photog.)* belichten. **exposed** [ɪk-'spəʊzd] *adj. (unprotected)* ungeschützt; ~ **position** exponierte Stellung. **exposure** [ɪk'spəʊʒə(r)] *n.* **a)** *(to cold etc.)* die of/suffer from ~: an Unterkühlung *(Dat.)* sterben/leiden; **b)** *(Photog.) (exposing time)* Belichtung, *die; (picture)* Aufnahme, *die.* **ex-'posure meter** *n.* Belichtungsmesser, *der*

**expound** [ɪk'spaʊnd] *v. t.* darlegen

**express** [ɪk'spres] **1.** *v. t.* ausdrücken; äußern *(Meinung, Wunsch, Dank, Bedauern)*; ~ **oneself** sich ausdrücken. **2.** *attrib. adj.* **a)** Eil*(brief, -bote usw.)*; Schnell*(paket, -sendung);* **b)** ausdrücklich *(Wunsch, Absicht).* **3.** *adv.* als Eilsache *(senden).* **4.** *n. (train)* Schnellzug, *der.* **expression** [ɪk-'spreʃn] *n.* Ausdruck, *der.* **expressive** [ɪk'spresɪv] *adj.* ausdrucksvoll

**express:** ~ **'train** *n.* D-Zug, *der;* ~**way** *n. (Amer.)* Schnellstraße, *die* **ex'pressly** *adv.* ausdrücklich

**expulsion** [ɪk'spʌlʃn] *n.* Ausweisung, *die* (**from** aus); *(from school)* Verweisung, *die* (**from** von)

**exquisite** ['ekskwɪzɪt, ɪk'skwɪzɪt] *adj.* erlesen. **ex'quisitely** *adv.* vorzüglich; kunstvoll *(verziert, geschnitzt)*

**extend** [ɪk'stend] **1.** *v. t.* verlängern; ausstrecken *(Arm, Bein, Hand);* ausziehen *(Leiter, Teleskop);* verlängern lassen *(Leihbuch, Visum);* ausdehnen *(Einfluß, Macht);* vergrößern *(Haus, Geschäft, Fabrik);* gewähren *([Gast]freundschaft, Hilfe, Kredit)* (**to** *Dat.);* ~ **the time limit** den Termin hinausschieben. **2.** *v. i.* sich erstrecken; **the season ~s from November to March** die Saison geht von November bis März

**extension** [ɪk'stenʃn] *n.* **a)** Verlängerung, *die;* **b)** *(part of house)* Anbau, *der;* **c)** *(telephone)* Nebenanschluß, *der; (number)* Apparat, *der.* **extensive** [ɪk'stensɪv] *adj.* ausgedehnt; umfangreich *(Reparatur, Wissen, Nachforschungen);* beträchtlich *(Schäden);* weitreichend *(Änderungen).* **ex'tensively** *adv.* beträchtlich *(ändern, beschädigen);* ausführlich *(berichten, schreiben)*

**extent** [ɪk'stent] *n.* Ausdehnung, *die; (scope)* Umfang, *der; (of damage)* Ausmaß, *das;* **to what ~?** inwieweit? **exterior** [ɪk'stɪərɪə(r)] **1.** *adj.* äußer...;

Außen*(fläche, -wand).* **2.** *n.* Äußere, *das; (of house)* Außenwände *Pl.*

**exterminate** [ɪk'stɜːmɪneɪt] *v. t.* ausrotten; vertilgen *(Ungeziefer).* **extermination** [ɪkstɜːmɪ'neɪʃn] *n.* Ausrottung, *die; (of pests)* Vertilgung, *die*

**external** [ɪk'stɜːnl] *adj.* äußer...; Außen*(fläche, -abmessungen);* purely ~: rein äußerlich; **for ~ use only** nur äußerlich anzuwenden

**extinct** [ɪk'stɪŋkt] *adj.* erloschen *(Vulkan);* ausgestorben *(Art, Rasse, Gattung).* **extinction** [ɪk'stɪŋkʃn] *n.* Aussterben, *das*

**extinguish** [ɪk'stɪŋgwɪʃ] *v. t.* löschen. **ex'tinguisher** *n.* Feuerlöscher, *der*

**extol** [ɪk'stɒl] *v. t.,* **-ll-** rühmen; preisen **extort** [ɪk'stɔːt] *v. t.* erpressen (**out of** von). **extortion** [ɪk'stɔːʃn] *n.* Erpressung, *die.* **extortionate** [ɪk'stɔːʃənət] *adj.* Wucher*(preis, -zinsen usw.),* maßlos überzogen *(Forderung)*

**extra** ['ekstrə] **1.** *adj.* zusätzlich; Mehr*(arbeit, -kosten, -ausgaben).* Sonder*(bus, -zug).* **2.** *adv.* **a)** *(more than usually)* besonders; extra *(lang, stark, fein);* **b)** *(additionally)* extra; **packing and postage** ~: zuzüglich Verpackung und Porto. **3.** *n.* **a)** *(added to services, salary, etc.)* zusätzliche Leistung; **b)** *(in play, film, etc.)* Statist *der*/Statistin, *die*

**extract 1.** ['ekstrækt] *n.* **a)** Extrakt, *der (fachspr. auch: das);* **b)** *(from book, music, etc.)* Auszug, *der.* **2.** [ɪk'strækt] *v. t.* ziehen *(Zahn);* herausziehen *(Dorn, Splitter usw.).* **extraction** [ɪk-'strækʃn] *n. (of tooth)* Extraktion, *die; (of thorn, splinter, etc.)* Herausziehen, *das.* **ex'tractor fan** *n.* Entlüfter, *der*

**extradite** ['ekstrədaɪt] *v. t.* ausliefern **extradition** [ekstrə'dɪʃn] *n.* Auslieferung, *die*

**extraordinary** [ɪk'strɔːdɪnərɪ] *adj.* außergewöhnlich; merkwürdig *(Benehmen);* **how ~!** wie seltsam!

**extravagance** [ɪk'strævəgəns] *n.* **a)** Extravaganz, *die;* **b)** *(extravagant thing)* Luxus, *der*

**extravagant** [ɪk'strævəgənt] *adj.* verschwenderisch; aufwendig *(Lebensstil);* teuer *(Geschmack)*

**extreme** [ɪk'striːm] **1.** *adj.* **a)** äußerst... *(Spitze, Rand, Ende);* extrem *(Gegensätze, Hitze, Kälte);* höchst... *(Gefahr);* äußerst... *(Notfall, Höflichkeit, Bescheidenheit);* stärkst... *(Schmerzen);* größt... *(Wichtigkeit);* **at the ~ edge/left** ganz am Rand/ganz links; **b**

*(not moderate)* extrem; drastisch ⟨*Maßnahme*⟩. **2.** *n.* Extrem, *das;* go to ~s vor nichts zurückschrecken; go from one ~ to the other von einem Extrem ins andere fallen. **ex'tremely** *adv.* äußerst. **extremist** [ɪk'striːmɪst] *n.* Extremist, *der/*Extremistin, *die; attrib.* extremistisch. **extremity** [ɪk-'stremɪtɪ] *n.* äußerstes Ende

**extricate** ['ekstrɪkeɪt] *v. t.* ~ sth. from sth. etw. aus etw. herausziehen; ~ oneself/sb. from sth. sich/jmdn. aus etw. befreien

**extrovert** ['ekstrəvɜːt] **1.** *n.* extrovertierter Mensch; **be an** ~: extrovertiert sein. **2.** *adj.* extrovertiert

**exuberant** [ɪg'zjuːbərənt] *adj.* **be** ~: sich überschwenglich freuen

**exude** [ɪg'zjuːd] *v. t.* absondern; *(fig.)* ausstrahlen

**exult** [ɪg'zʌlt] *v. i.* jubeln (**in, at, over** über + *Akk.*)

**eye** [aɪ] **1.** *n.* **a)** Auge, *das;* **keep an** ~ **on sb./sth.** auf jmdn./etw. aufpassen; **see** ~ **to** ~: einer Meinung sein; **with one's** ~s **shut** *(fig.)* blind; *(easily)* im Schlaf; **be up to one's** ~s **in work/debt** bis über beide Ohren in Arbeit/Schulden stecken *(ugs.);* **b)** *(of needle)* Öhr, *das; (metal loop)* Öse, *die.* **2.** *v. t.,* beäugen; ~ **sb. up and down** jmdn. von oben bis unten mustern

**eye:** ~**ball** *n.* Augapfel, *der;* ~**brow** *n.* Augenbraue, *die;* ~**lash** *n.* Augenwimper, *die;* ~**level** *n.* Augenhöhe, *die; attrib.* in Augenhöhe *nachgestellt;* **at** ~**level** in Augenhöhe; ~**lid** *n.* Augenlid, *das;* ~**shadow** *n.* Lidschatten, *der;* ~**sight** *n.* Sehkraft, *die;* **have good** ~**sight** er hat gute Augen haben; **his** ~**sight is poor** er hat schlechte Augen; ~**sore** *n.* Schandfleck, *der;* ~**witness** *n.* Augenzeuge, *der/*-zeugin, *die*

# F

**F, f** [ef] *n.* F, f, *das*
**fable** ['feɪbl] *n.* Fabel, *die; (myth, lie)* Märchen, *das*
**fabric** ['fæbrɪk] *n.* Gewebe, *das*

**fabricate** ['fæbrɪkeɪt] *v. t. (invent)* erfinden. **fabrication** [fæbrɪkeɪʃn] *n.* Erfindung, *die*

**fabulous** ['fæbjʊləs] *adj.* **a)** sagenhaft; **b)** *(coll.: marvellous)* fabelhaft *(ugs.)*

**face** [feɪs] **1.** *n.* **a)** Gesicht, *das;* **lie** ~ **down|ward]** ⟨*Person/Buch:*⟩ auf dem Bauch/Gesicht liegen; **make** *or* **pull a** ~/~s Grimassen schneiden; **on the** ~ **of it** dem Anschein nach; **in the** ~ **of sth.** trotz etw. *(Gen.);* **b)** *(of mountain, cliff)* Wand, *die; (of clock, watch)* Zifferblatt, *das; (of dice)* Seite, *die; (of coin, playing-card)* Vorderseite, *die.* **2.** *v. t.* **a)** sich wenden zu; **[stand] facing one another** sich *(Dat.)* gegenüber [stehen]; **b)** *(fig.)* ins Auge sehen (+ *Dat.*) ⟨*Tod, Vorstellung*⟩; stehen vor (+ *Dat.*) ⟨*Ruin, Entscheidung*⟩; ~ **the facts** den Tatsachen ins Gesicht sehen; **be** ~**d with sth.** sich einer Sache *(Dat.)* gegenübersehen; **c)** *(coll.: bear)* verkraften. **3.** *v. i. (in train etc.)* ~ **forwards/backwards** ⟨*Person:*⟩ in/entgegen Fahrtrichtung sitzen. **face 'up to** *v. t.* ins Auge sehen (+ *Dat.*); sich abfinden mit ⟨*Möglichkeit*⟩

**face:** ~-**cream** *n.* Gesichtscreme, *die;* ~-**flannel** *n. (Brit.)* Waschlappen, *der;* ~-**lift** *n.* **a)** Facelifting, *das;* **have** *or* **get a** ~-**lift** sich liften lassen; **b)** *(fig.)* Verschönerung, *die*

**facet** ['fæsɪt] *n.* Facette, *die; (fig.)* Aspekt, *der*

**facetious** [fə'siːʃəs] *adj.* [gewollt] witzig

**face:** ~-**to**-~: persönlich ⟨*Gespräch, Treffen*⟩; ~ **value** *n.* Nennwert, *der;* **accept sth. at |its|** ~ **value** *(fig.)* etw. für bare Münze nehmen

**facial** ['feɪʃl] *adj.* Gesichts-
**facile** ['fæsaɪl] *adj.* nichtssagend
**facilities** [fə'sɪlɪtɪz] *n. pl.* Einrichtungen; **cooking/washing** ~: Koch-/Waschgelegenheit, *die;* **sports** ~: Sportanlagen; **shopping** ~: Einkaufsmöglichkeiten

**facsimile** [fæk'sɪmɪlɪ] *n.* **a)** Faksimile, *das;* **b)** *see* **fax 1**

**fact** [fækt] *n.* Tatsache, *die;* ~s **and figures** Fakten und Zahlen; **the** ~ **remains that ...:** Tatsache bleibt: ...; **the true** ~s **of the case** *or* **matter** der wahre Sachverhalt; **know for a** ~ **that ...:** genau wissen, daß ...; **in** ~: tatsächlich

**faction** ['fækʃn] *n.* Splittergruppe, *die*
**factor** ['fæktə(r)] *n.* Faktor, *der*
**factory** ['fæktərɪ] *n.* Fabrik, *die.* '**factory farm** *n.* Agrarfabrik, *die*

**factual** ['fæktjʊəl] *adj.* sachlich
**faculty** ['fækəltı] *n.* **a)** Fähigkeit, *die;*
**mental ~:** geistige Kraft; **b)** *(Univ.)*
Fakultät, *die*
**fad** [fæd] *n.* Marotte, *die*
**fade** [feɪd] *v. i.* **a)** ⟨*Blätter, Blumen:*⟩
[ver]welken; **b)** ~ **|in colour|** [ver]blei-
chen; **the light ~d** es dunkelte; **c)**
⟨*Laut:*⟩ verklingen; **d)** *(fig.)* verblassen; ⟨*Schönheit:*⟩ verblühen; ⟨*Hoffnung:*⟩ schwinden; **e)** *(blend)* übergehen (**into** in + *Akk.*). **fade a'way** *v. i.*
schwinden; ⟨*Laut:*⟩ verklingen (**into** in
+ *Dat.*)
**faded** ['feɪdɪd] *adj.* welk ⟨*Blume, Blatt,
Laub*⟩; verblichen ⟨*Stoff, Farbe*⟩
**fag** [fæg] *n.* **a)** *(Brit. coll.)* Schinderei,
*die (ugs.);* **b)** *(sl.: cigarette)* Stäbchen,
*das (ugs.)*
**fail** [feɪl] **1.** *v. i.* **a)** scheitern; *(in examination)* nicht bestehen (**in** in + *Dat.*);
**b)** *(become weaker)*⟨*Augenlicht, Gehör,
Stärke:*⟩ nachlassen; **c)** *(break down,
stop)* ⟨*Versorgung:*⟩ zusammenbrechen; ⟨*Motor:*⟩ aussetzen; ⟨*Batterie,
Pumpe:*⟩ ausfallen; ⟨*Bremse:*⟩ versa-
gen. **2.** *v. t.* **a)** ~ **to do sth.** *(not succeed
in doing)* etw. nicht tun [können]; ~ **to
achieve one's purpose/aim** seine Ab-
sicht/sein Ziel verfehlen; **b)** *(be unsuccessful in)* nicht bestehen ⟨*Prüfung*⟩;
**c)** *(reject)* durchfallen lassen *(ugs.)*
⟨*Prüfling*⟩; **d)** ~ **to do sth.** *(not do)* etw.
nicht tun; *(neglect to do)* [es] versäumen, etw. zu tun; **not** ~ **to do sth.** etw.
tun; **e) words** ~ **me** mir fehlen die
Worte; **his courage ~ed him** ihn ver-
ließ der Mut. **3.** *n.* **without ~:** auf jeden Fall. **'failing 1.** *n.* Schwäche, *die.*
**2.** *prep.* ~ **that** andernfalls. **failure**
['feɪljə(r)] *n.* **a)** *(omission, neglect)* Ver-
säumnis, *das;* **b)** *(lack of success)*
Scheitern, *das;* **end in ~:** scheitern; **c)**
*(person or thing)* Versager, *der;* **our
plan/attempt was a ~:** unser Plan/Ver-
such war fehlgeschlagen
**faint** [feɪnt] **1.** *adj.* **a)** matt ⟨*Licht,
Farbe, Stimme, Lächeln*⟩; schwach
⟨*Geruch, Duft*⟩; leise ⟨*Flüstern, Geräusch, Stimme*⟩; entfernt ⟨*Ähnlichkeit*⟩; undeutlich ⟨*Umriß, Linie, Spur,
Fotokopie*⟩; *(giddy, weak)* matt; **she
felt** ~: ihr war schwindelig. **2.** *v. i.*
ohnmächtig werden (**from** vor +
*Dat.*). **3.** *n.* Ohnmacht, *die.* **'faintly**
*adv.* schwach; entfernt ⟨*sich ähneln*⟩
**¹fair** [feə(r)] *n. (fun-~)* Jahrmarkt, *der;*
*(exhibition)* Messe, *die;* **book/trade ~:**
Buch-/Handelsmesse, *die*

**²fair 1.** *adj.* **a)** *(just)* gerecht; begründet
⟨*Beschwerde, Annahme*⟩; fair ⟨*Spiel,
Kampf, Prozeß, Preis, Beurteilung,
Handel*⟩; ~ **play** Fairneß, *die;* **b)** *(not
bad, pretty good)* ganz gut ⟨*Bilanz, Anzahl, Chance*⟩; ziemlich ⟨*Maß, Geschwindigkeit*⟩; **c)** *(blond)* blond
⟨*Haar, Person*⟩; *(light)* hell ⟨*Haut*⟩;
*(~-skinned)* hellhäutig ⟨*Person*⟩; **d)**
schön ⟨*Wetter, Tag*⟩. **'fair-haired**
**1.** *adj.* blond. **2.** *adj.* fair ⟨*kämpfen,
spielen*⟩. **'fairly** *adv.* **a)** fair ⟨*kämpfen,
spielen*⟩; gerecht ⟨*bestrafen, beurteilen,
behandeln*⟩; **b)** *(rather)* ziemlich. **'fair-
ness** *n.* Gerechtigkeit, *die;* **in all ~ |to
sb.|** um fair [gegen jmdn.] zu sein
**fairy** ['feərı] *n.* Fee, *die*
**fairy:** ~ **'godmother** *n.* gute Fee; ~
**story,** ~**-tale** *ns.* Märchen, *das*
**faith** [feɪθ] *n.* **a)** *(reliance, trust)* Vertrauen, *das* (**in** zu); **have ~ in oneself**
Selbstvertrauen haben; **in good ~:** in
gutem Glauben; **b)** *(religious belief)*
Glaube, *der.* **faithful** ['feɪθfl] *adj.* **a)**
treu (**to** *Dat.*); **b)** *(conscientious)*
pflichtbewußt; [ge]treu ⟨*Diener*⟩; **c)**
*(accurate)* [wahrheits]getreu; original-
getreu ⟨*Wiedergabe, Kopie*⟩. **'faithfully** *adv.* **a)** treu ⟨*dienen*⟩; pflichtbewußt ⟨*überbringen, zustellen*⟩; hoch
und heilig ⟨*versprechen*⟩; **b)** *(accurately)* wahrheitsgetreu ⟨*erzählen*⟩; ori-
ginalgetreu ⟨*wiedergeben*⟩; genau ⟨*befolgen*⟩; **c) yours** ~: hochachtungsvoll
**fake** [feɪk] **1.** *adj.* unecht; gefälscht
⟨*Dokument, Banknote, Münze*⟩. **2.** *n.*
**a)** Imitation, *die; (painting)* Fälschung, *die;* **b)** *(person)* Schwindler,
*der*/Schwindlerin, *die.* **3.** *v. t.* fälschen
⟨*Unterschrift*⟩; vortäuschen ⟨*Krankheit, Unfall*⟩
**falcon** ['fɔ:lkn] *n.* Falke, *der*
**fall** [fɔ:l] **1.** *n.* **a)** Fallen, *das; (of person)*
Sturz, *der;* ~ **of snow/rain** Schnee-/
Regenfall, *der;* **have a ~:** stürzen; **b)**
*(collapse, defeat)* Fall, *der; (of dynasty,
empire)* Untergang, *der;* **c)** *(decrease)*
Rückgang, *der;* **d)** *(Amer.: autumn)*
Herbst, *der.* **2.** *v. i.,* **fell** [fel], ~**en**
['fɔ:ln] **a)** fallen; ⟨*Baum:*⟩ umstürzen;
⟨*Pferd:*⟩ stürzen; ~ **off sth.,** ~ **down
from sth.** von etw. [herunter]fallen; ~
**down |into| sth.** in etw. *(Akk.)* [hin-
ein]fallen; ~ **to the ground** auf den Boden fallen; ~ **down the stairs** *or* **downstairs** die Treppe herunter-/hinunter-
fallen; **b)** ⟨*Nacht, Dunkelheit:*⟩ hereinbrechen; ⟨*Abend:*⟩ anbrechen; **c)**
⟨*Blätter:*⟩ [ab]fallen; **d)** *(sink)* sinken;

⟨*Barometer:*⟩ fallen; ⟨*Absatz, Verkauf:*⟩ zurückgehen; ~ **by 10 per cent/ from 10[°C] to 0[°C]** um 10 %/von 10[°C] auf 0[°C] sinken; **e)** *(be killed)* ⟨*Soldat:*⟩ fallen; **f)** *(collapse)* einstürzen; ~ **to pieces**, ~ **apart** auseinanderfallen; **g)** *(occur)* fallen (**on** auf + *Akk.*). **fall 'back** *v. i.* zurückweichen. **fall 'back on** *v. t.* zurückgreifen auf ( + *Akk.*). **fall 'down** *v. i.* **a)** *see* **fall 2 a;** b) ⟨*Brücke, Gebäude:*⟩ einstürzen. **'fall for** *v. t. (coll.)* ~ **for sb.** sich in jmdn. verknallen *(ugs.);* ~ **for sth.** auf etw. *(Akk.)* hereinfallen *(ugs.).* **fall 'in** *v. i.* **a)** hineinfallen; **b)** *(Mil.)* antreten; ~ **in!** angetreten!; **c)** ⟨*Gebäude, Wand usw.:*⟩ einstürzen. **fall 'off** *v. i.* **a)** herunterfallen; **b)** *(diminish)* nachlassen. **fall 'out** *v. i.* **a)** herausfallen; ⟨*Haare, Federn:*⟩ ausfallen; **b)** *(quarrel)* ~ **out** |**with sb.**| sich |mit jmdm.| streiten. **fall 'over** *v. i.* umfallen; ⟨*Person:*⟩ [hin]fallen. **fall 'through** *v. i. (fig.)* ins Wasser fallen *(ugs.)*

**fallacy** ['fæləsɪ] *n.* Irrtum, *der*

**fallen** *see* **fall 2**

**fallible** ['fælɪbl] *adj.* nicht unfehlbar; fehlbar ⟨*Person*⟩

**'fall-out** *n.* radioaktiver Niederschlag

**fallow** ['fæləʊ] *adj.* brachliegend; ~ **ground/land** Brache, *die/*Brachland, *das;* **lie ~:** brachliegen

**false** [fɔːls, fɒls] *adj.* falsch; gefälscht ⟨*Urkunde, Dokument*⟩; künstlich ⟨*Wimpern*⟩; **under a ~ name** unter falschem Namen. **'falsely** *adv.* falsch; fälschlich[erweise] ⟨*annehmen, glauben, behaupten, beschuldigen*⟩

**false:** ~ **a'larm** *n.* blinder Alarm; ~ **'start** *n.* Fehlstart, *der;* ~ **'teeth** *n. pl.* [künstliches] Gebiß

**falsify** ['fɔːlsɪfaɪ] *v. t. (alter)* fälschen; *(misrepresent)* verfälschen ⟨*Tatsachen, Wahrheit*⟩

**falter** ['fɔːltə(r)] *v. i.* stocken

**fame** [feɪm] *n.* Ruhm, *der*

**familiar** [fə'mɪljə(r)] *adj.* **a)** *(taste, inclination)* bekannt ⟨*Gesicht, Name, Lied*⟩; **he looks ~:** er kommt mir bekannt vor; **b)** *(informal)* ungezwungen ⟨*Sprache, Art*⟩. **familiarity** [fəmɪlɪ'ærɪtɪ] *n.* Vertrautheit, *die.* **familiarize** [fə'mɪljəraɪz] *v. t.* vertraut machen (**with** mit)

**family** ['fæməlɪ] *n.* Familie, *die*

**family:** ~ **name** *n.* Familienname, *der;* ~ **'planning** *n.* Familienplanung, *die;* ~ **'tree** *n.* Stammbaum, *der*

**famine** ['fæmɪn] *n.* Hungersnot, *die*

**famished** ['fæmɪʃt] *adj.* ausgehungert; **I'm absolutely ~** *(coll.)* ich sterbe vor Hunger *(ugs.)*

**famous** ['feɪməs] *adj.* berühmt

**¹fan** [fæn] **1.** *n.* Fächer, *der; (apparatus)* Ventilator, *der.* **2.** *v. t.,* **-nn-** fächeln ⟨*Gesicht*⟩; anfachen ⟨*Feuer*⟩; ~ **oneself/sb.** sich/jmdm. Luft zufächeln. **fan 'out** *v. i.* fächern; ⟨*Soldaten:*⟩ ausfächern

**²fan** *n. (devotee)* Fan, *der*

**fanatic** [fə'nætɪk] *n.* Fanatiker, *der/*Fanatikerin, *die.* **fanatical** [fə'nætɪkl] *adj.* fanatisch. **fanaticism** [fə'nætɪsɪzm] *n.* Fanatismus, *der*

**'fan belt** *n.* Keilriemen, *der*

**fanciful** ['fænsɪfl] *adj.* überspannt ⟨*Vorstellung, Gedanke*⟩; phantastisch ⟨*Gemälde, Design*⟩

**'fan club** *n.* Fanklub, *der*

**fancy** ['fænsɪ] **1.** *n.* **a)** *(taste, inclination)* he has taken a ~ to a new car/her ein neues Auto/sie hat es ihm angetan; **take** *or* **catch sb.'s ~:** jmdn. gefallen; **b)** *(whim)* Laune, *die;* **tickle sb.'s ~:** jmdn. reizen. **2.** *attrib. adj.* kunstvoll ⟨*Arbeit, Muster*⟩; fein[st] ⟨*Kuchen, Spitzen*⟩. **3.** *v. t.* **a)** *(imagine)* sich *(Dat.)* einbilden; ~ **that!** *(coll.)* sieh mal einer an!; **b)** *(suppose)* glauben; **c)** *(wish to have)* mögen; **what do you ~ for dinner?** was hättest du gern zum Abendessen? **fancy 'dress** *n.* [Masken]kostüm, *das;* **in ~:** kostümiert; **fancy-dress party** Kostümfest, *das;* **fancy-dress ball** Maskenball, *der*

**fanfare** ['fænfeə(r)] *n.* Fanfare, *die*

**fang** [fæŋ] *n.* Reißzahn, *der; (of snake)* Giftzahn, *der*

**fan:** ~ **heater** *n.* Heizlüfter, *der;* ~**light** *n.* Oberlicht, *das;* ~ **mail** *n.* Fanpost, *die*

**fantastic** [fæn'tæstɪk] *adj.* **a)** *(grotesque, quaint)* bizarr; **b)** *(coll.: excellent)* phantastisch *(ugs.)*

**fantasy** ['fæntəzɪ] *n.* Phantasie, *die; (mental image)* Phantasiegebilde, *das*

**far** [fɑː(r)] **1.** *adv.* weit; ~ **above/below** hoch über/tief unter ( + *Dat.*); hoch oben/tief unten; **as ~ as Munich/the church** bis [nach] München/bis zur Kirche; ~ **and wide** weit und breit; **from ~ and wide** von fern und nah; ~ **too** viel zu; ~ **longer/better** weit[aus] länger/besser; **as ~ as I remember/ know** soweit ich mich erinnere/weiß; **go so ~ as to do sth.** so weit gehen und etw. tun; **so ~** *(until now)* bisher; **so ~ so good** so weit, so gut; **by ~:** bei wei-

tem; ~ **from easy/good** alles andere
als leicht/gut. **2.** *adj.* **a)** *(remote)* weit
entfernt; *(in time)* fern; **in the** ~ **distance** in weiter Ferne; **b)** *(more
remote)* weiter entfernt; **the** ~ **bank of
the river/side of the road** das andere
Flußufer/die andere Straßenseite; **the**
~ **door/wall** *etc.* die hintere Tür/
Wand *usw.*

**farce** [fɑːs] *n.* Farce, *die.* **farcical**
['fɑːsɪkl] *adj. (absurd)* farcenhaft

**fare** [feə(r)] *n.* **a)** *(price)* Fahrpreis, *der;
(money)* Fahrgeld, *das;* **what** *or* **how
much is the** ~**?** was kostet die Fahrt?;
**b)** *(food)* Kost, *die*

**Far:** ~ **'East** *n.* **the** ~ **East** der Ferne
Osten; ~ **'Eastern** *adj.* fernöstlich;
des Fernen Ostens *nachgestellt*

**farewell** [feə'wel] **1.** *int.* leb[e] wohl
*(veralt.).* **2.** *n. attrib.* ~ **speech/gift** Ab-
schiedsrede, *die/-*geschenk, *das*

**far-'fetched** *adj.* weit hergeholt

**farm** [fɑːm] **1.** *n.* [Bauern]hof, *der;
(larger)* Gut, *das;* ~ **animals** Nutzvieh,
*das.* **2.** *v. t.* bebauen ⟨*Land*⟩. **3.** *v. i.*
Landwirtschaft treiben. **'farmer** *n.*
Landwirt, *der/-*wirtin, *die*

**'farmhouse** *n.* Bauernhaus, *das;
(larger)* Gutshaus, *das*

**'farming** *n.* Landwirtschaft, *die*

**farm:** ~**land** *n.* Acker- und Weide-
land, *das;* ~**yard** *n.* Hof, *der*

**far:** ~**-'reaching** *adj.* weitreichend;
~**-sighted** *adj.* **a)** *(fig.)* weitblickend; **b)** *(Amer.: long-sighted)*
weitsichtig

**fart** [fɑːt] *(coarse)* **1.** *v. i.* furzen *(derb).*
**2.** *n.* Furz, *der (derb)*

**farther** ['fɑːðə(r)] *see* **further 1 a, 2**

**farthest** ['fɑːðɪst] *see* **furthest**

**fascinate** ['fæsɪneɪt] *v. t.* fesseln; bezaubern. **fascination** [fæsɪ'neɪʃn] *n.*
Zauber, *der;* **have a** ~ **for sb.** einen be-
sonderen Reiz auf jmdn. ausüben

**Fascism** ['fæʃɪzm] *n.* Faschismus, *der.*
**Fascist** ['fæʃɪst] **1.** *n.* Faschist,
*der/*Faschistin, *die.* **2.** *adj.* faschi-
stisch

**fashion** ['fæʃn] **1.** *n.* **a)** Mode, *die;* **b)**
*(manner)* Art [und Weise]; **talk/be-
have in a peculiar** ~: merkwürdig
sprechen/sich merkwürdig verhalten.
**2.** *v. t.* formen **(out of, from** aus; **[in]to**
zu). **fashionable** ['fæʃənəbl] *adj.*
modisch; vornehm ⟨*Hotel, Restaurant*⟩; Mode⟨*farbe, -autor*⟩. **fashionably** ['fæʃənəblɪ] *adv.* modisch

**¹fast** [fɑːst] **1.** *v. i.* fasten. **2.** *n.* Fasten,
*das*

**²fast** **1.** *adj.* **a)** *(fixed, attached)* fest;
**make |the boat|** ~: das Boot festma-
chen; **hard and** ~: fest; bindend
⟨*Regel*⟩; klar ⟨*Entscheidung*⟩; **b)**
*(rapid)* schnell; ~ **train** Schnellzug,
*der;* D-Zug, *der;* **c) be |ten minutes|** ~
⟨*Uhr:*⟩ [zehn Minuten] vorgehen. **2.**
*adv.* **a) be** ~ **asleep** fest schlafen;
*(when one should be awake)* fest eingeschlafen sein; **b)** *(quickly)* schnell

**fasten** ['fɑːsn] *v. t.* befestigen **(on, to**
an + *Dat.*); zumachen ⟨*Kleid,
Spange, Jacke*⟩; [ab]schließen ⟨*Tür*⟩;
anstecken ⟨*Brosche*⟩ **(to** an + *Akk.*); ~
**one's seat-belt** sich anschnallen. **'fastener, 'fastening** *ns.* Verschluß, *der*

**fastidious** [fæ'stɪdɪəs] *adj.* wählerisch; *(hard to please)* heikel

**'fast lane** *n.* Überholspur, *die;* **life in
the** ~ *(fig.)* Leben auf vollen Touren
*(ugs.)*

**fat** [fæt] **1.** *adj.* dick; rund ⟨*Wangen,
Gesicht*⟩. **2.** *n.* Fett, *das*

**fatal** ['feɪtl] *adj.* **a)** *(disastrous)* verheerend **(to** für); **it would be** ~: das wäre
das Ende; **b)** *(deadly)* tödlich ⟨*Unfall,
Verletzung*⟩. **fatality** [fə'tælɪtɪ] *n.* To-
desopfer, *das.* **'fatally** *adv.* tödlich;
**be** ~ **ill** todkrank sein

**fate** [feɪt] *n.* Schicksal, *das*

**'fat-head** *n.* Dummkopf, *der (ugs.)*

**father** ['fɑːðə(r)] *n.* Vater, *der.* **Father
'Christmas** *n.* der Weihnachtsmann.
**father-in-law** *n., pl.* ~**s-in-law**
Schwiegervater, *der.* **'fatherly** *adj.*
väterlich

**fathom** ['fæðəm] **1.** *n. (Naut.)* Faden,
*der.* **2.** *v. t. (comprehend)* verstehen; ~
**sb./sth. out** jmdn./etw. ergründen

**fatigue** [fə'tiːg] **1.** *n.* Ermüdung, *die.*
**2.** *v. t.* ermüden

**'fatness** *n.* Dicke, *die*

**fatten** ['fætn] *v. t.* herausfüttern ⟨*Person*⟩; mästen ⟨*Tier*⟩. **'fattening** *adj.*
**be** ~: dick machen

**fatty** ['fætɪ] *adj.* fett ⟨*Fleisch, Soße*⟩;
fetthaltig ⟨*Speise, Nahrungsmittel*⟩

**faucet** ['fɔːsɪt] *n. (Amer.)* Wasserhahn,
*der*

**fault** [fɔːlt, fɒlt] *n.* **a)** Fehler, *der;* **b)**
*(responsibility)* Schuld, *die;* **it's your**
~: du bist schuld; **it isn't my** ~: ich
habe keine Schuld; **be at** ~: im Unrecht sein; **c)** *(in machinery; also
Electr.)* Defekt, *der.* **'faultless** *adj.*
einwandfrei. **'faulty** *adj.* fehlerhaft;
defekt ⟨*Gerät, usw.*⟩

**fauna** ['fɔːnə] *n., pl.* ~**e** ['fɔːniː] *or* ~**s**
Fauna, *die*

**favor** etc. (Amer.) see **favour** etc.

**favour** ['feɪvə(r)] 1. n. a) Gunst, die; b) (kindness) Gefallen, der; ask sb. a ~, ask a ~ of sb. jmdn. um einen Gefallen bitten; do sb. a ~, do a ~ for sb. jmdm. einen Gefallen tun; as a ~: aus Gefälligkeit; c) be in ~ of sth. für etw. sein. 2. v. t. bevorzugen

**favourable** ['feɪvərəbl] adj. (Brit.) a) günstig ⟨Eindruck, Licht⟩; gewogen ⟨Haltung, Einstellung⟩; freundlich ⟨Erwähnung⟩; positiv ⟨Bericht[erstattung], Bemerkung⟩; b) (helpful) günstig (to für) ⟨Wetter, Wind, Umstand⟩.

**favourably** ['feɪvərəblɪ] adv. (Brit.) wohlwollend; be ~ disposed towards sb./sth. jmdm./einer Sache positiv gegenüberstehen

**favourite** ['feɪvərɪt] (Brit.) 1. adj. Lieblings-. 2. n. a) Liebling, der; (food/country etc.) Lieblingsessen, das/-land, das usw.; this/he is my ~: das/ihn mag ich am liebsten; b) (Sport) Favorit, der/Favoritin, die.

**favouritism** ['feɪvərɪtɪzm] n. (Brit.) Begünstigung, die; (when selecting sb. for a post etc.) Günstlingswirtschaft, die

**fawn** [fɔːn] 1. n. a) (colour) Rehbraun, das; b) (young deer) [Dam]kitz, das. 2. adj. rehfarben

**fax** [fæks] 1. n. [Tele]fax, das. 2. v. t. faxen. **'fax machine** n, Faxgerät, das

**FBI** abbr. (Amer.) Federal Bureau of Investigation FBI, das

**fear** [fɪə(r)] 1. n. Angst, die (of vor + Dat.); (instance) Befürchtung, die; ~ of death or dying/heights Todes-/Höhenangst, die; ~ of doing sth. Angst davor, etw. zu tun; in ~: angstvoll; no ~! (coll.) keine Bange! (ugs.). 2. v. t. a) ~ sb./sth. vor jmdm./etw. Angst haben; ~ to do or doing sth. Angst haben, etw. zu tun; b) (be worried about) befürchten; ~ [that ...] fürchten[, daß ...]. **fearful** ['fɪəfl] adj. a) (terrible) furchtbar; b) (frightened) ängstlich; be ~ of sth./sb. vor etw./jmdm. Angst haben. **'fearless** adj., **'fearlessly** adv. furchtlos

**easibility** [fiːzɪ'bɪlɪtɪ] n. Durchführbarkeit, die

**easible** ['fiːzɪbl] adj. durchführbar

**east** [fiːst] 1. n. a) (Relig.) Fest, das; b) (banquet) Festessen, das. 2. v. i. schlemmen; ~ on sth. sich an etw. (Dat.) gütlich tun

**eat** [fiːt] n. Meisterleistung, die

**eather** ['feðə(r)] n. Feder, die.

**'featherweight** n. (Boxing) Federgewicht, das

**feature** ['fiːtʃə(r)] 1. n. a) usu. in pl. (of face) Gesichtszug, der; b) (characteristic) [charakteristisches] Merkmal; be a ~ of sth. charakteristisch für etw. sein; c) (Journ.) Feature, das; d) (Cinemat.) ~ [film] Hauptfilm, der. 2. v. t. vorrangig vorstellen; (in film) in der Hauptrolle zeigen. 3. v. i. vorkommen; ~ in (be important) eine bedeutende Rolle haben bei

**Feb.** abbr. February Febr.

**February** ['februərɪ] n. Februar, der

**fed** [fed] 1. see **feed** 1, 2. 2. pred. adj. (sl.) be/get ~ up with sth./sb. jmdn./etw. satt haben/kriegen (ugs.); I'm ~ up Ich hab' die Nase voll (ugs.)

**federal** ['fedərl] adj. Bundes-; föderativ ⟨System⟩. **federation** [fedə'reɪʃn] n. Föderation, die

**fee** [fiː] n. Gebühr, die; (of doctor, lawyer, etc.) Honorar, das

**feeble** ['fiːbl] adj. schwach; wenig überzeugend ⟨Entschuldigung⟩; zaghaft ⟨Versuch⟩; lahm (ugs.) ⟨Witz⟩

**feed** [fiːd] 1. v. t., **fed** [fed] a) füttern; ~ sb./an animal with sth. jmdm. etw. zu essen/einem Tier [etw.] zu fressen geben; b) (provide food for) ernähren (on, with mit). 2. v. i., **fed** ⟨Tier:⟩ fressen (from aus); ⟨Person:⟩ essen (off von); ~ on sth. ⟨Tier:⟩ etw. fressen. 3. n. a) (for baby) Mahlzeit, die; b) (fodder) Futter, das. **'feedback** n. Reaktion, die

**feel** [fiːl] 1. v. t., **felt** [felt] a) (explore by touch) befühlen; b) (perceive by touch) fühlen; (become aware of) bemerken; (have sensation of) spüren; c) (experience) empfinden; verspüren ⟨Drang⟩; ~ the cold/heat unter der Kälte/Hitze leiden; ~ [that] ...: das Gefühl haben, daß ...; (think) glauben, daß ... 2. v. i., **felt** a) ~ [about] in sth. [for sth.] in etw. (Dat.) [nach etw.] [herum]suchen; b) (be conscious that one is) sich ... fühlen; ~ angry/sure/disappointed böse/sicher/enttäuscht sein; ~ like sth./doing sth. auf etw. (Akk.) Lust haben/Lust haben, etw. zu tun; c) (be consciously perceived as) sich ... anfühlen. **'feel for** v. t. ~ for sb. mit jmdm. Mitleid haben

**'feeler** n. Fühler, der. **'feeling** n. a) Gefühl, das; (sense of touch) [sense of] ~: Tastsinn, der; hurt sb.'s ~s jmdn. verletzen; b) (opinion) Ansicht, die

**feet** pl. of **foot**

**feign** [feɪn] v. t. vortäuschen; ~ **to do sth.** vorgeben, etw. zu tun

**¹fell** see **fall 2**

**²fell** [fel] v. t. fällen ⟨Baum⟩

**³fell** adj. **in one ~ swoop** auf einen Schlag

**fellow** ['felǝʊ] **1.** n. **a)** (comrade) Kamerad, der; **b)** (Brit. Univ.) Fellow, der; **c)** (of academy or society) Mitglied, das; **d)** (coll.: man, boy) Kerl, der (ugs.). **2.** attrib. adj. Mit-; ~ **man** or **human being** Mitmensch, der

**¹felt** [felt] n. Filz, der

**²felt** see **feel**

**felt[-tipped] 'pen** n. Filzstift, der

**female** ['fiːmeɪl] **1.** adj. weiblich; Frauen⟨stimme, -chor, -verein⟩. **2.** n. Frau, die; (foetus, child) Mädchen, das; (animal) Weibchen, das

**feminine** ['femɪnɪn] adj. weiblich; Frauen⟨angelegenheit, -leiden⟩; (womanly) feminin. **feminist** ['femɪnɪst] **1.** adj. feministisch; Feministen⟨bewegung, -gruppe⟩. **2.** n. Feministin, die/Feminist, der

**fence** [fens] **1.** n. Zaun, der. **2.** v. i. (Sport) fechten. **3.** v. t. ~ **|in|** einzäunen. **'fencer** n. Fechter, der/Fechterin, die. **fencing** ['fensɪŋ] n. (Sport) Fechten, das

**fend** [fend] v. i. ~ **for oneself** für sich selbst sorgen; (in hostile surroundings) sich allein durchschlagen. **fend 'off** v. t. abwehren

**fender** ['fendǝ(r)] n. **a)** (for fire) Kaminschutz, der; **b)** (Amer.) (car bumper) Stoßstange, die; (car mudguard) Kotflügel, der

**ferment** [fǝ'ment] **1.** v. i. gären. **2.** v. t. zur Gärung bringen. **fermentation** [fɜːmen'teɪʃn] n. Gärung, die

**fern** [fɜːn] n. Farnkraut, das

**ferocious** [fǝ'rǝʊʃǝs] adj. wild. **ferocity** [fǝ'rɒsɪtɪ] n. Wildheit, die

**ferret** ['ferɪt] n. Frettchen, das

**ferry** ['ferɪ] **1.** n. Fähre, die; (service) Fährverbindung, die. **2.** v. t. (in boat) ~ **|across or over|** übersetzen

**fertile** ['fɜːtaɪl] adj. (fruitful) fruchtbar; (capable of developing) befruchtet. **fertility** [fɜː'tɪlɪtɪ] n. Fruchtbarkeit, die **fertilize** ['fɜːtɪlaɪz] v. t. befruchten. **'fertilizer** n. Dünger, der

**fervent** ['fɜːvǝnt] adj. leidenschaftlich; inbrünstig ⟨Gebet, Wunsch, Hoffnung⟩. **fervour** (Brit.; Amer.: **fervor**) ['fɜːvǝ(r)] n. Leidenschaftlichkeit, die

**fester** ['festǝ(r)] v. i. eitern

**festival** ['festɪvl] n. **a)** (feast day) Fest, das; **b)** (of music etc.) Festival, das

**festive** ['festɪv] adj. festlich; fröhlich; **the ~ season** die Weihnachtszeit. **festivity** [fe'stɪvɪtɪ] n. **a)** (gaiety) Feststimmung, die; **b)** (celebration) Feier, die; **festivities** Feierlichkeiten Pl.

**festoon** [fe'stuːn] **1.** n. Girlande, die. **2.** v. t. schmücken (**with** mit)

**fetch** [fetʃ] v. t. **a)** holen; (collect) abholen (**from** von); ~ **sb. sth.**, ~ **sth. for sb.** jmdm. etw. holen; **b)** (be sold for) erzielen ⟨Preis⟩. **'fetching** adj. einnehmend

**fête** [feɪt] n. [Wohltätigkeits]basar, der

**fetish** ['fetɪʃ] n. Fetisch, der. **fetishism** ['fetɪʃɪzm] n. Fetischismus, der. **fetishist** ['fetɪʃɪst] n. Fetischist, der/Fetischistin, die

**fetter** ['fetǝ(r)] v. t. fesseln

**feud** [fjuːd] n. Fehde, die

**feudal** ['fjuːdl] adj. Feudal-; feudalistisch; ~ **system** Feudalsystem, das

**fever** ['fiːvǝ(r)] n. **a)** (high temperature) Fieber, das; **have a |high| ~:** [hohes] Fieber haben; **b)** (disease) Fieberkrankheit, die. **'feverish** adj. **a)** (Med.) fiebrig; **be ~:** Fieber haben; **b)** (excited) fiebrig

**few** [fjuː] **1.** adj. **a)** (not many) wenige abs. nur wenige; **with very ~ exceptions** mit ganz wenigen Ausnahmen; **his ~ belongings** seine paar Habseligkeiten; **a ~ ...:** wenige ...; **b)** (some) wenige; **a ~ ...:** ein paar ...; **a ~ more ...:** noch ein paar ... **2.** n. **a)** (no many) wenige; **a ~:** wenige; **just a ~ of you/her friends** nur ein paar von euch/ihrer Freunde; **b)** (some) **with a ~ of our friends** mit einigen unserer Freunde; **quite a ~:** ziemlich viele

**fiancé** [fɪ'ɑ̃seɪ] n. Verlobte, der

**fiancée** [fɪ'ɑ̃seɪ] n. Verlobte, die

**fiasco** [fɪ'æskǝʊ] n., pl. ~s Fiasko, das

**fib** [fɪb] **1.** n. Flunkerei, die (ugs.); **tell ~s** flunkern (ugs.). **2.** v. i., **-bb-** flunkern (ugs.)

**fibre** (Brit.; Amer.: **fiber**) ['faɪbǝ(r)] n. **a)** Faser, die; **b)** (material) [Faser]gewebe, das. **'fibreglass** n. (plastic) glasfaserverstärkter Kunststoff

**fiche** [fiːʃ] n., pl. **same** or ~s Mikrofiche, das od. der

**fickle** ['fɪkl] adj. unberechenbar

**fiction** ['fɪkʃn] n. erzählende Literatur; **a ~/~s** eine Erfindung. **fictional** ['fɪkʃǝnl] adj. erfunden ⟨Geschichte⟩; fiktiv ⟨Figur⟩

**fictitious** [fɪk'tɪʃəs] *adj.* fingiert; falsch ⟨*Name, Identität*⟩

**fiddle** ['fɪdl] **1.** *n.* **a)** *(Mus.) (coll./ derog.)* Fiedel, *die; (violin for traditional music)* Geige, *die;* |as| **fit as a ~:** kerngesund; **b)** *(sl.: swindle)* Gaunerei, *die.* **2.** *v.t. (sl.)* frisieren *(ugs.)* ⟨*Bücher, Rechnungen*⟩. **3.** *v.i.* herumspielen (with mit). **fiddler** ['fɪdlə(r)] *n.* Geiger, *der*/Geigerin, *die*

**fiddly** ['fɪdlɪ] *adj. (coll.)* knifflig

**fidelity** [fɪ'delɪtɪ] *n.* Treue, *die* (**to** zu)

**fidget** ['fɪdʒɪt] **1.** *v.i.* ~ |about| herumrutschen. **2.** *n. (person)* Zappelphilipp, *der (ugs.).* **'fidgety** *adj.* unruhig; zappelig ⟨*Kind*⟩

**field** [fiːld] *n.* **a)** Feld, *das;* **b)** *(for game)* Platz, *der;* [Spiel]feld, *das;* **c)** *(subject area)* [Fach]gebiet, *das;* **in the ~ of medicine** auf dem Gebiet der Medizin; **that is outside my ~:** das fällt nicht in mein Fach

**field:** **~-day** *n.* **have a ~-day** seinen großen Tag haben; **~ events** *n. pl.* technische Disziplinen; **~-glasses** *n. pl.* Feldstecher, *der;* **F~ 'Marshal** *n. (Brit. Mil.)* Feldmarschall, *der;* **~ mouse** *n.* Brandmaus, *die*

**fiend** [fiːnd] *n.* **a)** *(wicked person)* Scheusal, *das;* **b)** *(evil spirit)* böser Geist. **'fiendish** *adj.* **a)** teuflisch; **b)** *(very awkward)* höllisch

**fierce** ['fɪəs] *adj.* wild; erbittert ⟨*Widerstand, Kampf*⟩; scharf ⟨*Kritik*⟩. **'fiercely** *adv.* heftig ⟨*angreifen, Widerstand leisten*⟩; wütend ⟨*brüllen*⟩; aufs heftigste ⟨*kritisieren, bekämpfen*⟩

**fiery** ['faɪərɪ] *adj.* glühend; *(looking like fire)* feurig; *(blazing red)* feuerrot

**fifteen** [fɪf'tiːn] **1.** *adj.* fünfzehn. **2.** *n.* Fünfzehn, *die.* See also **eight.** **fifteenth** [fɪf'tiːnθ] **1.** *adj.* fünfzehnt... **2.** *n. (fraction)* Fünfzehntel, *das.* See also **eighth**

**fifth** [fɪfθ] **1.** *adj.* fünft... **2.** *n. (in sequence)* fünfte, *der/die/das; (in rank)* Fünfte, *der/die/das; (fraction)* Fünftel, *das.* See also **eighth**

**fiftieth** ['fɪftɪɪθ] *adj.* fünfzigst...

**fifty** ['fɪftɪ] **1.** *adj.* fünfzig. **2.** *n.* Fünfzig, *die.* See also **eight; eighty 2**

**fig** [fɪɡ] *n.* Feige, *die*

**fig.** *abbr.* **figure** Abb.

**fight** [faɪt] **1.** *v.i.,* fought [fɔːt] **a)** kämpfen; *(with fists)* sich schlagen; **b)** *(squabble)* [sich] streiten (**about** wegen). **2.** *v.t.,* fought **a)** ~ **sb./sth.** gegen jmdn./etw. kämpfen; *(using fists)* ~ **sb.** sich mit jmdm. schlagen; **b)** *(seek*

*to overcome)* bekämpfen; *(resist)* ~ **sb./sth.** gegen jmdn./etw. ankämpfen; **c)** ~ **a battle** einen Kampf austragen; **d)** kandidieren bei ⟨*Wahl*⟩. **3.** *n.* Kampf, *der* (**for** um). **'fight against** *v.t.* kämpfen gegen; ankämpfen gegen ⟨*Wellen, Wind*⟩. **fight 'back 1.** *v.i.* zurückschlagen. **2.** *v.t. (suppress)* zurückhalten. **fight 'off** *v.t.* abwehren. **'fight with** *v.t.* **a)** kämpfen mit; **b)** *(squabble with)* [sich] streiten mit

**'fighter** *n.* Kämpfer, *der*/Kämpferin, *die; (aircraft)* Kampfflugzeug, *das*

**'fighting** *n.* Kämpfe

**figment** ['fɪɡmənt] *n.* **a ~ of one's** *or* **the imagination** pure Einbildung

**'fig-tree** *n.* Feigenbaum, *der*

**figurative** ['fɪɡərətɪv] *adj.* übertragen

**figure** ['fɪɡə(r)] **1.** *n.* **a)** *(shape)* Form, *die;* **b)** *(carving, sculpture, one's bodily shape)* Figur, *die;* **c)** *(illustration)* Abbildung, *die;* **d)** *(person as seen)* Gestalt, *die; (literary ~)* Figur, *die;* **e)** *(numerical symbol)* Ziffer, *die; (number)* Zahl, *die; (amount of money)* Betrag, *der;* **f)** ~ **of speech** Redewendung, *die.* **2.** *v.i.* vorkommen; **b) that ~s** *(coll.)* das kann gut sein. **figure 'out** *v.t.* **a)** *(by arithmetic)* ausrechnen; **b)** *(understand)* verstehen

**filament** ['fɪləmənt] *n.* **a)** Faden, *der;* **b)** *(Electr.)* Glühfaden, *der*

**filch** ['fɪltʃ] *v.t.* stibitzen *(ugs.)*

**¹file** [faɪl] **1.** *n.* Feile, *die.* **2.** *v.t.* feilen ⟨*Fingernägel*⟩; mit der Feile bearbeiten ⟨*Holz, Eisen*⟩

**²file 1.** *n.* **a)** *(holder)* Ordner, *der; (box)* Kassette, *die;* **b)** *(papers)* Ablage, *die; (cards)* Kartei, *die.* **2.** *v.t.* **a)** [in die Kartei] einordnen/[in die Akten] aufnehmen; **b)** einreichen ⟨*Antrag*⟩

**³file 1.** *n. (Mil. etc.)* Reihe, *die;* |in| **single** *or* **Indian ~:** [im] Gänsemarsch. **2.** *v.i.* ~ |in/out| in einer Reihe [hinein-/hinaus]gehen

**filigree** ['fɪlɪɡriː] *n.* Filigran, *das*

**'filing-cabinet** *n.* Aktenschrank, *der*

**filings** ['faɪlɪŋz] *n. pl.* Späne

**fill** [fɪl] **1.** *v.t.* **a)** füllen; besetzen ⟨*Sitzplätze*⟩; *(fig.)* ausfüllen ⟨*Gedanken, Zeit*⟩; *(pervade)* erfüllen; **~ed with** voller ⟨*Reue, Bewunderung, Neid usw.*⟩; **b)** *(appoint sb. to)* besetzen ⟨*Posten*⟩. **2.** *v.i.* ~ |with sth.| sich [mit etw.] füllen. **3.** *n.* **eat/drink one's ~:** sich satt essen/trinken. **fill 'in 1.** *v.t.* **a)** füllen; zuschütten ⟨*Erdloch*⟩; **b)** *(complete)* ausfüllen; **c)** ~ **sb. in** |on sth.| *(coll.)* jmdn. [über etw. *(Akk.)*] ins

Bild setzen. 2. *v. i.* ~ **in** for sb. für jmdn. einspringen. **fill** '**out** *v. t.* ausfüllen. **fill** '**up** *v. t.* **a)** füllen (**with** mit); **b)** *(put petrol into)* tanken

**fillet** ['fɪlɪt] 1. *n.* Filet, *das.* 2. *v. t.* entgräten ⟨*Fisch*⟩

'**filling** *n.* **a)** *(for teeth)* Füllung, *die;* **b)** *(for pancakes etc.)* Füllung, *die; (for sandwiches etc.)* Belag, *der; (for spreading)* Aufstrich, *der.* '**filling station** *n.* Tankstelle, *die*

**filly** ['fɪlɪ] *n.* junge Stute

**film** [fɪlm] 1. *n.* **a)** Film, *der;* **b)** *(thin layer)* Schicht, *die.* 2. *v. t.* filmen; drehen ⟨*Kinofilm, Szene*⟩. '**film script** *n.* Drehbuch, *das.* '**film star** *n.* Filmstar, *der*

**Filofax, (P)** ['faɪləʊfæks] *n.* ≈ Terminplaner, *der*

**filter** ['fɪltə(r)] 1. *n.* Filter, *der.* 2. *v. t.* filtern. **filter** '**through** *v. t.* durchsickern

'**filter-tip** *n.* **a)** Filter, *der;* **b)** ~ |**cigarette**| Filterzigarette, *die*

**filth** [fɪlθ] *n.* Dreck, *der.* '**filthy** *adj.* schmutzig

**fin** [fɪn] *n.* Flosse, *die*

**final** ['faɪnl] 1. *adj.* letzt...; End⟨*spiel, -stadium, -stufe, -ergebnis*⟩; endgültig ⟨*Entscheidung*⟩. 2. *n.* **a)** *(Sport etc.)* Finale, *das;* **b)** ~**s** *pl. (university examination)* Examen, *das*

**finale** [fɪ'nɑːlɪ] *n.* Finale, *das*

**finalist** ['faɪnəlɪst] *n.* Teilnehmer/Teilnehmerin in der Endausscheidung; *(Sport)* Finalist, *der*/Finalistin, *die*

**finalize** ['faɪnəlaɪz] *v. t.* [endgültig] beschließen; *(complete)* zum Abschluß bringen

**finally** ['faɪnəlɪ] *adv.* **a)** *(in the end)* schließlich; *(expressing impatience etc.)* endlich; **b)** *(in conclusion)* abschließend; **c)** *(conclusively)* entschieden ⟨*sagen*⟩

**finance** [faɪ'næns, 'faɪnæns] 1. *n.* **a)** *in pl. (resources)* Finanzen *Pl.;* **b)** *(management of money)* Geldwesen, *das;* **c)** *(support)* Geldmittel *Pl.* 2. *v. t.* finanzieren. **financial** [faɪ'nænʃl] *adj.* finanziell; Finanz⟨*mittel, -experte, -lage*⟩; ~ **year** Geschäftsjahr, *das.* **financially** *adv.* finanziell. **financier** [faɪ'nænsɪə(r)] *n.* Finanzexperte, *der*/-expertin, *die*

**finch** [fɪntʃ] *n.* Fink[envogel], *der*

**find** [faɪnd] 1. *v. t., found* [faʊnd] finden; *(come across unexpectedly)* entdecken; auftreiben ⟨*Geld, Gegenstand*⟩; aufbringen ⟨*Kraft, Energie*⟩;

**want to** ~: suchen; ~ **that** ...: herausfinden, daß ...; ~ **sth. necessary** etw. für nötig erachten; ~ **sth./sb. to be** ...: herausfinden, daß etw./jmd. ... ist/ war; **you will** ~ |**that**| ...: Sie werden sehen, daß ... 2. *n.* Fund, *der.* **find** '**out** *v. t.* herausfinden

'**finder** *n.* Finder, *der*/Finderin, *die*

'**findings** *n. pl.* Ergebnisse

¹**fine** [faɪn] 1. *n.* Geldstrafe, *die.* 2. *v. t.* mit einer Geldstrafe belegen

²**fine** *adj.* **a)** hochwertig ⟨*Qualität, Lebensmittel*⟩; fein ⟨*Gewebe, Spitze*⟩; edel ⟨*Holz, Wein*⟩; **b)** *(delicate)* fein; zart ⟨*Porzellan*⟩; *(thin)* hauchdünn; **cut** *or* **run it** ~: knapp kalkulieren; **c)** *(in small particles)* [hauch]fein ⟨*Sand, Staub*⟩; ~ **rain** Nieselregen, *der;* **d)** *(sharp)* scharf ⟨*Spitze, Klinge*⟩; spitz ⟨*Nadel, Schreibfeder*⟩; **e)** *(excellent)* ausgezeichnet ⟨*Sänger, Schauspieler*⟩; **f)** *(satisfactory)* schön; **that's** ~ **by** *or* **with me** ja, ist mir recht; **g)** *(in good health or state)* gut; **feel** ~: sich wohl fühlen; **h)** schön ⟨*Wetter*⟩. **fine** '**arts** *n. pl.* schöne Künste

**finery** ['faɪnərɪ] *n.* Pracht, *die; (garments etc.)* Staat, *der*

**finger** ['fɪŋgə(r)] 1. *n.* Finger, *der.* 2. *v. t.* berühren; *(meddle with)* befingern

**finger:** ~-**mark** *n.* Fingerabdruck, *der;* ~**nail** *n.* Fingernagel, *der;* ~**print** *n.* Fingerabdruck, *der;* ~**tip** *n.* Fingerspitze, *die;* **have sth. at one's** ~**tips** *(fig.)* etw. im kleinen Finger haben *(ugs.)*

**finish** ['fɪnɪʃ] 1. *v. t.* **a)** beenden ⟨*Unterhaltung*⟩; erledigen ⟨*Arbeit*⟩; abschließen ⟨*Kurs, Ausbildung*⟩; **have** ~**ed sth.** etw. fertig haben; ~ **writing/ reading sth.** etw. zu Ende schreiben/ lesen; **b)** aufessen ⟨*Mahlzeit*⟩; auslesen ⟨*Buch, Zeitung*⟩; austrinken ⟨*Flasche, Glas*⟩. 2. *v. i.* **a)** aufhören; **have you** ~**ed?** sind Sie fertig?; **when does the concert** ~? wann ist das Konzert aus?; **b)** *(in race)* das Ziel erreichen. 3. *n.* **a)** Ende, *das;* **b)** *(~ing line)* Ziel, *das.* **finish** '**off** *v. t.* abschließen

'**finishing post** *n.* Zielpfosten, *der*

**finite** ['faɪnaɪt] *adj.* begrenzt

**Finland** ['fɪnlənd] *pr. n.* Finnland *(das)*

**Finn** [fɪn] *n.* Finne, *der*/Finnin, *die*

**Finnish** ['fɪnɪʃ] 1. *adj.* finnisch. 2. *n.* Finnisch, *das; see also* **English 2 a**

**fiord** [fɪ'ɔːd] *n.* Fjord, *der*

**fir** [fɜː(r)] *n.* Tanne, *die*

**fire** ['faɪə(r)] 1. *n.* **a)** Feuer, *das;* **be on**

~: brennen; **catch** ~: Feuer fangen; ⟨*Wald, Gebäude*:⟩ in Brand geraten; **set** ~ **to** sth. etw. anzünden; **b)** (*in grate*) [offenes] Feuer; (*electric or gas* ~) Heizofen, *der*; **light the** ~: den Ofen anstecken; (*in grate*) das [Kamin]feuer anmachen; **c)** (*destructive burning*) Brand, *der*; **d)** (*of guns*) **come/be under** ~: unter Beschuß geraten/beschossen werden. **2.** *v. t.* **a)** abschießen ⟨*Gewehr*⟩; abfeuern ⟨*Kanone*⟩; abgeben ⟨*Schuß*⟩; ~ **one's gun/pistol/rifle at** sb. auf jmdn. schießen; **two shots were** ~**d** es fielen zwei Schüsse; ~ **questions at** sb. jmdn. mit Fragen bombardieren; **b)** (*coll.: dismiss*) feuern (*ugs.*). **3.** *v. i.* feuern; ~ **at/on** schießen auf (+ *Akk.*); ~! Feuer!

**fire:** ~**-alarm** *n.* Feuermelder, *der*; ~**arm** *n.* Schußwaffe, *die*; ~ **brigade** (*Brit.*), ~ **department** (*Amer.*) *ns.* Feuerwehr, *die*; ~**-drill** *n.* Probe[feuer]alarm, *der*; ~**-engine** *n.* Löschfahrzeug, *das*; ~**-escape** *n.* (*staircase*) Feuertreppe, *die*; ~ **extinguisher** *n.* Feuerlöscher, *der*; ~ **hazard** *n.* Brandrisiko, *das*; ~**man** ['faɪəmən] *n., pl.* ~**men** [~mən] Feuerwehrmann, *der*; ~**place** *n.* Kamin, *der*; ~**side** *n.* **at** *or* **by the** ~**side** am Kamin; ~ **station** *n.* Feuerwache, *die*; ~**wood** *n.* Brennholz, *das*; ~**work** *n.* Feuerwerkskörper, *der*; ~**works** (*display*) Feuerwerk, *das*

¹**firm** [fɜ:m] *n.* Firma, *die*

²**firm** *adj.* **a)** fest; stabil ⟨*Konstruktion, Stuhl*⟩; **b)** (*resolute, strict*) bestimmt.

'**firmly** *adv.* **a)** fest; **b)** (*resolutely, strictly*) bestimmt

**first** [fɜ:st] **1.** *adj.* erst...; **he was** ~ **to arrive** er kam als erster an. **2.** *adv.* **a)** (*before anyone else*) zuerst; als erster/erste ⟨*sprechen, ankommen*⟩; (*before anything else*) an erster Stelle ⟨*stehen, kommen*⟩; ~ **come** ~ **served** wer zuerst kommt, mahlt zuerst (*Spr.*); **b)** (*beforehand*) vorher; **c)** (*for the* ~ *time*) zum ersten Mal; **d)** ~ **of all** zuerst; (*in importance*) vor allem. **3.** *n.* **a)** **the** ~ (*in sequence*) der/die/das erste; (*in rank*) der/die/das Erste; **b)** **at** ~: zuerst; **from the** ~: von Anfang an

**first:** ~ '**aid** *n.* erste Hilfe; ~**-aid box/kit** Verbandkasten, *der*/Erste-Hilfe-Ausrüstung, *die*; ~**-class 1.** ['--] *adj.* **a)** erster Klasse nachgestellt; Erste[r]-Klasse-⟨*Fahrkarte, Abteil, Post, Brief usw.*⟩; **b)** (*excellent*) erstklassig; **2.** [-'-] *adv.* erster Klasse ⟨*reisen*⟩

'**firstly** *adv.* zunächst [einmal]; (*followed by 'secondly'*) erstens

**first:** ~ **name** *n.* Vorname, *der*; ~**-rate** *adj.* erstklassig; ~ **school** *n.* (*Brit.*) ≈ Grundschule, *die*

'**fir tree** *n.* Tanne, *die*

**fish** [fɪʃ] **1.** *n.* Fisch, *der*. **2.** *v. i.* fischen; (*with rod*) angeln; **go** ~**ing** fischen/angeln gehen. **fish** '**out** *v. t.* (*coll.*) herausfischen (*ugs.*)

**fisherman** ['fɪʃəmən] *n., pl.* **fishermen** ['fɪʃəmən] Fischer, *der*; (*angler*) Angler, *der*

**fish:** ~ '**finger** *n.* Fischstäbchen, *das*; ~**-hook** *n.* Angelhaken, *der*

'**fishing** *n.* Fischen, *das*; (*with rod*) Angeln, *das*

**fishing:** ~ **boat** *n.* Fischerboot, *das*; ~**-net** *n.* Fischernetz, *das*; ~**-rod** *n.* Angelrute, *die*

**fish:** ~**monger** ['fɪʃmʌŋɡə(r)] *n.* (*Brit.*) Fischhändler, *der*/-händlerin, *die*; ~ **shop** *n.* Fischgeschäft, *das*

'**fishy** *adj.* **a)** fischartig; Fisch⟨*geschmack, -geruch*⟩; **b)** (*coll.: suspicious*) verdächtig

**fist** [fɪst] *n.* Faust, *die*

¹**fit** [fɪt] *n.* Anfall, *der*; (*fig.*) [plötzliche] Anwandlung; **be in** ~**s of laughter** sich vor Lachen biegen; **in a** ~ **of ...**: in einem Anfall von ...

²**fit 1.** *adj.* **a)** (*suitable*) geeignet; ~ **to eat** eßbar; **b)** (*worthy*) würdig; wert; **c)** (*proper*) richtig; **see** *or* **think** ~ |to do sth.| es für richtig halten[, etw. zu tun]; **d)** (*healthy*) fit (*ugs.*); **keep** ~: sich fit halten. **2.** *n.* Paßform, *die*; **it is a good/bad** ~: es sitzt *od.* paßt gut/nicht gut. **3.** *v. t.*, **-tt-:** **a)** ⟨*Kleider*:⟩ passen (+ *Dat.*); ⟨*Deckel, Bezug*:⟩ passen auf (+ *Akk.*); **b)** (*put into place*) anbringen (**to** an + *Dat. od. Akk.*); einbauen ⟨*Motor, Ersatzteil*⟩. **4.** *v. i.*, **-tt-** passen. **fit 'in 1.** *v. t.* unterbringen. **2.** *v. i.* **a)** ⟨*Person*:⟩ sich anpassen (**with** an + *Akk.*); **b)** (*be in accordance with*) ~ **in with** sth. mit etw. übereinstimmen

**fitful** ['fɪtfl] *adj.* unbeständig; unruhig ⟨*Schlaf*⟩; launisch ⟨*Brise*⟩

'**fitment** *n.* Einrichtung, *die*

'**fitness** *n.* **a)** (*physical*) Fitneß, *die*; **b)** (*suitability*) Eignung, *die*

'**fitted** *adj.* **a)** (*suited*) geeignet (**for** für, zu); **b)** (*shaped*) tailliert ⟨*Kleider*⟩; Einbau⟨*küche, schrank*⟩; ~ **carpet** Teppichboden, *der*

'**fitter** *n.* Monteur, *der*; (*of pipes*) Installateur, *der*; (*of machines*) Maschinenschlosser, *der*

**'fitting 1.** *adj.* *(appropriate)* passend; *(becoming)* schicklich *(geh.)* ⟨*Benehmen*⟩. **2.** *n.* **a)** usu. in *pl.* *(fixture)* Anschluß, *der;* ~s *(furniture)* Ausstattung, *die;* **b)** *(Brit.: size)* Größe, *die* **five** [faɪv] **1.** *adj.* fünf. **2.** *n.* Fünf, *die. See also* **eight. fiver** ['faɪvə(r)] *n.* *(Brit. coll.)* Fünfpfundschein, *der*

**fix** [fɪks] **1.** *v. t.* **a)** befestigen; **b)** festsetzen ⟨*Termin, Preis, Grenze*⟩; *(agree on)* ausmachen; **c)** *(repair)* reparieren; **d)** *(arrange)* arrangieren. **2.** *n.* *(coll.: predicament)* Klemme, *die (ugs.);* **be in a** ~: in der Klemme sitzen. **fix 'up** *v. t.* **a)** *(arrange)* arrangieren; festsetzen ⟨*Termin, Treffpunkt*⟩; **b)** *(provide)* versorgen; ~ **sb. up with sth.** jmdm. etw. verschaffen. **fixture** ['fɪkstʃə(r)] *n.* **a)** *(furnishing)* eingebautes Teil; **b)** *(Sport)* Veranstaltung, *die*

**fizz** [fɪz] *v. i.* [zischend] sprudeln **fizzle** ['fɪzl] *v. i.* zischen. **fizzle 'out** *v. i.* ⟨*Kampagne:*⟩ im Sande verlaufen **fizzy** ['fɪzɪ] *adj.* sprudelnd; ~ **lemonade** Brause[limonade], *die* **flabbergast** ['flæbəgɑːst] *v. t.* umhauen *(ugs.)* **flabby** ['flæbɪ] *adj.* schlaff **¹flag** [flæg] *n.* Fahne, *die; (national ~, on ship)* Flagge, *die* **²flag** *v. i.,* **-gg-** ⟨*Person:*⟩ abbauen; ⟨*Kraft, Begeisterung usw.:*⟩ nachlassen **flagon** ['flægn] *n.* Kanne, *die* **'flag-pole** *n.* Flaggenmast, *der* **flagrant** ['fleɪgrənt] *adj.* eklatant; flagrant ⟨*Verstoß*⟩ **'flagstone** *n.* Steinplatte, *die* **flair** [fleə(r)] *n.* Gespür, *das; (special ability)* Talent, *das* **flake** [fleɪk] **1.** *n.* Flocke, *die; (of dry skin)* Schuppe, *die.* **2.** *v. i.* abblättern. **flaky** ['fleɪkɪ] *adj.* blättrig ⟨*Kruste*⟩; ~ **pastry** Blätterteig, *der* **flamboyant** [flæm'bɔɪənt] *adj.* extravagant **flame** [fleɪm] *n.* Flamme, *die;* **be in** ~**s** in Flammen stehen **flan** [flæn] *n.* [fruit] ~: [Obst]torte, *die* **flank** [flæŋk] *n.* Seite, *die; (of animal; also Mil.)* Flanke, *die* **flannel** ['flænl] *n.* **a)** *(fabric)* Flanell, *der;* **b)** *(Brit.: for washing)* Waschlappen, *der* **flap** [flæp] **1.** *v. t.,* **-pp-:** ~ **its wings** mit den Flügeln schlagen. **2.** *v. i.,* **-pp-** ⟨*Flügel:*⟩ schlagen; ⟨*Segel, Fahne, Vorhang:*⟩ flattern. **3.** *n.* **a)** Klappe, *die; (envelope-seal, of shoe)* Lasche, *die;* **b)** *(fig. coll.)* **in a** ~: furchtbar aufgeregt

**flare** [fleə(r)] **1.** *v. i.* flackern; *(fig.)* ausbrechen; **tempers** ~**d** die Gemüter erhitzten sich. **2.** *n.* Leuchtsignal, *das.* **flare 'up** *v. i.* **a)** aufflackern; **b)** *(break out)* [wieder] ausbrechen **flash** [flæʃ] **1.** *n.* Aufleuchten, *das; (as signal)* Lichtsignal, *das;* ~ **of lightning** Blitz, *der;* **in a** ~: *(quickly)* im Nu. **2.** *v. t.* **a)** aufleuchten lassen; ~ **one's headlights** die Lichthupe betätigen; ~ **sb. a smile/glance** jmdm. ein Lächeln/einen Blick zuwerfen; **b)** *(display briefly)* kurz zeigen. **3.** *v. i.* aufleuchten; ~ **by** *or* **past** ⟨*Zeit, Ferien:*⟩ wie im Fluge vergehen **flash:** ~**back** *n.* Rückblende, *die* **(to auf + Akk.);** ~ **bulb** *n.* Blitzbirnchen, *das;* ~**-cube** *n.* Blitzwürfel, *der;* ~**-gun** *n.* Blitzgerät, *das;* ~**light** *n.* **a)** *(for signals)* Blinklicht, *das;* **b)** *(Amer.: torch)* Taschenlampe, *die* **'flashy** *adj.* auffällig **flask** [flɑːsk] *n.* **a)** *see* **Thermos; b)** *(for wine, oil)* [bauchige] Flasche; **c)** *(Chem.)* Kolben, *der* **¹flat** [flæt] *n.* *(Brit.)* Wohnung, *die* **²flat 1.** *adj.* **a)** flach; eben ⟨*Fläche*⟩; platt ⟨*Nase, Reifen*⟩; **b)** *(downright)* glatt *(ugs.)* ⟨*Absage, Weigerung, Widerspruch*⟩; **c)** *(Mus.)* [um einen Halbton] erniedrigt ⟨*Note*⟩; **d)** schal, abgestanden ⟨*Bier, Sekt*⟩; **e)** leer ⟨*Batterie*⟩. **2.** *adv.* *(Mus.)* zu tief **flat:** ~ **'feet** *n. pl.* Plattfüße; ~**-'fish** *n.* Plattfisch, *der;* ~**-'footed** *adj.* plattfüßig **'flatly** *adv.* rundweg **flatten** ['flætn] **1.** *v. t.* flach drücken ⟨*Schachtel*⟩; dem Erdboden gleichmachen ⟨*Stadt, Gebäude*⟩. **2.** *v. refl.* ~ **oneself against sth.** sich flach gegen etw. drücken **flatter** ['flætə(r)] *v. t.* schmeicheln (+ *Dat.*). **'flattering** *adj.* schmeichelhaft. **'flattery** *n.* Schmeichelei, *die* **flat 'tyre** *n.* Reifenpanne, *die* **flaunt** [flɔːnt] *v. t.* zur Schau stellen **flavor** *etc. (Amer.) see* **flavour** *etc.* **flavour** ['fleɪvə(r)] *(Brit.)* **1.** *n.* **a)** Geschmack, *der;* **b)** *(fig.)* Anflug, *der.* **2.** *v. t.* abschmecken. **'flavouring** *n.* *(Brit.)* Aroma, *das* **flaw** [flɔː] *n.* Fehler, *der; (imperfection)* Makel, *der; (in workmanship or goods)* Mangel, *der* **flax** [flæks] *n.* Flachs, *der* **flea** [fliː] *n.* Floh, *der.* **'flea market** *n.* *(coll.)* Flohmarkt, *der* **fled** *see* **flee**

**flee** [fli:] **1.** *v. i.*, **fled** [fled] fliehen; ~ **from sth./sb.** aus etw./vor jmdm. flüchten. **2.** *v. t.*, **fled** fliehen aus
**fleece** [fli:s] **1.** *n.* [Schaf]fell, *das.* **2.** *v. t. (fig.)* ausplündern. **fleecy** ['fli:sɪ] *adj.* flauschig
**fleet** [fli:t] *n.* Flotte, *die*
**fleeting** ['fli:tɪŋ] *adj.* flüchtig
**flesh** [fleʃ] *n.* Fleisch, *das; (of fruit, plant)* [Frucht]fleisch, *das.* **'fleshy** *adj.* fett; fleischig ⟨*Hände*⟩
**flew** *see* ²**fly** 1, 2
¹**flex** [fleks] *n. (Brit. Electr.)* Kabel, *das*
²**flex** *v. t.* beugen ⟨*Arm, Knie*⟩; ~ **one's muscles** seine Muskeln spielen lassen
**flexible** ['fleksɪbl] *adj.* **a)** biegsam; elastisch; **b)** *(fig.)* flexibel
**flick** [flɪk] *v. t.* schnippen; anknipsen ⟨*Schalter*⟩; verspritzen ⟨*Tinte*⟩. **'flick through** *v. t.* durchblättern
**flicker** ['flɪkə(r)] **1.** *v. i.* flackern; ⟨*Fernsehapparat:*⟩ flimmern. **2.** *n.* Flackern, *das; (of TV)* Flimmern, *das*
¹**flight** [flaɪt] *n.* **a)** Flug, *der;* **b)** ~ |of **stairs** *or* **steps**| Treppe, *die*
²**flight** *n. (fleeing)* Flucht, *die;* **take** ~: die Flucht ergreifen; **put to** ~: in die Flucht schlagen
**'flight attendant** *n.* Flugbegleiter, *der/*-begleiterin, *die*
**flimsy** ['flɪmzɪ] *adj.* **a)** dünn; nicht sehr haltbar ⟨*Verpackung*⟩; **b)** *(fig.)* fadenscheinig ⟨*Entschuldigung, Argument*⟩
**flinch** [flɪntʃ] *v. i.* zurückschrecken (**from** vor + *Dat.*); *(wince)* zusammenzucken
**fling** [flɪŋ] **1.** *n.* **have a** *or* **one's** ~: sich ausleben. **2.** *v. t.*, **flung** [flʌŋ] werfen; ~ **oneself into sth.** *(fig.)* sich in etw. *(Akk.)* stürzen
**flint** [flɪnt] *n.* Feuerstein, *der*
**flip** [flɪp] *v. t.*, **-pp-** schnipsen; ~ |**over**| *(turn over)* umdrehen. **'flip through** *v. t.* durchblättern
**flippant** ['flɪpənt] *adj.* leichtfertig
**flipper** ['flɪpə(r)] *n.* Flosse, *die*
**flirt** [flɜːt] *v. i.* flirten. **flirtation** [flɜː'teɪʃn] *n.* Flirt, *der*
**flit** [flɪt] *v. i.* huschen
**float** [fləʊt] **1.** *v. i.* treiben; *(in air)* schweben. **2.** *n. (for carnival)* Festwagen, *der.* **3.** *v. t. (set afloat)* flott machen; *(fig.)* lancieren ⟨*Plan, Idee*⟩. **floating 'voter** *n.* Wechselwähler, *der/*-wählerin, *die*
**flock** [flɒk] **1.** *n.* **a)** Herde, *die; (of birds)* Schwarm, *der;* **b)** *(of people)* Schar, *die.* **2.** *v. i.* strömen; ~ **round sb.** sich um jmdn. scharen

**flog** [flɒg] *v. t.*, **-gg-: a)** auspeitschen; **b)** *(Brit. sl.: sell)* verscheuern *(salopp)*
**flood** [flʌd] **1.** *n.* Überschwemmung, *die;* **the F~** *(Bibl.)* die Sintflut. **2.** *v. i.* ⟨*Fluß:*⟩ über die Ufer treten; *(fig.)* strömen. **3.** *v. t.* überschwemmen. **'floodlight 1.** *n.* Scheinwerfer, *der.* **2.** *v. t.*, **floodlit** ['flʌdlɪt] anstrahlen
**floor** [flɔ:(r)] **1.** *n.* **a)** Boden, *der;* **b)** *(storey)* Stockwerk, *das;* **first** ~ *(Amer.)* Erdgeschoß, *das;* **first** ~ *(Brit.)*, **second** ~ *(Amer.)* erster Stock; **ground** ~: Erdgeschoß, *das;* Parterre, *das.* **2.** *v. t.* **a)** *(confound)* überfordern; **b)** *(knock down)* zu Boden schlagen
**floor:** ~**board** *n.* Dielenbrett, *das;* ~-**cloth** *n. (Brit.)* Scheuertuch, *das;* ~-**polish** *n.* Bohnerwachs, *das;* ~ **show** *n.* ≈ Unterhaltungsprogramm, *das*
**flop** [flɒp] **1.** *v. i.*, **-pp-: a)** plumpsen; **b)** *(coll.: fail)* fehlschlagen; ⟨*Theaterstück, Show:*⟩ durchfallen. **2.** *n. (coll.: failure)* Reinfall, *der (ugs.)*
**floppy** ['flɒpɪ] *adj.* weich und biegsam
**flora** ['flɔ:rə] *n.* Flora, *die*
**floral** ['flɔ:rl, 'flɒrl] *adj.* geblümt ⟨*Kleid, Stoff*⟩; Blumen⟨*muster*⟩
**Florence** ['flɒrəns] *pr. n.* Florenz *(das)*
**florid** ['flɒrɪd] *adj.* blumig ⟨*Stil. Redeweise*⟩; gerötet ⟨*Teint*⟩
**florist** ['flɒrɪst] *n.* Florist, *der/*Floristin, *die*
**flotsam** ['flɒtsəm] *n.* ~ |**and jetsam**| Treibgut, *das*
**flounder** ['flaʊndə(r)] *v. i.* taumeln
**flour** ['flaʊə(r)] *n.* Mehl, *das*
**flourish** ['flʌrɪʃ] **1.** *v. i.* gedeihen; ⟨*Geschäft:*⟩ florieren, gutgehen. **2.** *v. t.* schwingen. **3.** *n.* **do sth. with a** ~: etw. schwungvoll tun
**flout** [flaʊt] *v. t.* mißachten
**flow** [fləʊ] **1.** *v. i.* fließen; ⟨*Körner, Sand:*⟩ rinnen, rieseln; ⟨*Gas:*⟩ strömen. **2.** *n.* **a)** Fließen, *das;* ~ **of water/people** Wasser-/Menschenstrom, *der;* ~ **of information** Informationsfluß, *der;* **b)** *(of tide, river)* Flut, *die*
**flower** ['flaʊə(r)] **1.** *n. (blossom)* Blüte, *die; (plant)* Blume, *die;* **come into** ~: zu blühen beginnen. **2.** *v. i.* blühen. **'flower-bed** *n.* Blumenbeet, *das.* **'flower-pot** *n.* Blumentopf, *der*
**'flowery** *adj.* geblümt ⟨*Stoff, Muster*⟩; *(fig.)* blumig ⟨*Sprache*⟩
**'flowing** *adj.* fließend; wallend ⟨*Haar*⟩
**flown** *see* ²**fly** 1, 2
**flu** [flu:] *n. (coll.)* Grippe, *die*

**fluctuate** ['flʌktjʊeɪt] *v.i.* schwanken. **fluctuation** [flʌktjʊ'eɪʃn] *n.* Schwankung, *die*

**fluency** ['fluːənsɪ] *n.* Gewandtheit, *die; (spoken)* Redegewandtheit, *die*

**fluent** ['fluːənt] *adj.* gewandt ⟨*Stil, Redeweise, Redner, Schreiber*⟩; **be ~ in Russian, speak ~ Russian** fließend Russisch sprechen

**fluff** [flʌf] *n.* Flusen; Fusseln

**fluffy** ['flʌfɪ] *adj.* [flaum]weich ⟨*Kissen, Küken*⟩; flauschig ⟨*Spielzeug, Decke*⟩

**fluid** ['fluːɪd] **1.** *n.* Flüssigkeit, *die.* **2.** *adj.* flüssig

**fluke** [fluːk] *n. (piece of luck)* Glücksfall, *der*

**flung** *see* **fling 2**

**fluorescent** [fluːə'resənt] *adj.* fluoreszierend. **fluorescent 'light** *n.* Leuchtstofflampe, *die*

**fluoride** ['fluːəraɪd] *n.* Fluorid, *das;* **fluoride toothpaste** fluorhaltige Zahnpasta

**flurry** ['flʌrɪ] *n.* **a)** Aufregung, *die;* **b)** *(of rain/snow)* [Regen-/Schnee]schauer, *der*

**¹flush** [flʌʃ] **1.** *v.i.* rot werden. **2.** *v.t.* ausspülen ⟨*Becken*⟩; **~ the toilet** *or* **lavatory** spülen. **3.** *n.* Rotwerden, *das*

**²flush** *adj. (level)* bündig; **be ~ with** sth. mit etw. bündig abschließen

**fluster** ['flʌstə(r)] *v.t.* aus der Fassung bringen. **flustered** ['flʌstəd] *adj.* nervös

**flute** [fluːt] *n.* Flöte, *die*

**flutter** ['flʌtə(r)] **1.** *v.i.* flattern. **2.** *v.t.* flattern mit ⟨*Flügel*⟩

**flux** [flʌks] *n.* **in a state of ~:** im Fluß

**¹fly** [flaɪ] *n.* Fliege, *die*

**²fly** *v.i.,* flew [fluː], flown [fləʊn] **a)** fliegen; **~ away** *or* **off** wegfliegen; **b)** *(fig.)* **~** |by *or* past| wie im Fluge vergehen; **c)** ⟨*Fahne:*⟩ gehißt sein. **2.** *v.t.,* flew, flown fliegen ⟨*Flugzeug, Fracht, Einsatz usw.*⟩; fliegen über (+ *Akk.*) ⟨*Strecke*⟩. **3.** *n.* in sing. or pl. *(on trousers)* Hosenschlitz, *der.* **fly 'in** *v.i.* [mit dem Flugzeug] eintreffen (**from** aus). **fly 'out** *v.i.* abfliegen (**of** von)

**flying** ['flaɪɪŋ]: **~ 'saucer** *n.* fliegende Untertasse; **~ 'start** *n. (Sport)* fliegender Start; **~ 'visit** *n.* Stippvisite, *die (ugs.)*

**fly:** **~leaf** *n.* Vorsatzblatt, *das;* **~over** *n. (Brit.)* [Straßen]überführung, *die*

**foal** [fəʊl] *n.* Fohlen, *das*

**foam** [fəʊm] **1.** *n.* Schaum, *der.* **2.** *v.i.* schäumen. **foam 'rubber** *n.* Schaumgummi, *der*

**fob** [fɒb] *v.t.,* **-bb-:** **~ sb. off with** sth. jmdn. mit etw. abspeisen *(ugs.)*

**focus** ['fəʊkəs] **1.** *n., pl.* **~es** *or* **foci** ['fəʊsaɪ] Brennpunkt, *der;* **out of/in ~:** unscharf/scharf eingestellt; unscharf/scharf ⟨*Foto, Film usw.*⟩; *(fig.)* **be the ~ of attention** im Brennpunkt des Interesses stehen. **2.** *v.t.,* **-s-** *or* **-ss-** einstellen (**on** auf + *Akk.*); bündeln ⟨*Licht, Strahlen*⟩. **3.** *v.i.,* **-s-** *or* **-ss-** *(fig.)* sich konzentrieren (**on** auf + *Akk.*)

**fodder** ['fɒdə(r)] *n.* [Vieh]futter, *das*

**foe** [fəʊ] *n. (poet./rhet.)* Feind, *der*

**foetus** ['fiːtəs] *n.* Fötus, *der*

**fog** [fɒg] *n.* Nebel, *der.* **'fog-light** *n. (Motor Veh.)* Nebelscheinwerfer, *der*

**foggy** ['fɒgɪ] *adj.* neblig

**fogy** ['fəʊgɪ] *n.* |old| **~:** [alter] Opa *(salopp)*/[alte] Oma *(salopp)*

**foible** ['fɔɪbl] *n.* Eigenheit, *die*

**¹foil** [fɔɪl] *n.* Folie, *die*

**²foil** *v.t.* vereiteln

**foist** [fɔɪst] *v.t.* **~** |off| **on to sb.** jmdm. andrehen *(ugs.)*; **auf jmdn. abwälzen** ⟨*Probleme, Verantwortung*⟩

**fold** [fəʊld] **1.** *v.t.* [zusammen]falten; **~ one's arms** die Arme verschränken. **2.** *v.i.* **a)** *(become ~ed)* sich zusammenfalten; **b)** *(be able to be ~ed)* sich falten lassen. **3.** *n.* Falte, *die; (line made by ~ing)* Kniff, *der.* **fold 'up** *v.t.* zusammenfalten ⟨*Laken*⟩; zusammenklappen ⟨*Stuhl*⟩

**'folder** *n.* Mappe, *die*

**foliage** ['fəʊlɪɪdʒ] *n.* Blätter *Pl.; (of tree also)* Laub, *das*

**folk** [fəʊk] *n.* **a)** Volk, *das;* **b)** *in pl.* **~|s|** *(people)* Leute *Pl.*

**folk:** **~-dance** *n.* Volkstanz, *der;* **~-lore** [**~**lɔː(r)] *n.* Folklore, *die;* **~-music** *n.* Volksmusik, *die;* **~-song** *n.* Volkslied, *das; (modern)* Folksong, *der*

**follow** ['fɒləʊ] **1.** *v.t.* **a)** folgen (+ *Dat.*); **b)** entlanggehen/-fahren ⟨*Straße usw.*⟩; **c)** *(come after)* folgen auf (+ *Akk.*); **d)** *(result from)* die Folge sein von; **e)** *(treat or take as guide)* sich orientieren an (+ *Dat.*); **f)** folgen (+ *Dat.*) ⟨*Prinzip, Instinkt, Trend*⟩; verfolgen ⟨*Politik*⟩; befolgen ⟨*Regel, Vorschrift, Rat, Warnung*⟩; sich halten an (+ *Akk.*) ⟨*Konventionen, Diät*⟩; **g)** *(grasp meaning of)* folgen (+ *Dat.*); **do you ~ me?** verstehst du, was ich meine? **2.** *v.i.* **a)** *(go, come)* **~ after** sb./sth. jmdm./einer Sache folgen; **b)** *(come next in order or time)* folgen; **as ~s** wie folgt; **c)** **~ from** sth.

*(result)* die Folge von etw. sein; *(be deducible)* aus etw. folgen. **follow 'on** *v. i. (continue)* ~ on from sth. die Fortsetzung von etw. sein. **follow 'up** *v. t.* a) ausbauen ⟨*Erfolg, Sieg*⟩; b) nachgehen (+ *Dat.*) ⟨*Hinweis*⟩

**'follower** *n.* Anhänger, *der*/Anhängerin, *die*

**'following 1.** *adj.* folgend; **the** ~: folgendes. **2.** *prep.* nach. **3.** *n.* Anhängerschaft, *die*

**folly** ['fɒlɪ] *n.* Torheit, *die (geh.)*

**fond** [fɒnd] *adj.* liebevoll; lieb ⟨*Erinnerung*⟩; **be** ~ **of sb.** jmdn. mögen; **be** ~ **of doing sth.** etw. gern tun

**fondle** ['fɒndl] *v. t.* streicheln

**'fondness** *n.* Liebe, *die*; ~ **for sth.** Vorliebe für etw.

**font** [fɒnt] *n.* Taufstein, *der*

**food** [fu:d] *n.* a) Nahrung, *die; (for animals)* Futter, *das*; b) *(as commodity)* Lebensmittel *Pl.*; c) *(in solid form)* Essen, *das*; d) *(particular kind)* Nahrungsmittel, *das*; Kost, *die*. **'food poisoning** *n.* Lebensmittelvergiftung, *die*. **'food processor** *n.* Küchenmaschine, *die*

**fool** [fu:l] **1.** *n.* Dummkopf, *der (ugs.).* **2.** *v. t.* ~ **sb. into doing sth.** jmdn. [durch Tricks] dazu bringen, etw. zu tun. **fool a'bout, fool a'round** *v. i.* Unsinn machen

**foolhardy** ['fu:lhɑːdɪ] *adj.* tollkühn

**foolish** *adj.* töricht; verrückt *(ugs.)* ⟨*Idee, Vorschlag*⟩

**foolproof** *adj. (infallible)* absolut sicher

**foot** [fʊt] **1.** *n., pl.* **feet** [fi:t] a) Fuß, *der*; **on** ~: zu Fuß; **put one's** ~ **in it** *(fig. coll.)* ins Fettnäpfchen treten *(ugs.)*; b) *(far end)* unteres Ende; *(of bed)* Fußende, *das*; c) *(measure)* Fuß, *der (30,48 cm).* **2.** *v. t.* ~ **the bill** die Rechnung bezahlen

**football** ['fʊtbɔːl] *n. (game, ball)* Fußball, *der*. **'football boot** *n.* Fußballschuh, *der*. **'footballer** *n.* Fußballspieler, *der*/-spielerin, *die*. **'football pools** *n. pl.* **the** ~: das Fußballtoto

**foot:** ~-**brake** *n.* Fußbremse, *die*; ~-**bridge** *n.* Fußgängerbrücke, *die*; ~**hold** *n.* Halt, *der*

**footing** *n.* a) *(fig.)* **be on an equal** ~ **[with sb.]** [jmdm.] gleichgestellt sein; b) *(foothold)* Halt, *der*

**foot:** ~-**note** *n.* Fußnote, *die*; ~-**path** *n.* Fußweg, *der*; ~-**print** *n.* Fußabdruck, *der*; ~-**step** *n.* Schritt, *der*; **follow in sb.'s** ~**steps** *(fig.)* in jmds. Fuß-

stapfen *(Akk.)* treten; ~-**wear** *n.* Schuhe *Pl.*

**for** [fə(r), *stressed* fɔ:(r)] **1.** *prep.* a) für; **what is it** ~? wofür ist das?; **reason** ~ **living** Grund zu leben; **a request** ~ **help** eine Bitte um Hilfe; **study** ~ **a university degree** auf einen Hochschulabschluß hin studieren; **take sb.** ~ **a walk** mit jmdm. einen Spaziergang machen; **be '**~ **doing sth.** *(in favour)* dafür sein, etw. zu tun; **cheque/bill** ~ **£5** Scheck/Rechnung über 5 Pfund; b) *(on account of, as penalty of)* wegen; **were it not** ~ **you/ your help** ohne dich/deine Hilfe; ~ **fear of** aus Angst vor (+ *Dat.*); c) *(in spite of)* ~ **all** ...: trotz ...; ~ **all that,** ...: trotzdem ...; d) ~ **all I know/care** ...: möglicherweise/ was mich betrifft, ...; ~ **one thing,** ...: zunächst einmal ...; e) *(during)* **stay** ~ **a week** eine Woche bleiben; **we've/we haven't been here** ~ **three years** wir sind seit drei Jahren hier/nicht mehr hier gewesen; f) **walk** ~ **20 miles** 20 Meilen gehen. **2.** *conj.* denn

**forage** ['fɒrɪdʒ] **1.** *n.* Futter, *das.* **2.** *v. i.* ~ **for sth.** auf der Suche nach etw. sein

**forbad, forbade** *see* **forbid**

**forbid** [fə'bɪd] *v. t.,* -**dd**-, **forbad** [fə-'bæd] *or* **forbade** [fə'bæd, fə'beɪd], **forbidden** [fə'bɪdn] ~ **sb. to do sth.** jmdm. verbieten, etw. zu tun; ~ **[sb.] sth.** [jmdm.] etw. verbieten; **it is** ~**den [to do sth.]** es ist verboten[, etw. zu tun]. **forbidden** *see* **forbid. for'bidding** *adj.* furchteinflößend

**force** [fɔ:s] **1.** *n.* a) *(strength, power)* Stärke, *die; (of explosion, storm)* Wucht, *die; (Phys.; physical strength)* Kraft, *die;* **in** ~: mit einem großen Aufgebot; b) *(validity)* Kraft, *die;* **in** ~: in Kraft; **come into** ~ ⟨*Gesetz usw.*:⟩ in Kraft treten; c) *(violence)* Gewalt, *die;* **by** ~: gewaltsam; d) *(group) (of workers)* Kolonne, *die;* Trupp, *der; (of police)* Einheit, *die; (Mil.)* Armee, *die;* **the** ~**s** die Armee; **be in the** ~**s** beim Militär sein. **2.** *v. t.* a) zwingen; ~ **sth. [up]on sb.** jmdm. etw. aufzwingen; b) ~ **[open]** aufbrechen; ~ **one's way in** sich *(Dat.)* mit Gewalt Zutritt verschaffen. **forced** [fɔ:st] *adj.* a) *(contrived, unnatural)* gezwungen; b) *(compelled by force)* erzwungen; Zwangs⟨*arbeit*⟩. **forced 'landing** *n.* Notlandung, *die.* **'force-feed** *v. t.* zwangsernähren. **forceful** ['fɔ:sfl] *adj.* stark ⟨*Persönlichkeit, Charakter*⟩;

energisch ⟨*Person, Art*⟩; eindrucksvoll ⟨*Sprache*⟩

**forceps** ['fɔːseps] *n., pl. same* |**pair of**| ~: Zange, *die*

**forcible** ['fɔːsɪbl] *adj.*, **forcibly** ['fɔːsɪblɪ] *adv.* gewaltsam

**ford** [fɔːd] **1.** *n.* Furt, *die*. **2.** *v. t.* durchqueren; *(wade through)* durchwaten

**fore** [fɔː(r)] **1.** *adj., esp. in comb.* vorder...; Vorder⟨*teil, -front usw.*⟩. **2.** *n.* to the ~: im Vordergrund

'**forearm** *n.* Unterarm, *der*

**foreboding** [fɔː'bəʊdɪŋ] *n.* Vorahnung, *die*

'**forecast 1.** *v. t.*, **forecast** *or* **forecasted** vorhersagen. **2.** *n.* Voraussage, *die*

'**forecourt** *n.* Vorhof, *der*

'**forefather** *n., usu. in pl.* Vorfahr, *der*

'**forefinger** *n.* Zeigefinger, *der*

'**forefront** *n.* |be| **in the** ~ **of** in vorderster Linie (+ *Gen.*) [stehen]

'**foregone** *adj.* **be a** ~ **conclusion** von vornherein feststehen; *(be certain)* so gut wie sicher sein

'**foreground** *n.* Vordergrund, *der*

**forehead** ['fɒrɪd, 'fɔːhed] *n.* Stirn, *die*

**foreign** ['fɒrɪn] *adj.* **a)** *(from abroad)* ausländisch; Fremd⟨*kapital, -sprache*⟩; **he is** ~: er ist Ausländer; **b)** *(abroad)* fremd; ~ **country** Ausland, *das*; Außen⟨*politik, -handel*⟩; **c)** *(from outside)* fremd; ~ **body** *or* **substance** Fremdkörper, *der*. '**foreigner** *n.* Ausländer, *der*/Ausländerin, *die*

**foreign:** ~ **ex'change** *n.* Devisen *Pl.*; **F~ Office** *n. (Brit. Hist./coll.)* Außenministerium, *das*; **F~ 'Secretary** *n. (Brit.)* Außenminister, *der*

**foreman** ['fɔːmən] *n., pl.* **foremen** ['fɔːmən] Vorarbeiter, *der*

**foremost** ['fɔːməʊst, 'fɔːməst] **1.** *adj.* **a)** vorderst...; **b)** *(fig.)* führend. **2.** *adv.* **first and** ~: zunächst einmal

'**forename** *n.* Vorname, *der*

'**forerunner** *n.* Vorläufer, *der*/Vorläuferin, *die*

**foresaw** *see* **foresee**

**foresee** [fɔː'siː] *v. t., forms as* **see** voraussehen. **foreseeable** [fɔː'siːəbl] *adj.* vorhersehbar; **in the** ~ **future** in nächster Zukunft

**foreseen** *see* **foresee**

'**foresight** *n.* Weitblick, *der*

**foreskin** *n. (Anat.)* Vorhaut, *die*

**forest** ['fɒrɪst] *n.* Wald, *der*; *(commercially exploited)* Forst, *der*

**fore'stall** *v. t.* zuvorkommen (+ *Dat.*)

**forestry** ['fɒrɪstrɪ] *n.* Forstwirtschaft, *die*

'**foretaste** *n.* Vorgeschmack, *der*

**fore'tell** *v. t.*, **fore'told** voraussagen

**forever** [fə'revə(r)] *adv. (constantly)* ständig

**fore'warn** *v. t.* vorwarnen

'**foreword** *n.* Vorwort, *das*

**forfeit** ['fɔːfɪt] **1.** *v. t.* verlieren; verwirken *(geh.)* ⟨*Recht, jmds. Gunst*⟩. **2.** *n.* Strafe, *die*; *(games)* Pfand, *das*

**forgave** *see* **forgive**

'**forge** [fɔːdʒ] **1.** *n.* **a)** *(workshop)* Schmiede, *die*; **b)** *(blacksmith's hearth)* Esse, *die*. **2.** *v. t.* **a)** schmieden (**into** zu); **b)** *(fig.)* schmieden ⟨*Plan*⟩; schließen ⟨*Vereinbarung, Freundschaft*⟩; **c)** *(counterfeit)* fälschen

²**forge** *v. i.* ~ **ahead** [das Tempo] beschleunigen; *(fig.)* Fortschritte machen

'**forger** *n.* Fälscher, *der*/Fälscherin, *die*

**forgery** ['fɔːdʒərɪ] *n.* Fälschung, *die*

**forget** [fə'get] **1.** *v. t.*, **-tt-**, **forgot** [fə'gɒt], **forgotten** [fə'gɒtn] vergessen; *(~ learned ability)* verlernen. **2.** *v. i.*, **-tt-**, **forgot**, **forgotten** es vergessen; ~ **about sth.** etw. vergessen; ~ **about it!** *(coll.)* schon gut! **forgetful** [fə'getfl] *adj.* vergeßlich. **for'getfulness** *n.* Vergeßlichkeit, *die*. **for'get-me-not** *n. (Bot.)* Vergißmeinnicht, *das*

**forgive** [fə'gɪv] *v. t.*, **forgave** [fə'geɪv], **forgiven** [fə'gɪvn] verzeihen; vergeben ⟨*Sünden*⟩; ~ **sb.** |**sth.** *or* **for sth.**| jmdm. [etw.] verzeihen. **for'giveness** *n.* Verzeihung, *die*; *(of sins)* Vergebung, *die*

**forgo** [fɔː'gəʊ] *v. t., forms as* **go** verzichten auf (+ *Akk.*)

**forgone** *see* **forgo**

**forgot, forgotten** *see* **forget**

**fork** [fɔːk] **1.** *n.* **a)** Gabel, *die*; **knives and ~s** Besteck, *das*; **b)** *(in road)* Gabelung, *die*; *(one branch)* Abzweigung, *die*. **2.** *v. i.* *(divide)* sich gabeln; *(turn)* abbiegen; ~ **left** links abbiegen. **fork 'out** *v. i. (sl.)* blechen *(ugs.)*

'**fork-lift truck** *n.* Gabelstapler, *der*

**forlorn** [fə'lɔːn] *adj.* **a)** *(desperate)* verzweifelt; **b)** *(forsaken)* verlassen

**form** [fɔːm] **1.** *n.* **a)** *(shape, type, style)* Form, *die*; **take ~:** Gestalt annehmen; **b)** *(printed sheet)* Formular, *das*; **c)** *(Brit. Sch.)* Klasse, *die*; **d)** *(bench)* Bank, *die*; **e)** *(Sport: physical condition)* Form, *die*; *(fig.)* **true to ~:** wie üblich. **2.** *v. t.* **a)** bilden; **b)** *(shape)* formen, gestalten (**into** zu); **c)** sich *(Dat.)* bilden ⟨*Meinung, Urteil*⟩; ge-

winnen ⟨*Eindruck*⟩; fassen ⟨*Plan*⟩;
entwickeln ⟨*Vorliebe, Gewohnheit*⟩;
schließen ⟨*Freundschaft*⟩; **d)** *(set up)*
bilden ⟨*Regierung*⟩; gründen ⟨*Bund,
Firma, Partei*⟩. **3.** *v. i.* sich bilden;
⟨*Idee:*⟩ Gestalt annehmen

**formal** ['fɔːml] *adj.* formell; förmlich
⟨*Person, Art, Einladung, Begrüßung*⟩;
*(official)* offiziell; **a ~ 'yes'/'no'** eine
bindende Zusage/endgültige Absage.
**formality** [fɔː'mælɪtɪ] *n.* **a)** *(requirement)* Formalität, *die;* **b)** *(being
formal)* Förmlichkeit, *die*

**format** ['fɔːmæt] *n.* Format, *das*

**formation** [fɔː'meɪʃn] *n.* **a)** *see* **form**
2 a, d: Bildung, *die;* Gründung, *die;* **b)**
*(Mil., Aeronaut.)* Formation, *die*

**former** ['fɔːmə(r)] *attrib. adj.* ehemalig; **in ~ times** früher; **the ~:** der/die/
das erstere; *pl.* die ersteren. '**formerly** *adv.* früher

**formidable** ['fɔːmɪdəbl] *adj.* gewaltig;
gefährlich ⟨*Herausforderung, Gegner*⟩

**formula** ['fɔːmjʊlə] *n.* Formel, *die.*
**formulate** ['fɔːmjʊleɪt] *v. t.* formulieren; *(devise)* entwickeln

**forsake** [fə'seɪk] *v. t.,* **forsook** [fə'sʊk],
**~n** [fə'seɪkn] **a)** *(give up)* verzichten
auf (+ *Akk.*); **b)** *(desert)* verlassen.
**for'saken** *adj.* verlassen

**fort** [fɔːt] *n. (Mil.)* Fort, *das*

**forte** ['fɔːteɪ] *n.* Stärke, *die*

**forth** [fɔːθ] *adv.* **and so ~:** und so weiter; *see also* **back 3**

**forthcoming** ['---, -'--] *adj.* **a)** *(ap-
proaching)* bevorstehend; in Kürze er-
scheinend ⟨*Buch usw.*⟩; **b)** *pred.* **be ~**
⟨*Geld, Antwort:*⟩ kommen; ⟨*Hilfe:*⟩ ge-
leistet werden; **not be ~:** ausbleiben;
**c)** *(responsive)* mitteilsam ⟨*Person*⟩

**forthright** *adj.* direkt

**forth'with** *adv.* unverzüglich

**fortieth** ['fɔːtɪɪθ] *adj.* vierzigst ...

**fortify** ['fɔːtɪfaɪ] *v. t.* **a)** *(Mil.)* befestigen; **b)** *(strengthen)* stärken

**fortitude** ['fɔːtɪtjuːd] *n.* innere Stärke

**fortnight** ['fɔːtnaɪt] *n.* vierzehn Tage

**fortress** ['fɔːtrɪs] *n.* Festung, *die*

**fortuitous** [fɔː'tjuːɪtəs] *adj.,* **for'tuit-
ously** *adv.* zufällig

**fortunate** ['fɔːtʃənət] *adj.* glücklich.
'**fortunately** *adv.* glücklicherweise

**fortune** ['fɔːtʃən, 'fɔːtʃuːn] *n.* **a)**
*(wealth)* Vermögen, *das;* **b)** *(luck)*
Schicksal, *das;* **bad/good ~:** Pech/
Glück, *das.* '**fortune-teller** *n.* Wahrsager, *der*/Wahrsagerin, *die*

**forty** ['fɔːtɪ] **1.** *adj.* vierzig; **have ~**
'**winks** ein Nickerchen machen *(ugs.).*

**2.** *n.* Vierzig, *die.* See *also* **eight;
eighty** 2

**forum** ['fɔːrəm] *n.* Forum, *das*

**forward** ['fɔːwəd] **1.** *adv.* **a)** *(in direction faced)* vorwärts; **b)** *(to the front)*
nach vorn; vor⟨*laufen, -rücken,
-schieben*⟩; **c)** *(closer)* heran; **he came
~ to greet me** er kam auf mich zu, um
mich zu begrüßen; **d) come ~** ⟨*Zeuge,
Helfer:*⟩ sich melden. **2.** *adj.* **a)** *(directed ahead)* vorwärts gerichtet; **b)** *(at
or to the front)* Vorder-; vorder... **3.** *n.*
*(Sport)* Stürmer, *der*/Stürmerin, *die.*
**4.** *v. t. (send on)* nachschicken ⟨*Post*⟩
(to an + *Akk.*)

**forwards** ['fɔːwədz] *see* **forward** 1 a, b

**forwent** *see* **forgo**

**fossil** ['fɒsɪl] *n.* Fossil, *das*

**foster** ['fɒstə(r)] **1.** *v. t.* **a)** fördern;
pflegen ⟨*Freundschaft*⟩; **b)** in Pflege
haben ⟨*Kind*⟩. **2.** *adj.* **~-:** Pflege⟨*kind,
-eltern; -sohn usw.*⟩

**fought** *see* **fight** 1, 2

**foul** [faʊl] **1.** *adj.* **a)** abscheulich ⟨*Geruch, Geschmack*⟩; **b)** *(polluted)* ver-
schmutzt ⟨*Wasser, Luft*⟩; *(putrid)* faulig ⟨*Wasser*⟩; stickig ⟨*Luft*⟩; **c)** *(sl.:
awful)* scheußlich *(ugs.);* anstößig
⟨*Sprache*⟩. **2.** *n. (Sport)* Foul, *das.*
**3.** *v. t.* **a)** beschmutzen; verpesten
⟨*Luft*⟩; **b)** *(Sport)* foulen. '**foul-
smelling** *adj.* übelriechend

¹**found** [faʊnd] *v. t.* **a)** *(establish)* gründen; stiften ⟨*Krankenhaus, Kloster*⟩;
begründen ⟨*Wissenschaft, Religion*⟩;
**b)** *(fig.: base)* begründen; **be ~ed** [up]-
**on sth.** [sich] auf etw. *(Akk.)* gründen

²**found** *see* **find** 1

**foundation** [faʊn'deɪʃn] *n.* **a)** Gründung, *die; (of hospital, monastery)*
Stiftung, *die;* **b)** *usu. in pl.* **~[s]** *(lit. or
fig.)* Fundament, *das;* **be without ~**
*(fig.)* unbegründet sein. **foun'dation
stone** *n.* Grundstein, *der*

¹'**founder** *n.* Gründer, *der*/Gründerin,
*die; (of hospital)* Stifter, *der*/Stifterin,
*die*

²'**founder** *v. i.* **a)** ⟨*Schiff:*⟩ sinken; **b)**
*(fig.: fail)* sich zerschlagen

**fountain** ['faʊntɪn] *n.* Fontäne, *die;
(structure)* Springbrunnen, *der; (fig.)*
Quelle, *die.* '**fountain-pen** *n.* Füllfe-
derhalter, *der*

**four** [fɔː(r)] **1.** *adj.* vier. **2.** *n.* Vier, *die;*
**on all ~s** auf allen vieren *(ugs.).* See
*also* **eight.** '**four-poster** *n.* **~ [bed]**
Himmelbett, *das.* **foursome** ['fɔːsəm]
*n.* Quartett, *das; (fig.)* **go in** *or* **as a ~:** zu
viert gehen

**fourteen** [fɔː'tiːn] **1.** *adj.* vierzehn. **2.** *n.* Vierzehn, *die. See also* **eight.**
**fourteenth** [fɔː'tiːnθ] **1.** *adj.* vierzehnt... **2.** *n.* (*fraction*) Vierzehntel, *das. See also* **eighth**
**fourth** [fɔːθ] **1.** *adj.* viert... **2.** *n.* (*in sequence*) vierte, *der/die/das;* (*in rank*) Vierte, *der/die/das;* (*fraction*) Viertel, *das. See also* **eighth.** '**fourthly** *adv.* viertens
**fowl** [faʊl] *n.* Haushuhn, *das;* (*collectively*) Geflügel, *das*
**fox** [fɒks] **1.** *n.* Fuchs, *der.* **2.** *v. t.* verwirren
**foyer** ['fɔɪeɪ] *n.* Foyer, *das*
**fraction** ['frækʃn] *n.* **a)** (*Math.*) Bruch, *der;* **b)** (*small part*) Bruchteil, *der*
**fracture** ['fræktʃə(r)] **1.** *n.* Bruch, *der.* **2.** *v. t.* brechen
**fragile** ['frædʒaɪl] *adj.* zerbrechlich
**fragment** ['frægmənt] *n.* Bruchstück, *das.* **fragmentary** ['frægməntərɪ] *adj.* bruchstückhaft
**fragrance** ['freɪgrəns] *n.* Duft, *der.* **fragrant** ['freɪgrənt] *adj.* duftend
**frail** [freɪl] *adj.* zerbrechlich; gebrechlich ⟨Greis, Greisin⟩
**frame** [freɪm] **1.** *n.* **a)** (*of vehicle*) Rahmen, *der;* (*of bed*) Gestell, *das;* **b)** (*border*) Rahmen, *der;* |spectacle| ~s [Brillen]gestell, *das.* **2.** *v. t.* **a)** rahmen; **b)** formulieren ⟨Frage, Antwort⟩; **c)** (*sl.: incriminate*) ~ sb. jmdm. etwas anhängen (*ugs.*). '**frame-up** *n.* (*coll.*) abgekartetes Spiel (*ugs.*). '**framework** *n.* Gerüst, *das*
**franc** [fræŋk] *n.* Franc, *der;* (*Swiss*) Franken, *der*
**France** [frɑːns] *pr. n.* Frankreich (*das*)
**franchise** ['fræntʃaɪz] *n.* **a)** Stimmrecht, *das;* **b)** (*Commerc.*) Lizenz, *die*
**¹frank** *adj.* offen; freimütig ⟨Geständnis, Äußerung⟩; **be ~ with sb.** zu jmdm. offen sein
**²frank** *v. t.* (*Post*) frankieren
**frankfurter** ['fræŋkfɜːtə(r)] (*Amer.:* **frankfurt** ['fræŋkfɜːt]) *n.* Frankfurter [Würstchen]
'**frankly** *adv.* offen; (*honestly*) offen gesagt
**frantic** ['fræntɪk] *adj.* **a)** verzweifelt ⟨Hilferufe, Gestikulieren⟩; **be ~ with fear/rage** *etc.* außer sich (*Dat.*) sein vor Angst/Wut *usw.;* **b)** hektisch ⟨Aktivität, Suche⟩. **frantically** ['fræntɪkəlɪ], '**franticly** *adv.* verzweifelt
**fraternize** ['frætənaɪz] *v. i.* ~ |with sb.| sich verbrüdern [mit jmdm.]
**fraud** [frɔːd] *n.* **a)** *no pl.* Betrug, *der;* **b)** (*trick*) Schwindel, *der;* **c)** (*person*) Betrüger, *der/*Betrügerin, *die.* **fraudulent** ['frɔːdjʊlənt] *adj.* betrügerisch
**fraught** [frɔːt] *adj.* **be ~ with danger** voller Gefahren sein
**¹fray** [freɪ] *n.* [Kampf]getümmel, *das;* **enter** *or* **join the ~:** sich in den Kampf stürzen
**²fray** *v. i.* [sich] durchscheuern; ⟨Hosenbein, Teppich, Seilende:⟩ ausfransen; **our nerves/tempers began to ~** (*fig.*) wir verloren langsam die Nerven/unsere Gemüter erhitzten sich
**freak** [friːk] *n.* **a)** Mißgeburt, *die; attrib.* ungewöhnlich ⟨Wetter, Ereignis⟩; **b)** (*sl.: fanatic*) Freak, *der*
**freckle** ['frekl] *n.* Sommersprosse, *die.* '**freckled** *adj.* sommersprossig
**free** [friː] **1.** *adj.,* **freer** ['friːə(r)], **freest** ['friːɪst] **a)** frei; **get ~:** freikommen; **set ~:** freilassen; **~ of charge/cost** gebührenfrei/kostenlos; **sb. is ~ to do sth.** es steht jmdm. frei, etw. zu tun; **~ time** Freizeit, *die;* **he's ~ in the mornings** er hat morgens Zeit; **b)** (*without payment*) kostenlos; frei ⟨Unterkunft, Verpflegung⟩; Frei⟨karte, -exemplar⟩; Gratis⟨probe⟩; '**admission ~**' „Eintritt frei"; **for ~** (*coll.*) umsonst. **2.** *adv.* gratis; umsonst. **3.** *v. t.* (*set at liberty*) freilassen; (*disentangle*) befreien (**of, from** von); ~ **sb./oneself from** jmdn./sich befreien aus ⟨Gefängnis, Sklaverei⟩. **freedom** ['friːdəm] *n.* Freiheit, *die*
**free: ~ 'gift** *n.* Gratisgabe, *die;* **~hold 1.** *n.* Besitzrecht, *das;* **2.** *adj.* Eigentums-; **~-lance 1.** *n.* freier Mitarbeiter/freie Mitarbeiterin; **2.** *adj.* freiberuflich
'**freely** *adv.* (*willingly*) großzügig; freimütig ⟨eingestehen⟩; (*without restriction*) frei; (*frankly*) offen
**free: F~mason** *n.* Freimaurer, *der;* **~-range** *adj.* freilaufend ⟨Huhn⟩; **~-range eggs** Eier von freilaufenden Hühnern; ~ **speech** *n.* Redefreiheit; **~way** *n.* (*Amer.*) Autobahn, *die;* **~-wheel** *v. i.* im Freilauf fahren
**freeze** [friːz] **1.** *v. i.,* **froze** [frəʊz], **frozen** ['frəʊzn] **a)** frieren; (*become covered with ice*) zufrieren; ⟨Straße:⟩ vereisen; ⟨Flüssigkeit:⟩ gefrieren; ⟨Rohr, Schloß:⟩ einfrieren; **b)** (*become rigid*) steif frieren. **2.** *v. t.,* **froze, frozen a)** (*preserve*) tiefkühlen; **b)** einfrieren ⟨Kredit, Löhne, Preise usw.⟩. '**freezer** *n.* Tiefkühltruhe, *die;* |upright| ~: Tiefkühlschrank, *der;* ~ com-

**partment** Tiefkühlfach, *das*. **freezing** ['fri:zɪŋ] **1.** *adj. (lit. or fig.)* frostig; **it's ~:** es ist eiskalt. **2.** *n.* **above/below ~:** über/unter dem/den Gefrierpunkt

**freight** [freɪt] *n.* Fracht, *die*. **'freighter** *n.* Frachter, *der*

**French** [frentʃ] **1.** *adj.* französisch; **he/ she is ~:** er ist Franzose/sie ist Französin. **2.** *n.* **a)** *(language)* Französisch, *das; see also* **English 2 a; b) the ~** *pl.* die Franzosen

**French: ~ 'bean** *n. (Brit.)* Gartenbohne, *die*; **~ 'dressing** *n.* Vinaigrette, *die*; **~ 'fries** *n. pl.* Pommes frites *Pl.* **~man** ['frentʃmən] *n., pl.* **~men** ['frentʃmən] Franzose, *der*; **~ 'window** *n.* französisches Fenster; **~woman** *n.* Französin, *die*

**frenzied** ['frenzɪd] *adj.* rasend

**frenzy** ['frenzɪ] *n.* **a)** Wahnsinn, *der*; *(fury)* Raserei, *die*

**frequency** ['fri:kwənsɪ] *n.* **a)** Häufigkeit, *die*; **b)** *(Phys.)* Frequenz, *die*

**frequent 1.** ['fri:kwənt] *adj.* **a)** häufig; **become less ~:** seltener werden; **b)** *(habitual)* eifrig. **2.** [fri:'kwent] *v.t.* häufig besuchen ⟨Café, Klub, usw.⟩. **frequently** ['fri:kwəntlɪ] *adv.* häufig

**fresco** *n. pl.* **~es** or **~s** Fresko, *das*

**fresh** [freʃ] *adj.* frisch; neu ⟨Beweise, Anstrich, Mut, Energie⟩; **~ supplies** Nachschub, *der* ⟨of an + *Dat.*⟩; **make a ~ start** noch einmal von vorne anfangen; *(fig.)* neu beginnen

**freshen** ['freʃn] *v.i.* auffrischen. **freshen 'up** *v.i.* sich auffrischen **'freshly** *adv.* frisch

**'freshness** *n.* Frische, *die*

**fresh 'water** *n.* Süßwasser, *das*

**fret** [fret] *v.i., -tt-* sich ⟨Dat.⟩ Sorgen machen. **fretful** ['fretfl] *adj.* verdrießlich; quengelig *(ugs.)*

**'fretsaw** *n.* Laubsäge, *die*

**Fri.** *abbr.* Friday Fr.

**friar** ['fraɪə(r)] *n.* Ordensbruder, *der*

**friction** ['frɪkʃn] *n.* Reibung, *die*

**Friday** ['fraɪdeɪ, 'fraɪdɪ] *n.* Freitag, *der*; **on ~:** [am] Freitag; **on a ~,** **on ~s** freitags; **~ 13 August** Freitag, der 13. August; *(at top of letter etc.)* Freitag, den 13. August; **next/last ~:** [am] nächsten/letzten Freitag; **Good ~:** Karfreitag, *der*

**fridge** [frɪdʒ] *n. (Brit. coll.)* Kühlschrank, *der*

**fried** *see* **¹fry**

**friend** [frend] *n.* **a)** Freund, *der*/ Freundin, *die*; **be ~s with sb.** mit jmdm. befreundet sein; **make ~s** [with

sb.] [mit jmdm.] Freundschaft schließen. **friendliness** ['frendlɪnɪs] *n.* Freundlichkeit, *die*. **'friendly 1.** *adj.* freundlich (**to** zu); freundschaftlich ⟨Rat, Beziehungen, Wettkampf⟩. **2.** *n. (Sport)* Freundschaftsspiel, *das*. **'friendship** *n.* Freundschaft, *die*

**frigate** ['frɪgət] *n. (Naut.)* Fregatte, *die*

**fright** [fraɪt] *n.* Schreck, *der*; **take ~:** erschrecken. **frighten** ['fraɪtn] *v.t.* ⟨Explosion, Schuß:⟩ erschrecken; ⟨Gedanke, Drohung:⟩ angst machen (+ *Dat.*); **be ~ed at** or **by sth.** vor etw. *(Dat.)* erschrecken. **'frightful** *adj.*, **'frightfully** *adv.* furchtbar

**frigid** ['frɪdʒɪd] *adj.* frostig; *(sexually)* frigid[e]

**frill** [frɪl] *n.* **a)** Rüsche, *die*; **b)** *in pl. (embellishments)* Beiwerk, *das*. **'frilly** *adj.* mit Rüschen besetzt; Rüschen- ⟨kleid, -bluse⟩

**fringe** [frɪndʒ] *n.* **a)** Fransenkante, *die* (**on an** + *Dat.*); **b)** *(hair)* [Pony]fransen *(ugs.)*; **c)** *(edge)* Rand, *der*

**frisk** [frɪsk] **1.** *v.i.* **~** [about] [herum]springen. **2.** *v.t. (coll.)* filzen *(ugs.)*. **'frisky** *adj.* munter

**¹fritter** ['frɪtə(r)] *n.* **apple** *etc.* **~s** Apfelstücke *usw.* in Pfannkuchenteig

**²fritter** *v.t.* **~ away** vergeuden

**frivolity** [frɪ'vɒlɪtɪ] *n.* Oberflächlichkeit, *die*

**frivolous** ['frɪvələs] *adj.* **a)** frivol; **b)** *(trifling)* belanglos

**frizzy** ['frɪzɪ] *adj.* kraus

**fro** [frəʊ] *adv.* see **to 2**

**frock** [frɒk] *n.* Kleid, *das*

**frog** [frɒg] *n.* Frosch, *der*. **frogman** ['frɒgmən] *n., pl.* **~men** ['frɒgmən] Froschmann, *der*. **'frog-spawn** *n.* Froschlaich, *der*

**frolic** ['frɒlɪk] *v.i.*, **-ck-: ~** [about or around] [herum]springen

**from** [frəm, *stressed* frɒm] *prep.* von; (**~ within; expr. origin**) aus; **~ Paris** aus Paris; **~ Paris to Munich** von Paris nach München; **be a mile ~ sth.** eine Meile von etw. entfernt sein; **where do you come ~?** **where are you ~?** woher kommen Sie?; **painted ~ life** nach dem Leben gemalt; **weak ~ hunger** schwach vor Hunger; **~ the year 1972** seit 1972; **~ [the age of] 18** ab 18 Jahre; **~ 4 to 6 eggs** 4 bis 6 Eier

**front** [frʌnt] **1.** *n.* **a)** Vorderseite, *die*; *(of house)* Vorderfront, *die*; **in** or **at the ~** [of sth.] vorn [in etw. *position: Dat., movement: Akk.*]; **to the ~:** nach vorn; **in ~:** vorn[e]; **be in ~ of sth./sb.**

vor etw./jmdm. sein; **b)** *(Mil.)* Front, *die;* **c)** *(at seaside)* Strandpromenade, *die;* **d)** *(Metereol.)* Front, *die;* **e)** *(bluff)* Fassade, *die.* **2.** *adj.* vorder...; Vorder- ⟨*rad, -zimmer, -zahn*⟩; ~ **garden** Vorgarten, *der;* ~ **row** erste Reihe.

**frontal** ['frʌntl] *adj.* Frontal-. **front 'door** *n.* *(of flat)* Wohnungstür, *die;* *(of house)* Haustür, *die*

**frontier** ['frʌntɪə(r)] *n.* Grenze, *die*

**front 'page** *n.* Titelseite, *die*

**frost** [frɒst] **1.** *n.* Frost, *der;* **ten degrees of** ~ *(Brit.)* zehn Grad minus. **2.** *v. t.* **~ed glass** Mattglas, *das.* '**frostbite** *n.* Erfrierung, *die.* '**frosting** *n.* *(esp. Amer.)* Glasur, *die.* '**frosty** *adj.* frostig

**froth** [frɒθ] **1.** *n.* Schaum, *der.* **2.** *v. i.* schäumen. '**frothy** *adj.* schaumig

**frown** [fraʊn] **1.** *v. i.* die Stirn runzeln **(lup|on** über + *Akk.*). **2.** *n.* Stirnrunzeln, *das*

**froze** *see* **freeze**

**frozen** ['frəʊzn] **1.** *see* **freeze. 2.** *adj.* **a)** zugefroren ⟨*Fluß, See*⟩; eingefroren ⟨*Wasserleitung*⟩; **I'm** ~ *(fig.)* ich bin eiskalt; **b)** *(to preserve)* tiefgekühlt; ~ **food** Tiefkühlkost, *die*

**frugal** ['fru:gl] *adj.* genügsam ⟨*Lebensweise, Mensch*⟩; frugal ⟨*Mahl*⟩

**fruit** [fru:t] *n.* Frucht, *die; collect.* Obst, *das*

**fruitful** ['fru:tfl] *adj.* fruchtbar

'**fruit juice** *n.* Obstsaft, *der*

'**fruitless** *adj.* nutzlos ⟨*Versuch, Gespräch*⟩; fruchtlos ⟨*Verhandlung, Suche*⟩

**fruit:** ~ **machine** *n.* *(Brit.)* Spielautomat, *der;* ~ '**salad** *n.* Obstsalat, *der*

'**fruity** *adj.* fruchtig ⟨*Geschmack, Wein*⟩

**frustrate** [frʌ'streɪt] *v. t.* vereiteln ⟨*Plan, Versuch*⟩; zunichte machen ⟨*Hoffnung, Bemühungen*⟩. '**frustrated** *adj.* frustriert. **frustration** [frʌ'streɪʃn] *n.* Frustration, *die*

¹**fry** [fraɪ] *v. t. & i.* braten; **fried egg** Spiegelei, *das*

²**fry** *n. (fishes)* Brut, *die;* **small** ~ *(fig.)* unbedeutende Leute

'**frying-pan** *n.* Bratpfanne, *die*

**ft.** *abbr.* **feet, foot** ft.

**fuck** [fʌk] *(coarse)* **1.** *v. t. & i.* ficken *(vulg.).* **2.** *n.* Fick, *der (vulg.)*

**fuddy-duddy** ['fʌdɪdʌdɪ] *(sl.)* **1.** *adj.* verkalkt *(ugs.).* **2.** *n.* Fossil, *das (fig.)*

**fudge** [fʌdʒ] *n.* Karamelbonbon, *der od. das*

**fuel** ['fju:əl] *n.* Brennstoff, *der; (for*

*vehicle)* Kraftstoff, *der; (for ship, aircraft)* Treibstoff, *der*

**fugitive** ['fju:dʒɪtɪv] *n.* Flüchtige, *der/die*

**fugue** [fju:g] *n. (Mus.)* Fuge, *die*

**fulfil** *(Amer.:* **fulfill)** [fʊl'fɪl] *v. t.,* **-ll-** erfüllen; halten ⟨*Versprechen*⟩. **ful'filment** *(Amer.:* **ful'fillment)** *n.* Erfüllung, *die*

**full** [fʊl] **1.** *adj.* **a)** voll; satt ⟨*Person*⟩; ~ **of** voller; **be** ~ **up** *(coll.)* voll [besetzt] sein; ⟨*Behälter:*⟩ randvoll sein; ⟨*Flug:*⟩ völlig ausgebucht sein; **I'm** ~ **[up]** *(coll.)* ich bin voll [bis obenhin] *(ugs.);* **be** ~ **of oneself** sehr von sich eingenommen sein; **b)** ausführlich ⟨*Bericht, Beschreibung*⟩; erfüllt ⟨*Leben*⟩; ganz ⟨*Stunde, Jahr, Monat, Seite*⟩; voll ⟨*Name, Bezahlung, Verständnis*⟩; ~ **details** alle Einzelheiten; **at** ~ **speed** mit Höchstgeschwindigkeit; **c)** voll ⟨*Gesicht*⟩; füllig ⟨*Figur*⟩; weit ⟨*Rock*⟩. **2.** *n.* **in** ~: vollständig. **3.** *adv. (exactly)* genau

**full:** ~ **back** *n.* Verteidiger, *der/*Verteidigerin, *die;* ~**-length** *adj.* lang ⟨*Kleid*⟩; ~ '**moon** *n.* Vollmond, *der;* ~**-scale** *adj.* **a)** in Originalgröße; **b)** großangelegt ⟨*Untersuchung, Suchaktion*⟩; ~ '**stop** *n.* Punkt, *der;* ~**-time** *adj.* ganztägig; ganztags⟨*arbeit*⟩

**fully** ['fʊlɪ] *adv.* voll [und ganz]; reich ⟨*belohnt*⟩; ausführlich ⟨*erklären*⟩

**fulsome** ['fʊlsəm] *adj.* übertrieben

**fumble** ['fʌmbl] *v. i.* ~ **at** *or* **with** [herum]fingern an (+ *Dat.*); ~ **in one's pockets for sth.** in seinen Taschen nach etw. kramen *(ugs.)*

**fume** [fju:m] **1.** *n. in pl.* ~s Dämpfe. **2.** *v. i.* vor Wut schäumen

**fumigate** ['fju:mɪgeɪt] *v. t.* ausräuchern

**fun** [fʌn] *n.* Spaß, *der;* **have** ~! viel Spaß!; **make** ~ **of sb.** sich über jmdn. lustig machen; **for** ~, **for the** ~ **of it** zum Spaß

**function** ['fʌŋkʃn] **1.** *n.* Aufgabe, *die,* Funktion, *die; (formal event)* Veranstaltung, *die.* **2.** *v. i.* ⟨*Maschine, System:*⟩ funktionieren; ~ **as** fungieren als; *(serve as)* dienen als. **functional** ['fʌŋkʃənl] *adj.* **a)** *(useful)* funktionell; **b)** *(working)* funktionsfähig

**fund** [fʌnd] **1.** *n.* **a)** *(money)* Fonds, *der;* **b)** *(fig.: stock)* Fundus, *der (od. von,* an + *Dat.*). **2.** *v. t.* finanzieren

**fundamental** [fʌndə'mentl] *adj.* grundlegend **(to** für); elementar ⟨*Bedürfnisse*⟩. **fundamentally** [fʌndə-

'mentəlı] *adv.* grundlegend; von Grund auf ⟨*verschieden, ehrlich*⟩

**funeral** ['fjuːnərl] *n.* Beerdigung, *die.* ~ **director** Bestattungsunternehmer, *der;* ~ **service** Trauerfeier, *die*

'**fun-fair** *n. (Brit.)* Jahrmarkt, *der*

**fungus** ['fʌŋgəs] *n., pl.* **fungi** ['fʌŋgaɪ, 'fʌndʒaɪ] *or* ~**es** Pilz, *der*

**funicular** [fjuː'nɪkjʊlə(r)] *adj. & n.* ~ |**railway**| [Stand]seilbahn, *die*

**funnel** ['fʌnl] *n.* Trichter, *der; (of ship etc.)* Schornstein, *der*

**funnily** ['fʌnɪlı] *adv.* komisch; ~ **enough** komischerweise

**funny** ['fʌnı] *adj.* **a)** komisch; lustig; witzig ⟨*Mensch, Einfall*⟩; **b)** *(strange)* komisch. '**funny-bone** *n.* Musikantenknochen, *der*

**fur** [fɜː(r)] *n.* **a)** Fell, *das; (garment)* Pelz, *der;* ~ **coat** Pelzmantel, *der;* **b)** *(in kettle)* Kesselstein, *der*

**furious** ['fjʊərɪəs] *adj.* wütend; heftig ⟨*Streit*⟩; wild ⟨*Tanz, Tempo, Kampf*⟩; **be** ~ **with sb.** wütend auf jmdn. sein. '**furiously** *adv.* wütend; wild ⟨*kämpfen*⟩: **wie wild** *(ugs.)* arbeiten

**furl** [fɜːl] *v. t.* einrollen ⟨*Segel, Flagge*⟩

**furnace** ['fɜːnıs] *n.* Ofen, *der*

**furnish** ['fɜːnıʃ] *v. t.* **a)** möblieren; **b)** *(supply)* liefern; ~ **sb. with sth.** jmdm. etw. liefern. '**furnishings** *n. pl.* Einrichtungsgegenstände

**furniture** ['fɜːnıtʃə(r)] *n.* Möbel *Pl.;* **piece of** ~: Möbel[stück], *das*

**furrow** ['fʌrəʊ] *n.* Furche, *die*

**furry** ['fɜːrı] *adj.* haarig; ~ **animal** *(toy)* Plüschtier, *das*

**further** ['fɜːðə(r)] **1.** *adj.* **a)** *(in space)* weiter entfernt; **b)** *(additional)* weiter... **2.** *adv.* weiter. **3.** *v. t.* fördern. **further'more** *adv.* außerdem. '**furthermost** *adj.* äußerst ...

**furthest** ['fɜːðıst] **1.** *adj.* am weitesten entfernt. **2.** *adv.* am weitesten ⟨*springen, laufen*⟩; am weitesten entfernt ⟨*sein, wohnen*⟩

**furtive** ['fɜːtıv] *adj.*, **furtively** *adv.* verstohlen

**fury** ['fjʊərı] *n.* Wut, *die; (of sea, battle)* Wüten, *das*

¹**fuse** [fjuːz] **1.** *v. t. (blend)* verschmelzen **(into zu).** **2.** *v. i.* ~ **together** miteinander verschmelzen

²**fuse** *n.* |time-|~: [Zeit]zünder, *der; (cord)* Zündschnur, *die*

³**fuse** *(Electr.)* **1.** *n.* Sicherung, *die.* **2.** *v. i.* **the lights have** ~**d** die Sicherung ist durchgebrannt. '**fuse box** *n.* Sicherungskasten, *der*

**fuselage** ['fjuːzəlɑːʒ] *n.* [Flugzeug]rumpf, *der*

**fusion** ['fjuːʒn] *n.* **a)** Verschmelzung, *die;* **b)** *(Phys.)* Fusion, *die*

**fuss** [fʌs] **1.** *n.* Theater, *das (ugs.);* **make a** ~ |**about sth.**| einen Wirbel |um etw.| machen. **2.** *v. i.* Wirbel machen; *(get agitated)* sich [unnötig] aufregen. '**fussy** *adj. (fastidious)* eigen; penibel; **I'm not** ~ *(I don't mind)* ich bin nicht wählerisch

**futile** ['fjuːtaıl] *adj.* vergeblich

**future** ['fjuːtʃə(r)] **1.** *adj.* [zu]künftig; **at some** ~ **date** zu einem späteren Zeitpunkt. **2.** *n.* **a)** Zukunft, *die;* **in** ~: in Zukunft; künftig; **b)** *(Ling.)* Futur, *das;* Zukunft, *die.* **futuristic** [fjuːtʃə'rıstık] *adj.* futuristisch

**fuze** [fjuːz] *see* ²**fuse**

**fuzzy** ['fʌzı] *adj.* **a)** *(frizzy)* kraus; **b)** *(blurred)* verschwommen

# G

**G, g** [dʒiː] *n.* G, g, *das*

**gab** [gæb] *n. (coll.)* **have the gift of the** ~: reden können

**gabble** ['gæbl] *v. i.* brabbeln *(ugs.)*

**gable** ['geıbl] *n.* Giebel, *der*

**gad** [gæd] *v. i.,* -dd- *(coll.)* ~ **about** herumziehen

**gadget** ['gædʒıt] *n.* Gerät, *das*

**Gaelic** ['geılık, 'gælık] **1.** *adj.* gälisch. **2.** *n.* Gälisch, *das*

**gaffe** [gæf] *n.* Fauxpas, *der*

**gag** [gæg] **1.** *n.* **a)** Knebel, *der;* **b)** *(joke)* Gag, *der.* **2.** *v. t.* -gg- knebeln

**gaiety** ['geıətı] *n.* Fröhlichkeit, *die*

**gaily** ['geılı] *adv.* fröhlich; in leuchtenden Farben ⟨*bemalt, geschmückt*⟩

**gain** [geın] **1.** *n.* **a)** Gewinn, *der;* **b)** *(increase)* Zunahme, *die* (**in** an + *Dat.*). **2.** *v. t.* **a)** gewinnen; finden ⟨*Zugang, Zutritt*⟩; erwerben ⟨*Wissen, Ruf*⟩; erlangen ⟨*Freiheit*⟩; erzielen ⟨*Vorteil, Punkte*⟩; verdienen ⟨*Lebensunterhalt, Geldsumme*⟩; ~ **weight/five pounds** |**in weight**| zunehmen/fünf Pfund zunehmen; ~ **speed** schneller werden; **b)** ⟨*Uhr:*⟩ vorgehen um. **3.** *v. i.* **a)** ~ **by**

**sth.** von etw. profitieren; **b)** ⟨*Uhr:*⟩ vorgehen

**gait** [geɪt] *n.* Gang, *der*

**gala** ['gɑ:lə, 'geɪlə] *n.* Festveranstaltung, *die; attrib.* Gala⟨*abend, -vorstellung*⟩; **swimming ~**: Schwimmfest, *das*

**galaxy** ['gæləksɪ] *n.* Galaxie, *die*

**gale** [geɪl] *n.* Sturm, *der*

**gall** [gɔ:l] *n. (sl.)* Unverschämtheit, *die*

**gallant** ['gælənt] *adj. (brave)* tapfer; *(chivalrous)* ritterlich. **gallantry** ['gæləntrɪ] *n. (bravery)* Tapferkeit, *die*

**'gall-bladder** *n.* Gallenblase, *die*

**gallery** ['gælərɪ] *n.* **a)** Galerie, *die;* **b)** *(Theatre)* dritter Rang

**galley** ['gælɪ] *n.* **a)** *(ship's kitchen)* Kombüse, *die;* **b)** *(Hist.)* Galeere, *die*

**gallivant** ['gælɪvænt] *v.i. (coll.)* herumziehen *(ugs.)*

**gallon** ['gælən] *n.* Gallone, *die*

**gallop** ['gæləp] **1.** *n.* Galopp, *der.* **2.** *v.i.* ⟨*Pferd, Reiter:*⟩ galoppieren

**gallows** ['gæləʊz] *n. sing.* Galgen, *der*

**galore** [gə'lɔ:(r)] *adv.* im Überfluß; in Hülle und Fülle

**galvanize** ['gælvənaɪz] *v.t.* wachrütteln; **~ sb. into action** jmdn. veranlassen, sofort aktiv zu werden

**gambit** ['gæmbɪt] *n.* Gambit, *das*

**gamble** ['gæmbl] *v.i.* **a)** [um Geld] spielen; **b)** *(fig.)* spekulieren; **~ on sth.** sich auf etw. *(Akk.)* verlassen. **gambler** ['gæmblə(r)] *n.* Glücksspieler, *der*

**'game** [geɪm] *n.* **a)** Spiel, *das; (of [table-]tennis, chess, cards, cricket)* Partie, *die;* **b)** *(fig.: scheme)* Vorhaben, *das;* **c)** *in pl. (athletic contests)* Spiele; *(in school) (sports)* Sport, *der; (athletics)* Leichtathletik, *die;* **d)** *(Hunting, Cookery)* Wild, *das*

**²game** *adj.* mutig; **be ~ to do sth.** bereit sein, etw. zu tun

**'gamekeeper** *n.* Wildheger, *der*

**gammon** ['gæmən] *n.* Räucherschinken, *der*

**gamut** ['gæmət] *n.* Skala, *die*

**gander** ['gændə(r)] *n.* Gänserich, *der*

**gang** [gæŋ] **1.** *n.* Bande, *die; (of workmen, prisoners)* Trupp, *der.* **2.** *v.i.* **~ up against** *or* **on** *(coll.)* sich verbünden gegen

**gangling** ['gæŋglɪŋ] schlaksig *(ugs.)*

**gangster** ['gæŋstə(r)] *n.* Gangster, *der*

**'gangway** *n.* Gangway, *die; (Brit.: between seats)* Gang, *der*

**gaol** [dʒeɪl] *see* **jail**

**gap** [gæp] *n.* **a)** Lücke, *die;* **b)** *(in time)* Pause, *die;* **c)** *(divergence)* Kluft, *die*

**gape** [geɪp] *v.i.* **a)** den Mund aufsperren; ⟨*Loch, Abgrund, Wunde:*⟩ klaffen; **b)** *(stare)* Mund und Nase aufsperren *(ugs.);* **~ at sb./sth.** jmdn./ etw. mit offenem Mund anstarren

**garage** ['gærɪdʒ] *n.* Garage, *die; (selling petrol)* Tankstelle, *die; (for repairing cars)* [Kfz-]Werkstatt, *die*

**garb** [gɑ:b] *n.* Tracht, *die*

**garbage** ['gɑ:bɪdʒ] *n.* **a)** Abfall, *der;* Müll, *der;* **b)** *(coll.: nonsense)* Quatsch, *der (salopp).* **'garbage can** *n. (Amer.)* Mülltonne, *die*

**garble** ['gɑ:bl] *v.t.* verstümmeln

**garden** ['gɑ:dn] *n.* Garten, *der.* **'garden centre** *n.* Gartencenter, *das.*

**gardener** ['gɑ:dnə(r)] *n.* Gärtner, *der*/Gärtnerin, *die.* **gardening** ['gɑ:dnɪŋ] *n.* Gartenarbeit, *die*

**gargle** ['gɑ:gl] *v.i.* gurgeln

**garish** ['geərɪʃ] *adj.* grell ⟨*Farbe, Licht*⟩; knallbunt ⟨*Kleidung*⟩

**garland** ['gɑ:lənd] *n.* Girlande, *die*

**garlic** ['gɑ:lɪk] *n.* Knoblauch, *der*

**garment** ['gɑ:mənt] *n.* Kleidungsstück, *das;* **~s** *pl. (clothes)* Kleidung, *die;* Kleider

**garnish** ['gɑ:nɪʃ] **1.** *v.t.* garnieren. **2.** *n.* Garnierung, *die*

**garret** ['gærɪt] *n.* Dachkammer, *die*

**garrison** ['gærɪsn] *n.* Garnison, *die*

**garter** ['gɑ:tə(r)] *n.* Strumpfband, *das*

**gas** [gæs] **1.** *n.* **a)** *pl.* **~es** ['gæsɪz] Gas, *das;* **b)** *(Amer. coll.: petrol)* Benzin, *das.* **2.** *v.t.,* **-ss-** mit Gas vergiften. **gas 'cooker** *n. (Brit.)* Gasherd, *der.* **gas 'fire** *n.* Gasofen, *der*

**gash** [gæʃ] **1.** *n.* Schnittwunde, *die.* **2.** *v.t.* aufritzen ⟨*Haut*⟩; **~ one's finger** sich *(Dat. od. Akk.)* in den Finger schneiden

**gas:** **~ mask** *n.* Gasmaske, *die;* **~ meter** *n.* Gaszähler, *der*

**gasoline (gasolene)** ['gæsəli:n] *n. (Amer.)* Benzin, *das*

**gasometer** [gæ'sɒmɪtə(r)] *n.* Gasometer, *der*

**gasp** [gɑ:sp] **1.** *v.i.* nach Luft schnappen (with vor); **he was ~ing for air** er rang nach Luft. **2.** *v.t.* **~ out** hervorstoßen. **3.** *n.* Keuchen, *das*

**'gas station** *n. (Amer.)* Tankstelle, *die*

**gastronomy** [gæ'strɒnəmɪ] *n.* Gastronomie, *die*

**'gasworks** *n. sing.* Gaswerk, *das*

**gate** [geɪt] *n.* Tor, *das; (barrier)* Sperre, *die; (to field etc.)* Gatter, *das; (of level crossing)* [Bahn]schranke, *die; (in airport)* Flugsteig, *der*

**gateau** ['gætəʊ] *n., pl.* ~s *or* ~x ['gæ-təʊz] Torte, *die*

**gate: ~crasher** ['geɪtkræʃə(r)] *n.* ungeladener Gast; **~way** *n.* Tor, *das*

**gather** ['gæðə(r)] **1.** *v.t.* **a)** sammeln; zusammentragen ⟨*Informationen*⟩; pflücken ⟨*Obst, Blumen*⟩; **b)** *(infer, deduce)* schließen **(from** aus); **c)** ~ **speed/force** schneller/stärker werden. **2.** *v.i.* sich versammeln; ⟨*Wolken:*⟩ sich zusammenziehen. **'gathering** *n.* Versammlung, *die*

**gaudy** ['gɔːdɪ] *adj.* protzig; grell ⟨*Farben*⟩

**gauge** [geɪdʒ] *n.* **1. a)** *(measure)* Maß, *das;* **b)** *(instrument)* Meßgerät, *das.* **2.** *v.t.* messen; *(fig.)* beurteilen

**gaunt** [gɔːnt] *adj.* hager

**gauntlet** ['gɔːntlɪt] *n.* Stulpenhandschuh, *der*

**gauze** [gɔːz] *n.* Gaze, *die*

**gave** *see* **give 1, 2**

**gay** [geɪ] **1.** *adj.* **a)** fröhlich; *(brightcoloured)* farbenfroh; **b)** *(coll.: homosexual)* schwul *(ugs.);* Schwulen⟨*lokal*⟩. **2.** *n. (coll.)* Schwule, *der (ugs.)*

**gaze** [geɪz] *v.i.* blicken; *(fixedly)* starren; ~ **at sb./sth.** jmdn./etw. anstarren

**GB** *abbr.* Great Britain GB

**GCSE** *abbr. (Brit.)* **General Certificate of Secondary Education**

**gear** [gɪə(r)] *n.* **1. a)** *(Motor Veh.)* Gang, *der;* **top/bottom** ~ *(Brit.)* der höchste/erste Gang; **change** *or* **shift** ~: schalten; **put the car into** ~: einen Gang einlegen; **out of** ~: im Leerlauf; **b)** *(coll.: clothes)* Aufmachung, *die;* **c)** *(equipment)* Gerät, *das;* Ausrüstung, *die.* **2.** *v.t.* ausrichten **(to** auf + *Akk.*). **'gearbox** *n.* Getriebekasten, *der.* **'gear-lever,** *(Amer.)* **'gear-shift** *ns.* Schalthebel, *der*

**geese** *pl. of* **goose**

**geezer** ['giːzə(r)] *(sl.: old man)* Opa, *der (ugs.)*

**gel** [dʒel] *n.* Gel, *das*

**gelatin** ['dʒelətɪn], *(Brit.)* **gelatine** ['dʒelətiːn] *n.* Gelatine, *die*

**gelignite** ['dʒelɪgnaɪt] *n.* Gelatinedynamit, *das*

**gem** [dʒem] *n.* Edelstein, *der*

**Gemini** ['dʒemɪnaɪ, 'dʒemɪnɪ] *n.* Zwillinge Pl.

**gender** ['dʒendə(r)] *n. (Ling.)* [grammatisches] Geschlecht

**gene** [dʒiːn] *n. (Biol.)* Gen, *das*

**general** ['dʒenrl] **1.** *adj.* allgemein; weitverbreitet ⟨*Ansicht*⟩; *(true of [nearly] all cases)* allgemeingültig; un-

gefähr ⟨*Vorstellung, Beschreibung usw.*⟩; **the** ~ **public** weite Kreise der Bevölkerung; **in** ~ **use** allgemein verbreitet; **as a** ~ **rule, in** ~: im allgemeinen. **2.** *n. (Mil.)* General, *der.*

**general e'lection** *see* **election**

**generalization** [dʒenrəlaɪ'zeɪʃn] *n.* Verallgemeinerung, *die*

**generalize** ['dʒenrəlaɪz] **1.** *v.t.* verallgemeinern. **2.** *v.i.* ~ **about sth.** [etw.] verallgemeinern

**generally** ['dʒenrəlɪ] *adv.* **a)** allgemein; ~ **available** überall erhältlich; ~ **speaking** im allgemeinen; **b)** *(usually)* im allgemeinen

**general prac'titioner** *n. (Med.)* Arzt/Ärztin für Allgemeinmedizin

**generate** ['dʒenəreɪt] *v.t.* erzeugen **(from** aus); *(result in)* führen zu.

**generation** [dʒenə'reɪʃn] *n.* **a)** Generation, *die;* **b)** *(production)* Erzeugung, *die.* **generator** ['dʒenəreɪtə(r)] *n.* Generator, *der*

**generosity** [dʒenə'rɒsɪtɪ] *n.* Großzügigkeit, *die*

**generous** ['dʒenərəs] *adj.* großzügig; reichlich ⟨*Vorrat, Portion*⟩. **'generously** *adv.* großzügig

**genetic** [dʒɪ'netɪk] *adj.* genetisch. **genetics** [dʒɪ'netɪks] *n.* Genetik, *die*

**Geneva** [dʒɪ'niːvə] **1.** *pr. n.* Genf *(das).* **2.** *attrib. adj.* Genfer

**genial** ['dʒiːnɪəl] *adj.* freundlich

**genitals** ['dʒenɪtlz] *n. pl.* Geschlechtsorgane

**genitive** ['dʒenɪtɪv] *adj. & n.* ~ |**case**| Genitiv, *der*

**genius** ['dʒiːnɪəs] *n.* **a)** *(person)* Genie, *das;* **b)** *(ability)* Talent, *das*

**genre** ['ʒɑ̃rə] *n.* Genre, *das*

**gent** [dʒent] *n.* **a)** *(coll./joc.)* Gent, *der (iron.);* **b)** **the G~s** *(Brit. coll.)* die Herrentoilette

**genteel** [dʒen'tiːl] *adj.* vornehm

**gentle** ['dʒentl] *adj.,* ~**r** ['dʒentlə(r)], ~**st** ['dʒentlɪst] sanft; liebenswürdig ⟨*Person, Verhalten*⟩; leicht, schwach ⟨*Brise*⟩; leise ⟨*Geräusch*⟩; gemächlich ⟨*Spaziergang, Tempo*⟩; mäßig ⟨*Hitze*⟩

**gentleman** ['dʒentlmən] *n., pl.* **gentlemen** ['dʒentlmən] Herr, *der;* *(well-mannered)* Gentleman, *der;* **Ladies and Gentlemen!** meine Damen und Herren!

**'gentleness** *n.* Sanftheit, *die; (of nature)* Sanftmütigkeit, *die*

**gently** ['dʒentlɪ] *adv. (tenderly)* zart; zärtlich; *(mildly)* sanft; *(carefully)* behutsam; *(quietly, softly)* leise

**genuine** ['dʒenjʊɪn] *adj.* **a)** *(real)* echt; **b)** *(true)* aufrichtig; wahr ⟨*Grund, Not*⟩. '**genuinely** *adv.* wirklich

**genus** ['dʒiːnəs, 'dʒenəs] *n., pl.* **genera** ['dʒenərə] *(Biol.)* Gattung, *die*

**geographical** [dʒiːə'græfɪkl] *adj.* geographisch

**geography** [dʒɪ'ɒgrəfɪ] *n.* Geographie, *die*; Erdkunde, *die (Schulw.)*

**geological** [dʒiːə'lɒdʒɪkl] *adj.* geologisch

**geologist** [dʒɪ'ɒlədʒɪst] *n.* Geologe, *der*/Geologin, *die*

**geology** [dʒɪ'ɒlədʒɪ] *n.* Geologie, *die*

**geometric** [dʒɪːə'metrɪk], **geometrical** [dʒɪːə'metrɪkl] *adj.* geometrisch

**geometry** [dʒɪ'ɒmɪtrɪ] *n.* Geometrie, *die*

**geranium** [dʒə'reɪnɪəm] *n.* Geranie, *die*; Pelargonie, *die*

**geriatric** [dʒerɪ'ætrɪk] *adj.* geriatrisch

**germ** [dʒɜːm] *n.* Keim, *der*

**German** ['dʒɜːmən] **1.** *adj.* deutsch; **he/she is** ∼: er ist Deutscher/sie ist Deutsche. **2.** *n.* **a)** *(person)* Deutsche, *der/die*; **b)** *(language)* Deutsch, *das*; *see also* **English 2 a**

**German Democratic Re'public** *pr. n. (Hist.)* Deutsche Demokratische Republik

**Germanic** [dʒɜː'mænɪk] *adj.* germanisch

**German 'measles** *n.* Röteln *Pl.*

**Germany** ['dʒɜːmənɪ] *pr. n.* Deutschland *(das)*; **Federal Republic of** ∼: Bundesrepublik Deutschland, *die*

**germinate** ['dʒɜːmɪneɪt] *v. i.* keimen

**gesticulate** [dʒe'stɪkjʊleɪt] *v. i.* gestikulieren. **gesticulation** [dʒestɪkjʊ-'leɪʃn] *n.* Gesten *Pl.*

**gesture** ['dʒestʃə(r)] *n.* Geste, *die*

**get** [get] **1.** *v. t.*, **-tt-**, **got** [gɒt], **got** *or (Amer.)* **gotten** ['gɒtn] **a)** *(obtain, receive)* bekommen; kriegen *(ugs.);* sich *(Dat.)* besorgen ⟨*Visum, Genehmigung*⟩; sich *(Dat.)* beschaffen ⟨*Geld*⟩; *(find)* finden ⟨*Zeit*⟩; *(fetch)* holen; *(buy)* kaufen; **where did you** ∼ **that?** wo hast du das her?; ∼ **sb. a job/taxi,** ∼ **a job/taxi for sb.** jmdm. einen Job verschaffen/ein Taxi besorgen; ∼ **oneself sth.** sich *(Dat.)* etw. zulegen; **b)** ∼ **the bus** *etc. (be in time for, catch)* den Bus *usw.* erreichen *od. (ugs.)* kriegen; *(travel by)* den Bus *usw.* nehmen; **c)** *(prepare)* machen *(ugs.),* zubereiten ⟨*Essen*⟩; **d)** *(win)* bekommen; finden ⟨*Anerkennung*⟩; erzielen ⟨*Tor, Punkt, Treffer*⟩; gewinnen ⟨*Spiel, Preis, Be-*

*lohnung*⟩; ∼ **permission** die Erlaubnis erhalten; **e)** finden ⟨*Schlaf, Ruhe*⟩; bekommen ⟨*Einfall, Vorstellung, Gefühl, Kopfschmerzen, Grippe*⟩; gewinnen ⟨*Eindruck*⟩; **f) have got** *(coll.: have)* haben; **have got a cold** eine Erkältung haben; **have got to do sth.** etw. tun müssen; **g)** *(succeed in placing, bringing, etc.)* bringen; kriegen *(ugs.);* ∼ **a message to sb.** jmdm. eine Nachricht zukommen lassen; ∼ **things going** *or* **started** die Dinge in Gang bringen; **h)** ∼ **everything packed/prepared** alles [ein]packen/vorbereiten; ∼ **sth. ready/done** etw. fertig machen; ∼ **one's feet wet** nasse Füße kriegen; ∼ **one's hands dirty** sich *(Dat.)* die Hände schmutzig machen; ∼ **one's hair cut** sich die Haare schneiden lassen; ∼ **sb. to do sth.** *(induce)* jmdn. dazu bringen, etw. zu tun; **i)** ∼ **sb. [on the telephone]** jmdn. [telefonisch] erreichen; **j)** *(coll.) (understand)* kapieren *(ugs.); (hear)* mitkriegen *(ugs.).* **2.** *v. i.,* **-tt-**, **got** *or (Amer.)* **gotten a)** *(succeed in coming or going)* kommen; ∼ **to London before dark** London vor Einbruch der Dunkelheit erreichen; **b)** *(come to be)* ∼ **working** sich an die Arbeit machen; ∼ **going** *or* **started** *(leave)* losgehen; *(become lively or operative)* in Schwung kommen; ∼ **going on** *or* **with sth.** mit etw. anfangen; **c)** ∼ **to know sb.** jmdn. kennenlernen; **d)** *(become)* werden; ∼ **ready/washed** sich fertigmachen/waschen; ∼ **frightened/hungry** Angst/Hunger kriegen. **get a'bout** *v. i.* **a)** *(travel)* herumkommen; **b)** ⟨*Gerücht:*⟩ sich verbreiten. '**get at** *v. t.* **a)** herankommen an (+ *Akk.*); **b)** *(find out)* [he]rausfinden ⟨*Wahrheit usw.*⟩; **what are you getting at?** worauf wollen Sie hinaus? **get a'way** *v. i.* **a)** *(leave)* wegkommen; **b)** *(escape)* entkommen. **get 'back 1.** *v. i.* zurückkommen; ∼ **back home** nach Hause kommen. **2.** *v. t. (recover)* zurückbekommen; ∼ **one's own back** *(sl.)* sich rächen. **get 'by** *v. i.* **a)** vorbeikommen; **b)** *(coll.: manage)* über die Runden kommen *(ugs.).* **get 'down 1.** *v. i.* hinunter-/heruntersteigen; ∼ **down to sth.** *(start)* sich an etw. *(Akk.)* machen. **2.** *v. t.* **a)** ∼ **sb./sth. down** jmdn./etw. hinunter-/herunterbringen; **b)** *(coll.: depress)* fertigmachen *(ugs.).* **get 'in 1.** *v. i. (into bus etc.)* einsteigen; *(arrive)* ankommen. **2.** *v. t. (fetch)* reinholen. **get 'off 1.** *v. i.* **a)** *(alight)* aussteigen; *(dismount)* absteigen; **b)** *(leave)* [weg]gehen; **c)** *(escape punishment)* davonkommen. **2.** *v. t.* **a)** *(remove)* ausziehen ⟨*Kleidung usw.*⟩; entfernen ⟨*Fleck usw.*⟩; abbekommen ⟨*Deckel usw.*⟩; **b)** aussteigen aus; absteigen von ⟨*Fahrrad*⟩; **c)** ~ **off the subject** vom Thema abkommen. **get 'on** *v. i.* **a)** *(mount)* aufsteigen; *(enter vehicle)* einsteigen; **b)** *(make progress)* vorankommen; **he's** ~**ting on well** es geht ihm gut; **c)** *(manage)* zurechtkommen. **get 'on with** *v. t.* **a)** weitermachen mit; **b)** ~ **on [well] with sb.** mit jmdm. [gut] auskommen. **get 'out** **1.** *v. i.* **a)** rausgehen/rausfahren *(of aus)*; **b)** *(alight)* aussteigen; **c)** *(escape)* ausbrechen *(of aus)*; *(fig.)* herauskommen; ~ **out of** *(avoid)* herumkommen um *(ugs.)*. **2.** *v. t.* **a)** *(cause to leave)* rausbringen; **b)** *(withdraw)* abheben ⟨*Geld*⟩ *(of von)*. **get 'over** *v. t.* **a)** *(cross)* gehen über (+ *Akk.*); *(climb)* klettern über (+ *Akk.*); **b)** *(recover from)* überwinden; hinwegkommen über (+ *Akk.*). **get 'round** *v. i.* ~ **round to doing sth.** dazu kommen, etw. zu tun. **get 'through** *v. i.* durchkommen. **get 'up** *v. i.* aufstehen. **get 'up to** *v. t.* ~ **up to mischief** etwas anstellen

**get:** ~**away** *n.* Flucht, *die; attrib.* Flucht⟨*plan, -wagen*⟩ **make one's** ~**-away** entkommen; ~**-up** *n. (coll.)* Aufmachung, *die*

**geyser** ['gi:zə(r)] *n.* **a)** *(spring)* Geysir, *der;* **b)** *(Brit.)* Durchlauferhitzer, *der*

**ghastly** ['gɑ:stlɪ] *adj.* grauenvoll; entsetzlich ⟨*Verletzungen*⟩; schrecklich ⟨*Fehler*⟩

**gherkin** ['gɜ:kɪn] *n.* Essiggurke, *die*

**ghetto** ['getəʊ] *n., pl.* ~**s** Getto, *das*

**ghost** [gəʊst] *n.* Geist, *der;* Gespenst, *das.* **'ghostly** *adj.* gespenstisch

**giant** ['dʒaɪənt] **1.** *n.* Riese, *der.* **2.** *attrib. adj.* riesig

**gibberish** ['dʒɪbərɪʃ] *n.* Kauderwelsch, *das*

**gibe** [dʒaɪb] *n.* Stichelei, *die*

**giblets** ['dʒɪblɪts] *n. pl.* [Geflügel]klein, *das*

**giddiness** ['gɪdɪnɪs] *n.* Schwindel, *der*

**giddy** ['gɪdɪ] *adj.* schwind[e]lig

**gift** [gɪft] *n.* **a)** Geschenk, *das;* **make sb. a** ~ **of sth., make a** ~ **of sth. to sb.** jmdm. etw. schenken; **a** ~ **box/pack** eine Geschenkpackung; **b)** *(talent)* Begabung, *die;* **have a** ~ **for languages/ mathematics** sprachbegabt/mathema-

tisch begabt sein. **'gifted** *adj.* begabt **(in, at** für). **'gift-wrap** *v. t.* als Geschenk einpacken

**gigantic** [dʒaɪ'gæntɪk] *adj.* gigantisch; riesig; enorm ⟨*Verbesserung, Appetit*⟩

**giggle** ['gɪgl] **1.** *n.* Kichern, *das.* **2.** *v. i.* kichern

**gild** [gɪld] *v. t.* vergolden

**gill** [gɪl] *n.* Kieme, *die*

**gilt** [gɪlt] **1.** *n.* Goldauflage, *die; (paint)* Goldfarbe, *die.* **2.** *adj.* vergoldet

**gimmick** ['gɪmɪk] *n. (coll.)* Gag, *der*

**gin** [dʒɪn] *n.* Gin, *der*

**ginger** ['dʒɪndʒə(r)] *n.* **a)** Ingwer, *der;* **b)** *(colour)* Rötlichgelb, *das.* **ginger 'beer** *n.* Ingwerbier, *das.* **'gingerbread** *n.* Pfefferkuchen, *der*

**gingerly** ['dʒɪndʒəlɪ] *adv.* vorsichtig

**gipsy** *see* gypsy

**giraffe** [dʒɪ'rɑ:f] *n.* Giraffe, *die*

**girder** ['gɜ:də(r)] *n.* Träger, *der*

**girdle** ['gɜ:dl] *n.* Hüfthalter, *der*

**girl** [gɜ:l] *n.* Mädchen, *das; (teenager)* junges Mädchen. **'girl-friend** *n.* Freundin, *die.* **'girlish** *adj.* mädchenhaft

**giro** ['dʒaɪərəʊ] *n.* **a)** Giro, *das; attrib.* Giro-; **bank** ~: Giroverkehr, *der;* **b)** *(coll.: cheque)* Scheck, *der*

**girth** [gɜ:θ] *n.* **a)** Umfang, *der;* **b)** *(for horse)* Bauchgurt, *der*

**gismo** ['gɪzməʊ] *n. (sl.)* Ding, *das (ugs.)*

**gist** [dʒɪst] *n.* Wesentliche, *das; (of tale, question, etc.)* Kern, *der*

**give** [gɪv] **1.** *v. t.,* **gave** [geɪv], **given** ['gɪvn] **a)** geben **(to** *Dat.*); **b)** *(as gift)* schenken; ~ **sb. sth.,** ~ **sth. to sb.** jmdm. etw. schenken; ~ **and take** *(fig.)* Kompromisse eingehen; **c)** *(assign)* aufgeben ⟨*Hausaufgaben usw.*⟩; *(grant, award, offer, allow to have)* geben; verleihen ⟨*Preis, Titel usw.*⟩; lassen ⟨*Wahl, Zeit*⟩; verleihen ⟨*Gewicht, Nachdruck*⟩; bereiten, machen ⟨*Freude, Mühe, Kummer*⟩; bieten ⟨*Schutz*⟩; leisten ⟨*Hilfe*⟩; gewähren ⟨*Unterstützung*⟩; **be** ~**n sth.** etw. bekommen; ~**n that** *(because)* da; *(if)* wenn; ~ **sb. hope** jmdm. Hoffnung machen; **d)** *(tell)* angeben ⟨*Namen, Anschrift, Alter, Grund*⟩; nennen ⟨*Einzelheiten*⟩; geben ⟨*Rat, Befehl, Anweisung, Antwort*⟩; fällen ⟨*Urteil, Entscheidung*⟩; sagen ⟨*Meinung*⟩; bekanntgeben ⟨*Nachricht*⟩; ~ **him my best wishes** richte ihm meine besten Wünsche aus; **e)** *(perform, sing, etc.)* geben ⟨*Vorstellung, Konzert*⟩; halten

⟨*Vortrag, Seminar*⟩; **f)** *(produce)* geben ⟨*Licht, Milch*⟩; ergeben ⟨*Zahlen, Resultat*⟩; **g)** *(make, show)* geben ⟨*Zeichen, Stoß, Tritt*⟩; machen ⟨*Satz, Ruck*⟩; ausstoßen ⟨*Schrei, Seufzer, Pfiff*⟩; ~ **sb. a [friendly] look** jmdm. einen [freundlichen] Blick zuwerfen; **h)** *(inflict)* versetzen ⟨*Schlag, Stoß*⟩; **sth. ~s me a headache** von etw. bekomme ich Kopfschmerzen; **i)** geben ⟨*Party, Essen usw.*⟩. **2.** *v. i.,* **gave, given** *(yield)* nachgeben; ⟨*Knie:*⟩ weich werden; ⟨*Bett:*⟩ federn. **3.** *n.* Nachgiebigkeit, *die; (elasticity)* Elastizität, *die.* **give a'way** *v. t.* **a)** verschenken; **b)** *(in marriage)* dem Bräutigam zuführen; **c)** *(betray)* verraten. **give 'back** *v. t.* zurückgeben. **give in 1.** ['--] *v. t.* abgeben. **2.** [-'-] *v. i.* nachgeben **(to** *Dat.*). **give 'off** *v. t.* ausströmen ⟨*Geruch*⟩; aussenden ⟨*Strahlen*⟩. **give 'up 1.** *v. i.* aufgeben. **2.** *v. t.* aufgeben; widmen ⟨*Zeit*⟩; ~ **sth. up** *(abandon habit)* sich *(Dat.)* etw. abgewöhnen; ~ **oneself up** sich stellen. **give 'way** *v. i.* **a)** *(yield)* nachgeben; **b)** *(in traffic)* ~ **way [to traffic from the right]** [dem Rechtsverkehr] die Vorfahrt lassen; **'G~ Way'** „Vorfahrt beachten"; **c)** *(collapse)* einstürzen

**given** *see* **give 1, 2**

**gizmo** *see* **gismo**

**glacier** ['glæsɪə(r)] *n.* Gletscher, *der*

**glad** [glæd] *adj.* froh; **be ~ of sth.** über etw. *(Akk.)* froh sein; **für etw. dankbar sein. gladden** ['glædn] *v. t.* erfreuen

**glade** [gleɪd] *n.* Lichtung, *die*

**'gladly** *adv.* gern

**glamor** *(Amer.) see* **glamour**

**glamorous** ['glæmərəs] *adj.* glanzvoll; glamourös ⟨*Filmstar*⟩

**glamour** ['glæmə(r)] *n.* Glanz, *der; (of person)* Ausstrahlung, *die*

**glance** [glɑ:ns] **1.** *n.* Blick, *der.* **2.** *v. i.* blicken; ~ **at sb./sth.** jmdn./etw. anblicken; ~ **at one's watch** auf seine Uhr blicken; ~ **at the newspaper** *etc.* einen Blick in die Zeitung *usw.* werfen; ~ **round [the room]** sich [im Zimmer] umsehen

**gland** [glænd] *n.* Drüse, *die.* **glandular** ['glændjʊlə(r)] *adj.* Drüsen-

**glare** [gleə(r)] **1.** *n.* **a)** grelles Licht; **b)** *(hostile look)* feindseliger Blick; **with a ~:** feindselig. **2.** *v. i. (glower)* [finster] starren; ~ **at sb./sth.** jmdn./etw. anstarren. **glaring** ['gleərɪŋ] *adj.* grell; *(fig.: conspicuous)* schreiend; grob ⟨*Fehler*⟩; kraß ⟨*Gegensatz*⟩

**glass** [glɑ:s] *n.* **a)** *(substance)* Glas, *das; pieces of/broken ~:* Glasscherben *Pl.; (smaller)* Glassplitter *Pl.;* **b)** *(drinking ~)* Glas, *das;* **a ~ of milk** ein Glas Milch; **c)** *(pane)* [Glas]scheibe, *die;* **d)** in *pl. (spectacles)* [a pair of] ~es eine Brille. **'glassy** *adj.* gläsern

**glaze** [gleɪz] **1.** *n.* Glasur, *die.* **2.** *v. t.* **a)** glasieren; **b)** *(fit with glass)* verglasen. **glazier** ['gleɪzɪə(r)] *n.* Glaser, *der*

**gleam** [gli:m] **1.** *n.* Schein, *der; (fainter)* Schimmer, *der;* ~ **of hope** Hoffnungsschimmer, *der.* **2.** *v. i.* ⟨*Licht:*⟩ scheinen; ⟨*Fußboden, Stiefel:*⟩ glänzen; ⟨*Zähne:*⟩ blitzen; ⟨*Augen:*⟩ leuchten. **'gleaming** *adj.* glänzend

**glean** [gli:n] *v. t.* zusammentragen ⟨*Informationen usw.*⟩; ~ **sth. from sth.** einer Sache *(Dat.)* etw. entnehmen

**glee** [gli:] *n.* Freude, *die; (gloating joy)* Schadenfreude, *die.* **gleeful** ['gli:fl] *adj.* freudig; *(gloating)* schadenfroh

**glen** [glen] *n.* [schmales] Tal

**glib** [glɪb] *adj.* aalglatt ⟨*Person*⟩; leicht dahingesagt ⟨*Antwort*⟩

**glide** [glaɪd] *v. i.* gleiten; *(through the air)* schweben. **'glider** *n.* Segelflugzeug, *das*

**glimmer** ['glɪmə(r)] **1.** *n.* Schimmer, *der* (**of** von); *(of fire)* Glimmen, *das.* **2.** *v. i.* glimmen

**glimpse** [glɪmps] **1.** *n.* [kurzer] Blick; **catch** *or* **have** *or* **get a ~ of sb./sth.** jmdn./etw. [kurz] zu sehen bekommen. **2.** *v. t.* flüchtig sehen

**glint** [glɪnt] **1.** *n.* Schimmer, *der.* **2.** *v. i.* blinken; glitzern

**glisten** ['glɪsn] *v. i.* glitzern

**glitter** ['glɪtə(r)] **1.** *v. i.* glitzern; ⟨*Juwelen, Sterne:*⟩ funkeln. **2.** *n.* Glitzern, *das; (of diamonds)* Funkeln, *das*

**gloat** [gləʊt] *v. i.* ~ **over sth.** sich hämisch über etw. *(Akk.)* freuen

**global** ['gləʊbl] *adj.* weltweit; ~ **warming** globaler Temperaturanstieg

**globe** [gləʊb] *n.* **a)** Kugel, *die;* **b)** Globus, *der;* **c)** *(world)* **the ~:** der Globus; der Erdball

**gloom** [glu:m] *n.* **a)** *(darkness)* Dunkel, *das (geh.);* **b)** *(despondency)* düstere Stimmung. **'gloomy** *adj.* **a)** düster; finster; **b)** *(depressing)* düster; *(depressed)* trübsinnig ⟨*Person*⟩

**glorify** ['glɔ:rɪfaɪ] *v. t.* verherrlichen; **a glorified messenger-boy** ein besserer Botenjunge

**glorious** ['glɔ:rɪəs] *adj.* **a)** *(illustrious)* ruhmreich ⟨*Held, Sieg*⟩; **b)** *(delightful)* wunderschön; herrlich

**glory** ['glɔ:rɪ] **1.** *n.* **a)** *(splendour)* Schönheit, *die; (majesty)* Herrlichkeit, *die;* **b)** *(fame)* Ruhm, *der.* **2.** *v.i.* ~ **in sth.** *(be proud of)* sich einer Sache *(Gen.)* rühmen

**gloss** [glɒs] *n.* Glanz, *der;* ~ **paint** Lackfarbe, *die.* '**gloss over** *v.t.* bemänteln; beschönigen ⟨*Fehler*⟩

**glossary** ['glɒsərɪ] *n.* Glossar, *das*

**glossy** *adj.* glänzend

**glove** [glʌv] *n.* Handschuh, *der.* '**glove compartment** *n.* Handschuhfach, *das*

**glow** [gləʊ] *v.i.* **a)** glühen; ⟨*Lampe, Leuchtfarbe:*⟩ schimmern, leuchten; **b)** *(fig.) (with warmth or pride)* ⟨*Gesicht, Wangen:*⟩ glühen (**with** vor + *Dat.*); *(with health or vigour)* strotzen (**with** vor + *Dat.*)

**glower** ['glaʊə(r)] *v.i.* finster dreinblicken; ~ **at sb.** jmdn. finster anstarren

'**glowing** *adj.* glühend; begeistert ⟨*Bericht*⟩

'**glow-worm** *n.* Glühwürmchen, *das*

**glucose** ['glu:kəʊz] *n.* Glucose, *die*

**glue** [glu:] **1.** *n.* Klebstoff, *der.* **2.** *v.t.* kleben; ~ **sth. to sth.** etw. an etw. *(Dat.)* an- *od.* festkleben

**glum** [glʌm] *adj.* verdrießlich

**glut** [glʌt] *n.* Überangebot, *das* (**of** an, von + *Dat.*)

**glutton** ['glʌtən] *n.* Vielfraß, *der (ugs.);* **a** ~ **for punishment** *(iron.)* ein Masochist *(fig.).* **gluttony** ['glʌtənɪ] *n.* Gefräßigkeit, *die*

**glycerine** ['glɪsəri:n] *(Amer.:* **glycerin** ['glɪsərɪn]) *n.* Glyzerin, *das*

**GMT** *abbr.* **Greenwich Mean Time** GMT; WEZ

**gnarled** [nɑːld] *adj.* knorrig; knotig ⟨*Hand*⟩

**gnash** [næʃ] *v.t.* ~ **one's teeth** mit den Zähnen knirschen

**gnat** [næt] *n.* [Stech]mücke, *die*

**gnaw** [nɔː] **1.** *v.i.* ~ **[away] at sth.** an etw. *(Dat.)* nagen. **2.** *v.t.* nagen an (+ *Dat.*); abnagen ⟨*Knochen*⟩

**gnome** [nəʊm] *n.* Gnom, *der*

**go** [gəʊ] **1.** *v.i., pres.* he goes [gəʊz], *p.t.* went [went], *pres. p.* going ['gəʊɪŋ], *p.p.* gone [gɒn] **a)** *(Fahrzeug:*⟩ fahren; ⟨*Flugzeug:*⟩ fliegen; ⟨*Vierfüßer:*⟩ laufen; *(on horseback etc.)* reiten; *(in lift)* fahren; *(on outward journey)* weg-, abfahren; *(travel regularly)* ⟨*Verkehrsmittel:*⟩ verkehren (**from** ... **to** zwischen + *Dat.* ... und); **go by bicycle/car/bus/train** *or* **rail/boat** *or* **sea**

*or* **ship** mit dem [Fahr]rad/Auto/Bus/Zug/Schiff fahren; **go by plane** *or* **air** fliegen; **go on foot** zu Fuß gehen; laufen *(ugs.);* **go on a journey** verreisen; **have far to go** es weit haben; **go to the toilet/cinema/a museum** auf die Toilette/ins Kino/ins Museum gehen; **go to the doctor['s]** *etc.* zum Arzt *usw.* gehen; **go bathing** baden gehen; **go cycling** radfahren; **go to see sb.** jmdn. aufsuchen; **go and see whether** ...: nachsehen [gehen], ob ...; **I'll go!** ich geh schon!; *(answer phone)* ich geh ran *od.* nehme ab; *(answer door)* ich mache auf; **b)** *(start)* losgehen; *(in vehicle)* losfahren; **c)** *(pass, circulate)* gehen; **a shiver went up** *or* **down my spine** ein Schauer lief mir über den Rücken; **go to** *(be given to)* ⟨*Preis, Gelder, Job:*⟩ gehen an (+ *Akk.*); ⟨*Titel, Besitz:*⟩ übergehen auf (+ *Akk.*); **go towards** *(be of benefit to)* zugute kommen (+ *Dat.*); **d)** *(act, function effectively)* gehen; ⟨*Mechanismus, Maschine:*⟩ laufen; **keep going** *(in movement)* weitergehen/-fahren; *(in activity)* weitermachen; *(not fail)* sich aufrecht halten; **keep sth. going** etw. in Gang halten; **make sth. go, get/set sth. going** etw. in Gang bringen; **e)** **go to work** zur Arbeit gehen; **go to school** in die Schule gehen; **go to a comprehensive school** auf eine Gesamtschule gehen; **f)** *(depart)* gehen; ⟨*Bus, Zug:*⟩ [ab]fahren; ⟨*Post:*⟩ rausgehen *(ugs.);* **g)** *(cease to function)* kaputtgehen; ⟨*Sicherung:*⟩ durchbrennen; *(break)* brechen; ⟨*Seil usw.:*⟩ reißen; **h)** *(disappear)* weggehen; ⟨*Mantel, Hut, Fleck:*⟩ verschwinden; ⟨*Geruch, Rauch:*⟩ sich verziehen; ⟨*Geld, Zeit:*⟩ draufgehen *(ugs.)* (**in, on** für); **i) to go** *(still remaining)* **have sth. [still] to go** [noch] etw. übrig haben; **one week** *etc.* **to go to** ...: noch eine Woche *usw.* bis ...; **there's hours to go** es dauert noch Stunden; **j)** *(be sold)* weggehen *(ugs.);* **verkauft werden; going! going! gone!** zum ersten! zum zweiten! zum dritten!; **go to sb.** an jmdn. gehen; **k)** *(run)* ⟨*Grenze, Straße usw.:*⟩ verlaufen, gehen; *(lead)* gehen; führen; *(extend)* reichen; **as** *or* **so far as he/it goes** soweit; **l)** *(turn out, progress)* ⟨*Projekt, Interview, Abend:*⟩ verlaufen; **how did your holiday go?** wie war Ihr Urlaub?; **things have been going well/badly** in der letzten Zeit läuft alles gut/schief; **m)** *(be, have form or nature)* sein;

⟨*Sprichwort, Gedicht, Titel:*⟩ lauten; **that's the way it goes** so ist es nun mal; **go hungry** hungern; **go without food/ water** es ohne Essen/Wasser aushalten; **n)** *(become)* werden; **the tyre has gone flat** der Reifen ist platt; **o)** *(have usual place)* kommen; *(belong)* gehören; **where does the box go?** wo kommt *od.* gehört die Kiste hin?; **p)** *(fit)* passen; **go in|to| sth.** in etw. *(Akk.)* gehen *od.* [hinein]passen; **go through sth.** durch etw. [hindurch]gehen; **q)** *(match)* passen (**with** zu); **r)** ⟨*Turmuhr, Gong:*⟩ schlagen; ⟨*Glocke:*⟩ läuten; **s)** *(coll.: be acceptable or permitted)* erlaubt sein; **it/that goes without saying** es/das ist doch selbstverständlich. *See also* **going** 2. **2.** *n., pl.* **goes** [gəʊz] *(coll.)* **a)** *(attempt, try)* Versuch, *der; (chance)* Gelegenheit, *die;* **have a go** es versuchen; **let me have a go/can I have a go?** laß mich [auch ein]mal/kann ich [auch ein]mal? *(ugs.);* **it's 'my go** ich bin an der Reihe *od.* dran; **at one go** auf einmal; **at the first go** auf Anhieb; **b)** *(vigorous activity)* **it's all go** es ist alles eine einzige Hetzerei *(ugs.);* **be on the go** auf Trab sein *(ugs.);* **c)** *(success)* **make a go of sth.** mit etw. Erfolg haben. **go a'head** *v. i.* **a)** *(in advance)* vorausgehen *(of Dat.);* **b)** *(proceed)* weitermachen; *(make progress)* ⟨*Arbeit:*⟩ fortschreiten, vorangehen. **go a'way** *v. i.* weggehen; *(on holiday or business)* verreisen. **go 'back** *v. i.* zurückgehen/-fahren; *(restart)* ⟨*Schule, Fabrik:*⟩ wieder anfangen; *(fig.)* zurückgehen; **go back to the beginning** noch mal von vorne anfangen. **go by 1.** ['--] *v. t.* **go by sth.** sich nach etw. richten; *(adhere to)* sich an etw. *(Akk.)* halten. **2.** [-'-] *v. i.* ⟨*Zeit:*⟩ vergehen. **go 'down** *v. i.* hinuntergehen/-fahren; ⟨*Sonne:*⟩ untergehen; ⟨*Schiff:*⟩ untergehen; *(fall to ground)* ⟨*Flugzeug usw.:*⟩ abstürzen. '**go for** *v. t.* **go for sb./sth.** *(go to fetch)* jmdn./etw. holen; *(apply to)* für jmdn./etw. gelten; *(like)* jmdn./etw. gut finden. **go 'in** *v. i.* hineingehen; reingehen *(ugs.).* **go 'off 1.** *v. i.* **a)** **go off with sb./sth.** sich mit jmdn./etw. auf- und davonmachen *(ugs.);* **b)** ⟨*Alarm, Schußwaffe:*⟩ losgehen; ⟨*Wecker:*⟩ klingeln; ⟨*Bombe:*⟩ hochgehen; **c)** *(turn bad)* schlecht werden; **d)** ⟨*Strom:*⟩ ausfallen. **2.** *v. t. (begin to dislike)* **go off sth.** von etw. abkommen. **go 'on** *v. i.* **a)** weitergehen/-fahren; **b)** *(continue)* weiterma-

chen; **c)** *(happen)* passieren. **go 'out** *v. i.* ausgehen; **go out to work/for a meal** arbeiten/essen gehen. **go over 1.** [-'--] *v. i.* hinübergehen. **2.** ['---, -'--] *v. t. (re-examine)* durchgehen. **go 'round** *v. i.* **a)** *(coll.)* **go round and** *od.* **to see sb.** bei jmdm. vorbeigehen *(ugs.);* **b)** *(look round)* sich umschauen; **c)** *(suffice)* reichen; langen *(ugs.).* **d)** *(spin)* sich drehen. **go through 1.** [-'-] *v. i.* ⟨*Ernennung:*⟩ durchkommen; ⟨*Antrag:*⟩ durchgehen. **2.** ['--] **a)** *(rehearse)* durchgehen; **b)** *(examine)* durchsehen; **c)** *(endure)* durchmachen. **go 'under** *v. i.* untergehen; *(fig.: fail)* eingehen. **go 'up** *v. i.* **a)** hinaufgehen/-fahren; ⟨*Ballon:*⟩ aufsteigen; *(Theatre)* ⟨*Vorhang:*⟩ aufgehen; ⟨*Lichter:*⟩ angehen; **b)** *(increase, ⟨Zahl:*⟩ wachsen; ⟨*Preis, Wert, Niveau:*⟩ steigen; *(in price)* ⟨*Ware:*⟩ teurer werden. **go without 1.** ['---] *v. t.* verzichten auf (+ *Akk.).* **2.** [-'--] *v. i.* verzichten

**goad** [gəʊd] *v. t.* ~ **sb. into sth./doing sth.** jmdn. zu etw. anstacheln/dazu anstacheln, etw. zu tun
'**go-ahead 1.** *adj.* unternehmungslustig; *(progressive)* fortschrittlich. **2.** *n.* **give sb./sth. the** ~: jmdm./einer Sache grünes Licht geben
**goal** [gəʊl] *n.* **a)** *(aim)* Ziel, *das;* **b)** *(Footb., Hockey)* Tor, *das;* **score/kick a** ~: einen Treffer erzielen. '**goalkeeper** *n.* Torwart, *der*
**goat** [gəʊt] *n.* Ziege, *die*
**gobble** ['gɒbl] **1.** *v. t.* ~ [**down** *or* **up**] hinunterschlingen. **2.** *v. i.* schlingen
'**go-between** *n.* Vermittler, *der/*Vermittlerin, *die*
**goblet** ['gɒblɪt] *n.* Kelchglas, *das*
**goblin** ['gɒblɪn] *n.* Kobold, *der*
**god** [gɒd] *n.* **a)** Gott, *der;* **b)** God *(Theol.)* Gott. '**godchild** *n.* Patenkind, *das.* '**god-daughter** *n.* Patentochter, *die*
**goddess** ['gɒdɪs] *n.* Göttin, *die*
**god:** ~**father** *n.* Pate, *der;* G~**forsaken** *adj.* gottverlassen; ~**mother** *n.* Patentante, *die;* ~**send** *n.* Gottesgabe, *die;* **be a** ~**send to sb.** für jmdn. ein Geschenk des Himmels sein; ~**son** *n.* Patensohn, *der*
**goggles** ['gɒglz] *n. pl.* Schutzbrille, *die*
**going** ['gəʊɪŋ] **1.** *n. (progress)* Vorankommen, *das;* **while the** ~ **is good** solange es noch geht. **2.** *adj.* **a)** *(available)* erhältlich; **there is sth.** ~: es gibt etw.; **b)** **be** ~ **to do sth.** etw. tun [wer-

den/wollen]; **I was ~ to say** ich wollte sagen; **it's ~ to snow** es wird schneien; **a ~ concern** eine gesunde Firma

**goings-'on** n. pl. Ereignisse

**gold** [gəʊld] 1. n. Gold, das. 2. attrib. adj. golden; Gold⟨münze, -kette usw.⟩

**golden** ['gəʊldn] adj. golden. **golden 'wedding** n. goldene Hochzeit

**gold: ~fish** n. Goldfisch, der; **~ 'medal** n. Goldmedaille, die; **~-mine** n. Goldmine, die; (fig.) Goldgrube, die; **~-plated** adj. vergoldet; **~smith** n. Goldschmied, der/-schmiedin, die

**golf** [gɒlf] n. Golf, das

**golf: ~ ball** n. Golfball, der; **~-club** n. a) (implement) Golfschläger, der; b) (association) Golfclub, der; **~-course** n. Golfplatz, der

**'golfer** n. Golfer, der/Golferin, die

**gondola** ['gɒndələ] n. Gondel, die

**gone** [gɒn] 1. see go 1. 2. pred. adj. a) (away) weg; **it's time you were ~**: es ist od. wird Zeit, daß du gehst; b) (of time: after) nach; **it's ~ ten o'clock** es ist zehn Uhr vorbei

**gong** [gɒn] n. Gong, der

**good** [gʊd] 1. adj., better ['betə(r)], best [best] a) gut; günstig ⟨Gelegenheit, Angebot⟩; ausreichend ⟨Vorrat⟩; ausgiebig ⟨Mahl⟩; **as ~ as** so gut wie; **his ~ eye/leg** sein gesundes Auge/Bein; **in ~ time** frühzeitig; **all in ~ time** alles zu seiner Zeit; **be ~ at sth.** in etw. (Dat.) gut sein; **too ~ to be true** zu schön, um wahr zu sein; **apples are ~ for you** Äpfel sind gesund; **be too much of a ~ thing** zuviel des Guten sein; **~ times** eine schöne Zeit; **feel ~**: sich wohl fühlen; **take a ~ look round** sich gründlich umsehen; **give sb. a ~ beating/scolding** jmdn. tüchtig verprügeln/ausschimpfen; **~ afternoon/day** guten Tag!; **~ evening/morning** guten Abend/Morgen!; **~ night** gute Nacht!; b) (enjoyable) schön ⟨Leben, Urlaub, Wochenende⟩; **the ~ life** das angenehme, sorglose Leben; **have a ~ time!** viel Spaß!; **have a ~ journey!** gute Reise!; c) (well-behaved) gut; brav; **be ~!, be a ~ girl/boy!** sei brav od. lieb!; [as] **~ as gold** ganz artig od. brav; d) (virtuous) rechtschaffen; (kind) nett; gut ⟨Absicht, Wünsche, Benehmen, Tat⟩; **be ~ to sb.** gut zu jmdm. sein; **would you be so ~ as to** or **~ enough to do that?** wären Sie so freundlich od. nett, das zu tun?; **that/it is ~ of you** das/es ist nett od. lieb von dir; e) (commendable) gut; **~ for 'you** etc. (coll.) bravo!; f) (attractive) schön; gut ⟨Figur⟩; **look ~**: gut aussehen; g) (considerable) [recht] ansehnlich ⟨Menschenmenge⟩; ganz schön, ziemlich (ugs.) ⟨Entfernung, Strecke⟩; gut ⟨Preis, Erlös⟩; h) **make ~** (succeed) erfolgreich sein; (compensate for) wiedergutmachen; (indemnify) ersetzen. 2. n. a) (use) Nutzen, der; **be some ~ to sb./sth.** jmdm./einer Sache nützen; **be no ~ to sb./sth.** für jmdn./etw. nicht zu gebrauchen sein; **it is no/not much ~ doing sth.** es hat keinen/kaum einen Sinn, etw. zu tun; **what's the ~ of ...?, what ~ is ...?** was nützt ...?; b) (benefit) **for your/his** etc. **own ~**: zu deinem/ seinem usw. Besten; **do no/little ~**: nichts/wenig helfen od. nützen; **do sb./sth. ~**: jmdm./einer Sache nützen; ⟨Ruhe, Erholung:⟩ jmdm./einer Sache guttun; ⟨Arznei:⟩ jmdm./einer Sache helfen; c) (goodness) Gute, das; **be up to no ~**: nichts Gutes im Sinn haben; d) **for ~** (finally) ein für allemal; (permanently) für immer; e) in pl. (wares etc.) Waren; (belongings) Habe, die; (Brit. Railw.) Fracht, die; attrib. Güter⟨wagen, -zug⟩

**good: ~bye** (Amer.: **~'by**) int. auf Wiedersehen!; (on telephone) auf Wiederhören!; **~-for-nothing** 1. adj. nichtsnutzig; 2. n. Taugenichts, der; **~-'looking** adj. gutaussehend

**'goodness** 1. n. Güte, die. 2. int. |my| **~!** meine Güte! (ugs.)

**good'will** n. guter Wille; attrib. Goodwill⟨botschaft, -reise usw.⟩

**'goody** n. (coll.: hero) Gute, der/die

**gooey** ['guːɪ] adj., gooier ['guːɪə(r)], gooiest ['guːɪɪst] (coll.) klebrig

**goose** [guːs] n., pl. geese [giːs] Gans, die

**gooseberry** ['gʊzbərɪ] n. Stachelbeere, die

**'goose: ~-pimples** n. pl. **have ~-pimples** eine Gänsehaut haben

**¹gore** [gɔː(r)] v. t. [mit den Hörnern] aufspießen od. durchbohren

**²gore** n. Blut, das

**gorge** [gɔːdʒ] 1. n. Schlucht, die. 2. v. i. & refl. ~ |oneself| sich vollstopfen (ugs.) (on mit)

**gorgeous** ['gɔːdʒəs] adj. prächtig; hinreißend ⟨Frau, Mann, Lächeln⟩

**gorilla** [gə'rɪlə] n. Gorilla, der

**gormless** ['gɔːmlɪs] adj. (Brit. coll.) dämlich (ugs.)

**gorse** [gɔːs] n. Stechginster, der

**gory** ['gɔːrɪ] *adj. (fig.)* blutrünstig

**gosh** [gɒʃ] *int. (coll.)* Gott!

**'go-slow** *n. (Brit.)* Bummelstreik, *der*

**gospel** ['gɒspl] *n.* Evangelium, *das*

**gossamer** ['gɒsəmə(r)] *n.* Altweibersommer, *der; attrib.* hauchdünn

**gossip** ['gɒsɪp] **1.** *n.* **a)** *(talk)* Klatsch, *der (ugs.);* **b)** *(person)* Klatschbase, *die (ugs.).* **2.** *v. i.* klatschen *(ugs.)*

**got** *see* **get**

**Gothic** ['gɒθɪk] *adj.* gotisch

**gotten** *see* **get**

**gouge** [gaʊdʒ] *v. t.* aushöhlen

**goulash** ['guːlæʃ] *n.* Gulasch, *das od. der*

**gourmet** ['gʊəmeɪ] *n.* Gourmet, *der*

**gout** [gaʊt] *n.* Gicht, *die*

**govern** ['gʌvn] **1.** *v. t.* **a)** regieren ⟨*Land, Volk*⟩; verwalten ⟨*Provinz*⟩; **b)** *(dictate)* bestimmen. **2.** *v. i.* regieren

**governess** ['gʌvənɪs] *n.* Gouvernante, *die (veraltet);* Hauslehrerin, *die*

**government** ['gʌvnmənt] *n.* Regierung, *die; attrib.* Regierungs-

**governor** ['gʌvənə(r)] *n.* **a)** *(of province etc.)* Gouverneur, *der;* **b)** *(of institution)* Direktor, *der*/Direktorin, *die;* |**board of**| ~s Vorstand, *der;* **c)** *(sl.: employer)* Boß, *der (ugs.)*

**gown** [gaʊn] *n.* **a)** [elegantes] Kleid; **b)** *(official or uniform robe)* Talar, *der*

**GP** *abbr.* **general practitioner**

**grab** [græb] **1.** *v. t.,* -bb- greifen nach; *(seize)* packen; ~ **the chance** die Gelegenheit ergreifen; ~ **hold of sb./sth.** sich *(Dat.)* jmdn./etw. schnappen *(ugs.).* **2.** *v. i.,* -bb-: ~ **at sth.** nach etw. greifen. **3.** *n.* **make a** ~ **at** *or* **for sb./sth.** nach jmdm./etw. greifen

**grace** [greɪs] *n.* **a)** *(charm)* Anmut, *die (geh.);* **b)** *(decency)* **have the** ~ **to do sth.** so anständig sein und etw. tun; **c)** *(delay)* Frist, *die;* **give sb. a day's** ~: jmdm. einen Tag Aufschub gewähren; **d)** *(prayers)* **say** ~: das Tischgebet sprechen. **graceful** ['greɪsfl] *adj.* elegant; graziös ⟨*Bewegung, Eleganz*⟩

**gracious** ['greɪʃəs] **1.** *adj.* **a)** liebenswürdig; **b)** *(merciful)* gnädig. **2.** *int.* **good** ~! [ach] du meine Güte!

**grade** [greɪd] **1.** *n.* **a)** Rang, *der; (Mil.)* Dienstgrad, *der;* **b)** *(position)* Stufe, *die;* **c)** *(Amer. Sch.: class)* Klasse, *die;* **d)** *(Sch., Univ.: mark)* Note, *die;* Zensur, *die.* **2.** *v. t.* **a)** einstufen ⟨*Schüler*⟩; [nach Größe/Qualität] sortieren ⟨*Eier, Kartoffeln*⟩; **b)** *(mark)* benoten

**gradient** ['greɪdɪənt] *n. (ascent)* Steigung, *die; (descent)* Gefälle, *das*

**gradual** ['grædʒʊəl] *adj.,* **'gradually** *adv.* allmählich

**graduate 1.** ['grædʒʊət] *n.* Graduierte, *der/die; (who has left university)* Akademiker, *der*/Akademikerin, *die;* **university** ~: Hochschulabsolvent, *der*/-absolventin, *die.* **2.** ['grædʒʊeɪt] *v. i.* einen akademischen Grad/Titel erwerben; *(Amer. Sch.)* die [Schul]abschlußprüfung bestehen (**from** an + *Dat.*)

**graffiti** [grə'fiːtiː] *n. sing. or pl.* Graffiti *Pl.*

**graft** [grɑːft] **1.** *n.* **a)** *(Bot.)* Edelreis, *das;* **b)** *(Med.) (operation)* Transplantation, *die; (thing ~ed)* Transplantat, *das;* **c)** *(Brit. sl.: work)* Plackerei, *die (ugs.).* **2.** *v. t.* **a)** *(Bot.)* pfropfen; **b)** *(Med.)* transplantieren. **3.** *v. i. (Brit. sl.)* schuften *(ugs.)*

**grain** [greɪn] *n.* **a)** Korn, *das; collect.* Getreide, *das;* **b)** *(particle)* Korn, *das;* **c)** *(in wood)* Maserung, *die; (in paper)* Faser, *die; (in leather)* Narbung, *die;* **go against the** ~ |**for sb.**| *(fig.)* jmdm. gegen den Strich gehen *(ugs.).* **'grainy** *adj.* körnig; gemasert ⟨*Holz*⟩; genarbt ⟨*Leder*⟩

**gram** [græm] *n.* Gramm, *das*

**grammar** ['græmə(r)] *n.* Grammatik, *die.* **'grammar book** *n.* Grammatik, *die.* **'grammar school** *n. (Brit.)* ≈ Gymnasium, *das*

**grammatical** [grə'mætɪkl] *adj.* **a)** grammati[kal]isch richtig *od.* korrekt; **b)** *(of grammar)* grammatisch. **grammatically** [grə'mætɪkəlɪ] *adv.* grammati[kal]isch ⟨*richtig, falsch*⟩

**gramme** *see* **gram**

**gramophone** ['græməfəʊn] *n.* Plattenspieler, *der*

**granary** ['grænərɪ] *n.* Getreidesilo, *der od. das;* Kornspeicher, *der*

**grand** [grænd] *adj.* **a)** *(most or very important)* groß; ~ **finale** großes Finale; **b)** *(splendid)* grandios; **c)** *(coll.: excellent)* großartig

**grand:** ~**child** *n.* Enkel, *der*/Enkelin, *die;* Enkelkind, *das;* ~~**dad[dy]** ['grændæd(ɪ)] *n. (coll./child lang.);* Opa, *der (Kinderspr./ugs.);* ~~**daughter** *n.* Enkelin, *die*

**grandeur** ['grændʒə(r), 'grændjə(r)] *n.* Erhabenheit, *die*

**'grandfather** *n.* Großvater, *der;* ~ **clock** *n.* Standuhr, *die*

**grandiose** ['grændɪəʊs] *adj.* grandios; *(pompous)* bombastisch

**grand:** ~**ma** *n. (coll./child lang.)* Oma,

*die (Kinderspr./ugs.);* ~**mother** *n.*
Großmutter, *die;* ~**pa** *n. (coll./child
lang.)* Opa, *der (Kinderspr./ugs.);*
~**parent** *n. (male)* Großvater, *der;
(female)* Großmutter, *die;* ~**parents**
Großeltern *Pl.;* ~ **pi'ano** *n.* [Kon-
zert]flügel, *der;* ~**son** *n.* Enkel, *der;*
~**stand** *n.* [Haupt]tribüne, *die*
**granite** ['grænɪt] *n.* Granit, *der*
**granny** ['grænɪ] *n. (coll./child lang.)*
Oma, *die (Kinderspr./ugs.)*
**grant** [grɑːnt] **1.** *v.t.* **a)** erfüllen
⟨*Wunsch*⟩; stattgeben (+ *Dat.*) ⟨*Gesuch*⟩; **b)** *(concede, give)* gewähren;
geben ⟨*Zeit*⟩; bewilligen ⟨*Geldmittel*⟩;
zugestehen ⟨*Recht*⟩; erteilen ⟨*Erlaubnis*⟩; **c)** *(in argument)* zugeben; **take
sb./sth. for** ~**ed** sich *(Dat.)* jmds. sicher sein/etw. für selbstverständlich
halten. **2.** *n.* Zuschuß, *der; (financial
aid [to student])* [Studien]beihilfe, *die;
(scholarship)* Stipendium, *das*
**granulated sugar** [grænjʊleɪtd 'ʃʊg-
ə(r)] *n.* Kristallzucker, *der*
**granule** ['grænjuːl] *n.* Körnchen, *das*
**grape** [greɪp] *n.* Weintraube, *die;* **a
bunch of** ~**s** eine Traube
'**grapefruit** *n., pl. same* Grapefruit,
*die*
**graph** [grɑːf] *n.* graphische Darstellung; ~ **paper** Diagrammpapier, *das*
**graphic** ['græfɪk] *adj.* **a)** graphisch; **b)**
*(vivid)* plastisch; anschaulich. **graphically** ['græfɪkəlɪ] *adv.* **a)** *(vividly)* plastisch; **b)** *(using graphics)* graphisch.
**graphics** ['græfɪks] *n. (use of dia-
grams)* graphische Darstellung; **computer** ~: Computergraphik, *die*
**grapple** ['græpl] *v.i.* handgemein werden; ~ **with** *(fig.)* sich auseinandersetzen mit
**grasp** [grɑːsp] **1.** *v.i.* ~ **at** ergreifen;
sich stürzen auf (+ *Akk.*) ⟨*Angebot*⟩.
**2.** *v.t.* **a)** *(seize)* ergreifen; **b)** *(hold
firmly)* festhalten; **c)** *(understand)* verstehen; erfassen ⟨*Bedeutung*⟩. **3.** *n.* **a)**
*(firm hold)* Griff, *der;* **b)** *(mental* ~*)*
**have a good** ~ **of sth.** etw. gut beherrschen. '**grasping** *adj.* habgierig
**grass** [grɑːs] *n.* **a)** Gras, *das;* **b)** *(lawn)*
Rasen, *der;* **c)** *(Brit. sl.: police informer)* Spitzel, *der.* '**grasshopper**
*n.* Grashüpfer, *der.* '**grass-root[s]**
*attrib. adj. (Polit.)* Basis-
¹**grate** [greɪt] *n.* Rost, *der; (recess)* Kamin, *der*
²**grate** *v.t.* **a)** reiben; *(less finely)* ras-
peln; **b)** *(grind)* ~ **one's teeth** mit den
Zähnen knirschen

**grateful** ['greɪtfl] *adj.* dankbar **(to**
*Dat.*). '**gratefully** *adv.* dankbar
'**grater** *n.* Reibe, *die;* Raspel, *die*
**gratify** ['grætɪfaɪ] *v.t.* freuen; **be grati-
fied by** *or* **with** *or* **at sth.** über etw.
*(Akk.)* erfreut sein. '**gratifying** *adj.*
erfreulich
**grating** ['greɪtɪŋ] *n.* Gitter, *das*
**gratitude** ['grætɪtjuːd] *n.* Dankbarkeit, *die* **(to** gegenüber)
**gratuitous** [grə'tjuːɪtəs] *adj. (motive-
less)* grundlos
**gratuity** [grə'tjuːɪtɪ] *n.* Trinkgeld, *das*
¹**grave** [greɪv] *n.* Grab, *das*
²**grave** *adj.* **a)** *(important, solemn)*
ernst; **b)** *(serious)* schwer ⟨*Fehler, Irrtum*⟩; ernst ⟨*Situation, Lage*⟩; groß
⟨*Gefahr*⟩; schlimm ⟨*Nachricht*⟩
'**grave-digger** *n.* Totengräber, *der*
**gravel** ['grævl] *n.* Kies, *der*
**grave:** ~**stone** *n.* Grabstein, *der;*
~**yard** *n.* Friedhof, *der*
**gravity** ['grævɪtɪ] *n.* **a)** *(of mistake, offence)* Schwere, *die; (of situation)*
Ernst, *der;* **b)** *(Phys., Astron.)* Gravitation, *die;* Schwerkraft, *die*
**gravy** ['greɪvɪ] *n.* **a)** *(juices)* Bratensaft,
*der;* **b)** *(dressing)* [Braten]soße, *die*
**gray** *etc. (Amer.)* see **grey** *etc.*
¹**graze** [greɪz] *v.i.* grasen; weiden
²**graze** **1.** *n.* Schürfwunde, *die.* **2.** *v.t.*
**a)** *(touch lightly)* streifen; **b)** *(scrape)*
abschürfen ⟨*Haut*⟩; zerkratzen ⟨*Oberfläche*⟩
**grease** [griːs] **1.** *n.* Fett, *das; (lubricant)* Schmierfett, *das.* **2.** *v.t.* einfet-
ten; *(lubricate)* schmieren. '**grease-
proof** *adj.* fettdicht; ~ **paper** Perga-
ment- *od.* Butterbrotpapier, *das*
**greasy** ['griːsɪ] *adj.* fettig; fett ⟨*Essen*⟩;
*(lubricated)* geschmiert; *(dirty with
lubricant)* schmierig
**great** [greɪt] *adj.* **a)** groß; **a** ~ **many**
sehr viele; sehr gut ⟨*Freund*⟩; *(impressive; coll.: splendid)* großartig; **be
a** ~ **one for sth.** etw. sehr gern tun; **b)**
Groß⟨*onkel, -tante, -neffe, -nichte*⟩;
Ur⟨*großmutter, -großvater, -enkel, -en-
kelin*⟩. **Great 'Britain** *pr. n.* Großbritannien *(das).* '**greatly** *adv.* sehr;
höchst ⟨*verärgert*⟩; stark ⟨*beeinflußt*⟩;
bedeutend ⟨*verbessert*⟩. '**greatness**
*n.* Größe, *die*
**Greece** [griːs] *pr. n.* Griechenland
*(das)*
**greed** [griːd] *n.* Gier, *die* **(for** nach);
*(gluttony)* Gefräßigkeit, *die.* '**greedy**
*adj.* gierig; *(gluttonous)* gefräßig
**Greek** [griːk] **1.** *adj.* griechisch; **sb. is**

~: jmd. ist Grieche/Griechin. **2.** *n.* **a)** *(person)* Grieche, *der*/Griechin, *die;* **b)** *(language)* Griechisch, *das; see also* **English 2 a**

**green** [gri:n] **1.** *adj.* **a)** grün; **b)** *(environmentally safe)* ökologisch; . **c)** *(gullible)* naiv; *(inexperienced)* grün; **d)** *(Polit.)* G~: grün; **the G~s** die Grü-. nen. **2.** *n.* **a)** *(colour)* Grün, *das;* **b)** *(piece of land)* Grünfläche, *die; village* ~: Dorfanger, *der;* **c)** *in pl.* *(~ vegetables)* Grüngemüse, *das.* '**green belt** *n.* Grüngürtel, *der.* **green 'card** *n.* *(Motor Veh.)* grüne Karte

**greenery** ['gri:nərɪ] *n.* Grün, *das*

**green:** **~fly** *n.* *(Brit.)* grüne Blattlaus; **~gage** ['gri:ngeɪdʒ] *n.* Reineclaude, *die;* **~grocer** *n.* *(Brit.)* Obst- und Gemüsehändler, *der*/-händlerin, *die;* **~house** *n.* Gewächshaus, *das;* **~house effect** Treibhauseffekt, *der*

**Greenland** ['gri:nlənd] *pr. n.* Grönland *(das)*

'**Green Party** *n.* *(Polit.)* die Grünen

**greet** [gri:t] *v. t.* begrüßen; *(in passing)* grüßen; *(receive)* empfangen. '**greeting** *n.* Begrüßung, *die; (in passing)* Gruß, *der; (words)* Grußformel, *die.* '**greetings card** *n.* Grußkarte, *die; (for birthday)* Glückwunschkarte, *die*

**gregarious** [grɪ'geərɪəs] *adj.* gesellig

**grenade** [grɪ'neɪd] *n.* Granate, *die*

**grew** *see* **grow**

**grey** [greɪ] **1.** *adj.* grau. **2.** *n.* Grau, *das.* '**greyhound** *n.* Windhund, *der*

**grid** [grɪd] *n.* **a)** *(grating)* Rost, *der;* **b)** *(of lines)* Gitter[netz], *das;* **c)** *(for supply)* Versorgungsnetz, *das*

**grief** [gri:f] *n.* Kummer, *der* **(over, at** über + *Akk.,* um); *(at loss of sb.)* Trauer, *die* **(for** um); **come to ~** *(fail)* scheitern

**grievance** ['gri:vəns] *n.* *(complaint)* Beschwerde, *die; (grudge)* Groll, *der*

**grieve** [gri:v] **1.** *v. t.* betrüben; bekümmern. **2.** *v. i.* trauern **(for** um)

**grievous** ['gri:vəs] *adj.* schwer ⟨*Verwundung, Krankheit*⟩

'**grill** [grɪl] **1.** *v. t.* *(cook)* grillen; *(fig.: question)* in die Mangel nehmen *(ugs.).* **2.** *n.* **a)** **mixed ~:** gemischte Grillplatte; **b)** *(on cooker)* Grill, *der*

**grille** (²**grill**) *n.* **a)** Gitter, *das;* **b)** *(Motor Veh.)* [Kühler]grill, *der*

**grim** [grɪm] *adj.* *(stern)* streng; grimmig ⟨*Lächeln, Schweigen*⟩; *(unrelenting)* erbittert ⟨*Widerstand, Kampf*⟩; *(ghastly)* grauenvoll ⟨*Aufgabe, Nachricht*⟩; trostlos ⟨*Aussichten*⟩

**grimace** [grɪ'meɪs] **1.** *n.* Grimasse, *die.* **2.** *v. i.* Grimassen schneiden; **~ with pain** vor Schmerz das Gesicht verziehen

**grime** [graɪm] *n.* Schmutz, *der.* **grimy** ['graɪmɪ] *adj.* schmutzig

**grin** [grɪn] **1.** *n.* Grinsen, *das.* **2.** *v. i.,* **-nn-** grinsen; **~ at sb.** jmdn. angrinsen

**grind** [graɪnd] **1.** *v. t.,* **ground** [graʊnd] **a)** ~ [up] zermahlen; mahlen ⟨*Kaffee, Pfeffer, Getreide*⟩; **b)** *(sharpen)* schleifen ⟨*Schere, Messer*⟩; schärfen ⟨*Klinge*⟩; **c)** *(rub harshly)* zerquetschen; **~ one's teeth** mit den Zähnen knirschen. **2.** *v. i., ground:* **~ to a halt** ⟨*Fahrzeug:*⟩ quietschend zum Stehen kommen; *(fig.)* ⟨*Verkehr:*⟩ zum Erliegen kommen. **3.** *n.* *(coll.)* Plackerei, *die (ugs.).* '**grinder** *n.* Schleifmaschine, *die; (coffee-~ etc.)* Mühle, *die.* '**grindstone** *n.* Schleifstein, *der*

**grip** [grɪp] **1.** *n.* **a)** *(firm hold)* Halt, *der; (fig.: power)* Umklammerung, *die;* **have a ~ on sth.** etw. festhalten; *(fig.)* etwas im Griff haben; **loosen one's ~:** loslassen; **lose one's ~** *(fig.)* nachlassen; **b)** *(strength or way of ~ping)* Griff, *der.* **2.** *v. t.,* **-pp-** [fest] halten; ⟨*Reifen:*⟩ greifen; *(fig.)* fesseln ⟨*Publikum, Aufmerksamkeit*⟩. **3.** *v. i.,* **-pp-** ⟨*Räder, Bremsen usw.:*⟩ greifen

**gripe** [graɪp] *v. i.* *(sl.)* meckern *(ugs.)* **(about** über + *Akk.)*

**gripping** ['grɪpɪŋ] *adj.* *(fig.)* packend

**grisly** ['grɪzlɪ] *adj.* grausig

**gristle** ['grɪsl] *n.* Knorpel, *der*

**grit** [grɪt] **1.** *n.* **a)** Sand, *der;* **b)** *(coll.: courage)* Schneid, *der (ugs.).* **2.** *v. t.,* **-tt-** **a)** streuen ⟨*Straßen*⟩; **b)** **~ one's teeth** die Zähne zusammenbeißen *(ugs.)*

**groan** [grəʊn] **1.** *n.* Stöhnen, *das; (of thing)* Ächzen, *das.* **2.** *v. i.* [auf]stöhnen **(at** bei); ⟨*Tisch, Planken:*⟩ ächzen. **3.** *v. t.* stöhnen

**grocer** ['grəʊsə(r)] *n.* Lebensmittelhändler, *der*/-händlerin, *die.* **grocery** ['grəʊsərɪ] *n.* **a)** *in pl. (goods)* Lebensmittel *Pl.;* **b)** **~ [store]** Lebensmittelgeschäft, *das*

**groggy** ['grɒgɪ] *adj.* groggy präd. *(ugs.)*

**groin** [grɔɪn] *n.* Leistengegend, *die*

**groom** [gru:m, grʊm] **1.** *n.* **a)** *(stableboy)* Stallbursche, *der;* **b)** *(bride~)* Bräutigam, *der.* **2.** *v. t.* striegeln ⟨*Pferd*⟩; *(fig.)* vorbereiten **(for** auf + *Akk.)*

**groove** [gru:v] *n.* Rille, *die*

**grope** [grəʊp] *v. i.* tasten **(for** nach)

**¹gross** [grəʊs] *adj.* **a)** *(flagrant)* grob ⟨*Fahrlässigkeit, Fehler*⟩; **b)** *(obese)* fett; **c)** *(total)* Brutto-

**²gross** *n., pl. same* Gros, *das*

**'grossly** *adj. (flagrantly)* äußerst; grob ⟨*übertreiben*⟩

**grotesque** [grəʊ'tesk] *adj.* grotesk

**grotto** ['grɒtəʊ] *n., pl.* ~es *or* ~s Grotte, *die*

**grotty** ['grɒtɪ] *adj. (Brit. sl.)* mies *(ugs.)*

**¹ground** [graʊnd] **1.** *n.* **a)** Boden, *der;* **get off the ~** *(coll.)* konkrete Gestalt annehmen; **b)** |sports| ~: Sportplatz, *der;* **c)** *in pl. (attached to house)* Anlage, *die;* **d)** *(reason)* Grund, *der;* **on the ~|s|** of auf Grund (+ *Gen.*); **on the ~|s| that** ...: unter Berufung auf die Tatsache, daß ...; **e)** *in pl. (sediment)* Satz, *der.* **2.** *v. t. (Aeronaut.)* am Boden festhalten

**²ground 1.** *see* grind 1, 2. **2.** *adj.* gemahlen ⟨*Kaffee, Getreide*⟩

**ground 'floor** *see* floor 1 b

**'grounding** *n.* Grundkenntnisse *Pl.*

**'groundless** *adj.* unbegründet

**ground:** ~**sheet** *n.* Bodenplane, *die;* ~**sman** ['graʊndzmən] *n., pl.* -**smen** ['graʊndzmən] *(Sport)* Platzwart, *der;* ~**work** *n.* Vorarbeiten *Pl.*

**group** [gru:p] **1.** *n.* Gruppe, *die.* **2.** *v. t.* gruppieren

**¹grouse** [graʊs] *n., pl. same* Rauhfußhuhn, *das;* |red| ~ *(Brit.)* Schottisches Moorschneehuhn

**²grouse** *v. i. (coll.)* meckern *(ugs.)*

**grove** [grəʊv] *n.* Wäldchen, *das*

**grovel** ['grɒvl] *v. i., (Brit.)* -ll- *(fig.)* katzbuckeln

**grow** [grəʊ] **1.** *v. i.,* grew [gru:], grown [grəʊn] **a)** wachsen; ~ **out of** *or* **from sth.** sich aus etw. entwickeln; *(from sth. abstract)* von etw. herrühren; ~ **in** gewinnen an (+ *Dat.*) ⟨*Größe, Bedeutung*⟩; **b)** *(become)* werden; ~ **apart** *(fig.)* sich auseinanderleben; ~ **to love/hate sb./sth.** jmdn./etw. liebenlernen/hassenlernen; ~ **to like sb./sth.** nach und nach Gefallen an jmdm./ etw. finden. **2.** *v. i.,* grew, grown ziehen; *(on a large scale)* anpflanzen; züchten ⟨*Blumen*⟩. **grow 'up** *v. i.* **a)** aufwachsen; *(become adult)* erwachsen werden; **b)** ⟨*Legende:*⟩ entstehen

**growl** [graʊl] **1.** *n.* Knurren, *das; (of bear)* Brummen, *das.* **2.** *v. i.* knurren; ⟨*Bär:*⟩ [böse] brummen

**grown** [grəʊn] **1.** *see* grow. **2.** *adj.* erwachsen. **'grown-up 1.** *n.* Erwachsene, *der/die.* **2.** *adj.* erwachsen

**growth** [grəʊθ] *n.* **a)** Wachstum, *das* (of, in *Gen.*); *(increase)* Zunahme, *die* (of, in *Gen.*); **b)** *(Med.)* Gewächs, *das*

**grub** [grʌb] *n.* **a)** Larve, *die; (maggot)* Made, *die;* **b)** *(sl.: food)* Fressen, *das (salopp)*

**grubby** ['grʌbɪ] *adj.* schmudd[e]lig *(ugs.)*

**grudge** [grʌdʒ] **1.** *v. t.* ~ **sb. sth.** jmdm. etw. mißgönnen; ~ **doing sth.** etw. ungern tun. **2.** *n.* Groll, *der;* **bear sb. a.** ~ *or* **a** ~ **against sb.** jmdm. gegenüber nachtragend sein. **grudging** ['grʌdʒɪŋ] *adj.* widerwillig; widerwillig gewährt ⟨*Zuschuß*⟩. **'grudgingly** *adv.* widerwillig

**gruelling** (*Amer.:* **grueling**) ['gru:əlɪŋ] *adj.* aufreibend; strapaziös ⟨*Reise*⟩

**gruesome** ['gru:səm] *adj.* grausig

**gruff** [grʌf] *adj.* barsch; rauh ⟨*Stimme*⟩

**grumble** ['grʌmbl] *v. i.* murren; ~ **about** *or* **over sth.** sich über etw. *(Akk.)* beklagen

**grumpy** ['grʌmpɪ] *adj.* unleidlich

**grunt** [grʌnt] **1.** *n.* Grunzen, *das.* **2.** *v. i.* grunzen

**guarantee** [gærən'ti:] **1.** *v. t.* **a)** garantieren für; [eine] Garantie geben auf (+ *Akk.*); **the clock is ~d for a year** die Uhr hat ein Jahr Garantie; **b)** *(promise)* garantieren *(ugs.); (ensure)* bürgen für ⟨*Qualität*⟩. **2.** *n.* **a)** *(Commerc. etc.)* Garantie, *die; (document)* Garantieschein, *der;* **b)** *(coll.: promise)* Garantie, *die (ugs.);* **give sb. a** ~ **that** ...: jmdm. garantieren, daß ...

**guard** [gɑ:d] **1.** *n.* **a)** *(guardsman)* Wachtposten, *der; (group of soldiers)* Wache, *die;* **be on** ~: Wache haben; **be on |one's|** ~ *(lit. or fig.)* sich hüten; **b)** *(Brit. Railw.)* [Zug]schaffner, *der/* -schaffnerin, *die;* **c)** *(Amer.: prison warder)* [Gefängnis]wärter, *der/*-wärterin, *die;* **d)** *(safety device)* Schutz, *der.* **2.** *v. t.* bewachen; hüten ⟨*Geheimnis*⟩; schützen ⟨*Leben*⟩; beschützen ⟨*Prominenten*⟩. **'guard against** *v. t.* sich hüten vor (+ *Dat.*); vorbeugen (+ *Dat.*) ⟨*Krankheit, Irrtum*⟩

**'guarded** *adj.* zurückhaltend

**guardian** ['gɑ:dɪən] *n.* **a)** Hüter, *der;* Wächter, *der;* **b)** *(Law)* Vormund, *der*

**guerrilla** [gə'rɪlə] *n.* Guerillakämpfer, *der/*-kämpferin, *die; attrib.* Guerilla-

**guess** [ges] **1.** *v. t.* **a)** *(estimate)* schätzen; *(surmise)* raten; *(surmise correctly)* erraten; raten ⟨*Rätsel*⟩; ~ **what!** *(coll.)* stell dir vor!; **b)** *(esp. Amer.:*

*suppose)* I ~: ich glaube. **2.** *v. i. (estimate)* schätzen; *(make assumption)* vermuten; *(surmise correctly)* es erraten; ~ **at sth.** etw. schätzen; **keep sb. ~ing** *(coll.)* jmdn. im unklaren lassen. **3.** *n.* Schätzung, *die;* **make** *or* **have a ~:** schätzen. '**guesswork** *n.* **be ~:** eine Vermutung sein

**guest** [gest] *n.* Gast, *der.* '**guesthouse** *n.* Pension, *die*

**guffaw** [gʌ'fɔː] **1.** *n.* brüllendes Gelächter. **2.** *v. i.* brüllend lachen

**guidance** ['gaɪdəns] *n.* **a)** *(leadership)* Führung, *die; (by teacher etc.)* [An]leitung, *die;* **b)** *(advice)* Rat, *der*

**guide** [gaɪd] **1.** *n.* **a)** Führer, *der/*Führerin, *die; (Tourism)* [Fremden]führer, *der/-*führerin, *die;* **b)** *(indicator)* **be a [good] ~ to sth.** ein [guter] Anhaltspunkt für etw. sein; **be no ~ to sth.** keine Rückschlüsse auf etw. *(Akk.)* zulassen; **c)** *(Brit.)* |**Girl**| **G~:** Pfadfinderin, *die;* **d)** *(handbook)* Handbuch, *das;* **e)** *(for tourists)* [Reise]führer, *der.* **2.** *v. t.* führen; *(fig.)* bestimmen ⟨*Handeln, Urteil*⟩; **be ~d by sth./sb.** sich von etw./jmdm. leiten lassen. '**guidebook** *n.* [Reise]führer, *der.* **guided** '**missile** *n.* Lenkflugkörper, *der.* '**guide-dog** *n.* Blinden[führ]hund, *der.* **guided** '**tour** *n.* Führung, *die* (of durch). '**guideline** *n.* Richtlinie, *die*

**guild** [gɪld] *n.* **a)** Verein, *der;* **b)** *(Hist.)* Gilde, *die;* Zunft, *die*

**guile** [gaɪl] *n.* Hinterlist, *die*

**guillotine** ['gɪlətiːn] *n.* Guillotine, *die*

**guilt** [gɪlt] *n.* **a)** Schuld, *die* (of, for an + *Dat.*); **b)** *(guilty feeling)* Schuldgefühle *Pl.* '**guilty** *adj.* **a)** schuldig; **be ~ of murder** des Mordes schuldig sein; **find sb. ~/not ~ |of sth.|** jmdn. [an etw. *(Dat.)*] schuldig sprechen/[von etw.] freisprechen; **feel ~** *(coll.)* ein schlechtes Gewissen haben; **b)** schuldbewußt ⟨*Miene, Blick, Verhalten*⟩; schlecht ⟨*Gewissen*⟩

**guinea-pig** ['gɪnɪpɪg] *n.* Meerschweinchen, *das; (fig.)* Versuchskaninchen, *das (ugs.)*

**guise** [gaɪz] *n.* Gestalt, *die;* **in the ~ of** in Gestalt (+ *Gen.*)

**guitar** [gɪ'tɑː(r)] *n.* Gitarre, *die.* **guitarist** [gɪ'tɑːrɪst] *n.* Gitarrist, *der/*Gitarristin, *die*

**gulf** [gʌlf] *n.* **a)** *(Geog.)* Golf, *der;* **b)** *(wide gap)* Kluft, *die*

**gull** [gʌl] *n.* Möwe, *die*

**gullet** ['gʌlɪt] *n.* **a)** Speiseröhre, *die;* **b)** *(throat)* Kehle, *die*

**gullible** ['gʌlɪbl] *adj.* leichtgläubig

**gully** ['gʌlɪ] *n. (artificial channel)* Abzugsrinne, *die; (drain)* Gully, *der*

**gulp** [gʌlp] **1.** *v. t.* hinunterschlingen; hinuntergießen ⟨*Getränk*⟩. **2.** *n.* **a)** Schlucken, *das;* **b)** *(large mouthful of drink)* kräftiger Schluck. **gulp** '**down** *v. t.* hinunterschlingen; hinuntergießen ⟨*Getränk*⟩

**¹gum** [gʌm] *n. (Anat.)* ~|s| Zahnfleisch, *das*

**²gum** **1.** *n.* **a)** Gummi, *das; (glue)* Klebstoff, *der;* **b)** *(Amer.)* see **chewing-gum.** **2.** *v. t.,* **-mm-:** **a)** *(smear with ~)* mit Klebstoff bestreichen; gummieren ⟨*Briefmarken, Etiketten usw.*⟩; **b)** *(fasten with ~)* kleben. '**gumboot** *n.* Gummistiefel, *der*

**gumption** ['gʌmpʃn] *n. (coll.)* Grips, *der*

**gun** [gʌn] *n.* Schußwaffe, *die; (rifle)* Gewehr, *das; (pistol)* Pistole, *die; (revolver)* Revolver, *der.* **gun** '**down** *v. t.* niederschießen

**gun:** ~-**fire** *n.* Geschützfeuer, *das;* ~**man** ['gʌnmən] *n., pl.* ~**men** ['gʌnmən] bewaffneter Mann

**gun:** ~**powder** *n.* Schießpulver, *das;* ~**shot** *n.* Schuß, *der*

**gurgle** ['gɜːgl] **1.** *n.* Gluckern, *das; (of brook)* Plätschern, *das.* **2.** *v. i.* gluckern; ⟨*Bach:*⟩ plätschern; ⟨*Baby:*⟩ lallen; *(with delight)* glucksen

**gush** [gʌʃ] **1.** *n.* Schwall, *der.* **2.** *v. i.* **a)** strömen; ~ **out** herausströmen; **b)** *(fig.: enthuse)* schwärmen

**gust** [gʌst] *n.* ~ |of wind| Bö[e], *die*

**gusto** ['gʌstəʊ] *n.* Genuß, *der; (vitality)* Schwung, *der*

'**gusty** *adj.* böig

**gut** [gʌt] **1.** *n.* **a)** *(material)* Darm, *der;* **b)** *in pl. (bowels)* Eingeweide *Pl.;* Gedärme *Pl.;* **c)** *in pl. (coll.: courage)* Schneid, *der (ugs.).* **2.** *v. t.,* **-tt-:** **a)** *(remove ~s of)* ausnehmen; **b)** *(remove fittings from)* ausräumen; **the house was ~ted |by fire|** das Haus brannte aus

**gutter** ['gʌtə(r)] *n. (below edge of roof)* Dachrinne, *die; (at side of street)* Rinnstein, *der;* Gosse, *die*

**guttural** ['gʌtərl] *adj.* guttural; kehlig

**guy** [gaɪ] *n.* **a)** *(sl.: man)* Typ, *der (ugs.);* **b)** *in pl. (Amer.: everyone)* |**listen,**| **you ~s!** [hört mal,] Kinder! *(ugs.)*

**guzzle** ['gʌzl] **1.** *v. t. (eat)* hinunterschlingen; *(drink)* hinuntergießen. **2.** *v. i.* schlingen

**gym** [dʒɪm] *n. (coll.)* **a)** *(gymnasium)* Turnhalle, *die;* **b)** *(gymnastics)* Turnen, *das*

**gymnasium** *n.* [dʒɪm'neɪzɪəm] *n., pl.* ~s *or* **gymnasia** [dʒɪm'neɪzɪə] Turnhalle, *die*

**gymnast** ['dʒɪmnæst] *n.* Turner, *der*/Turnerin, *die*

**gymnastic** [dʒɪm'næstɪk] *adj.* turnerisch ⟨*Können*⟩; ~ **equipment** Turngeräte. **gymnastics** [dʒɪm'næstɪks] *n.* Gymnastik, *die; (esp. with apparatus)* Turnen, *das*

'**gym-slip** *n.* Trägerrock, *der*

**gynaecologist** [gaɪnɪ'kɒlədʒɪst] *n.* Frauenarzt, *der*/Frauenärztin, *die*

**gynaecology** [gaɪnɪ'kɒlədʒɪ] *n.* Gynäkologie, *die*

**gypsy, Gypsy** ['dʒɪpsɪ] *n.* Zigeuner, *der*/Zigeunerin, *die*

**gyrate** [dʒaɪə'reɪt] *v. i.* sich drehen

# H

¹**H, h** [eɪtʃ] *n.* H, h, *das*

**haberdashery** ['hæbədæʃərɪ] *n. (goods)* Kurzwaren *Pl.; (Amer.: menswear)* Herrenmoden *Pl.*

**habit** ['hæbɪt] *n.* **a)** Gewohnheit, *die;* **good/bad** ~: gute/schlechte [An]gewohnheit; **get** *or* **fall into a** *or* **the** ~ **of doing sth.** [es] sich *(Dat.)* angewöhnen, etw. zu tun; **b)** *(coll.: addiction)* Süchtigkeit, *die*

**habitable** ['hæbɪtəbl] *adj.* bewohnbar

**habitat** ['hæbɪtæt] *n.* Habitat, *das*

**habitation** [hæbɪ'teɪʃn] *n.* **fit/unfit for human** ~: bewohnbar/unbewohnbar

**habitual** [hə'bɪtjʊəl] *adj.* **a)** gewohnt; **b)** *(given to habit)* gewohnheitsmäßig; Gewohnheits⟨*trinker*⟩. **ha'bitually** *adv. (regularly)* regelmäßig

¹**hack** [hæk] *v. t.* hacken ⟨*Holz*⟩; ~ **sth. to bits** *or* **pieces** etw. in Stücke hacken. **hack 'off** *v. t.* abhacken. **hack 'out** *v. t.* heraushauen (**from** aus)

²**hack** *n. (derog.: writer)* Schreiberling, *der*

**hackneyed** ['hæknɪd] *adj.* abgegriffen; abgedroschen *(ugs.)*

'**hack-saw** *n.* [Metall]bügelsäge, *die*

**had** *see* **have**

**haddock** ['hædək] *n., pl. same* Schellfisch, *der*

**hadn't** ['hædnt] *(coll.)* = **had not;** *see* **have**

**haemorrhage** ['hemərɪdʒ] *n.* Blutung, *die*

**haemorrhoid** ['hemərɔɪd] *n.* Hämorrhoide, *die*

**hag** [hæg] *n.* [alte] Hexe

**haggard** ['hægəd] *adj.* ausgezehrt; *(with worry)* abgehärmt

**haggle** ['hægl] *v. i.* sich zanken (**over, about** wegen); *(over price)* feilschen (**over, about** um)

**Hague** [heɪg] *pr. n.* **The** ~: Den Haag *(das)*

¹**hail** [heɪl] **1.** *n.* Hagel, *der.* **2.** *v. i.* **it** ~**s** *or* **is** ~**ing** es hagelt; ~ **down** *(fig.)* niederprasseln (**on** auf + *Akk.*)

²**hail** *v. t.* **a)** *(call out to)* anrufen; *(signal to)* anhalten ⟨*Taxi*⟩; **b)** *(acclaim)* zujubeln (+ *Dat.*); bejubeln (**as** als)

'**hailstone** *n.* Hagelkorn, *das*

**hair** [heə(r)] *n.* **a)** *(one strand)* Haar, *das;* **b)** *collect.* Haar, *das; Pl.; attrib.* Haar-; **have** *or* **get one's** ~ **done** sich *(Dat.)* das Haar *od.* die Haare machen lassen *(ugs.)*

**hair:** ~**brush** *n.* Haarbürste, *die;* ~-**conditioner** *n.* Frisiermittel, *das;* ~**cut** *n.* **a)** *(act)* Haareschneiden, *das;* **go for/need a** ~**cut** zum Friseur gehen/müssen; **get/have a** ~**cut** sich *(Dat.)* die Haare schneiden lassen; **b)** *(style)* Haarschnitt, *der;* ~-**do** *n. (style)* Frisur, *die;* ~**dresser** *n.* Friseur, *der*/Friseuse, *die;* **go to the** ~**dresser's** zum Friseur gehen; ~**pin** *n.* Haarnadel, *die;* ~**pin 'bend** *n.* Haarnadelkurve, *die;* ~-**raising** ['heəreɪzɪŋ] *adj.* haarsträubend; ~-**style** *n.* Frisur, *die*

'**hairy** *adj.* **a)** behaart; flauschig ⟨*Pullover, Teppich*⟩; **b)** *(sl.: difficult)* haarig

**hale** [heɪl] *adj.* ~ **and hearty** gesund und munter

**half** [hɑːf] **1.** *n., pl.* **halves** [hɑːvz] **a)** Hälfte, *die;* ~ **[of sth.]** die Hälfte [von etw.]; ~ **of Europe** halb Europa; **one and a** ~ **hours, one hour and a** ~: anderthalb *od.* eineinhalb Stunden; **divide sth. in** ~ *or* **into halves** etw. halbieren; **she is three and a** ~: sie ist dreieinhalb; **b)** *(Footb. etc.: period)* Halbzeit, *die.* **2.** *adj.* halb; ~ **the house/books/time** die Hälfte des Hauses/der Bücher/der Zeit; ~ **an hour** ei-

ne halbe Stunde. **3.** *adv.* **a)** zur Hälfte; halb ⟨*schließen, aufessen, fertig, voll, geöffnet*⟩; *(almost)* fast ⟨*ersticken, tot sein*⟩; ~ **as much/many** halb so viel/viele; **only** ~ **hear what ...**: nur zum Teil hören, was ...; **b)** ~ **past** *or (coll.)* ~ **one/two/three** *etc.* halb zwei/drei/vier *usw.*; ~ **past twelve** halb eins **half:** ~**-caste** *n.* Mischling, *der;* ~-'**hearted** *adj.* halbherzig; ~-'**hour** *n.* halbe Stunde; ~-'**mast** *n.* be [**flown**] **at** ~**-mast** auf Halbmast stehen; ~**-note** *n..(Amer. Mus.)* halbe Note; ~-'**price** **1.** *n.* halber Preis; **2.** *adj.* zum halben Preis *nachgestellt;* **3.** *adv.* zum halben Preis; ~-'**term** *n. (Brit.) (holiday)* ~**-term** [**holiday/ break**] Ferien in der Mitte des Trimesters; ~-'**time** *n. (Sport)* Halbzeit, *die;* ~-'**way** **1.** *adj.* ~**-way point** Mitte, *die;* **2.** *adv.* die Hälfte des Weges ⟨*begleiten, fahren*⟩
**hall** [hɔːl] *n.* **a)** Saal, *der; (building)* Halle, *die;* **b)** *(entrance* ~*)* Flur, *der*
'**hallmark** *n.* [Feingehalts]stempel, *der; (fig.)* Kennzeichen, *das*
**hallo** [hə'ləʊ] *int.* **a)** *(to call attention)* hallo; **b)** *(Brit.) see* **hello**
**Hallowe'en** [hæləʊ'iːn] *n.* Halloween, *das; Abend vor Allerheiligen*
**hallucination** [həluːsɪ'neɪʃn] *n.* Halluzination, *die*
'**hallway** *n.* Flur, *der*
**halo** ['heɪləʊ] *n., pl.* ~**es** Heiligenschein, *der*
**halt** [hɒlt, hɔːlt] **1.** *n.* **a)** Pause, *die; (interruption)* Unterbrechung, *die;* **call a** ~ **to sth.** mit etw. Schluß machen; **b)** *(Brit. Railw.)* Haltepunkt, *der.* **2.** *v.i.* **a)** stehenbleiben; ⟨*Fahrer:*⟩ anhalten; *(for a rest)* eine Pause machen; *(esp. Mil.)* haltmachen; ~, **who goes there?** *(Mil.)* halt, wer da?; **b)** *(end)* eingestellt werden. **3.** *v.t.* anhalten; einstellen ⟨*Projekt*⟩. '**halting** *adj.* schleppend; zögernd ⟨*Antwort*⟩
**halve** [hɑːv] *v.t.* halbieren
**halves** *pl. of* **half**
**ham** [hæm] *n.* Schinken, *der*
**hamburger** ['hæmbɜːgə(r)] *n.* Hacksteak, *das; (in roll)* Hamburger, *der*
**hamlet** ['hæmlɪt] *n.* Weiler, *der*
**hammer** ['hæmə(r)] **1.** *n.* Hammer, *der.* **2.** *v.t.* hämmern. **3.** *v.i.* hämmern (**at** an + *Dat.*). **hammer 'out** *v.t.* ausklopfen ⟨*Delle, Beule*⟩; *(fig.: devise)* ausarbeiten
**hammock** ['hæmək] *n.* Hängematte, *die*

¹**hamper** ['hæmpə(r)] *n.* [Deckel]korb, *der*
²**hamper** *v.t.* behindern
**hamster** ['hæmstə(r)] *n.* Hamster, *der*
**hand** [hænd] **1.** *n.* **a)** Hand, *die;* **by** ~ *(manually)* mit der *od.* von Hand; **give** *or* **lend** [**sb.**] **a** ~ [**with** *or* **in sth.**] [jmdm.] [**bei etw.**] helfen; **b)** *(share)* **have a** ~ **in sth.** bei etw. seine Hände im Spiel haben; **c)** *(worker)* Arbeiter, *der; (Naut.: seaman)* Matrose, *der;* **d)** *(of clock or watch)* Zeiger, *der;* **e) at** ~: in der Nähe; **on the one** ~ **...**, [**but**] **on the other** [~] **...**: einerseits ..., andererseits ...; **f)** *(Cards)* Karte, *die.* **2.** *v.t.* geben; ⟨*Überbringer:*⟩ übergeben ⟨*Sendung, Lieferung*⟩. **hand 'in** *v.t.* abgeben (**to**, **at** bei); einreichen ⟨*Petition*⟩. **hand 'out** *v.t.* austeilen. **hand 'over** *v.t.* übergeben (**to** *Dat.*)
**hand:** ~**bag** *n.* Handtasche, *die;* ~**-baggage** *n.* Handgepäck, *das;* ~**book** *n.* Handbuch, *das;* ~**-brake** *n.* Handbremse, *die;* ~**cuff** **1.** *n., usu. in pl.* Handschelle, *die;* **2.** *v.t.* ~**cuff sb.** jmdm. Handschellen anlegen
**handful** ['hændfʊl] *n.* Handvoll, *die;* **be a** ~ *(fig. coll.)* einen ständig auf Trab halten *(ugs.)*
**handicap** ['hændɪkæp] **1.** *n.* **a)** *(Sport, also fig.)* Handikap, *das;* **b)** *(physical)* Behinderung, *die.* **2.** *v.t.*, **-pp-** benachteiligen. **handicapped** ['hændɪkæpt] *adj.* [**mentally/physically**] ~: [geistig/körperlich] behindert
**handicraft** ['hændɪkrɑːft] *n.* [Kunst]handwerk, *das; (needlework, knitting, etc.)* Handarbeit, *die*
**handiwork** ['hændɪwɜːk] *n.* handwerkliche Arbeit; **it's all his own** ~: das hat er selbst gemacht
**handkerchief** ['hæŋkətʃɪf] *n., pl.* ~**s** *or* **handkerchieves** ['hæŋkətʃiːvz] Taschentuch, *das*
**handle** ['hændl] **1.** *n.* Griff, *der; (of door)* Klinke, *die; (of axe, brush, comb, broom, saucepan)* Stiel, *der; (of cup, jug)* Henkel, *der.* **2.** *v.t.* **a)** *(touch, feel)* anfassen; **b)** *(control)* handhaben ⟨*Fahrzeug, Flugzeug*⟩; **c)** *(deal/cope with)* umgehen/fertigwerden mit.
'**handlebars** *n. pl.* Lenkstange, *die*
**hand:** ~**-luggage** *n.* Handgepäck, *das;* ~**made** *adj.* handgearbeitet; ~**shake** *n.* Händedruck, *der*
**handsome** ['hænsəm] *adj.* gutaussehend
**hand:** ~**stand** *n.* Handstand, *der;* ~**writing** *n.* [Hand]schrift, *die*

**handy** ['hændɪ] *adj.* greifbar; **keep/ have sth. ~:** etw. greifbar haben.
'**handyman** *n.* Handwerker, *der;* [home] ~: Heimwerker, *der*
**hang** [hæŋ] **1.** *v. t.* **a)** *p. t., p. p.* **hung** [hʌŋ] hängen; aufhängen ‹*Bild, Gardinen*›; ankleben ‹*Tapete*›; **b)** *p. t., p. p.* **hanged** *(execute)* hängen (for wegen); ~ **oneself** sich erhängen. **2.** *v. i.,* **hung a)** hängen; ‹*Kleid usw.*:› fallen; **b)** *(be executed)* hängen. **3.** *n.* **get the ~ of sth.** *(coll.)* mit etw. klarkommen *(ugs.).* **hang a'bout, hang a'round** *v. i.* **a)** *(loiter)* herumlungern *(salopp);* **b)** *(coll.: wait)* warten. **hang 'on** *v. i.* **a)** sich festhalten (**to** an + *Dat.*); **b)** *(sl.: wait)* warten; **c)** ~ **on to** *(coll.: keep)* behalten. **hang 'out 1.** *v. t.* aufhängen ‹*Wäsche*›. **2.** *v. i.* **a)** heraushängen; **b)** *(sl.) (live)* wohnen; *(be often present)* sich herumtreiben *(ugs.).* **hang 'up** *v. t.* **1.** aufhängen. **2.** *v. i. (Teleph.)* auflegen
**hangar** ['hæŋə(r)] *n.* Hangar, *der*
'**hanger** *n.* Bügel, *der*
'**hang-glider** *n.* Drachen, *der*
'**hanging** *n. (execution)* Hinrichtung [durch den Strang]
**hang:** ~**man** [hæŋmən] *n., pl.* ~**men** [hæŋmən] Henker, *der;* ~**over** *n.* Kater, *der (ugs.);* ~**up** *n. (sl.)* Macke, *die (ugs.)*
**hanker** ['hæŋkə(r)] *v. i.* ~ **after** ein heftiges Verlangen haben nach
**hanky** ['hæŋkɪ] *n. (coll.)* Taschentuch, *das*
**Hanover** ['hænəʊvə(r)] *pr. n.* Hannover *(das)*
**haphazard** [hæp'hæzəd] *adj.,* **hap'hazardly** *adv.* willkürlich
**happen** ['hæpn] *v. i.* geschehen; ‹*Vorhergesagtes:*› eintreffen; ~ **to sb.** jmdm. passieren; ~ **to do sth./be sb.** zufällig etw. tun/jmd. sein; **as it** ~s *or* **it so** ~s **I have ...:** zufällig habe ich ...
'**happening** *n.* Ereignis, *das*
**happily** ['hæpɪlɪ] *adv.* **a)** glücklich ‹*lächeln*›; vergnügt ‹*spielen, lachen*›; **b)** *(gladly)* mit Vergnügen
**happiness** ['hæpɪnɪs] *n. see* **happy a:** Glück, *das;* Heiterkeit, *die;* Zufriedenheit, *die*
**happy** ['hæpɪ] *adj.* **a)** *(joyful)* glücklich; heiter ‹*Bild, Veranlagung*›; erfreulich ‹*Erinnerung, Szene*›; froh ‹*Ereignis*›; *(contented)* zufrieden; **b)** **be** ~ **to do sth.** *(glad)* etw. gern tun.
**happy-go-'lucky** *adj.* sorglos
**harass** ['hærəs] *v. t.* schikanieren.

'**harassment** *n.* Schikanierung, *die;* **sexual** ~: [sexuelle] Belästigung
**harbour** (*Brit.: Amer.:* **harbor**) ['hɑːbə(r)] **1.** *n.* Hafen, *der;* **in** ~: im Hafen. **2.** *v. t.* Unterschlupf gewähren (+ *Dat.*) ‹*Verbrecher, Flüchtling*›; hegen *(geh.)* ‹*Groll, Verdacht*›
**hard** [hɑːd] **1.** *adj.* **a)** hart; fest ‹*Gelee*›; stark ‹*Regen*›; streng ‹*Frost, Winter*›; gesichert ‹*Beweis, Daten*›; **b)** *(difficult)* schwer; **this is** ~ **to believe** das ist kaum zu glauben; **do sth. the** ~ **way** es sich *(Dat.)* bei etw. unnötig schwermachen; **c)** *(strenuous)* hart; **d)** *(vigorous)* kräftig ‹*Schlag, Stoß, Tritt*›; **e)** *(harsh)* hart. **2.** *adv.* **a)** *(strenuously)* hart ‹*arbeiten, trainieren*›; fleißig ‹*studieren, üben*›; genau ‹*überlegen*›; gut ‹*aufpassen, zuhören*›; **try** ~: sich sehr bemühen; **b)** *(vigorously)* heftig; fest ‹*schlagen, drücken, klopfen*›; **c)** *(severely)* hart; **be** ~ **up** knapp bei Kasse sein *(ugs.);* **feel** ~ **done by** sich schlecht behandelt fühlen
**hard:** ~**back** *n.* gebundene Ausgabe; ~**board** *n.* Hartfaserplatte, *die;* ~**-boiled** *adj.* **a)** hartgekocht ‹*Ei*›; **b)** *(tough)* hartgesotten
**harden** ['hɑːdn] **1.** *v. t.* härten; *(fig.)* abhärten (**to** gegen). **2.** *v. i.* hart werden; *(become confirmed)* sich verhärten. **hardened** ['hɑːdnd] *adj.* abgehärtet (**to** gegen); hartgesotten ‹*Verbrecher*›
**hard:** ~**-headed** *adj.* nüchtern; ~**-hearted** *adj.* hartherzig (**towards** gegenüber)
**hardly** ['hɑːdlɪ] *adv.* kaum; ~ **anyone** *or* **anybody/anything** fast niemand/ nichts; ~ **ever** so gut wie nie; ~ **at all** fast überhaupt nicht
'**hardness** *n.* Härte, *die*
'**hardship** *n.* **a)** Not, *die;* Elend, *das;* **b)** *(instance)* Notlage, *die*
**hard:** ~ '**shoulder** *n. (Brit.)* Standspur, *die;* ~**ware** *n.* **a)** *(goods)* Eisenwaren *Pl.; attrib.* Eisenwaren‹geschäft›; **b)** *(Computing)* Hardware, *die;* ~**-wearing** *adj.* strapazierfähig; ~**-working** *adj.* fleißig
**hardy** ['hɑːdɪ] *adj.* abgehärtet; zäh ‹*Rasse*›; winterhart ‹*Pflanze*›
**hare** [heə(r)] *n.* Hase, *der*
**hark** [hɑːk] *v. i.* [just] ~ **at him** hör ihn dir/hört ihn euch nur an!; ~ **back to** zurückkommen auf (+ *Akk.*)
**harm** [hɑːm] **1.** *n.* Schaden, *der;* **do sb.** ~, **do** ~ **to sb.** jmdm. schaden. **2.** *v. t.* etwas [zuleide] tun (+ *Dat.*); schaden

(+ *Dat.*) ⟨*Beziehungen, Land, Ruf*⟩.
**harmful** ['hɑːmfl] *adj.* schädlich (**to** für). '**harmless** *adj.* harmlos
**harmonica** [hɑːˈmɒnɪkə] *n.* Mundharmonika, *die*
**harmonious** [hɑːˈməʊnɪəs] *adj.* harmonisch
**harmonize** ['hɑːmənaɪz] 1. *v. t.* aufeinander abstimmen. 2. *v. i.* harmonieren (**with** mit)
**harmony** ['hɑːmənɪ] *n.* Harmonie, *die;* **be in** ~: harmonieren
**harness** ['hɑːnɪs] 1. *n.* Geschirr, *das.* 2. *v. t.* anschirren; *(fig.)* nutzen
**harp** [hɑːp] 1. *n.* Harfe, *die.* 2. *v. i.* ~ **on** [about] sth. immer wieder von etw. reden; *(critically)* auf etw. *(Dat.)* herumreiten *(salopp)*
**harpoon** [hɑːˈpuːn] *n.* Harpune, *die*
**harrowing** ['hærəʊɪŋ] *adj.* entsetzlich; grauenhaft ⟨*Anblick, Geschichte*⟩
**harsh** [hɑːʃ] *adj.* **a)** rauh ⟨*Gewebe, Klima*⟩; schrill ⟨*Ton, Stimme*⟩; grell ⟨*Licht*⟩; hart ⟨*Bedingungen, Leben*⟩; **b)** *(excessively severe)* [sehr] hart; ⟨äußerst⟩ streng ⟨*Disziplin*⟩; rücksichtslos ⟨*Tyrann, Herrscher, Politik*⟩. '**harshly** *adv.* [sehr] hart
**harvest** ['hɑːvɪst] 1. *n.* Ernte, *die.* 2. *v. t.* ernten
**has** *see* **have**
**hash** [hæʃ] *n.* **a)** *(Cookery)* Haschee, *das;* **b) make a** ~ **of** sth. *(coll.)* etw. verpfuschen *(ugs.)*
**hasn't** ['hæznt] = **has not**; *see* **have**
**hassle** ['hæsl] *(coll.)* 1. *n.* Ärger, *der.* 2. *v. t.* schikanieren
**haste** [heɪst] *n.* Eile, *die; (rush)* Hast, *die;* **make** ~: sich beeilen
**hasten** ['heɪsn] 1. *v. t.* beschleunigen. 2. *v. i.* eilen
**hastily** ['heɪstɪlɪ] *adv. (hurriedly)* eilig; *(rashly)* übereilt
**hasty** ['heɪstɪ] *adj.* eilig; flüchtig ⟨*Skizze, Blick*⟩; *(rash)* übereilt
**hat** [hæt] *n.* Hut, *der*
¹**hatch** [hætʃ] *n.* Luke, *die; (serving*~*)* Durchreiche, *die*
²**hatch** 1. *v. t.* ausbrüten. 2. *v. i.* [aus]schlüpfen. **hatch** '**out** 1. *v. i.* ausschlüpfen. 2. *v. t.* ausbrüten
'**hatchback** *n. (car)* Schräghecklimousine, *die*
**hatchet** ['hætʃɪt] *n.* Beil, *das;* **bury the** ~ *(fig.)* das Kriegsbeil begraben
**hate** [heɪt] 1. *n.* Haß, *der.* 2. *v. t.* hassen; **I** ~ **to say this** *(coll.)* ich sage das nicht gern. **hateful** ['heɪtfl] *adj.* abscheulich

**hatred** ['heɪtrɪd] *n.* Haß, *der*
**haughty** ['hɔːtɪ] *adj.* hochmütig
**haul** [hɔːl] 1. *v. i. & t.* ziehen. 2. *n.* **a)** Ziehen, *das;* **b)** *(catch)* Fang, *der; (fig.)* Beute, *die.* **haulage** ['hɔːlɪdʒ] *n.* Transport, *der*
**haunch** [hɔːntʃ] *n.* **sit on one's/its** ~**es** auf seinem Hinterteil sitzen
**haunt** [hɔːnt] *v. t.* ~ **a house/castle** in einem Haus/Schloß spuken; **a** ~**ed house** ein Haus, in dem es spukt. '**haunting** *adj.* sehnsüchtig
**have** 1. [hæv] *v. t., pres.* **he has** [hæz], *p. t. & p. p.* **had** [hæd] haben; *(obtain)* bekommen; *(take)* nehmen; bekommen ⟨*Kind*⟩; ~ **breakfast/dinner/lunch** frühstücken/zu Abend/zu Mittag essen; ~ **a cup of tea** eine Tasse Tee trinken; ~ **sb. to stay** jmdn. zu Besuch haben; **you've had it now** *(coll.)* jetzt ist es aus *(ugs.)*; ~ **a game of football** Fußball spielen. 2. [həv, əv, *stressed* hæv] *v. aux.*, **he has** [həz, əz, *stressed* hæz], **had** [həd, əd, *stressed* hæd] **I** ~**/I had read** ich habe/hatte gelesen; **I** ~**/I had gone** ich bin/war gegangen; **if I had known**...: wenn ich gewußt hätte...; ~ **sth. made** etw. machen lassen; ~ **to** müssen. **have** '**on** *v. t.* **a)** *(wear)* tragen; **b)** *(Brit. coll.: deceive)* ~ **sb. on** jmdn. auf den Arm nehmen *(ugs.)*. **have** '**out** *v. t.* **a)** ~ **a tooth/one's tonsils out** sich *(Dat.)* einen Zahn ziehen lassen/sich *(Dat.)* die Mandeln herausnehmen lassen; **b)** ~ **it out with sb.** mit jmdm. offen sprechen
**haven** ['heɪvn] *n.* geschützte Anlegestelle, *die; (fig.)* Zufluchtsort, *der*
**haven't** ['hævnt] = **have not**; *see* **have**
**haversack** ['hævəsæk] *n.* Brotbeutel, *der*
**havoc** ['hævək] *n.* **a)** *(devastation)* Verwüstungen; **cause** *or* **wreak** ~: Verwüstungen anrichten; **b)** *(confusion)* Chaos; **play** ~ **with** sth. etw. völlig durcheinanderbringen
¹**hawk** [hɔːk] *n.* Falke, *der*
²**hawk** *v. t.* hausieren mit. '**hawker** *n.* Hausierer, *der*/Hausiererin, *die*
**hay** [heɪ] *n.* Heu, *das*
**hay:** ~ **fever** *n.* Heuschnupfen, *der;* ~**stack** *n.* Heuschober, *der (südd.);* Heudieme, *die (nordd.);* ~**wire** *adj. (coll.)* **go** ~**wire** ⟨*Instrument:*⟩ verrückt spielen *(ugs.)*
**hazard** ['hæzəd] 1. *n.* Gefahr, *die.* 2. *v. t.* ~ **a guess** mit Raten probieren. **hazardous** ['hæzədəs] *adj.* gefährlich

**haze** [heɪz] *n.* Dunst[schleier], *der*
**hazelnut** ['heɪzlnʌt] *n.* Haselnuß, *die*
**hazy** ['heɪzɪ] *adj.* dunstig; *(fig.)* vage
**he** [hɪ, *stressed* hiː] *pron.* er
**head** [hed] **1.** *n.* **a)** Kopf, *der;* ~ **first** mit dem Kopf voran; ~ **over heels** kopfüber; **keep/lose one's** ~: einen klaren Kopf behalten/den Kopf verlieren; **in one's** ~: im Kopf; **enter sb.'s** ~: jmdm. in den Sinn kommen; **use your** ~: gebrauch deinen Verstand; **a** *or* **per** ~: pro Kopf; **b)** *in pl. (on coin)* ~s Kopf; ~s **or tails?** Kopf oder Zahl?; **c)** *(leader)* Leiter, *der*/Leiterin, *die;* **d)** *(on beer)* Blume, *die.* **2.** *attrib. adj.* ~ **waiter** Oberkellner, *der;* ~ **office** Hauptverwaltung, *die.* **3.** *v. t.* **a)** *(stand at top of)* anführen ⟨*Liste*⟩; *(lead)* leiten; führen ⟨*Bewegung*⟩; **b)** *(Football)* köpfen. **4.** *v. i.* steuern; ~ **for London** ⟨*Flugzeug, Schiff:*⟩ Kurs auf London nehmen; ⟨*Auto:*⟩ in Richtung London fahren; **you're** ~**ing for trouble** du wirst Ärger bekommen.
'**headache** *n.* Kopfschmerzen *Pl.*
'**header** *n. (Footb.)* Kopfball, *der*
'**headgear** *n.* Kopfbedeckung, *die*
'**heading** *n.* Überschrift, *die*
**head:** ~**lamp** *n.* Scheinwerfer, *der;* ~**land** *n.* Landspitze, *die;* ~**light** *n.* Scheinwerfer, *der;* ~**line** *n.* Schlagzeile, *die;* ~**long** *adv.* kopfüber; ~'**master** *n.* Schulleiter, *der;* ~'**mistress** *n.* Schulleiterin, *die;* ~~**on 1.** ['--] *adj.* frontal⟨*zusammenstoß*⟩; **2.** [-'-] *adv.* frontal; ~~**phones** *n. pl.* Kopfhörer, *der;* ~'**quarters** *n. sing. or pl.* Hauptquartier, *das;* ~~**rest** *n.* Kopfstütze, *die;* ~**room** *n.* [lichte] Höhe, *die;* ~**strong** *adj.* eigensinnig; ~**way** *n.* **make** ~**way** Fortschritte machen; ~ **wind** *n.* Gegenwind, *der*
'**heady** ['hedɪ] *adj.* berauschend
**heal** [hiːl] **1.** *v. t.* heilen. **2.** *v. i.* ~ |**up**| [ver]heilen
**health** [helθ] *n.* Gesundheit, *die;* **in good/very good** ~: bei guter/bester Gesundheit; **good** *or* **your** ~**!** auf deine Gesundheit!
**health:** ~ **centre** *n.* Poliklinik, *die;* ~ **food** *n.* Reformhauskost, *die;* ~~**food shop** Reformhaus, *das;* ~ **service** *n.* Gesundheitsdienst, *der*
'**healthy** ['helθɪ] *adj.* gesund
**heap** [hiːp] **1.** *n.* Haufen, *der;* ~**s of** *(coll.)* jede Menge *(ugs.).* **2.** *v. t.* aufhäufen
**hear** [hɪə(r)] **1.** *v. t.,* **heard** [hɜːd] **a)** hö-

ren; **b)** *(understand)* verstehen. **2.** *v. i.,* **heard:** ~ **about sb./sth.** von jmdm./ etw. [etwas] hören; **he wouldn't** ~ **of it** er wollte nichts davon hören. **3.** *int.* H~! H~! bravo!; richtig! **hear 'out** *v. t.* ausreden lassen
**heard** *see* **hear 1, 2**
'**hearing** *n.* Gehör, *das;* **be hard of** ~: schwerhörig sein. '**hearing-aid** *n.* Hörgerät, *das*
'**hearsay** ['hɪəseɪ] *n.* Gerücht, *das;* **it's only** ~: es ist nur ein Gerücht
**hearse** [hɜːs] *n.* Leichenwagen, *der*
**heart** [hɑːt] *n. (also Cards)* Herz, *das;* **by** ~: auswendig; **at** ~: im Grunde seines/ihres Herzens; **take/lose** ~: Mut schöpfen/verlieren; **my** ~ **sank** mein Mut sank; **the** ~ **of the matter** der wahre Kern der Sache; *see also* **club 1 c**
**heart:** ~ **attack** *n.* Herzanfall, *der; (fatal)* Herzschlag, *der;* ~**beat** *n.* Herzschlag, *der;* ~~**breaking** *adj.* herzzerreißend; ~~**broken** *adj.* **she was** ~~**broken** ihr Herz war gebrochen; ~**burn** *n.* Sodbrennen, *das*
**hearten** ['hɑːtn] *v. t.* ermutigen. '**heartening** *adj.* ermutigend
**heart:** ~ **failure** *n.* Herzversagen, *das;* ~**felt** *adj.* tiefempfunden ⟨*Beileid*⟩; aufrichtig ⟨*Dankbarkeit*⟩
**hearth** [hɑːθ] *n.* Platz vor dem Kamin. '**hearth-rug** *n.* Kaminvorleger, *der*
'**heartily** ['hɑːtɪlɪ] *adv.* von Herzen; **eat** ~: tüchtig essen
'**heartless** *adj.* herzlos
'**hearty** ['hɑːtɪ] *adj.* herzlich; ungeteilt ⟨*Zustimmung*⟩; herzhaft ⟨*Mahlzeit*⟩
**heat** [hiːt] **1.** *n.* **a)** *(hotness)* Hitze, *die;* **b)** *(Phys.)* Wärme, *die;* **c)** *(Sport)* Vorlauf, *der.* **2.** *v. t.* heizen. **heat 'up** *v. t.* heiß machen
'**heated** *adj. (angry)* hitzig
'**heater** *n.* Ofen, *der; (for water)* Boiler, *der*
**heath** [hiːθ] *n.* Heide, *die*
**heathen** ['hiːðn] **1.** *adj.* heidnisch. **2.** *n.* Heide, *der*/Heidin, *die*
**heather** ['heðə(r)] *n.* Heidekraut, *das*
'**heating** *n.* Heizung, *die*
**heat:** ~~**stroke** *n.* Hitzschlag, *der;* ~~**wave** *n.* Hitzewelle, *die*
**heave** [hiːv] **1.** *v. t.* **a)** heben; **b)** *(coll.: throw)* schmeißen *(ugs.);* **c)** ~ **a sigh** aufseufzen. **2.** *v. i. (pull)* ziehen. **3.** *n.* Zug, *der*
**heaven** ['hevn] *n.* Himmel, *der;* **in** ~: im Himmel; **for H~'s sake!** um Gottes willen! '**heavenly** *adj.* himmlisch

**heavily** ['hevɪlɪ] *adj.* schwer; *(to a great extent)* stark; schwer ⟨bewaffnet⟩; tief ⟨schlafen⟩; dicht ⟨bevölkert⟩; **smoke/drink** ~: ein starker Raucher/Trinker sein; **it rained/snowed** ~: es regnete/schneite stark

**heavy** ['hevɪ] *adj.* schwer; unmäßig ⟨Trinken, Rauchen⟩; **a** ~ **smoker/drinker** ein starker Raucher/Trinker; **be a** ~ **sleeper** sehr fest schlafen

**heavy:** ~**-duty** *adj.* strapazierfähig ⟨Kleidung, Material⟩; schwer ⟨Werkzeug, Maschine⟩; ~ '**goods vehicle** *n.* *(Brit.)* Schwerlastwagen, *der;* ~**weight** *n.* Schwergewicht, *das*

**Hebrew** ['hi:bru:] 1. *adj.* hebräisch. 2. *n. (language)* Hebräisch, *das*

**heckle** ['hekl] *v. t.* Zwischenrufe unterbrechen. **heckler** ['heklə(r)] *n.* Zwischenrufer, *der*

**hectic** ['hektɪk] *adj.* hektisch

**he'd** [hɪd, *stressed* hi:d] a) = **he had;** b) = **he would**

**hedge** [hedʒ] 1. *n.* Hecke, *die.* 2. *v. t.* ~ **one's bets** *(fig.)* nicht alles auf eine Karte setzen. 3. *v. i.* sich nicht festlegen

**hedgehog** ['hedʒhɒg] *n.* Igel, *der*

'**hedgerow** *n.* Hecke, *die* [als Feldbegrenzung]

**heed** [hi:d] 1. *v. t.* beachten; beherzigen ⟨Rat, Lektion⟩; ~ **the danger/risk** sich *(Dat.)* der Gefahr/des Risikos bewußt sein. 2. *n.* **give** *or* **pay** ~ **to, take** ~ **of** Beachtung schenken (+ *Dat.*). '**heedless** *adj.* unachtsam; **be** ~ **of sth.** auf etw. *(Akk.)* nicht achten

**heel** [hi:l] *n.* Ferse, *die; (of shoe)* Absatz, *der;* **Achilles'** ~ *(fig.)* Achillesferse, *die;* **down at** ~ *(fig.)* heruntergekommen; **take to one's** ~**s** Fersengeld geben *(ugs.)*

**hefty** ['heftɪ] *adj.* kräftig; *(heavy)* schwer

**height** [haɪt] *n.* a) Höhe, *die; (of person, animal, building)* Größe, *die;* b) *(fig.: highest point)* Höhepunkt, *der.* **heighten** ['haɪtn] *v. t.* aufstocken; *(fig.)* verstärken

**heir** [eə(r)] *n.* Erbe, *der*/Erbin, *die.* **heiress** ['eərɪs] *n.* Erbin, *die*

**heirloom** ['eəlu:m] *n.* Erbstück, *das*

**held** *see* ²**hold** 1, 2

**helicopter** ['helɪkɒptə(r)] *n.* Hubschrauber, *der*

**heliport** ['helɪpɔ:t] *n.* Heliport, *der*

**helium** ['hi:lɪəm] *n.* Helium, *das*

**hell** [hel] *n.* a) Hölle, *die;* b) *(coll.)* |oh| ~! verdammter Mist! *(ugs.);* **what the**

~! ach, zum Teufel! *(ugs.);* **run like** ~: wie der Teufel rennen *(ugs.)*

**he'll** [hɪl, *stressed* hi:l] = **he will**

**hello** [hə'ləʊ, he'ləʊ] *int. (greeting)* hallo; *(surprise)* holla

**hell's 'angel** *n.* Rocker, *der*

**helm** [helm] *n. (Naut.)* Ruder, *das*

**helmet** ['helmɪt] *n.* Helm, *der*

**help** [help] 1. *v. t.* a) ~ **sb.** |to do sth.| jmdm. helfen[, etw. zu tun]; **can I** ~ **you?** *(in shop)* was möchten Sie bitte?; b) *(serve)* ~ **oneself** sich bedienen; ~ **oneself to sth.** sich *(Dat.)* etw. nehmen; *(coll.: steal)* etw. mitgehen lassen *(ugs.);* c) *(avoid)* **if I/you can** ~ **it** wenn es irgend zu vermeiden ist; *(remedy)* **I can't** ~ **it** ich kann nichts dafür *(ugs.);* **it can't be** ~**ed** es läßt sich nicht ändern; d) *(refrain from)* **I can't** ~ **thinking** *or* **can't** ~ **but think that ...**: ich kann mir nicht helfen, ich glaube, ...; **I can't** ~ **laughing** ich muß einfach lachen. 2. *n.* Hilfe, *die;* **with the** ~ **of ...**: mit Hilfe ... (+ *Gen.*); **be of** |some|/**no**/**much** ~ **to sb.** jmdm. eine gewisse/keine/eine große Hilfe sein. **help 'out** 1. *v. i.* aushelfen. 2. *v. t.* ~ **sb. out** jmdm. helfen

'**helper** *n.* Helfer, *der*/Helferin, *die*

**helpful** ['helpfl] *adj. (willing)* hilfsbereit; *(useful)* hilfreich; nützlich

'**helping** 1. *adj.* **lend** |**sb.**| **a** ~ **hand** |**with sth.**| *(fig.)* |jmdm.| [bei etw.] helfen. 2. *n.* Portion, *die*

'**helpless** *adj.,* '**helplessly** *adv.* hilflos

**helter-skelter** [heltə'skeltə(r)] *n.* [spiralförmige] Rutschbahn

**hem** [hem] 1. *n.* Saum, *der.* 2. *v. t.,* -mm- säumen. **hem 'in** *v. t.* einschließen; **feel** ~**med in** sich eingeengt fühlen

**hemisphere** ['hemɪsfɪə(r)] *n.* Halbkugel, *die*

'**hem-line** *n.* Saum, *der*

**hemp** [hemp] *n.* Hanf, *der*

**hen** [hen] *n.* Huhn, *das;* Henne, *die*

**hence** [hens] *adv. (therefore)* daher. **hence'forth** *adv.* von nun an

**henchman** ['hentʃmən] *n., pl.* **henchmen** ['hentʃmən] Handlanger, *der*

**henpecked** ['henpekt] *adj.* **a** ~ **husband** ein Pantoffelheld, *der (ugs.);* **be** ~: unter dem Pantoffel stehen *(ugs.)*

¹**her** [hə(r), *stressed* hɜ:(r)] *pron.* sie; *as indirect object* ihr; **it was** ~: sie war's

²**her** *poss. pron. attr.* ihr

**herald** ['herəld] 1. *n.* Herold, *der.* 2. *v. t.* ankündigen. **heraldic** [he'rældɪk] *adj.* heraldisch. **heraldry** ['herəldrı] *n.* Heraldik, *die*

**herb** [hɜ:b] *n.* Kraut, *das.* **herbaceous** [hɜ:'beıʃəs] *adj.* krautartig; ~ **border** Staudenrabatte, *die.* **herbal** ['hɜ:bl] *attrib. adj.* Kräuter

**herd** [hɜ:d] **1.** *n.* Herde, *die; (of wild animals)* Rudel, *das.* **2.** *v. t.* **a)** treiben; ~ **people together** Menschen zusammenpferchen; **b)** *(tend)* hüten

**here** [hıə(r)] **1.** *adv.* **a)** *(in or at this place)* hier; **down/in/up** ~: hier unten/drin/oben; ~ **you are** *(coll.: giving sth.)* hier; **b)** *(to this place)* hierher; **in[to]** ~: hierherein; **come/bring** ~: [hier]herkommen/-bringen. **2.** *int. (attracting attention)* he. **here·by** *adv. (formal)* hiermit

**hereditary** [hı'redıtərı] *adj.* **a)** erblich ⟨*Titel, Amt*⟩; **b)** *(Biol.)* angeboren

**heresy** ['herısı] *n.* Ketzerei, *die*

**heretic** ['herıtık] *n.* Ketzer, *der/*Ketzerin, *die*

**here·with** *adv.* in der Anlage

**heritage** ['herıtıdʒ] *n.* Erbe, *das*

**hermetic** [hɜ:'metık] *adj.* luftdicht. **hermetically** [hɜ:'metıkəlı] *adv.* hermetisch

**hermit** ['hɜ:mıt] *n.* Einsiedler, *der/* Einsiedlerin, *die*

**hernia** ['hɜ:nıə] *n.* Bruch, *der*

**hero** ['hıərəʊ] *n., pl.* ~**es** Held, *der.* **heroic** [hı'rəʊık] *adj.* heldenhaft

**heroin** ['herəʊın] *n.* Heroin, *das*

**heroine** ['herəʊın] *n.* Heldin, *die*

**heroism** ['herəʊızm] *n.* Heldentum, *das*

**heron** ['hern] *n.* Reiher, *der*

**herring** ['herıŋ] *n.* Hering, *der*

**hers** [hɜ:z] *poss. pron. pred.* ihrer/ihre/ihres; **the book is** ~: das Buch gehört ihr

**her·self** *pron.* **a)** *emphat.* selbst; **[all] by** ~: [ganz] allein[e]; **b)** *refl.* sich; allein[e] ⟨*tun, wählen*⟩; **younger than/as heavy as** ~: jünger als/so schwer wie sie selbst

**he's** [hız, *stressed* hi:z] **a)** = **he is; b)** = **he has**

**hesitant** ['hezıtənt] *adj.* zögernd ⟨*Reaktion*⟩; stockend ⟨*Rede*⟩

**hesitate** ['hezıteıt] *v. i.* zögern; *(falter)* ins Stocken geraten; ~ **to do sth.** Bedenken haben, etw. zu tun. **hesitation** [hezı'teıʃn] *n.* **a)** *(indecision)* Unentschlossenheit, *die;* **without** ~: ohne zu zögern; **b)** *(instance of faltering)* Unsicherheit, *die;* **c)** *(reluctance)* Bedenken *Pl.*

**heterosexual** [hetərəʊ'seksjʊəl] **1.** *adj.* heterosexuell. **2.** *n.* Heterosexuelle, *der/die*

**het up** [het ˈʌp] *adj.* aufgeregt

**hew** [hju:] *v. t., p. p.* **hewn** [hju:n] *or* **hewed** [hju:d] hacken ⟨*Holz*⟩; losschlagen ⟨*Kohle, Gestein*⟩

**hewn** *see* **hew**

**hexagon** ['heksəgən] *n.* Sechseck, *das*

**hey** [heı] *int.* he; ~ **presto!** simsalabim!

**heyday** ['heıdeı] *n.* Blütezeit, *die*

**HGV** *abbr. (Brit.)* heavy goods vehicle

**hi** [haı] *int.* hallo *(ugs.)*

**hiatus** [haı'eıtəs] *n.* Unterbrechung, *die*

**hibernate** ['haıbəneıt] *v. i.* Winterschlaf halten. **hibernation** [haıbə'neıʃn] *n.* Winterschlaf, *der*

**hiccup** ['hıkʌp] **1.** *n.* **a)** Schluckauf, *der;* **have/get [the]** ~**s** den Schluckauf haben/bekommen; **b)** *(fig.: stoppage)* Störung, *die.* **2.** *v. i.* schlucksen *(ugs.)*

**hid** *see* ¹**hide**

**hidden** *see* ¹**hide**

¹**hide** [haıd] **1.** *v. t.,* **hid** [hıd], **hidden** ['hıdn] **a)** verstecken ⟨*Gegenstand, Person usw.*⟩ **(from** vor + *Dat.*); verbergen ⟨*Gefühle, Sinn usw.*⟩ **(from** vor + *Dat.*); verheimlichen ⟨*Tatsache, Absicht usw.*⟩ **(from** *Dat.*); **b)** *(obscure)* verdecken. **2.** *v. i.,* **hid, hidden** sich verstecken **(from** vor + *Dat.*)

²**hide** *n.* Haut, *die; (of furry animal)* Fell, *das; (dressed)* Leder, *das*

**hide-and-'seek** *n.* Versteckspiel, *das;* **play** ~: Verstecken spielen

**hideous** ['hıdıəs] *adj.* scheußlich

¹**hide-out** *n.* Versteck, *das*

¹**hiding** ['haıdıŋ] *n.* **go into** ~: sich verstecken; *(to avoid police, public attention)* untertauchen; **be in** ~: sich versteckt halten; *(to avoid police, public attention)* untergetaucht sein

²**hiding** *n. (coll.: beating)* Tracht Prügel; **give sb. a [good]** ~: jmdm. eine [ordentliche] Tracht Prügel verpassen *(ugs.)*

¹**hiding-place** *n.* Versteck, *das*

**hierarchy** ['haıərɑ:kı] *n.* Hierarchie, *die*

**hi-fi** ['haıfaı] *(coll.)* **1.** *adj.* Hi-Fi-. **2.** *n.* Hi-Fi-Anlage, *die*

**high** [haı] **1.** *adj.* **a)** hoch; groß ⟨*Höhe*⟩; stark ⟨*Wind*⟩; **b)** *(coll.: on a drug)* high *(ugs.);* **c) it's** ~ **time you left** es ist höchste Zeit, daß du gehst. **2.** *adv.* hoch; **search** *or* **look** ~ **and low** überall suchen. **3.** *n.* **a)** *(~est level/ figure)* Höchststand, *der;* **b)** *(Met-*

*eorol.)* Hoch, *das.* **'highbrow** *(coll.)*
**1.** *n.* Intellektuelle, *der/die.* **2.** *adj.* intellektuell ⟨*Person, Gerede usw.*⟩;
hochgestochen *(abwertend)* ⟨*Person,
Musik, Literatur usw.*⟩. **'high chair** *n.*
Hochstuhl, *der*
**higher edu'cation** *n.* Hochschulbil-
dung, *die*
**high:** ~-**'handed** *adj.* selbstherrlich;
~-**heeled** [haɪ'hiːld] *adj.* ⟨*Schuhe*⟩ mit
hohen Absätzen; ~ **jump** *n.* Hoch-
sprung, *der;* ~**land** *n.* Hochland,
*das;* ~**light 1.** *n.* a) Höhepunkt, *der;* b) *(bright area)* Licht, *das;*
**2.** *v.t.,* ~**lighted** ein Schlaglicht werfen auf (+ *Akk.*) ⟨*Probleme usw.*⟩
**'highly** *adv.* sehr; hoch⟨*interessant,
-angesehen, -bezahlt, -gebildet*⟩; leicht
⟨*entzündlich*⟩; stark ⟨*gewürzt*⟩; **think ~
of sb./sth.** eine hohe Meinung von
jmdm./etw. haben; **speak ~ of sb./sth.**
jmdn./etw. sehr loben. **highly-
strung** ['haɪlɪstrʌŋ] *adj.* übererregbar
**Highness** ['haɪnɪs] *n.* **His/her** *etc.* ~:
Seine/Ihre *usw.* Hoheit
**high:** ~-**pitched** ['haɪpɪtʃt] *adj.* hoch
⟨*Ton, Stimme*⟩; ~ **'pressure** *n.* a)
*(Meteorol.)* Hochdruck, *der;* b) *(Mech.
Engin.)* Überdruck, *der;* ~-**rise** *adj.*
~-**rise building** Hochhaus, *das;* ~-**rise
block of flats/office block** Wohn-/
Bürohochhaus, *das;* ~ **school** *n.*
≈ Oberschule, *die;* ~ **season** *n.*
Hochsaison, *die;* ~**way** *n.* öffentliche Straße
**hijack** ['haɪdʒæk] *v.t.* entführen. **'hijacker** *n.* Entführer, *der;* *(of aircraft)*
Hijacker, *der*
**hike** [haɪk] *n.* Wanderung, *die.* **'hiker**
*n.* Wanderer, *der*/Wanderin, *die*
**hilarious** [hɪ'leərɪəs] *adj.* urkomisch
**hill** [hɪl] *n.* Hügel, *der;* *(higher)* Berg,
*der;* *(slope)* Hang, *der*
**hill:** ~-**billy** ['hɪlbɪlɪ] *n.* *(Amer.)* Hinter-
wäldler, *der*/Hinterwäldlerin, *die;*
~**side** *n.* Hang, *der;* ~**top** *n.*
[Berg]gipfel, *der*
**'hilly** *adj.* hüg[e]lig
**hilt** [hɪlt] *n.* Griff, *der;* **[up] to the ~**
*(fig.)* voll und ganz
**him** [ɪm, *stressed* hɪm] *pron.* ihn; *as indirect object* ihm; **it was ~:** er war's
**Himalayas** [hɪmə'leɪəz] *pr. n. pl.* Hi-
malaya, *der*
**him'self** *pron.* a) *emphat.* selbst; b)
*refl.* sich. *See also* **herself**
**hind** [haɪnd] *adj.* hinter...; ~ **legs** Hin-
terbeine
**hinder** ['hɪndə(r)] *v.t.* *(impede)* behin-

dern; *(delay)* verzögern ⟨*Vollendung
einer Arbeit, Vorgang*⟩; aufhalten ⟨*Person*⟩; ~ **sb. from doing sth.** jmdn. daran hindern, etw. zu tun
**'hindquarters** *n. pl.* Hinterteil, *das*
**hindrance** ['hɪndrəns] *n.* Hindernis,
*das* (to für)
**'hindsight** *n.* **with [the benefit of]** ~:
im nachhinein
**Hindu** ['hɪnduː, hɪn'duː] **1.** *n.* Hindu,
*der.* **2.** *adj.* hinduistisch; Hindu⟨*gott,
-tempel*⟩
**hinge** [hɪndʒ] **1.** *n.* Scharnier, *das.* **2.**
*v.t.* mit Scharnieren versehen. **3.** *v.i.*
*(depend)* abhängen (**[up]on** von)
**hint** [hɪnt] **1.** *n.* a) *(suggestion)* Wink,
*der;* b) *(slight trace)* Spur, *die* (of von);
**the ~/no ~ of a smile** der Anflug/nicht
die Spur eines Lächelns; c) *(informa-
tion)* Tip, *der* (on für). **2.** *v.i.* ~ **at** andeuten
**hip** [hɪp] *n.* Hüfte, *die*
**hippie** ['hɪpɪ] *n.* *(coll.)* Hippie, *der*
**hippopotamus** [hɪpə'pɒtəməs] *n.*
Nilpferd, *das*
**hippy** *see* **hippie**
**hire** [haɪə(r)] **1.** *n.* Mieten, *das;* **be on ~
[to sb.]** [an jmdn.] vermietet sein; **for
~:** zu vermieten. **2.** *v.t.* a) *(employ)*
anwerben; engagieren ⟨*Anwalt, Berater usw.*⟩; b) *(obtain use of)* mieten;
~ **sth. from sb.** etw. bei jmdm. mieten;
c) *(grant use of)* ~ **[out]** vermieten; ~
**sth. [out] to sb.** etw. jmdm. *od.* an
jmdn. vermieten. **'hire-car** *n.* Miet-
wagen, *der.* **hire-'purchase** *n.* *(Brit.)*
Ratenkauf, *der; attrib.* Raten-; **pay
for/buy sth. on ~:** etw. in Raten be-
zahlen/auf Raten kaufen
**his** [ɪz, *stressed* hɪz] *poss. pron.* a) *attrib.* sein; b) *pred.* seiner/seine/sei-
n[e]s; *see also* **hers**
**hiss** [hɪs] **1.** *n.* Zischen, *das.* **2.** *v.i.* zischen
**historian** [hɪ'stɔːrɪən] *n.* Historiker,
*der*/Historikerin, *die*
**historic** [hɪ'stɒrɪk] *adj.* historisch.
**historical** [hɪ'stɒrɪkl] *adj.* historisch;
geschichtlich ⟨*Belege, Hintergrund*⟩
**history** ['hɪstərɪ] *n.* Geschichte, *die*
**hit** [hɪt] **1.** *v.t.,* **-tt-,** **hit** schlagen; *(with
missile)* treffen; ⟨*Geschoß, Ball usw.*:⟩
treffen; ⟨*Fahrzeug:*⟩ prallen gegen;
⟨*Schiff:*⟩ laufen gegen; ~ **one's head on
sth.** mit dem Kopf gegen etw. stoßen;
~ **it off with sb.** gut mit jmdm. aus-
kommen. **2.** *v.i.,* **-tt-,** **hit** schlagen. **3.**
*n.* a) *(blow)* Schlag, *der;* *(shot or bomb
striking target)* Treffer, *der;* b) *(suc-*

*cess)* Erfolg, *der; (in entertainment)* Schlager, *der;* Hit, *der (ugs.).* **hit 'back** *v. t. & i.* zurückschlagen. **'hit [up]on** *v. t.* kommen auf (+ *Akk.*) ⟨*Idee*⟩; finden ⟨*richtige Antwort, Methode*⟩

**hitch** [hɪtʃ] **1.** *v. t.* **a)** binden ⟨*Seil*⟩ **(round** um + *Akk.*); [an]koppeln ⟨*Anhänger usw.*⟩ **(to** an + *Akk.*); spannen ⟨*Zugtier usw.*⟩ **(to** vor + *Akk.*); **b)** ~ **a lift** *or* **ride** *(coll.)* per Anhalter fahren. **2.** *n. (problem)* Problem, *das.* **hitch 'up** *v. t.* hochheben ⟨*Rock*⟩

**'hitch-hike** *v. i.* per Anhalter fahren. **'hitch-hiker** *n.* Anhalter, *der*/Anhalterin, *die*

**'hit parade** *n.* Hitparade, *die*

**HIV** *abbr.* **human immuno-deficiency virus** HIV

**hive** [haɪv] *n.* [Bienen]stock, *der*

**HMS** *abbr. (Brit.)* **Her/His Majesty's Ship** H.M.S.

**hoard** [hɔːd] **1.** *n.* Vorrat, *der.* **2.** *v. t.* ~ **[up]** horten; hamstern ⟨*Lebensmittel*⟩

**hoarding** ['hɔːdɪŋ] *n. (fence)* Bauzaun, *der; (Brit.: for advertisements)* Reklamewand, *die*

**hoar-frost** ['hɔːfrɒst] *n.* [Rauh]reif, *der*

**hoarse** [hɔːs] *adj.* heiser

**hoax** [həʊks] **1.** *v. t.* anführen *(ugs.);* foppen. **2.** *n. (deception)* Schwindel, *der; (practical joke)* Streich, *der; (false alarm)* blinder Alarm

**hob** [hɒb] *n.* [Koch]platte, *die*

**hobble** ['hɒbl] *v. i.* ~ **[about]** [herum]humpeln

**hobby** ['hɒbɪ] *n.* Hobby, *das.* **'hobby-horse** *n.* Steckenpferd, *das*

**hobnailed** ['hɒbneɪld] *adj.* Nagel- ⟨*schuh, -stiefel*⟩

**hobo** ['həʊbəʊ] *n., pl.* **-es** *(Amer.)* Landstreicher, *der*/-streicherin, *die*

**hockey** ['hɒkɪ] *n.* Hockey, *das.* **'hockey-stick** *n.* Hockeyschläger, *der*

**hoe** [həʊ] **1.** *n.* Hacke, *die.* **2.** *v. t. & i.* hacken

**hog** [hɒg] **1.** *n.* [Mast]schwein. **2.** *v. t.,* **-gg-** *(coll.)* mit Beschlag belegen

**hoist** [hɔɪst] **1.** *v. t.* hochziehen, hissen ⟨*Flagge usw.*⟩; hieven ⟨*Last*⟩; setzen ⟨*Segel*⟩. **2.** *n.* [Lasten]aufzug, *der*

**¹hold** [həʊld] *n. (of ship)* Laderaum, *der; (of aircraft)* Frachtraum, *der*

**²hold 1.** *v. t.,* **held** [held] **a)** halten; *(carry)* tragen; *(keep fast)* festhalten; ~ **the door open for sb.** jmdm. die Tür aufhalten; ~ **sth. in place** etw. halten;

**b)** *(contain)* enthalten; *(be able to contain)* fassen ⟨*Liter, Personen usw.*⟩; **c)** *(possess)* besitzen; haben; **d)** *(keep possession of)* halten ⟨*Stützpunkt, Stadt, Stellung*⟩; ~ **the line** *(Teleph.)* am Apparat bleiben; ~ **one's own** sich behaupten; **e)** *(cause to take place)* stattfinden lassen; abhalten ⟨*Veranstaltung, Konferenz, Gottesdienst, Sitzung*⟩; veranstalten ⟨*Festival, Auktion*⟩; austragen ⟨*Meisterschaften*⟩; führen ⟨*Unterhaltung, Gespräch*⟩; durchführen ⟨*Untersuchung*⟩; halten ⟨*Vortrag, Rede*⟩; **f)** *(think, believe)* ~ **a view** *or* **an opinion** eine Ansicht haben (**on** über + *Akk.*); ~ **that ...:** der Ansicht sein, daß ...; ~ **oneself responsible for sth.** sich für etw. verantwortlich fühlen; ~ **sth. against sb.** jmdm. etw. vorwerfen. **2.** *v. i.,* **held** halten; ⟨*Wetter:*⟩ sich halten. **3.** *n.* **a)** *(grasp)* Griff, *der;* **grab** *or* **seize** ~ **of sth.** etw. ergreifen; **get** *or* **lay** *or* **take** ~ **of sth.** etw. fassen *od.* packen; **keep** ~ **of sth.** etw. festhalten; **get** ~ **of sth.** *(fig.)* etw. auftreiben; **get** ~ **of sb.** *(fig.)* jmdn. erreichen; **b)** *(influence)* Einfluß, *der* (**on, over** auf + *Akk.*); **c)** *(Sport)* Griff, *der.* **hold 'back 1.** *v. t.* zurückhalten. **2.** *v. i.* zögern. **hold 'on 1.** *v. t.* [fest]halten. **2.** *v. i.* **a)** sich festhalten; ~ **on to** sich festhalten an (+ *Dat.*); *(keep)* behalten; **b)** *(coll.: wait)* warten. **hold 'out 1.** *v. t.* ausstrecken ⟨*Hand, Arm usw.*⟩; hinhalten ⟨*Tasse, Teller*⟩. **2.** *v. i. (resist)* sich halten. **hold 'up** *v. t.* **a)** *(raise)* hochhalten; heben ⟨*Hand, Kopf*⟩; **b)** *(delay)* aufhalten; **c)** *(rob)* überfallen. **'hold with** *v. t.* not ~ **with sth.** etw. ablehnen

**'holdall** *n.* Reisetasche, *die*

**'holder** *n.* **a)** *(of post, title)* Inhaber, *der*/Inhaberin, *die;* **b)** ⟨*Zigaretten*⟩spitze, *die;* ⟨*Papier-, Zahnputzglas*⟩halter, *der*

**'hold-up** *n.* **a)** *(robbery)* [Raub]überfall, *der;* **b)** *(delay)* Verzögerung, *die*

**hole** [həʊl] *n.* Loch, *das; (of fox, badger, rabbit)* Bau, *der;* **pick** ~**s in** *(fig.)* zerpflücken *(ugs.)*

**holiday** ['hɒlɪdeɪ] *n.* **a)** [arbeits]freier Tag; *(public* ~*)* Feiertag, *der;* **b)** *in sing. or pl. (Brit.: vacation)* Urlaub, *der; (Sch.)* [Schul]ferien *Pl.* **'holiday-maker** *n.* Urlauber, *der*/Urlauberin, *die*

**Holland** ['hɒlənd] *pr. n.* Holland *(das)*

**hollow** ['hɒləʊ] **1.** *adj.* hohl; eingefallen ⟨*Wangen, Schläfen*⟩; *(fig.)* leer ⟨*Versprechen*⟩. **2.** *n.* [Boden]senke, *die.* **3.** *v. t.* ~ **out** aushöhlen

**holly** ['hɒlɪ] *n.* Stechpalme, *die*

**hologram** ['hɒləgræm] *n.* Hologramm, *der*

**holster** ['həʊlstə(r)] *n.* [Pistolen]halfter, *die od. das*

**holy** ['həʊlɪ] *adj.* heilig

**Holy:** ~ **'Ghost** *see* ~ **Spirit;** ~ **Land** *n.* **the** ~ **Land** das Heilige Land; ~ **'Spirit** *n.* Heiliger Geist

**homage** ['hɒmɪdʒ] *n.* Huldigung, *die* **(to an** + *Akk.*); **pay** *or* **do** ~ **to sb./sth.** jmdm./einer Sache huldigen

**home** [həʊm] **1.** *n.* **a)** Heim, *das; (flat)* Wohnung, *die; (house)* Haus, *das; (household)* [Eltern]haus, *das; (native country)* Heimat, *die;* **at** ~**:** zu Hause; **be/feel at** ~ *(fig.)* sich wohl fühlen; **make yourself at** ~**:** fühl dich wie zu Hause; **b)** *(institution)* Heim, *das.* **2.** *adj.* **a)** Haus-; **b)** *(Sport)* Heim-. **3.** *adv.* nach Hause

**home:** ~ **address** *n.* Privatanschrift, *die;* ~ **com'puter** *n.* Heimcomputer, *der;* ~**-grown** *adj.* selbstgezogen; ~**land** *n.* Heimat, *die*

**'homeless 1.** *adj.* obdachlos. **2.** *n.* **the** ~**:** die Obdachlosen. **'homelessness** *n.* Obdachlosigkeit, *die*

**homely** ['həʊmlɪ] *adj.* wohnlich ⟨*Zimmer usw.*⟩; behaglich ⟨*Atmosphäre*⟩

**home:** ~**-made** *adj.* selbstgemacht; selbstgebacken ⟨*Brot*⟩; hausgemacht ⟨*Lebensmittel*⟩; **H~ Office** *n. (Brit.)* Innenministerium, *das;* **H~ 'Secretary** *n. (Brit.)* Innenminister, *der;* ~**sick** *adj.* heimwehkrank; **become/be** ~**sick** Heimweh bekommen/haben; ~ '**town** *n.* Heimatstadt, *die;* ~**work** *n. (Sch.)* Hausaufgaben *Pl.;* **piece of** ~**work** Hausaufgabe, *die*

**homicide** ['hɒmɪsaɪd] *n.* Tötung, *die; (manslaughter)* Totschlag, *der*

**homosexual** [həʊməʊ'seksjʊəl] **1.** *adj.* homosexuell. **2.** *n.* Homosexuelle, *der/die*

**hone** [həʊn] *v. t.* wetzen

**honest** ['ɒnɪst] *adj.* ehrlich. '**honestly** *adv.* ehrlich; redlich ⟨*handeln*⟩; ~**!** ehrlich!; *(annoyed)* also wirklich! **honesty** ['ɒnɪstɪ] *n.* Ehrlichkeit, *die*

**honey** ['hʌnɪ] *n.* Honig, *der.* '**honeycomb** *n.* Honigwabe, *die.* '**honeymoon** *n.* Flitterwochen *Pl.; (journey)* Hochzeitsreise, *die*

**honk** [hɒŋk] **1.** *v. i.* ⟨*Fahrzeug, Fahrer:*⟩ hupen. **2.** *n.* Hupen, *das*

**honor, honorable** *(Amer.) see* **honour, honourable**

**honorary** ['ɒnərərɪ] *adj.* Ehren⟨*mitglied, -präsident, -doktor, -bürger*⟩

**honour** ['ɒnə(r)] *(Brit.)* **1.** *n.* **a)** Ehre, *die;* **b)** *(distinction)* Auszeichnung, *die.* **2.** *v. t.* ehren; *(Commerc.)* honorieren. **honourable** ['ɒnərəbl] *adj. (Brit.)* ehrenwert *(geh.)*

**hood** [hʊd] *n.* **a)** Kapuze, *die;* **b)** *(Amer. Motor Veh.)* Motorhaube, *die;* **c)** *(of pram)* Verdeck, *das*

**hoodlum** ['hu:dləm] *n.* Rowdy, *der*

**hoodwink** ['hʊdwɪŋk] *v. t.* hinters Licht führen

**hoof** [hu:f] *n., pl.* ~**s** *or* **hooves** [hu:vz] Huf, *der*

**hook** [hʊk] **1.** *n.* Haken, *der;* **by** ~ **or by crook** mit allen Mitteln. **2.** *v. t.* **a)** *(grasp)* mit Haken/mit einem Haken greifen; **b)** *(fasten)* mit Haken/mit einem Haken befestigen **(to an** + *Dat.*); **c) be** ~**ed** [**on sth.**] *(addicted)* [von etw.] abhängig sein; *(harmlessly)* auf etw. stehen *(ugs.).* **hook 'up** *v. t.* festhaken **(to an** + *Akk.*)

**hooligan** ['hu:lɪgən] *n.* Rowdy, *der.* **hooliganism** ['hu:lɪgənɪzm] *n.* Rowdytum, *das*

**hoop** [hu:p] *n.* Reifen, *der*

**hooray** [hʊ'reɪ] *int.* hurra

**hoot** [hu:t] **1.** *v. i.* **a)** *(call out)* johlen; **b)** ⟨*Eule:*⟩ schreien; **c)** ⟨*Fahrzeug, Fahrer:*⟩ hupen. **2.** *n.* **a)** *(shout)* ~**s of derision** verächtliches Gejohle; **b)** *(of owl)* Schrei, *der;* **c)** *(of vehicle)* Hupen, *das.* '**hooter** *n. (Brit.: siren)* Sirene, *die*

**hoover** ['hu:və(r)] *(Brit.)* **1.** *n.* **a)** **H~ (P)** [Hoover]staubsauger, *der;* **b)** *(made by any company)* Staubsauger, *der.* **2.** *v. t.* staubsaugen

**hooves** *pl. of* **hoof**

**'hop** [hɒp] *n.* **a)** *(plant)* Hopfen, *der;* **b)** *in pl. (Brewing)* Hopfen, *der*

**²hop 1.** *v. i.,* **-pp-: a)** hüpfen; ⟨*Hase:*⟩ hoppeln; **b)** *(fig. coll.)* ~ **out of bed** aus dem Bett springen; ~ **into the car/on** [**to**] **the bus/train** sich ins Auto/in den Bus/Zug schwingen *(ugs.).* **2.** *v. t.,* **-pp-** *(Brit. sl.)* ~ **it** sich verziehen *(ugs.).* **3.** *n.* **a)** Hüpfer, *der;* **b)** *(Brit. coll.)* **catch sb. on the** ~**:** jmdn. überraschen

**hope** [həʊp] **1.** *n.* Hoffnung, *die;* **sb.'s** ~[**s**] **of sth.** jmds. Hoffnung auf etw. *(Akk.);* **raise sb.'s** ~**s** jmdm. Hoffnung machen. **2.** *v. i. & t.* hoffen **(for** auf + *Akk.*); **I** ~ **so/not** hoffentlich/hoffent-

lich nicht; ~ **for the best** das Beste
hoffen. **hopeful** ['həʊpfl] *adj.* **a)** zuversichtlich; **be ~ of sth./of doing sth.**
auf etw. *(Akk.)* hoffen/voller Hoffnung sein, etw. zu tun; **b)** *(promising)*
vielversprechend. '**hopefully** *adv.* **a)**
*(expectantly)* voller Hoffnung; **b)**
*(coll.: it is hoped that)* hoffentlich.
'**hopeless** *adj.* **a)** hoffnungslos; **b)**
*(inadequate)* miserabel. '**hopelessly**
*adv.* **a)** hoffnungslos; **b)** *(inadequately)* miserabel

**hopscotch** ['hɒpskɒtʃ] *n.* Himmel-
und-Hölle-Spiel, *das*

**horde** [hɔːd] *n.* Horde, *die*

**horizon** [hə'raɪzn] *n.* Horizont, *der;* **on
the ~:** am Horizont

**horizontal** [hɒrɪ'zɒntl] *adj.* horizontal; waagerecht. **hori'zontally** *adv.*
horizontal; *(flat)* waagerecht

**hormone** ['hɔːməʊn] *n.* Hormon, *das*

**horn** [hɔːn] *n.* Horn, *das; (of vehicle)*
Hupe, *die*

**hornet** ['hɔːnɪt] *n.* Hornisse, *die*

'**horny** *adj. (hard)* hornig

**horoscope** ['hɒrəskəʊp] *n.* Horoskop, *das*

**horrible** ['hɒrɪbl] *adj.* grauenhaft;
grausig ⟨*Monster*⟩; grauenvoll ⟨*Verbrechen, Alptraum*⟩

**horrid** ['hɒrɪd] *adj.* scheußlich

**horrific** [hə'rɪfɪk] *adj.* schrecklich

**horrify** ['hɒrɪfaɪ] *v. t.* mit Schrecken erfüllen; **be horrified** *(shocked, scan-
dalized)* entsetzt sein (**at, by** über +
*Akk.*). '**horrifying** *adj.* grauenhaft

**horror** ['hɒrə(r)] *n.* **1.** Entsetzen, *das*
(**at** über + *Akk.*); *(repugnance)* Grausen, *das; (horrifying thing)* Greuel,
*der.* **2.** *attrib. adj.* Horror-. '**horror-
stricken**, '**horror-struck** *adjs.* von
Entsetzen gepackt

**hors-d'œuvre** [ɔː'dɜːvr] *n.* Hors-
d'œuvre, *das;* ≈ Vorspeise, *die*

**horse** [hɔːs] *n.* Pferd, *das*

**horse: ~back** *n.* **on ~back** zu Pferd;
**~man** ['hɔːsmən] *n., pl.* **~men**
['hɔːsmən] *([skilled] rider)* [guter] Reiter; **~play** *n.* Balgerei, *die; ~power*
*n., pl. same (Mech.)* Pferdestärke, *die;*
**~-racing** *n.* Pferderennsport, *der;*
**~radish** *n.* Meerrettich, *der; ~shoe*
*n.* Hufeisen, *das*

**horticulture** ['hɔːtɪkʌltʃə(r)] *n.* Gartenbau, *der*

**hose** [həʊz], '**hose-pipe** *ns.*
Schlauch, *der*

**hospice** ['hɒspɪs] *n. (Brit.: for the ter-
minally ill)* Sterbeklinik, *die*

**hospitable** [hɒ'spɪtəbl] *adj.* gastfreundlich ⟨*Person, Wesensart*⟩; **be ~
to sb.** jmdn. gastfreundlich aufnehmen

**hospital** ['hɒspɪtl] *n.* Krankenhaus,
*das;* **in ~** *(Brit.)*, **in the ~** *(Amer.)* im
Krankenhaus

**hospitality** [hɒspɪ'tælɪtɪ] *n.* Gast-
freundschaft, *die*

¹**host** [həʊst] *n. (large number)* Menge,
*die;* **a ~ of people/children** eine Menge Leute/eine Schar von Kindern

²**host** *n.* Gastgeber, *der/-geberin, die*

**hostage** ['hɒstɪdʒ] *n.* Geisel, *die*

**hostel** ['hɒstl] *n. (Brit.)* Wohnheim,
*das*

**hostess** ['həʊstɪs] *n.* Gastgeberin, *die;*
*(in night-club)* Animierdame, *die*

**hostile** ['hɒstaɪl] *adj.* **a)** feindlich; **b)**
*(unfriendly)* feindselig (**to[wards]** gegenüber); **be ~ to sth.** etw. ablehnen.
**hostility** [hɒ'stɪlɪtɪ] *n.* Feindseligkeit,
*die*

**hot** [hɒt] *adj.* **a)** heiß; warm ⟨*Mahlzeit,
Essen*⟩; **I am/feel ~:** mir ist heiß; **b)**
*(pungent)* scharf ⟨*Gewürz, Senf usw.*⟩;
scharf gewürzt ⟨*Essen*⟩; **c)** *(recent)*
noch warm ⟨*Nachrichten*⟩; **d)** *(sl.: illegally obtained)* heiß ⟨*Ware, Geld*⟩.
**hot 'air** *n. (sl.)* leeres Gerede *(ugs.).*
'**hotbed** *n. (Hort.)* Mistbeet, *das;*
*(fig.: of vice, corruption)* Brutstätte, *die*
(**of** für)

'**hot dog** *n. (coll.)* Hot dog, *der od. das*

**hotel** [həʊ'tel] *n.* Hotel, *das.* **ho'tel
room** *n.* Hotelzimmer, *das*

**hot: ~house** *n.* Treibhaus, *das; ~
line** *n. (Polit.)* heißer Draht

'**hotly** *adv.* heftig

**hot: ~plate** *n.* Kochplatte, *die; (to
keep food ~)* Warmhalteplatte, *die;*
**~-'water bottle** *n.* Wärmflasche, *die*

**hound** [haʊnd] **1.** *n.* Jagdhund, *der.* **2.**
*v. t.* verfolgen

**hour** ['aʊə(r)] *n.* **a)** Stunde, *die;* **half an
~:** eine halbe Stunde; **an ~ and a half**
anderthalb Stunden; **be paid by the ~:**
stundenweise bezahlt werden; **the
24-~ clock** die Vierundzwanzigstun-
denuhr; **b)** *(time o'clock)* Zeit, *die;* **the
small ~s [of the morning]** die frühen
Morgenstunden; **0100/0200/1700/
1800** **~s** *(on 24-~ clock)* 1.00/2.00/
17.00/18.00 Uhr. '**hourly** *adj., adv.*
stündlich; **be paid ~:** stundenweise
bezahlt werden

**house 1.** [haʊs] *n., pl.* **~s** ['haʊzɪz]
Haus, *das;* **to/at my ~:** zu mir [nach
Hause]/bei mir [zu Hause]. **2.** [haʊz]

*v.t.* **a)** ein Heim geben (+ *Dat.*); **b)** *(keep, store)* unterbringen. **houseboat** ['haʊsbəʊt] *n.* Hausboot, *das*

**household** ['haʊshəʊld] *n.* Haushalt, *der; attrib.* Haushalts-. **'householder** *n.* Wohnungsinhaber, *der/* -inhaberin, *die*

**house** [haʊs]: **~keeper** *n.* Haushälterin, *die;* **~keeping** *n.* Hauswirtschaft, *die;* **~-plant** *n.* Zimmerpflanze, *die;* **~-trained** *adj.* *(Brit.)* stubenrein ⟨*Hund, Katze*⟩; **~-warming** *n.* **~-warming |party|** Einzugsfeier, *die;* **~wife** *n.* Hausfrau, *die;* **~work** *n.* Hausarbeit, *die*

**housing** ['haʊzɪŋ] *n.* *(dwellings)* Wohnungen; *(provision of dwellings)* Wohnungsbeschaffung, *die.* **'housing estate** *n.* *(Brit.)* Wohnsiedlung, *die*

**hovel** ['hɒvl] *n.* [armselige] Hütte

**hover** ['hɒvə(r)] *v.i.* **a)** schweben; **b)** *(linger)* sich herumdrücken *(ugs.)*. **'hovercraft** *n., pl. same* Hovercraft, *das;* Luftkissenfahrzeug, *das.* **'hover mower** *n.* Luftkissenmäher, *der*

**how** [haʊ] *adv.* wie; **learn ~ to ride a bike/swim** radfahren/schwimmen lernen; **~ 'are you?** wie geht es dir?; *(greeting)* guten Morgen/Tag/ Abend!; **~ do you 'do?** *(formal)* guten Morgen/Tag/Abend!; **~ much?** wieviel?; **~ many?** wieviel?; wie viele?

**however** [haʊ'evə(r)] *adv.* **a)** wie ... auch; **b)** *(nevertheless)* jedoch; aber

**howl** [haʊl] **1.** *n.* *(of animal)* Heulen, *das;* *(of distress)* Schrei, *der;* **~s of laughter** brüllendes Gelächter. **2.** *v.i.* ⟨*Tier, Wind:*⟩ heulen; *(with distress)* schreien. **3.** *v.t.* [hinaus]schreien

**howler** ['haʊlə(r)] *n.* *(coll.: blunder)* Schnitzer, *der (ugs.)*

**HP** *abbr.* *(Brit.)* hire-purchase

**HQ** *abbr.* **headquarters** HQ

**hub** [hʌb] *n.* [Rad]nabe, *die;* *(fig.)* Mittelpunkt, *der*

**hubbub** ['hʌbʌb] *n.* Lärm, *der;* **a ~ of voices** ein Stimmengewirr

**'hub-cap** *n.* Radkappe, *die*

**huddle** ['hʌdl] *v.i.* sich drängen; **~ together** sich zusammendrängen. **huddle 'up** *v.i.* *(nestle up)* sich zusammenkauern; *(crowd together)* sich [zusammen]drängen

**¹hue** [hju:] *n.* Farbton, *der*

**²hue** *n.* **~ and cry** lautes Geschrei; *(protest)* Gezeter, *das*

**huff** [hʌf] **1.** *v.i.* **~ and puff** schnaufen und keuchen. **2.** *n.* **in a ~:** beleidigt

**hug** [hʌg] **1.** *n.* Umarmung, *die;* **give sb. a ~:** jmdn. umarmen. **2.** *v.t.,* **-gg-** umarmen

**huge** [hju:dʒ] *adj.* riesig; gewaltig ⟨*Unterschied, Verbesserung, Interesse*⟩

**hulking** ['hʌlkɪŋ] *adj.* *(coll.)* **~ great** klobig

**hull** [hʌl] *n.* *(Naut.)* Schiffskörper, *der*

**hum** [hʌm] **1.** *v.i.,* **-mm-:** **a)** summen; ⟨*Maschine:*⟩ brummen; **b)** **~ and haw** *(coll.)* herumdrucksen *(ugs.)*. **2.** *v.t.,* **-mm-** summen. **3.** *n.* **a)** Summen, *das;* *(of machinery)* Brummen, *das;* **b)** *(of voices, conversation)* Gemurmel, *das;* *(of traffic)* Brausen, *das*

**human** ['hju:mən] **1.** *adj.* menschlich; **the ~ race** die menschliche Rasse. **2.** *n.* Mensch, *der.* **human 'being** *n.* Mensch, *der*

**humane** [hju:'meɪn] *adj.* human

**humanitarian** [hju:mænɪ'teərɪən] *adj.* humanitär

**humanity** [hju:'mænɪtɪ] *n.* **a)** *(mankind)* Menschheit, *die; (people collectively)* Menschen; **b)** *(being humane)* Humanität, *die*

**humble** ['hʌmbl] **1.** *adj.* **a)** demütig; **b)** *(modest)* bescheiden; **c)** *(low-ranking)* einfach; niedrig ⟨*Status, Rang usw.*⟩. **2.** *v.t.* **a)** demütigen; **~ oneself** sich demütigen *od.* erniedrigen; **b)** *(defeat decisively)* [vernichtend] schlagen. **humbly** ['hʌmblɪ] *adv.* demütig

**humdrum** ['hʌmdrʌm] *adj.* alltäglich; eintönig ⟨*Leben*⟩

**humid** ['hju:mɪd] *adj.* feucht. **humidity** [hju:'mɪdɪtɪ] *n.* Feuchtigkeit, *die*

**humiliate** [hju:'mɪlɪeɪt] *v.t.* demütigen. **humiliation** [hju:mɪlɪ'eɪʃn] *n.* Demütigung, *die*

**humility** [hju:'mɪlɪtɪ] *n.* Demut, *die*

**humor** *(Amer.)* see **humour**

**humorous** ['hju:mərəs] *adj.* lustig, komisch ⟨*Geschichte, Name, Situation*⟩; witzig ⟨*Bemerkung*⟩

**humour** ['hju:mə(r)] *(Brit.)* **1.** *n.* **a)** Humor, *der;* **sense of ~:** Sinn für Humor; **b)** *(mood)* Laune, *die.* **2.** *v.t.* **~ sb.** jmdm. seinen Willen lassen

**hump** [hʌmp] **1.** *n.* **a)** *(of person)* Buckel, *der;* *(of animal)* Höcker, *der;* **b)** *(mound)* Hügel, *der.* **2.** *v.t.* *(Brit. sl.: carry)* schleppen. **humpback 'bridge** *n.* gewölbte Brücke

**¹hunch** [hʌntʃ] *v.t.* **~ |up|** hochziehen

**²hunch** *n.* *(feeling)* Gefühl, *das*

**'hunchback** *n.* *(back)* Buckel, *der;* *(person)* Bucklige, *der/die;* **be a ~:** einen Buckel haben

**hundred** ['hʌndrəd] **1.** *adj.* hundert; **a** *or* **one ~**: [ein]hundert; **two/several ~**: zweihundert/mehrere hundert; **a** *or* **one ~ and one** [ein]hundert[und]eins. **2.** *n.* **a)** *(number)* hundert; **a** *or* **one/ two ~**: [ein]hundert/zweihundert; **b)** *(written figure; group)* Hundert, *das;* **c)** *(indefinite amount)* ~s Hunderte. *See also* **eight. hundredth** ['hʌndrədθ] **1.** *adj.* hundertst...; **a ~ part** ein Hundertstel. **2.** *n. (fraction)* Hundertstel, *das;* *(in sequence)* hundertste, *der/die/das;(in rank)* Hundertste, *der/ die/das.* '**hundredweight** *n., pl. same (Brit.)* 50,8 kg; ≈ Zentner, *der*

**hung** *see* **hang 1, 2**

**Hungarian** [hʌŋ'geərɪən] **1.** *adj.* ungarisch; **sb. is ~**: jmd. ist Ungar/Ungarin. **2.** *n.* **a)** *(person)* Ungar, *der*/Ungarin, *die;* **b)** *(language)* Ungarisch, *das; see also* **English 2 a**

**Hungary** ['hʌŋgərɪ] *pr. n.* Ungarn *(das)*

**hunger** ['hʌŋgə(r)] **1.** *n.* Hunger, *der.* **2.** *v. i.* **~ after** *or* **for sth.** [heftiges] Verlangen nach jmdm./etw. haben.

'**hunger-strike** *n.* Hungerstreik, *der;* **go on ~**: in den Hungerstreik treten

**hungry** ['hʌŋgrɪ] *adj.* hungrig; **be ~**: Hunger haben; **go ~**: hungern

**hunk** [hʌŋk] *n.* [großes] Stück

**hunt** [hʌnt] **1.** *n.* Jagd, *die; (search)* Suche, *die.* **2.** *v. t.* jagen; *(search for)* Jagd machen auf (+ *Akk.*) ⟨*Mörder usw.*⟩. **3.** *v. i.* jagen; **go ~ing** auf die Jagd gehen; **~ after** *or* **for** Jagd machen auf (+ *Akk.*); *(seek)* suchen

'**hunter** *n.* Jäger, *der*

'**hunting** *n.* die Jagd (**of** auf + *Akk.*); *(searching)* Suche, *die* (**for** nach)

**hurdle** ['hɜːdl] *n.* Hürde, *die*

**hurl** [hɜːl] *v. t.* werfen; *(violently)* schleudern; **~ insults at sb.** jmdm. Beleidigungen ins Gesicht schleudern

**hurrah** [hʊ'rɑː], **hurray** [hʊ'reɪ] *int.* hurra

**hurricane** ['hʌrɪkən] *n.* Orkan, *der*

**hurried** ['hʌrɪd] *adj.* eilig; überstürzt ⟨*Abreise*⟩; **in Eile ausgeführt** ⟨*Arbeit*⟩

**hurry** ['hʌrɪ] **1.** *n.* Eile, *die;* **in a ~**: eilig; **be in a ~**: es eilig haben; **there's no ~**: es eilt nicht. **2.** *v. t.* antreiben ⟨*Person*⟩; hinunterschlingen ⟨*Essen*⟩; **~ one's work** seine Arbeit in zu großer Eile erledigen. **3.** *v. i.* sich beeilen; *(to or from place)* eilen. **hurry 'up 1.** *v. i.* sich beeilen. **2.** *v. t.* antreiben

**hurt** [hɜːt] **1.** *v. t.,* **hurt a)** weh tun (+ *Dat.*); *(injure)* verletzen; **~ oneself**

sich *(Dat.)* weh tun; *(injure oneself)* sich verletzen; **~ one's arm/back** sich *(Dat.)* am Arm/Rücken weh tun; *(injure)* sich *(Dat.)* den Arm/am Rücken verletzen; **b)** *(damage, be detrimental to)* schaden (+ *Dat.*); **c)** *(upset)* verletzen ⟨*Person, Stolz*⟩. **2.** *v. i.,* **hurt a)** weh tun; **b)** *(cause damage, be detrimental)* schaden. **3.** *adj.* gekränkt ⟨*Tonfall, Miene*⟩. **4.** *n. (emotional pain)* Schmerz, *der.* **hurtful** ['hɜːtfl] *adj.* verletzend

**hurtle** ['hɜːtl] *v. i.* rasen *(ugs.)*

**husband** ['hʌzbənd] *n.* Ehemann, *der;* **my/your/her ~**: mein/dein/ihr Mann; **~ and wife** Mann und Frau

**hush** [hʌʃ] **1.** *n. (silence)* Schweigen, *das; (stillness)* Stille, *die.* **2.** *v. t. (silence)* zum Schweigen bringen; *(still)* beruhigen. **3.** *v. i.* still sein; **~!** still! **hush 'up** *v. t.* vertuschen

**husk** [hʌsk] *n.* Spelze, *die*

'**husky** ['hʌskɪ] *adj.* heiser

²**husky** *n.* Eskimohund, *der*

**hustle** ['hʌsl] **1.** *v. t.* drängen (**into** zu). **2.** *n.* **~ and bustle** geschäftiges Treiben

**hut** [hʌt] *n.* Hütte, *die*

**hutch** [hʌtʃ] *n.* Stall, *der*

**hyacinth** ['haɪəsɪnθ] *n.* Hyazinthe, *die*

**hybrid** ['haɪbrɪd] **1.** *n.* Hybride, *die od. der* (**between** aus); *(fig.: mixture)* Mischung, *die.* **2.** *adj.* hybrid ⟨*Züchtung*⟩

**hydrangea** [haɪ'dreɪndʒə] *n.* Hortensie, *die*

**hydrant** ['haɪdrənt] *n.* Hydrant, *der*

**hydraulic** [haɪ'drɔːlɪk] *adj.* hydraulisch

**hydrochloric acid** [haɪdrəklɔːrɪk 'æsɪd] *n.* Salzsäure, *die*

**hydroelectric** [haɪdrəʊɪ'lektrɪk] *adj.* hydroelektrisch; **~ power station** Wasserkraftwerk, *das*

**hydrofoil** ['haɪdrəfɔɪl] *n.* Tragflächenboot, *das*

**hydrogen** ['haɪdrədʒən] *n.* Wasserstoff, *der.* '**hydrogen bomb** *n.* Wasserstoffbombe, *die*

**hyena** [haɪ'iːnə] *n.* Hyäne, *die*

**hygiene** ['haɪdʒiːn] *n.* Hygiene, *die.* **hygienic** [haɪ'dʒiːnɪk] *adj.* hygienisch

**hymn** [hɪm] *n.* Hymne, *die; (sung in service)* Kirchenlied, *das.* '**hymnbook** *n.* Gesangbuch, *das*

**hypermarket** ['haɪpəmɑːkɪt] *n. (Brit.)* Verbrauchermarkt, *der*

**hyphen** ['haɪfn] **1.** *n.* Bindestrich, *der.* **2.** *v. t.* mit Bindestrich schreiben

**hyphenate** ['haɪfəneɪt] *see* **hyphen** 2
**hypnosis** [hɪp'nəʊsɪs] *n., pl.* **hypnoses**
[hɪp'nəʊsiːz] Hypnose, *die; (act, process)* Hypnotisierung, *die;* **under ~ :** in
Hypnose *(Dat.).* **hypnotic** [hɪp-
'nɒtɪk] *adj.* hypnotisch. **hypnotism**
['hɪpnətɪzm] *n.* Hypnotik, *die; (act)*
Hypnotisieren, *das.* **hypnotist** ['hɪp-
nətɪst] *n.* Hypnotiseur, *der*/Hypnoti-
seuse, *die.* **hypnotize** ['hɪpnətaɪz]
*v. t.* hypnotisieren
**hypochondria** [haɪpə'kɒndrɪə] *n.* Hy-
pochondrie, *die.* **hypochondriac**
[haɪpə'kɒndrɪæk] *n.* Hypochonder,
*der*
**hypocrisy** [hɪ'pɒkrɪsɪ] *n.* Heuchelei,
*die.* **hypocrite** ['hɪpəkrɪt] *n.* Heuchler, *der*/Heuchlerin, *die.* **hypocritical** [hɪpə'krɪtɪkl] *adj.* heuchlerisch
**hypodermic** [haɪpə'dɜːmɪk] *adj. & n.*
~ |syringe| Injektionsspritze, *die*
**hypotenuse** [haɪ'pɒtənjuːz] *n.* Hypotenuse, *die*
**hypothesis** [haɪ'pɒθɪsɪs] *n., pl.* **hypo-
theses** [haɪ'pɒθɪsiːz] Hypothese, *die.*
**hypothetical** [haɪpə'θetɪkl] *adj.* hypothetisch
**hysteria** [hɪ'stɪərɪə] *n.* Hysterie, *die.*
**hysterical** [hɪ'sterɪkl] *adj.* hysterisch. **hysterics** [hɪ'sterɪks] *n. pl.
(laughter)* hysterischer Lachanfall;
*(crying)* hysterischer Weinkrampf;
**have ~ :** hysterisch lachen/weinen

# I

**¹I, i** [aɪ] *n.* I, i, *das*
**²I** *pron.* ich
**ice** [aɪs] **1.** *n.* **a)** Eis, *das;* **feel/be like ~
(be very cold)** eiskalt sein; **b)** *(~
cream)* [Speise]eis, *das;* **an ~/two ~s**
ein/zwei Eis. **2.** *v. t.* glasieren ⟨Ku-
chen⟩. **ice 'over, ice 'up** *v. i.* ⟨Gewäs-
ser:⟩ zufrieren
**'ice age** *n.* Eiszeit, *die*
**iceberg** ['aɪsbɜːg] *n.* Eisberg, *der*
**ice:** **~box** *n. (Amer.)* Kühlschrank,
*der;* **~-cold** *adj.* eiskalt; **~-'cream**
*n.* Eis, *das;* Eiscreme, *die;* **one
~-cream/two/too many ~-creams** ein/

zwei/zuviel Eis; **~-cube** *n.* Eiswür-
fel, *die;* ~ **hockey** *n.* Eishockey, *das*
**Iceland** ['aɪslənd] *pr. n.* Island *(das).*
**Icelandic** [aɪs'lændɪk] **1.** *adj.* isländisch. **2.** *n.* Isländisch, *das; see also*
**English 2 a**
**ice:** ~ **'lolly** *n.* Eis am Stiel; **~-rink** *n.*
Eisbahn, *die;* **~-skate 1.** *n.* Schlittschuh, *der;* **2.** *v. i.* Schlittschuh laufen; **~-skating** *n.* Schlittschuhlaufen, *das*
**icicle** ['aɪsɪkl] *n.* Eiszapfen, *der*
**icing** ['aɪsɪŋ] *n.* Zuckerguß, *der.* '**icing
sugar** *n. (Brit.)* Puderzucker, *der*
**icon** ['aɪkɒn] *n.* Ikone, *die*
**icy** ['aɪsɪ] *adj.* **a)** vereist ⟨Berge, Landschaft, Straße⟩; eisreich ⟨Region,
Land⟩; **in ~ conditions** bei Eis; **b)**
*(very cold)* eiskalt; eisig; *(fig.)* frostig
**I'd** [aɪd] **a)** = **I had; b)** = **I would**
**idea** [aɪ'dɪə] *n.* Idee, *die;* Gedanke,
*der; (mental picture)* Vorstellung, *die,
(vague notion)* Ahnung, *die;* **have you
any ~ |of| how ...?** weißt du ungefähr,
wie ...?; **have no ~ |of| where ...:** keine
Ahnung haben, wo ...; **not have the
slightest** *or* **faintest ~ :** nicht die leiseste Ahnung haben
**ideal** [aɪ'dɪəl] **1.** *adj.* ideal; vollendet
⟨Ehemann, Gastgeber⟩; vollkommen
⟨Welt⟩. **2.** *n.* Ideal, *das.* **idealism** [aɪ-
'dɪəlɪzm] *n.* Idealismus, *der.* **idealist**
[aɪ'dɪəlɪst] *n.* Idealist, *der*/Idealistin,
*die.* **idealistic** [aɪdɪə'lɪstɪk] *adj.* idealistisch. **idealize** [aɪ'dɪəlaɪz] *v. t.* idealisieren. **ideally** [aɪ'dɪəlɪ] *adv.* ideal;
~, ...: idealerweise *od.* im Idealfall
**identical** [aɪ'dentɪkl] *adj.* identisch;
**be ~ :** sich *(Dat.)* völlig gleichen; ~
**twins** eineiige Zwillinge
**identification** [aɪdentɪfɪ'keɪʃn] *n.*
Identifizierung, *die; (of plants, animals)* Bestimmung, *die*
**identify** [aɪ'dentɪfaɪ] *v. t.* identifizieren; bestimmen ⟨Pflanze, Tier⟩
**identity** [aɪ'dentɪtɪ] *n.* Identität, *die;*
**proof of ~ :** Identitätsnachweis, *der;*
|**case of| mistaken ~ :** [Personen]ver-
wechslung, *die.* **i'dentity card** *n.*
[Personal]ausweis, *der*
**idiocy** ['ɪdɪəsɪ] *n.* Idiotie, *die*
**idiom** ['ɪdɪəm] *n.* [Rede]wendung, *die.*
**idiomatic** [ɪdɪə'mætɪk] *adj.* idioma-
tisch
**idiosyncrasy** [ɪdɪə'sɪŋkrəsɪ] *n.* Eigentümlichkeit, *die.* **idiosyncratic** [ɪdɪə-
sɪŋ'krætɪk] *adj.* eigenwillig
**idiot** ['ɪdɪət] *n.* Idiot, *der (ugs.).*
**idiotic** [ɪdɪ'ɒtɪk] *adj.* idiotisch *(ugs.*

**idle** ['aɪdl] 1. *adj.* a) *(lazy)* faul; b) *(not in use)* außer Betrieb *nachgestellt;* **be ~** ‹*Maschinen, Fabrik:*› stillstehen; c) bloß ‹*Neugier, Spekulation*›; leer ‹*Geschwätz*›. 2. *v.i.* ‹*Motor:*› leerlaufen. **idle a'way** *v.t.* vertun

**idleness** *n.* Faulheit, *die*

**idol** ['aɪdl] *n.* Idol, *das.* **idolize** ['aɪdəlaɪz] *v.t.* vergöttern

**idyllic** [ɪ'dɪlɪk] *adj.* idyllisch

**i.e.** [aɪ'iː] *abbr.* that is d.h.; i.e.

**if** [ɪf] *conj.* a) wenn; **if anyone should ask ...**: falls jemand fragt, ...; **if I knew what to do ...**: wenn ich wüßte, was ich tun soll ...; **if I were you** an deiner Stelle; **if so/not** wenn ja/nein *od.* nicht; **if then/that/at all** wenn überhaupt; **as if** als ob; **if I only knew, if only I knew!** wenn ich das nur wüßte!; **if it isn't Ronnie!** das ist doch Ronnie!; b) *(whenever)* [immer] wenn; c) *(whether)* ob; d) *(though)* auch *od.* selbst wenn; e) *(despite being)* wenn auch

**igloo** ['ɪgluː] *n.* Iglu, *der od. das*

**ignite** [ɪg'naɪt] 1. *v.t.* anzünden. 2. *v.i.* sich entzünden. **ignition** [ɪg'nɪʃn] *n.* a) *(igniting)* Zünden, *das;* b) *(Motor Veh.)* Zündung, *die;* **~ key** Zündschlüssel, *der*

**ignorance** ['ɪgnərəns] *n.* Unwissenheit, *die;* **keep sb. in ~ of sth.** jmdn. in Unkenntnis über etw. *(Akk.)* lassen

**ignorant** ['ɪgnərənt] *adj.* unwissend; **be ~ of sth.** *(uninformed)* über etw. *(Akk.)* nicht informiert sein

**ignore** [ɪg'nɔː(r)] *v.t.* ignorieren; nicht befolgen ‹*Befehl, Rat*›; übergehen ‹*Frage, Bemerkung*›

**ill** [ɪl] 1. *adj.,* **worse** [wɜːs], **worst** [wɜːst] krank; **fall ~:** krank werden. 2. *adv.* **be ~ at ease** sich unwohl fühlen. 3. *n.* Übel, *das*

**I'll** [aɪl] a) = I shall; b) = I will

**'ill-advised** *adj.* unklug

**illegal** [ɪ'liːgl] *adj.,* **il'legally** *adv.* illegal

**illegible** [ɪ'ledʒɪbl] *adj.* unleserlich

**illegitimate** [ɪlɪ'dʒɪtɪmət] *adj.* unehelich ‹*Kind*›

**ill 'health** *n.* schwache Gesundheit

**illicit** [ɪ'lɪsɪt] *adj.* unerlaubt ‹*Beziehung, [Geschlechts]verkehr*›; Schwarz- ‹*handel, -verkauf, -arbeit*›

**'ill-informed** *adj.* schlecht informiert; auf Unkenntnis beruhend ‹*Bemerkung, Urteil*›

**illiteracy** [ɪ'lɪtərəsɪ] *n.* Analphabetentum, *das*

**illiterate** [ɪ'lɪtərət] *adj.* des Lesens und Schreibens unkundig; analphabetisch ‹*Bevölkerung*›

**illness** ['ɪlnɪs] *n.* Krankheit, *die*

**illogical** [ɪ'lɒdʒɪkl] *adj.* unlogisch

**ill-'treat** *v.t.* mißhandeln. **ill-'treatment** *n.* Mißhandlung, *die*

**illuminate** [ɪ'luːmɪneɪt] *v.t.* beleuchten. **illuminating** [ɪ'luːmɪneɪtɪŋ] *adj.* aufschlußreich. **illumination** [ɪluːmɪ'neɪʃn] *n.* Beleuchtung, *die*

**illusion** [ɪ'luːʒn] *n.* Illusion, *die;* **be under the ~ that ...**: sich *(Dat.)* einbilden, daß ... **illusory** [ɪ'luːsərɪ] *adj.* illusorisch

**illustrate** ['ɪləstreɪt] *v.t.* a) *(serve as example of)* veranschaulichen; b) illustrieren ‹*Buch, Erklärung*›. **illustration** [ɪlə'streɪʃn] *n.* a) *(example)* Beispiel, *das (of* für); b) *(picture)* Abbildung, *die*

**ill 'will** *n.* Böswilligkeit, *die*

**I'm** [aɪm] = I am

**image** ['ɪmɪdʒ] *n.* a) Bildnis, *das (geh.);* b) *(Optics)* Bild, *das;* c) [public] ~: Image, *das*

**imaginable** [ɪ'mædʒɪnəbl] *adj.* **the best solution ~:** die denkbar beste Lösung

**imaginary** [ɪ'mædʒɪnərɪ] *adj.* imaginär *(geh.);* eingebildet ‹*Krankheit*›

**imagination** [ɪmædʒɪ'neɪʃn] *n.* a) Phantasie, *die;* b) *(fancy)* Einbildung, *die*

**imaginative** [ɪ'mædʒɪnətɪv] *adj.* phantasievoll; *(showing imagination)* einfallsreich

**imagine** [ɪ'mædʒɪn] *v.t.* a) sich *(Dat.)* vorstellen; b) *(coll.: suppose)* glauben; c) *(get the impression)* **~ that ...**: sich *(Dat.)* einbilden[, daß ...]

**imbalance** [ɪm'bæləns] *n.* Unausgeglichenheit, *die*

**imbecile** ['ɪmbɪsiːl] *n.* Idiot, *der (ugs.)*

**imitate** ['ɪmɪteɪt] *v.t.* nachahmen. **imitation** [ɪmɪ'teɪʃn] *n.* a) Nachahmung, *die;* b) *(counterfeit)* Imitation, *die*

**immaculate** [ɪ'mækjʊlət] *adj.* *(spotless)* makellos; *(faultless)* tadellos

**immaterial** [ɪmə'tɪərɪəl] *adj.* unerheblich

**immature** [ɪmə'tjʊə(r)] *adj.* unreif; noch nicht voll entwickelt ‹*Lebewesen*›. **immaturity** [ɪmə'tjʊərɪtɪ] *n.* Unreife, *die*

**immediate** [ɪ'miːdjət] *adj.* a) unmittelbar; *(nearest)* nächst... ‹*Nachbar[schaft], Umgebung, Zukunft*›; engst... ‹*Familie*›; b) *(occurring at once)* prompt; unverzüglich ‹*Han-*

*deln, Maßnahmen*〉; umgehend 〈*Antwort*〉. **im'mediately 1.** *adv.* **a)** unmittelbar; **b)** *(without delay)* sofort. **2.** *conj. (coll.)* sobald

**immemorial** [ımı'mɔ:rıəl] *adj.* from time ~: seit undenklichen Zeiten

**immense** [ı'mens] *adj.* **a)** ungeheuer; **b)** *(coll.: great)* enorm. **im'mensely** *adv.* **a)** ungeheuer; **b)** *(coll.: very much)* unheimlich *(ugs.)*

**immerse** [ı'mɜ:s] *v. t.* [ein]tauchen; be ~d in thought/one's work in Gedanken versunken/in seine Arbeit vertieft sein. **immersion** [ı'mɜ:ʃn] *n.* Eintauchen, *das.* **im'mersion heater** *n.* Heißwasserbereiter, *der*

**immigrant** ['ımıgrənt] **1.** *n.* Einwanderer, *der*/Einwanderin, *die.* **2.** *adj.* Einwanderer-; ~ **workers** ausländische Arbeitnehmer

**immigration** [ımı'greıʃn] *n.* Einwanderung *die* (**into** nach, **from** aus); *attrib.* Einwanderungs〈*kontrolle, -gesetz*〉; ~ **officer** Beamter/Beamtin der Einwanderungsbehörde

**imminent** ['ımınənt] *adj.* unmittelbar bevorstehend; drohend 〈*Gefahr*〉; **be** ~: unmittelbar bevorstehen/drohen

**immobile** [ı'məʊbaıl] *adj. (immovable)* unbeweglich. **immobilize** [ı'məʊbəlaız] *v. t.* verankern; *(fig.)* lähmen

**immodest** [ı'mɒdıst] *adj.* unbescheiden; *(improper)* unanständig

**immoral** [ı'mɒrəl] *adj.* unmoralisch; *(in sexual matters)* sittenlos. **immorality** [ımə'rælıtı] *n.* Unmoral, *die; (in sexual matters)* Sittenlosigkeit, *die*

**immortal** [ı'mɔ:tl] *adj.* unsterblich. **immortality** [ımɔ:'tælıtı] *n.* Unsterblichkeit, *die.* **immortalize** [ı'mɔ:təlaız] *v. t.* unsterblich machen

**immovable** [ı'mu:vəbl] *adj.* unbeweglich; **be** ~: sich nicht bewegen lassen

**immune** [ı'mju:n] *adj.* **a)** *(exempt)* sicher (**from** vor + *Dat.*); **b)** *(not susceptible)* unempfindlich (**to** gegen); **c)** *(Med.)* immun (**to** gegen). **immunity** [ı'mju:nıtı] *n.* **a)** **diplomatic** ~: diplomatische Immunität; **b)** *(Med.)* Immunität, *die.* **immunize** ['ımjʊnaız] *v. t.* immunisieren

**imp** [ımp] *n.* **a)** Kobold, *der;* **b)** *(coll.: child)* Racker, *der (fam.)*

**impact** ['ımpækt] *n.* **a)** Aufprall, *der* (**on, against** auf + *Akk.*); *(collision)* Zusammenprall, *der;* **b)** *(fig.)* Wirkung, *die*

**impair** [ım'peə(r)] *v. t.* beeinträchtigen; schaden ( + *Dat.*) 〈*Gesundheit*〉

**impale** [ım'peıl] *v. t.* aufspießen

**impart** [ım'pɑ:t] *v. t.* **a)** *(give)* [ab]geben (**to an** + *Akk.*); **b)** *(communicate)* kundtun *(geh.)* (**to** *Dat.*); vermitteln 〈*Kenntnisse*〉 (**to** *Dat.*)

**impartial** [ım'pɑ:ʃl] *adj.* unparteiisch; gerecht 〈*Entscheidung, Urteil*〉

**impassable** [ım'pɑ:səbl] *adj.* unpassierbar (**to** für); *(to vehicles)* unbefahrbar (**to** für)

**impasse** ['æmpɑ:s] *n.* Sackgasse, *die*

**impassive** [ım'pæsıv] *adj.* ausdruckslos

**impatience** [ım'peıʃəns] *n.* Ungeduld, *die* (**at** über + *Akk.*)

**impatient** [ım'peıʃənt] *adj.* ungeduldig; ~ **at sth./with sb.** ungeduldig über etw. *(Akk.)*/mit jmdm. **im'patiently** *adv.* ungeduldig

**impeccable** [ım'pekəbl] *adj.* makellos; tadellos 〈*Manieren*〉

**impede** [ım'pi:d] *v. t.* behindern. **impediment** [ım'pedımənt] *n.* **a)** Hindernis, *das* (**to** für); **b)** *(speech defect)* Sprachfehler, *der*

**impel** [ım'pel] *v. t.,* **-ll-** treiben; **feel** ~**led to do sth.** sich genötigt *od.* gezwungen fühlen, etw. zu tun

**impending** [ım'pendıŋ] *adj.* bevorstehend

**impenetrable** [ım'penıtrəbl] *adj.* undurchdringlich (**by, to** für)

**imperative** [ım'perətıv] **1.** *adj.* dringend erforderlich. **2.** *n. (Ling.)* Imperativ, *der*

**imperceptible** [ımpə'septıbl] *adj.* nicht wahrnehmbar; *(very slight or gradual)* unmerklich

**imperfect** [ım'pɜ:fıkt] **1.** *adj.* **a)** *(incomplete)* unvollständig; **b)** *(faulty)* mangelhaft. **2.** *n. (Ling.)* Imperfekt, *das.* **imperfection** [ımpə'fekʃn] *n.* **a)** *(incompleteness)* Unvollständigkeit, *die;* **b)** *(fault)* Mangel, *der.* **im'perfectly** *adv.* **a)** *(incompletely)* unvollständig; **b)** *(faultily)* fehlerhaft

**imperial** [ım'pıərıəl] *adj.* kaiserlich. **imperialism** [ım'pıərıəlızm] *n.* Imperialismus, *der*

**imperil** [ım'perıl] *v. t., (Brit.)* **-ll-** gefährden

**imperious** [ım'pıərıəs] *adj.* herrisch

**impersonal** [ım'pɜ:sənl] *adj.* unpersönlich

**impersonate** [ım'pɜ:səneıt] *v. t.* sich ausgeben als; *(to entertain)* imitieren; nachahmen. **impersonator** [ım'pɜ:səneıtə(r)] *n. (entertainer)* Imitator, *der*/Imitatorin, *die*

**impertinence** [ɪmˈpɜːtɪnəns] *n.* Unverschämtheit, *die*

**impertinent** [ɪmˈpɜːtɪnənt] *adj.* unverschämt

**imperturbable** [ɪmpəˈtɜːbəbl] *adj.* gelassen; **be completely ~:** durch nichts zu erschüttern sein

**impervious** [ɪmˈpɜːvɪəs] *adj.* undurchlässig; **be ~ to sth.** *(fig.)* unempfänglich für etw. sein

**impetuous** [ɪmˈpetjʊəs] *adj.* unüberlegt; impulsiv ⟨*Person*⟩

**impetus** [ˈɪmpɪtəs] *n.* **a)** Kraft, *die;* **b)** *(fig.)* Motivation, *die*

**impinge** [ɪmˈpɪndʒ] *v.i.* **~ on sth.** auf etw. *(Akk.)* Einfluß nehmen

**impish** *adj.* lausbübisch

**implacable** [ɪmˈplækəbl] *adj.* unversöhnlich; erbittert ⟨*Gegner*⟩

**implausible** [ɪmˈplɔːzɪbl] *adj.* unglaubwürdig

**implement** 1. [ˈɪmplɪmənt] *n.* Gerät, *das.* 2. [ˈɪmplɪment] *v.t.* [in die Tat] umsetzen ⟨*Politik, Plan usw.*⟩

**implicate** [ˈɪmplɪkeɪt] *v.t.* belasten; **be ~d in a scandal** in einen Skandal verwickelt sein. **implication** [ɪmplɪˈkeɪʃn] *n.* Implikation, *die;* **by ~:** implizit

**implicit** [ɪmˈplɪsɪt] *adj.* **a)** *(implied)* implizit *(geh.);* unausgesprochen ⟨*Drohung, Zweifel*⟩; **b)** *(resting on authority)* unbedingt; blind ⟨*Vertrauen*⟩

**implore** [ɪmˈplɔː(r)] *v.t.* anflehen (for um)

**imply** [ɪmˈplaɪ] *v.t.* **a)** implizieren *(geh.);* *(say indirectly)* hindeuten auf *(+ Akk.);* **b)** *(insinuate)* unterstellen

**impolite** [ɪmpəˈlaɪt] *adj.* unhöflich

**import** 1. [ɪmˈpɔːt] *v.t.* importieren, einführen ⟨*Waren*⟩ **(from** aus, **into** nach). 2. [ˈɪmpɔːt] *n.* **a)** *(process)* Import, *der;* **b)** *(article)* Importgut, *das*

**importance** [ɪmˈpɔːtəns] *n.* Wichtigkeit, *die* **(to** für); *(significance)* Bedeutung, *die;* **be of ~:** wichtig sein; **full of one's own ~:** von seiner eigenen Wichtigkeit überzeugt

**important** [ɪmˈpɔːtənt] *adj.* wichtig **(to** für); *(significant)* bedeutend

**im'porter** *n.* Importeur, *der*

**impose** [ɪmˈpəʊz] *v.t.* auferlegen *(geh.)* ⟨*Bürde, Verpflichtung*⟩ (**up**|**on** *Dat.*); erheben ⟨*Steuer*⟩ **(on** auf + *Akk.*); verhängen ⟨*Kriegsrecht*⟩; anordnen ⟨*Rationierung*⟩. **im'pose on** *v.t.* ausnutzen ⟨*Gutmütigkeit, Toleranz usw.*⟩; **~ on sb.** sich jmdm. aufdrängen

**imposing** [ɪmˈpəʊzɪŋ] *adj.* imposant

**imposition** [ɪmpəˈzɪʃn] *n.* **a)** Auferlegung, *die;* *(of tax)* Erhebung, *die;* **b)** *(unreasonable demand)* Zumutung, *die*

**impossibility** [ɪmpɒsɪˈbɪlɪtɪ] *n.* Unmöglichkeit, *die*

**impossible** [ɪmˈpɒsɪbl] *adj.,* **impossibly** [ɪmˈpɒsɪblɪ] *adv.* unmöglich

**impostor** [ɪmˈpɒstə(r)] *n.* Hochstapler, *der/*-staplerin, *die; (swindler)* Betrüger, *der/*Betrügerin, *die*

**impound** [ɪmˈpaʊnd] *v.t.* beschlagnahmen

**impoverished** [ɪmˈpɒvərɪʃt] *adj.* **be/become ~:** verarmt sein/verarmen

**impracticable** [ɪmˈpræktɪkəbl] *adj.* undurchführbar

**impractical** [ɪmˈpræktɪkl] *adj.* **a)** *(unpractical)* unpraktisch; **b)** *see* **impracticable**

**imprecise** [ɪmprɪˈsaɪs] *adj.* ungenau

**impregnable** [ɪmˈpregnəbl] *adj.* uneinnehmbar ⟨*Festung, Bollwerk*⟩; *(fig.)* unanfechtbar ⟨*Ruf, Stellung*⟩

**impregnate** [ˈɪmpregneɪt] *v.t.* imprägnieren

**impress** [ɪmˈpres] *v.t.* beeindrucken; *abs.* Eindruck machen; **be ~ed by** or **with sth.** von etw. beeindruckt sein. **im'press [up]on** *v.t.* einschärfen (+ *Dat.*); **~ sth.** |**up**|**on sb.'s memory** jmdm. etw. einschärfen. **impression** [ɪmˈpreʃn] *n.* **a)** Eindruck, *der;* **form an ~ of sb.** sich *(Dat.)* ein Bild von jmdm. machen; **b)** *(impersonation)* **do an ~ of sb.** jmdn. imitieren; **do ~s** andere Leute imitieren. **impressionist** [ɪmˈpreʃənɪst] *n.* Impressionist, *der/* Impressionistin, *die*

**impressive** [ɪmˈpresɪv] *adj.* beeindruckend; imponierend

**imprint** 1. [ˈɪmprɪnt] *n.* Abdruck, *der; (fig.)* Stempel, *der.* 2. [ɪmˈprɪnt] *v.t.* aufdrucken; *(fig.)* einprägen **(on** *Dat.*)

**imprison** [ɪmˈprɪzn] *v.t.* in Haft nehmen; **be ~ed** sich in Haft befinden. **im'prisonment** *n.* Haft, *die;* **a long term of ~:** eine lange Haftstrafe

**improbable** [ɪmˈprɒbəbl] *adj.* unwahrscheinlich

**impromptu** [ɪmˈprɒmptjuː] 1. *adj.* improvisiert; **an ~ speech** eine Stegreifrede. 2. *adv.* aus dem Stegreif

**improper** [ɪmˈprɒpə(r)] *adj.* **a)** *(wrong)* unrichtig; **b)** *(unseemly)* unpassend; *(indecent)* unanständig. **im'properly** *adv. see* **improper:** unrichtig; unpassend; unanständig

**improvable** [ım'pru:vǝbl] *adj.* verbesserungsfähig

**improve** [ım'pru:v] **1.** *v. i.* besser werden; ⟨*Person, Wetter:*⟩ sich bessern. **2.**
*v. t.* verbessern. **3.** *v. refl.* ~ **oneself**
sich weiterbilden. **im'prove [up]on**
*v. t.* überbieten ⟨*Rekord, Angebot*⟩;
verbessern ⟨*Leistung*⟩. **improvement** [ım'pru:vmǝnt] *n.* Verbesserung, *die* (**on, over** gegenüber); **make
~s to sth.** Verbesserungen an etw.
*(Dat.)* vornehmen

**improvise** ['ımprǝvaız] *v. t.* improvisieren

**impudence** ['ımpjʊ:dǝns] *n.* Unverschämtheit, *die;* *(brazenness)* Dreistigkeit, *die*

**impudent** ['ımpjʊdǝnt] *adj.,* '**impud-
ently** *adv.* unverschämt; *(brazen[ly])*
dreist

**impulse** ['ımpʌls] *n.* Impuls, *der;* **on
[an]** ~: impulsiv. **impulsive** [ım'pʌl-
sıv] *adj.* impulsiv

**impunity** [ım'pju:nıtı] *v. t.* **with** ~: un-
gestraft

**impure** [ım'pjʊǝ(r)] *adj.* unrein. **im-
purity** [ım'pjʊǝrıtı] *n.* Unreinheit, *die;*
*(foreign body)* Fremdstoff, *der*

**impute** [ım'pju:t] *v. t.* zuschreiben (**to**
*Dat.*)

**in** [ın] **1.** *prep. (position; also fig.)* in
(+ *Dat.*); *(into)* in (+ *Akk.*); **in this
heat** bei dieser Hitze; **two feet in
diameter** mit einem Durchmesser von
zwei Fuß; **there are three feet in a yard**
ein Yard hat drei Fuß; **draw in crayon/
ink** mit Kreide/Tinte zeichnen; **pay in
pounds/dollars** in Pfund/Dollars bezahlen; **in fog/rain** *etc.* bei Nebel/Re-
gen *usw.;* **in the 20th century** im 20.
Jahrhundert; **4 o'clock in the morning/
afternoon** 4 Uhr morgens/abends; **in
1990** [im Jahre] 1990; **in three minutes/
years** in drei Minuten/Jahren; **in
doing this, he ...**; indem er das tut/tat,
er ...; **in that ...**; insofern als. **2.** *adv.* **a)**
*(inside)* hinein⟨*gehen usw.*⟩; herein-
⟨*kommen usw.*⟩; **b)** *(at home, work,
etc.)* **be in** dasein; **c) have it in for sb.** es
auf jmdn. abgesehen haben *(ugs.);* **sb.
is in for sth.** *(about to undergo)* jmdm.
steht etw. bevor. **3.** *adj. (coll.: in
fashion)* in *(ugs.).* **4.** *n.* **know the ins
and outs of sth.** sich in einer Sache genau auskennen

**ina'bility** *n.* Unfähigkeit, *die*

**inaccessible** [ınǝk'sesıbl] *adj.* unzu-
gänglich

**in'accuracy** *n.* **a)** *(incorrectness)* Un-

richtigkeit, *die;* **b)** *(imprecision)* Unge-
nauigkeit, *die*

**in'accurate** *adj.* **a)** *(incorrect)* unrichtig; **b)** *(imprecise)* ungenau

**in'active** *adj.* untätig. **inac'tivity** *n.*
Untätigkeit, *die*

**in'adequate** *adj.* unzulänglich; *(incompetent)* ungeeignet; **feel ~:**
überfordert fühlen

**inadvertent** [ınǝd'vɜ:tǝnt] *adj.,* **inad-
'vertently** *adv.* versehentlich

**inad'visable** *adj.* nicht ratsam

**inane** [ın'eın] *adj.* dümmlich

**in'animate** *adj.* unbelebt

**inap'plicable** *adj.* nicht zutreffend

**inap'propriate** *adj.* unpassend

**in'apt** *adj.* unpassend

**inar'ticulate** *adj.* **a) she's rather/very
~:** sie kann sich ziemlich/sehr
schlecht ausdrücken; **b)** *(indistinct)*
unverständlich

**inat'tentive** *adj.* unaufmerksam (**to**
gegenüber)

**in'audible** *adj.* unhörbar

**inau'spicious** *adj. (ominous)* unheil-
voll; *(unlucky)* unglücklich

**'inborn** *adj.* angeboren (**in** *Dat.*)

**in-'built** *adj.* jmdm./einer Sache eigen

**incalculable** [ın'kælkjʊlǝbl] *adj. (very
great)* unermeßlich

**in'capable** *adj.* **a) be ~ of doing sth.**
außerstande sein, etw. zu tun; **be ~ of
sth.** zu etw. unfähig sein; **b) be ~ of**
nicht zulassen ⟨*Beweis, Messung usw.*⟩

**incapacitate** [ınkǝ'pæsıteıt] *v. t.* unfähig machen

**incarcerate** [ın'kɑ:sǝreıt] *v. t.* einker-
kern *(geh.)*

**incendiary** [ın'sendıǝrı] *adj. & n.* ~
**device** Brandsatz, *der;* ~ [**bomb**]
Brandbombe, *die*

**'incense** ['ınsens] *n.* Weihrauch, *der*

**²incense** [ın'sens] *v. t.* erzürnen

**incentive** [ın'sentıv] *n.* Anreiz, *der*

**incessant** [ın'sesǝnt] *adj.,* **in'cess-
antly** *adv.* unablässig

**incest** ['ınsest] *n.* Inzest, *der.* **inces-
tuous** [ın'sestjʊǝs] *adj.* inzestuös

**inch** [ıntʃ] **1.** *n.* Inch, *der;* Zoll, *der
(veralt.).* **2.** *v. t. & i.* ~ [**one's way**] **forward** sich Zoll für Zoll vorwärtsbewe-
gen

**incident** ['ınsıdǝnt] *n.* **a)** *(notable
event)* Vorfall, *der;* **b)** *(clash)* Zwi-
schenfall, *der*

**incidental** [ınsı'dentl] *adj.* beiläufig
⟨*Bemerkung*⟩; Neben⟨*ausgaben, -ein-
nahmen*⟩. **incidentally** [ınsı'dentǝlı]
*adv.* nebenbei [bemerkt]

**incinerate** [ɪn'sɪnəreɪt] *v.t.* verbrennen. **incinerator** [ɪn'sɪnəreɪtə(r)] *n.* Verbrennungsofen, *der*

**incision** [ɪn'sɪʒn] *n.* Einschnitt, *der*

**incisive** [ɪn'saɪsɪv] *adj.* schneidend ⟨*Ton*⟩; scharf ⟨*Verstand*⟩; scharfsinnig ⟨*Kritik, Frage, Bemerkung, Argument*⟩

**incite** [ɪn'saɪt] *v.t.* anstiften; aufstacheln ⟨*Massen, Volk*⟩. **in'citement** *n.* Anstiftung, *die*/Aufstachelung, *die*

**inclination** [ɪnklɪ'neɪʃn] *n.* Neigung, *die*

**incline** 1. [ɪn'klaɪn] *v.t.* a) *(bend)* neigen; b) *(dispose)* veranlassen. 2. *v.i.* *(be disposed)* neigen (to|wards] zu). 3. ['ɪnklaɪn] *n.* Steigung, *die*. **inclined** [ɪn'klaɪnd] *adj.* geneigt; **they are ~ to be slow** sie neigen zur Langsamkeit; **if you feel [so] ~:** wenn Sie Lust dazu haben

**include** [ɪn'klu:d] *v.t.* einschließen; *(contain)* enthalten; **~d in the price** im Preis inbegriffen. **including** [ɪn'klu:dɪŋ] *prep.* einschließlich (+ *Gen.*); **~ VAT** inklusive Mehrwertsteuer. **inclusion** [ɪn'klu:ʒn] *n.* Aufnahme, *die*. **inclusive** [ɪn'klu:sɪv] *adj.* einschließlich; **be ~ of sth.** etw. einschließen; **from 2 to 6 January ~:** vom 2. bis einschließlich 6. Januar; **cost £50 ~:** 50 Pfund kosten, alles inbegriffen

**incognito** [ɪnkɒg'ni:təʊ] *adj., adv.* inkognito

**inco'herent** *adj.* zusammenhanglos

**income** ['ɪnkəm] *n.* Einkommen, *das*. **'income tax** *n.* Einkommensteuer, *die;* *(on wages, salary)* Lohnsteuer, *die*

**incoming** *adj.* ankommend; landend ⟨*Flugzeug*⟩; einfahrend ⟨*Zug*⟩; eingehend ⟨*Telefongespräch, Auftrag*⟩

**in'comparable** *adj.* unvergleichlich

**incom'patible** *adj.* unvereinbar; **be ~** ⟨*Menschen*⟩ nicht zueinander passen

**in'competence** [ɪn'kɒmpɪtəns] *n.* Unfähigkeit, *die;* Unvermögen, *das*

**in'competent** *adj.* unfähig

**incom'plete** *adj.* unvollständig

**incompre'hensible** *adj.* unbegreiflich; unverständlich ⟨*Rede, Argument*⟩

**incon'ceivable** *adj.* unvorstellbar

**incon'clusive** *adj.* ergebnislos; nicht schlüssig ⟨*Beweis, Argument*⟩

**incongruous** [ɪn'kɒŋgrʊəs] *adj.* unpassend

**inconsequential** [ɪnkɒnsɪ'kwenʃl] *adj.* belanglos

**incon'siderate** *adj.* rücksichtslos

**incon'sistency** *n. see* **inconsistent:** Widersprüchlichkeit, *die;* Inkonsequenz, *die;* Unbeständigkeit, *die*

**incon'sistent** *adj.* widersprüchlich; *(illogical)* inkonsequent; *(irregular)* unbeständig

**inconsolable** [ɪnkən'səʊləbl] *adj.* untröstlich

**incon'spicuous** *adj.* unauffällig

**incontinence** [ɪn'kɒntɪnəns] *n.* *(Med.)* Inkontinenz, *die*

**incontinent** [ɪn'kɒntɪnənt] *adj.* *(Med.)* inkontinent; **be ~:** an Inkontinenz leiden

**incontrovertible** [ɪnkɒntrə'vɜ:təbl] *adj.* unbestreitbar; unwiderlegbar ⟨*Beweis*⟩

**incon'venience** 1. *n.* Unannehmlichkeiten (to für); **put sb. to a lot of ~:** jmdm. große Unannehmlichkeiten bereiten. 2. *v.t.* Unannehmlichkeiten bereiten (+ *Dat.*); *(disturb)* stören

**incon'venient** *adj.* unbequem; ungünstig ⟨*Lage, Standort*⟩; **come at an ~ time** zu ungelegener Zeit kommen; **be ~ for sb.** jmdm. nicht passen

**incorporate** [ɪn'kɔ:pəreɪt] *v.t.* aufnehmen (in|to], **with in** + *Akk.*)

**incor'rect** *adj.* a) unrichtig; **be ~:** nicht stimmen; **it is ~ to say that ...:** es stimmt nicht, daß ...; b) *(improper)* inkorrekt. **incor'rectly** *adv.* a) unrichtigerweise; falsch ⟨*beantworten, aussprechen*⟩; b) *(improperly)* inkorrekt

**increase** 1. [ɪn'kri:s] *v.i.* zunehmen; ⟨*Lärm:*⟩ größer werden; ⟨*Preise, Nachfrage:*⟩ steigen; **~ in weight/size/price** schwerer/größer/teurer werden. 2. *v.t.* a) *(make greater)* erhöhen; b) *(intensify)* verstärken. 3. ['ɪnkri:s] *n.* Zunahme, *die* (in *Gen.*); **be on the ~:** ständig zunehmen. **increasing** [ɪn'kri:sɪŋ] *adj.* steigend; **an ~ number of people** mehr und mehr Menschen. **in'creasingly** *adv.* in zunehmendem Maße; **become ~ apparent** immer deutlicher werden

**in'credible** *adj.* *(also coll.: remarkable)* unglaublich. **in'credibly** *adv.* *(also coll.: remarkably)* unglaublich

**incredulous** [ɪn'kredjʊləs] *adj.* ungläubig

**incriminate** [ɪn'krɪmɪneɪt] *v.t.* belasten

**incubate** ['ɪŋkjʊbeɪt] *v.t.* bebrüten; *(to hatching)* ausbrüten. **incubation** [ɪŋkjʊ'beɪʃn] *n.* Bebrütung, *die*. **incubator** [ɪŋkjʊ'beɪtə(r)] *n.* Inkubator, *der;* *(for babies also)* Brutkasten, *der*

**incur** [ɪn'kɜ:(r)] *v. t.*, **-rr-** sich *(Dat.)* zuziehen ‹*Unwillen, Ärger*›; ~ **debts/expenses/risks** Schulden machen/Ausgaben haben/Risiken eingehen

**in'curable** *adj.* unheilbar

**incursion** [ɪn'kɜ:ʃn] *n.* Eindringen, *das; (by sudden attack)* Einfall, *der*

**indebted** [ɪn'detɪd] *pred. adj.* **be** |**much**| ~ **to sb. for sth.** jmdm. für etw. [sehr] zu Dank verpflichtet sein

**in'decency** *n.* Unanständigkeit, *die*

**in'decent** *adj.*, **in'decently** *adv.* unanständig

**inde'cision** *n.* Unentschlossenheit, *die*

**inde'cisive** *adj.* **a)** ergebnislos ‹*Streit, Diskussion*›; nichtssagend ‹*Ergebnis*›; **b)** *(hesitating)* unentschlossen

**indeed** [ɪn'di:d] *adv.* **a)** in der Tat; **thank you very much** ~: haben Sie vielen herzlichen Dank; ~ **it is** in der Tat; **b)** *(in fact)* ja sogar; ~, **he can ...:** ja, er kann sogar ...; **c)** *(admittedly)* zugegebenermaßen

**in'definite** *adj.* **a)** *(vague)* unbestimmt; **b)** *(unlimited)* unbegrenzt. **in'definitely** *adv.* **a)** *(vaguely)* unbestimmt; **b)** *(unlimitedly)* unbegrenzt; auf unbestimmte Zeit ‹*verschieben*›

**indelible** [ɪn'delɪbl] *adj.* unauslöschlich; ~ **ink** Wäschetinte, *die*

**indemnify** [ɪn'demnɪfaɪ] *v. t.* absichern **(against** gegen); *(compensate)* entschädigen. **indemnity** [ɪn'demnɪtɪ] *n.* Absicherung, *die; (compensation)* Entschädigung, *die*

**inde'pendence** *n.* Unabhängigkeit, *die*

**inde'pendent** *adj.*, **inde'pendently** *adv.* unabhängig **(of** von)

**indescribable** [ɪndɪ'skraɪbəbl] *adj.* unbeschreiblich

**indestructible** [ɪndɪ'strʌktɪbl] *adj.* unzerstörbar

**indeterminate** [ɪndɪ'tɜ:mɪnət] *adj.* unbestimmt; unklar ‹*Konzept*›

**index** ['ɪndeks] **1.** *n.* Register, *das.* **2.** *v. t.* mit einem Register versehen. **'index finger** *n.* Zeigefinger, *der*

**India** ['ɪndɪə] *n.* Indien *(das).*

**Indian** ['ɪndɪən] **1.** *adj.* **a)** indisch; **b)** |American| ~: indianisch. **2.** *n.* **a)** Inder, *der*/Inderin, *die;* **b)** |American| ~: Indianer, *der*/Indianerin, *die.* **Indian 'Ocean** *pr. n.* Indischer Ozean

**indicate** ['ɪndɪkeɪt] **1.** *v. t.* **a)** *(be a sign of)* erkennen lassen; **b)** *(state briefly)* andeuten; **c)** *(mark, point out)* anzeigen; **d)** *(suggest, make evident)* zum Ausdruck bringen **(to** gegenüber). **2.**

*v. i. (Motor Veh.)* blinken. **indication** [ɪndɪ'keɪʃn] *n.* [An]zeichen, *das (of Gen.,* für). **indicative** [ɪn'dɪkətɪv] **1.** *adj.* **a) be ~ of sth.** auf etw. *(Akk.)* schließen lassen; **b)** *(Ling.)* indikativisch. **2.** *n. (Ling.)* Indikativ, *der.* **indicator** ['ɪndɪkeɪtə(r)] *n. (on vehicle)* Blinker, *der*

**indict** [ɪn'daɪt] *v. t.* anklagen **(for, on a charge of** *Gen.*)

**in'difference** *n.* Gleichgültigkeit, *die* **(to**|**wards**| gegenüber)

**in'different** *adj.* **a)** gleichgültig; **b)** *(not good)* mittelmäßig

**indi'gestion** *n.* Magenverstimmung, *die; (chronic)* Verdauungsstörungen

**indignant** [ɪn'dɪgnənt] *adj.* entrüstet **(at, over, about** über + *Akk.*); indigniert ‹*Blick, Geste*›. **in'dignantly** *adv.* entrüstet; indigniert. **indignation** [ɪndɪg'neɪʃn] *n.* Entrüstung, *die* **(about, at, against, over** über + *Akk.*)

**in'dignity** *n.* Demütigung, *die*

**indigo** ['ɪndɪgəʊ] **1.** *adj.* ~ |**blue**| indigoblau. **2.** *n.* ~ |**blue**| Indigoblau, *das*

**indi'rect** *adj.* indirekt; ~ **speech** indirekte Rede. **indi'rectly** *adv.* indirekt. **indirect 'object** *n.* indirektes Objekt; *(in German)* Dativobjekt, *das*

**indi'screet** *adj.* indiskret. **indi'scretion** *n.* Indiskretion, *die*

**indiscriminate** [ɪndɪ'skrɪmɪnət] *adj.* unkritisch

**indi'spensable** *adj.* unentbehrlich **(to** für); unabdingbar ‹*Voraussetzung*›

**indisputable** [ɪndɪ'spju:təbl] *adj.*, **disputably** [ɪndɪ'spju:təblɪ] *adv.* unbestreitbar

**indi'stinct** *adj.*, **indi'stinctly** *adv.* undeutlich

**indi'stinguishable** *adj.* nicht unterscheidbar

**individual** [ɪndɪ'vɪdjʊəl] **1.** *adj.* **a)** einzeln; **b)** *(distinctive, characteristic)* individuell. **2.** *n.* einzelne, *der/die.* **indi'vidually** *adv.* einzeln

**indi'visible** *adj.* unteilbar

**indoctrinate** [ɪn'dɒktrɪneɪt] *v. t.* indoktrinieren

**indolence** ['ɪndələns] *n.* Trägheit, *die*

**indolent** ['ɪndələnt] *adj.* träge

**indomitable** [ɪn'dɒmɪtəbl] *adj.* unbeugsam

**Indonesia** [ɪndə'ni:ʃə] *pr. n.* Indonesien *(das)*

**'indoor** *adj.* ~ **swimming-pool/sports** Hallenbad, *das*/-sport, *der;* ~ **plants** Zimmerpflanzen; ~ **games** Spiele im Haus; *(Sport)* Hallenspiele

**indoors** [ɪn'dɔːz] *adv.* drinnen; im Haus; **go/come** ~: nach drinnen gehen/kommen
**induce** [ɪn'djuːs] *v. t.* ~ **sb. to do sth.** jmdn. dazu bringen, etw. zu tun. **in-'ducement** *n. (incentive)* Anreiz, *der*
**indulge** [ɪn'dʌldʒ] **1.** *v. t.* **a)** nachgeben (+ *Dat.*) ⟨*Wunsch, Verlangen, Verlockung*⟩; frönen *(geh.)* (+ *Dat.*) ⟨*Leidenschaft*⟩; **b)** *(please)* verwöhnen. **2.** *v. i.* ~ **in** frönen *(geh.)* (+ *Dat.*) ⟨*Leidenschaft*⟩. **indulgence** [ɪn'dʌl-dʒəns] *n.* **a)** Nachsicht, *die; (humouring)* Nachgiebigkeit, *die* (with gegenüber); *(thing indulged in)* Luxus, *der.* **indulgent** [ɪn'dʌldʒənt] *adj.* nachsichtig (**with, to|wards|** gegenüber)
**industrial** [ɪn'dʌstrɪəl] *adj.* industriell; Arbeits⟨*unfall, -medizin, -psychologie*⟩
**industrial:** ~ **'action** *n.* Arbeitskampfmaßnahmen; **take** ~ **action:** in den Ausstand treten; ~ **dispute** *n.* Arbeitskonflikt, *der;* ~ **estate** *n.* Industriegebiet, *das*
**industrialize** [ɪn'dʌstrɪəlaɪz] *v. t.* industrialisieren
**industrious** [ɪn'dʌstrɪəs] *adj.* fleißig; *(busy)* emsig
**industry** ['ɪndəstrɪ] *n.* **a)** Industrie, *die;* **b)** *see* **industrious:** Fleiß, *der;* Emsigkeit, *die*
**in'edible** *adj.* ungenießbar
**ineffective** *adj.* unwirksam; fruchtlos ⟨*Anstrengung, Versuch*⟩
**ineffectual** [ɪnɪ'fektjʊəl] *adj.* unwirksam; fruchtlos ⟨*Versuch, Bemühung*⟩; ineffizient ⟨*Methode, Person*⟩
**inefficiency** *n.* Leistungsschwäche, *die; (of organization, method)* schlechtes Funktionieren
**inefficient** *adj.* leistungsschwach; schlecht funktionierend ⟨*Organisation, Methode*⟩
**in'elegant** *adj.* unelegant
**in'eligible** *adj.* ungeeignet; **be** ~ **for** nicht in Frage kommen für ⟨*Beförderung, Position*⟩; nicht berechtigt sein zu ⟨*Leistungen des Staats usw.*⟩
**inept** [ɪ'nept] *adj.* unbeholfen
**ine'quality** *n.* Ungleichheit, *die*
**inert** [ɪ'nɜːt] *adj.* **a)** reglos; *(sluggish)* träge; **b)** *(Chem.)* inert; ~ **gas** Edelgas, *das.* **inertia** [ɪ'nɜːʃə] *n.* Trägheit, *die*
**inescapable** [ɪnɪ'skeɪpəbl] *adj.* unausweichlich
**ines'sential** *adj.* unwesentlich; *(dispensable)* entbehrlich
**inevitable** [ɪn'evɪtəbl] *adj.* unvermeidlich; unabwendbar ⟨*Ereignis, Krieg,*

*Schicksal*⟩; zwangsläufig ⟨*Ergebnis, Folge*⟩. **inevitably** [ɪn'evɪtəblɪ] *adv.* zwangsläufig
**ine'xact** *adj.* ungenau
**inex'cusable** *adj.* unverzeihlich
**inexhaustible** [ɪnɪg'zɔːstɪbl] *adj.* unerschöpflich; unverwüstlich ⟨*Person*⟩
**inexorable** [ɪn'eksərəbl] *adj.* unerbittlich
**inex'pensive** *adj.* preisgünstig
**inex'perience** *n.* Unerfahrenheit, *die.* **inex'perienced** *adj.* unerfahren; ~ **in sth.** wenig vertraut mit etw.
**inex'plicable** *adj.* unerklärlich
**in'fallible** *adj.* unfehlbar
**infamous** ['ɪnfəməs] *adj.* berüchtigt
**infancy** ['ɪnfənsɪ] *n.* frühe Kindheit; **be in its** ~ *(fig.)* noch in den Anfängen stecken
**infant** ['ɪnfənt] *n.* kleines Kind. **infantile** ['ɪnfəntaɪl] *adj.* kindlich; *(childish)* kindisch
**infantry** ['ɪnfəntrɪ] *n.* Infanterie, *die*
**'infant school** *n. (Brit.)* ≈ Vorschule, *die*
**infatuated** [ɪn'fætjʊeɪtɪd] *adj.* **be** ~ **with sb.** in jmdn. vernarrt sein
**infect** [ɪn'fekt] *v. t.* anstecken; infizieren; **the wound became** ~**ed** die Wunde entzündete sich. **infection** [ɪn'fekʃn] *n.* Infektion, *die;* **throat/ear/eye** ~: Hals-/Ohren-/Augenentzündung, *die.* **infectious** [ɪn'fekʃəs] *adj.* ansteckend; **be** ~ ⟨*Person:*⟩ eine ansteckende Krankheit haben
**infer** [ɪn'fɜː(r)] *v. t.,* **-rr-** schließen (**from** aus); ziehen ⟨*Schlußfolgerung*⟩. **inference** ['ɪnfərəns] *n.* [Schluß]folgerung, *die*
**inferior** [ɪn'fɪərɪə(r)] **1.** *adj. (of lower quality)* minderwertig ⟨*Ware*⟩; minder... ⟨*Qualität*⟩; unterlegen ⟨*Gegner*⟩; ~ **to sth.** schlechter als etw.; **feel** ~: Minderwertigkeitsgefühle haben. **2.** *n.* Untergebene, *der/die.* **inferiority** [ɪnfɪərɪ'ɒrɪtɪ] *n.* Minderwertigkeit, *die/* Unterlegenheit, *die.* **inferi'ority complex** *n.* Minderwertigkeitskomplex, *der*
**infernal** [ɪn'fɜːnl] *adj.* **a)** *(of hell)* höllisch; **b)** *(coll.)* verdammt *(salopp)*
**inferno** [ɪn'fɜːnəʊ] *n.* Inferno, *das*
**in'fertile** *adj.* unfruchtbar. **infer-'tility** *n.* Unfruchtbarkeit, *die*
**infest** [ɪn'fest] *v. t.* ⟨*Ungeziefer:*⟩ befallen; ⟨*Unkraut:*⟩ überwuchern; ~**ed with** befallen/überwuchert von
**infidelity** [ɪnfɪ'delɪtɪ] *n.* Untreue, *die* (**to** gegenüber)

**infiltrate** ['ınfıltreıt] v. t. **a)** infiltrieren; unterwandern ⟨Partei, Organisation⟩; **b)** einschleusen ⟨Agenten⟩

**infinite** ['ınfınıt] adj. **a)** (endless) unendlich; **b)** (very great) ungeheuer

**infinitive** [ın'fınıtıv] n. (Ling.) Infinitiv, der

**infinity** [ın'fınıtı] n. Unendlichkeit, die

**infirm** [ın'fɜ:m] adj. gebrechlich. **in-firmity** [ın'fɜ:mıtı] n. Gebrechlichkeit, die; (malady) Gebrechen, das

**inflamed** [ın'fleımd] adj. (Med.) **be/ become ~:** entzündet sein/sich entzünden

**inflammable** [ın'flæməbl] adj. feuergefährlich

**inflammation** [ınflə'meıʃn] n. (Med.) Entzündung, die

**inflammatory** [ın'flæmətərı] adj. aufrührerisch; **an ~ speech** eine Hetzrede

**inflatable** [ın'fleıtəbl] adj. aufblasbar; **~ dinghy** Schlauchboot, das

**inflate** [ın'fleıt] v. t. aufblasen; (with pump) aufpumpen

**inflation** [ın'fleıʃn] n. (Econ.) Inflation, die

**in'flexible** adj. **a)** (stiff) unbiegsam; **b)** (obstinate) [geistig] unbeweglich

**inflict** [ın'flıkt] v. t. zufügen ⟨Leid, Schmerzen⟩, beibringen ⟨Wunde⟩, versetzen ⟨Schlag⟩ (**on** Dat.)

**influence** ['ınflʊəns] **1.** n. Einfluß, der; **be a good/bad ~ [on sb.]** einen guten/schlechten Einfluß [auf jmdn.] ausüben. **2.** v. t. beeinflussen. **influential** [ınflʊ'enʃl] adj. einflußreich

**influenza** [ınflʊ'enzə] n. Grippe, die

**influx** ['ınflʌks] n. Zustrom, der

**inform** [ın'fɔ:m] **1.** n. informieren (of, **about** über + Akk.); **keep sb. ~ed** jmdn. auf dem laufenden halten. **2.** v. i. **~ against** or **on sb.** jmdn. denunzieren (to bei)

**in'formal** adj. **a)** zwanglos; **b)** (unofficial) informell. **infor'mality** n. Zwanglosigkeit, die

**informant** [ın'fɔ:mənt] n. Informant, der/Informantin, die

**information** [ınfə'meıʃn] n. Informationen Pl.; **give ~ on sth.** Auskunft über etw. (Akk.) erteilen; **piece** or **bit of ~:** Information, die; **~ centre** Auskunftsbüro, das

**informative** [ın'fɔ:mətıv] adj. informativ; **not very ~:** nicht sehr aufschlußreich ⟨Dokument, Schriftstück⟩

**informed** [ın'fɔ:md] adj. informiert

**in'former** n. Denunziant, der/Denunziantin, die

**infra-red** [ınfrə'red] adj. infrarot

**in'frequent** adj., **in'frequently** adv. selten

**infringe** [ın'frındʒ] v. t. & i. **~ [on]** verstoßen gegen. **in'fringement** n. Verstoß, der (of gegen)

**infuriate** [ın'fjʊərıeıt] v. t. wütend machen; **be ~d** wütend sein (by über + Akk.). **infuriating** [ın'fjʊərıeıtıŋ] adj. ärgerlich

**ingenious** [ın'dʒi:nıəs] adj. einfallsreich; genial ⟨Methode, Idee⟩; raffiniert ⟨Spielzeug, Maschine⟩. **ingenuity** [ındʒı'nju:ıtı] n. Genialität, die

**ingot** ['ıŋgət] n. Ingot, der

**ingratiate** [ın'greıʃıeıt] v. refl. **~ oneself with sb.** sich bei jmdm. einschmeicheln

**in'gratitude** n. Undankbarkeit, die (to[wards] gegenüber)

**ingredient** [ın'gri:dıənt] n. Zutat, die

**ingrowing** ['ıŋgrəʊıŋ] adj. eingewachsen ⟨Zehennagel usw.⟩

**inhabit** [ın'hæbıt] v. t. bewohnen. **inhabitable** [ın'hæbıtəbl] adj. bewohnbar. **inhabitant** [ın'hæbıtənt] n. Bewohner, der/Bewohnerin, die

**inhale** [ın'heıl] v. t. & i. einatmen; inhalieren (ugs.) ⟨Zigarettenrauch usw.⟩

**inherit** [ın'herıt] v. t. erben. **inheritance** [ın'herıtəns] n. Erbe, das; (inheriting) Erbschaft, die

**inhibit** [ın'hıbıt] v. t. hemmen. **in'hibited** adj. gehemmt. **inhibition** [ınhı'bıʃn] n. Hemmung, die

**inho'spitable** adj. ungastlich ⟨Person, Verhalten⟩; unwirtlich ⟨Gegend, Klima⟩

**in'human** adj. unmenschlich

**initial** [ı'nıʃl] **1.** adj. anfänglich; Anfangs⟨stadium, -schwierigkeiten⟩. **2.** n. esp. in pl. Initiale, die. **3.** v. t., (Brit.) -ll- abzeichnen ⟨Scheck, Quittung⟩; paraphieren ⟨Vertrag, Abkommen usw.⟩. **i'nitially** adv. anfangs; am Anfang

**initiate** [ı'nıʃıeıt] v. t. **a)** (introduce) einführen (into in + Akk.); (into knowledge, mystery) einweihen (into in + Akk.); **b)** (begin) einleiten. **initiation** [ınıʃı'eıʃn] n. **a)** (introduction) Einführung, die; (into knowledge, mystery) Einweihung, die

**initiative** [ı'nıʃətıv] n. Initiative, die; **lack ~:** keine Initiative haben

**inject** [ın'dʒekt] v. t. [ein]spritzen; injizieren (Med.). **injection** [ın'dʒekʃn] n. Spritze, die; Injektion, die

**injure** ['ındʒə(r)] v. t. **a)** verletzen; **his**

**leg was ~d** er wurde/*(state)* war am Bein verletzt; **b)** *(impair)* schaden (+ *Dat.*). **injured** ['ɪndʒəd] *adj.* verletzt; verwundet ⟨*Soldat*⟩. **injury** ['ɪndʒərɪ] *n.* Verletzung, *die* (**to** Gen.)

**in'justice** *n.* Ungerechtigkeit, *die*

**ink** [ɪŋk] *n.* Tinte, *die*

**inkling** ['ɪŋklɪŋ] *n.* Ahnung, *die;* **have an ~ of sth.** etw. ahnen

**inland** ['ɪnlənd, 'ɪnlænd] *adj.* Binnen-; binnenländisch. **Inland 'Revenue** *n.* *(Brit.)* ≈ Finanzamt, *das*

**'in-laws** *n pl. (coll.)* Schwiegereltern

**inlet** ['ɪnlət] *n.* [schmale] Bucht

**inmate** *n.* Insasse, *der*/Insassin, *die*

**inn** [ɪn] *n. (hotel)* Gasthof, *der; (pub)* Wirtshaus, *das*

**innate** [ɪ'neɪt] *adj.* angeboren

**inner** ['ɪnə(r)] *adj.* inner...; Innen⟨*hof, -tür, -fläche, -seite usw.*⟩; **~ tube** Schlauch, *der.* **innermost** ['ɪnəməʊst] *adj.* innerst...

**innocence** ['ɪnəsəns] *n.* **a)** Unschuld, *die;* **b)** *(naïvity)* Naivität, *die*

**innocent** ['ɪnəsənt] *adj.* **a)** unschuldig (**of** an + *Dat.*); **b)** *(naïve)* naiv

**innocuous** [ɪ'nɒkjʊəs] *adj.* harmlos

**innovation** [ɪnə'veɪʃn] *n.* Innovation, *die; (thing, change)* Neuerung, *die*

**innumerable** [ɪ'nju:mərəbl] *adj.* unzählig

**inoculate** [ɪ'nɒkjʊleɪt] *v. t.* impfen. **inoculation** [ɪnɒkjʊ'leɪʃn] *n.* Impfung, *die*

**inoffensive** *adj.* harmlos

**in'opportune** *adj.* unpassend; unangebracht ⟨*Bemerkung*⟩

**inordinate** [ɪ'nɔ:dɪnət] *adj.* unmäßig; ungeheuer ⟨*Menge*⟩

**inor'ganic** *adj.* anorganisch

**'in-patient** *n.* stationär behandelter Patient/behandelte Patientin

**'input** *n.* Input, *der od. das*

**inquest** ['ɪŋkwest] *n.* gerichtliche Untersuchung der Todesursache

**inquire** [ɪn'kwaɪə(r)] **1.** *v. i.* sich erkundigen (**about, after** nach, **of** bei); **~ into** untersuchen. **2.** *v. t.* sich erkundigen nach ⟨*Weg, Namen*⟩. **inquiry** [ɪn'kwaɪərɪ] *n.* **a)** *(question)* Erkundigung, *die* (**into** über + *Akk.*); **make inquiries** Erkundigungen einziehen; **b)** *(investigation)* Untersuchung, *die*

**inquisitive** [ɪn'kwɪzɪtɪv] *adj.* neugierig

**'inroad** *n.* Eingriff, *der* (**on, into** in + *Akk.*); **make ~s into sb.'s savings** jmds. Ersparnisse angreifen

**in'sane** *adj.* geisteskrank

**in'sanitary** *adj.* unhygienisch

**in'sanity** *n.* Geisteskrankheit, *die*

**insatiable** [ɪn'seɪʃəbl] *adj.* unersättlich; unstillbar ⟨*Verlangen*⟩

**inscribe** [ɪn'skraɪb] *v. t.* schreiben; *(on stone, rock)* einmeißeln; mit einer Inschrift versehen ⟨*Denkmal, Grabstein*⟩. **inscription** [ɪn'skrɪpʃn] *n.* Inschrift, *die; (on coin)* Aufschrift, *die*

**inscrutable** [ɪn'skru:təbl] *adj.* unergründlich; undurchdringlich ⟨*Miene*⟩

**insect** ['ɪnsekt] *n.* Insekt, *das.* **insecticide** [ɪn'sektɪsaɪd] *n.* Insektizid, *das.* **'insect repellent** *n.* Insektenschutzmittel, *das*

**inse'cure** *adj.* unsicher. **inse'curity** *n.* Unsicherheit, *die*

**in'sensitive** *adj.* **a)** gefühllos ⟨*Person, Art*⟩; *(unappreciative)* unempfänglich (**to** für); **b)** *(physically)* unempfindlich (**to** gegen)

**in'separable** *adj.* untrennbar; *(fig.)* unzertrennlich

**insert** [ɪn'sɜ:t] *v. t.* einlegen ⟨*Film*⟩; einwerfen ⟨*Münze*⟩; hineinstecken ⟨*Schlüssel*⟩; einstechen ⟨*Nadel*⟩. **insertion** [ɪn'sɜ:ʃn] *n. see* **insert:** Einlegen, *das;* Einwerfen, *das;* Hineinstecken, *das;* Einstechen, *das*

**inside 1.** [-'-, '--] *n.* **a)** *(internal side)* Innenseite, *die;* **on the ~:** innen; **to/from the ~:** nach/von innen; **b)** *(inner part)* Innere, *das.* **2.** ['--] *adj.* inner...; Innen⟨*wand, -einrichtung, -ansicht*⟩; *(fig.)* intern. **3.** [-'-] *adv. (on or in the ~)* innen; *(to the ~)* nach innen hinein/herein; *(indoors)* drinnen; **come ~:** hereinkommen; **take a look ~:** hineinsehen; **go ~:** [ins Haus] hineingehen; **turn a jacket ~ out** eine Jacke nach links wenden; **know sth. ~ out** etw. in- und auswendig kennen. **4.** [-'-] *prep. (position)* in (+ *Dat.*); *(direction)* in (+ *Akk.*) hinein

**insidious** [ɪn'sɪdɪəs] *adj.* heimtückisch

**'insight** *n. (discernment)* Verständnis, *das;* **gain an ~ into sth.** Einblick in etw. *(Akk.)* gewinnen

**insig'nificant** *adj.* unbedeutend; geringfügig ⟨*Summe*⟩

**insin'cere** *adj.* unaufrichtig. **insin'cerity** *n.* Unaufrichtigkeit, *die*

**insinuate** [ɪn'sɪnjʊeɪt] *v. t.* andeuten (**to sb.** jmdm. gegenüber). **insinuation** [ɪnsɪnjʊ'eɪʃn] *n.* Anspielung, *die* (**about** auf + *Akk.*)

**insipid** [ɪn'sɪpɪd] *adj.* fade

**insist** [ɪn'sɪst] *v. i.* bestehen (**[up]on** auf + *Dat.*); **~ on doing sth./on sb.'s doing sth.** darauf bestehen, etw. zu

tun/daß jmd. etw. tut; **if you** ~: wenn
du darauf bestehst. **insistence** [ın-
'sıstəns] *n.* Bestehen, *das* (**on** auf
+ *Dat.*). **insistent** [ın'sıstənt] *adj.* **be**
~ **that ...**: darauf bestehen, daß ...
**insolence** ['ınsələns] *n.* Unverschämtheit, *die;* Frechheit, *die*
**insolent** ['ınsələnt] *adj.,* **'insolently**
*adv.* unverschämt; frech
**in'soluble** *adj.* **a)** *(esp. Chem.)* unlös-
lich; **b)** *(not solvable)* unlösbar
**in'solvent** *adj.* zahlungsunfähig
**insomnia** [ın'sɒmnɪə] *n.* Schlaflosigkeit, *die.* **insomniac** [ın'sɒmnɪæk] *n.*
**be an** ~: an Schlaflosigkeit leiden
**inspect** [ın'spekt] *v.t.* prüfend betrachten; *(examine officially)* überprüfen; kontrollieren ⟨*Räumlichkeiten*⟩.
**inspection** [ın'spekʃn] *n.* Überprüfung, *die;* *(of premises)* Kontrolle, *die;*
Inspektion, *die;* **on |closer|** ~: bei nä-
herer Betrachtung. **inspector** [ın-
'spektə(r)] *n.* **a)** *(on bus, train, etc.)*
Kontrolleur, *der/*Kontrolleurin, *die;*
**b)** *(Brit.)* ≈ Polizeiinspektor, *der*
**inspiration** [ınspə'reıʃn] *n.* Inspiration, *die (geh.)*
**inspire** [ın'spaıə(r)] *v.t.* **a)** inspirieren
*(geh.)*⟨*Person*⟩; **b)** *(instil)* einflößen (**in**
*Dat.*). **inspiring** [ın'spaıərıŋ] *adj.* in-
spirierend *(geh.)*
**insta'bility** *n.* Instabilität, *die; (of person)* Labilität, *die*
**install** [ın'stɔ:l] *v.t.* installieren; einbauen ⟨*Badezimmer*⟩; anschließen
⟨*Telefon, Herd*⟩; ~ **oneself** sich installieren. **installation** [ınstə'leıʃn] *n.* **a)**
Installation, *die;* *(of bathroom)* Einbau, *der;* *(of telephone, cooker)* Anschluß, *der;* **b)** *(apparatus etc. in-
stalled)* Anlage, *die*
**instalment** *(Amer.:* **installment)**
[ın'stɔ:lmənt] *n.* **a)** *(part-payment)* Rate, *die;* **pay by** *or* **in** ~**s** in Raten zahlen; **b)** *(of serial, novel)* Fortsetzung,
*die; (Radio, Telev.)* Folge, *die*
**instance** ['ınstəns] *n. (example)* Beispiel, *das* (**of** für); **for** ~: zum Beispiel; **in many** ~**s** *(cases)* in vielen Fällen; **in the first** ~: zunächst einmal
**instant** ['ınstənt] **1.** *adj.* unmittelbar;
sofortig ⟨*Wirkung, Linderung, Ergeb-
nis*⟩; ~ **coffee/tea** Pulverkaffee/In-
stanttee, *der;* ~ **potatoes** fertiger Kartoffelbrei. **2.** *n.* Augenblick, *der;* **at
that very** ~: genau in dem Augenblick; **come here this** ~: komm sofort
her; **in an** ~: augenblicklich. **instant-
aneous** [ınstən'teınıəs] *adj.* unmittel-

bar; **his reaction was** ~: er reagierte
sofort. **'instantly** *adv.* sofort
**instead** [ın'sted] *adv.* statt dessen; ~
**of doing sth.** [an]statt etw. zu tun; ~ **of
sth.** anstelle einer Sache *(Gen.);* **I will
go** ~ **of you** ich gehe an deiner Stelle
**'instep** *n. (of foot)* Spann, *der;* Fuß-
rücken, *der; (of shoe)* Blatt, *das*
**instigate** ['ınstıgeıt] *v.t.* anstiften (**to**
zu); initiieren *(geh.)* ⟨*Reformen, Projekt usw.*⟩. **instigation** [ınstı'geıʃn] *n.*
Anstiftung, *die; (of reforms, project,
etc.)* Initiierung, *die;* **at sb.'s** ~: auf
jmds. Betreiben *(Akk.)*
**instil** *(Amer.:* **instill)** [ın'stıl] *v.t.,* **-ll-**
einflößen (**in** *Dat.*); beibringen ⟨*gutes
Benehmen, Wissen*⟩ (**in** *Dat.*)
**instinct** ['ınstıŋkt] *n.* Instinkt, *der.* **instinctive** [ın'stıŋktıv] *adj.,* **in'stinc-
tively** *adv.* instinktiv
**institute** ['ınstıtju:t] **1.** *n.* Institut, *das.*
**2.** *v.t.* einführen; einleiten ⟨*Suche,
Verfahren*⟩; anstrengen ⟨*Prozeß*⟩
**institution** [ınstı'tju:ʃn] *n.* Institution,
*die; (home)* Heim, *das;* Anstalt, *die*
**instruct** [ın'strʌkt] *v.t.* **a)** *(teach)* unterrichten ⟨*Klasse, Fach*⟩; **b)** *(direct,
command)* anweisen. **instruction**
[ın'strʌkʃn] *n.* **a)** *(teaching)* Unterricht, *der;* **b)** esp. in pl. *(direction,
order)* Anweisung, *die;* ~ **manual/**~**s
for use** Gebrauchsanleitung, *die.* **in-
structive** [ın'strʌktıv] *adj.* aufschlußreich; lehrreich ⟨*Erfahrung,
Buch*⟩. **instructor** [ın'strʌktə(r)] *n.*
Lehrer, *der/*Lehrerin, *die; (Mil.)* Ausbilder, *der*
**instrument** ['ınstrʊmənt] *n.* Instrument, *das.* **instrumental** [ınstrə-
'mentl] *adj.* **a)** *(Mus.)* Instrumental-;
**b)** *(helpful)* dienlich (**to** *Dat.*); **he was**
~ **in finding me a job** er hat mir zu einer Stelle verholfen
**insufferable** [ın'sʌfərəbl] *adj. (unbearably arrogant)* unausstehlich
**insuf'ficient** *adj.* nicht genügend;
unzulänglich ⟨*Beweise*⟩; unzureichend ⟨*Versorgung, Beleuchtung*⟩.
**insuf'ficiently** *adv.* ungenügend
**insulate** ['ınsjʊleıt] *v.t.* isolieren
(**against, from** gegen); **insulating tape**
Isolierband, *das.* **insulation** [ınsjʊ-
'leıʃn] *n.* Isolierung, *die*
**insulin** ['ınsjʊlın] *n.* Insulin, *das*
**insult 1.** ['ınsʌlt] *n.* Beleidigung, *die*
(**to** *Gen.*). **2.** [ın'sʌlt] *v.t.* beleidigen.
**insulting** [ın'sʌltıŋ] *adj.* beleidigend
**insuperable** [ın'su:pərəbl] *adj.* unüberwindlich

**insurance** [ɪnˈʃʊərəns] *n.* Versicherung, *die; (fig.)* Sicherheit, *die;* **take out ~ against/on sth.** eine Versicherung gegen etw. abschließen/etw. versichern lassen; **travel ~:** Reisegepäck- und -unfallversicherung, *die.* **inˈsurance policy** *n.* Versicherungspolice, *die*

**insure** [ɪnˈʃʊə(r)] *v. t.* versichern ⟨*Person*⟩; versichern lassen ⟨*Gepäck, Gemälde usw.*⟩; **~ [oneself] against sth.** [sich] gegen etw. versichern

**insurmountable** [ɪnsəˈmaʊntəbl] *adj.* unüberwindlich

**intact** [ɪnˈtækt] *adj.* **a)** *(entire)* unbeschädigt; intakt ⟨*Uhr, Maschine usw.*⟩; **b)** *(unimpaired)* unversehrt

**ˈintake** *n.* **a)** *(action)* Aufnahme, *die;* **b)** *(persons, things)* Neuzugänge; *(amount)* aufgenommene Menge

**inˈtangible** *adj.* nicht greifbar; *(mentally)* unbestimmbar

**integral** [ˈɪntɪgrl] *adj.* **a)** wesentlich ⟨*Bestandteil*⟩; **b)** *(whole)* vollständig

**integrate** [ˈɪntɪgreɪt] *v. t.* integrieren **(into in +** *Akk.***).** **integration** [ɪntɪˈgreɪʃn] *n.* Integration, *die* **(into in +** *Akk.***)**

**integrity** [ɪnˈtegrɪtɪ] *n.* Redlichkeit, *die*

**intellect** [ˈɪntəlekt] *n.* Verstand, *der;* Intellekt, *der.* **intellectual** [ɪntəˈlektjʊəl] **1.** *adj.* intellektuell; geistig anspruchsvoll ⟨*Person, Publikum*⟩. **2.** *n.* Intellektuelle, *der/die*

**intelligence** [ɪnˈtelɪdʒəns] *n.* **a)** Intelligenz, *die;* **b)** *(information)* Informationen *Pl.;* **c) military ~** *(organization)* militärischer Geheimdienst. **intelligent** [ɪnˈtelɪdʒənt] *adj.* intelligent

**intelligible** [ɪnˈtelɪdʒɪbl] *adj.* verständlich **(to für)**

**intend** [ɪnˈtend] *v. t.* beabsichtigen; **it was ~ed as a joke** das sollte ein Witz sein. **inˈtended** *adj.* beabsichtigt ⟨*Wirkung*⟩; **be ~ for sb./sth.** für jmdn./ etw. gedacht sein

**intense** [ɪnˈtens] *adj.* **a)** intensiv; groß ⟨*Hitze, Belastung, Interesse*⟩; stark ⟨*Schmerzen*⟩; **b)** *(earnest)* ernst. **inˈtensely** *adv.* äußerst; intensiv ⟨*studieren, fühlen*⟩

**intensify** [ɪnˈtensɪfaɪ] **1.** *v. t.* intensivieren. **2.** *v. i.* zunehmen

**intensity** [ɪnˈtensɪtɪ] *n. see* **intense a:** Intensität, *die;* Größe, *die;* Stärke, *die*

**intensive** [ɪnˈtensɪv] *adj.* intensiv; Intensiv⟨*kurs*⟩; **be in ~ care** auf der Intensivstation sein. **inˈtensively** *adv.* intensiv

**intent** [ɪnˈtent] **1.** *n.* Absicht, *die;* **to all ~s and purposes** im Grunde. **2.** *adj.* **be ~ on achieving sth.** etw. unbedingt erreichen wollen

**intention** [ɪnˈtenʃn] *n.* Absicht, *die.* **intentional** [ɪnˈtenʃənl] *adj.,* **inˈtentionally** *adv.* absichtlich

**inˈtently** *adv.* aufmerksam

**interact** [ɪntərˈækt] *v. i.* interagieren. **interaction** [ɪntərˈækʃn] *n.* Interaktion, *die*

**intercede** [ɪntəˈsiːd] *v. i.* sich einsetzen **(with** bei; **for, on behalf of** für**)**

**intercept** [ɪntəˈsept] *v. t.* abfangen

**interchange 1.** [ˈɪntətʃeɪndʒ] *n.* **a)** Austausch, *der;* **b)** *(road junction)* [Autobahn]kreuz, *das.* **2.** [ɪntəˈtʃeɪndʒ] *v. t.* austauschen. **interchangeable** [ɪntəˈtʃeɪndʒəbl] *adj.* austauschbar

**inter-city** [ɪntəˈsɪtɪ] *adj.* Intercity-; **~ train** Intercity[-Zug], *der*

**intercom** [ˈɪntəkɒm] *n. (coll.)* Gegensprechanlage, *die*

**interconnect** [ɪntəkəˈnekt] **1.** *v. t.* miteinander verbinden. **2.** *v. i.* miteinander in Zusammenhang stehen

**intercourse** [ˈɪntəkɔːs] *n. (sexual)* [Geschlechts]verkehr, *der*

**interest** [ˈɪntrəst] **1.** *n.* **a)** Interesse, *das;* **take** *or* **have an ~ in sb./sth.** sich für jmdn./etw. interessieren; **[just] for** *or* **out of ~:** [nur] interessehalber; **with ~:** interessiert; **act in one's own/sb.'s ~[s]** im eigenen/in jmds. Interesse handeln; **be of ~:** interessant sein **(to** für**)**; **b)** *(Finance)* Zinsen *Pl.* **2.** *v. t.* interessieren; **be ~ed** sich interessieren **(in** für**).** **ˈinteresting** *adj.* interessant

**interfere** [ɪntəˈfɪə(r)] *v. i.* sich einmischen **(in** + *Akk.***);** **~ with sth.** sich *(Dat.)* an etw. *(Dat.)* zu schaffen machen. **interference** [ɪntəˈfɪərəns] *n.* **a)** *(interfering)* Einmischung, *die;* **b)** *(Radio, Telev.)* Störung, *die*

**interim** [ˈɪntərɪm] **1.** *n.* **in the ~:** in der Zwischenzeit. **2.** *adj.* vorläufig

**interior** [ɪnˈtɪərɪə(r)] **1.** *adj.* inner...; Innen⟨*fläche, -wand*⟩. **2.** *n.* Innere, *das*

**interject** [ɪntəˈdʒekt] *v. t.* einwerfen. **interjection** [ɪntəˈdʒekʃn] *n.* Ausruf, *der*

**interloper** [ˈɪntələʊpə(r)] *n.* Eindringling, *der*

**interlude** [ˈɪntəluːd] *n.* Pause, *die; (music)* Zwischenspiel, *das*

**intermediate** [ɪntəˈmiːdjət] *adj.* Zwischen-

**interminable** [ɪnˈtɜːmɪnəbl] *adj.* endlos

**intermission** [ɪntə'mɪʃn] *n.* Pause, *die*
**intermittent** [ɪntə'mɪtənt] *adj.* in Abständen auftretend. **inter'mittently**
*adv.* in Abständen
**intern** [ɪn'tɜ:n] *v.t.* gefangenhalten
**internal** [ɪn'tɜ:nl] *adj.* inner...; Innen-
⟨*fläche, -abmessungen*⟩. **internally**
[ɪn'tɜ:nəlɪ] *adv.* innerlich
**international** [ɪntə'næʃənl] **1.** *adj.* international. **2.** *n.* **a)** *(Sport) (contest)*
Länderspiel, *das; (participant)* Nationalspieler, *der/*-spielerin, *die.* **inter-
'nationally** *adv.* international
**in'ternment** *n.* Internierung, *die*
**interplay** ['ɪntəpleɪ] *n.* Zusammenspiel, *das*
**interpret** [ɪn'tɜ:prɪt] **1.** *v.t.* **a)** interpretieren; deuten ⟨*Traum, Zeichen*⟩; **b)**
*(between languages)* dolmetschen. **2.**
*v.i.* dolmetschen. **interpretation**
[ɪntə:prɪ'teɪʃn] *n.* Interpretation, *die;*
*(of dream, symptoms)* Deutung, *die.*
**in'terpreter** *n.* Dolmetscher, *der/*
Dolmetscherin, *die*
**interrogate** [ɪn'terəgeɪt] *v.t.* verhören; ausfragen ⟨*Freund, Kind usw.*⟩.
**interrogation** [ɪnterə'geɪʃn] *n.* Verhör, *das*
**interrogative** [ɪntə'rɒgətɪv] *adj.*
*(Ling.)* Interrogativ-
**interrupt** [ɪntə'rʌpt] **1.** *v.t.* unterbrechen; **don't ~ me when I'm busy** stör
mich nicht, wenn ich zu tun habe. **2.**
*v.i.* unterbrechen; stören. **interruption** [ɪntə'rʌpʃn] *n.* Unterbrechung,
*die;* Störung, *die*
**intersect** [ɪntə'sekt] *v.i.* **a)** ⟨*Straßen:*⟩
sich kreuzen; **b)** *(Geom.)* sich schneiden. **intersection** [ɪntə'sekʃn] *n.* **a)**
*(road junction)* Kreuzung, *die;* **b)**
*(Geom.)* Schnittpunkt, *der*
**intersperse** [ɪntə'spɜ:s] *v.t.* **be ~d
with** durchsetzt sein mit
**interval** ['ɪntəvl] *n.* **a)** [Zeit]abstand,
*der;* **at ~s** in Abständen; **b)** *(break;
also Brit. Theatre etc.)* Pause, *die;*
**sunny ~s** Aufheiterungen *Pl.*
**intervene** [ɪntə'vi:n] *v.i.* **a)** [vermittelnd] eingreifen **(in** in + *Akk.*); **b) the
intervening years** die dazwischenliegenden Jahre. **intervention** [ɪntə-
'venʃn] *n.* Eingreifen, *das*
**interview** ['ɪntəvju:] **1.** *n.* **a)** *(for job)*
Vorstellungsgespräch, *das;* **b)** *(Journ.,
Radio, Telev.)* Interview, *das.* **2.** *v.t.*
ein Vorstellungsgespräch führen mit;
interviewen ⟨*Politiker, Filmstar usw.*⟩.
**'interviewer** *n.* Interviewer, *der/*Interviewerin, *die*

**intestine** [ɪn'testɪn] *n.* Darm, *der*
**intimacy** ['ɪntɪməsɪ] *n.* **a)** Vertrautheit,
*die;* **b)** *(sexual)* Intimität, *die*
**intimate 1.** ['ɪntɪmət] *adj.* **a)** eng
⟨*Freund, Verhältnis*⟩; genau, *(geh.)* intim ⟨*Kenntnis*⟩; **b)** *(sexually)* intim. **2.**
['ɪntɪmeɪt] *v.t. (imply)* andeuten. **in-
timately** ['ɪntɪmətlɪ] *adv.* genau-
[estens] ⟨*kennen*⟩; eng ⟨*verbinden*⟩
**intimidate** [ɪn'tɪmɪdeɪt] *v.t.* einschüchtern. **intimidation** [ɪntɪmɪ-
'deɪʃn] *n.* Einschüchterung, *die*
**into** [*before vowel* 'ɪntʊ, *before consonant* 'ɪntə] *prep.* in (+ *Akk.*); *(against)*
gegen; **I went out ~ the street** ich ging
auf die Straße hinaus; **translate sth. ~
English** etw. ins Englische übersetzen
**in'tolerable** *adj.* unerträglich
**in'tolerance** *n.* Intoleranz, *die*
**in'tolerant** *adj.* intolerant **(of** gegenüber)
**intonation** [ɪntə'neɪʃn] *n.* Intonation,
*die*
**intoxicate** [ɪn'tɒksɪkeɪt] *v.t.* betrunken machen. **intoxication** [ɪntɒksɪ-
'keɪʃn] *n.* Rausch, *der*
**intractable** [ɪn'træktəbl] *adj.* hartnäckig ⟨*Problem*⟩
**intransigent** [ɪn'trænsɪdʒənt] *adj.* unnachgiebig
**in'transitive** *adj. (Ling.)* intransitiv
**'in-tray** *n.* Eingangskorb, *der*
**intrepid** [ɪn'trepɪd] *adj.* unerschrocken
**intricacy** ['ɪntrɪkəsɪ] *n.* Kompliziertheit, *die*
**intricate** ['ɪntrɪkət] *adj.* kompliziert
**intrigue** [ɪn'tri:g] *v.t.* faszinieren. **in-
triguing** [ɪn'tri:gɪŋ] *adj.* faszinierend
**intrinsic** [ɪn'trɪnsɪk] *adj.* innewohnend; inner...; **~ value** innerer Wert
**introduce** [ɪntrə'dju:s] *v.t.* einführen;
**~ oneself/sb. [to sb.]** sich/jmdn.
[jmdm.] vorstellen. **introduction** [ɪn-
trə'dʌkʃn] *n.* Einführen, *das;* Einführung, *die; (to person)* Vorstellung, *die;*
*(to book)* Einleitung, *die.* **introduct-
ory** [ɪntrə'dʌktərɪ] *adj.* einleitend;
Einführungs⟨*kurs, -vortrag*⟩
**introspective** [ɪntrə'spektɪv] *adj.* in
sich *(Akk.)* gerichtet
**introvert** ['ɪntrəvɜ:t] **1.** *n.* Introvertierte, *der/die;* **be an ~:** introvertiert sein.
**2.** *adj.* introvertiert
**intrude** [ɪn'tru:d] *v.i.* stören. **in-
'truder** *n.* Eindringling, *der.* **intru-
sion** [ɪn'tru:ʒn] *n.* Störung, *die.* **in-
trusive** [ɪn'tru:sɪv] *adj.* aufdringlich
**intuition** [ɪntju:'ɪʃn] *n.* Intuition, *die*

**intuitive** [ɪn'tjuːɪtɪv] *adj.*, **in'tuitively** *adv.* intuitiv

**inundate** ['ɪnʌndeɪt] *v. t.* überschwemmen

**inure** [ɪ'njʊə(r)] *v. t.* gewöhnen (**to an** + *Akk.*)

**invade** [ɪn'veɪd] *v. t.* einfallen in (+ *Akk.*). **in'vader** *n.* Angreifer, *der*

**¹invalid** ['ɪnvəlɪd] *(Brit.)* **1.** *n.* Kranke, *der/die; (disabled)* Körperbehinderte, *der/die.* **2.** *adj.* körperbehindert

**²invalid** [ɪn'vælɪd] *adj.* nicht schlüssig ⟨*Argument, Theorie*⟩; ungültig ⟨*Fahrkarte, Garantie, Vertrag*⟩. **invalidate** [ɪn'vælɪdeɪt] *v. t.* aufheben; widerlegen ⟨*Theorie, These*⟩

**in'valuable** *adj.* unersetzlich ⟨*Person*⟩; unschätzbar ⟨*Dienst, Hilfe*⟩; außerordentlich wichtig ⟨*Rolle*⟩

**in'variable** *adj.* unveränderlich. **invariably** [ɪn'veərɪəblɪ] *adv.* immer; ausnahmslos ⟨*falsch, richtig*⟩

**invasion** [ɪn'veɪʒn] *n.* Invasion, *die*

**invective** [ɪn'vektɪv] *n.* Beschimpfungen *Pl.*

**invent** [ɪn'vent] *v. t.* erfinden. **invention** [ɪn'venʃn] *n.* Erfindung, *die.* **inventive** [ɪn'ventɪv] *adj.* **a)** schöpferisch ⟨*Person, Begabung*⟩; **b)** *(original)* originell. **inventor** [ɪn'ventə(r)] *n.* Erfinder, *der/*Erfinderin, *die*

**inventory** ['ɪnvəntərɪ] *n.* Bestandsliste, *die;* **make** *or* **take an ~ of sth.** von etw. ein Inventar aufstellen

**inverse** ['ɪnvɜːs] *adj.* umgekehrt

**invert** [ɪn'vɜːt] *v. t.* umstülpen

**in'vertebrate** *n.* wirbelloses Tier

**inverted 'commas** *n. pl. (Brit.)* Anführungszeichen *Pl.*

**invest** [ɪn'vest] *v. t.* **a)** *(Finance)* anlegen (**in** in + *Dat.*); investieren (**in** in + *Dat. od. Akk.*); **b)** *(fig.)* investieren; **~ sb. with sth.** jmdm. etw. übertragen; **~ sth. with sth.** einer Sache *(Dat.)* etw. verleihen

**investigate** [ɪn'vestɪgeɪt] *v. t.* untersuchen. **investigation** [ɪnvestɪ'geɪʃn] *n.* Untersuchung, *die.* **investigator** [ɪn'vestɪgeɪtə(r)] *n.* [**private**] **~:** [Privat]detektiv, *der/*-detektivin, *die*

**in'vestment** *n.* Investition, *die; (money invested)* angelegtes Geld; **be a good ~** *(fig.)* sich bezahlt machen. **investor** [ɪn'vestə(r)] *n.* [Kapital]anleger, *der/*-anlegerin, *die*

**inveterate** [ɪn'vetərət] *adj.* eingefleischt ⟨*Trinker, Raucher*⟩; unverbesserlich ⟨*Lügner*⟩

**invigorate** [ɪn'vɪgəreɪt] *v. t.* stärken; *(physically)* kräftigen. **invigorating** [ɪn'vɪgəreɪtɪŋ] *adj.* kräftigend ⟨*Getränk, Klima*⟩

**invincible** [ɪn'vɪnsɪbl] *adj.* unbesiegbar

**in'visible** *adj.* unsichtbar

**invitation** [ɪnvɪ'teɪʃn] *n.* Einladung, *die;* **at sb.'s ~:** auf jmds. Einladung *(Akk.)*

**invite** [ɪn'vaɪt] *v. t.* **a)** *(request to come)* einladen; **b)** *(request to do sth.)* auffordern; **c)** *(bring on)* herausfordern ⟨*Kritik, Verhängnis*⟩. **inviting** [ɪn'vaɪtɪŋ] *adj.* einladend; verlockend ⟨*Gedanke, Vorstellung*⟩

**invoice** ['ɪnvɔɪs] **1.** *n. (bill)* Rechnung, *die.* **2.** *v. t.* **~ sb.** jmdm. eine Rechnung schicken; **~ sb. for sth.** jmdm. etw. in Rechnung stellen

**invoke** [ɪn'vəʊk] *v. t.* anrufen

**in'voluntarily** *adv.*, **in'voluntary** *adj.* unwillkürlich

**involve** [ɪn'vɒlv] *v. t.* **a)** *(implicate)* verwickeln; **b)** **become** *or* **get ~d in a fight** in eine Schlägerei verwickelt werden; **get ~d with sb.** sich mit jmdm. einlassen; **c)** *(entail)* mit sich bringen. **involved** [ɪn'vɒlvd] *adj.* verwickelt; *(complicated)* kompliziert

**invulnerable** [ɪn'vʌlnərəbl] *adj.* unverwundbar; *(fig.)* unantastbar

**inward** ['ɪnwəd] **1.** *adj.* inner... **2.** *adv.* einwärts ⟨*gerichtet, gebogen*⟩; **open ~:** nach innen öffnen. **'inwardly** *adv.* im Inneren; innerlich. **inwards** ['ɪnwədz] *see* **inward** 2

**iodine** ['aɪədiːn] *n.* Jod, *das*

**ion** ['aɪən] *n.* Ion, *das*

**iota** [aɪ'əʊtə] *n.* **not one** *or* **an ~:** nicht ein Jota *(geh.)*

**IOU** [aɪəʊ'juː] *n.* Schuldschein, *der*

**Iran** [ɪ'rɑːn] *pr. n.* Iran, *der od. (das)*

**Iraq** [ɪ'rɑːk] *pr. n.* Irak, *der od. (das)*

**irate** [aɪ'reɪt] *adj.* wütend

**Ireland** ['aɪələnd] *pr. n.* Irland *(das)*

**iris** ['aɪərɪs] *n. (Bot., Anat.)* Iris, *die*

**Irish** ['aɪərɪʃ] **1.** *adj.* irisch; **sb. is ~:** jmd. ist Ire/Irin. **2.** *n.* **a)** *(language)* Irisch, *das; see also* **English** 2 a; **b)** *constr. as pl.* **the ~:** die Iren

**Irish: ~man** ['aɪərɪʃmən] *n., pl.* **~men** ['aɪərɪʃmən] Ire, *der;* **~ Re'public** *pr. n.* Irische Republik; **~ 'Sea** *pr. n.* Irische See; **~woman** *n.* Irin, *die*

**irk** [ɜːk] *v. t.* ärgern. **irksome** ['ɜːksəm] *adj.* lästig

**iron** ['aɪən] **1.** *n.* **a)** *(metal)* Eisen, *das;* **b)** *(for smoothing)* Bügeleisen, *das.* **2.** *attrib. adj.* eisern; Eisen⟨*platte usw.*⟩.

**3.** *v. t. & i.* bügeln. **iron 'out** *v. t.* herausbügeln; *(fig.)* aus dem Weg räumen

**Iron 'Curtain** *n.* *(Hist.)* Eiserner Vorhang

**ironic** [aɪ'rɒnɪk], **ironical** [aɪ'rɒnɪkl] *adj.* ironisch

**ironing** ['aɪənɪŋ] *n.* Bügeln, *das; (items)* Bügelwäsche, *die;* **do the ~:** bügeln. **'ironing-board** *n.* Bügelbrett, *das*

**ironmonger** ['aɪənmʌŋgə(r)] *n.* *(Brit.)* Eisenwarenhändler, *der/-*händlerin, *die*

**irony** ['aɪrəni] *n.* Ironie, *die;* **the ~ was that ...:** die Ironie lag darin, daß ...

**irradiate** [ɪ'reɪdɪeɪt] *v. t.* bestrahlen

**irrational** [ɪ'ræʃənl] *adj.* irrational

**irreconcilable** [ɪ'rekənsaɪləbl] *adj. (incompatible)* unvereinbar

**irrefutable** [ɪrɪ'fju:təbl] *adj.* unwiderlegbar

**irregular** [ɪ'regjʊlə(r)] *adj.* unregelmäßig; unkorrekt ‹*Verhalten, Handlung usw.*›. **irregularity** [ɪregjʊ'lærɪti] *n. see* **irregular:** Unregelmäßigkeit, *die;* Unkorrektheit, *die*

**irrelevant** [ɪ'relɪvənt] *adj.* belanglos; irrelevant *(geh.)*

**irreparable** [ɪ'repərəbl] *adj.* nicht wiedergutzumachend *nicht präd.;* irreparabel *(geh., Med.)*

**irreplaceable** [ɪrɪ'pleɪsəbl] *adj.* unersetzlich

**irrepressible** [ɪrɪ'presɪbl] *adj.* nicht zu unterdrücken *nicht präd.;* **she is ~:** sie ist nicht unterzukriegen *(ugs.)*

**irreproachable** [ɪrɪ'prəʊtʃəbl] *adj.* untadelig

**irresistible** [ɪrɪ'zɪstɪbl] *adj.* unwiderstehlich; bestechend ‹*Argument*›

**irresolute** [ɪ'rezəlu:t] *adj.* unentschlossen

**irrespective** [ɪrɪ'spektɪv] *adj.* **~ of** ungeachtet (+ *Gen.*)

**irresponsible** [ɪrɪ'spɒnsɪbl] *adj.* verantwortungslos ‹*Person*›; unverantwortlich ‹*Benehmen*›

**irretrievable** [ɪrɪ'tri:vəbl] *adj.* nicht mehr wiederzubekommen *nicht attr.*

**irreverent** [ɪ'revərənt] *adj.* respektlos

**irreversible** [ɪrɪ'vɜ:sɪbl], **irrevocable** [ɪ'revəkəbl] *adjs.* unwiderruflich

**irrigate** ['ɪrɪgeɪt] *v. t.* bewässern. **irrigation** [ɪrɪ'geɪʃn] *n.* Bewässerung, *die*

**irritable** ['ɪrɪtəbl] *adj. (quick to anger)* reizbar; *(temporarily)* gereizt

**irritant** ['ɪrɪtənt] *n.* Reizstoff, *der*

**irritate** ['ɪrɪteɪt] *v. t.* **a)** ärgern; **get ~d**

ärgerlich werden; **be ~d by sth.** sich über etw. *(Akk.)* ärgern; **b)** *(Med.)* reizen. **irritating** ['ɪrɪteɪtɪŋ] *adj.* lästig.

**irritation** [ɪrɪ'teɪʃn] *n.* **a)** Ärger, *der;* **b)** *(Med.)* Reizung, *die*

**is** *see* **be**

**Islam** ['ɪzlɑ:m] *n.* Islam, *der*

**island** ['aɪlənd] *n.* Insel, *die.* **'islander** *n.* Inselbewohner, *der/-*bewohnerin, *die*

**isle** [aɪl] *n.* Insel, *die*

**isn't** ['ɪznt] *(coll.)* = **is not;** *see* **be**

**isolate** ['aɪsəleɪt] *v. t.* isolieren. **isolated** ['aɪsəleɪtɪd] *adj.* **a)** *(single)* einzeln; ~ **cases/instances** Einzelfälle; **b)** *(remote)* abgelegen. **isolation** [aɪsə'leɪʃn] *n.* **a)** *(act)* Isolierung, *die;* **b)** *(state)* Isolation, *die*

**Israel** ['ɪzreɪl] *pr. n.* Israel *(das).* **Israeli** [ɪz'reɪli] **1.** *adj.* israelisch. **2.** *n.* Israeli, *der/die*

**issue** ['ɪʃu:, 'ɪsju:] **1.** *n.* **a)** *(point in question)* Frage, *die;* **make an ~ of sth.** etw. aufbauschen; **evade** *or* **dodge the** ~: ausweichen; **b)** *(of magazine etc.)* Ausgabe, *die;* **c)** *(result, outcome)* Ergebnis, *das.* **2.** *v. t.* **a)** *(give out)* ausgeben; ausstellen ‹*Paß*›; erteilen ‹*Lizenz, Befehl*›; ~ **sb. with sth.** etw. an jmdn. austeilen; **b)** *(publish)* herausgeben ‹*Publikation*›

**it** [ɪt] *pron.* **a)** es; **I can't cope with it any more** ich halte das nicht mehr länger aus; **what is it?** was ist los?; **b)** *(the thing, animal, young child previously mentioned)* er/sie/es; *as direct obj.* ihn/sie/es; *as indirect obj.* ihm/ihr/ihm; **c)** *(the person in question)* **who is it?** wer ist da?; **it was the children** es waren die Kinder; **is it you, Dad?** bist du es, Vater?

**Italian** [ɪ'tæljən] **1.** *adj.* italienisch; **sb. is ~:** jmd. ist Italiener/Italienerin. **2.** *n.* **a)** *(person)* Italiener, *der/*Italienerin, *die;* **b)** *(language)* Italienisch, *das; see also* **English 2 a**

**italic** [ɪ'tælɪk] **1.** *adj.* kursiv. **2.** *n. in pl.* Kursivschrift, *die;* **in ~s** kursiv

**Italy** ['ɪtəli] *pr. n.* Italien *(das)*

**itch** [ɪtʃ] **1.** *n.* Juckreiz, *der;* **I have an** ~: es juckt mich. **2.** *v. i.* **a)** einen Juckreiz haben; **it ~es** es juckt; **b)** ~ *or* **be** ~**ing to do sth.** darauf brennen, etw. zu tun. **'itchy** *adj.* kratzig; **be** ~: ‹*Körperteil:*› jucken

**it'd** ['ɪtəd] *(coll.)* **a)** = **it had;** **b)** = **it would**

**item** ['aɪtəm] *n.* **a)** Ding, *das;* Sache, *die; (in shop, catalogue)* Artikel, *der;*

*(on radio, TV)* Nummer, *die;* ~ **of clothing** Kleidungsstück, *das;* **b)** ~ |**of news**| Nachricht, *die.* **itemize** ['aɪtə-maɪz] *v.t.* einzeln aufführen

**itinerary** [aɪ'tɪnərərɪ] *n.* Reiseroute, *die*

**it'll** [ɪtl] *(coll.)* = it will

**its** [ɪts] *poss. pron. attrib.* sein/ihr/sein

**it's** [ɪts] **a)** = it is; **b)** = it has

**itself** [ɪt'self] *pron.* **a)** *emphat.* selbst; **b)** *refl.* sich

**I've** [aɪv] = I have

**ivory** ['aɪvərɪ] *n.* Elfenbein, *das; attrib.* elfenbeinern; Elfenbein-

**ivy** ['aɪvɪ] *n.* Efeu, *der*

# J

**J, j** [dʒeɪ] *n.* J, j, *das*

**jab** [dʒæb] **1.** *v.t.,* -bb- stoßen. **2.** *n.* **a)** Stoß, *der; (with needle)* Stich, *der;* **b)** *(Brit. coll.: injection)* Spritze, *die*

**jabber** ['dʒæbə(r)] *v.i.* plappern *(ugs.)*

**jack** [dʒæk] *n.* **a)** *(for car)* Wagenheber, *der;* **b)** *(Cards)* Bube, *der*

**jackal** ['dʒækl] *n.* Schakal, *der*

**jackdaw** ['dʒækdɔː] *n.* Dohle, *die*

**jacket** ['dʒækɪt] *n.* **a)** Jacke, *die; (of suit)* Jackett, *das;* **sports** ~: Sakko, *der;* **b)** *(of book)* Schutzumschlag, *der;* **c)** ~ **potatoes** in der Schale gebackene Kartoffeln

**'jackpot** *n.* Jackpot, *der;* **hit the** ~ *(fig.)* das große Los ziehen

**jaded** ['dʒeɪdɪd] *adj.* abgespannt

**jagged** ['dʒægɪd] *adj.* gezackt

**jaguar** ['dʒægjʊə(r)] *n.* Jaguar, *der*

**jail** [dʒeɪl] **1.** *n.* Gefängnis, *das.* **2.** *v.t.* ins Gefängnis bringen. **'jailbreak** *n.* Gefängnisausbruch, *der.* **jailer, jailor** ['dʒeɪlə(r)] *n.* Gefängniswärter, *der/*-wärterin, *die*

**'jam** [dʒæm] **1.** *v.t.,* -mm-: **a)** *(between two surfaces)* einklemmen; **b)** *(make immovable)* blockieren; *(fig.)* lähmen. **2.** *v.i.,* -mm-: **a)** *(become wedged)* sich verklemmen; **b)** ⟨*Maschine:*⟩ klemmen. **3.** *n.* **a)** *(crush, stoppage)* Blockierung, *die;* **b)** *(coll.: dilemma)* **be in a** ~: in der Klemme stecken

*(ugs.).* **jam 'on** *v.t.* ~ **the brakes |full| on** |voll| auf die Bremse steigen *(ugs.)*

**²jam** *n.* Marmelade, *die*

**Jamaica** [dʒə'meɪkə] *pr. n.* Jamaika *(das)*

**Jan.** *abbr.* **January** Jan.

**jangle** ['dʒæŋgl] **1.** *v.i.* klimpern; ⟨*Klingel:*⟩ bimmeln. **2.** *v.t.* rasseln mit

**janitor** ['dʒænɪtə(r)] *n.* Hausmeister, *der*

**January** ['dʒænjʊərɪ] *n.* Januar, *der; see also* **August**

**Japan** [dʒə'pæn] *n.* Japan *(das).* **Japanese** [dʒæpə'niːz] **1.** *adj.* japanisch. **2.** *n., pl. same* **a)** *(person)* Japaner, *der/*Japanerin, *die;* **b)** *(language)* Japanisch, *das; see also* **English 2 a**

**¹jar** [dʒɑː(r)] **1.** *v.i.,* -rr- quietschen; *(fig.)* ~ **on sb./sb.'s nerves** jmdm. auf die Nerven gehen. **2.** *v.t.,* -rr- erschüttern

**²jar** *n.* Topf, *der; (glass* ~*)* Glas, *das*

**jargon** ['dʒɑːgən] *n.* Jargon, *der*

**jasmin[e]** ['dʒæsmɪn] *n.* Jasmin, *der*

**jaundice** ['dʒɔːndɪs] *n. (Med.)* Gelbsucht, *die.* **jaundiced** ['dʒɔːndɪst] *adj. (fig.)* verbittert

**jaunt** [dʒɔːnt] *n.* Ausflug, *der*

**javelin** ['dʒævlɪn] *n.* **a)** Speer, *der;* **b)** *(Sport: event)* Speerwerfen, *das*

**jaw** [dʒɔː] *n.* Kiefer, *der.* **'jawbone** *n.* Kieferknochen, *der*

**jay** [dʒeɪ] *n.* Eichelhäher, *der*

**jazz** [dʒæz] **1.** *n.* Jazz, *der; attrib.* Jazz-. **2.** *v.t.* ~ **up** aufpeppen *(ugs.)*

**jealous** ['dʒeləs] *adj.* eifersüchtig **(of** auf + *Akk.*). **'jealousy** *n.* Eifersucht, *die*

**jeans** [dʒiːnz] *n. pl.* Jeans *Pl.*

**jeer** [dʒɪə(r)] *v.i.* höhnen *(geh.);* ~ **at sb.** jmdn. verhöhnen

**jelly** ['dʒelɪ] *n.* Gelee, *das; (dessert)* Götterspeise, *die.* **'jellyfish** *n.* Qualle, *die*

**jeopardize** ['dʒepədaɪz] *v.t.* gefährden

**jeopardy** ['dʒepədɪ] *n.* **in** ~: in Gefahr; gefährdet

**jerk** [dʒɜːk] **1.** *n.* Ruck, *der.* **2.** *v.t.* reißen an (+ *Dat.*). **3.** *v.i.* zucken

**jersey** ['dʒɜːzɪ] *n.* Pullover, *der; (Sport)* Trikot, *das*

**jest** [dʒest] **1.** *n.* Scherz, *der;* **in** ~: im Scherz. **2.** *v.i.* scherzen

**Jesus** ['dʒiːzəs] *pr. n.* Jesus *(der)*

**jet** [dʒet] *n.* **a)** *(stream)* Strahl, *der;* **b)** *(nozzle)* Düse, *die;* **c)** *(aircraft)* Düsenflugzeug, *das;* Jet, *der*

**jet:** ~-**black** *adj.* pechschwarz; ~ **en-**

**gine** n. Düsentriebwerk, das; ~ **lag** n. Jet-travel-Syndrom, das; ~-**propelled** adj. düsengetrieben

**jetsam** ['dʒetsəm] n. see **flotsam**

**'jet-set** n. Jet-set, der

**jettison** ['dʒetɪsən] v. t. über Bord werfen; (discard) wegwerfen

**jetty** ['dʒetɪ] n. Landungsbrücke, die

**Jew** [dʒuː] n. Jude, der/Jüdin, die

**jewel** ['dʒuːəl] n. Juwel, das od. der. **jeweller** (Amer.: **jeweler**) ['dʒuːələ(r)] n. Juwelier, der. **jewellery** (Brit.), **jewelry** ['dʒuːəlrɪ] n. Schmuck, der

**Jewish** ['dʒuːɪʃ] adj. jüdisch

**jib** [dʒɪb] v. i., -bb- sich sträuben (at gegen)

**jibe** see **gibe**

**jiffy** ['dʒɪfɪ] n. (coll.) **in a** ~: sofort

**jig** [dʒɪg] n. Jig, die

**'jigsaw** n. ~ |puzzle| Puzzle, das

**jilt** [dʒɪlt] v. t. sitzenlassen (ugs.)

**jingle** ['dʒɪŋgl] 1. n. (Commerc.) Werbespruch, der. 2. v. i. klimpern; ⟨Glöckchen:⟩ bimmeln. 3. v. t. klimpern mit ⟨Münzen, Schlüsseln⟩

**jinx** [dʒɪŋks] (coll.) 1. n. Fluch, der. 2. v. t. verhexen

**jitters** ['dʒɪtəz] n. pl. (coll.) großes Zittern. **jittery** ['dʒɪtərɪ] adj. (coll.) (nervous) nervös; (frightened) verängstigt

**job** [dʒɒb] n. a) (piece of work) Arbeit, die; I **have a** ~ **for you** ich habe eine Aufgabe für dich; b) (employment) Stelle, die; Job, der (ugs.). '**jobcentre** n. (Brit.) Arbeitsvermittlungsstelle, die. '**jobless** adj. arbeitslos

**jockey** ['dʒɒkɪ] n. Jockei, der

**jocular** ['dʒɒkjʊlə(r)] adj. lustig

**jodhpurs** ['dʒɒdpəz] n. pl. Reithose, die

**jog** [dʒɒg] 1. v. t., -gg-: a) (shake) rütteln; b) (nudge) [an]stoßen; c) ~ **sb.'s memory** jmds. Gedächtnis (Dat.) auf die Sprünge helfen. 2. v. i., -gg-: a) (up and down) auf und ab hüpfen; b) (trot) ⟨Pferd:⟩ [dahin]trotten; c) (Sport) joggen. 3. n. **go for a** ~: joggen gehen. '**jogging** n. Jogging, das

**join** [dʒɔɪn] 1. v. t. a) (connect) verbinden (**to** mit); b) (come into company of) sich gesellen zu; c) eintreten in (+ Akk.) ⟨Armee, Firma, Verein, Partei⟩. 2. v. i. ⟨Straßen:⟩ zusammenlaufen. **join in** 1. [-'-] v. i. mitmachen (**with** bei). 2. ['--] v. t. mitmachen bei. **join 'up** 1. v. i. (Mil.) einrücken. 2. v. t. miteinander verbinden

'**joiner** n. Tischler, der/Tischlerin, die

**joint** [dʒɔɪnt] 1. n. a) (Building) Fuge, die; b) (Anat.) Gelenk, das; c) **a** ~ |of meat| ein Stück Fleisch; (for roasting) ein Braten; d) (sl.: place) Laden, der. 2. adj. a) (of two or more) gemeinsam; b) Mit⟨autor, -erbe, -besitzer⟩. '**jointly** adv. gemeinsam

**joist** [dʒɔɪst] n. (Building) Deckenbalken, der; (steel) [Decken]träger, der

**joke** [dʒəʊk] 1. n. Witz, der; Scherz, der. 2. v. i. scherzen, Witze machen (**about** über + Akk.); **joking apart** Scherz beiseite! '**joker** n. a) Spaßvogel, der; b) (Cards) Joker, der

**jollity** ['dʒɒlɪtɪ] n. Fröhlichkeit, die; (merry-making) Festlichkeit, die

**jolly** ['dʒɒlɪ] 1. adj. fröhlich. 2. adv. (Brit. coll.) ganz schön (ugs.); ~ **good!** ausgezeichnet!

**jolt** [dʒəʊlt] 1. v. t. ⟨Fahrzeug:⟩ durchrütteln. 2. v. i. ⟨Fahrzeug:⟩ holpern. 3. n. a) (jerk) Stoß, der; Ruck, der; b) (fig.: shock) Schock, der

**Jordan** ['dʒɔːdn] pr. n. Jordanien (das)

**jostle** ['dʒɒsl] 1. v. i. ~ |against each other| aneinanderstoßen. 2. v. t. stoßen

**jot** [dʒɒt] n. |not| **a** ~: [k]ein bißchen. **jot 'down** v. t. [rasch] aufschreiben

**jotter** ['dʒɒtə(r)] n. Notizblock, der

**journal** ['dʒɜːnl] n. Zeitschrift, die

**journalism** ['dʒɜːnəlɪzm] n. Journalismus, der. **journalist** ['dʒɜːnəlɪst] n. Journalist, der/Journalistin, die

**journey** ['dʒɜːnɪ] n. a) Reise, die; b) (of vehicle) Fahrt, die

**jovial** ['dʒəʊvɪəl] adj. herzlich ⟨Gruß⟩; fröhlich ⟨Person⟩

**joy** [dʒɔɪ] n. Freude, die. **joyful** ['dʒɔɪfl] adj. froh[gestimmt] ⟨Person⟩; freudig ⟨Blick, Ereignis, Gesang⟩. **joyride** n. (coll.) Spritztour, die

**JP** abbr. Justice of the Peace

**jubilant** ['dʒuːbɪlənt] adj. jubelnd; **be** ~ ⟨Person:⟩ frohlocken. **jubilation** [dʒuːbɪ'leɪʃn] n. Jubel, der

**jubilee** ['dʒuːbɪliː] n. Jubiläum, das

**judge** [dʒʌdʒ] 1. n. a) Richter, der/Richterin, die; b) (in contest) Preisrichter, der/-richterin, die; c) (fig.: critic) Kenner, der/Kennerin, die. 2. v. t. a) (sentence) richten (geh.); b) (form opinion about) [be]urteilen. '**judg[e]ment** n. a) Urteil, das; b) (critical faculty) Urteilsvermögen, das

**judicial** [dʒuː'dɪʃl] adj. gerichtlich

**judicious** [dʒuː'dɪʃəs] adj. klarblickend

**judo** ['dʒuːdəʊ] n. Judo, das

**jug** [dʒʌg] *n.* Krug, *der; (with lid, water-~)* Kanne, *die*

**juggernaut** ['dʒʌgənɔ:t] *n. (Brit.: lorry)* schwerer Brummer *(ugs.)*

**juggle** ['dʒʌgl] *v. i.* jonglieren. **juggler** ['dʒʌglə(r)] *n.* Jongleur, *der*/Jongleuse, *die*

**juice** [dʒu:s] *n.* Saft, *der.* **juicy** ['dʒu:-sɪ] *adj.* saftig

**juke-box** ['dʒu:kbɒks] *n.* Jukebox, *die;* Musikbox, *die*

**Jul.** *abbr.* July Jul.

**July** [dʒʊ'laɪ] *n.* Juli, *der; see also* **August**

**jumble** ['dʒʌmbl] **1.** *v. t.* ~ **up** durcheinanderbringen. **2.** *n.* Durcheinander, *das.* '**jumble sale** *n. (Brit.)* Trödelmarkt, *der*

**jumbo jet** [dʒʌmbəʊ 'dʒet] *n.* Jumbo-Jet, *der*

**jump** [dʒʌmp] **1.** *n.* **a)** Sprung, *der;* **b)** *(in prices)* sprunghafter Anstieg. **2.** *v. i.* **a)** springen; ~ **for joy** einen Freudensprung machen; **b)** ~ **to conclusions** voreilige Schlüsse ziehen. **3.** *v. t.* **a)** überspringen; **b)** ~ **the queue** *(Brit.)* sich vordrängeln. **jump a'bout, jump a'round** *v. i.* herumspringen *(ugs.).* '**jump at** *v. t. (fig.)* sofort zugreifen bei ⟨*Angebot, Gelegenheit*⟩

'**jumper** *n.* Pullover, *der*

**jumpy** ['dʒʌmpɪ] *adj.* nervös

**Jun.** *abbr.* June Jun.

**junction** ['dʒʌŋkʃn] *n.* **a)** *(of railway lines, roads)* ≈ Einmündung, *die;* **b)** *(crossroads)* Kreuzung, *die*

**juncture** ['dʒʌŋktʃə(r)] *n.* **at this ~:** zu diesem Zeitpunkt

**June** [dʒu:n] *n.* Juni, *der; see also* **August**

**jungle** ['dʒʌŋgl] *n.* Dschungel, *der*

**junior** ['dʒu:nɪə(r)] *adj.* **a)** *(in age)* jünger; ~ **team** *(Sport)* Juniorenmannschaft, *die;* **b)** *(in rank)* rangniedriger ⟨*Person*⟩; niedriger ⟨*Rang*⟩. '**junior school** *n. (Brit.)* Grundschule, *die*

**junk** [dʒʌŋk] *n.* Trödel, *der (ugs.); (trash)* Ramsch, *der (ugs.).* '**junk food** *n.* minderwertige Kost. '**junk shop** *n.* Trödelladen, *der (ugs.)*

**Jupiter** ['dʒu:pɪtə(r)] *pr. n. (Astron.)* Jupiter, *der*

**jurisdiction** [dʒʊərɪs'dɪkʃn] *n.* Gerichtsbarkeit, *die*

**juror** ['dʒʊərə(r)] *n.* Geschworene, *der/die*

**jury** ['dʒʊərɪ] *n.* **a)** *(in court)* **the ~:** die Geschworenen; **b)** *(in competition)* Jury, *die*

**just** [dʒʌst] **1.** *adj. (morally right)* gerecht. **2.** *adv.* **a)** *(exactly)* genau; ~ **then/enough** gerade da/genug; ~ **as** *(exactly as)* genauso wie; *(when)* gerade, als; ~ **as you like** *or* **please** ganz wie Sie wünschen/du magst; ~ **as good** *etc.* genauso gut *usw.;* **b)** *(barely)* gerade [eben]; *(with little time to spare)* gerade noch; *(no more than)* nur; ~ **under £10** nicht ganz zehn Pfund; **c)** *(at this moment)* gerade; **not ~ now** im Moment nicht; **d)** *(coll.) (simply)* einfach; *(only)* nur; *esp. with imper.* mal [eben]; ~ **look at that!** guck dir das mal an!; ~ **a moment** einen Moment mal; ~ **in case** für alle Fälle

**justice** ['dʒʌstɪs] *n.* **a)** Gerechtigkeit, *die;* **b)** *(magistrate)* Schiedsrichter, *der/*-richterin, *die;* **J~ of the Peace** Friedensrichter, *der/*-richterin, *die*

**justifiable** [dʒʌstɪ'faɪəbl] *adj.* berechtigt. **justifiably** [dʒʌstɪ'faɪəblɪ] *adv.* zu Recht

**justification** [dʒʌstɪfɪ'keɪʃn] *n.* Rechtfertigung, *die*

**justify** ['dʒʌstɪfaɪ] *v. t.* rechtfertigen; **be justified in doing sth.** etw. zu Recht tun

**jut** [dʒʌt] *v. i.,* **-tt-:** ~ |**out**| [her]vorragen; herausragen

**juvenile** ['dʒu:vənaɪl] **1.** *adj.* **a)** jugendlich; **b)** *(immature)* kindisch. **2.** *n.* Jugendliche, *der/die.* **juvenile delinquency** [~ dɪ'lɪŋkwənsɪ] *n.* Jugendkriminalität, *die.* **juvenile delinquent** [~ dɪ'lɪŋkwənt] *n.* jugendlicher Straftäter/jugendliche Straftäterin

**juxtapose** [dʒʌkstə'pəʊz] *v. t.* nebeneinanderstellen (**with, to** und). **juxtaposition** [dʒʌkstəpə'zɪʃn] *n.* Nebeneinanderstellung, *die*

# K

**K, k** [keɪ] *n.* K, k, *das*

**kaleidoscope** [kə'laɪdəskəʊp] *n.* Kaleidoskop, *das*

**kangaroo** [kæŋgə'ru:] *n.* Känguruh, *das*

**karate** [kə'rɑːtɪ] n. Karate, das
**keel** [kiːl] n. (Naut.) Kiel, der
**keen** [kiːn] adj. a) (sharp) scharf; b) (cold) schneidend ⟨Wind, Kälte⟩; c) (eager) begeistert ⟨Fußballfan, Sportler⟩; lebhaft ⟨Interesse⟩; **be ~ to do sth.** darauf erpicht sein, etw. zu tun; d) (sensitive) scharf ⟨Augen⟩; fein ⟨Sinne⟩. **'keenly** adv. a) (sharply) scharf; b) (eagerly) eifrig; brennend ⟨interessiert sein⟩; c) (acutely) **be ~ aware of sth.** sich (Dat.) einer Sache (Gen.) voll bewußt sein
**keep** [kiːp] 1. v. t., kept [kept] a) halten ⟨Versprechen, Schwur, Sabbat, Fasten⟩; einhalten ⟨Verabredung, Vereinbarung⟩; begehen, feiern ⟨Fest⟩; b) (have charge of) aufbewahren; c) (retain) behalten; (not lose or destroy) aufheben ⟨Quittung, Rechnung⟩; d) halten ⟨Bienen, Hund usw.⟩; e) führen ⟨Tagebuch, Geschäft, Ware⟩; f) (support) versorgen ⟨Familie⟩; g) (detain) festhalten; **~ sb. waiting** jmdn. warten lassen; **what kept you?** wo bleibst du denn?; h) (reserve) aufheben. 2. v. i., kept a) (remain) bleiben; **are you ~ing well?** geht's dir gut?; b) **~ [to the] left/right** sich links/rechts halten; **~ doing sth.** (repeatedly) etw. immer wieder tun; **~ talking/working** etc. **until ...:** weiterreden/-arbeiten usw., bis ...; (remain good) ⟨Lebensmittel:⟩ sich halten. 3. n. a) (maintenance) Unterhalt, der; b) **for ~s** (coll.) auf Dauer; c) (Hist.: tower) Bergfried, der. **keep 'back** 1. v. i. zurückbleiben. 2. v. t. a) (restrain) zurückhalten ⟨Menschenmenge, Tränen⟩; b) (withhold) verschweigen ⟨Informationen, Tatsachen⟩ (from Dat.). **keep 'down** 1. v. i. unten bleiben. 2. v. t. a) niedrig halten ⟨Steuern, Preise usw.⟩; **keep one's weight down** nicht zunehmen; b) **keep your voice down!** rede nicht so laut! **keep 'off** 1. v. i. ⟨Person:⟩ wegbleiben. 2. v. t. fernhalten; **'keep off the grass'** „Betreten des Rasens verboten". **keep 'out** 1. v. i. **'keep out'** „Zutritt verboten". 2. v. t. nicht hereinlassen. **keep 'up** 1. v. i. **keep up with sb./ sth.** mit jmdm./etw. Schritt halten. 2. v. t. aufrechterhalten ⟨Freundschaft, jmds. Moral⟩; **keep one's strength up** sich bei Kräften halten; **keep it up!** weiter so!
**keep-'fit** n. Fitneßtraining, das
**'keeping** n. **be in ~ with sth.** einer Sache (Dat.) entsprechen

**'keepsake** n. Andenken, das
**keg** [keg] n. [kleines] Faß
**kennel** ['kenl] n. Hundehütte, die
**Kenya** ['kenjə] pr. n. Kenia (das)
**kept** see keep 1, 2
**kerb** [kɜːb], **'kerbstone** ns. (Brit.) Bordstein, der
**kernel** ['kɜːnl] n. Kern, der
**ketchup** ['ketʃʌp] n. Ketchup, der od. das
**kettle** ['ketl] n. [Wasser]kessel, der
**key** [kiː] n. a) Schlüssel, der; b) (on piano, typewriter, etc.) Taste, die; c) (Mus.) Tonart, die
**key:** **~board** n. (of piano etc.) Klaviatur, die; (of typewriter etc.) Tastatur, die; **~hole** n. Schlüsselloch, das; **~ring** n. Schlüsselring, der
**kg.** abbr. kilogram[s] kg
**khaki** ['kɑːkɪ] 1. adj. khakifarben. 2. n. (cloth) Khaki, der
**kick** [kɪk] 1. n. a) [Fuß]tritt, der; (Footb.) Schuß, der; **give sb. a ~:** jmdm. einen Tritt geben; b) (coll.: thrill) **do sth. for ~s** etw. zum Spaß tun; **he gets a ~ out of it** er hat Spaß daran. 2. v. i. treten; ⟨Pferd:⟩ ausschlagen. 3. v. t. einen Tritt geben (+ Dat.) ⟨Person, Hund⟩; treten gegen ⟨Gegenstand⟩; kicken (ugs.), schießen ⟨Ball⟩. **kick a'bout, kick a'round** v. t. [in der Gegend] herumkicken (ugs.). **kick 'off** v. i. (Footb.) anstoßen. **kick 'up** v. t. (coll.) **~ up a fuss/row** Krach schlagen/anfangen (ugs.)
**kid** [kɪd] 1. n. a) (young goat) Kitz, das; b) (coll.: child) Kind, das. 2. v. t., -dd- (coll.) auf den Arm nehmen (ugs.); **~ oneself** sich (Dat.) was vormachen
**kidnap** ['kɪdnæp] v. t., (Brit.) -pp- entführen. **'kidnapper** n. Entführer, der/Entführerin, die
**kidney** ['kɪdnɪ] n. Niere, die. **'kidney machine** n. künstliche Niere
**kill** [kɪl] v. t. a) töten; (deliberately) umbringen; **be ~ed in action** im Kampf fallen; **be ~ed in a car crash** bei einem Autounfall ums Leben kommen; b) **~ time** die Zeit totschlagen. **'killer** n. Mörder, der/Mörderin, die. **'killing** n. a) Töten, das; b) **make a ~** (coll.: great profit) einen [Mords]reibach machen (ugs.). **'killjoy** n. Spielverderber, der/-verderberin, die
**kiln** [kɪln] n. Brennofen, der
**kilo** ['kiːləʊ] n., pl. ~s Kilo, das
**kilogram, kilogramme** ['kɪləgræm] n. Kilogramm, das

**kilometre** (*Brit.; Amer.:* **kilometer**) ['kɪləmiːtə(r) (*Brit.*), kɪ'lɒmɪtə(r))] *n.* Kilometer, *der*

**kilowatt** *n.* ['kɪləwɒt] Kilowatt, *das*

**kilt** [kɪlt] *n.* Kilt, *der*

**kin** [kɪn] *n.* Verwandte

**¹kind** [kaɪnd] *n.* **a)** (*class, sort*) Art, *die;* **several ~s of apples** mehrere Sorten Äpfel; **all ~s of things/excuses** alles mögliche/alle möglichen Ausreden; **no ... of any ~:** keinerlei ...; **what ~ is it?** was für einer/eine/eins ist es?; **what ~ of [a] tree is this?** was für ein Baum ist das?; **b)** (*implying vagueness*) **a ~ of ...:** [so] eine Art ...; **~ of cute** (*coll.*) irgendwie niedlich (*ugs.*)

**²kind** *adj.* liebenswürdig; (*showing friendliness*) freundlich; **be ~ to animals** gut zu Tieren sein; **how ~!** wie nett [von ihm/Ihnen usw.]!

**kindergarten** ['kɪndəgɑːtn] *n.* Kindergarten, *der*

**kindle** ['kɪndl] (*fig.*) wecken

**kindly** ['kaɪndlɪ] **1.** *adv.* **a)** freundlich; nett; **b)** *in polite request etc.* freundlicherweise; **thank you ~:** herzlichen Dank. **2.** *adj.* freundlich; nett; (*kindhearted*) gütig

**'kindness** *n.* **a)** *no pl.* (*kind nature*) Freundlichkeit, *die;* **b) do sb. a ~** (*kind act*) jmdm. eine Gefälligkeit erweisen

**kindred** ['kɪndrɪd] *adj.* verwandt; **~ 'spirit** Gleichgesinnte, *der/die*

**king** [kɪŋ] *n.* König, *der.* **kingdom** ['kɪŋdəm] *n.* Königreich, *das*

**'kingfisher** *n.* Eisvogel, *der*

**'king-size[d]** *adj.* extragroß; Kingsize-(*Zigaretten*)

**kink** [kɪŋk] *n.* (*in pipe, wire, etc.*) Knick, *der;* (*in hair, wool*) Welle, *die*

**'kinky** *adj.* (*coll.*) spleenig; (*sexually*) abartig

**kiosk** ['kiːɒsk] *n.* **a)** Kiosk, *der;* **b)** (*telephone booth*) [Telefon]zelle, *die*

**kip** [kɪp] *n.* (*Brit. sl.: sleep*) **have a/get some ~:** eine Runde pennen (*salopp*)

**kipper** ['kɪpə(r)] *n.* Kipper, *der*

**kiss** [kɪs] **1.** *n.* Kuß, *der.* **2.** *v. t.* küssen; **~ sb. good night/goodbye** jmdm. einen Gutenacht-/Abschiedskuß geben. **3.** *v. i.* **they ~ed** sie küßten sich

**kit** [kɪt] *n.* **a)** (*Brit.: set of items*) Set, *das;* **b)** (*Brit.: clothing etc.*) **sports ~:** Sportzeug, *das;* **riding-/skiing-~:** Reit-/Skiausrüstung, *die.* **'kitbag** *n.* Tornister, *der*

**kitchen** ['kɪtʃɪn] *n.* Küche, *die; attrib.* Küchen-. **kitchen 'sink** *n.* [Küchen]ausguß, *der*

**kite** [kaɪt] *n.* Drachen, *der*

**kith** [kɪθ] *n.* **~ and kin** Freunde und Verwandte

**kitten** ['kɪtn] *n.* Kätzchen, *das*

**kitty** ['kɪtɪ] *n.* (*money*) Kasse, *die*

**kleptomania** [kleptə'meɪnɪə] *n.* Kleptomanie, *die.* **kleptomaniac** [kleptə-'meɪnɪæk] *n.* Kleptomane, *der/*Kleptomanin, *die*

**km.** *abbr.* **kilometre[s]** km

**knack** [næk] *n.* Talent, *das;* **get the ~ [of doing sth.]** den Bogen rauskriegen [, wie man etw. macht] (*ugs.*); **have lost the ~:** es nicht mehr zustande bringen

**knapsack** ['næpsæk] *n.* Rucksack, *der;* (*Mil.*) Tornister, *der*

**knead** [niːd] *v. t.* kneten

**knee** [niː] *n.* Knie, *das*

**knee:** **~cap** *n.* Kniescheibe, *die;* **~-deep** *adj.* knietief; **~-high** *adj.* kniehoch; **~-jerk reaction** *n.* (*fig.*) automatische Reaktion; **~-joint** *n.* Kniegelenk, *das*

**kneel** [niːl] *v. i.,* **knelt** [nelt] *or (esp. Amer.)* **kneeled** knien; **~ down** niederknien

**knelt** *see* **kneel**

**knew** *see* **know**

**knickers** ['nɪkəz] *n. pl.* (*Brit.*) [Damen]schlüpfer, *der*

**knife** [naɪf] **1.** *n., pl.* **knives** [naɪvz] Messer, *das.* **2.** *v. t.* (*stab*) einstechen auf (+ *Akk.*); (*kill*) erstechen

**knight** [naɪt] *n.* **a)** (*Hist.*) Ritter, *der;* **b)** (*Chess*) Springer, *der.* **'knighthood** *n.* Ritterwürde, *die*

**knit** [nɪt] *v. t.,* -tt- stricken; **~ one's brow** die Stirn runzeln. **'knitting** *n.* Stricken, *das;* (*work being knitted*) Strickarbeit, *die.* **'knitting needle** *n.* Stricknadel, *die.* **'knitwear** *n.* Strickwaren *Pl.*

**knives** *pl. of* **knife** 1

**knob** [nɒb] *n.* **a)** (*on door, walking-stick, etc.*) Knauf, *der;* **b)** (*control on radio etc.*) Knopf, *der;* **c)** (*of butter*) Klümpchen, *das*

**knock** [nɒk] **1.** *v. t.* **a)** (*strike*) (*lightly*) klopfen an (+ *Akk.*); (*forcefully*) schlagen gegen *od.* an (+ *Akk.*); **~ a hole in sth.** ein Loch in etw. (+ *Akk.*) schlagen; **b)** (*sl.: criticize*) herzziehen über (+ *Akk.*) (*ugs.*). **2.** *v. i.* klopfen (**at** an + *Akk.*). **3.** *n.* Klopfen, *das.* **knock 'down** *v. t.* **a)** (*in car*) umfahren; **b)** (*demolish*) abreißen. **knock 'off 1.** *v. t.* **a)** **~ off work** (*coll.: leave*) Feierabend machen; **b)** (*deduct*) **~ five pounds off the price** es fünf Pfund bil-

liger machen; c) *(coll.: do quickly)* aus
dem Ärmel schütteln *(ugs.)*; d) *(sl.:
steal)* klauen *(salopp)*. 2. *v. i. (coll.)*
Feierabend machen. **knock 'out** *v. t.*
a) *(make unconscious)* bewußtlos umfallen lassen; b) *(Boxing)* k. o. schlagen; c) *(sl.: exhaust)* kaputtmachen
*(ugs.)*. **knock 'over** *v. t.* umstoßen;.
⟨*Fahrer, Fahrzeug:*⟩ umfahren ⟨*Person*⟩
'**knock-down** *adj.* ~ **prices** Schleuderpreise
'**knocker** *n.* [Tür]klopfer, *der*
**knock: ~-kneed** ['nɒkni:d] *adj.*
X-beinig ⟨*Person*⟩; **~-out** *n. (Boxing)*
K.-o.-Schlag, *der*
**knot** [nɒt] 1. *n.* Knoten, *der*. 2. *v. t.*,
-tt- knoten ⟨*Seil, Faden usw.*⟩
'**knotty** *adj. (fig.: puzzling)* verwickelt
**know** [nəʊ] *v. t.*, **knew** [nju:], **known**
[nəʊn] a) *(recognize)* erkennen (**by** an
+ *Dat.*, **for** als + *Akk.*); b) *(be able to
distinguish)* ~ **sth. from sth.** etw. von
etw. unterscheiden können; c) *(be
aware of)* wissen; d) *(have understanding of)* können ⟨*ABC, Einmaleins,
Deutsch usw.*⟩; ~ **how to mend fuses**
wissen, wie man Sicherungen repa-
riert; ~ **how to drive a car** Auto fahren
können; e) kennen ⟨*Person*⟩. '**know-
all** *n.* Neunmalkluge, *der/die.*
'**know-how** *n.* praktisches Wissen
'**knowing** *adj.* a) wissend ⟨*Blick, Lächeln*⟩; b) *(cunning)* verschlagen.
'**knowingly** *adv.* a) *(intentionally)*
wissentlich; b) vielsagend ⟨*lächeln,
anblicken*⟩
**knowledge** ['nɒlɪdʒ] *n.* a) *(familiarity)* Kenntnisse (**of** in + *Dat.*); b)
*(awareness)* Wissen, *das;* **have no ~ of
sth.** nichts von etw. wissen; keine
Kenntnis von etw. haben *(geh.)*; c) |a|
~ **of languages/French** Sprach-/Fran-
zösischkenntnisse *Pl.* **knowledge-
able** ['nɒlɪdʒəbl] *adj.* **be ~ about** *or* **on
sth.** viel über etw. *(Akk.)* wissen
**known** [nəʊn] 1. *see* know. 2. *adj.* bekannt
**knuckle** ['nʌkl] *n.* [Finger]knöchel,
*der*
**Korea** [kə'rɪə] *pr. n.* Korea *(das)*
**kosher** ['kəʊʃə(r)] *adj.* koscher
**kudos** ['kju:dɒs] *n. (coll.)* Prestige, *das*
**kW** *abbr.* kilowatt|s| kW

# L

**L, l** [el] *n.* L, l, *das*
**£** *abbr.* pound|s| £; **cost £5** 5 £ od.
Pfund kosten
**l.** *abbr.* **litre|s|** l
**lab** [læb] *n. (coll.)* Labor, *das*
**label** ['leɪbl] 1. *n.* Schildchen, *das; (on
bottles, in clothes)* Etikett, *das; (tied/
stuck to an object)* Anhänger/Aufkle-
ber, *der*. 2. *v. t., (Brit.)* -ll-: a) etikettieren; auszeichnen ⟨*Waren*⟩; *(write on)*
beschriften; b) *(fig.)* ~ **sb./sth. |as| sth.**
jmdn./etw. als etw. etikettieren
**labor** *(Amer.) see* labour
**laboratory** [lə'bɒrətərɪ] *n.* Labor[ato-
rium], *das*
**labored, laborer** *(Amer.) see* labour-
**laborious** [lə'bɔ:rɪəs] *adj.* mühsam.
**la'boriously** *adv.* mühevoll
**labour** ['leɪbə(r)] *(Brit.)* 1. *n.* a) Arbeit,
*die;* b) *(workers)* Arbeiterschaft, *die;*
**immigrant ~:** ausländische Arbeitskräfte; c) **L~, the ~ Party** *(Polit.)* die
Labour Party; d) *(childbirth)* Wehen
*Pl.;* **be in ~:** in den Wehen liegen. 2.
*v. i.* hart arbeiten (**at, on** an + *Dat.*).
3. *v. t.* ~ **the point** sich lange darüber
verbreiten
**laboured** ['leɪbəd] *adj. (Brit.)* mühsam; schwerfällig ⟨*Stil*⟩; **his breathing
was ~:** er atmete schwer
'**labourer** *n. (Brit.)* Arbeiter, *der/*Arbeiterin, *die*
'**labour-saving** *adj.* arbeit[s]sparend
**labyrinth** ['læbərɪnθ] *n.* Labyrinth,
*das*
**lace** [leɪs] 1. *n.* a) *(for shoe)* Schnürsenkel, *der;* b) *(fabric)* Spitze, *die; attrib.*
Spitzen-. 2. *v. t.* ~ |up| [zu]schnüren
**lacerate** ['læsəreɪt] *v. t.* aufreißen
'**lace-up** 1. *attrib. adj.* Schnür-. 2. *n.*
Schnürschuh/-stiefel, *der*
**lack** [læk] 1. *n.* Mangel, *der* (**of** an +
*Dat.*). 2. *v. t.* **sb./sth. ~s sth.** jmdm./
einer Sache fehlt es an etw. *(Dat.)*
**lackey** ['lækɪ] *n.* Lakai, *der*
'**lacking** *adj.* **be ~:** fehlen
**laconic** [lə'kɒnɪk] *adj.* lakonisch

**lacquer** ['lækə(r)] *n*. Lack, *der*
**lacrosse** [lə'krɒs] *n*. Lacrosse, *das*
**lacy** ['leɪsɪ] *adj*. Spitzen-
**lad** [læd] *n*. Junge, *der*
**ladder** ['lædə(r)] **1.** *n*. **a)** Leiter, *die;* **b)** *(Brit.: in tights etc.)* Laufmasche, *die*. **2.** *v. i. (Brit.)* Laufmaschen/eine Laufmasche bekommen. **3.** *v. t. (Brit.)* Laufmaschen/eine Laufmasche machen in ( + *Akk.*)
**laden** ['leɪdn] beladen **(with** mit)
**ladle** ['leɪdl] *n*. Schöpfkelle, *die*
**lady** ['leɪdɪ] *n*. **a)** Dame, *die;* ~**-in-waiting** *(Brit.)* Hofdame, *die;* **b)** 'Ladies' *(WC)* „Damen"; **c)** *as form of address* **Ladies** meine Damen; **d)** *(Brit.) as title* **L~**: Lady
**lady:** ~**bird,** *(Amer.)* ~**bug** *ns.* Marienkäfer, *der;* ~**like** *adj*. damenhaft
**¹lag** [læg] *v. i.,* **-gg-:** ~ **[behind]** zurückbleiben; *(fig.)* im Rückstand sein
**²lag** *v. t.,* **-gg-** *(insulate)* isolieren
**lager** ['lɑ:gə(r)] *n*. Lagerbier, *das*
**lagging** *n*. Isolierung, *die*
**lagoon** [lə'gu:n] *n*. Lagune, *die*
**laid** *see* **²lay**
**laid-back** *adj. (coll.)* gelassen
**lain** *see* **²lie**
**lair** [leər] *n*. *(of wild animal)* Unterschlupf, *der;* *(of pirates, bandits)* Schlupfwinkel, *der*
**lake** [leɪk] *n*. See, *der*
**lamb** [læm] *n*. **a)** Lamm, *das;* **b)** *(meat)* Lamm[fleisch], *das*. **lamb 'chop** *n*. Lammkotelett, *das*. **lamb's-wool** *n*. Lambswool, *die*
**lame** [leɪm] *adj.,* **lamely** *adv*. lahm
**lament** [lə'ment] **1.** *n*. Klage, *die* (for um). **2.** *v. t.* ~ **that ...:** beklagen, daß ... **3.** *v. i.* klagen *(geh.);* ~ **over sth.** beklagen *(geh.)*. **lamentable** ['læməntəbl] *adj*. beklagenswert
**laminated** ['læmɪneɪtɪd] *adj*. lamelliert; ~ **glass** Verbundglas, *das*
**lamp** [læmp] *n*. Lampe, *die;* *(in street)* [Straßen]laterne, *die*. **lamppost** *n*. Laternenpfahl, *der*. **lampshade** *n*. Lampenschirm, *der*
**lance** [lɑ:ns] **1.** *n*. Lanze, *die*. **2.** *v. t. (Med.)* mit der Lanzette öffnen
**lance-'corporal** *n*. Obergefreite, *der*
**land** [lænd] **1.** *n*. Land, *das;* **have or own** ~: Grundbesitz haben. **2.** *v. t.* **a)** *(set ashore)* [an]landen; **b)** *(Aeronaut.)* landen; **c)** ~ **oneself in trouble** sich in Schwierigkeiten bringen; ~ **sb. with sth.,** ~ **sth. on sb.** jmdm. etw. aufhalsen *(ugs.)*. **3.** *v. i.* **a)** ⟨*Boot usw.:*⟩ anlegen, landen; ⟨*Passagier:*⟩ aussteigen

(from aus); **we** ~**ed at Dieppe** wir gingen in Dieppe an Land; **b)** *(Aeronaut.)* landen; **c)** ~ **on one's feet** *(fig.)* [wieder] auf die Füße fallen. **landed** *adj*. ~ **gentry/aristrocracy** Landadel, *der*.
**landing** *n*. **a)** *(of ship, aircraft)* Landung, *die;* **b)** *(on stairs)* Treppenabsatz, *der;* *(passage)* Treppenflur, *der*.
**landing-card** *n*. Landekarte, *die*.
**landing-stage** *n*. Landesteg, *der*
**land:** ~**lady** *n*. **a)** *(of rented property)* Vermieterin, *die;* **b)** *(of public house)* [Gast]wirtin, *die;* ~**-locked** *adj*. vom Land eingeschlossen ⟨Bucht, Hafen⟩; ⟨Staat⟩ ohne Zugang zum Meer; ~**lord** *n*. **a)** *(of rented property)* Vermieter, *der;* **b)** *(of public house)* [Gast]wirt, *der;* ~**mark** *n*. **a)** Orientierungspunkt, *der;* **b)** *(fig.)* Markstein, *der;* ~**owner** *n*. Grundbesitzer, *der/*-besitzerin, *die;* ~**scape** ['lændskeɪp] *n*. Landschaft, *die;* ~**slide** *n*. Erdrutsch, *der*
**lane** [leɪn] *n*. **a)** *(in the country)* Landsträßchen, *das;* Weg, *der;* **b)** *(in town)* Gasse, *die;* **c)** *(part of road)* [Fahr]spur, *die;* **'get in** ~" „bitte einordnen"; **d)** *(Sport)* Bahn, *die*
**language** ['læŋgwɪdʒ] *n*. Sprache, *die;* *(style)* Ausdrucksweise, *die*
**languid** ['læŋgwɪd] *adj*. träge
**languish** ['læŋgwɪʃ] *v. i.* **a)** *(lose vitality)* ermatten *(geh.);* **b)** ~ **under sth.** unter etw. *(Dat.)* schmachten *(geh.)*
**lank** [læŋk] *adj*. **a)** hager; **b)** glatt herabhängend ⟨Haar⟩
**lanky** ['læŋkɪ] *adj*. schlaksig *(ugs.)*
**lantern** ['læntən] *n*. Laterne, *die*
**¹lap** [læp] *n*. *(part of body)* Schoß, *der*
**²lap** *n*. *(Sport)* Runde, *die*
**³lap 1.** *v. i.,* **-pp-** schlecken. **2.** *v. t.,* **-pp-:** ~ **[up]** [auf]schlecken. **lap 'up** *v. t.* *(fig.)* schlucken
**lapel** [lə'pel] *n*. Revers, *das*
**Lapland** ['læplænd] *pr. n.* Lappland *(das)*
**lapse** [læps] **1.** *n*. **a)** *(interval)* **a/the** ~ **of ...:** eine/die Zeitspanne von ...; **b)** *(mistake)* Fehler, *der;* ~ **of memory** Gedächtnislücke, *die*. **2.** *v. i.* **a)** ⟨Vertrag, usw.:⟩ ungültig werden; **b)** ~ **into** verfallen in ( + *Akk.*)
**larceny** ['lɑ:sənɪ] *n*. Diebstahl, *der*
**lard** [lɑ:d] *n*. Schweineschmalz, *das*
**larder** ['lɑ:də(r)] *n*. Speisekammer, *die*
**large** [lɑ:dʒ] **1.** *adj*. groß. **2.** *n*. **at** ~ *(not in prison etc.)* auf freiem Fuß. **3.** *adv. see* **by 2 d**. **largely** *adv*. weitgehend
**large-size[d]** *adj*. groß

¹**lark** [lɑ:k] *n.* *(Ornith.)* Lerche, *die*

²**lark** *(coll.)* **1.** *n.* Jux, *der (ugs.)*. **2.** *v. i.*
~ [about *or* around] herumalbern
*(ugs.)*

**larva** ['lɑ:və] *n., pl.* ~e ['lɑ:vi:] Larve,
*die*

**laryngitis** [lærɪn'dʒaɪtɪs] *n.* Kehlkopf-
entzündung, *die*

**larynx** ['lærɪŋks] *n.* Kehlkopf, *der*

**lascivious** [lə'sɪvɪəs] *adj.* lüstern *(geh.)*

**laser** ['leɪzə(r)] *n.* Laser, *der.* '**laser
beam** *n.* Laserstrahl, *der*

**lash** [læʃ] **1.** *n.* **a)** *(stroke)* [Peit-
schen]hieb, *der;* **b)** *(on eyelid)* Wimper, *die.* **2.** *v. i.* ⟨*Welle, Regen:*⟩ peitschen (**against** gegen, **on** auf + *Akk.*).
**3.** *v. t.* **a)** *(fasten)* festbinden (**to** an +
*Dat.*); **b)** *(as punishment)* auspeitschen. **lash** '**down 1.** *v. t.* festbinden.
**2.** *v. i.* ⟨*Regen:*⟩ niederprasseln. **lash**
'**out** *v. i.* **a)** *(hit out)* um sich schlagen;
~ **out at sb.** nach jmdm. schlagen; **b)**
~ **out on sth.** *(coll.: spend freely)* sich
*(Dat.)* etw. leisten

**lashings** ['læʃɪŋz] *n. pl.* ~ **of sth.** Un-
mengen von etw.

**lass** [læs] *n.* Mädchen, *das*

**lasso** [lə'su:] Lasso, *das*

¹**last** [lɑ:st] **1.** *adj.* letzt...; **be** ~ **to arrive**
als letzter/letzte ankommen; ~ **night**
gestern nacht. **2.** *adv.* **a)** [ganz] zuletzt;
als letzter/letzte ⟨*sprechen, ankom-
men*⟩; **b)** *(on* ~ *previous occasion)* das
letzte Mal; zuletzt. **3.** *n.* **a)** *(person or
thing)* letzter...; **b)** **at** [long] ~: endlich

²**last** *v. i.* **a)** *(continue)* dauern; ⟨*Wetter,
Ärger:*⟩ anhalten; **b)** *(suffice)* reichen

'**last-ditch** *adj.* ~ **attempt** letzter ver-
zweifelter Versuch

'**lasting** *adj.* bleibend; dauerhaft ⟨*Beziehung*⟩; nachhaltig ⟨*Eindruck, Wirkung*⟩

'**lastly** *adv.* schließlich

**latch** [lætʃ] *n.* Riegel, *der;* **on the** ~:
nur eingeklinkt. **latch** '**on to** *v. t.*
*(coll.: understand)* kapieren *(ugs.)*

**late** [leɪt] **1.** *adj.* **a)** spät; **am I** ~? komme ich zu spät?; **be** ~ **for the train** den
Zug verpassen; **the train is** [an hour] ~:
der Zug hat [eine Stunde] Verspätung;
~ **shift** Spätschicht, *die;* ~ **summer**
Spätsommer, *der;* **b)** *(dead)* verstorben; **c)** *(former)* ehemalig. *See also*
**later** 1; **latest. 2.** *adv.* **a)** *(after proper
time)* verspätet; **b)** *(at/till a* ~ *hour)*
spät; **be up** ~: bis spät in die Nacht
aufbleiben; **work** ~ **at the office**
[abends] lange im Büro arbeiten; [a
bit] ~ **in the day** *(fig. coll.)* reichlich

spät. **3.** *n.* **of** ~: in letzter Zeit.
**latecomer** ['leɪtkʌmə(r)] *n.* Zuspät-
kommende, *der/die.* '**lately** *adv.* in
letzter Zeit. '**lateness** *n.* **a)** *(delay)*
Verspätung, *die;* **b) the** ~ **of the performance** der späte Beginn der Vorstellung

**latent** ['leɪtənt] *adj.* latent

**later** ['leɪtə(r)] **1.** *adv.* ~ [on] später. **2.**
*adj.* später; *(more recent)* neuer

**lateral** ['lætərl] *adj.* seitlich (**to** von); ~
**thinking** Querdenken, *das*

**latest** ['leɪtɪst] *adj.* **a)** *(modern)*
neu[e]st...; **b)** *(most recent)* letzt...; **c)**
**at** [the] ~/**the very** ~: spätestens/aller-
spätestens

**lathe** [leɪð] *n.* Drehbank, *die*

**lather** ['lɑ:ðə(r)] **1.** *n.* [Seifen]schaum,
*der.* **2.** *v. t.* einschäumen

**Latin** ['lætɪn] **1.** *adj.* lateinisch. **2.** *n.*
Latein, *das; see also* **English** 2 a.
**Latin A'merica** *pr. n.* Lateinamerika
*(das).* **Latin-A'merican** *adj.* latein-
amerikanisch

**latitude** ['lætɪtju:d] *n.* **a)** *(freedom)*
Freiheit, *die;* **b)** *(Geog.)* Breite, *die*

**latrine** [lə'tri:n] *n.* Latrine, *die*

**latter** ['lætə(r)] *attrib. adj.* letzter...; **the**
~: der/die/das letztere; *pl.* die letzte-
ren. '**latterly** *adv.* in letzter Zeit

**lattice** ['lætɪs] *n.* Gitter, *das*

**laudable** ['lɔ:dəbl] *adj.* lobenswert

**laugh** [lɑ:f] **1.** *n.* Lachen, *das;* *(continuous)* Gelächter, *das.* **2.** *v. i.* lachen; ~
**out loud** laut auflachen; ~ **at sb./sth.**
über jmdn./etw. lachen; *(jeer)* jmdn.
auslachen/etw. verlachen. **laugh** '**off**
*v. t.* mit einem Lachen abtun

**laughable** ['lɑ:fəbl] *adj.* lachhaft; lächerlich

'**laughing** *n.* **be no** ~ **matter** nicht zum
Lachen sein. '**laughing-gas** *n.* Lach-
gas, *das.* '**laughing-stock** *n.* **make
sb. a** ~, **make a** ~ **of sb.** jmdn. zum Gespött machen

**laughter** ['lɑ:ftə(r)] *n.* Lachen, *das;*
*(continuous)* Gelächter, *das*

**launch** [lɔ:ntʃ] *v. t.* **a)** zu Wasser lassen
⟨*Boot*⟩; vom Stapel lassen ⟨*neues
Schiff*⟩; abschießen ⟨*Harpune, Torpedo*⟩; schleudern ⟨*Speer*⟩; **b)** *(fig.)*
auf den Markt bringen ⟨*Produkt*⟩;
vorstellen ⟨*Buch, Schallplatte,
Sänger*⟩; ~ **an attack** einen Angriff
durchführen. '**launching pad,
launch pad** *ns.* [Raketen]abschuß-
rampe, *die*

**launder** ['lɔ:ndə(r)] *v. t.* waschen und
bügeln. **launderette** [lɔ:ndə'ret],

**laundrette** [lɔːn'dret], *(Amer.)* **laundromat** ['lɔːndrəmæt] *ns.* Waschsalon, *der.* **laundry** ['lɔːndrɪ] *n.* **a)** *(place)* Wäscherei, *die;* **b)** *(clothes etc.)* Wäsche, *die*

**lava** ['lɑːvə] *n.* Lava, *die*

**lavatory** ['lævətərɪ] *n.* Toilette, *die*

**lavender** ['lævɪndə(r)] *n.* Lavendel, *der*

**lavish** ['lævɪʃ] **1.** *adj.* großzügig. **2.** *v. t.* ~ sth. on sb. jmdn. mit·etw. überhäufen

**law** [lɔː] *n.* **a)** Gesetz, *das;* **break the ~**: gegen das Gesetz verstoßen; **take the ~ into one's own hands** sich *(Dat.)* selbst Recht verschaffen; **~ and order** Ruhe und Ordnung; **b)** *(of game)* Regel, *die;* **c)** *(as subject)* Jura *o.* Art.

**law:** **~-abiding** ['lɔːəbaɪdɪŋ] *adj.* gesetzestreu; **~court** *n.* Gerichtsgebäude, *das;* *(room)* Gerichtssaal, *der;* **~ful** ['lɔːfl] *adj.* rechtmäßig ⟨Besitzer, Erbe⟩; legal, gesetzmäßig ⟨Vorgehen, Maßnahme⟩; **~less** *adj.* gesetzlos

**lawn** [lɔːn] *n.* Rasen, *der.* **'lawn-mower** *n.* Rasenmäher, *der*

**'law suit** *n.* Prozeß, *der*

**lawyer** ['lɔːjə(r)] *n.* Rechtsanwalt, *der*/Rechtsanwältin, *die*

**lax** [læks] *adj.* lax

**laxative** ['læksətɪv] *n.* Abführmittel, *das*

**laxity** ['læksɪtɪ], **'laxness** *ns.* Laxheit, *die*

**¹lay** [leɪ] *adj.* Laien-

**²lay** *v. t.,* **laid** [leɪd] **a)** legen ⟨Teppichboden, Rohr, Kabel⟩; **b)** *(impose)* auferlegen ⟨Verantwortung, Verpflichtung⟩ (on *Dat.*); verhängen ⟨Strafe⟩ (on über + *Akk.*); **c)** ~ the table den Tisch decken; **d)** *(Biol.)* legen ⟨Ei⟩. **lay a'side** *v. t.* beiseite legen. **lay 'by** *v. t.* beiseite legen. **lay 'down** *v. t.* **a)** hinlegen; **b)** festlegen ⟨Regeln, Bedingungen⟩. **lay 'off 1.** *v. t. (from work)* vorübergehend entlassen. **2.** *v. i. (coll.: stop)* aufhören. **lay 'out** *v. t.* **a)** *(spread out)* ausbreiten; **b)** anlegen ⟨Garten⟩. **lay 'up** *v. t.* **a)** *(store)* lagern; **b)** I was laid up in bed for a week ich mußte eine Woche mein Bett hüten

**³lay** see **²lie**

**lay:** **~about** *n. (Brit.)* Gammler, *der (ugs.);* **~-by** *n., pl.* **~-bys** *(Brit.)* Parkbucht, *die;* Haltebucht, *die*

**layer** ['leɪə(r)] *n.* Schicht, *die*

**layette** [leɪ'et] *n.* |baby's| ~: Babyausstattung, *die*

**lay:** **~man** ['leɪmən] *n., pl.* **~men** ['leɪmən] Laie, *der;* **~out** *n. (of garden, park)* Anlage, *die; (of book, advertisement, etc.)* Layout, *das*

**laze** [leɪz] *v. i.* faulenzen; ~ **around** or **about** herumfaulenzen *(ugs.)*

**lazily** ['leɪzɪlɪ] *adv.* faul

**laziness** ['leɪzɪnɪs] *n.* Faulheit, *die*

**lazy** ['leɪzɪ] *adj.* faul. **'lazy-bones** *n. sing.* Faulpelz, *der*

**lb.** *abbr.* **pound|s|** ≈ Pfd.

**¹lead** [led] **1.** *n.* **a)** *(metal)* Blei, *das;* **b)** *(in pencil)* |Bleistift|mine, *die.* **2.** *attrib. adj.* Blei-

**²lead** [liːd] **1.** *v. t., led* [led] **a)** führen; ~ **sb. to do sth.** *(fig.)* jmdn. dazu bringen, etw. zu tun; **b)** *(fig.: influence)* ~ **sb. to do sth.** jmdn. veranlassen, etw. zu tun; **be easily led** sich leicht beeinflussen lassen; **he led me to believe that ...:** er machte mich glauben, daß ...; **c)** *(be first in)* anführen; **d)** *(direct)* anführen ⟨Bewegung, Abordnung⟩; leiten ⟨Diskussion, Orchester⟩. **2.** *v. i.,* **led a)** ⟨Straße usw., Tür:⟩ führen; **b)** *(be first)* führen; *(go in front)* vorangehen. **3.** *n.* **a)** *(precedent)* Beispiel, *das; (clue)* Anhaltspunkt, *der;* **follow sb.'s ~** jmds. Beispiel *(Dat.)* folgen; **b)** *(first place)* Führung, *die;* **be in the ~:** in Führung liegen; **c)** *(distance ahead)* Vorsprung, *der;* **d)** *(leash)* Leine, *die;* **on a ~:** an der Leine; **e)** *(Electr.)* Kabel, *das;* **f)** *(Theatre)* Hauptrolle, *die.* **lead a'way** *v. t.* abführen ⟨Gefangenen, Verbrecher⟩. **lead 'off 1.** *v. t.* abführen. **2.** *v. i.* beginnen. **lead 'on 1.** *v. t.* ~ **sb. on** *(entice)* jmdn. reizen; *(deceive)* jmdn. auf den Leim führen. **2.** *v. i.* ~ **on to** the next topic *etc.* zum nächsten Thema *usw.* führen. **lead 'up to** *v. t.* schließlich führen zu

**'leader** *n.* **a)** Führer, *der*/Führerin, *die; (of political party)* Vorsitzende, *der/die; (of expedition)* Leiter, *der*/Leiterin, *die;* **b)** *(Brit. Journ.)* Leitartikel, *der.* **'leadership** *n.* Führung, *die*

**lead-free** ['ledfriː] *adj.* bleifrei

**leading** ['liːdɪŋ] *adj.* führend

**leading:** ~ **'lady** *n.* Hauptdarstellerin, *die;* ~ **'man** *n.* Hauptdarsteller, *der;* ~ **'question** *n.* Suggestivfrage, *die;* ~ **role** *n.* Hauptrolle, *die; (fig.)* führende Rolle

**lead** [led]: **~-'pencil** *n.* Bleistift, *der;* **~-poisoning** *n.* Bleivergiftung, *die*

**leaf** [liːf] *n., pl.* **leaves** [liːvz] Blatt, *das; (of table)* Platte *die.* **leaf 'through** *v. t.* durchblättern

**leaflet** ['li:flɪt] *n.* [Hand]zettel, *der; (advertising)* Reklamezettel, *der; (political)* Flugblatt, *das*

'**leafy** *adj.* belaubt

**league** [li:g] *n.* **a)** *(agreement)* Bündnis, *das;* **be in ~ with** sb. mit jmdm. im Bunde sein; **b)** *(Sport)* Liga, *die*

**leak** [li:k] **1.** *n.* **a)** *(hole)* Leck, *das; (in roof, tent; also fig.)* undichte Stelle; **b)** *(escaping gas)* durch ein Leck austretendes Gas. **2.** *v. i.* **a)** *(escape)* austreten **(from** aus); **b)** ⟨*Faß, Tank, Schiff:*⟩ lecken; ⟨*Rohr, Leitung, Dach:*⟩ undicht sein; ⟨*Gefäß, Füller:*⟩ auslaufen; **c)** *(fig.)* ~ **[out]** durchsickern. **3.** *v. t.* ~ **sth. to** sb. jmdm. etw. zuspielen. **leakage** ['li:kɪdʒ] *n.* Auslaufen, *das; (of fluid, gas)* Ausströmen, *das; (fig.: of information)* Durchsickern, *das.*

'**leaky** *adj.* undicht; leck ⟨*Boot*⟩

¹**lean** [li:n] **1.** *adj.* mager. **2.** *n. (meat)* Magere, *das*

²**lean 1.** *v. i.,* **leaned** [li:nd, lent] *or (Brit.)* **leant** [lent] **a)** sich beugen; ~ **against the door** sich gegen die Tür lehnen; ~ **down/forward** sich herab-/vorbeugen; ~ **back** sich zurücklehnen; **b)** *(support oneself)* ~ **against/on** sth. sich gegen/an etw. *(Akk.)* lehnen; **c)** *(be supported)* lehnen **(against** an + *Dat.*); **d)** *(fig.)* ~ **[up]on** sb. *(rely)* auf jmdn. bauen; ~ **to[wards]** sth. *(tend)* zu etw. neigen. **2.** *v. t.,* **leaned** *or (Brit.)* **leant** lehnen **(against** gegen *od.* an + *Akk.*). **lean 'over** *v. i.* sich hinüberbeugen

'**leaning** *n.* Neigung, *die*

**leant** *see* ²**lean**

**leap** [li:p] **1.** *v. i.,* **leaped** [li:pt, lept] *or* **leapt** [lept] **a)** springen; ⟨*Herz:*⟩ hüpfen; **b)** *(fig.)* ~ **at the chance** die Gelegenheit beim Schopf packen. **2.** *v. t.,* **leaped** *or* **leapt** überspringen. **3.** *n.* Sprung, *der;* **with** *or* **in one ~:** mit einem Satz; **by ~s and bounds** *(fig.)* mit Riesenschritten. '**leap-frog 1.** *n.* Bockspringen, *das.* **2.** *v. i.,* **-gg-** Bockspringen machen

**leapt** *see* **leap** 1, 2

'**leap year** *n.* Schaltjahr, *das*

**learn** [lɜːn] **1.** *v. t.,* **learned** [lɜːnd, lɜːnt] *or* **learnt** [lɜːnt] **a)** lernen; ~ **to swim** schwimmen lernen; **b)** *(find out)* erfahren. **2.** *v. i.,* **learned** *or* **learnt a)** lernen; ~ **about sth.** etwas über etw. *(Akk.)* lernen; **b)** *(get to know)* erfahren **(of** von). **learned** ['lɜːnɪd] *adj.* gelehrt. '**learner** *n. (beginner)* Anfänger, *der*/Anfängerin, *die;* ~ **[driver]**

Fahrschüler, *der*/-schülerin, *die.* '**learning** *n. (of person)* Gelehrsamkeit, *die*

**learnt** *see* **learn**

**lease** [li:s] **1.** *n. (of land, business premises)* Pachtvertrag, *der; (of house, flat, office)* Mietvertrag, *der.* **2.** *v. t.* **a)** *(grant ~ on)* verpachten ⟨*Grundstück, Geschäft, Rechte*⟩; vermieten ⟨*Haus, Wohnung, Büro*⟩; **b)** *(take ~ on)* pachten ⟨*Grundstück, Geschäft*⟩; mieten ⟨*Haus, Wohnung, Büro*⟩. '**leasehold** *n. see* **lease** 2: **have the ~ of** *or* **on sth.** etw. gepachtet/gemietet haben

**leash** [li:ʃ] *n.* Leine, *die*

**least** [li:st] **1.** *adj. (smallest)* kleinst...; *(in quantity)* wenigst...; *(in status)* geringst... **2.** *n.* Geringste, *das;* **the ~ I can do** das mindeste, was ich tun kann; **at ~:** mindestens; *(anyway)* wenigstens; **at the [very] ~:** [aller]mindestens; **not [in] the ~:** nicht im geringsten. **3.** *adv.* am wenigsten

**leather** ['leðə(r)] **1.** *n.* Leder, *das.* **2.** *adj.* ledern; Leder(jacke, -mantel⟩. '**leather goods** *n.* Lederwaren *Pl.*

'**leathery** *adj.* ledern

¹**leave** [li:v] *n.* **a)** *(permission)* Erlaubnis, *die;* **b)** *(from duty or work)* Urlaub, *der;* ~ **[of absence]** Urlaub, *der;* **c)** **take one's ~** sich verabschieden

²**leave** *v. t.,* **left** [left] **a)** *(make or let remain)* hinterlassen; ~ **sb. to do sth.** es jmdm. überlassen, etw. zu tun; *(in will)* ~ **sb. sth.,** ~ **sth. to** sb. jmdm. etw. hinterlassen; **b)** *(refrain from doing, using, etc.)* stehenlassen ⟨*Abwasch, Essen*⟩; **c)** *(in given state)* lassen; ~ **sb. alone** *(allow to be alone)* jmdn. allein lassen; *(stop bothering)* jmdn. in Ruhe lassen; **d)** *(refer, entrust)* ~ **sth. to** sb./ **sth.** etw. jmdm./einer Sache überlassen; **e)** *(go away from, quit, desert)* verlassen; ~ **home at 6 a.m.** um 6 Uhr früh von zu Hause weggehen/-fahren; ~ **Bonn at 6 p.m.** *(by car, in train)* um 18 Uhr von Bonn abfahren; *(by plane)* um 18 Uhr in Bonn abfliegen; *abs.* **the train ~s at 8.30 a.m.** der Zug fährt *od.* geht um 8.30 Uhr; ~ **on the 8 a.m. train/flight** mit dem Acht-Uhr-Zug fahren/der Acht-Uhr-Maschine fliegen. **leave a'side** *v. t.* beiseite lassen. **leave be'hind** *v. t.* zurücklassen; *(by mistake)* vergessen; liegenlassen. **leave 'off** *v. t. (stop)* aufhören mit; *abs.* aufhören. **leave 'out** *v. t.* auslassen. **leave 'over** *v. t.* **be left over** übrig [geblieben] sein

**leaves** *pl. of* **leaf**

**Lebanon** ['lebənən] *pr. n.* |the| ~: [der] Libanon

**lecherous** ['letʃərəs] *adj.* lüstern *(geh.)*

**lecture** ['lektʃə(r)] **1. a)** *n.* Vortrag, *der; (Univ.)* Vorlesung, *die;* **b)** *(reprimand)* Strafpredigt, *die (ugs.).* **2.** *v. i.* ~ |to sb.| |on sth.| [vor jmdm.] einen Vortrag/*(Univ.)* eine Vorlesung [über etw. *(Akk.)*] halten. **3.** *v. t. (scold)* ~ jmdm. eine Strafpredigt halten. **'lecturer** *n.* Vortragende, *der/die;* senior ~: Dozent, *der/*Dozentin, *die*

**led** *see* ²**lead** 1, 2

**ledge** [ledʒ] *n.* Sims, *der od. das; (of rock)* Vorsprung, *der*

**ledger** ['ledʒə(r)] *n. (Commerc.)* Hauptbuch, *das*

**lee** [li:] *n.* **a)** *(shelter)* Schutz, *der;* **b)** ~ |side| *(Naut.)* Leeseite, *die*

**leech** [li:tʃ] *n.* [Blut]egel, *der*

**leek** [li:k] *n.* Stange Porree *od.* Lauch; ~s Porree, *der;* Lauch, *der*

**leer** [lɪə(r)] **1.** *n.* anzüglicher/spöttischer Blick. **2.** *v. i.* ~ at sb. jmdm. einen anzüglichen/spöttischen [Seiten]blick zuwerfen

**leeward** ['li:wəd] **1.** *adj.* to/on the ~ side of the ship nach/in Lee. **2.** *n.* Leeseite, *die;* to ~: leewärts

**'leeway** *n.* **a)** *(Naut.)* Leeweg, *der;* Abdrift, *die;* **b)** *(fig.)* Spielraum, *der*

**¹left** *see* ²**leave**

**²left** [left] **1.** *adj.* **a)** link...; on the ~ side auf der linken Seite; links; **b)** L~ *(Polit.)* link... **2.** *adv.* nach links. **3.** *n.* **a)** *(~-hand side)* linke Seite; on *or* to the ~ |of sb./sth.| links [von jmdm./etw.]; **b)** *(Polit.)* the L~: die Linke

**left:** ~-hand *adj.* link...; ~-'handed **1.** *adj.* linkshändig; ⟨Werkzeug⟩ für Linkshänder; be ~-handed Linkshänder/Linkshänderin sein; **2.** *adv.* linkshändig; ~-'luggage [office] *n. (Brit. Railw.)* Gepäckaufbewahrung, *die;* ~-overs *n. pl.* Reste; ~ 'wing *n.* linker Flügel; ~-'wing *adj. (Polit.)* linksgerichtet; Links⟨extremist, -intellektueller⟩; ~-'winger *n.* **a)** *(Sport)* Linksaußen, *der;* **b)** *(Polit.)* Angehöriger/Angehörige des linken Flügels

**leg** [leg] *n.* **a)** Bein, *das;* pull sb.'s ~ *(fig.)* jmdn. auf den Arm nehmen *(ugs.);* stretch one's ~s sich *(Dat.)* die Beine vertreten; **b)** ~ of lamb Lammkeule, *die;* **c)** *(of journey)* Etappe, *die*

**legacy** ['legəsɪ] *n.* Vermächtnis, *das (Rechtsspr.);* Erbschaft, *die*

**legal** ['li:gl] *adj.* **a)** *(concerning the law)* juristisch; Rechts⟨beratung, -streit, -experte, -schutz⟩; gesetzlich ⟨Vertreter⟩; rechtlich ⟨Gründe, Stellung⟩; Gerichts⟨kosten⟩; **b)** *(required by law)* gesetzlich ⟨Verpflichtung⟩; gesetzlich verankert ⟨Recht⟩; **c)** *(lawful)* legal; rechtsgültig ⟨Vertrag, Testament⟩.

**legality** [lɪ'gælɪtɪ] *n.* Legalität, *die.*

**legalize** ['li:gəlaɪz] *v. t.* legalisieren

**legend** ['ledʒənd] *n.* Sage, *die; (unfounded belief)* Legende, *die.* **legendary** ['ledʒəndərɪ] *adj.* legendär

**legibility** [ledʒɪ'bɪlɪtɪ] *n.* Leserlichkeit, *die*

**legible** ['ledʒɪbl] *adj.* leserlich; easily/scarcely ~: leicht/kaum lesbar

**legion** ['li:dʒn] *n.* Legion, *die*

**legislate** ['ledʒɪsleɪt] *v. i.* Gesetze verabschieden. **legislation** [ledʒɪs'leɪʃn] *n.* **a)** *(laws)* Gesetze; **b)** *(legislating)* Gesetzgebung, *die.* **legislative** ['ledʒɪslətɪv] *adj.* gesetzgebend. **legislator** ['ledʒɪsleɪtə(r)] *n.* Gesetzgeber, *der.* **legislature** ['ledʒɪsleɪtʃə(r)] *n.* Legislative, *die*

**legitimate** [lɪ'dʒɪtɪmət] *adj.* **a)** *(lawful)* legitim; rechtmäßig ⟨Besitzer, Regierung⟩; **b)** *(valid)* berechtigt; **c)** ehelich ⟨Kind⟩

**leisure** ['leʒə(r)] *n.* Freizeit, *die; attrib.* Freizeit-. **'leisurely** *adj.* gemächlich

**lemon** ['lemən] *n.* Zitrone, *die.* **lemonade** [lemə'neɪd] *n.* [Zitronen]limonade, *die*

**lend** [lend] *v. t.,* lent [lent] leihen; ~ sth. to sb. jmdm. etw. leihen. **'lender** *n.* Verleiher, *der/*Verleiherin, *die*

**length** [leŋθ, leŋkθ] *n.* **a)** *(also of time)* Länge, *die;* be six feet in ~: sechs Fuß lang sein; a short ~ of time kurze Zeit; **b)** at ~ *(for a long time)* lange; *(eventually)* schließlich; at |great| ~ *(in great detail)* lang und breit; at some ~: ziemlich ausführlich; **c)** go to any/great ~s alles nur/alles Erdenkliche tun; **d)** *(piece of material)* Länge, *die;* Stück, *das.* **lengthen** ['leŋθən] **1.** *v. i.* länger werden. **2.** *v. t.* verlängern; länger machen ⟨Kleid⟩. **lengthways** ['leŋθweɪz] *adv.* der Länge nach; längs. **'lengthy** *adj.* überlang

**lenient** ['li:nɪənt] *adj.* nachsichtig

**lens** [lenz] *n.* Linse, *die*

**Lent** [lent] *n.* Fastenzeit, *die*

**lent** *see* **lend**

**lentil** ['lentl] *n.* Linse, *die*

**Leo** ['li:əʊ] *n., pl.* ~s der Löwe

**leopard** ['lepəd] *n.* Leopard, *der*

**leotard** ['li:ətɑːd] *n.* Turnanzug, *der*
**leper** ['lepə(r)] *n.* Leprakranke, *der/die*
**leprosy** ['leprəsɪ] *n.* Lepra, *die*
**lesbian** ['lezbɪən] **1.** *n.* Lesbierin, *die.*
  **2.** *adj.* lesbisch
**less** [les] **1.** *adj.* weniger; **of ~ value/**
  **importance** weniger wertvoll/wichtig.
  **2.** *adv.* weniger; **~ and ~:** immer we-
  niger; **~ and ~** |often| immer seltener.
  **3.** *n.* weniger. **4.** *prep. (deducting)* **ten**
  **~ three** zehn weniger drei. **lessen**
  ['lesn] **1.** *v. t.* verringern. **2.** *v. i.* sich
  verringern. **lesser** ['lesə(r)] *attrib.*
  *adj.* geringer...
**lesson** ['lesn] *n.* **a)** *(class)* [Unter-
  richts]stunde, *die;* **b)** *(example, warning)* Lehre, *die;* **c)** *(Eccl.)* Lesung, *die*
**let** [let] **1.** *v. t.,* -tt-, **let a)** *(allow to)* lassen; **~ sb. do sth.** jmdn. etw. tun las-
  sen; **~ alone** *(far less)* geschweige
  denn; **b)** *(cause to)* **~ sb. know** jmdn.
  wissen lassen; **c)** *(Brit.: rent out)* vermieten. **2.** *v. aux.,* -tt-, **let** lassen; **Let's**
  **go to the cinema.** – Yes, **~'s/No,** **~'s**
  **not** Komm/Kommt, wir gehen ins Kino. – Ja, gut/Nein, lieber nicht; **~**
  **them come** in sie sollen hereinkommen. **let 'down** *v. t.* **a)** *(lower)* herun-
  ter-/hinunterlassen; **b)** *(Dressm.)* auslassen; **c)** *(disappoint, fail)* im Stich
  lassen. **let 'in** *v. t.* **a)** *(admit)* herein-/
  hineinlassen; **b)** **~ oneself in for sth.**
  sich auf etw. *(Akk.)* einlassen; **c)** **~ sb.**
  **in on a secret/plan** *etc.* jmdn. in ein
  Geheimnis/einen Plan *usw.* einwei-
  hen. **'let into** *v. t.* **a)** *(admit into)* lassen in *(+ Akk.)*; **b)** *(fig.: acquaint
  with)* **~ sb. into a secret** jmdn. in ein
  Geheimnis einweihen. **let 'off** *v. t.* **a)**
  *(excuse)* laufenlassen *(ugs.);* **~ sb. off**
  **sth.** jmdm. etw. erlassen; **b)** *(allow to
  alight)* aussteigen lassen; **c)** abbren-
  nen ⟨*Feuerwerk*⟩. **let 'on** *(sl.)* **1.** *v. i.*
  **don't ~ on!** nichts verraten! **2.** *v. t.* **sb.**
  **~ on to me that ...:** man hat mir ge-
  steckt, daß ... *(ugs.).* **let 'out** *v. t.* **a)** **~**
  **sb./an animal out** jmdn./ein Tier her-
  aus-/hinauslassen; **b)** ausstoßen
  ⟨*Schrei*⟩; **~ out a groan** aufstöhnen; **c)**
  verraten ⟨*Geheimnis*⟩; **d)** *(Dressm.)*
  auslassen; **e)** *(Brit.: rent out)* vermieten. **let 'through** *v. t.* durchlassen.
  **let 'up** *v. i. (coll.)* nachlassen
**'let-down** *n.* Enttäuschung, *die*
**lethal** ['li:θl] *adj.* tödlich
**lethargic** [lɪ'θɑːdʒɪk] *adj.* träge; *(apathetic)* lethargisch
**lethargy** ['leθədʒɪ] *n.* Trägheit, *die;*
  *(apathy)* Lethargie, *die*

**letter** ['letə(r)] **a)** Brief, *der* **(to an**
  **+ Akk.);** **b)** *(of alphabet)* Buchstabe,
  *der.* **'letter bomb** *n.* Briefbombe,
  *die.* **'letter-box** *n.* Briefkasten, *der*
  **'lettering** *n.* Typographie, *die*
**lettuce** ['letɪs] *n.* [Kopf]salat, *der*
**leukaemia,** *(Amer.)* **leukemia**
  [luː'kiːmɪə] *n.* Leukämie, *die*
**level** ['levl] **1.** *n.* **a)** Höhe, *die; (storey)*
  Etage, *die;* **b)** *(fig.: steady state)* Ni-
  veau, *das;* **be on a ~** |with sb./sth.| auf
  dem gleichen Niveau sein |wie jmd./
  etw.|. **2.** *adj.* **a)** waagerecht; eben
  ⟨*Boden, Land*⟩; **b)** *(on a ~)* **be ~** |with
  sth./sb.| auf gleicher Höhe |mit etw./
  jmdm.| sein; **c)** *(fig.)* **keep a ~ head** ei-
  nen kühlen Kopf bewahren; **do one's**
  **~ best** *(coll.)* sein möglichstes tun. **3.**
  *v. t., (Brit.)* -ll-: **a)** *(make ~)* ebnen; **b)**
  *(aim)* richten ⟨*Blick, Gewehr*⟩ **(at** auf
  **+ Akk.);** *(fig.)* richten ⟨*Kritik usw.*⟩
  **(at** gegen). **level 'crossing** *n. (Brit.
  Railw.)* [schienengleicher] Bahnüber-
  gang. **level-'headed** *adj.* besonnen
**lever** ['liːvə(r)] **1.** *n.* Hebel, *der.* **2.** *v. t.*
  **~ sth. open** etw. aufhebeln. **leverage**
  ['liːvərɪdʒ] *n.* Hebelwirkung, *die*
**levity** ['levɪtɪ] *n. (frivolity)* Unernst, *der*
**levy** ['levɪ] **1.** *n. (tax)* Steuer, *die.* **2.** *v. t.*
  erheben
**lewd** [ljuːd] geil; anzüglich ⟨*Geste*⟩;
  schlüpfrig ⟨*Witz*⟩
**liability** [laɪə'bɪlɪtɪ] *n.* **a)** Haftung, *die;*
  **b)** *(handicap)* Belastung, *die* **(to** für)
**liable** ['laɪəbl] *pred. adj.* **a)** *(legally
  bound)* **be ~ for sth.** für etw. haftbar
  sein *od.* haften; **b)** *(prone)* **be ~ to sth.**
  ⟨*Person:*⟩ zu etw. neigen; **be ~ to do**
  **sth.** ⟨*Sache:*⟩ leicht etw. tun; ⟨*Person:*⟩
  dazu neigen, etw. zu tun
**liaise** [lɪ'eɪz] *v. i. (coll.)* eine Verbindung herstellen; **~ on a project** bei einem Projekt zusammenarbeiten. **li-
  aison** [lɪ'eɪzɒn] *n. (co-operation)* Zusammenarbeit, *die*
**liar** ['laɪə(r)] *n.* Lügner, *der*/Lügnerin,
  *die*
**libel** ['laɪbl] **1.** *n.* Verleumdung, *die.* **2.**
  *v. t., (Brit.)* -ll- verleumden. **libellous**
  *(Amer.:* **libelous)** ['laɪbələs] *adj.* verleumderisch
**liberal** ['lɪbərl] **1.** *adj.* **a)** großzügig; **b)**
  *(Polit.)* liberal; **the L~ Democrats**
  *(Brit.)* die Liberaldemokraten. **2.** *n.*
  **L~** *(Polit.)* Liberale, *der/die*
**liberate** ['lɪbəreɪt] *v. t.* befreien **(from**
  aus). **liberation** [lɪbə'reɪʃn] *n.* Befreiung, *die.* **liberator** ['lɪbəreɪtə(r)] *n.*
  Befreier, *der*/Befreierin, *die*

**liberty** ['lɪbətɪ] *n.* Freiheit, *die;* **take the ~ of doing sth.** sich *(Dat.)* die Freiheit nehmen, etw. zu tun; **take liberties with sb.** sich *(Dat.)* Freiheiten gegen jmdn. herausnehmen *(ugs.)*
**Libra** ['li:brə] *n.* Waage, *die*
**librarian** [laɪ'breərɪən] *n.* Bibliothekar, *der/*Bibliothekarin, *die*
**library** ['laɪbrərɪ] *n.* Bibliothek, *die;* **public ~:** öffentliche Bücherei. **'library book** *n.* Buch aus der Bibliothek
**Libya** ['lɪbɪə] *pr. n.* Libyen *(das)*
**lice** *pl. of* **louse**
**licence** ['laɪsəns] **1.** *n.* [behördliche] Genehmigung; Lizenz, *die;* |driving-| ~**:** Führerschein, *der.* **2.** *v. t. see* **license 1**
**license** ['laɪsəns] **1.** *v. t.* ermächtigen; **get a car ~d** ≈ die Kfz-Steuer für ein Auto bezahlen. **2.** *n. (Amer.) see* **licence 1**
**licentious** [laɪ'senʃəs] *adj.* zügellos ⟨*Person*⟩; unzüchtig ⟨*Benehmen*⟩
**lichen** ['laɪkn, 'lɪtʃn] *n.* Flechte, *die*
**lick** [lɪk] **1.** *v. t.* **a)** lecken; **b)** *(sl.: beat)* verdreschen *(ugs.).* **2.** *n.* Lecken, *das.* **lick 'off** *v. t.* ablecken
**lid** [lɪd] *n.* **a)** Deckel, *der;* **b)** *(eyelid)* Lid, *das*
**lido** ['li:dəʊ] *n., pl.* ~s Freibad, *das*
**¹lie** [laɪ] **1.** *n.* Lüge, *die;* **tell ~s/a ~:** lügen. **2.** *v. i.,* lying ['laɪɪŋ] lügen; **~ to sb.** jmdn. be- *od.* anlügen
**²lie** *v. i.,* lying ['laɪɪŋ], lay [leɪ], lain [leɪn] **a)** liegen; *(assume horizontal position)* sich legen; **b) ~ idle** ⟨*Maschine, Fabrik:*⟩ stillstehen. **lie a'bout, lie a'round** *v. i.* herumliegen *(ugs.).* **lie 'back** *v. i.* sich zurücklegen; *(sitting)* sich zurücklehnen. **lie 'down** *v. i.* sich hinlegen
**lie-detector** ['laɪdɪˌtektə(r)] *n.* Lügendetektor, *der*
**'lie-in** *n. (coll.)* **have a ~:** [sich] ausschlafen
**lieu** [lju:] *n.* **in ~ of sth.** anstelle einer Sache *(Gen.);* **get holiday in ~:** statt dessen Urlaub bekommen
**lieutenant** [lef'tenənt] *n. (Army)* Oberleutnant, *der*
**life** [laɪf] *n., pl.* **lives** [laɪvz] Leben, *das;* **for ~:** lebenslänglich ⟨*inhaftiert*⟩; **true to ~:** wahrheitsgetreu
**life:** ~**belt** *n.* Rettungsring, *der;* ~**boat** *n.* Rettungsboot, *das;* ~**buoy** *n.* Rettungsring, *der;* ~ **cycle** *n.* Lebenszyklus, *der;* ~**guard** *n.* Rettungsschwimmer, *der/*-schwimmerin,

*die;* ~**-insurance** *n.* Lebensversicherung, *die;* ~**-jacket** *n.* Schwimmweste, *die;* ~**less** *adj.* leblos; *(fig.)* farblos; ~**like** *adj.* lebensecht; ~**line** *n.* Rettungsleine, *die;* *(fig.)* Rettungsanker, *der;* ~**long** *adj.* lebenslang; ~**-saving** *n.* Rettungsschwimmen, *das; attrib.* Rettungs-; ~ **sentence** *n.* lebenslängliche Freiheitsstrafe; ~**-size,** ~**-sized** *adj.* lebensgroß; **in** Lebensgröße *nachgestellt;* ~**-style** *n.* Lebensstil, *der;* ~**time** *n.* Lebenszeit, *die;* **during my ~time** während meines Lebens; **the chance of a ~time** eine einmalige Gelegenheit
**lift** [lɪft] **1.** *v. t.* heben; *(fig.)* erheben ⟨*Gemüt, Geist*⟩. **2.** *n.* **a)** *(in vehicle)* **get a ~:** mitgenommen werden; **give sb. a ~:** jmdn. mitnehmen; **b)** *(Brit.: elevator)* Aufzug, *der.* **3.** *v. i.* ⟨*Nebel:*⟩ sich auflösen. **'lift off** *v. t. & i.* abheben. **lift 'up** *v. t.* hochheben; heben ⟨*Kopf*⟩
**'lift-off** *n.* Abheben, *das*
**ligament** ['lɪgəmənt] *n.* Band, *das*
**¹light** [laɪt] **1.** *n.* **a)** Licht, *das;* **~ of day** Tageslicht, *das;* **b)** *(lamp)* Licht, *das;* *(fitting)* Lampe, *die;* **c)** *(signal to traffic)* Ampel, *die;* **d)** *(to ignite)* **have you got a ~?** haben Sie Feuer? **set ~ to sth.** etw. anzünden; **e)** **bring sth. to ~:** etw. ans [Tages]licht bringen; **throw** *or* **shed ~ |up|on sth.** Licht in etw. *(Akk.)* bringen; **f)** *(aspect)* **in that ~:** aus dieser Sicht; **seen in this ~:** so gesehen; **in the ~ of** angesichts (+ *Gen.*); **show sb. in a bad ~:** ein schlechtes Licht auf jmdn. werfen. **2.** *adj.* hell; ~**-blue/-brown** *etc.* hellblau/-braun *usw.* **3.** *v. t.,* **lit** [lɪt] *or* **lighted a)** *(ignite)* anzünden; **b)** *(illuminate)* erhellen. **light 'up 1.** *v. i.* **a)** *(become lit)* erleuchtet werden; **b)** *(become bright)* aufleuchten (with *vor*). **2.** *v. t.* **a)** *(illuminate)* erleuchten; **b)** anzünden ⟨*Zigarette*⟩
**²light 1.** *adj.* leicht; *(mild)* mild ⟨*Strafe*⟩. **2.** *adv.* **travel ~:** mit wenig *od.* leichtem Gepäck reisen
**'light-bulb** *n.* Glühbirne, *die*
**'lighted** *adj.* brennend ⟨*Kerze, Zigarette*⟩; angezündet ⟨*Streichholz*⟩
**¹lighten** ['laɪtn] *v. t. (make less heavy, difficult)* leichter machen
**²lighten 1.** *v. t. (make brighter)* aufhellen; heller machen ⟨*Raum*⟩. **2.** *v. i.* sich aufhellen
**'lighter** *n.* Feuerzeug, *das*
**light:** ~-'**headed** *adj.* leicht benommen; ~-'**hearted** *adj.* **a)** *(humorous)* unbeschwert; **b)** *(optimistic)* unbe-

kümmert; ~**house** *n.* Leuchtturm, *der*

'**lighting** *n.* Beleuchtung, *die*

'**lightly** *adv.* a) leicht; b) *(without serious consideration)* leichtfertig; c) *(cheerfully)* leichthin; **not treat sth.** ~: etw. nicht auf die leichte Schulter nehmen; d) **get off** ~: glimpflich davonkommen

¹**lightness** *n. (of weight; also fig.)* Leichtigkeit, *die*

²**lightness** *n. (of colour)* Helligkeit, *die*

**lightning** ['laɪtnɪŋ] *n.* Blitz, *der;* **flash of** ~: Blitz, *der.* '**lightning-conductor** *n.* Blitzableiter, *der*

'**lightweight** 1. *adj.* leicht. 2. *n.* Leichtgewicht, *das*

¹**like** [laɪk] 1. *adj.* a) *(resembling)* wie; **your dress is** ~ **mine** dein Kleid ist so ähnlich wie meins; **in a case** ~ **that** in so einem Fall; **what is sb./sth.** ~? wie ist jmd./etw.?; b) *(characteristic of)* typisch für ⟨*dich, ihn usw.*⟩; c) *(similar)* ähnlich. 2. *prep. (in the manner of)* wie; [**just**] ~ **that** [einfach] so. 3. *n.* a) *(equal)* **his/her** ~: seines-/ihresgleichen; b) *(similar things)* **the** ~: so etwas; **and the** ~: und dergleichen

²**like** 1. *v. t. (be fond of, wish for)* mögen; ~ **vegetables** Gemüse mögen; **gern Gemüse essen;** ~ **doing sth.** etw. gern tun; **would you** ~ **a drink?** möchtest du etwas trinken?; **would you** ~ **me to do it?** möchtest du, daß ich es tue?; **how do you** ~ **it?** wie gefällt es dir?; **if you** ~ *expr. assent* wenn du willst. 2. *n., in pl.* ~**s and dislikes** Vorlieben und Abneigungen. **likeable** ['laɪkəbl] *adj.* nett; sympathisch

**likelihood** ['laɪklɪhʊd] *n.* Wahrscheinlichkeit, *die*

**likely** ['laɪklɪ] 1. *adj.* wahrscheinlich; **there are** ~ **to be** [**traffic**] **hold-ups** man muß mit [Verkehrs]staus rechnen; **they are** [**not**] ~ **to come** sie werden wahrscheinlich [nicht] kommen; **is it** ~ **to rain tomorrow?** wird es morgen wohl regnen?; **this is not** ~ **to happen** es ist unwahrscheinlich, daß das geschieht. 2. *adv.* wahrscheinlich; **as** ~ **as not** höchstwahrscheinlich; **not** ~! *(coll.)* auf keinen Fall!

'**like-minded** *adj.* gleichgesinnt

**liken** ['laɪkn] *v. t.* ~ **sth./sb. to sth./sb.** etw./jmdn. mit etw./jmdm. vergleichen

'**likeness** *n.* Ähnlichkeit, *die* (to mit)

**likewise** ['laɪkwaɪz] *adv.* ebenso

**liking** ['laɪkɪŋ] *n.* Vorliebe, *die;* **take a** ~ **to sb./sth.** an jmdm./etw. Gefallen finden; **sth. is** [**not**] **to sb.'s** ~: etw. ist [nicht] nach jmds. Geschmack

**lilac** ['laɪlək] *n.* a) *(Bot.)* Flieder, *der;* b) *(colour)* Zartlila, *das*

**lily** ['lɪlɪ] *n.* Lilie, *die*

**limb** [lɪm] *n.* a) *(Anat.)* Glied, *das;* b) **be out on a** ~ *(fig.)* exponiert sein

**limber up** [lɪmbər 'ʌp] *v. i. (loosen up)* die Muskeln lockern

¹**lime** [laɪm] *n.* [**quick**]~: [ungelöschter] Kalk

²**lime** *n. (fruit)* Limone, *die*

³**lime** *see* lime-tree

'**limelight** *n.* **be in the** ~: im Rampenlicht [der Öffentlichkeit] stehen

**limerick** ['lɪmərɪk] *n.* Limerick, *der*

'**lime-tree** *n.* Linde, *die*

**limit** ['lɪmɪt] 1. *n.* a) Grenze, *die;* **set** *or* **put a** ~ **on sth.** etw. begrenzen; **be over the** ~ ⟨*Autofahrer:*⟩ zu viele Promille haben; **lower/upper** ~: Untergrenze/Höchstgrenze, *die;* **without** ~: unbegrenzt; **within** ~**s** inerhalb gewisser Grenzen; b) *(coll.)* **this is the** ~! das ist [doch] die Höhe!; **he/she is the** [**very**] ~: er/sie ist [einfach] unmöglich. 2. *v. t.* begrenzen (to auf + *Akk.*); einschränken ⟨*Freiheit*⟩. **limitation** [lɪmɪ'teɪʃn] *n.* Beschränkung, *die.* '**limited** *adj.* a) *(restricted)* begrenzt; b) *(intellectually narrow)* beschränkt. '**limitless** *adj.* grenzenlos

**limousine** ['lɪmʊziːn] *n.* Limousine, *die*

¹**limp** [lɪmp] 1. *v. i.* hinken. 2. *n.* Hinken, *das*

²**limp** *adj.* schlaff. '**limply** *adv.* schlaff; *(weakly)* schwach

**limpet** ['lɪmpɪt] *n. (Zool.)* Napfschnecke, *die*

**limpid** ['lɪmpɪd] *adj.* klar

**linctus** ['lɪŋktəs] *n.* Hustensaft, *der*

¹**line** [laɪn] 1. *n.* a) *(string, cord, rope, etc.)* Leine, *die;* b) *(telephone cable)* Leitung, *die;* c) *(long mark; also Math., Phys.)* Linie, *die;* d) *(row, series)* Reihe, *die;* e) *(Amer.: queue)* Schlange, *die;* **bring sb. into** ~: dafür sorgen, daß jmd. nicht aus der Reihe tanzt *(ugs.);* e) *(row of words on a page)* Zeile, *die;* f) *(wrinkle)* Falte, *die;* g) *(direction, course)* Richtung, *die;* **on the** ~**s of** nach Art (+ *Gen.*); **be on the right/wrong** ~**s** in die richtige/falsche Richtung gehen; **along** *or* **on the same** ~**s** in der gleichen Richtung; h) *(Railw.)* Bahnlinie, *die;* *(track)* Gleis, *das;* i) *(field of activity)*

Branche, *die;* **j)** *(Commerc.: product)* Artikel, *der;* Linie, *die (fachspr.).* **2.** *v. t.* **a)** linieren ⟨*Papier*⟩; **a ~d face** ein faltiges Gesicht; **b)** säumen *(geh.)* ⟨*Straße, Strecke*⟩. **line 'up 1.** *v. t.* antreten lassen ⟨*Gefangene, Soldaten usw.*⟩; [in einer Reihe] aufstellen ⟨*Gegenstände*⟩. **2.** *v. i.* ⟨*Gefangene, Soldaten:*⟩ antreten; *(queue up)* sich anstellen

²**line** *v. t.* füttern ⟨*Kleidungsstück*⟩; ausschlagen ⟨*Schublade usw.*⟩

**lineage** ['lɪnɪɪdʒ] *n.* Abstammung, *die*

**linear** ['lɪnɪə(r)] *adj.* linear

**linen** ['lɪnɪn] **1.** *n.* **a)** Leinen, *das;* **b)** *(shirts, sheets, etc.)* Wäsche, *die.* **2.** *adj.* Leinen⟨*faden, -bluse*⟩; Lein⟨*tuch*⟩

**liner** ['laɪnə(r)] Linienschiff, *das*

**'line-up** *n.* Aufstellung, *die*

**linger** ['lɪŋgə(r)] *v. i.* verweilen *(geh.);* bleiben

**lingerie** ['læʒərɪ] *n.* [women's] ~: Damenunterwäsche, *die*

**lingo** ['lɪŋgəʊ] *n. (coll.)* Sprache, *die*

**linguist** ['lɪŋgwɪst] *n.* Sprachkundige, *der/die*

**linguistic** [lɪŋ'gwɪstɪk] *adj. (of ~s)* linguistisch; *(of language)* sprachlich. **linguistics** [lɪŋ'gwɪstɪks] *n.* Linguistik, *die*

**lining** ['laɪnɪŋ] *n. (of clothes)* Futter, *das; (of objects, machines, etc.)* Auskleidung, *die*

**link** [lɪŋk] **1.** *n.* **a)** *(of chain)* Glied, *das;* **b)** *(connection)* Verbindung, *die.* **2.** *v. t.* verbinden; ~ **arms** sich unterhaken. **link 'up** *v. t.* miteinander verbinden

**links** [lɪŋks] *n.* [golf] ~: Golfplatz, *der*

**lino** ['laɪnəʊ] *n., pl.* **~s** Linoleum, *das*

**linseed** ['lɪnsiːd] *n.* Leinsamen, *der.* **linseed 'oil** *n.* Leinöl, *das*

**lint** [lɪnt] *n.* Mull, *der*

**lintel** ['lɪntl] *n. (Archit.)* Sturz, *der*

**lion** ['laɪən] *n.* Löwe, *der.* **lioness** ['laɪənɪs] *n.* Löwin, *die*

**lip** [lɪp] *n.* **a)** Lippe, *die;* **lower/upper** ~: Unter-/Oberlippe, *die;* **b)** *(of cup)* [Gieß]rand, *der; (of jug)* Schnabel, *der:* **lip: ~-read** *v. i.* von den Lippen lesen; **~-reading** *n.* Lippenlesen, *das;* **~-service** *n.* **pay ~-service to sth.** ein Lippenbekenntnis zu etw. ablegen; **~stick** *n.* Lippenstift, *der*

**liquefy** ['lɪkwɪfaɪ] **1.** *v. t.* verflüssigen. **2.** *v. i.* sich verflüssigen

**liqueur** [lɪ'kjʊə(r)] *n.* Likör, *der*

**liquid** ['lɪkwɪd] **1.** *adj.* flüssig. **2.** *n.* Flüssigkeit, *die*

**liquidate** ['lɪkwɪdeɪt] *v. t. (Commerc.)* liquidieren. **liquidation** [lɪkwɪ'deɪʃn] *n. (Commerc.)* Liquidation, *die*

**liquidize** ['lɪkwɪdaɪz] *v. t.* auflösen; *(Cookery)* [im Mixer] pürieren. **'liquidizer** *n.* Mixer, *der*

**liquor** ['lɪkə(r)] *n. (drink)* Alkohol, *der*

**liquorice** ['lɪkərɪs] *n.* Lakritze, *die*

**Lisbon** ['lɪzbən] *pr. n.* Lissabon *(das)*

**lisp** [lɪsp] **1.** *v. i. & t.* lispeln. **2.** *n.* Lispeln, *das*

¹**list** [lɪst] **1.** *n.* Liste, *die.* **2.** *v. t.* aufführen; auflisten; *(verbally)* aufzählen

²**list** *v. i. (Naut.)* Schlagseite haben

**listen** ['lɪsn] *v. i.* zuhören; ~ **to music/the radio** Musik/Radio hören; **they ~ed to his words** sie hörten ihm zu. **listener** ['lɪsnə(r)] *n.* Zuhörer, *der/*Zuhörerin, *die; (to radio)* Hörer, *der/*Hörerin, *die*

**listless** ['lɪstlɪs] *adj.* lustlos

**lit** *see* ¹**light 3**

**litany** ['lɪtənɪ] *n.* Litanei, *die*

**liter** *(Amer.) see* **litre**

**literacy** ['lɪtərəsɪ] *n.* Lese- und Schreibfertigkeit, *die*

**literal** ['lɪtərl] *adj.* **a)** wörtlich; **b)** *(not exaggerated)* buchstäblich. **literally** ['lɪtərəlɪ] *adv.* **a)** wörtlich; **b)** *(actually)* buchstäblich; **c)** *(coll.: with some exaggeration)* geradezu

**literary** ['lɪtərərɪ] *adj.* literarisch

**literate** ['lɪtərət] *adj.* des Lesens und Schreibens kundig; *(educated)* gebildet

**literature** ['lɪtrətʃə(r)] *n.* Literatur, *die*

**lithe** [laɪð] *adj.* geschmeidig

**litigation** [lɪtɪ'geɪʃn] *n.* Rechtsstreit, *der*

**litre** ['liːtə(r)] *n. (Brit.)* Liter, *der od. das*

**litter** ['lɪtə(r)] **1.** *n.* **a)** *(rubbish)* Abfall, *der;* **b)** *(of animals)* Wurf, *der.* **2.** *v. t.* verstreuen. **'litter-basket** *n.* Abfallkorb, *der.* **'litter-bin** Abfalleimer, *der*

**little** ['lɪtl] **1.** *adj.,* ~**r** ['lɪtlə(r)], ~**st** ['lɪtlɪst] (*Note: it is more common to use the compar. and superl. forms* **smaller, smallest**) **a)** klein; **a ~ way** ein kurzes Stück; **after a ~ while** nach kurzer Zeit; **b)** *(not much)* wenig; **there is very ~ tea left** es ist kaum noch Tee da; **a ~ ...** *(a small quantity of)* etwas ...; ein bißchen ... **2.** *n.* wenig; **a ~** *(a small quantity)* etwas; *(somewhat)* ein wenig; ~ **by** ~: nach und nach

**liturgy** ['lɪtədʒɪ] *n.* Liturgie, *die*

¹**live** [laɪv] **1.** *adj.* **a)** *attrib. (alive)* lebend; **b)** *(Radio, Telev.)* ~ **performance** Live-Aufführung, *die;* ~ **broad-**

cast Live-Sendung, *die;* c) *(Electr.)* stromführend. **2.** *adv. (Radio, Telev.)* live *⟨übertragen usw.⟩*

²**live** [lɪv] **1.** *v. i.* a) leben; b) *(make permanent home)* wohnen; leben. **2.** *v. t.* leben. **live 'down** *v. t.* Gras wachsen lassen über (+ *Akk.*); **he will never be able to ~ it down** das wird ihm ewig anhängen. **live on 1.** ['--] *v. t.* leben von. **2.** [-'-] *v. i.* weiterleben. **live 'up to** *v. t.* gerecht werden (+ *Dat.*)

**livelihood** ['laɪvlɪhʊd] *n.* Lebensunterhalt, *der*

**liveliness** ['laɪvlɪnɪs] *n.* Lebhaftigkeit, *die*

**lively** ['laɪvlɪ] *adj.* lebhaft; lebendig *⟨Schilderung⟩;* rege *⟨Handel⟩*

**liven up** [laɪvn 'ʌp] **1.** *v. t.* Leben bringen in (+ *Akk.*). **2.** *v. i.* *⟨Person:⟩* aufleben

**liver** ['lɪvə(r)] *n.* Leber, *die*

**livery** ['lɪvərɪ] *n.* Livree, *die*

**lives** *pl. of* **life**

**livestock** ['laɪvstɒk] *n. pl.* Vieh, *das*

**livid** ['lɪvɪd] *adj. (Brit. coll.)* fuchtig *(ugs.)*

**living** ['lɪvɪŋ] **1.** *n.* a) Leben, *das;* b) **make a ~:** seinen Lebensunterhalt verdienen; c) **the ~:** die Lebenden. **2.** *adj.* lebend; **within ~ memory** seit Menschengedenken. **'living-room** *n.* Wohnzimmer, *das*

**lizard** ['lɪzəd] *n.* Eidechse, *die*

**llama** ['lɑːmə] *n.* Lama, *das*

**load** [ləʊd] **1.** *n. (burden, weight; also fig.)* Last, *die; (amount carried)* Ladung, *die.* **2.** *v. t.* a) *(put ~ on)* beladen; *(put as load)* **~ sb. with work** *(fig.)* jmdm. Arbeit auftragen; b) laden *⟨Gewehr⟩;* **~ a camera** einen Film [in einen Fotoapparat] einlegen. **load 'up** *v. i.* laden (**with** *Akk.*)

**'loaded** *adj.* **a ~ question** eine suggestive Frage; **be ~** *(sl.: rich)* [schwer] Kohle haben *(salopp)*

¹**loaf** [ləʊf] *n., pl.* **loaves** [ləʊvz] Brot, *das;* [Brot]laib, *der;* **a ~ of bread** ein Laib Brot

²**loaf** *v. i.* **~ round town/the house** in der Stadt/zu Hause herumlungern *(ugs.)*

**loan** [ləʊn] **1.** *n.* a) *(thing lent)* Leihgabe, *die;* **be out on ~:** ausgeliehen sein; **have sth. on ~** [from sb.] etw. [von jmdm.] geliehen haben; b) *(money lent)* Darlehen, *das.* **2.** *v. t.* **~ sth. to sb.** jmdm. etw. leihen

**loath** [ləʊθ] *pred. adj.* **be ~ to do sth.** etw. ungern tun

**loathe** [ləʊð] *v. t.* verabscheuen.

**loathing** ['ləʊðɪŋ] *n.* Abscheu, *der* (**of,** **for** vor + *Dat.*). **loathsome** ['ləʊðsəm] *adj.* abscheulich; widerlich

**loaves** *pl. of* ¹**loaf**

**lobby** ['lɒbɪ] *n.* a) *(pressure group)* Lobby, *die;* b) *(of hotel)* Eingangshalle, *die; (of theatre)* Foyer, *das*

**lobe** [ləʊb] *n. (ear~)* Ohrläppchen, *das*

**lobster** ['lɒbstə(r)] *n.* Hummer, *der*

**local** ['ləʊkl] **1.** *adj.* lokal *(bes. Zeitungsw.);* Kommunal*⟨wahl, -abgaben⟩; (of this area)* hiesig; *(of that area)* dortig; ortsansässig *⟨Firma, Familie⟩; ⟨Wein, Produkt, Spezialität⟩* [aus] der Gegend; **she's a ~ girl** sie ist von hier/dort. **2.** *n.* a) *(person)* Einheimische, *der/die;* b) *(Brit. coll.: pub)* [Stamm]kneipe, *die*

**local: ~ anaes'thetic** *n.* Lokalanästhetikum, *das;* **~ au'thority** *n.* *(Brit.)* Kommunalverwaltung, *die;* **~ call** *n. (Teleph.)* Ortsgespräch, *das;* **~ 'government** *n.* Kommunalverwaltung, *die*

**locality** [ləʊ'kælɪtɪ] *n.* Ort, *der*

**'locally** *adv.* im/am Ort

**locate** [ləʊ'keɪt] *v. t.* a) **be ~d** liegen; b) *(determine position of)* ausfindig machen. **location** [ləʊ'keɪʃn] *n.* a) Lage, *die;* b) *(Cinemat.)* **be on ~:** bei Außenaufnahmen sein

**loch** [lɒx, lɒk] *n. (Scot.)* See, *der*

¹**lock** [lɒk] *n. (of hair)* [Haar]strähne, *die*

²**lock 1.** *n.* a) *(of door etc.)* Schloß, *das;* b) *(on canal etc.)* Schleuse, *die.* **2.** *v. t.* zuschließen. **3.** *v. i.* *⟨Tür, Kasten usw.:⟩* sich zuschließen lassen. **lock a'way** *v. t.* einschließen; einsperren *⟨Person⟩.* **lock 'in** *v. t.* einschließen; *(deliberately)* einsperren. **lock 'out** *v. t.* aussperren (**of** aus); **~ oneself out** sich aussperren. **lock 'up 1.** *v. i.* abschließen. **2.** *v. t.* a) abschließen *⟨Haus, Tür⟩;* b) *(imprison)* einsperren

**locker** ['lɒkə(r)] *n.* Schließfach, *das*

**locket** ['lɒkɪt] *n.* Medaillon, *das*

**lock: ~-jaw** *n. (Med.)* Kieferklemme, *die;* **~-out** *n.* Aussperrung, *die;* **~smith** *n.* Schlosser, *der*

**locomotive** [ləʊkə'məʊtɪv] *n.* Lokomotive, *die*

**locust** ['ləʊkəst] *n.* Heuschrecke, *die*

**lodge** [lɒdʒ] **1.** *n.* a) *(cottage)* Pförtner-/Gärtnerhaus, *das;* b) *(porter's room)* [Pförtner]loge, *die.* **2.** *v. t.* a) einlegen *⟨Beschwerde, Protest usw.⟩;* b) einreichen *⟨Klage⟩.* **3.** *v. i.* [zur Miete] wohnen. **'lodger** *n.* Untermieter,

*der*/Untermieterin, *die*. **lodging** ['lɒdʒɪŋ] *n*. [möbliertes] Zimmer
**loft** [lɒft] *n. (attic)* [Dach]boden, *der*
**lofty** ['lɒftɪ] *adj*. **a)** *(exalted)* hoch; **b)** *(haughty)* hochmütig
**log** [lɒg] *n*. **a)** *(timber)* [geschlagener] Baumstamm; *(as firewood)* [Holz]scheit, *das;* **b)** ~|-book| *(Naut.)* Logbuch, *das*. **log 'cabin** *n*. Blockhütte, *die*. **log-'fire** *n*. Holzfeuer, *das*
**loggerheads** ['lɒgəhedz] *n. pl*. **be at** ~ **with sb**. mit jmdm. im Clinch liegen
**logic** ['lɒdʒɪk] *n*. Logik, *die*. **logical** ['lɒdʒɪkl] *adj*. logisch; **she has a** ~ **mind** sie denkt logisch. **logically** ['lɒdʒɪkəlɪ] *adv*. logisch
**logo** ['ləʊgəʊ] *n., pl*. ~s Signet, *das*
**loin** [lɔɪn] *n*. Lende, *die*. **'loincloth** *n*. Lendenschurz, *der*
**loiter** ['lɔɪtə(r)] *v. i*. trödeln; *(linger suspiciously)* herumlungern
**loll** [lɒl] *v. i*. sich lümmeln *(ugs.)*
**lollipop** ['lɒlɪpɒp] *n*. Lutscher, *der*
**London** ['lʌndən] **1.** *pr. n*. London *(das)*. **2.** *attrib. adj*. Londoner. **'Londoner** *pr. n*. Londoner, *der*/Londonerin, *die*
**lone** [ləʊn] *attrib. adj*. einsam. **loneliness** ['ləʊnlɪnɪs] *n*. Einsamkeit, *die*
**lonely** ['ləʊnlɪ] *adj*. einsam
**loner** ['ləʊnə(r)] *n*. Einzelgänger, *der*/-gängerin, *die*
**lonesome** ['ləʊnsəm] *adj*. einsam
**¹long** [lɒŋ] **1.** *adj.,* ~**er** ['lɒŋgə(r)], ~**est** ['lɒŋgɪst] **a)** lang; weit ⟨*Reise, Weg*⟩; **b)** *(elongated)* länglich; schmal; **c) in the** '~ **run** auf die Dauer. **2.** *n*. (~ *interval)* **take** ~: lange dauern; **for** ~: lange; *(since* ~ *ago)* seit langem; **before** ~: bald. **3.** *adv.,* ~**er,** ~**est a)** lang[e]; **as or so** ~ **as** solange; **you should have finished** ~ **before now** du hättest schon längst fertig sein sollen; **much** ~**er** viel länger; **b) as** *or* **so** ~ **as** *(provided that)* solange; wenn
**²long** *v. i*. ~ **for sb./sth**. sich nach jmdm./etw. sehnen; ~ **to do sth**. sich danach sehnen, etw. zu tun
**long-distance 1.** ['---] *adj*. Fern⟨*gespräch, -verkehr usw.*⟩; Langstrecken⟨*läufer, -flug usw.*⟩. **2.** [-'--] *adv*. **phone** ~: ein Ferngespräch führen
**longevity** [lɒn'dʒevɪtɪ] *n*. Langlebigkeit, *die*
**'longhand** *n*. Langschrift, *die*
**'longing 1.** *n*. Sehnsucht, *die*. **2.** *adj*. sehnsüchtig. **'longingly** *adv*. sehnsüchtig
**longitude** ['lɒŋgɪtju:d] *n*. Länge, *die*

**long:** ~ **jump** *n. (Brit. Sport)* Weitsprung, *der;* ~**-lived** ['lɒŋlɪvd] *adj*. langlebig; ~**-playing 'record** *n*. Langspielplatte, *die;* ~**-range** *adj*. **a)** Langstrecken⟨*flugzeug, -rakete usw.*⟩; **b)** *(relating to time)* langfristig; ~**-sighted** [lɒŋ'saɪtɪd] *adj*. weitsichtig; *(fig.)* weitblickend; ~**-sleeved** ['lɒŋsli:vd] *adj*. langärmelig; ~**-standing** *attrib. adj*. seit langem bestehend; alt ⟨*Schulden, Streit*⟩; ~**-suffering** *adj*. schwer geprüft; ~**-term** *adj*. langfristig; ~ **wave** *n. (Radio)* Langwelle, *die;* ~**-winded** [lɒŋ'wɪndɪd] *adj*. langatmig
**loo** [lu:] *n. (Brit. coll.)* Klo, *das (ugs.)*
**look** [lʊk] **1.** *v. i*. **a)** sehen; gucken *(ugs.);* **b)** *(search)* nachsehen; **c)** *(face)* zugewandt sein (**to**|**wards** *Dat.*); **d)** *(appear)* aussehen; ~ **well/ill** gut/schlecht aussehen. **2.** *n*. **a)** Blick, *der;* **have** *or* **take a** ~ **at sb./sth**. *(Dat.)* jmdn./etw. ansehen; **b)** *(appearance)* Aussehen, *das*. **look 'after** *v. t. (care for)* sorgen für. **look a'head** *v. i. (fig.)* an die Zukunft denken. **'look at** *v. t*. **a)** *(regard)* ansehen; **b)** *(consider)* betrachten. **look 'back** *v. i*. **a)** sich umsehen; **b)** ~ **back on** *or* **to sth**. an etw. *(Akk.)* zurückdenken. **look 'down** [**up**]**on** *v. t*. **a)** herunter-/hinuntersehen auf (+ *Akk.*); **b)** *(fig.: despise)* herabsehen auf (+ *Akk.*). **'look for** *v. t*. **a)** *(seek)* suchen nach; **b)** *(expect)* erwarten. **look 'out** *v. i*. **a)** hinaus-/heraussehen (**of** aus); **b)** *(take care)* aufpassen; **c)** ~ **out on sth**. ⟨*Zimmer, Wohnung usw.*⟩ zu etw. hin liegen. **look 'out for** *v. t. (be prepared for)* achten auf (+ *Akk.*); *(keep watching for)* Ausschau halten nach ⟨*Arbeit, Gelegenheit, Sammelobjekt usw.*⟩. **look 'over** *v. t*. **a)** sehen über (+ *Akk.*); **b)** *(survey)* sich *(Dat.)* ansehen ⟨*Haus*⟩. **look 'round** *v. i*. sich umsehen. **'look through** *v. t*. **a)** ~ **through sth**. durch etw. [hindurch] sehen; **b)** *(inspect)* durchsehen ⟨*Papiere*⟩. **'look to** *v. t. (rely on)* ~ **to sb./sth. for sth**. etw. von jmdm./etw. erwarten. **look 'up 1.** *v. i*. **a)** aufblicken; **b)** *(improve)* besser werden. **2.** *v. t*. nachschlagen ⟨*Wort*⟩; heraussuchen ⟨*Telefonnummer, Zugverbindung usw.*⟩. **look 'up to** *v. t*. ~ **up to sb**. zu jmdm. aufsehen
**'look-alike** *n*. Doppelgänger, *der*/-gängerin, *die*
**looker-'on** *n*. Zuschauer, *der*/Zuschauerin, *die*

'**looking-glass** n. Spiegel, *der*

'**look-out** n., pl. ~s a) *(observation post)* Ausguck, *der;* b) *(person)* Wache, *die;* c) *(Brit. fig.)* that's a bad ~: das sind schlechte Aussichten; that's his ~: das ist sein Problem; d) keep a ~ |for sb./sth.| [nach etw./jmdm.] Ausschau halten

¹**loom** [lu:m] n. *(Weaving)* Webstuhl, *der*

²**loom** v. i. auftauchen

**loop** [lu:p] 1. n. a) Schleife, *die;* b) *(cord)* Schlaufe, *die.* 2. v. t. zu einer Schlaufe formen. '**loophole** n. *(fig.)* Lücke, *die*

**loose** [lu:s] adj. a) *(not firm)* locker ⟨Zahn, Schraube, Knopf⟩; b) *(not fixed)* lose ⟨Knopf, Buchseite, Brett, Stein⟩; offen ⟨Haar⟩; c) be at a ~ end *(fig.)* nichts zu tun haben; d) *(inexact)* ungenau. '**loose-fitting** adj. bequem geschnitten. '**loose-leaf** adj. Loseblatt-; ~ file Ringbuch, *das*

'**loosely** adv. locker; lose ⟨zusammenhängen⟩; frei ⟨übersetzen⟩

**loosen** ['lu:sn] v. t. lockern. **loosen 'up** v. i. sich auflockern; *(relax)* auftauen

'**looseness** n. Lockerheit, *die*

**loot** [lu:t] 1. v. t. plündern. 2. n. Beute, *die.* '**looter** n. Plünderer, *der*

**lop** [lɒp] v. t. ~ sth. |off or away| etw. abbauen *od.* abhacken

**lopsided** [lɒp'saɪdɪd] adj. schief

**lord** [lɔ:d] 1. n. a) *(master)* Herr, *der;* L~ *(Relig.)* Herr, *der;* c) *(Brit.: as title)* Lord, *der;* the House of L~s *(Brit.)* das Oberhaus. 2. int. *(coll.)* Gott; oh/good L~! du lieber Himmel! '**lordship** n. Lordschaft, *die*

**lore** [lɔ:(r)] n. Überlieferung, *die*

**lorry** ['lɒrɪ] n. *(Brit.)* Lastwagen, *der;* Lkw, *der.* '**lorry-driver** n. *(Brit.)* Lastwagenfahrer, *der;* Lkw-Fahrer, *der*

**lose** [lu:z] 1. v. t., lost [lɒst] a) verlieren; ~ one's way sich verlaufen/verfahren; b) ⟨Uhr:⟩ nachgehen; c) *(waste)* vertun ⟨Zeit⟩; *(miss)* versäumen ⟨Gelegenheit⟩; d) ~ weight abnehmen. 2. v. i., lost a) *(in match, contest)* verlieren; b) ⟨Uhr:⟩ nachgehen. '**loser** n. Verlierer, *der*/Verliererin, *die*

**loss** [lɒs] n. a) Verlust, *der* (of *Gen.*); sell at a ~: mit Verlust verkaufen; b) be at a ~: nicht [mehr] weiterwissen; be at a ~ for words um Worte verlegen sein; be at a ~ what to do nicht wissen, was zu tun ist

**lost** [lɒst] 1. *see* lose. 2. adj. a) verloren; get ~ ⟨Person:⟩ sich verlaufen/verfahren; get ~! *(sl.)* verdufte! *(salopp);* ~ cause aussichtslose Sache; b) *(wasted)* vertan ⟨Zeit⟩; *(missed)* versäumt ⟨Gelegenheit⟩

**lot** [lɒt] n. a) *(destiny)* Los, *das;* b) *(set of persons)* Haufen, *der;* the ~: [sie] alle; c) *(set of things)* Menge, *die;* the ~: alle/alles; d) *(coll.: large quantity)* ~s or a ~ of money etc. viel *od.* eine Menge Geld *usw.;* sing etc. a ~: viel singen *usw.;* like sth. a ~: etw. sehr mögen; have ~s to do viel zu tun haben; e) *(for choosing)* Los, *das;* draw/cast/throw ~s |for sth.| um etw. losen

**lotion** ['ləʊʃn] n. Lotion, *die*

**lottery** ['lɒtərɪ] n. Lotterie, *die*

**loud** [laʊd] 1. adj. a) laut; lautstark ⟨Protest, Kritik⟩; b) *(flashy, conspicuous)* aufdringlich; grell ⟨Farbe⟩. 2. adv. laut; laugh out ~: laut auflachen; say sth. out ~: etw. aussprechen. **loud 'hailer** n. Megaphon, *das*

'**loudly** adv. laut

'**loudness** n. Lautstärke, *die*

**loud'speaker** n. Lautsprecher, *der*

**lounge** [laʊndʒ] 1. v. i. ~ |about or around| [faul] herumliegen/-sitzen/ -stehen. 2. n. a) *(in hotel)* [Hotel]halle, *die;* *(at airport)* Wartehalle, *die;* b) *(sitting-room)* Wohnzimmer, *das*

**louse** [laʊs] n., pl. lice [laɪs] Laus, *die*

**lousy** ['laʊzɪ] adj. *(sl.)* a) *(disgusting)* ekelhaft; b) *(very poor)* lausig *(ugs.);* feel ~: sich mies *(ugs.)* fühlen

**lout** [laʊt] n. Rüpel, *der;* Flegel, *der*

**louver, louvre** ['lu:və(r)] n. ~ window Jalousiefenster, *das;* ~ door Jalousietür, *die*

**lovable** ['lʌvəbl] adj. liebenswert

**love** [lʌv] 1. n. a) Liebe, *die* (of, for zu); in ~ |with| verliebt [in (+ *Akk.*)]; fall in ~ |with| sich verlieben [in (+ *Akk.*)]; for ~: aus Liebe; ~ from Beth *(in letter)* herzliche Grüße von Beth; send one's ~ to sb. jmdn. grüßen lassen; b) *(sweetheart)* Geliebte, *der/ die;* |my| ~ *(coll.: form of address)* [mein] Liebling *od.* Schatz; c) *(Tennis)* fifteen/thirty ~: fünfzehn/dreißig null. 2. v. t. a) lieben; our/their ~d ones unsere/ihre Lieben; b) *(like)* I'd ~ a cigarette ich hätte sehr gerne eine Zigarette; ~ to do *or* ~ doing sth. etw. gern tun

**love:** ~ **affair** n. Liebesverhältnis, *das;* ~-**letter** n. Liebesbrief, *der;* ~-**life** n. Liebesleben, *das*

**loveliness** ['lʌvlɪnɪs] n. Schönheit, die
**lovely** ['lʌvlɪ] adj. [wunder]schön;
herrlich ⟨Tag, Essen⟩
**lover** ['lʌvə(r)] n. **a)** Liebhaber, der;
Geliebte, der; (woman) Geliebte, die;
**be ~s** ein Liebespaar sein; **b)** (person
who likes sth.) Freund, der/Freundin,
die
**love:** **~sick** adj. an Liebeskummer
leidend; liebeskrank (geh.); **~-song**
n. Liebeslied, das; **~-story** n. Liebesgeschichte, die
**loving** ['lʌvɪŋ] adj. **a)** (affectionate) liebend; **b)** (expressing love) liebevoll.
**'lovingly** adv. liebevoll
**low** [ləʊ] **1.** adj. **a)** niedrig; tief ausge-
schnitten ⟨Kleid⟩; tief ⟨Ausschnitt⟩;
tiefliegend ⟨Grund⟩; **b)** (of humble
rank) nieder...; niedrig; **c)** (inferior)
niedrig; gering ⟨Intelligenz, Bildung⟩;
**d)** (in pitch) tief; (in loudness) leise.
**2.** adv. **a)** (to a ~ position) tief; **b)** (not
loudly) leise; **c)** **lie ~** (hide) untertauchen. **'lowbrow** adj. (coll.) schlicht
⟨Person⟩; [geistig] anspruchslos ⟨Buch,
Programm⟩. **'low-cut** adj. [tief] aus-
geschnitten ⟨Kleid⟩
**¹lower** ['ləʊə(r)] v. t. **a)** herab-/hinab-
lassen; **b)** senken ⟨Blick⟩; auslassen
⟨Saum⟩; senken ⟨Preis, Miete, Zins
usw.⟩; **~ one's voice** leiser sprechen
**²lower 1.** compar. adj. unter...; Unter-
⟨grenze-, arm, -lippe usw.⟩. **2.** compar.
adv. tiefer
**low:** **~-fat** adj. fettarm; **~-grade**
adj. minderwertig; **~land** ['ləʊlənd]
n. Tiefland, das
**lowly** ['ləʊlɪ] adj. (modest) bescheiden
**low:** **~-lying** adj. tiefliegend; **~
point** n. Tiefpunkt, der; **~ pressure**
n. (Meteorol.) Tiefdruck, der
**loyal** ['lɔɪəl] adj. treu. **loyalty** ['lɔɪəltɪ]
n. Treue, die
**lozenge** ['lɒzɪndʒ] n. Pastille, die
**LP** abbr. **long-playing record** LP, die
**Ltd.** abbr. **Limited** GmbH
**lubricant** ['lu:brɪkənt] n. Schmiermit-
tel, das
**lubricate** ['lu:brɪkeɪt] v. t. schmieren.
**lubrication** [lu:brɪ'keɪʃn] n. Schmie-
rung, die; attrib. Schmier⟨system, -vor-
richtung⟩
**lucid** ['lu:sɪd] adj. klar. **lucidity** [lu:-
'sɪdɪtɪ] n. Klarheit, die
**luck** [lʌk] n. Glück, das; **good ~:**
Glück, das; **bad or hard ~:** Pech, das;
**good ~!** viel Glück!; **be in/out of ~:**
Glück/kein Glück haben; **no such ~:**
schön wär's. **luckily** ['lʌkɪlɪ] adv.

glücklicherweise. **lucky** ['lʌkɪ] adj. **a)**
glücklich; **be ~:** Glück haben; **b)**
(bringing good luck) Glücks⟨zahl, -tag
usw.⟩; **~ charm** Glücksbringer, der
**lucrative** ['lu:krətɪv] adj. einträglich;
lukrativ
**ludicrous** ['lu:dɪkrəs] adj. lächerlich;
lachhaft ⟨Angebot, Ausrede⟩
**lug** [lʌg] v. t., **-gg-** (drag) schleppen
**luggage** ['lʌgɪdʒ] n. Gepäck, das.
**'luggage-locker** n. [Gepäck]-
schließfach, das. **'luggage-rack** n.
Gepäckablage, die
**lugubrious** [lu:'gu:brɪəs] adj. (mournful) kummervoll; (dismal) düster
**lukewarm** ['lu:kwɔ:m] adj. lauwarm
**lull** [lʌl] **1.** v. t. **a)** (soothe) lullen; **b)**
(fig.) einlullen; **~ sb. into a false sense
of security** jmdn. in einer trügerischen
Sicherheit wiegen. **2.** n. Pause, die
**lullaby** ['lʌləbaɪ] n. Schlaflied, das
**lumbago** [lʌm'beɪgəʊ] n., pl. **~s**
(Med.) Hexenschuß, der
**lumber** ['lʌmbə(r)] **1.** n. **a)** (furniture)
Gerümpel, das; **b)** (useless material)
Kram, der (ugs.); **c)** (Amer.: timber)
[Bau]holz, das. **2.** v. t. **~ sb. with sth./
sb.** jmdm. etw./jmdn. aufhalsen (ugs.)
**'lumbering** adj. schwerfällig
**lumberjack** ['lʌmbədʒæk] n. (Amer.)
Holzfäller, der
**luminous** ['lu:mɪnəs] adj. [hell] leuchtend; Leucht⟨anzeige, -zeiger usw.⟩
**lump** [lʌmp] **1.** n. **a)** Klumpen, der; (of
sugar, butter, etc.) Stück, das; (of
wood) Klotz, der; (of dough) Kloß,
der; (of bread) Brocken, der; **b)** (swelling) Beule, die. **2.** v. t. **~ sth. with sth.**
etw. und etw. zusammentun. **lump
'sum** n. Pauschalsumme, die
**'lumpy** adj. klumpig ⟨Brei⟩; ⟨Kissen,
Matratze⟩ mit klumpiger Füllung
**lunacy** ['lu:nəsɪ] n. Wahnsinn, der
**lunar** ['lu:nə(r)] adj. Mond-
**lunatic** ['lu:nətɪk] **1.** adj. wahnsinnig.
**2.** n. Wahnsinnige, der/die; Irre, der/
die. **'lunatic asylum** n. (Hist.) Irren-
anstalt, die (veralt., ugs.)
**lunch** [lʌntʃ] **1.** n. Mittagessen, das;
**have or eat [one's] ~:** zu Mittag essen.
**2.** v. i. zu Mittag essen
**luncheon voucher** ['lʌntʃn vaʊtʃə(r)]
n. (Brit.) Essenmarke, die
**lunch:** **~-hour** n. Mittagspause, die;
**~-time** n. Mittagszeit, die; **at ~-time**
mittags
**lung** [lʌŋ] n. (right or left) Lungenflü-
gel, der; **~s** Lunge, die. **'lung cancer**
n. Lungenkrebs, der

**lunge** [lʌndʒ] **1.** *n.* Sprung nach vorn. **2.** *v. i.* ~ **at sb. with a knife** jmdn. mit einem Messer angreifen

**¹lurch** [lɜ:tʃ] *n.* **leave sb. in the** ~**:** jmdn. im Stich lassen

**²lurch 1.** *n.* Rucken, *das.* **2.** *v. i.* rucken; ⟨*Betrunkener:*⟩ torkeln

**lure** [ljʊə(r), lʊə(r)] **1.** *v. t.* locken. **2.** *n.* Lockmittel, *das*

**lurid** ['ljʊərɪd, 'lʊərɪd] *adj.* **a)** *(in colour)* grell; **b)** *(sensational)* reißerisch

**lurk** [lɜ:k] *v. i.* lauern

**luscious** ['lʌʃəs] *adj.* köstlich [süß]; saftig [süß] ⟨*Obst*⟩

**lush** [lʌʃ] *adj.* saftig ⟨*Wiese*⟩; grün ⟨*Tal*⟩; üppig ⟨*Vegetation*⟩

**lust** [lʌst] **1.** *n.* **a)** *(sexual)* Sinnenlust, *die;* **b)** *(strong desire)* Gier, *die* **(for** nach**). 2.** *v. i.* ~ **after** [lustvoll] begehren *(geh.).* **lustful** ['lʌstfl] *adj.* lüstern *(geh.)*

**lustily** ['lʌstɪlɪ] *adv.* kräftig; aus voller Kehle ⟨*rufen, singen*⟩

**lustre** ['lʌstə(r)] *n. (Brit.)* **a)** Schimmer, *der;* **b)** *(fig.: splendour)* Glanz, *der*

**lusty** ['lʌstɪ] *adj.* kräftig

**Luxembourg, Luxemburg** ['lʌksəmbɜ:g] *pr. n.* Luxemburg *(das)*

**luxuriant** [lʌg'zjʊərɪənt] *adj.* üppig

**luxuriate** [lʌg'zjʊərɪeɪt] *v. i.* ~ **in** sich aalen in (+ *Dat.*)

**luxurious** [lʌg'zjʊərɪəs] *adj.* luxuriös

**luxury** ['lʌkʃərɪ] *n.* **a)** Luxus, *der;* **b)** *(article)* Luxusgegenstand, *der;* **luxuries** Luxus, *der*

**LW** *abbr. (Radio)* **long wave** LW

**lying** ['laɪɪŋ] *adj.* verlogen ⟨*Person*⟩. *See also* ¹**lie 2**

**lynch** [lɪntʃ] *v. t.* lynchen

**lyric** ['lɪrɪk] **1.** *adj.* lyrisch; ~ **poetry** Lyrik, *die.* **2.** *n.* in pl. *(of song)* Text, *der.* **lyrical** ['lɪrɪkl] *adj.* **a)** lyrisch; **b)** *(coll.: enthusiastic)* gefühlvoll

# M

**M, m** [em] *n.* M, m, *das*

**m.** *abbr.* **a)** masculine m.; **b)** metre[s] m; **c)** million[s] Mill.; **d)** minute[s] Min.

**MA** *abbr.* **Master of Arts** M. A.

**mac** [mæk] *n. (Brit. coll.)* Regenmantel, *der*

**macaroni** [mækə'rəʊnɪ] *n.* Makkaroni *Pl.*

**machine** [mə'ʃi:n] *n.* Maschine, *die.* **ma'chine-gun** *n.* Maschinengewehr, *das*

**machinery** [mə'ʃi:nərɪ] *n.* **a)** *(machines)* Maschinen *Pl.;* **b)** *(mechanism)* Mechanismus, *der*

**machine:** ~ **tool** *n.* Werkzeugmaschine, *die;* ~-**washable** *adj.* waschmaschinenfest

**machinist** [mə'ʃi:nɪst] *n.* Maschinist, *der/*Maschinistin, *die;* |sewing-|~**:** [Maschinen]näherin, *die/*-näher, *der*

**macho** ['mætʃəʊ] *adj.* Macho-; **he is** ~**:** er ist ein Macho

**mackerel** ['mækərl] *n., pl. same or* ~**s** Makrele, *die*

**mackintosh** ['mækɪntɒʃ] *n.* Regenmantel, *der*

**mad** [mæd] *adj.* **a)** *(insane)* geisteskrank; **b)** *(frenzied)* wahnsinnig; **drive sb. mad** jmdn. um den Verstand bringen; **c)** *(foolish)* verrückt *(ugs.);* **d)** *(very enthusiastic)* **be** ~ **about** *or* **on sb./sth.** auf jmdn./etw. wild sein *(ugs.);* **e)** *(coll.: annoyed)* ~ |**with** *or* **at sb.**| sauer [auf jmdn.] *(ugs.);* **f)** *(with rabies)* toll[wütig]; |**run** *etc.*| **like** ~**:** wie wild [laufen *usw.*]

**madam** ['mædəm] *n.* gnädige Frau; **Dear M**~ *(in letter)* Sehr verehrte gnädige Frau

**madden** ['mædn] *v. t. (irritate)* [ver]ärgern. **maddening** ['mædənɪŋ] *adj. (irritating)* [äußerst] ärgerlich

**made** *see* **make 1**

'**madly** *adv. (coll.)* wahnsinnig *(ugs.)*

**madman** ['mædmən] *n., pl.* **madmen** ['mædmən] *n.* Wahnsinnige, *der*

'**madness** *n.* Wahnsinn, *der*

**magazine** [mægə'zi:n] *n.* **a)** Zeitschrift, *die;* **b)** *(of firearm)* Magazin, *das*

**maggot** ['mægət] *n.* Made, *die*

**magic** ['mædʒɪk] **1.** *n.* **a)** Magie, *die;* **work like** ~**:** wie ein Wunder wirken; **b)** *(conjuring)* Zauberei, *die.* **2.** *adj.* **a)** magisch; Zauber⟨*trank, -baum*⟩; **b)** *(fig.)* wunderbar. **magical** ['mædʒɪkl] *adj.* zauberhaft. **magician** [mə'dʒɪʃn] *n.* Magier, *der/*Magierin, *die; (conjurer)* Zauberer, *der/*Zauberin, *die*

**magistrate** ['mædʒɪstreɪt] *n.* Friedensrichter, *der/*-richterin, *die*

**magnanimity** [mægnə'nɪmɪtɪ] *n.* Großmut, *die*

**magnanimous** [mæg'nænɪməs] *adj.*
groẞmütig (**towards** gegen)

**magnate** ['mægneɪt] *n.* Magnat,
*der*/Magnatin, *die*

**magnesium** [mæg'ni:zɪəm] *n.* Magnesium, *das*

**magnet** ['mægnɪt] *n.* Magnet, *der.*
**magnetic** [mæg'netɪk] *adj.* magnetisch. **magnetic 'tape** *n.* Magnet-
band, *das*

**magnetism** ['mægnɪtɪzm] *n.* **a)** *(force,
lit. or fig.)* Magnetismus, *der;* **b)** *(fig.:
charm)* Anziehungskraft, *die*

**magnetize** ['mægnɪtaɪz] *v. t.* magneti-
sieren

**magnification** [mægnɪfɪ'keɪʃn] *n.*
Vergröẞerung, *die*

**magnificence** [mæg'nɪfɪsəns] *n.*
Pracht, *die; (beauty)* Herrlichkeit, *die;*
*(lavishness)* Üppigkeit, *die*

**magnificent** [mæg'nɪfɪsənt] *adj.* **a)**
prächtig; herrlich ⟨*Garten, Kunstwerk,
Wetter*⟩; *(lavish)* üppig ⟨*Mahl*⟩; **b)**
*(coll.: excellent)* fabelhaft *(ugs.)*

**magnify** ['mægnɪfaɪ] *v. t.* **a)** vergrö-
ẞern; **b)** *(exaggerate)* aufbauschen.
'**magnifying glass** *n.* Lupe, *die*

**magnitude** ['mægnɪtju:d] *n.* **a)** *(size)*
Gröẞe, *die;* **b)** *(importance)* Wichtigkeit, *die*

**magpie** ['mægpaɪ] *n.* Elster, *die*

**mahogany** [mə'hɒgənɪ] *n.* Mahagoni[holz], *das; attrib.* Mahagoni-

**maid** [meɪd] *n.* Dienstmädchen, *das*

**maiden** ['meɪdn] **1.** *n.* Jungfrau, *die.* **2.**
*adj.* **a)** *(unmarried)* unverheiratet; **b)**
*(first)* ~ **voyage/speech** Jungfernfahrt/
-rede, *die.* '**maiden name** *n.* Mäd-
chenname, *der*

**mail** [meɪl] **1.** *n. see* ²**post** 1. **2.** *v. t.* abschicken

**mail:** ~**bag** *n.* Postsack, *der;* ~**box** *n.*
*(Amer.)* Briefkasten, *der;* ~**ing list** *n.*
Adressenliste, *die;* ~**man** *n. (Amer.)*
Briefträger, *der;* ~ **order** *n.* Bestel-
lung per Post

**maim** [meɪm] *v. t.* verstümmeln

**main** [meɪn] **1.** *n.* **a)** *(channel, pipe)*
Hauptleitung, *die;* ~**s** *(Electr.)* Strom-
netz, *das;* **b) in the** ~: im groẞen und
ganzen. **2.** *attrib. adj.* Haupt-; **the** ~
**thing is that** ...: die Hauptsache ist,
daẞ ... **mainland** ['meɪnlənd] *n.* Festland, *das*

'**mainly** *adv.* hauptsächlich

**main:** ~**stay** *n.* [wichtigste] Stütze; ~
**street** [*Brit.* '-'-, *Amer.* '--] *n.* Haupt-
straẞe, *die*

**maintain** [meɪn'teɪn] *v. t.* **a)** *(keep up)*

aufrechterhalten; **b)** *(provide for)* ~ **sb.**
für jmds. Unterhalt aufkommen; **c)**
*(preserve)* instand halten; warten ⟨*Maschine*⟩; **d)** ~ **that** ...: behaupten,
daẞ ... **maintenance** ['meɪntənəns]
*n.* **a)** *(keeping up)* Aufrechterhaltung,
*die;* **b)** *(preservation)* Instandhaltung,
*die; (of machinery)* Wartung, *die;* **c)**
*(Law: money paid to support sb.)* Unterhalt, *der*

**maison[n]ette** [meɪzə'net] *n.* [zwei-
stöckige] Wohnung

**maize** [meɪz] *n.* Mais, *der*

**majestic** [mə'dʒestɪk] *adj.,* **majestically** [mə'dʒestɪkəlɪ] *adv.* majestätisch

**majesty** ['mædʒɪstɪ] *n.* Majestät, *die
(geh.);* **Your/Her** *etc.* **M~:** Eure/Seine
*usw.* Majestät

**major** ['meɪdʒə(r)] **1.** *adj.* **a)** *attrib.
(greater)* gröẞer...; **b)** *attrib. (important)* bedeutend...; *(serious)* schwer; ~
**road** Hauptverkehrsstraẞe, *die;* **C** ~:
*(Mus.)* Dur-; **C** ~: C-Dur. **2.** *n. (Mil.)*
Major, *der.* **3.** *v. i. (Amer. Univ.)* ~ **in**
**sth.** etw. als Hauptfach haben

**Majorca** [mə'jɔ:kə] *pr. n.* Mallorca
*(das)*

**majority** [mə'dʒɒrɪtɪ] *n.* Mehrheit,
*die;* **be in the** ~: in der Mehrzahl sein

**make** [meɪk] **1.** *v. t.,* **made** [meɪd] **a)**
machen (of aus); bauen ⟨*Straẞe,
Flugzeug*⟩; anlegen ⟨*Teich, Weg usw.*⟩;
zimmern ⟨*Tisch, Regal*⟩; basteln
⟨*Spielzeug, Vogelhäuschen usw.*⟩; nähen ⟨*Kleider*⟩; *(manufacture)* herstellen; *(prepare)* zubereiten ⟨*Mahlzeit*⟩;
machen, kochen ⟨*Kaffee, Tee*⟩;
backen ⟨*Brot, Kuchen*⟩; **b)** *(establish,
enact)* treffen ⟨*Unterscheidung, Über-
einkommen*⟩; ziehen ⟨*Vergleich*⟩; erlassen ⟨*Gesetz*⟩; aufstellen ⟨*Regeln,
Behauptung*⟩; stellen ⟨*Forderung*⟩; geben ⟨*Bericht*⟩; vornehmen ⟨*Zahlung*⟩;
erheben ⟨*Protest, Beschwerde*⟩; **c)**
*(cause to be or become)* ~ **happy/
known** *etc.* glücklich/bekannt *usw.*
machen; ~ **sb. captain** jmdn. zum Kapitän machen; **d)** ~ **sb. do sth.** *(cause)*
jmdn. dazu bringen, etw. zu tun;
*(compel)* jmdn. zwingen, etw. zu tun;
**be made to do sth.** etw. tun müssen; **e)**
*(earn)* machen ⟨*Profit, Verlust*⟩; verdienen ⟨*Lebensunterhalt*⟩; **f) what do
you** ~ **of him?** was hältst du von ihm?;
**g)** *(arrive at)* erreichen; **make it** *(succeed in arriving)* es schaffen; **h)** ~ '**do
with/without sth.** mit/ohne etw. auskommen. **2.** *n.*

*(brand)* Marke, *die.* 'make for *v. t.*
zusteuern auf (+ *Akk.*). make 'off
*v. i.* sich davonmachen. make 'off
with *v. t.* ~ off with sb./sth. sich mit
jmdm./etw. [auf und] davonmachen.
make 'out 1. *v. t.* a) *(write)* ausstellen; b) *(claim)* behaupten; c) *(manage
to see or hear)* ausmachen; *(manage to
read)* entziffern; d) *(pretend)* vorgeben. 2. *v. i. (coll.)* zurechtkommen (at
bei). make 'over *v. t.* überschreiben.
make 'up 1. *v. t.* a) *(assemble)* zusammenstellen; b) *(invent)* erfinden; c)
*(constitute)* bilden; be made up of ...:
bestehen aus ...; d) *(apply cosmetics to)*
schminken; ~ up one's face sich
schminken. 2. *v. i. (be reconciled)* sich
wieder vertragen. make 'up for *v. t.*
wiedergutmachen; ~ up for lost time
Versäumtes nachholen
'make-believe 1. *n.* it's only ~: das
ist bloß Phantasie. 2. *adj.* nicht echt
'maker *n. (manufacturer)* Hersteller,
*der*
make: ~shift *adj.* behelfsmäßig;
~-up *n. (Cosmetics)* Make-up, *das*
making ['meɪkɪŋ] *n.* in the ~: im Entstehen; have the ~s of a leader das
Zeug zum Führer haben *(ugs.)*
maladjusted [mælə'dʒʌstɪd] *adj.* ver-
haltensgestört
malady ['mælədɪ] *n.* Leiden, *das*
malaise [mə'leɪz] *n.* Unbehagen, *das*
malaria [mə'leərɪə] *n.* Malaria, *die*
Malaysia [mə'leɪzɪə] *pr. n.* Malaysia
*(das)*
male [meɪl] 1. *adj.* männlich; Männer-
⟨*stimme, -chor, -verein*⟩; ~ doctor/
nurse Arzt, *der*/Krankenpfleger, *der.*
2. *n. (person)* Mann, *der; (animal)*
Männchen, *das*
malevolence [mə'levələns] *n.* Boshaftigkeit, *die*
malevolent [mə'levələnt] *adj.* boshaft
malfunction [mæl'fʌŋkʃn] 1. *n.* Störung, *die; (Med.)* Funktionsstörung,
*die.* 2. *v. i.* nicht richtig funktionieren
malice ['mælɪs] *n.* Bosheit, *die.* malicious [mə'lɪʃəs] *adj.* böse
malign [mə'laɪn] *v. t.* verleumden
malignant [mə'lɪgnənt] *adj.* bösartig
malinger [mə'lɪŋgə(r)] *v. i.* simulieren.
ma'lingerer *n.* Simulant, *der*/Simu-
lantin, *die*
malleable ['mælɪəbl] *adj.* formbar
mallet ['mælɪt] *n.* Holzhammer, *der*
malnutrition [mælnju:'trɪʃn] *n.* Un-
terernährung, *die*
malt [mɔːlt] *n.* Malz, *das*

Malta ['mɔːltə] *pr. n.* Malta *(das)*
maltreat [mæl'triːt] *v. t.* mißhandeln.
mal'treatment *n.* Mißhandlung, *die*
mammal ['mæml] *n.* Säugetier, *das*
mammoth ['mæməθ] 1. *n.* Mammut,
*das.* 2. *adj.* Mammut-; gigantisch
⟨*Vorhaben*⟩
man [mæn] 1. *n.* a) *pl.* men [men]
Mann, *der;* b) *(human race)* der
Mensch. 2. *v. t.,* -nn- bemannen
⟨*Schiff*⟩; besetzen ⟨*Büro, Stelle usw.*⟩;
bedienen ⟨*Telefon, Geschütz*⟩
manacle ['mænəkl] 1. *n., usu. in pl.*
[Hand]fessel, *die.* 2. *v. t.* Handfesseln
anlegen (+ *Dat.*)
manage ['mænɪdʒ] 1. *v. t.* a) leiten
⟨*Geschäft*⟩; b) *(Sport)* betreuen
⟨*Mannschaft*⟩; c) *(cope with)* schaffen;
d) ~ to do sth. es fertigbringen, etw. zu
tun; he ~d to do it es gelang ihm, es zu
tun. 2. *v. i.* zurechtkommen; ~ without
sth. ohne etw. auskommen; I can ~:
es geht. manageable ['mænɪdʒəbl]
*adj.* leicht frisierbar ⟨*Haar*⟩; fügsam
⟨*Person, Tier*⟩; überschaubar ⟨*Größe,
Menge*⟩. 'management *n.* a) *(of a
business)* Leitung, *die;* b) *(managers)*
the ~: die Geschäftsleitung. 'manager *n. (of shop or bank)* Filialleiter,
*der*/-leiterin, *die; (of football team)*
[Chef]trainer, *der*/-trainerin, *die; (of
restaurant, shop, hotel)* Geschäftsführer, *der*/-führerin, *die.* manageress
[mænɪdʒə'res] *n.* Geschäftsführerin,
*die.* managing ['mænɪdʒɪŋ] *adj.* ~
director Geschäftsführer, *der*/-führe-
rin, *die*
¹mandarin ['mændərɪn] *n.* ~ [orange]
Mandarine, *die*
²mandarin *n. (bureaucrat)* Bürokrat,
*der*/Bürokratin, *die*
mandarine ['mændəriːn] *see* ¹mandarin
mandate ['mændeɪt] *n.* Mandat, *das*
mandatory ['mændətərɪ] *adj.* obligatorisch
mandolin[e] [mændə'lɪn] *n.* Mando-
line, *die*
mane [meɪn] *n.* Mähne, *die*
maneuver[able] *(Amer.) see* man-
œuvr-
manful ['mænfl] *adj.,* manfully
['mænfəlɪ] *adv.* mannhaft
manger ['meɪndʒə(r)] *n.* Krippe, *die*
mangle ['mæŋgl] *v. t.* verstümmeln
⟨*Person*⟩; demolieren ⟨*Sache*⟩
mangy ['meɪndʒɪ] *adj.* a) *(Vet. Med.)*
räudig; b) *(shabby)* schäbig
man: ~handle *v. t.* a) von Hand be-

wegen ⟨*Gegenstand*⟩; **b)** grob behandeln ⟨*Person*⟩; **~hole** *n.* Mannloch, *das*
'**manhood** *n.* Mannesalter, *das*
**man: ~-hour** *n.* Arbeitsstunde, *die;* **~-hunt** *n.* Verbrecherjagd, *die*
**mania** ['meɪnɪə] *n.* Manie, *die*
**manicure** [ˈmænɪkjʊə(r)] **1.** *n.* Maniküre, *die.* **2.** *v.t.* maniküren
**manifest** ['mænɪfest] **1.** *adj.* offenkundig. **2.** *v.t. (reveal)* offenbaren.
'**manifestly** *adv.* offenkundig
**manifesto** [mænɪˈfestəʊ] *n., pl.* ~s Manifest, *das*
**manifold** ['mænɪfəʊld] *adj. (literary)* mannigfaltig *(geh.)*
**manipulate** [məˈnɪpjʊleɪt] *v.t.* **a)** manipulieren; **b)** *(handle)* handhaben.
**manipulation** [mənɪpjʊ'leɪʃn] *n.* **a)** Manipulation, *die;* **b)** *(handling)* Handhabung, *die*
**mankind** [mæn'kaɪnd] *n.* Menschheit, *die*
**manly** ['mænlɪ] *adj.* männlich
'**man-made** *adj.* künstlich; *(synthetic)* Kunst⟨*faser, -stoff*⟩
**manned** [mænd] *adj.* bemannt
**manner** ['mænə(r)] *n.* **a)** Art, *die;* Weise, *die;* **in this ~:** auf diese Art und Weise; **b)** *(general behaviour)* Art, *die;* **c)** *in pl.* Manieren *Pl.* **mannerism** ['mænərɪzm] *n.* Eigenart, *die*
**manœuvrable** [məˈnuːvrəbl] *adj. (Brit.)* manövrierfähig
**manœuvre** [məˈnuːvə(r)] *(Brit.)* **1.** *n.* Manöver, *das.* **2.** *v.t. & i.* manövrieren
**manor** ['mænə(r)] *n.* **a)** *(land)* [Land]gut, *das;* **b)** *see* **manor-house.**
'**manor-house** *n.* Herrenhaus, *das*
'**manpower** *n.* Arbeitskräfte *Pl.*
**mansion** ['mænʃn] *n.* Herrenhaus, *das*
**manslaughter** ['mænslɔːtə(r)] *n.* Totschlag, *der*
**mantelpiece** ['mæntlpiːs] *n.* Kaminsims, *der od. das*
**mantle** ['mæntl] *n.* Umhang, *der*
**manual** ['mænjʊəl] **1.** *adj.* **a)** manuell; **~ work** Handarbeit; **b)** *(not automatic)* handbetrieben; ⟨*Bedienung, Schaltung*⟩ von Hand. **2.** *n.* Handbuch, *das*
**manufacture** [mænjʊ'fæktʃə(r)] **1.** *n.* Herstellung, *die.* **2.** *v.t.* herstellen. **manu'facturer** *n.* Hersteller, *der*
**manure** [məˈnjʊə(r)] **1.** *n.* Dung, *der.* **2.** *v.t.* düngen
**manuscript** ['mænjʊskrɪpt] *n.* Manuskript, *das*
**many** ['menɪ] **1.** *adj.* viele; **how ~**

**people/books?** wie viele *od.* wieviel Leute/Bücher? **2.** *n.* viele [Leute]; **~ of us** viele von uns; **a good/great ~:** eine Menge
**map** [mæp] **1.** *n.* [Land]karte, *die; (street plan)* Stadtplan, *der.* **2.** *v.t.,* **-pp-** kartographieren. **~ 'out** *v.t.* im einzelnen festlegen
**maple** ['meɪpl] *n.* Ahorn, *der*
**mar** [mɑː(r)] *v.t.* verderben
**marathon** ['mærəθən] *n.* **a)** Marathon[lauf], *der;* **b)** *(fig.)* Marathon, *das*
**marauder** [məˈrɔːdə(r)] *n.* Plünderer, *der*
**marble** ['mɑːbl] *n.* **a)** *(stone)* Marmor, *der;* **b)** *(toy)* Murmel, *die;* |**game of**| ~s Murmelspiel, *das*
**March** [mɑːtʃ] *n.* März, *der; see also* **August**
**march 1.** *n.* Marsch, *der;* |**protest**| ~: Protestmarsch, *der.* **2.** *v.i.* marschieren. **march 'off 1.** *v.i.* losmarschieren. **2.** *v.t.* abführen. **march 'past** *v.i.* vorbeimarschieren
'**marcher** *n.* |**protest**| ~: Demonstrant, *der*/Demonstrantin, *die*
**mare** [meə(r)] *n.* Stute, *die*
**margarine** [mɑːdʒəˈriːn], *(coll.)* **marge** [mɑːdʒ] *ns.* Margarine, *die*
**margin** ['mɑːdʒɪn] *n.* **a)** *(of page)* Rand, *der;* **b)** *(extra amount)* Spielraum, *der;* |**profit**| ~: [Gewinn]spanne, *die;* **by a narrow ~:** knapp. **marginal** ['mɑːdʒɪnl] *adj.,* '**marginally** *adv.* unwesentlich
**marigold** ['mærɪgəʊld] *n.* Ringelblume, *die*
**marijuana** [mærɪjʊ'ɑːnə] *n.* Marihuana, *das*
**marina** [məˈriːnə] *n.* Jachthafen, *der*
**marinade** [mærɪ'neɪd] **1.** *n.* Marinade, *die.* **2.** *v.t.* marinieren
**marine** [məˈriːn] **1.** *adj.* Meeres-; See⟨*versicherung, -recht usw.*⟩; Schiffs⟨*ausrüstung, -recht usw.*⟩. **2.** *n. (person)* Marineinfanterist, *der.* **mariner** ['mærɪnə(r)] *n.* Seemann, *der*
**marionette** [mærɪə'net] *n.* Marionette, *die*
**marital** ['mærɪtl] *adj.* ehelich; **~ status** Familienstand, *der*
**maritime** ['mærɪtaɪm] *adj.* See-
'**mark** [mɑːk] **1.** *n.* **a)** *(trace)* Spur, *die; (stain etc.)* Fleck, *der; (scratch)* Kratzer, *der;* **b)** *(sign)* Zeichen, *das;* **c)** *(Sch.)* Note, *die;* **d)** *(target)* Ziel, *das.* **2.** *v.t.* **a)** *(dirty)* schmutzig machen; *(scratch)* zerkratzen; **b)** *(put distinguishing ~ on)* kennzeichnen, markie-

ren (**with** mit); **c)** *(Sch.) (correct)* korrigieren; *(grade)* benoten; **d)** ~ **time** auf der Stelle treten. **mark** '**off** *v. t.* abgrenzen (**from** von, gegen). **mark** '**out** *v. t.* markieren

**²mark** *n. (monetary unit)* Mark, *die*
**marked** ['mɑːkt] *adj.,* **markedly** ['mɑːkɪdlɪ] *adv.* deutlich
'**marker** *n.* Markierung, *die.* '**marker pen** *n.* Markierstift, *der*
**market** ['mɑːkɪt] **1.** *n.* Markt, *der.* **2.** *v. t.* vermarkten. '**marketing** *n.* Marketing, *das.* '**market-place** *n.* Marktplatz, *der; (fig.)* Markt, *der*
'**marking** *n.* **a)** Markierung, *die;* **b)** *(on animal)* Zeichnung, *die*
**marksman** ['mɑːksmən] *n., pl.* **marksmen** ['mɑːksmən] Scharfschütze, *der*
**marmalade** ['mɑːməleɪd] *n.* |orange| ~: Orangenmarmelade, *die*
**¹maroon** [mə'ruːn] **1.** *adj.* kastanienbraun. **2.** *n.* Kastanienbraun, *das*
**²maroon** *v. t.* **a)** *(Naut.: put ashore)* aussetzen; **b)** ⟨*Flut, Hochwasser:*⟩ von der Außenwelt abschneiden
**marquee** [mɑː'kiː] *n.* Festzelt, *das*
**marquess, marquis** ['mɑːkwɪs] *n.* Marquis, *der*
**marriage** ['mærɪdʒ] *n.* **a)** Ehe, *die* (**to** mit); **b)** *(wedding)* Hochzeit, *die*
**married** ['mærɪd] *adj.* **a)** verheiratet; ~ **couple** Ehepaar, *das;* **b)** *(marital)* Ehe⟨*leben, -name*⟩
**marrow** ['mærəʊ] *n.* **a)** |vegetable| ~: Speisekürbis, *der;* **b)** *(Anat.)* [Knochen]mark, *das*
**marry** ['mærɪ] **1.** *v. t.* **a)** heiraten; **b)** *(join)* trauen; **they were** *or* **got/have got married** sie haben geheiratet. **2.** *v. i.* heiraten
**Mars** [mɑːz] *pr. n. (Astron.)* Mars, *der*
**marsh** [mɑːʃ] *n.* Sumpf, *der*
**marshal** ['mɑːʃl] **1.** *n.* **a)** *(officer in army)* Marschall, *der;* **b)** *(Sport)* Ordner, *der.* **2.** *v. t., (Brit.)* -ll- aufstellen ⟨*Truppen*⟩; ordnen ⟨*Fakten*⟩. '**marshalling yard** *n.* Rangierbahnhof, *der*
**marshmallow** [mɑː'ʃmæləʊ] *n. (sweet)* ≈ Mohrenkopf, *der*
'**marshy** *adj.* sumpfig
**marsupial** [mɑː'sjuːpɪəl] *n.* Beuteltier, *das*
**martial** ['mɑːʃl] *adj.* kriegerisch. **martial** '**law** *n.* Kriegsrecht, *das*
**martyr** ['mɑːtə(r)] **1.** *n.* Märtyrer, *der*/Märtyrerin, *die.* **2.** *v. t.* **be** ~**ed** den Märtyrertod sterben
**marvel** ['mɑːvl] **1.** *n.* Wunder, *das.* **2.**

*v. i., (Brit.)* -ll- *(literary)* ~ **at** sth. über etw. *(Akk.)* staunen. **marvellous** ['mɑːvələs] *adj.,* '**marvellously** *adv.* wunderbar
**marvelous[ly]** *(Amer.) see* **marvellous|ly|**
**Marxism** ['mɑːksɪzm] *n.* Marxismus, *der.* **Marxist** ['mɑːksɪst] **1.** *n.* Marxist, *der*/Marxistin, *die.* **2.** *adj.* marxistisch
**marzipan** ['mɑːzɪpæn] *n.* Marzipan, *das*
**mascara** |mæ'skɑːrə] *n.* Mascara, *das*
**mascot** ['mæskɒt] *n.* Maskottchen, *das*
**masculine** ['mæskjʊlɪn] *adj.* männlich. **masculinity** [mæskju'lɪnɪtɪ] *n.* Männlichkeit, *die*
**mash** [mæʃ] **1.** *n.* **a)** Brei, *der;* **b)** *(Brit. coll.:* ~*ed potatoes)* Kartoffelbrei, *der.* **2.** *v. t.* zerdrücken; ~**ed potatoes** Kartoffelbrei, *der*
**mask** [mɑːsk] **1.** *n.* Maske, *die.* **2.** *v. t.* maskieren
**masochism** ['mæsəkɪzm] *n.* Masochismus, *der.* **masochist** ['mæsəkɪst] *n.* Masochist, *der*/Masochistin, *die.* **masochistic** [mæsə'kɪstɪk] *adj.* masochistisch
**mason** ['meɪsn] *n.* **a)** Steinmetz, *der;* **b)** **M**~ *(Free*~*)* [Frei]maurer, *der.* **Masonic** [mə'sɒnɪk] *adj.* |frei|maurerisch; ~ **lodge** [Frei]maurerloge, *die.* **masonry** ['meɪsnrɪ] *n.* Mauerwerk, *das*
**masquerade** [mæskə'reɪd, mɑːskə'reɪd] **1.** *n.* Maskerade, *die.* **2.** *v. i.* ~ **as** sb./sth. sich als jmd./etw. ausgeben
**¹mass** [mæs] *n. (Eccl.)* Messe, *die*
**²mass** [mæs] **1.** *n.* **a)** Masse, *die;* **b)** **a** ~ **of** ...: eine Unmenge von ... **2.** *v. t.* anhäufen. **3.** *v. i.* sich ansammeln; ⟨*Truppen:*⟩ sich massieren
**massacre** ['mæsəkə(r)] **1.** *n.* Massaker, *das.* **2.** *v. t.* massakrieren
**massage** ['mæsɑːʒ] **1.** *n.* Massage, *die.* **2.** *v. t.* massieren
**massive** ['mæsɪv] *adj.* massiv; gewaltig ⟨*Aufgabe*⟩; enorm ⟨*Schulden*⟩
**mass:** ~ '**media** *n. pl.* Massenmedien *Pl.;* ~**-pro'duced** *adj.* serienmäßig produziert; ~ **pro'duction** *n.* Massenproduktion, *die*
**mast** [mɑːst] *n.* Mast, *der*
**master** ['mɑːstə(r)] **1.** *n.* **a)** Herr, *der;* **b)** *(of dog)* Herrchen, *das; (of ship)* Kapitän, *der;* **c)** *(Sch.: teacher)* Lehrer, *der;* **d)** *(expert, great artist)* Meister, *der* (**at** in + *Dat.*); **e)** **M**~ **of**

**Arts/Science** Magister Artium/rerum naturalium. **2.** *adj.* Haupt-. **3.** *v.t. (learn)* erlernen; **have ~ed a language** eine Sprache beherrschen. **masterful** ['mɑ:stəfl] *adj. (masterly)* meisterhaft

'**master-key** *n.* Hauptschlüssel, *der*

**masterly** ['mɑ:stəlɪ] *adj.* meisterhaft

**master:** ~**mind 1.** *n.* führender Kopf; **2.** *v.t.* ~**mind the plot** der Kopf des Komplotts sein; ~**piece** *n. (work of art)* Meisterwerk, *das;* ~**stroke** *n.* Meisterstück, *das;* ~ **switch** *n.* Hauptschalter, *der*

**mastery** ['mɑ:stərɪ] *n.* **a)** *(skill)* Meisterschaft, *die;* **b)** *(knowledge)* Beherrschung, *die (of Gen.)*

**masturbate** ['mæstəbeɪt] *v.i. & t.* masturbieren. **masturbation** [mæstə-'beɪʃn] *n.* Masturbation, *die*

**mat** [mæt] *n.* **a)** Matte, *die;* **b)** *(to protect table etc.)* Untersetzer, *der*

'**match** [mætʃ] **1.** *n.* **a) be no ~ for sb.** sich mit jmdm. nicht messen können; **meet one's ~:** seinen Meister finden; **b) be a [good** *etc.*] **~ for sth.** [gut *usw.*] zu etw. passen; **c)** *(Sport)* Spiel, *das; (Boxing)* Kampf, *der.* **2.** *v.t.* **a)** *(equal)* **~ sb. at chess** es mit jmdm. im Schach aufnehmen [können]; **b)** *(harmonize with)* passen zu; **a handbag and ~ing shoes** eine Handtasche und [dazu] passende Schuhe; **~ each other** zueinander passen. **3.** *v.i.* zusammenpassen

²**match** *n. (~stick)* Streichholz, *das*

'**matchless** *adj.* unvergleichlich

'**matchstick** *n.* Streichholz, *das*

'**mate** [meɪt] **1.** *n.* **a)** Kumpel, *der (ugs.);* **b)** *(Naut.)* ≈ Kapitänleutnant, *der;* **c)** *(workman's assistant)* Gehilfe, *der;* **d)** *(Zool.) (male)* Männchen, *das; (female)* Weibchen, *das.* **2.** *v.i.* sich paaren. **3.** *v.t.* paaren ⟨Tiere⟩

²**mate** *(Chess) see* **checkmate**

**material** [mə'tɪərɪəl] **1.** *adj.* **a)** materiell; **b)** *(relevant)* wesentlich. **2.** *n.* **a)** ~[s] Material, *das;* **building/writing ~s** Bau-/Schreibmaterial, *das;* **b)** *(cloth)* Stoff, *der.* **materialism** [mə'tɪərɪəlɪzm] *n.* Materialismus, *der.* **materialistic** [mətɪərɪə'lɪstɪk] *adj.* materialistisch. **materialize** [mə'tɪərɪəlaɪz] *v.i.* ⟨*Plan, Idee:*⟩ sich verwirklichen; ⟨*Treffen:*⟩ zustande kommen

**maternal** [mə'tɜ:nl] *adj.* mütterlich; Mutter⟨*instinkt*⟩

**maternity** [mə'tɜ:nɪtɪ] *n.* Mutterschaft, *die.* **ma'ternity dress** *n.*

Umstandskleid, *das.* **ma'ternity hospital** *n.* Entbindungsheim, *das*

**matey** ['meɪtɪ] *adj.,* **matier** ['meɪtɪə(r)],** **matiest** ['meɪtɪɪst] *(Brit. coll.)* kameradschaftlich

**math** [mæθ] *(Amer. coll.) see* **maths**

**mathematical** [mæθɪ'mætɪkl] *adj.,* **mathematically** [mæθɪ'mætɪkəlɪ] *adv.* mathematisch

**mathematician** [mæθəmə'tɪʃn] *n.* Mathematiker, *der/*Mathematikerin, *die*

**mathematics** [mæθɪ'mætɪks] *n.* Mathematik, *die*

**maths** [mæθs] *n. (Brit. coll.)* Mathe, *die (Schülerspr.)*

**matinée** ['mætɪneɪ] *n.* Nachmittagsvorstellung, *die*

**matrices** *pl. of* **matrix**

**matriculate** [mə'trɪkjʊleɪt] **1.** *v.t.* immatrikulieren (**in** an + *Dat.*). **2.** *v.i.* sich immatrikulieren. **matriculation** [mətrɪkjʊ'leɪʃn] *n.* Immatrikulation, *die*

**matrimonial** [mætrɪ'məʊnɪəl] *adj.* Ehe-

**matrimony** ['mætrɪmənɪ] *n.* Ehestand, *der*

**matrix** ['meɪtrɪks] *n., pl.* **matrices** ['meɪtrɪsi:z] *or* ~**es** Matrix, *die*

**matron** ['meɪtrən] *n. (in school)* ≈ Hausmutter, *die; (in hospital)* Oberschwester, *die*

**matt** [mæt] *adj.* matt

'**matted** *adj.* verfilzt

'**matter** ['mætə(r)] **1.** *n.* **a)** *(affair)* Angelegenheit, *die;* ~**s** die Dinge; **money** ~**s** Geldangelegenheiten; **b) it's a ~ of taste** das ist Geschmackssache; [**only**] **a ~ of time** [nur noch] eine Frage der Zeit; **c) what's the ~?** was ist [los]?; **d)** *(physical material)* Materie, *die.* **2.** *v.i.* etwas ausmachen; **what does it ~?** was macht das schon?; [**it**] **doesn't ~:** [das] macht nichts *(ugs.).* '**matter -of-fact** *adj.* sachlich

**mattress** ['mætrɪs] *n.* Matratze, *die*

**mature** [mə'tjʊə(r)] **1.** *adj.* reif; ausgereift ⟨*Stil, Käse, Portwein, Sherry*⟩. **2.** *v.t.* reifen lassen. **3.** *v.i.* reifen. **maturity** [mə'tjʊərɪtɪ] *n.* Reife, *die*

**Maundy Thursday** [mɔ:ndɪ 'θɜ:zdɪ] *n.* Gründonnerstag, *der*

**mausoleum** [mɔ:sə'li:əm] *n.* Mausoleum, *das*

**mauve** [məʊv] *adj.* mauve

**mawkish** ['mɔ:kɪʃ] *adj.* rührselig

**max.** *abbr.* **maximum** *(adj.)* max., *(n.)* Max.

**maxim** ['mæksım] *n.* Maxime, *die*
**maximum** ['mæksıməm] **1.** *n., pl.*
**maxima** ['mæksımə] Maximum, *das.*
**2.** *adj.* maximal; Maximal-; ~ **speed/**
**temperature** Höchstgeschwindigkeit,
*die*/-temperatur, *die*
**May** [meı] *n.* Mai, *der; see also* **August**
**may** *v. aux., only in pres.* **may,** *neg.*
*(coll.)* **mayn't** [meınt], *past* **might**
[maıt], *neg. (coll.)* **mightn't** ['maıtnt] **a)**
*expr. possibility* können; **it** ~ **be true**
das kann stimmen; **I** ~ **be wrong** vielleicht irre ich mich; **it** ~ **not be**
**possible** das wird vielleicht nicht möglich sein; **he** ~ **have missed his train**
vielleicht hat er seinen Zug verpaßt; **it**
~ *or* **might rain** es könnte regnen; **we**
~ *or* **might as well go** wir könnten eigentlich ebensogut [auch] gehen; **b)**
*expr. permission* dürfen; **c)** *expr. wish*
mögen; ~ **the best man win!** auf daß
der Beste gewinnt!
**maybe** ['meıbi:, 'meıbı] *adv.* vielleicht
**mayn't** [meınt] *(coll.)* **= may not;** *see*
**may**
**mayonnaise** [meıə'neız] *n.* Mayonnaise, *die*
**mayor** [meə(r)] *n.* Bürgermeister, *der*
**mayoress** ['meərıs] *n. (woman mayor)*
Bürgermeisterin, *die; (mayor's wife)*
[Ehe]frau des Bürgermeisters
**maze** [meız] *n.* Labyrinth, *das*
**me** [mı, *stressed* mi:] *pron.* mich; *as indirect object* mir; **who, me?** wer, ich?;
**not me** ich nicht; **it's me** ich bin's
**meadow** ['medəʊ] *n.* Wiese, *die*
**meagre** ['mi:gə(r)] *adj.* dürftig
**meal** [mi:l] *n.* Mahlzeit, *die;* **go out for**
**a** ~: essen gehen. 'mealtime *n.* Essenszeit, *die*
¹**mean** [mi:n] *n.* **a)** Mittelweg, *der;* **b)**
*(Math.)* Mittelwert, *der*
²**mean** *adj.* **a)** *(miserly)* geizig; **b)** *(unkind)* gemein; **c)** *(shabby)* schäbig
³**mean** *v. t.,* **meant** [ment] **a)** *(intend)*
beabsichtigen; ~ **to do sth.** etw. tun
wollen; **b)** *(design, destine)* **be ~t to do**
**sth.** etw. tun sollen; **c)** *(intend to convey)* meinen; **I [really]** ~ **it** ich meine
das ernst; **what do you** ~ **by that?** was
hast du damit gemeint?; **d)** *(signify)*
bedeuten
**meander** [mı'ændə(r)] *v. i.* **a)** *⟨Fluß:⟩*
sich winden; **b)** *⟨Person:⟩* schlendern
'**meaning** *n.* Bedeutung, *die; (of text*
*etc., life)* Sinn, *der.* **meaningful**
['mi:nıŋfl] *adj.* bedeutungsvoll *⟨Blick,*
*Ergebnis⟩;* sinnvoll *⟨Aufgabe, Gespräch⟩.* '**meaningless** *adj.* *⟨Wort,*

*Gespräch:⟩* ohne Sinn; sinnlos *⟨Aktivität⟩*
**means** [mi:nz] *n.* **a)** Möglichkeit, *die;*
[Art und] Weise; **by this** ~: hierdurch;
~ **of transport** Transportmittel, *das;* **b)**
*pl. (resources)* Mittel *Pl.;* **live within/**
**beyond one's** ~: seinen Verhältnissen
entsprechend/über seine Verhältnisse
leben; **c) by all** ~! selbstverständlich!;
**by no [manner of]** ~: ganz und gar
nicht; **by** ~ **of** durch; mit [Hilfe von]
'**means test** *n.* Überprüfung der Bedürftigkeit
**meant** *see* ³**mean**
**mean:** ~**time** *n.* **in the** ~**time** inzwischen; ~**time,** ~**while** *advs.* inzwischen
**measles** ['mi:zlz] *n.* Masern *Pl.*
**measly** ['mi:zlı] *adj. (coll.)* pop[e]lig
*(ugs.)*
**measurable** ['meʒərəbl] *adj.* meßbar
**measure** ['meʒə(r)] **1.** *n.* **a)** Maß, *das;*
**for good** ~: sicherheitshalber; *(as an*
*extra)* zusätzlich; **made to** ~: maßgeschneidert; **b)** *(degree)* **in some/large**
~: in gewisser Hinsicht/ in hohem
Maße; **c)** *(for measuring)* Maß, *das;* **d)**
*(step)* Maßnahme, *die;* **take** ~**s** Maßnahmen treffen. **2.** *v. t.* messen
*⟨Größe, Menge usw.⟩;* ausmessen
*⟨Raum⟩.* **3.** *v. i.* messen. **measure 'up**
**to** *v. t.* entsprechen ( + *Dat.*)
'**measured** ['meʒəd] *adj.* gemessen
*⟨Schritt, Worte⟩*
'**measurement** *n.* **a)** Messung, *die;* **b)**
*(dimension)* Maß, *das*
**meat** [mi:t] *n.* Fleisch, *das.* '**meaty**
*adj.* **a)** fleischig; **b)** *(fig.)* gehaltvoll
**mechanic** [mı'kænık] *n.* Mechaniker,
*der*/Mechanikerin, *die*
**mechanical** [mı'kænıkl] *adj.,*
**me'chanically** *adv.* mechanisch.
**mechanical 'pencil** *n.* *(Amer.)*
Drehbleistift, *der*
**me'chanics** *n.* **a)** Mechanik, *die;* **b)**
*pl. (mechanism)* Mechanismus, *der*
**mechanism** ['mekənızm] *n.* Mechanismus, *der*
**mechanization** [mekənaı'zeıʃn] *n.*
Mechanisierung, *die*
**mechanize** ['mekənaız] *v. t.* mechanisieren
**medal** ['medl] *n.* Medaille, *die; (decoration)* Orden, *der*
**medallion** [mı'dæljən] *n.* [große] Medaille
**medallist** ['medəlıst] *n.* Medaillengewinner, *der*/-gewinnerin, *die*
**meddle** ['medl] *v. i.* ~ **with sth.** sich

*(Dat.)* an etw. *(Dat.)* zu schaffen machen; ~ **in** sth. sich in etw. *(Akk.)* einmischen

**media** ['mi:dɪə] *see* **mass media; medium 1**

**mediaeval** *see* **medieval**

**mediate** ['mi:dɪeɪt] *v. i.* vermitteln. **mediator** ['mi:dɪeɪtə(r)] *n.* Vermittler, *der*/Vermittlerin, *die*

**medical** ['medɪkl] *adj.* medizinisch; ärztlich ⟨*Behandlung, Untersuchung*⟩

**medical:** ~ **certificate** *n.* Attest, *das;* ~ **school** *n.* medizinische Hochschule; ~ **student** *n.* Medizinstudent, *der*/-studentin *die*

**medicated** ['medɪkeɪtɪd] *adj.* medizinisch

**medication** [medɪ'keɪʃn] *n. (medicine)* Medikament, *das*

**medicinal** [mɪ'dɪsɪnl] *adj.* medizinisch

**medicine** ['medsən, 'medɪsɪn] *n.* **a)** *(science)* Medizin, *die;* **b)** *(preparation)* Medikament, *das*

**medieval** [medɪ'i:vl] *adj.* mittelalterlich

**mediocre** [mi:dɪ'əʊkə(r)] *adj.* mittelmäßig. **mediocrity** [mi:dɪ'ɒkrɪti] *n.* Mittelmäßigkeit, *die*

**meditate** ['medɪteɪt] *v. i.* nachdenken, *(esp. Relig.)* meditieren (**[up]on** über + *Akk.*). **meditation** [medɪ'teɪʃn] *n.* **a)** *(act)* Nachdenken, *das;* **b)** *(Relig.)* Meditation, *die*

**Mediterranean** [medɪtə'reɪnɪən] *pr. n.* the ~: das Mittelmeer

**medium** ['mi:dɪəm] **1.** *n., pl.* **media** ['mi:dɪə] *or* ~**s a)** *(substance)* Medium, *das;* **b)** *(means)* Mittel, *das;* **by** *or* **through the** ~ **of** durch; **c)** *pl.* ~**s** *(Spiritualism)* Medium, *das;* **d)** *in pl.* **media** *(mass media)* Medien *Pl.* **2.** *adj.* mittler ...; medium *nur präd.* ⟨*Steak*⟩.

**'medium-size[d]** *adj.* mittelgroß

**medley** ['medlɪ] *n.* **a)** buntes Gemisch; **b)** *(Mus.)* Potpourri, *das*

**meek** [mi:k] *adj.* **a)** *(humble)* sanftmütig; **b)** *(submissive)* zu nachgiebig

**meet** [mi:t] **1.** *v. t.,* met [met] **a)** treffen; *(collect)* abholen; **b)** *(make the acquaintance of)* kennenlernen; **pleased to** ~ **you** [sehr] angenehm; **c)** *(experience)* stoßen auf (+ *Akk.*) ⟨*Widerstand, Problem*⟩; **d)** *(satisfy)* entsprechen (+ *Dat.*) ⟨*Wunsch, Bedürfnis, Kritik*⟩; **e)** *(pay)* decken ⟨*Kosten*⟩; bezahlen ⟨*Rechnung*⟩. **2.** *v. i.,* met **a)** *(by chance)* sich *(Dat.)* begegnen; *(by arrangement)* sich treffen; **we've met before** wir kennen uns bereits; **b)** ⟨*Komi-*

*tee, Ausschuß usw.*:⟩ tagen. **meet 'up** *v. i.* sich treffen; ~ **up with** sb. *(coll.)* sich treffen. **'meet with** *v. t.* **a)** begegnen (+ *Dat.*); **b)** *(experience)* haben ⟨*Erfolg, Unfall*⟩; stoßen auf (+ *Akk.*) ⟨*Widerstand*⟩

**'meeting** *n.* **a)** Begegnung, *die;* *(by arrangement)* Treffen, *das;* **b)** *(assembly)* Versammlung, *die;* *(of committee etc.)* Sitzung, *die*

**megalomania** [megələ'meɪnɪə] *n.* Größenwahn, *der*

**megaphone** ['megəfəʊn] *n.* Megaphon, *das*

**melancholic** [melən'kɒlɪk] *adj.* melancholisch

**melancholy** ['melənkəlɪ] **1.** *n.* Melancholie, *die.* **2.** *adj.* melancholisch

**mellow** ['meləʊ] **1.** *adj.* **a)** *(softened by age or experience)* abgeklärt; **b)** *(ripe, well-matured)* reif. **2.** *v. i.* reifen

**melodic** [mɪ'lɒdɪk], **melodious** [mɪ'ləʊdɪəs] *adjs.,* **me'lodiously** *adv.* melodisch

**melodrama** ['melədrɑ:mə] *n.* Melodrama, *das.* **melodramatic** [melədrə'mætɪk] *adj.* melodramatisch

**melody** ['melədɪ] *n.* Melodie, *die*

**melon** ['melən] *n.* Melone, *die*

**melt** [melt] **1.** *v. i.* schmelzen. **2.** *v. t.* schmelzen; zerlassen ⟨*Butter*⟩. **melt a'way** *v. i.* [weg]schmelzen. **melt 'down 1.** *v. i.* schmelzen. **2.** *v. t.* einschmelzen

**melting:** ~-**point** *n.* Schmelzpunkt, *der;* ~-**pot** *n. (fig.)* Schmelztiegel, *der*

**member** ['membə(r)] *n.* **a)** Mitglied, *das;* **be a** ~: Mitglied sein; ~ **of a/the family** Familienangehörige, *der/die;* **b)** M~ **[of Parliament]** *(Brit.)* Abgeordnete [des Unterhauses], *der/die.* **'membership** *n.* **a)** Mitgliedschaft, *die* (**of** in + *Dat.*); **b)** *(number of members)* Mitgliederzahl, *die;* **c)** *(members)* Mitglieder *Pl.*

**membrane** ['membreɪn] *n. (Biol.)* Membran, *die*

**memento** [mɪ'mentəʊ] *n., pl.* ~**es** *or* ~**s** Andenken, *das* (**of** an + *Akk.*)

**memo** ['meməʊ] *n., pl.* ~**s** *(coll.) see* **memorandum**

**memoirs** ['memwɑ:z] *n. pl.* Memoiren *Pl.*

**memorable** ['memərəbl] *adj.* denkwürdig ⟨*Ereignis, Tag*⟩; unvergeßlich ⟨*Film, Buch, Aufführung*⟩

**memorandum** [memə'rændəm] *n., pl.* **memoranda** [memə'rændə] *or* ~**s** Mitteilung, *die*

**memorial** [mɪˈmɔːrɪəl] 1. *adj.* Gedenk-. 2. *n.* Denkmal, *das* (to für)

**memorize** [ˈmeməraɪz] *v. t.* sich *(Dat.)* merken *od.* einprägen; *(learn by heart)* auswendig lernen

**memory** [ˈmemərɪ] *n.* a) Gedächtnis, *das;* b) *(thing remembered, act of remembering)* Erinnerung, *die* (of an + *Akk.*); from ~: aus dem Gedächtnis; in ~ of zur Erinnerung an ( + *Akk.*); c) *(Computing)* Speicher, *der*

**men** *pl. of* **man**

**menace** [ˈmenɪs] 1. *v. t.* bedrohen. 2. *n.* Plage, *die.* ˈ**menacing** [ˈmenəsɪŋ] *adj.* drohend

**mend** [mend] 1. *v. t.* reparieren; ausbessern ⟨*Kleidung*⟩; kleben ⟨*Glas, Porzellan*⟩. 2. *v. i.* ⟨*Knochen, Bein usw.:*⟩ heilen. 3. *n.* be on the ~: auf dem Wege der Besserung sein

ˈ**menfolk** *n. pl.* Männer

**menial** [ˈmiːnɪəl] *adj.* niedrig; untergeordnet ⟨*Aufgabe*⟩

**meningitis** [menɪnˈdʒaɪtɪs] *n.* Hirnhautentzündung, *die*

**menopause** [ˈmenəpɔːz] *n.* Wechseljahre *Pl.*

**menstruate** [ˈmenstrʊeɪt] *v. i.* menstruieren. **menstruation** [menstrʊˈeɪʃn] *n.* Menstruation, *die*

**menswear** [ˈmenzweə(r)] *n.* Herrenbekleidung, *die*

**mental** [ˈmentl] *adj.* a) *(of the mind)* geistig; Geistes⟨*zustand, -störung*⟩; b) *(Brit. coll.: mad)* verrückt *(salopp)*

**mental:** ~ aˈrithmetic *n.* Kopfrechnen, *das;* ~ ˈhospital *n.* Nervenklinik, *die (ugs.);* ~ ˈillness *n.* Geisteskrankheit, *die*

**mentality** [menˈtælɪtɪ] *n.* Mentalität, *die*

ˈ**mentally** *adv.* geistig

**mention** [ˈmenʃn] 1. *n.* Erwähnung, *die.* 2. *v. t.* erwähnen (to gegenüber); don't ~ it keine Ursache

**menu** [ˈmenjuː] *n.* [Speise]karte, *die*

**mercenary** [ˈmɜːsɪnərɪ] 1. *adj.* gewinnsüchtig. 2. *n.* Söldner, *der*

**merchandise** [ˈmɜːtʃəndaɪz] *n.* [Handels]ware, *die*

**merchant** [ˈmɜːtʃənt] *n.* Kaufmann, *der.* **merchant ˈbank** *n.* Handelsbank, *die.* **merchant ˈnavy** *n. (Brit.)* Handelsmarine, *die*

**merciful** [ˈmɜːsɪfl] *adj.* gnädig. **mercifully** [ˈmɜːsɪfəlɪ] *adv. (fortunately)* glücklicherweise

**merciless** [ˈmɜːsɪlɪs] *adj.,* ˈ**mercilessly** *adv.* gnadenlos

**mercury** [ˈmɜːkjʊrɪ] 1. *n.* Quecksilber, *das.* 2. *pr. n.* M~ *(Astron.)* Merkur, *der*

**mercy** [ˈmɜːsɪ] *n.* Erbarmen, *das* (on mit); show sb. [no] ~: mit jmdm. [kein] Erbarmen haben; be at the ~ of sb./ sth. jmdm./einer Sache [auf Gedeih und Verderb] ausgeliefert sein

**mere** [mɪə(r)] *adj.,* ˈ**merely** *adv.* bloß

**merge** [mɜːdʒ] 1. *v. t.* a) *(combine)* zusammenschließen; b) *(blend gradually)* verschmelzen (with mit). 2. *v. i.* a) *(combine)* fusionieren (with mit); b) ⟨*Straße:*⟩ zusammenlaufen (with mit). **merger** [ˈmɜːdʒə(r)] *n.* Fusion, *die*

**meringue** [məˈræŋ] *n.* Meringe, *die;* Baiser, *das*

**merit** [ˈmerɪt] 1. *n.* a) *(worth)* Verdienst, *das;* b) *(good feature)* Vorzug, *der.* 2. *v. t.* verdienen

**mermaid** [ˈmɜːmeɪd] *n.* Nixe, *die*

**merrily** [ˈmerɪlɪ] *adv.* munter

**merriment** [ˈmerɪmənt] *n.* Fröhlichkeit, *die*

**merry** [ˈmerɪ] *adj.* fröhlich; ~ Christmas! frohe *od.* fröhliche Weihnachten! ˈ**merry-go-round** *n.* Karussell, *das.* ˈ**merry-making** *n.* Feiern, *das*

**mesh** [meʃ] *n.* a) Masche, *die;* b) *(netting; also fig.: network)* Geflecht, *das;* wire ~: Maschendraht, *der*

**mesmerize** [ˈmezməraɪz] *v. t.* faszinieren

**mess** [mes] *n.* a) *(dirty/untidy state)* [be] a ~ or in a ~: schmutzig/unaufgeräumt [sein]; what a ~! was für ein Dreck *(ugs.)*/Durcheinander!; b) *(bad state)* be [in] a ~: sich in einem schlimmen Zustand befinden; ⟨*Person:*⟩ schlimm dran sein; get into a ~: in Schwierigkeiten geraten; make a ~ of verpfuschen *(ugs.)* ⟨*Arbeit, Leben*⟩; c) *(Mil.)* Kasino, *das.* **mess aˈbout, mess aˈround** 1. *v. i. (potter)* herumwerken; *(fool about)* herumalbern. 2. *v. t.* ~ sb. about *or* around mit jmdm. nach Belieben umspringen. **mess ˈup** *v. t.* a) *(make dirty)* schmutzig machen; *(make untidy)* in Unordnung bringen; b) *(bungle)* ~ it/things up Mist bauen *(ugs.)*

**message** [ˈmesɪdʒ] *n.* Nachricht, *die;* give sb. a ~: jmdm. etwas ausrichten

**messenger** [ˈmesɪndʒə(r)] *n.* Bote, *der*/Botin, *die*

**Messiah** [mɪˈsaɪə] *n.* Messias, *der*

**Messrs** [ˈmesəz] *n. pl.* a) *(in name of firm)* ≈ Fa.; b) *pl. of* Mr; *(in list of names)* ~ A and B die Herren A und B '**messy** *adj. (dirty)* schmutzig; *(untidy)* unordentlich

**met** *see* **meet**

**metabolism** [mɪ'tæbəlɪzm] *n.* Stoffwechsel, *der*

**metal** ['metl] **1.** *n.* Metall, *das.* **2.** *adj.* Metall-. **metallic** [mɪ'tælɪk] *adj.* metallisch; **have a ~ taste** nach Metall schmecken. **metallurgy** [mɪ'tælədʒɪ] *n.* Metallurgie, *die*

**metamorphosis** [metə'mɔ:fəsɪs] *n., pl.* **metamorphoses** [metə'mɔ:fəsi:z] Metamorphose, *die*

**metaphor** ['metəfə(r)] *n.* Metapher, *die.* **metaphorical** [metə'fɒrɪkl] *adj.*, **metaphorically** [metə'fɒrɪkəlɪ] *adv.* metaphorisch

**meteor** ['mi:tɪə(r)] *n.* Meteor, *der.* **meteoric** [mi:tɪ'ɒrɪk] *adj. (fig.)* kometenhaft

**meteorological** [mi:tɪərə'lɒdʒɪkl] *adj.* meteorologisch ⟨*Instrument*⟩; Wetter⟨*ballon, -bericht*⟩

**meteorologist** [mi:tɪə'rɒlədʒɪst] *n.* Meteorologe, *der*/Meteorologin, *die*

**meteorology** [mi:tɪə'rɒlədʒɪ] *n.* Meteorologie, *die*

¹**meter** ['mi:tə(r)] *n.* **a)** Zähler, *der; (for coins)* Münzzähler, *der;* **b)** *(parking-~)* Parkuhr, *die*

²**meter** *(Amer.) see* ¹,²**metre**

**method** ['meθəd] *n.* Methode, *die.* **methodical** [mɪ'θɒdɪkl] *adj.*, **me-'thodically** *adv.* systematisch

**Methodist** ['meθədɪst] *n.* Methodist, *der*/Methodistin, *die*

**meths** [meθs] *n. (Brit. coll.)* [Brenn]-spiritus, *der*

**methylated spirit[s]** [meθɪleɪtɪd 'spɪrɪt(s)] *n. [pl.]* Brennspiritus, *der*

**meticulous** [mɪ'tɪkjʊləs] *adj.*, **me-'ticulously** *adv. (scrupulous[ly])* sorgfältig; *(over-scrupulous[ly])* übergenau

¹**metre** ['mi:tə] *n. (Brit.: poetic rhythm)* Metrum, *das*

²**metre** *n. (Brit.: unit)* Meter, *der od. das.* **metric** ['metrɪk] *adj.* metrisch; ~ **system** metrisches System. **metrication** [metrɪ'keɪʃn] *n.* Umstellung auf das metrische System

**metronome** ['metrənəʊm] *n.* Metronom, *das*

**metropolis** [mɪ'trɒpəlɪs] *n.* Metropole, *die.* **metropolitan** [metrə'pɒlɪtən] *adj.* ~ **New York** der Großraum New York; ~ **London** Großlondon *(das)*

**Mexican** ['meksɪkən] **1.** *adj.* mexikanisch. **2.** *n.* Mexikaner, *der*/Mexikanerin, *die*

**Mexico** ['meksɪkəʊ] *pr. n.* Mexiko *(das)*

**miaow** [mɪ'aʊ] **1.** *v. i.* miauen. **2.** *n.* Miauen, *das*

**mice** *pl. of* **mouse**

**microbe** ['maɪkrəʊb] *n.* Mikrobe, *die*

**micro** ['maɪkrəʊ]: ~**chip** *n.* Mikrochip, *der;* ~**computer** *n.* Mikrocomputer, *der;* ~**fiche** *n.* Mikrofiche, *das od. der;* ~**film 1.** *n.* Mikrofilm, *der;* **2.** *v. t.* auf Mikrofilm aufnehmen

**microphone** ['maɪkrəfəʊn] *n.* Mikrophon, *das*

**microprocessor** [maɪkrəʊ'prəʊsesə(r)] *n.* Mikroprozessor, *der*

**microscope** ['maɪkrəskəʊp] *n.* Mikroskop, *das.* **microscopic** [maɪkrə'skɒpɪk] *adj.* mikroskopisch; *(fig.: very small)* winzig

'**microwave** *n.* Mikrowelle, *die;* ~ **|oven|** Mikrowellenherd, *der*

**mid-** [mɪd] *in comb.* **in ~-air** in der Luft; **in ~-sentence** mitten im Satz; ~**July** Mitte Juli; **the ~-60s** die Mitte der sechziger Jahre; **a man in his ~-fifties** ein Mittfünfziger; **be in one's ~-thirties** Mitte Dreißig sein

**midday** ['mɪddeɪ, mɪd'deɪ] *n.* **a)** *(noon)* zwölf Uhr; **b)** *(middle of day)* Mittag, *der; attrib.* Mittags-

**middle** ['mɪdl] **1.** *attrib. adj.* mittler... **2.** *n.* **a)** Mitte, *die;* **in the ~ of the forest/night** mitten im Wald/in der Nacht; **b)** *(waist)* Taille, *die*

**middle:** ~ '**age** *n.* mittleres [Lebens]alter; ~**-aged** ['mɪdleɪdʒd] *adj.* mittleren Alters *nachgestellt;* **M~ 'Ages** *n. pl.* **the M~ Ages** das Mittelalter; ~ '**class** *n.* Mittelstand, *der;* ~**-class** *adj.* bürgerlich; **M~ 'East** *pr. n.* **the M~ East** der Nahe [und Mittlere] Osten; **M~ 'Eastern** *adj.* nahöstlich

**middling** ['mɪdlɪŋ] *adj.* mittelmäßig

**midge** [mɪdʒ] *n.* Stechmücke, *die*

**midget** ['mɪdʒɪt] **1.** *n.* Liliputaner, *der*/Liliputanerin, *die.* **2.** *adj.* winzig

**Midlands** ['mɪdləndz] *n. pl.* **the ~** *(Brit.)* Mittelengland

'**midnight** *n.* Mitternacht, *die*

'**midpoint** *n.* Mitte, *die*

**midriff** ['mɪdrɪf] *n.* Bauch, *der*

**midst** [mɪdst] *n.* **in the ~ of sth.** mitten in einer Sache; **in our/their/your ~:** in unserer/ihrer/eurer Mitte

**midsummer** ['---, -'--] *n.* die [Zeit der] Sommersonnenwende

**midway** ['--, -'-] *adv.* auf halbem Weg[e] ⟨*sich treffen, sich befinden*⟩

'**midwife** *n., pl.* '**midwives** Hebamme, *die*

**mid'winter** *n.* die [Zeit der] Wintersonnenwende

¹**might** [maɪt] *see* **may**

²**might** *n.* a) *(force)* Gewalt, *die;* b) *(power)* Macht, *die*

**mightn't** ['maɪtnt] *(coll.)* = **might not;** *see* **may**

**mighty** ['maɪtɪ] 1. *adj.* mächtig. 2. *adv. (coll.)* verdammt *(ugs.)*

**migraine** ['miːgreɪn] *n.* Migräne, *die*

**migrant** ['maɪgrənt] *n.* a) Auswanderer, *der*/Auswanderin, *die;* b) *(bird)* Zugvogel, *der*

**migrate** [maɪ'greɪt] *v. i.* a) *(to a town)* abwandern; *(to another country)* auswandern; b) ⟨*Vogel:*⟩ fortziehen. **migration** [maɪ'greɪʃn] *n.* a) *(to a town)* Abwandern, *das; (to another country)* Auswandern, *das;* b) *(of birds)* Zug, *der*

**mike** [maɪk] *n. (coll.)* Mikro, *das*

**Milan** [mɪ'læn] *pr. n.* Mailand *(das)*

**mild** [maɪld] *adj.* mild; sanft ⟨*Person*⟩

**mildew** ['mɪldjuː] *n.* a) Schimmel, *der;* b) *(on plant)* Mehltau, *der*

'**mildly** *adv.* a) *(gently)* mild[e]; b) *(slightly)* ein bißchen; c) **to put it ~:** gelinde gesagt

**mile** [maɪl] *n.* a) Meile, *die;* b) *(fig. coll.)* **~s better/too big** tausendmal besser/viel zu groß; **be ~s ahead of sb.** jmdm. weit voraus sein. **mileage** ['maɪlɪdʒ] *n.* [Anzahl der] Meilen; **a low ~:** ein niedriger Meilenstand.

'**milestone** *n.* Meilenstein, *der*

**militant** ['mɪlɪtənt] 1. *adj.* militant. 2. *n.* Militante, *der*/*die*

**military** ['mɪlɪtərɪ] 1. *adj.* militärisch; Militär⟨*regierung, -akademie, -uniform, -parade*⟩; **~ service** Militärdienst, *der.* 2. *n.* **the ~:** das Militär

**militate** ['mɪlɪteɪt] *v. i.* **~ against/in favour of sth.** [deutlich] gegen/für etw. sprechen

**militia** [mɪ'lɪʃə] *n.* Miliz, *die*

**milk** [mɪlk] 1. *n.* Milch, *die.* 2. *v. t.* melken

**milk: ~ 'chocolate** *n.* Milchschokolade, *die;* **~ jug** *n.* Milchkännchen, *das;* **~man** ['mɪlkmən] *n., pl.* **~men** ['mɪlkmən] Milchmann, *der;* **~ shake** *n.* Milchshake, *der;* **~-tooth** *n.* Milchzahn, *der*

'**milky** *adj.* milchig. **Milky 'Way** *n.* Milchstraße, *die*

**mill** [mɪl] 1. *n.* a) Mühle, *die;* b) *(factory)* Fabrik, *die.* 2. *v. t.* a) mahlen ⟨Getreide⟩; b) fräsen ⟨*Metallgegenstand*⟩. **mill a'bout** *(Brit.),* **mill a'round** *v. i.* durcheinanderlaufen

'**miller** *n.* Müller, *der*

**millet** ['mɪlɪt] *n.* Hirse, *die*

**milligram** ['mɪlɪgræm] *n.* Milligramm, *das*

**millilitre** (*Brit.; Amer.:* **milliliter**) ['mɪlɪliːtə(r)] *n.* Milliliter, *der od. das*

**millimetre** (*Brit.; Amer.:* **millimeter**) ['mɪlɪmiːtə(r)] *n.* Millimeter, *der*

**milliner** ['mɪlɪnə(r)] *n.* Modist, *der*/Modistin, *die.* '**millinery** *n.* Hutmacherei, *die*

**million** ['mɪljən] 1. *adj.* **a** *or* **one/two ~:** eine Million/zwei Millionen; **half a ~:** eine halbe Million. 2. *n.* a) Million, *die;* b) *(indefinite amount)* **~s of people** eine Unmenge Leute. **millionaire** [mɪljə'neə(r)] *n.* Millionär, *der*/Millionärin, *die.* **millionth** ['mɪljənθ] 1. *adj.* millionst... 2. *n. (fraction)* Millionstel, *das*

'**millstone** *n.* Mühlstein, *der*

**mime** [maɪm] 1. *n.* a) *(performance)* Pantomime, *die;* b) *(art)* Pantomimik, *die.* 2. *v. i.* pantomimisch agieren. 3. *v. t.* pantomimisch darstellen

**mimic** ['mɪmɪk] 1. *n.* Imitator, *der.* 2. *v. t.,* **-ck-** nachahmen

**min.** *abbr.* a) *(minute[s]* Min.; b) *(minimum (adj.)* mind., *(n.)* Min.

**mince** [mɪns] 1. *n.* Hackfleisch, *das.* 2. *v. t.* durch den [Fleisch]wolf drehen ⟨*Fleisch*⟩. '**mincemeat** *n.* a) Hackfleisch, *das;* b) *(sweet)* süße Pastetenfüllung aus Obst, Rosinen, Gewürzen, Nierenfett *usw.* **mince 'pie** *n.* mit „mincemeat b" gefüllte Pastete

'**mincer** *n.* Fleischwolf, *der*

**mind** [maɪnd] 1. *n.* a) Geist, *der;* b) *(remembrance)* **bear** *or* **keep sth. in ~:** an etw. *(Akk.)* denken; **have [got] sb./sth. in ~:** an jmdn./etw. denken; c) *(opinion)* **give sb. a piece of one's ~:** jmdm. gründlich die Meinung sagen; **to my ~:** meiner Meinung *od.* Ansicht nach; **change one's ~:** seine Meinung ändern; **I have a good ~ to do that** ich hätte große Lust, das zu tun; **make up one's ~, make one's ~ up** sich entscheiden; d) *(normal mental powers)* Verstand, *der;* **be out of one's ~:** den Verstand verloren haben; e) **frame of ~:** [seelische] Verfassung. 2. *v. t.* a) **I can't afford a bicycle, never ~ a car** ich kann mir kein Fahrrad leisten, geschweige denn ein Auto; b) *usu. neg.*

or *interrog. (object to)* would you ~
opening the door? würdest du bitte die
Tür öffnen?; I wouldn't ~ a walk ich
hätte nichts gegen einen Spaziergang;
c) *(take care)* ~ you don't go too near
the cliff-edge! paß auf, daß du nicht
zu nah an den Klippenrand gehst!; ~
how you go! paß auf! d) *(have charge
of)* aufpassen auf (+ *Akk.*). 3. *v.i.* a)
~! Vorsicht!; Achtung!; b) *(care, object)* do you ~ if I smoke? stört es Sie,
wenn ich rauche?; c) never ~ *(it's not
important)* macht nichts. mind 'out
*v.i.* aufpassen (for auf + *Akk.*); ~
out! Vorsicht!

'minded *adj.* mechanically ~: technisch veranlagt; not politically ~: un-
politisch

mindful ['maɪndfl] *adj.* be ~ of sth.
etw. berücksichtigen

'mindless *adj.* geistlos ‹*Person*›; sinnlos ‹*Gewalt*›

¹mine [maɪn] *n.* a) Bergwerk, *das;* b)
*(explosive)* Mine, *die*

²mine *poss. pron. pred.* meiner/meine/
mein[e]s; *see also* hers

'minefield *n.* Minenfeld, *das*

'miner *n.* Bergmann, *der*

mineral ['mɪnərl] 1. *adj.* mineralisch;
Mineral‹*salz, -quelle*›. 2. *n.* a) Mineral, *das;* b) *(Brit.: soft drink)* Erfri-
schungsgetränk, *das.* 'mineral water *n.* Mineralwasser, *das*

minesweeper ['maɪnswiːpə(r)] *n.* Mi-
nensuchboot, *das*

mingle ['mɪŋgl] 1. *v.t.* [ver]mischen. 2.
*v.i.* sich [ver]mischen (with mit)

mini ['mɪnɪ] *n. (coll.)* a) *(car)* M~, (P)
Mini, *der;* b) *(skirt)* Mini, *der (ugs.)*

mini- ['mɪnɪ] *in comb.* Mini-; Klein-
‹*bus, -wagen, -taxi*›

miniature ['mɪnɪtʃə(r)] 1. *n. (picture)*
Miniatur, *die.* 2. *adj.* Miniatur-

mini-: ~bus *n.* Kleinbus, *der;* ~cab *n.*
Minicar, *das*

minim ['mɪnɪm] *n. (Brit. Mus.)* halbe
Note

minimal ['mɪnɪml] *adj.* minimal

minimize ['mɪnɪmaɪz] *v.t.* a) *(reduce)*
auf ein Mindestmaß reduzieren; b)
*(understate)* bagatellisieren

minimum ['mɪnɪməm] 1. *n., pl.* minima
['mɪnɪmə] Minimum, *das* (of an +
*Dat.*). 2. *attrib. adj.* Mindest-

mining ['maɪnɪŋ] *n.* Bergbau, *der; attrib.* Bergbau-. 'mining industry *n.*
Bergbau, *der.* 'mining town *n.* Berg-
baustadt, *das*

minion ['mɪnjən] *n.* Lakai, *der*

minister ['mɪnɪstə(r)] 1. *n.* a) *(Polit.)*
Minister, *der*/Ministerin, *die;* b)
*(Eccl.)* Geistliche, *der/die;* Pfarrer,
*der*/Pfarrerin, *die.* 2. *v.i.* ~ to sb. sich
um jmdn. kümmern. ministerial [mɪ-
nɪ'stɪərɪəl] *adj.* *(Polit.)* Minister-; mini-
steriell. ministry ['mɪnɪstrɪ] *n.* a)
*(Polit.)* Ministerium, *das;* b) *(Eccl.)*
geistliches Amt

mink [mɪŋk] *n.* Nerz, *der*

minnow ['mɪnəʊ] *n.* Elritze, *die*

minor ['maɪnə(r)] 1. *adj.* a) *(lesser)*
kleiner...; b) *(unimportant)* weniger
bedeutend; *(not serious)* leicht; ~
road kleine Straße; c) *(Mus.)* Moll-; A
~: a-Moll. 2. *n.* Minderjährige, *der/
die.* minority [maɪ'nɒrɪtɪ, mɪ'nɒrɪtɪ]
*n.* Minderheit, *die;* in the ~: in der
Minderheit

minstrel ['mɪnstrl] *n.* fahrender Sänger

¹mint [mɪnt] 1. *n. (place)* Münzanstalt,
*die.* 2. *adj.* funkelnagelneu *(ugs.);* in
~ condition in tadellosem Zustand. 3.
*v.t.* prägen

²mint *n.* a) *(plant)* Minze, *die;* b) *(peppermint)* Pfefferminz, *das; attrib.*
Pfefferminz-

minuet [mɪnjʊ'et] *n.* Menuett, *das*

minus ['maɪnəs] *prep.* minus; weniger;
*(without)* abzüglich (+ *Gen.*)

minuscule ['mɪnəskjuːl] *adj.* winzig

¹minute ['mɪnɪt] *n.* a) Minute, *die; (moment)* Moment, *der;* b) ~s *(of meeting)*
Protokoll, *das;* take the ~s of a meeting bei einer Sitzung [das] Protokoll
führen

²minute [maɪ'njuːt] *adj. (tiny)* winzig

miracle ['mɪrəkl] *n.* Wunder, *das.*
miraculous [mɪ'rækjʊləs] *adj.* wunderbar

mirage ['mɪrɑːʒ] *n.* Fata Morgana, *die*

mirror ['mɪrə(r)] 1. *n.* Spiegel, *der.* 2.
*v.t.* [wider]spiegeln

misadventure [mɪsəd'ventʃə(r)] *n.*
Mißgeschick, *das*

misapprehension [mɪsæprɪ'henʃn]
*n.* Mißverständnis, *das;* be under a ~:
einem Irrtum unterliegen

misbehave [mɪsbɪ'heɪv] *v.i. & refl.*
sich schlecht benehmen. misbehav-
iour *(Amer.:* misbehavior) [mɪsbɪ-
'heɪvjə(r)] *n.* schlechtes Benehmen

miscalculate [mɪs'kælkjʊleɪt] 1. *v.t.*
falsch berechnen; *(misjudge)* falsch
einschätzen. 2. *v.i.* sich verrechnen.
miscalculation [mɪskælkjʊ'leɪʃn] *n.*
Rechenfehler, *der; (misjudgement)*
Fehleinschätzung, *die*

**miscarriage** [mɪs'kærɪdʒ] *n.* **a)** Fehlgeburt, *die;* **b)** ~ **of justice** Justizirrtum, *das*

**miscellaneous** [mɪsə'leɪnɪəs] *adj.* **a)** [kunter]bunt; **b)** *with pl. n.* verschieden. **miscellany** [mɪ'selənɪ] *n.* [bunte] Sammlung; [buntes] Gemisch

**mischief** ['mɪstʃɪf] *n.* **a)** Unfug, *der;* **get up to** ~: etwas anstellen; **b)** *(harm)* Schaden, *der.* **mischievous** ['mɪstʃɪvəs] *adj.* spitzbübisch; schelmisch

**misconception** [mɪskən'sepʃn] *n.* falsche Vorstellung (**about** von); **be |labouring| under a** ~ **about sth.** sich *(Dat.)* eine falsche Vorstellung von etw. machen

**misconduct** [mɪs'kɒndʌkt] *n.* unkorrektes Verhalten

**misconstrue** [mɪskən'stru:] *v. t.* mißverstehen

**miscount** [mɪs'kaʊnt] **1.** *v. i.* sich verzählen. **2.** *v. t.* falsch zählen

**misdeed** [mɪs'di:d] *n.* Missetat, *die (veralt., scherzh.)*

**misdemeanour** *(Amer.:* **misdemeanor)** [mɪsdɪ'mi:ne(r)] *n.* Missetat, *die (veralt., scherzh.)*

**misdirect** [mɪsdɪ'rekt, mɪsdaɪ'rekt] *v. t.* falsch adressieren ⟨*Brief*⟩; in die falsche Richtung schicken ⟨*Person*⟩

**miser** ['maɪzə(r)] *n.* Geizhals, *der*

**miserable** ['mɪzərəbl] *adj.* **a)** unglücklich; **feel** ~: sich elend fühlen; **b)** trist ⟨*Wetter, Urlaub*⟩. **miserably** ['mɪzərəblɪ] *adv.* unglücklich; jämmerlich ⟨*versagen*⟩; ~ **poor** bettelarm

**miserly** ['maɪzəlɪ] *adj.* geizig

**misery** ['mɪzərɪ] *n.* **a)** Elend, *das;* **b)** *(coll.: discontented person)* ~|-guts| Miesepeter, *der (ugs.)*

**misfire** [mɪs'faɪə(r)] *v. i.* **a)** ⟨*Motor:*⟩ Fehlzündungen haben; **b)** ⟨*Plan, Versuch:*⟩ fehlschlagen; ⟨*Streich, Witz:*⟩ danebengehen

**misfit** ['mɪsfɪt] *n.* Außenseiter, *der/* Außenseiterin, *die*

**misfortune** [mɪs'fɔ:tʃu:n] *n.* Mißgeschick, *das*

**misgiving** [mɪs'gɪvɪŋ] *n.* ~|s| Bedenken *Pl.*

**misguided** [mɪs'gaɪdɪd] *adj.* töricht

**mishandle** [mɪs'hændl] *v. t.* falsch behandeln

**mishap** ['mɪshæp] *n.* Mißgeschick, *das*

**mishear** [mɪs'hɪə(r)] **1.** *v. i.,* **misheard** [mɪs'hɜ:d] sich verhören. **2.** *v. t.,* **misheard** falsch verstehen

**mishit 1.** ['mɪshɪt] *n.* Fehlschlag, *der.*

**2.** [mɪs'hɪt] *v. t.,* **-tt-,** **mishit** verschlagen

**mishmash** ['mɪʃmæʃ] *n.* Mischmasch, *der (ugs.)* (of aus)

**misinform** [mɪsɪn'fɔ:m] *v. t.* falsch informieren

**misinterpret** [mɪsɪn'tɜ:prɪt] *v. t. (make wrong inference from)* falsch deuten; mißdeuten. **misinterpretation** [mɪsɪntɜ:prɪ'teɪʃn] *n.* **be open to** ~: leicht mißdeutet werden können

**misjudge** [mɪs'dʒʌdʒ] *v. t.* falsch einschätzen; falsch beurteilen ⟨*Person*⟩. **misjudgement,** **misjudgment** [mɪs'dʒʌdʒmənt] *n.* Fehleinschätzung, *die; (of person)* falsche Beurteilung

**mislay** [mɪs'leɪ] *v. t.,* **mislaid** [mɪs'leɪd] verlegen

**mislead** [mɪs'li:d] *v. t.,* **misled** [mɪs'led] irreführen. **mis'leading** *adj.* irreführend

**mismanage** [mɪs'mænɪdʒ] *v. t.* schlecht abwickeln ⟨*Geschäft, Projekt*⟩. **mismanagement** [mɪs'mænɪdʒmənt] *n.* schlechte Abwicklung

**misnomer** [mɪs'nəʊmə(r)] *n.* unzutreffende Bezeichnung

**misplace** [mɪs'pleɪs] *v. t.* an den falschen Platz stellen/legen/setzen *usw.*

**misprint 1.** ['mɪsprɪnt] *n.* Druckfehler, *der.* **2.** [mɪs'prɪnt] *v. t.* verdrucken

**mispronounce** [mɪsprə'naʊns] *v. t.* falsch aussprechen

**misread** [mɪs'ri:d] *v. t.,* **misread** [mɪs'red] falsch lesen

**misrepresent** [mɪsreprɪ'zent] *v. t.* falsch darstellen. **misrepresentation** [mɪsreprɪzen'teɪʃn] *n.* falsche Darstellung

**Miss** [mɪs] *n. (unmarried woman)* Frau; Fräulein *(veralt.); (girl)* Fräulein

**miss 1.** *n.* Fehlschlag, *der; (shot)* Fehlschuß, *der; (throw)* Fehlwurf, *der.* **2.** *v. t.* **a)** *(fail to hit)* verfehlen; **b)** *(let slip)* verpassen; ~ **an opportunity** sich *(Dat.)* eine Gelegenheit entgehen lassen; **c)** *(fail to catch)* verpassen ⟨*Zug*⟩; **d)** *(fail to take part in)* versäumen; ~ **school** in der Schule fehlen; **e)** *(fail to see)* übersehen; *(fail to hear)* nicht mitbekommen; **f)** *(feel the absence of)* vermissen; **she** ~**es him** er fehlt ihr. **3.** *v. i. (not hit sth.)* nicht treffen. **miss 'out 1.** *v. t.* weglassen. **2.** *v. i.* ~ **out on sth.** *(coll.)* sich *(Dat.)* etw. entgehen lassen

**misshapen** [mɪs'ʃeɪpn] *adj.* mißgebildet

**missile** ['mɪsaɪl] *n.* **a)** *(thrown)* [Wurf]geschoß, *das;* **b)** *(Mil.)* Rakete, *die.* '**missile base,** '**missile site** *ns.* Raketenbasis, *die*

'**missing** *adj.* fehlend; **be** ~: fehlen; ⟨*Person:*⟩ *(Mil. etc.)* vermißt werden; *(not present)* fehlen; ~ **person** Vermißte, *der/die*

**mission** ['mɪʃn] *n.* **a)** Mission, *die;* **b)** *(planned operation)* Einsatz, *der.* **missionary** ['mɪʃənərɪ] *n.* Missionar, *der/*Missionarin, *die*

**misspell** [mɪs'spel] *v. t., forms as* ¹**spell** falsch schreiben

**mist** [mɪst] *n.* *(fog)* Nebel, *der; (haze)* Dunst, *der; (on windscreen etc.)* Beschlag, *der.* **mist** '**up** *v. i.* [sich] beschlagen

**mistake** [mɪ'steɪk] **1.** *n.* Fehler, *der;* **by** ~: versehentlich. **2.** *v. t., forms as* take **1: a)** falsch verstehen; **b)** ~ **x for y** x mit y verwechseln. **mistaken** [mɪ'steɪkn] *adj.* **be** ~: sich täuschen; **a case of** ~ **identity** eine Verwechslung. **mi'stakenly** *adv.* irrtümlicherweise

**mistletoe** ['mɪsltəʊ] *n.* Mistel, *die* **mistook** *see* **mistake 2**

**mistress** ['mɪstrɪs] *n.* **a)** *(Brit. Sch.: teacher)* Lehrerin, *die;* **b)** *(lover)* Geliebte, *die*

**mistrust** [mɪs'trʌst] **1.** *v. t.* mißtrauen (+ *Dat.*). **2.** *n.* Mißtrauen, *das* (of gegenüber + *Dat.*). **mistrustful** [mɪs'trʌstfl] *adj.* mißtrauisch (**of** gegenüber)

'**misty** *adj.* dunstig

**misunderstand** [mɪsʌndə'stænd] *v. t., forms as* **understand** mißverstehen. **misunder'standing** *n.* Mißverständnis, *das*

**misuse 1.** [mɪs'ju:z] *v. t.* mißbrauchen. **2.** [mɪs'ju:s] *n.* Mißbrauch, *der*

**mite** [maɪt] *n.* **a)** *(Zool.)* Milbe, *die;* **b)** *(small child)* Würmchen, *das (fam.);* **poor little** ~: armes Kleines

**miter** *(Amer.) see* **mitre**

**mitigate** ['mɪtɪgeɪt] *v. t.* **a)** *(reduce)* lindern; **b)** *(make less severe)* mildern; **mitigating circumstances** mildernde Umstände

**mitre** ['maɪtə(r)] *n. (Brit. Eccl.)* Mitra, *die*

**mitten** ['mɪtn] *n.* Fausthandschuh, *der*

**mix** [mɪks] **1.** *v. t.* [ver]mischen; verrühren ⟨*Zutaten*⟩. **2.** *v. i.* **a)** *(become ~ed)* sich vermischen; **b)** *(be sociable, participate)* Umgang mit anderen [Menschen] haben; ~ **with** Umgang haben mit; ~ **well** kontaktfreudig sein. **3.** *n.*

*(coll.)* Mischung, *die;* |**cake-**|~: Backmischung, *die.* **mix** '**up** *v. t.* **a)** vermischen; **b)** *(muddle)* durcheinanderbringen; *(confuse)* verwechseln; **c) be/ get** ~**ed up in sth.** in etw. *(Akk.)* verwickelt sein/werden

**mixed** [mɪkst] *adj.* **a)** gemischt; **b)** *(diverse)* unterschiedlich. **mixed** '**grill** *n.* Mixed grill, *der.* **mixed** '**up** *adj. (coll.)* verwirrt ⟨*Person*⟩; **be/feel very** ~: völlig durcheinander sein

'**mixer** *n. (for food)* Mixer, *der*

**mixture** ['mɪkstʃə(r)] *n.* **a)** Mischung, *die* (**of** aus); **b)** *(Med.)* Mixtur, *die*

'**mix-up** *n.* Durcheinander, *das; (misunderstanding)* Mißverständnis, *das*

**mm.** *abbr.* **millimetre**[**s**] mm

**moan** [məʊn] **1.** *n.* **a)** Stöhnen, *das;* **b)** **have a** ~ *(complain)* jammern. **2.** *v. i.* **a)** stöhnen (**with** vor + *Dat.*); **b)** *(complain)* jammern (**about** über + *Akk.*). **3.** *v. t.* stöhnen

**moat** [məʊt] *n.* |**castle**| ~: Burggraben, *der*

**mob** [mɒb] **1.** *n.* **a)** *(rabble)* Mob, *der;* **b)** *(sl.: group)* **Peter and his** ~: Peter und seine ganze Blase *(salopp).* **2.** *v. t.,* **-bb-** belagern *(ugs.)* ⟨*Star*⟩

**mobile** ['məʊbaɪl] **1.** *adj.* beweglich; *(on wheels)* fahrbar. **2.** *n.* Mobile, *die.* **mobile** '**home** *n.* transportable Wohneinheit. **mobile** '**phone** *n.* Mobiltelefon, *das*

**mobility** [mə'bɪlɪtɪ] *n.* Beweglichkeit, *die*

**mobilization** [məʊbɪlaɪ'zeɪʃn] *n.* Mobilisierung, *die*

**mobilize** ['məʊbɪlaɪz] *v. t.* mobilisieren

**moccasin** ['mɒkəsɪn] *n.* Mokassin, *der*

**mocha** ['mɒkə] *n.* Mokka, *der*

**mock** [mɒk] **1.** *v. t.* sich lustig machen über (+ *Akk.*). **2.** *v. i.* sich lustig machen (**at** über + *Akk.*). **3.** *adj.* Schein- ⟨*kampf, -angriff, -ehe*⟩. **mockery** ['mɒkərɪ] *n.* Spott, *der;* **make a** ~ **of sth.** etw. zur Farce machen

'**mock-up** *n.* Modell [in Originalgröße]

**mode** [məʊd] *n.* **a)** Art [und Weise], *die;* **b)** *(fashion)* Mode, *die*

**model** ['mɒdl] **1.** *n.* **a)** Modell, *das;* **b)** *(example to be imitated)* Vorbild, *das;* **c)** *(Art)* Modell, *das; (Fashion)* Mannequin, *das; (male)* Dressman, *der.* **2.** *adj.* **a)** *(exemplary)* Muster-; **b)** *(miniature)* Modell-. **3.** *v. t., (Brit.)* **-ll-: a)** modellieren; ~ **sth. after** *or* |**up**|**on sth.** etw. einer Sache *(Dat.)* nachbilden; **b)**

*(Fashion)* vorführen. **4.** *v. i. (Fashion)* als Mannequin/Dressman arbeiten; *(Art)* Modell stehen/sitzen

**modem** ['məʊdem *n*. Modem, *der*

**moderate 1.** ['mɒdərət] *adj*. **a)** gemäßigt ⟨*Ansichten*⟩; maßvoll ⟨*Trinker, Forderungen*⟩; **b)** mittler... ⟨*Größe, Menge, Wert*⟩; *(reasonable)* angemessen ⟨*Preis, Summe*⟩. **2.** ['mɒdərət] *n*. Gemäßigte, *der/die*. **3.** ['mɒdəreɪt] *v. t.* mäßigen. **4.** ['mɒdəreɪt] *v.i.* nachlassen. **moderately** ['mɒdərətlɪ] *adv*. einigermaßen; mäßig ⟨*begeistert, groß, begabt*⟩. **moderation** [mɒdə'reɪ∫n] *n*. Mäßigkeit, *die;* **in ~**: mit Maßen

**modern** ['mɒdn] *adj*. modern; heutig ⟨*Zeit[alter], Welt, Mensch*⟩; **~ languages** neuere Sprachen. **modernize** ['mɒdənaɪz] *v. t.* modernisieren

**modest** ['mɒdɪst] *adj*. bescheiden; einfach ⟨*Haus, Kleidung*⟩. 'modestly *adv*. bescheiden. 'modesty *n*. Bescheidenheit, *die*

**modification** [mɒdɪfɪ'keɪ∫n] *n*. [Ab]änderung, *die*

**modify** ['mɒdɪfaɪ] *v. t.* [ab]ändern

**modulate** ['mɒdjʊleɪt] *v. t. & i.* modulieren. **modulation** [mɒdjʊ'leɪ∫n] *n*. Modulation, *die*

**module** ['mɒdjuːl] *n*. **a)** Bauelement, *das;* **b)** *(Astronaut.)* **command ~**: Kommandoeinheit, *die*

**mohair** ['məʊheə(r)] *n*. Mohair, *der*

**moist** [mɔɪst] *adj*. feucht **(with** von**)**. **moisten** ['mɔɪsn] *v. t.* anfeuchten. **moisture** ['mɔɪst∫ə(r)] *n*. Feuchtigkeit, *die*. **moisturizer** ['mɔɪst∫əraɪzə(r)], **moisturizing cream** ['mɔɪst∫əraɪzɪŋ kriːm] *ns*. Feuchtigkeitscreme, *die*

**molar** ['məʊlə(r)] *n*. Backenzahn, *der*

**molasses** [mə'læsɪz] *n*. Melasse, *die*

**mold** *(Amer.) see* [1,2]**mould**

**molder, molding, moldy** *(Amer.) see* **mould-**

[1]**mole** [məʊl] *n. (on skin)* Leberfleck, *der*

[2]**mole** *n. (animal)* Maulwurf, *der*

**molecular** [mə'lekjʊlə(r)] *adj*. molekular

**molecule** ['mɒlɪkjuːl] *n*. Molekül, *das*

'**molehill** *n*. Maulwurfshügel, *der*

**molest** [mə'lest] *v. t.* belästigen

**mollify** ['mɒlɪfaɪ] *v. t.* besänftigen

**mollusc,** *(Amer.)* **mollusk** ['mɒləsk] *n*. Weichtier, *das*

**mollycoddle** ['mɒlɪkɒdl] *v. t.* [ver]hätscheln

**molt** *(Amer.) see* **moult**

**molten** ['məʊltn] *adj*. geschmolzen

**mom** [mɒm] *(Amer. coll.) see* [2]**mum**

**moment** ['məʊmənt] *n*. Augenblick, *der;* **at any ~,** *(coll.)* **any ~**: jeden Augenblick; **one** *or* **just a** *or* **wait a ~!** einen Augenblick!; **in a ~** *(very soon)* sofort; **at the ~**: im Augenblick; **the ~ of truth** die Stunde der Wahrheit. **momentarily** ['məʊməntərɪlɪ] *adv*. einen Augenblick lang. **momentary** ['məʊməntərɪ] *adj*. kurz

**momentous** [mə'mentəs] *adj. (important)* bedeutsam; *(of consequence)* folgenschwer

**momentum** [mə'mentəm] *n*. Schwung, *der*

**Mon.** *abbr*. **Monday** Mo.

**monarch** ['mɒnək] *n*. Monarch, *der*/Monarchin, *die*. '**monarchy** *n*. Monarchie, *die*

**monastery** ['mɒnəstrɪ] *n*. Kloster, *das*. **monastic** [mə'næstɪk] *adj*. mönchisch

**Monday** ['mʌndeɪ, 'mʌndɪ] *n*. Montag, *der; see also* **Friday**

**monetary** ['mʌnɪtərɪ] *adj*. **a)** *(of currency)* monetär; Währungs⟨*politik, -system*⟩; **b)** *(of money)* finanziell

**money** ['mʌnɪ] *n*. Geld, *das;* **make ~** ⟨*Person:*⟩ [viel] Geld verdienen; ⟨*Geschäft:*⟩ etwas einbringen; **for 'my ~**: wenn man mich fragt

**money:** ~-**bag** *n*. Geldsack, *der;* ~-**box** *n*. Sparbüchse, *die;* ~-**making** *adj*. gewinnbringend; ~ **order** *n*. Postanweisung, *die*

**Mongolia** [mɒŋ'gəʊlɪə] *pr. n.* Mongolei, *die*. **Mongolian** [mɒŋ'gəʊlɪən] **1.** *adj*. mongolisch. **2.** *n. (person)* Mongole, *der*/Mongolin, *die*

**mongrel** ['mʌŋgrəl] *n*. ~ [**dog**] Promenadenmischung, *die*

**monitor** ['mɒnɪtə(r)] **1.** *n*. **a)** *(Sch.)* Aufsichtsschüler, *der*/-schülerin, *die;* **b)** *(Med., Telev., etc.)* Monitor, *der*. **2.** *v. t.* beobachten ⟨*Wetter, Flugzeug*⟩; abhören ⟨*Sendung, Telefongespräch*⟩

**monk** [mʌŋk] *n*. Mönch, *der*

**monkey** ['mʌŋkɪ] *n*. Affe, *der*

**monkey:** ~ **business** *n. (coll.: mischief)* Schabernack, *der;* ~-**nut** *n*. Erdnuß, *die;* ~-**wrench** *n*. Universalschraubenschlüssel, *der*

**mono** ['mɒnəʊ] *adj*. Mono-⟨*platte[nspieler], -wiedergabe*⟩

**monocle** ['mɒnəkl] *n*. Monokel, *das*

**monologue** *(Amer.:* **monolog)** ['mɒnəlɒg] *n*. Monolog, *der*

**monopolize** [mə'nɒpəlaɪz] *v.t.*

*(Econ.)* monopolisieren; *(fig.)* mit Beschlag belegen; ~ **the conversation** den/die anderen nicht zu Wort kommen lassen

**monopoly** [mə'nɒpəlɪ] *n.* **a)** *(Econ.)* Monopol, *das* (of auf + *Dat.*); **b)** *(exclusive possession)* alleiniger Besitz

**monotone** ['mɒnətəʊn] *n.* gleichbleibender Ton. **monotonous** [mə'nɒtənəs] *adj.,* **mo'notonously** *adv.* eintönig. **monotony** [mə'nɒtənɪ] *n.* Eintönigkeit, *die*

**monsoon** [mɒn'su:n] *n.* Monsun, *der*

**monster** ['mɒnstə(r)] *n.* **a)** *(creature)* Ungeheuer, *das; (huge thing)* Ungetüm, *das;* **b)** *(inhuman person)* Unmensch, *der.* **monstrosity** [mɒn'strɒsɪtɪ] *n.* **a)** *(outrageous thing)* Ungeheuerlichkeit, *die;* **b)** *(hideous building etc.)* Ungetüm, *das.* **monstrous** ['mɒnstrəs] *adj.* **a)** *(huge)* riesig; **b)** *(outrageous)* ungeheuerlich; **c)** *(atrocious)* scheußlich

**month** [mʌnθ] *n.* Monat, *der;* for a ~/~s einen Monat [lang]/monatelang. **'monthly 1.** *adj.* monatlich; Monats- ⟨*einkommen, -gehalt*⟩. **2.** *adv.* einmal im Monat. **3.** *n.* Monatsschrift, *die*

**monument** ['mɒnjʊmənt] *n.* Denkmal, *das.* **monumental** [mɒnjʊ'mentl] *adj.* **a)** *(massive)* monumental; **b)** gewaltig ⟨*Mißerfolg, Irrtum*⟩

**moo** [mu:] **1.** *n.* Muhen, *das.* **2.** *v.i.* muhen

**mooch** [mu:tʃ] *v.i. (sl.)* ~ **about** or **around/along** herumschleichen *(ugs.)*/ zockeln *(ugs.)*

**mood** [mu:d] *n.* **a)** Stimmung, *die;* be **in a good/bad** ~: [bei] guter/schlechter Laune sein; **I'm not in the** ~: ich hab' keine Lust dazu; **b)** *(bad* ~*)* Verstimmung, *die.* **'moody** *adj.* **a)** *(sullen)* mißmutig; **b)** *(subject to moods)* launenhaft

**moon** [mu:n] *n.* Mond, *der*

**moon:** ~**beam** *n.* Mondstrahl, *der;* ~**light 1.** *n.* Mondlicht, *das;* Mondschein, *der;* **2.** *v.i. (coll.)* nebenberuflich abends arbeiten; ~**lit** *adj.* mondbeschienen *(geh.)*

¹**moor** [mʊə(r), mɔ:(r)] *n. (Geog.)* [Hoch]moor, *das*

²**moor** *v.t. & i.* festmachen; vertäuen. **'mooring** *n.* ~[s] Anlegestelle, *die*

**moose** [mu:s] *n., pl. same* Amerikanischer Elch

**moot** [mu:t] **1.** *adj.* umstritten; offen ⟨*Frage*⟩; strittig ⟨*Punkt*⟩. **2.** *v.t.* erörtern ⟨*Frage, Punkt*⟩

**mop** [mɒp] **1.** *n.* **a)** Mop, *der;* **b)** ~ |of **hair**| Wuschelkopf, *der.* **2.** *v.t.,* -pp- moppen ⟨*Fußboden*⟩; *(wipe)* abwischen ⟨*Träne, Schweiß, Stirn*⟩. **mop 'up** *v.t.* aufwischen

**mope** [məʊp] *v.i.* Trübsal blasen

**moped** ['məʊped] *n.* Moped, *das*

**moral** ['mɒrl] **1.** *adj.* **a)** moralisch; sittlich ⟨*Wert*⟩; Moral⟨*begriff, -prinzip*⟩; **b)** *(virtuous)* moralisch ⟨*Leben, Person*⟩. **2.** *n.* **a)** Moral, *die;* **b)** in *pl.* *(habits)* Moral, *die*

**morale** [mə'rɑ:l] Moral, *die;* low/high ~: schlechte/gute Moral

**morality** [mə'rælɪtɪ] *n.* Moral, *die*

**morbid** ['mɔ:bɪd] *adj.* krankhaft; morbid *(geh.)* ⟨*Faszination, Neigung*⟩

**more** [mɔ:(r)] **1.** *adj.* mehr; any or some ~ *(apples, books, etc.)* noch welche; any or some ~ *(tea, paper, etc.)* noch etwas; any or some ~ **apples/tea** noch Äpfel/Tee; **I haven't any** ~ |**apples/tea**| ich habe keine [Apfel]/keinen [Tee] mehr; ~ and ~: immer mehr. **2.** *n.* mehr; ~ **and** ~: immer mehr; **six or** ~: mindestens sechs. **3.** *adv.* **a)** mehr; ~ **interesting** interessanter; **b)** *(nearer, rather)* eher; **c)** *(again)* wieder; **no** ~, **not any** ~: nicht mehr; **once** ~: noch einmal; **d)** ~ **and** ~: immer mehr; ~ **and** ~ **absurd** immer absurder; **e)** ~ **or less** *(fairly)* mehr oder weniger; *(approximately)* annähernd. **more'over** *adv.* und außerdem

**morgue** [mɔ:g] *see* **mortuary**

**morning** ['mɔ:nɪŋ] *n.* Morgen, *der; (not afternoon)* Vormittag, *der; attrib.* morgendlich; Morgen-; **this** ~: heute morgen; **tomorrow** ~, *(coll.)* **in the** ~: morgen früh; |**early**| **in the** ~: am [frühen] Morgen; *(regularly)* [früh] morgens

**Moroccan** [mə'rɒkən] **1.** *adj.* marokkanisch. **2.** *n.* Marokkaner, *der/*Marokkanerin, *die*

**Morocco** [mə'rɒkəʊ] *pr. n.* Marokko *(das)*

**moron** ['mɔ:rɒn] *n. (coll.)* Schwachkopf, *der*

**Morse [code]** [mɔ:s ('kəʊd)] *n.* Morsealphabet, *das*

**mortal** ['mɔ:tl] **1.** *adj.* **a)** sterblich; **b)** *(fatal)* tödlich (to für). **2.** *n.* Sterbliche, *der/die.* **mortality** [mɔ:'tælɪtɪ] *n.* **a)** Sterblichkeit, *die;* **b)** ~ |**rate**| Sterblichkeitsrate, *die.* **'mortally** *adv.* tödlich

**mortar** ['mɔ:tə(r)] *n.* Mörtel, *der*

**mortgage** ['mɔ:gɪdʒ] **1.** *n.* Hypothek,

*die.* 2. *v. t.* mit einer Hypothek belasten

**mortuary** ['mɔːtjʊərɪ] *n.* Leichenschauhaus, *das*

**mosaic** [məʊ'zeɪɪk] *n.* Mosaik, *das*

**Moscow** ['mɒskəʊ] *pr. n.* Moskau *(das)*

**Moselle** [məʊ'zel] *pr. n.* Mosel, *die*

**Moslem** ['mɒzləm] *see* **Muslim**

**mosque** [mɒsk] *n.* Moschee, *die*

**mosquito** [mɒs'kiːtəʊ] *n., pl.* **~es** Stechmücke, *die; (in tropics)* Moskito, *der*

**moss** [mɒs] *n.* Moos, *das.* '**mossy** *adj.* moosig

**most** [məʊst] **1.** *adj. (in number, majority of)* die meisten; *(in amount)* meist...; **make the ~ mistakes/the ~ noise** die meisten Fehler/den größten Lärm machen; **for the ~ part** größtenteils. **2.** *n.* **a)** *(greatest amount)* **the ~ it will cost is £10** es wird höchstens zehn Pfund kosten; **pay the ~:** am meisten bezahlen; **b)** *(greater part)* **~ of the girls** die meisten Mädchen; **~ of his friends** die meisten seiner Freunde; **~ of the poem** der größte Teil des Gedichts; **~ of the time** die meiste Zeit; **c)** *(on ~ occasions)* meistens. **3.** *adv.* **a)** am meisten; **the ~ interesting book** das interessanteste Buch; **~ often** am häufigsten; **b)** *(exceedingly)* äußerst. '**mostly** *adv. (most of the time)* meistens; *(mainly)* größtenteils

**MOT** *see* **MOT test**

**motel** [məʊ'tel] *n.* Motel, *das*

**moth** [mɒθ] *n.* Nachtfalter, *der; (in clothes)* Motte, *die.* '**mothball** *n.* Mottenkugel, *die.* '**moth-eaten** *adj.* von Motten zerfressen

**mother** ['mʌðə(r)] **1.** *n.* Mutter, *die.* **2.** *v. t. (over-protect)* bemuttern. '**motherhood** *n.* Mutterschaft, *die*

**mother: ~-in-law** *n., pl.* **~s-in-law** Schwiegermutter, *die;* **~land** *n.* Vaterland, *das*

**motherly** ['mʌðəlɪ] *adj.* mütterlich; **~ love** Mutterliebe, *die*

**mother: ~-of-'pearl** *n.* Perlmutt, *das;* **M~'s Day** *n.* Muttertag, *der; ~* '**tongue** *n.* Muttersprache, *die*

'**moth-proof** *adj.* mottenfest

**motif** [məʊ'tiːf] *n.* Motiv, *das*

**motion** ['məʊʃn] **1.** *n.* **a)** Bewegung, *die;* **b)** *(proposal)* Antrag, *der.* **2.** *v. t. & i. ~* |to| sb. to do sth. jmdm. bedeuten *(geh.),* etw. zu tun. **motionless** *adj.* bewegungslos

**motivate** ['məʊtɪveɪt] *v. t.* motivieren.

**motivation** [məʊtɪ'veɪʃn] *n.* Motivation, *die*

**motive** ['məʊtɪv] *n.* Beweggrund, *der;* **the ~ for the crime** das Tatmotiv

**motley** ['mɒtlɪ] *adj.* buntgemischt

**motor** ['məʊtə(r)] **1.** *n.* **a)** Motor, *der;* **b)** *(Brit.: ~ car)* Auto, *das.* **2.** *adj.* Motor〈mäher, -jacht usw.〉. **3.** *v. i. (Brit.)* [mit dem Auto] fahren

**motor: ~bike** *n. (coll.)* Motorrad, *das; ~* **boat** *n.* Motorboot, *das; ~* **car** *n. (Brit.)* Kraftfahrzeug, *das; ~* **cycle** *n.* Motorrad, *das*

'**motoring** *n. (Brit.)* Autofahren, *das*

'**motorist** *n.* Autofahrer, *der/*-fahrerin, *die*

**motorize** ['məʊtəraɪz] *v. t.* motorisieren

**motor: ~-racing** *n.* Autorennsport, *der; ~* **vehicle** *n.* Kraftfahrzeug, *das; ~way** *n. (Brit.)* Autobahn, *die*

**MOT test** *n. (Brit.)* ≈ TÜV, *der*

**mottled** ['mɒtld] *adj.* gesprenkelt

**motto** ['mɒtəʊ] *n., pl.* **~es** Motto, *das*

¹**mould** [məʊld] **1.** *n. (hollow container)* Form, *die.* **2.** *v. t.* formen (out of, from aus)

²**mould** *n. (Bot.)* Schimmel, *der*

**moulder** ['məʊldə(r)] *v. i. ~* |away| [ver]modern

'**moulding** *n.* **a)** Formteil, *das (of, in aus); (Archit.)* Zierleiste, *die;* **b)** *(wooden)* Leiste, *die*

'**mouldy** *adj.* schimmlig; **go ~:** schimmeln

**moult** [məʊlt] *v. i.* 〈Vogel:〉 sich mausern; 〈Hund, Katze:〉 sich haaren

**mound** [maʊnd] *n.* **a)** *(of earth)* Hügel, *der;* **b)** *(heap)* Haufen, *der*

**mount** [maʊnt] **1.** *n.* **a)** M~ **Vesuvius/ Everest** der Vesuv/der Mount Everest; **b)** *(animal)* Reittier, *das; (horse)* Pferd, *das;* **c)** *(of picture, photograph)* Passepartout, *das;* **d)** *(for gem)* Fassung, *die.* **2.** *v. t.* **a)** hinaufsteigen 〈Treppe〉; steigen auf (+ *Akk.*) 〈Plattform, Reittier, Fahrzeug〉; **b)** aufziehen 〈Bild〉; einfassen 〈Edelstein usw.〉; **c)** inszenieren 〈Stück, Oper〉; organisieren 〈Ausstellung〉; durchführen 〈Angriff, Operation〉. **3.** *v. i. ~* |up| *(increase)* steigen (to auf + *Akk.*)

**mountain** ['maʊntɪn] *n.* Berg, *der;* **in the ~s** im Gebirge. **mountaineer** [maʊntɪ'nɪə(r)] *n.* Bergsteiger, *der/* Bergsteigerin, *die.* **mountai'neering** *n.* Bergsteigen, *das.* **mountainous** ['maʊntɪnəs] *adj.* **a)** gebirgig; **b)** *(huge)* riesig

**mourn** [mɔːn] **1.** *v. i.* trauern; ~ **for** *or* **over** trauern um ⟨*Toten*⟩. **2.** *v. t.* betrauern. **'mourner** *n.* Trauernde, *der/ die.* **mournful** ['mɔːnfl] *adj.* klagend ⟨*Stimme, Ton, Schrei*⟩; trauervoll *(geh.)*⟨*Person*⟩. **'mourning** *n.* Trauer, *die;* **be in/go into** ~: Trauer tragen/anlegen

**mouse** [maʊs] *n., pl.* **mice** [maɪs] Maus, *die.* **'mouse trap** *n.* Mausefalle, *die*

**mousse** [muːs] *n.* Mousse, *die*

**moustache** [məˈstaːʃ] *n.* Schnurrbart, *der*

**mousy** ['maʊsɪ] *adj.* **a)** mattbraun ⟨*Haar*⟩; **b)** *(timid)* scheu

**mouth 1.** [maʊθ] *n.* **a)** *(of person)* Mund, *der;* *(of animal)* Maul, *das;* **with one's ~ open/full** mit offenem/ vollem Mund; **b)** *(harbour entrance)* [Hafen]einfahrt, *die;* *(of tunnel, cave)* Eingang, *der;* *(of river)* Mündung, *die.* **2.** [maʊð] *v. t.* mit Lippenbewegungen sagen. **mouthful** ['maʊθfʊl] *n.* Mundvoll, *der*

**mouth:** ~**-organ** *n.* Mundharmonika, *die;* ~**piece** *n.* **a)** Mundstück, *das;* **b)** *(fig.)* Sprachrohr, *das*

**movable** ['muːvəbl] *adj.* beweglich

**move** [muːv] **1.** *n.* **a)** *(change of home)* Umzug, *der;* **b)** *(action taken)* Schritt, *der;* *(Footb. etc.)* Spielzug, *der;* **c)** *(turn in game)* Zug, *der;* **make a ~:** ziehen; **it's your ~:** du bist am Zug; **d) be on the ~** ⟨*Person:*⟩ unterwegs sein; **e) make a ~** *(do sth.)* etwas tun; *(coll.: leave)* losziehen *(ugs.);* **f) get a ~ on** *(coll.)* einen Zahn zulegen *(ugs.);* **get a ~ on!** *(coll.)* [mach] Tempo! *(ugs.).* **2.** *v. t.* **a)** *(change position of)* bewegen; wegräumen ⟨*Hindernis, Schutt*⟩; *(transport)* befördern; ~ **sth. to a new position** etw. an einen neuen Platz bringen; ~ **house** umziehen; **b)** *(in game)* ziehen; **c)** *(affect)* bewegen; ~ **sb. to tears** jmdn. zu Tränen rühren; **be ~d by sth.** über etw. *(Akk.)* gerührt sein; **d)** *(prompt)* ~ **sb. to do sth.** jmdn. dazu bewegen, etw. zu tun; **e)** *(propose)* beantragen. **3.** *v. i.* **a)** sich bewegen; *(in vehicle)* fahren; **b)** *(in games)* ziehen; **c)** *(do sth.)* handeln; **d)** *(change home)* umziehen **(to** nach**);** ~ **into a flat** in eine Wohnung einziehen; ~ **out of a flat** aus einer Wohnung ausziehen; ~ **to London** nach London ziehen; **e)** *(change posture or state)* sich bewegen; **don't** ~**!** keine Bewegung! **move a'bout 1.** *v. i.* zu-

gange sein; *(travel)* unterwegs sein. **2.** *v. t.* herumräumen. **move a'long 1.** *v. i.* **a)** gehen/fahren; **b)** ~ **along, please!** gehen/fahren Sie bitte weiter! **2.** *v. t.* zum Weitergehen/-fahren auffordern. **move 'in 1.** *v. i.* **a)** *(to home etc.)* einziehen; **b)** ~ **on** ⟨*Truppen, Polizeikräfte:*⟩ vorrücken gegen. **2.** *v. t.* hineinbringen. **move 'off** *v. i.* sich in Bewegung setzen. **move 'on 1.** *v. i.* weitergehen/-fahren; ~ **on to another question** *(fig.)* zu einer anderen Frage übergehen. **2.** *v. t.* zum Weitergehen/-fahren auffordern. **move 'out** *v. t.* ausziehen **(of** aus**).** **move 'over** *v. i.* rücken. **move 'up** *v. i.* **a)** rücken; **b)** *(in queue, hierarchy)* aufrücken

**'movement** *n.* **a)** Bewegung, *die;* *(trend, tendency)* Tendenz, *die* **(towards** zu**);** **b)** *in pl.* Aktivitäten *Pl.;* **c)** *(Mus.)* Satz, *der*

**movie** ['muːvɪ] *n. (Amer. coll.)* Film, *der;* **the ~s** der Film; **go to the ~s** ins Kino gehen

**moving** ['muːvɪŋ] *adj.* **a)** beweglich; **b)** *(affecting)* ergreifend

**mow** [məʊ] *v. t., p.p.* **mown** [məʊn] *or* **mowed** [məʊd] mähen. **mow 'down** *v. t. (shoot)* niedermähen ⟨*Menschen*⟩

**'mower** *n.* Rasenmäher, *der*

**mown** *see* **mow**

**MP** *abbr.* **Member of Parliament**

**m.p.g.** *abbr.* **miles per gallon**

**m.p.h.** *abbr.* **miles per hour**

**Mr** ['mɪstə(r)] *n.* Herr; *(in an address)* Herrn

**Mrs** ['mɪsɪz] *n.* Frau

**Ms** [mɪz] *n.* Frau

**Mt.** *abbr.* **Mount**

**much** [mʌtʃ] **1.** *adj., more* [mɔː(r)], *most* [məʊst] viel; **too ~:** zuviel *indekl.* **2.** *n.* vieles; ~ **of the day** der Großteil des Tages; **not be ~ to look at** nicht sehr ansehnlich sein. **3.** *adv., more, most* **a)** viel ⟨*besser, schöner usw.*⟩; ~ **more lively/attractive** viel lebhafter/ attraktiver; **b)** mit Abstand ⟨*der/die/ das beste, klügste usw.*⟩; **c)** *(greatly)* sehr ⟨*lieben, genießen usw.*⟩; **(for** ~ **of the time)** viel ⟨*lesen, spielen usw.*⟩; *(often)* oft ⟨*sehen, besuchen usw.*⟩; **d)** [pretty *or* very] ~ **the same** fast [genau] der-/die-/dasselbe

**muck** [mʌk] *n.* **a)** *(coll.: something disgusting)* Dreck, *der (ugs.);* **b)** *(coll.: nonsense)* Mist, *der (ugs.).* **muck a'bout, muck a'round** *(Brit. sl.) v. i.* **a)** herumalbern *(ugs.);* **b)** *(tinker)* her-

umfummeln (**with** an + *Dat.*). **muck
'in** *v.i.* (*coll.*) mit anpacken (**with** bei).
**muck 'up** *v.t.* **a)** (*Brit. coll.: bungle*)
vermurksen (*ugs.*); **b)** (*make dirty*)
dreckig machen (*ugs.*); **c)** (*coll.: spoil*)
vermasseln (*salopp*)
'**mucky** *adj.* dreckig (*ugs.*)
'**mucus** ['mju:kəs] *n.* Schleim, *der*
**mud** [mʌd] *n.* Schlamm, *der*
**muddle** ['mʌdl] **1.** *n.* Durcheinander,
*das.* **2.** *v.t.* ~ |**up**| durcheinanderbrin-
gen; ~ **up** *(mix up)* verwechseln (**with**
mit). **muddle a'long, muddle 'on**
*v.i.* vor sich (*Akk.*) hin wursteln
(*ugs.*). **muddle 'through** *v.i.* sich
durchwursteln (*ugs.*)
**muddy** ['mʌdɪ] *adj.* schlammig; **get** *or*
**become** ~: verschlammen
'**mudguard** *n.* Schutzblech, *das; (of
car)* Kotflügel, *der*
¹**muff** [mʌf] *n.* Muff, *der*
²**muff** *v.t.* verpatzen (*ugs.*)
**muffle** ['mʌfl] *v.t.* **a)** (*envelop*) ~ |**up**|
einhüllen; **b)** dämpfen ⟨*Geräusch*⟩.
'**muffler** *n.* **a)** (*wrap, scarf*) Schal,
*der;* **b)** (*Amer. Motor Veh.*) Schalldämpfer, *der*
**mug** [mʌg] **1.** *n.* **a)** Becher, *der (meist
mit Henkel); (for beer etc.)* Krug, *der;*
**b)** (*sl.: face, mouth*) Visage, *die (salopp).* **c)** (*Brit. sl.: gullible person*) Trottel, *der (ugs.).* **2.** *v.t.,* -**gg**- (*rob*) überfallen und berauben. '**mugger** *n.*
Straßenräuber, *der/*-räuberin, *die.*
'**mugging** *n.* Straßenraub, *der*
'**muggy** ['mʌgɪ] *adj.* schwül
**mule** [mju:l] *n.* Maultier, *das*
**multicoloured** (*Brit., Amer.:* **multi-
colored**) ['mʌltɪkʌləd] *adj.* mehrfar-
big; bunt ⟨*Stoff, Kleid*⟩
**multinational** [mʌltɪ'næʃənl] **1.** *adj.*
multinational. **2.** *n.* multinationaler
Konzern, *der;* Multi, *der (ugs.)*
**multiple** ['mʌltɪpl] *adj.* mehrfach.
**multiple-'choice** *adj.* Multiple-
choice-⟨*Test, Frage*⟩. **multiple 'store**
*n.* (*Brit.: shop*) Kettenladen, *der*
**multiplication** [mʌltɪplɪ'keɪʃn] *n.*
Multiplikation, *die*
**multiply** ['mʌltɪplaɪ] **1.** *v.t.* multiplizieren, malnehmen (**by** mit). **2.** *v.i.*
sich vermehren
**multi-storey** ['mʌltɪstɔ:rɪ] *adj.* mehr-
stöckig; ~ **car park/block of flats**
Parkhaus/Wohnhochhaus, *das*
**multitude** ['mʌltɪtju:d] *n.* (*crowd*)
Menge, *die; (great number)* Vielzahl,
*die*
¹**mum** [mʌm] (*coll.*) **1.** *int.* ~'**s the word**

nicht weitersagen! **2.** *adj.* **keep** ~: den
Mund halten (*ugs.*)
²**mum** *n.* (*Brit. coll.: mother*) Mama, *die*
(*fam.*)
**mumble** ['mʌmbl] *v.i. & t.* nuscheln
(*ugs.*)
**mumps** [mʌmps] *n.* Mumps, *der*
**munch** [mʌntʃ] *v.t. & i.* ~ |**one's food**|
mampfen (*salopp*)
**mundane** [mʌn'deɪn] *adj.* **a)** (*dull*) banal; **b)** (*worldly*) weltlich
**Munich** ['mju:nɪk] *pr. n.* München
(*das*)
**municipal** [mju:'nɪsɪpl] *adj.* kommunal; Kommunal⟨*politik, -verwaltung*⟩
**mural** ['mjʊərl] *n.* Wandbild, *das*
**murder** ['mɜ:də(r)] **1.** *n.* Mord, *der* (of
an + *Dat.*). **2.** *v.t.* ermorden. '**murderer** *n.* Mörder, *der*/Mörderin, *die.*
**murderess** ['mɜ:dərɪs] *n.* Mörderin,
*die.* **murderous** ['mɜ:dərəs] *adj.* tödlich; Mord⟨*absicht, -drohung*⟩; mörderisch (*ugs.*) ⟨*Kampf*⟩
**murk** [mɜ:k] *n.* Dunkelheit, *die.*
'**murky** *adj.* **a)** (*dark*) düster; **b)**
(*dirty*) schmutzig-trüb ⟨*Wasser*⟩
**murmur** ['mɜ:mə(r)] **1.** *n.* **a)** (*subdued
sound*) Rauschen, *das;* **b)** (*expression
of discontent*) Murren, *das;* **c)** (*soft
speech*) Murmeln, *das.* **2.** *v.t.* murmeln. **3.** *v.i.* ⟨*Person:*⟩ murmeln; (*complain*) murren
**muscle** ['mʌsl] *n.* Muskel, *der.* **muscular** ['mʌskjʊlə(r)] *adj.* **a)** (*Anat.*)
Muskel-; **b)** (*strong*) muskulös
**muse** [mju:z] (*literary*) *v.i.* [nach]sin-
nen (*geh.*) (**on, over** über + *Akk.*)
**museum** [mju:'zi:əm] *n.* Museum, *das*
**mush** [mʌʃ] *n.* Brei, *der*
**mushroom** ['mʌʃrʊm, 'mʌʃru:m] **1.** *n.*
Pilz, *der; (cultivated)* Champignon,
*der.* **2.** *v.i.* wie Pilze aus dem Boden
schießen
'**mushy** *adj.* breiig
**music** ['mju:zɪk] *n.* **a)** Musik, *die;*
**piece of** ~: Musikstück, *das;* **set sth. to**
~: etw. vertonen; **b)** (*score*) Noten *Pl.*
**musical** ['mju:zɪkl] **1.** *adj.* musikalisch; Musik⟨*instrument, -verständnis,
-notation, -abend*⟩. **2.** *n.* Musical, *das*
**Muslim** ['mʊslɪm, 'mʌzlɪm] **1.** *adj.*
moslemisch. **2.** *n.* Moslem, *der*/Mos-
lime, *die*
**muslin** ['mʌzlɪn] *n.* Musselin, *der*
**mussel** ['mʌsl] *n.* Muschel, *die*
**must** [məst, *stressed* mʌst] **1.** *v. aux.,
only in pres., neg.* (*coll.*) **mustn't**
['mʌsnt] müssen; *with neg.* dürfen. **2.**
*n.* (*coll.*) Muß, *das*

**mustache** *see* **moustache**
**mustard** ['mʌstəd] *n.* Senf, *der*
**muster** ['mʌstə(r)] 1. *n.* **pass ~** : akzeptabel sein. 2. *v. t.* versammeln; *(Mil., Naut.)* [zum Appell] antreten lassen; *(fig.)* zusammennehmen ⟨*Kraft, Mut, Verstand*⟩. 3. *v. i.* sich [ver]sammeln. **muster 'up** *v. t.* aufbringen
**mustn't** ['mʌsnt] *(coll.)* = **must not**; *see* **must** 1
**musty** ['mʌstɪ] *adj.* muffig
**mutant** ['mju:tənt] 1. *adj.* mutiert. 2. *n.* Mutante, *die*
**mutation** [mju:'teɪʃn] *n.* Mutation, *die*
**mute** [mju:t] 1. *adj.* stumm. 2. *n.* Stumme, *der/die.* **'muted** *adj.* gedämpft
**mutilate** ['mju:tɪleɪt] *v. t.* verstümmeln. **mutilation** [mju:tɪ'leɪʃn] *n.* Verstümmelung, *die*
**mutinous** ['mju:tɪnəs] *adj.* meuternd
**mutiny** ['mju:tɪnɪ] 1. *n.* Meuterei, *die.* 2. *v. i.* meutern
**mutter** ['mʌtə(r)] *v. i. & t.* murmeln. **'muttering** *n.* Gemurmel, *das*
**mutton** ['mʌtn] *n.* Hammelfleisch, *das*
**mutual** ['mju:tjʊəl] *adj.* **a)** gegenseitig; **b)** *(coll.: shared)* gemeinsam. **mutually** *adv.* **a)** gegenseitig; **be ~ exclusive** sich [gegenseitig] ausschließen; **b)** *(in common)* gemeinsam
**muzzle** ['mʌzl] 1. *n.* **a)** *(of dog)* Schnauze, *die; (of horse, cattle)* Maul, *das;* **b)** *(of gun)* Mündung, *die;* **c)** *(put over animal's mouth)* Maulkorb, *der.* 2. *v. t.* **a)** einen Maulkorb anlegen (+ *Dat.*) ⟨*Hund*⟩; **b)** *(fig.)* mundtot machen *(ugs.)* (+ *Dat.*)
**MW** *abbr. (Radio)* **medium wave** MW
**my** [maɪ] *poss. pron. attrib.* mein; **my|, my|!, |my| oh my!** [ach du] meine Güte! *(ugs.)*
**myself** [maɪ'self] *pron.* **a)** *emphat.* selbst; **I thought so ~** : das habe ich auch gedacht; **b)** *refl.* mich/mir. *See also* **herself**
**mysterious** [mɪ'stɪərɪəs] *adj.* rätselhaft; geheimnisvoll ⟨*Fremder, Orient*⟩. **my'steriously** *adv.* auf rätselhafte Weise; geheimnisvoll ⟨*lächeln usw.*⟩
**mystery** ['mɪstərɪ] *n.* **a)** Rätsel, *das;* **b)** *(secrecy)* Geheimnis, *das.* **'mystery tour** *n.* Fahrt ins Blaue *(ugs.)*
**mystic** ['mɪstɪk] 1. *adj.* mystisch. 2. *n.* Mystiker, *der*/Mystikerin, *die.* **mystical** ['mɪstɪkl] *adj.* mystisch
**mystify** ['mɪstɪfaɪ] *v. t.* verwirren
**myth** [mɪθ] *n.* Mythos, *der.* **mythical** ['mɪθɪkl] *adj.* **a)** *(based on myth)* my-

thisch; **b)** *(invented)* fiktiv. **mythological** [mɪθə'lɒdʒɪkl] *adj.* mythologisch. **mythology** [mɪ'θɒlədʒɪ] *n.* Mythologie, *die*

# N

**N, n** [en] *n.* N, n, *das*
**N.** *abbr.* **a) north** N; **b) northern** n.
**NAAFI** ['næfɪ] *abbr. (Brit.)* **Navy, Army and Air Force Institutes** *Kaufhaus für Angehörige der britischen Truppen*
**nab** [næb] *v. t.,* **-bb-** *(sl.)* **a)** *(arrest)* schnappen *(ugs.);* **b)** *(seize)* sich *(Dat.)* schnappen
**nag** [næg] *v. i. & t.* **-gg-:** **~ [at]** sb. an jmdm. herumnörgeln; **~ [at]** sb. to do sth. jmdm. zusetzen *(ugs.),* daß er etw. tut. **'nagging** 1. *adj. (persistent)* quälend; bohrend ⟨*Schmerz*⟩. 2. *n.* Genörgel, *das*
**nail** [neɪl] 1. *n.* Nagel, *der;* **hit the ~ on the head** *(fig.)* den Nagel auf den Kopf treffen *(ugs.).* 2. *v. t.* nageln (**to** an + *Akk.*). **nail 'down** *v. t.* festnageln; zunageln ⟨*Kiste*⟩
**nail:** **~-brush** *n.* Nagelbürste, *die;* **~-clippers** *n. pl.* |pair of| **~-clippers** Nagelknipser, *der;* **~-file** *n.* Nagelfeile, *die;* **~ polish** *n.* Nagellack, *der;* **~-polish remover** Nagellackentferner, *der;* **~-scissors** *n. pl.* |pair of| **~-scissors** Nagelschere, *die;* **~ varnish** *(Brit.) see* **~ polish**
**naïve, naive** [naɪ'i:v] *adj.,* **na'ively, na'ively** *adv.* naiv
**naked** ['neɪkɪd] *adj.* nackt; **visible to** *or* **with the ~ eye** mit bloßem Auge zu erkennen. **'nakedness** *n.* Nacktheit, *die*
**name** [neɪm] 1. *n.* **a)** Name, *der;* **what's your ~/the ~ of this place?** wie heißt du/dieser Ort?; **my ~ is Jack** ich heiße Jack; **last ~** : Nachname, *der;* **by ~** : namentlich ⟨*erwähnen, aufrufen usw.*⟩; **know sb. by ~** : jmdn. mit Namen kennen; **b)** *(reputation)* Ruf, *der;* **make a ~ for oneself** sich *(Dat.)* einen Namen machen; **c) call** sb. **~s** jmdn. beschimpfen. 2. *v. t.* **a)** *(give ~ to)* ei-

nen Namen geben (+ *Dat.*); ~ **sb.**
**John** jmdn. John nennen; ~ **sb./sth.**
**after** *or (Amer.)* **for sb.** jmdn./etw.
nach jmdm. benennen; **be ~d John**
John heißen; **a man ~d Smith** ein
Mann namens Smith; **b)** *(call by right*
*~)* benennen; **c)** *(nominate)* ~ **sb. [as]**
**sth.** jmdn. zu etw. ernennen. **'name-**
**less** *adj.* namenlos. **'namely** *adv.*
nämlich. **'namesake** *n.* Namensvet-
ter, *der/-*schwester, *die*
**nanny** ['nænɪ] *n. (Brit.)* Kindermäd-
chen, *das.* **'nanny-goat** *n.* Ziege, *die*
**nap** [næp] **1.** *n.* Nickerchen, *das*
*(fam.);* **have a ~:** ein Nickerchen hal-
ten. **2.** *v. i.,* **-pp-** dösen *(ugs.);* **catch sb.**
**~ping** *(fig.)* jmdn. überrumpeln
**nape** [neɪp] *n.* ~ **|of the neck|** Nacken,
*der;* Genick, *das*
**napkin** ['næpkɪn] *n.* Serviette, *die*
**Naples** ['neɪplz] *pr. n.* Neapel *(das)*
**nappy** ['næpɪ] *n. (Brit.)* Windel, *die*
**narcissus** [nɑː'sɪsəs] *n., pl.* **narcissi**
[nɑː'sɪsaɪ] *or* **~es** Narzisse, *die*
**narcotic** [nɑː'kɒtɪk] **1.** *n.* **a)** *(drug)*
Rauschgift, *das;* **b)** *(active ingredient)*
Betäubungsmittel, *das.* **2.** *adj.* **a)** nar-
kotisch; ~ **drug** Rauschgift, *das;* **b)**
*(causing drowsiness)* einschläfernd
**narrate** [nə'reɪt] *v. t.* erzählen; kom-
mentieren ⟨*Film*⟩. **narration** [nə-
'reɪʃn] *n.* Erzählung, *die.* **narrative**
['nærətɪv] **1.** *n.* Erzählung, *die.* **2.** *adj.*
erzählend. **narrator** [nə'reɪtə(r)] *n.*
Erzähler, *der/*Erzählerin, *die*
**narrow** ['nærəʊ] **1.** *adj.* **a)** schmal;
schmal geschnitten ⟨*Rock, Hose,*
*Ärmel usw.*⟩; eng ⟨*Tal, Gasse*⟩; **b)**
*(limited)* eng; begrenzt ⟨*Auswahl*⟩; **c)**
knapp ⟨*Sieg, Mehrheit*⟩; **have a ~ es-**
**cape** mit knapper Not entkommen
**(from** *Dat.*); **d)** *(not tolerant)* engstirnig. **2.** *v. i.* sich verschmälern; ⟨*Tal:*⟩
sich verengen. **3.** *v. t.* verschmälern;
*(fig.)* einengen. **narrow 'down** *v. t.*
einengen **(to auf** + *Akk.*)
**narrow-'minded** *adj.* engstirnig
**nasal** ['neɪzl] *adj.* **a)** *(Anat.)* Nasen-; **b)**
näselnd; **speak in a ~ voice** näseln
**nastily** ['nɑːstɪlɪ] *adv.* **a)** *(unpleasantly)*
scheußlich; **b)** *(ill-naturedly)* gemein;
**behave ~:** häßlich sein
**nasty** ['nɑːstɪ] *adj.* **a)** *(unpleasant)*
scheußlich ⟨*Geruch, Geschmack*⟩; gemein ⟨*Trick, Person*⟩; häßlich ⟨*Ange-*
*wohnheit*⟩; **that was a ~ thing to say/**
**do** das war gemein; **b)** *(ill-natured)* böse; **be ~ to sb.** häßlich zu jmdm. sein;
**c)** *(serious)* übel; schlimm ⟨*Krankheit,*

*Husten, Verletzung*⟩; **she had a ~ fall**
sie ist übel gefallen
**nation** ['neɪʃn] *n.* Nation, *die; (people)*
Volk, *das.* **national** ['næʃənl] **1.** *adj.*
national; National⟨*flagge,* *-held,*
*-theater, -gericht, -charakter*⟩; Staats-
⟨*sicherheit,* *-religion*⟩; überregional
⟨*Rundfunkstation, Zeitung*⟩; landesweit ⟨*Streik*⟩. **2.** *n. (citizen)* Staatsbürger, *der/-*bürgerin, *die;* **foreign ~:**
Ausländer, *der/*Ausländerin, *die*
**national:** ~ **'anthem** *n.* National-
hymne, *die;* ~ **'costume** *n.* National-
tracht, *die;* **N~ 'Health [Service]** *n.*
*(Brit.)* staatlicher Gesundheitsdienst;
N~ **Health doctor/patient/spectacles**
≈ Kassenarzt, *der/-*patient, *der/-*brille, *die;* **N~ In'surance** *n. (Brit.)* Sozi-
alversicherung, *die*
**nationalism** ['næʃənəlɪzm] *n.* Nationalismus, *der.* **nationalist** ['næʃənə-
lɪst] **1.** *n.* Nationalist, *der/*Nationali-
stin, *die.* **2.** *adj.* nationalistisch
**nationality** [næʃə'nælɪtɪ] *n.* Staatsangehörigkeit, *die;* **what's his ~?** welche
Staatsangehörigkeit hat er?
**nationalization** [næʃənəlaɪ'zeɪʃn] *n.*
Verstaatlichung, *die*
**nationalize** ['næʃənəlaɪz] *v. t.* ver-
staatlichen
**'nationally** *adv.* landesweit
**native** ['neɪtɪv] **1.** *n.* **a)** *(of specified*
*place)* **a ~ of Britain** ein gebürtiger
Brite/eine gebürtige Britin; **b)** *(person*
*born in a place)* Eingeborene, *der/die;*
**c)** *(local inhabitant)* Einheimische,
*der/die.* **2.** *adj.* eingeboren; einheimisch ⟨*Pflanze, Tier*⟩; ~ **inhabitant**
Eingeborene/Einheimische, *der/die;*
~ **land** Geburts- *od.* Heimatland, *das;*
~ **language** Muttersprache, *die*
**nativity** [nə'tɪvɪtɪ] *n.* **the N~ [of Christ]**
die Geburt Christi. **na'tivity play** *n.*
Krippenspiel, *das*
**NATO, Nato** ['neɪtəʊ] *abbr.* North Atlantic Treaty Organization NATO, *die*
**natter** ['nætə(r)] *(Brit. coll.)* **1.** *v. i.*
quatschen *(ugs.).* **2.** *n.* **have a ~:** quatschen *(ugs.)*
**natural** ['nætʃrəl] *adj.* natürlich; Na-
tur⟨*zustand, -seide, -gewalt*⟩. **natural**
**'gas** *n.* Erdgas, *das.* **natural 'his-**
**tory** *n.* Naturkunde, *die*
**naturalism** ['nætʃrəlɪzm] *n.* Naturalismus, *der*
**naturalist** ['nætʃrəlɪst] *n.* Naturfor-
scher, *der/-*forscherin, *die*
**naturalization** [nætʃrəlaɪ'zeɪʃn] *n.*
Einbürgerung, *die*

**naturalize** ['nætʃrəlaɪz] v. t. einbürgern

**naturally** adv. **a)** (by nature) von Natur aus ⟨blaß, fleißig usw.⟩; (in a true-to-life way) naturgetreu; **b)** (of course) natürlich

**naturalness** n. Natürlichkeit, die

**nature** ['neɪtʃə(r)] n. **a)** Natur, die; **b)** (essential qualities) Beschaffenheit, die; in the ~ of things naturgemäß; **c)** (kind) Art, die; things of this ~: derartiges; **d)** (character) Wesen, das; be proud/friendly etc. by ~: ein stolzes/freundliches usw. Wesen haben. **'nature reserve** n. Naturschutzgebiet, das. **'nature study** n. Naturkunde, die. **'nature trail** n. Naturlehrpfad, der

**naught** [nɔːt] n. (arch./dial.) **come to ~:** zunichte werden

**naughtily** ['nɔːtɪlɪ] adv. ungezogen

**naughtiness** ['nɔːtɪnɪs] n. Ungezogenheit, die

**naughty** ['nɔːtɪ] adj. ungezogen; you ~ boy/dog du böser Junge/Hund

**nausea** ['nɔːzɪə] n. Übelkeit, die. **nauseate** ['nɔːzɪeɪt] v. t. (disgust) anwidern. **'nauseating** adj. (disgusting) widerlich. **nauseous** ['nɔːzɪəs] adj. sb. is or feels ~: jmdm. ist übel

**nautical** ['nɔːtɪkl] adj. nautisch. **nautical 'mile** n. Seemeile, die

**naval** ['neɪvl] adj. Marine-; See-⟨schlacht, -macht, -streitkräfte⟩; ~ ship Kriegsschiff, das

**nave** [neɪv] n. [Mittel]schiff, das

**navel** ['neɪvl] n. Nabel, der

**navigate** ['nævɪgeɪt] v. t. **a)** navigieren ⟨Schiff, Flugzeug⟩; **b)** befahren ⟨Fluß usw.⟩. **navigation** [nævɪ'geɪʃn] n. Navigation, die. **navigator** ['nævɪgeɪtə(r)] n. Navigator, der/Navigatorin, die

**navy** ['neɪvɪ] n. **a)** [Kriegs]marine, die; **b)** see navy blue. **navy 'blue** n. Marineblau, das. **'navy-blue** adj. marineblau

**Nazi** ['nɑːtsɪ] **1.** n. Nazi, der. **2.** adj. nazistisch; Nazi-

**NB** abbr. nota bene NB

**NCO** abbr. non-commissioned officer Uffz.

**NE** abbr. north-east NO

**near** [nɪə(r)] **1.** adv. nah[e]; **stand/live |quite| ~:** [ganz] in der Nähe stehen/wohnen; **come or draw ~/~er** ⟨Tag, Zeitpunkt:⟩ nahen/näherrücken; **get ~er together** näher zusammenrücken; **~ at hand** in Reichweite (Dat.); ⟨Ort⟩

ganz in der Nähe; ~ **to = 2. 2.** prep. **a)** (position) nahe an/bei (+ Dat.); (fig.) in der Nähe (+ Gen.); **keep ~ me** halte dich in meiner Nähe; it's ~ **here** es ist hier in der Nähe; **b)** (motion) nahe an (+ Akk.); (fig.) in der Nähe (+ Gen.); **don't come ~ me** komm mir nicht zu nahe. **3.** adj. **a)** (in space or time) nahe; **in the ~ future** in nächster Zukunft; **the ~est man** der am nächsten stehende Mann; **b)** (in nature) **£30 or ~/~est offer** 30 Pfund oder nächstbestes Angebot; ~ **escape** Entkommen mit knapper Not; **that was a ~ miss/thing!** das war knapp! **4.** v. t. sich nähern (+ Dat.); **the building is ~ing completion** das Gebäude steht kurz vor seiner Vollendung. **5.** v. i. ⟨Zeitpunkt:⟩ näherrücken. **'nearby** adj. nahe gelegen

**'nearly** adv. fast; **be ~ in tears** den Tränen nahe sein; **it is ~ six o'clock** es ist kurz vor sechs Uhr; **are you ~ ready?** bist du bald fertig?

**'nearness** n. Nähe, die

**'near-sighted** adj. (Amer.) kurzsichtig

**neat** [niːt] adj. **a)** (tidy) ordentlich; **b)** (undiluted) pur; **c)** (smart) gepflegt ⟨Erscheinung, Kleidung⟩; **d)** (deft) geschickt. **'neatly** adv. see neat a, c, d: ordentlich; gepflegt; geschickt. **'neatness** n. see neat a, c, d: Ordentlichkeit, die; Gepflegtheit, die; Geschicktheit, die

**necessarily** [nesɪ'serɪlɪ] adv. zwangsläufig; **it is not ~ true** es muß nicht [unbedingt] stimmen

**necessary** ['nesɪsərɪ] **1.** adj. nötig; notwendig; **do everything ~:** das Nötige od. Notwendige tun. **2.** n. **the necessaries of life** das Lebensnotwendige

**necessitate** [nɪ'sesɪteɪt] v. t. erforderlich machen

**necessity** [nɪ'sesɪtɪ] n. **a)** (need, necessary thing) Notwendigkeit, die; **do sth. out of or from ~:** etw. notgedrungen tun; **of ~:** notwendigerweise; **b)** (want) Not, der

**neck** [nek] n. **a)** Hals, der; **be a pain in the ~** (coll.) jmdm. auf die Nerven gehen (ugs.); **break one's ~** (fig. coll.) sich den Hals brechen; ~ **and ~:** Kopf an Kopf; **b)** (of garment) Kragen, der

**neck:** **~lace** ['neklɪs] n. [Hals]kette, die; (with jewels) Kollier, das; **~line** n. [Hals]ausschnitt, der; **~tie** n. Krawatte, die

**nectar** ['nektə(r)] *n.* Nektar, *der*
**née** (*Amer.:* **nee**) [neɪ] *adj.* geborene
**need** [niːd] **1.** *n.* **a)** Notwendigkeit, *die* (**for,** *of Gen.*); (*demand*) Bedarf, *der* (**for,** *of* an + *Dat.*); **as the ~ arises** nach Bedarf; **if ~ be** nötigenfalls; **there's no ~ for that** [das ist] nicht nötig; **there's no ~ to do sth.** es ist nicht nötig, etw. zu tun; **be in ~ of sth.** etw. brauchen; **there's no ~ for you to come** du brauchst nicht zu kommen; **b)** *no pl.* (*emergency*) Not, *die;* **in case of ~:** im Notfall; **c)** (*thing*) Bedürfnis, *das.* **2.** *v.t.* **a)** (*require*) brauchen; **sth. that urgently ~s doing** etw., was dringend gemacht werden muß; **it ~s a coat of paint** es muß gestrichen werden; **b)** *expr. necessity* müssen; **I ~ to do it** ich muß es tun; **it ~s/doesn't ~ to be done** es muß getan werden/es braucht nicht getan zu werden; **c)** *pres.* **he ~,** *neg.* **~ not** *or* (*coll.*) **~n't** ['niːdnt] *expr. desirability* müssen; *with neg.* brauchen zu
**needle** ['niːdl] **1.** *n.* Nadel, *die.* **2.** *v.t.* (*coll.*) nerven (*ugs.*)
**needless** ['niːdlɪs] *adj.* unnötig; **~ to add** *or* **say, ...:** überflüssig zu sagen, daß ... '**needlessly** *adv.* unnötig
'**needlework** *n.* Handarbeit, *die;* **do ~:** handarbeiten
**needn't** ['niːdnt] (*coll.*) = **need not;** *see* **need 2 c**
'**needy** *adj.* notleidend; bedürftig
**negation** [nɪ'geɪʃn] *n.* Verneinung, *die*
**negative** ['negətɪv] **1.** *adj.* negativ. **2.** *n.* **a)** (*Photog.*) Negativ, *das;* **b)** (*~ statement*) negative Aussage; (*answer*) Nein, *das.* '**negatively** *adv.* negativ
**neglect** [nɪ'glekt] **1.** *v.t.* vernachlässigen; **she ~ed to write** sie hat es versäumt zu schreiben. **2.** *n.* Vernachlässigung, *die;* **be in a state of ~** (*Gebäude:*) verwahrlost sein. **neglectful** [nɪ'glektfl] *adj.* gleichgültig (**of** gegenüber); **be ~ of** sich nicht kümmern um
**negligence** ['neglɪdʒəns] *n.* Nachlässigkeit, *die;* (*Law, Insurance, etc.*) Fahrlässigkeit, *die*
**negligent** ['neglɪdʒənt] *adj.* nachlässig; **be ~ about sth.** sich um etw. nicht kümmern
**negligible** ['neglɪdʒɪbl] *adj.* unerheblich
**negotiable** [nɪ'gəʊʃəbl] *adj.* **a)** verhandlungsfähig (*Forderung, Bedingungen*); **b)** passierbar (*Straße, Fluß*)
**negotiate** [nɪ'gəʊʃɪeɪt] **1.** *v.i.* verhandeln (**for, on, about** über + *Akk.*). **2.**

*v.t.* **a)** (*arrange*) aushandeln; **b)** überwinden (*Hindernis*); passieren (*Straße, Fluß*); nehmen (*Kurve*).
**negotiation** [nɪgəʊʃɪ'eɪʃn] *n.* Verhandlung, *die.* **negotiator** [nɪ'gəʊʃɪeɪtə(r)] *n.* Unterhändler, *der/*-händlerin, *die*
**Negress** ['niːgrɪs] *n.* Negerin, *die*
**Negro** ['niːgrəʊ] **1.** *n., pl.* **~es** Neger, *der.* **2.** *adj.* Neger-
**neigh** [neɪ] **1.** *v.i.* wiehern. **2.** *n.* Wiehern, *das*
**neighbor** *etc.* (*Amer.*) *see* **neighbour** *etc.*
**neighbour** ['neɪbə(r)] **1.** *n.* Nachbar, *der/*Nachbarin, *die;* **my next-door ~s** meine Nachbarn von nebenan. **2.** *v.t. & i.* **~ [upon]** grenzen an (+ *Akk.*). '**neighbourhood** *n.* (*district*) Gegend, *die;* (*neighbours*) Nachbarschaft, *die;* [**somewhere**] **in the ~ of £100** [so] um [die] 100 Pfund. '**neighbouring** *adj.* Nachbar-; angrenzend (*Felder*)
**neither** ['naɪðə(r), 'niːðə(r)] **1.** *adj.* keiner/keine/keins der beiden. **2.** *pron.* keiner/keine/keins von *od.* der beiden. **3.** *adv.* (*also not*) auch nicht; **~ am I,** (*sl.*) **me ~:** ich auch nicht. **4.** *conj.* (*not either*) weder; **~ ... nor ...:** weder ... noch ...
**neon** ['niːɒn] *n.* Neon, *das*
**neon: ~ 'light** *n.* Neonlampe, *die;* '**sign** *n.* Neonreklame, *die*
**nephew** ['nevjuː, 'nefjuː] *n.* Neffe, *der*
**nepotism** ['nepətɪzm] *n.* Vetternwirtschaft, *die*
**Neptune** ['neptjuːn] *pr. n.* (*Astron.*) Neptun, *der*
**nerve** [nɜːv] *n.* Nerv, *der;* **get on sb.'s ~s** jmdm. auf die Nerven gehen (*ugs.*); **lose one's ~:** die Nerven verlieren; **what [a] ~!** [so eine] Frechheit! '**nerve gas** *n.* Nervengas, *das.* '**nerve-racking** *adj.* nervenaufreibend
**nervous** ['nɜːvəs] *adj.* **a)** (*Anat., Med.*) Nerven-; **~ breakdown** Nervenzusammenbruch, *der;* **b)** (*having delicate nerves*) nervös; **be a ~ wreck** mit den Nerven völlig am Ende sein; **c)** (*Brit.: timid*) **be ~ of** *or* **about** Angst haben vor (+ *Dat.*); **be a ~ person** ängstlich sein. '**nervously** *adv.* nervös. '**nervousness** *n.* Ängstlichkeit, *die*
**nervy** ['nɜːvɪ] *adj.* **a)** nervös; **b)** (*Amer. coll.: impudent*) unverschämt
**nest 1.** *n.* Nest, *das.* **2.** *v.i.* nisten. '**nest-egg** *n.* (*fig.*) Notgroschen, *der*

**nestle** ['nesl] *v. i.* **a)** sich schmiegen **(to, up against** an + *Akk.*); **b)** *(lie half hidden)* eingebettet sein

¹**net** [net] **1.** *n.* Netz, *das.* **2.** *v. t.,* -tt- [mit einem Netz] fangen

²**net** *adj.* **a)** netto; Netto⟨*einkommen, -[verkaufs]preis usw.*⟩; ~ **weight** Nettogewicht, *das;* **b)** *(ultimate)* End⟨*ergebnis, -effekt*⟩

**net:** ~**ball** *n.* Netzball, *der.* ~ '**curtain** *n.* Store, *der*

**Netherlands** ['neðələndz] *pr. n. sing. or pl.* Niederlande *Pl.*

**nett** *see* ²**net** a

**netting** *n.* *([piece of] net)* Netz, *das;* **wire** ~: Maschendraht, *der*

**nettle** ['netl] *n.* Nessel, *die*

'**network** *n.* Netz, *das*

**neuralgia** [njʊə'rældʒə] *n.* Neuralgie, *die*

**neurosis** [njʊə'rəʊsɪs] *n., pl.* **neuroses** [njʊə'rəʊsiːz] Neurose, *die.* **neurotic** [njʊə'rɒtɪk] *adj.* **a)** nervenkrank; **b)** *(coll.)* neurotisch

**neuter** ['njuːtə(r)] *adj.* sächlich

**neutral** ['njuːtrl] **1.** *adj.* neutral. **2.** *n.* (~ **gear**) Leerlauf, *der.* **neutrality** [njuː'trælɪtɪ] *n.* Neutralität, *die*

**neutralize** ['njuːtrəlaɪz] *v. t.* neutralisieren

**neutron** ['njuːtrɒn] *n.* Neutron, *das*

**never** ['nevə(r)] *adv.* **a)** nie; ~-**ending** endlos; **b)** *(coll.)* **you ~ believed that, did you?** du hast das doch wohl nicht geglaubt?; **well, I ~ [did]!** [na] so was!

**nevertheˈless** *adv.* trotzdem

**new** [njuː] *adj.* neu

**new:** ~-**born** *adj.* neugeboren; ~**comer** ['njuːkʌmə(r)] *n.* Neuankömmling, *der;* ~-**fangled** ['njuːfæŋgld] *adj.* neumodisch; ~-**found** *adj.* neu; ~-**laid** *adj.* frisch [gelegt]

'**newly** *adv. (recently)* neu; ~ **married** seit kurzem verheiratet. '**newly-wed** *n.* Jungverheiratete, *der/die*

**new 'moon** *n.* Neumond, *der*

'**newness** *n.* Neuheit, *die*

**news** [njuːz] *n., no pl.* **a)** Nachricht, *die;* **be in the** ~: Schlagzeilen machen; **good/bad** ~: schlechte/gute Nachrichten; **b)** *(Radio, Telev.)* Nachrichten *Pl.*

**news:** ~**agent** *n.* Zeitungshändler, *der/*-händlerin, *die;* ~ **bulletin** *n.* Nachrichten *Pl.* ~**caster** *n.* Nachrichtensprecher, *der/*-sprecherin, *die;* ~**flash** *n.* Kurzmeldung, *die;* ~ '**headline** *n.* Schlagzeile, *die;* ~**letter** *n.* Rundschreiben, *das;*

~**paper** ['njuːspeɪpə(r)] *n.* **a)** Zeitung, *die;* **b)** *(material)* Zeitungspapier, *das;* ~**reader** *n.* Nachrichtensprecher, *der/*-sprecherin, *die;* ~-**reel** *n.* Wochenschau, *die;* ~-**sheet** *n.* Informationsblatt, *das;* ~ **summary** *n.* Kurznachrichten *Pl.;* ~**worthy** *adj.* [für die Medien] interessant

**newt** [njuːt] *n.* [Wasser]molch, *der*

**New: new 'year** *n.* Neujahr, *das;* **over the new year** über Neujahr; **a Happy ~ Year** ein glückliches *od.* gutes neues Jahr. ~ '**Year's** *(Amer.),* ~ **Year's 'Day** *ns.* Neujahrstag, *der;* ~ **Year's 'Eve** *n.* Silvester, *der od.* das; ~ **Zealand** [~ 'ziːlənd] *pr. n.* Neuseeland *(das);* ~ '**Zealander** *n.* Neuseeländer, *der/*-länderin, *die*

**next** [nekst] **1.** *adj.* nächst...; **the ~ but one** der/die/das übernächste; ~ **to** *(fig.: almost)* fast; nahezu; **[the] ~ time** das nächste Mal; **the ~ best** der/die/das nächstbeste; **am I ~?** komme ich jetzt dran? **2.** *adv. (in the ~ place)* als nächstes; *(on the ~ occasion)* das nächste Mal; **it's my turn ~:** ich komme als nächster dran; **sit/stand ~ to sb.** neben jmdm. stehen/sitzen; **place sth. ~ to sb./sth.** etw. neben jmdn./etw. stellen. **3.** *n.* **a) the week after ~:** [die] übernächste Woche; **b)** *(person)* ~ **of kin** nächster/nächste Angehörige; ~, **please!** der nächste, bitte!

'**next-door** *adj.* gleich nebenan *nachgestellt*

**NHS** *abbr. (Brit.)* **National Health Service**

**nib** [nɪb] *n.* Feder, *die*

**nibble** ['nɪbl] *v. t. & i.* knabbern **(at, on** an + *Dat.*)

**nice** [naɪs] *adj.* nett; angenehm ⟨*Stimme*⟩; schön ⟨*Wetter*⟩; *(iron.: disgraceful, difficult)* schön; ~ **[and] warm/fast** schön warm/schnell; ~-**looking** hübsch. '**nicely** *adv. (coll.)* **a)** *(well)* nett; gut ⟨*arbeiten, sich benehmen, plaziert sein*⟩; **b)** *(all right)* gut; **that will do ~:** das reicht völlig. **niceties** ['naɪsɪtɪz] *n. pl.* Feinheiten

**niche** [nɪtʃ, niːʃ] *n.* **a)** *(in wall)* Nische, *die;* **b)** *(fig.: suitable place)* Platz, *der*

**nick** *n.* **a)** *(notch)* Kerbe, *die;* **b)** *(sl. prison)* Knast, *der (salopp);* **c)** *(Brit.: police station)* Wache, *die;* **d) in good/poor ~** *(coll.)* gut/nicht gut im Schuß *(ugs.);* **e) in the ~ of time** gerade noch rechtzeitig. **2.** *v. t.* **a)** einkerben; **b)** *(Brit. sl.: arrest)* einlochen *(salopp);* **c)** *(Brit. sl.: steal)* klauen *(salopp)*

**nickel** ['nɪkl] *n.* **a)** Nickel, *das;* **b)** *(Amer. coll.: coin)* Fünfcentstück, *das*

**nickname** ['nɪkneɪm] *n.* Spitzname, *der; (affectionate)* Koseform, *die*

**nicotine** ['nɪkəti:n] *n.* Nikotin, *das*

**niece** [ni:s] *n.* Nichte, *die*

**Nigeria** [naɪ'dʒɪərɪə] *pr. n.* Nigeria *(das)*

**niggardly** ['nɪgədlɪ] *adj.* knaus[e]rig *(ugs.)*

**niggling** ['nɪglɪŋ] *adj.* **a)** *(petty)* belanglos; **b)** *(trivial)* nichtssagend; **c)** *(nagging)* nagend

**night** [naɪt] *n.* Nacht, *die; (evening)* Abend, *der;* **the following ~:** die Nacht/der Abend darauf; **the previous ~:** die vorausgegangene Nacht/der vorausgegangene Abend; **on Sunday ~:** Sonntag nacht/[am] Sonntag abend; **for the ~:** über Nacht; **at ~:** nachts/abends; **late at ~:** spätabends

**night:** **~cap** *n.* *(drink)* Schlaftrunk, *der;* **~club** *n.* Nachtklub, *der;* **~-dress** *n.* Nachthemd, *das;* **~fall** *n.* Einbruch der Dunkelheit

**nightie** ['naɪtɪ] *n.* *(coll.)* Nachthemd, *das*

**nightingale** ['naɪtɪŋgeɪl] *n.* Nachtigall, *die*

**night-life** *n.* Nachtleben, *das*

**nightly** ['naɪtlɪ] **1.** *adj. (happening every night/evening)* allnächtlich/allabendlich. **2.** *adv. (every night)* jede Nacht; *(every evening)* jeden Abend

**night:** **~mare** *n.* Alptraum, *der;* **~school** *n.* Abendschule, *die;* **~shift** *n.* Nachtschicht, *die;* **~-time** *n.* Nacht, *die;* **in the** *or* **at ~-time** nachts; **~-'watchman** *n.* Nachtwächter, *der*

**nil** [nɪl] *n.* null

**Nile** [naɪl] *pr. n.* Nil, *der*

**nimble** ['nɪmbl] *adj.,* **nimbly** ['nɪmblɪ] *adv.* flink

**nine** [naɪn] **1.** *adj.* neun. **2.** *n.* Neun, *die. See also* **eight**

**nineteen** [naɪn'ti:n] **1.** *adj.* neunzehn. **2.** *n.* Neunzehn, *die. See also* **eight**.

**nineteenth** [naɪn'ti:nθ] **1.** *adj.* neunzehnt... **2.** *n. (fraction)* Neunzehntel, *das. See also* **eighth**

**ninetieth** ['naɪntɪɪθ] *adj.* neunzigst...

**ninety** ['naɪntɪ] **1.** *adj.* neunzig. **2.** *n.* Neunzig, *die. See also* **eight; eighty 2**

**ninth** [naɪnθ] **1.** *adj.* neunt... **2.** *n. (in sequence)* neunte, *der/die/das; (in rank)* Neunte, *der/die/das; (fraction)* Neuntel, *das. See also* **eighth**

**nip** **1.** *v. t.,* **-pp-** zwicken. **2.** *v. i.,* **-pp-** *(Brit. sl.)* **~ in** hinein-/hereinflitzen *(ugs.);* **~ out** hinaus-/herausflitzen *(ugs.).* **3.** *n. (pinch, squeeze)* Kniff, *der; (bite)* Biß, *der.* **'nipper** *n. (Brit. coll.: child)* Balg, *das (ugs.)*

**nipple** ['nɪpl] *n.* **a)** Brustwarze, *die;* **b)** *(of feeding-bottle)* Sauger, *der*

**nitric acid** ['naɪtrɪk æsɪd] *n.* Salpetersäure, *die*

**nitrogen** ['naɪtrədʒən] *n.* Stickstoff, *der*

**nitwit** ['nɪtwɪt] *n. (coll.)* Trottel, *der (ugs.)*

**no** [nəʊ] **1.** *adj.* kein. **2.** *adv.* **a)** *(by no amount)* nicht; **no less [than]** nicht weniger [als]; **no more wine?** keinen Wein mehr?; **b)** *(as answer)* nein. **3.** *n., pl.* **noes** [nəʊz] Nein, *das*

**No.** *abbr.* **number** Nr.

**Noah's ark** [nəʊəz 'ɑ:k] *n.* die Arche Noah

**nobility** [nə'bɪlɪtɪ] *n.* Adel, *der;* **many of the ~:** viele Adlige

**noble** ['nəʊbl] **1.** *adj.* ad[e]lig; edel ⟨*Gedanken, Gefühle*⟩. **2.** *n.* Adlige, *der/die.* **nobleman** ['nəʊblmən] *n.., pl.* **noblemen** ['nəʊblmən] Adlige, *der*

**nobly** ['nəʊblɪ] *adv.* **a)** edel[gesinnt]; **b)** *(generously)* edelmütig *(geh.)*

**nobody** ['nəʊbədɪ] *n. & pron.* niemand; keiner; *(person of no importance)* Niemand, *der*

**nocturnal** [nɒk'tɜ:nl] *adj.* nächtlich; **~ animal/bird** Nachttier, *das/*-vogel, *der*

**nod** [nɒd] **1.** *v. i.,* **-dd-** nicken. **2.** *v. t.,* **-dd-:** **~ one's head [in greeting]** [zum Gruß] mit dem Kopf nicken. **3.** *n.* [Kopf]nicken, *das.* **nod 'off** *v. i.* einnicken *(ugs.)*

**noise** [nɔɪz] *n.* Geräusch, *das; (loud, harsh, unwanted)* Lärm, *der.* **'noiseless** *adj.,* **'noiselessly** *adv.* lautlos.

**noisily** ['nɔɪzɪlɪ] *adv.,* **noisy** ['nɔɪzɪ] *adj.* laut

**nomad** ['nəʊmæd] *n.* Nomade, *der.* **nomadic** [nəʊ'mædɪk] *adj.* nomadisch; **~ tribe** Nomadenstamm, *der*

**'no man's land** *n.* Niemandsland, *das*

**nominal** ['nɒmɪnl] *adj.* nominell; äußerst niedrig ⟨*Preis, Miete*⟩

**nominate** ['nɒmɪneɪt] *v. t.* **a)** *(propose)* nominieren; **b)** *(appoint)* ernennen. **nomination** [nɒmɪ'neɪʃn] *n. see* **nominate:** Nominierung, *die;* Ernennung, *die*

**nominative** ['nɒmɪnətɪv] *adj. & n.* **~ [case]** Nominativ, *der*

**nominee** [nɒmɪ'ni:] *n. (candidate)* Kandidat, *der/*Kandidatin, *die*

**non-** [nɒn] *pref.* nicht-
**nonchalant** ['nɒnʃələnt] *adj.* unbekümmert
**non-commissioned 'officer** *n.* Unteroffizier, *der*
**non-committal** [nɒnkə'mɪtl] *adj.* unverbindlich; **he was ~:** er hat sich nicht klar geäußert
**nondescript** ['nɒndɪskrɪpt] *adj.* unscheinbar; undefinierbar ⟨*Farbe*⟩
**none** [nʌn] **1.** *pron.* kein...; **~ of them** keiner/keine/keines von ihnen; **~ of this** nichts davon. **2.** *adv.* keineswegs; **I'm ~ the wiser now** jetzt bin ich um nichts klüger; **~ the less** nichtsdestoweniger
**nonentity** [nɒ'nɛntɪtɪ] *n.* Nichts, *das*
**non-existent** [nɒnɪg'zɪstənt] *adj.* nicht vorhanden
**non-'fiction** *n.* Sachliteratur, *die*
**non-'iron** *adj.* bügelfrei
**non-'member** *n.* Nichtmitglied, *das*
**nonplus** [nɒn'plʌs] *v. t.,* **-ss-** verblüffen
**nonsense** ['nɒnsəns] **1.** *n.* Unsinn, *der.* **2.** *int.* Unsinn. **nonsensical** [nɒn'sɛnsɪkl] *adj.* unsinnig
**non-'smoker** *n.* **a)** *(person)* Nichtraucher, *der/*-raucherin, *die;* **b)** *(train compartment)* Nichtraucherabteil, *das*
**non-'stick** *adj.* **~ frying-pan** *etc.* Bratpfanne *usw.* mit Antihaftbeschichtung
**non-stop 1.** ['--] *adj.* durchgehend ⟨*Zug, Busverbindung*⟩; Nonstop⟨*flug, -revue*⟩. **2.** [-'-] *adv.* ohne Unterbrechung ⟨*tanzen, reden, reisen, senden*⟩; nonstop ⟨*fliegen, tanzen, fahren*⟩
**noodle** ['nu:dl] *n., usu. pl.* Nudel, *die*
**nook** [nʊk] *n.* Winkel, *der;* Ecke, *die*
**noon** [nu:n] *n.* Mittag, *der;* zwölf Uhr [mittags]; **at/before ~:** um/vor zwölf [Uhr mittags]
**'no one** *pron. see* **nobody**
**noose** [nu:s] *n.* Schlinge, *die*
**nor** [nə(r), *stressed* nɔ:(r)] *conj.* noch; **neither/not ... ~ ...:** weder ... noch ...
**norm** [nɔ:m] *n.* Norm, *die*
**normal** ['nɔ:ml] **1.** *adj.* normal. **2.** *n.* **a)** (**~ value**) Normalwert, *der;* **b)** *(usual state)* normaler Stand; **everything is back to** *or* **has returned to ~:** es hat sich wieder alles normalisiert. **normality** [nɔ:'mælɪtɪ] Normalität, *die.* **'normally** *adv.* **a)** *(in normal way)* normal; **b)** *(ordinarily)* normalerweise
**north** [nɔ:θ] **1.** *n.* **a)** Norden, *der;* **in/to[wards]/from the ~:** im/nach/von Norden; **to the ~ of** nördlich von; **b)**

*usu.* **N~** *(Geog., Polit.)* Norden, *der.* **2.** *adj.* nördlich; Nord⟨*wind, -küste, -grenze*⟩. **3.** *adv.* nach Norden; **~ of** nördlich von
**north: N~ 'Africa** *pr. n.* Nordafrika *(das);* **N~ A'merica** *pr. n.* Nordamerika *(das);* **N~ A'merican 1.** *adj.* nordamerikanisch; **2.** *n.* Nordamerikaner, *der/*-amerikanerin, *die;* **~bound** *adj.* ⟨*Zug, Verkehr usw.*⟩ in Richtung Norden; **~-'east 1.** *n.* Nordosten, *der;* **2.** *adj.* nordöstlich; Nordost⟨*wind, -küste*⟩; **3.** *adv.* nordostwärts; nach Nordosten; **~-'eastern** *adj.* nordöstlich
**northerly** ['nɔ:ðəlɪ] *adj.* nördlich; ⟨*Wind*⟩ aus nördlichen Richtungen
**northern** ['nɔ:ðən] *adj.* nördlich; Nord⟨*grenze, -hälfte, -seite*⟩. **Northern 'Ireland** *pr. n.* Nordirland *(das)*
**North: ~ 'Germany** *pr. n.* Norddeutschland *(das);* **~ 'Pole** *pr. n.* Nordpol, *der;* **~ 'Sea** *pr. n.* Nordsee, *die*
**northward[s]** ['nɔ:θwəd(z)] *adv.* nordwärts
**north: ~-'west 1.** *n.* Nordwesten, *der;* **2.** *adj.* nordwestlich; Nordwest⟨*wind, -küste*⟩; **3.** *adv.* nordwestwärts; nach Nordwesten; **~-'western** *adj.* nordwestlich
**Norway** ['nɔ:weɪ] *pr. n.* Norwegen *(das).* **Norwegian** [nɔ:'wi:dʒn] **1.** *adj.* norwegisch; **sb. is ~:** jmd. ist Norweger/Norwegerin. **2.** *n.* **a)** *(person)* Norweger, *der/*Norwegerin, *die;* **b)** *(language)* Norwegisch, *das; see also* **English 2 a**
**Nos.** *abbr.* **numbers** Nrn.
**nose** [nəʊz] **1.** *n.* Nase, *die.* **2.** *v. t.* **~ one's way** sich *(Dat.)* vorsichtig seinen Weg bahnen. **3.** *v. i.* sich vorsichtig bewegen. **nose a'bout, nose a'round** *v. i.* *(coll.)* herumschnüffeln *(ugs.)*
**nose: ~bleed** *n.* Nasenbluten, *das;* **~dive 1.** *n.* Sturzflug, *der;* **2.** *v. i.* im Sturzflug hinuntergehen
**nosey** *see* **nosy**
**nostalgia** [nɒ'stældʒə] *n.* Nostalgie, *die;* **~ for sth.** Sehnsucht nach etw. **nostalgic** [nɒ'stældʒɪk] *adj.* nostalgisch
**nostril** ['nɒstrɪl] *n.* Nasenloch, *das; (of horse)* Nüster, *die*
**nosy** ['nəʊzɪ] *adj. (sl.)* neugierig
**not** [nɒt] *adv.* nicht; **he is ~ a doctor** er ist kein Arzt; **~ at all** überhaupt nicht; **~ ... but ...:** nicht ..., sondern ...; **~ a thing** gar nichts

**notable** ['nəʊtəbl] *adj.* bemerkenswert; **be ~ for sth.** für etw. bekannt
sein. **notably** ['nəʊtəblɪ] *adv.* besonders
**notation** [nəʊ'teɪʃn] *n.* Notierung, *die*
**notch** [nɒtʃ] **1.** *n.* Kerbe, *die.* **2.** *v.t.*
kerben. **notch 'up** *v.t.* erreichen
**note** [nəʊt] **1.** *n.* **a)** *(Mus.) (sign)* Note,
*die; (key of piano)* Taste, *die; (sound)*
Ton, *der;* **b)** *(jotting)* Notiz, *die;* **take**
*or* **make ~s** sich *(Dat.)* Notizen machen; **take** *or* **make a ~ of sth.** sich
*(Dat.)* etw. notieren; **c)** *(comment,
footnote)* Anmerkung, *die;* **d)** *(short
letter)* [kurzer] Brief; **e)** *(importance)* **a
person/something of ~:** eine bedeutende Persönlichkeit/etwas Bedeuten-
des; **be of ~:** bedeutend sein. **2.** *v.t.* **a)**
*(pay attention to)* beachten; **b)** *(notice)*
bemerken; **c)** *(write)* **~ |down]** [sich
*(Dat.)*] notieren. **'notebook** *n.* Notizbuch, *das*
**'noted** *adj.* bekannt **(for** für, wegen)
**note: ~pad** *n.* Notizblock, *der;*
**~paper** *n.* Briefpapier, *das;*
**~worthy** *adj.* bemerkenswert
**nothing** ['nʌθɪŋ] *n.* nichts; **~ interesting** nichts Interessantes; **~ much**
nichts Besonderes; **~ more than** nur;
**~ more, ~ less** nicht mehr, nicht weniger; **next to ~:** so gut wie nichts; **have
|got]** *or* **be ~ to do with sb./sth.** *(not
concern)* nichts zu tun haben mit
jmdm./etw.; **have ~ to do with sb.**
*(avoid)* jmdm. aus dem Weg gehen
**notice** ['nəʊtɪs] **1.** *n.* **a)** Anschlag, *der;
(in newspaper)* Anzeige, *die;* **b)** *(warning)* **at short/a moment's ~:** kurzfri-
stig/von einem Augenblick zum an-
dern; **c)** *(formal notification)* Ankün-
digung, *die;* **until further ~:** bis auf
weiteres; **d)** *(ending an agreement)*
Kündigung, *die;* **give sb. a month's ~:**
jmdm. mit einer Frist von einem Monat kündigen; **hand in one's ~, give ~**
*(Brit.),* **give one's ~** *(Amer.)* kündigen;
**e)** *(attention)* **bring sb./sth. to sb.'s ~:**
jmdm. auf jmdn./etw. aufmerksam
machen; **take no ~ of sb./sth.** *(disregard)* keine Notiz von jmdm./etw.
nehmen; **take no ~:** sich nicht darum
kümmern. **2.** *v.t.* bemerken. **noticeable** ['nəʊtɪsəbl] *adj.* wahrnehmbar
⟨*Fleck, Schaden, Geruch*⟩; merklich
⟨*Verbesserung*⟩; spürbar ⟨*Mangel*⟩.
**'notice-board** *n. (Brit.)* Anschlag-
brett, *das;* Schwarzes Brett
**notification** [nəʊtɪfɪ'keɪʃn] *n.* Mitteilung, *die* **(of sth.** über etw. *[Akk.]*)

**notify** ['nəʊtɪfaɪ] *v.t.* **a)** *(make known)*
ankündigen; **b)** *(inform)* benachrichtigen **(of** über *+ Akk.)*
**notion** ['nəʊʃn] *n.* Vorstellung, *die;*
**not have the faintest/least ~ of how/
what** *etc.* nicht die blasseste/geringste
Ahnung haben, wie/was usw.
**notoriety** [nəʊtə'raɪətɪ] *n.* traurige Berühmtheit
**notorious** [nə'tɔːrɪəs] *adj.* berüchtigt
**(for** wegen); notorisch ⟨*Lügner*⟩
**nougat** ['nuːgɑː] *n.* Nougat, *das od.
der*
**nought** [nɔːt] *n.* Null, *die*
**noun** [naʊn] *n. (Ling.)* Substantiv, *das*
**nourish** ['nʌrɪʃ] *v.t.* ernähren **(on** mit).
**'nourishing** *adj.* nahrhaft. **'nour-
ishment** *n.* Nahrung, *die*
**Nov.** *abbr.* November Nov.
**novel** ['nɒvl] **1.** *n.* Roman, *der.* **2.** *adj.*
neuartig. **novelist** ['nɒvəlɪst] *n.* Ro-
manautor, *der/*-autorin, *die*
**novelty** ['nɒvltɪ] *n.* **a)** **be a/no ~:** et-
was/nichts Neues sein; **b)** *(newness)*
Neuheit, *die;* **c)** *(gadget)* Überraschung, *die*
**November** [nə'vembə(r)] *n.* November, *der; see also* August
**novice** ['nɒvɪs] *n.* Anfänger, *der/*An-
fängerin, *die*
**now** [naʊ] **1.** *adv.* jetzt; *(nowadays)*
heutzutage; *(immediately)* [jetzt] sofort; **just ~** *(very recently)* gerade
eben; **|every] ~ and then** *or* **again** hin
und wieder; **well ~:** also; **~, ~:** na,
na; **~ then na** *(ugs.).* **2.** *conj.* **~
|that] ...:** jetzt, wo ... **3.** *n.* **before ~:** frü-
her; **by ~:** inzwischen; **a week from ~:**
[heute] in einer Woche. **nowadays**
['naʊədeɪz] *adv.* heutzutage
**nowhere** ['nəʊweə(r)] *adv.* nirgends;
nirgendwo; *(to no place)* nirgendwo-
hin
**nozzle** ['nɒzl] *n.* Düse, *die*
**nuance** ['njuːɑːs] *n.* Nuance, *die*
**nuclear** ['njuːklɪə(r)] *adj.* Atom-;
Kern⟨*explosion*⟩; atomar ⟨*Antrieb, Ge-
fechtskopf, Wettrüsten, Abrüstung*⟩;
nuklear ⟨*Abschreckung, Sprengkörper*⟩; atomgetrieben ⟨*Unterseeboot*⟩
**nucleus** ['njuːklɪəs] *n., pl.* **nuclei**
['njuːklɪaɪ] Kern, *der*
**nude** [njuːd] **1.** *adj.* nackt. **2.** *n.* **a)**
*(figure)* Akt, *der;* **b)** **in the ~:** nackt
**nudge** [nʌdʒ] **1.** *v.t.* anstoßen. **2.** *n.*
Stoß, *der*
**nudism** ['njuːdɪzm] *n.* Nudismus, *der;*
Freikörperkultur, *die.* **nudist** ['njuːd-
ɪst] *n.* Nudist, *der/*Nudistin, *die;* at-

*trib.* Nudisten-. **nudity** ['nju:dıtı] *n.* Nacktheit, *die*

**nugget** ['nʌgıt] *n.* Klumpen, *der; (of gold)* Goldklumpen, *der; (fig.)* ~**s of wisdom** goldene Weisheiten

**nuisance** ['nju:səns] *n.* Ärgernis, *das; what a* ~! so etwas Dummes!

**null** [nʌl] *adj.* ~ **and void** null und nichtig

**numb** [nʌm] **1.** *adj.* gefühllos, taub (**with** vor + *Dat.*); *(without emotion)* benommen. **2.** *v. t.* betäuben

**number** ['nʌmbə(r)] **1.** *n.* **a)** *(in series)* Nummer, *die;* **you've got the wrong** ~ *(Teleph.)* Sie sind falsch verbunden; **dial a wrong** ~: sich verwählen *(ugs.);* **b)** *(esp. Math.: numeral)* Zahl, *die;* **c)** *(sum, total, quantity)* [An]zahl, *die;* **a** ~ **of people/things** einige Leute/Dinge; **a** ~ **of times** mehrmals. **2.** *v. t.* **a)** *(assign* ~ *to)* numerieren; **b)** *(amount to, comprise)* zählen; **c)** *(include)* zählen (**among, with** zu); **d)** sb.'s days are ~ed jmds. Tage sind gezählt. '**number-plate** *n.* Nummernschild, *das*

**numeral** ['nju:mərl] *n.* Ziffer, *die*

**numerate** [nju:mərət] *adj.* be ~: rechnen können

**numerical** [nju:'merıkl] *adj.* numerisch; Zahlen⟨*wert, -folge*⟩; zahlenmäßig ⟨*Stärke, Überlegenheit*⟩

**numerous** ['nju:mərəs] *adj.* zahlreich

**nun** [nʌn] *n.* Nonne, *die*

**nurse** [nɜ:s] **1.** *n.* Krankenschwester, *die;* [**male**] ~: Krankenpfleger, *der.* **2.** *v. t.* **a)** pflegen ⟨*Kranke*⟩; **b)** *(fig.)* hegen *(geh.)* ⟨*Gefühl, Groll*⟩

**nursery** ['nɜ:sərı] *n.* **a)** *(room)* Kinderzimmer, *das;* **b)** *(crèche)* Kindertagesstätte, *die;* **c)** *see* **nursery school;** **d)** *(for plants)* Gärtnerei, *die.* '**nursery rhyme** *n.* Kinderreim, *der.* '**nursery school** *n.* Kindergarten, *der*

**nursing** ['nɜ:sıŋ] *n.* Krankenpflege, *die; attrib.* Pflege⟨*personal, -beruf*⟩. '**nursing home** *n.* Pflegeheim, *das*

**nurture** ['nɜ:tʃə(r)] *v. t. (rear)* aufziehen; *(fig.)* nähren

**nut** [nʌt] *n.* **a)** Nuß, *die;* **b)** *(Mech. Engin.)* [Schrauben]mutter, *die;* **c)** *(crazy person)* Verrückte, *der/die (ugs.).* '**nut-case** *n. (sl.)* Verrückte, *der/die (ugs.).* '**nutcrackers** *n. pl.* Nußknacker, *der*

**nutmeg** ['nʌtmeg] *n.* Muskat, *der*

**nutrient** ['nju:trıənt] *n.* Nährstoff, *der*

**nutrition** [nju:'trıʃn] *n.* Ernährung, *die; (food)* Nahrung, *die.* **nutritious** [nju:'trıʃəs] *adj.* nahrhaft

'**nutshell** *n.* Nußschale, *die;* **in a** ~ *(fig.)* in aller Kürze

**nutty** ['nʌtı] *adj.* **a)** *(in taste)* nussig; **b)** *(sl.: crazy)* verrückt *(ugs.)*

**nuzzle** ['nʌzl] *v. i.* sich kuscheln (**up to, against** an + *Akk.*)

**NW** *abbr.* north-west NW

**nylon** ['naılɒn] *n.* **a)** Nylon, *das; attrib.* Nylon-; **b)** *in pl. (stockings)* Nylonstrümpfe

**nymph** [nımf] *n.* Nymphe, *die*

# O

**O, o** [əʊ] *n.* O, o, *das*

**oaf** [əʊf] *n.* Stoffel, *der (ugs.)*

**oak** [əʊk] *n.* Eiche, *die*

**OAP** *abbr. (Brit.)* **old-age pensioner** Rentner, *der*/Rentnerin, *die*

**oar** [ɔ:(r)] *n.* Ruder, *das*

**oasis** [əʊ'eısıs] *n., pl.* **oases** [əʊ'eısi:z] Oase, *die*

**oat** [əʊt] *n.* ~**s** Hafer, *der*

**oath** [əʊθ] *n.* **a)** Eid, *der;* Schwur, *der;* **b)** *(swear-word)* Fluch, *der*

**obedience** [ə'bi:dıəns] *n.* Gehorsam, *der*

**obedient** [ə'bi:dıənt] *adj.* gehorsam; **be** ~ **to sb./sth.** jmdm./einer Sache gehorchen. **o'bediently** *adv.* gehorsam

**obelisk** ['ɒbəlısk] *n.* Obelisk, *der*

**obese** [əʊ'bi:s] *adj.* fettleibig. **obesity** [əʊ'bi:sıtı] *n.* Fettleibigkeit, *die*

**obey** [əʊ'beı] **1.** *v. t.* gehorchen (+ *Dat.*); sich halten an (+ *Akk.*) ⟨*Vorschrift, Regel*⟩; befolgen ⟨*Befehl*⟩. **2.** *v. i.* gehorchen

**obituary** [ə'bıtjʊərı] *n.* Nachruf, *der* (**to, of** auf + *Akk.*)

**object 1.** ['ɒbdʒıkt] *n.* **a)** *(thing)* Gegenstand, *der;* **b)** *(purpose)* Ziel, *das;* **c)** *(obstacle)* **money/time** *etc.* **is no** ~: Geld/Zeit *usw.* spielt keine Rolle; **d)** *(Ling.)* Objekt, *das.* **2.** [əb'dʒekt] *v. i.* **a)** Einwände/einen Einwand erheben (**to** gegen); **b)** *(have objection or dislike)* etwas dagegen haben; ~ **to sb./sth.** etwas gegen jmdn./etw. haben. **3.** *v. t.* einwenden. **objection** [əb-

'dʒekʃn] n. a) Einwand, *der;* **raise** *or* **make an ~ |to sth.|** einen Einwand [gegen etw.] erheben; b) *(dislike)* Abneigung, *die;* **have an/no ~ to sb./sth.** etw./nichts gegen jmdn./etw. haben; **have no ~s** nichts dagegen haben. **objectionable** [əb'dʒekʃənəbl] *adj.* unangenehm ⟨*Anblick, Geruch*⟩; anstößig ⟨*Bemerkung, Wort, Benehmen*⟩

**objective** [əb'dʒektɪv] 1. *adj.* objektiv. 2. *n. (goal)* Ziel, *das.* **ob'jectively** *adv.* objektiv. **objectivity** [ɒbdʒek-'tɪvɪtɪ] *n.* Objektivität, *die*

**obligation** [ɒblɪ'geɪʃn] *n.* Verpflichtung, *die;* **be under an ~ to sb.** jmdm. verpflichtet sein; **without ~:** unverbindlich

**obligatory** [ə'blɪgətərɪ] *adj.* obligatorisch; **it has become ~ to ...:** es ist jetzt Pflicht, zu ...

**oblige** [ə'blaɪdʒ] *v. t.* a) *(be binding on)* **~ sb. to do sth.** jmdm. vorschreiben, etw. zu tun; b) *(compel)* zwingen; **be ~d to do sth.** gezwungen sein, etw. zu tun; **feel ~d to do sth.** sich verpflichtet fühlen, etw. zu tun; c) *(be kind to)* **~ sb. by doing sth.** jmdm. den Gefallen tun und etw. tun; d) *(grateful)* **be much/greatly ~d to sb. [for sth.]** jmdm. [für etw.] sehr verbunden sein; **much ~d!** besten Dank! **obliging** [ə'blaɪdʒɪŋ] *adj.* entgegenkommend

**oblique** [ə'bliːk] *adj.* schief ⟨*Gerade, Winkel*⟩; *(fig.)* indirekt

**obliterate** [ə'blɪtəreɪt] *v. t.* auslöschen

**oblivion** [ə'blɪvɪən] *n.* Vergessenheit, *die;* **sink** *or* **fall into ~:** in Vergessenheit geraten

**oblivious** [ə'blɪvɪəs] *adj.* **be ~ to** *or* **of sth.** sich *(Dat.)* einer Sache *(Gen.)* nicht bewußt sein

**oblong** ['ɒblɒŋ] 1. *adj.* rechteckig. 2. *n.* Rechteck, *das*

**obnoxious** [əb'nɒkʃəs] *adj.* widerlich

**oboe** ['əʊbəʊ] *n.* Oboe, *die*

**obscene** [əb'siːn] *adj.* obszön. **obscenity** [əb'senɪtɪ] *n.* Obszönität, *die*

**obscure** [əb'skjʊə(r)] 1. *adj.* a) *(unexplained)* dunkel; b) *(hard to understand)* schwer verständlich ⟨*Argument, Dichtung, Autor, Stil*⟩; c) *(unknown)* unbekannt. 2. *v. t.* a) *(make indistinct)* verdunkeln; versperren ⟨*Aussicht*⟩; b) *(make unintelligible)* unverständlich machen

**obsequious** [əb'siːkwɪəs] *adj.* unterwürfig

**observance** [əb'zɜːvəns] *n.* Einhaltung, *die*

**observant** [əb'zɜːvənt] *adj.* aufmerksam

**observation** [ɒbzə'veɪʃn] *n.* a) Beobachtung, *die;* **be |kept| under ~:** beobachtet werden; *(by police)* überwacht werden; b) *(remark)* Bemerkung, *die* (on über + *Akk.*)

**observatory** [əb'zɜːvətərɪ] *n. (Astron.)* Sternwarte, *die*

**observe** [əb'zɜːv] *v. t.* a) *(watch)* beobachten; *(perceive)* bemerken; b) *(abide by, keep)* einhalten; c) *(say)* bemerken. **ob'server** *n.* Beobachter, *der*/Beobachterin, *die*

**obsess** [əb'ses] *v. t.* **~ sb.** von jmdm. Besitz ergreifen *(fig.);* **be/become ~ed with** *or* **by sb./sth.** von jmdm./etw. besessen sein/werden. **obsession** [əb-'seʃn] *n.* Zwangsvorstellung, *die.* **obsessive** [əb'sesɪv] *adj.* zwanghaft; **be ~ about sth.** von etw. besessen sein

**obsolete** ['ɒbsəliːt] *adj.* veraltet

**obstacle** ['ɒbstəkl] *n.* Hindernis, *das* (to für)

**obstinacy** ['ɒbstɪnəsɪ] *n. see* **obstinate:** Starrsinn, *der;* Hartnäckigkeit, *die*

**obstinate** ['ɒbstɪnət] *adj.* starrsinnig; *(adhering to particular course of action)* hartnäckig

**obstruct** [əb'strʌkt] *v. t.* a) *(block)* blockieren; behindern ⟨*Verkehr*⟩; **~ sb.'s view** jmdm. die Sicht versperren; b) *(fig.: impede; also Sport)* behindern. **obstruction** [əb'strʌkʃn] *n.* Blockierung, *die; (of progress; also Sport)* Behinderung, *die.* **obstructive** [əb-'strʌktɪv] *adj.* hinderlich; obstruktiv ⟨*Politik, Taktik*⟩; **be ~** ⟨*Person:*⟩ sich querlegen *(ugs.)*

**obtain** [əb'teɪn] *v. t.* bekommen; erzielen ⟨*Resultat, Wirkung*⟩. **obtainable** [əb'teɪnəbl] *adj.* erhältlich

**obtrusive** [əb'truːsɪv] *adj.* aufdringlich; *(conspicuous)* auffällig

**obtuse** [əb'tjuːs] *adj.* a) stumpf ⟨*Winkel*⟩; b) *(stupid)* begriffsstutzig

**obvious** ['ɒbvɪəs] *adj.* offenkundig; *(easily seen)* augenfällig; **be ~ [to sb.] that ...:** [jmdm.] klar sein, daß ... **'obviously** *adv.* offenkundig; sichtlich ⟨*enttäuschen, überraschen usw.*⟩

**occasion** [ə'keɪʒn] 1. *n.* a) Gelegenheit, *die;* **rise to the ~:** sich der Situation gewachsen zeigen; **on several ~s** bei mehreren Gelegenheiten; **on ~[s]** gelegentlich; b) *(special occurrence)* Anlaß, *der;* **it was quite an ~:** es war ein Ereignis; c) *(reason)* Grund, *der*

**(for** zu). **2.** *v. t.* verursachen. **occasional** [ə'keɪʒənl] *adj.* gelegentlich; vereinzelt ⟨*Regenschauer*⟩. **oc'casionally** *adv.* gelegentlich; |only| **very ~**: gelegentlich einmal

**occult** [ɒ'kʌlt, 'ɒkʌlt] *adj.* okkult; **the ~**: das Okkulte

**occupant** ['ɒkjʊpənt] *n.* Bewohner, *der*/Bewohnerin, *die*; (*of car, bus, etc.*) Insasse, *der*/Insassin, *die*

**occupation** [ɒkjʊ'peɪʃn] *n.* **a)** *(Mil.)* Besetzung, *die*; (*period*) Besatzungszeit, *die*; **b)** *(activity)* Beschäftigung, *die*; **c)** *(profession)* Beruf, *der*. **occupational** [ɒkjʊ'peɪʃənl] *adj.* Berufs-⟨*beratung, -risiko*⟩; **~ therapy** Beschäftigungstherapie, *die*

**occupier** ['ɒkjʊpaɪə(r)] *n.* (*Brit.*) Besitzer, *der*/Besitzerin, *die*; (*tenant*) Bewohner, *der*/Bewohnerin, *die*

**occupy** ['ɒkjʊpaɪ] *v. t.* **a)** *(Mil.; as demonstration)* besetzen; **b)** *(live in)* bewohnen; **c)** *(take up, fill)* einnehmen; belegen ⟨*Zimmer*⟩; in Anspruch nehmen ⟨*Zeit, Aufmerksamkeit*⟩; **d)** *(busy, employ)* beschäftigen

**occur** [ə'kɜː(r)] *v. i.*, **-rr-**: **a)** *(be met with)* vorkommen; ⟨*Gelegenheit:*⟩ sich bieten; ⟨*Problem:*⟩ auftreten; **b)** *(happen)* ⟨*Veränderung:*⟩ eintreten; ⟨*Unfall, Vorfall:*⟩ sich ereignen; **c) ~ to sb.** *(be thought of)* jmdm. in den Sinn kommen; ⟨*Idee:*⟩ jmdm. kommen.

**occurrence** [ə'kʌrəns] *n.* **a)** *(incident)* Ereignis, *das*; Begebenheit, *die*; **b)** *(occurring)* Vorkommen, *das*

**ocean** ['əʊʃn] *n.* Ozean, *der*; Meer, *das*

**o'clock** [ə'klɒk] *adv.* **it is two/six ~**: es ist zwei/sechs Uhr; **at two/six ~**: um zwei/sechs Uhr; **six ~** *attrib.* Sechs-Uhr-⟨*Zug, Maschine, Nachrichten*⟩

**Oct.** *abbr.* **October** Okt.

**octagon** ['ɒktəgən] *n.* Achteck, *das*

**octane** ['ɒkteɪn] *n.* Oktan, *das*

**octave** ['ɒktɪv] *n.* Oktave, *die*

**October** [ɒk'təʊbə(r)] *n.* Oktober, *der*; *see also* **August**

**octopus** ['ɒktəpəs] *n.* Tintenfisch, *der*

**odd** [ɒd] *adj.* **a)** *(surplus, spare)* übrig ⟨*Stück, Silbergeld*⟩; **£25 and a few ~ pence** 25 Pfund und ein paar Pence; **b)** *(occasional)* gelegentlich; **~ job/~-job man** Gelegenheitsarbeit, *die*/-arbeiter, *der*; **c)** *(one of pair or group)* einzeln; **~ socks** nicht zusammengehörende Socken; **be the ~ man out** ⟨*Gegenstand:*⟩ nicht dazu passen; **d)** *(uneven)* ungerade ⟨*Zahl, Seite, Hausnummer*⟩; **e)** *(plus something)*

**forty ~**: über vierzig; **twelve pounds ~**: etwas mehr als zwölf Pfund; **f)** *(strange, eccentric)* seltsam. **oddity** ['ɒdɪtɪ] *n.* *(object, event)* Kuriosität, *die*. **'oddly** *adv.* seltsam; **~ enough** seltsamerweise. **'odd-numbered** *adj.* ungerade

**odds** [ɒdz] *n. pl.* **a)** *(Betting)* Odds *Pl.*; **b)** |the| **~ are that she did it** wahrscheinlich hat sie es getan; **the ~ are against/in favour of sb./sth.** jmds. Aussichten/die Aussichten für etw. sind gering/gut; **c) ~ and ends** Kleinigkeiten; *(of food)* Reste; **d) be at ~ with sb. over sth.** mit jmdm. in etw. *(Dat.)* uneinig sein; **e) it makes no/little ~** |whether ...| es ist völlig/ziemlich gleichgültig|, ob ...|

**odious** ['əʊdɪəs] *adj.* widerwärtig

**odor** *etc.* (*Amer.*) *see* **odour** *etc.*

**odour** ['əʊdə(r)] *n.* Geruch, *der*. **'odourless** *adj.* geruchlos

**of** [əv, *stressed* ɒv] *prep.* von; *indicating material, substance* aus; **articles of clothing** Kleidungsstücke; **a friend of mine** ein Freund von mir; **where's that pencil of mine?** wo ist mein Bleistift?; **it was clever of you to do that** es war klug von dir, das zu tun; **the approval of sb.** jmds. Zustimmung; **the works of Shakespeare** Shakespeares Werke; **be made of ...**: aus ... |hergestellt| sein; **the fifth of January** der fünfte Januar; **his love of his father** seine Liebe zu seinem Vater; **person of extreme views** Mensch mit extremen Ansichten; **a boy of 14 years** ein vierzehnjähriger Junge; **the five of us** wir fünf

**off** [ɒf] **1.** *adv.* **a)** *(away)* **be a few miles ~**: wenige Meilen entfernt sein; **the lake is not far ~**: der See ist nicht weit |weg|; **I'm ~ now** ich gehe jetzt; **~ we go!** los geht's!; **b)** *(not on or attached or supported)* ab; **get the lid ~**: den Deckel abbekommen; **c) be ~** *(switched or turned ~)* ⟨*Wasser, Gas, Strom:*⟩ abgestellt sein; **the light/radio** *etc.* **is ~**: das Licht/Radio usw. ist aus; **d) the meat** *etc.* **is ~**: das Fleisch *usw.* ist schlecht |geworden|; **e) be ~** *(cancelled)* abgesagt sein; ⟨*Verlobung:*⟩ |auf|gelöst sein; **~ and on** immer und wieder *(ugs.)*; **f)** *(not at work)* frei; **on my day ~**: an meinem freien Tag; **have a week ~**: eine Woche Urlaub bekommen; **g)** *(no longer available)* |the| **soup** *etc.* **is ~**: es gibt keine Suppe *usw.* mehr; **h)** *(situated as regards money etc.)* **he is badly** *etc.* **~**: er

ist schlecht *usw.* gestellt. **2.** *prep.* von;
**be ~ school/work** in der Schule/am
Arbeitsplatz fehlen; **be ~ one's food**
keinen Appetit haben; **just ~ the
square** ganz in der Nähe des Platzes
**offal** ['ɒfl] *n.* Innereien *Pl.*
**offence** [ə'fens] *n.* *(Brit.)* **a)** *(hurting of
sb.'s feelings)* Kränkung, *die;* **I meant
no ~:** ich wollte Sie/ihn *usw.* nicht
kränken; **b)** *(annoyance)* **give ~:** Mißfallen erregen; **take ~:** verärgert sein;
**c)** *(crime)* Straftat, *die;* **criminal ~:**
strafbare Handlung
**offend** [ə'fend] **1.** *v.i.* verstoßen
**(against** gegen). **2.** *v.t.* **~ sb.** bei jmdm.
Anstoß erregen; *(hurt feelings of)*
jmdn. kränken. **offender** *n.* Straffäl-
lige, *der/die*
**offense** *(Amer.)* see offence
**offensive** [ə'fensɪv] **1.** *adj.* **a)** *(aggressive)* offensiv; Angriffs‹*waffe*›; **b)**
*(giving offence)* ungehörig; *(indecent)*
anstößig. **2.** *n.* Offensive, *die;* **take the
or go on the ~:** in die *od.* zur Offensive übergehen
**offer** ['ɒfə(r)] **1.** *v.t.* anbieten; vorbringen ‹*Entschuldigung*›; bieten
‹*Chance*›; aussprechen ‹*Beileid*›; **~ to
help** seine Hilfe anbieten; **~ resistance**
Widerstand leisten. **2.** *n.* Angebot,
*das;* [**have/be**] **on ~:** im Angebot [ha-
ben/sein]
**offhand** **1.** *adv.* **a)** *(without preparation)* auf Anhieb ‹*sagen, wissen*›;
spontan ‹*beschließen, entscheiden*›; **b)**
*(casually)* leichthin. **2.** *adj.* **a)** *(without
preparation)* spontan; **b)** *(casual)* beiläufig; **be ~ with sb.** zu jmdm. kurz angebunden sein
**office** ['ɒfɪs] *n.* **a)** Büro, *das;* **b)**
*(branch)* Zweigstelle, *die;* **c)** *(position)*
Amt, *das;* **hold ~:** amtieren. **'office
hours** *n. pl.* Dienststunden *Pl.*
**officer** ['ɒfɪsə(r)] *n.* **a)** *(Army etc.)* Offizier, *der;* **b)** *(official)* Beamte, *der/*Beamtin, *die;* **c)** *(constable)* Polizeibeam-
te, *der/*-beamtin, *die*
**official** [ə'fɪʃl] **1.** *adj.* offiziell; amtlich
‹*Verlautbarung*›; regulär ‹*Streik*›. **2.**
*n.* Beamte, *der/*Beamtin, *die; (party,
union, or sports ~)* Funktionär,
*der/*Funktionärin, *die.* **officially**
*adv.* offiziell
**officious** [ə'fɪʃəs] *adj.* übereifrig
**offing** ['ɒfɪŋ] *n.* **be in the ~:** bevorstehen; ‹*Gewitter:*› aufziehen
**off: ~-licence** *n. (Brit.)* ≈ Wein- und
Spirituosenladen, *der;* **~-load** *v.t.*
abladen; **~-putting** ['ɒfpʊtɪŋ] *adj.*

*(Brit. coll.)* abstoßend; **~-set** ['--, -'-]
*v.t., forms as* set: ausgleichen;
**~-shore** *adj.* küstennah; **~'side** *adj.*
Abseits-; **be ~-side** abseits sein;
**~-spring** *n., pl. same* Nachkommen-
schaft, *die; (of animal)* Junge *Pl.*
**often** ['ɒfn, 'ɒftn] *adv.* oft; **every so ~:**
gelegentlich
**oh** [əʊ] *int.* oh; *expr. pain* au
**oil** [ɔɪl] **1.** *n.* Öl, *das.* **2.** *v.t.* ölen
**oil: ~-field** *n.* Ölfeld, *das;* **~-
painting** *n.* Ölgemälde, *das;* **~ refinery** *n.* [Erd]ölraffinerie, *die;* **~ rig**
see ¹rig 1; **~-skins** *n. pl.* Ölzeug, *das;*
**~-slick** *n.* Ölteppich, *der;* **~-tanker**
*n.* Öltanker, *der;* **~ well** *n.* Ölquelle,
*die*
**oily** ['ɔɪlɪ] *adj.* ölig; ölverschmiert ‹*Gesicht, Hände*›
**ointment** ['ɔɪntmənt] *n.* Salbe, *die*
**OK** [əʊ'keɪ] *(coll.)* **1.** *adj.* in Ordnung;
okay *(ugs.).* **2.** *adv.* gut. **3.** *int.* okay
*(ugs.).* **4.** *v.t. (approve)* zustimmen
(+ *Dat.*); **be ~-d by sb.** von jmdm.
das Okay bekommen *(ugs.)*
**okay** [əʊ'keɪ] see OK
**old** [əʊld] *adj.* alt; **be [more than] 30
years ~:** [über] 30 Jahre alt sein
**old: ~ 'age** *n.* [fortgeschrittenes] Alter; **~-age** *attrib. adj.* Alters‹*rente,
-ruhegeld*›; **~-age pensioner** Rentner,
*der/*Rentnerin, *die;* **~-fashioned**
[əʊld'fæʃnd] *adj.* altmodisch
**olive** ['ɒlɪv] *n.* Olive, *die.* **olive 'oil** *n.*
Olivenöl, *das*
**Olympic** [ə'lɪmpɪk] *adj.* olympisch; **~
Games** Olympische Spiele
**omelette (omelet)** ['ɒmlɪt] *n.* Omelett, *das*
**omen** ['əʊmən] *n.* Vorzeichen, *das*
**ominous** ['ɒmɪnəs] *adj. (of evil omen)*
ominös; *(worrying)* beunruhigend
**omission** [ə'mɪʃn] *n.* Auslassung, *die;
(failure to act)* Unterlassung, *die*
**omit** [ə'mɪt] *v.t., -tt-* weglassen; **~ to
do sth.** es versäumen, etw. zu tun
**on** [ɒn] **1.** *prep.* auf *(position:* + *Dat.;
direction:* + *Akk.); (attached to)* an
(+ *Dat./Akk.); (concerning, about)*
über (+ *Akk.); in expressions of time*
an ‹*einem Abend, Tag usw.*›; **write sth.
on the wall** etw. an die Wand schreiben; **be hanging on the wall** an der
Wand hängen; **have sth. on one** etw.
bei sich haben; **on the bus/train** im
Bus/Zug; *(by bus/train)* mit dem Bus/
Zug; **on Oxford 56767** unter der
Nummer Oxford 56767; **on Sundays**
sonntags; **on [his] arrival** bei seiner

Ankunft; **on entering the room ...**: beim Betreten des Zimmers ...; **it's just on 9** es ist fast 9 Uhr; **the drinks are on me** *(coll.)* die Getränke gehen auf mich. **2.** *adv.* **with/without a hat/coat on** mit/ohne Hut/Mantel; **have a hat on** einen Hut aufhaben; **on and on** immer weiter; **speak/wait/work** *etc.* **on** weiterreden/-warten/-arbeiten *usw.;* **from now on** von jetzt an; **the light/radio** *etc.* **is on** das Licht/Radio *usw.* ist an; **is Sunday's picnic on?** findet das Picknick am Sonntag statt?; **what's on at the cinema?** was läuft im Kino?; **on and off** immer mal wieder *(ugs.)*; **on to, onto** auf ( + *Akk.*)

**once** [wʌns] **1.** *adv.* **a)** einmal; **~ a week/month/year** einmal die Woche/ im Monat/im Jahr; **~ again** *or* **more** noch einmal; **~ [and] for all** ein für allemal; **never/not ~**: nicht ein einziges Mal; **b)** *(multiplied by one)* ein mal; **c)** *(formerly)* früher einmal; **~ upon a time there lived a king** es war einmal ein König; **d) at ~** *(immediately)* sofort; *(at the same time)* gleichzeitig; **all at ~** *(suddenly)* plötzlich; *(simultaneously)* alle[s] zugleich. **2.** *conj.* wenn; *(with past tense)* als. **3.** *n.* [just or only] **this ~**: [nur] dieses eine Mal

**'oncoming** *adj.* entgegenkommend 〈Fahrzeug, Verkehr〉

**one** [wʌn] **1.** *adj.* ein; *see also* **eight 1;** *(single, only)* einzig; **no/not ~**: kein; **the ~ thing** das einzige; **at ~ time** einmal; **~ morning/night** eines Morgens/ Nachts. **2.** *n.* **a)** eins; **b)** *(number, symbol)* Eins, *die;* **c)** *(unit)* **in ~s** einzeln. **3.** *pron.* **a)** ein... *(of* + *Gen.)*; **big ~s and little ~s** große und kleine; **the older/younger ~**: der/die/das ältere/ jüngere; **this ~**: dieser/diese/dieses [da]; **that ~**: der/die/das [da]; **which ~?** welcher/welche/welches?; **which ~s?** welche?; **~ by ~**: einzeln; **love/ hate ~ another** sich lieben/hassen; **be kind to ~ another** nett zueinander sein; **b)** *(people in general; coll.: I, we)* man; *as indirect object* einem; *as direct object* einen; **~'s** sein

**one:** **~'self** *pron.* **a)** *emphat.* selbst; **be ~self** man selbst sein; **b)** *refl.* sich; *see also* **herself; ~-sided** *adj.* einseitig; **~-way** *adj.* **a)** in einer Richtung nachgestellt; Einbahn〈straße, -verkehr〉; **b)** einfach 〈Fahrpreis, Flug〉

**onion** ['ʌnjən] *n.* Zwiebel, *die*

**'onlooker** *n.* Zuschauer, *der*/Zuschauerin, *die*

**only** ['əʊnlɪ] **1.** *attrib. adj.* einzig...; **the ~ person** der/die einzige; **an ~ child** ein Einzelkind. **2.** *adv.* nur; **we had been waiting ~ 5 minutes when ...**: wir hatten erst 5 Minuten gewartet, als ...; **it's ~/~ just 6 o'clock** es ist erst 6 Uhr/ gerade erst 6 Uhr vorbei; **he ~ just made it** er hat es gerade noch geschafft; **~ if** nur [dann] ..., wenn; **~ the other day/week** erst neulich

**'onset** *n.* *(of winter)* Einbruch, *der; (of disease)* Ausbruch, *der*

**onslaught** ['ɒnslɔ:t] *n.* [heftige] Attacke *(fig.)*

**onus** ['əʊnəs] *n.* **the ~ is on him to do it** es ist seine Sache, es zu tun

**onward[s]** ['ɒnwədz] *adv. (in space)* vorwärts; **from X ~**: von X an; **from that day ~**: von diesem Tag an

**ooze** [u:z] **1.** *v. i.* sickern *(from* aus). **2.** *v. t.* triefen von *od.* vor ( + *Dat.*); *(fig.)* ausstrahlen

**opaque** [əʊ'peɪk] *adj.* lichtundurchlässig; opak *(fachspr.)*

**open** ['əʊpn] **1.** *adj.* **a)** offen; *(not blocked or obstructed)* frei; *(available)* frei 〈Stelle〉; **in the ~ air** im Freien; **be ~** 〈Laden, Museum, Bank *usw.*〉: geöffnet sein; **have an ~ mind about** *or* **on sth.** einer Sache gegenüber aufgeschlossen sein; **b)** unverhohlen 〈Bewunderung, Haß, Verachtung〉; **c)** *(frank, communicative)* offen 〈Wesen, Streit, Abstimmung, Regierungsstil〉; *(not secret)* öffentlich 〈Wahl〉; **d)** geöffnet 〈Regenschirm〉; aufgeblüht 〈Blume, Knospe〉; aufgeschlagen 〈Zeitung, Landkarte〉. **2.** *n.* **in the ~** *(outdoors)* unter freiem Himmel; [out] **in the ~** *(fig.)* öffentlich bekannt. **3.** *v. t.* **a)** öffnen; **b)** eröffnen 〈Konferenz, Diskussion, Laden〉; beginnen 〈Verhandlungen, Spiel〉; **c)** *(unfold, spread out)* aufschlagen 〈Zeitung, Landkarte〉; öffnen 〈Schirm〉. **4.** *v. i.* **a)** sich öffnen; **~ into/on to sth.** zu etw. führen; **b)** *(become ~ to customers)* öffnen; *(start trading etc.)* eröffnet werden; **c)** *(start)* beginnen; 〈Ausstellung:〉 eröffnet werden; 〈Theaterstück:〉 Premiere haben. **open 'up 1.** *v. t.* öffnen; *(establish)* eröffnen. **2.** *v. i.* sich öffnen; 〈Filiale:〉 eröffnet werden; 〈Firma:〉 sich niederlassen

**'open-air** *attrib. adj.* Openair〈konzert〉; ~ [swimming-]pool Freibad, *das*

**'opener** *n.* Öffner, *der*

**'opening 1.** *n.* **a)** Öffnen, *das; (becoming open)* Sichöffnen, *das; (of exhibi-*

*tion, new centre)* Eröffnen, *das;* **b)** *(establishment, ceremony)* Eröffnung, die; **c)** *(initial part)* Anfang, *der;* **d)** *(gap, aperture)* Öffnung, *die;* **e)** *(opportunity)* Möglichkeit, *die; (vacancy)* freie Stelle. **2.** *adj.* einleitend. **'opening hours** *n. pl.* Öffnungszeiten *Pl.*

**'openly** *adv.* **a)** *(publicly)* in der Öffentlichkeit; öffentlich ⟨*zugeben, verurteilen*⟩; **b)** *(frankly)* offen

**open:** ~-**'minded** *adj.* aufgeschlossen; ~-**'plan** *adj.* ~-**plan** office Großraumbüro, *das;* ~ **'sandwich** *n.* belegtes Brot

**opera** ['ɒpərə] *n.* Oper, *die*

**opera:** ~-**glasses** *n. pl.* Opernglas, *das;* ~-**house** *n.* Opernhaus, *das;* ~-**singer** *n.* Opernsänger, *der/*-sängerin, *die*

**operate** ['ɒpəreɪt] **1.** *v. i.* **a)** *(be in action)* in Betrieb sein; ⟨*Bus, Zug usw.:*⟩ verkehren; **b)** *(function)* arbeiten; **the torch ~s on batteries** die Taschenlampe arbeitet mit Batterien; **c)** ~ ⟨**on** *sb.*⟩ *(Med.)* [jmdn.] operieren. **2.** *v. t.* bedienen ⟨*Maschine*⟩; unterhalten ⟨*Busverbindung, Telefondienst*⟩; betätigen ⟨*Hebel, Bremse*⟩. **'operating-theatre** *n. (Brit. Med.)* Operationssaal, *der*

**operation** [ɒpə'reɪʃn] *n.* **a)** *(causing to work) (of machine)* Bedienung, *die; (of bus service, telephone service, etc.)* Unterhaltung, *die; (of lever, brake)* Betätigung, *die;* **b) come into ~** ⟨*Gesetz, Gebühr usw.:*⟩ in Kraft treten; **be in/out of ~** ⟨*Maschine, Gerät usw.:*⟩ in/außer Betrieb sein; **c)** *(Med.)* Operation, *die;* **have an ~:** operiert werden

**operational** [ɒpə'reɪʃənl] *adj. (esp. Mil.: ready to function)* einsatzbereit

**operative** ['ɒpərətɪv] *adj.* **become ~** ⟨*Gesetz:*⟩ in Kraft treten; **the scheme is ~:** das Programm läuft

**operator** ['ɒpəreɪtə(r)] *n.* [Maschinen]bediener, *der/*-bedienerin, *die; (Teleph.) (at exchange)* Vermittlung, *die; (at switchboard)* Telefonist, *der/* Telefonistin, *die*

**opinion** [ə'pɪnjən] *n.* Meinung, *die* **(on** über + *Akk.,* zu); **have a high/low ~ of sb.** eine/keine hohe Meinung von jmdm. haben; **in my ~:** meiner Meinung nach. **opinionated** [ə'pɪnjəneɪtɪd] *adj.* rechthaberisch

**opium** ['əʊpɪəm] *n.* Opium, *das*

**opponent** [ə'pəʊnənt] *n.* Gegner, *der/* Gegnerin, *die*

**opportune** ['ɒpətjuːn] *adj.* **a)** *(favour-*

*able)* günstig; **b)** *(well-timed)* zur rechten Zeit *nachgestellt*. **opportunism** [ɒpə'tjuːnɪzm] *n.* Opportunismus, *der*

**opportunist** [ɒpə'tjuːnɪst] *n.* Opportunist, *der/*Opportunistin, *die*

**opportunity** [ɒpə'tjuːnɪti] *n.* Gelegenheit, *die*

**oppose** [ə'pəʊz] **1.** *v. t.* sich wenden gegen. **2.** *v. i.* **the opposing team** die gegnerische Mannschaft. **opposed** [ə'pəʊzd] *adj.* **as ~ to** im Gegensatz zu; **be ~ to sth.** ⟨*Personen:*⟩ gegen etw. sein

**opposite** ['ɒpəzɪt] **1.** *adj.* gegenüberliegend ⟨*Straßenseite, Ufer*⟩; entgegengesetzt ⟨*Ende, Weg, Richtung*⟩; **the ~ sex** das andere Geschlecht. **2.** *n.* Gegenteil, *das (of* von). **3.** *adv.* gegenüber. **4.** *prep.* gegenüber

**opposition** [ɒpə'zɪʃn] *n.* **a)** Opposition, *die; (resistance)* Widerstand, *der* **(to** gegen); **in ~ to** entgegen; **b)** *(Brit. Polit.)* **the O~:** die Opposition

**oppress** [ə'pres] *v. t.* unterdrücken; *(fig.)* ⟨*Gefühl:*⟩ bedrücken. **oppression** [ə'preʃn] *n.* Unterdrückung, *die.* **oppressive** [ə'presɪv] *adj.* repressiv; *(fig.)* bedrückend ⟨*Ängste, Atmosphäre*⟩; *(hot and close)* drückend ⟨*Wetter, Klima, Tag*⟩

**opt** [ɒpt] *v. i.* sich entscheiden **(for** für); ~ **to do sth.** sich dafür entscheiden, etw. zu tun; ~ **out** nicht mitmachen/*(stop taking part)* nicht länger mitmachen **(of** bei)

**optical** ['ɒptɪkl] *adj.* optisch

**optician** [ɒp'tɪʃn] *n.* Optiker, *der/*Optikerin, *die*

**optima** *pl. of* **optimum**

**optimism** ['ɒptɪmɪzm] *n.* Optimismus, *der.* **optimist** ['ɒptɪmɪst] *n.* Optimist, *der/*Optimistin, *die.* **optimistic** [ɒptɪ'mɪstɪk] *adj.* optimistisch

**optimum** ['ɒptɪməm] **1.** *n., pl.* **optima** ['ɒptɪmə] Optimum, *das.* **2.** *adj.* optimal

**option** ['ɒpʃn] *n. (choice)* Wahl, *die; (thing)* Wahlmöglichkeit, *die.* **optional** ['ɒpʃənl] *adj.* nicht zwingend; ~ **subject** Wahlfach, *das*

**opulence** ['ɒpjʊləns] *n.* Wohlstand, *der*

**opulent** ['ɒpjʊlənt] *adj.* wohlhabend; feudal ⟨*Auto, Haus usw.*⟩

**or** [ə(r), *stressed* ɔː(r)] *conj.* **a)** oder; **he cannot read or write** er kann weder lesen noch schreiben; **without food or water** ohne Essen und Wasser; **15 or 20 minutes** 15 bis 20 Minuten; **in a day**

or two in ein, zwei Tagen; **b)** *introducing explanation* das heißt; **or rather** beziehungsweise

**oracle** ['ɒrəkl] *n.* Orakel, *das*

**oral** ['ɔ:rl] *adj.* mündlich; *(Med.)* oral

**orange** ['ɒrɪndʒ] **1.** *n.* **a)** *(fruit)* Orange, *die;* Apfelsine, *die;* **b)** *(colour)* Orange, *das.* **2.** *adj.* orange[farben]

**orator** ['ɒrətə(r)] *n.* Redner, *der*/Rednerin, *die*

**oratory** ['ɒrətərɪ] *n.* Redekunst, *die*

**orbit** ['ɔ:bɪt] **1.** *n. (Astron.)* [Umlauf]bahn, *die.* **2.** *v. i.* kreisen. **3.** *v. t.* umkreisen. **orbital** ['ɔ:bɪtl] *adj.* ~ **road** Ringstraße, *die*

**orchard** ['ɔ:tʃəd] *n.* Obstgarten, *der;* *(commercial)* Obstplantage, *die*

**orchestra** ['ɔ:kɪstrə] *n.* Orchester, *das.* **orchestral** [ɔ:'kestrl] *adj.* Orchester-

**orchid** ['ɔ:kɪd] *n.* Orchidee, *die*

**ordain** [ɔ:'deɪn] *v. t.* **a)** *(Eccl.)* ordinieren; **b)** *(decree)* verfügen

**ordeal** [ɔ:'di:l] *n.* Qual, *die*

**order** ['ɔ:də(r)] **1.** *n.* **a)** *(sequence)* Reihenfolge, *die;* out of ~: durcheinander; **b)** *(regular arrangement, normal state)* Ordnung, *die;* be/not be in ~: in Ordnung/nicht in Ordnung sein *(ugs.);* be out of/in ~ *(not in/in working condition)* nicht funktionieren/funktionieren; 'out of ~' „außer Betrieb"; in good/bad ~: in gutem/schlechtem Zustand; **c)** *(command)* Anweisung, *die; (Mil.)* Befehl, *der;* **d)** in ~ to do sth. um etw. zu tun; **e)** *(Commerc.)* Auftrag, *der* (for über + *Akk.*); *(to waiter, ~ed goods)* Bestellung, *die;* **f)** keep ~: Ordnung [be]wahren; *see also* law b; **g)** *(religious ~)* Orden, *der.* **2.** *v. t.* **a)** *(command)* befehlen; ⟨*Richter:*⟩ verfügen; ~ sb. to do sth. jmdn. anweisen/ *(Milit.)* jmdm. befehlen, etw. zu tun; **b)** *(Commerc.)* bestellen (**from** bei); **c)** *(arrange)* ordnen

**orderly** ['ɔ:dəlɪ] **1.** *adj.* friedlich; diszipliniert ⟨*Menge*⟩; *(methodical)* methodisch; *(tidy)* ordentlich. **2.** *n.* **a)** *(Mil.)* [Offiziers]bursche, *der;* **b)** medical ~: ≈ Krankenpflegehelfer, *der*

**ordinal** ['ɔ:dɪnl] *adj. & n.* ~ [number] Ordinalzahl, *die*

**ordinary** ['ɔ:dɪnərɪ] *adj. (normal)* normal ⟨*Gebrauch*⟩; üblich ⟨*Verfahren*⟩; *(not exceptional)* gewöhnlich

**ordination** [ɔ:dɪ'neɪʃn] *n. (Eccl.)* Ordination, *die;* Ordinierung, *die*

**ore** [ɔ:(r)] *n.* Erz, *das*

**organ** ['ɔ:gən] *n.* **a)** *(Mus.)* Orgel, *die;* **b)** *(Biol.)* Organ, *das*

**organic** [ɔ:'gænɪk] *adj.* organisch; biologisch-dynamisch ⟨*Ackerbau*⟩; biodynamisch ⟨*Nahrungsmittel*⟩

**organism** ['ɔ:gənɪzm] *n.* Organismus, *der*

**organist** ['ɔ:gənɪst] *n.* Organist, *der*/Organistin, *die*

**organization** [ɔ:gənaɪ'zeɪʃn] *n.* Organisation, *die;* ~ of time/work Zeit-/Arbeitseinteilung, *die*

**organize** ['ɔ:gənaɪz] *v. t.* organisieren; einteilen ⟨*Arbeit, Zeit*⟩; veranstalten ⟨*Konferenz, Festival*⟩; ~ into groups in Gruppen einteilen. **organizer** *n.* Organisator, *der*/Organisatorin, *die; (of event, festival)* Veranstalter, *der*/Veranstalterin, *die*

**orgasm** ['ɔ:gæzm] *n.* Orgasmus, *der*

**orgy** ['ɔ:dʒɪ] *n.* Orgie, *die*

**orient 1.** ['ɔ:rɪənt] *n.* the O~: der Orient. **2.** ['ɒrɪent] *v. t.* ausrichten (towards nach); ~ oneself sich orientieren

**oriental** [ɒrɪ'entl] **1.** *adj.* orientalisch. **2.** *n.* Asiat, *der*/Asiatin, *die*

**orientate** ['ɒrɪənteɪt] *see* orient 2. **orientation** [ɒrɪən'teɪʃn] *n.* Orientierung, *die*

**orienteering** [ɒrɪən'tɪərɪŋ] *n. (Brit.)* Orientierungsrennen, *das*

**orifice** ['ɒrɪfɪs] *n.* Öffnung, *die*

**origin** ['ɒrɪdʒɪn] *n. (derivation)* Herkunft, *die; (beginnings)* Anfänge *Pl.; (source)* Ursprung, *der;* country of ~: Herkunftsland, *das;* have its ~ in sth. seinen Ursprung in etw. *(Dat.)* haben.

**original** [ə'rɪdʒɪnl] **1.** *adj.* ursprünglich; Ur⟨*text, -fassung*⟩; eigenständig ⟨*Forschung*⟩; *(inventive)* originell; an ~ painting ein Original. **2.** *n.* Original, *das.* **originality** [ərɪdʒɪ'nælɪtɪ] *n.* Originalität, *die.* **originally** [ə'rɪdʒɪnəlɪ] *adv.* **a)** ursprünglich; **b)** originell ⟨*schreiben usw.*⟩. **originate** [ə'rɪdʒɪneɪt] *v. i.* ~ from entstehen aus; ~ in seinen Ursprung haben in (+ *Dat.*)

**ornament** ['ɔ:nəmənt] *n.* Ziergegenstand, *der.* **ornamental** [ɔ:nə'mentl] *adj.* dekorativ; Zier⟨*pflanze, -naht usw.*⟩

**ornate** [ɔ:'neɪt] *adj.* reich verziert; prunkvoll ⟨*Dekoration*⟩

**ornithology** [ɔ:nɪ'θɒlədʒɪ] *n.* Ornithologie, *die*

**orphan** ['ɔ:fn] **1.** *n.* Waise, *die.* **2.** *v. t.* be ~ed [zur] Waise werden. **orphanage** ['ɔ:fənɪdʒ] *n.* Waisenhaus, *das*

**orthodox** ['ɔ:θədɒks] *adj.* orthodox

**oscillate** ['ɒsɪleɪt] *v.i.* schwingen. **oscillation** [ɒsɪ'leɪʃn] *n.* Schwingen, *das; (single ~)* Schwingung, *die*

**ostensible** [ɒ'stensɪbl] *adj.* vorgeschoben. **ostensibly** [ɒ'stensɪblɪ] *adv.* vorgeblich

**ostentatious** [ɒsten'teɪʃəs] *adj.* prunkhaft ⟨*Kleidung, Schmuck*⟩; prahlerisch ⟨*Art*⟩

**osteopath** ['ɒstɪəpæθ] *n.* Spezialist für Knochenleiden

**ostrich** ['ɒstrɪtʃ] *n.* Strauß, *der*

**other** ['ʌðə(r)] **1.** *adj.* **a)** *(not the same)* ander...; **the ~ two/three** *etc. (the remaining)* die beiden/drei *usw.* anderen; **the ~ one** der/die/das andere; **some ~ time** ein andermal; **b)** *(further)* **one ~ thing** noch eins; **some/six ~ people** noch ein paar/noch sechs [andere *od.* weitere] Leute; **no ~ questions** keine weiteren Fragen; **c) ~ than** *(different from)* anders als; *(except)* außer; **d) the ~ day/evening** neulich; neulich abends. **2.** *n.* anderer/andere/anderes; **there are six ~s** es sind noch sechs andere da; **any ~:** irgendein anderer/-eine andere/-ein anderes; **not any ~:** kein anderer/keine andere/kein anderes; **one after the ~:** einer/eine/eins nach dem/der/dem anderen. **3.** *adv.* anders; **~ than that, ...:** abgesehen davon, ...

**otherwise** ['ʌðəwaɪz] **1.** *adv.* **a)** *(in a different way)* anders; **b)** *(or else)* anderenfalls; **c)** *(in other respects)* im übrigen. **2.** *pred. adj.* anders

**otter** ['ɒtə(r)] *n.* [Fisch]otter, *der*

**ouch** [aʊtʃ] *int.* autsch

**ought** [ɔ:t] *v. aux. only in pres. and past* ought, *neg. (coll.)* oughtn't ['ɔ:tnt] **I ~ to do/have done it** *expr. moral duty* ich müßte es tun/hätte es tun müssen; *expr. desirability* ich sollte es tun/hätte es tun sollen; **~ not** *or* **~n't you to have left by now?** müßtest du nicht schon weg sein?; **one ~ not to do it** man sollte es nicht tun; **he ~ to be hanged/in hospital** er gehört an den Galgen/ins Krankenhaus; **that ~ to be enough** das dürfte reichen; **he ~ to win** er müßte [eigentlich] gewinnen

**oughtn't** ['ɔ:tnt] *(coll.)* = **ought not**

**ounce** [aʊns] *n. (measure)* Unze, *die*

**our** ['aʊə(r)] *poss. pron. attrib.* unser

**ours** ['aʊəz] *poss. pron. pred.* unserer/unsere/unseres; *see also* **hers**

**ourselves** [aʊə'selvz] *pron.* **a)** *emphat.* selbst; **b)** *refl.* uns. See also **herself**

**oust** [aʊst] *v. t.* verdrängen; **~ sb. from his job/from power** jmdn. von seinem Arbeitsplatz vertreiben/jmdn. entmachten

**out** [aʊt] *adv.* **a)** *(away from place)* **~ here/there** hier/da draußen; **be ~ in the garden** draußen im Garten sein; **what's it like ~?** wie ist es draußen?; **go ~ shopping** *etc.* einkaufen *usw.* gehen; **be ~** *(not at home, not in one's office, etc.)* nicht dasein; **she was ~ all night** sie war eine/die ganze Nacht weg; **have a day ~ in London** einen Tag in London verbringen; **row ~ to ...:** hinaus-/herausrudern zu ...; **be ~ at sea** auf See sein; **b)** *(Sport, Games)* **be ~** ⟨*Ball:*⟩ aus *od.* im Aus sein; ⟨*Mitspieler:*⟩ ausscheiden; ⟨*Schlagmann:*⟩ aus[geschlagen] sein; **not ~:** nicht aus; **c) be ~** *(asleep)* weg sein *(ugs.)*; *(unconscious)* bewußtlos sein; **d)** *(no longer burning)* aus[gegangen]; **e)** *(in error)* **be 3 % ~ in one's calculations** sich um 3 % verrechnet haben; **this is £5 ~:** das stimmt um 5 Pfund nicht; **f)** *(not in fashion)* passé *(ugs.)*; out *(ugs.)*; **g) say it ~ loud** es laut sagen; **~ with it!** heraus mit der Sprache!; **their secret is ~:** ihr Geheimnis ist bekannt geworden; [**the**] **truth will ~:** die Wahrheit wird an den Tag kommen; **the sun/moon is ~:** die Sonne/der Mond scheint; **the third volume is just ~:** der dritte Band ist soeben erschienen; **the roses are ~:** die Rosen blühen; **h) be ~ for sth./to do sth.** auf etw. *(Akk.)* aussein/darauf aussein, etw. zu tun; **be ~ for trouble** Streit suchen; **i)** *(to or at an end)* **before the day/month was ~:** am selben Tag/vor Ende des Monats. *See also* **out of**

**out:** **~bid** *v.t.,* **~bid** überbieten; **~board** *adj.* **~board motor** Außenbordmotor, *der;* **~break** *n.* Ausbruch, *der;* **at the ~break of war** bei Kriegsausbruch; **an ~break of flu** eine Grippeepidemie; **~building** *n.* Nebengebäude, *das;* **~burst** *n.* Ausbruch, *der;* **an ~burst of weeping/laughter** ein Weinkrampf/Lachanfall; **an ~burst of temper** ein Wutanfall; **~cast** *n.* Ausgestoßene, *der/die;* **a social ~cast** ein Geächteter/eine Geächtete; **~come** *n.* Ergebnis, *das;* Resultat, *das;* **~cry** *n.* [Aufschrei der] Empörung; *adj.* überholt; **~do** *v. t.* überbieten (**in** an + *Dat.*); **~door** *adj.* **~door shoes/things** Stra-

ßenschuhe/-kleidung, *die;* ~**door games/pursuits** Spiele/Beschäftigungen im Freien; ~**door swimming-pool** Freibad, *das;* ~'**doors 1.** *adv.* draußen; **go** ~**doors** nach draußen gehen; **2.** *n.* **the |great|** ~**doors** die freie Natur
**outer** ['aʊtə(r)] *adj.* äußer...; Außen-⟨*fläche, -seite, -wand, -tür*⟩. **outer** '**space** *n.* Weltraum, *der*
**out:** ~**fit** *n.* **a)** *(clothes)* Kleider *Pl.;* **b)** *(equipment)* Ausrüstung, *die;* **c)** *(coll.: organization)* Laden, *der (ugs.);* ~**going 1.** *adj.* **a)** [aus dem Amt] scheidend ⟨*Regierung, Präsident*⟩; **b)** *(friendly)* kontaktfreudig ⟨*Person*⟩; **2.** *n., in pl.* ~**s** *(expenditure)* Ausgaben *Pl.;* ~'**grow** *v. t., forms as grow* herauswachsen aus ⟨*Kleider*⟩; *(leave behind)* entwachsen (+ *Dat.*); ~**house** *n.* Nebengebäude, *das*
'**outing** *n.* Ausflug, *der*
**out:** ~**landish** [aʊt'lændɪʃ] *adj.* ausgefallen; ~**law 1.** *n.* Bandit, *der*/Banditin, *die;* **2.** *v. t.* verbieten; ~**lay** *n.* Ausgaben *Pl.* (**on** für); ~**let** ['aʊtlet, 'aʊtlɪt] *n.* **a)** Ablauf, -fluß, *der;* **b)** *(fig.)* Ventil, *das;* ~**line 1.** *n.* **a)** *in sing. or pl.* Umriß, *der;* **b)** *(short account)* Grundriß, *der;* *(of topic)* Übersicht, *die* (**of** über + *Akk.*); **2.** *v. t. (describe)* umreißen; ~**live** [aʊt'lɪv] *v. t.* überleben; ~**look** *n.* **a)** *(view)* Aussicht, *die* (**over** über + *Akk.,* **on to** auf + *Akk.*); *(fig.; Meteorol.)* Aussichten *Pl.;* **b)** *(mental attitude)* Einstellung, *die* (**on** zu); ~**lying** *adj.* entlegen; ~**moded** [aʊt'məʊdɪd] *adj.* antiquiert; ~'**number** *v. t.* zahlenmäßig überlegen sein (+ *Dat.*)
**out of** *prep.* **a)** *(from within)* aus; **go** ~ **the door** zur Tür hinausgehen; **b)** *(not within)* **be** ~ **the country** im Ausland sein; **be** ~ **town/the room** nicht in der Stadt/im Zimmer sein; **feel** ~ **it** *or* **things** sich ausgeschlossen fühlen; **c)** *(from among)* **one** ~ **every three smokers** jeder dritte Raucher; **58** ~ **every 100** 58 von hundert; **d)** *(beyond range of)* außer ⟨*Reich-/Hörweite, Sicht, Kontrolle*⟩; **e)** *(from)* aus; **get money** ~ **sb.** Geld aus jmdm. herausholen; **do well** ~ **sb./sth.** von jmdm./ etw. profitieren; **f)** aus ⟨*Mitleid, Furcht, Neugier usw.*⟩; **g)** *(without)* ~ **money** ohne Geld; **we're** ~ **tea** wir haben keinen Tee mehr; **h)** *(away from)* von ... entfernt; **ten miles** ~ **London** 10 Meilen außerhalb von London
**out:** ~**-of-**'**date** *attrib. adj.* veraltet;

*(expired)* ungültig ⟨*Karte*⟩; ~-**patient** *n.* ambulanter Patient/ambulante Patientin; ~**patients'** **department|** Poliklinik, *die;* ~'**play** *v. t. (Sport)* besser spielen als; ~**post** *n.* Außenposten, *der; (of civilization etc.; also Mil.)* Vorposten, *der;* ~**put** *n.* Produktion, *die; (of liquid, electricity, etc.)* Leistung, *die; (Computing)* Ausgabe, *die*
**outrage 1.** ['aʊtreɪdʒ] *n.* **a)** *(deed)* Verbrechen, *das; (during war)* Greueltat, *die; (against decency)* grober Verstoß; **b)** *(strong resentment)* Empörung, *die* (**at** gegen). **2.** [aʊt'reɪdʒ] *v. t.* empören.
**outrageous** [aʊt'reɪdʒəs] *adj.* unverschämt; unverschämt hoch ⟨*Preis*⟩; unerhört ⟨*Frechheit, Skandal*⟩
**out:** ~**right 1.** [-'-] *adv.* **a)** ganz, komplett ⟨*kaufen, verkaufen*⟩; **b)** *(openly)* freiheraus ⟨*erzählen, sagen, lachen*⟩; **2.** ['--] *adj.* ausgemacht ⟨*Unehrlichkeit*⟩; glatt *(ugs.)* ⟨*Ablehnung, Absage, Lüge*⟩; klar ⟨*Sieg, Niederlage, Sieger*⟩; ~**set** *n.* Anfang, *der;* **at the** ~**set** zu Anfang; **from the** ~**set** von Anfang an
**outside 1.** [-'-, '--] *n.* **a)** Außenseite, *die;* **on the** ~: außen; **to/from the** ~: nach/von außen; **b)** *(external appearance)* Äußere, *das;* **c)** **at the |very|** ~ *(coll.)* äußerstenfalls; höchstens. **2.** ['--] *adj.* **a)** äußer...; Außen⟨*wand, -antenne, -kajüte, -toilette, -durchmesser*⟩; ~ **lane** Überholspur, *die;* **b)** **have only an** ~ **chance** nur eine sehr geringe Chance haben. **3.** [-'-] *adv. (on the* ~) draußen; *(to the* ~) nach draußen. **4.** [-'-] *prep.* **a)** *(position)* außerhalb (+ *Gen.*); ~ **the door** vor der Tür; **b)** *(to the* ~ *of)* aus ... hinaus; **go** ~ **the house** nach draußen gehen. **out**-'**sider** *n. (Sport; also fig.)* Außenseiter, *der*
**out:** ~**size** *adj.* überdimensional; ~**size clothes** Kleidung in Übergröße; ~**skirts** *n. pl.* Stadtrand, *der;* **the** ~**skirts of the town** die Außenbezirke der Stadt; ~'**spoken** *adj.* freimütig; **be** ~ **about sth.** sich freimütig über etw. äußern; ~-'**standing** *adj.* **a)** *(exceptional)* hervorragend; überragend ⟨*Bedeutung*⟩; außergewöhnlich ⟨*Person, Mut, Fähigkeit*⟩; **b)** *(not yet settled)* ausstehend ⟨*Schuld, Geldsumme*⟩; unbezahlt ⟨*Rechnung*⟩; ungelöst ⟨*Problem*⟩; ~'**standingly** *adv.* außergewöhnlich; ~-'**stretched** *adj.* ausgestreckt; *(spread out)* ausgebreitet; ~'**strip** *v. t. (pass in running)* überholen; *(in competition)* überflügeln;

**~-tray** *n*. Ablage für Ausgänge;
**~'vote** *v. t.* überstimmen

**outward** ['aʊtwəd] **1.** *adj.* **a)** *(external,
apparent)* [rein] äußerlich; äußere ⟨*Erscheinung, Bedingung*⟩; **b)** Hin⟨*reise,
-fracht*⟩. **2.** *adv.* nach außen ⟨*aufgehen, richten*⟩. **'outwardly** *adv.*
nach außen hin ⟨*Gefühle zeigen*⟩; öffentlich ⟨*Loyalität erklären*⟩. **'outwards** *see* **outward 2**

**out:** ~'**weigh** *v. t.* schwerer wiegen
als; überwiegen ⟨*Nachteile*⟩; ~'**wit**
*v. t.*, **-tt-** überlisten

**oval** ['əʊvl] **1.** *adj.* oval. **2.** *n.* Oval, *das*
**ovation** [əʊ'veɪʃn] *n.* Ovation, *die;* **a
standing** ~: stehende Ovationen
**oven** ['ʌvn] *n.* [Back]ofen, *der*
**oven:** **~-glove** *n.* Topfhandschuh,
*der;* **~-proof** *adj.* feuerfest;
**~-ready** *adj.* backfertig ⟨*Pommes
frites, Pastete*⟩; bratfertig ⟨*Geflügel*⟩

**over** ['əʊvə(r)] **1.** *adv.* **a)** *(outward and
downward)* hinüber; **climb/jump**
~: hinüber- *od.* (ugs.) rüberklettern/
-sehen/-springen; **b)** *(so as to cover
surface)* **board/cover** ~: zunageln/
-decken; **c)** *(across a space)* hinüber;
*(towards speaker)* herüber; **he swam ~
to us/the other side** er schwamm zu
uns herüber/hinüber zur anderen Seite; ~ **here/there** *(direction)* hier her-
über/dort hinüber; *(location)* hier/
dort; |**come in, please,**| ~ *(Radio)* über-
nehmen Sie bitte; ~ **and out** *(Radio)*
Ende; **d)** *(in excess etc.)* **children of 12
and** ~: Kinder im Alter von zwölf Jah-
ren und darüber; **be |left|** ~: übrig[ge-
blieben] sein; **e)** *(from beginning to
end)* von Anfang bis Ende; **say sth.
twice** ~: etw. zweimal sagen; |**all**| ~
**again,** *(Amer.)* ~: noch einmal [ganz
von vorn]; ~ **and** ~ |**again**| immer wie-
der; **f)** *(at an end)* vorbei; vorüber; **be**
~: vorbei sein; *(Aufführung:)* zu Ende
sein; **get sth.** ~ **with** etw. hinter sich
*(Akk.)* bringen; **be** ~ **and done with** erledigt sein; **g) all** ~ *(completely finished)* aus [und vorbei]; **I ache all** ~:
mir tut alles weh; **be shaking all** ~: am
ganzen Körper zittern. **2.** *prep.* **a)**
*(above, on, round about)* über *(position:* + *Dat.; direction:* + *Akk.);
(across)* über ( + *Akk.*); **look** ~ **a wall**
über eine Mauer sehen; **fall** ~ **a cliff**
von einem Felsen stürzen; **the pub** ~
**the road** die Wirtschaft gegenüber; **hit
sb.** ~ **the head** jmdm. auf den Kopf
schlagen; ~ **the page** auf der nächsten
Seite; **b)** *(in or across every part of)*

[überall] in ( + *Dat.*); *(to and fro upon)*
über ( + *Akk.*); *(all through)* durch;
**all** ~ *(in or on all parts of)* überall in
( + *Dat.*); **travel all** ~ **the country** das
ganze Land bereisen; **all** ~ **Spain** in
ganz Spanien; **all** ~ **the world** in der
ganzen Welt; **c)** *(on account of)* wegen; **d)** *(engaged with)* bei; **take
trouble** ~ **sth.** sich *(Dat.)* mit etw. Mühe geben; **be a long time** ~ **sth.** lange
für etw. brauchen; ~ **work/dinner** bei
der Arbeit/beim Essen; **e)** *(superior to,
in charge of)* über ( + *Akk.*); **have com-
mand/authority** ~ *sb.* Befehlsgewalt
über jmdn./Weisungsbefugnis gegenüber jmdm. haben; **be** ~ *sb. (in rank)*
über jmdm. stehen; **f)** *(beyond, more
than)* über ( + *Akk.*); ~ **and above** zusätzlich zu; **g)** *(throughout, during)*
über ( + *Akk.*); ~ **the weekend/sum-
mer** übers Wochenende/den Sommer
über; ~ **the past years** in den letzten
Jahren

**over:** **~all 1.** *n.* *(Brit.: garment)* Ar-
beitskittel, *der;* **2.** *adj.* **a)** Gesamt-
⟨*breite, -einsparung, -abmessung*⟩;
**have an ~all majority** die absolute
Mehrheit haben; **b)** *(general)* allge-
mein; **3.** ['---, --'-] *adv.* **a)** *(in all parts)*
insgesamt; **b)** *(taken as a whole)* im
großen und ganzen; ~'**awe** *v. t.* Ehrfurcht einflößen ( + *Dat.*); ~'**balance** *v. i.* das Gleichgewicht verlieren; ~'**bearing** *adj.* herrisch;
**~board** *adv.* über Bord; **fall ~board**
über Bord gehen; ~'**cast** *adj.* trübe;
bewölkt ⟨*Himmel*⟩; ~-'**charge** *v. t.* **a)**
*(beyond reasonable price)* zuviel abver-
langen ( + *Dat.*); **b)** *(beyond right
price)* zuviel berechnen ( + *Dat.*);
**~coat** *n.* Mantel, *der;* ~'**come** *v. t.*,
*forms as* **come: a)** überwinden; bezwingen ⟨*Feind*⟩; ⟨*Dämpfe:*⟩ betäuben; **b) he was ~come by grief/with
emotion** Kummer/Rührung überwäl-
tigte ihn; ~-'**cooked** *adj.* verkocht;
~'**crowded** *adj.* überfüllt; ~'**do** *v. t.*
*(carry to excess)* übertreiben; ~'**do it** *or*
**things** *(work too hard)* sich übernehmen; ~'**done** *adj.* **a)** *(exaggerated)*
übertrieben; **b)** *(~-cooked)* verkocht;
verbraten ⟨*Fleisch*⟩; ~'**dose** *n.* Über-
dosis, *die;* **~draft** *n.* Kontoüberzie-
hung, *die;* **have an ~draft of £50** sein
Konto um 50 Pfund überzogen ha-
ben; ~'**draw** *v. t.*, *forms as* **draw 1**
überziehen ⟨*Konto*⟩; ~'**drawn** *adj.*
überzogen ⟨*Konto*⟩; **I am ~drawn |at
the bank|** mein Konto ist überzogen;

**~drive** *n.* Schongang, *der;* **~'due** *adj.* überfällig; **the train is 15 minutes ~due** der Zug hat schon 15 Minuten Verspätung; **~'eat** *v. i., forms as* **eat** zuviel essen; **~estimate 1.** [~'estɪmeɪt] *v. t.* überschätzen; **2.** [~'estɪmət] *n.* zu hohe Schätzung; **~'fill** *v. t.* zu voll machen; **~flow 1.** [--'-] *v. t.* laufen über (+ *Akk.*) ⟨*Rand*⟩; *(flow over brim of)* überlaufen aus; **~flow its banks** ⟨*Fluß:*⟩ über die Ufer treten; **2.** [--'-] *v. i.* überlaufen; **3.** ['---] *n.* **~flow** |pipe| Überlauf, *der;* **~full** *adj.* zu voll; übervoll; **~grown** *adj.* überwachsen (with von); **~hang 1.** [--'-] *v. t.,* **~hung** [əʊvə'hʌŋ] ⟨*Felsen, Stockwerk:*⟩ hinausragen über (+ *Akk.*); **2.** ['---] *n.* Überhang, *der;* **~'hanging** *adj.* überhängend; **~haul 1.** [--'-] *v. t.* überholen; überprüfen ⟨*System*⟩; **2.** ['---] *n.* Überholung, *die;* **~head 1.** [--'-] *adv.* über mir/ihm/uns *usw.;* **2.** ['---] *adj.* **~head** wires Hochleitung, *die;* **3.** ['---] *n.* **~heads**, *(Amer.)* **~head** *(Commerc.)* Gemeinkosten *Pl.;* **~'hear** *v. t., forms as* **hear 1** *(accidentally)* zufällig [mit]hören; *(intentionally)* belauschen; **~'heat** *v. i.* zu heiß werden; ⟨*Maschine, Lager:*⟩ heißlaufen

**overjoyed** [əʊvə'dʒɔɪd] *adj.* überglücklich (**at** über + *Akk.*)

**over: ~lap 1.** [--'-] *v. t.* überlappen; **2.** [--'-] *v. i.* ⟨*Flächen, Dachziegel:*⟩ sich überlappen; ⟨*Aufgaben:*⟩ sich überschneiden; **3.** *n.* Überlappung, *die;* **~'leaf** *adv.* auf der Rückseite; **~'load** *v. t.* überladen; **~'look** *v. t.* **a)** ⟨*Hotel, Zimmer, Haus:*⟩ Aussicht bieten auf (+ *Akk.*); **b)** *(ignore, not see)* übersehen; *(allow to go unpunished)* hinwegsehen über (+ *Akk.*)

**'overly** *adv.* allzu

**over: ~night 1.** [--'-] *adv. (also fig.: suddenly)* über Nacht; **stay ~ night** übernachten; **2.** ['---] *adj.* **~night stay** Übernachtung, *die;* **be an ~night success** *(fig.)* über Nacht Erfolg haben; **~'pay** *v. t., forms as* **pay 2** überbezahlen; **~'power** *v. t.* überwältigen; **~'powering** *adj.* überwältigend; durchdringend ⟨*Geruch*⟩; **~'priced** *adj.* zu teuer; **~'rate** *v. t.* überschätzen; **~~re'act** *v. i.* unangemessen heftig reagieren (**to** auf + *Akk.*); **~~re'action** *n.* Überreaktion, *die* (**to** auf + *Akk.*); **~'ride** *v. t. forms as* **ride 3** sich hinwegsetzen über (+ *Akk.*); **~ripe** *adj.* überreif; **~'rule** *v. t.* aufheben ⟨*Entscheidung*⟩; zurückweisen ⟨*Einwand, Argument*⟩; **~rule** sb. jmds. Vorschlag ablehnen; **~'run** *v. t., forms as* **run 3: be ~run with** überlaufen sein von ⟨*Touristen*⟩; überwuchert sein von ⟨*Unkraut*⟩; **~seas 1.** [--'-] *adv.* in Übersee ⟨*leben, sein*⟩; nach Übersee ⟨*gehen*⟩; **2.** ['---] *adj.* Übersee-; **~'see** *v. t., forms as* **see 1** überwachen; *(manage)* leiten ⟨*Abteilung*⟩; **~'shadow** *v. t.* überschatten; **~'shoot** *v. t., forms as* **shoot 1** hinausschießen über (+ *Akk.*); **~shoot** |the runway| ⟨*Pilot, Flugzeug:*⟩ zu weit kommen; **~'sight** *n.* Versehen, *das;* **~'sleep** *v. i., forms as* **sleep 2** verschlafen; **~'spend** *v. i., forms as* **spend** zuviel [Geld] ausgeben; **~statement** *n.* Übertreibung, *die;* **~'step** *v. t.* überschreiten

**overt** [əʊ'vɜːt] *adj.* unverhohlen

**over: ~'take** *v. t.* überholen; **'no ~taking'** *(Brit.)* „Überholen verboten"; **~'throw 1.** [--'-] *v. t., forms as* **throw 1** stürzen; **2.** ['---] *n.* Sturz, *der;* **~time 1.** *n.* Überstunden; **2.** *adv.* **work ~time** Überstunden machen; **~tone** *n. (fig.)* Unterton, *der*

**overture** [əʊvətjʊə(r)] *n. (Mus.)* Ouvertüre, *die*

**over: ~'turn 1.** *v. t.* umstoßen; **2.** *v. i.* ⟨*Auto, Boot:*⟩ umkippen; ⟨*Boot:*⟩ kentern; **~~use** [əʊvə'juːz] *v. t.* zu oft verwenden; **~weight** *adj.* übergewichtig ⟨*Person*⟩; **be ~weight** Übergewicht haben

**overwhelm** [əʊvə'welm] *v. t.* überwältigen. **over'whelming** *adj.* überwältigend

**over: ~'work 1.** *v. t.* mit Arbeit überlasten; **2.** *v. i.* sich überarbeiten; **~'wrought** *adj.* überreizt

**owe** [əʊ] *v. t., owing* ['əʊɪŋ] schulden; **~ sb. sth., ~ sth. to sb.** jmdm. etw. schulden; *(fig.)* jmdm. etw. verdanken. **owing** ['əʊɪŋ] *pred. adj.* ausstehend; **be ~:** ausstehen. **'owing to** *prep.* wegen

**owl** [aʊl] *n.* Eule, *die*

**own** [əʊn] **1.** *adj.* eigen; **be sb.'s ~** |property| jmdm. selbst gehören; **a house/ideas of one's ~:** ein eigenes Haus/eigene Ideen; **on one's/its ~:** allein. **2.** *v. t.* besitzen; **be ~ed by sb.** jmdm. gehören. **own 'up** *v. i.* gestehen; **~ up to sth.** etw. zugeben

**'owner** *n.* Besitzer, *der/*Besitzerin, *die;* *(of shop, hotel, firm, etc.)* Inhaber, *der/*Inhaberin, *die.* **'ownership** *n.* Besitz, *der*

**ox** [ɒks] *n., pl.* **oxen** ['ɒksn] Ochse, *der*
**oxygen** ['ɒksɪdʒən] *n.* Sauerstoff, *der*
**oyster** ['ɔɪstə(r)] *n.* Auster, *die*
**oz.** *abbr.* **ounce|s|**
**ozone** ['əʊzəʊn] *n.* Ozon, *das.*
'**ozone-friendly** *adj.* ozonsicher;
*(not using (CFCs)* FCKW-frei. '**ozone
layer** *n.* Ozonschicht, *die*

# P

**P, p** [pi:] *n.* P, p, *das*
**p.** *abbr.* **a)** page S.; **b)** *(Brit.)* **penny/
pence** p
**pace** [peɪs] **1.** *n.* **a)** *(step)* Schritt, *der;*
**b)** *(speed)* Tempo, *das;* **keep ~ with**
Schritt halten mit. **2.** *v. i.* ~ **up and
down** auf und ab gehen. **3.** *v. t.* auf-
und abgehen in (+ *Dat.*)
'**pacemaker** *n.* *(Sport, Med.)* Schritt-
macher, *der*
**Pacific** [pə'sɪfɪk] **1.** *adj.* *(Geog.)* ~
**Ocean** Pazifischer *od.* Stiller Ozean.
**2.** *n.* **the** ~: der Pazifik
**pacifier** ['pæsɪfaɪə(r)] *n.* *(Amer.:
dummy)* Schnuller, *der*
**pacifism** ['pæsɪfɪzm] *n.* Pazifismus,
*der.* **pacifist** ['pæsɪfɪst] **1.** *n.* Pazifist,
*der/*Pazifistin, *die.* **2.** *adj.* pazifistisch
**pacify** ['pæsɪfaɪ] *v. t.* besänftigen
**pack** [pæk] **1.** *n.* **a)** *(bundle)* Bündel,
*das; (Mil.)* Tornister, *der; (rucksack)*
Rucksack, *der;* **b)** *(derog.: lot) (people)*
Bande, *die;* **a ~ of lies/nonsense** ein
Sack voll Lügen/eine Menge Unsinn;
**c)** *(Brit.)* ~ **|of cards|** [Karten]spiel,
*das;* **d)** *(wolves, wild dogs)* Rudel, *das;*
*(hounds)* Meute, *die;* **e)** *(packet)*
Packung, *die.* **2.** *v. t.* **a)** einpacken;
*(fill)* packen; ~ **one's bags** seine Koffer packen; **b)** *(cram)* vollstopfen
*(ugs.);* **c)** *(wrap)* verpacken (**in** in +
*Dat. od. Akk.*). **3.** *v. i* packen; **send sb.
~ing** *(fig.)* jmdn. rausschmeißen
*(ugs.).* **pack 'up 1.** *v. t.* zusammen-
packen ⟨*Sachen, Werkzeug*⟩; packen
⟨*Paket*⟩. **2.** *v. i. (coll.: stop)* aufhören
**package** ['pækɪdʒ] **1.** *n.* Paket, *das.* **2.**
*v. t.* verpacken
**package:** ~ **deal** *n.* Paket, *das;* ~

**holiday,** ~ **tour** *ns.* Pauschalreise,
*die*
**packed** [pækt] *adj.* **a)** gepackt; ~
**lunch** Lunchpaket, *das;* **b)** *(crowded)*
[über]voll; ~ **out** gerammelt voll *(ugs.)*
**packet** ['pækɪt] *n.* Päckchen, *das;*
*(box)* Schachtel, *die;* **a ~ of cigarettes**
ein Päckchen/eine Schachtel Zigaretten
'**packing** *n.* *(material)* Verpackungs-
material, *das;* **postage and** ~: Porto
und Verpackung. '**packing-case** *n.*
[Pack]kiste, *die*
**pact** [pækt] *n.* Pakt, *der*
'**pad** [pæd] **1.** *n.* Polster, *das; (block of
paper)* Block, *der.* **2.** *v. t.,* **-dd-** polstern ⟨*Jacke, Schulter*⟩. **pad 'out** *v. t.*
*(fig.)* auswalzen
'**pad** *v. i.,* **-dd-** tappen
**padding** ['pædɪŋ] *n.* Polsterung, *die;*
*(fig.)* Füllsel, *das*
'**paddle** ['pædl] **1.** *n.* [Stech]paddel,
*das.* **2.** *v. t. & i.* paddeln
'**paddle** **1.** *v. i. (with feet)* planschen.
**2.** *n.* **have a/go for a** ~: ein bißchen planschen/planschen gehen.
**paddling-pool** ['pædlɪŋpu:l] *n.*
Planschbecken, *das*
**paddock** ['pædək] *n.* Koppel, *die*
'**padlock** **1.** *n.* Vorhängeschloß, *das.*
**2.** *v. t.* [mit einem Vorhängeschloß]
verschließen
**pagan** ['peɪgən] **1.** *n.* Heide, *der/*Hei-
din, *die.* **2.** *adj.* heidnisch
'**page** [peɪdʒ] *n.* *(boy)* Page, *der*
'**page** *n. (of book etc.)* Seite, *die*
**pageant** ['pædʒənt] *n.* *(spectacle)*
Schauspiel, *das.* **pageantry** ['pæ-
dʒəntrɪ] *n.* Prunk, *der*
**paid** [peɪd] **1.** *see* **pay** 2, 3. **2.** *adj.* **a)** bezahlt ⟨*Urlaub, Arbeit*⟩; **b)** **put ~ to**
*(Brit. coll.)* zunichte machen; kurzen
Prozeß machen mit *(ugs.)* ⟨*Person*⟩
**pail** [peɪl] *n.* Eimer, *der*
**pain** [peɪn] *n.* **a)** *(suffering)* Schmerzen; *(mental* ~*)* Qualen; **be in** ~:
Schmerzen haben; **b)** *(instance)*
Schmerz, *der;* **I have a** ~ **in my knee/
stomach** mein Knie/Magen tut weh; **c)**
*in pl. (trouble taken)* Mühe, *die;* **take**
~**s** sich *(Dat.)* Mühe geben (**over** mit,
bei). **painful** ['peɪnfl] *adj.* **a)** schmerzhaft; **be** ~ ⟨*Körperteil:*⟩ weh tun; **b)**
*(distressing)* schmerzlich ⟨*Gedanke,
Erinnerung*⟩; traurig ⟨*Pflicht*⟩. '**pain-
killer** *n.* schmerzstillendes Mittel.
'**painless** *adj.* schmerzlos; *(fig.)* un-
problematisch. **painstaking** ['peɪnz-
teɪkɪŋ] *adj.* gewissenhaft

**paint** [peɪnt] 1. *n.* Farbe, *die; (on car)* Lack, *der.* 2. *v. t. (cover, colour)* [an]streichen; *(make picture of, make by ~ing)* malen; bemalen ⟨*Wand, Vase, Decke*⟩. **'paintbox** *n.* Malkasten, *der;* **~brush** *n.* Pinsel, *der*

**'painter** *n.* Maler, *der*/Malerin, *die*

**'painting** *n. (art)* Malerei, *die; (picture)* Gemälde, *das;* Bild, *das*

**pair** [peə(r)] 1. *n.* Paar, *das;* **a ~ of gloves/socks/shoes** *etc.* ein Paar Handschuhe/Socken/Schuhe *usw.;* **in ~s** paarweise; **a ~ of trousers/jeans** eine Hose/Jeans. 2. *v. t.* paaren. **pair 'off** *v. i.* Zweiergruppen bilden

**pajamas** [pə'dʒɑːməz] *(Amer.) see* pyjamas

**Pakistan** [pɑːkɪ'stɑːn] *pr. n.* Pakistan *(das)*. **Pakistani** [pɑːkɪ'stɑːnɪ] 1. *adj.* pakistanisch. 2. *n.* Pakistani, *der/die*

**pal** [pæl] *n. (coll.)* Kumpel, *der (ugs.)*

**palace** ['pælɪs] *n.* Palast, *der*

**palate** ['pælət] *n.* Gaumen, *der*

**palatial** [pə'leɪʃl] *adj.* palastartig

**¹pale** [peɪl] *adj.* blaß, *(nearly white)* bleich ⟨*Gesichtsfarbe, Haut, Gesicht*⟩; blaß ⟨*Farbe*⟩; fahl ⟨*Licht*⟩; **go ~:** blaß/bleich werden; *(fig.)* **~ imitation** schlechte Nachahmung

**²pale** *n.* **beyond the ~:** unmöglich

**Palestine** ['pælɪstaɪn] *pr. n.* Palästina *(das)*. **Palestinian** [pælɪ'stɪnɪən] 1. *adj.* palästinensisch. 2. *n.* Palästinenser, *der*/Palästinenserin, *die*

**palette** ['pælɪt] *n.* Palette, *die*

**¹pall** [pɔːl] *n.* **a)** *(over coffin)* Sargtuch, *das;* **b)** *(fig.)* Schleier, *der*

**²pall** *v. i.* **~ [on sb.]** [jmdm.] langweilig werden

**pallor** ['pælə(r)] *n.* Blässe, *die*

**¹palm** [pɑːm] *n. (tree)* Palme, *die*

**²palm** *n.* Handteller, *der.* **palm 'off** *v. t.* **~ sth. off on sb., ~ sb. off with sth.** jmdm. etw. andrehen *(ugs.)*

**palmistry** ['pɑːmɪstrɪ] *n.* Handlesekunst, *die*

**palm: P~ 'Sunday** *n.* Palmsonntag, *der;* **~-tree** *n.* Palme, *die*

**paltry** ['pɔːltrɪ, 'pɒltrɪ] *adj.* schäbig

**pamper** ['pæmpə(r)] *v. t.* verhätscheln; **~ oneself** sich verwöhnen

**pamphlet** ['pæmflɪt] *n. (leaflet)* Prospekt, *der; (booklet)* Broschüre, *die*

**pan** [pæn] *n.* [Koch]topf, *der; (for frying)* Pfanne, *die*

**panacea** [pænə'sɪə] *n.* Allheilmittel, *das*

**Panama** [pænə'mɑː] *pr. n.* Panama *(das);* **~ Ca'nal** Panamakanal, *der*

**'pancake** *n.* Pfannkuchen, *der*

**panda** ['pændə] *n.* Panda, *der*

**pandemonium** [pændɪ'məʊnɪəm] *n.* Chaos, *das; (uproar)* Tumult, *der*

**pander** ['pændə(r)] *v. i.* **~ to** allzu sehr entgegenkommen (+ *Dat.*)

**pane** [peɪn] *n.* Scheibe, *die*

**panel** ['pænl] *n.* **a)** Paneel, *das;* **b)** *(esp. Telev., Radio, etc.) (quiz team)* Rateteam, *das; (in public discussion)* Podium, *das*

**pang** [pæŋ] *n. (of pain)* Stich, *der;* **feel ~s of conscience/guilt** Gewissensbisse haben; **~[s] of hunger** quälender Hunger

**panic** ['pænɪk] 1. *n.* Panik, *die;* **hit the ~ button** *(fig. coll.)* Alarm schlagen; **(~)** durchdrehen *(ugs.)*. 2. *v. i.,* **-ck-** in Panik *(Akk.)* geraten; **don't ~!** nur keine Panik! **'panic-stricken, 'panic-struck** *adjs.* von Panik erfaßt

**panorama** [pænə'rɑːmə] *n.* Panorama, *das*

**pansy** ['pænzɪ] *n.* Stiefmütterchen, *das*

**pant** [pænt] *v. i.* keuchen; ⟨*Hund:*⟩ hecheln

**panther** ['pænθə(r)] *n.* Panther, *der*

**panties** ['pæntɪz] *n. pl. (coll.)* **[pair of] ~:** Schlüpfer, *der*

**pantomime** ['pæntəmaɪm] *n. (Brit.)* Märchenspiel *im Varietéstil, das um Weihnachten aufgeführt wird*

**pantry** ['pæntrɪ] *n.* Speisekammer, *die*

**pants** [pænts] *n. pl.* **a)** *(esp. Amer. coll.: trousers)* **[pair of] ~:** Hose, *die;* **b)** *(Brit. coll.: underpants)* Unterhose, *die*

**paper** ['peɪpə(r)] 1. *n.* **a)** *(material)* Papier, *das;* **b)** *in pl. (documents)* Unterlagen *Pl.; (to prove identity etc.)* Papiere *Pl.;* **c)** *(in examination) (Univ.)* Klausur, *die; (Sch.)* Arbeit, *die;* **d)** *(newspaper)* Zeitung, *die;* **e)** *(learned article)* Referat, *das.* 2. *adj.* aus Papier nachgestellt; Papier⟨*mütze, -taschentuch*⟩. 3. *v. t.* tapezieren

**paper: ~back** 1. *n.* Paperback, *das;* 2. *adj.* **~back book** Paperback, *das;* **~bag** *n.* Papiertüte, *die;* **~clip** *n.* Büroklammer, *die; (larger)* Aktenklammer, *die;* **~weight** *n.* Briefbeschwerer, *der;* **~work** *n.* Schreibarbeit, *die*

**par** [pɑː(r)] *n.* **feel below ~:** nicht ganz auf dem Posten sein *(ugs.);* **be on a ~ with sb./sth.** jmdm./einer Sache gleichkommen

**parable** ['pærəbl] *n.* Gleichnis, *das*

**parachute** ['pærəʃuːt] 1. *n.* Fallschirm, *der.* 2. *v. i.* ⟨*Truppen:*⟩ abspringen (**into** über + *Dat.*)

**parade** [pə'reɪd] **1.** *n.* **a)** *(display)* Zurschaustellung, *die;* **b)** *(Mil.)* Appell, *der;* **c)** *(procession)* Umzug, *der;* *(of troops)* Parade, *die.* **2.** *v. t.* zur Schau stellen. **3.** *v. i.* paradieren

**paradise** ['pærədaɪs] *n.* Paradies, *das*

**paradox** ['pærədɒks] *n.* Paradox[on], *das.* **paradoxical** [pærə'dɒksɪkl] *adj.* paradox

**paraffin** ['pærəfɪn] *n.* Paraffin, *das;* *(Brit.: fuel)* Petroleum, *das*

**paragon** ['pærəgən] Muster, *das* (of an + *Dat.*); ~ of virtue Tugendheld, *der*

**paragraph** ['pærəgrɑːf] *n.* Absatz, *der*

**parallel** ['pærəlel] **1.** *adj.* parallel; *(fig.: similar)* vergleichbar; ~ bars Barren, *der.* **2.** *n.* Parallele, *die;* ~ |of latitude| Breitenkreis, *der*

**paralyse** ['pærəlaɪz] *v. t.* lähmen; *(fig.)* lahmlegen ⟨*Verkehr, Industrie*⟩. **paralysis** [pə'rælɪsɪs] *n.* Lähmung, *die*

**paralyze** *(Amer.) see* **paralyse**

**paramount** ['pærəmaʊnt] *adj.* größt... ⟨*Wichtigkeit*⟩; Haupt⟨*überlegung*⟩; be ~: Vorrang haben

**paranoia** [pærə'nɔɪə] *n.* Paranoia, *die* *(Med.);* *(tendency)* Verfolgungswahn, *der.* **paranoid** ['pærənɔɪd] *adj.* be ~ ⟨*Person:*⟩ an Verfolgungswahn leiden

**parapet** ['pærəpɪt] *n.* Brüstung, *die*

**paraphernalia** [pærəfə'neɪlɪə] *n. sing.* Apparat, *der*

**paraphrase** ['pærəfreɪz] **1.** *n.* Umschreibung, *die.* **2.** *v. t.* umschreiben

**parasite** ['pærəsaɪt] *n.* Schmarotzer, *der.* **parasitic** [pærə'sɪtɪk] *adj.* **a)** *(Biol.)* parasitisch; **b)** *(fig.)* schmarotzerhaft

**parasol** ['pærəsɒl] *n.* Sonnenschirm, *der*

**paratroops** ['pærətruːps] *n. pl.* Fallschirmjäger *Pl.*

**parcel** ['pɑːsl] *n.* Paket, *das*

**parched** [pɑːtʃt] *adj.* ausgedörrt; trocken ⟨*Lippen*⟩

**parchment** ['pɑːtʃmənt] *n.* Pergament, *das*

**pardon** ['pɑːdn] **1.** *n.* Verzeihung, *die;* beg sb.'s ~: jmdn. um Entschuldigung bitten; I beg your ~: entschuldigen Sie bitte. **2.** *v. t.* **a)** ~ sb. |for| sth. jmdm. etw. verzeihen; **b)** *(excuse)* entschuldigen. **pardonable** ['pɑːdənəbl] *adj.* verzeihlich

**pare** [peə(r)] *v. t.* *(trim)* schneiden; *(peel)* schälen

**parent** ['peərənt] *n.* Elternteil, *der;* ~s Eltern *Pl.*

**parenthesis** [pə'renθɪsɪs] *n., pl.* **parentheses** [pə'renθɪsiːz] *(bracket)* runde Klammer

**Paris** ['pærɪs] *pr. n.* Paris *(das)*

**parish** ['pærɪʃ] *n.* Gemeinde, *die.* **parishioner** [pə'rɪʃənə(r)] *n.* Gemeinde[mit]glied, *das*

**park** [pɑːk] **1.** *n.* Park, *der.* **2.** *v. i.* parken. **3.** *v. t.* abstellen; parken ⟨*Kfz*⟩; a ~ed car ein parkendes Auto. **'parking** *n.* Parken, *das;* 'No ~' „Parken verboten"

**parking:** ~-light *n.* Parkleuchte, *die;* ~-lot *n.* *(Amer.)* Parkplatz, *der;* ~-meter *n.* Parkuhr, *die;* ~-space *n.* **a)** *no pl.* Parkraum, *der;* **b)** *(single space)* Parkplatz, *der;* ~-ticket *n.* Strafzettel [für falsches Parken]

**parliament** ['pɑːləmənt] *n.* Parlament, *das;* |Houses of| P~ *(Brit.)* Parlament, *das.* **parliamentary** [pɑːlə'mentərɪ] *adj.* parlamentarisch; Parlaments⟨*geschäfte, -wahlen, -reform*⟩

**parlour** *(Brit.; Amer.:* **parlor**) ['pɑːlə(r)] *n.* *(dated)* Wohnzimmer, *das*

**parochial** [pə'rəʊkɪəl] *adj.* krähwinklig

**parody** ['pærədɪ] **1.** *n.* Parodie, *die* (of auf + *Akk.*). **2.** *v. t.* parodieren

**parole** [pə'rəʊl] *n.* bedingter Straferlaß *(Rechtsw.);* on ~: auf Bewährung

**parquet** ['pɑːkɪ, 'pɑːkeɪ] *n.* ~ |floor/flooring| Parkett, *das*

**parrot** ['pærət] *n.* Papagei, *der*

**parry** ['pærɪ] *v. t.* abwehren ⟨*Faustschlag*⟩; *(Fencing; also fig.)* parieren

**parsley** ['pɑːslɪ] *n.* Petersilie, *die*

**parsnip** ['pɑːsnɪp] *n.* Gemeiner Pastinak, *der*

**parson** ['pɑːsn] *n.* Pfarrer, *der*

**part** [pɑːt] **1.** *n.* **a)** Teil, *der;* the greater ~: der größte Teil; der Großteil; for the most ~: größtenteils; in ~: teilweise; in large ~: groß[en]teils; in ~s zum Teil; **b)** *(of machine)* [Einzel]teil, *das;* **c)** *(share)* Anteil, *der;* **d)** *(Theatre)* Rolle, *die;* **e)** *(Mus.)* Part, *der;* Stimme, *die;* **f)** *usu. in pl. (region)* Gegend, *die;* *(of continent, world)* Teil, *der;* **g)** *(side)* Partei, *die;* take sb.'s ~: jmds. od. für jmdn. Partei ergreifen; **h)** take |no| ~ |in sth.| sich [an etw. *(Dat.)*] [nicht] beteiligen; **i)** take sth. in good ~: etw. nicht übelnehmen. **2.** *adv.* teils. **3.** *v. t.* **a)** *(divide into ~s)* teilen; scheiteln ⟨*Haar*⟩; **b)** *(separate)* trennen. **4.** *v. i.* ⟨*Seil, Tau, Kette:*⟩ reißen; ⟨*Wege, Personen:*⟩ sich trennen; ~ with sich trennen von ⟨*Besitz, Geld*⟩

**partial** ['pɑ:ʃl] *adj.* **a)** *(biased)* voreingenommen; **b) be/not be ~ to sth.** eine Schwäche/keine besondere Vorliebe für etw. haben; **c)** partiell ⟨*Lähmung, Sonnenfinsternis*⟩; **a ~ success** ein Teilerfolg. '**partially** *adv.* teilweise

**participant** [pɑ:'tısıpənt] *n.* Beteiligte, *der/die* (**in an** + *Dat.*)

**participate** [pɑ:'tısıpeıt] *v.i.* sich beteiligen (**in an** + *Dat.*); *(in arranged event)* teilnehmen (**in an** + *Dat.*).
**participation** [pɑ:tısı'peıʃn] *n.* Beteiligung, *die* (**in an** + *Dat.*); *(in arranged event)* Teilnahme, *die* (**in bei, an** + *Dat.*)

**participle** ['pɑ:tısıpl] *n.* Partizip, *das*

**particle** ['pɑ:tıkl] *n.* Teilchen, *das*

**particular** [pə'tıkjʊlə(r)] **1.** *adj.* **a)** besonder...; **here in ~:** besonders hier; **nothing/anything [in] ~:** nichts/irgend etwas Besonderes; **b)** *(fastidious)* genau; **I am not ~:** es ist mir gleich; **be ~ about sth.** es mit etw. genau nehmen. **2.** *n., in pl.* Einzelheiten; Details; *(of person)* Personalien *Pl.* **par'ticularly** *adv.* besonders

'**parting** **1.** *n.* **a)** [final] ~**:** Abschied, *der;* **b)** *(Brit.: in hair)* Scheitel, *der.* **2.** *attrib. adj.* Abschieds-

**partisan** ['pɑ:tızæn] *n.* Partisan, *der*/Partisanin, *die*

**partition** [pɑ:'tıʃn] **1.** *n.* **a)** *(Polit.)* Teilung, *die;* **b)** *(room-divider)* Trennwand, *die.* **2.** *v.t.* **a)** *(divide)* aufteilen ⟨*Land, Zimmer*⟩; **b)** *(Polit.)* teilen ⟨*Land*⟩. **partition 'off** *v.t.* abteilen

'**partly** *adv.* zum Teil; teilweise

**partner** ['pɑ:tnə(r)] *n.* Partner, *der*/Partnerin, *die.* '**partnership** *n.* Partnerschaft; **business ~:** [Personen]gesellschaft, *die*

**partridge** ['pɑ:trıdʒ] *n., pl. same or* ~**s** Rebhuhn, *das*

**part-time** **1.** ['-–] *adj.* Teilzeit⟨*arbeit, -arbeiter*⟩. **2.** ['-'-] *adv.* stundenweise; halbtags ⟨*arbeiten, studieren*⟩

**party** ['pɑ:tı] *n.* **a)** *(Polit., Law)* Partei, *die; attrib.* Partei-; **b)** *(group)* Gruppe, *die;* **c)** *(social gathering)* Party, *die*

**pass** [pɑ:s] **1.** *n.* **a)** *(passing of an examination)* bestandene Prüfung; '~' *(mark)* Ausreichend, *das;* **get a ~ in maths** die Mathematikprüfung bestehen; **b)** *(written permission)* Ausweis, *der;* **c)** *(Footb.)* Paß, *der (fachspr.);* Ballabgabe, *die;* **d)** *(in mountains)* Paß, *der.* **2.** *v.i.* **a)** *(go by)* ⟨*Fußgänger:*⟩ vorbeigehen; ⟨*Fahrer, Fahrzeug:*⟩ vorbeifahren; ⟨*Zeit, Se-*

*kunde:*⟩ vergehen; *(by chance)* ⟨*Person, Fahrzeug:*⟩ vorbeikommen; **b)** *(come to an end)* vorbeigehen; ⟨*Gewitter, Unwetter:*⟩ vorüberziehen; **c)** *(be accepted)* durchgehen (**as** als, **for** für); **d)** *(in exam)* bestehen. **3.** *v.t.* **a)** ⟨*Fußgänger:*⟩ vorbeigehen an (+ *Dat.*); ⟨*Fahrer, Fahrzeug:*⟩ vorbeifahren an (+ *Dat.*); *(by chance)* ⟨*Person, Fahrzeug:*⟩ vorbeikommen an (+ *Dat.*); **b)** *(overtake)* vorbeifahren an (+ *Dat.*); **c)** bestehen ⟨*Prüfung*⟩; **d)** *(approve)* verabschieden ⟨*Gesetzentwurf*⟩; annehmen ⟨*Vorschlag*⟩; bestehen lassen ⟨*Prüfungskandidaten*⟩; **e)** *(Footb. etc.)* abgeben (**to** an + *Akk.*); **f)** *(spend)* verbringen ⟨*Leben, Zeit, Tag*⟩; **g)** *(hand)* ~ **sb. sth.** jmdm. etw. reichen *od.* geben; **h)** fällen ⟨*Urteil*⟩; machen ⟨*Bemerkung*⟩; **i)** ~ **water** Wasser lassen. **pass a'way** *v.i. (euphem.)* die Augen schließen *(verhüll.).* **pass 'off** *v.t.* ~ **sth. off as sth.** etw. als etw. ausgeben. **pass 'on** *v.t.* weitergeben (**to** an + *Akk.*). **pass 'out** *v.i.* ohnmächtig werden. **pass 'up** *v.t.* entgehen lassen ⟨*Gelegenheit*⟩; ablehnen ⟨*Angebot*⟩

**passable** ['pɑ:səbl] *adj.* **a)** *(acceptable)* passabel; **b)** befahrbar ⟨*Straße*⟩

**passage** ['pæsıdʒ] *n.* **a)** *(voyage)* Überfahrt, *die;* **b)** *(way)* Durchgang, *der;* *(corridor)* Korridor, *der;* **c)** *(part of book etc.)* Textstelle, *die;* *(Mus.)* Stelle, *die*

**passenger** ['pæsındʒə(r)] *n.* Passagier, *der;* *(on train)* Reisende, *der/die;* *(on bus, in taxi)* Fahrgast, *der;* *(in car, on motor cycle)* Mitfahrer, *der*/Mitfahrerin, *die;* *(in front seat of car)* Beifahrer, *der*/Beifahrerin, *die.* '**passenger seat** *n.* Beifahrersitz, *der*

**passer-by** [pɑ:sə'baı] *n.* Passant, *der*/Passantin, *die*

'**passing** **1.** *n.* *(of time, years)* Lauf, *der;* **in ~:** beiläufig ⟨*bemerken usw.*⟩. **2.** *adj.* **a)** vorbeifahrend ⟨*Zug, Auto*⟩; vorbeikommend ⟨*Person*⟩; **b)** flüchtig ⟨*Blick*⟩; vorübergehend ⟨*Mode, Interesse*⟩; flüchtig ⟨*Bekanntschaft*⟩

**passion** ['pæʃn] *n.* Leidenschaft, *die;* *(enthusiasm)* leidenschaftliche Begeisterung; **he has a ~ for steam engines** Dampfloks sind seine Leidenschaft. **passionate** ['pæʃənət] *adj.* leidenschaftlich; heftig ⟨*Verlangen*⟩

**passive** ['pæsıv] **1.** *adj.* **a)** passiv; **b)** *(Ling.)* Passiv-. **2.** *n. (Ling.)* Passiv, *das*

**pass:** ~**port** n. a) [Reise]paß, der; attrib. Paß-; b) (fig.) Schlüssel, der (to zu); ~**word** n. a) Parole, die; Losung, die; b) (Computing) Paßwort, das

**past** [pɑːst] 1. adj. a) pred. (over) vorbei; b) attrib. (previous) früher; vergangen; ehemalig ⟨Präsident, Vorsitzende usw.⟩; c) attrib. (just gone by) letzt...; vergangen; **in the ~ few days** während der letzten Tage; (Ling.) ~ **tense** Vergangenheit, die. 2. n. Vergangenheit, die; **in the ~:** früher; in der Vergangenheit ⟨leben⟩; **be a thing of the ~:** der Vergangenheit angehören. 3. prep. (in time) nach; (in place) hinter (+ Dat.); **half ~ three** halb vier; **five [minutes] ~ two** fünf [Minuten] nach zwei; **gaze/walk ~ sb./sth.** an jmdm./etw. vorbeiblicken/vorbeigehen; ~ **repair** nicht mehr zu reparieren. 4. adv. vorbei; **hurry ~:** vorübereilen

**pasta** ['pæstə] n. Nudeln Pl.

**paste** [peɪst] 1. n. a) Brei, der; b) (glue) Kleister, der; c) (of meat, fish, etc.) Paste, die. 2. v. t. kleben; ~ **sth. into sth.** (Akk.) einkleben

**pastel** ['pæstl] 1. n. (crayon) Pastellstift, der. 2. adj. pastellfarben; Pastell⟨farben, -töne, -zeichnung⟩

**pasteurize** ['pɑːstʃəraɪz] v. t. pasteurisieren

**pastille** ['pæstɪl] n. Pastille, die

**pastime** ['pɑːstaɪm] n. Zeitvertreib, der; (person's specific ~) Hobby, das

**pastor** ['pɑːstə(r)] n. Pfarrer, der/Pfarrerin, die; Pastor, der/Pastorin, die

**pastoral** ['pɑːstərl] adj. Weide-; ländlich ⟨Reiz, Idylle, Umgebung⟩

**pastry** ['peɪstrɪ] n. Teig, der; (article of food) Gebäckstück, das; **pastries** collect. [Fein]gebäck, das

**pasture** ['pɑːstʃə(r)] n. Weide, die

**pasty** ['pæstɪ] n. Pastete, die

**¹pat** [pæt] 1. n. a) (tap) Klaps, der; b) (of butter) Stückchen, das. 2. v. t., -tt- leicht klopfen auf (+ Akk.); tätscheln, (once) einen Klaps geben (+ Dat.) ⟨Person, Hund, Pferd⟩; ~ **sb. on the arm/head** jmdm. den Arm/Kopf tätscheln

**²pat** adv. **have sth. off ~:** etw. parat haben

**patch** [pætʃ] 1. n. a) Stelle, die; **fog ~es** Nebelfelder; b) (on worn garment) Flicken, der; **be not a ~ on sth.** (fig. coll.) nichts gegen etw. sein. 2. v. t. flicken. **patch 'up** v. t. reparieren; (fig.) beilegen ⟨Streit⟩

**patchy** ['pætʃɪ] adj. uneinheitlich ⟨Qualität⟩; ungleichmäßig ⟨Arbeit⟩; sehr lückenhaft ⟨Wissen⟩

**pâté** ['pæteɪ] n. Pastete, die

**patent** ['peɪtənt, 'pætənt] 1. adj. (obvious) offenkundig. 2. n. Patent, das. 3. v. t. patentieren lassen. **patent 'leather** n. Lackleder, das; ~ **shoes** Lackschuhe. **'patently** adv. offenkundig; ~ **obvious** ganz offenkundig

**paternal** [pə'tɜːnl] adj. väterlich

**path** [pɑːθ] n. Weg, der; (line of motion) Bahn, die

**pathetic** [pə'θetɪk] adj. a) (pitiful) mitleiderregend; b) (contemptible) armselig ⟨Entschuldigung⟩; erbärmlich ⟨Person, Leistung⟩

**'pathway** n. Weg, der

**patience** ['peɪʃəns] n. Geduld, die

**patient** ['peɪʃənt] 1. adj. geduldig. 2. n. Patient, der/Patientin, die. **'patiently** adv. geduldig

**patio** ['pætɪəʊ] n., pl. ~**s** Veranda, die; Terrasse, die

**patriot** ['peɪtrɪət] n. Patriot, der/Patriotin, die. **patriotic** [peɪtrɪ'ɒtɪk] adj. patriotisch. **patriotism** ['peɪtrɪətɪzm] n. Patriotismus, der

**patrol** [pə'trəʊl] 1. n. (Police) Streife, die; (Mil.) Patrouille, die; **be on ~:** patrouillieren. 2. v. i., -ll- patrouillieren; ⟨Polizei:⟩ Streife laufen/fahren. 3. v. t., -ll- patrouillieren durch (+ Akk.); abpatrouillieren ⟨Straßen, Gegend, Lager⟩; patrouillieren vor (+ Dat.) ⟨Küste, Grenze⟩; ⟨Polizei:⟩ Streife laufen/fahren in (+ Dat.) ⟨Straßen, Stadtteil⟩. **pa'trol boat** n. Patrouillenboot, das. **pa'trol car** n. Streifenwagen, der

**patron** ['peɪtrən] n. a) Gönner, der/Gönnerin, die; (of institution, campaign) Schirmherr, der/Schirmherrin, die; b) (customer) (of shop) Kunde, der/Kundin, die; (of restaurant, hotel) Gast, der; (of theatre, cinema) Besucher, der/Besucherin, die; c) ~ [**saint**] Schutzheilige, der/die. **patronage** ['pætrənɪdʒ] n. Gönnerschaft, die; (for campaign, institution) Schirmherrschaft, die

**patronize** ['pætrənaɪz] v. t. a) (frequent) besuchen; b) (condescend to) ~ **sb.** jmdn. herablassend behandeln. **patronizing** ['pætrənaɪzɪŋ] adj. gönnerhaft; herablassend

**patter** ['pætə(r)] 1. n. (of rain) Prasseln, das; (of feet) Trappeln, das. 2. v. i. ⟨Regen:⟩ prasseln

**pattern** ['pætən] *n.* Muster, *das;* *(model)* Vorlage, *die;* *(for sewing)* Schnittmuster, *das;* *(for knitting)* Strickmuster, *das*

**paunch** [pɔ:ntʃ] *n.* Bauch, *der*

**pauper** ['pɔ:pə(r)] *n.* Arme, *der/die*

**pause** [pɔ:z] **1.** *n.* Pause, *die.* **2.** *v. i.* eine Pause machen; ⟨*Redner:*⟩ innehalten; *(hesitate)* zögern

**pave** [peɪv] *v. t.* befestigen; *(with stones)* pflastern; **~ the way for sth.** *(fig.)* einer Sache *(Dat.)* den Weg ebnen. '**pavement** *n.* **a)** *(Brit.: footway)* Bürgersteig, *der;* **b)** *(Amer.: roadway)* Fahrbahn, *die*

**pavilion** [pə'vɪljən] *n.* Pavillon, *der;* *(Brit. Sport)* Klubhaus, *das*

**paw** [pɔ:] *n.* Pfote, *die;* *(of bear, lion, tiger)* Pranke, *die*

¹**pawn** [pɔ:n] *n.* *(Chess)* Bauer, *der;* *(fig.)* Schachfigur, *die*

²**pawn** **1.** *n.* Pfand, *das;* **in ~:** verpfändet. **2.** *v. t.* verpfänden. '**pawnbroker** *n.* Pfandleiher, *der/*-leiherin, *die.* '**pawnshop** *n.* Leihhaus, *das*

**pay** [peɪ] **1.** *n.* *(wages)* Lohn, *der;* *(salary)* Gehalt, *das;* **be in the ~ of sb./sth.** für jmdn./etw. arbeiten. **2.** *v. t.,* **paid** [peɪd] bezahlen; zahlen ⟨*Geld*⟩; **~ sb. to do sth.** jmdn. dafür bezahlen, daß er etw. tut; **~ sb. £10** jmdm. 10 Pfund zahlen. **3.** *v. i.,* **paid** **a)** zahlen; **~ for sth./sb.** etw./für jmdn. bezahlen; **sth. ~s for itself** etw. macht sich bezahlt; **b)** *(be profitable)* sich lohnen; ⟨*Geschäft:*⟩ rentabel sein; **it ~s to be careful** es lohnt sich, vorsichtig zu sein. *See also* **paid.** **pay** '**back** *v. t.* zurückzahlen; **I'll ~ you back later** ich gebe dir das Geld später zurück. **pay** '**in** *v. t.* einzahlen. **pay** '**off** *v. t.* auszahlen ⟨*Arbeiter*⟩; abbezahlen ⟨*Schulden*⟩; ablösen ⟨*Hypothek*⟩; befriedigen ⟨*Gläubiger*⟩. **pay** '**out** *v. t.* auszahlen; *(spend)* ausgeben. **pay** '**up** *v. i.* zahlen

**payable** ['peɪəbl] *adj.* zahlbar; **be ~ to sb.** an jmdn. zu zahlen sein; **make a cheque ~ to the Post Office/to sb.** einen Scheck auf die Post/auf jmds. Namen ausstellen

**payee** [peɪ'i:] *n.* Zahlungsempfänger, *der/*-empfängerin, *die*

'**payment** *n.* **a)** *(of sum, bill, debt, fine)* Bezahlung, *die;* *(of interest, instalment, tax, fee)* Zahlung, *die;* **in ~ [for sth.]** als Bezahlung [für etw.]; **b)** *(amount)* Zahlung, *die*

**pay:** **~-packet** *n.* *(Brit.)* Lohntüte,

*die;* **~ phone** *n.* Münzfernsprecher, *der;* **~-rise** *n.* Lohn-/Gehaltserhöhung, *die;* **~-roll** *n.* Lohnliste, *die;* **be on sb.'s ~roll** für jmdn. arbeiten; **~-slip** *n.* Lohnstreifen, *der/*Gehaltszettel, *der;* **~ station** *n.* *(Amer.) see* **~ phone**

**PC** *abbr.* **a)** *(Brit.)* **police constable** Wachtm.; **b)** **personal computer** PC

**PE** *abbr.* **physical education**

**pea** [pi:] *n.* Erbse, *die*

**peace** [pi:s] *n.* Frieden, *der;* *(tranquillity)* Ruhe, *die;* **~ of mind** Seelenfrieden, *der.* **peaceable** ['pi:səbl] *adj.* friedfertig; *(calm)* friedlich. **peaceful** ['pi:sfl] *adj.* friedlich; friedfertig ⟨*Person, Volk*⟩. '**peacefully** *adv.* friedlich; **die ~:** sanft entschlafen

'**peacetime** *n.* Friedenszeiten *Pl.*

**peach** [pi:tʃ] *n.* Pfirsich, *der*

'**peacock** *n.* Pfau, *der*

**peak** [pi:k] **1.** *n.* **a)** *(of cap)* Schirm, *der;* **b)** *(of mountain)* Gipfel, *der;* *(fig.)* Höhepunkt, *der.* **2.** *attrib. adj.* Höchst-, Spitzen⟨*preise, -werte*⟩; **~-hour traffic** Stoßverkehr, *der.* **peaked** [pi:kt] *adj.* **~ cap** Schirmmütze, *die*

**peal** [pi:l] *n.* Läuten, *das;* **~ of bells** Glockenläuten, *das;* **a ~/~s of laughter** schallendes Gelächter

**peanut** ['pi:nʌt] *n.* Erdnuß, *die;* **~ butter** Erdnußbutter, *die;* **~s** *(coll.: little money)* ein paar Kröten *(salopp)*

**pear** [peə(r)] *n.* Birne, *die*

**pearl** [pɜ:l] *n.* Perle, *die*

'**pear-tree** *n.* Birnbaum, *der*

**peasant** ['pezənt] *n.* [armer] Bauer, *der;* Landarbeiter, *der*

**peat** [pi:t] *n.* Torf, *der*

**pebble** ['pebl] *n.* Kiesel[stein], *der*

**peck** [pek] **1.** *v. t.* hacken; picken ⟨*Körner*⟩. **2.** *v. i.* picken (**at** nach); **~ at one's food** in seinem Essen herumstochern. **3.** *n.* *(kiss)* flüchtiger Kuß.

'**pecking order** *n.* Hackordnung, *die*

**peckish** ['pekɪʃ] *adj.* *(coll.)* **feel/get ~:** Hunger haben/bekommen

**peculiar** [pɪ'kju:lɪə(r)] *adj.* **a)** *(strange)* seltsam; **I feel [slightly] ~:** mir ist [etwas] komisch; **b)** *(especial)* besonder...; **c)** *(belonging exclusively)* eigentümlich (**to** *Dat.*). **peculiarity** [pɪkju:lɪ'ærɪtɪ] *n.* **a)** *(odd trait)* Eigentümlichkeit, *die;* **b)** *(distinguishing characteristic)* [charakteristisches] Merkmal. **pe'culiarly** *adv.* **a)** *(strangely)* seltsam; **b)** *(especially)* besonders

**pedal** ['pedl] **1.** *n.* Pedal, *das.* **2.** *v. i.,*

*(Brit.)* **-ll-** in die Pedale treten.
'**pedal-bin** n. Treteimer, *der*
**pedant** ['pedənt] n. Pedant, *der*/Pedantin, *die*. **pedantic** [pɪ'dæntɪk] *adj*. pedantisch
**peddle** ['pedl] *v. t.* auf der Straße verkaufen; *(door to door)* hausieren mit
**pedestal** ['pedɪstl] n. Sockel, *der*
**pedestrian** [pɪ'destrɪən] **1.** *adj. (uninspired)* trocken; langweilig. **2.** n. Fußgänger, *der*/-gängerin, *die*. **pedestrian 'crossing** n. Fußgängerüberweg, *der*
**pedigree** ['pedɪgrɪ:] **1.** n. Stammbaum, *der*. **2.** *adj*. mit Stammbaum *nachgestellt*
**pedlar** ['pedlə(r)] n. Straßenhändler, *der*/-händlerin, *die; (door to door)* Hausierer, *der*/Hausiererin, *die*
**pee** [pi:] *(coll.)* **1.** *v. i.* pinkeln *(salopp);* Pipi machen *(Kinderspr.).* **2.** n. **a)** have a ~: pinkeln *(salopp);* **b)** *(urine)* Pipi, *das (Kinderspr.)*
**peek** [pi:k] *see* ²**peep**
**peel** [pi:l] **1.** *v. t.* schälen. **2.** *v. i.* ⟨Person, Haut:⟩ sich schälen; ⟨Farbe:⟩ abblättern. **3.** n. Schale, *die*. '**peelings** n. pl. Schalen
¹**peep** [pi:p] **1.** *v. i.* ⟨Maus, Vogel:⟩ piep[s]en. **2.** n. Piepsen, *das; (coll.: remark etc.)* Piep[s], *der*
²**peep 1.** *v. i.* gucken *(ugs.); (furtively)* verstohlen gucken *(ugs.).* **2.** n. kurzer/verstohlener Blick. '**peep-hole** n. Guckloch, *das*. **peeping 'Tom** n. Spanner, *der (ugs.)*
¹**peer** [pɪə(r)] n. Peer, *der; (equal)* Gleichgestellte, *der/die*
²**peer** *v. i.* forschend schauen; *(with difficulty)* angestrengt schauen; ~ at sth./sb. [sich *(Dat.)*] etw. genau ansehen/jmdn. forschend ansehen; *(with difficulty)* [sich *(Dat.)*] etw./jmdn. angestrengt ansehen
**peerage** ['pɪərɪdʒ] n. Peerswürde, *die*
**peevish** ['pi:vɪʃ] *adj*. nörgelig
**peg** [peg] n. *(for holding together)* Stift, *der; (for tying things to)* Pflock, *der; (for hanging things on)* Haken, *der; (clothes-~)* Wäscheklammer, *die; (tent-~)* Hering, *der;* off the ~ *(Brit.: ready-made)* von der Stange *(ugs.)*
**pejorative** [pɪ'dʒɒrətɪv] *adj.,* **pe'joratively** *adv*. abwertend
**pelican** ['pelɪkən] n. Pelikan, *der*. '**pelican crossing** n. *(Brit.)* Ampelübergang, *der*
**pellet** ['pelɪt] n. Kügelchen, *das*
**pelmet** ['pelmɪt] n. Blende, *die*

¹**pelt** [pelt] n. Fell, *das*
²**pelt 1.** *v. t.* ~ **sb. with sth.** jmdn. mit etw. bewerfen. **2.** *v. i.* **a)** it was ~ing down [with rain] es goß wie aus Kübeln *(ugs.);* **b)** *(run fast)* rasen *(ugs.)*
**pelvis** ['pelvɪs] n., pl. **pelves** ['pelvi:z] or ~**es** *(Anat.)* Becken, *das*
¹**pen** [pen] **1.** n. *(enclosure)* Pferch, *der*. **2.** *v. t.,* **-nn-:** ~ **sb. in a corner** jmdn. in eine Ecke drängen. **pen 'in** *v. t.* einpferchen
²**pen 1.** n. Federhalter, *der; (fountain-~)* Füller, *der; (ball-~)* Kugelschreiber, *der; (felt-tip ~)* Filzstift, *der*. **2.** *v. t.,* **-nn-** schreiben
**penal** ['pi:nl] *adj*. Straf-
**penalize** ['pi:nəlaɪz] *v. t.* bestrafen; *(Sport)* eine Strafe verhängen gegen
**penalty** ['penltɪ] n. **a)** Strafe, *die;* **pay the ~/the ~ for** or **of sth.** dafür/für etw. büßen [müssen]; **b)** *(Footb.)* Elfmeter, *der*
**penance** ['penəns] n. Buße, *die;* **act of ~**: Bußwerk, *das;* **do ~**: Buße tun
**pence** *see* **penny**
**pencil** ['pensl] **1.** n. Bleistift, *der;* **red/coloured ~**: Rot-/Buntstift, *der*. **2.** *v. t., (Brit.)* **-ll-** mit einem Bleistift/Farbstift schreiben. '**pencil-case** n. Griffelkasten, *der; (of soft material)* Federmäppchen, *das*. '**pencil-sharpener** n. Bleistiftspitzer, *der*
**pendant** ['pendənt] n. Anhänger, *der*
**pending** ['pendɪŋ] **1.** *adj*. unentschieden ⟨Angelegenheit, Sache⟩; schwebend ⟨Verfahren⟩. **2.** *prep*. ~ **his return** bis zu seiner Rückkehr
**pendulum** ['pendjʊləm] n. Pendel, *das*
**penetrate** ['penɪtreɪt] *v. t.* eindringen in ( + *Akk.*); *(pass through)* durchdringen. **penetrating** ['penɪtreɪtɪŋ] *adj*. durchdringend. **penetration** [penɪ'treɪʃn] n. Eindringen, *das* (**of** in + *Akk.*); *(passing through)* Durchdringen, *das*
'**pen-friend** n. Brieffreund, *der/*-freundin, *die*
**penguin** ['pengwɪn] n. Pinguin, *der*
**penicillin** [penɪ'sɪlɪn] n. Penizillin, *das*
**peninsula** [pɪ'nɪnsjʊlə] n. Halbinsel, *die*
**penis** ['pi:nɪs] n. Penis, *der*
**penitence** ['penɪtəns] n. Reue, *die*
**penitent** ['penɪtənt] *adj*. reuevoll *(geh.);* reuig *(geh.)* ⟨Sünder⟩
**penitentiary** [penɪ'tenʃərɪ] n. *(Amer.)* Straf[vollzugs]anstalt, *die*
'**penknife** n. Taschenmesser, *das*

**pennant** ['penənt] *n.* Wimpel, *der; (on official car etc.)* Ständer, *der*

**penniless** ['penɪlɪs] *adj.* mittellos

**penny** ['penɪ] *n., pl. usu.* **pennies** ['penɪz] *(for separate coins),* **pence** [pens] *(for sum of money)* Penny, *der;* **fifty pence** fünfzig Pence; **two/fifty pence |piece|** Zwei-/Fünfzigpencestück, *das*

**pension** ['penʃn] *n.* Rente, *die; (payment to retired civil servant also)* Pension, *die;* **be on a ~:** eine Rente beziehen; **widow's ~:** Witwenrente, *die.* **pension 'off** *v. t.* berenten *(Amtsspr.);* auf Rente setzen *(ugs.);* pensionieren ⟨*Lehrer, Beamten*⟩

'**pensioner** *n.* Rentner, *der*/Rentnerin, *die; (retired civil servant)* Pensionär, *der*/Pensionärin, *die*

**pensive** ['pensɪv] *adj.* nachdenklich

**pentagon** ['pentəgən] *n.* Fünfeck, *das*

**pent:** **~house** *n.* Penthaus, *das;* **~-up** *adj.* angestaut ⟨*Ärger, Wut*⟩; unterdrückt ⟨*Sehnsucht, Gefühle*⟩

**penultimate** [pe'nʌltɪmət] *adj.* vorletzt...

**people** ['pi:pl] *n.* **a)** *constr. as pl.* Leute *Pl.;* Menschen; *(as opposed to animals)* Menschen *Pl.;* **city/country ~** *(inhabitants)* Stadt-/Landbewohner; **local ~:** Einheimische; **working ~:** arbeitende Menschen; **coloured/white ~:** Farbige/Weiße; **~ say ...:** man sagt ...; **a crowd of ~** eine Menschenmenge; **b)** *(nation)* Volk, *das*

**pepper** ['pepə(r)] **1.** *n.* **a)** Pfeffer, *der;* **b)** *(vegetable)* Paprikaschote, *die;* **red/ green ~:** roter/grüner Paprika. **2.** *v. t.* **a)** pfeffern; **b)** *(pelt)* bombardieren *(ugs.)*

**pepper:** **~corn** *n.* Pfefferkorn, *das;* **~mint** *n. (sweet)* Pfefferminz, *das;* **~-pot** *n.* Pfefferstreuer, *der*

**per** [pə(r), *stressed* pɜ:(r)] *prep.* pro

**perceive** [pə'si:v] *v. t.* wahrnehmen; *(with the mind)* spüren; **~d** vermeintlich ⟨*Bedrohung, Gefahr, Wert*⟩

**per cent** *(Brit.; Amer.:* **percent)** [pə'sent] **1.** *adv.* **ninety ~ effective** zu 90 Prozent wirksam. **2.** *adj.* **a 5 ~ increase** ein Zuwachs von 5 Prozent. **3.** *n.* **a)** Prozent, *das;* **b)** *see* **percentage**

**percentage** [pə'sentɪdʒ] *n.* Prozentsatz, *der*

**perceptible** [pə'septɪbl] *adj.* wahrnehmbar

**perception** [pə'sepʃn] *n. (act)* Wahrnehmung, *die; (result)* Erkenntnis, *die; (faculty)* Wahrnehmungsvermögen, *das*

**perceptive** [pə'septɪv] *adj.* einfühlsam ⟨*Person, Bemerkung*⟩

**perch** [pɜ:tʃ] **1.** *n.* Sitzstange, *die.* **2.** *v. i.* **a)** sich niederlassen; **b)** *(be supported)* sitzen. **3.** *v. t.* setzen/stellen/legen

**percolate** ['pɜ:kəleɪt] *v. i.* [durch]sickern. **percolator** ['pɜ:kəleɪtə(r)] *n.* Kaffeemaschine, *die*

**percussion** [pə'kʌʃn] *n. (Mus.)* Schlagzeug, *das;* **~ instrument** Schlaginstrument, *das*

**perennial** [pə'renjəl] **1.** *adj.* **a)** *(Bot.)* ausdauernd; **b)** immer wieder auftretend ⟨*Problem*⟩. **2.** *n. (Bot.)* ausdauernde Pflanze

**perfect 1.** ['pɜ:fɪkt] *adj.* vollkommen; perfekt ⟨*Englisch, Timing*⟩; tadellos ⟨*Zustand*⟩; *(coll.: unmitigated)* absolut; **a ~ stranger** ein völlig Fremder. **2.** [pə'fekt] *v. t.* vervollkommnen. **perfection** [pə'fekʃn] *n.* Perfektion, *die;* **to ~:** perfekt. **perfectionism** [pə'fekʃənɪzm] *n.* Perfektionismus, *der.* **perfectionist** [pə'fekʃənɪst] *n.* Perfektionist, *der*/Perfektionistin, *die.* '**perfectly** *adv.* **a)** *(completely)* vollkommen; **be ~ entitled to do sth.** durchaus berechtigt sein, etw. zu tun; **b)** *(faultlessly)* perfekt; tadellos ⟨*sich verhalten*⟩

**perforate** ['pɜ:fəreɪt] *v. t.* perforieren; *(make opening into)* durchlöchern. **perforation** [pɜ:fə'reɪʃn] *n.* **a)** *(hole)* Loch, *das;* **b)** *in pl.* ~s Perforation, *die; (in sheets of stamps)* Zähnung, *die*

**perform** [pə'fɔ:m] **1.** *v. t.* ausführen ⟨*Arbeit, Operation*⟩; erfüllen ⟨*Pflicht, Aufgabe*⟩; vollbringen ⟨*[Helden]tat, Leistung*⟩; ausfüllen ⟨*Funktion*⟩; vollbringen ⟨*Wunder*⟩; anstellen ⟨*Berechnungen*⟩; durchführen ⟨*Experiment, Sektion*⟩; vorführen ⟨*Trick*⟩; aufführen ⟨*Theaterstück, Scharade*⟩; vortragen ⟨*Lied, Sonate usw.*⟩. **2.** *v. i.* eine Vorführung geben; *(sing)* singen; *(play)* spielen. **performance** [pə'fɔ:məns] *n.* **a)** *(of duty, task)* Erfüllung, *die;* **b)** *[notable] achievement; Motor Veh.)* Leistung, *die;* **c)** *(at theatre, cinema, etc.)* Vorstellung, *die;* **her ~ as Desdemona** ihre Darstellung der Desdemona; **the ~ of a play/opera** die Aufführung eines Theaterstücks/ einer Oper. **per'former** *n.* Künstler, *der*/Künstlerin, *die.* **per'forming** *attrib. adj.* dressiert ⟨*Tier*⟩

**perfume** ['pɜ:fju:m] *n.* Duft, *der; (fluid)* Parfüm, *das*

**perfunctory** [pə'fʌŋktərɪ] *adj.* oberflächlich ⟨*Arbeit, Überprüfung*⟩; flüchtig ⟨*Erkundigung, Bemerkung*⟩
**perhaps** [pə'hæps] *adv.* vielleicht
**peril** ['perl] *n.* Gefahr, *die.* **perilous**
['perələs] *adj.* gefahrvoll; **be** ~: gefährlich sein
**perimeter** [pə'rɪmɪtə(r)] *n.* [äußere]
Begrenzung; Grenze, *die*
**period** ['pɪərɪəd] **1.** *n.* **a)** *(of history or
life)* Periode, *die;* Zeit, *die; (any portion of time)* Zeitraum, *der;* **the Clas-
sical/Romantic** ~: die Klassik/Ro-
mantik; **b)** *(Sch.)* Stunde, *die;* **chem-
istry/English** ~: Chemie-/Englisch-
stunde, *die;* **c)** *(menstruation)* Periode,
*die;* **d)** *(punctuation mark)* Punkt, *der.*
**2.** *adj.* zeitgenössisch ⟨*Tracht, Kostüm*⟩; antik ⟨*Möbel*⟩. **periodic** [pɪərɪ-
'ɒdɪk] *adj.* regelmäßig; *(intermittent)*
gelegentlich. **periodical** [pɪərɪ'ɒdɪkl]
**1.** *adj. see* **periodic. 2.** *n.* Zeitschrift,
*die;* **weekly/monthly** ~: Wochenzeit-
schrift/Monatsschrift, *die.* **peri'od-
ically** *adv.* regelmäßig; *(intermittently)* gelegentlich
**peripheral** [pə'rɪfərl] *adj.* peripher
*(geh.);* Rand⟨*problem, -erscheinung*⟩
**periphery** [pə'rɪfərɪ] *n.* Peripherie, *die*
**periscope** ['perɪskəʊp] *n.* Periskop,
*das*
**perish** ['perɪʃ] *v.i.* **a)** *(die)* umkommen; **b)** *(rot)* verderben; ⟨*Gummi:*⟩ altern. **perishable** ['perɪʃəbl] *adj.*
[leicht] verderblich
'**perishing** *(coll.)* **1.** *adj.* mörderisch
⟨*Kälte*⟩; **it's/I'm** ~: es ist bitterkalt/
ich komme um vor Kälte *(ugs.).* **2.**
*adv.* mörderisch ⟨*kalt*⟩
**perjury** ['pɜːdʒərɪ] *n.* Meineid, *der;*
**commit** ~: einen Meineid leisten
¹**perk** [pɜːk] *(coll.)* **1.** *v.i.* ~ **up** munter
werden. **2.** *v.t.* ~ **up** aufmuntern
²**perk** *n. (Brit. coll.)* [Sonder]vergünsti-
gung, *die*
**perky** ['pɜːkɪ] *adj.* lebhaft; munter
**perm** [pɜːm] **1.** *n.* Dauerwelle, *die.* **2.**
*v.t.* **have one's hair** ~**ed** sich *(Dat.)* eine Dauerwelle machen lassen
**permanence** ['pɜːmənəns] *n.* Dauer-
haftigkeit, *die*
**permanent** ['pɜːmənənt] *adj.* fest
⟨*Sitz, Bestandteil, Mitglied*⟩; ständig
⟨*Wohnsitz, Adresse, Kampf*⟩; Dauer-
⟨*stellung, -visum*⟩; bleibend ⟨*Schaden*⟩. '**permanently** *adv.* dauernd;
auf Dauer ⟨*verhindern, bleiben*⟩
**permeable** ['pɜːmɪəbl] *adj.* durchläs-
sig; **be** ~ **to sth.** etw. durchlassen

**permeate** ['pɜːmɪeɪt] **1.** *v.t.* dringen
durch; **be** ~**d with** *or* **by sth.** *(fig.)* von
etw. durchdrungen sein. **2.** *v.i.* ~
**through sth.** etw. durchdringen
**permissible** [pə'mɪsɪbl] *adj.* zulässig;
**be** ~ **to** *or* **for sb.** jmdm. erlaubt sein
**permission** [pə'mɪʃn] *n.* Erlaubnis,
*die; (given by official body)* Genehmigung, *die;* **give sb.** ~ **to do sth.** jmdm.
erlauben, etw. zu tun
**permissive** [pə'mɪsɪv] *adj.* **the** ~ **society** die permissive Gesellschaft
**permit 1.** [pə'mɪt] *v.t.,* **-tt-** zulassen
⟨*Berufung, Einspruch usw.*⟩; ~ **sb. sth.**
jmdm. etw. erlauben; **sb. is** ~**ted to do
sth.** es ist jmdm. erlaubt, etw. zu tun.
**2.** *v.i.,* **-tt-** es zulassen. **3.** ['pɜːmɪt] *n.*
Genehmigung, *die*
**pernicious** [pə'nɪʃəs] *adj.* verderblich; bösartig ⟨*Krankheit*⟩
**perpendicular** [pɜːpən'dɪkjʊlə(r)]
*adj.* senkrecht
**perpetrate** ['pɜːpɪtreɪt] *v.t.* begehen;
verüben ⟨*Greuel*⟩
**perpetual** [pə'petjʊəl] *adj.* **a)** *(eternal)*
ewig; **b)** *(continuous; coll.: repeated)*
ständig. **per'petually** *adv.* **a)** *(eternally)* ewig; **b)** *(continuously; coll.: repeatedly)* ständig
**perpetuate** [pə'petjʊeɪt] *v.t.* aufrechterhalten
**perplex** [pə'pleks] *v.t.* verwirren. **per-
plexed** [pə'plekst] *adj.* verwirrt;
*(puzzled)* ratlos. **perplexity** [pə'plek-
sɪtɪ] *n.* Verwirrung, *die; (puzzlement)*
Ratlosigkeit, *die*
**persecute** ['pɜːsɪkjuːt] *v.t.* verfolgen.
**persecution** [pɜːsɪ'kjuːʃn] *n.* Verfolgung, *die*
**perseverance** [pɜːsɪ'vɪərəns] *n.* Beharrlichkeit, *die;* Ausdauer, *die*
**persevere** [pɜːsɪ'vɪə(r)] *v.i.* aushar-
ren; ~ **with** *or* **at** *or* **in sth.** bei etw. da-
beibleiben
**Persian** ['pɜːʃn] *adj.* persisch; Perser-
⟨*katze, -teppich*⟩
**persist** [pə'sɪst] *v.i.* **a)** nicht nachgeben; ~ **in doing sth.** etw. weiterhin [be-
harrlich] tun; **b)** *(continue to exist)* anhalten. **persistence** [pə'sɪstəns]
Hartnäckigkeit, *die.* **persistent** [pə-
'sɪstənt] *adj.* **a)** hartnäckig; **b)** *(constantly repeated)* dauernd; hartnäckig
⟨*Gerüchte*⟩. **per'sistently** *adv.* hartnäckig
**person** ['pɜːsn] *n.* Mensch, *der;* **in** ~:
persönlich; selbst
**personal** ['pɜːsənl] *adj.* persönlich;
Privat⟨*angelegenheit, -leben*⟩; ~ **com-**

**puter** Personalcomputer, *der;* ~ **stereo** Walkman, *der;* ~ **hygiene** Körperpflege, *die.* **personal as'sistant** *n.*persönlicher Referent/persönliche Referentin

**personality** [pɜːsə'nælɪtɪ] *n.* Persönlichkeit, *die*

'**personally** *adv.* persönlich

**personification** [pəsɒnɪfɪ'keɪʃn] *n.* Verkörperung, *die*

**personify** [pə'sɒnɪfaɪ] *v. t.* verkörpern; **be kindness personified** die Freundlichkeit in Person sein

**personnel** [pɜːsə'nel] *n.* Belegschaft, *die; (of shop, restaurant, etc.)* Personal, *das; attrib.* Personal-

**perspective** [pə'spektɪv] *n.* Perspektive, *die; (fig.)* Blickwinkel, *der*

**perspiration** [pɜːspɪ'reɪʃn] *n.* Schweiß, *der*

**perspire** [pə'spaɪə(r)] *v. i.* schwitzen

**persuade** [pə'sweɪd] *v. t.* **a)** *(convince)* überzeugen (of von); ~ **oneself** |**that**| ...: sich (*Dat.*) einreden, daß ...; **b)** *(induce)* überreden. **persuasion** [pə'sweɪʒn] *n.* Überzeugung, *die;* **it didn't take much** ~: es brauchte nicht viel Überredungskunst. **persuasive** [pə'sweɪsɪv] *adj.,* **per'suasively** *adv.* überzeugend

**pert** [pɜːt] *adj.* keck

**pertinent** ['pɜːtɪnənt] *adj.* relevant (**to** für)

**perturb** [pə'tɜːb] *v. t.* beunruhigen

**Peru** [pə'ruː] *pr. n.* Peru *(das).* **Peruvian** [pə'ruːvɪən] **1.** *adj.* peruanisch. **2.** *n.* Peruaner, *der*/Peruanerin, *die*

**pervade** [pə'veɪd] *v. t.* durchdringen. **pervasive** [pə'veɪsɪv] *adj.* durchdringend ⟨*Geruch, Kälte*⟩; weit verbreitet ⟨*Ansicht*⟩; sich ausbreitend ⟨*Gefühl*⟩

**perverse** [pə'vɜːs] *adj.* starrköpfig

**perversion** [pə'vɜːʃn] *n.* **a)** *(sexual)* Perversion, *die;* **b)** ~ **of justice** Rechtsbeugung, *die.* **pervert 1.** [pə'vɜːt] *v. t. (morally)* verderben. **2.** ['pɜːvɜːt] *n.* perverser Mensch. **perverted** [pə'vɜːtɪd] *adj. (sexually)* pervers

**pessimism** ['pesɪmɪzm] *n.* Pessimismus, *der.* **pessimist** ['pesɪmɪst] *n.* Pessimist, *der*/Pessimistin, *die.* **pessimistic** [pesɪ'mɪstɪk] *adj.* pessimistisch

**pest** [pest] *n. (thing)* Ärgernis, *das; (person)* Nervensäge, *die (ugs.); (animal)* Schädling, *der*

**pester** ['pestə(r)] *v. t.* belästigen; nerven *(ugs.);* ~ **sb. for sth.** jmdm. wegen etw. in den Ohren liegen

**pesticide** ['pestɪsaɪd] *n.* Pestizid, *das*

**pet** [pet] **1.** *n.* **a)** *(animal)* Haustier, *das;* **b)** *(as term of endearment)* Schatz, *der.* **2.** *adj. (favourite)* Lieblings-. **3.** *v. i.,* -tt- knutschen *(ugs.)*

**petal** ['petl] *n.* Blütenblatt, *das*

**peter** ['piːtə(r)] *v. i.* ~ **out** [allmählich] zu Ende gehen; ⟨*Weg:*⟩ sich verlieren

**petite** [pə'tiːt] *adj.* zierlich

**petition** [pə'tɪʃn] **1.** *n.* Petition, *die;* Eingabe, *die.* **2.** *v. t.* eine Eingabe richten an (+ *Akk.*)

**petrify** ['petrɪfaɪ] *v. t.* **be petrified with fear/shock** starr vor Angst/Schrecken sein

**petrol** ['petrl] *n. (Brit.)* Benzin, *das*

**petroleum** [pɪ'trəʊlɪəm] *n.* Erdöl, *das*

**petrol:** ~-**pump** *n. (Brit.)* Zapfsäule, *die;* ~-**station** *n. (Brit.)* Tankstelle, *die;* ~-**tank** *n. (Brit.)* Benzintank, *der;* ~-**tanker** *n. (Brit.)* Benzintankwagen, *der*

'**pet shop** *n.* Tierhandlung, *die*

**petticoat** ['petɪkəʊt] *n.* Unterrock, *der*

**petty** ['petɪ] *adj.* kleinlich ⟨*Vorschrift, Einwand*⟩; belanglos ⟨*Detail, Sorgen*⟩

**petulant** ['petjʊlənt] *adj.* bockig

**pew** [pjuː] *n. (Eccl.)* Kirchenbank, *die*

**pewter** ['pjuːtə(r)] *n.* Pewter, *der*

**phantom** ['fæntəm] *n.* Phantom, *das*

**pharmacist** ['fɑːməsɪst] *n.* Apotheker, *der*/Apothekerin, *die*

**pharmacy** ['fɑːməsɪ] *n. (dispensary)* Apotheke, *die*

**phase** [feɪz] *n.* Phase, *die.* **phase 'in** *v. t.* stufenweise einführen. **phase 'out** *v. t.* allmählich abschaffen ⟨*Verfahrensweise, Methode*⟩; *(stop producing)* [langsam] auslaufen lassen

**Ph.D.** [piːeɪtʃ'diː] *abbr.* **Doctor of Philosophy** Dr. phil.

**pheasant** ['fezənt] *n.* Fasan, *der*

**phenomenal** [fɪ'nɒmɪnl] *adj.* phänomenal

**phenomenon** [fɪ'nɒmɪnən] *n., pl.* **phenomena** [fɪ'nɒmɪnə] Phänomen, *das*

**phew** [fjuː] *int.* puh

**Philippines** ['fɪlɪpiːnz] *pr. n. pl.* Philippinen *Pl.*

**philistine** ['fɪlɪstaɪn] *n.* Banause, *der*/Banausin, *die*

**philosopher** [fɪ'lɒsəfə(r)] *n.* Philosoph, *der*/Philosophin, *die*

**philosophical** [fɪlə'sɒfɪkl] *adj.* **a)** philosophisch; **b)** *(resigned)* abgeklärt

**philosophy** [fɪ'lɒsəfɪ] *n.* Philosophie, *die*

**phlegm** [flem] *n.* Schleim, *der*

**phobia** ['fəʊbɪə] *n.* Phobie, *die*

**phone** [fəʊn] *(coll.)* **1.** *n.* Telefon, *das;*
by ~: telefonisch; **be on the ~:** Telefon haben; *(be phoning)* telefonieren.
**2.** *v. t. & i.* anrufen. **phone 'back**
*v. t. & i.* zurückrufen; *(make further
call)* wieder anrufen. **phone 'up** *v. t.
& i.* anrufen
**phone:** ~ **book** *n.* Telefonbuch, *das;*
~ **box** *n.* Telefonzelle, *die;* ~ **call** *n.*
Anruf, *der;* ~ **card** *n.* Telefonkarte,
*die;* ~ **number** *n.* Telefonnummer,
*die*
**phonetic** [fə'netɪk] *adj.* phonetisch.
**phonetics** [fə'netɪks] *n.* Phonetik,
*die*
**phoney** ['fəʊnɪ] *adj. (coll.) (sham)*
falsch; gefälscht ⟨*Brief, Dokument*⟩
**phonograph** ['fəʊnəɡrɑːf] *n. (Amer.)*
Plattenspieler, *der*
**phony** *see* **phoney**
**phosphorus** ['fɒsfərəs] *n.* Phosphor,
*der*
**photo** ['fəʊtəʊ] *n., pl.* ~**s** Foto, *das*
**photo-** ~**copier** *n.* Fotokopiergerät,
*das;* ~**copy 1.** *n.* Fotokopie, *die;* **2.**
*v. t.* fotokopieren
**photogenic** [fəʊtə'dʒiːnɪk] *adj.* fotogen
**photograph** ['fəʊtəɡrɑːf] **1.** *n.* Fotografie, *die;* Foto, *das;* **take a ~** |of sb./
sth.| [jmdn./etw.] fotografieren. **2.** *v. t.
& i.* fotografieren. **photographer**
[fə'tɒɡrəfə(r)] *n.* Fotograf, *der*/Fotografin, *die.* **photographic** [fəʊtə-
'ɡræfɪk] *adj.* fotografisch; Foto⟨*ausrüstung, -apparat, -ausstellung*⟩.
**photography** [fə'tɒɡrəfɪ] *n.* Fotografie, *die*
**phrase** [freɪz] **1.** *n.* [Rede]wendung,
*die.* **2.** *v. t.* formulieren. **'phrasebook** *n.* Sprachführer, *der*
**physical** ['fɪzɪkl] *adj.* **a)** physisch ⟨*Gewalt*⟩; dinglich ⟨*Welt, Universum*⟩; **b)**
*(of physics)* physikalisch; **c)** *(bodily)*
körperlich. **physical edu'cation** *n.*
*(Sch.)* Sport, *der.* **'physically** *adv.*
*(relating to the body)* körperlich
**physician** [fɪ'zɪʃn] *n.* Arzt, *der*/Ärztin,
*die*
**physicist** ['fɪzɪsɪst] *n.* Physiker, *der*/
Physikerin, *die*
**physics** ['fɪzɪks] *n.* Physik, *die*
**physiology** [fɪzɪ'ɒlədʒɪ] *n.* Physiologie, *die*
**physiotherapy** [fɪzɪəʊ'θerəpɪ] *n.* Physiotherapie, *die*
**physique** [fɪ'ziːk] *n.* Körperbau, *der*
**pianist** ['piːənɪst] *n.* Pianist, *der*/Pianistin, *die*

**piano** [pɪ'ænəʊ] *n., pl.* ~**s** *(upright)*
Klavier, *das; (grand)* Flügel, *der.*
**piano-ac'cordion** *n.* Akkordeon,
*das*
**¹pick** [pɪk] *n. (tool)* Spitzhacke, *die*
**²pick 1.** *n.* **a)** *(choice)* Wahl, *die;* **take
your ~:** du hast die Wahl; **b)** *(best
part)* Elite, *die;* **the ~ of** the fruit die
besten Früchte. **2.** *v. t.* **a)** pflücken
⟨*Blumen, Äpfel usw.*⟩; lesen ⟨*Trauben*⟩; **b)** *(select)* auswählen; ~ one's
way sich *(Dat.)* vorsichtig [s]einen
Weg suchen; **c)** ~ one's nose in der
Nase bohren; **d)** ~ sb.'s pocket jmdn.
bestehlen; **he had his pocket ~ed** er
wurde von einem Taschendieb bestohlen; **e)** ~ **a lock** ein Schloß
knacken *(salopp)*. **3.** *v. i.* ~ **and choose**
wählerisch sein. **'pick at** *v. t.* herumstochern in ( + *Dat.*) ⟨*Essen*⟩. **pick
on** *v. t. (victimize)* es abgesehen haben
auf ( + *Akk.*). **pick 'out** *v. t.* **a)**
*(choose)* auswählen; *(for oneself)* sich
*(Dat.)* aussuchen; **b)** *(distinguish)* entdecken ⟨*Detail, jmds. Gesicht in der
Menge*⟩. **pick up 1.** ['--] *v. t.* **a)** [in die
Hand] nehmen; hochnehmen ⟨*Baby*⟩;
*(after dropping)* aufheben ⟨*Masche*⟩; ~ **up the telephone** den [Telefon]hörer abnehmen; **b)** *(collect)*
mitnehmen; *(by arrangement)* abholen *(at, from* von); *(obtain)* holen; **c)**
*(become infected by)* sich *(Dat.)* holen
*(ugs.)* ⟨*Virus, Grippe*⟩; **d)** ⟨*Bus, Autofahrer:*⟩ mitnehmen; **e)** *(rescue from
the sea)* [aus Seenot] bergen; **f)** empfangen ⟨*Signal, Funkspruch usw.*⟩; **g)**
*(coll.: make acquaintance of)* aufreißen *(ugs.)*. **2.** [-'-] *v. i.* **a)** sich bessern;
**b)** ⟨*Wind:*⟩ auffrischen
**'pickaxe** *(Amer.:* **'pickax)** *see* **¹pick**
**picket** ['pɪkɪt] **1.** *n.* Streikposten, *der.*
**2.** *v. i.* Streikposten stehen. **3.** *v. t.*
Streikposten stellen vor ( + *Dat.*).
**'picket-line** *n.* Streikpostenkette, *die*
**pickle** ['pɪkl] **1.** *n., usu. in pl. (food)*
[Mixed] Pickles *Pl.* **2.** *v. t.* einlegen
⟨*Gurken, Zwiebeln, Eier*⟩; marinieren
⟨*Hering*⟩
**pick:** ~**-me-up** *n.* Stärkungsmittel,
*das;* ~**pocket** *n.* Taschendieb,
*der*/-diebin, *die;* ~**-up** *n.* **a)** ~ |truck|
Kleinlastwagen, *der;* **b)** *(of recordplayer, guitar)* Tonabnehmer, *der*
**picnic** ['pɪknɪk] **1.** *n.* Picknick, *das;* **go
for** *or* **on/have a ~:** ein Picknick machen. **2.** *v. i.,* **-ck-** picknicken; Picknick machen. **'picnic site** *n.* Picknickplatz, *der*

**pictorial** [pɪk'tɔːrɪəl] *adj.* illustriert ⟨*Bericht, Zeitschrift*⟩; bildlich ⟨*Darstellung*⟩

**picture** ['pɪktʃə(r)] **1.** *n.* **a)** Bild, *das*; **get the ~** *(coll.)* verstehen[, worum es geht]; **put sb. in the ~:** jmdn. ins Bild setzen; **b)** *(film)* Film, *der*; **c)** *in pl. (Brit.: cinema)* Kino, *das*; **go to the ~s** ins Kino gehen; **what's on at the ~s?** was läuft im Kino? **2.** *v. t.* **~** [to one**self**] sich *(Dat.)* vorstellen. '**picture-book** *n.* Bilderbuch, *das.* **picture 'postcard** *n.* Ansichtskarte, *die*

**picturesque** [pɪktʃə'resk] *adj.* malerisch

**pidgin** ['pɪdʒɪn] *n.* Pidgin, *das.* **pidgin 'English** *n.* Pidgin-Englisch, *das*

**pie** [paɪ] *n. (of meat, fish, etc.)* Pastete, *die; (of fruit etc.)* ≈ Obstkuchen, *der*

**piece** [piːs] **1.** *n.* **a)** Stück, *das; (of broken glass or pottery)* Scherbe, *die; (of jigsaw puzzle, crashed aircraft, etc.)* Teil, *der; (Amer.: distance)* [kleines] Stück; **a ~ of meat/cake** ein Stück Fleisch/Kuchen; **~ of furniture/luggage** Möbel-/Gepäckstück, *das;* **a three-~ suite** eine dreiteilige Sitzgarnitur; **~ of luck** Glücksfall, *der;* **~ of news/gossip/information** Nachricht, *die*/Klatsch, *der*/Information, *die;* **b)** *(Chess)* Figur, *die;* **c)** *(coin)* gold **~:** Goldstück, *das;* **a 10p ~:** ein 10-Pence-Stück; **d)** *(literary or musical composition)* Stück, *das; ~ of music* Musikstück, *das.* **2.** *v. t.* **~ to'gether** zusammenfügen **(from** aus)

**piece:** **~meal** *adv., adj.* stückweise; **~work** *n.* Akkordarbeit, *die*

**pier** [pɪə(r)] *n. (at seaside)* Pier, *der*

**pierce** [pɪəs] *v. t. (prick)* durchstechen; *(penetrate)* [ein]dringen in (+ *Akk.*) ⟨*Körper, Fleisch, Herz*⟩; **~ a hole in sth.** ein Loch in etw. *(Akk.)* stechen. **piercing** ['pɪəsɪŋ] *adj.* durchdringend ⟨*Stimme, Schrei, Blick*⟩

**piety** ['paɪətɪ] *n.* Frömmigkeit, *die*

**pig** [pɪg] *n.* **a)** Schwein, *das;* **~s might fly** *(iron.)* da müßte schon ein Wunder geschehen; **b)** *(coll.: greedy person)* Vielfraß, *der* *(ugs.)*

**pigeon** ['pɪdʒɪn] *n.* Taube, *die.* '**pigeon-hole** *n.* [Ablage]fach, *das; (for letters)* Postfach, *das*

**piggy** ['pɪgɪ]: **~back** *n.* **give sb. a ~back** jmdn. huckepack nehmen; **~ bank** *n.* Sparschwein[chen], *das*

**pig'headed** *adj.* dickschädelig *(ugs.)*

**pigment** ['pɪgmənt] *n.* Pigment, *das*

**pig:** **~sty** *n. (lit. or fig.)* Schweinestall,

*der;* **~tail** *n. (plaited)* Zopf, *der;* **~tails** *(at either side of head)* Rattenschwänzchen *Pl.* *(ugs.)*

**pike** [paɪk] *n., pl. same* Hecht, *der*

**pilchard** ['pɪltʃəd] *n.* Sardine, *die*

¹**pile** [paɪl] **1.** *n.* **a)** *(of dishes, plates)* Stapel, *der; (of paper, books, letters)* Stoß, *der; (of clothes)* Haufen, *der;* **b)** *(coll.: large quantity)* Haufen, *der* *(ugs.).* **2.** *v. t.* **a)** *(load)* [voll] beladen; **b)** *(heap up)* aufstapeln ⟨*Holz, Steine*⟩; aufhäufen ⟨*Abfall, Schnee*⟩. **pile 'in** *v. i. (seen from outside)* hineindrängen; *(seen from inside)* hereindrängen. **pile into** *v. t.* sich zwängen in (+ *Akk.*) ⟨*Auto, Zimmer, Zugabteil*⟩. **pile 'on 1.** *v. i. see* pile in. **2.** *v. t. (fig.)* **~ on the pressure** Druck machen. '**pile on to** *v. t.* drängen in (+ *Akk.*) ⟨*Bus usw.*⟩. **pile 'out** *v. i.* nach draußen drängen. **pile 'up 1.** *v. i.* **a)** ⟨*Waren, Post, Arbeit, Schnee:*⟩ sich auftürmen; ⟨*Verkehr:*⟩ sich stauen; **b)** *(crash)* aufeinander auffahren. **2.** *v. t.* aufstapeln ⟨*Steine, Bücher usw.*⟩; aufhäufen ⟨*Abfall, Schnee*⟩

²**pile** *n. (of fabric etc.)* Flor, *der*

³**pile** *n. (stake)* Pfahl, *der.* '**pile-driver** *n.* [Pfahl]ramme, *die*

**piles** [paɪlz] *n. pl. (Med.)* Hämorrhoiden *Pl.*

'**pile-up** *n.* Massenkarambolage, *die*

**pilfer** ['pɪlfə(r)] *v. t.* stehlen

**pilgrim** ['pɪlgrɪm] *n.* Pilger, *der*/Pilgerin, *die.* **pilgrimage** ['pɪlgrɪmɪdʒ] *n.* Pilgerfahrt, *die*

**pill** [pɪl] *n.* **a)** Tablette, *die;* Pille, *die* *(ugs.);* **b)** *(coll.: contraceptive)* **the ~** *or* **P~:** die Pille *(ugs.);* **be on the ~:** die Pille nehmen *(ugs.)*

**pillage** ['pɪlɪdʒ] *v. t.* [aus]plündern

**pillar** ['pɪlə(r)] *n.* Säule, *die.* '**pillar-box** *n. (Brit.)* Briefkasten, *der*

**pillion** ['pɪljən] *n.* Beifahrersitz, *der;* **ride ~:** als Beifahrer/Beifahrerin mitfahren

**pillow** ['pɪləʊ] *n.* [Kopf]kissen, *das.* '**pillowcase**, '**pillowslip** *ns.* [Kopf]kissenbezug, *der*

**pilot** ['paɪlət] **1.** *n.* **a)** *(Aeronaut.)* Pilot, *der*/Pilotin, *die;* **b)** *(Naut.)* Lotse, *der.* **2.** *adj.* Pilot⟨*programm, -studie, -projekt usw.*⟩. **3.** *v. t.* **a)** *(Aeronaut.)* fliegen; **b)** *(Naut.; fig.)* lotsen

'**pilot-light** *n.* Zündflamme, *die*

**pimp** [pɪmp] *n.* Zuhälter, *der*

**pimple** ['pɪmpl] *n.* Pickel, *der*

**pin 1.** *n.* **a)** Stecknadel, *die;* **~s and needles** *(fig.)* Kribbeln, *das;* **b)** *(peg)*

Stift, *der;* c) *(Electr.)* **a two-/three-~ plug** ein zwei-/dreipoliger Stecker. **2.** *v. t.,* **-nn-:** a) nageln ⟨*Knochen, Bein*⟩; **~ a badge to one's lapel** sich *(Dat.)* ein Abzeichen ans· Revers stecken; b) *(fig.)* **~ one's hopes on sb./sth.** seine [ganze] Hoffnung auf jmdn./etw. setzen; **~ the blame for sth. on sb.** jmdm. die Schuld an etw. *(Dat.)* zuschieben; c) **~ sb. against the wall** jmdn. an die Wand drängen. **pin 'down** *v. t.* **a)** *(fig.)* festnageln **(to** *or* **on auf +** *Akk.*); **b)** *(trap)·* festhalten. **pin 'up** *v. t.* aufhängen ⟨*Bild, Foto*⟩; anschlagen ⟨*Bekanntmachung, Liste*⟩; aufstecken ⟨*Haar*⟩; heften ⟨*Saum*⟩

**pinafore** [ˈpɪnəfɔː(r)] *n.* Schürze, *die (mit Oberteil)*

**pincers** [ˈpɪnsəz] *n. pl.* a) **|pair of|** **~:** Beißzange, *die;* b) *(of crab etc.)* Schere, *die*

**pinch** [pɪntʃ] **1.** *n.* a) *(squeezing)* Kniff, *der;* **give sb. a ~ on the arm/cheek** jmdn. *od.* jmdm. in den Arm/die Backe kneifen; b) *(fig.)* **feel the ~:** knapp bei Kasse sein *(ugs.);* **at a ~:** zur Not; c) *(small amount)* Prise, *die.* **2.** *v. t.* **a)** kneifen; **~ sb.'s cheek/bottom** jmdn. in die Wange/den Hintern *(ugs.)* kneifen; **b)** *(coll.: steal)* klauen *(salopp)*

**pincushion** *n.* Nadelkissen, *das*

¹**pine** [paɪn] *n. (tree)* Kiefer, *die*

²**pine** *v. i.* sich [vor Kummer] verzehren *(geh.).* **pine a'way** *v. i.* dahinkümmern

**pineapple** [ˈpaɪnæpl] *n.* Ananas, *die*

'**pine-tree** *n.* Kiefer, *die*

'**ping-pong** *(Amer.:* **Ping-Pong,** P) [ˈpɪŋpɒŋ] *n.* Tischtennis, *das*

**pink** [pɪŋk] **1.** *n.* Pink, *das;* Rosa, *das.* **2.** *adj.* pinkfarben; rosa

**pinkie** [ˈpɪŋkɪ] *n. (Amer., Scot.)* kleiner Finger

'**pin-money** *n.* Taschengeld, *das*

**pinnacle** [ˈpɪnəkl] *n.* Gipfel, *der; (fig.)* Höhepunkt, *der*

'**pin-point** *v. t.* genau festlegen

**pint** [paɪnt] *n.* Pint, *das;* ≈ halber Liter

'**pin-up** *(coll.) n.* Pin-up-Girl, *das; (picture) (of beautiful girl)* Pin-up[-Foto], *das; (of sports, film or pop star)* Starfoto, *das*

**pioneer** [paɪəˈnɪə(r)] **1.** *n.* Pionier, *der.* **2.** *v. t.* Pionierarbeit leisten für

**pious** [ˈpaɪəs] *adj.* fromm

**pip** [pɪp] *n. (seed)* Kern, *der*

**pipe** [paɪp] **1.** *n.* **a)** *(tube)* Rohr, *das;* b)

*(Mus.)* Pfeife, *die;* c) **|tobacco-|~:** [Tabaks]pfeife, *die.* **2.** *v. t.* [durch ein Rohr/durch Rohre] leiten. **pipe 'down** *v. i. (coll.)* ruhig sein. **pipe 'up** *v. i. (coll.)* etwas sagen

'**pipeline** *n.* Pipeline, *die;* **in the ~** *(fig.)* in Vorbereitung

**piper** [ˈpaɪpə(r)] *n.* Pfeifer, *der/*Pfeiferin, *die; (bagpiper)* Dudelsackspieler, *der/*-spielerin, *die*

**piping hot** [ˈpaɪpɪŋ hot] *adj.* kochendheiß

**piquant** [ˈpiːkənt] *adj.* pikant

**pique** [piːk] *n.* **in a |fit of| ~:** verstimmt

**piracy** [ˈpaɪrəsɪ] *n.* Seeräuberei, *die*

**pirate** [ˈpaɪrət] *n.* **a)** Pirat, *der;* Seeräuber, *der;* b) *(Radio)* **~ radio station** Piratensender, *der*

**Pisces** [ˈpaɪsiːz] *n.* Fische *Pl.*

**piss** [pɪs] *(coarse)* **1.** *n.* a) *(urine)* Pisse, *die (derb);* b) **have a/go for a ~:** pissen/pissen gehen *(derb).* **2.** *v. i.* pissen *(derb)*

**pistol** [ˈpɪstl] *n.* Pistole, *die*

**piston** [ˈpɪstən] *n.* Kolben, *der*

**pit** [pɪt] **1.** *n. (hole, mine)* Grube, *die; (natural)* Vertiefung, *die.* **2.** *v. t.,* **-tt-:** **~ one's wits/skill** *etc.* **against sth.** seinen Verstand/sein Können *usw.* an etw. *(Dat.)* messen

¹**pitch** [pɪtʃ] **1.** *n.* **a)** *(Brit.: usual place)* [Stand]platz, *der; (Sport: playing-area)* Feld, *das;* Platz, *der;* b) *(Mus.)* Tonhöhe, *die;* c) *(slope)* Neigung, *die.* **2.** *v. t.* **a)** *(erect)* aufschlagen; **~ camp** ein/das Lager aufschlagen; b) *(throw)* werfen. **3.** *v. i.* stürzen; ⟨*Schiff:*⟩ stampfen; **~ forward** vornüberstürzen

²**pitch** *n. (substance)* Pech, *das.* **pitch-'black** *adj.* pechschwarz; stockdunkel *(ugs.)* ⟨*Nacht*⟩. **pitch-'dark** *adj.* stockdunkel *(ugs.)*

**pitcher** [ˈpɪtʃə(r)] *n.* [Henkel]krug, *der*

'**pitchfork** *n.* Heugabel, *die*

'**pitfall** *n.* Fallstrick, *der*

**pith** [pɪθ] *n.* **a)** *(of orange etc.)* weiße Haut; **b)** *(fig.)* Kern, *der.* '**pithy** *adj. (fig.)* prägnant

**pitiable** [ˈpɪtɪəbl], **pitiful** [ˈpɪtɪfl] *adjs.* **a)** mitleiderregend; **b)** *(contemptible)* jämmerlich

'**pitiless** *adj.* unbarmherzig

**pittance** [ˈpɪtəns] *n.* Hungerlohn, *der*

**pity** [ˈpɪtɪ] **1.** *n.* Mitleid, *das;* **feel ~ for sb.** Mitgefühl für jmdn. empfinden; **have/take ~ on sb.** Erbarmen mit jmdm. haben; **|what a| ~!** [wie] schade! **2.** *v. t.* bemitleiden; **I ~ you** du tust mir leid

**pivot** ['pɪvət] **1.** *n.* [Dreh]zapfen, *der.* **2.** *v. i.* sich drehen

**pixie** ['pɪksɪ] *n.* Kobold, *der*

**pizza** ['piːtsə] *n.* Pizza, *die*

**placard** ['plækɑːd] *n.* Plakat, *das*

**placate** [plə'keɪt] *v. t.* beschwichtigen

**place** [pleɪs] **1.** *n.* **a)** *(spot)* Stelle, *der; (spot)* Stelle, *die;* **a [good]** ~ **to park/to stop** ein [guter] Platz zum Parken/eine [gute] Stelle zum Halten; **do you know a good/cheap** ~ **to eat?** weißt du, wo man gut/billig essen kann?; ~ **of worship** Andachtsort, *der;* **all over the** ~: überall; *(coll.: in a mess)* ganz durcheinander *(ugs.);* **b)** *(rank, position)* Stellung, *die;* **put sb. in his** ~: jmdn. in seine Schranken weisen; **c)** *(country, town)* Ort, *der;* ~ **of birth** Geburtsort, *der;* '**go** ~s *(coll.: fig.)* es [im Leben] zu was bringen *(ugs.);* **she is at his** ~: sie ist bei ihm; **e)** *(seat etc.)* [Sitz]platz, *der;* **change** ~s [with sb.] [mit jmdm.] die Plätze tauschen; *(fig.)* [mit jmdm.] tauschen; **f)** *(step, stage)* **in the first** ~: zuerst; **why didn't you say so in the first** ~? warum hast du das nicht gleich gesagt?; **g)** *(proper* ~*)* Platz, *der;* **everything fell into** ~ *(fig.)* alles wurde klar; **out of** ~: nicht am richtigen Platz; *(several things)* in Unordnung; **h)** *(position in competition)* Platz, *der.* **2.** *v. t.* **a)** *(vertically)* stellen; *(horizontally)* legen; **b)** *in p.p. (situated)* gelegen; **c)** *(find situation or home for)* unterbringen (with bei); **d)** *(class)* einordnen, einstufen; **be** ~**d second in the race** im Rennen den zweiten Platz belegen

**placid** ['plæsɪd] *adj.* ruhig

**plagiarism** ['pleɪdʒərɪzm] *n.* Plagiat, *das.* **plagiarize** ['pleɪdʒəraɪz] *v. t.* plagiieren

**plague** [pleɪg] **1.** *n.* **a)** *(esp. Hist.: epidemic)* Seuche, *die;* **the** ~ *(bubonic)* die Pest; **b)** *(infestation)* ~ **of rats** Rattenplage, *die.* **2.** *v. t.* plagen; ~**d with** *or* **by sth.** von etw. geplagt

**plaice** [pleɪs] *n., pl. same* Scholle, *die*

**plain** [pleɪn] **1.** *adj.* **a)** *(clear)* klar; *(obvious)* offensichtlich; **b)** *(frank)* offen; schlicht ⟨*Wahrheit*⟩; **be** ~ **sailing** *(fig.)* [ganz] einfach sein; **c)** *(unsophisticated)* einfach; schlicht ⟨*Kleidung*⟩; unliniert ⟨*Papier*⟩ ⟨*Stoff*⟩ ohne Muster; **d)** wenig attraktiv ⟨*Mädchen*⟩. **2.** *adv.* **a)** *(clearly)* deutlich; **b)** *(simply)* einfach. **plain** ~ **Ebene**, *die.* **plain** '**chocolate** *n.* halbbittere Schokolade. **plain** '**clothes** *n. pl.* **in** ~: in Zivil

**plainly** *adv.* **a)** *(clearly)* deutlich; **b)** *(obviously)* offensichtlich; *(undoubtedly)* eindeutig; **c)** *(frankly)* offen; **d)** *(simply)* schlicht

**plaintiff** ['pleɪntɪf] *n.* Kläger, *der*/Klägerin, *die*

**plaintive** ['pleɪntɪv] *adj.* klagend

**plait** [plæt] **1.** *n.* Zopf, *der.* **2.** *v. t.* flechten

**plan** [plæn] **1.** *n.* Plan, *der;* **[go] according to** ~: nach Plan [gehen]; planmäßig [verlaufen]. **2.** *v. t.,* -nn- planen; *(design)* entwerfen. **3.** *v. i.,* -nn- planen

**¹plane** [pleɪn] *n.* ~[-**tree**] Platane, *die*

**²plane** **1.** *n. (tool)* Hobel, *der.* **2.** *v. t.* hobeln

**³plane** *n.* **a)** *(Geom.: fig.)* Ebene, *die;* **b)** *(aircraft)* Flugzeug, *das;* Maschine, *die (ugs.)*

**planet** ['plænɪt] *n.* Planet, *der*

**plank** [plæŋk] *n.* Brett, *das; (thicker)* Bohle, *die; (on ship)* Planke, *die*

**plankton** ['plæŋktən] *n.* Plankton, *das*

**planner** *n.* Planer, *der*/Planerin, *die*

**planning** *n.* Planen, *das;* Planung, *die*

**plant** [plɑːnt] **1.** *n.* **a)** *(Bot.)* Pflanze, *die;* **b)** *no indef. art. (machinery)* Maschinen; **c)** *(factory)* Fabrik, *die;* Werk, *das.* **2.** *v. t.* **a)** pflanzen; **b)** *(sl.: conceal)* anbringen ⟨*Wanze*⟩; legen ⟨*Bombe*⟩; ~ **sth. on sb.** jmdm. etw. unterschieben. **plantation** [plɑːn'teɪʃn] *n.* Plantage, *die*

**plaque** [plɑːk, plæk] *n.* **a)** Platte, *die; (commemorating sb.)* [Gedenk]tafel, *die;* **b)** *(Dent.)* Plaque, *der*

**plaster** ['plɑːstə(r)] **1.** *n.* **a)** *(for walls etc.)* [Ver]putz, *der;* **b)** ~ **[of Paris]** Gips, *der;* **c)** *see* sticking-plaster. **2.** *v. t.* **a)** verputzen ⟨*Wand*⟩; **b)** *(daub)* ~ **sth. on sth.** etw. dick auf etw. *(Akk.)* auftragen. **plastered** ['plɑːstəd] *adj. (sl.: drunk)* voll *(salopp).* '**plasterer** *n.* Gipser, *der*

**plastic** ['plæstɪk] **1.** *n.* Plastik, *das;* Kunststoff, *der.* **2.** *adj.* aus Plastik *od.* Kunststoff *nachgestellt;* ~ **bag** Plastiktüte, *die;* ~ **surgery** plastische Chirurgie

**Plasticine, (P)** ['plæstɪsiːn] *n.* Plastilin, *das*

**plate** [pleɪt] **1.** *n.* **a)** Teller, *der; (serving* ~*)* Platte, *die;* **b)** *(metal* ~ *with name etc.)* Schild, *das;* **c)** *(for printing)* Platte, *die; (illustration)* [Bild]tafel, *die.* **2.** *v. t.* ~ **sth.** [**with gold/silver**] etw. vergolden/versilbern

**plateau** ['plætəʊ] *n., pl.* ~**x** ['plætəʊz] *or* ~**s** Hochebene, *die;* Plateau, *das*

**plate 'glass** n. Flachglas, das
**platform** ['plætfɔ:m] n. **a)** (Brit. Railw.) Bahnsteig, der; ~ 4 Gleis 4; **b)** (stage) Podium, das
**platinum** ['plætɪnəm] n. Platin, das
**platitude** ['plætɪtju:d] n. Platitüde, die (geh.); Gemeinplatz, der
**platoon** [plə'tu:n] n. (Mil.) Zug, der
**plausible** ['plɔ:zɪbl] adj. plausibel; einleuchtend
**play** [pleɪ] **1.** n. **a)** (Theatre) [Theater]stück, das; television ~: Fernsehspiel, das; **b)** (recreation) Spielen, das; Spiel, das; ~ **on words** Wortspiel, das; **c)** (Sport) Spiel, das; **d) come into ~, be brought** or **called into ~:** ins Spiel kommen. **2.** v.i. **a)** spielen; ~ **safe** sichergehen; ~ **for time** Zeit gewinnen wollen; **b)** (Mus.) spielen (**on** auf + Dat.). **3.** v.t. (also Sport, Theatre, Cards, Mus.) spielen; abspielen ⟨Schallplatte, Tonband⟩; schlagen ⟨Ball⟩; spielen gegen ⟨Mannschaft, Gegner⟩; ~ **the violin** etc. Geige usw. spielen; ~ **a trick/joke on sb.** jmdn. hereinlegen (ugs.)/jmdm. einen Streich spielen; ~ **one's cards right** (fig.) es richtig anfassen (fig.). **play a'bout, play a'round** v.i. spielen; **stop ~ing about** or **around** hör doch auf mit dem Unsinn! **play a'long** v.i. mitspielen. **play 'back** v.t. abspielen ⟨Tonband⟩. **play 'down** v.t. herunterspielen. **play 'up 1.** v.i. (coll.)⟨Kinder:⟩ nichts als Ärger machen. **2.** v.t. (coll.: annoy) ärgern
**'playboy** n. Playboy, der
**'player** n. Spieler, der/Spielerin, die
**playful** ['pleɪfl] adj. spielerisch; (frolicsome) verspielt
**play: ~-ground** n. Spielplatz, der; (Sch.) Schulhof, der; ~ **group** n. Spielgruppe, die
**playing: ~-card** n. Spielkarte, die; **~-field** n. Sportplatz, der
**play: ~mate** n. Spielkamerad, der/Spielkameradin, die; **~-off** n. Entscheidungsspiel, das; **~-pen** Laufgitter, der; **~thing** n. Spielzeug, das; **~wright** ['pleɪraɪt] n. Dramatiker, der/Dramatikerin, die
**PLC, plc** abbr. (Brit.) public limited company ≈ GmbH
**plea** [pli:] n. Appell, der (for zu)
**plead** [pli:d] **1.** v.i. **a)** inständig bitten (for um); (imploringly) flehen (for um); ~ **with sb. for sth.** jmdn. inständig um etw. bitten; **b)** (Law; also fig.) plädieren. **2.** v.t. **a)** inständig bitten;

(imploringly) flehen; **b)** (Law) ~ **guilty/not guilty** sich schuldig/nicht schuldig bekennen. **'pleading** adj. flehend
**pleasant** ['plezənt] adj. angenehm
**please** [pli:z] **1.** v.t. gefallen (+ Dat.); ~ **oneself** tun, was man will; ~ **yourself** ganz wie du willst. **2.** v.i. **I come and go as I ~:** ich komme und gehe, wie es mir gefällt; **if you ~:** bitte schön. **3.** int. bitte; ~ **do!** aber bitte od. gern! **pleased** [pli:zd] adj. (satisfied) zufrieden (**by** mit); (happy) erfreut (**by** über + Akk.); **be ~ at** or **about sth.** sich über etw. (Akk.) freuen. **pleasing** ['pli:zɪŋ] adj. gefällig
**pleasure** ['pleʒə(r)] n. (joy) Freude, die; (enjoyment) Vergnügen, das; **have the ~ of doing sth.** das Vergnügen haben, etw. zu tun; **with ~:** mit Vergnügen
**pleat** [pli:t] n. Falte, die. **'pleated** adj. gefältelt; Falten⟨rock⟩
**pledge** [pledʒ] **1.** n. Versprechen, das. **2.** v.t. versprechen; geloben ⟨Treue⟩
**plentiful** ['plentɪfl] adj. reichlich; **be ~:** reichlich vorhanden sein
**plenty** ['plentɪ] n. ~ **of** viel; **eine Menge;** (coll.: enough) genug
**pleurisy** ['plʊərɪsɪ] n. Pleuritis, die; Brustfellentzündung, die
**pliable** ['plaɪəbl] adj. biegsam
**plied** see **ply**
**pliers** ['plaɪəz] n. pl. **[pair of] ~:** Zange, die
**plight** [plaɪt] n. Notlage, die
**plimsoll** ['plɪmsl] n. (Brit.) Turnschuh, der
**plinth** [plɪnθ] n. Sockel, der
**plod** [plɒd] v.i., -dd- trotten. **plod 'on** v.i. (fig.) sich weiterkämpfen
**plonk** [plɒŋk] n. (sl.) [billiger] Wein
**plot** [plɒt] **1.** n. **a)** (conspiracy) Verschwörung, die; **b)** (of play, novel) Handlung, die; **c)** (of ground) Stück Land. **2.** v.t., -tt-: **a)** [heimlich] planen; **b)** (mark on map) einzeichnen. **3.** v.i., -tt-: ~ **against sb.** sich gegen jmdn. verschwören. **'plotter** n. Verschwörer, der/Verschwörerin, die
**plough** [plaʊ] **1.** n. Pflug, der. **2.** v.t. pflügen. **plough 'back** v.t. (Finance) reinvestieren
**plow** (Amer./arch.) see **plough**
**ploy** [plɔɪ] n. Trick, der
**pluck** [plʌk] **1.** v.t. **a)** pflücken ⟨Obst⟩; ~ **[out]** auszupfen ⟨Federn, Haare⟩; **b)** (pull at) zupfen an (+ Dat.); **c)** (strip of feathers) rupfen. **2.** v.i. ~ **at sth.** an

etw. *(Dat.)* zupfen. 3. *n.* Mut, *der.*
**pluck 'up** *v. t.* ~ **up |one's| courage** all
seinen Mut zusammennehmen
**pluckily** ['plʌkɪlɪ] *adv.,* '**plucky** *adj.*
tapfer
**plug** [plʌg] 1. *n.* a) *(filling hole)* Pfropfen, *der; (in cask)* Spund, *der; (for
basin etc.)* Stöpsel, *der;* b) *(Electr.)*
Stecker, *der.* 2. *v. t.,* -gg-: a) ~ |up| zu-
stopfen ⟨*Loch usw.*⟩; b) *(coll.: advertise)* Schleichwerbung machen für.
**plug 'in** *v. t.* anschließen
'**plug-hole** *n.* Abfluß, *der*
**plum** [plʌm] *n.* a) Pflaume, *die;* b)
*(fig.)* Leckerbissen, *der;* **a ~ job** ein
Traumjob *(ugs.)*
**plumage** ['plu:mɪdʒ] *n.* Gefieder, *das*
¹**plumb** [plʌm] 1. *v. t.* [aus]loten. 2.
*adv.* a) lotrecht; b) *(fig.)* genau
²**plumb** *v. t.* ~ **in** fest anschließen.
**plumber** ['plʌmə(r)] *n.* Klempner,
*der.* **plumbing** ['plʌmɪŋ] *n.* a)
Klempnerarbeiten *Pl.;* b) *(waterpipes)*
Wasserleitungen *Pl*
'**plumb-line** *n.* Lot, *das*
**plume** [plu:m] *n.* Feder, *die; (ornamental bunch)* Federbusch, *der*
**plummet** ['plʌmɪt] *v. i.* stürzen
**plump** [plʌmp] *adj.* mollig; rundlich.
'**plump for** *v. t.* sich entscheiden für
**plunder** ['plʌndə(r)] 1. *v. t.* [aus]plün-
dern ⟨*Gebäude, Gebiet*⟩. 2. *n.* Plünde-
rung, *die; (booty)* Beute, *die*
**plunge** [plʌndʒ] 1. *v. t.* stecken; *(into
liquid)* tauchen. 2. *v. i.* a) ~ **into sth.** in
etw. *(Akk.)* stürzen; b) ⟨*Straße usw.*⟩
steil abfallen. 3. *n.* Sprung, *der;* **take
the ~** *(fig. coll.)* den Sprung wagen
**plural** ['plʊərl] 1. *adj.* pluralisch; Plu-
ral-; ~ **noun** Substantiv im Plural. 2.
*n.* Mehrzahl, *die;* Plural, *der*
**plus** [plʌs] 1. *prep.* plus (+ *Dat.*). 2. *n.*
*(advantage)* Pluspunkt, *der*
**plush** [plʌʃ] 1. *n.* Plüsch, *der.* 2. *adj.*
*(coll.)* feudal *(ugs.)*
**Pluto** ['plu:təʊ] *pr. n. (Astron.)* Pluto,
*der*
**ply** [plaɪ] 1. *v. t.* a) *(use)* gebrauchen; b)
nachgehen (+ *Dat.*) ⟨*Handwerk, Ar-
beit*⟩; c) *(supply)* ~ **sb. with sth.** jmdn.
mit etw. versorgen; d) *(assail)* überhäufen. 2. *v. i.* ~ **between** zwischen
⟨*Orten*⟩ [hin- und her]pendeln
'**plywood** *n.* Sperrholz, *das*
**p.m.** [pi:'em] *adv.* nachmittags; **one ~:**
ein Uhr mittags
**pneumatic** [nju:'mætɪk] *adj.* pneuma-
tisch. **pneumatic 'drill** *n.* Preßluft-
bohrer, *der*

**pneumonia** [nju:'məʊnɪə] *n.* Lungen-
entzündung, *die*
**PO** *abbr.* a) postal order PA; b) Post
Office PA
¹**poach** [pəʊtʃ] *v. t.* a) *(catch illegally)*
wildern; illegal fangen ⟨*Fische*⟩; b)
stehlen, *(ugs.)* klauen ⟨*Idee*⟩
²**poach** *v. t. (Cookery)* pochieren ⟨*Ei*⟩;
dünsten ⟨*Fisch, Fleisch, Gemüse*⟩
'**poacher** *n.* Wilderer, *der*
**pocket** ['pɒkɪt] 1. *n.* a) Tasche, *die;*
*(fig.)* **be in ~:** Geld verdient haben; **be
out of ~:** draufgelegt haben. 2. *adj.*
Taschen⟨*rechner, -uhr, -ausgabe*⟩. 3.
*v. t.* a) einstecken; b) *(steal)* in die eigene Tasche stecken *(ugs.).* '**pocket-
book** *n. (wallet)* Brieftasche, *die;*
*(notebook)* Notizbuch, *das.* '**pocket-
money** *n.* Taschengeld, *das*
'**pock-marked** *adj.* a) pockennarbig
⟨*Gesicht, Haut*⟩; b) **a wall ~ with bullets** eine mit Einschüssen übersäte
Wand
**pod** [pɒd] *n.* Hülse, *die; (of pea)* Schote, *die*
**podgy** ['pɒdʒɪ] *adj.* dicklich
**poem** ['pəʊɪm] *n.* Gedicht, *das*
**poet** ['pəʊɪt] *n.* Dichter, *der.* **poetic**
[pəʊ'etɪk] *adj.* dichterisch
**poetry** ['pəʊɪtrɪ] *n.* [Vers]dichtung,
*die;* Lyrik, *die*
**poignant** ['pɔɪnjənt] *adj.* tief ⟨*Bedauern, Trauer*⟩; ergreifend ⟨*Anblick*⟩
**point** [pɔɪnt] 1. *n.* a) *(tiny mark, dot)*
Punkt, *der;* b) *(of tool, pencil, etc.)*
Spitze, *die;* c) *(single item; unit of scor-
ing)* Punkt, *der;* d) *(stage, degree)* **up
to a ~:** bis zu einem gewissen Grad;
**he gave up at this ~:** an diesem Punkt
gab er auf; e) *(moment)* Zeitpunkt,
*der;* **be on the ~ of doing sth.** etw. gerade tun wollen; f) *(distinctive trait)* Seite, *die;* **best/strong ~:** starke Seite;
Stärke, *die;* g) *(thing to be discussed)*
**come to** or **get to the ~:** zum Thema
kommen; **be beside the ~:** keine Rolle
spielen; **make a ~ of doing sth.** [gro-
ßen] Wert darauf legen, etw. zu tun;
h) *(of story, joke, remark)* Pointe, *die;*
i) *(purpose)* Zweck, *der;* Sinn, *der;* j)
*(precise place, spot)* Punkt, *der;* Stelle,
*die;* ~ **of view** *(fig.)* Standpunkt, *der;*
k) *(Brit.)* |**power or electric**| ~: Steck-
dose, *die;* l) *usu in pl. (Brit. Railw.)*
Weiche, *die.* 2. *v. i.* a) zeigen, weisen
(**to, at** auf + *Akk.*); b) ~ **towards** or **to**
*(fig.)* [hin]deuten auf (+ *Akk.*). 3. *v. t.*
richten ⟨*Waffe, Kamera*⟩ (**at** auf +
*Akk.*); ~ **one's finger at sth./sb.** mit

dem Finger auf etw./jmdn. zeigen.
**point 'out** *v.t.* hinweisen auf
(+ *Akk.*); ~ **sth./sb. out to sb.** jmdn.
auf etw./jmdn. hinweisen
**point-'blank 1.** *adj. (lit. or fig.)* direkt;
glatt ⟨*Weigerung*⟩; ~ **range** kürzeste
Entfernung. **2.** *adv. (at very close
range)* aus kürzester Entfernung
'**pointed** *adj.* **a)** spitz; **b)** *(fig.)* unmißverständlich
'**pointer** *n.* **a)** Zeiger, *der;* (*rod)* Zeige-
stock, *der;* **b)** *(coll.: indication)* Hinweis, *der* (**to** auf + *Akk.*)
'**pointless** *adj.* sinnlos; belanglos
⟨*Bemerkung, Geschichte*⟩
**poise** [pɔɪz] *n. (composure)* Haltung,
*die; (self-confidence)* Selbstvertrauen,
*das.* **poised** [pɔɪzd] *adj.* selbstsicher
**poison** ['pɔɪzn] **1.** *n.* Gift, *das.* **2.** *v.t.*
vergiften. '**poisoning** *n.* Vergiftung,
*die.* **poisonous** ['pɔɪzənəs] *adj.* giftig
**poke 1.** *v.t.* **a)** ~ **sth. |with sth.|** [mit
etw.] gegen etw. stoßen; ~ **sth. into
sth.** etw. in etw. *(Akk.)* stoßen; ~ **the
fire** das Feuer schüren; **b)** stecken
⟨*Kopf*⟩. **2.** *v.i.* **a)** [herum]stochern **(at,
in, among** in + *Dat.*); **b)** *(pry)* schnüffeln *(ugs.).* **3.** *n.* **a)** *(thrust)* Stoß, *der;*
**give sb. a** ~ **|in the ribs|** jmdm. einen
[Rippen]stoß versetzen; **give the fire a**
~: das Feuer [an]schüren. **poke
a'bout, poke a'round** *v.i.* herumschnüffeln *(ugs.)*
¹'**poker** *n.* Schüreisen, *das*
²'**poker** *n. (Cards)* Poker, *das od. der*
'**poker-faced** *adj.* mit unbewegter
Miene *nachgestellt*
**poky** ['pəʊkɪ] *adj.* winzig
**Poland** ['pəʊlənd] *pr. n.* Polen *(das)*
**polar** ['pəʊlə(r)] *adj.* polar ⟨*Kaltluft,
Gewässer*⟩; Polar⟨*eis, -gebiet, -fuchs*⟩.
**polar 'bear** *n.* Eisbär, *der*
**Pole** [pəʊl] *n.* Pole, *der*/Polin, *die*
¹'**pole** *n. (support)* Stange, *die;* **drive sb.
up the** ~ *(Brit. sl.)* jmdn. zum Wahnsinn treiben *(ugs.)*
²'**pole** *n. (Astron., Geog., Magn.,
Electr., fig.)* Pol, *der.* '**pole-star** *n.*
Polarstern, *der*
'**pole-vault** *n.* Stabhochsprung, *der*
**police** [pə'li:s] **1.** *n. pl.* Polizei, *die;
(members)* Polizisten *Pl.; attrib.* Poli-
zei-. **2.** *v.t.* [polizeilich] überwachen
⟨*Fußballspiel*⟩; kontrollieren ⟨*Gebiet*⟩
**police:** ~ **force** *n.* **the** ~ **force** die Polizei; ~**man** [pə'li:smən] *n., pl.* -**men**
[pə'li:smən] Polizist, *der;* ~ **station**
*n.* Polizeirevier, *das;* ~**woman** *n.*
Polizistin, *die*

¹'**policy** ['pɒlɪsɪ] *n.* Politik, *die*
²'**policy** *n. (Insurance)* Police, *die*
**polio** ['pəʊlɪəʊ] *n., no art.* Polio, *die;*
[spinale] Kinderlähmung
**Polish** ['pəʊlɪʃ] **1.** *adj.* polnisch; **sb. is**
~: jmd. ist Pole/Polin. **2.** *n.* Polnisch,
*das; see also* **English 2a**
**polish** ['pɒlɪʃ] **1.** *v.t.* **a)** polieren; bohnern ⟨*Fußboden*⟩; putzen ⟨*Schuhe*⟩; **b)**
*(fig.)* ausfeilen ⟨*Text, Theorie, Stil*⟩. **2.**
*n.* **a)** *(smoothness)* Glanz, *der;* **b)** *(substance)* Politur, *die;* **c)** *(fig.)* Schliff,
*der.* **polish 'off** *v.t. (coll.)* **a)** *(consume)* verdrücken *(ugs.);* **b)** *(complete
quickly)* durchziehen *(ugs.).* **polish
'up** *v.t.* **a)** polieren; **b)** ausfeilen
⟨*Stil*⟩; aufpolieren ⟨*Kenntnisse*⟩
**polite** [pə'laɪt] *adj.,* ~**r** [pə'laɪtə(r)], ~**st**
[pə'laɪtɪst] höflich. **po'liteness** *n.*
Höflichkeit, *die*
**political** [pə'lɪtɪkl] *adj.* politisch
**politician** [pɒlɪ'tɪʃn] *n.* Politiker,
*der*/Politikerin, *die*
**politics** ['pɒlɪtɪks] *n.* Politik, *die; (of
individual)* politische Einstellung
**polka** ['pɒlkə, 'pəʊlkə] *n.* Polka, *die.*
'**polka dot** *n.* [großer] Tupfen
**poll** [pəʊl] **1.** *n.* **a)** *(voting)* Abstimmung, *die; (to elect sb.)* Wahl, *die;* **go
to the** ~**s** zur Wahl gehen; **b)** *(opinion
~)* Umfrage, *die.* **2.** *v.t.* **a)** *(take vote[s]
of)* abstimmen/wählen lassen; **b)**
*(take opinion of)* befragen
**pollen** ['pɒlən] *n.* Pollen, *der;* Blüten-
staub, *der.* '**pollen count** *n.* Pollen-
menge, *die*
'**polling-booth** *n.* Wahlkabine, *die*
'**poll-tax** *n.* Kopfsteuer, *die*
**pollutant** [pə'lu:tənt] *n.* [Um-
welt]schadstoff, *der*
**pollute** [pə'lu:t] *v.t.* verschmutzen
⟨*Luft, Boden, Wasser*⟩. **pollution** [pə-
'lu:ʃn] *n.* [Umwelt]verschmutzung, *die*
**polo** ['pəʊləʊ] *n.* Polo, *das.* '**polo-
neck** *n.* Rollkragen, *der*
**polyester** [pɒlɪ'estə(r)] *n.* Polyester,
*der*
**polystyrene** [pɒlɪ'staɪri:n] *n.* Polystyr-
rol, *das;* ~ **foam** Styropor ⓌⓏ, *das*
**polytechnic** [pɒlɪ'teknɪk] *n. (Brit.)* ≈
technische Hochschule
**polythene** ['pɒlɪθi:n] *n.* Polyäthylen,
*das;* ~ **bag** Plastikbeutel, *der*
**pomegranate** ['pɒmɪgrænɪt] *n.* Gra-
natapfel, *der*
'**pommel-horse** *n.* Seitpferd, *das*
**pomp** [pɒmp] *n.* Pomp, *der*
**pom-pom** ['pɒmpɒm] *n.* Pompon,
*der;* ~ **hat** Pudelmütze, *die*

**pompous** ['pɒmpəs] *adj.* großspurig; gespreizt ⟨*Sprache*⟩

**pond** [pɒnd] *n.* Teich, *der*

**ponder** ['pɒndə(r)] **1.** *v. t.* nachdenken über (+ *Akk.*) ⟨*Frage, Ereignis*⟩; abwägen ⟨*Vorteile, Worte*⟩. **2.** *v. i.* nachdenken (**over, on** über + *Akk.*)

**ponderous** ['pɒndərəs] *adj.* schwer

**pong** [pɒŋ] *(Brit. coll.)* **1.** *n.* Mief, *der (ugs.).* **2.** *v. i.* miefen *(ugs.)*

**pony** ['pəʊnɪ] *n.* Pony, *das.* '**ponytail** *n.* Pferdeschwanz, *der.* **ponytrekking** ['pəʊnɪtrekɪŋ] *n. (Brit.)* Ponyreiten, *das*

**poodle** ['puːdl] *n.* Pudel, *der*

**¹pool** [puːl] *n.* **a)** Tümpel, *der;* **b)** *(temporary)* Lache, *die;* ~ **of blood** Blutlache, *die;* **c)** *(swimming-~)* Schwimmbecken, *das; (public)* Schwimmbad, *das; (in house or garden)* Pool, *der*

**²pool 1.** *n.* **a)** *(Gambling)* [gemeinsame Spiel]kasse; **the ~s** *(Brit.)* das Toto; **b)** *(common supply)* Topf, *der;* **a ~ of experience** ein Erfahrungsschatz; **c)** *(game)* Pool[billard], *das.* **2.** *v. t.* zusammenlegen ⟨*Geld, Ersparnisse*⟩; bündeln ⟨*Anstrengungen*⟩

**poor** [pʊə(r)] **1.** *adj.* **a)** arm; **b)** *(inadequate)* schlecht; schwach ⟨*Spiel, Gesundheit, Leistung, Rede*⟩; dürftig ⟨*Kleidung, Essen, Unterkunft*⟩; **of ~ quality** minderer Qualität; **c)** *(paltry)* schwach ⟨*Trost*⟩; schlecht ⟨*Aussichten*⟩; **d)** *(unfortunate)* arm *(auch iron.);* **e)** karg ⟨*Boden*⟩; **f)** *(deficient)* arm (**in an** + *Dat.*); ~ **in vitamins** vitaminarm. **2.** *n. pl.* **the ~:** die Armen. **poorly** ['pʊəlɪ] *adv., pred. adj.* schlecht

**¹pop** [pɒp] **1.** *v. i.,* **-pp-: a)** *(make sound)* knallen; **b)** *(coll.: go quickly)* **let's ~ round to Fred's** komm, wir gehen kurz bei Fred vorbei *(ugs.).* **2.** *v. t.,* **-pp-: a)** *(coll.: put)* ~ **the meat in the fridge** das Fleisch in den Kühlschrank tun; **b)** platzen ⟨*Luftballon*⟩. **3.** *n.* **a)** Knall, *der;* Knallen, *das;* **b)** *(coll.: drink)* Brause, *die (ugs.).* **4.** *adv.* **go ~:** knallen. **pop 'out** *v. i.* hervorschießen; ~ **out to the shops** schnell einkaufen gehen

**²pop** *(coll.)* **1.** *n.* Popmusik, *die;* Pop, *der.* **2.** *adj.* Pop⟨*star, -musik usw.*⟩

'**popcorn** *n.* Popcorn, *das*

**pope** [pəʊp] *n.* Papst, *der*/Päpstin, *die*

**poplar** ['pɒplə(r)] *n.* Pappel, *die*

**popper** ['pɒpə(r)] *n. (Brit. coll.)* Druckknopf, *der*

**poppy** ['pɒpɪ] *n.* Mohn, *der*

**popular** ['pɒpjʊlə(r)] *adj.* **a)** *(well liked)* beliebt; populär ⟨*Entscheidung, Maßnahme*⟩; **b)** verbreitet ⟨*Aberglaube, Irrtum, Meinung*⟩; allgemein ⟨*Wahl, Unterstützung*⟩. **popularity** [pɒpjʊ'lærɪtɪ] *n.* Beliebtheit, *die; (of decision, measure)* Popularität, *die.* **popularize** ['pɒpjʊləraɪz] *v. t.* **a)** *(make popular)* populär machen; **b)** *(make understandable)* breiteren Kreisen zugänglich machen. '**popularly** *adv.* allgemein

**populate** ['pɒpjʊleɪt] *v. t.* bevölkern; bewohnen ⟨*Insel*⟩. **population** [pɒpjʊ'leɪʃn] *n.* Bevölkerung, *die;* **Britain has a ~ of 56 million** Großbritannien hat 56 Millionen Einwohner

**porcelain** ['pɔːslɪn] *n.* Porzellan, *das*

**porch** [pɔːtʃ] *n.* Vordach, *das; (with side walls)* Vorbau, *der; (enclosed)* Windfang, *der*

**porcupine** ['pɔːkjʊpaɪn] *n.* Stachelschwein, *das*

**¹pore** [pɔː(r)] *n.* Pore, *die*

**²pore** *v. i.* ~ **over sth.** etw. [genau] studieren

**pork** [pɔːk] *n.* Schweinefleisch, *das; attrib.* Schweine-. **pork 'chop** *n.* Schweinekotelett, *das.* **pork 'pie** *n.* Schweinepastete, *die*

**porn** [pɔːn] *n. (coll.)* Pornographie, *die;* Pornos *(ugs.)*

**pornographic** [pɔːnə'græfɪk] *adj.* pornographisch; Porno- *(ugs.)*

**pornography** [pɔː'nɒgrəfɪ] *n.* Pornographie, *die*

**porous** ['pɔːrəs] *adj.* porös

**porridge** ['pɒrɪdʒ] *n.* [Hafer]brei, *der*

**¹port** [pɔːt] **1.** *n.* **a)** Hafen, *der;* **b)** *(Naut., Aeronaut.: left side)* Backbord, *das.* **2.** *adj. (Naut., Aeronaut.: left)* Backbord-; backbordseitig

**²port** *n. (wine)* Portwein, *der*

**portable** ['pɔːtəbl] *adj.* tragbar

**¹porter** ['pɔːtə(r)] *n. (Brit.: doorman)* Pförtner, *der; (of hotel)* Portier, *der*

**²porter** *n.* [Gepäck]träger, *der*/-trägerin, *die; (in hotel)* Hausdiener, *der*

**portfolio** [pɔːt'fəʊlɪəʊ] *n. pl.* ~**s a)** *(Polit.)* Geschäftsbereich, *der;* **b)** *(case, contents)* Mappe, *die*

**porthole** ['pɔːthəʊl] *n. (Naut.)* Seitenfenster, *das; (round)* Bullauge, *das*

**portion** ['pɔːʃn] *n.* **a)** *(part)* Teil, *der; (of ticket)* Abschnitt, *der;* **b)** *(of food)* Portion, *die*

**portly** ['pɔːtlɪ] *adj.* beleibt

**portrait** ['pɔːtrɪt] *n.* Porträt, *das*

**portray** [pɔː'treɪ] *v. t.* darstellen; *(make likeness of)* porträtieren

**Portugal** ['pɔ:tjʊgl] *pr. n.* Portugal *(das).* **Portuguese** [pɔ:tjʊ'gi:z] **1.** *adj.* portugiesisch; **sb. is ~ :** jmd. ist Portugiese/Portugiesin. **2.** *n.*, *pl. same* **a)** *(person)* Portugiese, *der/*Portugiesin, *die;* **b)** *(language)* Portugiesisch, *das; see also* **English 2 a**

**pose** [pəʊz] **1.** *v. t.* aufwerfen ⟨*Frage, Problem*⟩; darstellen ⟨*Bedrohung*⟩; mit sich bringen ⟨*Schwierigkeiten*⟩. **2.** *v. i.* **a)** *(assume attitude)* posieren; *(fig.)* sich geziert benehmen; **b)** **~ as** sich geben als. **3.** *n.* Pose, *die;* **strike a ~ :** eine Pose einnehmen. **poser** ['pəʊzə(r)] *n.* (*question)* knifflige Frage

**posh** [pɒʃ] *adj.* *(coll.)* vornehm; nobel *(spött.);* stinkvornehm *(salopp)*

**position** [pə'zɪʃn] **1.** *n.* **a)** *(place occupied)* Platz, *der;* *(of player in team, of plane, ship, etc.)* Position, *die;* *(of hands of clock, words, stars)* Stellung, *die;* *(of building)* Lage, *die;* **be in/out of ~ :** an seinem Platz/nicht an seinem Platz sein; **b)** *(Mil.)* Stellung, *die;* **c)** *(fig.: mental attitude)* Standpunkt, *der;* **d)** *(fig.: situation)* **be in a good ~ [financially]** [finanziell] gut gestellt sein; **be in a ~ of** strength eine starke Position haben; **e)** *(rank)* Stellung, *die;* **f)** *(job)* Stelle, *die;* **g)** *(posture)* Haltung, *die.* **2.** *v. t.* plazieren; postieren ⟨*Polizisten, Wachen*⟩; **~ oneself** sich stellen/*(sit)* setzen

**positive** ['pɒzɪtɪv] *adj.* **a)** *(also Math.)* positiv; konstruktiv ⟨*Vorschlag*⟩; *(definite)* eindeutig; *(convinced)* sicher; **I'm ~ of it** ich bin [mir] [dessen] ganz sicher; **b)** *(Electr.)* positiv ⟨*Elektrode, Ladung*⟩; Plus⟨*platte, -leiter*⟩; **c)** *as intensifier (coll.)* echt

**possess** [pə'zes] *v. t.* besitzen; *(as faculty or quality)* haben; ⟨*Furcht usw.:*⟩ ergreifen; **what ~ed you?** *(coll.)* was ist in dich gefahren? **possessed** [pə'zest] *adj.* besessen. **possession** [pə'zeʃn] *n.* **a)** *(thing possessed)* Besitz, *der;* **some of my ~s** einige meiner Sachen; **b)** *in pl. (property)* Besitz, *der;* **c)** *(possessing)* Besitz, *der;* **be in ~ of sth.** im Besitz einer Sache *(Gen.)* sein; **take ~ of** in Besitz nehmen; beziehen ⟨*Haus, Wohnung*⟩. **possessive** [pə'zesɪv] *adj.* **a)** besitzergreifend; **be ~ about sth./sb.** etw. eifersüchtig hüten/ an jmdn. Besitzansprüche stellen; **b)** *(Ling.)* possessiv. **possessor** [pə'zesə(r)] *n.* Besitzer, *der/*Besitzerin, *die* **possibility** [pɒsɪ'bɪlɪtɪ] *n.* Möglichkeit, *die*

**possible** ['pɒsɪbl] *adj.* möglich; *(likely)* [gut] möglich; **if ~ :** wenn möglich; **as ... as ~ :** so ... wie möglich; möglichst ... **possibly** ['pɒsɪblɪ] *adv.* **a)** **as often as I ~ can** so oft ich irgend kann; **I cannot ~ commit myself** ich kann mich unmöglich festlegen; **b)** *(perhaps)* möglicherweise

¹**post** [pəʊst] *n.* **a)** *(as support)* Pfosten, *der;* **b)** *(stake)* Pfahl, *der;* **c)** *(starting/ finishing ~)* Start-/Zielpfosten, *der*

²**post 1.** *n.* **a)** *(Brit.: one dispatch/delivery of letters)* Postausgang, *der/* Post[zustellung], *die;* **by return of ~ :** postwendend; **b)** *no indef. art. (Brit.: official conveying)* Post, *die;* **by ~ :** mit der Post; per Post; **c)** *(~ office)* Post, *die.* **2.** *v. t.* **a)** abschicken; **b)** *(fig. coll.)* **keep sb. ~ed** jmdn. auf dem laufenden halten

³**post 1.** *n.* **a)** *(job)* Stelle, *die;* Posten, *der;* **b)** *(Mil.; also fig.)* Posten, *der.* **2.** *v. t.* postieren; aufstellen

**postage** ['pəʊstɪdʒ] *n.* Porto, *das*

**postal** ['pəʊstl] *adj.* Post-; postalisch ⟨*Aufgabe, Einrichtung*⟩; *(by post)* per Post **nachgestellt.** '**postal order** *n.* ≈ Postanweisung, *die*

**post: ~-box** *n.* *(Brit.)* Briefkasten, *der;* **~card** *n.* Postkarte, *die;* **~code** *n.* *(Brit.)* Postleitzahl, *die;* **~-'date** *v. t. (give later date to)* vordatieren

**poster** ['pəʊstə(r)] *n.* Plakat, *das*

**posterior** [pɒ'stɪərɪə(r)] *n. (joc.)* Hinterteil, *das (ugs.)*

**posterity** [pɒ'sterɪtɪ] *n., no art.* Nachwelt, *die*

**posthumous** ['pɒstjʊməs] *adj.* postum

**post: ~man** ['pəʊstmən], *pl.* **~men** ['pəʊstmən] *n.* Briefträger, *der;* **~mark 1.** *n.* Poststempel, *der;* **2.** *v. t.* abstempeln

**post-mortem** [pəʊst'mɔ:təm] *n.* Obduktion, *die*

**post office** *n.* **a)** *(organization)* **the P~ Office** die Post; **b)** *(place)* Postamt, *das;* Post, *die*

**postpone** [pə'spəʊn] *v. t.* verschieben; *(for an indefinite period)* aufschieben. **post'ponement** *n.* Verschiebung, *die/*Aufschub, *der*

**postscript** ['pəʊskrɪpt] *n.* Nachschrift, *die;* *(fig.)* Nachtrag, *der*

**posture** ['pɒstʃə(r)] *n.* [Körper]haltung, *die*

'**post-war** *adj.* Nachkriegs-; der Nachkriegszeit **nachgestellt**

**posy** ['pəʊzɪ] *n.* Sträußchen, *das*

**pot** [pɒt] **1.** *n.* **a)** [Koch]topf, *der;* go to ~ *(coll.)* den Bach runtergehen *(ugs.);* **b)** *(container, contents)* Topf, *der; (tea-pot, coffee-pot)* Kanne, *die;* **c)** *(coll.: large sum)* **a** ~ **of/~s of** massenweise. **2.** *v. t.* ~ |up| eintopfen ⟨*Pflanze*⟩

**potassium** [pə'tæsɪəm] *n.* Kalium, *das*

**potato** [pə'teɪtəʊ] *n., pl.* ~**es** Kartoffel, *die*

**potent** ['pəʊtənt] *adj.* [hoch]wirksam ⟨*Droge*⟩; stark ⟨*Schnaps usw.*⟩; schlag-kräftig ⟨*Waffe*⟩

**potential** [pə'tenʃl] **1.** *adj.* potentiell *(geh.);* möglich. **2.** *n.* Potential, *das (geh.);* Möglichkeiten

'**pot-hole** *n.* **a)** Schlagloch, *das;* **b)** *(cave)* [tiefe] Höhle. '**pot-holer** *n.* Höhlenforscher, *der/*-forscherin, *die*

'**pot-shot** *n.* take a ~ |at sb./sth.| aufs Geratewohl [auf jmdn./etw.] schießen

'**potted** *adj.* **a)** *(planted)* Topf-; **b)** *(abridged)* kurzgefaßt

¹**potter** *n.* Töpfer, *der/*Töpferin, *die*

²**potter** *v. i.* ~ |about| [he]rumwerkeln *(ugs.)*

**pottery** ['pɒtərɪ] *n.* **a)** Töpferware, *die;* **b)** *(workshop, craft)* Töpferei, *die*

¹**potty** ['pɒtɪ] *adj.* *(Brit. sl.)* verrückt *(ugs.)* **(about, on** nach)

²**potty** *n. (Brit. coll.)* Töpfchen, *das*

**pouch** [paʊtʃ] *n.* Beutel, *der*

**pouffe** [pu:f] *n.* Sitzpolster, *das*

**poultry** ['pəʊltrɪ] *n.* Geflügel, *das*

**pounce** [paʊns] *v. i.* **a)** sich auf sein Opfer stürzen; ⟨*Raubvogel:*⟩ herabsto-ßen auf (+ *Akk.*); **b)** *(fig.)* ~ |up|on/at sich stürzen auf (+ *Akk.*)

¹**pound** [paʊnd] *n.* **a)** *(unit of weight)* [britisches] Pfund (453,6 *Gramm);* two ~|s| of apples 2 Pfund Äpfel; **b)** *(unit of currency)* Pfund, *das*

²**pound** *n. (enclosure)* Pferch, *der; (for stray dogs)* Zwinger; *(for cars)* Ab-stellplatz, *der*

³**pound 1.** *v. t. (crush)* zerstoßen. **2.** *v. i.* **a)** *(make one's way heavily)* stampfen; **b)** ⟨*Herz:*⟩ heftig schlagen

**pour** [pɔ:(r)] **1.** *v. t.* gießen; *(into cup, glass)* einschenken. **2.** *v. i.* **a)** *(flow)* strömen; ⟨*Rauch:*⟩ hervorquellen **(from** aus); ~ |with rain| in Strömen regnen; **b)** *(fig.)* strömen; ~ in her-ein-/hineinströmen; ~ **out** heraus-/hinausströmen. **pour** '**down** *v. i.* it's ~ing **down** es gießt [in Strömen] *(ugs.)*

**pout** [paʊt] **1.** *v. i.* einen Schmollmund machen. **2.** *v. t.* aufwerfen ⟨*Lippen*⟩

**poverty** ['pɒvətɪ] *n.* Armut, *die*

**powder** ['paʊdə(r)] **1.** *n.* **a)** Pulver, *das;* **b)** *(cosmetic)* Puder, *der.* **2.** *v. t.* **a)** pudern; **b)** *(reduce to* ~*)* pulverisie-ren; ~**ed milk** Milchpulver, *das.* '**powdery** *adj.* pulv[e]rig

**power** ['paʊə(r)] **1.** *n.* **a)** *(ability)* Kraft, *die;* do all in one's ~ **to help** sb. alles in seiner Macht Stehende tun, um jmdm. zu helfen; **b)** *(faculty)* Fä-higkeit, *die;* **c)** *(strength, intensity)* Kraft, *die; (of blow)* Wucht, *die;* **d)** *(authority, political* ~*)* Macht, *die* **(over** über + *Akk.*); come into ~: an die Macht kommen; **e)** *(authorization)* Vollmacht, *die;* **f)** *(State)* Macht, *die;* **g)** *(Math.)* Potenz, *die;* **h)** *(Mech., Electr.)* Kraft, *die; (electric current)* Strom, *der.* **2.** *v. t.* ⟨*Treibstoff, Strom:*⟩ antreiben; ⟨*Batterie:*⟩ mit Energie ver-sorgen. **powerful** ['paʊəfl] *adj.* **a)** *(strong)* stark; kräftig ⟨*Tritt, Schlag, Tier*⟩; heftig ⟨*Gefühl, Empfindung*⟩; hell, strahlend ⟨*Licht*⟩; **b)** mächtig ⟨*Clique, Person, Herrscher*⟩. '**power-less** *adj.* machtlos. '**power station** *n.* Kraftwerk, *das*

**p.p.** [pi:'pi:] *abbr.* **by proxy** pp[a].

**pp.** *abbr.* **pages**

**practicable** ['præktɪkəbl] *adj.* durch-führbar ⟨*Projekt, Plan*⟩

**practical** ['præktɪkl] *adj.* **a)** praktisch; praktisch veranlagt ⟨*Person*⟩; **b)** *(vir-tual)* tatsächlich; **c)** *(feasible)* mög-lich. **practical** '**joke** *n.* Streich, *der* '**practically** *adv.* praktisch; *(almost)* so gut wie; praktisch *(ugs.)*

¹**practice** ['præktɪs] *n.* **a)** *(repeated exercise)* Übung, *die;* be out of ~: au-ßer Übung sein; **b)** *(session)* Übungen *Pl.;* piano ~: Klavierüben, *das;* **c)** *(of doctor, lawyer, etc.)* Praxis, *die;* **d)** *(ac-tion)* put sth. into ~: etw. in die Praxis umsetzen; **e)** *(custom)* Gewohnheit, *die;* regular ~: Brauch, *der*

²**practice, practiced, practicing** *(Amer.)* see **practis-**

**practise** ['præktɪs] **1.** *v. t.* **a)** *(apply)* anwenden; praktizieren; **b)** ausüben ⟨*Beruf, Religion*⟩; **c)** trainieren in (+ *Dat.*) ⟨*Sportart*⟩; ~ **the piano/flute** Klavier/Flöte üben. **2.** *v. i.* üben.

**practised** ['præktɪst] *adj.* geübt.

**practising** ['præktɪsɪŋ] *adj.* prakti-zierend ⟨*Arzt, Katholik usw.*⟩

**pragmatic** [præg'mætɪk] *adj.* pragma-tisch

**Prague** [prɑ:g] *pr. n.* Prag *(das)*

**prairie** ['preərɪ] *n.* Grassteppe, *die; (in North America)* Prärie, *die*

**praise** [preiz] 1. *v.t.* loben; *(more strongly)* rühmen. 2. *n.* Lob, *das.* '**praiseworthy** *adj.* lobenswert

**pram** [præm] *n. (Brit.)* Kinderwagen, *der*

**prance** [prɑːns] *v.i.* **a)** ⟨*Pferd:*⟩ tänzeln; **b)** *(fig.)* stolzieren; ~ **about** *or* **around** herumhüpfen

**prank** [præŋk] *n.* Streich, *der*

**prattle** ['prætl] 1. *v.i.* plappern *(ugs.).* 2. *n.* Geplapper, *das (ugs.)*

**prawn** [prɔːn] *n.* Garnele, *die*

**pray** [prei] *v.i.* beten (for um). **prayer** [preə(r)] *n.* **a)** Gebet, *das;* **b)** *no art. (praying)* Beten, *das*

**preach** [priːtʃ] 1. *v.i.* predigen (to zu, vor + *Dat.;* on über + *Akk.*). 2. *v.t.* halten ⟨*Predigt*⟩; predigen ⟨*Evangelium, Botschaft*⟩. '**preacher** *n.* Prediger, *der*/Predigerin, *die*

**precarious** [prɪˈkeəriəs] *adj.* **a)** *(uncertain)* labil; prekär; **make a ~ living** eine unsichere Existenz haben; **b)** *(insecure, dangerous)* gefährlich

**precaution** [prɪˈkɔːʃn] *n.* Vorsichts-, Schutzmaßnahme, *die;* **as a ~:** vorsichtshalber

**precede** [prɪˈsiːd] *v.t. (in order or time)* vorangehen (+ *Dat.*). **precedence** ['presidəns] *n.* Priorität, *die (geh.),* Vorrang, *der* (over vor + *Dat.*). **precedent** ['presidənt] *n.* Präzedenzfall, *der*

**precinct** ['priːsɪŋkt] *n.* **a)** [**pedestrian**] **~:** Fußgängerzone, *die;* **b)** *(Amer.: district)* Bezirk, *der*

**precious** ['preʃəs] 1. *adj.* **a)** kostbar ⟨*Schmuckstück, Zeit*⟩; **b)** *(beloved)* lieb; **c)** *(affected)* affektiert. 2. *adv. (coll.)* herzlich ⟨*wenig, wenige*⟩

**precipice** ['presɪpɪs] *n.* Abgrund, *der*

**precipitate** 1. [prɪˈsɪpɪtət] *adj.* eilig ⟨*Flucht*⟩; übereilt ⟨*Entschluß*⟩. 2. [prɪˈsɪpɪteit] *v.t. (hasten)* beschleunigen; *(trigger)* auslösen

**precipitation** [prɪsɪpɪˈteiʃn] *n. (Meteorol.)* Niederschlag, *der*

**precipitous** [prɪˈsɪpɪtəs] *adj.* **a)** *(steep)* sehr steil; **b)** *see* precipitate 1

**précis** ['preisiː] *n., pl. same* [preisiːz] Zusammenfassung, *die*

**precise** [prɪˈsais] *adj.* genau; präzise; fein ⟨*Instrument*⟩; förmlich ⟨*Art*⟩; **be** [**more**] **~:** sich präzise[r] ausdrücken. **preˈcisely** *adv.* genau. **precision** [prɪˈsɪʒn] *n.* Genauigkeit, *die*

**preclude** [prɪˈkluːd] *v.t.* ausschließen

**precocious** [prɪˈkəʊʃəs] *adj.* frühreif ⟨*Kind*⟩; altklug ⟨*Äußerung*⟩

**preconceived** [priːkənˈsiːvd] *adj.* vorgefaßt ⟨*Ansicht, Vorstellung*⟩. **preconception** [priːkənˈsepʃn] *n.* vorgefaßte Meinung (of über + *Akk.*)

**precondition** [priːkənˈdɪʃn] *n.* Vorbedingung, *die* (of für)

**precursor** [priːˈkɜːsə(r)] *n.* Wegbereiter, *der*/-bereiterin, *die*

**predator** ['predətə(r)] *n.* Raubtier, *das; (fish)* Raubfisch, *der.* '**predatory** *adj.* räuberisch; ~ **animal** Raubtier, *das*

**predecessor** ['priːdisesə(r)] *n.* Vorgänger, *der*/-gängerin, *die*

**predestine** [priːˈdestɪn] *v.t.* von vornherein bestimmen (to zu)

**predicament** [prɪˈdɪkəmənt] *n.* Dilemma, *das*

**predicate** ['predɪkət] *n. (Ling.)* Prädikat, *das.* **predicative** [prɪˈdɪkətɪv] *adj. (Ling.)* prädikativ

**predict** [prɪˈdɪkt] *v.t.* voraus-, vorhersagen; vorhersehen ⟨*Folgen*⟩. **predictable** [prɪˈdɪktəbl] *adj.* voraussagbar; vorhersehbar ⟨*Ereignis, Reaktion*⟩; berechenbar ⟨*Person*⟩. **prediction** [prɪˈdɪkʃn] *n.* Vorhersage, *die*

**predominance** [prɪˈdɒmɪnəns] *n.* **a)** *(control)* Vorherrschaft, *die* (over über + *Akk.*); **b)** *(majority)* Überzahl, *die* (of von)

**predominant** [prɪˈdɒmɪnənt] *adj. (having more power)* dominierend; *(prevailing)* vorherrschend

**predominate** [prɪˈdɒmɪneit] *v.i. (be more powerful)* dominierend sein; *(be more important)* vorherrschen

**pre-eminent** [priːˈemɪnənt] *adj.* herausragend

**pre-empt** [priːˈempt] *v.t.* zuvorkommen (+ *Dat.*)

**preen** [priːn] *v.t.* putzen ⟨*Federn*⟩

**prefab** ['priːfæb] *n. (coll.)* Fertighaus, *das.* **prefabricated** [priːˈfæbrɪkeitɪd] *adj.* vorgefertigt

**preface** ['prefəs] 1. *n.* Vorwort, *das* (to Gen.). 2. *v.t. (introduce)* einleiten

**prefect** ['priːfekt] *n. (Sch.)* die Aufsicht führender älterer Schüler/führende ältere Schülerin

**prefer** [prɪˈfɜː(r)] *v.t.,* **-rr-** vorziehen; ~ **to do sth.** etw. lieber tun; ~ **sth. to sth.** etw. einer Sache (*Dat.*) vorziehen. **preferable** ['prefərəbl] *adj.* vorzuziehen *präd.;* vorzuziehend *attr.;* besser (to als). **preferably** ['prefərəbli] *adv.* am besten; *(as best liked)* am liebsten; **Wine or beer? – Wine, ~!** Wein oder Bier? – Lieber Wein! **preference**

['prefərəns] n. **a)** *(greater liking)* Vorliebe, *die; for* ~ *see* **preferably; have a** ~ **for sth.** |over sth.| etw. [einer Sache *(Dat.)*] vorziehen; **do sth. in** ~ **to sth.** else etw. lieber als etw. anderes tun; **b)** *(thing preferred)* **what are your** ~**s?** was wäre dir am liebsten?; **c) give** ~ **to sb.** jmdn. bevorzugen. **preferential** [prefə'renʃl] adj. bevorzugt ⟨Behandlung⟩

**prefix** ['pri:fɪks] n. Präfix, *das*

**pregnancy** ['pregnənsɪ] n. *(of woman)* Schwangerschaft, *die; (of animal)* Trächtigkeit, *die*

**pregnant** ['pregnənt] adj. schwanger ⟨Frau⟩; trächtig ⟨Tier⟩

**prehistoric** [pri:hɪ'stɒrɪk] adj. prähistorisch. **prehistory** [pri:'hɪstərɪ] Vorgeschichte, *die*

**prejudge** [pri:'dʒʌdʒ] v. t. vorschnell urteilen über (+ Akk.)

**prejudice** ['predʒʊdɪs] **1.** n. Vorurteil, *das.* **2.** v. t. beeinflussen. **prejudiced** ['predʒʊdɪst] adj. voreingenommen **(about** gegenüber, **against** gegen)

**preliminary** [prɪ'lɪmɪnərɪ] **1.** adj. Vor-; vorbereitend ⟨Forschung, Maßnahme⟩. **2.** n., usu. in pl. **preliminaries** Präliminarien Pl.; **as a** ~ **to sth.** als Vorbereitung auf etw. *(Akk.)*

**prelude** ['prelju:d] n. **a)** *(introduction)* Anfang, *der* **(to** Gen.); **b)** *(Theatre, Mus.)* Vorspiel, *das*

**premature** ['premətjʊə(r)] adj. **a)** *(hasty)* übereilt; **b)** *(early)* vorzeitig ⟨Altern, Ankunft⟩; verfrüht ⟨Bericht, Eile⟩; ~ **baby** Frühgeburt, *die.* **prematurely** adv. *(early)* vorzeitig; zu früh ⟨geboren werden⟩; *(hastily)* übereilt

**premeditated** [pri:'medɪteɪtɪd] adj. vorsätzlich

**premier** ['premɪə(r)] n. Premier[minister], *der*/Premierministerin, *die*

**première** ['premjeə(r)] n. Premiere, *die;* Erstaufführung, *die*

**premise** ['premɪs] n. **a)** ~s pl. *(building)* Gebäude, *das; (buildings and land)* Gelände, *das; (rooms)* Räumlichkeiten Pl.; **b)** see **premiss**

**premiss** ['premɪs] n. Prämisse, *die*

**premium** ['pri:mɪəm] n. Prämie, *die;* **be at a** ~ *(fig.)* sehr gefragt sein. **'Premium Bond** n. *(Brit.)* Prämienanleihe, *die;* Losanleihe, *die*

**premonition** [premə'nɪʃn] n. Vorahnung, *die*

**preoccupation** [prɪɒkjʊ'peɪʃn] n. Sorge, *die* **(with** um)

**preoccupied** [prɪ'ɒkjʊpaɪd] adj. *(lost in thought)* gedankenverloren; *(concerned)* besorgt **(with** um)

**pre-'packed** adj. abgepackt

**preparation** [prepə'reɪʃn] n. Vorbereitung, *die;* ~s pl. Vorbereitungen Pl. **(for** für). **preparatory** [prɪ'pærətərɪ] **1.** adj. vorbereitend ⟨Maßnahme, Schritt⟩; ~ **work** Vorarbeiten Pl. **2.** adv. ~ **to sth.** vor etw. *(Dat.)*

**prepare** [prɪ'peə(r)] **1.** v. t. **a)** vorbereiten; ausarbeiten ⟨Plan, Rede⟩; vorbereiten ⟨Person⟩ **(for** auf + Akk.); **be** ~**d to do sth.** *(be willing)* bereit sein, etw. zu tun; **b)** herstellen ⟨Chemikalie usw.⟩; zubereiten ⟨Essen⟩. **2.** v. i. sich vorbereiten **(for** auf + Akk.)

**prepaid** [pri:'peɪd] adj. ~ **envelope** frankierter Umschlag

**preponderance** [prɪ'pɒndərəns] n. Überlegenheit, *die* **(over** über + Akk.)

**preposition** [prepə'zɪʃn] n. *(Ling.)* Präposition, *die*

**prepossessing** [pri:pə'zesɪŋ] adj. einnehmend

**preposterous** [prɪ'pɒstərəs] adj. absurd; grotesk ⟨Äußeres, Kleidung⟩

**prerequisite** [pri:'rekwɪzɪt] **1.** n. [Grund]voraussetzung, *die.* **2.** adj. unbedingt erforderlich

**prerogative** [prɪ'rɒgətɪv] n. Privileg, *das;* Vorrecht, *das*

**Presbyterian** [prezbɪ'tɪərɪən] **1.** adj. presbyterianisch. **2.** n. Presbyterianer, *der*/Presbyterianerin, *die*

**prescribe** [prɪ'skraɪb] v. t. **a)** *(impose)* vorschreiben; **b)** *(Med.; also fig.)* verschreiben. **prescription** [prɪ'skrɪpʃn] n. **a)** Vorschreiben, *das;* **b)** *(Med.)* Rezept, *das*

**presence** ['prezəns] n. **a)** *(of person)* Anwesenheit, *die; (of things)* Vorhandensein, *das;* **in the** ~ **of** in Anwesenheit (+ Gen.); **b)** ~ **of mind** Geistesgegenwart, *die*

**¹present** ['prezənt] **1.** adj. **a)** anwesend **(at** bei); **all those** ~: alle Anwesenden; **b)** *(existing now)* gegenwärtig; jetzig ⟨Bischof, Chef usw.⟩; **c)** *(Ling.)* ~ **tense** Präsens, *das;* Gegenwart, *die.* **2.** n. **a) the** ~: die Gegenwart; **at** ~: zur Zeit; **for the** ~: vorläufig; **b)** *(Ling.)* Präsens, *das;* Gegenwart, *die*

**²present 1.** ['prezənt] n. *(gift)* Geschenk, *das.* **2.** [prɪ'zent] v. t. **a)** schenken; überreichen ⟨Preis, Medaille, Geschenk⟩; ~ **sth. to sb.** *or* **sb. with sth.** jmdm. etw. schenken/überreichen; ~

sb. with difficulties/a problem jmdn. vor Schwierigkeiten/ein Problem stellen; b) überreichen ⟨Gesuch⟩ (to bei); vorlegen ⟨Scheck, Bericht, Rechnung⟩ (to Dat.); ~ one's case seinen Fall darlegen; c) (exhibit) zeigen; bereiten ⟨Schwierigkeit⟩; d) (introduce) vorstellen (to Dat.); vorlegen ⟨Abhandlung⟩; moderieren ⟨Sendung⟩. 3. v. refl. ⟨Problem:⟩ auftreten; ⟨Möglichkeit:⟩ sich ergeben; ~ oneself for an interview zu einem Gespräch erscheinen.

**presentable** [prɪ'zentəbl] adj. ansehnlich; I'm not ~: ich kann mich nicht so zeigen. **presentation** [prezən'teɪʃn] n. a) (giving) Schenkung, die; (of prize, medal) Überreichung, die; b) (ceremony) Verleihung, die; c) (of petition) Überreichung, die; (of cheque, report, account) Vorlage, die; (of case) Darlegung, die

**present-'day** adj. heutig

**presenter** [prɪ'zentə(r)] n. (Radio, Telev.) Moderator, der/Moderatorin, die

**presentiment** [prɪ'zentɪmənt] n. Vorahnung, die

**presently** ['prezntlɪ] adv. bald; (Amer., Scot.: now) zur Zeit

**preservation** [prezə'veɪʃn] n. Erhaltung, die; (of leather, wood, etc.) Konservierung, die. **preservative** [prɪ'zɜːvətɪv] n. Konservierungsmittel, das

**preserve** [prɪ'zɜːv] 1. n. a) in sing. or pl. (fruit) Eingemachte, das; b) (fig.: special sphere) Domäne, die (geh.); c) wildlife/game ~: Tierschutzgebiet, das/Wildpark, der. 2. v. t. a) (keep safe) schützen (from vor + Dat.); b) bewahren ⟨Brauch⟩; wahren ⟨Anschein, Reputation⟩; c) (keep from decay) konservieren; einmachen ⟨Obst, Gemüse⟩; d) (protect) hegen ⟨Tierart, Wald⟩

**preside** [prɪ'zaɪd] v. i. präsidieren, vorsitzen (over Dat.); (at meeting etc.) den Vorsitz haben (at bei)

**presidency** ['prezɪdənsɪ] n. a) Präsidentschaft, die; b) (of society) Vorsitz, der

**president** ['prezɪdənt] n. a) Präsident, der/Präsidentin, die; b) (of society) Vorsitzende, der/die. **presidential** [prezɪ'denʃl] adj. Präsidenten-

**¹press** [pres] 1. n. a) (newspapers etc.) Presse, die; attrib. Presse-; b) see printing-press; c) (for flattening, compressing, etc.) Presse, die. 2. v. t. a) drücken; drücken auf (+ Akk.) ⟨Klin-

gel, Knopf⟩; treten auf (+ Akk.) ⟨Gas-, Brems-, Kupplungspedal usw.⟩; b) (urge) drängen ⟨Person⟩; (force) aufdrängen (|up|on Dat.); nachdrücklich vorbringen ⟨Forderung, Argument⟩; he did not ~ the point er ließ die Sache auf sich beruhen; c) (compress) pressen; auspressen ⟨Orangen, Saft⟩; keltern ⟨Trauben, Äpfel⟩; (iron) bügeln; e) be ~ed for time/money zu wenig Zeit/Geld haben. 3. v. i. a) (exert pressure) drücken; b) (be urgent) drängen; c) (make demand) ~ for sth. auf etw. (Akk.) drängen.

**press a'head, press 'on** v. i. (continue) [zügig] weitermachen; (continue travelling) [zügig] weitergehen/-fahren; ~ on with one's work sich mit der Arbeit ranhalten (ugs.)

**²press** v. t. ~ into service/use in Dienst nehmen; einsetzen

**'press conference** n. Pressekonferenz, die

**'pressing** adj. (urgent) dringend

**press: ~ release** n. Presseinformation, die; ~-up n. Liegestütz, der

**pressure** ['preʃə(r)] 1. n. Druck, der; put ~ on sb. jmdn. unter Druck setzen; atmospheric ~: Luftdruck, der. 2. v. t. unter Druck setzen ⟨Person⟩; ~ sb. into doing sth. jmdn. [dazu] drängen, etw. zu tun. **'pressure-cooker** n. Schnellkochtopf, der. **'pressure group** n. Pressure-group, die

**pressurize** ['preʃəraɪz] v. t. a) see pressure 2; b) ~d cabin Druckkabine, die

**prestige** [pre'stiːʒ] n. Prestige, das. **prestigious** [pre'stɪdʒəs] adj. angesehen

**presumably** [prɪ'zjuːməblɪ] adv. vermutlich

**presume** [prɪ'zjuːm] 1. v. t. a) ~ to do sth. sich (Dat.) anmaßen, etw. zu tun; (take the liberty) sich (Dat.) erlauben, etw. zu tun; b) (suppose) annehmen. 2. v. i. |up|on sth. etw. ausnützen. **presumption** [prɪ'zʌmpʃn] n. a) (arrogance) Anmaßung, die; b) (assumption) Annahme, die. **presumptuous** [prɪ'zʌmptjʊəs] adj. anmaßend

**presuppose** [priːsə'pəʊz] v. t. voraussetzen

**pretence** [prɪ'tens] n. (Brit.) a) (pretext) Vorwand, der; b) no art. (make-believe, insincere behaviour) Verstellung, die; it is all or just a ~: das ist alles nicht echt

**pretend** [prɪ'tend] 1. v. t. a) vorgeben;

she ~ed to be asleep sie tat, als ob sie schlief[e]; b) *(imagine in play)* ~ to be sth. so tun, als ob man etw. sei. 2. *v. i.* sich verstellen; she's only ~ing sie tut nur so

**pretense** *(Amer.) see* **pretence**

**pretension** [prɪ'tenʃn] *n.* a) Anspruch, *der* (to auf + *Akk.*); b) *(pretentiousness)* Überheblichkeit, *die.* **pretentious** [prɪ'tenʃəs] *adj.* hochgestochen; wichtigtuerisch ‹*Person*›; *(ostentatious)* großspurig

**pretext** ['pri:tekst] *n.* Vorwand, *der;* |up|on *or* under the ~ of doing sth. unter dem Vorwand, etw. tun zu wollen

**prettily** ['prɪtɪlɪ] *adv.* hübsch; sehr schön ‹*singen, tanzen*›

**pretty** ['prɪtɪ] 1. *adj. (also iron.)* hübsch. 2. *adv.* ziemlich; I am ~ well es geht mir ganz gut

**prevail** [prɪ'veɪl] *v. i.* a) die Oberhand gewinnen (against, over über + *Akk.*); ~ |up|on sb. to do sth. jmdn. dazu bewegen, etw. zu tun; b) *(predominate)* ‹*Zustand, Bedingung:*› vorherrschen; c) *(be current)* herrschen

**prevalence** ['prevələns] *n.* Vorherrschen, *das*

**prevalent** ['prevələnt] *adj.* a) *(existing)* herrschend; weit verbreitet ‹*Krankheit*›; b) *(predominant)* vorherrschend

**prevent** [prɪ'vent] *v. t. (hinder)* verhindern; *(forestall)* vorbeugen; ~ sb. from doing sth., ~ sb.'s doing sth., *(coll.)* ~ sb. doing sth. jmdn. daran hindern, etw. zu tun. **prevention** [prɪ'venʃn] *n.* Verhinderung, *die; (forestalling)* Vorbeugung, *die.* **preventive** [prɪ'ventɪv] *adj.* vorbeugend; Präventiv‹*maßnahme*›

**preview** ['pri:vju:] *n. (of film, play)* Voraufführung, *die; (of exhibition)* Vernissage, *die (geh.)*

**previous** ['pri:vɪəs] 1. *adj.* a) früher ‹*Anstellung, Gelegenheit*›; vorherig ‹*Abend*›; vorig ‹*Besitzer, Wohnsitz*›; the ~ page die Seite davor; b) *(prior)* ~ to vor (+ *Dat.*). 2. *adv.* ~ to vor (+ *Dat.*). **previously** *adv.* vorher

**pre-war** ['pri:wɔ:(r)] *adj.* Vorkriegs-

**prey** [preɪ] 1. *n., pl. same* a) *(animal[s])* Beute, *die;* beast/bird of ~: Raubtier, *das/*-vogel, *der;* b) *(victim)* Opfer, *das.* 2. *v. i.* ~ |up|on ‹*Raubtier, Raubvogel:*› schlagen; *(plunder)* ausplündern ‹*Person*›; Jagd machen auf (+ *Akk.*); ~ |up|on sb.'s mind jmdm. keine Ruhe lassen

**price** [praɪs] *n. (lit. or fig.)* Preis, *der;* at a ~ of zum Preis von; what is the ~ of this? was kostet das?; at/not at any ~: um jeden/keinen Preis. **'priceless** *adj.* a) *(invaluable)* unbezahlbar; b) *(coll.: amusing)* köstlich

**price:** ~-list *n.* Preisliste, *die;* ~-rise *n.* Preisanstieg, *der;* ~-tag *n.* Preisschild, *das*

**prick** [prɪk] 1. *v. t.* stechen; stechen in ‹*Ballon*›; aufstechen ‹*Blase*›. 2. *v. i.* stechen. 3. *n.* Stich, *der.* **'prick up** *v. t.* aufrichten ‹*Ohren*›; ~ up one's/its ears die Ohren spitzen

**prickle** ['prɪkl] 1. *n.* a) Dorn, *der;* b) *(Zool., Bot.)* Stachel, *der.* 2. *v. i.* kratzen. **prickly** ['prɪklɪ] *adj.* dornig; stachelig; *(fig.)* empfindlich

**pride** [praɪd] 1. *n.* a) Stolz, *der; (arrogance)* Hochmut, *der;* take |a| ~ in sb./ sth. auf jmdn./etw. stolz sein; sb's ~ and joy jmds. ganzer Stolz; b) *(of lions)* Rudel, *das.* 2. *v. refl.* ~ oneself |up|on sth. auf etw. *(Akk.)* stolz sein

**pried** *see* **pry**

**priest** [pri:st] *n.* Priester, *der.* **'priesthood** *n.* geistliches Amt

**prim** [prɪm] *adj.* spröde; *(prudish)* zimperlich

**primarily** ['praɪmərɪlɪ] *adv.* in erster Linie

**primary** ['praɪmərɪ] 1. *adj.* a) *(first)* primär *(geh.);* grundlegend; b) *(chief)* Haupt‹*rolle, -ziel, -zweck*›. 2. *n. (Amer.: election)* Vorwahl, *die.* **'primary school** *n.* Grundschule, *die*

**primate** ['praɪmeɪt] *n.* a) *(Eccl.)* Primas, *der;* b) *(Zool.)* Primat, *der*

**¹prime** [praɪm] 1. *n.* Höhepunkt, *der;* be in one's ~: in den besten Jahren sein. 2. *adj.* a) Haupt-; hauptsächlich; b) *(excellent)* erstklassig; vortrefflich ‹*Beispiel*›

**²prime** *v. t.* a) *(equip)* vorbereiten; ~ sb. with information/advice jmdn. instruieren/jmdm. Ratschläge erteilen; b) grundieren ‹*Wand, Decke*›; c) schärfen ‹*Sprengkörper*›

**prime:** ~ 'minister *n.* Premierminister, *der/*-ministerin, *die;* ~ 'number *n. (Math.)* Primzahl, *die*

**'primer** *n.* a) *(explosive)* Zündvorrichtung, *die;* b) *(paint)* Grundierlack, *der*

**primeval** [praɪ'mi:vl] *adj.* urzeitlich; Ur‹*zeiten, -wälder*›

**primitive** ['prɪmɪtɪv] *adj.* primitiv; *(prehistoric)* urzeitlich ‹*Mensch*›

**primrose** ['prɪmrəʊz] *n.* gelbe Schlüsselblume

**Primus, (P)** ['praɪməs] *n.* ~ |stove| Primuskocher, *der*

**prince** [prɪns] *n.* Prinz, *der.* '**princely** *adj.* fürstlich

**princess** [prɪn'ses] *n.* Prinzessin, *die; (wife of prince)* Fürstin, *die*

**principal** ['prɪnsɪpl] **1.** *adj.* Haupt-; *(most important)* wichtigst... **2.** *n. (of college)* Rektor, *der*/Rektorin, *die*

**principality** [prɪnsɪ'pælɪtɪ] *n.* Fürstentum, *das*

'**principally** *adv.* in erster Linie

**principle** ['prɪnsɪpl] *n.* Prinzip, *das;* **on the ~ that ...**: nach dem Grundsatz, daß ...; **in ~**: im Prinzip; **do sth. on ~** *or* **as a matter of ~**: etw. prinzipiell *od.* aus Prinzip tun

**print** [prɪnt] **1.** *n.* **a)** *(impression)* Abdruck, *der; (finger~)* Fingerabdruck, *der;* **b)** *(~ed lettering)* Gedruckte, *das; (type-face)* Druck, *der;* **c) be in/out of ~** ⟨*Buch:*⟩ erhältlich/vergriffen sein; **d)** *(~ed picture or design)* Druck, *der;* **e)** *(Photog.)* Abzug, *der.* **2.** *v. t.* **a)** drucken ⟨*Buch, Zeitschrift usw.*⟩; **b)** *(write)* in Druckschrift schreiben. **print 'out** *v. t. (Computing)* ausdrucken

'**printed** *adj.* **a)** gedruckt; **b)** *(published)* veröffentlicht. '**printed matter** *n. (Post)* Drucksachen *Pl.*

'**printer** *n.* **a)** *(worker)* Drucker, *der*/Druckerin, *die; (firm)* Druckerei, *die;* **b)** *(Computing)* Drucker, *der*

'**printing** *n.* **a)** Drucken, *das;* **b)** *(writing like print)* Druckschrift, *die;* **c)** *(edition)* Auflage, *die.* '**printingpress** *n.* Druckerpresse, *die*

'**printout** *n. (Computing)* Ausdruck, *der*

**prior** ['praɪə(r)] **1.** *adj.* vorherig ⟨*Warnung, Zustimmung usw.*⟩; früher ⟨*Verabredung*⟩; Vor⟨*geschichte, -kenntnis*⟩. **2.** *adv.* **~ to** vor (+ *Dat.*); **~ to doing sth.** bevor man etw. tut/tat; **~ to that** vorher. **priority** [praɪ'ɒrɪtɪ] *n.* **a)** *(precedence)* Vorrang, *der; attrib.* vorrangig; **have** *or* **take ~**: Vorrang haben (**over** vor + *Dat.*); **have ~** *(on road)* Vorfahrt haben; **give ~ to sb./ sth.** jmdm./einer Sache den Vorrang geben; **give top ~ to sth.** einer Sache *(Dat.)* höchste Priorität einräumen; **b)** *(matter)* vordringliche Angelegenheit

**prism** ['prɪzm] *n.* Prisma, *das*

**prison** ['prɪzn] *n.* **a)** Gefängnis, *das; attrib.* Gefängnis-; **b)** *(custody)* Haft, *die;* **in ~**: im Gefängnis; **go to ~**: ins Gefängnis gehen. '**prisoner** *n.* Ge-

fangene, *der/die;* **take sb. ~**: jmdn. gefangennehmen

**pristine** ['prɪstiːn] *adj.* unberührt; **in ~ condition** in tadellosem Zustand

**privacy** ['prɪvəsɪ] *n.* Privatsphäre, *die; (being undisturbed)* Ungestörtheit, *die;* **invasion of ~**: Eindringen in die Privatsphäre; **in the strictest ~**: unter strengster Geheimhaltung

**private** ['praɪvət] **1.** *adj.* **a)** *(outside State system)* privat; Privat⟨*schule, -industrie, -klinik usw.*⟩; **b)** persönlich ⟨*Dinge, Meinung, Interesse*⟩; nichtöffentlich ⟨*Versammlung, Sitzung*⟩; privat ⟨*Telefongespräch, Vereinbarung*⟩; Privat⟨*strand, -parkplatz, -leben*⟩; geheim ⟨*Verhandlung, Geschäft*⟩; persönlich ⟨*Gründe*⟩; *(confidential)* vertraulich. **2.** *n.* **a)** *(Brit. Mil.)* einfacher Soldat; **b) in ~**: privat; in kleinem Kreis ⟨*feiern*⟩; *(confidentially)* ganz im Vertrauen. '**privately** *adv.* privat ⟨*erziehen, zugeben*⟩; vertraulich ⟨*jmdn. sprechen*⟩; insgeheim ⟨*denken, glauben*⟩; **~ owned** in Privatbesitz

**privation** [praɪ'veɪʃn] *n.* Not, *die;* **suffer many ~s** viele Entbehrungen erleiden

**privatize** ['praɪvətaɪz] *v. t.* privatisieren

**privet** ['prɪvɪt] *n.* Liguster, *der*

**privilege** ['prɪvɪlɪdʒ] *n. (right, immunity)* Privileg, *das; (special benefit)* Sonderrecht, *das; (honour)* Ehre, *die.* '**privileged** *adj.* privilegiert

**privy** ['prɪvɪ] *adj.* **be ~ to sth.** in etw. *(Akk.)* eingeweiht sein

¹**prize** [praɪz] **1.** *n.* **a)** *(reward, money)* Preis, *der;* **win** *or* **take first ~**: den ersten Preis gewinnen; **b)** *(in lottery)* Gewinn, *der.* **2.** *v. t.* **~ sth. |highly|** etw. hoch schätzen

²**prize** *v. t.* **~ |open|** aufstemmen

**prize: ~-giving** *n.* Preisverleihung, *die;* **~-money** *n.* Geldpreis, *der; (Sport)* Preisgeld, *das;* **~-winner** *n.* Preisträger, *der*/-trägerin, *die; (in lottery)* Gewinner, *der*/Gewinnerin, *die*

**pro** [prəʊ] *n. in pl.* **the ~s and cons** das Pro und Kontra

**probability** [prɒbə'bɪlɪtɪ] *n.* Wahrscheinlichkeit, *die;* **in all ~**: aller Wahrscheinlichkeit nach

**probable** ['prɒbəbl] *adj.* wahrscheinlich; **highly ~**: höchstwahrscheinlich.

**probably** ['prɒbəblɪ] *adv.* wahrscheinlich

**probation** [prə'beɪʃn] *n.* **a)** Probezeit, *die;* **b)** *(Law)* Bewährung, *die;* **on ~**:

auf Bewährung. **probationary** [prə-'beɪʃənərɪ] *adj.* Probe-; ~ **period** Probezeit, *die*

**probe** [prəʊb] 1. *n.* a) Untersuchung, *die* (**into** *Gen.*); b) (*Med., Astron.*) Sonde, *die.* 2. *v. t.* untersuchen

**problem** ['prɒbləm] *n.* Problem, *das; (puzzle)* Rätsel, *das;* **what's the ~?** (*coll.*) wo fehlt's denn?; **the ~ about** *or* **with sb./sth.** das Problem mit jmdm./ bei etw. **problematic** [prɒblə'mætɪk], **problematical** [prɒblə'mætɪkl] *adj.* problematisch

**procedure** [prə'siːdjə(r)] *n.* Verfahren, *das*

**proceed** [prə'siːd] *v. i. (formal)* a) *(on foot)* gehen; *(as or by vehicle)* fahren; *(after interruption)* weitergehen/-fahren; b) *(begin and carry on)* beginnen; *(after interruption)* fortfahren; ~ **in** *or* **with sth.** *(begin)* [mit] etw. beginnen; *(continue)* etw. fortsetzen; c) *(be under way)* ⟨*Verfahren:*⟩ laufen; *(be continued after interruption)* fortgesetzt werden. **pro'ceedings** *n. pl.* a) *(events)* Vorgänge; b) *(Law)* Verfahren, *das;* **legal ~:** Gerichtsverfahren, *das;* **start/take [legal] ~:** gerichtlich vorgehen (**against** gegen)

**proceeds** ['prəʊsiːdz] *n. pl.* Erlös, *der* (**from** aus)

¹**process** ['prəʊses] 1. *n.* a) *(of time or history)* Lauf, *der;* **he learnt a lot in the ~:** er lernte eine Menge dabei; **be in the ~ of doing sth.** gerade etw. tun; b) *(proceeding, natural operation)* Vorgang, *der;* c) *(method)* Verfahren, *das.* 2. *v. t.* verarbeiten ⟨*Rohstoff, Signal*⟩; bearbeiten ⟨*Antrag, Akte*⟩; *(Photog.)* entwickeln ⟨*Film*⟩

²**process** [prə'ses] *v. i.* ziehen. **procession** [prə'seʃn] *n.* Zug, *der; (religious)* Prozession, *die; (festive)* Umzug, *der;* **go/march in ~:** ziehen

**proclaim** [prə'kleɪm] *v. t.* erklären ⟨*Absicht*⟩; geltend machen ⟨*Recht, Anspruch*⟩; verkünden ⟨*Amnestie*⟩; ausrufen ⟨*Republik*⟩. **proclamation** [prɒklə'meɪʃn] *n.* a) *(proclaiming)* Verkündung, *die;* b) *(notice)* Bekanntmachung, *die; (decree)* Erlaß, *der*

**procure** [prə'kjʊə(r)] *v. t.* beschaffen

**prod** 1. *v. t.,* **-dd-** *(poke)* stupsen *(ugs.);* stoßen mit ⟨*Stock, Finger usw.*⟩; ~ **sb. gently** jmdn. anstupsen. 2. *n.* Stupser, *der;* **give sb. a ~:** jmdm. einen Stupser geben

**prodigal** ['prɒdɪgl] *adj.* verschwenderisch; ~ **son** verlorener Sohn

**prodigious** [prə'dɪdʒəs] *adj.* ungeheuer

**prodigy** ['prɒdɪdʒɪ] *n.* [außergewöhnliches] Talent; **child ~:** Wunderkind, *das*

**produce** 1. ['prɒdjuːs] *n.* Produkte *Pl.;* Erzeugnisse *Pl.* 2. [prə'djuːs] *v. t.* a) vorzeigen ⟨*Paß, Fahrkarte*⟩; b) produzieren ⟨*Show, Film*⟩; inszenieren ⟨*Theaterstück, Hörspiel*⟩; herausgeben ⟨*Schallplatte, Buch*⟩; c) *(manufacture)* herstellen; *(in nature; Agric.)* produzieren; d) *(cause)* hervorrufen; bewirken ⟨*Änderung*⟩; e) *(bring into being)* erzeugen; führen zu ⟨*Situation*⟩; f) *(yield)* geben ⟨*Milch*⟩; legen ⟨*Eier*⟩; g) ⟨*Baum, Blume:*⟩ tragen ⟨*Früchte, Blüten*⟩; entwickeln ⟨*Triebe*⟩; bilden ⟨*Keime*⟩. **producer** [prə'djuːsə(r)] *n.* a) *(Cinemat., Theatre, Radio, Telev.)* Produzent, *der*/Produzentin, *die;* b) *(Brit. Theatre/Radio/Telev.)* Regisseur, *der*/Regisseurin, *die*

**product** ['prɒdʌkt] *n.* a) Produkt, *das; (of industrial process)* Erzeugnis, *das; (of art or intellect)* Werk, *das;* b) *(result)* Folge, *die;* c) *(Math.)* Produkt, *das* (**of** aus)

**production** [prə'dʌkʃn] *n.* a) *(Cinemat.)* Produktion, *die; (Theatre)* Inszenierung, *die; (of record, book)* Herausgabe, *die;* b) *(making)* Produktion, *die; (manufacturing)* Herstellung, *die; (thing produced)* Produkt, *das; (thing created)* Werk, *das;* c) *(yielding)* Produktion, *die; (yield)* Ertrag, *der.* **pro'duction line** *n.* Fertigungsstraße, *die*

**productive** [prə'dʌktɪv] *adj.* leistungsfähig ⟨*Betrieb, Bauernhof*⟩; fruchtbar ⟨*Gespräch, Verhandlungen*⟩. **productivity** [prɒdʌk'tɪvɪtɪ] *n.* Produktivität, *die*

**Prof.** [prɒf] *abbr.* Professor Prof.

**profane** [prə'feɪn] *adj.* a) *(irreligious)* gotteslästerlich; b) *(secular)* weltlich; c) *(irreverent)* respektlos ⟨*Bemerkung*⟩; profan ⟨*Sprache*⟩

**profess** [prə'fes] *v. t.* a) *(declare openly)* bekunden ⟨*Vorliebe, Abneigung*⟩; ~ **to be/do sth.** erklären, etw. zu sein/tun; b) *(claim)* vorgeben; ~ **to be/do sth.** behaupten, etw. zu sein/tun

**profession** [prə'feʃn] *n.* a) Beruf, *der;* **be a pilot by ~:** von Beruf Pilot sein; b) *(body of people)* Berufsstand, *der.*

**professional** [prə'feʃənl] 1. *adj.* a) Berufs⟨*ausbildung, -leben*⟩; beruflich ⟨*Qualifikation*⟩; b) *(worthy of profes-*

*sion) (in technical expertise)* fachmännisch; *(in attitude)* professionell; *(in experience)* routiniert; **c)** ~ **people** Angehörige hochqualifizierter Berufe; **d)** *(by profession)* gelernt; *(not amateur)* Berufs⟨musiker, -sportler⟩; Profi⟨sportler⟩; **e)** *(paid)* Profi⟨sport, -boxen⟩. **2.** *n. (trained person)* Fachmann, *der*/Fachfrau, *die; (non-amateur; also Sport)* Profi, *der*

**professor** [prə'fesə(r)] *n.* **a)** *(Univ.)* Professor, *der*/Professorin, *die* (of für); **b)** *(Amer.: teacher at university)* Dozent, *der*/Dozentin, *die*

**proficiency** [prə'fɪʃənsɪ] *n.* Können, *das*

**proficient** [prə'fɪʃənt] *adj.* fähig; gut ⟨*Pianist, Reiter usw.*⟩; geschickt ⟨*Radfahrer, Handwerker*⟩; **be ~ at** or **in maths** viel von Mathematik verstehen

**profile** ['prəʊfaɪl] *n.* **a)** *(side aspect)* Profil, *das;* **b)** *(biographical sketch)* Porträt, *das;* **c)** *(fig.)* **keep a low ~:** sich zurückhalten

**profit** ['prɒfɪt] *n.* Gewinn, *der;* Profit, *der;* **make a ~ from** or **out of sth.** mit etw. Geld verdienen; **make [a few pence] ~ on sth.** [ein paar Pfennige] an etw. *(Dat.)* verdienen. '**profit by** *v. t.* profitieren von; Nutzen ziehen aus ⟨*Fehler, Erfahrung*⟩. '**profit from** *v. t.* profitieren von

**profitable** ['prɒfɪtəbl] *adj.* rentabel; einträglich; *(fruitful)* nützlich

**profiteer** [prɒfɪ'tɪə(r)] **1.** *n.* Profitmacher, *der*/-macherin, *die.* **2.** *v. i.* sich bereichern. **profi'teering** *n.* Wucher, *der*

**profligate** ['prɒflɪgət] *adj.* verschwenderisch; **be ~ of** or **with sth.** verschwenderisch umgehen mit etw.

**profound** [prə'faʊnd] *adj.* tief; nachhaltig ⟨*Wirkung, Einfluß*⟩; tiefgreifend ⟨*Wandel, Veränderung*⟩; tiefempfunden ⟨*Beileid, Mitgefühl*⟩; tiefsitzend ⟨*Mißtrauen*⟩

**program** ['prəʊɡræm] **1.** *n.* **a)** *(Amer.)* see **programme 1; b)** *(Computing)* Programm, *das.* **2.** *v. t.,* **-mm-** *(Computing)* programmieren

**programme** ['prəʊɡræm] *n.* **a)** *([notice of] events)* Programm, *das;* **b)** *(Radio, Telev.)* Sendung, *die;* **c)** *(plan, instructions for machine)* Programm, *das*

**progress 1.** ['prəʊɡres] *n.* **a)** *no pl., no indef. art. (onward movement)* [Vorwärts]bewegung, *die; (advance)* Fortschritt, *der;* **make ~:** vorankommen; ⟨*Student, Patient:*⟩ Fortschritte ma

chen; **in ~:** im Gange. **2.** [prə'ɡres] *v. i.* **a)** *(move forward)* vorankommen; **b)** *(be carried on, develop)* Fortschritte machen. **progression** [prə'ɡreʃn] *n.* **a)** *(development)* Fortschritt, *der;* **b)** *(succession)* Folge, *die.* **progressive** [prə'ɡresɪv] *adj.* **a)** fortschreitend ⟨*Verbesserung, Verschlechterung*⟩; schrittweise ⟨*Reform*⟩; allmählich ⟨*Veränderung*⟩; **b)** *(favouring reform; in culture)* fortschrittlich; progressiv. **pro'gressively** *adv.* immer ⟨*schlechter, weiter*⟩

**prohibit** [prə'hɪbɪt] *v. t. (forbid)* verbieten; ~ **sb.'s doing sth.,** ~ **sb. from doing sth.** jmdm. verbieten, etw. zu tun. **prohibition** [prəʊhɪ'bɪʃn, prəʊɪ'bɪʃn] *n.* Verbot, *das.* **prohibitive** [prə'hɪbɪtɪv] *adj.* unerschwinglich ⟨*Preis, Miete*⟩; untragbar ⟨*Kosten*⟩

**project 1.** [prə'dʒekt] *v. t.* werfen ⟨*Schein*⟩; senden ⟨*Strahl*⟩; *(Cinemat.)* projizieren. **2.** [prə'dʒekt] *v. i. (jut out)* ⟨*Felsen:*⟩ vorspringen; ⟨*Zähne, Brauen:*⟩ vorstehen. **3.** ['prɒdʒekt] *n.* Projekt, *das*

**projectile** [prə'dʒektaɪl] *n.* Geschoß, *das*

**projection** [prə'dʒekʃn] *n.* **a)** *(protruding thing)* Vorsprung, *der;* **b)** *(estimate)* Hochrechnung, *die; (forecast)* Voraussage, *die*

**projector** [prə'dʒektə(r)] *n.* Projektor, *der*

**proliferate** [prə'lɪfəreɪt] *v. i. (increase)* sich ausbreiten. **proliferation** [prəlɪfə'reɪʃn] *n.* starke Zunahme

**prolific** [prə'lɪfɪk] *adj.* **a)** *(fertile)* fruchtbar; **b)** *(productive)* produktiv

**prologue** *(Amer.:* **prolog)** ['prəʊlɒɡ] *n.* Prolog, *der* (to zu)

**prolong** [prə'lɒŋ] *v. t.* verlängern. **prolonged** [prə'lɒŋd] *adj.* lang; lang anhaltend ⟨*Beifall*⟩

**promenade** [prɒmə'nɑ:d] *n.* Promenade, *die*

**prominence** ['prɒmɪnəns] *n.* **a)** *(conspicuousness)* Auffälligkeit, *die;* **b)** *(distinction)* Bekanntheit, *die*

**prominent** ['prɒmɪnənt] *adj.* **a)** *(conspicuous)* auffallend; **b)** *(foremost)* herausragend; **he was ~ in politics** er war ein prominenter Politiker; **c)** *(projecting)* vorspringend; vorstehend ⟨*Backenknochen, Brauen*⟩

**promiscuity** [prɒmɪ'skju:ɪtɪ] *n.* Promiskuität, *die (geh.)*

**promiscuous** [prə'mɪskjʊəs] *adj.* promiskuitiv *(geh.);* **a ~ man** ein Mann, der häufig die Partnerin wechselt

**promise** ['prɒmɪs] **1.** *n.* **a)** Versprechen, *das;* **sb.'s ~s** jmds. Versprechungen; **give** *or* **make a ~** |to sb.| [jmdm.] ein Versprechen geben; **give** *or* **make a ~** |to sb.| **to do sth.** [jmdm.] versprechen, etw. zu tun; **b)** *(fig.: reason for expectation)* Hoffnung, *die;* **a painter of** *or* **with ~:** ein vielversprechender Maler. **2.** *v.t.* **a)** versprechen; **~ sth. to sb., ~ sb. sth.** jmdm. etw. versprechen; **b)** *(fig.: give reason for expectation of)* verheißen *(geh.);* **~ sb. sth.** jmdm. etw. in Aussicht stellen. **3.** *v.i.* **~ well** *or* **favourably** vielversprechend sein; **I can't ~:** ich kann es nicht versprechen. **promising** ['prɒmɪsɪŋ] *adj.* vielversprechend

**promote** [prə'məʊt] *v.t.* **a)** *(to more senior job)* befördern; **b)** *(encourage)* fördern; **c)** *(publicize)* Werbung machen für; **d)** *(Footb.)* **be ~d** aufsteigen. **pro'moter** *n.* Veranstalter, *der/*Veranstalterin, *die.* **promotion** [prə'məʊʃn] *n.* **a)** Beförderung, *die;* **win** *or* **gain ~:** befördert werden; **b)** *(furtherance)* Förderung, *die;* **c)** *(publicization)* Werbung, *die; (instance)* Werbekampagne, *die;* **d)** *(Footb.)* Aufstieg, *der.* **promotional** [prə'məʊʃənl] *adj.* Werbe⟨*kampagne, -broschüre usw.*⟩

**prompt** [prɒmpt] **1.** *adj.* **a)** *(ready to act)* bereitwillig; **be ~ in doing sth.** *or* **to do sth.** etw. unverzüglich tun; **b)** *(done readily)* sofortig; **her ~ answer** ihre prompte Antwort; **take ~ action** sofort handeln; **c)** *(punctual)* pünktlich. **2.** *adv.* pünktlich; **at 6 o'clock ~:** Punkt 6 Uhr. **3.** *v.t.* **a)** *(incite)* veranlassen; **b)** *(supply with words)* soufflieren (+ *Dat.*); *(give suggestion to)* weiterhelfen (+ *Dat.*); **c)** hervorrufen ⟨*Kritik*⟩; provozieren ⟨*Antwort*⟩. **'promptly** *adv.* **a)** *(quickly)* prompt; **b)** *(punctually)* pünktlich

**prone** [prəʊn] *adj.* **a)** *(liable)* **be ~ to** anfällig sein für ⟨*Krankheiten*⟩; **be ~ to do sth.** dazu neigen, etw. zu tun

**prong** [prɒŋ] *n. (of fork)* Zinke, *die*

**pronoun** ['prəʊnaʊn] *n. (Ling.)* Pronomen, *das;* Fürwort, *das*

**pronounce** [prə'naʊns] **1.** *v.t.* **a)** *(declare)* verkünden; **~ sb./sth.** |to be| **sth.** jmdn./etw. für etw. erklären; **~ sb. fit for work** jmdn. für arbeitsfähig erklären; **b)** aussprechen ⟨*Wort, Buchstaben usw.*⟩. **2.** *v.i.* **~ on sth.** zu etw. Stellung nehmen; **~ for** *or* **in favour of/against sth.** sich für/gegen etw. aussprechen. **pronounced** [prə-

'naʊnst] *adj. (marked)* ausgeprägt. **pro'nouncement** *n.* Erklärung, *die;* **make a ~** |about sth.| eine Erklärung [zu etw.] abgeben

**pronunciation** [prənʌnsɪ'eɪʃn] *n.* Aussprache, *die;* **what is the ~ of this word?** wie wird dieses Wort ausgesprochen?

**proof** [pru:f] **1.** *n.* **a)** *(fact, evidence)* Beweis, *der;* **b)** *no indef. art. (Law)* Beweismaterial, *das;* **c)** *(proving)* **in ~ of** (+ *Gen.*); **d)** *no art. (standard of strength)* Proof *o.* Art.; **100° ~** *(Brit.)*, **128° ~** *(Amer.)* 64 Vol.-% Alkohol; **e)** *(Printing)* Abzug, *der.* **2.** *adj.* **a)** **be ~ against sth.** unempfindlich gegen etw. sein; *(fig.)* gegen etw. immun sein; **b)** *in comb.* ⟨*kugel-, einbruch-, idioten*⟩sicher; ⟨*schall-, wasser*⟩dicht; **flame-~:** nicht brennbar

**'proof-read** *v.t.* Korrektur lesen. **'proof-reader** *n.* Korrektor, *der/*Korrektorin, *die*

**prop** [prɒp] **1.** *n.* Stütze, *die; (Mining)* Strebe, *die.* **2.** *v.t.,* **-pp-** stützen; **the ladder was ~ped against the house** die Leiter war gegen das Haus gelehnt. **prop 'up** *v.t.* stützen; *(fig.)* vor dem Konkurs bewahren ⟨*Firma*⟩; stützen ⟨*Regierung*⟩

**propaganda** [prɒpə'gændə] *n.* Propaganda, *die*

**propagate** ['prɒpəgeɪt] **1.** *v.t.* **a)** *(Hort., Agric.)* vermehren **(from, by** durch); **b)** *(spread)* verbreiten. **2.** *v.i.* **a)** *(Bot.)* sich vermehren; **b)** *(spread)* sich ausbreiten. **propagation** [prɒpə'geɪʃn] *n.* **a)** *(Hort., Agric.)* Züchtung, *die;* **b)** *(Bot.)* Vermehrung, *die;* **c)** *(spreading)* Verbreitung, *die*

**propel** [prə'pel] *v.t.,* **-ll-** antreiben. **pro'peller** *n.* Propeller, *der.* **propelling 'pencil** *n. (Brit.)* Drehbleistift, *der*

**propensity** [prə'pensɪtɪ] *n.* **have a ~ to do sth.** *or* **for doing sth.** dazu neigen, etw. zu tun

**proper** ['prɒpə(r)] *adj.* **a)** *(accurate)* richtig; zutreffend ⟨*Beschreibung*⟩; eigentlich ⟨*Wortbedeutung*⟩; **b)** *postpos. (strictly so called)* im engeren Sinn nachgestellt; **in London ~:** in London selbst; **c)** *(genuine)* echt; richtig ⟨*Wirbelsturm, Schauspieler*⟩; **d)** *(satisfactory)* richtig; zufriedenstellend ⟨*Antwort*⟩; **e)** *(suitable)* angemessen; *(morally fitting)* gebührend; **do sth. the ~ way** etw. richtig machen; **f)** *attrib.*

**properly** *(coll.: thorough)* richtig. **'properly** *adv.* richtig; *(rightly)* zu Recht; ~ **speaking** genaugenommen

**proper:** ~ **'name,** ~ **'noun** *ns. (Ling.)* Eigenname, *der*

**property** ['prɒpətɪ] *n.* **a)** *(possession[s])* Eigentum, *das;* **b)** *(estate)* Besitz, *der;* Immobilie, *die (fachspr.);* **c)** *(attribute)* Eigenschaft, *die; (effect, special power)* Wirkung, *die*

**prophecy** ['prɒfɪsɪ] *n. (prediction)* Vorhersage, *die; (prophetic utterance)* Prophezeiung, *die*

**prophesy** ['prɒfɪsaɪ] *v. t. (predict)* vorhersagen; *(fig.)* prophezeien ⟨*Unglück*⟩; *(as fortune-teller)* weissagen

**prophet** ['prɒfɪt] *n.* Prophet, *der.* **prophetic** [prə'fetɪk] *adj.* prophetisch

**proportion** [prə'pɔːʃn] **1.** *n.* **a)** *(portion)* Teil, *der;* **b)** *(ratio)* Verhältnis, *das;* **the** ~ **of sth. to sth.** das Verhältnis von etw. zu etw.; **c)** *(correct relation; Math.)* Proportion, *die;* **be in** ~ |**to** *or* **with sth.**| im richtigen Verhältnis [zu *od.* mit etw.] stehen; **keep things in** ~ *(fig.)* die Dinge im richtigen Licht sehen; **be out of** ~/**all** *or* **any** ~ |**to** *or* **with sth.**| in keinem/keinerlei Verhältnis zu etw. stehen; **d)** *in pl. (size)* Dimension, *die.* **2.** *v. t.* proportionieren. **proportional** [prə'pɔːʃənl] *adj.* **a)** *(in proportion)* entsprechend; **be** ~ **to sth.** einer Sache *(Dat.)* entsprechen; **b)** *(Math.)* **be directly/indirectly** ~ **to sth.** einer Sache *(Dat.)* direkt/umgekehrt proportional sein. **proportionate** [prə'pɔːʃənət] *see* **proportional a**

**proposal** [prə'pəʊzl] *n.* Vorschlag, *der; (offer)* Angebot, *das;* ~ |**of marriage**| [Heirats]antrag, *der*

**propose** [prə'pəʊz] **1.** *v. t.* **a)** vorschlagen; ~ **sth. to sb.** jmdm. etw. vorschlagen; ~ **marriage** |**to sb.**| [jmdm.] einen Heiratsantrag machen; **b)** *(nominate)* ~ **sb. as/for sth.** jmdn. als/für etw. vorschlagen; **c)** *(intend)* ~ **doing** *or* **to do sth.** beabsichtigen, etw. zu tun. **2.** *v. i. (offer marriage)* ~ |**to sb.**| jmdm. einen Heiratsantrag machen. **proposition** [prɒpə'zɪʃn] *n.* **a)** *(proposal)* Vorschlag, *der;* **make** *or* **put a** ~ **to sb.** jmdm. einen Vorschlag machen; **b)** *(statement; Logic)* Aussage, *die*

**propound** [prə'paʊnd] *v. t.* darlegen

**proprietary** [prə'praɪətərɪ] *adj.* ~ **name** *or* **term** Markenname, *der*

**proprietor** [prə'praɪətə(r)] *n.* Inhaber, *der*/Inhaberin, *die*

**propriety** [prə'praɪətɪ] *n.* Anstand, *der;* **breach of** ~: Verstoß gegen die guten Sitten

**propulsion** [prə'pʌlʃn] *n.* Antrieb, *der*

**prosaic** [prə'zeɪk] *adj.* prosaisch *(geh.);* nüchtern

**proscribe** [prə'skraɪb] *v. t.* verbieten

**prose** [prəʊz] *n.* Prosa, *die; attrib.* Prosa⟨*werk, -stil*⟩

**prosecute** ['prɒsɪkjuːt] **1.** *v. t.* strafrechtlich verfolgen; ~ **sb. for sth.**/**doing sth.** jmdn. wegen etw. strafrechtlich verfolgen/jmdn. strafrechtlich verfolgen, weil er etw. tut/getan hat. **2.** *v. i.* Anzeige erstatten. **prosecution** [prɒsɪ'kjuːʃn] *n. (bringing to trial)* [strafrechtliche] Verfolgung; *(court procedure)* Anklage, *die; (prosecuting party)* Anklage[vertretung], *die;* **the** ~: die Anklage. **prosecutor** ['prɒsɪkjuːtə(r)] *n.* Ankläger, *der*/Anklägerin, *die;* **public** ~ ≈ Generalstaatsanwalt, *der*/-anwältin, *die*

**prospect 1.** ['prɒspekt] *n.* **a)** *(expectation)* Erwartung, *die (of* hinsichtlich*);* |**at the**| ~ **of sth.**/**doing sth.** [bei der] Aussicht auf etw.*(Akk.)*/[darauf], etw. zu tun; **b)** *in pl. (hope of success)* Zukunftsaussichten; **a man with** |**good**| ~**s** ein Mann mit Zukunft; **sb.'s** ~**s of sth.**/**doing sth.** jmds. Chancen auf etw. *(Akk.)*/darauf, etw. zu tun; **the** ~**s for sb.**/**sth.** die Aussichten für jmdn./etw. **2.** [prə'spekt] *v. i.* nach Bodenschätzen suchen. **prospective** [prə'spektɪv] *adj.* voraussichtlich; zukünftig ⟨*Erbe, Braut*⟩; potentiell ⟨*Käufer, Kandidat*⟩. **prospector** [prə'spektə(r)] *n.* Prospektor, *der; (for gold)* Goldsucher, *der*

**prospectus** [prə'spektəs] *n.* Prospekt, *der; (Brit. Univ.)* Studienführer, *der*

**prosper** ['prɒspə(r)] *v. i.* gedeihen; ⟨*Geschäft:*⟩ florieren; ⟨*Berufstätiger:*⟩ Erfolg haben. **prosperity** [prɒ'sperɪtɪ] *n.* Wohlstand, *der.* **prosperous** ['prɒspərəs] *adj.* wohlhabend; florierend ⟨*Unternehmen*⟩

**prostitute** ['prɒstɪtjuːt] *n.* Prostituierte, *die.* **prostitution** [prɒstɪ'tjuːʃn] *n.* Prostitution, *die*

**prostrate 1.** ['prɒstreɪt] *adj.* [auf dem Bauch] ausgestreckt. **2.** [prə'streɪt] *v. refl.* ~ **oneself** |**at sth.**/**before sb.**| sich [vor etw./jmdm.] niederwerfen

**protagonist** [prəʊ'tægənɪst] *n. (Lit.)* Protagonist, *der*/Protagonistin, *die*

**protect** [prə'tekt] *v. t.* **a)** schützen **(from** vor + *Dat.,* **against** gegen); **b)** *(preserve)* unter [Natur]schutz stellen

⟨*Pflanze, Tier*⟩. **protection** [prə-'tekʃn] *n.* Schutz, *der* (**from** vor + *Dat.*, **against** gegen). **protective** [prə'tektɪv] *adj.* schützend; Schutz-⟨*hülle, -anstrich, -vorrichtung, -maske*⟩; **be ~ towards sb.** fürsorglich genüber jmdm. sein

**protein** ['prəʊtiːn] *n.* Protein, *das* (*fachspr.*); Eiweiß, *das*

**protest** 1. ['prəʊtest] *n.* **a)** Beschwerde, *die*; **make** *or* **lodge a ~ |against sb./ sth.|** eine Beschwerde |gegen jmdn./ etw.| einreichen; **b)** *(gesture of disapproval)* ~|s| Protest, *der*; **under ~:** unter Protest; **in ~ |against sth.|** aus Protest |gegen etw.|; **c)** *no art. (dissent)* Protest, *der.* 2. [prə'test] *v. t. (affirm)* beteuern. 3. [prə'test] *v. i.* protestieren (**about** gegen); *(make written or formal ~)* Protest einlegen (**to** bei)

**Protestant** ['prɒtɪstənt] 1. *n.* Protestant, *der*/Protestantin, *die.* 2. *adj.* protestantisch; evangelisch

**pro'tester** *n.* Protestierende, *der/die*; *(at demonstration)* Demonstrant, *der*/ Demonstrantin, *die*

**protocol** ['prəʊtəkɒl] *n.* Protokoll, *das*

**proton** ['prəʊtən] *n.* Proton, *das*

**prototype** ['prəʊtətaɪp] *n.* Prototyp, *der*

**protract** [prə'trækt] *v. t.* verlängern.

**protractor** [prə'træktə(r)] *n. (Geom.)* Winkelmesser, *der*

**protrude** [prə'truːd] *v. i.* herausragen (**from** aus); ⟨*Zähne*⟩ vorstehen

**proud** [praʊd] 1. *adj.* **a)** stolz; **~ to do sth.** *or* **to be doing sth.** stolz darauf, etw. zu tun; **~ of sb./sth./doing sth.** stolz auf jmdn./etw./darauf, etw. zu tun; **b)** *(arrogant)* hochmütig. 2. *adv. (Brit. coll.)* **do sb. ~:** jmdn. verwöhnen. **'proudly** *adv.* stolz; *(arrogantly)* hochmütig

**prove** [pruːv] 1. *v. t., p.p.* ~**d** *or* **proven** ['pruːvn] beweisen; nachweisen ⟨*Identität*⟩; **~ one's ability** sein Können unter Beweis stellen; **~ sb. right/ wrong** ⟨*Ereignis:*⟩ jmdm. recht/unrecht geben; **be ~d wrong** *or* **to be false** ⟨*Theorie:*⟩ widerlegt werden; **~ one's/sb.'s case** *or* **point** beweisen, daß man recht hat/jmdm. recht geben. 2. *v. refl., p. p.* **proved** *or* **proven:** **~ oneself** sich bewähren. 3. *v. i., p. p.* **proved** *or* **proven:** **~ |to be|** sich erweisen als

**proven** *see* **prove**

**proverb** ['prɒvɜːb] *n.* Sprichwort, *das.* **proverbial** [prə'vɜːbɪəl] *adj.* sprichwörtlich

**provide** [prə'vaɪd] *v. t.* **a)** besorgen; liefern ⟨*Beweis*⟩; bereitstellen ⟨*Dienst, Geld*⟩; **~ a home/a car for sb.** jmdm. Unterkunft/ein Auto [zur Verfügung] stellen; **b)** ⟨*Vertrag, Gesetz:*⟩ vorsehen. **pro'vide for** *v. t.* **a)** *(make provision for)* vorsorgen für; ⟨*Plan, Gesetz:*⟩ vorsehen; **b)** *(maintain)* sorgen für, versorgen ⟨*Familie, Kind*⟩. **pro'vided** *conj.* **~ |that|** ...: vorausgesetzt, [daß] ...

**providence** ['prɒvɪdəns] *n.* **a) |divine| ~:** die [göttliche] Vorsehung; **b)** **P~** *(God)* der Himmel

**province** ['prɒvɪns] *n.* **a)** Provinz, *die*; **b) the ~s** *(regions outside capital)* die Provinz; **c)** *(sphere of action)* [Tätigkeits]bereich, *der*; *(area of responsibility)* Zuständigkeitsbereich, *der.*

**provincial** [prə'vɪnʃl] *adj.* Provinz-

**provision** [prə'vɪʒn] *n.* **a)** *(providing)* Bereitstellung, *die*; **make ~ for** vorsorgen *od*. Vorsorge treffen für ⟨*Notfall*⟩; **b)** **~s** *pl. (food)* Lebensmittel

**provisional** [prə'vɪʒənl] *adj.*, **provisionally** [prə'vɪʒənəlɪ] *adv.* vorläufig; provisorisch

**proviso** [prə'vaɪzəʊ] *n., pl.* **~s** Vorbehalt, *der*

**provocation** [prɒvə'keɪʃn] *n.* Provokation, *die*

**provocative** [prə'vɒkətɪv] *adj.* provozierend; *(sexually)* aufreizend

**provoke** [prə'vəʊk] *v. t.* **a)** provozieren ⟨*Person*⟩; reizen ⟨*Person, Tier*⟩; **~ sb. into doing sth.** jmdn. so sehr provozieren, daß er etw. tut; **b)** *(give rise to)* hervorrufen; erregen

**prow** [praʊ] *n. (Naut.)* Bug, *der*

**prowl** [praʊl] 1. *v. i.* streifen. 2. *v. t.* durchstreifen. 3. *n.* **be on the ~:** auf einem Streifzug sein

**proximity** [prɒk'sɪmɪtɪ] *n.* Nähe, *die*

**proxy** ['prɒksɪ] *n.* **by ~:** durch einen Bevollmächtigten/eine Bevollmächtigte

**prude** [pruːd] *n.* prüder Mensch

**prudence** ['pruːdəns] *n.* Besonnenheit, *die*

**prudent** ['pruːdənt] *adj.* **a)** *(careful)* besonnen; **b)** *(circumspect)* vorsichtig

**prudish** ['pruːdɪʃ] *adj.* prüde

**¹prune** [pruːn] *n.* Backpflaume, *die*

**²prune** *v. t.* **a)** *(trim)* [be]schneiden; **b)** *(fig.)* reduzieren

**pry** [praɪ] *v. i.* neugierig sein. **'pry into** *v. t.* seine Nase stecken in (+ *Akk.*) *(ugs.)* ⟨*Angelegenheit*⟩

**PS** *abbr.* **postscript** PS

**psalm** [sɑːm] *n.* Psalm, *der*

**pseudonym** ['sju:dənım] *n.* Pseudonym, *das*

**psychiatric** [saıkı'ætrık] *adj.* psychiatrisch

**psychiatrist** [saı'kaıətrıst] *n.* Psychiater, *der*/Psychiaterin, *die*

**psychiatry** [saı'kaıətrı] *n.* Psychiatrie, *die*

**psychic** ['saıkık] *adj.* be ~: übernatürliche Fähigkeiten haben

**psychoanalyse** [saıkəʊænəlaız] *v.t.* psychoanalysieren. **psychoa'nalysis** *n.* Psychoanalyse, *die.* **psycho'analyst** *n.* Psychoanalytiker, *der*/-analytikerin, *die*

**psychological** [saıkə'lɒdʒıkl] *adj.* psychologisch; psychisch ⟨*Problem*⟩

**psychologist** [saı'kɒlədʒıst] *n.* Psychologe, *der*/Psychologin, *die*

**psychology** [saı'kɒlədʒı] *n.* Psychologie, *die*

**psychopath** ['saıkəpæθ] *n.* Psychopath, *der*/Psychopathin, *die*

**PTO** *abbr.* please turn over b. w.

**pub** [pʌb] *n. (Brit. coll.)* Kneipe, *die (ugs.)*

**puberty** ['pju:bətı] *n., no art.* Pubertät, *die*

**public** ['pʌblık] **1.** *adj.* öffentlich; **make sth. ~:** etw. bekannt machen. **2.** *n., sing. or pl.* **a)** *(the people)* Öffentlichkeit, *die;* **b)** *(section of community)* Publikum, *das;* **c)** **in ~:** öffentlich

**publican** ['pʌblıkən] *n. (Brit.)* [Gast]wirt, *der*/-wirtin, *die*

**publication** [pʌblı'keıʃn] *n.* Veröffentlichung, *die*

**public:** **~ con'venience** *n.* öffentliche Toilette; **~ 'holiday** *n.* gesetzlicher Feiertag; **~ 'house** *n. (Brit.)* Gastwirtschaft, *die;* Gaststätte, *die*

**publicity** [pʌb'lısıtı] *n.* Publicity, *die; (advertising)* Werbung, *die;* **~ campaign** Werbekampagne, *die*

**publicize** ['pʌblısaız] *v.t.* publik machen ⟨*Ungerechtigkeit*⟩; werben für, Reklame machen für ⟨*Produkt*⟩

**public 'library** *n.* öffentliche Bücherei

**'publicly** *adv.* öffentlich; **~ owned** staatseigen

**public:** **~ re'lations** *n., sing. or pl.* Public Relations *Pl.;* **~ school** *n.* **a)** *(Brit.)* Privatschule, *die;* **b)** *(Scot., Amer.)* staatliche *od.* öffentliche Schule; **~ 'transport** *n.* öffentlicher Personenverkehr

**publish** ['pʌblıʃ] *v.t.* ⟨*Verlag:*⟩ verlegen ⟨*Buch, Zeitschrift, Musik usw.*⟩;

⟨*Autor:*⟩ veröffentlichen ⟨*Text*⟩. **'publisher** *n.* Verleger, *der*/Verlegerin, *die;* **~[s]** *(company)* Verlag, *der.* **'publishing** *n., no art.* Verlagswesen, *das*

**puck** [pʌk] *n. (Ice Hockey)* Puck, *der*

**pucker** ['pʌkə(r)] **1.** *v.t.* ~ |up| runzeln ⟨*Brauen, Stirn*⟩; kräuseln ⟨*Lippen*⟩. **2.** *v.i.* ~ |up| ⟨*Stoff:*⟩ sich kräuseln

**pudding** ['pʊdıŋ] *n.* **a)** Pudding, *der;* **b)** *(dessert)* süße Nachspeise

**puddle** ['pʌdl] *n.* Pfütze, *die*

**puerile** ['pjʊəraıl] *adj.* kindisch

**puff** [pʌf] **1.** *n.* **a)** Stoß, *der;* **~ of breath/wind** Atem-/Windstoß, *der;* **b)** **~ of smoke** Rauchstoß, *der;* **c)** *(pastry)* Blätterteigteilchen, *das.* **2.** *v.i.* **a)** ~ |and blow| schnaufen [und keuchen]; **b)** *(~ cigarette smoke etc.)* paffen *(ugs.)* (at an + *Dat.*); **c)** ⟨*Person:*⟩ keuchen; ⟨*Zug, Lokomotive:*⟩ schnaufend fahren. **3.** *v.t.* blasen ⟨*Rauch*⟩; stäuben ⟨*Puder*⟩. **puff 'out** *v.t.* **a)** bauschen ⟨*Segel*⟩; **b)** *(put out of breath)* außer Atem bringen ⟨*Person*⟩; **be ~ed |out|** außer Atem sein

**puff 'pastry** *n.* Blätterteig, *der*

**puffy** ['pʌfı] *adj.* verschwollen

**pugnacious** [pʌg'neıʃəs] *adj.* kampflustig

**pull** [pʊl] **1.** *v.t.* **a)** *(draw, tug)* ziehen an (+ *Dat.*); ziehen ⟨*Hebel*⟩; **~ sb.'s or sb. by the hair/ears/sleeve** jmdn. an den Haaren/Ohren/am Ärmel ziehen; **~ sth. over one's ears/head** sich *(Dat.)* etw. über die Ohren/den Kopf ziehen; **~ to pieces** in Stücke reißen; *(fig.)* zerpflücken ⟨*Argument usw.*⟩; **b)** *(extract)* [her]ausziehen; [heraus]ziehen ⟨*Zahn*⟩; **c)** *(strain)* sich *(Dat.)* zerren ⟨*Muskel*⟩. **2.** *v.i.* **a)** ziehen; **'P~'' „Ziehen''; **b)** ~ |to the left/right| ⟨*Auto, Boot:*⟩ [nach links/rechts] ziehen; **c)** *(pluck)* ~ **at** ziehen an (+ *Dat.*); ~ **at sb.'s sleeve** jmdn. am Ärmel ziehen. **3.** *n.* **a)** Zug, *der;* **b)** *(influence)* Einfluß, *der* (with auf + *Akk.,* bei). **pull a'part** *v.t.* **a)** *(take to pieces)* auseinandernehmen; **b)** *(fig.: criticize)* zerpflücken; verreißen ⟨*Buch, [literarisches] Werk*⟩. **pull 'down** *v.t.* **a)** herunterziehen; **b)** *(demolish)* abreißen. **pull 'in 1.** *v.t.* hereinziehen. **2.** *v.i.* **a)** ⟨*Zug:*⟩ einfahren; **b)** *(move to side of road)* an die Seite fahren; *(stop)* anhalten. **pull 'off** *v.t.* **a)** *(remove)* abziehen; *(violently)* abreißen; **b)** *(accomplish)* an Land ziehen *(ugs.).* **pull 'out 1.** *v.t.* herausziehen. **2.** *v.i.* **a)** *(depart)* abfahren; **b)**

*(away from roadside)* ausscheren. **pull 'through** *v. i.* ⟨*Patient:*⟩ durchkommen. **pull to'gether** *v. refl.* sich zusammennehmen. **pull up 1.** *v. t.* **a)** hochziehen; **b)** [he]rausziehen ⟨*Unkraut, Pflanze*⟩; **c)** *(reprimand)* zurechtweisen. **2.** *v. i. (stop)* anhalten.

**pulley** [ˈpʊlı] *n.* Rolle, *die*

**pullover** [ˈpʊləʊvə(r)] *n.* Pullover, *der*

**pulp** [pʌlp] **1.** *n.* Brei, *der.* **2.** *v. t.* zerdrücken ⟨*Rübe*⟩; einstampfen ⟨*Druckerzeugnis*⟩

**pulpit** [ˈpʊlpɪt] *n.* Kanzel, *die*

**pulsate** [pʊlˈseɪt] *v. i.* pulsieren

**¹pulse** [pʌls] *n.* Puls, *der; (single beat)* Pulsschlag, *der*

**²pulse** *n. (Cookery)* Hülsenfrucht, *die*

**pulverize** [ˈpʌlvəraɪz] *v. t.* pulverisieren

**puma** [ˈpjuːmə] *n.* Puma, *der*

**pumice** [ˈpʌmɪs] *n.* ~[-stone] Bimsstein, *der*

**pummel** [ˈpʌml] *v. t., (Brit)* -ll- einschlagen auf (+ *Akk.*)

**pump** [pʌmp] **1.** *n.* Pumpe, *die.* **2.** *v. i.* pumpen. **3.** *v. t.* pumpen; ~ sth. dry etw. leerpumpen; ~ sb. for **information** Auskünfte aus jmdm. herausholen; ~ up aufpumpen

**pumpkin** [ˈpʌmpkɪn] *n.* Kürbis, *der*

**pun** [pʌn] *n.* Wortspiel, *das*

**¹punch 1.** *v. t.* **a)** *(with fist)* boxen; **b)** *(pierce)* lochen; ~ a hole ein Loch stanzen; ~ a hole/holes in sth. etw. lochen. **2.** *n.* **a)** *(blow)* Faustschlag, *der;* **b)** *(for making holes) (in leather, tickets)* Lochzange, *die; (in paper)* Locher, *der*

**²punch** *n. (drink)* Punsch, *der*

**punch:** ~ line *n.* Pointe, *die;* ~-up *n. (Brit. coll.)* Prügelei, *die*

**punctual** [ˈpʌŋktjʊəl] *adj.* pünktlich. **punctuality** [pʌŋktjʊˈælɪtɪ] *n.* Pünktlichkeit, *die.* **punctually** *adv.* pünktlich

**punctuate** [pʌŋktjʊəɪt] *v. t.* mit Satzzeichen versehen. **punctuation** [pʌŋktjʊˈeɪʃn] *n.* Zeichensetzung, *die.* **punctu'ation mark** *n.* Satzzeichen, *das*

**puncture** [ˈpʌŋktʃə(r)] **1.** *n.* **a)** *(flat tyre)* Reifenpanne, *die;* **b)** *(hole)* Loch, *das.* **2.** *v. t.* durchstechen; be ~d ⟨*Reifen:*⟩ platt sein

**pundit** [ˈpʌndɪt] *n.* Experte, *der*/Expertin, *die*

**pungent** [ˈpʌndʒənt] *adj.* beißend, ätzend ⟨*Rauch*⟩; scharf ⟨*Soße*⟩; stechend riechend ⟨*Gas*⟩

**punish** [ˈpʌnɪʃ] *v. t.* bestrafen. **punishable** [ˈpʌnɪʃəbl] *adj.* strafbar. **'punishment** *n.* **a)** *(punishing)* Bestrafung, *die;* **b)** *(penalty)* Strafe, *die*

**punitive** [ˈpjuːnɪtɪv] *adj.* **a)** *(penal)* Straf-; **b)** *(severe)* [allzu] rigoros

**punk** [pʌŋk] *n.* **a)** *(Amer. sl.: worthless person)* Dreckskerl, *der (salopp);* **b)** *(admirer of ~ rock)* Punk, *der; (performer)* Punk[rock]er, *der*/-[rock]erin, *die;* **c)** *(music)* Punkrock, *der*

**punt** [pʌnt] *n.* Stechkahn, *der*

**puny** [ˈpjuːnɪ] *adj.* **a)** *(undersized)* zu klein ⟨*Baby, Junge*⟩; **b)** *(feeble)* gering ⟨*Kraft*⟩; schwach ⟨*Waffe, Person*⟩

**pup** [pʌp] *n.* Welpe, *der*

**pupa** [ˈpjuːpə] *n., pl.* ~e [ˈpjuːpiː] Puppe, *die.* **pupate** [pjuːˈpeɪt] *v. i.* sich verpuppen

**pupil** [ˈpjuːpɪl] *n.* **a)** Schüler, *der*/Schülerin, *die;* **b)** *(Anat.)* Pupille, *die*

**puppet** [ˈpʌpɪt] *n.* Puppe, *die; (marionette; also fig.)* Marionette, *die*

**puppy** [ˈpʌpɪ] *n.* Hundejunge, *das;* Welpe, *der*

**purchase** [ˈpɜːtʃəs] **1.** *n.* **a)** Kauf, *der;* **make a ~:** etwas kaufen; **b)** *(hold)* Halt, *der; (leverage)* Hebelwirkung, *die.* **2.** *v. t.* kaufen. **'purchaser** *n.* Käufer, *der*/Käuferin, *die*

**pure** [pjʊə(r)] *adj.* rein

**purée** [ˈpjʊəreɪ] *n.* Püree, *das*

**'purely** *adv.* **a)** *(solely)* rein; **b)** *(merely)* lediglich

**purgatory** [ˈpɜːgətərı] *n.* it was ~ *(fig.)* es war eine Strafe

**purge** [pɜːdʒ] **1.** *v. t.* **a)** *(cleanse)* reinigen (of von); **b)** *(remove)* entfernen; **c)** *(rid)* säubern ⟨*Partei*⟩ (of von). **2.** *n.* Säuberung[saktion], *die*

**purification** [pjʊərɪfɪˈkeɪʃn] *n.* Reinigung, *die*

**purify** [ˈpjʊərɪfaɪ] *v. t.* reinigen

**purist** [ˈpjʊərɪst] *n.* Purist, *der*/Puristin, *die*

**puritan,** *(Hist.)* **Puritan** [ˈpjʊərɪtn] *n.* Puritaner, *der*/Puritanerin, *die.* **puritanical** [pjʊərɪˈtænɪkl] *adj.* puritanisch

**purity** [ˈpjʊərɪtɪ] *n.* Reinheit, *die*

**purl** [pɜːl] **1.** *n.* linke Masche. **2.** *v. t.* ~ three [stitches] drei linke Maschen stricken

**purple** [ˈpɜːpl] **1.** *adj.* lila; violett. **2.** *n.* Lila, *das;* Violett, *das*

**purport** [pəˈpɔːt] *v. t.* ~ to do sth. *(profess)* [von sich] behaupten, etw. zu tun; *(be intended to seem)* den Anschein erwecken sollen, etw. zu tun

**purpose** ['pɜːpəs] n. a) (object) Zweck, der; (intention) Absicht, die; what is the ~ of doing that? was hat es für einen Zweck, das zu tun?; on ~: mit Absicht; absichtlich; b) (effect) to no ~: ohne Erfolg; to some/good ~: mit einigem/gutem Erfolg; c) (determination) Entschlossenheit, die. **purposeful** ['pɜːpəsfl] adj. zielstrebig; (with specific aim) entschlossen. 'purposely adv. absichtlich

**purr** [pɜː(r)] 1. v.i. schnurren. 2. n. Schnurren, das

**purse** [pɜːs] 1. n. Portemonnaie, das. 2. v.t. kräuseln ⟨Lippen⟩

**purser** ['pɜːsə(r)] n. Zahlmeister, der/ -meisterin, die

**pursue** [pə'sjuː] v.t. a) (chase) verfolgen; b) (look into) nachgehen (+ Dat.); c) (engage in) betreiben. **pursuer** [pə'sjuːə(r)] n. Verfolger, der/Verfolgerin, die. **pursuit** [pə'sjuːt] n. a) Verfolgung, die; (of knowledge, truth, etc.) Streben, das (of nach); in ~ of auf der Jagd nach ⟨Wild, Dieb usw.⟩; in Ausführung (+ Gen.) ⟨Beschäftigung⟩; with the police in |full| ~: mit der Polizei [dicht] auf den Fersen; b) (pastime) Beschäftigung, die

**pus** [pʌs] n. Eiter, der

**push** [pʊʃ] 1. v.t. a) schieben; (make fall) stoßen; drücken gegen ⟨Tür⟩; ~ one's way through/into/on to etc. sth. sich (Dat.) einen Weg durch/in/auf usw. etw. (Akk.) bahnen; b) (fig.: impel) drängen; c) (tax) ~ sb. |hard| jmdn. [stark] fordern; be ~ed for sth. (coll.: find it difficult to provide sth.) mit etw. knapp sein; be ~ed for money or cash knapp bei Kasse sein (ugs.); d) (sell illegally, esp. drugs) pushen (Drogenjargon). 2. v.i. a) schieben; (in queue) drängeln; (at door) drücken; ~ and shove schubsen und drängeln; b) (make demands) ~ for sth. etw. fordern; c) (make one's way) he ~ed between us er drängte sich zwischen uns; ~ through the crowd sich durch die Menge drängeln. 3. n. a) Stoß, der; give sth. a ~: etw. schieben; b) (effort) Anstrengungen Pl.; (Mil.: attack) Vorstoß, der; c) (crisis) when it comes to the ~, (Amer. coll.) when ~ comes to shove wenn es ernst wird; d) (Brit. sl.: dismissal) get the ~: rausfliegen (ugs.). **push a'head** v.i. ~ ahead with sth. etw. vorantreiben. **push 'in** v.i. sich hineindrängen. **push 'off** v.i. a)

(Boating) abstoßen; b) (sl.: leave) abhauen (salopp). **push 'on** 1. v.i. (with plans etc.) weitermachen. 2. v.t. draufdrücken ⟨Deckel usw.⟩. **push 'up** v.t. hochschieben; (fig.) hochtreiben

**push:** ~-**button** n. [Druck]knopf, der; Drucktaste; ~-**chair** n. (Brit.) Sportwagen, der; ~-**over** n. (coll.) Kinderspiel, das

**pushy** ['pʊʃɪ] adj. (coll.) [übermäßig] ehrgeizig ⟨Person⟩

**pussy** ['pʊsɪ] n. (child lang.: cat) Miezekatze, die (fam.)

**put** [pʊt] 1. v.t., -tt-, put a) (place) tun; (vertically) stellen; (horizontally) legen; ~ plates on the table Teller auf den Tisch stellen; ~ a stamp on the letter eine Briefmarke auf den Brief kleben; ~ the letter in an envelope/the letter-box den Brief in einen Umschlag/in den Briefkasten stecken; ~ sth. in one's pocket etw. in die Tasche stecken; ~ petrol in the tank Benzin in den Tank füllen; ~ the car in|to| the garage das Auto in die Garage stellen; ~ the plug in the socket den Stecker in die Steckdose stecken; ~ one's hands over one's eyes sich (Dat.) die Hände auf die Augen legen; where shall I ~ it? wo soll ich es hintun (ugs.)/-stellen/-legen usw.?; (fig.) be ~ in a difficult position in eine schwierige Lage geraten; ~ sb. on to sth. jmdn. auf etw. (Akk.) hinweisen; ~ sb. to work jmdn. arbeiten lassen; ~ sb. on antibiotics jmdn. auf Antibiotika setzen; ~ oneself in sb.'s place or situation sich in jmds. Lage (Akk.) versetzen; b) (submit) unterbreiten ⟨Vorschlag, Plan⟩ (to Dat.); c) (express) ausdrücken; let's ~ it like this: ...: sagen wir so: ...; ~ sth. into English etc. etw. ins Englische usw. übertragen; ~ sth. into words etw. in Worte fassen; d) (write) schreiben; ~ one's name on the list seinen Namen auf die Liste setzen; ~ sth. on the bill etw. auf die Rechnung setzen; e) (stake) setzen (on auf + Akk.); f) (estimate) ~ sb./sth. at jmdn./etw. schätzen auf (+ Akk.). 2. v.i. -tt-, put (Naut.) ~ |out| to sea in See stechen. **put a'cross** v.t. a) (communicate) vermitteln (to Dat.); b) (make acceptable) ankommen mit. **put a'way** v.t. a) wegräumen; reinstellen ⟨Auto⟩; (in file) abheften; b) (save) beiseite legen; c) (coll.) (eat) verdrücken (ugs.); (drink) runterkippen (ugs.); d) (coll.:

*confine)* einsperren *(ugs.).* **put 'back** *v. t.* **a)** ~ **the book back** das Buch zurücktun; **b)** ~ **the clock back** die Uhr zurückstellen; **c)** *(postpone)* verschieben. **put 'down** *v. t.* **a)** *(set down) (vertically)* hinstellen; *(horizontally)* hinlegen; auflegen ⟨*Hörer*⟩; **b)** *(suppress)* niederwerfen; **c)** *(humiliate)* herabsetzen; **d)** *(kill)* töten; **e)** *(write)* notieren; **f)** *(attribute)* ~ **sth. down to sth.** etw. auf etw. *(Akk.)* zurückführen. **put 'forward** *v. t.* **a)** *(propose)* aufwarten mit; **b)** *(nominate)* vorschlagen; **c)** ~ **the clock forward** die Uhr vorstellen. **put 'in 1.** *v. t.* **a)** *(install)* einbauen; **b)** *(submit)* stellen ⟨*Forderung*⟩; einreichen ⟨*Bewerbung*⟩; **c)** *(devote)* aufwenden ⟨*Mühe*⟩; *(perform)* einlegen ⟨*Sonderschicht, Überstunden*⟩. **2.** *v. i.* ~ **in for** sich bewerben um ⟨*Stellung*⟩; beantragen ⟨*Urlaub*⟩. **put 'off** *v. t.* **a)** *(postpone)* verschieben **(until** auf + *Akk.*); *(postpone engagement with)* vertrösten **(until** auf + *Akk.*); **b)** *(switch off)* ausmachen; **c)** *(repel)* abstoßen; ~ **sb. off sth.** jmdm. etw. verleiden; **d)** *(distract)* stören; **e)** *(dissuade)* ~ **sb. off doing sth.** jmdn. davon abbringen, etw. zu tun. **put 'on** *v. t.* **a)** anziehen ⟨*Kleidung, Hose usw.*⟩; aufsetzen ⟨*Hut, Brille*⟩; draufsetzen ⟨*Deckel*⟩; ~ **it on** *(coll.)* [nur] Schau machen *(ugs.);* **b)** anmachen ⟨*Radio, Licht*⟩; aufsetzen ⟨*Wasser, Kessel*⟩; **c)** *(gain)* ~ **on weight** zunehmen; **d)** *(stage)* spielen ⟨*Stück*⟩; zeigen ⟨*Film*⟩. **put 'out** *v. t.* **a)** rausbringen; **b)** ausmachen ⟨*Licht*⟩; löschen ⟨*Feuer*⟩; **c)** *(inconvenience)* in Verlegenheit bringen. **put 'through** *v. t.* **a)** *(carry out)* durchführen ⟨*Plan, Programm*⟩; **b)** *(Teleph.)* verbinden **(to** mit). **put 'up 1.** *v. t.* **a)** heben ⟨*Hand*⟩; errichten ⟨*Gebäude, Denkmal*⟩; aufstellen ⟨*Gerüst*⟩; **b)** *(display)* aushängen; **c)** hochnehmen ⟨*Fäuste*⟩; leisten ⟨*Widerstand, Gegenwehr*⟩; **d)** *(propose)* vorschlagen; *(nominate)* aufstellen; **e)** *(incite)* ~ **sb. up to sth.** jmdn. zu etw. anstiften; **f)** *(accommodate)* unterbringen; **g)** *(increase)* [he]raufsetzen ⟨*Preis, Miete*⟩. **2.** *v. i. (lodge)* übernachten. **put 'up with** *v. t.* sich *(Dat.)* bieten lassen ⟨*Beleidigung, Benehmen*⟩; sich abfinden mit ⟨*Lärm, Elend*⟩; sich abgeben mit ⟨*Person*⟩
**putrefy** [ˈpjuːtrɪfaɪ] *v. i.* sich zersetzen
**putrid** [ˈpjuːtrɪd] *adj. (rotten)* faul; ~ **smell** Fäulnisgeruch, *der*

**putt** [pʌt] *(Golf)* **1.** *v. i.* & *t.* putten. **2.** *n.* Putt, *der.* **'putter** *n.* Putter, *der*
**putty** [ˈpʌtɪ] *n.* Kitt, *der*
**'put-up** *adj.* **a** ~ **job** ein abgekartetes Spiel *(ugs.)*
**puzzle** [ˈpʌzl] **1.** *n. (problem, enigma)* Rätsel, *das; (toy)* Geduldsspiel, *das.* **2.** *v. t.* rätselhaft *od.* ein Rätsel sein (+ *Dat.*). **3.** *v. i.* ~ **over** *or* **about sth.** sich *(Dat.)* über etw. den Kopf zerbrechen. **puzzled** [ˈpʌzld] *adj.* ratlos. **puzzling** [ˈpʌzlɪŋ] *adj.* rätselhaft
**PVC** *abbr.* **p**oly**v**inyl **c**hloride PVC, *das*
**pygmy** [ˈpɪgmɪ] *n.* Pygmäe, *der*
**pyjamas** [pɪˈdʒɑːməz] *n. pl.* **[pair of]** ~: Schlafanzug, *der*
**pylon** [ˈpaɪlən] *n.* Mast, *der*
**pyramid** [ˈpɪrəmɪd] *n.* Pyramide, *die*
**Pyrenees** [pɪrəˈniːz] *pr. n. pl.* **the** ~: die Pyrenäen
**python** [ˈpaɪθən] *n.* Python, *die*

# Q

**Q, q** [kjuː] *n.* Q, q, *das*
**quack** [kwæk] **1.** *v. i.* ⟨*Ente:*⟩ quaken. **2.** *n.* Quaken, *das*
**quadrangle** [ˈkwɒdræŋgl] *n.* [viereckiger] Innenhof
**quadruped** [ˈkwɒdrʊped] *n.* Vierfüßler, *der*
**quadruple** [ˈkwɒdrʊpl] **1.** *adj.* vierfach. **2.** *v. t.* vervierfachen. **3.** *v. i.* sich vervierfachen
**quagmire** [ˈkwægmaɪə(r)] *n.* Sumpf, *der;* Morast, *der*
**'quail** [kweɪl] *n. (Ornith.)* Wachtel, *die*
**²quail** *v. i.* ⟨*Person:*⟩ [ver]zagen
**quaint** [kweɪnt] *adj.* drollig ⟨*Häuschen, Einrichtung*⟩; malerisch ⟨*Ort*⟩; *(odd)* kurios ⟨*Bräuche, Anblick*⟩
**quake** [kweɪk] **1.** *n. (coll.)* [Erd]beben, *das.* **2.** *v. i.* beben; ~ **with fear** vor Angst zittern
**Quaker** [ˈkweɪkə(r)] *n.* Quäker, *der/* Quäkerin, *die*
**qualification** [kwɒlɪfɪˈkeɪʃn] *n.* **a)** Qualifikation, *die; (condition)* Voraussetzung, *die;* **b)** *(limitation)* Vorbehalt, *der;* **without** ~: vorbehaltlos

**qualified** ['kwɒlɪfaɪd] *adj.* **a)** qualifiziert; *(by training)* ausgebildet; **b)** *(restricted)* nicht uneingeschränkt; **a** ~ **success** kein voller Erfolg; ~ **acceptance** bedingte Annahme

**qualify** ['kwɒlɪfaɪ] **1.** *v. t.* **a)** *(make competent)* berechtigen (**for** zu); **b)** *(modify)* einschränken. **2.** *v. i.* **a)** ~ **in law/medicine** seinen [Studien]abschluß in Jura/Medizin machen; ~ **as a doctor/lawyer** sein Examen als Arzt/Anwalt machen; **b)** *(fulfil a condition)* in Frage kommen (**for** für); **c)** *(Sport)* sich qualifizieren

**quality** ['kwɒlɪtɪ] **1.** *n.* **a)** Qualität, *die;* **b)** *(characteristic)* Eigenschaft, *die.* **2.** *adj.* Qualitäts-

**qualm** [kwɑ:m] *n.* Bedenken, *das* (**over, about** gegen)

**quandary** ['kwɒndərɪ] *n.* Dilemma, *das*

**quantity** ['kwɒntɪtɪ] *n.* **a)** Quantität, *die;* **b)** *(amount, sum)* Menge, *die*

**quarantine** ['kwɒrənti:n] *n.* Quarantäne, *die;* **be in** ~: unter Quarantäne stehen

**quarrel** ['kwɒrl] **1.** *n.* **a)** Streit, *der;* **have/pick a** ~ **with sb.** [about/over sth.] sich mit jmdm. [über etw. *(Akk.)*] streiten/Streit anfangen; **b)** *(cause of complaint)* Einwand, *der* (**with** gegen). **2.** *v. i., (Brit.)* **-ll-** [sich] streiten (**over** um, **about** über + *Akk.*); ~ **with each other** [sich] [miteinander] streiten; *(fall out)* sich [zer]streiten (**over** um, **about** über + *Akk.*). **quarrelsome** ['kwɒrlsəm] *adj.* streitsüchtig

**¹quarry** ['kwɒrɪ] *n.* Steinbruch, *der*

**²quarry** *n. (prey)* Beute, *die*

**quart** [kwɔ:t] *n.* Quart, *das*

**quarter** ['kwɔ:tə(r)] **1.** *n.* **a)** Viertel, *das;* **a** *or* **one** ~ **of** ein Viertel (+ *Gen.*); **a** ~ **of a mile/an hour** eine Viertelmeile/-stunde; **b)** *(of year)* Quartal, *das;* Vierteljahr, *das;* **c)** **[a]** ~ **to/past six** Viertel vor/nach sechs; **d)** *(direction)* Richtung, *die;* **e)** *(area of town)* [Stadt]viertel, *das;* **f)** ~**s** *pl. (lodgings)* Quartier, *das (bes. Milit.);* Unterkunft, *die;* **g)** *(Amer. coin)* Vierteldollar, *der.* **2.** *v. t.* **a)** *(divide)* vierteln; **b)** *(lodge)* einquartieren (*Soldaten*). **quarter-'final** *n.* Viertelfinale, *das.* '**quarterly 1.** *adj.* vierteljährlich. **2.** *n.* Vierteljahr[e]sschrift, *die*

**quartet** [kwɔ:'tet] *n.* Quartett, *das*

**quartz** [kwɔ:ts] *n.* Quarz, *der*

**quash** [kwɒʃ] *v. t.* **a)** *(annul)* aufheben; **b)** *(suppress)* niederschlagen

**quaver** ['kweɪvə(r)] **1.** *n. (Brit. Mus.)* Achtelnote, *die.* **2.** *v. i. (vibrate)* zittern

**quay** [ki:], '**quayside** *n.* Kai, *der*

**queasy** ['kwi:zɪ] *adj.* unwohl

**queen** [kwi:n] *n.* **a)** Königin, *die;* **b)** *(Chess, Cards)* Dame, *die.* **queen 'mother** *n.* Königinmutter, *die*

**queer** [kwɪə(r)] **1.** *adj.* **a)** *(strange)* sonderbar; *(eccentric)* verschroben; **b)** *(shady)* merkwürdig; **c)** *(out of sorts)* unwohl; **d)** *(sl. derog.: homosexual)* schwul *(ugs.).* **2.** *n. (sl. derog.: homosexual)* Schwule, *der (ugs.)*

**quell** [kwel] *v. t. (literary)* niederschlagen 〈*Aufstand*〉; zügeln 〈*Furcht*〉

**quench** [kwentʃ] *v. t.* löschen

**query** ['kwɪərɪ] **1.** *n.* Frage, *die.* **2.** *v. t.* in Frage stellen 〈*Anweisung, Glaubwürdigkeit*〉; beanstanden 〈*Rechnung*〉

**quest** [kwest] *n.* Suche, *die* (**for** nach)

**question** ['kwestʃn] **1.** *n.* **a)** Frage, *die;* **ask sb. a** ~: jmdm. eine Frage stellen; **b)** *(doubt, objection)* Zweifel, *der* (**about an** + *Dat.*); **there is no** ~ **about sth.** es besteht kein Zweifel an etw. *(Dat.);* **beyond all** *or* **without** ~: ohne Frage; **c)** *(problem, concern)* Frage, *die;* **sth./it is only a** ~ **of time** etw./es ist [nur] eine Frage der Zeit; **it is [only] a** ~ **of doing sth.** es geht [nur] darum, etw. zu tun; **the person/thing in** ~: die fragliche Person/Sache; **sth./it is out of the** ~: etw./es ist ausgeschlossen. **2.** *v. t.* **a)** befragen; 〈*Polizei, Gericht usw.:*〉 vernehmen; **b)** *(throw doubt upon, raise objections to)* bezweifeln. **questionable** ['kwestʃənəbl] *adj.* fragwürdig. '**question mark** *n.* Fragezeichen, *das*

**questionnaire** [kwestʃə'neə(r)] *n.* Fragebogen, *der*

**queue** [kju:] **1.** *n.* Schlange, *die.* **join the** ~: sich anstellen. **2.** *v. i.* ~ **[up]** Schlange stehen

**quibble** ['kwɪbl] **1.** *n.* Spitzfindigkeit, *die.* **2.** *v. i.* streiten

**quiche** [ki:ʃ] *n.* Quiche, *die*

**quick** [kwɪk] **1.** *adj.* schnell; kurz 〈*Rede, Pause*〉; flüchtig 〈*Kuß, Blick*〉; **be** ~! mach schnell! *(ugs.);* **be** ~ **to do sth.** etw. schnell tun; **a** ~ **temper** ein aufbrausendes Wesen. **2.** *adv.* schnell. **3.** *n.* empfindliches Fleisch; **be cut to the** ~ *(fig.)* tief getroffen sein. **quicken** ['kwɪkn] **1.** *v. t.* beschleunigen. **2.** *v. i.* sich beschleunigen. '**quickly** *adv.* schnell. '**quickness** *n.* **a)** *(speed)* Schnelligkeit, *die;* **b)** *(~ of perception)* Schärfe, *die*

**quick: ~sand** n. Treibsand, der;
  **~-tempered** [~'tempəd] adj. hitzig;
  **be ~-tempered** leicht aufbrausen;
  **~-witted** adj. geistesgegenwärtig
**quid** [kwɪd] n., pl. same (Brit. sl.)
  Pfund, das
**quiet** ['kwaɪət] 1. adj., ~er ['kwaɪə-
  tə(r)], ~est ['kwaɪətɪst] a) (silent) still;
  (not loud) leise; **keep ~ about sth.** (fig.)
  etw. geheimhalten; b) (peaceful, not
  busy) ruhig; c) (not overt) versteckt;
  **on the ~:** still und heimlich. 2. n. Ruhe, die; (silence, stillness) Stille, die.
**quieten** ['kwaɪətn] v.t. beruhigen.
**quieten 'down** v.i. sich beruhigen
'**quietly** adv. a) (silently) still; (not
  loudly) leise; b) (peacefully) ruhig
'**quietness** n. (absence of noise) Stille,
  die; (peacefulness) Ruhe, die
**quill** [kwɪl] n. (feather) Kielfeder, die;
  (of porcupine) Stachel, der
**quilt** [kwɪlt] 1. n. Schlafdecke, die. 2.
  v.t. wattieren
**quince** [kwɪns] n. Quitte, die
**quintet** [kwɪn'tet] n. Quintett, das
**quip** [kwɪp] 1. n. Witzelei, die. 2. v.i.,
  -pp- witzeln (**at** über + Akk.)
**quirk** [kwɜːk] n. Marotte, die; **a ~ of
  fate** eine Laune des Schicksals
**quit** [kwɪt] v.t., -tt-, (Amer.) quit (give
  up) aufgeben; (stop) aufhören mit; ~
  **doing sth.** aufhören, etw. zu tun; **they
  were given notice to ~ [the flat]** ihnen
  wurde [die Wohnung] gekündigt
**quite** [kwaɪt] adv. a) (entirely) ganz;
  völlig; fest (entschlossen); ~ **|so|!** [ja,]
  genau!; b) (to some extent) ziemlich;
  ganz (gern); ~ **a few** ziemlich viele
**quits** [kwɪts] pred. adj. **be ~ |with sb.|**
  [mit jmdm.] quitt sein (ugs.)
'**quiver** ['kwɪvə(r)] v.i. zittern (**with** vor
  + Dat.); (Stimme, Lippen:) beben
  (geh.); (Lid:) zucken
²**quiver** n. (for arrows) Köcher, der
**quiz** [kwɪz] 1. n., pl. ~**zes** Quiz, das. 2.
  v.t., -zz- ausfragen (**about sth.** nach
  etw., **about sb.** über jmdn.). **quizzical**
  ['kwɪzɪkl] adj. fragend
**quoit** [kɔɪt] n. [Gummi]ring, der
**quorum** ['kwɔːrəm] n. Quorum, das
**quota** ['kwəʊtə] n. a) (share) Anteil,
  der; b) (goods to be produced) Produk-
  tionsmindestquote, die; c) (maximum
  number) Höchstquote, die
**quotation** [kwəʊ'teɪʃn] n. a) Zitieren,
  das; (passage) Zitat, das; b) (estimate)
  Kosten[vor]anschlag, der. **quo'ta-
  tion-marks** n. pl. Anführungszeichen Pl.

**quote** [kwəʊt] 1. v.t. also abs. zitieren
  (**from** aus); zitieren aus (Buch, Text);
  (mention) anführen; nennen (Preis). 2.
  n. (coll.) a) (passage) Zitat, das; b) (estimate) Kosten[vor]anschlag, der; c)
  usu. in pl. (quotation-mark) Anführungszeichen, das

# R

**R, r** [ɑː(r)] n. R, r, das
**R.** abbr. **River** Fl.
**rabbi** ['ræbaɪ] n. Rabbi[ner], der; (as
  title) Rabbi, der
**rabbit** ['ræbɪt] n. Kaninchen, das
**rabbit: ~-burrow** n. Kaninchenbau,
  der; **~-hutch** n. (also fig.) Kanin-
  chenstall, der; **~-warren** n. Kanin-
  chengehege, das; (fig.) Labyrinth, das
**rabble** ['ræbl] n. Mob, der
**rabid** ['ræbɪd] adj. a) tollwütig; b) (extreme) fanatisch
**rabies** ['reɪbiːz] n. Tollwut, die
'**race** [reɪs] 1. n. Rennen, das; (fig.) **a ~
  against time** ein Wettlauf mit der Zeit.
  2. v.i. a) (in swimming, running, etc.)
  um die Wette schwimmen/laufen
  usw. (**with**, **against** mit); b) (Motor:)
  durchdrehen; (Puls:) jagen; c) (rush)
  sich sehr beeilen; ~ **after sb.** jmdn.
  hinterherhetzen. 3. v.t. um die Wette
  schwimmen/laufen usw. mit
²**race** n. (Anthrop., Biol.) Rasse, die;
  **the human ~:** die Menschheit
**race: ~-course** n. Rennbahn, die;
  **~-horse** n. Rennpferd, das; **~-track**
  n. Rennbahn, die
**racial** ['reɪʃl] adj. Rassen(diskriminierung, -konflikt, -gleichheit); rassisch
  (Gruppe, Minderheit). **racialism** ['reɪ-
  ʃəlɪzm] n. Rassismus, der. **racialist**
  ['reɪʃəlɪst] 1. n. Rassist, der/Rassistin,
  die. 2. adj. rassistisch
**racing** ['reɪsɪŋ] n. Rennsport, der; (with
  horses) Pferdesport, der. '**racing-car**
  n. Rennwagen, der. '**racing driver**
  n. Rennfahrer, der/-fahrerin, die
**racism** ['reɪsɪzm] n. Rassismus, der.
**racist** ['reɪsɪst] 1. n. Rassist, der/Ras-
  sistin, die. 2. adj. rassistisch

**rack** [ræk] **1.** *n. (for luggage)* Ablage, *die; (for toast, plates)* Ständer, *der; (on bicycle, motor cycle)* Gepäckträger, *der.* **2.** *v. t.* ~ **one's brain[s]** *(fig.)* sich *(Dat.)* den Kopf zerbrechen *(ugs.)*

¹**racket** ['rækɪt] *n.* Schläger, *der*

²**racket** *n.* **a)** *(disturbance)* Lärm, *der;* Krach, *der;* **b)** *(scheme)* Schwindelgeschäft, *das (ugs.).* **racketeer** [rækɪ'tɪə(r)] *n.* Ganove, *der; (profiteer)* Wucherer, *der*

**racoon** [rə'ku:n] *n.* Waschbär, *der*

**racy** ['reɪsɪ] *adj.* flott *(ugs.)* ⟨*Stil*⟩

**radar** ['reɪdɑ:(r)] *n.* Radar, *das od. der*

**radiant** ['reɪdɪənt] *adj.* strahlend; fröhlich ⟨*Stimmung*⟩; **be** ~: strahlen (**with** vor + *Dat.*)

**radiate** ['reɪdɪeɪt] **1.** *v. i.* **a)** ⟨*Hitze, Wärme:*⟩ ausstrahlen; ⟨*Schein, Wellen:*⟩ ausgehen (**from** von); **b)** *(from central point)* strahlenförmig ausgehen (**from** von). **2.** *v. t.* ausstrahlen ⟨*Licht, Wärme; Glück, Liebe*⟩; aussenden ⟨*Strahlen, Wellen*⟩. **radiation** [reɪdɪ'eɪʃn] *n. (of energy)* Emission, *die; (of signals)* Ausstrahlung, *die; (energy transmitted)* Strahlung, *die.* **radiator** ['reɪdɪeɪtə(r)] *n.* **a)** *(for heating)* Heizkörper, *der;* **b)** *(Motor Veh.)* Kühler, *der*

**radical** ['rædɪkl] *adj.* **1.** *(thorough; also Polit.)* radikal; drastisch ⟨*Maßnahme*⟩; **b)** *(progressive)* radikal; **c)** *(fundamental)* grundlegend. **2.** *n. (Polit.)* Radikale, *der/die*

**radio** ['reɪdɪəʊ] **1.** *n., pl.* ~**s a)** *no indef. art.* Funk, *der; (for private communication)* Sprechfunk, *der;* **b)** *no indef. art. (Broadcasting)* Rundfunk, *der;* **on the** ~: im Radio; **c)** *(apparatus)* Radio, *das.* **2.** *attrib. adj. (Broadcasting)* Rundfunk-; Radio⟨*welle, -teleskop*⟩; Funk⟨*mast, -turm, -taxi*⟩. **3.** *v. t.* funken

**radio:** ~**'active** *adj.* radioaktiv; ~**ac'tivity** *n.* Radioaktivität, *die;* ~**con'trolled** *adj.* funkgesteuert

**radish** ['rædɪʃ] *n.* Rettich, *der; (small, red)* Radieschen, *das*

**radius** ['reɪdɪəs] *n., pl.* **radii** ['reɪdɪaɪ] *or* ~**es** *(Math.)* Radius, *der; (fig.)* Umkreis, *der*

**RAF** [ɑ:reɪ'ef, *(coll.)* ræf] *abbr.* **Royal Air Force**

**raffle** ['ræfl] **1.** *n.* Tombola, *die;* ~ **ticket** Los, *das.* **2.** *v. t.* ~ [off] verlosen

**raft** [rɑ:ft] *n.* Floß, *das*

**rafter** ['rɑ:ftə(r)] *n.* Sparren, *der*

¹**rag** [ræg] *n.* **a)** [Stoff]fetzen, *der;* **b)**

*(old and torn clothes)* Lumpen *Pl.;* **c)** *(derog.: newspaper)* Käseblatt, *das (salopp)*

²**rag** *v. t.,* -**gg**- *(tease)* aufziehen

**rag:** ~**-bag** *n. (fig.)* Sammelsurium, *das;* ~ **doll** *n.* Stoffpuppe, *die*

**rage** [reɪdʒ] **1.** *n.* **a)** *(violent anger)* Wut, *die; (fit of anger)* Wutausbruch, *der;* **b)** **sth. is [all] the** ~: etw. ist [ganz] groß in Mode. **2.** *v. i.* **a)** *(rave)* toben; ~ **at** *or* **against sth./sb.** gegen etw./ jmdn. wüten; **b)** *(be violent, unchecked)* toben; ⟨*Krankheit:*⟩ wüten

**ragged** ['rægɪd] *adj.* zerrissen

**raid** [reɪd] **1.** *n.* Einfall, *der;* Überfall, *der; (Mil.)* Überraschungsangriff, *der; (by police)* Razzia, *die* (**on** in + *Dat.*). **2.** *v. t.* ⟨*Polizei:*⟩ eine Razzia machen auf (+ *Akk.*); ⟨*Räuber, Soldaten:*⟩ überfallen. **'raider** *n.* Räuber, *der/* Räuberin, *die*

**rail** [reɪl] *n.* **a)** Stange, *die; (on ship)* Reling, *die; (as protection against contact)* Barriere, *die;* **b)** *(Railw.: of track)* Schiene, *die;* **c)** *(~way)* [Eisen]bahn, *die; attrib.* Bahn-; **by** ~: mit der Bahn

**railing** ['reɪlɪŋ] *n. (round park)* Zaun, *der; (on staircase)* Geländer, *das*

**'railroad** *(Amer.),* **'railway** *ns.* **a)** *(track)* Bahnlinie, *die;* Bahnstrecke, *die;* **b)** *(system)* [Eisen]bahn, *die*

**railway:** ~ **carriage** *n.* Eisenbahnwagen, *der;* ~ **engine** *n.* Lokomotive, *die;* ~ **line** *n.* [Eisen]bahnlinie, *die;* ~ **station** *n.* Bahnhof, *der*

**rain** [reɪn] **1.** *n.* **a)** Regen, *der;* **b)** *(fig.: of arrows, blows, etc.)* Hagel, *der.* **2.** *v. i. impers.* **it is** ~**ing** es regnet. **3.** *v. t.* hageln lassen ⟨*Schläge, Hiebe*⟩

**rain:** ~**bow** ['reɪnbəʊ] *n.* Regenbogen, *der;* ~**-check** *n. (Amer. fig.)* **take a** ~**-check on sth.** auf etw. *(Akk.)* später wieder zurückkommen; ~**coat** *n.* Regenmantel, *der;* ~**fall** *n.* Niederschlag, *der;* ~**proof** *adj.* regendicht; ~**water** *n.* Regenwasser, *das*

**'rainy** *adj.* regnerisch ⟨*Tag, Wetter*⟩; regenreich ⟨*Gebiet, Sommer*⟩; ~ **season** Regenzeit, *die;* **keep sth. for a** ~ **day** *(fig.)* sich *(Dat.)* etw. für schlechte Zeiten aufheben

**raise** [reɪz] *v. t.* **a)** *(lift up)* heben; erhöhen ⟨*Temperatur, Miete, Gehalt*⟩; hochziehen ⟨*Fahne*⟩; aufziehen ⟨*Vorhang*⟩; hochheben ⟨*Arm*⟩; ~ **one's glass to sb.** das Glas auf jmdn. erheben; **b)** *(set upright)* aufrichten; erheben ⟨*Banner*⟩; ~ **sb.'s spirits** jmds. Stimmung heben; **c)** erheben ⟨*Forde-*

*rungen, Einwände⟩;* aufwerfen ⟨*Frage⟩;* zur Sprache bringen ⟨*Thema, Problem⟩;* **d)** aufziehen ⟨*Vieh, [Haus]tiere⟩;* großziehen ⟨*Familie, Kinder⟩;* **e)** aufbringen ⟨*Geld, Betrag⟩;* **f)** aufheben ⟨*Belagerung, Blockade, Embargo, Verbot⟩*

**raisin** ['reɪzn] *n.* Rosine, *die*

**rake** [reɪk] **1.** *n.* Rechen, *der;* Harke, *die.* **2.** *v. t.* **a)** harken; **b)** ~ **the fire** die Asche entfernen; **c)** *(with eyes, shots)* bestreichen. **rake 'in** *v. t. (coll.)* scheffeln *(ugs.).* **rake 'up** *v. t.* zusammenharken; *(fig.)* wieder ausgraben

**'rake-off** *n. (coll.)* [Gewinn]anteil, *der*

**rakish** ['reɪkɪʃ] *adj.* flott; keß

**rally** ['rælɪ] **1.** *v. i. (regain health)* sich wieder [ein wenig] erholen. **2.** *v. t.* **a)** *(reassemble)* wieder zusammenrufen; **b)** einigen ⟨*Partei, Kräfte⟩;* sammeln ⟨*Anhänger⟩.* **3.** *n.* **a)** *(mass meeting)* Versammlung, *die;* **b)** |motor| ~: Rallye, *die;* **c)** *(Tennis)* Ballwechsel, *der*

**ram** [ræm] **1.** *n. (Zool.)* Schafbock, *der;* Widder, *der.* **2.** *v. t.,* **-mm-: a)** *(force)* stopfen; ~ **a post into the ground** einen Pfosten in die Erde rammen; ~ **sth. home to sb.** jmdm. etw. deutlich vor Augen führen; **b)** *(collide with)* rammen

**ramble** ['ræmbl] **1.** *n.* |nature| ~: Wanderung, *die.* **2.** *v. i.* **a)** *(walk)* umherstreifen **(through, in** in + *Dat.);* **b)** *(in talk)* zusammenhangloses Zeug reden; **keep rambling on about sth.** sich endlos über etw. *(Akk.)* auslassen. **rambler** ['ræmblə(r)] *n.* Wanderer, *der*/Wanderin, *die.* **rambling** ['ræmblɪŋ] **1.** *n.* Wandern, *das.* **2.** *adj.* **a)** *(irregularly arranged)* verschachtelt; verwinkelt ⟨*Straßen⟩;* **b)** *(incoherent)* unzusammenhängend ⟨*Erklärung⟩;* **c)** ~ **rose** Kletterrose, *die*

**ramp** [ræmp] *n.* Rampe, *die*

**rampage 1.** ['ræmpeɪdʒ] *n.* Randale, *die (ugs.);* **be/go on the** ~ *(coll.)* randalieren. **2.** [ræm'peɪdʒ] *v. i.* randalieren

**rampant** ['ræmpənt] *adj.* zügellos ⟨*Gewalt, Rassismus⟩;* steil ansteigend ⟨*Inflation⟩;* üppig ⟨*Wachstum⟩*

**rampart** ['ræmpɑːt] *n.* Wehrgang, *der*

**'ramshackle** *adj.* klapprig ⟨*Auto⟩;* verkommen ⟨*Gebäude⟩*

**ran** *see* **run** 2, 3

**ranch** [rɑːntʃ] *n.* Ranch, *die*

**rancid** ['rænsɪd] *adj.* ranzig

**rancour** *(Brit.; Amer.:* **rancor)** ['ræŋkə(r)] *n.* [tiefe] Verbitterung

**random** ['rændəm] **1.** *n.* **at** ~: wahllos;

willkürlich; *(aimlessly)* ziellos; **choose at** ~: aufs Geratewohl wählen. **2.** *adj.* willkürlich

**randy** ['rændɪ] *adj.* geil; scharf *(ugs.)*

**rang** *see* **²ring** 2, 3

**range** [reɪndʒ] **1.** *n.* **a)** ~ **of mountains** Bergkette, *die;* **b)** *(of subjects)* Palette, *die;* *(of knowledge, voice)* Umfang, *der;* **c)** *(of missile etc.)* Reichweite, *die;* **at a** ~ **of 200 metres** auf eine Entfernung von 200 Metern; **d)** *(series, selection)* Kollektion, *die;* **e)** *(stove)* Herd, *der.* **2.** *v. i.* ⟨*Preise, Temperaturen:⟩* schwanken, sich bewegen **(from ... to** zwischen [+ *Dat.*] ... und)

**'ranger** *n.* Förster, *der*/Försterin, *die*

**¹rank** [ræŋk] **1.** *n.* **a)** *(position in hierarchy)* Rang, *der;* *(Mil. also)* Dienstgrad, *der;* **b)** *(social position)* [soziale] Stellung; **c)** *(row)* Reihe, *die;* **the** ~ **and file** *(fig.)* die breite Masse; **the** ~**s** *(enlisted men)* die Mannschaften und Unteroffiziere. **2.** *v. t.* ~ **among** zählen zu. **3.** *v. i.* ~ **among** zählen zu

**²rank** *adj.* **a)** kraß ⟨*Außenseiter⟩;* **b)** ~ **weeds** |wild|wucherndes Unkraut

**ransack** ['rænsæk] *v. t.* **a)** *(search)* durchsuchen **(for** nach); **b)** *(pillage)* plündern

**ransom** ['rænsəm] *n.* ~ |money| Lösegeld, *das;* **hold to** ~: als Geisel festhalten

**rant** [rænt] *v. i.* ~ |and rave| wettern *(ugs.)* **(about** über + *Akk.)*

**rap** [ræp] **1.** *n.* [energisches] Klopfen. **2.** *v. t.,* **-pp-** klopfen. **3.** *v. i.,* **-pp-** klopfen **(on** an + *Akk.)*

**¹rape** [reɪp] **1.** *n.* Vergewaltigung, *die.* **2.** *v. t.* vergewaltigen

**²rape** *n. (Bot., Agric.)* Raps, *der*

**rapid** ['ræpɪd] **1.** *adj.* schnell ⟨*Bewegung, Wachstum, Puls⟩;* rasch ⟨*Fortschritt, Ausbreitung⟩.* **2.** *n. in pl.* Stromschnellen. **rapidity** [rə'pɪdɪtɪ] *n.* Schnelligkeit, *die.* **'rapidly** *adv.* schnell

**rapist** ['reɪpɪst] *n.* Vergewaltiger, *der*

**rapport** [rə'pɔː(r)] *n.* [harmonisches] Verhältnis

**rapt** [ræpt] *adj.* gespannt ⟨*Miene⟩*

**rapture** ['ræptʃə(r)] *n.* |state of| ~: Verzückung, *die.* **rapturous** ['ræptʃərəs] *adj.* begeistert

**¹rare** [reə(r)] *adj.,* **'rarely** *adv.* selten

**²rare** *adj. (Cookery)* englisch gebraten

**rarity** ['reərɪtɪ] *n.* Seltenheit, *die*

**¹rash** [ræʃ] *n.* [Haut]ausschlag, *der*

**²rash** *adj.* voreilig ⟨*Urteil, Entscheidung⟩;* überstürzt ⟨*Versprechung⟩*

**rasher** ['ræʃə(r)] n. Speckscheibe, die
'**rashly** adv. voreilig
**rasp** [rɑ:sp] n. (tool) Raspel, die
**raspberry** ['rɑ:zbərɪ] n. Himbeere, die
**rat** [ræt] n. a) Ratte, die; smell a ~ (fig.) Lunte riechen (ugs.); b) (coll. derog.. person) Ratte, die (derb)
**rate** [reɪt] 1. n. a) (proportion) Rate, die; b) (tariff) Satz, der; ~ |of pay| Lohnsatz, der; c) (speed) Geschwindigkeit, die; Tempo, das; d) (Brit.: levy) |local or council| ~s Gemeindeabgaben; e) (coll.) at any ~ (at least) zumindest; wenigstens; (whatever happens) auf jeden Fall; at this ~ we won't get any work done so kriegen wir gar nichts fertig (ugs.). 2. v. t. a) einschätzen ⟨Intelligenz, Leistung⟩; b) (consider) betrachten; rechnen (among zu). 3. v. i. ~ as gelten als
**rather** ['rɑ:ðə(r)] adv. a) (by preference) lieber; b) (somewhat) ziemlich; I ~ think that ...: ich bin ziemlich sicher, daß ...; c) (more truly) vielmehr; or ~: beziehungsweise
**ratification** [rætɪfɪ'keɪʃn] n. Ratifizierung, die
**ratify** ['rætɪfaɪ] v. t. ratifizieren
**rating** ['reɪtɪŋ] n. a) (estimated standing) Einschätzung, die; b) (Radio, Telev.) |popularity| ~: Einschaltquote, die; c) (Brit. Navy) Matrose, der
**ratio** ['reɪʃɪəʊ] n., pl. ~s Verhältnis, das
**ration** ['ræʃn] 1'. n. ~|s| Ration, die (of an + Dat.). 2. v. t. rationieren ⟨Benzin, Zucker usw.⟩
**rational** ['ræʃənl] adj. (having reason) rational ⟨Wesen⟩; (sensible) vernünftig ⟨Person, Art usw.⟩
**rationalize** ['ræʃənəlaɪz] v. t. rationalisieren
'**rat race** n. erbarmungsloser Konkurrenzkampf
**rattle** ['rætl] 1. v. i. a) ⟨Fenster:⟩ klappern; ⟨Flaschen:⟩ klirren; ⟨Kette:⟩ rasseln; b) ⟨Zug, Bus:⟩ rattern. 2. v. t. a) klappern mit ⟨Würfel, Geschirr⟩; klirren lassen ⟨Fenster[scheiben]⟩; rasseln mit ⟨Kette⟩; b) (sl.: disconcert) ~ sb., get sb. ~d jmdn. durcheinanderbringen. 3. n. a) (of baby) Rassel, die; b) (sound) Klappern, das. **rattle** 'off v. t. (coll.) herunterrasseln (ugs.)
'**rattlesnake** n. Klapperschlange, die
**raucous** ['rɔ:kəs] adj. rauh
**ravage** ['rævɪdʒ] 1. v. t. heimsuchen ⟨Gebiet, Stadt⟩. 2. n. in pl. verheerende Wirkung
**rave** [reɪv] 1. v. i. a) (talk wildly) irrere-

den; b) (speak admiringly) schwärmen (about von). 2. attrib. adj. (coll.) begeistert ⟨Kritik⟩
**raven** ['reɪvn] n. Rabe, der
**ravenous** ['rævənəs] adj. I'm ~: ich habe einen Bärenhunger (ugs.)
**ravine** [rə'vi:n] n. Schlucht, die
**raving** ['reɪvɪŋ] 1. adj. irreredend ⟨Idiot⟩. 2. adv. be ~ mad völlig verrückt sein (ugs.)
**ravish** ['rævɪʃ] v. t. (charm) entzücken.
'**ravishing** adj. bildschön ⟨Anblick, Person⟩; hinreißend ⟨Schönheit⟩
**raw** [rɔ:] adj. a) (uncooked) roh; b) (inexperienced) unerfahren; c) (stripped of skin) blutig ⟨Fleisch⟩; offen ⟨Wunde⟩; d) (chilly) naßkalt. **raw** ma'terial n. Rohstoff, der
**ray** [reɪ] n. Strahl, der; ~ of sunshine/ light Sonnen-/Lichtstrahl, der
**raze** [reɪz] v. t. ~ to the ground dem Erdboden gleichmachen
**razor** ['reɪzə(r)] n. Rasiermesser, das; |electric| ~: [elektrischer] Rasierapparat. '**razor-blade** n. Rasierklinge, die
**RC** abbr. **Roman Catholic** r.-k.; röm.-kath.
**Rd.** abbr. **road** Str.
**RE** abbr. (Brit.) **Religious Education** Religionslehre, die
**re** [ri:] prep. (Commerc.) betreffs
**reach** [ri:tʃ] 1. v. t. a) (arrive at) erreichen; ankommen in (+ Dat.) ⟨Stadt, Land⟩; erzielen ⟨Übereinstimmung⟩; kommen zu ⟨Entscheidung; Ausgang, Eingang⟩; you can ~ her at this number du kannst sie unter dieser Nummer erreichen; b) (extend to) ⟨Straße:⟩ führen bis zu; ⟨Leiter, Haar:⟩ reichen bis zu. 2. v. i. a) (stretch out hand) ~ for sth. nach etw. greifen; ~ across the table über den Tisch langen; b) (be long/tall enough) sth. will/won't ~: etw. ist/ist nicht lang genug; I can't ~: ich komme nicht daran; c) (go as far as) ⟨Wasser, Gebäude, Besitz:⟩ reichen (|up| to bis [hinauf] zu). 3. n. Reichweite, die; be within easy ~: leicht erreichbar sein; be out of ~: nicht erreichbar sein. **reach** 'out v. i. die Hand ausstrecken (for nach)
**react** [rɪ'ækt] v. i. reagieren (to auf + Akk.). **reaction** [rɪ'ækʃn] n. Reaktion, die (to auf + Akk.)
**reactionary** [rɪ'ækʃənərɪ] (Polit.) 1. adj. reaktionär. 2. n. Reaktionär, der/Reaktionärin, die
**reactor** [rɪ'æktə(r)] n. |nuclear| ~: Kernreaktor, der

**read** [ri:d] **1.** *v. t.*, **read** [red] **a)** lesen; ~ **sb. sth.**, ~ **sth. to sb.** jmdm. etwas vorlesen; ~ **the gas meter** das Gas ablesen; **b)** *(interpret)* deuten; ~ **between the lines** zwischen den Zeilen lesen; **c)** *(study)* studieren. **2.** *v. i.*, **read a)** lesen; ~ **to sb.** jmdm. vorlesen; **b)** *(convey meaning)* lauten; **the contract** ~**s as follows** der Vertrag hat folgenden Wortlaut. **read 'out** *v. t.* laut vorlesen. **read 'over, read 'through** *v. t.* durchlesen. **read 'up** *v. t.* sich informieren (**on** über + *Akk.*)

**readable** ['ri:dəbl] *adj.* **a)** *(pleasant to read)* lesenswert; **b)** *(legible)* leserlich

'**reader** *n.* **a)** Leser, *der*/Leserin, *die;* **b)** *(book)* Lesebuch, *das*

'**readership** *n.* Leserschaft, *die*

**readily** ['redɪlɪ] *adv.* **a)** *(willingly)* bereitwillig; **b)** *(easily)* ohne weiteres

**readiness** ['redɪnɪs] *n.* Bereitschaft, *die;* **be in** ~: bereit sein (**for** für)

'**reading** *n.* **a)** Lesen, *das;* **b)** *(figure shown)* Anzeige, *die;* **c)** *(recital)* Lesung, *die* (**from** aus); **d)** *(Parl.)* Lesung, *die.* '**reading-lamp,** '**reading-light** *ns.* Leselampe, *die.* '**reading-matter** *n.* Lesestoff, *der;* Lektüre, *die*

**ready** ['redɪ] **1.** *adj.* **a)** *(prepared)* fertig; **be** ~ **to do sth.** bereit sein, etw. zu tun; **get** ~: sich fertigmachen; **b)** *(willing)* bereit; **c)** *(within reach)* griffbereit. **2.** *adv.* fertig. **3.** *n.* **at the** ~ ⟨*Schußwaffe*⟩ im Anschlag

**ready:** ~ '**cash** *see* ~ **money;** ~-'**made** *adj.* **a)** Konfektions⟨*anzug, -kleidung*⟩; **b)** *(fig.)* vorgefertigt; ~ '**money** *n.* Bargeld, *das*

**real** [rɪəl] *adj.* **a)** *(actually existing)* real ⟨*Ereignis, Lebewesen*⟩; wirklich ⟨*Macht*⟩; **b)** *(genuine)* echt ⟨*Interesse, Gold, Seide*⟩; **c)** *(complete)* total *(ugs.)* ⟨*Desaster, Enttäuschung*⟩; **d)** *(true)* wahr ⟨*Grund, Name, Glück*⟩; echt ⟨*Mitleid, Sieg*⟩; **the** ~ **thing** der/die/ das Echte; **e) be for** ~ *(sl.)* echt sein. '**real estate** *n.* Immobilien *Pl.*

**realism** ['rɪəlɪzm] *n.* Realismus, *der*

'**realist** *n.* Realist, *der*/Realistin, *die*

**realistic** [rɪə'lɪstɪk] *adj.* realistisch

**reality** [rɪ'ælɪtɪ] *n.* Realität, *die*

**realization** [rɪəlaɪ'zeɪʃn] *n.* Erkenntnis, *die*

**realize** ['rɪəlaɪz] *v. t.* **a)** *(be aware of)* bemerken; erkennen ⟨*Fehler*⟩; **I didn't** ~ *(abs.)* ich habe es nicht gewußt; ~ [**that**] ...: merken, daß ...; **b)** *(make happen)* verwirklichen; **c)** erbringen ⟨*Summe, Preis*⟩

**really** ['rɪəlɪ] *adv.* wirklich; **not** ~: eigentlich nicht; [**well,**] ~! [also] so was!

**realm** [relm] *n.* Königreich, *das*

**realtor** ['rɪəltə(r)] *(Amer.)* Grundstücksmakler, *der*

**reap** [ri:p] *v. t. (cut)* schneiden ⟨Getreide⟩; *(gather in)* einfahren ⟨Getreide, Ernte⟩

**reappear** [ri:ə'pɪə(r)] *v. i.* wieder auftauchen; *(come back)* [wieder] zurückkommen

¹**rear** [rɪə(r)] **1.** *n.* **a)** *(back part)* hinterer Teil; **b)** *(back)* Rückseite, *die;* **c)** *(Mil.)* Rücken, *der.* **2.** *adj.* hinter...; ~ **axle** Hinterachse, *die*

²**rear 1.** *v. t.* großziehen ⟨*Kind, Familie*⟩; halten ⟨*Vieh*⟩. **2.** *v. i. ⟨Pferd:⟩* sich aufbäumen

**rear:** ~**guard** *n. (Mil.)* Nachhut, *die;* ~**-light** *n.* Rücklicht, *das*

**rearm** [ri:'ɑ:m] *v. i. & t.* wiederaufrüsten

**rearrange** [ri:ə'reɪndʒ] *v. t.* umräumen ⟨*Möbel*⟩; verlegen ⟨*Spiel*⟩ (**for** auf + *Akk.*); ändern ⟨*Programm*⟩

**rear-view 'mirror** *n.* Rückspiegel, *der*

**reason** ['ri:zn] **1.** *n.* **a)** *(cause)* Grund, *der;* **have no** ~ **to complain** sich nicht beklagen können; **for that** [**very**] ~: aus [eben] diesem Grund; **b)** *(power to understand; sense)* Vernunft, *die; (power to think)* Verstand, *der;* **in** *or* **within** ~: innerhalb eines vernünftigen Rahmens. **2.** *v. i.* **a)** schlußfolgern (**from** aus); **b)** ~ **with** diskutieren mit (**about, on** über + *Akk.*); **you can't** ~ **with her** mit ihr kann man nicht vernünftig reden. **3.** *v. t.* schlußfolgern

**reasonable** ['ri:zənəbl] *adj.* **a)** vernünftig; **b)** *(inexpensive)* günstig.

**reasonably** ['ri:zənəblɪ] *adv.* **a)** *(within reason)* vernünftig; **b)** *(fairly)* ganz ⟨*gut*⟩; ziemlich ⟨*gesund*⟩

**reassurance** [ri:ə'ʃʊərəns] *n.* **a)** *(calming)* **give sb.** ~: jmdn. beruhigen; **b)** *(confirmation)* Bestätigung, *die*

**reassure** [ri:ə'ʃʊə(r)] *v. t.* beruhigen; ~ **sb. about his health.** jmdm. versichern, daß er gesund ist. **reassuring** [ri:ə'ʃʊərɪŋ] *adj.* beruhigend

**rebate** ['ri:beɪt] *n.* **a)** *(refund)* Rückzahlung, *die;* **b)** *(discount)* Preisnachlaß, *der* (**on** auf + *Akk.*)

**rebel 1.** ['rebl] *n.* Rebell, *der*/Rebellin, *die.* **2.** *attrib. adj.* Rebellen-. **3.** [rɪ'bel] *v. i.*, **-ll-** rebellieren. **rebellion** [rɪ'beljən] *n.* Rebellion, *die.* **rebellious** [rɪ'beljəs] *adj.* rebellisch

**rebound 1.** [rɪˈbaʊnd] *v. i.* **a)** *(spring back)* abprallen **(from** von); **b)** *(fig.)* zurückfallen **(upon** auf **+** *Akk.*). **2.** [ˈriːbaʊnd] *n.* Abprall, *der*
**rebuff** [rɪˈbʌf] **1.** *n.* [schroffe] Abweisung. **2.** *v. t.* [schroff] zurückweisen
**rebuild** [riːˈbɪld] *v. t.*, **rebuilt** [riːˈbɪlt] wieder aufbauen
**rebuke** [rɪˈbjuːk] **1.** *v. t.* tadeln, rügen **(for** wegen). **2.** *n.* Rüge, *die*
**recall 1.** [rɪˈkɔːl] *v. t.* **a)** *(remember)* sich erinnern an **(+** *Akk.*); **b)** *(serve as reminder of)* erinnern an **(+** *Akk.*); **c)** abberufen ⟨*Botschafter*⟩. **2.** [rɪˈkɔːl, ˈriːkɔːl] *n.* **a)** |powers of| ~: Gedächtnis, *das;* **b) beyond** ~: unwiderruflich
**recant** [rɪˈkænt] *v. i.* [öffentlich] widerrufen
**recap** [ˈriːkæp] *v. t. & i.*, **-pp-** *(coll.)* rekapitulieren
**recapitulate** [riːkəˈpɪtjʊleɪt] *v. t. & i.* rekapitulieren
**recapture** [riːˈkæptʃə(r)] *v. t.* wieder ergreifen ⟨*Gefangenen*⟩; wieder einfangen ⟨*Tier*⟩
**recede** [rɪˈsiːd] *v. i.* ⟨*Hochwasser, Flut:*⟩ zurückgehen; ~ |into the distance| in der Ferne verschwinden. **receding** [rɪˈsiːdɪŋ] *adj.* fliehend ⟨*Kinn, Stirn*⟩
**receipt** [rɪˈsiːt] *n.* **a)** *(receiving)* Empfang, *der;* **b)** *(written acknowledgement)* Quittung, *die;* **c)** in *pl. (amount received)* Einnahmen **(from** aus)
**receive** [rɪˈsiːv] *v. t.* **a)** *(get)* erhalten; beziehen ⟨*Gehalt, Rente*⟩; **b)** *(accept)* entgegennehmen ⟨*Buket, Lieferung*⟩; **c)** *(entertain)* empfangen ⟨*Gast*⟩. **re-ceiver** *n.* **a)** Empfänger, *der*/Empfängerin, *die;* **b)** *(Teleph.)* [Telefon]hörer, *der;* **c)** *(of stolen goods)* Hehler, *der*/Hehlerin, *die*
**recent** [ˈriːsənt] *adj.* jüngst ⟨*Ereignisse, Vergangenheit usw.*⟩; **the** ~ **closure of the factory** die kürzlich erfolgte Schließung der Fabrik. ˈ**recently** *adv. (a short time ago)* vor kurzem; *(in the recent past)* in der letzten Zeit
**receptacle** [rɪˈseptəkl] *n.* Behälter, *der;* Gefäß, *das*
**reception** [rɪˈsepʃn] *n.* **a)** *(welcome)* Aufnahme, *die;* **b)** *(party)* Empfang, *der;* **c)** *(Brit.: foyer)* die Rezeption. **re-ˈceptionist** *n. (in hotel)* Empfangschef, *der*/-dame, *die; (at doctor's)* Sprechstundenhilfe, *die.* **reˈception desk** *n.* Rezeption, *die*
**receptive** [rɪˈseptɪv] *adj.* aufgeschlossen, empfänglich **(to** für)
**recess** [rɪˈses, ˈriːses] *n.* **a)** *(alcove)* Ni-

sche, *die;* **b)** *(Brit. Parl.; Amer.: short vacation)* Ferien *Pl.; (Amer. Sch.; between classes)* Pause, *die*
**recharge** [riːˈtʃɑːdʒ] *v. t.* aufladen ⟨*Batterie*⟩
**recipe** [ˈresɪpɪ] *n.* Rezept, *das*
**recipient** [rɪˈsɪpɪənt] *n.* Empfänger, *der*/Empfängerin, *die*
**reciprocal** [rɪˈsɪprəkl] *adj.* gegenseitig ⟨*Abkommen, Zuneigung*⟩
**reciprocate** [rɪˈsɪprəkeɪt] *v. t.* erwidern
**recital** [rɪˈsaɪtl] *n. (performance)* [Solisten]konzert, *das; (of literature also)* Rezitation, *die*
**recitation** [resɪˈteɪʃn] *n.* Rezitation, *die*
**recite** [rɪˈsaɪt] *v. t.* **a)** rezitieren ⟨*Gedicht;*⟩; **b)** *(list)* aufzählen
**reckless** [ˈreklɪs] *adj.* unbesonnen; rücksichtslos ⟨*Fahrweise*⟩; ~ **of the dangers/consequences** ungeachtet der Gefahren/Folgen
**reckon** [ˈrekn] *v. t.* **a)** *(work out)* ausrechnen ⟨*Kosten*⟩; bestimmen ⟨*Position*⟩; **b)** *(consider)* halten **(as** für); *(estimate)* schätzen. ˈ**reckon on** *v. t.* **a)** *(rely on)* zählen auf **(+** *Akk.*); **b)** *(expect)* rechnen mit. ˈ**reckon with** *v. i.* rechnen mit
ˈ**reckoning** *n.* Berechnung, *die;* **by my** ~: nach meiner Rechnung
**reclaim** [rɪˈkleɪm] *v. t.* **a)** zurückbekommen ⟨*Steuern*⟩; **b)** urbar machen ⟨*Land*⟩
**recline** [rɪˈklaɪn] *v. i.* liegen; **reclining seat** Liegesitz, *der*
**recluse** [rɪˈkluːs] *n.* Einsiedler, *der*/Einsiedlerin, *die*
**recognition** [rekəgˈnɪʃn] *n.* **a)** Wiedererkennen, *das;* **be beyond all** ~: nicht wiederzuerkennen sein; **b)** *(acknowledgement)* Anerkennung, *die;* **in** ~ **of** als Anerkennung für
**recognize** [ˈrekəgnaɪz] *v. t.* **a)** *(know again)* wiedererkennen **(by** an **+** *Dat.*, **from** durch); **b)** *(acknowledge)* erkennen; anerkennen ⟨*Gültigkeit, Land*⟩; **be** ~**d as** gelten als
**recoil 1.** [rɪˈkɔɪl] *v. i.* zurückfahren. **2.** [ˈriːkɔɪl, rɪˈkɔɪl] *n.* Rückstoß, *der*
**recollect** [rekəˈlekt] **1.** *v. t.* sich erinnern an **(+** *Akk.*). **2.** *v. i.* sich erinnern. **recollection** [rekəˈlekʃn] *n.* Erinnerung, *die*
**recommend** [rekəˈmend] *v. t.* empfehlen. **recommendation** [rekəmenˈdeɪʃn] *n.* Empfehlung, *die;* **on sb.'s** ~: auf jmds. Empfehlung *(Akk.)*

**recompense** ['rekəmpens] 1. *v. t.* entschädigen. 2. *n.* Entschädigung, *die*

**reconcile** ['rekənsaɪl] *v. t.* **a)** *(restore to friendship)* versöhnen; **b)** ~ **oneself to sth.** sich mit etw. versöhnen

**reconnaissance** [rɪ'kɒnɪsəns] *n. (Mil.)* Aufklärung, *die*

**reconnoitre** *(Brit.; Amer.:* **reconnoiter)** [rekə'nɔɪtə(r)] *v. i.* auf Erkundung [aus]gehen

**reconsider** [ri:kən'sɪdə(r)] *v. t.* [noch einmal] überdenken

**reconstruct** [ri:kən'strʌkt] *v. t.* wieder aufbauen; *(fig.)* rekonstruieren. **reconstruction** [ri:kən'strʌkʃn] *n.* Wiederaufbau, *der; (thing reconstructed)* Rekonstruktion, *die*

**record** 1. [rɪ'kɔ:d] *v. t.* **a)** aufzeichnen; ~ **a new LP** eine neue LP aufnehmen; **b)** *(register officially)* dokumentieren; protokollieren ⟨*Verhandlung*⟩. 2. ['rekɔ:d] *n.* **a)** **be on** ~ ⟨*Prozeß, Verhandlung, Besprechung:*⟩ protokolliert sein; **have sth. on** ~: etw. dokumentiert haben; **b)** *(report)* Protokoll, *das;* **c)** *(document)* Dokument, *das;* |strictly| **off the** ~: [ganz] inoffiziell; **d)** *(for* ~*-player)* [Schall]platte, *die;* **e)** **have a** |criminal/police| ~: vorbestraft sein; **f)** *(Sport)* Rekord, *der*

**recorded** [rɪ'kɔ:dɪd] *adj.* aufgezeichnet ⟨*Konzert, Rede*⟩; ~ **music** Musikaufnahmen. **recorded de'livery** *n. (Brit. Post.)* eingeschriebene Sendung *(ohne Versicherung)*

**recorder** [rɪ'kɔ:də(r)] *n. (Mus.)* Blockflöte, *die*

**recording** [rɪ'kɔ:dɪŋ] *n.* **a)** *(process)* Aufzeichnung, *die;* **b)** *(what is recorded)* Aufnahme, *die.* **re'cording studio** *n.* Tonstudio, *das*

**record** ['rekɔ:d]: ~**-player** *n.* Plattenspieler, *der;* ~ **token** *n.* [Schall]plattengutschein, *der*

**re-count** 1. [ri:'kaʊnt] *v. t.* [noch einmal] nachzählen. 2. ['ri:kaʊnt] *n.* Nachzählung, *die*

**recoup** [rɪ'ku:p] *v. t.* [wieder] hereinbekommen ⟨*[Geld]einsatz*⟩

**recourse** [rɪ'kɔ:s] *n.* **have** ~ **to sb./sth.** bei jmdm./zu etw. Zuflucht nehmen

**recover** [rɪ'kʌvə(r)] 1. *v. t.* zurückbekommen. 2. *v. i.* ~ **from sth.** sich von etw. [wieder] erholen; **be |fully| ~ed** [völlig] wiederhergestellt sein. **recovery** [rɪ'kʌvərɪ] *n.* Erholung, *die;* **make a quick/good** ~: sich schnell/gut erholen

**recreation** [rekrɪ'eɪʃn] *n.* Freizeitbe-

schäftigung, *die;* Hobby, *das.* **recreational** [rekrɪ'eɪʃənl] *adj.* Freizeit-

**recruit** [rɪ'kru:t] 1. *n.* **a)** *(Mil.)* Rekrut, *der;* **b)** *(new member)* neues Mitglied. 2. *v. t.* *(Mil.: enlist)* anwerben; *(into party etc.)* werben ⟨*Mitglied*⟩; einstellen ⟨*neuen Mitarbeiter*⟩. **re'cruitment** *n. (Mil.)* Anwerbung, *die; (of new staff)* Neueinstellung, *die;* ~ **of members** Mitgliederwerbung, *die*

**rectangle** ['rektæŋgl] *n.* Rechteck, *das.* **rectangular** [rek'tæŋgjʊlə(r)] *adj.* rechteckig

**rector** ['rektə(r)] *n.* **a)** Pfarrer, *der;* **b)** *(Univ.)* Rektor, *der*/Rektorin, *die.* **rectory** ['rektərɪ] *n.* Pfarrhaus, *das*

**recuperate** [rɪ'kju:pəreɪt] *v. i.* sich erholen. **recuperation** [rɪkju:pə'reɪʃn] *n.* Erholung, *die*

**recur** [rɪ'kɜ:(r)] *v. i.,* **-rr-** sich wiederholen; ⟨*Krankheit:*⟩ wiederkehren; ⟨*Symptom:*⟩ wieder auftreten. **recurrence** [rɪ'kʌrəns] *n.* Wiederholung, *die; (of illness, thought, feeling)* Wiederkehr, *die; (of symptom)* Wiederauftreten, *das.* **recurrent** [rɪ'kʌrənt] *adj.* immer wiederkehrend

**recycle** [ri:'saɪkl] *v. t.* wiederverwerten. **recycling** [ri:'saɪklɪŋ] *n.* Recycling, *das*

**red** [red] 1. *adj.* rot. 2. *n.* Rot, *das.* **Red 'Cross** *n.* Rotes Kreuz. **red'currant** *n.* [rote] Johannisbeere

**redden** ['redn] *v. i.* ⟨*Gesicht, Himmel:*⟩ sich röten; ⟨*Person:*⟩ rot werden

**reddish** ['redɪʃ] *adj.* rötlich

**redecorate** [ri:'dekəreɪt] *v. t.* renovieren; *(with wallpaper)* neu tapezieren; *(with paint)* neu streichen

**redeem** [rɪ'di:m] *v. t.* **a)** [wieder] einlösen ⟨*Pfand*⟩; einlösen ⟨*Gutschein, Coupon*⟩; **b)** *(save)* retten. **redemption** [rɪ'dempʃn] *n. (from sin)* Erlösung, *die*

**redeploy** [ri:dɪ'plɔɪ] *v. t.* woanders einsetzen ⟨*Arbeitskräfte*⟩

**red:** ~**-'handed** *adj.* **catch sb.** ~**-handed** jmdn. auf frischer Tat ertappen; ~ **'herring** *n. (fig.)* Ablenkungsmanöver, *das;* ~**-hot** *adj.* [rot]glühend; **Red 'Indian** *(Brit.)* 1. *n.* Indianer, *der*/Indianerin, *die;* 2. *adj.* Indianer-

**redirect** [ri:daɪ'rekt] *v. t.* nachsenden ⟨*Post, Brief usw.*⟩; umleiten ⟨*Verkehr*⟩

**rediscover** [ri:dɪ'skʌvə(r)] *v. t.* wiederentdecken

**red:** ~**-'letter day** *n.* großer Tag; ~ **'light** *n.* rotes Warnlicht; *(traffic-*

*light)* rote Ampel; **drive through a ~ light** bei rot über die Ampel fahren; **~-'light district** *n.* Strich, *der (salopp)*

**redo** [riːˈduː] *v. t. forms as* **do** noch einmal machen ⟨*Bett, Hausaufgabe*⟩; neu frisieren ⟨*Haare*⟩

**redouble** [riːˈdʌbl] *v. t.* verdoppeln

**redress** [rɪˈdres] **1.** *n.* Entschädigung, *die.* **2.** *v. t.* wiedergutmachen; **~ the balance** das Gleichgewicht wiederherstellen

**red 'tape** *n. (fig.)* [unnötige] Bürokratie

**reduce** [rɪˈdjuːs] *v. t.* **a)** senken ⟨*Preis, Gebühr, Fieber, Aufwendungen, Blutdruck usw.*⟩; reduzieren ⟨*Geschwindigkeit, Gewicht*⟩; **at ~d prices** zu herabgesetzten Preisen; **b)** **~ to silence/tears** verstummen lassen/zum Weinen bringen. **reduction** [rɪˈdʌkʃn] *n. (in price, costs, speed, etc.)* Senkung, *die* (**in** *Gen.*); **~ in wages/weight** Lohnsenkung, *die/*Gewichtsabnahme, *die*

**redundancy** [rɪˈdʌndənsɪ] *n. (Brit.)* Arbeitslosigkeit, *die;* **redundancies** Entlassungen

**redundant** [rɪˈdʌndənt] *adj. (Brit.)* arbeitslos; **be made ~:** den Arbeitsplatz verlieren; **make ~:** entlassen

**red 'wine** *n.* Rotwein, *der*

**reed** [riːd] *n.* Schilf[rohr], *das*

**reef** [riːf] *n.* Riff, *das*

**'reef-knot** *n.* Kreuzknoten, *der*

**reek** [riːk] *v. i.* stinken **(of** nach)

**reel** [riːl] **1.** *n.* ⟨*Garn-, Angel*⟩rolle, *die;* ⟨*Film-, Tonband*⟩spule, *die.* **2.** *v. i.* **a)** *(be in a whirl)* sich drehen; **b)** *(sway)* torkeln

**refectory** [rɪˈfektərɪ] *n.* Mensa, *die*

**refer** [rɪˈfɜː(r)] **1.** *v. i.,* **-rr-:** **a)** **~ to** *(allude to)* sich beziehen auf (+ *Akk.*) ⟨*Buch, Person usw.*⟩; *(speak of)* sprechen von ⟨*Person, Problem usw.*⟩; **b)** **~ to** *(apply to, relate to)* betreffen; **c)** **~ to** *(consult, cite as proof)* nachsehen in (+ *Dat.*). **2.** *v. t.,* **-rr-:** **~ sb./sth. to sb./ sth.** jmdn./etw. an jmdn./auf etw. *(Akk.)* verweisen

**referee** [refəˈriː] *(Sport)* **1.** *n. (umpire)* Schiedsrichter, *der/*-richterin, *die; (Boxing)* Ringrichter, *der.* **2.** *v. t.* als Schiedsrichter/-richterin leiten

**reference** [ˈrefrəns] *n.* **a)** *(allusion)* Hinweis, *der* **(to** auf + *Akk.*); **make no ~ to sth.** etw. nicht ansprechen; **b)** *(testimonial)* Zeugnis, *das*

**referendum** [refəˈrendəm] *n.* Volksentscheid, *der*

**refill 1.** [riːˈfɪl] *v. t.* nachfüllen; **~ the glasses** nachschenken. **2.** [ˈriːfɪl] *n. (for ball-pen)* Ersatzmine, *die*

**refine** [rɪˈfaɪn] *v. t.* **a)** *(purify)* raffinieren; **b)** *(make cultured)* kultivieren; **c)** *(improve)* verbessern; verfeinern ⟨*Stil, Technik*⟩. **refined** [rɪˈfaɪnd] *adj.* kultiviert. **re'finement** *n.* Kultiviertheit, *die; (improvement)* Verbesserung, *die.*

**refinery** [rɪˈfaɪnərɪ] *n.* Raffinerie, *die*

**reflect** [rɪˈflekt] *v. t.* **a)** reflektieren; **b)** *(fig.)* widerspiegeln ⟨*Ansichten*⟩; **c)** *(contemplate)* nachdenken über (+ *Akk.*); **~ what/how ...:** überlegen, was/wie ... **re'flect [up]on** *v. t.* **a)** *(consider)* nachdenken über (+ *Akk.*); **b)** **~ badly [up]on sb./sth.** auf jmdn./etw. ein schlechtes Licht werfen. **reflection** [rɪˈflekʃn] *n.* **a)** Reflexion, *die; (by surface of water)* Spiegelung, *die;* **b)** *(image)* Spiegelbild, *das;* **c)** *(consideration)* Nachdenken, *das* **(upon** über + *Akk.*); **on ~:** bei weiterem Nachdenken. **reflective** [rɪˈflektɪv] *adj.* **a)** reflektierend; **b)** *(thoughtful)* nachdenklich. **reflector** [rɪˈflektə(r)] *n.* Rückstrahler, *der*

**reflex** [ˈriːfleks] **1.** *n.* Reflex, *der.* **2.** *adj.* **~ action** Reflexhandlung, *die*

**reflexive** [rɪˈfleksɪv] *adj. (Ling.)* reflexiv

**reform** [rɪˈfɔːm] **1.** *v. t. (make better)* bessern ⟨*Person*⟩; reformieren ⟨*Institution*⟩. **2.** *n.* Reform, *die* (**in** *Gen.*). **reformation** [refəˈmeɪʃn] *n. (of character)* Wandlung, *die;* **the R~** *(Hist.)* die Reformation. **re'former** *n.* [**political**] **~:** Reformpolitiker, *der/*Reformpolitikerin, *die*

**refract** [rɪˈfrækt] *v. t. (Phys.)* brechen

**'refrain** [rɪˈfreɪn] *n.* Refrain, *der*

**²refrain** *v. i.* **~ from doing sth.** es unterlassen, etw. zu tun

**refresh** [rɪˈfreʃ] *v. t.* erfrischen. **re'freshing** *adj.* erfrischend; wohltuend ⟨*Abwechslung*⟩. **re'freshment** *n.* Erfrischung, *die*

**refrigerate** [rɪˈfrɪdʒəreɪt] *v. t.* **a)** kühl lagern ⟨*Lebensmittel*⟩; **b)** *(chill)* kühlen; *(freeze)* einfrieren. **refrigeration** [rɪfrɪdʒəˈreɪʃn] *n.* kühle Lagerung; *(chilling)* Kühlung, *die; (freezing)* Einfrieren, *das.* **refrigerator** [rɪˈfrɪdʒəreɪtə(r)] *n.* Kühlschrank, *der*

**refuel** [riːˈfjuːəl] *(Brit.)* **-ll-: 1.** *v. t.* auftanken. **2.** *v. i.* [auf]tanken

**refuge** [ˈrefjuːdʒ] *n.* Zuflucht, *die;* **take ~ in** Schutz *od.* Zuflucht suchen in (+ *Dat.*) **(from** vor + *Dat.*)

**refugee** [refjʊ'dʒi:] *n.* Flüchtling, *der*
**refund 1.** [ri:'fʌnd] *v. t. (pay back)* zurückzahlen ⟨*Geld*⟩; erstatten ⟨*Kosten*⟩.
**2.** ['ri:fʌnd] *n.* Rückzahlung, *die; (of expenses)* [Rück]erstattung, *die*
**refusal** [rɪ'fju:zl] *n.* Ablehnung, *die; (after a period of time)* Absage, *die;* ~ **to do sth.** Weigerung, etw. zu tun
**¹refuse** [rɪ'fju:z] **1.** *v. t.* ablehnen; verweigern ⟨*Zutritt, Einreise, Erlaubnis*⟩; ~ **sb.** **admittance/entry/permission** jmdm. den Zutritt/die Einreise/die Erlaubnis verweigern; ~ **to do sth.** sich weigern, etw. zu tun. **2.** *v. i.* ablehnen; *(after request)* sich weigern
**²refuse** ['refju:s] *n.* Abfall, *der*
**refuse** ['refju:s]: ~ **collection** *n.* Müllabfuhr, *die;* ~ **collector** *n.* Müllwerker, *der;* ~ **disposal** *n.* Abfallbeseitigung, *die*
**refute** [rɪ'fju:t] *v. t.* widerlegen
**regain** [rɪ'ɡeɪn] *v. t.* zurückgewinnen ⟨*Zuversicht, Vertrauen, Augenlicht*⟩; ~ **one's strength** wieder zu Kräften kommen
**regal** ['ri:ɡl] *adj.* majestätisch
**regalia** [rɪ'ɡeɪlɪə] *n. pl. (of royalty)* Krönungsinsignien
**regard** [rɪ'ɡɑ:d] **1.** *v. t.* **a)** *(look at)* betrachten; **b)** *(give heed to)* beachten; **c)** *(fig.: look upon, contemplate)* betrachten; ~ **sb. as a friend/fool/genius** jmdn. als Freund betrachten/für einen Dummkopf/ein Genie halten; **be** ~**ed as** gelten als; **d)** *(concern, have relation to)* betreffen; **as** ~**s sb./sth.,** ~**ing sb./sth.** was jmdn./etw. angeht *od.* betrifft. **2.** *n.* **a)** *(attention)* **pay or have** ~ **to sb./sth.** jmdm./etw. Beachtung schenken; ~ **to** ohne Rücksicht auf (+ *Akk.*); **b)** *(esteem)* Achtung, *die;* **hold sb./sth. in high** ~: jmdn./etw. sehr schätzen; **c)** *in pl.* Grüße; **give her my** ~**s** grüße sie von mir; **with kind[est]** ~**s** mit herzlich[st]en Grüßen. **re'gardless** *adj.* ohne Rücksicht (**of** auf + *Akk.*)
**regatta** [rɪ'ɡætə] *n.* Regatta, *die*
**regenerate** [rɪ'dʒenəreɪt] *v. t.* erneuern
**regime, régime** [reɪ'ʒi:m] *n.* [Regierungs]system, *das*
**regiment** ['redʒɪmənt, 'redʒmənt] *n.* Regiment, *das.* **regimental** [redʒɪ'mentl] *adj.* Regiments-
**region** ['ri:dʒn] *n.* **a)** *(area)* Gebiet, *das;* **b)** *(administrative division)* Bezirk, *der;* **in the** ~ **of** *(fig.)* ungefähr. **regional** ['ri:dʒənl] *adj.* regional

**register** ['redʒɪstə(r)] **1.** *n.* Register, *das; (at school)* Klassenbuch, *das.* **2.** *v. t.* **a)** *(enter)* registrieren; *(cause to be entered)* registrieren lassen; anmelden ⟨*Auto, Patent*⟩; *(at airport)* einchecken ⟨*Gepäck*⟩; *abs. (at hotel)* sich ins Fremdenbuch eintragen; ~ **with the police** sich polizeilich anmelden; **b)** *(enrol)* anmelden; *(Univ.)* sich einschreiben; **c)** zum Ausdruck bringen ⟨*Überraschung*⟩; ~ **a protest** Protest anmelden. **registered** ['redʒɪstəd] *adj.* eingetragen ⟨*Firma*⟩; eingeschrieben ⟨*Student, Brief*⟩; ~ **trade mark** eingetragenes Warenzeichen; **by** ~ **post** per Einschreiben
**registrar** ['redʒɪstrɑ:(r), redʒɪ'strɑ:(r)] *n.* Standesbeamte, *der/*-beamtin, *die*
**registration** [redʒɪ'streɪʃn] *n.* Registrierung, *die; (enrolment)* Anmeldung, *die; (of students)* Einschreibung, *die.* **regi'stration document** *n.* *(Brit.)* Kraftfahrzeugbrief, *der.* **regi'stration number** *n.* amtliches Kennzeichen
**registry** ['redʒɪstrɪ] *n.* ~ |**office**| Standesamt, *das*
**regret** [rɪ'ɡret] **1.** *v. t.,* -tt- bedauern; **I** ~ **to say that ...:** ich muß leider sagen, daß ... **2.** *n.* Bedauern, *das;* **have no** ~**s** nichts bereuen. **regretfully** [rɪ'ɡretfəlɪ] *adv.* mit Bedauern. **regrettable** [rɪ'ɡretəbl] *adj.* bedauerlich. **regrettably** [rɪ'ɡretəblɪ] *adv.* bedauerlicherweise
**regroup** [ri:'ɡru:p] **1.** *v. t.* umgruppieren. **2.** *v. i.* **a)** *(form new group)* sich neu gruppieren; **b)** *(Mil.)* sich neu formieren
**regular** ['reɡjʊlə(r)] **1.** *adj.* regelmäßig; geregelt ⟨*Arbeit*⟩; fest ⟨*Anstellung*⟩; ~ **customer** Stammkunde, *der/*-kundin, *die;* ~ **army** reguläre Armee. **2.** *n. (coll.:* ~ *customer)* Stammkunde, *der/*-kundin, *die; (in pub)* Stammgast, *der.* **regularity** [reɡjʊ'lærɪtɪ] *n.* Regelmäßigkeit, *die.* **regularly** *adv.* regelmäßig
**regulate** ['reɡjʊleɪt] *v. t. (control)* regeln; *(restrict)* begrenzen; *(adjust)* regulieren. **regulation** [reɡjʊ'leɪʃn] *n.* **a)** *see* **regulate:** Regelung, *die;* Begrenzung, *die;* Regulierung, *die;* **b)** *(rule)* Vorschrift, *die*
**rehabilitate** [ri:hə'bɪlɪteɪt] *v. t.* rehabilitieren; ~ |**back into society**| wieder [in die Gesellschaft] eingliedern
**rehash 1.** [ri:'hæʃ] *v. t.* aufwärmen. **2.** ['ri:hæʃ] *n.* Aufguß, *der*

**rehearsal** [rɪ'hɜ:sl] *n.* Probe, *die.* **rehearse** [rɪ'hɜ:s] *v.t.* proben

**reign** [reɪn] 1. *n.* Herrschaft, *die.* 2. *v.i.* herrschen (over über + *Akk.*)

**rein** [reɪn] *n.* Zügel, *der*

**reincarnation** [ri:ɪnkɑ:'neɪʃn] *n.* *(Relig.)* Reinkarnation, *die*

**reindeer** ['reɪndɪə(r)] *n., pl. same* Ren[tier], *das*

**reinforce** [ri:ɪn'fɔ:s] *v.t.* verstärken; ~d concrete Stahlbeton, *der.* **rein'forcement** *n.* Verstärkung, *die;* ~[s] *(additional men etc.)* Verstärkung, *die*

**reinstate** [ri:ɪn'steɪt] *v.t. (in job)* wieder einstellen

**reinvigorate** [ri:ɪn'vɪgəreɪt] *v.t.* neu beleben; feel ~d sich gestärkt fühlen

**reiterate** [ri:'ɪtəreɪt] *v.t.* wiederholen

**reject** 1. [rɪ'dʒekt] *v.t.* ablehnen; zurückweisen ⟨*Bitte, Annäherungsversuch*⟩. 2. ['ri:dʒekt] *(thing)* Ausschuß, *der.* **rejection** [rɪ'dʒekʃn] *n.* Ablehnung, *die/*Zurückweisung, *die*

**rejoice** [rɪ'dʒɔɪs] *v.i.* sich freuen (over, at über + *Akk.*)

**¹rejoin** [rɪ'dʒɔɪn] *v.t. (reply)* erwidern (to auf + *Akk.*)

**²rejoin** [ri:'dʒɔɪn] *v.t.* wieder eintreten in (+ *Akk.*) ⟨*Partei, Verein*⟩

**rejoinder** [rɪ'dʒɔɪndə(r)] *n.* Erwiderung, *die* (to auf + *Akk.*)

**rejuvenate** [rɪ'dʒu:vəneɪt] *v.t.* verjüngen

**rekindle** [ri:kɪndl] *v.t.* wieder anfachen; wieder aufleben lassen ⟨*Verlangen, Hoffnungen*⟩

**relapse** [rɪ'læps] 1. *v.i.* ⟨*Kranker:*⟩ einen Rückfall bekommen. 2. *n.* Rückfall, *der*

**relate** [rɪ'leɪt] 1. *v.t.* a) erzählen ⟨*Geschichte*⟩; erzählen von ⟨*Abenteuer*⟩; b) *(bring into relation)* in Zusammenhang bringen (to, with mit). 2. *v.i.* a) ~ to *(have reference)* in Zusammenhang stehen mit; betreffen ⟨*Person*⟩; b) ~ to *(feel involved with)* eine Beziehung haben zu. **re'lated** *adj.* verwandt (to mit). **relation** [rɪ'leɪʃn] *n.* a) *(connection)* Beziehung, *die,* Zusammenhang, *der* (of ... and zwischen ... und); in *or* with ~ to in bezug auf (+ *Akk.*); b) *in pl. (dealings)* Verhältnis, *das* (with zu); c) *(relative)* Verwandte, *der/die.* **re'lationship** *n.* a) *(mutual tie)* Beziehung, *die* (with zu); b) *(kinship)* Verwandtschaftsverhältnis, *das;* c) *(connection)* Beziehung, *die; (between cause and effect)* Zusammenhang, *der;* d) *(sexual)* Verhältnis, *das*

**relative** ['relətɪv] 1. *n.* Verwandte, *der/die.* 2. *adj.* relativ. **'relatively** *adv.* relativ; verhältnismäßig. **relative 'pronoun** *n. (Ling.)* Relativpronomen, *das*

**relax** [rɪ'læks] 1. *v.t.* a) entspannen ⟨*Muskel, Körper[teil]*⟩; lockern ⟨*Griff*⟩; b) *(make less strict)* lockern ⟨*Gesetz, Disziplin*⟩. 2. *v.i.* sich entspannen. **relaxation** [ri:læk'seɪʃn] *n.* Entspannung, *die;* for ~: zur Entspannung. **relaxed** [rɪ'lækst] *adj.* entspannt, gelöst ⟨*Atmosphäre, Person*⟩. **re'laxing** *adj.* entspannend

**relay** 1. ['ri:leɪ] *n.* a) *(race)* Staffel, *die;* b) *(gang)* Schicht, *die;* work in ~s schichtweise arbeiten; c) *(Electr.)* Relais, *das.* 2. [ri:'leɪ] *v.t.* a) weiterleiten; b) *(Radio, Telev.)* übertragen. **'relay race** *n.* Staffellauf, *der; (Swimming)* Staffelschwimmen, *das*

**release** [rɪ'li:s] 1. *v.t.* a) *(free)* freilassen ⟨*Tier, Häftling, Sklaven*⟩; *(from jail)* entlassen (from aus); b) *(let go)* loslassen; lösen ⟨*Handbremse*⟩; c) *(make known)* veröffentlichen ⟨*Erklärung, Nachricht*⟩; *(issue)* herausbringen ⟨*Film, Schallplatte*⟩. 2. *n.* a) see 1a: Freilassung, *die;* Entlassung, *die;* b) *(of published item)* Veröffentlichung, *die;* c) *(handle, lever, button)* Auslöser, *der*

**relegate** ['relɪgeɪt] *v.t.* a) ~ sb. to the position of ...: jmdn. zu ... degradieren; b) *(Sport)* absteigen lassen; be ~d absteigen (to in + *Akk.*). **relegation** [relɪ'geɪʃn] *n. (Sport)* Abstieg, *der*

**relent** [rɪ'lent] *v.i.* nachgeben. **re'lentless** *adj.,* **re'lentlessly** *adv.* unerbittlich

**relevance** ['relɪvəns] *n.* Relevanz, *die* (to für)

**relevant** ['relɪvənt] *adj.* relevant (to für); wichtig ⟨*Information*⟩

**reliability** [rɪlaɪə'bɪlɪtɪ] *n.* Zuverlässigkeit, *die*

**reliable** [rɪ'laɪəbl] *adj.,* **reliably** [rɪ'laɪəblɪ] *adv.* zuverlässig

**reliance** [rɪ'laɪəns] *n.* Abhängigkeit, *die* (on von)

**reliant** [rɪ'laɪənt] *adj.* be ~ on sb./sth. auf jmdn./etw. angewiesen sein

**¹relief** [rɪ'li:f] *n.* a) Erleichterung, *die;* give [sb.] ~ [from pain] [jmdm.] [Schmerz]linderung verschaffen; what a ~!, that's a ~! da bin ich aber erleichtert!; b) *(assistance)* Hilfe, *die*

**²relief** *n. (Art)* Relief, *das*

**relief:** ~ **bus** *n.* Entlastungsbus, *der;*

*(as replacement)* Ersatzbus, *der;* ~ **map** *n.* Reliefkarte, *die;* ~ **road** *n.* Entlastungsstraße, *die*

**relieve** [rɪ'liːv] *v. t.* **a)** erleichtern; unterbrechen ⟨*Eintönigkeit*⟩; abbauen ⟨*Anspannung*⟩; stillen ⟨*Schmerzen*⟩; **I am** *or* **feel ~d to hear that ...:** es erleichtert mich zu hören, daß ...; **b)** ablösen ⟨*Wache, Truppen*⟩

**religion** [rɪ'lɪdʒn] *n.* Religion, *die*

**religious** [rɪ'lɪdʒəs] *adj.* religiös; Religions⟨*freiheit, -unterricht*⟩. **re'ligiously** *adv.* *(conscientiously)* gewissenhaft

**relinquish** [rɪ'lɪŋkwɪʃ] *v. t.* **a)** *(give up)* aufgeben; **b)** ~ **one's hold** *or* **grip on sb./sth.** jmdn./etw. loslassen

**relish** ['relɪʃ] **1.** *n.* **a)** *(liking)* Vorliebe, *die;* **do sth. with [great]** ~**:** etw. mit [großem] Genuß tun; **b)** *(condiment)* Relish, *das.* **2.** *v. t.* genießen

**relive** [riː'lɪv] *n.* noch einmal durchleben

**reload** [riː'ləʊd] *v. t.* nachladen ⟨*Schußwaffe*⟩

**reluctance** [rɪ'lʌktəns] *n.* Widerwille, *der;* **have a [great]** ~ **to do sth.** etw. nur mit Widerwillen tun

**reluctant** [rɪ'lʌktənt] *adj.* unwillig; **be** ~ **to do sth.** etw. nur ungern tun. **re'luctantly** *adv.* nur ungern

**rely** [rɪ'laɪ] *v. i.* *(have trust)* sich verlassen/*(be dependent)* angewiesen sein **(**[up]on auf + *Akk.***)**

**remain** [rɪ'meɪn] *v. i.* **a)** *(be left over)* übrigbleiben; **b)** *(stay)* bleiben; ~ **behind** noch dableiben; **c)** *(continue to be)* bleiben; **it ~s to be seen** es wird sich zeigen. **remainder** [rɪ'meɪndə(r)] *n.* Rest, *der.* **re'maining** *adj.* restlich. **re'mains** *n. pl.* **a)** Reste; **b)** *(human)* sterbliche [Über]reste *(verhüll.)*

**remand** [rɪ'mɑːnd] **1.** *v. t.* ~ **sb. [in custody]** jmdn. in Untersuchungshaft behalten. **2.** *n.* **on** ~**:** in Untersuchungshaft

**remark** [rɪ'mɑːk] **1.** *v. t.* bemerken **(to** gegenüber**). 2.** *v. i.* eine Bemerkung machen **(**[up]on zu, über + *Akk.***). 3.** *n.* Bemerkung, *die* **(on** über + *Akk.***)**

**remarkable** [rɪ'mɑːkəbl] *adj.* **a)** *(notable)* bemerkenswert; **b)** *(extraordinary)* außergewöhnlich. **remarkably** [rɪ'mɑːkəblɪ] *adv.* **a)** *(notably)* bemerkenswert; **b)** *(exceptionally)* außergewöhnlich

**remarry** [riː'mærɪ] *v. i. & t.* wieder heiraten

**remedy** ['remɪdɪ] **1.** *n.* [Heil]mittel,

*das* **(for gegen). 2.** *v. t.* beheben ⟨*Problem*⟩; retten ⟨*Situation*⟩

**remember** [rɪ'membə(r)] *v. t.* **a)** sich erinnern an (+ *Akk.*); **I ~ed to bring the book** ich habe daran gedacht, das Buch mitzubringen; **an evening to** ~**:** ein unvergeßlicher Abend; **b)** *(convey greetings)* ~ **me to them** grüße sie von mir. **remembrance** [rɪ'membrəns] *n.* Gedenken, *das;* **in** ~ **of sb.** zu jmds. Gedächtnis

**remind** [rɪ'maɪnd] *v. t.* erinnern **(of an** + *Akk.*); ~ **sb. to do sth.** jmdn. daran erinnern, etw. zu tun; **that ~s me, ...:** dabei fällt mir ein, ... **re'minder** *n.* Erinnerung, *die* **(of an** + *Akk.*); *(letter)* Mahnung, *die;* Mahnbrief, *der*

**reminisce** [remɪ'nɪs] *v. i.* sich in Erinnerungen *(Dat.)* ergehen **(about an** + *Akk.*). **reminiscences** [remɪ'nɪsənsɪz] *n. pl.* Erinnerungen; *(memoirs)* [Lebens]erinnerungen *Pl.* **reminiscent** [remɪ'nɪsənt] *adj.* **be** ~ **of sth.** an etw. *(Akk.)* erinnern

**remiss** [rɪ'mɪs] *adj.* nachlässig **(of** von**)**

**remission** [rɪ'mɪʃn] *n.* **a)** *(of debt, punishment)* Erlaß, *der;* **b)** *(of prison sentence)* Straferlaß, *der*

**remit** [rɪ'mɪt] *v. t.,* **-tt-** *(send)* überweisen ⟨*Geld*⟩. **remittance** [rɪ'mɪtəns] *n.* Überweisung, *die*

**remnant** ['remnənt] *n.* Rest, *der*

**remonstrate** ['remənstreɪt] *v. i.* protestieren **(against** gegen**);** ~ **with sb.** jmdm. Vorhaltungen machen **(about, on** wegen**)**

**remorse** [rɪ'mɔːs] *n.* Reue, *die* **(for, about** über + *Akk.*). **re'morseful** [rɪ'mɔːsfl] *adj.* reumütig. **re'morseless** *adj.* unerbittlich

**remote** [rɪ'məʊt] *adj.,* ~**r** [rɪ'məʊtə(r)], ~**st** [rɪ'məʊtɪst] **a)** fern ⟨*Vergangenheit, Zukunft, Zeit*⟩; abgelegen ⟨*Ort, Gebiet*⟩; ~ **from** weit entfernt von; **b)** *(slight)* gering ⟨*Chance*⟩. **remote con'trol** *n.* *(of vehicle)* Fernlenkung, *die;* *(for TV set)* Fernbedienung, *die.* **remote-con'trol[led]** *adj.* ferngelenkt; fernbedient ⟨*Anlage*⟩

**re'motely** *adv.* entfernt ⟨*verwandt*⟩; **they are not** ~ **alike** sie haben nicht die entfernteste Ähnlichkeit

**removable** [rɪ'muːvəbl] *adj.* abnehmbar; entfernbar ⟨*Trennwand*⟩; herausnehmbar ⟨*Futter*⟩

**removal** [rɪ'muːvl] *n.* **a)** Entfernung, *die;* *(of obstacle, problem)* Beseitigung, *die;* **b)** *(transfer of furniture)* Umzug, *der*

**removal:** ~ **firm** *n.* Spedition, *die;* ~ **man** *n.* Möbelpacker, *der;* ~ **van** *n.* Möbelwagen, *der*

**remove** [rɪ'muːv] *v. t.* entfernen; beseitigen ⟨*Spur, Hindernis*⟩; *(take off)* abnehmen; ausziehen ⟨*Kleidungsstück*⟩; ~ **a book from the shelf** ein Buch vom Regal nehmen. **re'mover** *n.* **a)** *(of paint/varnish/hair/rust)* Farb- / Lack- / Haar- / Rostentferner, *der;* **b)** *(man)* Möbelpacker, *der;* |**firm of**] ~**s** Spedition[sfirma], *die*

**remunerate** [rɪ'mjuːnəreit] *v. t.* bezahlen. **remuneration** [rɪmjuːnə'reɪʃn] *n.* Bezahlung, *die*

**Renaissance** [rə'neɪsəns, rɪ'neɪsəns] *n. (Hist.)* Renaissance, *die*

**rename** [rɪ'neɪm] *v. t.* umbenennen

**render** ['rendə(r)] *v. t.* **a)** *(make)* machen; **b)** erweisen ⟨*Dienst*⟩; **c)** *(translate)* übersetzen **(by mit).** '**rendering** *n. (translation)* Übersetzung, *die*

**rendezvous** ['rɒndeɪvuː] *n., pl. same* ['rɒndeɪvuːz] **a)** *(meeting-place)* Treffpunkt, *der;* **b)** *(meeting)* Verabredung, *die*

**renegade** ['renɪgeɪd] **1.** *n.* Abtrünnige, *der/die.* **2.** *adj.* abtrünnig

**renew** [rɪ'njuː] *v. t.* erneuern; fortsetzen ⟨*Angriff, Bemühungen*⟩; *(extend)* erneuern ⟨*Vertrag, Ausweis usw.*⟩; ~ **a library book** ⟨*Bibliothekar/Benutzer:*⟩ ein Buch [aus der Bücherei] verlängern/verlängern lassen. **renewal** [rɪ'njuːəl] *n.* Erneuerung, *die*

**renounce** [rɪ'naʊns] *v. t.* verzichten auf (+ *Akk.*); verstoßen ⟨*Person*⟩; ~ **the devil/one's faith** dem Teufel/seinem Glauben abschwören

**renovate** ['renəveɪt] *v. t.* renovieren ⟨*Gebäude*⟩; restaurieren ⟨*Möbel usw.*⟩. **renovation** [renə'veɪʃn] *n.* Renovierung, *die*/Restaurierung, *die*

**renown** [rɪ'naʊn] *n.* Renommee, *das.* **renowned** [rɪ'naʊnd] *adj.* berühmt (**for** wegen, für)

**rent** [rent] **1.** *n. (for house etc.)* Miete, *die; (for land)* Pacht, *die.* **2.** *v. t.* **a)** *(use)* mieten ⟨*Haus, Wohnung usw.*⟩; pachten ⟨*Land*⟩; mieten ⟨*Auto*⟩; **b)** *(let)* vermieten ⟨*Haus, Auto usw.*⟩ (**to** *Dat.,* an + *Akk.*); verpachten ⟨*Land*⟩ (**to** *Dat.,* an + *Akk.*). **rent 'out** *v. t. see* **rent 2 b**

**rental** ['rentl] *n.* Miete, *die*

**renunciation** [rɪnʌnsɪ'eɪʃn] *n. see* **renounce:** Verzicht, *der;* Verstoßung, *die*

**reopen** [rɪ'əʊpn] **1.** *v. t.* wieder öffnen; wieder aufmachen; wiedereröffnen

⟨*Geschäft, Lokal usw.*⟩; wiederaufnehmen ⟨*Diskussion, Verhandlung*⟩. **2.** *v. i.* ⟨*Geschäft, Lokal usw.:*⟩ wieder öffnen

**reorder** [rɪ'ɔːdə(r)] *v. t.* **a)** *(Commerc.)* nachbestellen ⟨*Ware*⟩; **b)** *(rearrange)* umordnen

**reorganization** [rɪ'ɔːgənaɪ'zeɪʃn] *n.* Umorganisation, *die; (of time, work)* Neueinteilung, *die*

**reorganize** [rɪ'ɔːgənaɪz] *v. t.* umorganisieren; neu einteilen ⟨*Zeit, Arbeit*⟩

**rep** [rep] *n. (coll.: representative)* Vertreter, *der*/Vertreterin, *die*

**repaid** *see* **repay**

**repair** [rɪ'peə(r)] **1.** *v. t. (mend)* reparieren; ausbessern ⟨*Kleidung, Straße*⟩. **2.** *n.* Reparatur, *die;* **be in good/bad** ~: in gutem/schlechtem Zustand sein. **re'pair man** *n.* Mechaniker, *der; (in house)* Handwerker, *der.* **re'pair shop** *n.* Reparaturwerkstatt, *die*

**repatriate** [rɪ'pætrieɪt] *v. t.* repatriieren. **repatriation** [rɪːpætrɪ'eɪʃn] *n.* Repatriierung, *die*

**repay** [rɪ'peɪ] *v. t.,* **repaid** [rɪ'peɪd] zurückzahlen ⟨*Schulden usw.*⟩; erwidern ⟨*Besuch, Gruß, Freundlichkeit*⟩; ~ **sb. for sth.** jmdm. etw. vergelten. **re'payment** *n.* Rückzahlung, *die*

**repeal** [rɪ'piːl] **1.** *v. t.* aufheben ⟨*Gesetz, Erlaß usw.*⟩. **2.** *n.* Aufhebung, *die*

**repeat** [rɪ'piːt] **1.** *n.* Wiederholung, *die.* **2.** *v. t.* wiederholen; **please** ~ **after me: ...:** sprich/sprecht/sprechen Sie mir bitte nach: ... **re'peated** *adj.* wiederholt; *(several)* mehrere; **make** ~ **efforts to ...:** wiederholt *od.* mehrfach versuchen, ...zu... **re'peatedly** *adv.* mehrmals

**repel** [rɪ'pel] *v. t.,* **-ll-: a)** *(drive back)* abwehren; **b)** *(be repulsive to)* abstoßen. **repellent** [rɪ'pelənt] *adj.* abstoßend

**repent** [rɪ'pent] *v. i.* bereuen (**of** *Akk.*). **repentance** [rɪ'pentəns] *n.* Reue, *die.* **repentant** [rɪ'pentənt] *adj.* reuig

**repercussion** [riːpə'kʌʃn] *n., usu. in pl.* Auswirkung, *die* (|**up**]**on** auf + *Akk.*)

**repertoire** ['repətwɑː(r)] *n.* Repertoire, *das*

**repertory** ['repətərɪ] *n. (Theatre)* Repertoiretheater, *das.* '**repertory company** *n.* Repertoiretheater, *das*

**repetition** [repɪ'tɪʃn] *n.* Wiederholung, *die*

**repetitious** [repɪ'tɪʃəs] *adj.* sich immer wiederholend *attr.*

**repetitive** [rɪ'petɪtɪv] *adj.* eintönig

**rephrase** [ri:'freɪz] *v. t.* umformulieren; **I'll ~ that** ich will es anders ausdrücken

**replace** [rɪ'pleɪs] *v. t.* **a)** *(vertically)* zurückstellen; *(horizontally)* zurücklegen; **b)** *(take place of)* ersetzen; **~ A with** *or* **by B** A durch B ersetzen; **c)** *(exchange)* austauschen, auswechseln ⟨*Maschinen[teile] usw.*⟩. **re'placement** *n.* **a)** *see* **replace a:** Zurückstellen, *das;* Zurücklegen, *das;* **b)** *(provision of substitute for)* Ersatz, *der; attrib.* Ersatz-; **c)** *(substitute)* Ersatz, *der;* **~ [part]** Ersatzteil, *das*

**replay 1.** [ri:'pleɪ] *v. t.* wiederholen ⟨*Spiel*⟩; nochmals abspielen ⟨*Tonband usw.*⟩. **2.** ['ri:pleɪ] *n.* Wiederholung, *die; (match)* Wiederholungsspiel, *das*

**replenish** [rɪ'plenɪʃ] *v. t.* auffüllen

**replica** ['replɪkə] *n.* Nachbildung, *die*

**reply** [rɪ'plaɪ] **1.** *v. i.* **~ [to sb./sth.]** [jmdm./auf etw. *(Akk.)*] antworten. **2.** *v. t.* **~ that …:** antworten, daß … **3.** *n.* Antwort, *die* (**to** auf + *Akk.*)

**report** [rɪ'pɔ:t] **1.** *v. t.* **a)** *(relate)* berichten/*(in writing)* einen Bericht schreiben über (+ *Akk.*); *(state formally also)* melden; **b)** *(name to authorities)* melden (**to** *Dat.*); *(for prosecution)* anzeigen (**to** bei). **2.** *v. i.* **a)** Bericht erstatten (**on** über + *Akk.*); berichten (**on** über + *Akk.*); **b)** *(present oneself)* sich melden (**to** bei). **3.** *n.* **a)** *(account)* Bericht, *der* (**on, about** über + *Akk.*); **b)** *(Sch.)* Zeugnis, *das;* **c)** *(of gun)* Knall, *der.* **reportedly** [rɪ'pɔ:tɪdlɪ] *adv.* wie verlautet. **reported 'speech** *n.* indirekte Rede. **re'porter** *n.* Reporter, *der/*Reporterin, *die*

**repossess** [ri:pə'zes] *v. t.* wieder in Besitz nehmen

**reprehensible** [reprɪ'hensɪbl] *adj.* tadelnswert

**represent** [reprɪ'zent] *v. t.* **a)** darstellen (**as** als); **b)** *(act for)* vertreten. **representation** [reprɪzen'teɪʃn] *n.* **a)** *(depicting, image)* Darstellung, *die;* **b)** *(acting for sb.)* Vertretung, *die;* **c)** **make ~s to sb.** bei jmdm. Protest einlegen. **representative** [reprɪ'zentətɪv] **1.** *n.* **a)** *(Commerc.)* Vertreter, *der/*Vertreterin, *die;* **b)** **R~** *(Amer. Polit.)* Abgeordneter/Abgeordnete. **2.** *adj. (typical)* repräsentativ (**of** für)

**repress** [rɪ'pres] *v. t.* unterdrücken. **repression** [rɪ'preʃn] *n.* Unterdrückung, *die.* **repressive** [rɪ'presɪv] *adj.* repressiv

**reprieve** [rɪ'pri:v] **1.** *v. t.* **~ sb.** *(postpone execution)* jmdm. Strafaufschub gewähren; *(remit execution)* jmdn. begnadigen. **2.** *n.* Strafaufschub, *der* (**of** für)/Begnadigung, *die; (fig.)* Gnadenfrist, *die*

**reprimand** ['reprɪmɑ:nd] **1.** *n.* Tadel, *der.* **2.** *v. t.* tadeln

**reprint 1.** [ri:'prɪnt] *v. t.* wieder abdrucken. **2.** ['ri:prɪnt] *n.* Nachdruck, *der*

**reprisal** [rɪ'praɪzl] *n.* Vergeltungsakt, *der* (**for** gegen)

**reproach** [rɪ'prəʊtʃ] **1.** *v. t.* **~ sb.** jmdm. Vorwürfe machen. **2.** *n.* Vorwurf, *der.* **reproachful** [rɪ'prəʊtʃfl] *adv.* vorwurfsvoll

**reproduce** [ri:prə'dju:s] **1.** *v. t.* wiedergeben. **2.** *v. i. (multiply)* sich fortpflanzen. **reproduction** [ri:prə-'dʌkʃn] *n.* **a)** Wiedergabe, *die;* **b)** *(producing offspring)* Fortpflanzung, *die;* **c)** *(copy)* Reproduktion, *die*

**reprove** [rɪ'pru:v] *v. t.* tadeln

**reptile** ['reptaɪl] *n.* Reptil, *das*

**republic** [rɪ'pʌblɪk] *n.* Republik, *die.* **republican** [rɪ'pʌblɪkən] **1.** *adj.* republikanisch. **2.** *n.* **R~** *(Amer. Polit.)* Republikaner, *der/*Republikanerin, *die*

**repudiate** [rɪ'pju:dɪeɪt] *v. t.* zurückweisen

**repugnance** [rɪ'pʌgnəns] *n.* Abscheu, *der* (**to[wards]** vor + *Dat.*)

**repugnant** [rɪ'pʌgnənt] *adj.* widerlich (**to** *Dat.*)

**repulse** [rɪ'pʌls] *v. t.* abwehren

**repulsion** [rɪ'pʌlʃn] *n. (disgust)* Widerwille, *der* (**towards** gegen)

**repulsive** [rɪ'pʌlsɪv] *adj.* abstoßend

**reputable** ['repjʊtəbl] *adj.* angesehen ⟨*Person, Beruf, Zeitung usw.*⟩; anständig ⟨*Verhalten*⟩; seriös ⟨*Firma*⟩

**reputation** [repjʊ'teɪʃn] *n.* **a)** Ruf, *der;* **have a ~ for** *or* **of doing/being sth.** in dem Ruf stehen, etw. zu tun/sein; **b)** *(good name)* Name, *der*

**repute** [rɪ'pju:t] **1.** *v. t. in pass.* **be ~d [to be] sth.** als etw. gelten; **she is ~d to have/make …:** man sagt, daß sie … hat/macht. **2.** *n.* Ruf, *der.* **reputed** [rɪ'pju:tɪd] *adj.,* **re'putedly** *adv.* angeblich

**request** [rɪ'kwest] **1.** *v. t.* bitten; **~ sth. of** *or* **from sb.** jmdn. um etw. bitten. **2.** *n.* Bitte, *die* (**for** um); **at sb.'s ~:** auf jmds. Bitte *(Akk.)* [hin]. **re'quest stop** *n. (Brit.)* Bedarfshaltestelle, *die*

**require** [rɪ'kwaɪə(r)] *v. t.* **a)** *(need)* brauchen; **b)** *(order, demand)* verlangen (of von); be ~d to do sth. etw. tun müssen. **re'quirement** *n.* **a)** *(need)* Bedarf, *der;* **b)** *(condition)* Erfordernis, *das*

**requisite** ['rekwızıt] **1.** *adj.* notwendig **(to,** for für). **2.** *n. in pl.* **toilet/travel ~s** Toiletten-/Reiseartikel *Pl.*

**requisition** [rekwı'zıʃn] **1.** *n. (order for sth.)* Anforderung, *die* **(for** *Gen.*). **2.** *v. t.* anfordern

**rescind** [rı'sınd] *v. t.* für ungültig erklären

**rescue** ['reskju:] . **1.** *v. t.* retten **(from** aus). **2.** *n.* Rettung, *die; attrib.* Rettungs〈*dienst, -mannschaft*〉; **go/come to the/sb.'s ~:** jmdm. zu Hilfe kommen. **rescuer** ['reskju:ə(r)] *n.* Retter, *der/*Retterin, *die*

**research** [rı'sɜ:tʃ, 'rı:sɜ:tʃ] **1.** *n.* Forschung, *die* **(into,** on über + *Akk.*); **~ work** Recherchen *Pl.* **2.** *v. i.* forschen; **~ into sth.** etw. erforschen. **researcher** [-'--, '---] *n.* Forscher, *der/* Forscherin, *die*

**resell** [ri:'sel] *v. t.,* **resold** [ri:'səʊld] weiterverkaufen **(to** an + *Akk.*)

**resemblance** [rı'zembləns] *n.* Ähnlichkeit, *die* **(to** mit)

**resemble** [rı'zembl] *v. t.* ähneln, gleichen (+ *Dat.*)

**resent** [rı'zent] *v. t.* übelnehmen. **resentful** [rı'zentfl] *adj.* übelnehmerisch, nachtragend 〈*Person, Art*〉; **be ~ of** *or* **feel ~ about sth.** etw. übelnehmen. **re'sentment** *n.* Groll, *der (geh.);* **feel ~ towards** *or* **against sb.** einen Groll auf jmdn. haben

**reservation** [rezə'veıʃn] *n.* **a)** Reservierung, *die;* **have a ~ [for a room]** ein Zimmer reserviert haben; **b)** *(doubt)* Vorbehalt, *der* **(about** gegen); Bedenken **(about** bezüglich + *Gen.*); **without ~:** ohne Vorbehalt

**reserve** [rı'zɜ:v] **1.** *v. t.* reservieren lassen 〈*Zimmer, Tisch, Platz*〉; *(set aside)* reservieren; **~ the right to do sth.** sich *(Dat.)* [das Recht] vorbehalten, etw. zu tun. **2.** *n.* **a)** *(extra amount)* Reserve, *die* **(of** an + *Dat.*). **have/hold** *or* **keep sth. in ~:** etw. in Reserve haben/ halten; **b)** *(place set apart)* Reservat, *das;* **c)** *(Sport)* Reservespieler, *der/*-spielerin, *die;* **the R~s** die Reserve; **d)** *(reticence)* Zurückhaltung, *die.* **reserved** [rı'zɜ:vd] *adj. (reticent)* reserviert

**reservoir** ['rezəvwɑ:(r)] *n. ([artificial] lake)* Reservoir, *das*

**reshape** [ri:'ʃeıp] *v. t.* umgestalten

**reshuffle** [ri:'ʃʌfl] **1.** *v. t.* **a)** umbilden 〈*Kabinett*〉; **b)** *(Cards)* neu mischen. **2.** *n.* Umbildung, *die*

**reside** [rı'zaıd] *v. i. (formal)* wohnen; wohnhaft sein *(Amtsspr.).* **residence** ['rezıdəns] *n.* **a)** *(abode)* Wohnsitz, *der; (of ambassador etc.)* Residenz, *die;* **b)** *(stay)* Aufenthalt, *der.* **'residence permit** *n.* Aufenthaltsgenehmigung, *die.* **resident** ['rezıdənt] **1.** *adj.* wohnhaft; **be ~ in England** sein Wohnsitz in England haben. **2.** *n. (inhabitant)* Bewohner, *der/*Bewohnerin, *die; (at hotel)* Hotelgast, *der.* **residential** [rezı'denʃl] *adj.* Wohn〈*gebiet, -siedlung, -straße*〉; **~ hotel** Hotel für Dauergäste

**residue** ['rezıdju:] *n.* **a)** Rest, *der;* **b)** *(Chem.)* Rückstand, *der*

**resign** [rı'zaın] **1.** *v. t.* zurücktreten von 〈*Amt*〉. **2.** *v. refl.* **~ oneself to sth./to doing sth.** sich mit etw. abfinden/sich damit abfinden, etw. zu tun. **3.** *v. i.* 〈*Arbeitnehmer:*〉 kündigen; 〈*Regierungsbeamter:*〉 zurücktreten **(from** von). **resignation** [rezıg'neıʃn] *n.* **a)** *see* **resign 3:** Kündigung, *die;* Rücktritt, *der;* **tender one's ~:** seine Kündigung/seinen Rücktritt einreichen; **b)** *(being resigned)* Resignation, *die;* **with ~:** resigniert. **resigned** [rı'zaınd] *adj.* resigniert; **be ~ to sth.** sich mit etw. abgefunden haben

**resilience** [rı'zılıəns] *n.* **a)** Elastizität, *die;* **b)** *(fig.)* Unverwüstlichkeit, *die*

**resilient** [rı'zılıənt] *adj.* elastisch; *(fig.)* unverwüstlich

**resin** ['rezın] *n.* Harz, *das*

**resist** [rı'zıst] **1.** *v. t.* **a)** standhalten (+ *Dat.*) 〈*Frost, Hitze, Feuchtigkeit usw.*〉; **b)** *(oppose)* sich widersetzen (+ *Dat.*); widerstehen (+ *Dat.*) 〈*Versuchung*〉. **2.** *v. i. see* **1 b:** sich widersetzen; widerstehen. **resistance** [rı'zıstəns] *n.* Widerstand, *der* **(to** gegen). **resistant** [rı'zıstənt] *adj.* **a)** *(opposed)* **be ~ to** sich widersetzen (+ *Dat.*); **b)** *(having power to resist)* widerstandsfähig **(to** gegen)

**resold** *see* **resell**

**resolute** ['rezəlu:t] *adj.* resolut, energisch 〈*Person*〉; entschlossen 〈*Tat*〉

**resolution** [rezə'lu:ʃn] *n.* **a)** *(firmness)* Entschlossenheit, *die;* **b)** *(decision)* Entschließung, *die; (Polit. also)* Resolution, *die;* **c)** *(resolve)* Vorsatz, *der;* **make a ~:** einen Vorsatz fassen

**resolve** [rı'zɒlv] **1.** *v. t.* **a)** lösen 〈*Problem, Rätsel*〉; ausräumen 〈*Schwierig-*

keit〉; **b)** *(decide)* beschließen; **c)** *(settle)* beilegen 〈*Streit*〉; regeln 〈*Angelegenheit*〉. **2.** *n.* **a)** Vorsatz, *der;* **b)** *(resoluteness)* Entschlossenheit, *die.*
**resolved** [rɪˈzɒlvd] *adj.* ~ |to do sth.| entschlossen[, etw. zu tun]
**resonant** [ˈrezənənt] *adj.* hallend 〈*Ton, Klang*〉
**resort** [rɪˈzɔːt] **1.** *n.* **a)** *(place)* Aufenthalt[sort], *der;* |holiday| ~: Ferienort, *der;* ski ~: Skiurlaubsort, *der;* seaside ~: Seebad, *das;* **b)** *(recourse)* **as a last** ~: als letzter Ausweg. **2.** *v. i.* ~ **to sth./ sb.** zu etw. greifen/sich an jmdn. wenden **(for** um**)**
**resound** [rɪˈzaʊnd] *v. i.* widerhallen.
**reˈsounding** *adj.* hallend 〈*Lärm*〉; überwältigend 〈*Sieg, Erfolg*〉
**resource** [rɪˈsɔːs, rɪˈzɔːs] *n. usu. in pl.* *(stock)* Mittel *Pl.;* Ressource, *die.* **resourceful** [rɪˈsɔːsfl, rɪˈzɔːsfl] *adj.* findig 〈*Person*〉
**respect** [rɪˈspekt] **1.** *n.* **a)** *(esteem)* Respekt, *der,* Achtung, *die* **(for** vor + *Dat.*); **show** ~ **for sb./etw.** zeigen; **b)** *(aspect)* Hinsicht, *die;* **in some** ~s in mancher Hinsicht; **c) with** ~ **to** ...: in bezug auf ... *(Akk.);* was ... [an]betrifft. **2.** *v. t.* respektieren; achten. **respectable** [rɪˈspektəbl] *adj.* angesehen 〈*Bürger usw.*〉; ehrenwert 〈*Motive*〉; *(decent)* ehrbar *(geh.)* 〈*Leute, Kaufmann*〉; anständig, respektabel 〈*Beschäftigung usw.*〉. **respectful** [rɪˈspektfl] *adj.* respektvoll **(to|wards|** gegenüber). **reˈspectfully** *adv.* respektvoll
**respective** [rɪˈspektɪv] *adj.* jeweilig. **reˈspectively** *adv.* beziehungsweise
**respiration** [respɪˈreɪʃn] *n.* Atmung, *die*
**respite** [ˈrespaɪt] *n.* Ruhepause, *die; (delay)* Aufschub, *der;* **without** ~: ohne Pause
**resplendent** [rɪˈsplendənt] *adj.* prächtig
**respond** [rɪˈspɒnd] **1.** *v. i.* **a)** *(answer)* antworten **(to** auf + *Akk.*); **b)** *(react)* reagieren **(to** auf + *Akk.*); 〈*Patient, Bremsen:*〉 ansprechen **(to** auf + *Akk.*). **2.** *v. t.* antworten; erwidern
**response** [rɪˈspɒns] *n.* **a)** *(answer)* Antwort, *die* **(to** auf + *Akk.*); **in** ~ |to| als Antwort [auf (+ *Akk.*)]; **b)** *(reaction)* Reaktion, *die*
**responsibility** [rɪspɒnsɪˈbɪlɪtɪ] *n.* **a)** *(being responsible)* Verantwortung, *die;* **b)** *(duty)* Verpflichtung, *die*
**responsible** [rɪˈspɒnsɪbl] *adj.* **a)** ver-

antwortlich; **be** ~ **to sb.** jmdm. gegenüber verantwortlich sein **(for** für**)**; **b)** *(trustworthy)* verantwortungsvoll. **reˈsponsibly** [rɪˈspɒnsɪblɪ] *adv.* verantwortungsbewußt
**responsive** [rɪˈspɒnsɪv] *adj.* aufgeschlossen 〈*Person*〉; **be** ~ **to sth.** auf etw. *(Akk.)* reagieren
¹**rest** [rest] **1.** *v. i.* ruhen; ~ **on** ruhen auf ( + *Dat.*); ~ **from sth.** sich von etw. ausruhen; ~ **assured that** ...: seien Sie versichert, daß ...; ~ **with sb.** 〈*Verantwortung:*〉 bei jmdm. liegen. **2.** *v. t.* **a)** ~ **sth. against sth.** etw. an etw. *(Akk.)* lehnen; **b)** ausruhen 〈*Augen*〉. **3.** *n.* **a)** *(repose)* Ruhe, *die;* **b)** *(break, relaxation)* Ruhe[pause], *die;* Erholung, *die* **(from** von**); take a** ~: sich ausruhen **(from** von**); c)** *(pause)* **have a** ~: [eine] Pause machen; ~ **period** [Ruhe]pause, *die*
²**rest** *n.* **the** ~: der Rest; **we'll do the** ~: alles Übrige erledigen wir
**restaurant** [ˈrestərɔ̃, ˈrestərɒnt] *n.* Restaurant, *das*
**rested** [ˈrestɪd] *adj.* ausgeruht
**restful** [ˈrestfl] *adj.* ruhig 〈*Tag, Woche*〉
**restive** [ˈrestɪv] *adj.* unruhig
ˈ**restless** *adj.* unruhig 〈*Nacht, Schlaf, Bewegung*〉; ruhelos 〈*Person*〉
**restoration** [restəˈreɪʃn] *n.* **a)** *(of peace, health)* Wiederherstellung, *die; (of work of art, building)* Restaurierung, *die;* **b) the R~** *(Brit. Hist.)* die Restauration
**restore** [rɪˈstɔː(r)] *v. t.* **a)** *(give back)* zurückgeben; **b)** restaurieren 〈*Bauwerk, Kunstwerk usw.*〉; ~ **sb. to health** jmdn. wiederherstellen; **c)** wiederherstellen 〈*Ordnung, Ruhe*〉
**restrain** [rɪˈstreɪn] *v. t.* zurückhalten 〈*Gefühl, Lachen, Person*〉; bändigen 〈*unartiges Kind, Tier*〉; ~ **sb./oneself from doing sth.** jmdn. davon abhalten/ sich zurückhalten, etw. zu tun. **reˈstrained** [rɪˈstreɪnd] *adj.* zurückhaltend 〈*Wesen, Kritik*〉; beherrscht 〈*Reaktion, Worte*〉. **restraint** [rɪˈstreɪnt] *n.* **a)** *(restriction)* Einschränkung, *die;* **b)** *(reserve)* Zurückhaltung, *die;* **c)** *(self-control)* Selbstbeherrschung, *die*
**restrict** [rɪˈstrɪkt] *v. t.* beschränken **(to** auf + *Akk.*). **reˈstricted** *adj.* beschränkt. **restriction** [rɪˈstrɪkʃn] *n.* Beschränkung, *die* **(on** *Gen.*). **reˈstrictive** [rɪˈstrɪktɪv] *adj.* restriktiv
ˈ**rest room** *n. (esp. Amer.)* Toilette, *die*
**result** [rɪˈzʌlt] **1.** *v. i.* **a)** *(follow)* ~ **from sth.** die Folge einer Sache *(Gen.)* sein;

b) *(end)* ~ **in sth.** in etw. *(Dat.)* resultieren. **2.** *n.* Ergebnis, *das;* **be the ~ of sth.** die Folge einer Sache *(Gen.)* sein; **as a ~** [of this] infolgedessen. **re'sultant** [rɪˈzʌltənt] *attrib. adj.* daraus resultierend

**resume** [rɪˈzjuːm] *v. t.* wiederaufnehmen; fortsetzen ⟨*Reise*⟩

**résumé** [ˈrezʊmeɪ] *n.* Zusammenfassung, *die*

**resumption** [rɪˈzʌmpʃn] *n.* Wiederaufnahme, *die*

**resurrection** [rezəˈrekʃn] *n. (Relig.)* Auferstehung, *die*

**resuscitate** [rɪˈsʌsɪteɪt] *v. t.* wiederbeleben

**retail** [ˈriːteɪl] **1.** *adj.* Einzel⟨*handel*⟩; Einzelhandels⟨*geschäft, -preis*⟩. **2.** *adv.* **buy/sell ~:** en détail kaufen/verkaufen. **'retailer** *n.* Einzelhändler, *der/*-händlerin, *die.* **retail 'price index** *n. (Brit.)* Preisindex des Einzelhandels

**retain** [rɪˈteɪn] *v. t.* behalten; ein-, zurückbehalten ⟨*Gelder*⟩

**retaliate** [rɪˈtælɪeɪt] *v. i.* Vergeltung üben **(against** an + *Dat.*). **retaliation** [rɪtælɪˈeɪʃn] *n.* Vergeltung, *die;* **in ~ for** als Vergeltung für

**retarded** [rɪˈtɑːdɪd] *adj.* [mentally] ~: [geistig] zurückgeblieben

**retch** [retʃ] *v. i.* würgen

**retentive** [rɪˈtentɪv] *adj.* gut ⟨*Gedächtnis*⟩

**rethink** [riːˈθɪŋk] *v. t.,* **rethought** [riːˈθɔːt] noch einmal überdenken

**reticence** [ˈretɪsəns] *n.* Zurückhaltung, *die*

**reticent** [ˈretɪsənt] *adj.* zurückhaltend **(on, about** in bezug auf + *Akk.*)

**retina** [ˈretɪnə] *n.* Netzhaut, *die*

**retinue** [ˈretɪnjuː] *n.* Gefolge, *das*

**retire** [rɪˈtaɪə(r)] *v. i.* **a)** ⟨*Angestellter, Arbeiter:*⟩ in Rente *(Akk.)* gehen; ⟨*Beamter, Militär:*⟩ in Pension *od.* den Ruhestand gehen; **b)** *(withdraw)* sich zurückziehen **(to** in + *Akk.*). **retired** [rɪˈtaɪəd] *adj.* aus dem Berufsleben ausgeschieden; ⟨*Beamter, Soldat:*⟩ im Ruhestand, pensioniert. **re'tirement** *n.* Ruhestand, *der*

**retiring** [rɪˈtaɪərɪŋ] *adj. (shy)* zurückhaltend

**retort** [rɪˈtɔːt] **1.** *n.* Entgegnung, *die* **(to** auf + *Akk.*). **2.** *v. t.* entgegnen

**retrace** [rɪˈtreɪs] *v. t.* zurückverfolgen; **~ one's steps** denselben Weg noch einmal zurückgehen

**retract** [rɪˈtrækt] *v. t.* zurücknehmen

**retrain** [riːˈtreɪn] **1.** *v. i.* [sich] umschulen [lassen]. **2.** *v. t.* umschulen

**retreat** [rɪˈtriːt] **1.** *n.* **a)** *(withdrawal)* Rückzug, *der;* **beat a ~** *(fig.)* das Feld räumen; **b)** *(place)* Zufluchtsort, *der.* **2.** *v. i.* sich zurückziehen

**retribution** [retrɪˈbjuːʃn] *n.* Vergeltung, *die*

**retrieval** [rɪˈtriːvl] *n.* **a)** *(of situation)* Rettung, *die;* **beyond** *or* **past ~:** hoffnungslos; **b)** *(rescue)* Rettung, *die; (from wreckage)* Bergung, *die*

**retrieve** [rɪˈtriːv] *v. t.* **a)** *(rescue)* retten **(from** aus); *(from wreckage)* bergen **(from** aus); **b)** *(recover)* zurückholen ⟨*Brief*⟩; wiederholen ⟨*Ball*⟩; wiederbekommen ⟨*Geld*⟩; **c)** *(Computing)* wiederauffinden ⟨*Informationen*⟩; **d)** ⟨*Hund:*⟩ apportieren; **e)** retten ⟨*Situation*⟩. **re'triever** *n.* Apportierhund, *der; (breed)* Retriever, *der*

**return** [rɪˈtɜːn] **1.** *v. i. (come back)* zurückkommen; *(go back)* zurückgehen; *(by vehicle)* zurückfahren. **2.** *v. t.* **a)** *(bring back)* zurückbringen; zurückgeben ⟨*geliehenen/gestohlenen Gegenstand*⟩; **~ed with thanks** mit Dank zurück; **b)** erwidern ⟨*Besuch, Gruß, Liebe*⟩; sich revanchieren für *(ugs.)* ⟨*Freundlichkeit, Gefallen*⟩; **c)** *(elect)* wählen ⟨*Kandidaten*⟩; **d)** **~ a verdict of guilty/not guilty** ⟨*Geschworene:*⟩ auf „schuldig"/„nicht schuldig" erkennen. **3.** *n.* **a)** Rückkehr, *die;* **many happy ~s** [of the day]! herzlichen Glückwunsch [zum Geburtstag]!; **b) by ~** [of post] postwendend; **c)** *(ticket)* Rückfahrkarte, *die; (for flight)* Rückflugschein, *der;* **d) ~[s]** *(proceeds)* Gewinn, *der* **(on, from** aus); **e)** *(bringing back)* Zurückbringen, *das; (of property, goods, book)* Rückgabe, *die* **(to** an + *Akk.*); **receive/get sth. in ~** [for sth.] etw. [für etw.] bekommen

**return: ~ 'fare** *n.* Preis für eine Rückfahrkarte/*(for flight)* einen Rückflugschein; **~ 'flight** *n.* Rückflug, *der;* **~ 'journey** *n.* Rückreise, *die;* Rückfahrt, *die;* **~ 'match** *n.* Rückspiel, *das;* **~ 'ticket** *n. (Brit.)* Rückfahrkarte, *die; (for flight)* Rückflugschein, *der*

**retype** [riːˈtaɪp] *v. t.* neu tippen

**reunion** [riːˈjuːnjən] *n. (gathering)* Treffen, *das*

**reunite** [riːjʊˈnaɪt] *v. t.* wieder zusammenführen

**reuse 1.** [riːˈjuːz] *v. t.* wiederverwenden. **2.** [riːˈjuːs] *n.* Wiederverwendung, *die*

**rev** [rev] *(coll.)* **1.** *n., usu. in pl.* Umdrehung, *die.* **2.** *v. i.,* -vv- hochtourig laufen. **3.** *v. t.,* -vv- aufheulen lassen. **rev 'up** *v. t.* aufheulen lassen

**Rev.** ['revərənd, *(coll.)* rev] *abbr.* Reverend Rev.

**reveal** [rɪ'viːl] *v. t.* enthüllen *(geh.);* be ~ed ⟨*Wahrheit:*⟩ ans Licht kommen. **re'vealing** *adj.* aufschlußreich

**revel** ['revl] *v. i., (Brit.)* -ll- genießen (in *Akk.*); ~ **in doing sth.** es [richtig] genießen, etw. zu tun

**revelation** [revə'leɪʃn] *n.* **a)** Enthüllung, *die (geh.);* **be a ~:** einem die Augen öffnen; **b)** *(Relig.)* Offenbarung, *die*

**revelry** ['revlrɪ] *n.* Feiern, *das*

**revenge** [rɪ'vendʒ] **1.** *v. t.* rächen ⟨*Person, Tat*⟩. **2.** *n. (action)* Rache, *die;* **take ~** *or* **have one's ~** [on sb.] [for sth.] Rache [an jmdm.] [für etw.] nehmen; **in ~ for sth.** als Rache für etw.

**revenue** ['revənjuː] *n.* ~[s] Einnahmen

**revere** [rɪ'vɪə(r)] *v. t.* verehren. **rev'erence** ['revərəns] *n.* Ehrfurcht, *die*

**Reverend** ['revərənd] *adj.* the ~ **John Wilson** Hochwürden John Wilson

**reverent** ['revərənt] *adj.* ehrfürchtig

**reverie** ['revərɪ] *n.* Träumerei, *die*

**reversal** [rɪ'vɜːsl] *n.* Umkehrung, *die*

**reverse** [rɪ'vɜːs] **1.** *adj.* entgegengesetzt ⟨*Richtung*⟩; Rück⟨*seite*⟩; umgekehrt ⟨*Reihenfolge*⟩. **2.** *n.* **a)** *(contrary)* Gegenteil, *das;* **b)** *(Motor Veh.)* Rückwärtsgang, *der;* **put the car into ~, go into ~:** den Rückwärtsgang einlegen. **3.** *v. t.* **a)** umkehren ⟨*Reihenfolge*⟩; ~ **the charge[s]** *(Brit.)* ein R-Gespräch anmelden; **b)** zurücksetzen ⟨*Fahrzeug*⟩. **4.** *v. i.* zurücksetzen; rückwärts fahren. **reverse 'gear** *n. (Motor Veh.)* Rückwärtsgang, *der; see also* **gear 1 a**

**reversible** [rɪ'vɜːsɪbl] *adj.* beidseitig tragbar ⟨*Kleidungsstück*⟩; Wende- ⟨*mantel, -jacke*⟩

**re'versing light** *n.* Rückfahrscheinwerfer, *der*

**revert** [rɪ'vɜːt] *v. i.* ~ **to** zurückkommen auf (+ *Akk.*) ⟨*Thema, Frage*⟩; ~ **to savagery** in den Zustand der Wildheit zurückfallen

**review** [rɪ'vjuː] **1.** *n.* **a)** *(survey)* Überblick, *der* (of über + *Akk.*); **b)** *(re-examination)* [nochmalige] Überprüfung; **c)** *(of book, play, etc.)* Kritik, *die;* Rezension, *die.* **2.** *v. t.* **a)** *(survey)* untersuchen; prüfen; **b)** *(re-examine)* überprüfen; **c)** *(Mil.)* inspizieren; **d)**

*(write a criticism of)* rezensieren. **re'viewer** *n.* Rezensent, *der*/Rezensentin, *der*

**revile** [rɪ'vaɪl] *v. t.* schmähen *(geh.)*

**revise** [rɪ'vaɪz] *v. t.* **a)** *(check over)* durchsehen ⟨*Manuskript*⟩; **b)** *(for exam)* wiederholen; *abs.* lernen. **re'vision** [rɪ'vɪʒn] *n.* **a)** *(checking over)* Durchsicht, *die;* **b)** *(amended version)* revidierte Fassung; **c)** *(for exam)* Wiederholung, *die*

**revisit** [riː'vɪzɪt] *v. t.* wieder besuchen

**revitalize** [riː'vaɪtəlaɪz] *v. t.* neu beleben

**revival** [rɪ'vaɪvl] *n.* Neubelebung, *die*

**revive** [rɪ'vaɪv] **1.** *v. i. (come back to consciousness)* wieder zu sich kommen; *(be reinvigorated)* zu neuem Leben erwachen. **2.** *v. t.* **a)** *(restore to consciousness)* wiederbeleben; *(reinvigorate)* wieder zu Kräften kommen lassen; **b)** wieder wecken ⟨*Lebensgeister, Interesse*⟩

**revoke** [rɪ'vəʊk] *v. t.* aufheben ⟨*Entscheidung*⟩; widerrufen ⟨*Befehl*⟩; widerrufen ⟨*Erlaubnis, Genehmigung*⟩

**revolt** [rɪ'vəʊlt] **1.** *v. i.* revoltieren (**against** gegen). **2.** *v. t.* mit Abscheu erfüllen. **3.** *n.* Revolte, *die (auch fig.);* Aufstand, *der.* **re'volting** *adj.* abscheulich; *(coll.: unpleasant)* widerlich

**revolution** [revə'luːʃn] *n.* Revolution, *die.* **revolutionary** [revə'luːʃənərɪ] **1.** *adj.* revolutionär. **2.** *n.* Revolutionär, *der*/Revolutionärin, *die*

**revolve** [rɪ'vɒlv] **1.** *v. t.* drehen. **2.** *v. i.* sich drehen (**round, about, on** um)

**revolver** [rɪ'vɒlvə(r)] *n.* [Trommel]revolver, *der*

**revolving** [rɪ'vɒlvɪŋ] *attrib. adj.* Dreh⟨*bühne, -tür*⟩

**revue** [rɪ'vjuː] *n.* Kabarett, *das; (musical show)* Revue, *die*

**revulsion** [rɪ'vʌlʃn] *n.* Abscheu, *der* (**at** vor + *Dat.,* gegen)

**reward** [rɪ'wɔːd] **1.** *n.* Belohnung, *die.* **2.** *v. t.* belohnen. **re'warding** *adj.* lohnend; **be ~/financially ~:** sich lohnen/einträglich sein

**rewind** [riː'waɪnd] *v. t.,* **rewound** [riː'waʊnd] **a)** wieder aufziehen ⟨*Uhr*⟩; **b)** zurückspulen ⟨*Film, Band*⟩

**reword** [riː'wɜːd] *v. t.* umformulieren

**rewrite** [riː'raɪt] *v. t.,* **rewrote** [riː'rəʊt], **rewritten** [riː'rɪtn] noch einmal [neu] schreiben; *(write differently)* umschreiben

**rhetoric** ['retərɪk] *n.* [art of] ~: Redekunst, *die;* Rhetorik, *die.* **rhetorical** [rɪˈtɒrɪkl] *adj.* rhetorisch

**rheumatic** [ruːˈmætɪk] *adj.* rheumatisch

**rheumatism** [ˈruːmətɪzm] *n.* Rheumatismus, *der;* Rheuma, *das (ugs.)*

**Rhine** [raɪn] *pr. n.* Rhein, *der*

**rhino** [ˈraɪnəʊ] *n., pl.* same *or* ~s *(coll.),* **rhinoceros** [raɪˈnɒsərəs] *n., pl.* same *or* ~es Nashorn, *das;* Rhinozeros, *das*

**rhododendron** [rəʊdəˈdendrən] *n.* Rhododendron, *der*

**rhubarb** [ˈruːbɑːb] *n.* Rhabarber, *der*

**rhyme** [raɪm] **1.** *n.* Reim, *der;* without ~ or reason ohne Sinn und Verstand. **2.** *v. i.* sich reimen (**with** auf + *Akk.*)

**rhythm** [ˈrɪðm] *n.* Rhythmus, *der.* **rhythmic** [ˈrɪðmɪk], **rhythmical** [ˈrɪðmɪkl] *adj.* rhythmisch

**rib** [rɪb] **1.** *n.* Rippe, *die.* **2.** *v. t.,* -bb- *(coll.)* aufziehen *(ugs.)*

**ribald** [ˈrɪbəld] *adj.* zotig

**ribbon** [ˈrɪbn] *n.* Band, *das; (on type-writer)* [Farb]band, *das*

**rice** [raɪs] *n.* Reis, *der.* **rice 'pudding** *n.* Milchreis, *der.* '**rice wine** *n.* Reiswein, *der*

**rich** [rɪtʃ] **1.** *adj.* **a)** reich (**in** an + *Dat.*); *(fertile)* fruchtbar ⟨*Land, Boden*⟩; **b)** *(splendid)* prachtvoll; **c)** *(containing much fat, oil, eggs, etc.)* gehaltvoll; **d)** *(deep, full)* voll[tönend] ⟨*Stimme*⟩; voll ⟨*Ton*⟩; satt ⟨*Farbe, Farbton*⟩. **2.** *n. pl.* the ~: die Reichen; ~ **and poor** Arm und Reich. **riches** [ˈrɪtʃɪz] *n. pl.* Reichtum, *der.* '**richly** *adv.* **a)** *(splendidly)* reich; üppig ⟨*ausgestattet*⟩; prächtig ⟨*gekleidet*⟩; **b)** *(fully)* voll und ganz; ~ **deserved** wohlverdient. '**richness** *n.* **a)** *(of food)* Reichhaltigkeit, *die;* **b)** *(of voice)* voller Klang; *(of colour)* Sattheit, *die*

**rickets** [ˈrɪkɪts] *n.* Rachitis, *die*

**rickety** [ˈrɪkɪtɪ] *adj.* wack[e]lig

**ricochet** [ˈrɪkəʃeɪ] **1.** *n.* **a)** Abprallen, *das;* **b)** *(hit)* Abpraller, *der.* **2.** *v. i.,* ~ed [ˈrɪkəʃeɪd] abprallen (**off** von)

**rid** [rɪd] *v. t.,* -dd-, rid: ~ **sth. of sth.** etw. von etw. befreien; ~ **oneself of sb./sth.** sich von jmdm./etw. befreien; **be** ~ **of sb./sth.** jmdn./etw. los sein *(ugs.);* **get** ~ **of sb./sth.** jmdn./etw. loswerden

**riddance** [ˈrɪdəns] *n.* good ~! Gott sei Dank ist er/es *usw.* weg!

**ridden** *see* ride 2, 3

¹**riddle** [ˈrɪdl] *n.* Rätsel, *das*

²**riddle** *v. t.* durchlöchern; ~d with bullets von Kugeln durchsiebt

**ride** [raɪd] **1.** *n. (on horseback)* [Aus]ritt,

*der; (in vehicle, at fair)* Fahrt, die; ~ **in a train/coach** Zug-/Busfahrt, die; **go for a** ~: ausreiten; **go for a |bi|cycle** ~: radfahren; **go for a** ~ |**in the car**| [mit dem Auto] wegfahren; **take sb. for a** ~ *(fig. sl.: deceive)* jmdn. reinlegen *(ugs.).* **2.** *v. i.,* rode [rəʊd], ridden [ˈrɪdn] *(on horse)* reiten; *(on bicycle, in vehicle)* fahren; ~ **to town on one's bike/in one's car/on the train** mit dem Rad/Auto/Zug in die Stadt fahren. **3.** *v. t.,* rode, ridden reiten ⟨*Pferd usw.*⟩; fahren mit ⟨*Fahrrad*⟩. **ride a'way, ride 'off** *v. i.* wegreiten/-fahren

'**rider** *n.* **a)** Reiter, *der*/Reiterin, *die; (of cycle)* Fahrer, *der*/Fahrerin, *die;* **b)** *(addition)* Zusatz, *der*

**ridge** [rɪdʒ] *n.* **a)** *(of roof)* First, *der;* **b)** *(long hilltop)* Grat, *der;* Kamm, *der;* **c)** *(Meteorol.)* ~ |**of high pressure**| langgestrecktes Hoch

**ridicule** [ˈrɪdɪkjuːl] **1.** *n.* Spott, *der.* **2.** *v. t.* verspotten

**ridiculous** [rɪˈdɪkjʊləs] *adj.* lächerlich

**riding** [ˈraɪdɪŋ] *n.* Reiten, *das.* '**riding lesson** *n.* Reitstunde, *die.* '**riding-school** *n.* Reitschule, *die*

**rife** [raɪf] *pred. adj.* weit verbreitet

**riff-raff** [ˈrɪfræf] *n.* Gesindel, *das*

**rifle** [ˈraɪfl] **1.** *n.* Gewehr, *das.* **2.** *v. t.* durchwühlen. **3.** *v. i.* ~ **through sth.** etw. durchwühlen

**rift** [rɪft] *n.* Unstimmigkeit, *die*

¹**rig** [rɪg] *n. (for oil-well)* [Öl]förderturm, *der; (off shore)* Förderinsel, *die.* **rig 'out** *v. t.* ausstaffieren. **rig 'up** *v. t.* aufbauen

²**rig** *v. t.,* -gg- manipulieren ⟨*[Wahl]-ergebnis*⟩; fälschen ⟨*Wahl*⟩

**rigging** [ˈrɪgɪŋ] *n.* Takelung, *die*

**right** [raɪt] **1.** *adj.* **a)** *(just, morally good, sound)* richtig; **b)** *(correct, true)* richtig; **you're |quite|** ~: du hast [völlig] recht; **be** ~ **in sth.** recht mit etw. haben; **is that clock** ~? geht die Uhr da richtig?; **put** *or* **set** ~: richtigstellen ⟨*Irrtum, Behauptung*⟩; wiedergutmachen ⟨*Unrecht*⟩; berichtigen ⟨*Fehler*⟩; richtig stellen ⟨*Uhr*⟩; **put** *or* **set sb.** ~: jmdn. berichtigen; **that's** ~: ja[wohl]; **so ist es; is that** ~? stimmt das?; *(indeed?)* aha!; |**am I**| ~? nicht [wahr?]; **c)** *(preferable, most suitable)* richtig; recht; **do sth. the** ~ **way** etw. richtig machen; **d)** *(opposite of left)* recht...; **on the** ~ **side** rechts; **e)** R~ *(Polit.)* recht... **2.** *v. t.* aus der Welt schaffen ⟨*Unrecht*⟩. **3.** *n.* **a)** *(fair claim, authority)* Recht, *das;* **have a/no** ~ **to sth.**

ein/kein Anrecht *od.* Recht auf etw. *(Akk.)* haben; **in one's own ~:** aus eigenem Recht; **~ of way** Vorfahrtsrecht, *das;* **have ~ of way** Vorfahrt haben; b) *(what is just)* Recht, *das;* **by ~|s|** von Rechts wegen; **in the ~:** im Recht; c) *(~-hand side)* rechte Seite; **on** *or* **to the ~ |of sb./sth.|** rechts [von jmdm./etw.]; d) *(Polit.)* **the R~:** die Rechte. **4.** *adv.* a) *(correctly)* richtig; b) *(to the ~-hand side)* nach rechts; c) *(completely)* ganz; d) *(exactly)* genau; **~ 'now** im Moment; jetzt sofort ⟨*handeln*⟩; e) *(straight)* direkt

'**right angle** *n.* rechter Winkel; **at ~s to sth.** rechtwinklig zu etw.

**righteous** ['raɪtʃəs] *adj.* rechtschaffen

**rightful** ['raɪtfl] *adj.* rechtmäßig ⟨*Besitzer, Herrscher*⟩

**right:** **~-hand** *adj.* recht...; **~-'handed 1.** *adj.* rechtshändig; ⟨*Werkzeug*⟩ für Rechtshänder; **be ~-handed** ⟨*Person:*⟩ Rechtshänder/ Rechtshänderin sein; **2.** *adv.* rechtshändig; **~-hand 'man** *n.* rechte Hand

'**rightly** *adv.* zu Recht

**right:** **~-'minded** *adj.* gerecht denkend; **~ 'wing** *n.* rechter Flügel; **~-wing** *adj. (Polit.)* rechtsgerichtet; Rechts⟨*extremist, -intellektueller*⟩; **~-winger** *n.* a) *(Sport)* Rechtsaußen, *der;* b) *(Polit.)* Rechte, *der/die*

**rigid** ['rɪdʒɪd] *adj.* a) starr; *(stiff)* steif; b) *(strict)* streng; unbeugsam ⟨*System*⟩. **rigidity** [rɪ'dʒɪtɪ] *n. see* **rigid:** Starrheit, *die;* Steifheit, *die;* Strenge, *die*

**rigmarole** ['rɪgmərəʊl] *n.* a) *(talk)* langatmiges Geschwafel *(ugs.);* b) *(procedure)* Zirkus, *der*

**rigor** ['rɪgə(r)] *(Amer.) see* **rigour**

**rigor mortis** [rɪgə 'mɔːtɪs] *n.* Totenstarre, *die*

**rigorous** ['rɪgərəs] *adj.* streng

**rigour** ['rɪgə(r)] *n. (Brit.)* Strenge, *die*

**rile** [raɪl] *v.t. (coll.)* ärgern

**rim** [rɪm] *n.* Rand, *der; (of wheel)* Felge, *die*

**rind** [raɪnd] *n. (of fruit)* Schale, *die; (of cheese)* Rinde, *die; (of bacon)* Schwarte, *die*

¹**ring** [rɪŋ] **1.** *n.* a) Ring, *der;* b) *(Boxing)* Ring, *der; (in circus)* Manege, *die.* **2.** *v.t. (surround)* umringen; einkreisen ⟨*Wort usw.*⟩

²**ring 1.** *n.* a) *(act of sounding bell)* Läuten, *das;* Klingeln, *das;* b) *(Brit. coll.: telephone call)* Anruf, *der;* **give sb. a**

**~:** jmdn. anrufen; c) *(fig.: impression)* **have the ~ of truth |about it|** glaubhaft klingen. **2.** *v.i.,* **rang** [ræŋ], **rung** [rʌŋ] a) *(sound clearly)* [er]schallen; ⟨*Hammer:*⟩ [er]dröhnen; b) *(be sounded)* ⟨*Glocke, Klingel, Telefon:*⟩ läuten; ⟨*Wecker, Telefon, Kasse:*⟩ klingeln; **the doorbell rang** es klingelte; c) *(~ bell)* läuten (for nach); d) *(Brit.: make telephone call)* anrufen. **3.** *v.t.,* **rang,** **rung** a) läuten ⟨*Glocke*⟩; **~ the |door|bell** läuten; klingeln; **it ~s a bell** *(fig. coll.)* es kommt mir [irgendwie] bekannt vor; b) *(Brit.: telephone)* anrufen. **ring 'back** *(Brit.) v.t. & i.* a) *(again)* wieder anrufen; b) *(in return)* zurückrufen. **ring 'off** *v.i. (Brit.)* auflegen. **ring 'out** *v.i.* ertönen

**ring:** **~ binder** *n.* Ringbuch, *das;* **~-finger** *n.* Ringfinger, *der*

**ringing** ['rɪŋɪŋ] *n.* Läuten, *das; (Brit. Teleph.:)* **~ tone** Freiton, *der*

'**ringleader** *n.* Anführer, *der/*Anführerin, *die*

**ringlet** ['rɪŋlɪt] *n.* [Ringel]löckchen, *das*

'**ring road** *n.* Ringstraße, *die*

**rink** [rɪŋk] *n. (for ice-skating)* Eisbahn, *die; (for roller-skating)* Rollschuhbahn, *die*

**rinse** [rɪns] **1.** *v.t.* a) *(wash out)* ausspülen ⟨*Mund, Gefäß usw.*⟩; b) [aus]spülen ⟨*Wäsche usw.*⟩; abspülen ⟨*Hände, Geschirr*⟩. **2.** *n.* Spülen, *das;* **give sth. a |good/quick|** ~: etw. [gut/schnell] ausspülen/abspülen/spülen. **rinse 'out** *v.t.* ausspülen

**riot** ['raɪət] **1.** *n.* Aufruhr, *der; ~s* Unruhen *Pl.;* **run ~:** randalieren. **2.** *v.i.* randalieren. '**rioter** *n.* Randalierer, *der.* **riotous** ['raɪətəs] *adj.* a) gewalttätig; b) *(unrestrained)* wild

**rip** [rɪp] **1.** *n.* Riß, *der.* **2.** *v.t.,* **-pp-** zerreißen; **~ open** aufreißen. **rip 'off** *v.t.* a) *(remove from)* reißen von; *(remove)* abreißen; b) *(sl.: defraud)* übers Ohr hauen *(ugs.).* **rip 'out** *v.t.* herausreißen (*out of* aus)

**RIP** *abbr.* **rest in peace** R.I.P.

'**rip-cord** *n.* Reißleine, *die*

**ripe** [raɪp] *adj.* reif (for zu). **ripen** ['raɪpn] **1.** *v.t.* zur Reife bringen. **2.** *v.i.* reifen. '**ripeness** *n.* Reife, *die*

'**rip-off** *n. (sl.)* Nepp, *der (ugs.)*

**riposte** [rɪ'pɒst] **1.** *n. (retort)* [rasche] Entgegnung. **2.** *v.i. (rasch)* antworten

**ripple** ['rɪpl] **1.** *n.* kleine Welle. **2.** *v.i.* ⟨*See:*⟩ sich kräuseln; ⟨*Welle:*⟩ plätschern. **3.** *v.t.* kräuseln

**rise** [raɪz] 1. *n.* **a)** *(advancement)* Aufstieg, *der;* **b)** *(in value, price, cost)* Steigerung, *die; (in population, temperature)* Zunahme, *die;* **c)** *(Brit.)* |pay| ~ *(in wages)* Lohnerhöhung, *die; (in salary)* Gehaltserhöhung, *die;* **d)** *(hill)* Anhöhe, *die;* **e)** give ~ to führen zu; Anlaß geben zu ⟨*Spekulation*⟩. 2. *v.i.,* rose [rəʊz], risen ['rɪzn] **a)** *(go up)* aufsteigen; **b)** ⟨*Sonne, Mond:*⟩ aufgehen; **c)** *(increase, reach higher level)* steigen; **d)** *(advance)* ⟨*Person:*⟩ aufsteigen; **e)** ⟨*Teig, Kuchen:*⟩ aufgehen; **f)** *(Theatre)* ⟨*Vorhang:*⟩ aufgehen; **g)** ⟨*Fluß:*⟩ entspringen. **rise 'up** *v.i.* **a)** ~ up |in revolt| aufbegehren *(geh.);* **b)** ⟨*Berg:*⟩ aufragen

**risen** *see* rise 2

**'riser** *n.* early ~: Frühaufsteher, *der*/Frühaufsteherin, *die*

**rising** ['raɪzɪŋ] 1. *n. (of sun, moon, etc.)* Aufgang, *der.* 2. *adj.* **a)** aufgehend ⟨*Sonne, Mond usw.*⟩; **b)** steigend ⟨*Kosten, Temperatur, Wasser, Flut*⟩; **c)** *(sloping upwards)* ansteigend

**risk** [rɪsk] 1. *n.* Gefahr, *die; (chance taken)* Risiko, *das;* at one's own ~: auf eigene Gefahr *od.* eigenes Risiko; take the ~ of doing sth. es riskieren, etw. zu tun; be at ~ ⟨*Zukunft, Plan:*⟩ gefährdet sein. 2. *v.t.* riskieren; I'll ~ it ich lasse es darauf ankommen. **'risky** *adj.* gefährlich; gewagt ⟨*Experiment, Projekt*⟩

**risqué** ['rɪskeɪ] *adj.* gewagt

**rissole** ['rɪsəʊl] *n.* Rissole, *die*

**rite** [raɪt] *n.* Ritus, *der*

**ritual** ['rɪtʃʊəl] 1. *adj.* rituell; Ritual-⟨*mord, -tötung*⟩. 2. *n.* Ritual, *das*

**rival** ['raɪvl] 1. *n. (competitor)* Rivale, *der*/Rivalin, *die;* business ~s Konkurrenten. 2. *v.t., (Brit.)* -ll- nicht nachstehen (+ *Dat.*). **rivalry** ['raɪvlrɪ] *n.* Rivalität, *die (geh.)*

**river** ['rɪvə(r)] *n.* Fluß, *der.* **'river-bed** *n.* Flußbett, *das.* **'riverside** 1. *n.* Flußufer, *das.* 2. *attrib. adj.* am Fluß gelegen; am Fluß *nachgestellt*

**rivet** ['rɪvɪt] 1. *n.* Niete, *die.* 2. *v.t.* **a)** [ver]nieten; **b)** *(fig.)* fesseln. **'riveting** *adj.* fesselnd

**RN** *abbr. (Brit.)* **Royal Navy** Königl. Mar.

**road** [rəʊd] *n.* Straße, *die;* across *or* over the ~ |from us| [bei uns] gegenüber; by ~ *(by car/bus/lorry)* per Auto/ Bus/Lkw; be on the ~: auf Reisen *od.* unterwegs sein; ⟨*Theaterensemble usw.:*⟩ auf Tournee *od.* Tour sein

**road:** ~ accident *n.* Verkehrsunfall, *der;* ~-block *n.* Straßensperre, *die;* ~-hog *n.* Verkehrsrowdy, *der;* ~-map *n.* Straßenkarte, *die* ~ safety *n.* Verkehrssicherheit, *die;* ~ sense *n.* Gespür für Verkehrssituationen; ~side *n.* Straßenrand, *der or* by/along the ~side am Straßenrand; ~ sign *n.* Verkehrszeichen, *das;* Straßenschild, *das (ugs.);* ~-sweeper *n.* Straßenkehrer, *der*/-kehrerin, *die;* ~-user *n.* Verkehrsteilnehmer, *der*/-teilnehmerin, *die;* ~way *n.* Fahrbahn, *die;* ~works *n. pl.* Straßenbauarbeiten *Pl.;* ~worthy *adj.* fahrtüchtig

**roam** [rəʊm] 1. *v.i.* umherstreifen. 2. *v.t.* streifen durch

**roar** [rɔː(r)] 1. *n. (of wild beast)* Gebrüll, *das; (of applause)* Tosen, *das; (of engine, traffic)* Dröhnen, *das;* ~s/a ~ |of laughter| dröhnendes Gelächter. 2. *v.i.* brüllen (with ~ + *Dat.*); ⟨*Motor:*⟩ dröhnen. **'roaring** *adj.* **a)** bullernd *(ugs.)* ⟨*Feuer*⟩; **b)** a ~ success ein Bombenerfolg; do a ~ trade ein Bombengeschäft machen

**roast** [rəʊst] 1. *v.t.* braten; rösten ⟨*Kaffeebohnen, Kastanien*⟩. 2. *attrib. adj.* gebraten ⟨*Fleisch, Ente usw.*⟩; Brat⟨*hähnchen, -kartoffeln*⟩; Röst⟨*kastanien*⟩; ~ beef *(sirloin)* Roastbeef, *das.* 3. *n.* Braten, *der*

**rob** [rɒb] *v.t.,* -bb- ausrauben ⟨*Bank, Safe, Kasse*⟩; berauben ⟨*Person*⟩. **robber** ['rɒbə(r)] *n.* Räuber, *der*/Räuberin, *die.* **robbery** ['rɒbərɪ] *n.* Raub, *der;* robberies Raubüberfälle

**robe** [rəʊb] *n.* Gewand, *das (geh.); (of judge, vicar)* Talar, *der*

**robin** ['rɒbɪn] *n.* ~ |redbreast| Rotkehlchen, *das*

**robot** ['rəʊbɒt] *n.* Roboter, *der*

**robust** [rəʊˈbʌst] *adj.* robust

**'rock** [rɒk] *n.* **a)** *(piece of ~)* Fels, *der;* **b)** *(large ~, hill)* Felsen, *der;* **c)** *(substance)* Fels, *der; (esp. Geol.)* Gestein, *das;* **d)** *(boulder)* Felsbrocken, *der; (Amer.: stone)* Stein, *der;* **e)** stick of ~: Zuckerstange, *die;* **f)** be on the ~s *(fig. coll.)* ⟨*Ehe, Firma:*⟩ kaputt sein *(ugs.)*

**²rock** 1. *v.t.* wiegen; *(in cradle)* schaukeln. 2. *v.i.* **a)** schaukeln; **b)** *(sway)* schwanken. 3. *n. (Mus.)* Rock, *der; attrib.* Rock-; ~ and *or* 'n' roll |music| Rock and Roll, *der*

**rock:** ~-'bottom *(coll.)* 1. *adj.* ~-bottom prices Schleuderpreise *(ugs.);* 2. *n.* reach *or* touch ~-bottom ⟨*Handel,*

*Preis:*) in den Keller fallen *(ugs.); her* **spirits reached ~-bottom** ihre Stimmung war auf dem Tiefpunkt; **~-climbing** n. [Fels]klettern, *das*
**rockery** ['rɒkərɪ] n. Steingarten, *der*
**rocket** ['rɒkɪt] 1. n. Rakete, *die.* 2. *v. i.* ⟨*Preise:*⟩ in die Höhe schnellen
**rocking: ~-chair** n. Schaukelstuhl, *der;* **~-horse** n. Schaukelpferd, *das*
'**rocky** adj. a) felsig; b) *(coll.: unsteady)* wackelig *(ugs.)*
**rod** [rɒd] n. Stange, *die; (for punishing)* Rute, *die; (for fishing)* [Angel]rute, *die*
**rode** see **ride** 2, 3
**rodent** ['rəʊdənt] n. Nagetier, *das*
'**roe** [rəʊ] n. *(of fish)* [**hard**] ~: Rogen, *der;* [**soft**] ~: Milch, *die*
²**roe** n. ~ [**deer**] Reh, *das*
**rogue** [rəʊg] n. Gauner, *der*
**role, rôle** [rəʊl] n. Rolle, *die*
'**roll** [rəʊl] n. a) Rolle, *die; (of cloth etc.)* Ballen, *der;* ~ **of film** Rolle Film; b) [**bread**] ~: Brötchen, *das*
²**roll** 1. n. *(of drum)* Wirbel, *der.* 2. *v. t.* a) rollen; *(between surfaces)* drehen; b) *(shape by ~ing)* rollen; drehen ⟨Zigarette⟩; c) walzen ⟨*Rasen, Metall usw.*⟩; ausrollen ⟨*Teig*⟩. 3. *v. i.* a) rollen; b) ⟨*Maschine:*⟩ laufen; **get sth. ~ing** *(fig.)* etw. ins Rollen bringen; c) **be ~ing in money** *or* **in it** *(coll.)* im Geld schwimmen *(ugs.).* **roll a'bout** *v. i.* herumrollen; ⟨*Schiff:*⟩ schlingern; ⟨*Kind, Hund:*⟩ sich wälzen. **roll 'back** *v. t.* zurückrollen. **roll 'by** *v. i.* ⟨*Zeit:*⟩ vergehen. **roll 'in** *v. i. (coll.)* ⟨*Briefe, Geldbeträge:*⟩ eingehen. **roll 'out** *v. t.* ausrollen ⟨*Teig, Teppich*⟩. **roll 'over** *v. i.* ⟨*Person:*⟩ sich umdrehen, *(to make room)* sich zur Seite rollen. **roll 'up** 1. *v. t.* aufrollen ⟨*Teppich*⟩; zusammenrollen ⟨*Landkarte, Dokument usw.*⟩; hochkrempeln ⟨*Ärmel*⟩. 2. *v. i. (coll.: arrive)* aufkreuzen *(salopp)*
'**roll-call** n. Ausrufen aller Namen; *(Mil.)* Zählappell, *der*
'**roller** n. a) Rolle, *die; (for lawn, road, etc.)* Walze, *die;* b) *(for hair)* Lockenwickler, *der*
**roller: ~ blind** n. Rouleau, *das;* **~-coaster** n. Achterbahn, *die;* **~-skate** 1. n. Rollschuh, *der;* 2. *v. i.* Rollschuh laufen; **~-skating** n. Rollschuhlaufen, *das*
'**rolling** adj. wellig ⟨*Gelände*⟩; ~ **hills** sanfte Hügel
**rolling: ~-pin** n. Teigrolle, *die;* **~-stock** n. *(Brit. Railw.)* Fahrzeugbestand, *der*

**ROM** [rɒm] *abbr. (Computing)* **read only memory** ROM
**Roman** ['rəʊmən] 1. n. Römer, *der/* Römerin, *die.* 2. *adj.* römisch.
**Roman 'Catholic** 1. *adj.* römischkatholisch. 2. n. Katholik, *der/*Katholikin, *die;* **sb. is a ~:** jmd. ist römischkatholisch
**romance** [rə'mæns] n. a) *(love affair)* Romanze, *die;* b) *(love-story)* [romantische] Liebesgeschichte
**Romania** [rəʊ'meɪnɪə] *pr. n.* Rumänien *(das).* **Romanian** [rəʊ'meɪnɪən] 1. *adj.* rumänisch. 2. n. a) *(person)* Rumäne, *der/*Rumänin, *die;* b) *(language)* Rumänisch, *das; see also* **English** 2 a
**Roman 'numeral** n. römische Ziffer
**romantic** [rəʊ'mæntɪk] *adj.* romantisch
**romanticism** [rəʊ'mæntɪsɪzm] n. *(Lit., Art., Mus.)* Romantik, *die*
**Romany** ['rɒmənɪ] 1. n. a) *(person)* Rom, *der;* b) *(language)* Romani, *das.* 2. *adj.* Roma-; *(Ling.)* Romani-
**Rome** [rəʊm] *pr. n.* Rom *(das)*
**romp** [rɒmp] 1. *v. i.* a) [herum]tollen; b) ~ **home** *or* **in** *(coll.: win easily)* spielend gewinnen. 2. n. Tollerei, *die*
**rompers** ['rɒmpəz] n. pl. Spielhöschen, *das*
**roof** [ru:f] 1. n. a) Dach, *das;* b) ~ **of the mouth** Gaumen, *der.* 2. *v. t.* bedachen. '**roofing** n. *(material)* Deckung, *die*
**roof: ~-rack** n. Dachgepäckträger, *der;* **~-top** n. Dach, *das*
'**rook** [rʊk] n. *(Ornith.)* Saatkrähe, *die*
²**rook** n. *(Chess)* Turm, *der*
**room** [ru:m, rʊm] n. a) *(in building)* Zimmer, *das; (for function)* Saal, *der;* b) *(space)* Platz, *der;* **make ~** [**for sb./ sth.**] [jmdm./einer Sache] Platz machen; **there is still ~ for improvement in his work** seine Arbeit ist noch verbesserungsfähig
**room: ~-mate** n. Zimmergenosse, *der/*-genossin, *die;* ~ **service** n. Zimmerservice, *der;* ~ **temperature** n. Zimmertemperatur, *die*
**roomy** ['ru:mɪ] *adj.* geräumig
**roost** [ru:st] 1. n. [Sitz]stange, *die.* 2. *v. i.* ⟨*Vogel:*⟩ sich [zum Schlafen] niederlassen
'**root** [ru:t] 1. n. Wurzel, *die;* **put down ~s/take ~:** Wurzeln schlagen. 2. *v. i.* ⟨*Pflanze:*⟩ wurzeln. 3. *v. t.* **stand ~ed to the spot** wie angewurzelt dastehen. **root 'out** *v. t.* ausrotten

**²root** *v. i* **a)** *(turn up ground)* wühlen (for nach); **b)** *(coll.)* ~ **for** *(cheer)* anfeuern

**rope** [rəʊp] **1.** *n.* **a)** *(cord)* Seil, *das;* **b)** **know the** ~s sich auskennen. **2.** *v. t.* festbinden. **rope 'in** *v. t. (fig.)* einspannen *(ugs.)*

**rope-'ladder** *n.* Strickleiter, *die*

**rosary** ['rəʊzəri] *n.* Rosenkranz, *der*

**¹rose** [rəʊz] *n.* **a)** *(plant, flower)* Rose, *die;* **b)** *(colour)* Rosa, *das*

**²rose** *see* rise 2

**rosé** [rəʊ'zeɪ, 'rəʊzeɪ] *n.* Rosé, *der*

**rose:** ~**-bed** *n.* Rosenbeet, *das;* ~**-bud** *n.* Rosenknospe, *die;* ~**-bush** *n.* Rosenstrauch, *der*

**rosemary** ['rəʊzməri] *n.* Rosmarin, *der*

**¹rose petal** *n.* Rosen[blüten]blatt, *das*

**rosette** [rəʊ'zet] *n.* Rosette, *die*

**roster** ['rɒstə(r)] *n.* Dienstplan, *der*

**rostrum** ['rɒstrəm] *n., pl.* **rostra** ['rɒstrə] *or* ~**s** Podium, *das*

**rosy** ['rəʊzɪ] *adj.* rosig

**rot** [rɒt] **1.** *n.* **a)** *see* 2: Verrottung, *die;* Fäulnis, *die; (fig.: deterioration)* Verfall, *der;* **stop the** ~ *(fig.)* dem Verfall Einhalt gebieten; **b)** *(sl.: nonsense)* Quark, *der (salopp).* **2.** *v. i.,* -tt- verrotten; ⟨*Fleisch, Gemüse, Obst:*⟩ verfaulen. **3.** *v. t.,* -tt- verrotten lassen; verfaulen lassen ⟨*Fleisch, Gemüse, Obst*⟩; zerstören ⟨*Zähne*⟩

**rota** ['rəʊtə] *n. (Brit.) (order of rotation)* Turnus, *der; (list)* Arbeitsplan, *der*

**rotary** ['rəʊtərɪ] *adj.* rotierend

**rotate** [rəʊ'teɪt] **1.** *v. i. (revolve)* rotieren; sich drehen. **2.** *v. t.* in Rotation versetzen. **rotation** [rəʊ'teɪʃn] *n.* **a)** Rotation, *die,* Drehung, *die* (**about** um); **b)** *(succession)* turnusmäßiger Wechsel; **in** *or* **by** ~: im Turnus

**rote** [rəʊt] *n.* **by** ~: auswendig

**rotten** ['rɒtn] *adj.,* ~**er** ['rɒtənə(r)], ~**est** ['rɒtənɪst] **a)** *(decayed)* verrottet; verfault ⟨*Obst, Gemüse*⟩; faul ⟨*Ei, Holz, Zähne*⟩; ~ **to the core** *(fig.)* verdorben bis ins Mark; **b)** *(corrupt)* verdorben; **c)** *(sl.: bad)* mies *(ugs.)*

**rotund** [rəʊ'tʌnd] *adj.* **a)** *(round)* rund; **b)** *(plump)* rundlich

**rouble** ['ru:bl] *n.* Rubel, *der*

**rouge** [ru:ʒ] *n.* Rouge, *das*

**rough** [rʌf] **1.** *adj.* **a)** *(coarse, uneven)* rauh; holp[e]rig ⟨*Straße usw.*⟩; uneben ⟨*Gelände*⟩; unruhig ⟨*Überfahrt*⟩; **b)** *(violent)* grob ⟨*Person, Worte, Behandlung*⟩; **c)** *(trying)* hart; **this is** ~ **on him** das ist hart für ihn; **sth. is** ~ **going**

etw. ist nicht einfach; **d)** *(approximate)* grob ⟨*Skizze, Schätzung*⟩; vag ⟨*Vorstellung*⟩; ~ **paper/notebook** Konzeptpapier, *das/*Kladde, *die;* **e)** *(coll.: ill)* angeschlagen *(ugs.).* **2.** *n.* **[be] in** ~: [sich] im Rohzustand [befinden]. **3.** *adv.* rauh ⟨*spielen*⟩; **sleep** ~: im Freien schlafen. **4.** *v. t.* ~ **it** primitiv leben.

**rough 'out** *v. t.* grob entwerfen.

**rough 'up** *v. t. (sl.)* anrempeln *(ugs.)*

**roughage** ['rʌfɪdʒ] *n.* Ballaststoffe *Pl.*

**rough:** ~**-and-ready** *adj.* provisorisch; ~**-and-'tumble** *n.* [milde] Rauferei; ~ **copy,** ~ **draft** *ns.* grobe Skizze; grober Entwurf

**roughen** ['rʌfn] *v. t.* aufrauhen

**¹roughly** *adv.* **a)** *(violently)* roh; grob; **b)** *(crudely)* leidlich; grob ⟨*skizzieren, bearbeiten, bauen*⟩; **c)** *(approximately)* ungefähr; grob ⟨*geschätzt*⟩

**¹roughness** *n.* **a)** Rauheit, *die; (unevenness)* Unebenheit, *die;* **b)** *(violence)* Roheit, *die*

**¹roughshod** *adj.* **ride** ~ **over sb./sth.** jmdn./etw. mit Füßen treten

**roulette** [ru:'let] *n.* Roulette, *das*

**round** [raʊnd] **1.** *adj.* rund; **in** ~ **figures** rund gerechnet. **2.** *n.* **a)** *(recurring series)* Serie, *die;* ~ **of talks/negotiations** Gesprächs-/Verhandlungsrunde, *die;* **the daily** ~: der Alltag; **b)** *(of ammunition)* Ladung, *die;* **50** ~s **[of ammunition]** 50 Schuß Munition; **c)** *(of game or contest)* Runde, *die;* **d)** *(burst)* ~ **of applause** Beifallssturm, *der;* **e)** ~ **[of drinks]** Runde, *die;* **f)** *(regular calls)* Runde, *die;* Tour, *die;* **go [on]** *or* **make one's** ~s seine Runden machen; **g) a** ~ **of toast/sandwiches** eine Scheibe Toast/eine Portion Sandwiches. **3.** *adv.* **a) all the year** ~: das ganze Jahr hindurch; **the third time** ~: beim dritten Mal; **have a look** ~: sich umsehen; **ask sb.** ~ **[for a drink]** jmdn. [zu einem Gläschen zu sich] einladen; **b)** *(by indirect way)* herum; **walk** ~: außen herum gehen; **c)** *(here)* hier; *(there)* dort; **I'll go** ~ **tomorrow** ich gehe morgen hin. **4.** *prep.* **a)** um [... herum]; **travel** ~ **England** durch England reisen; **run** ~ **the streets** durch die Straßen rennen; **walk** ~ **and** ~ **sth.** immer wieder um etw. herumgehen; **b)** *(in various directions from)* um [... herum]; rund um ⟨*einen Ort*⟩. **5.** *v. t.* ~ **a bend** um eine Kurve fahren/gehen/kommen *usw.* **round 'off** *v. t.* abrunden. **round 'up** *v. t.* verhaften ⟨*Verdächtige*⟩; zusammentreiben ⟨*Vieh*⟩

**round:** ~ **a'bout** adv. (on all sides)
ringsum; **~about 1.** n. **a)** (Brit.:
merry-go-round) Karussell, das; **b)**
(Brit.: road junction) Kreisverkehr,
der. **2.** adj. umständlich

**rounders** ['raʊndəz] n. sing. (Brit.)
Rounders, das

**round:** ~ **'number** n. runde Zahl;
~**-shouldered** [raʊnd'ʃəʊldəd] adj.
⟨Person⟩ mit einem Rundrücken; ~
**'trip** n. Rundreise, die

**rouse** [raʊz] v. t. wecken (from aus)

**rousing** ['raʊzɪŋ] adj. mitreißend
⟨Lied⟩; leidenschaftlich ⟨Rede⟩

**rout** [raʊt] **1.** n. [wilde] Flucht; (defeat)
verheerende Niederlage. **2.** v. t. auf-
reiben ⟨Feind, Truppen⟩; vernichtend
schlagen ⟨Gegner⟩

**route** [ruːt] n. Route, die; Weg, der

**routine** [ruː'tiːn] **1.** n. **a)** Routine, die;
**b)** (coll.: set speech) Platte, die (ugs.);
**c)** (Theatre) Nummer, die; (Dancing,
Skating) Figur, die. **2.** adj. routinemä-
ßig; Routine⟨arbeit⟩

**roux** [ruː] n. Mehlschwitze, die

**¹row** [raʊ] **1.** (coll.) n. **a)** (noise) Krach,
der; **make a ~:** Krach machen; **b)**
(quarrel) Krach, der (ugs.); **have/start
a ~:** Krach haben/anfangen (ugs.). **2.**
v. i sich streiten

**²row** [rəʊ] n. Reihe, die; **in a ~:** in einer Reihe

**³row** [rəʊ] v. i. & t. (with oars) rudern

**rowan** ['rəʊən] n. ~[-tree] Eberesche,
die

**row-boat** ['rəʊbəʊt] n. (Amer.) Ruderboot, das

**rowdy** ['raʊdɪ] **1.** adj. rowdyhaft; **the
party was ~:** auf der Party ging es laut
zu. **2.** n. Krawallmacher, der

**rowing-boat** ['rəʊɪŋbəʊt] n. (Brit.)
Ruderboot, das

**royal** ['rɔɪəl] adj. königlich

**royal:** **R~ 'Air Force** n. (Brit.) König-
liche Luftwaffe; ~ **'blue** n. (Brit.) Kö-
nigsblau, das; ~ **'family** n. königli-
che Familie; **R~ 'Navy** n. (Brit.) Kö-
nigliche Kriegsmarine

**royalty** ['rɔɪəltɪ] n. **a)** (payment) Tan-
tieme, die (on für); **b)** collect. (royal
persons) Mitglieder des Königshauses

**RSPCA** abbr. (Brit.) **R**oyal **S**ociety for
the **P**revention of **C**ruelty to **A**nimals
britischer Tierschutzverein

**rub** [rʌb] **1.** v. t., **-bb-** reiben (on,
against an + Dat.); (to remove dirt
etc.) abreiben; (to dry) trockenreiben;
~ **sth. off sth.** etw. von etw. reiben. **2.**
v. i., **-bb-** reiben (up∤on, against an +

Dat.). **3.** n. **give it a ~:** reib es ab;
**there's the ~** (fig.) da liegt der Haken
[dabei]. **rub 'down** v. t. abreiben. **rub 'in** v. t. einreiben; **there's no
need to** or **don't ~ it in** (fig.) reib es mir
nicht [dauernd] unter die Nase. **rub
'off** v. t. wegreiben; wegwischen. **rub
'out 1.** v. t. ausreiben; (using eraser)
ausradieren. **2.** v. i. sich ausreiben/
sich ausradieren lassen

**rubber** ['rʌbə(r)] n. **a)** Gummi, das od.
der; **b)** (eraser) Radiergummi, der

**rubber:** ~ **'band** n. Gummiband, das;
~ **plant** n. Gummibaum, der; ~
**'stamp** n. Gummistempel, der; ~
**-stamp** v. t. (fig.) absegnen (ugs.)

**rubbish** ['rʌbɪʃ] **1.** n. **a)** (refuse) Abfall,
der; (to be collected and dumped) Müll,
der; **b)** (worthless material) Plunder,
der (ugs.); **be ~:** nichts taugen; **c)**
(nonsense) Quatsch, der (ugs.). **2.** int.
Quatsch (ugs.). **'rubbish-bin** n. Ab-
fall-/Mülleimer, der. **'rubbish dump**
n. Müllkippe, die

**rubble** ['rʌbl] n. Trümmer Pl.

**ruby** ['ruːbɪ] n. Rubin, der

**rucksack** ['rʌksæk, 'rʊksæk] n. Rucksack, der

**rudder** ['rʌdə(r)] n. Ruder, das

**ruddy** ['rʌdɪ] adj. **a)** (reddish) rötlich;
**b)** (Brit. sl.: bloody) verdammt (salopp)

**rude** [ruːd] adj. **a)** unhöflich;
(stronger) rüde; **be ~ to sb.** zu jmdm.
grob unhöflich sein/jmdn. rüde behandeln; **b)** (abrupt) unsanft; ~
awakening böses Erwachen. **'rudely**
adv. **a)** (impolitely) unhöflich; rüde;
**b)** (abruptly) jäh (geh.). **'rudeness** n.
(bad manners) ungehöriges Beneh-
men

**rudimentary** [ruːdɪ'mentərɪ] elementar; primitiv ⟨Gebäude⟩

**rudiments** ['ruːdɪmənts] n. pl. Grundlagen Pl.

**rueful** ['ruːfl] adj. reumütig

**ruffian** ['rʌfɪən] n. Rohling, der

**ruffle** ['rʌfl] v. t. **a)** kräuseln; ~ **sb.'s
hair** jmdm. durch die Haare fahren;
**b)** (upset) aus der Fassung bringen

**rug** [rʌg] n. [kleiner, dicker] Teppich

**Rugby** ['rʌgbɪ] n. Rugby, das

**rugged** ['rʌgɪd] adj. **a)** (uneven) zer-
klüftet; unwegsam ⟨Land⟩; zerfurcht
⟨Gesicht⟩; **b)** (sturdy) robust

**ruin** ['ruːɪn] **1.** n. **a)** in sing. or pl. (remains) Ruine, die; **in ~s** in Trüm-
mern; **b)** (downfall) Ruin, der. **2.**
v. t. ruinieren; verderben ⟨Urlaub,
Abend⟩; ~**ed** (reduced to ruins) verfal-

len; **a ~ed castle/church** eine Burg-/
Kirchenruine. **ruinous** ['ruːɪnəs] *adj.*
ruinös

**rule** [ruːl] **1.** *n.* **a)** Regel, *die;* **the ~s of
the game** die Spielregeln; **be against
the ~s** regelwidrig sein; *(fig.)* gegen
die Spielregeln verstoßen; **as a ~:** in
der Regel; **~ of thumb** Faustregel, *die;*
**b)** *no pl. (government)* Herrschaft, *die*
(**over** über + *Akk.*). **2.** *v. t.* **a)** *(control)*
beherrschen; **b)** *(be the ruler of)* regieren; ⟨*Monarch, Diktator usw.:*⟩ herrschen über (+ *Akk.*). **3.** *v. i.* **a)** *(govern)* herrschen; **b)** *(decide)* entscheiden (**against** gegen; **in favour of** für).
**rule 'out** *v. t.* ausschließen; *(prevent)*
unmöglich machen
**ruled** [ruːld] *adj.* liniert ⟨*Papier*⟩
**ruler** ['ruːlə(r)] *n.* **a)** *(person)* Herrscher, *der*/Herrscherin, *die;* **b)** *(for
measuring)* Lineal, *das*
**ruling** ['ruːlɪŋ] **1.** *adj.* herrschend
⟨*Klasse*⟩; regierend ⟨*Partei*⟩. **2.** *n.* Entscheidung, *die*
**rum** [rʌm] *n.* Rum, *der*
**Rumania** *etc.* [ruː'meɪnɪə] *see* **Romania** *etc.*
**rumble** ['rʌmbl] **1.** *n.* Grollen, *das.* **2.**
*v. i.* **a)** grollen; ⟨*Magen:*⟩ knurren; **b)**
⟨*Fahrzeug:*⟩ rumpeln *(ugs.)*
**ruminate** ['ruːmɪneɪt] *v. i.* **~ on** *or* **over**
**sth.** über etw. *(Akk.)* grübeln
**rummage** ['rʌmɪdʒ] *v. i.* wühlen; **~
through sth.** etw. durchwühlen *(ugs.)*
**rummy** ['rʌmɪ] *n.* Rommé, *das*
**rumour** *(Brit.)*; *Amer.:* **rumor**]
['ruːmə(r)] **1.** *n.* Gerücht, *das;* **there is
a ~ that ...:** es geht das Gerücht, daß ...
**2.** *v. t.* **it is ~ed that ...:** es geht das Gerücht, daß ...
**rump** [rʌmp] *n.* **a)** *(buttocks)* Hinterteil, *das (ugs.);* **b)** *(remnant)* Rest, *der*
**rumple** ['rʌmpl] *v. t.* **a)** *(crease)* zerknittern; **b)** *(tousle)* zerzausen
**'rump steak** *n.* Rumpsteak, *das*
**rumpus** ['rʌmpəs] *n. (coll.)* Krach, *der*
*(ugs.);* **kick up** *or* **make a ~:** einen
Spektakel veranstalten *(ugs.)*
**run** [rʌn] **1.** *n.* **a)** Lauf, *der;* **on the ~:**
auf der Flucht; **b)** *(trip in vehicle)*
Fahrt, *die; (for pleasure)* Ausflug, *der;*
**c)** *(continuous stretch)* Länge, *die;*
*(spell)* **she has had a long ~ of success**
sie war lange [Zeit] erfolgreich; **have a
long ~** ⟨*Stück, Show:*⟩ viele Aufführ-
ungen erleben; **e)** *(succession)* Serie,
*die; (Cards)* Sequenz, *die;* **a ~ of vic-
tories** eine Siegesserie; **f)** *(use)* **have
the ~ of sth.** etw. zu seiner freien Ver-

fügung haben; **g)** *(enclosure)* Auslauf,
*der;* **h)** *(in stocking etc.)* Laufmasche,
*die.* **2.** *v. i.,* **-nn-,** ran [ræn], **run a)** laufen; **~ for the bus** laufen, um den Bus
zu kriegen *(ugs.);* **~ to help sb.** jmdm.
zu Hilfe eilen; **b)** *(roll, slide)* laufen;
⟨*Ball, Kugel:*⟩ rollen, laufen; ⟨*Schlitten, [Schiebe]tür:*⟩ gleiten; **c)** ⟨*Rad,
Maschine:*⟩ laufen; **d)** *(operate on a
schedule)* fahren; **~ between two places**
⟨*Zug, Bus:*⟩ zwischen zwei Orten verkehren; **e)** *(flow)* laufen; ⟨*Fluß:*⟩ fließen; ⟨*Augen:*⟩ tränen; **his nose was
~ning** ihm lief die Nase; **f)** ⟨*Vertrag,
Theaterstück:*⟩ laufen; **g)** *(have wording)* lauten; ⟨*Geschichte:*⟩ gehen *(fig.);*
**h)** ⟨*Butter, Eis:*⟩ zerlaufen; ⟨*Farben:*⟩
auslaufen; **i)** *(in election)* kandidieren.
**3.** *v. t.,* **-nn-,** ran, run **a)** laufen lassen;
*(drive)* fahren; **~ one's hand/fingers
through/along** *or* **over sth.** mit der
Hand/den Fingern durch etw. fahren/
über etw. *(Akk.)* streichen; **~ an** *or*
**one's eye along** *or* **down** *or* **over sth.**
*(fig.)* etw. überfliegen; **b)** *(cause to
flow)* [ein]laufen lassen; **~ a bath** ein
Bad einlaufen lassen; **c)** *(organize,
manage)* führen, leiten ⟨*Geschäft
usw.*⟩; veranstalten ⟨*Wettbewerb*⟩; **d)**
*(operate)* bedienen ⟨*Maschine*⟩; verkehren lassen ⟨*Verkehrsmittel*⟩; einsetzen ⟨*Sonderbus, -zug*⟩; laufen lassen ⟨*Motor*⟩; **e)** *(own and use)* sich
*(Dat.)* halten ⟨*Auto*⟩; **f)** **~ sb. into town**
*etc.* jmdn. in die Stadt *usw.* fahren.
**run a'cross** *v. t.* **~ across sb./sth.**
jmdn. treffen/auf etw. *(Akk.)* stoßen.
**run a'way** *v. i.* **a)** *(flee)* weglaufen;
fortlaufen; **b)** *(abscond)* **~ away [from
home]** [von zu Hause] weglaufen. **run
'down 1.** *v. t.* **a)** *(collide with)* überfahren; **b)** *(criticize)* heruntermachen
*(ugs.);* **c)** *(reduce)* abbauen. **2.** *v. i.* **a)**
hin-/herunterlaufen; **b)** *(decline)* sich
verringern; **c)** ⟨*Uhr, Spielzeug:*⟩ ablaufen; ⟨*Batterie:*⟩ leer werden. **'run into**
*v. t.* **a)** **~ into a tree** gegen einen Baum
fahren; **b)** *(meet)* **~ into sb.** jmdm. in
die Arme laufen *(ugs.);* **c)** stoßen auf
(+ *Akk.*) ⟨*Schwierigkeiten, Widerstand
usw.*⟩; **d)** *(amount to)* **~ into thousands**
in die Tausende gehen. **run 'off 1.** *v. i.*
weglaufen. **2.** *v. t.* abziehen ⟨*Kopien*⟩.
**run 'out** *v. i.* **a)** hin-/herauslaufen; **b)**
⟨*Vorräte, Bestände:*⟩ zu Ende gehen.
**run 'out of** *v. t.* **sb. ~s out of sth.**
jmdm. geht etw. aus; **I'm ~ning out of
patience** meine Geduld geht zu Ende.
**run 'over 1.** ['---] *v. t.* *(knock down)*

überfahren. 2. [-'--] *v. i.* überlaufen.
'run **through** *v. t.* durchspielen
⟨*Theaterstück*⟩. 'run **to** *v. t.* a) *(amount to)* sich belaufen auf ⟨*Akk.*⟩; b) *(be sufficient for)* sth. will ~ to sth. etw. reicht für etw. run 'up 1. *v. i.* hinlaufen; come ~ning up hingelaufen kommen. 2. *v. t.* a) rasch nähen ⟨*Kleidungsstück*⟩; b) zusammenkommen lassen ⟨*Schulden, Rechnung*⟩. run 'up against *v. t.* stoßen auf (+ *Akk.*) ⟨*Probleme, Widerstand usw.*⟩

run: ~**away** 1. *n.* Ausreißer, *der*/Ausreißerin, *die (ugs.);* 2. *attrib. adj.* durchgegangen ⟨*Pferd*⟩; außer Kontrolle geraten ⟨*Fahrzeug, Preise*⟩; galoppierend ⟨*Inflation*⟩; ~**-down** 1. ['--] *n. (coll.: briefing)* Übersicht, *die* (on über + *Akk.*); 2. [-'-] *adj. (tired)* mitgenommen

¹**rung** [rʌŋ] *n.* Sprosse, *die*

²**rung** *see* ²**ring** 2, 3

'**runner** *n.* a) Läufer, *der*/Läuferin, *die;* b) *(Bot.)* Ausläufer, *der;* c) *(on sledge)* Kufe, *die.* '**runner bean** *n.* *(Brit.)* Stangenbohne, *die.* **runner-**'up *n.* Zweite, *der/die;* the runners-up die Plazierten

'**running** 1. *n.* a) *(management)* Leitung, *die;* b) *(action)* Laufen, *das;* in/ out of the ~: im/aus dem Rennen. 2. *adj. (in succession)* hintereinander; win for the third year ~: schon drei Jahre hintereinander gewinnen. **running 'commentary** *n.* *(Broadcasting; also fig.)* Live-Kommentar, *der*

**runny** ['rʌnɪ] *adj.* a) laufend ⟨*Nase*⟩; b) zu dünn ⟨*Farbe, Marmelade*⟩

run: **-of-the-'mill** *adj.* ganz gewöhnlich; ~**-up** *n.* a) *during or* in the ~**-up to an event** im Vorfeld eines Ereignisses; b) *(Sport)* Anlauf, *der;* ~**way** *n.* *(for take-off)* Startbahn, *die; (for landing)* Landebahn, *die*

**rupture** ['rʌptʃə(r)] 1. *n.* Bruch, *der.* 2. *v. t.* ~ oneself sich *(Dat.)* einen Bruch zuziehen

**rural** ['rʊərl] *adj.* ländlich

**ruse** [ruːz] *n.* List, *die*

¹**rush** [rʌʃ] *n.* *(Bot.)* Binse, *die*

²**rush** 1. *n.* a) *(hurry)* Eile, *die;* what's all the ~? wozu diese Hast?; be in a [great] ~: in [großer] Eile sein; b) *(period of great activity)* Hochbetrieb, *der;* (~-hour) Stoßzeit, *die;* c) make a ~ for sth. sich auf etw. *(Akk.)* stürzen. 2. *v. t.* a) ~ sb./sth. somewhere jmdn./ etw. auf schnellstem Wege irgendwohin bringen; be ~ed *(have to hurry)* in

Eile sein; ~ sb. **into doing sth.** jmdn. dazu drängen, etw. zu tun; b) *(perform quickly)* auf die Schnelle erledigen; ~ it zu schnell machen. 3. *v. i.* a) *(move quickly)* eilen; ⟨*Hund, Pferd:*⟩ laufen; ~ to help sb. jmdm. zu Hilfe eilen; b) *(hurry unduly)* sich zu sehr beeilen; don't ~! nur keine Eile! **rush a'bout, rush a'round** *v. i.* herumhetzen

'**rush-hour** *n.* Stoßzeit, *die*

**rusk** [rʌsk] *n.* Zwieback, *der*

**Russia** ['rʌʃə] *pr. n.* Rußland *(das).* **Russian** ['rʌʃn] 1. *adj.* russisch; sb. is ~: jmd. ist Russe/Russin. 2. *n.* a) *(person)* Russe, *der*/Russin, *die;* b) *(language)* Russisch, *das; see also* **English** 2 a

**rust** [rʌst] 1. *n.* Rost, *der.* 2. *v. i.* rosten

**rustic** ['rʌstɪk] *adj.* a) ländlich; b) rustikal ⟨*Mobiliar*⟩

**rustle** ['rʌsl] 1. *n.* Rascheln, *das.* 2. *v. i.* rascheln. 3. *v. t.* a) rascheln lassen; b) *(Amer.: steal)* stehlen. **rustle 'up** *v. t.* zusammenzaubern ⟨*Mahlzeit*⟩

'**rust-proof** *adj.* rostfrei

'**rusty** *adj.* rostig

**rut** [rʌt] *n.* Spurrille, *die;* be in a ~ *(fig.)* aus dem [Alltags]trott nicht mehr herauskommen

**ruthless** ['ruːθlɪs] *adj.* rücksichtslos

**rye** [raɪ] *n.* Roggen, *der*

# S

**S, s** [es] *n.* S, s, *das*

**S.** *abbr.* a) south S; b) southern s.

**sabbath** ['sæbəθ] *n.* Sabbath, *der*

**sabbatical** [sə'bætɪkl] 1. *adj.* ~ term/ year Forschungssemester/-jahr, *das.* 2. *n.* Forschungsurlaub, *der*

**sabotage** ['sæbətɑːʒ] 1. *n.* Sabotage, *die.* 2. *v. t.* einen Sabotageakt verüben auf (+ *Akk.*); *(fig.)* sabotieren

**saccharin** ['sækərɪn] *n.* Saccharin, *das*

**sachet** ['sæʃeɪ] *n.* Beutel, *der;* *(cushion-shaped)* Kissen, *das*

**sack** [sæk] 1. *n.* a) Sack, *der;* b) *(coll.: dismissal)* Rausschmiß, *der (ugs.);* get the ~: rausgeschmissen werden *(ugs.);* give sb. the ~: jmdn. raus-

schmeißen *(ugs.)*. **2.** *v. t. (coll.)* rausschmeißen *(ugs.)* **(for wegen)**
**sacrament** ['sækrəmənt] *n.* Sakrament, *das*
**sacred** ['seıkrıd] *adj.* heilig
**sacrifice** ['sækrıfaıs] **1.** *n.* Opfer, *das*.
**2.** *v. t.* opfern
**sacrilege** [sækrılıdʒ] *n.* |act of| ~: Sa-
krileg, *das*
**sad** [sæd] *adj.* traurig **(at, about** über
+ *Akk.*); schmerzlich ⟨*Tod, Verlust*⟩;
**feel** ~: traurig sein. **sadden** ['sædn]
*v. t.* traurig stimmen
**saddle** ['sædl] **1.** *n.* Sattel, *der.* **2.** *v. t.*
**a)** satteln ⟨*Pferd usw.*⟩; **b)** *(fig.)* ~ **sb.**
**with sth.** jmdm. etw. aufbürden *(geh.)*.
**'saddle-bag** *n.* Satteltasche, *die*
**sadism** ['seıdızm] *n.* Sadismus, *der.*
**sadist** ['seıdıst] *n.* Sadist, *der*/Sadi-
stin, *die.* **sadistic** [sə'dıstık] *adj.*, **sa-**
**'distically** *adv.* sadistisch
**'sadly** *adv.* **a)** *(with sorrow)* traurig; **b)**
*(unfortunately)* leider
**'sadness** *n.* Traurigkeit, *die*
**safari** [sə'fɑːrı] *n.* Safari, *die;* **on** ~: auf
Safari
**safe** [seıf] **1.** *n.* Safe, *der;* Geld-
schrank, *der.* **2.** *adj.* **a)** *(out of danger)*
sicher **(from** vor + *Dat.*)**; he's** ~: er ist
in Sicherheit; ~ **and sound** sicher und
wohlbehalten; **b)** *(free from danger)*
ungefährlich; sicher ⟨*Ort, Hafen*⟩;
**wish sb. a** ~ **journey** jmdm. eine gute
Reise wünschen; **to be on the** ~ **side**
zur Sicherheit; **c)** *(reliable)* sicher
⟨*Methode, Investition*⟩. **'safeguard 1.**
*n.* Schutz, *der.* **2.** *v. t.* schützen.
**'safely** *adv.* sicher; **did the parcel ar-**
**rive** ~? ist das Paket heil angekom-
men? **safety** ['seıftı] *n.* Sicherheit, *die*
**safety:** ~**-belt** *n.* Sicherheitsgurt,
*der;* ~ **helmet** *n.* Schutzhelm, *der;* ~
**margin** *n.* Spielraum, *der;* ~**-pin** *n.*
Sicherheitsnadel, *die;* ~**-valve** *n.* Si-
cherheitsventil, *das; (fig.)* Ventil, *das*
**sag** [sæg] *v. i.,* **-gg-** durchhängen;
*(sink)* sich senken
**saga** ['sɑːgə] *n.* **a)** *(story of adventure)*
Heldenepos, *das; (medieval narrative)*
Saga, *die;* **b)** *(coll.: long involved story)*
[ganzer] Roman *(fig.)*
**¹sage** [seıdʒ] *n. (Bot.)* Salbei, *der od.*
*die*
**²sage 1.** *adj.* weis. **2.** *n.* Weise, *der*
**Sagittarius** [sædʒı'teərıəs] *n.* der
Schütze
**Sahara** [sə'hɑːrə] *pr. n.* **the** ~ |Desert|
die [Wüste] Sahara
**said** *see* **say** 1

**sail** [seıl] **1.** *n.* **a)** Segelfahrt, *die;* **b)**
*(piece of canvas)* Segel, *das.* **2.** *v. i.* **a)**
*(travel on water)* fahren; *(in sailing*
*boat)* segeln; **b)** *(start voyage)* auslaufen **(for** nach). **3.** *v. t.* **a)** steuern ⟨*Boot,*
*Schiff*⟩; segeln mit ⟨*Segeljacht,*
*-schiff*⟩; **b)** durchfahren/⟨*Segelschiff:*⟩
durchsegeln ⟨*Meer*⟩
**sail:** ~**board** *n.* Surfbrett, *das (zum*
*Windsurfen);* ~**-boarding** *n.* Windsurfen, *das;* ~**boat** *n. (Amer.)* Segelboot, *das*
**'sailing** *n.* Segeln, *das.* **'sailing boat**
*n.* Segelboot, *das.* **'sailing ship** *n.*
Segelschiff, *das*
**sailor** ['seılə(r)] *n.* Seemann, *der; (in*
*navy)* Matrose, *der*
**saint 1.** [sənt] *adj.* S~ **Michael** der heilige Michael; Sankt Michael. **2.** [seınt]
*n.* Heilige, *der/die.* **'saintly** ['seıntlı]
*adj.* heilig
**sake** [seık] *n.* **for the** ~ **of** um ... *(Gen.)*
willen; **for my** *etc.* ~: um meinetwil-
len *usw.;* mir *usw.* zuliebe
**salad** ['sæləd] *n.* Salat, *der.* **'salad**
**cream** *n.* ≈ Mayonnaise, *die.* **'salad**
**dressing** *n.* Salatsoße, *die*
**salary** ['sælərı] *n.* Gehalt, *das*
**sale** [seıl] *n.* **a)** Verkauf, *der; (at re-*
*duced prices)* Ausverkauf, *der;* |up| **for**
~: zu verkaufen; **b)** ~**s** *(amount sold)*
Verkaufszahlen *Pl.* **(of** für); Absatz,
*der;* **c)** |jumble *or* rummage| ~: [Wohl-
tätigkeits]basar, *der*
**salesman** ['seılzmən] *n., pl.* ~**men**
['seılzmən] Verkäufer, *der.* **'sales-**
**manship** *n.* Kunst des Verkaufens
**'saleswoman** *n.* Verkäuferin, *die*
**salient** ['seılıənt] *adj.* auffallend
**saliva** [sə'laıvə] *n.* Speichel, *der*
**sallow** ['sæləʊ] *adj.* blaßgelb
**salmon** ['sæmən] *n.* Lachs, *der*
**saloon** [sə'luːn] *n.* **a)** *(Brit.)* ~ |bar| se-
parater Teil eines Pubs mit mehr Kom-
fort; **b)** *(Brit.)* ~ |car| Limousine, *die*
**salt** [sɔːlt, sɒlt] **1.** *n.* |common| ~:
[Koch]salz, *das.* **2.** *adj. (containing or*
*tasting of* ~) salzig; *(preserved with* ~)
gepökelt ⟨*Fleisch*⟩; gesalzen ⟨*Butter*⟩.
**3.** *v. t.* **a)** salzen; **b)** *(cure)* [ein]pökeln;
**c)** ~ **the roads** Salz auf die Straßen
streuen. **salt-cellar** *n.* Salzstreuer,
*der.* **salt 'water** *n.* Salzwasser, *das*
**'salty** *adj.* salzig
**salute** [sə'luːt] **1.** *v. t.* grüßen. **2.** *v. i.*
*(Mil., Navy)* |militärisch| grüßen. **3.** *n.*
Salut, *der;* militärischer Gruß
**salvage** ['sælvıdʒ] **1.** *n.* Bergung, *die.*
**2.** *v. t.* bergen

**salvation** [sæl'veɪʃn] *n.* Erlösung, *die.*
**Salvation 'Army** *n.* Heilsarmee, *die*
**salvo** ['sælvəʊ] *n.* Salve, *die*
**Samaritan** [sə'mærɪtən] *n.* **good ~:**
[barmherziger] Samariter; **the ~s** *(organization)* ≈ die Telefonseelsorge
**same** [seɪm] **1.** *adj.* **the ~:** der/die/das
gleiche; **the ~ |thing|** *(identical)* der-/
die-/dasselbe. **2.** *adv.* **all** *or* **just the ~:**
trotzdem
**sample** ['sɑːmpl] **1.** *n.* *(example)* [Muster]beispiel, *das;* *(specimen)* Probe,
*die;* |**commercial**| **~:** Muster, *das.* **2.**
*v.t.* probieren
**sanctify** ['sæŋktɪfaɪ] *v.t.* heiligen
**sanctimonious** [sæŋktɪ'məʊnɪəs] *adj.*
scheinheilig
**sanction** ['sæŋkʃn] **1.** *n.* Sanktion,
*die.* **2.** *v.t.* sanktionieren
**sanctity** ['sæŋktɪtɪ] *n.* Heiligkeit, *die*
**sanctuary** ['sæŋktʃʊərɪ] *n.* **a)** *(holy
place)* Heiligtum, *das;* **b)** *(refuge)* Zufluchtsort, *der;* **c)** *(for animals)* Naturschutzgebiet, *das*
**sand** [sænd] **1.** *n.* Sand, *der.* **2.** *v.t.* **~
sth.** |**down**| etw. [ab]schmirgeln
**sandal** ['sændl] *n.* Sandale, *die*
**sand:** **~bag 1.** *n.* Sandsack, *der;* **2.**
*v.t.* mit Sandsäcken schützen;
**~bank** *n.* Sandbank, *die;* **~-castle**
*n.* Sandburg, *die;* **~paper 1.** *n.* Sandpapier, *das;* **2.** *v.t.* [mit Sandpapier]
[ab]schmirgeln; **~-pit** *n.* Sandkasten,
*der;* **~stone** *n.* Sandstein, *der*
**sandwich** ['sænwɪdʒ] **1.** *n.* Sandwich,
*der od. das;* ≈ [zusammengeklapptes]
belegtes Brot; **cheese ~:** Käsebrot,
*das.* **2.** *v.t.* einschieben (**between** zwischen + *Akk.;* **into** in + *Akk.*)
**'sandy** *adj.* **a)** sandig; Sand‹*boden,
-strand*›; **b)** rotblond ‹*Haar*›
**sane** [seɪn] *adj.* **a)** geistig gesund; **b)**
*(sensible)* vernünftig
**sang** *see* **sing**
**sanitary** ['sænɪtərɪ] *adj.* sanitär ‹*Verhältnisse, Anlagen*›. **'sanitary napkin** *(Amer.),* **'sanitary towel** *(Brit.)*
*ns.* Damenbinde, *die*
**sanitation** [sænɪ'teɪʃn] *n.* Kanalisation und Abfallbeseitigung
**sanity** ['sænɪtɪ] *n.* geistige Gesundheit; **lose one's ~:** den Verstand verlieren
**sank** *see* **sink 2, 3**
**Santa Claus** ['sæntə klɔːz] *n.* der
Weihnachtsmann
**sap** [sæp] **1.** *n.* Saft, *der.* **2.** *v.t.,* **-pp-**
zehren an (+ *Dat.*)
**sapling** ['sæplɪŋ] *n.* junger Baum

**sarcasm** ['sɑːkæzm] *n.* Sarkasmus,
*der.* **sarcastic** [sɑː'kæstɪk] *adj.* sarkastisch
**sardine** [sɑː'diːn] *n.* Sardine, *die*
**Sardinia** [sɑː'dɪnɪə] *pr. n.* Sardinien
*(das)*
**sardonic** [sɑː'dɒnɪk] *adj.* höhnisch;
sardonisch ‹*Lächeln*›
**sash** [sæʃ] *n.* Schärpe, *die*
**sat** *see* **sit**
**Sat.** *abbr.* Saturday Sa.
**Satan** ['seɪtən] *pr. n.* Satan, *der.* **satanic** [sə'tænɪk] *adj.* satanisch
**satchel** ['sætʃl] *n.* [Schul]ranzen, *der*
**satellite** ['sætəlaɪt] *n.* Satellit, *der*
**satellite:** **~ 'broadcasting** *n.* Satellitenfunk, *der;* **~-dish** *n.* Satellitenschüssel, *die;* **~ 'television** *n.* Satellitenfernsehen, *das*
**satin** ['sætɪn] *n.* Satin, *der*
**satire** ['sætaɪə(r)] *n.* Satire, *die* (**on** auf
+ *Akk.*). **satirical** [sə'tɪrɪkl] *adj.* satirisch
**satisfaction** [sætɪs'fækʃn] *n.* Befriedigung, *die* (**at, with** über + *Akk.*);
**meet with sb.'s |complete| ~:** jmdn. [in
jeder Weise] zufriedenstellen
**satisfactory** [sætɪs'fæktərɪ] *adj.* zufriedenstellend
**satisfy** ['sætɪsfaɪ] *v.t.* **a)** befriedigen;
zufriedenstellen ‹*Kunden*›; stillen
‹*Hunger, Durst*›; **b)** *(convince)* **~ sb.
|of sth.|** jmdn. |von etw.| überzeugen.
**'satisfying** *adj.* befriedigend; sättigend ‹*Gericht, Speise*›
**saturate** ['sætʃəreɪt] *v.t.* durchnässen;
[mit Feuchtigkeit durch]tränken
‹*Boden, Erde*›. **saturated** ['sætʃəreɪtɪd] *adj.* durchnäßt. **saturation** [sætʃə'reɪʃn] *n.* Durchnässung, *die*
**Saturday** ['sætədeɪ, 'sætədɪ] *n.* Sonnabend, *der;* Samstag, *der; see also* **Friday**
**Saturn** ['sætən] *pr. n.* (*Astron.*) Saturn,
*der*
**sauce** [sɔːs] *n.* **a)** Soße, *die;* **b)** *(impudence)* Frechheit, *die.* **saucepan**
['sɔːspən] *n.* Kochtopf, *der;* *(with
straight handle)* Kasserolle, *die*
**saucer** ['sɔːsə(r)] *n.* Untertasse, *die*
**saucy** ['sɔːsɪ] *adj.* **a)** *(rude)* frech; **b)**
*(pert, jaunty)* keck
**Saudi Arabia** [saʊdɪ ə'reɪbɪə] *pr. n.*
Saudi-Arabien *(das)*
**sauna** ['sɔːnə, 'saʊnə] *n.* Sauna, *die*
**saunter** ['sɔːntə(r)] *v.i.* schlendern
**sausage** ['sɒsɪdʒ] *n.* Wurst, *die.* **sausage 'roll** *n.* Blätterteig mit Wurstfüllung

**savage** ['sævɪdʒ] **1.** *adj.* **a)** *(uncivilized)* primitiv; wild ⟨*Volksstamm*⟩; unzivilisiert ⟨*Land*⟩; **b)** *(fierce)* brutal; wild ⟨*Tier*⟩. **2.** *n.* Wilde, *der/die (veralt.).*
**savagery** ['sævɪdʒrɪ] *n.* Brutalität, *die*
**save** [seɪv] **1.** *v.t.* **a)** *(rescue)* retten (**from** vor + *Dat.*); ~ **oneself from falling** sich [beim Hinfallen] fangen; **b)** *(put aside)* aufheben; sparen ⟨*Geld*⟩; sammeln ⟨*Briefmarken usw.*⟩; *(conserve)* sparsam umgehen mit; **c)** *(make unnecessary)* sparen ⟨*Geld, Zeit, Energie*⟩; ~ **sb./oneself sth.** jmdm./sich etw. ersparen; **d)** *(Sport)* abwehren ⟨*Schuß, Ball*⟩. **2.** *v.i.* sparen (**on** *Akk.*). **3.** *n. (Sport)* Abwehr, *die.*
**save 'up 1.** *v.t.* sparen. **2.** *v.i.* sparen (**for** für, auf + *Akk.*)
'**saver** *n.* Sparer, *der/*Sparerin, *die*
**saving** ['seɪvɪŋ] **1.** *n. in pl.* Ersparnisse *Pl.* **2.** *adj.* ⟨*kosten-, benzin*⟩sparend
**savings:** ~ **account** *n.* Sparkonto, *das;* ~ **bank** *n.* Sparkasse, *die*
**saviour** ['seɪvjə(r)] *n.* **a)** Retter, *der/*Retterin, *die;* **b)** *(Relig.)* **the S~:** der Heiland
**savor** *etc. (Amer.) see* **savour** *etc.*
**savour** ['seɪvə(r)] *(Brit.)* **1.** *n. (flavour)* Geschmack, *der.* **2.** *v.t.* genießen
**savoury** ['seɪvərɪ] *(Brit.)* **1.** *adj.* **a)** pikant; salzig; **b)** *(appetizing)* appetitanregend. **2.** *n.* [pikantes] Häppchen
'**saw** [sɔː] **1.** *n.* Säge, *die.* **2.** *v.t., p.p.* **sawn** [sɔːn] *or* **sawed** [zer]sägen; ~ **in half** in der Mitte durchsägen. **3.** *v.i., p.p.* **sawn** *or* **sawed** sägen; ~ **through sth.** etw. durchsägen
²**saw** *see* **see**
'**sawdust** *n.* Sägemehl, *das*
**sawn** *see* '**saw 2, 3**
**saxophone** ['sæksəfəʊn] *n.* Saxophon, *das*
**say** [seɪ] **1.** *v.t. pres. t.* **he says** [sez], *p.t. & p.p.* **said** [sed] **a)** sagen; **that is to ~:** das heißt; **do as** *or* **what I ~:** tun Sie, was ich sage; **when all is said and done** letzten Endes; **go without ~ing** sich von selbst verstehen; **she is said to be clever/to have done it** man sagt, sie sei klug/habe es getan; **b)** *(recite)* sprechen ⟨*Gebet, Text*⟩; **c)** *(have specified wording or reading)* sagen ⟨*Zeitung:*⟩ schreiben; ⟨*Uhr:*⟩ zeigen ⟨*Uhrzeit*⟩; **what does it ~ here?** was steht hier? **2.** *n.* **have a** *or* **some ~:** ein Mitspracherecht haben (**in** bei); **have no ~:** nichts zu sagen haben; **have one's ~:** seine Meinung sagen. '**saying** *n.* Redensart, *die*

**scab** [skæb] *n.* [Wund]schorf, *der*
**scaffold** ['skæfəld] *n.* Schafott, *das*
'**scaffolding** *n.* Gerüst, *das*
**scald** [skɔːld, skɒld] **1.** *n.* Verbrühung, *die.* **2.** *v.t.* verbrühen
'**scale** [skeɪl] *n.* **a)** *(of fish, reptile, etc.)* Schuppe, *die;* **b)** *(in kettle etc.)* Kesselstein, *der; (on teeth)* Zahnstein, *der*
²**scale** *n.* **a)** *in sing. or pl. (weighing-instrument)* ~|s] Waage, *die;* **b)** *(dish of balance)* Waagschale, *die*
³**scale 1.** *n.* **a)** *(series of degrees)* Skala, *die;* **b)** *(Mus.)* Tonleiter, *die;* **c)** *(dimensions)* Ausmaß, *das;* **be on a small** ~: bescheidenen Umfang haben; **d)** *(ratio of reduction)* Maßstab, *der;* **what is the ~ of the map?** welchen Maßstab hat diese Karte?; **e)** *(indication) (on map)* Maßstab, *der; (on thermometer)* [Anzeige]skala, *die.* **2.** *v.t.* ersteigen ⟨*Mauer, Leiter, Gipfel*⟩.
**scale 'down** *v.t.* [entsprechend] drosseln ⟨*Produktion*⟩; Abstriche machen bei ⟨*Planungen*⟩
**scalp** [skælp] *n.* Kopfhaut, *die*
**scalpel** ['skælpl] *n.* Skalpell, *das*
**scam** [skæm] *n. (Amer. sl.)* Masche, *die (ugs.)*
**scamper** ['skæmpə(r)] *v.i.* ⟨*Person:*⟩ flitzen; ⟨*Tier:*⟩ huschen
**scampi** ['skæmpɪ] *n. pl.* Scampi *Pl.*
**scan** [skæn] **1.** *v.t.,* **-nn-: a)** *(search thoroughly)* absuchen (**for** nach); **b)** *(look over cursorily)* flüchtig ansehen; überfliegen ⟨*Zeitung, Liste usw.*⟩ (**for** auf der Suche nach); **c)** *(Med.)* szintigraphisch untersuchen. **2.** *v.i.,* **-nn-** ⟨*Vers[zeile]:*⟩ das richtige Versmaß haben. **3.** *n. (Med.)* szintigraphische Untersuchung, *die*
**scandal** ['skændl] *n.* **a)** Skandal, *der* (**about/of** um); *(story)* Skandalgeschichte, *die;* **b)** *(outrage)* Empörung, *die;* **c)** *(gossip)* Klatsch, *der (ugs.).*
**scandalize** ['skændəlaɪz] *v.t.* schockieren. **scandalous** ['skændələs] *adj.* skandalös; schockierend ⟨*Bemerkung*⟩
**Scandinavia** [skændɪ'neɪvɪə] *pr. n.* Skandinavien *(das)*
**scant** [skænt] *adj.* wenig. **scanty** ['skæntɪ] *adj.* spärlich; knapp ⟨*Bikini*⟩
**scapegoat** ['skeɪpgəʊt] *n.* Sündenbock, *der;* **make sb. a** ~: jmdn. zum Sündenbock machen
**scar** [skɑː(r)] **1.** *n.* Narbe, *die.* **2.** *v.t.,* **-rr-:** ~ **sb./sb.'s face** bei jmdm./in jmds. Gesicht *(Dat.)* Narben hinterlassen

**scarce** [skeəs] *adj.* **a)** *(insufficient)* knapp; **b)** *(rare)* selten; **make oneself ~** *(coll.)* sich aus dem Staub machen *(ugs.).* '**scarcely** *adv.* kaum. **scarcity** ['skeəsɪtɪ] *n.* Knappheit, *die* (of an + *Dat.*)

**scare** [skeə(r)] **1.** *n.* **a)** *(sensation of fear)* Schreck[en], *der;* **give sb. a ~:** jmdm. einen Schreck[en] einjagen; **b)** *(general alarm)* [allgemeine] Hysterie; **bomb ~:** Bombendrohung, *die.* **2.** *v. t.* *(frighten)* Angst machen (+ *Dat.*); *(startle)* erschrecken. **scare a'way, scare 'off** *v. t.* verscheuchen

'**scarecrow** *n.* Vogelscheuche, *die*

**scared** [skeəd] *adj.* **be ~ of sb./sth.** vor jmdm./etw. Angst haben; **be ~ of doing/to do sth.** sich nicht [ge]trauen, etw. zu tun

**scarf** [skɑːf] *n., pl.* **~s** *or* **scarves** [skɑːvz] Schal, *der;* *(square)* Halstuch, *das;* *(worn over hair)* Kopftuch, *das*

**scarlet** ['skɑːlɪt] **1.** *n.* Scharlach, *der.* **2.** *adj.* scharlachrot. **scarlet 'fever** *n.* Scharlach, *der*

**scarves** *see* **scarf**

**scary** ['skeərɪ] *adj.* furchterregend ⟨*Anblick*⟩; schaurig ⟨*Film, Geschichte*⟩

**scatter** ['skætə(r)] **1.** *v. t.* **a)** vertreiben; auseinandertreiben ⟨*Menge*⟩; **b)** *(distribute irregularly)* verstreuen. **2.** *v. i.* sich auflösen; ⟨*Menge:*⟩ sich zerstreuen; *(in fear)* auseinanderstieben. **scattered** ['skætəd] *adj.* verstreut; vereinzelt ⟨*Regenschauer*⟩

**scavenge** ['skævɪndʒ] *v. i.* **~ for sth.** nach etw. suchen. '**scavenger** *n.* *(animal)* Aasfresser, *der;* *(fig. derog.: person)* Aasgeier, *der (ugs.)*

**scene** [siːn] *n.* **a)** *(place of event)* Schauplatz, *der;* **~ of the crime** Tatort, *der;* **b)** *(division of act)* Auftritt, *der;* **c)** *(view)* Anblick, *der;* **d) behind the ~s** hinter den Kulissen. **scenery** ['siːnə-rɪ] *n.* **a)** Landschaft, *die;* **b)** *(Theatre)* Bühnenbild, *das.* **scenic** ['siːnɪk] *adj.* landschaftlich schön

**scent** [sent] **1.** *n.* **a)** *(smell)* Duft, *der;* **b)** *(Hunting; also fig.: trail)* Fährte, *die;* **be on the ~ of sb./sth.** *(fig.)* jmdm./einer Sache auf der Spur sein; **c)** *(Brit.: perfume)* Parfüm, *das.* **2.** *v. t.* wittern

**sceptic** ['skeptɪk] *n.* Skeptiker, *der*/Skeptikerin, *die.* **sceptical** ['skeptɪkl] *adj.* skeptisch; **be ~ about** *or* **of sb./sth.** jmdm./einer Sache skeptisch gegenüberstehen. **scepticism** ['skeptɪsɪzm] *n.* Skepsis, *die*

**schedule** ['ʃedjuːl] **1.** *n.* **a)** *(list)* Tabelle, *die;* *(for event)* Programm, *das;* **b)** *(of work)* Zeitplan, *der;* **c) on ~:** plangemäß. **2.** *v. t.* zeitlich planen. '**scheduled flight** *n.* Linienflug, *der*

**scheme** [skiːm] *n.* **a)** *(arrangement)* Anordnung, *die;* **b)** *(plan)* Programm, *das;* *(project)* Projekt, *das;* **c)** *(dishonest plan)* Intrige, *die*

**schizophrenia** [skɪtsə'friːnɪə] *n.* Schizophrenie, *die.* **schizophrenic** [skɪtsə'frenɪk, skɪtsə'friːnɪk] *adj.* schizophren

**scholar** ['skɒlə(r)] *n.* Gelehrte, *der/ die.* '**scholarly** *adj.* wissenschaftlich; gelehrt ⟨*Person*⟩. '**scholarship** *n.* **a)** *(award)* Stipendium, *das;* **b)** *(scholarly work)* Gelehrsamkeit, *die*

**school** [skuːl] *n.* Schule, *die;* *(Amer.: college)* Hochschule, *die;* **be at** *or* **in ~:** in der Schule sein; *(attend ~)* zur Schule gehen; **go to ~:** zur Schule gehen; **~ holidays/exchange** Schulferien *Pl.*/Schüleraustausch, *der*

**school: ~boy** *n.* Schüler, *der;* **~girl** *n.* Schülerin, *die;* **~master** *n.* Lehrer, *der;* **~mistress** *n.* Lehrerin, *die;* **~teacher** *n.* Lehrer, *der*/Lehrerin, *die*

**sciatica** [saɪ'ætɪkə] *n.* Ischias, *die*

**science** ['saɪəns] *n.* Wissenschaft, *die.* **science 'fiction** *n.* Science-fiction, *die.* **scientific** [saɪən'tɪfɪk] *adj.* wissenschaftlich. **scientist** ['saɪəntɪst] *n.* Wissenschaftler, *der*/Wissenschaftlerin, *die*

**scintillating** ['sɪntɪleɪtɪŋ] *adj.* *(fig.)* geistsprühend

**scissors** ['sɪzəz] *n. pl.* **[pair of] ~:** Schere, *die*

¹**scoff** [skɒf] *v. i.* *(mock)* spotten; **~ at** sich lustig machen über (+ *Akk.*)

²**scoff** *v. t.* *(sl.: eat greedily)* verschlingen

**scold** [skəʊld] *v. t.* ausschimpfen **(for wegen); she ~ed him for being late** sie schimpfte ihn aus, weil er zu spät kam

**scone** [skɒn, skəʊn] *n.* weicher, oft zum Tee gegessener kleiner Kuchen

**scoop** [skuːp] **1.** *n.* **a)** Schaufel, *die;* *(for ice-cream etc.)* Portionierer, *der;* **b)** *(Journ.)* Knüller, *der (ugs.).* **2.** *v. t.* schaufeln ⟨*Kohlen, Zucker*⟩; schöpfen ⟨*Flüssigkeit*⟩. **scoop 'out** *v. t.* **a)** *(hollow out)* aushöhlen; schaufeln ⟨*Loch, Graben*⟩; **b)** [her]ausschöpfen ⟨*Flüssigkeit*⟩; auslöffeln ⟨*Fruchtfleisch*⟩; *(with a knife)* herausschneiden ⟨*Gehäuse, Fruchtfleisch*⟩. **scoop 'up** *v. t.*

schöpfen ⟨*Flüssigkeit, Suppe*⟩; schaufeln ⟨*Erde*⟩

**scooter** ['sku:tə(r)] *n.* **a)** *(toy)* Roller, *der;* **b)** |motor| ~: [Motor]roller, *der*

**scope** [skəʊp] *n.* **a)** Bereich, *der;* *(of discussion etc.)* Rahmen, *der;* **b)** *(opportunity)* Entfaltungsmöglichkeiten *Pl.*

**scorch** [skɔ:tʃ] *v. t.* versengen. '**scorching** *adj.* glühend heiß

**score** [skɔ:(r)] **1.** *n.* **a)** *(points)* [Spiel]stand, *der;* *(made by one player)* Punktzahl, *die;* keep |the| ~: zählen; **b)** *(Mus.)* Partitur, *die;* *(Cinemat.)* [Film]musik, *die;* **c)** *pl. same or* ~s *(group of 20)* zwanzig; **d)** *in pl. (great numbers)* ~s |and ~s| of zig *(ugs.);* Dutzende [von]; **e) on that** ~: was das betrifft; **f) pay off** *or* **settle an old** ~ *(fig.)* eine alte Rechnung begleichen. **2.** *v. t.* erzielen ⟨*Erfolg, Punkt usw.*⟩; ~ **a goal** ein Tor schießen. **3.** *v. i.* **a)** *(make* ~*)* Punkte/einen Punkt erzielen; *(*~ *goal/goals)* ein Tor/Tore schießen/werfen; **b)** *(keep* ~*)* aufschreiben. '**score-board** *n.* Anzeigetafel, *die.* '**scorer** *n.* **a)** *(recorder)* Anschreiber, *der/*Anschreiberin, *die;* **b)** *(Footb.)* Torschütze, *der/*-schützin, *die*

**scorn** [skɔ:n] **1.** *n.* Verachtung, *die.* **2.** *v. t.* verachten; in den Wind schlagen ⟨*Rat*⟩; ausschlagen ⟨*Angebot*⟩. **scornful** ['skɔ:nfl] *adj.* verächtlich ⟨*Lächeln, Blick*⟩; **be** ~ **of sth.** für etw. nur Verachtung haben

**Scorpio** ['skɔ:pɪəʊ] *n.* der Skorpion. **scorpion** ['skɔ:pɪən] *n.* Skorpion, *der*

**Scot** [skɒt] *n.* Schotte, *der/*Schottin, *die*

**Scotch** [skɒtʃ] **1.** *adj. see* **Scottish. 2.** *n.* Scotch, *der;* schottischer Whisky

**scotch** *v. t.* den Boden entziehen (+ *Dat.*) ⟨*Gerücht*⟩; zunichte machen ⟨*Plan*⟩

**Scotch:** ~ '**egg** *n. hartgekochtes Ei in Wurstbrät;* ~ '**whisky** *n.* schottischer Whisky

**scot-'free** *adj.* |get off/go| ~: ungeschoren |davonkommen *od.* bleiben|

**Scotland** ['skɒtlənd] *pr. n.* Schottland *(das)*

**Scots** [skɒts] **1.** *adj. (esp. Scot.)* schottisch; **sb. is** ~: jmd. ist Schotte/Schottin. **2.** *n. (dialect)* Schottisch, *das.* **Scotsman** ['skɒtsmən] *n., pl.* **Scotsmen** ['skɒtsmən] Schotte, *der.* '**Scotswoman** *n.* Schottin, *die*

**Scottish** ['skɒtɪʃ] *adj.* schottisch; **sb. is** ~: jmd. ist Schotte/Schottin

**scoundrel** ['skaʊndrl] *n.* Schuft, *der* '**scour** [skaʊə(r)] *v. t. (search)* durchkämmen *(for nach)*

²**scour** *v. t.* scheuern ⟨*Topf, Metall*⟩. '**scourer** *n.* Topfreiniger, *der*

**scourge** [skɜ:dʒ] *n.* Geißel, *die*

**scout** [skaʊt] **1.** *n.* **a)** |Boy| S~: Pfadfinder, *der;* **b)** *(Mil.)* Späher, *der.* **2.** *v. i.* ~ **for** Ausschau halten nach

**scowl** [skaʊl] **1.** *v. i.* ein mürrisches Gesicht machen. **2.** *n.* mürrischer [Gesichts]ausdruck

**scram** [skræm] *v. i.,* **-mm-** *(sl.)* abhauen *(salopp)*

**scramble** ['skræmbl] **1.** *v. i.* **a)** *(clamber)* klettern; ~ **through a hedge** sich durch eine Hecke zwängen; **b)** *(move hastily)* rennen *(ugs.);* ~ **for sth.** um etw. rangeln. **2.** *v. t. (Teleph., Radio)* verschlüsseln. **scrambled** '**egg** *n.* Rührei, *das*

¹**scrap** [skræp] **1.** *n.* **a)** *(of paper)* Fetzen, *der; (of food)* Bissen, *der;* **b)** *in pl. (odds and ends) (of food)* Reste *Pl.;* **c)** *(smallest amount)* **not a** ~ **of** kein bißchen; *(of sympathy, truth also)* nicht ein Fünkchen; **not a** ~ **of evidence** nicht die Spur eines Beweises; **d)** ~ |metal| Schrott, *der;* ~ **iron** Alteisen, *das.* **2.** *v. t.,* **-pp-** wegwerfen; *(send for* ~*)* verschrotten; *(fig.)* aufgeben

²**scrap** *(coll.)* **1.** *n. (fight)* Rauferei, *die.* **2.** *v. i.,* **-pp-** sich raufen

'**scrap-book** *n.* [Sammel]album, *das*

**scrape** [skreɪp] **1.** *v. t.* **a)** *(make smooth)* schaben ⟨*Häute, Möhren, Kartoffeln usw.*⟩; abziehen ⟨*Holz*⟩; *(damage)* verschrammen ⟨*Fußboden, Auto*⟩; **b)** *(remove)* [ab]kratzen ⟨*Farbe, Schmutz, Rost*⟩ **(off, from** von); **c)** *(draw along)* schleifen; **d)** ~ **together** *(raise)* zusammenkratzen *(ugs.); (save up)* zusammensparen. **2.** *v. i.* **a)** *(move with sound)* schleifen; **b)** *(emit scraping noise)* ein schabendes Geräusch machen; **c)** *(rub)* streifen **(against, over** *Akk.*). **3.** *n.* **a)** *(act, sound)* Kratzen, *das* **(against** an + *Dat.*); **b)** *(predicament)* Schwulitäten *Pl. (ugs.).* **scrape** '**by** *v. i. (fig.)* sich über Wasser halten **(on** mit). **scrape** '**out** *v. t.* **a)** *(excavate)* buddeln *(ugs.);* scharren; **b)** *(clean)* auskratzen. **scrape through 1.** ['--] *v. t.* sich zwängen durch; *(fig.)* mit Hängen und Würgen kommen durch ⟨*Prüfung*⟩. **2.** [-'-] *v. i.* sich durchzwängen; *(fig.: in examination)* mit Hängen und Würgen durchkommen

'**scraper** *n.* *(for shoes)* Kratzeisen, *das;* *(grid)* Abtreter, *der;* *(tool, kitchen utensil)* Schaber, *der;* *(for removing ice from car windows)* [Eis]kratzer, *der*

**scrap:** ~-**heap** *n.* Schutthaufen, *der;* ~ '**paper** *n.* Schmierpapier, *das*

**scrappy** ['skræpɪ] *adj.* lückenhaft

'**scrap-yard** *n.* Schrottplatz, *der*

**scratch** [skrætʃ] **1.** *v. t.* **a)** *(score surface of)* zerkratzen; *(score skin of)* kratzen; **b)** *(get scratch[es] on)* ~ **oneself/one's hands** *etc.* sich schrammen/ sich *(Dat.)* die Hände *usw.* zerkratzen; **c)** *(scrape without marking)* kratzen; kratzen an (+ *Dat.*) ⟨*Insektenstich usw.*⟩; ~ **oneself/one's arm** sich kratzen/sich *(Dat.)* den Arm *od.* am Arm kratzen. **2.** *v. i.* kratzen; *(~ oneself)* sich kratzen. **3.** *n.* **a)** *(mark, wound)* Kratzer, *der (ugs.);* Schramme, *die;* **b)** *(sound)* Kratzen, *das;* **c)** **have a [good]** ~: sich [ordentlich] kratzen; **d) start from** ~: bei Null anfangen *(ugs.);* **be up to** ~ ⟨*Arbeit, Leistung:*⟩ nichts zu wünschen übriglassen; ⟨*Person:*⟩ den Anforderungen genügen. **scratch a'bout, scratch a'round** *v. i.* scharren; *(fig.: search)* suchen (**for** nach). **scratch 'out** *v. t.* auskratzen ⟨*Auge*⟩

**scrawl** [skrɔ:l] **1.** *v. t.* hinkritzeln. **2.** *v. i.* kritzeln. **3.** *n.* Gekritzel, *das;* *(handwriting)* Klaue, *die (salopp)*

**scrawny** ['skrɔ:nɪ] *adj.* hager; dürr

**scream** [skri:m] **1.** *v. i.* schreien (**with** vor + *Dat.*). **2.** *v. t.* schreien. **3.** *n.* Schrei, *der;* *(of jet engine)* Heulen, *das;* ~**s of pain** Schmerzensschreie

**screech** [skri:tʃ] **1.** *v. i. & t.* kreischen. **2.** *n.* Kreischen, *das*

**screen** [skri:n] **1.** *n.* **a)** *(partition)* Trennwand, *die;* *(piece of furniture)* Wandschirm, *der;* **b)** *(of trees, persons, fog)* Wand, *die;* **c)** *(Cinemat.)* Leinwand, *die;* [TV] ~: Bildschirm, *der.* **2.** *v. t.* **a)** *(shelter)* schützen (**from** vor + *Dat.*); *(conceal)* verdecken; **b)** vorführen ⟨*Film*⟩; **c)** *(for disease)* untersuchen. '**screenplay** *n.* Drehbuch, *das*

**screw** [skru:] **1.** *n.* Schraube, *die.* **2.** *v. t.* schrauben (**to** an + *Akk.*); ~ **together** zusammenschrauben; ~ **down** festschrauben. **screw 'up** *v. t.* **a)** *(crumple up)* zusammenknüllen ⟨*Blatt Papier*⟩; **b)** verziehen ⟨*Gesicht*⟩; zusammenkneifen ⟨*Augen, Mund*⟩; **c)** *(sl.: bungle)* vermurksen *(salopp);* ~ **it/ things up** Mist bauen *(salopp)*

**screw:** ~-**cap** *n.* Schraubverschluß,

*der;* ~-**driver** *n.* Schraubenzieher, *der;* ~-**top** *see* ~-**cap**

**screwy** ['skru:ɪ] *adj. (sl.)* spinnig *(ugs.)*

**scribble** ['skrɪbl] **1.** *v. t.* hinkritzeln. **2.** *v. i.* kritzeln. **3.** *n.* Gekritzel, *das*

**script** [skrɪpt] *n.* **a)** *(handwriting)* Handschrift, *die;* **b)** *(of play)* Regiebuch, *das;* *(of film)* [Dreh]buch, *das;* **c)** *(for broadcaster)* Manuskript, *das*

**scripture** ['skrɪptʃə(r)] *n.* **a)** [Holy] S~, **the** [Holy] S~**s** die [Heilige] Schrift; **b)** *(Sch.)* Religion, *die*

'**script-writer** *n.* *(of film)* Drehbuchautor, *der/*-autorin, *die*

**scroll** [skrəʊl] *n.* *(roll)* Rolle, *die*

**scrounge** ['skraʊndʒ] *(coll.)* **1.** *v. t.* schnorren *(ugs.)* (**off, from** von). **2.** *v. i.* schnorren *(ugs.)* (**from** bei). '**scrounger** *n.* *(coll.)* Schnorrer, *der/* Schnorrerin, *die (ugs.)*

'**scrub** [skrʌb] **1.** *v. t.,* -**bb**-**:** **a)** schrubben *(ugs.);* scheuern; **b)** *(coll.: cancel)* zurücknehmen ⟨*Befehl*⟩; sausenlassen *(ugs.)* ⟨*Plan*⟩. **2.** *v. i.,* -**bb**- schrubben *(ugs.);* scheuern. **3.** *n.* **give sth. a** ~**:** etw. schrubben *(ugs.) od.* scheuern

²**scrub** *n.* *(brushwood)* Buschwerk, *das;* *(area)* Buschland, *das*

'**scruff** [skrʌf] *n.* **by the** ~ **of the neck** beim Genick

²**scruff** *n.* *(Brit. coll.)* *(man)* vergammelter Typ *(ugs.);* *(woman, girl)* Schlampe, *die.* '**scruffy** *adj.* vergammelt *(ugs.)*

**scrum** [skrʌm] *n.* Gedränge, *das*

**scruple** ['skru:pl] *n.* Skrupel, *der;* **have no** ~**s about doing sth.** keine Skrupel haben, etw. zu tun

**scrupulous** ['skru:pjʊləs] *adj.* gewissenhaft ⟨*Person*⟩; unbedingt ⟨*Ehrlichkeit*⟩; peinlich ⟨*Sorgfalt*⟩

**scrutinize** ['skru:tɪnaɪz] *v. t.* [genau] untersuchen ⟨*[Forschungs]gegenstand*⟩; [über]prüfen ⟨*Rechnung, Paß, Fahrkarte*⟩; mustern ⟨*Person*⟩

**scrutiny** ['skru:tɪnɪ] *n.* **a)** *(critical gaze)* musternder Blick; **b)** *(examination)* *(of recruit)* Musterung, *die;* *(of bill, passport, ticket)* [Über]prüfung, *die*

**scuff** [skʌf] **1.** *v. t.* streifen; verschrammen ⟨*Schuhe, Fußboden*⟩. **2.** *n.* Schramme, *die*

**scuffle** ['skʌfl] **1.** *n.* Handgreiflichkeiten *Pl.* **2.** *v. i.* handgreiflich werden (**with** gegen)

**scullery** ['skʌlərɪ] *n.* Spülküche, *die*

**sculptor** ['skʌlptə(r)] *n.* Bildhauer, *der/*-hauerin, *die*

**sculpture** ['skʌlptʃə(r)] *n.* **a)** *(art)*

Bildhauerei, *die;* **b)** *(piece of work)* Skulptur, *die;* Plastik, *die; (pieces collectively)* Skulpturen

**scum** [skʌm] *n.* **a)** Schmutzschicht, *die; (film)* Schmutzfilm, *der;* **b)** *(fig. derog.)* Abschaum, *der*

**scurry** ['skʌrɪ] *v. i.* huschen

¹**scuttle** ['skʌtl] *n.* Kohlenfüller, *der*

²**scuttle** *(Naut.) v. t.* versenken

³**scuttle** *v. i.* rennen; flitzen *(ugs.);* ⟨*Maus, Krabbe:*⟩ huschen

**scythe** [saɪð] *n.* Sense, *die*

**SE** *abbr.* south-east SO

**sea** [siː] *n.* **a)** Meer, *das;* **the ~:** das Meer; die See; **by ~:** mit dem Schiff; **by the ~:** am Meer; **at ~:** auf See *(Dat.);* **be all at ~** *(fig.)* nicht mehr weiter wissen; **put |out| to ~:** in See *(Akk.)* gehen; **b)** *(specific tract of water)* Meer, *das*

**sea: ~ 'air** *n.* Seeluft, *die;* **~-'bed** *n.* Meeresboden, *der;* **~-gull** *n.* [See]möwe, *die*

¹**seal** [siːl] *n. (Zool.)* Robbe, *die;* |**common**| **~:** [Gemeiner] Seehund

²**seal 1.** *n. (wax etc., stamp, impression)* Siegel, *das.* **2.** *v. t.* **a)** *(stamp, affix ~ to)* siegeln ⟨*Dokument*⟩; *(fasten with ~)* verplomben ⟨*Tür, Stromzähler*⟩; **b)** *(close securely)* abdichten ⟨*Behälter, Rohr usw.*⟩; zukleben ⟨*Umschlag, Paket*⟩; **c)** *(stop up)* verschließen; abdichten ⟨*Leck*⟩; verschmieren ⟨*Riß*⟩. **seal 'off** *v. t.* abriegeln

**sea: ~-legs** *n. pl.* Seebeine *Pl. (Seemannsspr.);* **get** *or* **find one's ~-legs** sich *(Dat.)* Seebeine wachsen lassen; **~-level** *n.* Meeresspiegel, *der*

'**sealing-wax** *n.* Siegellack, *der*

'**sea-lion** *n.* Seelöwe, *der*

**seam** [siːm] *n.* **a)** Naht, *die;* **b)** *(of coal)* Flöz, *das*

**seaman** ['siːmən] *n., pl.* **seamen** ['siː-mən] Matrose, *der*

'**sea mist** *n.* Küstennebel, *der*

'**seamless** *adj.* nahtlos

'**seamy** *adj.* **the ~ side |of life etc.|** *(fig.)* die Schattenseite[n] [des Lebens *usw.*]

**seance** ['seɪəns], **séance** ['seɪãs] *n.* Séance, *die*

**sea: ~plane** *n.* Wasserflugzeug, *das;* **~port** *n.* Seehafen, *der*

**sear** ['sɪə(r)] *v. t.* versengen

**search** [sɜːtʃ] **1.** *v. t.* durchsuchen (**for** nach); absuchen ⟨*Gebiet, Fläche*⟩ (**for** nach); *(fig.: probe)* erforschen ⟨*Herz, Gewissen*⟩; suchen in (+ *Dat.*) ⟨*Gedächtnis*⟩ (**for** nach). **2.** *v. i.* suchen (**for** nach). **3.** *n.* Suche, *die* (**for** nach);

*(of building, room, etc.)* Durchsuchung, *die;* **in ~ of sb./sth.** auf der Suche nach jmdm./etw. '**searching** *adj.* prüfend, forschend ⟨*Blick*⟩; bohrend ⟨*Frage*⟩

**search: ~light** *n.* Suchscheinwerfer, *der;* **~-party** *n.* Suchtrupp, *der;* **~-warrant** *n.* Durchsuchungsbefehl, *der*

**sea: ~-shore** *n.* [Meeres]küste, *die; (beach)* Strand, *der;* **~sick** *adj.* seekrank; **~sickness** *n.* Seekrankheit, *die;* **~side** *n.* [Meeres]küste, *die;* **by/to/at the ~side** am/ans/am Meer; **~side town** Seestadt, *die*

**season** ['siːzn] **1.** *n.* **a)** Jahreszeit, *die;* **nesting ~:** Nistzeit, *die;* **b)** *(period of social activity)* |**opera/football**| **~:** [Opern-/Fußball]saison, *die;* **holiday** *or (Amer.)* **vacation ~:** Urlaubszeit, *die;* **tourist ~:** Reisezeit, *die;* **c)** **raspberries are in/out of** *or* **not in ~:** jetzt ist die/nicht die Saison *od.* Zeit für Himbeeren; **be in ~** *(on heat)* brünstig sein; **d)** *see* **season-ticket. 2.** *v. t.* würzen ⟨*Fleisch, Rede*⟩. **seasonable** ['siːzənəbl] *adj.* der Jahreszeit gemäß. '**seasoned** *adj. (fig.)* erfahren. '**seasoning** *n.* Gewürze *Pl.;* Würze, *die.* '**season-ticket** *n.* Dauerkarte, *die*

**seat** [siːt] **1.** *n.* **a)** Sitzgelegenheit, *die; (in vehicle, cinema, etc.)* Sitz, *der; (of toilet)* [Klosett]brille, *die (ugs.);* **b)** *(place)* Platz, *der; (in vehicle)* [Sitz]platz, *der;* **have** *or* **take a ~:** sich [hin]setzen; **c)** *(part of chair)* Sitzfläche, *die;* **d)** *(buttocks)* Gesäß, *das; (part of clothing)* Gesäßpartie, *die; (of trousers)* Sitz, *der.* **2.** *v. t.* **a)** *(cause to sit)* setzen; ⟨*Platzanweiser:*⟩ einen Platz anweisen (+ *Dat.*); **~ oneself** sich setzen; **b)** *(have ~s for)* Sitzplätze bieten (+ *Dat.*); **~ 500 people** 500 Sitzplätze haben. '**seat-belt** *n.* Sicherheitsgurt, *der.* '**seated** *adj.* sitzend; **remain ~:** sitzen bleiben. '**seating** *n.* Sitzplätze; *attrib.* Sitz⟨*ordnung, -plan*⟩

**sea: ~-urchin** *n.* Seeigel, *der;* **~-wall** *n.* Strandmauer, *die;* **~-water** *n.* Meerwasser, *das;* **~-weed** *n.* [See]tang, *der;* **~worthy** *adj.* seetüchtig

**secluded** [sɪ'kluːdɪd] *adj. (hidden)* versteckt; *(isolated)* abgelegen; zurückgezogen ⟨*Leben*⟩. **seclusion** [sɪ'kluːʒn] *n. (remoteness)* Abgelegenheit, *die; (privacy)* Zurückgezogenheit, *die*

'**second** ['sekənd] **1.** *adj.* zweit...; **~**

largest/highest *etc.* zweitgrößt.../ -höchst... *usw.;* **come/be** ~: zweiter/ zweite werden/sein. **2.** *n.* **a)** *(unit of time or angle)* Sekunde, *die;* **b)** *(coll.: moment)* Sekunde, *die (ugs.);* **wait a few ~s** einen Moment warten; **in a ~** *(immediately)* sofort *(ugs.); (very quickly)* im Nu *(ugs.);* **just a ~!** *(coll.)* einen Moment!; **c) the ~** *(in sequence)* der/die/das Zweite; **d)** *in pl. (helping of food)* zweite Portion. **3.** *v. t. (support)* unterstützen

²**second** [sɪ'kɒnd] *v. t. (transfer)* vorübergehend versetzen

**secondary** ['sekəndərı] *adj. (of less importance)* zweitrangig; Neben-〈*sache*〉; **be ~ to sth.** einer Sache *(Dat.)* untergeordnet sein. '**secondary school** *n.* höhere Schule

**second:** ~-**best 1.** ['---] *adj.* zweitbest...; **2.** [-'-'] *n.* Zweitbeste, *der/die/ das;* ~-**class 1.** ['---] *adj. (of lower class)* zweiter Klasse *nachgestellt;* Zweite[r]-Klasse-〈*Fahrkarte, Abteil, Post, Brief usw.*〉; ~-**class stamp** Briefmarke für einen Zweiter-Klasse-Brief; **2.** [-'-'] *adv.* zweiter Klasse *(fahren);* ~ '**floor** *see* **floor 1 b;** ~ **hand** *n.* Sekundenzeiger, *der;* ~-**hand 1.** ['---] *adj.* **a)** gebraucht 〈*Kleidung, Auto usw.*〉; antiquarisch 〈*Buch*〉; **b)** *(selling used goods)* Gebrauchtwaren-; Secondhand〈*laden*〉; **c)** 〈*Nachrichten, Bericht*〉 aus zweiter Hand; **2.** [-'-'] *adv.* aus zweiter Hand

'**secondly** *adv.* zweitens

**second:** ~ **name** *n.* Nachname, *der;* ~-'**rate** *adj.* zweitklassig; ~ '**thoughts** *n. pl.* **have ~ thoughts** es sich *(Dat.)* anders überlegen (**about** mit); **we've had ~ thoughts about buying it** wir wollen es nun doch nicht kaufen; **but on ~ thoughts ...:** wenn ich's mir [noch mal] überlege, ...

**secrecy** ['si:krısı] *n.* **a)** *(keeping of secret)* Geheimhaltung, *die;* **b)** *(secretiveness)* Heimlichtuerei, *die;* **c) in ~:** im geheimen

**secret** ['si:krıt] **1.** *adj.* geheim; Geheim〈*fach, -tür, -abkommen, -kode*〉; heimlich 〈*Trinker, Liebhaber*〉; **keep sth. ~:** etw. geheimhalten (**from** vor + *Dat.*). **2.** *n.* **a)** Geheimnis, *das;* **make no ~ of sth.** kein Geheimnis aus etw. machen; *(fig.)* keinen Hehl aus etw. machen; **keep ~s/ a ~:** schweigen *(fig.);* **b) in ~:** im geheimen. **secret 'agent** *n.* Geheimagent, *der/* -agentin, *die*

**secretarial** [sekrə'teərıəl] *adj.* Sekretärinnen〈*kursus, -tätigkeit*〉; 〈*Arbeit*〉 als Sekretärin

**secretary** ['sekrətərı] *n.* Sekretär, *der/*Sekretärin, *die*

**secretive** ['si:krıtıv] *adj.* verschlossen 〈*Person*〉; **be ~:** geheimnisvoll tun (**about** mit)

'**secretly** *adv.* heimlich; insgeheim 〈*etw. glauben*〉

**sect** [sekt] *n.* Sekte, *die*

**section** ['sekʃn] *n.* **a)** *(part cut off)* Abschnitt, *der;* Stück, *das; (part of divided whole)* Teil, *der;* **b)** *(of firm)* Abteilung, *die; (of organization)* Sektion, *die;* **c)** *(of chapter, book)* Abschnitt, *der; (of statute etc.)* Paragraph, *der*

**sector** ['sektə(r)] *n.* Sektor, *der*

**secular** ['sekjʊlə(r)] *adj.* weltlich

**secure** [sɪ'kjʊə(r)] **1.** *adj.* sicher; *(firmly fastened)* fest; ~ **against** burglars gegen Einbruch geschützt. **2.** *v. t.* **a)** sichern (**for** *Dat.*); beschaffen 〈*Auftrag*〉 (**for** *Dat.*); *(for oneself)* sich *(Dat.)* sichern; **b)** *(fasten)* sichern. **se**-'**curely** *adv. (firmly)* fest 〈*verriegeln, zumachen*〉; sicher 〈*befestigen, untergebracht sein*〉. **security** [sɪ'kjʊərıtı] *n.* **a)** Sicherheit, *die;* ~ |**measures**| Sicherheitsmaßnahmen; **b)** *(Finance)* securities *pl.* Wertpapiere

**security:** ~ **forces** *n. pl.* Sicherheitskräfte *Pl.;* ~ **guard** *n.* Wächter, *der/* Wächterin, *die;* ~ **risk** *n.* Sicherheitsrisiko, *das*

**sedan** [sɪ'dæn] *n. (Amer. Motor Veh.)* Limousine, *die*

**sedate** [sɪ'deıt] **1.** *adj.* bedächtig; gesetzt 〈*alte Dame*〉; gemächlich 〈*Tempo, Leben*〉. **2.** *v. t.* sedieren. **sedation** [sɪ'deıʃn] *n.* Sedation, *die;* **be under ~:** sediert sein. **sedative** ['sedətıv] **1.** *n.* Beruhigungsmittel, *das.* **2.** *adj.* sedativ

**sedentary** ['sedəntərı] *adj.* sitzend

**sediment** ['sedımənt] *n.* Ablagerung, *die; (of tea, coffee, etc.)* Bodensatz, *der*

**seduce** [sɪ'dju:s] *v. t.* verführen. **seduction** [sɪ'dʌkʃn] *n.* Verführung, *die.* **seductive** [sɪ'dʌktıv] *adj.* verführerisch; verlockend 〈*Angebot*〉

**see** [si:] **1.** *v. t.,* **saw** [sɔ:], **seen** [si:n] **a)** sehen; **I can ~ it's hard for you** ich verstehe, daß es nicht leicht für dich ist; **I ~ what you mean** ich verstehe[, was du meinst]; **b)** *(meet [with])* sehen; treffen; *(meet socially)* sich treffen mit; **I'll ~ you there/at five** wir sehen uns

dort/um fünf; ~ you!, [I'll] be ~ing
you! *(coll.)* bis bald! *(ugs.)*; c) *(speak
to)* sprechen ‹*Person*› (about wegen);
*(visit)* gehen zu ‹*Arzt, Anwalt usw.*›;
*(receive)* empfangen; d) *(find out)* feststellen; *(by looking)* nachsehen; e)
*(make sure)* ~ |that| ...: *(imagine)* sich *(Dat.)* vorstel-
daß ...; f) *(imagine)* sich *(Dat.)* vorstel-
len; g) *(escort)* begleiten. 2. *v. i.*, saw,
seen a) sehen; b) *(make sure)* nachsehen; c) I ~: ich verstehe; you ~: weißt
du/wißt ihr/wissen Sie. **see about**
*v. t.* sich kümmern um. **see 'off** *v. t.*
a) *(say goodbye to)* verabschieden; b)
*(chase away)* vertreiben. **see 'out** *v. t.*
*(escort)* hinausbegleiten (of aus); ~
**oneself out** allein hinausfinden. **see
through** *v. t.* a) ['--] hindurchsehen
durch; *(fig.)* durchschauen; b) [-'-]
*(not abandon)* zu Ende bringen. **'see
to** *v. t.* sich kümmern um
**seed** [si:d] 1. *n.* a) Samen, *der; (of
grape etc.)* Kern, *der;* b) *no pl., no
indef. art. (~s collectively)* Samen[kör-
ner] *Pl.; (as collected for sowing)* Saat-
gut, *das; (for birds)* Körner *Pl.;* go or
run to ~: Samen bilden; *(fig.)* herunterkommen *(ugs.);* c) *(Sport)* gesetzter
Spieler/gesetzte Spielerin. 2. *v. t.* a)
*(place ~s in)* besäen; b) *(Sport)* setzen
‹*Spieler*›; **be ~ed number one** als Nummer eins gesetzt werden/sein. **'seedless** *adj.* kernlos
**seedling** ['si:dlɪŋ] *n.* Sämling, *der*
**'seedy** *adj.* a) *(coll.: unwell)* feel ~:
sich [leicht] angeschlagen fühlen; b)
*(shabby)* schäbig, *(ugs.)* vergammelt
‹*Aussehen*›; heruntergekommen
‹*Stadtteil*›; c) *(disreputable)* zweifelhaft
**'seeing** *conj.* ~ [that] ...: da ...; wo ...
*(ugs.)*
**seek** [si:k] *v. t.*, **sought** [sɔ:t] suchen;
anstreben ‹*Posten, Amt*›; sich bemü-
hen um ‹*Anerkennung, Interview, Einstellung*›; *(try to reach)* aufsuchen
**seem** [si:m] *v. i.* scheinen; you ~ tired
du wirkst müde; she ~s nice sie
scheint nett zu sein. **'seeming** *adj.*
scheinbar. **'seemingly** *adv.* a) *(evidently)* offensichtlich; b) *(to outward
appearance)* scheinbar
**seemly** ['si:mlɪ] *adj.* schicklich
**seen** *see* see
**seep** [si:p] *v. i.* ~ [away] [ab]sickern
**'see-saw** *n.* Wippe, *die*
**seethe** [si:ð] *v. i.* a) ~ [with anger/in-
wardly] vor Wut/innerlich schäumen;
b) ‹*Straßen usw.*:› wimmeln (with von)

**'see-through** *adj.* durchsichtig
**segment** ['segmənt] *n. (of orange,
pineapple, etc.)* Scheibe, *die*
**segregate** ['segrɪgeɪt] *v. t.* trennen;
*(racially)* absondern. **segregation**
[segrɪ'geɪʃn] *n.* Trennung, *die;* |racial|
~: Rassentrennung, *die*
**seismic** ['saɪzmɪk] *adj.* seismisch
**seize** [si:z] 1. *v. t.* a) ergreifen; ~ **power**
die Macht ergreifen; ~ **sb. by the arm/
collar** jmdn. am Arm/Kragen packen;
~ **the opportunity |to do sth.|** die Gele-
genheit ergreifen [und etw. tun]; ~
**any/a** *or* **the chance |to do sth.|** jede/
die Gelegenheit nutzen[, um etw. zu
tun]; **be ~d with remorse/panic** von
Gewissensbissen geplagt/von Panik
ergriffen werden; b) *(capture)* gefangennehmen ‹*Person*›; kapern ‹*Schiff*›;
mit Gewalt übernehmen ‹*Flugzeug,
Gebäude*›; einnehmen ‹*Festung,
Brücke*›; c) *(confiscate)* beschlagnahmen. 2. *v. i. see* ~ up. **'seize on** *v. t.*
sich *(Dat.)* vornehmen ‹*Einzelheit, Aspekt, Schwachpunkt*›; aufgreifen
‹*Idee, Vorschlag*›. **seize 'up** *v. i.* sich
festfressen
**seizure** ['si:ʒə(r)] *n.* a) *see* seize 1 b, c:
Gefangennahme, *die;* Kapern, *das;*
Übernahme, *die;* Einnahme, *die;* Beschlagnahme, *die;* b) *(Med.)* Anfall,
*der*
**seldom** ['seldəm] *adv.* selten
**select** [sɪ'lekt] 1. *adj.* ausgewählt. 2.
*v. t.* auswählen. **selection** [sɪ'lekʃn]
*n.* a) *(what is selected [from])* Auswahl,
*die* (of an + *Dat.*, from aus); b) *(act of
choosing)* [Aus]wahl, *die.* **selective**
[sɪ'lektɪv] *adj. (using selection)* selek-
tiv; *(careful in one's choice)* wählerisch
**self** [self] *n., pl.* **selves** [selvz] Selbst,
*das (geh.);* Ich, *das*
**self-** *in comb.* selbst-/Selbst-
**self:** ~-**ad'dressed** *adj.* ~-**addressed
envelope** adressierter Rückumschlag;
~-**ad'hesive** *adj.* selbstklebend;
~-**ap'pointed** *adj.* selbsternannt;
~-**as'surance** *n.* Selbstsicherheit,
*die;* ~-**as'sured** *adj.* selbstsicher;
~-'**catering** 1. *adj.* mit Selbstversor-
gung *nachgestellt;* 2. *n.* Selbstversor-
gung, *die;* ~-'**centred** *adj.* egozen-
trisch; ~-'**confidence** *n.* Selbstbewußtsein, *das;* ~-'**confident** *adj.*
selbstbewußt; ~-'**conscious** *adj.* unsicher; ~-'**consciousness** *n.* Unsicherheit, *die;* ~-'**contained** *adj.* abgeschlossen ‹*Wohnung*›; ~-**con'trol**
*n.* Selbstbeherrschung, *die;* ~-

con'trolled *adj.* voller Selbstbeherrschung *nachgestellt*; ~-de'ception *n.* Selbsttäuschung, *die*; ~-de'fence *n.* Notwehr, *die*; **in** ~-**defence** aus Notwehr; ~-**drive** *adj.* ~-**drive hire** |**company**| Autovermietung, *die*; ~-**drive vehicle** Mietwagen, *der*; ~-**em-**'**ployed** *adj.* selbständig; ~-'**evident** *adj.* offenkundig; ~-**ex**'**planatory** *adj.* ohne weiteres verständlich; **be** ~-**explanatory** für sich selbst sprechen; ~-'**help** *n.* Selbsthilfe, *die*; ~-**im**'**portant** *adj.* eingebildet; ~-**in**'**dulgent** *adj.* maßlos; ~-'**interest** *n.* Eigeninteresse, *das*

'**selfish** *adj.*, '**selfishly** *adv.* selbstsüchtig. '**selfishness** *n.* Selbstsucht, *die*

**self:** ~-'**pity** *n.* Selbstmitleid, *das*; ~-'**portrait** *n.* Selbstporträt, *das*; ~-**pos**'**sessed** *adj.* selbstbeherrscht; ~-'**raising flour** *n.* (*Brit.*) mit Backpulver versetztes Mehl; ~-**re**'**spect** *n.* Selbstachtung, *die*; ~-**re**'**specting** *adj.* **no** ~-**respecting person** ...: niemand, der etwas auf sich hält, ...; ~-'**righteous** *adj.* selbstgerecht; ~-'**sacrifice** *n.* Selbstaufopferung, *die*; ~-'**satisfied** *adj.* selbstzufrieden; (*smug*) selbstgefällig; ~-'**service** *n.* Selbstbedienung, *die*; *attrib.* Selbstbedienungs-; ~-'**sufficient** *adj.* unabhängig; selbständig (*Person*); ~-'**willed** *adj.* eigenwillig

**sell** [sel] **1.** *v.t.*, **sold** [səʊld] ~ **sth. to sb.**, ~ **sb. sth.** jmdm. etw. verkaufen; **be sold out** ausverkauft sein. **2.** *v.i.*, **sold** sich verkaufen; (*Person:*) verkaufen. **sell** '**off** *v.t.* verkaufen. **sell** '**out 1.** *v.t.* **a)** ausverkaufen; **b)** (*coll.:* betray) verpfeifen (*ugs.*). **2.** *v.i.* **we have** **or are sold out** wir sind ausverkauft

'**sell-by date** *n.* ≈ Mindesthaltbarkeitsdatum, *das*

'**seller** *n.* **a)** Verkäufer, *der*/Verkäuferin, *die*; **b)** (*product*) **be a good/slow** ~ : sich gut/nur langsam verkaufen

**Sellotape,** (P) ['seləteɪp] *n.* ≈ Tesafilm, *der* ⓌⓁ

'**sellotape** *v.t.* mit Tesafilm kleben

'**sell-out** *n.* **be a** ~: ausverkauft sein; (*coll.:* betrayal) Verrat sein

**selves** *pl.* of **self**

**semaphore** ['seməfɔ:(r)] **1.** *n.* (*system*) Winken, *das.* **2.** *v.i.* ~ **to sb.** jmdm. ein Winksignal übermitteln

**semblance** ['sembləns] *n.* Anschein, *der*

**semen** ['si:mən] *n.* Samen, *der*

**semi-** [semɪ] *pref.* halb-/Halb-

**semi:** ~**breve** *n.* (*Brit. Mus.*) ganze Note; ~**circle** *n.* Halbkreis, *der*; ~'**circular** *adj.* halbkreisförmig; ~'**colon** *n.* Semikolon, *das*; ~-**de**'**tached** *adj. & n.* ~-**detached** |**house**| Doppelhaushälfte, *die*; ~'**final** *n.* Halbfinale, *das*

**seminar** ['semɪnɑ:(r)] *n.* Seminar, *das*

'**semitone** *n.* (*Mus.*) Halbton, *der*

**semolina** [semə'li:nə] *n.* Grieß, *der*

**senate** ['senət] *n.* Senat, *der.* **senator** ['senətə(r)] *n.* Senator, *der*

**send** [send] *v.t.*, **sent** [sent] schicken; senden (*geh.*). **send a**'**way 1.** *v.t.* wegschicken. **2.** *v.i.* ~ **away** |**to sb.**| **for sth.** etw. [bei jmdm.] anfordern. **send** '**back** *v.t.* zurückschicken. '**send for** *v.t.* **a)** (*tell to come*) holen lassen; rufen (*Polizei, Arzt usw.*); **b)** (*order from elsewhere*) anfordern. **send** '**off** *v.t.* **1. a)** (*dispatch*) abschicken (*Sache*); **b)** (*Sport*) vom Platz stellen. **2.** *v.i.* see **send away 2. send** '**up** *v.t.* (*Brit. coll.:* parody) parodieren

'**sender** *n.* Absender, *der*

'**send-off** *n.* Verabschiedung, *die*

**senile** ['si:naɪl] *adj.* senil. **senility** [sɪ'nɪlɪtɪ] *n.* Senilität, *die*

**senior** ['si:nɪə(r)] **1.** *adj.* **a)** (*older*) älter; **b)** höher (*Rang, Beamter, Stellung*); leitend (*Angestellter, Stellung*). **2.** *n.* (*older*) Ältere, *der/die*; (*of higher rank*) Vorgesetzte, *der/die.* **senior** '**citizen** *n.* Senior, *der*/Seniorin, *die.* **seniority** [si:nɪ'ɒrɪtɪ] *n.* (*greater length of service*) höheres Dienstalter; (*higher rank*) höherer Rang

**sensation** [sen'seɪʃn] *n.* **a)** (*feeling*) Gefühl, *das*; **b)** (*person, event, etc.*) Sensation, *die.* **sensational** [sen'seɪʃənl] *adj.* sensationell

**sense** [sens] **1.** *n.* **a)** (*faculty*) Sinn, *der*; ~ **of smell/touch/taste** Geruchs-/Tast-/Geschmackssinn, *der*; **come to one's** ~**s** das Bewußtsein wiedererlangen; **b)** *in pl.* (*normal state of mind*) Verstand, *der*; **have taken leave of one's** ~**s** den Verstand verloren haben; **c)** (*consciousness*) Gefühl, *das*; ~ **of responsibility/guilt** Verantwortungs-/Schuldgefühl, *das*; **d)** (*practical wisdom*) Verstand, *der*; **sound or good** ~: [gesunder Menschen]verstand; **not have the** ~ **to do sth.** nicht so schlau sein, etw. zu tun; **there is no** ~ **in doing that** es hat keinen Sinn, das zu tun; **e)** (*meaning*) Sinn, *der*; (*of word*) Bedeutung, *die*; **make** ~: einen

Sinn ergeben; **in a** or **one ~:** in gewisser Hinsicht; **make ~ of sth.** etw. verstehen. **2.** v. t. spüren. **'senseless** adj. **a)** (unconscious) bewußtlos; **b)** (purposeless) sinnlos

**sensible** ['sensɪbl] adj. **a)** (reasonable) vernünftig; **b)** (practical) zweckmäßig. **sensibly** ['sensɪblɪ] adv. **a)** (reasonably) vernünftig; **b)** (practically) zweckmäßig

**sensitive** ['sensɪtɪv] adj. empfindlich; **be ~ to sth.** empfindlich auf etw. (Akk.) reagieren. **sensitivity** [sensɪ-'tɪvɪtɪ] n. Empfindlichkeit, die

**sensory** ['sensərɪ] adj. Sinnes-

**sensual** ['sensjʊəl] adj. sinnlich

**sensuous** ['sensjʊəs] adj. sinnlich

**sent** see **send**

**sentence** ['sentəns] **1.** n. **a)** (Law) [Straf]urteil, das; **b)** (Ling.) Satz, der. **2.** v. t. verurteilen (**to** zu)

**sentiment** ['sentɪmənt] n. **a)** Gefühl, das; **b)** (sentimentality) Sentimentalität, die; **c)** (opinion) Gedanke, der. **sentimental** [sentɪ'mentl] adj. sentimental. **sentimentality** [sentɪmen-'tælɪtɪ] n. Sentimentalität, die

**sentry** ['sentrɪ] n. Wache, die

**separable** ['sepərəbl] adj. trennbar

**separate 1.** ['sepərət] adj. verschieden ⟨Fragen, Probleme, Gelegenheiten⟩; gesondert ⟨Teil⟩; separat ⟨Eingang, Toilette, Blatt Papier, Abteil⟩; (one's own, individual) eigen ⟨Zimmer, Identität, Organisation⟩; **keep two things ~:** zwei Dinge auseinanderhalten. **2.** ['sepəreɪt] v. t. trennen; **they are ~d** (no longer live together) sie leben getrennt. **3.** v. i. **a)** (disperse) sich trennen; **b)** ⟨Ehepaar:⟩ sich trennen. **separately** ['sepərətlɪ] adv. getrennt. **separation** [sepə'reɪʃn] n. Trennung, die

**Sept.** abbr. **September** Sept.

**September** [sep'tembə(r)] n. September, der; see also **August**

**septic** ['septɪk] adj. septisch; **go ~:** eitrig werden

**sequel** ['si:kwl] n. **a)** (consequence, result) Folge, die (**to** von); **b)** (continuation) Fortsetzung, die

**sequence** ['si:kwəns] n. **a)** Reihenfolge, die; **b)** (part of film) Sequenz, die

**sequin** ['si:kwɪn] n. Paillette, die

**serenade** [serə'neɪd] **1.** n. Ständchen, das. **2.** v. t. **~ sb.** jmdm. ein Ständchen bringen

**serene** [sɪ'ri:n] adj. gelassen. **serenity** [sɪ'renɪtɪ] n. Gelassenheit, die

**sergeant** ['sɑ:dʒənt] n. (Mil.) Unterof-

fizier, der; (police officer) ≈ Polizeimeister, der. **sergeant-'major** n. ≈ [Ober]stabsfeldwebel, der

**serial** ['sɪərɪəl] n. Fortsetzungsgeschichte, die; (Radio, Telev.) Serie, die. **serialize** ['sɪərɪəlaɪz] v. t. in Fortsetzungen veröffentlichen; (Radio, Telev.) in Fortsetzungen senden

**series** ['sɪəri:z, 'sɪərɪz] n., pl. same **a)** (sequence) Reihe, die; (of events, misfortunes) Folge, die; **b)** (set of successive issues) Serie, die; **radio/TV ~:** Hörfunkreihe/Fernsehserie, die; **c)** (set of books) Reihe, die

**serious** ['sɪərɪəs] adj. **a)** (earnest) ernst; **b)** (important, grave) ernst ⟨Angelegenheit, Lage, Problem, Zustand⟩; ernsthaft ⟨Frage, Einwand, Kandidat⟩; schwer ⟨Krankheit, Unfall, Fehler, Niederlage⟩; ernstzunehmend ⟨Rivale⟩; ernstlich ⟨Gefahr, Bedrohung⟩; bedenklich ⟨Mangel⟩. **'seriously** adv. **a)** (earnestly) ernst; **take sth./sb. ~:** etw./jmdn. ernst nehmen; **b)** (severely) ernstlich; schwer ⟨verletzt⟩. **'seriousness** n. Ernst, der; **in all ~:** ganz im Ernst

**sermon** ['sɜ:mən] n. Predigt, die

**serrated** [se'reɪtɪd] adj. gezackt; **~ knife** Sägemesser, das

**serum** ['sɪərəm] n. Serum, das

**servant** ['sɜ:vənt] n. Diener, der/Dienerin, die

**serve** [sɜ:v] **1.** v. t. **a)** (work for) dienen (+ Dat.); **b)** (be useful to) dienlich sein (+ Dat.); **c)** (meet needs of) nutzen (+ Dat.); **~ a/no purpose** einen Zweck erfüllen/keinen Zweck haben; **d)** durchlaufen ⟨Lehre⟩; verbüßen ⟨Haftstrafe⟩; **e)** (dish up) servieren; (pour out) einschenken (**to** Dat.); **f)** **~|s|** or **it ~s him right!** (coll.) [das] geschieht ihm recht! **2.** v. i. **a)** dienen; **~ as chairman** das Amt des Vorsitzenden innehaben; **~ as a Member of Parliament** Mitglied des Parlaments sein; **~ on a jury** Geschworener/Geschworene sein; **b)** (be of use) **~ to do sth.** dazu dienen, etw. zu tun; **~ to show sth.** etw. zeigen; **~ for** or **as** dienen als; **c)** (Sport) aufschlagen. **3.** n. see **service 1g. serve 'up** v. t. **a)** servieren; **b)** (offer for consideration) auftischen (ugs.)

**service** ['sɜ:vɪs] **1.** n. **a)** Dienst, der; **do sb. a ~:** jmdm. einen guten Dienst erweisen; **b)** (Eccl.) Gottesdienst, der; **c)** (attending to customer) Service, der; (in shop, garage, etc.) Bedienung, die;

**d)** *(system of transport)* Verbindung, *die;* **there is no** |bus| **~ on Sundays** Sonntags verkehren keine Busse; **e)** *(provision of maintenance)* |after-sale| **~:** Kundendienst, *der;* **take one's car in for a ~:** sein Auto zur Inspektion bringen; **f)** *(operation)* Betrieb, *der;* **out of ~:** außer Betrieb; **g)** *(Sport)* Aufschlag, *der;* **whose ~ is it?** wer hat Aufschlag?; **h)** *(crockery set)* Service, *das;* **i)** *(assistance)* **can I be of ~** |to you|? kann ich Ihnen behilflich sein?; **I'm at your ~:** ich stehe zu Ihren Diensten; **j)** *(Mil.)* **the** |armed *or* fighting| **~s** die Streitkräfte; **in the ~s** beim Militär; **k)** |motorway| **~s** |Autobahn|raststätte, *die.* **2.** *v. t.* warten ⟨*Wagen, Waschmaschine, Heizung*⟩. **serviceable** ['sɜːvɪsəbl] *adj.* **a)** *(useful)* nützlich; **b)** *(durable)* haltbar

**service: ~ area** *n.* Raststätte, *die;* **~ charge** *n.* Bedienungsgeld, *das;* **~ industry** *n.* Dienstleistungsbetrieb, *der;* **~ man** ['sɜːvɪsmən] *n., pl.* **~ men** ['sɜːvɪsmən] Militärangehörige, *der;* **~ station** *n.* Tankstelle, *die*

**serviette** [sɜːvɪ'et] *n. (Brit.)* Serviette, *die*

**servile** ['sɜːvaɪl] *adj.* unterwürfig

**serving** ['sɜːvɪŋ] *n.* Portion, *die.* **'serving spoon** *n.* Vorlegelöffel, *der*

**session** ['seʃn] *n. (meeting)* Sitzung, *die;* **be in ~:** tagen

**set** [set] **1.** *v. t.,* -tt-, set **a)** *(put)* *(horizontally)* legen; *(vertically)* stellen; **~ sb. ashore** jmdn. an Land setzen; **~ sth./things right** *or* **in order** etw./die Dinge in Ordnung bringen; **b)** *(apply)* setzen; **~ a match to sth.** ein Streichholz an etw. *(Akk.)* halten; *see also* **fire 1 a;** ¹**light 1 d;** **c)** *(adjust)* einstellen **(at** auf + *Akk.*); aufstellen ⟨*Falle*⟩; stellen ⟨*Uhr*⟩; **~ the alarm for 5.30 a.m.** den Wecker auf 5.30 Uhr stellen; **d)** **be ~** ⟨*Buch, Film:*⟩ spielen; **e)** *(specify)* festlegen ⟨*Bedingungen*⟩; festsetzen ⟨*Termin, Ort usw.*⟩ **(for** auf + *Akk.*); **~ limits** Grenzen setzen; **f)** **~ sb. thinking that ...:** jmdn. auf den Gedanken bringen, daß ...; **g)** *(put forward)* stellen ⟨*Frage, Aufgabe*⟩; aufgeben ⟨*Hausaufgabe*⟩; aufstellen ⟨*Rekord*⟩; *(compose)* zusammenstellen ⟨*Rätsel, Fragen*⟩; **~ sb. an example, ~ an example to sb.** jmdm. ein Beispiel geben; **~ sb. a task/problem** jmdm. eine Aufgabe stellen/jmdn. vor ein Problem stellen; **~** |sb./oneself| **a target** |jmdm./sich| ein Ziel setzen; **h)** *(Med.:*

*put into place)* [ein]richten; einrenken ⟨*verrenktes Gelenk*⟩; **i)** legen ⟨*Haare*⟩; **j)** decken ⟨*Tisch*⟩; auflegen ⟨*Gedeck*⟩; **k)** fassen ⟨*Edelstein*⟩. **2.** *v. i.,* -tt-, set **a)** *(solidify)* fest werden; **b)** *(go down)* ⟨*Sonne, Mond:*⟩ untergehen. **3.** *n.* **a)** *(group)* Satz, *der;* **~** |of two| Paar, *das;* **a ~ of chairs** eine Sitzgruppe; **b)** *(radio, TV)* Gerät, *das;* **c)** *(Tennis)* Satz, *der;* **d)** *(of hair)* Legen, *das;* **e)** *(Theatre: scenery)* Bühnenbild, *das; (area of performance) (of film)* Drehort, *der; (of play)* Bühne, *die;* **f)** *(of people)* Kreis, *der;* **g)** *(Math.)* Menge, *die.* **4.** *adj.* **a)** *(fixed)* ⟨*Absichten, Zielvorstellungen, Zeitpunkt*⟩; **be ~ in one's ways** *or* **habits** in seinen Gewohnheiten festgefahren sein; **~ meal** *or* **menu** Menü, *das;* **b)** vorgeschrieben ⟨*Buch, Lektüre*⟩; **c)** *(ready)* **be** |all| **~ for sth.** zu etw. bereit sein; **be** |all| **~ to do sth.** bereit sein, etw. zu tun; **d)** *(determined)* **be ~ on sth./doing sth.** zu etw. entschlossen sein/entschlossen sein, etw. zu tun. '**set about** *v. t.* **~ about sth.** sich an etw. *(Akk.)* machen; **~ about doing sth.** sich daranmachen, etw. zu tun. **set a'side** *v. t.* **a)** beiseite legen; **b)** aufheben ⟨*Urteil, Entscheidung*⟩. **set 'back** *v. t.* **a)** aufhalten ⟨*Entwicklung*⟩; zurückwerfen ⟨*Projekt, Programm*⟩; **b)** *(coll.: cost)* kosten ⟨*Person*⟩; **c)** *(place at a distance)* zurücksetzen. **set 'down** *v. t.* **a)** absetzen ⟨*Fahrgast*⟩; **b)** *(record)* niederschreiben. **set 'off 1.** *v. i. (begin journey)* aufbrechen; *(start to move)* loslaufen; ⟨*Fahrzeug:*⟩ losfahren. **2.** *v. t.* **a)** *(cause to explode)* explodieren lassen; abbrennen ⟨*Feuerwerk*⟩; **b)** auslösen ⟨*Reaktion, Alarmanlage*⟩. **set 'out 1.** *v. i.* **a)** *(begin journey)* aufbrechen **(for** nach/zu); **b)** **~ out to do sth.** sich *(Dat.)* vornehmen, etw. zu tun. **2.** *v. t.* darlegen. **set 'up 1.** *v. t.* **a)** errichten ⟨*Straßensperre, Denkmal*⟩; aufbauen ⟨*Zelt, Klapptisch*⟩; **b)** *(establish)* gründen ⟨*Firma, Organisation*⟩; einrichten ⟨*Büro*⟩. **2.** *v. i.* **~ up in business** ein Geschäft aufmachen

'**set-back** *n.* Rückschlag, *der*

**settee** [se'tiː] *n.* Sofa, *das*

'**setting** *n.* **a)** *(Mus.)* Vertonung, *die;* **b)** *(surroundings)* Rahmen, *der; (of novel etc.)* Schauplatz, *der*

**settle** ['setl] **1.** *v. t.* **a)** *(horizontally)* [sorgfältig] legen; *(vertically)* [sorgfältig] stellen; *(at an angle)* [sorgfältig] lehnen; **b)** *(determine, resolve)* sich einigen auf ⟨*Preis*⟩; beilegen ⟨*Streit, Konflikt, Meinungsverschiedenheit*⟩; ausräumen ⟨*Zweifel*⟩; entscheiden ⟨*Frage, Spiel*⟩; c) bezahlen ⟨*Rechnung, Betrag*⟩; erfüllen ⟨*Forderung, Anspruch*⟩; ausgleichen ⟨*Konto*⟩. 2. *v. i.* **a)** *(become established)* sich niederlassen; *(as colonist)* sich ansiedeln; **b)** *(pay)* abrechnen; **c)** *(in chair, in front of fire, etc.)* sich niederlassen; *(to work etc.)* sich konzentrieren (**to** auf + *Akk.*); *(into way of life, retirement, etc.)* sich gewöhnen (**into** an + *Akk.*); **d)** *(subside)* ⟨*Haus, Fundament, Boden:*⟩ sich senken; ⟨*Schnee:*⟩ liegenbleiben. **settle 'down 1.** *v. i.* **a)** *(make oneself comfortable)* sich niederlassen (**in** in + *Dat.*); **b)** *(in town or house)* heimisch werden. **2.** *v. t.* **a)** ~ **oneself down** sich [gemütlich] hinsetzen; **b)** *(calm down)* beruhigen. **'settle for** *v. t.* *(agree to)* sich zufriedengeben mit. **settle 'in** *v. i.* *(in new home)* sich einleben. **'settle on** *v. t.* *(decide on)* sich entscheiden für. **settle 'up** *v. i.* abrechnen; ~ **up with the waiter** beim Kellner bezahlen

**'settlement** *n.* **a)** *(of argument, conflict, dispute, differences)* Beilegung, *die;* *(of question)* Klärung, *die;* *(of bill, account)* Bezahlung, *die;* *(of court case)* Vergleich, *der;* **b)** *(colony)* Siedlung, *die*

**settler** ['setlə(r)] *n.* Siedler, *der*/Siedlerin, *die*

**set:** ~**-to** *n., pl.* ~**-tos: have a** ~**-to** Streit haben; *(with fists)* sich prügeln; ~**-up** *n.* System, *das*

**seven** ['sevn] **1.** *adj.* sieben. **2.** *n.* Sieben, *die. See also* **eight**

**seventeen** [sevn'ti:n] **1.** *adj.* siebzehn. **2.** *n.* Siebzehn, *die. See also* **eight**.

**seventeenth** [sevn'ti:nθ] **1.** *adj.* siebzehnt... **2.** *n. (fraction)* Siebzehntel, *das. See also* **eighth**

**seventh** ['sevnθ] **1.** *adj.* sieb[en]t... **2.** *n. (in sequence)* sieb[en]te, *der/die/das;* *(in rank)* Sieb[en]te, *der/die/das;* *(fraction)* Sieb[en]tel, *das. See also* **eighth**

**seventieth** ['sevntɪɪθ] *adj.* siebzigst...

**seventy** ['sevntɪ] **1.** *adj.* siebzig. **2.** *n.* Siebzig, *die. See also* **eight**; **eighty 2**

**sever** ['sevə(r)] *v. t.* **a)** *(cut)* durchtrennen; *(fig.)* abbrechen ⟨*Beziehungen*⟩; **b)** *(separate)* abtrennen; *(with axe etc.)* abhacken

**several** ['sevrl] **1.** *adv.* mehrere; einige; ~ **times** mehrmals. **2.** *pron.* einige;

~ **of us** einige von uns; ~ **of the buildings** einige *od.* mehrere [der] Gebäude

**severe** [sɪ'vɪə(r)] *adj.,* ~**r** [sɪ'vɪərə(r)], ~**st** [sɪ'vɪərɪst] hart ⟨*Urteil, Strafe, Kritik, Test, Prüfung*⟩; streng ⟨*Frost, Stil, Schönheit*⟩; schwer ⟨*Dürre, Verlust, Behinderung, Verletzung, Krankheit*⟩; rauh ⟨*Wetter*⟩; heftig ⟨*Anfall, Schmerz*⟩; bedrohlich ⟨*Mangel, Knappheit*⟩; stark ⟨*Blutung*⟩. **se-'verely** *adv.* hart; schwer ⟨*verletzt, behindert*⟩. **severity** [sɪ'verɪtɪ] *n.* Strenge, *die;* *(of drought, shortage)* großes Ausmaß; *(of criticism)* Schärfe, *die*

**sew** [səʊ] *v. t. & i., p.p.* **sewn** [səʊn] *or* **sewed** [səʊd] nähen. **sew 'on** *v. t.* annähen ⟨*Knopf*⟩; aufnähen ⟨*Abzeichen, Band*⟩. **sew 'up** *v. t.* nähen ⟨*Saum, Naht, Wunde*⟩

**sewer** ['sju:ə(r), 'su:ə(r)] *n. (tunnel)* Abwasserkanal, *der;* *(pipe)* Abwasserleitung, *die*

**'sewing** *n.* Näharbeit, *die.* **'sewing-machine** *n.* Nähmaschine, *die*

**sewn** *see* **sew**

**sex** [seks] *n.* **a)** Geschlecht, *das;* **b)** *(sexuality; coll.: intercourse)* Sex, *der (ugs.);* **have** ~ **with sb.** *(coll.)* mit jmdm. schlafen

**sexism** ['seksɪzm] *n.* Sexismus, *der*

**sexist** ['seksɪst] *adj.* sexistisch

**'sex maniac** *n.* Triebverbrecher, *der*

**sexual** ['sekʃʊəl] *adj.* sexuell. **sexual 'intercourse** *n.* Geschlechtsverkehr, *der.* **sexuality** [sekʃʊ'ælɪtɪ] *n.* Sexualität, *die*

**'sexy** *adj.* sexy *(ugs.)*

**shabbily** ['ʃæbɪlɪ] *adv.,* **shabby** ['ʃæbɪ] *adj.* schäbig

**shack** [ʃæk] *n.* [armselige] Hütte

**shackle** ['ʃækl] **1.** *n., usu. in pl.* Fessel, *die.* **2.** *v. t.* anketten (**to** an + *Akk.*)

**shade** [ʃeɪd] **1.** *n.* **a)** Schatten, *der;* **b)** *(colour)* Ton, *der;* *(fig.)* Schattierung, *die;* **c)** *(lamp~)* [Lampen]schirm, *der.* **2.** *v. t.* **a)** *(screen)* beschatten; **b)** *(darken with lines)* ~ **[in]** [ab]schattieren. **3.** *v. i.* übergehen (**into** in + *Akk.*).

**shadow** ['ʃædəʊ] **1.** *n.* Schatten, *der.* **2.** *v. t. (follow)* beschatten. **'shadowy** *adj. (indistinct)* schattenhaft

**shady** ['ʃeɪdɪ] *adj.* **a)** schattig; **b)** *(disreputable)* zwielichtig

**shaft** [ʃɑːft] *n.* **a)** *(of tool, golf club)* Schaft, *der;* **b)** *(Mech. Engin.)* Welle, *die;* **c)** *(of mine, lift)* Schacht, *der;* **d)** *(of light, lightning)* Strahl, *der*

**shaggy** ['ʃægɪ] *adj.* zottelig

**shake** [ʃeɪk] **1.** *n.* Schütteln, *das;* **give**

sb./sth. a ~: jmdn./etw. schütteln. 2.
*v. t.*, **shook** [ʃʊk], **shaken** ['ʃeɪkn] a)
*(move violently)* schütteln; ~ **one's
fist/a stick at sb.** jmdm. mit der Faust/
einem Stock drohen; ~ **hands** sich
*(Dat.)* die Hand geben; b) *(cause to
tremble)* erschüttern *⟨Gebäude usw.⟩;*
~ **one's head** den Kopf schütteln; c)
*(shock)* erschüttern. 3. *v. i.*, **shook,
shaken** wackeln; *⟨Boden, Stimme:⟩* beben; *⟨Hand:⟩* zittern. **shake 'off** *v. t.*
abschütteln. **shake 'up** *v. t.* a) *(upset,
shock)* einen Schrecken einjagen
(+ *Dat.*); b) *(coll.: reorganize)* um-
krempeln *(ugs.)*
**shaken** *see* **shake** 2, 3
**shaky** ['ʃeɪkɪ] *adj.* wack[e]lig *⟨Möbel-
stück, Leiter⟩;* zittrig *⟨Hand, Stimme,
Greis⟩;* **feel** ~: sich zittrig fühlen
**shall** [ʃl, *stressed* ʃæl] *v. aux. only in
pres.* shall, *neg. (coll.)* **shan't** [ʃɑ:nt],
*past* **should** [ʃəd, *stressed* ʃʊd], *neg.
(coll.)* **shouldn't** ['ʃʊdnt] a) *expr. simple
future* werden; b) **should** *expr. conditional* würde/würdest/würden/wür-
det; **I should have been killed if I had
let go** ich wäre getötet worden, wenn
ich losgelassen hätte; **if we should be
defeated** falls wir unterliegen [sollten];
c) *expr. will or intention* **what ~ we do?**
was sollen wir tun?; **let's go in, ~ we?**
gehen wir dort hinein, oder?; **we
should be safe by now** jetzt dürften wir
in Sicherheit sein; **he shouldn't do
things like that!** er sollte so etwas
nicht tun!
**shallot** [ʃə'lɒt] *n.* Schalotte, *die*
**shallow** ['ʃæləʊ] *adj.* seicht *⟨Wasser,
Fluß⟩;* flach *⟨Schüssel, Teller, Was-
ser⟩; (fig.)* flach *⟨Person⟩*
**sham** [ʃæm] 1. *adj.* unecht; imitiert
*⟨Leder, Holz, Pelz⟩.* 2. *n. (pretence)*
Heuchelei, *die; (person)* Heuchler,
*der/*Heuchlerin, *die.* 3. *v. t.*, -mm- vortäuschen. 4. *v. i.*, -mm- simulieren
**shambles** ['ʃæmblz] *n. (coll.)* Chaos,
*das;* **the room was a ~:** das Zimmer
glich einem Schlachtfeld
**shame** [ʃeɪm] *n.* a) *(state)* Scham, *die;* b)
*(state of disgrace)* Schande, *die;* **put
sb./sth. to ~:** jmdn. beschämen/etw.
in den Schatten stellen; c) **what a ~!**
wie schade! **shamefaced** *adj.* betreten. **shameful** ['ʃeɪmfl] *adj.* beschämend. **'shameless** *adj.* schamlos
**shampoo** [ʃæm'pu:] 1. *v. t.* schampo-
nieren. 2. *n.* Shampoo[n], *das*
**shamrock** ['ʃæmrɒk] *n.* Klee, *der*
**shandy** ['ʃændɪ] *n.* Bier mit Limonade

**shan't** [ʃɑ:nt] *(coll.)* = **shall not**
**¹shanty** ['ʃæntɪ] *n. (hut)* [armselige]
Hütte
**²shanty** *n. (song)* Shanty, *das*
**'shanty town** *n.* Elendsviertel, *das*
**shape** [ʃeɪp] 1. *v. t.* formen; bearbeiten
*⟨Holz, Stein⟩* **(into** zu). 2. *n.* Form, *die;*
**take ~:** Gestalt annehmen. **shape
'up** *v. i.* sich entwickeln
**'shapeless** *adj.* formlos; unförmig
*⟨Kleid, Person⟩*
**shapely** ['ʃeɪplɪ] *adj.* wohlgeformt
*⟨Beine, Busen⟩;* gut *⟨Figur⟩*
**share** [ʃeə(r)] 1. *n.* a) *(portion)* Teil, *der
od. das;* |**fair**| ~: Anteil, *der;* **fair ~s**
gerechte Teile; **do more than one's
|fair| ~ of the work** mehr als seinen
Teil zur Arbeit beitragen. b) *(Commerc.)* Aktie, *die.* 2. *v. t.* teilen; gemeinsam tragen *⟨Verantwortung⟩.* 3.
*v. i.* ~ **in** teilnehmen an (+ *Dat.*); beteiligt sein an (+ *Dat.*) *⟨Gewinn⟩;* teilen *⟨Freude, Erfahrung⟩.* **share 'out**
*v. t.* aufteilen **(among** unter + *Akk.*)
**share:** ~**holder** *n.* Aktionär, *der/*
Aktionärin, *die;* ~-**out** *n.* Aufteilung,
*die*
**shark** [ʃɑ:k] *n.* Hai[fisch], *der*
**sharp** [ʃɑ:p] 1. *adj.* a) scharf; spitz
*⟨Nadel, Bleistift, Gipfel, Winkel⟩;*
deutlich *⟨Unterscheidung⟩;* sauer
*⟨Apfel⟩;* herb *⟨Wein⟩;* *(shrill, piercing)*
schrill *⟨Schrei, Pfiff⟩;* heftig *⟨Schmerz,
Krampf, Kampf⟩;* begabt *⟨Schüler,
Student⟩;* b) *(derog.: dishonest)* gerissen; c) *(Mus.)* [um einen Halbton] er-
höht *⟨Note⟩.* 2. *adv.* a) *(punctually)* **at
six o'clock ~:** Punkt sechs Uhr; b)
**turn ~ right/left** scharf nach rechts/
links abbiegen; c) **look ~!** halt dich
ran! *(ugs.);* d) *(Mus.)* zu hoch *⟨singen,
spielen⟩.* **sharpen** ['ʃɑ:pn] *v. t.* schärfen; [an]spitzen *⟨Bleistift⟩.* **'sharp-
ener** *n. (for pencils)* Spitzer, *der
(ugs.).* **'sharp-eyed** *adj.* scharfäu-
gig; **be ~:** scharfe Augen haben.
**'sharply** *adv.* scharf; in scharfem
Ton *⟨antworten⟩.* **'sharpness** *n.*
Schärfe, *die; (fineness of point)* Spitz-
heit, *die*
**shatter** ['ʃætə(r)] 1. *v. t.* zertrümmern;
zerbrechen *⟨Glas, Fenster⟩;* zerschlagen *⟨Hoffnungen⟩.* 2. *v. i.* zerbrechen.
**shattered** ['ʃætəd] *adj.* a) zerbrochen *⟨Glas, Fenster⟩; (fig.)* zerstört
*⟨Hoffnungen⟩;* zerrüttet *⟨Nerven⟩;* b)
*(coll.: greatly upset)* **she was ~ by the
news** die Nachricht hat sie schwer mitgenommen; **I'm ~!** ich bin ganz er-

schüttert!; *(Brit. coll.: exhausted)* ich
bin kaputt! *(ugs.)*. '**shattering** *adj.*
verheerend ⟨*Wirkung*⟩; vernichtend
⟨*Schlag, Niederlage*⟩
**shave** [ʃeɪv] **1.** *v. t.* rasieren; abrasieren ⟨*Haare*⟩. **2.** *v. i.* sich rasieren. **3.** *n.*
Rasur, *die;* **have a ~:** sich rasieren.
**shave 'off** *v. t.* abrasieren
'**shaven** [ˈʃeɪvn] *adj.* rasiert; [kahl]ge-
schoren ⟨*Kopf*⟩
'**shaver** *n.* Rasierapparat, *der.*
'**shaver point** *n.* Anschluß für den
Rasierapparat
**shaving** [ˈʃeɪvɪŋ] *n.* **a)** Rasieren, *das;*
**b)** *in pl. (of wood, metal, etc.)* Späne
**shaving: ~-brush** *n.* Rasierpinsel,
*der;* **~-cream** *n.* Rasiercreme, *die;*
**~-foam** *n.* Rasierschaum, *der*
**shawl** [ʃɔ:l] *n.* Schultertuch, *das*
**she** [ʃɪ, *stressed* ʃi:] *pron.* sie
**sheaf** [ʃi:f] *n., pl.* **sheaves** [ʃi:vz] *(of
corn etc.)* Garbe, *die; (of paper, arrows,
etc.)* Bündel, *das*
**shear** [ʃɪə(r)] *v. t., p.p.* **shorn** [ʃɔ:n] *or*
**sheared** *(clip)* scheren. **shears** [ʃɪəz] *n.
pl.* |**pair of**| **~:** Schere, *die;* **garden ~:**
Gartenschere, *die*
**sheath** [ʃi:θ] *n., pl.* **~s** [ʃi:ðz, ʃi:θs] **a)**
*(for knife, sword, etc.)* Scheide, *die;* **b)**
*(condom)* Gummischutz, *der*
**sheaves** *pl. of* **sheaf**
¹**shed** [ʃed] *v. t., -dd-,* **shed a)** verlieren;
abwerfen ⟨*Laub, Geweih*⟩; **b)** vergießen ⟨*Blut, Tränen*⟩; **c)** verbreiten
⟨*Licht*⟩
²**shed** *n.* Schuppen, *der*
**she'd** [ʃɪd, *stressed* ʃi:d] **a)** = she had;
**b)** = she would
**sheen** [ʃi:n] *n.* Glanz, *der*
**sheep** [ʃi:p] *n., pl. same* Schaf, *das.*
'**sheep-dog** *n.* Hütehund, *der*
**sheepish** [ˈʃi:pɪʃ] *adj.* verlegen
'**sheepskin** *n.* Schaffell, *das*
**sheer** [ʃɪə(r)] *adj.* **a)** rein; blank ⟨*Unsinn, Gewalt*⟩; **by ~ chance** rein zufällig; **b)** schroff ⟨*Felsen, Abfall*⟩
**sheet** [ʃi:t] *n.* **a)** Laken, *das;* **b)** *(of thin
metal or plastic)* Folie, *die; (of iron,
tin)* Blech, *das; (of glass)* Platte, *die;
(of paper)* Bogen, *der;* Blatt, *das;* **c)**
⟨*Eis-, Nebel*⟩decke, *die*
**sheik[h]** [ʃeɪk, ʃi:k] *n.* Scheich, *der*
**shelf** [ʃelf] *n., pl.* **shelves** [ʃelvz] Brett,
*das;* **shelves** *(set)* Regal, *das.* '**shelf-
life** *n.* Lagerfähigkeit, *die*
**shell** [ʃel] *n.* **a)** Schale, *die; (of snail)*
Haus, *das; (of turtle, tortoise)* Panzer,
*der; (on beach)* Muschel, *die;* **b)** *(Mil.)
(bomb)* Granate, *die.* **2.** *v. t.* **a)** *(take*

*out of ~)* schälen; **b)** *(Mil.)* [mit Artil-
lerie] beschießen. **shell 'out** *v. t. & i.
(sl.)* blechen *(ugs.)* (**on** für)
**she'll** [ʃɪl, *stressed* ʃi:l] = she will
'**shellfish** *n., pl. same* **a)** Schal[en]tier,
*das; (oyster, clam)* Muschel, *die; (crustacean)* Krebstier, *das;* **b)** *in pl.
(Gastr.)* Meeresfrüchte *Pl.*
**shelter** [ˈʃeltə(r)] **1.** *n.* **a)** *(shield)*
Schutz, *der* (**against** vor + *Dat.,* gegen); **bomb** *or* **air-raid ~:** Luftschutzraum, *der;* **get under ~:** sich unterstellen; **b)** *no pl. (place of safety)* Zuflucht,
*die.* **2.** *v. t.* schützen (**from** vor +
*Dat.*); Unterschlupf gewähren
(+ *Dat.*) ⟨*Flüchtling*⟩. **3.** *v. i.* Schutz
suchen (**from** vor + *Dat.*). '**sheltered** *adj.* geschützt; behütet ⟨*Leben*⟩
**shelve** [ʃelv] **1.** *v. t. (defer)* auf Eis legen *(ugs.)*. **2.** *v. i. (slope)* abfallen
**shelves** *pl. of* **shelf**
'**shelving** *n.* Regale *Pl.*
**shepherd** [ˈʃepəd] **1.** *n.* Schäfer, *der.*
**2.** *v. t.* führen. '**shepherdess** *n.*
Schäferin, *die*
**shepherd: ~'s 'crook** *n.* Schäfer-
stock, *der;* **~'s 'pie** *n.* Auflauf aus
*Hackfleisch mit einer Schicht Kartof-
felbrei darüber*
**sherry** [ˈʃerɪ] *n.* Sherry, *der*
**she's** [ʃɪz, *stressed* ʃi:z] **a)** = she is; **b)**
= she has
**shield** [ʃi:ld] **1.** *n.* Schild, *der.* **2.** *v. t.*
schützen (**from** vor + *Dat.*)
**shift** [ʃɪft] **1.** *v. t.* **a)** *(move)* umstellen
⟨*Möbel*⟩; wegnehmen ⟨*Arm, Hand,
Fuß*⟩; wegräumen ⟨*Schutt*⟩; entfernen
⟨*Schmutz, Fleck*⟩; **~ the responsibility/
blame onto sb.** die Verantwortung/
Schuld auf jmdn. schieben; **b)** *(Amer.
Motor Veh.)* **~ gears** schalten. **2.** *v. i.* **a)**
⟨*Wind:*⟩ drehen (**to** nach); ⟨*Ladung:*⟩
verrutschen; **b)** *(sl.: move quickly)* rasen. **3.** *n.* **a) ~ in emphasis** eine Ver-
lagerung des Akzents; **a ~ in public
opinion** ein Umschwung der öffentlichen Meinung; **b)** *(for work)* Schicht,
*die;* **eight-hour/late ~:** Achtstunden-/
Spätschicht, *die;* **do** *or* **work the late
~:** Spätschicht haben. '**shift work** *n.*
Schichtarbeit, *die*
**shifty** [ˈʃɪftɪ] *adj.* verschlagen
**shilling** [ˈʃɪlɪŋ] *n. (Hist.)* Shilling, *der*
**shilly-shally** [ˈʃɪlɪʃælɪ] *v. i.* zaudern;
**stop ~ing!** entschließ dich endlich!
**shimmer** [ˈʃɪmə(r)] **1.** *v. i.* schimmern.
**2.** *n.* Schimmer, *der*
**shin** [ʃɪn] **1.** *n.* Schienbein, *das.* **2.** *v. i.,
-nn-:* **~ up/down a tree** *etc.* einen

Baum *usw.* hinauf-/hinunterklettern.

'**shin-bone** *n.* Schienbein, *das*

'**shine** [ʃaɪn] **1.** *v. i.,* shone [ʃɒn]
⟨*Lampe, Licht, Stern:*⟩ leuchten;
⟨*Sonne, Mond:*⟩ scheinen; *(reflect
light)* glänzen. **2.** *v. t.,* shone: ~ a light
on sth./in sb.'s eyes etw. anleuchten/
jmdm. in die Augen leuchten. **3.** *n.*
Glanz, *der*

**shingle** ['ʃɪŋgl] *n. (pebbles)* Kies, *der*

'**shingles** *n. (Med.)* Gürtelrose, *die*

**shin:** ~-**guard,** ~-**pad** *ns.* Schien-
beinschutz, *der*

**shiny** ['ʃaɪnɪ] *adj.* glänzend

**ship** [ʃɪp] **1.** *n.* Schiff, *das.* **2.** *v. t.,* -**pp-**
*(transport by sea)* verschiffen; *(send
by road, train, or air)* verschicken
⟨*Waren*⟩. '**shipbuilding** *n.* Schiffbau,
*der*

'**shipment** *n.* **a)** Versand, *der; (by sea)*
Verschiffung, *die;* **b)** *(amount)* Sendung, *die*

'**shipowner** *n.* Schiffseigentümer,
*der*/-eigentümerin, *die; (of several
ships)* Reeder, *der*/Reederin, *die*

'**shipper** *n.* Spediteur, *der*/Spediteu-
rin, *die; (company)* Spedition, *die*

'**shipping** *n.* **a)** *(ships)* Schiffe; *(traffic)* Schiffahrt, *die;* **b)** *(transporting)*
Versand, *der*

**ship:** ~-**shape** *adj.* in bester Ordnung;
~-**wreck 1.** *n.* Schiffbruch, *der.* **2.** *v. t.*
be ~**wrecked** Schiffbruch erleiden;
~-**yard** *n.* [Schiffs]werft, *die*

**shirk** [ʃɜːk] *v. t.* sich drücken vor
(+ *Dat.*). '**shirker** *n.* Drückeberger,
*der (ugs.)*

**shirt** [ʃɜːt] *n.* |man's| ~: [Herren- *od.*
Ober]hemd, *das;* |woman's| ~: Hemd-
bluse, *die.* '**shirt-sleeve** *n.* Hemds-
ärmel, *der;* **in** ~**s** in Hemdsärmeln

**shit** [ʃɪt] *(coarse)* **1.** *v. i.,* -**tt-, shitted** *or*
**shit** scheißen *(derb).* **2.** *n.* **a)** Scheiße,
*die (derb);* **have** *(Brit.) or (Amer.)* **take
a** ~: scheißen *(derb);* **b)** *(person)*
Scheißkerl, *der (derb);* **c)** *(nonsense)*
Scheiß, *der (salopp)*

**shiver** ['ʃɪvə(r)] **1.** *v. i.* zittern **(with** *vor*
+ *Dat.).* **2.** *n.* Schau[d]er, *der (geh.)*

**shoal** [ʃəʊl] *n. (of fish)* Schwarm, *der*

**shock** [ʃɒk] **1.** *n.* **a)** Schock, *der;* **give
sb. a** ~: jmdm. einen Schock verset-
zen; **b)** *(violent impact)* Erschütterung,
*die* (of *durch*); **c)** *(Electr.)* Schlag, *der;*
**d)** *(Med.)* Schock, *der.* **2.** *v. t.* ~ **sb.**
|**deeply|** ein [schwerer] Schock für
jmdn. sein; *(scandalize)* jmdn.
schockieren. '**shock absorber** *n.*
Stoßdämpfer, *der*

'**shocking** *adj.* **a)** schockierend; **b)**
*(coll.: very bad)* fürchterlich *(ugs.)*

'**shock-proof** *adj.* stoßfest

**shod** *see* **shoe 2**

**shoddy** ['ʃɒdɪ] *adj.* schäbig; minderwertig ⟨*Arbeit, Stoff, Artikel*⟩

**shoe** [ʃuː] **1.** *n.* Schuh, *der; (of horse)*
[Huf]eisen, *das;* **put oneself into sb.'s**
~**s** *(fig.)* sich in jmds. Lage *(Akk.)* versetzen. **2.** *v. t.,* ~**ing, shod** [ʃɒd] beschlagen ⟨*Pferd*⟩

**shoe:** ~-**horn** *n.* Schuhlöffel, *der;*
~-**lace** *n.* Schnürsenkel, *der;*
~**maker** *n.* Schuhmacher, *der;*
~-**polish** *n.* Schuhcreme, *die;*
~-**shop** *n.* Schuhgeschäft, *das;*
~-**string** *n.* **on a** ~**string** *(coll.)* mit
ganz wenig Geld

**shone** *see* **shine 1, 2**

**shoo** [ʃuː] **1.** *int.* sch. **2.** *v. t.* scheuchen; ~ **away** fortscheuchen

**shook** *see* **shake 2, 3**

**shoot** [ʃuːt] **1.** *v. i.,* **shot** [ʃɒt] **a)** schießen **(at** *auf* + *Akk.*); **b)** *(move rapidly)*
schießen *(ugs.).* **2.** *v. t.,* **shot a)**
*(wound)* anschießen; *(kill)* erschießen; *(hunt)* schießen; ~ **sb. dead**
jmdn. erschießen; **b)** schießen mit
⟨*Bogen, Munition, Pistole*⟩; abschie-
ßen ⟨*Pfeil, Kugel*⟩ **(at** *auf* + *Akk.*); **c)**
*(Cinemat.)* drehen ⟨*Film, Szene*⟩. **3.** *n.*
*(Bot.)* Trieb, *der.* **shoot 'down** *v. t.*
niederschießen ⟨*Person*⟩; abschießen
⟨*Flugzeug*⟩. **shoot 'out** *v. i.* hervorschießen. **shoot 'up** *v. i.* in die Höhe
schießen ⟨*Preise, Kosten, Temperatur:*⟩ in die Höhe schnellen

**shooting:** ~-**range** *n.* Schießstand,
*der;* ~ '**star** *n.* Sternschnuppe, *die*

'**shoot-out** *n.* Schießerei, *die*

**shop** [ʃɒp] **1.** *n.* Laden, *der;* Geschäft,
*das;* **go to the** ~**s** einkaufen gehen;
**talk** ~: fachsimpeln *(ugs.).* **2.** *v. i.,*
-**pp-** einkaufen; **go** ~**ping** einkaufen
gehen. **shop a'round** *v. i.* sich umsehen **(for** *nach*)

**shop:** ~ **assistant** *n. (Brit.)* Verkäufer, *der*/Verkäuferin, *die;* ~-**keeper**
*n.* Ladenbesitzer, *der*/-besitzerin, *die;*
~-**lifter** *n.* Ladendieb, *der*/-diebin,
*die;* ~-**lifting** *n.* Ladendiebstahl,
*der;* ~**owner** *see* ~**keeper**

'**shopper** *n.* Käufer, *der*/Käuferin, *die*

'**shopping** *n.* **a)** Einkaufen, *das;* **do
the/one's** ~: einkaufen/[seine] Ein-
käufe machen; **b)** *(items bought)* Ein-
käufe *Pl.*

**shopping:** ~-**bag** *n.* Einkaufstasche,
*die;* ~-**basket** *n.* Einkaufskorb, *der;*

~ **centre** n. Einkaufszentrum, das; ~**-list** n. Einkaufszettel, der; ~ **mall** [~ mæl] n. Einkaufszentrum, das; ~ **street** n. Geschäftsstraße, die; ~ **trolley** n. Einkaufswagen, der

**shop:** ~**-soiled** adj. (Brit.) (slightly damaged) leicht beschädigt; (slightly dirty) angeschmutzt; ~ '**window** n. Schaufenster, das

**shore** [ʃɔː(r)] n. Ufer, das; (beach) Strand, der. **shore 'up** v.t. abstützen ⟨Mauer, Haus⟩; (fig.) stützen

**shorn** see **shear**

**short** [ʃɔːt] **1.** adj. **a)** kurz; **in a ~ time** or **while** (soon) bald; **in Kürze; a ~ time** or **while ago/later** vor kurzem/ kurze Zeit später; **in ~, ...:** kurz, ...; **b)** klein ⟨Person, Wuchs⟩; **c)** (deficient, scanty) knapp; **go ~ |of sth.|** [an etw. (Dat.)] Mangel leiden; **sb. is ~ of sth.** jmdm. fehlt es an etw. (Dat.); **time is getting/is ~:** die Zeit wird/ist knapp; **be in ~ supply** knapp sein; **be ~ |of cash|** knapp [bei Kasse] sein (ugs.). **2.** adv. **a)** (abruptly) plötzlich; **stop ~:** plötzlich abbrechen; **stop sb. ~:** jmdm. ins Wort fallen; **b)** **stop ~ of doing sth.** davor zurückschrecken, etw. zu tun. **shortage** ['ʃɔːtɪdʒ] n. Mangel, der (of an + Dat.); ~ of fruit/teachers Obstknappheit, die/ Lehrermangel, der

**short:** ~**bread** n. Shortbread, das; Keks aus Butterteig; ~ '**circuit** n. (Electr.) Kurzschluß, der; ~**coming** n., usu. in pl. Unzulänglichkeit, die; ~ 'cut n. Abkürzung, die; **take a ~ cut** den Weg abkürzen

**shorten** ['ʃɔːtn] **1.** v.i. kürzer werden. **2.** v.t. kürzen; verkürzen ⟨Besuch, Wartezeit⟩

**short:** ~**hand** n. Stenographie, die; ~**hand typist** Stenotypist, der/-typistin, die; ~ **list** n. (Brit.) engere Auswahl; **be on/put sb. on the ~ list** in der engeren Auswahl sein/jmdn. in die engere Auswahl nehmen; ~**-list** v.t. in die engere Auswahl nehmen; ~**-lived** adj. kurzlebig

'**shortly** adv. in Kürze; gleich (ugs.); ~ **before/after sth.** kurz vor/nach etw.

'**short-range** adj. **a)** Kurzstrecken- ⟨flugzeug, -rakete usw.⟩; **b)** (relating to time) kurzfristig

**shorts** [ʃɔːts] n. pl. **a)** (trousers) kurze Hose[n]; Shorts Pl.; **b)** (Amer.: underpants) Unterhose, die

**short:** ~-'**sighted** adj. kurzsichtig; ~**-sleeved** ['~sliːvd] adj. kurzärm[e]-

lig; ~**-staffed** [~'staːft] adj. **be |very| ~-staffed** [viel] zu wenig Personal haben; ~ '**story** n. Kurzgeschichte, die; ~**-term** adj. kurzfristig; (provisional) vorläufig ⟨Lösung⟩; ~ **wave** n. (Radio) Kurzwelle, die

**shot** [ʃɒt] **1.** n. **a)** Schuß, der; **fire a ~:** einen Schuß abgeben (**at** auf + Akk.); **like a ~** (fig.) wie der Blitz (ugs.); **I'd do it like a ~:** ich würde es auf der Stelle tun; **b)** (Athletics) **put the ~:** die Kugel stoßen; |**putting**| **the ~:** Kugelstoßen, das; **c)** (Sport: stroke, kick, throw) Schuß, der; **d)** (Photog.) Aufnahme, die; (Cinemat.) Einstellung, die. **2.** see **shoot** 1, 2, 3. adj. **be/get ~ of** (sl.) los sein/loswerden. '**shotgun** n. Schrotflinte, die

**should** see **shall**

**shoulder** ['ʃəʊldə(r)] **1.** n. Schulter, die. **2.** v.t. schultern; (fig.) übernehmen

**shoulder:** ~**-bag** n. Umhängetasche, die; ~**-blade** n. Schulterblatt, das; ~**-strap** n. (on garment) Schulterklappe, die; (on bag) Tragriemen, der

**shouldn't** ['ʃʊdnt] (coll.) = **should not;** see **shall**

**shout** [ʃaʊt] **1.** n. Ruf, der; (inarticulate) Schrei, der. **2.** v.i. & t. schreien. **shout 'down** v.t. niederschreien. **shout 'out 1.** v.i. aufschreien. **2.** v.t. [laut] rufen

'**shouting** n. Geschrei, das

**shove** [ʃʌv] **1.** n. Stoß, der. **2.** v.t. stoßen; schubsen (ugs.); (coll.: put) tun. **shove a'way** v.t. (coll.) wegschubsen (ugs.). **shove 'off** v.i. (sl.: leave) abschieben (ugs.)

**shovel** ['ʃʌvl] **1.** n. Schaufel, die. **2.** v.t., (Brit.) **-ll-** schaufeln

**show** [ʃəʊ] **1.** n. **a)** (entertainment, performance) Show, die; (Theatre) Vorstellung, die; (Radio, Telev.) [Unterhaltungs]sendung, die; **b)** (exhibition) Ausstellung, die; Schau, die; **put sth. on ~:** etw. ausstellen; **be on ~:** ausgestellt sein; **c)** (appearance) Anschein, der; **be for ~:** reine Angeberei sein (ugs.). **2.** v.t., p.p. **shown** [ʃəʊn] **a)** zeigen; vorzeigen ⟨Paß, Fahrschein usw.⟩; ~ **sb. sth., ~ sth. to sb.** jmdm. etw. zeigen; **b)** beweisen ⟨Mut, Urteilsvermögen usw.⟩; ~ **sb. that ...:** jmdm. beweisen, daß ...; ~ |**sb.**| **kindness/ mercy** freundlich [zu jmdm.] sein/Erbarmen [mit jmdm.] haben; **c)** ⟨Thermometer, Uhr usw.⟩ anzeigen; **d)** (exhibit in a show) ausstellen; zeigen

⟨*Film*⟩. **3.** *v. i., p. p.* **shown a)** *(be visible)* sichtbar *od.* zu sehen sein; *(come into sight)* sich zeigen; **b)** *(be ~n)* ⟨*Film:*⟩ laufen. **show 'in** *v. t.* hinein-/hereinführen. **show 'off** *v. i.* angeben *(ugs.);* prahlen. **show 'out** *v. t.* hinausführen. **show 'round** *v. t.* herumführen. **show 'through** *v. i.* durchscheinen. **show 'up 1.** *v. t.* **a)** *(make visible)* [deutlich] sichtbar machen; **b)** *(coll.: embarrass)* blamieren. **2.** *v. i.* **a)** *(be visible)* [deutlich] zu sehen sein; **b)** *(coll.: arrive)* sich blicken lassen *(ugs.)*

**show-down** *n. (fig.)* Kraftprobe, *die;* **have a ~** [with sb.] sich [mit jmdm.] auseinandersetzen

**shower** [ˈʃaʊə(r)] **1.** *n.* **a)** Schauer, *der;* **~ of rain/hail** Regen-/Hagelschauer, *der;* **b)** *(for washing)* Dusche, *die;* **have** *or* **take a** |cold/quick| **~:** [kalt/schnell] duschen. **2.** *v. t. (lavish)* **~ sth.** |up|on sb., **~ sb. with sth.** jmdn. mit etw. überhäufen. **3.** *v. i. (have a ~)* duschen

**shower: ~-curtain** *n.* Duschvorhang, *der;* **~ gel** *n.* Duschgel, *das;* **~-proof** *adj.* [bedingt] regendicht

**showery** *adj.* **it is ~:** es gibt immer wieder kurze Schauer; **a ~ day** ein Tag mit Schauerwetter

**show-jumping** *n.* Springreiten, *das*

**shown** *see* show 2, 3

**show: ~-off** *n. (coll.)* Angeber, *der/* Angeberin, *die;* **~-piece** *n. (of exhibition, collection)* Schaustück, *das;* *(highlight)* Paradestück, *das;* **~-room** *n.* Ausstellungsraum, *der*

**showy** *adj.* protzig *(ugs.)*

**shrank** *see* shrink

**shred** [ʃred] **1.** *n.* Fetzen, *der;* *(fig.)* Spur, *die;* **tear sth. to ~s** etw. zerfetzen; *(fig.)* etw. zerpflücken. **2.** *v. t.,* **-dd-** [im Reißwolf] zerkleinern

**shrew** [ʃruː] *n. (Zool.)* Spitzmaus, *die*

**shrewd** [ʃruːd] *adj.* klug; genau ⟨*[Ein]schätzung*⟩

**shriek** [ʃriːk] **1.** *n.* [Auf]schrei, *der.* **2.** *v. i.* [auf]schreien. **3.** *v. t.* schreien

**shrift** [ʃrɪft] *n.* **give sb. short ~:** jmdn. kurz abfertigen *(ugs.);* **get short ~** kurz abgefertigt werden *(ugs.)*

**shrill** [ʃrɪl] *adj.* schrill

**shrimp** [ʃrɪmp] *n.* Garnele, *die*

**shrine** [ʃraɪn] *n. (tomb)* Grab, *das*

**shrink** [ʃrɪŋk] **1.** *v. i.,* **shrank** [ʃræŋk], **shrunk** [ʃrʌŋk] **a)** schrumpfen; ⟨*Kleidung, Stoff:*⟩ einlaufen; ⟨*Metall, Holz:*⟩ sich zusammenziehen; **b)** *(recoil)* **~ from sb./sth.** vor jmdm. zurückweichen/vor etw. *(Dat.)* zurückschrecken; **~ from doing sth.** sich scheuen, etw. zu tun. **2.** *v. t.,* **shrank, shrunk** einlaufen lassen ⟨*Textilien*⟩

**shrivel** [ˈʃrɪvl] *v. i., (Brit.)* **-ll-:** ~ |up| verschrumpeln; ⟨*Pflanze, Blume:*⟩ welk werden

**shroud** [ʃraʊd] **1.** *n.* Leichentuch, *das.* **2.** *v. t.* **~ sth. in sth.** etw. in etw. *(Akk.)* hüllen

**Shrove** [ʃrəʊv] **'Tuesday** *n.* Fastnachtsdienstag, *der*

**shrub** [ʃrʌb] *n.* Strauch, *der*

**shrug** [ʃrʌg] **1.** *v. t. & i.,* **-gg-:** ~ |one's shoulders| die Achseln zucken. **2.** *n.* ~ |of one's *or* the shoulders| Achselzucken, *das.* **shrug 'off** *v. t.* in den Wind schlagen

**shrunk** *see* shrink

**shrunken** [ˈʃrʌŋkn] *adj.* verhutzelt *(ugs.)*⟨*Person*⟩; schrump[e]lig ⟨*Apfel*⟩

**shudder** [ˈʃʌdə(r)] **1.** *v. i.* zittern (**with** vor + *Dat.*). **2.** *n.* Zittern, *das*

**shuffle** [ˈʃʌfl] **1.** *n.* **a)** Schlurfen, *das;* **walk with a ~:** schlurfen; **b)** *(Cards)* Mischen, *das;* **give the cards a** |good| **~:** die Karten [gut] mischen. **2.** *v. t.* **a)** *(Cards)* mischen; **b)** ~ **one's feet** von einem Fuß auf den anderen treten

**shun** [ʃʌn] *v. t.,* **-nn-** meiden

**shunt** [ʃʌnt] *v. t. (Railw.)* rangieren

**shush** [ʃʊʃ] *int.* still

**shut** [ʃʌt] **1.** *v. t.,* **-tt-,** **shut** zumachen; schließen; zusammenklappen ⟨*Klappmesser, Fächer*⟩; ~ **one's finger in the door** sich *(Dat.)* den Finger in der Tür einklemmen. **2.** *v. i.,* **-tt-,** **shut** schließen; ⟨*Blüte:*⟩ sich schließen. **shut 'down 1.** *v. t.* **a)** schließen, zumachen ⟨*Deckel*⟩; **b)** stillegen ⟨*Fabrik*⟩; abschalten ⟨*Kernreaktor*⟩. **2.** *v. i.* ⟨*Laden, Fabrik:*⟩ geschlossen werden. **shut 'out** *v. t.* aussperren. **shut 'up 1.** *v. t.* abschließen; einsperren ⟨*Tier, Person*⟩. **2.** *v. i. (coll.: be quiet)* den Mund halten

**shutter** [ˈʃʌtə(r)] *n.* **a)** [Fenster]laden, *der;* **b)** *(Photog.)* Verschluß, *der;* ~ **release** Auslöser, *der;* ~ **speed** Verschlußzeit, *die*

**shuttle** [ˈʃʌtl] **1.** *n. (in loom)* Schiffchen, *das.* **2.** *v. i.* pendeln. **'shuttlecock** *n.* Federball, *der.* **'shuttle service** *n.* Pendelverkehr, *der*

**shy** [ʃaɪ] *adj.,* **~er** *or* **shier** [ˈʃaɪə(r)], **~est** *or* **shiest** [ˈʃaɪɪst] scheu; *(diffident)* schüchtern. **shy a'way** *v. i.* ~ **away from sth./doing sth.** etw. scheuen/sich scheuen, etw. zu tun

'**shyness** *n.* Scheuheit, *die; (diffidence)* Schüchternheit, *die*

**Siamese** [saɪə'miːz]: ~ '**cat** *n.* Siamkatze, *die;* ~ '**twins** *n. pl.* siamesische Zwillinge

**Siberia** [saɪ'bɪərɪə] *pr. n.* Siberien *(das)*

**Sicily** ['sɪsɪlɪ] *pr. n.* Sizilien *(das)*

**sick** [sɪk] *adj.* a) *(ill)* krank; **be off** ~: krank [gemeldet] sein; b) *(Brit.: vomiting or about to vomit)* be ~: sich erbrechen; **I'm going to be** ~: sich muß ich erbrechen; **sb. gets/feels** ~: jmdm. wird/ist [es] übel *od.* schlecht; **be/get** ~ **of sb./sth.** *(fig.)* jmdn./etw. satt haben/allmählich satt haben; **make sb.** ~ *(disgust)* jmdn. anekeln. '**sicken** ['sɪkn] **1.** *v. i.* be ~ing **for sth.** *(Brit.)* krank werden; etw. ausbrüten *(ugs.).* **2.** *v. t. (disgust)* anwidern. '**sickening** *adj.* ekelerregend, widerlich ⟨*Anblick, Geruch*⟩

**sickle** ['sɪkl] *n.* Sichel, *die*

'**sick-leave** *n.* Urlaub wegen Krankheit; **be on** ~ ≈ krank geschrieben sein

**sickly** ['sɪklɪ] *adj.* kränklich

'**sickness** *n.* Krankheit, *die; (nausea)* Übelkeit, *die*

**sick:** ~-**pay** *n.* Entgeltfortzahlung im Krankheitsfalle; *(paid by insurance)* Krankengeld, *das;* ~-**room** *n.* Krankenzimmer, *das*

**side** [saɪd] **1.** *n.* a) Seite, *die;* ~ **of beef** Rinderhälfte, *die;* ~ **of bacon** Speckseite, *die;* **walk/stand** ~ **by** ~: nebeneinander gehen/stehen; **work/fight** ~ **by** ~ [**with sb.**] Seite an Seite [mit jmdm.] arbeiten/kämpfen; **live** ~ **by** ~ [**with sb.**] in [jmds.] unmittelbarer Nachbarschaft leben; **to one** ~: zur Seite; **on one** ~: an der Seite; **on the** ~ *(as* ~*line)* nebenbei; **take** ~s [**with/against sb.**] [für/gegen] jmdn. Partei ergreifen; b) *(Sport: team)* Mannschaft, *die.* **2.** *v. i.* ~ **with sb.** sich auf jmds. Seite *(Akk.)* stellen. **3.** *adj.* Seiten-

**side:** ~-**board** *n.* Anrichte, *die;* ~-**car** *n.* Beiwagen, *der;* ~-**dish** *n.* Beilage, *die;* ~-**door** *n.* Seitentür, *die;* ~-**effect** *n.* Nebenwirkung, *die;* ~-**entrance** *n.* Seiteneingang, *der;* ~-**exit** *n.* Seitenausgang, *der;* ~-**light** *n.* Begrenzungsleuchte, *die;* **drive on** ~**lights** mit Standlicht fahren; ~-**line** *n. (occupation)* Nebenbeschäftigung, *die;* ~-**road** *n.* Seitenstraße, *die;* ~-**show** *n.* Nebenattraktion, *die;* ~-**step 1.** *n.* Schritt zur Seite; **2.** *v. t.*

ausweichen (+ *Dat.*); ~-**street** *n.* Seitenstraße, *die;* ~**track** *v. t.* get ~**tracked** abgelenkt werden; ~**walk** *n. (Amer.)* Bürgersteig, *der;* ~**ways** ['saɪdweɪz] **1.** *adv.* **look at sb./sth.** ~**ways** jmdn./etw. von der Seite ansehen; **2.** *adj.* seitlich

**siding** ['saɪdɪŋ] *n.* Abstellgleis, *das*

**sidle** ['saɪdl] *v. i.* schleichen [**up to zu**]

**siege** [siːdʒ] *n.* Belagerung, *die; (by police)* Umstellung, *die;* **lay** ~ **to sth.** etw. belagern

**sieve** [sɪv] **1.** *n.* Sieb, *das.* **2.** *v. t.* sieben

**sift** [sɪft] *v. t.* sieben; ~ **sth. from sth.** etw. von etw. trennen. **sift 'out** *v. t.* aussieben

**sigh** [saɪ] **1.** *n.* Seufzer, *der;* **breathe** *or* **give** *or* **heave a** ~: einen Seufzer ausstoßen; ~ **of relief/contentment** Seufzer der Erleichterung/Zufriedenheit. **2.** *v. i.* seufzen; ~ **with relief/despair** erleichtert/verzweifelt seufzen

**sight** [saɪt] **1.** *n.* a) *(faculty)* Sehvermögen, *das;* **know sb. by** ~: jmdn. vom Sehen kennen; b) *(act of seeing; spectacle)* Anblick, *der;* **catch/lose** ~ **of sb./sth.** jmdn./etw. erblicken/aus dem Auge verlieren; **at first** ~: auf den ersten Blick; c) *in pl.* ~**s** *(places of interest)* Sehenswürdigkeiten; **see the** ~**s** die Sehenswürdigkeiten ansehen; d) *(range)* Sichtweite, *die;* **in** ~: in Sicht; **within** *or* **in** ~ **of sb./sth.** *(able to see)* in jmds. Sichtweite *(Dat.)*/in Sichtweite einer Sache; **out of** ~: außer Sicht; e) *(of gun)* Visier, *das;* **set/have** [**set**] **one's** ~**s on sth.** *(fig.)* etw. anpeilen. **2.** *v. t.* sichten ⟨*Land, Schiff, Flugzeug*⟩; sehen ⟨*Entflohenen, Vermißten*⟩. '**sightseeing** *n.* **go** ~: Besichtigungen machen. **sightseer** ['saɪtsiːə(r)] *n.* Tourist *(der die Sehenswürdigkeiten besichtigt)*

**sign** [saɪn] **1.** *n.* a) *(symbol, signal, indication)* Zeichen, *das; (of future event)* Anzeichen, *das;* **as a** ~ **of** als Zeichen (+ *Gen.*); b) *(Astrol.)* ~ [**of the zodiac**] Sternzeichen, *das;* c) *(notice; on shop etc.)* Schild, *das.* **2.** *v. t. & i.* unterschreiben; ~ **one's name** [mit seinem Namen] unterschreiben. **sign 'on** *v. i. (as unemployed)* sich arbeitslos melden. **sign 'up** *v. i.* sich [vertraglich] verpflichten (**with** bei); *(for course)* sich einschreiben

**signal** ['sɪgnl] **1.** *n.* Signal, *das;* **a** ~ **for sth./to sb.** ein Zeichen zu etw./für jmdn. **2.** *v. i., (Brit.)* **-ll-** signalisieren; Signale geben; ⟨*Kraftfahrer:*⟩ blinken *(with hand)* anzeigen; ~ **to sb. |to do sth.|** jmdm. ein Zeichen geben[, etw. zu tun]. '**signal-box** *n.* Stellwerk, *das*

**signature** ['sɪgnətʃə(r)] *n.* Unterschrift, *die; (on painting)* Signatur, *die.* '**signature tune** *n.* Erkennungsmelodie, *die*

'**signboard** *n.* Schild, *das*

**signet-ring** ['sɪgnɪt rɪŋ] *n.* Siegelring, *der*

**significance** [sɪg'nɪfɪkəns] *n.* Bedeutung, *die;* **be of |no| ~:** [nicht] von Bedeutung sein

**significant** [sɪg'nɪfɪkənt] *adj.* **a)** *(noteworthy, important)* bedeutend; **b)** *(full of meaning)* bedeutsam. **sig'nificantly** *adv.* **a)** *(meaningfully)* bedeutungsvoll; ~ **|enough|** bedeutsamerweise; **b)** *(notably)* bedeutend

**signify** ['sɪgnɪfaɪ] *v.t.* bedeuten

'**signpost** *n.* Wegweiser, *der*

**silence** ['saɪləns] **1.** *n.* Schweigen, *das; (keeping a secret)* Verschwiegenheit, *die; (stillness)* Stille, *die;* **there was ~:** es herrschte Schweigen/Stille; **in ~:** schweigend. **2.** *v.t.* zum Schweigen bringen; *(fig.)* ersticken ⟨*Proteste*⟩; mundtot machen ⟨*Gegner*⟩. '**silencer** *n. (Arms; Brit. Motor Veh.)* Schalldämpfer, *der*

**silent** ['saɪlənt] *adj.* stumm; *(noiseless)* unhörbar; *(still)* still; **be ~** *(say nothing)* schweigen; ~ **film** Stummfilm, *der.* '**silently** *adv.* schweigend; stumm ⟨*weinen, beten*⟩; *(noiselessly)* lautlos

**silhouette** [sɪlʊ'et] **1.** *n.* **a)** *(picture)* Schattenriß, *der;* **b)** *(appearance against the light)* Silhouette, *die.* **2.** *v.t.* **be ~d against** sth. sich als Silhouette gegen etw. abheben

**silicon** ['sɪlɪkən] *n.* Silicium, *das;* ~ **chip** Siliciumchip, *der*

**silk** [sɪlk] **1.** *n.* Seide, *die.* **2.** *attrib. adj.* seiden; Seiden-. '**silkworm** *n.* Seidenraupe, *die.* '**silky** *adj.* seidig

**sill** [sɪl] *n. (of door)* [Tür]schwelle, *die; (of window)* Fensterbank, *die*

**silly** ['sɪlɪ] *adj.* dumm; *(imprudent, unwise)* töricht; *(childish)* albern

**silo** ['saɪləʊ] *n., pl.* ~s Silo, *der*

**silt** [sɪlt] *n.* Schlamm, *der;* Schlick, *der*

**silver** ['sɪlvə(r)] **1.** *n.* Silber, *das.* **2.** *attrib. adj.* silbern; Silber⟨*pokal, -münze*⟩

**silver:** ~ '**medal** *n.* Silbermedaille, *die;* ~ '**paper** *n.* Silberpapier, *das;* ~-**plated** *adj.* versilbert; ~ '**wedding** *n.* Silberhochzeit, *die*

**similar** ['sɪmɪlə(r)] *adj.* ähnlich **(to** *Dat.*). **similarity** [sɪmɪ'lærɪtɪ] *n.* Ähnlichkeit, *die* (to mit). '**similarly** *adv.* ähnlich; *(in exactly the same way)* ebenso

**simile** ['sɪmɪlɪ] *n.* Vergleich, *der*

**simmer** ['sɪmə(r)] **1.** *v.i.* ⟨*Flüssigkeit:*⟩ sieden. **2.** *v.t.* köcheln lassen. **simmer 'down** *v.i.* sich abregen *(ugs.)*

**simple** ['sɪmpl] *adj.* einfach; *(unsophisticated, not elaborate)* schlicht ⟨*Mobiliar, Schönheit, Kunstwerk, Kleidung*⟩; **it was a ~ misunderstanding** es war [ganz] einfach ein Mißverständnis. '**simple-minded** *adj.* **a)** *(unsophisticated)* schlicht; **b)** *(unintelligent)* beschränkt. **simpleton** ['sɪmpltən] *n.* Einfaltspinsel, *der (ugs.).* **simplicity** [sɪm'plɪsɪtɪ] *n.* Einfachheit, *die; (unpretentiousness, lack of sophistication)* Schlichtheit, *die.* **simplification** [sɪmplɪfɪ'keɪʃn] *n.* Vereinfachung, *die.* **simplify** ['sɪmplɪfaɪ] *v.t.* vereinfachen. **simplistic** [sɪm'plɪstɪk] *adj.* ¦all¦zu simpel. **simply** ['sɪmplɪ] *adv.* einfach; *(in an unsophisticated manner)* schlicht; *(merely)* nur; **it ~ isn't true** es ist einfach nicht wahr; **I was ~ trying to help** ich wollte nur helfen

**simulate** ['sɪmjʊleɪt] *v.t.* **a)** *(feign)* vortäuschen; **b)** simulieren ⟨*Bedingungen, Wetter usw.*⟩

**simultaneous** [sɪml'teɪnɪəs] *adj.,* **simul'taneously** *adv.* gleichzeitig

**sin** [sɪn] **1.** *n.* Sünde, *die.* **2.** *v.i.,* -**nn-** sündigen

**since** [sɪns] **1.** *adv.* seitdem. **2.** *prep.* seit; ~ **seeing you ...:** seit ich dich gesehen habe; ~ **then/that time** inzwischen. **3.** *conj.* **a)** seit; **it is a long time/ so long/not so long ~ ...:** es ist lange/so lange/gar nicht lange her, daß ...; **b)** *(seeing that, as)* da

**sincere** [sɪn'sɪə(r)] *adj.,* ~**r** [sɪn'sɪərə(r)], ~**st** [sɪn'sɪərɪst] aufrichtig; herzlich ⟨*Grüße, Glückwünsche usw.*⟩. **sin'cerely** *adv.* aufrichtig; **yours ~:** mit freundlichen Grüßen. **sincerity** [sɪn'serɪtɪ] *n.* Aufrichtigkeit, *die*

**sinew** ['sɪnju:] *n.* Sehne, *die*

**sinful** ['sɪnfl] *adj.* sündig; *(reprehensible)* sündhaft; **it is ~ to ...:** es ist eine Sünde, ... zu ...

**sing** [sɪŋ] *v.i. & t.,* **sang** [sæŋ], **sung** [sʌŋ] singen. **sing 'up** *v.i.* lauter singen

**singe** [sɪndʒ] *v.t. & i.,* ~**ing** versengen

**singer** ['sɪŋə(r)] *n.* Sänger, *der*/Sängerin, *die*

**single** ['sɪŋgl] 1. *adj.* **a)** einfach; *(sole)* einzig; *(separate, individual, isolated)* einzeln; **not a ~ one** kein einziger/keine einzige/kein einziges; **every ~ one** jeder/jede/jedes einzelne; **every ~ day** jeden Tag; **~ ticket** *(Brit.)* einfache Fahrkarte; **b)** *(for one person)* Einzel-⟨bett, -zimmer⟩; **c)** *(unmarried)* ledig; **a ~ man/woman** ein Lediger/eine Ledige; **~ people** Ledige. **2.** *n.* **a)** *(Brit.: ticket)* einfache Fahrkarte; **[a] two ~s to Manchester, please** einmal/zweimal einfach nach Manchester, bitte; **b)** *(record)* Single, *die;* **c)** in pl. *(Tennis etc.)* Einzel, *das.* **single 'out** *v.t.* **~ sb./sth. out as/for sth.** jmdn./etw. als/für etw. auswählen

**single:** **~-decker 1.** *n.* **be a ~-decker** ⟨Bus, Straßenbahn:⟩ nur ein Deck haben; **2.** *adj.* **~-decker bus/tram** Bus/Straßenbahn mit [nur] einem Deck; **~ [European] market** *n.* [europäischer] Binnenmarkt; **~-'handed** *adv.* allein; **~-minded** *adj.* zielstrebig

**singlet** ['sɪŋglɪt] *n. (Brit.) (vest)* Unterhemd, *das; (Sport)* Trikot, *das*

**singly** ['sɪŋglɪ] *adv.* einzeln

**singular** ['sɪŋgjʊlə(r)] 1. *adj.* **a)** *(Ling.)* singularisch; Singular-; **~ noun** Substantiv im Singular; **b)** *(extraordinary)* einmalig. **2.** *n. (Ling.)* Einzahl, *die;* Singular, *der.* **'singularly** *adv. (extraordinarily)* außerordentlich

**sinister** ['sɪnɪstə(r)] *adj.* finster; *(of evil omen)* unheilverkündend

**sink** [sɪŋk] 1. *n.* Spülbecken, *das.* **2.** *v.i.,* **sank** [sæŋk] *or* **sunk** [sʌŋk], **sunk** sinken. **3.** *v.t.,* **sank** *or* **sunk, sunk a)** versenken ⟨Schiff⟩; **b)** niederbringen ⟨Schacht⟩. **sink 'in** *v.i. (fig.)* jmdm. ins Bewußtsein dringen; ⟨Warnung, Lektion:⟩ verstanden werden

**'sinner** *n.* Sünder, *der*/Sünderin, *die*

**sinus** ['saɪnəs] *n.* Nebenhöhle, *die*

**sip** [sɪp] 1. *v.t.,* -pp-: **~ [up]** schlürfen. **2.** *v.i.,* -pp-: **~ at/from sth.** an etw. *(Dat.)* nippen. **3.** *n.* Schlückchen, *das*

**siphon** ['saɪfn] 1. *n.* Siphon, *der.* **2.** *v.t.* [durch einen Saugheber] laufen lassen

**sir** [sɜ:(r)] *n.* **a)** *(formal address)* der Herr; *(to teacher)* Herr Meier/Schmidt *usw.;* **b)** *(in letter)* **Dear Sir** Sehr geehrter Herr; **Dear Sirs** Sehr geehrte [Damen und] Herren; **Dear Sir or Madam** Sehr geehrte Dame/Sehr geehrter Herr; **c)** **Sir** [sə(r)] *(title of knight etc.)* Sir

**siren** ['saɪrən] *n.* Sirene, *die*

**sirloin** ['sɜ:lɔɪn] *n.* **a)** *(Brit.)* Roastbeef, *das;* **~ steak** Rumpsteak, *das;* **b)** *(Amer.)* Rumpsteak, *das*

**sissy** ['sɪsɪ] 1. *n.* Waschlappen, *der.* **2.** *adj.* feige

**sister** ['sɪstə(r)] *n.* **a)** Schwester, *die;* **b)** *(Brit.: nurse)* Oberschwester, *die.* **'sister-in-law** *n., pl.* **sisters-in-law** Schwägerin, *die*

**sit** [sɪt] 1. *v.i.,* -tt-, **sat** [sæt] **a)** *(become seated)* sich setzen; **~ on a chair/in an armchair** sich auf einen Stuhl/in einen Sessel setzen; **b)** *(be seated)* sitzen. **2.** *v.t.,* -tt-, **sat a)** setzen; **b)** *(Brit.)* machen ⟨Prüfung⟩. **sit 'back** *v.i.* sich zurücklehnen; *(fig.)* sich im Sessel zurücklehnen. **sit 'down** *v.i.* **a)** *(become seated)* sich setzen **(on/in** auf/in + *Akk.*); **b)** *(be seated)* sitzen. **sit 'up 1.** *v.i.* **a)** *(rise)* sich aufsetzen; **b)** *(be sitting erect)* [aufrecht] sitzen; **c)** *(stay up)* aufbleiben. **2.** *v.t.* aufsetzen

**site** [saɪt] 1. *n.* **a)** *(land)* Grundstück, *das;* **b)** *(location)* Sitz, *der; (of new factory etc.)* Standort, *der.* **2.** *v.t.* stationieren ⟨Raketen⟩; **~ a factory in London** London als Standort einer Fabrik wählen; **be ~d** gelegen sein

**'sitting** *n.* Sitzung, *die;* **the first ~ [for lunch]** der erste Schub [zum Mittagessen]

**situate** ['sɪtjʊeɪt] *v.t.* legen. **'situated** *adj.* gelegen; **be ~:** liegen. **situation** [sɪtjʊ'eɪʃn] *n.* **a)** *(location)* Lage, *die;* **b)** *(circumstances)* Situation, *die;* **c)** *(job)* Stelle, *die*

**six** [sɪks] 1. *adj.* sechs. **2.** *n.* Sechs, *die. See also* **eight**

**sixteen** [sɪks'ti:n] 1. *adj.* sechzehn. **2.** *n.* Sechzehn, *die. See also* **eight**. **sixteenth** [sɪks'ti:nθ] 1. *adj.* sechzehnt... **2.** *n. (fraction)* Sechzehntel, *das. See also* **eighth**

**sixth** [sɪksθ] 1. *adj.* sechst... **2.** *n. (in sequence)* sechste, *der/die/das; (in rank)* Sechste, *der/die/das; (fraction)* Sechstel, *das. See also* **eighth**

**sixtieth** ['sɪkstɪθ] *adj.* sechzigst...

**sixty** ['sɪkstɪ] 1. *adj.* sechzig. **2.** *n.* Sechzig, *die. See also* **eight; eighty 2**

**size** [saɪz] *n.* Größe, *die; (of paper)* Format, *das;* **be twice the ~ of sth.** zweimal so groß wie etw. sein; **a ~ 8 dress** ein Kleid [in] Größe 8; **be ~ 8** ⟨Person:⟩ Größe 8 haben. **size 'up** *v.t.* taxieren ⟨Lage⟩

**sizeable** ['saɪzəbl] *adj.* ziemlich groß; beträchtlich ⟨Summe, Einfluß⟩

**sizzle** ['sɪzl] *v.i.* zischen

**skate 1.** *n.* *(ice-~)* Schlittschuh, *der;* *(roller-~)* Rollschuh, *der.* **2.** *v.i.* *(ice-~)* Schlittschuh laufen; *(roller-~)* Rollschuh laufen. '**skateboard 1.** *n.* Skateboard, *das;* Rollerbrett, *das.* **2.** *v.i.* Skateboard fahren. '**skater** *n.* *(ice-~)* Eisläufer, *der*/Eisläuferin, *die;* *(roller-~)* Rollschuhläufer, *der*/-läuferin, *die.* **skating** ['skeɪtɪŋ] *n.* *(ice-~)* Schlittschuhlaufen, *das;* *(roller-~)* Rollschuhlaufen, *das.* '**skating rink** *n.* *(ice)* Eisbahn, *die;* *(for roller-skating)* Rollschuhbahn, *die*
**skeleton** ['skelɪtn] *n.* Skelett, *das.* '**skeleton key** *n.* Dietrich, *der.* '**skeleton staff** *n.* Minimalbesetzung, *die*
**skeptic** *etc.* *(Amer.)* see **sceptic** *etc.*
**sketch** [sketʃ] **1.** *n.* **a)** *(drawing)* Skizze, *die.* **b)** *(play)* Sketch, *der.* **2.** *v.t.* skizzieren. '**sketch-book** *n.* Skizzenbuch, *das.* '**sketch map** *n.* Faustskizze, *die*
'**sketchy** *adj.* skizzenhaft; lückenhaft ⟨*Informationen, Bericht*⟩
**skew** [skju:] **1.** *adj.* schräg. **2.** *n.* **on the ~:** schief
**skewer** ['skju:ə(r)] **1.** *n.* Bratspieß, *der.* **2.** *v.t.* aufspießen
**ski** [ski:] **1.** *n.* **a)** Ski, *der;* **b)** *(on vehicle)* Kufe, *die.* **2.** *v.i.* Ski laufen *od.* fahren. '**ski boot** *n.* Skistiefel, *der.* '**ski-lift** *n.* Skilift, *der*
**skid** [skɪd] **1.** *v.i.,* **-dd-** schlittern; *(from one side to the other; spinning round)* schleudern. **2.** *n.* Schlittern/Schleudern, *das.* '**skid marks** *n. pl.* Schleuderspur, *die*
**skier** ['ski:ə(r)] *n.* Skiläufer, *der*/-läuferin, *die*
**skiing** ['ski:ɪŋ] *n.* Skilaufen, *das;* *(Sport)* Skisport, *der*
**skilful** ['skɪlfl] *adj.* geschickt; gewandt ⟨*Redner*⟩; gut ⟨*Beobachter, Lehrer*⟩
**skill** [skɪl] *n.* **a)** *(expertness)* Geschick, *das;* *(of artist)* Können, *das;* **b)** *(technique)* Fertigkeit, *die;* *(of weaving, bricklaying)* Technik, *die.* **skilled** ['skɪld] *adj.* **a)** see **skilful;** **b)** qualifiziert ⟨*Arbeit, Tätigkeit*⟩; **~ trade** Ausbildungsberuf, *der;* **c)** *(trained)* ausgebildet. '**skillful** *(Amer.)* see **skilful**
**skim** [skɪm] *v.t.,* **-mm-: a)** *(remove)* abschöpfen; **b)** abrahmen ⟨*Milch*⟩; **c)** see **~ through. skim 'off** *v.t.* abschöpfen. '**skim through** *v.t.* überfliegen ⟨*Buch, Zeitung*⟩
**skimmed 'milk** *n.* entrahmte Milch
**skimp** [skɪmp] **1.** *v.t.* sparen an

(+ *Dat.*). **2.** *v.i.* sparen (**with, on** an + *Dat.*). '**skimpy** *adj.* winzig ⟨*Badeanzug*⟩; spärlich ⟨*Wissen*⟩
**skin** [skɪn] **1.** *n.* **a)** Haut, *die;* **b)** *(fur)* Fell, *das;* **c)** *(peel)* Schale, *die.* **2.** *v.t.,* **-nn-** häuten; schälen ⟨*Frucht*⟩
**skin: ~ cream** *n.* Hautcreme, *die;* **~-'deep** *adj.* *(fig.)* oberflächlich; **~-diver** *n.* Taucher, *der*/Taucherin, *die;* **~flint** *n.* Geizhals, *der;* **~head** *n.* *(Brit.)* Skinhead, *der*
**skinny** ['skɪnɪ] *adj.* mager
'**skin-tight** *adj.* hauteng
¹**skip** [skɪp] **1.** *v.i.,* **-pp-: a)** hüpfen; **b)** *(with skipping-rope)* seilspringen. **2.** *v.t.,* **-pp-** *(omit)* überspringen; **~ breakfast/lunch** das Frühstück/Mittagessen auslassen. **3.** *n.* Hüpfer, *der*
²**skip** *n.* *(Building)* Container, *der*
**ski: ~ pass** *n.* Skipaß, *der;* **~ pole** *n.* Skistock, *der*
**skipper** ['skɪpə(r)] *n.* Kapitän, *der*
'**skipping-rope** *(Brit.),* '**skip-rope** *(Amer.)* ns. Sprungseil, *das*
'**ski-resort** *n.* Skiurlaubsort, *der*
**skirmish** ['skɜːmɪʃ] *n.* *(Mil.)* **a)** Gefecht, *das;* **b)** *(argument)* Auseinandersetzung, *die*
**skirt** [skɜːt] **1.** *n.* Rock, *der.* **2.** *v.t.* herumgehen um. **skirt 'round** *v.t.* herumgehen um; *(fig.)* umgehen
'**skirting** *n.* **~-|-board|** *(Brit.)* Fußleiste, *die*
**ski: ~-run** *n.* Skihang, *der;* *(prepared)* [Ski]piste, *die;* **~-stick** *n.* Skistock, *der*
**skittle** ['skɪtl] *n.* **a)** Kegel, *der;* **b)** **~s** *sing.* *(game)* Kegeln, *das*
**skive** [skaɪv] *v.i.* *(Brit. sl.)* sich drücken *(ugs.).* **skive 'off** *(Brit. sl.)* **1.** *v.i.* sich verdrücken *(ugs.).* **2.** *v.t.* schwänzen *(ugs.)*
**skulk** [skʌlk] *v.i.* lauern
**skull** [skʌl] *n.* Schädel, *der*
**skunk** [skʌŋk] *n.* Stinktier, *das*
**sky** [skaɪ] *n.* Himmel, *der;* **in the ~:** am Himmel
**sky: ~-high 1.** *adj.* himmelhoch; astronomisch *(ugs.)* ⟨*Preise usw.*⟩; **2.** *adv.* **go ~-high** ⟨*Preise usw.*:⟩ in astronomische Höhen klettern *(ugs.);* **~light** *n.* Dachfenster, *das;* **~scraper** *n.* Wolkenkratzer, *der*
**slab** [slæb] *n.* **a)** *(flat stone etc.)* Platte, *die;* **b)** *(thick slice)* [dicke] Scheibe; *(of cake)* [dickes] Stück; *(of chocolate, toffee)* Tafel, *die*
**slack** [slæk] **1.** *adj.* **a)** *(lax)* nachlässig; schlampig *(ugs.);* **b)** *(loose)* schlaff;

locker ⟨*Verband*⟩. **2.** *n.* take in *or* up the ~: das Seil/die Schnur *usw.* straffen. **3.** *v. i. (coll.)* bummeln *(ugs.)*

**slacken** ['slækn] **1.** *v. i.* **a)** *(loosen)* sich lockern; **b)** *(diminish)* nachlassen; ⟨*Geschwindigkeit:*⟩ sich verringern. **2.** *v. t.* **a)** *(loosen)* lockern; **b)** *(diminish)* verringern

**slacks** [slæks] *n. pl.* |pair of| ~: lange Hose; Slacks *Pl. (Mode)*

**slag** [slæg] *n.* Schlacke, *die*

**slain** *see* **slay**

**slake** [sleɪk] *v. t.* stillen

**slam** [slæm] **1.** *v. t.*, -mm-: **a)** *(shut)* zuschlagen; **b)** *(put violently)* knallen *(ugs.)*. **2.** *v. i.*, -mm- zuschlagen

**slander** ['slɑːndə(r)] **1.** *n.* Verleumdung, *die* (on *Gen.*). **2.** *v. t.* verleumden. **slanderous** ['slɑːndərəs] *adj.* verleumderisch

**slang** [slæŋ] *n.* Slang, *der;* ⟨*Theater-, Soldaten-, Juristen*⟩jargon, *der; attrib.* Slang⟨*wort, -ausdruck*⟩

**slant** [slɑːnt] **1.** *v. i.* ⟨*Fläche:*⟩ sich neigen; ⟨*Linie:*⟩ schräg verlaufen. **2.** *v. t.* **a)** abschrägen; **b)** *(fig.: bias)* [so] hinbiegen *(ugs.)* ⟨*Meldung, Bemerkung*⟩. **3.** *n.* Schräge, *die;* on the *or* a ~: schräg

**slap** [slæp] **1.** *v. t.*, -pp-: **a)** schlagen; **b)** *(put)* knallen *(ugs.)*. **2.** *v. i.*, -pp- schlagen; klatschen. **3.** *n.* Schlag, *der.* **4.** *adv.* voll; ~ in the middle genau in der Mitte. **'slapdash** *adj.* schludrig *(ugs.).* **'slap-up** *attrib. adj. (sl.)* ⟨*Essen*⟩ mit allen Schikanen *(ugs.)*

**slash** [slæʃ] **1.** *v. t.* **a)** aufschlitzen; **b)** *(fig.)* [drastisch] reduzieren; [drastisch] kürzen ⟨*Gehalt, Umfang*⟩. **2.** *n.* **a)** *(slit)* Schlitz, *der;* **b)** *(~ing stroke)* Hieb, *der*

**slat** [slæt] *n.* Latte, *die*

**slate** [sleɪt] **1.** *n.* **a)** *(Geol.)* Schiefer, *der;* **b)** *(Building)* Schieferplatte, *die.* **2.** *v. t. (Brit. coll.: criticize)* in der Luft zerreißen *(ugs.)*

**slaughter** ['slɔːtə(r)] **1.** *n.* Schlachten, *das; (massacre)* Gemetzel, *das.* **2.** *v. t.* schlachten; *(massacre)* abschlachten

**slave** [sleɪv] **1.** *n.* Sklave, *der*/Sklavin, *die.* **2.** *v. i.* ~ |away| schuften *(ugs.);* sich abplagen (at mit). **'slave-driver** *n. (fig.)* Sklaventreiber, *der*/-treiberin, *die.* **slavery** ['sleɪvəri] *n.* Sklaverei, *die.* **slavish** ['sleɪvɪʃ] *adj.* sklavisch

**slay** [sleɪ] *v. t.*, slew [sluː], slain [sleɪn] *(literary)* ermorden

**sleazy** ['sliːzɪ] *adj.* schäbig; *(disreputable)* anrüchig

**sled** [sled], **sledge** [sledʒ] *ns.* Schlitten, *der.* **'sledge-hammer** *n.* Vorschlaghammer, *der*

**sleek** [sliːk] *adj. (glossy)* seidig

**sleep** [sliːp] **1.** *n.* Schlaf, *der;* get/go to ~: einschlafen; put to ~: einschläfern ⟨*Tier*⟩. **2.** *v. i.*, slept [slept] schlafen. **3.** *v. t.* slept: the hotel ~s 80 das Hotel hat 80 Betten. **'sleeper** *n.* **a)** be a heavy/light ~: einen tiefen/leichten Schlaf haben; **b)** *(Brit. Railw.: support)* Schwelle, *die;* **c)** *(Railw.) (coach)* Schlafwagen, *der; (train)* |night| ~: Nachtzug mit Schlafwagen

**sleeping:** ~-bag *n.* Schlafsack, *der;* ~-car *n.* Schlafwagen, *der;* ~-pill, ~-tablet *ns.* Schlaftablette, *die*

**sleep:** ~less *adj.* schlaflos; ~-walk *v. i.* schlafwandeln; ~-walker *n.* Schlafwandler, *der*/-wandlerin, *die*

**'sleepy** *adj.* schläfrig

**sleet** [sliːt] **1.** *n.* Schneeregen, *der.* **2.** *v. i. impers.* it is ~ing es gibt Schneeregen

**sleeve** [sliːv] *n.* **a)** Ärmel, *der; (fig.)* have sth. up one's ~: etw. in petto haben *(ugs.);* roll up one's ~s die Ärmel hochkrempeln *(ugs.);* **b)** *(for record)* Hülle, *die.* **'sleeveless** *adj.* ärmellos

**sleigh** [sleɪ] *n.* Schlitten, *der*

**sleight** [slaɪt] of 'hand *n.* Fingerfertigkeit, *die*

**slender** ['slendə(r)] *adj.* **a)** *(slim)* schlank; schmal ⟨*Buch, Band*⟩; **b)** gering ⟨*Chance, Mittel, Hoffnung*⟩

**slept** *see* **sleep** 2, 3

**sleuth** [sluːθ] *n.* Detektiv, *der*

**¹slew** [sluː] *v. i. & t.* schwenken

**²slew** *see* **slay**

**slice** [slaɪs] **1.** *n.* Scheibe, *die; (of apple, melon, peach, cake, pie)* Stück, *das;* a ~ of cake ein Stück Kuchen. **2.** *v. t.* in Scheiben schneiden; in Stücke schneiden ⟨*Bohnen, Apfel, Kuchen usw.*⟩; ~d bread Schnittbrot, *das*

**slick** [slɪk] **1.** *adj. (coll.)* **a)** *(dexterous)* professionell; **b)** *(pretentiously dexterous)* clever *(ugs.).* **2.** *n.* |oil-|~: Ölteppich, *der*

**slid** *see* **slide** 1, 2

**slide** [slaɪd] **1.** *v. i.*, slid [slɪd] rutschen; ⟨*Kolben, Schublade, Feder:*⟩ gleiten. **2.** *v. t.*, slid schieben. **3.** *n.* **a)** *(children's ~)* Rutschbahn, *die;* **b)** *(Photog.)* Dia[positiv], *das.* **sliding** ['slaɪdɪŋ] door *n.* Schiebetür, *die*

**slight** [slaɪt] **1.** *adj.* leicht; schwach ⟨*Hoffnung, Aussichten, Wirkung*⟩; not in the ~est nicht im geringsten. **2.** *n.*

Verunglimpfung, *die* (on *Gen.*); *(lack of courtesy)* Affront, *der* (on gegen).

**'slightly** *adv.* ein bißchen; leicht ⟨*verletzen, riechen nach, gewürzt sein, ansteigen*⟩; flüchtig ⟨*jmdn. kennen*⟩; oberflächlich ⟨*etw. kennen*⟩

**slim** [slɪm] **1.** *adj.* schlank; schmal ⟨*Band, Buch*⟩; schwach ⟨*Aussicht, Hoffnung*⟩; gering ⟨*Gewinn, Chancen*⟩. **2.** *v. i.*, **-mm-** abnehmen

**slime** [slaɪm] *n.* Schleim, *der.* **slimy** ['slaɪmɪ] *adj.* schleimig

**sling** [slɪŋ] **1.** *n. (Med.)* Schlinge, *die.* **2.** *v. t.*, **slung** [slʌŋ] *(coll.: throw)* schmeißen *(ugs.).* **sling 'out** *v. t. (coll.)* wegschmeißen *(ugs.);* ~ **sb. out** jmdn. rausschmeißen *(ugs.)*

**slink** [slɪŋk] *v. i.*, **slunk** [slʌŋk] schleichen. **slink a'way, slink 'off** *v. i.* davonschleichen

**slip** [slɪp] **1.** *v. i.*, **-pp-:** a) *(slide)* rutschen; ⟨*Messer:*⟩ abrutschen; *(and fall)* ausrutschen; b) *(escape)* schlüpfen; c) *(go)* ~ **to the butcher's** *etc.* [rasch] zum Fleischer *usw.* rüberspringen *(ugs.).* **2.** *v. t.*, **-pp-:** a) stecken; ~ **the dress over one's head das Kleid** über den Kopf streifen; b) ~ **sb.'s mind** *or* **memory** jmdm. entfallen. **3.** *n.* a) *(fall)* **after his** ~: nachdem er ausgerutscht [und gestürzt] war; b) *(mistake)* Versehen, *das;* ~ **of the tongue** Versprecher, *der;* c) *(underwear)* Unterrock, *der;* d) *(piece of paper)* Zettel, *der;* e) **give sb. the** ~: jmdm. entwischen *(ugs.).* **slip a'way** *v. i.* a) *(Person:)* sich fortschleichen; b) ⟨*Zeit:*⟩ verfliegen. **slip 'down** *v. i.* runterrutschen *(ugs.).* **slip 'in** *v. i.* ⟨*Person:*⟩ sich hineinschleichen. **slip into** *v. t.* schlüpfen in (+ *Akk.*) ⟨*Kleidungsstück*⟩. **slip 'off 1.** *v. i.* a) runterrutschen *(ugs.);* b) *see* **slip away** a. **2.** *v. t.* abstreifen ⟨*Schmuck, Handschuh*⟩; schlüpfen aus ⟨*Kleid, Schuh*⟩. **slip 'on** *v. t.* überstreifen ⟨*Handschuh, Ring*⟩; schlüpfen in (+ *Akk.*) ⟨*Kleid, Schuh*⟩. **slip 'out** *v. i.* ⟨*Person:*⟩ sich hinausschleichen. **slip 'over** *v. i. (fall)* ausrutschen. **slip 'up** *v. i. (coll.)* einen Schnitzer machen *(ugs.)*

**slipped** [slɪpt] **'disc** *n.* Bandscheibenvorfall, *der*

**'slipper** *n.* Hausschuh, *der*

**slippery** ['slɪpərɪ] *adj.* schlüpfrig

**slip:** ~**-road** *n. (Brit.) (to motorway)* Auffahrt, *die; (from motorway)* Ausfahrt, *die;* ~**shod** *adj.* schludrig *(ugs.);* ~**-up** *n. (coll.)* Schnitzer, *der*

**slit** [slɪt] **1.** *n.* Schlitz, *der.* **2.** *v. t.*, **-tt-,** **slit** aufschlitzen; ~ **sb.'s throat** jmdm. die Kehle durchschneiden

**slither** ['slɪðə(r)] *v. i.* rutschen

**sliver** ['slɪvə(r)] *n.* Splitter, *der*

**slobber** ['slɒbə(r)] *v. i.* sabbern *(ugs.)*

**slog** [slɒg] **1.** *v. t.*, **-gg-** *(in boxing, fight)* voll treffen. **2.** *v. i.*, **-gg-** *(work)* schuften *(ugs.).* **3.** *n.* a) *(hit)* wuchtiger Schlag; b) *(work)* Plackerei, *die (ugs.)*

**slogan** ['sləʊgən] *n.* Slogan, *der; (advertising* ~) Werbeslogan, *der*

**slop** [slɒp] **1.** *v. i.* schwappen (**out of, from** aus). **2.** *v. t.* schwappen; *(intentionally)* kippen. **slop 'over** *v. i.* überschwappen

**slope** [sləʊp] **1.** *n.* a) *(slant)* Neigung, *die;* b) *(slanting ground)* Hang, *der.* **2.** *v. i. (slant)* sich neigen; ⟨*Boden, Garten:*⟩ abschüssig sein; ~ **downwards/upwards** ⟨*Straße:*⟩ abfallen/ansteigen. **slope a'way** *v. i.* abfallen. **slope 'off** *v. i. (sl.)* sich verdrücken *(ugs.)*

**sloppy** ['slɒpɪ] *adj.* schludrig *(ugs.)*

**slosh** [slɒʃ] *adj.* **1.** *v. i.* platschen *(ugs.);* ⟨*Flüssigkeit:*⟩ schwappen. **2.** *v. t. (coll.: pour clumsily)* schwappen

**slot** [slɒt] **1.** *n.* a) *(hole)* Schlitz, *der;* b) *(groove)* Nut, *die.* **2.** *v. t.*, **-tt-:** ~ **sth. into place/sth.** etw. einfügen/in etw. *(Akk.)* einfügen. **slot in 1.** *v. t.* einfügen. **2.** *v. i.* sich einfügen

**sloth** [sləʊθ] *n.* a) *(lethargy)* Trägheit, *die;* b) *(Zool.)* Faultier, *das*

**'slot-machine** *n.* Automat, *der; (for gambling)* Spielautomat, *der*

**slouch** [slaʊtʃ] *v. i.* sich schlecht halten

**slovenly** ['slʌvnlɪ] *adj.* schlampig *(ugs.)*

**slow** [sləʊ] **1.** *adj.* langsam; langwierig ⟨*Arbeit*⟩; **be |ten minutes|** ~ ⟨*Uhr:*⟩ [zehn Minuten] nachgehen. **2.** *adv.* langsam. **3.** *v. i.* langsamer werden; ~ **to a halt** anhalten. **slow 'down, slow 'up** *v. i.* langsamer werden

**'slowcoach** *n.* Trödler, *der/*Trödlerin, *die (ugs.)*

**'slowly** *adv.* langsam

**slow 'motion** *n.* **in** ~: in Zeitlupe

**slowness** *n.* Langsamkeit, *die*

**sludge** [slʌdʒ] *n.* Schlamm, *der*

**slug** [slʌg] *n.* Nacktschnecke, *die*

**sluggish** ['slʌgɪʃ] *adj.* träge; schleppend ⟨*Nachfrage*⟩

**sluice** [sluːs] **1.** *n.* Schütz, *das.* **2.** *v. t.* ~ |**down**| abspritzen

**slum** [slʌm] *n.* Slum, *der; (single house or apartment)* Elendsquartier, *das*

**slumber** ['slʌmbə(r)] *(poet./rhet.)* **1.** *n.*
~|s| Schlummer, *der (geh.).* **2.** *v. i.*
schlummern *(geh.)*

**slump** [slʌmp] **1.** *n.* Sturz, *der (fig.); (in
demand, investment, sales)* starker
Rückgang **(in** *Gen.***);** *(economic depression)* Depression, *die.* **2.** *v. i.* **a)**
*(Commerc.)* stark zurückgehen; ⟨*Prei-
se, Kurse:*⟩ stürzen; **b)** *(collapse)* ⟨*Person:*⟩ fallen; **~ed in a chair** in einem
Sessel zusammengesunken

**slung** *see* **sling** 2

**slunk** *see* **slink**

**slur** [slɜ:(r)] **1.** *v. t.,* **-rr-: ~ one's words/
speech** undeutlich sprechen. **2.** *n.* Beleidigung, *die* **(on** für)

**slurp** [slɜ:p] *(coll.)* **1.** *v. t.* **~ |up|** schlür-
fen. **2.** *n.* Schlürfen, *das*

**slush** [slʌʃ] *n.* Schneematsch, *der.*
'**slushy** *adj.* **a)** matschig; **b)** *(sloppy)*
sentimental

**slut** [slʌt] *n.* Schlampe, *die (ugs.)*

**sly** [slaɪ] **1.** *adj.* schlau; gerissen *(ugs.)*
⟨*Geschäftsmann, Trick*⟩; verschlagen
⟨*Blick*⟩. **2.** *n.* **on the ~:** heimlich

**¹smack** [smæk] **1.** *n.* **a)** *(sound)*
Klatsch, *der;* **b)** *(blow)* Schlag, *der; (on
child's bottom)* Klaps, *der (ugs.).* **2.**
*v. t.* **a)** [mit der flachen Hand] schlagen; **b) ~ one's lips** [mit den Lippen]
schmatzen. **3.** *adv. (coll.)* direkt

**²smack** *v. i.* **~ of** schmecken nach;
*(fig.)* riechen nach *(ugs.)*

**small** [smɔ:l] **1.** *adj.* klein; gering ⟨*Wirkung, Appetit, Fähigkeit*⟩; schmal
⟨*Taille*⟩; dünn ⟨*Stimme*⟩; **make sb. feel
~:** jmdn. beschämen. **2.** *n.* **~ of the
back** Kreuz, *das.* **3.** *adv.* klein

**small: ~ ad** *n. (coll.)* Kleinanzeige,
*die;* **~ 'change** *n.* Kleingeld, *das;*
**~holding** *n.* landwirtschaftlicher
Kleinbetrieb; **~-'minded** *adj.* kleinlich; **~pox** *n.* Pocken *Pl.;* **~ talk** *n.*
leichte Unterhaltung; *(at parties)*
Smalltalk, *der;* **make ~ talk |with sb.|**
[mit jmdm.] Konversation machen

**smarmy** ['smɑ:mɪ] *adj. (coll.)* krieche-
risch

**smart** [smɑ:t] **1.** *adj.* **a)** *(clever)* clever;
*(ingenious)* raffiniert; **b)** *(neat)* schick;
schön ⟨*Haus, Garten, Auto*⟩; **c)** *attrib.*
*(fashionable)* elegant; smart. **2.** *v. i.*
schmerzen. **smart alec[k]** [smɑ:t
'ælɪk] *n. (coll.)* Besserwisser, *der.*

**smarten** ['smɑ:tn] *v. t.* herrichten; **~
oneself |up|** auf sein Äußeres achten.

'**smartly** *adv.* **a)** *(cleverly)* clever; **b)**
*(neatly)* schmuck ⟨*[an]gestrichen*⟩;
smart, flott ⟨*gekleidet, geschnitten*⟩

**smash** [smæʃ] **1.** *v. t.* **a)** zerschlagen;
**b) ~ sb. in the face/mouth** jmdm. [hart]
ins Gesicht/auf den Mund schlagen;
**c)** *(Tennis etc.)* schmettern. **2.** *v. i.* **a)**
zerbrechen; **b)** *(crash)* krachen **(into**
gegen). **3.** *n.* **a)** *(sound)* Krachen, *das;*
**b)** *see* **smash-up; c)** *(Tennis)* Schmet-
terball, *der.* **smash 'in** *v. t.* zer-
schmettern; einschlagen ⟨*Tür, Schädel*⟩. **smash 'up** *v. t.* zertrümmern

**smash-and-'grab [raid]** *n. (coll.)*
Schaufenstereinbruch, *der*

'**smashing** *adj. (coll.)* toll *(ugs.)*

'**smash-up** *n.* schwerer Zusammenstoß

**smattering** ['smætərɪŋ] *n.* **|have| a ~ of**
**German** *etc.* ein paar Brocken
Deutsch *usw.* [können]

**smear** [smɪə(r)] **1.** *v. t.* **a)** *(daub)* beschmieren; *(put on or over)* schmie-
ren; **b)** *(smudge)* verwischen; **c)** *(fig.)*
in den Schmutz ziehen. **2.** *n.* **a)**
*(blotch)* [Schmutz]fleck, *der;* **b)** *(fig.)*
Beschmutzung, *die* **(on** *Gen.*).

**smell** [smel] **1.** *n.* **a) have a good/bad
sense of ~:** einen guten/schlechten
Geruchssinn haben; **b)** *(odour)* Geruch, *der* **(of** nach); *(pleasant also)*
Duft, *der* **(of** nach); **a ~ of burning/
gas** ein Brand-/Gasgeruch; **c)** *(stink)*
Gestank, *der.* **2.** *v. t.,* **smelt** [smelt] *or*
**smelled** [smeld] **a)** *(perceive)* riechen;
**b)** *(inhale ~ of)* riechen an (+ *Dat.*). **3.**
*v. i.,* **smelt** *or* **smelled a)** *(emit ~)* riechen; *(pleasantly also)* duften; **b) ~ of**
*sth. (lit. or fig.)* nach etw. riechen; **c)**
*(stink)* riechen. '**smelly** *adj.* stin-
kend; **be ~:** stinken

**smelt** *see* **smell** 2, 3

**smile** [smaɪl] **1.** *n.* Lächeln, *das;* **give
sb. a ~:** jmdn. anlächeln. **2.** *v. i.* lächeln; **~ at sb./sth.** jmdn. anlächeln/
über etw. *(Akk.)* lächeln

**smirk** [smɜ:k] **1.** *v. t.* grinsen. **2.** *n.*
Grinsen, *das*

**smith** [smɪθ] *n.* Schmied, *der*

**smithereens** [smɪðə'ri:nz] *n. pl.* **blow/
smash sth. to ~:** etw. in tausend
Stücke sprengen/schlagen

**smock** [smɒk] *n.* Kittel, *der*

**smog** [smɒg] *n.* Smog, *der*

**smoke** [sməʊk] **1.** *n.* Rauch, *der.* **2.**
*v. i. & t.* rauchen. **smoked** [sməʊkt]
*adj. (Cookery)* geräuchert

**smoke: ~ detector** *n.* Rauchmelder,
*der;* **~less** *adj.* rauchlos; rauchfrei
⟨*Zone*⟩

'**smoker** *n.* **a)** Raucher, *der*/Rauche-
rin, *die;* **b)** *(Railw.)* Raucherabteil, *das*

'**smoke-screen** *n.* [künstliche] Nebelwand; *(fig.)* Vernebelung *die* (for *Gen.*)

**smoking** ['sməʊkıŋ] *n.* **a)** Rauchen, *das;* '**no ~**' „Rauchen verboten"; **b)** *(seating area)* [do you want to sit in] ~ or non-~? möchten Sie für Raucher oder Nichtraucher?

**smoky** ['sməʊkı] *adj. (emitting smoke)* rauchend; *(smoke-filled)* verräuchert

**smooth** [smu:ð] **1.** *adj.* **a)** *(even)* glatt; eben ⟨*Straße, Weg*⟩; **b)** *(mild)* weich; **c)** *(not jerky)* geschmeidig ⟨*Bewegung*⟩; ruhig ⟨*Fahrt, Flug*⟩; weich ⟨*Landung*⟩; **d)** *(without problems)* reibungslos. **2.** *v.t.* glätten. '**smoothly** *adv.* **a)** *(evenly)* glatt; **b)** *(not jerkily)* geschmeidig ⟨*sich bewegen*⟩; weich ⟨*landen*⟩; reibungslos ⟨*funktionieren*⟩

**smother** ['smʌðə(r)] *v.t.* ersticken; *(fig.)* unterdrücken ⟨*Gähnen*⟩; ersticken ⟨*Gelächter, Schreie*⟩

**smoulder** ['sməʊldə(r)] *v.i.* schwelen; she was ~ing with rage Zorn schwelte in ihr

**smudge** [smʌdʒ] **1.** *v.t.* verwischen. **2.** *v.i.* schmieren. **3.** *n.* Fleck, *der*

**smug** [smʌg] *adj.* selbstgefällig

**smuggle** ['smʌgl] *v.t.* schmuggeln. **smuggle** '**in** *v.t.* einschmuggeln; hinein-/hereinschmuggeln ⟨*Person*⟩. **smuggle** '**out** *v.t.* hinaus-/herausschmuggeln

**smuggler** ['smʌglə(r)] *n.* Schmuggler, *der*/Schmugglerin, *die*

**smuggling** ['smʌglıŋ] *n.* Schmuggel, *der*

**smutty** ['smʌtı] *adj. (lewd)* schmutzig

**snack** [snæk] *n.* Imbiß, *der.* '**snack-bar** *n.* Schnellimbiß, *der*

**snag** [snæg] *n. (problem)* Haken, *der;* what's the ~? wo klemmt es? *(ugs.)*

**snail** [sneıl] *n.* Schnecke, *die;* at [a] ~'s pace im Schneckentempo *(ugs.)*

**snake** [sneık] *n.* Schlange, *die*

**snap** [snæp] **1.** *v.t.,* -pp-: **a)** *(break)* zerbrechen; ~ sth. in two *or* in half etw. in zwei Stücke brechen; **b)** ~ one's fingers mit den Fingern schnalzen; **c)** ~ sth. home *or* into place etw. einschnappen lassen; ~ shut zuschnappen lassen; ~ shut zuschnappen ⟨*Portemonnaie, Schloß*⟩; zuklappen ⟨*Buch, Etui*⟩; ~ sth. open etw. aufschnappen lassen; **d)** *(take photograph of)* knipsen; **e)** *(say sharply)* fauchen; *(speak crisply or curtly)* bellen. **2.** *v.i.,* -pp-: **a)** *(break)* brechen; **b)** *(fig.: give way under strain)* ausrasten *(ugs.);* my patience

has finally ~ped nun ist mir der Geduldsfaden aber gerissen. **3.** *n. (Photog.)* Schnappschuß, *der.* '**snap at** *v.t. (speak sharply to)* anfauchen *(ugs.).* **snap** '**off** *v.t. & i.* abbrechen. **snap** '**up** *v.t. (fig. coll.)* [sich *(Dat.)*] schnappen *(ugs.)*

'**snapshot** *n.* Schnappschuß, *der*

**snare** [sneə(r)] **1.** *n.* Schlinge, *die.* **2.** *v.t.* [mit einer Schlinge] fangen

¹**snarl** [snɑ:l] **1.** *v.i.* knurren. **2.** *n.* Knurren, *das*

²**snarl** *n. (tangle)* Knoten, *der.* **snarl** '**up** *v.t. (bring to a halt)* zum Erliegen bringen; get ~ed up in the traffic im Verkehr steckenbleiben

'**snarl-up** *n.* Stau, *der*

**snatch** [snætʃ] **1.** *v.t.* **a)** *(grab)* schnappen; ~ sth. from sb. jmdm. etw. wegreißen; ~ some sleep ein bißchen schlafen; **b)** *(steal)* klauen *(ugs.).* **2.** *v.i.* einfach zugreifen. **3.** *n.* ~es of talk/conversation Gesprächsfetzen *Pl.*

**sneak** [sni:k] **1.** *v.t.* schmuggeln; ~ a look at schielen nach. **2.** *v.i.* **a)** schleichen; **b)** *(Brit. Sch. sl.: tell tales)* petzen *(Schülerspr.).* **3.** *n. (Brit. Sch. sl.)* Petzer, *der (Schülerspr.)*

**sneer** [snıə(r)] *v.i.* höhnisch lächeln/grinsen. '**sneer at** *v.t.* höhnisch anlächeln/angrinsen; *(scorn)* verhöhnen

**sneeze** [sni:z] **1.** *v.i.* niesen. **2.** *n.* Niesen, *das*

**sniff** [snıf] **1.** *n.* Schnuppern, *das; (with running nose, while crying)* Schniefen, *das.* **2.** *v.i.* schniefen; *(to detect a smell)* schnuppern. **3.** *v.t.* riechen *od.* schnuppern an (+ *Dat.*). '**sniff at** *v.t.* **a)** see sniff 3; **b)** *(show contempt for)* die Nase rümpfen über

**snigger** ['snıgə(r)] **1.** *v.i.* [boshaft] kichern. **2.** *n.* [boshaftes] Kichern

**snip** [snıp] **1.** *v.t.,* -pp- schnippeln *(ugs.),* schneiden ⟨*Loch*⟩; schnippeln *(ugs.) od.* schneiden an (+ *Dat.*) ⟨*Tuch, Haaren, Hecke*⟩; *(cut off)* abschnippeln *(ugs.);* abschneiden. **2.** *n. (cut)* Schnitt, *der;* Schnipser, *der (ugs.)*

**snipe** [snaıp] *v.i.* ~ at aus dem Hinterhalt beschießen. '**sniper** *n.* Heckenschütze, *der*

**snippet** ['snıpıt] *n. (of information in newspaper)* Notiz, *die; (of conversation)* Gesprächsfetzen, *der;* useful ~s of information nützliche Hinweise

**snivel** ['snıvl] *v.i., (Brit.)* -ll- schniefen

**snob** [snɒb] *n.* Snob, *der.* **snobbery** ['snɒbərı] *n.* Snobismus, *der.* **snobbish** ['snɒbıʃ] *adj.* snobistisch

**snooker** ['snu:kə(r)] *n.* Snooker, *das*

**snoop** [snu:p] *v. i.* schnüffeln *(ugs.)*

**snooty** ['snu:tɪ] *adj. (coll.)* hochnäsig *(ugs.)*

**snooze** [snu:z] *(coll.)* **1.** *v. i.* dösen *(ugs.).* **2.** *n.* Nickerchen, *das (fam.)*

**snore** [snɔ:(r)] **1.** *v. i.* schnarchen. **2.** *n.* Schnarcher, *der (ugs.);* ~s Schnarchen, *das*

**snorkel** ['snɔ:kl] *n.* Schnorchel, *der*

**snort** [snɔ:t] *v. i.* schnauben **(with, in** vor + *Dat.*)

**snot** [snɒt] *n. (sl.)* Rotz, *der (derb).* **snotty** *adj.* rotznäsig *(salopp);* ~ **child/nose** Rotznase, *die (salopp)*

**snout** [snaʊt] *n.* Schnauze, *die; (of pig)* Rüssel, *der*

**snow** [snəʊ] **1.** *n.* Schnee, *der.* **2.** *v. i. impers.* **it** ~**s/is** ~**ing** es schneit. **snow 'in** *v. t.* **they are** ~**ed in** sie sind eingeschneit. **snow 'under** *v. t.* **be** ~**ed under** *(with work)* erdrückt werden; *(with gifts, mail)* überschüttet werden **snow:** ~**ball 1.** *n.* Schneeball, *der;* **2.** *v. i. (fig.)* lawinenartig zunehmen; ~**bound** *adj.* eingeschneit; ~**drift** *n.* Schneewehe, *die;* ~**drop** *n.* Schneeglöckchen, *das;* ~**fall** *n.* Schneefall, *der;* ~**flake** *n.* Schneeflocke, *die;* ~**man** *n.* Schneemann, *der;* ~**plough** *n.* Schneepflug, *der;* ~**storm** *n.* Schneesturm, *der* **'snowy** *adj.* schneereich ⟨*Gegend*⟩; schneebedeckt ⟨*Berge*⟩

**snub** [snʌb] **1.** *v. t.,* **-bb-: a)** *(rebuff)* brüskieren; **b)** *(reject)* ablehnen. **2.** *n.* Abfuhr, *die*

**snub-'nosed** *adj.* stupsnasig

**¹snuff** [snʌf] *n.* Schnupftabak, *der;* **take a pinch of** ~: eine Prise schnupfen

**²snuff** *v. t.* ~ **|out|** löschen ⟨*Kerze*⟩

**snuffle** ['snʌfl] *v. i.* schnüffeln

**snug** [snʌg] *adj.* gemütlich; behaglich; **be a** ~ **fit** genau passen

**snuggle** ['snʌgl] *v. i.* ~ **up to sb.** sich an jmdn. kuscheln; ~ **together** sich aneinanderkuscheln; ~ **up** *or* **down in bed** sich ins Bett kuscheln

**so** [səʊ] **1.** *adv.* so; **as winter draws near, so it gets darker** je näher der Winter rückt, desto dunkler wird es; **so ... as so** ... wie; **so far** bis hierher; *(until now)* bisher; *(to such a distance)* so weit; **so much the better** um so besser; **so long!** bis dann! *(ugs.);* **and so on |and so forth|** und so weiter |und so fort|; **so as to** um ... zu; **so |that|** damit; **I'm so glad/tired!** ich bin ja so froh/müde!; **It's a rainbow! – So it is!** Es ist ein Regenbogen! – Ja, wirklich!; **'You suggested it. – So I did** Du hast es vorgeschlagen. – Das stimmt; **is that so?** so? *(ugs.);* wirklich?; **so am/have/would/could/will/do** I ich auch. **2.** *pron.* **he suggested that I take the train, and if I had done so, ...:** er riet mir, den Zug zu nehmen, und wenn ich es getan hätte, ...; **I'm afraid so** leider ja; **I told you so** ich habe es dir |doch| gesagt; **a week or so** etwa eine Woche; **very much so** in der Tat. **3.** *conj. (therefore)* daher; **so there you 'are!** ich habe also recht!; **so 'there!** |und| fertig!; **so?** na und?; **so you see ...:** du siehst also ...; **so where have you been?** wo warst du denn?

**soak** [səʊk] **1.** *v. t.* **a)** einweichen ⟨*Wäsche in Lauge*⟩; eintauchen ⟨*Brot in Milch*⟩; **b)** *(wet)* naß machen. **2.** *v. i.* **a)** *(steep)* put sth. in sth. to ~: etw. in etw. *(Dat.)* einweichen; **b)** *(drain)* ⟨*Feuchtigkeit, Nässe:*⟩ sickern. **'soaking** *adj. & adv.* ~ **|wet|** völlig durchnäßt

**'so-and-so** *n., pl.* ~**'s a)** *(person not named)* |Herr/Frau| Soundso; **b)** *(coll.: disliked person)* Biest, *das (ugs.)*

**soap** [səʊp] *n.* Seife, *die;* **with** ~ **and water** mit Wasser und Seife

**soap:** ~ **opera** *n.* Seifenoper, *die (ugs.);* ~ **powder** *n.* Seifenpulver, *das;* ~**suds** *n. pl.* Seifenschaum, *der* **'soapy** *adj.* seifig; ~ **water** Seifenlauge, *die*

**soar** [sɔ:(r)] *v. i.* aufsteigen; *(fig.)* ⟨*Preise, Kosten usw.:*⟩ in die Höhe schießen *(ugs.)*

**sob** [sɒb] **1.** *v. i.,* **-bb-** schluchzen **(with** vor + *Dat.*). **2.** *n.* Schluchzer, *der*

**sober** ['səʊbə(r)] *adj.* **a)** *(not drunk)* nüchtern; **b)** *(serious)* ernst. **sober 'up 1.** *v. i.* nüchtern werden. **2.** *v. t.* ausnüchtern

**'sobering** *adj.* ernüchternd

**so-called** ['səʊkɔ:ld] *adj.* sogenannt; *(alleged)* angeblich

**soccer** ['sɒkə(r)] *n.* Fußball, *der*

**sociable** ['səʊʃəbl] *adj.* gesellig

**social** ['səʊʃl] *adj.* **a)** sozial; gesellschaftlich; **b)** *(of* ~ *life)* gesellschaftlich; gesellig ⟨*Abend, Beisammensein*⟩

**socialism** ['səʊʃəlɪzm] *n.* Sozialismus, *der.* **socialist** ['səʊʃəlɪst] **1.** *n.* Sozialist, *der*/Sozialistin, *die.* **2.** *adj.* sozialistisch

**socialize** ['səʊʃəlaɪz] *v. i.* geselligen Umgang pflegen; ~ **with sb.** *(chat)* sich mit jmdm. unterhalten

'**socially** *adv*. **meet ~**: sich privat treffen; ~ **deprived** sozial benachteiligt
**social**: ~ **se'curity** *n*. a) *(Brit.: benefit)* Sozialhilfe, *die*; b) *(system)* soziale Sicherheit; ~ '**service** *n*. staatliche Sozialleistung; ~ **work** *n*. Sozialarbeit, *die*; ~ **worker** *n*. Sozialarbeiter, *der*/-arbeiterin, *die*
**society** [sə'saɪətɪ] *n*. a) Gesellschaft, *die*; **high ~**: High-Society, *die*; b) *(club, association)* Verein, *der*
**sociologist** [səʊsɪ'ɒlədʒɪst] *n*. Soziologe, *der*/Soziologin, *die*
**sociology** [səʊsɪ'ɒlədʒɪ] *n*. Soziologie, *die*
¹**sock** [sɒk] *n*. Socke, *die*
²**sock** *v. t.* *(coll.: hit)* hauen *(ugs.)*
**socket** ['sɒkɪt] *n*. a) *(Anat.)* *(of eye)* Höhle, *die*; *(of joint)* Pfanne, *die*; b) *(Electr.)* Steckdose, *die*
**soda** ['səʊdə] *n*. Soda, *das*. '**soda water** *n*. Soda[wasser], *das*
**sodden** ['sɒdn] *adj*. durchnäßt (**with** von)
**sodium** ['səʊdɪəm] *n*. Natrium, *das*
**sofa** ['səʊfə] *n*. Sofa, *das*
**soft** [sɒft] *adj*. weich; *(quiet)* leise; *(gentle)* sanft; **have a ~ spot for sb.** eine Vorliebe für jmdn. haben. '**soft-boiled** *adj*. weichgekocht ⟨Ei⟩. '**soft drink** *n*. alkoholfreies Getränk
**soften** ['sɒfn] 1. *v. i.* weicher werden. 2. *v. t.* aufweichen ⟨Boden⟩; enthärten ⟨Wasser⟩; mildern ⟨Farbe⟩
'**softly** *adv*. *(quietly)* leise; *(gently)* sanft
**soft**: ~ **toy** *n*. Stofftier, *das*; ~**ware** *n*. *(Computing)* Software, *die*
**soggy** ['sɒgɪ] *adj*. aufgeweicht
¹**soil** [sɔɪl] *n*. Erde, *die*; Boden, *der*
²**soil** *v. t.* beschmutzen
**solace** ['sɒləs] *n*. Trost, *der*; **take or find ~ in sth.** Trost in etw. *(Dat.)* finden
**solar** ['səʊlə(r)] *adj*. Sonnen-
**sold** *see* **sell**
**solder** ['səʊldə(r)] 1. *n*. Lot, *das*. 2. *v. t.* löten
**soldier** ['səʊldʒə(r)] *n*. Soldat, *der*
¹**sole** [səʊl] *n*. *(of foot/shoe)* Sohle, *die*
²**sole** *adj*. einzig; alleinig ⟨Verantwortung, Recht⟩; Allein⟨erbe, -eigentümer⟩. '**solely** *adv*. einzig und allein
**solemn** ['sɒləm] *adj*. feierlich; ernst ⟨Anlaß, Gespräch⟩
**solicitor** [sə'lɪsɪtə(r)] *n*. *(Brit.: lawyer)* Rechtsanwalt, *der*/-anwältin, *die*
**solid** ['sɒlɪd] 1. *adj*. a) *(rigid)* fest; b) *(of the same substance all through)*

massiv; c) *(well-built)* stabil; solide gebaut ⟨Haus, Mauer usw.⟩; d) *(complete)* ganz; **a good ~ meal** eine kräftige Mahlzeit. 2. *n*. fester Körper
**solidarity** [sɒlɪ'dærɪtɪ] *n*. Solidarität, *die*
**solidify** [sə'lɪdɪfaɪ] *v. i* fest werden
**solitary** ['sɒlɪtərɪ] *adj*. a) einsam; ~ **confinement** Einzelhaft, *die*; b) *(sole)* einzig
**solitude** ['sɒlɪtjuːd] *n*. Einsamkeit, *die*
**solo** ['səʊləʊ] 1. *n., pl.* ~**s** *(Mus.)* Solo, *das*. 2. *adj*. a) *(Mus.)* Solo-; b) ~ **flight** Alleinflug, *der*. 3. *adv*. a) *(Mus.)* solo; b) **go/fly ~** *(Aeronaut.)* einen Alleinflug machen. **soloist** ['səʊləʊɪst] *n*. *(Mus.)* Solist, *der*/Solistin, *die*
**solstice** ['sɒlstɪs] *n*. Sonnenwende, *die*
**soluble** ['sɒljʊbl] *adj*. a) *(esp. Chem.)* löslich; b) *(solvable)* lösbar
**solution** [sə'luːʃn] *n*. a) *(esp. Chem.)* Lösung, *die*; b) *([result of] solving)* Lösung, *die* (**to** Gen.); **find a ~ to sth.** eine Lösung für etw. finden; etw. lösen
**solvable** ['sɒlvəbl] *adj*. lösbar
**solve** [sɒlv] *v. t.* lösen
**solvent** ['sɒlvənt] 1. *adj*. a) *(esp. Chem.)* lösend; b) *(Finance)* solvent. 2. *n*. *(esp. Chem.)* Lösungsmittel, *das*
**sombre** *(Amer.*: **somber)** ['sɒmbə(r)] *adj*. dunkel; düster ⟨Stimmung, Atmosphäre⟩
**some** [səm, *stressed* sʌm] 1. *adj*. a) *(one or other)* [irgend]ein; ~ **day** eines Tages; b) *(a considerable quantity of)* einig...; c) *(a small quantity of)* ein bißchen; **would you like ~ wine/cherries?** möchten Sie [etwas] Wein/[ein paar] Kirschen?; **do ~ shopping/reading** einkaufen/lesen; d) *(to a certain extent)* ~ **guide** eine gewisse Orientierungshilfe. 2. *pron*. einig...; **would you like ~?** möchtest du etwas/*(plural)* welche?; ~ **..., others ...**: manche ..., andere ...
**somebody** ['sʌmbədɪ] *n. & pron.* jemand; ~ **or other** irgend jemand
'**somehow** *adv*. ~ |**or other**| irgendwie
**someone** ['sʌmwʌn] *see* **somebody**
**somersault** ['sʌməsɔːlt] *n*. Purzelbaum, *der (ugs.)*; Salto, *der (Sport)*; **turn a ~**: einen Purzelbaum schlagen *(ugs.)*/einen Salto springen
'**something** *n. & pron.* etwas; ~ **new** etwas Neues; ~ **or other** irgend etwas; **see ~ of sb.** jmdn. sehen
'**sometime** 1. *adj*. ehemalig. 2. *adv*. irgendwann
'**sometimes** *adv*. manchmal

'**somewhat** *adv.* ziemlich
'**somewhere 1.** *adv.* **a)** *(in a place)* irgendwo; **b)** *(to a place)* irgendwohin. **2.** *n.* look for ~ to stay sich nach einer Unterkunft umsehen
**son** [sʌn] *n.* Sohn, *der*
**sonata** [sə'nɑ:tə] *n.* Sonate, *die*
**song** [sɒŋ] *n.* **a)** Lied, *das;* **b)** *(bird cry)* Gesang, *der*
'**son-in-law** *n., pl.* **sons-in-law** Schwiegersohn, *der*
**soon** [su:n] *adv.* **a)** bald; *(quickly)* schnell; **b)** *(early)* früh; **none too ~:** keinen Augenblick zu früh; ~**er or later** früher oder später; **c) we'll set off as ~ as he arrives** sobald er ankommt, machen wir uns auf den Weg; **as ~ as possible** so bald wie möglich; **d)** *(willingly)* **just as ~** [as ...] genauso gern [wie ...]; **she would ~er die than ...:** sie würde lieber sterben, als ...
**soot** [sʊt] *n.* Ruß, *der*
**soothe** [su:ð] *v. t.* **a)** *(calm)* beruhigen; **b)** lindern ‹*Schmerz*›
'**sooty** *adj.* verrußt; rußig
**sophisticated** [sə'fɪstɪkeɪtɪd] *adj.* **a)** *(cultured)* kultiviert; **b)** *(elaborate, complex)* hochentwickelt; subtil ‹*Argument, System*›
**soporific** [sɒpə'rɪfɪk] *adj.* einschläfernd
**sopping** ['sɒpɪŋ] *adj. & adv.* ~ |wet| völlig durchnäßt
**soppy** ['sɒpɪ] *adj. (Brit. coll.)* rührselig; sentimental ‹*Person*›
**soprano** [sə'prɑ:nəʊ] *n.* Sopran, *der; (female also)* Sopranistin, *die*
**sordid** ['sɔ:dɪd] *adj.* dreckig; unerfreulich ‹*Detail, Geschichte*›
**sore** [sɔ:(r)] **1.** *adj.* weh; *(inflamed or injured)* wund; **a ~ throat** Halsschmerzen *Pl.;* **sb. has a ~ back/foot** *etc.* jmdm. tut der Rücken/Fuß *usw.* weh. **2.** *n.* wunde Stelle. '**sorely** *adv.* sehr; dringend ‹*nötig*›; ~ **tempted** stark versucht
**sorrow** ['sɒrəʊ] *n.* Kummer, *der*
**sorry** ['sɒrɪ] *adj.* **a) sb. is ~ that ...:** es tut jmdm. leid, daß ...; **sb. is ~ about sth.** jmdm. tut etwas leid; **I am *or* feel ~ for him** er tut mir leid; **sb. is *or* feels ~ for sth.** jmd. bedauert etw.; ~! Entschuldigung!; ~**?** wie bitte?; **I'm ~ to say** leider; **you'll be ~!** das wird dir noch leid tun; **b)** *(wretched)* traurig
**sort** [sɔ:t] **1.** *n.* **a)** Art, *die; (type)* Sorte, *die;* **a new ~ of bicycle** ein neuartiges Fahrrad; **all ~s of ...:** alle möglichen ...; **there are all ~s of things to do**

es gibt alles mögliche *od.* allerlei zu tun; ~ **of** *(coll.: more or less)* mehr oder weniger; **nothing of the ~:** nichts dergleichen; **b) be out of ~s** nicht in Form sein. **2.** *v. t.* sortieren. **sort 'out** *v. t.* **a)** *(settle)* klären; schlichten ‹*Streit*›; beenden ‹*Verwirrung*›; **b)** *(select)* aussuchen
'**sort code** *n.* Bankleitzahl, *die*
**sortie** ['sɔ:tɪ] *n.* Ausfall, *der; (flight)* Einsatz, *der*
**SOS** *n.* SOS, *das*
'**so so,** '**so-so** *adj., adv.* so lala *(ugs.)*
**soufflé** ['su:fleɪ] *n.* Soufflé, *das*
**sought** *see* **seek**
**soul** [səʊl] *n.* Seele, *die;* **not a ~:** keine Menschenseele
'**soul-destroying** *adj.* **a)** *(boring)* nervtötend; **b)** *(depressing)* deprimierend
**soulful** ['səʊlfl] *adj.* gefühlvoll; *(sad)* schwermütig
**soul:** ~ **mate** *n.* Seelenverwandte, *der/die;* ~-**searching** *n.* Gewissenskampf, *der*
¹**sound** [saʊnd] **1.** *adj.* **a)** *(healthy)* gesund; intakt ‹*Gebäude, Mauerwerk*›; **of ~ mind** im Vollbesitz der geistigen Kräfte; **b)** *(well-founded)* vernünftig ‹*Argument, Rat*›; klug ‹*Wahl*›; **it makes ~ sense** es ist sehr vernünftig; **c)** *(Finance: secure)* gesund, solide ‹*Basis*›; klug ‹*Investition*›. **2.** *adv.* fest, tief ‹*schlafen*›
²**sound 1.** *n.* **a)** *(Phys.)* Schall, *der;* **b)** *(noise)* Laut, *der; (of wind, sea, car, footsteps, breaking glass or twigs)* Geräusch, *das; (of voices, laughter, bell)* Klang, *der;* **do sth. without a ~:** etw. lautlos tun; **c)** *(Radio, Telev., Cinemat.)* Ton, *der;* **d)** *(fig.: impression)* **I like the ~ of your plan** ich finde, Ihr Plan hört sich gut an; **I don't like the ~ of this** das hört sich nicht gut an. **2.** *v. i.* klingen; **it ~s as if .../like ...:** es klingt, als .../wie ...; **that ~s a good idea to me** ich finde, die Idee hört sich gut an; **that ~s odd to me** das hört sich seltsam an, finde ich; ~**s good to me!** klingt gut! *(ugs.).* **3.** *v. t.* **a)** ertönen lassen; **b)** *(utter)* ~ **a note of caution** zur Vorsicht mahnen. **sound 'off** *v. i.* tönen *(ugs.),* schwadronieren **(on, about,** von**). sound 'out** *v. i.* ausfragen ‹*Person*›; ~ **sb. out on sth.** bei jmdm. wegen etw. vorfühlen
**sound:** ~ **barrier** *n.* Schallmauer, *die;* ~ **effect** *n.* Geräuscheffekt, *der*
'**sounding-board** *n.* **a)** *(Mus.)* Decke,

*die;* **b)** *(fig.: trial audience)* ≈ Test-gruppe, *die*

'**soundless** *adj.* lautlos

'**soundly** *adv.* **a)** *(solidly)* stabil, solide ⟨*bauen*⟩; **b)** *(deeply)* tief, fest ⟨*schlafen*⟩; **c)** *(thoroughly)* ordentlich *(ugs.)* ⟨*verhauen*⟩; vernichtend ⟨*schlagen, besiegen*⟩

**sound:** ~-**proof** 1. *adj.* schalldicht; 2. *v.t.* schalldicht machen; ~-**track** *n.* Soundtrack, *der;* ~-**wave** *n.* Schallwelle, *die*

**soup** [su:p] *n.* Suppe, *die;* **be/land in the** ~ *(fig. sl.)* in der Patsche sitzen/landen *(ugs.)*

**soup:** ~-**plate** *n.* Suppenteller, *der;* ~-**spoon** *n.* Suppenlöffel, *der*

**sour** ['saʊə(r)] *adj.* **a)** sauer; **b)** *(morose)* griesgrämig; säuerlich ⟨*Blick*⟩; **c)** *(unpleasant)* bitter

**source** [sɔ:s] *n.* Quelle, *die;* ~ **of income/infection** Einkommensquelle, *die*/Infektionsherd, *der;* **at** ~: an der Quelle

**south** [saʊθ] 1. *n.* **a)** Süden, *der;* **in/to|wards|/from the** ~: im/nach/von Süden; **to the** ~ **of** südlich von; **b)** *usu.* **S~** *(Geog., Polit.)* Süden, *der.* 2. *adj.* südlich; Süd⟨*küste, -wind, -grenze*⟩. 3. *adv.* nach Süden; ~ **of** südlich von

**South:** ~ '**Africa** *pr. n.* Südafrika *(das);* ~ '**African** *adj.* südafrika-nisch; ~ **A'merica** *pr. n.* Südamerika *(das);* ~ **A'merican** *adj.* südamerika-nisch; **s~-bound** *adj.* ⟨*Zug, Verkehr usw.*⟩ in Richtung Süden; **s~-'east** 1. *n.* Südosten, *der;* 2. *adj.* südöstlich; Südost⟨*wind, -küste*⟩; 3. *adv.* südost-wärts; nach Südosten; **s~-'eastern** *adj.* südöstlich

**southerly** ['sʌðəlɪ] *adj.* südlich; ⟨*Wind*⟩ aus südlichen Richtungen

**southern** ['sʌðən] *adj.* südlich; Süd-⟨*grenze, -hälfte, -seite*⟩

**South:** ~ '**Germany** *pr. n.* Süd-deutschland *(das);* ~ '**Pole** *pr. n.* Süd-pol, *der*

**southward[s]** ['saʊθwəd(s)] *adv.* südwärts

**south:** ~-'**west** 1. *n.* Südwesten, *der;* 2. *adj.* südwestlich; Südwest⟨*wind, -küste*⟩; 3. *adv.* südwestwärts; nach Südwesten; ~-'**western** *adj.* süd-westlich

**souvenir** [su:və'nɪə(r)] *n.* Souvenir, *das* (**of** aus)

**sovereign** ['sɒvrɪn] *n.* *(ruler)* Souve-rän, *der.* **sovereignty** ['sɒvrɪntɪ] *n.* Souveränität, *die*

**Soviet** ['səʊvɪət, 'sɒvɪət] *adj. (Hist.)* so-wjetisch; Sowjet⟨*bürger, -literatur*⟩

**Soviet 'Union** *pr. n. (Hist.)* Sowjet-union, *die*

¹**sow** [səʊ] *v.t., p.p.* **sown** [səʊn] *or* **sowed** *v.t.* **a)** *(plant)* [aus]säen; **b)** einsäen ⟨*Feld, Boden*⟩

²**sow** [saʊ] *n. (female pig)* Sau, *die*

**sown** *see* ¹**sow**

**soya [bean]** ['sɔɪə (bi:n)] *n.* Sojaboh-ne, *die*

**spa** [spa:] *n.* **a)** *(place)* Bad, *das;* Bade-ort, *der;* **b)** *(spring)* Mineralquelle, *die*

**space** [speɪs] *n.* **a)** Raum, *der;* **b)** *(interval between points)* Platz, *der;* **clear a** ~: Platz schaffen; **c) the wide open** ~**s** das weite, flache Land; **d)** *(Astron.)* Weltraum, *der;* **e)** *(blank between words)* Zwischenraum, *der;* **f)** *(interval of time)* Zeitraum, *der;* **in the** ~ **of a minute/an hour** innerhalb einer Minu-te/Stunde; **in a short** ~ **of time he was back** nach kurzer Zeit war er zurück.

**space 'out** *v.t.* verteilen

**space:** ~ **age** *n.* [Welt]raumzeitalter, *das;* ~-**bar** *n.* Leertaste, *die;* ~**craft** *n.* Raumfahrzeug, *das;* ~-**saving** *adj.* platzsparend; ~-**ship** *n.* Raum-schiff, *das;* ~-**suit** *n.* Raumanzug, *der;* ~ **travel** *n.* Raumfahrt, *die*

**spacious** ['speɪʃəs] *adj.* geräumig

**spade** [speɪd] *n.* **a)** Spaten, *der;* **b)** *(Cards)* Pik, *das; see also* **club** I c

**spaghetti** [spə'getɪ] *n.* Spaghetti *Pl.*

**Spain** [speɪn] *pr. n.* Spanien *(das)*

**span** [spæn] 1. *n.* **a)** Spanne, *die;* Zeit-spanne, *die;* **b)** *(of bridge)* Spannwei-te, *die.* 2. *v.t.,* -**nn**- überspannen ⟨*Fluß*⟩; umfassen ⟨*Zeitraum*⟩

**Spaniard** ['spænjəd] *n.* Spanier, *der*/Spanierin, *die*

**Spanish** ['spænɪʃ] 1. *adj.* spanisch; *sb.* **is** ~: jmd. ist Spanier/Spanierin. 2. *n.* **a)** *(language)* Spanisch, *das; see also* **English 2 a;** **b) the** ~ *pl.* die Spanier

**spank** [spæŋk] 1. *n.* ≈ Klaps, *der (ugs.).* 2. *v.t.* ~ **sb.** jmdm. den Hintern versohlen *(ugs.)*

**spanner** ['spænə(r)] *n. (Brit.)* Schrau-benschlüssel, *der*

**spar** [spa:(r)] *v.i.,* -**rr**-: **a)** *(Boxing)* sparren; **b)** *(fig.: argue)* [sich] zanken

**spare** [speə(r)] 1. *adj.* **a)** *(not in use)* übrig; ~ **time/moment** Freizeit, *die*/freier Augenblick; **there is one** ~ **seat** ein Platz ist noch frei; **b)** *(for use when needed)* zusätzlich, Extra⟨*bett, -tasse*⟩; ~ **room** Gästezimmer, *das.* 2. *n.* Ersatzteil, *das*/-reifen, *der usw.* 3.

*v. t.* **a)** entbehren; **we arrived with ten minutes to ~:** wir kamen zehn Minuten früher an; **b)** *(not inflict on)* **~ sb. sth.** jmdm. etw. ersparen; **c)** *(not hurt)* [ver]schonen; **d)** *(fail to use)* **not ~ any expense/pains** *or* **efforts** keine Kosten/Mühe scheuen; **no expense ~d** an nichts gespart

**spare:** **~ 'part** *n.* Ersatzteil, *das;* **~ 'tyre** *n.* Reserve-, Ersatzreifen, *der;* **~ 'wheel** *n.* Ersatzrad, *das*

**sparing** ['speərɪŋ] *adj.* sparsam

**spark** [spɑːk] **1.** *n.* **a)** Funke, *der; (fig.)* **a ~ of generosity/decency** ein Funke[n] Großzügigkeit/Anstand; **b) a bright ~** *(person, also iron.)* ein schlauer Kopf. **2.** *v. t.* **~ |off|** zünden; *(fig.)* auslösen

**sparkle** ['spɑːkl] **1.** *v. i.* **a)** ⟨*Diamant:*⟩ glitzern; ⟨*Augen:*⟩ funkeln; **b)** *(be lively)* sprühen **(with** vor + *Dat.).* **2.** *n.* Funkeln, *das.* **sparkling** ['spɑːklɪŋ] *adj.* glitzernd ⟨*Diamant*⟩; funkelnd ⟨*Augen*⟩. **sparkling 'wine** *n.* Schaumwein, *der*

**'spark-plug** *n.* Zündkerze, *die*

**sparrow** ['spærəʊ] *n.* Spatz, *der*

**sparse** [spɑːs] *adj.* spärlich; dünn ⟨*Besiedlung*⟩

**spasm** ['spæzm] *n.* Krampf, *der*

**spasmodic** [spæz'mɒdɪk] *adj.* **a)** *(marked by spasms)* krampfartig; **b)** *(intermittent)* sporadisch

**spastic** ['spæstɪk] **1.** *n.* Spastiker, *der/* Spastikerin, *die.* **2.** *adj.* spastisch

**spat** *see* spit 1, 2

**spate** [speɪt] *n.* **a) the river is in |full| ~:** der Fluß führt Hochwasser; **b)** *(fig.)* **a ~ of sth.** eine Flut von etw.; **a ~ of burglaries** eine Einbruchsserie

**spatial** ['speɪʃl] *adj.* räumlich

**spatter** ['spætə(r)] *v. t.* spritzen; **~ sb./sth. with sth.** jmdn./etw. mit etw. bespritzen

**spatula** ['spætjʊlə] *n.* Spachtel, *die*

**spawn** [spɔːn] **1.** *v. t. (fig.)* hervorbringen. **2.** *v. i. (Zool.)* laichen. **3.** *n. (Zool.)* Laich, *der*

**speak** [spiːk] **1.** *v. i.,* spoke [spəʊk], spoken ['spəʊkn] **a)** sprechen; **~ |with sb.| on** *or* **about sth.** [mit jmdm.] über etw. *(Akk.)* sprechen; **~ for/against sth.** sich für/gegen etw. aussprechen; **b)** *(on telephone)* **Is Mr Grant there? –** S~ing! Ist Mister Grant da? – Am Apparat!; **who is ~ing, please?** wer ist am Apparat, bitte? **2.** *v. t.,* spoke, spoken sprechen ⟨*Satz, Wort, Sprache*⟩; sagen ⟨*Wahrheit*⟩; **~ one's mind** sagen, was man denkt. **'speak**

**for** *v. t.* sprechen für; **sth. is spoken for** *(reserved)* etw. ist schon vergeben. **'speak of** *v. t.* sprechen von; **~ing of Mary** da wir gerade von Mary sprechen; **nothing to ~ of** nichts Besonderes. **'speak to** *v. t.* sprechen *od.* reden mit. **speak 'up** *v. i.* lauter sprechen

**'speaker** *n.* **a)** *(in public)* Redner, *der/*Rednerin, *die;* **b)** *(of a language)* Sprecher *der/*Sprecherin, *die;* **be a 'French ~:** Französisch sprechen; **c)** *(loudspeaker)* Lautsprecher, *der*

**'speaking 1.** *n.* Sprechen, *das;* **~ clock** *(Brit.)* telefonische Zeitansage. **2.** *adv.* **strictly/generally ~:** genaugenommen/im allgemeinen

**spear** [spɪə(r)] *n.* Speer, *der.* **'spearhead 1.** *n. (fig.)* Speerspitze, *die.* **2.** *v. t. (fig.)* anführen. **'spearmint** *n.* Grüne Minze; **~ chewing-gum** Pfefferminzkaugummi, *der od. das*

**special** ['speʃl] *adj.* speziell; besonder...; **nobody ~:** niemand Besonderer. **special de'livery** *n. (Post)* Eilzustellung, *die*

**specialist** ['speʃəlɪst] *n.* **a)** Spezialist, *der/*Spezialistin, *die* (in für); **b)** *(Med.)* Facharzt, *der/*-ärztin, *die*

**speciality** [speʃɪ'ælɪtɪ] *n.* Spezialität, *die*

**specialize** ['speʃəlaɪz] *v. i.* sich spezialisieren **(in** auf + *Akk.*)

**'specially** *adv.* **a)** speziell; **make sth. ~:** etw. speziell *od.* extra anfertigen; **b)** *(especially)* besonders

**special 'offer** *n.* Sonderangebot, *das;* **on ~:** im Sonderangebot

**specialty** ['speʃltɪ] *(esp. Amer.) see* speciality

**species** ['spiːʃiːz] *n., pl. same* Art, *die*

**specific** [spɪ'sɪfɪk] *adj.* bestimmt; **could you be more ~?** kannst du dich genauer ausdrücken? **specifically** [spɪ'sɪfɪkəlɪ] *adv.* ausdrücklich; eigens; extra *(ugs.)*

**specification** [spesɪfɪ'keɪʃn] *n., often pl. (details)* technische Daten; *(for building)* Baubeschreibung, *die*

**specify** ['spesɪfaɪ] *v. t.* ausdrücklich sagen; **unless otherwise specified** wenn nicht anders angegeben

**specimen** ['spesɪmən] *n.* **a)** *(example)* Exemplar, *das;* **b)** *(sample)* Probe, *die*

**speck** [spek] *n.* **a)** *(spot)* Fleck, *der;* **b)** *(particle)* Teilchen, *das;* **~ of soot/dust** Rußflocke, *die/*Staubkörnchen, *das*

**specs** [speks] *n. pl. (coll.: spectacles)* Brille, *die*

**spectacle** ['spektəkl] *n.* a) *in pl.* |pair of| ~s Brille, *die;* b) *(public show)* Spektakel, *das;* c) *(object of attention)* Anblick, *der.* '**spectacle case** *n.* Brillenetui, *das*

**spectacular** [spek'tækjʊlə(r)] *adj.* spektakulär

**spectator** [spek'teɪtə(r)] *n.* Zuschauer, *der*/Zuschauerin, *die*

**specter** *(Amer.) see* **spectre**

**spectra** *pl. of* **spectrum**

**spectre** ['spektə(r)] *n. (Brit.)* a) *(ghost)* Gespenst, *das;* b) *(fig.)* Schreckgespenst, *das*

**spectrum** ['spektrəm] *n., pl.* **spectra** ['spektrə] Spektrum, *das*

**speculate** ['spekjʊleɪt] *v.i.* spekulieren (**about, on** über + *Akk.*). **speculation** [spekjʊ'leɪʃn] *n.* Spekulation, *die* (**over** über + *Akk.*). **speculative** ['spekjʊlətɪv] *adj.* spekulativ. **speculator** ['spekjʊleɪtə(r)] *n.* Spekulant, *der*/Spekulantin, *die*

**sped** *see* **speed 2**

**speech** [spiːtʃ] *n.* a) *(public address)* Rede, *die;* **make** *or* **deliver** *or* **give a** ~: eine Rede halten; b) *(faculty or manner of speaking)* Sprache, *die.* '**speechless** *adj.* sprachlos (**with** vor + *Dat.*)

**speed** [spiːd] 1. *n.* Geschwindigkeit, *die;* Schnelligkeit, *die;* **at a** ~ **of ...:** mit einer Geschwindigkeit von ... 2. *v.i.* a) *p.t. & p.p.* **sped** [sped] *or* **speeded** schnell fahren; rasen *(ugs.);* b) *p.t. & p.p.* **speeded** *(go too fast)* zu schnell fahren; rasen *(ugs.).* '**speedboat** *n.* Rennboot, *das*

'**speeding** *n.* Geschwindigkeitsüberschreitung, *die*

'**speed limit** *n.* Geschwindigkeitsbeschränkung, *die*

**speedometer** [spiː'dɒmɪtə(r)] *n.* Tachometer, *der od. das*

'**speedy** *adj.* schnell; umgehend, prompt *(Antwort)*

¹**spell** [spel] 1. *v.t.,* **spelt** [spelt] *(Brit.) or* **spelled** a) schreiben; *(aloud)* buchstabieren; b) *(fig.: mean)* bedeuten. 2. *v.i.,* **spelt** *(Brit.) or* **spelled** *(say)* buchstabieren; *(write)* richtig schreiben

²**spell** *n. (period)* Weile, *die;* **a cold** ~**:** eine Kälteperiode

³**spell** *n.* a) *(magic charm)* Zauberspruch, *der;* **cast a** ~ **on sb.** jmdn. verzaubern; b) *(fascination)* Zauber, *der;* **break the** ~: den Bann brechen. '**spellbound** *adj.* verzaubert

'**spelling** *n.* Rechtschreibung, *die*

**spelt** *see* ¹**spell**

**spend** [spend] *v.t.,* **spent** [spent] a) *(pay out)* ausgeben; ~ **a penny** *(fig. coll.)* mal verschwinden *(ugs.);* b) verbringen ⟨*Zeit*⟩. '**spendthrift** *n.* Verschwender, *der*/Verschwenderin, *die*

**spent** 1. *see* **spend**. 2. *adj.* a) *(used up)* verbraucht; b) *(drained of energy)* erschöpft

**sperm** ['spɜːm] *n. pl* ~**s** *or same (Biol.)* Sperma, *der*

**spew** [spjuː] *v.t.* spucken

**sphere** [sfɪə(r)] *n.* a) *(field of action)* Bereich, *der;* Sphäre, *die (geh.);* b) *(Geom.)* Kugel, *die.* **spherical** ['sferɪkl] *adj.* kugelförmig

**spice** [spaɪs] 1. *n.* Gewürz, *das; (fig.)* Würze, *die.* 2. *v.t.* würzen. **spicy** ['spaɪsɪ] *adj.* pikant; würzig

**spider** ['spaɪdə(r)] *n.* Spinne, *die*

**spike** [spaɪk] *n.* Stachel, *der.* **spiky** ['spaɪkɪ] *adj.* stachelig

**spill** [spɪl] 1. *v.t.,* **spilt** [spɪlt] *or* **spilled** verschütten ⟨*Flüssigkeit*⟩; ~ **sth. on** ɜth. etw. auf etw. *(Akk.)* schütten; ~ **the beans** aus der Schule plaudern. 2. *v.i.,* **spilt** *or* **spilled** überlaufen

**spilt** *see* **spill**

**spin** [spɪn] 1. *v.t.,* **-nn-,** **spun** [spʌn] a) spinnen; ~ **yarn** Garn spinnen; b) *(in washing-machine etc.)* schleudern. 2. *v.i.,* **-nn-,** **spun** sich drehen; **my head is** ~**ning** *(fig.)* mir schwirrt der Kopf. **spin 'out** *v.t. (prolong)* in die Länge ziehen

**spinach** ['spɪnɪdʒ] *n.* Spinat, *der*

**spinal** ['spaɪnl] *adj.* Wirbelsäulen-; Rückgrat[s]-. **spinal 'column** *n.* Wirbelsäule, *die.* **spinal 'cord** *n.* Rückenmark, *das*

**spindle** ['spɪndl] *n.* Spindel, *die.* **spindly** ['spɪndlɪ] *adj.* spindeldürr

**spin-'drier** *n.* Wäscheschleuder, *die* **spin-'dry** *v.t.* schleudern

**spine** [spaɪn] *n.* a) *(backbone)* Wirbelsäule, *die;* b) *(Bot., Zool.)* Stachel, *der.* '**spineless** *adj. (fig.)* rückgratlos

'**spin-off** *n.* Nebenprodukt, *das*

**spinster** ['spɪnstə(r)] *n.* ledige Frau

**spiny** ['spaɪnɪ] *adj.* stachelig

**spiral** ['spaɪrl] 1. *adj.* spiralförmig. 2. *n.* Spirale, *die.* 3. *v.i., (Brit.)* **-ll-** ⟨*Weg:*⟩ sich hochwinden; ⟨*Kosten:*⟩ in die Höhe klettern; ⟨*Rauch:*⟩ in einer Spirale aufsteigen. **spiral 'staircase** *n.* Wendeltreppe, *die*

**spire** [spaɪə(r)] *n.* Turmspitze, *die*

**spirit** ['spɪrɪt] *n.* a) *in pl. (distilled liquor)* Spirituosen *Pl.;* b) *(mental atti-*

*tude)* Geisteshaltung, *die;* **in the right/
wrong ~:** mit der richtigen/falschen
Einstellung; **take sth. in the wrong ~:**
etw. falsch auffassen; **c)** *(courage)*
Mut, *der;* **d)** *(mental tendency)* Geist,
*der;* **high ~s** gehobene Stimmung; **in
poor** *or* **low ~s** niedergedrückt.
'**spirited** *adj.* beherzt
'**spirit-level** *n.* Wasserwaage, *die*
**spiritual** ['spɪrɪtʃʊəl] *adj.* spirituell
*(geh.)*
**spit** [spɪt] **1.** *v.i.,* -tt-, **spat** [spæt] *or* **spit**
spucken. **2.** *v.t.,* -tt-, **spat** *or* **spit**
spucken. **3.** *n.* Spucke, *die.* **spit 'out**
*v.t.* ausspucken
**spite** [spaɪt] **1.** *n.* **a)** Boshaftigkeit, *die;*
**b) in ~ of** trotz; **in ~ of oneself** obwohl
man es eigentlich nicht will. **2.** *v.t.* ärgern. **spiteful** ['spaɪtfl] *adj.* gehässig
**spittle** ['spɪtl] *n.* Spucke, *die*
**splash** [splæʃ] **1.** *v.t.* spritzen; **~ sth.
on |to|** *or* **over sb./sth.** jmdn./etw. mit
etw. bespritzen. **2.** *v.i.* **a)** spritzen; **b)**
*(in water)* platschen *(ugs.).* **3.** *n.* **a)**
*(liquid)* Spritzer, *der;* **b)** *(noise)* Plätschern, *das*
**splendid** ['splendɪd] *adj.* *(excellent)*
großartig; *(magnificent)* prächtig
**splendour** *(Brit.; Amer.:* **splendor)**
['splendə(r)] *n.* Pracht, *die*
**splint** [splɪnt] *n.* Schiene, *die*
**splinter** ['splɪntə(r)] *n.* Splitter, *der*
**split** [splɪt] **1.** *n.* **a)** *(tear)* Riß, *der;* **b)**
*(division into parts)* [Auf]teilung, *die;*
*(fig.)* Spaltung, *die.* **2.** *adj.* gespalten;
**be ~ on a question** [sich *(Dat.)*] in einer
Frage uneins sein. **3.** *v.t.,* -tt-, **split a)**
*(tear)* zerreißen; **b)** *(divide)* teilen. **4.**
*v.i.,* -tt-, **split a)** ⟨*Holz:*⟩ splittern;
⟨*Stoff, Seil:*⟩ reißen; **~ apart** zersplittern; **b)** *(divide into parts)* sich teilen.
**split 'up 1.** *v.t.* aufteilen. **2.** *v.i. (coll.)*
sich trennen; **~ up with sb.** sich von
jmdm. trennen
**splutter** ['splʌtə(r)] *v.i.* ⟨*Person:*⟩ pru-
sten; ⟨*Motor:*⟩ stottern
**spoil** [spɔɪl] **1.** *v.t.,* **spoilt** [spɔɪlt] *or*
**spoiled a)** *(impair)* verderben; **b)**
*(pamper)* verwöhnen; **be ~t for choice**
die Qual der Wahl haben. **2.** *v.i.,*
**spoilt** *or* **spoiled a)** verderben; **b) be
~ing for a fight** Streit suchen. **3.** *n.* **~|s**
*pl.|* Beute, *die.* '**spoilsport** *n.* Spiel-
verderber, *der/*-verderberin, *die*
**spoilt** *see* **spoil 1, 2**
'**spoke** [spəʊk] *n.* Speiche, *die*
²**spoke, spoken** *see* **speak**
**spokesman** ['spəʊksmən] *n.,* *pl.*
**spokesmen** ['spəʊksmən] Sprecher, *der*

**sponge** [spʌndʒ] **1.** *n.* Schwamm, *der.*
**2.** *v.t.* mit einem Schwamm waschen.
'**sponge on** *v.t.* **~ on sb.** bei *od.* von
jmdm. schnorren *(ugs.)*
**sponge: ~-bag** *n. (Brit.)* Kulturbeutel, *der;* **~-cake** *n.* Biskuitkuchen,
*der*
**sponger** ['spʌndʒə(r)] *n.* Schmarotzer, *der/*Schmarotzerin, *die*
**spongy** ['spʌndʒɪ] *adj.* schwammig
**sponsor** ['spɒnsə(r)] **1.** *n.* Sponsor,
*der.* **2.** *v.t.* **a)** sponsern; **b)** *(Polit.)* **~
sb.** jmds. Kandidatur unterstützen
**spontaneous** [spɒn'teɪnɪəs] *adj.*
spontan
**spooky** ['spuːkɪ] *adj.* gespenstisch
**spool** [spuːl] *n.* Spule, *die*
**spoon** [spuːn] *n.* **a)** Löffel, *der;* **b)**
*(amount) see* **spoonful. spoonful**
['spuːnfʊl] *n.* **a ~ of sugar** ein Löffel
[voll] Zucker
**sporadic** [spə'rædɪk] *adj.* sporadisch
**spore** [spɔː(r)] *n.* Spore, *die*
**sport** [spɔːt] **1.** *n.* **a)** Sport, *der;* **~s**
Sportarten; **water/indoor ~:** Wasser-/
Hallensport, *der;* **b)** *(fun)* Spaß, *der;*
**c) be a |real| ~** *(coll.)* ein prima Kerl
sein *(ugs.);* **be a ~!** sei kein Spielverderber! **2.** *v.t.* stolz tragen. '**sporting**
*adj.* **a)** sportlich; **b) give sb. a ~ chance**
jmdm. eine [faire] Chance geben
**sports: ~ car** *n.* Sportwagen, *der;* **~
jacket** *n.* sportlicher Sakko; **~man**
['spɔːtsmən] *n., pl.* **~men** ['spɔːtsmən]
Sportler, *der;* **~manship** ['spɔːts-
mənʃɪp] *n. (fairness)* [sportliche] Fairneß; **~wear** *n.* Sport[be]kleidung,
*die;* **~woman** *n.* Sportlerin, *die*
'**sporty** *adj.* sportlich
**spot** [spɒt] **1.** *n.* **a)** *(precise place)* Stelle, *die;* **on this ~:** an dieser Stelle; **be
in a tight ~** *(fig. coll.)* in der Klemme
sitzen *(ugs.);* **put sb. on the ~** *(fig. coll.)*
jmdn. in Verlegenheit bringen; **b)**
*(suitable area)* Platz, *der;* **c)** *(dot)* Tup-
fen, *der;* **d)** *(stain)* **~ |of blood/grease/
ink|** [Blut-/Fett-/Tinten]fleck, *der;* **e)**
*(Brit. coll.: small amount)* **do a ~ of**
work/sewing ein bißchen arbeiten/nä-
hen; **f)** *(drop)* **a ~** *or* **a few ~s of rain**
ein paar Regentropfen; **g)** *(Med.)*
Pickel, *der.* **2.** *v.t.,* -tt- *(detect)* entdecken; erkennen ⟨*Gefahr*⟩
**spot: ~ 'check** *n.* Stichprobe, *die;*
**~less** *adj.* fleckenlos; **her house is absolutely ~** *(fig.)* ihr Haus ist makellos
sauber; **~light** *n.* Scheinwerfer, *der;*
**be in the ~light** *(fig.)* im Rampenlicht
stehen

**spotted** ['spɒtɪd] *adj.* gepunktet
'**spotty** *adj. (pimply)* picklig
**spouse** [spaʊs] *n.* [Ehe]gatte, *der/*-gattin, *die*
**spout** [spaʊt] **1.** *n.* Schnabel, *der; (of tap)* Ausflußrohr, *das.* **2.** *v. i. (gush)* schießen (from aus)
**sprain** [spreɪn] **1.** *v. t.* verstauchen. **2.** *n.* Verstauchung, *die*
**sprang** see **spring** 2, 3
**sprawl** [sprɔ:l] *v. i.* **a)** sich ausstrecken; *(fall)* der Länge nach hinfallen; **b)** *(straggle)* sich ausbreiten
'**spray** [spreɪ] *(bouquet)* Strauß, *der*
²**spray** **1.** *v. t.* spritzen; sprühen ‹*Parfüm*›; besprühen ‹*Haar, Pflanze*›. **2.** *n.* **a)** *(drops)* Sprühnebel, *der;* **b)** *(liquid)* Spray, *der od. das*
**spread** [spred] **1.** *v. t.,* **spread a)** ausbreiten ‹*Tuch, Landkarte*› (**on** auf + *Dat.*); streichen ‹*Butter, Farbe, Marmelade*›; **b)** *(extend range of)* verbreiten; **c)** *(distribute)* verteilen. **2.** *v. i.,* **spread** sich ausbreiten. **3.** *n.* **a)** Verbreitung, *die; (of city, poverty)* Ausbreitung, *die;* **b)** *(coll.: meal)* Festessen, *das;* **c)** *(paste)* Brotaufstrich, *der.*
**spread 'out 1.** *v. t.* ausbreiten. **2.** *v. i.* sich verteilen
**spree** [spri:] *n.* **go on a shopping ~:** ganz groß einkaufen gehen
**sprig** [sprɪg] *n.* Zweig, *der*
**sprightly** ['spraɪtlɪ] *adj.* munter
**spring** [sprɪŋ] **1.** *n.* **a)** *(season)* Frühling, *der;* **in** [**the**] **~:** im Frühling *od.* Frühjahr; **b)** *(water)* Quelle, *die;* **c)** *(Mech.)* Feder, *die;* **d)** *(jump)* Sprung, *der.* **2.** *v. i.,* **sprang** [spræŋ] *or (Amer.)* **sprung** [sprʌŋ], **sprung a)** *(jump)* springen; **~ to life** *(fig.)* [plötzlich] zum Leben erwachen; **b)** *(arise)* entspringen (**from** *Dat.*). **3.** *v. t.,* **sprang** *or (Amer.)* **sprung, sprung; ~ sth. on sb.** jmdn. mit etw. überfallen
**spring:** **~board** *n.* Sprungbrett, *das;* **~-'clean 1.** *n.* Frühjahrsputz, *der;* **2.** *v. t.* Frühjahrsputz machen; **~ 'onion** *n.* Frühlingszwiebel, *die;* **~time** *n.* Frühling, *der*
**sprinkle** ['sprɪŋkl] *v. t.* streuen; sprengen ‹*Flüssigkeit*›. **sprinkler** ['sprɪŋklə(r)] *n. (Hort.)* Sprinkler, *der*
**sprint** [sprɪnt] **1.** *v. t. & i.* rennen; sprinten *(bes. Sport).* **2.** *n.* Sprint, *der*
**sprout** [spraʊt] **1.** *n.* **a)** Brussels **~s** Rosenkohl, *der;* **b)** *(Bot.)* Trieb, *der.* **2.** *v. i.* sprießen *(geh.)*
**spruce** [spru:s] **1.** *adj.* gepflegt. **2.** *n.* Fichte, *die*

**sprung** [sprʌŋ] **1.** *see* **spring** 2, 3. **2.** *attrib. adj.* gefedert
**spud** [spʌd] *n. (sl.)* Kartoffel, *die*
**spun** see **spin**
**spur** [spɜ:(r)] **1.** *n.* Sporn, *der; (fig.)* Ansporn, *der;* **on the ~ of the moment** ganz spontan. **2.** *v. t.,* **-rr-** *(fig.)* anspornen
**spurious** ['spjʊərɪəs] *adj.* gespielt ‹*Interesse*›; zweifelhaft ‹*Anspruch*›
**spurn** [spɜ:n] *v. t.* zurückweisen
'**spurt** [spɜ:t] *n.* Spurt, *der;* **put on a ~:** einen Spurt einlegen
²**spurt 1.** *v. i.* **~ out** |**from** *or* **of**| herausspritzen (aus). **2.** *n.* Strahl, *der*
**spy** [spaɪ] **1.** *n.* Spion, *der/*Spionin, *die.* **2.** *v. i.* spionieren; **~ on sb.** jmdm. nachspionieren
**squabble** ['skwɒbl] **1.** *n.* Streit, *der.* **2.** *v. i.* sich zanken (**over, about** wegen)
**squad** [skwɒd] *n.* **a)** *(Mil.)* Gruppe, *die;* **b)** *(group)* Mannschaft, *die*
**squadron** ['skwɒdrən] *n.* **a)** *(Navy)* Geschwader, *das;* **b)** *(Air Force)* Staffel, *die*
**squalid** ['skwɒlɪd] *adj.* **a)** *(dirty)* schmutzig; **b)** *(poor)* schäbig
**squall** [skwɔ:l] *n. (gust)* Bö, *die*
**squalor** ['skwɒlə(r)] *n.* Schmutz, *der*
**squander** ['skwɒndə(r)] *v. t.* vergeuden
**square** [skweə(r)] **1.** *n.* **a)** *(Geom.)* Quadrat, *das;* **b)** *(open area)* Platz, *der.* **2.** *adj.* **a)** quadratisch; **b)** **a ~ foot/mile** ein Quadratfuß/eine Quadratmeile. **3.** *v. t.* **a)** *(Math.)* quadrieren; **b)** **~ it with sb.** es mit jmdm. klären. **4.** *v. i. (agree)* übereinstimmen.
**square 'up** *v. i. (settle up)* abrechnen
**square 'root** *n.* Quadratwurzel, *die*
**squash** [skwɒʃ] **1.** *v. t. (crush)* zerquetschen; **~ sth. flat** etw. platt drücken. **2.** *n.* **a)** Fruchtsaftgetränk, *das;* **b)** *(Sport)* Squash, *das*
**squat** [skwɒt] *v. i.,* **-tt-:** **a)** *(crouch)* hocken; **b)** **~ in a house** ein Haus besetzen. '**squatter** *n.* Hausbesetzer, *der/*-besetzerin, *die*
**squawk** [skwɔ:k] *v. i.* ‹*Krähe:*› krähen; ‹*Huhn:*› kreischen
**squeak** [skwi:k] **1.** *n.* **a)** *(of animal)* Quieken, *das;* **b)** *(of brakes, hinge, etc.)* Quietschen, *das.* **2.** *v. i.* **a)** ‹*Tier:*› quieken; **b)** ‹*Scharnier, Tür, Bremse, Schuh usw.:*› quietschen
**squeal** [skwi:l] **1.** *v. i.* **a)** **~ with pain/in fear** ‹*Person:*› vor Schmerz/Angst aufschreien; ‹*Tier:*› vor Schmerz/Angst laut quieken; **b)** ‹*Bremsen, Räder:*›

kreischen; ⟨*Reifen:*⟩ quietschen. **2.** *n.*
Kreischen, *das; (of tyres)* Quietschen,
*das; (of animal)* Quieken, *das*

**squeamish** ['skwi:mıʃ] *adj.* be ~:
zartbesaitet sein

**squeeze** [skwi:z] **1.** *n.* Druck, *der;* give
sth. a small ~: etw. [leicht] drücken. **2.**
*v.t.* **a)** *(press)* drücken; drücken auf
( + Akk.)⟨*Tube, Plastikflasche*⟩*; (to get
juice)* auspressen; **b)** *(extract)* drücken
(out of aus); ~ out sth. etw. heraus-
drücken; **c)** *(force)* zwängen

**squelch** [skweltʃ] *v.i.* quatschen *(ugs.)*

**squid** [skwıd] *n.* Kalmar, *der*

**squiggle** ['skwıgl] *n.* Schnörkel, *der*

**squint** [skwınt] **1.** *n.* Schielen, *das.* **2.**
*v.i.* **a)** *(Med.)* schielen; **b)** *(with half-
closed eyes)* blinzeln

**squire** ['skwaıə(r)] *n.* ≈ Gutsherr, *der*

**squirm** [skwɜ:m] *v.i.* sich winden
(with vor + *Dat.*)

**squirrel** ['skwırl] *n.* Eichhörnchen, *das*

**squirt** [skwɜ:t] **1.** *v.t.* spritzen; sprühen ⟨*Spray, Puder*⟩; ~ sth. at sb. jmdn.
mit etw. bespritzen/besprühen. **2.** *v.i.*
spritzen. **3.** *n.* Spritzer, *der*

**St** *abbr.* Saint St.

**St.** *abbr.* Street Str.

**st.** *abbr. (Brit.: unit of weight)* **stone**

**stab** [stæb] **1.** *v.t.*, **-bb-** stechen; ~ sb.
in the chest jmdm. in die Brust ste-
chen. **2.** *v.i.*, **-bb-** stechen. **3.** *n.* **a)**
Stich, *der;* **b)** *(coll.: attempt)* make *or*
have a ~ [at it] [es] probieren

**stability** [stə'bılıtı] *n.* Stabilität, *die*

**stabilize** ['steıbılaız] **1.** *v.t.* stabilisieren. **2.** *v.i.* sich stabilisieren

¹**stable** ['steıbl] *adj.* stabil; gefestigt
⟨*Person*⟩

²**stable** *n.* Stall, *der*

**stack** [stæk] **1.** *n.* **a)** *(pile)* Stoß, *der;*
Stapel, *der;* **b)** *(coll.: large amount)*
Haufen, *der (ugs.);* **c)** [chimney-]~:
Schornstein, *der.* **2.** *v.t.* ~ [up]
[auf]stapeln

**stadium** ['steıdıəm] *n.* Stadion, *das*

**staff** [stɑ:f] **1.** *n.* **a)** *(stick)* Stock, *der;*
**b)** *(personnel)* Personal, *das; (of
school)* Lehrkollegium, *das.* **2.** *v.t.* mit
Personal ausstatten. '**staff-room** *n.*
*(Sch.)* Lehrerzimmer, *das*

**stag** [stæg] *n.* Hirsch, *der*

**stage** [steıdʒ] **1.** *n.* **a)** *(Theatre)* Bühne,
*die;* **b)** *(part of process)* Stadium, *das;*
at this ~: in diesem Stadium; do sth.
by ~s etw. abschnittsweise tun; in the
final ~s in der Schlußphase; **c)** *(distance)* Etappe, *die.* **2.** *v.t.* **a)** *(present)*
inszenieren; **b)** *(arrange)* veranstalten

**stage: ~-coach** *n.* Postkutsche, *die;*
~ **door** *n.* Bühneneingang, *der;* ~
**fright** *n.* Lampenfieber, *das;*
~-**manage** *v.t. (fig.)* veranstalten

**stagger** ['stægə(r)] **1.** *v.i.* schwanken.
**2.** *v.t. (astonish)* die Sprache verschlagen ( + *Dat.*)

**stagnant** ['stægnənt] *adj.* **a)** stehend
⟨*Gewässer*⟩*;* **b)** *(Econ.)* stagnierend

**stagnate** [stæg'neıt] *v.i.* **a)** ⟨*Wasser:*⟩
abstehen; **b)** ⟨*Wirtschaft, Geschäft:*⟩
stagnieren; ⟨*Person:*⟩ abstumpfen.
**stagnation** [stæg'neıʃn] *n.* **a)** *(of
water)* Stehen, *das;* **b)** *(Econ.)* Stagnation, *die*

**staid** [steıd] *adj.* gesetzt

**stain** [steın] **1.** *v.t.* **a)** verfärben; *(make
~s on)* Flecken hinterlassen auf
( + *Dat.*); **b)** *(colour)* beizen ⟨*Holz*⟩. **2.**
*n.* Fleck, *der.* **stained 'glass** *n.* far-
biges Glas; ~ '**window** Fenster mit
Glasmalerei

'**stainless** *adj.* fleckenlos. **stainless
'steel** *n.* Edelstahl, *der*

**stair** [steə(r)] *n. (step)* [Treppen]stufe,
*die;* ~s Treppe, *die.* '**staircase** *n.*
Treppenhaus, *das*

**stake** [steık] *n.* **a)** *(pointed stick)* Pfahl,
*der;* **b)** *(wager)* Einsatz, *der;* be at ~:
auf dem Spiel stehen

**stale** [steıl] *adj.* alt; muffig; abgestanden ⟨*Luft*⟩; alt[backen] ⟨*Brot*⟩; schal
⟨*Bier, Wein usw.*⟩

'**stalemate** *n.* Patt, *das*

¹**stalk** [stɔ:k] *v.t.* sich heranpirschen
an ( + *Akk.*)

²**stalk** *n. (Bot.) (main stem)* Stengel,
*der; (of leaf, flower, fruit)* Stiel, *der*

**stall** [stɔ:l] **1.** *n.* **a)** Stand, *der;* **b)** *(Brit.
Theatre)* ~s Parkett, *das.* **2.** *v.t.* ab-
würgen *(ugs.)* ⟨*Motor*⟩. **3.** *v.i.* ⟨*Motor:*⟩
stehenbleiben

**stallion** ['stæljən] *n.* Hengst, *der*

**stalwart** ['stɔ:lwət] *adj. (determined)*
entschieden; *(loyal)* treu

**stamina** ['stæmınə] *n.* Ausdauer, *die*

**stammer** ['stæmə(r)] **1.** *v.i.* stottern. **2.**
*v.t.* stammeln. **3.** *n.* Stottern, *das*

**stamp** [stæmp] **1.** *v.t.* **a)** *(impress, imprint sth. on)* [ab]stempeln; **b)** ~ one's
foot mit dem Fuß stampfen; **c)** *(put
postage ~ on)* frankieren; ~ed addressed envelope frankierter Rückumschlag; **d)** become *or* be ~ed on sb.'s
memory *or* mind sich jmdm. fest einprägen. **2.** *v.i.* aufstampfen. **3.** *n.* Marke, *die; (postage ~)* Briefmarke, *die;
(instrument for ~ing)* Stempel, *der.*
'**stamp on** *v.t.* **a)** zertreten ⟨*Insekt*⟩;

~ **on sb's foot** jmdm. auf den Fuß treten; **b)** *(suppress)* durchgreifen gegen. **stamp 'out** *v. t.* [aus]stanzen; *(fig.)* ausmerzen

**stamp:** ~ **album** *n.* Briefmarkenalbum, *das;* ~-**collecting** *n.* Briefmarkensammeln, *das*

**stampede** [stæm'pi:d] *n.* Stampede, *die*

**stand** [stænd] **1.** *v. i.,* **stood** [stʊd] **a)** stehen; **b) my offer/promise still** ~s mein Angebot/Versprechen gilt nach wie vor; **as it** ~s, **as things** ~: wie die Dinge [jetzt] liegen; **I'd like to know where I** ~ *(fig.)* ich möchte wissen, wo ich dran bin; **c)** *(be candidate)* kandidieren; **d)** [not] ~ **in sb.'s way** *(fig.)* jmdm. [keine] Steine in den Weg legen; **e)** *(be likely)* ~ **to win** *or* **gain/lose sth.** etw. gewinnen/verlieren können. **2.** *v. t.,* **stood a)** *(set in position)* stellen; **b)** *(endure)* ertragen; **I cannot** ~ [the **sight of**] **him/her** ich kann ihn/sie nicht ausstehen; **he can't** ~ **the pressure/strain** er ist dem Druck/den Strapazen nicht gewachsen; **I can't** ~ **it any longer!** ich halte es nicht mehr aus!; **c)** *(buy)* ~ **sb. sth.** jmdm. etw. ausgeben. **3.** *n.* **a)** *(support)* Ständer, *der;* **b)** *(stall; at exhibition)* Stand, *der;* **c)** *(raised structure)* Tribüne, *die.* **stand a'bout, stand a'round** *v. i.* herumstehen. **stand a'side** *v. i.* zur Seite treten. **'stand between** *v. t.* **sth.** ~s **between sb. and sth.** *(fig.)* etw. steht jmdm. bei etw. im Wege. **stand by 1.** [-'-] *v. i.* **a)** *(be near)* daneben stehen; **b)** *(be ready)* sich zur Verfügung halten. **2.** ['--] *v. t.* **a)** *(support)* ~ **by sb./ one another** jmdm./sich [gegenseitig] beistehen; **b)** *(adhere to)* ~ **by sth.** zu etw. stehen. **'stand for** *v. t.* **a)** *(signify)* bedeuten; **b)** *(coll.: tolerate)* sich *(Dat.)* bieten lassen. **stand 'in** *v. i.* aushelfen; ~ **in for sb.** für jmdn. einspringen. **stand 'out** *v. i.* *(be prominent)* herausragen; ~ **out a mile** *(fig.)* nicht zu übersehen sein. **'stand over** *v. t.* beaufsichtigen. **stand 'up** *v. i.* **a)** aufstehen; ~ **up straight** sich aufrecht hinstellen; **b)** ~ **up well** [in comparison **with sb./sth.**] [im Vergleich zu jmdm./ etw.] gut abschneiden; ~ **up for sb./ sth.** für jmdn./etw. Partei ergreifen; ~ **up to sb.** sich jmdm. entgegenstellen **standard** ['stændəd] **1.** *n.* **a)** Maßstab, *der;* **safety** ~s Sicherheitsnormen; **above/below/up to** ~: überdurchschnittlich [gut]/unter dem Durch-

schnitt/der Norm entsprechend; **b)** *(degree)* Niveau, *das;* ~ **of living** Lebensstandard, *der;* **c)** ~s *(morals)* Prinzipien; **d)** *(flag)* Standarte, *die.* **2.** *adj.* Standard-; **be** ~ **practice** allgemein üblich sein. **standardize** ['stændədaɪz] *v. t.* standardisieren

**'standard lamp** *n.* Stehlampe, *die*

**stand:** ~-**by 1.** *n.* **be on** ~-**by** einsatzbereit sein; **2.** *adj.* Ersatz-; ~-**in 1.** *n.* Ersatz, *der;* **2.** *adj.* Ersatz-

**'standing 1.** *n.* **a)** *(repute)* Ansehen, *das;* **b)** *(duration)* **of long/short** ~: von langer/kurzer Dauer. **2.** *adj.* **a)** *(erect)* stehend; **b)** fest ⟨*Regel, Brauch*⟩

**standing:** ~ **'order** *n.* Dauerauftrag, *der;* ~ **o'vation** *n.* stürmischer Beifall; ~-**room** *n.* Stehplätze

**stand:** ~-**pipe** *n.* Standrohr, *das;* ~-**point** *n.* *(fig.)* Standpunkt, *der;* ~-**still** *n.* Stillstand, *der;* **be at a** ~**still** stillstehen; **come to a** ~**still** zum Stehen kommen

**stank** *see* **stink 1**

**staple** ['steɪpl] **1.** *n.* [Heft]klammer, *die.* **2.** *v. t.* heften **(on to an** + *Akk.*). **stapler** ['steɪplə(r)] *n.* [Draht]hefter, *der*

**star** [stɑː(r)] **1.** *n.* **a)** Stern, *der;* **b)** *(prominent person)* Star, *der.* **2.** *v. i.* ~ **in a film** in einem Film die Hauptrolle spielen

**starboard** ['stɑːbəd] *n.* Steuerbord, *das*

**starch** [stɑːtʃ] *n.* Stärke, *die*

**stardom** ['stɑːdəm] *n.* Starruhm, *der*

**stare** [steə(r)] *v. i.* starren; ~ **at sb./sth.** jmdn./etw. anstarren

**'starfish** *n.* Seestern, *der*

**stark** [stɑːk] **1.** *adj.* scharf ⟨*Kontrast, Umriß*⟩. **2.** *adv.* völlig; ~ **naked** splitternackt *(ugs.)*

**starling** ['stɑːlɪŋ] *n.* Star, *der*

**starry** ['stɑːrɪ] *adj.* sternklar

**start** [stɑːt] **1.** *v. i.* **a)** *(begin)* anfangen; ~ **on sth.** etw. beginnen; **b)** *(set out)* aufbrechen; **c)** *(begin to function)* anlaufen; ⟨*Auto, Motor usw.:*⟩ anspringen. **2.** *v. t.* **a)** *(begin)* beginnen [mit]; ~ **doing** *or* **to do sth.** [damit] anfangen, etw. zu tun; **b)** *(cause)* auslösen; anfangen ⟨*Streit, Schlägerei*⟩; legen/*(accidentally)* verursachen ⟨*Brand*⟩; **c)** *(set up)* ins Leben rufen ⟨*Organisation, Projekt*⟩; **d)** *(switch on)* einschalten; anlassen ⟨*Motor, Auto*⟩. **3.** *n.* **a)** Anfang, *der;* Beginn, *der;* *(of race)* Start, *der;* **from the** ~: von Anfang an; **from** ~ **to finish** von Anfang bis Ende;

**make a ~:** anfangen (**on** mit); *(on journey)* aufbrechen; **b)** *(Sport: ~ingplace)* Start, *der.* '**starter** *n.* **a)** *(food)* Vorspeise, *die;* **b)** *(Sport)* Starter, *der*

**startle** ['stɑ:tl] *v.t.* erschrecken; **be ~d by sth.** über etw. *(Akk.)* erschrecken. **startling** ['stɑ:tlɪŋ] *adj.* erstaunlich

**starvation** [stɑ:'veɪʃn] *n.* Verhungern, *das*

**starve** [stɑ:v] *v.i.* **~** |**to death**| verhungern

**state** [steɪt] **1.** *n.* **a)** *(condition)* Zustand, *der;* **b)** *(nation)* Staat, *der;* **c) be in a ~:** aufgeregt sein; **d) lie in ~:** aufgebahrt sein. **2.** *v.t. (express)* erklären; angeben *(Alter usw.)*

**stately** ['steɪtlɪ] *adj.* majestätisch; stattlich *(Körperbau, Gebäude).* **stately 'home** *n.* Herrensitz, *der*

'**statement** *n.* **a)** *(stating, account)* Aussage, *die; (declaration)* Erklärung, *die;* **b)** |**bank**| **~:** Kontoauszug, *der*

**statesman** ['steɪtsmən] *n., pl.* **statesmen** ['steɪtsmən] Staatsmann, *der*

**static** ['stætɪk] *adj.* statisch

**station** ['steɪʃn] **1.** *n.* **a)** *see* **railwaystation;** **b)** *(status)* Rang, *der.* **2.** *v.t.* aufstellen *(Wache)*

**stationary** ['steɪʃənərɪ] *adj.* stehend; **be ~:** stehen

**stationer** ['steɪʃənə(r)] *n.* **~'s** |**shop**| Schreibwarengeschäft, *das.* **stationery** ['steɪʃənərɪ] *n.* **a)** *(writing materials)* Schreibwaren *Pl.;* **b)** *(writingpaper)* Briefpapier, *das*

'**station-wagon** *n. (Amer.)* Kombiwagen, *der*

**statistical** [stə'tɪstɪkl] *attrib. adj.,* **statistically** [stə'tɪstɪkəlɪ] *adv.* statistisch

**statistics** [stə'tɪstɪks] *n.* Statistik, *die*

**statue** ['stætʃu:, 'stætju:] *n.* Statue, *die*

**stature** ['stætʃə(r)] *n.* Statur, *die; (fig.)* Format, *das*

**status** ['steɪtəs] *n.* Rang, *der;* **social ~:** [gesellschaftlicher] Status. '**status symbol** *n.* Statussymbol, *das*

**statute** ['stætju:t] *n.* Gesetz, *das.* **statutory** ['stætjʊtərɪ] *adj.* gesetzlich

**staunch** [stɔ:ntʃ] *adj.* treu *(Freund);* überzeugt *(Katholik usw.)*

**stave** [steɪv] *v.t.* **~ 'off** abwenden; stillen *(Hunger)*

**stay** [steɪ] **1.** *n.* Aufenthalt, *der; (visit)* Besuch, *der;* **come/go for a short ~ with sb.** jmdn. kurz besuchen. **2.** *v.i.* bleiben; **~ put** *(coll.) (Person:)* bleiben[, wo man ist]; **~ the night in a hotel** die Nacht in einem Hotel ver-

bringen. **3.** *v.t.* **~ the course** *(fig.)* durchhalten. **stay a'way** *v.i.* wegbleiben. **stay be'hind** *v.i.* zurückbleiben. **stay 'in** zu Hause bleiben. **stay 'out** *v.i.* **a)** *(not go home)* wegbleiben *(ugs.);* **b)** *(remain outside)* draußen bleiben. **stay 'up** *v.i.* aufbleiben

**stead** [sted] *n.* **a) in sb.'s ~:** an jmds. Stelle *(Dat.);* **b) stand sb. in good ~:** jmdm. zustatten kommen

**steadfast** ['stedfɑ:st] *adj.* standhaft; zuverlässig *(Freund)*

**steadily** ['stedɪlɪ] *adv.* **a)** *(stably)* fest; **b)** *(continuously)* stetig

**steady** ['stedɪ] **1.** *adj.* **a)** *(stable)* stabil; *(not wobbling)* standfest; **b)** *(still)* ruhig; **c)** *(regular, constant)* stetig; gleichmäßig *(Arbeit, Tempo);* stabil *(Preis, Lohn);* gleichbleibend *(Temperatur);* **we had ~ rain/drizzle** wir hatten Dauerregen/es nieselte [bei uns] ständig; **d) a ~ job** eine feste Stelle; **a ~ boy-friend** ein fester Freund. **2.** *v.t.* festhalten *(Leiter);* beruhigen *(Nerven)*

**steak** [steɪk] *n.* Steak, *das*

**steal** [sti:l] **1.** *v.t.,* **stole** [stəʊl], **stolen** ['stəʊln] stehlen (**from** *Dat.*). **2.** *v.i.,* **stole, stolen a)** stehlen; **~ from sb.** jmdn. bestehlen; **b) ~ in/out** sich hinein-/hinausstehlen

**stealth** [stelθ] *n.* Heimlichkeit, *die;* **by ~:** heimlich. **stealthy** ['stelθɪ] *adj.* heimlich

**steam** [sti:m] **1.** *n.* Dampf, *der;* **let off ~** *(fig.)* Dampf ablassen *(ugs.);* **run out of ~** *(fig.)* den Schwung verlieren; **under one's own ~** *(fig.)* aus eigener Kraft. **2.** *v.t. (Cookery)* dämpfen; dünsten. **3.** *v.i.* dämpfen; **~ing hot** dampfend heiß. **steam 'up** *v.i.* beschlagen

'**steam engine** *n.* Dampflok[omotive], *die*

'**steamer** *n.* Dämpfer, *der*

'**steamroller** *n.* Dampfwalze, *die*

'**steam train** *n.* Dampfzug, *der*

'**steamy** *adj.* dunstig; beschlagen *(Glas)*

**steel** [sti:l] **1.** *n.* Stahl, *der.* **2.** *attrib. adj.* stählern; Stahl*(helm, -block, -platte).* **3.** *v.t.* **~ oneself for/against sth.** sich für/gegen etw. wappnen *(geh.);* **~ oneself to do sth.** allen Mut zusammennehmen, um etw. zu tun. '**steelworks** *n. sing. or pl.* Stahlwerk, *das*

¹**steep** [sti:p] *adj.* **a)** steil; **b)** *(coll.: ex-*

*cessive)* happig *(ugs.);* **the bill is | a bit|**
~: die Rechnung ist [ziemlich] gesalzen *(ugs.)*

²**steep** *v. t. (soak)* einweichen

**steeple** ['sti:pl] *n.* Kirchturm, *der*

**steer** [stɪə(r)] **1.** *v. t.* steuern; lenken. **2.** *v. i.* steuern; ~ **clear of sb./sth.** *(fig. coll.)* jmdm./einer Sache aus dem Weg[e] gehen. '**steering** *n. (Motor Veh.)* Lenkung, *die.* '**steering-wheel** *n.* Lenkrad, *das*

¹**stem** [stem] **1.** *n.* **a)** *(Bot.)* Stiel, *der;* **b)** *(Ling.)* Stamm, *der.* **2.** *v. i.,* -mm-: ~ **from sth.** auf etw. *(Akk.)* zurückzuführen sein

²**stem** *v. t.,* -mm- *(check, dam up)* aufhalten; eindämmen ⟨*Flut*⟩; stillen ⟨*Blutung*⟩

**stench** [stentʃ] *n.* Gestank, *der*

**stencil** ['stensl] *n.* Schablone, *die; (for duplicating)* Matritze, *die*

**step** [step] **1.** *n.* **a)** Schritt, *der;* **take a** ~ **back/forwards** einen Schritt zurücktreten/nach vorn treten; **b)** *(stair)* Stufe, *die;* **a flight of** ~s eine Treppe; |**pair of**| ~s *(ladder)* Stehleiter, *die;* **c) be in** ~: im Schritt sein; *(with music)* im Takt sein; **d) take** ~s **to do sth.** Schritte unternehmen, um etw. zu tun; **e)** *(stage)* ~ **by** ~: Schritt für Schritt; **what is the next** ~? wie geht es weiter?; **f)** *(grade)* Stufe, *die.* **2.** *v. i.,* -pp- treten; ~ **inside** eintreten; ~ **into sb's shoes** *(fig.)* an jmds. Stelle *(Akk.)* treten; ~ **over sb./sth.** über jmdn./etw. steigen. **step** '**back** *v. i.* zurücktreten. **step** '**in** *v. i.* **a)** eintreten; **b)** *(fig.) (take sb.'s place)* einspringen; *(intervene)* eingreifen. **step** '**up 1.** *v. i. (ascend)* hinaufsteigen. **2.** *v. t.* erhöhen; verstärken ⟨*Anstrengungen*⟩

**step:** ~**child** *n.* Stiefkind, *das;* ~**daughter** *n.* Stieftochter, *die;* ~**father** *n.* Stiefvater, *der;* ~**-ladder** *n.* Stehleiter, *die;* ~**mother** *n.* Stiefmutter, *die*

'**stepping-stone** *n.* Trittstein, *der; (fig.)* Sprungbrett, das (to für)

**stereo** ['steriəʊ] **1.** *n.* Stereo, *das; (equipment)* Stereoanlage, *die.* **2.** *adj.* stereo; Stereo⟨*aufnahme, -platte*⟩

**stereophonic** [steriə'fɒnɪk] *adj.* stereophon

**stereotype** ['steriətaɪp] **1.** *n.* Stereotyp, *das.* **2.** *v. t.* in ein Klischee zwängen; ~d stereotyp

**sterile** ['steraɪl] *adj.* steril

**sterilize** ['sterɪlaɪz] *v. t.* sterilisieren

**sterling** ['stɜ:lɪŋ] **1.** *n.* Sterling, *der;* **in** ~: in Pfund [Sterling]. **2.** *attrib. adj.* **a)** ~ **silver** Sterlingsilber, *das;* **b)** *(fig.)* gediegen

¹**stern** [stɜ:n] *adj.* streng; ernst ⟨*Warnung*⟩

²**stern** *n. (Naut.)* Heck, *das*

'**sternly** *adv.* streng

**steroid** ['steroɪd] *n.* Steroid, *das*

**stethoscope** ['steθəskəʊp] *n.* Stethoskop, *das*

**stew** [stju:] **1.** *n.* Eintopf, *der.* **2.** *v. t.* schmoren [lassen]

**steward** ['stju:əd] *n.* **a)** *(on ship, plane)* Steward, *der;* **b)** *(at public meeting etc.)* Ordner, *der.* '**stewardess** *n.* Stewardeß, *die*

**stick** [stɪk] **1.** *v. t.,* stuck [stʌk] **a)** *(thrust point of)* stecken; ~ **sth. in[to] sth.** mit etw. in etw. *(Akk.)* stechen; **b)** *(coll.: put)* stecken; ~ **a picture on the wall/a vase on the shelf** ein Bild an die Wand hängen/eine Vase aufs Regal stellen; ~ **sth. in the kitchen** etw. in die Küche tun *(ugs.);* **c)** *(with glue etc.)* kleben; **d) the car is stuck in the mud** das Auto ist im Schlamm steckengeblieben; **the door is stuck** die Tür klemmt [fest]. **2.** *v. i.,* stuck **a)** *(be fixed by point)* stecken; **b)** *(adhere)* kleben; ~ **to sth.** an etw. *(Dat.)* kleben; **c)** *(become immobile)* ⟨*Auto, Räder:*⟩ steckenbleiben; ⟨*Schublade, Tür, Griff, Bremse:*⟩ klemmen; ⟨*Schlüssel:*⟩ feststecken. **3.** *n.* Stock, *der;* **a** ~ **of chalk** ein Stück Kreide; **a** ~ **of celery/rhubarb** eine Stange Sellerie/Rhabarber. **stick a'bout, stick a'round** *v. i. (coll.)* dableiben; *(wait)* warten. '**stick by** *v. t. (fig.)* stehen zu. **stick** '**on** *v. t. (glue on)* aufkleben. **stick** '**out 1.** *v. t.* **a)** herausstrecken ⟨*Zunge*⟩; **b)** ~ **it out** *(coll.)* durchhalten. **2.** *v. i.* **a)** ⟨*Bauch:*⟩ vorstehen; **his ears** ~ **out** er hat abstehende Ohren; **b)** *(fig.: be obvious)* sich abheben; ~ **out a mile** *(sl.)* [klar] auf der Hand liegen; ~ **out like a sore thumb** *(coll.)* ins Auge springen. '**stick to** *v. t.* **a)** *(be faithful to)* halten ⟨*Versprechen*⟩; bleiben bei ⟨*Entscheidung*⟩; **b)** ~ **to the point** beim Thema bleiben. **stick** '**up 1.** *v. t.* **a)** *(coll.)* anschlagen ⟨*Poster*⟩; ~ **up one's hand** die Hand heben; **b)** *(seal)* zukleben. **2.** *v. i.* ~ **up for sb./sth.** für jmdn./etw. eintreten; ~ **up for yourself!** setz dich zur Wehr!

'**sticker** *n.* Aufkleber, *der*

'**sticking-plaster** *n.* Heftpflaster, *das*

'**sticky** *adj.* **a)** klebrig; ~ **label** Aufkleber, *der;* **b)** *(humid)* schwül ⟨*Klima, Luft*⟩

**stiff** [stɪf] *adj.* **a)** *(rigid)* steif; hart ⟨*Bürste, Stock*⟩; **be frozen ~:** steif vor Kälte sein; **b)** *(intense, severe)* hartnäckig; **c)** *(formal)* steif; **d)** *(difficult)* hart ⟨*Test*⟩; schwer ⟨*Frage, Prüfung*⟩; **e)** *(coll.)* **be bored/scared ~:** sich zu Tode langweilen/eine wahnsinnige Angst haben *(ugs.).* **stiffen** ['stɪfn] **1.** *v. t.* steif machen. **2.** *v. i.* steifer werden; ⟨*Person:*⟩ erstarren. **'stiffness** *n.* Steifheit, *die*

**stifle** ['staɪfl] **1.** *v. t.* ersticken; *(fig.)* unterdrücken. **2.** *v. i.* ersticken. **stifling** ['staɪflɪŋ] *adj.* stickig; drückend ⟨*Hitze*⟩

**stigma** ['stɪgmə] *n.* Stigma, *das (geh.)*

**stile** [staɪl] *n.* Zauntritt, *der*

**stiletto** [stɪ'letəʊ] *n.* ~ [**heel**] Stöckelabsatz, *der*

**¹still** [stɪl] **1.** *pred. adj.* still; **be ~:** [still] stehen; **hold sth. ~:** etw. ruhig halten; **keep** *or* **stay ~:** stillhalten; **stand ~:** stillstehen. **2.** *adv.* **a)** *(without change)* noch; *expr. surprise or annoyance* immer noch; **b)** *(nevertheless)* trotzdem; **c)** *with comparative (even)* noch

**²still** *n.* Destillierapparat, *der*

**still: ~born** *adj.* totgeboren; ~ **'life** *n. (Art)* Stilleben, *das*

**stilt** [stɪlt] *n.* Stelze, *die.* **'stilted** *adj.* gestelzt

**stimulant** ['stɪmjʊlənt] *n.* Stimulans, *das*

**stimulate** ['stɪmjʊleɪt] *v. t.* anregen. **stimulation** [stɪmjʊ'leɪʃn] *n.* Anregung, *die*

**stimulus** ['stɪmjʊləs] *n., pl.* **stimuli** ['stɪmjʊlaɪ] Ansporn, *der*

**sting** [stɪŋ] **1.** *n.* **a)** *(wounding)* Stich, *der;* *(by jellyfish, nettles)* Verbrennung, *die;* **b)** *(from ointment, wind)* Brennen, *das.* **2.** *v. t.,* **stung** [stʌŋ] stechen. **3.** *v. i.,* **stung** brennen. **'stinging-nettle** *n.* Brennessel, *die*

**stingy** ['stɪndʒɪ] *adj.* geizig; knaus[e]rig *(ugs.)*

**stink** [stɪŋk] **1.** *v. i.,* **stank** [stæŋk] *or* **stunk** [stʌŋk], **stunk** stinken **(of** nach). **2.** *n.* Gestank, *der*

**stint** [stɪnt] **1.** *v. i.* ~ **on sth.** an etw. *(Dat.)* sparen. **2.** *n.* [Arbeits]pensum, *das*

**stipulate** ['stɪpjʊleɪt] *v. t. (demand)* fordern; *(lay down)* festlegen. **stipulation** [stɪpjʊ'leɪʃn] *n. (condition)* Bedingung, *die*

**stir** [stɜː(r)] **1.** *v. t.,* **-rr-: a)** *(mix)* rüh-

ren; umrühren ⟨*Tee, Kaffee*⟩; **b)** *(move)* bewegen. **2.** *v. i.,* **-rr-** *(move)* sich rühren. **3.** *n.* Aufregung, *die.* **stir 'in** *v. t.* einrühren. **stir 'up** *v. t.* **a)** *(disturb)* aufrühren; **b)** *(fig.: arouse)* wecken ⟨*Interesse, Leidenschaft*⟩

**stirring** ['stɜːrɪŋ] *adj.* bewegend ⟨*Musik, Poesie*⟩; mitreißend ⟨*Rede*⟩

**stirrup** ['stɪrəp] *n.* Steigbügel, *der*

**stitch** [stɪtʃ] **1.** *n.* **a)** *(Sewing)* Stich, *der;* *(Knitting)* Masche, *die;* **b)** *(pain)* **have a ~:** Seitenstechen haben. **2.** *v. t.* nähen

**stoat** [stəʊt] *n.* Hermelin, *das*

**stock** [stɒk] **1.** *n.* **a)** *(origin, family, breed)* Abstammung, *die;* **b)** *(supply, store)* Vorrat, *der;* *(in shop etc.)* Warenbestand, *der;* **be in/out of ~** ⟨*Ware:*⟩ vorrätig/nicht vorrätig sein; **have sth. in ~:** etw. auf Lager haben; **take ~ of sth.** *(fig.)* über etw. *(Akk.)* Bilanz ziehen; **c)** *(Cookery)* Brühe, *die.* **2.** *v. t.* **a)** *(supply with ~)* beliefern; **b)** *(Commerc.: keep in ~)* auf Lager haben. **3.** *attrib. adj.* Standard-

**stock: ~broker** Effektenmakler, *der*/-maklerin, *die;* ~ **cube** *n.* Brühwürfel, *der;* ~ **exchange** *n.* Börse, *die*

**stocking** ['stɒkɪŋ] *n.* Strumpf, *der*

**'stockist** *n.* Fachhändler, *der*/-händlerin, *die*

**stock: ~-market** *n.* **a)** Börse, *die;* **b)** *(trading)* Börsengeschäft, *das;* **~pile 1.** *n.* Vorrat, *der;* *(weapons)* Arsenal, *das;* **2.** *v. t.* horten; anhäufen ⟨*Waffen*⟩; **~-'still** *pred. adj.* bewegungslos; **~-taking** *n.* Inventur, *die*

**stocky** ['stɒkɪ] *adj.* stämmig

**stodgy** ['stɒdʒɪ] *adj.* pappig

**stoical** ['stəʊɪkl] *adj.* stoisch

**stoke** [stəʊk] *v. t.* heizen ⟨*Ofen, Kessel*⟩; unterhalten ⟨*Feuer*⟩

**stole** *see* **steal**

**stolen** ['stəʊln] **1.** *see* **steal.** **2.** *attrib. adj.* heimlich ⟨*Vergnügen, Kuß*⟩

**stolid** ['stɒlɪd] *adj.* stur *(ugs.)*

**stomach** ['stʌmək] **1.** *n.* **a)** Magen, *der;* **b)** *(abdomen)* Bauch, *der.* **2.** *v. t.* *(fig.: tolerate)* ausstehen. **'stomachache** *n.* Magenschmerzen *Pl.* **'stomach upset** *n.* Magenverstimmung, *die*

**stone** [stəʊn] **1.** *n.* **a)** Stein, *der;* **a ~'s throw [away]** *(fig.)* nur einen Steinwurf weit entfernt; **b)** *(Brit.: weight unit)* Gewicht von *6,35 kg.* **2.** *adj.* steinern; Stein⟨*mauer, -brücke*⟩. **3.** *v. t.* mit Steinen bewerfen

**stone: S~ Age** *n.* Steinzeit, *die;* **~-cold** *adj.* eiskalt; **~-'deaf** *adj.* stocktaub *(ugs.)*

**stony** ['stəʊnɪ] *adj.* steinig

**stood** *see* stand 1, 2

**stool** [stu:l] *n.* Hocker, *der*

**stoop** [stu:p] **1.** *v. i.* ~ |down| sich bücken. **2.** *n.* **walk with a ~:** gebeugt gehen

**stop** [stɒp] **1.** *v. t.*, **-pp-: a)** anhalten ⟨*Person, Fahrzeug*⟩; aufhalten ⟨*Fortschritt, Verkehr, Feind*⟩; **b)** *(not let continue)* unterbrechen ⟨*Redner, Spiel, Gespräch*⟩; beenden ⟨*Krieg, Arbeit*⟩; stoppen ⟨*Produktion, Uhr*⟩; einstellen ⟨*Zahlung, Lieferung*⟩; ~ **that!** hör damit auf!; ~ **smoking/crying** aufhören zu rauchen/weinen; **c)** *(not let happen)* verhindern ⟨*Verbrechen, Unfall*⟩; ~ **sth. |from| happening** verhindern, daß etw. geschieht; **d)** *(switch off)* abstellen ⟨*Maschine*⟩; **e)** *(block up)* zustopfen ⟨*Loch*⟩; verschließen ⟨*Wasserhahn, Flasche*⟩; **f)** ~ **a cheque** einen Scheck sperren lassen. **2.** *v. i.*, **-pp-: a)** *(not extend further)* aufhören; ⟨*Zahlungen, Lieferungen:*⟩ eingestellt werden; **b)** *(not move further)* ⟨*Fahrzeug, Fahrer:*⟩ halten; ⟨*Maschine, Motor:*⟩ stillstehen; ⟨*Uhr, Fußgänger, Herz:*⟩ stehenbleiben. **3.** *n.* **a)** *(halt)* Halt, *der;* **bring to a ~:** zum Stehen bringen ⟨*Fahrzeug*⟩; zum Erliegen bringen ⟨*Verkehr*⟩; unterbrechen ⟨*Arbeit*⟩; **come to a ~:** stehenbleiben; ⟨*Fahrzeug:*⟩ zum Stehen kommen; ⟨*Arbeit, Verkehr:*⟩ zum Erliegen kommen; **put a ~ to** abstellen ⟨*Mißstände, Unsinn*⟩; **b)** *(place)* Haltestelle, *die.* **stop 'by** *v. i. (Amer.)* vorbeischauen *(ugs.).* **stop 'out** *v. i. (coll.)* draußen bleiben. **stop 'over** *v. i.* übernachten (at bei). **stop 'up 1.** *v. t.* zustopfen ⟨*Loch, Öffnung*⟩. **2.** *v. i. (coll.) see* **stay up**

**stop: ~gap** *n.* Notlösung, *die;* **~-light** *n. (traffic-light)* rotes Licht; **~over** *n.* Stopover, *der*

**stoppage** ['stɒpɪdʒ] *n.* **a)** *(halt)* Stillstand, *der;* *(strike)* Streik, *der;* **b)** *(deduction)* Abzug, *der*

**stopper** ['stɒpə(r)] *n.* Stöpsel, *der*

**stop: ~-press** *n.* letzte Meldung/ Meldungen; ~ **sign** *n.* Stoppschild, *das;* **~watch** *n.* Stoppuhr, *die*

**storage** ['stɔ:rɪdʒ] *n.* Lagerung, *die; (of films, books, documents)* Aufbewahrung, *die; (of data, water, electricity)* Speicherung, *die.* **'storage**

**heater** *n.* [Nacht]speicherofen, *der.* **'storage tank** *n.* Sammelbehälter, *der*

**store** [stɔ:(r)] **1.** *n.* **a)** *(Amer.: shop)* Laden, *der;* **b)** *(Brit.: large general shop)* Kaufhaus, *das;* **c)** *(warehouse)* Lager, *das;* **put sth. in ~:** etw. einlagern; **d)** *(stock)* Vorrat, *der* (of an + *Dat.*); **be** *or* **lie in ~ for sb.** jmdn. erwarten; **e)** **set |great| ~ by** *or* **on sth.** [großen] Wert auf etw. *(Akk.)* legen. **2.** *v. t.* einlagern; speichern ⟨*Getreide, Energie, Wissen, Daten*⟩. **store 'up** *v. t.* speichern; ~ **up provisions** sich *(Dat.)* Vorräte anlegen

**store: ~house** *n.* Lager[haus], *das;* **~-room** *n.* Lagerraum, *der*

**storey** ['stɔ:rɪ] *n.* Stockwerk, *das*

**stork** [stɔ:k] *n.* Storch, *der*

**storm** [stɔ:m] **1.** *n.* Unwetter, *das; (thunder~)* Gewitter, *das.* **2.** *v. t. & i.* stürmen. **'stormy** *adj.* stürmisch

**¹story** ['stɔ:rɪ] *n.* **a)** Geschichte, *die;* **b)** *(news item)* Bericht, *der;* **c)** *(coll.: lie)* Märchen, *das*

**²story** *(Amer.) see* **storey**

**stout** [staʊt] *adj.* **a)** *(strong)* fest; **b)** *(fat)* beleibt

**stove** [stəʊv] *n.* Ofen, *der; (for cooking)* Herd, *der*

**stow** [stəʊ] *v. t.* verstauen (into in + *Dat.*). **stow a'way 1.** *v. t.* verwahren. **2.** *v. i.* als blinder Passagier reisen

**straddle** ['strædl] *v. t.* ~ **a fence/chair** rittlings auf einem Zaun/Stuhl sitzen

**straggle** ['strægl] *v. i.* ~ |along| **behind the others** den anderen hinterherzockeln *(ugs.).* **straggler** ['stræglə(r)] *n.* Nachzügler, *der*

**straight** [streɪt] **1.** *adj.* **a)** gerade; glatt ⟨*Haar*⟩; **in a ~ line** in gerader Linie; **b)** *(undiluted)* **drink whisky ~:** Whisky pur trinken; **c)** *(direct)* direkt ⟨*Blick, Schuß, Weg*⟩; **be ~ with sb.** zu jmdm. offen sein; **get sth. ~** *(fig.)* etw. genau verstehen; **put** *or* **set the record ~:** die Sache richtigstellen. **2.** *adv.* **a)** gerade; **b)** *(directly)* geradewegs; ~ **after** sofort nach; **come ~ to the point** direkt zur Sache kommen; **look sb. ~ in the eye** jmdm. direkt in die Augen blicken; ~ **ahead** *or* **on** immer geradeaus; **c)** *(frankly)* aufrichtig; **d)** *(clearly)* klar ⟨*sehen, denken*⟩. **straight a'way** *adv. (coll.)* sofort

**straighten** ['streɪtn] **1.** *v. t.* **a)** geradeziehen ⟨*Teppich*⟩; glätten ⟨*Kleidung, Haare*⟩; **b)** *(put in order)* aufräumen. **2.** *v. i.* gerade werden. **straighten**

'**out 1.** *v. t.* **a)** geradebiegen; glätten ⟨*Decke, Teppich*⟩; **b)** *(clear up)* klären. **2.** *v. i.* gerade werden. **straighten** '**up 1.** *v. t. see* tidy up. **2.** *v. i.* sich aufrichten

**straight'forward** *adj.* **a)** *(frank)* freimütig; schlicht ⟨*Stil, Sprache, Bericht*⟩; klar ⟨*Anweisung, Vorstellungen*⟩; **b)** *(simple)* einfach

**strain** [streɪn] **1.** *n.* **a)** *(pull)* Belastung, *die;* *(on rope)* Spannung, *die;* **b)** *(tension)* Streß, *der;* **be under |a great deal of|** ~: unter großem Streß stehen; **c)** *(person, thing)* **be a** ~ **on sb./sth.** jmdn./etw. belasten; **d)** *(muscular injury)* Zerrung, *die.* **2.** *v. t.* **a)** *(overexert)* überanstrengen; zerren ⟨*Muskel*⟩; **b)** *(stretch tightly)* [fest] spannen; **c)** *(filter)* durchseihen; seihen **(through durch). 3.** *v. i.* *(strive intensely)* sich anstrengen. **strained** [streɪnd] *adj.* gezwungen ⟨*Lächeln*⟩; ~ **relations** gespannte Beziehungen

'**strainer** *n.* Sieb, *das*

**strait** [streɪt] *n.* **a)** *in sing. or pl.* *(Geog.)* Meerenge, *die;* **b)** *usu. in pl.* *(distress, difficulty)* Schwierigkeiten. '**straitjacket** *n.* Zwangsjacke, *die.* **straitlaced** [streɪt'leɪst] *adj.* puritanisch

¹**strand** [strænd] *n.* *(thread)* Faden, *der;* *(of beads)* Kette, *die;* *(of hair)* Strähne, *die;* *(of rope)* Strang, *der*

²**strand** *v. t.* *(leave behind)* trocken setzen; **be |left|** ~**ed** *(fig.)* seinem Schicksal überlassen sein

**strange** [streɪndʒ] *adj.* *(peculiar)* seltsam; sonderbar; ~ **to say** seltsamerweise; **feel** ~: sich komisch fühlen. **stranger** ['streɪndʒə(r)] *n.* Fremde, *der/die;* **he is a** ~ **here/to the town** er ist hier/in der Stadt fremd

**strangle** ['stræŋgl] *v. t.* erwürgen. '**stranglehold** *n.* Würgegriff, *der.* **strangulation** [stræŋgjʊ'leɪʃn] *n.* Erwürgen, *das*

**strap** [stræp] **1.** *n.* **a)** *(leather)* Riemen, *der;* *(textile)* Band, *das;* *(shoulder-*~**)** Träger, *der;* *(for watch)* Armband, *das;* **b)** *(to grasp in vehicle)* Halteriemen, *der.* **2.** *v. t.,* **-pp-:** ~ **|into position|/down** festschnallen; ~ **oneself in** sich anschnallen. '**strapless** *adj.* trägerlos

**strapping** ['stræpɪŋ] *adj.* stramm

**strata** *pl. of* stratum

**strategic** [strə'tiːdʒɪk] *adj.* strategisch

**strategist** ['strætɪdʒɪst] *n.* Stratege, *der/*Strategin, *die*

**strategy** ['strætɪdʒɪ] *n.* Strategie, *die*

**stratosphere** ['strætəsfɪə(r)] *n.* Stratosphäre, *die*

**stratum** ['strɑːtəm] *n., pl.* **strata** ['strɑːtə] Schicht, *die*

**straw** [strɔː] *n.* **a)** *no pl.* Stroh, *das;* **b)** *(single stalk)* Strohhalm, *der;* **that's the last or final** ~: jetzt reicht's aber; **c)** |**drinking-**|~: Strohhalm, *der*

**strawberry** ['strɔːbərɪ] *n.* Erdbeere, *die*

**stray** [streɪ] **1.** *v. i.* **a)** *(wander)* streunen; **b)** *(deviate)* abweichen **(from** von). **2.** *n.* *(animal)* streunendes Tier. **3.** *adj.* **a)** streunend; **b)** *(occasional)* vereinzelt

**streak** [striːk] *n.* Streifen, *der;* *(in hair)* Strähne, *die;* **have a jealous/cruel** ~: zur Eifersucht/Grausamkeit neigen. '**streaky** *adj.* streifig; ~ **bacon** durchwachsener Speck

**stream** [striːm] **1.** *n.* *(of water)* Wasserlauf, *der;* *(brook)* Bach, *der.* **2.** *v. i.* strömen; ⟨*Sonnenlicht:*⟩ fluten. '**streamline** *v. t.* [eine] Stromlinienform geben **(+ *Dat.*)**; **be** ~**lined** eine Stromlinienform haben

**street** [striːt] *n.* Straße, *die;* **in the** ~: auf der Straße; **in** *(Brit.)* **or on ... Street** in der ...straße

**street:** ~**car** *n.* *(Amer.)* Straßenbahn, *die;* ~**lamp** *n.* Straßenlaterne, *die;* ~**lighting** *n.* Straßenbeleuchtung, *die;* ~**map** *n.* Stadtplan, *der;* ~**market** *n.* Markt, *der;* ~**plan** *n.* Stadtplan, *der;* ~**wise** *(coll.)* **be** ~**wise** wissen, wo es langgeht

**strength** [streŋθ] *n.* *(power)* Kraft, *die;* *(strong point, force, intensity, amount of ingredient)* Stärke, *die;* *(of poison, medicine)* Wirksamkeit, *die;* **not know one's own** ~: nicht wissen, wie stark man ist; **give sb.** ~: jmdn. stärken; **go from** ~ **to** ~: immer erfolgreicher werden; **on the** ~ **of sth./that** auf Grund einer Sache *(Gen.)*/dessen; **in full** ~: in voller Stärke; **the police were there in** ~: es war ein starkes Polizeiaufgebot war da. **strengthen** ['streŋθən] *v. t.* stärken; *(reinforce, intensify)* verstärken

**strenuous** ['strenjʊəs] *adj.* **a)** *(energetic)* energisch; gewaltig ⟨*Anstrengung*⟩; **b)** *(requiring exertion)* anstrengend

**stress** [stres] **1.** *n.* **a)** *(strain)* Streß, *der;* **be under** ~: unter Streß *(Dat.)* stehen; **b)** *(emphasis)* Betonung, *die.* **2.** *v. t.* *(emphasize)* betonen

**stretch** [stretʃ] **1.** *v. t.* **a)** *(lengthen)* strecken ⟨*Arm, Hand*⟩; recken ⟨*Hals*⟩;

dehnen *(Gummiband)*; *(tighten)* spannen; b) *(widen)* dehnen. 2. a) *v. i. (extend in length)* sich dehnen; b) ~ to sth. *(be sufficient for)* für etw. reichen. 3. *v. refl.* sich strecken. 4. *n.* a) have a ~: sich strecken; b) at a ~ *(fig.)* wenn es sein muß; c) *(expanse)* Abschnitt, *der;* a ~ of road ein Stück Straße; d) *(period)* a four-hour ~: eine [Zeit]spanne von vier Stunden; at a ~: ohne Unterbrechung. 5. *adj.* Stretch-*(hose, -gewebe)*

**stretcher** ['stretʃə(r)] *n.* [Trag]bahre, *die*

**strew** [stru:] *v. t., p. p.* strewed [stru:d] *or* strewn [stru:n] streuen

**stricken** ['strɪkn] *adj. (afflicted)* heimgesucht; havariert *(Schiff)*; be ~ with fear/grief angsterfüllt/grambeugt

**strict** [strɪkt] *adj.* a) *(firm)* streng; in ~ confidence streng vertraulich; b) *(precise)* streng. **'strictly** *adv.* streng; ~ |speaking| strenggenommen

**stride** [straɪd] 1. *n.* Schritt, *der;* put sb. off his ~ *(fig.)* jmdn. aus dem Konzept bringen; take sth. in one's ~ *(fig).* mit etw. gut fertig werden. 2. *v. i.,* strode [strəʊd], stridden ['strɪdn] [mit großen Schritten] gehen

**strident** ['straɪdnt] *adj.* schrill

**strife** [straɪf] *n.* Streit, *der*

**strike** [straɪk] 1. *n. (Industry)* Streik, *der;* Ausstand, *der;* be on/go |out| *or* come out on ~: in den Streik getreten sein/in den Streik treten. 2. *v. t.,* struck [strʌk] a) *(hit)* schlagen; *(Schlag, Geschoß:)* treffen; *(Blitz:)* [ein]schlagen in (+ *Akk.*); b) *(delete)* streichen (from, off aus); c) *(ignite)* anzünden *(Streichholz)*; d) *(chime)* schlagen; e) *(impress)* beeindrucken; ~ sb. as |being| silly jmdm. dumm erscheinen; it ~s sb. that ...: es scheint jmdm., daß ...; f) *(occur to)* einfallen (+ *Dat.*). 3. *v. i.,* struck a) *(deliver a blow)* zuschlagen; *(Blitz:)* einschlagen; *(Unheil, Katastrophe:)* hereinbrechen *(geh.)*; *(hit)* schlagen (against gegen, |up|on auf + *Akk.*); b) *(ignite)* zünden; c) *(chime)* schlagen; d) *(Industry)* streiken. **strike 'back** *v. i.* zurückschlagen. **strike 'off** *v. t.* (~ off list) streichen *(Namen)*; *(from professional body)* die Zulassung entziehen (+ *Dat.*). **'strike up** *v. t.* beginnen *(Unterhaltung)*; schließen *(Freundschaft)*

**'strike pay** *n.* Streikgeld, *das*

**'striker** *n.* Streikende, *der/die*

**striking** ['straɪkɪŋ] *adj.* auffallend; erstaunlich *(Ähnlichkeit)*; schlagend *(Beispiel)*

**string** [strɪŋ] 1. *n.* a) *(thin cord)* Schnur, *die;* *(to tie up parcels etc. also)* Bindfaden, *der;* pull |a few *or* some| ~s *(fig.)* seine Beziehungen spielen lassen; with no ~s attached ohne Bedingung[en]; b) *(of bow)* Sehne, *die;* *(of racket, musical instrument)* Saite, *die.* 2. *v. t.,* strung [strʌŋ] *(thread)* auffädeln. **string a'long** *v. t. (deceive)* an der Nase herumführen *(ugs.).* **string to'gether** *v. t.* auffädeln; miteinander verknüpfen *(Wörter)*. **string 'up** *v. t.* aufhängen

**string 'bag** *n.* [Einkaufs]netz, *das*

**stringent** ['strɪndʒənt] *adj.* streng

**'strip** [strɪp] 1. *v. t.,* -pp- ausziehen *(Person)*. 2. *v. i.,* -pp- sich ausziehen

**'strip** *n. (narrow piece)* Streifen, *der*

**stripe** · [straɪp] *n.* Streifen, *der.*

**striped** [straɪpt] *adj.* gestreift

**strip-light** *n.* Neonröhre, *die;* ~ lighting *n.* Neonbeleuchtung, *die*

**stripper** ['strɪpə(r)] *n.* Stripper, *der/* Stripperin, *die (ugs.)*

**stripy** ['straɪpɪ] *adj.* gestreift; Streifen-*(muster)*

**strive** [straɪv] *v. i.,* strove [strəʊv], striven ['strɪvn] sich bemühen; ~ after *or* for sth. nach etw. streben

**strode** *see* stride 2

**'stroke** [strəʊk] *n.* a) *(act of striking)* Schlag, *der;* b) *(Med.)* Schlaganfall, *der;* c) *(sudden impact)* ~ of lightning Blitzschlag, *der;* ~ of |good| luck Glücksfall, *der;* d) at a *or* one ~: auf einen Schlag; not do a ~ |of work| keinen [Hand]schlag tun; ~ of genius genialer Einfall, *der;* e) *(in swimming)* Zug, *der;* f) *(of clock)* Schlag, *der;* on the ~ of nine Punkt neun [Uhr]

**'stroke** 1. *v. t.* streicheln. 2. *n.* give sb./sth. a ~: jmdn./etw. streicheln

**stroll** [strəʊl] 1. *v. i.* spazierengehen. 2. *n.* go for a ~: einen Spaziergang machen

**strong** [strɒŋ] *adj.,* ~er ['strɒŋgə(r)], ~est ['strɒŋgɪst] stark; fest *(Fundament, Schuhe)*; robust *(Konstitution, Magen)*; kräftig *(Arme, Muskeln, Tritt, Zähne)*; leistungsfähig *(Wirtschaft)*; gut, handfest *(Grund, Beispiel, Argument)*; glühend *(Anhänger)*; kräftig *(Geruch, Geschmack, Stimme)*; there is a ~ possibility that ...: es ist sehr wahrscheinlich, daß ...; take ~ measures/action energisch vorgehen.

'**stronghold** *n.* Festung, *die;* *(fig.)* Hochburg, *die.* **strong** '**language** *n.* derbe Ausdrucksweise

'**strongly** *adv.* stark; solide ⟨*gearbeitet*⟩; energisch ⟨*protestieren, bestreiten*⟩; nachdrücklich ⟨*unterstützen*⟩; dringend ⟨*raten*⟩; fest ⟨*glauben*⟩

**strong:** **~man** *n.* Muskelmann, *der (ugs.);* **~-'minded** *adj.* willensstark; **~-room** *n.* Tresorraum, *der*

**strove** *see* **strive**

**struck** *see* **strike** 2, 3

**structural** ['strʌktʃərl] *adj.* baulich

**structure** ['strʌktʃə(r)] *n.* **a)** Struktur, *die;* **b)** *(something constructed)* Konstruktion, *die; (building)* Bauwerk, *das*

**struggle** ['strʌgl] **1.** *v. i.* kämpfen; **~ to do sth.** sich abmühen, etw. zu tun; **~ against** *or* **with sb./sth.** mit jmdm./ etw. *od.* gegen jmdn./etw. kämpfen; **~ with sth.** *(try to cope)* mit etw. kämpfen. **2.** *n.* Kampf, *der*

**strum** [strʌm] **1.** *v. i.,* **-mm-** klimpern *(ugs.)* (on auf + *Dat.*). **2.** *v. t.,* **-mm-** klimpern *(ugs.)* auf (+ *Dat.*)

**strung** *see* **string** 2

¹**strut** [strʌt] **1.** *v. i.,* **-tt-** stolzieren. **2.** *n.* stolzierender Gang

²**strut** *n.* *(support)* Strebe, *die*

**stub** [stʌb] **1.** *n.* **a)** *(remaining portion)* Stummel, *der; (of cigarette)* Kippe, *die;* **b)** *(counterfoil)* Abschnitt, *der.* **2.** *v. t.,* **-bb-: a)** **~ one's toe [against** *or* **on sth.]** sich *(Dat.)* den Zeh [an etw. *(Dat.)*] stoßen; **b)** ausdrücken ⟨*Zigarette*⟩. **stub** '**out** *v. t.* ausdrücken

**stubble** ['stʌbl] *n.* Stoppeln *Pl.*

**stubborn** ['stʌbən] *adj.* **a)** *(obstinate)* starrköpfig; störrisch ⟨*Tier, Gesicht, Haltung*⟩; **b)** *(resolute)* hartnäckig.

'**stubbornness** *n.* *see* **stubborn:** Starrköpfigkeit, *die;* Hartnäckigkeit, *die*

**stuck** *see* **stick** 1, 2

'**stuck up** *adj.* *(conceited)* eingebildet

**student** ['stju:dənt] *n.* Student, *der/* Studentin, *die; (in school or training establishment)* Schüler, *der/*Schülerin, *die;* **be a ~ of sth.** etw. studieren

**studio** ['stju:dɪəʊ] *n., pl.* **~s a)** *(workroom)* Atelier, *das;* **b)** *(Cinemat., Radio, Telev.)* Studio, *das*

**studious** ['stju:dɪəs] *adj.* lerneifrig

**study** ['stʌdɪ] **1.** *n.* **a)** Studium, *das;* **b)** *(room)* Arbeitszimmer, *das.* **2.** *v. t.* studieren; sich *(Dat.)* [sorgfältig] durchlesen ⟨*Prüfungsfragen, Bericht*⟩

**stuff** [stʌf] **1.** *n.* *(material[s])* Zeug, *das (ugs.).* **2.** *v. t.* **a)** stopfen; zustopfen

⟨*Loch, Ohren*⟩; *(Cookery)* füllen; **~ sth. with** *or* **full of sth.** etw. mit etw. vollstopfen *(ugs.);* **b)** *(sl.)* **~ him!** zum Teufel mit ihm! '**stuffing** *n.* **a)** *(material)* Füllmaterial, *das;* **b)** *(Cookery)* Füllung, *die*

**stuffy** ['stʌfɪ] *adj.* stickig

**stumble** ['stʌmbl] *v. i.* stolpern (over über + *Akk.*). **stumbling-block** ['stʌmblɪŋblɒk] *n.* Stolperstein, *der*

**stump** [stʌmp] **1.** *n.* *(of tree, branch, tooth)* Stumpf, *der; (of cigar, pencil)* Stummel, *der.* **2.** *v. t.* verwirren; **be ~ed** ratlos sein. '**stumpy** *adj.* gedrungen; **~ tail** Stummelschwanz, *der*

**stun** [stʌn] *v. t.,* **-nn-** *(knock senseless)* betäuben; **be ~ned at** *or* **by sth.** *(fig.)* von etw. wie betäubt sein

**stung** *see* **sting** 2, 3

**stunk** *see* **stink** 1

¹**stunt** [stʌnt] *v. t.* hemmen

²**stunt** *n.* halsbrecherisches Kunststück; *(Cinemat.)* Stunt, *der*

**stupendous** [stju:'pendəs] *adj.* gewaltig

**stupid** ['stju:pɪd] *adj.* dumm; *(ridiculous)* lächerlich; **it would be ~ to do sth.** es wäre töricht, etw. zu tun. **stupidity** [stu:'pɪdɪtɪ] *n.* Dummheit, *die.* '**stupidly** *adv.* dumm

**stupor** ['stju:pə(r)] *n.* Benommenheit, *die;* **in a drunken ~:** sinnlos betrunken

**sturdy** ['stɜ:dɪ] *adj.* kräftig; stämmig ⟨*Beine, Arme*⟩

**stutter** ['stʌtə(r)] **1.** *v. i.* stottern. **2.** *n.* Stottern, *das*

¹**sty** [staɪ] *see* **pigsty**

²**sty, stye** [staɪ] *n.* *(Med.)* Gerstenkorn, *das*

**style** [staɪl] *n.* Stil, *der;* **dress in the latest ~:** sich nach der neuesten Mode kleiden; **|hair-]~:** Frisur, *die*

**styli** *pl. of* **stylus**

**stylish** ['staɪlɪʃ] *adj.* stilvoll; elegant ⟨*Kleidung, Auto, Person*⟩

**stylist** ['staɪlɪst] *n.* *(hair-~)* Haarstilist, *der/*-stilistin, *die*

**stylus** ['staɪləs] *n., pl.* **styli** ['staɪlaɪ] *or* **~es** [Abtast]nadel, *die*

**suave** [swɑ:v] *adj.* gewandt

**sub-** [sʌb] *pref.* unter-; sub-

**subconscious** *(Psych.)* **1.** *adj.* unterbewußt. **2.** *n.* Unterbewußtsein, *das*

'**subcontract** *v. t.* an einen Subunternehmer vergeben

**subdivide** ['---, --'-] *v. t.* unterteilen

**subdue** [səb'dju:] *v. t.* bändigen ⟨*Kind, Tier*⟩; dämpfen ⟨*Zorn, Lärm, Licht*⟩.

**subdued** [səb'dju:d] *adj.* gedämpft

**subject 1.** ['sʌbdʒɪkt] *n.* **a)** Staatsbürger, *der/*-bürgerin, *die; (to monarch)* Untertan, *der/*Untertanin, *die;* **b)** *(topic)* Thema, *das; (of study)* Fach, *das;* **change the ~:** das Thema wechseln. **2.** ['sʌbdʒɪkt] *adj.* **be ~ to sth.** von etw. abhängen. **3.** [səb'dʒekt] *v. t.* unterwerfen **(to** *Dat.*)*; (expose)* **~ sb./ sth. to sth.** jmdn./etw. einer Sache *(Dat.)* aussetzen

**subjective** [səb'dʒektɪv] *adj.* subjektiv

**subjugate** ['sʌbdʒʊgeɪt] *v. t.* unterjochen **(to** unter + *Akk.*)

**subjunctive** [səb'dʒʌŋktɪv] *(Ling.) n.* Konjunktiv, *der*

**sub'let** *v. t.,* **-tt-, sublet** untervermieten

**sublime** [sə'blaɪm] *adj.* erhaben

**submarine** [sʌbmə'ri:n] *n.* Unterseeboot, *das;* U-Boot, *das*

**submerge** [səb'mɜ:dʒ] *v. t.* **a) ~ sth.** [in the water] etw. eintauchen; **b)** *(flood)* 〈*Wasser:*〉 überschwemmen; **be ~d in water** unter Wasser stehen

**submission** [səb'mɪʃn] *n.* **a)** *(surrender, meekness)* Unterwerfung, *die;* **b)** *(presentation)* Einreichung, *die* **(to** bei)

**submissive** [səb'mɪsɪv] *adj.* gehorsam

**submit** [səb'mɪt] *v. t.,* **-tt-** *(present)* einreichen; vorbringen 〈*Vorschlag*〉; **~ sth. to sb.** jmdm. etw. vorlegen

**subordinate 1.** [sə'bɔ:dɪnət] *adj.* untergeordnet. **2.** [sə'bɔ:dɪnət] *n.* Untergebene, *der/die.* **3.** [sə'bɔ:dɪneɪt] *v. t.* unterordnen **(to** *Dat.*)

**subscribe** [səb'skraɪb] *v. i.* **a)** *(support)* **~ to sth.** sich einer Sache *(Dat.)* anschließen; **b)** *(make contribution)* **~ to sth.** eine Spende für etw. zusichern. **sub'scriber** *n. (to newspaper etc.)* Abonnent, *der/*Abonnentin, *die* **(to** *Gen.*). **subscription** [səb'skrɪpʃn] *n. (membership fee)* Mitgliedsbeitrag, *der* **(to** für)*; (to newspaper etc.)* Abonnement, *das*

**subsequent** ['sʌbsɪkwənt] *adj.* folgend; später 〈*Gelegenheit*〉

**subservient** [səb'sɜ:vɪənt] *adj.* untergeordnet **(to** *Dat.*)*; (servile)* unterwürfig

**subside** [səb'saɪd] *v. i.* **a)** *(sink lower)* 〈*Flut, Fluß:*〉 sinken; 〈*Boden, Haus:*〉 sich senken; **b)** *(abate)* nachlassen

**subsidiary** [səb'sɪdɪərɪ] **1.** *adj.* untergeordnet 〈*Funktion, Stellung*〉; Neben〈*fach, -aspekt*〉. **2.** *n. (Commerc.)* Tochtergesellschaft, *die*

**subsidize** ['sʌbsɪdaɪz] *v. t.* subventionieren. **subsidy** ['sʌbsɪdɪ] *n.* Subvention, *die*

**subsist** [səb'sɪst] *v. i.* **~ on sth.** von etw. leben. **subsistence** [səb'sɪstəns] *n.* [Über]leben, *das*

**substance** ['sʌbstəns] *n.* **a)** Stoff, *der;* **b)** *(solidity)* Substanz, *die;* **c)** *(content)* Inhalt, *der*

**sub'standard** *adj.* unzulänglich

**substantial** [səb'stænʃl] *adj.* **a)** *(considerable)* beträchtlich; **b)** gehaltvoll 〈*Essen*〉; **c)** *(solid)* solide 〈*Möbel, Haus*〉; wesentlich 〈*Unterschied*〉. **sub'stantially** *adv.* **a)** *(considerably)* wesentlich; **b)** *(solidly)* solide; **c)** *(essentially)* im wesentlichen

**substitute** ['sʌbstɪtjuːt] **1.** *n.* ~[s *pl.*] Ersatz, *der.* **2.** *v. t.* **~ A for B B durch A ersetzen. substitution** [sʌbstɪ'tjuːʃn] *n.* Ersetzung, *die*

**'subtitle** *n.* Untertitel, *der*

**subtle** ['sʌtl] *adj.* subtil *(geh.);* zart 〈*Duft, Parfüm, Hinweis*〉; fein 〈*Geschmack, Unterschied, Humor*〉

**subtract** [səb'trækt] *v. t.* abziehen. **subtraction** [səb'trækʃn] *n.* Subtraktion, *die*

**suburb** ['sʌbɜ:b] *n.* Vorort, *der.* **suburban** [sə'bɜ:bən] *adj.* Vorort-; 〈*Leben, Haus*〉 am Stadtrand

**subversive** [səb'vɜ:sɪv] *adj.* subversiv

**'subway** *n.* **a)** *(passage)* Unterführung, *die;* **b)** *(Amer.: railway)* Untergrundbahn, *die;* U-Bahn, *die*

**succeed** [sək'si:d] *v. i.* **a)** Erfolg haben; **sb. ~s in sth.** jmdm. gelingt etw.; jmd. schafft etw.; **sb. ~s in doing sth.** es gelingt jmdm., etw. zu tun; jmd. schafft es, etw. zu tun; **~ in business/ college** geschäftlich/im Studium erfolgreich sein; **I did not ~ in doing it** ich habe es nicht geschafft; **b)** *(come next)* die Nachfolge antreten

**success** [sək'ses] *n.* Erfolg, *der;* **make a ~ of sth.** bei etw. Erfolg haben. **successful** [sək'sesfl] *adj.* erfolgreich; **be ~ in sth./doing sth.** Erfolg bei etw. haben/dabei haben, etw. zu tun. **suc'cessfully** *adv.* erfolgreich

**succession** [sək'seʃn] *n.* **a)** Folge, *die;* **in ~:** hintereinander; **b)** *(series)* Serie, *die;* **c)** *(to throne)* Erbfolge, *die*

**successive** [sək'sesɪv] *adj.* aufeinanderfolgend. **suc'cessively** *adv.* hintereinander

**successor** [sək'sesə(r)] *n.* Nachfolger, *der/*Nachfolgerin, *die*

**succinct** [sək'sɪŋkt] *adj.* **a)** *(terse)* knapp; **b)** *(clear)* prägnant

**succulent** ['sʌkjʊlənt] *adj.* saftig

**succumb** [sə'kʌm] *v. i.* unterliegen; ~ **to** sth. einer Sache *(Dat.)* erliegen

**such** [sʌtʃ] **1.** *adj.* **a)** *(of that kind)* solch...; ~ **a person** ein solcher Mensch; ~ **a book** ein solches Buch; ~ **people** solche Leute; ~ **things** so etwas; **I said no** ~ **thing** ich habe nichts dergleichen gesagt; **there is no** ~ **bird** einen solchen Vogel gibt es nicht; **or some** ~ **thing** oder so etwas; **you'll do no** ~ **thing** das wirst du nicht tun; **experiences** ~ **as these** solche Erfahrungen; **b)** *(so great)* solch...; derartig; **I got** ~ **a fright that** ...: ich bekam einen derartigen *od. (ugs.)* so einen Schrecken, daß ...; ~ **was the force of the explosion that** ...: die Explosion war so stark, daß ...; **to** ~ **an extent** dermaßen; **c)** *with adj.* so; ~ **a big house** ein so großes Haus; ~ **a long time** so lange. **2.** *pron.* **as** ~: als solcher/solche/solches; *(strictly speaking)* im Grunde genommen; **an sich**; ~ **as** wie [zum Beispiel]; ~ **is life** so ist das Leben. **such-and-such** ['sʌtʃən-sʌtʃ] *adj.* **at** ~ **a time** um die und die Zeit. **'suchlike** *pron.* derlei

**suck** [sʌk] *v. t.* saugen (out of aus); lutschen ⟨*Bonbon*⟩. **suck 'up 1.** *v. t.* aufsaugen. **2.** *v. i.* ~ **up to sb.** *(sl.)* jmdm. in den Hintern kriechen *(salopp)*

**'sucker** *n.* **a)** *(suction pad)* Saugfuß, *der;* *(Zool.)* Saugnapf, *der;* **b)** *(sl.: dupe)* Dumme, *der/die*

**suckle** ['sʌkl] *v. t.* säugen

**suction** ['sʌkʃn] *n.* Saugwirkung, *die*

**Sudan** [suː'dɑːn] *pr. n.* |the| ~: [der] Sudan

**sudden** ['sʌdn] **1.** *adj.* **a)** *(unexpected)* plötzlich; **b)** *(abrupt)* jäh ⟨*Abgrund, Übergang, Ruck*⟩; **there was a** ~ **bend in the road** plötzlich machte die Straße eine Biegung. **2.** *n.* **all of a** ~: plötzlich. **'suddenly** *adv.* plötzlich. **'suddenness** *n.* Plötzlichkeit, *die*

**suds** [sʌdz] *n.* |soap-|~: [Seifen]lauge, *die;* *(froth)* Schaum, *der*

**sue** [suː] **1.** *v. t.* verklagen (for auf + *Akk.*). **2.** *v. i.* klagen (for auf + *Akk.*)

**suede** [sweɪd] *n.* Wildleder, *das*

**suet** ['suːɪt] *n.* Talg, *der*

**Suez** ['suɪz, 'sjuːɪz] *pr. n.* Suez *(das);* ~ **Canal** Suez-Kanal, *der*

**suffer** ['sʌfə(r)] **1.** *v. t.* erleiden; durchmachen ⟨*Schweres, Kummer*⟩; dulden ⟨*Unverschämtheit*⟩. **2.** *v. i.* leiden. **'suffer from** *v. t.* leiden unter (+ *Dat.*); leiden an (+ *Dat.*) ⟨*Krankheit*⟩

**sufferance** ['sʌfərəns] *n.* Duldung, *die;* **he remains here on** ~ **only** er ist hier bloß geduldet

**'suffering** *n.* Leiden, *das*

**suffice** [sə'faɪs] **1.** *v. i.* genügen; ~ **it to say** ...: nur soviel sei gesagt: ... **2.** *v. t.* genügen (+ *Dat.*)

**sufficiency** [sə'fɪʃənsɪ] *n.* Zulänglichkeit, *die*

**sufficient** [sə'fɪʃənt] *adj.* genug; ~ **money/food** genug Geld/genug zu essen; **be** ~: genügen; ~ **reason** Grund genug; **have you had** ~? *(food, drink)* haben Sie schon genug? **sufficiently** *adv.* genug; *(adequately)* ausreichend; ~ **large** groß genug; **a** ~ **large number** eine genügend große Zahl

**suffix** ['sʌfɪks] *n.* Nachsilbe, *die*

**suffocate** ['sʌfəkeɪt] **1.** *v. t.* ersticken; **he was** ~**d by the smoke** der Rauch erstickte ihn. **2.** *v. i.* ersticken. **suffocation** [sʌfə'keɪʃn] *n.* Erstickung, *die;* **a feeling of** ~: das Gefühl, zu ersticken

**sugar** ['ʃʊgə(r)] **1.** *n.* Zucker, *der;* **two** ~**s, please** *(lumps)* zwei Stück Zucker, bitte; *(spoonfuls)* zwei Löffel Zucker, bitte. **2.** *v. t.* zuckern

**sugar:** ~ **basin** *see* ~**-bowl;** ~**-beet** *n.* Zuckerrübe, *die;* ~**-bowl** *n.* Zuckerschale, *die;* *(covered)* Zuckerdose, *die;* ~**-cane** *n.* Zuckerrohr, *das;* ~**-coated** *adj.* gezuckert; mit Zucker überzogen ⟨*Dragee usw.*⟩; ~**-lump** *n.* Zuckerstück, *das;* *(when counted)* Stück Zucker

**'sugary** *adj.* süß; *(fig.)* süßlich

**suggest** [sə'dʒest] *v. t.* **a)** *(propose)* vorschlagen; ~ **sth. to sb.** jmdm. etw. vorschlagen; **he** ~**ed going to the cinema** er schlug vor, ins Kino zu gehen; **b)** *(assert)* **are you trying to** ~ **that he is lying** wollen Sie damit sagen, daß er lügt?; **c)** *(make one think of)* suggerieren ⟨*Symptome, Tatsachen:*⟩ schließen lassen auf (+ *Akk.*). **suggestion** [sə'dʒestʃn] *n.* **a)** Vorschlag, *der;* **at** *or* **on sb.'s** ~: auf jmds. Vorschlag *(Akk.);* **b)** *(insinuation)* Andeutungen *Pl.;* **c)** *(fig.: trace)* Spur, *die.* **suggestive** [sə'dʒestɪv] *adj.* **a)** **be** ~ **of sth.** auf etw. *(Akk.)* schließen lassen; **b)** *(indecent)* anzüglich

**suicidal** [suːɪ'saɪdl] *adj.* selbstmörderisch; **I felt** *or* **was quite** ~: ich hätte mich am liebsten gleich umgebracht

**suicide** ['suːɪsaɪd] *n.* Selbstmord, *der.* **'suicide attempt** *n.* Selbstmordversuch, *der*

**suit** [suːt] **1.** *n.* **a)** *(for men)* Anzug, *der;* *(for women))* Kostüm, *das;* **b)** *(Law)* ~ |**at law**| Prozeß, *der;* **c)** *(Cards)* Farbe, *die;* **follow ~** *(fig.)* das Gleiche tun. **2.** *v. t.* **a)** anpassen (**to** *Dat.*); **b)** be **~ed** |**to sth./one another**| [zu etw./zueinander] passen; **c)** *(satisfy needs of)* passen (+ *Dat.*); **will Monday ~ you?** paßt Ihnen Montag?; **does the climate ~ you?** bekommt Ihnen das Klima?; **d)** *(go well with)* passen zu; **does this hat ~ me?** steht mir dieser Hut?; **black ~s her** Schwarz steht ihr gut. **3.** *v. refl.* **~ oneself** tun, was man will; **~ yourself!** [ganz] wie du willst!

**suitability** [suːtəˈbɪlɪtɪ] *n.* Eignung, *die* (**for** für)

**suitable** [ˈsuːtəbl] *adj.* geeignet; angemessen ⟨*Kleidung*⟩; *(convenient)* passend; **Monday is the most ~ day** |**for me**| Montag paßt |mir| am besten. **suitably** [ˈsuːtəblɪ] *adv.* angemessen; entsprechend ⟨*gekleidet*⟩

'**suitcase** *n.* Koffer, *der*

**suite** [swiːt] *n.* **a)** *(of furniture)* Garnitur, *die;* **three-piece ~:** Polstergarnitur, *die;* **b)** *(of rooms)* Suite, *die*

**suitor** [ˈsuːtə(r)] *n.* Freier, *der*

**sulfur, sulfuric** *(Amer.) see* **sulph-**

**sulk** [sʌlk] *v. i.* schmollen. '**sulky** *adj.* schmollend; eingeschnappt *(ugs.)*

**sullen** [ˈsʌlən] *adj.* mürrisch

**sulphur** [ˈsʌlfə(r)] *n.* Schwefel, *der.* **sulphuric** [sʌlˈfjʊərɪk] *adj.* **~ acid** Schwefelsäure, *die*

**sultan** [ˈsʌltən] *n.* Sultan, *der*

**sultana** [sʌlˈtɑːnə] *n.* Sultanine, *die*

**sultry** [ˈsʌltrɪ] *adj.* schwül

**sum** [sʌm] *n.* **a)** Summe, *die* (**of** aus); **~** |**total**| Ergebnis, *das;* **b)** *(Arithmetic)* Rechenaufgabe, *die;* **do ~s** *(coll.)* rechnen; **she is good at ~s** *(coll.)* sie kann gut rechnen. **sum 'up 1.** *v. t.* **a)** zusammenfassen; **b)** *(Brit.: assess)* einschätzen. **2.** *v. i.* ein Fazit ziehen

**summarily** [ˈsʌmərɪlɪ] *adv.* summarisch; **~ dismissed** fristlos entlassen

**summarize** [ˈsʌməraɪz] *v. t.* zusammenfassen

**summary** [ˈsʌmərɪ] **1.** *adj.* summarisch; fristlos ⟨*Entlassung*⟩. **2.** *n.* Zusammenfassung, *die*

**summer** [ˈsʌmə(r)] *n.* Sommer, *der;* **in** |**the**| **~:** im Sommer. '**summerhouse** *n.* [Garten]laube, *die.* '**summertime** *n.* Sommer, *der*

'**summery** *adj.* sommerlich

**summing 'up** *n.* Zusammenfassung, *die*

**summit** [ˈsʌmɪt] *n.* Gipfel, *der*

**summon** [ˈsʌmən] *v. t.* **a)** rufen (**to** zu); holen ⟨*Hilfe*⟩; **b)** *(Law)* vorladen.

**summon 'up** *v. t.* aufbringen

**summons** [ˈsʌmənz] *n.* Vorladung, *die*

**sump** [sʌmp] *n.* Ölwanne, *die*

**sumptuous** [ˈsʌmptjʊəs] *adj.* üppig; luxuriös ⟨*Möbel, Kleidung*⟩

**sun** [sʌn] **1.** *n.* Sonne, *die;* **catch the ~** *(be in sunny position)* viel Sonne abbekommen; *(get ~burnt)* einen Sonnenbrand bekommen. **2.** *v. refl.,* **-nn-** sich sonnen

**Sun.** *abbr.* **Sunday** So.

**sun: ~bathe** *v. i.* sonnenbaden; **~bathing** *n.* Sonnenbaden, *das;* **~beam** *n.* Sonnenstrahl, *der;* **~-bed** *n. (with UV lamp)* Sonnenbank, *die;* *(in garden)* Gartenliege, *die;* **~burn** *n.* Sonnenbrand, *der;* **~burnt** *adj.* **be/get ~burnt** einen Sonnenbrand haben/bekommen

**sundae** [ˈsʌndeɪ] *n.* |**ice-cream**| **~:** Eisbecher, *der*

**Sunday** [ˈsʌndeɪ, ˈsʌndɪ] *n.* Sonntag, *der; see also* **Friday**

'**sundial** *n.* Sonnenuhr, *die*

**sundry** [ˈsʌndrɪ] **1.** *adj.* verschieden. **2.** *n. in pl.* Verschiedenes

'**sunflower** *n.* Sonnenblume, *die*

**sung** *see* **sing**

**sun: ~-glasses** *n. pl.* Sonnenbrille, *die;* **~-hat** *n.* Sonnenhut, *der*

**sunk** *see* **sink** 2, 3

**sun: ~-lamp** *n.* Höhensonne, *die;* **~lit** *adj.* sonnenbeschienen; **~light** *n.* Sonnenlicht, *das*

**sunny** [ˈsʌnɪ] *adj.* sonnig; **~ intervals** Aufheiterungen

**sun: ~rise** *n.* Sonnenaufgang, *der;* **~-roof** *n. (Motor Veh.)* Schiebedach, *das;* **~set** *n.* Sonnenuntergang, *der;* **~shade** *n.* Sonnenschirm, *der;* **~shine** *n.* Sonnenschein, *der;* **~stroke** *n.* Sonnenstich, *der;* **~-tan** *n.* [Sonnen]bräune, *die;* **get a ~-tan** braun werden; **~-tan lotion** *n.* Sonnencreme, *die;* **~-tanned** *adj.* braun[gebrannt]; **~-tan oil** *n.* Sonnenöl, *das*

**super** [ˈsuːpə(r)] *adj. (coll.)* super *(ugs.)*

**superb** [suːˈpɜːb] *adj.* einzigartig; erstklassig ⟨*Essen*⟩

**supercilious** [suːpəˈsɪlɪəs] *adj.* hochnäsig

**superficial** [suːpəˈfɪʃl] *adj.* oberflächlich

**superfluous** [sʊˈpɜːflʊəs] *adj.* überflüssig

**super:** **~glue** n. Sekundenkleber, der; **~human** adj. übermenschlich
**superintendent** [su:pərɪn'tendənt] n. (Brit. Police) Kommissar, der/Kommissarin, die
**superior** [su:'pɪərɪə(r)] 1. adj. **a)** (of higher quality) besonders gut ⟨Restaurant, Qualität, Stoff⟩; überlegen ⟨Technik, Intelligenz⟩; **he thinks he is ~ to us** er hält sich für besser als wir; **b)** (having higher rank) höher...; **be ~ to sb.** einen höheren Rang als jmd. haben. 2. n. Vorgesetzte, der/die. **superiority** [su:pɪərɪ'ɒrɪtɪ] n. Überlegenheit, die (to über + Akk.)
**superlative** [su:'pɜ:lətɪv] 1. adj. **a)** unübertrefflich; **b)** (Ling.) **a ~ adjective/ adverb** ein Adjektiv/Adverb im Superlativ. 2. n. (Ling.) Superlativ, der
**super:** **~market** n. Supermarkt, der; **~'natural** adj. übernatürlich; **~power** n. (Polit.) Supermacht, die
**supersede** [su:pə'si:d] v.t. ablösen (by durch)
**supersonic** [su:pə'sɒnɪk] adj. Überschall-
**superstition** [su:pə'stɪʃn] n. Aberglaube, der. **superstitious** [su:pə'stɪʃəs] adj. abergläubisch
**supervise** ['su:pəvaɪz] v.t. beaufsichtigen. **supervision** [su:pə'vɪʒn] n. Aufsicht, die. **supervisor** ['su:pəvaɪzə(r)] n. Aufseher, der/Aufseherin, die
**supper** ['sʌpə(r)] n. Abendessen, das; **have ⎪one's⎪ ~:** zu Abend essen. **'supper-time** n. Abendbrotzeit, die; **it's ~:** es ist Zeit zum Abendessen
**supplant** [sə'plɑ:nt] v.t. ablösen, ersetzen (by durch)
**supple** ['sʌpl] adj. geschmeidig
**supplement** ['sʌplɪmənt] 1. n. **a)** Ergänzung, die (to + Gen.); (addition) Zusatz, der; **b)** (of book) Nachtrag, der; **c)** (to fare) Zuschlag, der. 2. v.t. ergänzen. **supplementary** [sʌplɪ'mentərɪ] adj. zusätzlich; **~ fare/ charge** Zuschlag, der
**supplier** [sə'plaɪə(r)] n. (Commerc.) Lieferant, der/Lieferantin, die
**supply** [sə'plaɪ] 1. v.t. liefern ⟨Waren usw.⟩; beliefern ⟨Kunden, Geschäft⟩; **~ sth. to sb., ~ sb. with sth.** jmdn. mit etw. versorgen/(Commerc.) beliefern. 2. n. Vorräte Pl.; **military/medical supplies** militärischer/medizinischer Nachschub; **~ and demand** (Econ.) Angebot und Nachfrage
**support** [sə'pɔ:t] 1. v.t. **a)** (hold up) stützen ⟨Mauer, Verletzten⟩; (bear

weight of) tragen; **b)** unterstützen ⟨Politik, Verein⟩; (Footb.) **~ Spurs** Spurs-Fan sein; **c)** (provide for) ernähren ⟨Familie, sich selbst⟩; **d)** (speak in favour of) befürworten. 2. n. **a)** Unterstützung, die; **in ~:** zur Unterstützung; **speak in ~ of sb./sth.** jmdn. unterstützen/etw. befürworten; **b)** (money) Unterhalt, der; **c)** (sb./sth. that ~s) Stütze, die. **sup'porter** n. Anhänger, der/Anhängerin, die; **football ~:** Fußballfan, der. **sup'porting** adj. (Cinemat., Theatre) **~ role** Nebenrolle, die; **~ actor/actress** Schauspieler/-spielerin in einer Nebenrolle; **~ film** Vorfilm, der. **supportive** [sə'pɔ:tɪv] adj. hilfreich; **be very ~ ⎪to sb.⎪** ⎪jmdm.⎪ eine große Hilfe od. Stütze sein
**suppose** [sə'pəʊz] v.t. **a)** (assume) annehmen; **~ or supposing ⎪that⎪ he ...:** angenommen, ⎪daß⎪ er ...; **b)** (presume) vermuten; **I ~ so** (doubtfully) ja, vermutlich; (more confidently) ich glaube schon; **be ~d to do/be sth.** (be generally believed to do/be sth.) etw. tun/ sein sollen; **d)** (allow) **you are not ~d to do that** das darfst du nicht; **I'm not ~d to be here** ich dürfte eigentlich gar nicht hier sein. **supposedly** [sə'pəʊzɪdlɪ] adv. angeblich
**supposition** [sʌpə'zɪʃn] n. Annahme, die; Vermutung, die
**suppress** [sə'pres] v.t. unterdrücken. **suppression** [sə'preʃn] n. Unterdrückung, die
**supremacy** [su:'preməsɪ] n. **a)** (supreme authority) Souveränität, die; **b)** (superiority) Überlegenheit, die
**supreme** [su:'pri:m] adj. höchst...
**surcharge** ['sɜ:tʃɑ:dʒ] n. Zuschlag, der
**sure** [ʃʊə(r)] 1. adj. sicher; **be ~ of sth.** sich (Dat.) einer Sache (Gen.) sicher sein; **~ of oneself** selbstsicher; **don't be too ~:** da wäre ich mir nicht so sicher; **there is ~ to be a garage** es gibt bestimmt eine Tankstelle; **don't worry, it's ~ to turn out well** keine Sorge, es wird schon alles gutgehen; **for ~** (coll.) auf jeden Fall; **make ~ ⎪of sth.⎪** sich [einer Sache] vergewissern; **make or be ~ you do it, be ~ to do it** (do not fail to do it) sieh zu, daß du es tust; (do not forget) vergiß nicht, es zu tun; **a ~ winner** ein todsicherer Tip (ugs.). 2. adv. **~ enough** tatsächlich. 3. int. **~!, ~ thing!** (Amer.) na klar! (ugs.). **sure-footed** ['ʃʊəfʊtɪd] adj. trittsi-

cher. **'surely 1.** *adv.* **a)** *as sentence-modifier* doch; ~ **we've met before?** wir kennen uns doch, oder?; **b)** *(steadily)* sicher; **slowly but** ~: langsam, aber sicher; **c)** *(certainly)* sicherlich. **2.** *int. (Amer.)* natürlich

**surf** [sɜːf] *n.* Brandung, *die*

**surface** ['sɜːfɪs] **1.** *n.* Oberfläche, *die;* **outer** ~: Außenfläche, *die;* **the earth's** ~: die Erdoberfläche; **on the** ~: an der Oberfläche; *(fig.)* oberflächlich betrachtet. **2.** *v. i.* auftauchen; *(fig.)* hochkommen. **'surface area** *n.* Oberfläche, *die.* **'surface mail** *n.* gewöhnliche Post

**'surfboard** *n.* Surfbrett, *das*

**surfeit** ['sɜːfɪt] *n.* Übermaß, *das*

**'surfer** *n.* Surfer, *der*/Surferin, *die*

**'surfing** *n.* Surfen, *das*

**surge** [sɜːdʒ] *v. i.* ⟨*Wellen:*⟩ branden; **the crowd** ~**d forward** die Menschenmenge drängte sich nach vorn

**surgeon** ['sɜːdʒən] *n.* Chirurg, *der*/Chirurgin, *die*

**surgery** ['sɜːdʒərɪ] *n.* **a)** Chirurgie, *die;* **undergo** ~: sich einer Operation *(Dat.)* unterziehen; **b)** *(Brit.: place)* Praxis, *die;* **doctor's/dental** ~: Arzt-/Zahnarztpraxis, *die;* **c)** *(Brit.: time)* Sprechstunde, *die*

**surgical** ['sɜːdʒɪkl] *adj.* chirurgisch; ~ **treatment** Operation, *die*/Operationen

**surly** ['sɜːlɪ] *adj.* mürrisch

**surmise** [sə'maɪz] **1.** *n.* Vermutung, *die.* **2.** *v. t.* mutmaßen

**surmount** [sə'maʊnt] *v. t.* überwinden

**surname** ['sɜːneɪm] *n.* Nachname, *der;* Zuname, *der*

**surpass** [sə'pɑːs] *v. t.* übertreffen; ~ **oneself** sich selbst übertreffen

**surplus** ['sɜːpləs] **1.** *n.* Überschuß, *der* (**of** an + *Dat.*). **2.** *adj.* überschüssig; **be** ~ **to sb.'s requirements** von jmdm. nicht benötigt werden

**surprise** [sə'praɪz] **1.** *n.* **a)** Überraschung, *die;* **take sb. by** ~: jmdn. überrumpeln; **to my great** ~, **much to my** ~: zu meiner großen Überraschung; **it came as a** ~ **to us** es war für uns eine Überraschung; **b)** *attrib.* überraschend, unerwartet ⟨*Besuch*⟩; **a** ~ **attack** ein Überraschungsangriff. **2.** *v. t.* überraschen; überrumpeln ⟨*Feind*⟩; **I shouldn't be** ~**d if** ...: es würde mich nicht wundern, wenn ...; **be** ~**d at sb./sth.** sich über jmdn./etw. wundern. **surprising** [sə'praɪzɪŋ] *adj.* überraschend

**surreal** [sə'riːəl] *adj.* surrealistisch

**surrealism** [sə'riːəlɪzm] *n.* Surrealismus, *der*

**surrender** [sə'rendə(r)] **1.** *n.* *(to enemy)* Kapitulation, *die;* *(of possession)* Aufgabe, *die.* **2.** *v. i.* kapitulieren. **3.** *v. t.* aufgeben

**surreptitious** [sʌrəp'tɪʃəs] *adj.* heimlich; verstohlen ⟨*Blick*⟩

**surrogate** ['sʌrəgət] *n.* Ersatz, *der*

**surround** [sə'raʊnd] *v. t.* **a)** *(come or be all round)* umringen; ⟨*Truppen, Heer:*⟩ umzingeln ⟨*Stadt, Feind*⟩; **b)** *(encircle)* umgeben; **be** ~**ed by** *or* **with sth.** von etw. umgeben sein. **sur'rounding** *adj.* umliegend; **the** ~ **countryside** die [Landschaft in der] Umgebung. **sur'roundings** *n. pl.* Umgebung, *die*

**surveillance** [sə'veɪləns] *n.* Überwachung, *die;* **be under** ~: überwacht werden

**survey 1.** [sə'veɪ] *v. t.* betrachten; überblicken ⟨*Landschaft*⟩; inspizieren ⟨*Gebäude*⟩; bewerten ⟨*Situation*⟩. **2.** ['sɜːveɪ] *n.* Überblick, *der* (**of** über + *Akk.*); *(poll)* Umfrage, *die;* *(Surv.)* Vermessung, *die.* **surveyor** [sə'veɪə(r)] *n.* *(of building)* Gutachter, *der*/Gutachterin, *die;* *(of land)* Landvermesser, *der*/-vermesserin, *die*

**survival** [sə'vaɪvl] *n.* Überleben, *das;* **fight for** ~: Existenzkampf, *der*

**survive** [sə'vaɪv] **1.** *v. t.* überleben. **2.** *v. i.* ⟨*Person:*⟩ überleben; ⟨*Schriften, Traditionen:*⟩ erhalten bleiben. **survivor** [sə'vaɪvə(r)] *n.* Überlebende, *der/die*

**susceptible** [sə'septɪbl] *adj.* empfänglich (**to** für); *(to illness)* anfällig (**to** für)

**suspect 1.** [sə'spekt] *v. t.* **a)** *(imagine to be likely)* vermuten; ~ **the worst** das Schlimmste befürchten; ~ **sb. to be sth.,** ~ **that sb. is sth.** glauben *od.* vermuten, daß jmd. etw. ist; **b)** *(mentally accuse)* verdächtigen; ~ **sb. of sth./of doing sth.** jmdn. einer Sache verdächtigen/jmdn. verdächtigen, etw. zu tun. **2.** ['sʌspekt] *adj.* fragwürdig; verdächtig ⟨*Stoff, Paket*⟩. **3.** ['sʌspekt] *n.* Verdächtige, *der/die*

**suspend** [sə'spend] *v. t.* **a)** *(hang up)* [auf]hängen; **b)** *(stop)* suspendieren; **c)** *(from work)* ausschließen (**from** von); sperren ⟨*Sportler*⟩. **suspended 'sentence** *n.* *(Law)* Strafe mit Bewährung

**suspender belt** [sə'spendə belt] *n.* *(Brit.)* Strumpfbandgürtel, *der*

**suspenders** [sə'spendəz] *n. pl.* **a)**
*(Brit.: for stockings)* Strumpfbänder;
**b)** *(Amer.: for trousers)* Hosenträger
**suspense** [sə'spens] *n.* Spannung,
*die;* **keep sb. in ~:** jmdn. auf die Folter
spannen. **suspension** [sə'spenʃn] *n.*
*(Motor Veh.)* Federung, *die.* **su'spen-
sion bridge** *n.* Hängebrücke, *die*
**suspicion** [sə'spɪʃn] *n.* **a)** *(uneasy feeling)* Mißtrauen, *das (of* gegenüber);
*(unconfirmed belief)* Verdacht, *der;*
**have a ~ that ...:** den Verdacht haben,
daß ...; **b)** *(suspecting)* Verdacht, *der*
*(of* auf *+ Akk.);* **on ~ of murder** wegen Mordverdachts; **be under ~:** ver-
dächtigt werden
**suspicious** [sə'spɪʃəs] *adj.* **a)** *(tending
to suspect)* mißtrauisch *(of* gegenüber); **be ~ of sb./sth.** jmdm./einer
Sache mißtrauen; **b)** *(arousing suspicion)* verdächtig
**sustain** [sə'steɪn] *v. t.* **a)** *(support)* tragen ⟨*Gewicht*⟩; *(fig.)* aufrechterhalten;
**b)** erleiden ⟨*Verlust, Verletzung*⟩
**sustenance** ['sʌstɪnəns] *n.* Nahrung,
*die*
**SW** *abbr.* **a)** south-west SW; **b)** *(Radio)*
short wave KW
**swab** [swɒb] *n. (Med.: pad)* Tupfer,
*der*
**swagger** ['swægə(r)] *v. i.* großspurig
stolzieren
**¹swallow** ['swɒləʊ] **1.** *v. t.* schlucken;
*(by mistake)* verschlucken. **2.** *v. i.*
schlucken. **3.** *n.* Schluck, *der.* **swallow 'up** *v. t.* verschlucken
**²swallow** *n.* Schwalbe, *die*
**swam** *see* swim 1
**swamp** [swɒmp] **1.** *n.* Sumpf, *der.* **2.**
*v. t.* überschwemmen. **'swampy** *adj.*
sumpfig
**swan** [swɒn] *n.* Schwan, *der*
**swap** [swɒp] **1.** *v. t.,* -pp- tauschen *(for*
gegen). **2.** *v. i.,* -pp- tauschen. **3.** *n.*
Tausch, *der*
**swarm** [swɔ:m] **1.** *n.* Schwarm, *der.*
**2.** *v. i.* schwärmen; *(teem)* wimmeln
*(with* von)
**swarthy** ['swɔ:ðɪ] *adj.* dunkel
**swastika** ['swɒstɪkə] *n.* Hakenkreuz,
*das*
**swat** [swɒt] *v. t.,* -tt- totschlagen
**sway** [sweɪ] **1.** *v. i.* [hin und her]
schwanken; *(gently)* sich wiegen. **2.**
*v. t.* **a)** wiegen; **b)** *(influence)* beeinflussen. **3.** *n. (fig.)* Herrschaft, *die;*
**hold ~ over sb.** über jmdn. herrschen
**swear** [sweə(r)] **1.** *v. t.,* swore [swɔ:(r)],
sworn [swɔ:n] schwören ⟨*Eid usw.*⟩. **2.**

*v. i.,* swore, sworn **a)** fluchen; **b)** **~ to**
**sth.** etw. beschwören. **'swear at** *v. t.*
beschimpfen. **'swear by** *v. t. (coll.)*
schwören auf *(+ Akk.)*
**'swear-word** *n.* Kraftausdruck, *der*
**sweat** [swet] **1.** *n.* Schweiß, *der.* **2.** *v. i.*
schwitzen
**sweater** ['swetə(r)] *n.* Pullover, *der*
**'sweaty** *adj.* schweißig
**Swede** [swi:d] *n.* Schwede, *der/*
Schwedin, *die*
**swede** *n.* Kohlrübe, *die*
**Sweden** ['swi:dn] *pr. n.* Schweden
*(das)*
**Swedish** ['swi:dɪʃ] **1.** *adj.* schwedisch; **sb. is ~** er/sie: jmd. ist Schwede/
Schwedin. **2.** *n.* Schwedisch, *das; see*
*also* **English 2 a**
**sweep** [swi:p] **1.** *v. t.,* swept [swept] **a)**
fegen; kehren; **b)** **~ the country**
⟨*Epidemie, Mode:*⟩ das Land überrol-
len. **2.** *v. i.,* swept **a)** fegen; kehren; **b)**
*(go fast)* ⟨*Person, Auto:*⟩ rauschen;
⟨*Wind usw.:*⟩ fegen. **3.** *n.* **a) give sth. a**
**~:** etw. fegen *od.* kehren; **b)** *(curve)*
Bogen, *der.* **sweep 'up** *v. t.* zusam-
menfegen; zusammenkehren
**'sweeping** *adj.* pauschal; weitreichend ⟨*Einsparung*⟩; umwälzend ⟨*Veränderung*⟩
**sweet** [swi:t] **1.** *adj.* süß; reizend
⟨*Wesen, Gesicht, Mädchen*⟩; **have a ~**
**tooth** gern Süßes mögen; **how ~ of**
**you!** wie nett *od.* lieb von dir! **2.** *n.*
*(Brit.)* **a)** *(candy)* Bonbon, *das od. der;*
**b)** *(dessert)* Nachtisch, *der.* **sweet-
and-'sour** *attrib. adj.* süßsauer.
**'sweet corn** *n.* Zuckermais, *der*
**sweeten** ['swi:tn] *v. t.* süßen. **'sweetener** *n.* Süßstoff, *der*
**'sweetheart** *n.* Schatz, *der*
**'sweetness** *n.* Süße, *die*
**sweet:** **~ 'pea** *n.* Wicke, *die;* **~-shop**
*n. (Brit.)* Süßwarengeschäft, *das*
**swell** [swel] **1.** *v. t.,* **swelled, swollen**
['swəʊlən] *or* **swelled** anschwellen las-
sen. **2.** *v. i.,* **swelled, swollen** *or* **swelled**
**a)** *(expand)* ⟨*Körperteil:*⟩ anschwellen;
⟨*Segel:*⟩ sich blähen; ⟨*Material:*⟩ auf-
quellen; **b)** ⟨*Anzahl:*⟩ zunehmen.
**'swelling** *n.* Schwellung, *die*
**swelter** ['sweltə(r)] *v. i.* **~ing** glühend
heiß ⟨*Tag, Wetter*⟩; **~ing heat** Bruthit-
ze, *die*
**swept** *see* sweep 1, 2
**swerve** [swɜ:v] **1.** *v. i.* einen Bogen
machen; **~ to the right/left** nach
rechts/links [aus]schwenken. **2.** *n.* Bogen, *der*

**swift** [swɪft] **1.** *adj.* schnell. **2.** *n.* Mauersegler, *der.* '**swiftly** *adv.* schnell

**swig** [swɪg] *(coll.)* Schluck, *der*

**swill** [swɪl] *v. t.* ~ |out| [aus]spülen

**swim** [swɪm] **1.** *v. i.,* **-mm-,** swam [swæm], swum [swʌm] schwimmen; **my head was** ~ming mir war schwindelig. **2.** *n.* **have a/go for a** ~: schwimmen/schwimmen gehen. '**swimmer** *n.* Schwimmer, *der*/Schwimmerin, *die;* **be a good/poor** ~: gut/schlecht schwimmen können. '**swimming** *n.* Schwimmen, *das*

**swimming:** ~-**baths** *n. pl.* Schwimmbad, *das;* ~-**costume** *n.* Badeanzug, *der;* ~-**pool** *n.* Schwimmbecken, *das; (building)* Schwimmbad, *das;* ~-**trunks** *n. pl.* Badehose, *die*

'**swim-suit** *n.* Badeanzug, *der*

**swindle** ['swɪndl] **1.** *v. t.* betrügen; ~ **sb. out of sth.** jmdn. um etw. betrügen. **2.** *n.* Schwindel, *der;* Betrug, *der.* **swindler** ['swɪndlə(r)] *n.* Schwindler, *der*/Schwindlerin, *die*

**swine** [swaɪn] *n.* Schwein, *das*

**swing** [swɪŋ] **1.** *n.* **a)** Schaukel, *die;* **b)** (~ing) Schaukeln; **in full** ~ *(fig.)* in vollem Gang[e]. **2.** *v. i.,* swung [swʌn] **a)** schwingen; *(in wind)* schaukeln; **b)** *(go in sweeping curve)* schwenken. **3.** *v. t.,* swung schwingen. **swing-'door** *n.* Pendeltür, *die*

**swipe** [swaɪp] *(coll.) v. t.* **a)** *(hit)* knallen *(ugs.);* **b)** *(sl.: steal)* klauen *(ugs.)*

**swirl** [swɜ:l] **1.** *v. i.* wirbeln. **2.** *v. t.* umherwirbeln. **3.** *n.* Spirale, *die*

**swish** [swɪʃ] **1.** *v. i.* zischen. **2.** *n.* Zischen, *das.* **3.** *adj. (coll.)* schick *(ugs.)*

**Swiss** [swɪs] **1.** *adj.* Schweizer; schweizerisch; **he is** ~: jmd. ist Schweizer/Schweizerin. **2.** *n.* Schweizer, *der*/Schweizerin, *die;* **the** ~ *pl.* die Schweizer. **Swiss 'roll** *n.* Biskuitrolle, *die*

**switch** [swɪtʃ] **1.** *n.* **a)** *(esp. Electr.)* Schalter, *der;* **b)** *(change)* Wechsel, *der.* **2.** *v. t.* **a)** *(change)* ~ sth. |over| **to sth.** etw. auf etw. *(Akk.)* umstellen *od. (Electr.)* umschalten; **b)** *(exchange)* tauschen. **3.** *v. i.* wechseln; ~ |over| **to sth.** auf etw. *(Akk.)* umstellen *od. (Electr.)* umschalten. **switch 'off** *v. t. & i.* ausschalten; *(also fig. coll.)* abschalten. **switch 'on 1.** *v. t.* einschalten; anschalten. **2.** *v. i.* sich anschalten

**switch:** ~**back** *n.* Achterbahn, *die;* ~**board** *n.* [Telefon]zentrale, *die*

**Switzerland** ['swɪtsələnd] *pr. n.* die Schweiz

**swivel** ['swɪvl] **1.** *v. i.,* **-ll-** sich drehen. **2.** *v. t.,* **-ll-** drehen. '**swivel chair** *n.* Drehstuhl, *der*

**swollen** ['swəʊlən] **1.** *see* swell. **2.** *adj.* geschwollen; angeschwollen ‹Fluß›

**swoon** [swu:n] *(literary) v. i.* ohnmächtig werden

**swoop** [swu:p] **1.** *n.* **a)** Sturzflug, *der;* **b)** *(coll.: raid)* Razzia, *die.* **2.** *v. i.* herabstoßen; ~ **on sb.** sich auf jmdn. stürzen

**sword** [sɔ:d] *n.* Schwert, *das.* '**swordfish** *n.* Schwertfisch, *der*

**swore, sworn** *see* swear

**swot** [swɒt] *(Brit. coll.)* **1.** *n.* Streber, *der*/Streberin, *die.* **2.** *v. i.,* **-tt-** büffeln *(ugs.)*

**swum** *see* swim 1

**swung** *see* swing 2, 3

**sycamore** ['sɪkəmɔ:(r)] *n.* Bergahorn, *der*

**sycophant** ['sɪkəfænt] *n.* Kriecher, *der*

**syllable** ['sɪləbl] *n.* Silbe, *die*

**syllabus** ['sɪləbəs] *n.* Lehrplan, *der; (for exam)* Studienplan, *der*

**symbol** ['sɪmbl] *n.* Symbol, *das* (**of** für)

**symbolic** [sɪm'bɒlɪk], **symbolical** [sɪm'bɒlɪkl] *adj.* symbolisch. **symbolism** ['sɪmbəlɪzm] *n.* Symbolik, *die.* **symbolize** ['sɪmbəlaɪz] *v. t.* symbolisieren

**symmetrical** [sɪ'metrɪkl] *adj.* symmetrisch

**symmetry** ['sɪmɪtrɪ] *n.* Symmetrie, *die*

**sympathetic** [sɪmpə'θetɪk] *adj.* mitfühlend

**sympathize** ['sɪmpəθaɪz] *v. i.* **a)** ~ **with sb.** mit jmdm. [mit]fühlen; **b)** ~ **with** *(understand)* Verständnis haben für

**sympathy** ['sɪmpəθɪ] *n.* Mitgefühl, *das;* **in deepest** ~: mit aufrichtigem Beileid

**symphonic** [sɪm'fɒnɪk] *adj.* sinfonisch

**symphony** ['sɪmfənɪ] *n.* Sinfonie, *die*

**symptom** ['sɪmptəm] *n.* Symptom, *das.* **symptomatic** [sɪmptə'mætɪk] *adj.* symptomatisch (**of** für)

**synagogue** *(Amer.:* **synagog)** ['sɪnəgɒg] *n.* Synagoge, *die*

**synchromesh** ['sɪŋkrəmeʃ] *n. (Motor Veh.)* Synchrongetriebe, *das*

**synchronize** ['sɪŋkrənaɪz] *v. t.* synchronisieren; gleichstellen ‹Uhren›

**syndicate** ['sɪndɪkət] *n.* Syndikat, *das*

**syndrome** ['sɪndrəʊm] *n.* Syndrom, *das*

**synonym** ['sɪnənɪm] *n.* Synonym, *das.*

**synonymous** [sɪ'nɒnɪməs] *adj.* **a)** *(Ling.)* synonym (**with** mit); **b)** ~ **with** *(fig.)* gleichbedeutend mit

**synopsis** [sɪ'nɒpsɪs] *n., pl.* **synopses** [sɪ'nɒpsi:z] Inhaltsangabe, *die*

**syntactic** [sɪn'tæktɪk] *adj.* syntaktisch

**syntax** ['sɪntæks] *n.* Syntax, *die*

**synthesis** ['sɪnθɪsɪs] *n., pl.* **syntheses** ['sɪnθɪsi:z] Synthese, *die*

**synthesize** ['sɪnθɪsaɪz] *v.t.* zur Synthese bringen; *(Chem.)* synthetisieren.

**synthesizer** ['sɪnθɪsaɪzə(r)] *n. (Mus.)* Synthesizer, *der*

**synthetic** [sɪn'θetɪk] *adj.* synthetisch

**syphilis** ['sɪfɪlɪs] *n.* Syphilis, *die*

**syphon** *see* siphon

**Syria** ['sɪrɪə] *pr. n.* Syrien *(das)*

**syringe** [sɪ'rɪndʒ] **1.** *n.* Spritze, *die.* **2.** *v.t.* spritzen; ausspritzen ⟨*Ohr*⟩

**syrup** ['sɪrəp] *n.* Sirup, *der*

**system** ['sɪstəm] *n.* System, *das.* **systematic** [sɪstə'mætɪk] *adj.,* **systematically** [sɪstə'mætɪkəlɪ] *adv.* systematisch. **systematize** ['sɪstəmətaɪz] *v.t.* systematisieren. **'systems analyst** *n.* Systemanalytiker, *der*/ -analytikerin, *die*

# T

**T, t** [ti:] *n.* T, t, *das;* **to a T** ganz genau; **T-junction** Einmündung, *die;* **T-bone steak** T-bone-Steak, *das;* **T-shirt** T-shirt, *das*

**ta** [tɑ:] *int. (Brit. coll.)* danke

**tab** [tæb] *n.* **a)** *(projecting flap)* Zunge, *die; (on clothing)* Etikett, *das; (with name)* Namensschild, *das;* **b) pick up the** ~ *(Amer. coll.)* die Zeche bezahlen; **c) keep** ~s *or* **a** ~ **on** *(watch)* [genau] beobachten

**tabby** ['tæbɪ] *n.* ~ [**cat**] Tigerkatze, *die*

**table** ['teɪbl] **1.** *n.* **a)** Tisch, *der;* **b)** *(list)* Tabelle, *die;* ~ **of contents** Inhaltsverzeichnis, *das.* **2.** *v.t.* einbringen

**tableau** ['tæbləʊ] *n., pl.* ~**x** ['tæbləʊz] Tableau, *das*

**table:** ~**-cloth** *n.* Tischdecke, *die;* ~ **manners** *n. pl.* Tischmanieren *Pl.;* ~**-mat** *n.* Set, *das;* ~ **salt** *n.* Tafelsalz, *das;* ~**spoon** *n.* Servierlöffel, *der;* ~**spoonful** *n.* ≈ Eßlöffel[voll], *der*

**tablet** ['tæblɪt] *n.* **a)** Tablette, *die;* **b)** *(of soap)* Stück, *das*

**table:** ~ **tennis** *n.* Tischtennis, *das;* ~ **tennis bat** Tischtennisschläger, *der;* ~ **wine** *n.* Tischwein, *der*

**tabloid** ['tæblɔɪd] *n.* Boulevardzeitung, *die*

**taboo, tabu** [tə'bu:] **1.** *n.* Tabu, *das.* **2.** *adj.* Tabu⟨*wort*⟩; **be** ~: tabu sein

**tabulate** ['tæbjʊleɪt] *v.t.* tabellarisch darstellen. **tabulator** ['tæbjʊleɪtə(r)] *n.* Tabulator, *der*

**tacit** ['tæsɪt] *adj.,* **'tacitly** *adv.* stillschweigend

**taciturn** ['tæsɪtɜ:n] *adj.* schweigsam; wortkarg

**tack** [tæk] **1.** *n.* **a)** *(nail)* kleiner Nagel; **b)** *(stitch)* Heftstich, *der;* **c)** *(Naut., also fig.)* Kurs, *der.* **2.** *v.t.* **a)** *(nail)* festnageln; **b)** *(stitch)* heften. **3.** *v.i. (Naut.)* kreuzen

**tackle** ['tækl] **1.** *v.t.* **a)** angehen ⟨*Problem usw.*⟩; ~ **sb. about/on/over sth.** jmdn. auf etw. *(Akk.)* ansprechen; *(ask for sth.)* jmdn. um etw. angehen; **b)** *(Sport)* angreifen ⟨*Spieler*⟩; *(Amer. Footb.; Rugby)* fassen. **2.** *n.* **a)** *(equipment)* Ausrüstung, *die;* **b)** *(Sport)* Angriff, *der; (sliding* ~*)* Tackling, *das; (Amer. Footb.; Rugby)* Fassen und Halten

**tacky** ['tækɪ] *adj.* klebrig

**tact** [tækt] *n.* Takt, *der;* **he has no** ~: er hat kein Taktgefühl. **tactful** ['tæktfl] *adj.,* **'tactfully** *adv.* taktvoll

**tactical** ['tæktɪkl] *adj.* taktisch

**tactics** ['tæktɪks] *n. pl.* Taktik, *die*

**'tactless** *adj.,* **'tactlessly** *adv.* taktlos

**tadpole** ['tædpəʊl] *n.* Kaulquappe, *die*

**¹tag** [tæg] *n.* Schild, *das.* **tag a'long** *v.i.* mitkommen

**²tag** *n. (game)* Fangen, *das*

**tail** [teɪl] **1.** *n.* **a)** Schwanz, *der;* **b)** *in pl. (on coin)* ~**s** [**it is**] Zahl. **2.** *v.t. (sl.: follow)* beschatten. **tail 'back** *v.i.* sich stauen. **tail 'off** *v.i.* **a)** zurückgehen; **b)** *(into silence)* verstummen

**tail:** ~**back** *n. (Brit.)* Rückstau, *der;* ~**-end** *n.* Ende, *das;* ~**-gate** *n. (Motor Veh.)* Heckklappe, *die;* ~**-light** *n.* Rücklicht, *das*

**tailor** ['teɪlə(r)] *n.* Schneider, *der*/

Schneiderin, *die*. '**tailor-made** *adj.*
maßgeschneidert

'**tail wind** *n.* Rückenwind, *der*

**taint** [teɪnt] *v. t.* verderben; **be ~ed with
sth.** mit etw. behaftet sein *(geh.)*

**Taiwan** [taɪ'wɑːn] *pr. n.* Taiwan *(das)*

**take** [teɪk] **1.** *v. t.*, **took** [tʊk], **taken**
['teɪkn] **a)** *(get hold of, grasp, seize)*
nehmen; **b)** *(capture)* einnehmen
⟨*Stadt, Festung*⟩; machen ⟨*Gefangenen*⟩; **c)** *(gain, earn)* ⟨*Laden:*⟩
einbringen; ⟨*Person:*⟩ einnehmen;
⟨*Film, Stück:*⟩ einspielen; *(win)* gewinnen ⟨*Satz, Spiel, Preis, Titel*⟩; **d)** *(~
away with one)* mitnehmen; *(steal)*
mitnehmen *(verhüll.)*; **~ place** stattfinden; *(spontaneously)* sich ereignen;
⟨*Wandlung:*⟩ sich vollziehen; **e)** *(avail
oneself of, use)* nehmen; machen
⟨*Pause, Ferien, Nickerchen*⟩; **~ the opportunity to do/of doing sth.** die Gelegenheit dazu benutzen, etw. zu tun; **f)**
*(carry, guide, convey)* bringen; **~ sb. to
visit sb.** jmdn. zu Besuch bei jmdm.
mitnehmen; **~ home** mit nach Hause
nehmen; *(earn)* nach Hause bringen
⟨*Geld*⟩; *(accompany)* nach Hause bringen; **g)** *(remove)* nehmen; *(deduct)* abziehen; **~ sth./sb. from sb.** jmdm.
etw./jmdn. wegnehmen; **h)** *(make)*
machen ⟨*Foto, Kopie*⟩; *(photograph)*
aufnehmen; aufnehmen ⟨*Brief,
Diktat*⟩; machen ⟨*Prüfung, Sprung,
Spaziergang, Reise*⟩; ablegen ⟨*Gelübde, Eid*⟩; treffen ⟨*Entscheidung*⟩; **i)**
*(conduct)* halten ⟨*Gottesdienst, Unterricht*⟩; **Ms X ~s us for maths** in Mathe
haben wir Frau X; **j)** *(eat, drink)* nehmen ⟨*Zucker, Milch, Tabletten, Über-
dosis*⟩; trinken ⟨*Tee, Kaffee, Kognak
usw.*⟩; **k)** *(need, require)* brauchen
⟨*Platz, Zeit*⟩; haben ⟨*Objekt, Plural-s*⟩;
gebraucht werden mit ⟨*Kasus*⟩; **sth.
~s an hour/a year/all day** etw. dauert
eine Stunde/ein Jahr/einen ganzen
Tag; **l)** *(ascertain and record)* notieren
⟨*Namen, Adresse, Autonummer usw.*⟩;
fühlen ⟨*Puls*⟩; messen ⟨*Temperatur,
Größe usw.*⟩; **m)** *(assume)* **~ it [that]...:**
annehmen, daß...; **~ sb./sth. for/to be
sth.** jmdn./etw. für etw. halten; **n)**
*(react to)* aufnehmen; **~ sth. well/
badly** etw. gut/nur schwer verkraften;
**~ sth. calmly** *or* **coolly** etw. gelassen
[auf]nehmen; **o)** *(accept)* annehmen;
**p)** *(adopt, choose)* ergreifen ⟨*Maßnahmen*⟩; unternehmen ⟨*Schritte*⟩; **~
the wrong road** die falsche Straße nehmen; **q) be ~n ill** krank werden; **r) ~**

**sth. to bits** *or* **pieces** etw. auseinander-
nehmen. **2.** *v. i.*, **took, taken a)** ⟨*Transplantat:*⟩ vom Körper angenommen
werden; ⟨*Sämling, Pflanze:*⟩ angehen;
**b)** *(detract)* **~ from sth.** etw. schmälern. '**take after** *v. t. (resemble)*
jmdm. ähnlich sein; (**~ as one's
example)** es jmdm. gleichtun. **take
a'way** *v. t.* **a)** *(remove)* wegnehmen;
*(to a distance)* mitnehmen; **~ sth.
away from sb.** jmdm. etw. abnehmen;
**to ~ away** ⟨*Pizza, Snack usw.*⟩ zum
Mitnehmen; **b)** *(Math.: deduct)* abziehen. **take a'way from** *v. t.* schmälern. **take 'back** *v. t.* zurücknehmen;
*(return)* zurückbringen. **take 'down**
*v. t.* **a)** *(carry or lead down)* hinunter-
bringen; **b)** abnehmen ⟨*Bild, Ankündi-
gung, Weihnachtsschmuck*⟩; herunter-
ziehen ⟨*Hose*⟩; **~ sth. down from a
shelf** etw. von einem Regal herunter-
nehmen; **c)** *(write down)* aufnehmen.
**take 'in** *v. t.* **a)** hineinbringen; *(bring
indoors)* hereinholen; **b)** enger machen ⟨*Kleidungsstück*⟩; **c)** *(understand)* begreifen; **d)** *(cheat)* hereinlegen *(ugs.)*; *(deceive)* täuschen. **take
'off 1.** *v. t.* **a)** abnehmen ⟨*Deckel, Hut,
Tischtuch, Verband*⟩; abziehen ⟨*Kis-
senbezug*⟩; ausziehen ⟨*Schuhe, Hand-
schuhe*⟩; ablegen ⟨*Mantel, Schmuck*⟩;
**b)** *(deduct)* abziehen; **~ sth. off sth.**
etw. von etw. abziehen; **c) ~ a day** *etc.*
**off** sich *(Dat.)* einen Tag *usw.* frei
nehmen *(ugs.)*; **d)** *(mimic)* nachahmen. **2.** *v. i. (Aeronaut.)* starten. **take
'on** *v. t.* **a)** *(undertake)* übernehmen;
auf sich *(Akk.)* nehmen ⟨*Bürde*⟩; **b)**
*(employ)* einstellen; **c)** *(as opponent)* es
aufnehmen mit; *(Sport: meet)* antre-
ten gegen. **take 'out** *v. t.* **a)** *(remove)*
herausnehmen; ziehen ⟨*Zahn*⟩; **~ sth.
out of sth.** etw. aus etw. [heraus]neh-
men; **b)** *(withdraw)* abheben ⟨*Geld*⟩;
**c)** *(go out with)* **~ sb. out** mit jmdm.
ausgehen; **~ sb. out to** *or* **for lunch**
jmdn. zum Mittagessen einladen; **d)**
*(get issued)* abschließen ⟨*Versicherung*⟩; ausleihen ⟨*Bücher*⟩; **~ out a
subscription to sth.** etw. abonnieren;
**e) ~ it out on sb.** seine Wut an jmdm.
auslassen. **take 'over 1.** *v. t.* übernehmen. **2.** *v. i.* übernehmen; ⟨*Manager, Firmenleiter:*⟩ die Geschäfte
übernehmen; ⟨*Regierung, Präsident:*⟩
die Amtsgeschäfte übernehmen; **~
over from sb.** jmdn. ersetzen; *(temporarily)* jmdn. vertreten. '**take to** *v. t.* **a)**
*(get into habit of)* **~ to doing sth.** es

sich *(Dat.)* angewöhnen, etw. zu tun;
b) *(like)* sich hingezogen fühlen zu
⟨*Person*⟩; sich erwärmen für ⟨*Sache*⟩.
**take 'up 1.** *v. t.* **a)** *(lift up)* hochheben; *(pick up)* aufheben; herausreißen
⟨*Dielen*⟩; aufreißen ⟨*Straße*⟩; **b)** *(carry
or lead up)* hinaufbringen; **c)** in Anspruch nehmen ⟨*Zeit*⟩; brauchen/*(un-
desirably)* wegnehmen ⟨*Platz*⟩; **d)**
*(start)* ergreifen ⟨*Beruf*⟩; anfangen
⟨*Tennis, Schach, Gitarre usw.*⟩; aufnehmen ⟨*Arbeit, Kampf*⟩; antreten
⟨*Stelle*⟩; ~ **up a hobby** sich *(Dat.)* ein
Hobby zulegen; **e)** *(pursue further)* ~
**sth. up with sb.** sich in einer Sache an
jmdn. wenden. **2.** *v. i.* ~ **up with sb.**
*(coll.)* sich mit jmdm. einlassen
'**take-away** *n. (meal)* Essen zum Mitnehmen; *(restaurant)* Restaurant mit
Straßenverkauf
**taken** *see* **take**
**take:** ~**-off** *n.* **a)** *(Aeronaut.)* Start,
*der;* **b)** *(coll.: caricature)* Parodie, *die;*
~**-over** *n.* Übernahme, *die*
**takings** ['teɪkɪŋz] *n. pl.* Einnahmen
**talcum** ['tælkəm] *n.* ~ |**powder**| Kör-
perpuder, *der*
**tale** [teɪl] *n.* Erzählung, *die;* Geschichte, *die* (of von, about über + *Akk.*)
**talent** ['tælənt] *n.* Talent, *das;* **have**
|**great/no** *etc.*| ~ |**for sth.**| |viel/kein
*usw.*| Talent [zu *od.* für etw.] haben.
'**talented** *adj.* talentiert
**talk** [tɔːk] **1.** *n.* **a)** *(discussion)* Ge-
spräch, *das;* **have a** ~ |**with sb.**| |**about
sth.**| [mit jmdm.] [über etw. *(Akk.)*]
sprechen; **have** *or* **hold** ~**s** |**with sb.**|
[mit jmdm.] Gespräche führen; **b)**
*(speech, lecture)* Vortrag, *der.* **2.** *v. i.*
sprechen (**with, to** mit); *(lecture)* sprechen; *(converse)* sich unterhalten;
*(have* ~*s)* Gespräche führen; *(gossip)*
reden; ~ **on the phone** telefonieren. **3.**
*v. t.* reden; ~ **sb. into/out of sth.** jmdn.
zu etw. überreden/jmdm. etw. ausre-
den. **talk 'over** *v. t.* besprechen. **talk
'round** *v. t.* ~ **sb. round** jmdn. überreden
**talkative** ['tɔːkətɪv] *adj.* gesprächig
**talking:** ~ **point** *n.* Gesprächsthema,
*das;* ~**-to** *n. (coll.)* Standpauke, *die*
*(ugs.)*
**tall** [tɔːl] *adj.* hoch; groß ⟨*Person,
Tier*⟩; **that's a** ~ **order** das ist ziemlich
viel verlangt; ~ **story** unglaubliche
Geschichte
**tally** ['tælɪ] **1.** *n.* **keep a** ~ **of sth.** über
etw. *(Akk.)* Buch führen. **2.** *v. i.* übereinstimmen

**talon** ['tælən] *n.* Klaue, *die*
**tambourine** |tæmbə'riːn| *n.* Tambu-
rin, *das*
**tame** [teɪm] **1.** *adj.* zahm; *(fig.: spir-
itless)* lahm *(ugs.).* **2.** *v. t.* zähmen
**tamper** ['tæmpə(r)] *v. i.* ~ **with** sich
*(Dat.)* zu schaffen machen an
(+ *Dat.*)
**tampon** ['tæmpɒn] *n.* Tampon, *der*
**tan** [tæn] **1.** *v. t.,* -nn- gerben ⟨*Tierhaut,
Fell*⟩. **2.** *v. i.,* -nn- braun werden. **3.** *n.*
**a)** *(colour)* Gelbbraun, *das;* **b)** *(sun-*~*)*
Bräune, *die;* **have/get a** ~: braun sein/
werden. **4.** *adj.* gelbbraun
**tandem** ['tændəm] *n.* ~ |**bicycle**| Tan-
dem, *das*
**tang** [tæŋ] *n. (taste)* Geschmack, *der;*
*(smell)* Geruch, *der*
**tangent** ['tændʒənt] *n.* Tangente, *die;*
**go off at a** ~ *(fig.)* plötzlich vom Thema abschweifen
**tangible** ['tændʒɪbl] *adj.* greifbar;
spürbar ⟨*Unterschied, Verbesserung*⟩;
handfest ⟨*Beweis*⟩
**tangle** ['tæŋgl] **1.** *n.* Gewirr, *das; (in
hair)* Verfilzung, *die.* **2.** *v. t.* verheddern *(ugs.);* verfilzen ⟨*Haar*⟩. **tangle
'up** *v. t.* verheddern *(ugs.)*
**tango** ['tæŋgəʊ] *n., pl.* ~**s** Tango, *der*
**tank** [tæŋk] *n.* **a)** Tank, *der;* **b)** *(Mil.)*
Panzer, *der*
**tankard** ['tæŋkəd] *n.* Krug, *der*
**tanker** ['tæŋkə(r)] *n. (ship)* Tanker,
*der; (vehicle)* Tank[last]wagen, *der*
**tanned** [tænd] *adj.* braungebrannt
**tantalize** ['tæntəlaɪz] *v. t.* reizen. **tan-
talizing** ['tæntəlaɪzɪŋ] *adj.* verlockend
**tantamount** ['tæntəmaʊnt] *adj.* **be** ~
**to sth.** gleichbedeutend mit etw. sein
**tantrum** ['tæntrəm] *n.* Wutanfall, *der;
(of child)* Trotzanfall, *der;* **throw a** ~:
einen Wutanfall/Trotzanfall bekom-
men
'**tap** [tæp] **1.** *n.* Hahn, *der;* **hot/
cold|-water|** ~: Warm-/Kaltwasser-
hahn, *der;* **be on** ~ *(fig.)* zur Verfügung stehen. **2.** *v. t.,* -pp-: **a)** erschließen ⟨*Reserven, Markt*⟩; **b)** *(Teleph.)*
abhören; anzapfen *(ugs.)*
²**tap 1.** *v. t.,* -pp- klopfen an (+ *Akk.*);
*(on upper surface)* klopfen auf
(+ *Akk.*). **2.** *v. i.,* -pp-: ~ **at/on sth.** an
etw. *(Akk.)* klopfen; *(on upper surface)*
auf etw. *(Akk.)* klopfen. **3.** *n.* Klopfen,
*das.* '**tap-dance 1.** *n.* Step[tanz], *der.*
**2.** *v. i.* steptanzen; steppen
**tape** [teɪp] **1.** *n.* **a)** Band, *das;* **adhesive**
*or (coll.)* **sticky** ~: Klebeband, *das;* **b)**

*(for recording)* [Ton]band, *das* (of mit); **make a ~ of sth.** etw. auf Band aufnehmen. 2. *v. t.* **a)** *(record on ~)* [auf Band] aufnehmen; **b)** *(bind with ~)* [mit Klebeband] zukleben; **c) have got sb./sth. ~d** *(sl.)* jmdn. durchschaut haben/etw. im Griff haben

**tape: ~ cassette** *n.* Tonbandkassette, *die;* **~ deck** *n.* Tapedeck, *das;* **~-measure** *n.* Bandmaß, *das*

**taper** ['teɪpə(r)] 1. *v. i.* sich verjüngen; **~ |to a point|** spitz zulaufen. 2. *n.* |wax| **~:** Wachsstock, *der*

**tape: ~ recorder** *n.* Tonbandgerät, *das;* **~ recording** *n.* Tonbandaufnahme, *die*

**tapestry** ['tæpɪstrɪ] *n.* Gobelingewebe, *das; (wall-hanging)* Bildteppich, *der*

'**tapeworm** *n.* Bandwurm, *der*

'**tap-water** *n.* Leitungswasser, *das*

**tar** [tɑː(r)] 1. *n.* Teer, *der.* 2. *v. t.,* **-rr-** teeren

**target** ['tɑːgɪt] *n.* **a)** Ziel, *das;* **hit/miss the/its ~:** [das Ziel] treffen/das Ziel verfehlen; **b)** *(Sport)* Zielscheibe, *die*

**tariff** ['tærɪf] *n.* **a)** *(tax)* Zoll, *der;* **b)** *(list of charges)* Tarif, *der*

**tarnish** ['tɑːnɪʃ] 1. *v. t.* stumpf werden lassen ⟨*Metall*⟩; *(fig.)* beflecken ⟨*Ruf*⟩. 2. *v. i.* stumpf werden

**tarpaulin** [tɑːˈpɔːlɪn] *n.* Persenning, *die*

¹**tart** [tɑːt] *adj.* herb; sauer ⟨*Obst*⟩; *(fig.)* scharfzüngig

²**tart** *n.* **a)** *(Brit.) (filled pie)* ≈ Obstkuchen, *der; (small pastry)* Obsttörtchen, *das;* **b)** *(sl.: prostitute)* Nutte, *die (salopp).* **tart 'up** *v. t. (Brit. coll.)* **~ oneself up, get ~ed up** sich auftakeln *(ugs.)*

**tartan** ['tɑːtən] 1. *n.* Schotten[stoff], *der.* 2. *adj.* Schotten⟨*rock, -jacke*⟩

**tartar** ['tɑːtə(r)] *n.* Zahnstein, *der*

**tartar sauce** ['tɑːtə 'sɔːs] *n.* Remoulade[nsoße], *die*

**task** [tɑːsk] *n.* Aufgabe, *die;* **take sb. to ~:** jmdm. eine Lektion erteilen. '**task force** *n.* Sonderkommando, *das*

**tassel** ['tæsl] *n.* Quaste, *die*

**taste** [teɪst] 1. *v. t.* **a)** schmecken; *(try a little)* probieren; **b)** *(recognize flavour of)* [heraus]schmecken. 2. *v. i.* schmecken (of nach); **not ~ of anything** nach nichts schmecken. 3. *n.* **a)** *(flavour)* Geschmack, *der;* |sense of| **~:** Geschmack[ssinn], *der;* **b)** *(discernment)* Geschmack, *der;* **c)** *(sample)* Kostprobe, *die.* **tasteful** ['teɪstfl]

*adj.,* '**tastefully** *adv.* geschmackvoll.

'**tasteless** *adj.* geschmacklos. **tasty** ['teɪstɪ] *adj.* lecker

**tat** [tæt] *n. see* ²**tit**

**tattered** ['tætəd] *adj.* zerlumpt ⟨*Kleidung*⟩; zerfleddert ⟨*Buch*⟩. **tatters** ['tætəz] *n. pl.* Fetzen; **be in ~:** in Fetzen sein; *(fig.)* ruiniert sein

**tattoo** [təˈtuː] 1. *v. t.* tätowieren. 2. *n.* Tätowierung, *die*

**tatty** ['tætɪ] *adj. (coll.)* schäbig

**taught** *see* **teach**

**taunt** [tɔːnt] 1. *v. t.* verspotten (**about** wegen). 2. *n.* spöttische Bemerkung

**Taurus** ['tɔːrəs] *n.* der Stier

**taut** [tɔːt] *adj.* straff ⟨*Seil, Kabel*⟩; gespannt ⟨*Muskel*⟩

**tavern** ['tævən] *n.* Schenke, *die*

**tawny** ['tɔːnɪ] *adj.* gelbbraun

**tax** [tæks] 1. *n.* Steuer, *die.* 2. *v. t.* **a)** besteuern; versteuern ⟨*Einkommen*⟩; **b)** *(fig.)* strapazieren ⟨*Kräfte, Geduld*⟩. **taxable** ['tæksəbl] *adj.* steuerpflichtig. **taxation** [tækˈseɪʃn] *n.* Besteuerung, *die; (taxes payable)* Steuern. '**tax-free** *adj.* steuerfrei

**taxi** ['tæksɪ] 1. *n.* Taxi, *das.* 2. *v. i.,* **~ing** *or* **taxying** ⟨*Flugzeug:*⟩ rollen. '**taxi-driver** *n.* Taxifahrer, *der/*-fahrerin, *die*

'**tax inspector** *n.* Steuerinspektor, *der/*-inspektorin, *die*

**taxi: ~-rank** *(Brit.),* **~ stand** *(Amer.)* *ns.* Taxistand, *der*

**tax: ~payer** *n.* Steuerzahler, *der/*-zahlerin, *die;* **~ return** *n.* Steuererklärung, *die*

**tea** [tiː] *n.* **a)** Tee, *der;* **b)** *(meal)* |high| **~:** Abendessen, *das.* '**tea-bag** *n.* Teebeutel, *der.* '**tea-break** *n. (Brit.)* Teepause, *die*

**teach** [tiːtʃ] 1. *v. t.,* **taught** [tɔːt] unterrichten; *(at university)* lehren; **~ sb./oneself/an animal sth.** jmdm./sich/einem Tier etw. beibringen; **~ sb. to ride** jmdm. das Reiten beibringen. 2. *v. i.,* **taught** unterrichten. '**teacher** *n.* Lehrer, *der/*Lehrerin, *die*

**tea: ~-cloth** *n.* Geschirrtuch, *das;* **~cup** *n.* Teetasse, *die*

**teak** [tiːk] *n.* Teak[holz], *das*

'**tea-leaf** *n.* Teeblatt, *das*

**team** [tiːm] *n.* Team, *das; (Sport also)* Mannschaft, *die.* **team 'up** *v. i.* sich zusammentun *(ugs.)*

'**team-work** *n.* Teamarbeit, *die*

'**teapot** *n.* Teekanne, *die*

¹**tear** [teə(r)] 1. *n.* Riß, *der.* 2. *v. t.,* **tore** [tɔː(r)], **torn** [tɔːn] **a)** *(rip)* zerreißen;

*(pull apart)* auseinanderreißen; *(damage)* aufreißen; ~ **open** aufreißen ⟨*Brief, Paket*⟩; **b)** ~ **sth. out of sb.'s hands** jmdm. etw. aus der Hand reißen. **3.** *v. i.,* tore, torn **a)** *(rip)* [zer]reißen; **b)** *(move hurriedly)* rasen *(ugs.)*. **tear a'way** *v. t.* wegreißen; ~ **oneself away** *(fig.)* sich losreißen. **tear 'up** *v. t.* zerreißen

²**tear** [tɪə(r)] *n.* Träne, *die.* **tearful** ['tɪəfl] *adj.* weinend

**tear** [tɪə(r)]: ~**-drop** *n.* Träne, *die;* ~**-gas** *n.* Tränengas, *das*

**tease** [tiːz] **1.** *v. t.* necken (**about** wegen); aufziehen *(ugs.)* (**about** mit). **2.** *v. i.* seine Späße machen

**tea:** ~**-shop** *n. (Brit.)* ≈ Café, *das;* ~**spoon** *n.* Teelöffel, *der;* ~**-strainer** *n.* Teesieb, *das*

**teat** [tiːt] *n.* **a)** Zitze, *die;* **b)** *(of rubber or plastic)* Sauger, *der*

**tea:** ~**-time** *n.* Teezeit, *die;* ~**-towel** *n.* Geschirrtuch, *das*

**technical** ['teknɪkl] *adj.* technisch ⟨*Problem, Daten, Fortschritt*⟩; Fach-⟨*kenntnis, -sprache, -begriff, -wörterbuch*⟩; ~ **term** Fachbegriff, *der;* Fachausdruck, *der.* **technicality** [teknɪ'kælɪtɪ] *n.* technisches Detail

**technician** [tek'nɪʃn] *n.* Techniker, *der*/Technikerin, *die*

**technique** [tek'niːk] *n.* Technik, *die;* *(procedure)* Methode, *die*

**technological** [teknə'lɒdʒɪkl] *adj.* technisch; technologisch

**technology** [tek'nɒlədʒɪ] *n.* Technik, *die;* *(application of science)* Technologie, *die*

**teddy** ['tedɪ] *n.* ≈ [**bear**] Teddy[bär], *der*

**tedious** ['tiːdɪəs] *adj.* langwierig ⟨*Reise, Arbeit*⟩; *(uninteresting)* langweilig

**tee** [tiː] *(Golf)* Tee, *das*

**teem** [tiːm] *v. i.* wimmeln (**with** von)

**teenage[d]** ['tiːneɪdʒ(d)] *attrib. adj.* im Teenageralter *nachgestellt.* **teenager** ['tiːneɪdʒə(r)] *n.* Teenager, *der;* *(loosely)* Jugendliche, *der/die*

**teens** [tiːnz] *n. pl.* Teenagerjahre

**teeter** ['tiːtə(r)] *v. i.* wanken; ~ **on the edge of sth.** schwankend am Rande einer Sache *(Gen.)* stehen

**teeth** *pl. of* **tooth**

**teething troubles** ['tiːðɪŋ trʌblz] *n. pl.* have ~ *(fig.)* Anfangsschwierigkeiten haben

**teetotal** [tiː'təʊtl] *adj.* abstinent lebend. **teetotaller** [tiː'təʊtələ(r)] *n.* Abstinenzler, *der*/Abstinenzlerin, *die*

**telecommunications** [telɪkəmjuːnɪ'keɪʃnz] *n. pl.* Fernmelde- *od.* Nachrichtentechnik, *die*

**telegram** ['telɪgræm] *n.* Telegramm, *das*

**telegraph** ['telɪgrɑːf] *n.* Telegraf, *der;* ~ **pole** Telegrafenmast, *der*

**telepathy** [tɪ'lepəθɪ] *n.* Telepathie, *die*

**telephone** ['telɪfəʊn] **1.** *n.* Telefon, *das; attrib.* Telefon-; **answer the** ~: Anrufe entgegennehmen; *(on one occasion)* ans Telefon gehen; *(speak)* sich melden; **be on the** ~: Telefon haben; *(be speaking)* telefonieren (**to** mit). **2.** *v. t.* anrufen. **3.** *v. i.* anrufen; ~ **for a taxi** nach einem Taxi telefonieren

**telephone:** ~ **book** *n.* Telefonbuch, *das;* ~ **booth,** *(Brit.)* ~**-box** *ns.* Telefonzelle, *die;* ~ **call** *n.* Telefongespräch, *das;* ~ **directory** *n.* Telefonverzeichnis, *das;* ~ **exchange** *n.* Fernmeldeamt, *das;* ~ **number** *n.* Telefonnummer, *die;* ~ **operator** *n.* Telegrafist, *der*/Telegrafistin, *die*

**telephoto** [telɪ'fəʊtəʊ] *adj. (Photog.)* ~ **lens** Teleobjektiv, *das*

**teleprinter** ['telɪprɪntə(r)] *n.* Fernschreiber, *der*

**telescope** ['telɪskəʊp] *n.* Teleskop, *das;* Fernrohr, *das.* **telescopic** [telɪ'skɒpɪk] *adj. (collapsible)* ausziehbar; Teleskop⟨*antenne*⟩

**televise** ['telɪvaɪz] *v. t.* im Fernsehen senden *od.* übertragen

**television** ['telɪvɪʒn, telɪ'vɪʒn] *n.* **a)** *no art.* das Fernsehen; **on** ~: im Fernsehen; **watch** ~: fernsehen; **b)** *(~ set)* Fernsehapparat, *der;* Fernseher, *der (ugs.)*

**television:** ~ **channel** *n.* [Fernseh]kanal, *der;* ~ **programme** *n.* Fernsehsendung, *die;* ~ **set** *n.* Fernsehgerät, *das*

**Telex, telex** ['teleks] **1.** *n.* Telex, *das.* **2.** *v. t.* ein Telex schicken (+ *Dat.*); telexen ⟨*Nachricht*⟩

**tell** [tel] **1.** *v. t.,* told [təʊld] **a)** *(relate)* erzählen; *(make known)* sagen ⟨*Name, Adresse*⟩; anvertrauen ⟨*Geheimnis*⟩; ~ **sb. sth.** *or* **sth. to sb.** jmdm. etw. erzählen/sagen/anvertrauen; ~ **sb. the way to the station** jmdm. den Weg zum Bahnhof beschreiben; ~ **sb. the time** jmdm. die Uhrzeit sagen; ~ **tales** *(lie)* Lügengeschichten erzählen; *(gossip)* tratschen *(ugs.);* **b)** *(instruct)* sagen; ~ **sb. [not] to do sth.** jmdm. sagen, er soll[e] etw. [nicht] tun; **c)** *(determine)* feststellen; *(see, recognize)* erkennen **(by an +** *Dat.*)*;* *(with reference to the future)* [vorher]sagen; **d)** *(distinguish)* unterscheiden; **e) all told** insgesamt. **2.** *v. i., told* **a)** *(determine)* **how can you ~?** wie kann man das feststellen *od.* wissen?; **you never can ~:** man kann nie wissen; **b)** *(give information)* erzählen **(of, about** von); **c)** *(reveal secret)* es verraten; **time will ~:** das wird sich zeigen; **d)** *(produce an effect)* sich auswirken. **tell a'part** *v. t.* auseinanderhalten. **tell 'off** *v. t. (coll.)* **~ sb.** off **[for sth.]** jmdn. [für *od.* wegen etw.] ausschimpfen

**teller** ['telə(r)] *n.* **a)** *(in bank) see* **cashier; b)** *(counting votes)* Stimmenzähler, *der/*-zählerin, *die*

**telly** ['telɪ] *n. (Brit. coll.)* Fernseher, *der (ugs.)*

**temp** [temp] *n. (Brit. coll.)* Zeitarbeitskraft, *die*

**temper** ['tempə(r)] **1.** *n.* **a)** Naturell, *das; be* **in a good/bad ~:** gute/schlechte Laune haben; **keep/lose one's ~:** sich beherrschen/die Beherrschung verlieren; **b)** *(anger)* **fit of ~:** Wutanfall, *der;* **have a ~:** jähzornig sein. **2.** *v. t.* mäßigen; mildern ‹*Kritik*›

**temperament** ['temprəmənt] *n. (nature)* Veranlagung, *die;* Natur, *die; (disposition)* Temperament, *das.*

**temperamental** [temprə'mentl] *adj.* launenhaft

**temperate** ['tempərət] *adj.* gemäßigt

**temperature** ['temprɪtʃə(r)] *n.* Temperatur, *die;* **have or run a ~** *(coll.)* Temperatur *od.* Fieber haben

**template** ['templɪt] *n.* Schablone, *die*

**¹temple** ['templ] *n.* Tempel, *der*

**²temple** *n. (Anat.)* Schläfe, *die*

**tempo** ['tempəʊ] *n., pl.* **~s** *or* **tempi** ['tempi:] Tempo, *das*

**temporary** ['tempərərɪ] *adj.* vorübergehend; provisorisch ‹*Gebäude, Büro*›

**tempt** [tempt] *v. t.* **a) ~ sb. to do sth.** jmdn. geneigt machen, etw. zu tun; **be ~ed to do sth.** versucht sein, etw. zu tun; **~ sb. out** jmdn. hinauslocken; **b)** *(provoke)* herausfordern; **~ fate** das Schicksal herausfordern. **temptation** [temp'teɪʃn] *n.* **a)** *no pl. (attracting)* Verlockung, *die; (being attracted)* Versuchung, *die;* **b)** *(thing)* Verlockung, *die.* '**tempting** *adj.* verlockend

**ten** [ten] **1.** *adj.* zehn. **2.** *n.* Zehn, *die. See also* **eight**

**tenable** ['tenəbl] *adj.* haltbar ‹*Theorie*›; vertretbar ‹*Standpunkt*›

**tenacious** [tɪ'neɪʃəs] *adj.* hartnäckig. **tenacity** [tɪ'næsɪtɪ] *n.* Hartnäckigkeit, *die*

**tenant** ['tenənt] *n. (of flat, residential building)* Mieter, *der/*Mieterin, *die; (of farm, shop)* Pächter, *der/*Pächterin, *die*

**¹tend** [tend] *v. i.* **~ to do sth.** dazu neigen *od.* tendieren, etw. zu tun; **~ to sth.** zu etw. neigen; **he ~s to get upset if ...:** er regt sich leicht auf, wenn ...

**²tend** *v. t.* sich kümmern um; hüten ‹*Schafe*›; bedienen ‹*Maschine*›

**tendency** ['tendənsɪ] *n. (inclination)* Tendenz, *die;* **have a ~ to do sth.** dazu neigen, etw. zu tun

**¹tender** ['tendə(r)] *adj.* **a)** *(not tough)* zart; **b)** *(loving)* zärtlich; **c)** *(sensitive)* empfindlich

**²tender 1.** *v. t.* **a)** *(present)* einreichen ‹*Rücktritt*›; vorbringen ‹*Entschuldigung*›; **b)** *(offer as payment)* anbieten. **2.** *n.* Angebot, *das*

'**tenderly** *adv. (gently)* behutsam; *(lovingly)* zärtlich

'**tenderness** *n. see* **¹tender:** Zartheit, *die;* Zärtlichkeit, *die;* Empfindlichkeit, *die*

**tendon** ['tendən] *n. (Anat.)* Sehne, *die*

**tenement** ['tenɪmənt] *n.* Mietshaus, *das*

**tenet** ['tenɪt] *n.* Grundsatz, *der*

**tenner** ['tenə(r)] *n. (Brit. coll.)* Zehnpfundschein, *der*

**tennis** ['tenɪs] *n.* Tennis, *das*

**tennis:** **~-ball** *n.* Tennisball, *der;* **~-court** *n. (for lawn ~)* Tennisplatz, *der;* *(indoor)* Tennishalle, *die;* **~-racket** *n.* Tennisschläger, *der*

**tenor** ['tenə(r)] *n. (Mus.)* Tenor, *der*

**¹tense** [tens] *n. (Ling.)* Zeit, *die*

**²tense 1.** *adj.* gespannt. **2.** *v. i.* **sb. ~s** jmds. Muskeln spannen sich an. **3.** *v. t.* anspannen. **tension** ['tenʃn] *n.* **a)** Spannung, *die;* **b)** *(mental strain)* Anspannung, *die*

**tent** [tent] *n.* Zelt, *das*

**tentacle** ['tentəkl] *n.* Tentakel, *der od. das*

**tentative** ['tentətɪv] *adj.* **a)** *(not definite)* vorläufig; **b)** *(hesitant)* zaghaft

**tenterhooks** ['tentəhʊks] *n. pl.* **be on ~:** [wie] auf glühenden Kohlen sitzen

**tenth** [tenθ] **1.** *adj.* zehnt... **2.** *n. (in sequence)* zehnte, *der/die/das; (in rank)* Zehnte, *der/die/das; (fraction)* Zehntel, *das. See also* **eighth**

'**tent-peg** *n.* Zeltpflock, *der*

**tenuous** ['tenjʊəs] *adj.* dünn ‹*Atmo-*

*sphäre*⟩; dürftig ⟨*Argument*⟩; unbegründet ⟨*Anspruch*⟩

**tepid** ['tepɪd] *adj.* lauwarm

**term** [tɜ:m] **1.** *n.* **a)** [Fach]begriff, *der;* **b)** *in pl. (conditions)* Bedingungen; **come to ~s with sth.** mit etw. zurechtkommen; *(resign oneself to sth.)* sich mit etw. abfinden; **c)** *in pl. (charges)* Konditionen; **d) in the short/long/medium ~:** kurz-/lang-/mittelfristig; **e)** *(Sch.)* Halbjahr, *das; (Univ.: one of two/three divisions per year)* Semester, *das*/Trimester, *das;* **f)** *(limited period)* Zeitraum, *der;* **~ |of office|** Amtszeit, *die;* **g)** *in pl. (mode of expression)* Worte; **h)** *in pl. (relations)* **be on good/bad ~s with sb.** jit jmdm. auf gutem/ schlechtem Fuß stehen. **2.** *v. t.* nennen

**terminal** ['tɜ:mɪnl] **1.** *n.* **a)** *(for train or bus)* Bahnhof, *der; (for airline passengers)* Terminal, *der od. das;* **b)** *(Teleph., Computing)* Terminal, *das.* **2.** *adj. (Med.)* unheilbar

**terminate** ['tɜ:mɪneɪt] *v. t.* **a)** beenden; lösen ⟨*Vertrag*⟩; **b)** *(Med.)* unterbrechen ⟨*Schwangerschaft*⟩. **termination** [tɜ:mɪ'neɪʃn] *n.* **a)** *no pl.* Beendigung, *die; (of lease)* Ablauf, *der;* **b)** *(Med.)* Schwangerschaftsabbruch, *der*

**termini** *pl. of* **terminus**

**terminology** [tɜ:mɪ'nɒlədʒɪ] *n.* Terminologie, *die*

**terminus** ['tɜ:mɪnəs] *n., pl.* **~es** *or* **termini** ['tɜ:mɪnaɪ] Endstation, *die*

**terrace** ['terəs, 'terɪs] *n.* Häuserreihe, *die.* **terraced house** ['terəst haʊs], 'terɪst haʊs] *n.* Reihenhaus, *das*

**terrain** [te'reɪn] *n.* Gelände, *das*

**terrible** ['terɪbl] *adj.* **a)** *(coll.: very great or bad)* schrecklich *(ugs.);* **b)** *(coll.: incompetent)* schlecht; **c)** *(causing terror)* furchtbar. **terribly** ['terɪblɪ] *adv.* **a)** *(coll.: very)* unheimlich *(ugs.);* **b)** *(coll.: appallingly)* furchtbar *(ugs.);* **c)** *(coll.: incompetently)* schlecht; **d)** *(fearfully)* auf erschreckende Weise

**terrier** ['terɪə(r)] *n.* Terrier, *der*

**terrific** [tə'rɪfɪk] *adj. (coll.)* **a)** *(great, intense)* irrsinnig *(ugs.);* **b)** *(magnificent)* sagenhaft *(ugs.);* **c)** *(highly expert)* klasse *(ugs.)*

**terrify** ['terɪfaɪ] *v. t.* **a)** angst machen (+ *Dat.*); **be terrified that ...:** Angst haben, daß ...; **b)** *(scare)* Angst einjagen (+ *Dat.*). **terrifying** *adj.* entsetzlich ⟨*Erlebnis, Buch*⟩; furchterregend ⟨*Anblick*⟩; beängstigend ⟨*Geschwindigkeit*⟩

**territorial** [terɪ'tɔ:rɪəl] *adj.* territorial;

Gebiets⟨*anspruch usw.*⟩. **territory** ['terɪtrɪ] *n.* Gebiet, *das*

**terror** ['terə(r)] *n.* [panische] Angst; Schrecken, *der.* **terrorism** ['terərɪzm] *n.* Terrorismus, *der; (terrorist acts)* Terror, *der.* '**terrorist** *n.* Terrorist, *der*/Terroristin, *die.* **terrorize** ['terəraɪz] *v. t.* **a)** *(frighten)* in [Angst und] Schrecken versetzen; **b)** *(coerce)* terrorisieren

**terse** [tɜ:s] *adj.* **a)** *(concise)* kurz und bündig; **b)** *(curt)* knapp

**test** [test] **1.** *n.* **a)** *(Sch.)* Klassenarbeit, *die; (Univ.)* Klausur, *die;* **put sb./sth. to the ~:** jmdn./etw. erproben; **b)** *(analysis)* Test, *der.* **2.** *v. t.* untersuchen ⟨*Wasser, Augen*⟩; testen ⟨*Gehör, Augen*⟩; prüfen ⟨*Schüler*⟩; **~ sb. for Aids** jmdn. auf Aids untersuchen. '**test out** *v. t.* ausprobieren ⟨*Produkte*⟩ (**on** an + *Dat.*); erproben ⟨*Theorie, Idee*⟩

**Testament** ['testəmənt] *n.* **Old/New ~** *(Bibl.)* Altes/Neues Testament

**testicle** ['testɪkl] *n.* Testikel, *der (fachspr.);* Hoden, *der*

**testify** ['testɪfaɪ] **1.** *v. i.* **a)** **~ to sth.** etw. bezeugen; **b)** *(Law)* **~ against sb.** gegen jmdn. aussagen. **2.** *v. t.* bestätigen

**testimonial** [testɪ'məʊnɪəl] Zeugnis, *das;* Referenz, *die*

**testimony** ['testɪmənɪ] *n.* Aussage, *die*

'**test-tube** *n.* Reagenzglas, *das*

**testy** ['testɪ] *adj.* leicht reizbar ⟨*Person*⟩; gereizt ⟨*Antwort*⟩

**tetanus** ['tetənəs] *n.* Tetanus, *der*

**tetchy** ['tetʃɪ] *adj.* leicht reizbar; gereizt

**tether** ['teðə(r)] **1.** *n.* **be at the end of one's ~:** am Ende [seiner Kraft] sein. **2.** *v. t.* anbinden (**to** an + *Dat. od. Akk.*)

**text** [tekst] *n.* Text, *der.* '**textbook** *n.* Lehrbuch, *das*

**textile** ['tekstaɪl] *n.* Stoff, *der;* **~s** Textilien *Pl.*

**texture** ['tekstʃə(r)] *n.* Beschaffenheit, *die; (of fabric)* Struktur, *die*

**Thai** [taɪ] **1.** *adj.* thailändisch. **2.** *n.* **a)** *pl. same or* **~s** Thai, *der/die;* **b)** *(language)* Thai, *das.* **Thailand** ['taɪlænd] *pr. n.* Thailand *(das)*

**Thames** [temz] *pr. n.* Themse, *die*

**than** [ðən, *stressed* ðæn] *conj.* als; **I know you better ~ |I do|** him ich kenne dich besser als ihn

**thank** [θæŋk] *v. t.* **~ sb. |for sth.|** jmdm. [für etw.] danken; **~ God** *or* **goodness** *or* **heaven|s|** Gott sei Dank; **|I| ~ you**

danke; **no**, ~ **you** nein, danke; **yes**, ~
**you** ja, bitte; ~ **you very much** vielen
herzlichen Dank. **thankful** ['θæŋkfl]
*adj.* dankbar. **'thankless** *adj.* undankbar. **thanks** [θæŋks] *n. pl.* **a)**
*(gratitude)* Dank, *der;* ~ **to** *(with the
help of)* dank; *(on account of the bad
influence of)* wegen; **b)** *(formula expr.
gratitude)* danke; **no**, ~: nein, danke;
**yes**, ~: ja, bitte; **many** ~ *(coll.)* vielen
Dank. **'thank-you** *n. (coll.)* Danke-
schön, *das*

**that 1.** [ðæt] *adj., pl.* **those** [ðəʊz] **a)**
dieser/diese/dieses; **b)** *(coupled or
contrasted with 'this')* der/die/das. **2.**
[ðæt] *pron., pl.* **those a)** der/die/das;
**what bird is** ~? was für ein Vogel ist
das?; **like** ~: so; **|just| like** ~ *(without
effort, thought)* einfach so; ~**'s right!**
gut *od.* recht so; *(iron.)* nur so weiter!;
~ **will do** das reicht; **b)** *(Brit.)* **who is**
~? wer ist da?; *(on telephone)* wer ist
am Apparat? **3.** [ðət] *rel. pron., pl.*
**same** der/die/das; **everyone** ~ **I know**
jeder, den ich kenne; **this is all |the
money|** ~ **I have** das ist alles [Geld],
was ich habe. **4.** [ðæt] *adv. (coll.)* so. **5.**
[ðət] *rel. adv.* der/die/das; **the day** ~ **I
first met her** der Tag, an dem ich sie
zum ersten Mal sah. **6.** [ðət, *stressed*
ðæt] *conj.* daß; **|in order|** ~: damit

**thatch** [θætʃ] *n. (of straw)* Strohdach,
*das; (of reeds)* Schilfdach, *das; (roofing)* Dachbedeckung, *die.* **thatched**
[θætʃt] *adj.* stroh-/schilfgedeckt

**thaw** [θɔː] **1.** *n.* Tauwetter, *das.* **2.** *v. i.*
**a)** tauen; **b)** *(melt)* auftauen. **3.** *v. t.*
auftauen. **thaw 'out** *see* thaw 2, 3

**the** [*before vowel* ðɪ, *before consonant*
ðə, *when stressed* ðiː] **1.** *def. art.* der/
die/das. **2.** *adv.* ~ **more I practise** ~
**better I play** je mehr ich übe, desto *od.*
um so besser spiele ich; **so much** ~
**worse for sb./sth.** um so schlimmer für
jmdn./etw.

**theatre** *(Amer.:* **theater)** ['θɪətə(r)] *n.*
**a)** Theater, *das;* **b)** *(lecture* ~*)* Hör-
saal, *der;* **c)** *(Brit. Med.) see* **operating
theatre. theatrical** [θɪ'ætrɪkl] *adj.* **a)**
schauspielerisch; **b)** *(showy)* theatra-
lisch

**theft** [θeft] *n.* Diebstahl, *der*

**their** [ðeə(r)] *poss. pron. attrib.* ihr

**theirs** [ðeəz] *poss. pron. pred.* ihrer/ih-
re/ihres

**them** [ðəm, *stressed* ðem] *pron.* sie; *(as
indirect object)* ihnen; *see also* ¹**her**

**theme** [θiːm] *n.* Thema, *das*

**themselves** [ðəm'selvz] *pron.* **a)** em-

*phat.* selbst; **b)** *refl.* sich ⟨*waschen
usw.*⟩*;* sich selbst ⟨*die Schuld geben,
regieren*⟩*. See also* **herself**

**then** [ðen] **1.** *adv.* **a)** *(at that time)* damals; ~ **and there** auf der Stelle; **b)**
*(after that)* dann; ~ **|again|** *(and also)*
außerdem; **but** ~ *(after all)* aber
schließlich; **c)** *(in that case)* dann; **but**
~ **again** aber andererseits. **2.** *n.* **before**
~: vorher; davor; **since** ~: seitdem. **3.**
*adj.* damalig

**theological** [θiːə'lɒdʒɪkl] *adj.* theologisch; Theologie⟨*student*⟩

**theology** [θɪ'ɒlədʒɪ] *n.* Theologie, *die*

**theoretical** [θɪə'retɪkl] *adj.* theoretisch

**theory** ['θɪərɪ] *n.* Theorie, *die;* **in** ~:
theoretisch

**therapeutic** [θerə'pjuːtɪk] *adj.* therapeutisch

**therapist** ['θerəpɪst] *n.* Therapeut,
*der/*Therapeutin, *die*

**therapy** ['θerəpɪ] *n.* Therapie, *die*

**there** [ðeə(r)] **1.** *adv.* **a)** *(in/at that
place)* da; dort; *(fairly close)* da; **be
down/in/up** ~: da unten/drin/oben
sein; **b)** *(calling attention)* **hello** *or* **hi**
~! hallo!; **you** ~! Sie da!; **c)** *(in that respect)* da; **so** ~: und damit basta
*(ugs.);* **d)** *(to that place)* dahin, dorthin
⟨*gehen, fahren, rücken*⟩; **down/up**
~: dort hinunter/hinauf; **e)** [ðə(r),
*stressed* ðeə(r)] **was** ~ **anything in it?**
war da irgendwas drin?; ~ **was once es**
war einmal; ~ **is enough food** es gibt
genug zu essen. **2.** *int.* ~, ~: na, na
*(ugs.);* ~ **|you are|!** da, siehst du! **3.** *n.*
da; dort; **near** ~: da *od.* dort in der
Nähe. **thereabouts** ['ðeərəbaʊts]
*adv.* **a)** da [in der Nähe]; **b)** *(near that
number)* ungefähr. **therefore** ['ðeə-
fɔː(r)] *adv.* deshalb; also

**thermal** ['θɜːml] *adj.* thermisch; ~
**underwear** kälteisolierende Unterwäsche

**thermometer** [θə'mɒmɪtə(r)] *n.* Thermometer, *das*

**Thermos, thermos, (P)** ['θɜːməs] *n.*
~ **|flask/jug/bottle|** Thermosflasche,
*die* ⓌⓏ

**thermostat** ['θɜːməstæt] *n.* Thermostat, *der*

**these** *pl. of* **this**

**thesis** ['θiːsɪs] *n., pl.* **theses** ['θiːsiːz] **a)**
*(proposition)* These, *die;* **b)** *(dissertation)* Dissertation, *die* (**on** über
+ *Akk.*)

**they** [ðeɪ] *pron.* **a)** sie; **b)** *(people in
general)* man

**they'd** [ðeɪd] a) = **they would**; b) = **they had**

**they'll** [ðeɪl] = **they will**

**they're** [ðeə(r)] = **they are**

**they've** [ðeɪv] = **they have**

**thick** [θɪk] 1. *adj.* a) dick; **a rope two inches ~, a two-inch ~ rope** ein zwei Zoll starkes *od.* dickes Seil; b) *(dense)* dicht ⟨*Haar, Nebel, Wolken usw.*⟩; c) *(filled)* ~ **with** voll von; d) dickflüssig ⟨*Sahne*⟩; dick ⟨*Suppe, Schlamm, Kleister*⟩; e) *(stupid)* dumm. 2. *n.* **in the** ~ **of** mitten in (+ *Dat.*). **thick 'ear** *n.* **give sb. a** ~ *(Brit. sl.)* jmdm. ein paar hinter die Ohren geben *(ugs.)*

**thicken** ['θɪkn] 1. *v. t.* dicker machen; eindicken ⟨*Sauce*⟩. 2. *v. i.* a) dicker werden; b) ⟨*Nebel:*⟩ dichter werden; c) **the plot ~s** die Sache wird kompliziert

**'thickly** *adv.* a) *(in a thick layer)* dick; b) *(densely)* dicht

**'thickness** *n.* a) Dicke, *die;* **be two metres in** ~: zwei Meter dick sein; b) *(denseness)* Dichte, *die*

**thick:** **~-set** *adj.* gedrungen; **~skinned** *adj. (fig.)* dickfellig *(ugs.)*

**thief** [θiːf] *n., pl.* **thieves** [θiːvz] Dieb, *der*/Diebin, *die*

**thieve** [θiːv] *v. i.* stehlen

**thieves** *pl. of* **thief**

**thigh** [θaɪ] *n.* Oberschenkel, *der*

**thimble** ['θɪmbl] *n.* Fingerhut, *der*

**thin** [θɪn] 1. *adj.* a) dünn; **a tall, ~ man** ein großer, hagerer Mann; b) *(sparse)* dünn, schütter ⟨*Haar*⟩. 2. *adv.* dünn. 3. *v. t.* -nn-: a) dünner machen; b) *(dilute)* verdünnen. **thin 'out** *v. i.* ⟨*Menschenmenge:*⟩ sich verlaufen; ⟨*Verkehr:*⟩ abnehmen

**thing** [θɪŋ] *n.* a) Sache, *die;* Ding, *das;* **what's that ~ in your hand?** was hast du da in der Hand?; **be a rare ~:** etwas Seltenes sein; b) *(action)* **it was the right ~ to do** es war das einzig Richtige; **that was a foolish/friendly ~ to do** das war eine große Dummheit/ das war sehr freundlich; c) *(fact)* [Tat]sache, *die;* **it's a strange ~ that ...:** es ist seltsam, daß ...; **the best/worst ~ about her** das Beste/Schlimmste an ihr; d) *(idea)* **say the first ~ that comes into one's head** das sagen, was einem gerade so einfällt; **what a ~ to say!** wie kann man nur so etwas sagen!; e) *(task)* **she has a reputation for getting ~s done** sie ist für ihre Tatkraft bekannt; **a big ~ to undertake** ein großes Unterfangen; f) *(affair)* Sache, *die;* Angelegenheit, *die;* g) *(circumstance)*

**take ~s too seriously** alles zu ernst nehmen; **how are ~s?** wie geht's [dir]?; h) *(individual, creature)* Ding, *das;* i) *in pl. (personal belongings, clothes)* Sachen; j) *(product of work)* Sache, *die;* **the latest ~:** der letzte Schrei; k) *(what is important or proper)* das Richtige; **the ~ is ...** *(question)* die Frage ist ...

**think** [θɪŋk] 1. *v. t.,* **thought** [θɔːt] a) *(consider)* meinen; **we ~ [that] he will come** wir denken *od.* glauben, daß er kommt; **what do you ~?** was meinst du? **do you really ~ so?** findest du wirklich?; **what do you ~ of him/it?** was hältst du von ihm/davon?; ..., **don't you ~?** ... , findest *od.* meinst du nicht auch?; **I ~ so/not** ich glaube schon/nicht; **I ~ I'll try** ich glaube, ich werde es versuchen; b) *(imagine)* sich *(Dat.)* vorstellen. 2. *v. i.,* **thought** [nach]denken; **I need time to ~:** ich muß es mir erst überlegen; **I've been ~ing** ich habe nachgedacht; **~ twice** es sich *(Dat.)* zweimal überlegen. **'think of** *v. t.* a) denken an (+ *Akk.*); **he ~ of everything** er denkt einfach an alles; b) *(have as idea)* **we'll ~ of something** wir werden uns etwas einfallen lassen; **can you ~ of anyone who ...?** fällt dir jemand ein, der ...?; c) *(remember)* sich erinnern an (+ *Akk.*); **I just can't ~ of her name** ich komme einfach nicht auf ihren Namen; d) ~ **little/nothing of sb./sth.** *(consider contemptible)* wenig/nichts von jmdm./ etw. halten. **think 'over** *v. t.* sich *(Dat.)* überlegen. **think 'through** *v. t.* [gründlich] durchdenken. **think 'up** *v. t. (coll.)* sich *(Dat.)* ausdenken

**'thinker** *n.* Denker, *der*/Denkerin, *die*

**third** [θɜːd] 1. *adj.* dritt... 2. *n. (in sequence)* dritte, *der/die/das;* *(in rank)* Dritte, *der/die/das;* *(fraction)* Drittel, *das.* See also **eighth.** **'thirdly** *adv.* drittens

**'third-rate** *adj.* drittklassig

**Third 'World** *n.* dritte Welt

**thirst** [θɜːst] 1. *n.* Durst, *der;* **die of ~:** verdursten. 2. *v. i.* ~ **for revenge/ knowledge** nach Rache/Wissen dürsten *(geh.).* **'thirsty** *adj.* durstig; **be ~:** Durst haben

**thirteen** [θɜː'tiːn] 1. *adj.* dreizehn. 2. *n.* Dreizehn, *die.* See also **eight.**

**thirteenth** [θɜː'tiːnθ] *adj.* dreizehnt... See also **eighth**

**thirtieth** ['θɜːtɪɪθ] 1. *adj.* dreißigst... 2. *n. (fraction)* Dreißigstel, *das.* See also **eighth**

**thirty** ['θɜːtɪ] 1. *adj.* dreißig. 2. *n.* Dreißig, *die. See also* **eight; eighty** 2

**this** [ðɪs] 1. *adj., pl.* **these** [ðiːz] dieser/diese/dieses; *(with less emphasis)* der/die/das; **at ~ time** zu dieser Zeit; **by ~ time** inzwischen; mittlerweile; **these days** heut[zutag]e; **before ~ time** vorher; zuvor; **all ~ week** die[se] ganze Woche; **~ morning/evening** *etc.* heute morgen/abend *usw.;* **these last three weeks** die letzten drei Wochen; **~ Monday** *(to come)* nächsten Montag. 2. *pron., pl.* **these** a) **what's ~?** was ist [denn] das?; **fold it like ~!** falte es so!; b) *(the present)* **before ~:** bis jetzt; c) *(Brit. Teleph.: person speaking)* **~ is Andy hier** [spricht *od.* ist] Andy; *(Amer. Teleph.)* **who did you say ~ was?** wer ist am apparat?; d) **~ and that** dies und das

**thistle** ['θɪsl] *n.* Distel, *die*

**thorn** [θɔːn] *n.* a) *(part of plant)* Dorn, *der;* b) *(plant)* Dornenstrauch, *der.* **'thorny** *adj.* a) dornig; b) *(fig.)* heikel

**thorough** ['θʌrə] *adj.* gründlich

**thorough:** **~bred** *n.* reinrassiges Tier; *(horse)* Rassepferd, *das;* **~fare** *n.* Durchfahrtsstraße, *die;* **'no ~fare'** „Durchfahrt verboten"; *(on foot)* „kein Durchgang"

**'thoroughly** *adv.* gründlich *(untersuchen);* gehörig *(erschöpft);* so richtig *(genießen);* zutiefst *(beschämt);* total *(verdorben, verwöhnt);* **be ~ fed up with sth.** *(sl.)* von etw. die Nase gestrichen voll haben *(ugs.).* **'thoroughness** *n.* Gründlichkeit, *die*

**those** *see* **that** 1, 2

**though** [ðəʊ] 1. *(conj.)* a) *(despite the fact that)* obwohl; **late ~ it was** obwohl es so spät war; **the car, ~ powerful, is also economical** der Wagen ist zwar stark, aber [zugleich] auch wirtschaftlich; b) *(but nevertheless)* aber; **a slow ~ certain method** eine langsame, aber *od.* wenn auch sichere Methode; c) *(even if)* [even] **~:** auch wenn; d) *(and yet)* **~ you never know** obwohl man nie weiß. 2. *adv. (coll.)* trotzdem

**thought** [θɔːt] 1. *see* **think.** 2. *n.* a) *no pl.* Denken, *das;* b) *no pl., no art. (reflection)* Überlegung, *die;* Nachdenken, *das;* c) *(consideration)* Rücksicht, *die* (for auf + *Akk.*); d) *(idea, conception)* Gedanke, *der;* **it's the ~ that counts** der gute Wille zählt; **give up all ~[s] of sth.** sich *(Dat.)* etw. aus dem Kopf schlagen. **thoughtful** ['θɔːtfl] *adj.* a) nachdenklich; b) *(considerate)*

rücksichtsvoll; *(helpful)* aufmerksam. **'thoughtfully** *adv.* a) nachdenklich; b) *(considerately)* rücksichtsvollerweise. **'thoughtless** *adj.* a) gedankenlos; b) *(inconsiderate)* rücksichtslos. **'thoughtlessly** *adv.* a) gedankenlos; b) *(inconsiderately)* aus Rücksichtslosigkeit

**thousand** ['θaʊznd] 1. *adj.* a) tausend; **a** *or* **one ~:** eintausend; **two/several ~:** zweitausend/mehrere tausend; **a** *or* **one ~ and one** [ein]tausend[und]eins; b) **a ~** [and one] *(fig.: innumerable)* tausend *(ugs.).* 2. *n.* a) *(number)* tausend; **a** *or* **one/two ~:** ein-/zweitausend; b) *(written figure; group)* Tausend, *das;* c) *(indefinite amount)* **~s** Tausende. **thousandth** ['θaʊzndθ] 1. *adj.* tausendst... 2. *n. (fraction)* Tausendstel, *das; (in sequence)* Tausendste, *der/die/das*

**thrash** [θræʃ] *v.t.* a) verprügeln; b) *(defeat)* vernichtend schlagen. **thrash 'out** *v.t.* ausdiskutieren

**thread** [θred] 1. *n.* a) Faden, *der;* b) *(of screw)* Gewinde, *das.* 2. *v.t.* a) einfädeln; auffädeln *(Perlen);* b) **~ one's way through sth.** sich durch etw. schlängeln. **'threadbare** *adj.* a) abgenutzt; abgetragen *(Kleidung); (fig.)* abgedroschen *(Argument)*

**threat** [θret] *n.* Drohung, *die.* **threaten** ['θretn] *v.t.* a) bedrohen; **~ sb. with sth.** jmdm. etw. androhen; b) **~ to do sth.** damit drohen, etw. zu tun; c) drohen mit *(Gewalt, Rache usw.).* **threatening** ['θretnɪŋ] *adj.* drohend

**three** [θriː] 1. *adj.* drei. 2. *n.* Drei, *die. See also* **eight**

**three:** **~-dimensional** [θriːdɪ'menʃənl] *adj.* dreidimensional; **~fold** *adj., adv.* dreifach; **a ~fold increase** ein Anstieg auf das Dreifache; **~-quarters** 1. *n.* a) drei Viertel *pl.* (of + *Gen.*); **~-quarters of an hour** eine Dreiviertelstunde; 2. *adv.* dreiviertel *(voll);* **~some** ['θriːsəm] *n.* Dreigespann, *das;* Trio, *das*

**thresh** [θreʃ] *v.t.* dreschen

**threshold** ['θreʃəʊld] *n.* Schwelle, *die*

**threw** *see* **throw** 1

**thrift** [θrɪft] *n.* Sparsamkeit, *die.* **'thrifty** *adj.* sparsam

**thrill** [θrɪl] 1. *v.t.* a) *(excite)* faszinieren; b) *(delight)* begeistern. 2. *n.* a) Erregung, *die;* b) *(exciting experience)* aufregendes Erlebnis. **'thriller** *n.* Thriller, *der.* **'thrilling** *adj.* aufregend; spannend *(Buch, Film)*

**thrive** [θraɪv] *v. i.,* thrived *or* throve [θrəʊv], thrived *or* thriven ['θrɪvn] **a)** ⟨*Pflanze:*⟩ wachsen und gedeihen; **b)** *(prosper)* aufblühen ⟨on bei⟩

**throat** [θrəʊt] *n.* Hals, *der;* (*esp. inside*) Kehle, *die;* **a** |sore| ~: Halsschmerzen

**throb** [θrɒb] **1.** *v. i.,* -bb- pochen; ⟨*Motor:*⟩ dröhnen. **2.** *n.* Pochen, *das;* (*of engine*) Dröhnen, *das*

**throes** [θrəʊz] *n. pl.* Qual, *die;* **be in the ~ of sth.** *(fig.)* mitten in etw. *(Dat.)* stecken *(ugs.)*

**thrombosis** [θrɒm'bəʊsɪs] *n., pl.* **thromboses** [θrɒm'bəʊsi:z] Thrombose, *die*

**throne** [θrəʊn] *n.* Thron, *der*

**throng** [θrɒŋ] *n.* [Menschen]menge, *die*

**throttle** ['θrɒtl] *v. t.* erdrosseln

**through** [θru:] **1.** *prep.* **a)** durch; **b)** *(Amer.: up to and including)* bis [einschließlich]; **c)** *(by reason of)* durch; infolge von ⟨*Vernachlässigung, Einflüssen*⟩. **2.** *adv.* **a)** let sb. ~: jmdn. durchlassen; **b)** *(Teleph.)* be ~: durch sein *(ugs.);* be ~ to sb. mit jmdm. verbunden sein. **3.** *attrib. adj.* durchgehend ⟨*Zug*⟩. **through**'**out** **1.** *prep.* ~ **the war/period** den ganzen Krieg/die ganze Zeit hindurch; ~ **the country** im ganzen Land. **2.** *adv. (entirely)* ganz; *(always)* stets; die ganze Zeit [hindurch]

**throve** *see* **thrive**

**throw** [θrəʊ] **1.** *v. t.,* threw [θru:], thrown [θrəʊn] **a)** werfen; ~ sth. to sb. jmdm. etw. zuwerfen; ~ sth. at sb. etw. nach jmdm. werfen; **b)** *(bring to the ground)* zu Boden werfen; abwerfen ⟨*Reiter*⟩; **c)** *(coll.: disconcert)* ⟨*Frage:*⟩ aus der Fassung bringen. **2.** *n.* Wurf, *der.* **throw a**'**way** *v. t.* **a)** wegwerfen; **b)** *(lose by neglect)* verschenken ⟨*Vorteil, Spiel usw.*⟩. **throw** '**up** **1.** *v. t.* **a)** hochwerfen ⟨*Arme, Hände*⟩; **b)** *(produce)* hervorbringen ⟨*Ideen usw.*⟩. **2.** *v. i. (coll.)* brechen *(ugs.)*

'**throw-away** *adj.* **a)** Wegwerf-; Einweg-; **b)** beiläufig ⟨*Bemerkung*⟩

**thrown** *see* **throw** 1

**thrush** [θrʌʃ] *n. (Ornith.)* Drossel, *die*

**thrust** [θrʌst] **1.** *v. t.,* thrust stoßen; ~ aside *(fig.)* beiseite schieben. **2.** *n.* Stoß, *der*

**thud** [θʌd] *n.* dumpfer Schlag

**thug** [θʌg] *n.* Schläger, *der*

**thumb** [θʌm] **1.** *n.* Daumen, *der;* get the ~s up ⟨*Person, Projekt:*⟩ akzeptiert werden; **be under sb.'s** ~: unter jmds. Fuchtel stehen. **2.** *v. t.* ~ **a lift** per Anhalter fahren. '**thumb through** *v. t.* durchblättern

**thumb:** ~ **index** *n.* Daumenregister, *das;* ~**tack** *n. (Amer.)* Reißzwecke, *die*

**thump** [θʌmp] **1.** *v. t.* [mit Wucht] schlagen. **2.** *v. i.* **a)** hämmern ⟨at, on gegen⟩; **b)** ⟨*Herz:*⟩ heftig pochen. **3.** *n. (blow)* Schlag, *der;* (*sound*) Bums, *der (ugs.);* dumpfer Schlag

**thunder** ['θʌndə(r)] **1.** *n.* Donner, *der.* **2.** *v. i.* donnern. '**thunderclap** *n.* Donnerschlag, *der.* '**thunderstorm** *n.* Gewitter, *das.* '**thundery** *adj.* gewittrig

**Thurs.** *abbr.* **Thursday** Do.

**Thursday** ['θɜ:zdeɪ, 'θɜ:zdɪ] *n.* Donnerstag, *der; see also* **Friday**

**thus** [ðʌs] *adv.* so

**thwart** [θwɔ:t] *v. t.* durchkreuzen ⟨*Pläne*⟩; vereiteln ⟨*Versuch*⟩; ~ sb. jmdm. einen Strich durch die Rechnung machen

**thyme** [taɪm] *n.* Thymian, *der*

**thyroid** ['θaɪrɔɪd] *n.* Schilddrüse, *die*

**tiara** [tɪ'ɑ:rə] *n.* Diadem, *das*

**tick** [tɪk] **1.** *v. i.* ticken. **2.** *v. t.* **a)** mit einem Häkchen versehen; **b)** see ~ off a. **3.** *n.* **a)** *(of clock etc.)* Ticken, *das;* **b)** *(mark)* Häkchen, *das.* **tick** '**off** *v. t.* **a)** *(cross off)* abhaken; **b)** *(coll.: reprimand)* rüffeln *(ugs.)*

**ticket** ['tɪkɪt] *n.* Karte, *die;* (*for bus, train*) Fahrschein, *der;* (*for aeroplane*) Flugschein, *der;* (*for lottery, raffle*) Los, *das;* (*for library*) Ausweis, *der;* price ~: Preisschild, *das.* '**ticketcollector** *n. (on train)* Schaffner, *der*/Schaffnerin, *die;* (*on station*) Fahrkartenkontrolleur, *der*/-kontrolleurin, *die.* '**ticket-office** *n.* Fahrkartenschalter, *der;* (*for advance booking*) Kartenvorverkaufsstelle, *die*

**tickle** ['tɪkl] **1.** *v. t.* kitzeln. **2.** *v. i.* kitzeln. **ticklish** ['tɪklɪʃ] *adj.* kitzlig

**tidal** ['taɪdl] *adj.* Gezeiten-. '**tidal wave** *n.* Flutwelle, *die*

**tiddly-winks** ['tɪdlɪwɪŋks] *n. sing. (game)* Flohhüpfen, *das*

**tide** [taɪd] **1.** *n.* Tide, *die (nordd.);* **high** ~: Flut, *die;* **low** ~: Ebbe, *die;* **the ~s** die Gezeiten; **the ~ is in/out** es ist Flut/Ebbe. **2.** *v. t.* ~ **sb. over** jmdm. über die Runden helfen *(ugs.)*

**tidiness** ['taɪdɪnɪs] *n.* Ordentlichkeit, *die*

**tidy** ['taɪdɪ] **1.** *adj.* ordentlich; aufgeräumt ⟨*Zimmer, Schreibtisch*⟩. **2.** *v. t.* aufräumen; **~ oneself** sich zurechtmachen. **tidy 'up** *v. i.* aufräumen

**tie** [taɪ] **1.** *v. t.*, **tying** ['taɪɪŋ] binden (**to** an + *Akk.*, **into** zu); **~ a knot** einen Knoten machen; *(Sport)* **~ the match** unentschieden spielen. **2.** *v. i.*, **tying a)** *(be fastened)* **it ~s at the back** es wird hinten gebunden; **b)** *(have equal scores)* **~ for second place** mit gleicher Punktzahl den zweiten Platz erreichen. **3.** *n.* **a)** Krawatte, *die;* **b)** *(bond)* Band, *das; (restriction)* Bindung, *die;* **c)** *(equality of scores)* Punktgleichheit, *die;* **d)** *(Sport: match)* Begegnung, *die.* **tie 'in** *v. i.* **~ in with sth.** zu etw. passen. **tie 'up** *v. t.* **a)** festbinden; **~ up a parcel** ein Paket verschnüren; **b)** *(keep busy)* beschäftigen

**tier** [tɪə(r)] *n.* **a)** Rang, *der;* **b)** *(unit)* Stufe, *die*

**tiger** ['taɪgə(r)] *n.* Tiger, *der*

**tight** [taɪt] **1.** *adj.* **a)** *(firm)* fest; fest angezogen ⟨*Schraube, Mutter*⟩; festsitzend ⟨*Deckel*⟩; *(close-fitting)* eng ⟨*Kleid, Schuh usw.*⟩; **c)** *(impermeable)* **~ seal/joint** dichter Verschluß/dichte Fuge; **d)** *(taut)* straff; **e)** *(difficult to negotiate)* **a ~ corner** eine enge Kurve; **be in a ~ corner** *(fig.)* in der Klemme sein *(ugs.);* **f)** *(strict)* streng ⟨*Kontrolle, Disziplin*⟩; **g)** *(coll.: stingy)* knauserig *(ugs.);* **h)** *(coll.: drunk)* voll *(salopp).* **2.** *adv.* fest; **hold ~!** halt dich fest! **3.** *n.* **in** *pl.* **a)** *(Brit.)* |**pair of**| **~s** Strumpfhose, *die;* **b)** *(of dancer etc.)* Trikothose, *die.* **tighten** ['taɪtn] **1.** *v. t.* **a)** |fest| anziehen ⟨*Knoten, Schraube*⟩; straffziehen ⟨*Seil*⟩; **b)** verschärfen ⟨*Kontrolle*⟩. **2.** *v. i.* sich spannen. **tight-fisted** [taɪt'fɪstɪd] *adj.* geizig. **'tightrope** *n.* Drahtseil, *das*

**tile** [taɪl] **1.** *n.* *(on roof)* Ziegel, *der; (on floor, wall)* Fliese, *die;* Kachel, *die.* **2.** *v. t.* [mit Ziegeln] decken ⟨*Dach*⟩; fliesen ⟨*Wand, Fußboden*⟩; kacheln ⟨*Wand*⟩

**¹till** [tɪl] **1.** *prep.* bis; *(followed by article + noun)* bis zu; **not** […] **~:** erst. **2.** *conj.* bis

**²till** *n.* Kasse, *die*

**tilt** [tɪlt] **1.** *v. i.* kippen. **2.** *v. t.* kippen; neigen ⟨*Kopf*⟩. **3.** *n.* **a)** Schräglage, *die;* **a 45° ~:** eine Neigung von 45°; **b)** |**at**| **full ~:** mit voller Wucht

**timber** ['tɪmbə(r)] *n.* [Bau]holz, *das*

**time** [taɪm] **1.** *n.* **a)** Zeit, *die;* **in** |**the course of**| **~, as ~ goes on/went on** mit der Zeit; im Laufe der Zeit; **in ~, with**

**~** *(sooner or later)* mit der Zeit; **in** |**good**| **~** *(not late)* rechtzeitig; **all the ~ or this ~:** die ganze Zeit; *(without ceasing)* ständig; **a short ~ ago** vor kurzem; **~ off** *or* **out** freie Zeit; **in 'no ~:** im Handumdrehen; **in a week's/year's ~:** in einer Woche/in einem Jahr; **harvest/Christmas ~:** Ernte-/Weihnachtszeit, *die;* **on** *(punctually)* pünktlich; **ahead of ~:** zu früh ⟨*ankommen*⟩; vorzeitig ⟨*fertig werden*⟩; **have a good ~:** sich amüsieren; Spaß haben *(ugs.);* **b)** *(occasion)* Mal, *das;* **for the first ~:** zum ersten Mal; **at ~s** gelegentlich; **~ and again, ~ after ~:** immer |und immer| wieder; **at one ~, at** |**one and**| **the same ~** *(simultaneously)* gleichzeitig; **one at a ~:** einzeln; **two at a ~:** jeweils zwei; **c)** *(point in day etc.)* [Uhr]zeit, *die;* **tell the ~:** die Uhr lesen; **what ~ is it?, what is the ~?** wie spät ist es?; **by this/that ~:** inzwischen; **by the ~** |**that**| **we arrived** bis wir hinkamen; **d)** *(multiplication)* mal; **three ~s four** drei mal vier; **e)** *(Mus.)* Takt, *der;* **in ~:** im Takt. **2.** *v. t.* **a)** zeitlich abstimmen; **be well ~d** zur richtigen Zeit kommen; **b)** *(set to operate at correct ~)* einstellen; **c)** *(measure ~ taken by)* stoppen

**time: ~ bomb** *n.* Zeitbombe, *die;* **~-lag** *n.* zeitliche Verzögerung; **~-limit** *n.* Frist, *die*

**timely** ['taɪmlɪ] *adj.* rechtzeitig

**time: ~-scale** *n.* Zeitskala, *die;* **~-switch** *n.* Zeitschalter, *der;* **~table** *n.* **a)** *(scheme of work)* Zeitplan, *der; (Educ.)* Stundenplan, *der;* **b)** *(Transport)* Fahrplan, *der;* **~-zone** *n.* Zeitzone, *die*

**timid** ['tɪmɪd] *adj.* **a)** scheu ⟨*Tier*⟩; **b)** zaghaft ⟨*Mensch*⟩; *(shy)* schüchtern

**timing** ['taɪmɪŋ] *n.* **a)** **that was perfect ~!** du kommst gerade im richtigen Augenblick!; **b)** *(Theatre, Sport)* Timing, *das*

**tin** [tɪn] **1.** *n.* **a)** *(metal)* Zinn, *das;* **~-|-plate|** Weißblech, *das;* **b)** *(Brit.: for preserving)* [Konserven]dose, *die.* **2.** *v. t.*, **-nn-** *(Brit.)* zu Konserven verarbeiten. **tin 'foil** *n.* Stanniol, *das;* Alufolie, *die*

**tinge** [tɪndʒ] **1.** *v. t.*, **~ing** ['tɪndʒɪŋ] tönen. **2.** *n.* [leichte] Färbung; *(fig.)* Hauch, *der*

**tingle** ['tɪŋgl] *v. i.* kribbeln

**tinker** ['tɪŋkə(r)] **1.** *n.* Kesselflicker, *der.* **2.** *v. i.* **~ with sth.** an etw. *(Dat.)* herumbasteln *(ugs.)*

**tinkle** ['tɪŋkl] 1. *n.* Klingeln, *das.* 2. *v. i.* klingeln

**tinned** [tɪnd] *adj. (Brit.)* Dosen-

**tin:** ~**-opener** *n. (Brit.)* Dosenöffner, *der.* ~**pot** *attrib. adj. (derog.)* schäbig

**tinsel** ['tɪnsl] *n.* Lametta, *das*

**tint** [tɪnt] 1. *n.* Farbton, *der.* 2. *v. t.* tönen; kolorieren ⟨*Zeichnung*⟩

**tiny** ['taɪnɪ] *adj.* winzig

¹**tip** [tɪp] *n. (end, point)* Spitze, *die*

²**tip** 1. *v. i.,* -pp- *(lean, fall)* kippen; ~ **over** umkippen. 2. *v. t.,* -pp-: a) *(make tilt)* kippen; b) *(make overturn)* umkippen; *(Brit.: discharge)* kippen; c) voraussagen ⟨*Sieger*⟩; ~ **sb. to win** auf jmds. Sieg tippen; d) *(reward)* ~ **sb.** jmdm. Trinkgeld geben. 3. *n.* a) *(money)* Trinkgeld, *das;* b) *(special information)* Hinweis, *der;* Tip, *der (ugs.);* c) *(Brit.)* Müllkippe, *die.* **tip 'off** *v. t.* ~ **sb. off** jmdm. einen Hinweis *od. (ugs.)* Tip geben

'**tip-off** *n.* Hinweis, *der*

**tipsy** ['tɪpsɪ] *adj. (coll.)* angeheitert; beschwipst *(ugs.)*

**tip:** ~**toe** 1. *v. i.* auf Zehenspitzen gehen; 2. *n.* **on** ~**toe|s|** auf Zehenspitzen; ~**top** *adj.* tipptopp *(ugs.)*

¹**tire** ['taɪə(r)] *(Amer.) see* **tyre**

²**tire** 1. *v. t.* ermüden. 2. *v. i.* müde werden; ermüden; ~ **of sth./doing sth.** einer Sache *(Gen.)* überdrüssig werden. **tire 'out** *v. t.* erschöpfen; ~ **oneself out doing sth.** etw. bis zur Erschöpfung tun

**tired** ['taɪəd] *adj.* a) *(weary)* müde; b) *(fed up)* **be** ~ **of sth./doing sth.** etw. satt haben/es satt haben etw. zu tun. '**tireless** *adj.* unermüdlich. **tiresome** ['taɪəsəm] *adj.* a) *(wearisome)* mühsam; b) *(annoying)* lästig. **tiring** ['taɪərɪŋ] *adj.* ermüdend

**tissue** ['tɪʃuː, 'tɪsjuː] *n.* a) Gewebe, *das;* b) |**paper**| ~: Papiertuch, *das; (handkerchief)* Papiertaschentuch, *das;* c) ~ |**paper**| Seidenpapier, *das*

¹**tit** [tɪt] *n. (Ornith.)* Meise, *die*

²**tit** *n.* **it's** ~ **for tat** wie du mir, so ich dir

'**titb..‹** *n.* a) *(food)* Häppchen, *das (ugs.);* b) *(piece of news)* Neuigkeit, *die*

**title** ['taɪtl] *n.* Titel, *der.* '**title-role** *n.* Titelrolle, *die*

**tittle-tattle** ['tɪtltætl] *n.* Klatsch, *der (ugs.)*

**to** 1. *[before vowel* tʊ, *before consonant* tə, *stressed* tuː] *prep.* a) *(in the direction of and reaching)* zu; *(with name of place)* nach; **go to work/to the theatre** zur Arbeit/ins Theater gehen; **to France** nach Frankreich; b) *(as far as)* bis zu; **from London to Edinburgh** von London [bis] nach Edinburgh; **increase from 10 % to 20 %** von 10 % auf 20 % steigen; c) *introducing relationship or indirect object* **to sb./sth.** jmdm./einer Sache *(Dat.);* **lend/explain** *etc.* **sth. to sb.** jmdm. etw. leihen/erklären *usw.;* **speak to sb.** mit jmdm. sprechen; **that's all there is to it** mehr ist nicht dazu zu sagen; **what's that to you?** was geht das dich an?; **to me** *(in my opinion)* meiner Meinung nach; **14 miles to the gallon** 14 Meilen auf eine Gallone; d) *(until)* bis; **to the end** bis zum Ende; **to this day** bis heute; **five |minutes| to eight** fünf [Minuten] vor acht; e) *with infinitive of a verb* zu; *expr. purpose, or after* **too** um [...] zu; **want to know** wissen wollen; **do sth. to annoy sb.** etw. tun, um jmdn. zu ärgern; **too hot to drink** zu heiß zum Trinken; **he would have phoned but forgot to** er hätte angerufen, aber er vergaß es. 2. [tuː] *adv.* **to and fro** hin und her

**toad** [təʊd] *n. (also fig. derog.)* Kröte, *die*

'**toadstool** *n.* Giftpilz, *der*

**toast** [təʊst] 1. *n.* a) *no pl.* Toast, *der;* **a piece of** ~: eine Scheibe Toast; b) *(call to drink)* Toast, *der;* **drink a** ~ **to sb./sth.** auf jmdn./etw. trinken. 2. *v. t.* a) rösten; toasten ⟨*Brot*⟩; b) *(drink to)* trinken auf (+ *Akk.*). '**toaster** *n.* Toaster, *der*

**tobacco** [tə'bækəʊ] *n., pl.* ~**s** Tabak, *der.* **tobacconist** [tə'bækənɪst] *n.* Tabak[waren]händler, *der/*-händlerin, *die*

**toboggan** [tə'bɒgən] 1. *n.* Schlitten, *der.* 2. *v. i.* Schlitten fahren

**today** [tə'deɪ] 1. *n.* heute; ~'**s newspaper** die Zeitung von heute. 2. *adv.* heute

**toddler** ['tɒdlə(r)] *n.* ≈ Kleinkind, *das*

**to-do** [tə'duː] *n.* Getue, *das (ugs.)*

**toe** [təʊ] 1. *n.* Zeh, *der;* Zehe, *die; (of footwear)* Spitze, *die.* 2. *v. t.,* ~**ing** *(fig.)* ~ **the line** *or (Amer.)* **mark** sich einordnen. '**toe-nail** *n.* Zeh[en]nagel, *der*

**toffee** ['tɒfɪ] *n.* Karamel, *der; (Brit.: piece)* Toffee, *das;* Sahnebonbon, *das*

**together** [tə'geðə(r)] *adv.* a) *(in or into company)* zusammen; b) *(simultaneously)* gleichzeitig; c) *(one another)* miteinander

**toil** [tɔɪl] **1.** *v. i.* schwer arbeiten. **2.** *n.* [harte] Arbeit

**toilet** ['tɔɪlɪt] *n.* Toilette, *die.* 'toilet-bag *n.* Kulturbeutel, *der.* 'toilet-paper *n.* Toilettenpapier, *das*

**toiletries** ['tɔɪlɪtrɪz] *n. pl.* Körperpflegemittel; Toilettenartikel

**toilet:** ~-roll *n.* Rolle Toilettenpapier; ~ **water** *n.* Toilettenwasser, *das;* Eau de Toilette, *das*

**token** ['təʊkn] **1.** *n.* **a)** *(voucher)* Gutschein, *der;* **b)** *(counter, disc)* Marke, *die;* **c)** *(sign)* Zeichen, *das.* **2.** *attrib. adj.* symbolisch 〈*Preis*〉

**Tokyo** ['təʊkjəʊ] *pr. n.* Tokio *(das)*

**told** *see* tell

**tolerable** ['tɒlərəbl] *adj.* **a)** *(endurable)* erträglich **(to, for** für**)**; **b)** *(fairly good)* leidlich; annehmbar. **tolerance** ['tɒlərəns] *n.* Toleranz, *die.* **tolerant** ['tɒlərənt] *adj.* tolerant **(of, towards** gegen[über]**). tolerate** ['tɒləreɪt] *v. t.* dulden; *(bear)* ertragen 〈*Schmerzen*〉. **toleration** [tɒlə'reɪʃn] *n.* Tolerierung, *die (geh.)*

¹**toll** [təʊl] *n.* **a)** Gebühr, *die;* **b)** *(damage etc.)* Aufwand, *der;* **take its** ~ **of** sth. einen Tribut an etw. *(Dat.)* fordern *(fig.)*

²**toll** *v. i.* 〈*Glocke:*〉 läuten

'**toll-bridge** *n.* gebührenpflichtige Brücke

**tom** [tɒm] *n. (cat)* Kater, *der*

**tomato** [tə'mɑ:təʊ] *n., pl.* ~es Tomate, *die.* **to'mato juice** *n.* Tomatensaft, *der.* **tomato 'purée** *n.* Tomatenmark, *das*

**tomb** [tu:m] *n.* Grab, *das; (monument)* Grabmal, *das*

'**tomboy** *n.* Wildfang, *der*

'**tombstone** *n.* Grabstein, *der*

'**tom-cat** *n.* Kater, *der*

**tome** [təʊm] *n.* dicker Band; Wälzer, *der (ugs.)*

**tomfoolery** [tɒm'fu:lərɪ] *n.* Blödsinn, *der (ugs.)*

**tomorrow** [tə'mɒrəʊ] **1.** *n.* morgen; ~ **morning/afternoon/evening/night** morgen früh od. vormittag/nachmittag/abend/nacht; ~'s **newspaper** die morgige Zeitung. **2.** *adv.* morgen; **see you** ~! *(coll.)* bis morgen!; **the day after** ~: übermorgen

**ton** [tʌn] *n.* Tonne, *die*

**tone** [təʊn] **1.** *n.* **a)** *(sound)* Klang, *der;* *(Teleph.)* Ton, *der;* **b)** *(style of speaking)* Ton, *der;* **c)** *(tint, shade)* [Farb]ton, *der;* **d)** *(fig.: character)* **lower/raise the** ~ **of** sth. das Niveau

einer Sache *(Gen.)* senken/erhöhen; **set the** ~: den Ton angeben. **2.** *v. t.* tönen; abtönen 〈*Farbe*〉. **tone 'down** *v. t.* [ab]dämpfen 〈*Farbe*〉; *(fig.)* mäßigen 〈*Sprache*〉

**tongs** [tɒŋz] *n. pl.* |pair of| ~: Zange, *die*

**tongue** [tʌŋ] *n.* Zunge, *die;* **bite one's** ~ *(lit. or fig.)* sich auf die Zunge beißen; **find one's** ~: seine Sprache wiederfinden; **hold one's** ~: stillschweigen; **he made the remark** ~ **in cheek** *(fig.)* er meinte die Bemerkung nicht ernst. '**tongue-twister** *n.* Zungenbrecher, *der (ugs.)*

**tonic** ['tɒnɪk] **1.** *n.* **a)** *(Med.)* Tonikum, *das;* **b)** *(fig.: invigorating influence)* Wohltat, *die (geh.);* **c)** (~ **water**) Tonic, *das.* **2.** *attrib. adj.* kräftigend; *(fig.)* wohltuend 〈*Wirkung*〉. '**tonic water** *n.* Tonic[wasser], *das*

**tonight** [tə'naɪt] **1.** *n.* **a)** *(this evening)* heute abend; ~'s **performance** die heutige [Abend]vorstellung; **b)** *(this or the coming night)* heute nacht. **2.** *adv.* **a)** *(this evening)* heute abend; **b)** *(during this or the coming night)* heute nacht; **|I'll| see you** ~! bis heute abend!

**tonne** [tʌn] *n.* [metrische] Tonne

**tonsil** ['tɒnsl] *n.* [Gaumen]mandel, *die;* **have one's** ~s **out** sich *(Dat.)* die Mandeln herausnehmen lassen. **tonsillitis** [tɒnsə'laɪtɪs] *n.* Mandelentzündung, *die*

**too** [tu:] *adv.* **a)** *(excessively)* zu; ~ **difficult a task** eine zu schwierige Aufgabe; **b)** *(also)* auch; **c)** *(coll.: very)* besonders; **not** ~ **pleased** nicht gerade erfreut

**took** *see* take

**tool** [tu:l] *n.* Werkzeug, *das; (garden* ~) Gerät, *das;* |set of| ~s Werkzeug, *das.* '**tool box** *n.* Werkzeugkasten, *der.* '**tool kit** *n.* Werkzeug, *das*

**toot** [tu:t] **1.** *v. i. (on car etc. horn)* hupen. **2.** *n.* Tuten, *das*

**tooth** [tu:θ] *n., pl.* **teeth** [ti:θ] **a)** Zahn, *der;* **b)** *(of rake, fork, comb)* Zinke, *die; (of cog-wheel, saw)* Zahn, *der*

**tooth:** ~**ache** *n.* Zahnschmerzen *Pl.;* ~**brush** *n.* Zahnbürste, *die;* ~**paste** *n.* Zahnpasta, *die;* ~**pick** *n.* Zahnstocher, *der*

¹**top** [tɒp] **1.** *n.* **a)** *(highest part)* Spitze, *die; (of table)* Platte, *die;* (~ *end)* oberes Ende; *(of tree)* Wipfel, *der;* (~ *floor)* oberstes Stockwerk; *(rim of glass)* Rand, *der;* **on** ~ **of one another**

aufeinander; **on ~ of sth.** *(fig.: in addition)* zusätzlich zu etw.; **from ~ to bottom** von oben bis unten; **at the ~:** oben; **at the ~ of the building/hill/pile/stairs** oben im Gebäude/[oben] auf dem Hügel/[oben] auf dem Stapel/oben an der Treppe; **b)** *(highest rank)* Spitze, *die;* **~ of the table** *(Sport)* Tabellenspitze, *die;* **be |at the| ~ of the class** der/die Klassenbeste sein; **c)** *(upper surface)* Oberfläche, *die; (of cupboard, chest)* Oberseite, *die;* **on ~ of sth.** [oben] auf etw. *(position: Dat.; direction: Akk.);* **d)** *(folding roof)* Verdeck, *das;* **e)** *(upper deck of bus)* Oberdeck, *das;* **f)** *(cap of pen)* [Verschluß]kappe, *die;* **g)** *(upper garment)* Oberteil, *das;* **h)** *(lid)* Deckel, *der; (of bottle)* Stöpsel, *der.* **2.** *adj.* oberst...; höchst... ⟨*Ton, Preis*⟩; **~ end** oberes Ende; **the ~ pupil** der beste Schüler; **~ speed** Spitzen- *od.* Höchstgeschwindigkeit, *die.* **3.** *v. t.* **a)** *(be taller than)* überragen; **b)** *(surpass)* übertreffen. **top 'up** *(Brit. coll.) v. t.* auffüllen ⟨*Tank, Flasche, Glas*⟩

**²top** *n. (toy)* Kreisel, *der*

**top:** **~ 'hat** *n.* Zylinder[hut], *der;* **~-heavy** *adj.* oberlastig

**topic** ['tɒpɪk] *n.* Thema, *das.* **topical** ['tɒpɪkl] *adj.* aktuell

**'topless** *adj.* **a ~ dress/swimsuit** ein busenfreies Kleid/ein Oben-ohne-Badeanzug

**topmost** ['tɒpməʊst, 'tɒpməst] *adj.* oberst...; höchst... ⟨*Gipfel, Note*⟩

**topple** ['tɒpl] **1.** *v. i.* fallen. **2.** *v. t.* stürzen. **topple 'down** *v. i.* hinab-/herabfallen. **topple 'over** *v. i.* umfallen

**top 'secret** *adj.* streng geheim

**topsy-turvy** [tɒpsɪ'tɜːvɪ] *adv.* verkehrtrum *(ugs.);* **turn sth. ~:** etw. auf den Kopf stellen *(ugs.)*

**torch** [tɔːtʃ] *n. (Brit.)* Taschenlampe, *die*

**tore, torn** *see* **¹tear 2, 3**

**tornado** [tɔː'neɪdəʊ] *n., pl.* **~es** Wirbelsturm, *der; (in North America)* Tornado, *der*

**torpedo** [tɔː'piːdəʊ] **1.** *n., pl.* **~es** Torpedo, *der.* **2.** *v. t.* torpedieren

**torrent** ['tɒrənt] *n.* reißender Bach; *(fig.)* Flut, *die.* **torrential** [tə'renʃl] *adj.* wolkenbruchartig ⟨*Regen*⟩

**torso** ['tɔːsəʊ] *n., pl.* **~s** Rumpf, *der;* **bare ~:** nackter Oberkörper

**tortoise** ['tɔːtəs] *n.* Schildkröte, *die.* **tortoiseshell** ['tɔːtəsʃel] *n.* Schildpatt, *das*

**tortuous** ['tɔːtjʊəs] *adj.* verschlungen; *(fig.)* umständlich

**torture** ['tɔːtʃə(r)] **1.** *n.* Folter, *die.* **2.** *v. t.* foltern; *(fig.)* quälen

**toss** [tɒs] **1.** *v. t.* **a)** *(throw upwards)* hochwerfen; **~ a pancake** einen Pfannkuchen [durch Hochwerfen] wenden; **b)** *(throw casually)* werfen; schmeißen *(ugs.);* **c)** **~ a coin** eine Münze werfen; **d)** *(Cookery: mix)* wenden; mischen ⟨*Salat*⟩. **2,** *v. i.* **a)** **~ and turn** sich [schlaflos] im Bett wälzen; **b)** ⟨*Schiff:*⟩ hin und her geworfen werden; **c)** **(~ coin)** eine Münze werfen; **~ for sth.** mit einer Münze um etw. losen. **3.** *n.* **a)** **~ of a coin** Hochwerfen einer Münze; **b)** *(throw)* Wurf, *der.* **toss 'up** *v. i.* eine Münze werfen; **~ up for sth.** mit einer Münze um etw. losen

**¹tot** [tɒt] *n. (coll.)* **a)** kleines Kind; **b)** *(of liquor)* Gläschen, *das*

**²tot** *(coll.) v. t.,* **-tt-:** **~ 'up** zusammenziehen *(ugs.)*

**total** ['təʊtl] **1.** *adj.* **a)** gesamt; Gesamt- ⟨*gewicht, -wert, usw.*⟩; **b)** *(absolute)* völlig *nicht präd.;* **a ~ beginner** ein absoluter Anfänger. **2.** *n. (number)* Gesamtzahl, *die; (amount)* Gesamtbetrag, *der; (result of addition)* Summe, *die;* **a ~ of 200** insgesamt 200; **in ~:** insgesamt. **3.** *v. t., (Brit.)* **-ll-:** **a)** addieren, zusammenzählen ⟨*Zahlen*⟩; **b)** *(amount to)* [insgesamt] betragen

**totalitarian** [təʊtælɪ'teərɪən] *adj.* totalitär

**'totally** *adv.* völlig

**totter** ['tɒtə(r)] *v. i.* wanken; taumeln

**touch** [tʌtʃ] **1.** *v. t.* **a)** berühren; **b)** *(harm)* anrühren; **c)** *(fig.: rival)* **~ sth. an etw.** *(Akk.)* heranreichen; **d)** *(affect emotionally)* rühren. **2.** *v. i.* sich berühren; **don't ~!** nicht anfassen! **3.** *n.* **a)** Berührung, *die;* **b)** *no art. (faculty)* |sense of| **~:** Tastsinn, *der;* **c)** *(small amount)* **a ~ of salt/pepper** *etc.* eine Spur Salz/Pfeffer *usw.;* **a ~ of irony** *etc.* ein Anflug von Ironie *usw.;* **d)** *(fig.)* Detail, *das;* **e)** *(communication)* **be in/out of ~ |with sb.|** [mit jmdm.] Kontakt/keinen Kontakt haben; **get in ~:** mit jmdm. Kontakt aufnehmen. **touch 'down** *v. i.* ⟨*Flugzeug:*⟩ landen. **'touch on** *v. t. (mention)* ansprechen. **touch 'up** *v. t. (improve)* ausbessern. **'touch:** **~-and-go** *adj.* **it is ~-and-go |whether...|** es steht auf des Messers Schneide [, ob...]; **~down** *n. (Aeronaut.)* Landung, *die*

**'touching** adj. rührend. **touchy** ['tʌ-tʃɪ] adj. empfindlich; heikel ⟨Thema⟩

**tough** [tʌf] adj. **a)** fest ⟨Material, Stoff⟩; zäh ⟨Fleisch; fachspr.: Werkstoff, Metall⟩; widerstandsfähig ⟨Belag, Glas, Haut⟩; strapazierfähig ⟨Kleidung⟩; **b)** (hardy) zäh ⟨Person⟩; **c)** (difficult) schwierig; **d)** (severe, harsh) hart; **e)** (coll.) ~ luck Pech, das. **toughen** ['tʌfn] v. t. ~ |up| abhärten ⟨Person⟩; verschärfen ⟨Gesetz⟩

**tour** [tʊə(r)] **1.** n. **a)** [Rund]reise, die; Tour, die (ugs.); **b)** (Theatre, Sport) Tournee, die; **c)** (of house etc.) Besichtigung, die; **d)** ~ |of duty| Dienstzeit, die. **2.** v. i. **a)** ~/**go** ~**ing in** or **through a country** eine Reise od. (ugs.) Tour durch ein Land machen; **b)** (Theatre, Sport) eine Tournee machen. **3.** v. t. **a)** besichtigen ⟨Stadt, Gebäude⟩; ~ **a country/region** eine Reise od. (ugs.) Tour durch ein Land/Gebiet machen; **b)** (Theatre, Sport) ~ **a country/the provinces** eine Tournee durch das Land/die Provinz machen

**tourism** ['tʊərɪzm] n. **a)** Tourismus, der; **b)** (operation of tours) Touristik, die. **tourist** ['tʊərɪst] **1.** n. Tourist, der/Touristin, die. **2.** attrib. adj. Touristen-. **tourist infor'mation centre, 'tourist office** ns. Fremdenverkehrsbüro, das

**tournament** ['tʊənəmənt] n. (Hist.; Sport) Turnier, das

**'tour operator** n. Reiseveranstalter, der/-veranstalterin, die

**tousle** ['taʊzl] v. t. zerzausen

**tout** [taʊt] **1.** v. i. ~ **for customers** Kunden anreißen (ugs.) od. werben. **2.** n. Anreißer, der/Anreißerin, die (ugs.); **ticket** ~: Kartenschwarzhändler, der/-händlerin, die

**tow** [təʊ] **1.** v. t. schleppen; ziehen ⟨Anhänger, Wasserskiläufer⟩. **2.** n. Schleppen, das; **give a car a** ~: einen Wagen schleppen; **on** ~: im Schlepp[tau]. **tow a'way** v. t. abschleppen

**toward** [tə'wɔːd], **towards** [tə'wɔːdz] prep. **a)** (in direction of) ~ **sb./sth.** auf jmdn./etw. zu; **turn** ~ **sb.** sich zu jmdm. umdrehen; **b)** (in relation to) gegenüber; **feel sth.** ~ **sb.** jmdm. gegenüber etw. empfinden; **c)** (for) **a contribution** ~ **sth.** ein Beitrag zu etw.; **proposals** ~ **solving a problem** Vorschläge zur Lösung eines Problems; **d)** (near) gegen; ~ **the end of May** [gegen] Ende Mai

**towel** ['taʊəl] n. Handtuch, das

**tower** ['taʊə(r)] **1.** n. Turm, der. **2.** v. i. in die Höhe ragen. **'tower above** v. t. ~ **above sb./sth.** jmdn./etw. überragen

**'tower block** n. Hochhaus, das

**'towering** attrib. adj. hoch aufragend; (fig.) herausragend ⟨Leistung⟩

**town** [taʊn] n. Stadt, die; **the** ~ **of Cambridge** die Stadt Cambridge; **in |the|** ~: in der Stadt; **the** ~ (people) die Stadt; **be in/out of** ~: in der Stadt/nicht in der Stadt sein

**town:** ~ **'centre** n. Stadtmitte, die; Stadtzentrum, das; ~ **'hall** n. Rathaus, das; ~ **'planning** n. Stadtplanung, die

**tow:** ~~-**path** n. Leinpfad, der; ~~-**rope** n. Abschleppseil, das

**toxic** ['tɒksɪk] adj. giftig

**toy** [tɔɪ] **1.** n. Spielzeug, das; ~s Spielzeug, das. **2.** adj. Spielzeug-. **3.** v. i. ~ **with the idea of doing sth.** mit dem Gedanken spielen, etw. zu tun. **'toy-shop** n. Spielwarengeschäft, das

**trace** [treɪs] **1.** v. t. **a)** (copy) durchpausen; abpausen; **b)** zeichnen ⟨Linie⟩; **c)** (follow track of) folgen (+ Dat.); verfolgen; **d)** (find) finden. **2.** n. Spur, die. **'tracing paper** ['treɪsɪŋ peɪpə(r)] n. Pauspapier, das

**track** [træk] **1.** n. **a)** Spur, die; (of wild animal) Fährte, die; ~s (footprints) [Fuß]spuren; (of animal also) Fährte, die; **keep** ~ **of sb./sth.** jmdn./etw. im Auge behalten; **b)** (path) Weg, der; (footpath) Pfad, der; **c)** (Sport) Bahn, die; **cycling/greyhound** ~: Radrennbahn, die/Windhundrennbahn, die; **d)** (Railw.) Gleis, das; **e)** (course taken) Route, die; (of rocket, satellite) Bahn, die. **2.** v. t. ~ **an animal** die Spur/Fährte eines Tieres verfolgen; **the police** ~**ed him |to Paris|** die Polizei folgte seiner Spur [bis nach Paris]. **track 'down** v. t. aufspüren

**track:** ~ **events** n. pl. Laufwettbewerbe; ~ **suit** n. Trainingsanzug, der

**¹tract** [trækt] n. (area) Gebiet, das

**²tract** n. (pamphlet) [Flug]schrift, die

**tractor** ['træktə(r)] n. Traktor, der

**trade** [treɪd] **1.** n. **a)** (line of business) Gewerbe, das; **he's a butcher/lawyer etc. by** ~: er ist von Beruf Metzger/Rechtsanwalt usw.; **b)** no indef. art (commerce) Handel, der; **c)** (craft) Handwerk, das. **2.** v. i. (buy and sell) Handel treiben. **3.** v. t. tauschen; austauschen ⟨Waren, Grüße⟩; sich (Dat.)

sagen ⟨*Beleidigungen*⟩; ~ sth. for sth.
etw. gegen etw. tauschen. **trade 'in**
*v. t.* in Zahlung geben
'**trade mark** *n.* Warenzeichen, *das;*
**leave one's ~ on sth.** *(fig.)* einer Sache
*(Dat.)* seinen Stempel aufdrücken
'**trader** *n.* Händler, *der/*Händlerin, *die*
**trade:** ~ '**union** *n.* Gewerkschaft, *die;*
*attrib.* Gewerkschafts-; ~-'**unionist**
*n.* Gewerkschaft[l]er, *der/*Gewerkschaft[l]erin, *die*
**trading** ['treɪdɪŋ] *n.* Handel, *der.*
'**trading estate** *n. (Brit.)* Gewerbe-
gebiet, *das.* '**trading stamp** *n.* Ra-
battmarke, *die*
**tradition** [trə'dɪʃn] *n.* Tradition, *die.*
**traditional** [trə'dɪʃənl] *adj.* traditionell; herkömmlich ⟨*Erziehung, Methode*⟩. **tra'ditionally** *adv.* traditionell
**traffic** ['træfɪk] **1.** *n.* **a)** *no indef. art.*
Verkehr, *der;* **b)** *(trade)* Handel, *der.*
**2.** *v. i.,* -ck-: ~ **in sth.** mit etw. handeln
**traffic:** ~ **circle** *n. (Amer.)* Kreisverkehr, *der;* ~ **jam** *n.* [Verkehrs]stau,
*der;* ~ **lights** *n. pl.* [Verkehrs]ampel,
*die;* ~ **sign** *n.* Verkehrszeichen, *das;*
~ **signals** *see* ~ **lights;** ~ **warden** *n.*
*(Brit.)* Hilfspolizist, *der; (woman)*
Hilfspolizistin, *die;* Politesse, *die*
**tragedy** ['trædʒɪdɪ] *n.* Tragödie, *die.*
**tragic** ['trædʒɪk] *adj.* tragisch
**trail** [treɪl] **1.** *n.* **a)** Spur, *die;* ~ **of**
*smoke/dust* Rauch-/Staubfahne, *die;*
**b)** *(Hunting)* Spur, *die;* Fährte, *die;* **c)**
*(path)* Pfad, *der;* Weg, *der.* **2.** *v. t.* **a)**
*(pursue)* verfolgen; **b)** *(drag)* ~ **sth.**
[after *or* behind one] etw. hinter sich
*(Dat.)* herziehen. **3.** *v. i.* **a)** *(be
dragged)* schleifen; **b)** *(lag)* hinterher-
trotten; **c)** ⟨*Pflanze:*⟩ kriechen
**trailer** ['treɪlə(r)] *n.* **a)** Anhänger, *der;*
*(Amer.: caravan)* Wohnanhänger, *der;*
**b)** *(Cinemat., Telev.)* Trailer, *der*
**train** [treɪn] **1.** *v. t.* **a)** ausbilden (**in** in
+ *Dat.*); erziehen ⟨*Kind*⟩; abrichten
⟨*Hund*⟩; dressieren ⟨*Tier*⟩; **b)** *(Sport)*
trainieren; **c)** *(Hort.)* ziehen. **2.** *v. i.* **a)**
eine Ausbildung machen; **he is ~ing
as** *or* **to be a doctor/engineer** er macht
eine Arzt-/Ingenieursausbildung; **b)**
*(Sport)* trainieren. **3.** *n.* **a)** *(Railw.)*
Zug, *der;* **on the ~:** im Zug; **b)** *(of skirt
etc.)* Schleppe, *die;* **c)** ~ **of thought**
Gedankengang, *der.* '**train-driver** *n.*
Lokomotivführer, *der/*-führerin, *die*
**trained** [treɪnd] *adj.* ausgebildet ⟨*Arbeiter, Lehrer, Arzt, Stimme*⟩; abge-
richtet ⟨*Hund*⟩; dressiert ⟨*Tier*⟩; ge-
schult ⟨*Geist, Auge, Ohr*⟩

**trainee** [treɪ'ni:] *n.* Auszubildende,
*der/die*
'**trainer** *n.* [Konditions]trainer, *der/*
-trainerin, *die*
'**train fare** *n.* Fahrpreis, *der*
'**training** *n.* **a)** Ausbildung, *die;* **b)**
*(Sport)* Training, *das*
**train:** ~ **journey** *n.* Bahnfahrt, *die;*
*(long)* Bahnreise, *die;* ~ **set** *n.* [Mo-
dell]eisenbahn, *die;* ~ **station** *n.*
*(Amer.)* Bahnhof, *der*
**trait** [treɪt] *n.* Eigenschaft, *die*
**traitor** ['treɪtə(r)] *n.* Verräter, *der/*Verräterin, *die*
**tram** [træm] *n. (Brit.)* Straßenbahn,
*die;* ~**lines** Straßenbahnschienen
**tramp** [træmp] **1.** *n.* Landstreicher,
*der/*-streicherin, *die; (in city)* Stadtstreicher, *der/*-streicherin, *die.* **2.** *v. i.*
**a)** *(tread heavily)* trampeln; **b)** *(walk)*
marschieren
**trample** ['træmpl] **1.** *v. t.* zertrampeln.
**2.** *v. i.* trampeln. '**trample on** *v. t.*
herumtrampeln auf (+ *Dat.*)
**trampoline** ['træmpəli:n] *n.* Trampo-
lin, *das*
**trance** [trɑːns] *n.* Trance, *die;* **be in a**
~: in Trance sein
**tranquil** ['træŋkwɪl] *adj.* ruhig. **tranquillity** [træŋ'kwɪlɪtɪ] Ruhe, *die.*
**tranquillizer** ['træŋkwɪlaɪzə(r)] *n.*
Beruhigungsmittel, *das*
**transact** [træn'zækt] *v. t.* ~ **business**
Geschäfte tätigen. **transaction**
[træn'zækʃn] *n.* Geschäft, *das; (financial)* Transaktion, *die*
**transcend** [træn'send] *v. t.* übersteigen
**transcript** ['trænskrɪpt] *n.* Abschrift,
*die; (of trial)* Protokoll, *das*
**transfer** **1.** ['trænsfɜ:(r)] *v. t.,* -rr-: **a)**
*(move)* verlegen (**to** nach); überweisen
⟨*Geld*⟩ (**to** auf + *Akk.*); übertragen
⟨*Befugnis, Macht*⟩ (**to** *Dat.*); **b)** übereignen ⟨*Gegenstand, Grundbesitz*⟩ (**to**
*Dat.*); **c)** versetzen ⟨*Arbeiter, Angestellte*⟩; *(Footb.)* transferieren. **2.**
[træns'fɜ:(r)] *v. i.,* -rr-: **a)** *(when travelling)* umsteigen; **b)** *(change job etc.)*
wechseln. **3.** ['trænsfɜ:(r)] *n.* **a)** *(moving)* Verlegung, *die; (of powers)* Übertragung, *die* (**to** an + *Akk.*); *(of
money)* Überweisung, *die;* **b)** *(of employee etc.)* Versetzung, *die; (Footb.)*
Transfer, *der;* **c)** *(picture)* Abziehbild,
*das.* **transferable** [træns'fɜ:rəbl]
*adj.* übertragbar
**transform** [træns'fɔ:m] *v. t.* verwandeln. **transformation** [trænsfə-

'meɪʃn] *n.* Verwandlung, *die.* **trans-**
**'former** *n. (Electr.)* Transformator, *der*
**transfusion** [træns'fju:ʒn] *n. (Med.)*
Transfusion, *die*
**transient** ['trænzɪənt] *adj.* kurzlebig;
vergänglich
**transistor** [træn'zɪstə(r)] *n.* Transistor, *der*
**transit** ['trænsɪt] *n.* **in ~:** auf der
Durchreise; ⟨*Waren*⟩ auf dem Transport; **passengers in ~:** Transitreisende
**transition** [træn'sɪʒn, træn'zɪʃn] *n.*
Übergang, *der;* Wechsel, *der*
**transitive** ['trænsɪtɪv] *adj. (Ling.)*
transitiv
**transitory** ['trænsɪtərɪ] *adj.* vergänglich; *(fleeting)* flüchtig
**translate** [træns'leɪt] *v. t.* übersetzen.
**translation** [træns'leɪʃn] *n.* Übersetzung, *die.* **translator** [træns'leɪtə(r)]
*n.* Übersetzer, *der/*Übersetzerin, *die*
**translucent** [træns'lu:sənt] *adj.*
durchscheinend
**transmission** [træns'mɪʃn] *n.* **a)**
Übertragung, *die;* **b)** *(Motor Veh.)* Antrieb, *der; (gearbox)* Getriebe, *das*
**transmit** [træns'mɪt] *v. t.,* **-tt-: a)** *(pass on)* übersenden; übertragen; **b)**
durchlassen ⟨*Licht*⟩; leiten ⟨*Wärme*⟩.
**trans'mitter** *n.* Sender, *der*
**transparency** [træns'pærənsɪ] *n.* **a)**
Durchsichtigkeit, *die;* **b)** *(Photog.)*
Transparent, *das; (slide)* Dia, *das*
**transparent** [træns'pærənt] *adj.*
durchsichtig
**transpire** [træn'spaɪə(r)] *v. i.* sich herausstellen; *(coll.: happen)* passieren
**transplant** **1.** [træns'plɑ:nt] *v. t.* **a)**
verpflanzen ⟨*Organ*⟩; **b)** *(plant in another place)* umpflanzen. **2.** ['trænsplɑ:nt] *n. (Med.)* Transplantation, *die;*
Verpflanzung, *die*
**transport** **1.** [træns'pɔ:t] *v. t.* transportieren; befördern. **2.** ['trænspɔ:t] *n.* **a)**
Transport, *der;* Beförderung, *die; attrib.* Beförderungs-; **b)** *(means of conveyance)* Verkehrsmittel, *das;* **be without ~:** kein [eigenes] Fahrzeug haben
**transpose** [træns'pəʊz] *v. t.* vertauschen; umstellen
**transvestite** [træns'vestaɪt] *n.* Transvestit, *der*
**trap** [træp] **1.** *n.* **a)** Falle, *die;* **set** *or* **lay**
**a ~ for an animal** eine Falle für ein
Tier legen *od.* aufstellen; **set** *or* **lay a**
**~ for sb.** *(fig.)* jmdm. eine Falle stellen; **fall into a/sb.'s ~** *(fig.)* in die/
jmdm. in die Falle gehen; **b)** *(sl.:*
*mouth)* Klappe, *die (salopp).* **2.** *v. t.,*

**-pp-: a)** [in *od.* mit einer Falle] fangen
⟨*Tier*⟩; *(fig.)* in eine Falle locken ⟨*Person*⟩; **be ~ped** *(fig.)* in eine Falle gehen/in der Falle sitzen; **be ~ped in a**
**cave/by the tide** in einer Höhle festsitzen/von der Flut abgeschnitten sein;
**b)** *(confine)* einschließen; einklemmen ⟨*Körperteil*⟩. **trap'door** *n.* Falltür, *die*
**trapeze** [trə'pi:z] *n.* Trapez, *das*
**trash** [træʃ] *n., no indef. art.* **a)** *(rubbish)* Abfall, *der;* **b)** *(badly made*
*thing)* Mist, *der (ugs.); (bad literature)*
Schund, *der (ugs.)*
**trauma** ['trɔ:mə] *n., pl.* **-ta** ['trɔ:mətə]
*or* **~s** Trauma, *das.* **traumatic**
[trɔ:'mætɪk] *adj.* traumatisch
**travel** ['trævl] **1.** *n.* Reisen, *das; attrib.*
Reise-. **2.** *v. i., (Brit.)* **-ll-** reisen; *(go in*
*vehicle)* fahren. **3.** *v. t., (Brit.)* **-ll-** zurücklegen ⟨*Strecke, Entfernung*⟩; benutzen ⟨*Weg, Straße*⟩; **we had ~led 10**
**miles** wir waren 10 Meilen gefahren.
**'travel agency** *n.* Reisebüro, *das.*
**'travel agent** *n.* Reisebürokaufmann, *der/*-kauffrau, *die*
**traveler, traveling** *(Amer.) see*
**travell-**
**traveller** ['trævlə(r)] *n. (Brit.)* **a)** Reisende, *der/die;* **b)** *in pl. (gypsies etc.)*
fahrendes Volk. **'traveller's**
**cheque** *n.* Reisescheck, *der*
**travelling** ['trævlɪŋ] *attrib. adj. (Brit.)*
Wander⟨*zirkus, -ausstellung*⟩
**trawler** ['trɔ:lə(r)] *n.* [Fisch]trawler, *der*
**tray** [treɪ] *n.* Tablett, *das; (for correspondence)* Ablagekorb, *der*
**treacherous** ['tretʃərəs] *adj.* **a)** treulos ⟨*Person*⟩; **b)** *(deceptive)* tückisch.
**treachery** ['tretʃərɪ] *n.* Verrat, *der*
**treacle** ['tri:kl] *n. (Brit.)* Sirup, *der*
**tread** [tred] **1.** *n.* **a)** *(of tyre, boot, etc.)*
Lauffläche, *die;* **2 millimetres of ~ on**
**a tyre** 2 Millimeter Profil auf einem
Reifen; **b)** *(sound of walking)* Schritt, *der.* **2.** *v. i.,* trod [trɒd], **trodden** ['trɒdn]
*or* **trod** treten **(in/on** in/auf + *Akk.*);
*(walk)* gehen. **3.** *v. t.* trod, **trodden** *or*
**trod** treten auf (+ *Akk.*); stampfen
⟨*Weintrauben*⟩
**treason** ['tri:zn] *n.* **[high] ~:** Hochverrat, *der*
**treasure** ['treʒə(r)] **1.** *n.* Schatz, *der;*
Kostbarkeit, *die;* **art ~s** Kunstschätze.
**2.** *v. t.* in Ehren halten. **'treasure-**
**hunt** *n.* Schatzsuche, *die*
**treasurer** ['treʒərə(r)] *n.* Kassenwart, *der/*-wartin, *die.* **treasury** ['treʒərɪ] *n.*
**the T~:** das Finanzministerium

**treat** [tri:t] 1. *n.* **a)** [besonderes] Vergnügen; **b)** *(entertainment)* Vergnügen, *für dessen Kosten jmd. anderes aufkommt;* **lay on a special ~ for sb.** jmdm. etwas Besonderes bieten. 2. *v. t.* **a)** behandeln; **~ sth. as a joke** etw. als Witz nehmen; **~ sth. with contempt** für etw. nur Verachtung haben; **b)** *(Med.)* behandeln; **~ sb. for sth.** jmdn. wegen etw. behandeln; *(before confirmation of diagnosis)* jmdn. auf etw. *(Akk.)* behandeln; **c)** klären ⟨*Abwässer*⟩; **d)** *(provide with at own expense)* einladen; **~ sb. to sth.** jmdm. etw. spendieren; **~ oneself to a new hat** sich *(Dat.)* einen neuen Hut leisten

**treatise** ['tri:tɪs, 'tri:tɪz] *n.* Abhandlung, *die*

'**treatment** *n.* Behandlung, *die*

**treaty** ['tri:tɪ] *n.* [Staats]vertrag, *der*

**treble** ['trebl] 1. *adj.* **a)** dreifach; **b)** *(Brit. Mus.)* **~ voice** Sopranstimme, *die.* 2. *n.* **a)** *(~ quantity)* Dreifache, *das;* **b)** *(Mus.)* **he is a ~:** er singt Sopran. 3. *v. t.* verdreifachen. 4. *v. i.* sich verdreifachen. '**treble clef** *n. (Mus.)* Violinschlüssel, *der*

**tree** [tri:] *n.* Baum, *der*

**trek** [trek] 1. *v. i.,* **-kk-** ziehen **(across** durch). 2. *n.* [schwierige] Reise

**trellis** ['trelɪs] *n.* Gitter, *das; (for plants)* Spalier, *das*

**tremble** ['trembl] *v. i.* zittern **(with** vor **+ Dat.)**

**tremendous** [trɪ'mendəs] *adj.* gewaltig; *(coll.: wonderful)* großartig

**tremor** ['tremə(r)] *n.* **a)** Zittern, *das;* **b)** |earth| **~:** leichtes Erdbeben

**trench** [trentʃ] *n.* Graben, *der; (Mil.)* Schützengraben, *der*

**trend** [trend] *n.* **a)** Trend, *der;* **upward ~:** steigende Tendenz; **b)** *(fashion)* Mode, *die;* [Mode]trend, *der.* '**trendy** *adj. (Brit. coll.)* modisch; Schickimicki⟨*kneipe*⟩ *(ugs.)*

**trepidation** [trepɪ'deɪʃn] *n.* Beklommenheit, *die*

**trespass** ['trespəs] *v. i.* **~ on** unerlaubt betreten ⟨*Grundstück*⟩. '**trespasser** *n.* Unbefugte, *der/die*

**trial** ['traɪəl] *n.* **a)** *(Law)* [Gerichts]verfahren, *das;* **be on ~** |for murder| [wegen Mordes] angeklagt sein; **b)** *(testing)* Test, *der;* **employ sb. on ~:** jmdn. probeweise einstellen; [by] **~ and error** [durch] Ausprobieren; **c)** *(trouble)* Problem, *das;* **d)** *(Sport) (competition)* Prüfung, *die; (for selection)* Testspiel, *das*

**triangle** ['traɪæŋgl] *n.* **a)** Dreieck, *das;* **b)** *(Mus.)* Triangel, *das od. der.* **triangular** [traɪ'æŋgjʊlə(r)] *adj.* dreieckig

**tribe** [traɪb] *n.* Stamm, *der*

**tribulation** [trɪbjʊ'leɪʃn] *n.* Kummer, *der*

**tribunal** [traɪ'bju:nl] *n.* Schiedsgericht, *das*

**tributary** ['trɪbjʊtərɪ] *n.* Nebenfluß, *der*

**tribute** ['trɪbju:t] *n.* Tribut, *der* (**to an + Akk.**); **pay ~ to sb./sth.** jmdm./einer Sache den schuldigen Tribut zollen *(geh.)*

**trice** [traɪs] *n.* **in a ~:** im Handumdrehen

**trick** [trɪk] 1. *n.* **a)** Trick, *der;* **it was all a ~:** das war [alles] nur Bluff; **b)** *(feat of skill etc.)* Kunststück, *das;* **that should do the ~** *(coll.)* damit dürfte es klappen *(ugs.);* **c)** *(knack)* **get** *or* **find the ~** |of doing sth.| den Dreh finden[, wie man etw. tut]; **d)** *(prank)* Streich, *der;* **play a ~ on sb.** jmdm. einen Streich spielen; **e)** *(Cards)* Stich, *der.* 2. *v. t.* täuschen; hereinlegen; **~ sb. out of/into sth.** jmdm. etw. ablisten. 3. *adj.* **~ photograph** Trickaufnahme, *die;* **~ question** Fangfrage, *die.* **trickery** ['trɪkərɪ] *n.* [Hinter]list, *die*

**trickle** ['trɪkl] *v. i.* rinnen; *(in drops)* tröpfeln

**trickster** ['trɪkstə(r)] *n.* Schwindler, *der*/Schwindlerin, *die*

'**tricky** *adj.* verzwickt *(ugs.)*

**tricycle** ['traɪsɪkl] *n.* Dreirad, *das*

**tried** *see* try 2, 3

**trifle** ['traɪfl] *n.* **a)** *(Brit. Gastron.)* Trifle, *das;* **b)** *(thing of slight value)* Kleinigkeit, *die.* **trifling** ['traɪflɪŋ] *adj.* unbedeutend ⟨*Angelegenheit*⟩; gering ⟨*Wert*⟩

**trigger** ['trɪgə(r)] 1. *n.* **a)** *(of gun)* Abzug, *der; (of machine)* Drücker, *der;* **b)** *(fig.)* Auslöser, *der.* 2. *v. t.* ~ |off| auslösen

**trigonometry** [trɪgə'nɒmɪtrɪ] *n.* Trigonometrie, *die*

**trim** [trɪm] 1. *v. t.,* **-mm-:** **a)** schneiden ⟨*Hecke*⟩; [nach]schneiden ⟨*Haar*⟩; beschneiden ⟨*Papier, Hecke, Budget*⟩; **b)** *(ornament)* besetzen **(with** mit**).** 2. *adj.* proper; gepflegt ⟨*Garten*⟩. 3. *n.* **a)** **be in ~** *(healthy)* in Form *od.* fit sein; **b)** *(cut)* Nachschneiden, *das.* '**trimming** *n.* **a)** *(decorations)* Verzierung, *die;* **b)** **in** *pl. (coll.: accompaniments)* Beilagen; **with all the ~s** mit allem Drum und Dran *(ugs.)*

**Trinity** ['trɪnɪtɪ] *n. (Theol.)* **the |Holy| ~:** die Heilige Dreieinigkeit

**trinket** ['trɪŋkɪt] *n.* kleines, billiges Schmuckstück

**trio** ['triːəʊ] *n., pl.* **~s** Trio, *das*

**trip** [trɪp] **1.** *n.* **a)** Reise, *die; (shorter)* Ausflug, *der;* **b)** *(coll.: drug-induced hallucinations)* Trip, *der.* **2.** *v. i.,* **-pp-** stolpern **(on** über + *Akk.).* **trip 'up 1.** *v. i.* **a)** stolpern; **b)** *(fig.)* einen Fehler machen. **2.** *v. t.* **a)** stolpern lassen; **b)** *(fig.)* aufs Glatteis führen *(fig.)*

**tripe** [traɪp] *n.* **a)** Kaldaunen *Pl.;* **b)** *(sl.: rubbish)* Quatsch, *der (ugs.)*

**triple** ['trɪpl] **1.** *adj.* **a)** *(threefold)* dreifach; **b)** *(three times greater than)* ~ **the ...:** der/die/das dreifache ... **2.** *n.* Dreifache, *das.* **3.** *v. i.* sich verdreifachen. **4.** *v. t.* verdreifachen

**triplet** ['trɪplɪt] *n.* Drilling, *der*

**triplicate** ['trɪplɪkət] *n.* **in ~:** in dreifacher Ausfertigung

**tripod** ['traɪpɒd] *n.* Dreibein, *das*

**'tripper** *n. (Brit.)* Ausflügler, *der/* Ausflüglerin, *die*

**trite** [traɪt] *adj.* banal

**triumph** ['traɪəmf, 'traɪʌmf] **1.** *n.* Triumph, *der* **(over** über + *Akk.).* **2.** *v. i.* triumphieren **(over** über + *Akk.).* **triumphant** [traɪʌmfənt] *adj.* **a)** siegreich; **b)** triumphierend ⟨*Blick*⟩

**trivial** ['trɪvɪəl] *adj.* belanglos. **triviality** [trɪvɪ'ælɪtɪ] *n.* Belanglosigkeit, *die*

**trod, trodden** *see* **tread** 2, 3

**trolley** ['trɒlɪ] *n.* **a)** *(for serving food)* Servierwagen, *der;* **b)** |**supermarket**| **~:** Einkaufswagen, *der*

**trombone** [trɒm'bəʊn] *n.* Posaune, *die*

**troop** [truːp] **1.** *n.* **a)** *in pl.* Truppen; **b)** *(fig.)* Schar, *die.* **2.** *v. i.* **~ in/out** hinein-/hinausströmen

**trophy** ['trəʊfɪ] *n.* Trophäe, *die*

**tropic** ['trɒpɪk] *n.* **the T~s** *(Geog.)* die Tropen; **the ~ of Cancer/Capricorn** *(Astron., Geog.)* der Wendekreis des Krebses./Steinbocks. **tropical** ['trɒpɪkl] *adj.* tropisch; Tropen⟨*krankheit, -kleidung*⟩

**trot** [trɒt] **1.** *n. (coll.)* **on the ~:** hintereinander; **be on the ~:** auf Trab sein *(ugs.).* **2.** *v. i.,* **-tt-** traben

**trouble** ['trʌbl] **1.** *n.* **a)** Ärger, *der;* Schwierigkeiten *Pl.;* **there'll be ~ |if ...|** es wird Ärger geben, [wenn ...]; **what's the ~?** was ist denn?; **b) engine/brake ~:** Probleme mit dem Motor/der Bremse; **suffer from heart/liver ~:**

Probleme mit dem Herz/der Leber haben; **c)** *(inconvenience)* Mühe, *die;* **take a lot of ~:** sich *(Dat.)* sehr viel Mühe geben; **it's more ~ than it's worth** es lohnt sich nicht; **d)** *in sing. or pl. (unrest)* Unruhen. **2.** *v. t.* **a)** *(agitate)* beunruhigen; **don't let it ~ you** mach dir deswegen keine Sorgen; **b)** *(inconvenience)* stören. **3.** *v. i. (make an effort)* sich bemühen. **troubled** ['trʌbld] *adj.* **a)** *(worried)* besorgt; **b)** *(restless)* unruhig. **'trouble-maker** *n.* Unruhestifter *der/*-stifterin, *die.* **troublesome** ['trʌblsəm] *adj.* schwierig; lästig ⟨*Krankheit*⟩

**trough** [trɒf] *n.* Trog, *der*

**troupe** [truːp] *n.* Truppe, *die*

**trousers** ['traʊzəz] *n. pl.* |**pair of**| **~:** Hose, *die*

**'trouser suit** *n. (Brit.)* Hosenanzug, *der*

**trousseau** ['truːsəʊ] *n., pl.* **~s** *or* **~x** ['truːsəʊz] Aussteuer, *die*

**trout** [traʊt] *n., pl. same* Forelle, *die*

**trowel** ['traʊəl] *n.* Kelle, *die; (Hort.)* Pflanzkelle, *die*

**truant** ['truːənt] *n.* **play ~:** [die Schule] schwänzen *(ugs.)*

**truce** [truːs] *n.* Waffenstillstand, *der*

**truck** [trʌk] *n.* **a)** Last[kraft]wagen, *der;* Lkw, *der;* **b)** *(Brit. Railw.)* offener Güterwagen

**truculent** ['trʌkjʊlənt] *adj.* aufsässig

**trudge** [trʌdʒ] *v. i.* trotten; *(through snow etc.)* stapfen

**true** [truː] *adj.,* **~r** ['truːə(r)], **~st** ['truːɪst] **a)** wahr; wahrheitsgetreu ⟨*Bericht*⟩; richtig ⟨*Vorteil*⟩; *(rightly so called)* eigentlich; echt, wahr ⟨*Freund*⟩; **is it ~ that ...?** stimmt es, daß ...?; **~ to life** lebensecht; **b)** *(loyal)* treu

**truffle** ['trʌfl] *n.* Trüffel, *die od. (ugs.) der*

**truism** ['truːɪzm] *n.* Binsenweisheit, *die*

**truly** ['truːlɪ] *adv.* **a)** wirklich; **b)** *(accurately)* zutreffend; **yours ~:** mit freundlichen Grüßen

**trump** [trʌmp] *(Cards)* **1.** *n.* Trumpf, *der.* **2.** *v. t.* übertrumpfen. **'trump up** *v. t. (coll.)* konstruieren

**trumpet** ['trʌmpɪt] *n.* Trompete, *die.* **'trumpeter** *n.* Trompeter, *der/*Trompeterin, *die*

**truncheon** ['trʌntʃn] *n.* Schlagstock, *der*

**trundle** ['trʌndl] *v. t. & i.* rollen

**trunk** [trʌŋk] *n.* **a)** *(of elephant etc.)*

Rüssel, *der;* **b)** *(large box)* Schrankkoffer, *der;* **c)** *(of tree)* Stamm, *der;* **d)** *(of body)* Rumpf, *der;* **e)** *(Amer.: of car)* Kofferraum, *der;* **f)** *in pl. (Brit.)* |swimming| ~s Badehose, *die*

**truss** [trʌs] *n. (Med.)* Bruchband, *das*

**trust** [trʌst] **1.** *n.* **a)** Vertrauen, *das;* **place** *or* **put one's** ~ **in sb./sth.** sein Vertrauen auf *od.* in jmdn./etw. setzen; **take sth. on** ~: etw. einfach glauben; **b)** *(organization managed by trustees)* Treuhandgesellschaft, *die;* |charitable| ~: Stiftung, *die; (association of companies)* Trust, *der;* **c)** *(Law)* **hold in** ~: treuhänderisch verwalten. **2.** *v.t. (rely on)* trauen (+ *Dat.*); vertrauen (+ *Dat.*) ⟨*Person*⟩; ~ **sb. with sth.** jmdm. etw. anvertrauen. **3.** *v.i.* **a)** ~ **to** sich verlassen auf (+ *Akk.*); **b)** *(believe)* ~ **in sb./sth.** auf jmdn./etw. vertrauen. **trustee** [trʌˈstiː] *n.* Treuhänder, *der/*Treuhänderin, *die.* **trustful** [ˈtrʌstfl], **trusting** *adjs.* vertrauensvoll. **trustworthy** *adj.* vertrauenswürdig

**truth** [truːθ] *n., pl.* ~s [truːðz, truːθs] Wahrheit, *die;* **tell the** |whole| ~: die |ganze| Wahrheit sagen. **truthful** [ˈtruːθfl] *adj.* ehrlich

**try** [traɪ] **1.** *n.* Versuch, *der;* **have a** ~ **at sth./doing sth.** etw. versuchen/versuchen, etw. zu tun; **give it a** ~, **have a** ~: es versuchen. **2.** *v.t.* **a)** *(attempt)* versuchen; **b)** *(test usefulness of)* probieren; **c)** *(test)* auf die Probe stellen ⟨*Fähigkeit, Kraft, Geduld*⟩; **d)** *(Law.: take to trial)* ~ **a case** einen Fall verhandeln; ~ **sb.** |for sth.| jmdn. [wegen einer Sache] vor Gericht stellen. **3.** *v.i.* es versuchen; ~ **hard/harder** sich *(Dat.)* viel/mehr Mühe geben. **try** 'on *v.t.* anprobieren ⟨*Kleidungsstück*⟩. **try** 'out *v.t.* ausprobieren

'**trying** *adj.* **a)** *(testing)* schwierig; **b)** *(difficult to endure)* anstrengend

**T-shirt** *n.* T-Shirt, *das*

**tub** [tʌb] *n.* Kübel, *der; (for ice-cream etc.)* Becher, *der*

**tuba** [ˈtjuːbə] *n. (Mus.)* Tuba, *die*

**tubby** [ˈtʌbɪ] *adj.* rundlich

**tube** [tjuːb] *n.* **a)** *(for conveying liquids etc.)* Rohr, *das;* **b)** *(small cylinder)* Tube, *die; (for sweets, tablets)* Röhrchen, *das;* **c)** *(Anat., Zool.)* Röhre, *die;* **d)** *(of TV etc.)* Röhre, *die;* **e)** *(Brit. coll.: underground railway)* U-Bahn, *die*

**tuber** [ˈtjuːbə(r)] *n. (Bot.)* Knolle, *die*

**tuberculosis** [tjuːbɜːkjʊˈləʊsɪs] *n.* Tuberkulose, *die*

**tube:** ~ **station** *n. (Brit. coll.)* U-Bahnhof, *der;* ~ **train** *n. (Brit. coll.)* U-bahn-Zug, *der*

**tubing** [ˈtjuːbɪŋ] *n.* Rohre *Pl.*

**tubular** [ˈtjuːbjʊlə(r)] *adj.* rohrförmig

**tuck** [tʌk] **1.** *v.t.* stecken. **2.** *n. (in fabric) (for decoration)* Biese, *die; (to tighten)* Abnäher, *der.* **tuck** 'in **1.** *v.t.* hineinstecken. **2.** *v.i. (coll.)* zulangen *(ugs.).* **tuck** 'up *v.t.* **a)** hochkrempeln ⟨*Ärmel, Hose*⟩; hochnehmen ⟨*Rock*⟩; **b)** *(cover snugly)* zudecken

**Tue., Tues.** *abbrs.* Tuesday Di.

**Tuesday** [ˈtjuːzdeɪ, ˈtjuːzdɪ] *n.* Dienstag, *der; see also* **Friday**

**tuft** [tʌft] *n.* Büschel, *das*

**tug** [tʌg] **1.** *n.* **a)** Ruck, *der;* ~ **of war** Tauziehen, *das;* **b)** ~ |boat| Schlepper, *der.* **2.** *v.t.,* -gg- ziehen. **3.** *v.i.,* -gg- zerren (**at** an + *Dat.*)

**tuition** [tjuːˈɪʃn] *n.* Unterricht, *der*

**tulip** [ˈtjuːlɪp] *n.* Tulpe, *die*

**tumble** [ˈtʌmbl] **1.** *v.i.* stürzen; fallen. **2.** *n.* Sturz, *der.* '**tumble-drier** *n.* Wäschetrockner, *der.* '**tumble-dry** *v.t.* im Automaten trocknen

**tumbler** [ˈtʌmblə(r)] *n. (short)* Whiskyglas, *das; (long)* Wasserglas, *das*

**tummy** [ˈtʌmɪ] *n. (child lang./coll.)* Bäuchlein, *das.* '**tummy-ache** *n. (child lang./coll.)* Bauchweh, *das*

**tumour** *(Brit.; Amer.:* **tumor**) [ˈtjuːmə(r)] *n.* Tumor, *der*

**tumult** [ˈtjuːmʌlt] *n.* Tumult, *der*

**tuna** [ˈtjuːnə] *n., pl. same or* ~s Thunfisch, *der*

**tune** [tjuːn] **1.** *n.* **a)** *(melody)* Melodie, *die;* **change one's** ~ *(fig.)* sein Verhalten ändern; **call the** ~: den Ton angeben; **b)** *(correct pitch)* **sing in/out of** ~: richtig/falsch singen; **be in/out of** ~ ⟨*Instrument:*⟩ richtig gestimmt/verstimmt sein. **2.** *v.t.* **a)** *(Mus.: put in* ~) stimmen; **b)** *(Radio, Telev.)* einstellen (**to** auf + *Akk.*); **c)** einstellen ⟨*Motor, Vergaser*⟩. **tune** 'in *(Radio, Telev.)* ~ **to a station** einen Sender einstellen

**tuneful** [ˈtjuːnfl] *adj.* melodisch

**tunic** [ˈtjuːnɪk] *n. (of soldier)* Uniformjacke, *die; (of schoolgirl)* Kittel, *der*

'**tuning-fork** [ˈtjuːnɪŋfɔːk] *n.* Stimmgabel, *die*

**Tunisia** [tjuːˈnɪzɪə] *pr. n.* Tunesien *(das)*

**tunnel** [ˈtʌnl] **1.** *n.* Tunnel, *der; (dug by animal)* Gang, *der.* **2.** *v.i., (Brit.)* -lleinen Tunnel graben

**turban** [ˈtɜːbən] *n.* Turban, *der*

**turbine** [ˈtɜːbaɪn] *n.* Turbine, *die*

**turbulence** ['tɜ:bjʊləns] *n.* **a)** Aufgewühltheit, *die;* *(fig.)* Aufruhr, *der;* **b)** *(Phys.)* Turbulenz, *die*

**turbulent** ['tɜ:bjʊlənt] *adj.* **a)** aufgewühlt; **b)** *(Phys.)* turbulent

**tureen** [tjʊə'ri:n] *n.* Terrine, *die*

**turf** [tɜ:f] *n., pl.* ~s *or* turves [tɜ:vz] **a)** *no pl.* Rasen, *der;* **b)** *(segment)* Rasenstück, *das.* **turf 'out** *v. t. (sl.)* rausschmeißen *(ugs.)*

**Turk** [tɜ:k] *n.* Türke, *der*/Türkin, *die*

**Turkey** ['tɜ:kɪ] *pr. n.* die Türkei

**turkey** *n.* Truthahn, *der*/Truthenne, *die; (esp. as food)* Puter, *der*/Pute, *die*

**Turkish** ['tɜ:kɪʃ] **1.** *adj.* türkisch; *sb. is* ~: jmd. ist Türke/Türkin. **2.** *n.* Türkisch, *das; see also* **English 2 a**

**turmoil** ['tɜ:mɔɪl] *n.* Aufruhr, *der*

**turn** [tɜ:n] **1.** *n.* **a)** it is sb.'s ~ to do sth. jmd. ist an der Reihe, etw. zu tun; **it's your** ~ **|next|** du bist als nächster/ nächste dran *(ugs.) od.* an der Reihe; **out of** ~: außer der Reihe; *(fig.)* an der falschen Stelle ⟨*lachen*⟩; **take |it in|** ~s sich abwechseln; **b)** *(rotary motion)* Drehung, *die;* **c)** *(change of direction)* Wende, *die;* **take a** ~ **to the right/left,** do *or* **take a right/left** ~: nach rechts/ links abbiegen; *(fig.)* **take a favourable** ~ sich zum Guten wenden; **the** ~ **of the year/century** die Jahres-/Jahrhundertwende; **d)** *(bend)* Kurve, *die; (corner)* Ecke, *die;* **e)** *(short performance)* Nummer, *die;* **f)** *(service)* do sb. **a good** ~: jmdm. einen guten Dienst erweisen; **g)** *(coll.: fright)* give sb. quite **a** ~: jmdm. einen gehörigen Schrekken einjagen *(ugs.).* **2.** *v. t.* **a)** *(make revolve)* drehen; **b)** *(reverse)* umdrehen; wenden ⟨*Pfannkuchen, Auto, Heu*⟩; ~ **sth. upside down** *or* **on its head** *(lit. or fig.)* etw. auf den Kopf stellen; ~ **the page** umblättern; **c)** *(give new direction to)* drehen, wenden ⟨*Kopf*⟩; ~ **a hose/ gun on sb./sth.** einen Schlauch/ein Gewehr auf jmdn./etw. richten; ~ **one's attention/mind to sth.** sich/seine Gedanken einer Sache *(Dat.)* zuwenden; **d)** ~ **sb. loose on sb./sth.** jmdn. auf jmdn./etw. loslassen; **e)** *(cause to become)* verwandeln; ~ **the lights |down|** low das Licht dämpfen; ~ **a play/book into a film** ein Theaterstück/Buch verfilmen; **f)** *(shape in lathe)* drechseln ⟨*Holz*⟩; drehen ⟨*Metall*⟩; **g)** drehen ⟨*Pirouette*⟩; schlagen ⟨*Purzelbaum*⟩. **3.** *v. i.* **a)** *(revolve)* sich drehen; **b)** *(reverse direction)* ⟨*Person:*⟩ sich herumdrehen; ⟨*Auto:*⟩ wenden;

**c)** *(take new direction)* sich wenden; *(~ round)* sich umdrehen; ~ **to the left/ right** nach links/rechts abbiegen; **d)** *(become)* werden; ~ **|in|to sth.** zu etw. werden; *(be transformed)* sich in etw. *(Akk.)* verwandeln; **e)** *(become sour)* ⟨*Milch:*⟩ sauer werden. **2. turn a'way 1.** *v. i.* sich abwenden. **2.** *v. t.* **a)** *(avert)* abwenden; **b)** *(send away)* wegschikken. **turn 'down** *v. t.* **a)** herunterschlagen ⟨*Kragen*⟩; **b)** niedriger stellen ⟨*Heizung*⟩; herunterdrehen ⟨*Gas*⟩; leiser stellen ⟨*Ton, Radio, Fernseher*⟩; **c)** *(reject)* ablehnen; abweisen ⟨*Kandidaten usw.*⟩. **turn 'in 1.** *v. t.* **a)** nach innen drehen; **b)** *(hand in)* abgeben. **2.** *v. i.* **a)** *(enter)* einbiegen; **b)** *(coll.: go to bed)* in die Falle gehen *(salopp).* **turn 'off 1.** *v. t.* abschalten; abstellen ⟨*Wasser, Gas*⟩; zudrehen ⟨*Wasserhahn*⟩. **2.** *v. i.* abbiegen. **turn on** *v. t.* **a)** [-'-] anschalten; aufdrehen ⟨*Wasserhahn, Gas*⟩; **b)** ['--] *(attack)* angreifen. **turn 'out 1.** *v. t.* **a)** *(expel)* hinauswerfen *(ugs.);* **b)** *(switch off)* ausschalten; abdrehen ⟨*Gas*⟩; **c)** *(produce)* produzieren; **d)** *(Brit.) (empty)* ausräumen; leeren; *(get rid of)* wegwerfen. **2.** *v. i.* **a)** *(prove to be)* sb./sth. ~s out to be sth. jmd./etw. stellt sich als jmd./etw. heraus; **everything** ~ed **out well/all right in the end** alles endete gut; **b)** *(appear)* ⟨*Fans usw.:*⟩ erscheinen. **turn 'over 1.** *v. t.* umdrehen. **2.** *v. i.* **a)** *(tip over)* umkippen; ⟨*Boot:*⟩ kentern; ⟨*Auto, Flugzeug:*⟩ sich überschlagen; **b)** *(from one side to the other)* sich umdrehen; **c)** *(~ a page)* weiterblättern. **turn 'round** *v. i.* sich umdrehen. **'turn to** *v. t. (fig.)* ~ **to sb.** sich an jmdn. wenden; ~ **to sb. for help/advice** bei jmdm. Hilfe/Rat suchen; ~ **to drink** sich in den Alkohol flüchten. **turn 'up 1.** *v. i.* **a)** ⟨*Person:*⟩ erscheinen; **b)** *(present itself)* auftauchen; ⟨*Gelegenheit:*⟩ sich bieten. **2.** *v. t.* **a)** hochschlagen ⟨*Kragen*⟩; **b)** lauter stellen ⟨*Ton, Radio, Fernseher*⟩; aufdrehen ⟨*Heizung, Gas*⟩; heller machen ⟨*Licht*⟩

**'turning** *n.* Abzweigung, *die.* **'turning-point** *n.* Wendepunkt, *der*

**turnip** ['tɜ:nɪp] *n.* Kohlrübe, *die*

**turn:** ~-**out** *n. (of people)* Beteiligung, *die* (**for** an + *Dat.*); ~**over** *n.* **a)** *(Commerc.)* Umsatz, *der; (of stock)* Umschlag, *der;* **b)** *(of staff)* Fluktuation, *die;* ~**pike** *n. (Amer.)* gebührenpflichtige Autobahn; ~**stile** *n.* Drehkreuz, *das;* **~table** *n.* Plattenteller, *der;* **~-up** *n. (Brit. Fashion)* Aufschlag, *der*

**turpentine** ['tɜ:pntaɪn] *n.* Terpentin, *das*

**turquoise** ['tɜ:kwɔɪz] 1. *n.* a) Türkis, *der;* b) *(colour)* Türkis, *das.* 2. *adj.* türkis[farben]

**turret** ['tʌrɪt] *n.* Türmchen, *das*

**turtle** ['tɜ:tl] *n.* a) Meeresschildkröte, *die;* b) *(Amer.: freshwater reptile)* Wasserschildkröte, *die*

**turves** *see* turf b·

**tusk** [tʌsk] *n.* Stoßzahn, *der*

**tussle** ['tʌsl] 1. *n.* Gerangel, *das (ugs.).* 2. *v. i.* sich balgen

**tutor** ['tju:tə(r)] *n.* |private| ~: [Privat]lehrer, *der/*-lehrerin, *die*

**tuxedo** [tʌk'si:dəʊ] *n., pl.* ~s *or* ~es *(Amer.)* Smoking, *der*

**TV** [ti:'vi:] *n.* a) Fernsehen, *das;* b) *(television set)* Fernseher, *der (ugs.)*

**twaddle** ['twɒdl] *n.* Gewäsch, *das (ugs.)*

**twang** [twæŋ] 1. *v. t.* zupfen ⟨*Saite*⟩. 2. *n.* |nasal| ~: Näseln, *das*

**tweed** [twi:d] *n.* Tweed, *der*

**tweezers** ['twi:zəz] *n. pl.* |pair of| ~: Pinzette, *die*

**twelfth** [twelfθ] 1. *adj.* zwölft... 2. *n. (fraction)* Zwölftel, *das. See also* eighth

**twelve** [twelv] 1. *adj.* zwölf. 2. *n.* Zwölf, *die. See also* eight

**twentieth** ['twentɪθ] 1. *adj.* zwanzigst... 2. *n. (fraction)* Zwanzigstel, *das. See also* eighth

**twenty** ['twentɪ] 1. *adj.* zwanzig. 2. *n.* Zwanzig, *die. See also* eight; eighty 2

**twice** [twaɪs] *adv.* a) zweimal; b) *(doubly)* doppelt

**twiddle** ['twɪdl] *v. t.* herumdrehen an (+ *Dat.*) *(ugs.)*

¹**twig** [twɪg] *n.* Zweig, *der*

²**twig** *(coll.)* 1. *v. t.,* -gg- kapieren *(ugs.).* 2. *v. i.,* -gg- es kapieren *(ugs.)*

**twilight** ['twaɪlaɪt] *n.* a) *(evening light)* Dämmerlicht, *das;* b) *(period of half-light)* Dämmerung, *die*

**twin** [twɪn] 1. *attrib. adj.* a) Zwillings-; b) *(forming a pair)* Doppel-. 2. *n.* Zwilling, *der.* **twin 'beds** *n. pl.* zwei Einzelbetten

**twine** [twaɪn] 1. *n.* Bindfaden, *der.* 2. *v. i.* sich winden (**about, around** um)

**twinge** [twɪndʒ] *n.* Stechen, *das;* ~|s| **of conscience** *(fig.)* Gewissensbisse

**twinkle** ['twɪŋkl] 1. *v. i.* funkeln (**with** vor + *Dat.*). 2. *n.* Funkeln, *das*

**twinkling** ['twɪŋklɪŋ] *n.* **in a ~, in the ~ of an eye** im Handumdrehen

'**twin town** *n. (Brit.)* Partnerstadt, *die*

**twirl** [twɜ:l] 1. *v. t.* [schnell] drehen. 2. *v. i.* wirbeln (**around** über + *Akk.*)

**twist** [twɪst] 1. *v. t.* a) verdrehen ⟨*Worte, Bedeutung*⟩; ~ **one's ankle** sich *(Dat.)* den Knöchel verrenken; ~ **sb.'s arm** jmdm. den Arm umdrehen; *(fig.)* jmdm. [die] Daumenschrauben anlegen; b) *(rotate)* drehen. 2. *v. i.* sich winden. 3. *n.* a) *(motion)* Drehung, *die;* b) *(unexpected occurrence)* überraschende Wendung

**twit** [twɪt] *n. (Brit. sl.)* Trottel, *der (ugs.)*

**twitch** [twɪtʃ] 1. *v. i.* ⟨*Mund, Lippe:*⟩ zucken. 2. *n.* Zucken, *das*

**twitter** ['twɪtə(r)] 1. *n.* Zwitschern, *das.* 2. *v. i.* zwitschern

**two** [tu:] 1. *adj.* zwei. 2. *n.* Zwei, *die. See also* eight

**two:** ~-**faced** ['tu:feɪst] *adj. (fig.)* falsch; ~**fold** *adj., adv.* zweifach; a ~**fold increase** ein Anstieg auf das Doppelte; ~-**piece** 1. *n.* Zweiteiler, *der;* 2. *adj.* zweiteilig; ~**some** ['tu:səm] *n.* Paar, *das;* ~-**way** *adj.* a) zweibahnig *(Verkehrsw.);* '~-**way** traffic ahead' „Achtung Gegenverkehr"; b) ~-**way** mirror Einwegspiegel, *der*

**tycoon** [taɪ'ku:n] *n.* Magnat, *der*

**tying** *see* tie 1, 2

**type** [taɪp] 1. *n.* a) Art, *die; (person)* Typ, *der; what* ~ **of car ...?** was für ein Auto ...?; b) *(Printing)* Drucktype, *die.* 2. *v. t.* [mit der Maschine] schreiben; tippen *(ugs.).* 3. *v. i.* maschineschreiben. **type 'out** *v. t.* [mit der Schreibmaschine] abschreiben; abtippen *(ugs.)*

'**typewriter** *n.* Schreibmaschine, *die.*

'**typewritten** *adj.* maschine[n]geschrieben

**typhoid** ['taɪfɔɪd] *n.* ~ Typhus, *der*

**typhoon** [taɪ'fu:n] *n.* Taifun, *der*

**typical** ['tɪpɪkl] *adj.* typisch (**of** für)

**typify** ['tɪpɪfaɪ] *v. t.* ~ **sth.** als typisches Beispiel für etw. dienen

**typing** ['taɪpɪŋ] *n.* Maschineschreiben, *das*

**typist** ['taɪpɪst] *n.* Schreibkraft, *die*

**tyrannical** [tɪ'rænɪkl] *adj.* tyrannisch

**tyranny** ['tɪrənɪ] *n.* Tyrannei, *die*

**tyrant** ['taɪərənt] *n.* Tyrann, *der*

**tyre** ['taɪə(r)] *n.* Reifen, *der*

# U

**U, u** [ju:] *n*. U, u, *das*

**ubiquitous** [ju:'bɪkwɪtəs] *adj*. allgegenwärtig

**udder** ['ʌdə(r)] *n*. Euter, *das*

**ugliness** ['ʌglɪnɪs] *n*. Häßlichkeit, *die*

**ugly** ['ʌglɪ] *adj*. a) häßlich; b) *(nasty)* übel ⟨*Wunde, Laune usw.*⟩

**UK** *abbr*. United Kingdom

**Ukraine** [ju:'kreɪn] *pr. n*. Ukraine, *die*

**ulcer** ['ʌlsə(r)] *n*. Geschwür, *das*

**ulterior** [ʌl'tɪərɪə(r)] *adj*. hintergründig; ~ **motive** Hintergedanke, *der*

**ultimate** ['ʌltɪmət] **1.** *attrib. adj.* **a)** *(final)* letzt...; *(eventual)* endgültig ⟨*Sieg*⟩; **b)** *(fundamental)* tiefst... **2.** *n*. **the ~ in comfort/luxury** der Gipfel an Bequemlichkeit/Luxus. '**ultimately** *adv*. **a)** *(in the end)* schließlich; **b)** *(in the last analysis)* letzten Endes

**ultimatum** [ʌltɪ'meɪtəm] *n., pl.* ~**s** *or* **ultimata** [ʌltɪ'meɪtə] Ultimatum, *das*

**ultra·violet** *adj*. *(Phys.)* ultraviolett; UV-⟨*Lampe, Filter*⟩

**umbilical cord** [ʌm'bɪlɪkl kɔ:d] *n*. Nabelschnur, *die*

**umbrage** ['ʌmbrɪdʒ] *n*. **take ~ [at sth.]** [an etw. (+ *Dat.*)] Anstoß nehmen

**umbrella** [ʌm'brelə] *n*. [Regen]schirm, *der*

**umpire** ['ʌmpaɪə(r)] *n*. Schiedsrichter, *der*/-richterin, *die*

**umpteen** [ʌmp'ti:n] *adj*. *(coll.)* zig *(ugs.)*; x *(ugs.)*

**unabashed** [ʌnə'bæʃt] *adj*. ungeniert

**unable** [ʌn'eɪbl] *pred. adj*. **be ~ to do sth.** etw. nicht tun können

**unabridged** [ʌnə'brɪdʒd] *adj*. ungekürzt

**unac·ceptable** *adj*. unannehmbar

**unac·countable** *adj*. unerklärlich. **unaccountably** [ʌnə'kaʊntəblɪ] *adv*. unerklärlicherweise

**unac·customed** *adj*. ungewohnt; **be ~ to sth.** etw. *(Akk.)* nicht gewöhnt sein

**unadulterated** [ʌnə'dʌltəreɪtɪd] *adj*. **a)** *(pure)* unverfälscht; **b)** *(utter)* völlig

**unaided** [ʌn'eɪdɪd] *adj*. ohne fremde Hilfe

**unanimity** [ju:nə'nɪmɪtɪ] *n*. Einmütigkeit, *die*

**unanimous** [ju:'nænɪməs] *adj*. einstimmig; **be ~ in doing sth.** etw. einmütig tun

**unarmed** [ʌn'ɑ:md] *adj*. unbewaffnet; ~ **combat** Kampf ohne Waffen

**unassuming** [ʌnə'sju:mɪŋ] *adj*. bescheiden

**unattached** [ʌnə'tætʃt] *adj*. **a)** nicht befestigt; **b)** *(without a partner)* ungebunden

**unat·tended** *adj*. **a)** ~ **to** *(not dealt with)* unerledigt; nicht bedient ⟨*Kunde*⟩; nicht behandelt ⟨*Patient*⟩; **b)** *(not supervised)* unbewacht ⟨*Parkplatz, Gepäck*⟩

**unat·tractive** *adj*. unattraktiv

**unauthorized** [ʌn'ɔ:θəraɪzd] *adj*. unbefugt; **no entry for ~ persons** Zutritt für Unbefugte verboten

**una·vailable** *adj*. nicht erhältlich ⟨*Ware*⟩; **be ~ for comment** zur Stellungnahme nicht zur Verfügung stehen

**una·voidable** *adj*. unvermeidlich

**unaware** [ʌnə'weə(r)] *adj*. **be ~ of sth.** sich *(Dat.)* einer Sache *(Gen.)* nicht bewußt sein. **unawares** [ʌnə'weəz] *adv*. **catch sb. ~:** jmdn. überraschen

**unbalanced** [ʌn'bælənst] *adj*. **a)** unausgewogen; **b)** *(mentally ~)* unausgeglichen

**un·bearable** *adj., **unbearably** [ʌn'beərəblɪ] *adv*. unerträglich

**unbeatable** [ʌn'bi:təbl] *adj*. unschlagbar *(ugs.)*

**un·beaten** *adj*. **a)** ungeschlagen; **b)** *(not surpassed)* unerreicht; ungebrochen ⟨*Rekord*⟩

**unbe·lievable** *adj*. **a)** unglaublich; **b)** *(tremendous)* unwahrscheinlich

**unbiased, unbiassed** [ʌn'baɪəst] *adj*. unvoreingenommen

**unblemished** [ʌn'blemɪʃt] *adj*. makellos ⟨*Haut, Ruf*⟩

**un·block** *v. t*. frei machen

**un·bolt** *v. t*. aufriegeln ⟨*Tür*⟩

**unborn** [ʌn'bɔ:n, *attrib*. 'ʌnbɔ:n] *adj*. ungeboren

**un·breakable** *adj*. unzerbrechlich

**unburden** [ʌn'bɜ:dn] *v. t*. ~ **oneself** sein Herz ausschütten

**un·button** *v. t*. aufknöpfen

**uncalled-for** [ʌn'kɔ:ldfɔ:(r)] *adj*. unangebracht

**uncanny** [ʌn'kænɪ] *adj*. unheimlich

**uncaring** [ʌn'keərɪŋ] *adj.* gleichgültig

**unceasing** [ʌn'siːsɪŋ] *adj.* unaufhörlich

**unceremonious** [ʌnserɪ'məʊnɪəs] *adj.* **a)** *(informal)* formlos; **b)** *(abrupt)* brüsk. **uncere'moniously** *adv.* ohne Umschweife

**un'certain** *adj.* **a)** *(not sure)* be ~ [whether ...] sich *(Dat.)* nicht sicher sein[, ob ...]; **b)** *(not clear)* ungewiß ⟨Ergebnis, Zukunft⟩; of ~ **age/origin** unbestimmten Alters/unbestimmter Herkunft; **c)** *(ambiguous)* vage; **in no ~ terms** ganz eindeutig. **uncertainty** [ʌn'sɜːtntɪ] *n.* **a)** Ungewißheit, *die;* **b)** *(hesitation)* Unsicherheit, *die*

**unchanged** [ʌn'tʃeɪndʒd] *adj.* unverändert

**un'charitable** *adj.* **uncharitably** [ʌn'tʃærɪtəblɪ] *adv.* lieblos

**un'civil** *adj.* unhöflich

**uncle** ['ʌŋkl] *n.* Onkel, *der*

**un'comfortable** *adj.* **a)** unbequem; **b)** *(feeling discomfort)* be ~ : sich unbehaglich fühlen; **c)** *(uneasy, disconcerting)* unangenehm; peinlich ⟨Stille⟩. **un'comfortably** *adv.* unbequem; **be ~ aware of sth.** sich *(Dat.)* einer Sache peinlich bewußt sein

**un'common** *adj.* ungewöhnlich

**uncompli'mentary** *adj.* wenig schmeichelhaft

**uncompromising** [ʌn'kɒmprəmaɪzɪŋ] *adj.* kompromißlos

**uncon'ditional** *adj.* bedingungslos ⟨Kapitulation⟩; kategorisch ⟨Ablehnung⟩; ⟨Versprechen⟩ ohne Vorbehalte

**un'conscious** **1.** *adj.* **a)** *(Med.)* bewußtlos; **b)** *(unaware)* be ~ of sth. sich einer Sache *(Gen.)* nicht bewußt sein; **c)** *(not intended; Psych.)* unbewußt. **2.** *n.* Unbewußte, *das.* **un'consciously** *adv.* unbewußt

**uncon'ventional** *adj.,* **uncon'ventionally** *adv.* unkonventionell

**unco'operative** *adj.* unkooperativ; *(unhelpful)* wenig hilfsbereit

**un'cork** *v. t.* entkorken

**uncouth** [ʌn'kuːθ] *adj.* ungehobelt ⟨Person, Benehmen⟩; grob ⟨Bemerkung⟩

**un'cover** *v. t.* aufdecken

**undaunted** [ʌn'dɔːntɪd] *adj.* unverzagt

**undecided** [ʌndɪ'saɪdɪd] *adj.* **a)** *(not settled)* nicht entschieden; **b)** *(hesitant)* unentschlossen

**undeniably** [ʌndɪ'naɪəblɪ] *adv.* unbestreitbar

**under** ['ʌndə(r)] **1.** *prep.* **a)** *(underneath, below)* unter *(position: + Dat.; motion: + Akk.);* **from ~ the table/bed** unter dem Tisch/Bett hervor; **b)** *(undergoing)* ~ **treatment** in Behandlung; ~ **repair** in Reparatur; ~ **construction** im Bau; **c)** *(in conditions of)* bei ⟨Streß, hohen Temperaturen usw.⟩; **d)** *(subject to)* unter *(+ Dat.);* ~ **the terms of the contract** nach den Bestimmungen des Vertrags; **e)** *(with the use of)* unter *(+ Dat.);* ~ **an assumed name** unter falschem Namen; **f)** *(less than)* unter *(+ Dat.).* **2.** *adv.* **a)** *(in or to a lower or subordinate position)* darunter; **b)** *(in/into a state of unconsciousness)* be ~/put sb. ~ : in Narkose liegen/jmdn. in Narkose versetzen

**under:** ~**carriage** *n.* Fahrwerk, *das;* ~**clothes** *n. pl.,* ~**clothing** *see* **underwear;** ~**cover** *adj. (disguised)* getarnt; *(secret)* verdeckt; ~**cover agent** Geheimagent, *der;* ~**current** *n.* Unterströmung, *die;* *(fig.)* Unterton, *der;* ~'**cut** *v. t.,* ~**cut** unterbieten; ~**dog** *n.* **a)** *(in fight)* Unterlegene, *der/die;* **b)** *(fig.)* Benachteiligte, *der/die;* ~'**done** *adj.* halbgar; ~**estimate** [ʌndər'estɪmeɪt] **1.** *v. t.* unterschätzen; **2.** [ʌndər'estɪmət] *n.* Unterschätzung, *die;* ~'**fed** *adj.* unterernährt; ~'**foot** *adv.* am Boden; **be trampled ~foot** mit Füßen zertrampelt werden; ~'**go** *v. t., forms as* **go** 1 durchmachen; ~**go treatment** sich einer Behandlung unterziehen; ~**go a change** sich verändern; ~'**graduate** *n.* ~**graduate [student]** Student/Studentin vor der ersten Prüfung; ~**ground** **1.** [--'-] *adj.* **a)** unter der Erde; *(Mining)* unter Tage; **b)** *(fig.) (in hiding)* im Untergrund; *(into hiding)* in den Untergrund; **2.** ['---] *adj.* unterirdisch ⟨Höhle, See⟩; ~**ground railway** Untergrundbahn, *die;* U-Bahn, *die;* ~**ground car-park** Tiefgarage, *die.* **3.** *n. (railway)* U-Bahn, *die;* ~ **station/ train** U-Bahnhof, *der*/U-Bahn-Zug, *der;* ~**growth** *n.* Unterholz, *das;* ~**hand,** ~**handed** *adj.* **a)** *(secret)* heimlich; **b)** *(crafty)* hinterhältig; ~**lay** *n.* Unterlage, *die;* ~'**lie** *v. t., forms as* ²**lie:** ~**lie sth.** *(fig.)* einer Sache *(Dat.)* zugrundeliegen; ~**lying cause** eigentliche Ursache; ~'**line** *v. t.* unterstreichen

**underling** ['ʌndəlɪŋ] *n.* Untergebene, *der/die*

**under:** ~'**lying** *see* **underlie;** ~'**mine**

*v. t.* **a)** unterhöhlen; **b)** *(fig.)* untergraben; unterminieren ⟨*Autorität*⟩

**underneath** [ʌndəˈniːθ] **1.** *prep.* unter *(position:* + *Dat.; motion:* + *Akk.).* **2.** *adv.* darunter

**under:** ~**'paid** *adj.* unterbezahlt; ~**pants** *n. pl.* Unterhose, *die;* ~**pass** *n.* Unterführung, *die;* ~'**play** *v. t.* herunterspielen; ~'**privileged** *adj.* unterprivilegiert; ~'**rate** *v. t.* unterschätzen; ~**seal** *n.* Unterbodenschutz, *der*

**understand** [ʌndəˈstænd] **1.** *v. t.*, **understood** [ʌndəˈstʊd] **a)** verstehen; **make oneself understood** sich verständlich machen; **b)** *(have heard)* gehört haben; **c)** *(take as implied)* **it was understood that ...:** es wurde allgemein angenommen, daß ... **2.** *v. i.*, **understood a)** verstehen; **b)** *(gather, hear)* **if I ~ correctly** wenn ich mich nicht irre; **he is, I ~, no longer here** er ist, wie ich höre, nicht mehr hier. **understandably** [ʌndəˈstændəblɪ] *adv.* verständlicherweise. **under-'standing 1.** *adj.* verständnisvoll. **2.** *n.* **a)** *(agreement)* Verständigung, *die;* **reach an ~ with sb.** sich mit jmdm. verständigen; **on the ~ that ...:** unter der Voraussetzung, daß ...; **b)** *(intelligence)* Verstand, *der;* **c)** *(insight)* Verständnis, *das (of, for für)*

**under:** ~**statement** *n.* Untertreibung, *die;* ~**study** *n.* Ersatzspieler, *der/*-spielerin, *die;* ~'**take** *v. t., forms as take* 1 unternehmen; ~**take a task** eine Aufgabe übernehmen; ~**take to do sth.** sich verpflichten, etw. zu tun; ~**taker** *n.* Leichenbestatter, *der/*-bestatterin, *die;* ~'**taking** *n.* **a)** *(task)* Aufgabe, *die;* **b)** *(pledge)* Versprechen, *das;* ~**tone** *n.* **in ~tones** *or* **an ~tone** mit gedämpfter Stimme; ~**tone of criticism** kritischer Unterton; ~**tow** *n.* Unterströmung, *die;* ~'**value** *v. t.* unterbewerten; ~**water 1.** [`----`] *attrib. adj.* Unterwasser-; **2.** [`--'--`] *adv.* unter Wasser; ~**wear** *n.* Unterwäsche, *die;* ~'**weight** *adj.* untergewichtig; ~**world** *n.* Unterwelt, *der* **unde'sirable** *adj.* unerwünscht; **it is ~ that ...:** es ist nicht wünschenswert, daß ...

**undeveloped** [ʌndɪˈveləpt] *adj.* **a)** *(immature)* nicht voll ausgebildet; **b)** *(not built on)* nicht bebaut

**undies** [ˈʌndɪz] *n. pl. (coll.)* Unterwäsche, *die*

**un'dignified** *adj.* blamabel

**undo** [ʌnˈduː] *v. t.*, **undoes** [ʌnˈdʌz], **un-**doing [ʌnˈduːɪŋ], **undid** [ʌnˈdɪd], **undone** [ʌnˈdʌn] *(unfasten)* aufmachen

**un'done** *adj.* **a)** *(not accomplished)* unerledigt; **b)** *(not fastened)* offen

**undoubted** [ʌnˈdaʊtɪd] *adj.* unzweifelhaft. **un'doubtedly** *adv.* zweifellos

**un'dress 1.** *v. t.* ausziehen; **get ~ed** sich ausziehen **2.** *v. i.* sich ausziehen

**un'due** *attrib. adj.* übertrieben; übermäßig

**undulating** [ˈʌndjʊleɪtɪŋ] *adj.* Wellen-⟨*linie*⟩; **~ country** sanfte Hügellandschaft

**unduly** [ʌnˈdjuːlɪ] *adv.* übermäßig

**undying** [ʌnˈdaɪɪŋ] *adj.* ewig; unsterblich ⟨*Ruhm*⟩

**unearth** [ʌnˈɜːθ] *v. t.* **a)** ausgraben; **b)** *(fig.: discover)* aufdecken

**unearthly** [ʌnˈɜːθlɪ] *adj.* unheimlich; **at an ~ hour** in aller Herrgottsfrühe

**un'easy** *adj.* **a)** *(anxious)* besorgt; **he felt ~:** ihm war unbehaglich zumute; **b)** *(restless)* unruhig

**uneatable** [ʌnˈiːtəbl] *adj.* ungenießbar

**uneco'nomic** *adj.* unrentabel. **uneco'nomical** *adj.* **~ |to run|** unwirtschaftlich

**unemployed** [ʌnɪmˈplɔɪd] **1.** *adj.* arbeitslos. **2.** *n. pl.* **the ~:** die Arbeitslosen. **unem'ployment** *n.* Arbeitslosigkeit, *die.* **unem'ployment benefit** *n.* Arbeitslosengeld, *das*

**un'ending** *adj.* endlos

**un'equal** *adj.* unterschiedlich; ungleich ⟨*Kampf*⟩; **be ~ to sth.** einer Sache *(Dat.)* nicht gewachsen sein. **un'equalled** (*Amer.:* **unequaled**) [ʌnˈiːkwld] *adj.* unerreicht

**une'quivocal** *adj.* eindeutig

**unerring** [ʌnˈɜːrɪŋ] *adj.* unfehlbar

**un'ethical** *adj.* unmoralisch

**un'even** *adj.* **a)** *(not smooth)* uneben; **b)** *(not uniform)* ungleichmäßig; **c)** *(odd)* ungerade ⟨*Zahl*⟩. **un'evenly** *adv.* ungleichmäßig

**unex'pected** *adj.* unerwartet

**un'fair** *adj.* unfair; ungerecht. **un-'fairly** *adv.* **a)** *(unjustly)* ungerecht; unfair ⟨*spielen*⟩; **b)** *(unreasonably)* zu Unrecht. **un'fairness** *n.* Ungerechtigkeit, *die*

**un'faithful** *adj.* untreu

**unfa'miliar** *adj.* **a)** *(strange)* unbekannt; ungewohnt ⟨*Arbeit*⟩; **b)** **be ~ with sth.** sich mit etw. nicht auskennen

**un'fasten** *v. t.* **a)** öffnen; **b)** *(detach)* lösen

**un'favourable** *adj.* ungünstig. **un'fa-vourably** *adv.* ungünstig; **be ~ disposed towards sb./sth.** jmdm./etw. gegenüber ablehnend eingestellt sein

**un'feeling** *adj.* gefühllos

**unfinished** [ʌn'fɪnɪʃt] *adj.* unvollendet ⟨*Werk*⟩; unerledigt ⟨*Arbeit*⟩

**un'fit** *adj.* **a)** ungeeignet; **b)** *(not physically fit)* nicht fit *(ugs.);* **~ for military service** [wehrdienst]untauglich

**un'flattering** *adj.* wenig schmeichelhaft

**un'flinching** *adj.* unerschrocken

**un'fold 1.** *v. t.* entfalten; ausbreiten ⟨*Zeitung, Landkarte*⟩. **2.** *v. i.* sich entfalten; *(develop)* sich entwickeln

**unfore'seen** *adj.* unvorhergesehen

**unforgettable** [ʌnfə'getəbl] *adj.* unvergeßlich

**un'fortunate** *adj.* unglücklich. **un'fortunately** *adv.* leider

**un'founded** *adj. (fig.)* unbegründet

**un'freeze** *v. t. & i.,* **unfroze** [ʌn'frəʊz], **unfrozen** [ʌn'frəʊzn] auftauen

**un'friendly** *adj.* unfreundlich; feindlich ⟨*Staat*⟩

**un'furl 1.** *v. t.* aufrollen; losmachen ⟨*Segel*⟩. **2.** *v. i.* sich aufrollen

**un'furnished** *adj.* unmöbliert

**ungainly** [ʌn'geɪnlɪ] *adj.* unbeholfen

**ungram'matical** *adj.* ungrammatisch

**un'grateful** *adj.* undankbar

**un'happily** *adv.* **a)** unglücklich; **b)** *(unfortunately)* leider

**un'happiness** *n.* Bekümmertheit, *die*

**un'happy** *adj.* unglücklich; *(not content)* unzufrieden (about with); **be or feel ~ about doing sth.** Bedenken haben, etw. zu tun

**un'harmed** *adj.* unbeschädigt; *(uninjured)* unverletzt

**un'healthy** *adj.* ungesund

**un'helpful** *adj.* wenig hilfsbereit ⟨*Person*⟩; ⟨*Bemerkung, Kritik*⟩ die einem nicht weiterhilft

**un'hook** *v. t.* vom Haken nehmen; aufhaken ⟨*Kleid*⟩

**un'hurt** *adj.* unverletzt

**unhy'gienic** *adj.* unhygienisch

**unicorn** ['ju:nɪkɔ:n] *n.* Einhorn, *das*

**uni'dentified** *adj.* nicht identifiziert; **~ flying object** unbekanntes Flugobjekt

**unification** [ju:nɪfɪ'keɪʃn] *n.* Einigung, *die*

**uniform** ['ju:nɪfɔ:m] **1.** *adj.* einheitlich; **be ~ in shape/size** die gleiche Form/Größe haben. **2.** *n.* Uniform, *die;* **in/out of ~:** in/ohne Uniform.

**uniformity** [ju:nɪ'fɔ:mɪtɪ] *n.* Einheitlichkeit, *die.* '**uniformly** *adv.* einheitlich

**unify** ['ju:nɪfaɪ] *v. t.* einigen

**unilateral** [ju:nɪ'lætərl] *adj.* einseitig

**uni'maginable** *adj.* unvorstellbar

**uni'maginative** *adj.* phantasielos

**unim'portant** *adj.* unwichtig; bedeutungslos

**unin'habitable** *adj.* unbewohnbar

**unin'habited** *adj.* unbewohnt

**unin'jured** *adj.* unverletzt

**uninspiring** [ʌnɪn'spaɪərɪŋ] *adj.* langweilig

**unin'telligent** *adj.* nicht intelligent

**unin'telligible** *adj.* unverständlich

**unin'tended** *adj.* unbeabsichtigt

**unin'tentional** *adj.,* **unin'tentionally** *adv.* unabsichtlich

**unin'terested** *adj.* desinteressiert (**in** an + *Dat.*)

**union** ['ju:nɪən] *n.* **a)** *(trade ~)* Gewerkschaft, *die;* **b)** *(Polit.)* Union, *die.* **Union 'Jack** *n. (Brit.)* Union Jack, *der*

**unique** [ju:'ni:k] *adj.* einzigartig

**unison** ['ju:nɪsən] *n.* Unisono, *das;* **in ~:** einstimmig; **act in ~** *(fig.)* vereint handeln

**unit** ['ju:nɪt] *n.* **a)** *(also Mil., Math.)* Einheit, *die;* **~ of length/monetary ~:** Längen-/Währungseinheit, *die;* **b)** *(piece of furniture)* Element, *das;* **kitchen ~:** Küchenelement, *das*

**unite** [ju:'naɪt] **1.** *v. t.* vereinigen; einen, einigen ⟨*Partei, Mitglieder*⟩. **2.** *v. i.* sich vereinigen. **u'nited** *adj.* **a)** *(harmonious)* einig; **b)** *(combined)* gemeinsam

**United: ~ 'Kingdom** *pr. n.* Vereinigtes Königreich [Großbritannien und Nordirland]; **~ 'Nations** *pr. n. sing.* Vereinte Nationen *Pl.;* **~ States [of A'merica]** *pr. n. sing.* Vereinigte Staaten [von Amerika]

**unity** ['ju:nɪtɪ] *n.* Einheit, *die*

**universal** [ju:nɪ'vɜ:sl] *adj.,* **uni'versally** *adv.* allgemein

**universe** ['ju:nɪvɜ:s] *n.* Universum, *das*

**university** [ju:nɪ'vɜ:sɪtɪ] *n.* Universität, *die; attrib.* Universitäts-

**un'just** *adj.* ungerecht

**unkempt** [ʌn'kempt] *adj.* ungepflegt

**un'kind** *adj.,* **un'kindly** *adv.* unfreundlich. **un'kindness** *n.* Unfreundlichkeit, *die*

**un'known 1.** *adj.* unbekannt. **2.** *adv.* **~ to sb.** ohne daß jmd. davon weiß/wußte

**un'lawful** *adj.* ungesetzlich

**unless** [ən'les] *conj.* es sei denn; wenn ... nicht

**un'like 1.** *adj.* nicht ähnlich. **2.** *prep.* **be ~ sb./sth.** jmdm./einer Sache nicht ähnlich sein; **~ him, ...:** im Gegensatz zu ihm ...

**un'likely** *adj.* unwahrscheinlich; **be ~ to do sth.** etw. wahrscheinlich nicht tun

**un'limited** *adj.* unbegrenzt

**un'load** *v. t.* entladen 〈*Lastwagen, Waggon*〉; löschen 〈*Schiff, Schiffsladung*〉; ausladen 〈*Gepäck*〉

**un'lock** *v. t.* aufschließen

**un'lucky** *adj.* **a)** unglücklich; *(not successful)* glücklos; **be |very| ~:** [großes] Pech haben; **b)** *(bringing bad luck)* **an ~ number** eine Unglückszahl; **be ~:** Unglück bringen

**un'manned** *adj.* unbemannt

**un'married** *adj.* unverheiratet; ledig

**un'mask** *v. t. (fig.)* entlarven

**unmi'stakable** *adj.* deutlich; unverwechselbar 〈*Handschrift, Stimme*〉. **unmistakably** [ʌnmɪ'stəɪkəblɪ] *adv.* unverkennbar

**un'mitigated** *adj.* vollkommen; **be an ~ disaster** *(coll.)* eine einzige Katastrophe sein

**un'natural** *adj.*, **un'naturally** *adv.* unnatürlich; *(abnormal)* nicht normal

**un'necessarily** *adv.*, **un'necessary** *adj.* unnötig

**unofficial** *adj.*, **unofficially** *adv.* inoffiziell

**un'pack** *v. t. & i.* auspacken

**un'paid** *adj.* unbezahlt; nicht bezahlt; **~ for** nicht bezahlt

**unpalatable** [ʌn'pælətəbl] *adj.* ungenießbar

**un'paralleled** *adj.* beispiellos

**un'pardonable** *adj.* unverzeihlich

**un'pleasant** *adj.*, **un'pleasantly** *adv.* unangenehm. **un'pleasantness** *n. (bad feeling)* Verstimmung, *die*

**un'plug** *v. t.*, **-gg-:** **~ a lamp** den Stecker einer Lampe herausziehen

**un'popular** *adj.* unbeliebt 〈*Lehrer, Regierung usw.*〉, unpopulär 〈*Maßnahme, Politik*〉 **(with bei)**

**un'precedented** *adj.* beispiellos

**unpre'dictable** *adj.* unberechenbar

**unpre'pared** *adj.* unvorbereitet

**unprepos'sessing** *adj.* wenig attraktiv

**unpre'tentious** *adj.* einfach 〈*Wein, Stil, Haus*〉; bescheiden 〈*Person*〉

**unprincipled** [ʌn'prɪnsɪpld] *adj.* skrupellos

**unprintable** [ʌn'prɪntəbl] *adj.* nicht druckreif

**unpro'ductive** *adj.* fruchtlos 〈*Diskussion, Nachforschung*〉; unproduktiv 〈*Zeit, Arbeit*〉

**unpro'fessional** *adj. (contrary to standards)* standeswidrig

**un'profitable** *adj.* unrentabel

**un'promising** *adj.* nicht sehr vielversprechend

**un'qualified** *adj.* **a)** unqualifiziert; **b)** *(absolute)* uneingeschränkt; voll 〈*Erfolg*〉

**un'questionable** *adj.* unbezweifelbar 〈*Tatsache*〉; unbestreitbar 〈*Recht, Ehrlichkeit*〉. **unquestionably** [ʌn'kwestʃənəblɪ] *adv.* ohne Frage

**unravel** [ʌn'rævl] **1.** *v. t.*, *(Brit.)* **-ll-** entwirren; *(undo)* aufziehen; *(fig.)* **~ a mystery/the truth** ein Geheimnis enträtseln/die Wahrheit aufdecken. **2.** *v. i.*, *(Brit.)* **-ll-** sich aufziehen

**un'real** *adj.* unwirklich

**unrea'listic** *adj.* unrealistisch

**un'reasonable** *adj.* unvernünftig; übertrieben 〈*Ansprüche, Forderung, Preis, Kosten*〉

**unrecognizable** [ʌn'rekəgnaɪzəbl] *adj.* **be |absolutely *or* quite| ~:** [überhaupt] nicht wiederzuerkennen sein

**unre'lated** *adj.* **be ~:** nicht miteinander zusammenhängen; *(by family)* nicht verwandt sein

**unre'liable** *adj.* unzuverlässig

**unrequited** [ʌnrɪ'kwaɪtɪd] *adj.* unerwidert

**unreservedly** [ʌnrɪ'zɜːvɪdlɪ] *adv.* uneingeschränkt

**un'rest** *n.* Unruhen *Pl.*

**un'ripe** *adj.* unreif

**un'rivalled** *(Amer.:* **un'rivaled)** *adj.* unübertroffen

**un'roll 1.** *v. t.* aufrollen. **2.** *v. i.* sich aufrollen

**unruly** [ʌn'ruːlɪ] *adj.* ungebärdig

**un'safe** *adj.* nicht sicher; **feel ~:** sich unsicher fühlen

**un'said** *adj.* ungesagt

**un'salted** *adj.* ungesalzen

**unsatis'factory** *adj.* unbefriedigend

**un'savoury** *(Amer.:* **un'savory)** *adj.* unangenehm; zweifelhaft 〈*Angelegenheit*〉; unerfreulich 〈*Einzelheiten*〉

**unscathed** [ʌn'skeɪðd] *adj.* unversehrt

**un'screw 1.** *v. t.* abschrauben. **2.** *v. i.* sich abschrauben lassen

**un'scrupulous** *adj.* skrupellos
**un'seemly** *adj.* unschicklich
**unself'conscious** *adj.* unbefangen
**un'selfish** *adj.* selbstlos. **un'selfish-
ress** *n.* Selbstlosigkeit, *die*
**un'settled** *adj. (changeable)* wechselhaft; *(fig.)* ruhelos ⟨*Leben*⟩; unruhig
⟨*Zeit, Land*⟩
**un'settling** *adj.* störend
**unshak[e]able** [ʌn'ʃeɪkəbl] *adj.* un-
erschütterlich
**un'shaven** *adj.* unrasiert
**un'sightly** *adj.* unschön
**un'skilled** *adj.* ungelernt ⟨*Arbeiter*⟩
**un'sociable** *adj.* ungesellig
**unso'phisticated** *adj.* einfach
**un'sound** *adj.* **a)** *(diseased)* nicht gesund; krank; **b)** baufällig ⟨*Gebäude*⟩;
**c)** *(ill-founded)* wenig stichhaltig;
nicht vertretbar ⟨*Ansicht, Methode*⟩;
**d)** of ~ **mind** unzurechnungsfähig
**unspeakable** [ʌn'spiːkəbl] *adj.* unbeschreiblich; *(very bad)* unsäglich
**un'stable** *adj.* nicht stabil; [**mentally/
emotionally**] ~: [psychisch] labil
**un'steadily** *adv.* unsicher
**un'steady** *adj.* unsicher; wackelig
⟨*Leiter, Tisch*⟩
**un'stuck** *adj.* come ~: sich lösen; *(fig.
coll.: fail)*⟨*Person:*⟩ baden gehen *(ugs.)*
(over mit)
**unsuc'cessful** *adj.* erfolglos; be ~:
keinen Erfolg haben. **unsuc'cessfully** *adv.* erfolglos
**un'suitable** *adj.* ungeeignet
**unsu'specting** *adj.* nichtsahnend
**un'sweetened** *adj.* ungesüßt
**unsympa'thetic** *adj.* wenig mitfühlend; be ~: kein Mitgefühl zeigen
**unthinkable** [ʌn'θɪŋkəbl] *adj.* unvorstellbar
**un'tidily** *adv.* unordentlich
**un'tidiness** *n. see* **untidy**: Ungepflegt-
heit, *die*; Unaufgeräumtheit, *die*
**un'tidy** *adj.* ungepflegt ⟨*Äußeres, Person, Garten*⟩; unaufgeräumt ⟨*Zimmer*⟩
**un'tie** *v. t.,* **un'tying** aufknüpfen ⟨*Seil,
Paket*⟩; aufbinden ⟨*Knoten*⟩; losbin-
den ⟨*Pferd, Boot*⟩
**until** [ən'tɪl] **1.** *prep.* bis; ~ [**the**] **evening**
bis zum Abend; ~ **then** bis dahin; **not**
~ |**Christmas/the summer**| erst [Weih-
nachten/im Sommer]. **2.** *conj.* bis
**un'timely** *adj.* **a)** ungelegen; **b)** *(premature)* vorzeitig
**un'tiring** *adj.* unermüdlich
**un'told** *adj.* unbeschreiblich; unermeßlich ⟨*Reichtümer, Anzahl*⟩
**untoward** [ʌntə'wɔːd, ʌn'təʊəd] *adj.*

ungünstig; **nothing** ~ **happened** es gab
keine Schwierigkeiten
**untranslatable** [ʌntræns'leɪtəbl] *adj.*
unübersetzbar
**un'true** *adj.* unwahr; **that's** ~: das ist
nicht wahr
**un'trustworthy** *adj.* unzuverlässig
**un'truth** *n.* Unwahrheit, *die*
**¹unused** [ʌn'juːzd] *adj. (new, fresh)* unbenutzt; *(not utilized)* ungenutzt
**²unused** [ʌn'juːst] *adj. (unaccustomed)*
be ~ **to sth./doing sth.** etw. *(Akk.)*
nicht gewohnt sein/nicht gewohnt
sein, etw. zu tun
**un'usual** *adj.,* **un'usually** *adv.* ungewöhnlich
**un'veil** *v. t.* enthüllen; *(fig.)* vorstellen
⟨*Produkt*⟩; enthüllen ⟨*Plan*⟩
**un'versed** *adj.* nicht bewandert (**in** in
+ *Dat.*)
**un'wanted** *adj.* unerwünscht
**un'warranted** *adj.* ungerechtfertigt
**un'welcome** *adj.* unwillkommen
**un'well** *adj.* unwohl; **look** ~: nicht
wohl *od.* gut aussehen; **he feels** ~
*(poorly)* er fühlt sich nicht wohl
**unwieldy** [ʌn'wiːldɪ] *adj.* sperrig
**un'willing** *adj.* widerwillig; **be** ~ **to do
sth.** etw. nicht tun wollen. **un'willingly** *adv.* widerwillig
**unwind** [ʌn'waɪnd] **1.** *v. t.,* **unwound**
[ʌn'waʊnd] abwickeln. **2.** *v. i.,* **unwound** **a)** sich abwickeln; **b)** *(coll.:
relax)* sich entspannen
**un'wise** *adj.* unklug
**unwitting** [ʌn'wɪtɪŋ] *adj.,* **un'wittingly** *adv.* unwissentlich
**un'workable** *adj.* undurchführbar
⟨*Plan*⟩
**un'worthy** *adj.* unwürdig; **be** ~ **of sth.**
einer Sache *(Gen.)* nicht würdig sein;
**be** ~ **of sb./sth.** ⟨*Verhalten:*⟩ einer Per-
son/Sache *(Gen.)* unwürdig sein
**un'wrap** *v. t.,* **-pp-** auswickeln
**un'written** *adj.* ungeschrieben
**un'zip** *v. t.,* **-pp-**: ~ **a dress/bag** etc. den
Reißverschluß eines Kleides/einer
Tasche *usw.* öffnen
**up** [ʌp] **1.** *adv.* **a)** *(to higher place)* nach
oben; *(in lift)* aufwärts; **the bird flew
up to the roof** der Vogel flog aufs
Dach [hinauf]; **up into the air** in die
Luft [hinauf]; **up here/there** hier her-
auf/dort hinauf; **higher/a little way up**
höher/ein kurzes Stück hinauf; **come
on up!** komm [hier/weiter] herauf!;
**b)** *(to upstairs)* herauf/hinauf; nach
oben; **c)** *(in higher place, upstairs)*
oben; **up here/there** hier/da oben; **the**

**next floor up** ein Stockwerk höher; d) *(out of bed)* **be up** aufsein; e) *(in price, value, amount)* **prices have gone up/are up** die Preise sind gestiegen; **butter is up |by ...|** Butter ist [...] teurer; f) *(as far as)* **up to sth.** bis zu etw.; **up to here/there** bis hier[hin]/bis dorthin; g) |**not**| **be/feel up to sth.** *(capable of sth.)* einer Sache *(Dat.)* [nicht] gewachsen sein/sich einer Sache *(Dat.)* [nicht] gewachsen fühlen; |**not**| **be/feel up to doing sth.** [nicht] in der Lage sein/sich [nicht] in der Lage fühlen, etw. zu tun; h) **be up to sth.** *(doing)* etw. anstellen *(ugs.);* **it is |not| up to sb. to do sth.** *(sb.'s duty)* es ist [nicht] jmds. Sache, etw. zu tun; i) **be three points/games up** mit drei Punkten/Spielen vorn liegen; j) **walk up and down** auf und ab gehen; k) **time is up** die Zeit ist abgelaufen. 2. *prep.* herauf/hinauf; **walk up the hill/road** den Berg/die Straße hinaufgehen; **walk up and down the platform** auf dem Bahnsteig auf und ab gehen; **further up the ladder/coast** weiter oben auf der Leiter/an der Küste; **live just up the road** ein Stück weiter oben in der Straße wohnen. 3. *adj.* *(coll.: amiss)* **what's up?** was ist los? *(ugs.);* **something is up** irgendwas ist los *(ugs.).* 4. *v. t.,* -pp- *(coll.: increase)* erhöhen

'**upbringing** *n.* Erziehung, *die*
**up'date** *v. t.* auf den aktuellen Stand bringen
**up'grade** *v. t.* a) aufwerten ⟨*Stellung*⟩; b) *(improve)* verbessern
**upheaval** [ʌp'hiːvl] *n.* Aufruhr, *der;* *(disturbance)* Durcheinander, *das*
**up'hill** 1. *adj. (fig.)* **an ~ task/struggle** eine mühselige Aufgabe/ein harter Kampf. 2. *adv.* bergauf
**uphold** *v. t.,* **upheld** unterstützen; wahren ⟨*Tradition*⟩
**upholster** [ʌp'həʊlstə(r)] *v. t.* polstern. **up'holsterer** *n.* Polsterer, *der*/Polsterin, *die.* **up'holstery** *n.* a) *(craft)* Polster[er]handwerk, *das;* b) *(padding)* Polsterung, *die*
'**upkeep** *n.* Unterhalt, *der*
'**up-market** *adj.* exklusiv
**upon** [ə'pɒn] *prep.* auf *(direction:* + *Akk.; position:* + *Dat.)*
**upper** ['ʌpə(r)] 1. *compar. adj.* ober...; Ober⟨*grenze, -lippe, -arm usw.*⟩; **~ circle** oberer Rang; **~ class|es|** Oberschicht, *die;* **have/get/gain the ~ hand** die Oberhand haben/gewinnen/erhalten. 2. *n.* Oberteil, *das.* **upper 'deck**

*n.* Oberdeck, *das.* '**uppermost** 1. *adj.* oberst... 2. *adv.* ganz oben
'**upright** 1. *adj.* aufrecht. 2. *n.* seitliche Leiste
'**uprising** *n.* Aufstand, *der*
'**uproar** *n.* Aufruhr, *der*
**up'root** *v. t.* [her]ausreißen; ⟨*Sturm:*⟩ entwurzeln
**upset** 1. [ʌp'set] *v. t.,* -tt-, **upset** a) *(overturn)* umkippen; *(accidentally)* umstoßen ⟨*Tasse, Milch usw.*⟩; b) *(distress)* erschüttern; *(make angry)* aufregen; **don't let it ~ you** nimm es nicht so schwer; c) *(make ill)* **sth. ~s sb.** etw. bekommt jmdm. nicht; d) durcheinanderbringen ⟨*Plan*⟩. 2. *v. i.,* -tt-, **upset** umkippen. 3. *adj. (distressed)* bestürzt; *(agitated)* aufgeregt; **get ~ |about/over sth.|** sich [über etw. *(Akk.)*] aufregen. 4. ['ʌpset] *n.* a) *(agitation)* Aufregung, *die; (annoyance)* Verärgerung, *die;* b) **stomach ~:** Magenstimmung, *die;* c) *(upheaval)* Aufruhr, *der.* **up'setting** *adj.* erschütternd; *(sad)* traurig; *(annoying)* ärgerlich
'**upshot** *n.* Ergebnis, *das*
**upside 'down** 1. *adv.* verkehrt herum; **turn sth. ~:** etw. auf den Kopf stellen. 2. *adj.* auf dem Kopf stehend ⟨*Bild*⟩; **be ~:** auf dem Kopf stehen
**upstairs** 1. [-'-'] *adv.* nach oben ⟨*gehen, kommen*⟩; oben ⟨*sein, wohnen*⟩. 2. ['--'] *adj.* im Obergeschoß *nachgestellt*
'**upstart** *n.* Emporkömmling, *der*
**up'stream** *adv.* flußaufwärts
'**uptake** *n.* **be quick/slow on the ~** *(coll.)* schnell begreifen/schwer von Begriff sein *(ugs.)*
**uptight** [-'-, '--] *adj. (coll.: tense)* nervös **(about wegen)**
**up to 'date** *adj.* **be/keep ~:** auf dem neusten Stand sein/bleiben; **bring sth. ~:** etw. auf den neusten Stand bringen. **up-to-'date** *attrib. adj. (current)* aktuell; *(modern)* modern
'**upturn** *n.* Aufschwung, *der* **(in Gen.)**
**upward** ['ʌpwəd] 1. *adj.* nach oben gerichtet. 2. *adv.* aufwärts ⟨*sich bewegen*⟩; nach oben ⟨*sehen, gehen*⟩. **upwards** ['ʌpwədz] *adv.* a) *see* **upward** 2; b) **~ of** über *(+ Akk.)*
**uranium** [jʊə'reɪnɪəm] *n.* Uran, *das*
**Uranus** ['jʊərənəs, jʊə'reɪnəs] *pr. n. (Astron.)* Uranus, *der*
**urban** ['ɜːbn] *adj.* städtisch; Stadt⟨*gebiet, -bevölkerung, -planung*⟩
**urchin** ['ɜːtʃɪn] *n.* Strolch, *der*
**urge** [ɜːdʒ] 1. *v. t.* **~ sb. to do sth.** jmdn. drängen, etw. zu tun. 2. *n.* Trieb, *der.*

**urge 'on** *v. t.* antreiben; *(encourage)* anfeuern

**urgency** ['ɜ:dʒənsɪ] *n.* Dringlichkeit, *die*

**urgent** ['ɜ:dʒənt] *adj.* dringend; *(to be dealt with immediately)* eilig; **be in ~ need of sth.** etw. dringend brauchen.

**'urgently** *adv.* dringend; *(immediately)* eilig

**urinate** ['jʊərɪneɪt] *v. i.* urinieren

**urine** ['jʊərɪn] *n.* Urin, *der;* Harn, *der*

**urn** [ɜ:n] *n.* **a)** tea/coffee **~:** Tee-/Kaffeemaschine, *die;* **b)** *(vessel)* Urne, *die*

**Uruguay** ['jʊərəgwaɪ] *pr. n.* Uruguay *(das)*

**US** *abbr.* United States USA

**us** [əs, *stressed* ʌs] *pron.* uns; **it's us** wir sind's *(ugs.)*

**USA** *abbr.* United States of America USA

**usage** ['ju:zɪdʒ, 'ju:sɪdʒ] *n.* **a)** Brauch, *der;* **b)** *(Ling.)* Sprachgebrauch, *der*

**use 1.** [ju:s] *n.* **a)** Gebrauch, *der;* *(of dictionary, calculator, room)* Benutzung, *die;* *(of word, pesticide, spice)* Verwendung, *die;* |**not**| **be in ~:** [nicht] in Gebrauch sein; **be no longer in ~:** nicht mehr verwendet werden; **make ~ of sb./sth.** jmdn./etw. gebrauchen/ *(exploit)* ausnutzen; **make good ~ of, turn** *or* **put to good ~:** gut nutzen ⟨*Zeit, Talent, Geld*⟩; **put sth. to ~:** etw. verwenden; **b)** *(usefulness)* Nutzen, *der;* **is it of** |**any**| **~?** ist das [irgendwie] von Nutzen?; **be** |**of**| **no ~** |**to sb.**| [jmdm.] nicht nützen; **it's no ~** |**doing that**| es hat keinen Sinn[, das zu tun]; **c)** *(purpose)* Verwendung, *die;* **have/find a ~ for sth./sb.** für etw./jmdn. Verwendung haben/finden; **have no/not much ~ for sth./sb.** etw./jmdn. nicht/kaum brauchen. **2.** [ju:z] *v. t.* **a)** benutzen; nutzen ⟨*Gelegenheit*⟩; anwenden ⟨*Gewalt*⟩; in Anspruch nehmen ⟨*Firma, Dienstleistung*⟩; nutzen ⟨*Zeit, Gelegenheit*⟩; verwenden ⟨*Kraftstoff, Butter, Wort*⟩; **b)** **~d to** ['ju:st tə]: **I ~d to live in London** früher habe ich in London gelebt. **use 'up** *v. t.* aufbrauchen; verbrauchen ⟨*Geld, Energie*⟩

**used 1.** *adj.* **a)** [ju:zd] gebraucht; gestempelt ⟨*Briefmarke*⟩; **~ car** Gebrauchtwagen, *der;* **b)** [ju:st] **~ to sth.** [an] etw. *(Akk.)* gewöhnt. **2.** [ju:st] *see* **use 2 b**

**useful** ['ju:sfl] *adj.* nützlich; praktisch ⟨*Werkzeug*⟩; hilfreich ⟨*Rat, Idee*⟩.

**'usefulness** *n.* Nützlichkeit, *die*

**'useless** *adj.* unbrauchbar ⟨*Werkzeug,* *Rat, Idee*⟩; nutzlos ⟨*Wissen, Information, Protest, Anstrengung, Kampf*⟩; zwecklos ⟨*Widerstand, Protest*⟩

**'user** *n.* Benutzer, *der*/Benutzerin, *die.*

**'user-friendly** *adj.* benutzerfreundlich

**usher** ['ʌʃə(r)] **1.** *n.* *(in court)* Gerichtsdiener, *der;* *(at cinema, church)* Platzanweiser, *der.* **2.** *v. t.* führen. **usher 'in** *v. t.* hineinführen; *(fig.)* einläuten

**usherette** [ʌʃə'ret] *n.* Platzanweiserin, *die*

**USSR** *abbr. (Hist.)* Union of Soviet Socialist Republics UdSSR, *die*

**usual** ['ju:ʒʊəl] *adj.* üblich. **usually** ['ju:ʒʊəlɪ] *adv.* gewöhnlich

**usurp** [ju:'zɜ:p] *v. t.* sich *(Dat.)* widerrechtlich aneignen

**utensil** [ju:'tensɪl] *n.* Utensil, *das;* **writing ~s** Schreibutensilien; **kitchen ~s** Küchengeräte

**uterus** ['ju:tərəs] *n.* Gebärmutter, *die*

**utility** [ju:'tɪlɪtɪ] *n.* **a)** Nutzen, *der;* **b)** |**public**| **~:** öffentlicher Versorgungsbetrieb. **u'tility room** *n.* Raum, *in den* [größere] *Haushaltsgeräte (z. B. Waschmaschine) installiert sind*

**utilize** ['ju:tɪlaɪz] *v. t.* nutzen

**utmost** ['ʌtməʊst] **1.** *adj.* äußerst...; größt... ⟨*Höflichkeit, Eleganz, Einfachheit, Geschwindigkeit*⟩. **2.** *n.* Äußerste, *das;* **do** *or* **try one's ~ to do sth.** mit allen Mitteln versuchen, etw. zu tun

**¹utter** ['ʌtə(r)] *adj.* völlig; vollkommen; **~ fool** Volliidiot, *der (ugs.)*

**²utter** *v. t.* **a)** von sich geben ⟨*Schrei, Seufzer*⟩; **b)** *(say)* sagen. **utterance** ['ʌtərəns] *n.* Worte *Pl.*

**'utterly** *adv.* völlig; vollkommen; äußerst ⟨*dumm, lächerlich*⟩

**'U-turn** *n.* Wende [um 180°]; *(fig.)* Kehrtwendung, *die;* **make a ~:** wenden; **'No ~s'** „Wenden verboten"

# V

**¹V, v** [vi:] *n.* V, v, *das*

**²V** *abbr.* volt|**s**| V

**v.** *abbr.* versus gg.

**vacancy** ['veɪkənsɪ] *n.* **a)** *(job)* freie

Stelle; **b)** *(room)* freies Zimmer; **'va-cancies'** „Zimmer frei"; **'no vacancies'** „belegt"

**vacant** ['veɪkənt] *adj.* **a)** frei; **'situ-ations ~'** „Stellenangebote"; **b)** *(mentally)* leer

**vacate** [vəˈkeɪt] *v. t.* räumen

**vacation** [vəˈkeɪʃn] *n.* **a)** *(Brit. Univ.)* Ferien *Pl.;* **b)** *(Amer.) see* **holiday** b

**vaccinate** ['væksɪneɪt] *v. t.* impfen. **vaccination** [væksɪˈneɪʃn] *n.* Impfung, *die;* **have a ~:** geimpft werden

**vaccine** ['væksiːn] *n.* Impfstoff, *der*

**vacuum** ['vækjʊəm] **1.** *n.* **a)** Vakuum, *das;* **live in a ~:** im luftleeren Raum leben; **b)** *(coll.: ~ cleaner)* Sauger, *der (ugs.).* **2.** *v. t. & i.* [staub]saugen

**vacuum: ~ cleaner** *n.* Staubsauger, *der;* **~ flask** *n. (Brit.)* Thermosflasche, *die;* **~-packed** *adj.* vakuumverpackt

**vagaries** ['veɪgərɪz] *n. pl.* Launen *Pl.*

**vagina** [vəˈdʒaɪnə] *n.* Scheide, *die*

**vagrant** ['veɪgrənt] *n.* Landstreicher, *der*/Landstreicherin, *die; (in cities)* Stadtstreicher, *der*/Stadtstreicherin, *die*

**vague** [veɪg] *adj.* vage; verschwommen ⟨*Form, Umriß*⟩; *(absent-minded)* geistesabwesend; **not have the ~st idea** *or* **notion** nicht die blasseste *od.* leiseste Ahnung haben. **'vaguely** *adv.* vage; entfernt ⟨*bekannt sein, erinnern an*⟩; schwach ⟨*sich erinnern*⟩

**vain** [veɪn] *adj.* **a)** *(conceited)* eitel; **b)** *(useless)* leer; vergeblich ⟨*Hoffnung, Versuch*⟩; **in ~:** vergeblich. **'vainly** *adv.* vergebens

**vale** [veɪl] *n. (arch./poet.)* Tal, *das*

**valentine** ['væləntaɪn] *n.* **~ [card]** Grußkarte zum Valentinstag

**valet** ['væleɪ] *n.* Kammerdiener, *der*

**valiant** ['vælɪənt] *adj.,* **'valiantly** *adv.* tapfer

**valid** ['vælɪd] *adj.* **a)** *(legally acceptable)* gültig; berechtigt ⟨*Anspruch*⟩; **b)** *(justifiable)* stichhaltig ⟨*Argument*⟩; triftig ⟨*Grund*⟩; begründet ⟨*Einwand, Entschuldigung*⟩. **validate** ['vælɪdeɪt] *v. t.* rechtskräftig machen. **validity** [vəˈlɪdɪtɪ] *n.* Gültigkeit, *die*

**valley** ['vælɪ] *n.* Tal, *das*

**valour** *(Amer.:* **valor)** ['vælə(r)] *n.* Tapferkeit, *die*

**valuable** ['væljʊəbl] **1.** *adj.* wertvoll; **be ~ to sb.** für jmdn. wertvoll sein. **2.** *n.* **~s** Wertsachen

**valuation** [væljʊˈeɪʃn] *n.* Schätzung, *die*

**value** ['væljuː] **1.** *n.* Wert, *der;* **be of great/little/some/no ~ |to sb.|** [für jmdn.] von großem/geringem/einigem/keinerlei Nutzen sein; **know the ~ of sth.** wissen, was etw. wert ist; **something/nothing of ~:** etwas/nichts Wertvolles. **2.** *v. t.* schätzen. **value added 'tax** *n.* Mehrwertsteuer, *die*

**valve** [vælv] *n.* **a)** Ventil, *das;* **b)** *(Anat.)* Klappe, *die*

**vampire** ['væmpaɪə(r)] *n.* Vampir, *der*

**van** [væn] *n.* **|delivery| ~:** Lieferwagen, *der*

**vandal** ['vændl] *n.* Rowdy, *der.* **vandalism** ['vændəlɪzm] *n.* Wandalismus, *der.* **vandalize** ['vændəlaɪz] *v. t.* [mutwillig] beschädigen

**vanilla** [vəˈnɪlə] **1.** *n.* Vanille, *die.* **2.** *adj.* Vanille-

**vanish** ['vænɪʃ] *v. i.* verschwinden

**vanity** ['vænɪtɪ] *n.* Eitelkeit, *die.* **'vanity bag** *n.* Kosmetiktäschchen, *das*

**vantage-point** ['vɑːntɪdʒ pɔɪnt] *n.* Aussichtspunkt, *der*

**vapour** *(Brit.;* **Amer.:** **vapor)** ['veɪpə(r)] *n.* Dampf, *der*

**variable** ['veərɪəbl] *adj.* **a)** *(alterable)* veränderbar; **be ~:** verändert werden können; **b)** *(inconsistent)* unbeständig ⟨*Wetter, Wind, Leistung*⟩; wechselhaft ⟨*Wetter, Launen, Qualität*⟩

**variance** ['veərɪəns] *n.* **be at ~ |with sth.|** [mit etw.] nicht übereinstimmen

**variant** ['veərɪənt] *n.* Variante, *die*

**variation** [veərɪˈeɪʃn] *n.* **a)** *(varying)* Veränderung, *die; (difference)* Unterschied, *der;* **b)** *(variant)* Variante, *die (of, on Gen.)*

**varicose vein** [værɪkəʊs 'veɪn] *n.* Krampfader, *die*

**varied** ['veərɪd] *adj.* unterschiedlich; abwechslungsreich ⟨*Diät, Leben*⟩

**variety** [vəˈraɪətɪ] *n.* **a)** *(diversity)* Vielfältigkeit, *die; (in diet, routine)* Abwechslung, *die;* **add** *or* **give ~ to sth.** etw. abwechslungsreicher gestalten; **b)** *(assortment)* Auswahl, *die* (of an + *Dat.,* von); **for a ~ of reasons** aus verschiedenen Gründen; **c)** *(Theatre)* Varieté, *das;* **d)** *(form)* Art, *die; (of fruit, vegetable)* Sorte, *die; (cultivated)* Züchtung, *die*

**various** ['veərɪəs] *adj.* **a)** pred. *(different)* verschieden; unterschiedlich; **b)** *attrib. (several)* verschiedene; **at ~ times** mehrere Male. **'variously** *adv.* unterschiedlich

**varnish** ['vɑːnɪʃ] **1.** *n.* Lasur, *die.* **2.** *v. t.* lasieren

**vary** ['veəri] 1. *v. t.* verändern; ändern ⟨*Bestimmungen, Programm, Methode, Route*⟩; *(add variety to)* abwechslungsreicher gestalten. 2. *v. i. (become different)* sich ändern; ⟨*Preis, Qualität:*⟩ schwanken; *(be different)* unterschiedlich sein. **varying** *adj.* wechselnd; *(different)* unterschiedlich

**vase** [vɑ:z] *n.* Vase, *die*

**vast** [vɑ:st] *adj.* **a)** *(huge)* riesig; weit ⟨*Fläche, Meer*⟩; **b)** *(coll.: great)* enorm; Riesen⟨*menge, -summe*⟩. **'vastly** *adv. (coll.)* enorm; weitaus ⟨*besser*⟩; weit ⟨*überlegen, unterlegen*⟩

**VAT** [vi:ei'ti:, væt] *abbr.* **value added tax** MwSt.

**vat** [væt] *n.* Bottich, *der*

**Vatican** ['vætɪkən] *pr. n.* Vatikan, *der*

**¹vault** [vɔ:lt, vɒlt] *n.* **a)** *(Archit.)* Gewölbe, *das;* **b)** *(in bank)* Tresorraum, *der;* **c)** *(tomb)* Gruft, *die*

**²vault** 1. *v. i.* sich schwingen. 2. *v. t.* sich schwingen über ( + *Akk.*). 3. *n.* Sprung, *der*

**VD** *n.* Geschlechtskrankheit, *die*

**VDU** *abbr.* **visual display unit**

**veal** [vi:l] *n.* Kalb[fleisch], *das; attrib.* Kalbs-

**veer** [vɪə(r)] *v. i.* ⟨*Auto:*⟩ ausscheren. **veer a'way, veer 'off** *v. i.* ⟨*Auto:*⟩ ausscheren; ⟨*Fahrer, Straße:*⟩ abbiegen

**veg** [vedʒ] *n., pl. same (coll.)* Gemüse, *das*

**vegetable** ['vedʒɪtəbl] *n.* Gemüse, *das;* fresh ~s frisches Gemüse; *attrib.* Gemüse⟨*suppe, -extrakt, -garten*⟩. **'vegetable oil** *n.* Pflanzenöl, *das*

**vegetarian** [vedʒɪ'teərɪən] 1. *n.* Vegetarier, *der*/Vegetarierin, *die.* 2. *adj.* vegetarisch

**vegetate** ['vedʒɪteɪt] *v. i.* nur noch [dahin]vegetieren. **vegetation** [vedʒɪ'teɪʃn] *n.* Vegetation, *die*

**vehement** ['vi:əmənt] *adj.,* **'vehemently** *adv.* heftig

**vehicle** ['vi:ɪkl] *n.* **a)** Fahrzeug, *das;* **b)** *(fig.: medium)* Vehikel, *das*

**veil** [veɪl] 1. *n.* Schleier, *der.* 2. *v. t.* verschleiern

**vein** [veɪn] *n.* **a)** Vene, *die; (any bloodvessel)* Ader, *die;* **b)** *(fig.: mood)* Stimmung, *die;* in a similar ~: vergleichbarer Art

**Velcro, (P)** ['velkrəʊ] *n.* Klettverschluß, *der* ⓦ

**velocity** [vɪ'lɒsɪtɪ] *n.* Geschwindigkeit, *die*

**velvet** ['velvɪt] 1. *n.* Samt, *der.* 2. *adj.*

aus Samt *nachgestellt;* Samt-. **'velvety** *adj.* samtig

**vendetta** [ven'detə] *n.* Hetzkampagne, *die; (feud)* Fehde, *die*

**vending-machine** ['vendɪŋ məʃi:n] *n.* [Verkaufs]automat, *der*

**vendor** ['vendə(r)] *n.* Verkäufer, *der*/Verkäuferin, *die*

**veneer** [vɪ'nɪə(r)] *n.* Furnier, *das*

**venerable** ['venərəbl] *adj.* ehrwürdig

**ve'nereal disease** *n. (Med.)* Geschlechtskrankheit, *die*

**venetian blind** [vɪ'ni:ʃn blaɪnd] *n.* Jalousie, *die*

**Venezuela** [venɪ'zweɪlə] *pr. n.* Venezuela *(das)*

**vengeance** ['vendʒəns] *n.* **a)** Rache, *die;* take ~ [up]on sb. [for sth.] sich an jmdm. [für etw.] rächen; **b)** with a ~ *(coll.)* gewaltig *(ugs.)*

**Venice** ['venɪs] *pr. n.* Venedig *(das)*

**venison** ['venɪsn, 'venɪzn] *n.* Hirsch, *der;* Hirschfleisch, *das; (roe deer)* Reh[fleisch], *das*

**venom** ['venəm] *n.* Gift, *das.* **venomous** ['venəməs] *adj.* giftig

**¹vent** [vent] 1. *n.* **a)** Öffnung, *die;* **b)** *(fig.)* Ventil, *das (fig.);* give ~ to Luft machen ( + *Dat.*). 2. *v. t. (fig.)* Luft machen ( + *Dat.*)

**²vent** *n. (in garment)* Schlitz, *der*

**ventilate** ['ventɪleɪt] *v. t.* belüften. **ventilation** [ventɪ'leɪʃn] *n.* Belüftung, *die.* **ventilator** ['ventɪleɪtə(r)] *n.* **a)** Ventilator, *der;* **b)** *(Med.)* Beatmungsgerät, *das*

**ventriloquist** [ven'trɪləkwɪst] *n.* Bauchredner, *der*/-rednerin, *die*

**venture** ['ventʃə(r)] 1. *n.* Unternehmung, *die.* 2. *v. i.* **a)** *(dare)* wagen; **b)** *(dare to go)* sich wagen. 3. *v. t.* wagen. **venture 'out** *v. i.* sich hinauswagen

**venue** ['venju:] *n. (Sport)* [Austragungs]ort, *der; (Mus., Theatre)* [Veranstaltungs]ort, *der; (meeting-place)* Treffpunkt, *der*

**Venus** ['vi:nəs] *pr. n. (Astron.)* Venus, *die*

**veranda[h]** [və'rændə] *n.* Veranda, *die*

**verb** [vɜ:b] *n.* Verb, *das.* **verbal** ['vɜ:bl] *adj.,* **verbally** ['vɜ:bəlɪ] *adv.* **a)** *(relating to words)* sprachlich; **b)** *(oral[ly])* mündlich

**verbatim** [və'beɪtɪm] *adj., adv.* [wort]wörtlich

**verbose** [və'bəʊs] *adj.* weitschweifig ⟨*Roman, Autor*⟩; langatmig ⟨*Rede, Redner*⟩

**verdict** ['vɜːdɪkt] n. Urteil, das; ~ of guilty/not guilty Schuld-/Freispruch, der; reach a ~: zu einem Urteil kommen

**verge** [vɜːdʒ] n. a) Rasensaum, der; (on road) Bankette, die; b) (fig.) be on the ~ of war/tears am Rande des Krieges stehen/den Tränen nahe sein; be on the ~ of doing sth. kurz davor stehen, etw. zu tun. 'verge on v.t. [an]grenzen an (+ Akk.)

**verger** ['vɜːdʒə(r)] n. Küster, der

**verification** [ˌverɪfɪˈkeɪʃn] n. a) (check) Überprüfung, die; b) (confirmation) Bestätigung, die

**verify** ['verɪfaɪ] v.t. a) (check) überprüfen; b) (confirm) bestätigen

**vermin** ['vɜːmɪn] n. Ungeziefer, das

**vernacular** [vəˈnækjʊlə(r)] n. Landessprache, die

**versatile** ['vɜːsətaɪl] adj. vielseitig; (having many uses) vielseitig verwendbar. **versatility** [ˌvɜːsəˈtɪlɪtɪ] n. Vielseitigkeit, die

**verse** [vɜːs] n. a) (stanza) Strophe, die; b) (poetry) Lyrik, die; write some ~: einige Verse schreiben; piece of ~: Gedicht, das; written in ~: in Versform; c) (in Bible) Vers, der. **versed** [vɜːst] adj. be [well] ~ in sth. sich in etw. (Dat.) [gut] auskennen

**version** ['vɜːʃn] n. Version, die; (in another language) Übersetzung, die; (of vehicle, machine, tool) Modell, das

**versus** ['vɜːsəs] prep. gegen

**vertebra** ['vɜːtɪbrə] n., pl. ~e ['vɜːtɪbriː] Wirbel, der. **vertebrate** ['vɜːtɪbrət] n. Wirbeltier, das

**vertical** ['vɜːtɪkl] adj. senkrecht; be ~: senkrecht stehen. **vertically** ['vɜːtɪkəlɪ] adv. senkrecht

**vertigo** ['vɜːtɪɡəʊ] n. Schwindel, der

**verve** [vɜːv] n. Schwung, der

**very** ['verɪ] 1. attrib. adj. a) (precise, exact) genau; you're the ~ person I wanted to see genau dich wollte ich sehen; at the ~ moment when ...: im selben Augenblick, als ...; at the ~ centre genau in der Mitte; the ~ thing genau das Richtige; b) (extreme) at the ~ back/front ganz hinten/vorn; at the ~ end/beginning ganz am Ende/Anfang; from the ~ beginning von Anfang an; only a ~ little nur ein ganz kleines bißchen; c) (mere) bloß ⟨Gedanke⟩; d) (absolute) absolut ⟨Minimum, Maximum⟩; the ~ most I can offer is ...: ich kann allerhöchstens ... anbieten; for the ~ last time zum allerletzten Mal;

e) emphat. before their ~ eyes vor ihren Augen. 2. adv. a) (extremely) sehr; it's ~ near es ist ganz in der Nähe; ~ probably höchstwahrscheinlich; not ~ much nicht sehr; ~ little [nur] sehr wenig ⟨verstehen, essen⟩; thank you [~,] ~ much [vielen,] vielen Dank; b) (absolutely) aller⟨best..., -letzt..., -leichtest...⟩; at the ~ latest allerspätestens; c) (precisely) the ~ same one genau der-/die-/dasselbe

**vessel** ['vesl] n. a) (receptacle) Gefäß, das; [drinking-]~: Trinkgefäß, das; b) (Naut.) Schiff, das

**vest** [vest] 1. n. a) (Brit.) Unterhemd, das; b) (Amer.: waistcoat) Weste, die. 2. v.t. ~ sb. with sth., ~ sth. in sb. jmdm. etw. verleihen. 'vested adj. have a ~ interest in sth. ein persönliches Interesse an etw. (Dat.) haben

**vestige** ['vestɪdʒ] n. Spur, die; not a ~ of truth kein Fünkchen Wahrheit

**vestment** ['vestmənt] n. [Priester]gewand, das

**vestry** ['vestrɪ] n. Sakristei, die

**vet** [vet] 1. n. Tierarzt, der/-ärztin, die. 2. v.t., -tt- überprüfen

**veteran** ['vetərən] n. Veteran, der/Veteranin, die. **veteran 'car** n. (Brit.) Veteran, der

**veterinarian** [ˌvetərɪˈneərɪən] n. (Amer.) Tierarzt, der/-ärztin, die

**veterinary** ['vetərɪnərɪ] adj. tiermedizinisch. **veterinary 'surgeon** n. (Brit.) Tierarzt, der/-ärztin, die

**veto** ['viːtəʊ] 1. n., pl. ~es Veto, das. 2. v.t. sein Veto einlegen gegen

**vex** [veks] v.t. [ver]ärgern; (cause to worry) beunruhigen; be ~ed with sb. sich über jmdn. ärgern. **vexation** [vekˈseɪʃn] n. Verärgerung, die. **vexed** [vekst] adj. a) verärgert; b) ~ question vieldiskutierte Frage

**VHF** abbr. Very High Frequency UKW

**via** ['vaɪə] prep. über (+ Akk.) ⟨Ort, Sender, Telefon⟩; durch ⟨Eingang, Schornstein, Person⟩; per ⟨Post⟩

**viability** [ˌvaɪəˈbɪlɪtɪ] n. (feasibility) Realisierbarkeit, die

**viable** ['vaɪəbl] adj. (feasible) realisierbar

**viaduct** ['vaɪədʌkt] n. Viadukt, das od. der

**vibrant** ['vaɪbrənt] adj. lebenssprühend ⟨Atmosphäre⟩; lebhaft ⟨Farbe⟩

**vibrate** [vaɪˈbreɪt] 1. v.i. vibrieren; (under strong impact) beben. 2. v.t. vibrieren lassen. **vibration** [vaɪˈbreɪʃn] n. Vibrieren/Beben, das

**vicar** ['vɪkə(r)] *n.* Pfarrer, *der.* **vicar-age** ['vɪkərɪdʒ] *n.* Pfarrhaus, *das*

**vicarious** [vɪ'keərɪəs] *adj.* nachempfunden

**¹vice** [vaɪs] *n.* Laster, *das*

**²vice** *n. (Brit.: tool)* Schraubstock, *der*

**vice:** ~-'**chairman** *n.* stellvertretender Vorsitzender; ~-'**president** *n.* Vizepräsident, *der*/-präsidentin, *die*

**vice versa** [vaɪsɪ 'vɜːsə] *adv.* umgekehrt

**vicinity** [vɪ'sɪnɪtɪ] *n.* Umgebung, *die;* **in the ~ [of a place]** in der Nähe [eines Ortes]

**vicious** ['vɪʃəs] *adj.* **a)** *(malicious)* böse; bösartig ⟨*Tier*⟩; **b)** *(violent)* brutal. **vicious 'circle** *n.* Teufelskreis, *der*

**viciously** *adv.* **a)** *(maliciously)* boshaft; **b)** *(violently)* brutal

**victim** ['vɪktɪm] *n.* Opfer, *das; (of sarcasm, abuse)* Zielscheibe, *die (fig.).* **victimization** [vɪktɪmaɪ'zeɪʃn] *n.* Schikanierung, *die.* **victimize** ['vɪktɪmaɪz] *v.t.* schikanieren

**victor** ['vɪktə(r)] *n.* Sieger, *der*/Siegerin, *die*

**victorious** [vɪk'tɔːrɪəs] *adj.* siegreich

**victory** ['vɪktərɪ] *n.* Sieg, *der* (**over** über + *Akk.*); *attrib.* Sieges-

**video** ['vɪdɪəʊ] **1.** *adj.* Video-. **2.** *n., pl.* ~**s** (~ *recorder)* Videorecorder, *der;* (~ *tape,* ~ *recording)* Video, *das (ugs.).* **3.** *v.t. see* **videotape 2**

**video:** ~ **camera** *n.* Videokamera, *die;* ~ **cas'sette** *n.* Videokassette, *die;* ~ **game** *n.* Videospiel, *das;* ~ '**nasty** *n.* Horrorvideo, *das;* ~ **recorder** *n.* Videorecorder, *der;* ~ **recording** *n.* Videoaufnahme, *die;* ~**tape 1.** *n.* Videoband, *das;* **2.** *v.t.* [auf Videoband *(Akk.)*] aufnehmen

**vie** [vaɪ] *v.i.,* **vying** ['vaɪɪŋ] ~ [**with sb.**] **for sth.** [mit jmdm.] um etw. wetteifern

**Vienna** [vɪ'enə] **1.** *pr. n.* Wien *(das).* **2.** *attrib. adj.* Wiener. **Viennese** [vɪə-'niːz] **1.** *adj.* Wiener. **2.** *n., pl. same* Wiener, *der*/Wienerin, *die*

**Vietnam** [viet'næm] *pr. n.* Vietnam *(das).* **Vietnamese** [vietnə'miːz] **1.** *adj.* vietnamesisch. **2.** *n., pl. same* **a)** *(person)* Vietnamese, *der*/Vietnamesin, *die;* **b)** *(language)* Vietnamesisch, *das*

**view** [vjuː] **1.** *n.* **a)** *(range of vision)* Sicht, *die;* **be out of/in ~:** nicht zu sehen/zu sehen sein; **b)** *(what is seen)* Aussicht, *die;* **c)** *(picture)* Ansicht, *die;* **d)** *(opinion)* Ansicht, *die;* **what is your ~ or are your ~s on this?** was meinst

du dazu?; **hold** *or* **take the ~ that ...:** der Ansicht sein, daß ...; **in my ~:** meiner Ansicht nach; **e)** **be on ~:** besichtigt werden können; **in ~ of sth.** *(fig.)* angesichts einer Sache; **with a ~ to doing sth.** in der Absicht, etw. zu tun. **2.** *v.t.* **a)** *(look at)* sich *(Dat.)* ansehen; **b)** *(consider)* betrachten; **c)** *(inspect)* besichtigen. **3.** *v.i. (Telev.)* fernsehen. '**viewer** *n.* **a)** *(Telev.)* [Fernseh]zuschauer, *der*/-zuschauerin, *die;* **b)** *(for slides)* Diabetrachter, *der*

**view:** ~**finder** *n.* Sucher, *der;* ~**point** *n.* Standpunkt, *der*

**vigil** ['vɪdʒɪl] *n.* Wachen, *das;* **keep ~:** wachen

**vigilance** ['vɪdʒɪləns] *n.* Wachsamkeit, *die*

**vigilant** ['vɪdʒɪlənt] *adj.* wachsam

**vigor** *(Amer.) see* **vigour**

**vigorous** ['vɪgərəs] *adj.* kräftig; heftig ⟨*Attacke, Protest*⟩; energisch ⟨*Versuch, Anstrengung, Leugnen, Maßnahme*⟩. '**vigorously** *adv.* heftig; kräftig ⟨*schrubben, drücken*⟩

**vigour** ['vɪgə(r)] *n. (Brit.) (of person)* Vitalität, *die; (of body)* Kraft, *die; (of protest, attack)* Heftigkeit, *die*

**vile** [vaɪl] *adj.* gemein ⟨*Verleumdung*⟩; vulgär ⟨*Sprache*⟩; *(repulsive)* widerwärtig; *(coll.: very unpleasant)* scheußlich *(ugs.)*

**villa** ['vɪlə] *n.* **a)** **[holiday] ~:** Ferienhaus, *das;* **b)** **[country] ~:** Landhaus, *das*

**village** ['vɪlɪdʒ] *n.* Dorf, *das; attrib.* Dorf-. '**villager** *n.* Dorfbewohner, *der*/-bewohnerin, *die*

**villain** ['vɪlən] *n.* **a)** Verbrecher, *der;* **b)** *(Theatre)* Bösewicht, *der.* **villainous** ['vɪlənəs] *adj.* gemein

**vindicate** ['vɪndɪkeɪt] *v.t.* **a)** *(justify)* rechtfertigen; **b)** *(clear)* rehabilitieren. **vindication** [vɪndɪ'keɪʃn] *n.* **a)** *(justification)* Rechtfertigung, *die;* **b)** *(clearing)* Rehabilitierung, *die*

**vindictive** [vɪn'dɪktɪv] *adj.* nachtragend

**vine** [vaɪn] *n.* Weinrebe, *die*

**vinegar** ['vɪnɪgə(r)] *n.* Essig, *der*

**vineyard** ['vɪnjɑːd, 'vɪnjəd] *n.* Weinberg, *der*

**vintage** ['vɪntɪdʒ] **1.** *n.* Jahrgang, *der.* **2.** *adj.* erlesen ⟨*Wein*⟩. **vintage 'car** *n. (Brit.)* Oldtimer, *der*

**vinyl** ['vaɪnɪl] *n.* Vinyl, *das*

**viola** [vɪ'əʊlə] *n.* Bratsche, *die*

**violate** ['vaɪəleɪt] *v.t.* **a)** verletzen; brechen ⟨*Vertrag, Versprechen, Gesetz*⟩;

**b)** *(profane, rape)* schänden. **violation** [vaɪə'leɪʃn] *n. see* **violate**: Verletzung, *die;* Bruch, *der;* Schändung, *die*

**violence** ['vaɪələns] *n.* **a)** *(force)* Heftigkeit, *die;* *(of blow)* Wucht, *die;* **b)** *(brutality)* Gewalt, *die;* *(at public event)* Gewalttätigkeiten; **resort to** *or* **use ~:** Gewalt anwenden

**violent** ['vaɪələnt] *adj.* gewalttätig; *(fig.)* heftig; wuchtig ⟨*Schlag, Stoß*⟩; Gewalt⟨*verbrecher, -tat*⟩. **'violently** *adv.* brutal; *(fig.)* heftig

**violet** ['vaɪələt] **1.** *n.* **a)** Veilchen, *das;* **b)** *(colour)* Violett, *das.* **2.** *adj.* violett

**violin** [vaɪə'lɪn] *n.* Violine, *die;* Geige, *die.* **vio'linist** *n.* Geiger, *der*/Geigerin, *die*

**VIP** [viːaɪ'piː] *n.* Prominente, *der/die;* **the ~s** die Prominenz

**viper** ['vaɪpə(r)] *n.* Viper, *die*

**virgin** ['vɜːdʒɪn] **1.** *n.* **a)** Jungfrau, *die;* **b) the [Blessed] V~ [Mary]** die [Heilige] Jungfrau [Maria]. **2.** *adj.* *(unspoiled)* unberührt. **virginity** [və'dʒɪnɪtɪ] *n.* Unschuld, *die*

**Virgo** ['vɜːgəʊ] *n., pl.* **~s** die Jungfrau

**virile** ['vɪraɪl] *adj.* männlich. **virility** [vɪ'rɪlɪtɪ] *n.* Männlichkeit, *die*

**virtual** ['vɜːtjʊəl] *adj.* **a ~ ...:** so gut wie ein/eine ...; **the traffic came to a ~ standstill** der Verkehr kam praktisch zum Stillstand *(ugs.).* **'virtually** *adv.* so gut wie; praktisch *(ugs.)*

**virtue** ['vɜːtjuː] *n.* **a)** *(moral excellence)* Tugend, *die;* **b)** *(advantage)* Vorteil, *der;* **c) by ~ of** auf Grund (+ *Gen.*)

**virtuoso** [vɜːtjʊ'əʊzəʊ] *n., pl.* **virtuosi** [vɜːtjʊ'əʊziː] *or* **~s** Virtuose, *der*/Virtuosin, *die*

**virtuous** ['vɜːtjʊəs] *adj.* rechtschaffen ⟨*Person*⟩; tugendhaft ⟨*Leben*⟩

**virulent** ['vɪrʊlənt] *adj.* **a)** *(Med.)* virulent; starkwirkend ⟨*Gift*⟩; **b)** *(fig.)* heftig; scharf ⟨*Angriff*⟩

**virus** ['vaɪərəs] *n.* Virus, *das*

**visa** ['viːzə] *n.* Visum, *das*

**vis-à-vis** [viːzaː'viː] *prep.* *(in relation to)* bezüglich (+ *Gen.*)

**viscount** ['vaɪkaʊnt] *n.* Viscount, *der*

**viscous** ['vɪskəs] *adj.* dickflüssig

**visibility** [vɪzɪ'bɪlɪtɪ] *n.* **a)** Sichtbarkeit, *die;* **b)** *(range of vision)* Sicht, *die;* *(Meteorol.)* Sichtweite, *die*

**visible** ['vɪzɪbl] *adj.* sichtbar. **'visibly** *adv.* sichtlich

**vision** ['vɪʒn] *n.* **a)** *(sight)* Sehkraft, *die;* **b)** *(dream)* Vision, *die;* **c)** *usu. pl.* *(imaginings)* Phantasien; **d)** *(insight, foresight)* Weitblick, *der*

**visit** ['vɪzɪt] **1.** *v. t.* besuchen; aufsuchen ⟨*Arzt*⟩. **2.** *v. i.* einen Besuch/Besuche machen. **3.** *n.* Besuch, *der;* **pay** *or* **make a ~ to sb., pay sb. a ~:** jmdm. einen Besuch abstatten *(geh.)*

**'visiting: ~ card** *n.* Visitenkarte, *die;* **~ hours** *n. pl.* Besuchszeiten

**visitor** ['vɪzɪtə(r)] *n.* Besucher, *der*/Besucherin, *die; (to hotel)* Gast, *der;* **have ~s/a ~:** Besuch haben

**visual** ['vɪzjʊəl, 'vɪʒjʊəl] *adj.* visuell; optisch ⟨*Eindruck, Darstellung*⟩. **visual 'aids** *n. pl.* Anschauungsmaterial, *das.* **visual dis'play unit** *n.* Bildschirmgerät, *das*

**visualize** ['vɪzjʊəlaɪz, 'vɪʒjʊəlaɪz] *v. t.* **a)** *(imagine)* sich (*Dat.*) vorstellen; **b)** *(envisage)* voraussehen

**'visually** *adv.* bildlich

**vital** ['vaɪtl] *adj.* **a)** *(essential to life)* lebenswichtig; **b)** *(essential)* unbedingt notwendig; **c)** *(crucial)* entscheidend (**to** für); **it is ~ that you ...:** es ist von entscheidender Bedeutung, daß Sie ...

**vitality** [vaɪ'tælɪtɪ] *n.* Vitalität, *die.* **'vitally** *adv.* **~ important** von allergrößter Wichtigkeit; *(crucial)* von entscheidender Bedeutung

**vitamin** ['vɪtəmɪn, 'vaɪtəmɪn] *n.* Vitamin, *das*

**vivacious** [vɪ'veɪʃəs] *adj.* lebhaft. **vivacity** [vɪ'væsɪtɪ] *n.* Lebhaftigkeit, *die*

**vivid** ['vɪvɪd] *adj.* lebhaft ⟨*Farbe, Erinnerung*⟩; lebendig ⟨*Schilderung*⟩. **'vividly** *adv.* lebendig ⟨*beschreiben*⟩; **remember sth. ~:** sich lebhaft an etw. (*Akk.*) erinnern

**vixen** ['vɪksn] *n.* Füchsin, *die*

**vocabulary** [və'kæbjʊlərɪ] *n.* **a)** *(list)* Vokabelverzeichnis, *das;* **learn ~:** Vokabeln lernen; **b)** *(range of language)* Wortschatz, *der*

**vocal** ['vəʊkl] *adj.* **a)** *(concerned with voice)* stimmlich; **b)** lautstark ⟨*Minderheit, Protest*⟩. **'vocal cords** *n. pl.* Stimmbänder

**vocalist** ['vəʊkəlɪst] *n.* Sänger, *der*/Sängerin, *die*

**vocation** [və'keɪʃn] *n.* Berufung, *die*. **vocational** [və'keɪʃənl] *adj.* berufsbezogen. **vocational 'guidance** *n.* Berufsberatung, *die.* **vocational 'training** *n.* berufliche Bildung

**vociferous** [və'sɪfərəs] *adj.* laut; lautstark ⟨*Forderung, Protest*⟩

**vodka** ['vɒdkə] *n.* Wodka, *der*

**vogue** [vəʊg] *n.* Mode, *die;* **be in/come into ~:** in Mode sein/kommen

**voice** [vɔɪs] **1.** *n.* Stimme, *die;* **in a**

**firm/loud/soft** ~: mit fester/lauter/ sanfter Stimme. **2.** *v. t.* zum Ausdruck bringen
**void** [vɔɪd] **1.** *adj.* **a)** *(empty)* leer; **b)** *(invalid)* ungültig; **c)** ~ **of** ohne [jeden/ jedes/jede]. **2.** *n.* Nichts, *das*
**volatile** ['vɒlətaɪl] *adj.* **a)** *(Chem.)* flüchtig; **b)** *(fig.)* impulsiv; brisant ⟨*Lage*⟩
**volcanic** [vɒl'kænɪk] *adj.* vulkanisch
**volcano** [vɒl'keɪnəʊ] *n., pl.* ~**es** Vulkan, *der*
**volition** [və'lɪʃn] *n.* Wille, *der;* **of one's own** ~: aus eigenem Willen
**volley** ['vɒlɪ] *n.* **a)** *(of missiles)* Salve, *die;* **a** ~ **of arrows** ein Hagel von Pfeilen; **b)** *(Tennis)* Volley, *der.* '**volley-ball** *n.* Volleyball, *der*
**volt** [vəʊlt] *n.* Volt, *das.* **voltage** ['vəʊltɪdʒ] *n.* Spannung, *die*
**voluble** ['vɒljʊbl] *adj.* redselig
**volume** ['vɒljuːm] *n.* **a)** *(book)* Band, *der;* **b)** *(loudness)* Lautstärke, *die; (of voice)* Volumen, *das;* **c)** *(space)* Rauminhalt, *der; (amount of substance)* Teil, *der.* '**volume control** *n.* Lautstärkeregler, *der*
**voluntarily** ['vɒləntərɪlɪ] *adv.,* **voluntary** ['vɒləntərɪ] *adj.* freiwillig
**volunteer** [vɒlən'tɪə(r)] **1.** *n.* Freiwillige, *der/die.* **2.** *v. t.* anbieten ⟨*Hilfe, Dienste*⟩; herausrücken mit ⟨*Informationen*⟩. **3.** *v. i.* sich [freiwillig] melden; ~ **to do** *or* ~ **for the shopping** sich zum Einkaufen bereiterklären
**voluptuous** [və'lʌptjʊəs] *adj.* üppig
**vomit** ['vɒmɪt] **1.** *v. t.* erbrechen. **2.** *v. i.* sich übergeben. **3.** *n.* Erbrochene, *das*
**voracious** [və'reɪʃəs] *adj.* gefräßig ⟨*Person*⟩; unbändig ⟨*Appetit*⟩
**vote** [vəʊt] **1.** *n.* **a)** *(individual* ~*)* Stimme, *die;* **b)** *(act of voting)* Abstimmung, *die;* **take a** ~ **on sth.** über etw. *(Akk.)* abstimmen; **c)** *(right to* ~*)* Stimmrecht, *das.* **2.** *v. i.* abstimmen; *(in election)* wählen; ~ **for/against** stimmen für/gegen; ~ **to do sth.** beschließen, etw. zu tun; ~ **Labour/Conservative** *etc.* Labour/die Konservativen *usw.* wählen. **3.** *v. t.* ~ **sb. Chairman/President** *etc.* jmdn. zum Vorsitzenden/Präsidenten *usw.* wählen. '**voter** *n.* Wähler, *der/*Wählerin, *die*
**vouch** [vaʊtʃ] **1.** *v. t.* ~ **that ...**: sich dafür verbürgen, daß ... **2.** *v. i.* ~ **for sb./ sth.** sich für jmdn./etw. verbürgen
'**voucher** *n.* Gutschein, *der*
**vow** [vaʊ] **1.** *n.* Gelöbnis, *das; (Relig.)* Gelübde, *das.* **2.** *v. t.* geloben

**vowel** ['vaʊəl] *n.* Vokal, *der*
**voyage** ['vɔɪdʒ] **1.** *n.* Reise, *die; (sea* ~*)* Seereise, *die;* **outward/homeward** ~, ~ **out/home** Hin-/Rückreise, *die;* **a** ~ **to the moon** ein Mondflug. **2.** *v. i.* *(literary)* reisen
**vulgar** ['vʌlgə(r)] *adj.* vulgär; ordinär ⟨*Person, Benehmen, Witz*⟩. **vulgarity** [vʌl'gærɪtɪ] *n.* Vulgarität, *die*
**vulnerable** ['vʌlnərəbl] *adj.* **a)** *(exposed to danger)* angreifbar; **be** ~ **to sth.** für etw. anfällig sein; **be** ~ **to attack/in a** ~ **position** leicht angreifbar sein; **b)** *(without protection)* schutzlos
**vulture** ['vʌltʃə(r)] *n.* Geier, *der*
**vying** *see* **vie**

# W

¹**W, w** ['dʌblju:] *n.* W, w, *das*
²**W** *abbr.* **watt**|**s**| W
**W.** *abbr.* **a)** **west** W.; **b)** **western** w.
**wad** [wɒd] *n.* **a)** Knäuel, *das; (smaller)* Pfropfen, *der;* **b)** *(of papers)* Bündel, *das.* '**wadding** *n.* Futter, *das*
**waddle** ['wɒdl] **1.** *v. i.* watscheln. **2.** *n.* watschelnder Gang
**wade** [weɪd] *v. i.* waten. '**wade through** *v. t.* *(fig. coll.)* durchackern *(ugs.)* ⟨*Buch*⟩
**wafer** ['weɪfə(r)] *n.* Waffel, *die.* '**wafer-thin** *adj.* hauchdünn
¹**waffle** ['wɒfl] *n.* *(Gastr.)* Waffel, *die*
²**waffle** *(Brit. coll.: talk)* **1.** *v. i.* schwafeln *(ugs.).* **2.** *n.* Geschwafel, *das (ugs.)*
**waft** [wɒft, wɑ:ft] **1.** *v. t.* weben. **2.** *v. i.* ziehen
**wag** [wæg] **1.** *v. t.,* -**gg**- ⟨*Hund:*⟩ wedeln mit ⟨*Schwanz*⟩; ~ **one's finger at sb.** jmdm. mit dem Finger drohen. **2.** *v. i.,* -**gg**- ⟨*Schwanz:*⟩ wedeln
**wage** [weɪdʒ] **1.** *n. in sing. or pl.* Lohn, *der.* **2.** *v. t.* führen. '**wage increase** *n.* Lohnerhöhung, *die.* '**wage packet** *n.* Lohntüte, *die*
**wager** ['weɪdʒə(r)] *(dated/formal)* **1.** *n.* Wette, *die;* **lay a** ~ **on sth.** auf etw. *(Akk.)* wetten. **2.** *v. t. & i.* wetten
**waggle** ['wægl] *(coll.)* **1.** *v. t.* ~ **its tail**

⟨*Hund:*⟩ mit dem Schwanz wedeln. 2. *v.i.* hin und her schlagen

**waggon** *(Brit.),* **wagon** ['wægən] *n.* Wagen, *der*

**wail** [weɪl] **1.** *v.i.* klagen *(geh.)* (for um); ⟨*Kind:*⟩ heulen. **2.** *n.* klagender Schrei; ~s Geheul, *das*

**waist** [weɪst] *n.* Taille, *die;* **tight round the ~:** eng in der Taille. **waistcoat** ['weɪskəʊt] *n. (Brit.)* Weste, *die.* '**waistline** *n.* Taille, *die;* **be bad for the ~:** schlecht für die schlanke Linie sein

**wait** [weɪt] **1.** *v.i.* **a)** warten; **~ [for] an hour** eine Stunde warten; **~ a moment** Moment mal; **keep sb. ~ing, make sb. ~:** jmdn. warten lassen; **b) ~ at table** servieren. **2.** *v.t. (await)* warten auf (+ *Akk.*); **~ one's turn** warten, bis man drankommt. **3.** *n.* **a)** *after a long/short* **~:** nach langer/kurzer Wartezeit; **b) lie in ~ for sb./sth.** jmdm./einer Sache auflauern. **wait be'hind** *v.i.* noch hier-/dableiben. **wait for** *v.t.* warten auf (+ *Akk.*); **~ for sb. to do sth.** darauf warten, daß jmd. etw. tut; **~ for the rain to stop** warten, bis der Regen aufhört. **wait on** *v.t. (serve)* bedienen. **wait 'up** *v.i.* aufbleiben (for wegen)

'**waiter** *n.* Kellner, *der;* **~! Herr Ober!**

'**waiting:** **~-list** *n.* Warteliste, *die;* **~-room** *n.* Wartezimmer, *das; (Railw.)* Warteraum, *der*

**waitress** ['weɪtrɪs] *n.* Serviererin, *die;* **~! Fräulein!** *(veralt.)*

**waive** [weɪv] *v.t.* verzichten auf (+ *Akk.*)

'**wake** [weɪk] **1.** *v.i.,* woke [wəʊk], woken ['wəʊkn] aufwachen. **2.** *v.t.,* woke, woken wecken. **3.** *n. (by corpse)* Totenwache, *die.* **wake 'up** *v.i.* aufwachen; **~ up to sth.** *(fig.: realize)* etw. erkennen. **2.** *v.t.* **a)** wecken; **b)** *(fig.: enliven)* wachrütteln

²**wake** *n.* Kielwasser, *das;* **in the ~ of sth.** *(fig.)* im Gefolge von etw.

**waken** ['weɪkn] **1.** *v.t.* wecken. **2.** *v.i.* aufwachen

**Wales** [weɪlz] *pr.n.* Wales *(das)*

**walk** [wɔːk] **1.** *v.i.* **a)** laufen; *(not run)* gehen; *(not drive)* zu Fuß gehen; **learn to ~:** laufen lernen; **b)** *(exercise)* gehen. **2.** *v.t.* **a)** *(lead)* führen; ausführen ⟨*Hund*⟩; **b)** *(accompany)* bringen. **3.** *n.* **a)** Spaziergang, *der;* **go [out] for or take or have a ~:** einen Spaziergang machen; **ten minutes' ~ from here** zehn Minuten zu Fuß von hier;

**b)** *(gait)* Gang, *der;* **c)** *(path)* [Spazier]weg, *der.* **walk a'way with** *v.t. (coll.: win easily)* spielend leicht gewinnen. '**walk into** *v.t. (hit by accident)* laufen gegen ⟨*Pfosten, Laternenpfahl*⟩; **~ into sb.** mit jmdm. zusammenstoßen; **~ into a trap** in eine Falle gehen. **walk 'off with** *v.t.* sich davonmachen mit. **walk 'out** *v.i.* **a)** *(leave in protest)* aus Protest den Saal verlassen; **b)** *(go on strike)* in den Streik treten. **walk 'out of** *v.t. (leave in protest)* aus Protest verlassen. **walk 'out on** *v.t. (coll.)* verlassen

'**walker** *n.* Spaziergänger, *der/*-gängerin, *die; (rambler)* Wanderer, *der/* Wanderin, *die*

**walkie-talkie** [wɔːkɪ'tɔːkɪ] *n.* Walkietalkie, *das*

'**walking** *n.* [Spazieren]gehen, *das;* **at ~ pace** im Schrittempo; **be within ~ distance** zu Fuß zu erreichen sein

**walking:** **~ holiday** *n.* Wanderurlaub, *der;* **~ shoe** *n.* Wanderschuh, *der;* **~-stick** *n.* Spazierstock, *der*

**walk:** **~-out** *n.* Arbeitsniederlegung, *die;* **~-over** *n. (fig.: easy victory)* Spaziergang, *der (ugs.)*

**wall** [wɔːl] **1.** *n.* Wand, *die; (freestanding)* Mauer, *die;* **drive sb. up the ~** *(fig. coll.)* jmdn. auf die Palme bringen *(ugs.);* **go to the ~** *(fig.)* an die Wand gedrückt werden. **wall 'up** *v.t.* zumauern

**wallet** ['wɒlɪt] *n.* Brieftasche, *die*

'**wallflower** *n.* Goldlack, *der*

**wallop** ['wɒləp] *(coll.)* **1.** *v.t.* schlagen. **2.** *n.* Schlag, *der*

**wallow** ['wɒləʊ] *v.i.* **a)** sich wälzen; **b)** *(fig.)* schwelgen (**in** in + *Dat.*)

**wall:** **~-painting** *n.* Wandgemälde, *das;* **~-paper 1.** *n.* Tapete, *die;* **2.** *v.t.* tapezieren; **~-to-~** *adj.* **~-to-~ carpeting** Teppichboden, *der*

**walnut** ['wɔːlnʌt] *n.* Walnuß, *die*

**walrus** ['wɔːlrəs] *n.* Walroß, *das*

**waltz** [wɔːlts, wɒːls] **1.** *n.* Walzer, *der.* **2.** *v.i.* Walzer tanzen

**wan** [wɒn] *adj.* bleich

**wand** [wɒnd] *n.* Stab, *der*

**wander** ['wɒndə(r)] **1.** *v.i. (go aimlessly)* umherirren; *(walk slowly)* bummeln. **2.** *v.t.* wandern durch. **3.** *n. (coll.)* Spaziergang, *der.* **wander a'bout** *v.i.* sich herumtreiben. **wander 'off** *v.i. (stray)* weggehen

**wane** [weɪn] *v.i.* abnehmen

**wangle** ['wæŋgl] *v.t. (coll.)* organisieren *(ugs.)*

**want** [wɒnt] **1.** *v. t.* **a)** *(desire)* wollen;
~ **to do sth.** etw. tun wollen; **I** ~ **it
done by tonight** ich will, daß es bis
heute abend fertig wird; **b)** *(require,
need)* brauchen; **'W~ed – cook'**
„Koch/Köchin gesucht"; **you're ~ed
on the phone** du wirst am Telefon verlangt; **the windows** ~ **painting** die Fenster müßten gestrichen werden; **you** ~
**to be [more] careful** du solltest vorsichtig[er] sein; **c)** ~**ed [by the police]** [poli-
zeilich] gesucht. **2.** *n. a)* *(lack)* Mangel, *der* (of an + *Dat.*); **for** ~ **of sth.**
aus Mangel an etw. *(Dat.)*; **b)** *(need)*
Not, *der*; **c)** *(desire)* Bedürfnis, *das*.
'**want for** *v. i.* **sb.** ~**s for nothing** *or*
**doesn't** ~ **for anything** jmdm. fehlt es
an nichts
'**wanting** *adj.* **be** ~: fehlen; **sb./sth. is**
~ **in sth.** jmdm./einer Sache fehlt es
an etw. *(Dat.)*; **be found** ~: für unzureichend befunden werden
**wanton** ['wɒntən] *adj.*, '**wantonly**
*adv.* mutwillig
**war** [wɔ:(r)] *n.* Krieg, *der*; **between the**
~**s** zwischen den Weltkriegen; **declare**
~: den Krieg erklären (**on** *Dat.*); **be at**
~: sich im Krieg befinden; **make** ~:
Krieg führen (**on** gegen)
**warble** ['wɔ:bl] *v. t. & i.* trällern
**ward** [wɔ:d] *n.* **a)** *(in hospital)* Station,
*die*; **she's in W~** 3 sie liegt auf Station
3; **b)** *(child)* Mündel, *das od. die*; **c)**
*(electoral division)* Wahlbezirk, *der*.
**ward 'off** *v. t.* abwehren
**warden** ['wɔ:dn] *n.* **a)** *(of hostel)*
Heimleiter, *der*/-leiterin, *die*; *(of youth
hostel)* Herbergsvater, *der*/-mutter,
*die*; **b)** *(supervisor)* Aufseher, *der*/Auf-
seherin, *die*
'**warder** *n.* *(Brit.)* Wärter, *der*
**wardrobe** ['wɔ:drəʊb] *n.* **a)** Kleider-
schrank, *der*; **b)** *(clothes)* Garderobe,
*die*
**warehouse** ['weəhaʊs] *n.* Lagerhaus,
*das*; *(part of building)* Lager, *das*
**wares** [weəz] *n. pl.* Ware, *die*
**warfare** ['wɔ:feə(r)] *n.* Krieg, *der*
'**warhead** *n.* Sprengkopf, *der*
'**warily** ['weərɪlɪ] *adv.* vorsichtig; *(suspiciously)* mißtrauisch
'**warlike** *adj.* kriegerisch
**warm** [wɔ:m] **1.** *adj.* **a)** warm; **I am
[very]** ~: mir ist [sehr] warm; **b)** *(enthusiastic)* herzlich ⟨*Grüße, Dank*⟩. **2.**
*v. t.* wärmen; **warm machen** ⟨*Flüssigkeit*⟩; ~ **one's hands** sich *(Dat.)* die
Hände wärmen. **3.** *v. i.* ~ **to sb./sth.**
*(come to like)* sich für jmdn./etw. er-

wärmen. **warm 'up 1.** *v. i.* warm werden; ⟨*Sportler:*⟩ sich aufwärmen. **2.**
*v. t.* aufwärmen ⟨*Speisen*⟩; erwärmen
⟨*Raum, Zimmer*⟩
**warm:** ~**-blooded** ['wɔ:mblʌdɪd] *adj.*
warmblütig; ~**-hearted** ['wɔ:mhɑ:t-
ɪd] *adj.* warmherzig ⟨*Person*⟩
'**warmly** *adv.* **a)** warm; **b)** *(fig.)* herzlich ⟨*willkommen heißen, gratulieren,
begrüßen, grüßen, danken*⟩
**warmonger** ['wɔ:mʌŋgə(r)] *n.* Kriegs-
hetzer, *der*/-hetzerin, *die*
**warmth** [wɔ:mθ] *n.* **a)** Wärme, *die*; **b)**
*(fig.)* Herzlichkeit, *die*
**warn** [wɔ:n] *v. t.* **a)** *(inform, give notice)*
warnen (**against, of, about** vor +
*Dat.*); ~ **sb. that ...:** jmdn. darauf hinweisen, daß ...; ~ **sb. not to do sth.**
jmdn. davor warnen, etw. zu tun; **b)**
*(admonish)* ermahnen; *(officially)* ab-
mahnen. '**warning 1.** *n.* **a)** *(advance
notice)* Vorwarnung, *die*; **b)** *(lesson)*
**let that be a** ~ **to you** laß dir das eine
Warnung sein; **c)** *(caution)* Verwarnung, *die*; *(less official)* Warnung, *die*.
**2.** *adj.* Warn⟨*schild, -signal usw.*⟩
**warp** [wɔ:p] **1.** *v. i.* sich verbiegen;
⟨*Holz, Schallplatte:*⟩ sich verziehen. **2.**
*v. t.* **a)** verbiegen; **b)** *(fig.)* **a** ~**ed sense
of humour** ein abartiger Humor
**war:** ~**-path** *n.* **be on the** ~**-path** *(fig.)*
in Rage sein; ~**plane** *n.* Kampfflug-
zeug, *das*
**warrant** ['wɒrənt] **1.** *n.* *(for sb.'s arrest)*
Haftbefehl, *der*; **[search]** ~: Durchsuchungsbefehl, *der*. **2.** *v. t.* **a)** *(justify)*
rechtfertigen; **b)** *(guarantee)* garantieren. '**warranty** *n.* Garantie, *die*
**warrior** ['wɒrɪə(r)] *n.* *(esp. literary)*
Krieger, *der* *(geh.)*
**Warsaw** ['wɔ:sɔ:] **1.** *pr. n.* Warschau
*(das)*. **2.** *attrib. adj.* Warschauer
'**warship** *n.* Kriegsschiff, *das*
**wart** [wɔ:t] *n.* Warze, *die*
'**wartime** *n.* **a)** Kriegszeit, *die*; **in** *or*
**during** ~: im Krieg; **b)** *attrib.* Kriegs-
⟨*rationierung, -evakuierung usw.*⟩
**wary** ['weərɪ] *adj.* vorsichtig; *(suspicious)* mißtrauisch (**of** gegenüber); **be**
~ **of sb./sth.** sich vor jmdm./etw. in
acht nehmen
**was** *see* **be**
**wash** [wɒʃ] **1.** *v. t.* **a)** waschen; ~ **oneself** sich waschen; ~ **one's hands/face/
hair** sich *(Dat.)* die Hände/das Ge-
sicht/die Haare waschen; ~ **the
clothes** Wäsche waschen; ~ **the dishes**
[Geschirr] spülen; ~ **the floor** den
Fußboden aufwischen; **b)** *(remove)*

waschen ⟨*Fleck*⟩ (**out of** aus); abwaschen ⟨*Schmutz*⟩ (**off** von); c) *(carry along)* spülen. 2. *v. i.* a) sich waschen; b) ⟨*Stoff, Kleidungsstück:*⟩ sich waschen lassen. 3. *n.* a) give sb./sth. a |good| ~: jmdn./etw. [gründlich] waschen; b) *(laundering)* Wäsche, *die;* c) *(of ship)* Sog, *der.* **wash 'down** *v. t.* abspritzen ⟨*Auto, Deck, Hof*⟩. **wash 'off 1.** *v. t.* ~ **sth. off** etw. abwaschen. **2.** *v. i.* abgehen; *(from fabric etc.)* herausgehen. **wash 'out** *v. t.* ausscheuern ⟨*Topf*⟩; ausspülen ⟨*Mund*⟩; ~ **dirt/ marks out of clothes** Schmutz/Flecken aus Kleidern [her]auswaschen. **wash 'up 1.** *v. t.* *(Brit.)* ~ **the dishes up** das Geschirr spülen. **2.** *v. i.* spülen

**washable** ['wɒʃəbl] *adj.* waschbar

'**wash-basin** *n.* Waschbecken, *das*

'**washing** *n.* Wäsche, *die;* **do the** ~: waschen

**washing:** ~-**machine** *n.* Waschmaschine, *die;* ~-**powder** *n.* Waschpulver, *das;* ~-'**up** *n.* *(Brit.)* Abwasch, *der;* **do the** ~-**up** spülen; ~-'**up liquid** *n.* Spülmittel, *das*

**wasn't** ['wɒznt] *(coll.)* = **was not;** *see* **be**

**wasp** *n.* Wespe, *die*

**waste** [weɪst] **1.** *n.* a) *(useless remains)* Abfall, *der;* **kitchen** ~: Küchenabfälle *Pl.;* b) *(extravagant use)* Verschwendung, *die;* **it's a** ~ **of** time/money/energy das ist Zeit-/Geld-/Energieverschwendung. **2.** *v. t.* *(squander)* verschwenden; **all his efforts were** ~**d** all seine Mühe war umsonst; **don't** ~ **my time!** stehlen Sie mir nicht die Zeit! **3.** *adj.* a) ~ **material** Abfall, *der;* b) **lay sth.** ~: etw. verwüsten. **waste a'way** *v. i.* immer mehr abmagern

**waste:** ~ **disposal** *n.* Abfallbeseitigung, *die;* ~-**disposal unit** *n.* Müllzerkleinerer, *der*

**wasteful** ['weɪstfl] *adj.* a) *(extravagant)* verschwenderisch; b) *(causing waste)* unwirtschaftlich

**waste:** ~-**land** *n.* Ödland, *das;* ~ '**paper** *n.* Papierabfall, *der;* ~-'**paper basket** *n.* Papierkorb, *der*

**watch** [wɒtʃ] **1.** *n.* a) |wrist-/pocket-|~: [Armband-/Taschen]uhr, *die;* b) **keep** ~: Wache halten; **keep** |a| ~ **for sb./ sth.** auf jmdn./etw. achten; c) *(Naut.)* Wache, *die.* **2.** *v. i.* ~ **for sb./sth.** auf jmdn./etw. warten. **3.** *v. t.* a) *(observe)* sich *(Dat.)* ansehen ⟨*Sportveranstaltung, Fernsehsendung*⟩; ~ |**the**| **television** *or* **TV** fernsehen; ~ **sb. do** *or*

doing **sth.** zusehen, wie jmd. etw. tut; **we are being** ~**ed** wir werden beobachtet; b) *(be careful of, look after)* achten auf (+ *Akk.*). **watch 'out** *v. i.* a) *(be careful)* aufpassen; ~ **out!** Vorsicht!; b) *(look out)* ~ **out for sb./sth.** auf jmdn./etw. achten

'**watch-dog** *n.* Wachhund, *der;* *(fig.)* |**public**| ~: *[Leiter/Leiterin einer] Aufsichtsbehörde*

**watchful** ['wɒtʃfl] *adj.* wachsam

**watch:** ~-**maker** *n.* Uhrmacher, *der/* Uhrmacherin, *die;* ~-**man** ['wɒtʃmən] *n., pl.* ~-**men** ['wɒtʃmən] Wachmann, *der;* ~-**strap** *n.* [Uhr]armband, *das;* ~-**tower** *n.* Wachturm, *der*

**water** ['wɔ:tə(r)] **1.** *n.* a) Wasser, *das;* b) *in pl.* *(part of the sea etc.)* Gewässer *Pl.* **2.** *v. t.* a) bewässern ⟨*Land*⟩; wässern ⟨*Pflanzen*⟩; ~ **the flowers** die Blumen [be]gießen; b) verwässern ⟨*Bier usw.*⟩; c) tränken ⟨*Tier*⟩. **3.** *v. i.* ⟨*Augen:*⟩ tränen; **my mouth was** ~**ing** mir lief das Wasser im Munde zusammen. **water 'down** *v. t.* verwässern

**water:** ~-**butt** *n.* Regentonne, *die;* ~-**colour** *n.* a) *(paint)* Wasserfarbe, *die;* b) *(picture)* Aquarell, *das;* ~-**cress** *n.* Brunnenkresse, *die;* ~-**fall** *n.* Wasserfall, *der*

'**watering-can** *n.* Gießkanne, *die*

**water:** ~-**lily** *n.* Seerose, *die;* ~-**line** *n.* *(Naut.)* Wasserlinie, *die;* ~-**logged** ['wɔ:təlɒgd] *adj.* naß ⟨*Boden*⟩; aufgeweicht ⟨*Sportplatz*⟩; ~-**main** *n.* Hauptwasserleitung, *die;* ~-**mark** *n.* Wasserzeichen, *das;* ~-**melon** *n.* Wassermelone, *die;* ~ **meter** *n.* Wasseruhr, *die;* ~ **polo** *n.* Wasserball, *der;* ~-**proof 1.** *adj.* wasserdicht; wasserfest ⟨*Farbe*⟩; **2.** *v. t.* wasserdicht machen; imprägnieren ⟨*Stoff*⟩; ~-**shed** *n.* *(fig.)* Wendepunkt, *der;* ~-**ski 1.** *n.* Wasserski, *der;* **2.** *v. i.* Wasserski laufen; ~-**skiing** *n.* Wasserskilaufen, *das;* ~-**tight** *adj.* wasserdicht; ~-**tower** *n.* Wasserturm, *der;* ~-**way** *n.* Wasserstraße, *die*

'**watery** *adj.* wäßrig

**watt** [wɒt] *n.* Watt, *das*

**wave** [weɪv] **1.** *n.* a) Welle, *die;* b) *(gesture)* give sb. a ~: jmdm. zuwinken; **with a** ~ **of one's hand** mit einem Winken. **2.** *v. i.* a) ⟨*Fahne, Flagge, Wimpel:*⟩ wehen; ⟨*Baum, Gras, Korn:*⟩ sich wiegen; b) *(with hand)* winken; ~ **at** *or* **to sb.** jmdm. winken. **3.** *v. t.* schwenken; schwingen ⟨*Schwert*⟩; ~ **one's hand at** *or* **to sb.** jmdm. winken;

~ **goodbye to sb.** jmdm. zum Abschied zuwinken. **wave a'side** v.t. **a)** abtun ⟨*Zweifel, Einwand*⟩; **b)** *(signal to move)* ~ **sb.** aside [jmdn.] abwinken

**wave:** ~**band** n. Wellenbereich, der; ~**length** n. Wellenlänge, die; **be on the same** ~**length** [as sb.] *(fig.)* die gleiche Wellenlänge [wie jmd.] haben

**waver** ['weɪvə(r)] v.i. schwanken

**wavy** ['weɪvɪ] adj. wellig; ~ **line** Schlangenlinie, die

¹**wax** [wæks] **1.** n. **a)** Wachs, das; **b)** *(in ear)* Schmalz, das. **2.** v.t. wachsen

²**wax** v.i. **a)** ⟨*Mond:*⟩ zunehmen; **b)** *(become)* werden

**wax:** ~**work** n. Wachsfigur, die; ~**works** n. sing., pl. same Wachsfigurenkabinett, das

'**waxy** adj. wachsweich

**way** [weɪ] **1.** n. **a)** Weg, der; **ask the** or **one's** ~: nach dem Weg fragen; '**W- In/Out**' „Ein-/Ausgang"; **by** ~ **of** Switzerland über die Schweiz; **lead the** ~: vorausgehen; **go out of one's** ~: einen Umweg machen; *(fig.)* keine Mühe scheuen; **b)** *(method)* Art und Weise, die; **do it this** ~: mach es so; **c)** *(distance)* Stück, das; **it's a long** ~ **off** or **a long** ~ **from here** es ist weit weg von hier; **all the** ~: den ganzen Weg; **d)** *(direction)* Richtung, die; **she went this/that/the other** ~: sie ist in diese/die/die andere Richtung gegangen; **stand sth. the right/wrong** ~ **up** etw. richtig/falsch herum stellen; **e)** *(respect)* in [exactly] **the same** ~: [ganz] genauso; **in some** ~s in gewisser Hinsicht; **in one** ~: auf eine Art; **in every** ~: in jeder Hinsicht; **in a** ~: auf eine Art; **f)** *(custom)* Art, die; **g) get** or **have one's own** ~, **have it one's [own]** ~: seinen Willen kriegen; **be in sb.'s** or **the** ~: [jmdm.] im Weg sein; **make** ~ **for sth.** für etw. Platz machen; *(fig.)* einer Sache *(Dat.)* Platz machen; **in a bad** ~: schlecht; **either** ~: so oder so; **by the** ~: übrigens. **2.** adv. weit; ~ **back** *(coll.)* vor langer Zeit. **way'lay** v.t., forms as ²**lay** **1. a)** *(ambush)* überfallen; **b)** *(stop for conversation)* abfangen. **way-'out** adj. *(coll.)* verrückt

**WC** abbr. **water-closet** WC, das

**we** [wɪ, stressed wiː] pl. pron. wir

**weak** [wiːk] adj. **a)** schwach; *(easily led)* labil ⟨*Charakter, Person*⟩; **b)** dünn ⟨*Getränk*⟩

**weaken** ['wiːkn] **1.** v.t. schwächen; beeinträchtigen ⟨*Augen*⟩. **2.** v.i. ⟨*Entschlossenheit, Kraft:*⟩ nachlassen

**weakling** ['wiːklɪŋ] n. Schwächling, der

'**weakly** adv. schwach

'**weakness** n. Schwäche, die

**wealth** [welθ] n. **a)** *(abundance)* Fülle, die; **b)** *(riches, being rich)* Reichtum, der. '**wealthy** **1.** adj. reich. **2.** n. pl. **the** ~: die Reichen

**wean** [wiːn] v.t. abstillen; ~ **sb.** [away] **from sth.** *(fig.)* jmdm. etw. abgewöhnen

**weapon** ['wepən] n. Waffe, die

**wear** [weə(r)] **1.** n. **a)** ~ [and tear] Abnutzung, die; **b)** *(clothes)* Kleidung, die. **2.** v.t., **wore** [wɔː(r)], **worn** [wɔːn] **a)** *(have on)* tragen ⟨*Schmuck, Brille, Kleidung, Perücke*⟩; **I haven't a thing to** ~: ich habe überhaupt nichts anzuziehen; **b)** *(rub)* abtragen ⟨*Kleidungsstück*⟩; abnutzen ⟨*Teppich*⟩; **a** [badly] **worn tyre** ein [stark] abgefahrener Reifen. **3.** v.i., **wore, worn** **a)** ⟨*Kleider:*⟩ sich durchscheuern; ⟨*Absätze:*⟩ sich ablaufen; ⟨*Teppich:*⟩ sich abnutzen; **b)** *(endure rubbing)* halten; ~ **well/badly** sich gut/schlecht tragen. **wear a'way** **1.** v.t. abschleifen. **2.** v.i. sich abnutzen. **wear 'down** v.t. *(fig.)* zermürben. **wear 'off** v.i. ⟨*Schicht:*⟩ abgehen; ⟨*Wirkung, Schmerz:*⟩ nachlassen. **wear 'out** **1.** v.t. **a)** aufbrauchen; auftragen ⟨*Kleidungsstück*⟩; **b)** *(fig.: exhaust)* kaputtmachen *(ugs.)*; **be worn out** kaputt sein *(ugs.)*. **2.** v.i. kaputtgehen *(ugs.)*

**wearable** ['weərəbl] adj. **sth. is** [not] ~: man kann etw. [nicht] anziehen

**wearily** ['wɪərɪlɪ] adv. müde

**weary** ['wɪərɪ] **1.** adj. **a)** *(tired)* müde; **b) be** ~ **of sth.** einer Sache *(Gen.)* überdrüssig sein. **2.** v.t. **be wearied by sth.** durch etw. erschöpft sein. **3.** v.i. ~ **of sth./sb.** einer Sache/jmds. überdrüssig werden

**weasel** ['wiːzl] n. Wiesel, das

**weather** ['weðə(r)] **1.** n. Wetter, das; **what's the** ~ **like?** wie ist das Wetter?; **in all** ~s bei jedem Wetter; **he is feeling under the** ~ *(fig.)* er ist [zur Zeit] nicht ganz auf dem Posten. **2.** v.t. abwettern ⟨*Sturm*⟩; *(fig.)* durchstehen ⟨*schwere Zeit*⟩

**weather:** ~-**beaten** adj. wettergegerbt ⟨*Gesicht*⟩; verwittert ⟨*Felsen, Gebäude*⟩; ~**cock** n. Wetterhahn, der; ~ **forecast** n. Wettervorhersage, die; ~**man** n. Meteorologe, der; ~-**report** n. Wetterbericht, der; ~-**vane** n. Wetterfahne, die

**'weave** [wi:v] **1.** *n.* Bindung, *die.* **2.** *v. t.,* **wove** [wəʊv], **woven** ['wəʊvn] **a)** weben; flechten ⟨*Korb, Kranz*⟩; **b)** *(fig.)* einflechten ⟨*Thema usw.*⟩ (**into** in + *Akk.*)

**²weave** *v. i. (take intricate course)* sich schlängeln

**'weaver** *n.* Weber, *der*/Weberin, *die*

**web** [web] *n.* Netz, *das;* spider's ~: Spinnennetz, *das;* **webbed feet** [webd 'fi:t] *n. pl.* Schwimmfüße

**we'd** [wɪd, *stressed* wi:d] **a)** = we had; **b)** = we would

**Wed.** *abbr.* Wednesday Mi.

**wedding** ['wedɪŋ] *n.* Hochzeit, *die*

**wedding:** ~ **anniversary** *n.* Hochzeitstag, *der;* ~-**cake** *n.* Hochzeitskuchen, *der;* ~ **day** *n.* Hochzeitstag, *der;* ~ **dress** *n.* Brautkleid, *das;* ~ **present** *n.* Hochzeitsgeschenk, *das;* ~-**ring** *n.* Ehering, *der*

**wedge** [wedʒ] **1.** *n.* Keil, *der.* **2.** *v. t.* verkeilen; ~ **a door/window open** eine Tür/ein Fenster festklemmen, damit sie/es offen bleibt. **'wedge-shaped** *adj.* keilförmig

**wedlock** ['wedlɒk] *n.* **born in/out of** ~: ehelich/unehelich geboren

**Wednesday** ['wenzdeɪ, 'wenzdɪ] *n.* Mittwoch, *der; see also* **Friday**

**¹wee** [wi:] *adj. (child lang./Scot.)* klein

**²wee** *see* **wee-wee**

**weed** [wi:d] **1.** *n.* ~**|s|** Unkraut, *das.* **2.** *v. t.* jäten. **weed 'out** *v. t. (fig.)* aussieben

**'weed-killer** *n.* Unkrautvertilgungsmittel, *das*

**'weedy** *adj.* spillerig *(ugs.)* ⟨*Person*⟩

**week** [wi:k] *n.* Woche, *die;* **for several** ~**s** mehrere Wochen lang; **once a** ~, **every** ~: einmal in der Woche; **three times a** ~: dreimal in der Woche; **a two-**~ **visit** ein zweiwöchiger Besuch; **a** ~ **today/tomorrow** heute/morgen in einer Woche; **a** ~ **on Monday, Monday** ~: Montag in einer Woche.

**'weekday** *n.* Wochentag, *der.* **weekend** [-'-, '--] *n.* Wochenende, *das;* **at the** ~: am Wochenende; **go away for the** ~: übers Wochenende wegfahren

**weekly** ['wi:klɪ] **1.** *adj.* wöchentlich; Wochen⟨*zeitung, -zeitschrift, -lohn*⟩. **2.** *adv.* wöchentlich. **3.** *n. (newspaper)* Wochenzeitung, *die; (magazine)* Wochenzeitschrift, *die*

**weep** [wi:p] *v. i. & t.,* **wept** [wept] weinen. **weeping 'willow** *n.* Trauerweide, *die*

**'wee-wee** *(coll.)* **1.** *n.* Pipi, *das (ugs.);*

**do a** ~: Pipi machen *(ugs.).* **2.** *v. i.* Pipi machen *(ugs.)*

**weigh** [weɪ] *v. t. & i.* wiegen. **weigh 'down** *v. t. (fig.: depress)* niederdrücken. **weigh 'up** *v. t.* abwägen

**weight** [weɪt] *n.* Gewicht, *das;* **what is your** ~? wieviel wiegen Sie?; **be under/over** ~: zuwenig/zuviel wiegen. **'weighting** *n.* Zulage, *die.* **'weightlessness** *n.* Schwerelosigkeit, *die*

**weight:** ~-**lifter** *n.* Gewichtheber, *der*/-heberin, *die;* ~-**lifting** *n.* Gewichtheben, *das*

**'weighty** *adj.* **a)** *(heavy)* schwer; **b)** *(important)* gewichtig

**weir** [wɪə(r)] *n.* Wehr, *das*

**weird** [wɪəd] *adj. (coll.: odd)* bizarr

**welcome** ['welkəm] **1.** *int.* willkommen; ~ **home/to England!** willkommen zu Hause/in England! **2.** *n.* **a)** Willkommen, *das;* **b)** *(reception)* Empfang, *der.* **3.** *v. t.* begrüßen. **4.** *adj.* **a)** willkommen; gefällig ⟨*Anblick*⟩; **b)** *pred.* **you are** ~ **to take it** du kannst es gern nehmen; **you're** ~: gern geschehen!

**weld** [weld] *v. t. (join)* verschweißen; *(repair, make, attach)* schweißen (**|on|** **to** an + *Akk.*). **'welder** *n.* Schweißer, *der*/Schweißerin, *die*

**welfare** ['welfeə(r)] *n.* Wohl, *das.* **Welfare 'State** *n.* Wohlfahrtsstaat, *der.* **'welfare work** *n.* Sozialarbeit, *die*

**¹well** [wel] *n.* **a)** Brunnen, *der;* **b)** *see* **oil well; c)** *(stair-~)* Treppenloch, *das*

**²well 1.** *int.* ~! meine Güte!; ~, **let's forget that** na ja, lassen wir das; ~, **who was it?** nun *od.* und, wer war's?; **oh** ~**|,** **never mind|** na ja|, macht nichts]; ~? na? **2.** *adv.,* **better** ['betə(r)], **best** [best] gut; gründlich ⟨*trocknen, schütteln*⟩; **the business/patient is doing** ~: das Geschäft geht gut/dem Patienten geht es gut; ~ **done!** großartig!; **he is** ~ **over forty** er ist weit über vierzig; **as** ~ *(in addition)* auch; **A as** ~ **as B:** B und auch |noch| A. **3.** *adj. (in good health)* **How are you feeling now?** – **Quite** ~, **thank you** Wie fühlen Sie sich jetzt? – Ganz gut, danke; **look** ~: gut aussehen; **feel** ~: sich wohl fühlen; **he isn't |very|** ~: es geht ihm nicht |sehr| gut; **get** ~ **soon!** gute Besserung!; **make sb.** ~: jmdn. gesund machen

**we'll** [wɪl, *stressed* wi:l] = we will

**well:** ~-**behaved** *see* **behave 1;** ~-**being** *n.* Wohl, *das;* ~-**bred** *adj.*

anständig; ~-**built** adj. ⟨Person:⟩ mit
guter Figur; be ~-**built** eine gute Figur
haben; ~ **done** adj. (Cookery) durch-
gebraten; ~-**dressed** adj. gutgeklei-
det; ~-**educated** adj. gebildet; ~-
**heeled** adj. (coll.) gutbetucht (ugs.)
**wellington** ['weliŋtən] n. ~ [**boot**]
Gummistiefel, der
**well:** ~-**known** adj. bekannt; ~-
**made** adj. gut [gearbeitet]; ~-**man-**
**nered** adj. ⟨Person⟩ mit guten Manieren; be ~-**mannered** gute Manieren
haben; ~-**meaning** adj. wohlmei-
nend; be ~-**meaning** es gut meinen;
~-**meant** adj. gutgemeint; ~ **off** adj.
wohlhabend; sb. is ~ **off** jmdm. geht
es [finanziell] gut; ~-**read** ['welred]
adj. belesen; ~-**timed** adj. zeitlich
gut gewählt; ~-**to-do** adj. wohlhabend; ~-**wisher** n. Sympathisant,
der/Sympathisantin, die
**Welsh** [welʃ] 1. adj. walisisch; sb. is
~: jmd. ist Waliser/Waliserin. 2. n. a)
(language) Walisisch, das; see also
**English 2a;** b) pl. the ~: die Waliser.
**Welshman** ['welʃmən] n., pl. ~**men**
['welʃmən] Waliser, der. ~ '**rabbit**, ~
**rarebit** ['reəbɪt] ns. Käsetoast, der
**went** see go 1
**wept** see weep
**were** see be
**we're** [wɪə(r)] = we are
**weren't** (coll.) = were not; see be
**west** [west] 1. n. a) Westen, der; in/
to|wards|/from the ~: im/nach/von
Westen; to the ~ of westlich von; b)
usu. W~ (Geog., Polit.) Westen, der.
2. adj. westlich; West⟨küste, -wind,
-grenze, -tor⟩. 3. adv. nach Westen; ~
of westlich von
**West:** ~ **Ber'lin** pr. n. (Hist.) West-
Berlin (das); **w~bound** adj. ⟨Zug,
Verkehr usw.⟩ in Richtung Westen; ~
**Country** n. (Brit.) Westengland, das;
~ '**End** n. (Brit.) Westend, das
**westerly** ['westəlɪ] adj. westlich;
⟨Wind⟩ aus westlichen Richtungen
**western** ['westən] 1. adj. westlich;
West⟨grenze, -hälfte, -seite⟩; ~ **Ger-**
**many** Westdeutschland, das. 2. n.
Western, der. **Western 'Europe** pr.
n. Westeuropa (das)
**West:** ~ '**German** (Hist.) 1. adj. west-
deutsch; 2. n. Westdeutsche, der/die;
~ '**Germany** pr. n. (Hist.) Westdeutschland (das); ~ '**Indian** 1. adj.
westindisch; 2. n. Westinder, der/-in-
derin, die; ~ '**Indies** pr. n. pl. westin-
dische Inseln

**westward[s]** ['westwəd(z)] adv.
westwärts
**wet** [wet] 1. adj. a) naß; b) (rainy) regnerisch; feucht ⟨Klima⟩; c) frisch
⟨Farbe⟩; '~ **paint**" „frisch gestrichen";
d) (sl.: feeble) schlapp (ugs.). 2. v. t.
wet or wetted befeuchten. 3. n. a)
(moisture) Feuchtigkeit, die; b) in the
~: im Regen. '**wetness** n. Nässe, die
'**wet suit** n. Tauchanzug, der
**we've** [wɪv, stressed wi:v] = we have
**whack** [wæk] (coll.) 1. v. t. hauen
(ugs.). 2. n. Schlag, der
**whale** [weɪl] n. a) Wal, der; b) (coll.)
we had a ~ of a |good| time wir haben
uns bombig (ugs.) amüsiert
**wharf** [wɔ:f] n., pl. **wharves** [wɔ:vz] or
~s Kai, der
**what** [wɒt] 1. adj. welch...; ~ **book?**
welches Buch?; ~ **time does it start?**
um wieviel Uhr fängt es an?; ~ **kind**
**of man is he?** was für ein Mensch ist
er?; ~ **a fool you are!** was für ein
Dummkopf du doch bist!; ~ **cheek/**
**luck!** was für eine Frechheit/ein
Glück!; **I will give you** ~ **help I can** ich
werde dir helfen, so gut ich kann. 2.
adv. ~ **do I care?** was kümmert's
mich?; ~ **does it matter?** was macht's?
3. pron. was; ~**?** wie?; was? (ugs.); ~
**is your name?** wie heißt du/heißen
Sie?; ~ **about ...?** (~ will become of ...?)
was ist mit ...?; ~ **about a game of**
**chess?** wie wär's mit einer Partie
Schach?; ~**'s-his/-her/-its-name** wie
heißt er/sie/es noch; ~ **for?** wozu?; ~
**is it like?** wie ist es?; **so** ~**?** na und?;
**do** ~ **I tell you** tu, was ich dir sage
**whatever** [wɒt'evə(r)] 1. adj. ~ **prob-**
**lems you have** was für Probleme Sie
auch haben; **nothing** ~: absolut
nichts. 2. pron. **do** ~ **you like** mach,
was du willst; ~ **happens, ...:** was auch
geschieht, ...; **or** ~: oder was auch immer; ~ **does he want?** (coll.) was will er
nur?
**wheat** [wi:t] n. Weizen, der
**wheedle** ['wi:dl] v. t. ~ **sb. into doing**
**sth.** jmdm. so lange gut zureden, bis er
etw. tut; ~ **sth. out of sb.** jmdm. etw.
abschwatzen (ugs.)
**wheel** [wi:l] 1. n. a) Rad, das; |potter's|
~: Töpferscheibe, die; b) (steering ~)
Lenkrad, das; (ship's ~) Steuerrad,
das; **at** or **behind the** ~ (of car) am
Steuer. 2. v. t. (push) schieben. 3. v. i.
a) (turn round) kehrtmachen; b)
(circle) kreisen
**wheel:** ~**barrow** n. Schubkarre, die;

**~chair** *n.* Rollstuhl, *der;* **~-clamp** *n.* Parkkralle, *die*

**wheeze** [wi:z] *v. t.* schnaufen

**when** [wen] **1.** *adv.* wann; **the time ~ ...:** die Zeit, zu der/*(with past tense)* als ...; **the day ~ ...:** der Tag, an dem/*(with past tense)* als ... **2.** *conj.* **a)** *(at the time that)* als; *(with present or future tense)* wenn; **~ reading [a newspaper]** beim Lesen [einer Zeitung]; **b)** *(whereas)* **why do you go abroad ~ it's cheaper here?** warum fährst du ins Ausland, wo es doch hier billiger ist? **3.** *pron.* **by/till ~ ...?;** bis wann ...?; **since ~ ...?** seit wann ...?

**whence** [wens] *adv., conj. (arch./ literary)* woher

**whenever** [wen'evə(r)] **1.** *adv.* wann immer; **or ~:** oder wann immer; **~ did he do it?** *(coll.)* wann hat er es nur getan? **2.** *conj.* jedesmal wenn

**where** [weə(r)] **1.** *adv.* **a)** *(position)* wo; **~ shall we sit?** wohin wollen wir uns setzen?; **b)** *(to ~)* wohin. **2.** *conj.* wo. **3.** *pron.* **near/not far from ~ it happened** nahe der Stelle/nicht weit von der Stelle, wo es passiert ist

**whereabouts 1.** [weərə'baʊts] *adv. (where)* wo; *(to where)* wohin. **2.** ['weərəbaʊts] *n., sing. or pl. (of thing)* Verbleib, *der;(of person)* Aufenthalt[sort], *der*

**where: ~'as** *conj.* während; **he is very quiet, ~as she is an extrovert** er ist sehr ruhig, sie dagegen ist eher extravertiert; **~'by** *adv.* mit dem/der/denen; **~upon** [weərə'pɒn] *adv.* worauf

**wherever** [weər'evə(r)] **1.** *adv.* **a)** *(position)* wo immer; **sit ~ you like** setz dich, wohin du magst; **or ~:** oder wo immer; **b)** *(direction)* wohin immer; **or ~:** oder wohin immer; **c)** **~ have you been?** *(coll.)* wo hast du bloß gesteckt? **2.** *conj.* **a)** *(position)* überall [da], wo; **~ possible** wo *od.* wenn [irgend] möglich; **b)** *(direction)* wohin auch; **~ he went** wohin er auch ging

**whet** [wet] *v. t.,* **-tt-: a)** *(sharpen)* wetzen; **b)** *(fig.)* anregen ⟨*Appetit*⟩

**whether** ['weðə(r)] *conj.* ob; **I don't know ~ to go [or not]** ich weiß nicht, ob ich gehen soll [oder nicht]

**which** [wɪtʃ] **1.** *adj.* welch...; **~ one** welcher/welche/welches; **~ ones** welche; **~ way** *(how)* wie; *(in ~ direction)* wohin. **2.** *pron.* **a)** *interrog.* welcher/welche/welches; **~ of you?** wer von euch?; **b)** *rel.* der/die/das; **of ~:** dessen/deren; **after ~:** worauf[hin]

**whichever** [wɪtʃ'evə(r)] **1.** *adj.* welcher/welche/welches ... auch. **2.** *pron.* **a)** welcher/welche/welches ... auch; **b)** *(coll.)* **~ could it be?** welcher/welche/welches könnte das nur sein?

**whiff** [wɪf] *n. (puff; fig.: trace)* Hauch, *der; (smell)* leichter Geruch

**while** [waɪl] **1.** *n.* Weile, *die;* [for] **a ~:** eine Weile; **a long ~:** lange; **for a little** *or* **short ~:** eine kleine Weile; **be worth sb.'s ~:** sich [für jmdn.] lohnen. **2.** *conj.* **a)** *(as long as)* solange; **b)** *(although)* obgleich; **c)** *(whereas)* während. **while a'way** *v. t.* **~ away the time** sich *(Dat.)* die Zeit vertreiben (by, with with)

**whilst** [waɪlst] *(Brit.) see* while 2

**whim** [wɪm] *n.* Laune, *die*

**whimper** ['wɪmpə(r)] **1.** *n.* **~[s]** Wimmern, *das; (of dog etc.)* Winseln, *das.* **2.** *v. i.* wimmern; ⟨*Hund:*⟩ winseln

**whimsical** ['wɪmzɪkl] *adj.* launenhaft; *(odd, fanciful)* spleenig

**whine** [waɪn] **1.** *v. i.* **a)** heulen; ⟨*Hund:*⟩ jaulen; **b)** *(complain)* jammern. **2.** *n.* **a)** Heulen, *das; (of dog)* Jaulen, *das;* **b)** *(complaint)* **~[s]** Gejammer, *das*

**whip** [wɪp] **1.** *n.* **a)** Peitsche, *die;* **b)** *(Brit. Parl.)* Fraktionsgeschäftsführer, *der/*-führerin, *die.* **2.** *v. t.,* **-pp-: a)** peitschen; **b)** *(Cookery)* schlagen; **c)** *(move quickly)* reißen; **d)** *(sl.: steal)* klauen *(ugs.).* **whip 'out** *v. t.* [blitzschnell] herausziehen. **whip 'up** *v. t.* **a)** *(arouse)* anheizen *(ugs.);* **b)** *(coll.: make quickly)* schnell hinzaubern ⟨*Gericht, Essen*⟩

**whipped 'cream** *n.* Schlagsahne, *die*

**whirl** [wɜːl] **1.** *v. t.* [im Kreis] herumwirbeln. **2.** *v. i.* wirbeln. **3.** *n.* **a)** Wirbeln, *das;* **she was** *or* **her thoughts were in a ~** *(fig.)* ihr schwirrte der Kopf; **b)** *(bustle)* Trubel, *der.* **whirl 'round 1.** *v. t.* [im Kreis] herumwirbeln. **2.** *v. i.* [im Kreis] herumwirbeln; ⟨*Rad, Rotor:*⟩ wirbeln

**whirl: ~pool** *n.* Strudel, *der; (bathing pool)* Whirlpool, *der;* **~wind** *n.* Wirbelwind, *der*

**whirr** [wɜː(r)] **1.** *v. i.* surren. **2.** *n.* Surren, *das*

**whisk** [wɪsk] **1.** *n. (Cookery)* Schneebesen, *der; (part of mixer)* Rührbesen, *der.* **2.** *v. t.* **a)** *(Cookery)* [mit dem Schnee-/Rührbesen] schlagen; **b)** *(convey rapidly)* in Windeseile bringen. **whisk a'way** *v. t.* **a)** *(remove suddenly)* **~ sth. away [from sb.]**

[jmdm.] etw. [plötzlich] wegreißen; **b)** *(convey rapidly)* in Windeseile wegbringen

**whisker** ['wɪskə(r)] *n.* **a)** ~s *(on man's cheek)* Backenbart, *der;* **b)** *(of cat, mouse, rat)* Schnurrhaar, *das*

**whiskey** *(Amer., Ir.)*, **whisky** ['wɪskɪ] *n.* Whisky, *der; (American or Irish)* Whiskey, *der*

**whisper** ['wɪspə(r)] **1.** *v. i.* flüstern; ~ **to sb.** jmdm. etwas zuflüstern. **2.** *v. t.* flüstern; ~ **sth. to sb.** jmdm. etw. zuflüstern. **3.** *n.* **a)** Flüstern, *das;* **in a** ~, **in** ~**s** im Flüsterton; **b)** *(rumour)* Gerücht, *das*

**whistle** ['wɪsl] **1.** *v. i.* pfeifen; ~ **at sb.** *(in disapproval)* jmdn. auspfeifen. **2.** *v. t.* pfeifen. **3.** *n.* **a)** *(sound)* Pfiff, *der; (whistling)* Pfeifen, *das;* **b)** *(instrument)* Pfeife, *die;* **blow a/one's** ~: pfeifen

**white** [waɪt] **1.** *adj.* weiß. **2.** *n.* **a)** *(colour)* Weiß, *das;* **b)** *(of egg)* Eiweiß, *das;* **c)** W~ *(person)* Weiße, *der/die*

**white:** ~ **bread** *n.* Weißbrot, *das;* ~ **'coffee** *n. (Brit.)* Kaffee mit Milch; ~-'**collar worker** *n.* Angestellte, *der/die;* **W~ House** *pr. n. (Amer. Polit.)* the W~ House das Weiße Haus

**whiten** ['waɪtn] **1.** *v. t.* weiß machen; weißen ⟨*Wand, Schuhe*⟩. **2.** *v. i.* weiß werden

**'whiteness** *n.* Weiß, *das*

**white:** W~ '**Paper** *n. (Brit.)* öffentliches Diskussionspapier über Vorhaben der Regierung; ~**wash 1.** *n.* [weiße] Tünche; *(fig.)* Schönfärberei, *die;* **2.** *v. t.* [weiß] tünchen; ~ '**wine** *n.* Weißwein, *der*

**Whit** [wɪt] '**Monday** *n.* Pfingstmontag, *der*

**Whitsun** ['wɪtsn] *n.* Pfingsten, *das od. Pl.;* **at** ~: zu *od.* an Pfingsten

**whittle** ['wɪtl]: ~ **a'way** *v. t.* ~ **away sb.'s rights/power** jmdm. nach und nach alle Rechte/Macht nehmen; ~ '**down** *v. t.* allmählich reduzieren ⟨*Anzahl, Gewinn*⟩; verkürzen ⟨*Liste*⟩

**whiz, whizz** [wɪz] **1.** *v. i.,* -**zz**- zischen. **2.** *n.* Zischen, *das.* '**whiz[z]-kid** *n. (coll.)* Senkrechtstarter, *der*

**who** [huː, *stressed* huː] *pron.* **a)** *interrog.* wer; *(coll.: whom)* wen; *(coll.: to whom)* wem; **b)** *rel.* der/die/das; *(coll.: whom)* den/die/das; *(coll.: to whom)* dem/der/denen; **anyone/ those** ~ ...: wer ...; **everybody** ~ ...: jeder, der ...

**whoa** [wəʊ] *int.* brr

**who'd** [hʊd, *stressed* huːd] **a)** = **who had; b)** = **who would**

**whoever** [huː'evə(r)] *pron.* **a)** wer [immer]; **b)** *(no matter who)* wer ... auch; **c)** *(coll.)* ~ **could it be?** wer könnte das nur sein?

**whole** [həʊl] **1.** *adj.* ganz; **the** ~ **lot** [of them] [sie] alle. **2.** *n.* Ganze, *das;* **the** ~: das Ganze; **the** ~ **of my money/the village/London** mein ganzes Geld/das ganze Dorf/ganz London; **as a** ~: als Ganzes; **on the** ~: im großen und ganzen

**whole:** ~-**hearted** [həʊl'hɑːtɪd] *adj.* herzlich ⟨*Dank[barkeit]*⟩; rückhaltlos ⟨*Unterstützung*⟩; ~**meal** *adj.* Vollkorn-; ~ **note** *n. (Amer. Mus.)* ganze Note; ~ '**number** *n.* ganze Zahl; ~**sale 1.** *adj.* **a)** Großhandels-; **b)** *(fig.: on a large scale)* massenhaft; Massen-; **2.** *adv.* **a)** en gros; **b)** *(fig.: on a large scale)* massenweise; ~**saler** ['həʊlseɪlə(r)] *n.* Großhändler, *der/*-händlerin, *die*

**wholesome** ['həʊlsəm] *adj.* gesund

**who'll** [hʊl, *stressed* huːl] = **who will**

**wholly** ['həʊllɪ] *adv.* völlig

**whom** [huːm] *pron.* **a)** *interrog.* wen; *as indirect object* wem; **b)** *rel.* den/die/das; *pl.* die; *as indirect object* dem/der/dem; *pl.* denen

**whooping cough** ['huːpɪŋ kɒf] *n.* Keuchhusten, *der*

**whopper** ['wɒpə(r)] *n. (coll.)* **a)** Riese, *der;* **b)** *(lie)* faustdicke Lüge

**whopping** ['wɒpɪŋ] *adj. (coll.)* riesig; Riesen- *(ugs.)*; faustdick ⟨*Lüge*⟩

**whore** [hɔː(r)] *n.* Hure, *die*

**who's** [huːz] **a)** = **who is; b)** = **who has**

**whose** [huːz] *pron.* **a)** *interrog.* wessen; ~ [**book**] **is that?** wem gehört das [Buch]?; **b)** *rel.* dessen/deren/dessen; *pl.* deren

**who've** [hʊv, *stressed* huːv] = **who have**

**why** [waɪ] **1.** *adv.* **a)** *(for what reason)* warum; *(for what purpose)* wozu; ~ **is that?** warum das?; **b)** *(on account of which)* **the reason** ~ **he did it** der Grund, warum er es tat. **2.** *int.* ~, **certainly/of course!** aber sicher!

**wick** [wɪk] *n.* Docht, *der*

**wicked** ['wɪkɪd] *adj.* böse. '**wickedness** *n.* Bosheit, *die*

**wicker** ['wɪkə(r)] *n.* Korbgeflecht, *das; attrib.* Korb⟨*waren,* -*stuhl*⟩. '**wickerwork** *n.* **a)** *(material)* Korbgeflecht, *das;* **b)** *(articles)* Korbwaren

**wicket** ['wɪkɪt] *n. (Cricket)* Tor, *das*

**wide** [waɪd] 1. *adj.* a) *(broad)* breit; groß ⟨*Abstand, Winkel*⟩; **three feet ~:** drei Fuß breit; b) *(extensive)* weit; umfassend ⟨*Lektüre, Wissen, Kenntnisse*⟩; reichhaltig ⟨*Auswahl, Sortiment*⟩; c) *(off target)* be ~ of sth. etw. verfehlen. 2. *adv.* a) ~ **awake** hellwach; b) *(off target)* **shoot ~:** danebenschießen; **go ~:** das Ziel verfehlen. **wide-angle 'lens** *n.* Weitwinkelobjektiv, *das*

**'widely** *adv.* a) *(over a wide area)* weit ⟨*verbreitet, gestreut*⟩; b) *(by many people)* weithin ⟨*bekannt, akzeptiert*⟩; **a ~ held view** eine weitverbreitete Ansicht; c) *(greatly)* erheblich ⟨*sich unterscheiden*⟩

**widen** ['waɪdn] 1. *v. t.* verbreitern. 2. *v. i.* sich verbreitern

**wide:** **~-open** *attrib. adj.*, **~ 'open** *pred. adj.* weit geöffnet ⟨*Fenster, Tür*⟩; weit aufgerissen ⟨*Mund, Augen*⟩; **be ~ open** ⟨*Fenster, Tür:*⟩ weit offenstehen; **~spread** *adj.* weitverbreitet *präd.* getrennt geschr.

**widow** ['wɪdəʊ] *n.* Witwe, *die.* **widowed** ['wɪdəʊd] *adj.* verwitwet. **widower** ['wɪdəʊə(r)] *n.* Witwer, *der*

**width** [wɪdθ] *n.* Breite, *die; (of garment)* Weite, *die*

**wield** [wiːld] *v. t.* schwingen; *(fig.)* ausüben ⟨*Macht, Einfluß*⟩

**wife** [waɪf] *n., pl.* **wives** [waɪvz] Frau, *die*

**wig** [wɪg] *n.* Perücke, *die*

**wiggle** ['wɪgl] *(coll.)* 1. *v. t.* hin und her bewegen. 2. *v. i.* wackeln

**wild** [waɪld] 1. *adj.* a) wildlebend ⟨*Tier*⟩; wildwachsend ⟨*Pflanze*⟩; b) wild ⟨*Landschaft*⟩; c) *(unrestrained)* wild ⟨*Erregung*⟩; **run ~** ⟨*Pferd, Hund:*⟩ frei herumlaufen; ⟨*Kind:*⟩ herumtoben; **send** or **drive sb. ~:** jmdn. rasend vor Erregung machen; d) *(coll.: very keen)* **be ~ about sb./sth.** wild auf jmdn./etw. sein. 2. *n.* the ~[s] die Wildnis; **see an animal in the ~:** ein Tier in freier Wildbahn sehen

**wilderness** ['wɪldənɪs] *n.* Wildnis, *die; (desert)* Wüste, *die*

**wild:** **~-'goose chase** *n. (fig.)* aussichtslose Suche; **~life** *n.* die Tierund Pflanzenwelt; **~life park/reserve/sanctuary** Naturpark, *der/*-reservat, *das/*-schutzgebiet, *das*

**'wildly** *adv.* wild; **be ~ excited about sth.** über etw. *(Akk.)* ganz aus dem Häuschen sein *(ugs.);* ~ **inaccurate** völlig ungenau

**wilful** ['wɪlfl] *adj.*, **wilfully** ['wɪlfəlɪ] *adv.* a) *(deliberate[ly])* vorsätzlich; b) *(obstinate[ly])* starrsinnig

**¹will** [wɪl] *v. aux., only in: pres.* **will**, *neg. (coll.)* **won't** [wəʊnt], *past* **would** [wʊd], *neg. (coll.)* **wouldn't** ['wʊdnt] **He won't help me. W~/Would you?** Er will mir nicht helfen. Bist du bereit?; **the car won't start** das Auto springt nicht an; **~/would you pass the salt, please?** gibst du bitte mal das Salz rüber?/würdest du bitte mal das Salz rübergeben?; **~ you be quiet!** willst du wohl ruhig sein!; **he ~ sit there hour after hour** er pflegt dort stundenlang zu sitzen; **he '~ insist on doing it** er besteht unbedingt darauf, es zu tun; **~ you have some more cake?** möchtest *od.* willst du noch etwas Kuchen?; **the box ~ hold 5 lb. of tea** in die Kiste gehen 5 Pfund Tee; **tomorrow he ~ be in Oxford** morgen ist er in Oxford; **I promise I won't do it again** ich verspreche, ich mach's nicht noch mal; **if he tried, he would succeed** wenn er es versuchen würde, würde er es erreichen; **~ you please tidy up** würdest du bitte aufräumen?

**²will** *n.* a) *(faculty)* Wille, *der;* b) *(Law: testament)* Testament, *das;* c) *(desire)* **at ~:** nach Belieben; **~ to live** Lebenswille, *der;* **against one's/sb.'s ~:** gegen seinen/jmds. Willen

**'willing** *adj.* willig; **ready and ~:** bereit; **be ~ to do sth.** bereit sein, etw. zu tun. **'willingly** *adv.* a) *(with pleasure)* gern[e]; b) *(voluntarily)* freiwillig. **'willingness** *n.* Bereitschaft, *die*

**willow** ['wɪləʊ] *n.* Weide, *die*

**'will-power** *n.* Willenskraft, *die*

**willy-nilly** [wɪlɪ'nɪlɪ] *adv.* wohl oder übel *(etw. tun müssen)*

**wilt** [wɪlt] *v. i.* ⟨*Pflanze, Blumen:*⟩ welk werden, welken

**wily** ['waɪlɪ] *adj.* listig; gewieft ⟨*Person*⟩

**wimp** [wɪmp] *n. (coll.)* Schlappschwanz, *der (ugs.)*

**win** [wɪn] 1. *v. t.,* -nn-, *won* [wʌn] gewinnen; bekommen ⟨*Stipendium, Vertrag, Recht*⟩; **~ sb. sth.** jmdm. etw. einbringen. 2. *v. i.,* -nn-, *won* gewinnen. 3. *n.* Sieg, *der;* **have a ~:** gewinnen. **win 'over, win 'round** *v. t.* bekehren; *(to one's side)* auf seine Seite bringen; *(convince)* überzeugen. **win 'through** *v. i.* Erfolg haben

**wince** [wɪns] *v. i.* zusammenzucken **(at** bei)

**winch** [wɪntʃ] **1.** *n.* Winde, *die.* **2.** *v. t.* winden; ~ **up** hochwinden

¹**wind** [wɪnd] **1.** *n.* Wind, *der; (Med.)* Blähungen; **get** ~ **of** sth. *(fig.)* Wind von etw. bekommen; **be in the** ~ *(fig.)* in der Luft liegen; **get/have the** ~ **up** *(sl.)* Manschetten *(ugs.)* kriegen/haben. **2.** *v. t.* **the blow** ~**ed him** der Schlag nahm ihm den Atem

²**wind** [waɪnd] **1.** *v. i.,* **wound** [waʊnd] **a)** *(curve)* sich winden; *(move)* sich schlängeln; **b)** *(coil)* sich wickeln. **2.** *v. t.,* **wound a)** *(coil)* wickeln; ~ sth. **on** [**to**] sth. etw. auf etw. *(Akk.)* [auf]wickeln; **b)** aufziehen ⟨*Uhr*⟩. **wind** '**down** *v. t.* **a)** herunterdrehen ⟨*Autofenster*⟩; **b)** *(fig.: reduce gradually)* einschränken. **wind** '**up 1.** *v. t.* **a)** hochdrehen ⟨*Autofenster*⟩; **b)** *(coil)* aufwickeln; **c)** aufziehen ⟨*Uhr*⟩; **d)** *(coll.: annoy deliberately)* auf die Palme bringen *(ugs.);* **e)** beschließen ⟨*Debatte*⟩; **f)** *(Finance, Law)* auflösen. **2.** *v. i.* **a)** *(conclude)* schließen; **b)** *(coll.: end up)* ~ **up in prison/hospital** [zum Schluß] im Gefängnis/Krankenhaus landen *(ugs.)*

**wind** [wɪnd]: ~**break** *n.* Windschutz, *der;* ~-**chill factor** *n.* Wind-chill-Index, *der (Meteor.)*

**winder** ['waɪndə(r)] *n. (of watch)* Krone, *die; (of clock, toy)* Aufziehschraube, *die*

**wind** [wɪnd]: ~**fall** *n.* **a)** *(fruit)* ~**falls** Fallobst, *das;* **b)** *(fig.)* warmer Regen *(ugs.);* ~ **farm** *n.* Windpark, *der;* Windfarm, *die;* ~ **instrument** *n. (Mus.)* Blasinstrument, *das;* ~**mill** *n.* Windmühle, *die*

**window** ['wɪndəʊ] *n.* Fenster, *das; (shop*~*)* [Schau]fenster, *das;* **break a** ~: eine Fensterscheibe zerbrechen

**window:** ~-**box** *n.* Blumenkasten, *der;* ~-**cleaner** *n.* Fensterputzer, *der/*-putzerin, *die;* ~-**dressing** *n. (fig.)* Schönfärberei, *die;* ~-**pane** *n.* Fensterscheibe, *die;* ~-**shopping** *n.* Schaufensterbummeln, *das;* **go** ~-**shopping** einen Schaufensterbummel machen; ~-**sill** *n. (inside)* Fensterbank, *die; (outside)* Fenstersims, *der od. das*

**wind** [wɪnd]: ~**pipe** *n. (Anat.)* Luftröhre, *die;* ~**screen,** *(Amer.)* ~**shield** *ns. (Motor Veh.)* Windschutzscheibe, *die;* ~**screen/**~**shield wiper** Scheibenwischer, *der;* ~**screen/**~**shield washer** Scheibenwaschanlage, *die;* ~**surfer** *n.* Windsurfer, *der;*

~**surfing** *n.* Windsurfen, *das;* ~**swept** *adj.* windgepeitscht; vom Wind zerzaust ⟨*Person, Haare*⟩; ~-**tunnel** *n.* Windkanal, *der*

**windward** ['wɪndwəd] *adj.* ~ **side** Windseite, *die*

'**windy** *adj.* windig

**wine** [waɪn] *n.* Wein, *der*

**wine:** ~-**bar** *n.* Weinstube, *die;* ~-**cellar** *n.* [Wein]keller, *das;* ~-**glass** *n.* Weinglas, *das;* ~-**list** *n.* Weinkarte, *die;* ~-**tasting** ['waɪnteɪstɪŋ] *n.* Weinprobe, *die*

**wing** [wɪŋ] *n.* **a)** *(Ornith., Archit., Sport)* Flügel, *der;* **b)** *(Aeronaut.)* Tragfläche, *die;* **c)** *(Brit. Motor. Veh.)* Kotflügel, *der*

**wink** [wɪŋk] **1.** *v. i.* **a)** blinzeln; *(as signal)* zwinkern; ~ **at** sb. jmdm. zuzwinkern; **b)** *(flash)* blinken. **2.** *n.* **a)** Blinzeln, *das; (signal)* Zwinkern, *das;* **give** sb. **a** ~: jmdm. zuzwinkern; **b)** **not sleep a** ~: kein Auge zutun

'**winner** *n.* Sieger, *der/*Siegerin, *die; (of competition or prize)* Gewinner, *der/*Gewinnerin, *die*

'**winning** *adj.* **a)** *attrib.* siegreich; ~ **number** Gewinnzahl, *die;* **b)** *(charming)* einnehmend; gewinnend ⟨*Lächeln*⟩. '**winning-post** *n.* Zielpfosten, *der.* '**winnings** *n. pl.* Gewinn, *der*

**winter** ['wɪntə(r)] *n.* Winter, *der;* **in** [**the**] ~: im Winter. **winter** '**sports** *n. pl.* Wintersport, *der*

**wintry** ['wɪntrɪ] *adj.* winterlich; ~ **shower** Schneegestöber, *das*

**wipe** [waɪp] **1.** *v. t.* **a)** abwischen; [auf]wischen ⟨*Fußboden*⟩; *(dry)* abtrocknen; ~ **one's mouth/eyes/nose** sich *(Dat.)* den Mund/die Tränen/die Nase abwischen; ~ **one's feet/shoes** [sich *(Dat.)*] die Füße/Schuhe abtreten; **b)** *(get rid of)* [ab]wischen; ~ **one's/sb.'s tears** sich/jmdm. die Tränen abwischen. **2.** *n.* **give** sth. **a** ~: etw. abwischen. **wipe** '**down** *v. t.* abwischen; *(dry)* abtrocknen. **wipe** '**off** *v. t.* **a)** *(remove)* wegwischen; löschen ⟨*Bandaufnahme*⟩; **b)** *(pay off)* zurückzahlen ⟨*Schulden*⟩. **wipe** '**out** *v. t.* **a)** *(remove)* wegwischen; *(erase)* auslöschen; **b)** *(cancel)* tilgen; zunichte machen ⟨*Vorteil, Gewinn usw.*⟩; **c)** *(destroy)* ausrotten ⟨*Rasse, Tierart, Feinde*⟩; ausmerzen ⟨*Seuche, Korruption*⟩. **wipe** '**up** *v. t.* **a)** aufwischen; **b)** *(dry)* abtrocknen

'**wiper** *n. (Motor Veh.)* Wischer, *der*

**wire** ['waɪə(r)] 1. *n.* **a)** Draht, *der;* **b)** *(Electr., Teleph.)* Leitung, *die;* **c)** *(coll.: telegram)* Telegramm, *das.* 2. *v. t.* **a)** *(fasten)* ~ sth. together etw. mit Draht verbinden; **b)** *(Electr.)* ~ sth. to sth. etw. an etw. *(Akk.)* anschließen; ~ a house in einem Haus die Stromleitungen legen; **c)** *(coll.: telegraph)* ~ sb. jmdm. *od.* an jmdn. telegrafieren. 'wireless *n.* *(Brit.)* Radio, *das.* wire 'netting *n.* Maschendraht, *der*

**wiring** ['waɪərɪŋ] *n.* [elektrische] Leitungen

**wisdom** ['wɪzdəm] *n.* **a)** Weisheit, *die;* **b)** *(prudence)* Klugheit, *die.* 'wisdom tooth *n.* Weisheitszahn, *der*

**wise** [waɪz] *adj.* **a)** weise; vernünftig ⟨*Meinung*⟩; **b)** *(prudent)* klug; **c)** be none the ~r kein bißchen klüger als vorher sein. 'wisely *adv.* weise; *(prudently)* klug

**wish** [wɪʃ] 1. *v. t.* wünschen; I ~ I was *or* were rich ich wollte, ich wäre reich; I ~ to go ich möchte gehen; ~ sb. luck/success etc. jmdm. Glück/Erfolg *usw.* wünschen; ~ sb. well jmdm. alles Gute wünschen. 2. *v. i.* wünschen; ~ for sth. sich *(Dat.)* etw. wünschen. 3. *n.* Wunsch, *der;* make a ~: sich *(Dat.)* etwas wünschen; get *or* have one's ~: seinen Wunsch erfüllt bekommen. wishful thinking [wɪʃfl 'θɪŋkɪŋ] *n.* Wunschdenken, *das*

**wishy-washy** ['wɪʃɪwɒʃɪ] *adj.* labberig *(ugs.);* *(fig.)* lasch

**wisp** [wɪsp] *n.* *(of straw)* Büschel, *das;* ~ of hair Haarsträhne, *die;* ~ of cloud/smoke Wolkenfetzen, *der/* Rauchfahne, *die*

**wistful** ['wɪstfl] *adj.,* 'wistfully *adv.* wehmütig

**wit** [wɪt] *n.* **a)** *(humour)* Witz, *der;* **b)** *(intelligence)* Geist, *der;* be at one's ~'s *or* ~s' end sich *(Dat.)* keinen Rat mehr wissen; be frightened *or* scared out of one's ~s Todesangst haben; have/keep one's ~s about one auf Draht *(ugs.)* sein/nicht den Kopf verlieren; **c)** *(person)* geistreicher Mensch

**witch** [wɪtʃ] *n.* Hexe, *die*

**witch:** ~craft *n.* Hexerei, *die;* ~-doctor *n.* Medizinmann, *der;* ~-hunt *n.* Hexenjagd, *die* (for auf + *Akk.*)

**with** [wɪð] *prep.* mit; put sth. ~ sth. etw. zu etw. stellen/legen; have nothing to write ~: nichts zum Schreiben haben; I'm not '~ you *(coll.)* ich komme nicht mit; tremble ~ fear vor Angst zittern; I have no money ~ me ich habe kein Geld dabei *od.* bei mir; sleep ~ the window open bei offenem Fenster schlafen

**with'draw** 1. *v. t.,* forms as draw 1 zurückziehen; abziehen ⟨*Truppen*⟩; ~ sth. from an account etw. von einem Konto abheben. 2. *v. i.,* forms as draw 1 sich zurückziehen. **withdrawal** [wɪð'drɔːəl] *n.* **a)** Zurücknahme, *die;* *(of troops)* Abzug, *der;* *(of money)* Abhebung, *die;* **b)** *(from drugs)* Entzug, *der;* ~ symptoms Entzugserscheinungen. **with'drawn** *adj.* *(unsociable)* verschlossen

**wither** ['wɪðə(r)] 1. *v. t.* verdorren lassen. 2. *v. i.* [ver]welken. **wither a'way** *v. i.* dahinwelken *(geh.)*

**with'hold** *v. t.,* forms as ²hold: ~ sth. from sb. jmdm. etw. vorenthalten

**within** [wɪ'ðɪn] *prep.* innerhalb; stay/be ~ the law den Boden des Gesetzes nicht verlassen; ~ eight miles of sth. acht Meilen im Umkreis von etw.

**without** [wɪ'ðaʊt] *prep.* ohne; ~ doing sth. ohne etw. zu tun; ~ his knowing ohne daß er davon weiß/wußte

**with'stand** *v. t.,* withstood [wɪθ'stʊd] standhalten (+ *Dat.*); aushalten ⟨*Beanspruchung, hohe Temperaturen*⟩

**witness** ['wɪtnɪs] 1. *n.* Zeuge, *der/* Zeugin, *die* (of, to Gen.). 2. *v. t.* **a)** *(see)* ~ sth. Zeuge/Zeugin einer Sache *(Gen.)* sein; **b)** bestätigen ⟨*Unterschrift*⟩. 'witness-box *(Brit.),* 'witness-stand *(Amer.) ns.* Zeugenstand, *der*

**witticism** ['wɪtɪsɪzm] *n.* Witzelei, *die*

**wittingly** ['wɪtɪŋlɪ] *adv.* wissentlich

**witty** ['wɪtɪ] *adj.* witzig; geistreich ⟨*Person*⟩

**wives** *pl. of* wife

**wizard** ['wɪzəd] *n.* Zauberer, *der.* **wizardry** ['wɪzədrɪ] *n.* Zauberei, *die*

**wizened** ['wɪzənd] *adj.* runz[e]lig

**wobble** ['wɒbl] *v. i.* wackeln. **wobbly** ['wɒblɪ] *adj.* wack[e]lig

**woe** [wəʊ] *n.* *(arch./literary/joc.)* ~[s] Jammer, *der;* ~ betide you! wehe dir!

**woke, woken** *see* ¹wake 1, 2

**wolf** [wʊlf] 1. *n., pl.* wolves [wʊlvz] Wolf, *der.* 2. *v. t.* ~ [down] verschlingen

**woman** ['wʊmən] *n., pl.* women ['wɪmɪn] Frau, *die;* ~ doctor Ärztin, *die;* ~ friend Freundin, *die.* **womanizer** ['wʊmənaɪzə(r)] *n.* Schürzenjäger, *der.* 'womanly *adj.* fraulich

**womb** [wu:m] *n.* Gebärmutter, *die*
**women** *pl. of* **woman**
**women:** ~**folk** *n. pl.* Frauen; **W~'s**
'**Lib** *(coll.),* **W~'s Libe'ration** *ns.* die
Frauenbewegung; ~'**s** '**rights** *n. pl.*
die Rechte der Frau
**won** *see* **win** 1, 2
**wonder** ['wʌndə(r)] 1. *n.* a) *(thing)*
Wunder, *das;* b) *(feeling)* Staunen,
*das.* 2. *adj.* Wunder-. 3. *v. i.* sich wundern; staunen (**at** über + *Akk.*). 4. *v. t.*
sich fragen; I ~ **what the time is** wieviel Uhr mag es wohl sein?; I ~
**whether I might open the window** dürfte
ich vielleicht das Fenster öffnen?
**wonderful** ['wʌndəfl] *adj.,* **won-**
**derfully** ['wʌndəfəlɪ] *adv.* wunderbar
**won't** [wəʊnt] *(coll.)* = **will not**; *see*
¹**will**
**woo** [wu:] *v. t.* a) *(literary: court)* ~ **sb.**
um jmdn. werben *(geh.);* b) umwer-
ben ⟨*Kunden, Wähler*⟩
**wood** [wʊd] *n.* a) Holz, *das;* **touch** ~
*(Brit.),* **knock on** ~ *(Amer.)* unberufen!; b) *(trees)* Wald, *der.* '**woodcut**
*n.* Holzschnitt, *der.* '**woodcutter** *n.*
Holzfäller, *der*
'**wooded** *adj.* bewaldet
**wooden** ['wʊdn] *adj.* a) hölzern;
Holz-; b) *(fig.: stiff)* hölzern
**wood:** ~**land** ['wʊdlənd] *n.* Wald-
land, *das;* ~**pecker** *n.* Specht, *der;*
~-**wind** *n.* the ~-**wind** |**section**| die
Holzbläser; ~-**wind instrument** Holz-
blasinstrument, *das;* ~-**work** *n.* a)
*(craft)* Arbeiten mit Holz; b) *(things)*
Holzarbeit[en]; ~**worm** *n.* Holz-
wurm; **it's got** ~**worm** da ist der Holz-
wurm drin *(ugs.)*
'**woody** *adj.* a) *(wooded)* waldreich; b)
*(consisting of wood)* holzig
**wool** [wʊl] *n.* Wolle, *die; attrib.* Woll-.
**woollen** *(Amer.:* **woolen**) ['wʊlən]
1. *adj.* wollen. 2. *n.* ~**s** Wollsachen *Pl.*
'**woolly** *adj.* a) wollig; Woll⟨*pullover,*
*-mütze*⟩; b) *(confused)* verschwommen
**word** [wɜ:d] 1. *n.* Wort, *das;* ~**s** *(of*
*song or actor)* Text, *der;* **in other** ~**s**
mit anderen Worten; ~ **for** ~: Wort
für Wort; **too funny** *etc.* **for** ~**s** unsag-
bar komisch *usw.;* **have** ~**s** einen
Wortwechsel haben; **have a** ~ |**with**
**sb.**| **about sth.** [mit jmdm.] über etw.
*(Akk.)* sprechen; **could I have a** ~ |**with**
**you**|**?** kann ich dich mal sprechen?;
**say a few** ~**s** ein paar Worte sprechen;
**keep/break one's** ~: sein Wort halten/
brechen; **by** ~ **of mouth** durch mündli-
che Mitteilung; **send** ~ **that** ...: Nach-

richt geben, daß ... 2. *v. t.* formulieren.
'**wording** *n.* Formulierung, *die*
**word:** ~ **order** *n.* Wortstellung, *die;*
~ **processing** *n.* Textverarbeitung,
*die;* ~ **processor** *n.* Textverarbei-
tungssystem, *das*
**wore** *see* **wear** 2, 3
**work** [wɜ:k] 1. *n.* a) Arbeit, *die;* **at** ~
*(engaged in* ~**ing**) bei der Arbeit; *(fig.:*
*operating)* am Werk; *(at job)* auf der
Arbeit; **out of** ~: arbeitslos; **be in** ~:
eine Stelle haben; b) ~**s** *sing. or pl.*
*(factory)* Werk, *das;* c) ~**s** *pl. (*~**ing**
*parts)* Werk, *das; (operations)* Arbeiten; d) *(thing made or achieved)* Werk,
*das;* **a** ~ **of art/literature** ein Kunst-
werk/literarisches Werk. 2. *v. i.* a) arbeiten; b) *(function effectively)* funktionieren; **make the television** ~: den
Fernsehapparat in Ordnung bringen;
c) *(have an effect)* wirken (**on** auf
+ *Akk.*); d) ~ **loose** sich lockern. 3.
*v. t.* a) bedienen ⟨*Maschine*⟩; betätigen ⟨*Bremse*⟩; b) *(get labour from)* arbeiten lassen; c) ausbeuten ⟨*Stein-*
*bruch, Grube*⟩; d) *(cause to go gradu-*
*ally)* führen; ~ **one's way up/into sth.**
sich hocharbeiten/in etw. hineinar-
beiten. **work 'off** *v. t.* a) *(get rid of)*
loswerden; abreagieren ⟨*Wut*⟩; b) ab-
arbeiten ⟨*Schuld*⟩. '**work on** *v. t.* a) ~
**on sth.** an etw. *(Dat.)* arbeiten; b) *(try*
*to persuade)* ~ **on sb.** jmdn. bearbeiten
*(ugs.).* **work 'out** 1. *v. t.* a) *(calculate)*
ausrechnen; b) *(solve)* lösen; c) *(de-*
*vise)* ausarbeiten. 2. *v. i.* a) **sth.** ~**s out**
**at £2** etw. ergibt 2 Pfund; b) *(have*
*result)* laufen; **things** ~**ed out** |**well**| **in**
**the end** es ist schließlich doch alles
gutgegangen. **work 'up** 1. *v. t. (excite)*
aufpeitschen ⟨*Menge*⟩; **get** ~**ed up** sich
aufregen. 2. *v. i.* ~ **up to sth.** ⟨*Musik:*⟩
sich zu etw. steigern; ⟨*Geschichte,*
*Film:*⟩ auf etw. *(Akk.)* zusteuern
**workable** ['wɜ:kəbl] *adj. (feasible)*
durchführbar
**workaholic** [wɜ:kə'hɒlɪk] *n. (coll.)* ar-
beitswütiger Mensch
'**worker** *n.* Arbeiter, *der*/Arbeiterin,
*die*
'**workforce** *n.* Belegschaft, *die*
'**working** *adj.* a) *(in work)* werktätig;
b) ~ **model** funktionsfähiges Modell
**working:** ~ '**class** *n.* Arbeiterklasse,
*die;* ~-**class** *adj.* der Arbeiterklasse
*nachgestellt;* **sb. is** ~-**class** jmd. gehört
zur Arbeiterklasse; ~ **clothes** *n. pl.*
Arbeitskleidung, *die;* ~ '**day** *n.* a)
*(portion of day)* Arbeitstag, *der;* b)

*(day when work is done)* Werktag, *der;* ~ 'order *n.* be in |good| ~ order betriebsbereit sein; *⟨Auto:⟩* fahrbereit sein

**workman** ['wɜːkmən] *n., pl.* ~men ['wɜːkmən] Arbeiter, *der.* 'workmanship *n. (quality)* Kunstfertigkeit, *die*

**work:** ~-out *n.* [Fitneß]training, *das;* ~shop *n.* a) *(room)* Werkstatt; *die,* b) *(building)* Werk, *das*

**world** [wɜːld] *n.* a) Welt, *die;* in the ~: auf der Welt; the tallest building in the ~: das höchste Gebäude der Welt; all over the ~: in *od.* auf der ganzen Welt; b) *(vast amount)* it will do him a *or* the ~ of good es wird ihm unendlich guttun; a ~ of difference ein weltweiter Unterschied. **world 'champion** *n.* Weltmeister, *der*/-meisterin, *die.* **world-'famous** *adj.* weltberühmt

'**worldly** *adj.* weltlich; weltlich eingestellt *⟨Person⟩*

**world-wide** 1. ['--] *adj.* weltweit *nicht präd.* 2. [-'-] *adv.* weltweit

**worm** [wɜːm] 1. *n.* Wurm, *der.* 2. *v. t.* a) ~ oneself into sb.'s favour sich in jmds. Gunst *(Akk.)* schleichen; b) ~ sth. out of sb. etw. aus jmdm. herausbringen *(ugs.).* '**worm-eaten** *adj.* wurmstichig

**worn** *see* wear 2, 3

'**worn-out** *adj.* a) abgetragen *⟨Kleidungsstück⟩;* abgenutzt *⟨Teppich⟩;* b) erschöpft *⟨Person⟩*

**worried** ['wʌrɪd] *adj.* besorgt

**worry** ['wʌrɪ] 1. *v. t.* a) beunruhigen; b) *(bother)* stören. 2. *v. i.* sich *(Dat.)* Sorgen machen. '**worrying** *adj.* a) *(causing worry)* beunruhigend; b) *(full of worry)* sorgenvoll *⟨Zeit, Woche⟩*

**worse** [wɜːs] 1. *adj.* schlechter; schlimmer *⟨Schmerz, Krankheit, Benehmen⟩.* 2. *adv.* schlechter/ schlimmer. 3. *n.* Schlimmeres. **worsen** ['wɜːsn] 1. *v. t.* verschlechtern. 2. *v. i.* sich verschlechtern

**worship** ['wɜːʃɪp] 1. *v. t., (Brit.)* -pp-: a) anbeten; b) *(idolize)* abgöttisch verehren. 2. *v. i., (Brit.)* -pp- am Gottesdienst teilnehmen. 3. *n.* a) Anbetung, *die; (service)* Gottesdienst, *der;* b) Your/His W~: ≈ Euer/seine Ehren. '**worshipper** *(Amer.:* **worshiper)** *n.* Gottesdienstbesucher, *der*/-besucherin, *die*

**worst** [wɜːst] 1. *adj.* schlechtest...; schlimmst... *⟨Schmerz, Krankheit, Benehmen⟩.* 2. *adv.* am schlechtesten/

schlimmsten. 3. *n.* a) the ~: der/die/ das Schlimmste; get *or* have the ~ of it *(suffer the most)* am meisten zu leiden haben; if the ~ comes to the ~: wenn es zum Schlimmsten kommt; b) *(poorest in quality)* Schlechteste, *der/ die/das*

**worsted** ['wʊstɪd] *n.* Kammgarn, *das*

**worth** [wɜːθ] 1. *adj.* wert; it's ~ £80 es ist 80 Pfund wert; is it ~ hearing/the effort? ist es hörenswert/der Mühe wert?; is it ~ doing? lohnt es sich?; it isn't ~ it es lohnt sich nicht. 2. *n.* Wert, *der;* ten pounds' ~ of petrol Benzin für zehn Pfund. '**worthless** *adj.* a) *(valueless)* wertlos; b) *(having bad qualities)* nichtswürdig. '**worthwhile** *adj.* lohnend

**worthy** ['wɜːðɪ] *adj.* würdig

**wouldn't** ['wʊdnt] *(coll.)* = would not; *see* ¹will

¹**wound** [wuːnd] 1. *n.* Wunde, *die.* 2. *v. t.* verwunden; *(fig.)* verletzen

²**wound** *see* ²wind

**wove, woven** *see* ¹weave 2

**wrangle** ['ræŋgl] 1. *v. i.* [sich] streiten. 2. *n.* Streit, *der*

**wrap** [ræp] 1. *v. t., -pp-* einwickeln; *(fig.)* hüllen; ~ped abgepackt *⟨Brot usw.⟩;* ~ sth. |a|round sth. etw. um etw. wickeln. 2. *n.* Umschlag[e]tuch, *das.* **wrap 'up** *v. t.* a) *see* wrap 1; b) *(conclude)* abschließen; c) be ~ped up in one's work in seine Arbeit völlig versunken sein

'**wrapper** *n.* a) sweet-/toffee-~|s| Bonbonpapier, *das;* b) *(of book)* Schutzumschlag, *der*

'**wrapping** *n.* Verpackung, *die.* '**wrapping-paper** *n. (strong)* Packpapier, *das; (decorative)* Geschenkpapier, *das*

**wrath** [rɒθ] *n.* Zorn, *der*

**wreak** [riːk] *v. t.* a) *(cause)* anrichten; b) ~ vengeance on sb. an jmdm. Rache nehmen

**wreath** [riːθ] *n., pl.* **wreaths** [riːðz, riːθs] Kranz, *der*

**wreck** [rek] 1. *n.* a) Wrack, *das; b) (destruction of ship)* Schiffbruch, *der.* 2. *v. t.* a) *(destroy)* ruinieren; zu Schrott fahren *⟨Auto⟩;* be ~ed *(shipwrecked)* Schiffbruch erleiden; b) *(fig.: ruin)* zerstören; ruinieren *⟨Gesundheit, Urlaub⟩.* **wreckage** ['rekɪdʒ] *n.* Wrackteile *Pl.; (fig.)* Trümmer *Pl.*

**wren** *n.* Zaunkönig, *der*

**wrench** [rentʃ] 1. *n.* a) *(tool)* verstellbarer Schraubenschlüssel; b) *(violent* *twist)* Verrenkung, *die;* c) *(fig.)* be a great ~ [for sb.] sehr schmerzhaft für jmdn. sein. 2. *v.t.* a) reißen; ~ sth. from sb. jmdm. etw. entreißen; b) ~ one's ankle sich *(Dat.)* den Knöchel verrenken

**wrest** [rest] *v.t.* ~ sth. from sb. jmdm. etw. entreißen

**wrestle** ['resl] *v.i.* ringen. **wrestler** ['reslə(r)] *n.* Ringer, *der/*Ringerin, *die.* **wrestling** ['reslɪŋ] *n.* Ringen, *das*

**wretch** [retʃ] *n.* Kreatur, *die*

**wretched** ['retʃɪd] *adj.* a) *(miserable)* unglücklich; b) *(coll.: damned)* elend; c) *(very bad)* erbärmlich

**wriggle** ['rɪgl] 1. *v.i.* a) sich winden; ⟨*Fisch:*⟩ zappeln; b) *(move)* sich schlängeln. 2. *v.t.* ~ one's way sich schlängeln. 3. *n.* Windung, *die*

**wring** [rɪŋ] *v.t.,* wrung [rʌŋ] a) wringen; ~ out auswringen; b) ~ sb.'s hand jmdm. fest die Hand drücken; ~ the neck of an animal einem Tier den Hals umdrehen; c) ~ sth. from *or* out of sb. *(fig.)* jmdm. etw. abpressen. **wringing** 'wet *adj.* tropfnaß

**wrinkle** ['rɪŋkl] 1. *n.* Falte, *die; (in paper)* Knick, *der.* 2. *v.t.* falten. 3. *v.i.* sich in Falten legen. **wrinkled** ['rɪŋkld], **wrinkly** ['rɪŋklɪ] *adjs.* runz[e]lig

**wrist** [rɪst] *n.* Handgelenk, *das.* 'wrist-watch *n.* Armbanduhr, *die*

**writ** [rɪt] *n. (Law)* Verfügung, *die*

**write** [raɪt] 1. *v.i.,* wrote [rəʊt], **written** ['rɪtn] schreiben; ~ to sb./a firm jmdm./an eine Firma schreiben. 2. *v.t.,* wrote, written schreiben; ausschreiben ⟨*Scheck*⟩; the written language die Schriftsprache; written applications schriftliche Anträge. **write** 'back *v.i.* zurückschreiben. **write** 'down *v.t.* aufschreiben. **write** 'off 1. *v.t.* a) abschreiben ⟨*Schulden, Verlust*⟩; b) *(destroy)* zu Schrott fahren. 2. *v.i.* ~ off for sth. etw. [schriftlich] anfordern

'write-off *n.* Totalschaden, *der*

**writer** ['raɪtə(r)] *n.* Schriftsteller, *der/*Schriftstellerin, *die; (of letter, article)* Verfasser, *der/*Verfasserin, *die*

'write-up *n. (by critic)* Kritik, *die*

**writhe** [raɪð] *v.i.* sich winden

**writing** ['raɪtɪŋ] *n.* a) Schreiben, *das;* put sth. in ~: etw. schriftlich machen *(ugs.);* b) *(handwriting, something written)* Schrift, *die.* 'writing paper *n.* Schreibpapier, *das*

**written** *see* write

**wrong** [rɒŋ] 1. *adj.* a) *(morally bad)* unrecht *(geh.); (unfair)* ungerecht; b) *(mistaken)* falsch; be ~ ⟨*Person:*⟩ sich irren; the clock is ~: die Uhr geht falsch; c) *(not suitable)* falsch; give the ~ answer eine falsche Antwort geben; [the] ~ way round verkehrt herum; d) *(out of order)* nicht in Ordnung; what's ~? ist etwas nicht in Ordnung? 2. *adv.* falsch. 3. *n.* Unrecht, *das;* do ~: unrecht tun. 4. *v.t.* ~ sb. jmdn. ungerecht behandeln. **wrongful** ['rɒŋfl] *adj.* a) *(unfair)* unrecht *(geh.);* b) *(unlawful)* rechtswidrig. 'wrongfully *adv.* a) *(unfairly)* unrecht *(geh.)* ⟨*handeln*⟩; zu Unrecht ⟨*beschuldigen*⟩; b) *(unlawfully)* rechtswidrig. 'wrongly *adv.* a) falsch; b) *(mistakenly)* zu Unrecht; c) *see* wrongfully a

**wrote** *see* write

**wrought iron** [rɔ:t 'aɪən] *n.* Schmiedeeisen, *das; attrib.* schmiedeeisern

**wrung** *see* wring

**wry** [raɪ] *adj.,* ~er *or* wrier ['raɪə(r)], ~est *or* wriest ['raɪɪst] ironisch ⟨*Blick*⟩; fein ⟨*Humor, Witz*⟩

# X

**X, x** [eks] *n.* X, x, *das*

**Xerox,** (P), **xerox** ['zɪərɒks] 1. *n. (copy)* Xerokopie, *die.* 2. xerox *v.t.* xerokopieren

**Xmas** ['krɪsməs, 'eksməs] *n. (coll.)* Weihnachten, *das*

'X-ray 1. *n. (picture)* Röntgenaufnahme, *die.* 2. *v.t.* röntgen; durchleuchten ⟨*Gepäck*⟩

# Y

**Y, y** [waɪ] *n.* Y, y, *das*

**yacht** [jɒt] *n.* a) *(for racing)* Segeljacht, *die;* b) *(for pleasure)* Jacht, *die.* 'yachting *n.* Segeln, *das*

**Yank** [jæŋk] *n. (Brit. coll.: American)* Ami, *der (ugs.)*

**yank** *(coll.)* 1. *v. t.* reißen an (+ *Dat.*). 2. *n.* Reißen, *das*

**yap** [jæp] *v. i.*, **-pp-** kläffen

**¹yard** [jɑ:d] *n. (measure)* Yard, *das*

**²yard** *n.* a) *(attached to building)* Hof, *der;* in the ~: auf dem Hof; b) *(for storage)* Lager, *das*

**'yardstick** *n. (fig.)* Maßstab, *der*

**yarn** [jɑ:n] *n.* a) *(thread)* Garn, *das;* b) *(coll.: story)* Geschichte, *die*

**yawn** [jɔ:n] 1. *n.* Gähnen, *das.* 2. *v. i.* gähnen. **'yawning** *adj.* gähnend

**year** [jɪə(r)] *n.* a) Jahr, *das;* for |many| ~s jahrelang; once a ~, every ~: einmal im Jahr; a ten-~-old ein Zehnjähriger/eine Zehnjährige; b) *(group of students, vintage of wine)* Jahrgang, *der.* **'yearbook** *n.* Jahrbuch, *das.* **'yearly** 1. *adj.* jährlich; Einjahres-⟨abonnement⟩. 2. *adv.* jährlich

**yearn** [jɜ:n] *v. i.* ~ for *or* after sth./for sb. sich nach etw./jmdm. sehnen; ~ to do sth. sich danach sehnen, etw. zu tun. **'yearning** *n.* Sehnsucht, *die*

**yeast** [ji:st] *n.* Hefe, *die*

**yell** [jel] 1. *n.* gellender Schrei. 2. *v. t. & i.* [gellend] schreien

**yellow** ['jeləʊ] 1. *adj.* gelb. 2. *n.* Gelb, *das.* **'yellowish** *adj.* gelblich

**yelp** [jelp] 1. *v. i.* jaulen. 2. *n.* Jaulen, *das*

**yen** [jen] *n. (coll.: longing)* sb. has a ~ to do sth. es drängt jmdn. danach, etw. zu tun

**yes** [jes] 1. *adv.* ja; *(in contradiction)* doch. 2. *n., pl.* ~es Ja, *das*

**yesterday** ['jestədeɪ, 'jestədɪ] 1. *n.* gestern; the day before ~: vorgestern; ~'s paper die gestrige Zeitung. 2. *adv.* gestern; the day before ~: vorgestern

**yet** [jet] 1. *adv.* a) *(still)* noch; ~ again noch einmal; b) *(hitherto)* bisher; his best ~: sein bisher bestes; c) *neg.* not |just| ~: [jetzt] noch nicht; d) *(before all is over)* doch noch; he could win ~: er könnte noch gewinnen; e) *with compar. (even)* noch; f) *(nevertheless)* doch. 2. *conj.* doch

**yew** [ju:] *n.* ~[-tree] Eibe, *die*

**Yiddish** ['jɪdɪʃ] 1. *adj.* jiddisch. 2. *n.* Jiddisch, *das; see also* **English 2 a**

**yield** [ji:ld] 1. *v. t. (give)* bringen; hervorbringen ⟨Ernte⟩; abwerfen ⟨Gewinn⟩. 2. *v. i.* a) sich unterwerfen; b) *(give right of way)* Vorfahrt gewähren. 3. *n.* Ertrag, *der*

**yodel** ['jəʊdl] *v. i. & t., (Brit.)* -ll- jodeln

**yoga** ['jəʊgə] *n.* Joga, *der od. das*

**yoghurt, yogurt** ['jɒgət] *n.* Joghurt, *der od. das*

**yoke** [jəʊk] *n.* Joch, *das*

**yokel** ['jəʊkl] *n.* [Bauern]tölpel, *der*

**yolk** [jəʊk] *n.* Dotter, *der;* Eigelb, *das*

**yonder** ['jɒndə(r)] *(literary)* 1. *adj.* ~ tree jener Baum dort *(geh.).* 2. *adv.* dort drüben

**you** [ju, *stressed* ju:] *pron.* a) *sing./pl.* du/ihr; *(polite) sing. or pl.* Sie; *as direct object* dich/euch/Sie; *as indirect object* dir/euch/Ihnen; *refl.* dich/dir/euch; *(polite)* sich; it was ~: du warst/ihr wart/Sie waren es; b) *(one)* man

**you'd** [jʊd, *stressed* ju:d] a) = you had; b) = you would

**you'll** [jʊl, *stressed* ju:l] a) = you will; b) = you shall

**young** [jʌŋ] 1. *adj.*, ~er ['jʌŋgə(r)], ~est ['jʌŋgɪst] jung. 2. *n. pl. (of animals)* Junge; the ~ (~ people) die jungen Leute. **youngster** ['jʌŋstə(r)] *n.* a) *(child)* Kleine, *der/die/das;* b) *(young person)* Jugendliche, *der/die*

**your** [jə(r), *stressed* jʊə(r), jɔ:(r)] *poss. pron. attrib.: sing.* dein; *pl.* euer; *(polite) sing. or pl.* Ihr

**you're** [jə(r), *stressed* jʊə(r), jɔ:(r)] = you are

**yours** [jʊəz, jɔ:z] *poss. pron. pred.: sing.* deiner/deine/dein[e]s; *pl.* eurer/eure/eures; *(polite) sing. or pl.* Ihrer/Ihre/Ihr[e]s; *see also* **hers**

**yourself** [jə'self, jʊə'self, jɔ:'self] *pron.* a) *emphat.* selbst; b) *refl.* dich/dir/*(polite)* sich. *See also* **herself**

**yourselves** [jə'selvz, jʊə'selvz, jɔ:'selvz] *pron.* a) *emphat.* selbst; b) *refl.* euch/*(polite)* sich. *See also* **herself**

**youth** [ju:θ] *n.* a) Jugend, *die;* b) *pl.* ~s [ju:ðz] *(young man)* Jugendliche, *der.* **'youth club** *n.* Jugendklub, *der*

**youthful** ['ju:θfl] *adj.* jugendlich

**youth hostel** *n.* Jugendherberge, *die*

**you've** [jʊv, *stressed* ju:v] = you have

**Yugoslav** ['ju:gəslɑ:v] *see* **Yugoslavian**

**Yugoslavia** [ju:gə'slɑ:vɪə] *pr. n. (Hist.)* Jugoslawien *(das).* **Yugoslavian** [ju:gə'slɑ:vɪən] *(Hist.)* 1. *adj.* jugoslawisch. 2. *n.* Jugoslawe, *der/* Jugoslawin, *die*

# Z

**Z, z** [zed, *(Amer.)* zi:] *n.* Z, z, *das*
**Zaire** [zɑː'ɪə(r)] *pr. n.* Zaire *(das)*
**Zambia** ['zæmbɪə] *pr. n.* Sambia *(das)*
**zany** ['zeɪnɪ] *adj.* irre komisch *(ugs.);*
  Wahnsinns‹*humor, -komiker*›
**zeal** [ziːl] *n.* Eifer, *der.* **zealous** ['zeləs]
  *adj.* eifrig
**zebra** ['zebrə, 'ziːbrə] *n.* Zebra, *das.*
  **zebra 'crossing** *n. (Brit.)* Zebrastreifen, *der*
**zenith** ['zenɪθ] *n.* Zenit, *der*
**zero** ['zɪərəʊ] *n., pl.* ~s Null, *die*
**zest** [zest] *n. (enthusiasm)* Begeisterung, *die;* ~ **for living** Lebenslust, *die*
**zigzag** ['zɪgzæg] **1.** *adj.* zickzackför-

mig; Zickzack‹*muster, -anordnung*›.
**2.** *n.* Zickzacklinie, *die*
**Zimbabwe** [zɪm'bɑːbwɪ] *pr. n.* Simbabwe *(das)*
**zinc** [zɪŋk] *n.* Zink, *das*
**zip** [zɪp] **1.** *n.* Reißverschluß, *der.* **2.**
  *v. t.,* **-pp-:** ~ |up| sth. den Reißver-
  schluß an etw. *(Dat.)* zuziehen
**'Zip code** *n. (Amer.)* Postleitzahl, *die*
**zip-fastener** *see* zip 1
**zipper** ['zɪpə(r)] *see* zip 1
**zither** ['zɪðə(r)] *n.* Zither, *die*
**zodiac** ['zəʊdɪæk] *n.* Tierkreis, *der;*
  **sign of the** ~: Tierkreiszeichen, *das*
**zombie** *(Amer.:* **zombi**) ['zɒmbɪ] *n.*
  Zombie, *der*
**zone** [zəʊn] *n.* Zone, *die*
**zoo** [zuː] *n.* Zoo, *der*
**zoological** [zəʊə'lɒdʒɪkl] *adj.* zoologisch
**zoologist** [zəʊ'ɒlədʒɪst] *n.* Zoologe,
  *der/*Zoologin, *die*
**zoology** [zəʊ'ɒlədʒɪ] *n.* Zoologie, *die*
**zoom** [zuːm] *v. i.* rauschen. **zoom 'in
  on** *v. t. (Cinemat., Telev.)* zoomen auf
  *(+ Akk.)*
**'zoom lens** *n.* Zoomobjektiv, *das*

# A

**a, A** [a:] *das;* ~, ~ **a)** *(Buchstabe)* a/A; **das A und O** *(fig.)* the essential thing/ things (*Gen.* for); **von A bis Z** *(fig. ugs.)* from beginning to end; **b)** *(Musik)* [key of] A

**a** *Abk.* Ar, Are

**à** [a] *Präp. mit Nom., Akk. (Kaufmannsspr.)* **zehn Marken à 50 Pfennig** ten stamps at 50 pfennigs each

**A** *Abk.* Autobahn ≈ M

**Aal** *der;* ~|e|s, ~e eel; ~ **grün** *(Kochk.)* green eels; stewed eels; **aalen** *refl. V. (ugs.)* stretch out; **aal·glatt** *(abwertend)* **1.** *Adj.* slippery; ~ **sein** be as slippery as an eel; **2.** *adv.* smoothly

**Aas** *das;* ~es, ~e *od.* Äser **a)** *o. Pl.* carrion *no art.;* **b)** *Pl.* ~e *[rotting]* carcass; **c)** *Pl.* Äser *(salopp) (abwertend)* swine; *(anerkennend)* devil

**ab 1.** *Präp. mit Dat.* **a)** from; **ab 1980** as from 1980; **ab Werk** *(Kaufmannsspr.)* ex works; **ab Frankfurt fliegen** fly from Frankfurt; **b)** *([Rang]folge)* from ... on[wards]; **ab 20 DM** from 20 DM [upwards]; **2.** *Adv.* **a)** *(weg)* off; away; **b)** *(ugs.: Aufforderung)* off; away; **ab nach Hause** get off home; **c)** **Gewehr ab!** *(milit. Kommando)* order arms!; **d) ab und zu** *od.* **an** now and then

**ab|ändern** *tr. V.* alter; amend ⟨*text*⟩; **Ab·änderung** *die* alteration; *(eines Textes)* amendment

**ab|arbeiten** *tr. V.* work for ⟨*meal*⟩; work off ⟨*debt, amount*⟩

**ab·artig** *Adj.* deviant; abnormal

**Abb.** *Abk.* Abbildung Fig.

**Ab·bau** *der* **a)** dismantling; *(von Zelten, Lagern)* striking; **b)** *s.* **abbauen c:** cutback (*Gen.* in); pruning; reduction; **c)** *(Bergbau)* mining; *(von Stein)* quarrying

**ab|bauen** *tr. V.* **a)** dismantle; strike ⟨*tent, camp*⟩; **b)** *(beseitigen)* gradually remove; break down ⟨*prejudices, inhibitions*⟩; **c)** *(verringern)* cut back

⟨*staff*⟩; prune ⟨*jobs*⟩; reduce ⟨*wages*⟩; **d)** *(Bergbau)* mine; quarry ⟨*stone*⟩

**ab|beißen 1)** *unr. tr. V.* bite off; **2.** *unr. itr. V.* have a bite

**ab|bekommen** *unr. tr. V.* **a)** get; **b) einen Schlag/ein paar Kratzer ~:** get hit/get a few scratches; **etwas ~** *(getroffen werden)* be hit; *(verletzt werden)* be hurt; **c)** *(los-, herunterbekommen)* get ⟨*paint, lid, chain*⟩ off

**ab|berufen** *unr. tr. V.* recall ⟨*ambassador, envoy*⟩ (aus, von from)

**ab|bestellen** *tr. V.* cancel

**ab|bezahlen** *tr. V.* pay off

**ab|biegen** *unr. itr. V.; mit sein* turn off; **links/rechts ~:** turn [off] left/right

**Ab·bild** *das (eines Menschen)* likeness; *(eines Gegenstandes)* copy; *(fig.)* portrayal; **ab|bilden** *tr. V.* copy; reproduce ⟨*object, picture*⟩; depict ⟨*person, landscape*⟩; *(fig.)* portray; **Abbildung** *die* illustration

**ab|binden** *unr. tr. V.* **a)** *(losbinden)* untie; undo; **b)** *(abschnüren)* put a tourniquet on ⟨*artery, arm, leg, etc.*⟩; tie ⟨*umbilical cord*⟩

**ab|blasen** *unr. tr. V. (ugs.)* call off

**ab|blättern** *itr. V.; mit sein* flake off

**ab|blenden** *itr. V.* dip *(Brit.)* or *(Amer.)* dim one's headlight; **Abblend·licht** *das* dipped *(Brit.)* or *(Amer.)* dimmed beam

**ab|blitzen** *itr. V.; mit sein (ugs.)* **sie ließ alle Verehrer ~:** she gave all her admirers the brush-off

**ab|brausen** *tr. V.: s.* abduschen

**ab|brechen 1.** *unr. tr. V.* **a)** break off; break ⟨*needle, pencil*⟩; **b)** *(zerlegen)* strike ⟨*tent, camp*⟩; **c)** *(abreißen)* demolish, pull down ⟨*building*⟩; **d)** *(beenden)* break off ⟨*negotiations, [diplomatic] relations, discussion, activity*⟩; *(vorzeitig)* cut short ⟨*conversation, holiday, activity*⟩; **2.** *unr. itr. V.* **a)** *mit sein* break [off]; **b)** *(aufhören)* break off

**ab|bremsen** 1. *tr. V.* a) brake; b) retard ⟨*motion*⟩; 2. *itr. V.* brake

**ab|brennen** 1. *unr. itr. V.; mit sein* a) be burned down; **das Haus ist abgebrannt** the house has burned down; b) ⟨*fuse*⟩ burn away; ⟨*candle*⟩ burn down; 2. *unr. tr. V.* a) let off ⟨*firework*⟩; b) burn down ⟨*building*⟩

**ab|bringen** *unr. tr. V.* **jmdn. davon ~, etw. zu tun** dissuade sb. from doing sth. **jmdn. vom Kurs ~:** make sb. change course

**ab|bröckeln** *itr. V.; mit sein (auch fig.)* crumble away

**Ab·bruch** *der* a) *o. Pl.* demolition; pulling down; b) *(Beendigung)* breaking-off; c) **einer Sache** *(Dat.)* **[keinen] ~ tun** do [no] harm to sth.

**ab|buchen** *tr. V.* ⟨*bank*⟩ debit (**von** to); ⟨*creditor*⟩ claim by direct debit (**von** to)

**ab|bürsten** *tr. V.* a) brush off; b) *(säubern)* brush ⟨*garment*⟩

**ab|büßen** *tr. V.* serve [out] ⟨*prison sentence*⟩

**Abc** [a(:)be(:)'tse:] *das;* **~** *(auch fig.)* ABC; **Abc-Schütze** *der* child just starting school

**ab|dampfen** *itr. V.; mit sein (ugs.: abfahren)* set off

**ab|danken** *itr. V.* ⟨*ruler*⟩ abdicate; ⟨*government, minister*⟩ resign; **Abdankung** *die;* **~, ~en** *s.* **abdanken:** abdication; resignation

**ab|decken** 1. *tr. V.* a) open up; ⟨*gale*⟩ take the roof/roofs off ⟨*house*⟩, take the tiles off ⟨*roof*⟩; b) *(herunternehmen, -reißen)* take off; c) *(abräumen)* clear ⟨*table*⟩; clear away ⟨*dishes*⟩; d) *(schützen)* cover ⟨*person*⟩

**ab|dichten** *tr. V.* seal

**ab|drängen** *tr. V.* push away

**ab|drehen** 1. *tr. V.* a) *(ausschalten)* turn off; **den Hahn ~** *(fig.)* turn off the supply; b) *(abtrennen)* twist off; 2. *itr. V.; meist mit sein* turn off

**Ab·druck** *der; Pl.* **Abdrücke** mark; *(Fuß~)* footprint; *(Wachs~)* impression; *(Gips~)* cast; **ab|drücken** 1. *itr. V.* pull the trigger; shoot; 2. *tr. V. (zudrücken)* constrict

**ab|dunkeln** *tr. V.* darken ⟨*room*⟩; dim ⟨*light*⟩

**ab|duschen** *tr. V.* **sich/jmdn. [warm] ~:** take/give sb. a [hot] shower

**abend** *Adv.* **heute/morgen/gestern ~:** this/tomorrow/yesterday evening; **Abend** *der;* **~s, ~e** evening; **guten ~!** good evening; **am [frühen/späten] ~:** [early/late] in the evening; **zu ~ essen** have dinner; *(allgemeiner)* have one's evening meal; **ein bunter ~:** a social [evening]

**Abend-:** **~an·zug** *der* evening suit; **~brot** *das* supper; **~essen** *das* dinner; **~kasse** *die* box-office *(open on the evening of the performance);* **~kleid** *das* evening dress; **~kurs[us]** *der* evening class; **~land** *das; o. Pl.* West

**abendlich** *Adj.* evening; ⟨*quiet, coolness*⟩ of the evening

**Abend-:** **~mahl** *das; o. Pl. (Rel.)* Communion; *(N.T.)* Last Supper; **~programm** *das* evening programmes *pl.;* **~rot** *das* red glow of the sunset sky

**abends** *Adv.* in the evenings; **um sechs Uhr ~:** at six o'clock in the evening

**Abend-:** **~schule** *die* night school; **~stern** *der* evening star; **~stunde** *die* evening hour; **~vorstellung** *die* evening performance

**Abenteuer** *das;* **~s, ~** a) *(auch fig.)* adventure; b) *(Unternehmen)* venture; c) *(Liebesaffäre)* affair; **abenteuerlich** *Adj.* a) *(riskant)* risky; b) *(bizarr)* bizarre; **Abenteuer·roman** *der* adventure novel; **Abenteurer** *der;* **~s, ~:** adventurer

**aber** 1. *Konj.* but; 2. *Partikel* **~ ja/nein!** why, yes/no! **~ natürlich!** but of course!; **du bist ~ groß!** aren't you tall!

**Aber·glaube[n]** *der* superstition; **aber·gläubisch** *Adj.* superstitious

**abermals** *Adv.* once again; once more

**Abf.** *Abk.* **Abfahrt** dep.

**ab|fahren** 1. *unr. itr. V.; mit sein* a) *(wegfahren)* leave; **wo fährt der Zug nach Paris ab?** where does the Paris train leave from?; b) *(hinunterfahren)* drive down; *(Skisport)* ski down; 2. *unr. tr. V.* a) *(abtransportieren)* take away; b) *(abnutzen)* wear out; **abgefahrene Reifen** worn tyres; **Ab·fahrt** *die* a) departure; b) *(Skisport)* descent; *(Strecke)* run; **Abfahrtslauf** *der (Skisport)* downhill [racing]; **Abfahrt[s]·zeit** *die* time of departure; departure time

**Ab·fall** *der (Küchen~ o. ä.)* rubbish, *(Amer.)* trash *no indef. art., no pl.;* *(Fleisch~)* offal *no indef. art., no pl.;* *(Industrie~)* waste *no indef. art.;* *(auf der Straße)* litter *no indef. art., no pl.;* **Abfall·eimer** *der* rubbish bin; trash can *(Amer.);* *(auf der Straße)* litter bin;

trash can *(Amer.)*; **ab|fallen** *unr. itr. V.; mit sein* **a)** fall off; **b)** *(abschüssig sein)* ⟨*land, road, etc.*⟩ drop away, slope; **c)** *(übrigbleiben)* be left [over]; **für dich wird [dabei] auch etwas ~:** you'll get something out of it too; **d) von jmdm. ~:** leave sb.; **vom Glauben ~:** desert the faith; **ab · fällig 1.** *Adj.* disparaging; **2.** *adv.* **sich ~ über jmdn. äußern** make disparaging remarks about sb.

**ab|fangen** *unr. tr. V.* catch; intercept ⟨*agent, message, aircraft*⟩; **b)** repel ⟨*charge, assault*⟩; ward off ⟨*blow, attack*⟩

**ab|färben** *itr. V.* **a)** ⟨*colour, garment, etc.*⟩ run; **b) auf jmdn./etw. ~** *(fig.)* rub off on sb./sth.

**ab|fassen** *tr. V.* write ⟨*report, letter, etc.*⟩; draw up ⟨*will*⟩

**ab|fegen** *tr. V.* **a)** brush off; **etw. von etw. ~:** brush sth. off sth.; **b)** *(säubern)* **etw. ~:** brush sth. clean

**ab|fertigen** *tr. V.* dispatch ⟨*mail*⟩; deal with ⟨*applicant*⟩; handle ⟨*passengers*⟩; serve ⟨*customer*⟩; clear ⟨*ship*⟩ for sailing; clear ⟨*aircraft*⟩ for take-off; clear ⟨*lorry*⟩ for departure

**ab|feuern** *tr. V.* fire

**ab|finden 1.** *unr. tr. V.* **a) jmdn. mit etw. ~:** compensate sb. with sth.; **seine Gläubiger ~:** settle with one's creditors; **2.** *unr. refl. V.* **sich ~:** resign oneself; **sich ~ mit** come to terms with; learn to live with ⟨*noise, heat*⟩; **Abfindung die; ~, ~en** settlement; **eine ~ in Höhe von ... zahlen** make a settlement of ...

**ab|flauen** *itr. V.; mit sein* die down; subside; ⟨*interest, conversation*⟩ flag; ⟨*business*⟩ become slack; ⟨*noise*⟩ abate

**ab|fliegen** *unr. itr. V.; mit sein* leave

**ab|fließen** *unr. itr. V.; mit sein* flow off

**Ab · flug der** departure

**Ab · fluß der** drain; *(Rohr)* drain-pipe; *(für Abwasser)* waste-pipe

**ab|fragen** *tr. V.* test; **jmdn. od. jmdm. die Vokabeln ~:** test sb. on his/her vocabulary

**Abfuhr die; ~, ~en a)** removal; **b) jmdm. eine ~ erteilen** *(fig. ugs.)* rebuff sb.; **ab|führen 1.** *tr. V.* **a)** *(nach Festnahme)* take away; **b)** *(zahlen)* pay out; **c)** *(abbringen)* take away; **2.** *itr. V.* *(für Stuhlgang sorgen)* be a laxative; **Abführ · mittel das** laxative

**ab|füllen** *tr. V.* *(in Flaschen)* bottle; *(in Dosen)* can

**Ab · gabe die a)** handing in; *(eines Briefes, Pakets, Telegramms)* delivery; *(eines Gesuchs, Antrags)* submission; **b)** *(Steuer, Gebühr)* tax; *(auf Produkte)* duty; **c)** *(Ausstrahlung)* release; emission; **d)** *(Sport: Abspiel)* pass

**Ab · gang der a)** leaving; departure; *(Abfahrt)* departure; *(Theater)* exit; **b)** *(jmd., der ausscheidet)* departure; *(Schule)* leaver; **c)** *(bes. Amtsspr.: Todesfall)* death; **d)** *(Turnen)* dismount

**Ab · gas das** exhaust

**abgearbeitet** *Adj.* work-worn ⟨*hands*⟩

**ab|geben 1.** *unr. tr. V.* **a)** *(aushändigen)* hand over; deliver ⟨*letter, parcel, telegram*⟩; hand in, submit ⟨*application*⟩; hand in ⟨*school work*⟩; **den Mantel in der Garderobe ~:** leave one's coat in the cloakroom; **b)** *auch itr.* **jmdm. [etwas] von etw. ~:** let sb. have some of sth.; **c)** *(abfeuern)* fire; **2.** *unr. refl. V.* **sich mit jmdm./etw. ~:** spend time on sb./sth.; *(geringschätzig)* waste one's time on sb./sth

**ab · gebrannt** *Adj.* *(ugs.)* broke *(coll.)*

**abgebrüht** *Adj.* *(ugs.)* hardened

**ab · gedroschen** *Adj.* *(ugs.)* hackneyed

**ab · gegriffen** *Adj.* battered

**ab|gehen** *unr. itr. V.; mit sein* **a)** *(sich entfernen)* leave; *(Theater)* exit; **b)** *(ausscheiden)* leave; **c)** *(abfahren)* ⟨*train, ship, bus*⟩ leave, depart; **d)** *(abgeschickt werden)* ⟨*message, letter*⟩ be sent [off]; **e)** *(abzweigen)* branch off; **f)** *(sich lösen)* come off

**abgehetzt** *Adj.* exhausted

**ab · gelegen** *Adj.* remote; *(einsam)* isolated; out-of-the-way ⟨*district*⟩

**ab · geneigt** *Adj.* averse *(Dat.* to); **[nicht] ~ sein, etw. zu tun** [not] be averse to doing sth.

**Abgeordnete der/die;** *adj. Dekl.* member [of parliament]; *(z. B. in Frankreich)* deputy

**ab · gerissen** *Adj.* ragged

**ab · geschlagen** *Adj.* *(Sport)* [well] beaten

**ab · geschlossen** *Adj.* secluded

**ab · gesehen** *Adv.* **~ von** apart from; **~ davon, daß ...** apart from the fact that ...

**ab · gespannt** *Adj.* weary; exhausted

**ab · gestanden** *Adj.* flat

**ab · gestorben** *Adj.* dead ⟨*branch, tree*⟩; numb ⟨*fingers, legs, etc.*⟩

**ab · getreten** *Adj.* worn down

**abgewetzt** *Adj.* well-worn; battered ⟨*case etc.*⟩

**ab|gewöhnen** *tr. V.:* jmdm. etw. ~:
make sb. give up sth.; **sich** *(Dat.)* etw.
~: give up sth.

**ab|gießen** *unr. tr. V.* pour away ⟨*li-
quid*⟩; drain ⟨*potatoes*⟩

**abgöttisch** *Adj.* idolatrous

**ab|grenzen** *tr. V.* a) bound; etw. gegen
*od.* von etw. ~: separate sth. from sth.;
b) *(unterscheiden)* distinguish

**Ab·grund** der abyss; chasm; *(Abhang)*
precipice

**ab|hacken** *tr. V.* chop off; jmdm. die
Hand *usw.* ~: chop sb.'s hand *etc.* off

**ab|haken** *tr. V.* tick off; check off
*(Amer.)*

**ab|halten** *unr. tr. V.* a) jmdn./etw. |von
jmdm./etw.| ~: keep sb./sth. off
[sb./sth.]; b) jmdn. davon ~, etw. zu tun
stop sb. doing sth.; c) *(durchführen)*
hold ⟨*elections, meeting, referendum*⟩

**ab|handeln** *tr. V.* a) jmdm. etw. ~: do a
deal with sb. for sth.; b) *(darstellen)*
deal with

**abhanden** *Adv.* ~ kommen get lost; go
astray; etw. kommt jmdm. ~: sb. loses
sth.

**Ab·handlung** die treatise (über +
*Akk.* on)

**Ab·hang** der slope; incline; ¹**ab|hän-
gen** *unr. itr. V.* von jmdm./etw. ~: de-
pend on sb./sth.; ²**ab|hängen** 1. *tr. V.*
a) take down; b) *(abkuppeln)* un-
couple; c) *(ugs.)* shake off *(coll.)* ⟨*pur-
suer, competitor*⟩. 2. *itr. V. (den Hörer
auflegen)* hang up; **abhängig** *Adj.*
dependent (**von** on); *(süchtig)* addicted
(**von** to); **von** jmdm./etw. ~ **sein** depend
on sb./sth.; **Abhängigkeit** die; ~,
~en dependence; *(Sucht)* addiction

**ab|härten** *tr. V.* harden

**ab|hauen** 1. *unr. tr. V.* a) *Prät.* **haute
ab** knock off; b) *Prät.* **hieb** *(geh.) od.*
**haute ab** *(mit Schwert, Axt usw.)* chop
off; 2. *unr. itr. V.; mit sein; Prät.* **haute
ab** *(salopp)* beat it *(sl.)*

**ab|heben** 1. *unr. tr. V.* a) lift off ⟨*lid,
cover, etc.*⟩; |den Hörer| ~: answer [the
telephone]; b) *(von einem Konto)* withdraw ⟨*money*⟩; 2. *unr. itr. V.* ⟨*balloon*⟩
rise; ⟨*aircraft, bird*⟩ take off; ⟨*rocket*⟩
lift off; 3. *unr. refl. V.* stand out (**von**
against)

**ab|heften** *tr. V.* file

**ab|hetzen** *refl. V.* rush [around]; *s.
auch* abgehetzt

**Ab·hilfe** die; *o. Pl.* action to improve
matters; ~ **schaffen** put things right

**ab|holen** *tr. V.* collect, pick up ⟨*parcel,
book, tickets, etc.*⟩; pick up ⟨*person*⟩

**ab|hören** *tr. V.* a) jmdm. *od.* jmdn. Vo-
kabeln ~: test sb.'s vocabulary [orally];
das Einmaleins ~: ask questions on the
multiplication table; b) tap ⟨*telephone
conversation, telephone*⟩; bug *(coll.)*
⟨*conversation, premises*⟩; jmdn. ~: tap
sb.'s telephone

**Abi** das; ~s, ~s *(Schülerspr.)*, **Abitur**
das; ~s, ~e Abitur *(school-leaving examination at grammar school needed
for entry to higher education);* ≈ A
levels *(Brit.);* **Abiturient** der; ~en,
~en sb. who is taking/has passed the
'Abitur'

**ab|jagen** *tr. V.* jmdm. etw. ~: finally
get sth. away from sb.

**Abk.** *Abk.* Abkürzung abbr.

**ab|kaufen** *tr. V.* jmdm. etw. ~: buy sth.
from sb.

**ab|klopfen** *tr. V.* a) knock off; b) *(säu-
bern)* knock the dirt/snow/crumbs *etc.*
off; c) *(untersuchen)* tap

**ab|knicken** 1. *tr. V.* snap off; 2. *itr. V.;
mit sein* snap

**ab|kochen** *tr. V.* boil

**ab|kommen** *unr. itr. V.; mit sein* a)
vom Weg ~: lose one's way; vom Kurs
~: go off course; von der Fahrbahn ~:
leave the road; vom Thema ~: stray
from the topic; b) von einem Plan ~:
abandon a plan; **Ab·kommen das**;
~s, ~: agreement; **abkömmlich** *Adj.*
free; available

**ab|kratzen** 1. *tr. V.* a) *(mit den Fin-
gern)* scratch off; *(mit einem Werkzeug)* scrape off; b) *(säubern)* scrape
[clean]; 2. *itr. V.; mit sein (derb)* snuff it
*(sl.)*

**ab|kriegen** *tr. V. (ugs.) s.* abbekommen

**ab|kühlen** 1. *tr. V.* cool down; 2. *itr.,
refl. V.; itr. meist mit sein* cool down;
**Ab·kühlung die** cooling

**ab|kürzen** *tr., itr. V.* a) *(räumlich)*
shorten; den Weg ~: take a shorter
route; b) *(zeitlich)* cut short; c) *(kürzer
schreiben)* abbreviate (**mit** to); **Abkürzung die** a) *(Weg)* short cut; b) *(Wort)*
abbreviation

**ab|laden** *unr. tr., itr. V.* unload

**ab|lagern** *tr. V.* deposit

**ab|lassen** 1. *unr. tr. V.* let out (**aus** of);
let off ⟨*steam*⟩; 2. *unr. itr. V.* a) von
jmdm./etw. ~: leave sb./sth. alone; b)
von etw. ~ *(etw. aufgeben)* give sth. up

**Ab·lauf der** a) *(Verlauf)* course; *(einer
Veranstaltung)* passing off; b) *o. Pl.
(Ende)* **nach ~ eines Jahres** after a year;
**nach ~ einer Frist** at the end of a
period of time; **ab|laufen** *unr. itr. V.;*

*mit sein* **a)** flow away; *(aus einem Behälter)* run out; **b)** *(verlaufen)* pass off; **c)** ⟨*alarm clock*⟩ run down; ⟨*parking meter*⟩ expire; **d)** ⟨*period, contract, passport*⟩ expire

**ạb|lecken** *tr. V.* **a)** lick off; **b)** *(säubern)* lick clean

**ạb|legen 1.** *tr. V.* **a)** lay *or* put down; **b)** *(Bürow.)* file; **c)** stop wearing ⟨*clothes*⟩; **d)** give up ⟨*habit*⟩; lose ⟨*shyness*⟩; **e)** swear ⟨*oath*⟩; sit ⟨*examination*⟩; make ⟨*confession*⟩; **2.** *tr., itr. V.* take off; **möchten Sie ~?** would you like to take your coat off?; **3.** *itr. V.* |vom Kai| ~: cast off; **Ạbleger der;** ~s, ~: layer; *(Steckling)* cutting

**ạb|lehnen** *tr. V.* **a)** decline; decline, turn down ⟨*money, invitation, position*⟩; reject ⟨*suggestion, applicant*⟩; **b)** *(mißbilligen)* diapprove of; **Ạblehnung die;** ~, ~**en a)** rejection; **b)** *(Mißbilligung)* disapproval

**ạb|leiten** *tr. V.* **a)** divert; **b)** *(herleiten)* etw. aus/von etw. ~: derive sth. from sth.; **Ạb·leitung die** derivation

**ạb|lenken** *tr. V.* **a)** deflect; **b)** jmdn. von etw. ~: distract sb. from sth.; **c)** *(zerstreuen)* divert; **sich** ~: amuse oneself; **Ạb·lenkung die** *s.* **ablenken:** deflection; distraction; diversion

**ạb|lesen** *unr. tr. V.* **a)** read ⟨*speech, lecture*⟩; **werden Sie frei sprechen oder** ~? will you be talking from notes or reading your speech?; **b)** read ⟨*gas meter, thermometer, etc.*⟩; check ⟨*time, speed, temperature*⟩; **c)** *(erkennen)* see

**ạb|liefern** *tr., itr. V.* hand in; deliver ⟨*goods*⟩

**ạb|lösen 1.** *tr. V.* **a)** etw. |von etw.| ~: get sth. off [sth.]; **b)** jmdn. ~: relieve sb.; **sich** *od.* **einander** ~: take turns; **2.** *refl. V.* sich |von etw.| ~: come off [sth.]

**Ạb·lösung die** *(eines Postens)* changing; **ich schicke Ihnen jemanden zur** ~: I'll send someone to relieve you

**ạb|machen** *tr. V.* **a)** *(ugs.)* take off; take down ⟨*sign, rope*⟩; **b)** *(vereinbaren)* agree; **Ạbmachung die;** ~, ~**en** agreement

**ạb|magern** *itr. V.; mit sein* become thin; *(absichtlich)* slim; **Ạbmagerungs·kur die** reducing diet

**ạb|marschieren** *itr. V.; mit sein* depart; *(Milit.)* march off

**ạb|melden** *tr. V.* **a)** sich/jmdn. ~: report that one/sb. is leaving; **b)** *(Umzug melden)* notify the authorities that one is moving from an address; **c)** ein Auto ~: cancel a car's registration; **Ạb·meldung die a)** *(beim Weggehen)* report that one is leaving; **b)** *(beim Umzug)* registration of a move with the authorities at one's old address; **c)** ~ **eines Autos** cancellation of a car's registration

**Ạb·messung die** *meist Pl. (Dimension)* dimension; measurement

**ạb|montieren** *tr. V.* take off ⟨*part*⟩; dismantle ⟨*machine, equipment*⟩

**ạb|mühen** *refl. V.* toil; **sie mühte sich mit dem schweren Koffer ab** she struggled with the heavy suitcase

**Ạbnahme die;** ~, ~**n a)** *o. Pl. (das Entfernen)* removal; **b)** *(Verminderung)* decrease; **ạb|nehmen 1.** *unr. tr. V.* **a)** *(entfernen)* take off; take down ⟨*picture, curtain, lamp*⟩; **b)** jmdm. den Koffer ~: take sb.'s suitcase; jmdm. eine Arbeit ~: save sb. a job; **c)** jmdm. ein Versprechen/einen Eid ~: make sb. give a promise/swear an oath; **d)** *(prüfen)* inspect and approve; test and pass ⟨*vehicle*⟩; **e)** jmdm. etw. ~ *(wegnehmen)* take sth. off sb.; **f)** *(beim Telefon)* answer ⟨*telephone*⟩; pick up ⟨*receiver*⟩; **g)** *(Handarb.)* decrease; **h)** **das nehme ich dir/ihm** *usw.* **nicht ab** I won't buy that *(coll.)*; **2.** *unr. itr. V.* **a)** *(Gewicht verlieren)* lose weight; **b)** *(sich verringern)* decrease; drop; ⟨*attention, interest*⟩ flag; ⟨*brightness*⟩ diminish; **wir haben** ~**den Mond** there is a waning moon; **c)** *(beim Telefon)* answer the telephone

**Ạb·neigung die** dislike **(gegen for)**

**ạb|nutzen,** *(landsch.:)* **ạb|nützen** *tr., refl. V.* wear out; **abgenutzt** worn

**Abonnement** [abɔnə'mã:] **das;** ~s, ~s subscription *(Gen.* to); **abonnieren** *tr. V.* subscribe to

**Ạb·ordnung die** delegation

**ạb|passen** *tr. V.* **a)** *(abwarten)* wait for; **b)** *(aufhalten)* catch

**ạb|pausen** *tr. V.* trace

**ạb|pfeifen** *(Sport)* **1.** *itr. V.* blow the whistle; **2.** *tr. V.* [blow the whistle to] stop; **Ạb·pfiff der** *(Sport)* final whistle; *(Halbzeit~)* half-time whistle

**ạb|pflücken** *tr. V.* pick

**ạb|plagen** *refl. V.* slave away

**ạb|prallen** *itr. V.; mit sein* rebound; ⟨*bullet, missile*⟩ ricochet

**ạb|putzen** *tr. V. (ugs.);* **a)** wipe off; **b)** *(säubern)* wipe; **jmdm./sich das Gesicht** ~: clean sb.'s/one's face

**ạb|quälen** *refl. V.* **sich |mit etw.|** ~: struggle [with sth.]

**ạb|rackern** *refl. V. (ugs.)* flog oneself to death *(coll.)*

**ab|rasieren** *tr. V.* shave off

**ab|raten** *unr. itr. V.* **jmdm. von etw. ~:** advise sb. against sth.

**ab|räumen** *tr. V.* **a)** clear away; **b)** *(leer machen)* clear ⟨*table*⟩

**ab|rechnen 1.** *itr. V.* cash up; **mit jmdm. ~** *(fig.)* call sb. to account; **2.** *tr. V.* **die Kasse ~:** reckon up the till; **seine Spesen ~:** claim one's expenses; **Ab·rechnung die a)** cashing up *no art.; (Aufstellung)* statement; **b)** *(fig.: Vergeltung)* reckoning

**ab|reiben** *unr. tr. V.* **a)** rub off; **b)** *(säubern)* rub

**Ab·reise die** departure **(nach** for); **bei meiner ~:** when I left/leave; **ab|reisen** *itr. V.; mit sein* leave **(nach** for)

**ab|reißen 1.** *unr. tr. V.* **a)** tear off; tear down ⟨*poster, notice*⟩; pull off ⟨*button*⟩; **b)** *(niederreißen)* demolish, pull down ⟨*building*⟩; **2.** *unr. itr. V.; mit sein* **a)** fly off; ⟨*shoe-lace*⟩ break off; **b)** *(aufhören)* come to an end; ⟨*connection, contact*⟩ be broken off

**ab|richten** *tr. V.* train

**Ab·riß der a)** *o. Pl.: s.* **abreißen 1 b:** demolition; pulling down; **b)** *(knappe Darstellung)* outline

**ab|rollen 1.** *tr. V.* unwind; **2.** *itr. V.; mit sein* unwind [itself]

**ab|rücken 1.** *tr. V. (wegschieben)* move away; **2.** *itr. V.; mit sein* move away

**Ab·ruf der: auf ~:** on call; *(DV)* in retrievable form; **ab|rufen** *unr. tr. V.* summon; call

**ab|runden** *tr. V.* **a)** *(auch fig.)* round off; **b)** round ⟨*figure*⟩ up/down **(auf +** **Akk.** to); **etw. nach oben/unten ~:** round sth. up/down

**abrupt** [ap'rʊpt] **1.** *Adj.* abrupt; **2.** *adv.* abruptly

**ab|rüsten** *itr., tr. V.* disarm; **Ab·rüstung die; ~:** disarmament

**ab|rutschen** *itr. V.; mit sein* **a)** slip; **b)** *(nach unten rutschen)* slide down

**Abs.** *Abk.* **a)** Absender; **b)** Absatz

**Ab·sage die** *(auf eine Einladung)* refusal; *(auf eine Bewerbung)* rejection; **ab|sagen 1.** *tr. V.* cancel; withdraw ⟨*participation*⟩; **2.** *itr. V.* **jmdm. ~:** tell sb. one cannot come

**ab|sägen** *tr. V.* saw off

**Ab·satz der a)** *(am Schuh)* heel; **b)** *(Textunterbrechung)* break; **c)** *(Textabschnitt)* paragraph; **d)** *(Kaufmannsspr.)* sales *pl.*

**ab|saufen** *unr. itr. V.; mit sein (ugs.)* ⟨*engine, car*⟩ flood

**ab|saugen** *tr. V.* **a)** suck away; **b)** *(säubern)* hoover *(Brit. coll.)*

**ab|schaben** *tr. V.* **a)** scrape off; **b)** *(säubern)* scrape [clean]

**ab|schaffen** *tr. V.* **a)** *(beseitigen)* abolish ⟨*capital punishment, regulation, customs duty, institution*⟩; repeal ⟨*law*⟩; put an end to ⟨*injustice, abuse*⟩; **b)** *(weggeben)* get rid of; **Ab·schaffung die** abolition; *(von Gesetzen)* repeal; *(von Unrecht, Mißstand)* ending

**ab|schalten** *tr., itr. V.* switch off; shut down ⟨*power-station*⟩

**abschätzig 1.** *Adj.* derogatory; **2.** *adv.* derogatorily

**Ab·scheu der; ~s** detestation; abhorrence; **abscheulich 1.** *Adj.* **a)** disgusting ⟨*smell, taste*⟩; repulsive ⟨*sight*⟩; **b)** *(verwerflich)* disgraceful ⟨*behaviour*⟩; abominable ⟨*crime*⟩; **2.** *adv.* disgracefully

**ab|schicken** *tr. V.* send [off]

**ab|schieben** *unr. tr. V.* **a)** push away; **b)** *(abwälzen)* shift ⟨*responsibility, blame*⟩; **c)** *(außer Landes bringen)* deport

**Abschied der; ~[e]s, ~e** parting *(von* from); farewell **(von** to); **~ nehmen** take one's leave **(von** of)

**Abschieds-: ~brief der** farewell letter; **~geschenk das** parting gift; **~gruß der** goodbye; farewell

**ab|schießen** *unr. tr. V.* **a)** shoot down ⟨*aeroplane*⟩; **b)** fire ⟨*arrow*⟩; launch ⟨*spacecraft*⟩; **c)** *(töten)* take

**ab|schirmen** *tr. V.* **a)** *(schützen)* shield; **b)** *(fernhalten)* screen off ⟨*light, radiation*⟩

**ab|schlachten** *tr. V.* slaughter

**Ab·schlag der a)** *(Kaufmannsspr.)* discount; **b)** *(Teilzahlung)* interim payment; *(Vorschuß)* advance; **c)** *(Fußball)* goalkeeper's kick out; **ab|schlagen 1.** *unr. tr. V.* **a)** knock off; *(mit dem Beil, Schwert usw.)* chop off; **b)** *(ablehnen)* refuse; **c)** *(abwehren)* beat off; **2.** *unr. itr. V. (Fußball)* kick the ball out

**ab|schleifen** *unr. tr. V. (von Holz)* sand off; *(von Metall, Glas usw.)* grind off

**Abschlepp·dienst der** breakdown recovery service; tow[ing] service *(Amer.);* **ab|schleppen** *tr. V.* tow away; take ⟨*ship*⟩ in tow; **ein Auto zur Werkstatt ~:** tow a car to the garage; **Abschlepp·seil das** tow-rope; *(aus Draht)* towing cable

**ab|schließen 1.** *unr. tr. V.* **a)** *auch itr.*

*(zuschließen)* lock ⟨*door, gate, cupboard*⟩; lock [up] ⟨*house, flat, room, park*⟩; b) *(verschließen)* seal; etw. **luftdicht** ~: seal sth. hermetically; c) *(begrenzen)* border; d) *(zum Abschluß bringen)* conclude; e) *(vereinbaren)* strike ⟨*bargain, deal*⟩; make ⟨*purchase*⟩; enter into ⟨*agreement*⟩; 2. *unr. itr. V. (aufhören, enden)* end; ~**d sagte er ...**: in conclusion he said ...; **Abschluß der** *(Beendigung)* conclusion; end

**ab|schmecken** *tr. V.* a) *(kosten)* taste; try; b) *(würzen)* season

**ab|schmieren** *tr. V. (Technik)* grease

**ab|schminken** *tr. V.* jmdn./sich ~: remove sb.'s/one's make-up

**ab|schmirgeln** *tr. V.* rub off with emery; *(mit Sandpapier)* sand off

**ab|schnallen** *tr. V.* unfasten

**ab|schneiden** 1. *unr. tr. V.* a) *(auch fig.: isolieren)* cut off; cut down ⟨*sth. hanging*⟩; etw. von etw. ~: cut sth. off sth.; sich *(Dat.)* eine Scheibe Brot ~: cut oneself a slice of bread; b) *(kürzer schneiden)* cut; c) jmdm. den Weg ~: take a short cut to get ahead of sb.; 2. *unr. itr. V.* bei etw. gut/schlecht ~: do well/badly in sth.; **Ab·schnitt der** a) *(Kapitel)* section; b) *(Zeitspanne)* phase; d) *(Teil eines Formulars)* [detachable] portion

**ab|schrauben** *tr. V.* unscrew [and remove]

**ab|schrecken** *tr. V.* a) deter; b) *(fernhalten)* scare off; c) *(Kochk.)* pour cold water over; **Abschreckung die;** ~, ~en deterrence

**ab|schreiben** 1. *unr. tr. V.* a) copy out; etw. bei *od.* von jmdm. ~ *(in der Schule)* copy sth. off sb.; *(als Plagiator)* plagiarize sth. from sb.; b) *(Wirtsch.)* amortize; 2. *unr. itr. V.* bei *od.* von jmdm. ~ *(in der Schule)* copy off sb.; *(als Plagiator)* copy from sb.; **Ab·schreibung die** *(Wirtsch.)* amortization; **Ab·schrift die** copy

**ab|schürfen** *tr. V.* graze

**Ab·schuß der** a) *(eines Flugzeugs)* shooting down; b) *(von Geschossen)* firing; *(eines Raumschiffs)* launching

**abschüssig** *Adj.* downward sloping ⟨*land*⟩

**ab|schütteln** *tr. V.* shake off; *(herunterschütteln)* shake down

**ab|schwächen** 1. *tr. V.* a) *(mildern)* tone down ⟨*statement, criticism*⟩; b) *(verringern)* lessen ⟨*effect, impression*⟩; cushion ⟨*blow, impact*⟩; 2. *refl.*

*V.* ⟨*interest, demand*⟩ wane; **Abschwächung die;** ~, ~en a) *(Milderung)* toning down; b) *(eines Aufpralls, Stoßes usw.)* cushioning

**ab|schweifen** *itr. V.*; mit sein digress; **Abschweifung die;** ~, ~en digression

**ab|schwören** *unr. itr. V.* dem Teufel/seinem Glauben ~: renounce the Devil/one's faith; dem Alkohol/Laster ~: forswear alcohol/vice

**absehbar** *Adj.* foreseeable; in ~er Zeit within the foreseeable future; **ab|sehen** 1. *unr. tr. V.* a) *(voraussehen)* predict; foresee ⟨*event*⟩; b) es auf etw. *(Akk.)* abgesehen haben be after sth.; er hat es darauf abgesehen, uns zu ärgern he's out to annoy us; der Chef hat es auf ihn abgesehen the boss has got it in for him; 2. *unr. itr. V.* a) von etw. ~: *(etw. nicht beachten)* leave aside sth.; *s. auch* abgesehen; b) von etw. ~ *(auf etw. verzichten)* refrain from sth.

**ab|seilen** 1. *tr. V.* lower [with a rope]. 2. *refl. V. (Bergsteigen)* abseil

**ab|sein** *unr. itr. V.*; mit sein *(Zusschr. nur im Inf. u. Part.) (abgegangen sein)* have come off

**abseits** 1. *Präp. mit Gen.* away from; 2. *Adv.* a) far away; b) *(Ballspiele)* ~ sein *od.* stehen be offside; **Abseits das;** ~, ~: das war ein klares ~: that was clearly offside

**ab|senden** *unr. od. regelm. tr. V.* dispatch; **Ab·sender der** sender; *(Anschrift)* sender's address

**ab|setzen** 1. *tr. V.* a) take off ⟨*hat, glasses, etc.*⟩; b) *(hinstellen)* put down ⟨*bag, suitcase*⟩; c) *(aussteigen lassen)* jmdn. ~ *(im öffentlichen Verkehr)* put sb. down; let sb. out *(Amer.)*; *(im privaten Verkehr)* drop sb. [off]; d) remove ⟨*chancellor, judge*⟩ from office; depose ⟨*king, emperor*⟩; 2. *refl. V.* a) *(sich ablagern)* be deposited; b) *(flüchten)* get away

**Absetzung die;** ~, ~en *s.* absetzen 1 d: removal; deposition

**ab|sichern** 1. *tr. V.* make safe; 2. *refl. V.* safeguard oneself

**Ab·sicht die;** ~, ~en intention; etw. mit ~ tun do sth. intentionally; etw. ohne *od.* nicht mit ~ tun do sth. unintentionally; **ab·sichtlich** 1. *Adj.* intentional; deliberate; 2. *adv.* intentionally; deliberately

**ab|sinken** *unr. itr. V.*; mit sein sink

**absolut** *Adj.* absolute; **Absolutismus der;** ~ *(hist.)* absolutism *no art.*

**Absolvent** der; ~en, ~en *(einer Schule)* one who has taken the leaving *or (Amer.)* final examination; *(einer Akademie)* graduate; **absolvieren** *tr. V.* complete; **Absolvierung die;** ~: completion

**ab·sonderlich** *Adj.* strange; odd; **ab|sondern 1.** *tr. V.* exude; *(Physiol.)* secrete; **2.** *refl. V.* isolate oneself

**absorbieren** *tr. V.* absorb

**ab|speisen** *tr. V.* jmdn. mit etw. ~: fob sb. off with sth.

**abspenstig** *Adj.* jmdm. etw. ~ **machen** get sb. to part with sth.

**ab|sperren** *tr. V.* seal off; close off

**Ab·spiel** das *(Ballspiele)* passing; **ab|spielen 1.** *tr. V.* **a)** play ⟨record, tape⟩; **b)** vom Blatt ~: play ⟨piece of music⟩ at sight; **c)** *(Ballspiele)* pass; **2.** *refl. V.* take place

**Ab·sprache** die arrangement; eine ~ **treffen** make an arrangement; **ab|sprechen** *unr. tr. V.* **a)** jmdm. etw. ~: deny that sb. has sth.; **b)** *(vereinbaren)* arrange

**ab|springen** *unr. itr. V.; mit sein* jump off; *(herunterspringen)* jump down; **vom Fahrrad** ~: jump off one's bicycle; **Ab·sprung** der take-off; *(das Herunterspringen)* jump

**ab|spülen 1.** *tr. V.* **a)** wash off; **b)** *(reinigen)* rinse off; sich *(Dat.)* die Hände usw. ~: rinse one's hands *etc.*; das Geschirr ~ *(bes. südd.)* wash the dishes; **2.** *itr. V. (bes. südd.)* wash up

**ab|stammen** *itr. V.* be descended (von from); **Abstammung die;** ~, ~en descent

**Ab·stand** der **a)** distance; **in 20 Meter** ~: at a distance of 20 metres; **b)** *(Unterschied)* gap

**ab|stauben** *tr., itr. V.* dust

**Abstecher** der; ~s, ~: side-trip

**ab|stehen** *unr. itr. V.* ⟨hair⟩ stand up; ⟨pigtail[s]⟩ stick out; ~**de Ohren** protruding ears

**Ab·steige** die; ~, ~n *(ugs. abwertend)* cheap and crummy hotel *(sl.)*; **ab|steigen** *unr. itr. V.; mit sein* **a)** |vom Pferd/Fahrrad| ~: get off [one's horse/bicycle]; **b)** *(abwärts gehen)* go down

**ab|stellen** *tr. V.* **a)** put down; **b)** *(unterbringen)* put; *(parken)* park; **c)** *(ausschalten, abdrehen)* turn off; **d)** *(unterbinden)* put a stop to

**Abstell-:** ~**kammer** die, ~**raum** der lumber-room

**ab|stempeln** *tr. V.* **a)** frank ⟨letter⟩;

cancel ⟨stamp⟩; **b)** *(fig.)* label, brand **(zu, als** as)

**ab|sterben** *unr. itr. V.; mit sein* **a)** [gradually] die; **b)** *(gefühllos werden)* go numb

**Abstieg** der; ~|e|s, ~e **a)** descent; **b)** *(Niedergang)* decline

**ab|stimmen 1.** *itr. V.* vote (über + Akk. on); **2.** *tr. V.* etw. mit jmdm. ~: discuss and agree on sth. with sb.; **Ab·stimmung die a)** vote; während der ~; during the voting; **b)** *(Absprache)* agreement

**abstinent** [apsti'nɛnt] *Adj.* teetotal; ~ **sein** be a teetotaller; **Abstinenz die;** ~: teetotalism; **Abstinenzler** der; ~s, ~: teetotaller

**ab|stoppen 1.** *tr. V.* halt; stop; check ⟨advance⟩; **2.** *itr. V.* come to a halt; ⟨person⟩ stop

**Ab·stoß** der *(Fußball)* goal-kick; **ab|stoßen** *unr. tr. V.* **a)** push off; **b)** *(beschädigen)* chip ⟨crockery, paintwork, plaster⟩; **c)** *(verkaufen)* sell off; **d)** *(anwidern)* repel; put off; **abstoßend** *Adj.* repulsive

**abstrakt** [ap'strakt] *Adj.* abstract

**ab|streifen** *tr. V.* pull off; strip off ⟨berries⟩; die Asche |von der Zigarette/Zigarre| ~: remove the ash [from one's cigarette/cigar]

**ab|streiten** *unr. tr. V.* deny

**Ab·strich** der **a)** *(Med.)* swab; einen ~ **machen** take a swab; **b)** *(Streichung, Kürzung)* cut; ~**e machen** make cuts **(an +** *Dat.* in)

**ab|stumpfen** *itr. V.; mit sein* jmd. stumpft ab *(wird unsensibel)* sb.'s mind becomes deadened

**Ab·sturz** der fall; *(eines Flugzeugs)* crash; **ab|stürzen** *itr. V.; mit sein* fall; ⟨aircraft, pilot, passenger⟩ crash

**ab|stützen 1.** *refl. V.* support oneself **(mit on, an +** *Dat.* against); **2.** *tr. V.* support

**ab|suchen** *tr. V.* search **(nach** for)

**absurd** *Adj.* absurd

**Abszeß** der; Abszesses, Abszesse **a)** *(Med.)* abscess; **b)** *(Geschwür)* ulcer

**Abszisse** die; ~, ~en *(Math.)* abscissa

**Abt** der; ~|e|s, Äbte abbot

**Abt.** *Abk.* Abteilung

**ab|tasten** *tr. V.* etw. ~: feel sth. all over

**ab|tauen 1.** *itr. V.; mit sein (eis-/schneefrei werden)* become clear of ice/snow; ⟨refrigerator⟩ defrost; **2.** *tr. V.* melt; thaw; defrost ⟨refrigerator⟩

**Abtei** die; ~, ~en abbey

**Abteil** das; ~|e|s, ~e compartment; **Ab·teilung** die department; **Abteilungs·leiter** der head of department

**ab|tippen** tr. V. (ugs.) type out

**Äbtissin** die; ~, ~nen abbess

**ab|tönen** tr. V. tint

**ab|töten** tr. V. destroy ⟨parasites, germs⟩; deaden ⟨nerve, feeling⟩

**ab|tragen** unr. tr. V. (abnutzen) wear out; **abgetragen** well worn

**abträglich** Adj. (geh.) einer Sache (Dat.) ~ sein be detrimental to sth.

**Ab·transport** der s. abtransportieren: taking away; removal; **ab|transportieren** tr. V. take away; remove ⟨dead, injured⟩

**ab|treiben** 1. unr. tr. V. a) carry away; jmdn./ein Schiff vom Kurs ~: drive sb./a ship off course; b) abort ⟨foetus⟩; ein Kind ~ lassen have an abortion; 2. unr. itr. V.; mit sein be carried away; ⟨ship⟩ be drives off course; **Abtreibung** die; ~, ~en abortion

**ab|trennen** tr. V. detach

**ab|treten** 1. unr. tr. V. a) sich (Dat.) die Füße/Schuhe ~: wipe one's feet; b) jmdm. etw. ~: let sb. have sth.; 2. unr. itr. V.; mit sein a) (Theater) exit; (fig.) make one's exit; b) (zurücktreten) step down; ⟨monarch⟩ abdicate; **Abtreter** der; ~s, ~ doormat

**ab|trocknen** tr. V. dry; sich (Dat.) die Hände/die Tränen ~: dry one's hands/tears

**ab|tropfen** itr. V.; mit sein drip off

**abtrünnig** Adj. (einer Partei) renegade; (einer Religion, Sekte) apostate; der Kirche/dem Glauben ~ werden desert the Church/the faith

**ab|tun** unr. tr. V. dismiss

**ab|wägen** unr. od. regelm. tr., itr. V. weigh up; **abgewogen** carefully weighted; balanced ⟨judgement⟩

**ab|wählen** tr. V. vote out; drop ⟨school subject⟩

**ab|wandeln** tr. V. adapt

**ab|wandern** itr. V.; mit sein migrate; (in ein anderes Land) emigrate; **Abwanderung** die migration; (in ein anderes Land) emigration

**Ab·wandlung** die adaptation

**ab|warten** 1. itr. V. wait; sie warteten ab they awaited events; **warte ab!** wait and see; (als Drohung) just you wait!; 2. tr. V. wait for

**abwärts** Adv. downwards; (bergab) downhill; den Fluß ~: downstream

**Abwasch** der; ~|e|s washing-up (Brit.); washing dishes (Amer.); den ~ machen do the washing-up/wash the dishes; **abwaschbar** Adj. washable; **ab|waschen** 1. unr. tr. V. a) wash off; b) (reinigen) wash down; wash [up] ⟨dishes⟩; 2. unr. itr. V. wash up (Brit.); wash the dishes (Amer.)

**Ab·wasser** das; Pl. -wässer sewage

**ab|wechseln** refl., itr. V. alternate; wir wechselten uns ab we took turns; **abwechselnd** Adv. alternately; **Abwechslung** die; ~, ~en variety; (Wechsel) change; zur ~: for a change

**Ab·weg** der: auf ~e kommen od. geraten go astray; **abwegig** erroneous; false ⟨suspicion⟩

**Ab·wehr** die; ~ a) repulsion; (von Schlägen) fending off; (Sport) clearance; clearing (Amer.); b) (Sport: Hintermannschaft) defence; **ab|wehren** tr. V. a) repulse; fend off ⟨blow⟩; (Sport) clear ⟨ball, shot⟩; b) avert ⟨danger, consequences⟩

**ab|weichen** unr. itr. V.; mit sein a) deviate; b) (sich unterscheiden) differ; **Abweichung** die; ~, ~en a) deviation; b) (Unterschied) difference

**ab|weisen** unr. tr. V. turn away; turn down ⟨applicant, suitor⟩; **abweisend** Adj. cold ⟨look, tone of voice⟩; in ~em Ton coldly; **Ab·weisung** die; ~, ~en s. abweisen: turning away; turning down

**ab|wenden** 1. unr. od. regelm. tr. V. a) turn away; b) nur regelm. (verhindern) avert. 2. unr. od. regelm. refl. V. turn away

**ab|werben** unr. tr. V. lure away

**ab|werfen** 1. unr. tr. V. a) drop; throw off ⟨clothing⟩; jettison ⟨ballast⟩; throw ⟨rider⟩; b) (ins Spielfeld werfen) throw out ⟨ball⟩; c) (einbringen) bring in; 2. unr. itr. V. (Sport) throw the ball out

**ab|werten** tr., itr. V. devalue; **abwertend** Adj. derogatory ⟨term⟩; **Ab·wertung** die devaluation

**abwesend** Adj. absent; **Abwesenheit** die; ~ absence

**ab|wickeln** tr. V. a) unwind; b) (erledigen) deal with ⟨case⟩; do ⟨business⟩; **Abwicklung** die; ~, ~en s. abwickeln 1 b: dealing (Gen. with); doing

**ab|wiegen** unr. tr. V. weigh out; weigh ⟨single item⟩

**ab|wimmeln** tr. V. (ugs.) get rid of

**ab|wischen** tr. V. a) wipe away; b) (säubern) wipe

**Ab·wurf** der **a)** dropping; *(von Ballast)* jettisoning; **b) beim ~ stolperte der Torwart** the goalkeeper stumbled as he threw the ball out

**ab|zahlen** *tr. V.* pay off ⟨*debt, loan*⟩

**ab|zählen** *tr. V.* count

**Ab·zahlung** die paying off; **etw. auf ~ kaufen/verkaufen** buy/sell sth. on easy terms

**Ab·zeichen** das emblem; *(Anstecknadel, Plakette)* badge

**ab|zeichnen 1.** *tr. V.* **a)** *(kopieren)* copy; **b)** *(signieren)* initial; **2.** *refl. V.* stand out; *(fig.)* begin to emerge

**Abzieh·bild** das transfer; **ab|ziehen 1.** *unr. tr. V.* **a)** pull off; peel off ⟨*skin*⟩; strip ⟨*bed*⟩; **b)** *(Fot.)* make a print/prints of; **c)** *(Milit., auch fig.)* withdraw; **d)** *(subtrahieren)* subtract; take away; *(abrechnen)* deduct; **2.** *unr.. itr. V.; mit sein (sich verflüchtigen)* escape; **b)** *(Milit.)* withdraw; **Ab·zug** der **a)** *(an einer Schußwaffe)* trigger; **b)** *(Fot.)* print; **c)** *(Verminderung)* deduction; **abzüglich** *Präp. mit Gen. (Kaufmannsspr.)* less

**ab|zweigen 1.** *itr. V.; mit sein* branch off; **2.** *tr. V.* put aside; **Abzweigung** die; ~, ~en turn-off; *(Gabelung)* fork

**ach** *Interj.* **a)** *(betroffen, mitleidig)* oh [dear]; **b)** *(bedauernd, unwirsch)* oh; **c)** *(klagend)* ah; **d)** *(erstaunt)* oh; ~, **wirklich?** no, really?; ~, **der!** oh, him!; **e)** ~ **so!** oh, I see; ~ **was** *od.* **wo!** of course not

**Achat** der; ~[e]s, ~e *(Min.)* agate

**Achse** die; ~, ~n **a)** *(Rad~)* axle; **b)** *(Dreh~, Math., Astron.)* axis

**Achsel** die; ~, ~n *(Schulter)* shoulder; *(~höhle)* armpit

**Achsel-: ~haare** *Pl.* armpit hair *sing.*; **~höhle** die armpit

**¹acht** *Kardinalz.* eight; **um ~ [Uhr]** at eight [o'clock]; **um halb ~:** at half past seven; **dreiviertel ~, Viertel vor ~:** [a] quarter to eight; **es steht ~ zu ~/~ zu 2** *(Sport)* the score is eight all/eight to two; **²acht: sie waren zu ~:** there were eight of them

**³acht: etw. außer ~ lassen** disregard sth.; **sich in ~ nehmen** be careful; **sich vor jmdm./etw. in ~ nehmen** be wary of sb./sth.

**acht...** *Ordinalz.* eighth; **der ~e September** the eighth of September; **München, [den] 8. Mai 1984** Munich, 8 May 1984; **Acht** die; ~, ~en **a)** eight; **b)** *(Figur)* figure eight; **c)** *(Verbiegung)* buckle; **mein Rad hat eine ~:** my

wheel is buckled; **Achte** der/die; adj. *Dekl.* eighth

**acht-, Acht-:** ~**eck** das; ~s, ~e octagon; ~**eckig** *Adj.* octagonal; ~**einhalb** *Bruchz.* eight and a half

**achtel** *Bruchz.* eighth; **Achtel** das *(schweiz. meist* der); ~s, ~ eighth; **Achtel·note** die *(Musik)* quaver

**achten 1.** *tr. V.* respect; **2.** *itr. V.* **auf etw. (Akk.) ~:** pay heed to sth.

**achtens** *Adv.* eighthly; **Achterbahn** die roller-coaster; **acht·fach** *Vervielfältigungsz.* eightfold; **die ~fache Menge** eight times the quantity; **~fach vergrößert/verkleinert** magnified/reduced eight times; **das Achtfache** kosten cost eight times as much

**acht|geben** *unr. itr. V.* **a)** auf jmdn./etw. ~: take care of sb./sth.; **b)** *(vorsichtig sein)* be careful

**acht-:** ~**hundert** *Kardinalz.* eight hundred; ~**jährig** *Adj. (8 Jahre alt)* eight-year-old *attrib.*; eight years old *pred.; (8 Jahre dauernd)* eight-year *attrib.;* ~**köpfig** *Adj.* ⟨*family, committee*⟩ of eight

**acht·los 1.** *Adj.* heedless; **2.** *adv.* heedlessly

**acht-:** ~**mal** *Adv.* eight times; ~**spurig** *Adj.* eight-lane ⟨*road*⟩; eight-track ⟨*cassette*⟩; ~**stellig** *Adj.* eight-figure *attrib.;* ~**stellig sein** have eight figures; ~**stimmig** 1. *Adj.* eight-part *attrib.;* 2. *adv.* in eight parts; ~**stöckig** *Adj.* eight-storey *attrib.;* ~**tägig** *Adj. (8 Tage alt)* eight-day-old *attrib.; (8 Tage dauernd)* eight-day[-long] *attrib.;* ~**tausend** *Kardinalz.* eight thousand; ~**teilig** *Adj.* eight-piece ⟨*tea-service, tool-set, etc.*⟩; eight-part ⟨*series, serial*⟩

**Achtung** die; ~ **a)** respect (vor + *Dat., Gen.* for); **b)** ~! watch out!; ~, **fertig, los!** on your marks, get set, go!

**acht·zehn** *Kardinalz.* eighteen; **18 Uhr 33** 6.33 p.m.; *(auf der 24-Stunden-Uhr)* 1833; **achtzehn·jährig** *Adj. (18 Jahre alt)* eighteen-year-old *attrib.;* eighteen years old *pred.; (18 Jahre dauernd)* eighteen-year *attrib.*

**achtzig** *Kardinalz.* eighty; **mit ~ [km/h] fahren** drive at *or (coll.)* do eighty [k.p.h.]; **über/etwa ~ [Jahre alt] sein** be over/about eighty [years old]; **mit ~ [Jahren]** *od.* **Achtzig** at eighty [years of age]; **achtzig·jährig** *Adj. (80 Jahre alt)* eighty-year-old *attrib.;* eighty years old *pred.; (80 Jahre dauernd)* eighty-year *attrib.*

**ächzen** *itr. V.* groan

**Acker** der; ~s, **Äcker** field; **Acker-bau** der; *o. Pl.* arable farming *no indef. art.*

**A. D.** *Abk.* Anno Domini AD

**ADAC** [a:de:a:'tse:] der; ~ *Abk.* Allgemeiner Deutscher Automobilclub

**Adams·apfel** der *(ugs.)* Adam's apple

**adäquat** [at|ɛ'kva:t] *Adj.* ap- propriate (*Dat.* to); suitable (*Dat.* for)

**addieren** 1. *tr. V.* add [up]; 2. *itr. V.* add; **Addition** die; ~, ~en addition

**ade** *Interj. (veralt., landsch.)* farewell *(dated);* bye *(coll.)*

**Adel** der; ~s nobility; **der niedere/hohe** ~: the lesser nobility/the aristocracy; **adelig** *s.* **adlig**; **Adelige** *s.* **Adlige**; **adeln** *tr. V.* jmdn. ~: give sb. a title; *(in den hohen Adel erheben)* raise sb. to the peerage

**Adels-:** ~**geschlecht** das noble family; ~**stand** der nobility; *(hoher Adel)* nobility; ~**titel** der title of nobility

**Ader** die; ~, ~n a) blood-vessel; b) *o. Pl. (Anlage, Begabung)* streak; c) *(Bot., Geol.)* vein; d) *(Elektrot.)* core

**adieu** [a'djø:] *Interj. (veralt.)* adieu

**Adjektiv** das; ~s, ~e *(Sprachw.)* adjective

**Adjutant** der; ~en, ~en adjutant

**Adler** der; ~s, ~: eagle

**adlig** *Adj.* noble; ~ **sein** be a noble [man/woman]; **Adlige** der/die *adj. Dekl.* noble [man/woman]

**Admiral** der; ~s, ~e *od.* **Admiräle** admiral

**adoptieren** *tr. V.* adopt; **Adoption** die; ~, ~en adoption

**Adoptiv-:** ~**eltern** *Pl.* adoptive parents; ~**kind** das adopted child

**Adressat** der; ~en, ~en, **Adressatin** die; ~, ~nen addressee; **Adreß-buch** das directory; **Adresse** die; ~, ~n address; **bei jmdm. an die falsche** ~ **kommen** *od.* **geraten** *(fig. ugs.)* come to the wrong address *(fig.);* **adressieren** *tr. V.* address

**adrett** 1. *Adj.* smart. 2. *adv.* smartly

**Advent** [at'vɛnt] der; ~s **a)** Advent; b) *(Adventssonntag)* Sunday in Advent

**Advents-:** ~**kalender** der Advent calendar; ~**kranz** der *garland of evergreens with four candles for the Sundays in Advent*

**Adverb** [at'vɛrp] das; ~s, ~ien *(Sprachw.)* adverb; **adverbial** *(Sprachw.)* 1. *Adj.* adverbial; 2. *adv.* adverbially

**Advokat** [atvo'ka:t] der; ~en, ~en *(österr., schweiz., sonst veralt.)* lawyer; advocate *(arch.)*

**Aero-** [aero- *od.* ɛ:ro-]: ~**gramm** das air[-mail] letter; ~**sol** das; ~s, ~e aerosol

**Affäre** die; ~, ~n affair; **sich aus der** ~ **ziehen** *(ugs.)* get out of it

**Affe** der; ~n, ~n **a)** monkey; *(Menschen~)* ape; b) *(salopp) (dummer Kerl)* oaf; clot *(Brit. sl.);* *(Geck)* dandy

**Affekt** der; ~[e]s, ~e emotion; **im** ~: in the heat of the moment; **affektiert** *(abwertend)* 1. *Adj.* affected; 2. *adv.* affectedly

**Affen·theater** das *(salopp)* farce

**Afghane** [af'ga:nə] der; ~n, ~n **a)** Afghan; b) *(Hund)* Afghan hound; **afghanisch** *Adj.* Afghan; **Afghanistan** [af'ga:nιsta:n] (das); ~s Afghanistan

**Afrika·** (das); ~s Africa; **Afrikaner** der; ~s, ~ African; **afrikanisch** *Adj.* African

**After** der; ~s, ~: anus

**AG** [a:'ge:] *Abk.* die; ~, ~s Aktiengesellschaft PLC *(Brit.);* Ltd. *(private company) (Brit.);* Inc. *(Amer.)*

**Agent** der; ~en, ~en; **Agentin** die; ~, ~nen agent; **Agentur** die; ~, ~en agency

**Aggregat** das; ~[e]s, ~e *(Technik)* unit; *(Elektrot.)* set; **Aggregat·zustand** der *(Chemie)* state

**Aggression** die; ~, ~en aggression; **aggressiv** 1. *Adj.* aggressive; 2. *adv.* aggressively; **Aggressivität** die; ~: aggressiveness; **Aggressor** der; ~s, ~en aggressor

**Agitation** die; ~: agitation; **agitieren** *itr. V.* agitate

**Agrar·land** das; *Pl.* ~länder agrarian country

**Ägypten** (das); ~s Egypt; **Ägypter** der; ~s, ~ Egyptian; **ägyptisch** *Adj.* Egyptian

**ah** *Interj. (verwundert)* oh; *(freudig, genießerisch)* ah; *(verstehend)* oh; ah

**äh** [ɛ(:)] *Interj.* **a)** *(angeekelt)* ugh; b) *(stotternd)* er; hum

**aha** [a'ha(:)] *Interj. (verstehend)* oh[, I see]; *(triumphierend)* aha

**Ahn** der; ~[e]s, *od.* ~en, ~en *(geh.)*, **Ahne** der; ~n, ~n forebear; ancestor

**ähneln** *itr. V.* jmdm. ~: resemble *or* be like sb.; **jmdm. sehr/wenig** ~: strongly resemble *or* be very like sb./bear little resemblance to sb.; **einer Sache** *(Dat.)* ~: be similar to sth.; be like sth.; **sich**

*(Dat.)* ~: resemble one another; be alike

**ahnen** *tr. V.* a) *(im voraus fühlen)* have a premonition of; b) *(vermuten)* suspect; **das konnte ich doch nicht ~!** I had no way of knowing that

**ähnlich** 1. *Adj.* similar; **jmdm.** ~ **sein** be like sb.; ~ **wie** like; 2. *adv.* similarly; ⟨*answer, react*⟩ in a similar way; 3. *Präp. mit Dat.* like; **Ähnlichkeit die**; ~, ~**en** similarity; **mit jmdm.** ~ **haben** be like sb.

**Ahnung die**; ~, ~**en** a) *(Vorgefühl)* premonition; b) *(ugs.: Kenntnisse)* knowledge; **von etw. |viel|** ~ **haben** know [a lot] about sth.; **keine** ~! [I've] no idea; **ahnungs·los** *Adj. (nichts ahnend)* unsuspecting; *(naiv, unwissend)* naïve

**ahoi** *Interj. (Seemannsspr.)* ahoy

**Ahorn** ['aːhɔrn] *der*; ~s, ~e maple

**Ähre die**; ~, ~n ear

**Aids** [eːts] *das*; ~: Aids

**Aids-**: ~**kranke** der/die person suffering from Aids; ~**test der** Aids test

**Akademie die**; ~, ~n academy; *(Bergbau, Forst~, Bau~)* school; college; **Akademiker der**; ~s, ~, **Akademikerin die**; ~, ~**nen** [university/college] graduate; **akademisch** 1. *Adj.* academic; 2. *adv.* academically

**Akazie** [aˈkaːtsi̯ə] *die*; ~, ~n acacia

**akklimatisieren** *refl. V.* become or get acclimatized

**Akkord der**; ~|e|s, ~e a) *(Musik)* chord; b) *(Wirtsch.) (~arbeit)* piecework; *(~lohn)* piece-work pay *no indef. art., no pl.; (~satz)* piece-rate

**Akkordeon das**; ~s, ~s accordion

**Akku der**; ~s, ~s *(ugs.)*, **Akkumulator der**; ~s, ~en accumulator *(Brit.)*; storage battery

**akkurat** 1. *Adj.* meticulous; 2. *adv.* meticulously

**Akkusativ der**; ~s, ~e *(Sprachw.)* accusative [case]; **Akkusativ·objekt das** *(Sprachw.)* accusative or direct object

**Akne die**; ~, ~n *(Med.)* acne

**Akrobat der**; ~en, ~en acrobat; **Akrobatik die**; ~ acrobatics *pl.*; **akrobatisch** *Adj.* acrobatic

**Akt der**; ~|e|s, ~e a) *(auch Theater, Zirkus~, Varieté~)* act; b) *(Zeremonie)* ceremony; c) *(Geschlechts~)* sexual act; d) *(bild. Kunst)* nude; **Akt·bild das** nude [picture]

**Akte die**; ~, ~n file

**Akten-**: ~**deckel** der folder; ~**kof-**

**fer** der attaché case; ~**mappe** die brief-case; ~**ordner** der file; ~**tasche** die brief-case; ~**zeichen** das reference

**Akteur** [akˈtøːɐ̯] *der*; ~s, ~e person involved

**Akt·foto das** nude photo

**Aktie** ['aktsi̯ə] *die*; ~, ~n *(Wirtsch.)* share; ~**n** shares *(Brit.)*; stock *(Amer.)*; **die** ~**n fallen/steigen** share or stock prices are falling/rising; **Aktien·gesellschaft die** joint-stock company

**Aktion die**; ~, ~**en** a) action *no indef. art.; (militärisch)* operation; b) *(Kampagne)* campaign

**Aktionär der**; ~s, ~e shareholder

**aktiv** 1. *Adj.* a) active; b) *(Milit.)* serving *attrib.* ⟨*officer, soldier*⟩; 2. *adv.* actively; **Aktiv das**; ~s, ~e *(Sprachw.)* active; **Aktive der/die**; *adj. Dekl. (Sport)* participant; **aktivieren** *tr. V.* mobilize ⟨*party members, group, class, etc.*⟩; **den Kreislauf** ~: stimulate the circulation; **Aktivität die**; ~, ~**en** activity

**Akt·modell das** nude model

**Aktualität die**; ~, ~**en** a) *(Gegenwartsbezug)* relevance [to the present]; b) *(von Nachrichten usw.)* topicality; **aktuell** *Adj.* topical; *(gegenwärtig)* current; *(neu)* up-to-the-minute; **eine** ~**e Sendung** *(Ferns., Rundf.)* a [news and] current affairs programme

**Akupunktur die**; ~, ~**en** *(Med.)* acupuncture

**Akustik die**; ~ a) *(Lehre vom Schall)* acoustics *sing., no art.*; b) *(Schallverhältnisse)* acoustics *pl.*; **akustisch** 1. *Adj.* acoustic. 2. *adv.* acoustically

**akut** *Adj. (auch Med.)* acute; pressing, urgent ⟨*question, issue*⟩

**Akzent der**; ~|e|s, ~e a) *(Sprachw.) (Betonung)* stress; *(Betonungszeichen)* accent; b) *(Sprachmelodie, Aussprache)* accent

**akzeptabel** 1. *Adj.* acceptable; 2. *adv.* acceptably; **akzeptieren** *tr. V.* accept

**à la** [a la] *(Gastr., ugs.)* à la

**Alabaster der**; ~s, ~: alabaster

**à la carte** [ala'kart] *(Gastr.)* à la carte

**Alarm der**; ~|e|s, ~e alarm; *(Flieger~)* air-raid warning; ~ **geben/**(fig. ugs.) **schlagen** raise the alarm; **blinder** ~: false alarm

**alarm-, Alarm-**: ~**anlage** die alarm system; ~**bereit** *Adj.* on alert *postpos.*; ~**bereitschaft** die alert

**alarmieren** *tr. V.* **a)** alarm; **b)** *(zu Hilfe rufen)* call [out] ⟨*doctor, police, fire brigade, etc.*⟩

**Alarm-:** **~sirene** die warning siren; **~stufe** die alert stage

**Albaner** der; ~s, ~Albanian; **Albanien** [al'ba:niən] *(das)*; ~s Albania; **albanisch** *Adj.* Albanian

**Albatros** der; ~, ~se *(Zool.)* albatross

**Alben** *s.* Album

**albern** *Adj.* **a)** silly; **sich ~ benehmen** act silly; **b)** *(ugs.: nebensächlich)* silly; stupid; **Albernheit** die; ~, ~en silliness

**Albino** der; ~s, ~s albino

**Album** das; ~s, Alben album

**Alge** die; ~, ~n alga

**Algebra** [*österr.:* al'ge:bra] die; ~: algebra

**Algerien** [al'ge:riən] *(das)*; ~s Algeria; **Algerier** der; ~s, ~: Algerian; **algerisch** *Adj.* Algerian

**alias** *Adv.* alias

**Alibi** das; ~s, ~s alibi

**Alkohol** der; ~s, ~e alcohol; **alkohol·frei** *Adj.* non-alcoholic; **Alkoholiker** der; ~s, ~: alcoholic; **alkoholisch** *Adj.* alcoholic; **Alkoholismus** der; ~: alcoholism *no art.*

**all** *Indefinitpron. u. unbest. Zahlw.* **1.** *attr. (ganz, gesamt...)* all; **~es andere/ Weitere/übrige** everything else; **~es Schöne** everything *or* all that is beautiful; **~es Gute!** all the best!; **wir/ihr/sie ~e** all of us/you/them; **~e Anwesenden** all those present; **~e Bewohner der Stadt** all the inhabitants of the town; **~e Jahre wieder** every year; **~e fünf Minuten/Meter** every five minutes/ metres; **Bücher ~er Art** all kinds of books; **in ~er Ruhe** in peace and quiet; **2.** *alleinstehend* **a)** ~e all; **~e, die ...**: all those who ...; **b)** ~es *(auf Sachen bezogen)* everything; *(auf Personen bezogen)* everybody; **das ~es** all that; **trotz ~em** in spite of everything; **~es in ~em** all in all; **vor ~em** above all; **das ist ~es** that's all *or (coll.)* it; **ist das ~es?** is that all *or (coll.)* it?; **~es mal herhören!** *(ugs.)* listen everybody!; **~es aussteigen!** *(ugs.)* everyone out!; *(vom Schaffner gesagt)* all change!

**All das;** ~s *s.* Weltall

**alle** *Adj.; nicht attr.:* **~ sein** be all gone; **~ werden** run out

**alle·dem** *Pron.* **trotz ~:** in spite of *or* despite all that

**Allee** die; ~, ~n avenue

**allein** [a'lain] **1.** *Adj.; nicht attr.* **a)** *(für sich)* alone; on one's/its own; by oneself/itself; **ganz ~:** all on one's/its own; **b)** *(einsam)* alone; **2.** *adv. (ohne Hilfe)* by oneself/itself; on one's/its own; **etw. ~ tun** do sth. oneself; **von ~** *(ugs.)* by oneself/itself; **3.** *Adv.* **a)** *(geh.: ausschließlich)* alone; **b)** |schon| **~ der Gedanke/|schon| der Gedanke ~:** the mere thought [of it]; **alleine** *(ugs.)* *s.* allein 1a, 2, 3b; **alleinig** *Adj.; nicht präd.* sole

**allein-, Allein-:** **~gang** der *(fig.)* independent initiative; **im ~gang** off one's own bat; **~stehend** *Adj.* ⟨*person*⟩ living alone; *(ledig)* single ⟨*person*⟩; **~stehende** der/die; *adj. Dekl.* person living alone; *(Ledige[r])* single person

**alle·mal** *Adv.* **a)** *(ugs.)* any time *(coll.)*; **was der kann, das kann ich doch ~:** anything he can do, I can do too; **b)** **ein für ~:** once and for all; **allen·falls** *Adv.* **a)** *(höchstens)* at [the] most; **b)** *(bestenfalls)* at best

**aller-:** **~dings** *Adv.* **a)** *(einschränkend)* though; **es stimmt ~dings, daß ...**: it's true though that ...; **b)** *(zustimmend)* [yes,] certainly; **das war ~dings Pech** that was bad luck, to be sure; **~erst...** *Adj.; nicht präd.* very first; **der/die/das ~erste** the very first; **b)** *(best...)* very best

**Allergie** die; ~, ~n *(Med.)* allergy; **allergisch 1.** *Adj. (Med.)* allergic; **2.** *adv.* **auf etw.** *(Akk.)* **~ reagieren** have an allergic reaction to sth.

**aller-, Aller-:** **~größt...** *Adj.* utmost ⟨*trouble, care, etc.*⟩; biggest ⟨*car, house, town, etc.*⟩ of all; tallest ⟨*person*⟩ of all; **am ~größten** sein be [the] biggest/tallest of all; **~hand** *indekl. unbest. Gattungsz. (ugs.)* **a)** *attr.* all kinds *or* sorts of; **b)** *alleinstehend* all kinds *or* sorts of things; **das ist ~hand** *(viel)* that's a lot; **das ist ja ~hand!** that's just not on! *(Brit. coll.)*; **~heiligen** das; **~** *(bes. kath. Kirche)* All Saints' Day; **~herzlichst 1.** *Adj.* warmest ⟨*thanks, greetings, congratulations*⟩; most cordial ⟨*reception, welcome, invitation*⟩; **2.** most warmly; **~höchst...** **1.** *Adj.* highest ⟨*building, tree, etc.*⟩ of all; **2.** *adv.* **am ~höchsten** ⟨*fly, jump, etc.*⟩ the highest of all; **~höchstens** *Adv.* at the very most

**allerlei** *indekl. unbest. Gattungsz.: attr.* all kinds *or* sorts of; *alleinstehend* all kinds *or* sorts of things; **Al-**

lerl**ei** das; ~s, ~s *(Gemisch)* potpourri; *(Durcheinander)* jumble

**aller-, Aller-:** ~l**e**tzt... *Adj.; nicht präd.* **a)** very last; **b)** *(ugs. abwertend)* most dreadful *(coll.);* **das ist das Allerletzte** that is the absolute limit; ~l**ie**bst... 1) *Adj.* most favourite; **es wäre mir am ~liebsten** *od.* **das ~liebste, wenn ...:** I should like it best of all if ...; 2. *adv.* **etw. am ~liebsten tun** like doing sth. best of all; ~m**ei**st... 1. *Indefinitpron. u. unbest. Zahlw.* by far the most *attrib.;* **das ~meiste/am ~meisten** most of all/by far the most; 2. *Adv.* **am ~meisten** most of all; ~m**i**ndest... *Adj.*slightest; least; **das ~mindeste** the very least; ~n**ä**chst... 1. *Adj.* very nearest *attrib.; (Reihenfolge ausdrückend)* very next *attrib.;* 2. *adv.* **am ~nächsten** nearest of all; ~n**eu**[e]st... *Adj.* very latest *attrib.;* **das Allerneu[e]ste** the very latest; ~schl**i**mmst... *Adj.* very worst *attrib.:* ~sch**ö**nst... 1. *Adj.* most beautiful *attrib.;* loveliest *attrib.; (angenehmst...)* very nicest *attrib.;* 2. *adv.* **er singt am ~schönsten** his singing is the most beautiful of all; ~s**ei**ts *Adv.* **guten Morgen ~seits!** good morning everyone

**Allerwelts-:** ~g**e**sicht das nondescript face; ~w**o**rt das hackneyed word

**aller**w**e**nigst... 1. *Adj.* lest ... of all; *Pl.* fewest ... of all; 2. *adv.* **am ~wenigsten** least of all

**alle·s**a**mt** *Indefinitpron. u. unbest. Zahlw. (ugs.)* all [of you/us/them]; **wir ~:** we all

**Alles·kleber** der all-purpose adhesive

**all·gem**e**in** 1. *Adj.* general; universal ⟨*conscription, suffrage*⟩; **im ~en Interesse** in the common interest; **im ~en** in general; 2. *adv.* **a)** generally; *(ausnahmslos)* universally; **es ist ~ bekannt, daß ...:** it is common knowledge that ...; **b)** *(unverbindlich)* ⟨*write, talk, discuss*⟩ in general terms

**Allgem**e**in-:** ~b**e**finden das *(Med.)* general state of health; ~b**i**ldung die; *o. Pl.* general education

**Allgem**e**inheit die;** ~ **a)** generality; **b) die ~:** the general public

**Allgem**e**in-:** ~med**i**zin die; *o. Pl.* general medicine; ~w**o**hl das public good

**All·h**e**ilmittel** das *(auch fig.)* cureall; panacea

**Allig**a**tor** der; ~s, ~en alligator

**All**ii**erte** der; *adj. Dekl.* ally; **die ~n** the Allies

**all-:** ~j**ä**hrlich 1. *Adj.* annual; yearly; 2. *adv.* annually; every year; ~m**ä**chtig *Adj.* all-powerful

**all·mählich** 1. *Adj.* gradual; 2. *adv.* gradually; 3. *Adv.* **wir sollten ~ gehen** it's time we got going

**all-, All-:** ~m**o**rgendlich 1. *Adj.* regular morning; 2. *adv.* every morning; ~s**ei**tig 1. *Adj.* general; allround, *(Amer.)* all-around *attrib.;* 2. *adv.* generally; ~s**ei**ts *Adv.* on all sides; ~t**a**g der **a)** *(Werktag)* weekday; **b)** *o. Pl. (Einerlei)* daily routine; **der graue ~:** the dull routine of everyday life; ~t**ä**glich *Adj.* ordinary ⟨*face, person, appearance, etc.*⟩; everyday ⟨*topic, event, sight*⟩; commonplace ⟨*remark*⟩; **ein nicht ~täglicher Anblick** a sight one doesn't see every day; ~t**a**gs *Adv.* [on] weekdays; ~zu *Adv.* all too; **nicht ~zu viele** not too many

**allzu-:** ~fr**ü**h *Adv.* all too early; *(~bald)* all too soon; ~l**a**ng[e] *Adv.* too long; ~**o**ft *Adv.* too often; ~s**e**hr *Adv.* too much; **nicht ~sehr** not too much; ~v**ie**l *Adv.* too much

**Alm** die; ~, ~en mountain pasture; Alpine pasture; **Alm·hütte die** Alpine hut

**Almosen** das; ~s, ~ alms *pl.*

**Alp** die; ~, ~en *(bes. schweiz.) s.* **Alm**

**Alp**a**ka** das; ~s, ~s alpaca

**Alpen** *Pl.* **die ~:** the Alps

**Alpen-:** ~r**o**se die rhododendron; ~v**ei**lchen das cyclamen

**Alpha** das; ~[s], ~[s] alpha; **Alphab**e**t** das; ~[e]s, ~e alphabet; **alphab**e**tisch** 1. *Adj.* alphabetical; 2. *adv.* alphabetically

**Alp·horn** das alpenhorn; **alp**i**n** *Adj.* Alpine; **Alpin**i**st** der; ~en, ~en Alpinist

**als** *Konj.* **a)** *(zeitlich)* when; **damals, ~:** [in the days] when; **gerade ~:** just as; **b)** *(kausal)* **um so mehr, ~:** all the more since *or* in that; **c)** *Vergleichspartikel* **größer/älter/mehr/weniger ~:** bigger/older/more/less than; **anders ~ wir sein/leben** be different/live differently from us; **soviel/soweit ~ möglich** as much/as far as possible; **so bald/ schnell ~ möglich** as soon/as quickly as possible; **~ [wenn** *od.* **ob]** *(+ Konjunktiv II)* as if; as though; **~ ob ich das nicht wüßte!** as if I didn't know; **d)**

~ **Rentner/Arzt** as a pensioner/a doctor sich ~ **wahr/Lüge erweisen** prove to be true/a lie

**also** 1. *Adv.* so; therefore; **2.** *Partikel* **a)** *(das heißt)* that is; **b)** *(nach Unterbrechung)* well [then]; **c)** *(verstärkend)* **na** ~! there you are[, you see]; ~ **schön** well all right then

**alt, älter, ältest...** *Adj.* **a)** old; ~ **und jung** old and young; **seine** ~**en Eltern** his aged parents; **wie** ~ **bist du?** how old are you?; **mein älterer/ältester Bruder** my elder/eldest brother; **b)** *(nicht mehr frisch)* old; ~**es Brot** stale bread; **c)** *(vom letzten Jahr)* old; ~**e Äpfel/Kartoffeln** last year's apples/potatoes; **d)** *(langjährig)* long-standing ⟨*acquaintance*⟩; **e)** *(antik, klassisch)* ancient; **f)** *(vertraut)* old familiar ⟨*streets, sights, etc.*⟩; **ganz der/die** ~**e sein** be just the same

¹**Alt** der; ~**s**, ~**e** *(Musik)* alto; *(Frauenstimme)* contralto; *(im Chor)* contraltos *pl.*

²**Alt** das; ~|**s**|, ~: *top fermented, dark beer*

**Altar** der; ~|**e**|**s**, **Altäre** altar

**alt-, Alt-:** ~**bau · wohnung die** flat *(Brit.)* or *(Amer.)* apartment in an old building; ~**bekannt** *Adj.* wellknown; ~**bier** das *s.* ²**Alt**

**Alte** der/die; *adj. Dekl.* **a)** *(alter Mensch)* old man/woman; *Pl.* old people; **b)** *(salopp)* *(Vater, Ehemann)* old man *(coll.)*; *(Mutter, Ehefrau)* old woman *(coll.)*; *(Chef)* governor *(sl.)*; *(Chefin)* boss *(coll.)*; **die** ~**n** *(Eltern)* my/his *etc.* old man and old woman 4(coll.); **c)** *Pl. (Tiereltern)* parents

**alt · ehrwürdig** *Adj. (geh.)* venerable; time-honoured ⟨*customs*⟩; **Alt · englisch** das Old English

**Alter** das; ~**s**, ~: age; *(hohes* ~*)* old age; **im** ~: in one's old age; **im** ~ **von** at the age of; **älter** 1. *s.* **alt**; 2. *Adj. (nicht mehr jung)* elderly; **altern** *itr. V.; mit sein* age

**alters-, Alters-:** ~**genosse** der, ~**genossin** die contemporary; ~**gruppe** die age-group; ~**schwach** *Adj.* old and infirm ⟨*person*⟩; old and weak ⟨*animal*⟩; ~**schwäche** die; *o. Pl. (bei Menschen)* [old] age and infirmity; *(bei Tieren)* [old] age and weakness; ~**stufe** die age; ~**unterschied** der age difference; ~**versorgung** die provision for one's old age; *(System)* pension scheme

**Altertum** das; ~**s** antiquity *no art.*

**Älteste** der/die; *adj. Dekl.* **a)** *(Dorf~, Vereins~, Kirchen~ usw.)* elder; **b)** *(Sohn, Tochter)* eldest

**alt-, Alt-:** ~**griechisch** das classical or ancient Greek; ~**hochdeutsch** das Old High German; ~**klug;** ~**kluger,** ~**klugst...** 1. *Adj.* precocious; **2.** *adv.* precociously; ~**last** die *(Ökologie)* old, improperly disposed of harmful waste; *(fig.)* inherited problem

**ältlich** *Adj.* rather elderly

**alt-, Alt-:** ~**modisch** 1. *Adj.* oldfashioned; **2.** *adv.* in an old-fashioned way; ~**rosa** *Adj.* old rose; ~**stadt** die old [part of the] town; ~**waren · händler** der second-hand dealer

**Alu** das; ~**s** *(ugs.)* aluminium; **Alufolie** die aluminium foil; **Aluminium** das; ~**s** aluminium

**am** *Präp.* + *Art.* **a)** = **an dem;** **b)** **Frankfurt am Main** Frankfurt on [the] Main; **am Marktplatz** on the market square; **am Meer/Fluß** by the sea/on *or* by the river; **am Anfang/Ende** at the beginning/end; **am 19. November** on 19 November; **am schnellsten laufen** run [the] fastest; **am Verwelken sein** be wilting

**Amateur** [ama'tø:ɐ̯] der; ~**s**, ~**e** amateur

**Amazonas** der; ~: Amazon

**Amboß** der; **Ambosses, Ambosse** anvil

**ambulant** *(Med.)* 1. *Adj.* out-patient *attrib.*; 2. *adv.* jmdn. ~ **behandeln** give sb. out-patient treatment; **Ambulanz** die; ~, ~**en a)** *(in Kliniken)* out-patient[s'] department; **b)** *(Krankenwagen)* ambulance

**Ameise** die; ~, ~**n** ant

**Ameisen-:** ~**bär** der ant-eater; ~**haufen** der anthill

**amen** *Adv.* amen; **Amen** das; ~**s**, ~: Amen

**Amerika** (das); ~**s** America; **Amerikaner** der; ~**s**, ~ **a)** American; **b)** *(Gebäck) small, flat iced cake;* **Amerikanerin** die; ~, ~**nen** American; **amerikanisch** *Adj.* American

**Amino · säure** die *(Chemie)* amino acid

**Ammann** der; ~|**e**|**s**, **Ammänner** *(schweiz.) (Gemeinde~, Bezirks~)* ≈ mayor; *(Land~)* cantonal president

**Amme** die; ~, ~**n** wet-nurse

**Amnestie** [amnɛs'ti:] die; ~, ~**n** amnesty; **amnestieren** *tr. V.* grant an amnesty to

**Amöbe** die; ~, ~n *(Biol.)* amoeba
**Amok** der: ~ **laufen** run amok;
**Amok·läufer** der madman
**Ampel** die; ~, ~n a) *(Verkehrs~)* traffic lights *pl.;* b) *(für Pflanzen)* hanging flowerpot
**Amphibie** [am'fi:biə] die; ~, ~n *(Zool.)* amphibian; **Amphibien·fahrzeug** das amphibious vehicle
**Amphi·theater** das amphitheatre
**Ampulle** die; ~, ~n *(Med.)* ampoule
**Amputation** die; ~, ~en *(Med.)* amputation; **amputieren** *tr. V.* amputate
**Amsel** die; ~, ~n blackbird
**Amt** das; ~|e|s, Ämter a) *(Stellung)* post; position; *(hohes politisches od. kirchliches ~)* office; **im ~ sein** be in office; b) *(Aufgabe)* task; job; c) *(Behörde)* office; d) *(Fernsprechvermittlung)* exchange; **amtieren** *itr. V.* a) hold office; b) *(vorübergehend)* act **(als** as); **amtlich** 1. *Adj.* a) *(ugs.: sicher)* definite; 2. *adv.* officially; **Amt·mann** der; *Pl.* ...männer *od.* ...leute, **Amt·männin** die; ~, ~nen senior civil servant
**Amts-:** ~**arzt** der medical officer; ~**gericht** das local *or* district court; ~**geschäfte** *Pl.* official duties; ~**leitung** die *(Fernspr.)* exchange line
**Amulett** das; ~|e|s, ~e amulet; charm
**amüsant** 1. *Adj.* entertaining; 2. *adv.* in an entertaining way; **amüsieren** 1. *refl. V.* a) *(sich vergnügen)* enjoy oneself; **sich mit jmdm.** ~: have fun *or* a good time with sb.; b) *(belustigt sein)* be amused; **sich über jmdn./etw.** ~: find sb./sth. funny; 2. *tr. V.* amuse
**an** 1. *Präp. mit Dat.* a) *(räumlich)* at; *(auf)* on; **Frankfurt an der Oder** Frankfurt on [the] Oder; **Tür an Tür** next door to one another; **an ... vorbei** past; b) *(zeitlich)* on; **an jedem Sonntag** every Sunday; **an Ostern** *(bes. südd.)* at Easter; c) **arm/reich an Vitaminen** low/rich in vitamins; **jmdn. an etw. erkennen** recognize sb. by sth.; **an etw. leiden** suffer from sth.; **an einer Krankheit sterben** die of a disease; d) **an |und für| sich** actually; 2. *Präp. mit Akk.* a) to; *(auf, gegen)* on; b) **an etw./ jmdn. glauben** believe in sth./sb.; **an etw. denken** think of sth.; **sich an etw. erinnern** remember sth.; 3. *Adv.* a) *(Verkehrsw.)* **Köln an:** 9.15 arriving Cologne 09.15; b) *(ugs.: in Betrieb)* on; **die Waschmaschine/der Fernseher**
ist an the washing-machine/television is on; *s. auch* **ansein**; c) *(ugs.: ungefähr)* around; about; **an |die| 20 000 DM** around *or* about 20,000 DM
**Analyse** die; ~, ~n analysis; **analysieren** *tr. V.* analyse; **analytisch** 1. *Adj.* analytical; 2. *adv.* analytically
**Ananas** die; ~, ~ *od.* ~se pineapple
**Anarchie** die; ~, ~n anarchy; **Anarchist** der; ~en, ~en anarchist
**Anatomie** die; ~, ~n anatomy; **anatomisch** *Adj.* anatomical
**an|bahnen** 1. *tr. V.* initiate ⟨*negotiations, talks, process, etc.*⟩; develop ⟨*relationship, connection*⟩; 2. *refl. V.* ⟨*development*⟩ be in the offing; ⟨*friendship, relationship*⟩ start to develop
**an|bändeln** *itr. V.* **mit jmdm.** ~ *(ugs.)* get off with sb. *(Brit. coll.);* pick sb. up
**An·bau** der; *Pl.* **Anbauten** a) *o. Pl.* building; b) *(Gebäude)* extension; c) *o. Pl. (das Anpflanzen)* growing
**an|bauen** 1. *tr. V.* a) build on; b) *(anpflanzen)* grow; 2. *itr. V. (das Haus vergrößern)* build an extension
**an·bei** *Adv. (Amtsspr.)* herewith; **Rückporto** ~: return postage enclosed
**an|beißen** 1. *unr. tr. V.* bite into; take a bite of; 2. *unr. itr. V. (auch fig. ugs.)* bite
**an|belangen** *tr. V.* **was mich/dies usw. anbelangt** as far as I am/this matter is *etc.* concerned
**an|beten** *tr. V. (auch fig.)* worship
**An·betracht** der: **in ~ einer Sache** *(Gen.)* in view of sth.
**an|betreffen** *unr. tr. V. s.* **anbelangen**
**an|betteln** *tr. V.* **jmdn.** ~: beg from sb.; **jmdn. um etw.** ~: beg sb. for sth.
**Anbetung** die; ~, ~en *(auch fig.)* worship
**an|biedern** *refl. V.* **sich |bei jmdm.|** ~: curry favour [with sb.]
**an|bieten** 1. *unr. tr. V.* offer; **jmdm. etw.** ~: offer sb. sth.; 2. *unr. refl. V.* a) offer one's services; **sich ~, etw. zu tun** offer to do sth.; b) *(fig.)* ⟨*possibility, solution*⟩ suggest itself
**an|binden** *unr. tr. V.* tie [up] (an + Dat. od. Akk. to); tie up, moor ⟨*boat*⟩ (an + Dat. od. Akk. to); tether ⟨*animal*⟩ (an + Dat. od. Akk. to)
**an|blasen** *unr. tr. V.* a) blow at; b) *(anfachen)* blow on
**An·blick** der sight; **an|blicken** *tr. V.* look at
**an|blinzeln** *tr. V.* a) blink at; b) *(zuzwinkern)* wink at

**an|brechen 1.** *unr. tr. V.* **a)** crack; **b)** *(öffnen)* open; **c)** *(zu verbrauchen beginnen)* break into *(supplies, reserves)*; **2.** *unr. itr. V.; mit sein (geh.: beginnen) (dawn, day)* break; *(age, epoch)* dawn

**an|brennen 1.** *unr. tr. V. (anzünden)* light; **2.** *unr. itr. V.; mit sein* burn

**an|bringen** *unr. tr. V.* **a)** *(befestigen)* put up *(sign, aerial, curtain, plaque)* **(an** + *Dat.* on); **b)** *(äußern)* make *(request, complaint, comment)*; **c)** *(zeigen)* demonstrate *(knowledge, experience)*; **d)** *(ugs.: herbeibringen)* bring

**An·bruch** *der o. Pl. (geh.: Beginn)* dawn[ing]; **der ~ des Tages** daybreak

**an|brüllen** *tr. V. (ugs.)* bellow at

**Andacht die; ~, ~en a)** *o. Pl. (Sammlung)* rapt attention; *(im Gebet)* silent worship; **b)** *(Gottesdienst)* prayers *pl.*;

**andächtig 1.** *Adj.* rapt; *(ins Gebet versunken)* devout; **2.** *adv.* with rapt attention; *(ins Gebet versunken)* devoutly

**an|dauern** *itr. V. (negotiations)* continue, go on; *(weather, rain)* last

**andauernd 1.** *Adj.* continual; constant; **2.** *adv.* continually; constantly

**Anden** *Pl.* **die ~:** the Andes

**An·denken das; ~s, ~ a)** *o. Pl.* memory; **zum ~ an jmdn./etw.** to remind you/us *etc.* of sb./sth.; **b)** *(Erinnerungsstück)* memento; *(Reise~)* souvenir

**ander...** *Indefinitpron.* **1.** *attr.* **a)** other; **ein ~er/eine ~e/ein ~es** another; **das Kleid gefällt mir nicht, haben Sie noch ~e/ein ~es?** I don't like that dress, do you have any others/another?; **jemand ~er** *od.* **~es** someone else; *(in Fragen)* anyone else; **niemand ~er** *od.* **~es** nobody else; **etwas ~es** something else; *(in Fragen)* anything else; **nichts ~es** nothing else; not anything else; **b)** *(verschieden)* different; **2.** *alleinstehend* **ein ~/eine ~e:** another [one]; **nicht drängeln, einer nach dem ~n** don't push, one after the other; **ein ~er/eine ~e/ein ~es** another [one]; **ein[e]s nach dem ~[e]n** first things first; **ich will weder das eine noch das ~e** I don't want either; **anderen·falls** *Adv.* otherwise; **anderer·seits** *Adv.* on the other hand; **ander·mal** *Adv.* **ein ~:** another time; **andern·falls** *Adv.* otherwise

**ändern 1.** *tr. V.* change; alter; alter *(garment)*; change *(person)*; **2.** *refl. V.* change

**anders** *Adv.* **a)** *(verschieden) (think,*

*act, feel, do)* differently **(als from** *or esp. Brit.* to); *(be, look, sound, taste)* different **(als from** *or esp. Brit.* to); **es war alles ganz ~:** it was all quite different; **b)** *(sonst)* else; **niemand ~:** nobody else; **jemand ~:** someone else; *(in Fragen)* anyone else

**anders-, Anders-:** **~artig** *Adj.* different; **~farbig** *Adj.* different-coloured *attrib.;* of a different colour *postpos.;* **~gläubige** *der/die* person of a different religion; **~herum** *Adv.* the other way round *or (Amer.)* around; **~herum gehen/fahren** go/drive round *or (Amer.)* around the other way; **~wo** *Adv. (ugs.)* elsewhere; **~woher** *Adv. (ugs.)* from somewhere else; **~wohin** *Adv. (ugs.)* somewhere else

**andert·halb** *Bruchz.* one and a half; **~ Stunden** an hour and a half

**Änderung die; ~, ~en** change *(Gen.* in); alteration *(Gen.* to)

**anderweitig 1.** *Adj.* other; **2.** *adv.* in another way

**an|deuten 1.** *tr. V.* **a)** *(zu verstehen geben)* hint; **b)** *(nicht vollständig ausführen)* outline; *(kurz erwähnen)* indicate; **2.** *refl. V.* be indicated; **An·deutung die** hint

**An·drang der;** *o. Pl.* crowd; *(Gedränge)* crush

**andre...** *s.* **ander...**

**an|drehen** *tr. V.* **a)** *(einschalten)* turn on; **b)** **jmdm. etw. ~** *(ugs.)* palm sb. off with sth.

**andrer·seits** *Adv.* on the other hand

**an|drohen** *tr. V.* **jmdm. etw. ~:** threaten sb. with sth.; **An·drohung die** threat

**an|drücken** *tr. V.* press down

**an|ecken** *itr. V.; mit sein* **bei jmdm. ~** *(fig. ugs.)* rub sb. [up *(Brit.)*] the wrong way

**an|eignen** *refl. V.* **a)** appropriate; **b)** *(lernen)* acquire; learn

**an·einander** *Adv.* **~ denken** think of each other *or* one another; **~ vorbeigehen** pass each other *or* one another

**aneinander:** **~|binden** *unr. tr. V.* tie together; **~|legen** *tr. V.* put *or* place next to each other *or* one another; **~|liegen** *unr. itr. V.* lie next to each other

**Anekdote die; ~, ~n** anecdote

**an|ekeln** *tr. V.* disgust

**Anemone die; ~, ~n** anemone

**an|erkennen** *unr. tr. V.* **a)** recognize *(country, record, verdict, qualification,* *document*); acknowledge ⟨*debt*⟩; accept ⟨*demand, bill, conditions, rules*⟩; allow ⟨*claim, goal*⟩; b) *(nicht leugnen)* acknowledge; c) *(würdigen)* appreciate; respect ⟨*viewpoint, opinion*⟩; ein ~der Blick an appreciative look; **an-erkennens·wert** *Adj.* commendable; **Anerkennung die**; ~, ~en *s.* **anerkennen: a)** recognition; acknowledgement; acceptance; allowance; b) acknowledgement; c) appreciation; respect *(Gen.* for)

**an|fachen** *tr. V.* fan; *(fig.)* arouse ⟨*anger, curiosity, enthusiasm*⟩; inflame ⟨*passion*⟩; stir up ⟨*hatred*⟩; inspire ⟨*hope*⟩; ferment ⟨*discord, war*⟩

**an|fahren 1.** *unr. tr. V.* **a)** run into; hit; b) *(herbeifahren)* deliver; c) *(ansteuern)* stop at ⟨*village etc.*⟩; ⟨*ship*⟩ put in at ⟨*port*⟩; d) *(zurechtweisen)* shout at; **2.** *unr. itr. V.; mit sein* **a)** *(starten)* start off; b) **angefahren kommen** come driving/riding up; **An·fahrt die a)** *(das Anfahren)* journey; b) *(Weg)* approach

**An·fall der** attack; *(epileptischer ~, fig.)* fit; **einen ~ bekommen** *od. (ugs.)* **kriegen** have an attack/a fit; **an·fallen 1.** *unr. tr. V.* attack; **2.** *unr. itr V.; mit sein* ⟨*costs*⟩ be incurred; ⟨*interest*⟩ accrue; ⟨*work*⟩ come up; **an·fällig** *Adj.* ⟨*person*⟩ with a delicate constitution; ⟨*machine*⟩ susceptible to faults; **gegen** *od.* **für etw. ~ sein** be susceptible to sth.

**An·fang der** beginning; start; *(erster Abschnitt)* beginning; **am** *od.* **zu ~:** at first; **von ~ an** from the outset; **~ 1984/der Woche** *usw.* at the beginning of 1984/of the week *etc.;* **an·fangen 1.** *unr. itr. V.* **a)** begin; start; **mit etw. ~:** start [on] sth.; **~, etw. zu tun** start to do sth.; b) *(zu sprechen ~)* begin; **von etw. ~:** start on about sth.; c) *(eine Stelle antreten)* start; **2.** *unr. tr. V.* **a)** begin; start; *(anbrechen)* start; b) *(machen)* do; **An·fänger der;** ~s, ~: beginner; **anfänglich** *Adj.* initial; **anfangs** *Adv.* at first; initially

**Anfangs-:** ~**buchstabe der** initial [letter]; ~**stadium das** initial stage **an|fassen 1.** *tr. V.* **a)** *(fassen, halten)* take hold of; b) *(berühren)* touch; c) **jmdn. ~** *(an der Hand nehmen)* take sb.'s hand; d) *(angehen)* tackle ⟨*problem, task, etc.*⟩; e) *(behandeln)* treat ⟨*person*⟩; **2.** *itr. V.* |**mit**| ~: lend a hand **anfechtbar** *Adj.: s.* **anfechten a:** disputable; contestable; challengeable;

**an|fechten** *unr. tr. V.* **a)** dispute ⟨*statement, contract*⟩; contest ⟨*will*⟩; challenge ⟨*decision, law, opinion*⟩; b) *(beunruhigen)* trouble

**an|fertigen** *tr. V.* make

**an|feuchten** *tr. V.* moisten ⟨*lips, stamp*⟩; dampen ⟨*ironing, cloth, etc.*⟩

**an|feuern** *tr. V.* spur on

**an|flehen** *tr. V.* beseech; implore

**an|fliegen 1.** *unr. itr. V.; mit sein* fly in; **angeflogen kommen** come flying in; **gegen den Wind ~:** fly into the wind; **2.** *unr. tr. V.* fly to ⟨*city, country, airport*⟩; **An·flug der a)** approach; b) *(Hauch)* hint; c) *(Anwandlung)* fit; **in einem ~ von Großzügigkeit** in a fit of generosity

**an|fordern** *tr. V.* ask for; order ⟨*goods, materials*⟩; send for ⟨*ambulance*⟩; **An·forderung die a)** *o. Pl.* *(das Anfordern)* request *(Gen.* for); b) *(Anspruch)* demand

**An·frage die** inquiry; *(Parl.)* question; **an|fragen** *itr. V.* inquire; ask

**an|freunden** *refl. V.* become friends

**an|fügen** *tr. V.* add

**an|fühlen** *refl. V.* feel

**an|führen** *tr. V.* **a)** lead; b) *(zitieren)* quote; c) *(nennen)* give ⟨*example, reason, details, proof*⟩; d) *(ugs.: hereinlegen)* have on *(Brit. coll.);* dupe; **An·führer der** leader; *(Rädelsführer)* ringleader; **An·führung die a)** *(das Zitieren, Zitat)* quotation; b) *(Nennung)* giving

**Anführungs-:** ~**strich der,** ~**zeichen das** quotation-mark

**An·gabe die a)** *(das Mitteilen)* giving; b) *(Information)* piece of information; ~**n** information *sing.;* c) *(Ballspiele)* service; serve; **an|geben 1.** *unr. tr. V.* **a)** give ⟨*reason*⟩; declare ⟨*income, dutiable goods*⟩; name ⟨*witness*⟩; b) *(bestimmen)* set ⟨*course, direction*⟩; **den Takt ~:** keep time; **2.** *unr. itr. V.* **a)** *(prahlen)* boast; brag; *(sich angeberisch benehmen)* show off; b) *(Ballspiele)* serve; **Angeber der;** ~s, ~ braggart; **Angeberei die;** ~: showing-off; **angeblich 1.** *Adj.* alleged; **2.** *adv.* supposedly; allegedly **an·geboren** *Adj.* innate ⟨*characteristic*⟩; congenital ⟨*disease*⟩

**An·gebot das a)** offer; b) *(Wirtsch.)* supply; *(Sortiment)* range

**an·gebracht** *Adj.* appropriate

**an·gegriffen** *Adj.* weakened ⟨*health, stomach*⟩; strained ⟨*nerves, voice*⟩

**angeheitert** *Adj.* tipsy

**an|gehen** 1. *unr. itr. V.; mit sein* **a)** ⟨*radio, light, heating*⟩ come on; ⟨*fire*⟩ catch; **b)** *(anwachsen, wachsen)*⟨*plant*⟩ take root; **e)** **es mag noch** ~: it's [just about] acceptable; **f)** **gegen etw./jmdn.** ~: fight sth./sb.; 2. *unr. tr. V.* **a)** *(angreifen)* attack; **b)** *(in Angriff nehmen)* tackle ⟨*problem, difficulty*⟩; take ⟨*fence, bend*⟩; **c)** *(bitten)* ask (**um** for); **d)** *(betreffen)* concern; **das geht dich nichts an** it's none of your business; **angehend** *Adj.* budding; *(zukünftig)* prospective

**an|gehören** *itr. V.* **jmdm./einer Sache** ~: belong to sb./sth.; **der Regierung/ einer Familie** ~: be a member of the government/a family; **an·gehörig** *Adj.* belonging (*Dat.* to); **Angehörige der/die;** *adj. Dekl.* **a)** *(Verwandte)* relative; relation; **b)** *(Mitglied)* member

**Angeklagte der/die;** *adj. Dekl.* accused; defendant

**Angel die;** ~, ~n **a)** fishing-rod; **b)** *(Tür~, Fenster~ usw.)* hinge; **etw. aus den ~n heben** *(fig.)* turn sth. upside down

**An·gelegenheit die** matter; *(Aufgabe, Problem)* affair

**Angel·haken der** fish-hook; **angeln** 1. *tr. V. (zu fangen suchen)* fish for; *(fangen)* catch. 2. *itr. V.* angle; fish; **Angel·rute die** fishing-rod **Angel·sachse der** Anglo-Saxon **Angel·schnur die** fishing-line

**an·gemessen** *Adj.* appropriate; reasonable, fair ⟨*price, fee*⟩

**an·genehm** 1. *Adj.* pleasant; **~e Reise/Ruhe!** [have a] pleasant journey/ have a good rest; |**sehr**| ~! delighted to meet you; 2. *adv.* pleasantly

**an·gesehen** *Adj.* respected

**angesichts** *Präp. mit Gen. (geh.)* **a)** in the face of; **b)** *(fig.: in Anbetracht)* in view of

**angespannt** *Adj.* **a)** close ⟨*attention*⟩; taut ⟨*nerves*⟩; **b)** tense ⟨*situation*⟩; tight ⟨*market, economic situation*⟩

**angestellt** *Adj.* **bei jmdm.** ~ **sein** be employed by sb.; work for sb.; **Angestellte der/die;** *adj. Dekl.* [salaried] employee

**an·getan** *Adj.* **von jmdm./etw.** ~ **sein** be taken with sb./sth.

**an·getrunken** *Adj.* [slightly] drunk **an·gewiesen** *Adj.* **auf jmdn./etw.** ~ **sein** have to rely on sb./sth.

**an|gewöhnen** *tr. V.* **jmdm. etw.** ~: get sb. used to sth.; **jmdm.** ~, **etw. zu tun**

get sb. used to doing sth.; **sich** *(Dat.)* **etw.** ~: get into the habit of sth.; |**es**| **sich** *(Dat.)* ~, **etw. zu tun** get into the habit of doing sth.; **An·gewohnheit die** habit

**an|gleichen** 1. *unr. tr. V.* **etw. einer Sache** *(Dat.)* *od.* **an etw.** *(Akk.)* ~: bring sth. into line with sth.; 2. *unr. refl. V.* **sich jmdm./einer Sache** *od.* **an jmdn./etw.** ~: become like sb./sth.; **An·gleichung die: die ~ der Löhne an die Preise** bringing wages into line with prices

**Angler der;** ~s, ~ angler

**Anglistik die;** ~: English studies *pl.,* no art.

**Angola (das);** ~s Angola

**Angora-:** ~**katze die** angora cat; ~**wolle die** angora [wool]

**an|greifen** 1. *unr. tr. V.* **a)** *(auch fig.)* attack; **b)** *(schwächen)* affect ⟨*health, heart, stomach, intestine, voice*⟩; weaken ⟨*person*⟩; 2. *unr. itr. V. (auch fig.)* attack; **An·greifer der** *(auch fig.)* attacker; **An·griff der** **a)** attack; **zum** ~ **blasen** *(auch fig.)* sound the attack; **b)** **etw. in** ~ **nehmen** tackle sth.

**angst** *Adj.* **jmdm. ist/wird** |**es**| ~ |**und bange**| sb. is/becomes frightened; **Angst die;** ~, **Ängste a)** *(Furcht)* fear; ~ **bekommen** *od.* *(ugs.)* **kriegen** become frightened; ~ **haben** be frightened (**vor** + *Dat.* of); **b)** *(Sorge)* anxiety; ~ **haben** be anxious (**um** about); **keine** ~, **ich vergesse es schon nicht!** don't worry, I won't forget [it]!; **ängstigen** 1. *tr. V.* frighten; *(beunruhigen)* worry; 2. *refl. V.* be frightened; *(sich sorgen)* worry; **ängstlich** 1. *Adj.* anxious; 2. *adv.* anxiously; **Ängstlichkeit die;** ~: timidity

**an|gucken** *tr. V. (ugs.)* look at; **sich** *(Dat.)* **etw./jmdn.** ~: have a look at sth./ sb.

**an|gurten** *tr. V.* strap in; **sich** ~: put on one's seat-belt

**an|haben** *unr. tr. V.* **a)** *(ugs.: am Körper tragen)* have on; **b)** **jmdm./einer Sache etwas** ~ **können** be able to harm sb./sth.

**an|halten** 1. *unr. tr. V.* **a)** stop; **b)** *(auffordern)* urge; 2. *unr. itr. V.* **a)** stop; **b)** *(andauern)* go on; last; **anhaltend** 1. *Adj.* constant; continuous; 2. *adv.* constantly; continuously; **An·halter der** hitch-hiker; **per** ~ **fahren** hitch[-hike]; **An·halterin die** hitch-hiker; **Anhalts·punkt der** clue (**für** to); *(für eine Vermutung)* grounds *pl.*

**an·hand 1.** *Präp. mit Gen.* with the help of; **2.** *Adv.* ~ **von** with the help of **An·hang der a)** *(Buchw.)* appendix; **b)** *(Anhängerschaft)* following; **c)** *(Verwandtschaft)* family; **an|hängen 1.** *tr. V.* **a)** hang up **(an +** *Akk.* on); **b)** *(ankuppeln)* couple on **(an +** *Akk.* to); hitch up *⟨trailer⟩* **(an +** *Akk.* to); **c)** *(anfügen)* add **(an +** *Akk.* to); **2.** *refl. V.* **a)** hang on **(an +** *Akk.* to); **b)** *(ugs.: sich anschließen)* **sich [an jmdn.** *od.* **bei jmdm.]** ~: tag along [with sb.] *(coll.);* **An·hänger der a)** *(Mensch)* supporter; **b)** *(Wagen)* trailer; **c)** *(Schmuckstück)* pendant; **d)** *(Schildchen)* tag; **Anhängerschaft die;** ~, ~en supporters *pl.;* **anhänglich** *Adj.* devoted *⟨dog, friend⟩;* **Anhänglichkeit die;** ~: devotion **an|hauchen** *tr. V.* breathe on *⟨mirror, glasses⟩;* blow on *⟨fingers, hands⟩* **an|häufen** *tr. V.* accumulate; **Anhäufung die** accumulation **an|heben** *unr. tr. V.* **a)** lift [up]; **b)** *(erhöhen)* raise *⟨prices, wages, etc.⟩* **an|heften** *tr. V.* attach *⟨label, list⟩;* put up *⟨sign, notice⟩* **anheim|stellen** *(geh.) tr. V.* **|es| jmdm.** ~, **etw. zu tun** leave it to sb. to do sth. **An·hieb der: auf** ~ *(ugs.)* straight off **an|himmeln** *tr. V.* worship **An·höhe die** rise **an|hören 1.** *tr. V.* listen to; **sich** *(Dat.)* **jmdn./etw.** ~: listen to sb./sth.; **2.** *refl. V.* sound **animieren** *tr. V.* encourage **Anis der;** ~**|es|** aniseed **Ank.** *Abk.* Ankunft arr. **An·kauf der** purchase; **an|kaufen** *tr. V.* purchase; buy **Anker der;** ~**s,** ~ anchor; **vor** ~ **gehen/liegen** drop anchor/lie at anchor; ~ **werfen** drop anchor; **ankern** *itr. V.* **a)** anchor; **b)** *(vor Anker liegen)* be anchored; **Anker·platz der** anchorage **An·klage die a)** charge; **unter** ~ **stehen** have been charged **(wegen** with); **b)** *(~vertretung)* prosecution; **Anklage·bank die** dock; **auf der** ~ **sitzen** *(auch fig.)* be in the dock; **an|klagen** *tr. V.* **a)** *(Rechtsw.)* charge *(Gen.,* **wegen** with); accuse; **b)** *(geh.: beschuldigen)* accuse; **An·kläger der** prosecutor **an|klammern 1.** *tr. V.* peg *(Brit.),* pin *(Amer.)* *⟨clothes, washing⟩* up; clip *⟨sheet etc.⟩;* **(mit Heftklammern)** staple *⟨sheet etc.⟩;* **2.** *refl. V.* **sich an jmdn./etw.** ~: cling to sb./sth.

**An·klang der: |bei jmdm.|** ~ **finden** meet with [sb.'s] approval **an|kleben 1.** *tr. V.* stick up *⟨poster, etc.⟩;* **2.** *itr. V.; mit sein* stick **an|kleiden** *tr. V. (geh.)* dress; **sich** ~: dress **an|klopfen** *itr. V.* knock **an|knüpfen 1.** *tr. V.* **a)** tie on **(an +** *Akk.* to); **b)** *(beginnen)* start up *⟨conversation⟩;* establish *⟨relations, business links⟩;* form *⟨relationship⟩;* **2.** *itr. V.* **an etw.** *(Akk.)* ~: take sth. up; **ich knüpfe dort an, wo ...** I'll pick up where ... **an|kommen** *unr. itr. V.; mit sein* **a)** *(eintreffen)* arrive; **seid ihr gut angekommen?** did you arrive safely?; **b)** **|bei jmdm.| |gut|** ~ *(fig. ugs.)* go down [very] well [with sb.]; **c) gegen jmdn./etw.** ~: be able to deal with sb./fight sth.; **d)** *unpers.* **es kommt auf jmdn./etw. an** *(jmd./etw. ist ausschlaggebend)* it depends on sb./sth.; **es kommt auf etw.** *(Akk.)* **an** *(etw. ist wichtig)* sth. matters *(Dat.* to); **es kommt |ganz| darauf** *od.* **drauf an** *(ugs.)* it [all] depends; **e)** *unpers.* **es darauf** *od.* **drauf** ~ **lassen** *(ugs.)* chance it; **es auf etw.** *(Akk.)* ~ **lassen** [be prepared to] risk sth. **an|koppeln 1.** *tr. V.* couple *⟨carriage⟩* up; hitch *⟨trailer⟩* up; dock *⟨spacecraft⟩;* **2.** *itr. V. ⟨spacecraft⟩* dock **an|kreuzen** *tr. V.* mark with a cross **an|kündigen 1.** *tr. V.* announce; **2.** *refl. V.* announce itself; **An·kündigung die** announcement **Ankunft die;** ~, **Ankünfte** arrival; **„~"** 'arrivals' **Ankunfts-:** ~**halle die** arrival[s] hall; ~**tafel die** arrivals board **an|kuppeln** *tr. V. s.* ankoppeln 1 **an|kurbeln** *tr. V.* **a)** crank [up]; **b)** *(fig.)* boost *⟨economy, production, etc.⟩* **Anl.** *Abk.* Anlage encl. **an|lächeln** *tr. V.* smile at; **an|lachen 1.** *tr. V.* smile at. **2.** *refl. V.* **sich** *(Dat.)* **jmdn.** ~ *(ugs.)* get off with sb. *(Brit. coll.);* pick sb. up **An·lage die a)** *o. Pl. (das Anlegen) (einer Kartei)* establishment; *(eines Parks, Gartens usw.)* laying out; *(eines Parkplatzes, Stausees)* construction; **b)** *(Grün~)* park; *(um ein Schloß usw. herum)* grounds *pl.;* **c)** *(Einrichtung)* facilities *pl.;* **militärische** ~**n** military installations; **d)** *(Werk)* plant; **e)** *(Musik~, Lautsprecher~ usw.)* system; **f)** *(Geld~)* investment; **g)** *(Konzeption)* conception; *(Struktur)* structure; **h)**

*(Veranlagung)* aptitude; *(Neigung)* tendency; **i)** *(Beilage zu einem Brief)* enclosure

**Anlaß** der; **Anlasses, Anlässe a)** cause (zu for); **etw. zum ~ nehmen, etw. zu tun** take sth. as an opportunity to do sth.; **aus aktuellem ~:** because of current events; **b)** *(Gelegenheit)* occasion

**an|lassen 1.** *unr. tr. V.* **a)** leave ⟨*light, radio, heating, etc.*⟩ on; leave ⟨*engine*⟩ running; leave ⟨*candle*⟩ burning; **b)** keep ⟨*coat, gloves, etc.*⟩ on; **c)** *(in Gang setzen)* start [up]; **2.** *unr. refl. V.* **sich gut/schlecht ~:** get off to a good/bad start; **Anlasser** der; **~s, ~** starter

**an·läßlich** *Präp. mit Gen.* on the occasion of

**An·lauf** der **a)** run-up; [mehr] **~ nehmen** take [more of] a run-up; **b)** *(Versuch)* attempt; **beim** *od.* **im ersten/dritten ~:** at the first/third attempt; **an|laufen 1.** *unr. itr. V.;* mit sein **a) angelaufen kommen** come running along; *(auf einen zu)* come running up; **b) gegen jmdn./etw. ~:** run at sb./sth.; **c)** *(Anlauf nehmen)* take a run-up; **d)** *(zu laufen beginnen)* ⟨*engine*⟩ start [up]; *(fig.)* ⟨*film*⟩ open; ⟨*production, campaign, search*⟩ start; **e) rot/dunkel** *usw.* **~:** go *or* turn red/dark *etc.;* **f)** *(beschlagen)* mist up; **2.** *unr. tr. V.* put in at ⟨*port*⟩

**an|legen 1.** *tr. V.* **a)** put *or* lay ⟨*domino, card*⟩ [down] (**an** + *Akk.* next to); place, position ⟨*ruler, protractor*⟩ (**an** + *Akk.* on); put ⟨*ladder*⟩ up (**an** + *Akk.* against); **b) die Flügel/Ohren ~:** close its wings/lay its ears back; **die Arme ~:** put one's arms to one's sides; **c)** *(geh.: anziehen, umlegen)* don; **d)** *(schaffen, erstellen)* lay out ⟨*town, garden, plantation, street*⟩; start ⟨*file, album*⟩; compile ⟨*statistics, index*⟩; **e)** *(investieren)* invest; **f)** *(ausgeben)* spend (**für** on); **g) es darauf ~, etw. zu tun** be determined to do sth.; **2.** *itr. V.* **a)** *(landen)* moor; **b)** *(Kartenspiele)* lay a card/cards; **c)** *(Domino)* play [a domino/dominoes]; **d)** *(das Gewehr ~)* aim (**auf** + *Akk.* at); **3.** *refl. V.* **sich mit jmdm. ~:** pick an argument with sb.

**Anlege-:** **~platz** der berth; **~steg** der jetty

**an|lehnen 1.** *tr. V.* **a)** lean (**an** + *Akk. od. Dat.* against); **b)** leave ⟨*door, window*⟩ slightly open; **2.** *refl. V.* **sich [an jmdn.** *od.* **jmdm./etw.] ~:** lean [on sb./ against sth.]; **Anlehnung** die; **~,**

**~en: in ~an** (+ *Akk.*) in imitation of; following

**Anleihe** die; **~, ~n** loan

**an|leiten** *tr. V.* instruct; **An·leitung** die instructions *pl.*

**an|lernen** *tr. V.* train

**an|liegen** *unr. itr. V.* **a)** ⟨*pullover etc.*⟩ fit tightly; **b)** *(ugs.: vorliegen)* be on; **An·liegen** das; **~s, ~** *(Bitte)* request; *(Angelegenheit)* matter; **anliegend** *Adj.* **a)** *(angrenzend)* adjacent; **b)** *(beiliegend)* enclosed; **Anlieger** der; **~s, ~:** resident; „**~ frei**" 'except for access'

**an|locken** *tr. V.* attract ⟨*customers, tourists, etc.*⟩; lure ⟨*bird, animal*⟩

**an|lügen** *tr. V.* lie to

**an|machen** *tr. V.* **a)** put ⟨*light, radio, heating*⟩ on; light ⟨*fire*⟩; **b)** mix ⟨*cement, plaster, paint, etc.*⟩; dress ⟨*salad*⟩

**an|malen** *tr. V.* paint

**an|maßen** *refl. V.* **sich** *(Dat.)* **etw. ~:** claim sth. [for oneself]; **an·maßend 1.** *Adj.* presumptuous; *(arrogant)* arrogant; **2.** *adv.* presumptuously; *(arrogant)* arrogantly; **Anmaßung** die; **~, ~en** presumption; *(Arroganz)* arrogance

**an|melden** *tr. V.* **a)** *(als Teilnehmer)* enrol (**zu** for); **sich ~:** enrol (**zu** for); **b)** *(melden, anzeigen)* license ⟨*radio, television*⟩; apply for ⟨*patent*⟩; register ⟨*domicile, car, trade mark*⟩; **sich ~:** register one's new address; **c)** *(ankündigen)* announce; **sind Sie angemeldet?** do you have an appointment?; **sich beim Arzt ~:** make an appointment to see the doctor; **d)** *(geltend machen)* express ⟨*reservation, doubt, wish*⟩; put forward ⟨*demand*⟩; **An·meldung** die **a)** *(zur Teilnahme)* enrolment; **b)** *s.* **anmelden b:** licensing; application (*Gen.* for); registration; **c)** *(Ankündigung)* announcement; *(beim Arzt, Rechtsanwalt usw.)* making an appointment

**an|merken** *tr. V.* **a) jmdm. seinen Ärger/seine Verlegenheit** *usw.* **~:** notice that sb. is annoyed/embarrassed *etc.;* **man merkt ihm [nicht] an, daß er krank ist** you can[not] tell that he is ill; **sich nichts ~ lassen** not let it show; **b)** *(geh.: bemerken)* note; **Anmerkung** die; **~, ~en a)** *(Fußnote)* note; **b)** *(geh.: Bemerkung)* comment

**An·mut** die; **~** *(geh.)* grace; **an·mutig** *(geh.)* **1.** *Adj.* graceful ⟨*girl, movement, dance*⟩; charming, delightful

⟨*girl, smile, picture, landscape*⟩; **2.** *adv.* ⟨*move, dance*⟩ gracefully; ⟨*smile, greet*⟩ charmingly

**an|nähen** *tr. V.* sew on

**an|nähern 1.** *refl. V.* get closer *(Dat.* to sth); **2.** *tr. V.* bring closer *(Dat.* to); **annähernd 1.** *Adv.* almost; *(ungefähr)* approximately; **2.** *adj.* approximate

**Annahme die;** ~, ~n **a)** *(das Annehmen)* acceptance; **b)** *(Vermutung)* assumption; **in der** ~, **daß** ...: on the assumption that ...; **annehmbar 1.** *Adj.* **a)** acceptable; **b)** *(recht gut)* reasonable; **2.** *adv.* reasonably [well]; **an|nehmen 1.** *unr. tr. V.* **a)** accept; take; accept ⟨*alms, invitation, condition, help*⟩; take ⟨*food, telephone call*⟩; accept, take up ⟨*offer, challenge*⟩; **b)** *(Sport)* take ⟨*ball, pass, etc.*⟩; **c)** *(billigen)* approve; **d)** *(aufnehmen)* take on ⟨*worker, patient, pupil*⟩; **e)** *(hinnehmen)* accept ⟨*fate, verdict, punishment*⟩; **f)** *(adoptieren)* adopt; **g)** *(haften lassen)* take ⟨*dye, ink*⟩; **h)** *(sich aneignen)* adopt ⟨*habit, mannerism, name, attitude*⟩; **i)** *(bekommen)* take on ⟨*look, appearance, form, dimension*⟩; **j)** *(vermuten, voraussetzen)* assume; **angenommen, [daß]** ...: assuming [that] ...; **2.** *unr. refl. V. (geh.)* **sich jmds./einer Sache** ~: look after sb./ sth.; **Annehmlichkeit die;** ~, ~en comfort; *(Vorteil)* advantage

**annektieren** *tr. V.* annex

**Annonce** [a'nõːsə] **die;** ~, ~n advertisement; advert *(Brit. coll.)*; **annoncieren** *itr. V.* advertise

**annullieren** *tr. V.* annul

**anonym 1.** *Adj.* anonymous; **2.** *adv.* anonymously; **Anonymität die;** ~: anonymity

**Anorak der;** ~s, ~s anorak

**an|ordnen** *tr. V.* **a)** *(arrangieren)* arrange; **b)** *(befehlen)* order; **An·ordnung die** *s.* **anordnen: a)** arrangement; **b)** order

**an·organisch** *Adj.* inorganic

**an|packen 1.** *tr. V.* **a)** *(ugs.: anfassen)* grab hold of; **b)** *(angehen)* tackle; **2.** *itr. V.* **[mit]** ~ *(ugs.: mithelfen)* lend a hand

**an|passen 1.** *tr. V.* **a)** *(passend machen)* fit; **b)** *(abstimmen)* suit *(Dat.* to); **2.** *refl. V.* adapt [oneself] *(Dat.* to); ⟨*animal*⟩ adapt; **Anpassung die;** ~, ~en adaptation **(an** + *Akk.* to); **anpassungs·fähig** *Adj.* adaptable

**an|pfeifen 1.** *unr. tr. V.* **das Spiel/die zweite Halbzeit** ~: blow the whistle to start the game/the second half; **2.** *unr. itr. V.* blow the whistle; **An·pfiff der a)** *(Sport)* whistle for the start of play; **b)** *(salopp: Zurechtweisung)* bawling-out *(coll.)*

**an|pflanzen** *tr. V.* **a)** plant; **b)** *(anbauen)* grow

**an|pöbeln** *tr. V.* *(ugs.)* abuse

**an|prangern** *tr. V.* denounce **(als** as)

**an|preisen** *unr. tr. V.* extol

**An·probe die** fitting; **an|probieren** *tr. V.* try on

**an|rechnen** *tr. V.* **a)** count; **b)** jmdm. etw. ~ *(in Rechnung stellen)* charge sb. for sth.

**An·recht das** right; **ein** ~ **auf etw.** *(Akk.)* **haben** be entitled to sth.

**An·rede die** form of address; **an|reden** *tr. V.* address

**an|regen** *tr. V.* **a)** stimulate ⟨*imagination, digestion*⟩; whet ⟨appetite⟩; **b)** *(ermuntern)* prompt; *(vorschlagen)* propose; **anregend** *Adj.* stimulating; **An·regung die a)** *s.* **anregen a:** stimulation; whetting; **b)** *(Denkanstoß)* stimulus; **c)** *(Vorschlag)* proposal

**an|reichern 1.** *tr. V.* enrich; **2.** *refl. V.* accumulate

**An·reise die** journey [there/here]; **an|reisen** *itr. V.; mit sein* travel there/here; **mit der Bahn** ~: go/come by train

**An·reiz der** incentive

**an|rempeln** *tr. V.* barge into; *(absichtlich)* jostle

**Anrichte die;** ~, ~n sideboard; **an|richten** *tr. V.* **a)** arrange ⟨*food*⟩; *(servieren)* serve; **b)** cause ⟨*disaster, confusion, devastation, etc.*⟩

**anrüchig** *Adj.* **a)** disreputable; **b)** *(unanständig)* indecent

**an|rücken** *itr. V.; mit sein* ⟨*troops*⟩ advance; ⟨*firemen, police*⟩ move in

**An·ruf der** call; **Anruf·beantworter der;** ~s, ~: [telephone-]answering machine; **an|rufen** *unr. tr. V.* **a)** call or shout to ⟨*friend, passer-by*⟩; call ⟨*sleeping person*⟩; **b)** *(geh.: angehen, bitten)* appeal to ⟨*person, court*⟩ **(um** for); call upon ⟨*God*⟩; **c)** *auch itr. (telefonisch* ~) call; **Anrufer der;** ~s, ~: caller

**an|rühren** *tr. V.* **a)** touch; **b)** *(bereiten)* mix

**ans** *Präp. + Art.* **a)** = **an das; b) sich** ~ **Arbeiten machen** set to work

**An·sage** die announcement; **an|sagen** tr. V. **a)** announce; **b)** *(Kartenspiele)* bid

**an|sammeln 1.** tr. V. accumulate; amass ⟨*riches, treasure*⟩; **2.** refl. V. accumulate; *(fig.)* ⟨*anger, excitement*⟩ build up; **An·sammlung** die **a)** collection; **b)** *(Auflauf)* crowd

**ansässig** Adj. resident

**An·satz** der *(erstes Zeichen, Beginn)* beginnings pl.

**an|schaffen** tr. V. [sich *(Dat.)*] etw. ~ get [oneself] sth.; **An·schaffung** die purchase

**an|schalten** tr. V. switch on

**an|schauen** tr. V. *(bes. südd., österr., schweiz.)* s. ansehen; **anschaulich 1.** vivid; **2.** adv. vividly; **Anschauung** die; ~, ~en **a)** *(Wahrnehmung)* experience; **b)** *(Auffassung)* view

**An·schein** der appearance; **allem** od. **dem** ~ **nach** to all appearances; **an·scheinend** Adv. apparently

**an|schieben** unr. tr. V. push ⟨*vehicle*⟩

**an|schießen** unr. tr. V. shoot and wound

**An·schlag** der **a)** *(Bekanntmachung)* notice; *(Plakat)* poster; **b)** *(Attentat)* assassination attempt; *(auf ein Gebäude, einen Zug o. ä.)* attack; **c)** *(Texterfassung)* keystroke; **d) mit dem Gewehr im** ~: with rifle/rifles levelled; **an|schlagen** unr. tr. V. put up, ⟨*notice, announcement, message*⟩ **(an** + *Akk.* on); **b)** *(beschädigen)* chip

**an|schließen 1.** unr. tr. V. **a)** connect **(an** + *Akk. od. Dat.* to); connect up ⟨*electrical device*⟩; **b)** *(festschließen)* lock, secure **(an** + *Dat. od. Akk.* to); **2.** unr. refl. V. sich jmdm./einer Sache ~: join sb./sth.; **An·schluß** der connection; **Anschluß·zug** der connecting train

**an|schnallen** tr. V. put on ⟨*skis, skates*⟩; **sich** ~ *(im Auto)* put on one's seatbelt; *(im Flugzeug)* fasten one's seatbelt

**an|schrauben** tr. V. screw on **(an** + *Akk.* to)

**an|schreien** unr. tr. V. shout at

**An·schrift** die address

**Anschuldigung** die; ~, ~en accusation

**an|schwellen** unr. itr. V.; mit sein **a)** swell [up]; *(fig.)* swell; ⟨*water, river*⟩ rise; **b)** *(lauter werden)* grow louder; ⟨*noise*⟩ rise

**an|schwemmen** tr. V. wash ashore

**an|sehen** unr. tr. V. **a)** look at; watch ⟨*television programme*⟩; see ⟨*play, film*⟩; jmdn. **groß/böse** ~: stare at sb./give sb. an angry look; **hübsch** usw. **anzusehen** be pretty etc. to look at; **sieh |mal| |einer| an!** *(ugs.)* well, I never! *(coll.)*; **b)** *(erkennen)* **man sieht ihm sein Alter nicht an** he does not look his age; **man sieht ihr die Strapazen an** she's showing the strain; **c)** *(zusehen bei)* etw. |mit| ~: watch sth.; **das kann man doch nicht |mit|** ~: I/you can't just stand by and watch that; **Ansehen das;** ~s [high] standing; **an·sehnlich** Adj. **a)** *(beträchtlich)* considerable; **b)** *(gut aussehend, stattlich)* handsome

**an|sein** unr. itr. V.; mit sein *(ugs.)* ⟨*light, gas, etc.*⟩ be on

**an|setzen** unr. tr. V. **a)** *(in die richtige Stellung bringen)* position ⟨*ladder, jack, drill, saw*⟩; **b)** *(anfügen)* attach, put on **(an** + *Akk. od. Dat.* to); **c)** *(festlegen)* fix ⟨*meeting etc.*⟩ **(für, auf** + *Akk.* for); fix, set ⟨*deadline, date, price*⟩; **d)** *(veranschlagen)* estimate; **e)** *(anrühren)* mix

**An·sicht** die **a)** *(Meinung)* opinion; view; **meiner** ~ **nach** in my opinion or view; **b)** *(Bild)* view; **Ansichts·karte** die picture postcard

**an|spannen 1.** tr. V. **a)** harness ⟨*horse etc.*⟩ **(an** + *Akk.* to); yoke up ⟨*oxen*⟩ **(an** + *Akk.* to); hitch up ⟨*carriage, cart, etc.*⟩ **(an** + *Akk.* to); **b)** *(anstrengen)* strain; **An·spannung** die strain

**an|spielen** itr. V. auf jmdn./etw. ~: allude to sb./sth.; **Anspielung** die; ~, ~en allusion **(auf** + *Akk.* to); *(verächtlich, böse)* insinuation **(auf** + *Akk.* about)

**An·sporn** der incentive; **an|spornen** tr. V. spur on

**An·sprache** die speech; address; **an|sprechen 1.** unr. tr. V. **a)** speak to; **b)** *(gefallen)* appeal to; **2.** unr. itr. V. *(reagieren)* respond **(auf** + *Akk.* to)

**an|springen 1.** unr. itr. V.; mit sein ⟨*car, engine*⟩ start; **2.** unr. tr. V. jump up at

**An·spruch** der **a)** claim; *(Forderung)* demand; **[keine] Ansprüche stellen** make [no] demands; **in** ~ **nehmen** take advantage of ⟨*offer*⟩; exercise ⟨*right*⟩; take up ⟨*time*⟩; **b)** *(Anrecht)* right

**an·spruchs-:** ~**los 1.** Adj. **a)** *(genügsam)* undemanding; **b)** *(schlicht)* unpretentious; **2.** adv. **a)** *(genügsam)* undemandingly; ⟨*live*⟩ modestly; **b)** *(schlicht)* unpretentiously; ~**voll 1.** Adj. discriminating ⟨*reader, audience,* *gourmet⟩; ⟨schwierig⟩* demanding; ambitious *⟨subject⟩*

**an|spucken** *tr. V.* spit at

**Anstalt die;** ~, ~en institution

**An·stand** der *o. Pl.* decency; **anständig 1.** *Adj.* **a)** decent; *(ehrbar)* respectable; **2.** *adv.* decently; *(ordentlich)* properly

**an|starren** *tr. V.* stare at

**an·statt** *Konj.* ~ **zu arbeiten/**~**, daß er arbeitet** instead of working

**an|stecken 1.** *tr. V.* **a)** pin on *⟨badge, brooch⟩;* put on *⟨ring⟩;* **b)** *(infizieren, auch fig.)* infect; **2.** *itr. V.* be infectious; **ansteckend** *Adj.* infectious; *(durch Berührung)* contagious; **Ansteckung die;** ~, ~en infection; *(durch Berührung)* contagion

**an|stehen** *unr. itr. V. (Schlange stehen)* queue [up], *(Amer.)* stand in line **(nach for)**

**an·stelle 1.** *Präp. mit Gen.* instead of; **2.** *Adv.* ~ **von** instead of

**an|stellen 1.** *refl. V.* queue [up], *(Amer.)* stand in line **(nach for); 2.** *tr. V.* **a)** *(aufdrehen)* turn on; **b)** *(einschalten)* switch on; **c)** *(einstellen)* employ; **An·stellung die a)** *o. Pl.* employment; **b)** *(Stellung)* job

**Anstieg der;** ~**[e]s** rise, increase (+ *Gen.* in)

**an|stiften** *tr. V.* incite; **An·stifter der, An·stifterin die** instigator; **An·stiftung die** incitement

**an|stimmen** *tr. V.* start singing *⟨song⟩;* start playing *⟨piece of music⟩;* **ein Geschrei** ~ : start shouting

**An·stoß der a)** stimulus **(zu for); den |ersten|** ~ **zu etw. geben** initiate sth.; **b)** ~ **erregen** cause offence **(bei to); |keinen|** ~ **an etw.** *(Dat.)* **nehmen** [not] object to sth.; **an|stoßen 1.** *unr. itr. V.* **a)** *mit sein* **an etw.** *(Akk.)* ~ : bump into sth.; **b)** |**mit den Gläsern**| ~ : clink glasses; **auf jmdn./etw.** ~ : drink to sb./sth.; **2.** *unr. tr. V.* **jmdn./etw.** ~ : give sb./sth. a push; **jmdn. aus Versehen** ~ : knock into sb. inadvertently; **anstößig 1.** *Adj.* offensive; **2.** *adv.* offensively

**an|strahlen** *tr. V.* **a)** illuminate; *(mit Scheinwerfer)* floodlight; **b)** *(anblicken)* beam at

**an|streben** *tr. V. (geh.)* aspire to; *(mit großer Anstrengung)* strive for

**an|streichen** *unr. tr. V.* **a)** paint; **b)** *(markieren)* mark

**an|strengen 1.** *refl. V.* make an effort; **sich mehr/sehr** ~ : make more of an ef-

fort/a great effort; **2.** *tr. V.* strain *⟨eyes, ears, voice⟩;* be a strain on *⟨person⟩;* **seine Phantasie** ~ : exercise one's imagination; **anstrengend** *Adj. (körperlich)* strenuous; *(geistig)* demanding; **Anstrengung die;** ~, ~en **a)** effort; **große** ~**en machen, etw. zu tun** make every effort to do sth.; **b)** *(Strapaze)* strain

**An·strich der** paint

**An·sturm der** rush **(auf** + *Akk.* **to);** *(auf Banken, Waren)* run **(auf** + *Akk.* **on)**

**Antarktika (das);** ~**s** Antarctica; **Antarktis die;** ~ : **die** ~ : the Antarctic; **antarktisch** *Adj.* Antarctic

**An·teil der** share **(an** + *Dat.* of); ~ **an etw.** *(Dat.)* **nehmen** take an interest in sth.; **An·teilnahme die a)** interest **(an** + *Dat.* in); **b)** *(Mitgefühl)* sympathy **(an** + *Dat.* with)

**Antenne die;** ~, ~**n** aerial; antenna *(Amer.)*

**anthrazit** [antra'tsi:t] *Adj.; nicht attr.* anthracite[-grey]; **anthrazit·grau** *Adj.* anthracite-grey

**anti-, Anti-** anti-; **Anti·alkoholiker der** teetotaller; **Antibiotikum das;** ~**s, Antibiotika** *(Med.)* antibiotic

**antik** *Adj.* **a)** classical; **b)** *(aus vergangenen Zeiten)* antique *⟨furniture, fittings, etc.⟩;* **Antike die;** ~ classical antiquity *no art.*

**Antilope die;** ~, ~**n** antelope

**Antipathie die;** ~, ~**n** antipathy

**Antiquariat das** antiquarian bookshop/department; *(mit neueren gebrauchten Büchern)* second-hand bookshop/department; **Antiquität die;** ~, ~**en** antique

**Antlitz das;** ~**es,** ~**e** *(dichter., geh.)* countenance *(literary);* face

**Antrag der;** ~**[e]s, Anträge a)** application **(auf** + *Akk.* for); **einen** ~ **stellen** make an application; **b)** *(Formular)* application form

**an|treffen** *unr. tr. V.* find; *(zufällig)* come across

**an|treiben** *unr. tr. V.* **a)** drive *⟨animals, column of prisoners⟩* on or along; *(fig.)* urge; **b)** *(in Bewegung setzen)* drive; power *⟨ship, aircraft⟩*

**an|treten 1.** *unr. itr. V.; mit sein* **a)** form up; *(in Linie)* line up; *(Milit.)* fall in; **b)** *(sich stellen)* meet one's opponent; *(als Mannschaft)* line up; **gegen jmdn.** ~ : meet sb./line up against sb.; **2.** *unr. tr. V.* **a)** start *⟨job, apprenticeship⟩;* take up *⟨position, appoint-*

*ment*); set out on ⟨*journey*⟩; begin ⟨*prison sentence*⟩; come into ⟨*inheritance*⟩

**An·trieb** der drive

**An·tritt** der: vor ~ Ihres Urlaubs before you go on holiday *(Brit.) or (Amer.)* vacation; vor ~ der Reise before setting out on the journey

**an|tun** *unr. tr. V.* **a)** jmdm. ein Leid ~: hurt sb.; jmdm. etwas Böses/ein Unrecht ~: do sb. harm/an injustice; **b)** jmd./etw. hat es jmdm. angetan sb. was taken with sb./sth.; *s. auch* **angetan**

**Antwort** die; ~, ~en **a)** answer; reply; er gab mir keine ~: he didn't answer [me] *or* reply; **b)** *(Reaktion)* response; **antworten** *itr. V.* **a)** answer; reply; auf etw. *(Akk.)* ~: answer sth.; reply to sth.; jmdm. ~: answer sb.; reply to sb.; **b)** *(reagieren)* respond (**auf** + *Akk.* to)

**an|vertrauen** 1. *tr. V.* jmdm. etw. ~: entrust sb. with sth.; *(fig.: mitteilen)* confide sth. to sb.; 2. *refl. V.* sich jmdm./einer Sache ~: put one's trust in sb./sth.; sich jmdm. ~ *(fig.: sich jmdm. mitteilen)* confide in sb.

**an|wachsen** *unr. itr. V.;* *mit sein* **a)** grow on; **b)** *(Wurzeln schlagen)* take root; **c)** *(zunehmen)* grow

**Anwalt** der; ~[e]s, Anwälte, **Anwältin** die; ~, ~nen **a)** *(Rechts~)* lawyer; solicitor *(Brit.);* attorney *(Amer.); (vor Gericht)* barrister *(Brit.);* attorney[-at-law] *(Amer.);* advocate *(Scot.);* **b)** *(Fürsprecher)* advocate

**An·wärter** der candidate (**auf** + *Akk.* for); *(Sport)* contender (**auf** + *Akk.* for)

**an|weisen** *unr. tr. V.* instruct; *s. auch* **angewiesen; An·weisung** die instruction

**an|wenden** *unr. (auch regelm.) tr. V.* use, employ ⟨*process, trick, method, violence, force*⟩; use ⟨*medicine, money, time*⟩; apply ⟨*rule, paragraph, proverb, etc.*⟩ (**auf** + *Akk.* to); **An·wendung** die *s.* **anwenden**: use; employment; application

**An·wesen** das property

**anwesend** *Adj.* present (**bei** at); die Anwesenden those present; **Anwesenheit** die; ~: presence

**an|widern** *tr. V.* nauseate

**An·zahl** die; ~: number; eine ganze ~: a whole lot

**an|zahlen** *tr. V.* put down ⟨*sum*⟩ as a deposit (**auf** + *Akk.* on); *(bei Ratenzahlung)* make a down payment of ⟨*sum*⟩ (**auf** + *Akk.* on); **An·zahlung** die deposit; *(bei Ratenzahlung)* down payment

**An·zeichen** das sign; indication

**Anzeige** die; ~, ~n **a)** *(Straf~)* report; **b)** *(Inserat)* advertisement; **c)** *(eines Instruments)* display; **an|zeigen** *tr. V.* **a)** *(Strafanzeige erstatten)* jmdn./etw. ~: report sb./sth. to the police/ the authorities; **b)** *(zeigen)* show; indicate; show ⟨*time, date*⟩; **Anzeigen·teil** der advertisement section *or* pages *pl.*

**an|ziehen** *unr. tr. V.* **a)** *(auch fig.)* attract; **b)** draw up ⟨*knees, feet, etc.*⟩; **c)** tighten ⟨*rope, wire, screw, knot, belt, etc.*⟩; put on ⟨*handbrake*⟩; **d)** *(ankleiden)* dress; sich ~: get dressed; **e)** *(anlegen)* put on ⟨*clothes*⟩; **anziehend** *Adj.* attractive; **An·zug** der **a)** suit; **b)** im ~ sein ⟨*storm*⟩ be approaching; ⟨*fever, illness*⟩ be coming on; ⟨*enemy*⟩ be advancing; **anzüglich** 1. *Adj.* insinuating ⟨*remark, question*⟩; 2. *adv.* in an insinuating way

**an|zünden** *tr. V.* light; set fire to ⟨*building etc.*⟩

**an|zweifeln** *tr. V.* doubt; question

**apart** 1. *Adj.* individual *attrib.;* 2. *adv.* in an individual style

**Apartment** das; ~s, ~s studio flat *(Brit.);* studio apartment *(Amer.)*

**Apathie** die; ~, ~n apathy; **apathisch** 1. *Adj.* apathetic; 2. *adv.* apathetically

**Aperitif** [aperi'ti:f] der; ~s, ~s aperitif

**Apfel** der; ~s, Äpfel apple

**Apfel-:** ~baum der apple-tree; ~kuchen der apple-cake; *(mit Äpfeln belegt)* apple flan; ~mus das apple purée; ~saft der apple-juice

**Apfelsine** die; ~, ~n orange

**Apfel-:** ~strudel der apfelstrudel; ~wein der cider

**Apostel** der; ~s, ~: apostle

**Apotheke** die; ~, ~n **a)** chemist's [shop] *(Brit.);* drugstore *(Amer.);* **b)** *(Haus~)* medicine cabinet; *(Reise~, Bord~)* first-aid kit; **Apotheker** der; ~s, ~, **Apothekerin** die; ~, ~nen [dispensing] chemist *(Brit.);* druggist

**App.** *Abk.* Apparat ext.

**Apparat** der; ~[e]s, ~e **a)** apparatus *no pl.; (Haushaltsgerät)* appliance; *(kleiner)* gadget; **b)** *(Radio~)* radio; *(Fernseh~)* television; *(Foto~)* camera; **c)** *(Telefon)* telephone; *(Nebenstelle)* extension; **d)** *(Personen und Hilfsmittel)* organization; *(Verwaltungs~)* system

**Appartement** [apartə'mã:, *schweiz.
auch:* -'mɛnt] *das;* ~s, ~s *(schweiz.
auch:* ~e) a) *s.* Apartment; b) *(Hotel-
suite)* suite
**Appell** der; ~s, ~e a) appeal (zu for,
an + *Akk.* to); b) *(Milit.)* muster; *(An-
wesenheits~)* roll-call; **appellieren**
*itr. V.* appeal (an + *Akk.* to)
**Appetit** der; ~|e|s, ~e appetite (auf +
*Akk.* for); **guten** ~! enjoy your meal!;
**appetitlich** *Adj.* a) appetizing; b)
*(sauber, ansprechend)* attractive and
hygienic; **Appetit·losigkeit die;** ~:
lack of appetite
**applaudieren** *itr. V.* applaud; **Applaus** der; ~es, ~e applause
**Aprikose** die; ~, ~n apricot
**April** der; ~|s|, ~e April; der ~: April
**Aquädukt** der *od.* das; ~|e|s, ~e aque-
duct
**Aquaplaning das;** ~|s| aquaplaning
**Aquarell** das; ~s, ~e water-colour
[painting]
**Aquarium das;** ~s, **Aquarien** aquarium
**Äquator** der; ~s equator
**Ar** das *od.* der; ~s, ~e are
**Ära** die; ~, **Ären** era
**Araber** der; ~s, ~ Arab; **Arabien**
[a'ra:biən] (das); ~s Arabia; **arabisch** *Adj.* Arabian; Arabic *(language, numeral, literature, etc.)*
**Arbeit** die; ~, ~en a) work *no indef.
art.;* **vor/nach der** ~ *(ugs.)* before/
after work; b) *(Produkt, Werk)* work;
c) *(Aufgabe)* job; d) *(Klassen~)* test;
**arbeiten** 1. *itr. V.* work; 2. *tr. V. (herstellen)* make; **Arbeiter der;** ~s, ~:
worker; *(Bau~, Land~)* labourer;
**Arbeiter·klasse die** working
class[es *pl.*]; **Arbeiterschaft die;** ~:
workers *pl.;* **Arbeit·geber der;** ~:
~: employer; **Arbeitnehmer der;**
~s, ~: employee
**arbeits-, Arbeits-:** ~**amt** das job
centre *(Brit.);* ~**bedingungen** *Pl.*
working conditions; ~**fähig** *Adj.* fit
for work *postpos.; (grundsätzlich)* able
to work *postpos.;* ~**gang** der operation; ~**kraft die** a) capacity for work;
b) *(Mensch)* worker; ~**los** *Adj.* unemployed; ~**lose** der/die; *adj. Dekl.*
unemployed person/man/woman
*etc.;* **die** ~**n** the unemployed; ~**losigkeit die;** ~: unemployment *no indef.
art.;* ~**markt** der labour market;
~**platz der** a) work-place; b) *(~stätte)*
place of work; c) *(~verhältnis)* job;
~**scheu** *Adj.* work-shy; ~**tag** der

working day; ~**teilung die** division
of labour; ~**unfähig** *Adj.* unfit for
work *postpos.; (grundsätzlich)* unable
to work *postpos.;* ~**zeit die** working
hours *pl.;* **die tägliche** ~**zeit** the working day
**Archäologe** der; ~n, ~n archaeologist; **Archäologie die;** ~: archaeology *no art.;* **archäologisch** *Adj.*
archaeological
**Arche die;** ~, ~n ark; **die** ~ **Noah**
Noah's Ark
**Architekt** der; ~en, ~en architect;
**Architektur die;** ~ architecture
**Archiv das;** ~s, ~e archives *pl.;*
archive
**Ären** *s.* **Ära**
**Arena die;** ~, **Arenen** arena; *(Stier-
kampf~, Manege)* ring
**arg, ärger, ärgst...** *(geh., landsch.)*
*Adj.* a) *(schlimm)* bad; **im** ~**en liegen**
be in a sorry state; b) *(unangenehm
groß, stark)* severe ⟨pain, hunger,
shock, disappointment⟩; serious ⟨error,
dilemma⟩; extreme ⟨embarrassment⟩;
gross ⟨exaggeration, injustice⟩; 2. *adv.*
*(äußerst, sehr)* extremely
**Ärger** der; ~s a) annoyance; b) *(Unannehmlichkeiten)* trouble; ~ **bekommen**
get into trouble; **ärgerlich** 1. *Adj.* a)
annoyed; b) *(Ärger erregend)* annoying; 2. *adv.* a) with annoyance; b)
*(Ärger erregend)* annoyingly; **ärgern**
1. *tr. V.* a) annoy; b) *(reizen)* tease; 2.
*refl. V.* sich |über jmdn./etw.| ~: be/get
annoyed [at sb./about sth.]; **Ärgernis**
das; ~ses, ~se annoyance; *(etw. An-
stößiges)* nuisance
**arg-, Arg-:** ~**listig** *Adj.* deceitful;
*(heimtückisch)* malicious; ~**los** 1.
*Adj.* unsuspecting; 2. *adv.* unsuspect-
ingly; ~**losigkeit die;** ~: unsuspecting nature
**ärgst...** *s.* **arg**
**Argument** das; ~|e|s, ~e argument;
**Argumentation die;** ~, ~en argumentation; **argumentieren** *itr. V.*
argue
**Argwohn** der; ~|e|s suspicion; **arg-
wöhnisch** *(geh.)* 1. *Adj.* suspicious;
2. *adv.* suspiciously
**Arie** ['a:riə] die; ~, ~n aria
**Aristokrat** der; ~en, ~en aristocrat;
**Aristokratin die;** ~, ~nen aristocrat; **Aristokratie die;** ~, ~n aristocracy; **aristokratisch** 1. *Adj.* aristocratic; 2. *adv.* aristocratically
**arithmetisch** 1. *Adj.* arithmetical; 2.
*adv.* arithmetically

**Arkade** die; ~, ~n arcade

**Arktis** die; ~: Arctic; **arktisch** Adj. Arctic; (fig.) arctic

**arm,** ärmer, ärmst... Adj. poor; ~ und reich (veralt.) rich and poor [alike]; ~ an Nährstoffen poor in nutrients; der/ die Ärmste od. Arme the poor man/ boy/woman/girl

**Arm** der; ~[e]s, ~e arm; jmdm. [mit etw.] unter die ~e greifen help sb. out [with sth.]; ein Hemd mit halbem ~: a short-sleeved shirt

**Armaturen·brett** das instrument panel; (im Kfz) dashboard

**Arm-:** ~band das bracelet; (Uhr~) strap; ~band·uhr die wrist-watch

**Armee** die; ~, ~n (auch fig.) army

**Ärmel** der; ~s, ~: sleeve; [sich (Dat.)] etw. aus dem ~ schütteln (ugs.) produce sth. just like that

**Ärmel·kanal** der [English] Channel

**ärmer** s. arm; **ärmlich** 1. Adj. cheap ⟨clothing⟩; shabby ⟨flat, office⟩; meagre ⟨meal⟩. 2. adv. cheaply ⟨furnished, dressed⟩

**Arm·reif** der armlet

**arm·selig** Adj. a) miserable; pathetic ⟨result, figure⟩; meagre ⟨meal, food⟩; paltry ⟨return, salary, sum, fee⟩; b) (abwertend: erbärmlich) miserable; **ärmst...** s. arm; **Armut** die; ~ poverty

**Aroma** das; ~s, Aromen (Duft) aroma; (Geschmack) flavour; **aromatisch** Adj. aromatic; distinctive ⟨taste⟩; ~ duften give off an aromatic fragrance

**arrangieren** [arãˈziːrən] 1. tr. V. (geh., Musik) arrange; 2. refl. V. sich ~: adapt; sich mit jmdm. ~: come to an accommodation with sb.

**Arrest** der; ~[e]s, ~e detention

**arrogant** 1. Adj. arrogant; 2. adv. arrogantly; **Arroganz** die; ~ arrogance

**Arsch** der; ~[e]s, Ärsche (derb) a) arse (Brit. coarse); ass (Amer. sl.); leck mich am ~! (fig.) piss off (coarse); im ~ sein (fig.) be buggered (coarse); b) (widerlicher Mensch) arse-hole (Brit. coarse); ass-hole (Amer. sl.); **Arsch-loch** das (derb) s. Arsch b

**Art** die; ~, ~en a) kind; sort; Bücher aller ~: all kinds or sorts of books; [so] eine ~ ...: a sort of ...; aus der ~ schlagen not be true to type; (in einer Familie) be different from all the rest of the family; b) (Biol.) species; c) o. Pl. (Wesen) nature; (Verhaltensweise) way; (gutes Benehmen) behaviour; die feine englische ~ (ugs.) the proper way

to behave; d) (Weise) way; auf diese ~: in this way; ~ und Weise way; (Kochk.) nach ~ des Hauses à la maison; nach Schweizer ~: Swiss style

**Arterie** [arˈteːri̯ə] die; ~, ~n artery

**artig** Adj. well-behaved; sei ~: be a good boy/girl/dog etc.

**Artikel** der; ~s, ~ a) article; b) (Ware) item

**Artillerie** die; ~, ~n artillery

**Artischocke** die; ~, ~n artichoke

**Artist** der; ~en, ~en [variety/circus] performer

**Arznei** die; ~, ~en (veralt.), **Arznei·mittel** das medicine

**Arzt** der; ~es, Ärzte, **Ärztin** die; ~, ~nen doctor; **ärztlich** 1. Adj. medical; auf ~e Verordnung on doctor's orders; 2. adv. sich ~ behandeln lassen have medical treatment

**As** das; ~ses, ~se ace

**Asbest** der; ~[e]s, ~e asbestos

**Asche** die; ~, ~n ash[es pl.]; (sterbliche Reste) ashes pl.

**Aschen-:** ~becher der ashtray; ~brödel das; ~s, ~ (auch fig.) Cinderella

**Ascher·mittwoch** der Ash Wednesday

**Äser** s. Aas

**Asiat** der; ~en, ~en, **Asiatin** die; ~, ~nen Asian; **asiatisch** Adj. Asian; **Asien** [ˈaːzi̯ən] (das); ~s Asia

**Askese** die; ~: asceticism; **Asket** der; ~en, ~en ascetic; **asketisch** 1. Adj. ascetic; 2. adv. ascetically

**asozial** 1. Adj. asocial; 2. adv. asocially

**Aspekt** der; ~[e]s, ~e aspect

**Asphalt** der; ~[e]s, ~e asphalt

**Aspik** der (österr. auch das); ~s, ~e aspic

**aß** 1. u. 3. Pers. Sg. Prät. v. essen

**Assistent** der; ~en, ~en, **Assistentin** die; ~, ~nen assistant

**Ast** der; ~[e]s, Äste branch; sich (Dat.) einen ~ lachen (ugs.) split one's sides [with laughter]

**Aster** die; ~, ~n aster; (Herbst~) Michaelmas daisy

**ästhetisch** 1. Adj. aesthetic; 2. adv. aesthetically

**Asthma** das; ~s asthma

**Astrologe** der; ~n, ~n astrologer; **Astrologie** die; ~: astrology no art.; **astrologisch** Adj. astrological

**Astronaut** der; ~en, ~en; **Astronautin** die; ~, ~nen astronaut

**Astronom** der; ~en, ~en astronomer;

**Astronomie** die; ~: astronomy *no art.;* **astronomisch** *Adj.* astronomical

**Asyl** das; ~s, ~e a) asylum; b) *(Obdachlosen~)* hostel; **Asylant** der; ~en, ~en, **Asylantin** die; ~, ~nen person granted [political] asylum; **Asyl·bewerber** der person seeking [political] asylum

**Atelier** [atə'lie:] das; ~s, ~s studio

**Atem** der; ~s breath; **außer** ~ **sein/geraten** be/get out of breath

**atem-, Atem-**: ~**beraubend** 1. *Adj.* breath-taking; 2. *adv.* breath-takingly; ~**los** 1. *Adj.* breathless; 2. *adv.* breathlessly; ~**pause** die breathing space; ~**zug** der breath

**Atheismus** der; ~: atheism *no art.;* **Atheist** der; ~en, ~en atheist; **atheistisch** 1. *Adj.* atheistic; 2. *adv.* atheistically

**Athen** (das); ~s Athens

**Äther** der; ~s, ~ ether

**Äthiopien** [ε'tio:piən] (das); ~s Ethiopia

**Athlet** der; ~en, ~en a) *(Sportler)* athlete; b) *(ugs.: kräftiger Mann)* muscleman; **athletisch** *Adj.* athletic

**Atlanten** s. ¹Atlas

**Atlantik** der; -s Atlantic; **atlantisch** *Adj.* Atlantic; **der Atlantische Ozean** the Atlantic Ocean

**Atlas** der; ~ *od.* ~ses, **Atlanten** *od.* ~se atlas

**atmen** *itr., tr. V.* breathe

**Atmosphäre** [atmo'sfε:rə] die; ~, ~n *(auch fig.)* atmosphere

**Atmung** die; ~: breathing

**Atom** das; ~s, ~e atom; **atomar** *Adj.* atomic; *(Atomwaffen betreffend)* nuclear

**Atom-**: ~**bombe** die atom bomb; ~**energie** die; *o. Pl.* nuclear energy *no indef. art.;* ~**kern** der atomic nucleus; ~**kraft** die; *o. Pl.* nuclear power *no indef. art.;* ~**kraftwerk** das nuclear power-station; ~**krieg** der nuclear war; ~**müll** der nuclear waste; ~**physik** die nuclear physics *sing., no art.;* ~**pilz** der mushroom cloud; ~**reaktor** der nuclear reactor; ~**waffe** die nuclear weapon; ~**waffen·frei** *Adj.* nuclear-free; ~**zeitalter** das; *o. Pl.* nuclear age

**Attacke** die; ~, ~n *(auch Med.)* attack (auf + *Akk.* on)

**Attentat** das; ~[e]s, ~e assassination attempt; *(erfolgreich)* assassination; **Attentäter** der; ~s, ~, **Attentäterin** die; ~, ~nen would-be assassin; *(erfolgreich)* assassin

**Attest** das; ~[e]s, ~e medical certificate

**Attraktion** die; ~, ~en attraction; **attraktiv** 1. *Adj.* attractive; 2. *adv.* attractively; **Attraktivität** die; ~: attractiveness

**Attrappe** die; ~, ~n dummy

**Attribut** das; ~[e]s, ~e attribute

**ätzen** 1. *tr. V.* etch; 2. *itr. V.* corrode; **ätzend** 1. *Adj.* corrosive; *(fig.)* caustic ⟨wit, remark, criticism⟩; pungent ⟨smell⟩; 2. *adv.* caustically ⟨ironic, critical⟩

**au** *Interj.* a) *(bei Schmerz)* ouch; b) *(bei Überraschung, Begeisterung)* oh

**Aubergine** [obɛr'ʒi:nə] die; ~, ~n aubergine *(Brit.);* egg-plant

**auch** 1. *Adv.* a) as well; too; also; Klaus war ~ dabei Klaus was there as well *or* too; Klaus was also there; **Ich gehe jetzt. – Ich** ~: I'm going now – So am I; **Mir ist warm. – Mir** ~: I feel warm – So do I; **das weiß ich** ~ **nicht** I don't know either; b) *(sogar, selbst)* even; ~ **wenn, wenn** ~: even if; 2. *Partikel* a) etwas anderes habe ich ~ **nicht** erwartet I never expected anything else; **nun hör aber** ~ **zu**! now listen!; b) **bist du dir** ~ **im klaren, was das bedeutet?** are you sure you understand what that means?; **bist du** ~ **glücklich?** are you truly happy?; **lügst du** ~ **nicht?** you're not lying, are you?; c) **wo**.../**wer**.../**was**... *usw.* ~: wherever/whoever/whatever *etc.* ...; **wie dem** ~ **sei** however that may be; d) **mag er** ~ **noch so klug sein** no matter how clever he is

**Audienz** die; ~, ~en audience

**auf** 1. *Präp. mit Dat.* a) on; ~ **See** at sea; ~ **dem Baum** in the tree; ~ **der Erde** on earth; ~ **der Welt** in the world; ~ **der Straße** in the street; b) at ⟨post office, town, hall, police station⟩; ~ **seinem Zimmer** *(ugs.)* in his room; **Geld** ~ **der Bank haben** have money in the bank; ~ **der Schule/Uni** at school/university; c) at ⟨party, wedding⟩; on ⟨course, trip, walk, holiday, tour⟩; 2. *Präp. mit Akk.* a) on; ~ **einen Berg steigen** climb up a mountain; ~ **die Straße gehen** go [out] into the street; b) ~ **die Schule/Uni gehen** go to school/university; ~ **einen Lehrgang gehen** go on a course; c) ~ **10 km [Entfernung]** for [a distance of] 10 km; **wir näherten uns der Hütte [bis]** ~ **30 m we**

approached to within 30 m of the hut; **d) ~ Jahre |hinaus|** for years [to come]; **etw. ~ nächsten Mittwoch verschieben** postpone sth. until next Wednesday; **die Nacht von Sonntag ~ Montag** Sunday night; **das fällt ~ einen Montag** it falls on a Monday; **e) ~ diese Art und Weise** in this way; **~ deutsch** in German; **~ das sorgfältigste** *(geh.)* most carefully; **f) ~ Wunsch** on request; **~ meine Bitte** at my request; **~ Befehl** on command; **g) ein Teelöffel ~ einen Liter Wasser** one teaspoon to one litre of water; **~ die Sekunde/den Millimeter |genau|** [precise] to the second/ millimetre; **~ deine Gesundheit!** your health; **~ bald/morgen!** *(bes. südd.)* see you soon/tomorrow; **3. *Adv.* a) ~!** *(steh/steht auf!)* up you get!; **b) sie waren längst ~ und davon** they had made off long before; **c) ~!** *(bes. südd.: los)* come on; **~ geht's** off we go; **~ ins Schwimmbad!** come on, off to the swimming-pool!; **d) ~ und ab** *(hin und her)* up and down; to and fro; **e) Helm/Hut/Brille ~!** helmet/hat/ glasses on!; **f) Fenster/Mund ~!** open the window/your mouth!

**auf|atmen** *itr. V.* breathe a sigh of relief

**auf|bahren** *tr. V.* lay out; **aufgebahrt sein** lie in state

**Auf·bau der; ~|e|s, ~ten a)** *o. Pl.* building; **b)** *o. Pl. (Struktur)* structure; **c)** *Pl. (Schiffbau)* superstructure *sing.*

**auf|bauen** *tr. V.* **a)** erect ⟨*hut, kiosk, podium*⟩; set up ⟨*equipment, train set*⟩; build ⟨*house, bridge*⟩; put up ⟨*tent*⟩; **b)** *(hinstellen, arrangieren)* lay or set out ⟨*food, presents, etc.*⟩; **c)** *(fig.: schaffen)* build ⟨*state, economy, etc.*⟩; build up ⟨*business, organization, army, spy network*⟩; **d)** *(fig.: strukturieren)* structure

**auf|bäumen** *refl. V.* rear up; **sich gegen jmdn./etw. ~** *(fig.)* rise up against sb./sth.

**auf|bessern** *tr. V.* improve; increase ⟨*pension, wages, etc.*⟩

**auf|bewahren** *tr. V.* keep; **etw. kühl ~:** store sth. in a cool place; **Auf·bewahrung die** keeping

**auf|bieten** *unr. tr. V.* exert ⟨*strength, energy, will-power, influence, authority*⟩; call on ⟨*skill, wit, powers of persuasion or eloquence*⟩

**auf|blasen** *unr. tr. V.* blow up; inflate

**auf|bleiben** *unr. itr. V.; mit sein* **a)** *(geöffnet bleiben)* stay open; **b)** *(nicht zu Bett gehen)* stay up

**auf|blenden** *itr. V.* switch to full beam

**auf|blicken** *itr. V.* **a)** look up; *(kurz)* glance up; **b) zu jmdm. ~** *(fig.)* look up to sb.

**auf|blühen** *itr. V.; mit sein* **a)** come into bloom; ⟨*bud*⟩ open; **b)** *(fig.: aufleben)* blossom [out]

**auf|brauchen** *tr. V.* use up

**auf|brechen 1.** *unr. tr. V.* break open ⟨*lock, safe, box, crate, etc.*⟩; break into ⟨*car*⟩; force [open] ⟨*door*⟩; **2.** *unr. itr. V.; mit sein* **a)** ⟨*bud*⟩ open; ⟨*ice [sheet], surface, ground*⟩ break up; ⟨*wound*⟩ open; **b)** *(losgehen, -fahren)* set off

**auf|bringen** *unr. tr. V.* **a)** find; raise ⟨*money*⟩; *(fig.)* summon [up] ⟨*strength, energy, courage*⟩; find ⟨*patience*⟩; **b)** *(kreieren)* start ⟨*fashion, custom, rumour*⟩; introduce ⟨*slogan, theory*⟩; **c)** **jmdn. ~:** make sb. angry; **d) jmdn. gegen jmdn./etw. ~:** set sb. against sb./ sth.

**Auf·bruch der** departure

**auf|brühen** *tr. V.* brew [up]

**auf|decken** *tr. V.* **a)** uncover; **b)** *(Kartenspiele)* show; **c)** *(fig.)* reveal; uncover; *(enthüllen)* expose

**auf|drängen 1.** *tr. V.* **jmdm. etw. ~:** force sth. on sb.; **2.** *refl. V.* **sich jmdm. ~:** force oneself on sb.

**auf|drehen** *tr. V.* **a)** unscrew ⟨*bottle-cap, nut*⟩; undo ⟨*screw*⟩; turn on ⟨*tap, gas, water*⟩; open ⟨*valve, bottle, vice*⟩; **b)** *(ugs.)* turn up ⟨*radio, record-player, etc.*⟩

**auf·dringlich 1.** *Adj.* pushy *(coll.)* ⟨*person*⟩; *(fig.)* insistent ⟨*music, advertisement*⟩; pungent ⟨*perfume, smell*⟩; loud ⟨*colour, wallpaper*⟩; **2.** *adv.* ⟨*behave*⟩ pushily, *(coll.)*; **Aufdringlichkeit die; ~s. aufdringlich:** pushiness *(coll.)*; insistent manner; pungency

**auf·einander** *Adv.* on top of one another

**aufeinander-: ~|folgen** *itr. V.; mit sein* follow one another; **~folgend** successive; **~|legen 1.** *tr. V.* lay ⟨*planks etc.*⟩ one on top of the other; **2.** *refl. V.* lie on top of one another; **~|liegen** *unr. V.* lie on top of each other *or* one another; **~|prallen** *itr. V.; mit sein* crash into one another; collide; *(fig.)* ⟨*opinions*⟩ clash; **~|treffen** *unr. itr. V.; mit sein (fig.)* meet

**Aufenthalt der; ~|e|s, ~e a)** stay; **b)** *(Fahrtunterbrechung)* stop

**Aufenthalts-: ~erlaubnis die** residence permit; **~raum der** *(in einer*

*Schule o. ä.)* common-room *(Brit.); (in einer Jugendherberge)* day-room; *(in einem Betrieb o. ä.)* recreation-room

**auf|essen** *unr. tr. (auch itr.) V.* eat up

**auf|fahren** 1. *unr. itr. V.; mit sein* **a)** **auf ein anderes Fahrzeug ~** *(aufprallen)* drive into the back of another vehicle; **b)** **auf den Vordermann zu dicht ~**: drive too close to the car in front; **c)** *(vorfahren)* drive up; **d)** *(in Stellung gehen)* move up [into position]; 2. *unr. tr. V.* **a)** *(in Stellung bringen)* move up; **b)** *(ugs.: auftischen)* serve up; **Auf·fahrt die a)** drive up; **b)** *(Weg)* drive; **c)** *(Autobahn~)* slip-road *(Brit.);* access road *(Amer.);* **d)** *(schweiz.) s.* **Himmelfahrt**

**auf|fallen** *unr. itr. V.; mit sein* stand out; **jmdm. fällt etw. auf** sb. notices sth.; **auffallend** 1. *Adj.* conspicuous; *(eindrucksvoll, bemerkenswert)* striking; 2. *adv.* conspicuously; *(eindrucksvoll, bemerkenswert)* strikingly; **auf·fällig** 1. *Adj.* conspicuous; garish *(colour);* 2. *adv.* conspicuously

**auf|fangen** *unr. tr. V.* **a)** catch; **b)** *(aufnehmen, sammeln)* collect

**auf|fassen** *tr. V.* grasp; **a)** **etw. als etw. ~**: regard sth. as sth.; **etw. persönlich/falsch ~**: take sth. personally/misunderstand sth.; **Auf·fassung die** *(Ansicht)* view; *(Begriff)* conception; **der ~ sein, daß ...**: take the view that ...

**auffindbar** *Adj.* findable; **auf|finden** *unr. tr. V.* find

**auf|fordern** *tr. V.* **jmdn. ~, etw. zu tun** call upon sb. to do sth.; *(einladen, ermuntern)* ask sb. to do sth.; **jmdn. [zum Tanz] ~**: ask sb. to dance; **Auf·forderung die** request; *(nachdrücklicher)* demand; *(Einladung, Ermunterung)* invitation

**auf|fressen** *unr. tr. V. (auch fig.)* eat up

**auf|führen** 1. *tr. V.* **a)** put on *(film);* stage *(play, ballet, opera);* perform *(piece of music);* **b)** *(auflisten)* list; 2. *refl. V.* behave; **Auf·führung die** performance

**Auf·gabe die a)** task; **b)** *(fig.: Zweck, Funktion)* function; **c)** *(Schulw.)* *(Übung)* exercise; *(Prüfungs~)* question; *(Haus~) s.* **Haus~**; **d)** *(Rechen~, Mathematik~)* problem; **e)** *(Kapitulation)* retirement; *(im Schach)* resignation; **jmdn. zur ~ zwingen** force sb. to retire/resign; **f)** *(das Aufgeben a)* giving up; **g)** *(einer Postsendung)* posting *(Brit.);* mailing *(Amer.); (eines Tele-*

*gramms)* handing in; *(einer Bestellung, einer Annonce)* placing; **h)** *(von Gepäck)* checking in

**Auf·gang der a)** *(eines Gestirns)* rising; **b)** *(Treppe)* stairs *pl.;* staircase; stairway; *(in einem Bahnhof, zu einer Galerie, einer Tribüne)* steps *pl.*

**auf|geben** 1. *unr. tr. V.* **a)** give up; *(Sport)* retire from *(race, competition);* **b)** *(übergeben, übermitteln)* post *(Brit.),* mail *(letter, parcel);* hand in, *(telefonisch)* phone in *(telegram);* place *(advertisement, order);* check *(luggage, baggage);* **c)** *(Schulw.: als Hausaufgabe)* set *(Brit.);* assign *(Amer.);* **d)** **jmdm. ein Rätsel ~**: set *(Brit.)* or *(Amer.)* assign sb. a puzzle; 2. *unr. itr. V.* **a)** give up; *(im Sport)* retire; *(im Schach)* resign

**Auf·gebot das a)** contingent; **ein gewaltiges ~ an Polizisten/Fahrzeugen/Material** a huge force of police/array of vehicles/materials; **b)** *(zur Heirat)* notice of an/the intended marriage; *(kirchlich)* banns *pl.*

**auf|gehen** *unr. itr. V.; mit sein* **a)** rise; **b)** *(sich öffnen [lassen])* *(door, parachute, wound)* open; *(stage curtain)* go up; *(knot, button, zip, bandage, shoelace, stitching)* come undone; *(boil, pimple, blister)* burst; *(flower, bud)* open [up]; **c)** *(keimen)* come up; **d)** *(aufgetrieben werden)* *(dough, cake)* rise; **e)** *(Math.)* *(calculation)* work out; *(equation)* come out; **f)** **etw. geht jmdm. auf** sb. realizes sth.

**aufgeklärt** *Adj.* enlightened; **~ sein** *(sexualkundlich)* know the facts of life

**auf·gelegt** *Adj.* gut/schlecht *usw.* **~ sein** be in a good/bad *etc.* mood; **zu etw. ~ sein** be in the mood for sth.

**auf·gelöst** *Adj.* distraught *(person)*

**aufgeregt** 1. *Adj.* excited; *(nervös, beunruhigt)* agitated; 2. *adv.* excitedly; *(nervös, beunruhigt)* agitatedly

**auf·geschlossen** *Adj.* open-minded *(gegenüber as regards, about);* *(interessiert, empfänglich)* receptive *(Dat., für to);* *(zugänglich)* approachable; **Auf·geschlossenheit die** *s.* **aufgeschlossen:** open-mindedness; receptiveness; approachableness

**aufgeweckt** *Adj.* bright; **Aufgewecktheit die; ~**: brightness

**auf|gießen** *unr. tr. V.* make *(coffee, tea)*

**auf|gliedern** *tr. V.* subdivide, break down **(in** + *Akk.* into); **Auf·gliederung die** subdivision; breakdown

**auf|greifen** *unr. tr. V.* pick up

**auf Grund, aufgrund** *s.* **Grund c**

**auf|haben** *(ugs.)* **1.** *unr. tr. V.* **a)** *(aufgesetzt haben)* have on; **b)** *(geöffnet haben)* have ⟨*zip*⟩ undone; have ⟨*door, window, jacket, blouse*⟩ open; **2.** *unr. itr. V.* ⟨*shop, office*⟩ be open

**auf|halten** **1.** *unr. tr. V.* **a)** halt; **b)** *(stören)* hold up; **c)** *(ugs.: geöffnet halten)* hold ⟨*sack, door, etc.*⟩ open; **die Augen [und Ohren]** ~: keep one's eyes [and ears] open; **2.** *unr. refl. V.* **a)** stay; **b)** **sich mit jmdm./etw.** ~: spend [a long] time on sb./sth.

**auf|hängen** **1.** *tr. V.* **a)** hang up; hang ⟨*picture, curtains*⟩; **b)** *(erhängen)* hang; **2.** *refl. V.* hang oneself; **Aufhänger** *der;* ~**s,** ~ loop

**auf|heben** *unr. tr. V.* **a)** pick up; **b)** *(aufbewahren)* keep; **c)** *(abschaffen)* abolish; repeal ⟨*law*⟩; rescind ⟨*order, instruction*⟩; cancel ⟨*contract*⟩; lift ⟨*ban, prohibition*⟩; **d)** *(ausgleichen)* cancel out; neutralize ⟨*effect*⟩; **Aufheben** *das;* ~**s: viel** ~**[s]/kein** ~ **von jmdm./etw. machen** make a great fuss/not make any fuss about sb./sth.

**auf|heitern** **1.** *tr. V.* cheer up; **2.** *refl. V.* ⟨*weather*⟩ brighten up

**auf|hetzen** *tr. V.* incite

**auf|holen** **1.** *tr. V.* make up ⟨*time, delay*⟩; pull back ⟨*lead*⟩; **2.** *itr. V.* catch up; ⟨*athlete, competitor*⟩ make up ground

**auf|horchen** *itr. V.* prick up one's ears

**auf|hören** *itr. V.* stop; **[damit]** ~, **etw. zu tun** stop doing sth.

**auf|kaufen** *tr. V.* buy up

**auf|klappen** *tr. V.* open, fold open ⟨*chair, table*⟩; open [up] ⟨*suitcase, trunk*⟩; open ⟨*book, knife*⟩

**auf|klären** **1.** *tr. V.* **a)** clear up ⟨*matter, mystery, question, misunderstanding, error, confusion*⟩; solve ⟨*crime, problem*⟩; explain ⟨*event, incident, cause*⟩; resolve ⟨*contradiction, disagreement*⟩; **b)** *(unterrichten)* enlighten; **ein Kind** ~ *(sexualkundlich)* tell a child the facts of life; **2.** *refl. V.* **a)** ⟨*misunderstanding, mystery*⟩ be cleared up; **b)** ⟨*weather*⟩ brighten [up]; ⟨*sky*⟩ brighten; **Auf·klärung** *die s.* **aufklären 1: a)** clearing up; solution; explanation; resolution; **b)** enlightenment; **die** ~ **der Kinder** *(über Sexualität)* telling the children the facts of life

**auf|kleben** *tr. V.* stick on; *(mit Klei-*

*ster)* paste on; **Auf·kleber** *der* sticker

**auf|knöpfen** *tr. V.* unbutton; undo

**auf|kochen** **1.** *tr. V.* bring to the boil; **2.** *itr. V.* **mit sein** come to the boil

**auf|kommen** *unr. itr. V.; mit sein* **a)** ⟨*wind*⟩ spring up; ⟨*storm, gale*⟩ blow up; ⟨*fog*⟩ come down; ⟨*rumour*⟩ start; ⟨*suspicion, doubt, feeling*⟩ arise; ⟨*fashion, style, invention*⟩ come in; ⟨*boredom*⟩ set in; ⟨*mood, atmosphere*⟩ develop; **b)** ~ **für** *(bezahlen)* bear ⟨*costs*⟩; pay for ⟨*damage*⟩; pay ⟨*expenses*⟩; be liable for ⟨*debts*⟩; stand ⟨*loss*⟩; **c)** ~ **für** *(Verantwortung tragen für)* be responsible for

**auf|krempeln** *tr. V.* roll up

**auf|laden** **1.** *unr. tr. V.* **a)** load **(auf + Akk.** on [to]); **b)** **jmdm. etw.** ~ *(ugs.)* load sb. with sth.; *(fig.)* saddle sb. with sth.; **c)** charge [up] ⟨*battery*⟩; **2.** *unr. refl. V.* ⟨*battery*⟩ charge

**Auf·lage** *die* **a)** *(Buchw.)* edition; **b)** *(Verpflichtung)* condition

**auf|lassen** *unr. tr. V. (ugs.)* **a)** leave ⟨*door, window, jacket, etc.*⟩ open; **b)** keep on ⟨*hat, glasses, etc.*⟩

**auf|lauern** *itr. V.* **jmdm.** ~: lie in wait for sb.

**Auf·lauf** *der* **a)** *(Menschen~)* crowd; **b)** *(Speise)* soufflé

**auf|leben** *itr. V.; mit sein* revive; *(fig.: wieder munter werden)* come to life

**auf|legen** **1.** *tr. V.* **a)** put on; **den Hörer** ~: put down the receiver; **b)** *(Buchw.)* publish; **2.** *itr. V. (den Hörer* ~*)* hang up

**auf|lehnen** *refl. V.* rebel; **Auflehnung** *die;* ~, ~**en** rebellion

**auf|leuchten** *itr. V.; auch mit sein* light up; *(für kurze Zeit)* flash

**auf|lockern** *tr. V.* **a)** loosen; break up ⟨*soil*⟩; **b)** *(fig.)* introduce some variety into ⟨*landscape, lesson, lecture*⟩; relieve ⟨*pattern, façade*⟩; make ⟨*mood, atmosphere, evening*⟩ more relaxed; **Auf·lockerung** *die* **a)** *s.* **auflockern a:** loosening; breaking up; **b) zur** ~ **der Stimmung/des Abends** to make the mood/evening more relaxed

**auf|lösen** **1.** *tr. V.* dissolve; resolve ⟨*difficulty, contradiction*⟩; solve ⟨*puzzle, equation*⟩; break off ⟨*engagement*⟩; cancel ⟨*arrangement, contract, agreement*⟩; dissolve ⟨*organization*⟩; **2.** *refl. V.* dissolve **(in + Akk.** into); ⟨*parliament*⟩ dissolve itself; ⟨*crowd, demonstration*⟩ break up; ⟨*fog, mist*⟩ lift; *(fig.)* ⟨*empire, social order*⟩ disintegrate; **Auf·lösung die a)** *s.* **auflösen 1**: dissolving; resolution; solution; breaking off; cancellation; dissolution; **b)** *s.* **auflösen 2**: dissolving; breaking up lifting; disintegration

**auf|machen 1.** *tr. V.* **a)** open; undo ⟨*button, knot*⟩; **b)** *(ugs.: eröffnen)* open [up] ⟨*shop, business, etc.*⟩; **2.** *itr. V.* **a)** ⟨*shop, office, etc.*⟩ open; **b)** *(ugs.: die Tür öffnen)* open the door; **jmdm. ~:** open the door to sb.; **c)** *(ugs.: eröffnet werden)* ⟨*shop, business*⟩ open [up]; **Aufmachung die; ~, ~en** presentation; *(Kleidung)* get-up

**auf|marschieren** *itr. V.; mit sein* assemble; *(heranmarschieren)* march up; **Truppen sind an der Grenze aufmarschiert** troops were deployed along the border

**aufmerksam 1.** *Adj.* **a)** attentive; sharp ⟨*eyes*⟩; **jmdn. auf jmdn./etw. ~ machen** draw sb.'s attention to sb./ sth.; **auf jmdn./etw. ~ werden** become aware of sb./sth.; **~ werden** notice; **b)** *(höflich)* attentive; **2.** *adv.* attentively; **Aufmerksamkeit die; ~, ~en a)** *o. Pl.* attention; **b)** *(Höflichkeit)* attentiveness; **c)** *(Geschenk)* small gift

**auf|muntern** *tr. V.* **a)** cheer up; **b)** *(beleben)* liven up; **c)** *(ermutigen)* encourage; **Aufmunterung die; ~** *s.* **aufmuntern**: cheering up; livening up; encouragement

**Aufnahme die; ~, ~n a)** *s.* **aufnehmen b**: opening; establishment; taking up; **b)** *(Empfang)* reception; **c)** *s.* **aufnehmen d**: admission (**in** + *Akk.* into); **d)** *(Einschließung)* inclusion; **e)** *(Finanzw.)* raising; **f)** *(Aufzeichnung)* taking down; *(von Personalien, eines Diktats)* taking [down]; **g)** *s.* **aufnehmen k**: taking: photographing; filming; **h)** *(Bild)* shot; **i)** *(das Aufnehmen auf Tonträger, das Aufgenommene)* recording; **j)** *(Anklang)* reception; response (*Gen.* to); **k)** *(Einverleibung, Absorption)* absorption

**auf|nehmen** *unr. tr. V.* **a)** *(aufheben)* pick up; *(fig.)* take up ⟨*idea, theme, etc.*⟩; **es mit jmdm./etw. ~/nicht ~ können** *(fig.)* be a/no match for sb./ sth.; **b)** *(beginnen mit)* open ⟨*negotiations, talks*⟩; establish ⟨*relations, contacts*⟩; take up ⟨*studies, activity, occupation*⟩; start ⟨*production, investigation*⟩; **c)** *(empfangen)* receive; *(beherbergen)* take in; **d)** *(beitreten lassen)* admit (**in** + *Akk.* to); **e)** *(einschließen, verzeichnen)* include; **f)** *(erfassen)*

take in ⟨*impressions, information, etc.*⟩; **g)** *(absorbieren)* absorb; **h)** *(Finanzw.)* raise ⟨*mortgage, money, loan*⟩; **i)** *(reagieren auf)* receive; **j)** *(aufschreiben)* take down; take [down] ⟨*dictation, particulars*⟩; **k)** *(fotografieren)* take ⟨*picture*⟩; photograph, take a photograph of ⟨*scene, subject*⟩; *(filmen)* film; **l)** *(auf Tonträger)* record

**auf|opfern** *refl. V.* devote oneself sacrificingly (**für** to); **aufopfernd 1.** *Adj.* self-sacrificing; **2.** *adv.* self-sacrificingly

**auf|passen** *itr. V.* **a)** watch out; *(konzentriert sein)* pay attention; **paß mal auf!** *(ugs.: hör mal zu!)* now listen; **b)** **auf jmdn./etw. ~:** keep an eye on sb./ sth.

**auf|platzen** *itr. V.; mit sein* burst open; ⟨*seam, cushion*⟩ split open; ⟨*wound*⟩ open up

**Auf·prall der; ~[e]s, ~e** impact; **auf|prallen** *itr. V.; mit sein* **auf etw.** *(Akk.)* **~:** hit sth.

**Auf·preis der** additional charge

**auf|pumpen** *tr. V.* pump up

**auf|putschen** *tr. V.* stimulate; arouse ⟨*passions, urge*⟩; **Aufputsch·mittel das** stimulant

**auf|räumen** *tr., itr. V.* clear up

**auf·recht 1.** *Adj. (auch fig.)* upright; **2.** *adv.* ⟨*walk, sit, hold oneself*⟩ straight; **aufrecht|erhalten** *unr. V.* maintain; keep up ⟨*deception, fiction, contact, custom*⟩

**auf|regen 1.** *tr. V.* excite; *(ärgern)* annoy; irritate; *(beunruhigen)* agitate; **2.** *refl. V.* get worked up (**über** + *Akk.* about); **Auf·regung die** excitement *no pl.; (Beunruhigung)* agitation *no pl.;* **jmdn. in ~ versetzen** make sb. excited/agitated

**auf|reißen 1.** *unr. tr. V.* **a)** *(öffnen)* tear open; wrench open ⟨*drawer*⟩; fling open ⟨*door, window*⟩; **die Augen/ den Mund ~:** open one's eyes/mouth wide; **b)** *(beschädigen)* tear open; tear ⟨*clothes*⟩; break up ⟨*road, soil*⟩; **2.** *itr. V.; mit sein* ⟨*clothes*⟩ tear; ⟨*seam*⟩ split; ⟨*wound*⟩ open; ⟨*cloud*⟩ break up

**auf|reizen** *tr. V.* excite; **auf·reizend 1.** *Adj.* provocative; **2.** *adv.* provocatively

**auf|richten 1.** *tr. V.* erect; put up; **den Oberkörper ~:** raise one's upper body; **jmdn. [wieder] ~** *(fig.)* give fresh heart to sb.; **2.** *refl. V.* stand up [straight]; **sich an jmdn./etw. [wieder] ~** *(fig.)* take heart from sb./sth.

**auf·richtig** 1. *Adj.* sincere; 2. *adv.* sincerely; **Auf·richtigkeit** die sincerity

**auf|rücken** *itr. V.; mit sein* move up

**Auf·ruf** der a) call; b) *(Appell)* appeal (**an** + *Akk.* to); **auf|rufen** *unr. tr. V.* a) call; b) jmdn. ~, etw. **zu tun** call upon sb. to do sth.; c) *(Rechtsw.)* appeal for ⟨witnesses⟩

**Aufruhr** der; ~s, ~e a) *(Widerstand)* rebellion; b) *o. Pl. (Erregung)* turmoil; **aufrührerisch** *Adj.* inflammatory

**Auf·rüstung** die armament

**aufs** *Präp.* + *Art.* = **auf das**

**auf|sagen** *tr. V.* recite

**auf|sammeln** *tr. V.* gather up

**aufsässig** 1. *Adj.* recalcitrant; 2. *adv.* recalcitrantly

**Auf·satz** der *(Text)* essay

**auf|saugen** *unr. (auch regelm.) tr. V.* soak up; *(fig.)* absorb

**auf|schieben** *unr. tr. V.* postpone

**Auf·schlag** der a) *(Aufprall)* impact; b) *(Preis~)* surcharge; c) *(Ärmel~)* cuff; *(Hosen~)* turn-up; *(Revers)* lapel; d) *(Tennis usw.)* serve

**auf|schlagen** 1. *unr. itr. V.* a) *mit sein* **auf etw.** *(Dat. od. Akk.)* ~: hit sth.; b) *(teurer werden)* ⟨price, rent, costs⟩ go up; c) *(Tennis usw.)* serve.; 2. *unr. tr. V.* a) *(öffnen)* crack ⟨nut, egg⟩ [open]; knock a hole in ⟨ice⟩; **sich** *(Dat.)* **das Knie/den Kopf** ~: cut one's knee/head; b) open ⟨book, newspaper, one's eyes⟩; **schlagt S. 15 auf!** turn to page 15; c) turn up ⟨collar, sleeve, trouserleg⟩; d) *(aufbauen)* set up ⟨camp⟩; pitch ⟨tent⟩; put up ⟨bed, hut, scaffolding⟩; e) **5% auf etw.** *(Akk.)* ~: put 5% on sth.

**auf|schließen** 1. *unr. tr. V.* unlock; 2. *unr. itr. V.* [jmdm.] ~: unlock the door/gate etc. [for sb.]; **Auf·schluß** der information *no pl.*

**auf|schneiden** 1. *unr. tr. V.* a) cut open; b) *(zerteilen)* cut; 2. *unr. itr. V.* *(ugs.: prahlen)* boast (**mit** about); **Auf·schnitt** der; *o. Pl.* [assorted] cold meats *pl.*/cheeses *pl.*

**auf|schnüren** *tr. V.* undo

**auf|schrauben** *tr. V.* unscrew; unscrew the top of ⟨bottle, jar, etc.⟩

**auf|schreiben** *unr. tr. V.* write down; [sich *(Dat.)*] etw. ~: make a note of sth.; **Auf·schrift** die inscription

**Auf·schub** der postponement; **die Sache duldet keinen** ~: the matter brooks no delay

**Auf·schwung** der upturn *(Gen.* in)

**Aufsehen** das; ~s stir; [großes] ~ erregen cause a [great] stir; **Auf·seher** der *(im Gefängnis)* warder *(Brit.);* [prison] guard *(Amer.); (im Park)* park-keeper; *(im Museum, auf dem Parkplatz)* attendant; *(auf einem Gut, Sklaven~)* overseer

**auf|sein** *unr. itr. V.; mit sein; nur im Inf. und Part. zusammengeschrieben (ugs.)* a) be open; b) *(nicht im Bett sein)* be up

**auf|setzen** 1. *tr. V.* a) put on; b) *(verfassen)* draw up ⟨text⟩; 2. *refl. V.* sit up

**Auf·sicht** die supervision; *(bei Prüfungen)* invigilation *(Brit.);* proctoring *(Amer.)*

**auf|springen** *unr. itr. V.; mit sein* a) jump up; b) *(hinaufspringen)* jump on (**auf** + *Akk.* to); c) *(rissig werden)* crack

**Auf·stand** der rebellion; **auf·ständisch** *Adj.* rebellious

**auf|stehen** *unr. itr. V. mit sein* stand up; *(aus dem Liegen)* get up

**auf|steigen** *unr. itr. V.; mit sein* a) *(auf ein Fahrzeug)* get on; **auf etw.** *(Akk.)* ~: get on [to] sth.; b) *(bergan steigen)* climb; c) *(hochsteigen)* ⟨sap, smoke, mist⟩ rise; d) *(beruflich, gesellschaftlich)* rise (**zu** to); **zum Direktor** ~: rise to be manager

**auf|stellen** 1. *tr. V.* a) put up (**auf** + *Akk.* on); set up ⟨skittles⟩; *(postieren)* post; b) *(aufrecht hinstellen)* stand up; c) *(Sport)* select, pick ⟨team, player⟩; d) *(bilden)* put together ⟨team of experts⟩; raise ⟨army⟩; e) *(nominieren)* nominate; put up; 2. *refl. V.* position oneself; **Auf·stellung** die a) *s.* **aufstellen 1a:** putting up; setting up; posting; b) *s.* **aufstellen b:** standing up; c) *s.* **aufstellen c:** selection; picking; d) *s.* **aufstellen d:** putting together; raising; d) *(Nominierung)* nomination

**Aufstieg** der; ~[e]s, ~e a) climb; b) *s.* **aufsteigen d:** rise

**auf|stoßen** 1. *unr. tr. V.* push open; 2. *unr. itr. V.* belch; ⟨baby⟩ bring up wind

**Auf·strich** der spread

**auf|stützen** 1. *tr. V.* rest ⟨one's arms etc.⟩; 2. *refl. V.* support oneself; **die Arme auf etw.** *(Akk. od. Dat.)* ~: rest one's arms on sth.

**auf|suchen** *tr. V.* call on; go to ⟨doctor⟩

**Auf·takt** der *(fig.)* start

**auf|tauchen** *itr. V.; mit sein* a) surface; b) *(sichtbar werden)* appear

**auf|tauen** 1. *tr. V.* thaw; 2. *itr. V.; mit sein (auch fig.)* thaw

**auf|teilen** *tr. V.* a) divide [up]; b) *(verteilen)* share out

**Auftrag** der; ~[e]s, **Aufträge** a) instructions *pl.;* **in** jmds. ~ *(Dat.)* on sb.'s instructions; *(für jmdn.)* on behalf of sb; b) *(Bestellung)* order; *(bei Künstlern, Architekten usw.)* commission; c) *(Mission)* task; *(Aufgabe)* job; **auf|tragen** *unr. tr. V.* a) jmdm. ~, etw. zu tun instruct sb. to do sth.; b) *(aufstreichen)* put on *(paint, make-up, etc.);* **Auftrag·geber** der client

**auf|treten** *unr. itr. V.; mit sein* a) tread; b) *(sich benehmen)* behave; c) *(eine Vorstellung geben)* appear; **als Zeuge/Kläger ~:** appear as a witness/a plaintiff; d) *(auftauchen) (problem, difficulty, difference of opinion)* arise; *(symptom, danger, pest)* appear; **Auftreten** das; ~s *(Benehmen)* manner

**Auf·trieb** der a) *(Physik) (statischer ~)* buoyancy; *(dynamischer ~)* lift; b) *(fig.)* impetus; **das hat ihm ~/neuen ~ gegeben** that has given him a lift/given him new impetus

**Auf·tritt** der a) *(Vorstellung)* appearance; b) *(Theater: das Auftreten)* entrance; *(Szene)* scene

**auf|tun** *unr. refl. V. (geh.)* open; *(fig.)* open up

**auf|wachen** *itr. V.; mit sein* wake up, awaken (**aus** from); *(aus Ohnmacht, Narkose)* come round (**aus** from)

**auf|wachsen** *unr. itr. V.; mit sein* grow up

**Auf·wand** der; ~[e]s cost; expense

**auf|wärmen** 1. *tr. V.* heat or warm up *(food);* 2. *refl. V.* warm oneself up

**aufwärts** *Adv.* upwards

**auf|wecken** *tr. V.* wake [up]; waken

**auf|weichen** 1. *tr. V.* soften; 2. *itr. V.; mit sein* become soft; soften up

**auf·wendig** 1. *Adj.* lavish; *(kostspielig)* costly; expensive; 2. *adv.* lavishly; *(kostspielig)* expensively

**auf|wiegeln** *tr. V.* incite; stir up

**auf|wirbeln** *tr. V.* swirl up

**auf|wischen** *tr. V.* a) wipe or mop up; b) *(säubern)* wipe *(floor);* *(mit Wasser)* wash *(floor)*

**auf|zählen** *tr. V.* list; **Auf·zählung** die a) *(Vorgang)* of; b) *(Liste)* list

**auf|zeichnen** *tr. V.* a) record; b) *(zeichnen)* draw; **Auf·zeichnung** die record; *(Film~, Ton~)* recording; ~en *(Notizen)* notes

**auf|ziehen** 1. *unr. tr. V.* a) pull open *(drawer);* open, draw [back] *(curtains);* undo *(zip);* b) wind up *(clock, toy, etc.).* 2. *unr. itr. V.; mit sein* come up; *(clouds, storm)* gather

**Auf·zucht** die raising; rearing

**Auf·zug** der a) *(Lift)* lift *(Brit.);* elevator *(Amer.);* b) *(abwertend: Aufmachung)* get-up; c) *(Theater: Akt)* act

**Aug·apfel** der eyeball; **Auge** das; ~s, ~n eye; **gute/schlechte ~n haben** have good/poor eyesight; **auf einem ~ blind** blind in one eye; **da wird er ~n machen** *(fig. ugs.)* his eyes will pop out of his head; **ich traute meinen ~n nicht** *(ugs.)* I couldn't believe my eyes; **ein ~ od. beide ~n zudrücken** *(fig.)* turn a blind eye; **jmdn./etw. nicht aus den ~n lassen** not take one's eyes off sb./sth.; **ins ~ gehen** *(fig. ugs.)* end in disaster; **unter vier ~n** *(fig.)* in private

**Augen-:** ~**arzt** der eye specialist; ~**blick** [*auch:* --'-] der *s.* ¹**Moment;** ~**blicklich** [*auch:* --'--] 1. *Adj.* a) *(sofortig)* immediate; b) *(gegenwärtig)* present; 2. *adv.* a) *(sofort)* at once; b) *(zur Zeit)* at the moment; ~**braue** die eyebrow; ~**lid** das eyelid; ~**zeuge** der eyewitness

**August** der; ~[e]s od. ~, ~e August

**Auktion** die; ~, ~en auction

**Aula** die; ~, Aulen od. ~s hall

**aus** 1. *Präp. mit Dat.* a) *(aus dem Inneren von)* out of; b) *(Herkunft, Quelle, Ausgangspunkt angebend, auch zeitlich)* from; ~ **Spanien/Köln** *usw.* from Spain/Cologne *etc.;* c) ~ **der Mode/ Übung sein** be out of fashion/training; d) *(Grund, Ursache angebend)* out of; **etw. ~ Erfahrung wissen** know sth. from experience; ~ **Versehen** by mistake; e) *(bestehend ~)* of; *(hergestellt ~)* made of; ~ **etw. bestehen** consist of sth.; f) ~ **ihm ist ein guter Arzt geworden** he made a good doctor; 2. *Adv.* a) *(ugs.: vorbei)* ~ **jetzt!** that's enough; b) „~" *(an Lichtschaltern)* 'out'; *(an Geräten)* 'off'; c) **vom Fenster/obersten Stockwerk ~:** from the window/top storey; **von mir ~** *(ugs.)* if you like; **von sich** *(Dat.)* ~: of one's own accord

**aus|atmen** *itr., tr. V.* breathe out

**Aus·bau** der; ~[e]s a) *(Erweiterung)* extension; b) *(Ausgestaltung)* conversion (**zu** into); **aus|bauen** *tr. V.* a) *(demontieren)* remove (**aus** from); b) *(erweitern)* extend

**Aus·beute** die yield; **aus|beuten** tr. V. exploit

**aus|bilden** tr. V. **a)** train; **b)** (entwickeln) develop; **Aus·bildung** die **a)** training; **b)** (Entwicklung) development

**Aus·blick** der view (auf + Akk. of)

**aus|brechen** unr. itr. V.; mit sein **a)** break out (aus of); (fig.) break free (aus from); **b)** jmdm. bricht der Schweiß aus sb. breaks into a sweat; **c)** ⟨volcano⟩ erupt; **d)** (beginnen) break out; ⟨crisis⟩ break; **e)** in Gelächter/Weinen ~: burst out laughing/crying; in Beifall/Tränen ~: burst into applause/tears

**aus|breiten** **1.** tr. V. spread; spread [out] ⟨map, cloth, sheet, etc.⟩; open out ⟨fan, newspaper⟩; (nebeneinanderlegen) spread out; **2.** refl. V. spread

**Aus·bruch** der **a)** (Flucht) escape (aus from); **b)** (Beginn) outbreak; **c)** (Gefühls~) outburst; **d)** (eines Vulkans) eruption

**aus|brüten** tr. V. hatch out; (im Brutkasten) incubate

**Aus·dauer** die stamina; **aus·dauernd** Adj. with stamina postpos.

**aus|dehnen** **1.** tr. V. **a)** stretch; (fig.) extend (auf + Akk. to); (zeitlich) prolong; **2.** refl. V. expand; (zeitlich) go on; **Aus·dehnung** die expansion; (fig.) extension; (zeitlich) prolongation

**aus|denken** unr. refl. V. sich (Dat.) etw. ~: think sth. up

**Aus·druck** der; ~[e]s, **Ausdrücke** expression; (Terminus) term; etw. zum ~ bringen express sth.; **aus|drücken** **1.** tr. V. **a)** (auspressen) squeeze ⟨juice⟩ out; squeeze [out] ⟨lemon, grape, orange, etc.⟩; squeeze out ⟨sponge⟩; squeeze ⟨boil, pimple⟩; **b)** stub out ⟨cigarette⟩; **c)** (mitteilen) express; **2.** refl. V. **a)** express oneself; **b)** (offenbar werden) be expressed; **ausdrücklich** [od. -'--] **1.** Adj. express attrib. ⟨command, wish, etc.⟩; explicit ⟨reservation⟩; **2.** adv. expressly; ⟨mention⟩ explicitly; **ausdrucks·los** **1.** Adj. expressionless; **2.** adv. expressionlessly; **ausdrucks·voll** **1.** Adj. expressive; **2.** adv. expressively

**aus einander** Adv. apart; etw. ~ schreiben write sth. as separate words **auseinander-, Auseinander-:** ~|brechen **1.** unr. itr. V.; mit sein (auch fig.) break up; **2.** unr. tr. V. break ⟨sth.⟩ up; ~|gehen unr. itr. V.;

mit sein **a)** part; ⟨crowd⟩ disperse; **b)** (fig.) ⟨opinions, views⟩ differ; ~|halten unr. tr. V. tell ⟨things, people⟩ apart; ~|nehmen unr. tr. V. take ⟨sth.⟩ apart; ~|setzen **1.** tr. V. jmdm. etw. ~setzen explain sth. to sb.; **2.** refl. V. sich mit jmdm. ~setzen have it out with sb.; sich mit etw. ~setzen concern oneself with sth.; ~**setzung** die; ~, ~en (Streit) argument; **b)** (Kampfhandlungen) clash

**Aus·fahrt** die exit

**Aus·fall** der **a)** (das Nichtstattfinden) cancellation; **b)** (Einbuße, Verlust) loss; **c)** (eines Motors) failure; (einer Maschine, eines Autos) breakdown; **aus|fallen** unr. itr. V.; mit sein **a)** fall out; **b)** (nicht stattfinden) be cancelled; etw. ~ lassen cancel sth.; **c)** (ausscheiden) drop out; **d)** (nicht mehr funktionieren) ⟨engine, brakes, signal⟩ fail; ⟨machine, car⟩ break down; **e)** (ein bestimmtes Ergebnis zeigen) turn out; **ausfallend** Adj. [gegen jmdn.] ~ sein/werden be/become abusive [towards sb.]; **Ausfall·straße** die main road out of the/a town/city

**aus·findig** Adv. jmdn./etw. ~ machen find sb./sth.

**Aus·flug** der outing; **Ausflügler** der; ~s, ~: day-tripper; excursionist (Amer.)

**Ausflugs-:** ~**dampfer** der pleasure steamer; ~**lokal** das restaurant/café catering for [day-]trippers

**aus|fragen** tr. V. jmdn. ~: question sb., ask sb. questions (nach, über + Akk. about)

**aus|fransen** itr. V.; mit sein fray

**Aus·fuhr** die; ~, ~en s. Export; **aus|führen** tr. V. **a)** (ausgehen mit) take ⟨person⟩ out; **b)** (spazierenführen) take ⟨person, animal⟩ for a walk; **c)** (exportieren) export; **d)** (durchführen) carry out; (Sport) take ⟨penalty, free kick, corner⟩; **ausführlich** [auch: -'--] **1.** Adj. detailed; full; **2.** adv. in detail; **Aus·führung** die (Durchführung) carrying out; (Sport) taking

**aus|füllen** tr. V. **a)** fill; fill in ⟨form, crossword puzzle⟩; **b)** (beanspruchen, einnehmen) take up ⟨space⟩

**Aus·gabe** die **a)** o. Pl. giving out; (von Essen) serving; **b)** (Geld~) item of expenditure; ~n expenditure sing. (für on); **c)** (Edition) edition

**Aus·gang** der **a)** o. Pl. (Erlaubnis zum Ausgehen) time off; (von Soldaten) leave; **b)** (Tür ins Freie) exit (Gen.

from); c) *(Anat.)* outlet; d) *(Ende)* end; *(eines Romans, Films usw.)* ending; e) o. Pl. *(Ergebnis)* outcome; *(eines Wettbewerbs)* result; **ein Unfall mit tödlichem** ~: an accident with fatal consequences; **Ausgangspunkt der** starting-point

**aus|geben** *unr. tr. V.* **a)** give out; serve *(food, drinks)*; **b)** *(verbrauchen)* spend *(money)* (**für** on)

**ausgebucht** *Adj.* booked up

**aus·gefallen** *Adj.* unusual

**ausgeglichen** *Adj.* balanced; well-balanced *(person)*; equable *(climate)*

**aus|gehen** *unr. itr. V.; mit sein* **a)** go out; **b)** *(fast aufgebraucht sein)* run out; **c)** *(enden)* end; **gut/schlecht** ~: turn out well/badly; *(story, film)* end happily/unhappily; **d) von jmdm./etw.** ~: come from sb./sth.; **e) von etw.** ~ *(etw. zugrunde legen)* take sth. as one's starting-point; *(etw. annehmen)* assume sth.

**aus·gelassen 1.** *Adj.* exuberant *(mood, person)*; lively *(party, celebration)*; *(wild)* boisterous; **2.** *adv.* exuberantly; *(wild)* boisterously

**aus·genommen** *Konj.* except

**ausgeprägt** *Adj.* marked

**ausgerechnet** *Adv.* *(ugs.)* ~ **heute/ morgen** today/tomorrow of all days; ~ **hier** here of all places; ~ **Sie** you of all people

**aus·geschlossen** *Adj.* **das ist** ~: that is out of the question

**aus·geschnitten** *Adj.* low-cut *(dress, blouse, etc.)*

**aus·gestorben** *Adj.* |wie| ~: deserted

**ausgezeichnet** [*od.* '--'--] **1.** *Adj.* excellent; outstanding *(expert)*; **2.** *adv.* excellently

**ausgiebig 1.** *Adj.* substantial *(meal)*; **2.** *adv.* *(profit)* handsomely; *(read)* extensively; **von etw.** ~ **Gebrauch machen** make full use of sth.

**aus|gießen** *unr. tr. V.* **a)** pour out (**aus** of); **b)** *(leeren)* empty

**Ausgleich** *der;* ~|e|s, ~e **a)** *s.* **ausgleichen a**: evening out; reconciliation; **b)** *(Schadensersatz)* compensation; **als** *od.* **zum** ~ **für etw.** to make up sth.; **aus|gleichen** *unr. tr. V.* **a)** even out; reconcile *(differences of opinions, contradictions)*; **b)** compensate for *(damage)*; make up for *(misfortune, lack)*; **etw. durch etw.** ~: make up for sth. with sth.; **sich** ~: balance out; *(sich gegenseitig aufheben)* cancel each other out

**aus|graben** *unr. tr. V.* dig up; *(Archäol.)* excavate; **Aus·grabung die** *(Archäol.)* excavation

**aus|halten** *unr. tr. V.* stand; bear; endure; withstand *(attack, load, pressure, test, wear and tear)*; **er konnte es zu Hause nicht mehr** ~: he couldn't stand it at home any more; **es ist nicht zum Aushalten** it is unbearable

**aus|handeln** *tr. V.* negotiate

**aus|händigen** *tr. V.* hand over

**Aus·hang der** notice

**aus|heben** *unr. tr. V.* dig out *(earth etc.)*; dig *(trench, grave, etc.)*

**aus|helfen** *unr. itr. V.* help out; **jmdm.** ~: help sb. out (**mit, bei** with); **Aus·hilfe die a)** o. Pl. *(das Aushelfen)* help; **b)** *s.* **Aushilfskraft**; **Aushilfs·kraft die** temporary worker; *(in Läden, Gaststätten)* temporary assistant; *(Sekretärin)* temporary secretary; temp *(coll.)*

**aus|holen** *itr. V.* |mit dem Arm| ~: draw back one's arm; *(zum Schlag)* raise one's arm

**aus|kennen** *unr. refl. V.* (an einem Ort *usw.*) know one's way around; *(in einem Fach, einer Angelegenheit usw.)* know what's what; **sie kennt sich in dieser Stadt aus** she knows her way around the town; **sich** |gut| **mit/in etw.** *(Dat.)* ~: know [a lot] about sth.

**Aus·klang der** *(geh.)* end; **zum** ~ **des Festes** to end *or* close the festival

**aus|kleiden** *tr. V.* *(geh.)* undress; **sich** ~: undress

**aus|klingen** *unr. itr. V. mit sein* end

**aus|klopfen** *tr. V.* **a)** beat out (**aus** + *Dat.* of); **b)** *(säubern)* beat *(carpet)*; knock *(pipe)* out

**aus|kochen** *tr. V.* boil; *(keimfrei machen)* sterilize *(instruments etc.)* [in boiling water]

**aus|kommen** *unr. itr. V.; mit sein* **a)** manage (**mit** on); **b) mit jmdm.** |gut| ~: get on [well] with sb.

**Auskommen das;** ~s livelihood

**Auskunft die;** ~, **Auskünfte** piece of information; **Auskünfte** information *sing.*; |jmdm. über etw. *(Akk.)*| ~ **geben** give [sb.] information [about sth.]; **b)** o. Pl. *(Stelle)* information desk/counter/office/centre *etc.*; *(Fernspr.)* directory enquiries *no art.* *(Brit.)*; directory information *no art.* *(Amer.)*

**aus|lachen** *tr. V.* laugh at

**aus|laden** *unr. tr. V.* unload *(goods etc.)*

**Aus·lage die a)** Pl. *(Unkosten)* expenses; **b)** *(ausgestellte Ware)* item on display; **~n** goods on display

**Aus·land das;** o. Pl. foreign countries pl.; **im/ins ~:** abroad; **aus dem ~:** from abroad; **Ausländer der;** ~s, ~, **Ausländerin die;** ~, ~nen foreigner; **ausländisch** Adj. foreign

**Auslands-:** **~aufenthalt der** stay abroad; **~gespräch das** *(Fernspr.)* international call; **~korrespondent der** foreign correspondent; **~reise die** trip abroad

**aus|lassen** unr. tr. V. **a)** *(weglassen)* leave out; **b)** *(versäumen)* miss ⟨opportunity, chance, etc.⟩

**Auslauf der a)** o. Pl. **keinen/zuwenig ~ haben** have no/too little chance to run around outside; **b)** *(Raum)* space to run around in; **aus|laufen** unr. itr. V.; mit sein **a)** run out **(aus** of); **b)** *(leer laufen)* empty; ⟨egg⟩ run out; **c)** *(in See stechen)* sail **(nach** for); **d)** *(erlöschen)* ⟨contract, agreement, etc.⟩ run out; **Aus·läufer der a)** *(Geogr.)* foothill usu. in pl.; **b)** *(Met.) (eines Hochs)* ridge; *(eines Tiefs)* trough

**aus|legen** tr. V. **a)** *(hinlegen)* lay out; display ⟨goods, exhibits⟩; **b)** etw. mit **Fliesen/Teppichboden ~:** tile/carpet sth.; **c)** *(leihen)* lend; **d)** *(interpretieren)* interpret; etw. **falsch ~:** misinterpret sth.; **Auslegung die;** ~, ~en interpretation

**aus|leihen** unr. tr. V. s. **leihen**

**aus|liefern** tr. V. **jmdm. etw.** od. etw. **an jmdn. ~:** hand sth. over to sb.

**aus|löschen** tr. V. **a)** extinguish; **b)** *(beseitigen)* erase ⟨drawing, writing⟩

**aus|losen** tr. V. etw. **~:** draw lots for sth.

**aus|lösen** tr. V. **a)** trigger ⟨mechanism, device, alarm, etc.⟩; release ⟨camera shutter⟩; **b)** provoke ⟨discussion, anger, laughter, reaction, outrage, heart attack⟩; cause ⟨sorrow, horror, surprise, disappointment, panic, war⟩; excite, arouse ⟨interest, enthusiasm⟩; **Auslöser der;** ~s, ~ *(Fot.)* shutter release

**aus|machen** tr. V. **a)** *(ugs.)* put out ⟨light, fire, cigarette, candle⟩; switch off ⟨television, radio, hi-fi⟩; turn off ⟨gas⟩; **b)** *(vereinbaren)* agree [on]; **~, daß ...:** agree that ...; **c)** *(auszeichnen, kennzeichnen)* make up; **d) wenig/ nichts/viel ~:** make little/no/a great difference; **e) das macht mir nichts aus** I don't mind

**Aus·maß das a)** *(Größe)* size; **b)** *(Grad)* extent

**aus|messen** unr. tr. V. measure up

**Aus·nahme die;** ~, ~n exception; **mit ~ von** with the exception of; **bei jmdm. eine ~ machen** make an exception in sb.'s case; **Ausnahme·zustand der** state of emergency; **ausnahms·weise** Adv. by way of an exception; **Dürfen wir mitkommen? – Ausnahmsweise [ja]** May we come too? – Yes, just this once

**aus|nehmen** unr. tr. V. **a)** gut ⟨fish, rabbit, chicken⟩; **b)** *(ausschließen von)* exclude; *(gesondert behandeln)* make an exception of

**aus|nutzen,** *(bes. südd., österr.)* **aus|nützen** tr. V. **a)** take advantage of; **b)** *(ausbeuten)* exploit

**aus|packen** tr., itr. V. unpack; *(auswickeln)* unwrap

**aus|pressen** tr. V. squeeze out ⟨juice⟩; squeeze ⟨orange, lemon⟩; *(keltern)* press ⟨grapes etc.⟩

**aus|probieren** tr. V. try out

**Aus·puff der** exhaust

**aus|radieren** tr. V. rub out; erase

**aus|rauben** tr. V. rob

**aus|räumen** **1.** tr. V. **a)** clear out **(aus** of); **b)** *(fig.)* clear up; dispel ⟨prejudice, suspicion, misgivings⟩; **2.** itr. V. clear everything out

**aus|rechnen** tr. V. work out; **das kannst du dir leicht ~** *(ugs.)* you can easily work that out [for yourself]

**Aus·rede die** excuse; **aus|reden** **1.** itr. V. finish [speaking]; **2.** tr. V. **jmdm. etw. ~:** talk sb. out of sth.

**aus|reichen** itr. V. be enough or sufficient **(zu** for); **ausreichend** **1.** Adj. sufficient; enough; *(als Note)* fair. **2.** adv. sufficiently

**aus|reißen** **1.** unr. tr. V. tear out; pull out ⟨plants, weeds⟩; **2.** unr. itr. V.; mit sein **a)** *(sich lösen)* come off; **b)** *(ugs.: weglaufen)* run away *(Dat.* from)

**aus|renken** tr. V. dislocate

**aus|richten** tr. V. **a)** **jmdm. etw. ~:** tell sb. sth.; **b)** *(einheitlich anordnen)* line up; **c)** *(erreichen)* achieve

**aus|rollen** tr. V. roll out

**aus|rotten** tr. V. eradicate

**Aus·ruf der** cry; **aus|rufen** unr. tr. V. **a)** call out; „**Schön!" rief er aus** 'Lovely', he exclaimed; **b)** *(offiziell verkünden)* proclaim; declare ⟨state of emergency⟩; **c)** *(zum Kauf anbieten)* cry; **Ausrufe·zeichen das** exclamation mark

**aus|ruhen** *refl., itr. V.* have a rest; |sich| ein wenig/richtig ~: rest a little/ have a good rest; **ausgeruht sein** be rested

**aus|rüsten** *tr. V.* equip; **Aus·rü·stung die a)** *o. Pl.* equipping; **b)** (~sgegenstände) equipment *no pl.*

**aus|rutschen** *itr. V.; mit sein* slip

**Aus·sage die** statement; **aus|sagen 1.** *tr. V.* **a)** say; **c)** (vor Gericht, vor der Polizei) state; (unter Eid) testify; **2.** *itr. V.* make a statement; (unter Eid) testify

**aus|schalten** *tr. V.* **a)** switch *or* turn off; **b)** (fig.) eliminate; exclude ⟨emotion, influence⟩; dismiss ⟨doubt, objection⟩; shut out ⟨feeling, thought⟩

**Aus·schank der;** ~|e|s, serving

**Aus·schau die:** nach jmdm./etw. ~ halten keep a look-out for sb./sth.; **aus|schauen** *itr. V.* nach jmdm./etw. ~ look out for sb./sth.

**aus|scheiden 1.** *unr. itr. V.; mit sein* **a)** aus etw. ~: leave sth.; aus dem Amt ~: leave office; **b)** (Sport) be eliminated; **c)** diese Möglichkeit/dieser Kandidat scheidet aus this possibility/candidate has to be ruled out; **2.** *unr. tr. V.* (Physiol.) excrete ⟨waste⟩; eliminate, expel ⟨poison⟩; exude ⟨sweat⟩; **Aus·scheidung die a)** (Physiol.) *s.* **ausscheiden 2:** excretion; elimination; expulsion; exudation; ~en (Ausgeschiedenes) excreta; **b)** (Sport) qualifier

**aus|schenken** *tr. V.* serve

**aus|schimpfen** *tr. V.* jmdn. ~: tell sb. off

**aus|schlafen 1.** *unr. itr., refl. V.* have a good sleep; **2.** *unr. tr. V.* seinen Rausch ~: sleep off the effects of alcohol

**Aus·schlag der a)** (Haut~) rash; **b)** (eines Zeigers, einer Waage) deflection; (eines Pendels) swing; den ~ geben (fig.) tip the scales (fig.); **aus|schlagen 1.** *unr. tr. V.* **a)** knock out; **b)** (ablehnen) turn down; **2.** *unr. itr. V.* **a)** ⟨horse⟩ kick; **b)** ⟨needle, pointer⟩ be deflected, swing; **c)** (sprießen) come out [in bud]; **aus·schlag·gebend** *Adj.* decisive

**aus|schließen** *unr. tr. V.* **a)** (ausstoßen) expel (aus from); **b)** (nicht teilnehmen lassen) exclude (aus from); **c)** (fig.) rule out ⟨possibility⟩; jeden Irrtum ~: rule out all possibility of error; **e)** (aussperren) lock out; **ausschließlich** [od. '-'--, -'--] **1.** *Adj.* exclusive; **2.** *Adv.* exclusively; **3.** *Präp. mit Gen.* excluding; **Aus·schluß der** exclusion (von from); (aus einer Gemeinschaft) expulsion (aus from); unter ~ der Öffentlichkeit with the public excluded; (Rechtsw.) in camera

**aus|schmücken** *tr. V.* deck out

**aus|schneiden** *unr. tr. V.* cut out; **Aus·schnitt der a)** (Zeitungs~) cutting; clipping; **b)** (Hals~) neck; ein tiefer ~: a plunging neck-line; **c)** (Teil) part; (eines Textes) excerpt; (eines Films) clip; (Bild~) detail

**aus|schreiben** *unr. tr. V.* **a)** (nicht abgekürzt schreiben) etw. ~: write sth. out in full; **b)** (ausstellen) make out ⟨cheque, invoice, receipt⟩; **c)** (bekanntgeben) call ⟨election, meeting⟩; advertise ⟨idea⟩; put ⟨supply order etc.⟩ out to tender; **Aus·schreibung die** *s.* **ausschreiben c:** calling; advertisement; invitation to tender

**Ausschreitungen** *Pl.* acts of violence

**Aus·schuß der** committee

**aus|schütten** *tr. V.* tip out ⟨water, sand, coal, etc.⟩; (ausleeren) empty ⟨bucket, bowl, container⟩

**ausschweifend 1.** *Adj.* wild ⟨imagination, emotion, hope, desire, orgy⟩; extravagant ⟨idea⟩; riotous, wild ⟨enjoyment⟩; dissolute ⟨life, person⟩; **2.** *adv.* ~ leben lead a dissolute life; **Ausschweifung die** ~, ~en (im Genießen) dissolution

**aus|sehen** *unr. itr. V.* look (wie like); so siehst du aus! (ugs.) that's what you think!; **Aussehen das;** ~s appearance

**aus|sein** *unr. itr. V.; mit sein; nur im Inf. und Part. zusammengeschrieben* **a)** ⟨play, film, war⟩ be over; wann ist die Vorstellung aus? what time does the performance end?; die Schule ist aus school is out; **b)** ⟨fire, candle, etc.⟩ be out; **c)** ⟨radio, light, etc.⟩ be off

**außen** *Adv.* outside; die Vase ist ~ bemalt the vase is painted on the outside; das Fenster geht nach ~ auf the window opens outwards; von ~: from the outside

**außen-, Außen-:** ~handel der; *o. Pl.* foreign trade *no art.;* ~minister der Foreign Minister; ~ministerium das Foreign Ministry; ~politik die foreign politics *sing.;* ~politisch **1.** *Adj.* ⟨question⟩ relating to foreign policy; **2.** *adv.* as regards foreign policy; ~seite die outside

**Außenseiter** der; ~s, ~, **Außenseiterin** die; ~, ~nen outsider

**außer** 1. *Präp. mit Dat.* **a)** *(abgesehen von)* apart from; aside from *(Amer.)*; **b)** *(außerhalb von)* out of; ~ **sich sein** be beside oneself (**vor** + *Dat.* with); **c)** *(zusätzlich zu)* in addition to; 2. *Präp. mit Akk.* ~ **sich geraten** become beside oneself (**vor** + *Dat.* with); 3. *Konj.* except; **äußer...** *Adj.* outer; outside *(pocket)*; outlying *(district, area)*; external *(injury, form, circumstances, cause, force)*; outward *(appearance, similarity, effect, etc.)*; foreign *(affairs)*

**außer·dem** [*auch:* --'-] *Adv.* as well; *(überdies)* besides

**Äußere** das; ~n [outward] appearance

**außer-:** ~**ehelich** 1. *Adj.* extramarital; illegitimate *(child, birth)*; 2. *adv.* outside marriage; ~**gewöhnlich** 1. *Adj.* **a)** unusual; **b)** *(das Gewohnte übertreffend)* exceptional; 2. *adv.* **a)** unusually; **b)** *(sehr)* exceptionally; ~**halb** *Präp. mit Gen.* outside

**äußerlich** 1. *Adj.* external *(use, injury)*; outward *(appearance, calm, similarity, etc.)*; 2. *adv.: s. Adj.:* externally; outwardly

**äußern** 1. *tr. V.* express, voice *(opinion, view, criticism, reservations, disapproval, doubt)*; express *(wish)*; voice *(suspicion)*; 2. *refl. V.* **a)** **sich über etw.** *(Akk.)* ~: give one's view on sth.; **b)** *(illness)* manifest itself (**in** + *Dat.*, **durch** in)

**außer·ordentlich** 1. *Adj.* **a)** extraordinary; **b)** *(das Gewohnte übertreffend)* exceptional; 2. *adv.* *(sehr)* exceptionally; extremely *(pleased, relieved)*

**äußerst** *Adv.* extremely; **äußerst...** *Adj.* **a)** extreme; **b)** *(letztmöglich)* latest possible *(date, deadline)*; *(höchst...)* highest *(price)*; *(niedrigst...)* lowest *(price)*; **c)** *(schlimmst...)* worst

**außerstande** *Adv.* ~ **sein, etw. zu tun** *(nicht befähigt)* be unable to do sth.; *(nicht in der Lage)* not be in a position to do sth.

**Äußerung** die; ~, ~en comment

**aus|setzen** 1. *tr. V.* **a)** expose (*Dat.* to); **Belastungen ausgesetzt sein** be subject to strains; **b)** *(sich selbst überlassen)* abandon *(baby, animal)*; *(auf einer einsamen Insel)* maroon; **c)** **an jmdm./etw. etwas auszusetzen haben** find fault with sb./sth.; 2. *itr. V.* **a)** *(aufhören)* stop; *(engine, machine)* cut

out; **b)** *(pausieren)* *(player)* miss a turn; **mit der Arbeit/dem Training [ein paar Wochen]** ~: stop work/training [for a few weeks]

**Aus·sicht** die **a)** view (**auf** + *Akk.* of); **b)** *(fig.)* prospect; ~ **auf etw.** *(Akk.)* **haben,** etw. **in** ~ **haben** have the prospect of sth.

**aussichts-, Aussichts-:** ~**los** 1. *Adj.* hopeless. 2. *adv.* hopelessly; ~**reich** *Adj.* promising; ~**turm** der look-out tower

**aus|sortieren** *tr. V.* sort out

**aus|spannen** *itr. V.* take *or* have a break

**aus|sperren** 1. *tr. V.* lock out; shut *(animal)* out; 2. *itr. V.* lock the workforce out; **Aus·sperrung** die lockout

**aus|spielen** *tr. V.* **a)** *auch itr.* *(Kartenspiel)* lead; **b)** **jmdn./etw. gegen jmdn./etw.** ~: play sb./sth. off against sb./sth.

**Aus·sprache** die **a)** pronunciation; **b)** *(Gespräch)* discussion

**aus|sprechen** 1. *unr. tr. V.* **a)** pronounce; **b)** *(ausdrücken)* express; voice *(suspicion, request)*; 2. *unr. refl. V.* **a) b) sich lobend/mißbilligend** usw. **über jmdn./etw.** ~: speak highly/disapprovingly of etc. sb./sth.; **c)** *(offen sprechen)* say what's on one's mind; **sich bei jmdm.** ~: have a heart-to-heart talk with sb.; **d)** *(Strittiges klären)* talk things out (**mit** with); 3. *unr. itr. V.* *(zu Ende sprechen)* finish [speaking]; **Aus·spruch** der remark

**aus|spucken** 1. *itr. V.* spit.; 2. *tr. V.* spit out

**aus|spülen** *tr. V.* rinse out

**Aus·stand** der strike

**aus|statten** ['au̯sʃtatn̩] *tr. V.* provide (**mit** with); *(mit Gerät)* equip; *(mit Möbeln, Teppichen, Gardinen usw.)* furnish; **Ausstattung** die; ~, ~en **a)** *s.* ausstatten provision; equipping; furnishing; **b)** *(Ausrüstung)* equipment; *(Innen– eines Autos)* trim; **c)** *(Einrichtung)* furnishings *pl.*

**aus|stehen** 1. *unr. itr. V.* **noch** ~ *(debt)* be outstanding; *(decision)* be still to be taken; *(solution)* be still to be found; 2. *unr. tr. V.* **ich kann ihn/das nicht** ~: I can't stand him/it

**aus|steigen** *unr. itr. V.; mit sein* get out; *(aus einem Zug, Bus)* get off

**aus|stellen** *tr. V.* **a)** put on display; display; *(im Museum, auf einer Messe)* exhibit; **b)** *(ausfertigen)* make out

⟨*cheque, prescription, receipt, bill*⟩; issue ⟨*visa, passport, certificate*⟩; **c)** *(ugs.: ausschalten)* switch off ⟨*cooker, radio, heating, engine*⟩; **Aus·stel·lung die a)** exhibition; **b)** *s.* **ausstellen b:** making out; issuing

**aus|sterben** *unr. itr. V.; mit sein* die out; ⟨*species*⟩ become extinct

**Aus·steuer die** trousseau *(consisting mainly of household linen)*

**Ausstieg der:** ~|e|s, ~e *(Tür)* exit

**aus|stopfen** *tr. V.* stuff

**aus|stoßen** *unr. tr. V.* **a)** expel; give off, emit ⟨*gas, fumes, smoke*⟩; **b)** give ⟨*cry, whistle, laugh, sigh, etc.*⟩; let out ⟨*cry, scream, yell*⟩; utter ⟨*curse, threat, etc.*⟩

**aus|strahlen 1.** *tr. V.* **a)** *(auch fig.)* radiate; ⟨*lamp*⟩ give out ⟨*light*⟩; **b)** *(Rundf., Ferns.)* broadcast; **2.** *itr. V.* **a)** radiate; ⟨*light*⟩ be given out; *(fig.)* ⟨*pain*⟩ spread; **b)** auf jmdn./etw. ~ *(fig.)* communicate itself to sb./influence sth.; **Aus·strahlung die** *(fig.)* charisma

**aus|strecken 1.** *tr. V.* stretch out; put out ⟨*feelers*⟩; **2.** *refl. V.* stretch out

**aus|streichen** *unr. tr. V.* cross out

**aus|strömen** *itr. V.; mit sein* pour out; ⟨*gas, steam*⟩ escape

**aus|suchen** *tr. V.* choose; pick

**Aus·tausch der a)** exchange; **im ~ für** *od.* **gegen** in exchange for; **b)** *(das Ersetzen)* replacement **(gegen** with); **aus|tauschen** *tr. V.* **a)** exchange **(gegen** for); **b)** *(ersetzen)* replace **(gegen** with); **Austausch·motor der** replacement engine

**aus|teilen** *tr. V.* distribute **an** + *Akk.* to); *(aushändigen)* hand out ⟨*books, post, etc.*⟩ **(an** + *Akk.* to); give ⟨*orders*⟩; deal [out] ⟨*cards*⟩; give out ⟨*marks, grades*⟩; serve ⟨*food etc.*⟩

**Auster die;** ~, ~n oyster

**aus|tragen** *unr. tr. V.* **a)** deliver ⟨*newspapers, post*⟩; **b)** ⟨*pregnant woman*⟩ carry ⟨*child*⟩ to full term; *(nicht abtreiben)* have ⟨*child*⟩; **c)** *(ausfechten)* settle ⟨*conflict, differences*⟩; fight out ⟨*battle*⟩

**Australien** [aus'tra:liən] **(das);** ~s Australia; **Australier der;** ~s, ~: Australian; **australisch** *Adj.* Australian

**aus|treiben** *unr. tr. V.* **a)** exorcize, cast out ⟨*evil spirit, demon*⟩; **b)** jmdm. etw. ~: cure sb. of sth.

**aus|treten 1.** *unr. tr. V.* **a)** tread out ⟨*spark, cigarette-end*⟩; trample out

⟨*fire*⟩; **b)** *(bahnen)* tread out ⟨*path*⟩; **c)** wear out ⟨*shoes*⟩; **2.** *unr. itr. V.; mit sein* **a)** *(ugs.: zur Toilette gehen)* pay a call *(coll.)*; **b)** **aus etw.** ~ *(ausscheiden)* leave sth.

**aus|trinken** *tr. V.* drink up ⟨*drink*⟩; finish ⟨*glass, cup, etc.*⟩

**Aus·tritt der** leaving

**aus|trocknen 1.** *tr. V.* dry out; dry up ⟨*river bed, marsh*⟩; **2.** *itr. V.; mit sein* dry out; ⟨*river bed, pond, etc.*⟩ dry up; ⟨*skin, hair*⟩ become dry

**aus|üben** *tr. V.* practise ⟨*art, craft*⟩; follow ⟨*profession*⟩; carry on ⟨*trade*⟩; do ⟨*job*⟩; hold ⟨*office*⟩; wield ⟨*power, right, control*⟩

**Aus·verkauf der** sale; **ausverkauft** *Adj.* sold out

**Aus·wahl die a)** choice; **b)** *(Sortiment)* range; **viel/wenig ~ haben** have a wide/limited selection **(an** + *Dat.,* **von** of); **aus|wählen** *tr. V.* choose **(aus** from)

**Aus·wanderer der** emigrant; **aus|wandern** *itr. V.; mit sein* emigrate; **Aus·wanderung die** emigration

**auswärtig** *Adj.* **a)** non-local; **b)** *(das Ausland betreffend)* foreign; **auswärts** *Adv.* **a)** *(nach außen)* outwards; **b)** *(nicht zu Hause)* ⟨*sleep*⟩ away from home; **~essen** eat out; **c)** *(nicht am Ort)* in another town; *(Sport)* away; **Auswärts·spiel das** *(Sport)* away match

**aus|waschen** *unr. tr. V.* wash out

**aus|wechseln** *tr. V.* **a)** change **(gegen** + *Akk.* for); **b)** *(ersetzen)* replace **(gegen** with); *(Sport)* substitute ⟨*player*⟩

**Aus·weg der** way out **(aus** of); **ausweg·los 1.** *Adj.* hopeless. **2.** *adv.* hopelessly

**aus|weichen** *unr. itr. V.; mit sein* get out of the way **(Dat.** of); *(Platz machen)* make way **(Dat.** for); **einem Schlag/Angriff** ~: dodge a blow/evade an attack; **dem Feind** ~: avoid [contact with] the enemy; **einer Frage** ~: evade a question; **eine ~de Antwort** an evasive answer

**Ausweis der;** ~es, ~e card; *(Personal~)* identity card; **aus|weisen 1.** *unr. tr. V.* **a)** expel **(aus** from); **b)** **jmdn. als etw.** ~: show that sb. is/was sth.; **2.** *unr. refl. V.* prove *or* establish one's identity [by showing one's papers]; **können Sie sich ~?** do you have any means of identification?; **Aus·weisung die** expulsion **(aus** from)

**aus|weiten** *tr. V.* stretch

**aus·wendig** *Adv.* etw. ~ können/lernen know/learn sth. [off] by heart

**aus|werten** *tr. V.* analyse and evaluate; **Aus·wertung die** analysis and evaluation

**aus|wirken** *refl. V.* have an effect (auf + *Akk.* on); **sich günstig ~:** have a favourable effect; **Aus·wirkung die** effect (auf + *Akk.* on)

**Aus·wuchs der a)** *(Wucherung)* growth; excrescence *(Med., Bot.);* **b)** *(fig.)* unhealthy product; *(Exzeß)* excess

**aus|zahlen 1.** *tr. V.* **a)** pay out ⟨*money*⟩; **b)** pay off ⟨*employee, worker*⟩; buy out ⟨*business partner*⟩; **2.** *refl. V.* pay

**aus|zählen** *tr. V.* **a)** count [up] ⟨*votes etc.*⟩; **b)** *(Boxen)* count out

**aus|zeichnen** *tr. V.* **a)** *(mit einem Preisschild)* mark; **b)** *(ehren)* honour; **Aus·zeichnung die a)** *o. Pl. (von Waren)* marking; **b)** *(Ehrung)* honouring; *(Orden)* decoration; *(Preis)* award

**aus|ziehen 1.** *unr. tr. V.* **a)** pull out ⟨*couch*⟩; extend ⟨*table, tripod, etc.*⟩; **b)** *(ablegen)* take off ⟨*clothes*⟩; **c)** *(entkleiden)* undress; **sich ~:** get undressed; **2.** *unr. itr. V.; mit sein* move out (aus of); **Aus·zug der a)** *(das Ausziehen)* move; **b)** *(Bankw.)* statement; **c)** *(Textpassage)* extract

**Auto** das; ~s, ~s car; automobile *(Amer.);* **~ fahren** drive; *(mitfahren)* go in the car

**Auto-:** **~bahn** die motorway *(Brit.);* expressway *(Amer.);* **~biographie** [-----'-] die autobiography; **~bus der** *s.* Bus; **~fähre** die car ferry; **~fahren** das driving; motoring; **~fahrer der** [car-]driver; **~fahrt die** drive; **~gramm** [--'-] das; ~s, ~e autograph; **~kino** das drive-in cinema

**Automat der;** ~en, ~en **a)** *(Verkaufs~)* [vending-] machine; *(Spiel~)* slot-machine; **b)** *(in der Produktion)* robot; **Automatik die;** ~, ~en automatic control mechanism; *(Getriebe~)* automatic transmission; **automatisch** *(auch fig.)* **1.** *Adj.* automatic; **2.** *adv.* automatically; **automatisieren** *tr. V.* automate; **Automatisierung die;** ~, ~en automation

**auto-, Auto-:** **~mobil** [---'-] das; ~s, ~e *(geh.)* motor car; automobile *(Amer.);* **~nom** [--'-] **1.** *Adj.* autonomous; **2.** *adv.* autonomously; **~nomie**

[---'-] die; ~, ~n autonomy; **~nummer die** [car] registration number

**Autopsie** [autɔ'psi:] die; ~, ~n postmortem [examination]

**Autor der;** ~s, ~en author

**Auto-:** **~radio das** car radio; **~reifen der** car tyre; **~reisezug der** Motorail train *(Brit.);* auto train *(Amer.)*

**Autorin die;** ~, ~nen authoress; author

**autoritär** *Adj.* authoritarian; **Autorität die;** ~, ~en authority

**Auto-:** **~schlange die** queue of cars; **~schlüssel der** car key; **~stopp der** hitch-hiking; **per ~stopp fahren, ~stopp machen** hitch-hike; **~unfall der** car accident; **~vermietung die** car rental firm; **~werkstatt die** garage

**Avocado** [avo'ka:do] die; ~, ~s avocado [pear]

**Axt die;** ~, Äxte axe

**Azalee** [atsa'le:ə] die; ~, ~n azalea


# B


**b, B** [be:] das; ~, ~ **a)** *(Buchstabe)* b/B; **b)** *(Musik)* [key of] B flat

**B** *Abk.* Bundesstraße ≈ A *(Brit.)*

**Baby** ['be:bi] das; ~s, ~s baby; **Baby·sitter** [-sɪtɐ] der; ~s, ~: babysitter

**Bach der;** ~[e]s, Bäche **a)** stream; brook; **b)** *(Rinnsal)* stream [of water]

**Back·blech das** baking-sheet

**Back·bord das** *(Seew., Luftf.)* port [side]; **Backe die;** ~, ~n cheek

**backen 1.** *unr. itr. V.* bake; **2.** *unr. tr. V.* **a)** bake; **b)** *(bes. südd.) s.* braten

**Backen·zahn der** molar

**Bäcker der;** ~s, ~: baker; **er ist ~:** he is a baker; **zum/beim ~:** to the/at the baker's; **Bäckerei die;** ~, ~en baker's [shop]

**Back-:** **~fisch der** fried fish *(in breadcrumbs);* **~form die** baking-tin *(Brit.);* baking-pan *(Amer.);* **~hähnchen das, ~hendl das** *(österr.),* **~huhn das** fried chicken *(in breadcrumbs);* **~ofen der** oven; **~pulver**

**das** baking-powder; **~stein** der brick; **~waren** *Pl.* bread, cakes, and pastries

**Bad** das; ~|e|s, **Bäder a)** bath; *(das Schwimmen)* swim; *(im Meer o. ä.)* bathe; **ein ~ nehmen** *(geh.)* take a bath; *(schwimmen)* go for a swim; *(im Meer o. ä.)* bathe; **b)** *(Badezimmer)* bathroom; **ein Zimmer mit ~:** a room with [private] bath; **c)** *(Schwimm~)* [swimming-]pool; **d)** *(Heil~)* spa; *(See~)* [seaside] resort

**Bade-:** **~an·zug** der bathing costume; **~hose** die bathing trunks *pl;* **~mantel** der dressing-gown; bathrobe; **~meister** der swimming-pool attendant; **~mütze** die bathing cap

**baden 1.** *itr. V.* **a)** have a bath; **b)** *(schwimmen)* bathe; **~ gehen** go for a bathe; **2.** *tr. V.* bath ⟨*child, patient, etc.*⟩; bathe ⟨*wound, eye, etc.*⟩

**Bäder** *s.* **Bad**

**Bade-:** **~strand** der bathing-beach; **~tuch** das bath towel; **~wanne** die bath[-tub]; **~wasser** das bath water; **~zimmer** das bathroom

**Bagatelle** die; ~, **~n** trifle

**Bagger** der; **~s,** ~: excavator; *(Schwimm~)* dredger; **Bagger·see** der flooded gravel-pit

**Bahn** die; ~, **~en a)** *(Weg)* path; **b)** *(Route)* path; *(eines Geschosses)* trajectory; **c)** *(Sport)* track; *(für Pferderennen)* course *(Brit.);* track *(Amer.);* *(für einzelne Teilnehmer)* lane; *(Kegel~)* alley; *(Bowling~)* lane; **d)** *(Eisen~)* railways *pl.;* railroad *(Amer.);* *(Zug)* train; **jmdn. zur ~ bringen** take sb. to the station; **|mit der| ~ fahren** go by train; **f)** *(Straßen~)* tram; streetcar *(Amer.)*

**bahn-, Bahn-:** **~brechend** *Adj.* pioneering; **~bus** der railway bus; **~damm** der railway embankment

**bahnen** *tr. V.* clear ⟨*way, path*⟩; **jmdm./einer Sache einen Weg ~** *(fig.)* pave the way for sb./sth.

**Bahn-:** **~fahrt** die train journey; **~hof** der [railway *or* *(Amer.)* railroad] station; **~reise** die train journey; **~schranke** die level-crossing *(Brit.)* *or* *(Amer.)* grade crossing barrier/gate; **~steig** der; **~|e|s,** ~**e** [station] platform; **~übergang** der level-crossing *(Brit.);* grade crossing *(Amer.);* **~verbindung** die train connection

**Bahre** die; ~, **~n a)** *(Kranken~)* stretcher; **b)** *(Toten~)* bier

**Baiser** [bɛ'ze:] das; ~s, ~s meringue
**Bajonett** das; ~|e|s, ~e bayonet
**Bakterie** [bak'te:rɪə] die; ~, ~n bacterium
**Balance** [ba'laŋsə] die; ~, ~n balance; **balancieren** *itr., tr. V.; itr. mit sein* balance

**bald** *Adv.* **a)** soon; *(leicht, rasch)* quickly; easily; **wird's ~?** get a move on, will you; **bis ~!** see you soon; **b)** *(ugs.: fast)* almost

**Baldrian** ['baldria:n] der; ~s, ~e valerian

**Balkan** ['balka:n] der; ~s: der ~: the Balkans *pl.;* *(Gebirge)* the Balkan Mountains *pl.* **auf dem ~:** in the Balkans

**Balken** der; ~s, ~: beam
**Balkon** [bal'kɔŋ, bal'ko:n] der; ~s, ~s [bal'kɔŋs] *od.* ~e [bal'ko:nə] **a)** balcony; **b)** *(im Theater, Kino)* circle

**Ball** der; ~|e|s, **Bälle a)** ball; **~ spielen** play ball; **b)** *(Fest)* ball

**Ballade** die; ~, ~n ballad
**Ballast** der; ~|e|s, ~e ballast
**ballen 1.** *tr. V.* clench ⟨*fist*⟩; **2.** *refl. V.* ⟨*fist*⟩ clench; **Ballen** der; ~s, ~ **a)** *(Packen)* bale; **b)** *(Hand~, Fuß~)* ball

**Ballett** das; ~|e|s, ~e ballet
**Ball-:** **~junge** der ballboy; **~kleid** das ball gown

**Ballon** [ba'lɔŋ] der; ~s, ~s balloon
**Ball-:** **~saal** der ballroom; **~spiel** das ball game; **~spielen** das; ~s playing ball *no art.*

**Ballungs·gebiet** das conurbation
**Balsam** der; ~s, ~e balsam; *(fig.)* balm

**Balte** der; ~n, ~n, **Baltin** die; ~, ~nen Balt; **Baltikum** das; ~s Baltic States *pl.;* **baltisch** *Adj.* Baltic

**Bambus** der; ~ *od.* ~ses, ~se bamboo
**banal** *Adj.* **a)** banal; **b)** *(gewöhnlich)* commonplace

**Banane** die; ~, ~n banana
**Banause** der; ~n, ~n *(abwertend)* philistine

**band** *1. u. 3. Pers. Sg. Prät. v.* **binden**
**¹Band** das; ~|e|s, **Bänder a)** ribbon; *(Haar~, Hut~)* band; *(Schürzen~)* string; **b)** *(Klebe~, Isolier~, Ton~ usw.)* tape; **etw. auf ~** *(Akk.)* **aufnehmen** tape[-record] sth.; **c)** *s.* **Förderband; d)** *s.* **Fließband; e) am laufenden ~** *(ugs.)* nonstop; **f)** *(Anat.)* ligament
**²Band** der; ~|e|s, **Bände** ['bɛndə] volume
**³Band** [bɛnt] die; ~, ~s band; *(Beat~, Rock~ usw.)* group

¹**Bande** die; ~, ~n a) gang; b) *(ugs.: Gruppe)* mob *(sl.)*

²**Bande** die; ~, ~n *(Sport)* [perimeter] barrier; *(mit Reklame)* billboards *pl.; (Billard)* cushion

**Bänder** *s.* ¹**Band**

**bändigen** *tr. V.* tame ⟨*animal*⟩; control ⟨*person, anger, urge*⟩

**Bandit** der; ~en, ~en bandit

**Band·scheibe** die [intervertebral] disc

**bang, bange; banger, bangst... od. bänger, bängst...:** 1. *Adj.* afraid; scared; *(besorgt)* anxious; mir ist/wurde ~ [zumute] I am/became scared; 2. *adv.* anxiously; **bangen** *itr. V.* be anxious

¹**Bank** die; ~, Bänke bench; *(mit Lehne)* bench seat; *(Kirchen~)* pew; etw. auf die lange ~ schieben *(ugs.)* put sth. off

²**Bank** die; ~, ~en bank

¹**Bankett** das; ~|e|s, ~e banquet

²**Bankett** das; ~|e|s, ~e *(an Straßen)* shoulder; *(unbefestigt)* verge

**Bankier** [baŋ'kịe:] der; ~s, ~s banker

**Bank-: ~konto** das bank account; **~leitzahl** die bank sorting code number; **~note** die banknote; bill *(Amer.);* **~raub** der bank robbery; **~räuber** der bank robber

**bankrott** *Adj.* bankrupt; ~ gehen go bankrupt; **Bankrott** der; ~|e|s, ~e bankruptcy; ~ machen go bankrupt

**Bann** der; ~|e|s *(fig. geh.)* spell

**bar** 1. *Adj.* cash; 2. *adv.* in cash

**Bar** die; ~, ~s bar

**Bär** der; ~en, ~en bear

**Baracke** die; ~, ~n hut

**Barbar** der; ~en, ~en barbarian; **Barbarei** die; ~, ~en a) *(Roheit)* barbarity; b) *(Kulturlosigkeit)* barbarism *no indef. art.;* **barbarisch** 1. *Adj.* a) *(roh)* barbarous; b) *(unzivilisiert)* barbaric; 2. *adv.* a) *(roh)* barbarously; b) *(unzivilisiert)* barbarically

**Bar·dame** die barmaid

**Barett** das; ~|e|s, ~e *(eines Geistlichen)* biretta; *(eines Richters, Professors)* cap; *(Baskenmütze)* beret

**bar·fuß** *indekl. Adj.; nicht attr.* barefooted; ~ herumlaufen/gehen run about/go barefoot

**barg** *1. u. 3. Pers. Sg. Prät. v.* bergen

**Bar-: ~geld** das cash; **~hocker** der bar stool

**Bariton** ['ba(:)ritɔn] der; ~s, ~e baritone

**Barkasse** die; ~, ~n launch

**barmherzig** *(geh.)* 1. *Adj.* merciful; 2. *adv.* mercifully; **Barmherzigkeit** die; ~ *(geh.)* mercy

**Barock** das *od.* der; ~|s| a) baroque; b) *(Zeit)* baroque age

**Baro·meter** das barometer

**Baron** der; ~s, ~e baron; *(als Anrede)* [Herr] ~: ≈ my lord; **Baronin** die; ~, ~nen baroness; *(als Anrede)* [Frau] ~: ≈ my Lady

**Barren** der; ~s, ~ a) *(Gold~, Silber~ usw.)* bar; b) *(Turngerät)* parallel bars *pl.*

**Barriere** [ba'rịe:rə] die; ~, ~n *(auch fig.)* barrier

**Barrikade** die; ~, ~n barricade

**barsch** 1. *Adj.* curt; 2. *adv.* curtly

**Barsch** der; ~|e|s, ~e perch

**barst** *1. u. 3. Pers. Sg. Prät. v.* bersten

**Bart** der; ~|e|s, Bärte a) beard; *(Oberlippen~, Schnurr~)* moustache; b) *(von Katzen, Mäusen, Robben)* whiskers *pl.;* c) *(am Schlüssel)* bit; **bärtig** *Adj.* bearded; **Bart·wuchs** der growth of beard

**Bar·zahlung** die cash payment

**Basalt** der; ~|e|s, ~e basalt

**Basar** der; ~s, ~e bazaar

**Basis** die; ~, Basen a) *(Grundlage)* basis; b) *(Math., Archit., Milit.)* base

**Baske** der; ~n, ~n, **Baskin** die; ~, ~nen Basque

**Basken-: ~land** das Basque region; **~mütze** die beret

**Basket·ball** ['ba(:)skət-] der basketball

**Baß** der; Basses, Bässe *(Musik)* a) bass; b) *(Instrument)* double-bass

**Bassin** [ba'sɛ̃:] das; ~s, ~s *(Schwimm~)* pool; *(im Garten)* pond

**Bassist** der; ~en, ~en *(Musik)* a) *(Sänger)* bass; b) *(Instrumentalist)* double-bass player; bassist; *(in einer Rockband)* bass guitarist

**Bast** der; ~|e|s, ~e bast; *(Raffia~)* raffia

**basta** *Interj. (ugs.)* that's enough; und damit ~! and that's that!

**Bastelei** die; ~, ~en; a) *(Gegenstand)* piece of handicraft work; b) *(ugs.: das Basteln)* handicraft work; **basteln** 1. *tr. V.* make; 2. *itr. V.* make things [with one's hands]

**Bastion** die; ~, ~en bastion

**bat** *1. u. 3. Pers. Sg. Prät. v.* bitten

**Bataillon** [batal'jo:n] das; ~s, ~e *(Milit.)* battalion

**Batik** der; ~s, ~en *od.* die; ~, ~en batik

**Batist** der; ~[e]s, ~e batiste

**Batterie** die; ~, ~n battery

**Batzen** der; ~s, ~ *(ugs.)* a) *(Klumpen)* lump; b) *(Menge)* pile *(coll.)*

¹**Bau** der; ~[e]s, ~ten a) *o. Pl. (Errichtung)* building; im ~ sein be under construction; b) *(Gebäude)* building; c) auf dem ~ arbeiten *(Bauarbeiter sein)* be in the building trade; d) *o. Pl. (Struktur)* structure

²**Bau** der; ~[e]s, ~e *(Kaninchen~)* burrow; hole; *(Fuchs~)* earth

**Bau·arbeiten** *Pl.* building work *sing.*

**Bauch** der; ~[e]s, Bäuche *(auch fig.: von Schiffen, Flugzeugen)* belly; **bauchig** *Adj.* bulbous

**Bauch-:** ~**laden** der vendor's tray; ~**landung** die belly-landing; ~**nabel** der *(ugs.)* belly-button *(coll.);* ~**redner** der ventriloquist; ~**schmerzen** *Pl.* stomach-ache *sing.;* ~**speichel·drüse** die pancreas; ~**tanz** der belly-dance; ~**tänzerin** die belly-dancer; ~**weh** das *(ugs.)* tummy-ache *(coll.);* stomach-ache

**bauen** 1. *tr. V.* build; 2. *itr. V.* a) build; wir wollen ~: we want to build a house; *(bauen lassen)* we want to have a house built; b) auf jmdn./etw. ~ *(fig.)* rely on sb./sth.

¹**Bauer** der; ~n, ~n a) farmer; *(mit niedrigem sozialem Status)* peasant; b) *(Schachfigur)* pawn; c) *(Kartenspiele)* s. Bube

²**Bauer** das *od.* der; ~s, ~: [bird-]cage

**Bäuerin** die; ~, ~nen a) s. ¹ Bauer a: [lady] farmer; peasant [woman]; b) *(Frau eines Bauern)* farmer's wife; **bäuerlich** *Adj.* farming *attrib.; (ländlich)* rural

**Bauern-:** ~**haus** das farmhouse; ~**hof** der farm

**bau-, Bau-:** ~**fällig** *Adj.* ramshackle; unsafe ⟨*roof, ceiling*⟩; ~**jahr** das year of construction; *(bei Autos)* year of manufacture; ~**kasten** der construction set; *(mit Holzklötzen)* box of bricks; ~**klotz** der building-brick

**baulich** *Adj.; nicht präd.* structural

**Baum** der; ~[e]s, Bäume tree; **Bäumchen** das; ~s, ~ small tree

**Bau·meister** der *(hist.)* [architect and] master builder

**baumeln** *itr. V. (ugs.)* dangle (**an** + *Dat.* from)

**Baum-:** ~**schule** die tree nursery; ~**stamm** der tree-trunk; ~**stumpf** der tree-stump; ~**wolle** die cotton

**Bau·platz** der site for building

**bäurisch** *(abwertend)* 1. *Adj.* boorish; 2. *adv.* boorishly

**Bau·satz** der kit

**Bausch** der; ~[e]s, ~e *od.* Bäusche a) *(Watte~)* a wad; b) etw. in ~ und Bogen verwerfen/verdammen reject/condemn sth. wholesale; **bauschen** 1. *tr. V.* billow ⟨*sail, curtains, etc.*⟩; 2. *refl. V.* ⟨*dress, sleeve*⟩ puff out; *(ungewollt)* bunch up; *(im Wind)* ⟨*curtain, flag, etc.*⟩ billow [out]; **bauschig** *Adj.* puffed ⟨*dress*⟩; baggy ⟨*trousers*⟩

**bau-, Bau-:** ~**sparen** *itr. V.; nur Inf. gebr.* save with a building society; ~**spar·kasse** die ≈ building society; ~**stein** der a) building stone; b) *(Bestandteil)* element; *(Elektronik, DV)* module; c) *(~klotz)* building-brick; ~**stelle** die building site; *(beim Straßenbau)* road-works *pl.*

**Bauten** *Pl.: s.* Bau

**Bau-:** ~**unternehmer** der building contractor; ~**weise** die method of construction; ~**werk** das building; *(Brücke, Staudamm)* structure

**Bayer** der; ~n, ~n Bavarian; **bay[e]risch** *Adj.* Bavarian; **Bayern (das)**; ~s Bavaria

**Bazille** die; ~, ~n *(ugs.) s.* Bazillus a; **Bazillus** der; ~, Bazillen a) bacillus; b) *(fig.)* cancer

**Bd.** *Abk.* Band Vol.

**beabsichtigen** *tr. V.* intend

**beachten** *tr. V.* a) follow ⟨*rule, regulations, instruction*⟩; heed, follow ⟨*advice*⟩; obey ⟨*traffic signs*⟩; observe ⟨*formalities*⟩; b) *(berücksichtigen)* take account of; *(achten auf)* pay attention to; **beachtlich** 1. *Adj.* considerable; 2. *adv.* considerably; **Beachtung** die a) *s.* beachten a: following; heeding; obeying; b) *(Berücksichtigung)* consideration; c) *(Aufmerksamkeit)* attention

**Beamte** der; *adj. Dekl.* official; *(Staats~)* [permanent] civil servant; *(Kommunal~)* [established] local government officer; *(Polizei~)* [police] officer; **Beamtin** die; ~, ~nen *s.* Beamte

**beängstigend** *Adj.* worrying

**beanspruchen** *tr. V.* a) claim; etw. ~ können be entitled to expect sth.; b) *(ausnutzen)* make use of ⟨*person, equipment*⟩; take advantage of ⟨*hospitality, services*⟩; c) *(erfordern)* demand ⟨*energy, attention, stamina*⟩; take up ⟨*time, space, etc.*⟩; **Bean-**

**spruchung** die; ~, ~en demands pl. (Gen. on); die ~ durch den Beruf the demands of his/her job

**beanstanden** tr. V. take exception to; (sich beklagen über) complain about; **Beanstandung** die; ~, ~en complaint

**beantragen** tr. V. apply for

**beantworten** tr. V. answer; reply to ⟨letter⟩; return ⟨greeting⟩

**bearbeiten** tr. V. a) deal with; handle ⟨case⟩; b) (adaptieren) adapt (für for); **Bearbeitung** die; ~, ~en a) die ~ eines Antrags/eines Falles usw. dealing with an application/handling a case etc.; b) (Adaption) adaptation

**beaufsichtigen** tr. V. supervise; look after ⟨child⟩

**beauftragen** tr. V. entrust

**bebauen** tr. V. build on; develop; **Bebauung** die; ~, ~en a) development; b) (Gebäude) buildings pl.

**beben** itr. V. shake; **Beben** das; ~s, ~ (Erd~) earthquake

**bebildern** tr. V. illustrate

**Becher** der; ~s, ~ (Glas~, Porzellan~) glass; tumbler; (Plastik~) beaker; cup; (Eis~) (aus Glas, Metall) sundae dish; (aus Pappe) tub; (Joghurt~) carton

**Becken** das; ~s, ~ a) (Wasch~) basin; (Abwasch~) sink; (Toiletten~) pan; b) (Anat.) pelvis; c) Pl. (Musik) cymbals

**bedacht** Adj. auf etw. (Akk.) ~ sein be intent on sth.; **bedächtig** 1. Adj. a) deliberate; measured ⟨steps, stride, speech⟩; b) (besonnen) thoughtful; well-considered ⟨words⟩; 2. adv. a) deliberately; b) (besonnen) thoughtfully

**bedanken** refl. V. say thank you; sich bei jmdm. [für etw.] ~: thank sb. [for sth.]

**Bedarf** der; ~[e]s need (an + Dat. of); requirement (an + Dat. for); (Bedarfsmenge) needs pl.; requirements pl.; bei ~: if required

**bedauerlich** Adj. regrettable; **bedauerlicher·weise** Adv. regrettably; **bedauern** tr., itr. V. a) feel sorry for; sie läßt sich gerne ~: she likes being pitied; b) (schade finden) regret; ich bedaure sehr, daß ...: I am very sorry that ...; **Bedauern** das; ~s regret; zu meinem ~: to my regret; **bedauerns·wert** Adj. (geh.) unfortunate ⟨person⟩

**bedecken** tr. V. cover; **bedeckt** Adj. overcast ⟨sky⟩

**bedenken** unr. tr. V. a) consider; b) (beachten) take into consideration; **Bedenken** das; ~s, ~ reservation (gegen about); ohne ~: without hesitation; **bedenken·los** 1. Adj. unhesitating; (skrupellos) unscrupulous; 2. adv. without hesitation; (skrupellos) unscrupulously; **bedenklich** 1. Adj. a) dubious ⟨methods, transactions, etc.⟩; b) (bedrohlich) alarming; 2. adv. alarmingly; **Bedenk·zeit** die; o. Pl. time for reflection

**bedeuten** tr. V. a) mean; was soll das ~? what does that mean?; b) (sein) represent; das bedeutet ein Wagnis that is being really daring; **bedeutend** 1. Adj. a) important; b) (groß) substantial; considerable ⟨success⟩; 2. adv. considerably; **Bedeutung** die; ~, ~en a) meaning; b) o. Pl. (Wichtigkeit) importance

**bedeutungs-**: **~los** Adj. insignificant; **~voll** 1. Adj. a) significant; b) (vielsagend) meaningful; meaning ⟨look⟩; 2. adv. meaningfully

**bedienen** 1. tr. V. a) serve; werden Sie schon bedient? are you being served?; b) (handhaben) operate ⟨machine⟩; 2. itr. V. serve; 3. refl. V. help oneself; sich selbst ~ (im Geschäft, Restaurant usw.) serve oneself; **Bedienung** die; ~, ~en a) o. Pl. (das Bedienen) service; ~ inbegriffen service included; b) o. Pl. (das Handhaben) operation; c) (Serviererin) waiter/waitress; **Bedienungs·anleitung** die operating instructions pl.

**bedingen** tr. V. cause; **Bedingung** die; ~, ~en condition; unter der ~, daß ...: on condition that ...; **bedingungs·los** Adj. unconditional

**bedrängen** tr. V. a) besiege ⟨town, fortress, person⟩; put ⟨opposing player⟩ under pressure; b) (belästigen) pester; **bedrohen** tr. V. threaten; **bedrohlich** 1. Adj. (unheilverkündend) ominous; (gefährlich) dangerous; 2. adv. (unheilverkündend) ominously; (gefährlich) dangerously; **Bedrohung** die threat (Gen. to)

**bedrucken** tr. V. print

**bedrücken** tr. V. depress

**Beduine** der; ~n, ~n Bed[o]uin

**bedürfen** unr. itr. V. jmds./einer Sache ~ (geh.) require or need sb./sth.; **Bedürfnis** das; ~ses, ~se need (nach for); das ~ haben, etw. zu tun feel a need to do sth.; **bedürftig** Adj. needy

**Beef·steak** ['biːf-] **das** [beef]steak; **deutsches ~:** ≈ beefburger
**beehren** *tr. V. (geh.)* honour
**beeiden** *tr. V. ~,* **daß ...:** swear [on oath] that ...; **eine Aussage ~:** swear to the truth of a statement
**beeilen** *refl. V.* hurry [up *(coll.)*]
**beeindrucken** *tr. V.* impress; **beeindruckend** *Adj.* impressive
**beeinflussen** *tr. V.* influence; **Beeinflussung die; ~, ~en** influencing
**beeinträchtigen** *tr. V.* restrict ⟨*sights, freedom*⟩; detract from ⟨*pleasure, enjoyment, value*⟩; spoil ⟨*appetite, good humour*⟩; impair ⟨*quality, reactions, efficiency, vision, hearing*⟩; damage, harm ⟨*sales, reputation*⟩
**beenden** *tr. V.* end; finish ⟨*piece of work etc.*⟩; complete ⟨*studies*⟩
**beengen** *tr. V.* restrict
**beerben** *tr. V.* **jmdn. ~:** inherit sb's estate
**beerdigen** *tr. V.* bury; **Beerdigung die; ~, ~en** burial; *(Trauerfeier)* funeral; **Beerdigungs·institut das** [firm *sing.* of] undertakers *pl.*
**Beere die; ~, ~n** berry
**Beet das; ~[e]s, ~e** *(Blumen~)* bed; *(Gemüse~)* plot
**befahrbar** *Adj.* passable; **befahren** *unr. tr. V.* **a)** drive on ⟨*road*⟩; drive across ⟨*bridge*⟩; use ⟨*railway line*⟩; **die Straße ist stark/wenig ~:** the road is heavily/little used; **eine stark ~e Straße** a busy road; **b)** sail ⟨*sea*⟩; navigate, sail up/down ⟨*river, canal*⟩
**befallen** *unr. tr. V.* **a)** overcome; ⟨*misfortune*⟩ befall; **von Panik/Angst ~ werden** be seized with panic/fear; **b)** ⟨*pests*⟩ attack
**befangen 1.** *Adj.* **a)** self-conscious ⟨*person*⟩; **b)** *(voreingenommen)* biased; **2.** *adv.* self-consciously; **Befangenheit die; ~ a)** self-consciousness; **b)** *(Voreingenommenheit)* bias
**befassen** *refl. V.* **sich mit etw. ~:** occupy oneself with sth.; ⟨*article, book*⟩ deal with sth.; *(etw. studieren)* study sth.
**Befehl der; ~[e]s, ~e a)** order; **b) den ~ über jmdn./etw. haben** be in command of sb./sth.; **befehlen 1.** *unr. tr., itr. V.* order; *(Milit.)* order; **man befahl ihm zu warten** he was told to wait; **2.** *unr. itr. V.* **über jmdn./etw. ~:** have command of *or* be in command of sb./sth.; **Befehls·haber der; ~s, ~** *(Milit.)* commander

**befestigen** *tr. V.* **a)** fix; **etw. an der Wand ~:** fix sth. to the wall; **b)** *(haltbar machen)* stabilize ⟨*bank, embankment*⟩; make up ⟨*road, path, etc.*⟩; **c)** *(sichern)* fortify ⟨*town etc.*⟩; strengthen ⟨*border*⟩; **Befestigung die; ~, ~en a)** fixing; **b)** *(Milit.)* fortification
**befeuchten** *tr. V.* moisten; damp ⟨*hair, cloth*⟩
**befiehlst, befiehlt** *2., 3. Pers. Sg. Präsens v.* **befehlen**
**befinden** *unr. refl. V.* be; **Befinden das; ~s** health; *(eines Patienten)* condition
**beflecken** *tr. V.* stain
**befohlen** *2. Part. v.* **befehlen**
**befolgen** *tr. V.* follow, obey ⟨*instruction, grammatical rule*⟩; obey, comply with ⟨*law, regulation*⟩; follow ⟨*advice, suggestion*⟩
**befördern** *tr. V.* **a)** carry; transport; **b)** *(aufrücken lassen)* promote; **Beförderung die a)** *o. Pl.* carriage; transport; *(Personen~)* transport; **b)** *(das Aufrückenlassen)* promotion
**befragen** *tr. V.* **a)** question (über + *Akk.* about); **b)** *(konsultieren)* ask; **Befragung die; ~, ~en a)** questioning; **b)** *(Konsultation)* consultation; **c)** *(Umfrage)* opinion poll
**befreien 1.** *tr. V.* **a)** free; liberate ⟨*country, people*⟩ (von from); **b)** *(freistellen)* exempt (von from); **c)** jmdn. von Schmerzen ~: free sb. of pain; **2.** *refl. V.* free oneself (von from); **Befreier der** liberator; **Befreiung die; ~ a)** *s.* befreien 1a: freeing; liberation; **b)** *(Freistellung)* exemption; **c)** die ~ von Schmerzen release from pain
**befremden** *tr. V.* jmdn. ~: put sb. off
**befreunden** *refl. V. s.* **anfreunden**; [gut *od.* eng] befreundet sein be [good *or* close] friends (mit with)
**befriedigen** *tr. V.* **a)** satisfy; gratify ⟨*lust*⟩; **b)** *(ausfüllen)* ⟨*job, occupation, etc.*⟩ fulfil; **c)** *(sexuell)* satisfy; sich [selbst] ~: masturbate; **befriedigend 1.** *Adj.* satisfactory; **2.** *adv.* satisfactorily; **Befriedigung die; ~ a)** *s.* befriedigen a: satisfaction; gratification; **b)** *(Genugtuung)* satisfaction
**befristet** *Adj.* temporary ⟨*visa*⟩; fixed-term ⟨*ban, contract*⟩
**befruchten** *tr. V.* fertilize ⟨*egg*⟩; pollinate ⟨*flower*⟩; impregnate ⟨*female*⟩; **Befruchtung die; ~, ~en** *s.* befruchten: fertilization; pollination; impregnation

**Befugnis** die; ~, ~se authority
**befühlen** tr. V. feel
**Befund** der (bes. Med.) result[s pl.]
**befürchten** tr. V. fear; **ich befürchte, daß ...:** I am afraid that ...
**befürworten** tr. V. support
**begabt** Adj. talented; **Begabung** die; ~, ~en talent
**begann** 1. u. 3. Pers. Sg. Prät. v. beginnen
**begatten** tr. V. mate with; ⟨man⟩ copulate with; **sich ~:** mate; ⟨persons⟩ copulate; **Begattung die** mating; (bei Menschen) copulation
**begeben** unr. refl. V. (geh.) proceed; make one's way; go; **sich zu Bett ~:** retire to bed; **sich an die Arbeit ~:** commence work
**begegnen** itr. V.; mit sein jmdm. ~: meet sb.; **sich** (Dat.) ~: meet [each other]; **Begegnung die; ~, ~en a)** meeting; **b)** (Sport) match
**begehen** unr. tr. V. **a)** commit ⟨crime, adultery, indiscretion, sin, suicide, faux-pas, etc.⟩; make ⟨mistake⟩; **eine |furchtbare| Dummheit ~:** do something [really] stupid; **b)** (geh.: feiern) celebrate
**begehren** tr. V. desire; **begehrens·wert** Adj. desirable; **begehrlich** 1. Adj. greedy; **2.** adv. greedily; **begehrt** Adj. much sought-after
**begeistern** 1. tr. V. jmdn. [für etw.] ~: fire sb. with enthusiasm [for sth.]; **2.** refl. V. get enthusiastic (für about); **begeistert** 1. Adj. enthusiastic (von about); **2.** adv. enthusiastically; **Begeisterung die; ~:** enthusiasm
**Begierde** die; ~, ~n desire (nach for); **begierig** 1. Adj. eager; **2.** adv. eagerly
**begießen** unr. tr. V. water ⟨plants⟩
**Beginn** der; ~[e]s beginning; [gleich] **zu ~:** [right] at the beginning; **beginnen** 1. unr. itr. V. start; begin; **mit dem Bau ~:** start or begin building; **dort beginnt der Wald** the forest starts there; **2.** unr. tr. V. start; begin; start ⟨argument⟩; ~, **etw. zu tun** start to do sth.
**beglaubigen** tr. V. certify; **Beglaubigung die; ~, ~en** certification
**begleichen** unr. tr. V. settle ⟨bill, debt⟩; pay ⟨sum⟩
**begleiten** tr. V. accompany; **jmdn. nach Hause ~:** see sb. home; **Begleiter** der; ~s, ~, **Begleiterin** die; ~, ~nen companion; (zum Schutz) escort; (Führer[in]) guide; **Begleitung**

die; ~, ~en **a)** o. Pl. **er bot uns seine ~ an** he offered to accompany us; **in ~ eines Erwachsenen** accompanied by an adult; **b)** (Musik) accompaniment
**beglückwünschen** tr. V. congratulate (zu on)
**begnadet** Adj. (geh.) divinely gifted;
**begnadigen** tr. V. pardon; reprieve;
**Begnadigung die; ~, ~en** reprieving; (Straferlaß) pardon; reprieve
**begnügen** refl. V. content oneself
**Begonie** [be'go:niə] die; ~, ~n begonia
**begonnen** 2. Part. v. beginnen
**begraben** unr. tr. V. bury; **Begräbnis das; ~ses, ~se** burial; (~feier) funeral
**begreifen** 1. unr. tr. V. understand; **er konnte nicht ~, was geschehen war** he could not grasp what had happened; **2.** itr. V. understand; **schnell** od. **leicht/langsam** od. **schwer ~:** be quick/ slow on the uptake; **begreiflich** Adj. understandable
**begrenzen** tr. V. limit, restrict (auf + Akk. to)
**Begriff** der **a)** concept; (Terminus) term; **b)** (Auffassung) idea; **sich** (Dat.) **keinen ~ von etw. machen können** not be able to imagine sth.; **ein/kein ~ sein/be not be well known; **c)** **im ~ sein** od. **stehen, etw. zu tun** be about to do sth.; **begriffs·stutzig** Adj. (abwertend) obtuse
**begründen** tr. V. **a)** give reasons for; **b)** (gründen) found; establish ⟨fame, reputation⟩; **Begründer** der founder; **begründet** Adj. well-founded; reasonable ⟨demand, objection, complaint⟩; **Begründung die; ~, ~en** reason[s]; **mit der ~, daß ...:** on the grounds that ...
**begrüßen** tr. V. **a)** greet; ⟨hostess, host⟩ welcome; **b)** (fig.) welcome; **Begrüßung die; ~, ~en** greeting; (von Gästen) welcoming; (Zeremonie) welcome (Gen. for)
**begünstigen** tr. V. favour
**begutachten** tr. V. **a)** examine and report on; **b)** (ugs.) have a look at
**begütert** Adj. wealthy
**begütigen** tr. V. placate
**behäbig** 1. Adj. slow and ponderous; **2.** adv. slowly and ponderously
**behagen** itr. V. **etw. behagt jmdm.** sb. likes sth.; **Behagen das; ~s** pleasure; **behaglich** 1. Adj. comfortable; **2.** adv. comfortably; **Behaglichkeit die; ~:** comfortableness

**behалten** *unr. tr. V.* **a)** keep; etw. für sich ~: keep sth. to oneself; **b)** *(zurück~)* be left with ⟨*scar, defect, etc.*⟩; **c)** *(sich merken)* remember

**Behälter** der; ~s, ~ container; *(für Abfälle)* receptacle

**behandeln** *tr. V. (auch Med.)* treat; handle ⟨*matter, machine, device*⟩; deal with ⟨*subject, question etc.*⟩

**Behandlung** die; ~, ~en treatment

**behängen** *tr. V.* hang

**beharren** *itr. V.* **auf etw.** *(Dat.)* ~ *(etw. nicht aufgeben)* persist in sth.; *(auf etw. bestehen)* insist on sth.; **beharrlich** 1. *Adj.* dogged; 2. *adv.* doggedly; **Beharrlichkeit** die; ~: doggedness

**behauen** *unr. tr. V.* hew

**behaupten** 1. *tr. V.* **a)** maintain; assert; ~, jmd. zu sein/etw. zu wissen claim to be sb./know sth.; **b)** *(verteidigen)* maintain ⟨*position*⟩; retain ⟨*record*⟩; 2. *refl. V.* **a)** assert oneself; *(nicht untergehen)* hold one's ground; *(dableiben)* survive; **b)** *(Sport)* win through; **Behauptung** die; ~, ~en assertion

**Behausung** die; ~, ~en dwelling

**beheben** *unr. tr. V.* remove ⟨*danger, difficulty*⟩; repair ⟨*damage*⟩; remedy ⟨*abuse, defect*⟩; **Behebung** die; ~, ~en *s.* beheben: removal; repair; remedying

**beheimatet** *Adj.* **an einem Ort/in einem Land** *usw.* ~ sein be native to a place/to a country *etc.*

**beheizen** *tr. V.* heat

**behelfen** *unr. refl. V.* make do

**behelfs·mäßig** 1. *Adj.* makeshift; 2. *adv.* in a makeshift way

**behelligen** *tr. V.* bother; *(zudringlich werden gegen)* pester

**behend, behende** 1. *Adj. (geschickt)* deft; *(flink)* nimble; 2. *adv.; s. Adj.:* deftly; nimbly

**beherbergen** *tr. V.* accommodate

**beherrschen** 1. *tr. V.* **a)** control; rule ⟨*country, people*⟩; **b)** *(meistern)* control ⟨*vehicle, animal*⟩; be in control of ⟨*situation*⟩; **c)** *(bestimmen, dominieren)* dominate ⟨*townscape, landscape, discussions*⟩; **d)** *(zügeln)* control ⟨*feelings*⟩; control, curb ⟨*impatience*⟩; **e)** *(gut können)* have mastered ⟨*instrument, trade*⟩; have a good command of ⟨*language*⟩; 2. *refl. V.* control oneself; **beherrscht** 1. *Adj.* self-controlled; 2. with self-control; **Beherrschung** die; ~ **a)** control; *(eines*

*Volks, Landes usw.)* rule; **b)** *(das Meistern)* control; **c)** *(Beherrschtheit)* self-control; **d)** *(das Können)* mastery

**beherzigen** *tr. V.* take ⟨*sth.*⟩ to heart

**beherzt** 1. *Adj.* spirited; 2. *adv.* spiritedly

**behilflich** *Adj.* [jmdm.] ~ sein help [sb.] (bei with)

**behindern** *tr. V.* **a)** hinder; impede ⟨*movement*⟩; hold up ⟨*traffic*⟩; **b)** *(Sport, Verkehrsw.)* obstruct; **behindert** *Adj.* handicapped; **Behinderte** der/die; adj. Dekl. handicapped person; **die ~n** the handicapped; **WC für** ~: toilet for disabled persons; **Behinderung** die; ~, ~en **a)** hindrance; **b)** *(Sport, Verkehrsw.)* obstruction; **c)** *(Gebrechen)* handicap

**Behörde** die; ~, ~n authority; *(Amt, Abteilung)* department; **behördlich** 1. *Adj.* official; 2. *adv.* officially

**behüten** *tr. V.* protect (vor + *Dat.* from); *(bewachen)* guard

**behutsam** 1. *Adj.* careful; 2. *adv.* carefully

**bei** *Präp. mit Dat.* **a)** *(nahe)* near; *(dicht an, neben)* by; **wer steht da ~ ihm?** who is standing there with him?; **etw.** ~ **sich haben** have sth. with *or* on one; **sich** ~ **jmdm. entschuldigen** apologize to sb.; **b)** *(unter)* among; **war heute ein Brief für mich** ~ **der Post?** was there a letter for me in the post today?; **c)** *(an)* by; **jmdn.** ~ **der Hand nehmen** take sb. by the hand; **d)** *(im Wohn-/Lebens-/Arbeitsbereich von)*; ~ **uns tut man das nicht** we don't do that; ~ **mir [zu Hause]** at my house; ~ **uns um die Ecke/gegenüber** round the corner from us/opposite us; ~ **seinen Eltern leben** live with one's parents; **wir sind** ~ **ihr eingeladen** we have been invited to her house; **wir treffen uns** ~ **uns/Peter** we'll meet at our/Peter's place; ~ **uns in der Firma** in our company; ~ **Schmidt** *(auf Briefen)* c/o Schmidt; ~ **einer Firma sein** be with a company; ~ **jmdm./einem Verlag arbeiten** work for sb./a publishing house; **e)** *(im Bereich eines Vorgangs)* at; ~ **einer Hochzeit/einem Empfang** *usw.* be at a wedding/reception *etc.*; ~ **einem Unfall** in an accident; **f)** *(im Werk von)* ~ **Goethe** in Goethe; **g)** *(im Falle von)* in the case of; **wie** ~ **den Römern** as with the Romans; ~ **der Hauskatze** in the domestic cat; **h)** *(modal)* ~ **Tag/Nacht** by day/night; ~ **Tageslicht** by daylight; ~ **Nebel** in fog; **i)** *(im Falle des Auftretens von)* „~ **Nässe Schleudergefahr"** 'slippery when wet'; **j)** *(angesichts)* with; ~ **dieser Hitze** in this heat; ~ **deinen guten Augen/ihrem Talent** with your good eyesight/her talent; **k)** *(trotz)* ~ **all seinem Engagement/seinen Bemühungen** in spite of *or* despite *or* for all his commitment/efforts

**bei|behalten** *unr. tr. V.* keep; retain; keep up ⟨*custom, habit*⟩; keep to ⟨*course, method*⟩; preserve, maintain ⟨*way of life; attitude*⟩

**bei|bringen** *unr. tr. V.* **a)** jmdm. etw. ~: teach sb. sth.; **b)** *(ugs.: mitteilen)* jmdm. ~, daß ...: break it to sb. that ...; **c)** *(zufügen)* jmdm./sich etw. ~: inflict sth. on sb./oneself

**Beichte die;** ~, ~n confession *no def. art.;* **beichten 1.** *itr. V.* confess; **2.** *tr. V. (auch fig.)* confess

**Beicht-:** ~**stuhl der** confessional; ~**vater der** father confessor

**beid...** *Indefinitpron. u. Zahlw.* **1.** *Pl.* ~e both; *(der/die/das eine oder der/die/das andere)* either *sing.;* **die** ~**en** the two; **die/seine** ~**en Brüder** the/his two brothers; **die** ~**en ersten Strophen** the first two verses; **kennst du die** ~**en?** do you know those two?; **alle** ~e both of us/you/them; **ihr/euch** ~e you two; **ihr/euch** ~e **nicht** neither of you; **wir/uns** ~e the two of us/both of us; **er hat** ~e **Eltern verloren** he has lost both [his] parents; **mit** ~**en Händen** with both hands; **ich habe** ~e **gekannt** I knew both of them; **einer/eins von** ~**en** one of the two; **keiner/keins von** ~**en** neither [of them]; **2.** *Neutr. Sg.;* ~es both *pl.; (das eine oder das andere)* either; ~**es ist möglich** either is possible; **ich glaube** ~**es/**~**es nicht** I believe both things/neither thing; **das ist** ~**es nicht richtig** neither of those is correct; **beiderlei** *Gattungsz., indekl.* ~ **Geschlechts** of both sexes; **beider·seits 1.** *Präp. mit Gen.* on both sides of; **2.** *Adv.* on both sides

**bei·einander** *Adv.* together; ~ **Trost suchen** seek comfort from each other

**Bei·fahrer der, Bei·fahrerin die a)** passenger; **b)** *(berufsmäßig)* co-driver; *(im LKW)* driver's mate; **Beifahrer·sitz der** passenger seat; *(eines Motorrads)* pillion

**Bei·fall der;** *o. Pl.* **a)** applause; **b)** *(Zustimmung)* approval; **bei·fällig 1.** *Adj.* approving; **2.** *adv.* approvingly

**beige** [be:ʃ] *Adj.* beige; **Beige das;** ~, ~ *od. (ugs.)* ~s beige

**Bei·geschmack der:** einen bitteren usw. ~ **haben** have a slightly bitter *etc.* taste [to it]

**Bei·hilfe die a)** aid; *(Zuschuß)* allowance; **b)** *o. Pl. (Rechtsw.: Mithilfe)* aiding and abetting

**Beil das;** ~[e]s, ~e axe; *(kleiner)* hatchet

**Bei·lage die a)** *(Zeitungs~)* supplement; **b)** *(zu Speisen)* side-dish; *(Gemüse~)* vegetables *pl.*

**bei·läufig 1.** *Adj.* casual; **2.** *adv.* casually

**bei|legen** *tr. V.* **a)** enclose; **b)** *(schlichten)* settle ⟨*dispute etc.*⟩

**Bei·leid das** sympathy; [mein] herzliches *od.* aufrichtiges ~! please accept my sincere condolences

**bei|liegen** *unr. itr. V.* einem Brief ~: be enclosed with a letter; **bei·liegend** *Adj.* enclosed; ~ **senden wir ...:** please find enclosed ...

**beim** *Präp. + Art.* **a)** = bei dem; **b)** ~ **Film sein** be in films; **c)** er will ~ **Arbeiten nicht gestört werden** he doesn't want to be disturbed when working; ~ **Duschen sein** be taking a shower

**bei|messen** *unr. tr. V.* attach

**Bein das;** ~[e]s, ~e leg; **jmdm. ein** ~ **stellen** trip sb.; *(fig.)* put *or* throw a spanner *or (Amer.)* a monkey-wrench in sb.'s works; **wieder auf den** ~**en sein** be back on one's feet again

**bei·nah[e]** *Adv.* almost

**Bei·name der** epithet

**Bein·bruch der:** das ist [doch] kein ~ *(ugs.)* it's not the end of the world

**beinhalten** *tr. V. (Papierdt.)* involve

**-beinig** *adj.* -legged

**bei|pflichten** *itr. V.* agree (*Dat.* with)

**beirren** *tr. V.* sich durch nichts/von niemandem ~ **lassen** not be deterred by anything/anybody

**beisammen** *Adv.* together; **beisammen|haben** *unr. tr. V.* **a)** have got together; **b)** er hat [sie] nicht alle beisammen *(ugs.)* he's not all there *(coll.);* **Beisammen·sein das** get-together

**Bei·schlaf der** sexual intercourse

**Bei·sein das:** in jmds. ~: in the presence of sb. *or* in sb.'s presence

**bei·seite** *Adv.* aside

**Beis[e]l das;** ~s, ~ *od.* ~n *(österr.)* pub *(Brit. coll.);* bar *(Amer.)*

**bei|setzen** *tr. V.* lay to rest; inter ⟨*ashes*⟩; **Bei·setzung die;** ~, ~en funeral; burial

15*

**Bei·spiel** das example (für of); **zum ~:** for example; **mit gutem ~ vorangehen** set a good example; **beispielhaft** *Adj.* exemplary; **beispiel·los** *Adj.* unparalleled; **beispiels·weise** *Adv.* for example

**beißen 1.** *unr. tr., itr. V. (auch fig.)* bite; **2.** *unr. refl. V. (ugs.)* ⟨*colours, clothes*⟩ clash; **beißend** *Adj.* biting ⟨*cold*⟩; acrid ⟨*smoke, fumes*⟩; sharp ⟨*frost*⟩; **Beiß·zange** die *s.* Kneifzange

**Bei·stand** der *o. Pl. (geh.: Hilfe)* aid; **bei|stehen** *unr. itr. V.* jmdm. **~:** aid sb.

**bei|steuern** *tr. V.* contribute

**Beitrag** der; **~[e]s, Beiträge** contribution; *(Versicherungs~)* premium; *(Mitglieds~)* subscription; **bei|tragen** *unr. tr., itr. V.* contribute (zu to)

**bei|treten** *unr. itr. V.; mit sein* join ⟨*union, club, etc.*⟩; **einem Abkommen/ Pakt** accede to ⟨*pact, agreement*⟩; **Bei·tritt** der joining

**Bei·wagen** der side-car

**Bei·werk** das; *o. Pl.* accessories *pl.*

**bei|wohnen** *itr. V.* einer Sache *(Dat.)* **~** *(geh.)* be present at sth.

**Beize** die; **~, ~n** *(Holzbearb.)* [wood]-stain

**beizeiten** *Adv.* in good time

**beizen** *tr. V. (Holzbearb.)* stain

**bejahen** [bə'ja:ən] *tr. V.* **a)** *auch itr.* answer ⟨*sth.*⟩ in the affirmative; **b)** *(gutheißen)* approve of; **das Leben ~:** have a positive *or* an affirmative attitude to life; **Bejahung** die; **~, ~en a)** affirmative reply; **b)** *(das Gutheißen)* approval

**bejammern** *tr. V.* lament

**bejubeln** *tr. V.* cheer; acclaim

**bekämpfen** *tr. V.* **a)** fight against; **b)** combat ⟨*disease, epidemic, pest, unemployment, crime, etc.*⟩; **Bekämpfung** die; **~ a)** fight (*Gen.* against); **b)** *s.* bekämpfen b: combating

**bekannt** *Adj.* well-known; **b)** jmd./ etw. ist jmdm. **~:** sb. knows sb./sth.; **Darf ich ~ machen? Meine Eltern** may I introduce my parents?; **Bekannte** der/die; *adj. Dekl.* acquaintance

**Bekannt·gabe** die; **~:** announcement; **bekannt|geben** *unr. tr. V.* announce

**bekanntlich** *Adv.* as is well known; **etw. ist ~ der Fall** sth. is known to be the case

**bekannt|machen** *tr. V.* announce; *(der Öffentlichkeit)* make public; **Bekannt·machung** die; **~, ~en** announcement

**Bekanntschaft** die; **~, ~en** acquaintance

**bekannt|werden** *unr. itr. V.; mit sein (nur im Inf. und 2. Part. zusammengeschr.)* become known

**bekehren 1.** *tr. V.* convert; **2.** *refl. V.* become converted; **Bekehrung** die; **~, ~en** *(auch fig.)* conversion (zu to)

**bekennen 1.** *unr. tr. V.* **a)** confess; **~, daß ...** admit that ...; **b)** *(Rel.)* profess; **2.** *refl. V.* **sich zum Islam ~:** profess Islam; **sich zu Buddha ~:** profess one's faith in Buddha; **sich zu seiner Schuld ~:** confess one's guilt; **sich schuldig/nicht schuldig ~:** confess/not confess one's guilt; *(vor Gericht)* plead guilty/not guilty; **Bekenntnis** das; **~ses, ~se a)** confession; **b)** *(Eintreten)* **ein ~ zum Frieden** a declaration for peace; **c)** *(Konfession)* denomination

**beklagen 1.** *tr. V. (geh.)* **a)** *(betrauern)* mourn; **b)** *(bedauern)* lament; **2.** *refl. V.* complain

**bekleckern** *tr. V. (ugs.)* etw./sich |mit Soße usw.| **~:** drop *or* spill sauce *etc.* down sth./oneself

**bekleiden** *tr. V.* **a)** clothe; **mit etw. bekleidet sein** be wearing sth.; **b)** *(geh.: innehaben)* occupy ⟨*office, position*⟩; **Bekleidung** die clothing; clothes *pl.*

**beklemmend** *Adj.* oppressive; **Beklemmung** die; **~, ~en** oppressive feeling; **beklommen** *Adj.* uneasy; *(stärker)* apprehensive

**beklopft** *Adj. (salopp)* barmy *(Brit. sl.);* loony *(sl.)*

**beknien** *tr. V. (ugs.)* beg

**bekommen 1.** *unr. tr. V.* **a)** get; get; receive ⟨*money, letter, reply, news, orders*⟩; *(erreichen)* catch ⟨*train, bus, flight*⟩; **was ~ Sie?** *(im Geschäft)* can I help you?; *(im Lokal, Restaurant)* what would you like?; **was ~ Sie |dafür|?** how much is that?; **Hunger/ Durst ~:** get hungry/thirsty; **Angst/ Mut ~:** become frightened/take heart; **er bekommt einen Bart** he's growing a beard; **sie bekommt eine Brust** her breasts are developing; **Zähne ~:** ⟨*baby*⟩ teethe; **sie bekommt ein Kind** she's expecting a baby; **b)** etw. durch die Tür/ins Auto **~:** get sth. through the door/into the car; **2.** *unr. V.; in der Funktion eines Hilfsverbs zur Umschreibung des Passivs* get; **etw. geschenkt ~:** get [given] sth. *or* be given sth. as a present; **3.** *unr. itr. V.; mit sein* jmdm. **gut** ~: do sb. good; jmdm. |gut| ~: ⟨*food, medicine*⟩ agree with sb.; **wohl bekomm's!** your [very good] health!

**bekömmlich** *Adj.* easily digestible
**beköstigen** *tr. V.* cater for
**bekräftigen** *tr. V.* reinforce ⟨*statement*⟩; reaffirm ⟨*promise*⟩
**bekreuzigen** *refl. V.* (*kath. Kirche*) cross oneself
**bekriegen** *tr. V.* wage war on; (*fig.*) fight; **sich** ~: be at war; (*fig.*) fight
**bekümmern** *tr. V.* jmdn. ~: cause sb. worry; **bekümmert** *Adj.* worried; (*stärker*) distressed
**bekunden** *tr. V.* express
**belächeln** *tr. V.* smile [pityingly/ tolerantly *etc.*] at
**beladen** *unr. tr. V.* load ⟨*ship*⟩; load [up] ⟨*car, wagon*⟩; load up ⟨*horse, donkey*⟩
**Belag** der; ~|e|s, **Beläge a)** coating; **b)** (*Fußboden~*) covering; (*Straßen~*) surface; (*Brems~*) lining; **c)** (*von Kuchen, Scheibe Brot usw.*) topping; (*von Sandwiches*) filling
**belagern** *tr. V.* (*auch fig.*) besiege; **Belagerung** die; ~, ~en siege; (*fig.*) besieging
**Belang** der; ~|e|s, ~e **a)** von/ohne ~ sein be of importance/of no importance; **b)** *Pl.* (*Interessen*) interests
**belangen** *tr. V.* (*Rechtsw.*) sue; (*strafrechtlich*) prosecute
**belang·los** *Adj.* (*trivial*) trivial; (*unerheblich*) of no importance (**für** for); **Belanglosigkeit** die; ~, ~en unimportance; (*Trivialität*) triviality
**belassen** *unr. tr. V.* leave
**belasten** *tr. V.* **a)** etw. ~: put sth. under strain; (*durch Gewicht*) put weight on sth.; **b)** (*beeinträchtigen*) pollute ⟨*atmosphere*⟩; put pressure on ⟨*environment*⟩; **c)** (*in Anspruch nehmen*) burden (**mit** with); **d)** jmdn. ~ ⟨*responsibility, guilt*⟩ weigh upon sb.; ⟨*thought*⟩ weigh upon sb.'s mind; **e)** (*Rechtsw.*) incriminate
**belästigen** *tr. V.* bother; (*sehr aufdringlich*) pester; (*sexuell*) molest
**Belastung** die; ~, ~en **a)** strain; (*das Belasten*) straining; (*durch Gewicht*) loading; (*Last*) load; **b)** die ~ der Atmosphäre/Umwelt durch Schadstoffe the pollution of the atmosphere by harmful substances/the pressure on the environment caused by harmful substances; **c)** (*Bürde, Sorge*) burden

**belaufen** *unr. refl. V.* sich auf ...(*Akk.*) ~: come to ...
**belauschen** *tr. V.* eavesdrop on
**beleben 1.** *tr. V.* enliven; stimulate ⟨*economy*⟩; **2.** *refl. V.* ⟨*market, economic activity*⟩ revive, pick up; **belebend 1.** *Adj.* invigorating; **2.** *adv.* ~ wirken have an invigorating effect; **belebt** *Adj.* busy ⟨*street, crossing, town, etc.*⟩
**Beleg** der; ~|e|s, ~e (*Beweisstück*) piece of [supporting] documentary evidence; (*Quittung*) receipt
**belegen** *tr. V.* **a)** (*Milit.: beschießen*) bombard; (*mit Bomben*) attack; **b)** (*mit Belag versehen*) cover ⟨*floor*⟩ (**mit** with); fill ⟨*flan base, sandwich*⟩; top ⟨*open sandwich*⟩; **eine Scheibe Brot mit Käse** ~: put some cheese on a slice of bread; **c)** (*in Besitz nehmen*) occupy ⟨*seat, room, etc.*⟩; **d)** (*Hochschulw.*) enrol for ⟨*seminar, lecture-course*⟩; **e)** den ersten/letzten Platz ~ (*Sport*) take first place/come last; **f)** (*nachweisen*) prove; give a reference for ⟨*quotation*⟩
**Belegschaft** die; ~, ~en staff
**belegt** *Adj.* **a)** ein ~es Brot an open *or* (*Amer.*) openface sandwich; (*zugeklappt*) a sandwich; **ein ~es Brötchen** a roll with topping; an open-face roll (*Amer.*); (*zugeklappt*) a filled roll; a sandwich roll (*Amer.*); **b)** (*mit Belag bedeckt*) furred ⟨*tongue, tonsils*⟩; **c)** (*heiser*) husky ⟨*voice*⟩; **d)** (*nicht mehr frei*) ⟨*room, flat*⟩ occupied
**belehren** *tr. V.* teach; instruct; (*aufklären*) enlighten; (*informieren*) inform; **ich lasse mich gern** ~: I'm quite willing to believe otherwise; **Belehrung** die; ~, ~en instruction; (*Zurechtweisung*) lecture
**beleibt** *Adj.* (*geh.*) portly
**beleidigen** *tr. V.* insult; **beleidigt** *Adj.* insulted; (*gekränkt*) offended; **Beleidigung** die; ~, ~en **a)** insult; **b)** (*Rechtsw.*) (*schriftlich*) libel; (*mündlich*) slander
**belesen** *Adj.* well-read
**beleuchten** *tr. V.* light up; light ⟨*stairs, room, street, etc.*⟩; **Beleuchtung** die; ~, ~en **a)** lighting; (*Anstrahlung*) illumination
**beleumdet** *Adj.* übel/gut ~ sein have a bad/good reputation
**Belgien** ['bɛlgiən] (*das*); ~s Belgium; **Belgier** der; ~s, ~ Belgian; **belgisch** *Adj.* Belgian
**belichten** *tr. V.* (*Fot.*) expose; *itr.* **richtig/falsch/kurz** ~: use the right/

wrong exposure/a short exposure time; **Belichtung die** *(Fot.)* exposure
**Belieben das**; ~s: **nach** ~: just as you/they *etc.* like
**beliebig** 1. *Adj.* any; 2. *adv.* as you like/he likes *etc.*; ~ **lange/viele** as long/many as you like/he likes *etc.*
**beliebt** *Adj.* popular; favourite *attrib.*; **Beliebtheit die**; ~: popularity
**beliefern** *tr. V.* supply
**bellen** *itr. V.* bark
**belohnen** *tr. V.* reward ⟨*person, thing*⟩; **Belohnung die**; ~, ~en reward
**belügen** *unr. tr. V.* lie to
**belustigen** *tr. V.* amuse; **Belustigung die**; ~, ~en amusement
**bemächtigen** *refl. V.* sich jmds./einer Sache ~ *(geh.)* seize sb./sth.
**bemalen** *tr. V.* paint; *(verzieren)* decorate
**bemängeln** *tr. V.* find fault with
**bemerkbar** *Adj.* sich ~ machen attract attention [to oneself]; *(erkennbar werden)* become apparent; *(spürbar werden)* make itself felt; **bemerken** *tr. V.* a) *(wahrnehmen)* notice; **ich wurde nicht bemerkt** I was unobserved; b) *(äußern)* remark; **bemerkenswert** 1. *Adj.* remarkable; 2. *adv.* remarkably; **Bemerkung die**; ~, ~en a) *(Äußerung)* remark; comment; b) *(Notiz)* note; *(Anmerkung)* comment
**bemitleiden** *tr. V.* pity; feel sorry for; **bemitleidens·wert** *Adj.* pitiable
**bemogeln** *tr. V. (ugs.)* cheat; diddle *(Brit. sl.)*
**bemühen** *refl. V.* make an effort; **sich ~, etw. zu tun** endeavour to do sth.; **sich um etw. ~**: try to obtain sth.; **sich um eine Stelle ~**: try to get a job; **sich um jmdn. ~** *(kümmern)* seek to help sb.; **Bemühung die**; ~, ~en effort
**benachbart** *Adj.* neighbouring *attrib.*
**benachrichtigen** *tr. V.* notify (von of); **Benachrichtigung die**; ~, ~en notification
**benachteiligen** *tr. V.* put at a disadvantage; *(diskriminieren)* discriminate against
**benehmen** *unr. refl. V.* behave; **Benehmen das**; ~s behaviour; **kein ~ ›haben** have no manners *pl.*
**beneiden** *tr. V.* envy; **jmdn. um etw. ~**: envy sb. sth.; **beneidens·wert** *Adj.* enviable
**Benelux·länder** *Pl.* Benelux countries
**benennen** *unr. tr. V.* name

**Bengel der**; ~s, ~ *od. (nordd.)* ~s a) *(abwertend: junger Bursche)* young rascal; b) *(fam.: kleiner Junge)* little lad
**benommen** *Adj.* dazed; *(durch Fieber, Alkohol)* muzzy
**benoten** *tr. V.* mark *(Brit.)*; grade *(Amer.)*; **einen Test mit „gut" ~**: mark a test 'good' *(Brit.)*; assign a grade of 'good' to a test *(Amer.)*
**benötigen** *tr. V.* need; require
**benutzen** *tr. V.* use; **Benutzer der**; ~s, ~: user; **Benutzung die**; ~: use
**Benzin das**; ~s petrol *(Brit.)*; gasoline *(Amer.)*; gas *(Amer. coll.)*; *(Wasch~)* benzine
**Benzol das**; ~s, ~e *(Chemie)* benzene
**beobachten** *tr. V.* observe; watch; **Beobachter der**; ~s, ~: observer; **Beobachtung die**; ~, ~en observation
**bepacken** *tr. V.* load
**bepflanzen** *tr. V.* plant
**bequem** 1. *Adj.* a) comfortable; b) *(abwertend: träge)* idle; 2. *adv.* a) comfortably; b) *(leicht)* easily; **bequemen** *refl. V.* sich dazu ~, etw. zu tun *(geh.)* condescend to do sth.; **Bequemlichkeit die**; ~ a) comfort; b) *(Trägheit)* idleness
**berappen** *tr., itr. V. (ugs.)* s. **blechen**
**beraten** 1. *unr. tr. V.* a) advise; **jmdn. gut/schlecht ~**: give sb. good/bad advice; b) *(besprechen)* discuss ⟨*plan, matter*⟩; 2. *unr. itr. V.* über etw. *(Akk.)* ~: discuss sth. 3. *unr. refl. V.* sich mit jmdm. ~, ob ...: discuss with sb. whether ...; **Berater der**; ~s, ~: adviser; **beratschlagen** 1. *tr. V.* discuss; 2. *itr. V.* über etw. *(Akk.)* ~: discuss sth.; **Beratung die**; ~, ~en a) advice *no indef. art.*; *(durch Arzt, Rechtsanwalt)* consultation; b) *(Besprechung)* discussion
**berauben** *tr. V. (auch fig.)* rob (Gen. of)
**berauschen** *(geh.)* 1. *tr. V. (auch fig.)* intoxicate; 2. *refl. V.* become intoxicated (an + *Dat.* with)
**berechnen** *tr. V.* a) *(auch fig.)* calculate; predict ⟨*behaviour, consequences*⟩; b) *(anrechnen)* charge; **jmdm. 10 Mark für etw. od. jmdm. etw. mit 10 Mark ~**: charge sb. 10 marks for sth.; **jmdm. zuviel ~**: overcharge sb.; **Berechnung die** a) calculation; b) *o. Pl. (Eigennutz)* [calculating] self-interest
**berechtigen** *tr. V.* entitle; *itr. die*

**Karte berechtigt zum Eintritt** the ticket entitles the bearer to admission; **berechtigt** *Adj.* **a)** *(gerechtfertigt)* justified; **b)** *(befugt)* authorized; **Berechtigung die**; ~, ~en **a)** *(Befugnis)* entitlement; *(Recht)* right; **b)** *(Rechtmäßigkeit)* legitimacy

**bereden** *tr. V.* **a)** *(besprechen)* discuss; **b)** jmdn. ~, etw. zu tun talk sb. into doing sth.

**Bereich der**; ~|e|s, ~e area; **im privaten/staatlichen ~**: in the private/public sector

**bereichern** *refl. V.* get rich; **Bereicherung die**; ~, ~en **a)** moneymaking; **b)** *(Nutzen)* valuable acquisition

**bereifen** *tr. V.* put tyres on ⟨*car*⟩; put a tyre on ⟨*wheel*⟩; **Bereifung die**; ~, ~en [set *sing.* of] tyres *pl.*

**bereinigen** *tr. V.* clear up ⟨*misunderstanding*⟩; settle, resolve ⟨*dispute*⟩

**bereit** *Adj.* ready; ~ **sein, etw. zu tun** be ready *or* willing to do sth.

**bereiten** *tr. V.* **a)** prepare; make ⟨*tea, coffee*⟩; **b)** *(verursachen)* cause ⟨*trouble, sorrow, difficulty, etc.*⟩

**bereit-**: ~|**halten** *unr. tr. V.* have ready; ~|**legen** *tr. V.* lay out ready; ~|**liegen** *unr. itr. V.* be ready

**bereits** *Adv.* already

**Bereitschaft die**; ~: readiness; willingness; **Bereitschafts·dienst der**: ~**dienst haben** ⟨*doctor, nurse*⟩ be on call; ⟨*policeman, fireman*⟩ be on stand-by duty; ⟨*chemist's*⟩ be on rota duty *(for dispensing outside normal hours)*

**bereit-**: ~|**stehen** *unr. itr. V.* be ready; ~|**stellen** *tr. V.* place ready; get ready ⟨*food, drinks*⟩; ready, make ⟨*money, funds*⟩ available; ~**willig 1.** *Adj.* willing. **2.** *adv.* readily

**bereuen 1.** *tr. V.* regret; **2.** *itr. V.* be sorry; *(Rel.)* repent

**Berg der**; ~|e|s, ~e **a)** hill; *(im Hochgebirge)* mountain; **b)** *(Haufen)* huge pile; *(von Akten, Abfall auch)* mountain

**berg-, Berg-**: ~**ab** [-'-] *Adv.* downhill; ~**auf** [-'-] *Adv.* uphill; ~**bahn die** mountain railway; *(Seilbahn)* mountain cableway; ~**bau der**; *o. Pl.* mining

**bergen** *unr. tr. V.* **a)** rescue, save ⟨*person*⟩; salvage ⟨*ship, cargo, belongings*⟩; **b)** *(geh.: enthalten)* hold

**Berg-**: ~**führer der** mountain guide; ~**hütte die** mountain hut

**bergig** *Adj.* hilly; *(mit hohen Bergen)* mountainous

**Berg-**: ~**kristall der** rock crystal; ~**land das** hilly country *no indef. art;* *(mit hohen Bergen)* mountainous country *no indef. art.;* ~**mann der** *Pl.* ~**leute** miner; ~**station die** top station; ~**steigen das**; ~s mountaineering *no art.;* ~**steiger der** mountaineer

**Bergung die**; ~, ~en **a)** rescue; **b)** *(von Schiffen, Gut)* salvaging

**Berg-**: ~**wacht die** mountain rescue service; ~**werk das** mine

**Bericht der**; ~|e|s, ~e report; **berichten** *tr., itr. V.* report

**Bericht-**: ~**erstatter der**; ~s, ~: reporter; ~**erstattung die** reporting *no indef. art.*

**berichtigen** *tr. V.* correct; **Berichtigung die**; ~, ~en correction

**berieseln** *tr. V.* **a)** *(bewässern)* irrigate; **b) sich ständig mit Musik ~ lassen** *(ugs. abwertend)* constantly have music on in the background

**Berlin (das)**; ~s Berlin; **Berliner 1.** *Adj.; nicht präd.* Berlin; **2. der**; ~s, ~: **a)** Berliner; **b)** (~ *Pfannkuchen*) [jam *(Brit.)* or *(Amer.)* jelly] doughnut; **berlinisch** *Adj.* Berlin *attrib.*

**Bern (das)**; ~s Bern[e]

**Bernhardiner der**; ~s, ~: St. Bernard [dog]

**Bern·stein der**; *o. Pl.* amber

**bersten** *unr. itr. V.; mit sein (geh.)* ⟨*ice*⟩ break up; ⟨*glass*⟩ shatter [into pieces]; ⟨*wall*⟩ crack up

**berüchtigt** *Adj.* notorious (**wegen** for); *(verrufen)* disreputable

**berücksichtigen** *tr. V.* take into account; consider ⟨*applicant, application, suggestion*⟩; **Berücksichtigung die**; ~: **bei** ~ **aller Umstände** taking all the circumstances into account

**Beruf der**; ~|e|s, ~e occupation; *(akademischer)* profession; *(handwerklicher)* trade; **was sind Sie von** ~? what do you do for a living?

**¹berufen 1.** *unr. tr. V.* **a)** *(einsetzen)* appoint; **b) berufe es nicht!** *(ugs.)* don't speak too soon!; **2.** *unr. refl. V.* **sich auf etw.** *(Akk.)* ~: refer to sth.; **sich auf jmdn.** ~: quote *or* mention sb.'s name

**²berufen** *Adj.* **a)** competent; **aus** ~**em Munde** from somebody qualified to speak; **b) sich dazu** ~ **fühlen, etw. zu tun** feel called to do sth.

**beruflich 1.** *Adj.; nicht präd.* vocational ⟨*training etc.*⟩; *(bei akademischen Berufen)* professional ⟨*training etc.*⟩; **2.** *adv.* ~ **erfolgreich sein** be successful in one's career; **sich** ~ **weiterbilden** undertake further job training

**berufs-, Berufs-:** ~**ausbildung die** vocational training; ~**beratung die** vocational guidance; ~**erfahrung die;** *o. Pl.* [professional] experience; ~**geheimnis das** professional secret; *(Schweigepflicht)* professional secrecy; ~**krankheit die** occupational disease; ~**leben das** working life; ~**schule die** vocational school; ~**soldat der** regular soldier; ~**sportler der** professional sportsman; ~**tätig** *Adj.* working *attrib.;* ~**tätige der/die;** *adj. Dekl.* working person; ~**tätige** *Pl.* working people; ~**verkehr der** rush-hour traffic

**Berufung die;** ~, ~**en a)** *(für ein Amt)* offer of an appointment **(auf, in, an +** *Akk.* to); **b)** *(innerer Auftrag)* vocation; **c)** *(das Sichberufen)* **unter** ~ *(Dat.)* **auf jmdn./etw.** referring *or* with reference to sb./sth.); **d)** *(Rechtsw.: Einspruch)* appeal; ~ **einlegen** lodge an appeal

**beruhen** *itr. V.* **auf etw.** *(Dat.)* ~: be based on sth.; **etw. auf sich** ~ **lassen** let sth. rest

**beruhigen** [bə'ruːɪgn̩] **1.** *tr. V.* calm [down]; pacify ⟨*child, baby*⟩; salve ⟨*conscience*⟩; *(trösten)* soothe; *(von einer Sorge befreien)* reassure; **2.** *refl. V.* ⟨*person*⟩ calm down; ⟨*sea*⟩ become calm; **Beruhigung die;** ~ *s.* **beruhigen 1:** calming [down]; pacifying; salving; soothing; reassurance; **Beruhigungs·mittel das** tranquillizer

**berühmt** *Adj.* famous; **berühmt·berüchtigt** *Adj.* notorious; **Berühmtheit die;** ~, ~**en a)** *o. Pl.* *(Ruhm)* fame; **b)** *(Mensch)* celebrity

**berühren** *tr. V.* **a)** touch; *(fig.)* touch on ⟨*topic, issue. etc.*⟩; **sich** ~: touch; **b)** *(beeindrucken)* affect; **das berührt mich nicht** it's a matter of indifference to me; **Berührung die;** ~, ~**en** touch; **mit jmdm./etw. in** ~ *(Akk.)* **kommen** *(auch fig.)* come into contact with sb./sth.

**besagen** *tr. V.* say; *(bedeuten)* mean

**besänftigen** *tr. V.* calm [down]; pacify; calm, soothe ⟨*temper*⟩

**Besatz der** *(Borte)* trimming *no indef. art.*

**Besatzung die a)** *(Mannschaft)* crew;

**b)** *(Milit.: Verteidigungstruppe)* garrison; **c)** *(Milit.: Okkupationstruppen)* occupying forces *pl.*

**besaufen** *unr. refl. V. (salopp)* get canned *(Brit. sl.)* or bombed *(Amer. sl.);* **Besäufnis das;** ~ses, ~se *(salopp)* booze-up *(Brit. sl.):* blast *(Amer. sl.)*

**beschädigen** *tr. V.* damage; **Beschädigung die a)** *o. Pl.* damaging; **b)** *(Schaden)* damage

**¹beschaffen** *tr. V.* obtain, get *(Dat.* for)

**²beschaffen** *Adj.* **so** ~ **sein, daß ...:** be such that ...; **Beschaffenheit die;** ~: properties *pl.*

**Beschaffung die** *s.* **beschaffen:** obtaining; getting

**beschäftigen 1.** *refl. V.* occupy oneself; **sich viel mit Musik/den Kindern** ~: devote a great deal of one's time to music/the children; **sehr beschäftigt sein** be very busy; **2.** *tr. V.* **a)** *(geistig in Anspruch nehmen)* **jmdn.** ~: preoccupy sb.; **b)** *(angestellt haben)* employ ⟨*workers, staff*⟩; **c)** *(zu tun geben)* occupy; **jmdn. mit etw.** ~: give sb. sth. to occupy him/her; **Beschäftigte der/die;** *adj. Dekl.* employee; **Beschäftigung die;** ~, ~**en a)** *(Tätigkeit)* activity; **b)** *(Anstellung, Stelle)* job; **c)** *(mit einer Frage, einem Problem)* consideration (mit of); *(Studium)* study (mit of); **d)** *o. Pl. (von Arbeitskräften)* employment

**beschämen** *tr. V.* shame; **beschämend 1.** *Adj.* **a)** *(schändlich)* shameful; **b)** *(demütigend)* humiliating; **2.** *adv.* shamefully; **beschämt** *Adj.* ashamed; **Beschämung die;** ~: shame

**beschatten** *tr. V.* **a)** *(geh.)* shade; **b)** *(überwachen)* shadow

**beschaulich 1.** *Adj.* peaceful ⟨*life, manner, etc.*⟩; **2.** *adv.* peacefully

**Bescheid der;** ~[e]s, ~e **a)** *(Auskunft)* information; *(Antwort)* answer; reply; **jmdm.** ~ **geben** *od.* **sagen[, ob ...]** let sb. know or tell sb. [whether ...]; **sage bitte im Hotel** ~**, daß ...:** please let the hotel know that ...; **[über etw.** *(Akk.)***]** ~ **wissen** know [about sth.]; **b)** *(Entscheidung)* decision

**¹bescheiden 1.** *unr. tr. V.* **jmdn./etw. abschlägig** ~: turn sb./sth. down; **2.** *unr. refl. V. (geh.)* be content

**²bescheiden 1.** *Adj.* modest; **2.** *adv.* modestly; **Bescheidenheit die;** ~: modesty

**bescheinigen** *tr. V.* confirm ⟨*sth.*⟩ in writing; **Bescheinigung die; ~, ~en** written confirmation *no indef. art.; (Schein, Attest)* certificate

**beschenken** *tr. V.* give ⟨*sb.*⟩ a present/presents

**bescheren** *tr. V.* jmdn. [mit etw.] ~: give sb. [sth. as] a Christmas present/Christmas presents

**Bescherung die; ~, ~en a)** *(zu Weihnachten)* giving out of the Christmas presents; **b) das ist ja eine schöne ~** *(ugs.)* this is a pretty kettle of fish

**beschießen** *unr. tr. V.* fire at; *(mit Artillerie)* bombard

**beschimpfen** *tr. V.* abuse; swear at; **Beschimpfung die; ~, ~en** insult; **~en** abuse *sing.;* insults

**Beschlag der** a) fitting; b) jmdn./etw. mit ~ belegen *od.* in ~ nehmen monopolize sb./sth.; **¹beschlagen 1.** *unr. tr. V.* shoe ⟨*horse*⟩; **2.** *unr. itr. V.; mit sein* ⟨*window*⟩ mist up *(Brit.),* fog up *(Amer.); (durch Dampf)* steam up

**²beschlagen** *Adj.* knowledgeable

**Beschlag·nahme die; ~, ~n** confiscation; **beschlag·nahmen** *tr. V.* confiscate

**beschleunigen 1.** *tr. V.* accelerate; speed up ⟨*work, delivery*⟩; quicken ⟨*pace, step[s], pulse*⟩; **2.** *refl. V.* ⟨*heartrate*⟩ increase; ⟨*pulse*⟩ quicken; **3.** *itr. V.* ⟨*driver, car, etc.*⟩ accelerate; **Beschleunigung die; ~, ~en** *s.* beschleunigen 1: acceleration; speeding up; quickening

**beschließen** *unr. tr. V.* a) decide; pass ⟨*law*⟩; ~, etw. zu tun decide *or* resolve to do sth.; b) *(beenden)* end

**Beschluß der** decision; *(gemeinsam gefaßt)* resolution; **einen ~ fassen** come to a decision/pass a resolution; **beschluß·fähig** *Adj.* quorate; **Beschluß·fähigkeit die;** *o. Pl.* presence of a quorum

**beschmieren** *tr. V.* etw./sich ~: get sth./oneself in a mess

**beschmutzen** *tr. V.* make ⟨*sth.*⟩ dirty

**beschneiden** *unr. tr. V.* a) cut ⟨*hedge*⟩; prune ⟨*bush*⟩; cut back ⟨*tree*⟩; einem Vogel die Flügel ~: clip a bird's wings; *(Med., Rel.)* circumcise; **Beschneidung die; ~, ~en a)** *s.* beschneiden a: cutting; pruning; cutting back; b) *(Med., Rel.)* circumcision

**beschönigen** *tr. V.* gloss over

**beschränken 1.** *tr. V.* restrict (auf + Akk. to); **2.** *refl. V.* sich auf etw. *(Akk.)* ~: restrict oneself to sth.; **beschränkt 1.** *Adj.* a) *(dumm)* dullwitted; b) *(engstirnig)* narrowminded; **2.** *adv.* narrow-mindedly; **Beschränktheit die; ~:** a) *(Dummheit)* lack of intelligence; b) *(Engstirnigkeit)* narrow-mindedness; **Beschränkung die; ~, ~en** restriction

**beschreiben** *unr. tr. V.* a) write on; *(vollschreiben)* write ⟨*page, side, etc.*⟩; b) *(darstellen)* describe; **Beschreibung die; ~, ~en** description

**beschriften** *tr. V.* label; inscribe ⟨*stone*⟩; letter ⟨*sign, label, etc.*⟩; *(mit Adresse)* address

**beschuldigen** *tr. V.* accuse (*Gen.* of); **Beschuldigte der/die;** *adj. Dekl.* accused; **Beschuldigung die; ~, ~en** accusation

**beschummeln** *tr. V.* *(ugs.)* cheat; diddle *(Brit. coll.)*

**Beschuß der** fire

**beschützen** *tr. V.* protect (vor + *Dat.* from); **Beschützer der; ~s, ~, Beschützerin die; ~, ~nen** protector

**Beschwerde die; ~, ~n a)** complaint (gegen, über + *Akk.* about); b) *Pl. (Schmerz)* pain *sing.; (Leiden)* trouble *sing.*

**beschweren 1.** *refl. V.* complain (über + *Akk.,* wegen about); **2.** *tr. V.* weight down; **beschwerlich** *Adj.* arduous; *(ermüdend)* exhausting

**beschwichtigen** *tr. V.* pacify; mollify ⟨*anger etc.*⟩; **Beschwichtigung die; ~, ~en** pacification; *(des Zorns usw.)* mollification

**beschwingt** *Adj.* lively

**beschwipst** *Adj.* *(ugs.)* tipsy

**beschwören** *unr. tr. V.* a) swear to; ~, daß ...: swear that ...; eine Aussage ~: swear a statement on oath; b) charm ⟨*snake*⟩; c) *(erscheinen lassen)* invoke ⟨*spirit*⟩; d) *(bitten)* implore; **Beschwörung die; ~, ~en a)** *(Zauberspruch)* spell; incantation; b) *s.* beschwören c: invoking; c) *(Bitte)* entreaty

**beseitigen** *tr. V.* remove; eliminate ⟨*error, difficulty*⟩; dispose of ⟨*rubbish*⟩; **Beseitigung die; ~:** *s.* beseitigen: removal; elimination; disposal

**Besen der; ~s, ~** broom; **ich fress' einen ~, wenn das stimmt** *(salopp)* I'll eat my hat if that's right *(coll.);* **neue ~ kehren gut** *(Spr.)* a new broom sweeps clean *(prov.)*

**besessen** *Adj.* a) possessed; b) *(fig.)* obsessive ⟨*gambler*⟩; von einer Idee ~

sein be obsessed with an idea; **Be-sessenheit die;** ~ a) possession; b) obsessiveness

**besetzen** *tr. V.* a) *(mit Pelz, Spitzen)* edge; trim; **mit Perlen besetzt** set with pearls; b) *(belegen; auch Milit.: erobern)* occupy; c) *(vergeben)* fill ⟨*post, position, role, etc.*⟩; **besetzt** *Adj.* occupied; ⟨*table, seat*⟩ taken *pred.*; *(gefüllt)* full; *(Fernspr.)* engaged; busy *(Amer.)*; **Besetzung die;** ~, ~**en** a) *(einer Stellung)* filling; b) *(Film, Theater usw.)* cast; c) *(Eroberung)* occupation

**besichtigen** *tr. V.* see ⟨*sights*⟩; see the sights of ⟨*town*⟩; view ⟨*house etc. for sale*⟩; **Besichtigung die;** ~, ~**en** **zur** ~ **der Stadt/des Schlosses/der Wohnung** to see the sights of the town/to see the castle/to view the flat

**besiedeln** *tr. V.* settle

**besiegen** *tr. V.* defeat

**besinnen** *unr. refl. V.* a) think it over; b) **sich [auf jmdn./etw.]** ~: remember [sb./sth.]; **Besinnung die;** ~: consciousness; **die** ~ **verlieren** faint; [**wieder] zur** ~ **kommen** regain consciousness; **besinnungs·los** 1. *Adj.* unconscious; 2. *adv.* mindlessly

**Besitz der** a) property; b) *(das Besitzen)* possession; **im** ~ **einer Sache** *(Gen.)* **sein** be in possession of sth.; **besitzen** *unr. tr. V.* own; have ⟨*quality, talent, etc.*⟩; *(nachdrücklicher)* possess; **Besitzer der;** ~**s,** ~, **Besitzerin die;** ~, ~**nen** owner

**besoffen** *Adj. (salopp)* canned *(Brit. sl.)*; bombed *(Amer. sl.)*; **Besoffene der/die;** *adj. Dekl. (salopp)* drunk

**besohlen** *tr. V.* sole; **neu** ~: resole

**besonder...** *Adj.; nicht präd.* special; **ein** ~**es Ereignis** an unusual *or* a special event; **keine** ~**e Leistung** no great achievement; **Besonderheit die;** ~, ~**en** special feature; *(Eigenart)* peculiarity; **besonders** 1. *Adv.* particularly; 2. *Adj.; nicht attr.; nur verneint (ugs.)* **nicht** ~ **sein** be nothing special

**besonnen** 1. *Adj.* prudent; 2. *adv.* prudently; **Besonnenheit die;** ~: prudence

**besorgen** *tr. V.* a) get; *(kaufen)* buy; b) *(erledigen)* take care of; **Besorgnis die;** ~, ~**se** concern; **besorgt** 1. *Adj.* concerned (**um** about); 2. *adv.* with concern; **Besorgung die;** ~, ~**en** purchase

**bespitzeln** *tr. V.* spy on

**besprechen** *unr. tr. V.* discuss; *(rezensieren)* review; **Besprechung die;** ~, ~**en** discussion; *(Konferenz)* meeting; *(Rezension)* review

**bespritzen** *tr. V.* a) splash; *(mit einem Wasserstrahl)* spray; b) *(beschmutzen)* bespatter

**besprühen** *tr. V.* spray

**besser** 1. *Adj.* a) better; **um so** ~: so much the better; b) *(sozial höher gestellt)* superior; 2. *adv.* [**immer**] **alles** ~ **wissen** always know better; **es** ~ **haben** be better off; ~ **gesagt** to be [more] precise; 3. *Adv. (lieber)* **das läßt du** ~ **sein** *od. (ugs.)* **bleiben** you'd better not do that

**besser|gehen** *unr. itr. V.; mit sein* **jmdm. geht es besser** sb. feels better

**bessern** 1. *refl. V.* improve; ⟨*person*⟩ mend one's ways; 2. *tr. V.* improve; reform ⟨*criminal*⟩; **Besserung die;** ~: recovery; **gute** ~! get well soon

**best...** 1. *Adj.* a) best; **bei** ~**er Gesundheit/Laune sein** be in the best of health/spirits *pl.*; **im** ~**en Falle** at best; **in den** ~**en Jahren, im** ~**en Alter** in one's prime; ~**e Grüße an ...** *(Akk.)* best wishes to ...; **mit den** ~**en Grüßen** *od.* **Wünschen** with best wishes; *(als Briefschluß)* ≈ yours sincerely; b) **es ist** *od.* **wäre das** ~**e, wenn ...:** it would be best if ...; **der/die/das nächste** ~**e ...:** the first ... one comes across; **einen Witz zum** ~**en geben** entertain [those present] with a joke; **das Beste vom Besten** the very best; **sein Bestes tun** do one's best; **zu deinem Besten** for your benefit; 2. *adv.* **am** ~**en** best; 3. *Adv.* **am** ~**en fährst du mit dem Zug** it would be best for you to go by train

**Bestand der** a) *o. Pl.* existence, *(Fort~)* continued existence; b) *(Vorrat)* stock (**an** + *Dat.* of)

**bestanden** *Adj.* **von** *od.* **mit etw.** ~ **sein** have sth. growing on it; **mit Tannen** ~**e Hügel** fir-covered hills

**beständig** 1. *Adj.* a) *nicht präd.* constant; b) *(gleichbleibend)* constant; steadfast ⟨*person*⟩; settled ⟨*weather*⟩; c) *(widerstandsfähig)* resistant (**gegen** to); 2. *adv.* constantly; **Beständigkeit die;** ~ a) steadfastness; b) *(Widerstandsfähigkeit)* resistance (**gegen** to)

**Bestand·teil der** component

**bestärken** *tr. V.* confirm

**bestätigen** 1. *tr. V.* confirm; endorse ⟨*document*⟩; acknowledge ⟨*receipt*⟩; 2. *refl. V.* be confirmed; ⟨*rumour*⟩ prove to be true; **Bestätigung die;** ~, ~**en**

confirmation; *(des Empfangs)* acknowledgement; *(schriftlich)* letter of confirmation

**bestatten** *tr. V. (geh.)* inter *(formal)*; bury; **Bestattung die;** ~, ~en *(geh.)* interment *(formal)*; burial; *(Feierlichkeit)* funeral

**bestäuben** *tr. V.* **a)** dust; **b)** *(Biol.)* pollinate

**bestaunen** *tr. V.* marvel at

**bestechen** *unr. tr. V.* bribe; **bestechlich** *Adj.* corruptible; open to bribery *postpos.*; **Bestechung die;** ~, ~en bribery *no indef. art.*; **Bestechungs·geld das** bribe

**Besteck das;** ~[e]s, ~e cutlery setting; *(ugs.: Gesamtheit der Bestecke)* cutlery

**bestehen** **1.** *unr. itr. V.* **a)** exist; **es besteht [die] Aussicht/Gefahr, daß ...:** there is a prospect/danger that ...; **noch besteht die Hoffnung, daß ...:** there is still hope that ...; **b)** *(fortdauern)* survive; last; **c) aus etw.** ~: consist of sth.; *(hergestellt sein)* be made of sth.; **d) auf etw.** *(Dat.)* ~: insist on sth.; **2.** *unr. tr. V.* pass *⟨test, examination⟩*; **Bestehen das;** ~s existence; **die Firma feiert ihr 10jähriges** ~: the firm is celebrating its tenth anniversary

**bestehen|bleiben** *unr. itr. V.; mit sein* remain; *⟨regulation⟩* remain in force

**bestehend** *Adj.* existing; current *⟨conditions⟩*

**bestehlen** *unr. tr. V.* rob

**besteigen** *unr. tr. V.* **a)** climb; mount *⟨horse, bicycle⟩*; ascend *⟨throne⟩*; **b)** board *⟨ship, aircraft⟩*; get on *⟨bus, train⟩*; **Besteigung die** ascent

**bestellen** *tr. V.* **a)** *auch itr.* order (bei from); **würden Sie mir bitte ein Taxi** ~? would you order me a taxi?; **b)** *(reservieren lassen)* reserve *⟨tickets, table⟩*; **c)** jmdn. [für 10 Uhr] zu sich ~: ask sb. to go/come to see one [at 10 o'clock]; **d)** *(ausrichten)* jmdm. etw. ~: tell sb. sth.; **bestell deinem Mann schöne Grüße von mir** give your husband my regards; **Bestellung die a)** order; **b)** *(Reservierung)* reservation

**besten·falls** *Adv.* at best; **bestens** *Adv.* extremely well

**besteuern** *tr. V.* tax

**bestialisch** **1.** *Adj.* **a)** bestial; **b)** *nicht präd.* *(ugs.: schrecklich)* ghastly *(coll.)*; **2.** *adv.* **a)** in a bestial manner; **b)** *(ugs.: schrecklich)* awfully *(coll.)*; **Bestialität die;** ~: bestiality

**besticken** *tr. V.* embroider

**Bestie** ['bɛstiə] **die;** ~, ~n beast

**bestimmen** **1.** *tr. V.* **a)** *(festsetzen)* decide on; fix *⟨price, time, etc.⟩*; **b)** *(vorsehen)* intend; **das ist für dich bestimmt** that is meant for you; **c)** *(identifizieren)* identify; determine *⟨age, position⟩*; define *⟨meaning⟩*; **d)** *(prägen)* determine the character of; **2.** *itr. V.* **a)** make the decisions; **b)** über jmdn. ~: tell sb. what to do; **[frei] über etw.** *(Akk.)* ~: do as one wishes with sth.; **bestimmend** **1.** *Adj.* decisive; **2.** *adv.* decisively; **bestimmt 1.** *Adj.* **a)** *(speziell)* particular; *(gewiß)* certain; *(genau)* definite; **b)** *(festgelegt)* fixed; given *⟨quantity⟩*; **c)** *(Sprachw.)* definite *⟨article etc.⟩*; **d)** *(entschieden)* firm; **2.** *adv.* **a)** *(deutlich)* clearly; *(genau)* precisely; **b)** *(entschieden)* firmly **3.** *Adv.* for certain; **du weißt es doch [ganz]** ~ **noch** I'm sure you must remember it; **ich habe das** ~ **liegengelassen** I must have left it behind; **Bestimmtheit die;** ~: firmness; *(im Auftreten)* decisiveness; **Bestimmung die a)** *o. Pl. (das Festsetzen)* fixing; **b)** *(Vorschrift)* regulation; **c)** *o. Pl. (Zweck)* purpose; **d)** *s.* bestimmen 1 c: identification; determination; definition; **e)** *(Sprachw.)* modifier; **adverbiale** ~: adverbial qualification

**best·möglich** *Adj.* best possible

**bestrafen** *tr. V.* punish (für, wegen for); **es wird mit Gefängnis bestraft** it is punishable by imprisonment; **Bestrafung die;** ~, ~en punishment

**bestrahlen** *tr. V.* **a)** illuminate; floodlight *⟨building⟩*; **b)** *(Med.)* treat *⟨tumour, part of body⟩* using radiotherapy; **Bestrahlung die;** ~, ~en *(Med.)* radiation [treatment] *no indef. art.*

**Bestreben das** endeavour[s *pl.* ]; **bestrebt** *Adj.:* ~ **sein, etw. zu tun** endeavour to do sth.; **Bestrebung die;** ~, ~en effort; *(Versuch)* attempt

**bestreichen** *unr. tr. V.* **A mit B** ~: spread B on A

**bestreiten** *unr. tr. V.* **a)** dispute; *(leugnen)* deny; **b)** *(finanzieren)* finance *⟨studies⟩*; pay for *⟨studies, sb.'s keep⟩*; meet *⟨costs, expenses⟩*; **c)** *(gestalten)* carry *⟨programme, conversation, etc.⟩*

**bestreuen** *tr. V.* sprinkle

**Bestseller der;** ~s, ~: best seller

**bestürzt** **1.** *Adj.* dismayed; **2.** *adv.* with dismay

**Besuch** der; ~|e|s, ~e **a)** visit (*Gen.*, **bei** to); **ein ~ bei jmdm.** a visit to sb.; *(kurz)* a call on sb.; **b)** *(Teilnahme)* attendance (*Gen.* at); **c)** *(Gast)* visitor; *(Gäste)* visitors *pl.*; ~ **haben** have visitors/a visitor; **besuchen** *tr. V.* **a)** visit; *(weniger formell)* go to see (*person*); go to (*exhibition, theatre, museum, etc.*); *(zur Besichtigung)* go to see (*church, exhibition, etc.*); **b) die Schule/Universität ~:** go to school/university; **Besucher** der; ~s, ~, **Besucherin** die; ~, ~nen visitor; **besucht** *Adj.* **gut/schlecht ~:** well/poorly attended (*lecture, performance, etc.*); much/little frequented (*restaurant etc.*)

**betagt** *Adj. (geh.)* elderly

**betasten** *tr. V.* feel [with one's fingers]

**betätigen** 1. *refl. V.* occupy oneself; **sich politisch/körperlich ~:** engage in political/physical activity; 2. *tr. V.* operate (*lever, switch, flush, etc.*); apply (*brake*); **Betätigung** die; ~, ~en: **a)** activity; **b)** *o. Pl. s.* betätigen 2: operation; application

**betäuben** *tr. V.* **a)** *(Med.)* anaesthetize; deaden (*nerve*); **jmdn. örtlich ~:** give sb. a local anaesthetic; **b)** *(unterdrücken)* deaden (*pain*); still (*unease, fear*); **c)** *(benommen machen)* daze; *(mit einem Schlag)* stun; **Betäubung** die; ~, ~en: **a)** *(Med.)* anaesthetization; *(Narkose)* anaesthesia; **b)** *(Benommenheit)* daze; **Betäubungsmittel** das narcotic; *(Med.)* anaesthetic

**beteiligen** 1. *refl. V.* take part (**an +** *Dat.* in); 2. *tr. V.* **jmdn. |mit 10%| an etw.** *(Dat.)* **~:** give sb. a [10%] share of sth.; **beteiligt** *Adj.* **a)** involved (**an +** *Dat.* in); **b)** *(finanziell)* **an einem Unternehmen/am Gewinn ~ sein** have a share in a business/in the profit; **Beteiligte** der/die; *adj. Dekl.* person involved; **Beteiligung** die; ~, ~en **a)** participation (**an +** *Dat.* in); **b)** *(Anteil)* share (**an +** *Dat.* in)

**beten** 1. *itr. V.* pray (**für, um** for); 2. *tr. V.* say (*prayer*)

**beteuern** *tr. V.* affirm; protest (*one's innocence*); **Beteuerung** die; ~, ~en *s.* beteuern: affirmation; protestation

**Beton** [be'tɔŋ, *bes. österrr.:* be'to:n] der; ~s, ~s [-ɔŋs] *od.* (*bes. österr.:*) ~e [-o:nə] concrete

**betonen** *tr. V.* **a)** stress (*word, syllable*); **b)** *(hervorheben)* emphasize

**betonieren** *tr. V.* concrete; surface (*road etc.*) with concrete

**betont** 1. *Adj.* **a)** stressed; **b)** *(bewußt)* studied; 2. *adv.* studiedly; **Betonung** die; ~, ~en **a)** stressing; **b)** *(Akzent)* stress; *(Intonation)* intonation; **c)** *(Hervorhebung)* emphasis

**betören** *tr. V. (geh.)* captivate

**betr.** *Abk.* betreffs, betrifft re; **Betr.** *Abk.* Betreff re

**Betracht: jmdn./etw. in ~ ziehen** consider sb./sth.; **jmdn./etw. außer ~ lassen** disregard sb./sth.; **betrachten** *tr. V.* **a)** look at; **b) jmdn./etw. als etw. ~:** regard sb./sth. as sth.; **c)** *(beurteilen)* consider; **Betrachter** der; ~s, ~: observer

**beträchtlich** 1. *Adj.* considerable; 2. *adv.* considerably

**Betrachtung** die; ~, ~en **a)** contemplation; *(Untersuchung)* examination; **b)** *(Überlegung)* reflection

**Betrag** der; ~|e|s, Beträge amount; „~ dankend erhalten" 'received with thanks'; **betragen** 1. *unr. itr. V.* be; *(bei Geldsummen)* come to; 2. *unr. refl. V.* behave; **Betragen** das; ~s behaviour

**Betreff** der; ~|e|s, ~e *(im Brief)* heading; **betreffen** *unr. tr. V.* concern; (*new rule, change, etc.*) affect; **betreffend** *Adj.* concerning; **der ~e Sachbearbeiter** the person dealing with this matter; **in dem ~en Fall** in the case in question; **betreffs** *Präp. mit Gen. (Amtsspr., Kaufmannsspr.)* concerning

**betreiben** *unr. tr. V.* **a)** proceed with, *(energisch)* press ahead with (*task, case, etc.*); pursue (*policy, studies*); carry on (*trade*); go in for (*sport*); **b)** run (*business, shop*); **c)** *(in Betrieb halten)* operate

¹**betreten** *unr. tr. V. (hineintreten in)* enter; *(treten auf)* step on to; *(begehen)* walk on (*carpet, grass, etc.*); „Betreten verboten" 'Keep off'; *(kein Eintritt)* 'Keep out'

²**betreten** 1. *Adj.* embarrassed; 2. *adv.* with embarrassment

**betreuen** *tr. V.* look after; care for (*invalid*); supervise (*youth group*); see to the needs of (*tourists, sportsmen*); **Betreuung** die; ~ care *no indef. art.*

**Betrieb** der; ~|e|s, ~e **a)** business; *(Firma)* firm; **b)** *o. Pl. (das In-Funktion-Sein)* operation; **außer ~ sein** not operate; *(wegen Störung)* be out of order; **in/außer ~ setzen** start up/stop

⟨*machine etc.*⟩; c) *o. Pl. (ugs.: Treiben)*
bustle; *(Verkehr)* traffic; **es herrscht
großer** ~, **es ist viel** ~: it's very busy;
**betrieblich** *Adj.* firm's; company
**Betriebs-**: ~**angehörige der/die**
employee; ~**anleitung die**, ~**anweisung die** operating instructions
*pl.;* ~**ausflug der** staff outing;
~**ferien** *Pl.* firm's annual close-down
*sing.;* „**Wegen** ~**ferien geschlossen"**
'closed for annual holidays'; ~**klima
das** working atmosphere; ~**rat der a)**
works committee; **b)** *(Person)* member
of a/the works committee; ~**wirt der**
graduate in business management;
~**wirtschaft die;** *o. Pl.* business
management
**betrinken** *unr. refl. V.* get drunk
**betroffen 1.** *Adj.* upset; *(bestürzt)* dismayed; **2.** *adv.* in dismay; **Betrof-
fenheit die;** ~: dismay
**betrüblich** *Adj.* gloomy; **betrübt 1.**
*Adj.* sad; gloomy ⟨*face etc.*⟩; **2.** sadly;
*(schwermütig)* gloomily
**Betrug der;** ~|e|s deception; *(Delikt)*
fraud; **betrügen 1.** *unr. tr. V.* deceive; be unfaithful to ⟨*husband, wife*⟩; *(Rechtsw.)* defraud; *(beim Spielen)* cheat; **jmdn. um 100 DM** ~: cheat
or *(coll.)* do sb. out of 100 marks; *(arg-
listig)* swindle sb. out of 100 marks; **2.**
*unr. itr. V.* cheat; *(bei Geschäften)*
swindle people; **Betrüger der;** ~s,
~: swindler; *(Hochstapler)* con man
*(coll.); (beim Spielen)* cheat; **Betrü-
gerei die;** ~, ~**en** deception; *(beim
Spielen usw.)* cheating; *(bei Geschäften)* swindling; **Betrügerin die;** ~,
~**nen** swindler; *(beim Spielen)* cheat
**betrunken** *Adj.* drunken *attrib.;*
drunk *pred.;* **Betrunkene der/die;**
*adj. Dekl.* drunk
**Bett das;** ~|e|s, ~**en a)** bed; **ins** *od.* **zu**
~ **gehen** go to bed; **die Kinder ins** ~
**bringen** put the children to bed; **b)**
*(Feder~)* duvet
**Bett-:** ~**bezug der** duvet cover;
~**decke die** blanket; *(gesteppt)* quilt
**Bettelei die;** ~, ~**en** begging *no art.;*
**betteln** *itr. V.* beg (um for)
**bett·lägerig** *Adj.* bedridden
**Bett·laken das** sheet
**Bettler der;** ~s, ~, **Bettlerin die;** ~,
~**nen** beggar
**Bett-:** ~**ruhe die** bed rest; ~**wäsche
die** bed-linen; ~**zeug das;** *o. Pl. (ugs.)*
bedclothes *pl.*
**betucht** *Adj. (ugs.)* well-heeled *(coll.);*
well-off

**betupfen** *tr. V.* dab
**Beuge die;** ~, ~**n** *(Turnen)* bend;
**beugen 1.** *tr. V.* **a)** bend; bow
⟨*head*⟩; **b)** *(Sprachw.: flektieren)* in-
flect ⟨*word*⟩; **2.** *refl. V.* **a)** bend over;
**sich nach vorn/hinten** ~: bend for-
wards/bend over backwards; **sich aus
dem Fenster** ~: lean out of the window; **b)** *(sich fügen)* give way;
**Beugung die;** ~, ~**en** *(Sprachw.)* in-
flexion
**Beule die;** ~, ~**n** bump; *(Vertiefung)*
dent; **beulen** *itr. V.* bulge
**beunruhigen** *tr., refl. V.* worry
**beurlauben** *tr. V.* **a)** jmdn. |für zwei
Tage| ~: give sb. [two days'] leave of
absence; **b)** *(suspendieren)* suspend
**beurteilen** *tr. V.* judge; assess ⟨*situation etc.*⟩; **Beurteilung die;** ~, ~**en**
**a)** judgement; *(einer Lage usw.)* assessment; **b)** *(Gutachten)* assessment
**Beute die;** ~, ~**n** *(Gestohlenes)* haul;
loot *no indef. art.;* **b)** *(von Raubtieren)*
prey; *(eines Jägers)* bag
**Beutel der;** ~s, ~ bag; *(kleiner, für Tabak usw.)* pouch
**bevölkern** *tr. V.* populate; **Bevölkerung die;** ~, ~**en** population; *(Volk)*
people
**bevollmächtigen** *tr. V.* authorize;
**Bevollmächtigte der/die;** *adj.
Dekl.* authorized representative
**bevor** *Konj.* before; ~ **du nicht unter-
schrieben hast** until you have signed;
**bevor|stehen** *unr. itr. V.* be near;
**unmittelbar** ~: be imminent; **jmdm.
steht etw. bevor** sth. is in store for sb.;
**bevorstehend** *Adj.* forthcoming;
**unmittelbar** ~: imminent
**bevorzugen** *tr. V.* **a)** *(vorziehen)*
prefer (vor + *Dat.* to); **b)** *(begünstigen)* favour; give preference *or* preferential treatment to (vor + *Dat.*
over); **bevorzugt 1.** *Adj.* favoured;
*(privilegiert)* privileged; preferential
⟨*treatment*⟩; **2.** *adv.* jmdn. ~ **behandeln** give sb. preferential treatment;
**Bevorzugung die;** ~, ~**en** *(Begünstigung)* preferential treatment
**bewachen** *tr. V.* guard; **bewachter
Parkplatz** car park with an attendant;
**Bewacher der;** ~s, ~: guard; **Be-
wachung die;** ~, ~**en** guarding
**bewaffnen: 1.** *tr. V.* arm; **2.** *refl. V.
(auch fig.)* arm oneself (mit with); **Be-
waffnung die;** ~, ~**en a)** arming; **b)**
*(Waffen)* weapons *pl.*
**bewahren** *tr. V.* **a)** protect (vor
+ *Dat.* from); **b)** *(erhalten)* **seine Fas-**

sung ~: retain one's composure; **Still-schweigen** ~: remain silent
**bewähren** *refl. V.* prove oneself/itself; **bewährt** *Adj.* proven ⟨*method, design, etc.*⟩; well-tried ⟨*recipe, cure*⟩; reliable ⟨*worker*⟩; **Bewährung die;** ~, ~en *(Rechtsw.)* probation
**bewaldet** *Adj.* wooded
**bewältigen** *tr. V.* cope with; overcome ⟨*difficulty, problem*⟩; cover ⟨*distance*⟩; **Bewältigung die;** ~, ~en *s.* bewältigen: coping with; overcoming; covering
**bewandert** *Adj.* well-versed
**Bewandtnis die;** ~, ~se: mit etw. hat es |s|eine eigene/besondere ~: there's a [special] story behind sth.
**bewässern** *tr. V.* irrigate; **Bewässerung die;** ~, ~en irrigation
**¹bewegen** 1. *tr. V.* a) move; b) *(ergreifen)* move; c) *(innerlich beschäftigen)* preoccupy; 2. *refl. V.* move
**²bewegen** *unr. tr. V.* jmdn. dazu ~, etw. zu tun ⟨*thing*⟩ induce sb. to do sth.; ⟨*person*⟩ prevail upon sb. to do sth.; **Beweg·grund der** motive
**beweglich** *Adj.* a) movable; moving ⟨*target*⟩; b) *(rege)* agile ⟨*mind*⟩; **bewegt** *Adj.* eventful; *(unruhig)* turbulent; **Bewegung die;** ~, ~ a) *(bes. Technik, Physik)* motion; b) *(körperliche ~)* exercise; c) *(Ergriffenheit)* emotion; d) *(Bestreben, Gruppe)* movement; **Bewegungs·freiheit die;** *o. Pl.* freedom of movement; **bewegungs·los** *Adj.* motionless
**Beweis der;** ~es, ~e proof *(Gen., für of)*; belastende ~e incriminating evidence; **beweisbar** *Adj.* provable; **beweisen** *unr. tr. V.* prove; **Beweis·material das** evidence
**bewenden** *unr. V.* es bei od. mit etw. ~ lassen content oneself with sth.
**bewerben** *unr. refl. V.* apply (bei to, um for); **Bewerber der** applicant; **Bewerbung die** application
**bewerfen** *unr. tr. V.* jmdn./etw. mit etw. ~: throw sth. at sb./sth.
**bewerten** *tr. V.* assess; rate; *(dem Geldwert nach)* value (mit at); **Bewertung die** assessment; *(dem Geldwert nach)* valuation
**bewilligen** *tr. V.* grant; **Bewilligung die;** ~, ~en granting
**bewirken** *tr. V.* bring about; cause
**bewirten** *tr. V.* feed; jmdn. mit etw. ~: serve sb. sth.
**bewirtschaften** *tr. V.* a) manage

⟨*estate, farm, restaurant, business, etc.*⟩; b) farm ⟨*fields, land*⟩
**Bewirtung die;** ~, ~en provision of food and drink
**bewog** *1. u. 3. Pers. Sg. Prät. v.* ²**bewegen**
**bewohnbar** *Adj.* habitable; **bewohnen** *tr. V.* inhabit, live in ⟨*house, area*⟩; live in ⟨*room, flat*⟩; **Bewohner der;** ~s, ~, **Bewohnerin die;** ~, ~nen *(eines Hauses, einer Wohnung)* occupant; *(einer Stadt, eines Gebietes)* inhabitant; **bewohnt** *Adj.* occupied ⟨*house etc.*⟩; inhabited ⟨*area*⟩
**bewölken** *refl. V.* cloud over; become overcast; **bewölkt** *Adj.* cloudy; overcast; **Bewölkung die;** ~, ~en cloud [cover]
**Bewunderer der;** ~s, ~, **Bewunderin die;** ~, ~nen admirer; **bewundern** *tr. V.* admire (wegen, für for); **bewunderns·wert** *Adj.* a) admirable; 2. *adv.* admirably; **Bewunderung die;** ~: admiration
**bewußt** 1. *Adj.* conscious ⟨*reaction, behaviour, etc.*⟩; *(absichtlich)* deliberate ⟨*lie, deception, attack, etc.*⟩; etw. ist/wird jmdm. ~: sb. is/becomes aware of sth.; sb. realizes sth.; sich *(Dat.)* einer Sache *(Gen.)* ~ sein/werden be/become aware of something; 2. *adv.* consciously; *(absichtlich)* deliberately; **bewußt·los** *Adj.* unconscious; **Bewußtlosigkeit die;** ~: unconsciousness; **Bewußt·sein das** a) consciousness; das ~ verlieren/wiedererlangen lose/regain consciousness; bei vollem ~ sein be fully conscious; b) *(deutliches Wissen)* awareness
**bezahlbar** *Adj.* affordable; **bezahlen** 1. *tr. V.* pay ⟨*person, bill, taxes, rent, amount*⟩; pay for ⟨*goods etc.*⟩; das macht sich bezahlt it pays off; 2. *itr. V.* pay; Herr Ober, ich möchte ~ od. bitte ~: waiter, the bill *or (Amer.)* check please; **Bezahlung die** payment; *(Lohn, Gehalt)* pay
**bezaubernd** 1. *Adj.* enchanting; 2. *adv.* enchantingly
**bezeichnen** *tr. V.* a) jmdn./sich/etw. als etw. ~: call sb./oneself/sth. sth.; b) *(Name, Wort sein für)* denote; **bezeichnend** *Adj.* characteristic (für of); **Bezeichnung die** a) marking; *(Angabe durch Zeichen)* indication; b) *(Name)* name
**bezeugen** *tr. V.* testify to
**bezichtigen** *tr. V.* accuse

**beziehen 1.** *unr. tr. V.* **a)** cover ⟨*seat, cushion, etc.*⟩; **die Betten frisch ~:** put clean sheets on the beds; **b)** *(einziehen in)* move into ⟨*house, office*⟩; **c)** *(Milit.)* take up ⟨*position, post*⟩; **d)** *(erhalten)* obtain ⟨*goods*⟩; draw ⟨*pension, salary*⟩; **e)** *(in Beziehung setzen)* apply **(auf +** *Akk.* **to); 2.** *unr. refl. V.* **a) es/der Himmel bezieht sich it/the sky** is clouding over *or* becoming overcast; **b) sich auf jmdn./ etw. ~** *(sich berufen auf)* ⟨*person, letter, etc.*⟩ refer to sb./sth.; *(betreffen)* ⟨*question, statement, etc.*⟩ relate to sb./sth.; **wir ~ uns auf Ihr Schreiben vom 28. 8.** with reference to your letter of 28 August; **Beziehung die a)** relation; *(Zusammenhang)* connection **(zu** with); **zwischen A und B besteht keine/eine ~:** there is no/a connection between A and B; **b)** *(Freundschaft, Liebes~)* relationship; **c)** *(Hinsicht)* respect; **in mancher ~:** in many respects; **beziehungs·weise** *Konj.* and ... respectively; *(oder)* or

**Bezirk der; ~|e|s, ~e** district

**bezug: in ~ auf jmdn./etw.** regarding sb./sth.

**Bezug der a)** *(für Kissen usw.)* cover; *(für Polstermöbel)* loose cover; slipcover *(Amer.)*; *(für Betten)* duvet cover; *(für Kopfkissen)* pillowcase; **b)** *o. Pl. (Erwerb)* obtaining; *(Kauf)* purchase; **~ einer Zeitung** taking a newspaper; **c)** *Pl.* salary *sing.*; **d)** *(Papierdt.)* **mit** *od.* **unter ~ auf etw.** *(Akk.)* with reference to sth.; **~ nehmend auf unser Telex** with reference to our telex; **bezüglich** *Präp. mit Gen.* regarding

**bezwecken** *tr. V.* aim to achieve

**bezweifeln** *tr. V.* doubt

**bezwingen** *unr. tr. V.* conquer ⟨*enemy, mountain, pain, etc.*⟩; defeat ⟨*opponent*⟩; capture ⟨*fortress*⟩

**BH** [be:'ha:] **der; ~|s|, ~|s|** *Abk.:* Büstenhalter bra

**Bibel die; ~, ~n** *(auch fig.)* Bible

**Biber der; ~s, ~:** beaver

**Bibliothek die; ~, ~en** library

**biblisch** *Adj.* biblical

**Bidet** [bi'de:] **das; ~s, ~s** bidet

**bieder** *Adj.* unsophisticated; *(langweilig)* stolid; *(treuherzig)* trusting

**biegen 1.** *unr. tr. V.* bend; **2.** *unr. refl. V.* bend; *(nachgeben)* give; **3.** *unr. itr. V.; mit sein* turn; **biegsam** *Adj.* flexible; pliable ⟨*material*⟩; **Biegung die; ~, ~en** bend

**Biene die; ~, ~n** bee

**Bienen-: ~honig der** bees' honey; **~königin die** queen bee; **~korb der** straw hive; **~stock der** beehive

**Bier das; ~|e|s, ~e** beer

**Bier-: ~deckel der** beer-mat; **~dose die** beer can; **~faß das** beer-barrel; **~flasche die** beer-bottle; **~garten der** beer garden; **~glas das** beerglass; **~kasten der** beer-crate; **~zelt das** beer tent

**Biest das; ~|e|s, ~er** *(ugs. abwertend)* **a)** *(Tier, Gegenstand)* wretched thing; **b)** *(Mensch)* wretch

**bieten 1.** *unr. tr. V.* **a)** offer; put on ⟨*programme etc.*⟩; provide ⟨*shelter, guarantee, etc.*⟩; **b) ein schreckliches Bild ~:** present a terrible picture; **einen prächtigen Anblick ~:** be a splendid sight; **2.** *unr. refl. V.* **sich jmdm. ~:** present itself to sb.; **3.** *unr. itr. V.* bid

**Bigamie die; ~:** bigamy *no def. art.*

**Bikini der; ~s, ~s** bikini

**Bilanz die; ~, ~en** **a)** balance sheet; **b)** *(Ergebnis)* outcome; **~ ziehen** take stock

**Bild das; ~|e|s, ~er** **a)** picture; **b)** *(Anblick)* sight; **c)** *(Metapher)* image

**bilden 1.** *tr. V.* **a)** form **(aus** from); *(modellieren)* mould **(aus** from); **eine Gasse ~:** make a path; **sich** *(Dat.)* **ein Urteil ~:** form an opinion; **b)** *(ansammeln)* build up ⟨*fund, capital*⟩; **c)** *(darstellen)* be ⟨*exception etc.*⟩; **d)** *(erziehen)* educate; **2.** *refl. V.* **a)** form; **b)** *(lernen)* educate oneself

**Bilder·buch das** picture-book *(for children)*

**Bild·hauer der** sculptor

**bild·hübsch** *Adj.* really lovely; stunningly beautiful ⟨*girl*⟩

**bildlich 1.** *Adj.* pictorial; *(übertragen)* figurative; **2.** *adv.* pictorially; *(übertragen)* figuratively; **Bildnis** ['bɪltnɪs] **das; ~ses, ~se** portrait

**Bild·schirm der** *(Ferns., Informationst.)* screen; **Bildschirm·gerät das** VDU; visual display unit

**bild·schön** *Adj.* really lovely; stunningly beautiful ⟨*girl, woman*⟩

**Bildung die; ~, ~en a)** *(Erziehung)* education; *(Kultur)* culture; **b)** *(das Formen)* formation; **Bildungslücke die** gap in one's education

**Billard** ['bɪljart, *österr.:* bi'jaːɐ̯] **das; ~s, ~e** billiards

**Billard-: ~kugel die** billiard-ball; **~stock der** billiard-cue; **~tisch der** billiard-table

**Billett** [bɪl'jɛt] das; ~|e|s, ~e od. ~s ⟨schweiz., veralt.⟩ ticket

**Billiarde** die; ~, ~n thousand million million; quadrillion ⟨Amer.⟩

**billig** 1. Adj. a) cheap; b) ⟨abwertend: primitiv⟩ cheap ⟨trick⟩; feeble ⟨excuse⟩; 2. adv. cheaply

**billigen** tr. V. approve; **Billigung** die; ~: approval

**Billion** die; ~, ~en million million; trillion ⟨Amer.⟩

**bimmeln** itr. V. ⟨ugs.⟩ ring

**bin** 1. Pers. Sg. Präsens v. ¹sein

**Binde** die; ~, ~n a) ⟨Verband⟩ bandage; ⟨Augen~⟩ blindfold; b) ⟨Arm~⟩ armband

**Binde-:** ~gewebe das ⟨Anat.⟩ connective tissue; ~haut die ⟨Anat.⟩ conjunctiva

**binden** 1. unr. tr. V. a) ⟨auch fig.⟩ tie; knot ⟨tie⟩; make up ⟨wreath, bouquet⟩; **jmdn. an sich** ⟨Akk.⟩ ~ ⟨fig.⟩ make sb. dependent on one; b) ⟨fesseln, festhalten, zusammenhalten, fig.: verpflichten, Buchw.⟩ bind; c) ⟨Kochk.: legieren⟩ thicken ⟨sauce⟩; 2. unr. refl. V. tie oneself down; **Binder** der; ~s, ~ tie; **Bindestrich** der hyphen; **Bind·faden** der string

**Bindung** die; ~, ~en a) ⟨Beziehung⟩ relationship ⟨an + Akk. to⟩; b) ⟨Verbundenheit⟩ attachment ⟨an + Akk. to⟩; c) ⟨Ski~⟩ binding

**binnen** Präp. mit Dat. od. ⟨geh.⟩ Gen. within

**Binsen·weisheit** die truism

**bio-, Bio:** ~chemie die biochemistry; ~graph der; ~en, ~en biographer; ~graphie die; ~, ~n biography; ~graphisch Adj. biographical; ~loge der; ~n, ~n biologist; ~logie die; ~: biology no art.; ~logisch Adj. a) biological; b) ⟨natürlich⟩ natural ⟨medicine, cosmetic, etc.⟩; ~top der od. das; ~s, ~e ⟨Biol.⟩ biotope

**Birke** die; ~, ~n birch[-tree]; ⟨Holz⟩ birch[wood]

**Birma** (das); ~s Burma

**Birn·baum** der pear-tree; **Birne** die; ~, ~n a) pear; b) ⟨Glüh~⟩ [light-]bulb; c) ⟨salopp: Kopf⟩ nut ⟨sl.⟩

**bis** 1. Präp. mit Akk. a) ⟨zeitlich⟩ until; till; ⟨die ganze Zeit über und bis zu einem bestimmten Zeitpunkt⟩ up until; up till; ⟨nicht später als⟩ by; b) ⟨räumlich⟩ to; **dieser Zug fährt nur ~ Offenburg** this train only goes as far as Offenburg; **~ 5 000 Mark** up to 5,000

marks; c) ~ **auf** ⟨einschließlich⟩ down to; ⟨mit Ausnahme von⟩ except for; 2. Adv. ~ **zu 6 Personen** up to six people. 3. Konj. a) ⟨nebenordnend⟩ to; b) ⟨unterordnend⟩ until; till; ⟨österr.: sobald⟩ when

**Bisam·ratte** die musk-rat

**Bischof** der; ~s, Bischöfe bishop; **bischöflich** Adj. episcopal

**bis·her** Adv. up to now; ⟨aber jetzt nicht mehr⟩ until now; till now; **bisherig** Adj. ⟨vorherig⟩ previous; ⟨momentan⟩ present

**Biskaya** [bɪs'ka:ja] die; ~: the Bay of Biscay

**Biskuit** [bɪs'kvi:t] das od. der; ~|e|s, ~s od. ~e a) sponge biscuit; b) ⟨~teig⟩ sponge

**bis·lang** Adv.: s. bisher

**Bison** der; ~s, ~s bison

**Biß** der; Bisses, Bisse bite

**bißchen** indekl. Indefinitpron. a) adj. **ein** ~ **Geld/Wasser** a bit of or a little money/a drop of or a little water; **ein/ kein** ~ **Angst haben** be a bit/not a bit frightened; b) adv. **ein/kein** ~: a bit or a little/not a or one bit; c) subst. **ein** ~: a bit; a little; ⟨bei Flüssigkeiten⟩ a drop; a little; **das/kein** ~: the little [bit]/not a or one bit

**Bissen** der; ~s, ~: mouthful

**bissig** 1. Adj. a) ~ **sein** ⟨dog⟩ bite; **ein ~er Hund** a dog that bites; „**Vorsicht, ~er Hund**" 'beware of the dog'; b) cutting ⟨remark, tone, etc.⟩; 2. adv. ⟨say⟩ cuttingly

**Biß·wunde** die bite

**bist** 2. Pers. Sg. Präsens v. ¹sein

**Bistum** ['bɪstu:m] das; ~s, Bistümer bishopric; diocese

**bis·weilen** Adv. ⟨geh.⟩ from time to time

**bitte** 1. Adv. please; 2. Interj. a) ⟨Bitte, Aufforderung⟩ please; **zwei Tassen Tee,** ~: two cups of tea, please; ~|, **nehmen Sie doch Platz**|! do take a seat; **Noch eine Tasse Tee?** – |Ja| ~! Another cup of tea? – Yes, please; b) ⟨Aufforderung, etw. entgegenzunehmen⟩ ~ |schön od. sehr|! there you are!; c) ⟨Ausdruck des Einverständnisses⟩ ~ |gern|! certainly; of course; **Entschuldigung!** – **Bitte!** [I'm] sorry! – That's all right!; d) ~ |schön od. sehr|! ⟨im Laden, Lokal⟩ yes, please?; e) |wie| ~? ⟨Nachfrage⟩ sorry; f) **Vielen Dank!** – **Bitte |schön od. sehr|** Many thanks! – Not at all or you're welcome

**Bitte die;** ~, ~n request; *(inständig)* plea; **bitten** *unr. tr. V.* **a)** *auch itr.* ask (um for); **darf ich Sie um Feuer/ein Glas Wasser** ~? could I ask you for a light/a glass of water, please?; **b)** *(einladen)* ask

**bitter 1.** *Adj.* **a)** bitter; plain *(chocolate)*; **b)** *(fig.) (verbittert)* bitter; **c)** *(schmerzlich)* bitter, painful, hard *(loss)*; hard *(time, fate, etc.)*; dire *(need)*; desperate *(poverty)*; grievous *(injustice, harm)*; **2.** *adv. (sehr stark)* desperately; *(regret)* bitterly

**bitter-:** ~**böse 1.** *Adj.* furious; **2.** *adv.* furiously; ~**kalt** *Adj.; präd. getrennt geschr.* bitterly cold

**bitterlich 1.** *Adj.* slightly bitter *(taste)*. **2.** *adv. (heftig)* *(cry, complain, etc.)* bitterly; **bitter·süß** *Adj. (auch fig.)* bitter-sweet

**Bitt·steller der;** ~s, ~petitioner

**Biwak das;** ~s, ~s *(bes. Milit., Bergsteigen)* bivouac

**bizarr 1.** *Adj.* bizarre; **2.** *adv.* bizarrely

**Bizeps der;** ~[es], ~e biceps

**Blähung die;** ~, ~en flatulence *no art., no pl.*

**Blamage** [bla'maːʒə] **die;** ~, ~n disgrace; **blamieren 1.** *tr. V.* disgrace; **2.** *refl. V.* disgrace oneself; *(sich lächerlich machen)* make a fool of oneself

**blank** *Adj.* shiny

**Blanko-:** ~**scheck der** *(auch fig.)* blank cheque; ~**vollmacht die** *(auch fig.)* carte blanche

**Bläschen** ['blɛːsçən] **das;** ~s, ~ **a)** [small] bubble; **b)** *(in der Haut)* [small] blister; **Blase die;** ~, ~n **a)** bubble; **b)** *(in der Haut)* blister; **c)** *(Harn~)* bladder; **Blase·balg der** bellows *pl.*; **blasen 1.** *unr. itr. V.* blow; **2.** *unr. tr. V.* **a)** blow; **b)** *(spielen)* play *(musical instrument, tune, melody, etc.)*; **Bläser der;** ~s, ~ *(Musik)* wind player

**blasiert** *(abwertend)* **1.** *Adj.* blasé; **2.** *adv.* in a blasé way

**Blas-:** ~**instrument das** wind instrument; ~**kapelle die** brass band; ~**musik die** brass-band music

**Blasphemie** [blasfe'miː] **die;** ~, ~n blasphemy

**Blas·rohr das** blowpipe

**blaß 1.** *Adj.* pale; **2.** *adv.* palely; **Blässe die;** ~: paleness

**Blatt das;** ~[es], Blätter **a)** *(von Pflanzen)* leaf; **b)** *(Papier)* sheet; **c)** *(Buchseite usw.)* page; etw. vom ~ spielen sight-read sth.; **d)** *(Zeitung)* paper; **e)**

*(Spielkarten)* hand; **f)** *(am Werkzeug, Ruder)* blade; **Blättchen das;** ~s, ~ **a)** *(von Pflanzen)* [small] leaf; **b)** *(Papier)* [small] sheet; **blättern** *itr. V.* in einem Buch ~: leaf through a book; **Blätter·teig der** puff pastry

**Blatt-:** ~**gold das;** *o. Pl.* gold leaf; ~**laus die** aphid

**blau** *Adj.* blue; ein ~er Fleck a bruise; ~ sein *(fig. ugs.)* be tight *(coll.)*; das Blaue vom Himmel herunterlügen *(ugs.)* lie like anything; **Blau das;** ~s, ~ *od. (ugs.:)* ~s blue

**blau-, Blau-:** ~**äugig** *Adj.* **a)** blueeyed; **b)** *(naiv)* naive; ~**beere die** bilberry; ~**grau** *Adj.* blue-grey; ~**grün** *Adj.* blue-green

**bläulich** *Adj.* bluish

**blau-, Blau-:** ~**licht das** flashing blue light; ~|**machen** *itr. V. (ugs.)* skip work; ~**mann der;** *Pl.* ~männer *(ugs.)* boiler suit; ~**säure die;** *o. Pl.* *(Chemie)* prussic acid; ~**stichig** *Adj. (Fot.)* with a blue cast *postpos., not pred.*; ~**stichig sein** have a blue cast

**Blazer** ['bleːzɐ] **der;** ~s, ~: blazer

**Blech das;** ~[es], ~e **a)** sheet metal; *(Stück Blech)* metal sheet; **b)** *(Back~)* [baking] tray

**Blech-:** ~**büchse die,** ~**dose die** tin

**blechen** *tr., itr. V. (ugs.)* cough up *(sl.)*

**blechern** *Adj.* **1.** *(metallisch klingend)* tinny *(sound, voice)*; **2.** *adv.* tinnily

**Blech-:** ~**musik die** *(abwertend)* brass-band music; ~**napf der** metal bowl

**Blechner der;** ~s, ~ *(südd.) s.* Klempner

**Blech-:** ~**schaden der** *(Kfz-W.)* damage *no indef. art.* to the bodywork; ~**trommel die** tin drum

**blecken** *tr. V.* die Zähne ~: bare one's/its teeth

**Blei das;** ~[es], ~e lead

**Bleibe die;** ~, ~n place to stay; **bleiben** *unr. itr. V.; mit sein* **a)** stay; remain; ~ Sie bitte am Apparat hold the line please; wo bleibt er so lange? where has he got to?; auf dem Weg ~: keep to the path; sitzen ~: stay *or* remain sitting down *or* seated; bei etw. ~: *(fig.: an etw. festhalten)* keep to sth.; **b)** *(übrigbleiben)* be left; remain; **bleibend** *Adj.* lasting; permanent *(damage)*; **bleiben|lassen** *unr. tr. V.* etw. ~: give sth. a miss

**bleich** *Adj.* pale; ¹**bleichen** *tr. V.* bleach; ²**bleichen** *regelm., veralt. auch unr. itr. V.* become bleached

**blei-, Blei-:** ~**frei** *Adj.* unleaded ⟨*fuel*⟩; ~**kristall** das lead crystal; ~**kugel die** lead ball; *(Geschoß)* lead bullet; ~**schwer** *Adj.* heavy as lead *postpos.;* ~**stift** der pencil; **mit** ~: in pencil; ~**stift·spitzer** der pencil-sharpener

**Blende die;** ~, ~**n a)** *(Lichtschutz)* shade; *(am Fenster)* blind; **b)** *(Optik, Film, Fot.)* diaphragm; *(Blendenzahl)* aperture setting; **blenden 1.** *tr. V.* **a)** *(auch fig.)* dazzle; **b)** *(blind machen)* blind; **2.** *itr. V.* ⟨*light*⟩ be dazzling; **blendend 1.** *Adj.* es geht mir ~: I feel wonderfully well; **2.** *adv.* wir haben uns ~ amüsiert we had a marvellous time

**blich** *1. u. 3. Pers. Sg. Prät. v.* ²**bleichen**
**Blick der;** ~**[e]s,** ~**e a)** look; *(flüchtig)* glance; **b)** *o. Pl. (Ausdruck)* look in one's eyes; **mit mißtrauischem** ~: with a suspicious look in one's eye; **c)** *(Aussicht)* view; **ein Zimmer mit** ~ **aufs Meer** a room with a sea view; **d)** *o. Pl. (Urteil[skraft])* eye; **blicken 1.** *itr. V.* look; *(flüchtig)* glance; **2.** *tr. V.* **sich** ~ **lassen** put in an appearance
**Blick-:** ~**feld** das field of vision; ~**punkt** der view; ~**winkel** der **a)** angle of vision; **b)** *(fig.)* point of view; viewpoint

**blieb** *1. u. 3. Pers. Sg. Prät. v.* **bleiben**
**blies** *1. u. 3. Pers. Sg. Prät. v.* **blasen**
**blind 1.** *Adj.* **a)** *(auch fig.)* blind; ~ **werden** go blind; **b)** *(trübe)* clouded ⟨*glass*⟩; **c)** **ein** ~**er Passagier** a stowaway; **d)** ~**er Alarm** a false alarm; **2.** *adv.* **a)** *(ohne hinzusehen)* without looking; *(wahllos)* blindly; **b)** *(unkritisch)* ⟨*trust*⟩ implicitly; ⟨*obey*⟩ blindly; **Blind·darm der a)** caecum; **b)** *(volkst.: Wurmfortsatz)* appendix; **Blinde der/die;** *adj. Dekl.* blind person; **blind man/woman; die** ~**n** the blind; **Blinde·kuh** *o. Art.* blind man's buff

**Blinden-:** ~**hund** der guide-dog; ~**schrift die** Braille
**Blindheit die;** ~ *(auch fig.)* blindness; **blindlings** *Adv.* blindly; ⟨*trust*⟩ implicitly; **Blind·schleiche die;** ~, ~**n** slowworm; **blind·wütig 1.** *Adj.* raging ⟨*anger, hatred, fury, etc.*⟩; wild ⟨*rage*⟩; **2.** *adv.* in a blind rage
**blinken 1.** *itr. V.* **a)** ⟨*light, glass, crystal*⟩ flash; ⟨*star*⟩ twinkle; ⟨*metal, fish*⟩ gleam; **b)** *(Verkehrsw.)* indicate; **2.** *tr. V.* flash; **Blinker der;** ~**s,** ~ indicator [light]

**Blink-:** ~**licht das a)** flashing light; **b)** *s.* **Blinker;** ~**zeichen** das flashlight signal
**blinzeln** *itr. V.* blink; *(mit einem Auge, um ein Zeichen zu geben)* wink
**Blitz der;** ~**es,** ~**e a)** lightning *no indef. art.;* **ein** ~: a flash of lightning; **|schnell| wie der** ~: like lightning; **b)** *(~licht)* flash
**blitz-, Blitz-:** ~**ableiter** der lightning-conductor; ~**artig 1.** *Adj.* lightning; **2.** *adv.* like lightning; ⟨*disappear*⟩ in a flash; ~**blank** *Adj. (ugs.)* ~**blank |geputzt|** sparkling clean; brightly polished ⟨*shoes*⟩
**blitzeblank** *s.* **blitzblank; blitzen** *itr. V.* **a)** *unpers.* es blitzte *(einmal)* there was a flash of lightning; *(mehrmals)* there was lightning; **b)** *(glänzen)* ⟨*light, glass, crystal*⟩ flash; ⟨*metal*⟩ gleam
**blitz-, Blitz-:** ~**gerät** das flash [unit]; ~**licht das;** *Pl.* ~**lichter** flash[light]; ~**schnell 1.** *Adj.* lightning *attrib.;* ~**schnell sein** be like lightning; **2.** *adv.* like lightning; ⟨*disappear*⟩ in a flash; ~**start** der lightning start
**Block der;** ~**[e]s, Blöcke** *od.* ~**s a)** *Pl. nur* **Blöcke** *(Brocken)* block; **b)** *(Wohn~)* block; **c)** *Pl. nur* **Blöcke** *(Gruppierung von politischen Kräften, Staaten)* bloc; **d)** *(Schreib~)* pad
**Blockade die;** ~, ~**n** blockade
**Block-:** ~**flöte die** recorder; ~**haus das,** ~**hütte das** log cabin
**blockieren** *tr. V.* block; jam ⟨*telephone line*⟩; halt ⟨*traffic*⟩; lock ⟨*wheel, machine, etc.*⟩
**Block·schrift die** block capitals *pl.*
**blöd[e]** *(ugs.)* **1.** *Adj.* **a)** *(dumm)* stupid; idiotic *(coll.);* **b)** *(unangenehm)* stupid; **2.** *adv.* stupidly; idiotically *(coll.);* **Blödelei die;** ~, ~**en** silly joke; **blödeln** *itr. V.* make silly jokes; **Blödheit die;** ~, ~**en** stupidity
**blöd-, Blöd-:** ~**mann** der; *Pl.* ~**männer** *(salopp)* stupid idiot *(coll.);* ~**sinn** der; *o. Pl. (ugs.)* nonsense; **mach doch keinen** ~**sinn!** don't be stupid; ~**sinnig** *(ugs.)* **1.** *Adj.* idiotic *(coll.);* **2.** *adv.* idiotically *(coll.)*
**blöken** *itr. V.* ⟨*sheep*⟩ bleat; ⟨*cattle*⟩ low
**blond** *Adj.* fair-haired, blond ⟨*man, race*⟩; blonde ⟨*woman*⟩; blond/blonde, fair ⟨*hair*⟩; **Blondine die;** ~, ~**n** blonde
**bloß 1.** *Adj.* **a)** *(nackt)* naked; **b)** *(nichts als)* mere ⟨*words, promises, tri-*⟩

*viality, suspicion, etc.*)*;* der ~e **Gedanke daran** the mere thought of it; **2.** *Adv. (ugs.: nur)* only; **3.** *Partikel* **was hast du dir ~ dabei gedacht?** what on earth were you thinking of?; **Blöße die;** ~: **sich** *(Dat.)* **eine/keine ~ geben** show a/not show any weakness; **bloß|stellen** *tr. V.* show up; expose ⟨*swindler, criminal, etc.*⟩

**Blouson** [blu'zõ:] *das od.* der; ~[s], ~s blouson

**blubbern** *itr. V. (ugs.)* bubble

**Bluejeans, Blue jeans** ['blu:dʒi:ns] *Pl. od.* die; ~, ~: [blue] jeans *pl.*

**Blues** [blu:s] der; ~, ~: blues *pl.*

**Bluff** der; ~s, ~s bluff; **bluffen** *tr., itr. V.* bluff

**blühen** *itr. V.* **a)** ⟨*plant*⟩ flower, be in flower *or* bloom; ⟨*flower*⟩ be in bloom, be out; ⟨*tree*⟩ be in blossom; **~de Gärten** gardens full of flowers; **b)** *(florieren)* thrive; **c)** *(ugs.: bevorstehen)* jmdm. ~: be in store for sb.; **das kann dir auch noch ~:** the same could happen to you; **blühend** *Adj.* **a)** *(frisch, gesund)* glowing ⟨*colour, complexion, etc.*⟩; radiant ⟨*health*⟩; **b)** *(übertrieben)* vivid ⟨*imagination*⟩

**Blümchen** das; ~s, ~: [little] flower; **Blume die;** ~, ~n **a)** flower; **b)** *(des Weines)* bouquet; **c)** *(des Biers)* head

**blumen-, Blumen-:** **~beet das** flower-bed; **~erde die** potting compost; **~geschäft das** florist's; **~geschmückt** *Adj.* flower-bedecked; adorned with flowers *postpos.;* **~kasten der** flower-box; *(vor einem Fenster)* window box; **~kohl** der cauliflower; **~strauß der** bunch of flowers; *(Bukett)* bouquet of flowers; **~topf der** flowerpot; **~vase die** [flower] vase; **~zwiebel die** bulb

**Bluse die;** ~, ~n blouse

**Blut das;** ~[e]s blood

**blut-, Blut-:** **~arm** *Adj. (Med.)* anaemic; **~armut die** *(Med.)* anaemia; **~bad das** blood-bath; **~bahn die** bloodstream; **~befleckt** *Adj.* bloodstained; **~beschmiert** *Adj.* smeared with blood *postpos.;* **~buche die** copper beech; **~druck der** blood pressure

**Blüte die;** ~, ~n **a)** flower; bloom; *(eines Baums)* blossom; **~n treiben** flower; ⟨*tree*⟩ blossom; **b)** *(das Blühen)* flowering; *(Baum~)* blossoming

**Blut·egel** der leech; **bluten** *itr. V.* bleed **(aus** from)

**blüten-, Blüten-:** **~blatt das** petal;

**~honig** der blossom honey; **~staub** der pollen; **~weiß** *Adj.* sparkling white

**Bluter** der; ~s, ~ *(Med.)* haemophiliac

**Blut-:** **~erguß** der haematoma; *(blauer Fleck)* bruise; **~fleck[en]** der blood-stain; **~gefäß das** *(Anat.)* blood-vessel; **~gerinnsel das** blood-clot; **~gruppe die** blood group; **~hochdruck der** high blood pressure; **~hund der** bloodhound

**blutig a)** bloody; **jmdn. ~ schlagen** beat sb. to a pulp; **b)** *(fig. ugs.: völlig)* complete ⟨*beginner, layman, etc.*⟩

**blut-, Blut-:** **~jung** *Adj.* very young; **~konserve die** container of stored blood; **~konserven** stored blood; **~körperchen das** blood corpuscle; **rote/weiße ~körperchen** red/white corpuscles; **~krebs der** leukaemia; **~kreislauf der** blood circulation; **~lache die** pool of blood; **~leer** *Adj.* bloodless; **~leere die** restricted blood supply; **~orange die** blood orange; **~probe die a)** *(~entnahme, ~untersuchung)* blood test; **b)** *(kleine ~menge)* blood sample; **~rache die** blood revenge; **~rot** *Adj.* blood-red; **~rünstig 1.** *Adj.* bloodthirsty; **2.** *adv.* bloodthirstily; **~schande die** incest; **~spende die** *(das Spenden)* giving no indef. art. of blood; *(~menge)* blood-donation; **~spender der** blood-donor; **~spur die** trail of blood; **~stillend** *Adj.* styptic

**bluts-, Bluts-:** **~tropfen der** drop of blood; **~verwandt** *Adj.* related by blood *postpos.;* **~verwandtschaft die** blood relationship

**Blut-:** **~tat die** *(geh.)* bloody deed; **~transfusion die** blood-transfusion

**Blutung die;** ~, ~en **a)** bleeding *no indef. art., no pl.;* **b)** *(Regel~)* period

**blut-, Blut-:** **~unterlaufen** *Adj.* suffused with blood *postpos.;* bloodshot ⟨*eyes*⟩; **~vergießen das;** ~s bloodshed; **~vergiftung die** blood-poisoning *no indef. art., no pl.;* **~wurst die** black pudding

**Bö die;** ~, ~en gust [of wind]

**Bob der;** ~, ~s bob[-sleigh]

**Bob-:** **~bahn die** bob[-sleigh] run; **~fahrer der** bobber

¹**Bock der;** ~[e]s, Böcke **a)** *(Reh~, Kaninchen~)* buck; *(Ziegen~)* billy-goat; he-goat; *(Schafs~)* ram; **b)** *(Gestell)* trestle; **c)** *(Turngerät)* buck

²**Bock das;** ~s *(Bier)* bock [beer]; **Bock·bier das** bock [beer]

**bocken** *itr. V.* refuse to go on; *(vor einer Hürde)* refuse; *(sich aufbäumen)* buck; **bockig 1.** *Adj.* stubborn and awkward; *(coll.).* **2.** *adv.* stubbornly [and awkwardly]; **Bocks·horn das:** sich ins ~horn jagen lassen *(ugs.)* let oneself be browbeaten

**Bock-:** ~**springen das** *(Turnen)* vaulting [over the buck]; ~**wurst die** bockwurst

**Boden der;** ~**s, Böden a)** *(Erd~)* ground; *(Fuß~)* floor; **am ~ zerstört |sein|** *(ugs.)* [be] shattered *(coll.);* bleiben wir doch auf dem ~ der Tatsachen *(fig.)* let's stick to the facts; **b)** *(unterste Fläche)* bottom; *(Torten~)* base; **c)** *(Dach~, Heu~)* loft

**boden-, Boden-:** ~**belag der** floor-covering; ~**frost der** ground frost; ~**kammer die** attic; ~**los** *Adj.* **a)** bottomless; **b)** *(ugs.: unerhört)* incredible *(foolishness, meanness, etc.);* ~**nebel der** ground fog/mist; ~**satz der** sediment; ~**schätze** *Pl.* mineral resources

**Boden·see der;** *o. Pl.* Lake Constance

**boden-, Boden-:** ~**ständig** *Adj.* indigenous *(culture, population, etc.);* ~**turnen das** floor exercises *pl.;* ~**welle die** bump

**Bodybuilding** [bɔdibɪldɪŋ] **das;** ~s body-building *no art.*

**Böe die;** ~, ~**n** *s.* Bö

**bog** *1. u. 3. Pers. Sg. Prät. v.* biegen

**Bogen der;** ~**s, ~,** *(südd., österr.:)* **Bögen a)** curve; *(Math.)* arc; **b)** *(Archit.)* arch; **c)** *(Waffe, Musik: Geigen~ usw.)* bow; **d)** *(Papier~)* sheet

**bogen-, Bogen-:** ~**fenster das** arched window; ~**förmig** *Adj.* arched; ~**schießen das** archery *no art.*

**Boheme** [boˈeːm] **die;** ~: bohemian society; **Bohemien** [boeˈmjɛ̃ː] **der;** ~**s, ~s** bohemian

**Bohle die;** ~, ~**n** [thick] plank

**Böhnchen das;** ~**s, ~:** [small] bean; **Bohne die;** ~, ~**n** bean; **nicht die ~** *(ugs.)* not one little bit

**Bohnen-:** ~**eintopf der** bean stew; ~**kaffee der** real coffee; ~**kraut das** savory; ~**stange die** *(auch ugs.: Mensch)* beanpole; ~**stroh das:** dumm wie ~stroh *(ugs.)* as thick as two short planks *(coll.);* ~**suppe die** bean soup

**bohnern** *tr., itr. V.* polish; **Bohnerwachs das** floor-polish

**bohren 1.** *tr. V.* **a)** bore; *(mit Bohrer, Bohrmaschine)* drill, bore 〈*hole*〉; sink 〈*well, shaft, pole, post etc.*〉 (in + Akk. into); **b)** *(bearbeiten)* drill 〈*wood, concrete, etc.*〉; **c)** *(drücken in)* poke (in + Akk. in[to]); **2.** *itr. V.* **a)** drill; in der Nase ~: pick one's nose; **nach Öl/ Wasser usw. ~:** drill for oil/water *etc.;* **b)** *(ugs.: drängen, fragen)* keep on; **3.** *refl. V.* bore its way; **bohrend** *Adj.* **a)** gnawing 〈*pain, hunger, remorse*〉; **b)** *(hartnäckig)* piercing 〈*look etc.*〉; probing 〈*question*〉; **Bohrer der;** ~**s, ~** drill; **Bohr·turm der** derrick; **Bohrung die;** ~, ~**en** drill-hole

**böig** *Adj.* gusty

**Boiler** [ˈbɔylɐ] **der;** ~**s, ~:** water-heater

**Boje die;** ~, ~**n** buoy

**Bolivien** [boˈliːviən] **(das);** ~s Bolivia

**Böller·schuß der** gun salute

**Boll·werk das** bulwark; *(fig.)* bulwark; bastion; stronghold

**Bolschewik der;** ~**en, ~i,** *(abwertend:)* ~**en** Bolshevik; **Bolschewismus der;** ~: Bolshevism *no art.;* **Bolschewist der;** ~**en, ~en** Bolshevist; **bolschewistisch** *Adj.* Bolshevik

**bolzen** *(ugs.)* *itr. V.* kick the ball about

**Bolzen der;** ~**s, ~** bolt

**bombardieren** *tr. V.* **a)** bomb; **b)** *(fig. ugs.)* bombard; **Bombardierung die;** ~, ~**en a)** *(Milit.)* bombing; **b)** *(fig. ugs.)* bombardment

**bombastisch 1.** *Adj.* bombastic; **2.** *adv.* bombastically

**Bombe die;** ~, ~**n** bomb

**Bomben-:** ~**angriff der** bomb attack; ~**anschlag der** bomb attack; ~**drohung die** bomb threat; ~**erfolg der** *(ugs.)* smash hit *(sl.);* ~**form die** *(ugs.)* top form

**Bomber der;** ~**s, ~:** bomber

**Bon** [bɔŋ] **der;** ~**s, ~s a)** voucher; coupon; **b)** *(Kassenzettel)* receipt

**Bonbon** [bɔŋˈbɔŋ] **der od. (österr. nur) das;** ~**s, ~s** sweet *(Brit.);* candy *(Amer.);* *(fig.)* treat

**bongen** *tr. V. (ugs.)* ring up

**Bongo das;** ~**|s|, ~s od. die;** ~, ~**s** bongo [drum]

**Bonmot** [bõˈmoː] **das;** ~**s, ~s** bon mot

**Bonze der;** ~**n, ~n** bigwig *(coll.)*

**Boom** [buːm] **der;** ~**s, ~s** boom

**Boot das;** ~**|e|s, ~e** boat

**Boots-:** ~**fahrt die** boat trip; ~**haus das** boathouse; ~**steg der** landing-stage; ~**verleih der** boat-hire

¹**Bord das;** ~**|e|s, ~e** shelf

²**Bord der;** ~**|e|s, ~e** *(eines Schiffes)*

side; **an** ~: on board; **über** ~: over-
board

**Bordell** das; ~s, ~e brothel

**Bord·stein** der kerb

**Bordüre** die; ~, ~n edging

**borgen** tr. V.: s. **leihen**

**Borke** die; ~, ~n bark

**borniert** 1. Adj. bigoted; 2. adv. in a
bigoted way

**Börse** die; ~, ~n stock market; (Gebäude) stock exchange

**Börsen-**: ~**krach** der stock-market
crash; ~**makler** der stockbroker

**Borste** die; ~, ~n bristle; **borstig**
Adj. bristly

**Borte** die; ~, ~n braiding no indef.
art.; edging no indef. art.

**bös** s. **böse**; **bös·artig** 1. Adj. a)
malicious ⟨person, remark, etc.⟩; vicious ⟨animal⟩; b) (Med.) malignant;
2. adv. maliciously; **Bös·artigkeit**
die a) maliciousness; (von Tieren) vi-
ciousness; b) (Med.) malignancy

**Böschung** die; ~, ~en embankment

**böse** 1. Adj. a) wicked; evil; b) (übel)
bad ⟨times, illness, dream, etc.⟩; nasty
⟨experience, affair, situation, trick, surprise, etc.⟩; c) (ugs.) (wütend) mad
(coll.); (verärgert) cross (coll.); d)
(fam.: ungezogen) naughty; f) (ugs.:
arg) terrible (coll.) ⟨pain, fall, shock,
disappointment, storm, etc.⟩; 2. adv. a)
(übel) ⟨end⟩ badly; **es war doch nicht** ~
**gemeint** I didn't mean it nastily; b)
(ugs.) (wütend) angrily; (verärgert)
crossly (coll.); c) (ugs.: sehr) terribly
(coll.); **boshaft** 1. Adj. malicious; 2.
adv. maliciously; **Boshaftigkeit**
die; ~, ~en a) o. Pl. maliciousness; b)
(Bemerkung) malicious remark; **Bosheit** die; ~, ~en a) o. Pl. malice; b)
(Bemerkung) malicious remark

**Boß** der; Bosses, Bosse (ugs.) boss
(coll.)

**bös·willig** 1. Adj. malicious; wilful
⟨desertion⟩; 2. adv. maliciously; wilfully ⟨desert⟩; **Bös·willigkeit** die;
~: malice; maliciousness

**bot** 1. u. 3. Pers. Sg. Prät. v. **bieten**

**Botanik** die; ~ botany no art.; **botanisch** 1. Adj. botanical; 2. adv.
botanically

**Bötchen** das; ~s, ~ little boat

**Bote** der; ~n, ~n a) messenger; b)
(Laufbursche) errand-boy; **Botschaft** die; ~, ~en a) message; b) (diplomatische Vertretung) embassy;
**Botschafter** der; ~s, ~: ambassador

**Böttcher** der; ~s, ~: cooper

**Bottich** der; ~s, ~e tub

**Bouillon** [bul'jɔŋ] die; ~, ~s bouillon

**Boulevard** [bulə'va:ɐ̯] der; ~s, ~s
boulevard

**Bourgeoisie** [bʊrʒoa'zi:] die; ~, ~n
bourgeoisie

**Boutique** [bu'ti:k] die; ~, ~s od. ~n
boutique

**Bowle** ['bo:lə] die; ~, ~n punch (made
of wine, champagne, sugar, and fruit or
spices)

**bowlen** ['boʊlən] itr. V. bowl; **Bowling** ['boʊlɪŋ] das; ~s, ~s [ten-pin]
bowling; **Bowling·bahn** die bowling-alley

**Box** die; ~, ~en a) box; b) (Lautsprecher) speaker; c) (Pferde-) [loose] box;
d) (Motorsport) pit

**boxen** 1. itr. V. box; **gegen jmdn.** ~:
fight sb.; box [against] sb.; 2. tr. V.
punch; **Boxer** der; ~s, ~ (Sportler,
Hund) boxer

**Box-**: ~**handschuh** der boxing
glove; ~**kampf** der boxing match;
(im Streit) fist-fight; ~**ring** der boxing
ring; ~**sport** der; o. Pl. boxing no art.

**Boy** [bɔy] der; ~s, ~s servant; (im Hotel) page-boy

**Boykott** [bɔy'kɔt] der; ~|e|s, ~s boy-
cott; **boykottieren** tr. V. boycott

¹**brach** 1. u. 3. Pers. Sg. Prät. v. **brechen**

²**brach** Adj. fallow; (auf Dauer) uncul-
tivated

**Brachial·gewalt** die; o. Pl. brute
force

**Brach·land** das fallow [land]; (auf
Dauer) uncultivated land; **brach|lie-
gen** unr. itr. V. (auch fig.) lie fallow;
(auf Dauer) lie waste

**brachte** 1. u. 3. Pers. Sg. Prät. v. **bringen**

**Branche** ['brã:ʃə] die; ~, ~n [branch
of] industry

**Brand** der; ~|e|s, Brände fire; **beim** ~
**der Scheune** when the barn caught
fire; **etw. in** ~ **stecken** set fire to sth.

**branden** itr. V. (geh.) break

**Branden·burg** (das); ~s Branden-
burg

**brand-, Brand-**: ~**marken** tr. V.
brand ⟨person⟩; denounce ⟨thing⟩;
~**neu** Adj. (ugs.) brand-new; ~**salbe**
die ointment for burns; ~**schaden**
der fire damage no pl., no indef. art.;
~**stelle** die burn; ~**stifter** der arsonist; ~**stiftung** die arson

**Brandung** die; ~, ~en surf

**Brand·wunde** die burn
**brannte** *1. u. 3. Pers. Sg. Prät. v.* **brennen**
**Brannt·wein** der spirits *pl.; (Sorte)* spirit
**Brasilianer** der; ~s, ~, Brazilian; **brasilianisch** *Adj.* Brazilian; **Brasilien** [bra'zi:liən] (das); ~s Brazil
**brät** *3. Pers. Sg. Präsens v.* **braten**; **Brat·apfel** der baked apple; **braten** *unr. tr., itr. V.* fry; *(im Backofen)* roast; **Braten** der; ~s, ~ a) joint; b) *o. Pl.* roast [meat] *no indef. art.*
**Braten-:** ~**saft** der meat juice[s *pl.*]; ~**soße** die gravy
**Brat-:** ~**fett** das *[cooking]* fat; ~**fisch** der fried fish; ~**hähnchen** das, *(südd., österr.)* ~**hendl** das roast chicken; *(gegrillt)* broiled chicken; ~**hering** der fried herring; ~**kartoffeln** *Pl.* fried potatoes; home fries *(Amer.);* ~**pfanne** die frying-pan; ~**spieß** der spit; ~**wurst** die *[fried/ grilled]* sausage
**Brauch** der; ~[e]s, Bräuche custom
**brauchbar** *Adj.* useful; *(benutzbar)* usable; wearable ⟨*clothes*⟩; **brauchen** *1. tr. V.* a) *(benötigen)* need; b) *(aufwenden müssen)* mit dem Auto braucht er zehn Minuten it takes him ten minutes by car; wie lange brauchst du dafür? how long will it take you?; *(im allgemeinen)* how long does it take you?; c) *(benutzen, gebrauchen)* use; ich könnte es gut ~: I could do with it; *2. mod. V.; 2. Part ~:* need; du brauchst nicht zu helfen there is no need [for you] to help; du brauchst doch nicht gleich zu weinen there's no need to start crying
**Brauchtum** ['brauxtu:m] das; ~s, Brauchtümer custom
**Braue** die; ~, ~n [eye]brow
**brauen** *tr. V.* brew; **Brauerei** die; ~, ~en brewery
**braun** *Adj.* brown; ~ werden *(sonnengebräunt)* get a tan; **Braun** das; ~s, ~, *(ugs.)* ~s brown; **Braun·bär** der brown bear; **Bräune** die; ~: [sun]tan; **bräunen** *tr. V.* a) tan; sich ~: get a tan; b) *(Kochk.)* brown; **braun·gebrannt** *Adj.* [sun-]tanned; **Braunkohle** die brown coal; lignite; **bräunlich** *Adj.* brownish; **Bräunung** die; ~, ~en browning
**Braus** *s.* **Saus**
**Brause** die; ~, ~n a) fizzy drink; *(~pulver)* sherbet; b) *(veralt.: Dusche)* shower; **brausen** *1. itr. V.* a) ⟨*wind,*

*water, etc.*⟩ roar; b) *(sich schnell bewegen)* race; c) *auch refl.: s.* **duschen 1; 2. tr. V. s.** **duschen 2**
**Brause-:** ~**pulver** das sherbet; ~**tablette** die effervescent tablet
**Braut** die; ~, Bräute bride
**Bräutigam** der; ~s, ~e [bride]groom
**Braut-:** ~**jungfer** die bridesmaid; ~**kleid** das wedding dress; ~**paar** das bride and groom
**brav** *1. Adj.* a) *(artig)* good; b) *(redlich)* honest; *2. adv.* nun iß schön ~ deine Suppe be a good boy/girl and eat up your soup
**bravo** ['bra:vo] *Interj.* bravo; **Bravo** das; ~s, ~s cheer; **Bravo·ruf** der cheer
**BRD** [be:|ɛr'de:] die; ~ *Abk.* Bundesrepublik Deutschland FRG
**Brech-:** ~**bohne** die green bean; ~**eisen** das crowbar
**brechen** *1. unr. tr. V.* a) break; sich *(Dat.)* den Arm/das Genick ~: break one's arm/neck; b) *(ablenken)* break ⟨*waves*⟩; refract ⟨*light*⟩; c) *(bezwingen)* overcome ⟨*resistance*⟩; break ⟨*will, silence, record, blockade, etc.*⟩; d) *(nicht einhalten)* break ⟨*agreement, contract, promise, the law, etc.*⟩; e) *(ugs.: erbrechen)* bring up. *2. unr. itr. V.* a) *mit sein* break; brechend voll sein be full to bursting; b) mit jmdm. ~: break with sb.; c) *mit sein durch etw.* ~: break through sth.; d) *(ugs.: sich erbrechen)* throw up. *3. unr. refl. V.* ⟨*waves etc.*⟩ break; ⟨*rays etc.*⟩ be refracted; **Brecher** der; ~s, ~: breaker
**Brech-:** ~**mittel** das emetic; ~**reiz** der nausea; ~**stange** die crowbar
**Brei** der; ~[e]s, ~e *(Hafer~)* porridge *(Brit.)*, oatmeal *(Amer.) no indef. art.* *(Reis~)* rice pudding; *(Grieß~)* semolina *no indef. art.;* **breiig** *Adj.* mushy
**breit** *1. Adj.* a) wide; broad, wide ⟨*hips, face, shoulders, forehead, etc.*⟩; etw. ~er machen widen sth.; die Beine ~ machen open one's legs; ein 5 cm ~er Saum a hem 5 cm wide; b) *(groß)* die ~e Masse the general public; *2. adv.* ~ gebaut sturdily built; **breit·beinig** *1. Adj.* rolling ⟨*gait*⟩; *2. adv.* with one's legs apart; **Breite** die; ~, ~n a) *s.* **breit 1 a:** width; breadth; b) *(Geogr.)* latitude; **breiten** *(geh.) tr., refl. V.* spread
**Breiten-:** ~**grad** der degree of latitude; parallel *(~kreis);* ~**kreis** der parallel

**breit-, Breit-:** ~|**machen** refl. V. (ugs.) **a)** take up room; **b)** (sich ausbreiten) be spreading; ~**schult[e]-rig** Adj. broad-shouldered; ~**seite** die long side; (eines Schiffes) side; ~|**treten** unr. tr. V. (ugs. abwertend) go on about; ~**wand** die (Kino) big screen

**Brems-:** ~**backe** die brake-shoe; ~**belag** der brake lining

¹**Bremse** die; ~, ~n brake

²**Bremse** die; ~, ~n (Insekt) horse-fly

**bremsen** tr. V. **a)** auch itr. brake; **b)** (fig.) slow down ⟨rate, development, production, etc.⟩; restrict ⟨imports etc.⟩

**Brems-:** ~**klotz** der brake pad; ~**licht** das; Pl. ~**lichter** brake-light; ~**pedal** das brake-pedal; ~**spur** die skid-mark; ~**weg** der braking distance

**brenn·bar** Adj. combustible; **brennen 1.** unr. itr. V. **a)** burn; ⟨house etc.⟩ be on fire; **schnell/leicht** ~: catch fire quickly/easily; **es brennt!** fire!; **b)** (glühen) be alight; **c)** (leuchten) be on; **das Licht** ~ **lassen** leave the light on; **d) die Sonne brannte** the sun was burning down; **e)** (schmerzen) ⟨wound etc.⟩ sting; ⟨feet etc.⟩ be sore; **f) darauf** ~, **etw. zu tun** be dying to do sth.; **2.** unr. tr. V. **a)** burn ⟨hole, pattern, etc.⟩; **einem Tier ein Zeichen ins Fell** ~: brand an animal; **b)** (mit Hitze behandeln) fire ⟨porcelain etc.⟩; distil ⟨spirits⟩; **c)** (rösten) roast ⟨coffee-beans, almonds, etc.⟩; **brennend 1.** Adj. (auch fig.) burning; lighted ⟨cigarette⟩; urgent ⟨topic⟩; **2.** adv. **es interessiert mich** ~, **ob** ...: I'm dying to know whether ...; **Brennessel** die; ~, ~n stinging nettle

**Brenn-:** ~**glas** das burning-glass; ~**holz** das; o. Pl. firewood; ~**material** das fuel; ~**nessel** die s. Brennessel; ~**punkt** der focus; ~**spiritus der** methylated spirits; ~**stoff** der fuel

**brenzlig** Adj. **a)** ⟨smell, taste, etc.⟩ of burning not pred.; **b)** (ugs.: gefährlich) dicey (sl.)

**Bresche** die; ~, ~n gap; breach; |für jmdn.| **in die** ~ **springen** stand in [for sb.]

**Brett** das; ~[e]s, ~er **a)** board; (lang und dick) plank; (Diele) floorboard; **Schwarzes** ~: notice-board; **ein** ~ **vor dem Kopf haben** (fig. ugs.) be thick; **b)** Pl. (Ski) skis

**Bretter-:** ~**wand** die wooden partition; ~**zaun** der wooden fence

**Brett·spiel das** board game

**Brezel** die; ~, ~n pretzel

**Bridge** [brɪtʃ] das; ~: bridge

**Brief** der; ~[e]s, ~e letter

**Brief-:** ~**beschwerer** der; ~s, ~: paperweight; ~**block** der; Pl. ~**blocks** writing-pad; ~**bogen** der sheet of writing-paper; ~**freund** der pen-friend; pen-pal (coll.); ~**geheimnis das** privacy of the post; ~**karte** die correspondence card; ~**kasten** der **a)** post-box; **b)** (privat) letter-box; ~**kopf** der **a)** letter-heading; **b)** (aufgedruckt) letter-head; ~**kuvert** das (veralt.) s. ~umschlag

**brieflich 1.** Adj. written; **2.** adv. by letter; **Brief·marke** die [postage] stamp

**Briefmarken-:** ~**album** das stamp-album; ~**sammler** der stamp-collector; ~**sammlung** die stamp-collection

**Brief-:** ~**öffner** der letter-opener; ~**papier** das writing-paper; ~**partner** der, ~**partnerin** die pen-friend; ~**schreiber** der [letter-]writer; ~**tasche** die wallet; ~**taube** die carrier pigeon; ~**träger** der postman; letter-carrier (Amer.); ~**trägerin** die postwoman; [female] letter-carrier (Amer.); ~**um·schlag** der envelope; ~**waage** die letter-scales pl.; ~**wahl** die postal vote; ~**wechsel** der correspondence

**Bries** das; ~es, ~e (Kochk.) sweetbreads pl.

**briet** 1. u. 3. Pers. Sg. Prät. v. **braten**

**Brigade** die; ~, ~n (Milit.) brigade

**Brikett** das; ~s, ~s briquette

**brillant** [brɪl'jant] **1.** Adj. brilliant. **2.** adv. brilliantly; **Brillant** der; ~en, ~en brilliant

**Brillant-:** ~**ring** der (brilliant-cut) diamond ring; ~**schmuck** der; o. Pl. (brilliant-cut) diamond jewellery

**Brillanz** [brɪl'jants] die; ~ brilliance

**Brille** die; ~, ~n **a)** glasses pl.; spectacles pl.; **eine** ~ a pair of glasses or spectacles; **eine** ~ **tragen** wear glasses or spectacles; **b)** (ugs.: Klosett~) [lavatory] seat

**Brillen-:** ~**etui** das, ~**futteral** das glasses-case; spectacle-case; ~**glas** das [spectacle-]lens; ~**schlange** die spectacled cobra; ~**träger** der person who wears glasses; ~ **sein** wear glasses

**Brimborium** das; ~s (ugs. abwertend) hoo-ha (coll.)

**bringen** *unr. tr. V.* **a)** *(her~)* bring; *(hin~)* take; **jmdm. Glück/Unglück ~:** bring sb. [good] luck/bad luck; **jmdm. eine Nachricht ~:** bring sb. news; **b)** *(begleiten)* take; **jmdn. nach Hause/ zum Bahnhof ~:** take sb. home/to the station; **c) es zu etwas/nichts ~:** get somewhere/get nowhere; **d) jmdn. ins Gefängnis ~** ⟨*crime, misdeed*⟩ land sb. in gaol; **jmdn. wieder auf den rechten Weg ~** *(fig.)* get sb. back on the straight and narrow; **jmdn. zum Lachen/zur Verzweiflung ~:** make sb. laugh/drive sb. to despair; **jmdn. dazu ~, etw. zu tun** get sb. to do sth.; **etw. hinter sich ~** *(ugs.)* get sth. over and done with; **e) jmdn. um seinen Besitz ~:** do sb. out of his property; **f)** *(präsentieren)* present; *(veröffentlichen)* publish; *(senden)* broadcast; **g) ein Opfer ~:** make a sacrifice; **h) einen großen Gewinn/hohe Zinsen ~:** make a large profit/earn high interest; **i) das bringt es mit sich, daß ...:** that means that ...; **j)** *(verursachen)* cause
**brisant** *Adj.* explosive; **Brisanz die;** **~:** explosiveness
**Brise die; ~, ~n** breeze
**Britannien (das); ~s** Britain; *(hist.)* Britannia; **Brite der; ~n, ~n** Briton; **die ~n** the British; **er ist [kein] ~:** he is [not] British; **Britin die; ~, ~nen** Briton; British girl/woman; **britisch** *Adj.* British; **die Britischen Inseln** the British Isles
**bröckelig** *Adj.* crumbly; **bröckeln** **1.** *itr. V.* **a)** crumble; **b)** *mit sein von der Wand ~:* crumble away from the wall; **2.** *tr. V.* crumble; **Brocken der; ~s, ~** *(von Brot)* hunk; *(von Fleisch)* chunk; *(von Lehm, Kohle, Erde)* lump; **ein paar ~ Englisch** *(fig.)* a smattering of English
**brodeln** *itr. V.* bubble
**Broiler** ['brɔylɐ] **der; ~s, ~** *(regional) s.* **Brathähnchen**
**Brokat der; ~[e]s, ~e** brocade
**Brokkoli** *Pl.* broccoli *sing.*
**Brom · beere die** blackberry
**Bronchie** ['brɔnçiə] **die; ~, ~n** bronchial tube; **Bronchitis die; ~,** bronchitis
**Bronze** ['brõːsə] **die; ~:** bronze; **Bronze · medaille die** bronze medal
**Brosche die; ~, ~n** brooch
**Broschüre die; ~, ~n** booklet
**Brösel der; ~s, ~:** breadcrumb; **bröselig** *Adj.* crumbly; **bröseln** *itr. V.* crumble

**Brot das; ~[e]s, ~e** bread *no pl., no indef. art.; (Laib ~)* loaf [of bread]; *(Scheibe ~)* slice [of bread]
**Brot-: ~aufstrich der** spread; **~belag der** topping; *(im zusammengeklappten Brot)* filling
**Brötchen das; ~s, ~:** roll
**Brot-: ~erwerb der** way to earn a living; **~korb der** bread-basket; **~laib der** loaf [of bread]; **~messer das** bread-knife; **~rinde die** [bread] crust; **~zeit die** *(südd.)* **a)** *(Pause)* [tea-/ coffee-/lunch-]break; **b)** *o. Pl. (Vesper)* snack; *(Vesperbrot)* sandwiches *pl.*
**Bruch der; ~[e]s, Brüche a)** break; **in die Brüche gehen** *(zerbrechen)* get broken; *(fig.)* break up; **b)** *(Med.: Knochen~)* fracture; break; **c)** *(Med.: Eingeweide~)* hernia; **d)** *(fig.) (eines Versprechens)* breaking; *(eines Abkommens, Gesetzes)* violation; **e)** *(Math.)* fraction; **brüchig** *Adj.* **a)** brittle ⟨*rock, brickwork*⟩; **b)** *(fig.)* crumbling ⟨*relationship, marriage, etc.*⟩
**Bruch-: ~landung die** crash-landing; **~rechnen das** fractions *pl.;* **~strich der** fraction line; **~stück das** fragment; **~teil der** fraction; **im ~teil einer Sekunde** in a split second
**Brücke die; ~, ~n a)** *(auch: Kommando-, Zahnmed., Bodenturnen, Ringen)* bridge; **b)** *(Landungs~)* gangway; **c)** *(Teppich)* rug
**Brücken-: ~bogen der** arch [of a/the bridge]; **~geländer das** parapet
**Bruder der; ~s, Brüder** brother; **Brüderchen das; ~s, ~:** little brother; **brüderlich 1.** *Adj.* brotherly; **2.** *adv.* in a brotherly way; **Brüderlichkeit die; ~:** brotherliness; **Brüderschaft die; ~:** [mit jmdm.] ~ trinken drink to close friendship [with sb.] *(agreeing to use the familiar 'du' form)*
**Brühe die; ~, ~n a)** stock; *(als Suppe)* clear soup; **b)** *(ugs. abwertend) (Getränk)* muck; *(verschmutztes Wasser)* filthy water; **brühen** *tr. V.* **a)** blanch; **b)** *(auf~)* brew, make ⟨*tea*⟩; make ⟨*coffee*⟩
**brüh-, Brüh-: ~warm** *Adj.* etw. ~warm weitererzählen *(ugs.)* pass sth. on straight away; **~würfel der** stock cube
**brüllen 1.** *itr. V.* **a)** ⟨*bull, cow, etc.*⟩ bellow; ⟨*lion, tiger, etc.*⟩ roar; **b)** *(ugs.) (schreien)* roar; *(weinen)* howl; **2.** *tr. V.* yell
**brummen** *tr., itr. V.* **a)** ⟨*insect*⟩ buzz; ⟨*bear*⟩ growl; ⟨*engine etc.*⟩ drone; **b)**

*(unmelodisch singen)* drone; c) *(mürrisch sprechen)* mumble; **Brummer** der; ~s, ~ *(ugs.)* a) *(Fliege)* bluebottle; b) *(Lkw)* heavy lorry *(Brit.)* or truck; **brummig** Adj. *(ugs.)* grumpy

**Brumm-**: ~**kreisel** der humming top; ~**schädel** der *(ugs.)* thick head

**brünett** Adj. dark-haired *(person)*; dark *(hair)*; **Brünette** die; ~, ~n brunette

**Brunnen** der; ~s, ~ a) well; b) *(Spring~)* fountain; **Brunnen·kresse** die watercress

**Brunst** die; ~, **Brünste** *(von männlichen Tieren)* rut; *(von weiblichen Tieren)* heat; **Brunst·zeit** die *(bei männlichen Tieren)* rutting season; *(bei weiblichen Tieren)* [season of] heat

**brüsk** 1. Adj. brusque; 2. adv. brusquely; **brüskieren** tr. V. offend; *(stärker)* insult; *(schneiden)* snub

**Brüssel** (das); ~s Brussels

**Brust** die; ~, **Brüste** a) chest; b) *(der Frau)* breast; c) *(Hähnchen~)* breast; *(Rinder~)* brisket; d) o. Pl. *(~schwimmen)* breast-stroke

**brüsten** refl. V. sich mit etw. ~: boast about sth.

**Brust-**: ~**kasten** *(ugs.)* chest; ~**korb** der *(Anat.)* thorax *(Anat.)*; ~**krebs** der breast cancer; ~**schwimmen** unr. itr. V.; nur im Inf. do [the] breast-stroke; ~**schwimmen** das breast-stroke; ~**tasche** die breast pocket

**Brüstung** die; ~, ~en parapet; *(Balkon~)* balustrade

**Brust·warze** die nipple

**Brut** die; ~, ~en a) brooding; b) *(Jungtiere, auch fig. scherzh.: Kinder)* brood

**brutal** 1. Adj. brutal; violent *(attack, programme, etc.)*; brute *(force, strength)*; 2. adv. brutally; **Brutalität** die; ~, ~en a) o. Pl. brutality; b) *(Handlung)* act of brutality

**brüten** itr. V. a) brood; b) *(grübeln)* ponder (über + Dat. over); **brütend·heiß** Adj. *(ugs.)* boiling hot; **Brüter** der; ~s, ~ *(Kernphysik)* breeder

**Brut-**: ~**kasten** der incubator; ~**stätte** die *(auch fig.)* breeding-ground

**brutto** Adv. gross

**Brutto-**: ~**einkommen** das gross income; ~**gehalt** das gross salary; ~**sozialprodukt** das *(Wirtsch.)* gross national product

**brutzeln** 1. itr. V. sizzle. 2. tr. V. *(ugs.)* fry [up]

**Bub** der; ~en, ~en *(südd., österr., schweiz.)* boy; lad; **Bube** der; ~n, ~n *(Kartenspiele)* jack; knave; **Bubi** der; ~s, ~s a) [little] boy or lad; b) *(salopp: Schnösel)* young lad

**Buch** das; ~[e]s, **Bücher** book; *(Dreh~)* script; über etw. *(Akk.)* ~ führen keep a record of sth.

**Buch-**: ~**binder** der bookbinder; ~**druck** der; o. Pl. letterpress printing

**Buche** die; ~, ~n a) beech[-tree]; b) o. Pl. *(Holz)* beech[wood]

**Buch·ecker** die beech-nut

**buchen** tr. V. a) enter; b) *(vorbestellen)* book

**Bücher·brett** das bookshelf

**Bücherei** die; ~, ~en library

**Bücher-**: ~**regal** das bookshelves pl.; ~**schrank** der bookcase; ~**wurm** der *(scherzh.)* bookworm

**Buch-**: ~**fink** der chaffinch; ~**führung** die bookkeeping; ~**halter** der bookkeeper; ~**haltung** die a) accountancy; b) *(Abteilung)* accounts department; ~**händler** der bookseller; ~**handlung** die bookshop; ~**klub** der book club; ~**laden** der bookshop; ~**messe** die book fair; ~**rücken** der spine

**Buchs·baum** ['buks-] der box[-tree]

**Buchse** ['buksə] die; ~, ~n a) *(Elektrot.)* socket; b) *(Technik)* bush

**Büchse** ['byksə] die; ~, ~n a) tin; b) *(ugs.: Sammel~)* [collecting-]box; c) *(Gewehr)* rifle; *(Schrot~)* shotgun; **Büchsen-** s. **Dosen-**

**Buchstabe** der; ~ns, ~n letter; *(Druckw.)* character; ein großer/kleiner ~: a capital [letter]/small letter; **buchstabieren** tr. V. spell; **buchstäblich** Adv. literally

**Bucht** die; ~, ~en bay

**Buchung** die; ~, ~en a) entry; b) *(Vorbestellung)* booking

**Buckel** der; ~s, ~ a) hump; einen ~ machen *(cat)* arch its back; *(person)* hunch one's shoulders; b) *(ugs.: Rücken)* back; rutsch mir den ~ runter! *(salopp)* get lost! *(sl.)*; **buckeln** itr. V. *(ugs.)* bow and scrape; vor jmdm. ~: kowtow to sb.

**bücken** refl. V. bend down

**bucklig** Adj. hunchbacked; **Bucklige** der/die; adj. Dekl. hunchback

**¹Bückling** der; ~s, ~e *(ugs. scherzh.: Verbeugung)* bow

**²Bückling** der; ~s, ~e *(Hering)* bloater

**buddeln** *itr., tr. V. (ugs.)* dig
**Buddha** ['bʊda] der; ~s, ~s Buddha;
**Buddhismus** der; ~: Buddhism *no
art.;* **Buddhist** der; ~en, ~en Buddhist; **buddhistisch** *Adj.* Buddhist
*attrib.*
**Bude** die; ~, ~n a) kiosk; *(Markt~)*
stall; *(Jahrmarkts~)* booth; b) *(Bau~)*
hut; c) *(ugs.) (Haus)* dump *(coll.);
(Zimmer)* room; digs *pl. (Brit. coll.)*
**Budget** [by'dʒe:] das; ~s, ~s budget
**Büfett** das; ~[e]s, ~s *od.* ~e a) sideboard; b) *(Schanktisch)* bar; c) *(Verkaufstisch)* counter; d) **kaltes** ~: cold
buffet
**Büffel** der; ~s, ~: buffalo
**büffeln** *(ugs.)* 1. *itr. V.* swot *(Brit. sl.);*
cram; 2. *tr. V.* swot up *(Brit. sl.);* cram
**Buffet** [by'fe:] das; ~s, ~s *s.* Büfett
**Bug** der; ~[e]s, ~e *u.* Büge bow
**Bügel** der; ~s, ~ a) *(Kleider~)* hanger;
b) *(Brillen~)* ear-piece; c) *(an einer
Tasche, Geldbörse)* frame
**bügel-, Bügel-:** ~**brett** das ironing-
board; ~**eisen** das iron; ~**falte** die
[trouser] crease; ~**frei** *Adj.* non-iron
**bügeln** *tr., itr. V.* iron
**bugsieren** [bʊ'ksi:rən] *tr. V. (ugs.)*
shift; manœuvre; steer ⟨person⟩
**buh** *Interj.* boo; **Buh** das; ~s, ~s
*(ugs.)* boo; **buhen** *itr. V. (ugs.)* boo
**buhlen** *itr. V. (geh. abwertend)* **um
jmds. Gunst** ~: court sb.'s favour
**Buh·mann** der; *Pl.* Buhmänner *(ugs.)*
whipping-boy
**Bühne** die; ~, ~n a) stage; b) *(Theater)*
theatre
**bühnen-, Bühnen-:** ~**arbeiter** der
stage-hand; ~**bildner** der; ~s, ~:
stage designer; ~**reif** *Adj.* ⟨play etc.⟩
ready for the stage; ⟨imitation etc.⟩
worthy of the stage; dramatic ⟨entrance etc.⟩
**Buh·ruf** der boo
**buk** *1. u. 3. Pers. Sg. Prät. v.* **backen**
**Bukett** das; ~s, ~s *od.* ~e *(geh.)* bouquet
**Bulette** die; ~, ~n *(bes. berl.)* rissole
**Bulgare** der; ~n, ~n Bulgarian; **Bulgarien** [bʊl'ga:riən] *(das);* ~s Bulgaria; **bulgarisch** *Adj.* Bulgarian
**Bull-:** ~**auge** das circular porthole;
~**dogge** die bulldog; ~**dozer**
[-do:zɐ] der; ~s, ~: bulldozer
**Bulle** der; ~n, ~n a) bull; b) *(salopp:
Polizist)* cop *(sl.);* **Bullen·hitze** die
*(ugs.)* sweltering *or* boiling heat
**Bulletin** [byl'tɛ̃:] das; ~s, ~s bulletin
**bullig** 1. *Adj.* a) beefy ⟨person, appear-

ance, etc.⟩; chunky ⟨car⟩; b) *(drükkend)* sweltering ⟨heat⟩; 2. *adv.* ~ **heiß**
boiling hot
**Bull·terrier** der bull-terrier
**bum** *Interj.* bang
**Bumerang** der; ~s, ~e *od.* ~s
boomerang
**Bummel** der; ~s, ~ a) stroll **(durch**
around); b) *(durch Lokale)* pub-crawl
*(coll.);* **Bummelei** die; ~, ~en *(ugs.)*
a) dawdling; b) *(Faulenzerei)* loafing
about; **bummelig** *(ugs.)* 1. *Adj.* a)
slow; b) *(nachlässig)* slipshod; 2. *adv.*
a) slowly; b) *(nachlässig)* in a slipshod
way; **bummeln** *itr. V.* a) **mit sein**
stroll **(durch** around); **durch die Kneipen** ~: go on a pub-crawl *(Brit. coll.);*
b) *(trödeln)* dawdle; c) *(faulenzen)*
laze about
**bums** *Interj.* bang; **Bums** der; ~es,
~e *(ugs.)* bang; *(dumpfer)* thud;
**bumsen** *itr. V. (ugs.)* a) bang; *(dumpfer)* thump; *unpers.* **es bumste ganz
furchtbar** there was a terrible bang/
thud; b) **mit sein** *(stoßen)* bang
¹**Bund** der; ~[e]s, Bünde a) *(Vereinigung)* association; *(Bündnis, Pakt)* alliance; b) *(föderativer Staat)* federation; c) *(an Röcken, Hosen)* waist-
band
²**Bund** das; ~[e]s, ~e bunch; **Bündchen** das; ~s, ~ band; **Bündel** das;
~s, ~ bundle; **bündeln** *tr. V.* bundle
up ⟨newspapers, old clothes, rags, etc.⟩;
tie ⟨banknotes etc.⟩ into bundles/a
bundle; tie ⟨flowers, radishes, carrots,
etc.⟩ into bunches/a bunch; sheave
⟨straw, hay, etc.⟩
**Bundes-** federal; *(in Namen, Titeln)*
Federal
**bundes-, Bundes-:** ~**bürger** der
*(veralt.)* West German citizen;
~**deutsch** *Adj. (veralt.)* West German; ~**land** das [federal] state;
*(österr.)* province; ~**liga** die national
division; ~**rat** der Bundesrat; ~**republik** die federal republic; **die ~republik Deutschland** The Federal Republic of Germany; ~**straße** die
federal highway; ≈ A road *(Brit.);*
~**tag** der Bundestag
**Bundestags-:** ~**abgeordnete** der/
die member of parliament; member of
the Bundestag; ~**wahl** die parliamentary *or* general election
**bundes-, Bundes-:** ~**trainer** der national team manager; ~**wehr** die
[Federal] Armed Forces *pl.;* ~**weit**
*Adj., adv.* nation-wide

**Bund-:** **~falten** *Pl.* pleats; **~hose** die knee-breeches

**bündig** 1. *Adj.* **a)** succinct; **b)** *(schlüssig)* conclusive; **2.** *adv.* **a)** succinctly; **b)** *(schlüssig)* conclusively

**Bündnis** das; **~ses**, **~se** alliance

**Bungalow** ['bʊŋgalo] der; **~s**, **~s** bungalow

**Bunker** der; **~s**, **~ a)** bunker; **b)** *(Luftschutz~)* air-raid shelter

**bunt** 1. *Adj.* **a)** colourful; *(farbig)* coloured; **~e Farben/Kleidung** bright colours/brightly coloured clothes; **b)** *(fig.)* varied ⟨*programme etc.*⟩; **2.** *adv.* **a)** colourfully; **b)** *(fig.)* **ein ~ gemischtes Programm** a varied programme

**bunt-, Bunt-:** **~bemalt** *Adj.* brightly painted; **~papier** das coloured paper; **~specht** der spotted woodpecker; **~stift** der coloured pencil/crayon

**Bürde** die; **~**, **~n** *(geh.)* weight; load

**Burg** die; **~**, **~en a)** castle; **b)** *(Strand~)* wall of sand

**Bürge** der; **~n**, **~n** guarantor; **bürgen** *itr. V.* **a) für jmdn./etw. ~:** vouch for sb./sth.; **b)** *(fig.)* guarantee

**Bürger** der; **~s**, **~**, **Bürgerin** die; **~**, **~nen** citizen

**Bürger-:** **~initiative** die citizens' action group; **~krieg** der civil war

**bürgerlich** *Adj.* **a)** nicht präd. *(staats~)* civil ⟨*rights, marriage, etc.*⟩; civic ⟨*duties*⟩; **b)** *(dem Bürgertum zugehörig)* middle-class; **die ~e Küche** good plain cooking; **c)** *(Polit.)* non-socialist; *(nicht marxistisch)* non-Marxist

**bürger-, Bürger-:** **~meister** der mayor; **~nah** *Adj.* which/who reflects the general public's interests *postpos., not pred.;* **~pflicht** die duty as a citizen; **~steig** der pavement *(Brit.);* sidewalk *(Amer.)*

**Bürgertum** ['--tu:m] das; **~s a)** middle class; **b)** *(Groß~)* bourgeoisie

**Bürgin** die; **~**, **~nen** *s.* Bürge; **Bürgschaft** die; **~**, **~en a)** guarantee; **b)** *(Betrag)* penalty

**Büro** das; **~s**, **~s** office

**Büro-:** **~angestellte** der/die office-worker; **~artikel** der item of office equipment; **~haus** das office-block; **~klammer** die paper-clip

**Bürokrat** der; **~en**, **~en** bureaucrat; **Bürokratie** die; **~**, **~n** bureaucracy; **bürokratisch** 1. *Adj.* bureaucratic; **2.** *adv.* bureaucratically

**Bürschchen** ['byrʃçən] das; **~**, **~:** little fellow; **Bursche** der; **~n**, **~n a)** boy; lad; **b)** *(abwertend: Kerl)* guy *(sl.)*

**burschikos** 1. *Adj.* **a)** sporty ⟨*look, clothes*⟩; [tom]boyish ⟨*behaviour, girl, haircut*⟩; **b)** *(ungezwungen)* casual ⟨*comment, behaviour, etc.*⟩; **2.** *adv.* **a)** [tom]boyishly; **b)** *(ungezwungen)* in a colloquial way

**Bürste** die; **~**, **~n** brush; **bürsten** *tr. V.* brush

**Bus** der; **~ses**, **~se** bus; **Bus·bahnhof** der bus station

**Busch** der; **~[e]s**, **Büsche** bush; **auf den ~ klopfen** *(fig. ugs.)* sound things out

**Büschel** das; **~s**, **~:** tuft; *(von Heu, Stroh)* handful

**Busen** der; **~s**, **~** bust

**Bus-:** **~fahrer** der bus-driver; **~haltestelle** die bus-stop; **~linie** die bus-route

**Bussard** der; **~s**, **~e** buzzard

**Buße** die; **~**, **~n** *(Rel.)* penance *no art.;* **büßen** 1. *tr. V.* **a)** atone for; **b)** *(fig.)* pay for; **2.** *itr. V.* **a) für etw. ~:** atone for sth.; **b)** *(fig.)* pay; **Buß·geld** das *(Rechtsw.)* fine

**Büsten·halter** der bra; brassière *(formal)*

**Butan·gas** das butane gas

**Butt** der; **~[e]s**, **~e** flounder; butt

**Bütten·papier** das handmade paper *(with deckle-edge)*

**Butter** die; **~:** butter; **es ist alles in ~** *(ugs.)* everything's fine

**butter-, Butter-:** **~blume** die *(Sumpfdotterblume)* marsh marigold; *(Hahnenfuß)* buttercup; **~brot** das slice of bread and butter; *(zugeklappt)* sandwich; **~creme** die butter-cream; **~milch** die buttermilk; **~weich** *Adj.* beautifully soft

**b.w.** *Abk.* bitte wenden p.t.o.

**bzw.** *Abk.* beziehungsweise

# C

**c, C** [tse:] das; **~**, **~: a)** *(Buchstabe)* c/C; **b)** *(Musik)* [key of] C

**ca.** *Abk.* cirka c.

**Café** das; **~s**, **~s** café

**Cafeteria** die; ~, ~s cafeteria

**cal** *Abk.* |Gramm|kalorie cal.

**Callgirl** ['kɔːlgəːl] das; ~s, ~s call-girl

**Camp** [kɛmp] das; ~s, ~s camp; **campen** *itr. V.* camp; **Camping** das; ~s camping

**Camping-:** ~**bus** der motor caravan; camper; ~**platz** der campsite; campground *(Amer.)*

**Canasta** das; ~s canasta

**Caravan** ['ka(:)ravan] der; ~s, ~s *(Wohnwagen)* caravan; trailer *(Amer.)*

**Cayenne·pfeffer** [ka'jɛn-] der cayenne [pepper]

**CD** [tseːˈdeː] die; ~, ~s CD

**CDU** [tseːdeːˈuː] die; ~ *Abk.* Christlich-Demokratische Union |Deutschlands| [German] Christian Democratic Party

**C-Dur** ['tseː-] das; ~: C major

**Cello** ['tʃɛlo] das; ~s, ~s *od.* **Celli** cello

**Celsius** *o. Art.* **20 Grad** ~: 20 degrees Celsius *or* centigrade

**Cembalo** ['tʃɛmbalo] das; ~s, ~s *od.* **Cembali** harpsichord

**Ceylon** ['tsailɔn] **(das)**; ~s *(hist.)* Ceylon *(Hist.)*

**Champagner** [ʃamˈpamjɐ] der; ~s, ~ champagne *(from Champagne)*

**Champignon** ['ʃampɪnjɔn] der; ~s, ~s mushroom

**Chance** ['ʃãːsə] die; ~, ~n a) chance; b) *Pl. (Aussichten)* prospects; |bei jmdm| ~n haben stand a chance [with sb.]

**Chaos** das; ~: chaos *no art.*

**Charakter** der; ~s, ~e [...ˈteːrə] character; **charakterisieren** *tr. V.* characterize; **charakteristisch** *Adj.* characteristic (für of); **charakterlich** 1. *Adj.* character *attrib.;* 2. *adv.* in [respect of] character; **charakter·los** *Adj.* unprincipled; *(niederträchtig)* despicable; *(labil)* spineless

**charmant** [ʃarˈmant] 1. *Adj.* charming; 2. *adv.* charmingly; **Charme** [ʃarm] der; ~s charm

**Charter-** ['tʃartɐ-]: ~**flug** der charter flight; ~**maschine** die chartered aircraft

**Chassis** [ʃaˈsiː] das; ~ [ʃaˈsiː(s)], ~ [ʃaˈsiːs] chassis

**Chauffeur** [ʃoˈføːɐ̯] der; ~s, ~e driver; *(privat angestellt)* chauffeur

**Chef** [ʃɛf] der; ~s, ~s, **Chefin** die; ~, ~nen *(Leiter[in])* head; *(der Polizei, des Generalstabs)* chief; *(einer Partei, Bande)* leader; *(Vorgesetzte[r])* superior; boss *(coll.)*

**Chef-:** ~**koch** der chef; head cook; ~**sekretärin** die director's secretary

**Chemie** die; ~ a) chemistry *no art.;* b) *(ugs.: Chemikalien)* chemicals *pl.;* **Chemiker** der; ~s, ~, **Chemikerin** die; ~, ~nen *(graduate)* chemist; **chemisch** 1. *Adj.* chemical; 2. *adv.* chemically

**Chicorée** ['ʃikore] der; ~s *od.* die; ~: chicory

**Chiffon** ['ʃɪfõ] der; ~s, ~s chiffon

**Chiffre** ['ʃɪfrə] die; ~, ~n a) *(Zeichen)* symbol; b) *(Geheimzeichen)* cipher; c) *(in Annoncen)* box number

**Chile** ['tʃiːle, 'çiːlə] **(das)**; ~s Chile; **Chilene** [tʃiˈleːnə, çiˈleːnə] der; ~n, ~n, **Chilenin** die; ~, ~nen Chilean; **chilenisch** *Adj.* Chilean

**Chili** ['tʃiːli] der; ~s, ~es a) *Pl. (Schoten)* chillies; b) *o. Pl. (Gewürz)* chilli [powder]

**China (das)**; ~s China; **Chinese** der; ~n, ~n, **Chinesin** die; ~, ~nen Chinese; **chinesisch** *Adj.* Chinese

**Chip** [tʃɪp] der; ~s, ~s a) *(Spielmarke)* chip; b) *(Kartoffel~)* [potato] crisp *(Brit.)* or *(Amer.)* chip; c) *(Elektronik)* [micro]chip

**Chirurg** der; ~en, ~en surgeon; **Chirurgie** die; ~, ~n a) *o. Pl.* surgery *no art.;* b) *(Abteilung)* surgical department; *(Station)* surgical ward; **chirurgisch** 1. *Adj.* surgical; 2. *adv.* surgically; by surgery

**Chlor** das; ~s chlorine; **Chloroform** das; ~s chloroform; **Chlorophyll** das; ~s chlorophyll

**Cholera** die; ~: cholera

**cholerisch** *Adj.* irascible; choleric ⟨temperament⟩

**Cholesterin** das; ~s cholesterol

**Chor** der; ~[e]s, **Chöre** ['køːrə] *(auch Archit.)* choir; *(in Oper, Sinfonie, Theater; Komposition)* chorus; **im** ~ **rufen** shout in chorus; **Choral** der; ~s, **Choräle** *(Kirchenlied)* chorale

**Choreographie** die; ~, ~n choreography

**Chose** ['ʃoːzə] die; ~, ~n *(ugs.)* stuff; **die ganze** ~: the whole lot *(coll.)* or *(sl.)* shoot

**Chow-Chow** [tʃau 'tʃau] der; ~s, ~s chow

**Christ** der; ~en, ~en Christian

**Christ-:** ~**baum** der *(bes. südd.)* Christmas tree; ~**demokrat** der *(Politik)* Christian Democrat

**Christenheit** die; ~ Christendom *no art.;* **Christentum** das; ~s Chris-

tianity *no art.; (Glaube)* Christian
faith

**Christin** die; ~, ~nen Christian;
**Christ·kind** das; *o. Pl.* Christ-child
*(as bringer of Christmas gifts);* **christlich 1.** *Adj.* Christian. **2.** *adv.* in a
[truly] Christian spirit

**Christ-:** ~**messe** die *(kath. Rel.)*
Christmas Mass; ~**mette** die *(kath.
Rel.)* Christmas Mass; *(ev. Rel.)* midnight service [on Christmas Eve];
~**rose** die Christmas rose; ~**stollen**
der [German] Christmas loaf *(with
candied fruit, almonds, etc.)*

**Christus (der);** ~ *od.* **Christi** Christ

**Chrom** das; ~s chromium

**Chromosom** das; ~s, ~en *(Biol.)*
chromosome

**Chronik** die; ~, ~en chronicle; **chronisch** *Adj.* chronic

**Chrysantheme** die; ~, ~n chrysanthemum

**City** ['sɪtɪ] die; ~, ~s city centre

**clever** ['klɛvɐ] **1.** *Adj. (raffiniert)*
shrewd; *(intelligent, geschickt)* clever;
**2.** *adv.: s. Adj.:* shrewdly; cleverly

**Clique** ['klɪkə] die; ~, ~n a) *(abwertend)* clique; b) *(Freundeskreis)* set;
*(größere Gruppe)* crowd *(coll.)*

**Clown** [klaun] der; ~s, ~s clown

**Club** *s.* **Klub**

**cm** *Abk.:* **Zentimeter** cm.

**Co.** *Abk.:* **Compagnie** Co.

**Cockpit** das; ~s, ~s cockpit

**Cocktail** ['kɔkteɪl] der; ~s, ~s cocktail

**Cognac** Ⓦ der; ~s, ~s Cognac

**Color-** *(Fot.)* colour *(film, slide, etc.)*

**Colt** Ⓦ der; ~s, ~s Colt **(P)** [revolver]

**Comic·heft** *das* comic

**Computer** [kom'pjuːtɐ] der; ~s, ~:
computer

**Container** [kɔn'teːnɐ] der; ~s, ~: container; *(für Müll)* [refuse] skip

**cool** [kuːl] *(ugs.)* **1.** *Adj.* cool; ~ **bleiben** keep one's cool *(sl.);* **2.** *adv.*
coolly *(coll.)*

**Cord** der; ~[e]s, ~e *od.* ~s cord;
*(~samt)* corduroy

**Corned beef** ['kɔːnd 'biːf] das; ~ ~:
corned beef

**Couch** [kautʃ] die, *(schweiz. auch:)*
der; ~, ~es sofa

**Coup** [kuː] der; ~s, ~s coup

**Coupon** [ku'põː] der; ~s, ~s coupon;
voucher

**Courage** [ku'raːʒə] die; ~ *(ugs.)* courage

**Cousin** [ku'zɛ̃ː] der; ~s, ~s, **Cousine**
die; ~, ~n cousin

**Cowboy** ['kaubɔy] der; ~s, ~s cowboy

**Credo** *s.* **Kredo**

**Creme** [kreːm] die; ~, ~s, *(schweiz.:)*
~n cream

**ČSFR** [tʃeː|ɛs|ɛf'|ɛr] die; ~ : die ~ : Cze-
choslovakia

**CSU** [tseː|ɛs'|uː] die; ~ *Abk.:* **Christ-
lich-Soziale Union** CSU

**Curry** ['kœri] das; ~s, ~s curry-powder

# D

**d, D** [deː] das; ~, ~ **a)** *(Buchstabe)*
d/D; **b)** *(Musik)* [key of] D

**D** *Abk.* **Damen**

**da 1.** *Adv.* **a)** *(dort)* there; **da draußen/
drinnen/drüben/unten** out/in/over/
down there; **da, wo where; b)** *(hier)*
here; **c)** *(zeitlich)* then; *(in dem Augenblick)* at that moment; **d)** *(deshalb)* **der
Zug war schon weg, da habe ich den
Bus genommen** the train had already
gone, so I took the bus; **e)** *(ugs.: in diesem Fall)* **da kann man nichts machen**
there's nothing one can do about it; **2.**
*Konj. (weil)* as; since

**da·bei** *Adv.* **a)** with it/him/her/them;
**nahe** ~: close by; **b)** *(währenddessen)*
at the same time; *(bei diesem Anlaß)*
then; on that occasion; **die** ~ **entste-
henden Kosten** the expense involved;
**c)** *(außerdem)* ~ |**auch**| what is more;
**d)** *(hinsichtlich dessen)* about it/them;
**was hast du dir denn** ~ **gedacht?** what
'were you thinking of

**dabei-:** ~|**bleiben** *unr. itr. V.; mit
sein* stay there; be there; ~|**haben**
*unr. tr. V.* have with one; ~|**sein** *unr.
itr. V.; mit sein (Zusschr. nur im Inf. u.
2. Part.)* **a)** *(anwesend sein)* be there;
be present (**bei** at); *(teilnehmen)* take
part (**bei** in); **b)** |**gerade**| ~**sein, etw. zu
tun** be just doing sth.; ~|**stehen** *unr.
itr. V.* stand there

**da|bleiben** *unr. itr. V.; mit sein* stay
there; *(hier bleiben)* stay here

**Dach** das; ~[e]s, **Dächer** roof

**Dach-:** ~**decker** [~dɛkɐ] der; ~s, ~:
roofer; ~**garten** der roof-garden;
~**kammer** die attic [room]; ~**luke**

**die** skylight; ~**pappe die** roofing-felt; ~**rinne die** gutter

**Dachs** [daks] der; ~es, ~e badger

**dachte** *1. u. 3. Pers. Sg. Prät. v. denken*

**Dach-:** ~**terrasse die** roof-terrace; ~**ziegel der** roof-tile

**Dackel der;** ~s, ~: dachshund

**da·durch** *Adv.* **a)** through it/them; **b)** *(durch diesen Umstand)* as a result; *(durch dieses Mittel)* by this [means]

**da·für** *Adv.* **a)** for it/them; ~, **daß** ... *(wenn man berücksichtigt, daß)* considering that ...; *(damit)* so that ...; ~ **sorgen [, daß ...]** see to it [that ...]; **b)** ~ **sein** be in favour [of it]; **ein Beispiel** ~ **ist ...:** an example of this is ...; **c)** *(als Gegenleistung)* in return [for it]; *(beim Tausch)* in exchange; *(statt dessen)* instead

**dafür|können** *unr. tr. V.* **etwas/nichts** ~: be/not be responsible

**dagegen** *Adv.* **a)** against it/them; **etwas ~ haben** have sth. against it; **ich habe nichts** ~: I've no objection; ~ **sein** be against it; **b)** *(im Vergleich dazu)* by or in comparison

**da·heim** *Adv.* **a)** *(bes. südd., österr., schweiz.)* **a)** *(zu Hause)* at home; *(nach Präp.)* home; **b)** *(in der Heimat)* [back] home

**da·her** *Adv.* **a)** from there; **b)** *(durch diesen Umstand)* hence; **c)** *(deshalb)* therefore; so

**daher|kommen** *unr. itr. V.* come along

**da·hin a)** there; **b)** *(fig.)* ~ **mußte es kommen** it had to come to that; **c)** **bis** ~: to there; *(zeitlich)* until then; **d)** ~ **sein** be or have gone; **e)** *(in diesem Sinne)* ~ **[gehend], daß ...:** to the effect that ...

**da·hinten** *Adv.* over there

**da·hinter** *Adv.* behind it/them; *(folgend)* after it/them

**Dahlie** ['da:liə] **die;** ~, ~n dahlia

**da-:** ~**lassen** *unr. tr. V. (ugs.)* leave [there]; *(hier lassen)* leave here; ~**liegen** *unr. itr. V.* lie there

**dalli** *Adv. (ugs.)* **|~| ~!** get a move on!

**damalig** *Adj.; nicht präd.* at that or the time *postpos*; **damals** *Adv.* at that time

**Damast der;** ~[e]s, ~e damask

**Dame die;** ~, ~n **a)** *(Frau)* lady; **b)** *(Schach, Kartenspiele)* queen; **c)** *o. Pl.* *(Spiel)* draughts *(Brit.)*; checkers *(Amer.)*

**Damen-:** ~**binde die** sanitary towel *(Brit.) or (Amer.)* napkin; ~**friseur der** ladies' hairdresser; ~**rad das** lady's bicycle; ~**toilette die** ladies' toilet

**da·mit 1.** *Adv.* **a)** with it/them; **b)** *(gleichzeitig)* with that; **c)** *(daher)* thus; **2.** *Konj.* so that

**dämlich** *(ugs. abwertend)* **1.** *Adj.* stupid; **2.** *adv.* stupidly

**Damm der;** ~[e]s, **Dämme** embankment; levee *(Amer.)*; *(Deich)* dike; *(Stau~)* dam

**dämmern** *itr. V.* **es dämmert** *(morgens)* it is getting light; *(abends)* it is getting dark; **Dämmerung die;** ~, ~**en a)** *(Abend~)* twilight; dusk; **b)** *(Morgen~)* dawn

**Dämon der;** ~s, ~**en** [dɛ'mo:nən] demon; **dämonisch** *Adj.* daemonic

**Dampf der;** ~[e]s, **Dämpfe** steam *no pl., no indef. art ;* **dampfen** *itr. V.* steam **(vor + Dat.** with)

**dämpfen** *tr. V.* **a)** *(garen)* steam ⟨*fish, vegetables, potatoes*⟩; **b)** *(mildern)* muffle ⟨*sound*⟩; cushion, absorb ⟨*blow, impact, shock*⟩

**Dampfer der;** ~s, ~: steamer

**Dampf-:** ~**maschine die** steam engine; ~**nudel die** *(südd., Kochk.)* steamed yeast dumpling; ~**walze die** steamroller

**da·nach** *Adv.* **a)** *(zeitlich)* after it/that; then; **b)** *(räumlich)* after it/them; **c)** *(entsprechend)* in accordance with it/them

**Däne der;** ~n, ~n Dane

**da·neben** *Adv.* **a)** beside him/her/it/them *etc.;* **b)** *(im Vergleich dazu)* in comparison

**daneben-:** ~**|benehmen** *unr. refl. V. (ugs.)* blot one's copybook *(coll.)*; ~**|gehen** *unr. itr. V.; mit sein* miss [the target]; ~**|schießen** *unr. itr. V.* miss [the target]

**Dänemark (das);** ~s Denmark; **Dänin die;** ~, ~**nen** Dane; Danish woman/girl; **dänisch** *Adj.* Danish; *s. auch* **deutsch, Deutsch**

**dank** *Präp. mit Dat. u. Gen.* thanks to; **Dank der;** ~[e]s thanks *pl.;* **mit [vielem od. bestem]** ~ **zurück** thanks for the loan; *(bes. geschrieben)* returned with thanks!; **vielen/besten/herzlichen** ~! thank you very much; **dankbar 1.** *Adj.* grateful; *(anerkennend)* appreciative ⟨*child, audience, etc.*⟩; **|jmdm.| für etw.** ~ **sein** be grateful [to sb.] for sth.; **2.** *adv.* gratefully; **Dankbarkeit die;** ~: gratitude; **danke** *Höflich-*

*keitsformel* thank you; *(ablehnend)* no, thank you; ~ **schön/sehr/vielmals** thank you very much; **danken 1.** *itr. V. (Dank aussprechen)* thank; **ich danke Ihnen vielmals** thank you very much; **na, ich danke!** *(ugs.)* no, 'thank you!; **2.** *tr. V.* |**aber bitte,**| **nichts zu ~:** don't mention it; **Danke·schön das; ~s** thank-you

**dann** *Adv.* **a)** then; **was ~?** what happens then?; **noch drei Tage, ~ ist Ostern** another three days and it will be Easter; **bis ~:** see you then; **~ und wann** now and then; **b)** *(in diesem Falle)* then; in that case; **~ will ich nicht weiter stören** in that case I won't disturb you any further; |**na,**| **~ eben nicht!** in that case, forget it!; **nur ~, wenn ...**: only if ...

**daran** [da'ran] *Adv.* **a)** *(an dieser/diese Stelle, an diesem/diesen Gegenstand)* on it/them; **dicht ~:** close to it/them; **nahe ~ sein, etw. zu tun** be on the point of doing sth.; **b)** *(hinsichtlich dieser Sache)* about it/them; **~ ist nichts zu machen** there's nothing one can do about it; **kein Wort ~ ist wahr** not a word of it is true; **mir liegt viel ~:** it means a lot to me; **c) ich wäre beinahe ~ erstickt** I almost choked on it; **er ist ~ gestorben** he died of it

**daran|setzen** *tr. V.* devote ⟨*energy etc.*⟩ to it; summon up ⟨*ambition*⟩ for it; *(aufs Spiel setzen)* risk ⟨*one's life, one's honour*⟩ for it

**darauf** *Adv.* **a)** on it/them; *(oben ~)* on top of it/them; **b) er hat ~ geschossen** he shot at it/them; **c)** *(danach)* after that; **ein Jahr ~ / kurz ~ starb er** he died a year later/shortly afterwards

**darauf-: ~folgend** *Adj.* following; **~hin** [--'-] *Adv.* **a)** thereupon; **b)** *(unter diesem Gesichtspunkt)* with a view to this/that

**daraus** *Adv.* **a)** from it/them; out of it/them; **b) mach dir nichts ~** don't worry about it; **was ist ~ geworden?** what has become of it?

**darf** *1. u. 3. Pers. Sg. Präsens v.* **dürfen**

**darfst** *2. Pers. Sg. Präsens v.* **dürfen**

**darin** *Adv.* **a)** in it/them; **b)** *(in dieser Hinsicht)* in that respect

**dar|legen** *tr. V.* explain; set forth ⟨*reasons, facts*⟩

**Darm** der; **~|e|s, Därme** intestines *pl.*; bowels *pl.*

**dar|stellen** *tr. V.* **a)** depict; portray; **etw. graphisch ~:** present sth. graphically; **b)** *(verkörpern)* play; act; **c)**

*(schildern)* describe ⟨*person, incident, etc.*⟩; present ⟨*matter, argument*⟩; **d)** *(sein, bedeuten)* represent

**Darsteller** der; **~s, ~** actor; **Darstellerin** die; **~, ~nen** actress; **Darstellung** die **a)** representation; *(Schilderung)* portrayal; *(Bild)* picture; **graphische/schematische ~:** diagram; *(Graph)* graph; **b)** *(Beschreibung, Bericht)* description; account

**darüber** *Adv.* **a)** over it/them; **b) ~ hinaus** in additon [to that]; *(noch obendrein)* what is more; **c)** *(über dieser/diese Angelegenheit)* about it/them; **d)** *(über diese Grenze, dieses Maß hinaus)* over [that]

**darüber|stehen** *unr. itr. V. (fig.)* be above such things

**darum** *Adv.* **a)** [a]round it/them; **b)** *(diesbezüglich)* **ich sorge mich ~:** I worry about it; **c)** ['--] *(deswegen)* for that reason

**darunter** *Adv.* **a)** *(unter dem Genannten/das Genannte)* under it/them; **b)** *(unter dieser Grenze, diesem Maß)* less; **Bewerber im Alter von 40 Jahren und ~:** applicants aged 40 and under

**das 1.** *best. Art. Nom. u. Akk.* the; **2.** *Demonstrativpron.* **a)** *attr.* **das Kind war es** it was 'that child'; **b)** *alleinstehend* **das** |**da**| that one; **das** |**hier**| this one [here]; **3.** *Relativpron. (Mensch)* who; that; *(Sache, Tier)* which; that

**da|sein** *unr. itr. V.; mit sein; Zusschr. nur im Inf. u. Part.* **a)** be there; *(hier sein)* be here; **noch ~** *(übrig sein)* be left; **ist Herr X da?** is Mr X about *or* available?; **ich bin gleich wieder da** I'll be right back; **b)** *(fig.)* ⟨*case*⟩ occur; ⟨*moment*⟩ have arrived; ⟨*situation*⟩ have arisen

**Da·sein** das existence

**da|sitzen** *unr. itr. V.* sit there

**dasjenige** *s.* **derjenige**

**daß** *Konj.* **a)** that; **entschuldigen Sie bitte, ~ ich mich verspätet habe** please forgive me for being late; **ich verstehe nicht, ~ sie ihn geheiratet hat** I don't understand why she married him; **b)** *(nach Pronominaladverbien o. ä.)* [the fact] that; **das liegt daran, ~ du nicht aufgepaßt hast** that comes from your not paying attention; **c)** *(im Konsekutivsatz)* that; |**so**| **~:** so that; **d)** *(im Finalsatz)* so that; **e)** *(im Ausruf)* **~ mir das passieren mußte!** why did it have to [go and] happen to me!

**dasselbe** *s.* **derselbe**

**da|stehen** *unr. itr. V.* **a)** stand there;

**b)** *(fig.)* **gut ~:** be in a good position; **|ganz| allein ~:** be [all] alone in the world

**Daten 1.** *s.* **Datum; 2.** *Pl.* data

**Daten-:** **~schutz** der data protection; **~verarbeitung die** data processing *no def. art.*

**datieren** *tr. V.* date

**Dativ** der; **~s, ~e** *(Sprachw.)* dative [case]; **Dativ·objekt das** *(Sprachw.)* indirect object

**Dattel die; ~, ~n** date; **Dattel·palme die** date-palm

**Datum das; ~s, Daten** date

**Dauer die; ~ a)** length; **für die ~ eines Jahres** *od.* **von einem Jahr** for a period of one year; **b)** *(Fortbestehen)* **von ~ sein** last [long]; **auf die ~:** in the long run; **auf ~:** permanently

**dauer-, Dauer-:** **~auftrag** der *(Bankw.)* standing order; **~haft 1.** *Adj.* **a)** [long-]lasting ⟨peace, friendship, etc.⟩; **b)** *(haltbar)* durable; **2.** *adv.* lastingly; **~karte die** season ticket; **~lauf** der jogging *no art.;* **ein ~lauf** a jog

**¹dauern** *itr. V.* last; ⟨job etc.⟩ take; **einen Moment, es dauert nicht lange** just a minute, it won't take long

**dauernd 1.** *Adj.* constant ⟨noise, interruptions, etc.⟩; permanent ⟨institution⟩; **2.** *adv.* constantly; **er kommt ~ zu spät** he keeps on arriving late

**Dauer-:** **~stellung die** permanent position; **~welle die** perm; **~wurst die** smoked sausage *(with good keeping properties, esp. salami)*

**Daumen** der; **~s, ~:** thumb

**Daune die; ~, ~n** down [feather]; **~n** down *sing.*

**davon** *Adv.* **a)** *(von dieser Stelle entfernt, weg)* from it/them; *(von dort)* from there; *(mit Entfernungsangabe)* away [from it/them]; **b)** *(hinsichtlich dieser Sache)* about it/them; **c)** *(durch diese Angelegenheit verursacht)* by it/them; **das kommt ~!** *(ugs.)* [there you are,] that's what happens; **d) ich hätte gern ein halbes Pfund ~:** I would like half a pound of that/those; **e) ~ kann man nicht leben** you can't live on that

**davon-:** **~|fahren** *unr. itr. V.; mit sein* leave; *(mit dem Auto)* drive off; *(mit dem Fahrrad, Motorrad)* ride off; **~|kommen** *unr. itr. V.; mit sein* get away; **~|laufen** *unr. itr. V.; mit sein* run away; **~|tragen** *unr. itr. V.* **a)** carry away; take away ⟨rubbish⟩; **b)** *(geh.: erringen)* gain ⟨a victory, fame⟩;

**c)** *(geh.: sich zuziehen)* receive ⟨injuries⟩

**da·vor** *Adv.* **a)** in front of it/them; **b)** *(zeitlich)* before [it/them]

**davor-:** **~|liegen** *unr. itr. V.* lie in front of it/them; **~|schieben 1.** *unr. tr. V.* push in front of it/them; **2.** *unr. refl. V.* move in front of it/them; **~|stehen** *unr. itr. V.* stand in front of it/them; **~|stellen 1.** *tr. V.* put in front of it/them; **2.** *refl. V.* plant oneself in front of it/them

**da·zu** *Adv.* **a)** *(zusätzlich zu dieser Sache)* with it/them; *(gleichzeitig)* at the same time; *(außerdem)* what is more; **b)** *(diesbezüglich)* about it/them; **c)** *(zu diesem Zweck)* for it; **d)** *(zu diesem Ergebnis)* to it; **~ reicht unser Geld nicht** we haven't enough money for that

**dazu-:** **~|geben** *unr. tr. V.* add; **~|gehören** *tr. V.* belong to it/them; **~|kommen** *unr. itr. V.; mit sein* **a)** *(hinzukommen)* arrive; **b)** *(hinzukommen)* **kommt noch etwas dazu?** is there anything else [you would like]?; **~ kommt daß ...** *(fig.)* what's more, ...; on top of that ...; **~|rechnen** *tr. V.* add on; **~|tun** *unr. tr. V. (ugs.)* add

**da·zwischen** *Adv.* in between; between them; *(darunter)* among them

**dazwischen-:** **~|kommen** *unr. itr. V.; mit sein* **a) mit dem Finger ~kommen** get one's finger caught [in it]; **b)** *(es verhindern)* prevent it; **es ist mir etwas ~gekommen** I had problems; **~|reden** *itr. V.* interrupt

**DDR** [deːdeːˈ|ɛr] die; **~** *Abk.* *(1949–1990)* Deutsche Demokratische Republik GDR; East Germany *(in popular use)*

**Debatte die; ~, ~n** debate **(über +** *Akk.* **on); zur ~ stehen** be under discussion

**Debüt** [deˈbyː] **das; ~s, ~s** debut

**Deck das; ~|e|s, ~s** deck

**Deck·bett das** *s.* **Oberbett; Decke die; ~, ~n a)** *(Tisch~)* tablecloth; **b)** *(Woll~, Pferde~, fig.)* blanket; *(Reise~)* rug; **c)** *(Zimmer~)* ceiling

**Deckel** der; **~s, ~ a)** lid; *(auf Flaschen, Gläsern usw.)* top; *(Schacht~, Uhr~, Buch~ usw.)* cover; **b)** *(Bier~)* beer-mat

**decken 1.** *tr. V.* **a) etw. über etw.** *(Akk.)* **~:** spread sth. over sth. **b)** roof ⟨house⟩; cover ⟨roof⟩; **c) den Tisch ~:** lay the table; **d)** *(schützen; Finanzw., Versicherungsw.)* cover; **e)** *(befriedigen)* meet ⟨need, demand⟩; **2.** *itr. V.*

*(den Tisch ~ )* lay the table; **Deckmantel** der; *o. Pl.* cover; **Deckung** die; ~, ~en a) *(Schutz; auch fig.)* cover *(esp. Mil.); (Boxen)* guard; *(bes. Fußball)* defence; **in ~ gehen** take cover; **b)** *(Befriedigung)* meeting; **c)** *(Finanzw., Versicherungsw.)* cover[ing]; **deckungs·gleich** *Adj. (Geom.)* congruent

**defekt** *Adj.* defective; faulty; **~ sein** have a defect; be faulty; *(nicht funktionieren)* not be working; **Defekt** der; ~[e]s, ~e defect, fault **(an +** *Dat.* **in)**

**defensiv** 1. *Adj.* defensive; 2. *adv.* defensively; **Defensive** die; ~, ~n defensive; **in der ~:** on the defensive; **die ~** *(Sport)* defensive play

**definieren** *tr. V.* define; **Definition** die; ~, ~en definition

**definitiv** 1. *Adj.* definitive; 2. *adv.* finally

**Defizit** das; ~s, ~e a) deficit; b) *(Mangel)* deficiency

**deformieren** *tr. V.* a) *(verformen)* distort; b) *(entstellen)* deform *(also fig.)*

**deftig** *Adj. (ugs.)* a) [good] solid *attrib.* ⟨meal etc.⟩; [nice] big ⟨sausage etc.⟩; b) *(derb)* crude, coarse ⟨joke, speech, etc.⟩

**Degen** der; ~s, ~ a) *(Waffe)* [light] sword; b) *(Fechtsport)* épée

**degradieren** *tr. V.* demote

**dehnbar** *Adj.* a) *(elastisch)* ⟨material etc.⟩ that stretches *not pred.*; elastic ⟨waistband etc.⟩; **Dehnbarkeit** die; ~: elasticity; **dehnen** *tr., refl. V.* stretch

**Deich** der; ~[e]s, ~e dike

**Deichsel** ['daiksl] die; ~, ~n shaft; **deichseln** *tr. V. (ugs.)* fix

**dein** *Possessivpron.* your; **viele Grüße von Deinem Emil** with best wishes, yours Emil; **das Buch dort, ist das ~[e]s?** that book over there, is it yours?; **du und die Deinen** *(geh.)* you and yours; **deiner** *Gen. des Personalpronomens* du *(geh.)* of you; **deinerseits** *Adv. (von deiner Seite)* on your part; *(auf deiner Seite)* for your part; **deinet·wegen** *Adv.* because of you; *(für dich)* on your behalf; *(dir zuliebe)* for your sake

**dekadent** *Adj.* decadent; **Dekadenz** die; ~: decadence

**deklamieren** *tr., itr. V.* recite

**Deklination** die; ~, ~en *(Sprachw.)* declension; **deklinieren** *tr. V. (Sprachw.)* decline

**Dekolleté** [dekɔl'te:] das; ~s, ~s low[-cut] neckline; décolletage

**Dekor** das; ~s, ~s *od.* ~e decoration; *(Muster)* pattern; **Dekorateur** [dekora'tø:ɐ̯] der; ~s, ~e, **Dekorateurin** die; ~, ~nen *(Schaufenster~)* window-dresser; *(von Innenräumen)* interior designer; **Dekoration** die; ~, ~en decorations *pl.; (Schaufenster~)* window display; **dekorativ** 1. *Adj.* decorative; 2. *adv.* decoratively; **dekorieren** *tr. V.* decorate ⟨room etc.⟩; dress ⟨shop-window⟩

**Deko·stoff** der furnishing fabric

**Dekret** das; ~[e]s, ~e decree

**Delegation** die; ~, ~en delegation; **delegieren** *tr. V.* a) send as a delegate/as delegates; b) delegate ⟨task etc.⟩ (an + *Akk.* to); **Delegierte** der/ die; *adj. Dekl.* delegate

**delikat** *Adj.* a) delicious; *(fein)* delicate ⟨bouquet, aroma⟩; b) *(heikel)* delicate; **Delikatesse** die; ~, ~n delicacy

**Delikt** das; ~[e]s, ~e offence

**Delinquent** der; ~en, ~en offender

**Delirium** das; ~s, **Delirien** delirium

**Delle** die; ~, ~n *(ugs.)* dent

**Delphin** der; ~s, ~e dolphin

**dem** 1. *best. Art., Dat. Sg. v.* ¹**der** 1 *u.* **das** 1 to the; *(nach Präp.)* the; 2. *Demonstrativpron., Dat. Sg. v.* ¹**der** 2 *u.* **das** 2: a) *attr.* that; **gib es dem Mann** give it to 'that man; b) *alleinstehend* **gib es nicht dem, sondern dem da!** don't give it to him, give it to that man/child *etc.*; 3. *Relativpron., Dat. Sg. v.* ¹**der** 3 *u.* **das** 3 *(Person)* that/ whom; *(Sache)* that/which; **der Mann/das Kind, dem ich das Geld gab** the man/the child I gave the money to

**Demagoge** der; ~n, ~n demagogue

**demagogisch** *Adj.* demagogic

**Dementi** das; ~s, ~s denial; **dementieren** 1. *tr. V.* deny; 2. *itr. V.* deny it

**dem-:** **~entsprechend** 1. *Adj.* appropriate; 2. *adv.* accordingly; *(vor Adjektiven)* correspondingly; **~gemäß** *Adv.* a) *(infolgedessen)* consequently; b) *(entsprechend)* accordingly; **~jenigen** *s.* derjenige; **~nach** *Adv.* therefore; **~nächst** *Adv.* shortly

**Demokrat** der; ~en, ~en democrat; *(Parteimitglied)* Democrat; **Demokratie** die; ~, ~n democracy; **demokratisch** 1. *Adj.* democratic; 2. *adv.* democratically; **demokratisieren** *tr. V.* democratize

**demolieren** *tr. V.* wreck; smash up (*furniture*)

**Demonstrant** der; ~en, ~en demonstrator; **Demonstrantin** die; ~, ~nen demonstrator; **Demonstration** die; ~, ~en demonstration (für in support of, **gegen** against); **demonstrativ** 1. *Adj.* a) pointed; b) (*Sprachw.*) demonstrative; 2. *adv.* pointedly; **Demonstrativ·pronomen** das (*Sprachw.*) demonstrative pronoun; **demonstrieren** 1. *itr. V.* demonstrate (**für** in support of, **gegen** against); 2. *tr. V.* demonstrate

**dem·selben** s. derselbe

**Demut** die; ~: humility; **demütig** 1. *Adj.* humble; 2. *adv.* humbly; **demütigen** 1. *tr. V.* humiliate; 2. *refl. V.* humble oneself; **Demütigung** die; ~, ~en humiliation

**dem·zufolge** *Adv.* consequently

¹**den** 1. *best. Art., Akk. Sg. v.* ¹**der** 1: the; 2. *Demonstrativpron., Akk. Sg. v.* ¹**der** 2: a) *attr.* that; **ich meine den Mann** I mean 'that man; b) *alleinstehend* **ich meine den [da]** I mean 'that one; 3. *Relativpron., Akk. Sg. v.* ¹**der** 3 (*Person*) that/whom; (*Sache*) that/which; **der Mann, den ich gesehen habe** the man that I saw

²**den** 1. *best. Art., Dat. Pl. v.* ¹**der** 1, ¹**die** 1, **das** 1 the; 2. *Demonstrativpron. Dat. Pl. v.* ¹**der** 2 a, ¹**die** 2 a, **das** 2 a those.

**denen** 1. *Demonstrativpron., Dat. Pl. v.* ¹**der** 2 b, ¹**die** 2 b, **das** 2 b them; **gib es ~, nicht den anderen** give it to 'them, not to the others; 2. *Relativpron., Dat. Pl. v.* ¹**der** 3, ¹**die** 3, **das** 3 (*Personen*) that/whom; (*Sachen*) that/which; **die Menschen, ~ wir Geld gegeben haben** the people to whom we gave money; **die Tiere, ~ er geholfen hat** the animals that he helped

**denjenigen** s. derjenige

**denkbar** 1. *Adj.* conceivable; 2. *adv.* (*sehr, äußerst*) extremely; **denken** 1. *unr. itr. V.* think (**an** + *Akk.* of, **über** + *Akk.* about); **wie denkst du darüber?** what do you think about it?; what's your opinion of it?; **schlecht von jmdm. ~:** think badly of sb.; **denk daran, daß .../zu ...:** don't forget that .../to ...; **ich denke nicht daran!** no way!; not on your life!; **ich denke nicht daran, das zu tun** I've no intention of doing that; 2. *unr. tr. V.* think; **wer hätte das gedacht?** who would have thought it?; **eine gedachte Linie** an imaginary line; 3. *unr. refl. V.* a)

(*sich vorstellen*) imagine; b) **sich** (*Dat.*) **bei etw. etwas ~:** mean something by sth.; **ich habe mir nichts [Böses] dabei gedacht** I didn't mean any harm [by it]; **Denken** das; ~s thinking; (*Denkweise*) thought; **Denker** der; ~s, ~: thinker

**denk-, Denk- ~faul** *Adj.* mentally lazy; **~mal** das; **~mals, ~mäler** od. **~male** monument; **~vermögen** das ability to think [creatively]; **~würdig** *Adj.* memorable; **~zettel** der lesson

**denn** 1. *Konj.* (*kausal*) for; because; b) (*geh.: als*) than; 2. *Adv.* **es sei ~, ...:** unless ...; 3. *Partikel* (*in Fragesätzen*) **wie geht es dir ~?** tell me, how are you?; **wie heißt du ~?** tell me your name; **warum ~ nicht?** why ever not?

**dennoch** *Adv.* nevertheless

**denselben** s. derselbe

**Denunziant** der; ~en, ~en informer; grass (*sl.*); **denunzieren** *tr. V.* denounce; (*bei der Polizei*) inform against; grass on (*sl.*) (**bei** to)

**Deo** das; ~s, ~s, **Deodorant** das; ~s, ~s (*auch:*) ~e deodorant

**Deponie** die; ~, ~n tip (*Brit.*); dump; **deponieren** *tr. V.* put; (*im Safe o. ä.*) deposit

**Deportation** die; ~, ~en transportation; (*ins Ausland*) deportation; **deportieren** *tr. V.* transport; (*ins Ausland*) deport; **Deportierte** der/die; *adj. Dekl.* transportee; (*ins Ausland*) deportee

**Depot** [de'po:] das; ~s, ~s a) depot; (*Lagerhaus*) warehouse; (*für Möbel usw.*) depository; (*im Freien, für Munition o. ä.*) dump; (*in einer Bank*) strong-room; safe deposit; b) (*hinterlegte Wertgegenstände*) deposits *pl.*

**Depp** der; ~en (*auch:*) ~s, ~en (*auch:*) ~e (*bes. südd., österr., schweiz. abwertend*) s. Dummkopf

**Depression** die; ~, ~en depression; **depressiv** 1. *Adj.* depressive; 2. *adv.* **~ veranlagt sein** have a tendency towards depression; **deprimieren** *tr. V.* depress; **deprimierend** *Adj.* depressing; **deprimiert** 1. *Adj.* depressed; 2. *adv.* dejectedly

¹**der** 1. *best. Art. Nom.* the; **der Tod** death; **der „Faust"** 'Faust'; **der Bodensee/Mount Everest** Lake Constance/Mount Everest; **der Iran/Sudan** Iran/the Sudan; **der Mensch/Mann ist ...:** man is .../men are ...; 2. *Demonstrativpron.* a) *attr.* that; **der Mann war es** it was 'that man; b) *al-*

*leinstehend* he; **der war es** it was 'him; **der |da|** *(Person)* that man/boy; *(Sache)* that one; **der |hier|** *(Person)* this man/boy; *(Sache)* this one; 3. *Relativpron. (Person)* who/that; *(Sache)* which/that; **der Mann, der da drüben entlanggeht** the man walking along over there; 4. *Relativ- u. Demonstrativpron.* the one who

**²der** 1. *best. Art.* a) *Gen. Sg. v.* ¹**die** 1: **der Hut der Frau** the woman's hat; **der Henkel der Tasse** the handle of the cup; b) *Dat. Sg. v.* ¹**die** 1 to the; *(nach Präp.)* the; c) *Gen. Pl. v.* ¹**der** 1, ¹**die** 1, **das** 1: **das Haus der Freunde** our/their *etc.* friends' house; **das Bellen der Hunde** the barking of the dogs; 2. *Demonstrativpron.* a) *Gen. Sg. v.* ¹**die** 2: of the; of that; b) *Dat. Sg. v.* ¹**die** 2 *attr.* **der Frau |da/hier|** gehört es it belongs to that woman there/this woman here; c) *Gen. Pl. v.* ¹**der** 2 a, ¹**die** 2 a, **das** 2 a of those; 3. *Relativpron.; Dat. Sg. v.* ¹**die** 3: **die Frau, der ich es gegeben habe** the woman I gave it to; **die Katze, der er einen Tritt gab** the cat [that] he kicked

**der·art** *Adv.* so; **es hat lange nicht mehr ~ geregnet** it hasn't rained as hard as that for a long time; **sie hat ~ geschrien, daß ...:** she screamed so much that ...; **der·artig** 1. *Adj.* such; 2. *adv. s.* derart

**derb** 1. *Adj.* a) tough ‹*material*›; stout, ‹*shoes*›; b) *(kraftvoll, deftig)* earthy ‹*scenes, humour*›; 2. *adv.* a) strongly ‹*made, woven, etc.*›; b) *(kraftvoll, deftig)* earthily

**deren** 1. *Relativpron.* a) *Gen. Sg. v.* ¹**die** 3 *(Personen)* whose; *(Sachen)* of which; b) *Gen. Pl. v.* ¹**der** 3, ¹**die** 3, **das** 3 *(Personen)* whose; *(Sachen)* **Maßnahmen, ~ Folgen wir noch nicht absehen können** measures, the consequences of which we cannot yet foresee; 2. *Demonstrativpron.* a) *Gen. Sg. v.* ¹**die** 2: **meine Tante, ihre Freundin und ~ Hund** my aunt, her friend and 'her dog; b) *Gen. Pl. v.* ¹**der** 2, ¹**die** 2, **das** 2: **meine Verwandten und ~ Kinder** my relatives and their children

**derent-:** ~**wegen** *Adv.* 1. *relativ (Personen)* because of whom; *(Sachen)* because of which; 2. *demonstrativ* because of them; ~**willen** *Adv.* um ~**willen** *(Personen)* for whose sake; *(Sachen)* for the sake of which

**derer** *Demonstrativpron.; Gen. Pl. v.* ¹**der** 2, ¹**die** 2, **das** 2 of those

**der·gleichen** *indekl. Demonstrativpron.* a) *attr.* such; like that *postpos., not pred.;* b) *alleinstehend* that sort of thing

**der·jenige, die·jenige, das·jenige** *Demonstrativpron.* a) *attr.* that; *Pl.* those; b) *alleinstehend* that one; *Pl.* those

**derlei** *indekl. Demonstrativpron.: s.* dergleichen

**der·maßen** *Adv.* ~ **schön** *usw.,* **daß ...:** so beautiful *etc.* that ...

**derselbe, dieselbe, dasselbe** *Demonstrativpron.* a) *attr.* the same; b) *alleinstehend* the same one; *Pl.* the same people; **er sagt immer dasselbe** he always says the same thing; **noch einmal dasselbe, bitte** *(ugs.)* [the] same again please

**der·zeit** *Adv.* at present; **der·zeitig** *Adj.* present; current

**des** 1. *best. Art.; Gen. Sg. v.* ¹**der** 1, **das** 1: **die Mütze des Jungen** the boy's cap; **das Klingeln des Telefons** the ringing of the telephone; 2. *Demonstrativpron.; Gen. Sg. v.* ¹**der** 2, **das** 2: **er ist der Sohn des Mannes, der ...:** he's the son of the man who ...

**Deserteur** [dezɛrˈtøːɐ̯] **der;** ~**s,** ~**e** deserter; **desertieren** *itr. V.; mit sein* desert

**des·gleichen** *Adv.* likewise; **er ist Arzt, ~ sein Sohn** he is a doctor, as is his son

**des·halb** *Adv.* for that reason; ~ **bin ich zu dir gekommen** that is why I came to you

**Des·infektion die** disinfection; **Desinfektions·mittel das** disinfectant; **des·infizieren** *tr. V.* disinfect

**Des·interesse das** lack of interest

**Despot** [dɛsˈpoːt] **der;** ~**en,** ~**en** despot; *(fig. abwertend)* tyrant; **despotisch** 1. *Adj.* despotic; 2. *adv.* despotically

**des·selben** *s.* derselbe

**dessen** 1. *Relativpron.; Gen. Sg. v.* ¹**der** 3, **das** 3 *attr. (Person)* whose; *(Sache)* of which; 2. *Demonstrativpron.; Gen. Sg. v.* ¹**der** 2, **das** 2: **mein Onkel, sein Sohn und ~ Hund** my uncle, his son, and 'his dog

**Dessert** [dɛˈseːɐ̯] **das;** ~**s,** ~**s** dessert

**destillieren** *tr. V. (Chemie)* distil

**desto** *Konj., vor Komp.* **je eher, ~ besser** the sooner the better

**des·wegen** *Adv. s.* deshalb

**Detail** [deˈtai] **das;** ~**s,** ~**s** detail; **de-**

**tailliert** 1. *Adj.* detailed; 2. *adv.* in detail; **sehr ~:** in great detail

**Detektiv** der; ~s, ~e [private] detective

**Detonation** die; ~, ~en detonation; explosion

**Deut** *in* **keinen ~:** not one bit

**deuten** 1. *itr. V.* point; |mit dem Finger| auf jmdn./etw. ~: point [one's finger] at sb./sth.; 2. *tr. V.* interpret

**deutlich** 1. *Adj.* clear; 2. *adv.* clearly; **Deutlichkeit** die; ~a) clarity; b) *(Eindeutigkeit)* clearness

**deutsch** 1. *Adj.* German; **Deutsche Mark** Deutschmark; German mark; **auf** *od.* **in ~:** in German; **auf** |gut| **~** *(ugs.)* in plain English; 2. *adv.* **~ sprechen/schreiben** speak/write German; **Deutsch** das; ~-|s| German; **gutes/ fließend ~ sprechen** speak good/fluent German; **¹Deutsche** der/die; *adj. Dekl.* German; **~|r| sein** be German; **²Deutsche** das; *adj. Dekl.* **das ~:** German; **aus dem ~n/ins ~ übersetzen** translate from/into German; **Deutschland (das)** ~s Germany

**deutsch-, Deutsch-:** **~lehrer** der German teacher; **~sprachig** *Adj.* a) German-speaking; b) German-language *attrib.*; **~unterricht** der German teaching; *(Unterrichtsstunde)* German lesson

**Deutung** die; ~, ~en interpretation

**Devise** die; ~, ~n motto; **Devisen** *Pl.* foreign currency *sing.*

**Dezember** der; ~s, ~: December

**dezent** 1. *Adj.* quiet *(colour, pattern, suit)*; subdued *(lighting, music)*; 2. *adv.* discreetly; *(dress)* unostentatiously

**dezimal** *Adj.* decimal

**Dezimal-:** **~system** das decimal system; **~zahl** die decimal [number]

**dezimieren** *tr. V.* decimate

**dgl.** *Abk.* dergleichen, desgleichen

**d. h.** *Abk.* das heißt i. e.

**Di.** *Abk.* Dienstag Tue[s].

**Dia** das; ~s, ~s slide

**Diabetiker** der; ~s, ~, **Diabetikerin,** die; ~, ~nen diabetic

**Diagnose** [dia'gno:zə] die; ~, ~n diagnosis

**diagonal** 1. *Adj.* diagonal; 2. *adv.* diagonally; **Diagonale** die; ~, ~n diagonal

**Dialekt** der; ~|e|s, ~e dialect

**Dialog** der; ~|e|s, ~e dialogue

**Diamant** der; ~en, ~en diamond

**diät** *adv.* **~ kochen** cook according to

a/one's diet; **~ essen** be on a diet; **Diät die; ~, ~en** diet; **eine ~ einhalten** keep to a diet; **Diäten** *Pl.* [parliamentary] allowance *sing.*

**dich** 1. *Akk. von* du you; 2. *Akk. des Reflexivpron. der 2. Pers. Sg.* yourself

**dicht** 1. *Adj.* a) thick; dense *(forest, hedge, crowd)*; heavy, dense *(traffic)*; b) *(undurchlässig)* *(für Luft)* airtight; *(für Wasser)* watertight; 2. *adv.* a) densely *(populated, wooded)*; b) *(undurchlässig)* tightly; c) *mit Präp. (nahe)* **~ neben** right next to

**dicht·besiedelt** *Adj.* *(präd. getrennt geschrieben)* densely populated

**Dichte** die; ~ *(Physik, fig.)* density

**dichten** 1. *itr. V.* write poetry; 2. *tr. V. (verfassen)* write; compose; **Dichter** der; ~s, ~: poet; *(Schriftsteller)* writer; author; **Dichterin** die; ~, ~nen poet[ess]; *(Schriftstellerin)* writer; author[ess]; **dichterisch** *Adj.* poetic; *(schriftstellerisch)* literary

**dicht|machen** *tr., itr. V. (ugs.)* shut; *(endgültig)* shut down

**¹Dichtung** die; ~, ~en seal; *(am Hahn usw.)* washer; *(am Vergaser, Zylinder usw.)* gasket

**²Dichtung** die; ~, ~en a) work of literature; *(in Versform)* poetic work; poem; b) *o. Pl. (Dichtkunst)* literature; *(in Versform)* poetry

**dick** 1. *Adj.* a) thick; stout *(tree)*; fat *(person, legs, etc.)*; swollen *(cheek, ankle, tonsils, etc.)*; **~ werden** get fat; **5 cm ~ sein** be 5 cm thick; b) *(ugs.: groß)* big *(mistake)*; hefty, *(coll.)* fat *(salary)*; 2. *adv.* thickly; **etw. ~ unterstreichen** underline sth. heavily; **sich ~ anziehen** wrap up warm[ly]; **etw. 5 cm ~ schneiden** cut sth. 5 cm. thick; **~ geschwollen** *(ugs.)* badly swollen; **¹Dicke** die; ~: thickness; *(von Menschen, Körperteilen)* fatness; **²Dicke** der/die; *adj. Dekl. (ugs.)* fatty *(coll.)*; **dick·fellig** *(ugs.)* *Adj.* thick-skinned; **Dickicht** ['dıkıçt] das; ~|e|s, ~e thicket

**dick-, Dick-:** **~kopf** der *(ugs.)* mule *(coll.)*; **ein ~kopf sein** be stubborn as a mule; **einen ~kopf haben** be pig-headed; **~köpfig** *Adj. (ugs.)* pig-headed; **~milch** die sour milk

**¹die** 1. *best. Art. Nom.* the; **die Helga** *(ugs.)* Helga; **die Frau/Menschheit** women *pl.*/mankind; 2. *Demonstrativpron.* a) *attr.* **die Frau war es** it was 'that woman; b) *alleinstehend* **sie; die war es** it was 'her; **die |da|** *(Person)* that woman/girl; *(Sache)* that one; **3.** *Relativpron. Nom. (Person)* who; that; *(Sache, Tier)* which; that; **4.** *Relativ-u. Demonstrativpron.* the one who

**²die 1.** *best. Art.* a) *Akk. Sg. v.* **¹die 1** the; **ich sah die Frau** I saw the women; b) *Nom. u. Akk. Pl. v.* **¹der 1, ¹die 1, das 1** the; **2.** *Demonstrativpron. Nom. u. Akk. Pl. v.* **¹der 1, ¹die 1, das 1:** *attr.* **ich meine die Männer, die** ... I mean those men who ...; *alleinstehend* **ich meine die |da|** I mean 'them; **3.** *Relativpron.* a) *Akk. Sg. v.* **¹die 3** *(Person)* who; *(Sache)* that; b) *Nom. u. Akk. Pl. v.* **¹der 3, ¹die 3, das 3** *(Personen)* whom; *(Sachen)* which; **die Männer, die ich gesehen habe** the men I saw

**Dieb** der; ~|e|s, ~e thief; **Diebin** die; ~, ~nen [woman] thief; **diebisch 1.** *Adj.* a) thieving; b) *(verstohlen)* mischievous; **2.** *adv.* mischievously; **Diebstahl** der; ~|e|s, Diebstähle theft

**die · jenige** *s.* derjenige

**Diele** die; ~, ~n hall[way]

**dienen** *itr. V.* serve; **womit kann ich ~?** what can I do for you?; **Diener** der; ~s, ~ servant; **einen ~ machen** *(ugs.)* bow; make a bow; **Dienerin** die; ~, ~nen maid; servant

**dienlich** *Adj.* helpful; **Dienst** der; ~|e|s, ~e a) *o. Pl. (Tätigkeit)* work; *(von Soldaten, Polizeibeamten, Krankenhauspersonal usw.)* duty; **seinen ~ antreten** start work/go on duty; **~ haben** be at work/on duty; *(doctor)* be on call; *(chemist)* be open; b) *(Arbeitsverhältnis)* post; **Major außer ~:** retired major; c) *o. Pl. (Tätigkeitsbereich)* service; *s. auch* **öffentlich;** d) *(Hilfe)* service

**Diens · tag** der Tuesday; **am ~:** on Tuesday; **~, der 1. Juni** Tuesday, 1 June; **er kommt ~:** he is coming on Tuesday; **ab nächsten ~:** from next Tuesday [onwards]; **~ in einer Woche** a week on Tuesday; **~ vor einer Woche** a week last Tuesday; **diens · tags** *Adv.* on Tuesday[s]

**dienst-, Dienst-:** **~bereit** *Adj.* *(chemist)* open *pred.;* *(doctor)* on call; *(dentist)* on duty; **~bote** der servant; **~eifrig** *Adj.* zealous; **~frei** *Adj.* free *(time)*; **~geheimnis** das a) professional secret; *(im Staatsdienst)* official secret; b) *o. Pl.* professional secrecy; *(im Staatsdienst)* official secrecy; **~grad** der *(Milit.)* rank; **~leistung** die *(auch Wirtsch.)* service

**dienstlich 1.** *Adj.* business *(call)*; *(im Staatsdienst)* official *(letter, call, etc.)*; **2.** *adv.* on business; *(im Staatsdienst)* on official business

**dienst-, Dienst-:** **~reise** die business trip; **~stelle** die office; **~wagen** der official car; *(Geschäftswagen)* company car; **~weg** der official channels *pl.;* **~zeit** die a) period of service; b) *(tägliche Arbeitszeit)* working hours *pl.*

**dies** *s.* dieser

**dies · bezüglich** *adv.* regarding this

**diese** *s.* dieser

**Diesel** der; ~|s|, ~: diesel

**die · selbe** *s.* derselbe

**Diesel · motor** der diesel engine

**dieser, diese, dieses, dies** *Demonstrativpron.* a) *attr.* this; *Pl.* these; b) *alleinstehend* this one; *Pl.* these; **dies alles** all this; **dies und das,** *(geh.)* **dieses und jenes** this and that

**diesig** *Adj.* hazy

**dies-:** **~mal** *Adv.* this time; **~seits 1.** *Präp. mit Gen.* on this side of; **2.** *Adv.* **~seits von** on this side of

**Dietrich** der; ~s, ~e picklock

**diffamieren** *tr. V.* defame; **Diffamierung** die; ~, ~en defamation

**Differenz** die; ~, ~en difference; *(Meinungsverschiedenheit)* difference [of opinion]; **differenziert** *Adj.* complex; subtly differentiated *(methods, colours)*; sophisticated *(taste)*

**diffus** *Adj. (Physik, Chemie)* diffuse; b) *(geh.)* vague; vague and confused *(idea, statement, etc.)*; **2.** *adv.* in a vague and confused way

**Digital-** digital *(clock, display, etc.)*

**digitalisieren** *tr. V. (DV)* digitalize

**Diktat** das; ~|e|s, ~e dictation

**Diktator** der; ~s, ~en dictator; **diktatorisch 1.** *Adj.* dictatorial; **2.** *adv.* dictatorially; **Diktatur** die; ~, ~en dictatorship

**diktieren** *tr. V.* dictate

**Diktier · gerät das** dictating machine

**Dilemma** das; ~s, ~s dilemma

**Dilettant** [dilɛ'tant] der; ~en, ~en, Dilettantin die; ~, ~nen dilettante; **dilettantisch 1.** *Adj.* dilettante; amateurish; **2.** *adv.* amateurishly

**Dill** der; ~|e|s, ~e dill

**Dimension** die; ~, ~en *(Physik, fig.)* dimension

**DIN** [di:n] *Abk.* **Deutsche Industrie-Norm|en|** *German Industrial Standard[s];* DIN; **DIN-A4-Format** A4

**¹Ding** das; ~[e]s, ~e a) thing; b) *meist Pl.* **nach Lage der** ~e the way things are; **persönliche/private** ~e personal/private matters; **ein** ~ **der Unmöglichkeit sein** be quite impossible; **vor allen** ~**en** above all; c) **guter** ~**e sein** *(geh.)* be in good spirits; **²Ding** das; ~[e]s, ~er *(ugs.)* thing; **das ist ja ein** ~! that's really something

**Diözese** die; ~, ~n diocese

**Dipl.-Ing.** *Abk.* Diplomingenieur *academically qualified engineer*

**Diplom** das; ~s, ~e ≈ [first] degree *(in a scientific or technical subject); (für einen Handwerksberuf)* diploma; **Diplom-:** qualified

**Diplomat** der; ~en, ~en, **Diplomatin** die; ~, ~nen diplomat; **diplomatisch** 1. *Adj.* diplomatic; 2. *adv.* diplomatically

**dir** 1. *Dat. von* **du** to you; *(nach Präp.)* you; **Freunde von** ~: friends of yours; 2. *Dat. des Reflexivpron. der 2. Pers. Sg.* yourself

**direkt** 1. *Adj.* direct; 2. *adv.* straight; directly; **etw.** ~ **übertragen** broadcast sth. live; **Direkt·flug** der direct flight

**Direktion** die; ~, ~en management; *(Büroräume)* managers' offices *pl.;* **Direktor** der; ~s, ~en, **Direktorin** die; ~, ~nen director; *(einer Schule)* headmaster/headmistress; *(einer Strafanstalt)* governor; *(einer Abteilung)* manager

**Direkt·übertragung** die live broadcast

**Dirigent** der; ~en, ~en conductor; **dirigieren** *tr. V.* a) *auch itr.* conduct; b) *(führen)* steer

**Disco** ['dısko:] die; ~, ~s disco

**Diskette** die; ~, ~n *(DV)* floppy disc

**Diskont·satz** der *(Finanzw.)* discount rate

**Diskothek** die; ~, ~en discothèque

**Diskrepanz** die; ~, ~en discrepancy

**diskret** 1. *Adj. (vertraulich)* confidential; *(taktvoll)* discreet; tactful; 2. *adv. (vertraulich)* confidentially; *(taktvoll)* discreetly; tactfully; **Diskretion** die; ~ a) *(Verschwiegenheit, Takt)* discretion; b) *(Unaufdringlichkeit)* discreetness

**diskriminieren** *tr. V.* discriminate against; **Diskriminierung** die; ~, ~en discrimination

**Diskussion** die; ~, ~en discussion; **zur** ~ **stehen** be under discussion

**Diskussions-:** ~**beitrag** der contribution to a/the discussion; ~**leiter** der chairman [of the discussion]

**diskutieren** 1. *itr. V.* **über etw.** *(Akk.)* ~: discuss sth.; 2. *tr. V.* discuss

**disqualifizieren** *tr. V.* disqualify

**Distanz** die; ~, ~en *(auch fig.)* distance; **distanzieren** *refl. V.* **sich von jmdm./etw.** ~ *(fig.)* dissociate oneself from sb./sth.; **distanziert** *Adj.* reserved

**Distel** die; ~, ~n thistle

**Distel·fink** der goldfinch

**Disziplin** die; ~, ~en discipline; *(Selbstbeherrschung)* [self-]discipline; **disziplinieren** 1. *tr. V.* discipline; 2. *refl. V.* discipline oneself; **diszipliniert** 1. *Adj.* well-disciplined; *(beherrscht)* disciplined; 2. *adv.* in a well-disciplined way; *(beherrscht)* in a disciplined way

**divers...** [di'vɛrs...] *Adj.; nicht präd.* various; *(mehrer...)* several

**Dividende** [divi'dɛndə] die; ~, ~n *(Wirtsch.)* dividend

**dividieren** *tr. V.* divide; **Division** die; ~, ~en *(auch Milit.)* division

**DM** *Abk.* Deutsche Mark DM

**Do.** *Abk.* Donnerstag Thur[s].

**doch** 1. *Konj.* but; 2. *Adv.* a) *(jedoch)* but; b) *(dennoch)* all the same; still; c) *(geh.: nämlich)* **wußte er** ~, **daß** ...: because he knew that ...; d) *(entgegen allen gegenteiligen Behauptungen, Annahmen)* **er war also** ~ **der Mörder!** so he 'was the murderer!; e) *(ohnehin)* in any case; 3. *Interj.* **Das stimmt nicht. – Doch!** That's not right. – [Oh] yes it is!; **Hast du keinen Hunger? – Doch!** Aren't you hungry? – Yes [I am]!; 4. *Partikel* a) *(Ungeduld ausdrückend)* **paß** ~ **auf!** [oh] do be careful!; **das ist** ~ **nicht zu glauben** that's just incredible; b) *(Zweifel ausdrückend)* **du hast** ~ **meinen Brief erhalten?** you did get my letter, didn't you?; c) *(Überraschung ausdrückend)* **das ist** ~ **Karl!** there's Karl! d) *(verstärkt Bejahung/Verneinung ausdrückend)* **gewiß/sicher** ~: [why] certainly; of course; **ja** ~: [yes,] all right; **nicht** ~! *(abwehrend)* [no,] don't!; e) *(Wunsch verstärkend)* **wäre es** ~ ...: if only it were ...

**Docht** der; ~[e]s, ~ wick

**Dock** das; ~s, ~s dock

**Dogge** die; ~, ~n: [deutsche] ~: Great Dane

**Dogma** das; ~s, **Dogmen** *(auch fig.)* dogma; **dogmatisch** *(Theol., auch fig.) Adj.* dogmatic

**Dohle** die; ~, ~n jackdaw

**Doktor** der; ~s, ~en *(auch ugs. Arzt)* doctor; *(Titel)* Doctor; **Doktor·arbeit** die doctoral thesis

**Doktrin** die; ~, ~en doctrine

**Dokument** das; ~|e|s, ~e document

**Dokumentar-**: ~**bericht** der documentary report; ~**film** der documentary [film]

**Dokumentation** die; ~, ~en *o. Pl.* documentation; b) *(Bericht)* documentary report

**dokumentieren** *tr. V.* a) document; *(fig.)* demonstrate; b) *(festhalten)* record

**Dolch** der; ~|e|s, ~e dagger

**Dolde** die; ~, ~n *(Bot.)* umbel

**doll** *(bes. nordd., salopp)* 1. *Adj.* a) *(ungewöhnlich)* incredible; b) *(großartig)* great *(coll.)*; 2. *adv.* a) *(großartig)* fantastically [well] *(coll.)*; b) *(sehr)* ⟨hurt⟩ dreadfully *(coll.)*, like mad

**Dollar** der; ~|s|, ~s dollar; **zwei ~** : two dollars

**dolmetschen** *itr. V.* act as interpreter; **Dolmetscher** der; ~s, ~, **Dolmetscherin** die; ~, ~nen interpreter

**Dom** der; ~|e|s, ~e cathedral

**dominieren** *itr. V.* dominate

**dominikanisch** *Adj.* Dominican; **die Dominikanische Republik** the Dominican Republic

**Domizil** das; ~s, ~e *(geh.)* domicile; residence

**Dom·pfaff** der; ~en *od.* ~s, ~en *(Zool.)* bullfinch

**Dompteur** [dɔmp'tøːɐ] der; ~s, ~e, **Dompteuse** [dɔmp'tøːzə] die; ~, ~n tamer

**Donau** die; ~ : Danube

**Donner** der; ~s, ~ : thunder; **donnern** *itr. V.* a) *(unpers.)* thunder; b) *(fig.)* thunder; ⟨engine⟩ roar

**Donners·tag** der Thursday; *s. auch* Dienstag; **donnerstags** *Adv.* on Thursday[s]; *s. auch* dienstags

**Donner·wetter** das *(ugs.)* a) *(Krach)* row; b) ['--'--] zum ~ [noch einmal]! damn it!; ~! my word

**doof** *(ugs.)* 1. *Adj.* stupid; dumb *(coll.)*; 2. *adv.* stupidly

**Doppel** das; ~s, ~ a) *(Kopie)* duplicate; copy; b) *(Sport)* doubles *sing. or pl.*

**doppel-, Doppel-**: ~**bett** das double bed; ~**bock** das extra-strong bock beer; ~**decker** der; ~s, ~ : biplane; ~**deutig** [~dɔytɪç] 1. *Adj.* a)

ambiguous; b) *(anzüglich)* suggestive; 2. *adv.* a) ambiguously; b) *(anzüglich)* suggestively; ~**fenster** das double-glazed window; ~**gänger** der; ~s, ~, ~**gängerin** die; ~, ~nen double; ~**kinn** das double chin; ~**punkt** der colon

**doppelt** 1. *Adj.* double; **die ~e Menge** twice the quantity; **mit ~er Kraft arbeiten** work with twice as much energy; 2. *adv.* a) **so groß/alt wie ...**: twice as large/old as ...; **sich ~ anstrengen** try twice as hard; **Doppelte** das; *adj. Dekl.* **das ~ bezahlen** pay twice as much; pay double

**Doppel-**: ~**tür** die double door; ~**zentner** der 100 kilograms; ~**zimmer** das double room

**Dorf** das; ~|e|s, **Dörfer** village; **auf dem ~**: in the country; **Dorf·bewohner** der villager

**Dorn** der; ~|e|s, ~en thorn; **jmdm. ein ~ im Auge sein** annoy sb. intensely; **dornig** *Adj.* thorny; **Dorn·röschen** ⟨das⟩ the Sleeping Beauty

**dörren** *tr. V.* dry

**Dörr-**: ~**fleisch** das *(südd.)* lean bacon; ~**obst** das dried fruit

**Dorsch** der; ~|e|s, ~e cod

**dort** *Adv.* there; *s. auch* da 1 a

**dort-**: ~|**bleiben** *intr. V.; mit sein* stay there; ~**her** *Adv.* |von| ~her from there; ~**hin** *Adv.* there

**dortig** *Adj.; nicht präd.* there

**Dose** die; ~, ~n a) *(Blech~)* tin; *(Pillen~)* box; *(Zucker~)* bowl; b) *(Konserven~)* can; tin *(Brit.)*; *(Bier~)* can

**dösen** *itr. V. (ugs.)* doze

**Dosen-**: ~**bier** das canned beer; ~**milch** die canned *or (Brit.)* tinned milk; ~**öffner** der can opener; tin-opener *(Brit.)*

**dosieren** *tr. V.* etw. ~ : measure out the required dose of sth.; **Dosis** die; ~, **Dosen** dose

**Dotter** der *od.* das; ~s, ~ : yolk

**Dotter·blume** die marsh marigold

**Dozent** der; ~en, ~en, **Dozentin** die; ~, ~nen lecturer (für in)

**Dr.** *Abk.*: Doktor Dr

**Drache** der; ~n, ~n *(Myth.)* dragon; **Drachen** der; ~s, ~ a) kite; b) *(Fluggerät)* hang-glider

**Dragée, Dragee** [dra'ʒe:] das; ~s, ~s dragée

**Draht** der; ~|e|s, **Drähte** a) wire; b) *(Leitung)* wire; *(Telefonleitung)* line; wire; c) *(Telefonverbindung)* line

**draht-, Draht-**: ~**los** *(Nachrichtenw.)*

**1.** *Adj.* wireless; **2.** *adv.* etw. ~los telegrafieren/übermitteln radio sth.; ~seil das [steel] cable; ~seil·bahn die cable railway; ~zieher der *(fig.)* wire puller

dr**a**ll *Adj.* strapping ⟨*girl*⟩; full, rounded ⟨*cheeks, face, bottom*⟩

Dr**a**ma das; ~s, Dr**a**men drama; *(fig., ugs.)* disaster; **dramatisch 1.** *Adj.* dramatic. **2.** *adv.* dramatically; **dramatisieren** *tr. V.* dramatize

dr**a**n *Adv. (ugs.)* **a)** häng das Schild ~! put the sign up!; **b)** arm ~ sein be in a bad way; gut/schlecht ~ sein be well off/badly off; früh/spät ~ sein be early/late; ich bin ~: it's my turn; **dran|bleiben** *unr. itr. V.; mit sein (ugs.) (am Telefon)* hang on *(coll.)*

dr**a**ng *1. u. 3. Pers. Sg. Prät. v.* dringen

Dr**a**ng der; ~[e]s, Dr**ä**nge urge

dr**ä**nge *1. u. 3. Pers. Sg. Konjunktiv II v.* dringen

dr**ä**ngeln *(ugs.)* **1.** *itr. V.* **a)** push [and shove]; **b)** *(auf jmdn. einreden)* go on *(coll.)*; **2.** *tr. V.* **a)** push; shove; **b)** *(einreden auf)* go on at *(coll.)*; **3.** *refl. V.* sich nach vorn ~: push one's way to the front

dr**ä**ngen **1.** *itr. V.* **a)** push; **b)** die Zeit drängt time is pressing; **2.** *tr. V.* **a)** push; **b)** *(antreiben)* press; urge; **3.** *refl. V.* crowd

drangsal**ie**ren *tr. V. (quälen)* torment; *(plagen)* plague

dr**a**n-: ~|halten *unr. refl. V. (ugs.)* get a move on *(coll.);* ~|kommen *unr. itr. V.; mit sein (ugs.)* have one's turn; ~|nehmen *unr. tr. V. (ugs.) (beim Friseur usw.)* see to; *(beim Arzt)* see

dr**a**stisch **1.** *Adj.* drastic ⟨*measure, means*⟩; **2.** *adv.* drastically; ⟨*punish*⟩ severely

dr**au**f *Adv. (ugs.)* on it

dr**au**f-, Dr**au**f-: ~gänger der daredevil; ~gängerisch *Adj.* daring; ~|gehen *unr. itr. V.; mit sein (ugs.)* **a)** *(umkommen)* kick the bucket *(sl.);* **b)** *verbraucht werden)* go *(für* on*);* ~|zahlen *(ugs.)* **1.** *tr. V.* noch etwas/ 1 250 DM ~zahlen fork out *(sl.) or* pay a bit more/an extra 1,250 marks; **2.** *itr. V. (Unkosten haben)* ich zahle dabei noch ~: it's costing me money

dr**au**ßen *Adv.* outside; hier/da ~: out here/there; von/nach ~: from outside/ outside

Dr**e**ck der; ~[e]s **a)** *(ugs.)* dirt; *(sehr viel)* filth; *(Schlamm)* mud; **b)** *(salopp abwertend: Angelegenheit)* mach dei-

nen ~ allein do it yourself; das geht dich einen [feuchten] ~ an *(salopp)* none of your damned business *(sl.);* **c)** *(salopp abwertend: Zeug)* junk *no indef. art.;* Dr**e**ck·arbeit die *(auch fig.)* dirty work *no indef. art., no pl.*/dirty job; **dreckig 1.** *Adj.* **a)** *(ugs., auch fig.)* dirty; *(sehr schmutzig)* filthy; **b)** *(salopp: unverschämt)* cheeky; **2.** *adv.* **a)** es geht ihm ~ *(ugs.)* he's in a bad way; **b)** *(salopp: unverschämt)* cheekily

Dr**e**ck-: ~sau die, ~schwein das *(derb)* filthy swine

Dr**e**h der; ~s, ~s *(ugs.)* **a)** den ~ heraushaben have [got] the knack; **b)** [so] um den ~: about that

Dr**e**h-: ~arbeiten *Pl. (Film)* shooting *sing.* (zu of); ~bank die lathe; ~buch das screenplay; [film] script

dr**e**hen **1.** *tr. V.* **a)** turn; **b)** *(formen)* twist ⟨*rope, thread*⟩; roll ⟨*cigarette*⟩; **c)** *(Film)* shoot ⟨*scene*⟩; film ⟨*report*⟩; make; ⟨*film*⟩; **2.** *itr. V.* **a)** ⟨*car*⟩ turn; ⟨*wind*⟩ change; **b)** an etw. *(Dat.)* ~: turn sth.; **c)** *(Film)* film; **3.** *refl. V.* **a)** turn; **b)** *(ugs.: zum Gegenstand haben)* sich um etw. ~: be about sth.

Dr**e**h-: ~orgel die barrel-organ; ~restaurant das revolving restaurant; ~stuhl der swivel chair; ~tür die revolving door

Dr**e**hung die; ~, ~en turn; *(um einen Mittelpunkt)* revolution

dr**ei** *Kardinalz.* three; Dr**ei** die; ~, ~en three; eine ~ schreiben *(Schulw.)* get a C

dr**ei**-, Dr**ei**-: ~eck das; ~s, ~e *(Geom.)* triangle; ~eckig *Adj.* triangular; ~ein·halb *Bruchz.* three and a half

Dr**ei**er der; ~s, ~ *(ugs.)* three; dr**ei**erlei *Gattungsz.; indekl.* **a)** *attr.* three kinds *or* sorts of; three different; **b)** *subst.* three [different] things

dr**ei**-, Dr**ei**-: ~fach *Vervielfältigungsz.* triple; die ~fache Menge three times the amount; ~fache das; *adj. Dekl.* das ~fache kosten cost three times as much; das ~fache von 3 ist 9 three times three is nine; ~hundert *Kardinalz.* three hundred; ~jährig *Adj.* (3 Jahre alt) three-year-old *attrib.;* (3 Jahre dauernd) three-year *attrib.;* ~kampf der *(Sport)* triathlon; ~klang der triad; ~köpfig *Adj.* (family, crew) of three; ~mal *Adv.* three times; ~malig *Adj.* eine ~malige Wiederholung three repeats

**drein** *(ugs.) s.* **darein**
**drein-:** ~|**blicken,** ~|**schauen** *itr. V.* look
**drei-, Drei-:** ~**rad** das tricycle; ~**satz** der; rule of three; ~**seitig** *Adj.* three-sided *(figure);* three-page ⟨*letter, leaflet, etc.*⟩
**dreißig** *Kardinalz.* thirty; *s. auch* achtzig; **dreißigjährig** *Adj. (30 Jahre alt)* thirty-year-old *attrib.; (30 Jahre dauernd)* thirty-year *attrib.;* **dreißigst...** *Ordinalz.* thirtieth; **Dreißigstel** das; ~**s,** ~: thirtieth
**dreist** 1. *Adj.* brazen; barefaced ⟨*lie*⟩; 2. *adv.* brazenly
**drei·stellig** *Adj.* three-figure *attrib.*
**Dreistigkeit** die; ~, ~**en a)** *o. Pl.* brazenness; **b)** *(Handlung)* brazen act
**drei-, Drei-:** ~**tausend** *Kardinalz.* three thousand; ~**teilig** *Adj.* three-part *attrib.;* three-piece *attrib.* ⟨*suit*⟩; ~**viertel** *Bruchz.* three-quarters; ~**viertel·stunde** [---'--] die three-quarters of an hour; ~**viertel·takt** [-'---] der three-four time; ~**zehn** *Kardinalz.* thirteen; *s. auch* achtzehn
**Dresche** die; ~ *(salopp)* walloping *(sl.);* thrashing; **dreschen** 1. *unr. tr. V.* **a)** thresh; **b)** *(salopp: schlagen)* wallop *(sl.);* thrash; 2. *unr. itr. V.* thresh
**dressieren** *tr. V.* train ⟨*animal*⟩; **Dressur** die; ~, ~**en** training
**Drill** der; ~|e|s drilling; *(Milit.)* drill; **drillen** *tr. V. (auch Milit.)* drill
**Drilling** der; ~**s,** ~**e** triplet
**drin** *Adv. (ugs.)* **a)** in it; **b)** *s.* drinnen
**dringen** *unr. itr. V.* **a)** *mit sein durch/ in etw.* ~: penetrate sth.; **b)** *mit sein in* jmdn. ~ *(geh.)* press sb.; **c)** *auf etw. (Akk.)* ~: insist upon sth.; **dringend** 1. *Adj.* urgent; strong ⟨*suspicion, advice*⟩; 2. *adv.* urgently; ⟨*advise, suspect*⟩ strongly; ~ **erforderlich** essential; **dringlich** 1. *Adj.* urgent; 2. *adv.* urgently; **Dringlichkeit** die; ~: urgency
**drinnen** *Adv.* inside; *(im Haus)* indoors; inside
**dritt** *in* wir waren zu ~: there were three of us
**dritt...** *Ordinalz.* third; **Drittel** das, *(schweiz. meist der);* ~**s,** ~: third; **dritteln** *tr. V.* split *or* divide three ways; **drittens** *Adv.* thirdly
**DRK** [de:|ɛr'ka:] das; ~ *Abk.* **Deutsches Rotes Kreuz** German Red Cross
**Dr. med.** *Abk.* doctor medicinae MD
**droben** *Adv. (südd., österr., sonst geh.)* up there

**Droge** die; ~, ~**n** drug
**drogen-:** ~**abhängig,** ~**süchtig** *Adj.* addicted to drugs *postpos.*
**Drogerie** die; ~, ~**n** chemist's [shop] *(Brit.);* drugstore *(Amer.);* **Drogist** der; ~**en,** ~**en, Drogistin** die; ~, ~**nen** chemist *(Brit.);* druggist *(Amer.)*
**drohen** *itr., mod. V.* threaten; *(bevorstehen)* be threatening; jmdm. droht etw. sb. is threatened with sth.; **drohend** *Adj.* threatening; *(bevorstehend)* impending
**Drohne** die; ~, ~**n** drone
**dröhnen** *itr. V.* boom; ⟨*machine*⟩ roar
**Drohung** die; ~, ~**en** threat
**drollig** 1. *Adj.* funny; comical; *(niedlich)* sweet; cute *(Amer.);* 2. *adv.: s. Adj.:* comically; sweetly; cutely *(Amer.)*
**Dromedar** das; ~**s,** ~**e** dromedary
**Drops** der *od.* das; ~, ~: fruit *or (Brit.)* acid drop
**drosch** *1. u. 3. Pers. Sg. Prät. v.* **dreschen**
**Drossel** die; ~, ~**n** thrush
**drosseln** *tr. V.* **a)** turn down ⟨*heating, air-conditioning*⟩; throttle back ⟨*engine*⟩; **b)** *(herabsetzen)* reduce
**Dr. phil.** *Abk.* doctor philosophiae Dr
**drüben** *Adv.* dort *od.* da ~: over there; ~ **auf der anderen Seite** over on the other side
¹**Druck** der; ~|e|s, **Drücke a)** *(auch fig.)* pressure; **b)** *o. Pl.* ein ~ auf den Knopf a touch of the button; ²**Druck** der; ~|e|s, ~**e a)** *o. Pl.* printing; in ~ gehen go to press; **b)** *(Produkt)* print; **Druck·buchstabe** der printed letter; **drucken** *tr., itr. V.* print
**drücken** 1. *tr. V.* **a)** press; press, push ⟨*button*⟩; squeeze ⟨*juice, pus*⟩ (**aus** out of); jmdm. die Hand ~: squeeze sb.'s hand; **b)** *(liebkosen)* jmdn. ~: hug [and squeeze] sb.; **c)** ⟨*shoe etc.*⟩ pinch; **d)** *(herabsetzen)* push down ⟨*price, rate*⟩; depress ⟨*sales*⟩; bring down ⟨*standard*⟩; 2. *itr. V.* **a)** press; auf den Knopf ~: press *or* push the button; „bitte ~": 'push'; **b)** *(Druck verursachen)* ⟨*shoe etc.*⟩ pinch; 3. *refl. V. (ugs.: sich entziehen)* shirk; sich vor etw. *(Dat.)* ~: get out of sth.; **drückend** *Adj.* heavy ⟨*debt, taxes*⟩; serious ⟨*worries*⟩; grinding ⟨*poverty*⟩; **b)** *(schwül)* oppressive
**Drucker** der; ~**s,** ~: printer; **Druckerei** die; ~, ~**en** printing-works; *(Firma)* printing-house; printer's

**druck-, Druck-:** ~**fehler** der misprint; printer's error; ~**knopf** der press-stud *(Brit.);* snap-fastener; ~**luft** die compressed air; ~**mittel** das means of bringing pressure to bear (gegenüber on); ~**reif** 1. *Adj.* ready for publication; *(~fertig)* ready for press; 2. *adv.* ⟨*speak*⟩ in a polished manner; ~**sache** die *(Postw.)* printed matter; ~**schrift** die **a)** printed writing; **b)** *(Schriftart)* type[-face]; **c)** *(Schriftwerk)* pamphlet

**drum** *Adv. (ugs.)* **a)** *s.* **darum; b)** [a]round; **alles** *od.* **das |ganze| Drum und Dran** *(bei einer Mahlzeit)* all the trimmings; *(bei einer Feierlichkeit)* all the palaver that goes with it *(coll.);* **Drum·herum** das; ~s everything that goes/went with it

**drunter** *Adv. (ugs.)* underneath; **es** *od.* **alles geht** ~ **und drüber** everything is topsy-turvy

**Drüse** die; ~, ~n gland

**Dschungel** ['dʒʊŋ]] der; ~s, ~ *(auch fig.)* jungle

**dt.** *Abk.* deutsch G.

**Dtzd.** *Abk.* Dutzend doz.

**du** *Personalpron.;* 2. *Pers. Sg. Nom.* you; *(in Briefen)* Du you; **du zueinander sagen** use the familiar form in addressing one another; *s. auch (Gen.)* **deiner,** *(Dat.)* **dir,** *(Akk.)* **dich**

**Dübel** der; ~s, ~: plug

**ducken** 1. *refl. V.* duck; 2. *itr. V. (fig. abwertend)* humble oneself (vor + *Dat.* before)

**Dudel·sack** der bagpipes *pl.*

**Duell** das; ~s, ~e duel; **duellieren** *refl. V.* fight a duel

**Duett** das; ~|e|s, ~e *(Musik)* duet; **im** ~ **singen** sing a duet

**Duft** der; ~|e|s, Düfte scent; *(von Parfüm, Blumen)* scent; fragrance; *(von Kaffee usw.)* aroma; **duften** *itr. V.* smell (**nach** of)

**dulden** *tr. V.* tolerate; put up with; **duldsam** 1. *Adj.* tolerant (**gegen** towards); 2. *adv.* tolerantly

**dumm, dümmer, dümmst...** 1. *Adj.* **a)** stupid; **b)** *(unvernünftig)* foolish; **c)** *(ugs.: töricht, albern)* idiotic; silly; **d)** *(ugs.: unangenehm)* nasty *(feeling);* **das wird mir jetzt zu** ~ *(ugs.)* I've had enough of it; 2. *adv. (ugs.)* idiotically; **Dumme** der/die; *adj. Dekl.* fool; **der** ~ **sein** *(ugs.)* be the loser; **dummer·weise** *Adv.* **a)** unfortunately; *(ärgerlicherweise)* annoyingly; **b)** *(törichterweise)* foolishly;

**Dummheit** die; ~, ~en **a)** *o. Pl.* stupidity; **b)** *(unkluge Handlung)* stupid thing; **Dumm·kopf** der *(ugs.)* nitwit *(coll.)*

**dumpf** 1. *Adj.* **a)** dull ⟨*thud, rumble of thunder*⟩; muffled ⟨*sound, thump*⟩; **b)** *(muffig)* musty; **c)** *(stumpfsinnig)* dull; 2. *adv.* **a)** ⟨*echo*⟩ hollowly; **b)** *(stumpfsinnig)* apathetically

**Düne** die; ~, ~n dune

**düngen** 1. *tr. V.* fertilize ⟨*soil, lawn*⟩; spread fertilizer on ⟨*field*⟩; scatter fertilizer around ⟨*plants*⟩; 2. *itr. V.* **gut** ~ ⟨*substance*⟩ be a good fertilizer; **Dünger** der; ~s, ~: fertilizer

**dunkel** 1. *Adj. (auch fig.)* dark; *(tief)* deep ⟨*voice, note*⟩; *(undeutlich)* vague; 2. *adv. (tief)* ⟨*speak*⟩ in a deep voice; **b)** *(undeutlich)* vaguely

**Dünkel** der; ~s *(geh.)* arrogance; *(Einbildung)* conceit[edness]

**dunkel-:** ~**blond** *Adj.* light brown ⟨*hair*⟩; ⟨*person*⟩ with light brown hair; ~**häutig** *Adj.* dark-skinned

**Dunkelheit** die; ~: darkness; **Dunkel·kammer** die dark-room; **dunkeln** *itr. V. (unpers.)* **es dunkelt** *(geh.)* it is growing dark; **Dunkel·ziffer** die number of unrecorded cases

**dünn** 1. *Adj.* thin; slim ⟨*book*⟩; fine ⟨*stocking*⟩; watery ⟨*coffee, tea, beer*⟩; 2. *adv.* thinly ⟨*sliced, populated*⟩; lightly ⟨*dressed*⟩

**Dunst** der; ~|e|s, Dünste **a)** *o. Pl.* haze; *(Nebel)* mist; **b)** *(Geruch)* smell; **dünsten** *tr. V.* steam ⟨*fish, vegetables*⟩; braise ⟨*meat*⟩; stew ⟨*fruit*⟩; **dunstig** *Adj.* hazy

**Duo** das; ~s, ~s *(Musik)* duet; *(fig. scherzh.)* duo; pair

**Duplikat** das; ~|e|s, ~e duplicate

**Dur** das; ~ *(Musik)* major [key]

**durch** 1. *Präp. mit Akk.* **a)** *(räumlich)* through; **b)** *(modal)* by; ~ **Boten** by courier; **zehn |geteilt|** ~ **zwei** ten divided by two; 2. *Adv.* **a)** *(hin~)* **das ganze Jahr** ~: throughout the whole year; **b)** *(ugs.: vorbei)* **es war 3 Uhr** ~: it was gone 3 o'clock; **c)** ~ **und** ~ **naß/überzeugt** wet through [and through]/completely totally convinced

**durch|arbeiten** 1. *tr. V.* work through; 2. *itr. V.* work through; **die Nacht** ~: work through the night

**durch·aus** *Adv.* absolutely; perfectly; quite ⟨*correct, possible, understandable*⟩; **das ist** ~ **richtig** that is entirely right; ~ **nicht** by no means

**durch|beißen** *unr. tr. V.* bite through

**durch|blättern** *tr. V.* leaf through

**Durch·blick der** *(ugs.)* **den |absoluten| ~ haben** know [exactly] what's going on; **durch|blicken** *itr. V.* **a)** look through; **durch etw. ~:** look through sth.; **b)** **~ lassen, daß .../wie ...:** hint that .../at how ...

**Durch·blutung die;** *o. Pl.* flow of blood (+ *Gen.* to); [blood-]circulation

¹**durch|bohren** *tr. V.* drill through ⟨*wall, plank*⟩; drill ⟨*hole*⟩; ²**durch·bohren** *tr. V.* pierce

¹**durch|brechen 1.** *unr. tr. V.* etw. ~: break sth. in two; **2.** *unr. itr. V.; mit sein* **a)** break in two; **b)** *(hervorkommen)* ⟨*sun*⟩ break through; **c)** *(einbrechen)* fall through ⟨*ice, floor, etc.*⟩; ²**durch·brechen** *unr. tr. V.* break through

**durch|brennen** *unr. itr. V.; mit sein* **a)** ⟨*heating coil, light bulb*⟩ burn out; ⟨*fuse*⟩ blow; **b)** *(ugs.: weglaufen) (von zu Hause)* run away; *(mit der Kasse, mit dem Geliebten/der Geliebten)* run off

**durch|bringen** *unr. tr. V.* get through; *(bei Wahlen)* jmdn. ~: get sb. elected; **seine Familie/sich ~:** support one's family/ oneself

**Durch·bruch der** *(fig.)* breakthrough

**durch|drehen 1.** *tr. V.* put ⟨*meat*⟩ through the mincer *or* (Amer.) grinder; **2.** *itr. V. auch mit sein (ugs.)* crack up *(coll.)*

¹**durch|dringen** *unr. tr. V.; mit sein* ⟨*rain, sun*⟩ come through; ²**durch·dringen** *unr. tr. V.* penetrate; **jmdn. ~** ⟨*idea*⟩ take hold of sb.

**durch·einander** *Adv.* ~ **sein** ⟨*papers, desk, etc.*⟩ be in a muddle; *(verwirrt sein)* be confused; *(aufgeregt sein)* be flustered; **Durcheinander das;** ~**s a)** muddle; mess; **b)** *(Wirrwarr)* confusion

**durcheinander|bringen** *unr. tr. V.* **a)** get ⟨*room, flat*⟩ into a mess; get ⟨*papers, file*⟩ into a muddle; muddle up ⟨*papers, file*⟩; **b)** *(verwirren)* confuse; **c)** *(verwechseln)* confuse ⟨*names etc.*⟩; get ⟨*names etc.*⟩ mixed up

**durch|fahren** *unr. itr. V.; mit sein* **a)** |durch etw.| ~: drive through [sth.]; **b)** *(nicht anhalten)* go straight through; *(mit dem Auto)* drive straight through; **der Zug fährt |in H.| durch** the train doesn't stop [at H.]; **Durch·fahrt die a)** „**~ verboten**" 'no entry except for access'; **auf der ~ sein** be passing through; **b)** *(Weg)* thoroughfare; „**bitte |die| ~ freihalten**" 'please do not obstruct'

**Durch·fall der** diarrhoea *no art.;* **durch|fallen** *unr. itr. V.; mit sein* **a)** fall through; **b)** *(ugs.: nicht bestehen)* fail

**durch|finden** *unr. refl. V.* find one's way through

**durchführbar** *Adj.* practicable; **durch|führen 1.** *tr. V.* carry out; put into effect ⟨*decision, programme*⟩; perform ⟨*operation*⟩; hold ⟨*meeting, election, examination*⟩; **2.** *itr. V.* durch etw./unter etw. *(Dat.)* ~ ⟨*track, road*⟩ go through/under sth.; **Durch·führung die** carrying out; *(einer Operation)* performing; *(einer Versammlung, Wahl, Prüfung)* holding; *(eines Wettbewerbs)* staging

**Durch·gang der a)** passage[way]; „**kein ~**", „~ **verboten**" 'no thoroughfare'; **b)** *(Phase)* stage; *(einer Versuchsreihe)* run; *(Sport, Wahlen)* round

**Durchgangs-:** ~**straße die** through road; ~**verkehr der** through traffic

**durch|geben** *unr. tr. V.* announce ⟨*news*⟩; give ⟨*results, weather report*⟩; **eine Meldung im Radio/Fernsehen ~:** make an announcement on the radio/ on television

**durch·gefroren** *Adj.* frozen stiff; chilled to the bone

**durch|gehen 1.** *unr. itr. V.; mit sein* **a)** |durch etw.| ~: go *or* walk through [sth.]; **b)** *(hindurchdringen)* |durch etw.| ~:⟨*rain, water*⟩ come through [sth.]; **c)** *(direkt zum Ziel führen)* ⟨*train etc.*⟩ go [right] through (**bis** to); ⟨*flight*⟩ go direct; **d)** *(andauern)* go on (**bis zu** until); **e)** *(hingenommen werden)* ⟨*discrepancy*⟩ be tolerated; ⟨*mistake, discourtesy*⟩ be allowed to pass; **jmdm. etw. ~ lassen** let sb. get away with sth. **f)** ⟨*horse*⟩ bolt; **2.** *unr. tr. V.; mit sein* go through ⟨*newspaper, text*⟩

**durch·gehend 1.** *Adj.* **a)** continuous ⟨*line, pattern, etc.*⟩; constantly recurring ⟨*motif*⟩; **b)** *(direkt)* through *attrib.* ⟨*train, carriage*⟩; direct ⟨*flight, connection*⟩; **2.** *adv.* ~ **geöffnet haben/bleiben** be/stay open all day

**durch|greifen** *unr. itr. V.* |hart| ~: take drastic measures *or* steps

**durch|halten 1.** *unr. itr. V.* hold out; *(bei einer schwierigen Aufgabe)* see it through; **2.** *unr. tr. V.* stand

**durch|hängen** *unr. itr. V.* sag
**durch|kämmen** *tr. V.* **a)** comb ⟨*hair*⟩ through; **b)** *(durchsuchen)* comb ⟨*area etc.*⟩
**durch|kommen** *unr. itr. V.; mit sein* **a)** come through; *(mit Mühe)* get through; **b)** *(ugs.: beim Telefonieren)* get through; **c)** *(durchgehen, -fahren usw.)* **durch etw. ~:** come through sth.; **d)** *(ugs.: überleben)* pull through
¹**durch|kreuzen** *tr. V.* cross out;
²**durch·kreuzen** *tr. V. (vereiteln)* frustrate
**durch|lassen** *unr. tr. V.* **a)** jmdn. |durch etw.| ~: let sb. through [sth.]; **b)** *(durchlässig sein)* let ⟨*light, water, etc.*⟩ through; **durchlässig** *Adj.* permeable; *(porös)* porous; *(undicht)* leaky; ⟨*raincoat, shoe*⟩ that lets in water
**Durch·lauf** der *(Sport, DV)* run;
¹**durch|laufen** 1. *unr. itr. V.; mit sein* **a)** |durch etw.| ~: run through [sth.]; *(durchrinnen)* trickle through [sth.]; **b)** *(passieren)* ⟨*runners*⟩ run *or* pass through; **c)** *(ohne Pause laufen)* run without stopping; 2. *unr. tr. V.* go through ⟨*soles*⟩; ²**durch·laufen** *unr. tr. V.* go through ⟨*phase, stage*⟩; **durchlaufend** 1. *Adj.* continuous; 2. *adv.* ⟨*numbered, marked*⟩ in sequence
**durch|lesen** *unr. tr. V.* **etw. |ganz| ~:** read sth. [all the way] through
**durch·leuchten** *tr. V.* x-ray; *(fig.)* investigate ⟨*case, matter, problem, etc.*⟩ thoroughly
**durch·löchern** *tr. V.* make holes in
**durch|machen** *(ugs.)* 1. *tr. V.* **a)** undergo ⟨*change*⟩; complete ⟨*training course*⟩; go through ⟨*stage, phase*⟩; serve ⟨*apprenticeship*⟩; **b)** *(erleiden)* go through; **c)** *(durcharbeiten)* work through ⟨*lunch-break etc.*⟩; 2. *itr. V. (durcharbeiten)* work [right] through; *(durchfeiern)* celebrate all night/day *etc.*; keep going all night/day *etc.*
**Durchmesser** der; ~s, ~: diameter
**durch|nehmen** *unr. tr. V. (Schulw.: behandeln)* do
**durch|probieren** *tr. V.* taste ⟨*wines, cakes, etc.*⟩ one after another
**durch·queren** *tr. V.* cross; travel across ⟨*country*⟩; ⟨*train*⟩ go through ⟨*country*⟩
**durch|rechnen** *tr. V.* calculate ⟨*costs etc.*⟩ [down to the last penny]; check ⟨*bill*⟩ thoroughly
**Durch·reise** die journey through;
**durch|reisen** *itr. V.; mit sein* travel

through; **Durchreise·visum** das transit visa
**durch|reißen** 1. *unr. tr. V.* **etw. ~:** tear sth. in two *or* in half; 2. *unr. itr. V.; mit sein* ⟨*fabric, garment*⟩ rip, tear; ⟨*thread, rope*⟩ snap [in two]
**durch|rosten** *itr. V.; mit sein* rust through
**durchs** *Präp. + Art.* = **durch das**
**Durch·sage** die announcement; *(an eine bestimmte Person)* message
**durchschaubar** *Adj.* transparent; **leicht ~** easy to see through; **durchschauen** *tr. V.* **a)** see through ⟨*person, plan, etc.*⟩; see ⟨*situation*⟩ clearly
**durch|schlafen** *unr. itr. V.* sleep [right] through
**Durch·schlag** der **a)** *(Kopie)* carbon [copy]; **b)** *(Küchengerät)* strainer; **durch|schlagen** *unr. tr. V.* **etw. ~:** chop sth. in two; **durchschlagend** *Adj.* resounding ⟨*success*⟩; decisive ⟨*effect, measures*⟩; conclusive ⟨*evidence*⟩
**durch|schneiden** *unr. tr. V.* cut through ⟨*thread, cable*⟩; cut ⟨*ribbon, sheet of paper*⟩ in two; cut ⟨*throat, umbilical cord*⟩; **etw. in der Mitte ~:** cut sth. in half; **Durch·schnitt** der average; **im ~:** on average; **über/unter dem ~** liegen be above/below average; **durchschnittlich** 1. *Adj.* **a)** *nicht präd.* average ⟨*growth, performance, output*⟩; **b)** *(ugs.: nicht außergewöhnlich)* ordinary ⟨*life, person, etc.*⟩; **c)** *(mittelmäßig)* modest; ordinary ⟨*appearance*⟩; 2. *adv.* ⟨*earn etc.*⟩ on [an] average; **~ groß** of average height
**Durchschnitts-:** **~alter** das average age; **~geschwindigkeit** die average speed
**Durch·schrift** die carbon [copy]
**durch|sehen** 1. *unr. itr. V.* |durch etw.| ~: look through [sth.]; 2. *unr. tr. V.* look through
**durch|sein** *unr. itr. V., mit sein; nur im Inf. u. Part. zusammengeschrieben (ugs.)* **a)** |durch etw.| ~: be through [sth.]; **b)** *(abgefahren sein)* ⟨*train, bus, etc.*⟩ have gone; **c)** *(fertig sein)* have finished; **durch etw. ~:** have got through sth.; **d)** ⟨*cheese*⟩ be ripe; ⟨*meat*⟩ be well done
**durch|setzen** 1. *tr. V.* carry through; achieve ⟨*objective*⟩; enforce ⟨*demand, claim*⟩; 2. *refl. V.* assert oneself; ⟨*idea etc.*⟩ find *or* gain acceptance
**Durch·sicht** die: **nach ~ der Unterlagen** after looking *or* checking through

the documents; **dụrchsichtig** *Adj.*
*(auch fig.)* transparent

**dụrch|sprechen** *unr. tr. V.* talk ⟨*matter etc.*⟩ over; discuss ⟨*matter etc.*⟩
thoroughly

**dụrch|stehen** *unr. tr. V.* stand ⟨*pace,
boring job*⟩; come through ⟨*difficult
situation*⟩; get over ⟨*illness*⟩

**dụrch|stellen** *tr. V.* put ⟨*call*⟩ through
(in + *Akk.*, auf + *Akk.* to)

**dụrch|streichen** *unr. tr. V.* cross out;
*(in Formularen)* delete

**durch·sụchen** *tr. V.* search (**nach**
for); search, scour ⟨*area*⟩ (**nach** for);
**Durchsụchung die; ~, ~en** search

**dụrch|treten** *unr. tr. V.* press ⟨*clutch-,
brake-pedal*⟩ right down

**durchtrịeben** *(abwertend)* 1. *Adj.*
crafty; sly; 2. *adv.* craftily; slyly

**durch·wạchsen** *Adj.* ~er Speck
streaky bacon

**Dụrchwahl die; a)** direct dialling;
**mein Apparat hat keine ~:** I don't
have an outside line; **b)** *s.* **Durchwahl-
nummer; dụrch|wählen** *itr. V.* **a)**
dial direct; **b)** *(bei Nebenstellenanla-
gen)* dial straight through; **Dụrch-
wahl·nummer die** number of the/
one's direct line

**dụrch|zählen** *tr. V.* count; count up

**dụrch|ziehen 1.** *unr. tr. V.* **jmdn./etw.
|durch etw.|** ~: pull sb./sth. through
[sth.]; **ein Gummiband |durch etw.|** ~:
draw an elastic through [sth.]; 2. *unr.
itr. V.; mit sein* pass through; ⟨*soldiers*⟩ march through

**Durch·zug der** *o. Pl.* draught

**dụrfen 1.** *unr. Modalverb; 2. Part.* ~ **a)**
etw. tun ~: be allowed to do sth.; **darf
ich rauchen?** may I smoke?; **was darf
es sein?** can I help you?; **b)** *Konjunktiv
II + Inf.* das dürfte der Grund sein
that is probably the reason; 2. *unr. tr.,
itr. V.* er hat nicht gedurft he was not
allowed to; **dụrfte,** *1. u. 3. Pers. Sg.
Prät. v.* dürfen; **dụrfte** *1. u. 3. Pers.
Sg. Konjunktiv II v.* dürfen

**dụrr** *Adj.* **a)** withered; arid, barren
⟨*ground, earth*⟩; **b)** *(mager)* scrawny;
**Dụrre die; ~, ~n** drought

**Dụrst der; ~|e|s** thirst; ~ **haben** be
thirsty; **ich habe ~ auf ein Bier** I could
just drink a beer; **dụrstig** *Adj.*
thirsty; **durst·stillend** *Adj.* thirst-
quenching

**Dụsche die; ~, ~n** shower; **dụschen**
*itr., refl. V.* have a shower

**Dụse die; ~, ~n** *(Technik)* nozzle; *(eines Vergasers)* jet

**Dụsen-:** ~**flugzeug das** jet aircraft;
~**motor der** jet engine

**dụster 1.** *Adj.* **a)** dark; gloomy; dim
⟨*light*⟩; **b)** *(fig.)* gloomy; sombre ⟨*colour, music*⟩; 2. *adv. (fig.)* gloomily

**Dụtzend das; ~s, ~e** dozen; zwei ~:
two dozen; **dụtzend·weise** *Adv.* in
[their] dozens *(coll.)*

**dụzen** *tr. V.* call ⟨*sb.*⟩ 'du' *(the familiar
form of address)*

**dynạmisch 1.** *Adj.* **a)** *(auch fig.)* dynamic; 2. *adv.* dynamically

**Dynamịt das; ~s** dynamite

**Dynạmo der; ~s, ~s** dynamo

**Dynastịe die; ~, ~n** dynasty

**D-Zug** ['de:-] **der** express train

# E

**e, E** [e:] **das; ~, ~ a)** *(Buchstabe)* e/E;
**b)** *(Musik)* [key of] E

**Ẹbbe die; ~, ~n** ebb tide; *(Zustand)*
low tide; **es ist ~:** the tide is out

**ẹben 1.** *Adj.* **a)** flat; **b)** *(glatt)* level; 2.
*adv.* **a)** *(gerade jetzt)* just; **b)** *(kurz)*
[for] a moment; **Ẹbene die; ~, ~n a)**
plain; **in der ~:** on the plain; **b)** *(Geom., Physik)* plane; **c)** *(fig.)* level

**ẹben·falls** *Adv.* likewise; as well;
**danke, ~:** thank you, [and] [the] same
to you

**Ẹben·holz das** ebony

**ẹben·so** *Adv.* **a)** *mit Adjektiven* just
as; **b)** *mit Verben* in exactly the same
way

**ẹbenso-:** ~**gern** *Adv.* ~**gern mag ich
Erdbeeren |wie ...|** I like strawberries
just as much [as ...]; ~**gern würde ich
an den Strand gehen** I would just as
soon go to the beach; ~**gut** *Adv.* just
as well; ~**sehr** *Adv.* **a)** *mit Adjektiven*
just as; **b)** *mit Verben* just as much

**Ẹber der; ~s, ~:** boar

**Ẹber·esche die** rowan; mountain ash

**ẹbnen** *tr. V.* level ⟨*ground*⟩

**Ẹcho das; ~s, ~s** echo

**ẹcht 1.** *Adj.* **a)** genuine; real ⟨*love,
friendship*⟩; **b)** *nicht präd. (typisch)*
real, typical; 2. *adv.* **a)** *(ugs. verstärkend)* really; **b)** *(typisch)* typically

**Eck-:** ~**ball** der *(Sport)* corner[-kick/ -hit/-throw]; einen ~**ball treten** take a corner; ~**bank** die corner seat

**Ecke** die; ~, ~**n** corner; **an der** ~: on *or* at the corner; **um die** ~: round the corner; **eckig** *Adj.* square; angular

**Eck·zahn** der canine tooth

**edel** *Adj.* a) *nicht präd.* thoroughbred ⟨*horse*⟩; species ⟨*rose*⟩; b) *(großmütig)* noble[-minded], high-minded ⟨*person*⟩; noble ⟨*thought, gesture, feelings, deed*⟩; honourable ⟨*motive*⟩

**Edel-:** ~**metall** das precious metal; ~**stahl** der stainless steel; ~**stein** der precious stone; gem[stone]

**Editiọn** die; ~, ~**en** edition

**EDV** *Abk.* elektronische Datenverarbeitung EDP

**Efeu** der; ~s ivy

**Effẹkt** der; ~[e]s, ~e effect; **effẹkt-voll** *Adj.* effective; dramatic ⟨*pause, gesture, entrance*⟩

**EG** ['e:'ge:] die; ~ *Abk.* a) **Europäische Gemeinschaft** EC; b) **Erdgeschoß**

**egal** *Adj. nicht attr. (ugs.: einerlei)* **es ist jmdm.** ~: it's all the same to sb.; [**ganz**] ~, **wie/wer** *usw.* ...: no matter how/who *etc.* ...

**Egge** die; ~, ~**n** harrow

**ehe** *Konj.* before

**Ehe** die; ~, ~**n** marriage

**Ehe-:** ~**bett** das marriage-bed; *(Doppelbett)* double bed; ~**frau** die wife; *(verheiratete Frau)* married woman; ~**krach** der *(ugs.)* row; ~**leute** *Pl.* married couple

**ehelich** *Adj.* marital; matrimonial; conjugal ⟨*rights, duties*⟩; legitimate ⟨*child*⟩

**ehemalig** *Adj.* former

**Ehe-:** ~**mann** der; *Pl.* ~**männer** husband; *(verheirateter Mann)* married man; ~**paar** das married couple

**eher** *Adv.* a) *(früher)* earlier; sooner; b) *(lieber)* rather; sooner

**Ehe-:** ~**ring** der wedding-ring; ~**scheidung** die divorce

**Ehre** die; ~, ~**n** honour; **jmdm.** ~ **antun** pay tribute to sb.; **ehren** *tr. V.* a) honour; **Sehr geehrter Herr Müller!/Sehr geehrte Frau Müller!** Dear Herr Müller/Dear Frau Müller; b) *(Ehre machen)* **deine Hilfsbereitschaft ehrt dich** your willingness to help does you credit; **ehrenhaft** *Adj.* honourable

**ehren-, Ehren-:** ~**rührig** *Adj.* defamatory ⟨*allegations*⟩; ~**sache** die: **das ist** ~**sache** that is a point of

honour; ~**sache!** you can count on me!; ~**voll** *Adj.* honourable; ~**wert** *Adj. (geh.)* worthy; ~**wort** das; *pl.* ~**worte:** ~**wort** [!/?] word of honour [!/?]

**ehrerbietig** *Adj. (geh.)* respectful

**Ehr·furcht** die reverence (vor + *Dat.* for); **ehrfürchtig** *Adj.* reverent

**ehr-, Ehr-:** ~**gefühl** das; *o. Pl.* sense of honour; ~**geiz** der ambition; ~**geizig** *Adj.* ambitious

**ehrlich** *Adj.* honest; genuine ⟨*concern, desire, admiration*⟩; upright ⟨*character*⟩; **Ehrlichkeit** die; ~ *s.* ehrlich: honesty; genuineness; uprightness

**ehr·los** *Adj.* dishonourable

**Ehrung** die; ~, ~**en:** **die** ~ **der Preisträger** the prize-giving *(Brit.)* or *(Amer.)* awards ceremony; **bei der** ~ **der Sieger** when the winners were awarded their medals/trophies

**ehr·würdig** *Adj.* venerable

**Ei** das; ~[e]s, ~**er** egg

**Eiche** die; ~, ~**n** oak[-tree]; *(Holz)* oak[-wood]

**Eichel** die; ~, ~**n** acorn

**eichen** *tr. V.* calibrate ⟨*measuring instrument, thermometer*⟩; standardize ⟨*weights, measures, containers, products*⟩; adjust ⟨*weighing-scales*⟩

**Eich·hörnchen** das squirrel

**Eid** der; ~[e]s, ~**e** oath

**Eidechse** ['aidɛksə] die; ~, ~**n** lizard

**eide·stattlich** *Adj. (Rechtsw.)* **eine** ~**e Erklärung** a statutory declaration

**Ei·dotter** der *od.* das egg yolk

**Eier-:** ~**becher** der egg-cup; ~**kuchen** der pancake; *(Omelett)* omelette; ~**likör** der egg-liqueur; ~**stock** der *(Physiol., Zool.)* ovary; ~**uhr** die egg-timer

**Eifer** der; ~s eagerness

**Eifer·sucht** die jealousy (auf + *Akk.* of); **eifer·süchtig** *Adj.* jealous (auf + *Akk.* of)

**eifrig** *Adj.* eager

**Ei·gelb** das; ~[e]s, ~**e** egg yolk

**eigen-, Eigen-:** ~**art** die *(Wesensart)* particular nature; *(Zug)* peculiarity; **eine** ~**art dieser Stadt** one of the characteristic features of this city; ~**artig** *Adj.* peculiar; strange; odd; ~**händig** 1. *Adj.* personal ⟨*signature*⟩; holographic ⟨*will, document*⟩; 2. *adv.* ⟨*present, sign*⟩ personally; ~**heim** das house of one's own

**Eigenheit** die; ~, ~**en** peculiarity

**eigen-, Eigen-:** ~**lob** das self-praise;

**~mächtig** *Adj.* unauthorized; **~name der** proper name; **~nützig** *Adj.* self-seeking; selfish ⟨*motive*⟩
**eigens** *Adv.* specially
**Eigenschaft die**; ~, **~en** quality; characteristic; *(von Sachen, Stoffen)* property
**Eigenschafts·wort das** adjective
**eigen-, Eigen-:** **~sinn der**; *o. Pl.* obstinacy; **~sinnig** *Adj.* obstinate; **~ständig** *Adj.* independent
**eigentlich** 1. *Adj. (wirklich)* actual; real; *(wahr)* true; *(ursprünglich)* original; 2. *Adv.* actually; 3. *Partikel* **wie spät ist es ~?** tell me, what time is it?; **was willst du ~?** what exactly do you want?
**Eigen·tor das** *(Ballspiele, fig.)* own goal
**Eigentum das**; **~s** property; *(einschließlich Geld usw.)* assets *pl.*
**Eigentümer der**; **~s,** ~: owner; *(Hotel~, Geschäfts~)* proprietor; **Eigentümerin die**; ~, **~nen** owner; *(Hotel~, Geschäfts~)* proprietress; proprietor; **Eigentums·wohnung die** owner-occupied flat *(Brit.)*; condominium apartment *(Amer.)*
**eigen·willig** *Adj.* self-willed
**eignen** *refl. V.* be suitable; **Eignung die**; ~: suitability; **seine ~ zum Fliegen** his aptitude for flying
**Eignungs-:** **~prüfung die, ~test der** aptitude test
**Eil-:** **~bote der** special messenger; **„durch od. per ~boten"** *(veralt.)* 'express'; **~brief der** express letter
**Eile die**; ~: hurry; **in ~ sein** be in a hurry; **eilen** *itr. V.* a) *mit sein* hurry; *(besonders schnell)* rush; b) *(dringend sein)* be urgent; **„eilt!"** 'urgent'; **eilig** 1. *Adj.* a) hurried; **es ~ haben** be in a hurry; b) *(dringend)* urgent; 2. *adv.* hurriedly; **Eil·zug der** semi-fast train
**Eimer der**; **~s,** ~: bucket; *(Milch~)* pail; *(Abfall~)* bin; **ein ~ |voll| Wasser** a bucket of water; **im ~ sein** *(salopp)* be up the spout *(sl.)*
**¹ein** 1. *Kardinalz.* one; 2. *unbest. Art.* a/an; 3. *Indefinitpron; s.* **irgendein a**; *s. auch* **einer**
**²ein** *(elliptisch)* **~ - aus** *(an Schaltern)* on – off
**Einakter der**; **~s,** ~: one-act play
**einander** *reziprokes Pron.; Dat. u. Akk. (geh.)* each other; one another
**ein|arbeiten** *tr. V.* train ⟨*employee*⟩
**ein·armig** *Adj.* one-armed
**ein|äschern** *tr. V.* cremate

**ein|atmen** *tr., itr. V.* breathe in
**ein·äugig** *Adj.* one-eyed
**Ein·bahn·straße die** one-way street
**Ein·band der**; *Pl.* **-bände** binding
**Ein·bau der**; **~s, ~ten** fitting; *(eines Motors)* installation; **ein|bauen** *tr. V.* build in, fit; install ⟨*engine, motor*⟩; **Einbau·küche die** fitted kitchen
**ein·beinig** *Adj.* one-legged
**ein|berufen** *unr. tr. V.* summon; call; **Ein·berufung die** a) *(das Einberufen)* calling; b) *(zur Wehrpflicht)* call-up; conscription; draft *(Amer.)*
**Einbett·zimmer das** single room
**ein|beziehen** *unr. tr. V.* include
**ein|biegen** *unr. itr. V.; mit sein* turn
**ein|bilden** *refl. V.* a) **sich** *(Dat.)* **etw. ~:** imagine sth.; b) *(ugs.)* **sich** *(Dat.)* **etwas ~:** be conceited (**auf +** *Akk.* about); **Ein·bildung die**; ~, **~en** a) imagination; b) *(falsche Vorstellung)* fantasy; c) *(Hochmut)* conceitedness
**ein|binden** *unr. tr. V.* bind ⟨*book*⟩; **etw. neu ~:** rebind sth.
**ein|blenden** *tr. V. (Rundf., Ferns., Film)* insert
**Ein·blick der** a) view; **~ in etw.** *(Akk.)* **haben** be able to see into sth.; b) *(Durchsicht)* **jmdm. ~ in etw.** *(Akk.)* **gewähren** allow sb. to look at *or* examine sth.; c) *(Kenntnis)* insight
**ein|brechen** *unr. itr. V.* a) *mit haben od. sein* break in; **in eine Bank ~:** break into a bank; **bei jmdm. ~:** burgle sb.; b) *mit sein (einstürzen)* ⟨*roof, ceiling*⟩ cave in; c) *mit sein (durchbrechen)* fall through; **Einbrecher der**; **~s,** ~: burglar
**ein|bringen** *unr. tr. V.* a) bring in ⟨*harvest*⟩; b) *(verschaffen)* **Gewinn/Zinsen ~:** yield a profit/bring in interest; **jmdm. Ruhm ~:** bring sb. fame; c) *(Parl.: vorlegen)* introduce ⟨*bill*⟩; d) invest ⟨*capital, money*⟩
**Ein·bruch der** a) burglary; **ein ~ in eine Bank** a break-in at a bank; b) *(das Einstürzen)* collapse
**einbürgern** 1. *tr. V.* naturalize; 2. *refl. V.* ⟨*custom, practice*⟩ become established; ⟨*person, plant, animal*⟩ become naturalized; **Einbürgerung die**; ~, **~en** naturalization
**Einbuße die** loss; **ein|büßen** *tr. V.* lose; *(durch eigene Schuld)* forfeit
**ein|checken** *tr., itr. V. (Flugw.)* check in
**ein|cremen** *tr. V.* put cream on ⟨*hands etc.*⟩; **sich ~:** put cream on
**ein|dämmen** *tr. V. (fig.)* check; stem

**ein|decken** 1. *refl. V.* stock up; 2. *tr. V.* (*ugs.: überhäufen*) jmdn. mit Arbeit ~: swamp sb. with work

**eindeutig** *Adj.* clear; **Eindeutigkeit die;** ~, ~en clarity

**ein|dringen** *unr. itr. V.; mit sein* in etw. (*Akk.*) ~: penetrate into sth.; ⟨*bullet*⟩ pierce sth.; (*allmählich*) ⟨*water, sand, etc.*⟩ seep into sth.; **ein·dringlich** *Adj.* urgent; impressive ⟨*voice*⟩; forceful, powerful ⟨*words*⟩; **Eindringling der;** ~s, ~e intruder

**Ein·druck der;** ~[e]s, **Eindrücke** impression; **ein|drücken** *tr. V.* smash in (*mudguard, bumper*); stave in ⟨*side of ship*⟩; smash ⟨*pier, column, support*⟩; break ⟨*window*⟩; crush ⟨*ribs*⟩; flatten ⟨*nose*⟩; **eindrucks·voll** 1. *Adj.* impressive; 2. *adv.* impressively

**eine** *s.* ¹**ein**

**ein|ebnen** *tr. V.* level

**eineiig** ['ain|aiiç] *Adj.* identical ⟨*twins*⟩

**ein·ein·halb** *Bruchz.* one and a half; ~ **Stunden** an hour and a half

**ein|engen** *tr. V.* a) jmdn. ~: restrict sb.'s movement[s]; b) (*fig.*) restrict

**einer, eine, eines, eins** *Indefinitpron.* (*man*) one; (*jemand*) someone; somebody; (*fragend, verneint*) anyone; anybody; **kaum einer** hardly anybody; **ein[e]s ist sicher** one thing is for sure

**Einer der;** ~s, ~ a) (*Math.*) unit; b) (*Sport*) single sculler; **im** ~: in the single sculls

**einerlei** *Adj.* ~, **ob/wo/wer** *usw.* no matter whether/where/who *etc.*; **es ist** ~: it makes no difference

**Einerlei das;** ~s monotony

**einerseits** *Adv.* on the one hand

**ein·fach** 1. *Adj.* a) simple; b) (*nicht mehrfach*) single ⟨*knot, ticket, journey*⟩; 2. *Partikel* simply; just; **Einfachheit die;** ~: simplicity

**ein|fädeln** 1. *tr. V.* thread (**in** + *Akk.* into); 2. *refl. V.* (*Verkehrsw.*) filter in

**ein|fahren** 1. *unr. itr. V.; mit sein* come in; ⟨*train*⟩ pull in; **in den Bahnhof** ~: pull into the station; 2. *unr. tr. V.* a) bring in ⟨*harvest*⟩; b) (*beschädigen*) knock down ⟨*wall*⟩; smash in ⟨*mudguard*⟩; **Ein·fahrt die** a) (*das Hineinfahren*) entry; **Vorsicht bei der** ~ **des Zuges!** stand clear [of the edge of the platform], the train is approaching; b) (*Zufahrt*) entrance; (*Autobahn*~) slip road; „**keine** ~" 'no entry'

**Ein·fall der** a) (*Idee*) idea; b) *o. Pl.*

(*Licht*~) incidence (*Optics*); **ein|fallen** *unr. itr. V.; mit sein* a) jmdm. ~: occur to sb.; **was fällt dir denn ein!** what do you think you're doing?; b) (*in Erinnerung kommen*) **ihr Name fällt mir nicht ein** I cannot think of her name; **plötzlich fiel ihr ein, daß** ...: suddenly she remembered that ...; c) (*von Licht*) come in

**einfalls-:** ~**los** *Adj.* unimaginative; lacking in ideas; ~**reich** *Adj.* imaginative; full of ideas

**Einfalt die;** ~: simpleness; simplemindedness; **einfältig** *Adj.* simple; naïve; naïve ⟨*remarks*⟩

**ein|fangen** *unr. tr. V.* catch

**ein|fassen** *tr. V.* border; edge; frame ⟨*picture*⟩; set ⟨*gem*⟩; edge ⟨*grave, lawn, etc.*⟩; **Ein·fassung die** *s.* **einfassen:** border; edging; frame; setting

**ein|finden** *unr. refl. V.* arrive; (*sich treffen*) meet; ⟨*crowd*⟩ gather

**ein|fliegen** *unr. tr. V.* fly in

**ein|flößen** *tr. V.* a) jmdm. Tee ~: pour tea into sb.'s mouth; b) (*fig.*) jmdm. Angst ~: put fear into sb.

**Ein·fluß der** influence; **Einfluß·bereich der** sphere of influence; **einfluß·reich** *Adj.* influential

**ein·förmig** *Adj.* monotonous

**ein|frieren** 1. *unr. itr. V.; mit sein* freeze; ⟨*pipes*⟩ freeze up; 2. *unr. tr. V.* a) deep-freeze ⟨*food*⟩; b) (*fig.*) freeze

**ein|fügen** *tr. V.* fit in; **etw. in etw.** (*Akk.*) ~: fit sth. into sth.

**ein|fühlen** *refl. V.* **sich in jmdn.** ~: empathize with sb.; **einfühlsam** *Adj.* understanding; **Ein·fühlung die;** ~: empathy (**in** + *Akk.* with)

**Ein·fuhr die;** ~, ~**en** *s.* **Import;** **ein|führen** *tr. V.* a) (*als Neuerung*) introduce ⟨*fashion, method, technology*⟩; b) (*importieren*) import; **Ein·führung die** introduction

**Ein·gabe die** petition; (*Beschwerde*) complaint

**Ein·gang der** entrance; „**kein** ~" 'no entry'; **ein·gängig** *Adj.* catchy; **eingangs** *Adv.* at the beginning; pedes

**Eingangs-:** ~**halle die** entrance hall; (*eines Hotels, Theaters*) foyer; ~**tür die** (*von Kaufhaus, Hotel usw.*) [entrance] door; (*von Wohnung, Haus usw.*) front door

**ein·gebildet** *Adj.* a) imaginary ⟨*illness*⟩; b) (*arrogant*) conceited

**Eingeborene der/die;** *adj. Dekl.* (*veralt.*) native

**ein|gehen 1.** *unr. itr. V.; mit sein* **a)** arrive; **b)** *(fig.)* **in die Geschichte ~:** go down in history; **c)** *(schrumpfen)* shrink; **d) auf eine Frage ~/nicht ~:** go into *or* deal with/ignore a question; **auf jmdn. ~:** be responsive to sb.; **auf jmdn. nicht ~:** ignore sb.'s wishes; **2.** *unr. tr. V.* enter into ⟨*contract, matrimony*⟩; take ⟨*risk*⟩; accept ⟨*obligation*⟩

**eingehend** *Adj.* detailed

**Ein·gemachte das; ~n** preserved fruit/vegetables

**ein|gemeinden** *tr. V.* incorporate ⟨*village*⟩ (**in** + *Akk.,* **nach** into)

**ein·geschnappt** *Adj. (ugs.)* huffy

**Ein·geständnis das** confession; admission; **ein|gestehen** *unr. tr. V.* admit

**Eingeweide das; ~s, ~;** *meist Pl.* entrails *pl.;* innards *pl.*

**ein|gewöhnen** *refl. V.* get used to one's new surroundings

**ein|gießen** *unr. tr. V., itr. V.* pour in

**ein|gliedern** *tr. V.* integrate (**in** + *Akk.* into); incorporate ⟨*village, company*⟩ (**in** + *Akk.* into); *(einordnen)* include (**in** + *Akk.* into)

**ein|graben** *unr. tr. V.* bury (**in** + *Akk.* in); sink ⟨*pile, pipe*⟩ (**in** + *Akk.* into)

**ein|gravieren** *tr. V.* engrave (**in** + *Akk.* on)

**ein|greifen** *unr. itr. V.* intervene (**in** + *Akk.* in); **Ein·griff der a)** intervention (**in** + *Akk.* in); **b)** *(Med.)* operation

**ein|haken 1.** *tr. V.* **a)** *(mit Haken befestigen)* fasten; **b) sich ~:** link arms; **2.** *refl. V.* **sich bei jmdm. ~:** link arms with sb.

**Ein·halt der: jmdm./einer Sache ~ gebieten** *od.* **tun** *(geh.)* halt sb./sth.; **ein|halten 1.** *unr. tr. V.* keep ⟨*appointment*⟩; meet ⟨*deadline, commitments*⟩; keep to ⟨*diet, speed-limit, agreement*⟩; observe ⟨*regulation*⟩; **2.** *unr. itr. V. (geh.)* stop

**ein·heimisch** *Adj.* native; home *attrib.* ⟨*team*⟩; **Einheimische der/die;** *adj. Dekl.* local

**Einheit die; ~, ~en** unity; **einheitlich 1.** *Adj.* unified; *(unterschiedslos)* uniform ⟨*dress*⟩; standard ⟨*procedure, practice*⟩; **2.** *adv.* **~ gekleidet sein** be dressed the same

**einhellig 1.** *Adj.* unanimous; **2.** *adv.* unanimously

**ein|holen 1.** *tr. V.* **a)** catch up with ⟨*person, vehicle*⟩; **b)** make up ⟨*arrears, time*⟩; **2.** *itr. V. (ugs.)* s. **einkaufen 1**

**ein·hundert** *Kardinalz. s.* **hundert**

**einig** *Adj.* **sich** *(Dat.)* **~ sein** be agreed; **sich** *(Dat.)* **~ werden** reach agreement

**einig...** *Indefinitpron. u. unbest. Zahlwort* some; **~e wenige** a few; **~e hundert** several hundred

**einigen 1.** *tr. V.* unite; **2.** *refl. V.* reach an agreement

**einigermaßen** *Adv.* somewhat

**Einigkeit die; ~ a)** unity; **b)** *(Übereinstimmung)* agreement

**ein·jährig** *Adj.* one-year-old *attrib.;* one year old *pred.;* ⟨*ein Jahr dauernd*⟩ one-year *attrib.*

**Ein·kauf der a) Einkäufe machen** do some shopping; **b)** *(eingekaufte Ware)* purchase; **c)** *o. Pl. (Abteilung)* purchasing department; **ein|kaufen 1.** *itr. V.* shop; **~ gehen** go shopping; **2.** *tr. V.* buy; purchase; **Ein·käufer der** buyer; purchaser

**Einkaufs-: ~bummel der** [leisurely] shopping expedition; **~zentrum das** shopping centre

**ein|kehren** *itr. V.; mit sein* stop; **in einem Wirtshaus ~:** stop at an inn

**ein|klammern** *tr. V.* **etw. ~:** put sth. in brackets; bracket sth.

**Ein·klang der** harmony; **in** *od.* **im ~ stehen** accord

**ein|kleben** *tr. V.* stick in

**ein|kleiden** *tr. V.* clothe

**ein|klemmen** *tr. V.* **a)** *(quetschen)* catch; **b)** *(fest einfügen)* clamp

**ein|kochen** *tr. V.* preserve ⟨*fruit etc.*⟩

**Einkommen das; ~s, ~:** income

**ein|kreisen** *tr. V.* **a) etw. ~:** put a circle round sth.; **b)** *(umzingeln)* surround

**Einkünfte** *Pl.* income *sing.;* **feste ~:** a regular income

¹**ein|laden** *unr. tr. V.* load ⟨*goods*⟩

²**ein|laden** *unr. tr. V.* invite ⟨*person*⟩ (**zu** for); **einladend** *Adj.* inviting; **Ein·ladung die** invitation

**Ein·lage die a)** *(in Brief)* enclosure; **b)** *(Kochk.)* vegetables, dumplings, etc. added to a clear soup; **c)** *(Schuh~)* arch-support; **d)** *(Programm~)* interlude

**ein|lagern** *tr. V.* store; lay in ⟨*stores*⟩

**Einlaß der; Einlasses, Einlässe** admission; **ein|lassen** *unr. tr. V.* **a)** *(hereinlassen)* admit; let in; **b)** *(einfüllen)* run ⟨*water*⟩

**Ein·lauf der** *(Med.)* enema; **ein|laufen 1.** *unr. itr. V.; mit sein* **a)** ⟨*ship*⟩ come in; **b)** *(kleiner werden)* shrink; **2.** *unr. tr. V.* wear in ⟨*shoes*⟩

**ein|leben** *refl. V.* settle down

**ein|legen** *tr. V.* a) load ⟨*film*⟩; engage ⟨*gear*⟩; b) *(Kochk.)* pickle

**ein|leiten** *tr. V.* a) introduce; b) induce ⟨*birth*⟩; c) lead in; etw. in etw. *(Akk.)* ~: lead sth. into sth.; **Ein·leitung die** a) introduction; b) *(einer Geburt)* induction

**ein|leuchten** *itr. V.* jmdm. ~: be clear to sb.; **ein·leuchtend** *Adj.* plausible

**ein|liefern** *tr. V.* take ⟨*letter, person*⟩ (**bei, in** + **Abk.** to)

**ein|lösen** *tr. V.* cash ⟨*cheque*⟩

**ein|machen** *tr. V.* preserve ⟨*fruit etc.*⟩; *(in Gläser)* bottle

**einmal** 1. *Adv.* a) once; **noch ~ so groß |wie|** twice as big [as]; etw. noch ~ tun do sth. again; b) ['-'-] *(später)* one day; *(früher)* once; **es war ~ ...**: once upon a time there was ...; 2. *Partikel* **nicht ~**: not even; **wieder ~**: yet again; **Einmal·eins das; ~**: [multiplication] tables *pl.;* **einmalig** 1. *Adj.* a) unique; one-off ⟨*payment, purchase*⟩; b) *(ugs.)* fantastic *(coll.)*; 2. *adv. (ugs.)* really fantastically *(coll.)*

**Ein·marsch der** a) entry; b) *(Besetzung)* invasion (**in** + *Akk.* of); **ein|marschieren** *itr. V.; mit sein* march in

**ein|mischen** *refl. V.* interfere (**in** + *Akk.* in)

**einmütig** 1. *Adj.* unanimous; 2. *adv.* unanimously

**ein|nähen** *tr. V.* sew in

**Einnahme die; ~, ~en** a) income; *(Staats~)* revenue; *(Kassen~)* takings *pl.;* b) *(von Arzneimitteln)* taking; c) *(einer Stadt, Burg)* taking; **ein|nehmen** *unr. tr. V.* a) take; *(verdienen)* earn; b) *(ausfüllen)* take up ⟨*amount of room*⟩; c) *(beeinflussen)* jmdn. für sich ~: win sb. over

**Ein·öde die** barren waste

**ein|ordnen** 1. *tr. V.* arrange; put in order; 2. *refl. V.* a) *(Verkehrsw.)* get into the correct lane; „~" 'get in lane'; b) *(sich einfügen)* fit in

**ein|packen** 1. *tr. V.* pack (**in** + *Akk.* in); *(einwickeln)* wrap [up]; 2. *itr. V. (ugs.)* **er kann ~**: he's had it *(coll.)*

**ein|parken** *tr., itr. V.* park

**ein|pflanzen** *tr. V.* a) plant; b) *(Med., fig.)* implant

**ein|prägen** *tr. V.* a) stamp (**in** + *Akk.* into, on); b) *(fig.)* sich *(Dat.)* etw. ~: memorize sth.; **jmdm. etw. ~**: impress sth. on sb.; **einprägsam** *Adj.* easily remembered

**ein|rahmen** *tr. V.* frame

**ein|räumen** *tr. V.* a) put away; b) *(füllen)* seinen Schrank ~: put one's things away in one's cupboard; **ein Zimmer ~**: put the furniture into a room; c) *(zugestehen)* admit

**ein|reden** 1. *tr. V.* jmdm. etw. ~: talk sb. into believing sth.; sich *(Dat.)* ~, daß ...: persuade oneself that ...; 2. *itr. V.* **auf jmdn. ~**: talk insistently to sb.

**ein|regnen** *refl. V.; unpers.* **es hat sich eingeregnet** it's begun to rain steadily.

**ein|reiben** *unr. tr. V.* rub ⟨*substance*⟩ in; etw. mit Öl ~: rub oil into sth.

**ein|reichen** *tr. V.* submit; lodge ⟨*complaint*⟩; tender ⟨*resignation*⟩

**ein|reihen** 1. *refl. V.* sich in etw. *(Akk.)* ~: join sth.; 2. *tr. V.* jmdn. in eine Kategorie ~: place sb. in a category

**Einreiher der; ~s, ~**: single-breasted suit/jacket

**Ein·reise die** entry; **Einreise·erlaubnis die** entry permit; **ein|reisen** *itr. V.; mit sein* enter; **nach Schweden ~**: enter Sweden

**ein|reißen** 1. *unr. tr. V.* a) pull down ⟨*building*⟩; b) *(einen Riß machen in)* tear; rip; 2. *unr. itr. V.; mit sein* tear; rip

**ein|renken** *tr. V.* a) *(Med.)* set; b) *(ugs.: bereinigen)* sort out

**ein|richten** 1. *refl. V.* sich schön ~: furnish one's home beautifully; sich häuslich ~: make oneself at home; 2. *tr. V.* furnish ⟨*flat, house*⟩; fit out ⟨*shop*⟩; equip ⟨*laboratory*⟩; **Ein·richtung die** a) *o. Pl.* furnishing; b) *(Mobiliar)* furnishings *pl.*

**ein|rollen** 1. *tr. V.* roll up ⟨*carpet etc.*⟩; put ⟨*hair*⟩ in curlers; 2. *itr. V.; mit sein* roll in

**ein|rosten** *itr. V.; mit sein* go rusty

**ein|rücken** 1. *itr. V.; mit sein (einmarschieren)* move in; 2. *tr. V.* indent ⟨*line, heading, etc.*⟩

**eins** 1. *Kardinalz.* one; **es ist ~**: it is one o'clock; ~ zu null one-nil; ~ zu ~: one all; „~, zwei, drei!" 'ready, steady, go'; 2. *Adj.* mir ist alles ~: it's all the same to me; 3. *Indefinitpron. s.* irgendein u. **Eins die; ~, ~en** a) one; b) *(Schulnote)* one; A

**einsam** *Adj.* a) lonely ⟨*person, decision*⟩; b) *(einzeln)* solitary ⟨*tree, wanderer*⟩; c) *(abgelegen)* isolated; d) *(menschenleer)* deserted; **Einsamkeit die; ~** a) loneliness; b) *(Alleinsein)* solitude; c) *(Abgeschiedenheit)* isolation

**ein|sammeln** *tr. V.* **a)** *(auflesen)* pick up; gather up; **b)** *(sich aushändigen lassen)* collect in; collect ⟨*tickets*⟩
**Ein·satz** der **a)** *(aus Stoff)* inset; *(in Kochtopf, Nähkasten usw.)* compartment; **b)** *(Betrag)* stake; **c)** *(Gebrauch)* use; *(von Truppen)* deployment
**Einsatz-:** ~**befehl** der order to go into action; **den** ~**befehl haben** have operational command; ~**leiter** der head of operations; ~**wagen** der *(der Polizei)* police car; *(der Feuerwehr)* fire-engine; *(Notarztwagen)* ambulance
**ein|saugen** *unr. (auch regelm.) tr. V.* suck in; breathe [in] ⟨*fresh air*⟩
**ein|schalten 1.** *tr. V.* **a)** switch on ⟨*radio, TV, electricity, etc.*⟩; **b)** *(fig.)* call in ⟨*press, police, expert, etc.*⟩; **2.** *refl. V.* **a)** switch [itself] on; **b)** *(eingreifen)* intervene (**in** + *Akk.* in)
**ein|schärfen** *tr. V.* **jmdm. etw.** ~: impress sth. [up]on sb.
**ein|schätzen** *tr. V.* judge ⟨*person*⟩; assess ⟨*situation, income, damages*⟩; *(schätzen)* estimate; **Ein·schätzung** die *s.* **einschätzen**: judging; assessment; estimation
**ein|schenken** *tr., itr. V.* **a)** *(eingießen)* pour [out]; **jmdm. etw.** ~: pour out sth. for sb.; **b)** *(füllen)* fill [up] ⟨*glass, cup*⟩
**ein|scheren** *itr. V.; mit sein* **auf eine Fahrspur** ~: get *or* move into a lane
**ein|schicken** *tr. V.* send in
**ein|schieben** *unr. tr. V.* **a)** push in; **b)** *(einfügen)* insert; put on ⟨*trains, buses*⟩
**ein|schiffen** *tr., refl. V.* embark
**ein|schlafen** *unr. itr. V.; mit sein* **a)** fall asleep; **b)** *(verhüll.: sterben)* pass away; **c)** *(gefühllos werden)* go to sleep; **ein|schläfern** *tr. V.* **a)** **jmdn.** ~: send sb. to sleep, *(betäuben)* put sb. to sleep; **b)** *(schmerzlos töten)* **ein Tier** ~: put an animal to sleep; **einschläfernd 1.** *Adj.* soporific; **2.** *adv.* ~ **wirken** have a soporific effect
**ein|schlagen 1.** *unr. tr. V.* **a)** knock in; **b)** *(zertrümmern)* smash [in]; **c)** *(einwickeln)* wrap up ⟨*present*⟩; cover ⟨*book*⟩; **2.** *unr. itr. V.* **a)** ⟨*bomb*⟩ land; ⟨*lightning*⟩ strike; **b)** **auf jmdn./etw.** ~: rain blows on sb./sth.
**einschlägig 1.** *Adj.* specialist ⟨*journal, shop*⟩; relevant ⟨*literature, passage*⟩; **2.** *adv.* **er ist** ~ **vorbestraft** he has previous convictions for a similar offence/similar offences
**ein|schleichen** *unr. refl. V.* steal in

**ein|schließen** *unr. tr. V.* **a)** **etw. in etw.** *(Dat.)* ~: lock sth. up [in sth.]; **jmdn./sich** ~: lock sb./oneself in; **b)** *(umgeben)* surround; **einschließlich 1.** *Präp. mit Gen.* including; ~ **der Unkosten** including expenses; **2.** *adv.* **bis** ~ **30. Juni** up to and including 30 June
**ein|schmeicheln** *refl. V.* **sich bei jmdm.** ~: ingratiate oneself with sb.
**ein|schmuggeln** *tr. V.* smuggle in
**ein|schneiden** *unr. tr. V.* **a)** make a cut in; **b)** *(einritzen)* carve; **einschneidend** *Adj.* drastic
**ein|schneien** *itr. V.; mit sein* get snowed in
**Ein·schnitt** der cut
**ein|schränken 1.** *tr. V.* **a)** reduce, curb ⟨*expenditure, consumption*⟩; **b)** *(einengen)* limit; restrict; **jmdn. in seinen Rechten** ~: limit *or* restrict sb.'s rights; **2.** *refl. V.* economize; **Einschränkung** die ~, ~**en a)** restriction; limitation; **b)** *(Vorbehalt)* reservation
**ein|schreiben** *unr. tr. V.* **a)** *(Postw.)* register ⟨*letter*⟩; **b)** *(eintragen)* **sich/jmdn.** ~: enter one's/sb.'s name; **Ein·schreiben** das *(Postw.)* registered letter; **per** ~: by registered mail
**ein|schreiten** *unr. itr. V.* intervene
**ein|schüchtern** *tr. V.* intimidate
**ein|schulen** *tr. V.* **eingeschult werden** start school
**ein|sehen** *unr. tr. V.* **a)** *(überblicken)* see into; **b)** *(prüfend lesen)* look at; **c)** *(erkennen)* realize; **d)** *(begreifen)* see
**ein|seifen** *tr. V.* lather
**ein·seitig 1.** *Adj.* **a)** on one side *postpos.*; **b)** *(tendenziös)* one-sided; **2.** *adv.* **a)** on one side; **b)** *(tendenziös)* one-sidedly
**ein|senden** *unr. tr. V.* **a)** *(auch regelm.) tr. V.* send [in]
**ein|setzen 1.** *tr. V.* **a)** *(hineinsetzen)* put in; **b)** put on ⟨*special train etc.*⟩; **c)** *(ernennen)* appoint; **d)** *(in Aktion treten lassen)* use; **e)** *(aufs Spiel setzen)* stake ⟨*money*⟩; **f)** *(riskieren)* risk; **2.** *itr. V.* begin; ⟨*storm*⟩ break. **3.** *refl. V.* *(sich engagieren)* **ich werde mich dafür** ~, **daß ...**: I shall do what I can to see that ...; **sich nicht genug** ~: ⟨*pupil*⟩ be lacking application; ⟨*minister*⟩ be lacking in commitment
**Ein·sicht** die **a)** view (**in** + *Akk.* into); **b)** *(Einblick)* ~ **in die Akten nehmen** take *or* have a look at the files; **c)** *(Erkenntnis)* insight; **einsichtig** *Adj.* **a)**

*(verständnisvoll)* understanding; **b)** *(verständlich)* comprehensible

**Ein·siedler der** hermit

**ein·silbig** *Adj.* **a)** monosyllabic ⟨*word*⟩; **b)** *(fig.)* taciturn ⟨*person*⟩

**ein|sinken** *unr. itr. V.* sink in

**Einsitzer der**; ~s, ~: single-seater; **einsitzig** *Adj.* single-seater *attrib.*

**ein|spannen** *tr. V.* harness ⟨*horse*⟩; put in ⟨*paper*⟩; fix ⟨*fabric*⟩; clamp ⟨*work*⟩

**ein|sparen** *tr. V.* save

**ein|sperren** *tr. V.* lock up

**einsprachig** *Adj.* monolingual

**ein|springen** *unr. itr. V.; mit sein* stand in; *(aushelfen)* step in and help out

**ein|spritzen** *tr. V.* inject; **jmdm. etw. ~:** inject sb. with sth.; **Einspritz·motor der** fuel-injection engine

**Ein·spruch der** objection (**gegen** to)

**einspurig 1.** *Adj.* single-track ⟨*road*⟩; **2.** *adv.* **die Autobahn ist nur ~ befahrbar** only one lane of the motorway is open

**einst** *Adv. (geh.)* once

**ein|stampfen** *tr. V.* pulp ⟨*books*⟩

**Ein·stand der: seinen ~ geben** celebrate starting a new job

**ein|stecken** *tr. V.* **a)** put in; **b)** *(mitnehmen)* put ⟨*sth.*⟩ in one's pocket/bag *etc.*

**ein|stehen** *unr. itr. V.* **für jmdn. ~:** vouch for sb.; **für etw. ~:** take responsibility for sth.

**ein|steigen** *unr. itr. V.; mit sein* **a)** *(in ein Fahrzeug)* get in; **in ein Auto ~:** get into a car; **in den Bus ~:** get on the bus; **b)** *(eindringen)* climb in

**einstellbar** *Adj.* adjustable; **ein|stellen 1.** *tr. V.* **a)** *(einordnen)* put away ⟨*books etc.*⟩; **b)** *(unterstellen)* put in ⟨*car, bicycle*⟩; **c)** *(beschäftigen)* take on ⟨*workers*⟩; **d)** *(regulieren)* adjust; **e)** *(beenden)* stop; call off ⟨*search, strike*⟩; **f)** *(Sport)* equal ⟨*record*⟩; **2.** *refl. V.* **a)** arrive; **b)** ⟨*pain, worry*⟩ begin; ⟨*success*⟩ come; ⟨*symptoms, consequences*⟩ appear; **c) sich auf etw.** *(Akk.)* **~:** prepare oneself for sth.; **sich schnell auf neue Situationen ~:** adjust quickly to new situations

**ein·stellig** *Adj.* single-figure *attrib.*

**Ein·stellung die a)** *(von Arbeitskräften)* employment; **b)** *(Regulierung)* adjustment; **c)** *(Beendigung)* stopping; **d)** *(Sport)* **die ~ eines Rekordes** the equalling of a record; **e)** *(Ansicht)*

attitude; **ihre politische/religiöse ~:** her political/religious views *pl.*; **f)** *(Film)* take

**Ein·stich der a)** insertion; **b)** *(~stelle)* puncture; prick

**Ein·stieg der**; ~[e]s, ~e *(Eingang)* entrance; *(Tür)* door/doors

**ein|stimmen 1.** *itr. V.* join in. **2.** *tr. V.* **jmdn. auf etw.** *(Akk.)* **~:** get sb. in the [right] mood for sth.

**einstimmig 1.** *Adj.* **a)** *(Musik)* for one voice; **b)** *(einmütig)* unanimous ⟨*decision, vote*⟩; **2.** *adv.* **a)** *(Musik)* in unison; **b)** *(einmütig)* unanimously

**ein·stöckig** *Adj.* single-storey *attrib.*

**ein|studieren** *tr. V.* rehearse

**ein|stufen** *tr. V.* classify; categorize

**ein·stündig** *Adj.* one-hour *attrib.*

**ein|stürmen** *itr. V.* **mit Fragen auf jmdn. ~:** besiege sb. with questions

**Ein·sturz der** collapse; **ein|stürzen** *itr. V.; mit sein* collapse

**einst·weilen** *Adv.* for the time being

**eintägig** *Adj.* one-day *attrib.*; **Eintags·fliege die** *(Zool.)* mayfly; *(fig. ugs.)* seven-day wonder

**ein|tauchen 1.** *tr. V.* dip; *(untertauchen)* immerse; **2.** *itr. V.; mit sein* dive in; ⟨*submarine*⟩ dive

**ein|tauschen** *tr. V.* exchange (**gegen** for)

**ein·tausend** *Kardinalz.: s.* tausend

**ein|teilen** *tr. V.* **a)** divide up; classify ⟨*plants, species*⟩; **b)** *(disponieren, verplanen)* organize

**einteilig** *Adj.* one-piece

**eintönig 1.** *Adj.* monotonous; **2.** *adv.* monotonously; **Eintönigkeit die**; ~: monotony

**Ein·topf der** stew

**Ein·tracht die**; *o. Pl.* harmony; **ein·trächtig** *Adj.* harmonious

**Eintrag der**; ~[e]s, **Einträge** entry; **ein|tragen** *unr. tr. V.* **a)** enter; **b)** *(Amtsspr.)* register

**einträglich** *Adj.* lucrative

**ein|treffen** *unr. itr. V.; mit sein* **a)** arrive; **b)** *(verwirklicht werden)* come true

**ein|treiben** *unr. tr. V.* collect ⟨*taxes, debts*⟩; *(durch Gerichtsverfahren)* recover ⟨*debts, money*⟩

**ein|treten 1.** *unr. itr. V.; mit sein* **a)** enter; **bitte, treten Sie ein!** please come in; **b)** *(Mitglied werden)* **in einen Verein/einen Orden ~:** join a club/enter a religious order; **c)** *(Raumfahrt)* enter; **2.** *unr. tr. V.* kick in ⟨*door, window, etc.*⟩

ein|trichtern *tr. V. (salopp)* jmdm. etw. ~: drum sth. into sb.

Ein·tritt der a) entry; entrance; vor dem ~ in die Verhandlungen *(fig.)* before entering into negotiations; b) *(Beitritt)* der ~ in einen Verein/einen Orden joining a club/entering a religious order; c) *(von Raketen)* entry; d) *(Zugang, Eintrittsgeld)* admission; e) *(Beginn)* onset; ~ der Dunkelheit nightfall

Eintritts-: ~geld das admission fee; ~karte die admission ticket; ~preis der admission charge

ein|trocknen *itr. V.; mit sein* dry; ⟨water, toothpaste⟩ dry up; ⟨leather⟩ dry out; ⟨berry, fruit⟩ shrivel

ein|üben *tr. V.* practise

einverstanden *Adj.* ~ sein agree; mit jmdm./etw. ~ sein approve of sb./sth.

Ein·verständnis das consent

ein|wachsen *unr. itr. V.; mit sein* grow into the flesh; eingewachsen ingrown ⟨toe-nail⟩

Einwand der; ~[e]s, Einwände objection (gegen to)

Ein·wanderer der immigrant; ein|wandern *itr. V.; mit sein* immigrate (in + *Akk.* into); Ein·wanderung die immigration

einwand·frei 1. *Adj.* flawless; impeccable ⟨behaviour⟩; indisputable ⟨proof⟩; 2. *adv.* flawlessly; ⟨behave⟩ impeccably; ⟨prove⟩ beyond question

ein|wechseln *tr. V.* a) change ⟨money⟩; b) *(Sport)* substitute ⟨player⟩

ein|wecken *tr. V.* preserve; bottle

Ein·weg·flasche die non-returnable bottle

ein|weichen *tr. V.* soak

ein|weihen *tr. V.* open [officially] ⟨bridge, road⟩; dedicate ⟨monument⟩; Einweihung die; ~, ~en *s.* einweihen: [official] opening; dedication

ein|weisen *unr. tr. V.* a) *(in eine Tätigkeit)* introduce; b) *(in ein Amt)* install

ein|wenden *unr. (auch regelm.) tr. V.* dagegen läßt sich vieles ~: there is a lot to be said against that

ein|werfen *unr. tr. V.* a) mail ⟨letter⟩; insert ⟨coin⟩; b) smash ⟨window⟩; c) throw in ⟨ball⟩; d) *(bemerken, sagen)* throw in ⟨remark⟩

ein|wickeln *tr. V.* wrap [up]

ein|willigen *itr. V.* agree (in + *Akk.* to); Einwilligung die; ~, ~en agreement

ein|winken *tr. V. (Verkehrsw.)* guide in ⟨aircraft, car⟩

ein|wirken a) *(beeinflussen)* auf jmdn. ~: influence sb.; b) *(eine Wirkung ausüben)* have an effect (auf + *Akk.* on); Ein·wirkung die *(Einfluß)* influence; *(Wirkung)* effect

Einwohner der; ~s, ~, Einwohnerin die; ~, ~nen inhabitant

Ein·wurf der a) insertion; *(von Briefen)* mailing; b) *(Ballspiele)* throw-in; c) *(Bemerkung)* interjection

Ein·zahl die; *o. Pl.* singular

ein|zahlen *tr. V.* pay in; Ein·zahlung die payment

ein|zäunen *tr. V.* fence in; enclose; Einzäunung die; ~, ~en fencing-in

ein|zeichnen *tr. V.* draw *or* mark in

einzeilig *Adj.* one-line *attrib.*

Einzel das; ~s, ~ *(Sport)* singles *pl.*

Einzel-: ~bett das single bed; ~fall der a) particular case; b) *(Ausnahme)* isolated case; ~gänger [-gɛŋɐ] der; ~s, ~: loner; ~haft die solitary confinement; ~handel der retail trade; ~händler der retailer

Einzelheit die; ~, ~en a) detail; b) *(einzelner Umstand)* particular

Einzel·kind das only child

einzeln *Adj.* a) *(für sich allein)* individual; b) *(alleinstehend)* solitary ⟨building, tree⟩; single ⟨lady, gentleman⟩; c) ~e *(wenige)* a few; *(einige)* some; d) *substantivisch* der/jeder ~e the/each individual; ~es some things *pl.*; das Einzelne the particular

Einzel-: ~teil das individual part; ~zelle die single cell; ~zimmer das single room

ein|ziehen 1. *unr. tr. V.* a) put in; thread in ⟨tape, elastic⟩; b) *(einholen)* haul in ⟨net⟩; c) *(einatmen)* breathe in ⟨scent, fresh air⟩; inhale ⟨smoke⟩; d) *(einberufen)* call up ⟨recruits⟩; e) *(beitreiben)* collect; 2. *unr. itr. V.; mit sein* a) ⟨liquid⟩ soak in; b) *(einkehren)* enter; c) *(in eine Wohnung)* move in

einzig 1. *Adj.* only; kein ~es Wort not a single word; 2. *adv.* a) *intensivierend bei Adj.* extraordinarily; b) *(ausschließlich)* only; das ~ Wahre the only thing; einzig·artig 1. *Adj.* unique; 2. *adv.* uniquely

Ein·zug der a) entry (in + *Akk.* into); b) *(in eine Wohnung)* move; Einzugs·bereich der catchment area

Eis das; ~es a) ice; b) *(Speise~)* ice-cream; ein ~ am Stiel an ice-lolly *(Brit.)* or *(Amer.)* ice pop

Eis-: ~bahn die ice-rink; ~bär der polar bear; ~becher der ice-cream sundae; ~**bein** das *(Kochk.)* knuckle of pork; ~**berg** der iceberg; ~**beutel** der ice-bag; ~**café** das ice-cream parlour

**Ei·schnee** der stiffly beaten eggwhite

**Eisen** das; ~s, ~: iron

**Eisen·bahn** die a) railway; railroad *(Amer.);* mit der ~ **fahren** go by train; b) *(Bahnstrecke)* railway line; railroad track *(Amer.);* **Eisenbahner** der; ~s, ~: railwayman; railroader *(Amer.);* **Eisenbahn·unglück** das train crash

**Eisen-:** ~**erz** das iron ore; ~**kette** die iron chain; ~**ring** der iron ring; ~**stange** die iron bar; ~**waren** Pl. ironmongery *sing.;* ~**zeit** die Iron Age

**eisern** 1. *Adj. (auch fig.)* iron; 2. *adv.* resolutely; ⟨save, train⟩ with iron determination; ~ **durchgreifen** take drastic measures

**eis-, Eis-:** ~**fach** das freezing compartment; ~**frei** *Adj.* ice-free; ~**gekühlt** *Adj.* iced; ~**glatt** *Adj.* icy; ~**glätte** die black ice; ~**hockey** das ice hockey

**eisig** 1. *Adj.* a) icy ⟨wind, cold⟩; icy [cold] ⟨water⟩; b) *(fig.)* frosty; 2. *adv.* a) ~ **kalt** sein be icy cold; b) *(fig.)* ⟨smile⟩ frostily; **eisig·kalt** *Adj. s.* eiskalt 1 a

**eis-, Eis-:** ~**kaffee** der iced coffee; ~**kalt** 1. *Adj.* a) ice-cold ⟨drink⟩; freezing cold ⟨weather⟩; b) *(gefühllos)* icy; ice-cold ⟨look⟩; 2. *adv.* es lief mir ~**kalt** über den Rücken a cold shiver went down my spine; ~**kunstlauf** der figure skating; ~**kunst·läufer** der figure skater; ~**lauf** der ice-skating; ~|**laufen** *unr. itr. V.; mit sein* ice-skate; ~**laufen** das ice-skating; ~**läufer** der ice-skater; ~**schrank** der refrigerator; ~**sport** der ice sports *pl.;* ~**tanz** der *(Sport)* ice-dancing; ~**waffel** die [ice-cream] wafer; ~**wein** der *wine made from grapes frozen on the vine;* ~**würfel** der ice cube; ~**zapfen** der icicle; ~**zeit** die ice age

**eitel** *Adj.* vain; **Eitelkeit** die; ~, ~en vanity

**Eiter** der; ~s pus; **eitern** *itr. V.* suppurate; **eitrig** *Adj.* suppurating

**Ei·weiß** das a) egg-white; b) *(Protein)* protein

¹**Ekel** der; ~s revulsion; |einen| ~ vor etw. *(Dat.)* haben have a revulsion for

sth.; ²**Ekel** das; ~s, ~ *(ugs. abwertend)* horror; er ist ein |altes| ~: he is quite obnoxious; **ekelhaft** *Adj.* revolting ⟨sight⟩; horrible ⟨weather, person⟩ **ekeln** 1. *refl. V.* be disgusted; sich vor etw. *(Dat.)* ~: find sth. repulsive; 2. *tr., itr. V. (unpers.)* es ekelt mich *od.* mir ekelt davor I find it revolting; **eklig** *Adj.* a) *s.* ekelhaft; b) *(ugs.: gemein)* nasty

**Ekstase** [εk'staːzə] die; ~, ~n ecstasy

**Ekzem** das; ~s, ~e *(Med.)* eczema

**Elan** der; ~s zest; vigour

**elastisch** *Adj.* elasticated ⟨material⟩; springy ⟨surface⟩; supple ⟨person, body⟩; **Elastizität** die; ~: elasticity; *(Federkraft)* springiness; *(Geschmeidigkeit)* suppleness

**Elch** der; ~|e|s, ~e elk; *(in Nordamerika)* moose

**Elefant** der; ~en, ~en elephant

**elegant** 1. *Adj.* elegant; 2. *adv.* elegantly; **Eleganz** die; ~: elegance

**elektrifizieren** *tr. V.* electrify; **Elektrifizierung** die; ~, ~en electrification

**Elektriker** der; ~s, ~: electrician; **elektrisch** 1. *Adj.* electric; electrical ⟨resistance, wiring, system⟩; 2. *adv.* ~ **kochen** cook with electricity; ~ **geladen sein** be electrically charged; **elektrisieren** 1. *tr. V. (Med.)* treat using electricity; 2. *refl. V.* get an electric shock; **Elektrizität** die; ~ electricity

**Elektrizitäts·werk** das power station

**Elektro-:** ~**artikel** der electrical appliance; ~**auto** das electric car; ~**gerät** das electrical appliance; ~**geschäft** das electrical shop *or (Amer.)* store; ~**herd** der electric cooker; ~**mobil** das electric car; ~**motor** der electric motor

**Elektron** das; ~s, ~en [-'troːnən] electron

**Elektronen-:** ~**[ge]hirn** das *(ugs.)* electronic brain *(coll.);* ~**rechner** der electronic computer

**Elektronik** die; ~ a) electronics *sing., no art.;* b) *(Teile)* electronics *pl.;* **elektronisch** 1. *Adj.* electronic; 2. *adv.* electronically

**Elektro-:** ~**rasierer** der electric shaver; ~**technik** die electrical engineering *no art.;* ~**techniker** der a) electronics engineer; b) *(Elektriker)* electrician

**Element** das; ~|e|s, ~e element; **ele-**

ment**a**r *Adj.* **a)** *(grundlegend)* fundamental; **b)** *(einfach)* elementary 〈*knowledge*〉*;* **c)** *(naturhaft)* elemental 〈*force*〉*;* **Element**a**r·teilchen** das *(Physik)* elementary particle

**e**lend *Adj.* wretched; miserable; **E**lend das; ~s misery

**E**lends-: ~**quartier** das slum [dwelling]; ~**viertel** das slum area

**e**lf *Kardinalz.* eleven; **E**lf die; ~, ~en **a)** eleven; **b)** *(Sport)* team; side

**E**lfe die; ~, ~n fairy

**E**lfen·bein das ivory

**E**lfenbein-: ~**schnitzerei** die *o. Pl.* ivory-carving; ~**turm** der *(fig.)* ivory tower

**E**lf·m**e**ter der *(Fußball)* penalty; einen ~ schießen take a penalty; **E**lfm**e**ter·schießen das *(Fußball)* durch ~schießen by *or* on penalties

elimin**ie**ren *tr. V.* eliminate

**E**l**i**te die; ~, ~n élite

**E**ll·bogen der; ~s, ~: elbow

**E**lle die; ~, ~n **a)** *(Anat.)* ulna; **b)** *(frühere Längeneinheit)* cubit; **c)** *(veralt.: Maßstock)* ≈ yardstick; **E**llen·bogen *s.* Ellbogen

**E**ll**i**pse die; ~, ~n ellipse

**E**lsaß das; ~ *od.* **E**lsasses Alsace

**E**lster die; ~, ~n magpie

**e**lterlich *Adj.* parental; **E**ltern *Pl.* parents *pl.*

**e**ltern-, **E**ltern-: ~**abend** der *(Schulw.)* parents' evening; ~**haus** das home; ~**los** *Adj.* orphaned; ~**teil** der parent

**E**mail [e'mai̯] das; ~s, ~s, **E**maille [e'maljə] die; ~, ~n enamel

**E**manzipation die; ~, ~en emancipation; **emanzip**ie**ren** *refl. V.* emancipate; **emanzip**ie**rt** *Adj.* emancipated

**E**mb**a**rgo das; ~s, ~s embargo

**E**mbl**e**m das; ~s, ~e emblem

**E**mbryo der; ~s, ~nen [-y'o:nən] *od.* ~s embryo

**E**migr**a**nt der; ~en, ~en emigrant; *(Flüchtling)* émigré; **E**migr**a**tion die; ~, ~en *(das Emigrieren)* emigration; **emigr**ie**ren** *itr. V.; mit sein* emigrate

**E**mot**i**on die; ~, ~en emotion; **emot**io**nal** **1.** *Adj.* emotional; emotive 〈*topic, question*〉*;* **2.** *adv.* emotionally

**E**mpfang der; ~|e|s, Empfänge reception; *(Entgegennahme)* receipt; **empf**a**ngen** *unr. tr. V.* receive; **E**mpf**ä**nger der; ~s, ~ **a)** recipient; *(eines Briefs)* addressee; **b)** *(Empfangsgerät)* receiver

empf**ä**nglich *Adj.* **a)** receptive (für to); **b)** *(beeinflußbar)* susceptible; **E**mpf**ä**ngnis die; ~: conception; **E**mpf**ä**ngnis·verhütung die contraception

empf**a**ngs-, **E**mpf**a**ngs-: ~**berechtigt** *Adj.* authorized to receive payment/goods *postpos.;* ~**chef** der head receptionist; ~**dame** die receptionist; ~**halle** die reception lobby

empf**e**hlen **1.** *unr. tr. V.* recommend; **2.** *unr. refl. V.* **a)** take one's leave; **b)** *unpers.* es empfiehlt sich, ... zu ...: it's advisable to ...; **empf**e**hlens·wert** *Adj.* **a)** to be recommended *postpos.;* recommendable; **b)** *(ratsam)* advisable; **E**mpf**e**hlung die; ~, ~en **a)** recommendation; **b)** *(Empfehlungsschreiben)* letter of recommendation; **empf**ie**hl** *Imperativ Sg. v.* empfehlen; **empf**ie**hlst** *2. Pers. Sg. Präsens v.* empfehlen; **empf**ie**hlt** *3. Pers. Sg. Präsens v.* empfehlen

empf**i**nden *unr. tr. V.* **a)** *(wahrnehmen)* feel; **b)** *(auffassen)* etw. als Beleidigung ~: feel sth. to be an insult; **E**mpf**i**nden das; ~s feeling; für mein *od.* nach meinem ~: to my mind; **empf**i**ndlich** **1.** *Adj.* **a)** sensitive; fast 〈*film*〉*;* **b)** *(leicht beleidigt)* sensitive; **c)** *(anfällig)* zart und ~: delicate; **d)** *(spürbar)* severe 〈*punishment, shortage*〉*;* **2.** *adv.* ~ auf etw. *(Akk.)* reagieren *(sensibel)* be susceptible to sth.; *(beleidigt)* react oversensitively to sth.; **E**mpf**i**ndlichkeit die; ~, ~en *s.* empfindlich: sensitivity; severity; *(eines Films)* speed

empf**i**ndsam *Adj.* sensitive 〈*nature*〉*;* **E**mpf**i**ndung die; ~, ~en *(Gefühl)* feeling

empf**i**ng *1. u. 3. Pers. Sg. Prät. v.* empfangen

empf**o**hlen **1.** *2. Part. v.* empfehlen; **2.** *Adj.* recommended

emp**i**risch **1.** *Adj.* empirical; **2.** *adv.* empirically

emp**o**r *Adv. (geh.)* upwards

Emp**o**re die; ~, ~n gallery

emp**ö**ren **1.** *tr. V.* fill with indignation; outrage; **2.** *refl. V.* become indignant *or* outraged; **emp**ö**rend** *Adj.* outrageous; **emp**ö**rt** *Adj.* outraged

**e**msig **1.** *Adj.* industrious 〈*person*〉*;* bustling 〈*activity*〉*;* **2.** *adv.* industriously

**E**mu der; ~s, ~s *(Zool.)* emu

**E**nde das; ~s, ~n end; am ~ der Stra-

ße/Stadt at the end of the road/town;
**am/bis/gegen** ~ **des Monats** at/by/towards the end of the month; ~ **April**
at the end of April; **zu** ~ **sein** ⟨*patience, war*⟩ be at an end; ⟨*school*⟩ be
over; ⟨*film, game*⟩ have finished; ~
**gut, alles gut** all's well that ends well
*(prov.);* **enden** *itr. V.* **a)** end; ⟨*programme*⟩ finish; **b) in der Gosse** ~:
end up in the gutter; *(dort sterben)* die
in the gutter

**end·gültig 1.** *Adj.* final ⟨*consent, decision*⟩; conclusive ⟨*evidence*⟩; **2.** *adv.*
**das ist** ~ **vorbei** that's all over and
done with; **sich** ~ **trennen** separate for
good

**End-:** ~**kampf der** *(Sport)* final; *(Milit.)* final battle; ~**lauf der** *(Sport)*
final

**endlich 1.** *Adv.* **a)** *(nach langer Zeit)* at
last; **b)** *(schließlich)* in the end; **2.** *Adj.*
finite

**end-, End-:** ~**los 1.** *Adj.* **a)** *(ohne Ende)* infinite; *(ringförmig)* continuous;
**b)** *(nicht enden wollend)* endless; interminable ⟨*speech*⟩; **2.** *adv.* ~**los lange**
**dauern** be interminably long; ~**runde**
**die** *(Sport)* final; ~**spiel das** *(Sport)*
final; ~**spurt der** *(bes. Leichtathletik)*
final spurt; ~**stadium das** final
stage; *(Med.)* terminal stage;
~**station die** terminus

**Endung die;** ~, ~**en** *(Sprachw.)* ending
**Energie die;** ~, ~**n** energy

**Energie-:** ~**politik die** energy policy;
~**quelle die** energy source; ~**versorgung die** energy supply

**energisch 1.** *Adj.* **a)** energetic ⟨*person*⟩; firm ⟨*action*⟩; **b)** forceful ⟨*voice,
words*⟩; **2.** *adv.* **a)** energetically; ~
**durchgreifen** take drastic action; **b)**
⟨*reject, say*⟩ forcefully; ⟨*stress*⟩ emphatically; ⟨*deny*⟩ strenuously

**eng** [ɛŋ] **1.** *Adj.* **a)** *(schmal)* narrow **b)**
*(dicht)* close ⟨*writing*⟩; **c)** *(fest anliegend)* close-fitting **d)** *(beschränkt)*
narrow; **e)** *(nahe)* close ⟨*friend*⟩; **2.**
*adv.* **a)** *(dicht)* ~ **[zusammen] sitzen/
stehen** sit/stand close together; **b)** *(fest
anliegend)* ~ **anliegen/sitzen** fit
closely; **c)** *(beschränkt)* **etw. zu** ~ **auslegen** interpret sth. too narrowly; **d)**
*(nahe)* closely; **Enge die;** ~, ~**n** confinement

**Engel der;** ~**s,** ~: angel
**eng·herzig** *Adj.* petty
**England (das);** ~**s** England; **Engländer der;** ~**s,** ~: Englishman/English
boy; **er ist** ~: he is English; **die** ~: the

English; **Engländerin die;** ~, ~**nen**
Englishwoman/English girl; **englisch 1.** *Adj.* English; **die** ~**e Sprache/
Literatur** the English language/English literature; **2.** *adv.* ~ **sprechen**
speak English; **Englisch das;** ~[s]
English

**englisch-, Englisch-:** ~**lehrer der**
'English teacher; ~**sprachig** *Adj.* **a)**
English-language ⟨*book, magazine*⟩;
**b)** *(~ sprechend)* English-speaking
⟨*population, country*⟩; ~**unterricht
der** English teaching; *(Unterrichtsstunde)* English lesson

**Eng·paß der a)** defile; **b)** *(fig.)* bottleneck; **eng·stirnig** *Adj.* narrowminded

**Enkel der;** ~**s,** ~: grandson; **Enkelin
die;** ~, ~**nen** granddaughter; **Enkel·kind das** grandchild

**enorm 1.** *Adj.* enormous ⟨*sum, costs*⟩;
tremendous *(coll.)* ⟨*effort*⟩; immense
⟨*strain*⟩; **2.** *adv.* tremendously *(coll.)*

**Ensemble** [ã'sã:bl] **das** ensemble;
*(Theater~)* company

**entarten** *itr. V.; mit sein* degenerate
**entbehren** *tr. V. (verzichten auf)* do
without; **entbehrlich** *Adj.* dispensable; **Entbehrung die;** ~, ~**en** privation

**entbinden 1.** *unr. tr. V.* **a) jmdn. von
einem Versprechen** ~: release sb. from
a promise; **seines Amtes** *od.* **von seinem Amt entbunden werden** be relieved
of [one's] office; **b) jmdn.** ~ *(Med.)* deliver sb.'s baby; **2.** *unr. itr. V.* give
birth; **Entbindung die** *(Med.)* delivery

**entblößen 1.** *refl. V.* take one's
clothes off; ⟨*exhibitionist*⟩ expose
oneself; **2.** *tr. V.* uncover ⟨*one's arm
etc.*⟩

**entdecken** *tr. V.* **a)** discover; **b)** *(ausfindig machen)* **jmdn.** ~: find sb.; **etw.**
~: find *or* discover sth.; **Entdecker
der;** ~**s,** ~: discoverer; **Entdeckung
die;** ~, ~**en** discovery

**Ente die;** ~, ~**n** duck
**entehren** *tr. V.* dishonour; ~**d** degrading

**enteignen** *tr. V.* expropriate; **Enteignung die** expropriation

**enterben** *tr. V.* disinherit
**entern** *tr., itr. V.* board ⟨*ship*⟩
**entfachen** *tr. V. (geh.)* **a)** kindle, light
⟨*fire*⟩; **b)** *(fig.)* provoke ⟨*quarrel, argument*⟩; arouse ⟨*passion, enthusiasm*⟩

**entfallen** *unr. itr. V.; mit sein* **a)** *(aus
dem Gedächtnis)* **es ist mir** ~: it es-

capes me; **b)** *(zugeteilt werden)* **auf jmdn./etw.** ~: be allotted to sb./sth.; **c)** *(wegfallen)* lapse
**entfalten 1.** *tr. V.* **a)** open [up]; unfold ⟨*map etc.*⟩; **b)** *(fig.)* display ⟨*ability, talent*⟩; **2.** *refl. V.* **a)** open [up]; **b)** *(fig.)* ⟨*personality, talent, etc.*⟩ develop; **Entfaltung die;** ~, ~**en** *(fig.)* **a)** *(Entwicklung)* development; **b)** *s.* **entfalten 1 b:** display
**entfernen 1.** *tr. V.* remove; take out ⟨*tonsils etc.*⟩; **2.** *refl. V.* go away; **entfernt 1.** *Adj.* **a)** *(fern)* remote; **das ist od. liegt weit ~ von der Stadt** it is a long way from the town; **10 km/zwei Stunden ~:** 10 km/two hours away; **b)** slight ⟨*acquaintance*⟩; distant ⟨*relation*⟩; slight ⟨*resemblance*⟩; **2.** *adv.* **a)** *(fern)* remotely; **b)** slightly ⟨*acquainted*⟩; distantly ⟨*related*⟩; **Entfernung die;** ~, ~**en a)** *(Abstand)* distance; **b)** *(das Beseitigen)* removal
**entfesseln** *tr. V.* unleash
**entflammen 1.** *tr. V.* arouse ⟨*enthusiasm etc*⟩; **2.** *itr. V.; mit sein* flare up
**entfliehen** *unr. itr. V.; mit sein* escape; **jmdm.** ~: escape from sb.
**entfremden 1.** *tr. V.* **a)** etw. seinem Zweck ~: use sth. for a different purpose; **b)** *(Philos., Soziol.)* entfremdet alienated; **2.** *refl. V.* sich jmdm./einer Sache ~: become estranged from sb./ unfamiliar with sth.; **Entfremdung die;** ~, ~**en** alienation; estrangement
**entführen** *tr. V.* kidnap ⟨*child etc.*⟩; hijack ⟨*plane, lorry, etc.*⟩; **Entführer der** *s.* **entführen:** kidnapper; hijacker; **Entführung die** *s.* **entführen:** kidnapping; hijacking
**entgegen 1.** *Adv.* towards; **2.** *Präp. mit Dat.* ~ **meinem Wunsch** against my wishes; ~ **dem Befehl** contrary to orders
**entgegen-, Entgegen-:** ~|**bringen** *unr. tr. V.* *(fig.)* show ⟨*love, understanding*⟩; ~|**fahren** *unr. itr. V.; mit sein* **jmdm.** ~**fahren** come/go to meet sb.; ~|**gehen** *unr. itr. V.; mit sein* **a)** **jmdm.** ~**gehen** go to meet sb.; **b)** *(fig.)* be heading for ⟨*catastrophe, hard times*⟩; ~**gesetzt 1.** *Adj.* **a)** *(umgekehrt)* opposite ⟨*end, direction*⟩; **b)** *(gegensätzlich)* opposing; **2.** *adv.* **genau** ~**gesetzt handeln/denken** do/think exactly the opposite; ~|**kommen** *unr. itr. V.; mit sein* **jmdm.** ~**kommen** come to meet sb.; *(Zugeständnisse machen)* be accommodating towards sb.; ~**kommen das** co-operation;

*(Zugeständnis)* concession; ~**kommend** *Adj.* obliging; ~|**nehmen** *unr. itr. V.* receive; ~|**treten** *unr. itr. V.; mit sein* go/come up to; *(fig.)* stand up to ⟨*difficulties*⟩
**entgegnen** *tr. V.* retort; reply
**entgehen** *unr. itr. V.; mit sein* **a)** *(entkommen)* escape; **b)** **jmdm. entgeht etw.** sb. misses sth.
**entgeistert** *Adj.* dumbfounded
**Entgelt das;** ~|**e**|**s**, ~**e** payment; fee
**entgiften** *tr. V.* decontaminate ⟨*substance etc.*⟩; detoxicate ⟨*body etc.*⟩
**entgleisen** *itr. V.; mit sein* **a)** be derailed; **b)** *(fig.)* make a/some faux pas
**entgräten** *tr. V.* fillet
**enthaaren** *tr. V.* remove hair from; **Enthaarungs·mittel das** hair remover
¹**enthalten 1.** *unr. tr. V.* contain; **2.** *unr. refl. V.* **sich einer Sache** *(Gen.)* ~: abstain from sth.; **sich der Stimme** ~: abstain; ²**enthalten** *Adj.* **in etw.** *(Dat.)* ~ **sein** be contained in sth.; **das ist im Preis** ~: that is included in the price; **enthaltsam 1.** *Adj.* abstemious; *(sexuell)* abstinent; **2.** *adv.* ~ **leben** live in abstinence; **Enthaltsamkeit die;** ~: abstinence; **Enthaltung die** abstention
**enthaupten** *tr. V. (geh.)* behead
**enthäuten** *tr. V.* skin
**entheben** *unr. tr. V. (geh.)* relieve
**enthemmt** *Adj.* uninhibited
**enthüllen** *tr. V.* unveil ⟨*monument etc.*⟩; reveal ⟨*face, truth, secret*⟩; **Enthüllung die;** ~, ~**en** *s.* **enthüllen:** unveiling; revelation
**Enthusiasmus** [entu'ziasmʊs] **der;** ~: enthusiasm; **enthusiastisch 1.** *Adj.* enthusiastic; **2.** *adv.* enthusiastically
**entkalken** *tr. V.* decalcify
**entkleiden** *tr. V. (geh.)* **a)** undress; **b)** *(berauben)* strip
**entkommen** *unr. itr. V.; mit sein* escape
**entkorken** *tr. V.* uncork ⟨*bottle*⟩
**entkräften** *tr. V.* **a)** weaken; **völlig** ~: exhaust; **b)** *(fig.)* refute ⟨*argument etc.*⟩; **Entkräftung die;** ~, ~**en** debility; **völlige** ~: exhaustion; **b)** *(fig.)* refutation
**entladen 1.** *unr. tr. V.* unload; **2.** *unr. refl. V.* **a)** ⟨*storm*⟩ break; **b)** *(fig.)* ⟨*anger etc.*⟩ erupt; ⟨*aggression etc.*⟩ be released
**entlang 1.** *Präp. mit Akk. u. Dat.* along; **2.** *Adv.* along; **hier/dort** ~, **bitte!** this/that way please!

**entlang-:** ~|**fahren** *unr. itr. V.; mit sein* **a)** *(streichen)* drive along; **b)** *(streichen)* go along; ~|**gehen** *unr. itr. V.; mit sein* ⟨*person*⟩ go *or* walk along; ~|**laufen** *unr. itr. V.; mit sein* **a)** walk/run along; **b)** *(verlaufen)* go *or* run along

**entlarven** *tr. V.* expose

**entlassen** *unr. tr. V.* **a)** *(aus dem Gefängnis)* release; *(aus dem Krankenhaus, der Armee)* discharge; **b)** *(aus einem Arbeitsverhältnis)* dismiss; *(wegen Arbeitsmangels)* make redundant *(Brit.)*; lay off; **Entlassung die**; ~, ~**en** *s.* **entlassen**: release; discharge; dismissal; redundancy *(Brit.)*; laying off

**entlasten** *tr. V.* **a)** relieve; **b)** *(Rechtsw.)* exonerate ⟨*defendant*⟩; **Entlastung die**; ~, ~**en a)** relief; **b)** *(Rechtsw.)* exoneration; defence

**entlaufen** *unr. itr. V.; mit sein* run away; **ein ~er Sträfling/Sklave** an escaped convict/a runaway slave

**entlausen** *tr. V.* delouse

**entledigen** *refl. V.* **sich jmds./einer Sache** *(Gen.)* ~ *(geh.)* rid oneself of sb./sth.

**entleeren** *tr. V.* empty; evacuate ⟨*bowels, bladder*⟩

**entlegen** *Adj.* remote

**entleihen** *unr. tr. V.* borrow

**entlocken** *tr. V. (geh.)* **jmdm. etw.** ~: elicit sth. from sb.

**entlohnen** *tr.V.* pay; **Entlohnung die**; ~, ~**en** payment; *(Lohn)* pay

**entlüften** *tr. V.* ventilate; **Entlüfter der**; ~s, ~: ventilator

**entmachten** *tr. V.* deprive of power

**entmilitarisieren** *tr. V.* demilitarize

**entmündigen** *tr. V.* incapacitate; **Entmündigung die**; ~, ~**en** incapacitation

**entmutigen** *tr. V.* discourage

**Entnahme die**; ~, ~**n** *(von Wasser)* drawing; *(von Blut)* extraction

**entnehmen** *unr. tr. V.* **a)** etw. [einer Sache *(Dat.)*] ~: take sth. [from sth.]; **b)** *(ersehen aus)* gather *(Dat.* from)

**entnervend** *Adj.* nerve-racking

**entpuppen** *refl. V.* **sich als etw./jmd.** ~: turn out to be sth./sb.

**entrahmen** *tr. V.* skim ⟨*milk*⟩

**entreißen** *unr. tr. V.* **jmdm. etw.** ~: snatch sth. from sb.

**entrichten** *tr. V. (Amtsspr.)* pay ⟨*fee*⟩

**entrümpeln** *tr. V.* clear out; **Entrümpelung die**; ~, ~**en** clear-out

**entrüsten 1.** *refl. V.* **sich [über etw.** *(Akk.)*] ~: be indignant [at *or* about

sth.]; **2.** *tr. V. (empören)* **jmdn.** ~: make sb. indignant; **Entrüstung die** indignation *(über + Akk.* at, about)

**Entsafter der**; ~s, ~: juice-extractor

**entsagen** *itr. V.* **einer Sache** *(Dat.)* ~ *(geh.)* renounce sth.; **Entsagung die**; ~, ~**en** *(geh.)* renunciation

**entschädigen** *tr. V.* compensate (für for); **jmdn. für etw.** ~ *(fig.)* make up for sth.; **Entschädigung die** compensation

**entschärfen** *tr. V.* defuse; tone down ⟨*discussion, criticism*⟩

**entscheiden 1.** *unr. refl. V.* **a)** decide; **b)** *(unpers.)* **morgen entscheidet es sich, ob ...:** I/we/you will know tomorrow whether ...; **2.** *unr. itr. V.* **über etw.** *(Akk.)* ~: settle sth; **3.** *unr. tr. V.* decide on ⟨*dispute*⟩; decide ⟨*outcome, result*⟩; **entscheidend 1.** *Adj.* crucial; decisive ⟨*action*⟩; **2.** *adv.* **jmdn./etw.** ~ **beeinflussen** have a decisive influence on sb./sth.; **Entscheidung die** decision

**entschieden 1.** *Adj.* **a)** *(entschlossen)* determined; resolute; **b)** *(eindeutig)* definite; **2.** *adv.* resolutely; **das geht ~ zu weit** that is going much too far

**entschlafen** *unr. itr. V.; mit sein* pass away

**entschließen** *unr. refl. V.* decide; **Entschließung die** resolution; **entschlossen** *Adj.* determined; **Entschlossenheit die**; ~: determination; **Entschluß der** decision

**entschlüsseln** *tr. V.* decipher

**entschuldigen 1.** *refl. V.* apologize; **2.** *tr. (auch itr.) V.* excuse ⟨*person*⟩; **sich ~ lassen** ask to be excused; ~ **Sie [bitte]!** *(bei Fragen, Bitten)* excuse me; *(bedauernd)* I'm sorry; **Entschuldigung die**; ~, ~**en a)** apology; **b)** *(Grund)* excuse; **c)** *(Höflichkeitsformel)* ~! *(bei Fragen, Bitten)* excuse me; *(bedauernd)* [I'm] sorry

**entschwinden** *unr. itr. V.; mit sein (geh.)* disappear; vanish

**entsetzen 1.** *refl. V.* be horrified; **2.** *tr. V.* horrify; **Entsetzen das**; ~s horror; **entsetzlich 1.** *Adj.* **a)** horrible ⟨*accident, crime, etc.*⟩; **b)** nicht präd. *(ugs.: stark)* terrible ⟨*thirst, hunger*⟩; **2.** *adv.* terribly *(coll.)*

**entsinnen** *unr. refl. V.* **sich jmds./einer Sache** ~: remember sb./sth.

**entspannen 1.** *tr. V.* relax; **2.** *refl. V.* **a)** ⟨*person*⟩ relax; **b)** *(fig.)* ⟨*situation, tension*⟩ ease; **Entspannung die**; *o. Pl.* **a)** relaxation; **b)** *(politisch)* easing

of tension; détente; **Entspạn-
nungs·politik die** policy of détente
**entsprẹchen** *unr. itr. V.* **a)** *(übereinstimmen mit)* **einer Sache** *(Dat.)* ~:
correspond to sth.; **b)** *(nachkommen)*
**einem Wunsch** ~: comply with a request; **den Anforderungen** ~: meet the
requirements; **entsprẹchend 1.**
*Adj.* **a)** corresponding; *(angemessen)*
appropriate; **b)** *nicht attr. (dem~)* in
accordance *postpos.*; **2.** *adv.* **a)** *(angemessen)* appropriately; **b)** *(dem~)* accordingly; **3.** *Präp. mit Dativ:* ~ **einer
Sache** in accordance with sth.
**entsprịngen** *unr. itr. V.; mit sein* **a)**
⟨*river*⟩ rise; **b)** *(entstehen aus)* **einer Sache** *(Dat.)* ~: spring from sth.
**entstẹhen** *unr. itr. V.; mit sein* **a)** originate; ⟨*quarrel, friendship, etc.*⟩ arise;
**b)** *(gebildet werden)* be formed (**aus**
from, **durch** by); **c)** *(sich ergeben)*
occur; *(als Folge)* result; **Entstẹ-
hung die;** ~: origin
**entstẹinen** *tr. V.* stone
**entstẹllen** *tr. V.* **a)** disfigure; **b)** *(verfälschen)* distort ⟨*text, facts*⟩; **Ent-
stẹllung die a)** disfigurement; **b)**
*(Verfälschung)* distortion
**entstören** *tr. V. (Elektrot.)* suppress
⟨*engine, electrical appliance*⟩
**enttạrnen** *tr. V.* uncover
**enttäuschen** *tr. V.* disappoint; **enttäuscht** *Adj.* disappointed; dashed
⟨*hopes*⟩; **Enttäuschung die** disappointment
**entwạchsen** *unr. itr. V.; mit sein* **einer Sache** *(Dat.)* ~: grow out of sth.
**entwạffnen** *tr. V. (auch fig.)* disarm;
**entwạffnend** *Adj.* disarming
**entwạrnen** *itr. V.* sound the all-clear;
**Entwạrnung die** all-clear
**entwässern** *tr. V.* drain; **Entwässerung die;** ~, ~**en** drainage
**ẹntweder** *Konj.:* ~ ... **oder** either ... **or**
**entwẹichen** *unr. itr. V.; mit sein* escape
**entwẹnden** *tr. V. (geh.)* purloin
**entwẹrfen** *unr. itr. V.* design ⟨*furniture, dress*⟩; draft ⟨*novel etc.*⟩; draw
up ⟨*plans etc.*⟩
**entwẹrten** *tr. V.* **a)** cancel ⟨*ticket,
postage stamp*⟩; **b)** devalue ⟨*currency*⟩
**entwịckeln 1.** *refl. V.* develop; **2.** *tr.
V.* produce ⟨*vapour, smell*⟩; display
⟨*ability, characteristic*⟩; develop
⟨*equipment, photograph, film*⟩; elaborate ⟨*theory, ideas*⟩; **Entwịcklung
die;** ~, ~**en a)** development; *(von
Dämpfen usw.)* production; **in der** ~

**sein** ⟨*young person*⟩ be adolescent; **b)**
*(Darlegung)* elaboration; **c)** *(Fot.)* developing
**Entwịcklungs-:** ~**helfer der** development aid worker; ~**hilfe die** [devel-
opment] aid; ~**land das;** *Pl.* ~**länder**
developing country; ~**politik die** development aid policy
**entwịrren** *tr. V.* disentangle
**entwịschen** *itr. V.; mit sein (ugs.)* get
away
**entwöhnen** *tr. V.* wean
**entwürdigend** *Adj.* degrading
**Entwụrf der a)** design; **b)** *(Konzept)*
draft
**entwụrzeln** *tr. V.* uproot
**entziẹhen 1.** *unr. tr. V.* **a)** take away;
**b)** *(nicht zugestehen)* withdraw; **2.** *unr.
refl. V.* **sich seinen Pflichten** *(Dat.)* ~:
evade one's duty; **das entzieht sich
meiner Kontrolle** that is beyond my
control; **Entziẹhung die a)** withdrawal; **b)** *(Entziehungskur)* withdrawal
treatment *no indef. art.*
**entziffern** *tr. V.* decipher
**entzụ̈ckend** *Adj.* delightful; **ent-
zụ̈ckt** *Adj.* delighted
**Entzug der;** ~[e]s withdrawal
**entzụ̈ndbar** *Adj.* [in]flammable; **ent-
zụ̈nden 1.** *tr. V.* light ⟨*fire*⟩; strike
⟨*match*⟩; **2.** *refl. V.* **a)** ignite; **b)** *(anschwellen)* become inflamed; **ent-
zụ̈ndlich** *Adj.* **a)** [in]flammable ⟨*substance*⟩; **b)** *(Med.)* inflammatory;
**Entzụ̈ndung die;** ~, ~**en** inflammation
**entzwẹi** *Adj. (geh.)* in pieces; **ent-
zwẹien** *refl. V.* fall out; **ent-
zwei‖gehen** *unr. itr. V.; mit sein
(geh.)* break
**Enzian** ['ɛntsiaːn] *der;* ~**s,** ~**e** gentian
**Enzyklika die;** ~, **Enzykliken** encycli-
cal
**Enzyklopạ̈die die;** ~, ~**n** encyclopaedia; **enzyklopạ̈disch** *Adj.* ency-
clopaedic
**Epen** *s.* **Epos**
**Epidemie die;** ~, ~**n** epidemic
**Epilepsịe die;** ~, ~**n** *(Med.)* epilepsy
*no art.;* **Epilẹptiker der;** ~**s,** ~: epileptic; **epilẹptisch** *Adj.* epileptic
**episch** *Adj.* epic
**Episọde die;** ~, ~**n** episode
**Epọche die;** ~, ~**n** epoch
**Epos** ['eːpɔs] *das;* ~, **Epen** epic [poem];
epos
**er** *Personalpron. 3. Pers. Sg. Nom.
Mask.* he; *(betont)* him; *(bei Dingen/
Tieren)* it; *s. auch* **ihm; ihn; seiner**

**erachten** *tr. V. (geh.)* consider; etw. **als** *od.* **für seine Pflicht** ~: consider sth. [to be] one's duty

**erarbeiten** *tr. V.* work for

**Erb·anlage die** hereditary disposition

**erbarmen** *refl. V. (geh.)* take pity (*Gen.* on); **Erbarmen das;** ~s pity; **erbärmlich 1.** *Adj.* **a)** *(elend)* wretched; **b)** *(unzulänglich)* pathetic; **c)** *(abwertend: gemein)* mean; wretched; **d)** *(sehr groß)* terrible 〈*hunger, fear, etc.*〉; **2.** *adv.* terribly

**erbauen 1.** *tr. V.* **a)** build; **b)** *(geh.: erheben)* uplift; **2.** *refl. V.* **sich an etw.** *(Dat.)* ~: be uplifted by sth.; **Erbauer der;** ~s, ~: architect

**¹Erbe das;** ~s **a)** inheritance; **b)** *(Vermächtnis)* legacy; **²Erbe der;** ~n ~n heir; **erben** *tr. (auch itr.) V.* inherit

**erbetteln** *tr. V.* get by begging

**erbeuten** *tr. V.* carry off, get away with 〈*valuables, prey, etc.*〉; capture 〈*enemy plane, tank, etc.*〉

**Erb-:** ~**folge die** succession; ~**gut das** *(Biol.)* genetic make-up

**Erbin die;** ~, ~**nen** heiress

**erbitten** *unr. tr. V. (geh.)* request

**erbittern** *tr. V.* enrage; **erbittert 1.** *Adj.* bitter; **2.** *adv.* ~ **kämpfen** wage a bitter struggle

**erblassen** *itr. V.; mit sein (geh.)* turn pale; blanch *(literary)*

**erbleichen** *itr. V.; mit sein (geh.) s.* **erblassen**

**erblich** *Adj.* hereditary 〈*title, disease*〉

**erblicken** *tr. V. (geh.)* catch sight of; *(fig.)* see

**erblinden** *itr. V.; mit sein* lose one's sight

**erblühen** *itr. V.; mit sein (geh.)* bloom; blossom

**Erb·masse die** *(Biol.)* genetic make-up

**erbost** *Adj.* furious

**erbrechen 1.** *unr. tr. V.* bring up 〈*food*〉; **2.** *unr. itr., refl. V.* vomit; **Erbrechen das;** ~s vomiting

**erbringen** *unr. tr. V.* produce

**Erbschaft die;** ~, ~**en** inheritance; **Erbschaft[s]·steuer die** estate *or* death duties *pl.*

**Erbse die;** ~, ~**n** pea

**Erb-:** ~**stück das** heirloom; ~**sünde die** original sin; ~**teil das** share of an/ the inheritance

**Erd-:** ~**achse die** earth's axis; ~**apfel der** *(bes. österr.) s.* Kartoffel; ~**beben das** earthquake; ~**beere die** strawberry; ~**boden der** ground; earth;

**etw. dem** ~**boden gleichmachen** raze sth. to the ground

**Erde die;** ~, ~**n a)** *(Erdreich)* soil; earth; **b)** *o. Pl. (fester Boden)* ground; **c)** *o. Pl. (Welt)* earth; world; **d)** *o. Pl. (Planet)* Earth

**erdenklich** *Adj.* conceivable

**Erd-:** ~**gas das** natural gas; ~**geschoß das** ground floor; first floor *(Amer.)*; ~**kunde die** geography; ~**nuß die** peanut; ~**oberfläche die** earth's surface; ~**öl das** oil

**erdöl-, Erdöl-:** ~**exportierend** *Adj.* oil-exporting 〈*country*〉; ~**gewinnung die** oil production; ~**leitung die** oil pipeline

**erdrosseln** *tr. V.* strangle

**erdrücken** *tr. V.* **a)** crush; **b)** *(fig.: belasten)* overwhelm; **erdrückend** *Adj.* overwhelming; oppressive 〈*heat, silence*〉

**Erd-:** ~**rutsch der** landslide; ~**teil der** continent

**erdulden** *tr. V.* endure 〈*sorrow, misfortune*〉; tolerate 〈*insults*〉; *(über sich ergehen lassen)* undergo

**ereifern** *refl. V.* get excited

**ereignen** *refl. V.* happen; 〈*accident, mishap*〉 occur; **Ereignis das;** ~**ses,** ~**se** event; occurrence

**Eremit der;** ~**en,** ~**en** hermit

**ererbt** *Adj.* inherited

**¹erfahren** *unr. tr. V.* **a)** find out; learn; *(hören)* hear; **b)** *(geh.: erleben)* experience; *(erleiden)* suffer; **²erfahren** *Adj.* experienced; **Erfahrung die;** ~, ~**en** experience; ~**en sammeln** gain experience *sing.;* **etw. in** ~ **bringen** discover sth.; **erfahrungs·gemäß** *Adv.* in our/my experience

**erfassen** *tr. V.* **a)** *(mitreißen)* catch; **b)** *(begreifen)* grasp 〈*situation, etc.*〉; **c)** *(registrieren)* record; **Erfassung die** registration

**erfinden** *unr. tr. V.* invent; **das ist alles erfunden** it is pure fabrication; **Erfinder der;** ~**s,** ~ **a)** inventor; **b)** *(Urheber)* creator; **erfinderisch** *Adj.* inventive; *(schlau)* resourceful; **Erfindung die;** ~, ~**en** invention

**erflehen** *tr. V. (geh.)* beg

**Erfolg der;** ~**[e]s,** ~**e** success; **keinen** ~ **haben** be unsuccessful

**erfolgen** *itr. V.; mit sein* take place; occur; **es erfolgte keine Reaktion** there was no reaction

**erfolg-:** ~**los 1.** *Adj.* unsuccessful; **2.** *adv.* unsuccessfully; ~**reich 1.** *Adj.* successful; **2.** *adv.* successfully

**Erfolgs·erlebnis das** feeling of achievement

**erfolg·versprechend** *Adj.* promising

**erforderlich** *Adj.* required; necessary; **erfordern** *tr. V.* require; demand

**erforschen** *tr. V.* discover ⟨*facts, causes, etc.*⟩; explore ⟨*country*⟩; **Erforschung die** research (+ *Gen.* into); *(eines Landes usw.)* exploration

**erfreuen 1.** *tr. V.* please; **2.** *refl. V.* sich an etw. *(Dat.)* ~: take pleasure in sth.; **erfreulich** *Adj.* pleasant

**erfrieren 1.** *unr. itr. V.; mit sein* freeze to death; ⟨*plant, harvest, etc.*⟩ be damaged by frost; **2.** *unr. refl. V.* sich *(Dat.)* die Finger ~: get frostbite in one's fingers

**erfrischen 1.** *tr. (auch itr.) V.* refresh; **2.** *refl. V.* freshen oneself up; **erfrischend** *(auch fig.) Adj.* refreshing; **Erfrischung die;** ~, ~en *(auch fig.)* refreshment; **Erfrischungs·raum der** refreshment room

**erfüllen 1.** *tr. V.* grant ⟨*wish, request*⟩; fulfil ⟨*contract*⟩; carry out ⟨*duty*⟩; meet ⟨*condition*⟩; **2.** *refl. V.* ⟨*wish*⟩ come true; **Erfüllung die: in ~ gehen** come true

**erfunden** *Adj.* fictional ⟨*story*⟩

**ergänzen** *tr. V.* **a)** *(vervollständigen)* complete; *(erweitern)* add to; **b)** *(hinzufügen)* add ⟨*remark*⟩; **Ergänzung die;** ~, ~en **a)** *(Vervollständigung)* completion; *(Erweiterung)* enlargement; **b)** *(Zusatz)* addition; *(zu einem Gesetz)* amendment

**ergattern** *tr. V. (ugs.)* manage to grab

**ergaunern** *tr. V.* get by underhand means

¹**ergeben 1.** *unr. refl. V.* **a)** sich in etw. *(Akk.)* ~: submit to sth.; **b)** *(kapitulieren)* surrender *(Dat.* to); **c)** *(folgen, entstehen)* arise *(aus* from); **2.** *unr. tr. V.* result in; ²**ergeben** *Adj.* **a)** *(zugeneigt)* devoted; **b)** *(resignierend)* mit ~er Miene with an expression of resignation; **Ergebnis das;** ~ses, ~se result; **ergebnis·los** *Adj.* fruitless

**ergehen** *unr. refl. V.* sich in etw. *(Dat.)* ~: indulge in sth.

**ergiebig** *Adj.* rich ⟨*deposits, resources*⟩; fertile ⟨*topic*⟩

**ergötzen** *(geh.)* **1.** *tr. V.* enthrall; **2.** *refl. V.* sich an etw. *(Dat.)* ~: be delighted by sth.

**ergrauen** *itr. V.; mit sein* go grey

**ergreifen** *unr. tr. V.* **a)** *(greifen)* grab;

**b)** *(festnehmen)* catch ⟨*thief etc.*⟩; **c)** *(fig.: erfassen)* seize; **d)** *(fig.: aufnehmen)* take up ⟨*career*⟩; take ⟨*initiative, opportunity*⟩; **e)** *(fig.: bewegen)* move; **ergreifend** *Adj.* moving; **ergriffen** *Adj.* moved

**ergründen** *tr. V.* ascertain; discover ⟨*cause*⟩

**erhaben** *Adj.* solemn ⟨*moment*⟩; awe-inspiring ⟨*sight*⟩; sublime ⟨*beauty*⟩; über etw. *(Akk.)* ~ sein be above sth.

**Erhalt der;** ~[e]s *(Amtsdt.)* receipt; **erhalten** *unr. tr. V.* **a)** receive ⟨*letter, news, gift*⟩; be given ⟨*order*⟩; get ⟨*good mark, impression*⟩; **b)** *(bewahren)* preserve ⟨*town, building*⟩ **erhältlich** *Adj.* obtainable; **Erhaltung die;** ~: preservation; *(des Friedens)* maintenance

**erhängen** *tr. V.* hang

**erhärten** *tr. V.* strengthen ⟨*suspicion, assumption*⟩; substantiate ⟨*claim*⟩

**erheben 1.** *tr. V.* **a)** raise **b)** *(verlangen)* levy ⟨*tax*⟩; charge ⟨*fee*⟩; **2.** *unr. refl. V.* **a)** rise; **b)** *(rebellieren)* rise up (**gegen** against); **erhebend** *Adj.* uplifting; **erheblich 1.** *Adj.* considerable; **2.** *adv.* considerably

**erheitern** *tr. V.* jmdn. ~: cheer sb. up

**erhellen** *tr. V.* light up

**erhitzen 1.** *tr. V.* heat ⟨*liquid*⟩; jmdn. ~: make sb. hot; **2.** *refl. V.* heat up; ⟨*person*⟩ become hot

**erhoffen** *tr. V.* sich *(Dat.)* viel/wenig von etw. ~: expect a lot/little from sth.

**erhöhen 1.** *tr. V.* increase ⟨*prices, productivity, etc.*⟩; **2.** *refl. V.* ⟨*rent, prices*⟩ rise; **Erhöhung die;** ~, ~en increase (*Gen.* in)

**erholen** *refl. V. (auch fig.)* recover (**von** from); *(sich ausruhen)* have a rest; **erholsam** *Adj.* restful; **Erholung die;** ~: *s.* erholen: recovery; rest; ~ brauchen need a rest; **erholungs·bedürftig** *Adj.* in need of a rest *postpos.*

**erhören** *tr. V. (geh.)* hear

**Erika die;** ~, ~s *od.* Eriken *(Bot.)* erica

**erinnern 1.** *refl. V.* sich an jmdn./etw. ~: remember sb./sth.; sich [daran] ~, daß ...: remember *or* recall that ...; **2.** *tr. V.* jmdn. an etw./jmdn. ~: remind sb. of sth./sb.; **Erinnerung die;** ~, ~en memory (**an** + *Akk.* of); etw. [noch gut] in ~ haben [still] remember sth. [well]; zur ~ an jmdn./etw. in memory of sb./sth.

**erjagen** *tr. V.* **a)** catch; **b)** *(gewinnen)* win ⟨*fame*⟩; make ⟨*money, fortune*⟩

**erkalten** *tr. V.; mit sein* cool; **erkäl-**

ten *refl. V.* catch cold; **Erkältung die**; ~, ~en cold

**erkämpfen** *tr. V.* win; **den Sieg ~**: gain a victory

**erkaufen** *tr. V.* a) *(durch Opfer)* win; b) *(durch Geld)* buy

**erkennbar** *Adj.* recognizable; *(sichtbar)* visible; **erkennen** *unr. tr. V.* a) recognize; b) *(deutlich sehen)* make out; **erkenntlich** *Adj.* a) **sich [für etw.]** ~ **zeigen** show one's appreciation for sth.; b) *s.* erkennbar; **Erkenntnis die**; ~, ~se discovery; **zu der ~ kommen, daß ...**: come to the realization that ...

**Erker der**; ~s, ~: bay window; **Erker·fenster das** bay window

**erklärbar** *Adj.* explicable; **erklären** 1. *tr. V.* a) explain; b) *(mitteilen)* state; declare; c) **jmdn. für tot ~**: pronounce someone dead; **jmdn. zu etw. ~**: name sb. as sth; 2. *refl. V.* **sich einverstanden/bereit ~**: declare oneself [to be] in agreement/willing; **erklärlich** *Adj.* understandable; **erklärt** *Adj.* declared; **Erklärung die**; ~, ~en a) *(Darlegung)* explanation; b) *(Mitteilung)* statement

**erklimmen** *unr. tr. V. (geh.)* climb

**erklingen** *unr. itr. V.; mit sein* ring out

**erkranken** *itr. V.; mit sein* become ill **(an + Dat.** with); **schwer erkrankt sein** be seriously ill; **Erkrankung die**; ~, ~en illness; *(eines Körperteils)* disease

**erkunden** *tr. V.* reconnoitre *(terrain)*; **erkundigen** *refl. V.* **sich nach jmdm./ etw.** ~: ask after sb./enquire about sth.; **Erkundigung die**; ~, ~en enquiry

**erlahmen** *itr. V.; mit sein* tire; *(strength)* flag

**erlangen** *tr. V.* gain; obtain *(credit, visa)*; reach *(age)*

**Erlaß der; Erlasses, Erlasse** decree; **erlassen** *unr. tr. V.* a) enact *(law)*; declare *(amnesty)*; issue *(warrant)*; b) *(verzichten auf)* remit *(sentence)*

**erlauben** 1. *tr. V.* a) allow; b) *(ermöglichen)* permit; 2. *refl. V.* **sich (Dat.) etw.** ~: permit oneself sth.; **Erlaubnis die**; ~, ~se permission; *(Schriftstück)* permit

**erläutern** *tr. V.* explain; comment on *(picture etc.)*; annotate *(text)*; **Erläuterung die** explanation

**Erle die**; ~, ~n alder

**erleben** *tr. V.* experience; **etwas Schreckliches** ~: have a terrible experience; **er wird das nächste Jahr**

**nicht mehr** ~: he won't see next year; **du kannst was** ~! *(ugs.)* you won't know what's hit you!; **Erlebnis das**; ~ses, ~se experience

**erledigen** 1. *tr. V.* deal with *(task)*; settle *(matter)*; **ich muß noch einige Dinge erledigen** I must see to a few things; **sie hat alles pünktlich erledigt** she got everything done on time; 2. *refl. V.(matter, problem)* resolve itself; **vieles erledigt sich von selbst** a lot of things sort them'selves out; **erledigt** *Adj.* closed *(case)*; *(ugs.)* worn out *(person)*

**erlegen** *tr. V.* shoot *(animal)*

**erleichtern** *tr. V.* a) make easier; b) *(befreien)* relieve; **Erleichterung die**; ~, ~en a) **zur ~ der Arbeit** to make the work easier; b) *(Befreiung)* relief; c) *(Verbesserung, Milderung)* alleviation

**erleiden** *unr. tr. V.* suffer

**erlernbar** *Adj.* learnable; **erlernen** *tr. V.* learn

**erlesen** *Adj.* superior *(wine)*; choice *(dish)*

**erleuchten** *tr. V.* a) light; b) *(geh.: mit Klarheit erfüllen)* inspire; **Erleuchtung die**; ~, ~en inspiration

**erliegen** *unr. itr. V.; mit sein* succumb *(Dat.* to); **einem Irrtum** ~: be misled; **einer Krankheit** *(Dat.)* ~: die from an illness

**erlogen** *Adj.* made up

**Erlös der**; ~es, ~e proceeds *pl.*

**erlöschen** *unr. itr. V.; mit sein (fire)* go out; **ein erloschener Vulkan** an extinct volcano

**erlösen** *tr. V.* save, rescue **(von** from); **Erlöser der**; ~s, ~ a) saviour; b) *(christl. Rel.)* redeemer; **Erlösung die** release **(von** from)

**ermächtigen** *tr. V.* authorize; **Ermächtigung die**; ~, ~en authorization

**ermahnen** *tr. V.* admonish; tell *(coll.)*; *(warnen)* warn; **Ermahnung die** admonition; *(Warnung)* warning

**Ermang[e]lung die**; ~: **in** ~ *(+ Gen.) (geh.)* in the absence of

**ermäßigen** *tr. V.* reduce; **Ermäßigung die** reduction

**ermatten** *(geh.)* 1. *itr. V.; mit sein* become exhausted; 2. *tr. V.* exhaust, tire

**ermessen** *unr. tr. V.* estimate, gauge; **Ermessen das**; ~s estimation

**ermitteln** 1. *tr. V.* ascertain *(facts)*; discover *(culprit, address)*; establish

⟨*identity, origin*⟩; decide ⟨*winner*⟩; calculate ⟨*quota, rates, data*⟩; **2.** *itr. V. (Rechtsw.)* investigate; **Ermittlung die;** ∼, ∼**en a)** *(das Ermitteln) s.* ermitteln **a**: ascertainment; discovery; establishment; **b)** *(Untersuchung)* investigation

**ermöglichen** *tr. V.* enable

**ermorden** *tr. V.* murder; **Ermordung die;** ∼, ∼**en** murder

**ermüden 1.** *itr. V.; mit sein* tire; **2.** *tr. V.* tire; make tired; **ermüdend** *Adj.* tiring; **Ermüdung die;** ∼, ∼**en** tiredness

**ermuntern** *tr. V.* encourage; **ermunternd** *Adj.* encouraging

**ermutigen** *tr. V.* encourage; **Ermutigung die;** ∼, ∼**en** encouragement

**ernähren 1.** *tr. V.* **a)** feed ⟨*young, child*⟩; **b)** *(unterhalten)* keep ⟨*family, wife*⟩; **2.** *refl. V.* feed oneself; **Ernährer der;** ∼**s,** ∼, **Ernährerin die;** ∼, ∼**nen** breadwinner; **Ernährung die;** ∼: feeding; *(Nahrung)* diet

**ernennen** *unr. tr. V.* appoint; **Ernennung die** appointment (**zu** as)

**erneuern** *tr. V.* **a)** replace; **b)** *(wiederherstellen)* renovate ⟨*roof, building*⟩; *(fig.)* thoroughly reform ⟨*system*⟩; **Erneuerung die a)** replacement; **b)** *(Wiederherstellung)* renovation; **erneut 1.** *Adj.* renewed; **2.** *adv.* once again

**erniedrigen** *tr. V.* humiliate; **Erniedrigung die;** ∼, ∼**en** humiliation

**ernst 1.** *Adj.* **a)** serious; **b)** *(aufrichtig)* genuine ⟨*intention, offer*⟩; **c)** *(gefahrvoll)* serious ⟨*injury*⟩; grave ⟨*situation*⟩; **2.** *adv.* seriously

**Ernst der;** ∼[e]**s a)** seriousness; **das ist mein |voller|** ∼: I mean that [quite] seriously; **b)** *(Wirklichkeit)* **daraus wurde |blutiger/bitterer|** ∼: it became [deadly] serious; **der** ∼ **des Lebens** the serious side of life

**ernst-, Ernst-:** ∼**fall der: im** ∼: when the real thing happens; ∼**gemeint** *Adj. (präd. getrennt geschrieben)* serious; sincere ⟨*wish*⟩; ∼**haft 1.** *Adj.* serious; **2.** *adv.* seriously; ∼**haftigkeit die;** ∼: seriousness

**ernstlich 1.** *Adj.* **a)** serious; **b)** *(aufrichtig)* genuine ⟨*wish*⟩; **2.** *adv.* **a)** seriously; **b)** *(aufrichtig)* genuinely ⟨*sorry, repentant*⟩

**Ernte die;** ∼, ∼**n a)** harvest; **b)** *(Ertrag)* crop; **die** ∼ **einbringen** bring in the harvest; **Ernte·dank·fest das** harvest festival; **ernten** *tr. V.* harvest

**ernüchtern** *tr. V.* sober up; *(fig.)* bring down to earth; ∼**d** sobering; **Ernüchterung die;** ∼, ∼**en** *(fig.)* disillusionment

**Eroberer der;** ∼**s,** ∼, **Eroberin die;** ∼, ∼**nen** conqueror; **erobern** *tr. V.* **a)** conquer; take ⟨*town, fortress*⟩; seize ⟨*power*⟩; **Eroberung die;** ∼, ∼**en** conquest; *(einer Stadt, Festung)* taking

**eröffnen** *tr. V.* **a)** open; start ⟨*business, practice*⟩; **b)** *(mitteilen)* **jmdm. etw.** ∼: reveal sth. to sb.; **c) ein Testament** ∼: read a will; **Eröffnung die a)** opening; *(einer Sitzung)* start; **b)** *(Mitteilung)* revelation; **c)** *(Testaments∼)* reading

**erörtern** *tr. V.* discuss; **Erörterung die;** ∼, ∼**en** discussion

**Erotik die;** ∼: eroticism; **erotisch** *Adj.* erotic

**Erpel der;** ∼**s,** ∼: drake

**erpicht** *Adj.* **in auf etw.** *(Akk.)* ∼ **sein** be keen on sth.

**erpressen** *tr. V.* **a)** *(nötigen)* blackmail; **b)** *(erlangen)* extort ⟨*money etc.*⟩; **Erpresser der;** ∼**s,** ∼: blackmailer; **Erpressung die** blackmail *no indef. art.; (von Geld, Geständnis)* extortion

**erproben** *tr. V.* test ⟨*medicine*⟩ (**an** + *Akk.* on)

**erraten** *unr. tr. V.* guess

**errechnen** *tr. V.* calculate

**erregen 1.** *tr. V.* **a)** annoy; **b)** *(sexuell)* arouse; **c)** *(verursachen)* arouse; **2.** *refl. V.* get excited; **erregend** *Adj.* exciting; *(sexuell)* arousing; **Erreger der;** ∼**s,** ∼ *(Med.)* pathogen; **erregt** *Adj.* excited; *(sexuell)* aroused; **Erregung die** excitement

**erreichbar** *Adj.* **a)** within reach *postpos.;* **b) der Ort ist mit dem Zug** ∼: the place can be reached by train; **erreichen** *tr. V.* **a)** reach; **den Zug** ∼: catch the train; **er ist telefonisch zu** ∼: he can be contacted by telephone; **b)** *(durchsetzen)* achieve ⟨*goal, aim*⟩

**errichten** *tr. V.* **a)** build ⟨*house, bridge, etc.*⟩; **b)** *(aufstellen)* erect

**erringen** *unr. tr. V.* gain ⟨*victory*⟩; reach ⟨*first etc. place*⟩

**erröten** *itr. V.; mit sein* blush

**Errungenschaft die;** ∼, ∼**en** achievement

**Ersatz der;** ∼**es a)** replacement; **b)** *(Entschädigung)* compensation

**Ersatz-:** ∼**kasse die** private health insurance company; ∼**mann der;** *Pl.* ∼**männer,** ∼**leute** replacement; *(Sport)*

substitute; **~rad das** spare wheel; **~reifen der** spare tyre; **~teil das** *(bes. Technik)* spare part; spare *(Brit.)*

**ersaufen** *unr. itr. V.; mit sein (salopp)* drown; **ersäufen** *tr. V.* drown

**erschaffen** *unr. tr. V.* create; **Erschaffung die** creation

**erscheinen** *unr. itr. V.; mit sein* ⟨*book*⟩ be published; **Erscheinung die**; **~, ~en a)** *(Vorgang)* phenomenon; **b)** *(äußere Gestalt)* appearance; **c)** *(Vision)* apparition; **eine ~ haben** see a vision

**Erscheinungs-:** **~bild das** appearance; **~form die** manifestation

**erschießen** *unr. tr. V.* shoot dead; **Erschießung die**; **~, ~en** shooting

**erschlaffen** *itr. V.; mit sein* ⟨*muscle, limb*⟩ become limp; ⟨*skin*⟩ grow slack

¹**erschlagen** *unr. tr. V.* strike dead; kill; ²**erschlagen** *Adj. (ugs.)* **a)** *(erschöpft)* worn out; **b)** *(verblüfft)* **wie ~ sein** be flabbergasted *(coll.)* or thunderstruck

**erschließen** *unr. tr. V.* develop ⟨*area, building land*⟩; tap ⟨*resources*⟩

**erschöpfen** *tr. V.* exhaust; **erschöpfend** *Adj.* exhaustive; **erschöpft** *Adj.* exhausted; **Erschöpfung die** exhaustion

¹**erschrecken** *unr. itr. V.; mit sein* be startled; **vor etw.** *(Dat.) od.* **über etw.** *(Akk.)* **~:** be startled by sth.; ²**erschrecken** *tr. V.* frighten; scare; ³**erschrecken** *unr. od. regelm. refl. V.* get a fright; **erschreckend** *Adj.* alarming; **erschrocken 1. 2. Part. v.** ¹**erschrecken;** **2.** *Adj.* frightened

**erschüttern** *tr. V. (auch fig.)* shake; **erschütternd** *Adj.* deeply distressing; deeply shocking ⟨*conditions*⟩; **Erschütterung die**; **~, ~en a)** vibration; *(der Erde)* tremor; **b)** *(Ergriffenheit)* shock; *(Trauer)* distress

**erschweren** *tr. V.* **etw. ~:** make sth. more difficult; **erschwerend 1.** *Adj.* complicating ⟨*factor*⟩; **2.** *adv.* **es kommt ~ hinzu, daß er ...:** to make matters worse he ...

**erschwinglich** *Adj.* reasonable

**ersehen** *unr. tr. V.* see; **aus etw. zu ~ sein** be evident from sth.

**ersetzen** *tr. V.* **a)** replace **(durch** by); **b)** *(erstatten)* reimburse ⟨*expenses*⟩; **jmdm. einen Schaden ~:** compensate sb. for damages

**ersichtlich** *Adj.* apparent

**erspähen** *tr. V. (geh.)* espy *(literary)*; catch sight of

**ersparen** *tr. V.* save; **Ersparnis die; ~, ~se** saving

**ersprießlich** *Adj. (geh.)* fruitful ⟨*contacts, collaboration*⟩

**erst 1.** *Adv.* **a)** *(zu~)* first; **~ einmal** first [of all]; **b)** *(nicht eher als)* **eben ~:** only just; **~ nächste Woche** not until next week; **er war ~ zufrieden, als ...:** he was not satisfied until ...; **c)** *(nicht mehr als)* only; **2.** *Partikel* **so was lese ich gar nicht ~:** I dont even start reading that sort of stuff

**erst...** *Ordinalz.* **a)** first; **etw. das ~e Mal tun** do sth. for the first time; **am Ersten [des Monats]** on the first [of the month]; **als ~er/~e etw. tun** be the first to do sth.; **b)** *(best...)* **das ~e Hotel** the best hotel; **der/die Erste [der Klasse]** the top boy/girl [of the class]

**erstarren** *itr. V.; mit sein* ⟨*jelly, plaster*⟩ set; ⟨*limbs, fingers*⟩ grow stiff

**erstatten** *tr. V.* **a)** reimburse ⟨*expenses*⟩; **b) Anzeige gegen jmdn. ~:** report sb. [to the police]; **Erstattung die;** **~, ~en** *(von Kosten)* reimbursement

**Erst·aufführung die** première

**erstaunen** *tr. V.* astonish; **Erstaunen das;** **~s** astonishment; **erstaunlich 1.** *Adj.* astonishing; **2.** *adv.* astonishingly

**Erst·ausgabe die** first edition

**erstechen** *unr. tr. V.* stab [to death]

**erstehen** *(geh.)* **1.** *unr. tr. V. (kaufen)* purchase; **2.** *unr. itr. V.; mit sein* ⟨*difficulties, problems*⟩ arise

**ersteigen** *unr. tr. V.* climb

**ersteigern** *tr. V.* buy [at an auction]

**erstellen** *tr. V. (Papierdt.)* **a)** *(bauen)* build; **b)** *(anfertigen)* make ⟨*assessment*⟩; draw up ⟨*plan, report, list*⟩

**erste·mal** *Adv.* **das ~:** for the first time; **ersten·mal** *Adv.* **zum ~:** for the first time; **beim ~:** the first time

**erstens** *Adv.* firstly; in the first place; **erster...** *Adj.* the former

**erst·geboren** *Adj.* first-born

**ersticken 1.** *itr. V.; mit sein* suffocate; *(sich verschlucken)* choke; **2.** *tr. V.* **a)** *(töten)* suffocate; **b)** smother ⟨*flames*⟩

**erstklassig 1.** *Adj.* first-class; **2.** *adv.* superbly; **erstmals** *Adv.* for the first time; **erstrangig** *Adj.* **a)** first-class; **b)** *(vordringlich)* of top priority *postpos.*

**erstreben** *tr. V.* strive for; **erstrebens·wert** *Adj.* ⟨*ideals etc.*⟩ worth striving for; desirable ⟨*situation*⟩

**erstrecken** *refl. V.* **a)** *(sich ausdeh-*

*nen)* stretch; **b)** *(dauern)* **sich über 10 Jahre ~:** carry on for 10 years

**erstürmen** *tr. V.* take by storm

**ersuchen** *tr. V.* *(geh.)* ask; **jmdn. ~. etw. zu tun** request sb. to do sth.

**ertappen** *tr. V.* catch ⟨thief, burglar⟩

**erteilen** *tr. V.* give ⟨advice, information⟩; give, grant ⟨permission⟩; **Erteilung die** giving; *(einer Genehmigung)* granting

**ertönen** *itr. V.; mit sein* sound

**Ertrag der; ~[e]s, Erträge a)** yield; **b)** *(Gewinn)* return

**ertragen** *unr. tr. V.* bear; **erträglich** *Adj.* tolerable; bearable ⟨pain⟩

**ertrag·reich** *Adj.* lucrative ⟨business⟩; productive ⟨land, soil⟩

**ertränken** *tr. V.* drown; **ertrinken** *unr. itr. V.; mit sein* be drowned; drown

**erübrigen 1.** *tr. V.* spare ⟨money, time⟩; **2.** *refl. V.* be unnecessary

**erwachen** *itr. V.; mit sein (geh.)* awake

**Erwachen das; ~s** *(auch fig.)* awakening

**¹erwachsen** *unr. itr. V.; mit sein* **a)** grow **(aus** out of); ⟨rumour⟩ spread; **b)** *(sich ergeben)* ⟨difficulties, tasks⟩ arise; **²erwachsen** *Adj.* grown-up *attrib.;* **~ sein** be grown up; **Erwachsene der/die;** *adj. Dekl.* grown-up

**erwägen** *unr. tr. V.* consider; **Erwägung die; ~, ~en** consideration; **etw. in ~ ziehen** take sth. into consideration

**erwählen** *tr. V. (geh.)* choose

**erwähnen** *tr. V.* mention; **erwähnens·wert** *Adj.* worth mentioning *postpos.;* **Erwähnung die; ~, ~en** mention

**erwärmen 1.** *tr. V.* heat; **2.** *refl. V.* *(warm werden)* ⟨air, water⟩ warm up

**erwarten** *tr. V.* expect; **jmdn. am Bahnhof ~:** wait for sb. at the station; **Erwartung die; ~, ~en** expectation

**erwartungs-: ~gemäß** *Adv.* as expected; **~voll** *Adj.* expectant

**erwecken** *tr. V.* **a)** *(auf~)* wake; **b)** *(erregen)* arouse ⟨longing, pity⟩

**erweichen** *tr. V.* soften

**erweisen 1.** *unr. tr. V.* **a)** prove; **b)** *(bezeigen)* **jmdm. Achtung ~:** show respect to sb.; **2.** *unr. refl. V.* **sich als etw. ~:** prove to be sth.

**erweitern 1.** *tr. V.* widen ⟨river, road⟩; expand ⟨library, business⟩; enlarge ⟨collection⟩; dilate ⟨pupil, blood vessel⟩; **2.** *refl. V.* ⟨road, river⟩ widen;

⟨pupil, blood vessel⟩ dilate; **Erweiterung die; ~, ~en** *s.* **erweitern:** widening; expansion; enlargement; dilation

**Erwerb der; ~[e]s a)** *(Aneignung)* acquisition; **b)** *(Kauf)* purchase; **erwerben** *unr. tr. V.* **a)** *(verdienen)* earn; **b)** *(sich aneignen)* gain; **c)** *(kaufen)* acquire

**erwerbs-: ~los** *Adj.: s.* **arbeitslos; ~tätig** *Adj.* gainfully employed; **~unfähig** *Adj.* incapable of gainful employment *postpos.;* unable to work *postpos.*

**Erwerbung die** acquisition; *(Gekauftes)* purchase

**erwidern** *tr. V.* **a)** reply; **b)** *(reagieren auf)* return ⟨greeting, visit⟩; reciprocate ⟨sb.'s feelings⟩; **Erwiderung die; ~, ~en a)** reply **(auf +** *Akk.* to); **b)** *s.* **erwidern b:** return; reciprocation

**erwiesen** *Adj.* proved; proven ⟨fact⟩; **erwiesener·maßen** *Adv.* as has been proved

**erwirken** *tr. V.* obtain

**erwirtschaften** *tr. V.* **etw. ~:** obtain sth. by careful management

**erwischen** *tr. V. (ugs.)* **a)** catch ⟨culprit, train, bus⟩; **b)** *(greifen)* grab; **c)** *(bekommen)* manage to get; **d)** *(unpers.)* **es hat ihn erwischt** *(ugs.)* *(er ist tot)* he's bought it *(sl.);* *(er ist krank)* he's got it; *(er ist verletzt)* he's been hurt; *(scherzh.: er ist verliebt)* he's got it bad *(coll.)*

**erwünscht** *Adj.* wanted

**erwürgen** *tr. V.* strangle

**Erz** [e:rts *od.* e:rts] **das; ~es, ~e** ore

**erzählen** *tr. (auch itr.) V.* tell ⟨joke, story⟩; **jmdm. etw. ~:** tell sb. sth.; **Erzähler der** story-teller; *(Autor)* writer [of stories]; narrative writer; **Erzählung die; ~, ~en** narration; *(Bericht)* account; *(Literaturw.)* story

**Erz-: ~bischof der** archbishop; **~bistum das, ~diözese die** archbishopric; archdiocese; **~engel der** archangel

**erzeugen** *tr. V.* produce; generate ⟨electricity⟩; **Erzeuger der; ~s, ~** *(Vater)* father; **Erzeugnis das** product; **Erzeugung die** *(von Lebensmitteln usw.)* production; *(von Industriewaren)* manufacture; *(Strom~)* generation

**Erz·feind der** arch enemy

**erziehen** *unr. tr. V.* bring up; *(in der Schule)* educate; **ein Kind zu Sauberkeit und Ordnung ~:** bring a child up to be clean and tidy; **Erzieher** der; ~s, ~, **Erzieherin** die; ~, ~nen educator; *(Pädagoge)* educationalist; *(Lehrer)* teacher; **Erziehung** die; *o. Pl.* upbringing; *(Schul~)* education; **Erziehungs·berechtigte** der/die; *adj. Dekl.* parent or [legal] guardian

**erzielen** *tr. V.* reach ⟨*agreement, compromise, speed*⟩; achieve ⟨*result, effect*⟩; make ⟨*profit*⟩; obtain ⟨*price*⟩

**erzürnen** *(geh.) tr. V.* anger; *(stärker)* incense

**erzwingen** *unr. tr. V.* force

**es** *Personalpron.; 3. Pers. Sg. Nom. u. Akk. Neutr.* a) *(s. auch Gen.* **seiner**; *Dat.* **ihm**) *(Sache)* it; *(weibliche Person)* she/her; *(männliche Person)* he/him; b) *ohne Bezug auf ein bestimmtes Subst., mit unpers. Verben, als formales Satzglied* it; **ich bin es** it's me; **wir sind traurig, ihr seid es auch** we are sad, and so are you; **es sei denn, |daß| ...**: unless ...; **es ist genug!** that's enough; **es hat geklopft** there was a knock; **es klingelt** someone is ringing; **es wird schöner** the weather is improving; **es geht ihm gut/schlecht** he is well/unwell; **es wird gelacht** there is laughter; **es läßt sich aushalten** it is bearable; **er hat es gut** he has it good; **er meinte es gut** he meant well

**Esche** die; ~, ~n *(Bot.)* ash

**Esel** der; ~s, ~ a) donkey; ass; b) *(ugs.: Dummkopf)* ass *(coll.)*

**Esels-**: ~**brücke** die *(ugs.)* mnemonic; ~**ohr** das *(ugs.: umgeknickte Stelle)* dog-ear

**Eskalation** die; ~, ~en escalation

**Eskimo** der; ~|s|, ~|s| Eskimo

**Eskorte** die; ~, ~n escort; **eskortieren** *tr. V.* escort

**Espe** die; ~, ~n aspen

**eßbar** *Adj.* edible; **nicht** ~: inedible; **essen** *unr. tr., itr. V.* eat; **etw. gern** ~: like sth.; **sich satt** ~: eat one's fill; **gut** ~: have a good meal; *(immer)* eat well; ~ **gehen** go out for a meal; **Essen** das; ~s, ~ *(Mahlzeit)* meal; *(Speise)* food; |das| ~ **machen/kochen** get/cook the meal

**Essen|s|-**: ~**marke** die meal-ticket; ~**zeit** die mealtime

**Essenz** die; ~, ~en essence

**Esser** der; ~s, ~: **er ist ein schlechter** ~: he has a poor appetite

**Essig** der; ~s, ~e vinegar; **Essiggurke** die pickled gherkin

**Eß-**: ~**kastanie** die sweet chestnut; ~**löffel** der *(Suppenlöffel)* soup-

spoon; *(für Nach-, Vorspeise)* dessert-spoon; ~**stäbchen** das chopstick; ~**teller** der dinner plate; ~**tisch** der dining-table; ~**waren** *Pl.* food *sing.*; ~**zimmer** das dining-room

**Establishment** [ɪs'tɛblɪʃmənt] das; ~s, ~s Establishment

**Este** der; ~n, ~n Estonian; **Est·land** (das); ~s Estonia

**Estragon** ['ɛstragɔn] der; ~s tarragon

**Estrich** ['ɛstrɪç] der; ~s, ~e composition floor

**etablieren** *tr. V.* establish; set up; **etabliert** *Adj.* established

**Etage** [e'ta:ʒə] die; ~, ~n floor; storey

**Etappe** die; ~, ~n stage

**Etat** [e'ta:] der; ~s, ~s budget

**etepetete** [e:tǝpe'te:tǝ] *Adj. (ugs.)* fussy; finicky

**Ethik** die; ~, ~en a) ethics *sing.*; b) *o. Pl. (sittliche Normen)* ethics *pl.*; **ethisch** *Adj.* ethical

**Etikett** das; ~|e|s, ~en *od.* ~e *od.* ~s label; **Etikette** die; ~, ~n etiquette; **etikettieren** *tr. V.* label

**etlich...** *Indefinitpron. u. unbest. Zahlwort: Sg.* quite a lot of; *Pl.* quite a few

**Etüde** die; ~, ~n *(Musik)* étude

**Etui** [ɛt'vi:] das; ~s, ~s case

**etwa** 1. *Adv.* a) *(ungefähr)* about; ~ **so groß wie ...**: about as large as ...; ~ **roughly like this**; b) *(beispielsweise)* for example; 2. *Partikel* **störe ich** ~? am I disturbing you at all?; **etwaig...** ['ɛtva(:)ɪg...] *Adj.* possible

**etwas** *Indefinitpron.* a) something; *(fragend, verneinend)* anything; **irgend** ~: something; b) *(Bedeutsames)* **aus ihm wird** ~: he'll make something of himself; c) *(ein Teil)* some; *(fragend, verneinend)* any; ~ **von dem Geld** some of the money; d) *(ein wenig)* a little; ~ **lauter/besser** a little louder/better

**Etymologie** die; ~, ~n etymology

**euch** 1. *Dat. u. Akk. Pl. des Personalpron.* **ihr** you; 2. *Dat. u. Akk. Pl. des Reflexivpron. der 2. Pers. Pl.* yourselves

¹**euer** *Possessivpron.* your; **Grüße von Eu|e|rer Helga/Eu|e|rem Hans** Best wishes, Yours, Helga/Hans; ²**euer** *Gen. des Personalpron.* **ihr** *(geh.)* **wir werden** ~ **gedenken** we will remember you

**Eule** die; ~, ~n owl; ~**n nach Athen tragen** carry coals to Newcastle

**Eunuch** der; ~en, ~en eunuch

**Euphorie** die; ~, ~n *(bes. Med., Psych.)* euphoria

**eure** s. ¹euer; **eurer·seits** s. deinerseits; **euret·wegen** Adv. s. deinetwegen

**Eurocheque** ['ɔyroʃɛk] der; ~s, ~s Eurocheque

**Europa (das)**; ~s Europe

**Europäer** der; ~s, ~, **Europäerin** die; ~, ~nen European; **europäisch** Adj. European; **die Europäische Gemeinschaft** the European Community

**Europa-**: ~**meister** der (Sport) European champion; ~**meisterschaft** die (Sport) a) (Wettbewerb) European Championship; b) (Sieg) European title; ~**parlament** das; o. Pl. European Parliament; ~**pokal** der (Sport) European cup; ~**rat** der; o. Pl. Council of Europe; ~**straße** die European long-distance road

**Euro·scheck** der s. Eurocheque

**Euter** das od. der; ~s, ~: udder

**e. V., E. V.** Abk. eingetragener Verein

**ev.** Abk. evangelisch ev.

**evakuieren** [evaku'i:rən] tr. V. evacuate; **Evakuierung** die; ~, ~en evacuation

**evangelisch** [evaŋ'ge:lɪʃ] Adj. Protestant; **Evangelium** das; ~s, Evangelien a) (auch fig.) gospel; b) (christl. Rel.) Gospel ·

**eventuell** [evɛn'tu̯ɛl] 1. Adj. possible; 2. adv. possibly; perhaps

**Evolution** [evolu'tsi̯o:n] die; ~, ~en evolution

**evtl.** Abk. eventuell

**EWG** [e:ve:'ge:] die; ~: EEC

**ewig** 1. Adj. eternal; (abwertend) never-ending; 2. adv. eternally; for ever; **Ewigkeit** die; ~, ~en a) eternity; b) (ugs.) es dauert eine ~: it takes ages (coll.).

**ex** Adv. (ugs.) etw. ex trinken drink sth. down in one (coll.); **Ex-** (vor Personenbez.: vormalig) ex-

**exakt** Adj. exact; precise

**Examen** das; ~s, ~ od. **Examina** examination

**Exekution** die; ~, ~en execution; **Exekutive** die; ~, ~n (Rechtsw., Politik) executive

**Exempel** das; ~s, ~: example; **Exemplar** das; ~s, ~e specimen; (Buch, Zeitung usw.) copy

**exerzieren** tr., itr. V. drill

**Exil** das; ~s, ~e exile

**Existenz** die; ~, ~en a) existence; b) (Lebensgrundlage) livelihood; c) (Mensch) character

**Existenz-**: ~**grundlage** die basis of

one's livelihood; ~**minimum** das subsistence level

**existieren** itr. V. exist

**Exitus** der; ~ (Med.) death

**exkl.** Abk. exklusive excl.

**exklusiv** 1. Adj. exclusive; 2. adv. exclusively; **exklusive** Präp. + Gen. exclusive of

**Ex·kommunikation** die excommunication

**Exkursion** die; ~, ~en study trip

**exotisch** 1. Adj. exotic; 2. adv. exotically

**expandieren** tr., itr. V. expand; **Expansion** die; ~, ~en expansion

**Expedition** die; ~, ~en expedition

**Experiment** das; ~[e]s, ~e experiment; **experimentell** 1. Adj. experimental; 2. adv. experimentally; **experimentieren** itr. V. experiment

**Experte** der; ~n, ~n, **Expertin** die; ~, ~nen expert (für in)

**explodieren** itr. V.; mit sein (auch fig.) explode; ⟨costs⟩ rocket; **Explosion** die; ~, ~en explosion; **explosiv** 1. Adj. (auch fig.) explosive; 2. adv. explosively

**Exponent** der; ~en, ~en (Math.) exponent; **exponiert** Adj. exposed

**Export** der; ~[e]s, ~e export

**Export-**: ~**artikel** der export; ~**bier** das export beer

**Exporteur** [ɛkspɔr'tø:ɐ̯] der; ~s, ~e (Wirtsch.) exporter

**Export-**: ~**firma** die exporter; ~**handel** der export trade

**exportieren** tr., itr. V. export

**Expreß·gut** das express freight

**Expressionismus** der; ~: expressionism no art.; **expressionistisch** Adj. expressionist

**extra** Adv. a) (gesondert) ⟨pay⟩ separately; b) (zusätzlich, besonders) extra; c) (eigens) especially; **Extra** das; ~s, ~s extra; **Extra·blatt** das special edition

**Extrakt** der; ~[e]s, ~e extract

**extravagant** [-va'gant] Adj. flamboyant; flamboyantly furnished ⟨flat⟩

**extrem** Adj. extreme; **Extrem** das; ~s, ~e extreme; **Extrem·fall** der extreme case; **Extremismus** der; ~: extremism; **Extremist** der; ~en, ~en extremist; **extremistisch** Adj. extremist

**Exzellenz** die; ~, ~en Excellency

**exzentrisch** 1. Adj. eccentric; 2. adv. eccentrically

**Exzeß** der; Exzesses, Exzesse excess

# F

f, F [ɛf] das; ~, ~ a) *(Buchstabe)* f/F; b) *(Musik)* [key of] F
f. *Abk.* folgend f.
Fa. *Abk.* Firma
**Fabel** die; ~, ~n fable; *(Kern einer Handlung)* plot
**fabelhaft 1.** *Adj. (ugs.: großartig)* fantastic *(coll.)*; **2.** *adv. (ugs.)* fantastically *(coll.)*
**Fabrik** die; ~, ~en factory
**Fabrikant** der; ~en, ~en manufacturer; **Fabrikat** das; ~[e]s, ~e product; *(Marke)* make; **Fabrikation** die; ~: production
**Fabrik-:** ~besitzer der factory-owner; ~direktor der works manager
**fabrizieren** *tr. V. (ugs. abwertend)* knock together *(coll.)*
**Fach** das; ~[e]s, Fächer a) compartment; *(für Post)* pigeon-hole; b) *(Studien~, Unterrichts~)* subject; *(Wissensgebiet)* field; *(Berufszweig)* trade; **ein Mann vom ~:** an expert
**Fach-:** ~arbeiter der skilled worker; ~arzt der specialist (für in); ~geschäft das specialist shop
**fachlich** *Adj.* specialist ⟨knowledge, work⟩; technical ⟨problem, explanation, experience⟩
**Fach-:** ~mann der expert; ~werk das o. Pl. *(Bauweise)* half-timbered construction; ~werk·haus das half-timbered house
**Fackel** die; ~, ~n torch
**fade** *Adj.* insipid
**Faden** der; ~s, Fäden thread; **ein ~:** a piece of thread
**faden·scheinig** *Adj.* threadbare; flimsy ⟨excuse⟩
**Fagott** das; ~[e]s, ~e bassoon
**fähig** *Adj.* a) *(begabt)* able; capable; b) zu etw. ~ sein be capable of sth.; **Fähigkeit** die; ~, ~en a) *meist Pl.* ability; capability; geistige ~en intellectual faculties; b) o. Pl. *(Imstandesein)* ability (zu to)

**fahl** *Adj.* pale; pallid; wan ⟨light⟩
**fahnden** *itr. V.* search (nach for)
**Fahne** die; ~, ~n flag
**Fahr·bahn** die carriageway
**Fähre** die; ~, ~n ferry
**fahren 1.** *unr. itr. V.; mit sein* a) *(als Fahrzeuglenker)* drive; *(mit dem Fahrrad, Motorrad usw.)* ride; b) *(als Mitfahrer; mit öffentlichem Verkehrsmittel)* go (mit by); *(mit dem Aufzug/der Rolltreppe/der Seilbahn)* take the lift *(Brit.)* or *(Amer.)* elevator/escalator/cable-car; *(per Anhalter)* hitch-hike; c) *(reisen)* go; in Urlaub ~: go on holiday; d) *(los~)* go; leave; e) ⟨motor vehicle, train, lift, cable-car⟩ go; ⟨ship⟩ sail; mein Auto fährt nicht my car won't go; f) *(verkehren)* ⟨train etc.⟩ run; **2.** *unr. tr. V.* a) *(fortbewegen)* drive ⟨car, lorry, train, etc.⟩; ride ⟨bicycle, motor cycle⟩; b) 50/80 km/h ~: do 50/80 k.p.h.; hier muß man 50 km/h ~: you've got to keep to 50 k.p.h. here; sail ⟨boat⟩; Auto ~: drive [a car]; Kahn od. Boot/Kanu ~: boating/canoeing; Ski ~: ski; U-Bahn ~: ride on the underground *(Brit.)* or *(Amer.)* subway; c) *(befördern)* take
**Fahrenheit** o. Art. 70 Grad ~: 70 degrees Fahrenheit
**fahren|lassen** *unr. tr. V.* let go; **Fahrer** der; ~s, ~: driver; **Fahrerflucht** die: ~ begehen fail to stop after [being involved in] an accident; **Fahrerin** die; ~, ~nen driver
**Fahr-:** ~gast der passenger; ~geld das fare
**fahrig** *Adj.* nervous
**fahr-, Fahr-:** ~karte die ticket; ~karten·automat der ticket machine; ~karten·schalter der ticket window; ~lässig **1.** *Adj.* negligent ⟨behaviour⟩; ~e Tötung/Körperverletzung *(Rechtsw.)* causing death/injury through [culpable] negligence; **2.** *adv.* negligently; ~lehrer der driving instructor
**Fähr·mann** der ferryman
**Fahr-:** ~plan der timetable; schedule *(Amer.)*; ~preis der fare; ~prüfung die driving test; ~rad das bicycle; cycle; mit dem ~ fahren cycle; ride a bicycle; ~rad·ständer der bicycle rack; ~schein der ticket; ~schein·automat der ticket machine; ~schein·entwerter der ticket cancelling machine; ~schule die driving school; ~spur die traffic-lane
**fährst** 2. *Pers. Sg. Präsens v.* **fahren**

**Fahr-:** **~stuhl** der lift *(Brit.);* elevator *(Amer.); (für Lasten)* hoist; **~stunde** die driving lesson

**Fahrt** die; **~, ~en a)** journey; freie **~ haben** have a clear run; *(Schiffsreise)* voyage; *(kurze Reise, Ausflug)* trip; **b)** *o. Pl. (Geschwindigkeit)* **in voller ~:** at full speed; **fährt** *3. Pers. Sg. Präsens v.* **fahren**

**Fährte** die trail; jmds. **~ verfolgen** track sb.

**Fahrt·kosten** *Pl. (für öffentliche Verkehrsmittel)* fare/fares; *(für Autoreisen)* travel costs; **Fahr·treppe** die escalator; **Fahrt·richtung** die direction; **in ~ parken** park in the direction of the traffic; **die ~ ändern** change direction; **fahr·tüchtig** *Adj.* ⟨*driver*⟩ fit to drive; ⟨*vehicle*⟩ roadworthy

**Fahrt-:** **~wind** der airflow; **~ziel** das destination

**Fahr-:** **~werk** das *(Flugw.)* undercarriage; **~zeit** die travelling time; **~zeug** das vehicle; *(Luft~)* aircraft; *(Wasser~)* vessel

**fair** [fɛːɐ̯] **1.** *Adj.* fair (**gegen** to); **2.** *adv.* fairly

**Fakten** *s.* **Faktum**; **faktisch 1.** *Adj.* real; actual; **2.** *adv.* **das bedeutet ~ ...:** it means in effect ...

**Faktor** der; **~s, ~en** *(auch Math.)* factor

**Faktum** das; **~s, Fakten** fact

**Fakultät** die; **~, ~en** *(Hochschulw.)* faculty

**Falke** der; **~n, ~n** *(auch Politik fig.)* hawk

**Fall** der; **~|e|s, Fälle a)** *(Sturz)* fall; **zu ~ kommen** have a fall; **jmdn. zu ~ bringen** *(fig.)* bring about sb.'s downfall; **b)** *(das Fallen)* descent; **der freie ~:** free fall; **c)** *(Ereignis; Rechtsw., Med., Grammatik)* case; *(zu erwartender Umstand)* eventuality; **es ist |nicht| der ~:** it is [not] the case; **gesetzt den ~:** assuming; **auf jeden ~, in jedem ~, auf alle Fälle** in any case; **auf keinen ~:** on no account; **Falle** die; **~, ~n** *(auch fig.)* trap; **fallen** *unr. itr. V.; mit sein* **a)** fall; **etw. ~ lassen** drop sth.; **b)** *(hin~, stürzen)* fall [over]; **über einen Stein ~:** trip over a stone; **c)** ⟨*prices, light, glance, choise*⟩ fall; ⟨*temperature, water level*⟩ fall, drop; ⟨*fever*⟩ subside; ⟨*shot*⟩ be fired; **d)** *(im Kampf sterben)* die; fall *(literary);* **fällen** *tr. V.* **a)** fell ⟨*tree, timber*⟩; **ein Urteil ~** ⟨*judge*⟩ pass sentence; ⟨*jury*⟩ return a verdict; **fällig** *Adj.* due; **falls** *(Konj.)*

**a)** *(wenn)* if; **b)** *(für den Fall, daß)* in case; **Fall·schirm** der parachute; **mit dem ~ abspringen** *(im Notfall)* parachute out; *(als Sport)* make a [parachute] jump

**falsch 1.** *Adj.* **a)** *(unecht, imitiert)* false ⟨*teeth, plait*⟩; imitation ⟨*jewellery*⟩; **b)** *(gefälscht)* forged; assumed ⟨*name*⟩; **c)** *(irrig, fehlerhaft)* wrong; **2.** *adv.* wrongly; **die Uhr geht ~:** the clock is wrong; **fälschen** *tr. V.* forge; **Fälscher** der; **~s, ~** forger; **Falschgeld** das counterfeit money; **fälschlich 1.** *Adj.* false; **2.** *adv.* falsely; **Falschmeldung** die false report; **Fälschung** die; **~, ~en** fake

**Falt·blatt** das leaflet; *(in Zeitungen, Zeitschriften, Büchern)* insert; **Falte** die; **~, ~n a)** crease; **b)** *(im Stoff)* fold; *(mit scharfer Kante)* pleat; **c)** *(Haut~)* wrinkle; **falten 1.** *tr. V.* fold; **die Hände ~:** fold one's hands; **2.** *refl. V. (auch Geol.)* fold; ⟨*skin*⟩ become wrinkled; **Falten·rock** der pleated skirt; **Falter** der; **~s, ~** *(Nacht~)* moth; *(Tag~)* butterfly; **faltig a)** *Adj.* ⟨*clothes*⟩ gathered [in folds]; wrinkled ⟨*skin, hands*⟩; **b)** *(zerknittert)* creased **-fältig** *Adj., adv.* -fold

**familiär** *Adj.* **a)** family ⟨*problems, worries*⟩; **b)** *(zwanglos)* familiar; informal; **Familie** [fa'miːliə] die; **~, ~n** family; **~ Meyer** the Meyer family

**Familien-:** **~angehörige** der/die; *adj. Dekl.* member of the family; **~feier** die family party; **~leben** das; *o. Pl.* family life; **~name** der surname; **~planung** die; *o. Pl.* family planning *no art.;* **~stand** der marital status; **~vater** der: **~vater sein** be the father of a family; **ein guter ~vater** a good husband and father

**Fan** [fɛn] der; **~s, ~s** fan

**Fanatiker** der; **~s, ~:** fanatic; *(religiös)* fanatic; zealot; **fanatisch 1.** *Adj.* fanatical; **2.** *adv.* fanatically

**fand** *1. u. 3. Pers. Sg. Prät. v.* **finden**

**Fanfare** die; **~, ~n** *(Signal)* fanfare

**Fang** der; **~|e|s, Fänge a)** *(Tier~)* trap; *(von Fischen)* catching; **b)** *(Beute)* bag; *(von Fischen)* catch; **fangen 1.** *unr. tr. V.* catch; capture ⟨*fugitive etc.*⟩; **2.** *unr. refl. V.* **a)** *(in eine Falle geraten)* be caught; **b)** *(wieder in die normale Lage kommen)* **sich |gerade| noch ~:** [just] manage to steady oneself; **Fang·frage** die catch question

**Farb-:** **~bild** das *(Foto)* colour photo; **~dia** das colour slide

**Fạrbe** die; ~, ~n a) colour; b) *(für Textilien)* dye; *(zum Malen, Anstreichen)* paint; ~n **mischen/auftragen** mix/ apply paint; **fạrb·echt** *Adj.* colourfast; **fạrben 1.** *tr. V.* dye; **2.** *refl. V.* change colour; **sich schwarz/rot** *usw.* ~: turn black/red *etc;* **3.** *itr. V. (ugs.: ab~)* ⟨*material, blouse etc.*⟩ run; **-fạrben** *Adj.* coloured
**fạrben-:** ~**blind** *Adj.* colour-blind; ~**froh** *Adj.* colourful; ~**prächtig** *Adj.* vibrant with colour *postpos.*
**Fạrb-:** ~**fernsehen** das colour television; ~**fernseher** der *(ugs.)* colour telly *(coll.)* or television; ~**film** der colour film; ~**foto** das colour photo
**fạrbig 1.** *Adj.* **a)** coloured; **b)** *(bunt, auch fig.)* colourful; **2.** *adv.* colourfully; **-farbig** *Adj.* -coloured; **Fạrbige** der/die; *adj. Dekl.* coloured man/woman; *Pl.* coloured people
**fạrblich 1.** *Adj.* in colour *postpos.;* as regards colour *postpos;* **2.** *adv.* **etw.** ~ **abstimmen** match sth. in colour
**fạrb-, Fạrb-:** ~**los** *Adj. (auch fig.)* colourless; clear ⟨*varnish*⟩; neutral ⟨*shoe polish*⟩; ~**stift** der coloured pencil; ~**stoff** der **a)** *(Med., Biol.)* pigment; **b)** *(für Textilien)* dye; **c)** *(für Lebensmittel)* colouring; ~**ton** der shade
**Fạrbung** die; ~, ~en colouring
**Fạrn** der; ~|e|s, ~e, **Fạrn·kraut** das fern
**Fasạn** der; ~|e|s, ~e|n| pheasant
**Fạsching** der; ~s, ~e od. ~s [preLent] carnival
**Faschịsmus** der; ~: fascism *no art.* **Faschịst** der; ~en, ~en fascist; **faschịstisch** *Adj.* fascist
**fạseln** *itr. V. (ugs. abwertend)* drivel
**Fạser** die; ~, ~n fibre; **fạsern** *itr. V.* fray
**Fạß** das; **Fạsses, Fässer** barrel; *(Öl~)* drum; *(kleines Bier~)* keg; *(kleines Sherry~* usw.*)* cask; **Bier vom** ~: draught beer; **ein** ~ **ohne Boden** an endless drain on sb.'s resources
**Fassạde** die; ~, ~n façade
**fạßbar** *Adj.* **a)** tangible ⟨*results*⟩; **b)** *(verständlich)* comprehensible
**Fạß·bier** das draught beer; beer on draught
**fạssen 1.** *tr. V.* **a)** *(greifen)* grasp; take hold of; **b)** *(festnehmen)* catch ⟨*thief, culprit*⟩; **c)** *(aufnehmen können)* ⟨*hall, tank*⟩ hold; **d)** *(begreifen)* **ich kann es nicht** ~: I cannot take it in; **e)** **einen Entschluß** ~: make *or* take a decision; **2.** *itr. V.* **a)** *(greifen)* **nach etw.** ~: reach

for sth.; **in etw.** *(Akk.)* ~: put one's hand in sth.; **fạßlich** *Adj.* comprehensible
**Fasson** [fa'sõ:] die; ~, ~s style; shape
**Fạssung** die; ~, ~en **a)** *(Form)* version; **b)** *o. Pl. (Selbstbeherrschung)* composure; **die** ~ **bewahren** keep one's composure; **die** ~ **verlieren** lose one's self-control; **jmdn. aus der** ~ **bringen** upset sb.; **c)** *(für Glühlampen)* holder; **fạssungs·los** *Adj.* stunned
**fạst** *Adv.* almost; nearly; ~ **nie** hardly ever
**fạsten** *itr. V.* fast; **Fạst·nacht** die carnival
**faszinịeren** *tr. V.* fascinate
**fatạl** *Adj.* **a)** *(peinlich, mißlich)* awkward; **b)** *(verhängnisvoll)* fatal
**fauchen** *itr. V.* **a)** ⟨*cat*⟩ hiss; ⟨*tiger, person*⟩ snarl
**faul** *Adj.* **a)** *(verdorben)* rotten; bad ⟨*food, tooth*⟩; foul ⟨*water, air*⟩; **b)** *(träge)* lazy; **Fäule** die; ~: foulness; **faulen** *itr. V.; meist mit sein* rot; ⟨*water*⟩ go foul; ⟨*meat, fish*⟩ go off
**faulenzen** *itr. V.* laze about; loaf about *(derog.);* **Faulenzer** der; ~s, ~: idler; lazy-bones *sing. (coll.)*
**Faulheit** die; ~: laziness; **faulig** *Adj.* stagnating ⟨*water*⟩; ~ **schmecken/riechen** taste/smell off; **Fäulnis** die; ~: rottenness
**Faul-:** ~**pelz** der *(fam.)* lazy-bones *sing. (coll.);* ~**tier** das **a)** *(Zool.)* sloth; **b)** *(ugs.: Faulenzer) s.* ~**pelz**
**Faust** die; ~, **Fäuste** fist; **eine** ~ **machen** clench one's fist; **das paßt wie die** ~ **aufs Auge** *(ugs.) (paßt nicht)* that clashes horribly; *(paßt)* that matches perfectly; **auf eigene** ~: on one's own initiative; **Fäustchen** das; ~s, ~; **sich** *(Dat.)* **ins** ~ **lachen** laugh up one's sleeve; **faust·dick** *Adj.* as thick as a man's fist *postpos.; (fig.)* bare-faced ⟨*lie*⟩; **Fäustling** der; ~s, ~e mitten; **Faust·regel** die rule of thumb
**Favorịt** [favo'ri:t] der; ~en, ~en favourite
**Fạx** das; ~, ~|e| fax; **fạxen** *tr. V.* fax
**Fạxen** *Pl. (ugs.)* fooling around
**Fazịt** ['fa:tsit] das; ~s, ~s od. ~e result
**Februar** der; ~|s|, ~e February
**fẹchten** *unr. itr., tr. V.* fence; **Fẹchter** der; ~s, ~: fencer
**Fẹder** die; ~, ~n **a)** *(Vogel~)* feather; **b)** *(zum Schreiben)* nib; **c)** *(Technik)* spring
**feder-, Fẹder-:** ~**ball** der **a)** *(Spiel)* badminton; **b)** *(Ball)* shuttlecock;

~**bett** das duvet *(Brit.)*; stuffed quilt *(Amer.)*; ~**führend** *Adj.* in charge *postpos.*; ~**halter** der fountain-pen; ~**leicht** *Adj.* ⟨*person*⟩ as light as a feather; featherweight ⟨*object*⟩; ~**lesen** das: **nicht viel** ~**lesen[s] mit jmdm./etw. machen** give sb./sth. short shrift

**fedeɾn** 1. *itr. V.* ⟨*springboard, floor, etc.*⟩ be springy; 2. *tr. V. (mit einer Federung versehen)* spring; **das Bett ist gut gefedert** the bed is well-sprung; **Federung** die; ~, ~**en** *(Kfz-W.)* suspension

**Fee** die; ~, ~**n** fairy

**Fege·feuer** das purgatory; **fegen** 1. *tr. V.* **a)** *(bes. nordd.: säubern)* sweep; **b)** *(schnell entfernen)* brush; 2. *itr. V.* sweep up

**fehl** *Adv.* ~ **am Platz[e] sein** be out of place; **Fehl·anzeige** die: ~! *(ugs.)* no chance! *(coll.)*; **fehlen** *itr. V.* **a)** *(nicht vorhanden sein)* **ihm fehlt das Geld** he has no money; **b)** *(ausbleiben)* be absent; **c)** *(verschwunden sein)* be missing; **in der Kasse fehlt Geld** money is missing from the till; **d)** *(vermißt werden)* **er/das wird mir** ~: I shall miss him/that; **e)** *(erforderlich sein)* be needed; **ihm** ~ **noch zwei Punkte zum Sieg** he needs only two points to win; **es fehlte nicht viel, und ich wäre eingeschlafen** I all but fell asleep; **f)** *unpers. (mangeln)* **es fehlt an Lehrern** there is a lack of teachers; **g)** *(krank sein)* **was fehlt Ihnen?** what seems to be the matter?; **fehlt dir etwas?** is there something wrong?; **Fehler** der; ~**s**, ~ **a)** *(Irrtum)* mistake; error; *(Sport)* fault; **b)** *(schlechte Eigenschaft)* fault; **fehler·frei** *Adj.* faultless; **fehlerhaft** *Adj.* faulty; defective; imperfect ⟨*pronunciation*⟩; **Fehler·quelle** die source of error

**fehl-, Fehl-:** ~**geburt** die miscarriage; ~**schlag** der failure; ~**|schlagen** *unr. itr. V.; mit sein* fail; ~**start** der *(Leichtathletik)* false start; ~**tritt** der *(fig. geh.)* slip; ~**zündung** die *(Technik)* misfire

**Feier** die; ~, ~**n a)** *(Veranstaltung)* party; *(aus festlichem Anlaß)* celebration; **b)** *(Zeremonie)* ceremony; **Feier·abend** der *(Arbeitsschluß)* finishing time; **nach** ~: after work; ~ **machen** finish work; **feierlich** 1. *Adj.* ceremonial ⟨*act etc.*⟩; solemn ⟨*silence*⟩; 2. *adv.* solemnly; ceremoniously; **Feierlichkeit** die; ~, ~**en a)** o.

*Pl.* solemnity; **b)** *meist Pl. (Veranstaltung)* celebration; **feiern** 1. *tr. V.* **a)** celebrate ⟨*birthday, wedding, etc.*⟩; **b)** acclaim ⟨*artist, sportsman, etc.*⟩; 2. *itr. V.* celebrate

**Feier·tag** der holiday; **ein gesetzlicher/kirchlicher** ~ a public holiday/religious festival

**feig[e]** 1. *Adj.* cowardly; 2. *adv.* in a cowardly way

**Feige** die; ~, ~**n** fig

**Feigheit** die; ~: cowardice; **Feigling** der; ~**s**, ~**e** coward

**Feile** die; ~, ~**n** file; **feilen** *tr., itr. V.* file

**feilschen** *itr. V.* haggle (**um** over)

**fein** 1. *Adj.* **a)** fine; finely-ground ⟨*flour*⟩; finely-granulated ⟨*sugar*⟩; **b)** *(hochwertig)* high-quality ⟨*fruit, soap, etc.*⟩; fine ⟨*silver, gold, etc.*⟩; fancy ⟨*cakes, pastries, etc.*⟩; **c)** *(ugs.: erfreulich)* great *(coll.)*; 2. *adv.* ~ **[he]raussein** *(ugs.)* be sitting pretty *(coll.)*

**Feind** der; ~**[e]s**, ~**e** enemy; **feindlich** 1. *Adj.* **a)** hostile; **b)** *(Milit.)* enemy ⟨*attack, activity*⟩; 2. *adv.* in a hostile manner; **Feindschaft** die; ~, ~**en** enmity; **feind·selig** *Adj.* hostile

**Feinheit** die; ~, ~**en a)** fineness; delicacy; **b)** *(Nuance)* subtlety

**fein-, Fein-:** ~**kost·geschäft** das delicatessen; ~**|machen** *refl. V. (ugs.)* dress up; ~**schmecker** der; ~**s**, ~**gourmet**; ~**sinnig** *Adj.* sensitive and subtle; ~**waschmittel** das mild detergent

**feist** *Adj. (meist abwertend)* fat

**Feld** das; ~**[e]s**, ~**er a)** field; **b)** *(Sport: Spiel*~*)* pitch; field; **c)** *(auf Formularen)* box; space; *(auf Brettspielen)* space; *(auf dem Schachbrett)* square; **d)** *o. Pl. (Tätigkeitsbereich)* field; sphere

**Feld-:** ~**herr** der *(veralt.)* commander; ~**marschall** der Field Marshal; ~**salat** der corn salad; ~**stecher** der binoculars *pl.*; ~**webel** der; ~**s**, ~ *(Milit.)* sergeant; ~**weg** der path; track; ~**zug** der *(Milit., fig.)* campaign

**Felge** die; ~, ~**n** [wheel] rim

**Fell** das; ~**[e]s**, ~**e a)** *(Haarkleid)* fur; *(Pferde*~, *Hunde*~, *Katzen*~*)* coat; *(Schaf*~*)* fleece; **b)** *(Material)* fur; **c)** *(abgezogen)* hide; **ein dickes** ~ **haben** *(ugs.)* be thick-skinned

**Fels** der; ~**en**, ~**en** rock; **Felsen** der; ~**s**, ~: rock; *(an der Steilküste)* cliff; **felsen·fest** *Adj.* firm; unshakeable

⟨*opinion, belief*⟩; **fẹlsig** *Adj.* rocky; **Fẹls·wand** die rock face

**femini̱n** *Adj.* feminine; **Femini̱smus** der; ~ feminism *no art.;* **Femini̱stin** die; ~, ~nen feminist

**Fẹnchel** der; ~s fennel

**Fẹnster** das; ~s, ~: window

**Fẹnster-:** ~**bank** die window-sill; ~**laden** der [window] shutter; ~**leder** das wash-leather; ~**platz** der window-seat; ~**putzer** der window-cleaner; ~**rahmen** der window-frame; ~**scheibe** die window-pane

**Ferien** ['fe:riən] *Pl.* **a)** holiday[s *pl.*] *(Brit.)*; vacation *(Amer.);* **in die ~ fahren** go on holiday/vacation; ~ **haben** have a *or* be on holiday/vacation; **Ferien·haus** das holiday/vacation house

**Fẹrkel** das; ~s, ~: piglet

**fẹrn 1.** *Adj.* distant; **2.** *adv.* ~ **von der Heimat** far from home; **3.** *Präp. mit Dat. (geh.)* far [away] from; **fẹrn|bleiben** *unr. itr. V.; mit sein (geh.)* stay away; **Fẹrne** die; ~, ~n distance; **fẹrner** *Adv.* furthermore

**fẹrn-, Fẹrn-:** ~**fahrer** der long-distance lorry-driver *(Brit.)* or *(Amer.)* trucker; ~**gespräch** das long-distance call; ~**glas** das binoculars *pl.;* ~|**halten** *unr. tr., refl. V.* keep away; ~**heizung** die district heating system; ~**licht** das *(Kfz-W.)* full beam; ~**melde·amt** das telephone exchange; ~**ọst** *o. Art.* Far East; ~**rohr** das telescope; ~**ruf** der telephone number; ~**schreiben** das telex [message]; ~**schreiber** der telex [machine]

**Fẹrnseh-:** ~**antenne** die television aerial *(Brit.)* or *(Amer.)* antenna; ~**apparat** der television [set]

**fẹrn|sehen** *unr. itr. V.* watch television; **Fẹrn·sehen** das; ~s television; **im ~:** on television; **Fẹrn·seher** der; ~s, ~ *(ugs.)* telly *(Brit. coll.);* TV

**Fẹrnseh-:** ~**gebühren** *Pl.* television licence fee; ~**gerät** das television [set]; ~**programm** das **a)** *(Sendungen)* television programmes *pl.;* **b)** *(Kanal)* television channel; **c)** *(Blatt, Programmheft)* television [programme] guide; ~**sendung** die television programme; ~**spiel** das television play; ~**zuschauer** der television viewer

**Fẹrn·sprecher** der telephone

**Fẹrnsprech-:** ~**gebühren** *Pl.* tele-

phone charges; ~**teilnehmer** der telephone subscriber; telephone customer *(Amer.)*

**Fẹrn-:** ~**steuerung** die *(Technik)* remote control; ~**straße** die major road; ~**verkehr** der long-distance traffic; ~**zug** der long-distance train

**Fẹrse** die; ~, ~n heel

**fẹrtig** *Adj.* **a)** finished ⟨*manuscript, picture, etc.*⟩; **das Essen ist ~:** lunch/dinner *etc.* is ready; |**mit etw.**| ~ **sein/werden** have finished/finish [sth.]; **b)** *(bereit, verfügbar)* ready (**zu, für** for); **c)** *(ugs.: erschöpft)* shattered *(coll.)*

**fẹrtig-, Fẹrtig-:** ~**bau** der; *Pl.* ~**ten** prefabricated building; ~**bauweise** die prefabricated construction; prefabrication ~|**bringen** *unr. tr. V.* manage

**fẹrtigen** *tr. V.* make

**Fẹrtig-:** ~**gericht** das ready-to-serve meal; ~**haus** das prefabricated house; prefab *(coll.)*

**Fẹrtigkeit** die; ~, ~en skill

**fẹrtig-, Fẹrtig-:** ~|**machen** *tr. V. (ugs.)* finish ⟨*task, job, etc.*⟩; get ⟨*meals, beds*⟩ ready; **jmdn.** ~**machen** *(erschöpfen)* wear sb. out; *(durch Schikanen)* wear sb. down; *(deprimieren)* get sb. down; ~|**stellen** *tr. V.* complete; ~**stellung** die completion

**Fẹssel** die; ~, ~n fetter; shackle; *(Kette)* chain; **fẹsseln** *tr. V.* **a)** tie up; **b)** *(faszinieren)* ⟨*book*⟩ grip; ⟨*work, person*⟩ fascinate

**fẹst 1.** *Adj.* **a)** *(nicht flüssig od. gasförmig)* solid; **b)** firm ⟨*bandage*⟩; sound ⟨*sleep*⟩; sturdy ⟨*shoes*⟩; strong ⟨*fabric*⟩; solid ⟨*house, shell*⟩; steady ⟨*voice*⟩; **der ~en Überzeugung sein, daß ...:** be of the firm opinion that ...; **c)** *(dauernd)* permanent ⟨*address*⟩; fixed ⟨*income*⟩; **2.** *adv.* **a)** ⟨*tie, grip*⟩ tight[ly]; **b)** ⟨*ugs.: auch* ~**e**⟩ ⟨*work*⟩ with a will; ⟨*eat*⟩ heartily; ⟨*sleep*⟩ soundly; **c)** ⟨*believe, be convinced*⟩ firmly; **sich auf jmdn./etw.** ~ **verlassen** rely one hundred per cent on sb./sth.; **d)** *(endgültig)* firmly; **etw.** ~ **vereinbaren** come to a firm arrangement about sth.; **e)** *(auf Dauer)* permanently; ~ **befreundet sein** be close friends; *(als Paar)* be going steady

**Fẹst** das; ~[e]s, ~e **a)** celebration; *(Party)* party; **b)** *(Feiertag)* festival; **frohes ~!** happy Christmas/Easter!

**fẹst-:** ~|**binden** *unr. tr. V.* tie [up]; ~|**bleiben** *unr. itr. V.; mit sein* stand firm; ~|**fahren** *unr. itr., refl. V. (itr. V.*

*mit sein)* get stuck; *(fig.)* get bogged down; ~|**halten 1.** *unr. tr. V.* **a)** *(halten, packen)* hold on to; **b)** *(nicht weiterleiten)* withhold ⟨*letter, parcel, etc.*⟩; **c)** *(verhaftet haben)* hold, detain ⟨*suspect*⟩; **2.** *unr. refl. V.* **sich an** jmdm./etw. ~**halten** hold on to sb./sth.

**fęstigen 1.** *tr. V.* strengthen; consolidate ⟨*position*⟩; **2.** *refl. V.* ⟨*friendship, ties*⟩ become stronger

**Festival** ['fɛstivəl] *das*; ~s, ~s festival

**fęst-, Fęst-:** ~|**kleben** *tr., itr. V.; mit sein* stick (**an** + *Dat.* to); ~|**land** *das*; *o. Pl. (Kontinent)* continent; *(im Gegensatz zu den Inseln)* mainland; ~|**legen** *tr. V.* **a)** fix ⟨*time, deadline, price*⟩; arrange ⟨*programme*⟩; **b)** *(verpflichten)* **sich [auf etw. (Akk.)]** ~**legen [lassen]** commit oneself [to sth.]; jmdn. **[auf etw. (Akk.)]** ~**legen** tie sb. down [to sth.]

**fęstlich 1.** *Adj.* festive ⟨*atmosphere*⟩; formal ⟨*dress*⟩; **2.** *adv.* festively; formally

**fęst-:** ~|**machen** *tr. V.* **a)** *(befestigen)* fix; **b)** *(fest vereinbaren)* arrange ⟨*meeting etc.*⟩; ~|**nageln** *tr. V.* **a)** *(befestigen)* nail (**an** + *Dat.* to); **b)** *(ugs.: festlegen)* jmdn. **[auf etw. (Akk.)]** ~**nageln** tie sb. down [to sth.]; ~|**nehmen** *unr. tr. V.* arrest

**Fęst·rede** *die* speech

**fęst-, Fęst-:** |**schnallen** *tr. V.* tie (**an** + *Dat.* to); ~|**sitzen** *unr. itr. V.* be stuck; ~|**stehen** *unr. itr. V.* ⟨*order, appointment, etc.*⟩ have been fixed; ⟨*decision*⟩ be definite; ⟨*fact*⟩ be certain; ~|**stellen** *tr. V.* **a)** establish ⟨*identity, age, facts*⟩; **b)** *(wahrnehmen)* detect; diagnose ⟨*illness*⟩; ~**stellung** *die* **a)** establishment; **b)** *(Wahrnehmung)* realization; **die** ~**stellung machen, daß** ...: realize that ...

**Fęst·tag** *der* holiday; *(Ehrentag)* special day

**Fęstung** *die*; ~, ~en fortress

**Fęst·zelt** *das* marquee

**fęst|ziehen** *unr. tr. V.* pull tight

**Fęte** *die*; ~, ~n *(ugs.)* party

**fętt 1.** *Adj.* **a)** fatty ⟨*food*⟩; ~**er Speck** fat bacon; **b)** *(sehr dick)* fat; **2.** *adv.* ~ **essen** eat fatty foods; **Fętt** *das*; ~[e]s, ~e fat; ~ **ansetzen** ⟨*animal*⟩ fatten up; ⟨*person*⟩ put on weight

**fętt-, Fętt-:** ~**arm** *Adj.* low-fat ⟨*food*⟩; low in fat *pred.*; ~**auge** *das* speck of fat; ~**fleck[en]** *der* grease mark; ~**gedruckt** *Adj. (präd. getrennt geschrieben)* bold

**fęttig** *Adj.* greasy

**fętt-, Fętt-:** ~**leibig** *Adj.* obese; ~**leibigkeit** *die*; ~: obesity; ~**näpfchen** *das:* **ins** ~**näpfchen treten** *(scherzh.)* put one's foot in it; ~**reich** *Adj.* high-fat

**Fętzen** *der*; ~s, ~: scrap

**feucht** *Adj.* damp; humid ⟨*climate*⟩; **feucht·fröhlich** *Adj. (ugs. scherzh.)* merry ⟨*company*⟩; boozy *(coll.)* ⟨*evening*⟩; **Feuchtigkeit** *die* moisture

**feucht-:** ~**kalt** *Adj.* cold and damp; ~**warm** *Adj.* muggy

**feudal** *Adj.* **a)** feudal ⟨*system*⟩; **b)** aristocratic ⟨*regiment etc.*⟩; **c)** *(ugs.: vornehm)* plush ⟨*hotel etc.*⟩

**Feuer** *das*; ~s, ~ **a)** fire; jmdm. ~ **geben** give sb. a light; **b)** *(Brand)* fire; blaze; ~! fire!; **c)** *o. Pl. (Milit.)* **das** ~ **einstellen** cease fire

**feuer-, Feuer-:** ~**eifer** *der* enthusiasm; zest; ~**fest** *Adj.* heat-resistant ⟨*dish, plate*⟩; fire-proof ⟨*material*⟩; ~**gefährlich** *Adj.* [in]flammable; ~**holz** *das*; *o. Pl.* firewood; ~**leiter** *die (bei Häusern)* fire escape; *(beim* ~*wehrauto)* [fireman's] ladder; ~**löscher** *der*; ~s, ~: fire extinguisher; ~**melder** *der* fire alarm

**feuern 1.** *tr. V.* **a)** *(ugs.: entlassen)* fire *(coll.)*; sack *(coll.)*; **b)** *(ugs.: schleudern, werfen)* fling; **2.** *itr. V. (Milit.)* fire (**auf** + *Akk.* at)

**feuer-, Feuer-:** ~**rot** *Adj.* fiery red; ~**schlucker** *der* fire-eater; ~**sirene** *die* fire siren; ~**stein** *der* flint; ~**versicherung** *die* fire insurance; ~**waffe** *die* firearm; ~**wehr** *die*; ~, ~**en** fire service; ~**wehr·auto** *das* fire engine; ~**wehr·mann** *der*; *Pl.* ~**männer** *od.* ~**leute** fireman; ~**werk** *das* firework display; *(~werkskörper)* fireworks *pl.*; ~**werks·körper** *der* firework; ~**zeug** *das* lighter

**Feuilleton** [fœjə'tõː] *das*; ~s, ~s arts section

**feurig** *Adj.* fiery

**ff.** *Abk.* **folgende [Seiten]** ff.

**Ffm.** *Abk.* **Frankfurt am Main**

**Fiaker** ['fjakɐ] *der*; ~s, ~ *(österr.)* cab

**Fiasko** *das*; ~s, ~s fiasco

**Fibel** *die*; ~, ~n reader; primer

**ficht** [fɪçt] *Imperativ Sg. u. 3. Pers. Sg. Präsens v.* **fechten**

**Fichte** *die*; ~, ~n spruce

**ficken** *tr., itr. V. (vulg.)* fuck *(coarse)*

**fidel** *Adj. (ugs.)* jolly

**Fieber** *das*; ~s **[high]** temperature; *(über 38 °C)* fever; ~ **haben** have a

[high] temperature/a fever; **bei jmdm. ~ messen** take sb's temperature; **fieber·frei** *Adj.* ⟨*person*⟩ free from fever; **fieberhaft** *Adj.* feverish; **fieberig** *Adj.* feverish; **fiebern** *itr. V.* have a temperature; **Fieber·thermometer** das [clinical] thermometer; **fiebrig** *Adj.* feverish

**Fiedel** die; ~, ~n *(veralt., scherzh.)* fiddle

**fiel** *1. u. 3. Pers. Sg. Prät. v.* **fallen**

**fiepen** *itr. V.* ⟨*dog*⟩ whimper; ⟨*bird*⟩ cheep

**fies** 1. *Adj.* *(ugs.)* nasty ⟨*person, character*⟩; 2. *adv.* in a nasty way

**Figur** die; ~, ~en **a)** *(einer Frau)* figure; *(eines Mannes)* physique; **b)** *(Bildwerk)* figure; **c)** *(geometrisches Gebilde)* shape

**fiktiv** *Adj.* fictitious

**Filet** [fiˈleː] das; ~s, ~s fillet

**Filiale** die; ~, ~n branch

**Filigran** das; ~s, ~e filigree

**Film** der; ~[e]s, ~e **a)** *(Fot.)* film; **b)** *(Kino~)* film; movie *(Amer. coll.);* **filmen** *tr., itr. V.* film

**Film-:** **~kamera** die film camera; *(Schmalfilmkamera)* cine-camera; **~produzent** der film producer; **~regisseur** der film director; **~schau·spieler** der film actor

**Filter** der, ~s, ~: filter; **filtern** *tr. V.* filter

**Filter-:** **~papier** das filter paper; **~zigarette** die [filter-]tipped cigarette

**Filz** der; ~es, ~e felt

**Fimmel** der; ~s, ~: **einen ~ für etw. haben** *(ugs. abwertend)* have a thing about sth. *(coll.)*

**Finale** das; ~s, ~[s] **a)** *(Sport)* final; **b)** finale

**Finanz** die; ~: finance *no art.*

**Finanz-:** **~amt** das **a)** *(Behörde)* ≈ Inland Revenue; **b)** *(Gebäude)* tax office; **~beamte** der tax officer

**Finanzen** *Pl.* finances; **finanziell** [finanˈtsi̯ɛl] *Adj.* financial; **finanzieren** *tr. V.* finance; **Finanzierung** die; ~, ~en financing

**Finanz-:** **~minister** der minister of finance; **~politik** die *(des Staates, eines Unternehmens)* financial policy; *(allgemeine)* politics of finance

**Findel·kind** das foundling

**finden** *unr. tr. V.* find; **Freunde ~:** make friends; **Finder** der; ~s, ~: finder; *s. auch* **ehrlich 1 a**; **Finder·lohn** der reward [for finding sth.]; **findig** *Adj.* resourceful; **Findling** der; ~s,

~e **a)** *(Findelkind)* foundling; **b)** *(Geol.)* erratic block

**fing** *1. u. 3. Pers. Sg. Prät. v.* **fangen**

**Finger** der; ~s, ~: finger; **lange ~ machen** *(ugs.)* get itchy fingers

**Finger-:** **~abdruck** der fingerprint; **~fertigkeit** die; *o. Pl.* dexterity; **~hut** der thimble

**fingern** *itr. V.* fiddle; **an etw.** *(Dat.)* **~:** fiddle with sth.; **nach etw. ~:** fumble [around] for sth.

**Finger-:** **~nagel** der fingernail; **~spitze** die fingertip; **~spitzen·gefühl** das; *o. Pl.* feeling

**fingieren** *tr. V.* fake; **ein fingierter Name** a false name

**Fink** der; ~en, ~en finch

**Finne** der; ~n, ~n, **Finnin** die; ~, ~nen Finn; **finnisch** *Adj.* Finnish; **Finnland (das);** ~s Finland

**finster** 1. *Adj.* dark; dimly-lit ⟨*pub, district*⟩; 2. *adv.* **jmdn. ~ ansehen** give sb. a black look; **Finsternis** die; ~, ~se darkness; *(auch bibl., fig.)* dark

**Finte** die; ~, ~n trick; **jmdn. durch eine ~ täuschen** deceive sb. by trickery

**firm** *Adj.* **in etw.** *(Dat.)* **~ sein** be well up in sth.

**Firma** die; ~, **Firmen** firm; company

**Firmen-:** **~inhaber** der owner of the/a company; **~schild** das company's name plate; **~zeichen** das trademark

**Firmung** die; ~, ~en confirmation

**First** der; ~[e]s, ~e ridge

**Fisch** der; ~[e]s, ~e **a)** fish; **[fünf] ~e fangen** catch [five] fish; **kleine ~e** *(fig.)* small fry; **b)** *(Astrol.)* **die ~e** Pisces; **er ist [ein] ~:** he is a Piscean; **fischen** 1. *tr. V.* **a)** fish for; **b)** *(ugs.)* **etw. aus etw. ~:** fish sth. out of sth.; 2. *itr. V.* fish; **nach etw. ~:** fish for sth.; **Fischer** der; ~s, ~ fisherman

**Fischer·boot** das fishing boat

**Fischerei** die; ~: fishing

**Fisch-:** **~fang** der; *o. Pl.* **vom ~ leben** make a/one's living by fishing; **auf ~ gehen** go fishing; **~geschäft** das fishmonger's [shop] *(Brit.);* fish store *(Amer.);* **~grät[en]·muster** das *(Textilw.)* herringbone pattern; **~konserve** die canned fish; **~kutter** der fishing trawler; **~stäbchen** das *(Kochk.)* fish finger

**Fiskus** der; ~, **Fisken** *od.* ~se Government *(as managing the State finances)*

**Fittich** der; ~[e]s, ~e *(dichter.)* wing

**fix** 1. *Adj.* *(ugs.)* quick; **ein ~er Bursche** a bright lad; **~ und fertig** quite finished; *(völlig erschöpft)* completely shattered *(coll.);* **2.** *adv. (ugs.)* quickly; **mach ~!** hurry up!

**fixen** *itr. V. (Drogenjargon)* fix *(sl.);* **Fixer der; ~s, ~** *(Drogenjargon)* fixer

**fixieren** *tr. V.* **a)** fix one's gaze on; **jmdn. scharf ~:** gaze sharply at sb.; **b)** *(geh.: schriftlich niederlegen)* take down

**Fix·stern der** *(Astron.)* fixed star

**Fjord** [fjɔrt] **der; ~|e|s, ~e** fiord

**FKK** [ɛf ka: 'ka:] *Abk.* Freikörperkultur nudism *no art.;* naturism *no art.;* **FKK-Strand der** nudist beach

**flach** *Adj.* **a)** flat; **b)** *(niedrig)* low; **c)** *(nicht tief)* shallow ⟨*water, dish*⟩; **Flä·che die; ~, ~n a)** area; **b)** *(Ober~)* surface; **c)** *(Geom.)* area; *(einer dreidimensionalen Figur)* side

**Flächen-: ~inhalt der** area; **~maß das** unit of square measure

**flach|fallen** *itr. V.; mit sein (ugs.)* ⟨*trip*⟩ fall through; ⟨*event*⟩ be cancelled; **Flach·land das;** *o. Pl.* lowland

**Flachs der; ~es** flax

**flachsen** *itr. V.* **mit jmdm. ~** *(ugs.)* joke with sb.

**flackern** *itr. V.* flicker

**Fladen der; ~s, ~** *flat, round unleavened cake made with oat or barley flour*

**Flagge die; ~, ~n** flag; **flaggen** *itr. V.* put out the flags

**flambieren** *tr. V. (Kochk.)* flambé

**Flamme die; ~, ~n a)** flame; **b)** *(Brennstelle)* burner

**Flanell der; ~s, ~e** flannel

**flanieren** *itr. V.; mit Richtungsangabe mit sein* stroll

**Flanke die; ~, ~n a)** *(Weiche)* flank; **b)** *(Ballspiele: Vorlage)* centre; **c)** *(Teil des Spielfeldes)* wing

**Flasche die; ~, ~n** bottle; **eine ~ Wein** a bottle of wine; **dem Kind die ~ geben** feed the baby

**Flaschen-: ~bier das** bottled beer; **~öffner der** bottle-opener; **~zug der** block and tackle

**flatterhaft** *Adj.* fickle; **flattern** *itr. V. mit Richtungsangabe mit sein* flutter

**flau** *Adj.* **a)** slack ⟨*breeze*⟩; **b)** *(leicht übel)* queasy ⟨*feeling*⟩

**Flaum der; ~|e|s** fuzz

**Flausch der; ~|e|s, ~e** brushed wool; **flauschig** *Adj.* fluffy

**Flause die; ~, ~n;** *meist Pl. (ugs.)* **er hat nur ~n im Kopf** he can never think of anything sensible

**Flaute die; ~, ~n a)** *(Seemannsspr.)* calm; **b)** *(Kaufmannsspr.)* fall[-off] in trade

**Flechte die; ~, ~n a)** *(Bot.)* lichen; **b)** *(Med.)* eczema

**flechten** *unr. tr. V.* plait ⟨*hair*⟩; weave ⟨*basket, mat*⟩

**Fleck der; ~|e|s, ~e a)** stain; *(andersfarbige Stelle)* patch; **flecken** *itr. V.* stain; **flecken·los 1.** *Adj.* spotless; **2.** *adv.* spotlessly

**Fleck·entferner der** stain *or* spot remover

**fleckig** *Adj.* stained; blotchy ⟨*face, skin*⟩

**Fleder·maus die** bat

**Flegel der; ~s, ~** *(abwertend)* lout; **flegelhaft** *Adj. (abwertend)* loutish

**flehen** ['fle:ən] *itr. V.* plead (um for)

**Fleisch das; ~|e|s a)** flesh; **b)** *(Nahrungsmittel)* meat; **Fleisch·brühe die** bouillon; consommé; **Fleischer der; ~s, ~:** butcher; **Fleischerei die; ~, ~en** butcher's shop

**fleischig** *Adj.* plump ⟨*hands, face*⟩; fleshy ⟨*leaf, fruit*⟩

**Fleisch-: ~käse der** meat loaf; **~klößchen das** small meat ball; **~pastete die** *(Kochk.)* pâté; **~salat der** *(Kochk.)* meat salad; **~vergiftung die** food poisoning [from meat]; **~waren** *Pl.* meat products; **~wolf der** mincer; **~wunde die** flesh-wound; **~wurst die** pork sausage

**Fleiß der; ~es** hard work; *(Eigenschaft)* diligence; **fleißig 1.** *Adj.* hard-working; **2.** *adv.* hard; **~ lernen** learn as much as one can

**flennen** *itr. V. (ugs.)* blubber

**fletschen** *tr., itr. V.* **die Zähne** *od.* **mit den Zähnen ~:** bare one's teeth

**Fleurop** ⓌⓏ ['flɔyrɔp] **die** Interflora **(P)**

**flexibel 1.** *Adj.* flexible; **2.** *adv.* flexibly

**flicht** *Imperativ Sg. u. 3. Pers. Sg. Präsens v.* flechten

**flicken** *tr. V.* mend; repair ⟨*engine, cable*⟩; **Flicken der; ~s, ~:** patch

**Flick-: ~werk das;** *o. Pl. (abwertend)* botched-up job; **~zeug das** repair kit

**Flieder der; ~s, ~:** lilac

**Fliege die; ~, ~n a)** fly; **b)** *(Schleife)* bow-tie; **fliegen 1.** *unr. itr. V.; mit sein* **a)** fly; **b)** *(ugs.: fallen)* **vom Pferd/ Fahrrad ~:** fall off a/the horse/bicycle; **c)** *(ugs.: entlassen werden)* get the sack *(coll.);* **von der Schule ~:** be chucked out [of the school] *(coll.);* **2.** *unr. tr. V.* fly

**Fliegen-:** ~**fenster** das wire-mesh window; ~**gewicht** das *(Schwerathletik)* flyweight; ~**pilz** der fly agaric; **Flieger** der; ~s, ~ pilot; **Fliegeralarm** der air-raid warning; **fliegerisch** *Adj.* aeronautical

**fliehen** ['fli:ən] *unr. itr. V.; mit sein* flee (vor + *Dat.* from); *(aus dem Gefängnis usw.)* escape (**aus** from); **ins Ausland/über die Grenze** ~: flee the country/escape over the border

**Flieh·kraft** die *(Physik)* centrifugal force

**Fliese** die; ~, ~n tile

**Fließ·band** das conveyor belt; **am** ~**band arbeiten** *od. (ugs.)* **stehen** work on the assembly line

**fließen** *unr. itr. V.; mit sein* flow; ~**des Wasser** running water; **eine Sprache** ~**d sprechen** speak a language fluently

**flimmern** *itr. V.; mit Richtungsangabe mit sein* shimmer

**flink** 1. *Adj.* nimble *⟨fingers⟩*; sharp *⟨eyes⟩*; quick *⟨hands⟩*; 2. *adv.* quickly

**Flinte** die; ~, ~n shotgun; **die** ~ **ins Korn werfen** *(fig.)* throw in the towel

**Flirt** der; ~s, ~s flirtation; **flirten** *itr. V.* flirt

**Flitter** der; ~s frippery; trumpery

**Flitter·wochen** *Pl.* honeymoon *sing.*

**flitzen** *itr. V.; mit sein (ugs.)* shoot; dart; **Flitzer** der; ~s, ~ *(ugs.)* sporty job *(coll.)*

**floaten** ['flɔʊtn̩] *tr., itr. V. (Wirtsch.)* float

**flocht** *1. u. 3. Pers. Sg. Prät. v.* flechten

**Flocke** die; ~, ~n a) flake; b) *(Staub~)* piece of fluff; **flockig** *Adj.* fluffy

**flog** *1. u. 3. Pers. Sg. Prät. v.* fliegen

**floh** *1. u. 3. Pers. Sg. Prät. v.* fliehen

**Floh** der; ~|e|s, Flöhe flea

**Floh-:** ~**markt** der flea market; ~**zirkus** der flea-circus

**Flora** die; ~, Floren flora

**Florett** das; ~|e|s, ~e foil

**florieren** *itr. V.* flourish

**Florist** der; ~en, ~en, **Floristin** die; ~, ~nen [qualified] flower-arranger

**Floskel** die; ~, ~n cliché

**floß** *1. u. 3. Pers. Sg. Prät. v.* fließen

**Floß** das; ~es, **Flöße** raft

**Flosse** die; ~, ~n a) *(Zool., Flugw.)* fin; b) *(zum Tauchen)* flipper

**flößen** *tr., itr. V.* float

**Flößer** der; ~s, ~: raftsman

**Flöte** die; ~, ~n flute; *(Block~)* recorder; **flöten** 1. *itr. V. ⟨bird⟩* flute; 2. *tr. V.* whistle; **flöten|gehen** *unr. itr.*

*V.; mit sein (ugs.) ⟨money⟩* go down the drain; *⟨time⟩* be wasted

**flott** 1. *Adj.* a) *(schwungvoll)* lively; b) *(schick)* smart; 2. *adv. ⟨work⟩* quickly; *⟨dance, write⟩* in a lively manner; *⟨be dressed⟩* smartly

**Flotte** die; ~, ~n fleet

**flott|machen** *tr. V.* refloat *⟨ship⟩*; get *⟨car⟩* back on the road

**Flöz** das; ~es, ~e *(Bergbau)* seam

**Fluch** der; ~|e|s, **Flüche** curse; oath; **fluchen** *itr. V.* curse; swear

**Flucht** die; ~: flight; **flucht·artig** 1. *Adj.* hurried; hasty; 2. *adv.* hurriedly; hastily; **flüchten** 1. *itr. V.; mit sein* **vor jmdm./etw.** ~: flee from sb./sth.; **vor der Polizei** ~: run away from the police; 2. *refl. V.* take refuge; **flüchtig** 1. *Adj.* a) fugitive; b) cursory; superficial *⟨insight⟩*; 2. *adv.* a) *(oberflächlich)* cursorily; b) *(eilig)* hurriedly; **Flüchtigkeit** die; ~, ~en cursoriness;

**Flüchtigkeits·fehler** der slip; **Flüchtling** der; ~s, ~e refugee; **Flucht·weg** der escape route

**Flug** der; ~|e|s, **Flüge** flight

**Flug-:** ~**bahn** die trajectory; ~**blatt** das pamphlet; leaflet

**Flügel** der; ~s, ~ a) wing; b) *(Klavier)* grand piano

**Flug·gast** der [air] passenger

**flügge** *Adj.* fully-fledged

**Flug-:** ~**gesellschaft** die airline; ~**hafen** der airport; ~**linie** die a) *(Strecke)* air route; b) *(Gesellschaft)* airline; ~**lotse** der air traffic controller; ~**platz** der airfield; ~**schein** der air ticket; ~**verkehr** der air traffic

**Flug·zeug** das; ~|e|s, ~e aeroplane *(Brit.)*; airplane *(Amer.)*; aircraft

**Flugzeug-:** ~**absturz** der plane crash; ~**entführer** der [aircraft] hijacker; ~**entführung** die [aircraft] hijack[ing]; ~**träger** der aircraft carrier

**Flunder** die; ~, ~n flounder

**flunkern** *itr. V.* tell stories

**Fluor** das; ~s *(Chemie)* fluorine

**[1]Flur** der; ~|e|s, ~e *(Korridor)* corridor; *(Diele)* [entrance] hall; **im/auf dem** ~: in the corridor/hall

**[2]Flur** die; ~, ~en farmland *no indef. art.*

**Fluß** der; Flusses, Flüsse river; *(fließende Bewegung)* flow

**fluß-, Fluß-:** ~**ab[wärts]** *Adv.* downstream; ~**auf[wärts]** *Adv.* upstream; ~**bett** das river bed

**Flüßchen** das; ~s, ~: small river

**flüssig 1.** *Adj.* **a)** liquid; **b)** *(fließend, geläufig)* fluent; **2.** *adv.* ⟨*write, speak*⟩ fluently; **Flüssigkeit** die; ~, ~en **a)** liquid; *(auch Gas)* fluid; **b)** *(Geläufigkeit)* fluency; **flüssig|machen** *tr. V.* make available ⟨*money, funds*⟩

**Fluß·pferd** das hippopotamus

**flüstern** *itr., tr. V.* whisper

**Flut** die; ~, ~en **a)** *o. Pl.* tide; **b)** *meist Pl. (geh.: Wassermasse)* flood; **fluten** *itr. V.; mit sein (geh.)* flood; **Flut·licht** das; *o. Pl.* floodlight

**focht** *1. u. 3. Pers. Sg. Prät. v.* **fechten**

**Föderalismus** der; ~: federalism *no art.;* **föderalistisch** *Adj.* federalist

**Fohlen** das; ~s, ~: foal

**Föhn** der; ~[e]s, ~e föhn

**Folge** die; ~, ~n **a)** *(Auswirkung)* consequence; *(Ergebnis)* consequence; result; **b)** *(Aufeinander~)* succession; *(zusammengehörend)* sequence; **c)** *(Fortsetzung) (einer Sendung)* episode; *(eines Romans)* instalment; **Folgeerscheinung** die consequence; **folgen** *itr. V.; mit sein* follow; jmdm. im Amt/in der Regierung ~: succeed sb. in office/in government; **auf** etw. *(Akk.)* ~: follow sth.; **aus** etw. ~: follow from sth.; **folgend** *Adj.* der/die/das ~e the next in order; im ~en *od.* in ~em in [the course of] the following discussion/passage *etc.;* **folgendermaßen** *Adv.* as follows; *(so)* in the following way; **folge·richtig 1.** *Adj.* logical; consistent ⟨*behaviour, action*⟩; **2.** *adv.* logically; ⟨*act, behave*⟩ consistently; **folgern 1.** *tr. V.* etw. **aus** etw. ~: infer sth. from sth.; **2.** *itr. V.* richtig ~: draw a/the correct conclusion; **Folgerung** die; ~, ~en conclusion

**folglich** *Adv.* consequently; **folgsam 1.** *Adj.* obedient; **2.** *adv.* obediently

**Folie** ['foːliə] die; ~, ~n *(Metall~)* foil; *(Plastik~)* film

**Folklore** die; ~ **a)** folklore; **b)** *(Musik)* folk-music

**Folter** die; ~, ~n torture; **foltern** *tr. V.* torture; *(fig.)* torment; **Folterung** die; ~, ~en torture

**Fön** ⓦ der; ~[e]s, ~e hair-drier

**Fond** [fõː] der; ~s, ~s *(geh.)* back

**Fonds** [fõː] der; ~ [fõː(s)], ~ [fõːs] fund

**Fondue** [fõ'dyː] die; ~, ~s *od.* das; ~s, ~s *(Kochk.)* fondue

**fönen** *tr. V.* blow-dry

**Fontäne** die; ~, ~n jet; *(Springbrunnen)* fountain

**forcieren** [fɔr'siːrən] *tr. V.* step up ⟨*production*⟩; intensify ⟨*efforts*⟩; push forward ⟨*developments*⟩

**Förderer** der; ~s, ~: patron

**fordern** *tr. V.* **a)** demand; **b)** *(in Anspruch nehmen)* make demands on

**fördern** *tr. V.* **a)** promote; patronize, support ⟨*artist, art*⟩; further ⟨*investigation*⟩; foster ⟨*talent, tendency*⟩; improve ⟨*appetite*⟩; aid ⟨*digestion, sleep*⟩; **b)** *(Bergbau, Technik)* mine ⟨*coal, ore*⟩; extract ⟨*oil*⟩

**Forderung** die; ~, ~en **a)** demand; **b)** *(Kaufmannsspr.)* claim (**an** + *Akk.* against)

**Förderung** die; ~, ~en *o. Pl. s.* **fördern a:** promotion; patronage; support; furthering; fostering; improvement; aiding; **b)** *(Bergbau, Technik)* output; *(das Fördern)* mining; *(von Erdöl)* extraction

**Forelle** die; ~, ~n trout

**Form** die; ~, ~en **a)** shape; **in** ~ **von** Tabletten in the form of tablets; **b)** *(bes. Sport: Verfassung)* form; **in** ~ **sein** be on form; **c)** *(vorgeformtes Modell)* mould; *(Back~)* baking tin; **d)** *(Darstellungs~, Umgangs~)* form

**formal 1.** *Adj.* formal; **2.** *adv.* formally; **formalisieren** *tr. V.* formalize

**Formalität** die; ~, ~en formality

**Format** das; ~[e]s, ~e a) size; *(Buch~, Papier~, Bild~)* format; **b)** *o. Pl. (Persönlichkeit)* stature

**formbar** *Adj.* malleable

**Formel** die; ~, ~n formula

**formell** *Adj.* formal

**formen** *tr. V.* **a)** *(gestalten)* form; shape; **b)** *(bilden, prägen)* mould; form ⟨*character, personality*⟩; **Form·fehler** der irregularity

**formieren** *tr., refl. V.* form

**förmlich 1.** *Adj.* **a)** formal; **b)** *(regelrecht)* positive; **2.** *adv.* **a)** formally; **b)** *(geradezu)* sich ~ **fürchten** be really afraid

**form·los** *Adj.* **a)** informal; **b)** *(gestaltlos)* shapeless

**Form·sache** die formality

**Formular** das; ~s, ~e form; **formulieren** *tr. V.* formulate; **Formulierung** die; ~, ~en **a)** *o. Pl. (das Formulieren)* formulation; *(eines Entwurfes, Gesetzes)* drafting; **b)** *(formulierter Text)* formulation

**form·vollendet 1.** *Adj.* perfectly executed ⟨*pirouette, bow, etc.*⟩; ⟨*poem*⟩ perfect in form; **2.** *adv.* faultlessly

**forsch** *Adj.* forceful

**forschen** itr. V. **a) nach** jmdm./etw. ~:
search or look for sb./sth.; **b)** (als Wissenschaftler) research; **Forscher** der;
~s, **Forscherin** die; ~, ~nen researcher; **Forschung** die; ~, ~en research; **Forschungs·reisende** der/
die explorer

**Forst** der; ~|e|s, ~e|n| forest; **Förster**
der; ~s, ~: forest warden

**Forst·wirtschaft** die forestry

**Forsythie** [fɔr'zy:tsiə] die; ~, ~n forsythia

**fort** Adv. **a)** s. weg; **b)** (weiter) und so
~: and so on

**fort-, Fort-:** ~**an** [-'-] Adv. from now/
then on; ~**bestand** der; o. Pl. continuation; (eines Staates) continued
existence; ~|**bewegen** 1. tr. V.
move; shift; 2. refl. V. move [along];
~|**bleiben** unr. itr. V.; mit sein fail to
come; ~|**bringen** unr. tr. V.: s. wegbringen; ~|**dauern** itr. V. continue;
~|**fahren** 1. unr. itr. V. **a)** mit sein
leave; **b)** auch mit sein (weitermachen)
continue; go on; 2. unr. tr. V. drive
away; ~|**führen** tr. V. **a)** lead away;
**b)** (fortsetzen) continue; ~**gang** der;
o. Pl. **a)** departure (aus from); **b)** (Weiterentwicklung) progress; ~|**gehen**
unr. itr. V.; mit sein leave; geh ~! go
away!; ~**geschritten** Adj. advanced; ~**geschrittene** der/die;
adj. Dekl. advanced student/player;
~|**kommen** unr. itr. V.; mit sein s.
wegkommen a, b; ~|**laufen** unr. itr.
V.; mit sein a) s. weglaufen; **b)** (sich
~setzen) continue; ~**laufend** 1. Adj.
continuous; 2. adv. continuously;
~|**pflanzen** refl. V. **a)** reproduce
[oneself/itself]; **b)** (sich verbreiten)
⟨idea, mood⟩ spread; ⟨sound, light⟩
travel; ~**pflanzung** die reproduction; ~|**schaffen** tr. V. take away;
~|**schreiten** unr. itr. V.; mit sein ⟨process⟩ continue; ⟨time⟩ move on;
~**schritt** der progress; ~**schritte** progress sing.; **ein** ~**schritt** a step forward; ~**schrittlich** 1. Adj. progressive; 2. adv. progressively;
~**schrittlichkeit** die; ~: progressiveness; ~|**setzen** 1. tr. V. continue;
2. refl. V. continue; ~**setzung** die; ~,
~en a) (das ~setzen) continuation; **b)**
(anschließender Teil) instalment;
~|**während** 1. Adj.; nicht präd.
continual; 2. adv. continually;
~|**werfen** unr. tr. V.: s. wegwerfen

**Foto** das; ~s, ~s photo; ~s **machen**
take photos

**Foto-:** ~**album** das photo album;
~**apparat** der camera

**fotogen** Adj. photogenic **Foto·graf**
der; ~en, ~en photographer; **Fotografie** die; ~, ~n **a)** o. Pl. photography no art.; **b)** (Lichtbild) photograph; **fotografieren** tr. V. photograph; take a photograph/photographs of; **Fotografin** die; ~, ~nen
photographer

**foto-, Foto-:** ~**kopie** die photocopy;
~**kopieren** tr., itr. V. photocopy;
~**kopierer** der photocopier; ~**labor**
das photographic laboratory; ~**modell** das photographic model

**Foul** [faul] das; ~s, ~s (Sport) foul (**an**
+ Dat. on)

**Foyer** [foa'je:] das; ~s, ~s foyer

**FPÖ** Abk. **Freiheitliche Partei Österreichs**

**Fr.** Abk. **a) Franken** SFr.; **b) Frau**; **c)**
**Freitag** Fri.

**Fracht** die; ~, ~en (Schiffs~, Luft~)
cargo; freight; (Bahn~, LKW~)
goods pl.; freight; **Frachter**
der; ~s, ~: freighter

**Fracht-:** ~**gut** das slow freight; slow
goods pl.; ~**schiff** das cargo ship

**Frack** der; ~|e|s, Fräcke tails pl.; evening dress

**Frage** die; ~, ~n question; (Angelegenheit) issue; **in** ~ **kommen** be
possible; **das kommt nicht in** ~ (ugs.)
that is out of the question; **Fragebogen** der questionnaire; (Formular)
form; **fragen** 1. tr., itr. V. **a)** ask; **b)**
(sich erkundigen) **nach etw.** ~: ask or
inquire about sth.; **c)** (nachfragen) ask
for; 2. refl. V. **sich** ~, **ob** ...: wonder
whether ...; **Frage·zeichen** das
question mark; **fraglich** Adj. **a)**
doubtful; **b)** nicht präd. (betreffend) in
question postpos.; relevant

**Fragment** das; ~|e|s, ~e fragment

**frag·würdig** Adj. **a)** questionable; **b)**
(zwielichtig) dubious

**Fraktion** die; ~, ~en parliamentary
party; (mit zwei Parteien) parliamentary coalition

**Fraktions-** (Parl.): ~**führer** der
leader of the parliamentary party/
coalition; ~**zwang** der obligation to
vote in accordance with party policy

**frank** Adv. ~ **und frei** frankly and
openly; openly and honestly

**Franken** der; ~s ~: [Swiss] franc

**Frankfurter** die; ~, ~ (Wurst) frankfurter

**frankieren** *tr. V.* frank
**Frank·reich (das);** ~s France
**Franse** die; ~, ~n strand [of a/the fringe]
**Franzose** der; ~n, ~n Frenchman; **er ist** ~: he is French; **die** ~n the French; **Französin** die; ~, ~nen Frenchwoman; **französisch** *Adj.* French; **Französisch das;** ~[s] French
**Fräse** die; ~, ~n *(für Holz)* moulding machine; *(für Metall)* milling machine
**fraß** *1. u. 3. Pers. Sg. Prät. v.* **fressen;** **Fraß** der; ~es *(derb)* muck
**Fratze** die; ~, ~n a) hideous face; b) *(ugs.: Grimasse)* grimace
**Frau** die; ~, ~en a) woman; b) *(Ehe~)* wife; c) *(Titel, Anrede)* ~ Schulze Mrs Schulze; *(in Briefen)* **Sehr geehrte** ~ **Schulze** Dear Madam; *(bei persönlicher Bekanntschaft)* Dear Mrs/Miss/Ms Schulze
**Frauen-:** ~arzt der, ~ärztin die gynaecologist; ~**bewegung die** *o. Pl.* women's movement; ~**rechtlerin** die; ~, ~nen feminist; Women's Libber *(coll.)*
**Fräulein** das; ~s, ~ *(ugs.* ~s) a) *(junges* ~) young lady; *(ältliches* ~) spinster; b) *(Titel, Anrede)* ~ **Mayer/ Schulte** Miss Mayer/Schulte
**fraulich** 1. *Adj.* feminine; 2. *adv.* in a feminine way
**frech** 1. *Adj.* a) impertinent; cheeky; bare-faced 〈*lie*〉; b) *(keck, keß)* saucy; 2. *adv.* impertinently; cheekily; **Frechheit** die; ~, ~en a) *o. Pl.* impertinence; cheek; b) *(Äußerung)* impertinent *or* cheeky remark
**frei** 1. *Adj.* a) *(unabhängig)* free; b) *(nicht angestellt)* free-lance; c) *(ungezwungen)* free and easy; d) *(nicht mehr in Haft)* free; e) *(offen)* open; f) *(unbesetzt)* vacant; free; g) *(kostenlos)* free 〈*food, admission*〉; h) *(verfügbar)* spare; free 〈*time*〉; 2. *adv.* freely
**frei-, Frei-:** ~**bad** das open-air swimming-pool; ~|**bekommen** 1. *unr. itr. V. (ugs.)* get time off; 2. *unr. tr. V.* **jmdn./etw.** ~**bekommen** get sb./ sth. released; ~**beruflich** 1. *Adj.* self-employed; free-lance; 〈*doctor, lawyer*〉 in private practice; 2. *adv.* ~**beruflich tätig sein/arbeiten** work free-lance/practise privately; ~**betrag der** *(Steuerw.)* [tax] allowance
**Freier** der; ~s, ~ *(veralt.)* suitor
**frei-, Frei-:** ~**exemplar das** *(Buch)* free copy; *(Zeitung)* free issue; ~|**geben unr. tr. V.** release; ~**gebig** *Adj.*

generous; open-handed; ~**gehege** das outdoor enclosure; ~**gepäck das** baggage allowance; ~**hafen der** free port; ~|**halten** *unr. tr. V.* a) treat; b) *(offenhalten)* keep 〈*entrance, roadway*〉 clear; **Einfahrt** ~**halten!** no parking in front of entrance; ~**handels·zone die** free-trade zone; ~**händig** *adv.* 〈*cycle*〉 without holding on
**Freiheit** die; ~, ~en a) freedom; ~, **Gleichheit, Brüderlichkeit** Liberty, Equality, Fraternity; b) *(Vorrecht)* freedom; privilege; **freiheitlich** 1. *Adj.* liberal 〈*philosophy, conscience*〉; ~ **und demokratisch** free and democratic; 2. *adv.* liberally
**Freiheits-:** ~**beraubung die** *(jur.)* wrongful detention; ~**strafe die** term of imprisonment
**frei-, Frei-:** ~**herr der** baron; ~**karte die** complimentary ticket; ~|**kaufen** *tr. V.* ransom 〈*hostage*〉; buy the freedom of 〈*slave*〉; ~|**kommen** *unr. itr. V.* **aus dem Gefängnis** ~**kommen** be released from prison; ~**körper·kultur die;** *o. Pl.* nudism *no art.;* naturism *no art.;* ~|**lassen** *unr. tr. V.* set free; release; ~|**legen** *tr. V.* uncover
**freilich** *Adv.* of course
**Frei·licht-:** ~**bühne die,** ~**theater das** open-air theatre
**frei-, Frei-:** ~|**machen** 1. *refl. V. (ugs.: frei nehmen)* take time off; 2. *tr. V. (Postw.)* frank; **etw. mit 0,50 DM** ~**machen** put a 50-pfennig stamp on sth.; ~**marke die** postage stamp; ~**mütig** 1. *Adj.* frank; 2. *adv.* frankly; ~**schaffend** *Adj.* free-lance; ~|**schwimmen** *unr. refl. V.* **sich** ~**schwimmen** pass the 15-minute swimming test; ~|**sprechen** *unr. tr. V.* a) *(Rechtsw.)* acquit; b) *(für unschuldig erklären)* exonerate (**von** from); ~**spruch der** *(Rechtsw.)* acquittal; ~|**stellen** *tr. V.* a) jmdm. etw. ~**stellen** leave sth. up to sb.; b) *(befreien)* release 〈*person*〉; **jmdn. vom Wehrdienst** ~**stellen** exempt sb. from military service; ~**stoß der** *(Fußball)* free kick
**Frei·tag der** Friday; *s. auch* **Dienstag, Dienstag-;** **freitags** *Adv.* on Friday[s]; *s. auch* **dienstags**
**frei-, Frei-:** ~**tod der** *(verhüll.)* suicide *no art.;* ~**treppe die** [flight of] steps; ~**übung die,** *meist Pl.* *(Sport)* keep-fit exercise; ~**wild das** fair game; ~**willig** 1. *Adj.* voluntary

⟨*decision*⟩; optional ⟨*subject*⟩; **2.** *adv.* voluntarily; **sich ~willig melden** volunteer; **~zeichen das** ringing tone; **~zeit die**; *o. Pl.* spare time; **~zügig** *Adj.* **a)** generous; **b)** *(gewagt, unmoralisch)* risqué ⟨*remark, film, dress*⟩; **~zügigkeit die** generosity

**fremd** *Adj.* **a)** foreign; **b)** *(nicht eigen)* other people's; of others *postpos.*; **c)** *(unbekannt)* strange

**fremd·artig** *Adj.* strange

**¹Fremde der/die**; *adj. Dekl.* **a)** stranger; **b)** *(Ausländer)* foreigner; **²Fremde die**; ~ *(geh.)* **die ~:** foreign parts *pl.*

**Fremden-:** **~führer der** tourist guide; **~verkehr der** tourism *no art.;* **~zimmer das** room

**fremd-, Fremd-:** **~|gehen** *unr. itr. V.; mit sein (ugs.)* be unfaithful; **~herrschaft die** foreign domination; **~ländisch** *Adj.* foreign; *(exotisch)* exotic

**Fremdling der**; ~s, ~e *(veralt.)* stranger

**fremd-, Fremd-:** **~sprache die** foreign language; **~sprachig** *Adj.* bilingual/multilingual ⟨*staff, secretary*⟩; foreign ⟨*literature*⟩; foreign-language ⟨*edition, teaching*⟩; **~sprachlich** *Adj.* foreign-language ⟨*teaching*⟩; foreign ⟨*word*⟩; **~wort das**; *Pl.* **~wörter** foreign word

**frenetisch 1.** *Adj.* frenetic; **2.** *adv.* frenetically

**Frequenz die**; ~, ~en *(Physik)* frequency; *(Med.: Puls~)* rate

**Fresse die**; ~, ~n *(derb)* **a)** *(Mund)* gob *(sl.);* **b)** *(Gesicht)* mug *(sl.);* **fressen 1.** *unr. tr. V.* **a)** *(animal)* eat; *(sich ernähren von)* feed on; **b)** *(ugs.: verschlingen)* swallow up ⟨*money, time, distance*⟩; drink ⟨*petrol*⟩; **c)** *(zerstören)* eat away; **d)** *(derb: von Menschen)* guzzle; **2.** *unr. itr. V. (von Tieren)* feed; *(derb: von Menschen)* stuff one's face *(sl.);* **Fressen das**; ~s **a)** *(für Hunde, Katzen usw.)* food; *(für Vieh)* feed; **b)** *(derb: Essen)* grub *(sl.);* **Fresserei die**; ~, ~en *(derb)* guzzling

**Freude die**; ~, ~n joy; *(Vergnügen)* pleasure; **~ an etw.** *(Dat.)* **haben** take pleasure in sth.

**Freuden-:** **~haus das** house of pleasure; **~tag der** happy day; **freudestrahlend** *Adj.* beaming with joy; **freudig** *Adj.* joyful; joyous ⟨*heart*⟩; delightful ⟨*surprise*⟩; **freud·los** *Adj.* joyless; **freuen 1.** *refl. V.* be glad

*(über + Akk.* about); *(froh sein)* be happy; **sich auf etw.** *(Akk.)* **~:** look forward to sth.; **2.** *tr. V.* please

**Freund der**; ~es, ~e **a)** friend; **b)** *(Verehrer, Geliebter)* boy-friend; **Freundin die**; ~, ~nen **a)** friend; **b)** *(Geliebte)* girl-friend; *(älter)* lady-friend; **freundlich 1.** *Adj.* **a)** kind ⟨*face*⟩; friendly ⟨*reception*⟩; **b)** *(angenehm)* pleasant; **c)** *(freundschaftlich)* friendly; **2.** *adv.* **jmdm. ~ danken** thank sb. kindly; **Freundlichkeit die**; ~: kindness; **Freundschaft die**; ~, ~en friendship; **mit jmdm. ~ schließen** make friends with sb.; **freundschaftlich 1.** *Adj.* friendly; **2.** *adv.* in a friendly way

**Frevel** ['freːfl̩] **der**; ~s, ~ *(geh., veralt.)* crime; outrage

**Friede der**; ~ns, ~n *(älter, geh.)* s. **Frieden**; **Frieden der**; ~s, ~: peace

**Friedens-:** **~forschung die** peace studies *pl., no art.;* **~konferenz die** peace conference; **~nobelpreis der** Nobel Peace Prize; **~pfeife die** pipe of peace; **~richter der** *lay magistrate dealing with minor offences;* ≈ Justice of the Peace; **~taube die** dove of peace; **~verhandlungen** *Pl.* peace negotiations; **~vertrag der** peace treaty

**fried·fertig** *Adj.* peaceable ⟨*person, character*⟩; **Fried·hof der** cemetery; *(Kirchhof)* graveyard; **friedlich 1.** *Adj.* peaceful; **2.** *adv.* peacefully; **fried·liebend** *Adj.* peace-loving

**frieren** *unr. itr. V.* **a)** be or feel cold; **b)** *mit sein (ge~)* freeze

**Frikadelle die**; ~, ~n rissole

**frisch 1.** *Adj.* fresh; new-laid ⟨*egg*⟩; clean ⟨*linen, underwear*⟩; wet ⟨*paint*⟩; **2.** *adv.* freshly; **Frische die**; ~ freshness; **geistige ~:** mental alertness; **körperliche ~:** physical fitness; **Frisch·halte·beutel der** airtight bag

**Friseur** [friˈzøːɐ̯] **der**; ~s, ~e, **Friseuse** [friˈzøːzə] **die**; ~, ~n hairdresser; **frisieren** *tr. V.* **jmdn./sich ~:** do sb.'s/one's hair; **sich ~ lassen** have one's hair done

**friß** *Imperativ Sg. v.* **fressen**

**frißt** *2. u. 3. Pers. Sg. Präsens v.* **fressen**

**Frist die**; ~, ~en **a)** time; period; **die ~ verlängern** extend the deadline; **b)** *(begrenzter Aufschub)* extension

**frist-:** **~gemäß**, **~gerecht** *Adj., adv.* within the specified time *postpos.; (bei Anmeldung usw.)* before the

closing date *postpos.;* ~**los 1.** *Adj.* instant; **2.** *adv.* without notice
**Frisur die;** ~, ~**en** hairstyle
**fritieren** *tr. V.* deep-fry
**frivol** [fri'vo:l] *Adj.* a) *(schamlos)* suggestive ⟨*remark, picture, etc.*⟩; risqué ⟨*joke*⟩; earthy ⟨*man*⟩; flighty ⟨*woman*⟩; b) *(leichtfertig)* frivolous
**froh** *Adj.* a) happy; cheerful ⟨*person, mood*⟩; good ⟨*news*⟩; b) *(ugs.: erleichtert)* pleased, glad (**über** + *Akk.* about)
**fröhlich** *Adj.* cheerful; happy
**Fröhlichkeit die;** ~: cheerfulness; *(eines Festes, einer Feier)* gaiety
**Froh·sinn der;** *o. Pl.* cheerfulness; gaiety
**fromm;** ~**er** *od.* **frömmer,** ~**st...** *od.* **frömmst...** 1. *Adj.* pious, devout ⟨*person*⟩; devout ⟨*Christian*⟩; 2. *adv.* piously; **Frömmigkeit die;** ~: piety; devoutness
**Fron·leichnam** [fro:n-] *o. Art.* [the feast of] Corpus Christi
**Front die;** ~, ~**en** a) *(Gebäude~)* front; façade; b) *(Kampfgebiet)* front [line]; **frontal** 1. *Adj.* head-on ⟨*collision*⟩; frontal ⟨*attack*⟩; 2. *adv.* ⟨*collide*⟩ head-on; ⟨*attack*⟩ from the front; **Front·an·trieb der** *(Kfz-W.)* front-wheel drive
**fror** *1. u. 3. Pers. Sg. Prät. v.* **frieren**
**Frosch der;** ~[e]s, **Frösche** frog
**Frosch-:** ~**mann der;** *Pl.* ~**männer** frogman; ~**perspektive die** worm's-eye view; ~**schenkel der** frog's leg
**Frost der;** ~[e]s, **Fröste** frost; **Frost·beule die** chilblain; **frösteln** *itr. V.* feel chilly; **frostig** 1. *Adj.* frosty *(auch fig.)*; 2. *adv.* frostily; **Frost·schutz·mittel das** a) frost protection agent; b) *(Kfz-W.)* antifreeze
**Frottee das u. der;** ~s, ~s terry towelling; **Frottee·handtuch das** terry towel; **frottieren** *tr. V.* rub; towel
**frotzeln** 1. *tr. V.* tease; 2. *itr. V.* über jmdn./etw. ~: make fun of sb./sth.
**Frucht die;** ~, **Früchte** fruit; **frucht·bar** *Adj.* fertile; fruitful ⟨*work, idea, etc.*⟩; **Fruchtbarkeit die;** ~: fertility; fruitfulness **Frucht·becher der** fruit sundae; **fruchten** *tr. V.* **nichts** ~: be no use; **fruchtig** *Adj.* fruity; **frucht·los** *Adj.* fruitless, vain ⟨*efforts*⟩; **Frucht·saft der** fruit juice
**früh** 1. *Adj.* a) early; b) *(vorzeitig)* premature; 2. *adv.* early; **heute** ~: this

morning; **früh·auf: von** ~**auf** from early childhood on[wards]; **Frühaufsteher der;** ~s, ~: early riser; **Frühe die;** ~: **in aller** ~: at the crack of dawn; **früher** ['fry:ɐ] 1. *Adj., nicht präd.* a) *(vergangen)* earlier; former; b) *(ehemalig)* former ⟨*owner, occupant, friend*⟩; 2. *adv.* formerly; ~ **war er ganz anders** he used to be quite different; **Früh·erkennung die** *(Med.)* early recognition
**frühestens** *Adv.* at the earliest; **Früh·geburt die** a) premature birth; b) *(Kind)* premature baby
**Früh·jahr das** spring; **Frühjahrs·müdigkeit die** springtime tiredness
**Frühling der;** ~s, ~e spring; **Frühlings·anfang der** first day of spring
**früh-, Früh-:** ~**reif** *Adj.* precocious ⟨*child*⟩; ~**schoppen der** morning drink; *(um Mittag)* lunchtime drink; ~**sport der** early-morning exercise
**Früh·stück das;** ~s, ~e breakfast; **frühstücken** *itr. V.* have breakfast; **Frühstücks·pause die** morning break; coffee break
**früh·zeitig** 1. *Adj.* early; *(vorzeitig)* premature; 2. *adv.* early; *(vorzeitig)* prematurely
**Frustration die;** ~, ~**en** *(Psych.)* frustration; **frustrieren** *tr. V.* frustrate
**Fuchs der;** ~es, **Füchse** fox; **fuchsen** *tr. V.* annoy; vex; **fuchs·teufels·wild** *Adj.* *(ugs.)* livid *(coll.)*
**Fuchtel die;** ~: **unter jmds.** ~ *(ugs.)* under sb.'s thumb; **fuchteln** *itr. V.* *(ugs.)* **mit etw.** ~: wave sth. about
**Fuder das;** ~s, ~: cart-load
¹**Fuge die;** ~, ~**n** joint; *(Zwischenraum)* gap; ²**Fuge die;** ~, ~**n** *(Musik)* fugue
**fügen** 1. *tr. V.* place; set; **etw zu etw.** ~ *(fig.)* add sth. to sth.; 2. *refl. V.* a) *(sich ein~)* **sich in etw.** *(Akk.)* ~: fit into sth.; b) *(gehorchen)* **sich** ~: fall into line; **fügsam** *Adj.* obedient
**fühlbar** *Adj.* noticeable; **fühlen** 1. *tr., itr. V.* feel; 2. *refl. V.* **sich krank** ~: feel sick; **Fühler der;** ~s, ~: feeler; antenna; **Fühlungnahme die;** ~: initial contact
**fuhr** *1. u. 3. Pers. Sg. Prät. v.* **fahren**
**Fuhre die;** ~, ~**n** load
**führen** 1. *tr. V.* a) lead; b) *(verkaufen)* stock, sell ⟨*goods*⟩; c) *(durch~)* **Gespräche/Verhandlungen** ~: hold conversations/negotiations; **eine glückliche Ehe** ~: be happily married; d) *(leiten)* manage, run ⟨*company, business,*

*pub, etc.*⟩; lead ⟨*party, country*⟩; command ⟨*regiment*⟩; **e)** *(Amtsspr.)* drive ⟨*train, motor, vehicle*⟩; **f)** *(als Kennzeichnung, Bezeichnung haben)* bear; **einen Titel/Künstlernamen** ~: have a title/use a stage name; **g)** *(angelegt haben)* keep ⟨*diary, list, file*⟩; **h)** *(registrieren)* **jmdn. in einer Liste/Kartei** ~: have sb. on a list/on file; **i)** *(tragen)* **etw. bei** *od.* **mit sich** ~: have sth. on one; **eine Waffe/einen Ausweis bei sich** ~: carry a weapon/a pass; **2.** *itr. V.* **a)** lead; **b)** *(an der Spitze liegen)* lead; be ahead; **führend** *Adj.* leading; high-ranking ⟨*official*⟩; prominent ⟨*position*⟩

**Führer** der; ~s, ~ **a)** *(Leiter)* leader; **b)** *(Fremden~)* guide; **Führerin** die; ~, ~nen *s.* Führer; **führer·los** **1.** *Adj.* leaderless; *(ohne Lenker)* driverless ⟨*car*⟩; **2.** *adv.: s.* **1**; without a leader; without a driver; **Führer·schein** der driving licence *(Brit.)*; driver's license *(Amer.)*; **Führung** die; ~, ~en **a)** *o. Pl. s.* führen **1 d**: management; running; leadership; command; **b)** *(Fremden~)* guided tour; **c)** *o. Pl. (führende Position)* lead

**Führungs-:** ~**kraft** die manager; ~**spitze** die *(Politik)* top leadership; *(im Betrieb)* top management; ~**zeugnis** das *document issued by police certifying that holder has no criminal record*

**Fuhr-:** ~**unternehmer** der haulage contractor; ~**werk** das cart

**Fülle** die; ~ **a)** wealth; abundance; **b)** *(Körper~)* corpulence; **füllen** **1.** *tr. V.* fill; *(Kochk.)* stuff; **b)** *(fig.)* fill in ⟨*gap, time*⟩; **2.** *refl. V.* *(voll werden)* fill [up]; **Füller** der; ~s, ~ *(ugs.)* [fountain-]pen; **Füll·federhalter** der fountain-pen; **füllig** *Adj.* corpulent, portly ⟨*person*⟩; ample ⟨*figure, bosom*⟩; **Füllung** die; ~, ~en stuffing; *(Kochk.; Zahnmed.)* filling; *(in Schokolade)* centre

**fummeln** *itr. V. (ugs.)* **a)** *(fingern)* fiddle; **b)** *(erotisch)* pet

**Fund** der; ~[e]s, ~e *(auch Archäol.)* find

**Fundament** das; ~[e]s, ~e **a)** *(Bauw.)* foundations *pl.;* **b)** *(Basis)* base; basis; **fundamental** *Adj.* fundamental

**Fund-:** ~**büro** das lost property office *(Brit.)*; lost and found office *(Amer.)*; ~**grube** die treasure-house

**fundieren** *tr. V.* underpin

**fündig** *Adj.* ~ **sein** yield something; ~ **werden** make a find; *(bei Bohrungen)* make a strike

**Fund·ort** der place *or* site where sth. is/was found

**fünf** *Kardinalz.* five; **Fünf** die; ~, ~en five; *(Schulnote)* E

**fünf-, Fünf-:** ~**eck** das; ~s, ~e pentagon; ~**fach** *Vervielfältigungsz.* fivefold; ~**fache** das; *adj. Dekl.* five times as much; ~**hundert** *Kardinalz.* five hundred; ~**kampf** der *(Sport)* pentathlon

**Fünfling** der; ~s, ~e quintuplet; quin *(coll.)*

**fünf-:** ~**mal** *Adv.* five times; ~**stellig** *Adj.* five-figure

**fünft...** *Ordinalz.* fifth; **Fünf·tagewoche** die five-day [working] week; **fünf·tausend** *Kardinalz.* five thousand

**fünftel** *Bruchz.* fifth; **Fünftel** das *(schweiz. meist* der*)*; ~s, ~: fifth; **fünftens** *Adv.* fifthly; **fünf·zehn** *Kardinalz.* fifteen; **fünfzig** *Kardinalz.* fifty; **Fünfzig** die; ~: fifty; **fünfziger** *indekl. Adj.; nicht präd.* **die** ~ **Jahre** the fifties; **Fünfziger** der; ~s, ~ **a)** *(ugs.)* fifty-pfennig piece; **b)** *(50jähriger)* fifty-year-old; **fünfzigst...** *Ordinalz.* fiftieth

**fungieren** *itr. V.* **als etw.** ~ ⟨*person*⟩ act as sth.; ⟨*word etc.*⟩ function as sth.

**Funk** der; ~s radio; **Funk·ausstellung** die radio and television exhibition

**Funke** der; ~ns, ~n *(auch fig.)* spark

**funkeln** *itr. V.* ⟨*light, star*⟩ twinkle; ⟨*gold, diamonds*⟩ glitter; ⟨*eyes*⟩ blaze

**funken** *tr. V.* radio; ⟨*transmitter*⟩ broadcast; **Funker** der; ~s, ~: radio operator

**Funk-:** ~**gerät** das radio set; *(tragbar)* walkie-talkie; ~**haus** das broadcasting centre; ~**kolleg** das radio-based [adult education] course; ~**sprech·gerät** das radiophone; *(tragbar)* walkie-talkie; ~**spruch** der radio signal; *(Nachricht)* radio message; ~**stille** die radio silence; ~**streife** die [police] radio patrol; ~**taxi** das radio taxi

**Funktion** die; ~, ~en function; **Funktionär** der; ~s, ~e official; functionary; **funktionieren** *itr. V.* work; function; **funktions·tüchtig** *Adj.* working; sound ⟨*organ*⟩

**Funk-:** ~**turm** der radio tower; ~**verbindung** die radio contact

**Funzel** die; ~, ~n *(ugs.)* useless light

**für** 1. *Präp. mit Akk.* for; etw. ~ ungültig erklären declare sth. invalid *s. auch* was 1

**Furche** die; ~, ~n a) furrow; b) *(Wagenspur)* rut

**Furcht** die; ~: fear; ~ vor jmdm./etw. haben fear sb./sth.; **furchtbar** 1. *Adj.* a) dreadful; b) *(ugs.: unangenehm)* terrible *(coll.)*; 2. *adv. (ugs.)* terribly *(coll.)*; **fürchten** 1. *refl. V.* sich [vor jmdm./etw.] ~: be afraid *or* frightened [of sb./sth.]; 2. *tr. V.* be afraid of; ich fürchte, [daß] ...: I'm afraid [that] ...; **fürchterlich** *Adj. s.* furchtbar; **furcht·los** 1. *Adj.* fearless; 2. *adv.* fearlessly; **furchtsam** 1. *Adj.* timid; 2. *adv.* timidly

**für·einander** *Adv.* for one another; for each other

**Furie** ['fuːrjə] die; ~, ~n Fury

**Furnier** das; ~s, ~e veneer

**Für·sorge** die; ~ a) care; b) *(veralt.: Sozialhilfe)* welfare; c) *(veralt.: Sozialamt)* social services *pl.*; **für·sorglich** 1. *Adj.* considerate; 2. *adv.* considerately

**Für·sprache** die support; **Für·sprecher** der advocate

**Fürst** der; ~en, ~en prince; **Fürstentum** das; ~s, Fürstentümer principality; **fürstlich** 1. *Adj.* a) royal; b) *(fig.: üppig)* lavish; 2. *adv.* lavishly

**Furt** die; ~, ~en ford

**Furunkel** der *od.* das; ~s, ~: boil; furuncle

**Für·wort** das; *Pl.* -wörter pronoun

**Fusion** die; ~, ~en amalgamation; *(von Konzernen)* merger; **fusionieren** *itr. V.* merge

**Fuß** der; ~es, Füße foot; *(einer Lampe, Säule)* base; *(von Möbeln)* leg; zu ~ gehen go on foot; walk; bei ~! heel!; *(fig.)* auf freiem ~ sein be at large; auf großem ~ leben live in great style

**Fuß·ball** der a) *o. Pl. (Ballspiel)* [Association] football; b) *(Ball)* football; **Fußballer** der; ~s, ~: footballer

**Fußball-:** ~platz der football ground; *(Spielfeld)* football pitch; ~spiel das a) football match; b) *o. Pl. (Sportart)* football *no art.*; ~spieler der football player

**Fuß·boden** der floor; **fußen** *itr. V.* auf etw. *(Dat.)* ~: be based on sth.; **Fuß·ende** das foot; **Fußgänger** der; ~s, ~, **Fußgängerin** die; ~, ~nen pedestrian

**Fußgänger-:** ~brücke die footbridge; ~übergang der, ~überweg der pedestrian crossing; ~unterführung die pedestrian subway; ~zone die pedestrian precinct

**Fuß-:** ~nagel der toe-nail; ~note die footnote; ~stapfen der; ~s, ~: footprint; ~tritt der kick; ~volk das a) *(hist.)* footmen *pl.*; b) *(abwertend: Untergeordnete)* lower ranks *pl.*; ~weg der footpath

**futsch** *Adj.(salopp)* ~ sein have gone for a burton *(Brit. sl.)*

**¹Futter** das; ~s *(Tiernahrung)* feed; *(für Pferde, Kühe)* fodder

**²Futter** das; ~s *(von Kleidungsstücken)* lining

**Futteral** das; ~s, ~e case

**¹füttern** *tr. V.* feed

**²füttern** *tr. V. (mit ²Futter ausstatten)* line

**Fütterung** die; ~, ~en feeding

**Futur** das; ~s, ~e *(Sprachw.)* future [tense]

# G

**g, G** [geː] das; ~, ~ a) *(Buchstabe)* g/G; b) *(Musik)* [key of] G

**g** *Abk.* a) **Gramm** g; b) **Groschen**

**gab** *1. u. 3. Pers. Sg. Prät. v.* geben

**Gabe** die; ~, ~n a) *(geh.: Geschenk, Talent)* gift; *(Almosen, Spende)* alms *pl.*

**Gabel** die; ~, ~n fork; *(Telefon~)* cradle; **gabeln** *refl. V.* fork; **Gabel·stapler** der; ~s, ~: fork-lift truck; **Gabelung** die; ~, ~en fork

**Gaben·tisch** der gift table

**gackern** *itr. V.* a) cluck; b) *(ugs.: lachen)* cackle

**gaffen** *itr. V. (abwertend)* gape; gawp *(coll.)*

**Gag** [gɛk] der; ~s, ~s a) *(Theater, Film)* gag; b) *(Besonderheit)* gimmick

**Gage** ['gaːʒə] die; ~, ~n salary; *(für einzelnen Auftritt)* fee

**gähnen** *itr. V. (auch fig.)* yawn

**Gala** ['gaːla, *auch* 'gala] die; ~: formal dress

**galant** 1. *Adj.* gallant; *(amourös)* amorous; 2. *adv.* gallantly

**Gala·vorstellung** die gala performance

**Galeere** die; ~, ~n galley

**Galerie** die; ~, ~n gallery

**Galgen** der gallows *sing.*

**Galgen-:** ~**frist** die reprieve; ~**humor** der gallows humour

**Galle** die; ~, ~n a) *(Gallenblase)* gall[-bladder]; b) *(Sekret) (bei Tieren)* gall; *(bei Menschen)* bile

**Galopp** der; ~s, ~s *od.* ~e gallop; **galoppieren** *itr. V.; meist mit sein* gallop

**galt** *1. u. 3. Pers. Sg. Prät. v.* **gelten**

**galvanisch** [gal'va:nɪʃ] *Adj.* galvanic

**Gamasche** die; ~, ~n gaiter; *(bis zum Knöchel reichend)* spat

**Gambe** die; ~, ~n *(Musik)* viola da gamba

**Gamma·strahlen** *Pl. (Physik, Med.)* gamma rays

**gammelig** *Adj. (ugs.)* a) bad; rotten; b) *(unordentlich)* scruffy; **gammeln** *itr. V.* a) *(ugs.)* go off; b) *(nichts tun)* loaf around; bum around *(Amer. coll.)*; **Gammler** der; ~s, ~ *(ugs.)* drop-out *(coll.)*

**gäng:** ~ **und gäbe sein** be quite usual

**Gang** der; ~[e]s, **Gänge** a) walk; gait; b) *(Besorgung)* errand; c) *o. Pl. (Verlauf)* course; d) *(Technik)* gear; e) *(Flur) (in Zügen, Gebäuden usw.)* corridor; *(Verbindungs~)* passage[-way]; *(im Theater, Kino, Flugzeug)* aisle; f) *(Kochk.)* course; **gangbar** *Adj.* passable; *(fig.)* practicable

**Gängel·band** das *in* jmdn. am ~ führen keep sb. in leading-reins; **gängeln** *tr. V. (ugs.)* jmdn. ~: boss sb. around

**gängig** *Adj.* a) *(üblich)* common; *(aktuell)* current; b) *(leicht verkäuflich)* popular

**Gang·schaltung** die *(Technik)* gear system; *(Art)* gear-change

**Gangway** ['gæŋweɪ] die; ~, ~s gangway

**Ganove** [ga'no:və] der; ~n, ~n *(ugs. abwertend)* crook *(coll.)*

**Gans** die; ~, **Gänse** goose

**Gänse-:** ~**blümchen** das daisy; ~**braten** der roast goose; ~**füßchen** das; *meist Pl. (ugs.) s.* **Anführungszeichen**; ~**haut** die *(fig.)* goose-flesh; goose pimples *pl.*; ~**marsch** *in* im ~**marsch** in single *or* Indian file

**Gänserich** der; ~s, ~e gander

**ganz** 1. *Adj.* a) *(gesamt)* whole; entire; **den ~en Tag/das ~e Jahr** all day/year; b) *(ugs.: alle)* die ~**en Kinder/Leute/Gläser** *usw.* all the children/people/glasses *etc.*; c) *(vollständig)* whole; d) *(ugs.: ziemlich [viel])* **eine ~e Menge/ein ~er Haufen** quite a lot/quite a pile; e) *(ugs.: unversehrt)* intact; **etw. wieder ~ machen** mend sth.; 2. *adv.* quite; **Ganze** das; *adj. Dekl.* a) whole; b) *(alles)* das ~: the whole thing; **gänzlich** *Adv.* entirely

**ganz-:** ~**tägig** 1. *Adj.* all-day; **eine ~tägige Arbeit** a full-time job; 2. *adv.* all day; ~**tags** *Adv.* ~ **arbeiten** work full-time

¹**gar** *Adj.* cooked; done *pred.*

²**gar** *Partikel* a) *(überhaupt)* ~ **nicht** [wahr] not [true] at all; ~ **nichts** nothing at all; ~ **niemand** *od.* **keiner** nobody at all; ~ **keines** not a single one; ~ **kein Geld** no money at all; b) *(südd., österr., schweiz.: verstärkend)* ~ **zu** only too; c) *(geh.: sogar)* even

**Garage** [ga'ra:ʒə] die; ~, ~n garage

**Garant** der; ~en, ~en guarantor; **Garantie** die; ~, ~n guarantee; **garantieren** 1. *tr. V.* guarantee; 2. *itr. V.* **für etw. ~:** guarantee sth.; **garantiert** *Adv. (ugs.)* **wir kommen ~ zu spät** we're dead certain to arrive late *(coll.)*; **Garantie·schein** der guarantee [certificate]

**Garaus** ['ga:ʀlaʊs] jmdm. den ~ machen do sb. in *(coll.)*

**Garbe** die; ~, ~n a) sheaf; b) *(Geschoß~)* burst of fire

**Garde** die; ~, ~n guard

**Garderobe** die; ~, ~n a) *o. Pl.* wardrobe; clothes *pl.*; b) *(Flur~)* coatrack; c) *(im Theater o. ä.)* cloakroom; checkroom *(Amer.)*; **Garderobenfrau** die cloakroom *or (Amer.)* checkroom attendant

**Gardine** die; ~, ~n a) net curtain; b) *(landsch., veralt.)* curtain

**Gardinen-:** ~**predigt** die *(ugs.)* telling-off *(coll.)*; *(einer Ehefrau zu ihrem Mann)* curtain lecture; ~**stange** die curtain rail

**garen** *tr., itr. V.* cook

**gären** *regelm. (auch unr.) itr. V.* ferment; *(fig.)* seethe

**Garn** das; ~[e]s, ~e a) thread; *(Näh~)* cotton; b) *(Seew.)* yarn

**Garnele** die; ~, ~n shrimp

**garnieren** *tr. V.* a) decorate; b) *(Gastr.)* garnish

**Garnison** die; ~, ~en garrison

**Garnitur** die; ~, ~en **a)** set; *(Wäsche)* set of [matching] underwear; *(Möbel)* suite; **b)** *(ugs.)* die erste/zweite ~: the first/second-rate people *pl.*

**garstig** *Adj.* **a)** nasty; bad *(behaviour)*

**Gärtchen** das; ~s, ~: little garden; **Garten** der; ~s, **Gärten** garden

**Garten-:** ~**arbeit** die gardening; ~**bau** der; *o. Pl.* horticulture; ~**fest** das garden party; ~**haus** das summer-house; ~**laube** die summerhouse; garden house; ~**lokal** das beer garden; *(Restaurant)* open-air café; ~**schau** die horticultural show; ~**zwerg** der **a)** garden gnome; **b)** *(salopp abwertend)* little runt

**Gärtner** der; ~s, ~: gardener; **Gärtnerei** die; ~, ~en nursery; **Gärtnerin** die; ~, ~nen gardener

**Gärung** die; ~, ~en fermentation

**Gas** das; ~es, ~e **a)** gas; **b)** *(Treibstoff)* petrol *(Brit.)*; gasoline *(Amer.)*; gas *(Amer. coll.)*; ~ **wegnehmen** take one's foot off the accelerator; ~ **geben** accelerate; put one's foot down *(coll.)*

**gas-, Gas-:** ~**flasche** die gas-cylinder; *(für einen Herd, Ofen)* gas bottle; ~**förmig** *Adj.* gaseous; ~**hahn** der gas tap; ~**herd** der gas cooker; ~**leitung** die gas pipe; *(Hauptrohr)* gas main; ~**maske** die gas mask; ~**pedal** das accelerator [pedal]; gas pedal *(Amer.)*; ~**pistole** die pistol that fires gas cartridges

**Gasse** die; ~, ~n lane; *(österr.)* street; **Gassen·junge** der *(abwertend)* street urchin

**Gast** der; ~[e]s, **Gäste a)** guest; **b)** *(Besucher eines Lokals)* patron; **c)** *(Besucher)* visitor; **Gast·arbeiter** der immigrant *or* guest worker

**Gäste-:** ~**buch** das guest book; ~**zimmer** das *(privat)* guest room; spare room; *(im Hotel)* room

**gast-, Gast-:** ~**freundlich** *Adj.* hospitable; ~**freundschaft** die hospitality; ~**geber** der host; ~**geberin,** die hostess; ~**haus** das, ~**hof** der inn

**gastieren** *itr. V.* give a guest performance

**gastlich** *Adj.* hospitable; **Gastlichkeit** die; ~: hospitality

**Gastronom** der; ~en, ~en restaurateur; **Gastronomie** die; ~: catering *no art.*; *(Gaststättengewerbe)* restaurant trade

**Gast-:** ~**spiel** das guest performance; ~**stätte** die public house; *(Speiselokal)* restaurant; ~**wirt** der publican;

landlord; *(eines Restaurants)* [restaurant] proprietor; *(Pächter)* restaurant manager; ~**wirtschaft** die *s.* ~**stätte**

**Gas-:** ~**vergiftung** die gas-poisoning *no indef. art.*; ~**versorgung** die gas supply; ~**werk** das gasworks *sing.*; ~**zähler** der gas meter

**Gatte** der; ~n, ~n husband

**Gatter** das; ~s, ~ **a)** *(Zaun)* fence; *(Lattenzaun)* fence; paling; **b)** *(Tor)* gate;

**Gattin** die; ~, ~nen *(geh.)* wife

**Gattung** die; ~, ~en **a)** kind; sort; *(Kunst~)* genre; form; **b)** *(Biol.)* genus

**Gaudi** das; ~s *(bayr., österr.)* die; ~ *(ugs.)* bit of fun

**Gaukler** der; ~s, ~ **a)** *(veralt.: Taschenspieler)* itinerant entertainer; **b)** *(geh.: Betrüger)* charlatan

**Gaul** der; ~[e]s, **Gäule** nag *(derog.)*

**Gaumen** der; ~s, ~: palate

**Gauner** der; ~s, ~ *(abwertend)* crook *(coll.)*; rogue; **Gaunerei** die; ~, ~en swindle; **Gauner·sprache** die thieves' cant *or* Latin

**Gaze** ['gaːzə] die; ~, ~n gauze

**geachtet** *Adj.* respected

**Geäst** das; ~[e]s branches *pl.*

**geb.** *Abk.* **a)** geboren; **b)** geborene

**Gebäck** das; ~[e]s, ~e cakes and pastries *pl.*; *(Kekse)* biscuits *pl.*; *(Törtchen)* tarts *pl.*

**gebacken** 2. *Part. v.* **backen**

**Gebälk** das; ~[e]s, ~e beams *pl.*; *(Dach~)* rafters *pl.*

**gebar** 1. u. 3. *Pers. Sg. Prät. v.* **gebären**

**Gebärde** die; ~, ~n gesture; **gebärden** *refl. V.* behave

**gebären** *unr. tr. V.* bear; give birth to; *s. auch* **geboren**

**Gebäude** das; ~s, ~ **a)** building; **b)** *(Gefüge)* structure

**gebaut** *Adj.* gut ~ sein have a good figure

**Gebein** das; ~[e]s, ~e *Pl. (geh.)* bones *pl.*; *(sterbliche Reste)* [mortal] remains

**Gebell** das; ~[e]s barking; *(der Jagdhunde)* baying

**geben** 1. *unr. tr. V.* give; jmdm. die Hand ~: shake sb.'s hand; ~ Sie mir bitte Herrn N. please put me through to Mr N.; Unterricht ~: teach; eins plus eins gibt zwei one and one is *or* makes two; etw. von sich ~: utter sth.; 2. *unr. tr. V. (unpers.)* es gibt there is/ are; *(coll.)*; heute gibt's Fisch we're having fish today; morgen gibt es Schnee it'll snow tomorrow; 3. *unr. itr.*

*V.* **a)** *(Karten austeilen)* deal; **b)** *(Sport: aufschlagen)* serve; **4.** *unr. refl. V.* **a)** **sich |natürlich/steif|** ~: act *or* behave [naturally/stiffly]; **b)** **das gibt sich noch** it will get better

**Gebet** das; ~|e|s, ~e prayer

**gebeten** *2. Part. v.* **bitten**

**Gebets-:** ~**mühle** die prayer wheel; ~**teppich** der *(islam. Rel.)* prayer mat

**gebiert** *3. Pers. Sg. Präsens v.* **gebären**

**Gebiet** das; ~|e|s, ~e region; area; *(Staats~)* territory; *(Bereich, Fach)* field

**gebieten** *(geh.)* **a)** command; order; **b)** *(erfordern)* demand; **Gebieter** der; ~s, ~ *(veralt.)* master; **gebieterisch** *(geh.) Adj.* imperious; *(herrisch)* domineering; peremptory ⟨*tone*⟩

**Gebilde** das; ~s, ~: object; *(Bauwerk)* structure

**gebildet** *Adj.* educated

**Gebirge** das; ~s, ~: mountain range; **im** ~: in the mountains; **gebirgig** *Adj.* mountainous

**Gebiß** das; Gebisses, Gebisse **a)** set of teeth; teeth *pl.;* **b)** *(Zahnersatz)* denture; plate *(coll.); (für beide Kiefer)* dentures *pl.;* **gebissen** *2. Part. v.* **beißen**

**geblasen** *2. Part. v.* **blasen**

**geblichen** *2. Part. v.* **bleichen**

**geblümt** *Adj.* flowered

**Geblüt** das; ~|e|s *(geh.)* blood

**gebogen** *2. Part. v.* **biegen**

**geboren 1.** *2. Part. v.* **gebären; 2.** *Adj.* **blind/taub** ~ **sein** be born blind/deaf; **Frau Anna Schmitz** ~**e Meyer** Mrs Anna Schmitz née Meyer

**geborgen 1.** *2. Part. v.* **bergen; 2.** *Adj.* safe; secure; **Geborgenheit** die; ~: security

**geborsten** *2. Part. v.* **bersten**

**gebot** *1. u. 3. Pers. Sg. Prät. v.* **gebieten; Gebot** das; ~|e|s, ~e **a)** *(Grundsatz)* precept; **die Zehn** ~**e** *(Rel.)* the Ten Commandments; **b)** *(Vorschrift)* regulation; **geboten 1.** *2. Part. v.* **bieten, gebieten; 2.** *Adj. (ratsam)* advisable; *(notwendig)* necessary

**Gebr.** *Abk.* Gebrüder Bros.

**gebracht** *2. Part. v.* **bringen**

**gebrannt** *2. Part. v.* **brennen**

**gebraten** *2. Part. v.* **braten**

**Gebrauch** der **a)** *o. Pl.* use; **b)** *meist Pl. (Brauch)* custom; **gebrauchen** *tr. V.* use; **gebräuchlich** *Adj.* **a)** normal; customary; **b)** *(häufig)* common

**gebrauchs-, Gebrauchs-:** ~**an-**weisung** die instructions *pl.* [for use]; ~**fertig** *Adj.* ready for use *pred.;* ~**gegenstand** der item of practical use

**gebraucht** *Adj.* second-hand; used ⟨*car*⟩ **Gebraucht·wagen** der used car

**Gebrechen** das; ~s, ~ *(geh.)* affliction; **gebrechlich** *Adj.* infirm; **Gebrechlichkeit** die; ~: infirmity

**gebrochen 1.** *2. Part. v.* **brechen; 2.** *Adj.* ~**es Englisch/Deutsch** broken English/German; **3.** *adv.* ~ **Deutsch sprechen** speak broken German

**Gebrüder** *Pl.:* **die** ~ **Meyer** Meyer Brothers

**Gebrüll** das; ~|e|s roaring

**Gebrumm** das; ~|e|s *(von Bären)* growling; *(von Flugzeugen, Bienen)* droning; *(von Insekten)* buzz[ing]

**gebückt** *Adj.* **in** ~**er Haltung** bending forward

**Gebühr** die; ~, ~**en** charge; *(Maut)* toll; *(Anwalts~)* fee

**gebühren** *(geh.) itr. V.* **jmdm. gebührt Achtung** *usw.* sb. deserves respect *etc.;* **gebührend 1.** *Adj.* fitting; **2.** *adv.* fittingly

**gebühren-, Gebühren-:** ~**ermäßi-**gung** die: reduction of charges/fees; ~**frei 1.** *Adj.* free of charge *pred.;* **2.** *adv.* free of charge; ~**pflichtig** *Adj.* **eine** ~**pflichtige Verwarnung** a fine and a caution

**gebunden 1.** *2. Part. v.* **binden; 2.** *Adj. (verpflichtet)* bound

**Geburt** die; ~, ~**en** birth; **Geburten·kontrolle** die; *o. Pl.* birth control; **gebürtig** *Adj.* **ein** ~**er Schwabe** a Swabian by birth

**Geburts-:** ~**anzeige** die birth announcement; ~**datum** das date of birth; ~**helfer** der *(Arzt)* obstetrician; ~**ort** der place of birth; ~**tag** der birthday; **jmdm. zum** ~ **gratulieren** wish sb. many happy returns of the day; ~**ur·kunde** die birth certificate

**Gebüsch** das; ~|e|s, ~e bushes *pl.*

**gedacht** *2. Part. v.* **denken, gedenken**

**Gedächtnis** das; ~ses, ~se **a)** memory; **b)** *(Andenken)* memory

**Gedächtnis-:** ~**lücke** die gap in one's memory; ~**schwund** der loss of memory

**gedämpft** *Adj.* subdued ⟨*mood*⟩; subdued, soft ⟨*light*⟩; muffled ⟨*sound*⟩

**Gedanke** der; ~ns, ~n **a)** thought; **der** ~ **an etw.** *(Akk.)* the thought of sth.; **b)** *Pl. (Meinung)* ideas; **c)** *(Einfall)* idea

**gedanken-, Gedanken-:** ~**gang** der train of thought; ~**los 1.** *Adj.* unconsidered; *(zerstreut)* absentminded; **2.** *adv.* without thinking; *(zerstreut)* absent-mindedly; ~**losigkeit** die *(Zerstreutheit)* absentmindedness; *(Unüberlegtheit)* lack of thought; ~**strich** der dash; ~**verloren** *Adv.* lost in thought; ~**voll 1.** *Adj.* pensive; **2.** *adv.* pensively
**gedanklich 1.** *Adj.* intellectual; **2.** *adv.* intellectually
**Gedärm** das; ~|e|s, ~e intestines *pl.*; bowels *pl.*, *(eines Tieres)* entrails *pl.*
**Gedeck** das; ~|e|s, ~e **a)** place setting; cover; **b)** *(Menü)* set meal; **c)** *(Getränk)* drink [with a cover charge]
**gedeihen** *unr. itr. V.*; *mit sein* **a)** thrive; **b)** *(fortschreiten)* progress
**gedenken** *unr. itr. V.* **a)** jmds./einer Sache ~ *(geh.)* remember sb./sth.; *(in einer Feier)* commemorate sb./sth.; **b)** etw. zu tun ~: intend to do *or* doing sth.
**Gedenk·stätte** die memorial
**Gedicht** das; ~|e|s, ~e poem
**gediegen 1.** *Adj.* solid ⟨*furniture*⟩; sound ⟨*piece of work*⟩; **2.** *adv.* ~ gebaut/verarbeitet solidly built/made
**gedieh** *1. u. 3. Pers. Sg. Prät. v.* **gedeihen; gediehen** *2. Part. v.* **gedeihen**
**Gedränge** das; ~s pushing and shoving; *(Menge)* crush; crowd
**gedroschen** *2. Part. v.* **dreschen**
**gedrungen 1.** *2. Part. v.* **dringen; 2.** *Adj.* stocky; thick-set
**Geduld** die; ~: patience; **gedulden** *refl. V.* be patient; **geduldig 1.** *Adj.* patient; **2.** *adv.* patiently; **Geduldsspiel** das puzzle
**gedurft** *2. Part. v.* **dürfen**
**geeignet** *Adj.* suitable; *(richtig)* right
**Gefahr** die; ~, ~en **a)** danger; *(Bedrohung)* danger; threat (für to); **bei** ~: in case of emergency; **b)** *(Risiko)* risk; **auf eigene** ~: at one's own risk; **gefährden** *tr. V.* endanger; jeopardize ⟨*enterprise, success, position, etc.*⟩
**gefahren** *2. Part. v.* **fahren**
**gefährlich 1.** *Adj.* dangerous; *(gewagt)* risky; **2.** *adv.* dangerously
**gefahr·los** *Adj.* safe; **2.** *adv.* safely
**Gefährt** das; ~|e|s, ~e *(geh.)* vehicle
**Gefährte** der; ~n, ~n, **Gefährtin** die; ~, ~nen *(geh.)* companion; *(Ehemann/Ehefrau)* partner in life
**Gefälle** das; ~s, ~: slope; incline; *(einer Straße)* gradient
**¹gefallen** *unr. itr. V.* **a)** das gefällt mir

|gut| I like it [a lot]; **b)** sich *(Dat.)* etw. ~ lassen put up with sth.
**²gefallen** *2. Part. v.* **fallen, gefallen**
**¹Gefallen** der; ~s, ~: favour
**²Gefallen** das; ~s pleasure
**Gefallene** der; *adj. Dekl.* soldier killed in action; **die** ~**n** the fallen
**gefällig 1.** *Adj.* **a)** obliging; helpful; **b)** *(anziehend)* pleasing; agreeable ⟨*programme, behaviour*⟩; **2.** *adv.* pleasingly; agreeably; **Gefälligkeit** die; ~, ~en favour; **gefälligst** *Adv.* *(ugs.)* kindly
**gefangen** *2. Part. v.* **fangen; Gefangene** der/die; *adj. Dekl.* prisoner
**gefangen-:** ~|**halten** *unr. tr. V.* jmdn./ein Tier ~**halten** hold sb. prisoner/keep an animal in captivity; ~|**nehmen** *unr. tr. V.* jmdn. ~**nehmen** take sb. prisoner
**Gefangenschaft** die; ~, ~en captivity
**Gefängnis** das; ~ses, ~se **a)** prison; gaol; **b)** *(Strafe)* imprisonment
**Gefängnis-:** ~**strafe** die prison sentence; ~**wärter** der [prison] warder
**Gefasel** das; ~s *(ugs. abwertend)* twaddle *(coll.)*; drivel *(derog.)*
**Gefäß** das; ~es, ~e **a)** vessel; container; **b)** *(Anat.)* vessel
**gefaßt** *Adj.* **a)** calm; composed; **b)** *in* auf etw. *(Akk.)* |nicht| ~ sein [not] be prepared for sth.
**Gefecht** das; ~|e|s, ~e battle
**Gefieder** das; ~s, ~: plumage; feathers *pl.*; **gefiedert** *Adj.* feathered
**geflissentlich 1.** *Adj.* deliberate; **2.** *adv.* deliberately
**geflochten** *2. Part. v.* **flechten**
**geflogen** *2. Part. v.* **fliegen**
**geflohen** *2. Part. v.* **fliehen**
**geflossen** *2. Part. v.* **fließen**
**Geflügel** das; ~s poultry
**gefochten** *2. Part. v.* **fechten**
**Gefolge** das; ~s, ~: entourage
**gefragt** *Adj.* in great demand *postpos.*; sought-after
**gefräßig** *Adj.* *(abwertend)* greedy
**Gefreite** der; *adj. Dekl. (Milit.)* lancecorporal *(Brit.)*; private first class *(Amer.)*; *(Marine)* able seaman; *(Luftw.)* aircraftman first class *(Brit.)*; airman third class *(Amer.)*
**gefressen** *2. Part. v.* **fressen**
**gefrieren** *unr. itr. V.*; *mit sein* freeze
**gefrier-, Gefrier-:** ~**fach** das freezing compartment; ~**punkt** der freezing-point; ~**schrank** der freezer;

~|**trocknen** tr. V.; meist im Inf. u. 2.
Part. freeze-dry
**gefroren** 2. Part. v. **frieren, gefrieren**
**Gefüge** das; ~s, ~: structure; **gefü-
gig** Adj. compliant; docile ⟨animal⟩
**Gefühl** das; ~s, ~e a) sensation; feeling; b) (Gemütsverfassung) feeling;
**gefühl·los** Adj. a) numb; b) (herzlos,
kalt) unfeeling
**gefühls-, Gefühls-:** ~**betont** Adj.
emotional; ~**duselei** die; ~ (ugs. abwertend) mawkishness; ~**mäßig** Adj.
emotional ⟨reaction⟩; ⟨action⟩ based
on emotion
**gefühl·voll** 1. Adj. sensitive; (ausdrucksvoll) expressive; 2. adv. sensitively; expressively
**gefüllt** 2. Part. v. **füllen**
**gefunden** 2. Part. v. **finden**; s. auch
**Fressen** b
**gegangen** 2. Part. v. **gehen**
**gegeben** 2. Part. v. **geben**
**gegen** Präp. mit Akk. a) against; ~
etw. stoßen knock into sth.; ein Mittel
~ Krebs a cure for cancer; ~ die Abmachung contrary to the agreement;
b) ~ Abend/Morgen towards evening/
dawn; ~ vier Uhr around 4 o'clock; c)
(im Vergleich zu) compared with; d)
(im Ausgleich für) for; ~ Quittung
against a receipt
**Gegen-:** ~**angriff** der counter-
attack; ~**argument** das counter-
argument; ~**besuch** der return visit
**Gegend** die; ~, ~en a) area; b) (Kör-
perregion) region
**Gegen-:** ~**darstellung** die: eine
~darstellung |der Sache| an account
[of the matter] from an opposing point
of view; ~**druck** der counter-
pressure
**gegen·einander** Adv. against each
other or one another
**Gegen-:** ~**gewicht** das counter-
weight; ein ~gewicht zu od. gegen etw.
bilden (fig.) counterbalance sth.;
~**leistung** die service in return;
~**mittel** das (gegen Gift) antidote;
(gegen Krankheit) remedy; ~**probe**
die cross-check; ~**satz** der a) (Gegenteil) opposite; b) (Widerspruch) conflict; ~**sätzlich** Adj. conflicting;
~**seitig** 1. Adj. (wechselseitig) mutual; 2. adv. sich ~seitig helfen/über-
bieten help/outdo each other or one
another; ~**seitigkeit** die reciprocity;
auf ~seitigkeit (Dat.) beruhen be mutual; ~**spieler** der opponent; (Sport)
opposite number

**Gegen·stand** der object; (Thema)
subject; topic; **gegenständlich** Adj.
(Kunst) representational; (Philos.) objective; **gegenstands·los** Adj. a)
(hinfällig) invalid; b) (grundlos, unbegründet) unfounded ⟨accusation, complaint, jealousy⟩; baseless ⟨fear⟩
**gegen-, Gegen-:** ~**stimme** die vote
against; ohne ~stimme unanimously;
~**stück** das companion piece; (fig.)
counterpart; ~**teil** das opposite; im
~teil on the contrary; ~**teilig** Adj.
opposite; contrary
**gegen·über** Präp. mit Dat. a) opposite; b) (in bezug auf) ~ jmdm. od.
jmdm. ~ freundlich sein be kind to sb.;
c) (im Vergleich zu) compared with
**gegenüber-, Gegenüber-:** ~|**ste-
hen** unr. itr. V. a) jmdm./einer Sache
~stehen stand facing sb./sth.; (fig.)
face sb./sth.; b) jmdm./einer Sache
feindlich/wohlwollend ~stehen be ill/
well disposed towards sb./sth.;
~|**stellen** tr. V. confront; ~**stellung**
die confrontation; b) (Vergleich) com-
parison; ~|**treten** unr. itr. V.; mit sein
jmdm./einer Sache treten (auch fig.)
face sb./sth.
**Gegen·verkehr** der oncoming traffic
**Gegenwart** die; ~ a) present; b) (Anwesenheit) presence; c) (Grammatik)
present [tense]; **gegenwärtig** 1. Adj.
present; 2. adv. at present; at the moment
**Gegen-:** ~**wehr** die; o. Pl. resistance;
~**wind** der head wind; ~**zug** der
(Brettspiele, fig.) countermove
**gegessen** 2. Part. v. **essen**
**geglichen** 2. Part. v. **gleichen**
**geglitten** 2. Part. v. **gleiten**
**Gegner** der; ~s, ~ a) adversary; opponent; b) (Sport) opponent; **gegne-
risch** Adj. opposing; opponents'
⟨goal⟩
**gegolten** 2. Part. v. **gelten**
**gegoren** 2. Part. v. **gären**
**gegossen** 2. Part. v. **gießen**
**gegriffen** 2. Part. v. **greifen**
**gehabt** 2. Part. v. **haben**
¹**Gehalt** der; ~|e|s, ~e a) meaning; b)
(Anteil) content
²**Gehalt** das, österr. auch: der; ~|e|s,
Gehälter salary
**gehalten** 2. Part. v. **halten**
**Gehalts-:** ~**empfänger** der salary
earner; ~**erhöhung** die salary increase
**gehalt·voll** Adj. nutritious ⟨food⟩;
⟨novel, speech⟩ rich in substance

**gehässig** *Adj. (abwertend)* spiteful; **Gehässigkeit die; ~, ~en a)** *(Wesen)* spitefulness; **b)** *(Äußerung)* spiteful remark

**gehauen** *2. Part. v.* **hauen**

**gehäuft** *Adj.* ein ~er Teelöffel/Eßlöffel a heaped teaspoon/tablespoon

**Gehäuse das; ~s, ~** *(einer Maschine)* casing; housing; *(einer Kamera, Uhr)* case

**geh·behindert** *Adj.* able to walk only with difficulty *postpos.;* disabled

**Gehege das; ~s, ~ a)** *(Jägerspr.)* preserve; **b)** *(im Zoo)* enclosure

**geheim 1.** *Adj.* **a)** secret; **b)** *(mysteriös)* mysterious; **2.** *adv.* ~ **abstimmen** vote by secret ballot

**geheim-, Geheim-:** ~**agent** der secret agent; ~**dienst** der secret service; ~|**halten** *unr. tr. V.* keep secret

**Geheimnis das; ~ses, ~se** secret; **Geheimnis·tuerei die;** ~ *(ugs.)* secretiveness; **geheimnis·voll** *Adj.* mysterious

**Geheiß das: auf jmds.** ~ *(geh.)* at sb.'s behest

**gehen** *unr. itr. V.;* **mit sein a)** walk; go; **über die Straße** ~: cross the street; **b)** *(sich irgendwohin begeben)* go; **c)** *(regelmäßig besuchen)* attend; **d)** *(weg~)* go; leave; **e)** *(in Funktion sein)* work; **meine Uhr geht falsch** my watch is wrong; **f)** *(möglich sein)* **ja, das geht** yes, I/we can manage that; **das geht nicht** that can't be done; **g)** *(ugs.: gerade noch angehen)* **Hast du gut geschlafen? – Es geht** Did you sleep well? – Not too bad; **h)** *(sich entwickeln)* **der Laden/das Geschäft geht gut/gar nicht** the shop/business is doing well/not doing well at all; **i)** *(unpers.)* **wie geht es dir?** How are you?; **jmdm. geht es gut/schlecht** *(gesundheitlich)* sb. is well/not well; *(geschäftlich)* sb. is doing well/badly; **j)** *(unpers.) (sich um etw. handeln)* ; **worum geht es hier?** what is this all about?; **2.** *unr. tr. V. (zurücklegen)* **10 km** ~: walk 10 km.

**gehen|lassen** *unr. refl. V. (sich nicht beherrschen)* lose control of oneself; *(sich vernachlässigen)* let oneself go

**geheuer** *Adj.* **a)** in diesem Gebäude ist **es nicht** ~: this building is eerie; **b)** ihr **war doch nicht |ganz|** ~: she felt [a little] uneasy; **c)** **die Sache ist |mir| nicht ganz** ~: [I feel] there's something odd about this business

**Gehilfe der;** ~**n,** ~**n** assistant

**Gehirn das;** ~|e|s, ~e brain

**Gehirn-:** ~**erschütterung die** concussion; ~**schlag der** stroke; ~**wäsche die** brainwashing *no indef. art.*

**gehoben 1.** *2. Part. v.* **heben; 2.** *Adj.* **a)** higher; senior ⟨*position*⟩; **b)** *(gewählt)* elevated, refined

**geholfen** *2. Part. v.* **helfen**

**Gehör das;** ~|e|s [sense of] hearing

**gehorchen** *itr. V.* **jmdm.** ~: obey sb.

**gehören 1.** *itr. V.* **a) jmdm.** ~: belong to sb.; **b)** *(Teil eines Ganzen sein)* **zu jmds. Freunden/Aufgaben** ~: be one of sb.'s friends/part of sb.'s duties; **c)** *(passend sein)* **dein Roller gehört nicht in die Küche!** your scooter does not belong in the kitchen!; **d)** *(nötig sein)* **es hat viel Fleiß dazu gehört** it took a lot of hard work; **dazu gehört sehr viel** that takes a lot; **2.** *refl. V. (sich schikken)* be fitting; **es gehört sich |nicht|, ... zu ...:** it is [not] good manners to ...; **gehörig 1.** *Adj.* **a)** proper; **b)** *(ugs.: beträchtlich)* **ein** ~**er Schrecken/eine** ~**e Portion Mut** a good fright/a good deal of courage; **2.** *adv. (ugs.: beträchtlich)* ~ **essen/trinken** eat/drink heartily

**gehorsam** *Adj.* obedient; **Gehorsam der;** ~s obedience

**Geh·steig der** pavement *(Brit.);* sidewalk *(Amer.)*

**Geier der;** ~**s,** ~: vulture

**Geige die;** ~, ~**n** violin

**Geiger·zähler der** *(Physik)* Geiger counter

**geil** *Adj. (oft abwertend: sexuell erregt)* randy; horny *(sl.); (lüstern)* lecherous

**Geisel die;** ~, ~**n** hostage

**Geißel die;** ~, ~**n** *(hist., auch fig.)* scourge

**Geist der;** ~|e|s, ~**e a)** *o. Pl. (Verstand)* mind; **b)** *o. Pl. (Scharfsinn)* wit; **c)** *o. Pl. (innere Einstellung)* spirit; **d)** *(denkender Mensch)* mind; intellect; **ein großer/kleiner** ~: a great mind/a person of limited intellect; **e)** *(überirdisches Wesen)* spirit; **der Heilige** ~ *(christl. Rel.)* the Holy Ghost *or* Spirit; **f)** *(Gespenst)* ghost; **Geisterfahrer der** *person driving on the wrong side of the road or the wrong carriageway;* **geisterhaft** *Adj.* ghostly; eerie ⟨*atmosphere*⟩

**geistes-, Geistes-:** ~**abwesend 1.** *Adj.* absent-minded; **2.** *adv.* absentmindedly; ~**blitz der** *(ugs.)* brainwave; ~**gegenwart die** presence of mind; ~**gegenwärtig 1.** *Adj.* quickwitted; **2.** *adv.* with great presence of

mind; ~**krank** *Adj.* mentally ill;
~**wissenschaften** *Pl.* arts; humanities; ~**zustand** der; *o. Pl.* mental state
**geistig** 1. *Adj.* a) intellectual; *(Psych.)*
mental; b) alcoholic ⟨*drinks*⟩; 2. *adv.*
intellectually; *(Psych.)* mentally;
**geistlich** *Adj.* sacred ⟨*song, music*⟩;
religious ⟨*order, book, writings*⟩;
**Geistliche** der; *adj. Dekl.* clergyman
**geist**-: ~**los** *Adj.* dim-witted; *(trivial)*
trivial; ~**reich** 1. *Adj.* witty; *(klug)*
clever; 2. *adv.:* wittily; cleverly
**Geiz** der; ~es meanness; *(Knauserigkeit)* miserliness; **geizen** *itr. V.* be
mean; **Geiz·hals** der *(abwertend)*
skinflint; **geizig** *Adj.* mean; *(knauserig)* miserly
**gekannt** 2. *Part. v.* kennen
**Gekicher** das; ~s giggling
**geklungen** 2. *Part. v.* klingen
**geknickt** *Adj.* (ugs.) dejected
**gekniffen** 2. *Part. v.* kneifen
**gekommen** 2. *Part. v.* kommen
**gekonnt** 1. 2. *Part. v.* können; 2. *Adj.*
accomplished; *(hervorragend ausgeführt)* masterly
**gekrochen** 2. *Part. v.* kriechen
**gekünstelt** 1. *Adj.* artificial; 2. *adv.*
er lächelte ~: he gave a forced smile
**Gelächter** das; ~s, ~: laughter
**geladen** 2. *Part. v.* laden
**Gelände** das; ~s, ~ a) *(Landschaft)*
ground; terrain; b) *(Grundstück)* site;
*(von Schule, Krankenhaus usw.)*
grounds *pl.*
**Geländer** das; ~s, ~: banisters *pl.*;
handrail; *(am Balkon, an einer
Brücke)* railing[s *pl.*]; *(aus Stein)*
parapet
**gelang** 3. *Pers. Sg. Prät. v.* gelingen
**gelangen** *itr. V.*; *mit sein* an etw.
*(Akk.)/zu etw.* ~: reach sth.; *(fig.)* zu
Ansehen ~: gain esteem
**gelassen** 1. 2. *Part. v.* lassen; 2. *Adj.*
calm; *(gefaßt)* composed; **Gelassenheit** die; ~: calmness; *(Gefaßtheit)* composure
**Gelatine** [ʒela'tiːnə] die; ~: gelatine
**gelaufen** 2. *Part. v.* laufen
**geläufig** *Adj.* (vertraut) common ⟨*expression, concept*⟩
**gelaunt** gut/schlecht ~ sein be in a
good/bad mood
**gelb** *Adj.* yellow; **Gelb** das; ~s, ~ *od.*
(ugs.) ~s yellow; **gelblich** *Adj.* yellowish; yellowed ⟨*paper*⟩; sallow
⟨*skin*⟩; **Gelb·sucht** die; *o. Pl. (Med.)*
jaundice

**Geld** das; ~es, ~er money; **großes** ~:
large denominations *pl.*; **kleines/bares** ~: change/cash
**geld**-, **Geld**-: ~**automat** der cash
dispenser ~**beutel** der *(bes. südd.)*
purse; ~**börse** die purse; ~**gier** die
avarice; ~**gierig** *Adj.* avaricious;
~**mittel** *Pl.* financial resources;
~**schein** der banknote; bill *(Amer.)*;
~**schrank** der safe; ~**strafe** die
fine; ~**stück** das coin; ~**wechsel**
der exchanging of money; „~**wechsel**" 'bureau de change'
**Gelee** [ʒe'leː] der *od.* das; ~s, ~s jelly
**gelegen** 1. 2. *Part. v.* liegen; 2. *Adj.* a)
*(passend)* convenient; **Gelegenheit**
die; ~, ~en opportunity; *(Anlaß)* occasion
**Gelegenheits**-: ~**arbeit** die casual
work; ~**kauf** der bargain
**gelegentlich** 1. *Adj.* occasional; 2.
*adv.* occasionally
**gelehrig** *Adj.* ⟨*child*⟩ who is quick to
learn; ⟨*animal*⟩ that is quick to learn;
**gelehrt** *Adj.* learned; **Gelehrte** der/
die; *adj. Dekl.* scholar
**Geleit** das; ~[e]s, ~e *(geh.)* sie bot uns
ihr ~ an she offered to accompany us;
**geleiten** *tr. V. (geh.)* escort; **Geleit·schutz** der *(Milit.)* escort
**Gelenk** das; ~[e]s, ~e joint; **gelenkig**
1. *Adj.* agile ⟨*person*⟩; supple ⟨*limb*⟩;
2. *adv.* agilely; **Gelenkigkeit** die; ~:
agility; *(von Gliedmaßen)* suppleness
**gelernt** *Adj.* qualified
**gelesen** 2. *Part. v.* lesen
**Geliebte** der/die; *adj. Dekl.* lover/
mistress
**geliefert** *Adj.:* ~ sein *(salopp)* have
had it *(coll.)*
**geliehen** 2. *Part. v.* leihen
**gelind[e]** 1. *Adj.* mild; 2. *adv.* mildly;
~e gesagt to put it mildly
**gelingen** *unr. itr. V.*; *mit sein* succeed;
**Gelingen** das; ~s success
**gelitten** 2. *Part. v.* leiden
**gellen** *itr. V.* a) *(hell schallen)* ring out;
b) *(nachhallen)* ring
**geloben** *tr. V. (geh.)* vow; **das Gelobte
Land** the Promised Land
**gelogen** 2. *Part. v.* lügen
**gelöst** *Adj.* relaxed
**gelten** 1. *unr. itr. V.* a) *(gültig sein)* be
valid; ⟨*banknote, coin*⟩ be legal tender; ⟨*law etc.*⟩ be in force; b) *(angesehen werden)* als etw. ~: be regarded as
sth.; c) (+ *Dat.*) *(bestimmt sein für)* be
directed at; 2. *unr. tr. V.* a) *(wert sein)*
sein Wort gilt viel/wenig his word car

ries a lot of/little weight; **b)** *unpers.* es gilt, etw. zu tun it is essential to do sth.; **geltend: etw. ~ machen** assert sth.; **Geltung die; ~ a)** validity; für jmdn. **~ haben** apply to sb.; **b)** *(Wirkung)* recognition; **zur ~ kommen** show to [its best] advantage; **Geltungs·bedürfnis das** need for recognition

**gelungen 1.** *2. Part. v.* gelingen; **2.** *Adj.* **a)** *(ugs.: spaßig)* priceless; **b)** *(ansprechend)* inspired

**gemächlich** [gə'mɛ(:)çlıç] **1.** *Adj.* leisurely; **2.** *adv.* in a leisurely manner

**gemacht** *in ein* ~**er Mann sein** *(ugs.)* be a made man

**Gemahl der; ~s, ~e** *(geh.)* consort; husband; **Gemahlin die; ~, ~nen** *(geh.)* consort; wife

**Gemälde das; ~s, ~:** painting

**gemäß** *Präp. + Dat.* in accordance with

**gemäßigt** *Adj.* moderate; qualified ⟨*optimism*⟩; temperate ⟨*climate*⟩

**gemein 1.** *Adj.* **a)** vulgar ⟨*joke, expression*⟩; nasty ⟨*person*⟩; **b)** *(niederträchtig)* mean; dirty ⟨*lie*⟩; mean ⟨*trick*⟩; **2.** *adv.* in a mean *or* nasty way

**Gemeinde die; ~, ~n a)** municipality; *(Bewohner)* community; **b)** *(Pfarr~)* parish; **c)** *(versammelte Gottesdienstteilnahme)* congregation

**Gemeinde-: ~rat der a)** *(Gremium)* local council; **b)** *(Mitglied)* local councillor; **~schwester die** district nurse; **~verwaltung die** local administration

**gemein·gefährlich** *Adj.* dangerous to the public; **Gemein·gut das;** *o. Pl. (geh.)* common property

**Gemeinheit die; ~, ~en a)** *o. Pl.* meanness; **b)** *(Handlung)* mean trick

**gemein·nützig** *Adj.* serving the public good *postpos., not pred.; (wohltätig)* charitable

**gemeinsam 1.** *Adj.* **a)** common ⟨*interests, characteristics*⟩; mutual ⟨*acquaintance, friend*⟩; joint ⟨*property, account*⟩; shared ⟨*experience*⟩; **b)** *(miteinander unternommen)* joint; **2.** *adv.* together; **Gemeinsamkeit die; ~, ~en** common feature

**Gemeinschaft die; ~, ~en a)** community; **b)** *o. Pl. (Verbundenheit)* coexistence; **gemeinschaftlich** *s.* gemeinsam

**gemein·verständlich** *Adj.* generally comprehensible; **Gemein·wohl das** public good

**gemessen 1.** *2. Part. v.* messen; **2.** *Adj. (würdevoll)* measured ⟨*steps, tones, language*⟩; deliberate ⟨*words, manner of speaking*⟩

**Gemetzel das; ~s, ~:** massacre

**gemieden** *2. Part. v.* meiden

**Gemisch das; ~|e|s, ~e** mixture **(aus, von** of)

**gemocht** *2. Part. v.* mögen

**gemolken** *2. Part. v.* melken

**Gemse die; ~, ~n** chamois

**Gemurmel das; ~s** murmuring

**Gemüse das; ~s, ~:** vegetables *pl.*

**gemußt** *2. Part. v.* müssen

**Gemüt das; ~|e|s, ~er a)** nature; **b)** *(Empfindungsvermögen)* heart; **c)** *(Mensch)* soul

**gemütlich 1.** *Adj.* snug; cosy; *(bequem)* comfortable; *(ungezwungen)* informal; **2.** *adv.* cosily; *(bequem)* comfortably; **~ beisammensitzen** sit pleasantly together; **Gemütlichkeit die; ~:** snugness; *(Zwanglosigkeit)* informality

**gemüts·krank** *Adj. (Med., Psych.)* emotionally disturbed; **Gemüts·mensch der** *(ugs.)* even-tempered person; **gemüt·voll** *Adj.* warm-hearted; *(empfindsam)* sentimental

**Gen das; ~s, ~e** *(Biol.)* gene

**genannt** *2. Part. v.* nennen

**genas** *1. u. 3. Pers. Sg. Prät. v.* genesen

**genau 1.** *Adj.* **a)** *(exakt)* exact; precise; **b)** *(sorgfältig, gründlich)* meticulous, ⟨*person*⟩; careful ⟨*study*⟩; **2.** *adv.* **a)** exactly; precisely; **~ um 8⁰⁰** at 8 o'clock precisely; **b)** *(gerade, eben)* just; **c)** *(als Verstärkung)* just; **d)** *(als Zustimmung)* exactly; precisely; **e)** *(sorgfältig)* **~ arbeiten/etw. ~ durchdenken** work/think sth. out meticulously

**genau·genommen** *Adv.* strictly speaking

**Genauigkeit die; ~ a)** *(Exaktheit)* exactness; precision; *(einer Waage)* accuracy; *(Sorgfalt)* meticulousness; **genau·so** *Adv.* **a)** *mit Adjektiven* just as; **b)** *mit Verben* in exactly the same way; *(in demselben Maße)* just as much

**genehm** *Adj. in* jmdm. **~ sein** *(geh.) (jmdm. passen)* be convenient to sb.; *(jmdm. angenehm sein)* be acceptable to sb.

**genehmigen** *tr. V.* approve ⟨*plan, alterations, application*⟩; authorize ⟨*stay*⟩; grant ⟨*request*⟩; give per-

mission for ⟨*demonstration*⟩; **sich**
*(Dat.)* **etw. ~** *(ugs.)* treat oneself to
sth.; **Genehmigung** die; ~, ~en a) *s.*
**genehmigen**; approval; authorization;
granting; permission (*Gen.* for); b)
*(Schriftstück)* permit; *(Lizenz)* licence
**geneigt** *Adj.* **in ~ sein, etw. zu tun** be
inclined to do sth.
**General** der; ~s, ~e *od.* **Generäle**
general
**General-:** ~**direktor** der chairman;
president *(Amer.)*; ~**probe** die *(auch
fig.)* dress rehearsal; ~**streik** der general strike; ~**vertreter** der general
representative
**Generation** die; ~, ~en generation;
**Generations·konflikt** der generation gap
**Generator** der; ~s, ~en generator
**generell** 1. *Adj.* general; 2. *adv.*
generally
**genesen** *unr. itr. V.; mit sein (geh.)* recover; **Genesung** die; ~, ~en *(geh.)*
recovery
**genetisch** *(Biol.) Adj.* genetic
**Genf** (das); ~s Geneva; **Genfer** 1.
der; ~s, ~: Genevese; 2. *Adj.* Genevese; **der ~ See** Lake Geneva
**genial** *Adj.* brilliant; **Genialität** die;
~: genius
**Genick** das; ~[e]s, ~e back *or* nape of
the neck
**Genie** [ʒe'niː] das; ~s, ~s genius
**genieren** [ʒe'niːrən] *refl. V.* be embarrassed
**genießbar** *Adj.* *(eßbar)* edible; *(trinkbar)* drinkable; **genießen** *unr. tr. V.*
enjoy; **Genießer** der; ~s, ~: **er ist ein
richtiger ~:** he is a regular 'bon vi-
veur'
**Genitale** das; ~s, **Genitalien** [geni'taː-
liən], **Genital·organ** das genital
organ
**Genitiv** der; ~s, ~e *(Sprachw.)* gen-
itive [case]
**genommen** 2. *Part. v.* **nehmen**
**genoß** *1. u. 3. Pers. Sg. Prät. v.* **genießen**
**Genosse** der; ~n, ~n comrade
**genossen** 2. *Part. v.* **genießen**
**Genossenschaft** die; ~, ~en co-
operative; **Genossin** die; ~, ~nen
comrade
**genug** *Adv.* enough
**genügen** *itr. V.* a) be enough; b) **einer
Sache** *(Dat.)* ~: satisfy sth.; **genügend** 1. *Adj.* a) enough; b) *(befriedigend)* satisfactory; 2. *adv.* enough;
**genügsam** *Adj.* modest

**Genugtuung** [-tuːʊŋ] die; ~, ~en satisfaction
**Genus** das; ~, **Genera** *(Sprachw.)* gender
**Genuß** der; **Genusses, Genüsse** a) *o.
Pl.* consumption; b) *(Wohlbehagen)*
**etw. mit ~ essen/lesen** eat sth. with
relish/enjoy reading sth.
**genüßlich** *Adv.* ⟨*eat, drink*⟩ with relish
**Geograph** der; ~en, ~en geographer;
**Geographie** die; ~: geography *no
art.;* **geographisch** *Adj.* geo-
graphic[al]
**Geologe** der; ~n, ~n geologist; **Geologie** die; ~: geology *no art.;* **geologisch** *Adj.* geological
**Geometrie** die; ~: geometry *no art.;*
**geometrisch** *Adj.* geometric[al]
**Gepäck** das; ~[e]s luggage *(Brit.)*;
baggage *(Amer.)*; *(am Flughafen)* baggage
**Gepäck-:** ~**annahme** die a) checking in the luggage/baggage; b) *(Schalter)* [in-counter of the] luggage office
*(Brit.)* or baggage office *(Amer.)*; *(zur
Aufbewahrung)* [in-counter of the]
left-luggage office *(Brit.)* or checkroom *(Amer.)*; *(am Flughafen)* baggage check-in; ~**aufbewahrung** die
left-luggage office *(Brit.)*; checkroom
*(Amer.)*; *(Schließfächer)* luggage
lockers *(Brit.)*; baggage lockers
*(Amer.)*; ~**ausgabe** die [out-counter
of the] luggage office *(Brit.) or (Amer.)*
baggage office; *(zur Aufbewahrung)*
[out-counter of the] left-luggage office
*(Brit.)* or *(Amer.)* checkroom; *(am
Flughafen)* baggage reclaim; ~**kontrolle** die baggage check; ~**netz** das
luggage rack *(Brit.)*; baggage rack
*(Amer.)* ~**schalter** der s. ~**annahme**
b; ~**schein** der luggage ticket *(Brit.)*,
baggage check *(Amer.)*; ~**träger** der
a) porter; b) *(am Fahrrad)* carrier;
rack
**gepfeffert** *Adj.* *(ugs.)* steep *(coll.*
⟨*price, rent, etc.*⟩
**gepfiffen** 2. *Part. v.* **pfeifen**
**gepflegt** *Adj.* a) well-groomed spruce
⟨*appearance*⟩; neat ⟨*clothing*⟩; b)
*(hochwertig)* choice ⟨*food, drink*⟩
**Gepflogenheit** die; ~, ~en *(geh.)*
custom; *(Gewohnheit)* habit
**gepriesen** 2. *Part. v.* **preisen**
**gequält** *Adj.* forced ⟨*smile, gaiety*⟩,
pained ⟨*expression*⟩
**gequollen** 2. *Part. v.* **quellen**
**gerade,** *(ugs.)* **grade** 1. *Adj.* a)

straight; **b)** *(nicht schief)* upright; **c)** *(aufrichtig)* forthright; direct; **d)** *(Math.)* even ⟨*number*⟩; **2.** *Adv.* just; *(direkt)* right; **Gerade die; ~n, ~n** *(Geom.)* straight line

**gerade-: ~aus** *Adv.* straight ahead; **~|biegen** *unr. tr. V.* **a)** bend straight; straighten [out]; **b)** *(ugs.: bereinigen)* straighten out; **~heraus** [----'-] *(ugs.)* *Adv.* etw. ~heraus **sagen** say sth. straight out; **~so** *Adv.* **~so groß/lang wie ...**: just as big/long as ...; **~|stehen** *unr. itr. V.* **a)** stand up straight; **b)** *(fig.: einstehen)* für etw. ~stehen accept responsibility for sth.; **~zu** *Adv.* really; *(beinahe)* almost

**Geranie** [ge'ra:niǝ] **die; ~, ~n** geranium

**gerann** *3. Pers. Sg. Prät. v.* **gerinnen**

**gerannt** *2. Part. v.* **rennen**

**gerät** *3. Pers. Sg. Präsens v.* **geraten**

**Gerät das; ~|e|s, ~e a)** piece of equipment; *(Fernseher, Radio)* set; *(Garten~)* tool; **b)** *(Turnen)* piece of apparatus

**¹geraten** *unr. itr. V.; mit sein* **a)** *(gelangen)* get; **b)** *(werden)* turn out; *(gut~)* turn out well

**²geraten 1.** *2. Part. v.* **raten, ¹geraten; 2.** *Adj.* advisable

**Geratewohl: aufs ~** *(ugs.)* ⟨*select*⟩ at random; **wir fuhren aufs ~ los** *(ugs.)* we went for a drive just to see where we ended up

**gerät** *3. Pers. Sg. Präsens v.* **¹geraten**

**geraum** *Adj. (geh.)* considerable

**geräumig** *Adj.* spacious ⟨*room*⟩; roomy ⟨*cupboard etc.*⟩

**Geräusch das; ~|e|s, ~e** sound; *(unerwünscht)* noise

**geräusch-: ~arm 1.** *Adj.* quiet; **2.** *adv.* quietly **~los 1.** *Adj.* silent; **2.** *adv.* **a)** silently; **b)** *(fig. ugs.)* without [any] fuss; **~voll** *Adj.* noisy

**gerben** *tr. V.* tan ⟨*hides, skins*⟩

**gerecht 1.** *Adj.* just *(unparteiisch)* fair; **2.** *adv.* justly

**gerechtfertigt** *Adj.* justified

**Gerechtigkeit die; ~**: justice; **Gerechtigkeits·sinn der** sense of justice

**Gerede das; ~s** *(abwertend)* **a)** *(ugs.)* talk; **b)** *(Klatsch)* gossip

**geregelt** *Adj.* regular, steady ⟨*job*⟩

**gereizt** *Adj.* irritable

**¹Gericht das; ~|e|s, ~e** court; *(Richter)* bench; *(Gebäude)* court[-house]; **das Jüngste ~** *(Rel.)* the Last Judgement

**²Gericht das; ~|e|s, ~e** dish

**gerichtlich 1.** *Adj.* judicial; legal ⟨*proceedings*⟩; **2.** *adv.* jmdn. ~ **verfolgen** take sb. to court

**Gerichts-: ~hof der** Court of Justice; **~kosten** *Pl.* legal costs; **~saal der** courtroom; **~verfahren das** legal proceedings *pl.*; **~vollzieher der; ~s, ~**: bailiff

**gerieben** *2. Part. v.* **reiben**

**gering** *Adj.* **a)** low; little ⟨*value*⟩; small ⟨*quantity, amount*⟩; short ⟨*distance, time*⟩; **b)** *(unbedeutend)* slight; minor ⟨*role*⟩

**geringfügig 1.** *Adj.* slight; minor ⟨*alteration, injury*⟩; trivial ⟨*amount, detail*⟩; **2.** *adv.* slightly; **Geringfügigkeit die; ~, ~en** triviality; **gering|-schätzen** *tr. V.* think very little of ⟨*person, achievement*⟩; set little store by ⟨*success, riches*⟩; **geringschätzig** *Adj.* disdainful; disparaging ⟨*remark*⟩

**gerinnen** *unr. itr. V.; mit sein* ⟨*blood*⟩ clot; ⟨*milk*⟩ curdle

**Gerippe das; ~s, ~**: skeleton

**gerippt** *Adj.* ribbed; fluted ⟨*glass, column*⟩

**gerissen 1.** *2. Part. v.* **reißen; 2.** *Adj.* *(ugs.)* crafty

**geritten** *2. Part. v.* **reiten**

**Germane der; ~n, ~n** *(hist.)* ancient German; Teuton; **germanisch** *Adj.* *(auch fig.)* Germanic; Teutonic; **Germanistik die; ~**: German studies *pl.*, no art.

**gern[e]; lieber, am liebsten** *Adv.* **a)** etw. ~ **tun** like *or* enjoy doing sth.; **er spielt lieber Tennis als Golf** he prefers playing tennis to golf; **etw. ~/am liebsten essen** like sth./like sth. best; **ja, ~/aber ~**: yes, of course; certainly!; **b)** *(durchaus)* **das glaube ich ~**: I can well believe that

**gerochen** *2. Part. v.* **riechen**

**Geröll das; ~s, ~e** debris; *(größer)* boulders *pl.*

**geronnen** *2. Part. v.* **rinnen, gerinnen**

**Gerste die; ~**: barley; **Gersten-korn das** *(Med.)* sty

**Gerte die; ~, ~n** switch

**Geruch der; ~|e|s, Gerüche** smell; *(von Blumen)* scent

**Gerücht das; ~|e|s, ~e** rumour

**gerufen** *2. Part. v.* **rufen**

**geruhsam 1.** *Adj.* peaceful; leisurely ⟨*stroll*⟩; **2.** *adv.* leisurely; quietly

**Gerümpel das; ~s** junk

**gerungen** *2. Part. v.* **ringen**

**Gerüst das; ~|e|s, ~e** scaffolding *no pl., no indef. art.*

**gesamt** *Adj.*whole; entire; **gesamt-deutsch** *Adj.* all-German; **Gesamt·eindruck der** general impression; **Gesamtheit die: die ~ der Bevölkerung** the entire population **Gesamt-:** ~**schule die** comprehensive [school]; ~**werk das** œuvre; *(Bücher)* complete works *pl.*
**gesandt** *2. Part. v.* **senden**
**Gesandte der/die;** *adj. Dekl.* envoy; **Gesandtschaft die;** ~, ~**en** legation
**Gesang der;** ~|e|s, **Gesänge a)** singing; **b)** *(Lied)* song
**Gesang-:** ~**buch das** hymn-book; ~**verein der** choral society
**Gesäß das;** ~**es,** ~**e** backside; buttocks *pl.*
**geschaffen** *2. Part. v.* **schaffen 1**
**Geschäft das;** ~|e|s, ~**e a)** business; *(Transaktion)* [business] deal; **ein gutes ~ machen** make a good profit; **b)** *(Laden)* shop; store *(Amer.)*
**Geschäfte·macher der** *(abwertend)* profit-seeker
**geschäftig** *Adj.* bustling
**geschäftlich 1.** *Adj.* business *attrib.;* **2.** *adv.* on business
**geschäfts-, Geschäfts-:** ~**freund der** business associate; ~**führer der** manager; *(Vereinswesen)* secretary; ~**führung die;** *o. Pl.* management; ~**inhaber der** owner of the/a business; ~**jahr das** financial year; ~**kosten** *Pl.* **auf** ~**kosten** on expenses; ~**lage die** [business] position; ~**leitung die** *s.* ~**führung;** ~**leute** *s.* ~**mann;** ~**mann der;** *Pl.* ~**leute** businessman; ~**ordnung die** standing orders *pl.; (im Parlament)* [rules *pl.* of] procedure; ~**partner der** business partner; ~**reise die** business trip; ~**schluß der** closing-time; ~**stelle die** branch; *(einer Partei, eines Vereins)* office; ~**straße die** shopping-street; ~**tüchtig** *Adj.* able, ⟨*businessman, landlord, etc.*⟩; ~**viertel das** business quarter; *(Einkaufszentrum)* shopping district; ~**wagen der** company car; ~**zeit die** business hours *pl.; (im Büro)* office hours *pl.*
**geschah** *3. Pers. Sg. Prät. v.* **geschehen**
**geschehen** *unr. itr. V.; mit sein* happen; occur; *(ausgeführt werden)* be done; **jmdm. geschieht etw.** sth. happens to sb.
**gescheit** *Adj.* **a)** *(intelligent)* clever; **b)** *(ugs.: vernünftig)* sensible
**Geschenk das;** ~|e|s, ~**e** present; gift

**Geschenk-:** ~**artikel der** gift; ~**packung die** gift pack
**Geschichte die;** ~, ~**n a)** history; **b)** *(Erzählung)* story; **geschichtlich** *Adj.* **a)** historical; **b)** *(bedeutungsvoll)* historic
¹**Geschick das;** ~|e|s, ~**e** *(geh.)* fate
²**Geschick das;** ~|e|s skill; **Geschicklichkeit die;** ~: skilfulness; skill; **geschickt 1.** *Adj.* **a)** skilful; **b)** *(klug)* clever; adroit; **2.** *adv.* **a)** *(gewandt)* skilfully; **b)** *(klug)* cleverly; adroitly
**geschieden** *2. Part. v.* **scheiden**
**geschienen** *2. Part. v.* **scheinen**
**Geschirr das;** ~|e|s, ~**e a)** crockery; *(benutzt)* dishes *pl.;* **b)** *(für Zugtier)* harness
**Geschirr-:** ~**spül·maschine die** dishwasher; ~**tuch das;** *Pl.* -**tücher** tea-towel; dish towel *(Amer.)*
**geschissen** *2. Part. v.* **scheißen**
**geschlafen** *2. Part. v.* **schlafen**
**geschlagen** *2. Part. v.* **schlagen**
**Geschlecht das;** ~|e|s, ~**er a)** sex; **b)** *(Generation)* generation; **c)** *(Sippe)* family; **d)** *(Sprachw.)* gender; **geschlechtlich** *Adj.* sexual
**geschlechts-, Geschlechts-:** ~**krank** *Adj.* ⟨person⟩ suffering from VD; ~**krankheit die** venereal disease; ~**teil das** genitals *pl.;* ~**verkehr der** sexual intercourse; ~**wort das** *s.* **Artikel a**
**geschlichen** *2. Part. v.* **schleichen**
**geschliffen 1.** *2. Part. v.* **schleifen; 2.** *Adj.* polished
**geschlossen 1.** *2. Part. v.* **schließen; 2.** *Adj.* united ⟨*action, front*⟩; unified ⟨*procedure*⟩; **eine** ~**e Ortschaft** a built-up area
**geschlungen** *2. Part. v.* **schlingen**
**Geschmack der;** ~|e|s, **Geschmäcke** taste; **geschmacklos 1.** *Adj.* tasteless; **2.** *adv.* tastelessly; **Geschmacklosigkeit die;** ~, ~**en** lack of [good] taste; bad taste; *(Äußerung)* tasteless remark; **Geschmack[s]·sache die in das ist** ~: that is a question *or* matter of taste
**geschmack·voll 1.** *Adj.* tasteful. **2.** *adv.* tastefully
**Geschmeide das;** ~**s,** ~ *(geh.)* jewellery *no pl.*
**geschmeidig 1.** *Adj.* **a)** sleek ⟨*hair, fur*⟩; soft ⟨*leather, boots, skin*⟩; **b)** *(gelenkig)* supple ⟨*fingers*⟩; lithe ⟨*body, movement, person*⟩; **2.** *adv. (gelenkig)* agilely

**geschmịssen** 2. *Part. v.* **schmeißen**
**geschmọlzen** 2. *Part. v.* **schmelzen**
**Geschnẹtzelte** das; *adj. Dekl.: small, thin slices of meat [cooked in sauce]*
**geschnịtten** 2. *Part. v.* **schneiden**
**geschọben** 2. *Part. v.* **schieben**
**geschọllen** 2. *Part. v.* **schallen**
**geschọlten** 2. *Part. v.* **schelten**
**Geschọ̈pf** das; ~|e|s, ~e creature
**geschọren** 2. *Part. v.* **scheren**
**¹Geschọß** das; **Geschọsses, Geschọsse** projectile; *(Kugel)* bullet; *(Rakete)* missile
**²Geschọß** das; **Geschọsses, Geschọsse** floor; storey
**geschọssen** 2. *Part. v.* **schießen**
**Geschrẹi** das; ~s a) shouting; *(von Verletzten, Tieren)* screaming; screams *pl.; (ugs. fig)* fuss
**geschrịeben** 2. *Part. v.* **schreiben**
**geschrịe[e]n** 2. *Part. v.* **schreien**
**geschrịtten** 2. *Part. v.* **schreiten**
**geschụnden** 2. *Part. v.* **schinden**
**Geschụ̈tz** das; ~es, ~e [big] gun; **Geschụ̈tz·feuer** das artillery-fire; shell-fire
**geschụ̈tzt** *Adj.* sheltered
**Geschwạder** das; ~s, ~ *(Marine)* squadron; *(Luftwaffe)* wing *(Brit.)*; group *(Amer.)*
**Geschwạ̈tz** das; ~es *(ugs. abwertend)* prattling; *(Klatsch)* gossip; **geschwạ̈tzig** *Adj. (abwertend)* talkative
**geschwịegen** 2. *Part. v.* **schweigen**
**geschwịnd** *(bes. südd.)* 1. *Adj.* swift; quick; 2. *adv.* swiftly; quickly
**Geschwịndigkeit** die; ~, ~en speed
**Geschwịndigkeits-:** **~begrenzung** die, **~beschränkung** die speed limit
**Geschwịster** *Pl.* brothers and sisters
**geschwọllen** 1. 2. *Part. v.* **schwellen**; 2. *Adj.* a) swollen; b) *(fig. abwertend)* pompous; 3. *adv.* pompously
**geschwọmmen** 2. *Part. v.* **schwimmen**
**geschwọren** 2. *Part. v.* **schwören**; **Geschwọrene** der/die; *adj. Dekl.* juror
**Geschwụlst** die; ~, **Geschwụlste** tumour
**geschwụnden** 2. *Part. v.* **schwinden**
**geschwụngen** 1. 2. *Part. v.* **schwingen**; 2. *Adj.* curved
**Geschwụ̈r** das; ~s, ~e ulcer; *(Furunkel)* boil
**gesẹhen** 2. *Part v. sehen*

**Gesẹlle** der; ~n, ~n journeyman; *(Kerl)* fellow; **gesẹllen** *refl. V.* sich zu jmdm. ~: join sb.; **gesẹllig** *Adj.* sociable; ein ~er Abend/~es Beisammensein a convivial evening/a friendly get-together; **Gesẹlligkeit** die; ~: die ~ lieben enjoy [good] company
**Gesẹllschaft** die; ~, ~en a) society; b) *(Veranstaltung)* party; c) *(Kreis von Menschen)* group of people; d) *(Wirtschaft)* company; **Gesẹllschafter** der; ~s, ~ a) ein guter ~ sein be good company; b) *(Wirtsch.)* partner; *(Teilhaber)* shareholder; **Gesẹllschafterin** die; ~, ~nen a) [lady] companion; b) *(Wirtsch.)* partner; *(Teilhaber)* shareholder; **gesẹllschaftlich** *Adj.* social
**gesẹllschafts-, Gesẹllschafts-:** **~fähig** *Adj. (auch fig.)* socially acceptable; **~ordnung** die social order; **~reise** die group tour; **~schicht** die stratum of society; **~spiel** das party game
**gesẹssen** 2. *Part. v.* **sitzen**
**Gesẹtz** das; ~es, ~e a) law; *(geschrieben)* statute; b) *(Regel)* rule
**Gesẹtz-:** **~buch** das statute-book; **~geber** der legislator; *(Organ)* legislature; **~gebung** die; ~: legislation
**gesẹtzlich** 1. *Adj.* legal; statutory ⟨holiday⟩; lawful ⟨heir, claim⟩; 2. *adv.* legally; **gesẹtz·mäßig** 1. *Adj.* a) law-governed; ~ sein be governed by or obey a [natural] law/[natural] laws; b) *(gesetzlich)* legal; *(rechtmäßig)* lawful; 2. *adv.* in accordance with a [natural] law/[natural] laws; **Gesẹtz·mäßigkeit** die a) conformity to a [natural] law/[natural] laws; b) *(Gesetzlichkeit)* legality; *(Rechtmäßigkeit)* lawfulness
**gesẹtzt** *Adj.* staid
**gesẹtz·widrig** *Adj.* illegal; unlawful
**Gesịcht** das; ~|e|s, ~er face; *(fig.)* das ~ einer Stadt the appearance of a town
**Gesịchts-:** **~ausdruck** der expression; look; **~creme** die face-cream; **~punkt** der point of view; **~wasser** das face-lotion; **~züge** *Pl.* features
**Gesịndel** das; ~s *(abwertend)* rabble
**gesịnnt** *Adj.* christlich/sozial ~ |sein| [be] Christian-minded/public-spirited; jmdm. freundlich ~ sein be well-disposed towards sb.; **Gesịnnung** die; ~, ~en [basic] convictions *pl.;* [fundamental] beliefs *pl.;* **gesịn-**

**nungs·los** *(abwertend) Adj.* unprincipled; **Gesinnungs·wandel** der change of attitude

**gesittet 1.** *Adj.* well-behaved; well-mannered

**gesogen** 2. *Part. v.* **saugen**

**gesondert 1.** *Adj.* separate; **2.** *adv.* separately

**gesonnen** *Adj.* ~ **sein, etw. zu tun** feel disposed to do sth.

**gesotten** 2. *Part. v.* **sieden**

**Gespann** das; ~[e]s, ~e a) *(Zugtiere)* team; b) *(Wagen)* horse and carriage; c) *(Menschen)* couple; pair

**gespannt** *Adj.* a) eager; rapt ⟨attention⟩; ~ **zuhören** listen with rapt attention; b) tense ⟨situation, atmosphere⟩; strained ⟨relationships⟩

**Gespenst** das; ~[e]s, ~er a) ghost; b) *(geh.: Gefahr)* spectre

**gespenstig, gespenstisch** *Adj.* ghostly; eerie ⟨building, atmosphere⟩

**gespie[e]n** 2. *Part. v.* **speien**

**gesponnen** 2. *Part. v.* **spinnen**

**Gespött** das; ~[e]s mockery; ridicule

**Gespräch** das; ~[e]s, ~e conversation; *(Diskussion)* discussion; *(Telefon~)* call (mit to); **gesprächig** *Adj.* talkative

**Gesprächs-:** ~**partner** der: mein heutiger ~**partner wird X sein** today I shall be talking to X; ~**stoff** der topics *pl.* of conversation; ~**thema** das topic of conversation

**gesprochen** 2. *Part. v.* **sprechen**

**gesprossen** 2. *Part. v.* **sprießen**

**gesprungen** 2. *Part. v.* **springen**

**Gespür** das; ~s feel

**gest.** *Abk.* **gestorben** d.

**Gestalt** die; ~, ~en a) build; b) *(Mensch, Persönlichkeit)* figure; c) *(in der Dichtung)* character; d) *(Form)* form; **gestalten** *tr. V.* fashion; lay out ⟨public gardens⟩; shape ⟨character, personality⟩; arrange ⟨party, conference, etc.⟩; **Gestaltung** die; ~, ~en s. **gestalten**: fashioning; laying out; arranging

**gestand** *1. u. 3. Pers. Sg. Prät. v.* **gestehen**

**gestanden** 2. *Part. v.* **stehen, gestehen**

**geständig** *Adj.:* ~ **sein** have confessed; **Geständnis** das; ~ses, ~se confession

**Gestank** der; ~[e]s *(abwertend)* stench; stink

**gestatten 1.** *tr., itr. V.* permit; allow; ~ **Sie, daß ich ...:** may I ...?; **2.** *refl. V.* sich *(Dat.)* etw. ~: allow oneself sth.

**Geste** ['gɛstə, 'geːstə] die; ~, ~n *(auch fig.)* gesture

**Gesteck** das; ~[e]s, ~e flower arrangement

**gestehen** *tr., itr. V.* confess

**Gestein** das; ~[e]s, ~e rock

**Gestell** das; ~[e]s, ~e a) *(für Weinflaschen)* rack; *(zum Wäschetrocknen)* horse; b) *(Unterbau)* frame

**gestern** *Adv.* yesterday

**gestiegen** 2. *Part. v.* **steigen**

**gestikulieren** *itr. V.* gesticulate

**Gestirn** das; ~[e]s, ~e star

**gestochen 1.** 2. *Part. v.* **stechen; 2.** *Adj.* extremely neat ⟨handwriting⟩

**gestohlen** 2. *Part. v.* **stehlen**

**gestorben** 2. *Part. v.* **sterben**

**gestoßen** 2. *Part. v.* **stoßen**

**Gesträuch** das; ~[e]s, ~e shrubbery; bushes *pl.*

**gestreift** *Adj.* striped

**gestrichen 1.** 2. *Part. v.* **streichen; 2.** *Adj.* level ⟨measure⟩

**gestrig** *Adj.* yesterday's

**gestritten** 2. *Part. v.* **streiten**

**Gestrüpp** das; ~[e]s, ~e undergrowth

**gestunken** 2. *Part. v.* **stinken**

**Gestüt** das; ~[e]s, ~e stud[-farm]

**Gesuch** das; ~[e]s, ~e request (um for); *(Antrag)* application (um for); **gesucht** *Adj.* a) [much] sought-after; b) *(gekünstelt)* laboured

**gesund; gesünder, seltener: ~er, gesündest..., seltener: ~est...** *Adj.* healthy; wieder ~ **werden** get better; **bleib** ~! look after yourself!; **Gesundheit** die; ~: health; ~! *(ugs.)* bless you!; **gesundheitlich 1.** *Adj.; nicht präd.* ~e **Betreuung** health care; **sein** ~er **Zustand** [the state of] his health; **2.** *adv.* **wie geht es Ihnen** ~? how are you?

**gesundheits-, Gesundheits-:** ~**amt** das [local] public health department; ~**schädlich** *Adj.* detrimental to [one's] health *postpos.*; ~**zeugnis** das certificate of health; ~**zustand** der state of health

**gesungen** 2. *Part. v.* **singen**

**gesunken** 2. *Part. v.* **sinken**

**getan** 2. *Part. v.* **tun**

**Getier** das; ~[e]s *(geh.)* animals *pl.*

**Getöse** das; ~s [thunderous] roar; *(von vielen Menschen)* din

**getragen** 2. *Part. v.* **tragen**

**Getränk** das; ~[e]s, ~e drink; beverage *(formal)*

**getrauen** *refl. V.* dare

**Getreide** das; ~s grain

**Getreide-:** ~**anbau** der growing of cereals; ~**handel** der corn-trade

**getrennt 1.** *Adj.* separate; **2.** *adv.* ⟨*pay*⟩ separately; ⟨*sleep*⟩ in separate rooms

**getreten** *2. Part. v.* **treten**

**getreu 1.** *Adj. (geh.)* exact; faithful ⟨*image*⟩; **2.** *adv. (geh.)* ⟨*report, describe*⟩ faithfully

**Getriebe** das; ~s, ~ gears *pl.; (in einer Maschine)* gear system; **getrieben** *2. Part. v.* **treiben**

**getroffen** *2. Part. v.* **treffen, triefen**

**getrogen** *2. Part. v.* **trügen**

**getrost 1.** *Adj.* confident; **2.** *adv.* confidently; **du kannst es mir ~ glauben** you can take my word for it

**getrunken** *2. Part. v.* **trinken**

**Getto** das; ~s, ~s ghetto

**Getue** das; ~s *(ugs. abwertend)* fuss (**um** about)

**Getümmel** das; ~s tumult

**geübt** *Adj.* accomplished; practised ⟨*eye, ear*⟩

**Gewächs** das; ~es, ~e plant; **gewachsen 1.** *2. Part. v.* **wachsen; 2. in jmdm./einer Sache ~ sein** be a match for sb./be equal to sth.

**gewagt** *Adj.* daring; *(gefährlich)* risky; *(fast anstößig)* risqué ⟨*joke etc.*⟩

**gewählt** *Adj.* refined; **2.** *adv.* in a refined manner

**Gewähr** die; ~: guarantee; **keine ~ übernehmen** be unable to guarantee sth.; **gewähren** *tr. V.* **a)** grant; give ⟨*pleasure, joy*⟩; **gewähr·leisten** *tr. V.* guarantee

**Gewahrsam** der; ~s **a)** *(Obhut)* safekeeping; **b)** *(Haft)* custody

**Gewährs·mann** der; *Pl.* ~**männer** *od.* ~**leute** informant; source

**Gewalt** die; ~, ~en **a)** power; **b)** *o. Pl. (Willkür)* force; **c)** *o. Pl. (körperliche Kraft)* force; violence; **Gewalt·anwendung** die use of force *or* violence; **Gewalten·teilung** die separation of powers; **gewaltig 1.** *Adj.* **a)** *(immens)* huge; **b)** *(imponierend)* mighty, huge, massive ⟨*building etc*⟩; monumental ⟨*literary work etc.*⟩; **2.** *adv. (ugs.)* very much; **gewalt·los 1.** *Adj.* non-violent; **2.** *adv.* without violence; **Gewalt·losigkeit** die; ~: non-violence; **gewaltsam 1.** *Adj.* forcible ⟨*expulsion*⟩; enforced ⟨*separation*⟩; violent ⟨*death*⟩; **2.** *adv.* forcibly; **gewalt·tätig** *Adj.* violent

**Gewand** das; ~|e|s, **Gewänder** *(geh.)* robe; gown

**gewandt 1.** *2. Part. v.* **wenden; 2.** *Adj.* skilful; *(körperlich)* agile; **3.** *adv.* skilfully; *(körperlich)* agilely; **Gewandtheit** die; ~: *s.* **gewandt 2:** skill; skilfulness; agility

**gewann** *1. u. 3. Pers. Sg. Prät. v.* **gewinnen**

**gewaschen** *2. Part. v.* **waschen**

**Gewässer** das; ~s, ~: stretch of water

**Gewebe** das; ~s, ~ **a)** *(Stoff)* fabric; **b)** *(Med., Biol.)* tissue

**Gewehr** das; ~|e|s, ~e rifle; *(Schrot~)* shotgun

**Geweih** das; ~|e|s, ~e antlers *pl.*

**Gewerbe** das; ~s, ~: business; *(Handel, Handwerk)* trade

**Gewerbe-:** ~**freiheit** die right to carry on a business *or* trade; ~**ordnung** die laws *pl.* governing trade and industry; ~**schein** der licence to carry on a business *or* trade; ~**treibende** der/die; *adj. Dekl.* tradesman/tradeswoman; ~**zweig** der branch of trade

**gewerblich 1.** *Adj.* commercial; business *attrib.; (industriell)* industrial; **2.** *adv.* ~ **tätig sein** work; **gewerbs·mäßig** *Adj.* professional

**Gewerkschaft** die; ~, ~en trade union; **Gewerkschaft[l]er** der; ~s, ~: trade unionist; **gewerkschaftlich 1.** *Adj.* [trade] union *attrib.;* **2.** *adv.:* ~ **organisiert sein** belong to a [trade] union; **Gewerkschaftsfunktionär** der [trade] union official

**gewesen** *2. Part. v.* ¹**sein**

**gewichen** *2. Part. v.* **weichen**

**Gewicht** das; ~|e|s, ~e *(auch fig.)* weight; |**nicht**| **ins ~ fallen** be of [no] consequence; **Gewicht·heben** das; ~s weight-lifting; **gewichtig** *Adj.* weighty; **Gewichts·klasse** die *(Sport)* weight [division *or* class]

**gewieft** *Adj. (ugs.)* cunning

**gewiesen** *2. Part. v.* **weisen**

**gewillt** *Adj.* **in ~** |**nicht**| ~ **sein, etw. zu tun** be [un]willing to do sth.

**Gewimmel** das; ~s throng; *(von Insekten)* teeming mass

**Gewinde** das; ~s, ~ *(Technik)* thread

**Gewinn** der; ~|e|s, ~e **a)** profit; **b)** *(Preis einer Lotterie)* prize; *(beim Spiel)* winnings *pl.;* **c)** *(Sieg)* win; **Gewinn·beteiligung** die *(Wirtsch.)* profit-sharing; *(Betrag)* profit-sharing bonus; **gewinn·bringend** *Adj.* lucrative

**gewinnen 1.** *unr. tr. V.* win; gain

⟨*time, influence, validity, etc.*⟩; **2.** *unr. itr. V.* win (**bei** at); **gewinnend** *Adj.* winning; **Gewinner der**; ~s, ~: winner
**Gewinn-**: ~**spanne** die profit margin; ~**sucht** die greed for profit; ~**zahl** die winning number
**Gewirr** das; ~[e]s **a)** tangle; **b)** *(Durcheinander)* ein ~ von Ästen a maze of branches
**gewiß 1.** *Adj.* certain; **2.** *adv.* certainly
**Gewissen** das; ~s, ~: conscience; **gewissenhaft 1.** *Adj.* conscientious; **2.** *adv.* conscientiously; **gewissen·los** *Adj.* unscrupulous; **Gewissens·bisse** *Pl.* pangs of conscience
**gewissermaßen** *Adv.* *(sozusagen)* as it were; *(in gewissem Sinne)* to a certain extent; **Gewißheit die**; ~, ~en certainty
**Gewitter** das; ~s, ~: thunderstorm; **Gewitter·wolke die** thundercloud; **gewittrig** *Adj.* thundery
**gewitzt** *Adj.* shrewd
**gewoben** *2. Part. v.* weben
**gewogen 1.** *2. Part. v.* wiegen; **2.** *Adj.* *(geh.)* well disposed (+ *Dat.* towards)
**gewöhnen 1.** *tr. V.* jmdn. an jmdn./etw. ~: get sb. used to sb./sth.; accustom sb. to sb./sth.; **2.** *refl. V.* sich an jmdn./etw. ~: get used *or* get *or* become accustomed to sb./sth.; accustom oneself to sb./sth.; **Gewohnheit die**; ~, ~en habit; **gewohnheits·mäßig 1.** *Adj.* habitual ⟨*drinker etc.*⟩; automatic ⟨*reaction etc.*⟩; **2.** *adv.* *(regelmäßig)* habitually; **gewöhnlich 1.** *Adj.* **a)** normal; ordinary; **b)** *(gewohnt, üblich)* usual; **c)** *(abwertend: ordinär)* common; **2.** *adv.* **a)** [für] ~: usually; **wie** ~: as usual; **b)** *(abwertend: ordinär)* in a common way
**gewohnt** *Adj.* **a)** usual; **b)** etw. *(Akk.)* ~ sein be used to sth.
**Gewölbe** das; ~s, ~: vault
**gewonnen** *2. Part. v.* gewinnen
**geworben** *2. Part. v.* werben
**geworfen** *2. Part. v.* werfen
**gewrungen** *2. Part. v.* wringen
**Gewühl** das; ~[e]s milling crowd
**gewunden** *2. Part. v.* winden
**Gewürz** das; ~es, ~e spice; *(würzende Zutat)* seasoning
**Gewürz-**: ~**gurke** die pickled gherkin; ~**nelke** die clove
**gewußt** *2. Part. v.* wissen

**gez.** *Abk.* gezeichnet sgd.
**Gezeiten** *Pl.* tides
**gezielt 1.** *Adj.* specific ⟨*questions, measures, etc.*⟩; deliberate ⟨*insult, indiscretion*⟩; well-directed ⟨*advertising campaign*⟩; **2.** *adv.* ⟨*proceed, act*⟩ purposefully
**geziemen** *(geh. veralt.)* **1.** *itr. V.* jmdm. [nicht] ~: [ill] befit sb; **2.** *refl. V.* be proper; sich für jmdn. ~: befit sb.
**geziert 1.** *Adj.* *(abwertend)* affected; **2.** *adv.* *(abwertend)* affectedly
**gezogen** *2. Part. v.* ziehen
**Gezwitscher** das; ~s twittering
**gezwungen 1.** *2. Part. v.* zwingen; **2.** *Adj.* forced; **gezwungenermaßen** *Adv.* of necessity
**gib** *Imperativ Sg. Präsens v.* geben; **gibst** *2. Pers. Sg. Präsens v.* geben; **gibt** *3. Pers. Sg. Präsens v.* geben
**Gicht** die; ~: gout
**Giebel** der; ~s, ~: gable
**Gier** die; ~: greed (**nach** for); **gierig 1.** *Adj.* greedy; **2.** *adv.* greedily
**gießen 1.** *unr. tr. V.* **a)** pour (**in** + *Akk.* into, **über** + *Akk.* over); **b)** *(verschütten)* spill (**über** + *Akk.* over); **c)** *(begießen)* water; **2.** *(unpers., ugs.)* pour [with rain]
**Gießer** der; ~s, ~: caster; **Gießerei** die; ~, ~en foundry
**Gift** das; ~[e]s, ~e **a)** poison; *(Schlangen~)* venom; **gift·grün** *Adj.* garish green; **giftig** *Adj.* poisonous; venomous ⟨*snake*⟩; toxic, poisonous ⟨*substance, gas, chemical*⟩; *(fig.)* venomous
**Gift-**: ~**müll** der toxic waste; ~**schlange** die venomous snake; ~**zahn** der poison fang
**Gigant** der; ~en, ~en giant; **gigantisch** *Adj.* gigantic
**Gilde** die; ~, ~n *(hist.)* guild
**gilt** *3. Pers. Sg. Präsens v.* gelten
**Gimpel** der; ~s, ~: bullfinch
**Gin** [dʒɪn] der; ~s gin
**ging** *1. u. 3. Pers. Sg. Prät. v.* gehen
**Ginster** der; ~s, ~: broom
**Gipfel** der; ~s, ~: peak; *(höchster Punkt des Berges)* summit; *(fig.)* height; **Gipfel·konferenz die** summit conference; **gipfeln** *itr. V.* in etw. *(Dat.)* ~: culminate in sth.
**Gips** der; ~es, ~e plaster; gypsum *(Chem.)*; **Gips·abdruck der** plaster cast; **gipsen** *tr. V.* plaster; put ⟨*leg, arm, etc.*⟩ in plaster; **Gips·verband** der plaster cast
**Giraffe** die; ~, ~n giraffe

**Girlande** die; ~, ~n festoon
**Giro** ['ʒiːro] das; ~s, ~s, österr. auch
  **Giri** (Finanzw.) giro; **Giro·konto**
  das (Finanzw.) current account
**gis, Gis** das; ~, ~ (Musik) G sharp
**Gischt** der; ~|e|s, ~e od. die; ~, ~en
  spray
**Gitarre** die; ~, ~n guitar
**Gitter** das; ~s, ~: bars pl.; (vor Fen-
  ster-, Türöffnungen) grille; (in der
  Straßendecke, im Fußboden) grating;
  (Geländer) railing[s pl.]; **Gitter·fen-
  ster** das barred window
**Glacé·hand·schuh** [gla'seː...] der
  kid glove
**Gladiole** die; ~, ~n gladiolus
**Glanz** der; ~es a) (von Licht, Sternen,
  Augen) brightness; (von Haar, Metall,
  Perlen, Leder usw.) lustre; sheen; b)
  (der Jugend, Schönheit) radiance; (des
  Adels usw.) splendour; **glänzen** itr.
  V. a) (Glanz ausstrahlen) shine; ⟨hair,
  metal, etc.⟩ gleam; ⟨elbows, trousers,
  etc.⟩ be shiny; b) (Bewunderung erregen) shine (bei at); **glänzend** (ugs.)
  1. Adj. a) shining; gleaming ⟨hair,
  metal, etc.⟩; b) shiny ⟨elbows, trousers,
  etc.⟩; b) (bewundernswert) brilliant;
  splendid ⟨references, marks, results,
  etc.⟩; 2. adv. ~ mit jmdm. auskommen
  get on very well with sb.; **es geht mir/
  uns** ~: I am/we are very well
**glanz-, Glanz-:** ~**leistung** die (auch
  iron.) brilliant performance; ~**los**
  Adj. dull; lacklustre; ~**nummer** die
  star turn; ~**voll** 1. Adj. brilliant;
  sparkling ⟨variety number⟩; 2. adv.
  brilliantly
**Glas** das; ~es, Gläser a) o. Pl. glass; b)
  (Trinkgefäß) glass; zwei ~ od. Gläser
  Wein two glasses of wine; c) (Behälter) jar; **Glas·bläser** der glass-
  blower; **Gläschen** ['glɛːsçən] das;
  ~s, ~ a) [little] glass; b) (kleines Gefäß) [little] [glass] jar; **Glaser** der; ~s,
  ~: glazier; **gläsern** Adj. glass;
  **Glas·faser** die; meist Pl. glass fibre;
  **glasieren** tr. V. a) glaze; b) (Kochk.)
  ice; glaze ⟨meat⟩; **glasig** Adj. a)
  glassy; b) (Kochk.) transparent;
  **Glas·malerei** die stained glass;
  **Glasur** die; ~, ~en a) glaze; b)
  (Kochk.) icing; (auf Fleisch) glaze
**glatt** 1. Adj. a) smooth; (rutschig) slippery; b) (ugs.: offensichtlich) downright ⟨lie⟩; outright ⟨deception, fraud⟩;
  flat ⟨refusal⟩; 2. adv. a) smoothly; b)
  (ugs.: rückhaltlos) jmdm. etw. ~ ins
  Gesicht sagen tell sb. sth. straight to

his/her face; ⟨reject, deny⟩ flatly;
**Glätte** die; ~: smoothness; (Rut-
  schigkeit) slipperiness; **Glatt·eis** das
  glaze; ice; (auf der Straße) black ice;
**glätten** tr. V. smooth out ⟨piece of
  paper, etc.⟩; smooth [down] ⟨feathers,
  fur, etc.⟩; plane ⟨wood etc.⟩
**glatt-:** ~|**gehen** unr. itr. V.; mit sein
  (ugs.) go smoothly; ~**weg** Adv. (ugs.)
  etw. ~**weg** ablehnen/ignorieren turn
  sth. down flat/simply ignore sth.; **das
  ist** ~**weg** erlogen/erfunden that's a
  downright lie/that's pure invention
**Glatze** die; ~, ~n bald head
**Glaube** der; ~ns faith (an + Akk. in);
  (Überzeugung, Meinung) belief (an +
  Akk. in); **glauben** 1. tr. V. (meinen)
  think; 2. itr. V. believe (an + Akk. in)
**Glaubens-:** ~**bekenntnis** das creed;
  ~**freiheit** die; o. Pl. religious freedom
**glaubhaft** 1. Adj. credible; 2. adv.
  convincingly; **gläubig** 1. Adj. devout; (vertrauensvoll) trusting; 2. adv.
  devoutly; (vertrauensvoll) trustingly;
  **Gläubige** der/die; adj. Dekl. be-
  liever; **Gläubiger** der; ~s, ~ creditor
**glaub·würdig** 1. Adj. credible; 2.
  adv. convincingly
**gleich** 1. Adj. a) (identisch, von derselben Art) same; (~berechtigt, ~wertig,
  Math.) equal; b) (ugs.: gleichgültig) es
  ist mir völlig od. ganz ~: I couldn't
  care less (coll.); ganz ~, wer anruft, ...:
  no matter who calls, ...; 2. adv. a)
  (übereinstimmend) ~ groß/alt usw.
  sein be the same height/age etc.; ~
  gut/schlecht usw. equally good/bad
  etc.; b) (in derselben Weise) ~ aufge-
  baut/gekleidet having the same struc-
  ture/wearing identical clothes; c) (sofort) at once; straight away; (bald) in
  a moment; d) (räumlich) right; just; ~
  rechts/links immediately on the right/
  left
**gleich-, Gleich-:** ~**alt[e]rig**
  [~alt[ə]rɪç] Adj. of the same age (mit
  as); ~**artig** 1. Adj. of the same kind
  postpos. (+ Dat. as); (sehr ähnlich)
  very similar (+ Dat. to); 2. adv. in the
  same way; ~**berechtigt** Adj. having
  equal rights postpos.; ~**berechtigte
  Partner** equal partners; ~**berechti-
  gung** die equal rights pl.; ~|**bleiben**
  unr. itr. V.; mit sein remain the same;
  ⟨speed, temperature, etc.⟩ remain constant; ~**bleibend** Adj. constant,
  steady ⟨temperature, speed, etc.⟩;
  **gleichen** unr. itr. V. jmdm./einer Sa-

**che** ~: be like *or* resemble sb./sth.;
**gleichermaßen** *Adv.* equally
**gleich-, Gleich-:** ~**falls** *Adv. (auch)*
also; *(ebenfalls)* likewise; **danke**
~**falls**! thank you, [and] the same to
you; ~**förmig** 1. *Adj.* a) *(einheitlich)*
uniform; b) *(monoton)* monotonous;
2. *adv.* a) *(einheitlich)* uniformly; b)
*(monoton)* monotonously; ~**ge-
schlechtlich** *Adj.* homosexual;
~**gewicht das**; *o. Pl.* balance; ~**ge-
wichts·störung** die disturbance of
one's sense of balance; ~**gültig** 1.
*Adj.* indifferent (**gegenüber** towards);
*(belanglos)* trivial; **das ist mir |voll-
kommen|** ~: it's a matter of [complete]
indifference to me; 2. *adv.* indifferently; ~**gültigkeit** die indifference
(**gegenüber** towards)
**Gleichheit** die; ~, ~en a) identity;
*(Ähnlichkeit)* similarity; b) *o. Pl. (gleiche Rechte)* equality; **Gleichheitszeichen** das equals sign
**gleich-, Gleich-:** ~**|kommen** *unr.
itr. V.; mit sein* a) *(entsprechen)* be tantamount to; b) *(die gleiche Leistung erreichen)* jmdm./einer Sache [an etw.
*(Dat.)*] ~**kommen** equal sb./sth. [in
sth.]; ~**|machen** *tr. V.* make equal;
~**mäßig** 1. *Adj.* regular ⟨*interval,
rhythm*⟩; uniform ⟨*acceleration, distribution*⟩; even ⟨*heat*⟩; 2. *adv.* ⟨*breathe*⟩
regularly; **etw.** ~**mäßig verteilen/auf-
tragen** distribute sth. equally/apply
sth. evenly; ~**mut der** equanimity
**Gleichnis** das; ~**ses,** ~**se** *(Allegorie)*
allegory; *(Parabel)* parable; **gleich-
sam** *Adv. (geh.)* as it were
**gleich-, Gleich-:** ~**|schalten** *tr. V.*
force into line; ~**schenk[e]lig** *Adj.
(Math.)* isosceles; ~**schritt** der; *o. Pl.*
marching in step; ~**seitig** *Adj.
(Math.)* equilateral; ~**|setzen** *tr. V.*
equate; ~**|stellen** *tr. V.* equate;
~**strom der** *(Elektrot.)* direct current
**Gleichung** die; ~, ~en equation
**gleich-:** ~**wertig** *Adj.* of the same
value *postpos.;* ~**wohl** [·'- *od.* '--] *Adv.*
nevertheless; ~**zeitig** 1. *Adj.* simultaneous; 2. *adv.* at the same time
**Gleis** das; ~**es,** ~**e** track; *(Bahnsteig)*
platform; *(einzelne Schiene)* rail
**gleiten** *unr. itr. V.; mit sein* glide;
⟨*hand*⟩ slide; **Gleit·flug** der glide
**Gletscher** der; ~**s,** ~: glacier; **Glet-
scher·spalte** die crevasse
**glich** *1. u. 3. Pers. Sg. Prät. v.* gleichen
**Glied** das; ~**[e]s,** ~**er** a) limb; *(Finger~,
Zehen~)* joint; b) *(Ketten~, auch fig.)*

link; c) *(Teil eines Ganzen)* section;
*(Mitglied)* member; **gliedern** 1. *tr. V.*
structure; organize ⟨*thoughts*⟩; 2. *refl.
V.* **sich in Gruppen/Abschnitte** *usw.* ~:
be divided into groups/sections *etc.;*
**Gliederung** die; ~, ~en structure
**Glied-:** ~**maße** [-ma:sə] die; ~, ~n
limb; ~**satz der** *(Sprachw.)* subordinate clause
**glimmen** *unr. od. regelm. itr. V.* glow;
**Glimm·stengel** der *(ugs. scherzh.)*
fag *(sl.);* ciggy *(coll.)*
**glimpflich** 1. *Adj.* a) **der Unfall nahm
ein** ~**es Ende** the accident turned out
not to be too serious; b) *(mild)* lenient
⟨*sentence, punishment*⟩; 2. *adv.* a) *(ohne Schaden)* ~ **davonkommen** get off
lightly; b) *(mild)* leniently
**glitschig** *Adj. (ugs.)* slippery
**glitt** *1. u. 3. Pers. Sg. Prät. v.* gleiten
**glitzern** *itr. V.* ⟨*star*⟩ twinkle; ⟨*diamond, decorations*⟩ sparkle; ⟨*snow,
eyes, tears*⟩ glisten
**global** 1. *Adj.* a) global; world-wide;
b) *(umfassend)* all-round ⟨*education*⟩;
overall ⟨*control, planning, etc.*⟩; c) *(allgemein)* general; 2. *adv.* a) world-
wide; b) *(umfassend)* in overall terms;
c) *(allgemein)* in general terms; **Globen** *s.* Globus
**Globetrotter** der; ~**s,** ~: globetrotter
**Globus** der; ~ *od.* ~**ses,** **Globen** globe
**Glöckchen** das; ~**s,** ~: [little] bell;
**Glocke** die; ~, ~n bell
**Glocken-:** ~**blume** die *(Bot.)* cam-
panula; ~**rock** der widely flared
skirt; ~**spiel** das a) carillon; *(mit einer Uhr gekoppelt auch)* chimes *pl.;* b)
*(Instrument)* glockenspiel
**glomm** *1. u. 3. Pers. Sg. Prät. v.* glimmen
**Glorien·schein** der glory; *(um den
Kopf, fig.)* halo; **glorifizieren** *tr. V.*
glorify; **Glorifizierung** die; ~, ~en
glorification; **glor·reich** 1. *Adj.*
glorious; 2. *adv.* gloriously
**Glossar** das; ~**s,** ~**e** glossary
**Glosse** die; ~, ~n commentary; *(spöttische Bemerkung)* sneering comment
**glotzen** *itr. V. (abwertend)* goggle;
gawp *(coll.)*
**Glück das;** ~**[e]s** a) luck; **|es ist|** ein ~,
**daß** ...: it's lucky that ...; **|kein|** ~ **haben**
be [un]lucky; **viel** ~! [the] best of
luck!; b) happiness
**Glucke** die; ~, ~n brood-hen
**glücken** *tr. V.; mit sein* succeed; **etw.
glückt** jmdm. sb. is successful with sth.
**gluckern** *itr. V.* gurgle; glug

**glücklich** 1. *Adj.* **a)** happy (über + *Akk.* about); **b)** *(erfolgreich)* lucky ⟨*winner*⟩; successful ⟨*outcome*⟩; safe ⟨*journey*⟩; **c)** *(vorteilhaft)* fortunate; 2. *adv.* **a)** *(erfolgreich)* successfully; **b)** *(vorteilhaft, zufrieden)* happily ⟨*chosen, married*⟩; **glücklicher·weise** *Adv.* fortunately; luckily; **glück·selig** 1. *Adj.* blissfully happy; 2. *adv.* blissfully; **Glück·seligkeit** die; ~: bliss

**glucksen** *itr. V.* **a)** *s.* gluckern; **b)** *(lachen)* chuckle

**Glücks-:** ~**klee** der four-leaf clover; ~**pfennig** der lucky penny; ~**pilz** der *(ugs.)* lucky devil *(coll.)*

**Glück[s]·sache** die: das ist ~: it's a matter of luck; **Glücks·spiel** das game of chance; **glück·strahlend** *Adj.* radiantly happy; **Glücks·zahl** die lucky number; **Glück·wunsch** der congratulations *pl.;* **herzlichen ~ zum Geburtstag!** happy birthday!

**Glüh·birne** die light-bulb; **glühen** *itr. V.* glow; **glühend** 1. *Adj.* red-hot ⟨*metal etc.*⟩; blazing ⟨*heat*⟩; ardent ⟨*admirer etc.*⟩; passionate ⟨*words, letter, etc.*⟩; 2. *adv.* ⟨*love*⟩ passionately; ⟨*admire*⟩ ardently; ~ **heiß** blazing hot; **Glüh·wein** der mulled wine

**Glut** die; ~, ~**en a)** embers *pl.;* **b)** *(geh.: Leidenschaft)* passion; **glut·rot** *Adj.* fiery red

**Glyzerin** das; ~s glycerine

**GmbH** *Abk.* Gesellschaft mit beschränkter Haftung ≈ p.l.c.

**Gnade** die; ~, ~**n** *(Gunst)* favour; *(Rel.)* grace; *(Milde)* mercy

**gnaden-, Gnaden-:** ~**brot** das: jmdm./einem Tier das ~**brot** geben keep sb./an animal in his/ her/its old age; ~**frist** die reprieve; ~**gesuch** das plea for clemency; ~**los** *(auch fig.)* 1. *Adj.* merciless; 2. *adv.* mercilessly; ~**schuß** der coup de grâce *(by shooting)*

**gnädig** *Adj.* gracious; *(glimpflich)* lenient ⟨*sentence etc.*⟩

**Gnom** der; ~**en**, ~**en** gnome

**Gockel** der; ~**s**, ~ *(bes. südd., sonst ugs. scherzh.)* cock

**Gold** das; ~[e]s gold; **Gold·barren** der gold bar; **golden** 1. *Adj. (aus Gold)* gold; *(herrlich)* golden ⟨*days, memories, etc.*⟩; 2. *adv.* like gold

**Gold-:** ~**grube** die *(auch fig.)* gold-mine; ~**hamster** der golden hamster

**goldig** *Adj.* sweet

**gold-, Gold-:** ~**richtig** *(ugs.) Adj.*

absolutely right; ~**schmied** der goldsmith; ~**schnitt** der gilt; ~**währung, die** *(Wirtsch.)* currency tied to the gold standard

¹**Golf** der; ~[e]s, ~e gulf

²**Golf** das; ~s *(Sport)* golf

**Golf-:** ~**platz** der golf-course; ~**schläger** der golf club; ~**spieler** der, ~**spielerin** die golfer; ~**strom** der Gulf Stream

**Gondel** die; ~, ~**n** gondola; **gondeln** *itr. V.; mit sein (ugs.)* **a)** *(mit einem Boot)* cruise; **b)** *(reisen)* travel around; **c)** *(herumfahren)* cruise around

**Gong** der; ~**s**, ~**s** gong; **gongen** *itr. V.* es hat gegongt the gong has sounded

**gönnen** *tr. V.* jmdm. etw. ~: not begrudge sb. sth.; sich/jmdm. etw. ~: allow oneself/sb. sth.; **Gönner** der; ~**s**, ~: patron; **gönnerhaft** *(abwertend) Adj.* patronizing

**gor** 3. *Pers. Sg. Prät. v.* gären

**Göre** die; ~, ~**n** *(nordd., oft abwertend)* kid *(coll.)*

**Gorilla** der; ~**s**, ~**s** gorilla

**goß** 1. u. 3. *Pers. Sg. Prät. v.* gießen

**Gosse** die; ~, ~**n** gutter

**Gotik** die; ~ *(Stil)* Gothic [style]; *(Epoche)* Gothic period; **gotisch** *Adj.* Gothic

**Gott** der; ~**es**, **Götter a)** *o. Pl.; o. Art.* God; grüß [dich] ~! *(landsch.)* hello!; um ~**es Willen** *(bei Erschrecken)* for God's sake; *(bei einer Bitte)* for heaven's sake; **b)** *(übermenschliches Wesen)* god

**Gottes-:** ~**dienst** der service; ~**haus** das *(geh.)* house of God; ~**lästerung** die blasphemy

**Gottheit** die; ~, ~**en** deity; **Göttin** die; ~, ~**nen** goddess; **göttlich** 1. *Adj. (auch fig.)* divine; 2. *adv.* divinely

**gott-, Gott-:** ~**lob** *adv.* thank goodness; ~**los** 1. *Adj.* **a)** ungodly ⟨*life etc.*⟩; impious ⟨*words, speech, etc.*⟩; **b)** *(Gott leugnend)* godless ⟨*theory etc.*⟩; 2. *adv. (verwerflich)* irreverently; ~**va·ter** der God the Father; ~**vertrauen** das trust in God

**Götze** der; ~**n**, ~**n** *(auch fig.)* idol; **Götzen-:** ~**bild** das idol; ~**diener** der idolater

**Gouverneur** [guvɛr'nøːɐ̯] der; ~**s**, ~**e** governor

**Grab** das; ~[e]s, **Gräber** grave; das **Heilige ~:** the Holy Sepulchre; das ~

des Unbekannten Soldaten the tomb of
the Unknown Warrior; **graben** *unr.*
*tr., itr. V.* dig; **Graben der;** ~s, **Grä-**
**ben** ditch; *(Schützen~)* trench; *(Fe-*
*stungs~)* moat
**Grab-:** ~**kammer** die burial cham-
ber; ~**mal das;** *Pl.* ~**mäler,** *geh.* ~**ma-**
**le** monument; ~**stein** der gravestone
**gräbst** *2. Pers. Sg. Präsens v.* **graben;**
**gräbt** *3. Pers. Sg. Präsens v.* **graben**
**Gracht** die; ~, ~en canal
**Grad der;** ~[e]s, ~e degree; *(Milit.)*
rank; **Grad·messer** der gauge,
yardstick (für of)
**graduell** 1. *Adj.* gradual; slight ⟨*differ-*
*ence etc.*⟩; 2. *adv.* gradually; ⟨*differ-*
*ent*⟩ in degree; **graduiert** *Adj.* graduate; **ein** ~**er Ingenieur** an engineering
graduate
**Graf der;** ~en, ~en count; *(britischer*
~*)* earl
**Grafik** *usw. s.* **Graphik** *usw.*
**Gräfin** die; ~, ~**nen** countess; **Graf-**
**schaft** die; ~, ~**en a)** count's land;
*(in Großbritannien)* earldom; **b)** *(Ver-*
*waltungsbezirk)* county
**Gram der;** ~[e]s *(geh.)* grief; sorrow;
**grämen** 1. *tr. V.* grieve; 2. *refl. V.*
grieve (über + *Akk.,* um over)
**Gramm das;** ~s, ~e gram
**Grammatik** die; ~, ~en grammar;
**grammatisch** 1. *Adj.* grammatical;
2. *adv.* grammatically
**Grammophon** ⓦ **das;** ~s, ~e gramophone; phonograph *(Amer.)*
**Granat der;** ~[e]s, ~e *(Schmuckstein)*
garnet; **Granat·apfel** der pomegranate
**Granate** die; ~, ~n shell; *(Hand~)*
grenade
**grandios** 1. *Adj.* magnificent; 2. *adv.*
magnificently
**Granit der;** ~s, ~e granite
**grantig** *(südd., österr. ugs.)* 1. *Adj.*
bad-tempered; 2. *adv.* badtemperedly
**Graphik** die; ~, ~en graphic art[s *pl.*];
*(Kunstwerk)* graphic; *(Druck)* print;
**Graphiker der;** ~s, ~, **Graphikerin**
**die;** ~, ~**nen** [graphic] designer;
*(Künstler[in])* graphic artist; **gra-**
**phisch** 1. *Adj.* graphic; 2. *adv.*
graphically
**Gras das;** ~es, **Gräser** grass; **über etw.**
*(Akk.)* ~ **wachsen lassen** *(ugs.)* let the
dust settle on sth.; **grasen** *itr. V.*
graze; **Gras·halm** der blade of grass
**gräßlich** 1. *Adj.* **a)** *(abscheulich)* horrible; terrible ⟨*accident*⟩; **b)** *(ugs.: un-*

*angenehm)* dreadful *(coll.);* **c)** *(ugs.:*
*sehr stark)* terrible *(coll.);* 2. *adv.* **a)**
*(abscheulich)* horribly; terribly; **b)**
*(ugs.: unangenehm)* terribly *(coll.);* **c)**
*(ugs.: sehr)* terribly *(coll.)*
**Grat der;** ~[e]s, ~e ridge
**Gräte** die; ~, ~n [fish-]bone
**Gratifikation** die; ~, ~en bonus
**gratis** *Adv.* free [of charge]; gratis
**Grätsche** die; ~, ~n *(Turnen)*
straddle; *(Sprung)* straddle-vault
**Gratulant der;** ~en, ~en, **Gratulan-**
**tin die;** ~, ~**nen** well-wisher; **Gratu-**
**lation die;** ~, ~en congratulations
*pl.;* **gratulieren** *itr. V.* jmdm. ~: congratulate sb.; **jmdm. zum Geburtstag**
~: wish sb. many happy returns [of
the day]
**grau** *Adj.* grey; *(trostlos)* dreary; drab
**¹grauen** *itr. V. (geh.)* **der Morgen/der**
**Tag graut** morning/day is breaking
**²grauen** *itr. V. (unpers.)* **ihm graut** [es]
**davor/vor ihr** he dreads [the thought
of] it/he's terrified of her; **Grauen**
**das;** ~s, ~: horror (vor + *Dat.* of);
**grauen·haft** 1. *Adj.* horrifying;
*(ugs.: sehr unangenehm)* terrible
*(coll.);* 2. *adv.* horrifyingly; *(ugs.: sehr*
*unangenehm)* terribly *(coll.)*
**grau-:** ~**haarig** *Adj.* grey-haired;
~**meliert** *Adj. (präd. getrennt ge-*
*schrieben)* greying ⟨*hair*⟩
**Graupe** die; ~, ~n **a)** grain of pearl
barley; **b)** *Pl. (Gericht)* pearl barley
*sing.*
**graupeln** *itr. V. (unpers.)* **es graupelt**
there's soft hail falling
**grausam** 1. *Adj.* **a)** cruel; **b)** *(furcht-*
*bar)* terrible; dreadful; 2. *adv.* **a)**
cruelly; **b)** *(furchtbar)* terribly, dreadfully; **Grausamkeit die;** ~, ~**en a)** *o.*
*Pl.* cruelty; **b)** *(Handlung)* act of
cruelty
**grausen** 1. *tr., itr. V. (unpers.)* **es grau-**
**ste ihm** *od.* **ihn davor/vor ihr** he
dreaded it/he was terrified of her; 2.
*refl. V.* **sich vor etw./jmdm.** ~: dread
sth./be terrified of sb.; **Grausen das;**
~s horror; **grausig** *s.* **grauenhaft**
**gravieren** *tr. V.* engrave; **gra-**
**vierend** *Adj.* serious, grave; **Gra-**
**vierung die;** ~, ~en engraving
**Gravitation** die; ~ *(Physik, Astron.)*
gravitation
**Gravur** [gra'vuːɐ̯] die; ~, ~en engraving
**Grazie** ['graːtsiə] **die;** ~, ~**n a)** *o. Pl.*
*(Anmut)* gracefulness; **b)** *Pl. (Myth.)*
Graces

**greifen** 1. *unr. tr. V.* a) *(er~)* take hold of; grasp; *(rasch ~)* seize; b) *(fangen)* catch; 2. *unr. itr. V.* a) **in/unter/hinter etw./sich** *(Akk.)* ~: reach into/under/behind sth./one; **nach etw.** ~: reach for sth.; *(hastig)* make a grab for sth.; b) *(Technik)* grip

**Greis** der; ~es, ~e old man; **Greisin** die; ~, ~nen old woman

**grell** 1. *Adj.* a) *(hell)* glaring, ⟨*light, sun, etc.*⟩; b) *(auffallend)* garish ⟨*colour etc.*⟩; loud ⟨*dress, pattern, etc.*⟩; c) *(schrill)* shrill, ⟨*cry, voice, etc.*⟩; 2. *adv.* a) *(hell)* with glaring brightness; b) *(auffallend)* **gegen** *od.* **von etw.** ~ **abstechen** contrast sharply with sth.; c) *(schrill)* shrilly

**Gremium** das; ~s, Gremien committee

**Grenze** die; ~, ~n a) boundary; *(Staats~)* border; *(gedachte Trennungslinie)* borderline; b) *(fig.)* limit; **grenzen** *itr. V.* **an etw.** *(Akk.)* ~: border [on] sth.; **grenzen·los** 1. *Adj.* boundless; *(fig.)* boundless, unbounded ⟨*joy, wonder, jealousy, grief, etc.*⟩; unlimited ⟨*wealth, power*⟩; limitless ⟨*patience, ambition*⟩; extreme ⟨*tiredness, anger, foolishness*⟩; 2. *adv.* endlessly; *(fig.)* beyond all measure; **Grenzen·losigkeit** die; ~: boundlessness

**Grenz-:** ~**übergang** der border crossing-point; ~**verkehr** der [cross-]border traffic

**Greuel** der; ~s, ~ a) etw./jmd. ist jmdm. ein ~: sb. loathes *or* detests sth./sb.; b) *meist Pl. (geh.)* *(~tat)* atrocity; **Greuel·tat** die atrocity; **greulich** 1. *Adj.* a) horrifying; b) *(unangenehm)* awful; 2. *adv.* a) horrifyingly; b) *(unangenehm)* terribly

**Grieche** der; ~n, ~n Greek; **Griechen·land** (das); ~s Greece; **griechisch** 1. *Adj.* Greek; 2. *adv.* ⟨*speak, write*⟩ in Greek; **Griechisch** das; ~[s] Greek *no art.*

**griesgrämig** 1. *Adj.* grumpy; 2. *adv.* in a grumpy manner

**Grieß** der; ~es, ~e semolina; **Grieß·brei** der semolina

**griff** *1. u. 3. Pers. Sg. Prät. v.* greifen; **Griff** der; ~[e]s, ~e a) grip; grasp; b) *(Knauf, Henkel)* handle; **griff·bereit** *Adj.* ready to hand *postpos.*

**Griffel** der; ~s, ~: slate-pencil

**griffig** *Adj.* a) *(handlich)* handy; b) *(gut greifend)* that grips well *postpos., not pred.;* non-slip ⟨*surface, floor*⟩

**Grill** der; ~s, ~s grill; *(Rost)* barbecue

**Grille** die; ~, ~n a) cricket; b) *(sonderbarer Einfall)* whim

**grillen** 1. *tr. V.* grill; 2. *itr. V.* **im Garten** ~: have a barbecue in the garden

**Grimasse** die; ~, ~n grimace

**grimmig** 1. *Adj.* furious ⟨*person*⟩; grim ⟨*expression*⟩; 2. *adv.* grimly

**grinsen** *itr. V.* grin; *(höhnisch)* smirk

**Grippe** die; ~, ~n a) influenza; flu *(coll.)*; b) *(volkst.: Erkältung)* cold

**Grips** der; ~es brains *pl.*

**grob** 1. *Adj.* a) coarse; thick ⟨*wire*⟩; rough ⟨*work*⟩; b) *(ungefähr)* rough; c) *(schwerwiegend)* gross; flagrant ⟨*lie*⟩; d) *(barsch)* rude; 2. *adv.* a) coarsely; b) *(ungefähr)* roughly; c) *(schwerwiegend)* grossly; d) *(barsch)* rudely; **Grobheit** die; ~, ~en a) *o. Pl.* rudeness; b) *(Äußerung)* rude remark

**Grobian** der; ~[e]s, ~e lout

**Grog** der; ~s, ~s grog

**grölen** 1. *tr. V. (ugs. abwertend)* bawl [out]; roar, howl ⟨*approval*⟩; 2. *itr. V.* bawl

**Groll** der; ~[e]s *(geh.)* rancour; **grollen** *itr. V. (geh.)* a) |mit| jmdm. ~: bear a grudge against sb.; b) ⟨*thunder*⟩ rumble

**Grönland** (das); ~s Greenland

**Gros** [gro:] das; ~ [gro:s], ~ [gro:s] bulk

**Groschen** der; ~s, ~ a) *(österreichische Münze)* groschen; b) *(ugs.: Zehnpfennigstück)* ten-pfennig piece; *(fig.)* penny; cent *(Amer.)*

**groß**; größer, größt... 1. *Adj.* a) big; large; great ⟨*length, width, height*⟩; tall ⟨*person*⟩; wide ⟨*selection*⟩; 1 m² ~: 1 m² in area; im ~en und ganzen by and large; b) *(älter)* big ⟨*brother, sister*⟩; *(erwachsen)* grown-up; c) *(lange dauernd)* long, lengthy; d) intense ⟨*heat, cold*⟩; high ⟨*speed*⟩; great, major ⟨*event, artist, work*⟩; 2. *adv.* ein Wort ~ schreiben write a word with a capital; *(ugs.: besonders)* greatly; **groß·artig** 1. *Adj.* magnificent; 2. *adv.* magnificently

**Großbritannien** (das); ~s the United Kingdom; [Great] Britain

**Groß·buchstabe** der capital [letter]

**Größe** die; ~, ~n size; *(Höhe, Körper~)* height; *(fig.)* greatness; **die ~ der Katastrophe** the [full] extent of the catastrophe

**Groß·eltern** *Pl.* grandparents; **Größen·wahn** der delusions *pl.* of grandeur; **größer** *s.* groß

**Groß-:** ~**fahndung** die large-scale

search; ~**handel** der wholesale trade; ~**händler** der wholesaler; ~**industrielle** der/die; *adj. Dekl.* big industrialist

**Grossist** der; ~en, ~en *(Kaufmannsspr.)* wholesaler

**groß-, Groß-**: ~**macht** die great power; ~**maul** das *(ugs. abwertend)* big-mouth *(coll.)*; ~**mut** die; ~: generosity; ~**mütig** *Adj.* generous; ~**mutter** die grandmother; ~**reinemachen** das *(ugs.)* thorough cleaning; ~|**schreiben** *unr. tr. V. (ugs.) in* ~**geschrieben werden** be stressed; *s. auch* **groß** 2; ~**spurig** *(abwertend)* 1. *Adj.* boastful; *(hochtrabend)* pretentious; 2. *adv.* boastfully; *(hochtrabend)* pretentiously; ~**stadt** die city; large town; ~**städter** der city-dweller

**größt...** *s.* **groß**; **Groß·teil** der a) *(Hauptteil)* major part; b) *(nicht unerheblicher Teil)* large part; **größtenteils** *Adv.* for the most part; **größt·möglich** *Adj.* greatest possible

**groß-, Groß-**: ~|**tun** *unr. itr. V.* boast; ~**vater** der grandfather; ~|**ziehen** *unr. tr. V.* bring up; raise; rear ⟨*animal*⟩; ~**zügig** 1. *Adj.* generous; grand and spacious ⟨*building, garden, etc.*⟩; 2. *adv.* a) generously; ~**zügigkeit** die generosity

**grotesk** 1. *Adj.* grotesque; 2. *adv.* grotesquely

**Grotte** die; ~, ~n grotto

**grub** *1. u. 3. Pers. Sg. Prät. v.* **graben**; **Grübchen** das; ~s, ~: dimple; **Grube** die; ~, ~n pit; *(Bergbau)* mine

**grübeln** *itr. V.* ponder (**über** + *Dat.* on, over)

**Gruben·arbeiter** der miner; mineworker

**grüezi** *Adv. (schweiz.)* hallo

**Gruft** die; ~, **Grüfte** vault; *(in einer Kirche)* crypt

**grün** *Adj.* green; **Grün** das; ~s, ~ *od.* *(ugs.)* ~s a) green; b) *o. Pl. (Pflanzen)* greenery; **Grün·anlage** die green space; *(Park)* park

**Grund** der; ~|e|s, **Gründe** a) ground; *(eines Gewässers)* bottom; b) *(Ursache, Veranlassung)* reason

**Grund-**: ~**besitz** der a) *(Eigentum an Land)* ownership of land; b) *(Land)* land; ~**buch** das land register

**gründen** 1. *tr. V.* a) found; set up, establish ⟨*business*⟩; start [up] ⟨*club*⟩; b) *(aufbauen)* base ⟨*plan, theory, etc.*⟩

(**auf** + *Akk.* on); 2. *itr. V.* **auf** *od.* **in** etw. *(Dat.)* ~: be based on sth. 3. *refl. V.* **sich auf etw.** *(Akk.)* ~: be based on sth.; **Gründer** der; ~s, ~, **Gründerin** die; ~, ~nen: founder

**grundieren** *tr. V.* prime

**Grund-, Grund-**: ~**gesetz** das Basic Law; ~**kenntnis** die; *meist Pl.* basic knowledge *no pl.* (**in** + *Dat.* of); ~**lage** die basis; foundation; ~**legend** 1. *Adj.* fundamental, basic (**für** to); seminal ⟨*idea, work*⟩; 2. *adv.* fundamentally

**gründlich** 1. *Adj.* thorough; 2. *adv.* thoroughly; **Gründlichkeit** die; ~: thoroughness

**grund·los** 1. *Adj.* groundless; 2. *adv.* **sich ~los aufregen/ängstigen** be needlessly agitated/alarmed; **Grundnahrungs·mittel** das basic food[stuff]

**Grün·donnerstag** der Maundy Thursday

**Grund-**: ~**prinzip** das fundamental principle; ~**recht** das basic *or* constitutional right; ~**riß** der a) *(Bauw.)* [ground-] plan; b) *(Leitfaden)* outline; ~**satz** der principle

**grund·sätzlich** 1. *Adj.* a) fundamental ⟨*difference, question, etc.*⟩; b) *(aus Prinzip)* ⟨*opponent etc.*⟩ on principle; c) *(allgemein)* ⟨*agreement etc.*⟩ in principle; 2. *adv.* a) fundamentally; b) *(aus Prinzip)* on principle; c) *(allgemein)* in principle

**Grund-**: ~**schule** die primary school; ~**stein** der foundation-stone; ~**stück** das plot [of land]

**Gründung** die; ~, ~en *s.* **gründen** 1 a: foundation; setting up; establishing; starting [up]

**Grund-**: ~**wasser** das *(Geol.)* ground water; ~**zug** der essential feature

**Grüne** das; *adj. Dekl.* green; **im ~n/ins ~**: [out] in/into the country

**Grün-**: ~**fläche** die green space; *(im Park)* lawn; ~**span** der verdigris; ~**streifen** der central reservation *(grassed and often with trees and bushes)*

**grunzen** *tr., itr. V.* grunt

**Gruppe** die; ~, ~n a) group; b) *(Klassifizierung)* class; category

**Gruppen-**: ~**reise** die *(Touristik)* group travel *no pl., no art.*; ~**sieg** der *(Sport)* top place in the group

**gruppieren** 1. *tr. V.* arrange; 2. *refl. V.* form a group/groups; **Gruppierung** die; ~, ~en grouping

**gruselig** *Adj.* eerie; creepy; **gruseln**
**1.** *tr., itr. V. (unpers.)* es gruselt jmdn.
*od.* **jmdm.** sb.'s flesh creeps; **2.** *refl. V.*
be frightened

**Gruß** der; ~es, Grüße a) greeting; *(Milit.)* salute; b) *(im Brief)* mit herzlichen
Grüßen [with] best wishes; **mit bestem
~/freundlichen Grüßen** yours sincerely; **grüßen 1.** *tr. V.* a) greet; *(Milit.)* salute; b) *(Grüße senden)* **grüße
deine Eltern [ganz herzlich]** von mir
please give your parents my [kindest]
regards; **2.** *itr. V.* say hello; *(Milit.)* salute

**Grütze** die; ~, ~n groats *pl.*; **rote ~:**
red fruit pudding *(made with fruit
juice, fruit and cornflour, etc.)*

**gucken** *itr. V. (ugs.)* a) look; *(heimlich)* peep; b) *(hervorsehen)* stick out;
c) *(dreinschauen)* look; **Guck·loch
das** spy-hole

**Guerilla** [ge'rɪlja] die; ~, ~s guerrilla
war; *(Einheit)* guerrilla unit

**Gulasch** ['gʊlaʃ, 'gu:laʃ] das *od.* der;
~[e]s, ~e *od.* ~s goulash

**Gulden** der; ~s, ~: guilder

**gültig** *Adj.* valid; current *(note, coin)*;
**Gültigkeit** die; ~: validity; **~ haben/
erlangen** be/become valid

**Gummi** der *od.* das; ~s, ~[s] rubber

**Gummi-:** ~**band das;** *Pl.* ~**bänder**
rubber *or* elastic band; *(in Kleidung)*
elastic *no indef. art.;* ~**bärchen das**
jelly baby; ~**baum** der rubber plant

**gummieren** *tr. V.* gum

**Gummi-:** ~**handschuh** der rubber
glove; ~**knüppel** der [rubber]
truncheon; ~**sohle** die rubber sole;
~**stiefel** der rubber boot; *(für Regenwetter)* wellington [boot] *(Brit.)*

**Gunst** die; ~: favour; goodwill; **günstig 1.** *Adj.* favourable; propitious
*(sign)*; auspicious *(moment)*; beneficial *(influence)*; good; **2.** *adv.* favourably; **etw. ~ beeinflussen** have *or* exert
a beneficial influence on sth.

**Gurgel** die; ~, ~n throat; **jmdm. die ~
zudrücken** throttle sb.; **gurgeln** *itr.
V.* gargle

**Gurke** die; ~, ~n cucumber; *(einge-
legt)* gherkin

**gurren** *itr. V. (auch fig.)* coo

**Gurt** der; ~[e]s, ~e strap; *(im Auto,
Flugzeug)* [seat-]belt; **Gürtel** der; ~s,
~: belt

**Gürtel-:** ~**linie** die waist[line]; ~**reifen** der radial[-ply] tyre

**GUS** [ge:|u:'|ɛs] *Abk.* **Gemeinschaft
Unabhängiger Staaten** CIS

**Guß** der; Gusses, Güsse a) *(das Gießen)* casting; b) *(ugs.: Regenschauer)*
downpour

**Guß·eisen das** cast iron; **guß·ei-
sern** *Adj.* cast-iron

**gut; besser, best... 1.** *Adj.* good; fine
*(wine)*; **ein ~es neues Jahr** a happy
new year; **mir ist nicht ~:** I'm not feeling well; ~**en Appetit!** enjoy your
lunch/dinner *etc.!;* **eine ~e Stunde [von
hier]** a good hour [from here]; **2.** *adv.*
a) well; b) *(mühelos)* easily; *s. auch*
**besser, best...**

**Gut das;** ~[e]s, Güter a) property; *(Be-
sitztum, auch fig.)* possession; b)
*(landwirtschaftlicher Grundbesitz)* estate; c) *(Fracht~, Ware)* item; Güter
goods; *(Fracht~)* freight *sing.;* goods
*(Brit.)*;

**gut-, Gut-:** ~**achten das;** ~**s,** ~**:** [ex-
pert's] report; ~**artig** *Adj.* a) good-
natured; b) *(nicht gefährlich)* benign;
~**aussehend** *Adj.* good-looking;
~**bürgerlich** *Adj.* good middle-
class; ~**bürgerliche Küche** good plain
cooking; ~**dünken das;** ~**s** discretion

**Güte** die; ~: goodness; kindness;
*(Qualität)* quality

**Güter-:** ~**abfertigung** die a) *(Abfertigung von Waren)* dispatch of freight
*or (Brit.)* goods; b) *(Annahmestelle)*
freight *or (Brit.)* goods office;
~**bahnhof** der freight depot; goods
station *(Brit.);* ~**wagen** der goods
wagon *(Brit.);* freight car *(Amer.);*
~**zug** der goods train *(Brit.);* freight
train *(Amer.)*

**gut-, Gut-:** ~**[gehen** *unr. itr. V.; mit
sein* a) *(unpers.)* es geht jmdm. gut sb.
is well; b) *(~ ausgehen)* turn out well;
~**gelaunt** *Adj. (präd. getrennt geschrieben)* cheerful; ~**gemeint** *Adj.
(präd. getrennt geschrieben)* well-
meant; ~**gläubig** *Adj.* innocently
trusting; ~**haben das;** ~**s,** ~**:** credit
balance; ~**[heißen** *unr. tr. V.* approve of; ~**herzig** *Adj.* kind-hearted

**gütig 1.** *Adj.* kindly; **2.** *adv.* ~ **lächeln**
give a kindly smile; **gütlich** *Adj.*
amicable

**gut-, Gut-:** ~**[machen** *tr. V.* make
good *(damage);* put right *(omission,
mistake, etc.);* ~**mütig** *Adj.* good-natured; ~**mütigkeit** die; ~: good nature

**Guts·besitzer** der owner of a/the estate; landowner

**gut-, Gut-:** ~**schein** der voucher,

coupon (für, auf + *Akk.* for); ~|-
**schreiben** *unr. tr. V.* credit;
**~schrift die** credit

**Guts·hof der** estate; manor

**gut-:** ~|**tun** *unr. itr. V.* do good;
**~willig** 1. *Adj.* willing; *(entgegenkommend)* obliging; 2. *adv. etw.* **~wil-
lig herausgeben/versprechen** hand sth.
over voluntarily/promise sth. willingly

**Gymnasium das;** ~s, **Gymnasien** ≈
grammar school

**Gymnastik die;** ~: physical exercises
*pl.; (Turnen)* gymnastics *sing.*

**Gynäkologe der;** ~n, ~n gynaecologist

# H

---

**h, H** [ha:] **das;** ~, ~ a) *(Buchstabe)*
h/H; b) *(Musik)* [key of] B

**h** *Abk.* a) **Uhr** hrs; b) **Stunde** hr[s]

**H** *Abk.* a) **Herren;** b) **Haltestelle**

**¹ha** [ha(:)] *Interj.* a) *(Überraschung)* ah;
b) *(Triumph)* aha

**²ha** *Abk.* **Hektar** ha

**Haar das;** ~[e]s, ~e hair; **blonde** ~e *od.*
**blondes** ~ **haben** have fair hair; *(fig.)*
**~e auf den Zähnen haben** *(ugs.
scherzh.)* be a tough customer; **um ein**
~ *(ugs.)* very nearly

**Haar-:** **~ausfall der** hair loss; **~bür-
ste die** hairbrush; **~büschel das** tuft
of hair

**haaren** *itr. V.* moult; **Haares·breite
die** *in* **um** ~: by a hair's breadth;
**Haar·festiger der** setting lotion;
**haar·genau** *(ugs.)* 1. *Adj.* exact; 2.
*adv.* exactly; **haarig** *Adj.* hairy

**haar-, Haar-:** **~klemme die** hair-
grip; **~nadel die** hairpin; **~na-
del·kurve die** hairpin bend;
**~schnitt der** haircut; *(modisch)* hairstyle; **~spange die** hair-slide;
**~sträubend** *Adj.* a) *(grauenhaft)*
hair-raising; b) *(empörend)* outrageous; shocking; **~teil das** hair-
piece; **~wasch·mittel das** shampoo; **~wasser das;** *Pl.* ~wässer hair
lotion

**Habe die;** ~ *(geh.)* possessions *pl.;*
**haben** 1. *unr. tr. V.* have; have got;
**heute** ~ **wir schönes Wetter** the
weather is fine today; **es gut/schlecht/
schwer** ~: have it good *(coll.)/*have a
bad time [of it]/have a difficult time;
**du hast zu gehorchen** you must obey;
**das Jahr hat 12 Monate** there are 12
months in a year; 2. *refl. V. (ugs.: sich
aufregen)* make a fuss; 3. *Hilfsverb*
have; **ich habe/hatte ihn eben gesehen**
I've/I'd just seen him; **er hat es gewußt**
he knew it; 4. *mod. V.* **du hast zu gehorchen** you must obey; **er hat sich
nicht einzumischen** he's not to interfere; **Haben das;** ~s, ~ *(Kaufmannsspr.)* credit; **Habe·nichts
der;** ~, ~e pauper; **Hab·gier die** *(abwertend)* greed; **hab·gierig** 1. *Adj.
(abwertend)* greedy; 2. *adv.* greedily

**Habicht der;** ~s, ~e hawk

**Hab-:** **~seligkeiten** *Pl.* [meagre] belongings; **~sucht die;** ~ *(abwertend)*
greed; avarice

**Hachse die;** ~, ~n *(südd.)* knuckle

**Hack das;** ~s *(ugs., bes. nordd.)*
mince; **Hack·braten der** meat loaf

**¹Hacke die;** ~, ~n hoe; *(Pickel)*
pick[axe]

**²Hacke die;** ~, ~n *(bes. nordd. u. md.)*
heel

**hacken** 1. *itr. V.* a) hoe; b) *(picken)*
peck; 2. *tr. V.* a) hoe ⟨garden, flower-
bed, etc.⟩; b) *(zerkleinern)* chop; chop
[up] ⟨meat, vegetables, etc.⟩

**Hack·fleisch das** minced meat;
mince

**Häcksel der** *od.* **das;** ~s *(Landw.)*
chaff

**hadern** *itr. V. (geh.)* **mit etw.** ~: be at
odds with sth.

**Hafen der;** ~s, **Häfen** harbour; port

**Hafen-:** **~arbeiter der** dock-worker;
docker; **~kneipe die** dockland pub
*(Brit. coll.)* or *(Amer.)* bar; **~rund-
fahrt die** trip round the harbour;
**~stadt die** port; **~viertel das** dock
area

**Hafer der;** ~s oats *pl.*

**Hafer-:** **~brei der** porridge;
**~flocken** *Pl.* porridge oats

**Haff das;** ~[e]s, ~s *od.* ~e lagoon

**Haft die;** ~ a) *(Gewahrsam)* custody;
*(aus politischen Gründen)* detention;
b) *(Freiheitsstrafe)* imprisonment

**-haft** *Adj., adv.* -like

**haftbar** *Adj. (bes. Rechtsspr.)* **für etw.**
~ **sein** be liable for sth.; **Haft·befehl
der** *(Rechtsw.)* warrant [of arrest]

**¹haften** *itr. V.* stick; *(sich festsetzen)* ⟨*smell, dirt, etc.*⟩ cling (**an** + *Dat.* to)
**²haften** *itr. V.* **für** jmdn./etw. ~ : be responsible for sb./liable for sth.; *(Rechtsw., Wirtsch.)* be liable
**haften|bleiben** *unr. itr. V.; mit sein* stick (**an/auf** + *Dat.* to); ⟨*smell, smoke*⟩ cling (**an/auf** + *Dat.* to); *(ugs.: im Gedächtnis bleiben)* stick
**Häftling** der; ~s, ~e prisoner
**Haft·pflicht** die liability (für for); **Haftpflicht·versicherung** die personal liability insurance; *(für Autofahrer)* third party insurance
**Haft·schale** die contact lens
**Haftung** die; ~, ~en liability; Gesellschaft mit [un]beschränkter ~ : [un]limited [liability] company
**Hagebutte** die; ~, ~n a) *(Frucht)* rose-hip; b) *(ugs.: Heckenrose)* dog-rose
**Hagel** der; ~s, ~ *(auch fig.)* hail; **hageln** *itr., tr. V. (unpers.)* hail
**hager** *Adj.* gaunt
**haha** [ha'ha(:)] *Interj.* ha ha
**Häher** der; ~s, ~ : jay
**¹Hahn** der; ~|e|s, Hähne cock; *(Wetter~)* weathercock
**²Hahn** der; ~|e|s, Hähne, *fachspr.:* ~en a) tap; faucet *(Amer.);* b) *(bei Waffen)* hammer
**Hähnchen** das; ~s, ~ : chicken; **Hahnen·fuß** der buttercup
**Hai** der; ~s, ~e shark
**Häkchen** das; ~s, ~ a) [small] hook; b) *(Zeichen)* mark; *(beim Abhaken)* tick; **häkeln** *tr., itr. V.* crochet; **Häkel·nadel** die crochet-hook
**haken** 1. *tr. V.* hook (**an** + *Akk.* on to); 2. *itr. V. (klemmen)* be stuck; **Haken** der; ~s, ~ a) hook; b) *(Zeichen)* tick; c) *(ugs.: Schwierigkeit)* catch; d) *(Boxen)* hook; **Haken·kreuz** das swastika
**halb** 1. *Adj. u. Bruchz.* half; eine ~e Stunde/ein ~er Meter half an hour/a metre; zum ~en Preis [at] half price; ~ Europa/die ~e Welt half of Europe/half the world; es ist ~ eins it's half past twelve; die ~e Wahrheit half [of] the truth; [noch] ein ~es Kind sein be hardly more than a child; 2. *adv.* ~ voll/leer half-full/-empty; ~ angezogen half dressed; **Halb·dunkel** das semi-darkness; **Halbe** der. die od. das; *adj. Dekl. (ugs.)* half litre *(of beer etc.);* **Halb·edelstein** der *(veralt.)* semi-precious stone
**halber** *Präp. mit Gen.; nachgestellt*

*(wegen)* on account of; *(um ... willen)* for the sake of
**halb-, Halb-:** ~finale das *(Sport)* semi-final; ~gar *Adj.* half-cooked; ~gefror[e]ne das; *adj. Dekl.* soft ice cream
**halbieren** *tr. V.* cut/tear ⟨*object*⟩ in half; halve ⟨*amount, number*⟩
**halb-, Halb-:** ~insel die peninsula; ~jahr das six months *pl.;* half year; ~jährlich 1. *Adj.* six-monthly; 2. *adv.* every six months; ~kreis der semicircle; ~kugel die hemisphere; ~lang *Adj.* mid-length ⟨*hair*⟩; mid-calf length ⟨*coat, dress, etc.*⟩; ~links [-'-] *Adv. (Fußball)* ⟨*play*⟩ [at] inside left; ~mast *Adv.* at half-mast; ~mond der a) *(Mond)* half-moon; b) *(Figur)* crescent; ~offen *Adj. (präd. getrennt geschrieben)* half-open; ~pension die half-board; ~rechts [-'-] *Adv. (Fußball)* ⟨*play*⟩ [at] inside right; ~schuh der shoe; ~starke der; *adj. Dekl. (ugs. abwertend)* [young] hooligan; ~tags *Adv.* ⟨*work*⟩ part-time; *(morgens/nachmittags)* ⟨*work*⟩ [in the] mornings/afternoons; ~voll *Adj. (präd. getrennt geschrieben)* half-full; ~wegs *Adv.* to some extent; ~wüchsig [~vy:ksıç] *Adj.* adolescent; ~wüchsige der/die; *adj. Dekl.* adolescent; ~zeit die *(bes. Fußball)* a) half; b) *(Pause)* half-time
**Halde** die; ~, ~n *(Bergbau)* slag-heap
**half** *1. u. 3. Pers. Sg. Prät. v.* helfen
**Hälfte** die; ~, ~n a) half; b) *(ugs.: Teil)* part
**¹Halfter** der od. das; ~s, ~ : halter
**²Halfter** die; ~, ~n; *auch* das; ~s, ~ : holster
**Hall** der; ~|e|s, ~e a) *(geh.)* reverberation; b) *(Echo)* echo
**Halle** die; ~, ~n hall; *(Fabrik~)* shed; *(Hotel~, Theater~)* foyer
**hallen** *itr. V.* a) reverberate; ⟨*shot, bell, cry*⟩ ring out; b) *(widerhallen)* echo
**Hallen-** indoor ⟨*swimming-pool, handball*⟩
**Hallig** die; ~, ~en small low island *(particularly one of those off Schleswig-Holstein)*
**hallo** *Interj.* hello; **Hallo** das; ~s, ~s cheering
**Halluzination** die; ~, ~en hallucination
**Halm** der; ~|e|s, ~e stalk; stem
**Hals** der; ~es, Hälse *(Kehle)* throat; ~ über Kopf *(ugs.)* in a rush
**Hals-:** ~ab·schneider der *(ugs. ab-*

*wertend)* shark; ~**band** das; *Pl.*
~**bänder** *(für Tiere)* collar; ~**bruch**
der *s.* ~- **und Beinbruch;** ~**entzündung** die inflammation of the throat;
~**-Nasen-Ohren-Arzt** der ear, nose,
and throat specialist; ~**schlagader**
die carotid [artery]; ~**schmerzen** *Pl.*
sore throat *sing.;* ~**starrig** [~ʃtarɪç]
*Adj. (abwertend)* stubborn; obstinate;
~**tuch** das cravat; ~- **und Beinbruch** *Interj. (scherzh.)* good luck;
~**weh** das *(ugs.) s.* ~schmerzen
**halt** *Interj.* stop; **Halt** der; ~|e|s, ~e
hold
**haltbar** *Adj.* a) ~ **sein** *⟨food⟩* keep
[well]; ~ **bis 5. 3.** use by 5 March; b)
*(nicht verschleißend)* hard-wearing
*⟨material, clothes⟩;* c) *(aufrechtzuer-
halten)* tenable *⟨hypothesis etc.⟩;*
**Haltbarkeit** die; ~ *(Strapazierfähig-
keit)* durability
**halten 1.** *unr. tr. V.* a) *(auch Milit.)*
hold; **die Hand vor den Mund** ~: put
one's hand in front of one's mouth; b)
*(Ballspiele)* save *⟨shot, penalty, etc.⟩;*
c) *(bewahren)* keep; *(beibehalten, aufrechterhalten)* keep up *⟨speed etc.⟩;*
maintain *⟨temperature, equilibrium⟩;*
d) *(erfüllen)* keep; **sein Wort/ein Versprechen** ~: keep one's word/a
promise; e) *(besitzen, beschäftigen, beziehen)* keep *⟨chickens etc.⟩;* take
*⟨newspaper, magazine, etc.⟩;* f) *(einschätzen)* **jmdn. für reich/ehrlich** ~:
think sb. is rich/honest; **viel von
jmdm.** ~: think a lot of sb.; g) *(ab~,
veranstalten)* give, *⟨speech, lecture⟩;* 2.
*unr. itr. V.* a) *(stehenbleiben)* stop; b)
*(unverändert, an seinem Platz bleiben)*
last; c) *(Sport)* save; d) *(beistehen)* **zu
jmdm.** ~: stand by sb.; 3. *unr. refl. V.*
a) *(sich durchsetzen, behaupten)* **wir
werden uns/die Stadt wird sich nicht
länger ~ können** we/the town won't be
able to hold out much longer; b) *(sich
bewähren)* **sich gut** ~: do well; c) *(unverändert bleiben)* *⟨weather, flowers,
etc.⟩* last; *⟨milk, meat, etc.⟩* keep; d)
*(Körperhaltung haben)* **sich schlecht/
gerade** ~: hold oneself badly/straight;
e) *(bleiben)* **sich auf den Beinen/im
Sattel** ~: stay on one's feet/in the
saddle; **sich links/rechts** ~: keep [to
the] left/right; **sich an etw.** *(Akk.)* ~:
keep to sth.
**Halter** der; ~s, ~ a) *(Fahrzeug~)*
keeper; b) *(Tier~)* owner; c) *(Vorrichtung)* holder; **Halterung** die; ~, ~en
support

**Halte-:** ~**stelle** die stop; ~**verbot**
das a) „~**verbot**" 'no stopping'; **hier
ist** ~**verbot** this is a no-stopping zone;
b) *(Stelle)* no-stopping zone; ~**ver-
bots·schild** das no-stopping sign
**-haltig,** *(österr.)* -**hältig:** **vit-
amin~/silber~** *usw.* containing vit-
amins/silver *etc. postpos., not pred.;*
**vitamin~ sein** contain vitamins
**halt-:** ~**los** *Adj.* a) *(labil)* ~**los sein** be
a weak character; **ein** ~**loser Mensch** a
weak character; b) *(unbegründet)* un-
founded; ~|**machen** *itr. V.* stop
**Haltung** die; ~, ~en a) *(Körper~)* posture; b) *(Pose)* manner; c) *(Einstellung)* attitude; d) *(Fassung)* composure
**Halunke** der; ~n, ~n scoundrel; villain
**Hamburger** der; ~s, ~ od. ~s *(Frikadelle)* hamburger
**hämisch 1.** *Adj.* malicious; 2. *adv.*
maliciously
**Hammel** der; ~s, ~ a) wether; b)
*(Fleisch)* mutton; **Hammel·fleisch**
das mutton
**Hammer** der; ~s, Hämmer a) hammer; *(Holz~)* mallet; ~ **und Sichel**
hammer and sickle; b) *(Technik)* ram;
**hämmern** *itr., tr. V.* hammer
**Hämorrhoiden** [hɛmɔro'iːdn̩] *Pl.*
*(Med.)* haemorrhoids; piles
**Hampel·mann** der; ~|e|s, Hampel-
männer a) jumping jack; b) *(ugs. abwertend)* puppet
**hampeln** *itr. V. (ugs.)* jump about
**Hamster** der; ~s, ~: hamster
**hamstern** *tr., itr. V.* a) *(horten)* hoard;
b) *(Lebensmittel tauschen)* barter
goods for [food]
**Hand** die; ~, Hände hand; **jmdm. die** ~
**geben** shake sb.'s hand; ~ **und Fuß/
weder** ~ **noch Fuß haben** *(ugs.)* make
sense/no sense; **alle** *od.* **beide Hände
damit voll haben,** etw. **zu tun** *(ugs.)*
have one's hands full doing sth.; **die
Hände in den Schoß legen** sit back and
do nothing; **etw. aus der** ~ **geben** let
sth. out of one's hands; ~ **in** ~ **arbeiten** work hand in hand; **etw. zur** ~ **ha-
ben** have sth. handy; **zu Händen |von|
Herrn Müller** attention Herr Müller
**Hand-:** ~**arbeit** die a) handicraft;
**etw. in** ~**arbeit herstellen** make sth. by
hand; b) *(Gegenstand)* handmade article; c) *(Nadelarbeit)* [piece of] needlework; ~**ball** der handball; ~**besen**
der brush; ~**betrieb** der; *o. Pl.* manual operation; ~**bewegung** die a)

movement of the hand; b) *(Geste)* gesture; **~bremse** die handbrake; **~buch** das handbook; *(technisches ~buch)* manual

**Händchen** das; ~s, ~: [little] hand; **Hände** s. Hand

**Hände-:** **~druck** der; *Pl.* ~drücke handshake; **~klatschen** das; ~s clapping

**Handel** der; ~s trade; **handeln 1.** *itr. V.* **a)** trade; deal; **b)** *(feilschen)* haggle; **c)** *(agieren)* act; **d)** *(sich verhalten)* behave; **e) von etw.** *od.* **über etw.** *(Akk.)* ~ ⟨*book, film, etc.*⟩ be about *or* deal with sth.; **2.** *refl. V. (unpers.)* **es handelt sich um ...**: it is a matter of ...; *(es dreht sich um)* it's about ...

**handels-, Handels-:** **~abkommen** das trade agreement; **~bank** die merchant bank; **~bilanz** die **a)** *(eines Betriebes)* balance-sheet; **b)** *(eines Staates)* balance of trade; **~einig, ~eins in** mit jmdm. **~einig** *od.* **~eins werden/ sein** agree/have agreed terms with sb.; **~flotte** die merchant fleet; **~gesellschaft** die company; **~klasse** die grade; **~marine** die merchant navy; **~partner** der trading partner; **~register** das register of companies; **~schiff** das merchant ship; **~schule** die commercial college; **~straße** die *(hist.)* trade route; **~üblich** *Adj.* **~übliche Praktiken/Größen** standard business practices/standard [commercial] sizes; **~unternehmen** das trading concern; **~vertreter** der [sales] representative; travelling salesman/ saleswoman; **~vertretung** die trade mission; **~zentrum** das trading centre

**hände·ringend** *Adv. (ugs.: dringend)* ⟨*need*⟩ urgently; ⟨*search for sb./sth.*⟩ desperately

**hand-, Hand-:** **~feger** der brush; **~fest** *Adj.* robust; sturdy; substantial ⟨*meal etc.*⟩; **c)** solid ⟨*proof*⟩; concrete ⟨*suggestion*⟩; complete ⟨*lie*⟩; well-founded ⟨*argument*⟩; **~fläche** die palm [of one's/the hand]; flat of one's/the hand; **~gas** das *(Kfz-W.)* hand throttle; **~gearbeitet** *Adj.* hand-made; **~gelenk** das wrist; **~gemenge** das fight; **~gepäck** das hand-baggage; **~geschrieben** *Adj.* handwritten; **~granate** die hand-grenade; **~greiflich** *Adj.* **a)** *(tätlich)* **~greiflich werden** start using one's fists; **b)** tangible ⟨*success, advantage, proof, etc.*⟩; palpable ⟨*contradiction,*

*error*⟩; obvious ⟨*fact*⟩; **~griff** der **a)** mit einem **~griff/wenigen ~griffen** in one movement/without much trouble; *(schnell)* in no time at all/next to no time; **b)** *(am Koffer, an einem Werkzeug)* handle; **~habe** die ~, ~n: eine ⟨rechtliche⟩ **~habe** [gegen jmdn.] a legal handle [against sb.]; **~haben** *tr. V.* **a)** handle; operate ⟨*device, machine*⟩; **b)** *(praktizieren)* implement ⟨*law etc.*⟩; **~habung** die ~, ~en **a)** handling; *(eines Gerätes, einer Maschine)* operation; **b)** *(Durchführung)* implementation

**Handikap** ['hɛndikɛp] das; ~s, ~s *(auch Sport)* handicap; **handikapen** ['hɛndikɛpn] *tr. V.* handicap

**Hand-:** **~käse** der *(landsch.)* small, hand-formed curd cheese; **~koffer** der [small] suitcase; **~kuß** der kiss on sb.'s hand; **~langer** der; ~s, ~ *(ungelernter·Arbeiter)* labourer; *(abwertend)* lackey; **~lauf** der handrail

**Händler** der; ~s, ~: trader

**handlich** *Adj.* handy; easily carried ⟨*parcel, suitcase*⟩; easily portable ⟨*television, camera*⟩

**Handlung** die; ~, ~en **a)** *(Vorgehen)* action; *(Tat)* act; **b)** *(Fabel)* plot

**handlungs-, Handlungs-:** **~fähig** *Adj.* able to act *pred.*; working *attrib.* ⟨*majority*⟩; **~freiheit** die; *o. Pl.* freedom of action; **~reisende** der/die s. **Handelsvertreter**; **~weise** die conduct

**hand-, Hand-:** **puppe** die glove *or* hand puppet; **~schelle** die handcuff; **~schlag** der handshake; **~schrift** die handwriting; **~schriftlich 1.** *Adj.* hand-written; **2.** *adv.* by hand; **~schuh** der glove; **~schuhfach** das glove compartment; **~signiert** *Adj.* signed; **~spiegel** der hand-mirror; **~stand** der *(Turnen)* handstand; **~tasche** die handbag; **~tuch** das; *Pl.* -tücher towel; **~umdrehen:** im **~umdrehen** in no time at all; **~voll** die; ~ *(auch fig.)* handful

**Hand·werk** das craft; *(als Beruf)* trade; **sein** ~ **kennen** *od.* **verstehen/beherrschen** know one's job; **Handwerker** der; ~s, ~: tradesman; **handwerklich** *Adj.* **ein ~er Beruf** a [skilled] trade; **Handwerks·zeug** das tools *pl.*

**Hand·zeichen** das sign [with one's hand]; *(eines Autofahrers)* hand signal; *(Abstimmung)* show of hands

**Hanf** der; ~[e]s hemp

**Hang** der; ~|e|s, **Hänge** slope; *(Neigung)* tendency

**Hänge-**: ~**brücke** die suspension bridge; ~**lampe** die pendant-light; ~**matte** die hammock

¹**hängen** *unr. itr. V.; südd., österr., schweiz. mit sein* hang (**an** + *Dat.* from); *(an einem Fahrzeug)* be hitched (**an** + *Dat.* to); ²**hängen** 1. *tr. V.* a) hang (**in/über** + *(Akk.)* in/over; **an/ auf** + *Akk.* on); *(befestigen)* hitch up (**an** + *Akk.* to); couple on ⟨*railway carriage, etc.*⟩ (**an** + *Akk.* to); 2. *refl. V.* a) **sich an etw.** *(Akk.)* ~: hang on to sth.; b) *(sich festsetzen)* cling (**an** + *Akk.* to); **hängen|bleiben** *unr. itr. V.; mit sein (ugs.)* a) *(festgehalten werden)* [mit dem Ärmel *usw.*] **an/in etw.** *(Dat.)* ~: get one's sleeve *etc.* caught on/in sth.; b) *(verweilen)* get stuck *(coll.);* c) *(haften)* **an/auf etw.** *(Dat.)* ~: stick to sth.; **hängend** *Adj.* hanging; **Hänge·schrank** der wall-cupboard

**hänseln** *tr. V.* tease

**Hanse·stadt** die Hanseatic city

**Hantel** die; ~, ~n *(Sport)(kurz)* dumbbell; *(lang)* barbell

**hantieren** *itr. V.* be busy

**Häppchen** das; ~s, ~ a) [small] morsel; b) *(Appetithappen)* canapé

**Happen** der; ~s, ~: morsel

**happig** *Adj. (ugs.)* ~**e Preise** fancy prices *(coll.)*

**Happy-End** [ˈhɛpiˈlɛnt] das; ~|s|, ~s happy ending

**Harfe** die; ~, ~n harp

**Harke** die; ~, ~n rake; **harken** *tr. V.* rake

**harm·los** 1. *Adj.* a) *(ungefährlich)* harmless; slight ⟨*injury, cold, etc.*⟩; mild ⟨*illness*⟩; safe ⟨*medicine, bend, road, etc.*⟩; b) *(arglos)* innocent; harmless ⟨*fun, pastime, etc.*⟩; 2. *adv.* a) *(ungefährlich)* harmlessly; b) *(arglos)* innocently; **Harmlosigkeit** die; ~ a) *(Ungefährlichkeit)* harmlessness *(einer Krankheit)* mildness; *(eines Medikamentes)* safety; b) *(Arglosigkeit, harmloses Verhalten)* innocence

**Harmonie** die; ~, ~n *(auch fig.)* harmony; **harmonieren** *itr. V.* a) harmonize; b) *(miteinander auskommen)* get on well

**Harmonika** die; ~, ~s *od.* **Harmoniken** harmonica

**harmonisch** 1. *Adj.* harmonious; *(Musik)* harmonic; 2. *adv.* harmoniously; *(Musik)* harmonically

**Harmonium** das; ~s, **Harmonien** harmonium

**Harn** der; ~|e|s, ~e *(Med.)* urine; **Harn·blase** die bladder

**Harnisch** der; ~s, ~e armour

**Harpune** die; ~, ~n harpoon

**harren** *itr. V. (geh.)* **jmds./einer Sache** *od.* **auf jmdn./etw.** ~: await sb./sth.

**harsch** 1. *Adj.* a) *(vereist)* crusted; b) *(barsch)* harsh; 2. *adv.* harshly; **Harsch** der; ~|e|s crusted snow

**hart; härter, härtest...** 1. *Adj.* a) hard; b) tough ⟨*situation, job*⟩; harsh ⟨*reality, truth*⟩; c) *(streng)* harsh ⟨*penalty, punishment, judgement*⟩; tough ⟨*measure, law, course*⟩; d) *(rauh)* rough ⟨*game, opponent*⟩; 2. *adv.* hard chair; a) *(mühevoll)* ⟨*work*⟩ hard; b) *(streng)* harshly; c) *(nahe)* close (**an** + *Dat.* to); **Härte** die; ~, ~n a) *(auch Physik)* hardness; b) *(Widerstandsfähigkeit)* toughness; c) *(schwere Belastung)* hardship; d) *(Strenge)* harshness; e) *(Heftigkeit)* ⟨*eines Aufpralls usw.*⟩ force; *(eines Streits)* violence; f) *(Rauheit)* roughness; **Härte·fall** der a) case of hardship; b) *(ugs.: Person)* hardship case; **härten** *tr., itr. V.* harden; **härter** *s.* **hart; härtest...** *s.* **hart**

**hart-, Hart-**: ~**gekocht** *Adj.* hardboiled ⟨*egg*⟩; ~**geld** das coins *pl.*; ~**herzig** 1. *Adj.* hard-hearted; 2. *adv.* hard-heartedly; ~**herzigkeit** die; ~: hard-heartedness; ~**näckig** 1. *Adj.* a) *(eigensinnig)* obstinate; stubborn; b) *(ausdauernd)* dogged; 2. *adv.* a) *(eigensinnig)* obstinately; stubbornly; b) *(ausdauernd)* doggedly; ~**näckigkeit** die; ~ a) *(Eigensinn)* obstinacy; stubbornness; b) *(Ausdauer)* doggedness; ~**wurst** die dry sausage

**Harz** das; ~es, ~e resin

**Harzer Käse** der; ~ ~s, ~ ~: Harz [Mountain] cheese

**Haschee** *(Kochk.)* das; ~s, ~s hash

¹**haschen** *tr. V. (veralt.)* catch

²**haschen** *itr. V. (ugs.)* smoke [hash] *(coll.)*

**Häschen** [ˈhɛːsçən] das; ~, ~: bunny

**Haschisch** das *od.* der; ~|s| hashish

**Hase** der; ~n, ~n a) hare; b) *(landsch.) s.* **Kaninchen**

**Hasel·nuß** die hazel-nut

**Hasen-**: ~**fuß** der *(spöttisch abwertend)* coward; chicken *(sl.);* ~**scharte** die *(Med.)* harelip

**Haspel** die; ~, ~n *(Technik)(für Garn)* reel; *(für ein Seil, Kabel)* drum

**Haß** der; **Hasses** hatred (**auf** + *Akk.*, **gegen** of, for); **hassen** *tr.*, *itr. V.* hate; **haß·erfüllt** *Adj.* filled with hatred *postpos.*

**häßlich** 1. *Adj.* **a)** ugly; **b)** *(gemein)* nasty; **c)** *(unangenehm)* awful ⟨*weather, cold, situation, etc.*⟩; 2. *adv.* **a)** ⟨*dress*⟩ unattractively; **b)** *(gemein)* nastily; **Häßlichkeit** die; ~, ~**en a)** *o. Pl. (Aussehen)* ugliness; **b)** *o. Pl. (Gesinnung)* nastiness

**hast** 2. *Pers. Sg. Präsens v.* **haben**

**Hast** die; ~: haste; **hasten** *itr. V.; mit sein* hurry; **hastig** 1. *Adj.* hasty; hurried; 2. *adv.* hastily; hurriedly

**hat** 3. *Pers. Sg. Präsens v.* **haben**

**hätscheln** *tr. V.* caress

**hatschi** *Interj.* atishoo

**hatte** *1. u. 3. Pers. Sg. Prät. v.* **haben**; **hätte** *1. u. 3. Pers. Sg. Konjunktiv II v.* **haben**

**Haube** die; ~, ~**n a)** bonnet; *(einer Krankenschwester)* cap; **b)** *(Kfz-W.)* bonnet *(Brit.)*; hood *(Amer.)*

**Hauch** der; ~|e|s, ~e *(geh.)* **a)** *(Atem, auch fig.)* breath; **b)** *(Luftzug)* breath of wind; **c)** *(leichter Duft)* delicate smell; **d)** *(dünne Schicht)* [gossamer-]thin layer; **hauch·dünn** *Adj.* gossamer-thin ⟨*material, dress*⟩; wafer-thin ⟨*layer, slice, majority*⟩; **hauchen** *itr. V.* breathe (**gegen, auf** + *Akk.* on)

**Haue** die; ~, ~**n a)** *(südd., österr.: Hakke)* hoe; **b)** *(ugs.: Prügel)* a hiding *(coll.)*; **hauen** 1. *unr. tr. V.* **a)** *(ugs.: schlagen)* belt; clobber *(coll.)*; **b)** *(ugs.: auf einen Körperteil)* belt *(coll.)*; hit; **c)** *(herstellen)* carve ⟨*figure, statue, etc.*⟩ (**in** + *Akk.* in); 2. *unr. itr. V.* **a)** *(ugs.: prügeln)* **er haut immer gleich** he's quick to hit out; **b)** *(auf einen Körperteil)* belt *(coll.)*; hit; **c)** *(ugs.: auf/gegen etw. schlagen)* thump; 3. *unr. refl. V. (ugs.: sich prügeln)* have a punch-up *(coll.)*

**Haufen** der; ~s, ~: heap; pile; *(Gruppe)* bunch *(coll.)*; **häufen** 1. *tr. V.* heap, pile (**auf** + *Akk.* on to); *(aufheben)* hoard ⟨*money, supplies*⟩; 2. *refl. V. (sich mehren)* pile up

**häufig** 1. *Adj.* frequent; 2. *adv.* frequently; often; **Häufigkeit** die; ~, ~**en** frequency; **Häufung** die; ~, ~**en** increasing frequency

**Haupt** das; ~|e|s, **Häupter** *(geh., auch fig.)* head

**haupt-, Haupt-:** ~**bahnhof** der main station; ~**beruflich** 1. *Adj.* sei-

ne ~**berufliche Tätigkeit** his main occupation; 2. *adv.* **er ist** ~**beruflich als Elektriker tätig** his main occupation is that of electrician; ~**darsteller** der *(Theater, Film)* male lead; ~**darstellerin** die *(Theater, Film)* female lead; ~**eingang** der main entrance; ~**fach** das major; ~**figur** die main character; ~**film** der main feature; ~**gebäude** das main building; ~**gericht** das main course; ~**gewinn** der first prize

**Häuptling** der; ~s, ~e chief[tain]

**haupt-, Haupt-:** ~**mahlzeit** die main meal; ~**mann** der; *Pl.* ~**leute** *(Milit.)* captain; ~**person** die central figure; ~**postamt** das main post office; ~**quartier** das *(Milit., auch fig.)* headquarters *sing. or pl.*; ~**rolle** die main role; lead; ~**sache** die main thing; ~**sächlich** 1. *Adv.* mainly; principally; 2. *Adj.; nicht präd.* main; principal; ~**saison** die high season; ~**satz** der main clause; *(alleinstehend)* sentence; ~**schlagader** die aorta; ~**schul·abschluß** der ≈ secondary school leaving certificate; ~**schule** die ≈ secondary modern school; ~**stadt** die capital [city]; ~**städtisch** *Adj.* metropolitan; ~**straße** die main street; ~**verkehr** der bulk of the traffic

**Hauptverkehrs-:** ~**straße** die main road; ~**zeit** die rush hour

**Haupt-:** ~**wache** die main police station; ~**wort** das *(Sprachw.)* noun

**hau ruck** *Interj.* heave[-ho]

**Haus** das; ~es, **Häuser** house; *(Amts-, Firmengebäude usw.)* building; *(Heim)* home; **nach** ~e home; **zu** ~e at home; **das erste** ~ **am Platze** the best hotel in the town

**haus-, Haus-:** ~**angestellte** der/die domestic servant; ~**apotheke** die medicine cabinet; ~**arbeit** die housework; *(Schulw.)* homework; ~**arrest** der house arrest; ~**arzt** der family doctor; ~**aufgabe** die homework; ~**backen** 1. *Adj.* plain; unadventurous ⟨*clothes*⟩; 2. *adv.* ⟨*dress*⟩ unadventurously; ~**besetzer** der squatter; ~**besitzer** der house-owner; *(Vermieter)* landlord; ~**besitzerin** die house-owner; *(Vermieterin)* landlady; ~**besuch** der house-call; ~**boot** das houseboat

**Häuschen** ['hɔysçən] das; ~s, ~: small house; **aus dem** ~ **sein** *(ugs.)* be over the moon *(coll.)*; **hausen** *itr. V.*

*(ugs. abwertend)* live; **b)** *(Verwüstungen anrichten)* |**furchtbar**| ~: wreak havoc; **Häuser·block der** block [of houses]

**haus-, Haus-:** ~**flur der** hall[way]; *(im Obergeschoß)* landing; ~**frau die** housewife; ~**freund der a)** friend of the family; *(verhüll.: Liebhaber)* man-friend *(euphem.)*; ~**friedensbruch der** *(Rechtsw.)* trespass; ~**gebrauch der** domestic use; **das reicht für den** ~**gebrauch** *(ugs.)* it's good enough to get by *(coll.)*; ~**gehilfin die** [home] help; ~**gemacht** *Adj.* home-made

**Haus·halt der a)** household; **b)** *(Arbeit im* ~*)* housekeeping; **jmdm. den** ~ **führen** keep house for sb.; **c)** *(Politik)* budget; **haus|halten** *unr. itr. V.* be economical (mit with); **Haushälterin die;** ~, ~**nen** housekeeper

**Haushalts-:** ~**debatte, die** *(Politik)* budget debatte; ~**geld das;** *o. Pl.* housekeeping money; ~**jahr das** financial year; ~**kasse die** housekeeping money; ~**plan der** budget; ~**waren** *Pl.* household goods

**Haus·herr der a)** *(Familienoberhaupt)* head of the household; **b)** *(als Gastgeber)* host; **c)** *(Rechtsspr.) (Eigentümer)* owner; *(Mieter)* occupier; **haushoch 1.** *Adj.* as high as a house; *(fig.)* overwhelming; **2.** *adv. (fig.)* ~ **gewinnen** win hands down

**hausieren** *itr. V.* |mit etw.| ~: hawk [sth.]; peddle [sth.]; „**Hausieren verboten**" 'no hawkers'; **Hausierer der;** ~s, ~: pedlar; hawker

**häuslich** *Adj.* **a)** domestic; **b)** *(das Zuhause liebend)* home-loving

**Hausmacher·art die: nach** ~: home-made-style *attrib.*

**Hausmanns·kost die** plain cooking

**Haus-:** ~**marke die a)** house wine; **b)** *(ugs.: bevorzugtes Getränk)* favourite tipple *(coll.)*; ~**meister der,** ~**meisterin die** caretaker; ~**mittel das** household remedy; ~**musik die** music at home; ~**nummer die** house number; ~**ordnung die** house rules *pl.*; ~**putz der** spring-clean; *(regelmäßig)* clean-out; ~**rat der** household goods *pl.*; ~**schlüssel der** front-door key; house-key; ~**schuh der** slipper

**Haussuchung die;** ~, ~**en** house search; **Haussuchungs·befehl der** search warrant

**Haus-:** ~**tier das a)** pet; **b)** *(Nutztier)* domestic animal; ~**tür die** front door; ~**verbot das** ban on entering the house/pub/restaurant *etc.;* ~**verwalter der** manager [of the block]; ~**wirt der** landlord; ~**wirtin die** landlady; ~**wirtschaft die;** *o. Pl.* domestic science and home economics

**Haut die;** ~, **Häute** skin; **aus der** ~ **fahren** *(ugs.)* go up the wall *(coll.)*; **Haut·arzt der** skin specialist; **häuten 1.** *tr. V.* skin; flay; **2.** *refl. V.* shed its skin/their skins

**haut-, Haut-:** ~**eng** *Adj.* skin-tight; ~**farbe die** [skin] colour; ~**krankheit die** skin disease

**Haxe die;** ~, ~**n** *s.* Hachse

**he** *Interj.* *(ugs.)* hey

**Heb·amme die** midwife

**Hebel der;** ~s, ~: lever

**heben** *unr. tr. V.* **a)** lift; raise 〈baton, camera, glass〉; **b)** *(verbessern)* raise 〈standard, level〉; increase 〈turnover, self-confidence〉; improve 〈mood〉; enhance 〈standing〉; boost 〈morale〉

**¹hecheln** *itr. V.* *(ugs. abwertend)* gossip

**²hecheln** *itr. V.* pant [for breath]

**Hecht der;** ~|e|s, ~e pike; **Hecht·sprung der a)** *(Turnen)* Hecht vault; **b)** *(Schwimmen)* racing dive; *(vom Sprungturm)* pike-dive

**Heck das;** ~|e|s, ~e *od.* ~s stern; *(Flugzeug* ~*)* tail; *(Auto* ~*)* rear

**Hecke die;** ~, ~**n a)** hedge; **b)** *(wildwachsend)* thicket

**Hecken-:** ~**rose die** dogrose; ~**schütze der** sniper

**Heck·scheibe die** rear window

**Heer das;** ~|e|s, ~e armed forces *pl.;* *(für den Landkrieg, fig.)* army

**Hefe die;** ~, ~**n** yeast

**¹Heft das;** ~|e|s, ~e *(geh.)* haft; handle

**²Heft das;** ~|e|s, ~e **a)** *(bes. Schule)* exercise-book; **b)** *(Nummer einer Zeitschrift)* issue; **Heftchen das;** ~s, ~: book [of tickets/stamps *etc.* ]; **heften 1.** *tr. V.* **a)** *(mit einer Nadel)* pin; *(mit einer Klammer)* clip; *(mit Klebstoff)* stick; **b)** *(Schneiderei)* tack; **c)** *(Buchbinderei)* stitch; *(mit Klammern)* staple; **2.** *refl. V.* **sich an jmds. Fersen** *(Akk.)* ~: stick hard on sb.'s heels

**heftig 1.** *Adj.* violent; heavy 〈rain, shower, blow〉; severe 〈pain〉; 〈person〉 with a violent temper; **2.** *adv.* 〈rain, snow, breathe〉 heavily; 〈hit〉 hard; 〈quarrel〉 violently

**Heft-:** ~**klammer die** staple; ~**pflaster das** sticking plaster; ~**zwecke die** *s.* Reißzwecke

**hegen** *tr. V.* **a)** *(bes. Forstw., Jagdw.)*

look after, tend; **b)** *(geh.: umsorgen)* look after; **c)** *(fig.)* feel ⟨contempt, hatred, mistrust⟩; cherish ⟨hope, wish, desire⟩; harbour ⟨grudge, suspicion⟩

**Hehl** der *od.* das: kein|en| ~ aus etw. machen make no secret of sth.; **Hehler** der; ~s, ~: receiver [of stolen goods]; **Hehlerei** die; ~, ~en *(Rechtsw.)* receiving [stolen goods] *no art.*

**¹Heide** der; ~n, ~n heathen

**²Heide** die; ~, ~n **a)** heath; *(~landschaft)* heathland; **Heide·kraut** das; *o. Pl.* heather

**Heidel·beere** die bilberry

**heidnisch** *Adj.* heathen

**heikel** *Adj.* **a)** *(schwierig)* delicate, ticklish ⟨matter, subject⟩; ticklish tricky ⟨problem, question, situation⟩; **b)** *(wählerisch)* fussy **(in bezug auf +** *Akk.* about)

**heil** *Adj. (nicht entzwei)* in one piece; wieder ~ sein ⟨injured part⟩ have healed [up]; **Heil** das; ~s **a)** *(Wohlergehen)* benefit; **b)** *(Rel.)* salvation; **Heiland** der; ~|e|s, ~e Saviour

**Heil·anstalt** die *(Anstalt für Kranke od. Süchtige)* sanatorium; *(psychiatrische Klinik)* mental hospital; **heilbar** *Adj.* curable

**Heil·butt** der halibut

**heilen** 1. *tr. V.* cure; heal ⟨wound⟩; 2. *itr. V.; mit sein* ⟨wound⟩ heal [up]; ⟨fracture⟩ mend

**heil·froh** *Adj.* very glad

**heilig** *Adj.* **a)** holy; **die Heilige Schrift** the Holy Scriptures *pl.;* **der Heilige Abend** Christmas Eve **b)** *(geh.: unantastbar)* sacred ⟨right, tradition, cause, etc.⟩; **Heilig·abend** der Christmas Eve; **Heilige** der/die; *adj. Dekl.* saint; **heiligen** *tr. V.* keep ⟨tradition, Sabbath, etc.⟩; **der Zweck heiligt die Mittel** the end justifies the means; **Heiligen·schein** der gloriole; *(um den Kopf)* halo; **Heiligkeit** die; ~: holiness; **Heiligtum** das; ~s, **Heiligtümer** shrine

**Heil-:** ~kraut das medicinal herb; ~mittel das *(auch fig.)* remedy (gegen for); *(Medikament)* medicament; ~praktiker der non-medical practitioner

**heilsam** *Adj.* salutary; **Heils·armee** die Salvation Army; **Heilung** die; ~, ~en *(einer Wunde)* healing; *(von Krankheit, Kranken)* curing

**Heim** das; ~|e|s, ~e **a)** *(Zuhause)* home; **b)** *(Anstalt, Alters~)* home; *(für*

Obdachlose) hostel; **Heim·arbeit** die outwork

**Heimat** die; ~, ~en **a)** *(~ort)* home; home town/village; *(~land)* home; homeland; **b)** *(Ursprungsland)* natural habitat

**Heimat-:** ~kunde die local history, geography, and natural history; ~land das native land; *(fig.)* home

**heimatlich** *Adj.* native ⟨dialect⟩; nostalgic ⟨emotions⟩

**heimat-, Heimat-:** ~los *Adj.* homeless; ~museum das museum of local history; ~ort der home town/village; ~vertriebene der/die; *adj. Dekl.* expellee [from his/her homeland]

**heim-, Heim-:** ~|bringen *unr. tr. V.* **a)** jmdn. ~: take *or.* see sb. home; **b)** bring home; ~|fahren 1. *unr. itr. V.; mit sein* drive home; 2. *unr. tr. V.* drive home; ~fahrt die journey home; *(mit dem Auto)* drive home; ~|gehen *unr. itr. V.; mit sein* go home

**heimisch** *Adj. (einheimisch)* indigenous, native ⟨plants, animals, etc.⟩ **(in** + *Dat.* to); domestic ⟨industry⟩; **sich** ~ fühlen feel at home; ~ **werden [in (** + *Dat.*)] settle in[to]

**heim-, Heim-:** ~kehr die; ~: return home; homecoming; ~|kehren *itr. V.; mit sein* return home **(aus** from); ~|kommen *unr. itr. V.; mit sein* come home

**heimlich** 1. *Adj.* secret; 2. *adv.* secretly; **Heimlichkeit** die; ~, ~en; *meist Pl.* secret

**heim-, Heim-:** ~reise die journey home; ~|suchen *tr. V.* ⟨storm, earthquake, epidemic⟩ strike; ⟨disease⟩ afflict; ⟨nightmares, doubts⟩ plague; ~tückisch 1. *Adj. (bösartig)* malicious; *(fig.)* insidious ⟨disease⟩; 2. *adv.* maliciously; ~wärts *Adv. (nach Hause zu)* home; *(in Richtung Heimat)* homeward[s]; ~weg der way home-; ~weh das homesickness; ~weh haben be homesick **(nach** for); ~|zahlen *tr. V.* jmdm. etw. ~zahlen pay sb. back for sth.

**Heinzel·männchen** das brownie

**Heirat** die; ~, ~en marriage; **heiraten** 1. *itr. V.* get married; 2. *tr. V.* marry

**Heirats-:** ~antrag der: jmdm. einen ~antrag machen propose to sb.; ~anzeige die announcement of a/the forthcoming marriage; ~schwindler der *person who makes a spurious offer of marriage for purposes of fraud*

**heiser** 1. *Adj.* hoarse; 2. *adv.* in a hoarse voice; **Heiserkeit die;** ~ *s.* heiser: hoarseness

**heiß** 1. *Adj.* hot; **jmdm. ist** ~: sb. feels hot; **etw.** ~ **machen** heat sth. up; heated ⟨*debate, argument*⟩; fierce ⟨*fight, battle*⟩; ardent ⟨*wish, love*⟩; **ein** ~**es Thema** a controversial subject; 2. *adv.* ⟨*fight*⟩ fiercely; ⟨*love*⟩ dearly; ⟨*long*⟩ fervently

**heißen** *unr. itr. V.* ⟨*den Namen tragen*⟩ be called; ⟨*bedeuten*⟩ mean; ⟨*lauten*⟩ ⟨*saying*⟩ go; ⟨*unpers.*⟩ **es heißt, daß ...**: they say that ...; **in dem Artikel heißt es ...**: in the article it says that ...

**heiter** *Adj.* cheerful; fine ⟨*weather, day*⟩; **Heiterkeit die;** ~ a) ⟨*Frohsinn*⟩ cheerfulness; b) ⟨*Belustigung*⟩ merriment

**heizbar** *Adj.* heated; **Heiz·decke die** electric blanket; **heizen** 1. *itr. V.* have the heating on; 2. *tr. V.* heat ⟨*room etc.*⟩; **Heizer der;** ~s, ~ ⟨*einer Lokomotive*⟩ fireman; ⟨*eines Schiffes*⟩ stoker

**Heiz-:** ~**kissen das** heating pad; ~**körper der** radiator; ~**ofen der** stove; heater; ~**platte die** hotplate

**Heizung die;** ~, ~**en** a) [central] heating *no pl., no indef. art.;* b) ⟨*ugs.: Heizkörper*⟩ radiator

**Hektar das** *od.* **der;** ~s, ~**e** hectare

**Hektik die;** ~: hectic rush; ⟨*des Lebens*⟩ hectic pace; **hektisch** *Adj.* hectic

**Held der;** ~**en,** ~**en** hero; **heldenhaft** 1. *Adj.* heroic; 2. *adv.* heroically; **Heldentum das;** ~s heroism; **Heldin die;** ~, ~**nen** heroine

**helfen** *unr. itr. V.* help; **jmdm. [bei etw.]** ~: help sb. [with sth.]; ⟨*unpers.*⟩ **es hilft nichts** it's no use *or* good; **Helfer der;** ~s, ~: helper; ⟨*Mitarbeiter*⟩ assistant; ⟨*eines Verbrechens*⟩ accomplice

**Helikopter der;** ~s, ~: helicopter

**hell** 1. *Adj.* a) ⟨*von Licht erfüllt*⟩ light; well-lit ⟨*stairs*⟩; b) ⟨*klar*⟩ bright ⟨*day, sky, etc.*⟩; c) ⟨*viel Licht spendend*⟩ bright ⟨*light, lamp, star, etc.*⟩; d) ⟨*blaß*⟩ light ⟨*colour*⟩; fair ⟨*skin, hair*⟩; light-coloured ⟨*clothes*⟩; e) ⟨*akustisch*⟩ high, clear ⟨*sound, voice*⟩; ringing ⟨*laugh*⟩; f) ⟨*klug*⟩ bright; g) ⟨*ugs.: absolut*⟩ sheer, utter ⟨*madness, foolishness, despair*⟩; 2. *adv.* brightly

**hell-:** ~**blau** *Adj.* light blue; ~**blond** *Adj.* very fair; light blonde

**Helle das;** *adj. Dekl.* ≈ lager

**Heller der;** ~s, ~: heller; **bis auf den letzten** ~/**bis auf** ~ **und Pfennig** ⟨*ugs.*⟩ down to the last penny *or* ⟨*Amer.*⟩ cent

**hell-:** ~**grün** *Adj.* light green; ~**häutig** *Adj.* fair-skinned

**Helligkeit die;** ~, ~**en** ⟨*auch Physik*⟩ brightness

**hell-, Hell-:** ~**rot** *Adj.* light red; ~**sehen** *unr. itr. V.; nur im Inf.* ~**sehen können** have second sight; ~**seher der** clairvoyant; ~**wach** *Adj.* wide awake

**Helm der;** ~[e]s, ~e helmet

**Hemd das;** ~[e]s, ~**en** shirt; ⟨*Unterhemd*⟩ [under]vest; undershirt; **Hemds·ärmel der** shirt-sleeve

**hemmen** *tr. V.* a) ⟨*verlangsamen*⟩ slow [down]; b) ⟨*aufhalten*⟩ check; stem ⟨*flow*⟩; c) ⟨*beeinträchtigen*⟩ hinder; **Hemmung die;** ~, ~**en** a) ⟨*Gehemmtheit*⟩ inhibition; b) ⟨*Bedenken*⟩ scruple; **hemmungs·los** 1. *Adj.* unrestrained; 2. *adv.* unrestrainedly

**Hendl das;** ~s, ~[n] ⟨*bayr., österr.*⟩ chicken; ⟨*Brathähnchen*⟩ [roast] chicken

**Hengst der;** ~[e]s, ~**e** ⟨*Pferd*⟩ stallion

**Henkel der;** ~s, ~: handle

**Henker der;** ~s, ~: hangman; ⟨*Scharfrichter, auch fig.*⟩ executioner

**Henne die;** ~, ~**n** hen

**her** [he:ɐ̯] *Adv.* ~ **damit** give it to me; give it here ⟨*coll.*⟩; **vom Fenster** ~: from the window; **von ihrer Kindheit** ~: since childhood; **von der Konzeption** ~: as far as the last basic design is concerned

**herab** *Adv.* down; **von oben** ~ ⟨*fig.*⟩ condescendingly

**herab-:** ~**hängen** *unr. itr. V.* hang [down] ⟨*von* from⟩; ~**hängende Schultern** drooping shoulders; ~**lassen** 1. *unr. tr. V.* let down; lower; 2. *unr. refl. V.* ⟨*iron.: bereit sein*⟩ **sich** ~**lassen, etw. zu tun** condescend to do sth.; ~**lassend** 1. *Adj.* condescending; patronizing ⟨*zu* towards⟩; 2. *adv.* condescendingly; patronizingly; ~**sehen** *unr. itr. V.* **auf jmdn.** ~**sehen** look down on sb.; ~**setzen** *tr. V.* a) reduce; b) ⟨*abwerten*⟩ belittle

**heran** *Adv.* **an etw.** ⟨*Akk.*⟩ ~: right up to sth.

**heran-, Heran-:** ~**bilden** *tr. V.* train [up]; ⟨*auf der Schule, Universität*⟩ educate; ~**bringen** *unr. tr. V.* a) bring [up] ⟨**an** + *Akk.,* **zu** to⟩; b) ⟨*vertraut machen*⟩ **jmdn. an etw.** ⟨*Akk.*⟩ ~**bringen** introduce sb. to sth.; ~**fahren**

*unr. itr. V.; mit sein* drive up (**an** + *Akk.* to); ~|**kommen** *unr. itr. V.; mit sein* **an etw.** *(Akk.)* ~**kommen** come near to sth.; *(erreichen)* reach sth.; *(erwerben)* obtain sth.; ~|**reifen** *itr. V.; mit sein* 〈*fruit, crops*〉 ripen; **zur Frau** ~**reifen** mature into a woman; ~|**treten** *unr. itr. V.; mit sein (sich wenden)* **an jmdn.** ~**treten** approach sb.; ~|**wachsen** *unr. itr. V.; mit sein* grow up; ~**wachsende der/die;** *adj. Dekl.* young person; ~|**ziehen** *unr. tr. V.* pull over; pull up 〈*chair*〉; **etw. zu sich** ~**ziehen** pull sth. towards one

**herauf** *Adv.* up

**herauf-:** ~|**beschwören** *tr. V.* a) *(verursachen)* cause 〈*disaster, war, crisis*〉; b) *(erinnern)* evoke 〈*memories etc.*〉; ~|**kommen** *unr. itr. V.; mit sein (nach oben kommen)* come up; ~|**setzen** *tr. V.* increase, put up 〈*prices, rents, interest rates, etc.*〉

**heraus** *Adv.* ~ **aus den Federn!/dem Bett!** rise and shine!/out of bed!

**heraus-:** ~|**bekommen** *unr. tr. V.* a) *(entfernen)* get out (**aus** of); b) *(ugs.: lösen)* work out 〈*problem, answer, etc.*〉; solve 〈*puzzle*〉; c) *(ermitteln)* find out; d) *(als Wechselgeld bekommen)* **5 DM** ~**bekommen** get back 5 marks change; **ich bekomme noch 5 DM** ~**:** I still have 5 marks [change] to come; ~|**bringen** *unr. tr. V.* a) *(nach außen bringen)* bring out (**aus** of); b) *(nach draußen begleiten)* show out; c) *(veröffentlichen)* bring out; *(aufführen)* put on, stage 〈*play*〉; screen 〈*film*〉; d) *(auf den Markt bringen)* bring out; e) *(populär machen)* make widely known; ~|**fahren 1.** *unr. itr. V.; mit sein* a) *(nach außen fahren)* **aus etw.** ~**fahren** drive/ride out of sth.; b) *(fahrend* ~**kommen**) come out; **2.** *unr. tr. V.* **den Wagen |aus dem Hof|** ~**fahren** drive the car out [of the yard]; **jmdn.** ~**fahren** drive sb. out (**zu** to); ~|**finden 1.** *unr. tr. V.* find out; trace 〈*fault*〉; **2.** *unr. itr. V.* find one's way out (**aus** of); ~|**fordern 1.** *tr. V.* a) *(auch Sport)* challenge; b) *(heraufbeschwören)* provoke 〈*person, resistance, etc.*〉; invite 〈*criticism*〉; court 〈*danger*〉; **2.** *itr. V.* **zu etw.** ~**fordern** provoke sth.; ~**forderung die** *(auch Sport)* challenge; *(Provokation)* provocation; ~|**geben 1.** *unr. tr. V.* a) *(aushändigen)* hand over 〈*property, person, hostage, etc.*〉; *(zurückgeben)* give back; b) *(als Wechselgeld zurückgeben)* **5 DM/zuviel** ~**ge-**

**ben** give 5 marks/too much change; c) *(veröffentlichen)* publish; d) issue 〈*stamp, coin, etc.*〉; **2.** *itr. V.* give change; ~**geber der** publisher; *(Redakteur)* editor; ~|**gehen** *unr. itr. V.; mit sein* a) go out (**aus** of); b) *(sich entfernen lassen)* 〈*stain etc.*〉 come out; ~|**halten** *unr. refl. V.* keep out; ~|**hängen** *tr. V.* hang out (**aus** of); ~|**helfen** *unr. itr. V.* **jmdm.** ~**helfen** *(auch fig.)* help sb. out (**aus** of); ~|**holen** *tr. V.* a) *(nach außen holen)* bring out; b) *(ugs.: erwirken)* win 〈*wage increase, advantage, etc.*〉; ~|**kommen** *unr. itr. V.; mit sein* a) come out (**aus** of); b) *(erscheinen; ugs.: auf den Markt kommen, bekannt werden)* come out; ~|**nehmen** *unr. tr. V.* a) take out (**aus** of); b) *(ugs.: entfernen)* take out 〈*appendix, tonsils, tooth, etc.*〉; ~|**reden** *refl. V. (ugs.)* talk one's way out (**aus** of); ~|**reißen** *unr. tr. V.* a) tear out (**aus** of); pull up 〈*plant*〉; ~|**rutschen** *itr. V.; mit sein (ugs.)* 〈*remark etc.*〉 slip out; ~|**stellen** *refl. V.* **es stellte sich** ~**, daß** ...: it turned out that ...; ~|**suchen** *tr. V.* pick out; look out 〈*file*〉

**herb** *Adj.* [slightly] sharp 〈*taste*〉; dry 〈*wine*〉; [slightly] sharp 〈*smell, perfume*〉; bitter 〈*disappointment*〉; severe 〈*face, features*〉; austere 〈*beauty*〉; harsh 〈*words, criticism*〉

**herbei-:** ~|**eilen** *itr. V.; mit sein* hurry over; ~|**laufen** *unr. itr. V.; mit sein* come running up

**Herberge die;** ~, ~**n** *(veralt.: Gasthaus)* inn

**her|bringen** *unr. tr. V.* **etw.** ~**:** bring sth. [here]

**Herbst der;** ~|e|s, ~e autumn; fall *(Amer.); s. auch* **Frühling; Herbstanfang der** beginning of autumn; **herbstlich** *Adj.* autumn *attrib.;* autumnal

**Herd der;** ~|e|s, ~e cooker; *(fig.)* centre *(of disturbance/rebellion)*

**Herde die;** ~, ~**n** herd

**herein-:** ~|**bitten** *unr. tr. V.* **jmdn.** ~**bitten** ask *or* invite sb. in; ~|**brechen** *unr. itr. V.; mit sein (geh.)* 〈*night, evening, dusk*〉 fall; 〈*winter*〉 set in; 〈*storm*〉 strike, break; ~|**bringen** *unr. tr. V.* bring in; ~|**fallen** *unr. itr. V.; mit sein (ugs.)* be taken for a ride *(coll.);* be done *(coll.);* ~|**kommen** *unr. itr. V.; mit sein* come in; ~|**lassen** *unr. tr. V.* let in; ~|**legen** *tr. V. (ugs.)* **jmdn.** ~**legen** take sb. for a ride *(coll.)* (**mit, bei** with); ~|**platzen** *itr.*

*V.; mit sein (ugs.)* burst in; ~|**schnei-
en** *unr. itr. V.; mit sein (ugs.)* turn up
out of the blue *(coll.)*

**her-, Her-:** ~**fahrt** die journey here;
~|**fallen** *unr. itr. V.; mit sein* über
jmdn. ~**fallen** attack sb.; *(gierig zu essen beginnen)* über etw. *(Akk.)* ~**fallen**
fall upon sth.; ~**gang** der: der ~**gang**
der Ereignisse the sequence of events;
~|**geben** *unr. tr. V.* hand over; *(weg-
geben)* give away; ~|**gehen** *unr. itr.
V.; mit sein* neben/vor/hinter jmdn.
~**gehen** walk along beside/in front of/
behind sb.; ~|**haben** *unr. tr. V. (ugs.)*
wo hat er/sie das ~? where did he/she
get that from?; ~|**halten** *unr. itr. V.*
~**halten müssen [für jmdn./etw.]** be the
one to suffer [for sb./sth.]; ~|**hören**
*itr. V.* listen

**Hering** der; ~s, ~e a) herring; b) *(Zeltpflock)* peg

**her-:** ~|**kommen** *unr. itr. V.; mit sein*
come here; ~**kömmlich** *Adj.* conventional; traditional ⟨*custom*⟩

**Herkunft** die; ~, **Herkünfte** origin

**her-:** ~|**laufen** *unr. itr. V.; mit sein*
vor/hinter/neben jmdn. ~**laufen** run
[along] in front of/behind/alongside
sb.; *(nachlaufen)* hinter jmdm. ~**laufen**
run after sb.; *(fig.)* chase sb. up;
~|**leiten** *tr., refl. V.* derive (**aus,** von
from); ~|**machen** *(ugs.) refl. V.* sich
über etw. *(Akk.)* ~**machen** get stuck
into sth. *(coll.)*

**Hermelin** der; ~s, ~e *(Pelz)* ermine

**hermetisch** 1. *Adj.* hermetic; 2. *adv.*
hermetically

**Heroin** das; ~s heroin

**Herr** der; ~n, ~en a) *(Mann)* gentleman; b) *(Titel, Anrede)* ~ Schulze Mr
Schulze; **Sehr geehrter ~ Schulze!**
Dear Sir; *(bei persönlicher Bekanntschaft)* Dear Mr Schulze; **meine ~en**
gentlemen; c) *(Gebieter)* master

**herren-, Herren-:** ~**ausstatter** der
[gentle]men's outfitter; ~**los** *Adj.*
abandoned ⟨*car, luggage*⟩; stray ⟨*dog,
cat*⟩; ~**salon** der men's hairdressing
salon; ~**schuh** der man's shoe;
~**schuhe** men's shoes; ~**toilette** die
[gentle]men's toilet

**Herr·gott** der; ~s: der [liebe]/unser ~:
the Lord [God]; God; **Herrgottsfrühe** die *in* in aller ~: at the crack of
dawn

**her|richten** *tr. V. (bereitmachen)* get
⟨*room, refreshments, etc.*⟩ ready; arrange ⟨*table*⟩; *(in Ordnung bringen)*
renovate

**Herrin** die; ~, ~en mistress; **herrisch**
1. *Adj.* overbearing; imperious; 2.
*adv.* imperiously; **herrlich** 1. *Adj.*
marvellous; magnificent ⟨*view,
clothes*⟩; 2. *adv.* marvellously; **Herrlichkeit** die; ~, ~en a) o. Pl. *(Schönheit)* magnificence; splendour; b)
*meist Pl. (herrliche Sache)* marvellous
thing; **Herrschaft** die; ~, ~en a) o.
Pl. rule; *(Macht)* power; b) Pl. *(Damen u. Herren)* ladies and gentlemen;
**herrschen** *itr. V.* rule; ⟨*monarch*⟩
reign, rule; **draußen ~ 30° Kälte** it's
30° below outside; **Herrscher** der;
~s, ~: ruler; **herrsch·süchtig** *Adj.*
domineering

**her-:** ~|**rühren** *itr. V.* von jmdm./etw.
~**rühren** come from sb./stem from
sth.; ~|**sein** *unr. itr. V.; mit sein* einen
Monat/lange ~**sein** be a month/a long
time ago; **es ist lange ~, daß wir ...:** it
is a long time since we ...; **von Köln
~sein** be from Cologne; hinter jmdm.
*(ugs.)*/etw. ~**sein** be after sb./sth.;
~|**stellen** *tr. V.* produce

**Her·steller** der; ~s, ~: producer;
**Her·stellung** die production

**herüber** *Adv.* over

**herum** *Adv.* um ... ~ *(Richtung)*
round; *(Anordnung)* around; um
Weihnachten ~: around Christmas

**herum-:** ~|**ärgern** *refl. V. (ugs.)* sich
mit jmdm./etw. ~**ärgern** keep getting
annoyed with sb./sth.; ~|**drehen** 1.
*tr. V. (ugs.)* turn ⟨*key*⟩; turn over ⟨*coin,
mattress, hand, etc.*⟩; 2. *refl. V.* turn
[a]round; ~|**fahren** *(ugs.)* 1. *unr. itr.
V.; mit sein (sich plötzlich herumdrehen)* spin round; 2. *unr. tr. V.* jmdn. [in
der Stadt] ~**fahren** drive sb. around
the town; ~|**führen** 1. *tr. V.* jmdn. [in
der Stadt] ~**führen** show sb. around
the town; 2. *itr. V.* um etw. ~**führen**
⟨*road etc.*⟩ go round sth.; ~|**gehen**
*unr. itr. V.; mit sein (vergehen)* pass;
um etw. ~**gehen** go round sth.; etw.
~**gehen lassen** circulate sth.; pass;
~|**kommen** *unr. itr. V.; mit sein (ugs.)*
a) *(vermeiden können)* um etw. [nicht]
~**kommen** [not] be able to get out of
sth.; b) *(viel reisen)* get around *or*
about; in der Welt ~**kommen** see a lot
of the world; ~|**laufen** *unr. itr. V.; mit
sein* a) walk/*(schneller)* run around *or*
about; um etw. ~**laufen** go round sth.;
b) *(gekleidet sein)* wie ein Hippie ~**laufen** go about looking like a hippie;
~|**lungern** *itr. V. (salopp)* loaf
around; ~|**schlagen** *unr. refl. V.*

*(ugs.)* **sich mit Problemen/Einwänden ~schlagen** grapple with problems/ battle against objections; **~|sein** *unr. itr. V.; mit sein; Zusammenschreibung nur im Inf. und Part. (ugs.) (vergangen sein)* have passed; **~|sitzen** *unr. itr. V. (ugs.)* sit around *or* about; **~|sprechen** *unr. refl. V.* get around *or* about; **~|stöbern** *itr. V. (ugs.)* keep rummaging around *or* about (in + *Dat.* in); **~|treiben** *unr. refl. V. (ugs. abwertend)* **sich auf den Straßen/in Discos ~treiben** hang around the streets/in discos; **sich in der Welt ~treiben** roam about the world

**herunter** *Adv.* **a)** *(nach unten)* down; **b)** *(fort)* off; **~ vom Sofa!** [get] off the sofa!

**herunter-:** **~|bringen** *unr. tr. V.* bring down; **~|fallen** *unr. itr. V.; mit sein* fall down; **vom Tisch/Stuhl ~fallen** fall off the table/chair; **~|gehen** *unr. itr. V.; mit sein* **a)** come down; **b)** *(niedriger werden) (temperature)* drop; ⟨*prices*⟩ come down, fall; **~gekommen** 1. *2. Part. v.* **~kommen**; 2. *Adj.* poor ⟨*health*⟩; dilapidated ⟨*building*⟩; run-down ⟨*area*⟩; down and out ⟨*person*⟩; **~|handeln** *tr. V. (ugs.)* **einen Preis ~handeln** beat down a price; **~|hängen** *unr. itr. V.* hang down; **~|hauen** *unr. tr. V. (ugs.)* **jmdm. eine ~hauen** give sb. a clout round the ear *(coll.)*; **~|kommen** *unr. itr. V.; mit sein* **a)** come down; **b)** *(ugs.: verfallen)* go to the dogs *(coll.)*; **~|lassen** *unr. tr. V.* lower; **~|schlucken** *tr. V.* swallow; **~|sein** *unr. itr. V.; mit sein; Zusammenschreibung nur im Inf. und Part. (ugs.)* be down; **|körperlich| ~sein** be in poor health; **~|spielen** *tr. V. (ugs.)* play down *(coll.)*

**hervor** *Adv.* **aus ... ~:** out of

**hervor-:** **~|heben** *unr. tr. V.* stress; **~ragend** 1. *Adj.* outstanding[ly good]; 2. *adv.* **~ragend geschult** outstandingly well trained; **~ragend spielen/arbeiten** play/work outstandingly well; **~|tun** *unr. refl. V.* distinguish oneself; *(wichtig tun)* show off

**Herz** *das;* ~ens, ~en **a)** heart; *(Kartenspiel)* hearts *pl.;* **von ~en kommen** come from the heart; **ein ~ für die Armen haben** feel for the poor; **ein ~ für Kinder haben** have a love of children; **schweren ~ens** with a heavy heart; **etw. auf dem ~en haben** have sth. on one's mind; **es nicht übers ~ bringen, etw. zu tun** not have the heart to do sth.; **sich**

*(Dat.)* **etw. zu ~en nehmen** take sth. to heart; **Herz·anfall** *der* heart attack; **herzens·gut** ['--'-] *Adj.* kindhearted; **Herzens·lust** *die:* **nach ~:** to one's heart's content; **herzhaft** 1. *Adj.* hearty; *(nahrhaft)* hearty ⟨*meal*⟩; *(von kräftigem Geschmack)* tasty; 2. *adv.* heartily; *(nahrhaft)* **er ißt gern ~:** he likes to have a hearty meal

**her|ziehen** *unr. itr. V.; mit sein od. haben (ugs.)* **über jmdn./etw. ~:** run sb./ sth. down

**herzig** 1. *Adj.* sweet; delightful; 2. *adv.* sweetly; delightfully

**herz-, Herz-:** **~infarkt** *der* heart attack; **~klopfen** *das;* **~s:** **jmd. hat ~klopfen** sb.'s heart is pounding; **~krank** *Adj.* ⟨*person*⟩ with a heart condition

**herzlich** 1. *Adj.* warm ⟨*smile, reception*⟩; kind ⟨*words, regards*⟩; *(ehrlich gemeint)* sincere; **~en Dank** many thanks; 2. *adv.* warmly; *(ehrlich gemeint)* sincerely; ⟨*congratulate*⟩ heartily; **~ wenig** very *or (coll.)* precious little; **Herzlichkeit** *die* warmth; kindness; *(Aufrichtigkeit)* sincerity; **herz·los** 1. *Adj.* heartless; 2. *adv.* heartlessly

**Herzog** *der;* ~s, Herzöge duke; **Herzogin** *die;* ~, ~nen duchess

**herz-, Herz-:** **~schlag** *der* heartbeat; *(Herzversagen)* heart failure; **~schmerz** *der; meist Pl.* pain in the region of the heart; **~transplantation** *die (Med.)* heart transplantation; **~zerreißend** 1. *Adj.* heart-rending; 2. *adv.* heart-rendingly

**Hessen (das);** ~s Hesse

**Hetze** *die;* ~ **a)** [mad] rush; **b)** *o. Pl. (abwertend)* smear campaign; **hetzen** 1. *tr. V.* **a)** hunt; **b)** *(antreiben)* rush; 2. *itr. V.* **a)** *(in großer Eile sein)* rush; **b)** *mit sein (hasten)* rush; *(rennen)* dash; race; **Hetz·rede** *die (abwertend)* inflammatory speech

**Heu** *das;* ~[e]s hay

**Heuchelei** *die;* ~: hypocrisy; **heucheln** 1. *itr. V.* be a hypocrite; 2. *tr. V.* feign; **Heuchler** *der;* ~s, ~: hypocrite; **heuchlerisch** 1. *Adj.* hypocritical; 2. *adv.* hypocritically

**heuer** *Adv. (südd., österr., schweiz.)* this year

**Heuer** *die;* ~, ~n *(Seemannsspr.)* pay; wages *pl.*

**Heu·ernte** *die* **a)** hay harvest; **b)** *(Ertrag)* hay crop

**heulen** *itr. V.* **a)** howl; ⟨*siren etc.*⟩ wail; **b)** (*ugs.: weinen*) howl; bawl

**Heurige** der; *adj. Dekl.* (*bes. österr.*) **a)** (*Wein*) new wine; **b)** (*Weinlokal*) inn with new wine on tap

**Heu-:** ~**schnupfen** der hay fever; ~**schrecke** die grasshopper

**heute** *Adv.* today; ~ **früh** early this morning; ~ **morgen/abend** this morning/evening; ~ **mittag** [at] midday today; ~ **nacht** tonight; (*letzte Nacht*) last night; ~ **in einer Woche** a week [from] today; today week; ~ **vor einer Woche** a week ago today; **heutig** *Adj.* **a)** (*von diesem Tag*) today's; der ~**e** **Tag** today; **b)** (*gegenwärtig*) today's; of today *postpos.*; **in der** ~**en Zeit** nowadays; **heut·zu·tage** *Adv.* nowadays

**Hexe** die; ~, ~n witch; **hexen** *itr. V.* work magic

**Hexen·schuß** der; *o. Pl.* lumbago *no indef. art.;* **Hexerei** die; ~, ~en witchcraft; (*von Kunststücken usw.*) magic

**hieb** *1. u. 3. Pers. Sg. Prät. v.* **hauen;** **Hieb** der; ~|e|s, ~e **a)** (*Schlag*) blow; (*mit der Peitsche*) lash; **b)** *Pl.* (*ugs.: Prügel*) hiding *sing.;* **hieb·fest** *Adj.:* hieb- und stichfest watertight; castiron

**hielt** *1. u. 3. Pers. Sg. Prät. v.* **halten**

**hier** *Adv.* **a)** here; |von| ~ **oben/unten** [from] up/down here; **b)** (*jetzt*) now; **von** ~ **an** from now on

**hieran** *Adv.* here; **sich** ~ **festhalten** hold on to this; (*fig.*) **im Anschluß** ~: immediately after this

**Hierarchie** [hierar'çi:] die; ~, ~n hierarchy

**hierauf** *Adv.* **a)** on here; (*darauf*) on this; **wir werden** ~ **zurückkommen** we'll come back to this; **b)** (*danach*) after that; then; **c)** (*infolgedessen*) whereupon; **hieraus** *Adv.* out of here; (*aus dieser Tatsache, Quelle*) from this

**hier-:** ~|**behalten** *unr. tr. V.* jmdn./etw. ~: keep sb./sth. here; ~**bei** *Adv.* **a)** (*bei dieser Gelegenheit*) Diese Übung ist sehr schwierig. Man kann sich ~ leicht verletzen. This exercise is very difficult. You can easily injure yourself doing it; **b)** (*bei der erwähnten Sache*) here; ~|**bleiben** *unr. itr. V.; mit sein* stay here; ~**durch** *Adv.* through here; (*auf Grund dieser Sache*) because of this; ~**für** *Adv.* for this

**hier·her** *Adv.* here; **ich gehe bis** ~ **und nicht weiter** I'm going this far and no further

**hierher-:** ~|**gehören** *itr. V.* belong here; (*hierfür wichtig sein*) be relevant [here]; ~|**kommen** *unr. itr. V.; mit sein* come here

**hier·hin** *Adv.* here; **bis** ~: up to here

**hier-:** ~**in** *Adv.* **a)** (*räumlich*) in here; **b)** in this; ~|**lassen** *unr. tr. V.* etw. ~: leave sth. here; ~**mit** *Adv.* with this/these; ~**mit ist der Fall erledigt** that puts an end to the matter; ~**nach** *Adv.* (*anschließend*) after that

**Hieroglyphe** die; ~, ~n hieroglyph

**hier-:** ~**sein** *unr. itr. V.; mit sein; Zusammenschreibung nur im Inf. und Part.* be here; ~**über** *Adv.* **a)** (*über dem Erwähnten*) above here; (*über das Erwähnte*) over here; **b)** (*das Erwähnte betreffend*) about this/these; ~**von** *Adv.* of this/these; ~**zu** *Adv.* with this; (*hinsichtlich dieser Sache*) about this; ~**zu gehört/gehören** ...: this includes/these include; ~**zu reicht mein Geld nicht** I haven't got enough money for that; ~**zu·lande** *Adv.* [here] in this country

**hiesig** *Adj.; nicht präd.* local

**hieß** *1. u. 3. Pers. Sg. Prät. v.* **heißen**

**Hi-Fi-Anlage** ['haifi-] die hi-fi system

**Hilfe** die; ~, ~n **a)** help; (*für Notleidende*) aid; relief; **zu** ~! help!; **b)** (*Hilfskraft*) help; (*im Geschäft*) assistant

**Hilfe-:** ~**leistung** die help; ~**ruf** der cry for help; ~**stellung** die (*Turnen*) jmdm. ~**stellung geben** act as spotter for sb.

**hilflos** **1.** *Adj.* helpless; **2.** *adv.* helplessly; **Hilflosigkeit** die; ~ helplessness

**hilfs-, Hilfs-:** ~**bedürftig** *Adj.* **a)** (*schwach*) in need of help *postpos.;* **b)** (*notleidend*) in need; needy; ~**bereit** *Adj.* helpful; ~**bereitschaft** die helpfulness; ~**kraft** die assistant; ~**mittel** das aid; ~**zeit·wort** das (*Sprachw.*) auxiliary [verb]

**Himalaja** der; ~|s|: der/im ~: the/in the Himalayas *pl.*

**Him·beere** die raspberry

**Himmel** der; ~s, ~ sky; (*Rel.*) heaven; ~ **noch** [ein]mal! for Heaven's sake!

**Himmel·bett** das four-poster bed; **himmel·blau** *Adj.* sky-blue; clear blue ⟨*eyes*⟩

**Himmels-:** ~**richtung** die point of the compass; ~**schlüsselchen** das cowslip

**hịmmel·weit** *Adj.* enormous, vast ⟨*difference*⟩; **hịmmlisch** *Adj. (auch fig.)* heavenly

**hin** *Adv.* **a)** *(räumlich)* **zur Straße ~ liegen** face the road; **b)** *(zeitlich)* **gegen Mittag ~:** towards midday; **c)** *(in Verbindungen)* **nach außen ~:** outwardly; **auf meinen Rat ~:** on my advice; **auf seine Bitte ~:** at his request; **d)** *(in Wortpaaren)* **~ und zurück** there and back; **einmal Köln ~ und zurück** a return [ticket] to Cologne; **~ und her** to and fro; back and forth; **~ und wieder** [every] now and then

**hinạb** *Adv. s.* **hinunter**

**hinạb|-** *s.* **hinunter|-**

**hinạuf** *Adv.* up; **bis ~ zu** up to

**hinạuf-:** **~|fahren** *unr. itr. V.; mit sein* go up; *(im Auto)* drive up; *(mit einem Motorrad)* ride up; **~|gehen** *unr. itr. V.; mit sein* **a)** *(nach oben gehen)* go up; **b)** *(nach oben führen)* lead up; **c)** *(ugs.: steigen)* ⟨*prices, taxes, etc.*⟩ go up; rise; **~|klettern** *itr. V.; mit sein* climb up; **~|steigen** *unr. itr. V.; mit sein* climb up; **~|ziehen** **1.** *unr. tr. V.* pull up; **2.** *unr. itr. V.; mit sein* move up; **3.** *unr. refl. V. (sich erstrecken)* stretch up

**hinạus** *Adv.* **a)** *(räumlich)* out; **b)** *(zeitlich)* **auf Jahre ~:** for years to come; **c)** *(etw. überschreitend)* **über etw.** *(Akk.)* **~:** in addition to sth.

**hinạus-:** **~|bringen** *unr. tr. V.* **jmdn./etw. ~bringen** see sb. out/take sth. out (aus of); **~|fahren** **1.** *unr. itr. V.; mit sein* **aus etw. ~fahren** *(mit dem Auto)* drive out of sth.; *(mit dem Zweirad)* ride out of sth.; ⟨*car, bus*⟩ go out of sth.; ⟨*train*⟩ pull out of sth.; **zum Flugplatz ~fahren** drive out to the airport; **2.** *unr. tr. V.* **jmdn./etw. ~fahren** drive sb./take sth. out; **~|fallen** *unr. itr. V.; mit sein* fall out (aus of); **~|finden** *unr. itr. V.* find one's way out (aus of); **~|gehen** *unr. itr. V.; mit sein* **a)** go out (aus of); **b)** *(gerichtet sein)* **das Zimmer geht zum Garten/nach Westen ~:** the room looks out on to the garden/faces west; **~|kommen** *unr. itr. V.; mit sein* come out (aus of); **~|laufen** *unr. itr. V.; mit sein* **a)** run out (aus of); **b)** *(als Ergebnis haben)* **auf etw.** *(Akk.)* **~laufen** lead to sth.; **~|sehen** *unr. itr. V.* look out; **zum Fenster ~sehen** look out of the window; **~|sein** *unr. itr. V.; mit sein* **über etw.** *(Akk.)* **~sein** be past sth.; **~|tragen** *unr. tr. V.* **jmdn./etw. ~tragen** carry

sb./sth. out; **~|werfen** *unr. tr. V. (auch ugs. fig.)* throw out (**aus** of); **~|ziehen 1.** *unr. tr. V.* **a)** *(nach draußen ziehen)* **jmdn./etw. ~ziehen** pull sb./sth. out (**aus** of); tow ⟨*ship*⟩ out; **b)** *(verzögern)* put off; delay; **2.** *unr. refl. V.* be delayed; **~|zögern 1.** *tr. V.* delay; **2.** *refl. V.* be delayed

**hin-, Hịn-:** **~blick** der *in* **im** *od.* **in ~blick auf etw.** *(Akk.)* *(wegen)* in view of; *(hinsichtlich)* with regard to; **~|bringen** *unr. tr. V.* **jmdn./etw. ~bringen** take sb./sth. [there]; **~|denken** *unr. itr. V.* **wo denkst du hin?** *(ugs.)* whatever are you thinking of?

**hịnderlich** *Adj.* **~ sein** get in the way; **hịndern** *tr. V.* **a)** *(abhalten)* **jmdn. ~:** stop sb. (**an** + *Dat.* from); **b)** *(behindern)* hinder; **Hịndernis** *das;* **~ses, ~se** obstacle

**hịn|deuten** *itr. V.* **a)** **auf jmdn./etw.** *od.* **zu jmdm./etw. ~:** point to sb./sth.; **b)** **auf etw.** *(Akk.)* **~** *(fig.)* point to sth.

**hin·dụrch** *Adv.* **a)** *(räumlich)* **durch den Wald ~:** through the wood; **b)** *(zeitlich)* **das ganze Jahr ~:** throughout the year

**hinein** *Adv.* **a)** *(räumlich)* in; **in etw.** *(Akk.)* **~:** into sth.; **b)** *(zeitlich)* **bis in den Morgen/tief in die Nacht ~:** till morning/far into the night

**hinein-:** **~|bringen** *unr. tr. V.* take in; **~|fahren** *(mit dem Auto)* drive in; *(mit dem Zweirad)* ride in; **in etw.** *(Akk.)* **~fahren** drive/ride into sth.; **~|fallen** *unr. itr. V.; mit sein* fall in; **in etw.** *(Akk.)* **~fallen** fall into sth.; **~|gehen** *unr. itr. V.; mit sein* go in; **in etw.** *(Akk.)* **~gehen** go into sth.; **~|gucken** *itr. V. (ugs.)* look in; **in etw.** *(Akk.)* **~gucken** look in[to] sth.; **~|kommen** *unr. itr. V.; mit sein* **a)** come in; **in etw.** *(Akk.)* **~kommen** come into sth.; **b)** *(gelangen, auch fig.)* get in; **in etw.** *(Akk.)* **~kommen** get into sth.; **~|reden** *itr. V.* **jmdm. in seine Angelegenheiten/Entscheidungen** *usw.* **~reden** interfere in sb.'s affairs/ decisions *etc.*; **~|sehen** *unr. itr. V.* look in; **in etw.** *(Akk.)* **~sehen** look into sth.; **~|versetzen** *refl. V.* **sich in jmdn.** *od.* **jmds. Lage ~versetzen** put oneself in sb.'s position

**hin-, Hịn-:** **~|fahren 1.** *unr. itr. V.; mit sein* go there; **2.** *unr. tr. V.* **jmdn. ~fahren** drive sb. there; **~fahrt die** journey there; *(Seereise)* voyage out; **~|fallen** *unr. itr. V.; mit sein* **a)** fall over; **b)** **jmdm. fällt etw. ~:** sb. drops sth.; etw. ~**fallen lassen** drop sth.; ~**fällig** *Adj.* a) infirm; frail; b) *(ungültig)* invalid; ~|**fliegen** *unr. itr. V.; mit sein* fly there; ~**flug der** outward flight

**hing** *1. u. 3. Pers. Sg. Prät. v.* hängen

**Hin·gabe die;** ~: devotion; *(Eifer)* dedication; **Hingebung die;** ~: devotion; **hingebungs·voll 1.** *Adj.* devoted; **2.** *adv.* devotedly; with devotion; *⟨listen⟩* with rapt attention; *⟨dance, play⟩* with abandon

**hin·gegen** *Konj., Adv. (jedoch)* however; *(andererseits)* on the other hand

**hin-:** ~|**gehen** *unr. itr. V.; mit sein* a) go [there]; *zu jmdm./etw.* ~**gehen** go to sb./sth.; b) *(verstreichen)* ⟨*time*⟩ go by; ~|**halten** *unr. tr. V.* a) hold out; b) *(warten lassen)* jmdn. ~**halten** keep sb. waiting; ~|**hören** *itr. V.* listen

**hinken** ['hɪŋkn̩] *itr. V.* a) walk with a limp; b) *mit sein (hinkend gehen)* limp

**hin-:** ~|**kommen** *unr. itr. V.; mit sein* a) get there; b) *(an einen Ort gehören)* go; belong; c) *(ugs.: stimmen)* be right; ~**länglich 1.** *Adj.* sufficient; *(angemessen)* adequate; **2.** *adv.* sufficiently; *(angemessen)* adequately; ~|**legen 1.** *tr. V.* put; *(weglegen)* put down; **2.** *refl. V.* lie down; ~**reichend 1.** *Adj.* sufficient; *(angemessen)* adequate; **2.** *adv.* sufficiently; *(angemessen)* adequately; ~**reise die** journey there; *(mit dem Schiff)* voyage out; ~**reißend** *Adj.* enchanting ⟨*person, picture, view*⟩; captivating ⟨*speaker, play*⟩; ~|**richten** *tr. V.* execute; ~**richtung die** execution

**Hinrichtungs·kommando das** firing-squad

**hin-, Hin-:** ~|**sehen** *unr. itr. V.* look; ~|**sein** *unr. itr. V.; mit sein (nur im Inf. u. Part. zusammengeschrieben) (ugs.)* a) *(verloren sein)* be gone; b) *(nicht mehr brauchbar sein)* have had it *(coll.);* ⟨*car*⟩ be a write-off; c) *(salopp: tot sein)* have snuffed it *(sl.);* d) *(ugs.: hingerissen sein)* von jmdm./etw. ganz ~**sein** be mad about sb./bowled over by sth.; ~|**setzen 1.** *tr. V.* put; **2.** *refl. V.* sit down; ~**sicht die;** *o. Pl.* in gewisser ~**sicht** in a way/in some respect *or* ways; **in jeder** ~**sicht** in every respect; **in finanzieller** ~**sicht** financially; ~**sichtlich** *Präp. mit Gen. (Amtsspr.)* with regard to; *(in Anbetracht)* in view of; ~|**stellen 1.** *tr. V.* put; put up ⟨*building*⟩; *(absetzen)* put down; **2.** *refl. V.* stand

**hinten** *Adv.* at the back; **sich** ~ **anstellen** join the back of the queue *(Brit.) or (Amer.)* line; **weiter** ~: further back; *(in einem Buch)* further on; **die Adresse steht** ~ **auf dem Brief** the address is on the back of the envelope; **nach** ~ **hinaus liegen/gehen** be at the back; **die anderen sind ganz weit** ~: the others are a long way back

**hinter 1.** *Präp. mit Dat.* behind; *(nach)* after; **3 km** ~ **der Grenze** 3 km beyond the frontier; **eine Prüfung** ~ **sich haben** *(fig.)* have got an examination over [and done] with; **viele Enttäuschungen/eine Krankheit** ~ **sich haben** have experienced many disappointments/ have got over an illness; **2.** *Präp. mit Akk.* behind

**hinter...** *Adj.; nicht präd.* back

**hinter-, Hinter-:** ~**einander** *Adv.* a) *(räumlich)* one behind the other; b) *(zeitlich)* one after another *or* the other; ~**gedanke der** ulterior motive; ~**gehen** [--'--] *unr. tr. V.* deceive; ~**grund der** background; ~**gründig 1.** *Adj.* enigmatic; **2.** *adv.* enigmatically; ~**halt der** ambush; ~**hältig 1.** *Adj.* underhand; **2.** *adv.* in an underhand manner; ~**her** *Adv. (räumlich)* behind; *(nachher)* afterwards; ~**hof der** courtyard; ~**land das** hinterland; *(Milit.)* back area; ~**lassen** [--'--] *unr. tr. V.* leave; ~**legen** [--'--] *tr. V.* deposit **(bei** with); ~**list die** guile; deceit; ~**listig** *Adj.* deceitful; ~**mann der;** *Pl.* ~**männer** a) person behind; b) *(Gewährsmann)* [secret] informant

**Hintern der;** ~s, ~ *(ugs.)* backside; bottom

**hinter-, Hinter-:** ~**rad das** rear wheel; ~**teil das** backside; behind; ~**treffen das** *(ugs.)* **in ins** ~**treffen geraten** *od.* **kommen** fall behind; ~**treiben** [--'--] *unr. tr. V.* foil ⟨*plan*⟩; prevent ⟨*marriage, promotion*⟩; block ⟨*law, investigation, reform*⟩; ~**treppe die** back stairs *pl.;* ~**tür die** back door; ~**wäldler** [~vɛltlɐ] **der;** ~s, ~ *(spött.)* backwoodsman

**hinüber** *Adv.* over; across

**Hin- und Rück·fahrt die** journey there and back; round trip *(Amer.)*

**hinunter** *Adv.* down

**hinunter-:** ~|**fahren 1.** *unr. itr. V.; mit sein* go down; *(mit dem Auto)* drive down; *(mit dem Fahrrad)* ride down; **2.** *unr. tr. V.* jmdn./ein Auto/eine Ladung ~**fahren** drive sb. down/

drive a car down/take a load down;
~|**gehen** *unr. itr. V.; mit sein* go
down; *⟨aircraft⟩* descend; ~|**klettern**
*itr. V.; mit sein* climb down; ~|**rei-
chen** 1. *tr. V.* hand down; 2. *itr. V.*
*(sich bis hinunter erstrecken)* reach
down (**bis auf** + *Akk.* to)
**Hin·weg** der way there
**hin·weg** *Adv.* a) *(geh.)* ~ **mit dir!**
away with you!; b) **über etw.** ~: over
sth.
**hinweg-:** ~|**gehen** *unr. itr. V.; mit*
*sein* **über etw.** *(Akk.)* ~**gehen** pass over
sth.; ~|**kommen** *unr. itr. V.; mit sein*
**über etw.** *(Akk.)* ~**kommen** get over
sth.; ~|**setzen** *refl. V.* **sich über etw.**
*(Akk.)* ~**setzen** ignore sth.
**Hinweis** ['hɪnvaɪs] *der;* ~**es,** ~**e** hint;
**unter** ~ **auf** ( + *Akk.*) with reference
to
**hin-:** ~|**weisen** 1. *unr. itr. V.* **auf**
**jmdn./etw.** ~**weisen** point to sb./sth.;
2. *unr. tr. V.* **jmdn. auf etw.** *(Akk.)*
~**weisen** point sth. out to sb.; ~|**wei-
send** *Adj. (Grammatik)* demonstrat-
ive; ~|**werfen** *unr. tr. V.* throw
down; ~|**ziehen** 1. *unr. tr. V.* pull,
draw (**zu** to, towards); 2. *unr. itr. V.;*
*mit sein* a) *(umziehen)* move there; **wo**
**ist sie** ~**gezogen?** where did she move
to?; 3. *unr. refl. V.* a) *(sich erstrecken)*
drag on (**über** + *Akk.* for); b) *(sich*
*verzögern)* be delayed
**hinzu-:** ~|**fügen** *tr. V.* add; ~|**kom-
men** *unr. itr. V.; mit sein* a) come
along; b) *(hinzugefügt werden)* **zu etw.**
~**kommen** be added to sth.; **es kommt**
**noch** ~, **daß** ... *(fig.)* there is also the
fact that...; ~|**tun** *unr. tr. V. (ugs.)* add
**Hirn** das; ~**|e|s,** ~**e** a) brain; b) *(Speise;*
*ugs.: Verstand)* brains *pl.*
**Hirsch** der; ~**|e|s,** ~**e** deer; *(Rothirsch)*
red deer; *(männlicher Rothirsch)* stag;
*(Speise)* venison
**Hirse** die; ~, ~**n** millet
**Hirt** der; ~**en,** ~**en, Hirte** der; ~**n,** ~**n**
herdsman; *(Schaf*~*)* shepherd
**hissen** *tr. V.* hoist
**historisch** *Adj.* a) historical; b) *(geschichtlich bedeutungsvoll)* historic
**Hit** der; ~**|s|,** ~**s** *(ugs.)* hit
**Hitze** die; ~: heat
**hitze-, Hitze-:** ~**beständig** *Adj.*
heat-resistant; ~**frei** *Adj.* ~**frei haben**
have the rest of the day off [school/
work] because of excessively hot
weather; ~**welle** die heat wave
**hitzig** *Adj.* a) hot-tempered; b) *(erregt)*
heated *⟨discussion etc.⟩*

**hitz-, Hitz-:** ~**kopf** der hothead;
~**köpfig** *Adj.* hot-headed; ~**schlag**
der heat-stroke
**hl** *Abk.* Hektoliter hl
**hob** *1. u. 3. Pers. Sg. Prät. v.* **heben**
**Hobby** das; ~**s,** ~**s** hobby
**Hobel** der; ~**s,** ~ **a)** plane; b) *(Küchengerät)* [vegetable] slicer; **Ho-
bel·bank** die woodworker's bench;
**hobeln** *tr., itr. V.* a) plane; b) *(schneiden)* slice
**hoch, höher, höchst...** 1. *Adj.* high; tall
*⟨tree, mast⟩;* long *⟨grass⟩;* deep *⟨snow,*
*water⟩;* heavy *⟨fine⟩;* large *⟨sum,*
*amount⟩;* severe, extensive *⟨damage⟩;*
senior *⟨official, officer, post⟩;* high-
level *⟨diplomacy, politics⟩;* **höchste Gefahr** extreme danger; **es ist höchste**
**Zeit, daß ...:** it is high time that ...; **das**
**hohe C** top C; **vier** ~ **zwei** *(Math.)* four
to the power [of] two; four squared; 2.
*adv. (in großer Höhe)* high; *(nach*
*oben)* up; *(zahlenmäßig viel, sehr)*
highly; ~ **verschuldet/versichert** heavily in debt/insured for a large sum [of
money]; **etw.** ~ **und heilig versprechen**
promise sth. faithfully; **Hoch** das;
~**s,** ~**s a)** *(Hochruf)* **ein |dreifaches|** ~
**auf jmdn. ausbringen** give three cheers
for sb.; b) *(Met.)* high
**Hoch·achtung** die great respect;
**hochachtungs·voll** *Adv. (Briefschluß)* yours faithfully
**hoch-, Hoch-:** ~**aktuell** *Adj.* highly
topical; ~**amt** das *(kath. Rel.)* high
mass; ~|**arbeiten** *refl. V.* work one's
way up; ~**begabt** *Adj. (präd. getrennt*
*geschrieben)* highly gifted; ~**betagt**
*Adj.* aged; ~**betrieb** der; *o. Pl. (ugs.)*
**es herrschte** ~ **betrieb im Geschäft** the
shop was at its busiest; ~**blüte** die
golden age; ~**burg** die stronghold;
~**deutsch** *Adj.* High German;
~**deutsch** das, ~**deutsche** das
High German, ~**druck** der *(Physik,*
*Met.)* high pressure; ~**empfindlich**
*Adj.* highly sensitive *⟨instrument, de-
vice, material, etc.⟩;* extremely delicate *⟨fabric⟩;* ~|**fahren**
*unr. itr. V.; mit sein* a) *(ugs.)* go up;
*(mit dem Auto)* drive up; *(mit dem*
*Fahrrad, Motorrad)* ride up; b) *(auffahren)* start up; **aus dem Sessel** ~**fahren** start [up] from one's chair; c) *(aufbrausen)* flare up; ~**finanz** die high
finance; ~**fliegend** *Adj.* ambitious;
~**form** die top form; ~**gebirge** das
[high] mountains *pl.;* ~**gefühl** das
[feeling of] elation; ~|**gehen** *unr. itr.*

*V.; mit sein (ugs.)* go up; *(zornig werden)* blow one's top *(coll.)*; explode; *(explodieren)* ⟨*bomb, mine*⟩ go off; **~genuß** der *in* ein **~genuß** sein be a real delight; **~geschlossen** *Adj.* high-necked ⟨*dress*⟩; **~gestellt** *Adj.*; *nicht präd.* ⟨*person*⟩ in a high position; important ⟨*person*⟩; **~glanz** der: etw. auf **~glanz bringen** give sth. a high polish; *(fig.)* make sth. spick and span; **~gradig** 1. *Adj.* extreme; 2. *adv.* extremely; **~|halten** *unr. tr. V.* hold up; **~haus** das high-rise-building; **~|heben** *unr. tr. V.* lift up; raise ⟨*arm, leg, hand*⟩; **~interessant** *Adj.* extremely interesting; **~kant** *Adv.* *(ugs.)* in jmdn. **~kant hinauswerfen** chuck sb. out *(sl.)*; throw sb. out on his/her ear *(coll.)*; **~|kommen** *unr. itr. V.; mit sein (ugs.)* come up; *(vorwärtskommen)* get on; **~|krempeln** *tr. V.* roll up; **~|leben** *itr. V. in* jmdn./ etw. **~leben lassen** cheer sb./sth.; **er lebe ~!** three cheers for him; **~leistungs·sport** der top-level sport; **~modern** *Adj.* ultra-modern; **~mut** der arrogance; **~mütig** *Adj.* arrogant; **~näsig** *Adj. (abwertend)* stuck-up; **~|nehmen** *unr. tr. V. (ugs.: verspotten)* jmdn. **~nehmen** pull sb.'s leg; **~ofen** der blast furnace; **~prozentig** *Adj.* high-proof ⟨*spirits*⟩; **~rechnung** die *(Statistik)* projection; **~ruf** der cheer; **~saison** die high season; **~|schlagen** 1. *unr. tr. V.* turn up ⟨*collar, brim*⟩; 2. *unr. itr. V.; mit sein* ⟨*water, waves*⟩ surge up; ⟨*flames*⟩ leap up; **~schule** die college; *(Universität)* university

**Hochsee·fischerei** die deep-sea fishing *no art.*

**hoch-, Hoch-:** **~sitz** der *(Jagdw.)* raised hide; **~sommer** der high summer; **~spannung** die *(Elektrot.)* high voltage; **~|spielen** *tr. V.* blow up

**höchst** [hø:çst] *Adv.* extremely; most; **höchst...** *s.* **hoch**

**Hoch·stapler** [~∫ta:plɐ] der; **~s, ~** confidence trickster; con-man *(coll.)*; *(Aufschneider)* fraud

**höchstens** *Adv.* at most; *(bestenfalls)* at best

**Höchst-:** **~fall** der *in* im **~fall** at [the] most; **~form** die *(bes. Sport)* peak form; **~geschwindigkeit** die top speed; *(Geschwindigkeitsbegrenzung)* speed limit

**Hoch·stimmung** die high spirits *pl.*

**höchst-, Höchst-:** **~leistung** die

supreme performance; *(Ergebnis)* supreme achievement; **~maß** das: ein **~maß** an etw. *(Dat.)* a very high degree of sth.; **~wahrscheinlich** *Adv.* very probably

**hoch-, Hoch-:** **~tour** die: auf **~touren laufen** run at full speed; *(intensiv betrieben werden)* be in full swing; **~trabend** *(abwertend)* 1. *Adj.* high-flown; 2. *adv.* in a high-flown manner; **~|treiben** *unr. tr. V.* force up ⟨*prices etc.*⟩; **~verrat** der high treason; **~wasser** das *(Flut)* high tide; *(Überschwemmung)* flood; **~wertig** *Adj.* high-quality ⟨*goods*⟩; highly nutritious ⟨*food*⟩; **~würden** o. *Art.; ~|s|* *(veralt.)* Reverend Father

**Hochzeit** die; **~, ~en** wedding

**Hochzeits-:** **~feier** die wedding; **~nacht** die wedding night; **~reise** die honeymoon [trip]

**Hocke** die; **~, ~n a)** *(Körperhaltung)* squat; crouch; **b)** *(Turnen)* squat vault; **hocken** 1. *itr. V.* **a)** *mit haben od. (südd.) sein* squat; crouch; **b)** *mit haben od. (südd.) sein (ugs.: sich aufhalten)* sit around; 2. *refl. V.* crouch down; **Hocker** der; **~s, ~**: stool

**Höcker** der; **~s, ~**: hump; *(auf der Nase)* bump; *(auf dem Schnabel)* knob

**Hockey** ['hɔki] das; **~s** hockey

**Hoden** der; **~s, ~**: testicle

**Hof** der; **~[e]s, Höfe a)** courtyard; *(Schul~)* playground; *(Gefängnis~)* [prison] yard; **b)** *(Bauern~)* farm; **c)** *(Herrscher, Hofstaat)* court

**Hof·dame** die lady of the court; *(Begleiterin der Königin)* lady-in-waiting; **hof·fähig** *Adj.* presentable at court *pred.*

**hoffen** 1. *tr. V.* hope; 2. *itr. V.* hope; **auf etw.** *(Akk.)* **~**: hope for sth.; *(Vertrauen setzen auf)* **auf jmdn./etw. ~**: put one's faith in sb./sth.; **hoffentlich** *Adv.* hopefully; **~!** let's hope so; **Hoffnung** die; **~, ~en** hope

**hoffnungs-, Hoffnungs-:** **~los** 1. *Adj.* hopeless; despairing ⟨*person*⟩; 2. *adv.* hopelessly; **~losigkeit** die; **~**: despair; *(der Lage)* hopelessness; **~voll** 1. *Adj.* **a)** hopeful; full of hope *pred.*; **b)** *(erfolgversprechend)* promising; 2. *adv.* **a)** full of hope; **b)** *(erfolgversprechend)* promisingly

**höflich** 1. *Adj.* polite; 2. *adv.* politely; **Höflichkeit** die; **~**: politeness

**hohe** ['ho:ə] *s.* **hoch**; **Höhe** ['hø:ə] die; **~, ~n** height; etw. in die **~ heben**

lift sth. up; **das ist ja die ~!** *(fig. ugs.)* that's the limit

**Hoheit die; ~, ~en** sovereignty (**über** + *Akk.* over); **Seine/Ihre ~:** His/Your Highness

**Hoheits-: ~gebiet das** [sovereign] territory; **~gewässer das;** *meist Pl.* territorial waters

**Höhen-: ~flug der** *(fig.)* flight; **~lage die** altitude; **~luft die;** *o. Pl.* mountain air; **~messer der** altimeter; **~sonne die** *(Med.)* sun lamp; **~unterschied der** difference in altitude

**Höhepunkt der** high point; *(einer Veranstaltung)* high spot; *(einer Laufbahn, des Ruhms)* pinnacle; *(Orgasmus)* climax

**höher** ['hø:ɐ] *s.* **hoch**

**hohl** *Adj.* hollow; **Höhle die; ~, ~n a)** cave; *(größer)* cavern; **b)** *(Tierbau)* lair

**Hohl-: ~maß das** measure of capacity; **~raum der** cavity; [hollow] space; **~spiegel der** concave mirror

**Hohn der; ~[e]s** scorn; derision; **höhnen** *(geh.) itr. V.* jeer; **höhnisch 1.** *Adj.* scornful; **2.** *adv.* scornfully

**Hokuspokus der; ~:** hocus-pocus; *(abwertend: Drum und Dran)* fuss

**hold** *Adj. (dichter. veralt.)* fair; lovely; lovely ⟨*sight, smile*⟩

**holen 1.** *tr. V.* **a)** fetch; get; **b)** *(ab~)* fetch; **c)** *(ugs.: erlangen)* get ⟨*prize etc.*⟩; carry off ⟨*medal, trophy, etc.*⟩; **2.** *refl. V. (ugs.: sich zuziehen)* catch; **sich** *(Dat.)* **|beim Baden| einen Schnupfen ~:** catch a cold [swimming]

**Holland (das); ~s** Holland; **Holländer der; ~s, ~:** Dutchman; **holländisch** *Adj.* Dutch

**Hölle die; ~, ~n** hell *no art.;* **Höllenlärm der** *(ugs.)* diabolical noise or row *(coll.);* **höllisch 1.** *Adj.* **a)** infernal; ⟨*spirits, torments*⟩ of hell; **b)** *(ugs.: sehr groß)* tremendous *(coll.);* **2.** *adv. (ugs.: sehr)* hellishly *(coll.)*

**Holm der; ~[e]s, ~e a)** *(Turnen)* bar

**holpern** *itr. V. mit sein (fahren)* jolt; bump; **holprig** *Adj.* **a)** bumpy; rough; **b)** *(stockend)* halting ⟨*speech*⟩; clumsy ⟨*verses, style, language, etc.*⟩

**Holunder der; ~s, ~:** elder

**Holz das; ~es, Hölzer** wood; *(Bau-, Tischler~)* timber; wood; **Holz·bein das** wooden leg; **hölzern** *Adj. (auch fig.)* wooden; **Holz·fäller der** woodcutter; lumberjack *(Amer.);* **holzfrei** *Adj.* wood-free ⟨*paper*⟩; **holzig** *Adj.* woody

**Holz-: ~klotz der** block of wood; *(als Spielzeug)* wooden block; **~kohle die** charcoal; **~kopf der** *(salopp abwertend)* blockhead; **~pantoffel der** clog; **~scheit das** piece of wood; *(Brenn~)* piece of firewood; **~schnitt der a)** *o. Pl.* woodcutting *no art.;* **b)** *(Blatt)* woodcut; **~schuh der** clog; **~stoß der** pile of wood; **~weg der: auf dem ~weg sein** be on the wrong track *(fig.);* **~wolle die;** *o. Pl.* wood-wool; **~wurm der** the woodworm

**homogen** *Adj.* homogeneous

**homöopathisch** *Adj.* homoeopathic

**Homo·sexualität die; ~:** homosexuality; **homo·sexuell 1.** *Adj.* homosexual; **2.** *adv.* **~ veranlagt sein** have homosexual tendencies

**Honig der; ~s, ~e** honey; **Honig·kuchen der** honey cake; **Honig·wabe die** honeycomb

**Honorar das; ~s, ~e** fee; *(Autoren~)* royalty; **Honoratioren** [honora-'tsi̯o:rən] *Pl.* notabilities; **honorieren** *tr. V.* **a)** jmdn. **~:** pay sb. [a/his/her fee]; **b)** *(würdigen)* appreciate; *(belohnen)* reward

**Hopfen der; ~s, ~:** hop

**hopp** *Interj.* quick; look sharp; **hoppeln** *itr. V.; mit sein* hop; (**über** + *Akk.* across, over); **hoppla** *Interj.* oops; whoops; **hopsen** *itr. V.; mit sein (ugs.) (springen)* jump; *(hüpfen)* ⟨*animal*⟩ hop; ⟨*child*⟩ skip; ⟨*ball*⟩ bounce; **Hopser der; ~s, ~** *(ugs.)* [little] jump

**Hör·apparat der** hearing-aid; **hörbar 1.** *Adj.* audible; **2.** *adv.* audibly; *(geräuschvoll)* noisily; **horchen** *itr. V.* listen (**auf** + *Akk.* to); *(heimlich zuhören)* eavesdrop

**Horde die; ~, ~n** horde; *(von Halbstarken)* mob

**hören 1.** *tr. V.* hear; *(anhören)* listen to; **2.** *itr. V.* hear; *(zuhören)* listen; **auf jmdn./jmds. Rat ~:** listen to sb./sb.'s advice; **Hören·sagen das: vom ~:** from hearsay; **Hörer der; ~s, ~ a)** listener; **b)** *(Telefon~)* receiver

**Hör-: ~fehler der a) das war ein ~fehler** he/she *etc.* misheard; **b)** *(Schwerhörigkeit)* hearing defect; **~funk der** radio; **im ~funk** on the radio; **~gerät das** hearing-aid

**hörig** *Adj.:* jmdm. **~ sein** be submissively dependent on sb.; *(sexuell)* be sexually enslaved to sb.

**Horizont der; ~[e]s, ~e** *(auch Geol., fig.)* horizon; **horizontal 1.** *Adj.*

horizontal; **2.** *adv.* horizontally; **Horizontale die;** ~, ~**n a)** *(Linie)* horizontal line; **b)** *o. Pl. (Lage)* **die** ~: the horizontal

**Hormon das;** ~s, ~e hormone

**Horn das;** ~|e|s, **Hörner** horn; **Hörnchen das;** ~s, ~ *(Gebäck)* croissant; **Horn · haut die a)** callus; hard skin *no indef. art.;* **b)** *(am Auge)* cornea

**Hornisse die;** ~, ~n hornet

**Horoskop das;** ~s, ~e horoscope

**Hör · rohr das** stethoscope

**Horror der;** ~s horror

**Hör-:** ~**saal der** lecture theatre *or* hall; ~**spiel das** radio play

**Horst der;** ~|e|s, ~e eyrie

**Hort der;** ~|e|s, ~e *s.* **Kinderhort; horten** *tr. V.* hoard; stockpile ⟨*raw materials*⟩

**Hortensie die;** ~, ~n hydrangea

**Hör · weite die:** in/außer ~weite in/ out of earshot

**Höschen** ['høːsçən] **das;** ~s, ~: trousers *pl.;* pair of trousers; *(kurzes* ~*)* shorts *pl.;* pair of shorts; **Hose die;** ~, ~n **a)** trousers *pl.;* pants *pl. (Amer.); (Unter*~*)* pants *pl.; (Freizeit*~*)* slacks *pl.; (Bund*~*)* breeches *pl.; (Reit*~*)* riding breeches *pl.;* **eine** ~: a pair of trousers/pants/slacks *etc.* **Hosen-:** ~**an · zug der** trouser suit *(Brit.);* pant suit; ~**matz der** *(ugs. scherzh.)* toddler; ~**rock der** culottes *pl.;* ~**tasche die** trouser-pocket; pants pocket *(Amer.);* ~**träger** *Pl.* braces; suspenders *(Amer.);* pair of braces/suspenders

**Hospital das;** ~s, ~e *od.* **Hospitäler** hospital

**Hostie** ['hɔstiə] **die;** ~, ~n *(christl. Rel.)* host

**Hotel das;** ~s, ~s hotel; **Hotel · bar die** hotel bar; **Hotel garni** [~ gar'ni:] **das;** ~ ~, ~s ~s bed-and-breakfast hotel; **Hotelier** [hotɛ'li̯e:] **der;** ~s, ~s hotelier

**hüben** *Adv.* over here

**hübsch 1.** *Adj.* pretty; nice ⟨*area, flat, voice, tune, etc.*⟩; nice-looking ⟨*boy, person*⟩; **ein** ~**es Sümmchen** *(ugs.)* a tidy sum *(coll.);* a nice little sum; **das ist eine** ~**e Geschichte** *(ugs. iron.)* this is a fine *or* pretty kettle of fish *(coll.);* **2.** *adv.* prettily; *(ugs.: sehr)* ~ **kalt** perishing cold

**Hub · schrauber der;** ~s, ~: helicopter

**huckepack** *Adv.* jmdn. ~ **tragen** *(ugs.)* give sb. a piggyback

**hudeln** *itr. V. (bes. südd., österr.)* be sloppy (**bei** in)

**Huf der;** ~|e|s, ~e hoof

**Huf-:** ~**eisen das** horseshoe; ~**schmied der** farrier

**Hüfte die;** ~, ~n hip

**Hüft-:** ~**gelenk das** *(Anat.)* hip-joint; ~**gürtel der** girdle

**Hügel der;** ~s, ~ hill; **hügelig** *Adj.* hilly

**Huhn das;** ~|e|s, **Hühner a)** chicken; *(Henne)* chicken; hen; **Hühnchen das;** ~s, ~: small chicken; **mit jmdm. |noch| ein** ~ **zu rupfen haben** *(ugs.)* [still] have a bone to pick with sb.

**Hühner-:** ~**auge das** *(am Fuß)* corn; ~**brühe die** chicken broth

**hui** [hui] *Interj.* whoosh

**huldigen** *itr. V.* jmdm. ~: pay tribute to sb.; **Huldigung die;** ~, ~en tribute

**Hülle die;** ~, ~n cover; **hüllen** *tr. V. (geh.)* wrap

**Hülse die;** ~, ~n **a)** case; **b)** *(Bot.)* pod

**human** *Adj.* humane; **Humanismus der;** ~: humanism; *(Epoche)* Humanism *no art.;* **humanitär** *Adj.* humanitarian

**Humbug** ['hʊmbʊk] **der;** ~s *(ugs.)* humbug

**Hummel die;** ~, ~n bumble-bee

**Hummer der;** ~s, ~: lobster

**Humor der;** ~s humour; *(Sinn für* ~*)* sense of humour; **den** ~ **nicht verlieren** remain good-humoured; **Humorist der;** ~en, ~en **a)** *(Autor)* humorist; **b)** *(Vortragskünstler)* comedian; **humoristisch** *Adj.* humorous

**humor-:** ~**los** *Adj.* humourless; ~**voll** *Adj.* humorous

**humpeln** *itr. V.* **a)** *auch mit sein* walk with a limp; **b)** *mit sein (sich* ~*d fortbewegen)* limp

**Hund der;** ~es, ~e **a)** dog; **auf den** ~ **kommen** *(ugs.)* go to the dogs *(coll.);* **vor die** ~**e gehen** *(ugs.)* go to the dogs *(coll.); (sterben)* kick the bucket *(sl.);* **b)** *(abwertend)* bastard *(coll.)*

**hunde-, Hunde-:** ~**elend** *Adj.; nicht attr. (ugs.)* [really] wretched *or* awful; ~**hütte die** [dog-]kennel; ~**kuchen der** dog-biscuit; ~**müde** *Adj.; nicht attr. (ugs.)* dog-tired; ~**rasse die** breed of dog

**hundert** *Kardinalz.* **a)** a *or* one hundred; **b)** *(ugs.: viele)* hundreds of; **¹Hundert das;** ~s, ~e hundred; **²Hundert die;** ~, ~en hundred; **Hunderter der;** ~s, ~ *(ugs.)* hundred-mark/-dollar *etc.* note; **hun-**

**dert·mal** *Adv.* a hundred times; **auch wenn du dich ~ beschwerst** *(ugs.)* however much you complain

**Hundert-:** **~mark·schein** der hundred-mark note; **~meter·lauf** der *(Leichtathletik)* hundred metres *sing.*

**hundert·prozentig** 1. *Adj.* **a)** *(von 100 %)* [one-]hundred per cent *attrib.;* **b)** *(ugs.: völlig)* a hundred per cent; **c)** *(ugs.: ganz sicher)* absolutely reliable; 2. *adv. (ugs.)* **ich bin nicht ~ sicher** I'm not a hundred per cent sure; **hundertst...** ['hʊndɐtst...] *Ordinalz.* hundredth; **hundertstel** ['hʊndɐtst|l] *Bruchz.* hundredth; **Hundertstel** das *(schweiz. meist* der*);* **~s, ~:** hundredth; **hundert·tausend** *Kardinalz.* a *or* one hundred thousand

**Hüne** der; **~n, ~n** giant; **Hünen·grab** das megalithic tomb; *(Hügelgrab)* barrow

**Hunger** der; **~s a) ~ bekommen/haben** get/be hungry; **b)** *(geh.: Verlangen)* hunger; *(nach Ruhm, Macht)* craving; **Hunger·kur** die starvation diet; **hungern** *itr. V.* go hungry; starve; **nach etw. ~:** *(fig.)* hunger for sth.; **Hungers·not** die famine; **Hunger·streik** der hunger-strike; **hungrig** *Adj. (auch geh. fig.)* hungry **(nach** for**)**

**Hupe** die; **~, ~n** horn; **hupen** *itr. V.* sound one's horn; **dreimal ~:** hoot three times

**hüpfen** *itr. V.;* **mit sein** hop; ⟨*ball*⟩ bounce

**Hürde** die; **~, ~n** hurdle; **Hürden·lauf** der *(Leichtathletik)* hurdling; *(Wettbewerb)* hurdles *pl.*

**Hure** die; **~, ~n** *(abwertend)* whore; **huren** *itr. V. (abwertend)* whore

**hurra** *Interj.* hurray; hurrah; **~ schreien** cheer; **Hurra** das; **~s, ~s** cheer

**hurtig** 1. *Adj.* rapid; 2. *adv.* quickly

**huschen** *itr. V.;* **mit sein** *(lautlos u. leichtfüßig)* ⟨*person*⟩ steal; *(lautlos u. schnell)* dart; ⟨*mouse, lizard, etc.*⟩ dart; ⟨*smile*⟩ flit; ⟨*light*⟩ flash; ⟨*shadow*⟩ slide quickly

**hüsteln** *itr. V.* give a slight cough; **husten** 1. *itr. V.* cough; *(Husten haben)* have a cough; 2. *tr. V.* cough up ⟨*blood, phlegm*⟩; **Husten** der; **~s, ~:** cough

**Husten-:** **~bonbon** das cough-drop; **~tropfen** *Pl.* cough-drops

¹**Hut** der; **~es, Hüte** hat; *(fig.)* **da geht einem/mir der ~ hoch** *(ugs.)* it makes you/me mad *(coll.);* **das kann er sich**

*(Dat.)* **an den ~ stecken** *(ugs. abwertend)* he can keep it *(coll.)*

²**Hut** die; **~** *(geh.)* keeping;. care; **auf der ~ sein** be on one's guard; **hüten** 1. *tr. V.* look after; tend ⟨*sheep, cattle, etc.*⟩; 2. *refl. V.* be on one's guard

**Hut·schnur** die *in* das geht mir über die **~** *(ugs.)* that's going too far

**Hütte** die; **~, ~n a)** hut; *(ärmliches Haus)* shack; hut; **b)** *(Eisen~)* iron [and steel] works *sing. or pl.;* **c)** *(Jagd~)* [hunting-]lodge

**Hütten-:** **~käse** der cottage cheese; **~schuh** der slipper-sock

**Hyäne** die; **~, ~n** hyena

**Hyazinthe** die; **~, ~n** hyacinth

**Hydrant** der; **~en, ~en** hydrant; **Hydraulik** die; **~** *(Technik)* **a)** *(Theorie)* hydraulics *sing., no art.;* **b)** *(Vorrichtungen)* hydraulics *pl.;* **hydraulisch** *(Technik)* 1. *Adj.* hydraulic; 2. *adv.* hydraulically; **Hydro·kultur** die; **~, ~en** *(Gartenbau)* hydroponics *sing.*

**Hygiene** die; **~ a)** *(Gesundheitspflege)* health care; **b)** *(Sauberkeit)* hygiene; **hygienisch** 1. *Adj.* hygienic; 2. *adv.* hygienically

**Hymne** ['hʏmnə] die; **~, ~n** hymn; *(National~)* national anthem

**Hypnose** die; **~, ~n** hypnosis; **hypnotisieren** *tr. V.* hypnotize

**Hypochonder** [hypo'xɔndɐ] der; **~s, ~:** hypochondriac

**Hypotenuse** die; **~, ~n** *(Math.)* hypotenuse

**Hypothek** die; **~, ~en** *(Bankw.)* mortgage; *(fig.)* burden

**Hypothese** die; **~, ~n** hypothesis; **hypothetisch** 1. *Adj.* hypothetical; 2. *adv.* hypothetically

**Hysterie** die; **~, ~n** hysteria; **hysterisch** 1. *Adj.* hysterical; 2. *adv.* hysterically

# I

**i, I** das; **~, ~:** i/I; **das Tüpfelchen auf dem i** *(fig.)* the final touch

**i** *Interj.* ugh; **i bewahre, i wo** *(ugs.)* [good] heavens, no!

**i. A.** *Abk.* **im Auftrag|e|** p.p.

**IC** *Abk.* **Intercity** IC

**ich** *Personalpron.; 1. Pers. Sg. Nom.* I;
**immer ~** *(ugs.)* [it's] always me; **~
nicht** not me; **Menschen wie du und ~:**
people like you and me; *s. auch (Gen.)*
**meiner**, *(Dat.)* **mir**, *(Akk.)* **mich**

**Ich das;** ~|s|, ~|s| **a)** self; **b)** *(Psych.)*
ego

**Ich-Form die;** *o. Pl.* first person

**ideal** 1. *Adj.* ideal; 2. *adv.* ideally;
**Ideal das;** ~s, ~e ideal

**Ideal-:** ~**bild das** ideal; ~**fall der**
ideal case; ~**gewicht das** ideal
weight

**idealisieren** *tr. V.* idealize; **Idealismus der;** ~ *(auch Philos.)* idealism;
**Idealist der;** ~en, ~en idealist;
**idealistisch** *(auch Philos.)* 1. *Adj.*
idealistic; 2. *adv.* idealistically; **Idee
die;** ~, ~n **a)** idea; **b)** *(ein bißchen)* ei-
ne ~: a shade; **eine ~ |Salz/Pfeffer|** a
touch [of salt/pepper]; **ideell** *Adj.*
non-material; *(geistig-seelisch)* spiritual; **ideen·los** *Adj.* [completely]
lacking in ideas *postpos.*

**Identifikation** [identifika'tsĭo:n] **die;**
~, ~en *(auch Psych.)* identification;
**identifizieren** 1. *tr. V.* identify; 2.
*refl. V. (auch Psych.)* **sich mit jmdm./
etw. ~:** identify with sb./sth.; **identisch** *Adj.* identical; **Identität die;**
~: identity

**Ideologe der;** ~n, ~n ideologue;
**Ideologie die;** ~, ~|n [-i:ən] ideology;
**ideologisch** 1. *Adj.* ideological; 2.
*adv.* ideologically

**Idiot der;** ~en, ~en *(auch ugs. abwertend)* idiot; **Idioten·hügel der** *(ugs.
scherzh.)* nursery slope; **Idiotie die;**
~, ~n [-i:ən] **a)** idiocy; **b)** *(ugs. abwertend: Dummheit)* madness; **Idiotin
die;** ~, ~nen *(auch ugs. abwertend)*
**idiotisch** 1. *Adj.* **a)** *(Psych.)* severely
subnormal; **b)** *(ugs. abwertend)* idiotic; 2. *adv. (auch ugs. abwertend)*
idiotically

**Idol das;** ~s, ~e *(auch bild. Kunst)* idol

**Idyll das;** ~s, ~e idyll; **Idylle die;** ~,
~n idyll; **idyllisch** *Adj.* idyllic

**Igel der;** ~s, ~: hedgehog

**Iglu der** *od.* **das;** ~s, ~s igloo

**Ignoranz** [ɪgno'rants] **die;** ~: ignorance; **ignorieren** *tr. V.* ignore

**ihm** *Dat. von* **er**, **es:** *(bei männlichen
Personen)* him; *(bei weiblichen Personen)* her; *(bei Dingen, Tieren)* it; **gib es
~:** give it to him; give him it; **Freunde
von ~:** friends of his

**ihn** *Akk. von* **er** *(bei männlichen Personen)* him; *(bei Dingen, Tieren)* it

**ihnen** *Dat. von* **sie**, *Pl.* them; **gib es ~:**
give it to them; give them it; **Freunde
von ~:** friends of theirs

**Ihnen** *Dat. von* **Sie** you; **ich habe es ~
gegeben** I gave it to you; **Freunde von
~:** friends of yours

**¹ihr** [i:ɐ̯] *Dat. von* **sie**, *Sg. (bei Personen)*
her; *(bei Dingen, Tieren)* it

**²ihr**, *(in Briefen)* **Ihr** *Personalpron.; 2.
Pers. Pl. Nom.* you

**³ihr** *Possessivpron.* **a)** *Sg. (einer Person)*
her; *(eines Tieres, einer Sache)* its; **b)**
*Pl.* their

**Ihr** *Possessivpron. (Anrede)* your; ~
**Hans Meier** *(Briefschluß)* yours, Hans
Meier; **welcher Mantel ist ~er?** which
coat is yours?

**ihrer a)** *Gen. von* **sie**, *Sg. (geh.)* **wir ge-
dachten ~:** we remembered her; **b)**
*Gen. von* **sie**, *Pl. (geh.)* **wir werden ~
gedenken** we will remember them; **es
waren ~ zwölf** there were twelve of
them

**Ihrer** *Gen. von* **Sie** *(geh.)* **wir werden ~
gedenken** we will remember you

**ihrerseits** *Adv.* for her/their part;
*(von ihr/ihnen)* on her/their part

**Ihrerseits** *Adv. s.* **deinerseits**

**ihres·gleichen** *indekl. Pron.* people
*pl.* like her/them; *(abwertend)* the
likes of her/them

**Ihresgleichen** *indekl. Pron.* people
*pl.* like you; *(abwertend)* the likes of
you

**ihret·wegen** *Adv.: s.* **meinetwegen:**
because of her/them; for her/their
sake; about her/them; as far as she is/
they are concerned

**Ihretwegen** *Adv.: s.* **deinetwegen**

**Ikone die;** ~, ~n icon

**illegal** 1. *Adj.* illegal; 2. *adv.* illegally
**Illegalität die;** ~, ~en illegality; **ille-
gitim** ['ɪlegiti:m] *Adj. (geh.)* illegitimate

**illuminieren** *tr. V.* illuminate

**Illusion die;** ~, ~en illusion; **illusorisch** *Adj.* illusory; *(zwecklos)* pointless

**Illustration** [ɪlustra'tsĭo:n] **die;** ~, ~en
illustration; **illustrieren** *tr. V.* illustrate; **Illustrierte die;** *adj. Dekl.* magazine

**Iltis der;** ~ses, ~se polecat; *(Pelz)* fitch
**im** *Präp. + Art.* **a)** = **in dem; b)** *(räumlich)* in the; **im Theater** at the theatre;
**im Fernsehen** on television; **im Bett** in
bed; **c)** *(zeitlich)* **im Mai** in May; **im**

letzten **Jahr** last year; im **Alter von ...** at the age of ...; **d)** *(Verlauf)* etw. im Sitzen tun do sth. [while] sitting down; im Gehen sein be going

**Image** ['ɪmɪtʃ] das; ~[s], ~s ['ɪmɪtʃs] image; **imaginär** *Adj. (geh., Math.)* imaginary

**Imbiß** der; Imbisses, Imbisse **a)** *(kleine Mahlzeit)* snack; **b)** *s.* **Imbißstube**; **Imbiß·stube** die café

**Imitation** die; ~, ~en imitation; **imitieren** *tr. V.* imitate

**Imker** der; ~s, ~: bee-keeper

**Immatrikulation** [ɪmatrikula'tsi̯oːn] die; ~, ~en *(Hochschulw.)* registration; **immatrikulieren** *tr., refl. V. (Hochschulw.)* register

**immer** *Adv.* **a)** always; **schon** ~: always; ~ **wieder** time and time again; ~, **wenn** every time that; **b)** ~ + *Komp.* ~ **dunkler** darker and darker; ~ **mehr** more and more; **c)** *(ugs.: jeweils)* ~ **drei Stufen auf einmal** three steps at a time; **d)** *(auch)* **wo/wer/ wann/wie** [auch] ~: wherever/whoever/whenever/however; **e)** *(verstärkend)* ~ **noch, noch** ~: still; **f)** *(ugs.: bei Aufforderung)* ~ **geradeaus!** keep [going] straight on

**immer-, Immer-:** ~**fort** *Adv.* all the time; ~**grün** *Adj.* evergreen; ~**grün** das periwinkle; ~**hin** *Adv.* **a)** *(wenigstens)* at any rate; **b)** *(trotz allem)* all the same; **c)** *(schließlich)* after all; ~**zu** *Adv. (ugs.)* the whole time

**Immigrant** der; ~en, ~en immigrant; **Immigration** [ɪmigra'tsi̯oːn] die; ~, ~en immigration; **immigrieren** *itr. V.; mit sein* immigrate

**Immobilien** *Pl.* property *sing.;* real estate *sing.*

**immun a)** *(Med., fig.)* immune (**gegen** to); **b)** *(Rechtsspr.)* ~ **sein** have immunity; **Immunität** die; ~, ~en **a)** *(Med.)* immunity (**gegen** to); **b)** *(Rechtsspr.)* immunity (**gegen** from)

**Imperativ** der; ~s, ~e **a)** *(Sprachw.)* imperative; **b)** *(Philos.)* [kategorischer] ~: [categorical] imperative

**Imperfekt** das; ~s, ~e*(Sprachw.)* imperfect [tense]

**Imperialismus** der; ~: imperialism *no art.;* **imperialistisch** *Adj.* imperialistic

**Imperium** das; ~s, Imperien *(hist., fig.)* empire

**impfen** *tr. V.* vaccinate; inoculate

**Impf-:** ~**paß** der vaccination certificate; ~**stoff** der vaccine

**Impfung** die; ~, ~en vaccination

**implantieren** *tr. V. (Med.)* implant

**imponieren** *itr. V.* impress; **imponierend** **1.** *Adj.* impressive; **2.** *adv.* impressively

**Import** der; ~[e]s, ~e import; **Importeur** [ɪmpɔr'tøːɐ̯] der; ~s, ~e importer; **importieren** *tr., itr. V.* import

**imposant** **1.** *Adj.* imposing; impressive ⟨*achievement*⟩; **2.** *adv.* imposingly

**impotent** *Adj.* impotent; **Impotenz** die; ~: impotence

**imprägnieren** *tr. V.* impregnate; *(wasserdicht machen)* waterproof

**Improvisation** die; ~, ~en improvisation; **improvisieren** *tr., itr. V.* improvise

**Impuls** der; ~es, ~e stimulus; *(innere Regung)* impulse; **impulsiv** **1.** *Adj.* impulsive; **2.** *adv.* impulsively

**imstande** *Adv.* ~ **sein, etw. zu tun** be able to do sth.

**in** **1.** *Präp. mit Dat.* **a)** *(auf die Frage: wo?/wann?/wie?)* in; **er hat** ~ **Tübingen studiert** he studied at Tübingen; *s. auch* **im; 2.** *Präp. mit Akk. (auf die Frage: wohin?)* into; *s. auch* **ins**

**In·anspruchnahme** die; ~, ~n *(starke Belastung)* demands *pl.*

**In·begriff** der quintessence; **inbegriffen** *Adj.* included

**In·betriebnahme** die; ~, ~n, **In·betriebsetzung** die; ~, ~en *(Amtsspr.)* opening; *(von Maschinen)* bringing into service

**In·brunst** die; ~ *(geh.)* fervour; *(der Liebe)* ardour; **in·brünstig** *(geh.)* **1.** *Adj.* fervent; ardent ⟨*love*⟩; **2.** *adv.* fervently; ⟨*love*⟩ ardently

**in·dem** *Konj.* **a)** *(während)* while; *(gerade als)* as; **b)** *(dadurch, daß)* ~ **man etw. tut** by doing sth.

**Inder** ['ɪndɐ] der; ~s, ~: Indian

**in·dessen** **1.** *Konj. (geh.)* **a)** *(während)* while; **b)** *(wohingegen)* whereas; **2.** *Adv.* **a)** *(inzwischen)* meanwhile; in the mean time; **b)** *(jedoch)* however

**Index** der; ~ od. ~es, ~e od. Indizes **a)** *Pl.* ~e od. Indizes *(Register)* index; **b)** *Pl.* ~e *(kath. Kirche)* Index

**Indianer** der; ~s, ~: [American] Indian; **Indianer·häuptling** der Indian chief

**Indien** ['ɪndi̯ən] (das) India

**in·different** *Adj.* indifferent

**Indikativ** der; ~s, ~e [-iːvə] *(Sprachw.)* indicative [mood]

**in·direkt 1.** *Adj.; nicht präd.* indirect; **2.** *adv.* indirectly

**indisch** *Adj.* Indian

**in·diskret** *Adj.* indiscreet; **In·diskretion die; ~, ~en** indiscretion

**Individualist der; ~en, ~en** *(geh.)* individualist; **Individualität die; ~, ~en** *(geh.)* **a)** *o. Pl.* individuality; **b)** *(Persönlichkeit)* personality; **individuell 1.** *Adj.* individual; private *(property, vehicle, etc.)*; **2.** *adv.* individually; **Individuum das; ~s, Individuen** *(auch Chemie, Biol.)* individual

**Indiz das; ~es, ~ien a)** *(Rechtsw.)* piece of circumstantial evidence; **~ien** circumstantial evidence *sing.*; **b)** *(Anzeichen)* sign **(für** of)

**indoktrinieren** *tr. V.* indoctrinate

**Indonesien** [ɪndoˈneːzi̯ən] **(das)** Indonesia; **Indonesier der; ~s, ~** Indonesian; **indonesisch** *Adj.* Indonesian

**industrialisieren** *tr. V.* industrialize; **Industrialisierung die; ~:** industrialization; **Industrie die; ~, ~n** industry

**Industrie-: ~betrieb der** industrial firm; **~gebiet das** industrial area; **~kaufmann der** *person with three years' business training employed on the business side of an industrial company*

**industriell 1.** *Adj.* industrial; **2.** *adv.* industrially; **Industrielle der/die;** *adj. Dekl.* industrialist

**Industrie-: ~staat der** industrial nation; **~stadt die** industrial town; **~zweig der** branch of industry

**in·einander** *Adv.* ~ **verliebt sein** be in love with each other *or* one another; ~ **verschlungene Ornamente** intertwined decorations; **ineinander|greifen** *unr. itr. V.* mesh together *(lit. or fig.)*

**infam 1.** *Adj.* disgraceful; **2.** *adv.* disgracefully

**Infanterie die; ~, ~n** *(Milit.)* infantry

**Infarkt der; ~[e]s, ~e** *(Med.)* infarction

**Infekt der; ~[e]s, ~e** *(Med.)* infection

**Infektion** [ɪnfɛkˈtsi̯oːn] **die; ~, ~en** *(Med.)* **a)** *(Ansteckung)* infection; **b)** *(ugs.: Entzündung)* inflammation

**Infektions-: ~gefahr die** *(Med.)* risk of infection; **~herd der** *(Med.)* seat of the/an infection; **~krankheit die** *(Med.)* infectious disease

**Inferno das; ~s** *(geh.)* inferno

**Infinitiv der; ~s, ~e** *(Sprachw.)* infinitive

**infizieren 1.** *tr. V.* infect; **2.** *refl. V.* become infected; **sich bei jmdm. ~:** be infected by sb.

**in flagranti** *Adv.* *(geh.)* in flagrante [delicto]

**Inflation die; ~, ~en** *(Wirtsch.)* inflation; *(Zeit der ~)* period of inflation

**in·folge 1.** *Präp.* + *Gen.* as a result of; **2.** *Adv.* ~ **von etw.** *(Dat.)* as a result of sth.

**infolge·dessen** *Adv.* consequently

**Informatik die; ~:** computer science *no art.;* **Information die; ~, ~en a)** information *no pl., no indef. art.* **(über** + *Akk.* about, on); **eine ~:** [a piece of] information; **b)** *(Büro)* information bureau; *(Stand)* information desk

**Informations-: ~material das** informational literature; **~quelle die** source of information

**informativ** *Adj.* informative; **informieren 1.** *tr. V.* inform **(über** + *Akk.* about); **2.** *refl. V.* inform oneself, find out **(über** + *Akk.* about)

**Infra·rot das; ~s** *(Physik)* infra-red radiation; **Infra·struktur die** infrastructure

**Infusion die; ~, ~en** *(Med.)* infusion

**Ing.** *Abk.* Ingenieur; **Ingenieur** [ɪnʒeˈni̯øːɐ̯] **der; ~s, ~e** [qualified] engineer

**Ingwer der; ~s, ~** ginger

**Inhaber der; ~s, ~ a)** holder; **b)** *(Besitzer)* owner

**inhaftieren** *tr. V.* take into custody; detain; **Inhaftierung die; ~, ~en** detention

**inhalieren** *tr. V.* inhale

**In·halt der; ~[e]s, ~e a)** contents *pl.;* **b)** *(einer Geschichte usw.)* content; **c)** *(bes. Math.)* *(Flächen~)* area; *(Raum~)* volume

**Inhalts-: ~angabe die** summary [of contents]; synopsis; *(eines Films, Dramas)* synopsis; **~verzeichnis das** table of contents; *(auf einem Paket)* list of contents

**in·human** *Adj.* **a)** *(unmenschlich)* inhuman; **b)** *(rücksichtslos)* inhumane

**Initiale die; ~, ~n** initial [letter]

**Initiative die; ~, ~n** initiative; **Initiator** [iniˈtsi̯aːtor] **der; ~s, ~en** initiator; *(einer Organisation)* founder

**Injektion die; ~, ~en** *(Med.)* injection; **injizieren** *tr. V.* *(Med.)* inject

**inkl.** *Abk.* inklusive incl.

**inklusive** [ɪnkluˈziːvə] **1.** *Präp.* + *Gen.* *(bes. Kaufmannsspr.)* including; **2.** *Adv.* inclusive

**inkognito** *Adv.* *(geh.)* incognito

**in·kompetent** *Adj.* incompetent; **In·kompetenz** die incompetence
**in·konsequent** 1. *Adj.* inconsistent; 2. *adv.* inconsistently; **In·konsequenz** die inconsistency
**in·korrekt** 1. *Adj.* incorrect; 2. *adv.* incorrectly
**In·kraft·treten** das; ~s: mit [dem] ~ des Gesetzes when the law comes/came into force
**In·land** das; ~[e]s **a)** im ~: at home; **b)** *(Binnenland)* interior; inland; im/ins ~: inland; **inländisch** *Adj.* domestic; home-produced *(goods)*
**Inlands-:** ~markt der domestic market; ~porto das inland postage
**in·mitten** 1. *Präp.* + *Gen. (geh.)* in the midst of; 2. *Adv.* ~ von in the midst of
**inne|haben** *unr. tr. V.* hold, occupy *(position)*; hold *(office)*
**innen** *Adv.* inside; *(auf/an der Innenseite)* on the inside
**innen-, Innen-:** ~architekt der interior designer; ~aufnahme die *(Fot.)* indoor photo[graph]; *(Film)* interior shot; ~einrichtung die furnishings *pl.*; ~hof der inner courtyard; ~leben das; *o. Pl.* **a)** [inner] thoughts and feelings *pl.*; **b)** *(oft scherzh.: Ausstattung)* inside; ~minister der Minister of the Interior; ≈ Home Secretary *(Brit.)*; ≈ Secretary of the Interior *(Amer.)*; ~politik die *(eines Staates)* home affairs *pl.*; *(einer Regierung)* domestic policy/policies *pl.*; ~politisch *s.* ~politik: 1. *Adj.* ~politische Fragen matters of domestic policy; 2. *adv.* as regards home affairs/domestic policy; ~stadt die town centre; downtown *(Amer.)*; *(einer Großstadt)* city centre
**inner...** *Adj.* inner; *(inländisch; Med.)* internal; inside *(pocket, lane)*; **Innere** das; *adj. Dekl.; o. Pl.* inside; *(eines Gebäudes, Wagens, Schiffes)* interior; inside; *(eines Landes)* interior; **Innereien** *Pl.* entrails; *(Kochk.)* offal *sing.*; **inner·halb** 1. *Präp.* + *Gen.* **a)** within; ~ der Familie/Partei *(fig.)* within the family/party; **b)** *(binnen)* within; ~ einer Woche within a week; 2. *Adv.* **a)** ~ von within; **b)** *(im Verlauf)* ~ von zwei Jahren within two years; **innerlich** 1. *Adj.* inner; 2. *adv.* inwardly; **innerst...** *Adj.* innermost; **Innerste** das; *adj. Dekl.; o. Pl.* innermost being
**inne|wohnen** *itr. V. (geh.)* etw. wohnt

jmdm./einer Sache ~: sb./sth. possesses sth.
**innig** 1. *Adj.* deep *(affection, sympathy)*; fervent *(wish)*; intimate *(friendship)*; mein ~ster Dank my sincerest thanks; 2. *adv. (love)* with all one's heart; **Innigkeit** die; ~: depth; *(einer Beziehung)* intimacy
**Innung** ['ɪnʊŋ] die; ~, ~en [trade] guild
**in·offiziell** 1. *Adj.* unofficial; 2. *adv.* unofficially
**in puncto** as regards
**ins** *Präp.* + *Art.* = in das
**Insasse** der; ~n, ~n **a)** *(Fahrgast)* passenger; **b)** *(Bewohner)* inmate
**ins·besond[e]re** *Adv.* particularly; in particular
**In·schrift** die inscription
**Insekt** [ɪn'zɛkt] das; ~s, ~en insect
**Insel** die; ~, ~n island
**Inserat** das; ~[e]s, ~e advertisement *(in a newspaper)*; **Inserent** der; ~en, ~en advertiser; **inserieren** *itr. V.* advertise
**ins·geheim** *Adv.* secretly
**ins·gesamt** *Adv.* in all; altogether; *(alles in allem)* all in all
**insofern** 1. *Adv.* [ɪn'zo:fɛrn] *(in dieser Hinsicht)* to this extent; 2. *Konj.* [ɪnzo'fɛrn] *(falls)* provided [that]
**insoweit** [ɪn'zo:vait/ɪnzo'vait] *Adv./Konj. s.* insofern
**in spe** [ɪn 'spe:] future *attrib.*; mein Schwiegersohn ~ ~: my future son-in-law
**Inspektion** [ɪnspɛk'tsi̯o:n] die; ~, ~en inspection; *(Kfz-W.)* service
**Inspiration** [ɪnspira'tsi̯o:n] die; ~, ~en inspiration; **inspirieren** *tr. V.* inspire
**inspizieren** *tr. V.* inspect
**Installateur** [ɪnstala'tø:ɐ̯] der; ~s, ~e plumber; *(Gas~)* [gas-]fitter; *(Heizungs~)* heating engineer; *(Elektro~)* electrician; **Installation** [ɪnstala'tsi̯o:n] die; ~, ~en installation; *(Rohre)* plumbing *no pl.*; **installieren** *tr. V.* install
**in·stand** *Adv.* etw. ist gut/schlecht ~: sth. is in good/poor condition; etw. ~ halten keep sth. in good condition; etw. ~ setzen/bringen repair sth.; **Instand·haltung** die maintenance
**in·ständig** 1. *Adj.* urgent; 2. *adv.* urgently
**Instanz** [ɪn'stants] die; ~, ~en **a)** authority; **b)** *(Rechtsw.)* [die] erste/zweite/dritte ~: the court of original jurisdiction/the appeal court/the court of

final appeal; **durch alle ~en gehen** go through all the courts

**Instinkt** [ɪn'stɪŋkt] der; ~[e]s, ~e instinct; **instinktiv** 1. *Adj.* instinctive; 2. *adv.* instinctively

**Institut** das; ~[e]s, ~e a) institute; **Institution** [ɪnstitu'tsi̯oːn] die; ~, ~en *(auch fig.)* institution

**Instruktion** [ɪnstrʊk'tsi̯oːn] die; ~, ~en instruction

**Instrument** [ɪnstru'mɛnt] das; ~[e]s, ~e instrument; **instrumental** *(Musik)* 1. *Adj.* instrumental; 2. *adv.* instrumentally

**Insulin** das; ~s insulin

**inszenieren** *tr. V.* stage; put on; *(Regie führen bei)* direct; *(fig.) (einfädeln)* engineer; *(organisieren)* stage; **Inszenierung** die; ~, ~en staging; *(Regie)* direction; *(Aufführung)* production

**intakt** *Adj.* a) *(unbeschädigt)* intact; b) *(funktionsfähig)* in [proper] working order *postpos.;* healthy *(economy)*

**integer** *Adj.* **eine integre Persönlichkeit** a person of integrity; ~ **sein** be a person of integrity

**Integral** das; ~s, ~s *(Math.)* integral **integrieren** *tr. V.* integrate

**Intellekt** der; ~[e]s intellect; **intellektuell** *Adj.* intellectual; **Intellektuelle** der/die; *adj. Dekl.* intellectual; **intelligent** 1. *Adj.* intelligent; 2. *adv.* intelligently; **Intelligenz** die; ~a) intelligence; b) *(Gesamtheit der Intellektuellen)* intelligentsia; **Intelligenz·quotient** der intelligence quotient

**Intendant** der; ~en, ~en *(Theater)* manager and artistic director; *(Fernseh~, Rundfunk~)* director-general

**Intensität** die; ~: intensity

**intensiv** 1. *Adj. (gründlich)* intensive *(kräftig)* intense; 2. *adv.* intensively; **intensivieren** *tr. V.* intensify; increase *(exports);* strengthen *(connections);* **Intensiv·station die** intensive-care unit

**Intercity-Zug** der inter-city train

**interessant** 1. *Adj.* interesting; 2. *adv.* ~ **schreiben** write in an interesting way; **interessanterweise** *Adv.* interestingly enough; **Interesse das;** ~s, ~n interest; ~ **an jmdm./etw. haben** be interested in sb./sth.; **interesse·halber** *Adv.* out of interest; **Interessen·gebiet das** field of interest; **Interessent** der; ~en, ~en interested person; *(möglicher Käufer)* potential buyer; **Interessen·ver-**

**band der** [organized] interest group; **Interessen·vertretung die a)** representation; b) *(Vertreter von Interessen)* representative body; **interessieren** 1. *refl. V.* **sich für jmdn./etw.** ~: be interested in sb./sth. 2. *tr. V.* interest; **das interessiert mich nicht** I'm not interested [in it]; **interessiert** *Adj.* interested **(an** + *Dat.* in)

**Interjektion** [ɪntɛɪ̯ɛk'tsi̯oːn] die; ~, ~en *(Sprachw.)* interjection

**Interkontinental·rakete die** *(Milit.)* intercontinental ballistic missile

**intern** 1. *Adj.* internal; 2. *adv.* internally

**Internat** das; ~[e]s, ~e boarding-school

**inter·national** 1. *Adj.* international; 2. *adv.* internationally; **Inter·nationale die;** ~, ~n a) International; Internationale; b) *(Lied)* Internationale

**Internats-:** ~**schüler** der, ~**schülerin** die boarding-school pupil; boarder

**internieren** *tr. V. (Milit.)* intern; **Internierung** die; ~, ~en internment **Internist** der; ~en, ~en *(Med.)* internist

**Interpol** die; ~: Interpol *no art.*

**Interpret** der; ~en, ~en interpreter *(of music, text, events, etc.);* **Interpretation** [ɪntɛprɛta'tsi̯oːn] die; ~, ~en interpretation *(of music, text, events, etc.);* **interpretieren** *tr. V.* interpret *(music, texts, events, etc.);* **Interpretin die;** ~, ~nen *s.* Interpret

**Interpunktion** [ɪntɛpʊŋk'tsi̯oːn] die; ~ *(Sprachw.)* punctuation

**Intervall** [ɪntɛ'val] das; ~s, ~e *(Musik, Math.)* interval

**intervenieren** *itr. V. (geh., Politik)* intervene; **Intervention** [ɪntɛvɛn'tsi̯oːn] die; ~, ~en *(geh., Politik)* intervention; *(Protest)* representations *pl.*

**Interview** [ɪntɐ'vju:] das; ~s, ~s interview; **interviewen** [ɪntɐ'vju:ən] *tr. V.* interview

**intim** 1. *Adj.* intimate; 2. *adv.* ~ **befreundet sein** be intimate friends; **Intimität** [ɪntimi'tɛːt] die; ~, ~en intimacy; **Intim·sphäre die** private life

**in·tolerant** *Adj.* intolerant

**intransitiv** 1. *Adj. (Sprachw.)* intransitive; 2. *adv.* intransitively

**Intrige** [ɪn'tri:gə] die; ~, ~n intrigue

**Intuition** [ɪntui̯'tsi̯oːn] die; ~, ~en intuition; **intuitiv** 1. *Adj.* intuitive; 2. *adv.* intuitively

**intus** ['ɪntʊs] *in etw.* ~ **haben** *(ugs.) (begriffen haben)* have got sth. into one's head; *(gegessen od. getrunken haben)* have put sth. away *(coll.)*

**Invalide** der; *adj. Dekl.* invalid

**Invasion** die; ~, ~en invasion

**Inventar** das; ~s, ~e *(einer Firma)* fittings and equipment *pl.; (eines Hauses, Büros)* furnishings and fittings *pl.;* **Inventur** die; ~, ~en stocktaking

**investieren** *tr., itr. V. (auch fig.)* invest (in + *Akk.* in); **Investition** [ɪnvɛsti'tsi̯oːn] die; ~, ~en investment; **Investitions·güter** *Pl. (Wirtsch.)* capital goods; **Investor** [ɪn'vɛstɔr] der; ~s, ~en [-'toːrən] *(Wirtsch.)* investor

**in·wie·fern** *Adv.* in what way; *(bis zu welchem Grade)* to what extent; **in·wie·weit** *Adv.* to what extent

**Inzest** der; ~[e]s, ~e incest; **In·zucht** die; ~: inbreeding

**in·zwischen** *Adv.* a) *(seither)* in the meantime; since [then]; b) *(bis zu einem Zeitpunkt) (in der Gegenwart)* by now; *(in der Vergangenheit/Zukunft)* by then; c) *(währenddessen)* meanwhile

**IOK** [ioː'kaː] das; ~[s] Internationales Olympisches Komitee IOC

**Ion** das; ~s, ~en *(Physik, Chemie)* ion

**Irak** (das); ~s *od.* der; ~[s] Iraq; **Ira-ker** der; ~s, ~Iraqi; **irakisch** Iraqi

**Iran** (das); ~s *od.* der; ~[s] Iran; **Ira-ner** der; ~s, ~; **iranisch** *Adj.* Iranian

**irden** *Adj.* earthen[ware]; **irdisch** *Adj.* a) earthly; worldly ⟨*goods, pleasures, possessions*⟩; b) *(zur Erde gehörig)* terrestrial; das ~e Leben life on earth

**Ire** der; ~n, ~n Irishman

**irgend** *Adv.* a) ~ **jemand** someone; somebody; *(fragend, verneinend)* anyone; anybody; ~ **etwas** something; *(fragend, verneinend)* anything; ~ **so etwas** something like that; b) *(irgendwie)* wenn ~ möglich if at all possible

**irgend-:** ~**ein** *Indefinitpron.* a) *(attr.)* some; *(fragend, verneinend)* any; b) *(subst.)* ~**einer**/~**eine** someone; somebody; *(fragend, verneinend)* anyone; anybody; ~**eines** *od. (ugs.)* ~**eins** any one; ~**einmal** *Adv.* sometime; ~**wann** *Adv.* [at] some time [or other]; *(zu jeder beliebigen Zeit)* [at] any time; ~**was** *Indefinitpron. (ugs.)*

something [or other]; *(fragend, verneinend)* anything; ~**welch** *Indefinitpron.* some; *(fragend, verneinend)* any; ~**wer** *Indefinitpron. (ugs.)* somebody or other *(coll.); (fragend, verneinend)* anyone; anybody; ~**wie** *Adv.* somehow; ~**wo** *Adv.* somewhere; *(fragend, verneinend)* anywhere; ~**woher** *Adv.* from somewhere; *(fragend, verneinend)* from anywhere; ~**wohin** *Adv.* somewhere; *(fragend, verneinend)* anywhere

**Irin** die; ~, ~nen Irishwoman

**Iris** die; ~, ~ *(Bot., Anat.)* iris

**irisch** *Adj.* Irish; **Irland** (das); ~s Ireland

**Ironie** die; ~, ~n irony; **ironisch** 1. *Adj.* ironic; ironical; 2. *adv.* ironically

**irre** 1. *Adj.* insane; 2. *adv. (salopp)* terribly *(coll.);* **Irre** der/die; *adj. Dekl.* madman/madwoman; lunatic; *(fig.)* lunatic

**irre|führen** *tr. V.* mislead; *(täuschen)* deceive; **Irreführung** die: eine bewußte ~führung a deliberate attempt to mislead; ~**führung der Öffentlichkeit** misleading the public

**irrelevant** ['ɪrelevant] *Adj.* irrelevant (für to)

**irre|machen** *tr. V.* disconcert; put off; **irren** 1. *refl. V.* be mistaken; Sie haben sich in der Nummer geirrt you've got the wrong number; 2. *itr. V.* a) da ~ Sie you are wrong there; b) *mit sein (ziellos umherstreifen)* wander

**Irren-:** ~**anstalt** die *(veralt. abwertend)* mental home; ~**haus** das *(abwertend)* [lunatic] asylum

**Irr·fahrt** die wandering; **irriger-weise** *Adv.* mistakenly

**irritieren** *tr., itr. V.* a) *(verwirren)* put off; b) *(stören)* disturb

**Irr-, Irr-:** ~**licht** das will o' the wisp; ~**sinn** der; *o. Pl.* a) insanity; madness; b) *(ugs. abwertend)* lunacy; ~**sinnig** 1. *Adj.* a) *(geistig gestört)* insane; mad; *(absurd)* idiotic; b) *(ugs.: extrem)* terrible *(coll.);* terrific *(coll.)* ⟨*speed, heat, cold*⟩; 2. *adv. (ugs.)* terribly *(coll.)*

**Irrtum** der; ~s, Irrtümer mistake; ~! wrong!; im ~ sein be wrong *or* mistaken; **irrtümlich** 1. *Adj.* incorrect; 2. *adv.* by mistake

**Ischias** ['ɪʃi̯as] der *od.* das *od. Med.* die; ~: sciatica

**Islam** [ɪs'laːm *od.* 'ɪslam] der; ~[s]: der ~: Islam; **islamisch** *Adj.* Islamic

**Island** (das); ~s Iceland; **Isländer der**; ~s, ~ Icelander; **isländisch** *Adj.* Icelandic

**Isolation die**; ~, ~en *s.* Isolierung; **Isolator der**; ~s, ~en insulator; **Isolier·band das**; *Pl.* ~bänder insulating tape; **isolieren** *tr. V.* **a)** isolate; **b)** *(Technik)* insulate ⟨*wiring, wall, etc.*⟩; lag ⟨*boilers, pipes, etc.*⟩; **Isolier·station die** *(Med.)* isolation ward; **Isolierung die**; ~, ~en **a)** isolation; **b)** *(Technik) s.* isolieren **b:** insulation; lagging

**Isotop das**; ~s, ~e isotope

**Israel** ['ısraeːl] (das); ~s Israel; **Israeli der**; ~[s], ~[s]/die; ~, ~[s] Israeli; **israelisch** *Adj.* Israeli; **Israelit der**; ~en, ~en Israelite; **israelitisch** *Adj.* Israelite

**iß** *Imperativ Sg. v.* essen

**ißt** *2. u. 3. Pers. Sg. Präsens v.* essen

**ist** *3. Pers. Sg. Präsens v.* sein

**Italien** [i'taːli̯ən] (das); ~s Italy; **Italiener** [ita'li̯eːnɐ] der; ~s, ~: Italian; **italienisch** *Adj.* Italian

**I-Tüpfel[chen] das**; ~s, ~: final touch; **bis aufs [letzte]** ~: down to the last detail

**i. V.** [iːˈfaʊ̯] *Abk.* in Vertretung

# J

—————

**j, J** [jɔt, *österr.:* jeː] das; ~, ~: j/J

**ja** 1. *Interj.* yes; *(nachgestellt: nicht wahr?)* won't you/doesn't it *etc.*?; 2. *Partikel* **Sie wissen ja, daß** ...: you know, of course, that ...; **da seid ihr ja!** there you are!; **Ja das**; ~[s], ~[s] yes; **mit** ~ **stimmen** vote yes

**Jacht die**; ~, ~en yacht

**Jacke die**; ~, ~n jacket; *(gestrickt)* cardigan; **Jacken·kleid das** dress and jacket combination; **Jacket-krone** ['dʒɛkɪt-] **die** *(Zahnmed.)* jacket crown; **Jackett** [ʒa'kɛt] **das**; ~s, ~s jacket

**Jade die**; ~: jade

**Jagd die**; ~, ~en **a)** *o. Pl.* **die** ~: shooting; hunting; **auf die** ~ **gehen** go hunting/shooting; **b)** *(Veranstaltung)* shoot; *(Hetzjagd)* hunt; **c)** *(Verfolgung)* hunt; *(Verfolgungsjagd)* chase; **auf jmdn./etw.** ~ **machen** hunt for sb./sth.

**Jagd-:** ~**beute die** bag; kill; ~**bomber der** *(Luftwaffe)* fighter-bomber; ~**flieger der** *(Luftwaffe)* fighter pilot; ~**flugzeug das** *(Luftwaffe)* fighter aircraft; ~**gewehr das** sporting gun; ~**horn das** hunting-horn; ~**hund der** gun-dog; ~**hütte die** shooting box; ~**revier das** preserve; shoot; ~**schein der** game licence; ~**wurst die** chasseur sausage; ~**zeit die** open season

**jagen** 1. *tr. V.* **a)** hunt ⟨*game, fugitive, criminal, etc.*⟩; shoot ⟨*game, game birds*⟩; *(hetzen)* chase ⟨*fugitive, criminal, etc.*⟩; **b)** *(treiben)* drive; **jmdn. aus dem Haus** ~: throw sb. out of the house; 2. *itr. V. (die Jagd ausüben)* go shooting *or* hunting; **Jäger der**; ~s, ~: **a)** hunter; **b)** *(Milit.)* rifleman; **c)** *(Soldatenspr.: Jagdflugzeug)* fighter; **Jäger·hut der** huntsman's hat

**Jäger-:** ~**latein das** *(scherzh.)* [hunter's] tall story/stories; **das ist das reinste** ~**latein** that's all wild exaggeration; ~**rock der** hunting jacket; ~**schnitzel das** *(Kochk.)* escalope chasseur

**Jaguar der**; ~s, ~e jaguar

**jäh** [jɛː] 1. *Adj. (geh.)* **a)** sudden; abrupt ⟨*change, movement, stop*⟩; sudden, sharp ⟨*pain*⟩; **b)** *(steil)* steep; precipitous; 2. *adv.* **a)** ⟨*change*⟩ abruptly; **b)** *(steil)* ⟨*fall, drop*⟩ steeply; **jählings** *Adv. (geh.)* **a)** *(plötzlich)* ⟨*change, end, stop*⟩ suddenly, abruptly; ⟨*die*⟩ suddenly; **b)** *(steil)* steeply

**Jahr das**; ~[e]s, ~e year; **ein halbes** ~: six months; **im** ~[e] **1908** in [the year] 1908; **er ist zwanzig** ~e **[alt]** he is twenty years old; **Kinder bis zu zwölf** ~**en** children up to the age of twelve; **zwischen den** ~**en** between Christmas and the New Year; **jahr·aus** *Adv.* ~, **jahrein** year in, year out; **jahre·lang** 1. *Adj.; nicht präd.* [many] years of; long-standing ⟨*feud, friendship*⟩; 2. *adv.* for [many] years

**jähren** *refl. V.* **heute jährt sich zum zehntenmal, daß** ...: it is ten years ago today that ...

**Jahres-:** ~**bilanz die** *(Wirtsch., Kaufmannsspr.)* annual balance [of accounts]; *(Dokument)* annual balance sheet; ~**einkommen das** annual income; ~**ende das** end of the year;

~**frist**; *o. Art.; o. Pl.* in *od.* **innerhalb** *od.* **binnen** ~**frist** within [a period of] a *or* one year; ~**hälfte die**: **die erste/ zweite** ~**hälfte** the first/secound half *or* six months of the year; ~**karte die** yearly season ticket; ~**tag der** anniversary; ~**urlaub der** annual holiday *or (formal)* leave *or (Amer.)* vacation; ~**wechsel der** turn of the year; **zum** ~**wechsel die besten Wünsche** best wishes for the New Year; ~**zahl die** date; ~**zeit die** season

**Jahr·gang der a)** *(Altersklasse)* year; **der** ~ **1900** those born in 1900; **b)** *(eines Weines)* vintage; **c)** *(einer Zeitschrift)* set [of issues] for a/the year; **Jahr·hundert das** century; **Jahrhundert·wende die** turn of the century; -**jährig a)** *(... Jahre alt)* **ein elfjähriges Kind** an eleven-year-old child; **b)** *(... Jahre dauernd)* ...year's/years'; **nach vierjähriger Vorbereitung** after four years' preparation; **mit dreijähriger Verspätung** three years late; **jährlich 1.** *Adj.; nicht präd.* annual; yearly; **2.** *adv.* annually; yearly; **zweimal** ~: twice a year

**Jahr-**: ~**markt der** fair; fun-fair; ~**tausend das** thousand years; millennium; ~**zehnt das** decade

**jahrzehnte·lang 1.** *Adj.; nicht präd.* decades of ⟨*practice, experience, etc.*⟩; **2.** *adv.* for decades

**Jäh·zorn der** violent anger; **jäh·zornig 1.** *Adj.* violent-tempered; **2.** *adv.* in a blind rage

**ja·ja** *Part. (ugs.)* **a)** *(seufzend)* ~[, so ist das Leben] o well[, that's life]; **b)** *(ungeduldig)* ~[, ich komme schon]! all right, all right[, I'm coming]!

**Jalousie** [ʒalu'zi:] **die**; ~, ~**n** Venetian blind

**Jamaika (das)**; -**s** Jamaica; **Jamaikaner der**; ~**s**, ~ Jamaican

**Jammer der**; ~**s** [mournful] wailing; *(Elend)* misery; **jämmerlich 1.** *Adj.* pitiful; **b)** wretched ⟨*appearance, existence, etc.*⟩; paltry, meagre ⟨*quantity*⟩; **2.** *adv.* pitifully; **jammern** *itr. V.* wail; *(sich beklagen)* moan; **jammer·schade** *Adj.; nicht attr. (ugs.)* **es ist** ~**schade, daß** ...: it's a crying shame that ...; **es ist** ~**schade um ihn** it's a great pity about him

**Janker der**; ~**s**, ~ *(südd., österr.)* Alpine jacket

**Januar der**; ~[s], ~**e** January

**Japan (das)**; ~**s** Japan; **Japaner der**;

~**s**, ~**Japanese**; **japanisch** *Adj.* Japanese

**japsen** *itr. V. (ugs.)* pant

**Jargon** [jar'gõ:] **der**; ~**s**, ~**s** jargon

**Jasmin der**; ~**s**, ~**e** jasmine

**Ja·stimme die** yes-vote

**jäten** *tr., itr. V.* weed; **Unkraut** ~: weed

**Jauche die**; ~, ~**n** liquid manure; **Jauche·grube die** liquid-manure reservoir

**jauchzen** *itr. V.* cheer; **vor Freude** ~: shout for joy; **Jauchzer der**; ~**s**, ~: cry of delight

**jaulen** *itr. V.* howl

**Jause die**; ~, ~**n** *(österr.)* **a)** snack; **eine** ~ **machen** have a snack; **b)** *(Nachmittagskaffee)* [afternoon] tea

**ja·wohl** *Part.* certainly; **Ja·wort das** consent; **jmdm. das** ~ **geben** consent to marry sb.

**Jazz** [dʒæz *od.* dʒɛs *od.* jats] **der**; ~: jazz; **Jazz·keller der** jazz cellar

¹**je 1.** *Adv.* **a)** *(jemals)* ever; **mehr/besser denn je** more/better than ever; **b)** *(jeweils)* **je zehn Personen** ten people at a time; **sie kosten je 30 DM** they cost 30 DM each; **c)** *(entsprechend)* **je nach Gewicht** according to weight; **2.** *Präp. mit Akk.* per; for each; **3.** *Konj.* **je länger, je lieber** the longer the better; **je nachdem** it all depends

²**je** *Interj.* **ach je, wie schade!** oh dear, what a shame!

**Jeans** [dʒi:nz] *Pl. od.* **die**; ~, ~: jeans *pl.*; denims *pl.*

**jede** *s.* **jeder**; **jeden·falls** *Adv.* **a)** in any case; **b)** *(zumindest)* at any rate; **jeder, jede, jedes** *Indefinitpron. u. unbest. Zahlwort* **1.** *attr.* **a)** *(alle)* every; **b)** *(alle einzeln)* each; **c)** *(jeglicher)* all; **2.** *alleinstehend* **a)** *(alle)* everyone; everybody; **b)** *(alle einzeln)* **jedes der Kinder** each of the children

**jeder-**: ~**mann** *Indefinitpron. u. unbest. Zahlwort; nur alleinstehend* everyone; everybody; ~**zeit** *Adv.* [at] any time

**jedes** *s.* **jeder**; **jedes·mal** *Adv.* every time

**je·doch** *Konj., Adv.* however

**je·her** [*od.* '-'-] *Adv.* **seit** *od.* **von** ~: always; since time immemorial

**jemals** *Adv.* ever

**jemand** *Indefinitpron.* someone; somebody; *(fragend, verneinend)* anyone; anybody

**Jemen (das)**; ~**s** *od.* **der**; ~[s] Yemen

**jener, jene, jenes** *Demonstrativpron.*

*(geh.)* 1. *attr.* that; *(im Pl.)* those; 2. *alleinstehend* that one; *(im Pl.)* those

**jenseits** 1. *Präp. mit Gen.* on the other side of; *(in größerer Entfernung)* beyond; 2. *Adv.* on the other side; ~ **vom Rhein** on the other side of the Rhine; **Jenseits das;** ~: hereafter; beyond

**¹Jersey** ['dʒøːɐ̯zi] **der;** ~|s|, ~s *(Textilind.)* jersey

**²Jersey das;** ~s, ~s *(Sport: Trikot)* jersey

**Jesus (der);** Jesu Jesus

**Jet** [dʒɛt] **der;** ~|s|, ~s jet; **mit einem ~ fliegen/reisen** fly/travel by jet

**jetzig** *Adj.; nicht präd.* current

**jetzt** *Adv.* **a)** just now; **bis ~:** up to now; **bis ~ noch nicht** not yet; **von ~ an** *od.* **ab** from now on[wards]; **erst ~** *od.* **~ erst** only just; **schon ~:** already; **b)** *(heutzutage)* now; nowadays

**jeweilig** *Adj.; nicht präd.* **a)** *(in einem bestimmten Fall)* particular; **b)** *(zu einer bestimmten Zeit)* current; of the time *postpos., not pred.;* **c)** *(zugehörig, zugewiesen)* respective; **jeweils** *Adv.* **a)** *(jedesmal)* ~ **am ersten/letzten Mittwoch des Monats** on the first/last Wednesday of each month; **b)** *(zur Zeit)* at the time

**Jg.** *Abk.* **Jahrgang**

**Jh.** *Abk.* **Jahrhundert** c.

**jiddisch** ['jɪdɪʃ] *Adj.* Yiddish

**Job** [dʒɔp] **der;** ~s, ~s *(ugs.; auch DV)* job; **jobben** [dʒɔbn̩] *itr. V. (ugs.)* do a job/jobs

**Joch das;** ~|e|s, ~e yoke

**Jockei, Jockey** ['dʒɔke *od.* 'dʒɔki] **der;** ~s, ~s jockey

**Jod** [joːt] **das;** ~|e|s iodine

**jodeln** *itr., tr. V.* yodel

**jod·haltig** *Adj.* iodiferous

**Joga der** *od.* **das;** ~|s| yoga

**joggen** ['dʒɔgn̩] *itr. V.; mit Richtungsangabe mit sein* jog

**Joghurt** ['joːgʊrt] **der** *od.* **das;** ~|s|, ~|s| yoghurt; **Joghurt·becher der** yoghurt pot *(Brit.)* or *(Amer.)* container

**Johannis·beere die** currant; **rote/weiße/schwarze ~n** redcurrants/white currants/blackcurrants

**johlen** *itr. V.* yell; *(vor Wut)* howl

**Joint** [dʒɔɪnt] **der;** ~s, ~s *(ugs.)* joint *(sl.)*

**Jolle die;** ~, ~n keel-centre-board yawl

**Jongleur** [ʒɔŋˈløːɐ̯] **der;** ~s, ~e juggler; **jonglieren** *tr., itr. V.* juggle

**Joppe die;** ~, ~n heavy jacket

**Jordanien (das);** ~s Jordan; **Jorda-**

**nier der;** ~s, ~: Jordanian; **jordanisch** *Adj.* Jordanian

**Jot das;** ~, ~: j, J

**Journalismus der;** ~: journalism *no art.;* **Journalist der;** ~en, ~en journalist; **journalistisch** 1. *Adj.; nicht präd.* journalistic; **eine ~e Ausbildung** a training in journalism; 2. *adv.* journalistically; ~ **tätig sein** be a journalist

**jr.** *Abk.* **junior** Jr.

**Jubel der;** ~s rejoicing; jubilation; *(laut)* cheering; **jubeln** *itr. V.* cheer; **über etw.** *(Akk.)* ~: rejoice over sth.; **Jubilar der;** ~s, ~e man celebrating his anniversary/birthday; **Jubiläum das;** ~s, **Jubiläen** anniversary; *(eines Monarchen)* jubilee; **jubilieren** *itr. V. (geh.)* jubilate *(literary);* rejoice

**juchzen** ['jʊxtsn̩] *itr. V. (ugs.)* shout with glee

**jucken** 1. *tr., itr. V.* **a)** **mir juckt die Haut** I itch; **es juckt mich hier** I've got an itch here; **b)** *(Juckreiz verursachen)* irritate; 2. *tr. V. (reizen, verlocken)* **es juckt mich, das zu tun** I am itching to do it; 3. *refl. V. (ugs.: sich kratzen)* scratch; **Juck·reiz der** itch

**Jude der;** ~n, ~n Jew; **Juden·stern der** *(ns.)* Star of David; **Judentum das;** ~s **a)** *(Volk)* Jewry; Jews *pl.;* **b)** *(Kultur u. Religion)* Judaism; **Jüdin die;** ~, ~nen Jewess; **jüdisch** *Adj.* Jewish

**Judo** ['juːdo] **das;** ~|s| judo *no art.*

**Jugend die;** ~ **a)** youth; **b)** *(Jugendliche)* young people

**jugend-, Jugend-:** ~**amt das** youth office *(agency responsible for education and welfare of young people);* ~**arrest der** detention in a community home; ~**bewegung die** *(hist.)* [German] youth Movement; ~**buch das** book for young people; ~**frei** *Adj. ⟨film, book, etc.⟩* suitable for persons under 18; **nicht ~frei** ⟨*film*⟩ not U-certificate *pred.;* ~**gefährdend** *Adj.* liable to have an undesirable influence on the moral development of young people *postpos.;* ~**heim das** youth centre; ~**herberge die** youth hostel; ~**kriminalität die** juvenile delinquency

**jugendlich** 1. *Adj.* **a)** *nicht präd.* young ⟨*offender, customer, etc.*⟩; **b)** *(für Jugendliche charakteristisch)* youthful; **Jugendliche der/die;** *adj. Dekl.* young person; **die ~n** the young people

**Jugend-:** ~**liebe** die sweetheart of one's youth; ~**schutz** der protection of young people; ~**schutz·gesetz** das laws *pl.* protecting young people; ~**sprache** die young people's language *no art.*; ~**stil** der art nouveau; *(in Deutschland)* Jugendstil; ~**strafe** die youth custody sentence; ~**sünde** die youthful folly; ~**zeit** die youth; ~**zentrum** das youth centre

**Jugo·slawe** der Yugoslav; **Jugoslawien** (das); ~s Yugoslavia; **jugo·slawisch** *Adj.* Yugoslav[ian]

**Julei** der; ~|s|, ~s *s.* Juli

**Juli** der; ~|s|, ~s July; *s. auch* April

**jung** *Adj.*; jünger, jüngst... **a)** young; new ⟨*project, undertaking, sport, marriage, etc.*⟩; **b)** *(letzt...)* recent; **in jüngster Zeit** recently

¹**Junge** der; ~n, ~n *od. (ugs.)* Jung|en|s boy; ²**Junge** das; *adj. Dekl.* **ein** ~s one of the young; ~ **kriegen** give birth to young; **jungen** *itr. V.* give birth; ⟨*cat*⟩ have kittens; ⟨*dog*⟩ have pups; **jungenhaft** *Adj.* boyish; **jünger** *Adj.* youngish; **sie ist noch** ~: she is still quite young; *s. auch* jung; **Jünger** der; ~s, ~: follower; **Jungfer** die; ~, ~n *(abwertend: ältere ledige Frau)* spinster; **Jungfern·fahrt** die maiden voyage; **Jungfern·häutchen** das hymen; **Jung·frau** die **a)** virgin; **b)** *(Astrol.)* Virgo; **jung·fräulich** *Adj. (geh., auch fig.)* virgin; **Jung·geselle** der bachelor; **Junggesellin** die; ~, ~nen bachelor girl

**Jüngling** der; ~s, ~e *(geh., spött.)* youth; boy; **jüngst** *Adv. (geh.)* recently; **jüngst...** *s.* jung; **Jüngste** der/die; *adj. Dekl.* youngest [one]

**Jung-:** ~**verheiratete** der/die; *adj. Dekl.*, young married man/woman; **die** ~**verheirateten** the newly-weds; ~**wähler** der first-time voter

**Juni** der; ~|s|, ~s June; *s. auch* April

**junior** *indekl. Adj.*; **nach Personennamen** junior; **Junior** der; ~s, ~en **a)** *(oft scherzh.)* junior *(joc.)*; **b)** *(Kaufmannsspr.)* junior partner; **Junior·chef** der owner's *or (coll.)* boss's son

**Juno** der; ~|s|, ~s *s.* Juni

**Junta** ['xʊnta] die; ~, **Junten** junta

**Jura** *o. Art., o. Pl.* law; ~ **studieren** read Law; **Jurist** der; ~en, ~en, **Juristin** die; ~, ~nen lawyer; jurist; **juristisch** *Adj.* legal

**Jury** [ʒyˈriː] die; ~, ~s **a)** *(Preisrichter)* panel [of judges]; jury; **b)** *(Sachverständige)* panel [of experts]

**Justiz** die; ~: justice; *(Behörden)* judiciary

**Justiz-:** ~**irrtum** der miscarriage of justice; ~**minister** der Minister of Justice; ~**vollzugs·anstalt** die *(Amtsspr.)* penal institution *(formal)*; prison

**Jute** ['juːtə] die; ~: jute

**Juwel** das *od.* der; ~s, ~en piece of jewellery; *(Edelstein)* jewel; **Juwelier** [juvəˈliːɐ̯] der; ~s jeweller; **Juwelier·geschäft** das jeweller's shop

**Jux** der; ~es, ~e *(ugs.)* joke

# K

**k, K** [kaː] das; ~, ~: k/K

**Kabarett** das; ~s, ~s *od.* ~e **a)** satirical revue; **b)** *(Ensemble)* cabaret act; **Kabarettist** der; ~en, ~en revue performer

**kabbeln** *refl. V. (ugs.)* bicker **(mit with)**

**Kabel** das; ~s, ~: cable; *(für kleineres Gerät)* flex

**Kabeljau** der; ~s, ~e *od.* ~s cod

**kabeln** *tr., itr. V. (veralt.)* cable

**Kabine** die; ~, ~n **a)** cabin; **b)** *(Umkleideraum, abgeteilter Raum)* cubicle; **c)** *(einer Seilbahn)* [cable-]car; **Kabinett** das; ~s, ~e Cabinet

**Kabrio** das; ~s, ~s, **Kabriolett** das; ~s, ~s convertible

**Kachel** die; ~, ~n [glazed] tile; **kacheln** *tr. V.* tile

**Kadaver** der; ~s, ~: carcass

**Kader** der *od. (schweiz.)* das; ~s, ~ cadre; **b)** *(Sport)* squad

**Käfer** der; ~s, ~: beetle

**Kaff** das; ~s, ~s *od.* **Käffer** *(ugs. abwertend)* dump *(coll.)*

**Kaffee** ['kafe *od. (österr.)* kaˈfeː] der; ~s, ~s **a)** coffee; **b)** *(Nachmittags~)* afternoon coffee; ~ **trinken** have afternoon coffee

**Kaffee-:** ~**kanne** die coffee-pot; ~**kränzchen** das *(veralt.)* **a)** *(Zusammentreffen)* coffee afternoon; **b)** *(Gruppe)* coffee circle; ~**maschine**

die coffee-maker; ~**mühle** die coffee-grinder; ~**satz** der coffee-grounds *pl.;* ~**tante die** *(ugs. scherzh.)* coffee addict

**Käfig** der; ~s, ~e cage

**kahl** *Adj.* a) *(ohne Haare)* bald; b) *(ohne Grün, schmucklos)* bare

**kahl-, Kahl-:** ~|**fressen** *unr. tr. V.* etw. ~fressen strip sth. bare; ~**köpfig** *Adj.* bald[-headed]; ~|**scheren** *unr. tr. V.* jmdn. ~scheren shave sb.'s head; ~**schlag** der a) clear-felling *no indef. art.;* b) *(Waldfläche)* clear-felled area

**Kahn** der; ~|e|s, **Kähne** a) *(Ruder~)* rowing-boat; *(Stech~)* punt; b) *(Lastschiff)* barge

**Kai** der; ~s, ~s quay

**Kaiser** der; ~s, ~: emperor; **Kaiserin** die; ~, ~**nen** empress

**Kaiser-:** ~**krone** die imperial crown; ~**reich** das empire; ~**schnitt** der Caesarean section

**Kajüte** die; ~, ~**n** *(Seemannsspr.)* cabin

**Kakao** [ka'kau] der; ~s, ~s cocoa

**Kakerlak** der; ~s *od.* ~**en,** ~**en** cockroach

**Kaktus** der; ~, **Kakteen** cactus

**Kalauer** der; ~s, ~: corny joke *(coll.);* *(Wortspiel)* atrocious *or (coll.)* corny pun

**Kalb** das; ~|e|s, **Kälber** a) calf; b) *(ugs.:* ~*fleisch)* veal; **kalben** *itr. V.* calve; **Kalb·fleisch das** veal

**Kalbs-:** ~**braten** der *(Kochk.)* roast veal *no indef. art.; (Gericht)* roast of veal; ~**leder** das calfskin; ~**schnitzel das** veal cutlet

**Kalender** der; ~s, ~: calendar; *(Taschen~)* diary; **Kalender·jahr das** calendar year

**Kalesche** die; ~, ~**n** *(hist.)* barouche

**Kali** das; ~s, ~s potash

**Kaliber** das; ~s, ~: a) *(Technik, Waffenkunde)* calibre; b) *(ugs., oft abwertend)* sort; kind

**Kalifornien** [kali'fɔrniən] **(das);** ~s California

**Kalium** *(Chemie)* das; ~s potassium

**Kalk** der; ~|e|s, ~e calcium carbonate; *(Baustoff)* lime; quicklime; **kalken** *tr. V.* whitewash

**Kalk-:** ~**mangel** der; *o. Pl.* calcium deficiency; ~**stein** der limestone

**Kalkül** das *od.* der; ~s, ~e *(geh.)* calculation; **Kalkulation** die; ~, ~**en** *(auch Wirtsch.)* calculation; **kalkulieren** *tr. V.* calculate ⟨*cost, price*⟩; cost ⟨*product, article*⟩

**Kalorie** die; ~, ~**n** calorie; **kalorienarm** 1. *Adj.* low-calorie *attrib.;* ~**arm sein** be low in calories; 2. *adv.* ~**arm kochen** cook low-calorie meals

**kalt; kälter, kältest...** 1. *Adj.* cold; frosty ⟨*atmosphere, smile*⟩; 2. *adv.* a) ~ **duschen** have a cold shower **Getränke/Sekt** ~ **stellen** cool drinks/chill champagne; b) *(nüchtern)* coldly; c) *(abweisend, unfreundlich)* frostily

**kalt-, Kalt-:** ~|**bleiben** *unr. itr. V.;* mit sein remain unmoved; ~**blütig** 1. *Adj.* a) cool-headed; b) *(abwertend: skrupellos)* cold-blooded; 2. *adv.* a) coolly; b) *(abwertend: skrupellos)* cold-bloodedly; ~**blütigkeit die;** ~: *s.* ~**blütig a, b:** cool-headedness; cold-bloodedness

**Kälte** die; ~ cold; *(fig.)* coldness

**Kälte-:** ~**einbruch** der *(Met.)* sudden onset of cold weather; ~**grad** der degree of frost

**kälter** *s.* **kalt; kältest...** *s.* **kalt; Kälte·welle** die cold spell

**kalt-, Kalt-:** ~**herzig** *Adj.* cold-hearted; ~**lächelnd** *Adv. (ugs. abwertend)* etw. ~lächelnd tun take callous pleasure in doing sth.; ~|**lassen** *unr. tr. V. (ugs.)* jmdn. ~lassen leave sb. unmoved; *(nicht interessieren)* leave sb. cold *(coll.);* ~|**machen** *V. (salopp)* jmdn. ~machen do sb. in *(sl.);* ~**miete** die rent exclusive of heating; ~**schale** die *cold sweet soup made with fruit, beer, wine, or milk;* ~**schnäuzig** [~ʃnɔytsɪç] *(ugs.)* 1. *Adj.* cold and insensitive; *(frech)* insolent; 2. *adv.* coldly and insensitively; *(frech)* insolently; ~|**stellen** *tr. V. (ugs.)* jmdn. ~stellen put sb. out of the way *(coll. joc.)*

**kam** *1. u. 3. Pers. Prät. v.* **kommen**

**Kambodscha** [kam'bɔdʒa] **(das);** ~s Cambodia

**käme** *1. u. 3. Pers. Konjunktiv II v.* **kommen**

**Kamel** das; ~s, ~e camel

**Kamera** die; ~, ~s camera

**Kamerad** der; ~**en,** ~**en** companion; *(Freund)* friend; *(Mitschüler)* mate; *(Soldat)* comrade; *(Sport)* team-mate; **Kameradschaft die;** ~: comradeship; **kameradschaftlich** 1. *Adj.* comradely; 2. *adv.* in a comradely way

**Kamera·mann der** *Pl.* ~**männer** *od.* ~**leute** cameraman

**Kamerun** ['kaməru:n] **(das);** ~s Cameroon; the Cameroons *pl.*

**Kamille** die; ~, ~n camomile

**Kamin** der, *schweiz.: das*; ~s, ~e fireplace; **Kamin·feger** der *(bes. südd.) s.* **Schornsteinfeger**

**Kamm** der; ~[e]s, **Kämme a)** comb; **b)** *(bei Hühnern usw.)* comb; **c)** *(Gebirgs~)* ridge; **kämmen** *tr. V.* comb

**Kammer** die; ~, ~n **a)** store-room; **b)** *(Biol., Med., Technik, Waffenkunde)* chamber; **c)** *(Parl.)* chamber

**Kammer-:** ~**diener** der *(veralt.)* valet; ~**jäger** der pest controller; ~**musik** die; *o. Pl.* chamber music; ~**sänger** der *title awarded to singer of outstanding merit*; ~**zofe** die *(veralt.)* lady's maid

**Kamm·garn** das worsted

**Kampagne** [kam'panjə] die; ~, ~n campaign

**Kampf** der; ~[e]s, **Kämpfe a)** *(militärisch)* battle (**um** for); **b)** *(zwischen persönlichen Gegnern)* fight; *(fig.)* struggle; **c)** *(Wett~)* contest; *(Boxen)* contest; bout; **d)** *(Einsatz aller Mittel)* fight (**um, für** for; **gegen** against); **kampf·bereit** *Adj.* ready to fight *postpos.*; ⟨*army, troops*⟩ ready for battle; **kämpfen** *itr. V.* **a)** fight; **b)** *(Sport: sich messen)* ⟨*team*⟩ play; ⟨*wrestler, boxer*⟩ fight

**Kampfer** der; ~s camphor

**Kämpfer** der; ~s, ~, **Kämpferin** die; ~, ~nen fighter

**kampf-, Kampf-:** ~**fähig** *Adj.* ⟨*troops*⟩ fit for action; ⟨*boxer etc.*⟩ fit to fight; ~**handlungen** *Pl.* fighting *sing.*; ~**richter** der *(Sport)* judge; ~**unfähig** *Adj.* ⟨*troops*⟩ unfit for action; ⟨*boxer etc.*⟩ unfit to fight

**kampieren** *itr. V.* camp

**Kanada (das)**; ~s Canada; **Kanadier** [ka'na:diɐ] der; ~s, ~ Canadian; **kanadisch** *Adj.* Canadian

**Kanal** der; ~s, **Kanäle a)** canal; **b)** *(Geogr.)* der ~: the [English] Channel; **c)** *(für Abwässer)* sewer; **d)** *(zur Entwässerung, Bewässerung)* channel; *(Graben)* ditch; **e)** *(Rundf., Ferns., Weg der Information)* channel; **Kanalisation** die; ~, ~en sewerage system; sewers *pl.*; **kanalisieren** *tr. V.* **a)** *(lenken)* channel ⟨*energies, goods, etc.*⟩; **b)** *(schiffbar machen)* canalize

**Kanaren** *Pl.* Canaries; **Kanarien·vogel** [ka'na:riən-] der canary; **Kanarische Inseln** *Pl.* Canary Islands

**Kandare** die; ~, ~n curb bit; **jmdn. an die** ~ **nehmen** *(fig.)* take sb. in hand

**Kandidat** der; ~en, ~en **a)** candidate; **b)** *(beim Quiz usw.)* contestant; **Kandidatur** die; ~, ~en candidature (**auf** + *Akk.* for); **kandidieren** *itr. V.* stand [as a candidate] (**für** for)

**kandieren** *tr. V.* candy; **kandiert** crystallized ⟨*orange, petal*⟩; glacé ⟨*cherry, pear*⟩; candied ⟨*peel*⟩; **Kandis** der; ~, **Kandis·zucker** der rock candy

**Känguruh** ['kɛŋguru] das; ~s, ~s kangaroo

**Kaninchen** das; ~s, ~: rabbit

**Kanister** der; ~s, ~: can; [metal/plastic] container

**kann** *1. u. 3. Pers. Sg. Präsens v.* **können**

**Kännchen** das; ~s, ~: [small] pot; *(für Milch)* [small] jug; **Kanne** die; ~, ~n **a)** pot; *(für Milch, Wein, Wasser)* jug; **b)** *(Henkel~)* can; *(für Milch)* pail; *(beim Melken)* churn

**kannst** *2. Pers. Sg. Präsens v.* **können**

**kannte** *1. u. 3. Pers. Sg. Prät. v.* **kennen**

**Kanon** der; ~s, ~s canon

**Kanone** die; ~, ~n cannon; *(fig. ugs.: Könner)* ace

**Kantate** die; ~, ~n *(Musik)* cantata

**Kante** die; ~, ~n edge; **kantig** *Adj.* square-cut ⟨*timber, stone*⟩; roughedged ⟨*rock*⟩; angular ⟨*face*⟩; square ⟨*chin*⟩

**Kantine** die; ~, ~n canteen

**Kanton** der; ~s, ~e canton

**Kantor** der; ~s, ~en choirmaster and organist

**Kanu** das; ~s, ~s canoe

**Kanüle** die; ~, ~n *(Med.)* cannula

**Kanzel** die; ~, ~n **a)** pulpit; **b)** *(Flugw.)* cockpit

**Kanzlei** die; ~, ~en **a)** *(veralt.: Büro)* office; **b)** *(Anwalts~)* chambers *pl. (of barrister)*; office *(of lawyer)*

**Kanzler** der; ~s, ~ chancellor

**Kap** das; ~s, ~s cape

**Kapazität** die; ~, ~en **a)** capacity; **b)** *(Experte)* expert

**Kapelle** die; ~, ~n **a)** *(Archit.)* chapel; **b)** *(Musik~)* band; [light] orchestra

**Kapell·meister** der bandmaster; *(im Orchester)* conductor; *(im Theater usw.)* musical director

**Kaper** die; ~, ~n caper *usu. in pl.*

**kapern** *tr. V.* **a)** *(hist.)* capture; **b)** *(ugs.)* jmdn. [für etw.] ~ : rope sb. in[to sth.]

**kapieren** *(ugs.)* **1.** *tr. V. (ugs.)* get *(coll.)*; **2.** *itr. V.* **kapiert?** got it? *(coll.)*

**Kapital** das; ~s, ~e *od.* ~ien a) capital; b) *(fig.)* asset; **Kapitalismus** der; ~: capitalism *no art.;* **Kapitalist** der; ~en, ~en capitalist; **kapitalistisch** *Adj.* capitalistic
**Kapital·verbrechen** das serious offence; *(mit Todesstrafe bedroht)* capital offence
**Kapitän** der; ~s, ~e *(Seew.)* captain
**Kapitel** das; ~s, ~: chapter
**Kapitulation** die; ~, ~en surrender; capitulation; **seine ~ erklären** admit defeat; **kapitulieren** *itr. V.* a) surrender; capitulate; b) *(fig.: aufgeben)* give up; **vor etw.** *(Dat.)* ~: give up in the face of sth.
**Kaplan** der; ~s, **Kapläne** *(kath. Kirche)* chaplain; *(Hilfsgeistlicher)* curate
**Kappe** die; ~, ~n cap
**kappen** *tr. V.* a) *(Seemannsspr.)* cut; b) *(beschneiden)* cut back ⟨hedge etc.⟩; *(abschneiden)* cut off ⟨branches etc.⟩
**Käppi** das; ~s, ~s garrison cap
**Kapsel** die; ~, ~n capsule
**Kapstadt** (das) Cape Town
**kaputt** *Adj.* a) broken; **das Telefon ist** ~: the phone is not working; b) *(ugs.: erschöpft)* shattered *(coll.)*
**kaputt-:** ~|gehen *unr. itr. V.; mit sein (ugs.) (entzweigehen)* break; ⟨machine⟩ break down, *(sl.)* pack up; ⟨light-bulb⟩ go; *(zerbrechen)* be smashed; ~|lachen *refl. V. (ugs.)* kill oneself [laughing] *(coll.)*; ~|machen (ugs.) 1. *tr. V.* break; spoil ⟨sth. made with effort⟩; ruin ⟨clothes, furniture, etc.⟩; finish ⟨person⟩ off; 2. *refl. V.* wear oneself out
**Kapuze** die; ~, ~n hood; *(bei Mönchen)* cowl; hood; **Kapuziner** der; ~s, ~: Capuchin [friar]
**Karabiner** der; ~s, ~: carbine
**Karaffe** die; ~, ~n carafe; *(mit Glasstöpsel)* decanter
**Karambolage** [karambo'la:ʒə] die; ~, ~n *(ugs.)* crash; collision
**Karamel** der *(schweiz.: das)*; ~s caramel; **Karamel·bonbon** der *od.* das caramel [toffee]
**Karat** das; ~|e|s, ~e carat
**Karate** das; ~|s| karate
**Karawane** die; ~, ~n caravan
**Kardinal** der; ~s, **Kardinäle** *(kath. Kirche)* cardinal
**Kardinal-:** ~tugend die; *meist Pl.* cardinal virtue; ~zahl die cardinal [number]
**Karenz** die; ~, ~en, **Karenz·zeit** die waiting period

**Kar·freitag** der Good Friday
**karg 1.** *Adj.* meagre ⟨wages etc.⟩; frugal ⟨meal etc.⟩; poor ⟨light, accommodation⟩; *(wenig fruchtbar)* barren; **2.** *adv.* ~ **bemessen sein** ⟨helping⟩ be mingy *(Brit. coll.);* ⟨supply⟩ be scanty; ~ **leben** live frugally; **kärglich 1.** *Adj.* meagre, poor ⟨wages etc.⟩; poor ⟨light⟩; frugal ⟨meal⟩; scanty ⟨supply⟩; **2.** *adv.* poorly ⟨lit, paid, rewarded⟩
**karibisch** *Adj.* Caribbean
**kariert** *Adj.* check, checked ⟨material, pattern⟩; check ⟨jacket etc.⟩; squared ⟨paper⟩
**Karies** ['ka:riɛs] die; ~: caries
**Karikatur** die; ~, ~en cartoon; *(Porträt)* caricature; **Karikaturist** der; ~en, ~en cartoonist; *(Porträtist)* caricaturist; **karikieren** *tr. V.* caricature
**karitativ** *Adj.* charitable
**Karl** [karl] (der) Charles; ~ **der Große** Charlemagne
**Karneval** ['karnəval] der; ~s, ~e *od.* ~s carnival; ~ **feiern** join in the carnival festivities
**Karnickel** das; ~s, ~ *(landsch.)* rabbit
**Kärnten** (das); ~s Carinthia
**Karo** das; ~s, ~s a) square; *(auf der Spitze stehend)* diamond; b) *o. Pl. (~muster)* check; c) *o. Art.; o. Pl. (Kartenspiel: Farbe)* diamonds *pl.*; *(Kartenspiel: Karte)* diamond; **Karo·as** das ace of diamonds
**Karosse** die; ~, ~n [state-]coach; **Karosserie** die; ~, ~n bodywork
**Karotte** die; ~, ~n small carrot
**Karpaten** *Pl.* Carpathians; Carpathian Mountains
**Karpfen** der; ~s, ~: carp
**Karre** die; ~, ~n *(bes. nordd.)* a) s. **Karren**; b) *(abwertend: Fahrzeug)* [old] heap *(coll.)*
**Karree** das; ~s, ~s: ums ~ **gehen/fahren** walk/drive round the block
**karren** *tr. V.* a) cart; b) *(salopp: mit einem Auto)* run *(coll.);* **Karren** der; ~s, ~ *(bes. südd., österr.)* cart; *(zweirädrig)* barrow
**Karriere** [ka'riɛːrə] die; ~, ~n career; ~ **machen** make a [successful] career for oneself
**Kar·samstag** der Easter Saturday
**Karte** die; ~, ~n card; *(Speise~)* menu; *(Fahr~, Flug~, Eintritts~)* ticket; *(Land~)* map; **alles auf eine ~ setzen** stake everything on one chance; **Kartei** die; ~, ~en card file
**Kartei-:** ~karte die file card; ~kasten der file-card box

**Kartell** das; ~s, ~e *(Wirtsch., Politik)* cartel

**Kartell-:** ~amt das *government body concerned with the control and supervision of cartels;* ≈ Monopolies and Mergers Commission *(Brit.);* ~gesetz das *law relating to cartels;* ≈ monopolies law *(Brit.)*

**Karten-:** ~haus das house of cards; ~spiel das a) *(Spiel mit Karten)* card-game; b) *(Satz Spielkarten)* pack *or (Amer.)* deck [of cards]; ~vor·verkauf der; *o. Pl.* advance booking

**Kartoffel** die; ~, ~n potato

**Kartoffel-:** ~brei der mashed potatoes *pl.;* mash *(coll.);* ~chips *Pl.* [potato] crisps *(Brit.) or (Amer.)* chips; ~käfer der Colorado beetle; ~kloß der potato dumpling; ~puffer der potato pancake *(made from grated raw potatoes);* ~püree das; *s.* ~brei

**Karton** [kar'tɔŋ] der; ~s, ~s a) *(Pappe)* card[board]; b) *(Schachtel)* cardboard box

**Karussell** das; ~s, ~s *od.* ~e merry-go-round; carousel *(Amer.); (kleineres)* roundabout

**Kar·woche** die Holy Week

**Karzinom** das; ~s, ~e *(Med.)* carcinoma

**kaschieren** *tr. V.* conceal; hide; disguise ⟨fault⟩

¹**Kaschmir (das)**; ~s Kashmir; ²**Kaschmir** der; ~s, ~e *(Textilw.)* cashmere

**Käse** der; ~s, ~: cheese; *(ugs. abwertend: Unsinn)* rubbish

**Käse-:** ~blatt das *(salopp abwertend)* rag; ~glocke die cheese dome

**Kaserne** die; ~, ~n barracks *sing. or pl.*

**käse·weiß** *Adj. (ugs.)* [as] white as a sheet; **käsig** *Adj. (ugs.)* pasty; pale

**Kasino** das; ~s, ~s a) *(Spiel~)* casino; b) *(Offiziers~)* [officers'] mess; c) *(Speiseraum)* canteen

**Kasko·versicherung** die *(Voll~)* comprehensive insurance; *(Teil~)* insurance against theft, fire, or act of God

**Kasper** der; ~s, ~: ≈ Punch; *(fig. ugs.)* clown; **Kasperl** das; ~s, ~[n] *(österr.),* **Kasperle** das *od.* der; ~s, ~: *s.* Kasper

**Kasper-:** ~puppe die ≈ Punch and Judy puppet; ~theater das ≈ Punch and Judy show; *(Puppenbühne)* ≈ Punch and Judy theatre

**Kasse** die; ~, ~n a) cash-box; *(Regi-strier~)* till; b) *(Ort zum Bezahlen)* cash desk; *(im Supermarkt)* checkout; *(in einer Bank)* counter; c) *(Kassenraum)* cashier's office; d) *(Theater~, Kino~)* box-office

**Kasseler** das; ~s smoked loin of pork

**Kassen-:** ~arzt der *doctor who treats members of health insurance schemes;* ~bon der sales slip; receipt; ~patient der *patient who is a member of a health insurance scheme;* ~zettel der *s.* ~bon

**Kassette** die; ~, ~n a) box; case; b) *(mit Büchern, Schallplatten)* boxed set; *(Tonband~, Film~)* cassette; **Kassetten·recorder** der cassette recorder

**kassieren** 1. *tr. V.* a) collect; b) *(ugs.: wegnehmen)* confiscate; take away ⟨driving licence⟩; 2. *itr. V.* a) bei jmdm. ~: give sb. his/her bill *or (Amer.)* check; *(ohne Rechnung)* settle up with sb.; **darf ich bei Ihnen ~?** would you like your bill?/can I settle up with you?; **Kassierer** der; ~s, ~, **Kassiererin** die; ~, ~nen cashier; *(bei einem Verein)* treasurer

**Kastanie** [kas'ta:niə] die; ~, ~n chestnut; **kastanien·braun** *Adj.* chestnut

**Kästchen** das; ~s, ~ a) small box; b) *(vorgedrucktes Quadrat)* square; *(auf Fragebögen)* box

**Kaste** die; ~, ~n caste

**kasteien** *refl. V.* a) *(als Bußübung)* chastise oneself; b) *(sich Entbehrungen auferlegen)* deny oneself; **Kasteiung** die; ~, ~en a) *(als Bußübung)* self-chastisement; b) *(Auferlegung von Entbehrungen)* self-denial

**Kastell** das; ~s, ~e a) *(hist.: röm. Lager)* fort; b) *(Burg)* castle

**Kasten** der; ~s, Kästen a) box; *(für Flaschen)* crate; b) *(ugs.: Briefkasten)* post-box; c) *(ugs. abwertend) (Gebäude)* barracks *sing. or pl.; (Auto)* heap *(coll.); (fig. ugs.)* etw. auf dem ~ haben have got it up top *(coll.);* **Kastenbrot** das tin[-loaf]

**Kastration** [kastra'tsio:n] die; ~, ~en castration; **kastrieren** *tr. V.* castrate

**Katalog** der; ~[e]s, ~e *(auch fig.)* catalogue; **katalogisieren** *tr. V.* catalogue

**Katalysator** der; ~s, ~en [-za'to:rən] *(Chemie, fig.)* catalyst; *(Kfz-W.)* catalytic converter

**katapultieren** *tr. V. (auch fig.)* catapult; eject ⟨pilot⟩

**Katarrh** [ka'tar] der; ~s, ~e *(Med.)* catarrh

**katastrophal** [katastro'fa:l] **1.** *Adj.* disastrous; *(stärker)* catastrophic; **2.** *adv.* disastrously; *(stärker)* catastrophically; **Katastrophe** [katas-'tro:fə] die; ~, ~n *(Unglück)* disaster; *(stärker, auch Literaturw.)* catastrophe

**Katastrophen-:** ~alarm der disaster alert; ~gebiet das disaster area; ~schutz der *(Organisation)* emergency services *pl.; (Maßnahmen)* disaster procedures *pl.*

**Kategorie** die; ~, ~n category; **kategorisch 1.** *Adj.* categorical; **2.** *adv.* categorically

**Kater** der; ~s, ~ **a)** tom-cat; **b)** *(ugs.)* hangover

**Kathedrale** die; ~, ~n cathedral

**Katholik** der; ~en, ~en, **Katholikin** die; ~, ~nen [Roman] Catholic; **katholisch** *Adj.* [Roman] Catholic; **Katholizismus** der; ~: [Roman] Catholicism *no art.*

**Kätzchen** das; ~s, ~ **a)** little cat; pussy; *(junge Katze)* kitten; **b)** *meist Pl.* catkin; **Katze** die; ~, ~n cat

**katzen-, Katzen-:** ~auge das reflector; Cat's-eye (P); ~jammer der **a)** *(Kater)* hangover; **b)** *(fig.)* mood of depression; ~musik die *(ugs. abwertend)* terrible row *(coll.);* ~sprung der stone's throw; ~wäsche die *(ugs.)* ~wäsche machen have a lick and a promise *(coll.)*

**Kauderwelsch** das; ~[s] gibberish *no indef. art.*

**kauen** *tr., itr. V.* chew; |die] Nägel ~: bite one's nails

**kauern 1.** *itr., refl. V.* crouch [down]; *(ängstlich)* cower

**Kauf** der; ~[e]s, **Käufe a)** *(das Kaufen)* buying; purchasing *(formal);* **b)** *(das Gekaufte)* purchase; **kaufen 1.** *tr. V.* buy; purchase; **2.** *itr. V. (einkaufen)* shop; **Käufer** der; ~s, ~: buyer; purchaser *(formal)*

**Kauf-:** ~haus das department store; ~kraft die *(Wirtsch.)* **a)** *(Wert des Geldes)* purchasing power; **b)** *(Zahlungsfähigkeit)* spending power

**käuflich 1.** *Adj.* **a)** for sale *postpos.;* **b)** *(bestechlich)* venal; ~ **sein** be easily bought; **2.** *adv.* etw. ~ erwerben/erstehen purchase sth.; **Kauf·mann** der; *Pl.* **Kaufleute a)** *(Geschäftsmann)* businessman; *(Händler)* trader; **b)** *(Besitzer)* shopkeeper; *(eines Lebens-*

*mittelladens)* grocer; **kaufmännisch** *Adj.* commercial; business *attrib.;* **Kauf·preis** der purchase price

**Kau·gummi** der *od.* das; ~s, ~s chewing gum

**Kaukasus** der; ~: the Caucasus

**Kaulquappe** die; ~, ~n tadpole

**kaum** *Adv.* hardly; scarcely; ~ **hatte er Platz genommen, als ...:** no sooner had he sat down than ...

**kausal** *Adj. (geh., Sprachw.)* causal

**Kau·tabak** der chewing tobacco

**Kaution** [kau'tsio:n] die; ~, ~en **a)** *(bei Freilassung eines Gefangenen)* bail; **b)** *(beim Mieten einer Wohnung)* deposit

**Kautschuk** der; ~s, ~e rubber

**Kauz** der; ~es, **Käuze a)** *(Wald~)* tawny owl; *(Stein~)* little owl; **b)** *(Sonderling)* strange fellow; oddball *(coll.)*

**Kavalier** [kava'li:g] der; ~s, ~e gentleman; **Kavaliers·delikt** das trifling offence

**Kavallerie** die; ~, ~n *(Milit. hist.)* cavalry; **Kavallerist** der; ~en, ~en cavalryman

**Kaviar** ['ka:viar] der; ~s, ~e caviare

**kcal** *Abk.* Kilo|gramm|kalorie kcal

**keck 1.** *Adj.* **a)** cheeky; saucy *(Brit.);* **b)** *(veralt.: verwegen)* bold; **c)** *(flott)* jaunty, pert ⟨hat etc.⟩; **2.** *adv.* **a)** cheekily; saucily *(Brit.);* **b)** *(veralt.: verwegen)* boldly; **c)** *(flott)* jauntily; **Keckheit** die; ~, ~en **a)** cheek; sauce *(Brit.);* **b)** *(veralt.: Kühnheit)* boldness

**Kegel** der; ~s, ~ **a)** cone; **b)** *(Spielfigur)* skittle; *(beim Bowling)* pin; **Kegel·bahn** die skittle alley; **kegelförmig** *Adj.* conical; **kegeln 1.** *itr. V.* play skittles *or* ninepins; **2.** *tr. V.* eine Partie ~: play a game of skittles *or* ninepins; **eine Neun** ~: score a nine

**Kehle** die; ~, ~n throat; **Kehl·kopf** der *(Anat.)* larynx

**Kehre** die; ~, ~n sharp bend; ¹**kehren 1.** *tr. V.* turn; **2.** *refl. V.* turn

²**kehren 1.** *itr. V. (bes. südd.)* sweep; do the sweeping; **2.** *tr. V.* sweep; *(mit einem Handfeger)* brush; **Kehricht** der *od.* das; ~s *(schweiz.: Müll)* refuse; garbage *(Amer.)*

**Kehr·seite** die **a)** back; *(einer Münze, Medaille)* reverse; *(scherzh.) (Gesäß)* backside; **b)** *(nachteiliger Aspekt)* drawback; disadvantage; **kehrt|machen** *itr. V. (ugs.)* turn [round and go] back

**keifen** *itr. V. (abwertend)* nag

**Keil** der; ~|e|s, ~e a) *(zum Spalten)* wedge; b) *(zum Festklemmen)* chock; *(unter einer Tür)* wedge; **keilen** *refl. V. (ugs.: sich prügeln)* fight; scrap; **Keiler** der; ~s, ~ *(Jägerspr.)* wild boar; **Keilerei** die; ~, ~en *(ugs.)* punch-up *(coll.);* fight

**Keil-:** ~**riemen** der *(Technik)* V-belt; ~**schrift** die cuneiform script

**Keim** der; ~|e|s, ~e *(Bot.)* shoot; *(Biol.)* embryo; **keimen** *itr. V.* germinate; *(fig.) ⟨hope⟩* stir; **keim·frei** *Adj.* germ-free; sterile; **Keim·zelle** die nucleus

**kein** *Indefinitpron.* a) no; b) *(ugs.: nicht ganz, nicht einmal)* less than; **kein...** *Indefinitpron.* ~**er**/~**e** nobody; no one; ~s **von beiden** neither [of them]; **keinerlei** *indekl. unbest. Gattungsz.* no ... what[so]ever

**keines-:** ~**falls** *Adv.* on no account; ~**wegs** *Adv.* by no means

**kein·mal** *Adv.* not [even] once

**Keks** der; ~ *od.* ~es, ~ *od.* ~e biscuit *(Brit.);* cookie *(Amer.)*

**Kelch** der; ~|e|s, ~e goblet; *(Rel.)* chalice

**Kelle** die; ~, ~n a) ladle; b) *(Signalstab)* signalling disc; c) *(Maurer~)* trowel

**Keller** der; ~s, ~ cellar; *(~geschoß)* basement; **Keller·assel** die woodlouse; **Kellerei** die; ~, ~en winery; *(Kellerräume)* [wine] cellars *pl.;* **Keller·geschoß** das basement

**Kellner** der; ~s, ~ waiter; **kellnern** *itr. V. (ugs.)* work as a waiter/waitress

**Kelte** der; ~n, ~n Celt

**Kelter** die; ~, ~n winepress; **keltern** *tr. V.* press *⟨grapes etc.⟩*

**keltisch** *Adj.* Celtic

**Kenia** (das); ~s Kenya; **Kenianer** der; ~s, ~: Kenyan

**kennen** *unr. tr. V.* a) know; b) *(bekannt sein mit)* know; **kennen|lernen** *tr. V.* get to know; *(erstmals begegnen)* meet; *(in Berührung gebracht werden mit)* come to know; **Kenner** der; ~s, ~: expert (+ *Gen.* on); *(von Wein, Speisen)* connoisseur; **Kennerblick** der expert eye; **mit** ~: with an expert eye; **Kenn·marke** die [police] identification badge; ≈ [police] warrant card *or (Amer.)* ID card; **kenntlich** *Adj.:* ~ **sein** be recognizable (**an** by); **etw./jmdn.** ~ **machen** mark sth./make sb. [easily] identifiable; **Kenntnis** die; ~, ~se knowledge

**kenn-, Kenn-:** ~**wort** das; *Pl.* ~**wörter** code-word; *(Parole)* password; code-word; ~**zahl** die index; ~**zeichen** das a) sign; b) *(Erkennungszeichen)* badge; *(auf einem Behälter, einer Ware usw.)* label; *(am Fahrzeug)* registration number; ~**zeichnen** *tr. V.* a) mark; label; mark *⟨way⟩;* b) *(charakterisieren)* characterize; ~**zeichnend** *Adj.* typical, characteristic (**für** of)

**kentern** *itr. V. mit sein* capsize

**Keramik** die; ~, ~en *o. Pl.* ceramics *pl.;* pottery; *(~gegenstand)* piece of pottery

**Kerbe** die; ~, ~n notch

**Kerbel** der; ~s chervil

**Kerb·holz** das: **etwas auf dem** ~**holz haben** *(ugs.)* have done a job *(sl.)*

**Kerker** der; ~s, ~ *(hist.)* dungeons *pl.; (einzelne Zelle)* dungeon

**Kerl** der; ~s, ~e *(nordd., md. auch:* ~s*)* *(ugs.)* fellow *(coll.);* bloke *(Brit. sl.)*

**Kern** der; ~|e|s, ~e pip; *(von Steinobst)* stone; *(von Nüssen usw.)* kernel; *(Atom~)* nucleus; *(fig.)* **der** ~ **einer Sache** the heart of a matter; **der harte** ~: the hard core

**kern-, Kern-:** ~**energie** die nuclear energy *no art.;* ~**gehäuse** das core; ~**gesund** *Adj.* fit as a fiddle *pred.*

**kernig** *Adj.* earthy *⟨language⟩;* forceful *⟨speech⟩;* pithy *⟨saying⟩*

**kern-, Kern-:** ~**kraft** die nuclear power; ~**kraftwerk** das nuclear power station *or* plant; ~**los** *Adj.* seedless; ~**obst** das pomaceous fruit; ~**physik** die nuclear physics *sing., no art.;* ~**reaktor** der nuclear reactor; ~**seife** die washing soap; ~**spaltung** die *(Physik)* nuclear fission *no art.;* ~**waffe** die; *meist Pl.* nuclear weapon

**Kerze** die; ~, ~n candle

**kerzen-, Kerzen-:** ~**gerade**, *(ugs.)* ~**grade** 1. *Adj.* dead straight; 2. *adv.* bolt upright; ~**halter** der candleholder; ~**leuchter** der candlestick

**keß** 1. *Adj.* a) pert; jaunty *⟨hat, dress, etc.⟩;* b) *(frech)* cheeky; 2. *adv.* a) *(flott)* jauntily; b) *(frech)* cheekily

**Kessel** der; ~s, ~ a) kettle; *(zum Kochen)* pot; *(Wasch~)* copper; b) *(Berg~)* basin-shaped valley; c) *(Milit.)* encircled area

**Kessel-:** ~**stein** der; *o. Pl.* scale; ~**treiben** das *(Hetzkampagne)* witchhunt

**Kette** die; ~, ~n chain; *(Hals~)* necklace; *(von Ereignissen)* string; **ketten** *tr. V.* chain (**an** + *Akk.* to)

**Ketten-:** ~**hund** der guard-dog *(kept on a chain);* ~**raucher** der chain-smoker

**Ketzer** der; ~s, ~ *(auch fig.)* heretic; **Ketzerei** die; ~, ~en *(auch fig.)* heresy

**keuchen** *itr. V.* gasp for breath; **Keuch·husten** der whooping cough *no art.*

**Keule** die; ~, ~n a) club; b) *(Kochk.)* leg

**keusch** 1. *Adj.* chaste; 2. *adv.* ~ leben lead a chaste life; **Keuschheit** die; ~ chastity

**Kfz** [ka:|ɛf'tsɛt] *Abk.* **Kraftfahrzeug**

**kg** *Abk.* **Kilogramm** kg

**KG** *Abk.* **Kommanditgesellschaft**

**kichern** *itr. V.* giggle

**kicken** *(ugs.)* 1. *itr. V.* play football; 2. *tr. V.* kick

**kidnappen** ['kɪtnɛpn̩] *tr. V.* kidnap; **Kidnapper** der; ~s, ~: kidnapper

**Kiebitz** der; ~es, ~e lapwing; peewit

**¹Kiefer** der; ~s, ~: jaw; *(~knochen)* jaw-bone

**²Kiefer** die; ~, ~n pine[tree]

**Kiefer·höhle** die *(Anat.)* maxillary sinus

**Kiefern·holz** das pine[-wood]

**Kiel** der; ~|e|s, ~e keel; **kiel·holen** *tr. V. (Seemannsspr.)* keel-haul ⟨*person*⟩; **Kiel·wasser** das wake

**Kieme** die; ~, ~n; *meist Pl.* gill

**Kien** der; ~|e|s resinous wood

**Kies** der; ~es, ~e gravel; *(auf dem Strand)* shingle; **Kiesel** der; ~s, ~: pebble; **Kiesel·stein** der pebble

**Kies-:** ~**grube** die gravel pit; ~**weg** der gravel path

**kiffen** *itr. V. (ugs.)* smoke pot *(sl.)* or grass *(sl.);* **Kiffer** der; ~s, ~ *(ugs.)* pot-head *(sl.)*

**kikeriki** [kikəri'ki:] *Interj. (Kinderspr.)* cock-a-doodle-doo

**Killer** der; ~s, ~ *(salopp)* killer; *(gegen Bezahlung)* hit man *(sl.)*

**Kilo** das; ~s, ~|s| kilo; **Kilo·gramm** das kilogram; **Kilometer** der; ~s, ~: kilometre; **kilometer·lang** 1. *Adj.* miles long *pred.;* 2. *adv.* for miles [and miles]; **Kilometer·stand** der mileage reading

**Kimme** die; ~, ~n sighting notch

**Kimono** der; ~s, ~s kimono

**Kind** das; ~|e|s, ~er a) child; **ein** ~ erwarten be expecting; |~er,| ~er! my goodness!

**Kinder-:** ~**arzt** der paediatrician; ~**bett** das cot; *(für größeres Kind)* child's bed; ~**dorf** das children's village

**Kinderei** die; ~, ~en childishness *no indef. art., no pl.*

**kinder-, Kinder-:** ~**feindlich** *Adj.* hostile to children *pred.;* ~**freundlich** *Adj.* fond of children *pred.;* ⟨*town, resort*⟩ which caters for children; ⟨*planning, policy*⟩ which caters for the needs of children; ~**garten** der nursery school; ~**gärtnerin** die nusery-school teacher; ~**heilkunde** die paediatrics *sing., no art.;* ~**hort** der day-home for schoolchildren; ~**lähmung** die poliomyelitis; ~**leicht** *(ugs.) Adj.* childishly simple; dead easy; **das ist** ~**leicht** it's kid's stuff *(coll.);* it's child's play; ~**lieb** *Adj.* fond of children *pred.;* ~**los** *Adj.* childless; ~**reich** *Adj.* with many children *postpos., not pred.;* ~**sterblichkeit** die child mortality; ~**stube** die; *o. Pl.* **eine gute/schlechte** ~**stube gehabt haben** have been well/badly brought up; ~**teller** der *(auf der Speisekarte)* children's menu; ~**wagen** der pram *(Brit.);* baby carriage *(Amer.);* *(Sportwagen)* push-chair *(Brit.);* stroller *(Amer.)*

**Kindes-:** ~**alter** das; *o. Pl.* childhood; ~**mißhandlung** die *(Rechtsw.)* child abuse

**Kindheit** die; ~: childhood; **kindisch** 1. *Adj.* childish, infantile; naïve ⟨*ideas*⟩; 2. *adv.* childishly; **kindlich** 1. *Adj.* childlike; 2. *adv.* ⟨*behave*⟩ in a childlike way

**Kinkerlitzchen** *Pl. (ugs.)* trifles

**Kinn** das; ~|e|s, ~e chin

**Kinn-:** ~**haken** der hook to the chin; ~**lade** die jaw

**Kino** das; ~s, ~s cinema *(Brit.);* movie theater *(Amer.);* **Kino·karte** die cinema ticket *(Brit.);* movie ticket *(Amer.)*

**Kiosk** der; ~|e|s, ~e kiosk

**¹Kippe** die; ~, ~n *(ugs.)* cigarette end; dog-end *(sl.)*

**²Kippe** die; ~, ~n a) *(Bergmannsspr.)* slag-heap; **etw. steht auf der** ~ *(fig.)* it's touch and go with sth.; *(etw. ist noch nicht entschieden)* sth. hangs in the balance; **kippen** 1. *tr. V.* a) tip [up]; b) *(ausschütten)* tip [out]; 2. *itr. V.; mit sein* tip over; ⟨*top-heavy object*⟩ topple over; ⟨*person*⟩ topple; ⟨*boat*⟩ overturn; ⟨*car*⟩ roll over

**Kipp-:** ~**fenster** das horizontally pivoted window; ~**schalter** der tumbler switch

**Kirche** die; ~, ~n church; **in die ~ gehen** go to church

**Kirchen-:** ~**fest** das church festival; ~**lied** das hymn; ~**musik** die church music; ~**steuer** die church tax

**Kirch·hof** der *(veralt.)* churchyard; **kirchlich** 1. *Adj.* ecclesiastical; church *attrib.* ⟨*wedding, funeral*⟩; 2. *adv.* ~ **getraut/begraben werden** have a church wedding/funeral

**Kirch-:** ~**turm** der [church] steeple; *(ohne Turmspitze)* church tower; ~**weih** die; ~, ~**en** fair *(held on the anniversary of the consecration of a church)*

**Kirmes** die; ~, **Kirmessen** *(bes. md., niederd.)* s. **Kirchweih**

**Kirsch·baum** der cherry[-tree]; **Kirsche** die; ~, ~n cherry

**Kirsch-:** ~**torte** die cherry gateau; *(mit Tortenboden)* cherry flan; ~**wasser** das kirsch

**Kissen** das; ~s, ~: cushion; *(Kopf~)* pillow

**Kiste** die; ~, ~n box; *(Truhe)* chest; *(Latten~)* crate

**Kitsch** der; ~[e]s kitsch; **kitschig** *Adj.* kitschy

**Kitt** der; ~[e]s, ~e putty; *(für Porzellan, Kacheln usw.)* cement

**Kittchen** das; ~s, ~ *(ugs.)* clink *(sl.)*

**Kittel** der; ~s, ~ **a)** overall; *(eines Arztes usw.)* white coat; **b)** *(hemdartige Bluse)* smock

**kitten** *tr. V.* cement [together]

**Kitz** das; ~es, ~e *(Reh~)* fawn; *(Ziegen~, Gemsen~)* kid

**kitzeln** *tr., itr. V.* tickle; **kitzlig** *Adj. (auch fig.)* ticklish

**KKW** [ka:ka:'|ve:] *Abk.* **Kernkraftwerk**

**Klacks** der; ~es, ~e *(ugs.)* dollop *(coll.)*; *(~ Senf)* dab

**Kladde** die; ~, ~n rough book

**Kladderadatsch** der; ~[e]s, ~e *(ugs.)* unholy mess *(coll.)*

**klaffen** *itr. V.* yawn; ⟨*hole, wound*⟩ gape; **kläffen** *itr. V. (abwertend)* yap

**Klafter** ['klaftɐ] der *od.* das; ~s, ~ *(Raummaß für Holz)* cord

**Klage** die; ~, ~n **a)** *(Äußerung der Trauer)* lament; **b)** *(Beschwerde)* complaint; **c)** *(Rechtsw.)* action; *(im Strafrecht)* charge; **klagen** 1. *itr. V.* **a)** *(geh.: jammern)* wail; *(stöhnend)* moan; **b)** *(sich beschweren)* complain *(über + Akk.* about); **c)** *(bei Gericht)*

take legal action; 2. *tr. V.* **jmdm. sein Leid/seine Not ~:** pour out one's sorrows *pl.*/troubles *pl.*; **Kläger** der; ~s, ~, **Klägerin** die; ~, ~**nen** *(im Zivilrecht)* plaintiff; *(im Strafrecht)* prosecuting party; *(bei einer Scheidung)* petitioner; **kläglich** *Adj.* **a)** *(mitleiderregend)* pitiful; **b)** *(minderwertig)* pathetic; **c)** *(erbärmlich)* despicable ⟨*behaviour, role, compromise*⟩; pathetic ⟨*result, defeat*⟩

**Klamauk** der; ~s *(ugs. abwertend)* fuss; *(Lärm, Krach)* row *(coll.)*

**klamm** *Adj.* **a)** *(feucht)* cold and damp; **b)** *(steif)* numb; **Klammer** die; ~, ~n *(Wäsche~)* peg; *(Haar~)* [hair-]grip; *(Zahn~)* brace; *(Büro~)* paper-clip; *(Heft~)* staple; *(Schriftzeichen)* bracket; **klammern** 1. *refl. V.* **sich an jmdn./etw.** ~ *(auch fig.)* cling to sb./sth.; 2. *tr. V.* **a) eine Wunde ~:** close a wound with a clip/clips; **b)** *(mit einer Büroklammer)* clip; *(mit einer Heftmaschine)* staple; *(mit Wäscheklammern)* peg

**Klamotten** *Pl. (salopp) (Kleidung)* gear *sing. (sl.); (Kram)* stuff *sing.*

**Klampfe** die; ~, ~n *(volkst.: Gitarre)* guitar

**klang** *1. u. 3. Pers. Sg. Prät. v.* **klingen**

**Klang** der; ~[e]s, **Klänge a)** *(Ton)* sound; **b)** *(~farbe)* tone

**Klapp·bett** das folding bed; **Klappe** die; ~, ~n **a)** [hinged] lid; *(am LKW)* tail-gate; *(seitlich)* side-gate; *(am Kombiwagen)* back; *(am Ofen)* [drop-] door; **b)** *(an Musikinstrumenten)* key; *(an einer Trompete)* valve; **c)** *(Filmjargon)* clapper-board; **d)** *(salopp: Mund)* trap *(sl.)*; **klappen** 1. *tr. V.* **nach oben/unten ~:** turn up/down ⟨*collar, hat-brim*⟩; lift up/put down ⟨*lid*⟩; **nach vorne/hinten ~:** tilt forward/back ⟨*seat*⟩; 2. *itr. V.* **a)** ⟨*door, shutter*⟩ bang; **b)** *(stoßen)* bang; **c)** *(ugs.: gelingen)* work out all right; **klapperig** *Adj.* rickety; **klappern** *itr. V.* **a)** rattle; **b)** *(ein Klappern erzeugen)* make a clatter; **Klapperschlange** die rattlesnake; **klapprig** *Adj.* rickety

**Klapp-:** ~**sitz** der tip-up seat; ~**stuhl** der folding chair

**Klaps** der; ~es, ~e *(ugs.)* smack; slap; **Klaps·mühle** die *(salopp)* loony-bin *(sl.)*

**klar** 1. *Adj.* **a)** clear; straight ⟨*question, answer*⟩; **sich** *(Dat.)* **über etw.** *(Akk.)* **im ~en sein** realize sth.; **b)** *nicht attr.*

*(fertig)* ready; **2.** *adv.* clearly; **Klär-anlage** die sewage treatment plant; **Klare** der; ~n, ~n schnapps; **klären 1.** *tr. V.* **a)** settle ⟨*question, issue, matter*⟩; clarify ⟨*situation*⟩; clear up ⟨*case, affair, misunderstanding*⟩; **b)** *(reinigen)* purify; treat ⟨*effluent, sewage*⟩; **2.** *refl. V.* **a)** ⟨*situation*⟩ become clear; ⟨*question, issue, matter*⟩ be settled; **b)** *(rein werden)* ⟨*liquid, sky*⟩ clear; ⟨*weather*⟩ clear [up]; **klar|gehen** *unr. itr. V.; mit sein (ugs.)* go OK *(coll.);* **Klarheit** die; ~: clarity; **sich** *(Dat.)* **über etw.** *(Akk.)* ~ **verschaffen** clarify sth.

**Klarinette** die; ~, ~n clarinet

**klar-:** ~**|machen** *tr. V.* **a)** *(ugs.)* make clear; **b)** *(Seemannsspr.)* get ready; ~**|sehen** *unr. itr. V.* understand the matter

**Klarsicht·folie** die transparent film; **klar|stellen** *tr. V.* clear up; clarify; **Klar·text** der *(auch DV)* clear text; **im** ~**text** *(fig.)* in plain language; **Klärung** die; ~, ~en **a)** clarification; **b)** *(Reinigung)* purification; *(von Abwässern)* treatment; **klar|werden** *unr. V.; mit sein; nur im Inf. und Part. zusammengeschrieben* **1.** *refl. V.* **sich** *(Dat.)* **über etw.** *(Akk.)* ~: realize sth.; **2.** *itr. V.* **jmdm. wird etw. klar** sth. becomes clear to sb.

**klasse** *(ugs.)* **1.** *indekl. Adj.* great *(coll.);* **2.** *adv.* marvellously; **Klasse** die; ~, ~n **a)** *(Schul~)* class; *(Raum)* class-room; *(Stufe)* year; grade *(Amer.);* **b)** *(Sport)* league; *(Boxen)* division; **c)** *(Fahrzeug~, Boots~, Qualitätsstufe)* class

**klassen-, Klassen-:** ~**arbeit** die *(Schulw.)* [written] class test; ~**gesellschaft** die *(Soziol.)* class society; ~**kampf** der *(marx.)* class struggle; ~**lehrer** der, ~**lehrerin** die*(Schulw.)* class teacher; ~**los** *Adj. (Soziol.)* classless; ~**sprecher** der, ~**sprecherin** die *(Schulw.)* class spokesman; ~**treffen das** *(Schulw.)* class reunion; ~**ziel das** *(Schulw.)* required standard *(for pupils in a particular class);* ~**zimmer das** *(Schulw.)* class-room

**klassifizieren** *tr. V.* classify **(als** as); **Klassifizierung** die; ~, ~en classification; **Klassik** die; ~ **a)** *(Antike)* classical antiquity *no art.;* **b)** *(Zeit kultureller Höchstleistung)* classical period **Klassiker** der; ~s, ~: classical writer/

composer; **klassisch** *Adj.* classical; *(vollendet, zeitlos; auch iron.)* classic; **Klassizismus** der; ~: classicism

**Klatsch** der; ~|e|s, ~e **a)** *o. Pl. (ugs. abwertend)* gossip; **b)** *(Geräusch)* smack; **Klatsch·base** die *(ugs. abwertend)* gossip; **klatschen** *itr. V.* **a)** *auch mit sein* ⟨*waves, wet sails*⟩ slap; **b)** *(mit den Händen; applaudieren)* clap; **c)** *(schlagen)* slap; **d)** *(ugs. abwertend: reden)* gossip (**über** + *Akk.* about); **klatschhaft** *Adj.* gossipy; fond of gossip *pred.;* **Klatsch·mohn** der corn-poppy; **klatsch·naß** *Adj. (ugs.)* sopping wet; dripping wet ⟨*hair*⟩

**Klaue** die; ~, ~n **a)** claw; *(von Raubvögeln)* talon; *(salopp: Hand)* mitt *(sl.);* **b)** *o. Pl. (salopp abwertend: Schrift)* scrawl; **klauen** *(ugs.)* **1.** *tr. V.* pinch *(sl.);* **jmdm. etw.** ~: pinch sth. from sb.; **2.** *itr. V.* pinch *(sl.)* things

**Klause** die; ~, ~n hermitage; *(Klosterzelle)* cell; **Klausel** die; ~, ~n clause; *(Bedingung)* condition; *(Vorbehalt)* proviso

**Klavier** [kla'vi:ɐ̯] das; ~s, ~e piano **Klebe·folie** die adhesive film; **kleben 1.** *itr. V.* **a)** stick **(an** + *Dat.* to); **b)** *(ugs.: klebrig sein)* be sticky *(von, vor* + *Dat.* with); **2.** *tr. V.* **a)** *(befestigen)* stick; *(mit Klebstoff)* glue; **jmdm. eine** ~ *(salopp)* belt sb. one *(coll.);* **b)** *(reparieren)* stick *or* glue ⟨*vase etc.*⟩ back together; **Kleber** der; ~s, ~: adhesive; glue; **klebrig** *Adj.* sticky

**Kleb-:** ~**stoff** der adhesive; glue; ~**streifen** der adhesive *or* sticky tape **kleckern** *(ugs.)* itr. V. make a mess; **Klecks** der; ~es, ~e **a)** stain; *(nicht aufgesogen)* blob; *(Tintenfleck)* [ink-] blot; **b)** *(ugs.: kleine Menge)* spot; *(von Senf, Mayonnaise)* dab; **klecksen** *itr. V.* **a)** make a stain/stains; *(mit Tinte)* make a blot/blots; ⟨*pen*⟩ blot; **b)** *(ugs. abwertend: schlecht malen)* daub

**Klee** der; ~s clover; **Klee·blatt** das clover-leaf

**Kleid** das; ~es, ~er **a)** dress; **b)** *Pl. (Kleidung)* clothes; **kleiden 1.** *refl. V.* dress; **2.** *tr. V.* **a)** dress; **b)** *(jmdm. stehen)* suit

**Kleider-:** ~**bügel** der clothes-hanger; coat-hanger; ~**bürste** die clothes-brush; ~**haken** der coat-hook; ~**schrank** der wardrobe; ~**ständer** der coat-stand

**kleidsam** *Adj.* becoming; **Kleidung** die; ~: clothes *pl.*

**Kleidungs·stück** das garment

**klein** 1. *Adj.* **a)** little; small; **er ist ~er als ich** he is shorter than me; **b)** *(jung)* little; **von ~ auf** from an early age; **c)** *(von kurzer Dauer)* little, short ⟨*while*⟩; short ⟨*walk, break, holiday*⟩; brief ⟨*moment*⟩; **d)** *(von geringer Menge)* small; low ⟨*price*⟩; **~es Geld haben** have some [small] change; **e)** *(von geringem Ausmaß)* small ⟨*party, gift*⟩; scant ⟨*attention*⟩; slight ⟨*cold, indisposition, mistake, irregularity*⟩; minor ⟨*event, error*⟩; **f)** *(unbedeutend)* lowly ⟨*employee*⟩; minor ⟨*official*⟩; **~ anfangen** *(ugs.)* start off in a small way; **2.** *adv.* **die Heizung ~/~er einstellen** turn the heating down low/lower; **ein Wort ~ schreiben** write a word with a small initial letter

**klein-, Klein-:** **~anzeige die** *(Zeitungsw.)* small *or* classified advertisement; **~asien (das)** Asia Minor; **~bürgerlich** *Adj.* **a)** *(das Kleinbürgertum betreffend)* lower middle-class; **b)** *(abwertend: spießbürgerlich)* petit bourgeois

¹**Kleine der;** *adj. Dekl.* **a)** *(kleiner Junge)* little boy; **b)** *(ugs. Anrede)* little man; ²**Kleine die;** *adj. Dekl.* **a)** *(kleines Mädchen)* little girl; **b)** *(ugs. Anrede)* love; *(abwertend)* little madam

**klein-, Klein-:** **~familie die** *(Soziol.)* nuclear family; **~geld das;** *o. Pl.* [small] change; **~gläubig** sceptical

**Kleinigkeit die;** **~, ~en** small thing; *(Einzelheit)* [small] detail; **ich habe noch eine ~ zu erledigen** I still have a small matter to attend to; **eine ~ essen** have a [small] bite to eat; **eine ~ für jmdn. sein** be no trouble for sb.

**klein-, Klein-:** **~kind das** small child; **~kram der** *(ugs.)* odds and ends *pl.*; *(unbedeutende Dinge)* trivial matters *pl.*; **~|kriegen** *tr. V. (ugs.)* **a)** *(zerkleinern)* crush [to pieces]; **b)** *(zerstören)* smash; break; **c)** *(aufbrauchen)* get through; **d)** **jmdn. ~kriegen** get sb. down *(coll.)*; *(durch Drohungen)* intimidate sb.; *(gefügig machen)* bring sb. into line; **~laut** **1.** *Adj.* subdued; *(verlegen)* sheepish; **2.** *adv.* in a subdued fashion; *(verlegen)* sheepishly

**kleinlich** *(abwertend)* **1.** *Adj.* pernickety; *(ohne Großzügigkeit)* mean; *(engstirnig)* small-minded; petty; **2.** *adv.* meticulously

**Kleinod das;** **~|e|s, ~e** *od.* **~ien** *(geh.)* **a)** *(Schmuckstück)* piece of jewellery;

*(Edelstein)* jewel; **b)** *(Kostbarkeit)* gem

**klein-, Klein-:** **~|schneiden** *unr. tr. V.* cut into small pieces; chop up ⟨*onion*⟩ [small]; **~stadt die** small town; **~städter der** small-town dweller

**Kleinste der/die/das;** *adj. Dekl.* youngest boy/girl/child

**klein|stellen** *tr. V.* turn down [low]

**Kleister der;** **~s, ~:** paste

**Klementine die;** **~, ~n** clementine

**Klemme die;** **~, ~n** clip; **in der ~ sein** *od.* **sitzen** *(ugs.)* be in a fix *(coll.)*; **klemmen 1.** *tr. V.* **a)** *(befestigen)* tuck; stick *(coll.)*; **b)** *(quetschen)* **sich** *(Dat.)* **den Fuß/die Hand ~:** get one's foot/hand caught *or* trapped; **2.** *refl. V.* **sich hinter etw.** *(Akk.)* **~** *(fig. ugs.)* put some hard work into sth.; **3.** *itr. V.* ⟨*door, drawer, etc.*⟩ stick

**Klempner der;** **~s, ~:** tinsmith; *(~ und Installateur)* plumber

**Kleptomanie die;** **~** *(Psych.)* kleptomania *no art.*

**klerikal** *Adj. (auch abwertend)* clerical; church ⟨*property*⟩; **Klerus der;** **~:** clergy

**Klette die;** **~, ~n** bur; *(Pflanze)* burdock

**klettern** *itr. V.; mit sein (auch fig.)* climb; **auf einen Baum ~:** climb a tree; **Kletter·pflanze die** creeper; *(Bot.)* climbing plant; climber

**klicken** *itr. V.* click

**Klient der;** **~en, ~en, Klientin die;** **~, ~nen** client

**Klima das;** **~s, ~s** *od.* **Klimate** climate; **Klima·an·lage die** air-conditioning *no indef. art.*; **klimatisch** *Adj.* climatic; **klimatisieren** *tr. V.* air-condition; **Klima·wechsel der** change of climate

**Klimm·zug der** *(Turnen)* pull-up

**klimpern 1.** *itr. V.* jingle; **2.** *tr. V. (ugs. abwertend)* plunk out ⟨*tune etc.*⟩

**Klinge die;** **~, ~n** blade

**Klingel die;** **~, ~n** bell

**Klingel-:** **~beutel der** offertory-bag; collection-bag; **~knopf der** bell-push

**klingeln** *itr. V.* ring; ⟨*alarm clock*⟩ go off; **es klingelt** *(an der Tür)* there is a ring at the door; *(Telefon)* the telephone is ringing

**klingen** *unr. itr. V.* sound; **die Glocken klangen** the bells were ringing

**Klinik die;** **~, ~en** hospital; *(spezialisiert)* clinic

**Klinke die;** **~, ~n** door-handle

**Klinker der;** **~s, ~:** [Dutch] clinker

**klipp** 594

**klipp** *Adv.:* ~ **und klar** *(ugs.)* quite plainly

**Klippe** die; ~, ~n rock

**klirren** *itr. V.* clink; ⟨*weapons in fight*⟩ clash; ⟨*window-pane*⟩ rattle; ⟨*chains, spurs*⟩ rattle; ⟨*harness*⟩ jingle

**Klischee** das; ~s, ~s cliché

**klitsch·naß** *Adj. (ugs.)* sopping wet; *(tropfnaß)* dripping wet

**klitze·klein** *Adj. (ugs.)* teeny[-weeny] *(coll.)*

**Klo** das; ~s, ~s *(ugs.)* loo *(Brit. coll.);* john *(Amer. coll.)*

**Kloake** die; ~, ~n cesspit; *(Kanal)* sewer

**klobig** *Adj.* heavy and clumsy [-looking] ⟨*shoes, furniture*⟩; bulky ⟨*figure*⟩; *(plump)* clumsy

**Klo·papier** das *(ugs.)* loo-paper *(Brit. coll.);* toilet-paper

**klopfen** 1. *itr. V.* **a)** *(schlagen)* knock; **b)** *(pulsieren)* ⟨*heart*⟩ beat; ⟨*pulse*⟩ throb; 2. *tr. V.* beat ⟨*carpet*⟩

**Klöppel** der; ~s, ~ *(Glocken~)* clapper; **klöppeln** *tr., itr. V.* ⟨etw.⟩ ~: make [sth. in] pillow-lace

**Klops** der; ~es, ~e *(nordostd.)* meat ball

**Klosett** das; ~s, ~s *od.* ~e lavatory

**Kloß** der; ~es, **Klöße** dumpling; *(Fleisch~)* meat ball

**Kloster** das; ~s, **Klöster** *(Mönchs~)* monastery; *(Nonnen~)* convent

**Klotz** der; ~es, **Klötze** block [of wood]; *(Stück eines Baumstamms)* log

**Klub** der; ~s, ~s club; **Klub·sessel** der club chair

**¹Kluft** die; ~, ~en *(ugs.)* gear *(coll.);* *(Uniform)* garb

**²Kluft** die; ~, **Klüfte** *(veralt.)* *(Spalte)* cleft; *(im Gletscher)* crevasse; *(Abgrund)* chasm; *(fig.)* gulf

**klug; klüger, klügst...** *Adj.* clever; bright ⟨*child, pupil*⟩; intelligent ⟨*eyes*⟩; *(vernünftig)* wise; sound ⟨*advice*⟩; *(geschickt)* shrewd ⟨*politician, negotiator, question*⟩; astute ⟨*businessman*⟩; **klüger** *s.* klug; **Klugheit** die; ~ *s.* klug: cleverness; brightness; intelligence; wisdom; soundness; shrewdness; astuteness; **klügst...** *s.* klug

**klumpen** *itr. V.* go lumpy; **Klumpen** der; ~s, ~: lump; **ein** ~ **Gold** a gold nugget

**km** *Abk.* Kilometer km.

**knabbern** 1. *tr. V.* nibble; 2. *itr. V.* **an** etw. *(Dat.)* ~: nibble [at] sth.

**Knabe** der; ~n, ~n *(geh. veralt./ südd., österr., schweiz.)* boy; *(ugs.: Bursche)*

chap *(coll.);* **knabenhaft** 1. *Adj.* boyish; 2. *adv.* boyishly

**Knäcke·brot** das crispbread; *(Scheibe)* slice of crispbread; **knacken** 1. *itr. V.* **a)** ⟨*bed, floor, etc.*⟩ creak; **b)** *mit sein (ugs.: zerbrechen)* snap; ⟨*window*⟩ crack; 2. *tr. V.* **a)** crack ⟨*nut, shell*⟩; *(salopp: aufbrechen)* crack ⟨*safe*⟩ [open]; break into ⟨*car, bank, etc.*⟩; **knackig** *Adj.* **a)** crisp; **b)** *(ugs.: attraktiv)* delectable; **Knacks** der; ~es, ~e *(ugs.)* crack; *(fig.: Defekt)* **einen** ~ **bekommen** ⟨*person*⟩ have a breakdown; ⟨*health*⟩ suffer

**Knall** der; ~[e]s, ~e bang; **knallen** 1. *itr. V.* **a)** ⟨*shot*⟩ ring out; ⟨*firework*⟩ go bang; ⟨*cork*⟩ pop; ⟨*door*⟩ slam; ⟨*whip, rifle*⟩ crack; **mit der Tür** ~: slam the door; **b)** *(ugs.: schießen)* shoot, fire **(auf** + *Akk.* at); **c)** *(Ballspiele ugs.)* **aufs Tor** ~: belt the ball/puck at the goal *(coll.);* 2. *tr. V.* **a)** *(ugs.)* slam down; *(werfen)* sling *(coll.);* **b)** *(ugs.: schlagen)* **jmdm. eine** ~ *(salopp)* belt sb. one *(coll.)*

**knall-: ~hart** *(ugs.)* 1. *Adj.* very tough ⟨*demands, measures, etc.*⟩; ⟨*person*⟩ as hard as nails; 2. *adv.* brutally; **gegen etw. ~hart vorgehen** take very tough action against sth.; **~rot** *Adj.* bright or vivid red; **sie wurde ~rot** she turned as red as a beetroot

**knapp** 1. *Adj.* **a)** meagre; narrow ⟨*victory, lead*⟩; narrow, bare ⟨*majority*⟩; **die Vorräte wurden** ~: supplies ran short; **vor einer ~en Stunde** just under an hour ago; **b)** *(eng)* tight-fitting ⟨*garment*⟩; *(zu eng)* tight ⟨*garment*⟩; **c)** *(kurz)* terse ⟨*reply, greeting*⟩; succinct ⟨*description, account, report*⟩; 2. *adv.* **a)** ~ **bemessen sein** be meagre, ⟨*time*⟩ be limited; ~ **gewinnen/verlieren** win/lose narrowly; **er ist** ~ **fünfzig** he is just this side of fifty; **b)** *(eng)* ~ **sitzen** fit tightly; *(zu eng)* be a tight fit; **c)** *(kurz)* ⟨*reply*⟩ tersely; ⟨*describe, summarize*⟩ succinctly; **Knappheit** die; ~ ~ **a)** *(Mangel)* shortage **(an** + *Dat.* of); **b)** *(Kürze)* *(einer Antwort, eines Grußes)* terseness; *(einer Beschreibung, eines Berichts)* succinctness

**knarren** *itr. V.* creak

**Knast** der; ~[e]s, **Knäste** *od.* ~e *(ugs.)* **a)** *o. Pl. (Strafe)* bird *(sl.);* time; **b)** *(Gefängnis)* clink *(sl.);* prison

**knattern** *itr. V.* clatter; ⟨*sail*⟩ flap; ⟨*radio*⟩ crackle

**Knäuel** der *od.* das; ~s, ~ ball; *(wirres ~)* tangle

**Knauf** der; ~[e]s, **Knäufe** knob; *(eines Schwertes, Dolches)* pommel

**knauserig** *Adj. (ugs. abwertend)* stingy; tight-fisted; **knausern** *itr. V. (ugs. abwertend)* be stingy; skimp

**knautschen** *(ugs.)* 1. *tr. V.* crumple; crease *(dress)*; 2. *itr. V. (dress, material)* crease

**Knebel** der; ~s, ~ a) gag; b) *(Griff)* toggle; **knebeln** *tr. V.* gag

**Knecht** der; ~[e]s, ~e farm-labourer; **knechten** *tr. V. (geh.)* reduce to slavery; enslave; *(unterdrücken)* oppress; **Knechtschaft** die; ~, ~en *(geh.)* bondage; slavery

**kneifen** 1. *unr. tr., itr. V.* pinch; 2. *unr. itr. V.* a) *(clothes)* be too tight; b) *(ugs.: sich drücken)* chicken *(sl.)* out (vor + *Dat.* of); **Kneif·zange** die pincers *pl.*

**Kneipe** die; ~, ~n *(ugs.)* pub *(Brit. coll.)*; bar *(Amer.)*

**kneippen** *itr. V. (ugs.)* take a Kneipp cure; **Kneipp·kur** die Kneipp cure

**kneten** *tr. V.* a) *(bearbeiten)* knead *(dough, muscles)*; work *(clay)*; b) *(formen)* model *(figure)*; **Knet·masse** die Plasticine (P)

**Knick** der; ~[e]s, ~e sharp bend; *(Falz)* crease; **knicken** 1. *tr. V.* a) *(brechen)* snap; b) *(falten)* crease *(page, paper, etc.)*; 2. *itr. V.; mit sein* snap

**Knicks** der; ~es, ~e curtsy; **knicksen** *itr. V.* curtsy (vor + *Dat.* to)

**Knie** das; ~s, ~ ['kni:(ə)] a) knee; b) *(Biegung)* sharp bend

**knie-, Knie-:** ~**beuge** die kneebend; ~**fall** der: einen ~fall tun *od.* machen *(auch fig.)* go down on one's knees (vor + *Dat.* before); ~**kehle** die hollow of the knee

**knien** ['kni:(ə)n] 1. *itr. V.* kneel; 2. *refl. V.* kneel [down]

**Knie-:** ~**scheibe** die kneecap; ~**strumpf** der knee-length sock

**Kniff** der; ~[e]s, ~e a) pinch; b) *(Falte)* crease; c) *(Kunstgriff)* trick

**knipsen** *tr. V.* a) *(entwerten)* clip; punch; b) *(fotografieren)* take a snap[shot] of

**Knirps** der; ~es, ~e a) (Ⓦ *Taschenschirm)* telescopic umbrella; b) *(ugs.: Junge)* nipper *(coll.)*

**knirschen** *itr. V.* crunch; **mit den Zähnen** ~: grind one's teeth

**knistern** *itr. V.* rustle; *(wood, fire)* crackle

**knittern** *tr., itr. V.* crease; crumple

**knobeln** *itr. V. (mit Würfeln)* play dice

**Knob·lauch** der garlic; **Knob·lauch·zehe** die clove of garlic

**Knöchel** der; ~s, ~: ankle; *(am Finger)* knuckle; **Knochen** der; ~s, ~: bone

**knochen-, Knochen-:** ~**bau** der; o. *Pl.* bone structure; ~**bruch** der fracture; ~**hart** *Adj. (ugs.)* rock-hard; ~**mark** das bone marrow

**knochig** *Adj.* bony

**Knödel** der; ~s, ~ *(bes. südd., österr.)* dumpling

**Knolle** die; ~, ~n tuber

**Knopf** der; ~[e]s, **Knöpfe** button; *(Knauf)* knob; **knöpfen** *tr. V.* button [up]; **Knopf·loch** das buttonhole

**Knorpel** der; ~s, ~ *(Anat.)* cartilage; *(im Steak o. ä.)* gristle

**knorrig** *Adj.* gnarled

**Knospe** die; ~, ~n bud; **knospen** *itr. V.* bud

**knoten** *tr. V.* knot; **Knoten** der; ~s, ~: knot; *(Haartracht)* bun; knot; *(Med.)* lump; **Knoten·punkt** der junction; intersection

**knuffen** *tr. V.* poke

**Knüller** der; ~s, ~ *(ugs.)* sensation; *(Angebot, Verkaufsartikel)* sensational offer

**knüpfen** *tr. V.* a) tie (**an** + *Akk.* to); **Bedingungen an etw.** *(Akk.)* ~: attach conditions to sth.; b) *(durch Knoten herstellen)* knot; make *(net)*;

**Knüppel** der; ~s, ~ cudgel; *(Polizei~)* truncheon; **knüppel·dick** *Adv. (ugs.)* **es kam ~dick** it was one disaster after the other; **Knüppel·schaltung** die *(Kfz-W.)* floor[-type] gearchange

**knurren** 1. *itr. V.* a) *(animal)* growl; *(wütend)* snarl; *(fig.)* *(stomach)* rumble; b) *(murren)* grumble (**über** + *Akk.* about)

**knusprig** *Adj.* crisp; crusty *(bread, roll)*

**knutschen** *(ugs.)* 1. *tr. V.* smooch with *(coll.)*; *(sexuell berühren)* pet; **sich** ~: smooch *(coll.)*/pet; 2. *itr. V.* smooch *(coll.)*; *(sich sexuell berühren)* pet

**k. o.** [ka:'|o:] *Adj.; nicht attr.* a) *(Boxen)* jmdn. **k. o. schlagen** knock sb. out; b) *(ugs.: übermüdet)* all in *(coll.)*

**koalieren** *itr. V. (Politik)* form a coalition (**mit** with); **Koalition** die; ~, ~en coalition

**Kobalt** das; ~s *(Chemie)* cobalt

**Kobold** der; ~[e]s, ~e goblin

**Kobra** die; ~, ~s cobra
**Koch** der; ~|e|s, Köche cook; *(Küchenchef)* chef; **Koch·buch** das cookery book *(Brit.)*; cookbook *(Amer.)*; **kochen** 1. *tr. V.* **a)** boil; *(zubereiten)* cook *(meal)*; make ⟨purée, jam⟩; Tee ~: make some tea; **b)** *(waschen)* boil; 2. *itr. V.* **a)** *(Speisen zubereiten)* cook; **b)** *(sieden)* ⟨water, milk, etc.⟩ boil; **Kocher** der; ~s, ~ [small] stove; *(Kochplatte)* hotplate
**Köcher** der; ~s, ~ *(für Pfeile)* quiver
**Köchin** die; ~, ~nen cook
**Koch-**: ~**löffel** der wooden spoon; ~**nische** die kitchenette; ~**topf** der [cooking] pot
**Köder** der; ~s, ~: bait; **ködern** *tr. V.* lure
**Koffein** das; ~s caffeine; **koffeinfrei** *Adj.* decaffeinated
**Koffer** der; ~s, ~: [suit]case
**Koffer-**: ~**kuli** der luggage trolley; ~**radio** das portable radio; ~**raum** der boot *(Brit.)*; trunk *(Amer.)*
**Kognak** ['kɔnjak] der; ~s, ~s brandy; *s. auch* **Cognac**
**Kohl** der; ~|e|s **a)** cabbage; **b)** *(ugs. abwertend: Unsinn)* rubbish; rot *(sl.)*; **Kohl·dampf** der; *o. Pl. (salopp)* |einen| ~ haben be ravenously hungry
**Kohle** die; ~, ~n coal; [1]**kohlen** *itr. V.* smoulder; ⟨wick⟩ smoke
[2]**kohlen** *itr. V. (fam.) (lügen)* tell fibs; *(übertreiben)* exaggerate
**Kohlen-**: ~**grube** die coal-mine; ~**händler** der coal merchant ~**monoxyd** [--'---] das *(Chemie)* carbon monoxide; ~**säure** die carbonic acid; ~**stoff** der; *o. Pl.* carbon
**Kohle·papier** das carbon paper
**Köhler** der; ~s, ~: charcoal burner
**Kohl-**: ~**kopf** der [head of] cabbage; ~**rübe** die swede
**Koitus** der; ~, Koitus *(geh.)* sexual intercourse; coitus *(formal)*
**Koje** die; ~, ~n **a)** *(Seemannsspr.)* bunk; berth; **b)** *(Ausstellungsstand)* stand
**Kokain** das; ~s cocaine
**kokett** 1. *Adj.* coquettish; 2. *adv.* coquettishly
**Kokos·nuß** die coconut
**Koks** der; ~es coke
**Kolben** der; ~s, ~ **a)** *(Technik)* piston; **b)** *(Chemie: Glas~)* flask; **c)** *(Teil des Gewehrs)* butt
**Kolchose** [kɔl'çoːzə] die; ~, ~n kolkhoz; Soviet collective farm
**Kolibri** der; ~s, ~s humming-bird

**Kolik** die; ~, ~en colic
**Kollaborateur** [kɔlabora'tøːɐ̯] der; ~s, ~e collaborator
**Kollaps** der; ~es, ~e collapse
**Kolleg** das; ~s, ~s lecture
**Kollege** der; ~n, ~n colleague; **kollegial** 1. *Adj.* helpful and considerate; 2. *adv.* ⟨act etc.⟩ like a good colleague/good colleagues; **Kollegium** das; ~s, Kollegien **a)** *(Gruppe)* group; *(unmittelbar zusammenarbeitend)* team; **b)** *(Lehrkörper)* [teaching] staff
**Kollekte** die; ~, ~n collection; **Kollektion** [kɔlɛk'tsi̯oːn] die; ~, ~en collection; *(Sortiment)* range; **kollektiv** 1. *Adj.* collective; 2. *adv.* collectively
**kollidieren** *itr. V.* **a)** *mit sein* collide; **b)** *(fig.)* conflict
**Kollier** [kɔ'li̯eː] das; ~s, ~s necklace
**Kollision** die; ~, ~en collision
**Köln (das)**; ~s Cologne; **Kölner** 1. *indekl. Adj.* Cologne attrib.; *(in Köln)* in Cologne postpos., not pred; ⟨suburb, archbishop, mayor, speciality⟩ of Cologne; 2. der; ~s, ~: inhabitant of Cologne; *(von Geburt)* native of Cologne; **Kölnerin** die; ~, ~nen *s.* **Kölner 2**
**Kolonialismus** der; ~: colonialism *no art.*; **Kolonie** die; ~, ~n colony; **kolonisieren** *tr. V.* colonize
**Kolonne** die; ~, ~n column
**Koloß** der; Kolosses, Kolosse *(auch fig. ugs.)* giant; **kolossal** 1. *Adj.* **a)** colossal; gigantic; **b)** *(ugs.: sehr groß)* tremendous *(coll.)*; incredible *(coll.)* ⟨rubbish, nonsense⟩; 2. *adv. (ugs.)* tremendously *(coll.)*
**Kolumbianer** der; ~s, ~: Colombian; **Kolumbien** [ko'lʊmbi̯ən] **(das)**; ~s Colombia
**Kombination** die; ~, ~en **a)** combination; **b)** *(gedankliche Verknüpfung)* deduction; piece of reasoning; **c)** *(Kleidungsstücke)* ensemble; suit; *(Herren~)* suit; **kombinieren** 1. *tr. V.* combine; 2. *itr. V.* deduce; reason
**Kombi-**: ~**wagen** der estate [car]; station wagon *(Amer.)*; ~**zange** die combination pliers *pl.*
**Komet** der; ~en, ~en comet
**Komfort** der; ~s comfort; **komfortabel** 1. *Adj.* comfortable; 2. *adv.* comfortably
**Komik** die; ~: comic effect; *(komisches Element)* comic element; **Komiker** der; ~s, ~ **a)** *(Vortragskünstler)* comedian; **b)** *(Darsteller)* comic actor; **komisch** *Adj.* **a)** comical; funny; **b)** *(seltsam)* funny

**Komitee** das; ~s, ~s committee
**Komma** das; ~s, ~s od. ~ta comma;
*(Math.)* decimal point; **zwei ~ acht**
two point eight
**Kommandant** der; ~en, ~en *(Milit.)*
commanding officer; **Kommandeur**
[kɔman'døːɐ̯] der; ~s, ~e *(Milit.) s.*
Kommandant; **kommandieren** 1. *tr.
V.* **a)** command; be in command of;
order ⟨*retreat, advance*⟩; **b)** *(ugs.)*
**jmdn. ~:** boss sb. about *(coll.)*; 2. *itr.
V. (ugs.)* boss people about *(coll.)*
**Kommandit·gesellschaft** die
*(Wirtsch.)* limited partnership
**Kommando** das; ~s, ~s command
**kommen** *unr. itr. V.; mit sein* **a)** come;
**angelaufen ~:** come running along;
*(auf jmdn. zu)* come running up; **b)**
*(gelangen, geraten)* get; **unter ein Auto
~:** be knocked down by a car; **wie
kommst du darauf?** what gives you
that idea? **c) ~ lassen** *(bestellen)*
order ⟨*taxi*⟩; **den Arzt/die Polizei ~
lassen** send for a doctor/the police; **d)**
*(aufgenommen werden)* **zur Schule/
aufs Gymnasium ~:** start school/
grammar school; **e)** *(auftauchen)*
⟨*seeds, plants*⟩ come up; ⟨*buds,
flowers*⟩ come out; ⟨*teeth*⟩ come
through; **f)** *(seinen festen Platz haben)*
go; belong; **in die Schublade~:** go *or*
belong in the drawer; *(seinen Platz erhalten)* **in die Mannschaft ~:** get into
the team; **auf den ersten Platz ~:** go
into first place; **g)** *(Gelegenheit haben)*
**dazu ~, etw. zu tun** get round to doing
sth.; **h)** *(sich ereignen)* come about;
**wie kommt es, daß ...:** how is it that ...;
**how come that ...** *(coll.)*; **i)** *(etw. erlangen)* **zu Geld ~:** become wealthy; **zu
Erfolg/Ruhm** *usw.* **~:** gain success/
fame *etc.*
**kommend** *Adj.* **a)** *(folgend)* next; **b)**
*(mit großer Zukunft)* der ~e **Mann/
Meister** the coming man/future champion
**Kommentar** der; ~s, ~e commentary; *(Stellungnahme)* comment; **kein
~!** no comment!; **Kommentator**
der; ~s, ~en commentator; **kom-
mentieren** *tr. V.* **a)** *(erläutern)* furnish with a commentary ⟨*text, work*⟩;
**b)** *(Stellung nehmen zu)* comment on
**kommerziell** 1. *Adj.* commercial; 2.
*adv.* commercially
**Kommiß** der; Kommisses *(Soldatenspr.)* army; **Kommissar** der; ~s,
~e **a)** *(Beamter der Polizei)* detective
superintendent; **b)** *(staatlicher Beauf-*

*tragter)* commissioner; **Kommission** die; ~, ~en **a)** *(Gremium)* committee; *(Prüfungs~)* commission; **b) etw.
in ~ nehmen/haben/geben** *(Wirtsch.)*
take/have sth. on commission/give
sth. to a dealer for sale on commission
**Kommode** die; ~, ~n chest of drawers
**kommunal** *Adj.* local; *(bei einer städ-
tischen Gemeinde)* municipal; local;
**Kommunal·wahl** die local [govern-
ment] elections *pl.*; **Kommunikati-
on** ['kɔmunika'tsi̯oːn] die; ~, ~en
*(Sprachw., Soziol.)* communication;
**Kommunion** die; ~, ~en *(kath. Kirche)* [Holy] Communion; **Kommuni-
qué** [kɔmyni'keː] das; ~s, ~s communiqué; **Kommunismus** der; ~:
communism; **Kommunist** der; ~en,
~en communist; **kommunistisch** 1.
*Adj.* communist; 2. *adv.* Communist-
⟨*influenced, led, ruled, etc.*⟩; **kommunizieren** *itr. V.* **a)** *(geh.)* communicate; **b)** *(kath. Kirche)* receive [Holy]
Communion
**Komödiant** der; ~en, ~en *(veralt.)*
actor; player; *(abwertend: Heuchler)*
play-actor; **Komödie** [ko'møːdi̯ə]
die; ~, ~n comedy; *(Theater)* comedy
theatre
**Kompagnon** [kɔmpan'jõː] der; ~s, ~s
*(Wirtsch.)* partner; associate
**kompakt** *Adj.* solid
**Kompanie** die; ~, ~n company
**Komparativ** der; ~s, ~e *(Sprachw.)*
comparative
**Kompaß** der; Kompasses, Kompasse
compass
**kompensieren** *tr. V.* **etw. mit etw.** *od.*
**durch etw. ~:** compensate for sth. by
sth.
**kompetent** *Adj.* competent; **Kom-
petenz** die; ~, ~en competence; *(bes.
Rechtsw.)* authority
**komplett** 1. *Adj.* complete; 2. *adv.*
fully ⟨*furnished, equipped*⟩; *(ugs.: ganz
und gar)* completely
**Komplex** der; ~es, ~e *(auch Psych.)*
complex
**Komplikation** [kɔmplika'tsi̯oːn] die;
~, ~en *(auch Med.)* complication
**Kompliment** das; ~[e]s, ~e compliment
**Komplize** der; ~n, ~n *(abwertend)* accomplice
**komplizieren** *tr. V.* complicate;
**kompliziert** 1. *Adj.* complicated; 2.
*adv.* ~ **aufgebaut sein** have a complicated *or* complex structure

**Komplott** das; ~|e|s, ~e plot; conspiracy

**komponieren** tr., itr. V. compose; **Komponist** der; ~en, ~en composer; **Komposition** [kɔmpozi'tsi̯oːn] die; ~, ~en composition; **Kompost** der; ~|e|s, ~e compost; **Kompott** das; ~|e|s, ~e stewed fruit; compote

**Kompresse** die; ~, ~n (Med.) a) (Umschlag) [wet] compress; b) (Mull) [gauze] pad; **Kompressor** der; ~s, ~en (Technik) compressor

**Kompromiß** der; Kompromisses, Kompromisse compromise

**kompromiß-, Kompromiß-:** ~**bereit** Adj. willing to compromise pred.; ~**los** 1. Adj. uncompromising; 2. adv. uncompromisingly; ~**vorschlag** der compromise proposal

**kompromittieren** tr. V. compromise **Kondensation** [kɔndɛnza'tsi̯oːn] die; ~, ~en (Physik, Chemie) condensation; **Kondensator** der; ~s, ~en (Elektrot.) capacitor; **kondensieren** tr., itr. V. (itr. auch mit sein) (Physik, Chemie) condense

**Kondens-:** ~**milch** die condensed milk; ~**streifen** der condensation trail; ~**wasser** das condensation

**Kondition** [kɔndi'tsi̯oːn] die; ~, ~en condition; **Konditional·satz** der (Sprachw.) conditional clause; **Konditions·training** das fitness training **Konditor** der; ~s, ~en pastry-cook; **Konditorei** die; ~, ~en cake-shop; (Lokal) café

**kondolieren** itr. V. offer one's condolences; jmdm. [zu jmds. Tod] ~: offer one's condolences to sb. [on sb.'s death]

**Kondom** das od. der; ~s, ~e condom **Konfekt** das; ~|e|s a) confectionery; sweets pl. (Brit.); candies pl. (Amer.); b) (bes. südd., österr., schweiz.: Teegebäck) [small] fancy biscuits pl. (Brit.) or (Amer.) cookies pl.

**Konfektion** die; ~, ~en ready-made garments pl.

**Konferenz** die; ~, ~en conference; (Besprechung) meeting; **konferieren** 1. itr. V. confer (über + Akk. on, about)

**Konfession** die; ~, ~en denomination; **konfessionell** 1. Adj.; nicht präd. denominational; 2. adv. as regards denomination; ~ |un|gebunden sein have [no] denominational ties

**Konfetti** das; ~|s| confetti

**Konfirmand** der; ~en, ~en (ev. Rel.) confirmand; **Konfirmation** [kɔnfirma'tsi̯oːn] die; ~, ~en (ev. Rel.) confirmation; **konfirmieren** tr. V. (ev. Rel.) confirm

**konfiszieren** tr. V. (bes. Rechtsw.) confiscate

**Konfitüre** die; ~, ~n jam

**Konflikt** der; ~|e|s, ~e conflict

**Konföderation** die; ~, ~en confederation

**konform** Adj. concurring attrib.; ~ gehen be in agreement; **Konformist** der; ~en, ~en conformist

**Konfrontation** die; ~, ~en confrontation; **konfrontieren** tr. V. confront

**konfus** 1. Adj. confused; 2. adv. in a confused fashion

[1]**Kongo** der; ~|s| (Fluß) Congo; [2]**Kongo** (das); ~s od. der; ~|s| (Staat) the Congo

**Kongreß** der; Kongresses, Kongresse congress; conference; der ~ (USA): Congress; **Kongreß·halle** die conference hall

**König** der; ~s, ~e king; **Königin** die; ~, ~nen queen; **königlich** 1. Adj. a) royal; b) (vornehm) regal; c) (reichlich) princely ⟨gift, salary, wage⟩; 2. adv. ⟨pay⟩ handsomely; (ugs.: außerordentlich) ⟨enjoy oneself⟩ immensely (coll.); **König·reich** das kingdom; **Königs·haus** das royal house; **Königtum** das; ~s, Königtümer a) o. Pl. (Monarchie) monarchy; b) (veralt.: Reich) kingdom

**Konjugation** [kɔnjuga'tsi̯oːn] die; ~, ~en (Sprachw.) conjugation; **konjugieren** tr. V. (Sprachw.) conjugate; **Konjunktion** [kɔnjʊŋk'tsi̯oːn] die; ~, ~en (Sprachw.) conjunction; **Konjunktiv** der; ~s, ~e (Sprachw.) subjunctive; **Konjunktur** die; ~, ~en (Wirtsch.) a) (wirtschaftliche Lage) [level of] economic activity; economy; (Tendenz) economic trend; b) (Hoch~) boom; (Aufschwung) upturn [in the economy]; **konjunkturell** Adj. economic; **Konjunktur·politik** die (Wirtsch.) measures pl. aimed at avoiding violent fluctuations in the economy

**konkav** (Optik) 1. Adj. concave; 2. adv. concavely

**konkret** 1. Adj. concrete; 2. adv. in concrete terms

**Konkurrent** der; ~en, ~en, Konkurrentin die; ~, ~nen (Sport, Wirtsch.)

competitor; **Konkurrenz** die; ~, ~en *(Sport, Wirtsch.)* competition; **konkurrenz·fähig** *Adj.* competitive; **Konkurrenz·kampf** der competition; *(zwischen zwei Menschen)* rivalry; **konkurrieren** *itr. V.* compete; **Konkurs** der; ~es, ~e a) *(Bankrott)* bankruptcy; b) *(gerichtliches Verfahren)* bankruptcy proceedings *pl.*
**können** 1. *unr. Modalverb; 2. Part.* ~ **a)** be able to; **er kann gut reden/tanzen** he is a good talker/dancer; **ich kann nicht schlafen** I cannot *or (coll.)* can't sleep; **kann das explodieren?** could it explode?; **man kann nie wissen** you never know; **es kann sein, daß ...**: it could be that ...; **kann ich Ihnen helfen?** can I help you?; b) *(Grund haben)* du kannst ganz ruhig sein you don't have to worry; **das kann man wohl sagen!** you could well say that; c) *(dürfen)* **kann ich gehen?** can I go?; ~ **wir mit[kommen]?** can we come too?; 2. *unr. tr. V. (beherrschen)* know ⟨language⟩; be able to play ⟨game⟩; **sie kann das [gut]** she can do that [well]; **etw./nichts für etw.**~: be/not be responsible for sth.; 3. *unr. itr. V.* **a)** *(fähig sein)* **er kann nicht anders** there's nothing else he can do; *(es ist seine Art)* he can't help it *(coll.)*; b) *(Zeit haben)* **ich kann heute nicht** I can't today *(coll.)*; c) *(ugs.: Kraft haben)* **kannst du noch [weiter]?** can you go on?; d) *(ugs.: umgehen ~)* **[gut] mit jmdm.** ~: get on [well] with sb.; **Können** das; ~s ability; **Könner** der; ~s, ~: expert; **konnte** *1. u. 3. Pers. Sg. Prät. v.* können; **könnte** *1. u. 3. Pers. Sg. Konjunktiv II v.* können
**konsequent** 1. *Adj.* consistent; *(folgerichtig)* logical; 2. *adv.* consistently; *(folgerichtig)* logically; **Konsequenz** die; ~, ~en a) *(Folge)* consequence; b) *o. Pl. (Unbeirrbarkeit)* determination
**konservativ** 1. *Adj.* conservative; 2. *adv.* conservatively; **Konservative** der/die; *adj. Dekl.* conservative; **Konservatorium** das; ~s, Konservatorien conservatoire; conservatory *(Amer.)*; **Konserve** die; ~, ~n a) *(Büchse)* can; tin *(Brit.)*; b) *(konservierte Lebensmittel)* preserved food; *(in Dosen)* canned *or (Brit.)* tinned food
**Konserven-:** ~**büchse** die, ~**dose** die can; tin *(Brit.)*
**konservieren** *tr. V.* preserve; conserve ⟨work of art⟩; **Konservierung**

die; ~, ~en preservation; **Konservierungs·mittel** das preservative
**konsolidieren** *tr. V.* consolidate
**Konsonant** der; ~en, ~en consonant
**Konsortium** [kɔn'zɔrtsiʊm] das; ~s, Konsortien *(Wirtsch.)* consortium
**konspirativ** [kɔnspira'ti:f] *Adj.* conspiratorial
**konstant** [kɔn'stant] 1. *Adj.* a) constant; b) *(beharrlich)* persistent; 2. *adv.* a) constantly; b) *(beharrlich)* persistently
**Konstellation** [kɔnstɛla'tsio:n] die; ~, ~en a) *(von Parteien usw.)* grouping; *(von Umständen)* combination; b) *(Astron., Astrol.)* constellation
**konstituieren** [kɔnstitu'i:rən] 1. *tr. V. (gründen)* constitute; set up; 2. *refl. V.* be constituted; **Konstitution** [kɔnstitu'tsio:n] die; ~, ~en constitution
**konstruieren** [kɔnstru'i:rən] *tr. V.* a) *(entwerfen)* design; b) *(aufbauen, Geom, Sprachw.)* construct; c) *(abwertend)* fabricate; **Konstrukteur** [kɔnstrʊk'tø:ɐ̯] der; ~s, ~e designer; design engineer; **Konstruktion** [kɔnstrʊk'tsio:n] die; ~, ~en a) *(Aufbau, Geom., Sprachw.)* construction; *(das Entwerfen)* designing; b) *(Entwurf)* design; *(Bau)* construction; **konstruktiv** 1. *Adj.* constructive; 2. *adv.* constructively
**Konsul** der; ~s, ~n *(Dipl., hist.)* consul; **Konsulat** das; ~[e]s, ~e *(Dipl., hist.)* consulate; **konsultieren** *tr. V. (auch fig.)* consult
**Konsum** der; ~s consumption; **Konsument** der; ~en, ~en consumer; **Konsum·gesellschaft** die consumer society; **konsumieren** *tr. V.* consume
**Kontakt** der; ~[e]s, ~e contact; **mit** *od.* **zu jmdm.** ~ **haben/halten** be/remain in contact with sb.
**Kontakt-:** ~**linse** die contact lens; ~**mann** der; *Pl.:* ~**männer** *od.* ~**leute** *(Agent)* contact
**Konten** *s.* Konto
**kontern** *tr., itr. V. (Boxen, auch fig.)* counter; *(Ballspiele)* counter-attack; **Konter·revolution** die counter-revolution
**Kontinent** der; ~[e]s, ~e continent; **kontinental** *Adj.* continental
**Kontingent** das; ~[e]s, ~e quota
**kontinuierlich** 1. *Adj.* steady; 2. *adv.* steadily; **Kontinuität** die; ~: continuity
**Konto** das; ~s, Konten *od.* Konti ac-

count; **ein laufendes** ~: a current account

**Konto-:** ~**aus·zug** der *(Bankw.)* [bank] statement; ~**nummer** die account number

**Kontor** das; ~**s,** ~**e** branch; *(einer Reederei)* office

**Konto·stand** der *(Bankw.)* balance; state of an/one's account

**kontra** 1. *Präp. mit Akk. (Rechtsspr., auch fig.)* versus; 2. *Adv.* against

**Kontra** das; ~**s,** ~**s** *(Kartenspiele)* double; **jmdm.** ~ **geben** *(fig. ugs.)* flatly contradict sb.

**Kontrahent** der; ~**en,** ~**en** adversary; opponent

**konträr** *Adj.* contrary; opposite; **Kontrast** der; ~|**e**|**s,** ~**e** contrast

**Kontroll·abschnitt** der stub; **Kontrolle** die; ~, ~**n** a) *(Überwachung)* surveillance; b) *(Überprüfung)* check; *(bei Waren, bei Lebensmitteln)* inspection; c) *(Herrschaft)* control; **die** ~ **über etw.** *(Akk.)* **verlieren** lose control of sth.; **Kontrolleur** [kɔntrɔ'løːɐ̯] der; ~**s,** ~**e** inspector; **Kontrollgang** der tour of inspection; *(eines Nachtwächters)* round; *(eines Polizisten)* patrol; **kontrollieren** *tr. V.* a) *(überwachen)* check; monitor; b) *(überprüfen)* check; inspect 〈*goods, food*〉; c) *(beherrschen)* control; **Kontrollturm** der control tower

**Kontroverse** [kɔntro'vɛr] die; ~, ~**n** controversy (**um, über** + *Akk.* about)

**Kontur** die; ~, ~**en;** *meist Pl.* contour; outline

**Konvention** [kɔnvɛn'tsi̯oːn] die; ~, ~**en** convention; **konventionell** 1. *Adj.* a) conventional; b) *(förmlich)* formal; 2. *adv.* a) conventionally; b) *(förmlich)* formally

**Konversation** [kɔnvɛrza'tsi̯oːn] die; ~, ~**en** conversation; **Konversations·lexikon das** encyclopaedia

**konvertieren** [kɔnvɛr'tiːrən] *itr. V.; auch mit sein (Rel.)* be converted

**konvex** [kɔn'vɛks] *(Optik)* 1. *Adj.* convex; 2. *adv.* convexly

**Konvoi** [kɔn'vɔ̯y] der; ~**s,** ~**s** *(bes. Milit.)* convoy

**Konzentration** [kɔntsɛntra'tsi̯oːn] die; ~, ~**en** concentration

**Konzentrations-:** ~**fähigkeit** die; *o. Pl.* ability to concentrate; ~**lager** das *(bes. ns.)* concentration camp

**konzentrieren** 1. *refl., tr. V.* concentrate; **sich auf etw.** *(Akk.)* ~: concentrate on sth.; **konzentriert** 1. *Adj.*

concentrated; 2. *adv.* with concentration

**Konzept** das; ~|**e**|**s,** ~**e** a) [rough] draft; b) *(Programm)* programme; *(Plan)* plan

**Konzern** der; ~|**e**|**s,** ~**e** *(Wirtsch.)* group [of companies]

**Konzert** das; ~|**e**|**s,** ~**e** a) *(Komposition)* concerto; b) *(Veranstaltung)* concert; **Konzert·saal** der concert-hall

**Konzession** die; ~, ~**en** a) *(Amtsspr.)* licence; b) *(Zugeständnis)* concession

**Konzil** das; ~**s,** ~**e** od. ~**ien** *(kath. Kirche)* council

**konzipieren** *tr. V.* draft; design 〈*device, car, etc.*〉

**kooperativ** 1. *Adj.* co-operative; 2. *adv.* co-operatively; **kooperieren** *tr. V.* co-operate

**Koordinate** die; ~, ~**n** coordinate; **Koordinaten·system das** *(Math.)* system of coordinates; **koordinieren** *tr. V.* coordinate

**Kopenhagen (das);** ~**s** Copenhagen

**Kopf** der; ~|**e**|**s,** **Köpfe** a) head; **ein** ~ **Salat** a lettuce; ~ **an** ~: shoulder to shoulder; *(im Wettlauf)* neck and neck; *(fig.)* **nicht wissen, wo einem der** ~ **steht** not know whether one is coming or going; ~ **hoch!** chin up!; **den** ~ **hängen lassen** become disheartened; b) *(Person)* person; **ein kluger/fähiger** ~ **sein** be a clever/able man/woman; **pro** ~: per head; **die führenden Köpfe der Wirtschaft** the leading minds in the field of economics; c) *(Wille)* **seinen** ~ **durchsetzen** make sb. do what one wants; d) *(Verstand)* mind; head; **sich** *(Dat.)* **den** ~ **zerbrechen** *(ugs.)* rack one's brains (**über** + *Akk.* over)

**Kopf-:** ~**bahn·hof** der terminal station; ~**bedeckung die** headgear; **ohne** ~**bedeckung** without anything on one's head

**Köpfchen** das; ~**s,** ~: brains *pl.;* ~ **muß man haben** you've got to have it up here *(coll.);* **köpfen** *tr. V.* a) decapitate; *(hinrichten)* behead; b) *(Fußball)* head

**Kopf-:** ~**ende** das head end; ~**haut die** [skin of the] scalp; ~**hörer** der headphones *pl.;* ~**kissen das** pillow; ~**lastig** *Adj.* down by the head *pred.;* ~**los** 1. *Adj.* rash; *(in Panik)* panic-stricken; 2. *adv.* rashly; ~**los davonrennen** flee in panic; ~**rechnen** *itr. V.; nur im Inf. gebr.* do mental arithmetic; ~**rechnen das** mental arithmetic; ~**salat** der head lettuce;

~**schmerz** der; *meist Pl.* headache; ~**schmerzen haben** have a headache *sing.; ~***sprung*** der header; ~**stand** der headstand; ~|**stehen** *unr. itr. V. (ugs.: überrascht sein)* be bowled over; ~**stein·pflaster das** cobblestones *pl.; ~***tuch*** das headscarf; ~**weh das;** *o. Pl. (ugs.)* headache; ~**weh haben** have a headache; ~**zerbrechen das;** ~**s:** etw. bereitet *od.* macht jmdm. ~**zerbrechen** sb. has to rack his/her brains about sth.; *(etw. macht jmdm. Sorgen)* sth. is a worry to sb.

**Kopie** die; ~, ~**n** copy; *(Durchschrift)* carbon copy; *(Fotokopie)* photocopy; *(Fot., Film)* print; **kopieren** *tr. V.* copy; *(fotokopieren)* photocopy; *(Fot., Film)* print; **Kopier·gerät das** photocopier

¹**Koppel das;** ~**s,** ~, *österr.:* die; ~, ~**n** *(Gürtel)* [leather] belt *(as part of a uniform);* ²**Koppel die;** ~, ~**n** paddock

**koppeln** *tr. V.* couple (an + *Akk.* to); dock ⟨*spacecraft*⟩

**Koppelung** *s.* Kopplung; **Kopplung die;** ~, ~**en** coupling; *(Raumf.)* docking

**kopulieren** *itr. V.* copulate

**Koralle** die; ~, ~**n** coral

**Koran** der; ~**s,** ~**e** Koran

**Korb** der; ~**es,** Körbe **a)** basket; **b)** jmdm. einen ~ geben turn sb. down; **Korb·ball der;** *o. Pl.* netball

**Kord** der; ~|**e**|**s a)** corduroy; cord; **b)** *s.* Kordsamt

**Kordel** die; ~, ~**n** cord

**Kord·samt** der cord velvet

**Korea** (das); ~**s** Korea; **Koreaner** der; ~**s,** ~: Korean; **koreanisch** *Adj.* Korean

**Korinthe** die; ~, ~**n** currant

**Kork** der; ~**s,** ~**e** cork; **Korken der;** ~**s,** ~: cork; **Korken·zieher der** corkscrew

¹**Korn das;** ~|**e**|**s,** Körner **a)** *(Frucht)* grain; *(Getreide~)* grain [of corn]; *(Pfeffer~)* corn; **b)** *o. Pl. (Getreide)* corn; grain; **c)** *(Salz~, Sand~)* grain; *(Hagel~)* stone; ²**Korn der;** ~|**e**|**s,** ~ *(ugs.)* corn·schnapps; corn liquor *(Amer.);* **Korn·blume** die cornflower; **Körnchen das;** ~**s,** ~: tiny grain; *(von Sand usw.)* [tiny] grain; granule; **Körner** *s.* Korn; **Korn·feld das** cornfield; **körnig** *Adj.* granular

**Korona** die; ~, Koronen crowd *(coll.)*

**Körper** der; ~**s,** ~: body

**körper-, Körper-:** ~**bau** der; *o. Pl.* physique; ~**behindert** *Adj.* physic-

ally handicapped; ~**behinderte** der/die physically handicapped person; ~**behinderte** *Pl.* physically handicapped people; ~**geruch** der body odour; BO *(coll.);* ~**größe** die height **körperlich** 1. *Adj.* physical; 2. *adv.* physically

**Körper-:** ~**pflege** die body care *no art.;* ~**spray** der *od.* das deodorant spray; ~**teil** der part of the/one's body; ~**verletzung** die *(Rechtsw.)* bodily harm *no indef. art.*

**Korps** [koːɐ̯] **das;** ~ [koːɐ̯(s)], ~ [koːɐ̯s] **a)** *(Milit.)* corps; **b)** *(Studentenverbindung)* student duelling society

**korpulent** *Adj.* corpulent

**korrekt** 1. *Adj.* correct; 2. *adv.* correctly; **korrekter·weise** *Adv.* to be [strictly] correct; **Korrektheit die;** ~: correctness; **Korrektor** der; ~**s,** ~**en** [-ˈtoːrən] proof-reader; **Korrektur** die; ~, ~**en** correction

**Korrespondent** der; ~**en,** ~**en** correspondent; **Korrespondenz die;** ~, ~**en** correspondence; **korrespondieren** *itr. V.* correspond (mit with)

**Korridor** der; ~**s,** ~**e** corridor

**korrigieren** *tr. V.* correct; revise ⟨*opinion, view*⟩

**korrupt** *Adj.* corrupt; **Korruption** [kɔrʊpˈtsi̯oːn] **die;** ~, ~**en** corruption

**Korsett das;** ~**s,** ~**s** *od.* ~**e** corset

**Korsika** (das); ~**s** Corsica

**koscher** *Adj.* kosher

**Kose-:** ~**form** die familiar form; ~**name** der pet name

**Kosinus** der; ~, ~ *od.* ~**se** *(Math.)* cosine

**Kosmetik** die; ~ **a)** beauty culture *no art.;* **b)** *(fig.)* cosmetic procedures *pl.;* **Kosmetikerin** die; ~, ~**nen** cosmetician; beautician; **kosmetisch** 1. *Adj. (auch fig.)* cosmetic; 2. *adv.* jmdn. ~ beraten give sb. advice on beauty care; sich ~ behandeln lassen have beauty treatment

**kosmisch** *Adj.* cosmic ⟨*ray, dust, etc.*⟩; space ⟨*age, station, research, etc.*⟩; meteoric ⟨*iron*⟩; **Kosmos** der; ~: cosmos

**Kost** die; ~: food; ~ **und Logis** board and lodging

**kostbar** 1. *Adj.* valuable; precious ⟨*time*⟩; 2. *adv.* expensively ⟨*dressed*⟩; luxuriously ⟨*decorated*⟩; **Kostbarkeit** die; ~, ~**en a)** *(Sache)* treasure; **b)** *o. Pl. (Eigenschaft)* value

¹**kosten** 1. *tr. V.* **a)** taste; try; 2. *itr. V. (probieren)* have a taste

²**kosten** *tr. V.* **a)** cost; **b)** *(erfordern)* take; cost ⟨*lives*⟩; **Kosten** *Pl.* cost *sing.*; costs; *(Auslagen)* expenses; *(Rechtsw.)* costs

**kosten-, Kosten-: ~deckend** *Adj.* that covers/cover [one's] costs *postpos., not pred.;* **~erstattung** die reimbursement of costs; **~los 1.** *Adj.* free; **2.** *adv.* free of charge; **~pflichtig** *(Rechtsw.)* **1.** *Adj.* eine **~pflichtige Verwarnung** a fine and a caution; **2.** *adv.* eine Klage **~pflichtig abweisen** dismiss a case with costs; ein Auto **~pflichtig abschleppen** tow a car away at the owner's expense; **~voran·schlag** der estimate

**Kost·geld** das payment for [one's] board

**köstlich 1.** *Adj.* delicious; *(unterhaltsam)* delightful; **2.** *adv.* ⟨*taste*⟩ delicious; **sich ~ amüsieren/unterhalten** enjoy oneself enormously *(coll.);* **Köstlichkeit** die; **~, ~en** *(Sache)* delicacy

**Kost·probe** die; **~, ~n** taste

**kost·spielig** *Adj.* costly

**Kostüm** das; **~s, ~e a)** suit; **b)** *(Theater~, Verkleidung)* costume; **kostümieren** *tr. V.* dress up

**Kot** der; **~[e]s, ~e** excrement

**Kotangens** der; **~, ~** *(Math.)* cotangent

**Kotelett** [kɔt'lɛt] das; **~s, ~s** chop; *(vom Nacken)* cutlet; **Koteletten** *Pl.* side-whiskers

**Köter** der; **~s, ~** *(abwertend)* cur

**Kot·flügel** der *(Kfz-W.)* wing

**kotzen** *itr. V. (derb)* puke *(coarse)*

**KP** [ka:'pe:] *Abk.* Kommunistische Partei CP

**Krabbe** die; **~, ~n a)** *(Zool.)* crab; **b)** *(ugs.: Garnele)* shrimp; *(größer)* prawn; **krabbeln 1.** *itr. V.; mit sein* crawl; **2.** *tr. V. (ugs.: kraulen)* tickle

**Krach** der; **~[e]s, Kräche a)** *o. Pl. (Lärm)* noise; row; **b)** *(lautes Geräusch)* crash; **c)** *(ugs.: Streit)* row; **krachen 1.** *itr. V.* **a)** *(Krach auslösen)* ⟨*thunder*⟩ crash; ⟨*shot*⟩ ring out; **b)** *mit sein (ugs.: bersten)* ⟨*ice*⟩ crack; ⟨*bed*⟩ collapse; **c)** *mit sein (ugs.: mit Krach auftreffen)* crash; **2.** *refl. V. (ugs.)* row *(coll.);* **krächzen** *itr. V.* ⟨*raven, crow*⟩ caw; ⟨*parrot*⟩ squawk; ⟨*person*⟩ croak

**kraft** *Präp. + Gen. (Amtsspr.)* **~ [meines]** Amtes by virtue of my office; **~ Gesetzes** by law; **Kraft** die; **~, Kräfte** strength; *(Wirksamkeit)* power; *(Physik)* force; *(Arbeits~)* employee; **mit**

**letzter ~:** with one's last ounce of strength; **aus eigener ~:** by one's own efforts; **mit vereinten Kräften werden wir ...:** if we join forces *or* combine our efforts we will ...; **außer ~ setzen** repeal ⟨*law*⟩; countermand ⟨*order*⟩; **außer ~ sein/treten** no longer be/cease to be in force; **in ~ treten/sein/bleiben** come into/be in/remain in force

**Kraft-: ~aufwand** der effort; **~brühe** die strong meat broth; **~fahrer** der driver; motorist; **~fahrzeug** das motor vehicle

**Kraftfahrzeug-: ~brief** der vehicle registration document; log-book *(Brit.);* **~schein** der vehicle registration document; **~steuer** die vehicle tax

**kräftig 1.** *Adj.* strong; vigorous ⟨*plant, shoot*⟩; powerful, hefty ⟨*blow, kick, etc.*⟩; nourishing ⟨*soup, bread, meal, etc.*⟩; **2.** *adv.* powerfully ⟨*built*⟩; ⟨*rain, snow*⟩ heavily; ⟨*eat*⟩ heartily; **kräftigen** *tr. V.* ⟨*holiday, air, etc.*⟩ invigorate; ⟨*food etc.*⟩ fortify

**kraft-, Kraft-: ~meier** der; **~s, ~** *(ugs.: abwertend)* muscleman; **~probe** die trial of strength; **~rad** das *(Amtsspr.)* motorcycle; **~stoff** der *(Kfz-W.)* fuel; **~stoff·verbrauch** der fuel consumption; **~voll 1.** *Adj.* powerful; **2.** *adv.* powerfully; **~wagen** der motor vehicle; **~werk** das power station

**Kragen** der; **~s, ~, südd., österr. u. schweiz. auch: Krägen** collar; **Kragen·weite** die collar size

**Krähe** ['krɛ:ə] die; **~, ~n** crow; **krähen** *itr. V. (auch fig.)* crow; **Krähen·füße** *Pl. (ugs.)* crow's feet

**krakeelen** *itr. V. (ugs.)* kick up a row *(coll.)*

**krakeln** *tr., itr. V. (ugs.)* scrawl; **kraklig** *Adj. (ugs. abwertend)* scrawly

**Kralle** die; **~, ~n** claw; **krallen 1.** *refl. V.* **sich an etw. (Akk.) ~** ⟨*cat*⟩ dig its claws into sth.; ⟨*person*⟩ clutch sth. [tightly]; **2.** *tr. V. (fest greifen)* **die Finger in/um etw. (Akk.) ~:** dig one's fingers into sth./clutch sth. [tightly] with one's fingers

**Kram** der; **~[e]s *(ugs.)* a)** stuff; *(Gerümpel)* junk; **b)** *(Angelegenheit)* affair; **kramen 1.** *itr. V.* **in etw. (Dat.) ~:** rummage about in sth.; **2.** *tr. V. (ugs.)* **etw. aus etw. ~:** fish *(coll.)* sth. out of sth.; **Krämer** der; **~s, ~:** grocer; **Kram·laden** der *(ugs. abwertend)* junk shop

**Krampf** der; ~|e|s, Krämpfe a) cramp; *(Zuckung)* spasm; b) *o. Pl.* painful strain; *(sinnloses Tun)* senseless waste of effort; **Krampf·ader** die varicose vein; **krampfhaft 1.** *Adj.* convulsive; *(verbissen)* desperate; 2. *adv.* convulsively; *(verbissen)* desperately

**Kran** der; ~|e|s, Kräne a) crane; b) *(südwestd.: Wasserhahn)* tap; faucet *(Amer.)*

**Kranich** der; ~s, ~e crane

**krank;** kränker, kränkst... *Adj.* ill *usu. pred.;* sick; bad ⟨*leg, tooth*⟩; diseased ⟨*plant, organ*⟩; *(fig.)* ailing ⟨*economy, business*⟩; ~ werden be taken ill; jmdn. ~ schreiben give sb. a medical certificate; **Kranke** der/die; *adj. Dekl.* sick man/woman; *(Patient)* patient; **kränkeln** *itr. V.* be in poor health; **kränken** *tr. V.* jmdn. ~: hurt sb. *or* sb.'s feelings

**Kranken-:** ~**geld** das sickness benefit; ~**haus** das hospital; ~**kasse** die health insurance scheme; *(Körperschaft)* health insurance institution; *(privat)* health insurance company; ~**pfleger** der male nurse; ~**schein** der health insurance certificate; ~**schwester** die nurse; ~**versicherung** die a) *(Versicherung)* health insurance; b) *(Unternehmen)* health insurance company; ~**wagen** der ambulance

**krank|feiern** *itr. V. (ugs.)* skive off work *(sl.)* [pretending to be ill]; **kränker** s. krank; **krankhaft 1.** *Adj.* pathological; morbid ⟨*growth, state, swelling, etc.*⟩; 2. *adv.* pathologically; morbidly ⟨*swollen, sensitive*⟩; **Krankheit** die; ~, ~en a) illness; *(bestimmte Art, von Pflanzen, Organen)* disease; b) *o. Pl. (Zeit des Krankseins)* illness; **Krankheits·erreger** der pathogen; **kränklich** *Adj.* ailing; **kränkst...** s. krank; **Kränkung** die; ~, ~en: eine ~: an injury to one's/sb.'s feelings

**Kranz** der; ~es, Kränze wreath; garland; *(auf einem Grab usw.)* wreath; **Kränzchen** das; ~s, ~: coffee circle; coffee klatch *(Amer.)*

**Krapfen** der; ~s, ~: doughnut

**kraß 1.** *Adj.* blatant ⟨*case*⟩; flagrant ⟨*injustice*⟩; stark ⟨*contrast*⟩; complete ⟨*contradiction*⟩; sharp ⟨*difference*⟩; out-and-out ⟨*egoist*⟩; 2. *adv.* sich ~ ausdrücken put sth. bluntly; sich von etw. ~ unterscheiden be in stark contrast to sth.

**Krater** der; ~s, ~: crater

**Kratz·bürste** die *(ugs. scherzh.)* prickly so-and-so; **kratzen 1.** *tr. V.* scratch; *(entfernen)* scrape; 2. *itr. V.* a) scratch; b) *(jucken)* itch; **Kratzer** der; ~s, ~ *(ugs.)* scratch; **kratzig** *Adj.* itchy ⟨*material*⟩

**Kraul** das; ~s *(Sport)* crawl; ¹**kraulen 1.** *itr. V.* do the crawl; 2. *tr. V.; auch mit sein* eine Strecke ~: cover a distance using the crawl

²**kraulen** *tr. V.* jmdm. das Kinn ~: tickle sb. under the chin; jmdn. in den Haaren ~: run one's fingers through sb.'s hair

**kraus** *Adj.* creased ⟨*skirt etc.*⟩; frizzy ⟨*hair*⟩; **Krause** die; ~, ~n *(Kragen)* ruff; *(am Ärmel)* ruffle

**kräuseln 1.** *tr. V.* ruffle ⟨*water, surface*⟩; gather ⟨*material etc.*⟩; frizz ⟨*hair*⟩; 2. *refl. V.* ⟨*hair*⟩ go frizzy; ⟨*water*⟩ ripple; ⟨*smoke*⟩ curl up

**Kraut** das; ~|e|s, Kräuter a) herb; b) *o. Pl. (bes. südd., österr.: Kohl)* cabbage

**Krawall** der; ~s, ~e a) riot; b) *o. Pl. (ugs.: Lärm)* row *(coll.)*

**Krawatte** die; ~, ~n tie

**kreativ 1.** *Adj.* creative; 2. *adv.* ~ veranlagt sein have a creative bent

**Kreatur** die; ~, ~en creature

**Krebs** der; ~es, ~e a) crustacean; *(Fluß~)* crayfish; *(Krabbe)* crab; b) *(Krankheit)* cancer

**krebs-, Krebs-:** ~**erregend,** ~**erzeugend** *Adj.* carcinogenic; ~**krank** *Adj.* ~**krank** sein have cancer; ~**rot** *Adj.* as red as a lobster *postpos.*

**Kredit** der; ~|e|s, ~e credit; *(Darlehen)* loan; **Kredit·karte** die credit card; mit ~karte bezahlen pay by credit card; **kredit·würdig** *Adj.* *(Finanzw.)* credit-worthy

**Kreide** die; ~, ~n chalk; **kreidebleich** *Adj.* as white as a sheet *postpos.;* **Kreide·felsen** der chalk cliff

**kreieren** [kre'i:rən] *tr. V.* create

**Kreis** der; ~es, ~e circle; *(Verwaltungsbezirk)* district; *(Wahl~)* ward; **Kreis·bahn** die orbit

**kreischen** *itr. V.* screech; ⟨*door*⟩ creak

**Kreisel** der; ~s, ~ *(Kinderspielzeug)* top; *(ugs.: Kreisverkehr)* roundabout; **kreisen** *itr. V.; auch mit sein* ⟨*planet*⟩ revolve (um around); ⟨*satellite etc.*⟩ orbit; ⟨*aircraft, bird*⟩ circle

**kreis-, Kreis-:** ~**förmig** *Adj.* circular; ~**lauf** der *(Physiol.)* circulation; *(der Natur, des Lebens usw.)* cycle;

~lauf·störungen *Pl.* *(Med.)* circulatory trouble *sing.;* ~rund *Adj.* [perfectly] round; ~säge die circular saw
**Kreiß·saal** der *(Med.)* delivery room
**Kreis-:** ~stadt die chief town of a/the district; ~verkehr der roundabout
**Krem** die; ~, ~s *s.* Creme
**Krematorium** das; ~s, Krematorien crematorium
**kremig** *s.* cremig
**Krempe** die; ~, ~n brim
**Krempel** der; ~s *(ugs. abwertend)* stuff; *(Gerümpel)* junk
**krepieren** *itr. V.; mit sein (salopp)* ⟨*person*⟩ snuff it *(sl.)*
**Krepp** der; ~s, ~s *od.* ~e crêpe
**Kresse** die; ~, ~n *(Bot.)* cress
**Kreta (das)** ~s Crete
**Kreuz** das; ~es, ~e a) cross; *(Kreuzzeichen)* sign of the cross; b) *(Teil des Rückens)* small of the back; jmdn. aufs ~ legen *(salopp)* take sb. for a ride *(sl.);* c) *o. Art., o. Pl. (Kartenspiel) (Farbe)* clubs *pl.;* *(Karte)* club; d) *(Autobahn)* interchange; e) *(Musik)* sharp;
**kreuzen** 1. *tr. V. (auch Biol.)* cross; 2. *refl. V.* a) *(überschneiden)* cross; b) *(zuwiderlaufen)* clash (mit with); 3. *itr. V.; mit haben od. sein (fahren)* cruise
**Kreuz-:** ~fahrer der *(hist.)* crusader; ~fahrt die cruise; ~feuer das *(Milit., auch fig.)* cross-fire; ~gang der cloister
**kreuzigen** *tr. V.* crucify; **Kreuzigung** die; ~, ~en crucifixion
**Kreuz-:** ~otter die adder; [common] viper; ~ritter der *(hist.)* crusader; ~schmerzen *Pl.* pain *sing.* in the small of the back
**Kreuzung** die; ~, ~en a) crossroads *sing.;* b) *(Biol.)* crossing; cross-breeding; *(Ergebnis)* cross
**kreuz-, Kreuz-:** ~verhör das cross-examination; ~weise crosswise; ~wort·rätsel das crossword [puzzle]; ~zug der *(hist., fig.)* crusade
**kribbelig** *Adj. (ugs.) (vor Ungeduld)* fidgety; *(nervös)* edgy; **kribbeln** *itr. V. (jucken)* tickle; *(prickeln)* tingle
**kriechen** *unr. itr. V.* a) *mit sein* ⟨*insect, baby*⟩ crawl; ⟨*plant*⟩ creep; ⟨*person, animal*⟩ creep, crawl; b) *auch mit sein (fig. abwertend)* crawl (vor + *Dat.* to); **Kriecher** der; ~s, ~ *(abwertend)* crawler; **Kriech·spur** die *(Verkehrsw.)* crawler lane
**Krieg** der; ~[e]s, ~e war
**kriegen** *tr. V. (ugs.)* get; *(erreichen)* catch ⟨*train, bus, etc.*⟩

**Krieger** der; ~s, ~: warrior; **kriegerisch** *Adj.* a) *(kampflustig)* warlike; b) *(militärisch)* military; eine ~e Auseinandersetzung an armed conflict
**kriegs-, Kriegs-:** ~beil das tomahawk; das ~beil begraben *(scherzh.)* bury the hatchet; ~bemalung die *(Völkerk.)* war-paint; ~beschädigt *Adj.* war-disabled; ~beschädigte der/die war invalid; ~dienst der a) *(im Krieg)* active service; b) *(Wehrdienst)* military service; den ~dienst verweigern be a conscientious objector; ~dienst·verweigerer der conscientious objector; ~erklärung die declaration of war; ~gefangene der prisoner of war; POW; ~gefangenschaft die captivity; ~schiff das warship; ~verbrechen das *(Rechtsw.)* war crime
**Krimi** der; ~[s], ~[s] *(ugs.)* crime thriller; **Kriminal·beamte** der [plain-clothes] detective; **Kriminalität** die; ~: crime *no art.*
**Kriminal-:** ~polizei die criminal investigation department; ~roman der crime novel; *(mit Detektiv als Held)* detective novel
**kriminell** 1. *Adj.* criminal; 2. *adv.* ~ veranlagt sein have criminal tendencies; ~ handeln act illegally; **Kriminelle** der/die; *adj. Dekl.* criminal
**Krimskrams** der; ~[es] *(ugs.)* stuff
**Kringel** der; ~s, ~ *(Kreis)* [small] ring; *(Kritzelei)* round squiggle; *(Gebäck)* [ring-shaped] biscuit; **kringeln** *refl. V.* curl [up]; ⟨*hair*⟩ go curly; sich ~ [vor Lachen] *(ugs.)* kill oneself [laughing] *(coll.)*
**Kripo** die; ~ *(ugs.)* die ~: ≈ the CID
**Krippe** die; ~, ~n a) *(Futtertrog)* manger; crib; b) *(Weihnachts~)* model of a nativity scene; c) *(Kinder~)* crèche
**Krise** die; ~, ~n *(auch Med.)* crisis; **kriseln** *itr. V. (unpers.)* es kriselt in ihrer Ehe/in der Partei their marriage is in trouble/the party is in a state of crisis; **Krisen·herd** der trouble spot
[1]**Kristall** der; ~s, ~e crystal; [2]**Kristall** das; ~s crystal *no indef. art.*
**Kriterium** das; ~s, Kriterien criterion
**Kritik** die; ~, ~en a) criticism *no indef. art.* (an + *Dat.* of); an jmdm./etw. ~ üben criticize sb./sth.; b) *(Besprechung)* review; **Kritiker** der; ~s, ~: critic; **kritik·los** 1. *Adj.* uncritical; 2. *adv.* uncritically; **kritisch** 1. *Adj.* critical; 2. *adv.* critically; **kritisieren**

*tr. V.* criticize; review ⟨*book, play, etc.*⟩
**kritzeln 1.** *itr. V. (schreiben)* scribble; *(zeichnen)* doodle; **2.** *tr. V.* scribble
**Kroatien** [kro'a:tsiən] *(das)*; ~s Croatia; **kroatisch** *Adj.* Croatian
**kroch** *1. u. 3. Pers. Sg. Prät. v.* **kriechen**
**Krokant** der; ~s praline
**Krokette** die; ~, ~n *(Kochk.)* croquette
**Krokodil** das; ~s, ~e crocodile; **Krokodils·tränen** *Pl. (ugs.)* crocodile tears
**Krokus** der; ~, ~ *od.* ~se crocus
**Krone** die; ~, ~n crown; *(eines Baumes)* top; crown; *(einer Welle)* crest; **die ~ der Schöpfung** the pride of creation; **krönen** *tr. V. (auch fig.)* crown; **Kronen·korken** der crown cork
**Kron-**: ~**juwel das** *od.* der; *meist Pl.* die ~juwelen the crown jewels; ~**leuchter** der chandelier; ~**prinz** der crown prince
**Krönung** die; ~, ~en coronation; *(fig.)* culmination; **Kron·zeuge** der *(Rechtsw.)* person who turns Queen's/King's evidence; **als ~ auftreten** turn Queen's/King's evidence
**Kropf** der; ~|e|s, **Kröpfe** *(Med.)* goitre
**Kröte** die; ~, ~n **a)** toad; **b)** *Pl. (salopp: Geld)* **ein paar/eine ganze Menge ~n verdienen** earn a few bob *(Brit. sl.)*/a fair old whack *(sl.)*
**Krücke** die; ~, ~n crutch; **Krückstock** der walking-stick
**Krug** der; ~|e|s, **Krüge** jug; *(größer)* pitcher; *(Bier~)* mug
**Krume** die; ~, ~n crumb; **Krümel** der; ~s, ~: crumb; **krümeln** *itr. V.* **a)** crumble; **b)** *(Krümel machen)* make crumbs
**krumm 1.** *Adj.* **a)** bent ⟨*nail, back*⟩; crooked ⟨*stick, branch, etc.*⟩; bandy ⟨*legs*⟩; **b)** *nicht präd. (ugs.: unrechtmäßig)* crooked; **2.** *adv.* crookedly; **krümmen 1.** *tr. V.* bend; **2.** *refl. V.* **a)** *(sich winden)* writhe; **b)** *(krumm verlaufen)* ⟨*road, path, river*⟩ bend
**krumm-**: ~|**lachen** *refl. V. (ugs.)* **sich über etw.** *(Akk.)* ~**lachen** fall about laughing over sth.; ~|**nehmen** *unr. tr. V. (ugs.)* **etw.** ~**nehmen** take sth. the wrong way
**Krümmung** die; ~, ~en bend
**Krüppel** der; ~s, ~: cripple
**Kruste** die; ~, ~n crust; *(vom Braten)* crisp

**Kruzifix** das; ~es, ~e crucifix
**Krypta** die; ~, **Krypten** *(Archit.)* crypt
**Kuba** *(das)*; ~s Cuba; **Kubaner** der; ~s, ~: Cuban
**Kübel** der; ~s, ~: pail
**Kubik-** cubic ⟨*metre, foot, etc.*⟩
**Küche** die; ~, ~n kitchen; *(Einrichtung)* kitchen furniture *no indef. art.*; *(Kochk.)* cooking; cuisine; **kalte/warme ~**: cold/hot food
**Kuchen** der; ~s, ~: cake; *(Obst~)* flan; *(Torte)* gateau
**Kuchen-**: ~**form** die cake-tin; ~**gabel** die pastry-fork
**Küchen·gerät** das kitchen utensil; *(als Kollektivum)* kitchen utensils *pl.*
**Kuckuck** der; ~s, ~e **a)** cuckoo; **zum ~ |noch mal|!** *(salopp)* for crying out loud! *(coll.)*; **b)** *(scherzh.: Pfandsiegel)* bailiff's seal *(placed on distrained goods)*; **Kuckucks·uhr** die cuckoo clock
**Kufe** die; ~, ~n runner; *(von Flugzeugen, Hubschraubern)* skid
**Kugel** die; ~, ~n **a)** ball; *(Geom.)* sphere; *(Kegeln)* bowl; *(beim Kugelstoßen)* shot; **b)** *(ugs.: Geschoß)* bullet; **Kugel·lager das** *(Technik)* ball-bearing; **kugeln** *tr. V.* roll; **2.** *refl. V.* **sich |vor Lachen| ~** *(ugs.)* double *or* roll up |laughing|
**kugel-, Kugel-**: ~**rund** [-'-'-] *Adj.* round as a ball *postpos.*; *(scherzh.: dick)* rotund; tubby; ~**schreiber** der ball-pen; Biro (P); ~**sicher** *Adj.* bullet-proof; ~**stoßen das** ~s shot[-put]; *(Disziplin)* putting the shot *no art.*
**Kuh** die; ~, **Kühe** cow
**Kuh-**: ~**fladen** der cow-pat; ~**haut** die: **das geht auf keine ~haut** *(fig. salopp)* it's absolutely staggering
**kühl 1.** *Adj.* cool; **etw.** ~ **lagern** keep sth. in a cool place; **2.** *adv.* coolly
**Kuhle** die; ~, ~n *(ugs.)* hollow
**Kühle** die; ~: coolness
**kühlen** *tr. V.* cool; chill ⟨*wine*⟩; refrigerate ⟨*food*⟩; **2.** *itr. V.* ⟨*cold compress, ointment, breeze, etc.*⟩ have a cooling effect; **Kühler** der; ~s, ~ **a)** *(am Auto)* radiator; *(~haube)* bonnet *(Brit.)*; hood *(Amer.)*; **b)** *(Sekt~)* ice-bucket; **Kühler·haube** die bonnet *(Brit.)*; hood *(Amer.)*
**Kühl-**: ~**schrank** der refrigerator; fridge *(Brit. coll.)*; icebox *(Amer.)*; ~**truhe** die |chest| freezer; *(im Lebensmittelgeschäft)* freezer |cabinet|
**Kühlung** die; ~, ~en cooling; *(Vor-*

*richtung)* cooling system; *(für Lebensmittel)* refrigeration system; **Kühl·wasser das** cooling water
**kühn 1.** *Adj.* bold; *(dreist)* audacious; **2.** *adv.* boldly; *(gewagt)* daringly; *(dreist)* audaciously; **Kühnheit die; ~:** boldness; *(Gewagtheit)* daringness; *(Dreistigkeit)* audacity
**Kuh·stall der** cowshed
**Küken das; ~s, ~:** chick
**kulant** *Adj.* obliging; fair ⟨*terms*⟩; **Kulanz die; ~:** willingness to oblige
**Kuli der; ~s, ~s a)** coolie; **b)** *(ugs.)* ball-point; Biro **(P)**
**kulinarisch** *Adj.* culinary
**Kulisse die; ~, ~n** piece of scenery; flat; *(Hintergrund)* backdrop; **die ~n** the scenery *sing.*
**kullern** *(ugs.) itr. V. mit sein* roll
**Kult der; ~[e]s, ~e** *(auch fig.)* cult; **kultivieren** *tr. V. (auch fig.)* cultivate; **kultiviert 1.** *Adj.* cultured; *(vornehm)* refined; **2.** *adv.* in a cultured manner; *(vornehm)* in a refined manner; **Kultur die; ~, ~en a)** *o. Pl.* culture; *(kultivierte Lebensart)* refinement; **ein Mensch von ~:** a cultured person; **b)** *(Zivilisation, Lebensform)* civilization
**Kultur-: ~abkommen das** cultural agreement; **~austausch der** cultural exchange; **~beutel der** sponge-bag *(Brit.);* toilet-bag
**kulturell 1.** *Adj.* cultural; **2.** *adv.* culturally
**Kultur-: ~film der** documentary film; **~geschichte die a)** *o. Pl.* history of civilization; *(einer bestimmten Kultur)* cultural history; **~politik die** cultural and educational policy
**Kultus·minister der** minister for education and cultural affairs
**Kümmel der; ~s, ~:** caraway [seed]; *(Branntwein)* kümmel
**Kummer der; ~s** sorrow; grief; *(Ärger, Sorgen)* trouble; **~ um** *od.* **über jmdn.** grief for sb.; **jmdm. ~ machen** give sb. trouble; **kümmerlich** *Adj.* **a)** *(schwächlich)* puny; stunted ⟨*vegetation, plants*⟩; **b)** *(ärmlich)* wretched; miserable; **c)** *(abwertend: gering)* miserable; meagre ⟨*knowledge, left-overs*⟩; **kümmern 1.** *refl. V.* **a)** sich um jmdn./etw. ~: take care of sb./sth.; **b)** *(sich befassen mit)* **sich nicht um Politik ~:** not be interested in politics; **2.** *tr. V.* concern
**Kumpan der; ~s, ~e** *(ugs.)* **a)** pal *(coll.);* buddy *(coll.);* **b)** *(abwertend:*

*Mittäter)* accomplice; **Kumpel der; ~s, ~ a)** *(Bergmannsspr.)* miner; **b)** *(salopp: Kamerad)* pal *(coll.);* buddy *(coll.)*
**kündbar** *Adj.* terminable ⟨*contract*⟩; redeemable ⟨*loan, mortgage*⟩; **¹Kunde der; ~n, ~n** customer; *(eines Architekten-, Anwaltbüros, einer Versicherung usw.)* client
**²Kunde die; ~** *(geh.)* tidings *pl. (literary);* **Kunden·dienst der** *o. Pl.* service to customers; *(Wartung)* after-sales service; **Kundgebung die; ~, ~en** rally; **kundig** *Adj. (kenntnisreich)* knowledgeable; *(sachverständig)* expert; **kündigen 1.** *tr. V.* cancel ⟨*subscription, membership*⟩; terminate ⟨*contract, agreement*⟩; **seine Stellung ~:** hand in one's notice **(bei** to); **2.** *unr. itr. V.* **a)** *(ein Mietverhältnis beenden)* ⟨*tenant*⟩ give notice; **jmdm. ~** ⟨*landlord*⟩ give sb. notice to quit; **zum 1. Juli ~:** give notice for 1 July; **b)** *(ein Arbeitsverhältnis beenden)* ⟨*employee*⟩ hand in one's notice **(bei** to); **jmdm. ~** ⟨*employer*⟩ give sb. his/her notice; **Kündigung die; ~, ~en a)** *(der Mitgliedschaft, eines Abonnements)* cancellation; *(eines Vertrags)* termination; **b)** *(eines Arbeitsverhältnisses)* **jmdm. die ~ aussprechen** give sb. his/her notice; **Kundin die; ~, ~nen** customer/client; **Kundschaft die; ~, ~en** *o. Pl.; s.* **¹Kunde a:** customers *pl.;* clientele; **Kundschafter der; ~s, ~:** scout; **kund|tun** *(geh.) unr. tr. V.* announce
**künftig 1.** *Adj.* future; **2.** *adv.* in future
**Kunst die; ~, Künste a)** art; **b)** *(das Können)* skill; **die ärztliche ~:** medical skill; **das ist keine ~!** *(ugs.)* there's nothing 'to it
**kunst-, Kunst-: ~aus·stellung die** art exhibition; **~buch das** art book; **~erzieher der, ~erzieherin die** art teacher; **~faser die** synthetic fibre; **~führer der** guide to cultural and artistic monuments [of an/the area]; **~genuß der** enjoyment of art; *(Ereignis)* artistic treat; **~gerecht 1.** *Adj.* expert; **2.** *adv.* expertly; **~geschichte die** *o. Pl.* art history; **~geschichtlich 1.** *Adj.* art historical ⟨*studies, evidence, expertise*⟩; ⟨*work*⟩ on art history; **2.** *adv.* **~geschichtlich interessiert/versiert** interested/well versed in art history; **~gewerbe das** arts and crafts *pl.;* **~griff der** trick; dodge;

~**halle** die art gallery; ~**händler** der [fine-]art dealer; ~**handwerk** das craftwork; ~**kritiker** der art critic; ~**leder** imitation leather

**Künstler** der; ~s, ~, **Künstlerin** die; ~, ~**nen a)** artist; *(Zirkus~, Varieté~)* artiste; **b)** *(Könner)* genius (**in** + *Dat.* at); **künstlerisch 1.** *Adj.* artistic; **2.** *adv.* artistically; **Künstler·name** der stage-name; **künstlich 1.** *Adj.* **a)** artificial; **b)** *(gezwungen)* forced ⟨*laugh, cheerfulness, etc.*⟩; **2.** *adv.* artificially

**kunst-, Kunst-:** ~**los** *Adj.* plain; ~**post·karte** die art postcard; ~**sammler** der art collector; ~**sammlung** die art collection; ~**stoff** der synthetic material; plastic; ~**stück** das trick; **das ist kein ~stück** *(ugs.)* it's no great feat; ~**turnen** das gymnastics *sing.;* ~**voll 1.** *Adj.* ornate and artistic; *(kompliziert)* elaborate; **2.** *adv.* **a)** ornately or elaborately and artistically; **b)** *(geschickt)* skilfully; ~**werk** das work of art

**kunter·bunt 1.** *Adj.* multi-coloured; *(abwechslungsreich)* varied; *(ungeordnet)* jumbled ⟨*confusion, muddle, etc.*⟩; **2.** *adv.* ⟨*painted, printed*⟩ in many colours; ~ **durcheinander sein** be higgledy-piggledy

**Kupfer** das; ~s **a)** copper; **b)** *(~geschirr)* copperware; *(~geld)* coppers *pl.*

**Kupfer-:** ~**geld** das coppers *pl.;* ~**stich** der **a)** *o. Pl.* copperplate engraving *no art.;* **b)** *(Blatt)* copperplate print *or* engraving

**Kuppe** die; ~, ~n **a)** [rounded] hilltop; **b)** *(Finger~)* tip; end

**Kuppel** die; ~, ~n dome; *(kleiner)* cupola

**Kuppelei** die; ~: procuring; **kuppeln** *itr. V.* operate the clutch; **Kuppelung** *s.* Kupplung; **Kuppler** der; ~s, ~: procurer; **Kupplerin** die; ~, ~nen procuress; **Kupplung** die; ~, ~en **a)** *(Kfz-W.)* clutch; **b)** *(Technik: Vorrichtung zum Verbinden)* coupling

**Kur** die; ~, ~en [health] cure; *(ohne Aufenthalt im Badeort)* course of treatment

**Kür** die; ~, ~en *(Eiskunstlauf)* free programme; *(Turnen)* optional exercises *pl.*

**Kurbel** die; ~, ~n crank [handle]; *(an Spieldosen, Grammophonen)* winder; *(an einem Brunnen)* [winding-]handle; **kurbeln** *tr. V.* etw. **nach oben/unten**

~: wind sth. up/down; **Kurbel·welle** die *(Technik)* crankshaft

**Kürbis** der; ~ses, ~se pumpkin

**Kurde** der; ~n, ~n Kurd

**Kur-:** ~**fürst** der *(hist.)* Elector; ~**gast** der visitor to a/the spa; *(Patient)* patient at a/the spa

**Kurier** der; ~s, ~e courier

**kurieren** *tr. V. (auch fig.)* cure (**von** of)

**kurios 1.** *Adj.* curious; **2.** *adv.* curiously; strangely; oddly; **Kuriosität** die; ~, ~en **a)** *o. Pl.* strangeness; **b)** *(Gegenstand)* curiosity; curio

**Kur-:** ~**konzert** das concert [at a spa]; ~**ort** der spa; ~**pfuscher** der *(ugs. abwertend)* quack

**Kurs** der; ~es, ~e **a)** *(Richtung)* course; **ein harter/weicher** ~ *(fig.)* a hard/soft line; **b)** *(von Wertpapieren)* price; *(von Devisen)* exchange rate; **der** ~ **des Dollars** the dollar rate; **c)** *(Lehrgang)* course; *(Teilnehmer)* class

**Kürschner** der; ~s, ~: furrier

**kursieren** *itr. V.; auch mit sein* circulate; **Kurs·teilnehmer** der course participant; **Kursus** der; ~, **Kurse** *s.* Kurs; **Kurs·wagen** der *(Eisenb.)* through carriage

**Kur·taxe** die visitors' tax *(at a spa)*

**Kurve** die; ~, ~n **a)** *(einer Straße)* bend; **b)** *(Geom.)* curve; **c)** *(in der Statistik, Temperatur~ usw.)* graph; **kurven** *itr. V.; mit sein* **a)** ⟨*aircraft*⟩ circle; ⟨*tanks etc.*⟩ circle [round]; **b)** *(ugs.: fahren)* drive around; **kurven·reich** *Adj.* winding; twisting

**kurz; kürzer, kürzest... 1.** *Adj.* short; *(zeitlich; knapp)* short, brief; quick ⟨*look*⟩; **2.** *adv.* **a)** *(zeitlich)* briefly; *(knapp)* ~ **gesagt** in a word; **b)** *(wenig)* just; ~ **vor/hinter der Kreuzung** just before/past the crossroads; ~ **vor/nach Pfingsten** just before/after Whitsun; **Kurz·arbeit** die short-time working; **kurz·ärm[e]lig** *Adj.* short-sleeved; **Kürze** die; ~ **a)** shortness; **b)** *(geringe Dauer)* shortness; brevity; **in** ~: shortly; **c)** *(Knappheit)* brevity; **Kürzel** das; ~s, ~: shorthand symbol; **kürzen** *tr. V.* shorten; abridge ⟨*article, book*⟩; cut ⟨*pension, budget*⟩; **kürzer** *s.* kurz; **kurzerhand** *Adv.* without more ado; **kürzest...** *s.* kurz

**kurz-, Kurz-:** ~**fristig 1.** *Adj.* **a)** ⟨*refusal, resignation, etc.*⟩ at short notice; **b)** *(für kurze Zeit)* short-term; **2.** *adv.* **a)** at short notice; **b)** *(für kurze Zeit)* for a short time; *(auf kurze Sicht)* in the short term; *(in kurzer Zeit)* without delay; **~geschichte** die short story; **~lebig** *Adj. (auch fig.)* short-lived

**kürzlich** *Adv.* recently; not long ago

**kurz-, Kurz-:** **~parker** der short-stay *(Brit.) or* short-term parker; **~schluß** der *(Elektrot.)* short-circuit; **~sichtig** *(auch fig.)* 1. *Adj.* short-sighted; 2. *adv.* short-sightedly

**Kürzung** die; **~, ~en** cut

**kurz-, Kurz-:** **~waren** *Pl.* haberdashery *sing. (Brit.);* notions *(Amer.);* **~welle** die *(Physik, Rundf.)* short wave; **~zeitig** 1. *Adj.* brief; 2. *adv.* briefly

**kuscheln** *refl. V.* **sich an jmdn. ~:** snuggle up to sb.

**kuschen** *itr. V.* knuckle under **(vor +** *Dat.* **to)**

**Kusine** die; **~, ~n** *s.* Cousine

**Kuß** der; **Kusses, Küsse** kiss; **kußecht** *Adj.* kissproof; **küssen** *tr., itr. V.* kiss; **Kuß·hand** die: **jmdm. eine ~ zuwerfen** blow sb. a kiss; **mit ~** *(ugs.)* gladly

**Küste** die; **~, ~n** coast; **Küsten·wache** die coastguard [service]

**Küster** der; **~s, ~:** sexton

**Kutsche** die; **~, ~n** coach; **Kutscher** der; **~s, ~:** coach-driver; **kutschieren** *itr. V.; mit sein* drive, ride [in a coach]; 2. *tr. V.* **jmdn. ~:** drive sb. [in a coach]

**Kutte** die; **~, ~n** [monk's/nun's] habit

**Kutter** der; **~s, ~:** cutter

**Kuvert** [ku'veːɐ̯] das; **~s, ~s** envelope; *(geh.: Gedeck)* cover

**Kuwait** [ku'vait] **(das);** **~s** Kuwait

**Kybernetik** die; **~:** cybernetics *sing.*

# L

**l, L** [ɛl] **das;** **~, ~:** l/L

**l** *Abk.* Liter l.

**laben** *(geh.)* 1. *tr. V.* **jmdn. ~:** give sb. refreshment; 2. *refl. V.* refresh oneself **(an +** *Dat.,* **mit** with)

**labil** *Adj.* **a)** *(Med.)* delicate ‹*constitution, health*›; poor ‹*circulation*›; **b)**

*(auch Psych.)* unstable ‹*person, character, situation, etc.*›

**Labor** das; **~s, ~s,** *auch:* **~e** laboratory; **Laboratorium** das; **~s, Laboratorien** laboratory

**Labyrinth** das; **~[e]s, ~e** maze; labyrinth

[1]**Lache** die; **~, ~n** *(ugs.)* laugh

[2]**Lache** ['la(ː)xə] die; **~, ~n** puddle; *(von Blut, Öl)* pool

**lächeln** *itr. V.* smile **(über +** *Akk.* at); **Lächeln** das; **~s** smile; **lachen** 1. *itr. V.* laugh **(über +** *Akk.* at); 2. *tr. V.* **was gibt es denn zu ~?** what's so funny?; **Lachen** das; **~s** laughter; **ein lautes ~:** a loud laugh; **lächerlich** 1. *Adj.* ridiculous; ludicrous ‹*argument, statement*›; 2. *adv.* ridiculously; **Lächerlichkeit** die; **~:** ridiculousness; *(von Argumenten, Behauptungen usw.)* ludicrousness; **lachhaft** *Adj.* ridiculous

**Lachs** der; **~es, ~e** salmon

**Lack** der; **~[e]s, ~e a)** varnish; *(für Metall, Lackarbeiten)* lacquer; **lackieren** *tr. V.* varnish; spray ‹*car*›; **Lack·leder** das patent leather

**Lade** die; **~, ~n** *(landsch.)* drawer; **Lade·hemmung** die jam; [1]**laden** 1. *unr. tr. V.* load; *(Physik)* charge; 2. *unr. itr. V.* load [up]

[2]**laden** *unr. tr. V.* **a)** *(Rechtsspr.)* summon; **b)** *(geh.: ein~)* invite

**Laden** der; **~s, Läden a)** shop; store *(Amer.);* **der ~ läuft** *(ugs.)* business is good; **b)** *(Fenster~)* shutter

**Laden-:** **~diebstahl** der shop-lifting; **~schluß** der shop *or (Amer.)* store closing-time; **~tisch** der [shop-]counter

**Lade-:** **~rampe** die loading ramp; **~raum** der *(beim Auto)* luggage-space; *(beim Flugzeug, Schiff)* hold; *(bei LKWs)* payload space

**lädieren** *tr. V.* damage

**lädst** 2. *Pers. Sg. Präsens v.* **laden; lädt** 3. *Pers. Sg. Präsens v.* **laden**

**Ladung** die; **~, ~en a)** *(Schiffs~, Flugzeug~)* cargo; *(LKW~)* load; **b)** *(beim Sprengen, Schießen; Physik)* charge; **c)** *(Rechtsspr.: Vor~)* summons *sing.*

**lag** 1. *u.* 3. *Pers. Sg. Prät. v.* **liegen; Lage** die; **~, ~n a)** situation; **eine gute ~ haben** be well situated; **b)** *(Art des Liegens)* position; **c)** *(Situation)* situation; **Lage·plan** der map of the area; **Lager** das; **~s, ~ a)** camp; **b)** store-room; *(in Geschäften, Betrieben)* stock-room; **c)** *(Warenbestand)* stock

**Lager-:** ~**feuer** das camp-fire; ~**halle** die warehouse

**lagern 1.** *tr. V.* **a)** store; **b)** *(hinlegen)* lay down; **2.** *itr. V.* **a)** camp; **b)** *(liegen)* lie; ⟨*foodstuffs, medicines, etc.*⟩ be kept

**Lager-:** ~**platz** der campsite; ~**raum** store-room; *(im Geschäft, Betrieb)* stock-room

**Lagerung** die; ~, ~en storage

**Lagune** die; ~, ~n lagoon

**lahm** *Adj.* **a)** *(gelähmt)* lame; *(ugs.: unbeweglich)* stiff; **b)** *(ugs.: unzureichend)* lame ⟨*excuse, explanation, etc.*⟩; **c)** *(ugs. abwertend: matt)* dreary; **lahmen** *itr. V.* be lame; **lähmen** *tr. V.* paralyse; *(fig.)* paralyse ⟨*economy, industry*⟩; bring ⟨*traffic*⟩ to a standstill; **Lähmung** die; ~, ~en paralysis; *(fig.) (der Wirtschaft, Industrie)* paralysis; **zu einer ~ des Verkehrs führen** bring traffic to a standstill

**Laib** der; ~[e]s, ~e loaf; **ein [halber] ~ Brot** [half] a loaf of bread

**Laich** der; ~[e]s, ~e spawn; **laichen** *itr. V.* spawn

**Laie** der; ~n, ~n *(Mann)* layman; *(Frau)* laywoman

**Lakai** der; ~en, ~en lackey; liveried footman

**Lake** die; ~, ~n brine

**Laken** das; ~s, ~ *(bes. nordd.)* sheet

**Lakritze** die; ~, ~n liquorice

**lallen** *tr., itr. V.* ⟨*baby*⟩ babble; ⟨*drunk/drowsy person*⟩ mumble

**Lamelle** die; ~, ~n *(einer Jalousie)* slat; *(eines Heizkörpers)* rib

**lamentieren** *itr. V. (ugs.)* moan (**über** + *Akk.* about)

**Lametta** das; ~s lametta

**Lamm** das; ~[e]s, **Lämmer** lamb

**lamm-, Lamm-:** ~**fell** das lambskin; ~**fleisch** das lamb; ~**fromm 1.** *Adj.* ⟨*person*⟩ as meek as a [little] lamb; **2.** *adv.* ⟨*answer*⟩ like a lamb

**Lampe** die; ~, ~n light; *(Tisch~, Öl~, Signal~)* lamp

**Lampen-:** ~**fieber** das stage fright; ~**schirm** der [lamp]shade

**Lampion** [lamˈpjɔŋ] der; ~s, ~s Chinese lantern

**Land** das; ~es, **Länder** od. *(veralt.)* ~**e a)** *o. Pl.* land *no indef. art.; (dörfliche Gegend)* country *no indef. art.;* **an ~:** ashore; **auf dem ~ wohnen** live in the country; **b)** *(Staat)* country; **c)** *(Bundesland)* Land; state; *(österr.)* province; **Land · bevölkerung** die rural population

**Lande-:** ~**an · flug** der *(Flugw.)* [landing] approach; ~**bahn** die *(Flugw.)* [landing] runway

**landen 1.** *itr. V.; mit sein* **a)** land; *(ankommen)* arrive; **b)** *(ugs.: gelangen)* land up; **2.** *tr. V.* **a)** land ⟨*aircraft, troops, passengers, fish, etc.*⟩; **b)** *(ugs.: zustande bringen)* pull off ⟨*victory, coup*⟩; have ⟨*smash hit*⟩

**Ländereien** *Pl.* estates

**Länder-:** ~**kampf** der *(Sport)* international match; ~**spiel** das *(Sport)* international [match]

**Landes-:** ~**innere** das interior [of the country]; ~**kunde** die; *o. Pl.* regional studies *pl., no art.;* ~**regierung** die government of a/the Land/province; ~**sprache** die language of the country; ~**tracht** die national costume *or* dress; ~**verrat** der *(Rechtsw.)* treason; ~**währung** die currency of a/the country

**land-, Land-:** ~**flucht** die migration from the countryside [to the towns]; ~**gewinnung** die reclamation of land; ~**haus** das country house; ~**karte** die map; ~**kreis** der district; ~**läufig** *Adj.* widely accepted

**ländlich** *Adj.* rural; country *attrib.* ⟨*life*⟩

**Land-:** ~**plage** die *(fig.)* pest; nuisance; ~**ratte** die *(ugs.)* landlubber

**Landschaft** die; ~, ~en landscape; *(ländliche Gegend)* countryside; **landschaftlich 1.** *Adj.* regional; **2.** *adv.* ~ **herrlich gelegen sein** be in a glorious natural setting

**Lands · mann** der; *Pl.* ~**leute** fellow-countryman; compatriot

**Land-:** ~**straße** die country road; *(im Gegensatz zur Autobahn)* ordinary road; ~**streicher** der tramp; ~**strich** der area; ~**tag** der Landtag; state parliament; *(österr.)* provincial parliament; **Landung** die; ~, ~en landing; **Landungs · brücke** die [floating] landing-stage

**land-, Land-:** ~**weg** der overland route; **auf dem ~weg** overland; ~**wirt** der farmer; ~**wirtschaft** die *o. Pl.* agriculture *no art.;* farming *no art.;* ~**wirtschaftlich 1.** *Adj.* agricultural; **2.** *adv.* ~ **genutzt werden** be used for agricultural purposes; ~**zunge** die *(Geogr.)* tongue of land

**lang; länger, längst... 1.** *Adj.* long; *(ugs.: groß)* tall; **2.** *adv.* [for] a long time; **eine Sekunde/mehrere Stunden ~:** for a second/several hours

**lang-:** ~**ärm[e]lig** *Adj.* long-sleeved; ~**atmig 1.** *Adj.* long-winded; **2.** *adv.* long-windedly; ⟨*relate*⟩ at great length
**lange;** länger, am längsten *Adv.* **a)** a long time; **bist du schon** ~ **hier?** have you been here long?; **b)** *(bei weitem)* **ich bin noch** ~ **nicht fertig** I'm no-where near finished; **hier is es** ~ **nicht so schön** it isn't nearly as nice here; **Länge die;** ~, ~**n** length; *(Geogr.)* longitude
**langen** *(ugs.)* **1.** *itr. V.* **a)** be enough; **b)** *(greifen)* reach (**in** + *Akk.* into; **auf** + *Akk.* on to; **nach** for); **2.** *tr. V.* **jmdm. eine** ~ *(ugs.)* give sb. a clout [around the ear] *(coll.)*
**Längen·grad der** *(Geogr.)* degree of longitude
**länger 1.** *s.* **lang, lange; 2.** *Adj.* **seit** ~**er Zeit** for quite some time
**Lange·weile die;** ~ *od.* **Langenweile** boredom; ~ **haben** be bored
**lang-, Lang-:** ~**fristig 1.** *Adj.* long-term; long-dated ⟨*loan*⟩; **2.** *adv.* on a long-term basis; ~**jährig** *Adj.* ⟨*customer, friend*⟩ of many years' standing; long-standing ⟨*friendship*⟩; ~**jährige Erfahrung** many years of experience; ~**lauf der** *(Skisport)* cross-country
**länglich** *Adj.* oblong; **längs 1.** *Präp.* + *Gen. od. (selten) Dat.* along; **2.** *Adv.* lengthways; **Längs·achse die** longitudinal axis
**langsam 1.** *Adj.* slow; **2.** *adv.* **a)** slowly; ~, **aber sicher** *(ugs.)* slowly but surely; **b)** *(allmählich)* gradually
**Lang-:** ~**schläfer der** late riser; ~**spiel·platte die** long-playing record; LP
**Längs·schnitt der** longitudinal section
**längst** *Adv.* **a)** *(schon lange)* a long time ago; **b)** *(bei weitem)* **hier ist es** ~ **nicht so schön** it isn't nearly as nice here; **längst...** *s.* **lang; längstens** *Adv. (ugs.) (höchstens)* at [the] most; *(spätestens)* at the latest
**Languste die;** ~, ~**n** spiny lobster
**lang-, Lang-:** ~**weilen 1.** *tr. V.* bore; **2.** *refl. V.* be bored; ~**weilig 1.** *Adj.* boring; dull ⟨*place*⟩; **2.** *adv.* boringly; ~**welle die** *(Physik, Rundf.)* long wave; ~**wierig** *Adj.* lengthy; prolonged ⟨*search*⟩
**Lanze die;** ~, ~**n** lance; *(zum Werfen)* spear
**Laos** ['laːɔs] **(das); Laos'** Laos; **Laote** [laˈoːtə] **der;** ~**n,** ~**n** Laotian

**lapidar 1.** *Adj. (kurz, aber wirkungsvoll)* succinct; *(knapp)* terse; **2.** *adv.* succinctly/tersely
**Lappalie die;** ~, ~**n** trifle
**Lappe der;** ~**n,** ~**n** Lapp
**Lappen der;** ~**s,** ~: cloth; *(Fetzen)* rag; *(Wasch~)* flannel
**läppisch** *Adj.* silly
**Lapp·land (das)** Lapland
**Lärche die;** ~, ~**n** larch
**Lärm der;** ~**[e]s** noise; *(Krach)* din; row *(coll.);* **Lärm·belästigung die** disturbance caused by noise; **lärmen** *itr. V.* make a noise *or* *(coll.)* row
**Larve die;** ~, ~**n** grub; larva
**las** *1. u. 3. Pers. Sg. Prät. v.* **lesen**
**lasch 1.** *Adj.* limp ⟨*handshake*⟩; feeble ⟨*action, measure*⟩; lax ⟨*upbringing*⟩; **2.** *adv. s. Adj.:* limply; feebly; laxly
**Lasche die;** ~, ~**n** *(Gürtel~)* loop; *(eines Briefumschlags)* flap; *(Schuh~)* tongue
**Laser** ['leizə] **der;** ~**s,** ~ *(Physik)* laser
**laß** *Imperativ Sg. v.* **lassen; lassen 1.** *unr. tr. V.* **a)** *mit Inf.* + *Akk. (2. Part.* ~*) (veranlassen)* **etw. tun/machen/bauen/waschen** ~: have *or* get sth. done/made/built/washed; **jmdn. warten** ~: keep sb. waiting; **jmdn. grüßen** ~: send one's regards to sb.; **jmdn. kommen/rufen** ~: send for sb.; **b)** *mit Inf.* + *Akk. (2. Part.* ~*) (erlauben)* **jmdn. etw. tun** ~: let sb. do sth.; allow sb. to do sth.; **c)** *(belassen)* **jmdn. in Frieden** ~: leave sb. in peace; **d)** *(hinein~/heraus~)* let *or* allow (**in** + *Akk.* into, **aus** out of); **e)** *(unterlassen)* stop; **f)** *(zurück~; bleiben* ~*)* leave; **g)** *(überlassen)* **jmdm. etw.** ~: let sb. have sth.; **h)** *(als Aufforderung)* **laß/laßt uns gehen/fahren!** let's go!; **i)** *(verlieren)* lose; *(ausgeben)* spend; **2.** *unr. refl. V.* **die Tür läßt sich leicht öffnen** the door opens easily; **das läßt sich nicht beweisen** it can't be proved; **3.** *unr. itr. V.* **a)** *(ugs.)* **Laß mal. Ich mache das schon** Leave it. I'll do it; **b)** *(veranlassen)* **ich lasse bitten** would you ask him/her/them to come in
**lässig 1.** *Adj.* casual; **2.** *adv.* casually
**läßt** *3. Pers. Sg. Präsens v.* **lassen**
**Last die;** ~, ~**en** load; *(Gewicht)* weight; *(Bürde)* burden; **lasten** *itr. V.* be a burden; **auf jmdm./etw.** ~: weigh heavily [up]on sb./sth.; **¹Laster der;** ~**s,** ~ *(ugs.: Lkw)* truck; lorry *(Brit.)*
**²Laster das;** ~**s,** ~: vice; **lasterhaft** *Adj. (abwertend)* depraved; **lästern**

**1.** *itr. V. (abwertend)* über jmdn./etw. ~: make malicious remarks about sb./sth.; **2.** *tr. V. (veralt.)* blaspheme against

**lästig** *Adj.* tiresome; troublesome ⟨*illness, cough, etc.*⟩

**Last-:** ~**schrift** die debit; ~**wagen** der truck; lorry *(Brit.)*

**Lasur** die; ~, ~en varnish; *(farbig)* glaze

**Latein** das; ~s Latin; **Latein·amerika (das)** Latin America; **lateinisch** *Adj.* Latin

**latent** *Adj.* latent

**Laterne** die; ~, ~n a) *(Leuchte)* lamp; lantern *(Naut.);* b) *(Straßen~)* street light; **Laternen·pfahl** der lamppost

**Latrine** die; ~, ~n latrine

**latschen** *itr. V.; mit sein (salopp)* trudge; *(schlurfend)* slouch; **Latschen** der; ~s, ~ *(ugs.)* old worn-out shoe/slipper

**Latte** die; ~, ~n a) lath; *(Zaun~)* pale; b) *(Sport: Quer~ des Tores)* [cross]bar; c) *(Leichtathletik)* bar; **Latten·zaun** der paling fence

**Latz** der; ~es, Lätze bib; **Lätzchen** das; ~s, ~: bib

**lau** *Adj.* tepid, lukewarm ⟨*water etc.*⟩; mild ⟨*wind, air, evening, etc.*⟩

**Laub** das; ~[e]s leaves *pl.;* **dichtes** ~: thick foliage; **Laub·baum** der broad-leaved tree

**Laube** die; ~, ~n summer-house; *(überdeckter Sitzplatz)* bower; arbour

**Laub-:** ~**frosch** der tree frog; ~**säge** die fretsaw; ~**wald** der deciduous wood/forest

**Lauch** der; ~[e]s *(Porree)* leek

**Lauer** die; ~: auf der ~ liegen *od.* sein *(ugs.) (jmdm. auflauern)* lie in wait; **lauern** *itr. V. (auch fig.)* lurk

**Lauf** der; ~[e]s, Läufe a) *o. Pl.* running; b) *(Sport: Wettrennen)* heat; c) *o. Pl. (Ver~)* course; im ~[e] der Zeit in the course of time; im ~[e] der Jahre/ des Tages over the years/during the day; d) *(von Schußwaffen)* barrel; **Lauf·bahn** die a) *(Werdegang)* career; b) *(Leichtathletik)* running-track; **laufen 1.** *unr. itr. V.; mit sein* a) run; *(beim Eislauf)* skate; *(beim Ski~)* ski; *(gehen)* go; *(zu Fuß gehen)* walk; in *(Akk.)*/gegen etw. ~: walk into sth.; **dauernd zum Arzt ~** *(ugs.)* keep running to the doctor; b) *(im Gang sein)* ⟨*machine*⟩ be running; ⟨*radio, television, etc.*⟩ be on; *(funktionie-*

*ren)* ⟨*machine*⟩ run; ⟨*radio, television, etc.*⟩ work; c) *(gelten)* ⟨*contract, agreement, engagement, etc.*⟩ run; d) *(gespielt werden)* ⟨*programme, play, etc.*⟩ be on; **2.** *unr. tr. u. itr. V.* a) *mit sein (zurücklegen) (zu Fuß)* walk; *(rennen)* run; b) *mit sein (erzielen)* einen Rekord ~: set up a record; c) *mit haben od. sein* Ski/Schlittschuh/Rollschuh ~: ski/skate/roller-skate; **laufend 1.** *Adj.* a) *(ständig)* regular ⟨*interest, income*⟩; recurring ⟨*costs*⟩; b) *(gegenwärtig)* current ⟨*issue, year, month, etc.*⟩; **2.** *adv.* constantly; ⟨*increase*⟩ steadily; **Läufer** der; ~s, ~ a) *(Sport)* runner; *(Handball; Fußball veralt.)* half-back; b) *(Teppich) (long narrow)* carpet; **Lauf·feuer** das brush fire; **wie ein** ~: like wildfire

**Lauf-:** ~**masche** die ladder; ~**paß** der: er hat seiner Freundin den ~paß gegeben *(ugs.)* he finished with his girl-friend *(coll.);* ~**schritt** der: im ~schritt, marsch, marsch! at the double, quick march!

**läufst** *2. Pers. Sg. Präsens v.* laufen; **Lauf·stall** der playpen; **läuft** *3. Pers. Sg. Präsens v.* laufen

**Lauge** die; ~, ~n a) soapy water; b) *(Chemie)* alkaline solution; **Laugen·brezel** die *(südd.)* pretzel

**Laune** die; ~, ~n mood; **launenhaft** *Adj.* temperamental; *(unberechenbar)* capricious; **launig** witty; **launisch** *Adj.: s.* launenhaft

**Laus** die; ~, Läuse louse

**Laus·bub** der little rascal

**lauschen** *itr. V.* a) *(horchen)* listen; b) *(zuhören)* listen [attentively]; **Lauscher** der; ~s, ~: eavesdropper; **lauschig** *Adj.* cosy, snug ⟨*corner*⟩

**lausig 1.** *Adj. (ugs.)* a) *(abwertend: unangenehm, schäbig)* lousy *(sl.);* rotten *(coll.);* b) *(sehr groß)* perishing *(Brit. sl.),* freezing ⟨*cold*⟩; terrible *(coll.)* ⟨*heat*⟩; **2.** *adv.* terribly *(coll.)*

¹**laut 1.** *Adj.* loud; *(geräuschvoll)* noisy; **2.** *adv.* loudly; *(geräuschvoll)* noisily

²**laut** *Präp. + Gen. od. Dat. (Amtsspr.)* according to

**Laut** der; ~[e]s, ~e sound

**Laute** die; ~, ~n lute

**lauten** *itr. V.* ⟨*answer, instruction, slogan*⟩ be, run; ⟨*letter, passage, etc.*⟩ read, go; ⟨*law*⟩ state; **läuten 1.** *tr., itr. V.* ring; ⟨*alarm clock*⟩ go off; **2.** *itr. V. (bes. südd.: klingeln)* ring; es läutete the bell rang *or* went (zu for)

¹**lauter** *Adj. (geh.)* honourable ⟨*person, intentions, etc.*⟩; honest ⟨*truth*⟩

²**lauter** *indekl. Adj.* nothing but; sheer ⟨*nonsense, joy, etc.*⟩

**läutern** *tr. V. (geh.)* reform ⟨*character*⟩; purify ⟨*soul*⟩; **Läuterung** die; ~, ~en *(geh.)* reformation; *(der Seele)* purification

**laut·hals** *Adv.* at the top of one's voice; ~ **lachen** roar with laughter

**lautlich** 1. *Adj.* phonetic; 2. *adv.* phonetically

**laut-, Laut-:** ~**los** 1. *Adj.* silent; soundless; *(wortlos)* silent; 2. *adv.* silently; soundlessly; ~**schrift** die *(Phon.)* phonetic alphabet; *(Umschrift)* phonetic transcription; ~**sprecher** der loudspeaker; *(einer Stereoanlage usw.)* speaker; ~**stark** 1. *Adj.* loud; vociferous, loud ⟨*protest*⟩; 2. *adv.* loudly; ⟨*protest*⟩ vociferously; ~**stärke** die volume

**lau·warm** *Adj.* lukewarm

**Lava** die; ~, **Laven** *(Geol.)* lava

**Lavendel** der; ~s, ~: lavender

**Lawine** die; ~, ~n *(auch fig.)* avalanche; **eine ~ von Protesten** *(fig.)* a storm of protest; **Lawinen·gefahr** die danger of avalanches

**lax** 1. *Adj.* lax; 2. *adv.* laxly

**Lazarett** das; ~[e]s, ~e military hospital

**leben** *itr. V.* live; *(lebendig sein)* be alive; **leb[e] wohl!** farewell!; **von seiner Rente/seinem Gehalt ~:** live on one's pension/salary; **Leben** das; ~s, ~ a) life; **das ~:** life; **sich** *(Dat.)* **das ~ nehmen** take one's [own] life; **am ~ sein/ bleiben** be/stay alive; **ums ~ kommen** lose one's life; b) *(Betriebsamkeit)* **auf dem Markt herrschte ein reges ~:** the market was bustling with activity; **das ~ auf der Straße** the comings and goings in the street; **lebend** *Adj.* living; live ⟨*animal*⟩; **lebendig** 1. *Adj.* living; *(lebhaft)* lively; 2. *adv. (lebhaft)* in a lively way

**lebens-, Lebens-:** ~**abend** der *(geh.)* evening of one's life *(literary)*; ~**art** die a) way of life; b) *o. Pl. (Umgangsformen)* manners *pl.;* ~**aufgabe** die life's work; ~**bejahend** *Adj.* ⟨*person*⟩ with a positive attitude to life; ~**bereich** der area of life; ~**dauer** die life-span; ~**ende** das end [of one's life]; ~**erinnerungen** *Pl.* memories of one's life; *(aufgezeichnet)* memoirs; ~**erwartung** die life expectancy; ~**fähig** *Adj. (auch fig.)*

viable; ~**freude** die; *o. Pl.* zest for life; ~**froh** *Adj.* full of zest for life *postpos.;* ~**gefahr** die mortal danger; „**Achtung, ~gefahr!**" 'danger'; ~**gefährlich** 1. *Adj.* highly dangerous; critical ⟨*injury*⟩; 2. *adv.* critically ⟨*injured, ill*⟩; ~**geister** *Pl.* jmds. ~**geister |wieder| wecken** put new life into sb.; ~**groß** *Adj.* life-size; ~**größe** die: **eine Statue in ~größe** a life-size statue

**Lebenshaltungs·kosten** *Pl.* cost of living *sing.*

**lebens-, Lebens-:** ~**jahr** das year of [one's] life; ~**kraft** die vitality; ~**künstler** der: **ein |echter/wahrer| ~künstler** a person who always knows how to make the best of things; ~**lage** die situation [in life]; ~**länglich** 1. *Adj.* ~**länglicher Freiheitsentzug** life imprisonment; 2. *adv.* jmdn. ~**länglich gefangenhalten** keep sb. imprisoned for life; ~**lauf** der curriculum vitae; c.v.; ~**lustig** *Adj.* ⟨*person*⟩ full of the joys of life

**Lebens·mittel** das; *meist Pl.* food[stuff]; ~ *Pl.* food *sing.;* **Lebensmittel·geschäft** das food shop

**lebens-:** ~**müde** *Adj.* weary of life *pred.;* ~**notwendig** *Adj.* essential; ~**raum** der a) *(Umkreis)* lebensraum; b) *(Biol.)* s. Biotop; ~**retter** der rescuer; ~**standard** der standard of living; ~**unterhalt** der: **seinen ~unterhalt verdienen/bestreiten** earn one's living/support oneself; ~**versicherung** die life insurance; ~**wandel** der way of life; ~**weg** der [journey through] life; ~**weise** die way of life; ~**zeichen** das sign of life; ~**zeit** die life[-span]; **auf ~zeit** for life

**Leber** die; ~, ~n liver

**Leber-:** ~**fleck** der liver spot; ~**käse** der; *o. Pl.* meat loaf made with mincemeat, [minced liver,] eggs, and spices; ~**tran** der fish-liver oil; *(des Kabeljaus)* cod-liver oil; ~**wurst** die liver sausage

**Lebe-:** ~**wesen** das living being; ~**wohl** [--'-] das; ~[e]s, ~ *od.* ~e *(geh.)* farewell

**lebhaft** 1. *Adj.* a) lively; busy ⟨*traffic*⟩; brisk ⟨*business*⟩; b) *(deutlich)* vivid ⟨*idea, picture, etc.*⟩; c) *(kräftig)* bright ⟨*colour*⟩; vigorous ⟨*applause, opposition*⟩. 2. *adv.* a) in a lively way; b) *(deutlich)* vividly; c) *(kräftig)* brightly ⟨*coloured*⟩

**leb-, Leb-:** ~**kuchen** der ≈ ginger-bread; ~**los** Adj. lifeless; ~**zeiten** Pl. **bei** od. **zu jmds.** ~**zeiten** during sb.'s lifetime

**lechzen** itr. V. (geh.) **nach einem Trunk** ~: long for a drink; **nach Rache** usw. ~: thirst for revenge etc.

**leck** Adj. leaky; ~ **sein** leak; **Leck** das; ~|e|s, ~s leak

¹**lecken** 1. tr. V. lick; 2. itr. V. **an etw.** (Dat.) ~: lick sth.

²**lecken** itr. V. (leck sein) leak

**lecker** Adj. tasty (meal); delicious (cake etc.); good (smell, taste); **Leckerbissen** der delicacy; **Leckerei** die; ~, ~**en** (ugs.) dainty; (Süßigkeit) sweet [meat]

**led.** Abk. ledig

**Leder** das; ~s, ~: leather; **Lederwaren** Pl. leather goods

**ledig** Adj. single; **eine** ~**e Mutter** an unmarried mother; **Ledige** der/die; adj. Dekl. single person; **lediglich** Adj. merely

**leer** Adj. empty; clean (sheet of paper); **Leere** die; ~ (auch fig.) emptiness; **leeren** tr., refl. V. empty

**leer-, Leer-:** ~**gefegt** Adj. deserted (street, town); **wie** ~**gefegt** deserted; ~**lauf** der; o. Pl. **im** ~**lauf den Berg hinunterfahren** (driver) coast down the hill in neutral; (cyclist) freewheel down the hill; ~**stehend** Adj. empty, unoccupied; ~**taste** die space-bar

**Leerung** die; ~, ~**en** emptying; (von Briefkästen) collection

**Lefze** die; ~, ~**n** lip

**legal** 1. Adj. legal; 2. adv. legally; **legalisieren** tr. V. legalize; **Legalität** die; ~: legality

**legen** 1. tr. V. **a)** lay [down]; **b)** (verlegen) lay (pipe, cable, carpet, tiles, etc.); 2. tr., itr. V. (hen) lay; 3. refl. V. **a)** lie down; **b)** (nachlassen) die down; abate; (enthusiasm) wear off, subside

**legendär** Adj. legendary

**Legende** die; ~, ~**n** legend

**leger** [le'ʒeːɐ̯] 1. Adj. casual; 2. adv. casually

**legieren** tr. V. alloy; **Legierung** die; ~, ~**en** alloy

**Legislative** die; ~, ~**n** (Politik) legislature; **Legislaturperiode** die legislative period; **legitim** Adj. legitimate; **Legitimation** [legitima-'tsioːn] die; ~, ~**en a)** legitimation; **b)** (Ausweis) proof of identity; **legitimieren** 1. tr. V. **a)** (rechtfertigen) justify; **b)** (bevollmächtigen) authorize; **c)**

(für legitim erklären) legitimize (child, relationship); 2. refl. V. show proof of one's identity

**Lehm** der; ~s loam; (Ton) clay

**Lehne** die; ~, ~**n** (Rücken~) back; (Arm~) arm; **lehnen** 1. tr., refl. V. lean (**an** + Akk., **gegen** against); 2. itr. V. be leaning (**an** + Dat. against); **Lehnstuhl** der armchair

**Lehrbuch** das textbook

**Lehre** die; ~, ~**n a)** apprenticeship; **b)** (Weltanschauung) doctrine; **c)** (Theorie, Wissenschaft) theory; **d)** (Erfahrung) lesson; **lehren** tr., itr. V. teach; **Lehrer** der; ~s, ~ (auch fig.) teacher; (Ausbilder) instructor; **Lehrerin** die; ~, ~**nen** teacher

**Lehr-:** ~**gang** der course (**für, in** + Dat. in); ~**jahr** das year as an apprentice; ~**körper** der (Amtsspr.) teaching staff; faculty (Amer.)

**Lehrling** der; ~s, ~**e** apprentice; (in kaufmännischen Berufen) trainee

**lehr-, Lehr-:** ~**reich** Adj. informative; ~**stelle** die apprenticeship; (in kaufmännischen Berufen) trainee post; ~**stoff** der (Schulw.) syllabus

**Leib** der; ~|e|s, ~**er** (geh.) body; **Leibgericht** das favourite dish; **leibhaftig** Adj. in person postpos.; (echt) real; **leiblich** Adj. physical (well-being); (blutsverwandt) real

**Leib-:** ~**schmerzen** Pl. abdominal pain sing.; ~**wächter** der bodyguard

**Leiche** die; ~, ~**n** [dead] body; corpse; **leichenblaß** Adj. deathly pale; **Leichnam** der; ~s, ~**e** (geh.) body

**leicht** 1. Adj. light; lightweight (suit, material); easy (task, question, job, etc.); slight (accent, illness, wound, doubt, etc.); mild (cigar, cigarette); 2. adv. lightly (built); (einfach, schnell, spielend) easily; (geringfügig) slightly

**leicht-, Leicht-:** ~**athletik** die [track and field] athletics sing.; ~**fallen** unr. itr. V.; mit sein be easy; **das fällt mir** ~: its easy for me; ~**fertig** 1. Adj. careless (behaviour, person); rash (promise); ill-considered, slapdash (plan); 2. adv. carelessly; ~**gläubig** Adj. gullible

**Leichtigkeit** die; ~ (geringes Gewicht) lightness; (Mühelosigkeit) ease

**leicht-, Leicht-:** ~|**machen** tr. V. **jmdm./sich etw.** ~**machen** make sth. easy for sb./oneself; ~|**nehmen** unr. tr. V. **etw.** ~**nehmen** make light of sth.; ~**sinn** der; o. Pl. carelessness no in-

*def. art.; (mit Gefahr verbunden)* recklessness *no indef. art.; ~***sinnig** 1. *Adj.* careless; *(sich, andere gefährdend)* reckless; *(fahrlässig)* negligent; 2. *adv.* carelessly; *(gefährlich)* recklessly; *(promise)* rashly; *~***verletzt** *Adj.; präd. getrennt geschrieben* slightly injured

**leid** *Adj.; nicht attr.* a) es tut mir ~ [, daß ...] I'm sorry [that ...]; er tut mir ~: I feel sorry for him; b) *(überdrüssig)* etw./jmdn. ~ sein/werden *(ugs.)* be/get fed up with sth./sb. *(coll.); **Leid** das; ~[e]s a) *(Schmerz)* suffering; *(Kummer)* grief; sorrow; b) *(Unrecht)* wrong; *(Böses)* harm; **leiden** 1. *unr. itr. V.* suffer **(an, unter** + *Dat.* from); 2. *unr. tr. V.* a) jmdn. [gut] ~ können *od.* mögen like sb.; b) *(geh.: ertragen müssen)* suffer *(hunger, thirst, etc.);* **Leiden** das; ~s, ~ a) *(Krankheit)* illness; *(Gebrechen)* complaint; b) *(Qual)* suffering; **leidend** *Adj.* a) *(krank)* ailing; b) *(schmerzvoll)* strained *(voice);* martyred *(expression)*

**Leidenschaft** die; ~, ~en passion (zu, für for); **leidenschaftlich** 1. *Adj.* passionate; vehement *(protest);* 2. *adv.* passionately; *(eifrig)* dedicatedly; etw. ~ gern tun adore doing sth.

**leider** *Adv.* unfortunately; **leidig** *Adj.* tiresome; **leidlich** *Adj.* reasonable

**Leier** die; ~, ~n lyre

**leihen** *unr. tr. V.* a) jmdm. etw. ~: lend sb. sth.; b) *(entleihen)* borrow

**Leih-:** ~**gebühr** die hire *or (Amer.)* rental charge; *(bei Büchern)* borrowing fee; ~**haus** das pawnbroker's; pawnshop; ~**mutter** die surrogate mother; ~**wagen** der hire *or (Amer.)* rental car

**Leim** der; ~[e]s glue; **leimen** *tr. V.* glue **(an** + *Akk.* to)

**Leine** die; ~, ~n rope; *(Wäsche~, Angel~)* line; *(Hunde~)* lead *(esp. Brit.);* leash; **Leinen** das; ~s a) *(Gewebe)* linen; b) *(Buchw.)* cloth; **Lein·wand** die a) *o. Pl.* linen; *(grob)* canvas; b) *(des Malers)* canvas; c) *(für Filme und Dias)* screen

**leise** 1. *Adj.* a) quiet; soft *(steps, music, etc.);* b) *(leicht)* faint; slight; slight, gentle *(touch);* 2. *adv.* a) quietly; b) *(leicht; kaum merklich)* slightly; *(touch, rain)* gently

**Leiste** die; ~, ~n strip; *(Holz~)* batten; *(profiliert)* moulding

**leisten** 1. *tr. V.* do *(work);* *(schaffen)* achieve *(a lot, nothing);* jmdm. Hilfe ~: help sb.; 2. *refl. V. (ugs.)* sich *(Dat.)* etw. ~: treat oneself to sth.; sich *(Dat.)* etw. [nicht] ~ können [not] be able to afford sth.; **Leistung** die; ~, ~en a) *o. Pl. (Qualität bzw. Quantität der Arbeit)* performance; b) *(Errungenschaft)* achievement; *(im Sport)* performance; c) *o. Pl. (Leistungsvermögen, Physik: Arbeits~)* power; d) *(Zahlung, Zuwendung)* payment; *(Versicherungsw.)* benefit; e) *(Dienst~)* service

**leistungs-, Leistungs-:** ~**fähig** *Adj.* capable *(person);* *(körperlich)* able-bodied; ~**gesellschaft** die competitive society; ~**prinzip** das; *o. Pl.* competitive principle; ~**sport** der competitive sport *no art.*

**Leit·artikel** der *(Zeitungsw.)* leading article; **leiten** *tr. V.* a) *(anführen)* lead; head; be head of *(school);* *(verantwortlich sein für)* be in charge of *(project, expedition, etc.);* manage *(factory, enterprise);* *(den Vorsitz führen bei)* chair; conduct *(orchestra, choir);* ~**der Angestellter** manager; b) *(begleiten, führen)* lead; c) *(lenken)* direct; route *(traffic);* *(um~)* divert; ¹**Leiter** der; ~s, ~: leader; *(einer Abteilung)* head; *(eines Instituts)* director; *(einer Schule)* head teacher; headmaster *(Brit.);* principal *(esp. Amer.);* *(Vorsitzender)* chair[man]

²**Leiter** die; ~, ~n ladder

**Leiterin** die; ~, ~nen *s.* ¹**Leiter;** *(einer Schule)* head teacher; headmistress *(Brit.);* principal *(esp. Amer.)*

**Leit·planke** die crash barrier; guardrail *(Amer.)*

**Leitung** die; ~, ~en a) *o. Pl. s.* **leiten a:** leading; heading; being in charge; management; chairing; b) *o. Pl. (einer Expedition usw.)* leadership; *(Verantwortung)* responsibility *(Gen.* for); *(eines Betriebes, Unternehmens)* management; *(einer Sitzung, Diskussion)* chairmanship; c) *(leitende Personen)* management; *(einer Schule)* head and senior staff; d) *(Rohr~)* pipe; *(Haupt~)* main; e) *(Draht, Kabel)* cable; *(für ein Gerät)* lead; f) *(Telefon~)* line

**Leitungs·wasser** das tap-water

**Lektion** [lɛk'tsi̯oːn] die; ~, ~en lesson

**Lektüre** die; ~, ~n a) *o. Pl.* reading; b) *(Lesestoff)* reading [matter]

**Lende** die; ~, ~n loin

**lenken** *tr. V.* **a)** *auch itr.* steer; be at the controls of ⟨*aircraft*⟩; guide ⟨*missile*⟩; *(fahren)* drive ⟨*car etc.*⟩; **b)** direct ⟨*thoughts etc.*⟩ (**auf** + *Akk.* to); turn ⟨*attention*⟩ (**auf** + *Akk.* to); **c)** *(kontrollieren)* control ⟨*person, press, economy*⟩; govern ⟨*state*⟩; **Lenker der;** ~s, ~ **a)** handlebars *pl.;* **b)** *(Fahrer)* driver

**Lenk-:** ~**rad** das steering-wheel; ~**stange** die handlebars *pl.*

**Lenz der;** ~es, ~e *(dichter. veralt.)* spring

**Leopard der;** ~en, ~en leopard

**Lepra die;** ~: leprosy *no art.*

**Lerche die;** ~, ~n lark

**lernen** 1. *itr. V.* study; *(als Lehrling)* train; 2. *tr. V.* learn (**aus** from)

**lesbar** *Adj.* legible; *(klar)* lucid ⟨*style*⟩; *(verständlich)* comprehensible

**Lesbe die;** ~, ~n *(ugs.)* Lesbian; **Lesbierin** ['lɛsbiərɪn] **die;** ~, ~nen Lesbian; **lesbisch** *Adj.* Lesbian

**Lese·buch** das reader; ¹**lesen** *unr. tr., itr. V.* read; ²**lesen** *unr. tr. V.* **a)** pick ⟨*grapes, berries, fruit*⟩; gather ⟨*firewood*⟩; **Ähren** ~: glean [ears of corn]; **b)** *(aussondern)* pick over; **Leser der;** ~s, ~, **Leserin die;** ~, ~nen reader; **leserlich** 1. *Adj.* legible; 2. *adv.* legibly; **Lese·zeichen** das bookmark; **Lesung die;** ~, ~en reading

**Lette der;** ~n, ~n, **Lettin die;** ~, ~nen Latvian; **lettisch** *Adj.* Latvian; Lettish ⟨*language*⟩; **Lett·land (das);** ~s Latvia

**Letzt:** zu guter ~: in the end; **letzt...** *Adj.* last; ~en Endes in the end; *(äußerst...)* ultimate; *(neuest...)* latest ⟨*news*⟩; **letzte·mal: das** ~: [the] last time; **letzten·mal: beim** ~: last time; **zum** ~: for the last time; **letzter...** *Adj.* latter; **letztlich** *Adv.* ultimately; in the end

**Leuchte die;** ~, ~n light; **leuchten** *itr. V.* **a)** ⟨*moon, sun, star, etc.*⟩ be shining; ⟨*fire, face*⟩ glow; **b)** shine a/the light; jmdm. ~: light the way for sb.; **leuchtend** *Adj.* **a)** shining ⟨*eyes*⟩; brilliant ⟨*colours*⟩; bright ⟨*blue, red, etc.*⟩; **b)** *(großartig)* shining ⟨*example*⟩; **Leuchter der;** ~s, ~: candelabrum; *(für eine Kerze)* candlestick

**Leucht-:** ~**reklame** die neon sign; ~**turm** der lighthouse; ~**zifferblatt** das luminous dial

**leugnen** 1. *tr. V.* deny; 2. *itr. V.* deny it

**Leukämie die;** ~, ~n *(Med.)* leukaemia

**Leumund der;** ~[e]s *(geh.)* reputation

**Leute** *Pl.* people; die reichen/alten ~: the rich/the old

**Leutnant der;** ~s, ~s second lieutenant *(Milit.)*

**leut·selig** 1. *Adj.* affable; 2. *adv.* affably

**Lexikon** das; ~s, **Lexika** *od.* **Lexiken** encyclopaedia *(Gen.,* für of)

**Libanese der;** ~n, ~n, **Libanesin die;** ~, ~nen Lebanese; **Libanon (das)** *od.* **der;** ~s Lebanon

**Libelle die;** ~, ~n dragon-fly

**liberal** 1. *Adj.* liberal; 2. *adv.* liberally; **Liberale der/die;** *adj. Dekl.* liberal; **liberalisieren** *tr. V.* liberalize; relax ⟨*import controls*⟩

**Libero der;** ~s, ~s *(Fußball)* sweeper

**Libyen (das);** ~s Libya; **libysch** *Adj.* Libyan

**licht** *Adj.* **a)** light; **b)** *(dünn bewachsen)* sparse; thin; **Licht das;** ~[e]s, ~er **a)** *o. Pl.* light; **b)** *(elektrisches* ~*)* light; **c)** *Pl. auch* ~e *(Kerze)* candle; **Licht·bild** das [small] photograph *(for passport etc.)*; **licht·empfindlich** *Adj.* sensitive to light; ¹**lichten** 1. *tr. V.* thin out ⟨*trees etc.*⟩; 2. *refl. V.* ⟨*trees*⟩ thin out; ⟨*hair*⟩ grow thin; ⟨*fog, mist*⟩ lift

²**lichten** *tr. V. (Seemannsspr.)* den/die Anker ~: weigh anchor

**lichterloh** 1. *Adj.* blazing ⟨*fire*⟩; leaping ⟨*flames*⟩; 2. *adv.* ~ brennen be blazing fiercely

**Licht-:** ~**hupe** die headlight flasher; ~**reklame** die neon sign; ~**schalter** der light-switch

**Lichtung die;** ~, ~en clearing

**Lid** das; ~[e]s, ~er eyelid

**lieb** 1. *Adj.* **a)** *(liebevoll)* kind ⟨*words, gesture*⟩; **b)** *(liebenswert)* likeable; nice; *(stärker)* lovable ⟨*child, girl, pet*⟩; ~ aussehen look sweet *or (Amer.)* cute; **c)** *(artig)* good ⟨*child, dog*⟩; **d)** *(geschätzt)* dear; sein liebstes Spielzeug his favourite toy; ~er Hans/~e Else! *(am Briefanfang)* dear Hans/Else; **e)** *(angenehm)* welcome; es wäre mir ~/~er, wenn ...: I should be glad/should prefer it if ...; 2. *adv.* **a)** *(liebenswert)* kindly; **b)** *(artig)* nicely; **Liebe die;** ~, ~n **a)** *o. Pl.* love; ~ zu jmdm./zu etw. love for sb./of sth.; aus ~ [zu jmdm.] for love [of sb.]; tu mir die ~ und ...: do me a favour and ...; mit ~: lovingly; with loving care; **b)** *(ugs.:*

*geliebter Mensch)* love; **Liebelei** die; ~, ~en flirtation; **lieben** 1. *tr. V.* **a)** **jmdn.** ~: love sb.; *(sexuell)* make love to sb.; **sich** ~: be in love; *(sexuell)* make love; **b)** etw. ~: be fond of sth.; *(stärker)* love sth.; 2. *itr. V.* be in love; **liebend** *Adv.* etw. ~ **gern tun** [simply] love doing sth.; **liebenswürdig** *Adj.* kind; charming ⟨*smile*⟩; **lieber** *Adv.* **a)** *s.* **gern; b)** better; **laß das** ~: better not do that

**Liebes-: ~brief** der love-letter; **~paar** das courting couple; **~roman** der romantic novel

**liebe·voll** 1. *Adj.* loving *attrib.* ⟨*care*⟩; affectionate ⟨*embrace, gesture, person*⟩; 2. *adv.* lovingly; affectionately; *(mit Sorgfalt)* lovingly; **lieb|haben** *unr. tr. V.* love; *(gern haben)* be fond of; **Liebhaber** der; ~s, ~ a) lover; **b)** *(Interessierter, Anhänger)* enthusiast *(Gen.* for); *(Sammler)* collector; **lieblich** 1. *Adj.* **a)** charming; *(angenehm)* sweet ⟨*scent, sound*⟩; 2. *adv.* sweetly; *(angenehm)* pleasingly; **Liebling** der; ~s, ~e *(bes. als Anrede)* darling; *(bevorzugte Person)* favourite; **Lieblings-** favourite; **lieb·los** 1. *Adj.* loveless. 2. *adv.* **a)** without affection; **b)** *(ohne Sorgfalt)* without proper care; **liebsten: am** ~: *s.* **gern**

**Liechtenstein (das);** ~s Liechtenstein

**Lied** das; ~[e]s, ~er song

**liederlich** *Adj.* slovenly; messy ⟨*hairstyle, person*⟩

**Lieder-: ~macher** der; ~s, ~, **~macherin** die; ~, **~nen** singer-songwriter

**lief** 1. *u.* 3. *Pers. Sg. Prät. v.* **laufen**

**Lieferant** der; ~en, ~en supplier; **lieferbar** *Adj.* available; *(vorrätig)* in stock; **liefern** *tr. V.* **a)** *(bringen)* deliver (**an** + *Akk.* to); *(zur Verfügung stellen)* supply; **b)** *(hervorbringen)* produce; provide ⟨*eggs, honey, examples, raw material, etc.*⟩

**Liefer-: ~schein** der delivery note; **~termin** der delivery date

**Lieferung** die; ~, ~en delivery

**Liefer-: ~wagen** der [delivery] van; **~zeit** die delivery time

**Liege** die; ~, ~n day-bed; *(zum Ausklappen)* bed-settee; *(als Gartenmöbel)* sun-lounger; **liegen** *unr. itr. V.* lie; ⟨*person*⟩ be lying down; *(sich befinden)* be; ⟨*object*⟩ be [lying]; ⟨*town, house, etc.*⟩ be [situated]; **im Bett** ~:

lie in bed; **das liegt an ihm** *od.* **bei ihm** it is up to him; *(ist seine Schuld)* it is his fault; **es liegt mir nicht** it doesn't suit me; *(es spricht mich nicht an)* I doesn't appeal to me; *(ich mag es nicht)* I don't like it; **daran liegt ihm viel/wenig/nichts** he sets great/little/no store by that

**liegen-: ~|bleiben** *unr. itr. V.; mit sein* **a)** stay [lying]; **[im Bett]** ~: stay in bed; **b)** ⟨*things*⟩ stay, be left; *(vergessen werden)* be left behind; *(nicht erledigt werden)* be left undone; **~|lassen** *unr. tr. V.* **a)** leave; *(vergessen)* leave [behind]; **b)** *(unerledigt lassen)* leave ⟨*work*⟩ undone; leave ⟨*letters*⟩ unposted/unopened

**Liege-: ~stuhl** der deck-chair; **~wagen** der couchette car

**lieh** 1. *u.* 3. *Pers. Sg. Prät. v.* **leihen**

**lies** *Imperativ Sg. v.* **lesen**

**ließ** 1. *u.* 3. *Pers. Sg. Prät. v.* **lassen**

**liest** 3. *Pers. Sg. Präsens v.* **lesen**

**Lift** der; ~[e]s, ~e *od.* ~s **a)** lift *(Brit.)*; elevator *(Amer.)*; **b)** *Pl.:* ~e *(Ski~, Sessel~)* lift

**Liga** die; ~, **Ligen** league; *(Sport)* division

**Likör** der; ~s, ~e liqueur

**lila** *indekl. Adj.* mauve; *(dunkel~)* purple; **Lila** das; ~s *od. (ugs.)* ~s mauve; *(Dunkel~)* purple

**Lilie** ['li:li̯ə] die; ~, ~n lily

**Liliputaner** der; ~s, ~: dwarf

**Limit** das; ~s, ~s limit

**Limo** die, *auch:* das; ~, ~[s] *(ugs.)* fizzy drink; **Limonade** die; ~, ~n fizzy drink; *(Zitronen~)* lemonade

**Linde** die; ~, ~n lime[-tree]

**lindern** *tr. V.* relieve ⟨*suffering, pain*⟩; slake ⟨*thirst*⟩

**Lineal** das; ~s, ~e ruler

**Linie** ['li:ni̯ə] die; ~, ~n line; *(Verkehrsstrecke)* route; **die** ~ **12** *(Verkehrsw.)* the number 12; **auf die |schlanke|** ~ **achten** *(ugs. scherzh.)* watch one's figure; **auf der ganzen** ~ *(fig.)* all along the line

**linien-, Linien-: ~bus** der regular bus; **~flug** der scheduled flight; **~richter** der *(Fußball usw.)* linesman; *(Tennis)* line judge; *(Rugby)* touch judge; **~treu** 1. *Adj.* loyal to the party line *postpos.;* 2. *adv.* ⟨*act*⟩ in accordance with the party line

**linieren, liniieren** *tr. V.* rule

**link...** *Adj.* **a)** left; **b)** *(innen, nicht sichtbar)* wrong, reverse ⟨*side*⟩; **c)** *(in der Politik)* left-wing; **linkisch** 1.

*Adj.* awkward; **2.** *adv.* awkwardly; **links** *Adv.* on the left; *(Politik)* on the left wing

**links-, Links-:** ~**abbieger** der *(Verkehrsw.)* motorist/cyclist/car *etc.* turning left; ~**außen** der; ~, ~ *(Ballspiele)* left wing; outside left; ~**händer** der; ~s, ~: left-hander; ~**kurve** die left-hand bend; ~**verkehr** der driving *no art.* on the left

**Linoleum** das; ~s linoleum; lino

**Linse** die; ~, ~n a) *(Bot., Kochk.)* lentil; b) *(Med., Optik)* lens

**Lippe** die; ~, ~n lip; **Lippen·stift** der lipstick

**liquid** *Adj. (Wirtsch.)* liquid *(funds, resources)*; solvent *(business)*; **liquidieren** *(verhüll.: töten; Wirtsch.)* liquidate

**lispeln** *itr. V.* lisp

**Lissabon (das);** ~s Lisbon

**List** die; ~, ~en a) [cunning] trick; b) *(listige Art)* o. *Pl.* cunning

**Liste** die; ~, ~n list; **schwarze** ~: blacklist

**listig 1.** *Adj.* cunning; crafty; **2.** *adv.* cunningly; craftily

**Litauen (das);** ~s Lithuania; **Litauer** der; ~s, ~: Lithuanian; **litauisch** *Adj.* Lithuanian

**Liter** der, *auch:* das; ~s, ~: litre

**literarisch** *Adj.* literary; **Literatur** die; ~, ~en literature

**Litfaß·säule** die advertising column

**Lithographie** die; ~, ~n *(Druck)* lithograph

**litt** *1. u. 3. Pers. Sg. Prät. v.* leiden

**Litze** die; ~, ~n braid

**Lizenz** die; ~, ~en licence

**Lkw, LKW** [ɛlka:'ve:] der; ~[s], ~[s] *Abk.* **Lastkraftwagen** truck; lorry *(Brit.)*

**Lob** das; ~[e]s, ~e praise *no indef. art.*

**Lobby** ['lɔbi] die; ~, ~s *od.* **Lobbies** lobby

**loben** *tr.V.* praise; **löblich** *Adj.* commendable; **Lob·lied** das song of praise

**Loch** das; ~[e]s, **Löcher** hole; **lochen** *tr. V.* punch holes/a hole in; punch *(ticket)*; **Locher** der; ~s, ~: punch; **löcherig** *Adj.* full of holes *pred.*

**Locke** die; ~, ~n curl

**locken** *tr.V.* a) lure; b) *(reizen)* tempt

**Locken·wickler** der [hair] curler

**locker 1.** *Adj.* loose; *(entspannt)* relaxed *(position, muscles)*; slack *(rope, rein)*; **2.** *adv.* ~ sitzen *(tooth, screw, nail)* be loose; *(entspannt, ungezwun-*

*gen)* loosely; **locker|lassen** *unr. itr. V. (ugs.)* **nicht** ~: not give up; **lockern 1.** *tr. V.* loosen; slacken [off] *(rope etc.)*; relax *(muscles, limbs)*; **2.** *refl. V. (brick, tooth, etc.)* work itself loose; *(person)* loosen up

**lockig** *Adj.* curly

**Lock·vogel** der decoy

**Loden·mantel** der loden coat

**Löffel** der; ~s, ~: spoon; *(als Maßangabe)* spoonful; *(Jägerspr.)* ear; **löffeln** *tr. V.* spoon [up]

**log** *1. u. 3. Pers. Sg. Prät. v.* lügen

**Logarithmus** der; ~, **Logarithmen** *(Math.)* logarithm; log

**Loge** ['lo:ʒə] die; ~, ~n box; **logieren** *itr. V. (veralt.)* stay

**Logik** die; ~: logic; **logisch 1.** *Adj.* logical; **2.** *adv.* logically

**Lohn** der; ~[e]s, **Löhne** a) wage[s *pl.*]; pay *no indef. art.*, *no pl.*; b) o. *Pl. (Belohnung)* reward; **Lohn·büro** das payroll office

**lohnen 1.** *refl., itr. V.* be worth it; **2.** *tr. V.* be worth; **lohnend** *Adj.* rewarding

**Lohn·steuer** die income tax; **Lohnsteuer·karte** die income-tax card; **Lohn·tüte** die pay-packet *(Brit.)*; wage packet

**Lokal** das; ~s, ~e pub *(Brit. coll.)*; bar *(Amer.)*; *(Speise~)* restaurant; **Lokalität** die; ~, ~en locality

**Lokal-:** ~**blatt** das local paper; ~**termin** der *(Rechtsspr.)* visit to the scene [of the crime]

**Lokomotive** [lokomo'ti:və] die; ~, ~n locomotive; **Lokomotiv·führer** der engine-driver *(Brit.)*; engineer *(Amer.)*

**Lokus** der; ~ *od.* ~ses, ~ *od.* ~se *(salopp)* loo *(Brit. coll.)*; john *(Amer. coll.)*

**London (das);** ~s London; **Londoner 1.** *indekl. Adj.* London; **2.** der; ~s, ~: Londoner

**Lorbeer** der; ~s, ~en a) laurel; b) *(Gewürz)* bay-leaf

**Lore** die; ~, ~n car; *(kleiner)* tub

**los 1.** *Adj.* a) *(gelöst, ab)* off; b) es ist etwas ~: there is something going on; c) jmdn./etw. ~ sein be rid of sb./sth.; **2.** *Adv. (als Aufforderung)* come on!

**Los** das; ~es, ~e a) lot; b) *(Lotterie~)* ticket

**Lösch·blatt** das piece of blotting-paper; **löschen** *tr. V.* a) put out; extinguish; **seinen Durst** ~ *(fig.)* quench one's thirst; b) *(tilgen)* delete *(entry)*; erase *(recording, memory, etc.)*; **Lösch·papier** das blotting paper

**lose** 1. *Adj.* loose; 2. *adv.* loosely
**Löse·geld** das ransom
**losen** *itr. V.* draw lots (**um** for)
**lösen** 1. *tr. V.* a) remove ⟨*stamp, wall-paper*⟩; etw. von etw. ~: remove sth. from sth.; b) *(lockern)* undo ⟨*screw, belt, tie*⟩; c) *(klären)* solve; resolve ⟨*contradiction, conflict*⟩; d) *(annullieren)* break off ⟨*engagement*⟩; cancel ⟨*contract*⟩; sever ⟨*relationship*⟩; e) *(kaufen)* buy, obtain ⟨*ticket*⟩; 2. *refl. V.* a) *(lose werden)* come off; *(sich lockern)* ⟨*wallpaper, plaster*⟩ come off; ⟨*packing, screw*⟩ come loose; b) *(sich klären)* ⟨*puzzle, problem*⟩ be solved; c) *(sich auflösen)* dissolve
**los-:** ~|**fahren** *unr. itr. V.; mit sein* set off; *(wegfahren)* move off; ~|**gehen** *unr. itr. V.; mit sein* a) *(aufbrechen)* set off; b) *(ugs.: beginnen)* start; c) *(ugs.: abgehen)* ⟨*button, handle, etc.*⟩ come off; ~|**kommen** *unr. itr. V.; mit sein* *(ugs.)* a) get away; b) *(freikommen)* get free; ~|**lassen** *unr. tr. V.* a) *(nicht festhalten)* let go of; b) *(freilassen)* let ⟨*person, animal*⟩ go; ~|**legen** *itr. V.* *(ugs.)* get going
**löslich** *Adj.* soluble
**los-:** ~|**machen** 1. *tr. V.* *(ugs.)* let ⟨*animal*⟩ loose; untie ⟨*string, line, rope*⟩; unhitch ⟨*trailer*⟩; ~|**reißen** *unr. refl. V.* break free *or* loose; ~|**sagen** *refl. V.* sich von jmdm./etw. ~sagen break with sb./sth.; ~|**schlagen** *unr. itr. V.* *(bes. Milit.)* attack; launch one's attack
**Losung** die; ~, ~en slogan; *(Milit.: Kennwort)* password
**Lösung** die; ~, ~en a) solution *(Gen., für* to); b) *s.* lösen 1 d: breaking off; cancellation; severing
**los|werden** *unr. tr. V.; mit sein* get rid of
**Lot** das; ~|e|s, ~e plumb[-bob]; [nicht] im ~ sein be [out of] plumb
**löten** *tr. V.* solder
**Lotion** [lo'tsio:n] die; ~, ~en lotion
**Lotse** der; ~n, ~n *(Seew.)* pilot; **lotsen** *tr. V.* guide
**Lotterie** die; ~, ~n lottery; **Lotto** das; ~s, ~s national lottery
**Lotto-:** ~**schein** der national-lottery coupon; ~**zahlen** *Pl.* winning national-lottery numbers
**Löwe** der; ~n, ~n a) lion; b) *(Astrol.)* Leo; the Lion
**Löwen-:** ~**anteil** der lion's share, ~**mäulchen** das snapdragon; ~**zahn** der dandelion

**Löwin** die; ~, ~nen lioness
**loyal** [loa'ja:l] 1. *Adj.* loyal; 2. *adv.* loyally; **Loyalität** die; ~: loyalty
**LP** [ɛl'pe:] die; ~, ~|s| *Abk.* **Langspielplatte** LP
**Luchs** der; ~es, ~e lynx
**Lücke** die; ~, ~n gap; **Lücken·büßer** der; ~s, ~ *(ugs.)* stopgap; **lückenhaft** *Adj.* sketchy; **lückenlos** *Adj.* complete
**lud** *1. u. 3. Pers. Sg. Prät. v.* laden
**Luft** die; ~, Lüfte air; **an die frische ~ gehen** get out in[to] the fresh air; **die ~ anhalten** hold one's breath; **tief ~ holen** take a deep breath; **in die ~ gehen** *(fig. ugs.)* blow one's top *(coll.)*
**luft-, Luft-:** ~**ballon** der balloon; ~**brücke** die airlift; ~**dicht** *Adj.* airtight; ~**druck** der a) *(Physik)* air pressure; b) *(Druckwelle)* blast
**lüften** 1. *tr. V.* a) air ⟨*room, clothes, etc.*⟩; b) raise ⟨*hat*⟩; c) disclose ⟨*secret*⟩; 2. *itr. V.* air the room/house *etc.*
**luft-, Luft-:** ~**fahrt** die; *o. Pl.* aviation *no art.;* ~**feuchtigkeit** die [atmospheric] humidity; ~**gekühlt** *Adj.* air-cooled; ~**gewehr** das air rifle; airgun
**luftig** *Adj.* airy ⟨*room, building, etc.*⟩; light ⟨*clothes*⟩
**Luftkissen·boot** das hovercraft
**luft-, Luft-:** ~**leer** *Adj.* ein ~leerer Raum a vacuum; ~**linie** die *o. Pl.* 1 000 km ~linie 1,000 km. as the crow flies; ~**loch** das air-hole; ~**matratze** die air-bed; air mattress; Lilo (P); ~**pirat** der [aircraft] hijacker; ~**post** die airmail; etw. per *od.* mit ~post schicken send sth. [by] airmail; ~**pumpe** die air pump; *(für Fahrrad)* [bicycle-]pump; ~**röhre** die *(Anat.)* windpipe; ~**schiff** das airship; ~**schloß** das castle in the air; ~**schutz** der air-raid protection *no art.;* ~**schutz·keller** der air-raid shelter; ~**verschmutzung** die air pollution; ~**waffe** die air force
**Lüge** die; ~, ~n lie; **lügen** 1. *itr., tr. V.* lie; das ist gelogen! that's a lie!; **Lügner** der; ~s, ~: liar
**Luke** die; ~, ~n *(Dach~)* skylight; *(bei Schiffen)* hatch; *(Keller~)* trap-door
**lukrativ** 1. *Adj.* lucrative; 2. *adv.* lucratively
**Lümmel** der; ~s, ~: lout; *(ugs., fam.: Bengel)* rascal
**Lump** der; ~en, ~en scoundrel; **lumpen** *(ugs.)* tr. V. sich nicht ~ lassen splash out *(coll.)*; **Lumpen** der; ~s,

~: rag; **Lumpen·sammler** der rag-and-bone man

**Lunge** die; ~, ~n lungs *pl.*

**Lungen-**: **~entzündung** die pneumonia *no indef. art.*; **~krebs** der lung cancer; **~zug** der inhalation

**Lunte** die; ~, ~n fuse; match

**Lupe** die; ~, ~n magnifying glass

**Lurch** der; ~[e]s, ~e amphibian

**Lust** die; ~ a) ~ **haben, etw. zu tun** feel like doing sth.; b) *(Vergnügen)* pleasure; joy; **lustig** 1. *Adj.* a) merry; jolly; enjoyable ⟨*time*⟩; b) *(komisch)* funny; 2. *adv.* a) merrily; b) *(komisch)* funnily

**lust-, Lust-**: **~los** 1. *Adj.* listless; 2. *adv.* listlessly; **~spiel** das comedy

**lutherisch** *Adj.* Lutheran

**lutschen** 1. *tr. V.* suck; 2. *itr. V.* suck; **an etw.** *(Dat.)* ~: suck sth.

**Luxemburg** (das); ~s Luxembourg

**luxuriös** 1. *Adj.* luxurious; 2. *adv.* luxuriously; **Luxus** der; ~: luxury

**Lymph·knoten** der lymph node

**lynchen** *tr. V.* lynch

**Lyrik** die; ~: lyric poetry; **lyrisch** *Adj.* lyrical; lyric ⟨*poetry*⟩

**Lyzeum** das; ~s, Lyzeen girls' high school

# M

**m, M** [ɛm] **das**; ~, ~: m/M

**m** *Abk.* Meter m

**machen** 1. *tr. V.* a) make; **aus Plastik/ Holz** *usw.* **gemacht** made of plastic/ wood *etc.*; **sich** *(Dat.)* **etw.** ~ **lassen** have sth. made; **etw. aus jmdm.** ~: make sb. into sth.; **jmdn. zum Präsidenten** *usw.* ~: make sb. president *etc.*; **jmdm./sich [einen] Kaffee** ~: make [some] coffee for sb./oneself; b) *(verursachen)* **jmdm. Arbeit** ~: make [extra] work for sb.; **das macht das Wetter** that's [because of] the weather; c) *(ausführen)* do ⟨*job, repair, etc.*⟩; **einen Spaziergang** ~: go for a walk; **eine Reise** ~: go on a journey; **einen Besuch [bei jmdm.]** ~: pay [sb.] a visit; d) *(tun)* do; **was machst du da?**

what are you doing?; **so etwas macht man nicht** that [just] isn't done; e) **was macht ...?** *(wie ist es um ... bestellt?)* how is ...?; **was macht die Gesundheit/ Arbeit?** how are you keeping/ how ist the job [getting on]?; f) *(ergeben) (beim Rechnen)* be; *(bei Geldbeträgen)* come to; **zwei mal zwei macht vier** two times two is four; **das macht 12 DM** that is 12 marks; *(Endsumme)* that comes to 12 marks; g) *(schaden)* **was macht das schon?** what does it matter?; **macht nichts!** *(ugs.)* it doesn't matter; h) *(teilnehmen an)* **einen Kursus** *od.* **Lehrgang** ~: take a course; **i) mach's gut!** *(ugs.)* look after yourself!; *(auf Wiedersehen)* so long!; 2. *refl. V.* a) **sich an etw.** *(Akk.)* ~: get down to sth.; b) *(ugs.: sich entwickeln)* do well; c) **mach dir nichts daraus!** *(ugs.)* don't let it bother you; 3. *itr. V.* a) **mach schon!** *(ugs.)* get a move on! *(coll.)*; b) **das macht hungrig/durstig** it makes you hungry/thirsty; **das macht dick** it's fattening; **Machenschaften** *Pl. (abwertend)* wheeling and dealing *sing.*

**Macht** die; ~, **Mächte** power; **an die** ~ **kommen** come to power; **Macht·haber** der; ~s, ~: ruler; **mächtig** 1. *Adj.* a) powerful; b) *(beeindruckend groß)* mighty; 2. *adv.* *(ugs.)* terribly *(coll.)*

**macht-, Macht-**: **~kampf** der power struggle; **~los** *Adj.* powerless; **gegen etw. ~los sein** be powerless in the face of sth.; **~probe** die trial of strength

**Mädchen** das; ~s, ~ a) girl; b) *(Haus~)* maid; **mädchenhaft** *Adj.* girlish; **Mädchen·name** der a) girl's name; b) *(Name vor der Ehe)* maiden name

**Made** die; ~, ~n maggot; **madig** *Adj.* maggoty; **jmdn./etw.** ~ **machen** *(ugs.)* run sb./sth. down

**Madonna** die; ~, **Madonnen** madonna

**mag** *1. u. 3. Pers. Sg. Präsens v.* **mögen**

**Magazin** das; ~s, ~e a) *(Lager)* store; *(für Waren)* stock-room; b) *(für Patronen, Dias, Film usw.; Zeitschrift)* magazine

**Magen** der; ~s, **Mägen** *od.* ~: stomach

**magen-, Magen-**: **~bitter** der; ~s, ~: bitters *pl.*; **~schmerzen** *Pl.* stomach-ache *sing.*

**mager** *Adj.* a) thin; b) *(fettarm)* low-fat; low in fat *pred.*; lean ⟨*meat*⟩; c) *(fig.)* poor ⟨*soil, harvest*⟩; meagre ⟨*profit, increase, success, report, etc.*⟩; thin ⟨*programme*⟩

**Mager-:** ~**milch** die skim[med] milk; ~**quark** der low-fat curd cheese

**Magie** die; ~: magic; **Magier** ['maːgiɐ] der; ~s, ~ *(auch fig.)* magician; **magisch** *Adj.* magic ⟨*powers*⟩; *(geheimnisvoll)* magical

**Magistrat** der; ~[e]s, ~e City Council

**Magnet** der; ~en *od.* ~[e]s, ~e magnet; **magnetisch** 1. *Adj.* magnetic; 2. *adv.* magnetically; **Magnetismus** der; ~: magnetism; **Magnet·nadel** die [compass] needle

**Mahagoni** das; ~s mahogany

**Mäh·drescher** der combine harvester; **mähen** 1. *tr. V.* mow; cut ⟨*corn*⟩; 2. *itr. V.* mow; *(Getreide ~)* reap

**Mahl** das; ~[e]s, **Mähler** *(geh.)* meal; repast *(formal)*

**mahlen** *unr. tr., itr. V.* grind

**Mahl·zeit** meal

**Mähne** die; ~, ~n mane

**mahnen** *tr. V.* urge; remind ⟨*debtor*⟩

**Mahn-:** ~**mal** das memorial *(erected as a warning to future generations)*; ~**schreiben** das reminder

**Mahnung** die; ~, ~en a) exhortation; *(Warnung)* admonition; b) *s.* **Mahnschreiben**

**Mai** der; ~[e]s *od.* ~: May

**Mai~:** ~**baum** der maypole; ~**glöckchen** das lily of the valley; ~**käfer** der May-bug

**Mais** der; ~es maize; corn *(esp. Amer.); (als Gericht)* sweet corn; **Mais·kolben** der corn-cob; *(als Gericht)* corn on the cob

**Majestät** die; ~, ~en a) *(Titel)* Majesty; Eure ~: Your Majesty; b) *o. Pl. (geh.)* majesty; **majestätisch** 1. *Adj.* majestic; 2. *adv.* majestically

**Major** der; ~s, ~e *(Milit.)* major

**Majoran** der; ~s, ~e marjoram

**makaber** *Adj.* macabre

**Makedonien** [makeˈdoːni̯ən] *(das)*; ~s Macedonia

**Makel** der; ~s, ~ *(geh.)* a) *(Schmach)* stigma; b) *(Fehler)* blemish; **makel·los** 1. *Adj.* flawless; spotless ⟨*white, cleanness*⟩; 2. *adv.* immaculately; spotlessly ⟨*clean*⟩

**Make-up** [meːkˈlap] das; ~s, ~s make-up

**Makkaroni** *Pl.* macaroni *sing.*

**Makler** der; ~s, ~: estate agent *(Brit.)*; realtor *(Amer.)*

**Makrele** die; ~, ~n mackerel

**Makrone** die; ~, ~n macaroon

**mal** 1. *Adv.* times; *(bei Flächen)* by; 2. *Partikel* **komm ~ her!** come here!; ¹**Mal** das; ~[e]s, ~e time; **mit einem** ~[e] all at once; ²**Mal** das; ~[e]s, ~e *od.* **Mäler** mark; *(Muttermal)* birthmark; *(braun)* mole

**Malaie** der; ~n, ~n Malay; **Malaysia** *(das)*; ~s Malaysia

**Mal·buch** das colouring-book; **malen** *tr., itr. V.* paint; decorate ⟨*flat, room, walls*⟩; **Maler** der; ~s, ~: painter; **Malerei** die; ~, ~en painting; **malerisch** 1. *Adj.* picturesque; 2. *adv.* picturesquely

**mal|nehmen** *unr. tr., itr. V.* multiply *(mit by)*

**Malz·bier** das malt beer

**Mama** die; ~, ~s *(fam.)* mamma; **Mami** die; ~, ~s *(fam.)* mummy *(Brit. coll.)*; mommy *(Amer. coll.)*

**Mammut** das; ~s, ~e *od.* ~s mammoth

**man** *Indefinitpron. im Nom.* one; you *2nd person; (irgend jemand)* somebody; *(die Behörden; die Leute dort)* they *pl.; (die Menschen im allgemeinen)* people *pl;* ~ **hat mir gesagt** ...: I was told ...

**Management** ['mænɪdʒmənt] das; ~s, ~s management; **managen** ['mɛnɪdʒn] *tr. V.* a) *(ugs.)* fix; organize; b) *(betreuen)* manage ⟨*singer, artist, player*⟩; **Manager** ['mɛnɪdʒɐ] der; ~s, ~: manager; *(eines Fußballvereins)* club secretary

**manch** *Indefinitpron.* a) *attr.* many a; in [so] ~**er Beziehung** in many respects; b) *alleinstehend* ~**er** many a person/man; ~**e** *Pl.* some; *(viele)* many; [so] ~**es** a number of things; *(allerhand Verschiedenes)* all kinds of things; **mancherlei** *unbest. Gattungsz.* a) *attr.* various; a number of; b) *alleinstehend* various things; **manch·mal** *Adv.* sometimes

**Mandant** der; ~en, ~en client

**Mandarine** die; ~, ~n mandarin [orange]

**Mandel** die; ~, ~n a) almond; b) *(Anat.)* tonsil; **Mandel·entzündung** die tonsillitis *no indef. art.*

**Manege** [maˈneːʒə] die; ~, ~n *(im Zirkus)* ring; *(in der Reitschule)* arena

¹**Mangel** der; ~s, **Mängel** a) *o. Pl. (Fehlen)* lack **(an** + *Dat.* of); *(Knappheit)* shortage, lack **(an** + *Dat.* of); b) *(Fehler)* defect

²**Mangel** die; ~, ~n [large] mangle

**mangelhaft 1.** *Adj.* faulty ⟨*goods, German, English, etc.*⟩; *(unzulänglich)* inadequate ⟨*knowledge, lighting*⟩; *(Schulw.)* **die Note „~"** the mark 'unsatisfactory'; *(bei Prüfungen)* the fail mark; **2.** *adv.* faultily; *(unzulänglich)* inadequately; **¹mangeln** *itr. V.; unpers.* **es mangelt an etw.** *(Dat.)* *(etw. fehlt)* there is a lack of sth.; *(etw. ist unzureichend vorhanden)* there is a shortage of sth.; **jmdm./einer Sache mangelt es an etw.** *(Dat.)* sb./sth. lacks sth.

**²mangeln** *tr. V.* mangle

**mangels** *Präp. mit Gen.* in the absence of

**Manie die; ~, ~n** mania

**Manier die; ~, ~en** a) manner; b) *Pl.* *(Umgangsformen)* manners; **manierlich 1.** *Adj.* a) *(fam.)* well-mannered; well-behaved ⟨*child*⟩; b) *(ugs.: einigermaßen gut)* decent; **2.** *adv.* a) *(fam.)* nicely; b) *(ugs.: einigermaßen gut)* **ganz/recht ~:** quite/really nicely

**Manifest das; ~[e]s, ~e** manifesto

**Maniküre die; ~:** manicure; **maniküren** *tr. V.* manicure

**manipulieren** *tr. V.* manipulate; rig ⟨*election result etc.*⟩

**Manko das; ~s, ~s** shortcoming; deficiency

**Mann der; ~[e]s, Männer** a) man; b) *(Ehemann)* husband; **Männchen das; ~s, ~** a) little man; b) *(Tier~)* male; **~ machen** ⟨*animal*⟩ sit up and beg

**Mannequin** ['manəkē] **das; ~s, ~s** mannequin; [fashion] model

**mannig·fach** *Adj.* multifarious

**männlich 1.** *Adj.* a) male; b) *s.* **maskulin 1; 2.** *adv.* in a masculine way; **Mannschaft die; ~, ~en** *(Sport, auch fig.)* team; *(Schiffs-, Flugzeugbesatzung)* crew; *(Milit.)* unit

**Manöver das; ~s, ~** a) *(Milit.)* exercise; **~** *Pl.* manœuvres; b) *(Bewegung; fig. abwertend: Trick)* manœuvre; **manövrieren** *itr., tr. V.* manœuvre

**Mansarde die; ~, ~n** attic; *(Zimmer)* attic room

**Manschette die; ~, ~n** cuff; **Manschetten·knopf der** cuff-link

**Mantel der; ~s, Mäntel** coat

**Manuskript das; ~[e]s, ~e** a) manuscript; *(Typoskript)* typescript; b) *(Notizen)* notes *pl.*

**Mappe die; ~, ~n** a) folder; b) *(Aktentasche)* briefcase; *(Schul~)* schoolbag

**Marathon·lauf** [...ton...] **der** marathon

**Märchen das; ~s, ~:** fairy story; fairy-tale; *(ugs.: Lüge)* [tall] story *(coll.)*; **Märchen·buch das** book of fairy stories; **märchenhaft 1.** *Adj.* magical; **2.** *adv.* magically; *(ugs.)* fantastically *(coll.)*

**Margarine die; ~:** margarine

**Margerite die; ~, ~n** ox-eye daisy

**Maria (die); ~s** *od. (Rel.)* **Mariä** Mary; **Marien·käfer der** ladybird

**Marihuana das; ~s** marijuana

**Marinade die; ~, ~n** *(Kochk.)* marinade; *(Salatsauce)* [marinade] dressing

**Marine die; ~, ~n** fleet; *(Kriegs~)* navy

**Marionette die; ~, ~n** puppet; marionette; **Marionetten·theater das** puppet theatre

**¹Mark die; ~, ~:** mark; **Deutsche ~:** Deutschmark

**²Mark das; ~[e]s** a) *(Knochen~)* marrow; b) *(Frucht~)* pulp

**markant** *Adj.* striking; prominent ⟨*figure, nose, chin*⟩; clear-cut ⟨*features, profile*⟩

**Marke die; ~, ~n** a) *(Waren~)* brand; *(Fabrikat)* make; b) *(Brief~, Rabatt~, Beitrags~)* stamp; c) *(Essen~)* meal-ticket; d) *(Erkennungs~)* [identification] disc; *(Dienst~)* [police] identification badge; ≈ warrant card *(Brit.)* or *(Amer.)* ID card

**Marken-: ~artikel der** proprietary *or* *(Brit.)* branded article; **~zeichen das** trade mark

**markieren** *tr. V.* a) mark; b) *(ugs.: vortäuschen)* sham ⟨*illness, breakdown, etc.*⟩; **2.** *itr. V. (ugs.: simulieren)* put it on *(coll.)*; **Markierung die; ~, ~en** marking

**Markt der; ~[e]s, Märkte** market; *(~platz)* market-place *or* -square; **freitags ist ~:** Friday is market-day

**Markt-: ~forschung die** market research *no def. art.*; **~frau die** market-woman; **~halle die** covered market; **~lücke die** gap in the market; **~platz der** market-place; **~stand der** market stall; **~wirtschaft die** market economy

**Marmelade die; ~, ~n** jam; *(Orangen~)* marmalade

**Marmor der; ~s** marble

**Marokkaner der; ~s, ~:** Moroccan; **marokkanisch** *Adj.* Moroccan; **Marokko (das); ~s** Morocco

**Marone** die; ~, ~n [sweet] chestnut

**Mars** der; ~: Mars *no def. art.*

**Marsch** der; ~|e|s, **Märsche** march; *(Wanderung)* [long] walk; **marschieren** *itr. V.; mit sein* march; *(wandern)* walk

**Mars·mensch** der Martian

**Marter** die; ~, ~n *(geh.)* torture; *(seelisch)* torment; **martern** *tr. V. (geh.)* torture

**Märtyrer** der; ~s, ~: martyr; **Martyrium** das; ~s, Martyrien martyrdom

**Marxismus** der; ~: Marxism *no art.;* **Marxist** der; ~en, ~en Marxist; **marxistisch** *Adj.* Marxist

**März** der; ~|es| March

**Marzipan** das; ~s marzipan

**Masche** die; ~, ~n stitch; *(Lauf~)* run; ladder *(Brit.); (beim Netz)* mesh; **Maschen·draht** der wire netting

**Maschine** die; ~, ~n a) *(auch ugs.: Motorrad)* machine; b) *(ugs.: Automotor)* engine; c) *(Flugzeug)* [aero]plane; d) *(Schreib~)* typewriter; **maschine·geschrieben** *Adj.* typewritten; **maschinell** 1. *Adj.* machine *attrib.;* by machine *postpos.;* 2. *adv.* by machine; ~ **hergestellt** machine-made

**Maschinen-:** ~**gewehr** das machine-gun; ~**pistole** die sub-machine-gun

**maschine|schreiben** *unr. itr. V.; nur im Inf. u. Part.* type

**Masern** *Pl.* measles *sing. or pl.*

**Maserung** die; ~, ~en [wavy] grain

**Maske** die; ~, ~n mask; **Masken·ball** der masked ball; **Maskerade** die; ~, ~n [fancy-dress] costume; **maskieren** 1. *tr. V.* mask; 2. *refl. V.* put on a mask/masks

**Maskottchen** das; ~s, ~: [lucky] mascot

**maskulin** [*auch* '---] 1. *Adj. (auch Sprachw.)* masculine; 2. *adv.* in a masculine way

**maß** *1. u. 3. Pers. Sg. Prät. v.* **messen**; ¹**Maß** das; ~es, ~e a) measure (*für* of); *(fig.)* das ~ ist **voll** enough is enough; b) *(Größe)* measurement; c) *(Grad)* degree (**an** + *Dat.* of); **in großem/gewissem** ~e to a great/certain extent; ²**Maß** die; ~, ~|e| *(bayr., österr.)* litre [of beer]

**Massage** [ma'sa:ʒə] die; ~, ~n massage

**Massaker** das; ~s, ~: massacre

**Maß-:** ~**anzug** der made-to-measure suit; ~**arbeit** die a) custom-made item; *(Kleidungsstück)* made-to-

measure item; b) *(genaue Arbeit)* neat work

**Masse** die; ~, ~n a) mass; b) *(Gemisch)* mixture

**Maß·einheit** die unit of measurement

**Massen·grab** das mass grave; **massenhaft** 1. *Adj.; nicht präd.* in huge numbers *postpos.;* 2. *adv.* on a huge scale

**massen-, Massen-:** ~**karambolage** die multiple crash; ~**medium** das mass medium; ~**mörder** der mass murderer; ~**produktion** die mass production; ~**weise** *Adv.* in huge numbers

**Masseur** [ma'søːʀ] der; ~s, ~e masseur; **Masseurin** die; ~, ~nen, **Masseuse** [ma'søːzə] die; ~, ~n masseuse

**maß·gebend, maß·geblich** 1. *Adj.* authoritative ⟨book, expert, opinion⟩; definitive ⟨text⟩; influential ⟨person, circles, etc.⟩; decisive ⟨factor, influence, etc.⟩; 2. *adv.* ⟨influence⟩ to a considerable extent; *(entscheidend)* decisively; **maß|halten** *unr. itr. V.* exercise moderation

**massieren** *tr. V.* massage

**mäßig** 1. *Adj.* moderate; *(mittel~)* mediocre; 2. *adv.* in moderation; moderately ⟨gifted, talented⟩; *(mittel~)* indifferently; **mäßigen** *refl. V. (geh.)* a) practise *or* exercise moderation; b) *(sich beherrschen)* control *or* restrain oneself; **Mäßigkeit** die; ~: moderation; **Mäßigung** die; ~: moderation

**massiv** 1. *Adj.* a) solid; b) *(heftig)* massive ⟨demand⟩; crude ⟨accusation, threat⟩; strong ⟨attack, criticism, pressure⟩; 2. *adv.* ⟨attack⟩ strongly; ⟨accuse, threaten⟩ crudely

**maß-, Maß-:** ~**krug** der *(südd., österr.)* litre beer-mug; *(aus Steingut)* stein; ~**los** 1. *Adj.* extreme; gross ⟨exaggeration, insult⟩; excessive ⟨demand, claim⟩; boundless ⟨ambition, greed, sorrow, joy⟩; 2. *adv.* extremely; ⟨exaggerate⟩ grossly; ~**nahme** die; ~, ~n measure; ~**regel** die regulation; *(Maßnahme)* measure; ~**regeln** *tr. V. (zurechtweisen)* reprimand; *(bestrafen)* discipline; ~**stab** der a) standard; b) *(einer Karte, eines Modells usw.)* scale; ~**voll** 1. *Adj.* moderate; 2. *adv.* in moderation

**Mast** der; ~|e|s, ~en, *auch:* ~e *(Schiffs~, Antennen~)* mast; *(Stange,*

*Fahnen~)* pole; *(Hochspannungs~)* pylon

**mästen** *tr. V.* fatten

**masturbieren** *itr., tr. V.* masturbate

**Match** [mɛtʃ] *das od.* der; *~[e]s, ~s od. ~e* match

**Material** das; *~s, ~ien* material; *(Bau~; Hilfsmittel)* materials *pl.;* **Materialismus** der; *~:* materialism; **Materialist** der; *~en, ~en* materialist; **materialistisch** 1. *Adj.* materialistic; 2. *adv.* materialistically

**Materie** die; *~, ~n* a) matter; b) *(geh.: Thema, Gegenstand)* subjectmatter; **materiell** 1. *Adj. (finanziell)* financial; 2. *adv.* materially; *(finanziell)* financially

**Mathematik** die; *~:* mathematics *sing., no art.;* **mathematisch** 1. *Adj.* mathematical; 2. *adv.* mathematically

**Matjes** der; *~, ~:* matie [herring]

**Matratze** die; *~, ~n* mattress

**Matrose** der; *~n, ~n* sailor; seaman

**Matsch** der; *~[e]s (ugs.)* mud; *(breiiger Schmutz)* sludge; *(Schnee~)* slush; **matschig** *Adj. (ugs.)* a) muddy; slushy *⟨snow⟩;* b) *(weich)* mushy; squashy *⟨fruit⟩*

**matt** 1. *Adj.* a) weak; feeble *⟨applause, reaction⟩;* b) *(glanzlos)* matt; dull *⟨metal, mirror, etc.⟩;* c) *(undurchsichtig)* frosted *⟨glass⟩;* pearl *⟨light-bulb⟩;* d) subdued; *(Schach)* checkmated; *~!* checkmate!; 2. *adv.* a) *(kraftlos)* weakly; b) *(mäßig) ⟨protest, contradict⟩* feebly

**Matte** die; *~, ~n* mat

**Matt·scheibe** die *(ugs.)* telly *(Brit. coll.);* box *(coll.)*

**Mätzchen** das; *~s, ~: ~ machen (ugs.)* fod about *or* around

**Mauer** die; *~, ~n* wall; **mauern** 1. *tr. V.* build; 2. *itr. V.* lay bricks; **Mauer·werk** das a) masonry; *(aus Ziegeln)* brickwork; b) *(Mauern)* walls *pl.*

**Maul** das; *~[e]s, Mäuler (von Tieren)* mouth; *(derb: Mund)* gob *(sl.)*

**Maul-:** *~esel* der mule; *~korb* der *(auch fig.)* muzzle; *~tier* das mule; *~wurf* der mole

**Maurer** der; *~s, ~:* bricklayer

**Maus** die; *~, Mäuse* mouse

**Mauschelei** die; *~, ~en (ugs. abwertend)* shady wheeling and dealing *no indef. art.;* **mauscheln** *itr. V. (ugs. abwertend)* engage in shady wheeling and dealing

**Mäuschen** das; *~s, ~:* little mouse; **mäuschen·still** *Adj. ~ sein* be as quiet as a mouse; **Mause·falle** die mousetrap

**Maut** die; *~, ~en* toll

**maximal** 1. *Adj.* maximum; 2. *adv. ~ zulässige Geschwindigkeit* maximum permitted speed; **Maxime** die; *~, ~n* maxim; **Maximum** das; *~s, Maxima* maximum *(an + Dat. of)*

**Mayonnaise** [majo'nɛːzə] die; *~, ~n* mayonnaise

**Mäzen** der; *~s, ~e (geh.)* patron

**MdB, M.d.B.** *Abk.* Mitglied des Bundestages Member of the Bundestag

**m.E.** *Abk.* meines Erachtens in my opinion *or* view

**Mechanik** die; *~:* mechanics *sing., no art.;* **Mechaniker** der; *~s, ~:* mechanic; **mechanisch** 1. *Adj.* mechanical; power *attrib. ⟨loom, press⟩;* 2. *adv.* mechanically; **Mechanismus** der; *~, Mechanismen* mechanism

**meckern** *itr. V.* a) *(auch fig.)* bleat; b) *(ugs.: nörgeln)* grumble; moan

**Mecklenburg-Vorpommern (das);** *~s* Mecklenburg-Western Pomerania

**Medaille** [me'daljə] die; *~, ~n* medal; **Medaillon** [medal'jöː] das; *~s, ~s* a) locket; b) *(Kochk., bild. Kunst)* medallion

**Medikament** das; *~[e]s, ~e* medicine; *(Droge)* drug

**meditieren** *itr. V.* meditate *(über + Akk.* [up]on)

**Medium** das; *~s, Medien* medium

**Medizin** die; *~, ~en* medicine; **Mediziner** der; *~s, ~:* doctor; *(Student)* medical student; **medizinisch** 1. *Adj.* medical; medicinal *⟨bath etc.⟩;* medicated *⟨toothpaste, soap, etc.⟩;* 2. *adv.* medically

**Meer** das; *~[e]s, ~e (auch fig.)* sea; *am ~:* by the sea; **Meer·enge** die straits *pl.;* strait

**Meeres-:** *~bucht* die bay; *~früchte* Pl. *(Kochk.)* seafood *sing.;* *~spiegel* der sea-level

**Meer-:** *~jungfrau* die mermaid; *~rettich* der horse-radish; *~schweinchen* das guinea-pig

**Megaphon** das; *~s, ~e* megaphone; loud hailer

**Mehl** das; *~[e]s* flour; **mehlig** *Adj.* a) floury; b) mealy *⟨potato, apple, etc.⟩*

**mehr** 1. *Indefinitpron.* more; 2. *Adv.* a) more; b) **nicht ~:** not ... any more; no longer; *es war niemand ~ da* there was no one left; *das wird nie ~ vorkommen* it will never happen again; *da ist* nichts ~ zu machen there is nothing more to be done

**mehr-: ~bändig** *Adj.* in several volumes *postpos.*; **~deutig 1.** *Adj.* ambiguous; **2.** *adv.* ambiguously

**mehren** *(geh.) refl. V.* increase; **mehrer...** *Indefinitpron. u. unbest. Zahlwort* **a)** *attr.* several; **b)** *alleinstehend* ~e several people; ~es several things *pl.;* **mehr·fach 1.** *Adj.* multiple; *(wiederholt)* repeated; **2.** *adv.* several times; *(wiederholt)* repeatedly; **Mehrheit die;** ~, ~en majority

**mehr-, Mehr-: ~jährig** *Adj.* lasting several years *postpos.;* **~malig** *Adj.; nicht präd.* repeated; **~mals** *Adv.* several times; *(wiederholt)* repeatedly; **~sprachig** *Adj.* multilingual; **~stimmig** *(Musik)* **1.** *Adj.* for several voices *postpos.;* ein ~stimmiges Lied a part-song; **2.** *adv.* ~stimmig singen sing in harmony; **~teilig** *Adj.* in several parts *postpos.;* **~wert der** *(Wirtsch.)* surplus value; **~wertsteuer die** *(Wirtsch.)* value added tax *(Brit.);* VAT *(Brit.);* sales tax *(Amer.);* **~zahl die** *(o. Pl. a) (Sprachw.)* plural; **b)** *(Mehrheit)* majority

**meiden** *unr. tr. V. (geh.)* avoid

**Meile die;** ~, ~n mile

**mein** *Possessivpron.* my; ~e Damen und Herren ladies and gentlemen; das Buch dort, ist das ~[e]s? that book over there, is it mine?

**Mein·eid der** perjury *no indef. art.;* einen ~ schwören commit perjury

**meinen 1.** *itr. V.* think; **2.** *tr. V.* **a)** think; **b)** *(sagen wollen, im Sinn haben)* mean; **c)** *(beabsichtigen)* mean; intend; es gut mit jmdm. ~: mean well by sb.; **d)** *(sagen)* say

**meiner** *Gen. von ich (geh.)* gedenkt ~: remember me; erbarme dich ~: have mercy upon me; **meinerseits** *Adv.* for my part; ganz ~: the pleasure is [all] mine; **meinetwegen** *Adv.* **a)** because of me; *(mir zuliebe)* for my sake; *(um mich)* about me; **b)** *[auch --'--] (von mir aus)* as far as I'm concerned; ~! if you like

**Meinung die;** ~, ~en opinion (zu über + *Akk.* about); meiner ~ nach in my opinion; ganz meine ~: I agree entirely; einer ~ sein be of the same opinion

**Meinungs-: ~forschung die** opinion research; **~freiheit die** freedom to form and express one's own opinions; *(Redefreiheit)* freedom of

speech; **~umfrage die** [public] opinion poll; **~verschiedenheit die** difference of opinion

**Meise die;** ~, ~n tit[mouse]

**Meißel der;** ~s, ~: chisel; **meißeln** *tr. V.* chisel; carve ⟨*statue, sculpture*⟩ with a chisel

**meist** *Adv.* mostly; **meist...** *Indefinitpron. u. unbest. Zahlw.* most; die ~en Leute ...: most people ...; am ~en most; **meistens** *Adv. s.* meist

**Meister der;** ~s, ~ **a)** master; **b)** *(Werk~, Polier)* foreman; **c)** *(Sport)* champion; **meisterhaft 1.** *Adj.* masterly; **2.** *adv.* in a masterly manner; **meistern** *tr. V.* master; **Meisterschaft die;** ~, ~en **a)** *o. Pl.* mastery; **b)** *(Sport)* championship

**Meister-: ~stück das** masterpiece (an + *Dat.* of); **~titel der** *(Sport)* championship [title]; **~werk das** masterpiece (an + *Dat.* of)

**Melancholie** [melaŋko:'li:] die; ~*(Gemützustand)* melancholy; *(Psych.)* melancholia; **melancholisch 1.** *Adj.* melancholy; melancholy, melancholic ⟨*person, temperament*⟩; **2.** *adv.* melancholically

**melden 1.** *tr. V.* report; *(registrieren lassen)* register ⟨*birth, death, etc.*⟩ *(Dat.* with); **2.** *refl. V.* **a)** report; **b)** *(am Telefon)* answer; **c)** *(ums Wort bitten)* put one's hand up; **d)** *(von sich hören lassen)* get in touch (bei with); **Meldung die;** ~, ~en **a)** report; *(Nachricht)* piece of news; **b)** *(Wort~)* request to speak

**meliert** *Adj.* mottled; [grau] ~es Haar hair streaked with grey

**melken** *regelm. (auch unr.) tr. V.* milk

**Melodie die;** ~, ~n melody; *(Weise)* tune; **melodisch 1.** *Adj.* melodic; **2.** *adv.* melodically

**Melone die;** ~, ~n **a)** melon; **b)** *(ugs.: Hut)* bowler [hat]

**Membran die;** ~, ~en **a)** *(Technik)* diaphragm; **b)** *(Biol., Chemie)* membrane

**Memoiren** [me'mǫa:rən] *Pl.* memoirs

**Menge die;** ~, ~n **a)** quantity; amount; **b)** *(große ~)* lot *(coll.);* eine ~ *(ugs.)* lots [of it/them] *(coll.);* **c)** *(Menschen~)* crowd; **d)** *(Math.)* set

**Mengen-: ~lehre die;** *o. Pl.* set theory *no art.;* **~rabatt der** bulk discount

**Mensa die;** ~, ~s *od.* Mensen refectory *(of university, college)*

**Mensch der;** ~en, ~en **a)** *(Gattung)*

der ~: man; die ~en man *sing.;* human beings; mankind *sing.;* b) *(Person)* person; man/woman; ~en people

**menschen-, Menschen-:** ~**affe** der anthropoid [ape]; ~**auflauf** der crowd [of people]; ~**feind** der misanthropist; ~**fresser** der *(ugs.)* cannibal; ~**freund** der philanthropist; ~**handel** der trade *or* traffic in human beings; ~**kenner** der judge of human nature; ~**kenntnis** die; *o. Pl.* ability to judge human nature; ~**leben** das life; ~**leer** *Adj.* deserted; ~**menge** die crowd [of people]; ~**recht** das human right; ~**schlag** der breed [of people]; ~**seele** die: keine ~seele not a [living] soul

**Menschens·kind:** ~! *(salopp) (erstaunt)* good heavens; good grief; *(vorwurfsvoll)* for heaven's sake

**menschen·unwürdig 1.** *Adj.* ⟨*accommodation*⟩ unfit for human habitation; ⟨*conditions*⟩ unfit for human beings; ⟨*behaviour*⟩ unworthy of a human being; **2.** *adv.* ⟨*treat*⟩ in a degrading and inhumane way; ⟨*live, be housed*⟩ in conditions unfit for human beings; **Menschen·verstand** der human intellect; **Menschheit** die; ~: mankind *no art.;* humanity *no art.;* human race; **menschlich 1.** *Adj.* a) human; b) *(annehmbar)* civilized; c) *(human)* humane ⟨*person, treatment, etc.*⟩; **2.** *adv.* a) er ist mir ~ sympathisch I like him as a person; b) *(human)* humanely; **Menschlichkeit** die humanity *no art.*

**Mensen** *s.* Mensa

**Mentalität** die; ~, ~en mentality

**Menü** das; ~s, ~s *(auch DV)* menu

**merkbar 1.** *Adj.* noticeable; **2.** *adv.* noticeably; **Merk·blatt** leaflet; **merken 1.** *tr. V.* notice; **2.** *refl. V.* sich *(Dat.)* etw. ~: remember sth.; **merklich** *s.* merkbar; **Merkmal** das; ~s, ~e feature

**Merkur** der; ~s Mercury

**merkwürdig 1.** *Adj.* strange; odd; **2.** *adv.* strangely; oddly

**meßbar** *Adj.* measurable

¹**Messe** die; ~, ~n *(Gottesdienst, Musik)* mass

²**Messe** die; ~, ~n *(Ausstellung)* [trade] fair

**messen 1.** *unr. tr. V.* **a)** *auch itr.* measure; **b)** *(beurteilen)* judge (**nach** by); **2.** *unr. refl. V. (geh.)* compete (**mit** with)

**Messer** das; ~s, ~: knife

**messer-, Messer-:** ~**scharf 1.** *Adj.* razor-sharp; *(fig.)* incisive ⟨*logic*⟩; razor-sharp ⟨*wit, intellect*⟩; **2.** *adv. (fig. ugs.)* ⟨*argue*⟩ incisively; ~**stich** der knife-thrust; *(Wunde)* knife-wound

**Messias** der; ~, ~se Messiah

**Messing** das; ~s brass

**Messung** die; ~, ~en measurement

**Metall** das; ~s, ~e metal; **Metall·industrie** die metal-processing and metal-working industries *pl.;* **metallisch** *Adj.* metallic; metal *attrib.,* metallic ⟨*conductor*⟩

**Metapher** die; ~, ~n metaphor

**Meta·physik** die; ~: metaphysics *sing., no art.*

**Meteor** der; ~s, ~e meteor; **Meteorit** der; ~en *od.* ~s, ~e[n] meteorite

**Meteorologe** der; ~n, ~n meteorologist; **Meteorologie** die; ~: meteorology *no art.*

**Meter** der *od.* das; ~s, ~: metre

**meter-, Meter-:** ~**dick** *Adj. (sehr dick)* metres thick *postpos.;* ~**hoch** *Adj.* metres high *postpos.;* ⟨*snow*⟩ metres deep; ~**maß** das tape-measure; *(Stab)* [metre] rule

**Methode** die; ~, ~n method; **methodisch 1.** *Adj.* methodological; *(nach einer Methode vorgehend)* methodical; **2.** *adv.* methodologically; *(nach einer Methode)* methodically

**Metier** [me'tje:] das; ~s, ~s profession

**Metrik** die; ~, ~en metrics

**Metropole** die; ~, ~n metropolis

**Mett·wurst** die *soft smoked sausage made of minced pork and beef*

**Metzger** der; ~s, ~ *(bes. westmd., südd., schweiz.)* butcher; **Metzgerei** die; ~, ~en *(bes. westmd., südd., schweiz.)* butcher's [shop]

**Meute** die; ~, ~n **a)** *(Jägerspr.)* pack; **b)** *(ugs. abwertend)* mob; **Meuterei** die; ~, ~en mutiny; **meutern** *itr. V.* **a)** mutiny; ⟨*prisoners*⟩ riot; **b)** *(ugs.: Unwillen äußern)* moan

**Mexikaner** der; ~s, ~: Mexican; **mexikanisch** *Adj.* Mexican; **Mexiko (das)**; ~s Mexico

**MEZ** *Abk.* **mitteleuropäische Zeit** CET

**mg** *Abk.* **Milligramm** mg

**MG** [ɛm'ge:] das; ~s, ~s *Abk.* **Maschinengewehr**

**Mi.** *Abk.* **Mittwoch** Wed.

**miau** *Interj.* miaow; **miauen** *itr. V.* miaow

**mich 1.** *Akk. von* **ich** me; **2.** *Akk. des Reflexivpron. der 1. Pers. Sg.* myself

**mick[e]rig** *Adj. (ugs.)* miserable; measly *(sl.)*; puny ⟨person⟩
**mied** *1. u. 3. Pers. Sg. Prät. v.* **meiden**
**Mieder·waren** *Pl.* corsetry *sing.*
**Miene** die; ~, ~n expression
**mies** *(ugs.)* 1. *Adj.* lousy *(sl.)*; 2. *adv.* lousily *(sl.)*
**Mies·muschel** die [common] mussel
**Miete** die; ~, ~n rent; *(für ein Auto, Boot)* hire charge; **zur ~ wohnen** live in rented accommodation; **mieten** *tr. V.* rent; *(für kürzere Zeit)* hire; **Mieter** der; ~s, ~: tenant; **Miets·haus** das block of rented flats *(Brit.)* or *(Amer.)* apartments
**Miet-:** ~**vertrag** der tenancy agreement; ~**wagen** der hire-car
**Migräne** die; ~, ~n migraine
**mikro-, Mikro-** micro-
**Mikrobe** die; ~, ~n microbe
**mikro-, Mikro-:** ~**film** der microfilm; ~**phon** [--'-] das; ~s, ~e microphone; ~**skop** [--'-] das; ~s, ~e microscope; ~**skopisch** --'--] 1. *Adj.* microscopic; 2. *adv.* microscopically
**Milbe** die; ~, ~n mite
**Milch** die; ~: milk; **Milch·flasche** die milk-bottle; **milchig** 1. *Adj.* milky; 2. *adv.* ~ **weiß** milky-white
**Milch-:** ~**kaffee** der coffee with plenty of milk; ~**kännchen** das milk-jug; ~**reis** der rice pudding; ~**straße** die Milky Way; Galaxy
**mild, milde** 1. *Adj.* mild; lenient ⟨judge, judgement⟩; soft ⟨light⟩; smooth ⟨brandy⟩; 2. *adv.* ⟨gütig⟩ leniently; *(gelinde)* mildly; **Milde** die; ~: mildness; *(Güte)* leniency; **mildern** *tr. V.* moderate; mitigate ⟨punishment⟩; **Milderung** die; ~: *s.* **mildern:** moderation; mitigation
**Milieu** [mi'liø:] das; ~s, ~s environment
**militant** *Adj.* militant; ¹**Militär** das; ~s armed forces *pl.;* military; *(Soldaten)* soldiers *pl.;* ²**Militär** der; ~s, ~s [high-ranking military] officer
**Militär-:** ~**dienst** der military service; ~**diktatur** die military dictatorship
**militärisch** *Adj.* military; **militarisieren** *tr. V.* militarize; **Military** ['mɪlɪtərɪ] die; ~, ~s *(Reiten)* three-day event; **Miliz** die; ~, ~en militia; *(Polizei)* police
**Mill.** *Abk.* Million m.
**milli- Milli-** milli-
**Milliarde** die; ~, ~n billion
**Milli-:** ~**gramm** das milligram;

~**meter** der *od.* das millimetre; ~**meter·papier** das [graph] paper ruled in millimetre squares
**Million** die; ~, ~en million; **Millionär** der; ~s, ~e millionaire
**Millionen-:** ~**schaden** der damage *no pl., no indef. art.* running into millions; ~**stadt** die town with over a million inhabitants
**millionst...** *Ordinalz.* millionth
**Milz** die; ~: spleen
**Mimik** die; ~: gestures and facial expressions *pl.*
**Mimose** die; ~, ~n a) mimosa; b) *(fig.)* over-sensitive person
**minder** *Adv. (geh.)* less; **minder...** *Adj.* inferior ⟨goods, brand⟩; **minder·bemittelt** *Adj.* without much money *postpos., not pred.;* ~**bemittelt sein** not have much money; geistig ~**bemittelt** *(fig. salopp abwertend)* not all that bright *(coll.);* **Minderheit** die; ~, ~en minority
**minder·jährig** *Adj.* ⟨child etc.⟩ who is/was a minor; **Minder·jährige** der/die; *adj. Dekl.* minor; **mindern** *tr. V. (geh.)* reduce; **Minderung** die; ~, ~en reduction *(Gen.* in); **minder·wertig** *Adj.* inferior; **mindest...** *Adj.* least; *(geringst...)* slightest; **das ist das ~e, was du tun kannst** it is the least you can do; **mindestens** *Adv.* at least
**Mine** die; ~, ~n a) *(Bergwerk, Sprengkörper)* mine; b) *(Bleistift~)* lead; *(Kugelschreiber~, Filzschreiber~)* refill
**Mineral** das; ~s, ~e *od.* **Mineralien** mineral; **Mineralogie** die; ~: mineralogy *no art.*
**Mineral-:** ~**öl** das mineral oil; ~**wasser** das mineral water
**Mini** das; ~s, ~s *(Mode)* mini *(coll.);* **Mini-** mini-; **Miniatur** die; ~, ~en miniature
**minimal** 1. *Adj.* minimal; marginal ⟨advantage, lead⟩; very slight ⟨benefit, profit⟩; 2. *adv.* minimally; **Minimum** das; ~s, **Minima** minimum (**an** + *Dat.* of)
**Minister** der; ~s, ~: minister (**für** for); *(eines britischen Hauptministeriums)* Secretary of State (**für** for); *(eines amerikanischen Hauptministeriums)* Secretary (**für** of); **Ministerium** das; ~s, **Ministerien** Ministry; Department *(Amer.);* **Minister·präsident** der a) *(eines deutschen Bundeslandes)* minister-president; b) *(Pre-*

*mierminister)* Prime Minister; **Ministrant** der; ~en, ~en *(kath. Kirche)* server

**Minorität** die; ~, ~en *s.* Minderheit

**minus** *Konj., Adv. (bes. Math.)* minus;

**Minus** das; ~: deficit; **Minus·zeichen** das minus sign

**Minute** die; ~, ~n minute; **minuten·lang** 1. *Adj.* lasting [for] several minutes *postpos.;* 2. *adv.* for several minutes; **Minuten·zeiger** der minute-hand

**Mio.** *Abk.* Million[en] m.

**mir** 1. *Dat. von* ich to me; *(nach Präpositionen)* me; Freunde von ~: friends of mine; gehen wir zu ~: let's got to my place; von ~ aus as far as I'm concerned; 2. *Dat. des Reflexivpron. der 1. Pers. Sg.* myself

**Mirabelle** die; ~, ~n mirabelle

**Misch-:** ~**brot** das bread made from wheat and rye flour; ~**ehe** die mixed marriage

**mischen** 1. *tr. V.* mix; 2. *refl. V.* a) *(sich ver~)* mix (**mit** with); ⟨*smell, scent*⟩ blend (**mit** with); b) *(sich ein~)* sich in etw. *(Akk.)* ~: interfere in sth.; **Misch·farbe** die non-primary colour; **Mischling** der; ~s, ~e halfcaste; **Mischmasch** der; ~[e]s, ~e *(ugs., meist abwertend)* hotchpotch; mishmash; **Mischung** die; ~, ~en mixture; *(Tee~, Kaffee~, Tabak~)* blend; *(Pralinen~)* assortment; **Misch·wald** der mixed [deciduous and coniferous] forest

**miserabel** *(ugs.)* 1. *Adj.* dreadful *(coll.);* 2. *adv.* dreadfully *(coll.);* **ihm geht es gesundheitlich ~**: he's in a bad way; **Misere** die; ~, ~n *(geh.)* wretched *or* dreadful state; *(Elend)* misery; *(Not)* distress

**miß** *Imperativ Sg. v.* messen

**miß·achten** *tr. V.* a) *(ignorieren)* disregard; ignore; b) *(geringschätzen)* be contemptuous of

**miß·billigen** *tr. V.* disapprove of; **Miß·billigung** die disapproval

**Miß·brauch** der *s.* mißbrauchen: abuse; misuse; **miß·brauchen** *tr. V.* abuse; misuse; abuse ⟨*trust*⟩

**missen** *tr. V. (geh.)* jmdn./etw. nicht ~ mögen not want to be without sb./sth.

**Miß·erfolg** der failure

**Misse·tat** die *(geh. veralt.)* misdeed

**miß·fallen** *unr. itr. V.* etw. mißfällt jmdm. sb. dislikes sth.; **Mißfallen** das; ~s displeasure; *(Mißbilligung)* disapproval

**Miß·geschick** das mishap

**miß·glücken** *itr. V.; mit sein* fail

**miß·gönnen** *tr. V.* jmdm. etw. ~: begrudge sb. sth.

**Miß·griff** der error of judgement

**miß·handeln** *tr. V.* maltreat; **Mißhandlung** die maltreatment

**Mission** die; ~, ~en mission; **Missionar** der; ~s, ~e, missionary

**Miß·kredit** der *in* jmdn./etw. in ~ bringen bring sb./sth. into discredit

**mißlang** *1. u. 3. Pers. Sg. Prät. v.* mißlingen

**mißliebig** *Adj.* unpopular

**mißlingen** *unr. itr. V.; mit sein* fail; **Mißlingen** das; ~s failure; **mißlungen** *2. Part. v.* mißlingen

**Miß·mut** der ill humour *no indef. art.;* **miß·mutig** 1. *Adj.* badtempered; sullen *(face);* 2. *adv.* badtemperedly

**Miß·stand** der deplorable state of affairs *no pl.*

**mißt** *2. u. 3. Pers. Sg. Präsens v.* messen

**miß·trauen** *itr. V.* jmdm./einer Sache ~: mistrust *or* distrust sb./sth.; **Mißtrauen** das; ~s mistrust, distrust (gegen of); **mißtrauisch** 1. *Adj.* mistrustful; distrustful; 2. *adv.* mistrustfully; distrustfully

**miß·verständlich** 1. *Adj.* unclear; ⟨*formulation, concept, etc.*⟩ that could be misunderstood; 2. *adv.* ⟨*express oneself, describe*⟩ in a way that could be misunderstood; **Miß·verständnis** das misunderstanding; **miß·verstehen**[1] *unr. tr. V.* misunderstand

**Mist** der; ~[e]s a) dung; *(Dünger)* manure; *(mit Stroh usw. gemischt)* muck; b) *(~haufen)* dung/manure/ muck heap; c) *(ugs. abwertend) (Unsinn)* rubbish *no indef. art.; (Minderwertiges)* junk *no indef. art.*

**Mistel** die; ~, ~n mistletoe

**Mist·haufen** der dung/manure/ muck heap

**mit** 1. *Präp. mit Dat.* with; **ein Zimmer ~ Frühstück** a room with breakfast included; **~ 50 [km/h] fahren** drive at 50 [k.p.h]; **~ der Bahn/dem Auto fahren** go by train/car; **~ 20 [Jahren]** at [the age of] twenty; 2. *Adv.* a) too; as well; b) **seine Arbeit war ~ am besten** *(ugs.)* his work was among the best

**Mit·arbeit** die; *o. Pl.* collaboration

---

[1] *ich mißverstehe, mißverstanden, mißzuverstehen*

(**bei/an** + *Dat.* on); *(Mithilfe)* assistance (**bei, in** + *Dat.* in); *(Beteiligung)* participation (**in** + *Dat.* in); **mit|arbeiten** *itr. V.* collaborate (**bei/an** + *Dat.* on) *(sich beteiligen)* participate (**in** + *Dat.* in); **Mit·arbeiter** der a) collaborator; **freier ~:** free-lance worker; b) *(Angestellter)* employee

**mit|bekommen** *unr. tr. V.* a) etw. ~: be given sth. to take with one; b) *(wahrnehmen)* be aware of; *(durch Hören, Sehen)* hear/see

**mit|bestimmen** 1. *itr. V.* have a say; 2. *tr. V.* have an influence on; **Mitbestimmung** die; *o. Pl.* participation (**bei** in); *(der Arbeitnehmer)* codetermination

**mit|bringen** *unr. tr. V.* a) etw. ~: bring sth. with one; **jmdm./sich etw. ~:** bring sth. with one for sb./bring sth. back for oneself; b) *(haben)* have ⟨ability, gift, etc.⟩; **Mitbringsel** das; **~s, ~:** [small] present; *(Andenken)* [small] souvenir

**mit·einander** *Adv.* a) with each other *or* one another; **~ sprechen** talk to each other *or* one another; b) *(gemeinsam)* together

**mit|erleben** *tr. V.* a) witness ⟨events etc.⟩; b) *(mitmachen)* be alive during

**mit|fahren** *unr. itr. V.; mit sein* bei jmdn. [im Auto] ~: go/travel with sb. [in his/her car]; *(mitgenommen werden)* get a lift with sb. [in his/her car]

**mit·fühlend** 1. *Adj.* sympathetic; 2. *adv.* sympathetically

**mit|führen** *tr. V.* a) *(Amtsspr.: bei sich tragen)* etw. ~: carry sth. [with one]; b) *(transportieren)* ⟨river, stream⟩ carry along

**mit|geben** *unr. tr. V.* jmdm. etw. ~: give sb. sth. to take with him/her; *(fig.)* provide sb. with sth.

**Mit·gefühl** das; *o. Pl.* sympathy

**mit|gehen** *unr. itr. V.; mit sein* a) go too; **mit jmdm. ~:** go with sb.; b) *(sich mitreißen lassen)* begeistert ~: respond enthusiastically

**Mit·gift** die; **~, ~en** *(veralt.)* dowry

**Mit·glied** das member *(Gen., in* + *Dat.* of)

**mit|halten** *unr. itr. V.* keep up (**bei** in, **mit** with)

**Mit·hilfe** die; *o. Pl.* help; assistance

**mit|hören** 1. *tr. V.* listen to; *(zufällig)* overhear ⟨conversation, argument, etc.⟩; *(abhören)* listen in on; 2. *itr. V.* listen; *(zufällig)* overhear

**mit|kommen** *unr. itr. V.; mit sein* a)

come too; **kommst du mit?** are you coming [with me/us]?; b) *(Schritt halten)* keep up

**Mit·läufer** der *(abwertend)* [mere] supporter

**Mit·laut** der consonant

**Mit·leid** das pity, compassion (**mit** for); *(Mitgefühl)* sympathy (**mit** for); **Mit·leidenschaft** die: jmdn./etw. in ~ ziehen affect sb./sth.; **mit·leidig** 1. *Adj.* compassionate; *(mitfühlend)* sympathetic; 2. *adv.* compassionately; *(mitfühlend)* sympathetically

**mit|machen** 1. *tr. V.* a) *(teilnehmen an)* go on ⟨trip⟩; join in ⟨joke⟩; follow ⟨fashion⟩; fight in ⟨war⟩; do ⟨course, seminar⟩; **das mache ich nicht mit** *(ugs.)* I can't go along with it; b) *(ugs.: erleiden)* **zwei Weltkriege/viele Bombenangriffe mitgemacht haben** have been through two world wars/many bomb attacks; 2. *itr. V.* a) *(sich beteiligen)* join in; b) *(ugs.: funktionieren)* **mein Herz/Kreislauf macht nicht mit** my heart/circulation can't take it

**Mit·mensch** der fellow human being

**mit|nehmen** *unr. tr. V.* a) jmdn. ~: take sb. with one; etw. ~: take sth. with one; *(verhüll.: stehlen)* walk off with sth. *(coll.)*; *(kaufen)* take sth.; **Essen/Getränke zum Mitnehmen** food/ drinks to take away *or (Amer.)* to go; b) *(in Mitleidenschaft ziehen)* jmdn. ~: take it out of sb.

**mit|reden** *itr. V.* a) join in the conversation; b) *(mitbestimmen)* have a say

**Mit·reisende** der/die fellow passenger

**mit|reißen** *unr. tr. V.* **die Begeisterung/seine Rede hat alle Zuhörer mitgerissen** the audience was carried away with enthusiasm/by his speech

**mit·samt** *Präp. mit Dat.* together with

**Mit·schuld** die share of the blame *or* responsibility (**an** + *Dat.* for)

**Mit·schüler** der, **Mit·schülerin** die schoolfellow

**mit|spielen** *itr. V.* a) join in the game; b) **in einem Film ~:** be in a film; **in einem Orchester/in** *od.* **bei einem Fußballverein ~:** play in an orchestra/for a football club; **Mit·spieler** der, **Mit·spielerin** die player; *(in derselben Mannschaft)* team-mate

**mittag** *Adv.* **heute/Montag ~:** at midday today/on Monday; **Mittag** der; **~s, ~e** midday *no art.;* **gegen ~:** around midday; **zu ~ essen** have lunch; **b)** *o. Pl. (ugs.: Mittagspause)* lunch-hour; **Mittag·essen das** lunch; **mittags** *Adv.* at midday; **12 Uhr ~:** 12 noon

**Mittags-: ~pause die** lunch-hour; **~ruhe die** period of quiet after lunch; **~zeit die a)** *o. Pl. (Zeit gegen 12 Uhr)* lunch-time *no art.;* **b)** *(~pause)* lunch-hour

**Mitte die; ~, ~n** middle; *(eines Kreises, einer Kugel, Stadt)* centre; **~ des Monats/Jahres** in the middle of the month/year

**mit|teilen** *tr. V.* **jmdm. etw. ~:** tell sb. sth.; *(informieren)* inform sb. of sth.; **mitteilsam** *Adj.* communicative; *(gesprächig)* talkative; **Mit·teilung die** communication; *(Bekanntgabe)* announcement

**Mittel das; ~s, ~ a)** means; *(Methode)* way; method; *(Werbe~, Propaganda~ usw.)* device *(Gen.* for); **mit allen ~n versuchen, etw. zu tun** try by every means to do sth.; **b)** *(Arznei)* **ein ~ gegen Husten** *usw.* a cure for coughs *etc.;* **c)** *Pl. (Geld~)* funds; *(Privat~)* means

**Mittel·alter das;** *o. Pl.* Middle Ages *pl.;* **mittel·alterlich** *Adj.* medieval

**mittelbar 1.** *Adj.* indirect; **2.** *adv.* indirectly

**mittel-, Mittel-: ~ding das;** *o. Pl.* **ein ~ding sein** be something in between; **~europa (das)** Central Europe; **~finger der** middle finger; **~gebirge das** low mountains *pl.;* **~linie die** centre line; *(Fußball)* half-way line; **~los** *Adj.* without means *postpos.;* **~mäßig** *Adj.* mediocre; **~meer das** Mediterranean [Sea]; **~punkt der a)** *(Geom.)* centre; *(einer Strecke)* midpoint; **b)** *(Mensch/Sache im Zentrum)* centre of attention; **~scheitel der** centre parting; **~schule die** *s.* Realschule; **~stand der;** *o. Pl.* middle class; **~weg der** middle course; **~welle die** *(Physik, Rundf.)* medium wave

**mitten** *Adv.* **~ an/auf etw.** *(Akk./Dat.)* in the middle of sth.; **~ durch die Stadt** right through the town

**mitten-: ~drin** *Adv.* [right] in the middle; **~durch** *Adv.* [right] through the middle

**Mitter·nacht die;** *o. Pl.* midnight *no art.;* **Mitternachts·sonne die** midnight sun

**mittler...** *Adj.* middle; moderate ⟨*speed*⟩; medium-sized ⟨*company,*

*town*⟩; medium ⟨*quality, size*⟩; *(durchschnittlich)* average

**mittler·weile** *Adv.* since then; *(bis jetzt)* by now; *(unterdessen)* in the meantime

**Mittwoch der; ~[e]s, ~e** Wednesday; **mittwochs** *Adv.* on Wednesday[s]

**mit·unter** *Adv.* from time to time

**mit·wirken** *itr. V.* **an etw.** *(Dat.)/***bei etw. ~:** collaborate on/be involved in sth.; **in einem Orchester/Theaterstück ~:** play in an orchestra/act *or* appear in a play; **Mitwirkende der/die** *adj. Dekl. (an einer Sendung)* participant; *(in einer Show)* performer; *(in einem Theaterstück)* actor

**Mit·wisser der; ~s ~: ~ einer Sache** *(Gen.)* **sein** be an accessory to sth.

**mixen** *tr. V.* mix; **sich** *(Dat.)* **einen Drink ~:** fix oneself a drink; **Mixer der; ~s, ~ a)** *(Bar~)* barman; bar-tender·*(Amer.);* **b)** *(Gerät)* blender and liquidizer

**mm** *Abk.* Millimeter mm.

**Mo.** *Abk.* Montag Mon.

**Mob der; ~s** *(abwertend)* mob

**Möbel das; ~s, ~ a)** *Pl.* furniture *sing., no indef. art.;* **b)** piece of furniture; **Möbel·wagen der** furniture van; removal van; **mobil** *Adj.* **a)** mobile; **~ machen** mobilize; **b)** *(ugs.) (lebendig)* lively; **Mobiliar das; ~s** furnishings *pl.;* **mobilisieren** *tr. V.* **a)** *(Milit., fig.)* mobilize; **b)** *(aktivieren)* activate; **Mobilmachung die; ~, ~en** mobilization; **Mobil·telefon das** cellular phone; **möblieren** *tr. V.* furnish

**mochte** *1. u. 3. Pers. Sg. Prät. v.* mögen; **möchte** *1. u. 3. Pers. Sg. Konjunktiv II v.* mögen

**Mode die; ~, ~n** fashion; **Mode·farbe die** fashionable colour

**Modell das; ~s, ~e** *(auch fig.)* model; **jmdm. ~ sitzen** *od.* **stehen** sit for sb.; **modellieren** *tr. V.* model, mould ⟨*figures, objects*⟩; mould ⟨*clay, wax*⟩; **Modell·kleid das** model dress

**Moden·schau die** fashion show

**Moder der; ~s** mould; *(~geruch)* mustiness

**Moderation die; ~, ~en** *(Rundf., Ferns.)* presentation; **Moderator der; ~s, ~en, Moderatorin die; ~, ~nen** *(Rundf., Ferns.)* presenter; **moderieren** *tr. V. (Rundf., Ferns.)* present ⟨*programme*⟩

**¹modern** *itr. V.; auch mit sein* go mouldy

²**modern 1.** *Adj.* modern; *(modisch)* fashionable; **2.** *adv.* in a modern manner; *(modisch)* fashionably; **modernisieren** *tr. V.* modernize

**Mode-:** ~**schöpfer** der couturier; ~**schöpferin die** couturière; ~**wort das;** *Pl.* ~**wörter** vogue-word; ~**zeitschrift die** fashion magazine

**modifizieren** *tr. V. (geh.)* modify

**modisch 1.** *Adj.* fashionable; **2.** *adv.* fashionably

**Mofa das;** ~**s,** ~**s** [low-powered] moped

**Mogelei die;** ~, ~**en** *(ugs.)* cheating *no pl.;* **mogeln** *itr. V.* cheat

**mögen 1.** *unr. Modalverb; 2. Part.* ~: **a)** *(wollen)* want to; **das hätte ich sehen** ~: I would have liked to see that; **b)** *(geh.: sollen)* **das mag genügen** that should be enough; **c)** *(Vermutung, Möglichkeit)* **sie mag/mochte vierzig sein** she must be/must have been [about] forty; |**das**| **mag sein** maybe; **d)** *Konjunktiv II (den Wunsch haben)* **ich/ sie möchte gern wissen ...**: I would/she would like to know ...; **2.** *unr. tr. V.* like; **sie mag keine Rosen** she does not like roses; **sie** ~ **sich** they're fond of one another; **möchten Sie ein Glas Wein?** would you like a glass of wine?; **ich möchte lieber Tee** I would prefer tea; **3.** *unr. itr. V.* **a)** *(es wollen)* like to; **b) ich möchte nach Hause** I want to go home; **er möchte zu Herrn A** he would like to see Mr A

**möglich** *Adj.* possible; **es war ihm nicht** ~ |**zu kommen**| he was unable [to come]; **alles** ~**e** *(ugs.)* all sorts of things; |**das ist doch**| **nicht** ~! impossible!; **sein** ~**stes tun** do one's utmost; **möglicherweise** *Adv.* possibly; **Möglichkeit die;** ~, ~**en a)** possibility; *(Methode)* way; **es besteht die** ~, **daß ...**: there is a possibility that ...; **b)** *(Gelegenheit)* opportunity; chance; **möglichst** *Adv.* **a)** if [at all] possible; **b)** ~ **schnell** as fast as possible

**Mohammed (der)** Muhammad; **Mohammedaner der;** ~**s,** ~: Muslim; Muhammadan; **mohammedanisch** *Adj.* Muslim; Muhammadan

**Mohn der;** ~**s** poppy; *(Samen)* poppy seed; *(auf Brot, Kuchen)* poppy seeds *pl.*

**Mohn-:** ~**blume die** poppy; ~**brötchen das** poppy-seed roll; ~**kuchen der** poppy-seed cake

**Möhre die;** ~, ~**n** carrot

**Mohren·kopf der** chocolate marshmallow

**Mohr·rübe die** carrot

**mokieren** *refl. V. (geh.)* **sich über etw.** *(Akk.)* ~: scoff at sth.; **sich über jmdn.** ~: mock sb.

**Mokka der;** ~**s** strong black coffee

**Molch der;** ~|**e**|**s,** ~**e** newt

**Mole die;** ~, ~**n** [harbour] mole

**Molekül das;** ~**s,** ~**e** molecule

**molk** *1. u. 3. Pers. Sg. Prät. v.* **melken**; **Molkerei die;** ~, ~**en** dairy

**Moll das;** ~ *(Musik)* minor [key]

**mollig 1.** *Adj.* **a)** *(rundlich)* plump; **b)** *(warm)* snug; **2.** *adv.* snugly; ~ **warm** warm and snug

¹**Moment der;** ~|**e**|**s,** ~**e** moment; **jeden** ~ *(ugs.)* [at] any moment; **im** ~: at the moment; ²**Moment das;** ~|**e**|**s,** ~**e** factor, element (**für** in); **momentan 1.** *Adj.* **a)** present; **b)** *(vorübergehend)* temporary; *(flüchtig)* momentary; **2.** *adv.* **a)** at present; **b)** *(vorübergehend)* temporarily

**Monaco (das);** ~**s** Monaco

**Monarch der;** ~**en,** ~**en** monarch; **Monarchie die;** ~, ~**n** monarchy; **Monarchin die;** ~, ~**nen** monarch

**Monat der;** ~**s,** ~**e** month; **im** ~ **April** in the month of April; **monatelang 1.** *Adj.* lasting for months *postpos., not pred.;* **2.** *adv.* for months [on end]; **monatlich 1.** *Adj.* monthly; **2.** *adv.* every month; *(pro Monat)* per month

**Monats-:** ~**erste der** first [day] of the month; ~**hälfte die** half of the month; ~**karte die** monthly season-ticket; ~**letzte der** last day of the month

**Mönch der;** ~|**e**|**s,** ~**e** monk

**Mond der;** ~|**e**|**s,** ~**e** moon; **auf** *od.* **hinter dem** ~ **leben** *(fig. ugs.)* be a bit behind the times *(coll.);* **nach dem** ~ **gehen** *(ugs.)* ⟨clock, watch⟩ be hopelessly wrong

**Mond-:** ~**finsternis die** eclipse of the moon; ~**landung die** moon landing

**Mongole der;** ~**n,** ~**n a)** Mongol; **b)** *(Bewohner der Mongolei)* Mongolian; **Mongolei die;** ~: Mongolia

**Monitor der;** ~**s,** ~**en** monitor

**Mono·gramm das;** ~**s,** ~**e** monogram; **Monographie die;** ~, ~**n** monograph

**Monolog der;** ~**s,** ~**e** monologue

**Monopol das;** ~**s,** ~**e** monopoly (**auf** + *Akk.,* **für** in, of)

**monoton 1.** *Adj.* monotonous; **2.** *adv.*

monotonously; **Monotonie** die; ~, ~n monotony

**Monster** das; ~s, ~: monster; *(häßlich)* [hideous] brute; **Monstren** s. **Monstrum**; **monströs** *Adj.* monstrous; **Monstrum** das; ~s, **Monstren a)** monster; **b)** *(Sache)* hulking great thing *(coll.)*

**Mon·tag** der Monday

**Montage** [mɔn'ta:ʒə] die; ~, ~n **a)** *(Zusammenbau)* assembly; *(Einbau)* installation; *(Aufstellen)* erection; *(Anbringen)* fitting (**an** + *Akk. od. Dat.* to); mounting (**auf** + *Akk. od. Dat.* on); **b)** *(Film, bild. Kunst, Literaturw.)* montage

**montags** *Adv.* on Monday[s]

**montieren** *tr. V.* **a)** *(zusammenbauen)* assemble (**aus** from); erect *(building)*; **b)** *(anbringen)* fit (**an** + *Akk. od. Dat.* to; **auf** + *Akk. od. Dat.* on); *(einbauen)* install (**in** + *Akk.* in); *(befestigen)* fix (**an** + *Akk. od. Dat.* to)

**Monument** das; ~|e|s, ~e monument; **monumental** *Adj.* monumental

**Moor** das; ~|e|s, ~e bog; *(Bruch)* marsh

**Moos** das; ~es, ~e moss

**Moped** ['mo:pɛt] das; ~s, ~s moped

**Mops** der; ~es, **Möpse** pug [dog]; *(salopp: dicke Person)* podge *(coll.)*

**Moral** die; ~ **a)** *(Norm)* morality; **b)** *(Sittlichkeit)* morals *pl.;* **c)** *(Selbstvertrauen)* morale; **d)** *(Lehre)* moral; **moralisch** 1. *Adj.* **a)** moral; **b)** *(tugendhaft)* virtuous; 2. *adv.* **a)** morally; **b)** *(tugendhaft)* virtuously; **moralisieren** *itr. V. (geh.)* moralize; **Moralist** der; ~en, ~en moralist

**Morast** der; ~|e|s, ~e *od.* **Moräste a)** bog; swamp; **b)** *o. Pl. (Schlamm)* mud

**Mord** der; ~|e|s, ~e murder (**an** + *Dat.* of); *(durch ein Attentat)* assassination; **einen ~ begehen** commit murder; **morden** *tr., itr. V.* murder; **Mörder** der; ~s, ~: murderer *(esp. Law);* killer; *(politischer ~)* assassin; **Mörderin** die; ~, ~nen murderer; murderess; *(politische ~)* assassin; **mörderisch** 1. *Adj.* **a)** murderous; 2. *adv. (ugs.)* dreadfully *(coll.);* **Mordfall** der murder case; **mords-, Mords-** *(ugs.)* terrific *(coll.)*

**Mord-:** ~**verdacht** der suspicion of murder; ~**versuch** der attempted murder; *(Attentat)* assassination attempt; ~**waffe** die murder weapon

**morgen** *Adv.* **a)** tomorrow; ~ **in einer Woche** tomorrow week; a week to-

morrow; ~ **um diese Zeit** this time tomorrow; **bis** ~! until tomorrow!; see you tomorrow!; **b)** *(am Morgen)* **heute** ~: this morning; |**am**| **Sonntag** ~: on Sunday morning; **Morgen** der; ~s, ~: morning; **am** ~: in the morning; **am folgenden** *od.* **nächsten** ~: next morning; **früh am** ~, **am frühen** ~: early in the morning; **morgendlich** *Adj.* morning

**Morgen-:** ~**grauen** das daybreak; ~**mantel** der dressing-gown; ~**rot** das *(geh.)* rosy dawn

**morgens** *Adv.* in the morning; *(jeden Morgen)* every morning; **Dienstag** *od.* **dienstags** ~: on Tuesday morning[s]; **von** ~ **bis abends** from morning to evening; **morgig** *Adj.* tomorrow's

**Morphium** das; ~s morphine; **morphium·süchtig** *Adj.* addicted to morphine *pred.*

**morsch** *Adj. (auch fig.)* rotten

**Mörser** der; ~s, ~ *(Gefäß, Geschütz)* mortar

**Mörtel** der; ~s mortar

**Mosaik** das; ~s, ~en *od.* ~e mosaic

**Mosambik** (das); ~s Mozambique

**Moschee** die; ~, ~n mosque

**Moschus** der; ~: musk

**Mosel** die; ~: Moselle; **Mosel·wein** der Moselle [wine]

**Moskau** (das); ~s Moscow; **Moskauer** 1. *indekl. Adj.* Moscow *attrib.;* 2. der; ~s, ~: Muscovite

**Moskito** der; ~s, ~s mosquito

**Moslem** der; ~s, ~s Muslim; **moslemisch** *Adj.* Muslim

**Most** der; ~|e|s, ~e **a)** [cloudy fermented] fruit-juice; **b)** *(landsch.: neuer Wein)* new wine; **Mostrich** der; ~s *(nordostd.)* mustard

**Motel** das; ~s, ~s motel

**Motiv** das; ~s, ~e **a)** motive; **b)** *(fachspr.: Thema)* motif; theme; *(bild. Kunst)* subject

**Motor** der; ~s, ~en engine; *(Elektro~)* motor; **Motor·haube** die *(Kfz-W.)* bonnet *(Brit.);* hood *(Amer.);* **motorisieren** *tr. V.* motorize; **Motor·rad** das motor cycle; **Motor·rad·fahrer** der motor-cyclist

**Motor-:** ~**roller** der motor scooter; ~**schaden** der engine trouble *no indef. art.*

**Motte** die; ~, ~n moth; **Motten·kugel** die moth-ball

**Motto** das; ~s, ~s motto; *(Schlagwort)* slogan

**Möwe** die; ~, ~n gull

**Mrd.** *Abk.* Milliarde bn.

**Mücke** die; ~, ~n midge; *(größer)* mosquito; **Mücken·stich** der midge/mosquito bite

**Mucks** der; ~es, ~e *(ugs.)* murmur [of protest]; **keinen ~ sagen** not utter a [single] word

**müde** 1. *Adj.* tired; *(ermattet)* weary; *(schläfrig)* sleepy; **jmdn./etw.** *od.* **jmds./einer Sache ~ sein** *(geh.)* be tired of sb./sth.; 2. *adv.* wearily; *(schläfrig)* sleepily; **Müdigkeit die;** ~: tiredness

**muffelig** *(ugs.)* 1. *Adj.* grumpy; 2. *adv.* grumpily

**muffig** *Adj.* musty

**Mühe** die; ~, ~n trouble; **sich** *(Dat.)* **mit jmdm./etw. ~ geben** take [great] pains over sb./sth.; **mit Müh und Not** with great difficulty; **mühelos** 1. *Adj.* effortless; 2. *adv.* effortlessly; **mühe·voll** *Adj.* laborious; painstaking ⟨*work*⟩

**Mühle** die; ~, ~n a) mill; *(Kaffee~)* [coffee-] grinder; b) *(Spiel)* o. *Art.*, o. *Pl.* nine men's morris

**Mühsal** die; ~, ~e *(geh.)* tribulation; *(Strapaze)* hardship; **mühsam** 1. *Adj.* laborious; 2. *adv.* laboriously; **müh·selig** *(geh.)* 1. *Adj.* laborious; arduous ⟨*journey, life*⟩; 2. *adv.* with [great] difficulty

**Mulde** die; ~, ~n hollow

**Mull** der; ~[e]s *(Stoff)* mull; *(Verband~)* gauze

**Müll** der; ~s refuse; rubbish; garbage *(Amer.)*; trash *(Amer.)*; *(Industrie~)* [industrial] waste

**Mull·binde** die gauze bandage

**Müller** der; ~s, ~: miller

**Müll-:** ~**halde** die refuse dump; ~**mann** der; *Pl.* ~**männer** *(ugs.)* dustman *(Brit.)*; garbage man *(Amer.)*; ~**sack** der refuse bag; ~**schlucker** der rubbish *or (Amer.)* garbage chute; ~**tonne** die dustbin *(Brit.)*; garbage *or* trash can *(Amer.)*; ~**wagen** der dust-cart *(Brit.)*; garbage truck *(Amer.)*

**mulmig** *Adj.* *(ugs.)* uneasy

**Multiplikation** die; ~, ~en *(Math.)* multiplication; **multiplizieren** *tr. V.* multiply **(mit** by**)**

**Mumie** ['mu:miə] die; ~, ~n mummy

**Mumm** der; ~s *(ugs.)* *(Mut)* guts *pl.* *(coll.)*; *(Tatkraft)* drive; zap *(sl.)*; *(Kraft)* muscle-power

**Mumps** der *od.* die; ~: mumps *sing.*

**München** **(das)**; ~s Munich;

**Münch[e]ner** 1. *indekl. Adj.* Munich *attrib;* 2. der; ~s, ~: inhabitant/native of Munich

**Mund** der; ~[e]s, Münder mouth; **er küßte sie auf den ~:** he kissed her on the lips; **mit vollem ~ sprechen** speak with one's mouth full; **den ~ nicht aufmachen** *(fig. ugs.)* not say anything; **den** *od.* **seinen ~ halten** *(ugs.)* *(zu sprechen aufhören)* shut up *(coll.)*; *(nichts sagen)* not say anything; *(nichts verraten)* keep quiet **(über +** *Akk.* about**); sie ist nicht auf den ~ gefallen** *(fig. ugs.)* she's never at a loss for words; **Mund·art** die dialect

**münden** *itr. V.;* **mit sein** **in etw.** *Akk.* ~: ⟨*river*⟩ flow into sth.; ⟨*corridor, street*⟩ lead into sth.

**mund-, Mund-:** ~**faul** *Adj.* *(ugs.)* uncommunicative; ~**gerecht** *Adj.* bite-sized; ~**geruch** der bad breath *no indef. art.;* ~**harmonika** die mouth-organ

**mündig** *Adj.* of age *pred.;* ~ **werden** come of age

**mündlich** 1. *Adj.* oral; 2. *adv.* orally; **Mund·stück** das mouthpiece; *(bei Zigaretten)* tip; **mund·tot** *Adj.* **jmdn. ~ machen** silence sb.; **Mündung** die; ~, ~en a) mouth; *(größere Trichter~)* estuary; b) *(bei Feuerwaffen)* muzzle

**Mund-zu-Mund-Beatmung** die mouth-to-mouth resuscitation

**Munition** die; ~: ammunition

**munkeln** *tr., itr. V.* *(ugs.)* **man munkelt, daß ...:** there is a rumour that ...

**Münster** das; ~s, ~: minster; *(Dom)* cathedral

**munter** 1. *Adj.* a) cheerful; *(lebhaft)* lively ⟨*eyes, game*⟩; b) *(wach)* awake; 2. *adv.* cheerfully; **Munterkeit die;** ~: cheerfulness

**Münz·automat** der slot-machine; **Münze** die; ~, ~n coin

**Münz-:** ~**fernsprecher** der pay-phone; pay station *(Amer.)*; ~**tankstelle** die coin-in-the-slot petrol *(Brit.)* *or (Amer.)* gas station; ~**wechsler** der change machine

**mürbe** *Adj.* crumbly ⟨*biscuit, cake, etc.*⟩; tender ⟨*meat*⟩; soft ⟨*fruit*⟩; **jmdn. ~ machen** *(fig.)* wear sb. down

**Murmel** die; ~, ~n marble

**murmeln** *tr., itr. V.* mumble; mutter; *(sehr leise)* murmur

**Murmel·tier** das marmot

**murren** *itr. V.* grumble; **mürrisch** 1. *Adj.* grumpy; 2. *adv.* grumpily

**Mus** das *od.* der; ~es, ~e purée
**Muschel** die; ~, ~n a) mussel; *(Schale)* [mussel-]shell; b) *(am Telefon) (Hör~)* ear-piece; *(Sprech~)* mouthpiece
**Muse** die; ~, ~n muse
**Museum** das; ~s, Museen museum
**Musik** die; ~, ~en music; **musikalisch** 1. *Adj.* musical; 2. *adv.* musically; **Musikant** der; ~en, ~en musician; **Musik·box** die juke-box; **Musiker** der; ~s, ~, **Musikerin** die; ~, ~nen musician
**Musik-:** ~hochschule die college of music; ~instrument das musical instrument; ~stunde die music-lesson
**musisch** 1. *Adj.* artistic; *(education)* in the arts; 2. *adv.* artistically; **musizieren** *itr. V.* play music; *(bes. unter Laien)* make music
**Muskat** der; ~[e]s, ~e nutmeg; **Muskat·nuß** die nutmeg
**Muskel** der; ~s, ~n muscle
**Muskel-:** ~kater der stiff muscles *pl.;* ~protz der *(ugs.)* muscleman
**Muskulatur** die; ~, ~en musculature; muscular system; **muskulös** *Adj.* muscular
**Müsli** das; ~s, ~s muesli
**muß** *1. u. 3. Pers. Sg. Präsens v.* **müssen**; **Muß** das; ~: necessity; must *(coll.)*
**Muße** die; ~: leisure
**müssen** 1. *unr. Modalverb*; 2. *Part.* ~ **a)** have to; **er muß es tun** he must do it; he has to *or (coll.)* has got to do it; **das muß 1968 gewesen sein** it must have been in 1968; **er muß gleich hier sein** he will be here at any moment; **b)** *Konjunktiv II* **es müßte doch möglich sein** it ought to be possible; **reich müßte man sein!** how nice it would be to be rich!; 2. *unr. itr. V.* **ich muß nach Hause** I have to *or* must go home; **ich muß mal** *(fam.)* I need to spend a penny *(Brit. coll.) or (Amer. coll.)* go to the john
**müßig** 1. *Adj.* idle *(person)*; *(hours, weeks, life)* of leisure; 2. *adv.* idly; **Müßig·gang** der *o. Pl.* leisure; *(Untätigkeit)* idleness
**müßte** *1. u. 3. Pers. Sg. Prät. v.* **müssen**
**Muster** das; ~s, ~ a) *(Vorlage)* pattern; b) *(Vorbild)* model **(an** + *Dat.* of); c) *(Verzierung)* pattern; d) *(Warenprobe)* sample; **muster·gültig** 1. *Adj.* exemplary; impeccable *(order)*; 2. *adv.* in an exemplary fashion
**mustern** *tr. V.* a) eye; b) *(Milit.: ärzt-*

*lich untersuchen)* **jmdn.** ~: give sb. his medical; **Musterung** die; ~, ~en a) scrutiny; b) *(Milit.: von Wehrpflichtigen)* medical examination; medical
**Mut** der; ~[e]s courage; **mutig** 1. *Adj.* brave; 2. *adv.* bravely; **mut·los** *Adj.* dejected; *(entmutigt)* disheartened; **Mut·losigkeit** die; ~: dejection
**mutmaßlich** *Adj.* supposed; suspected *(murderer etc.)*
**Mut·probe** die test of courage
**¹Mutter** die; ~, Mütter mother; **²Mutter** die; ~, ~n nut; **mütterlich** 1. *Adj.* a) maternal *(line, love, instincts, etc.)*; b) *(fürsorglich)* motherly *(woman, care)*; 2. *adv.* in a motherly way; **mütterlicher·seits** *Adv.* on the/ his/her *etc.* mother's side
**Mutter-:** ~liebe die motherly love *no art.;* ~mal das; *Pl.* ~male birthmark
**Mutterschaft** die; ~: motherhood
**mutter-, Mutter-:** ~seelen·allein *Adj.* all alone; ~söhnchen das mummy's *or (Amer.)* mama's boy; ~sprache die mother tongue; ~tag der; *o. Pl.* Mother's Day *no def. art.*
**Mutti** die; ~, ~s mummy *(Brit. coll.);* mum *(Brit. coll.);* mommy *(Amer. coll.);* mom *(Amer. coll.)*
**mut·willig** 1. *Adj.* wilful; wanton *(destruction)*; 2. *adv.* wilfully
**Mütze** die; ~, ~n cap
**MW** *Abk. (Rundf.)* Mittelwelle MW
**Mw.-St., MwSt.** *Abk.* Mehrwertsteuer VAT
**mysteriös** 1. *Adj.* mysterious; 2. *adv.* mysteriously; **Mystik** die; ~: mysticism
**Mythologie** die; ~, ~n mythology; **Mythos** der; ~, Mythen myth

# N

n, N [ɛn] das; ~, ~: n/N
N *Abk.* Nord[en] N
na *Interj. (ugs.)* well; **na so [et]was!** well I never!; **na und?** *(wennschon)* so what?; *(beschwichtigend)* **na, na, na!** now, now, come along; *(triumphierend)* **na also!** there you are!; *(unsi-*

*cher)* **na**, ich weiß nicht hmm, I'm not sure; *(ärgerlich)* **na**, was soll das denn? now what's all this about?; *(drohend)* **na warte!** just [you] wait!

**Nabel** der; ~s, ~: navel; **Nabelschnur** die umbilical cord

**nach** 1. *Präp. mit Dat.* **a)** *(räumlich)* to; der Zug ~ München the train for Munich *or* the Munich train; ~ Hause gehen go home; ~ Osten [zu] eastwards; [towards the] east; **b)** *(zeitlich)* after; **zehn [Minuten]** ~ **zwei** ten [minutes] past two; **c)** *(mit bestimmten Verben, bezeichnet das Ziel der Handlung)* for; **d)** *(bezeichnet [räumliche und zeitliche] Reihenfolge)* after; ~ **Ihnen/dir!** after you; **e)** *(gemäß)* according to; ~ **meiner Ansicht** *od.* **Meinung, meiner Ansicht** *od.* **Meinung** ~ : in my view *or* opinion;~ **der neusten Mode gekleidet** dressed in [accordance with] the latest fashion; **dem Gesetz** ~ : in accordance with the law; by law; ~ **etw. schmecken/riechen** taste/smell of sth.; 2. *Adv.* **a)** *(räumlich)* **[alle] mir** ~ ! [everybody] follow me!; **b)** *(zeitlich)* ~ **und** ~ : little by little; gradually; ~ **wie vor** still

**nach|ahmen** *tr. V.* imitate; **Nachahmung** die; ~, ~en imitation

**Nachbar** der; ~n , ~n neighbour; **Nachbar·haus** das house next door; **Nachbarin** die; ~, ~nen neighbour; **Nachbarschaft** die; ~ **a)** the whole neighbourhood; **b)** *(Beziehungen)* **gute** ~ : good neighbourliness; **c)** *(Gegend)* neighbourhood; *(Nähe)* vicinity

**nach|bestellen** *tr. V.* [noch] etw. ~ : order more of sth.; *⟨shop⟩* reorder sth.

**Nach·bildung** die **a)** *o. Pl.* copying; **b)** *(Gegenstand)* copy

**nach|blicken** *tr. V. (geh.)* jmdm./einer Sache ~ : gaze after sb./sth.

**nach|datieren** *tr. V.* backdate

**nach·dem** *Konj.* **a)** after; **b)** *s.* ¹**je** 3 b

**nach|denken** *unr. itr. V.* think; **denk mal [gut** *od.* **scharf] nach** have a [good] think; **Nach·denken** das thought; **nachdenklich** 1. *Adj.* thoughtful; 2. *adv.* thoughtfully

**Nach·druck** der; *Pl.* ~e a) *o. Pl.* mit ~ : emphatically; **b)** *(Druckw.)* reprint; **nachdrücklich** 1. *Adj.* emphatic; 2. *adv.* emphatically

**nach|eifern** *itr. V.* jmdm. ~ : emulate sb.

**nach·einander** *Adv.* one after the other

**nach|empfinden** *unr. tr. V.* empathize with *⟨feeling⟩*; share *⟨delight, sorrow⟩*

**Nach·erzählung** die retelling [of a story]; *(Schulw.)* reproduction

**Nachfahr** der; ~en , ~en *(geh.)* descendant

**Nach·folge** die succession; **Nachfolger** der; ~s, ~, **Nachfolgerin** die; ~, ~nen successor

**Nach·forschung** die investigation

**Nach·frage** die demand (nach for)

**nach|fühlen** *tr. V.* empathize with

**nach|füllen** *tr. V.* top up; **Salz/Wein** ~ : put [some] more salt/wine in

**nach|geben** *unr. itr. V.* give way

**Nach·gebühr** die excess postage

**nach|gehen** *unr. itr. V.; mit sein* **a)** jmdm./einer Sache ~ : follow sb./sth.; **einer Sache** ~ *(fig.)* look into a matter; **einem Beruf** ~ : practise a profession; **b)** *(nicht aus dem Kopf gehen)* jmdm. ~ : remain on sb.'s mind; **c)** *⟨clock, watch⟩* be slow; [um] eine Stunde ~ : be an hour slow

**Nach·geschmack** der after-taste

**nach·giebig** *Adj.* indulgent; **Nachgiebigkeit** die; ~ : indulgence

**nach·haltig** 1. *Adj.* lasting; 2. *adv. (auf längere Zeit)* for a long time

**Nach·hause·weg** der way home

**nach|helfen** *unr. itr. V.* help

**nach·her** [*auch:* '--] *Adv.* afterwards; *(später)* later [on]; **bis** ~ ! see you later!

**Nachhilfe·unterricht** der coaching

**nach|holen** *tr. V. (nachträglich erledigen)* catch up on *⟨work, sleep⟩*; make up for *⟨working hours missed⟩*

**Nachkomme** der; ~n, ~n descendant; **nach|kommen** *unr. itr. V.; mit sein* follow [later]; come [on] later; **Nachkommenschaft** die; ~ : descendants *pl.*; **Nachkömmling** der; ~s, ~e much younger child *(than the rest)*

**Nach·kriegs-** post-war *⟨generation, period, etc.⟩*

**Nach·laß** der; Nachlasses, Nachlasse *od.* Nachlässe **a)** estate; **b)** *(Kaufmannsspr.: Rabatt)* discount; **nach|lassen** 1. *unr. itr. V.* let up; *⟨pain, stress, pressure⟩* ease; *⟨effect⟩* wear off; *⟨interest, enthusiasm, strength, courage⟩* wane; *⟨health, hearing, memory⟩* deteriorate; *⟨business⟩* drop off; 2. *unr. tr. V. (Kaufmannsspr.)* give a discount of; **nach·lässig** 1. *Adj.* careless; 2. *adv.* carelessly; **Nachlässigkeit** die; ~, ~en carelessness

**nach|laufen** *unr. itr. V.; mit sein* jmdm./einer Sache ~: run after sb./ sth.

**nach|lesen** *unr. tr. V.* look up

**nach|lösen 1.** *tr. V.* eine Fahrkarte ~: buy a ticket [on the train, bus, etc.]; **2.** *itr. V.* pay the excess [fare]

**nach|machen** *tr. V. (auch tun)* copy; *(imitieren)* imitate; *(genauso herstellen)* reproduce ⟨*period furniture etc.*⟩; forge ⟨*signature*⟩

**nach·mittag** *Adv.* heute ~: this afternoon; |am| Sonntag ~: on Sunday afternoon; **Nach·mittag** der afternoon; **am** ~: in the afternoon; **am späten** ~: late in the afternoon; **nach·mittags** *Adv.* in the afternoon; **dienstags** *od.* Dienstag ~: on Tuesday afternoons; **um vier Uhr** ~: at four in the afternoon; at 4 p.m.

**Nachnahme** die; ~, ~n: per ~: cash on delivery; COD

**Nach·name** der surname

**nachprüfbar** *Adj.* verifiable; **nach|-prüfen** *tr., itr. V.* check

**nach|rechnen** *tr. V.* check ⟨*figures*⟩

**Nach·rede** die: üble ~: malicious gossip; *(Rechtsw.)* defamation [of character]

**Nachricht** die; ~, ~en a) news *no pl.;* eine ~ hinterlassen leave a message; **b)** *Pl. (Ferns., Rundf.)* news *sing.;* ~en hören listen to the news

**Nachrichten-:** ~sprecher der, ~sprecherin die news-reader

**nach|rücken** *itr. V.; mit sein* move up

**Nach·ruf** der; ~|e|s, ~e obituary (auf + *Akk.* of); **nach|rufen** *unr. tr., itr. V.* jmdm. |etw.| ~: call [sth.] after sb.

**nach|sagen** *tr. V.* a) *(wiederholen)* repeat; **b)** man sagt ihm nach, er sei ...: he is said to be ...; jmdm. Schlechtes ~: speak ill of sb.

**Nach·saison** die late season

**nach|schicken** *tr. V.* a) *(durch die Post o. ä.)* forward; **b)** jmdm. jmdn. ~: send sb. after sb.

**nach|schlagen 1.** *unr. tr. V.* look up; **2.** *unr. itr. V.* im Lexikon/Wörterbuch ~: consult the encyclopaedia/dictionary; **Nachschlage·werk** das work of reference

**Nach·schlüssel** der duplicate key

**Nach·schub** der *(Milit.)* a) supply (an + *Dat.* of); **b)** *(~material)* supplies *pl.* (an + *Dat.* of)

**nach|sehen 1.** *unr. itr. V.* a) jmdm./einer Sache ~: gaze after sb./sth.; **b)** *(kontrollieren)* check; **c)** *(nachschla-*

*gen)* have a look; **2.** *unr. tr. V.* a) *(nachlesen)* look up; **b)** *(überprüfen)* check [over]

**nach|senden** *unr. od. regelm. tr. V.* forward

**Nach·sicht** die leniency; **nachsichtig 1.** *Adj.* lenient (gegen, mit towards); **2.** *adv.* leniently

**nach|sitzen** *unr. itr. V.* be in detention; |eine Stunde| ~ müssen have [an hour's] detention

**Nach·speise** die dessert; sweet

**Nach·spiel** das: die Sache wird noch ein ~ haben this affair will have repercussions; ein gerichtliches ~ haben result in court proceedings

**nach|sprechen** *unr. tr. V.* |jmdm.| etw. ~: repeat sth. [after sb.]

**nächst... 1.** *Sup. zu* nahe; **2.** *Adj.* next; *(kürzest)* shortest ⟨*way*⟩; am ~en Tag the next day; beim ~en Mal, das ~e Mal the next time; der ~e bitte! next [one], please; wer kommt als ~er dran? whose turn is it next?; **Nächste** der; ~n, ~n *(geh.)* neighbour; **Nächsten·liebe** die charity [to one's neighbour]; **nächstens** *Adv.* a) shortly; **b)** *(ugs.: wenn es so weitergeht)* if it goes on like this

**nächst-:** ~liegend *Adj.; nicht präd.* first, immediate ⟨*problem*⟩; [most] obvious ⟨*explanation etc.*⟩; ~möglich *Adj.* earliest possible

**nach|suchen** *itr. V. (geh.)* um etw. ~: request sth.; *(bes. schriftlich)* apply for sth.

**nacht** *Adv.* gestern/morgen/Dienstag ~: last night/tomorrow night/on Tuesday night; heute ~: tonight; **Nacht** die; ~, Nächte night; bei ~, in der ~: at night[-time]; über ~ bleiben stay overnight

**Nacht-:** ~arbeit die; *o. Pl.* night work *no art.;* ~dienst der night duty; ~dienst haben be on night duty; ⟨*chemist's shop*⟩ be open late

**Nach·teil** der disadvantage; **nachteilig 1.** *Adj.* detrimental; harmful; **2.** *adv.* detrimentally; harmfully

**Nacht-:** ~essen das *(bes. südd., schweiz.)* s. Abendessen; ~hemd das night-shirt

**Nachtigall** die; ~, ~en nightingale

**Nach·tisch** der; *o. Pl.* dessert; sweet

**nächtlich** *Adj.* nocturnal; night ⟨*sky*⟩; ⟨*darkness, stillness*⟩ of the night; **Nacht·lokal** das night-spot *(coll.)*

**nach|tragen** *unr. tr. V. (schriftlich ergänzen)* insert; add; **nach·tragend**

*Adj.* unforgiving; *(rachsüchtig)* vindictive; **nachträglich 1.** *Adj.* later; subsequent ⟨*apology*⟩*; (verspätet)* belated ⟨*greetings, apology*⟩*;* **2.** *adv.* afterwards; subsequently; *(verspätet)* belatedly

**nach|trauern** *itr. V.* jmdm./einer Sache ~: bemoan the passing of sb./sth.

**Nacht·ruhe die** night's sleep; **nachts** *Adv.* at night; **Montag** *od.* **montags** ~: on Monday nights; **um 3 Uhr** ~: at 3 o'clock in the morning

**Nacht-:** ~**schicht die** night-shift; ~**schwester die** night nurse; ~**tisch der** bedside table; ~**tischlampe die** bedside light; ~**topf der** chamber-pot; ~**wächter der** night-watchman

**Nach·untersuchung die** follow-up examination; check-up

**nach|vollziehen** *unr. tr. V.* reconstruct; *(begreifen)* comprehend

**nach|wachsen** *unr. itr. V.; mit sein* |wieder| ~: grow again

**Nachweis der;** ~**es,** ~**e** proof *no indef. art.* (*Gen.,* über + *Akk.* of)*; (Zeugnis)* certificate (über + *Akk.* of); **nachweisbar 1.** *Adj.* demonstrable ⟨*fact, truth, error, defect, guilt*⟩*;* detectable ⟨*substance, chemical*⟩*;* **2.** *adv.* demonstrably; **nach|weisen** *unr. tr. V.* prove; **nachweislich** *Adv.* as can be proved

**nach|winken** *itr. V.* jmdm./einer Sache ~: wave after sb./sth.

**Nach·wirkung die** after-effect

**Nach·wort das;** *Pl.* ~**worte** afterword

**Nach·wuchs der;** *o. Pl* a) *(fam.: Kind[er])* offspring; b) *(junge Kräfte)* new blood; *(für eine Branche usw.)* new recruits *pl.; (in der Ausbildung)* trainees *pl.*

**nach|zahlen** *tr., itr. V.* a) pay later; b) *(zusätzlich zahlen)* **25 DM** ~: pay another 25 marks

**nach|zählen** *tr., itr. V.* [re]count

**Nach·zahlung die** additional payment

**Nachzügler der** straggler; *(spät Ankommender)* latecomer

**Nackedei der;** ~**s,** ~**s** *(fam. scherzh.)* |kleiner| ~: naked little thing

**Nacken der;** ~**s,** ~: back *or* nape of the neck; *(Hals)* neck

**nackt** *Adj.* naked; bare ⟨*feet, legs, arms, skin, fists*⟩*; (fig.)* plain ⟨*truth, fact*⟩*;* bare ⟨*existence*⟩*;* **Nackt·ba-**

**de·strand der** nudist beach; **Nackte der/die;** *adj. Dekl.* naked man/woman; **Nackt·foto das** nude photo

**Nadel die;** ~, ~**n** needle; *(Steck~, Hut~, Haar~)* pin

**Nadel-:** ~**baum der** conifer; coniferous tree; ~**wald der** coniferous forest

**Nagel der;** ~**s,** Nägel nail; **den** ~ **auf den Kopf treffen** *(fig. ugs.)* hit the nail on the head *(coll.)*

**Nagel-:** ~**bürste die** nailbrush; ~**feile die** nail-file; ~**lack der** nail varnish *(Brit.);* nail polish

**nageln** *tr. V.* nail (**an** + *Akk.* to, **auf** + *Akk.* on)*; (Med.)* pin; **nagel·neu** *Adj. (ugs.)* brand-new; **Nagel·schere die** nail-scissors *pl.*

**nagen 1.** *itr. V.* gnaw; **an etw.** *(Dat.)* ~: gnaw [at] sth.; **2.** *tr. V.* gnaw off; **ein Loch ins Holz** ~: gnaw a hole in the wood

**nah** *s.* nahe

**Nah·aufnahme die** *(Fot.)* close-up [photograph]

**nahe** ['naːə]; näher ['nɛːɐ], nächst... **1.** *Adj.* a) *(räumlich)* near *pred.;* close *pred.;* nearby *attrib.;* b) *(zeitlich)* imminent; near *pred.;* c) *(eng)* close ⟨*relationship etc.*⟩*;* **2.** *adv.* a) *(räumlich)* ~ **an** (+ *Dat./Akk.*), ~ **bei** close to; ~ **gelegen** nearby; **von** ~**m** from close up; b) *(zeitlich)* ~ **an die achtzig** *(ugs.)* pushing eighty *(coll.);* c) *(eng)* closely; **3.** *Präp. mit Dat. (geh.)* near; close to; **Nähe die;** ~: closeness

**nahe-:** ~**bei** *Adv.* nearby; close by; ~**|gehen** *unr. itr. V.; mit sein* jmdm. ~**gehen** affect sb. deeply; ~**|kommen** *unr. itr. V.; mit sein* einer Sache *(Dat.)* ~**kommen** come close to sth.; ⟨*amount*⟩ approximate to sth.; jmdm./sich |menschlich| ~**kommen** get to know sb./one another well; ~**|legen** *tr. V.* suggest; give rise to ⟨*suspicion, supposition, thought*⟩*;* ~**|liegen** *unr. itr. V.* ⟨*thought*⟩ suggest itself; ⟨*suspicion, question*⟩ arise; ~**liegend** *Adj.* obvious ⟨*reason, solution*⟩

**nähen 1.** *itr. V.* sew; *(Kleider machen)* make clothes; **2.** *tr. V.* a) sew ⟨*seam, hem*⟩*;* make ⟨*dress etc.*⟩*;* b) *(Med.)* stitch

**näher 1.** *Komp. zu* nahe; **2.** *Adj.* a) *(kürzer)* shorter ⟨*way, road*⟩*;* b) *(genauer)* more precise ⟨*information*⟩*;* closer ⟨*investigation, inspection*⟩*;* **3.** *adv.* a) **bitte treten Sie** ~! please come in/nearer/this way; b) *(genauer)* more closely; *(im einzelnen)* in [more] detail

**näher|kommen** *unr. itr. V.; mit sein* jmdm. |menschlich| ~**kommen** get on closer terms with sb.; **nähern** *refl. V.* approach; **sich jmdm./einer Sache** ~: approach sb./sth.

**nahe-:** ~|**stehen** *unr. itr. V.* jmdm. ~**stehen** be on intimate terms with sb.; ~**zu** *Adv.* almost; nearly; *(mit Zahlenangabe)* close on

**Näh-:** ~**garn** das [sewing] cotton; ~**kasten** der sewing-box

**nahm** *1. u. 3. Pers. Sg. Prät. v.* nehmen

**Näh-:** ~**maschine** die sewingmachine; ~**nadel** die sewing-needle

**nähren** 1. *tr. V.* feed (mit on); 2. *refl. V. (geh.)* **sich von etw.** ~: live on sth.; ⟨animal⟩ feed on sth.; **nahrhaft** *Adj.* nourishing; **Nahrung** die; ~: food; **Nahrungs·mittel** das food [item]; ~**mittel** *Pl.* foodstuffs; **Nähr·wert** der nutritional value

**Näh·seide** die sewing silk

**Naht** die; ~, Nähte seam

**Nah-:** ~**verkehr** der local traffic; ~**verkehrs·zug** der local train

**Näh·zeug** das sewing things *pl.*

**naiv** 1. *Adj.* naïve; 2. *adv.* naïvely; **Naivität** die; ~: naïvety

**Name** der; ~ns, ~n name; **namens** *Adv.* by the name of

**Namens-:** ~**schild** das a) *(an Türen usw.)* name-plate; b) *(zum Anstecken)* name-badge; ~**tag** der name-day

**namentlich** 1. *Adj.* by name *postpos.*; 2. *adv.* by name; 3. *Adv. (besonders)* particularly; **namhaft** *Adj.* a) *(berühmt)* noted; b) *(ansehnlich)* noteworthy ⟨sum, difference⟩; notable ⟨contribution, opportunity⟩; **nämlich** *Adv.* a) **er kann nicht kommen, er ist ~ krank** he cannot come, as he is ill; b) *(und zwar)* namely

**nannte** *1. u. 3. Pers. Sg. Prät. v.* nennen

**nanu** *Interj.* ~, **was machst du denn hier?** hello, what are you doing here?; ~, **Sie gehen schon?** what, you're going already?

**Napf** der; ~|e|s, Näpfe bowl *(esp. for animal's food)*

**Narbe** die; ~, ~n scar; **narbig** *Adj.* scarred

**Narkose** die; ~, ~n *(Med.)* narcosis

**Narr** der; ~en, ~en fool; **Narrenfreiheit** die freedom to do as one pleases; **Närrin** die; ~, ~nen fool; **närrisch** 1. *Adj.* crazy; carnivalcrazy ⟨season⟩; 2. *adv.* crazily

**Narzisse** die; ~, ~n narcissus

**naschen** 1. *itr. V. (Süßes essen)* eat sweet things; *(heimlich essen)* have a nibble; 2. *tr. V.* eat ⟨sweets, chocolate, etc.⟩; **er hat Milch genascht** he has been at the milk; **naschhaft** *Adj.* sweet-toothed; ~ **sein** have a sweet tooth

**Nase** die; ~, ~n nose; **die ~ voll haben** *(ugs.)* have had enough

**Nasen-:** ~**bluten** das; ~s bleeding from the nose; ~**loch** das nostril; ~**tropfen** *Pl.* nose-drops

**nase·weis** 1. *Adj.* precocious; pert ⟨remark, reply⟩; 2. *adv.* precociously; **Nas·horn** das rhinoceros

**naß**; nasser *od.* nässer, nassest... *od.* nässest...: *Adj.* wet; **sich/das Bett ~ machen** wet oneself/one's bed; **Nässe** die; ~: wetness; **naß·kalt** *Adj.* cold and wet; **Naß·rasur** die wet shaving *no art.*

**Nation** die; ~, ~en nation; **national** 1. *Adj.* a) national; 2. *adv.* nationally

**National-:** ~**elf** die *(Fußball)* national side; ~**hymne** die national anthem

**Nationalismus** der; ~: nationalism *usu. no art.*; **nationalistisch** 1. *Adj.* nationalist; nationalistic; 2. *adv.* nationalistically; **Nationalität** die; ~, ~en nationality

**national-,** **National-:** ~**mannschaft** die national team; ~**sozialismus** der National Socialism; ~**sozialist** der National Socialist; ~**sozialistisch** *Adj.* National Socialist

**NATO, Nato** die; ~: NATO, Nato *no art.*

**Natron** das; ~s |doppeltkohlensaures| ~: sodium bicarbonate; |kohlensaures| ~: sodium carbonate

**Natter** die; ~, ~n colubrid

**Natur** die; ~, ~en nature; **die freie ~:** [the] open countryside; **Naturalien** [natu'ra:li̯ən] *Pl.* natural produce *sing. (used as payment)*; **in ~** *(Dat.)* **bezahlen** pay in kind; **Naturalismus** der; ~: naturalism; **naturalistisch** 1. *Adj.* naturalistic; 2. *adv.* naturalistically; **Naturell** das; ~s, ~e temperament

**natur-,** **Natur-:** ~**erscheinung** die natural phenomenon; ~**farben** *Adj.* natural-coloured; ~**freund** der nature-lover; ~**gemäß** *Adv.* naturally; ~~**geschichte** die; *o. Pl.* natural history; ~**gesetz** das law of nature; ~**getreu** 1. *Adj.* lifelike ⟨portrait, imitation⟩; faithful ⟨reproduction⟩; 2. *adv.* ⟨draw⟩ true to life; ⟨reproduce⟩

faithfully; **~heilkunde die** naturopathy *no art.*; **~katastrophe die** natural disaster

**natürlich 1.** *Adj.* natural; **2.** *adv.* ⟨*laugh, behave*⟩ naturally; **3.** *Adv.* **a)** *(selbstverständlich, wie erwartet)* naturally; of course; **b)** *(zwar)* of course; **Natürlichkeit die** ~: naturalness

**Natur-:** **~park der** ≈ national park; **~produkt das** natural product; **~schutz der** [nature] conservation; **~schutz·gebiet das** nature reserve; **~verbunden** *Adj.* ⟨*person*⟩ in tune with nature; **~volk das** primitive people; **~wissenschaft die** natural science *no art.*; **~wissenschaftler der** [natural] scientist; **~wissenschaftlich 1.** *Adj.* scientific; **2.** *adv.* scientifically; **~wunder das** miracle *or* wonder of nature

**Navigation die** ~: navigation *no art.*

**n. Chr.** *Abk.* nach Christus AD

**Neandertaler der** ~s, ~: Neanderthal man

**Nebel der** ~s, ~: fog; *(weniger dicht)* mist; **nebelig** *s.* neblig

**Nebel-:** **~scheinwerfer der** foglamp; **~wand die** wall of fog

**neben 1.** *Präp. mit Dat.* **a)** *(Lage)* next to; beside; **b)** *(außer)* apart from; aside from *(Amer.)*; **c)** *(verglichen mit)* beside; **2.** *Präp. mit Akk. (Richtung)* next to; beside; **neben·an** *Adv.* next door; **neben·bei** *Adv.* **a)** ⟨*work*⟩ on the side; *(zusätzlich)* as well; **b)** *(beiläufig)* ⟨*remark, ask*⟩ by the way; ⟨*mention*⟩ in passing

**neben-, Neben-:** **~beruf der** second job; sideline; **~beruflich 1.** *Adj.* eine **~berufliche Tätigkeit** a second job; **2.** *adv.* on the side; **er arbeitet ~beruflich als Übersetzer** he translates as a sideline; **~beschäftigung die** second job; sideline; **~buhler der, ~buhlerin die** rival

**neben·einander** *Adv.* **a)** next to each other; *(fig.: zusammen)* ⟨*live, exist*⟩ side by side; **~ wohnen** live next door to each other; **b)** *(gleichzeitig)* together

**nebeneinander-:** **~|legen** *tr. V.* lay *or* place ⟨*objects*⟩ side by side; **~|setzen** *tr. V.* put *or* place ⟨*persons, objects*⟩ next to each other; **~|sitzen** *unr. itr. V.* sit next to each other; **~|stellen** *tr. V.* put *or* place ⟨*tables, chairs, etc.*⟩ next to each other

**Neben-:** **~erwerb der** secondary occupation; **~fach das** subsidiary subject; minor *(Amer.)*; **~fluß der** tributary; **~gebäude das a)** annexe; outbuilding; **b)** *(Nachbargebäude)* neighbouring building; **~geräusch das** background noise; **~haus das** house next door

**neben·her** *Adv. s.* nebenbei

**nebenher-:** **~|fahren** *unr. itr. V.; mit sein* drive/ride alongside; **~|gehen** *unr. itr. V.; mit sein* walk alongside

**neben-, Neben-:** **~kosten** *Pl.* **a)** additional costs; **b)** *(bei Mieten)* heating, lighting, and services; **~produkt das** by-product; **~rolle die** supporting role; **~sache die** minor matter; **~sachen** inessentials; **~sächlich** *Adj.* of minor importance *postpos.*; unimportant; minor ⟨*detail*⟩; **~satz der** *(Sprachw.)* subordinate clause; **~straße die** side street; **~tätigkeit die** second job; sideline; **~tisch der** next table; **~verdienst der** additional income; **~wirkung die** side-effect; **~zimmer das** next room

**neblig** *Adj.* foggy; *(weniger dicht)* misty

**Necessaire** [nesɛ'sɛːɐ̯] *das* ~s, ~s sponge-bag *(Brit.)*; toilet bag *(Amer.)*

**necken** *tr. V.* tease; **Neckerei die** ~: teasing

**nee** *(ugs.)* no; nope *(Amer. coll.)*

**Neffe der** ~n, ~n nephew

**negativ 1.** *Adj.* negative; **2.** *adv.* ⟨*answer*⟩ in the negative; **Negativ das** ~s, ~e *(Fot.)* negative

**Neger der** ~s, ~: Negro; **Negerin die** ~, ~nen Negress

**nehmen** *unr. tr. V.* take; **sich** *(Dat.)* **etw.** ~: take sth.; *(sich bedienen)* help oneself to sth.; **auf sich** *(Akk.)* ~: take on ⟨*responsibility, burden*⟩; **jmdm./einer Sache etw.** ~: deprive sb./sth. of sth.; **was nehmen Sie dafür?** how much do you charge for it?

**Neid der** ~[e]s envy; jealousy; **neiden** *tr. V. (geh.)* **jmdm. etw.** ~: envy sb. [for] sth.; **neidisch 1.** *Adj.* envious; **2.** *adv.* enviously

**neigen 1.** *tr. V.* tip; tilt; incline ⟨*head, upper part of body*⟩; **2.** *refl. V.:* ⟨*person*⟩ lean; ⟨*ship*⟩ heel over, list; ⟨*scales*⟩ tip; **3.** *itr. V.* **a) zu Erkältungen/Krankheiten** ~: be prone to colds/illnesses; **b)** *(tendieren)* tend; **Neigung die** ~, ~en **a)** *(Vorliebe)* inclination; **b)** *o. Pl. (Tendenz)* tendency

**nein** *Interj.* no; **Nein das** ~[s], ~[s] no; **Nein·stimme die** no-vote

**Nektar** der; ~s, ~e *(Bot.)* nectar; **Nektarine** die; ~, ~n nectarine

**Nelke** die; ~, ~n pink; *(Dianthus caryophyllus)* carnation; b) *(Gewürz)* clove

**nennen** 1. *unr. tr. V.* a) call; b) *(angeben)* give 〈*name, date of birth, address, reason, price, etc.*〉; c) *(anführen)* give 〈*example*〉; *(erwähnen)* mention 〈*person, name*〉; 2. *unr. refl. V.* 〈*person, thing*〉 be called

**neo-, Neo-:** neo-

**Neon** das; ~s neon

**Neon-:** ~licht das neon light; ~röhre die neon tube

**Nepal** (das); ~s Nepal

**Nepp** der; ~s *(ugs. abwertend)* daylight robbery *no art.*; rip-off *(sl.)*; **Nepp·lokal** das *(ugs. abwertend)* clip-joint *(sl.)*

**Nerv** der; ~s, ~en nerve; die ~en verlieren lose control [of oneself]; jmdm. auf die ~en gehen *od.* fallen get on sb.'s nerves

**nerven-, Nerven-:** ~aufreibend *Adj.* nerve-racking; ~bündel das *(ugs.)* bundle of nerves *(coll.)*; ~gift das neurotoxin; ~heilanstalt die *(veralt.)* psychiatric hospital; ~krank *Adj.* 〈*person*〉 suffering from a nervous disease; ~probe die mental trial; ~säge die *(salopp)* pain in the neck *(coll.)*; ~zusammenbruch der nervous breakdown

**nervlich** *Adj.* nervous 〈*strain*〉; **nervös** 1. *Adj. (auch Med.)* nervous; jittery 〈*person*〉; 2. *adv.* nervously; **Nervosität** die; ~ nervousness; **nerv·tötend** *Adj.* nerve-racking 〈*wait*〉; soul-destroying 〈*activity, work*〉

**Nerz** der; ~es, ~e mink; **Nerz·mantel** der mink coat

**Nessel** die; ~, ~n nettle

**Nest** das; ~[e]s, ~er a) nest; b) *(fam.: Bett)* bed; c) *(ugs. abwertend: kleiner Ort)* little place

**nett** 1. *Adj.* nice; *(freundlich)* kind; 2. *adv.* nicely; *(freundlich)* kindly; **netter·weise** *Adv.* kindly

**netto** *Adv.* 〈*weigh, earn, etc.*〉 net

**Netto-:** ~einkommen das net income; ~gehalt das net salary

**Netz** das; ~es, ~e a) net; *(Einkaufs~)* string bag; *(Gepäck~)* [luggage-]rack; b) *(Spinnen~)* web; c) *(Verteiler~, Verkehrs~ usw.)* network; *(für Strom, Wasser, Gas)* mains *pl.*; **Netz·haut** die *(Anat.)* retina

**neu** 1. *Adj.* new; die ~este Mode the latest fashion; das ist mir ~: that is news to me; der/die Neue the new man/woman/boy/girl; 2. *adv.* a) ~ tapeziert/gestrichen repapered/repainted; sich ~ einrichten refurnish one's home; b) *(gerade erst)* diese Ware ist ~ eingetroffen this item has just come in; **neu·artig** *Adj.* new; **Neu·bau** der; *Pl.* Neubauten new house/building; **Neubau·wohnung** die flat *(Brit.)* or *(Amer.)* apartment in a new block/house

**neuerdings** *Adv.* er trägt ~ eine Brille he has recently started wearing glasses; **neu·eröffnet** *Adj.* a) newly-opened; b) *(wiedereröffnet)* reopened; **Neu·eröffnung** die a) opening; b) *(Wiedereröffnung)* reopening; **Neuerung** die; ~, ~en innovation; **neu·geboren** *Adj.* newborn; **Neu·gier, Neugierde** die; ~: curiosity; *(Wißbegierde)* inquisitiveness; **neu·gierig** 1. *Adj.* curious; *(wißbegierig)* inquisitive; inquisitive 〈*person*〉; ich bin ~, was er dazu sagt I'm curious to know what he'll say about it; 2. *adv.* 〈*ask*〉 inquisitively; 〈*peer*〉 nosily *(coll. derog.)*; **Neuheit** die; ~, ~en a) *o. Pl.* novelty; b) *(Neues)* new product/gadget/article *etc.*; **Neuigkeit** die; ~, ~en piece of news; ~en news *sing.*; **Neu·jahr** das New Year's Day; **Neu·land** das *(fig.)* new ground; **neulich** *Adv.* recently; ~ morgens the other morning; **Neuling** der; ~s, ~e newcomer; *(auf einem Gebiet)* novice; **Neu·mond** der new moon

**neun** *Kardinalz.* nine; **Neun** die; ~, ~en nine

**neun-:** ~hundert *Kardinalz.* nine hundred; ~jährig *Adj. (9 Jahre alt)* nine-year-old *attrib.*; *(9 Jahre dauernd)* nine-year *attrib.*; ~mal *Adv.* nine times

**neunt...** *Ordinalz.* ninth

**neun·tausend** *Kardinalz.* nine thousand; **Neuntel** das *(schweiz. meist der)*; ~s, ~: ninth; **neuntens** *Adv.* ninthly; **neun·zehn** *Kardinalz.* nineteen; **neunzig** *Kardinalz.* ninety; **neunziger** *indekl. Adj.; nicht präd.* die ~ Jahre the nineties; **neunzigst...** *Ordinalz.* ninetieth

**neu·reich** *Adj.* nouveau riche

**Neurose** die; ~, ~n neurosis; **neurotisch** *Adj.* neurotic

**Neu·see·land** (das); ~s New Zealand; **Neuseeländer** der; ~s, ~: New Zealander

**neutral** 1. *Adj.* neutral; 2. *adv.* sich ~ verhalten remain neutral; **Neutralität** die; ~, ~en neutrality; **Neutron** das; ~s, ~en neutron; **Neutrum** das; ~s, **Neutra** *(österr. nur so) od.* **Neutren** *(Sprachw.)* neuter

**neu-, Neu-:** ~**wert** der value when new; ~**wertig** *Adj.* as new; ~**zeit** die; *o, Pl.* modern age; ~**zeitlich** *Adj.* modern

**nicht** *Adv.* a) not; ~! [no,] don't!; ~|**wahr**|? isn't it/he/she *etc.*; don't you/we/they *etc.*; **du magst das,** ~ |**wahr**|? you like that, don't you?; **was du ~ sagst!** you don't say!

**nicht-, Nicht-:** non-

**Nicht·angriffs·pakt** der non-aggression pact

**Nichte** die; ~, ~n niece

**nichtig** *Adj.* a) *(geh.)* vain ⟨things, pleasures, etc.⟩; trivial ⟨reason⟩; b) *(Rechtsspr.)* void; **Nicht·raucher** der non-smoker; „,~raucher" 'no smoking'; **nicht·rostend** *Adj.* non-rusting ⟨blade⟩; stainless ⟨steel⟩; **nichts** *Indefinitpron.* nothing; **ich möchte ~:** I don't want anything

**nichts-, Nichts-:** ~**nutz** der; ~es, ~e *(veralt.)* good-for-nothing; ~**nutzig** *Adj. (veralt.)* good-for-nothing attrib.; worthless ⟨existence⟩; ~**sagend** 1. *Adj.* empty; *(fig.: ausdruckslos)* expressionless ⟨face⟩; 2. *adv.* meaninglessly ⟨formulated⟩; ~**tun** das idleness *no art.*

**Nickel** das; ~s nickel

**nicken** *itr. V.* nod

**nie** *Adv.* never

**nieder** 1. *Adj.; nicht präd.* lower ⟨class, intelligence⟩; minor ⟨official⟩; lowly ⟨family, origins, birth⟩; menial ⟨task⟩; 2. *Adv.* down

**nieder-, Nieder-:** ~**gang** der fall; decline; ~|**gehen** *unr. itr. V.; mit sein* ⟨plane etc., rain, avalanche⟩ come down; ~**geschlagen** *Adj.* dejected; ~**geschlagenheit** die; ~: dejection; ~**lage** die defeat

**Nieder·lande** *Pl.:* die ~: the Netherlands; **Niederländer** der; ~s, ~: Dutchman; **Niederländerin** die; ~, ~**nen** Dutchwoman; **niederländisch** *Adj.* Dutch; Netherlands *attrib.* ⟨government, embassy, etc.⟩

**nieder-, Nieder-:** ~|**lassen** *unr. refl. V.* a) set up in business; ⟨doctor, lawyer⟩ set up in practice; b) *(seinen Wohnsitz nehmen)* settle; ~**lassung** die; ~, ~**en** *(Wirtsch.)* branch; ~|**le-**

**gen** *tr. V.* a) *(geh.: hinlegen)* lay *or* put down; lay ⟨wreath⟩; b) *(fig.)* resign [from] ⟨office⟩; relinquish ⟨command⟩

**Nieder·sachsen** (das) Lower Saxony

**nieder-, Nieder-:** ~**schlag** der precipitation; ~|**schlagen** *unr. tr. V.* a) **jmdn.** ~**schlagen** knock sb. down; b) *(beenden)* suppress, put down ⟨revolt, uprising, etc.⟩; c) *(senken)* lower ⟨eyes, eyelids⟩; ~**trächtig** 1. *Adj.* malicious ⟨person, slander, lie, etc.⟩; *(verachtenswert)* despicable ⟨person⟩; base ⟨misrepresentation, slander, lie⟩; 2. *adv.* ⟨betray, lie, treat⟩ in a despicable way; ~**trächtigkeit** die; ~, ~**en** a) *o. Pl. s.* ~**trächtig** 1: maliciousness; despicableness; baseness; b) *(gemeine Handlung)* despicable act

**Niederung** die; ~, ~**en** low-lying area; *(an Flußläufen, Küsten)* flats *pl.*; *(Tal)* valley

**niedlich** 1. *Adj.* sweet; cute *(Amer. coll.)*; 2. *adv.* sweetly

**niedrig** 1. *Adj.* low; lowly ⟨origins, birth⟩; base ⟨instinct, desire, emotion⟩; vile ⟨motive⟩; 2. *adv.* ⟨hang, fly⟩ low

**niemals** *Adv.* never; **niemand** *Indefinitpron.* nobody; no one

**Niere** die; ~, ~**n** kidney

**Nieren-:** ~**entzündung** die nephritis; ~**stein** der kidney stone

**Niesel·regen** der drizzle

**niesen** *itr. V.* sneeze

¹**Niete** die; ~, ~**n** a) *(Los)* blank; b) *(ugs.: Mensch)* dead loss *(coll.)* (**in** + *Dat.* at)

²**Niete** die; ~, ~**n** rivet; **nieten** *tr. V.* rivet

**Nikolaus·tag** der St Nicholas' Day

**Nikotin** das; ~s nicotine; **nikotin·arm** *Adj.* low-nicotine *attrib.*; low in nicotine *pred.*

**Nil** der; ~|s| Nile; **Nil·pferd** das hippopotamus

**nimm** *Imperativ Sg. v.* **nehmen**

**nippen** *itr. V.* sip

**nirgends, nirgend·wo** *Adv.* nowhere

**Nische** die; ~, ~**n** niche; *(Erweiterung eines Raumes)* recess

**nisten** *itr. V.* nest

**Nitrat** das; ~|e|s, ~**e** nitrate

**Niveau** [ni'vo:] das; ~s, ~s level; *(Qualitäts~)* standard

**Nixe** die; ~, ~**n** nixie; *(mit Fischschwanz)* mermaid

**nobel** *Adj.* a) *(geh.)* noble;

noble[-minded] ⟨*person*⟩; **b)** *(oft spött.: luxuriös)* elegant; posh *(coll.)*

**Nobel·preis** der Nobel prize

**noch 1.** *Adv.* **a)** *([wie] bisher)* still; ~ **nicht** not yet; **sie sind immer ~ nicht da** they're still not here; **ich habe Großvater ~ gekannt** I'm old enough to have known grandfather; **er hat ~ Glück gehabt** he was lucky; **das geht ~:** that's [still] all right; **b)** *(als Rest einer Menge)* **ich habe [nur] ~ zehn Mark** I've [only] ten marks left; **es sind ~ 10 km bis zur Grenze** it's another 10 km. to the border; **c)** *(bevor etw. anderes geschieht)* just; **ich will ~ [schnell] duschen** I just want to have a [quick] shower; **d)** *(irgendwann einmal)* some time; one day; **er wird ~ anrufen/kommen** he will still call/come; **e)** *(womöglich)* if you're/he's *etc.* not careful; **du kommst ~ zu spät!** you'll be late if you're not careful; **f)** *(drückt eine geringe zeitliche Distanz aus)* only; **gestern habe ich ihn ~ gesehen** I saw him only yesterday; **g)** *(nicht später als)* ~ **am selben Abend** the [very] same evening; **h)** *(außerdem, zusätzlich)* **wer war ~ da?** who else was there?; ~ **etwas Kaffee?** [would you like] some more coffee?; **Geld/Kleider** *usw.* ~ **und ~** heaps and heaps of money/clothes *etc. (coll.)*; **i) er ist ~ größer [als Karl]** he is even taller [than Karl]; **er will ~ mehr haben** he wants even more; **jeder ~ so dumme Mensch versteht das** anyone, however stupid, can understand that; **j) wie heißt sie [doch] ~?** [now] what's her name again?; **2.** *Partikel* **das ist ~ Qualität!** that's what I call quality; **der wird sich ~ wundern** *(ugs.)* he's in for a surprise; **er kann ~ nicht einmal lesen** he can't even read; **3.** *Konj. (und auch nicht)* nor; **weder ... noch** neither ... nor; **noch·mals** *Adv.* again

**Nominativ** der; ~s, ~e *(Sprachw.)* nominative [case]

**Nonne** die; ~, ~n nun

**Nord** *o. Art.; o. Pl. (bes. Seemannsspr., Met.) s.* Norden

**nord-, Nord-:** **~afrika (das)** North Africa; **~amerika (das)** North America; **~deutsch** *Adj.* North German

**Norden** der; ~s north; **der ~:** the North; **nach ~:** northwards; **Nordirland (das)** Northern Ireland; **nordisch** *Adj.* Nordic; **Nord·kap das** North Cape; **nördlich 1.** *Adj.* **a)** *(im*

*Norden gelegen)* northern; **b)** *(nach, aus dem Norden)* northerly; **c)** *(aus dem Norden kommend, für den Norden typisch)* Northern; **2.** *adv.* northwards; ~ **von ...:** [to the] north of ...; **3.** *Präp. mit Gen.* [to the] north of; **Nord·pol** ['--] der North Pole; **Nord·rhein-Westfalen (das); ~s** North Rhine-Westphalia; **Nord·see die;** *o. Pl.* North Sea; **nord·wärts** *Adv.* northwards; **Nord·wind** der northerly wind

**Nörgelei** die; ~ *(abwertend) o. Pl.* grumbling; **nörgeln** *itr. V. (abwertend)* moan, grumble (**an** + *Dat.* about)

**Norm** die; ~, ~en **a)** norm; **b)** *(geforderte Arbeitsleistung)* quota; **c)** *(Sport)* qualifying standard; **d)** *(technische, industrielle ~)* standard; **normal 1.** *Adj.* normal; **2.** *adv.* normally; **Normal·benzin das** ≈ two-star petrol *(Brit.)*; regular *(Amer.)*; **normalerweise** *Adv.* normally; **normalisieren 1.** *tr. V.* normalize; **2.** *refl. V.* return to normal

**Normandie** die; ~: Normandy

**normen** *tr. V.*, **normieren** *tr. V.* standardize

**Norwegen (das); ~s** Norway; **Norweger** der; ~s, ~, **Norwegerin die; ~, ~nen** Norwegian; **norwegisch** *Adj.* Norwegian

**Nostalgie** die; ~: nostalgia

**Not** die; ~, **Nöte a)** *(Gefahr)* **in ~ sein** be in desperate straits; **b)** *o. Pl. (Mangel, Armut)* need; poverty [and hardship]; ~ **leiden** suffer poverty [and hardship]; **in ~ geraten/sein** encounter hard times/be suffering want [and deprivation]; **c)** *o. Pl. (Verzweiflung)* distress; **d)** *(Sorge, Mühe)* trouble; **mit knapper ~:** by the skin of one's teeth; **f)** *o. Pl. (veralt.: Notwendigkeit)* necessity; **zur ~:** if need be

**Notar** der; ~s, ~e notary; **Notariat das; ~[e]s, ~e a)** *(Amt)* notaryship; **b)** *(Kanzlei)* notary's office

**not-, Not-:** **~arzt** der doctor on [emergency] call; **~ausgang** der emergency exit; **~bremse** die emergency brake; **~dienst** der *s.* Bereitschaftsdienst; **~dürftig 1.** *Adj.* makeshift ⟨*shelter, repair*⟩; scanty ⟨*cover, clothing*⟩; **2.** *adv.* scantily ⟨*clothed*⟩

**Note** die; ~, **~n a)** *(Zeichen)* note; **b)** *Pl. (Text)* music *sing.*; **c)** *(Schul~)* mark; **d)** *(Eislauf, Turnen)* score

**not-, Not-:** **~fall** der **a)** emergency; **b)**

im ~**fall** *(nötigenfalls)* if need be; ~**falls** *Adv.* if need be; ~**gedrungen** *Adv.* of necessity

**notieren** 1. *tr. V.* [sich *(Dat.)*] etw. ~: make a note of sth.; 2. *itr. V. (Börsenw., Wirtsch.)* be quoted (**mit** at)

**nötig** 1. *Adj.* necessary; etw./jmdn. ~ **haben** need sth./sb.; 2. *adv.* er **braucht** ~ **Hilfe** he is in urgent need of help; **nötigen** *tr. V.* compel; force; *(Rechtsspr.)* coerce

**Notiz** die; ~, ~**en** note; *(Zeitungs~)* brief report; **von jmdm./etw. [keine]** ~ **nehmen** take [no] notice of sb./sth.

**Notiz-:** ~**block** der, *Pl.* ~**blocks,** *schweiz.:* ~**blöcke** notepad; ~**buch** das notebook

**not-, Not-:** ~**lage** die serious difficulties *pl.;* ~**landen**[1] *itr. V.; mit sein* do an emergency landing; ~**landung** die emergency landing; ~**leidend** *Adj.* needy; ~**lösung** die stopgap; ~**lüge** die evasive lie; *(aus Rücksichtnahme)* white lie

**notorisch** 1. *Adj.* notorious; 2. *adv.* notoriously

**Not-:** ~**ruf der** a) *(Hilferuf)* emergency call; *(eines Schiffes)* Mayday call; b) *(Nummer)* emergency number; ~**ruf · nummer** die emergency number; ~**ruf · säule** die emergency telephone *(mounted in a pillar)*; ~**stand** der crisis; *(Staatsrecht)* state of emergency; ~**unterkunft** die emergency accommodation *no pl., no indef. art.;* ~**wehr** die self-defence

**not · wendig** *Adj.* necessary; **Not-wendigkeit** die; ~, ~**en** necessity

**Nougat** ['nu:gat] der; *auch* das; ~**s** nougat

**Novelle** die; ~, ~**n** *(Literaturw.)* novella

**November** der; ~[s], ~: November

**Nr.** *Abk.* Nummer No

**Nu** der: **im Nu** in no time

**Nuance** ['nÿã:sə] die; ~, ~**n** nuance; *(Grad)* shade

**nüchtern** 1. *Adj. (nicht betrunken; realistisch)* sober; *(ungeschminkt)* bare, plain ⟨*fact*⟩; **der Patient muß ~ sein** the patient's stomach must be empty; 2. *adv.* soberly

**nuckeln** *(ugs.) itr. V.* suck (**an** + *Dat.* at)

**Nudel** die; ~, ~**n** piece of spaghetti/vermicelli/tortellini *etc.; (als Suppen-*

*einlage)* noodle; ~**n** *(Teigwaren)* pasta *sing.; (als Suppeneinlage)* noodles

**nuklear** 1. *Adj.* nuclear; 2. *adv.* ~ **angetrieben** nuclear-powered

**null** *Kardinalz.* nought; ~ **Komma sechs** [nought] point six; **gegen** ~ **Uhr** around twelve midnight; **Null** die; ~, ~**en** a) nought; zero; **in** ~ **Komma nichts** *(ugs.)* in less than no time; **gleich** ~ **sein** *(fig.)* be practically zero; **auf** ~ **stehen** ⟨*indicator, needle, etc.*⟩ be at zero; b) *(ugs.: Versager)* failure; dead loss *(coll.);* **Null · punkt der** zero

**numerieren** *tr. V.* number; **Numerierung** die; ~, ~**en** numbering; **Nummer** die; ~, ~**n** a) number; **ein Wagen mit [einer] Münchner** ~: a car with a Munich registration; **ich bin unter der** ~ **24 26 79 zu erreichen** I can be reached on 24 26 79; b) *(Ausgabe)* issue; c) *(Größe)* size; **Nummern · schild das** number-plate; license plate *(Amer.)*

**nun** 1. *Adv.* now; 2. *Partikel* now; **das hast du ~ davon!** it serves you right!; **kommst du ~ mit oder nicht?** now are you coming or not?; ~ **gut** [well,] all right; ~, ~! now, come on; ~ **ja** ...: well, yes ...

**nur** 1. *Adv.* a) *(nicht mehr als)* only; just; b) *(ausschließlich)* only; **nicht** ~ ..., **sondern auch** ...: not only ..., but also ...; ~ **so zum Spaß** just for fun; 2. *Konj.* but; **ich kann dir das Buch leihen,** ~ **nicht heute** I can lend you the book, only not today; 3. *Partikel* **wenn er ~ hier wäre** if only he were here; ~ **zu!** go ahead; **laß dich ~ nicht erwischen** just don't let me/them *etc.* catch you; **was sollen wir ~ tun?** what on earth are we going to do?; **so schnell er ~ konnte** just as fast as he could

**Nürnberg** (das); ~**s** Nuremberg

**Nuß** die; ~, **Nüsse** a) nut; **Nuß · baum** der walnut-tree; **Nuß · knacker** der nutcrackers *pl.*

**Nutte** die; ~, ~**n** *(derb)* tart *(sl.);* hooker *(Amer. sl.)*

**nutz-:** ~**bar** *Adj.* usable; exploitable, utilizable ⟨*mineral resources, invention*⟩; cultivatable ⟨*land, soil*⟩; ~**bringend** 1. *Adj.* useful; *(gewinnbringend)* profitable; 2. *adv.* profitably

**nutzen** 1. *tr. V.* a) use; exploit, utilize ⟨*natural resources*⟩; cultivate ⟨*land, soil*⟩; harness ⟨*energy source*⟩; exploit ⟨*advantage*⟩; b) *(be~, aus~)* use; make use of; 2. *itr. V. s.* **nützen** 1;

---

[1] *ich notlande, notgelandet, notzulanden*

**Nutzen** der; ~s a) benefit; [jmdm.] **von ~ sein** be of use [to sb.]; b) *(Profit)* profit; **nützen** 1. *itr. V.* be of use *(Dat.* to); **nichts ~:** be no use; 2. *tr. V. s.* **nutzen** 1; **nützlich** *Adj.* useful; **nutzlos** 1. *Adj.* useless; *(vergeblich)* vain *attrib.;* in vain *pred.;* 2. *adv.* uselessly; *(vergeblich)* in vain; **Nutz·losigkeit** die; ~: uselessness; *(Vergeblichkeit)* futility; **Nutznießer** der; ~s, ~, **Nutznießerin** die; ~, ~nen beneficiary; **Nutzung** die; ~, ~en use; *(des Landes, des Bodens)* cultivation; *(von Bodenschätzen)* exploitation; utilization; *(einer Energiequelle)* harnessing

**Nylon** Ⓦ ['nailɔn] das; ~s nylon
**Nymphe** die; ~, ~n *(Myth., Zool.)* nymph
**Nymphomanin** die; ~, ~nen *(Psych.)* nymphomaniac

# O

—————

**o, O** das; ~, ~: o/O
**O** *Abk.* Ost[en] E
**ö, Ö** das; ~, ~: o/O umlaut
**o. ä.** *Abk.* **oder ähnlich[es]** or similar
**Oase** die; ~, ~n *(auch fig.)* oasis
**ob** *Konj.* a) whether; b) **und ob!** of course!
**OB** *Abk.* **Oberbürgermeister**
**Obacht** die; ~ *(bes. südd.)* caution; ~ **auf jmdn./etw. geben** take care of sb./ sth.; *(aufmerksam sein)* pay attention to sb./sth.
**Obdach** das; ~[e]s *(geh.)* shelter; **obdach·los** *Adj.* homeless; **Obdachlose** der/die; *adj. Dekl.* homeless person/man/woman; **die** ~n the homeless
**Obduktion** die; ~, ~en *(Med., Rechtsw.)* post-mortem [examination]; autopsy
**O-Beine** *Pl.* bandy legs; bow-legs
**oben** *Adv.* a) **hier/dort ~:** up here/ there; **weiter ~:** further up; **nach ~:** upwards; **von ~:** from above; **von ~ herab** *(fig.)* condescendingly; b) *(im Gebäude)* upstairs; **nach ~:** upstairs;

c) *(am oberen Ende, zum oberen Ende hin)* at the top; **nach ~ [hin]** towards the top; **von ~:** from the top; c) *(an der Oberseite)* on top; d) *(in einer Hierarchie, Rangfolge)* at the top; e) *([weiter] vorn im Text)* above; **oben·genannt** *Adj.* above-mentioned
**ober...** *Adj.* upper *attrib.;* top *attrib.*
**Ober** der; ~s, ~: waiter; **Herr ~!** waiter!
**Ober-:** ~**arm** der upper arm; ~**bekleidung** die outer clothing; ~**bürgermeister** der mayor
**Ober·fläche** die surface; *(Flächeninhalt)* surface area; **oberflächlich** 1. *Adj.* superficial; 2. *adv.* superficially
**ober·halb** 1. *Adv.* above; ~ **von** above; 2. *Präp. mit Gen.* above
**Ober-:** ~**haupt** das head; *(einer Verschwörung)* leader; ~**hemd** das shirt; ~**kiefer** der upper jaw; ~**körper** der upper part of the body; ~**schenkel** der thigh; ~**schicht** die *(Soziol.)* upper class; ~**schule** die secondary school; ~**seite** die top
**oberst...** *s.* **ober...**
**Ober·teil** das *od.* der top [part]; *(eines Bikinis, Anzugs, Kleids usw.)* top [half]
**ob·gleich** *Konj. s.* **obwohl**
**obig** *Adj.* above
**Objekt** das; ~s, ~e object; *(Kaufmannsspr.: Immobilie)* property; **objektiv** 1. *Adj.* objective; 2. *adv.* objectively; **Objektiv** das; ~s, ~e lens; **Objektivität** die; ~: objectivity
**Obrigkeit** die; ~, ~en authorities *pl.*
**ob·schon** *Konj. (geh.)* although
**Obst** das; ~[e]s fruit
**Obst-:** ~**baum** der fruit-tree; ~**garten** der orchard; ~**kuchen** der fruit flan; ~**saft** der fruit juice
**obszön** 1. *Adj.* obscene; 2. *adv.* obscenely; **Obszönität** die; ~, ~en obscenity
**ob·wohl** *Konj.* although; though
**Ochse** ['ɔksə] der; ~n, ~n a) ox; bullock; b) *(salopp)* numskull *(coll.);* **Ochsen·schwanz·suppe** die oxtail soup
**od.** *Abk.* **oder**
**öde** *Adj.* a) deserted; desolate ⟨area, landscape⟩; b) *(unfruchtbar)* barren; c) *(langweilig)* tedious; dreary ⟨life, time, existence⟩; **Öde** die; ~: *s.* **öde a–c:** desertedness; desolateness; barrenness; tediousness; dreariness
**oder** *Konj.* or; *(in Fragen)* **er ist doch hier, ~?** he is here, isn't he? *(zweifelnd)* he is here – or isn't he?

**OEZ** *Abk.* osteuropäische Zeit EET

**Ofen** der; ~s, **Ö**fen heater; *(Kohle~)* stove; *(Back~)* oven; *(Brenn~, Trokken~)* kiln; **Ofen·rohr** das [stove] flue

**offen 1.** *Adj.* **a)** open; **ein ~es Hemd** a shirt with the collar unfastened; ~ **haben** *od.* **sein** be open; ~**es Licht** a naked light; **b)** *(frei)* vacant ⟨*job, post*⟩; **c)** *(ungewiß, ungeklärt)* open ⟨*question*⟩; uncertain ⟨*result*⟩; **d)** *(noch nicht bezahlt)* outstanding ⟨*bill*⟩; **e)** *(freimütig, aufrichtig)* frank [and open] ⟨*person*⟩; frank, candid ⟨*look, opinion, reply*⟩; **2.** *adv.* openly; ~ **gesagt** frankly; to be frank; **offen·bar 1.** *Adj.* obvious; **2.** *adv.* obviously; **Offenbarung** die; ~, ~en revelation; **offen|bleiben** *unr. itr. V.; mit sein* **a)** stay open; **b)** *(ungeklärt bleiben)* remain open; ⟨*decision*⟩ be left open; **Offen·heit** die; ~: *s.* offen e: frankness [and openness]; candour

**offen-:** ~**kundig 1.** *Adj.* obvious; **2.** *adv.* obviously; ~**lassen** *unr. tr. V.* etw. ~**lassen** leave sth. open; ~**sichtlich 1.** *Adj.* obvious; **2.** *adv.* obviously

**offensiv 1.** *Adj.* **a)** offensive; **b)** *(Sport)* attacking; **2.** *adv.* **a)** offensively; **b)** *(Sport)* ~ **spielen** play an attacking game; **Offensive** die; ~, ~n *(auch Sport)* offensive

**offen|stehen** *unr. itr. V.* be open

**öffentlich 1.** *Adj.* public; state *attrib.,* [state-] maintained ⟨*school*⟩; **der** ~**e Dienst** the civil service; **2.** *adv.* publicly; ⟨*perform, appear*⟩ in public; **Öffentlichkeit** die; ~: public

**offiziell 1.** *Adj.* official; **2.** *adv.* officially

**Offizier** der; ~s, ~e officer

**öffnen 1.** *tr. V.* open; turn on ⟨*tap*⟩; undo ⟨*coat, blouse, button, zip*⟩; **2.** *itr. V.* **a)** [jmdm.] ~: open the door [to sb.]; **b)** *(geöffnet werden)* ⟨*shop, bank, etc.*⟩ open; **3.** *refl. V.* open; **Öffner** der; ~s, ~: opener; **Öffnung** die; ~, ~en opening; **Öffnungs·zeiten** *Pl.* opening times

**oft** *Adv.* öfter, **am** öftesten often; **wie oft soll ich dir noch sagen, daß ...?** how many [more] times do I have to tell you that ...?; **öfter** *Adv.* now and then; **oftmals** *Adv.* often; frequently

**OG** *Abk.* Obergeschoß

**ohne 1.** *Präp. mit Akk.* without; ~ **mich!** [you can] count me out!; ~ **weiteres** *(leicht, einfach)* easily; *(ohne Einwand)* readily; **2.** *Konj.* ~ **zu zögern** without hesitation; **ohne·hin** *Adv.* anyway

**Ohnmacht** die; ~, ~en **a)** faint; **in** ~ **fallen** faint; **b)** *(Machtlosigkeit)* powerlessness; impotence; **ohnmächtig 1.** *Adj.* **a)** unconscious; ~ **werden** faint; ~ **sein** have fainted; **b)** *(machtlos)* powerless; impotent; **2.** *adv.* impotently; ~ **zusehen** watch helplessly

**Ohr** das; ~[e]s, ~en ear; **gute/schlechte** ~**en haben** have good/poor hearing *sing.;* **jmdn. übers** ~ **hauen** *(fig. ugs.)* put one over on sb. *(coll.);* **Öhr** das, ~[e]s, ~e eye; **Ohren·schmerz** der earache; ~**schmerzen haben** have [an] earache *sing.*

**ohr-, Ohr-:** ~**feige** die box on the ears; ~**feigen** *tr. V.* jmdn. ~**feigen** box sb.'s ears; **ich könnte mich ~feigen!** *(ugs.)* I could kick myself!; ~**läppchen** das ear-lobe; ~**ring** der ear-ring

**okay** [o'ke] *(ugs.)* *Interj., Adj., adv.* OK *(coll.);* **okay** *(coll.)*

**öko-, Öko-:** eco-

**Ökologie** die; ~: ecology; **ökologisch 1.** *Adj.* ecological; **2.** *adv.* ecologically

**ökonomisch 1.** *Adj.* **a)** economic; **b)** *(sparsam)* economical; **2.** *adv.* economically

**Oktober** der; ~[s], ~: October

**Öl** das; ~[e]s, ~e oil; **in Öl malen** paint in oils; **ölen** *tr. V.* oil; **Öl·farbe** die **a)** oil-based paint; **b)** *(zum Malen)* oil-paint; **ölig** *Adj.* oily

**Olive** die; ~, ~n olive

**Öl-:** ~**ofen** der oil heater; ~**sardine** die sardine in oil; **eine Dose ~n** a tin of sardines; ~**wechsel** der *(bes. Kfz-W.)* oil-change

**Olympiade** die; ~, ~n Olympic Games *pl.;* Olympics *pl.;* **Olympia·stadion** das Olympic stadium; **olympisch** *Adj.* Olympic; **die Olympischen Spiele** the Olympic Games; the Olympics

**Oma** die; ~, ~s *(fam.)* granny *(coll./ child lang.)*

**Omelett** [ɔm[ə]'lɛt] das; ~[e]s, ~e *od.* ~s omelette

**Omnibus** der; ~ses, ~se omnibus *(formal);* *(Privat- und Reisebus auch)* coach

**Onkel** der; ~s, ~ *od. (ugs.)* ~s uncle

**OP** [o:'pe:] der; ~[s], ~[s] *Abk.* Operationssaal

**Opa** der; ~s, ~s *(fam.)* grandad *(coll./ child lang.)*

**Opal** der; ~s, ~e opal

**OPEC** ['o:pɛk] die; ~ *Abk.* OPEC

**Oper** die; ~, ~n opera; *(Opernhaus)* Opera; opera-house

**Operation** die; ~, ~en operation; **Operations·saal** der operating-theatre *(Brit.) or* -room

**Operette** die; ~, ~n operetta

**operieren** 1. *tr. V.* operate on ⟨*patient*⟩; 2. *itr. V.* operate

**Opern·glas** das opera-glass[es *pl.*]

**Opfer** das; ~s, ~: a) sacrifice; b) *(Geschädigter)* victim; **opfern** *tr. V.* *(auch fig.)* sacrifice; offer up ⟨*fruit, produce, etc.*⟩

**Opium** das; ~s opium

**opponieren** *itr. V.* **gegen jmdn./etw.** ~: oppose sb./sth.; **Opposition** die; ~, ~en opposition; **oppositionell** *Adj.* opposition *attrib.* ⟨*group, movement, etc.*⟩; ⟨*newspaper, writer, artist, etc.*⟩ opposed to the government

**Optik** die; ~: optics *sing., no art.;* **Optiker** der; ~s, ~: optician

**optimal** 1. *Adj.* optimal; optimum *attrib;* 2. *adv.* **jmdn.** ~ **beraten** give sb. the best possible advice; **Optimismus** der; ~: optimism; **Optimist** der; ~en, ~en, **Optimistin** die; ~, ~nen optimist; **optimistisch** 1. *Adj.* optimistic; 2. *adv.* optimistically

**optisch** 1. *Adj.* optical; visual ⟨*impression*⟩; **eine** ~**e Täuschung** an optical illusion; 2. *adv.* optically; visually ⟨*impressive, effective*⟩

**orange** [o'rã:ʒ(ə)] *indekl. Adj.* orange; **Orange** die; ~, ~n orange

**Orangen-:** ~**marmelade** die orange marmalade; ~**saft** der orange-juice

**Orchester** [or'kɛstə] das; ~s, ~: orchestra

**Orden** der; ~s, ~ a) order; b) *(Ehrenzeichen)* decoration

**ordentlich** 1. *Adj.* a) [neat and] tidy; neat ⟨*handwriting, clothes*⟩; b) *(anständig)* respectable; proper ⟨*manners*⟩; c) *(planmäßig)* ordinary ⟨*meeting*⟩; ~**es Mitglied** full member; d) *(ugs.: richtig)* proper; real; **ein** ~**es Stück Kuchen** a nice big piece of cake; e) *(ugs.: recht gut)* decent ⟨*wine, flat, marks, etc.*⟩; **ganz** ~: pretty good; 2. *adv.* a) tidily; neatly; ⟨*write*⟩ neatly; b) *(anständig)* properly; c) *(ugs.: gehörig)* ~ **feiern** have a real good celebration *(coll.)*; d) *(ugs.: recht gut)* ⟨*ski, speak, etc.*⟩ really well

**Ordinal·zahl** die ordinal [number]; **ordinär** 1. *Adj.* vulgar; 2. *adv.* vulgarly; **Ordinate** die; ~, ~n *(Math.)* ordinate

**ordnen** *tr. V.* arrange; **sein Leben/seine Finanzen** ~: straighten out one's life/put one's finances in order; **Ordner** der; ~s, ~: file; **Ordnung** die; ~, ~en order; *(geregelter Ablauf)* routine; ~ **halten** keep things tidy; **in** ~ **sein** *(ugs.)* be OK *(coll.) or* all right; **hier ist etw. nicht in** ~: there's something wrong here; **sie ist in** ~ *(ugs.)* she's OK *(coll.);* **in** ~! *(ugs.)* OK! *(coll.);* all right!

**ordnungs-, Ordnungs-:** ~**gemäß** 1. *Adj.* ⟨*conduct etc.*⟩ in accordance with the regulations; 2. *adv.* in accordance with the regulations; ~**halber** *Adv.* as a matter of form; ~**widrig** *(Rechtsw.)* 1. *Adj.* ⟨*actions, behaviour, etc.*⟩ contravening the regulations; illegal ⟨*parking*⟩; 2. *adv.* ~**widrig parken** park illegally; ~**zahl** die ordinal [number]

**Organ** das; ~s, ~e organ; *(ugs.: Stimme)* voice; **Organisation** die; ~, ~en organization; **Organisator** der; ~s, ~en organizer; **organisatorisch** *Adj.* organizational; **organisch** 1. *Adj.* organic; 2. *adv.* organically; **organisieren** 1. *tr. V.* organize; 2. *itr. V.* **gut** ~ **können** be a good organizer; 3. *refl. V.* organize; **Organismus** der; **Organismen** organism

**Organist** der; ~en, ~en, **Organistin** die; ~, ~nen organist

**Orgasmus** der; ~, **Orgasmen** orgasm

**Orgel** die; ~, ~n organ

**Orgie** ['orgiə] die; ~, ~n *(auch fig.)* orgy

**Orient** ['o:riɛnt] der; ~s Middle East and south-western Asia *(including Afghanistan and Nepal);* **der Vordere** ~: the Middle East; **orientalisch** *Adj.* oriental; **orientieren** 1. *refl. V.* a) get one's bearings; b) **sich über etw.** *(Akk.)* ~ *(fig.)* inform oneself about sth.; c) **sich an etw.** *(Dat.)* ~ *(fig.)* be oriented towards sth.; ⟨*policy, advertising*⟩ be geared towards sth; 2. *tr. V. (unterrichten)* inform **(über** + *Akk.* about); **Orientierung** die; ~ a) **die** ~ **verlieren** lose one's bearings; b) *(Unterrichtung)* **zu Ihrer** ~: for your information; **Orientierungs·sinn** der sense of direction

**original** 1. *Adj.* original; 2. *adv.* ~ **italienischer Espresso** genuine Italian es-

presso coffee; **etw. ~ übertragen**
broadcast sth. live; **Original das; ~s,
~e** original; **Original·fassung die**
original version; **Originalität die; ~:**
originality; **originell 1.** *Adj.* original;
**2.** *adv.* with originality

**Orkan** der; ~|e|s, ~e hurricane

**Ornament das; ~|e|s, ~e** ornament

**¹Ort** der; ~|e|s, ~e place; (Dorf) vil-
lage; *(Stadt)* town; **an ~ und Stelle**
there and then; **²Ort: vor ~** *(fig.)* on
the spot

**Orthographie** die; ~; ~n orthography; **orthographisch 1.** *Adj.* or-
thographic; **~e Fehler** spelling mistakes; **2.** *adv.* orthographically; **Or-
thopäde** der; ~n, ~n orthopaedic
specialist; **orthopädisch 1.** *Adj.* orthopaedic; **2.** *adv.* orthopaedically

**örtlich 1.** *Adj. (auch Med.)* local; **2.**
*adv. (auch Med.)* locally; **~ betäubt
werden** be given a local anaesthetic;
**Ortschaft** die; ~, ~en *(Dorf)* village;
*(Stadt)* town

**Orts-: ~gespräch das** *(Fernspr.)*
local call; **~name** der place-name;
**~netz·kennzahl die** *(Fernspr.)* dialling code; area code *(Amer.)*

**Öse** die; ~, ~n eye

**Ossi** der; ~s, ~s *(salopp)* East German

**Ost** *o. Art.; o. Pl. (bes. Seemannsspr.,
Met.) s.* Osten

**ost-, Ost-: ~block** der; *o. Pl.* East-
ern bloc; **~deutsch** *Adj.* Eastern
German; *(hist.: auf die DDR bezogen)*
East German; **~deutschland (das)**
Eastern Germany; *(hist.: DDR)* East
Germany

**Osten** der; ~s east; **der ~:** the East;
**der Ferne ~:** the Far East; **der Nahe ~:**
the Middle East

**Oster-: ~ei das** Easter egg; **~glocke
die** daffodil; **~hase** der Easter hare
*(said to bring children their Easter
Eggs)*

**Ostern das; ~, ~:** Easter; **Frohe** *od.*
**Fröhliche ~:** Happy Easter!; **zu ~:** at
Easter

**Österreich (das); ~s** Austria; **Österreicher** der; ~s, **Österreicherin die**
~, ~nen Austrian; **österreichisch**
*Adj.* Austrian

**Ost·europa (das)** Eastern Europe;
**östlich 1.** *Adj.* **a)** *(im Osten gelegen)*
eastern; **b)** *(nach, aus dem Osten)* easterly; **c)** *(aus dem Osten kommend, für
den Osten typisch; Politik)* Eastern;
⟨*influence, policies*⟩ of the East; **2.** *adv.*
eastwards; **~ von ...:** [to the] east of ...;

**3.** *Präp. mit Gen.* [to the] east of;
**Ost·see die;** *o. Pl.* Baltic [Sea];
**ost·wärts** *Adv.* eastwards;
**Ost·wind** der easterly wind

**¹Otter** der; ~s, ~ *(Fisch~)* otter

**²Otter** die; ~, ~n *(Viper)* adder; viper

**Otto·motor** der Otto engine

**Ouvertüre** [uvɛr'tyːrə] **die; ~, ~n**
*(auch fig.)* overture *(Gen.* to)

**oval** *Adj.* oval

**Ozean** der; ~s, ~e ocean; **Oze-
an·dampfer** der ocean liner

**Ozon** der *od.* das; ~s ozone

# P

---

**p, P** [pe] **das; ~, ~:** p/P

**paar** *indekl. Indefinitpron.* **ein ~ ...: a**
few ...; *(zwei od. drei)* a couple of ...;
**Paar das; ~|e|s, ~e** pair; *(Mann und
Frau)* couple; **ein ~ Würstchen** two
sausages; **paaren** *refl. V.* ⟨*animals*⟩
mate; ⟨*people*⟩ copulate; **Paar·lauf**
der pairs *pl.;* **paar·mal** *Adv.* **ein
~mal** a few times; *(zwei- oder dreimal)*
a couple of times; **paar·weise** *Adv.*
in pairs

**Pacht die; ~, ~en a)** lease; **etw. in ~
nehmen** lease sth.; **etw. in ~ haben**
have sth. on lease; **etw. in ~ geben**
lease sth.; **pachten** *tr. V.* lease;
**Pächter** der; ~s, ~, **Pächterin die;**
~, ~nen leaseholder; *(eines Hofes)*
tenant

**¹Pack** der; ~|e|s, ~e *od.* Päcke **a)** pack;
**b)** *s.* Packen; **²Pack das;** ~|e|s *(ugs.
abwertend)* rabble; **Päckchen das;**
~s, ~ **a)** package; *(auch Postw.)* small
parcel; *(Bündel)* packet; **b)** *s.* Pak-
kung **a; packen 1.** *tr. V.* **a)** pack; **b)**
*(fassen)* grab [hold of]; *(fig.)* **Furcht
packte ihn/er wurde von Furcht ge-
packt** he was seized with fear; **2.** *itr. V.*
*(Koffer usw. ~)* pack; **Packen der;**
~s, ~: pile; *(zusammengeschnürt)*
bundle; *(von Geldscheinen)* wad;
**Pack·papier das** [stout] wrapping-
paper; **Packung die; ~, ~en a)**
packet; pack *(esp. Amer.);* **b)** *(Med.,
Kosmetik)* pack

**Pädagoge** der; ~n, ~n *(Erzieher, Lehrer)* teacher; *(Wissenschaftler)* educationalist; **pädagogisch** 1. *Adj.* educational; **seine ~en Fähigkeiten** his teaching ability *sing.;* 2. *adv.* educationally ⟨*sound, wrong*⟩

**Paddel** das; ~s, ~: paddle; **Paddel·boot** das canoe; **paddeln** *itr. V.; mit sein* paddle; *(als Sport)* canoe

**paffen** 1. *tr. V.* puff at ⟨*pipe etc.*⟩; 2. *itr. V.* puff away

**Page** ['pa:ʒə] der; ~n, ~n bellboy

**Paket** das; ~⟨e⟩s, ~e pile; *(zusammengeschnürt)* bundle; *(Eingepacktes, Post~)* parcel; *(Packung)* packet; pack *(esp. Amer.)*

**Paket-:** ~**karte** die parcel dispatch form; ~**schalter** der parcels counter

**Pakistan** (das); ~s Pakistan; **Pakistaner** der; ~s, ~, **Pakistani** der; ~⟨s⟩, ~⟨s⟩ Pakistani; **pakistanisch** *Adj.* Pakistani

**Pakt** der; ~⟨e⟩s, ~e pact; **paktieren** *itr. V.* make *or* do a deal/deals

**Palast** der; ~⟨e⟩s, Paläste palace

**Palästina** (das); ~s Palestine; **Palästinenser** der; ~s, ~: Palestinian; **palästinensisch** *Adj.* Palestinian

**Palette** die; ~, ~n palette

**Palme** die; ~, ~n palm[-tree]

**Pampelmuse** die; ~, ~n grapefruit

**Panama** (das); ~s Panama; **Panama·kanal** der; *o. Pl.* Panama Canal

**panieren** *tr. V.* bread; coat ⟨*sth.*⟩ with breadcrumbs; **Panier·mehl** das breadcrumbs *pl.*

**Panik** die; ~, ~en panic; **panisch** *Adj.* panic *attrib.* ⟨*fear, terror*⟩; panic-stricken ⟨*flight*⟩

**Panne** die; ~, ~n a) breakdown; *(Reifen~)* puncture; flat [tyre]; b) *(Mißgeschick)* mishap; **Pannen·dienst** der breakdown service

**Panorama** das; ~s, Panoramen panorama

**Panther** der; ~s, ~: panther

**Pantoffel** der; ~s, ~n backless slipper

**Pantomime** die; ~, ~n mime

**Panzer** der; ~s, ~ a) *(Milit.)* tank; b) *(Zool.)* armour *no indef. art.; (von Schildkröten, Krebsen)* shell

**Panzer-:** ~**glas** das bullet-proof glass; ~**schrank** der safe

**Papa** der; ~s, ~s *(ugs.)* daddy *(coll.)*

**Papagei** der; ~en *od.* ~s, ~⟨e⟩n parrot

**Papi** der; ~s, ~s *(ugs.)* daddy *(coll.)*

**Papier** das; ~s, ~e a) paper; b) *Pl. (Ausweis[e])* [identity] papers; c) *(Finanzw.: Wert~)* security

**Papier-:** ~**geld** das paper money; ~**korb** der waste-paper basket

**Pappe** die; ~, ~n cardboard

**Pappel** die; ~, ~n poplar

**päppeln** *tr. V.* feed up

**Papp·karton** der cardboard box

**Paprika** der; ~s, ~⟨s⟩ a) pepper; b) *o. Pl. (Gewürz)* paprika

**Papst** der; ~⟨e⟩s, Päpste pope; **päpstlich** *Adj.* papal

**Parabel** die; ~, ~n a) *(bes. Literaturw.)* parable; b) *(Math.)* parabola

**Parade** die; ~, ~n parade

**Paradies** das; ~es, ~e paradise; **paradiesisch** *Adj.* paradisical; *(herrlich)* heavenly

**paradox** *Adj.* paradoxical

**Paragraph** der; ~en, ~en section; *(in Vertrag)* clause

**parallel** 1. *Adj.* parallel; 2. *adv.* ~ **verlaufen** run parallel (**mit, zu** to); **Parallele** die; ~, ~n parallel; **Parallelogramm** das; ~s, ~e parallelogram; **Parallel·straße** die street running parallel *(Gen.* to)

**Para·nuß** die Brazil-nut

**Parasit** der; ~en, ~en *(auch fig.)* parasite

**parat** *Adj.* ready

**Parfum** [par'fœ̃:], **Parfüm** das; ~s, ~s perfume; **Parfümerie** die; ~, ~en perfumery; **parfümieren** *tr. V.* perfume

**Pariser** 1. *indekl. Adj.* Parisian; Paris *attrib.;* 2. der; ~s, ~ Parisian; **Pariserin** die; ~, ~nen Parisian

**Parität** die; ~, ~en parity

**Park** der; ~s, ~s park; *(Schloß~ usw.)* grounds *pl.*

**Parka** der; ~s, ~s parka

**parken** *tr., itr. V.* park; „Parken verboten!" 'No Parking'

**Parkett** das; ~⟨e⟩s, ~e a) parquet floor; b) *(Theater)* [front] stalls *pl.;* parquet *(Amer.)*

**Park-:** ~**gebühr** die parking-fee; ~**haus** das multi-storey car-park; ~**lücke** die parking-space; ~**platz** der car-park; parking lot *(Amer.); (für ein einzelnes Fahrzeug)* parking-space; ~**scheibe** die parking-disc; ~**schein** der car-park ticket; ~**uhr** die parking-meter; ~**verbot** das ban on parking; **im ~verbot stehen** be parked illegally; ~**verbots·schild** das no-parking sign

**Parlament** das; ~⟨e⟩s, ~e parliament; **Parlamentarier** der; ~s, ~, **Parlamentarierin** die; ~, ~nen member of

parliament; **parlamentạrisch** *Adj.*
parliamentary
**Parodịe** die; ~, ~n parody (**auf** +
*Akk.* of)
**Parọle** die; ~, ~n a) *(Wahlspruch)*
motto; *(Schlagwort)* slogan; b) *(bes.
Milit.: Kennwort)* password
**Partẹi** die; ~, ~en a) *(Politik,
Rechtsw.)* party; b) *(Gruppe, Mann-
schaft)* side; **für jmdn. ~ ergreifen** *od.*
**nehmen** side with sb.; **parteiisch 1.**
*Adj.* biased; 2. *adv.* in a biased man-
ner; **partei·los** *Adj. (Politik)* inde-
pendent *⟨MP⟩*; **Partei·tag** der party
conference *or (Amer.)* convention
**Partẹrre** das; ~s, ~s ground floor;
first floor *(Amer.)*
**Partịe** die; ~, ~n a) part; b) *(Spiel,
Sport: Runde)* game; *(Golf)* round; c)
**eine gute ~ [für jmdn.] sein** be a good
match [for sb.]
**Partisạn** der; ~s *od.* ~en, ~en, **Parti-
sạnin** die, ~, ~nen guerrilla; *(gegen
Besatzungstruppen im Krieg)* partisan
**Partitụr** die; ~, ~en *(Musik)* score
**Partizịp** das; ~s, ~ien [-'tsi:pi̯ən]
*(Sprachw.)* participle
**Pạrtner** der; ~s, ~, **Pạrtnerin** die; ~,
~nen partner; **Pạrtnerschaft** die; ~,
~en partnership; **pạrtnerschaft-
lich 1.** *Adj. ⟨co-operation etc.⟩* on a
partnership basis; 2. *adv.* in a spirit of
partnership; **Pạrtner·stadt** die twin
town *(Brit.)*; sister city *or* town
*(Amer.)*
**Party** ['pa:ɐ̯ti] die; ~, ~s *od.* **Pạrties**
party
**Parzẹlle** die; ~, ~n [small] plot [of
land]
**Pạß** der; **Pạsses, Pạsse** a) *(Reise~)*
passport; b) *(Gebirgs~; Ballspiele)*
pass
**passạbel 1.** *Adj.* reasonable; presentable *⟨appearance⟩*; 2. *adv.* reasonably
well
**Passage** [pa'sa:ʒə] die; ~, ~n a) *[shop-
ping]* arcade; b) *(Abschnitt)* passage;
**Passagier** [pasa'ʒi:ɐ̯] der; ~s, ~e
passenger; **blinder ~:** stowaway
**Passagier-:** ~**dampfer** der passenger steamer; ~**flugzeug** das passenger aircraft; ~**liste** die passenger
list
**Pạß·amt** das passport office
**Passạnt** der; ~en, ~en, **Passạntin**
die; ~, ~nen passer-by
**Pạß·bild** das passport photograph
**Pạsse** *s.* Paß
**pạssen** *itr. V.* a) *(die richtige Größe/*

*Form haben)* fit; b) *(geeignet sein)* be
suitable (**auf** + *Akk.*, **zu** for); *(harmonieren) ⟨colour etc.⟩* match; **zu etw./
jmdm. ~:** go well with sth./be well
suited to sb.; **zueinander ~ ⟨things⟩** go
well together; *⟨two people⟩* be suited to
each other; c) *(genehm sein)* **jmdm. ~**
*⟨time⟩* suit sb.; d) *(Kartenspiel)* pass;
**pạssend** *Adj.* a) *(geeignet)* suitable
*⟨dress, present, etc.⟩*; right *⟨words, expression, moment⟩*; b) *(harmonierend)*
matching *⟨shoes etc.⟩*
**Pạß·foto** das *s.* Paßbild
**passịerbar** *Adj.* passable *⟨road⟩*; nav-
igable *⟨river⟩*; negotiable *⟨path⟩*; **pas-
sịeren 1.** *tr. V.* pass; **die Grenze ~:**
cross the border; 2. *itr. V.; mit sein*
happen
**Passiọn** die; ~, ~en a) passion; b)
*(christl. Rel.)* Passion
**passioniert** *Adj.* passionate *⟨col-
lector, card-player, huntsman⟩*
**passiv 1.** *Adj.* passive; 2. *adv.* pass-
ively; **Pạssiv** das; ~s, ~e *(Sprachw.)*
passive; **Passivität** die; ~: passivity
**Pạß-:** ~**kontrolle** die passport
check; ~**zwang** der obligation to
carry a passport
**Pạste** die; ~, ~n paste
**Pastẹll** das; ~[e]s, ~e a) *(Farbton)* pastel shade; b) *o. Pl. (Maltechnik)* pastel
*no art.*
**Pastẹll-:** ~**farbe** die pastel colour;
~**ton** der pastel shade
**Pastẹte** die; ~, ~n a) *(gefüllte ~)* vol-
au-vent; b) *(in einer Schüssel o. ä. ge-
gart)* pâté; *(in einer Hülle aus Teig gebacken)* pie
**pasteurisịeren** [pastøri'zi:rən] *tr. V.*
pasteurize
**Pastịlle** die; ~, ~n pastille
**Pạstor** der; ~s, ~en, **Pastọrin** die; ~,
~nen pastor
**Pạte** der; ~n, ~n godfather; *(männlich
od. weiblich)* godparent
**Pạten-:** ~**kind** das godchild; ~**onkel**
der godfather; ~**stadt** die *s.* Partnerstadt
**patẹnt** *(ugs.)* **1.** *Adj.* a) *(tüchtig)* capable; b) *(zweckmäßig)* ingenious; 2.
*adv.* ingeniously; neatly *⟨solved⟩*; **Patẹnt** das; ~[e]s, ~e a) *(Schutz)* patent;
**etw. zum** *od.* **als ~ anmelden** apply for
a patent for sth.; b) *(Erfindung)* [pa-
tented] invention
**Pạten·tante** die godmother
**patentịeren** *tr. V.* patent; **Patẹnt-
lösung** die patent remedy (**für, zu**
for)

**Pater** der; ~s, ~ *od.* **Patres** *(kath. Kirche)* Father; **Paternoster der**; ~s, ~ *(Aufzug)* paternoster [lift]
**pathetisch 1.** *Adj.* emotional ⟨*speech, manner*⟩; melodramatic ⟨*gesture*⟩; pompous ⟨*voice*⟩; **2.** *adv.* emotionally; *(dramatisch)* [melo]dramatically; **Pathos** das; ~: emotionalism
**Patient** [pa'tsiɛnt] der; ~en, ~en, **Patientin** die; ~, ~nen patient
**Patin** die; ~, ~nen godmother
**Patres** *s.* Pater
**Patriot** der; ~en, ~en, **Patriotin** die; ~, ~nen patriot; **patriotisch 1.** *Adj.* patriotic; **2.** *adv.* patriotically; **Patriotismus** der; ~: patriotism
**Patrone** die; ~, ~n cartridge
**Patrouille** [pa'trʊljə] die; ~, ~n patrol; **patrouillieren** [patrʊl'jiːrən] *itr. V.; auch mit sein* be on patrol
**Patsche** die; ~, ~n *(ugs.) s.* Klemme; **patschen** *itr. V., mit sein (ugs.)* splash; **patsch·naß** *Adj. (ugs.)* sopping wet
**patzig** *(ugs.)* **1.** *Adj.* snotty *(coll.); (frech)* cheeky; **2.** *adv.* snottily *(coll.); (frech)* cheekily
**Pauke** die; ~, ~n kettledrum; **auf die ~ hauen** *(ugs.) (feiern)* paint the town red *(sl.); (sich lautstark äußern)* come right out with it
**pausbäckig** *Adj.* chubby-faced; chubby ⟨*face*⟩
**pauschal 1.** *Adj.* **a)** all-inclusive ⟨*price, settlement*⟩; **b)** *(verallgemeinernd)* sweeping ⟨*judgement, criticism, statement*⟩; indiscriminate ⟨*prejudice*⟩; wholesale ⟨*discrimination*⟩; **2.** *adv.* **a)** ⟨*cost*⟩ all in all; ⟨*pay*⟩ in a lump sum; **b)** *(ohne zu differenzieren)* wholesale
**Pauschale** die; ~, ~n flat-rate payment
**Pauschal-:** ~**preis** der flat rate; *(Inklusivpreis)* all-in price; ~**reise** die package holiday; *(mit mehreren Reisezielen)* package tour
**Pause** die; ~, ~n break; *(Ruhe~)* rest; *(Theater)* interval *(Brit.);* intermission *(Amer.)*
**pausen** *tr. V.* trace; *(eine Lichtpause machen)* Photostat *(Brit.* P)
**pausen·los 1.** *Adj.;* incessant ⟨*noise, moaning, questioning*⟩; continous ⟨*work, operation*⟩; **2.** *adv.* incessantly; ⟨*work*⟩ non-stop
**Pavian** ['paːvi̯aːn] der; ~s, ~e baboon
**Pavillon** ['pavɪljɔn] der; ~s, ~s pavilion

**Pazifik** der; ~s Pacific; **pazifisch** *Adj.* Pacific ⟨*area*⟩; **der Pazifische Ozean** the Pacific Ocean
**Pech** das; ~[e]s, ~e **a)** pitch; **b)** *o. Pl. (Mißgeschick)* bad luck; **pech·schwarz** *Adj. (ugs.)* jet-black
**Pedal** das; ~s, ~e pedal
**Pediküre** die; ~, ~n pedicure; **pediküren** *tr. V.* pedicure
**Pegel** der; ~s, ~ **a)** water-level indicator; *(Tide~)* tide-gauge; **b)** *(Wasserstand)* water-level
**peilen** *tr. V.* take a bearing on ⟨*transmitter, fixed point*⟩
**Pein** die; ~ *(geh.)* torment; **peinigen** *tr. V. (geh.)* torment; *(foltern)* torture; **peinlich 1.** *Adj.* **a)** embarrassing; awkward ⟨*question, position, pause*⟩; **es ist mir sehr ~:** I feel very bad *(coll.)* or embarrassed about it; **b)** *(äußerst genau)* meticulous; **2.** *adv.* **a)** unpleasantly ⟨*surprised*⟩; **b)** *(überaus [genau])* meticulously; **Peinlichkeit** die; ~, ~en **a)** *o. Pl.* embarrassment; **die ~ der Situation** the awkwardness of the situation; **b)** *o. Pl. (Genauigkeit)* meticulousness; **c)** *(peinliche Situation)* embarrassing situation
**Peitsche** die; ~, ~n whip; **peitschen** *tr. V.* whip; *(fig.)* ⟨*storm, waves, rain*⟩ lash
**Pelikan** der; ~s, ~e pelican
**Pelle** die; ~, ~n *(bes. nordd.)* skin; *(abgeschält)* peel; **pellen** *(bes. nordd.) tr., refl. V.* peel; **Pell·kartoffel** die potato boiled in its skin
**Pelz** der; ~es, ~e **a)** fur; coat; *(des toten Tieres)* skin; pelt; **b)** *o. Pl. (Material)* fur; *(~mantel)* fur coat; **Pelz·mantel** der fur coat
**Pendel** das; ~s, ~: pendulum
**pendeln** *itr. V.* **a)** swing [to and fro]; *(mit weniger Bewegung)* dangle; **b)** *mit sein* ⟨*bus, ferry, etc.*⟩ operate a shuttle service; ⟨*person*⟩ commute
**penetrant 1.** *Adj.* **a)** penetrating ⟨*smell, taste*⟩; overpowering ⟨*stink, perfume*⟩; **b)** *(aufdringlich)* pushing, *(coll.)* pushy ⟨*person*⟩; overbearing ⟨*tone, manner*⟩; aggressive ⟨*question*⟩; **2.** *adv.* **a)** overpoweringly; **b)** *(aufdringlich)* overbearingly
**penibel 1.** *Adj.* over-meticulous ⟨*person*⟩; *(pedantisch)* pedantic; **2.** *adv.* painstakingly; over-meticulously ⟨*dressed*⟩
**Penis** der; ~, ~se penis
**Penner** der; ~s, ~ *(salopp)* tramp *(Brit.);* hobo *(Amer.)*

**Pensen** s. **Pensum**
**Pension** [pã'zjo:n] die; ~, ~en a) o. Pl.
*(Ruhestand)* in ~ gehen retire; in ~
sein be retired; b) *(Ruhegehalt)* [retire-
ment] pension; c) *(Haus für
[Ferien]gäste)* guest-house; d) o. Pl.
*(Unterkunft u. Verpflegung)* board;
**Pensionär** [pãzjo'nɛːɐ̯] der; ~s, ~e,
**Pensionärin** die; ~, ~nen retired
civil servant; **pensionieren** tr. V.
pension off; retire; sich [vorzeitig] ~
lassen take [early] retirement; **Pen-
sionierung** die; ~, ~en retirement
**Pensum** das; ~s, **Pensen** work quota
**per** *Präp. mit Akk.* a) *(mittels)* by; ~
Adresse X care of X; c/o X; b) *(Kaufmannsspr.: [bis] zum)* by; *(am)* on; c)
*(Kaufmannsspr.: pro)* per
**perfekt** 1. *Adj.* a) perfect ⟨*crime,
host*⟩; faultless ⟨*English, French, etc.*⟩;
b) ~ sein *(ugs.: abgeschlossen, fertig
sein)* be finalized; 2. *adv.* perfectly;
**Perfekt** das; ~s *(Sprachw.)* perfect
**Pergament·papier** das grease-proof
paper
**Periode** die; ~, ~n period
**Perle** die; ~, ~n a) *(auch fig.)* pearl; b)
*(aus Holz, Glas o. ä.)* bead; **Perlmutt**
das; ~s mother-of-pearl
**Perlon** ⓦ das; ~s ≈ nylon
**Perser** der; ~s, ~ a) Persian; b) s. Per-
serteppich; **Perserin** die; ~, ~nen
Persian; **Perser·teppich** der Per-
sian carpet; **Persianer** der; ~s, ~
*(~mantel)* Persian lamb coat; **Per-
sien** (das); ~s Persia; **persisch** *Adj.*
Persian
**Person** die; ~, ~en person; *(in der
Dichtung, im Film)* character; **Personal** das; ~s *(in einem Betrieb o. ä.)*
staff; *(im Haushalt)* domestic staff *pl.*;
**Personal·ausweis** der identity
card; **Personalien** *Pl.* personal particulars; **Personal·pronomen** das
*(Sprachw.)* personal pronoun
**Personen-:** ~**kraftwagen** der *(bes.
Amtsspr.)* private car *or (Amer.)* automobile; ~**name** der [personal name;
~**wagen** der *(Auto)* [private] car;
automobile *(Amer.)*; *(im Unterschied
zum Lastwagen)* passenger car *or
(Amer.)* automobile; ~**zug** der stopping train
**persönlich** 1. *Adj.* personal; ~ werden get personal; 2. *adv.* personally;
*(auf Briefen)* 'private [and confiden-
tial]'; **Persönlichkeit** die; ~, ~en a)
personality; b) *(Mensch)* person of
character; **eine** ~ **sein** have a strong

personality; ~**en des öffentlichen Le-
bens** public figures
**Perspektive** die; ~, ~n perspective;
*(Blickwinkel)* angle; *(Zukunftsaus-
sicht)* prospect
**Peru** (das); ~s Peru; **Peruaner** der;
~s, ~: Peruvian; **peruanisch** *Adj.*
Peruvian
**Perücke** die; ~, ~n wig
**pervers** *Adj.* perverted
**Pessimismus** der; ~: pessimism;
**Pessimist** der; ~en, ~en, **Pessimi-
stin** die; ~, ~nen pessimist; **pessi-
mistisch** 1. *Adj.* pessimistic; 2. *adv.*
pessimistically
**Pest** die; ~: plague
**Petersilie** [petɐ'ziːljə] die; ~: parsley
**Petroleum** [pe'troːleʊm] das; ~s par-
affin *(Brit.)*; kerosene *(Amer.)*
**Petrus** (der); **Petri** *(christl. Rel.: Apo-
stel)* St Peter
**Pf** *Abk.* **Pfennig**
**Pfad** der; ~[e]s, ~e path
**Pfad-:** ~**finder** der Scout; ~**finderin**
die; ~, ~nen Guide *(Brit.)*; girl scout
*(Amer.)*
**Pfaffe** der; ~n, ~n *(abwertend)* cleric;
Holy Joe *(derog.)*
**Pfahl** der; ~[e]s, **Pfähle** post; stake
**Pfand** das; ~[e]s, **Pfänder** a) security;
pledge *(esp. fig.)*; b) *(für Flaschen
usw.)* deposit (**auf** + *Dat.* on); **pfän-
den** tr. V. seize [under distress] *(Law)*
⟨*goods, chattels*⟩; attach ⟨*wages etc.*⟩
*(Law)*; **Pfänder** s. **Pfand**; **Pfän-
dung** die; ~, ~en seizure; distraint
*(Law)*; *(von Geldsummen, Vermögens-
rechten)* attachment *(Law)*
**Pfanne** die; ~, ~n [frying-]pan;
**Pfann·kuchen** der a) pancake; b)
*(Berliner ~)* doughnut
**Pfarrei** die; ~, ~en a) *(Bezirk)* parish;
b) *(Dienststelle)* parish office; c) s.
**Pfarrhaus**; **Pfarrer** der; ~s, ~ pastor;
*(anglikanisch)* vicar; *(von Freikirchen)*
minister; **Pfarrerin** die; ~, ~nen
[woman] pastor; *(in Freikirchen)*
[woman] minister; **Pfarr·haus** das
vicarage; *(katholisch)* presbytery; *(in
Schottland)* manse
**Pfau** der; ~[e]s, ~en peacock;
**Pfauen·auge** das peacock butterfly
**Pfd.** *Abk.* **Pfund** lb.
**Pfeffer** der; ~s, ~: pepper; **Pfeffer·-
kuchen** der ≈ gingerbread; **Pfefferminz** o. *Art., indekl.* peppermint;
**Pfeffer·minze** die peppermint
[plant]; **Pfefferminz·tee** der peppermint tea

**pfeffern** *tr. V.* season with pepper
**Pfeife die; ~, ~n** pipe; *(Triller~)*
whistle; **pfeifen 1.** *unr. itr. V.*
whistle; ⟨*bird*⟩ sing; *(auf einer Triller-
pfeife o.ä.)* ⟨*policeman, referee, etc.*⟩
blow one's whistle; **auf jmdn./etw. ~**
*(ugs.)* not give a damn about sb./sth.;
**2.** *unr. tr. V.* whistle ⟨*tune etc.*⟩; ⟨*bird*⟩
sing ⟨*song*⟩; *(auf einer Pfeife)* pipe,
play ⟨*tune etc.*⟩
**Pfeil** der; ~|e|s, ~e arrow
**Pfeiler** der; ~s, ~: pillar; *(Brücken~)*
pier
**Pfennig** der; ~s, ~e pfennig; **es kostet
20 ~:** it costs 20 pfennig[s]
**pferchen** *tr. V.* cram; pack
**Pferd** das; ~|e|s, ~e horse; *(Schachfi-
gur)* knight; **mit ihr kann man ~e stehlen** *(ugs.)* she's game for anything
**Pferde-: ~rennen** das horse-race;
*(Sportart)* horse-racing; **~schwanz**
der *(Frisur)* pony-tail; **~stall der**
stable
**pfiff** *1. u. 3. Pers. Sg. Prät. v.* pfeifen;
**Pfiff** der; ~|e|s, ~e a) whistle; b)
*(ugs.: besonderer Reiz)* style
**Pfifferling** der; ~s, ~e chanterelle;
**keinen** *od.* **nicht einen ~ wert sein**
*(ugs.)* be not worth a bean *(sl.)*
**pfiffig 1.** *Adj.* smart; bright ⟨*idea*⟩;
artful ⟨*smile, expression*⟩; **2.** *adv.* art-
fully
**Pfingsten** das; ~, ~: Whitsun
**Pfingst-: ~montag** der Whit Monday *no def. art.*; **~sonntag der** Whit
Sunday *no def. art.*
**Pfirsich** der; ~s, ~e peach
**Pflanze die; ~, ~n** plant; **pflanzen**
*tr. V.* plant; **Pflanzen·öl** das vegetable oil; **pflanzlich** *Adj.* plant *attrib.*
⟨*life, motif*⟩; vegetable ⟨*dye, fat*⟩
**Pflaster das; ~s, ~ a)** *(Straßen~)*
road surface; *(auf dem Gehsteig)*
pavement; **ein teures/gefährliches ~**
*(ugs.)* an expensive/dangerous place
*or* spot to be; **b)** *(Wund~)* sticking-
plaster; **pflastern** *tr. (auch itr.) V.*
surface; *(mit Kopfsteinpflaster, Stein-
platten)* pave; **Pflaster·stein der**
paving-stone; *(Kopfstein)* cobble-
stone
**Pflaume die; ~, ~n** plum; **getrocknete
~n** [dried] prunes
**Pflege die; ~:** care; *(Maschinen~,
Fahrzeug~)* maintenance; *(fig.: von
Beziehungen, Kunst, Sprache)* cultivation; **jmdn./etw. in ~ (Akk.) nehmen**
look after sb./sth.
**pflege-, Pflege-: ~eltern** *Pl.* foster-

parents; **~fall** der: **ein ~ sein** be in
[permanent] need of nursing; **~kind**
das foster-child; **~leicht** *Adj.* easy-
care *attrib.* ⟨*textiles, flooring*⟩
**pflegen 1.** *tr. V.* look after; care for;
take care of ⟨*skin, teeth, floor*⟩; look
after ⟨*bicycle, car, machine*⟩; look
after, tend ⟨*garden, plants*⟩; cultivate
⟨*relations, arts, interests*⟩; foster ⟨*contacts, co-operation*⟩; pursue ⟨*hobby*⟩;
**2.** *mod. V.* etw. zu tun ~: usually do
sth.; **Pfleger** der; ~s, ~ a) *(Kran-
ken~)* [male] nurse; b) *(Tier~)*
keeper; **Pflegerin** die; ~, ~nen a)
*(Kranken~)* nurse; b) *(Tier~)* keeper
**Pflicht** die; ~, ~en duty
**pflicht-, Pflicht-: ~bewußt 1.** *Adj.*
conscientious; **2.** *adv.* with a sense of
duty; **~bewußtsein das, ~gefühl
das;** *o. Pl.* sense of duty; **~übung** die
*(fig.)* ritual exercise
**Pflock** der; ~|e|s, Pflöcke peg
**pflücken** *tr. V.* pick
**Pflug** der; ~|e|s, Pflüge plough; **pflü-
gen** *tr., itr. V.* plough
**Pforte die; ~, ~n** *(Tor)* gate; *(Tür)*
door; *(Eingang)* entrance; **Pförtner**
der; ~s, ~ porter; *(eines Wohnblocks,
Büros)* door-keeper; *(am Tor)* gate-
keeper
**Pfosten** der; ~s, ~ post
**Pfote die; ~, ~n** paw
**Pfropf** der; ~|e|s, ~e blockage;
**pfropfen** *tr. V. (ugs.)* cram; stuff; ge-
pfropft voll crammed [full]; packed;
**Pfropfen** der stopper; *(Korken)*
cork; *(für Fässer)* bung
**pfui** *Interj.* ugh; **~ rufen** boo
**Pfund** das; ~|e|s, ~e pound
**Pfütze die; ~, ~n** puddle
**Phänomen** das; ~s, ~e phenomenon
**Phantasie die; ~, ~n a)** *o. Pl.* imagination; b) *meist Pl. (Produkt der ~)*
fantasy; **phantasie·los 1.** *Adj.* unimaginative; **2.** *adv.* unimaginatively;
**phantasie·voll 1.** *Adj.* imaginative;
**2.** *adv.* imaginatively; **phantastisch
1.** *Adj.* a) fantastic; ⟨*idea*⟩ divorced
from reality; b) *(ugs.: großartig)* fantastic *(coll.)*; **2.** *adv. (ugs.)* fantastically
*(coll.)*
**Phase die; ~, ~n** phase
**Philosoph** der; ~en, ~en philosopher; **Philosophie die; ~, ~n**
philosophy; **philosophieren** *itr.
(auch tr.) V.* philosophize; **philosophisch 1.** *Adj.* philosophical; ⟨*dictionary, principles*⟩ of philosophy; **2.**
*adv.* philosophically

**Photo** 652

**Photo** das; ~s, ~s *s.* Foto
**Phrase** die; ~, ~n *(abwertend)* [empty] phrase; cliché
**Physik** die; ~: physics *sing., no art.;* **physikalisch** *Adj.* physics *attrib.* ⟨*experiment, formula, research, institute*⟩; physical ⟨*map, process*⟩; **Physiker** der; ~s, ~ physicist; **physisch** 1. *Adj.* physical; 2. *adv.* physically
**Pianist** der; ~en, ~en, **Pianistin** die; ~, ~nen pianist
**Pickel** der; ~s, ~: pimple
**picken** 1. *itr. V.* peck (**nach** at; **an** + *Akk.,* **gegen** on, against); 2. *tr. V.* ⟨*bird*⟩ peck; *(ugs.)* ⟨*person*⟩ pick
**Picknick** das; ~s, ~e *od.* ~s picnic
**piep[s]en** *itr. V. (ugs.)* squeak; ⟨*small bird*⟩ cheep
**Pietät** [piɛ'tɛːt] die; ~: respect; *(Ehrfurcht)* reverence
**Pik** das; ~|s|, ~|s| *(Kartenspiel)* a) *(Farbe)* spades *pl.;* b) *(Karte)* spade
**pikant** 1. *Adj.* a) piquant; b) *(fig.: witzig)* ironical; c) *(verhüll.: schlüpfrig)* racy ⟨*joke, story*⟩; 2. *adv.* piquantly ⟨*seasoned*⟩
**pikiert** 1. *Adj.* piqued; 2. *adv.* ⟨*reply, say*⟩ in an aggrieved tone
**Pilger** der; ~s, ~: pilgrim; **pilgern** *itr. V.* go on a pilgrimage
**Pille** die; ~, ~n pill
**Pilot** der; ~en, ~en pilot
**Pils** das; ~, ~: Pils
**Pilz** der; ~es, ~e fungus; *(Speise~, auch fig.)* mushroom
**Pinguin** der; ~s, ~e penguin
**Pinie** ['piːniə] die; ~, ~n [stone- *or* umbrella] pine
**pinkeln** *itr. V. (salopp)* pee *(coll.)*
**Pinsel** der; ~s, ~: brush; *(Mal~)* paintbrush
**Pinzette** die; ~, ~n tweezers *pl.*
**Pionier** der; ~s, ~e *(Milit.)* sapper; *(fig.: Wegbereiter)* pioneer
**Pirat** der; ~en, ~en pirate
**pissen** *itr. V. (derb)* piss *(coarse)*
**Pistazie** [pɪs'taːtsiə] die; ~, ~n pistachio
**Piste** die; ~, ~n *(Ski~)* piste; *(Renn~)* course; *(Flugw.)* runway
**Pistole** die; ~, ~n pistol
**Pizza** die; ~, ~s *od.* Pizzen pizza
**Pkw, PKW** ['peːkaːveː] der; ~|s|, ~|s| [private] car; automobile *(Amer.)*
**plädieren** *itr. V. (Rechtsw.)* plead (**auf** + *Akk.* for); *(fig.)* argue; **Plädoyer** [plɛdoa'jeː] das; ~s, ~s *(Rechtsw.)* summing up *(for the defence/prosecution); (fig.)* plea

**Plage** die; ~, ~n a) nuisance; b) *(ugs.: Mühe)* bother; trouble; **plagen** 1. *tr. V.* a) torment; b) *(ugs.: bedrängen)* harass; *(mit Bitten, Fragen)* pester; 2. *refl. V.* a) *(sich abmühen)* slave away; b) *(leiden)* sich mit etw. ~: be bothered by sth.
**Plakat** das; ~|e|s, ~e poster; **Plakette** die; ~, ~n badge
**Plan** der; ~|e|s, Pläne a) plan; b) *(Karte)* map; plan
**Plane** die; ~, ~n tarpaulin
**planen** *tr., itr. V.* plan
**Planet** der; ~en, ~en planet
**planieren** *tr. V.* level; grade; **Planier·raupe** die bulldozer
**Planke** die; ~, ~n plank
**plan-:** ~los 1. *Adj.* aimless; *(ohne System)* unsystematic; 2. *adv. s.* 1: aimlessly; unsystematically; ~mäßig 1. *Adj.* a) scheduled ⟨*service, steamer*⟩; ~mäßige Ankunft/Abfahrt scheduled time of arrival/departure; b) *(systematisch)* systematic; 2. *adv.* a) *(wie geplant)* according to plan; *(pünktlich)* on schedule; b) *(systematisch)* systematically
**Plansch·becken** das paddling-pool; **planschen** *itr. V.* splash [about]
**Plantage** [plan'taːʒə] die; ~, ~n plantation
**Planung** die; ~, ~en planning; **Plan·wirtschaft** die planned economy
¹**Plastik** die; ~, ~en sculpture; ²**Plastik** das; ~s *(ugs.)* plastic
**Plastik-:** ~beutel der, ~tüte die plastic bag
**Platane** die; ~, ~n plane-tree
**Platin** das; ~s platinum
**plätschern** *itr. V.* a) splash; b) *mit sein (~d auftreffen)* splash (**an** + *Akk.,* **gegen** against); **plätschern** *itr. V.* a) splash; *(rain)* patter; ⟨*stream*⟩ burble; b) *mit sein* ⟨*stream*⟩ burble along
**platt** *Adj.* flat; **ein Platter** *(ugs.)* a flat *(coll.)*
**platt·deutsch** *Adj.* Low German
**Platte** die; ~, ~n a) *(Stein~)* slab; *(Metall~)* plate; sheet; *(Span~, Hartfaser~ usw.)* board; *(Tisch~)* [table-] top; *(Grab~)* [memorial] slab; b) *(Koch~)* hotplate; c) *(Schall~)* [gramophone] record; d) *(Teller)* plate; *(zum Servieren, aus Metall)* dish; **kalte** ~: selection of cold meats [and cheese]; **Platten·spieler** der record-player; **Platt·fuß** der a) flat foot; b) *(ugs.: Reifenpanne)* flat *(coll.)*

**Plątz** der; ~es, **Plätze** a) square; b)
*(Sport~)* ground; *(Spielfeld)* field;
*(Tennis~, Volleyball~ usw.)* court;
*(Golf~)* course; c) *(Stelle, wo jmd.,
etw. hingehört)* place; **nicht** od. **fehl
am** ~|e| **sein** *(fig.)* be out of place; d)
*(Sitz~)* seat; *(am Tisch, Steh~ usw.)*
place; ~ **nehmen** sit down; e) *(bes.
Sport: Plazierung)* place; f) *(Ort)*
place; **am** ~: in the town/village; g) *o.
Pl. (Raum)* space; room; ~ **machen**
make room *(Dat.* for); **Plätzchen
das**; ~s, ~ **a)** little place; b) *(Keks)*
biscuit *(Brit.)*; cookie *(Amer.)*
**plątzen** itr. V.; *mit sein* **a)** burst; *(explodieren)* explode; b) *(ugs.: scheitern)*
fall through; **der Wechsel/das Treffen
ist geplatzt** the bill has bounced
*(sl.)*/the meeting is off; **c) in eine Versammlung** ~ *(ugs.)* burst into a meeting
**Plątz-:** ~**karte** die reserved-seat
ticket; ~**konzert** das open-air concert *(by a military or brass band)*;
~**mangel** der lack of space; ~**regen**
der cloudburst; ~**wunde** die lacer-
ated wound
**plaudern** itr. V. chat
**plausibel** Adj. plausible
**pleite** *(ugs.)* ~ **sein** ⟨person⟩ be broke
*(coll.)*; ⟨company⟩ have gone bust
*(coll.)*; ~ **gehen** go bust *(coll.)*; **Pleite**
die; ~, ~n *(ugs.)* a) *(Bankrott)* bankruptcy *no def. art.*; ~ **machen** go bust
*(coll.)*; b) *(Mißerfolg)* wash-out *(sl.)*
**Plissee** das; ~s, ~s accordion pleats
*pl.*
**Plǫmbe** die; ~, ~n a) *(Siegel)* [lead]
seal; b) *(veralt.: Zahnfüllung)* filling;
**plombieren** tr. V. a) *(versiegeln)*
seal; b) *(veralt.)* fill ⟨tooth⟩
**plötzlich** 1. Adj. sudden; 2. adv. suddenly
**plump** 1. Adj. a) *(dick)* plump; *(unförmig)* ungainly ⟨shape⟩; *(rundlich)*
bulbous; b) *(schwerfällig)* clumsy ⟨mo-
vements, style⟩; c) *(fig.)* *(dreist)* crude
⟨lie, deception, trick⟩; *(leicht durchschaubar)* blatantly obvious; *(unbeholfen)* clumsy ⟨excuse, advances⟩;
crude ⟨joke, forgery⟩; 2. adv. a)
*(schwerfällig)* clumsily; b) *(fig.)* in a
blatantly obvious manner
**plündern** itr., tr. V. a) loot; plunder
⟨town⟩; b) *(scherzh.)* raid ⟨larder,
fridge, account⟩
**Plural** der; ~s, ~e plural
**plus** Konj., Adv. plus; **Plus** das; ~:
surplus; *(Vorteil)* advantage

**Plüsch** der; ~|e|s, ~e plush
**Plusquam·perfekt** das pluperfect
[tense]
**PLZ** Abk. **Postleitzahl**
**Po** der; ~s, ~s *(ugs.)* bottom
**Pöbel** der; ~s rabble
**pǫchen** itr. V. *(klopfen)* knock **(gegen/
an** + Akk. at, on); *(geh.: pulsieren)*
⟨heart⟩ pound
**Pǫcken** Pl. smallpox *sing.*
**Podęst** das od. der; ~|e|s, ~e rostrum;
**Podium** das; ~s, **Podien** *(Plattform)*
platform; *(Bühne)* stage; *(trittartige
Erhöhung)* rostrum
**Poesie** die; ~: poetry; **Poet** der; ~en,
~en *(veralt.)* poet; bard *(literary)*;
**poetisch** 1. Adj. poetic[al]; 2. adv.
poetically
**Pointe** ['poɛ̃:tə] die; ~, ~n *(eines Wit-
zes)* punch line; *(einer Geschichte)*
point; *(eines Sketches)* curtain line
**Pokal** der; ~s, ~e a) *(Trinkgefäß)* gob-
let; b) *(Siegestrophäe, ~wettbewerb)*
cup
**Pökel·fleisch** das salt meat; **pökeln**
tr. V. salt
**Poker** das od. der; ~s poker; **pokern**
itr. V. play poker
**Pol** der; ~s, ~e pole
**Pole** der; ~n, ~n Pole
**polemisch** 1. Adj. polemic[al]; 2. adv.
polemically
**Polen** das; ~s Poland
**Police** [po'li:sə] die; ~, ~n *(Versicherungsw.)* policy
**polieren** tr. V. polish
**Poli·klinik** die out-patients' clinic
**Polin** die; ~n, ~nen Pole
**Politik** die; ~, ~en **a)** o. Pl. politics
*sing., no art.;* b) *(eine spezielle ~)* policy; **Politiker** der; ~s, ~, **Politike-
rin** die; ~, ~nen politician; **politisch**
1. Adj. political; 2. adv. politically;
**politisieren** 1. itr. V. talk politics; 2.
tr. V. make politically active
**Politur** die; ~, ~en polish
**Polizei** die; ~, ~en police *pl.*
**Polizei-:** ~**auto** das police car; ~**beamte** der police officer; ~**kontrolle**
die police check
**polizeilich** 1. Adj. police; ~e **Melde-
pflicht** obligation to register with the
police; 2. adv. by the police
**Polizei-:** ~**präsidium** das police
headquarters *sing. or pl.;* ~**revier** das
police station; ~**streife** die police
patrol; ~**stunde** die closing time;
~**wache** die police station
**Polizist** der; ~en, ~en policeman

**polnisch** *Adj.* Polish
**Polster das**; ~s, ~: upholstery *no pl., no indef. art.;* **Polster·möbel** *Pl.* upholstered furniture *sing.;* **polstern** *tr. V.* upholster ⟨*furniture*⟩
**poltern** *itr. V.* **a)** crash about; **b)** *mit sein* **der** Karren polterte über das Pflaster the cart clattered over the cobblestones
**Polyp der**; ~en, ~en *(Zool., Med.)* polyp
**Pommern (das)**; ~s Pomerania
**Pommes frites** [pɔm'frit] *Pl.* chips *(Brit.);* French fries *(Amer.)*
**pompös** 1. *Adj.* grandiose; 2. *adv.* grandiosely
**¹Pony** ['pɔni] **das**; ~s, ~s pony; **²Pony der**; ~s, ~s *(Frisur)* fringe
**Popeline·mantel der** poplin coat
**populär** 1. *Adj.* popular (**bei** with); 2. *adv.* popularly; **Popularität die**; ~: popularity
**Pore die**; ~, ~n pore
**Pornographie die**; ~: pornography
**Porree der**; ~s leek
**Portal das**; ~s, ~e portal
**Portemonnaie** [pɔrtmɔ'ne:] **das**; ~s, ~s purse
**Porti** *Pl. s.* Porto
**Portier** [pɔr'tie:] **der**; ~s, ~s, *österr.:* [pɔr'tiːɐ] **der**; ~s, ~e porter
**Portion** [pɔr'tsioːn] **die**; ~, ~en **a)** *(beim Essen)* portion; helping; **b)** *(ugs.: Anteil)* amount
**Porto das**; ~s, ~s *od.* **Porti** postage (**für** on, for)
**Portugal (das)**; ~s Portugal; **Portugiese der**; ~n, ~n Portuguese; **portugiesisch** *Adj.* Portuguese
**Portwein der** port
**Porzellan das**; ~s porcelain; china
**Posaune die**; ~, ~n trombone
**Position** [pozi'tsioːn] **die**; ~, ~en position; **positiv** 1. *Adj.* positive; 2. *adv.* positively; **Positiv das**; ~s, ~e *(Fot.)* positive
**Possessiv·pronomen das** *(Sprachw.)* possessive pronoun
**Post die**; ~, ~en **a)** post *(Brit.);* mail; **etw. mit der** *od.* **per** ~ **schicken** send sth. by post *or* mail; **b)** *(~amt)* post office
**Post-:** ~**amt das** post office; ~**anweisung die** postal remittance form; ~**auto das** mail van; ~**bote der** *(ugs.)* postman *(Brit.);* mailman *(Amer.)*
**Posten der**; ~s, ~ **a)** post; **b)** *(bes. Milit.: Wachmann)* sentry

**post-, Post-:** ~**fach das** post-office *or* PO box; *(im Büro, Hotel o. ä.)* pigeon-hole; ~**karte die** postcard; ~**lagernd** *Adj., adv.* poste restante; general delivery *(Amer.);* ~**leitzahl die** postcode; Zip code *(Amer.);* ~**stempel der** *(Abdruck)* postmark; ~**wendend** *Adv.* by return [of post]
**potent** *Adj.* potent; **Potenz die**; ~, ~en **a)** *o. Pl.* potency; **b)** *(Math.)* power; **potenzieren** *tr. V. (Math.)* **mit 5** ~: raise to the power [of] 5
**Pracht die**; ~: splendour; **prächtig, pracht·voll** 1. *Adj.* splendid; 2. *adv.* splendidly
**prädestiniert** *Adj.* predestined
**Prädikat das**; ~[e]s, ~e **a)** *(Auszeichnung)* rating; **b)** *(Sprachw.)* predicate
**Prag (das)**; ~s Prague
**prägen** *tr. V.* **a)** emboss; **b)** mint ⟨*coin*⟩; **c)** *(fig.: beeinflussen)* shape
**prägnant** 1. *Adj.* concise; succinct; 2. *adv.* concisely; succinctly
**Prägung die**; ~, ~en embossing; *(von Münzen)* minting
**prahlen** *itr. V.* boast, brag (**mit** about)
**Praktik die**; ~, ~en practice; **Praktika** *s.* Praktikum; **Praktikant der**; ~en, ~en, **Praktikantin die**; ~, ~nen **a)** *(in einem Betrieb)* student trainee; **b)** *(an der Hochschule)* physics/chemistry student *(doing a period of practical training);* **Praktikum das**; ~s, **Praktika** period of practical training; **praktisch** 1. *Adj.* practical; ~**er** Arzt general practitioner; 2. *adv.* practically; *(auf die Praxis bezogen; wirklich)* in practice; **praktizieren** *tr. V.* practise
**Praline die**; ~, ~n [filled] chocolate
**prall** *Adj.* **a)** hard ⟨*ball*⟩; bulging ⟨*sack, wallet, bag*⟩; big strong *attrib.* ⟨*thighs, muscles, calves*⟩; well-rounded ⟨*breasts*⟩; **b)** *(intensiv)* blazing ⟨*sun*⟩; **prallen** *itr. V.; mit sein* crash (**gegen/auf/an** + *Akk.* into); collide (**gegen/auf/an** + *Akk.* with)
**Prämie** ['prɛːmiə] **die**; ~, ~n **a)** *(Leistungs~; Wirtschaft)* bonus; *(Belohnung)* reward; *(Spar~, Versicherungs~)* premium; **b)** *(einer Lotterie)* [extra] prize; **prämieren** *tr. V.* award a prize to ⟨*person, film*⟩; give an award for ⟨*best essay etc.*⟩
**Pranger der**; ~s, ~ *(hist.)* pillory
**Pranke die**; ~, ~n paw
**Präparat das**; ~[e]s, ~e preparation
**Präposition die**; ~, ~en *(Sprachw.)* preposition

**Prärie** die; ~, ~n prairie
**Präsens** ['prɛːzɛns] das; ~ *(Sprachw.)* present [tense]; **präsentieren** *tr. V.* present
**Präservativ** das; ~s, ~e condom
**Präsident** der; ~en, ~en; **Präsidentin** die; ~, ~nen president; **Präsidium** das; ~s, Präsidien a) committee; b) *(Vorsitz)* chairmanship; c) *(Polizei~)* police headquarters *sing. or pl.*
**prasseln** *itr. V.* pelt down; ⟨*shots*⟩ clatter; ⟨*fire*⟩ crackle
**prassen** *itr. V.* live extravagantly; *(schlemmen)* feast
**Präteritum** das; ~s *(Sprachw.)* preterite [tense]
**Praxis** die; ~, Praxen a) *o. Pl. (im Unterschied zur Theorie)* practice *no art.*; *(Erfahrung)* [practical] experience; b) *(eines Arztes, Anwalts usw.)* practice; *(~räume) (eines Arztes)* surgery *(Brit.)*; office *(Amer.); (eines Anwalts usw.)* office
**präzise** 1. *Adj.* precise; 2. *adv.* precisely; **Präzision** die; ~: precision
**predigen** 1. *itr. V.* deliver a/the sermon; 2. *tr. V.* preach; **Prediger** der; ~s, ~: preacher; **Predigt** die; ~, ~en sermon
**Preis** der; ~es, ~e a) *(Kauf~)* price (für of); b) *(Belohnung)* prize; **Preis·aus·schreiben** das [prize] competition
**Preisel·beere** die cowberry; cranberry *(Gastr.)*
**preisen** *unr. tr. V. (geh.)* praise
**preis-, Preis-:** ~**günstig** 1. *Adj.* ⟨*goods*⟩ available at unusually low prices; **das ist |sehr| ~günstig** that is [very] good value; 2. *adv.* at a low price; ~**nachlaß** der price reduction; ~**schild** das price-tag; ~**steigerung** die increase in prices; ~**träger** der prizewinner; ~**verleihung** die presentation [of prizes/awards]; ~**wert** 1. *Adj.* good value *pred.*; 2. *adv.* ⟨*eat*⟩ at a reasonable price; **dort kann man ~wert einkaufen** you get good value for money there
**Prellung** die; ~, ~en bruise
**Premiere** [prəˈmi̯eːrə] die; ~, ~n opening night
**Presse** die; ~, ~n a) press; *(Zitronen~)* squeezer; b) *o. Pl. (Zeitungen)* press
**Presse-:** ~**freiheit** die freedom of the press; ~**meldung** die press report
**pressen** *tr. V.* press
**Preß·luft-:** ~**bohrer** der pneumatic

drill; ~**hammer** der pneumatic hammer
**Prestige** [prɛsˈtiːʒə] das; ~s prestige
**prickeln** *itr. V.* tingle
**pries** *1. u. 3. Pers. Sg. Prät. v.* preisen
**Priester** der; ~s, ~: priest; **Priesterin** die; ~, ~nen priestess
**prima** *(ugs.)* 1. *indekl. Adj.* great *(coll.)*; 2. *adv.* ⟨*taste*⟩ great *(coll.)*; ⟨*sleep*⟩ fantastically well *(coll.)*
**primär** 1. *Adj.* primary; 2. *adv.* primarily
**Primel** die; ~, ~n primula; *(Schlüsselblume)* cowslip
**primitiv** 1. *Adj.* primitive; *(einfach, schlicht)* simple; 2. *adv.* primitively; *(einfach, schlicht)* in a simple manner
**Prinz** der; ~en, ~en prince; **Prinzessin** die; ~, ~nen princess
**Prinzip** das; ~s, ~ien [-ˈtsiːpi̯ən] principle; **aus** ~: on principle; **prinzipiell** 1. *Adj.* in principle *postpos., not pred.*; ⟨*rejection*⟩ on principle; 2. *adv.* *(im Prinzip)* in principle; *(aus Prinzip)* on principle
**Prise** die; ~, ~n pinch
**privat** 1. *Adj.* private; *(persönlich)* personal; 2. *adv.* privately
**Privat-:** ~**adresse** die private *or* home address; ~**angelegenheit** die private matter; ~**besitz** der private property; ~**eigentum** das private property; ~**leben** das; *o. Pl.* private life; ~**lehrer** der private tutor; ~**patient** der private patient; ~**unterricht** der private tuition
**pro** *Präp. mit Akk.* per; ~ **Stück** each; a piece
**pro-:** pro-; ~**westlich**/~**kommunistisch** pro-western/pro-communist
**Probe** die; ~, ~n a) test; b) *(Muster, Teststück)* sample; c) *(Theater~, Orchester~)* rehearsal
**Probe-:** ~**fahrt** die trial run; *(vor dem Kauf, nach einer Reparatur)* test drive; ~**jahr** das probationary year
**proben** *tr., itr. V.* rehearse; **probeweise** *Adv.* ⟨*employ*⟩ on a trial basis; **Probe·zeit** die probationary period; **probieren** 1. *tr. V.* a) try; have a go at; b) *(kosten)* taste; try; c) *(aus~)* try out; *(an~)* try on ⟨*clothes, shoes*⟩; 2. *itr. V.* a) *(versuchen)* try; b) *(kosten)* have a taste
**Problem** das; ~s, ~e problem; **problematisch** *Adj.* problematic[al]; **problem·los** 1. *Adj.* problem-free; 2. *adv.* without any problems
**Produkt** das; ~|e|s, ~e *(auch Math.,*

*fig.)* product; **Produktion die; ~,
~en** production; **produktiv 1.** productive; prolific ⟨*writer, artist, etc.*⟩;
**2.** *adv.* ⟨*work, co-operate*⟩ product-
ively; **Produktivität die; ~:** productivity; **Produzent der; ~en, ~en** producer; **produzieren** *tr. V.* produce
**Prof.** *Abk.* Professor Prof.; **professionell 1.** *Adj.* professional; **2.** *adv.*
professionally; **Professor der; ~s,
~en; Professorin die; ~, ~nen** professor; **Profi der; ~s, ~s** *(ugs.)* pro
*(coll.)*
**Profil das; ~s, ~e a)** *(Seitenansicht)*
profile; **im ~:** in profile; **b)** *(von Reifen, Schuhsohlen)* tread
**Profit der; ~|e|s, ~e** profit; **profi-
tieren** *itr. V.* profit **(von, bei** by**)**
**Prognose die; ~, ~n** prognosis; *(Wet-
ter~, Wirtschafts~)* forecast
**Programm das; ~s, ~e a)** programme; program *(Amer., Computing); (Ferns.: Sender)* channel
**Programm-: ~heft das** programme;
**~hinweis der** programme announcement
**programmieren** *tr. V.* **a)** *(DV)* program; **b)** *(auf etw. festlegen)* programme
**Programm-: ~vorschau die** *(im
Fernsehen)* preview [of the
week's/evening's *etc.* viewing]; *(im
Kino)* trailers *pl.;* **~zeitschrift die**
radio and television magazine
**progressiv 1.** *Adj.* progressive; **2.**
*adv.* progressively
**Projekt das; ~|e|s, ~e** project; **Pro-
jektor der; ~s, ~en** projector; **projizieren** *tr. V. (Optik)* project
**proklamieren** *tr. V.* proclaim
**Prolet der; ~en, ~en** *(abwertend)*
peasant; **Proletariat das; ~|e|s** pro-
letariat; **Proletarier** [prole'taːriɐ]
**der; ~s, ~** proletarian; **proleta-
risch** *Adj.* proletarian
**Promenade die; ~, ~n** promenade
**Promille das; ~s, ~:** [part] per thousand; **er fährt nur ohne ~** *(ugs.)* he
never drinks and drives; **er hatte 1,8
~:** he had a blood alcohol level of 1.8
per thousand; **Promille·grenze die**
*(ugs.)* legal [alcohol] limit
**prominent** *Adj.* prominent; **Prominenz die; ~:** prominent figures *pl.*
**prompt 1.** *Adj.* prompt; **2.** *adv.* **a)**
promptly; **b)** *(ugs., meist iron.: wie erwartet)* [and] sure enough
**Pronomen das; ~s, ~** *od.* **Pronomina**
*(Sprachw.)* pronoun

**Propaganda die; ~:** propaganda;
**propagieren** *tr. V.* propagate
**Propan·gas das;** *o. Pl.* propane
**Propeller der; ~s, ~** propeller
**Prophet der; ~en, ~en** prophet; **pro-
phezeien** *tr. V.* prophesy *(Dat.* for**)**;
predict ⟨*result, weather*⟩
**Proportion die; ~, ~en** proportion
**Prosa die; ~:** prose
**prosit** *Interj.* your [very good] health;
**~ Neujahr!** happy New Year!
**Prospekt der** *od. (bes. österr.)* **das
~|e|s, ~e** *(Werbeschrift)* brochure;
*(Werbezettel)* leaflet
**prost** *Interj. (ugs.)* cheers *(Brit. coll.)*
**Prostituierte die/der;** *adj. Dekl.*
prostitute; **Prostitution die; ~:**
prostitution *no art.*
**Protest der; ~|e|s, ~e** protest; **Prote-
stant der; ~en, ~en, Protestantin
die; ~, ~nen** Protestant; **protestantisch** *Adj.* Protestant; **protestieren**
*itr. V.* protest, make a protest **(gegen**
against, about**); Protest·kundge-
bung die** protest rally
**Prothese die; ~, ~n** artificial limb;
prosthesis *(Med.); (Zahn~)* set of
dentures; dentures *pl.*
**Protokoll das; ~s, ~e a)** *(wörtlich mit-
geschrieben)* transcript; *(Ergebnis~)*
minutes *pl.; (bei Gericht)* record; **etw.
zu ~ geben** make a statement about
sth.; **b)** *(diplomatisches Zeremoniell)*
protocol; **protokollieren 1.** *tr. V.*
take down; take the minutes of ⟨*meeting*⟩; minute ⟨*remark*⟩; **2.** *itr. V.* take
the minutes; *(bei Gericht)* keep the
record
**Proviant der; ~s, ~e** provisions *pl.*
**Provinz die; ~, ~en** province; **pro-
vinziell 1.** *Adj.* provincial; **2.** *adv.*
provincially
**Provision die; ~, ~en** *(Kaufmannsspr.)* commission; **provisorisch 1.** *Adj.* provisional; temporary;
**2.** *adv.* temporarily
**Provokation die; ~, ~en** provocation; **provozieren** *tr. V.* provoke
**Prozedur die; ~, ~en** procedure
**Prozent das; ~|e|s, ~e a)** *nach Zahlen-
angaben Pl. ungebeugt* per cent *sing.;*
**fünf ~:** five per cent; **b)** *Pl. (ugs.: Ge-
winnanteil)* share *sing.* of the profits;
*(Rabatt)* discount *sing.;* **auf etw.
***(Akk.)* **~e bekommen** get a discount on
sth.; **-prozentig** *adj.* -per-cent
**Prozent-: ~rechnung die** percentage calculation; **~satz der** percentage

**prozentual** 1. *Adj.* percentage; 2. *adv.* ~ **am Gewinn beteiligt sein** have a percentage share in the profits

**Prozeß** der; **Prozesses, Prozesse a)** trial; *(Fall)* [court] case; **einen ~ gewinnen/verlieren** win/lose a case; **b)** *(Vorgang)* process; **prozessieren** *itr. V.* go to court; **gegen jmdn. ~:** bring an action against sb.; **Prozeß·kosten** *Pl.* legal costs

**prüde** *(abwertend)* 1. *Adj.* prudish; 2. prudishly

**prüfen** *tr. V.* **a)** *auch itr.* examine *(pupil, student, etc.);* **mündlich/schriftlich geprüft werden** have an oral/a written examination; **b)** *(untersuchen)* examine (**auf** + *Akk.* for); check *(device, machine, calculation)* (**auf** + *Akk.* for); investigate *(complaint); (testen)* test (**auf** + *Akk.* for); **c)** *(kontrollieren)* check; examine *(accounts, books);* **d)** *(vor einer Entscheidung)* check *(price);* examine *(offer);* consider *(application);* **Prüfer** der; ~s, ~, **Prüferin** die; ~, ~**nen a)** inspector; *(Buch~)* auditor; **b)** *(im Examen)* examiner; **Prüfung** die; ~, ~**en a)** examination; exam *(coll.);* **eine ~ machen** *od.* **ablegen** take an examination; **b)** *s.* **prüfen b–d:** examination; check; investigation; test; consideration

**Prügel** *Pl. (Schläge)* beating *sing.; (als Strafe für Kinder)* hiding *(coll.);* **prügeln** 1. *tr. (auch itr.) V.* beat; 2. *refl. V.* **sich** ~: fight; **sich mit jmdm. |um etw.|** ~: fight sb. [over *or* for sth.]

**Prunk** der; ~[e]s splendour; magnificence

**PS** [pe:'|ɛs] das; ~, ~: *Abk.* Pferdestärke h.p.

**Psalm** der; ~s, ~en psalm

**Psychiater** der; ~s, ~: psychiatrist; **Psychiatrie** die; ~ psychiatry *no art.;* **psychisch** 1. *Adj.* psychological; mental *(process, illness);* 2. *adv.* psychologically; ~ **gesund/krank sein** be mentally fit/ill

**psycho-, Psycho-** [psy:ço-]: ~**loge** der; ~n, ~n psychologist; ~**logie** die; ~: psychology; ~**login** die psychologist; ~**logisch** 1. *Adj.* psychological; 2. *adv.* psychologically

**Pubertät** die; ~: puberty

**Publikum** das; ~s **a)** *(Zuschauer, Zuhörer)* audience; *(bei Sportveranstaltungen)* crowd; **b)** *(Kreis von Interessierten)* public; *(eines Schriftstellers)* readership; **c)** *(Besucher)* clientele; **publizieren** *tr. (auch itr.) V.* publish

**Pudding** der; ~s, ~e *od.* ~s thick, usually flavoured, milk-based dessert; ≈ blancmange

**Pudel** der; ~s, ~ poodle

**Puder** der; ~s, ~: powder; **Puderdose** die powder compact; **pudern** *tr. V.* powder; **Puder·zucker** der icing sugar *(Brit.);* confectioners' sugar *(Amer.)*

¹**Puff** der; ~[e]s, Püffe *(ugs.)* **a)** *(Stoß)* thump; *(leichter/kräftiger Stoß mit dem Ellenbogen)* nudge/dig; **b)** *(Knall)* bang; ²**Puff** der *od.* das; ~s, ~s *(salopp: Bordell)* knocking-shop *(Brit. sl.);* brothel; **puffen** *(ugs.) tr. V.: s.* ¹**Puff a:** thump; nudge; dig

**Pulli** der; ~s, ~s *(ugs.),* **Pullover** der; ~s, ~: pullover; sweater; **Pullunder** der; ~s, ~: slipover

**Puls** der; ~es, ~e pulse; **Puls·ader** die artery

**Pult** das; ~[e]s, ~e desk; *(Lese~)* lectern

**Pulver** das; ~s, ~ powder

**pumm[e]lig** *Adj. (ugs.)* chubby

**Pumpe** die; ~, ~n pump; **pumpen** *tr., itr. V.* **a)** *(auch fig.)* pump; **b)** *(salopp) s.* leihen a, b

**Punkt** der; ~[e]s, ~e **a)** *(Tupfen)* dot; *(größer)* spot; **b)** *(Satzzeichen)* full stop; **c)** *(I-Punkt)* dot; **d)** *(Stelle)* point; **ein schwacher/wunder ~** *(fig.)* a weak/sore point; **e)** *(Gegenstand, Thema, Abschnitt)* point; *(einer Tagesordnung)* item; **f)** *(Bewertungs~)* point; *(bei einer Prüfung)* mark

**pünktlich** 1. *Adj.* punctual; 2. *adv.* punctually; on time; **Pünktlichkeit** die; ~: punctuality

**Punsch** der; ~[e]s, ~e *od.* Pünsche punch

**Pupille** die; ~, ~n pupil

**Puppe** die; ~, ~n **a)** doll[y]; **b)** *(Marionette)* puppet; marionette

**Puppen-:** ~**stube** die doll's house; dollhouse *(Amer.);* ~**wagen** der doll's pram

**pur** *Adj.* **a)** *(rein)* pure; **b)** *(unvermischt)* neat *(whisky etc.);* straight

**Püree** das; ~s, ~s **a)** purée; **b)** *s.* **Kartoffelbrei**

**Purpur** der; ~s crimson

**Puste** die; ~ *(salopp)* puff; breath

**Pustel** die; ~, ~n pimple; pustule *(Med.)*

**pusten** *(ugs.) tr., itr. V.* blow

**Pute** die; ~, ~n turkey hen; *(als Braten)* turkey; **Puter** der; ~s, ~: turkeycock; *(als Braten)* turkey

**Putsch** der; ~[e]s, ~e putsch; coup [d'état]; **putschen** itr. V. organize a putsch or coup

**Putz** der; ~es plaster; *(für Außenmauern)* rendering; **putzen** tr. V. **a)** *(blank reiben)* polish; **b)** *(säubern)* clean; groom ⟨horse⟩; [sich *(Dat.)*] die **Zähne/die Nase** ~: clean or brush one's teeth/blow one's nose; **c)** *auch* itr. *(saubermachen)* clean ⟨room, shop, etc.⟩; ~ **gehen** work as a cleaner; **d)** *(vorbereiten)* wash and prepare ⟨vegetables⟩; **Putz·frau** die cleaner

**Puzzle** ['pazl] das; ~s, ~s, **Puzzlespiel** das jigsaw [puzzle]

**Pyjama** [py'dʒaːma] der *(österr., schweiz. auch:* das); ~s, ~s pyjamas *pl.*

**Pyramide** die; ~, ~n pyramid

# Q

**q, Q** [kuː] das; ~, ~: q, Q

**Quadrat** das; ~[e]s, ~e square; **quadratisch** Adj. square; **Quadratmeter** der od. das square metre

**quaken** itr. V. ⟨duck⟩ quack; ⟨frog⟩ croak

**Qual** die; ~, ~en a) o. Pl. torment; **b)** *meist Pl. (Schmerzen)* agony; ~en pain *sing.;* agony *sing.; (seelisch)* torment *sing.;* **quälen** tr. V. **a)** torment ⟨person, animal⟩; be cruel to ⟨animal⟩; *(foltern)* torture; **b)** *(plagen)* ⟨cough etc.⟩ plague; *(belästigen)* pester; **Quälerei** die; ~, ~en a) torment; *(Folter)* torture; *(Grausamkeit)* cruelty; **b)** *(das Belästigen)* pestering

**Qualifikation** die; ~, ~en a) *(Ausbildung)* qualifications pl.; **b)** *(Sport)* qualification; **qualifizieren** refl. V. **a)** gain qualifications; **b)** *(Sport)* qualify

**Qualität** die; ~, ~en quality; **qualitativ** 1. Adj. qualitative; ⟨difference, change⟩ in quality; 2. adv. with regard to quality; **Qualitäts·erzeugnis** das quality product

**Qualle** die; ~, ~n jellyfish

**Qualm** der; ~[e]s [thick] smoke; **qualmen** itr. V. a) give off clouds of [thick] smoke; b) *(ugs.: rauchen)* puff away

**qual·voll** 1. Adj. agonizing; 2. adv. agonizingly

**Quantität** die; ~, ~en quantity; **Quantum** das; ~s, Quanten quota (an + Dat. of); *(Dosis)* dose

**Quarantäne** [karan'tɛːnə] die; ~, ~n quarantine

**Quark** der; ~s quark

**Quartal** das; ~s, ~e quarter [of the year]

**Quartett** das; ~[e]s, ~e a) quartet; b) *(Spiel)* ≈ Happy Families; *(Satz von vier Karten)* set [of four]

**Quartier** das; ~s, ~e accommodation *no indef. art.;* accommodations *pl. (Amer.);* place to stay; *(Mil.)* quarters *pl.*

**Quarz** der; ~es, ~e quartz

**quasi** Adv. |so| ~: more or less; *(so gut wie)* as good as

**Quaste** die; ~, ~n tassel

**Quatsch** der; ~[e]s *(ugs.)* a) *(Äußerung)* rubbish; b) *(Handlung)* nonsense; *(Unfug)* messing about; laß den ~: stop that nonsense

**Queck·silber** das mercury

**Quelle** die; ~, ~n spring; *(eines Flusses; fig.)* source; **quellen** unr. itr. V.; *mit sein* a) ⟨liquid⟩ gush, stream; *(aus der Erde)* well up; ⟨smoke⟩ billow; b) *(sich ausdehnen)* swell [up]

**quer** Adv. sideways; *(schräg)* diagonally; *(rechtwinklig)* at right angles; ~ **durch/über** (+ Akk.) straight through/across

**quer-, Quer-:** ~**achse** die transverse axis; ~**schnitt** der *(auch fig.)* cross-section; ~**schnitt[s]·gelähmt** Adj. *(Med.)* paraplegic; ~**straße** die intersecting road

**quetschen** tr. V. crush; sich *(Dat.)* die **Hand** ~: get one's hand caught

**quietschen** itr. V. squeak; ⟨brakes, tyres⟩ squeal, screech; *(ugs.)* ⟨person⟩ squeal, shriek

**Quirl** der; ~[e]s, ~e long-handled blender with a star-shaped head

**quitt** Adj. *(ugs.)* quits

**Quitte** die; ~, ~n quince

**quittieren** tr. V. a) *auch* itr. acknowledge, confirm ⟨receipt, condition⟩; give a receipt for ⟨sum, invoice⟩; b) etw. mit etw. ~: react or respond to sth. with sth.; **Quittung** die; ~, ~en a) receipt; b) *(fig.)* come-uppance *(coll.)*

**Quiz** [kvɪs] **das;** ~, ~: quiz
**quoll** *1. u. 3. Pers. Sg. Prät. v.* **quellen**
**Quote** die; ~, ~n proportion; **Quo-**
**ten·regelung** die *requirement that*
*women should be adequately repres-*
*ented*

# R

**r, R** [ɛr] **das;** ~, ~: r, R
**Rabatt** der; ~|e|s, ~e discount
**Rabatte** die; ~, ~n border
**Rabe** der; ~n, ~n raven
**rabiat** 1. *Adj.* violent; brutal; ruthless
⟨*methods*⟩; 2. *adv. (gewalttätig)* violently; brutally
**Rache** die; ~: revenge; |an jmdm.| ~
nehmen take revenge [on sb.]
**Rachen** der; ~s, ~ a) *(Schlund)*
pharynx *(Anat.);* b) *(Maul)* mouth;
maw *(literary); (fig.)* jaws *pl.*
**rächen** 1. *tr. V.* avenge ⟨*person,*
*crime*⟩; take revenge for ⟨*insult,*
*crime*⟩; 2. *refl. V.* a) take one's
revenge; b)⟨*mistake etc.*⟩ take its/their
toll
**Rachitis** die; ~ *(Med.)* rickets *sing.*
**Rach·sucht** die; *o. Pl. (geh.)* lust for
revenge; **rach·süchtig** *(geh.)* 1. *Adj.*
vengeful; 2. *adv.* vengefully
**Rad** das; ~es, Räder ['rɛ:dɐ] a) wheel;
das fünfte ~ am Wagen sein *(fig. ugs.)*
be superfluous; b) *(Fahr~)* bicycle;
bike *(coll.)*
**Radar** der *od.* das; ~s radar
**Radar-:** ~**falle** die *(ugs.)* [radar] speed
trap; ~**kontrolle** die [radar] speed
check
**rad-, Rad-:** **dampfer** der paddle-
steamer; ~|**fahren** *unr. itr. V.* ; mit
*sein* cycle; ride a bicycle *or (coll.)*
bike; ~**fahrer** der cyclist
**Radien** *s.* Radius
**radieren** *tr. (auch itr.) V.* erase; **Ra-**
**dier·gummi** der rubber [eraser]
**Radieschen** das; ~s, ~: radish
**radikal** 1. *Adj.* radical; drastic ⟨*meas-*
*ure, method, cure*⟩; 2. *adv.* radically;
*(vollständig)* totally; **Radikalismus**
der; ~: radicalism

**Radio** das *(südd., schweiz. auch:* der);
~s, ~s radio; ~ hören listen to the
radio; **Radio·wecker** der radio
alarm clock
**Radius** der; ~, Radien radius
**Rad·kappe** die hub-cap
**Radler** der; ~s, ~: cyclist
**Rad-:** ~**rennbahn** die cycle-racing
track; ~**rennen** das cycle race;
*(Sport)* cycle-racing; ~**sport** der cycling *no def. art.;* ~**tour** die cycling
tour; ~**weg** der cycle-path *or* -track
**raffen** *tr. V.* a) snatch; rake in *(coll.)*
⟨*money*⟩; etw. |an sich| ~: seize sth.;
*(eilig)* snatch sth.; b) gather ⟨*material,*
*curtain*⟩
**Raffinerie** die; ~, ~n refinery; **Raffi-**
**nesse** die; ~, ~n a) *o. Pl. (Schlauheit)*
guile; ingenuity; b) *meist Pl. (Finesse)*
refinement; **raffiniert** 1. *Adj.* a) ingenious ⟨*plan, design*⟩; *(verfeinert)*
refined, subtle ⟨*colour, scheme, ef-*
*fect*⟩; sophisticated ⟨*dish, cut (of*
*clothes)*⟩; b) *(gerissen)* cunning ⟨*per-*
*son, trick*⟩; 2. *adv.* a) ingeniously;
*(verfeinert)* with great refinement/
sophistication; b) *(gerissen)* cunningly
**Rage** ['ra:ʒə] die; ~ *(ugs.)* fury
**ragen** *itr. V.* a) *(vertikal)* rise [up];
⟨*mountains*⟩ tower up; b) *(horizontal)*
project, stick out (in + *Akk.* into;
über + *Akk.* over)
**Ragout** [ra'gu:] das; ~s, ~s ragout
**Rahm** der; ~|e|s cream
**rahmen** *tr. V.* frame; **Rahmen** der;
~s, ~ a) frame; *(Fahrgestell)* chassis;
b) *(fig.)* framework
**Rakete** die; ~, ~n rocket; *(Lenkflug-*
*körper)* missile
**rammen** *tr. V.* ram
**Rampe** die; ~, ~n a) *(Lade~)* [load-
ing] platform; b) *(schiefe Fläche)*
ramp; **Rampen·licht** das: im ~ |der
Öffentlichkeit| stehen be in the lime-
light
**Ramsch** der; ~|e|s, ~e *(ugs.)* a) *(Ware)*
trashy goods *pl.;* b) *(Kram)* junk
**ran** *Adv. (ugs.)* a) *s.* heran; b) *(fang[t]*
*an)* off you go; *(fangen wir an)* let's
go; c) *(greif[t] an)* go at him/them!
**Rand** der; ~|e|s, Ränder a) edge; *(Ein-*
*fassung)* border; *(Hut~)* brim; *(Bril-*
*len~, Gefäß~, Krater~)* rim; *(eines*
*Abgrunds)* brink; *(auf einem Schrift-*
*stück)* margin; *(Weg~)* verge;
*(Stadt~)* outskirts *pl.;* b) *(Schmutz~)*
mark; *(rund)* ring
**randalieren** *itr. V.* riot

**Rand·bemerkung** die marginal note *or* comment

**rang** *1. u. 3. Pers. Sg. Prät. v.* ringen

**Rang** der; ~|e|s, **Ränge a)** rank; *(in der Gesellschaft)* status; **b)** *(im Theater)* circle; **erster ~:** dress circle; **zweiter ~:** upper circle; **dritter ~:** gallery

**rangieren** [raŋ'ʒiːrən] *tr. V.* shunt ⟨*trucks etc.*⟩; switch ⟨*cars*⟩ *(Amer.)*

**Rang·ordnung** die order of precedence; *(Verhaltensf.)* pecking order

**Ranke** die; ~, ~n *(Bot.)* tendril; **ranken** *refl. V.* climb, grow **(an +** *Dat.* up, **über +** *Akk.* over)

**rann** *1. u. 3. Pers. Sg. Prät. v.* rinnen

**rannte** *1. u. 3. Pers. Sg. Prät. v.* rennen

**Ranzen** der; ~s, ~: satchel

**ranzig** *Adj.* rancid

**Rappe** der; ~n, ~n black horse

**Rappen** der; ~s, ~: [Swiss] centime

**Raps** der; ~es *(Bot.)* rape

**rar** *Adj.* scarce; *(selten)* rare; **Rarität** die; ~, ~en rarity

**rasant** *(ugs.)* **1.** *Adj.* tremendously fast *(coll.)* ⟨*car, horse, etc.*⟩; **2.** *adv.* at terrific speed *(coll.)*

**rasch** **1.** *Adj.* quick; speedy, swift ⟨*end, action, decision, progress*⟩; **2.** *adv.* quickly; ⟨*decide, end, proceed*⟩ swiftly, rapidly

**rascheln** *itr. V.* rustle; ⟨*mouse etc.*⟩ make a rustling noise

**rasen** *itr. V.* **a)** *mit sein (ugs.: eilen)* dash *or* rush [along]; *(fahren)* tear *or* race along; *(fig.)* ⟨*pulse*⟩ race; **b)** *(toben)* ⟨*person*⟩ rage

**Rasen** der; ~s, ~: grass *no indef. art.; (gepflegte ~fläche)* lawn

**rasend** **1.** *Adj.* **a)** *(sehr schnell)* breakneck *attrib.* ⟨*speed*⟩; **b)** *(tobend)* raging; **c)** *(heftig)* violent; **2.** *adv. (ugs.)* incredibly *(coll.)*

**Rasen·mäher** der; ~s, ~: lawnmower

**Raserei** die; ~, ~en *(ugs.)* tearing along *no art.*

**Rasier·apparat** der [safety] razor; *(elektrisch)* electric shaver; **rasieren** *tr. V.* shave; **sich ~:** shave; **sich naß/ trocken/elektrisch ~:** have a wet shave/ have a dry shave/use an electric shaver

**Rasier-:** **~klinge** die razor-blade; **~wasser** das aftershave; *(vor der Rasur)* pre-shave lotion

**Rasse** die; ~, ~n **a)** breed; **b)** *(Menschen~)* race

**Rassel** die; ~, ~n rattle; **rasseln** *itr. V.* rattle

**Rassen-:** **~haß** der racial hatred *no art.;* **~trennung** die; *o. Pl.* racial segregation *no art.*

**Rassismus** der; ~: racism; racialism; **Rassist** der; ~en, ~en racist; racialist

**Rast** die; ~, ~en rest; **~ machen** stop for a break; **rasten** *itr. V.* rest; take a rest *or* break

**Rast-:** **~haus** das roadside café; *(an der Autobahn)* motorway restaurant; **~platz der a)** place to rest; **b)** *(an Autobahnen)* parking place *(with benches and WCs);* picnic area; **~stätte die** service area

**Rasur** die; ~, ~en shave

**Rat** der; ~|e|s, **Räte a)** *o. Pl.* advice; **ein ~:** a word of advice; **b)** *(Gremium)* council

**rät** *3. Pers. Sg. Präsens v.* raten

**Rate** die; ~, ~n **a)** *(Teilbetrag)* instalment; **etw. auf ~n kaufen** buy sth. by instalments *or (Brit.)* on hire purchase *or (Amer.)* on the installment plan; **b)** *(Statistik)* rate

**raten** **1.** *unr. itr. V.* **a)** jmdm. **~:** advise sb.; **b)** *(schätzen)* guess; **2.** *tr. V.* **a)** jmdm. **~, etw. zu tun** advise sb. to do sth.; **b)** *(er~)* guess

**Raten·zahlung** die payment by instalments

**Rat·haus** das town hall

**Ration** die; ~, ~en ration; **rational** *Adj.* rational; **rationalisieren** *tr., itr. V.* rationalize

**rationell** **1.** *Adj.* efficient; *(wirtschaftlich)* economic; **2.** *adv.* efficiently; *(wirtschaftlich)* economically; **rationieren** *tr. V.* ration

**rat·los** **1.** *Adj.* baffled; helpless ⟨*look*⟩; **2.** *adv.* helplessly; **Rat·losigkeit** die; ~: helplessness; **ratsam** *Adj.; nicht attr.* advisable; **Rat·schlag** der [piece of] advice

**Rätsel** das; ~s, ~ **a)** riddle; *(Bilder~, Kreuzwort~ usw.)* puzzle; **b)** *(Geheimnis)* mystery; **rätselhaft** **1.** *Adj.* mysterious; *(unergründlich)* enigmatic; **2.** *adv.* mysteriously; *(unergründlich)* enigmatically

**Ratte** die; ~, ~n *(auch fig.)* rat

**Raub** der; ~|e|s **a)** robbery; **b)** *(Beute)* stolen goods *pl.;* **rauben** *tr. V.* steal; kidnap ⟨*person*⟩; jmdm. etw. **~:** rob sb. of sth.; *(geh.: wegnehmen)* deprive sb. of sth.; **Räuber** der; ~s, ~: robber

**Raub-:** **~fisch** der predatory fish; **~mord** der *(Rechtsw.)* murder **(an +** *Dat.* of) in the course of a robbery *or* with robbery as motive; **~tier das**

predator; **~überfall** der robbery (**auf** + *Akk.* of); **~vogel** der bird of prey
**Rauch** der; **~|e|s** smoke; **rauchen 1.** *itr. V.* smoke; **2.** *tr. (auch itr.) V.* smoke ⟨*cigarette, pipe, etc.*⟩; „**Rauchen verboten**" 'No smoking'; **Raucher** der; **~s, ~**: smoker; **Raucher·abteil** das smoking-compartment; smoker; **Raucherin** die; **~, ~nen** smoker; **räuchern** *tr. V.* smoke ⟨*meat, fish*⟩; **rauchig** *Adj.* smoky; husky ⟨*voice*⟩; **Rauch·verbot** das ban on smoking
**räudig** *Adj.* mangy
**rauf** *Adv. (ugs.)* up; **~ mit euch!** up you go!; *s. auch* **herauf; hinauf**
**raufen 1.** *itr., refl. V.* fight; **2.** *tr. V.* **sich** *(Dat.)* **die Haare/den Bart ~**: tear one's hair/at one's beard
**rauh 1.** *Adj.* **a)** *(nicht glatt)* rough; **b)** *(nicht mild)* harsh ⟨*climate, winter*⟩; raw ⟨*wind*⟩; **c)** *(kratzig)* husky, hoarse ⟨*voice*⟩; **d)** *(entzündet)* sore ⟨*throat*⟩; **e)** *(grob, nicht feinfühlig)* rough; harsh ⟨*words, tone*⟩; **2.** *adv.* **a)** *(kratzig)* ⟨*speak etc.*⟩ huskily, hoarsely; **b)** *(grob, nicht feinfühlig)* roughly
**Rauh-:** **~faser·tapete** die woodchip wallpaper; **~reif** der hoar-frost
**Raum** der; **~|e|s, Räume** **a)** *(Wohn~, Nutz~)* room; **b)** *(Gebiet)* area; region; **c)** *o. Pl. (Platz)* room; space; **räumen** *tr. V.* **a)** clear [away]; clear ⟨*snow*⟩; **b)** *(an einen Ort)* clear; move; **c)** *(frei machen)* clear ⟨*street, building, warehouse, stocks, etc.*⟩; **d)** *(verlassen)* vacate; **Raum·fahrt** die; **~**: space travel; **räumlich 1.** *Adj.* **a)** spatial; **aus ~en Gründen** for reasons of space; **b)** *(dreidimensional)* three-dimensional; stereoscopic ⟨*vision*⟩; **2.** *adv.* **a)** spatially; **b)** *(dreidimensional)* three-dimensionally; **Raum·schiff** das spaceship; **Räumung** die; **~, ~en** **a)** clearing; **b)** *(das Verlassen)* vacation; vacating; **c)** *(wegen Gefahr)* evacuation; **d)** *(eines Lagers)* clearance
**raunen** *tr., itr. V. (geh.)* whisper
**Raupe** die; **~, ~n** caterpillar
**raus** *Adv. (ugs.)* out; **~ mit euch!** out you go!; *s. auch* **heraus; hinaus**
**Rausch** der; **~|e|s, Räusche** **a)** state of drunkenness; *(starkes Gefühl)* transport; **der ~ der Geschwindigkeit** the exhilaration *or* thrill of speed; **rauschen** *itr. V.* ⟨*water, wind, torrent*⟩ rush; ⟨*trees, leaves*⟩ rustle; ⟨*skirt, curtains, silk*⟩ swish; ⟨*waterfall, strong wind*⟩ roar; ⟨*rain*⟩ pour down;

**Rausch·gift** das drug; narcotic; **~ nehmen** take drugs; be on drugs
**räuspern** *refl. V.* clear one's throat
**raus|schmeißen** *unr. tr. V. (ugs.)* chuck (coll.) ⟨*objects*⟩ out *or* away; give ⟨*employee*⟩ the push *(coll.) or* sack *(coll.)*; chuck (coll.) *or* throw ⟨*customer, drunk, tenant*⟩ out (aus of)
**Raute** die; **~, ~n** *(Geom.)* rhombus
**Razzia** die; **~, Razzien** raid
**reagieren** *itr. V.* react (**auf** + *Akk.* to); **Reaktion** die; **~, ~en** reaction (**auf** + *Akk.* to); **reaktionär** *Adj.* reactionary; **Reaktionär** der; **~s, ~e** reactionary; **Reaktor** der; **~s, ~en** [-'to:rən] reactor
**real 1.** *Adj.* real; **2.** *adv.* actually; **realisieren** *tr. V. (geh.)* realize; **Realismus** der; **~**: realism; **Realist** der; **~en, ~en** realist; **realistisch 1.** *Adj.* realistic; **2.** *adv.* realistically; **Realität** die; **~, ~en** reality
**Rebe** die; **~, ~n** **a)** vine shoot; **b)** *(Weinstock)* [grape] vine
**Rebell** der; **~en, ~en** rebel; **rebellieren** *itr. V.* rebel (**gegen** against); **Rebellion** die; **~, ~en** rebellion; **rebellisch** *Adj.* rebellious
**Reb-:** **~huhn** das partridge; **~stock** der vine
**rechen** *tr. V. (bes. südd.)* rake; **Rechen** der; **~s, ~** *(bes. südd.)* rake
**Rechen-:** **~fehler** der arithmetical error; **~maschine** die calculator
**Rechenschaft** die; **~**: account; **jmdn. für etw. zur ~ ziehen** call *or* bring sb. to account for sth.
**rechnen 1.** *tr. V.* **a) eine Aufgabe ~**: work out a problem; **b)** *(veranschlagen)* reckon; estimate; **gut/rund gerechnet** at a generous/rough estimate; **c)** *(berücksichtigen)* take into account; **d)** *(einbeziehen)* count; **2.** *itr. V.* **a)** do *or* make a calculation/calculations; **gut/schlecht ~ können** be good/bad at figures; **b)** *(zählen)* reckon; **c)** *(ugs.: berechnen)* calculate; estimate; **d)** *(wirtschaften)* budget carefully; **e) auf jmdn./etw.** *od.* **mit jmdn./etw. ~**: count on sb./sth.; **f) mit etw. ~** *(etw. einkalkulieren)* reckon with sth.; *(etw. erwarten)* expect sth.; **Rechnen** das; **~s** arithmetic; **Rechner** der; **~s, ~**: calculator; *(Computer)* computer; **rechnerisch** *Adj.* arithmetical; **Rechnung** die; **~, ~en** **a)** calculation; **b)** *(schriftliche Kosten~)* bill; invoice *(Commerc.)*; **[jmdm.] etw. in ~ stellen** charge [sb.] for sth.

**recht 1.** *Adj.* **a)** *(geeignet, richtig)* right; **b)** *(gesetzmäßig, anständig)* right; proper; ~ **und billig** right and proper; **c)** *(wunschgemäß)* **jmdm.** ~ **sein** be all right with sb.; **d)** *(wirklich, echt)* real; **2.** *adv.* **a)** *(geeignet)* **du kommst gerade** ~: you are just in time; **b)** *(richtig)* correctly; **c)** *(gesetzmäßig, anständig)* properly; **d)** *(wunschgemäß)* **es jmdm.** ~ **machen** please sb.; **e)** *(wirklich, echt)* really; **f)** *(ziemlich)* quite; rather; *s. auch* **Recht d; recht...** *Adj.* **a)** right; right[-hand] ⟨*edge*⟩; **b)** *(außen, sichtbar)* right ⟨*side*⟩; **c)** *(in der Politik)* right-wing; **Recht das;** ~[**e**]**s,** ~**e a)** *(Rechtsordnung)* law; **b)** *(Rechtsanspruch)* right; **sein** ~ **fordern** *od.* **verlangen** demand one's rights; **c)** *o. Pl. (Berechtigung)* right **(auf** + *Akk.* **to); gleiches** ~ **für alle!** equal rights for all!; **im** ~ **sein** be in the right; **zu** ~: rightly; **d) recht haben** be right; **jmdm. recht geben** admit that sb. is right

**recht·fertigen** *tr. V.* justify **(vor** + *Dat.* to); **Recht·fertigung die** justification

**rechtlich 1.** *Adj.* legal; **2.** *adv.* legally; **recht·los** *Adj.* without rights *postpos.*; **rechtmäßig 1.** *Adj.* lawful; rightful; legitimate ⟨*claim*⟩; **2.** *adv.* lawfully; rightfully; **Rechtmäßigkeit die;** ~: legality; *(eines Anspruchs)* legitimacy

**rechts** *Adv.* **a)** on the right; **von** ~: from the right; **b)** *(Politik)* on the right wing

**Rechts-:** ~**abbieger der** *(Verkehrsw.)* motorist/cyclist/car *etc.* turning right; ~**anwalt der,** ~**anwältin die** lawyer; solicitor *(Brit.)*; attorney *(Amer.)*; *(vor Gericht)* barrister *(Brit.)*; attorney[-at-law] *(Amer.)*; advocate *(Scot.)*; ~**außen** [-'--] **der;** ~, ~ *(Ballspiele)* right wing; outside right

**recht-, Recht-:** ~**schaffen 1.** *Adj.* honest; **2.** *adv.* honestly; ~**schreibfehler der** spelling mistake; ~**schreibung die** orthography

**rechts-, Rechts-:** ~**händer der;** ~**s,** ~: right-hander; ~**kräftig** *(Rechtsw.)* **1.** *Adj.* final [and absolute] ⟨*decision, verdict, etc.*⟩; **2.** *adv.* **jmdn.** ~**kräftig verurteilen** pass a final sentence on sb.; ~**kurve die** right-hand bend

**Recht·sprechung die;** ~, ~**en** administration of justice; *(eines Gerichts)* jurisdiction

**rechts-, Rechts-:** ~**staat der** [constitutional] state founded on the rule of law; ~**staatlich** *Adj.* founded on the rule of law *postpos.*; ~**verkehr der** driving *no art.* on the right; ~**widrig 1.** *Adj.* unlawful; **2.** *adv.* unlawfully

**recht-:** ~**wink[e]lig** *Adj.* right-angled; ~**zeitig 1.** *Adj.* timely; ⟨*pünktlich*⟩ punctual; **2.** *adv.* in time; ⟨*pünktlich*⟩ on time

**Reck das;** ~[**e**]**s,** ~**e** *od.* ~**s** horizontal bar

**recken 1.** *tr. V.* stretch; **2.** *refl. V.* stretch oneself

**Redakteur** [redak'tø:ɐ̯] **der;** ~**s,** ~**e, Redakteurin die;** ~, ~**nen** editor; **Redaktion die;** ~, ~**en a)** *(Redakteure)* editorial staff; **b)** *(Büro)* editorial department *or* office/offices *pl.*

**Rede die;** ~, ~**n a)** *(Ansprache)* address; speech; **eine** ~ **halten** give *or* make a speech; **b)** *o. Pl. (Vortrag)* rhetoric; **c)** *(Äußerung, Ansicht)* **nicht der** ~ **wert sein** be not worth mentioning; **jmdn. zur** ~ **stellen** make someone explain himself/herself; **reden 1.** *tr. V.* talk; **Unsinn** ~: talk nonsense; **kein Wort** ~: not say *or* speak a word; **2.** *itr. V.* **a)** *(sprechen)* talk; speak; **viel/wenig** ~: talk a lot *(coll.)*/not talk much; **b)** *(sich äußern, eine Rede halten)* speak; **gut** ~ **können** be a good speaker; **c)** *(sich unterhalten)* talk; **mit jmdm./über jmdn.** ~: talk to/about sb.; **Redens·art die a)** expression; *(Sprichwort)* saying; **b)** *Pl. (Phrase)* empty *or* meaningless words

**Rede·wendung die** *(Sprachw.)* idiom

**redlich 1.** *Adj.* honest; **2.** *adv.* honestly; **Redlichkeit die;** ~: honesty

**Redner der;** ~**s,** ~, **Rednerin die** ~, ~**nen a)** speaker; **b)** *(Rhetoriker)* orator; **red·selig** *Adj.* talkative

**reduzieren 1.** *tr. V.* reduce **(auf** + *Akk.* to); **2.** *refl. V.* decrease; diminish

**Reeder der;** ~**s,** ~: shipowner; **Reederei die;** ~, ~**en** shipping firm

**reell 1.** *Adj.* honest, straight ⟨*person, deal, etc.*⟩; sound, solid ⟨*business, firm, etc.*⟩; straight ⟨*offer*⟩; **2.** *adv.* honestly

**Reet das;** ~**s** *(nordd.)* reeds *pl.*

**Referat das;** ~[**e**]**s,** ~**e a)** paper; **b)** *(kurzer schriftlicher Bericht)* report; **referieren** *itr. V.* **über etw.** *(Akk.)* ~: present a paper on sth.; *(zusammenfassend)* give a report on sth.

**reflektieren** *tr. V.* reflect
**Reflex** der; ~es, ~e reflex; **Refle-xiv·pronomen das** *(Sprachw.)* re-flexive pronoun
**Reform die**; ~, ~en reform; **Re-form·haus das** health-food shop; **reformieren** *tr. V.* reform
**Refrain** [rə'frɛ̄:] der; ~s, ~s chorus
**Regal das**; ~s, ~e [set *sing.* of] shelves *pl.*
**rege 1.** *Adj.* **a)** *(betriebsam)* busy ⟨traf-fic⟩; brisk ⟨demand, trade, business, etc.⟩; **b)** *(lebhaft)* lively; keen ⟨inter-est⟩; **2.** *adv.* **a)** *(betriebsam)* actively; **b)** *(lebhaft)* actively
**Regel die**; ~, ~n **a)** rule; **nach allen ~n der Kunst** *(fig.)* well and truly; **b)** rule; custom; **die ~ sein** be the rule; **in der** *od.* **aller ~:** as a rule; **c)** *(Menstruati-on)* period; **regel·mäßig 1.** *Adj.* regular; **2.** *adv.* regularly; **Re-gel·mäßigkeit die** regularity; **re-geln 1.** *tr. V.* **a)** settle ⟨matter, ques-tion, etc.⟩; put ⟨finances, affairs, etc.⟩ in order; **b)** *(einstellen, regulieren)* regulate; *(steuern)* control; **2.** *refl. V.* take care of itself; **Regelung die**; ~, ~en **a)** *o. Pl. s.* **regeln 1 a, b:** settle-ment; putting in order; regulation; control; **b)** *(Vorschrift)* regulation
**regen 1.** *tr. V.* *(geh.)* move; **2.** *refl. V.* **a)** *(sich bewegen)* move; **b)** *(geh.)* ⟨hope, doubt, desire, conscience⟩ stir
**Regen** der; ~s, ~ **a)** rain; **vom** *od.* **aus dem ~ in die Traufe kommen** *(fig.)* jump out of the frying-pan into the fire; **b)** *(fig.)* shower
**Regen-:** ~**bogen** der rainbow; ~**mantel** der raincoat; mackintosh; ~**schirm** der umbrella; ~**tag** der rainy day; ~**wetter das**; *o. Pl.* wet weather; ~**wolke die** rain cloud; ~**wurm** der earthworm
**Regie** [re'ʒi:] die; ~ **a)** *(Theater, Film, Ferns., Rundf.)* direction; **b)** *(Leitung, Verwaltung)* management
**regieren 1.** *itr. V.* rule (über + *Akk.* over); ⟨party, administration⟩ govern; **2.** *tr. V.* rule; govern; ⟨monarch⟩ reign over; **Regierung die**; ~, ~en **a)** *o. Pl.* *(Herrschaft)* rule; *(eines Monarchen)* reign; **b)** *(Kabinett)* government; **Re-gierungs·sitz** der seat of govern-ment
**Regiment das**; ~[e]s, ~e *od.* ~er **a)** *Pl.* ~e *(Herrschaft)* rule; **b)** *Pl.* ~er *(Milit.)* regiment
**Region die**; ~, ~en region; **regional 1.** *Adj.* regional; **2.** *adv.* regionally

**Regisseur** [reʒɪ'sø:ɐ̯] der; ~s, ~e, **Re-gisseurin die**; ~, ~nen director
**Register das**; ~s, ~ **a)** index; **b)** *(amt-liche Liste)* register; **c)** *(Musik) (bei In-strumenten)* register; *(Orgel~)* stop; **registrieren** *tr. V.* **a)** register; **b)** *(be-wußt wahrnehmen)* note; register
**Regler** der; ~s, ~ *(Technik)* regulator; *(Kybernetik)* control
**reg·los** *Adj.* motionless
**regnen 1.** *itr., tr. V. (unpers.)* rain; **es regnet** it is raining; **2.** *itr. V.; mit sein* *(fig.)* rain down; **regnerisch** *Adj.* rainy
**regulär** *Adj.* **a)** proper; normal ⟨work-ing hours⟩; **b)** *(normal, üblich)* nor-mal; **regulieren** *tr. V.* regulate; **Re-gulierung die**; ~, ~en regulation
**Regung die**; ~, ~en *(geh.: Gefühl)* stir-ring; **regungs·los** *Adj.* motionless
**Reh das**; ~[e]s, ~e roe-deer
**Reh-:** ~**bock** der roebuck; ~**kitz das** fawn [of a/the roe-deer]
**Reibe die**; ~, ~n, **Reib·eisen das** grater; **reiben 1.** *unr. tr. V.* **a)** rub; **b)** *(zerkleinern)* grate; **2.** *unr. itr. V.* rub (**an** + *Dat.* on); **Reibung die**; ~, ~en *(Physik, fig.)* friction; **reibungs·los 1.** *Adj.* smooth; **2.** *adv.* smoothly
**reich 1.** *Adj.* **a)** *(vermögend)* rich; **b)** *(prächtig)* costly ⟨goods, gifts⟩; rich ⟨décor, finery⟩; **c)** *(üppig)* rich; abun-dant ⟨harvest⟩; abundant ⟨mineral re-sources⟩; **~ an etw.** *(Dat.)* **sein** be rich in sth.; **d)** *(vielfältig)* rich ⟨collection, possibilities⟩; wide, large ⟨selection, choice⟩; wide ⟨knowledge, experience⟩; **2.** *adv.* richly
**Reich das**; ~[e]s, ~e **a)** empire; *(Kö-nig~)* kingdom; realm; **das |Deutsche| ~** *(hist.)* the German Reich *or* Em-pire; **das Dritte ~** *(hist.)* the Third Reich; **b)** *(fig.)* realm
**reichen 1.** *itr. V.* **a)** *(aus~)* be enough; **das Geld reicht nicht** I/we *etc.* haven't got enough money; **jetzt reicht's mir aber!** now I've had enough!; **danke, es reicht** that's enough, thank you; **b)** *(sich erstrecken)* reach; ⟨forest, fields, etc.⟩ extend; **2.** *tr. V.* **a)** pass; hand; **jmdm. die Hand ~:** hold out one's hand to sb.; **sich** *(Dat.)* **die Hand ~:** shake hands; **b)** *(servieren)* serve ⟨food, drink⟩
**reich·haltig** *Adj.* extensive; varied ⟨programme⟩; substantial ⟨meal⟩; **reichlich 1.** *Adj.* large; ample ⟨space, time⟩; good ⟨hour, year⟩; **2.** *adv.* **a)** amply; **b)** *(mehr als)* over; more than;

c) *(ugs.: ziemlich, sehr)* a bit too ⟨*cheeky, dear, late*⟩; **Reichtum** der; ~s, Reichtümer a) *o. Pl.* wealth (an + *Dat.* of); b) *Pl. (Vermögenswerte)* riches

**Reich·weite** die reach; *(eines Geschützes, Senders, Flugzeugs)* range

**reif** *Adj.* a) ripe ⟨*fruit, grain, cheese*⟩; mature ⟨*brandy, cheese*⟩; ~ für etw. sein *(ugs.)* be ready for sth.; b) *(erwachsen, ausgewogen)* mature

¹**Reif** der; ~|e|s hoar-frost

²**Reif** der; ~|e|s, ~e *(geh.)* ring; *(Arm~)* bracelet; *(Diadem)* circlet

**Reife** die; ~ a) ripeness; *(von Menschen, Gedanken, Produkten)* maturity; b) *(Reifung)* ripening; **reifen** 1. *itr. V.*; *mit sein* a) ⟨*fruit, cereal, cheese*⟩ ripen; b) *(geh.: älter, reifer werden)* mature (zu into); c) ⟨*idea, plan, decision*⟩ mature; 2. *tr. V.* ripen ⟨*fruit, cereal*⟩;

**Reifen** der; ~s, ~ a) hoop; b) *(Gummi~)* tyre; c) *s.* ²**Reif**

**Reifen-:** ~panne die puncture; ~wechsel der tyre change

**reiflich** 1. *Adj.* [very] careful; 2. *adv.* [very] carefully

**Reigen** der; ~s, ~ a) round dance; b) *(fig.)* den ~ eröffnen start off

**Reihe** die; ~, ~n a) row; in Reih und Glied *(Milit.)* in rank and file; aus der ~ tanzen *(fig. ugs.)* be different; b) *o. Pl. (Reihenfolge)* series; er/sie *usw.* ist an der ~: it's his/her *etc.* turn; der ~ nach, nach der ~: in turn; c) *(größere Anzahl)* number; **reihen** *(geh.) tr. V.* string; thread

**Reihen-:** ~folge die order; ~haus das terraced house

**Reiher** der; ~s, ~: heron

**Reim** der; ~|e|s, ~e rhyme; **reimen** 1. *itr. V.* make up rhymes; 2. *tr., refl. V.* rhyme (auf + *Akk.* with)

¹**rein** *Adv. (ugs.)* ~ mit dir! in you go/ come!

²**rein** 1. *Adj.* a) *(unvermischt)* pure; b) *(nichts anderes als)* pure; sheer; plain, unvarnished ⟨*truth*⟩; c) *(frisch, sauber)* clean; fresh ⟨*clothes, sheet of paper, etc.*⟩; pure, clean ⟨*water, air*⟩; clear ⟨*complexion*⟩; etw. ins ~e schreiben make a fair copy of sth.; etw. ins ~e bringen clear sth. up; 2. *Adv.* purely; ~ gar nichts *(ugs.)* absolutely nothing

**Rein·fall** der *(ugs.)* let-down

**Rein·gewinn** der net profit

**Reinheit** die; ~ a) purity; b) *(Sauberkeit)* cleanness; *(des Wassers, der*

Luft) purity; *(der Haut)* clearness; **reinigen** *tr. V.* clean; purify *(effluents, air, water, etc.)*; Kleider [chemisch] ~ lassen have clothes [dry-] cleaned; **Reinigung** die; ~, ~en a) *s.* reinigen: cleaning; purification; drycleaning; b) *(Betrieb)* [dry-]cleaner's; **reinlich** *Adj.* cleanly; **Reinlichkeit** die; ~: cleanliness

**rein·rassig** *Adj.* thoroughbred ⟨*animal*⟩; **Rein·schrift** die fair copy

**Reis** der; ~es rice

**Reise** die; ~, ~n journey; *(kürzere Fahrt, Geschäfts~)* trip; *(Ausflug)* outing; trip; *(Schiffs~)* voyage; eine ~ machen go on a trip/an outing; auf ~n sein travel; *(nicht zu Hause sein)* be away; glückliche *od.* gute ~! have a good journey

**Reise-:** ~an·denken das souvenir; ~büro das travel agent's; travel agency; ~bus der coach; ~führer der a) *(~leiter)* courier; b) *(Buch)* guidebook; ~führerin die courier; ~gepäck das luggage *(Brit.)*; baggage *(Amer.)*; *(am Flughafen)* baggage; ~gesellschaft die a) *(~gruppe)* party of tourists; *(ugs.: ~veranstalter)* tour operator; ~kosten *Pl.* travel expenses; ~leiter der, ~leiterin die courier

**reisen** *itr. V.*; *mit sein* a) travel; b) *(ab~)* leave; set off; **Reisende** der/ die; *adj. Dekl.* traveller; *(Fahrgast)* passenger

**Reise-:** ~paß der passport; ~scheck der traveller's cheque; ~tasche die hold-all; ~verkehr der holiday traffic; ~ziel das destination

**Reisig** das; ~s brushwood

**Reiß·brett** das drawing-board

**reißen** 1. *unr. tr. V.* a) tear; *(in Stücke)* tear up; b) *(ziehen an)* pull; *(heftig)* yank *(coll.)*; c) *(werfen, ziehen)* jmdn. zu Boden/in die Tiefe ~: knock sb. to the ground/drag sb. down into the depths; d) *(töten)* ⟨*wolf, lion, etc.*⟩ kill ⟨*prey*⟩; e) etw. an sich ~ *(fig.)* seize sth.; 2. *unr. itr. V.* a) *mit sein* ⟨*paper, fabric*⟩ tear, rip; ⟨*rope, thread*⟩ break, snap; ⟨*film*⟩ break; ⟨*muscle*⟩ tear; b) *(ziehen an)* etw. *(Dat.)* ~: pull at sth.; 3. *unr. refl. V. (ugs.: sich bemühen um)* sie ~ sich um die Eintrittskarten they are fighting each other to get tickets; **reißend** *Adj.* rapacious ⟨*animal*⟩; raging ⟨*torrent*⟩; ~en Absatz finden sell like hot cakes

**Reiß-:** ~leine die *(Flugw.)* rip-cord;

**~nagel** der s. **~zwecke; ~ver-schluß** der zip [fastener]; **~zwecke** die drawing-pin *(Brit.);* thumbtack *(Amer.)*

**reiten 1.** *unr. itr. V.; meist mit sein* ride; **2.** *unr. tr. V.; auch mit sein* ride; **Schritt/Trab/Galopp ~:** ride at a walk/trot/gallop; **Reiten** das; ~s riding *no art.;* **Reiter** der; ~s, ~, **Reiterin** die; ~, ~nen rider

**Reit-: ~hose** die riding breeches *pl.;* **~pferd** das saddle-horse; **~stiefel** der riding boot

**Reiz** der; ~es, ~e **a)** *(Physiol.)* stimulus; **b)** *(Anziehungskraft)* attraction; appeal *no pl.; (des Verbotenen, der Ferne usw.)* lure; **c)** *(Zauber)* charm; **reizbar** *Adj.* irritable; **Reizbarkeit** die; ~: irritability; **reizen 1.** *tr. V.* **a)** annoy; tease ‹*animal*›; *(herausfordern, provozieren)* provoke; *s. auch* **gereizt; b)** *(Physiol.)* irritate; **c)** *(Interesse erregen bei)* jmdn. ~: attract sb.; appeal to sb.; **d)** *(Kartenspiele)* bid; **2.** *itr. V. (Kartenspiele)* bid; **reizend 1.** *Adj.* charming; delightful, lovely ‹*child*›; **2.** *adv.* charmingly; **reizlos** *Adj.* unattractive; ‹landscape, scenery› lacking in charm; **reizvoll** *Adj.* **a)** *(hübsch)* charming; **b)** *(interessant)* attractive

**rekeln** *refl. V. (ugs.)* stretch

**Reklamation** [reklama'tsi̯o:n] die; ~, ~en complaint **(wegen** about); **Reklame** die; ~, ~n **a)** *o. Pl.* advertising *no indef. art.; ~* **für** jmdn./etw. **machen** promote sb./advertise *or* promote sth.; **b)** *(ugs.: Werbemittel)* advert *(Brit. coll.);* ad *(coll.); (im Fernsehen, Radio auch)* commercial; **reklamieren 1.** *itr. V.* complain; **2.** *tr. V.* **a)** complain about **(bei** to, **wegen** on account of); **b)** *(beanspruchen)* claim

**rekonstruieren** *tr. V.* reconstruct

**Rekord** der; ~|e|s, ~e record

**Rekrut** der; ~en, ~en *(Milit.)* recruit

**Rektor** der; ~s, ~en **a)** *(einer Schule)* head[master]; **b)** *(Universitäts~)* Rector; ≈ Vice-Chancellor *(Brit.); (einer Fachhochschule)* principal; **Rektorin** die; ~, ~nen **a)** *(einer Schule)* head[mistress]; **b)** *s.* **Rektor b**

**Relation** die; ~, ~en relation; **relativ 1.** *Adj.* relative; **2.** *adv.* relatively

**Relativ-: ~pronomen** das *(Sprachw.)* relative pronoun; **~satz** der *(Sprachw.)* relative clause

**Relief** das; ~s, ~s *od.* ~e relief

**Religion** die; ~, ~en religion; **religi-**

**ös 1.** *Adj.* religious; **2.** *adv.* in a religious manner

**Relikt** das; ~|e|, ~e relic

**Reling** die; ~, ~s *od.* ~e [deck-]rail

**Reliquie** die; ~, ~n relic

**Remis** das; ~ [rə'mi:(s)], ~ [rə'mi:s] *(bes. Schach)* draw

**Ren** das; ~s, ~s *od.* ~e reindeer

**Rendezvous** [rãde'vu:] das; ~ [...'vu:(s)], ~ ['rãde'vu:s] rendezvous

**Renn·bahn** die *(Sport)* race-track; *(für Pferde)* racecourse; **rennen** *unr. itr. V.; mit sein* run; **an/gegen** jmdn./ etw. ~: run *or* bang into sb./sth.; **Rennen** das; ~s, ~: running; *(Pferde~, Auto~)* racing; *(Wettbewerb)* race

**Renn-: ~fahrer** der racing driver; **~pferd** das racehorse; **~rad** das racing cycle; **~wagen** der racing car

**renommiert** *Adj.* renowned

**renovieren** *tr. V.* renovate; redecorate ‹*room, flat*›; **Renovierung** die; ~, ~en renovation; *(eines Zimmers, einer Wohnung)* redecoration

**rentabel 1.** *Adj.* profitable; **2.** *adv.* profitably

**Rente** die; ~, ~n **a)** pension; **b)** *(Kapitalertrag)* annuity

**Ren·tier** das reindeer

**rentieren** *refl. V.* be profitable; ‹*equipment, machinery*› pay its way

**Rentner** der; ~s, ~, **Rentnerin** die; ~, ~nen pensioner

**Reparatur** die; ~, ~en repair **(an +** *Dat.* to)

**Reparatur·werkstatt** die repair [work]shop; *(für Autos)* garage

**reparieren** *tr. V.* repair; mend

**Repertoire** [repɛ'toa:ɐ̯] das; ~s, ~s repertoire

**Report** der; ~|e|s, ~e, **Reportage** [repɔr'ta:ʒə] die; ~, ~n report; **Reporter** der; ~s, ~, **Reporterin** die; ~, ~nen reporter

**Repräsentant** der; ~en, ~en, **Repräsentantin** die; ~, ~nen representative; **repräsentativ** *Adj.* representative; **repräsentieren** *tr. V.* represent

**Repressalie** die; ~, ~n repressive measure

**Reproduktion** die reproduction; **reproduzieren** *tr. V.* reproduce

**Reptil** das; ~s, ~ien reptile

**Republik** die; ~, ~en republic; **republikanisch** *Adj.* republican

**Reservat** das; ~|e|s, ~e **a)** reservation; **b)** *(Naturschutzgebiet)* reserve; **Reserve** die; ~, ~n reserve

**Reserve-:** ~**rad** das spare wheel;
~**reifen** der spare tyre
**reservieren** tr. V. reserve; **Reser-**
**voir** [rεzεr'vọa:ẹ] das; ~s, ~e (auch
fig.) reservoir (an + Dat. of)
**Residenz** die; ~, ~en a) residence; b)
(Hauptstadt) [royal] capital
**Resignation** die; ~, ~en resignation;
**resignieren** itr. V. give up
**resolut** 1. Adj. resolute; 2. adv. resolutely; **Resolution** die; ~, ~en resolution
**Resonanz** die; ~, ~en resonance
**Respekt** der; ~[e]s a) (Achtung) respect (vor + Dat. for); b) (Furcht)
jmdm. ~ einflößen intimidate sb.; **re-**
**spektieren** tr. V. respect; **re-**
**spekt·los** 1. Adj. disrespectful; 2.
adv. disrespectfully; **Respektlosig-**
**keit** die; ~: disrespectfulness; **re-**
**spekt·voll** 1. Adj. respectful; 2. adv.
respectfully
**Ressort** [rε'so:ẹ] das; ~s, ~s area of responsibility; (Abteilung) department
**Rest** der; ~[e]s, ~e a) rest; ein ~ von a
little bit of; b) (Endstück) remnant; c)
(Math.) remainder
**Restaurant** [rεsto'rã:] das; ~s, ~s restaurant; **restaurieren** tr. V. restore
**restlich** Adj. remaining; **rest·los** 1.
Adj. complete; 2. adv. completely
**Resultat** das; ~[e]s, ~e result
**Retorte** die; ~, ~n retort
**retten** 1. tr. V. save; (vor Gefahr) save;
rescue; (befreien) rescue; jmdm. das
Leben ~: save sb.'s life; 2. refl. V. (fliehen) escape (aus from); **Retter** der;
~s, ~, **Retterin** die; ~, ~nen rescuer
**Rettich** der; ~s, ~e radish
**Rettung** die rescue; (vor Zerstörung)
saving
**rettungs-, Rettungs-:** ~**boot** das
lifeboat; ~**hubschrauber** der rescue
helicopter; ~**los** 1. Adj. hopeless;
inevitable ⟨disaster⟩; 2. adv. hopelessly; ~**ring** der lifebelt
**Reue** die; ~: remorse (über + Akk.
for); (Rel.) repentance; **reuen** tr. V.
etw. reut jmdn. sb. regrets sth.;
**reu·mütig** Adj. remorseful; repentant ⟨sinner⟩
**Reuse** die; ~, ~n fish-trap
**Revanche** [re'vã:ʃ(ə)] die; ~, ~n
revenge; (Sport) return match/fight/
game; **revanchieren** refl. V. **a)** get
one's revenge, (coll.) get one's own
back (bei on); b) **sich bei jmdm. für ei-**
**ne Einladung** ~ (ugs.) return sb.'s invitation

**Revers** [rə've:ẹ] das od. (österr.) der; ~
[rə'vε:ẹ(s)], ~ [rə'vε:ẹs] lapel
**Revier** das; ~s, ~e a) (Aufgabenbe-
reich) province; b) (Zool.) territory; c)
(Polizei~) (Dienststelle) [police] station; (Bereich) district; (des einzelnen
Polizisten) beat
**Revision** die; ~, ~en a) revision; (Änderung) amendment; b) (Rechtsw.)
appeal [on a point/points of law]; ~
einlegen, in die ~ gehen lodge an appeal [on a point/points of law]
**Revolte** die; ~, ~n revolt; **Revoluti-**
**on** die; ~, ~en (auch fig.) revolution;
**revolutionär** 1. Adj. revolutionary;
2. adv. in a revolutionary way; **Revo-**
**lutionär** der; ~s, ~e, **Revolutionä-**
**rin** die; ~, ~nen revolutionary
**Revolver** der; ~s, ~: revolver
**Rezept** das; ~[e]s, ~e a) (Med.) prescription; b) (Anleitung) recipe; **Re-**
**zeption** die; ~, ~en reception no
art.; **rezept·pflichtig** Adj. ⟨drug
etc.⟩ obtainable only on prescription
**R-Gespräch** ['εr-] das reverse-charge
call (Brit.); collect call (Amer.)
**Rhabarber** der; ~s rhubarb
**Rhein** der; ~[e]s Rhine; **rheinisch**
Adj. Rhenish; ⟨speciality etc.⟩ of the
Rhine region; **Rhein·land** das; ~[e]s
Rhineland; **Rheinland-Pfalz** (die);
~': the Rhineland-Palatinate
**Rhetorik** die; ~, ~en rhetoric
**Rheuma** das; ~s (ugs.) rheumatism;
**rheumatisch** (Med.) 1. Adj. rheumatic; 2. adv. rheumatically; **Rheu-**
**matismus** der; ~, Rheumatismen
(Med.) rheumatism
**Rhinozeros** das; ~[ses], ~se rhinoceros; rhino (coll.)
**Rhododendron** der od. das; ~s, Rho-
dodendren rhododendron
**rhythmisch** 1. Adj. rhythmical;
rhythmic; 2. adv. rhythmically;
**Rhythmus** der; ~, Rhythmen (auch
fig.) rhythm
**richten** 1. tr. V. **a)** direct ⟨gaze⟩ (auf +
Akk. at, towards); turn ⟨eyes, gaze⟩
(auf + Akk. towards); point ⟨torch,
telescope, gun⟩ (auf + Akk. at); aim
⟨gun, missile, telescope, searchlight⟩
(auf + Akk. on); (fig.) direct ⟨activity,
attention⟩ (auf + Akk. towards); address ⟨letter, remarks, words⟩ (an +
Akk. to); level ⟨criticism⟩ (an + Akk.
at); b) (gerade~) straighten; c) (abur-
teilen) judge; (verurteilen) condemn;
s. auch zugrunde a; 2. refl. V. **a)** (sich
hinwenden) sich auf jmdn./etw. ~

*(auch fig.)* be directed towards sb./ sth.; **b) sich an jmdn./etw.** ~ ⟨person⟩ turn on sb./sth.; ⟨appeal, explanation⟩ be directed at sb./sth.; **sich gegen jmdn./etw.** ~ ⟨person⟩ criticize sb./ sth.; ⟨criticism, accusations, etc.⟩ be aimed *or* levelled at sb./sth.; **c)** *(sich orientieren)* **sich nach jmdm./jmds. Wünschen** ~: fit in with sb./sb.'s wishes; **d)** *(abhängen)* **sich nach jmdm./etw.** ~: depend on sb./sth.; **3.** *itr. V. (urteilen)* judge; **Richter der;** ~s, ~, **Richterin die;** ~, ~nen judge
**Richt·geschwindigkeit die** recommended maximum speed
**richtig 1.** *Adj.* **a)** right; *(zutreffend)* right; correct; accurate ⟨prophecy, premonition⟩; **b)** *(ordentlich)* proper; **c)** *(wirklich, echt)* real; **2.** *adv.* **a)** right; correctly; **b)** *(ordentlich)* properly; **c)** *(richtiggehend)* really
**richtig|stellen** *tr. V.* correct
**Richt-:** ~**linie** die guideline; ~**schnur die;** *Pl.* ~**schnuren** *(fig.)* guiding principle
**Richtung die;** ~, ~en **a)** direction; **b)** *(fig.: Tendenz)* movement; trend
**rieb** *1. u. 3. Pers. Sg. Prät. v.* **reiben**
**riechen 1.** *unr. tr. V.* **a)** smell; **b)** *(wittern)* ⟨dog etc.⟩ pick up the scent of; **2.** *unr. itr. V.* **a)** smell; **an jmdm./etw.** ~: smell sb./sth.; **b)** *(einen Geruch haben)* smell (**nach** of)
**rief** *1. u. 3. Pers. Sg. Prät. v.* **rufen**
**Riegel der;** ~s, ~ **a)** bolt; **b) ein** ~ **Schokolade** a bar of chocolate
**Riemen der;** ~s, ~ **a)** strap; *(Treib~, Gürtel)* belt; **sich am** ~ **reißen** *(ugs.)* pull oneself together; get a grip on oneself; **b)** *(Ruder)* [long] oar
**Riese der;** ~n, ~n giant
**rieseln** *itr. V.; mit Richtungsangabe mit sein* trickle [down]; ⟨snow⟩ fall gently
**Riesen-** giant; enormous ⟨selection, profit, portion⟩; tremendous *(coll.)* ⟨effort, rejoicing, success⟩; terrific *(coll.)*, terrible *(coll.)* ⟨stupidity, scandal, fuss⟩
**riesen·groß** *Adj.* enormous; huge; terrific *(coll.)* ⟨surprise⟩; **Riesenschritt der** giant stride; **riesig 1.** *Adj.* enormous; huge; vast ⟨country⟩; tremendous ⟨effort, progress⟩; **2.** *adv. (ugs.)* tremendously *(coll.)*; terribly *(coll.)*
**Riesling der;** ~s, ~e Riesling
**riet** *1. u. 3. Pers. Sg. Prät. v.* **raten**
**Riff das;** ~[e]s, ~e reef
**Rille die;** ~, ~n groove

**Rind das;** ~[e]s, ~er **a)** cow; *(Stier)* bull; ~**er** cattle *pl.;* **b)** *(~fleisch)* beef
**Rinde die;** ~, ~n **a)** *(Baum~)* bark; **b)** *(Brot~)* crust; *(Käse~)* rind
**Rinder·braten der** roast beef *no indef. art.; (roh)* roasting beef *no indef. art.*
**Rind-:** ~**fleisch das** beef; ~**vieh das** cattle *pl.*
**Ring der;** ~[e]s, ~e ring; **Ringel·natter die** ring-snake
**ringen 1.** *unr. tr. V. (Sport, fig.)* wrestle; *(fig.: kämpfen)* struggle, fight **(um** for; **gegen, mit** with); **nach Luft** ~: struggle for breath; **2.** *unr. tr. V.* **die Hände** ~: wring one's hands; **Ringen das;** ~s *(Sport)* wrestling *no art.*
**Ring-:** ~**finger der** ring-finger; ~**kampf der a)** [stand-up] fight; **b)** *(Sport)* wrestling bout
**rings** *Adv.* all around; **rings·herum** *Adv.* all around [it/them *etc.*]
**Ring·straße die** ring road
**rings-:** ~**um**, ~**umher** *Adv.* all around
**Rinne die;** ~, ~n channel; *(Dach~, Rinnstein)* gutter; *(Abfluß)* drainpipe; **rinnen** *unr. itr. V.; mit sein* run; **Rinn·stein der** gutter
**Rippchen das;** ~s, ~ *(Kochk. südd.)* rib [of pork]; **Rippe die;** ~, ~n rib
**Risiko das;** ~s, **Risiken** risk; **riskant 1.** *Adj.* risky; **2.** *adv.* riskily; **riskieren** *tr. V.* risk
**riß** *1. u. 3. Pers. Sg. Prät. v.* **reißen**
**Riß der;** **Risses, Risse** tear; *(Spalt, Sprung)* crack; **rissig** *Adj.* cracked; chapped ⟨lips⟩
**ritt** *1. u. 3. Pers. Sg. Prät. v.* **reiten**; **Ritt der;** ~[e]s, ~e ride; **Ritter der;** ~s, ~: knight; **Ritter·sporn der** delphinium; **rittlings** *Adv.* astride
**Ritze die;** ~, ~n crack; [narrow] gap; **ritzen** *tr. V.* scratch
**Rivale der;** ~n, ~n, **Rivalin die;** ~, ~nen rival; **Rivalität die;** ~, ~en rivalry *no indef. art.*
**Robbe die;** ~, ~n seal
**Robe die;** ~, ~n robe; *(schwarz)* gown
**Roboter der;** ~s, ~: robot
**robust** *Adj.* robust
**roch** *1. u. 3. Pers. Sg. Prät. v.* **riechen**
**Rochade die;** ~, ~n *(Schach)* castling
**röcheln** *itr. V.* ⟨dying person⟩ give the death-rattle
**Rock der;** ~[e]s, **Röcke** skirt
**Rodel·bahn die** toboggan-run; *(Sport)* luge-run; **rodeln** *itr. V.; mit sein* sledge; toboggan

**roden** tr. V. clear ⟨wood, land⟩; (ausgraben) grub up ⟨tree⟩
**Rogen** der; ~s, ~: roe
**Roggen** der; ~s rye
**Roggen-:** ~**brot** das rye bread; ein
~**brot** a loaf of rye bread; ~**brötchen** das rye-bread roll
**roh** 1. Adj. **a)** raw ⟨food⟩; unboiled
⟨milk⟩; unfinished ⟨wood⟩; **b)** (ungenau) rough; **c)** (brutal) brutish; brute
attrib. ⟨force⟩; 2. adv. **a)** (ungenau)
roughly; **b)** (brutal) brutishly; (grausam) callously; (grob) coarsely
**Roh-:** ~**bau** der shell [of a/the build-
ing]; ~**kost** die raw fruit and vegetables pl.; ~**material** das raw material; ~**öl** das crude oil
**Rohr** das; ~|e|s, ~e **a)** (Leitungs~)
pipe; (als Bauteil) tube; **b)** o. Pl. (Röhricht) reeds pl.; **c)** o. Pl. (Werkstoff)
reed; **Röhre** die; ~, ~n tube; (Elek-
tronen~) valve (Brit.); tube (Amer.)
**Roh·stoff** der raw material
**Rokoko** das; ~|s| rococo
**Rolladen** der; ~s, **Rolläden** [roller]
shutter; **Roll·bahn** die (Flugw.) taxi-
way; **Rolle** die; ~, ~n **a)** (Spule) reel;
**b)** (zylindrischer [Hohl]körper; Zusam-
mengerolltes) roll; **c)** (Walze) roller; **d)**
(Rad) [small] wheel; (an Möbeln usw.)
castor; (für Gardine, Schiebetür usw.)
runner; **e)** (Turnen, Kunstflug) roll; **f)**
(Theater, Film usw., fig.) role; part;
(Soziol.) role; **es spielt keine ~:** it is of
no importance; (es macht nichts aus) it
doesn't matter; **rollen** 1. tr. V. roll; 2.
itr. V. **a)** mit sein⟨ball, wheel, etc.⟩ roll;
⟨vehicle⟩ move; ⟨aircraft⟩ taxi; **Roller**
der; ~s, ~: scooter
**Roll-:** ~**feld** das runway[s] and taxi-
way[s]; ~**kragen** der polo-neck;
~**laden** der s. Rolladen; ~**mops** der
rollmops; ~**schuh** der roller-skate;
~**schuh laufen** roller-skate; ~**splitt**
der loose chippings pl.; ~**stuhl** der
wheelchair; ~**treppe** die escalator
**Rom** (das); ~s Rome
**Roman** der; ~s, ~e novel
**Romantik** die; ~: romanticism; die
~: Romanticism; **romantisch** 1.
Adj. romantic; 2. adv. romantically
**Romanze** die; ~, ~n romance
**Römer** der; ~s, ~: Roman
**römisch-katholisch** Adj. Roman
Catholic
**röntgen** tr. V. X-ray
**Röntgen-:** ~**aufnahme** die, ~**bild**
das X-ray [image/photograph or pic-
ture]; ~**strahlen** Pl. X-rays

**rosa** 1. indekl. Adj. pink; 2. adv. pink;
**Rosa** das; ~s, ~ od. ~s pink; **Rose**
die; ~, ~n rose
**rosé** 1. indekl. Adj. pale pink; **Rosé**
der; ~s, ~s rosé [wine]
**Rosen-:** ~**kohl** der; o. Pl. [Brussels]
sprouts pl.; ~**kranz** der (kath. Kirche)
rosary; **einen** ~**kranz beten** say a rosary; ~**montag** der the day before
Shrove Tuesday
**rosig** Adj. **a)** rosy; pink ⟨piglet etc.⟩; **b)**
(fig.) rosy; optimistic ⟨mood⟩
**Rosine** die; ~, ~n raisin
**Rosmarin** der; ~s rosemary
**Roß** das; **Rosses, Rosse** od. **Rösser**
horse; steed (poet./joc.); **hoch zu ~:** on
horseback; **auf dem** od. **seinem hohen**
~ **sitzen** (fig.) be on one's high horse
**¹Rost** der; ~|e|s, ~e **a)** (Gitter) grating;
(eines Ofens, einer Feuerstelle) grate;
(Brat~) grill; **b)** (Bett~) base
**²Rost** der; ~|e|s rust
**Rost-:** ~**braten** der grilled steak;
~**bratwurst** die grilled sausage
**rosten** itr. V.; auch mit sein rust
**rösten** ['rœstn̩, 'rø:stn̩] tr. V. roast;
toast ⟨bread⟩
**rost·frei** Adj. stainless ⟨steel⟩
**Rösti** die; ~ (schweiz. Kochk.) thinly
sliced fried potatoes pl.
**rostig** Adj. rusty
**rot** 1. Adj. red; ~ **werden** turn red; ⟨per-
son⟩ blush; ⟨traffic-light⟩ change to
red; 2. adv. red; **Rot** das; ~s, ~ od.
~s red; **Rot·barsch** der rose-fish;
**Röte** die; ~: red[ness]; **röten** 1. tr. V.
redden; 2. refl. V. go or turn red;
**rot·haarig** Adj. red-haired; **Rothirsch** der red deer
**rotieren** itr. V. **a)** rotate; **b)** (ugs.: hektisch sein) get into a flap (coll.)
**Rot-:** ~**käppchen** (das) Little Red
Riding Hood; ~**kehlchen** das; ~s,
~: robin [redbreast]; ~**kohl** der, (bes.
südd., österr.) ~**kraut** das red cabbage
**rötlich** Adj. reddish; **Rot·stift** der
red pencil; **Rötung** die; ~, ~en red-
dening; **Rot·wein** der red wine
**Rotz** der; ~es (salopp) snot (sl.)
**Rouge** [ru:ʒ] das; ~s, ~s rouge
**Roulade** [ru:la:də] die; ~, ~n (Kochk.)
[beef/veal/pork] olive
**Route** ['ru:tə] die; ~, ~n route; **Routine** [ru'ti:nə] die; ~ **a)** (Erfahrung) experience; (Übung) practice; **b)** (Gewohnheit) routine no def. art.
**Rübe** die; ~, ~n turnip; **rote** ~: beetroot; **gelbe** ~ (südd.) carrot

**rüber** *Adv. (ugs.)* over

**Rubin** der; ~s, ~e ruby

**Rubrik** die; ~, ~en column; *(fig.: Kategorie)* category

**Ruck** der; ~|e|s, ~e jerk

**Rück·blick** der look back (**auf** + *Akk.* at); retrospective view (**auf** + *Akk.* of)

**rücken** *itr., tr. V.* move

**Rücken** der; ~s, ~: back; *(Buch~)* spine **Rücken-:** **~deckung die a)** *(bes. Milit.)* rear cover; b) *(fig.)* backing; **~lehne die** [chair/seat] back; **~mark das** *(Anat.)* spinal cord; **~schmerzen** *Pl.* backache *sing.;* **~schwimmen das** backstroke; **~wind der** tail wind

**rück-, Rück-:** ~|**erstatten** *tr. V.; nur im Inf. u. 2. Part.* repay; **~erstattung die** repayment; **~fahrkarte die, ~fahrschein der** return [ticket]; **~fahrt die** return journey; **~fall der** *(Med., auch fig.)* relapse; **~fällig** *Adj. (Med., auch fig.)* relapsed ⟨*patient, alcoholic, etc.*⟩; **~fällig werden** have a relapse ⟨*alcoholic etc.*⟩ go back to one's old ways; ⟨*criminal*⟩ commit a second offence; **~flug der** return flight; **~frage die** query; **~gabe die** return; **~gang der** drop, fall *(Gen.* in); **~gängig** *Adj.* **~gängig machen** cancel ⟨*agreement, decision, etc.*⟩; **~grat das** spine; *(bes. fig.)* backbone; **~halt der** support; backing; **~halt·los 1.** *Adj.* unreserved, unqualified ⟨*support*⟩; **2.** *adv.* unreservedly; **~kehr die; ~:** return; **~lage die** savings *pl.;* **~läufig** *Adj.* decreasing ⟨*number*⟩; declining ⟨*economic growth etc.*⟩; falling ⟨*rate, production, etc.*⟩; **~licht das** rear- *or* tail-light

**rücklings** *Adv.* on one's back

**Rück-:** **~nahme die** taking back; **~reise die** return journey; **~ruf der** *(Fernspr.)* return call

**Ruck·sack** der rucksack; *(Touren~)* back-pack

**rück-, Rück-:** **~schlag der** set-back; **~schritt der** retrograde step; **~seite die** back; *(einer Münze usw.)* reverse; far side; **~sicht auf jmdn. nehmen** show consideration for *or* towards sb.; **~sicht·nahme die; ~:** consideration; **~sichts·los 1.** *Adj.* inconsiderate; thoughtless; *(verantwortungslos)* reckless ⟨*driver*⟩; *(schonungslos)* ruthless; **2.** *adv. s. Adj:* inconsiderately;

recklessly; ruthlessly; **~sichts·losigkeit die;** ~, ~en *s.* rücksichtslos : lack of consideration; recklessness; ruthlessness; **~sichts·voll 1.** *Adj.* considerate; **2.** *adv.* considerately; **~sitz der** back seat; **~spiegel der** rear-view mirror; **~sprache die** consultation; **~stand der a)** *(Rest)* residue; b) *(ausstehende Zahlung)* arrears *pl.;* c) *(Zurückbleiben hinter dem gesetzten Ziel)* backlog; *(bes. Sport: hinter dem Gegner)* deficit; |mit etw.| **im ~stand sein/in ~stand** *(Akk.)* **geraten** be/get behind [with sth.]; **~ständig** *Adj.* a) backward; *(schon länger fällig)* outstanding ⟨*payment, amount*⟩; ⟨*wages*⟩ still owing; **~strahler der** reflector; **~tritt der** resignation (**von** from); *(von einer Kandidatur, einem Vertrag usw.)* withdrawal (**von** from)

**rückwärts** *Adv.* backwards; **Rückwärts·gang der** *(Kfz-W.)* reverse [gear]

**rück-, Rück-:** **~weg der** return journey; **~wirkend 1.** *Adj.* retrospective; backdated ⟨*pay increase*⟩; **2.** retrospectively; **~zahlung die** repayment; **~zug der** retreat

**Rüde** der; ~n, ~n [male] dog

**Rudel** das; ~s, ~: herd; *(von Wölfen, Hunden)* pack

**Ruder** das; ~s, ~ a) *(Riemen)* oar; b) *(Steuer~)* rudder; **Ruder·boot das** row-boat; rowing-boat *(Brit.);* **rudern 1.** *itr. V.; mit sein* row; **2.** *tr. V.* row

**Ruf** der; ~|e|s, ~e a) call; *(Schrei)* shout; cry; *(Tierlaut)* call; b) *o. Pl. (fig.: Forderung)* call (**nach** for); c) *o. Pl. (Telefonnummer)* telephone [number]; d) *(Leumund)* reputation; **rufen 1.** *unr. itr. V.* call (**nach** for); *(schreien)* shout (**nach** for); ⟨*animal*⟩ call; **2.** *unr. tr. V.* a) *(aus~)* call; *(schreien)* shout; b) *(herbei~, an~)* **jmdn.** ~: call sb.; **jmdn. zu Hilfe** ~: call to sb. to help

**Ruf-:** **~name der** first name *(by which one is generally known);* **~nummer die** telephone number

**Rüge die;** ~, ~n reprimand; **rügen** *tr. V.* reprimand ⟨*person*⟩ (**wegen** for); censure ⟨*carelessness etc.*⟩

**Ruhe die;** ~ a) *(Stille)* silence; ~ |bitte|! quiet *or* silence [please]!; b) *(Ungestörtheit)* peace; **jmdn. mit etw. in ~ lassen** stop bothering sb. with sth.; c) *(Unbewegtheit)* rest; d) *(Erholung)* rest *no def. art.;* e) *(Gelassenheit)*

calm[ness]; composure; |die| ~ bewah-
ren/die ~ verlieren keep calm/lose
one's composure; in |aller| ~: [really]
calmly; ruhe‧los 1. Adj. restless; 2.
adv. restlessly; ruhen itr. V. a)
(aus~) rest; b) (geh.: schlafen) sleep;
c) (stillstehen) ⟨work, business⟩ have
stopped; ⟨production, firm⟩ be at a
standstill

Ruhe-: ~pause die break; ~stand
der; o. Pl. retirement; ~störung die
disturbance; (Rechtsw.) disturbance
of the peace; ~tag der closing day;
„Dienstag ~tag" 'closed on Tuesdays'

ruhig 1. Adj. a) (still, leise) quiet; b)
(friedlich, ungestört) peaceful ⟨times,
life, valley, etc.⟩; quiet ⟨talk, reflection,
life⟩; c) (unbewegt) calm ⟨sea,
weather⟩; still ⟨air⟩; (fig.) peaceful
⟨melody⟩; (gleichmäßig) steady
⟨breathing, hand, steps⟩; smooth
⟨flight, crossing⟩; d) (gelassen) calm
⟨voice etc.⟩; quiet, calm ⟨person⟩; 2.
adv. a) (still, leise) quietly; sich ~ verhalten keep quiet; b) (friedlich, ohne
Störungen) peacefully; (ohne Zwi-
schenfälle) uneventfully; ⟨work, think⟩
in peace; c) (unbewegt) ⟨sit, lie, stand⟩
still; (gleichmäßig) ⟨burn, breathe⟩
steadily; ⟨run, fly⟩ smoothly; d) (gelassen) ⟨speak, watch, sit⟩ calmly; 3. Adv.
by all means

Ruhm der; ~|e|s fame; rühmen 1. tr.
V. praise; 2. refl. V. boast (+ Gen.
about; ruhm‧reich Adj. glorious
⟨victory, history⟩; celebrated ⟨general,
army, victory⟩

Ruhr die; ~, ~en dysentery no art.

Rühr‧ei das scrambled egg[s pl.]; rühren 1. tr. V. a) (um~) stir; (ein~) stir
⟨egg, powder, etc.⟩ ⟨an, in + Akk.
into⟩; b) (bewegen) move ⟨limb, fingers, etc.⟩; c) (fig.) move; touch; 2. itr.
V. a) (um~) stir; b) (geh.: her~) das
rührt daher, daß ...: that stems from
the fact that ...; 3. refl. V. a) (sich bewegen) move; b) (Milit.) rührt euch! at
ease!; rührend 1. Adj. touching; 2.
adv. touchingly; rühr‧selig 1. Adj.
a) emotional ⟨person⟩; b) (allzu gefühlvoll) over-sentimental; 2. adv. in an
over-sentimental manner; Rührung
die; ~: emotion

Ruine die; ~, ~n ruin; ruinieren tr.
V. ruin

rülpsen itr. V. (ugs.) burp

rum Adv. (ugs.) s. herum

Rum der; ~s, ~s rum

Rumäne der; ~n, ~n Romanian; Ru-

mänien (das); ~s Romania; rumänisch Adj. Romanian

Rummel der; ~s (ugs.) a) commotion;
(Aufhebens) fuss (um about); b) (Jahrmarkt) fair

Rumpf der; ~|e|s, Rümpfe a) trunk [of
the body]; b) (beim Schiff) hull; c)
(beim Flugzeug) fuselage

rümpfen tr. V. die Nase |bei etw.| ~:
wrinkle one's nose [at sth.]; über
jmdn./etw. die Nase rümpfen (fig.)
look down one's nose at sb./turn up
one's nose at sth.

rund 1. Adj. a) round; b) (dicklich)
plump ⟨arms etc.⟩; chubby ⟨cheeks⟩;
fat ⟨stomach⟩; c) (ugs.: ganz) round
⟨dozen, number, etc.⟩; 2. Adv. a) (ugs.:
etwa) about; b) ~ um jmdn./etw. [all]
around sb./sth.; Rund‧blick der
panorama; view in all directions;
Runde die; ~, ~n a) (Sport: Strecke)
lap; b) (Sport: Durchgang usw.)
round; über die ~n kommen (fig. ugs.)
get by; manage; c) (Personenkreis)
circle; (Gesellschaft) company; d)
(Rundgang) round; e) (Lage) round

rund-, Rund-: ~erneuern tr. V.
(Kfz-W.) remould; ~fahrt die tour
(durch of); ~funk der a) radio; b)
(Einrichtung, Gebäude) radio station

Rundfunk-: ~anstalt die broadcasting corporation; ~gerät das radio
set; ~sendung die radio programme; ~sprecher der radio announcer

rund-, Rund-: ~gang der round
(durch of); ~herum Adv. a) (ringsum)
all around; b) (völlig) completely

rundlich Adj. a) roundish; b) (mollig)
plump

Rund-: ~reise die [circular] tour
(durch of); ~weg der circular path or
walk

runter Adv. (ugs.) ~ |da|! get off
[there]; s. auch herunter; hinunter

Runzel die; ~, ~n wrinkle;
runz[e]lig Adj. wrinkled; runzeln
tr. V. die Stirn/die Brauen ~: wrinkle
one's brow/knit one's brows; (ärgerlich) frown

rupfen tr. V. a) pluck ⟨goose, hen,
etc.⟩; b) (abreißen) pull up ⟨weeds,
grass⟩; pull off ⟨leaves etc.⟩

Rüsche die; ~, ~n ruche; frill

Ruß der; ~es soot

Russe der; ~n, ~n Russian

Rüssel der; ~s, ~ (des Elefanten)
trunk; (des Schweins) snout; (bei Insekten u. ä.) proboscis

**rußen** *itr. V.* give off sooty smoke

**Russin** die; ~, ~nen Russian; **russisch** 1. *Adj.* Russian; 2. *adv. (auf ~)* in Russian; **Russisch das**; ~[s] Russian; **Ruß·land (das)**; ~s Russia

**rüsten** *itr. V.* arm

**rüstig** 1. *Adj.* sprightly; active

**rustikal** 1. *Adj.* country-style ⟨*food, inn, clothes, etc.*⟩; rustic ⟨*furniture*⟩; 2. *adv.* in [a] country style

**Rüstung** die; ~, ~en a) armament *no art.*; *(Waffen)* arms *pl.*; weapons *pl.*; b) *(hist.)* suit of armour

**Rüstungs-:** ~**industrie** die armaments *or* arms industry; ~**kontrolle** die arms control; ~**stopp** der arms freeze

**Rute** die; ~, ~n switch; *(Birken~, Angel~, Wünschel~)* rod

**Rutsch·bahn** die slide; **rutschen** *itr. V.;* *mit sein* slide; ⟨*clutch, carpet*⟩ slip; **rutschig** *Adj.* slippery

**rütteln** *tr., itr. V.* shake

# S

**s, S** [ɛs] das; ~, ~: s, S

**s** *Abk.* Sekunde sec.; s.

**S** *Abk.* a) Süden S.; b) *(österr.)* **Schilling** Sch.

**s.** *Abk.* siehe

**S.** *Abk.* Seite p.

**Sa.** *Abk.* Samstag Sat.

**Saal** der; ~[e]s, Säle a) hall; *(Ball~)* ballroom; b) *(Publikum)* audience

**Saar·land das**; ~[e]s Saarland; Saar *(esp. Hist.)*

**Saat** die; ~, ~en a) *(das Gesäte)* [young] crops *pl.*; b) *o. Pl. (das Säen)* sowing; c) *(Samenkörner)* seed[s *pl.*]

**Säbel** der; ~s, ~: sabre

**Sabotage** [zabo'ta:ʒə] die; ~, ~n sabotage *no art.*; **sabotieren** *tr. V.* sabotage

**sach·dienlich** *Adj.* useful; **Sache** die; ~, ~n a) *Pl.* things; b) *(Angelegenheit)* matter; business *(esp. derog.)*; **zur ~ kommen** come to the point; c) *(Rechts~)* case; d) *o. Pl. (Anliegen)* cause

**sach-, Sach-:** ~**gemäß**, ~**gerecht** 1. *Adj.* proper; correct; 2. *adv.* properly; correctly; ~**kenntnis** die expertise; ~**kundig** 1. *Adj.* with a knowledge of the subject *postpos., not pred.*; 2. *adv.* expertly

**sachlich** 1. *Adj.* a) *(objektiv)* objective; *(nüchtern)* functional ⟨*building, style, etc.*⟩; matter-of-fact ⟨*letter etc.*⟩; b) *nicht präd. (sachbezogen)* factual ⟨*error*⟩; 2. *adv. (objektiv)* objectively; ⟨*state*⟩ as a matter of fact; *(nüchtern)* ⟨*furnished*⟩ in a functional style; ⟨*written*⟩ in a matter-of-fact way; b) *(sachbezogen)* factually ⟨*wrong*⟩; **sächlich** *Adj. (Sprachw.)* neuter; **Sach·schaden** der damage [to property] *no indef. art.*

**Sachse** der; ~n, ~n Saxon; **Sachsen-Anhalt (das)**; ~s Saxony-Anhalt

**sacht, sachte** 1. *Adj.* a) *(behutsam)* gentle; b) *(leise)* quiet; 2. *adv.* a) gently; b) *(leise)* quietly

**Sach-:** ~**verhalt** der; ~[e]s, ~e facts *pl.* [of the matter]; ~**verstand** der expertise; grasp of the subject

**Sack** der; ~[e]s, Säcke sack; *(aus Papier, Kunststoff)* bag

**Sack-:** ~**gasse** die cul-de-sac; ~**hüpfen** das; ~s sack race

**Sadismus** der; ~: sadism *no art.*; **Sadist** der; ~en, ~en, **Sadistin** die; ~, ~nen sadist; **sadistisch** 1. *Adj.* sadistic; 2. *adv.* sadistically

**säen** *tr. (auch itr.) V.* sow

**Saft** der; ~[e]s, Säfte a) juice; b) *(in Pflanzen)* sap; **saftig** *Adj.* a) juicy; sappy ⟨*stem*⟩; lush ⟨*meadow, green*⟩; b) *(ugs.)* hefty ⟨*slap, blow*⟩; steep *(coll.)* ⟨*prices, bill*⟩; crude ⟨*joke, song, etc.*⟩; strongly-worded ⟨*letter etc.*⟩

**Sage** die; ~, ~n legend; *(bes. nordische)* saga

**Säge** die; ~, ~n saw

**sagen** 1. *tr. V.* a) say; **was ich noch ~ wollte** [oh] by the way; **unter uns gesagt** between you and me; b) *(mitteilen)* jmdm. etw. ~: say sth. to sb.; *(zur Information)* tell sb. sth.; c) *(nennen)* zu jmdm./etw. X ~: call sb./sth. X; d) *(anordnen, befehlen)* tell; 2. *refl. V.* sich *(Dat.)* etw. ~: say sth. to oneself

**sägen** *tr., itr. V.* saw

**sah** *1. u. 3. Pers. Sg. Prät. v.* sehen

**Sahne** die; ~: cream

**Saison** [zɛˈzõː] die; ~, ~s season

**Saite** die; ~, ~n string; **Saiten·instrument das** stringed instrument

**Sakko** der *od.* das; ~s, ~s jacket

**Sakrament** das; ~|e|s, ~e sacrament; **Sakristei** die; ~, ~en sacristy

**Salami** die; ~, ~|s| salami

**Salat** der; ~|e|s, ~e a) salad; b) *o. Pl.* |grüner| ~: lettuce; **ein Kopf** ~: a [head of] lettuce

**Salat-:** ~**besteck** das salad-servers *pl.;* ~**soße** die salad-dressing

**Salbe** die; ~, ~n ointment

**Salbei** der *od.* die; ~: sage

**Saldo** der; ~s, ~s *od.* **Saldi** *(Buchf., Finanzw.)* balance

**Säle** *s.* Saal

**Salmiak** der *od.* das; ~: sal ammoniac

**Salon** [za'lõ:] der; ~s, ~s a) *(Raum)* drawing-room; b) *(Geschäft)* [hair- *etc.*] salon

**salopp** 1. *Adj.* casual ⟨*clothes*⟩; informal ⟨*behaviour*⟩; 2. *adv.* ⟨*dress*⟩ casually

**Salto** der; ~s, ~s *od.* **Salti** somersault; *(beim Turnen auch)* salto

**salutieren** *itr. V. (bes. Milit.)* salute

**Salve** die; ~, ~n *(Milit.)* salvo; *(aus Gewehren)* volley

**Salz** das; ~es, ~e salt; **salzen** *tr. V.* salt; **salzig** *Adj.* salty

**Salz-:** ~**kartoffel** die; *meist Pl.* boiled potato; ~**säure** die; *o. Pl. (Chemie)* hydrochloric acid; ~**stange** die salt stick; ~**streuer** der; ~s, ~: salt-sprinkler; salt-shaker *(Amer.);* ~**wasser** das; *Pl.* ~wässer a) *o. Pl. (zum Kochen)* salted water; b) *(Meerwasser)* salt water

**Sambia** (das); ~s Zambia

**Samen** der; ~s, ~ a) *(~korn)* seed; b) *o. Pl. (~körner)* seed[s *pl.*]; c) *o. Pl. (Sperma)* sperm; semen

**sammeln** 1. *tr. (auch itr.) V.* a) collect; gather ⟨*honey, firewood, fig.: experiences, impressions, etc.*⟩; gather, pick ⟨*berries etc.*⟩; b) *(zusammenkommen lassen)* gather ⟨*people*⟩ [together]; assemble ⟨*people*⟩; cause ⟨*light rays*⟩ to converge; 2. *refl. V.* gather [together]; **Sammler** der; ~s, ~: collector; **Sammlung** die; ~, ~en collection; b) |innere| ~: composure

**Samstag** der; ~|e|s, ~e Saturday; *s. auch* Dienstag; Dienstag-; **samstags** *Adv.* on Saturdays

**samt** 1. *Präp. mit Dat.* together with; 2. *Adv.* ~ **und sonders** one and all

**Samt** der; ~|e|s, ~e velvet

**sämtlich** *Indefinitpron. u. unbest. Zahlwort* all the

**Sand** der; ~|e|s sand

**Sandale** die; ~, ~n sandal

**sandig** *Adj.* sandy

**Sand-:** ~**kasten** der [child's] sandpit; sand-box *(Amer.);* ~**kuchen** der Madeira cake; ~**mann** der, ~**männchen** das; *o. Pl.* sandman; ~**stein** der sandstone; ~**strand** der sandy beach

**sandte** *1. u. 3. Pers. Sg. Prät. v.* senden

**sanft** 1. *Adj.* gentle; *(leise)* soft; *(friedlich)* peaceful; 2. *adv.* gently; *(leise)* softly; *(friedlich)* peacefully

**sang** *1. u. 3. Pers. Sg. Prät. v.* singen; **Sänger** der; ~s, ~, **Sängerin** die; ~, ~nen singer

**sanieren** 1. *tr. V.* a) redevelop ⟨*area*⟩; rehabilitate ⟨*building*⟩; *(renovieren)* renovate [and improve] ⟨*flat etc.*⟩; b) *(Wirtsch.)* restore ⟨*firm*⟩ to profitability; 2. *refl. V.* ⟨*company etc.*⟩ restore itself to profitability; ⟨*person*⟩ get oneself out of the red; **Sanierung** die; ~, ~en a) *s.* sanieren a: redevelopment; rehabilitation; renovation; b) restoration to profitability; **sanitär** *Adj.* sanitary; **Sanitäter** der; ~s, ~: first-aid man; *(im Krankenwagen)* ambulance man

**sank** *1. u. 3. Pers. Sg. Prät. v.* sinken

**sann** *1. u. 3. Pers. Sg. Prät. v.* sinnen

**Saphir** der; ~s, ~e sapphire

**Sardelle** die; ~, ~n anchovy

**Sardine** die; ~, ~n sardine

**Sarg** der; ~|e|s, Särge coffin

**saß** *1. u. 3. Pers. Sg. Prät. v.* sitzen

**Satan** der *(bibl.)* Satan *no def. art.*

**Satellit** der; ~en, ~en satellite

**Satire** die; ~, ~n satire

**satt** *Adj.* a) full [up] *pred.;* well-fed; **sich** ~ **essen/trinken** eat/drink as much as one wants; eat/drink one's fill; b) **jmdn./etw.** ~ **haben** *(ugs.)* be fed up with sb./sth. *(coll.)*

**Sattel** der; ~s, Sättel a) saddle; **satteln** 1. *tr. V.* saddle; 2. *itr. V.* saddle the/one's horse

**sättigen** *itr. V.* be filling

**Sattler** der; ~s, ~: saddler; *(allgemein)* leather-worker

**Satz** der; ~es, Sätze a) *(sprachliche Einheit)* sentence; b) *(Musik)* movement; c) *(Tennis, Volleyball)* set; *(Tischtennis, Badminton)* game; d) *(Sprung)* leap; jump; e) *(Amtsspr.: Tarif)* rate; f) *(Set)* set; g) *(Boden~)* sediment; *(von Kaffee)* grounds *pl.*

**Satzung** die; ~, ~en articles of association *pl.;* statutes *pl.*

**Satz·zeichen** das punctuation mark

**Sau** die; ~, **Säue a)** *(weibliches Schwein)* sow; **b)** *(bes. südd.: Schwein)* pig

**sauber 1.** *Adj.* **a)** clean; **b)** *(sorgfältig)* neat; **2.** *adv.* **a)** *(sorgfältig)* neatly; **b)** *(fehlerlos)* |sehr| ~: [quite] perfectly; **Sauberkeit** die; ~: cleanness; **sauber|machen 1.** *tr. V.* clean; **2.** *itr. V.* clean; do the cleaning; **säubern** *tr. V.* clean; **Säuberung** die; ~, ~en cleaning

**Sauce** *s.* Soße

**Saudi** [zaudi] der; ~s, ~s Saudi; **Saudi-Arabien (das)** Saudi Arabia

**sauer 1.** *Adj.*'**a)** sour; pickled ⟨*herring, gherkin, etc.*⟩; acid[ic] ⟨*wine, vinegar*⟩; **saurer Regen** acid rain; **b)** *(ugs.: verärgert)* cross, annoyed (**auf** + *Akk.* with); **2.** *adv.* in vinegar; **Sauer · braten** der *braised beef marinated in vinegar and herbs;* sauerbraten *(Amer.)*

**Sauerei** die; ~, ~en *(salopp abwertend)* **a)** *(Unflätigkeit)* obscenity **b)** *(Gemeinheit)* bloody scandal *(sl.)*

**Sauer-:** ~**kirsche** die sour cherry; ~**kraut** das *o. Pl.* sauerkraut

**säuerlich** *Adj.* |leicht| ~: slightly sour; slightly sharp ⟨*sauce*⟩

**Sauer-:** ~**stoff** der; *o. Pl.* oxygen; ~**stoffgerät** das oxygen apparatus; ~**stoffmangel** der; *o. Pl.* lack of oxygen; ~**teig** der leaven

**saufen 1.** *unr. itr. V.* *(salopp: trinken)* drink; swig *(coll.); (Alkohol trinken)* drink; booze *(coll.);* **2.** *unr. tr. V. (salopp: trinken)* drink; **Säufer** der; ~s, ~ *(salopp)* boozer *(coll.);* **säuft** *3. Pers. Sg. Präsens v.* saufen

**saugen 1.** *tr. V.* **a)** *auch unr.* suck; **b)** *auch itr. (staub)* ~: vacuum; hoover *(coll.);* **2.** *regelm. (auch unr.) itr. V.* **an etw.** *(Dat.)* ~: suck [at] sth.; **3.** *unr. (auch regelm.) refl. V.* **sich voll etw.** ~: become soaked with sth.; **säugen** *tr. V.* suckle; **Säuge · tier** das *(Zool.)* mammal; **Säugling** der; ~s, ~e baby; **Säuglings · pflege die** baby care

**Säule** die; ~, ~n column; *(nur als Stütze, auch fig.)* pillar

**Saum** der; ~|e|s, **Säume** hem; **säumen** *tr. V.* hem; *(fig. geh.)* line

**säumig** *(geh.) Adj.* tardy

**Sauna** die; ~, ~s *od.* **Saunen** sauna

**Säure** die; ~, ~n **a)** *o. Pl. (von Früchten)* sourness; *(von Wein, Essig)* acidity; *(von Soßen)* sharpness; **b)** *(Chemie)* acid; **Saure · gurken · zeit die** *(ugs.)* silly season *(Brit.)*

**Saus:** in ~ **und Braus leben** live the high life

**säuseln 1.** *itr. V.* ⟨*leaves, branches, etc.*⟩ rustle; ⟨*wind*⟩ murmur; **2.** *tr. V.* *(iron.: sagen)* whisper; **sausen** *itr. V.* **a)** ⟨*wind*⟩ whistle; ⟨*storm*⟩ roar; ⟨*head, ears*⟩ buzz; **b)** *mit sein* ⟨*person*⟩ rush; ⟨*vehicle*⟩ roar; **c)** *mit sein* ⟨*whip, bullet, etc.*⟩ whistle

**Savanne** [za'vanə] die; ~, ~n savannah

**Saxophon** das; ~s, ~e saxophone

**S-Bahn** ['εs-] die city and suburban railway

**SB-** [εs'be:-] self-service *(attrib.)*

**Schabe** die; ~, ~n cockroach

**schaben** *tr., itr. V.* scrape; **Schaber** der; ~s, ~: scraper

**schäbig 1.** *Adj.* **a)** *(abgenutzt)* shabby; **b)** *(jämmerlich, gering)* pathetic; **c)** *(gemein)* shabby; **2.** *adv.* **a)** *(abgenutzt)* shabbily; **b)** *(jämmerlich)* miserably; **c)** *(gemein)* meanly

**Schach** das; ~s, ~s **a)** *o. Pl. (Spiel)* chess; **b)** *(Stellung)* check; **jmdn./etw. in** ~ **halten** *(ugs. fig.)* keep sb./sth. in check

**Schach-:** ~**brett** das chessboard; ~**figur** die chess piece; ~**spiel** das **a)** *o. Pl. (Spiel)* chess; *(das Spielen)* chess-playing; **b)** *(Brett und Figuren)* chess set

**Schacht** der; ~|e|s, **Schächte** shaft

**Schachtel** die; ~, ~n **a)** box; **eine** ~ **Zigaretten** a packet *or (Amer.)* pack of cigarettes; **b)** **alte** ~ *(salopp abwertend)* old bag *(sl.)*

**schade** *Adj.* |ach, wie| ~! [what a] pity *or* shame; |es ist| ~ **um jmdn./etw.** it's a pity *or* shame about sb./sth.; **für jmdn./für** *od.* **zu etw. zu** ~ **sein** be too good for sb./sth.

**Schädel** der; ~s, ~: skull; *(Kopf)* head; **Schädel · bruch** der *(Med.)* skull fracture

**schaden** *itr. V.* **jmdm./einer Sache** ~: damage *or* harm sb./sth.; **Schaden** der; ~s, **Schäden a)** damage *no pl., no indef. art.;* **ein kleiner/großer** ~: little/ major damage; **b)** *(Nachteil)* disadvantage

**schaden-, Schaden-:** ~**ersatz** der *(Rechtsw.)* damages *pl.;* ~**freude die** *o. Pl.* malicious pleasure; ~**froh 1.** *Adj.* gloating; ~**froh sein** gloat; **2.** *adv.* with malicious pleasure

**schadhaft** *Adj.* defective; **schädigen** *tr. V.* damage ⟨*health, reputation, interests*⟩; harm, hurt ⟨*person*⟩; cause

losses to ⟨*firm, industry, etc.*⟩; **Schädigung** die; ~, ~en damage *no pl., no indef. art.* (*Gen.* to); **schädlich** *Adj.* harmful; **Schädling** der; ~s, ~e pest
**Schaf** das; ~[e]s, ~e a) sheep; b) *(ugs.: Dummkopf)* twit (*Brit. sl.*);
**Schaf·bock** der ram; **Schäfchen** das; ~s, ~: [little] sheep; *(Lamm)* lamb; **Schäfer** der; ~s, ~: shepherd; **Schäfer·hund** der sheep-dog; |*deutscher*] ~: Alsatian; **Schaf·fell** das sheepskin
**schaffen** 1. *unr. tr. V.* a) create; b) *auch regelm. (herstellen)* create ⟨*conditions, jobs, situation, etc.*⟩; make ⟨*room, space, fortune*⟩; 2. *tr. V.* a) *(bewältigen)* manage; es ~, etw. zu tun manage to do sth.; b) *(ugs.: erschöpfen)* wear out; c) etw. aus etw./in etw. *(Akk.)* ~: get sth. out of/into sth.; 3. *itr. V.* a) *(südd.: arbeiten)* work; b) sich *(Dat.)* zu ~ machen busy oneself; jmdm. zu ~ machen cause sb. trouble
**Schaffner** der; ~s ~ *(im Bus)* conductor; *(im Zug)* guard *(Brit.)*; conductor *(Amer.)*; **Schaffnerin** die; ~, ~nen *(im Bus)* conductress *(Brit.)*; *(im Zug)* guard *(Brit.)*; conductress *(Amer.)*
**Schaffung** die; ~: creation
**Schafott** das; ~[e]s, ~e scaffold
**Schafs·käse** der sheep's milk cheese; **Schaf·wolle** die sheep's wool
**Schakal** der; ~s, ~e jackal
**schal** *Adj.* stale ⟨*drink, taste, smell, joke*⟩; empty ⟨*words, feeling*⟩
**Schal** der; ~s, ~s od. ~e scarf
**Schale** die; ~, ~n a) *(Obst~)* skin; *(abgeschälte ~)* peel *no pl.*; b) *(Nuß~, Eier~)* shell; c) *(Schüssel)* bowl; *(flacher)* dish; d) sich in ~ werfen *od.* schmeißen *(ugs.)* get dressed [up] to the nines; **schälen** 1. *tr. V.* peel ⟨*fruit, vegetable*⟩; shell ⟨*egg, nut, pea*⟩; 2. *refl. V.* peel
**Schall** der; ~[e]s, ~e od. Schälle sound; **Schall·dämpfer** der a) silencer; b) *(Musik)* mute; **schalldicht** *Adj.* sound-proof; **schallen** *regelm. (auch unr.) itr. V.* ring out; ~des Gelächter ringing laughter
**Schall-:** ~**geschwindigkeit** die speed *or* velocity of sound; ~**platte** die record
**Schalotte** die; ~, ~n shallot
**schalt** *1. u. 3. Pers. Sg. Prät. v.* schelten
**schalten** 1. *tr. V.* switch; 2. *itr. V.* a)

*(Schalter betätigen)* switch, turn (auf + *Akk.* to); b) ⟨*machine*⟩ switch (auf + *Akk.* to); c) *(im Auto)* change [gear]; d) ~ und walten manage one's affairs; e) *(ugs.: begreifen)* twig *(coll.)*; catch on *(coll.)*; **Schalter** der; ~s, ~ a) switch; b) *(Post~, Bank~ usw.)* counter
**Schalter-:** ~**beamte** der counter clerk; *(im Bahnhof)* ticket clerk; ~**halle** die hall; *(im Bahnhof)* booking-hall *(Brit.)*; ticket office
**Schaltjahr** das leap year; **Schaltung** die; ~, ~en *(Elektrot.)* circuit; wiring system
**Scham** die; ~: shame; **schämen** *refl. V.* be ashamed (*Gen.*, für, wegen of); **Scham·gefühl** das; *o. Pl.* sense of shame; **schamhaft** 1. *Adj.* bashful; 2. *adv.* bashfully; **scham·los** 1. *Adj.* a) *(skrupellos, dreist)* shameless; b) *(unanständig)* indecent; shameless ⟨*person*⟩; 2. *adv.* a) *(skrupellos, dreist)* shamelessly; b) *(unanständig)* indecently
**Schande** die; ~: disgrace; **schändlich** 1. *Adj.* disgraceful; 2. *adv.* disgracefully
**Schar** die; ~, ~en crowd; horde; **scharen·weise** *Adv.* in swarms *or* hordes
**scharf**; **schärfer, schärfst...** 1. *Adj.* a) sharp; b) *(stark gewürzt, brennend, stechend)* hot; strong ⟨*drink, vinegar, etc.*⟩; caustic ⟨*chemical*⟩; pungent ⟨*smell*⟩; c) *(durchdringend)* shrill; *(hell)* harsh; *(kalt)* biting ⟨*cold, wind, etc.*⟩; sharp ⟨*frost*⟩; d) *(deutlich wahrnehmend)* keen; e) *(schnell)* fast; hard ⟨*ride, gallop, etc.*⟩; f) *(explosiv)* live; *(Ballspiele)* powerful ⟨*shot*⟩; g) das ~e S *(bes. österr.)* the German letter 'ß'; h) ~ auf jmdn./etw. sein *(ugs.)* really fancy sb. *(coll.)*/be really keen on sth; 2. *adv.* a) ~ würzen/abschmecken season/flavour highly; ~ riechen smell pungent; b) *(durchdringend)* shrilly; *(hell)* harshly; *(kalt)* bitingly; c) *(deutlich wahrnehmend)* ⟨*listen, watch, etc.*⟩ closely, intently; ⟨*think, consider, etc.*⟩ hard; d) *(deutlich hervortretend)* sharply; e) *(schonungslos)* ⟨*attack, criticize, etc.*⟩ sharply, strongly; ⟨*watch, observe, etc.*⟩ closely; f) *(schnell)* fast; ~ bremsen brake hard *or* sharply; **Schärfe** die; ~ a) sharpness; b) *(von Geschmack)* hotness; *(von Chemikalien)* causticity; *(von Geruch)* pungency; c) *(Intensität)* shrillness; *(des*

*Frostes)* sharpness; **schärfen 1.** *tr. V. (auch fig.)* sharpen; **2.** *refl. V.* become sharper *or* keener

**scharf-:** ~**kantig** *Adj.* sharp-edged; ~**sichtig** *Adj.* sharp-sighted; perspicacious; ~**sinnig 1.** *Adj.* astute; **2.** *adv.* astutely

**Scharlach** der; ~s *(Med.)* scarlet fever

**Scharnier** das; ~s, ~e hinge

**scharren** *itr. V.* a) scrape; b) *(wühlen)* scratch; **2.** *tr. V.* scrape, scratch out ⟨*hole, hollow, etc.*⟩

**Schaschlik** der *od.* das; ~s, ~s *(Kochk.)* shashlik

**Schatten** der; ~s, ~ a) shadow; b) *o. Pl. (schattige Stelle)* shade; **schattig** *Adj.* shady

**Schatz** der; ~es, Schätze treasure *no indef. art.;* **schätzen 1.** *tr. V.* a) estimate; **sich glücklich** ~: deem oneself lucky; b) *(ugs.: annehmen)* reckon; c) *(würdigen, hochachten)* **jmdn.** ~: hold sb. in high esteem; **2.** *itr. V.* guess; **Schätzung** die; ~, ~en estimate

**Schau** die; ~, ~en a) *(Ausstellung)* exhibition; b) *(Vorführung)* show; c) **zur** ~ **stellen** *(ausstellen)* exhibit; display; *(offen zeigen)* display

**Schauder** der; ~s, ~: shiver; **schauderhaft 1.** *Adj.* terrible; **2.** *adv.* terribly; **schaudern** *itr. V.* a) *(vor Kälte)* shiver; b) *(vor Angst)* shudder

**schauen** *(bes. südd., österr., schweiz.)* **1.** *itr. V.* a) look; b) *(sich kümmern um)* **nach jmdm./etw.** ~: take *or* have a look at sb./sth.; c) *(achten)* **auf etw.** *(Akk.)* ~: set store by sth.; d) *(ugs.: sich bemühen)* **schau, daß du ...:** see *or* mind that you ...; e) *(nachsehen)* have a look; **2.** *tr. V.* **Fernsehen** ~: watch television

**Schauer** der; ~s, ~: shower

**Schauer·geschichte** die horror story; **schauerlich 1.** *Adj.* a) horrifying; b) *(ugs.: fürchterlich)* terrible *(coll.);* **2.** *(ugs.: fürchterlich)* terribly *(coll.)*

**Schaufel** die; ~, ~n shovel; *(Kehr~)* dustpan; **schaufeln** *tr. V.* shovel; *(graben)* dig

**Schau·fenster** das shop-window; **Schaufenster·bummel** der: **einen** ~ **machen** go window-shopping

**Schaukel** die; ~, ~n a) swing; b) *(Wippe)* see-saw; **schaukeln 1.** *itr. V.* a) swing; *(im Schaukelstuhl)* rock; b)

*(sich hin und her bewegen)* sway [to and fro]; *(sich auf und ab bewegen)* ⟨*ship, boat*⟩ pitch and toss; ⟨*vehicle*⟩ bump [up and down]; **2.** *tr. V.* rock

**Schaukel-:** ~**pferd** das rockinghorse; ~**stuhl** der rocking-chair

**Schau·lustige** der/die; *adj. Dekl.* curious onlooker

**Schaum** der; ~s, Schäume a) foam; *(von Seife usw.)* lather; *(von Getränken, Suppen usw.)* froth; b) *(Geifer)* foam; froth; **schäumen** *itr. V.* foam; froth; ⟨*soap etc.*⟩ lather; ⟨*beer, fizzy drink, etc.*⟩ froth [up]

**Schaum-:** ~**gummi** der foam rubber; ~**wein** der sparkling wine

**Schau-:** ~**spiel** das a) *o. Pl. (Drama)* drama *no art.;* b) *(ernstes Stück)* play; c) *(geh.: Anblick)* spectacle; ~**spieler** der actor; ~**spielerin** die actress; ~**steller** der; ~s, ~: showman

**Scheck** der; ~s, ~s cheque; **Scheckheft** das cheque-book; **Scheck·karte** die cheque card

**scheel** *(ugs.)* **1.** *Adj.* disapproving; *(neidisch)* envious; jealous; **2.** *adv.* disapprovingly; *(neidisch)* enviously; jealously

**Scheibe** die; ~, ~n a) disc; b) *(abgeschnittene* ~*)* slice; c) *(Glas~)* pane [of glass]; *(Fenster~)* [window-]pane; **Scheiben·wischer** der windscreen-wiper

**Scheide** die; ~, ~n a) sheath; b) *(Anat.)* vagina

**scheiden** *unr. tr. V.* dissolve ⟨*marriage*⟩; divorce ⟨*married couple*⟩; **sich** ~ **lassen** get divorced *or* get a divorce; **Scheidung** die; ~, ~en divorce

**Schein** der; ~[e]s, ~e a) *o. Pl. (Licht~)* light; b) *o. Pl. (An~)* appearances *pl.,* *no art.; (Täuschung)* pretence; **etw. nur zum** ~ **tun** [only] pretend to do sth.; make a show of doing sth.; c) *(Geld~)* note; **scheinbar 1.** *Adj.* apparent; seeming; **2.** *adv.* seemingly; **scheinen** *unr. itr. V.* a) shine; b) *(den Eindruck erwecken)* seem; appear; **mir scheint, [daß] ...:** it seems *or* appears to me that ...

**schein-, Schein-:** ~**heilig 1.** *Adj.* hypocritical; **2.** *adv.* hypocritically; ~**werfer** der floodlight; *(am Auto)* headlight

**Scheiße** die; ~ *(derb)* shit *(coarse);* crap *(coarse);* **scheißen** *unr. itr. V. (derb)* [have *or* (Amer.) take a] shit *(coarse);* crap *(coarse);* have a crap *(coarse)*

**Scheitel** der; ~s, ~: parting; **scheiteln** tr. V. part ⟨hair⟩

**scheitern** itr. V.; mit sein fail; ⟨talks, marriage⟩ break down; ⟨plan, project⟩ fail, fall through

**Schelle** die; ~, ~n bell; **schellen** itr. V. (westd.) s. **klingeln**

**Schell·fisch** der haddock

**Schelm** der; ~|e|s, ~e rascal; rogue; **schelmisch** 1. Adj. roguish; 2. adv. roguishly

**Schelte** die; ~, ~n (geh.) scolding; **schelten** (südd., geh.) 1. unr. itr. V. auf od. über jmdn./etw. ~: moan about sb./sth.; 2. unr. tr. V. scold

**Schema** das; ~s, ~s od. ~ta od. **Schemen** pattern; **schematisch** 1. Adj. a) diagrammatic; b) (mechanisch) mechanical; 2. adv. a) in diagram form; b) (mechanisch) mechanically

**Schemel** der; ~s, ~ a) stool; b) (südd.: Fußbank) footstool

**Schenkel** der; ~s, ~: thigh

**schenken** tr. V. a) give; jmdm. etw. [zum Geburtstag] ~: give sb. sth. or sth. to sb. [as a birthday present or for his/her birthday]; b) (ugs.: erlassen) jmdm./sich etw. ~: spare sb./oneself sth.

**Scherbe** die; ~, ~n fragment

**Schere** die; ~, ~n a) scissors pl.; eine ~: a pair of scissors; b) (Zool.) claw; ¹**scheren** unr. tr. V. crop; (von Haar befreien) shear, clip ⟨sheep⟩

²**scheren** tr., refl. V. sich um jmdn./ etw. nicht ~: not care about sb./sth.; **Schererelen** Pl. (ugs.) trouble no pl.

**Scherz** der; ~es, ~e joke; **scherzen** itr. V. joke; **scherzhaft** 1. Adj. jocular; 2. adv. jocularly

**scheu** 1. Adj. shy; timid ⟨animal⟩; (ehrfürchtig) awed; 2. adv. a) shyly; b) (von Tieren) timidly; **Scheu** die; ~ a) shyness; (Ehrfurcht) awe; b) (von Tieren) timidity

**scheuchen** tr. V. shoo; drive

**scheuen** 1. tr. V. shrink from; shun ⟨people, light, company, etc.⟩; 2. refl. V. sich vor etw. (Dat.) ~: be afraid of or shrink from sth. 3. itr. V. ⟨horse⟩ shy (vor + Dat. at)

**scheuern** 1. tr., itr. V. a) (reinigen) scour; scrub; b) (reiben) rub; chafe; 2. tr. V. (reiben an) rub

**Scheuer-**: ~pulver das scouring powder; ~tuch das; Pl. ~tücher scouring cloth

**Scheune** die; ~, ~n barn

**Scheusal** das; ~s, ~e monster;

**scheußlich** 1. Adj. a) dreadful; b) (ugs.: äußerst unangenehm) dreadful (coll.); ghastly (coll.) ⟨weather, taste, smell⟩; 2. adv. a) dreadfully; b) (ugs.: sehr) dreadfully (coll.)

**Schi** usw.: s. **Ski** usw.

**Schicht** die; ~, ~en a) (Lage) layer; (Geol.) stratum; (von Farbe) coat; (sehr dünn) film; b) (Gesellschafts~) stratum; c) (Arbeits~) shift; ~ arbeiten work shifts; be on shift work; **schichten** tr. V. stack

**schick** 1. Adj. a) stylish; chic ⟨clothes, fashions⟩; smart ⟨woman, girl, man⟩; b) (ugs.: großartig, toll) great (coll.); fantastic (coll.); 2. adv. a) stylishly; smartly ⟨furnished, decorated⟩

**schicken** 1. tr. V. send; jmdm. etw. ~, etw. an jmdn. ~: send sth. to sb.; send sb. sth.; 2. itr. V. nach jmdm. ~: send for sb; 3. refl. V. (veralt.: sich ziemen) be proper or fitting

**Schicksal** das; ~s, ~e: |das| ~: fate; destiny; (schweres Los) fate; **Schicksals·schlag** der stroke of fate

**Schiebe·dach** das sunroof; **schieben** 1. unr. tr. V. a) push; b) (stecken) put; c) etw. auf jmdn./etw. ~: blame sb./sth. for sth.; 2. unr. refl. V. sich durch die Menge ~: push one's way through the crowd; 3. unr. itr. V. push; (heftig) shove; **Schiebe·tür** die sliding door; **Schiebung** die; ~, ~en (ugs.) a) shady deal; b) (o. Pl.: Begünstigung) pulling strings

**schied** 1. u. 3. Pers. Sg. Prät. v. **scheiden**

**Schieds·richter** der referee; (Tennis, Hockey, Kricket) umpire

**schief** 1. Adj. a) (schräg) leaning ⟨wall, fence, post⟩; (nicht parallel) crooked; sloping ⟨surface⟩; worn[-down] ⟨heels⟩; b) (fig.: verzerrt) distorted ⟨picture, presentation, view, impression⟩; false ⟨comparison⟩; 2. adv. a) (schräg) das Bild hängt/der Teppich liegt ~: the picture/carpet is crooked; der Tisch steht ~: the table isn't level; b) (fig.: verzerrt) etw. ~ darstellen give a distorted account of sth.

**Schiefer** der; ~s (Gestein) slate

**schief-**: ~|gehen, ~|laufen unr. itr. V.; mit sein (ugs.) go wrong

**schielen** itr. V. a) squint; auf dem rechten Auge ~: have a squint in one's right eye; b) (ugs.: blicken) look out of the corner of one's eye

**schien** 1. u. 3. Pers. Sg. Prät. v. **scheinen**

**Schien·bein das** shinbone; **Schiene die; ~, ~n a)** rail; **b)** (Gleit~) runner; **c)** (Med.: Stütze) splint; **schienen** tr. V. jmds. Arm/ Bein ~: put sb.'s arm/leg in a splint/ splints

**schießen 1.** unr. itr. V. **a)** shoot; **auf** jmdn./etw. ~: shoot/fire at sb./sth.; **b)** mit sein (fließen, heraus~) gush; (spritzen) spurt; **c)** mit sein (schnell wachsen) shoot up; **2.** unr. tr. V. **a)** shoot; fire ⟨bullet, missile, rocket⟩; **b)** (Fußball) score ⟨goal⟩; **c)** (ugs.: fotografieren) einige Aufnahmen ~: take a few snaps; **Schießerei die; ~, ~en a)** shooting no indef. art., no pl.; **b)** (Schußwechsel) gun-battle

**Schiff das; ~⟨e⟩s, ~e a)** ship; **mit dem ~:** by ship or sea; **b)** (Archit.: Kirchen~) (Mittel~) nave; (Quer~) transept; (Seiten~) aisle; **Schiffahrt die;** o. Pl. shipping no indef. art.; (Schifffahrtskunde) navigation

**Schiff-: ~bruch der** (veralt.) shipwreck; **~brüchige der/die;** adj. Dekl. shipwrecked man/woman

**Schiffer der; ~s, ~:** boatman; (eines Lastkahns) bargee; (Kapitän) skipper

**Schiffs-: ~arzt der** ship's doctor; **~brücke die** pontoon bridge; **~junge der** ship's boy; **~reise die** voyage; (Vergnügungsreise) cruise; **~verkehr der** shipping traffic

**Schikane die; ~, ~n a)** harassment no indef. art.; **b) mit allen ~n** (ugs.) ⟨kitchen, house⟩ with all mod cons (Brit. coll.); ⟨car, bicycle, stereo⟩ with all the extras; **schikanieren** tr. V. jmdn. ~: harass sb.

**¹Schild der; ~⟨e⟩s, ~e** shield; **²Schild das; ~⟨e⟩s, ~er** sign; (Nummern~) number-plate; (Namens~) nameplate; (auf Denkmälern, Gebäuden usw.) plaque; (Etikett) label; **schildern** tr. V. describe; **Schild·kröte die** tortoise; (Seeschildkröte) turtle

**Schilf das; ~⟨e⟩s a)** reed; **b)** o. Pl. (Röhricht) reeds pl.

**schillern** itr. V. shimmer

**Schilling der; ~s, ~e** schilling

**schilt** 3. Pers. Sg. Präsens v. schelten

**Schimmel der; ~s, ~ a)** o. Pl. mould; (auf Leder, Papier) mildew; **b)** (Pferd) white horse; **schimmelig** Adj. mouldy; mildewy ⟨paper, leather⟩; **schimmeln** itr. V.; auch mit sein go mouldy; ⟨leather, paper⟩ get covered with mildew

**Schimmer der; ~s** (Schein) gleam;

(von Seide) shimmer; sheen; **keinen ~** [von etw.] **haben** (ugs.) not have the faintest idea [about sth.] (coll.); **schimmern** itr. V. gleam; ⟨water, sea⟩ glisten, shimmer; ⟨metal⟩ glint, gleam; ⟨silk etc.⟩ shimmer

**schimmlig** s. schimmelig

**Schimpanse der; ~n, ~n** chimpanzee

**schimpfen 1.** itr. V. **a)** carry on (coll.) (auf, über + Akk. about); (meckern) grumble, moan (auf, über + Akk. at); **b) mit jmdm. ~:** tell sb. off; scold sb.; **2.** tr. V. jmdn. ~: tell sb. off; **Schimpf·wort das** (Beleidigung) insult; (derbes Wort) swear-word

**schinden** unr. tr. V. maltreat; illtreat; **Zeit ~** (ugs.) play for time

**Schinken der; ~s, ~** ham; **Schinken·speck der** bacon

**Schippe die; ~, ~n** (Schaufel) shovel

**Schirm der; ~⟨e⟩s, ~e** umbrella; brolly (Brit. coll.); (Sonnen~) sunshade

**Schirm-: ~herr der** patron; **~herrin die** patroness; **~herrschaft die** patronage; **~ständer der** umbrella stand

**schiß 1. u. 3.** Pers. Sg. Prät. v. scheißen

**Schlacht die; ~, ~en** battle; **schlachten** tr. (auch itr.) V. slaughter; kill ⟨rabbit, chicken, etc.⟩; **Schlachter der; ~s, ~** (nordd.) butcher; **Schlachterei die; ~, ~en** (nordd.) butcher's [shop]

**Schlacht-: ~hof der** abattoir; **~vieh das** animals pl. kept for meat; (kurz vor der Schlachtung) animals pl. for slaughter

**Schlacke die; ~, ~n** cinders pl.; (Hochofen~) slag

**Schlaf der; ~⟨e⟩s** sleep; **einen leichten/ festen/gesunden ~ haben** be a light/ heavy/good sleeper; **Schlaf·an·zug der** pyjamas pl.; **Schläfchen das; ~s, ~:** nap; snooze (coll.)

**Schläfe die; ~, ~n** temple

**schlafen** unr. itr. V. **a)** (auch fig.) sleep; **tief od. fest ~:** be sound asleep; **lange ~:** sleep for a long time; (am Morgen) sleep in; **~ gehen** go to bed; **b)** (ugs.: nicht aufpassen) be asleep; **Schläfer der; ~s, ~:** sleeper

**schlaff 1.** Adj. **a)** slack; flabby ⟨stomach, muscles⟩; **b)** (schlapp, matt) limp ⟨body, hand, handshake⟩; shaky ⟨knees⟩; **2.** adv. **a)** slackly; **b)** (schlapp, matt) limply

**Schlaf-: ~gelegenheit die** place to sleep; **~mittel das** sleep-inducing drug

schläfrig 1. *Adj.* sleepy; 2. *adv.* sleepily
Schlaf-: ~saal der dormitory; ~sack sleeping-bag
schläft 3. *Pers. Sg. Präsens v.* schlafen
Schlaf-: ~tablette die sleeping-pill; ~wagen der sleeping-car; sleeper; ~zimmer das bedroom
Schlag der; ~[e]s, Schläge a) blow; *(Faust~)* punch; *(Klaps)* slap; *(Tennis~, Golf~)* stroke; shot; ~ auf ~ *(fig.)* in quick succession; b) *(Auf~, Aufprall)* bang; *(dumpf)* thud; *(Klopfen)* knock; c) *o. Pl. (des Herzens, Pulses)* beating; *(eines Pendels)* swinging; d) *(einzelne rhythmische Bewegung) (Herz~, Puls~, Takt~)* beat; *(eines Pendels)* swing; e) *o. Pl. (Töne) (einer Uhr)* striking; *(einer Glocke)* ringing; f) *(einzelner Ton) (Stunden~)* stroke; *(Glocken~)* ring; ~ acht Uhr on the stroke of eight
schlag-, Schlag-: ~ader die artery; ~anfall der stroke; ~artig 1. *Adj.* very sudden; 2. *adv.* quite suddenly; ~baum der barrier
schlagen 1. *unr. tr. V.* a) hit; beat; strike; *(mit der Faust)* punch; hit; *(mit der flachen Hand)* slap; b) *(mit Richtungsangabe)* hit *(ball)*; einen Nagel in etw. *(Akk.)* ~: knock a nail into sth.; c) *(rühren)* beat *(mixture)*; whip *(cream)*; *(mit einem Schneebesen)* whisk; d) *(läuten) (clock)* strike; *(bell)* ring; e) *(legen)* throw; f) *(einwickeln)* wrap (in + *Akk.* in); g) *(besiegen, übertreffen)* beat; 2. *unr. itr. V.* a) er schlug mit der Faust auf den Tisch he beat the table with his fist; b) mit den Flügeln ~ *(bird)* beat or flap its wings; c) *mit sein (prallen)* bang; mit dem Kopf auf etw. *(Akk.)/*gegen etw. ~: bang one's head on/against sth.; d) *mit sein* jmdm. auf den Magen ~: affect sb.'s stomach; e) *(pulsieren) (heart, pulse)* beat; *(heftig) (heart)* pound; *(pulse)* throb; f) *(läuten) (clock)* strike; *(bell)* ring; 3. *unr. refl. V.* fight; sich mit jmdm. ~: fight with sb.; Schlager der; ~s, ~ a) pop song; b) *(Erfolg) (Buch)* best seller; *(Ware)* best-selling line; *(Film, Stück, Lied)* hit
Schläger der; ~s, ~ a) *(Raufbold)* tough; thug; b) *(Tennis~, Federball~, Squash~)* racket; *(Tischtennis~, Kricket~)* bat; *([Eis]hockey~, Polo~)* stick; *(Golf~)* club; Schlägerei die; ~, ~en brawl; fight
Schlager·sänger der pop singer

schlag-, Schlag-: ~fertig *Adj.* quick-witted *(reply)*; *(person)* who is quick at repartee; ~fertigkeit die; *o. Pl.* quickness at repartee; ~loch das pothole; ~obers das; ~ *(österr.)*, ~rahm der *(bes. südd., österr., schweiz.)*, ~sahne die whipping cream; *(geschlagen)* whipped cream; ~zeile die headline; ~zeug das drums *pl.*
schlaksig *(ugs.) Adj.* gangling; lanky
Schlamassel der *od.* das; ~s *(ugs.)* mess
Schlamm der; ~[e]s, ~e *od.* Schlämme a) mud; b) *(Schlick)* sludge; schlammig *Adj.* a) muddy; b) *(schlickig)* sludgy; muddy
Schlamperei die; ~, ~en *(ugs. abwertend)* sloppiness; schlampig *(ugs. abwertend)* 1. *Adj.* a) *(liederlich)* slovenly; b) *(nachlässig)* sloppy; slipshod *(work)*; 2. *adv.* a) *(liederlich)* in a slovenly way; b) *(nachlässig)* sloppily
schlang *1. u. 3. Pers. Sg. Prät. v.* schlingen; Schlange die; ~, ~n a) snake; b) *(Menschen~)* queue; line *(Amer.)*; ~ stehen queue; stand in line *(Amer.)*; c) *(Auto~)* tailback *(Brit.)*; backup *(Amer.)*; schlängeln *refl. V.* *(snake)* wind [its way]; *(road)* wind, snake [its way]; Schlangen·linie die wavy line
schlank *Adj.* slim *(person)*; slim, slender *(build, figure)*; Schlankheits·kur die slimming diet
schlapp *Adj.* a) worn out; tired out; *(wegen Schwüle)* listless; *(wegen Krankheit)* run-down; b) *(ugs.: ohne Schwung)* wet *(sl.)*; feeble; c) slack *(rope, cable)*; loose *(skin)*; flabby *(stomach, muscles)*; Schlappe die; ~, ~n setback; schlapp|machen *itr. V. (ugs.)* flag; *(zusammenbrechen)* flake out *(coll.)*; *(aufgeben)* give up
schlau 1. *Adj.* a) shrewd; astute; *(gerissen)* wily; crafty; cunning; b) *(ugs.: gescheit)* clever; bright; smart; aus jmdm. nicht ~ werden *(ugs.)* not be able to make sb. out; 2. *adv.* shrewdly; astutely; *(gerissen)* craftily; cunningly
Schlauch der; ~[e]s, Schläuche a) hose; b) *(Fahrrad~, Auto~)* tube; Schlauch·boot das rubber dinghy; inflatable [dinghy]; schlauchen *(ugs.) tr., auch itr. V.* jmdn. ~: take it out of sb.; schlauch·los *Adj.* tubeless *(tyre)*
Schläue die; ~: shrewdness; astute-

ness; *(Gerissenheit)* wiliness; crafti-
ness; cunning

**Schlaufe die; ~, ~n** loop

**schlecht 1.** *Adj.* **a)** bad; poor, bad
⟨*food, quality, style, harvest, health,
circulation*⟩; poor ⟨*salary, eater, appetite*⟩; poor-quality ⟨*goods*⟩; bad, weak
⟨*eyes*⟩; **um jmdn./mit etw. steht es ~:**
sb./sth. is in a bad way; **b)** *(böse)* bad;
wicked; **c)** *nicht attr. (ungenießbar)*
off; **das Fleisch ist ~ geworden** meat
has gone off; **2.** *adv.* **a)** badly; **er
sieht/hört ~:** his sight is poor/he has
poor hearing; **über jmdn.** *od.* **von
jmdm. ~ sprechen** speak ill of sb.; **b)**
*(schwer)* **heute geht es ~:** today is difficult; **c) ~ und recht, mehr ~ als recht**
after a fashion

**schlecht-: ~bezahlt** *Adj. (präd. getrennt geschrieben)* badly *or* poorly
paid; **~|gehen** *unr. itr. V.; unpers.;
mit sein* **es geht ihr/mir ~:** she is/I am
doing badly; *(gesundheitlich)* she is/I
am ill *or* unwell *or* poorly; **~gelaunt**
*Adj. (präd. getrennt geschrieben)* bad-
tempered; **~|machen** *tr. V.* **jmdn.
~machen** run sb. down; disparage sb.

**schlecken** *(bes. südd., österr.) tr. V.*
lap up

**schleichen 1.** *unr. itr. V.; mit sein*
creep; *(heimlich)* creep; sneak; ⟨*cat*⟩
slink, creep; *(langsam fahren)* crawl
along; **2.** *unr. refl. V.* creep; sneak;
⟨*cat*⟩ slink, creep; **schleichend** *Adj.*
insidious ⟨*disease*⟩; slow[-acting]
⟨*poison*⟩; creeping ⟨*inflation*⟩; gradual
⟨*crisis*⟩

**Schleier der; ~s, ~:** veil; **schleier-
haft** *Adj.* **jmdm. ~haft sein/bleiben**
be/remain a mystery to sb.

**Schleife die; ~, ~n a)** bow; *(Fliege)*
bow-tie; **b)** *(starke Biegung)* loop

**¹schleifen** *unr. tr. V.* grind; cut ⟨*diamond, glass*⟩; *(mit Schleifpapier usw.)*
sand; *(schärfen)* sharpen

**²schleifen 1.** *tr. V.* **a)** *(auch fig.)* drag;
**b)** *(niederreißen)* raze ⟨*sth.*⟩ [to the
ground]; **2.** *itr. V.; auch mit sein* drag;
**die Kupplung ~ lassen** *(Kfz-W.)* slip
the clutch

**Schleim der; ~|e|s, ~e** mucus; *(im
Hals)* phlegm; *(von Schnecken)* slime;
**schleimig** *Adj. (auch fig.)* slimy;
*(Physiol., Zool.)* mucous

**schlemmen** *itr. V.* have a feast;
**Schlemmer der; ~s, ~:** gourmet

**schlendern** *itr. V.; mit sein* stroll

**Schlenker der; ~s, ~** *(ugs.)* swerve;
**einen ~ machen** swerve

**schlenkern** *tr., itr. V.* swing; **mit den
Armen ~:** swing one's arms

**Schleppe die; ~, ~n** train; **schleppen 1.** *tr. V.* **a)** *(ziehen)* tow ⟨*vehicle,
ship*⟩; **b)** *(tragen)* carry; lug; **c)** *(ugs.:
mitnehmen)* drag; **2.** *refl. V.* drag *or*
haul oneself; **Schlepper der; ~s, ~**
**a)** *(Schiff)* tug; **b)** *(Traktor)* tractor

**Schlepp-: ~lift der** T-bar [lift]; **~tau
das** tow-line

**Schleuder die; ~, ~n** sling; *(mit Gummiband)* catapult *(Brit.)*; slingshot
*(Amer.)*; **schleudern 1.** *tr. V.* hurl; **2.**
*itr. V.; mit sein* ⟨*vehicle*⟩ skid

**schleunigst** *Adv.* **a)** *(auf der Stelle)* at
once; immediately; straight away; **b)**
*(eilends)* hastily; with all haste

**Schleuse die; ~, ~n a)** sluice[-gate];
**b)** *(Schiffs~)* lock

**schlich** *1. u. 3. Pers. Sg. Prät. v.* **schleichen**

**schlicht 1.** *Adj.* **a)** simple; plain ⟨*pattern, furniture*⟩; **b)** *(unkompliziert)*
simple, unsophisticated ⟨*person, view,
etc.*⟩; **2.** *adv.* simply; simply, plainly
⟨*dressed, furnished*⟩

**schlichten 1.** *tr. V.* settle ⟨*argument
etc.*⟩; settle ⟨*industrial dispute etc.*⟩ by
mediation; **2.** *itr. V.* mediate

**Schlick der; ~|e|s, ~e** silt

**schlief** *1. u. 3. Pers. Sg. Prät. v.* **schlafen**

**Schließe die; ~, ~n** clasp; *(Schnalle)*
buckle; **schließen 1.** *unr. tr. V.* **a)**
close; shut; turn off ⟨*tap*⟩; fasten ⟨*belt,
bracelet*⟩; do up ⟨*button, zip*⟩; close
⟨*street, route, border, electrical circuit*⟩;
fill, close ⟨*gap*⟩; **b)** *(außer Betrieb setzen)* close [down] ⟨*shop, school*⟩; **c)**
*(ein~)* **etw./jmdn./sich in etw.** *(Akk.)*
**~:** lock sth./sb./oneself in sth.; **d)** *(beenden)* close ⟨*meeting, proceedings, debate*⟩; end, conclude ⟨*letter, speech,
lecture*⟩; **e)** *(eingehen, vereinbaren)*
conclude ⟨*treaty, pact, cease-fire,
agreement*⟩; reach ⟨*settlement, compromise*⟩; enter into ⟨*contract*⟩; **f)** *(folgern)* infer **(aus** from**); 2.** *unr. itr. V.* **a)**
close, shut; **b)** *(enden)* end; conclude;
**c)** **|aus etw.| auf etw.** *(Akk.)* **~:** infer
sth. [from sth.]; **3.** *unr. refl. V.* ⟨*door,
window*⟩ close, shut; ⟨*wound, circle*⟩
close; **Schließ·fach das** locker; *(bei
der Post)* PO box; *(bei der Bank)* safe-
deposit box; **schließlich** *Adv.* **a)** finally; in the end; **b)** *(immerhin, doch)*
after all

**schliff** *1. u. 3. Pers. Sg. Prät. v.* **schleifen**

**Schliff** der; ~[e]s, ~e a) o. Pl. cutting; (von Messern, Sensen usw.) sharpening; b) (Art, wie etw. geschliffen wird) cut; (von Messern, Scheren usw.) edge; c) o. Pl. **einem Brief/Text** usw. **den letzten ~ geben** put the finishing touches pl. to a letter/text etc.

**schlimm** 1. Adj. a) grave, serious ⟨error, mistake, accusation, offence⟩; bad, serious ⟨error, mistake⟩; b) (übel) bad; nasty, bad ⟨experience⟩; **[das ist alles] halb so ~**: it's not as bad as all that; **ist nicht ~!** [it] doesn't matter; 2. adv. **~ d[a]ran sein** be in a bad way; (in einer ~en Situation) be in dire straits; **schlimmsten·falls** Adv. if the worst comes to the worst

**Schlinge** die; ~, ~n a) loop; (für den Arm) sling; (zum Aufhängen) noose; b) (Fanggerät) snare

**schlingen** 1. unr. tr. V. etw. um etw. ~: loop sth. round sth.; 2. unr. refl. V. **sich um etw. ~**: wind itself round sth; 3. unr. itr. V. bolt one's food

**schlingern** itr. V.; mit sein ⟨ship, boat⟩ roll; ⟨train, vehicle⟩ lurch from side to side

**Schlips** der; ~es, ~e tie

**Schlitten** der; ~s, ~: sledge; sled; (Pferde~) sleigh; (Rodel~) toboggan; **~ fahren** go tobogganing

**schlittern** itr. V. slide

**Schlitt-:** ~**schuh** der [ice-]skate; ~**schuh laufen** od. **fahren** [ice-]skate; ~**schuh·laufen** das [ice-]skating no art.; ~**schuh·läufer** der [ice-]skater

**Schlitz** der; ~es, ~e a) slit; (Briefkasten~, Automaten~) slot; b) (Hosen~) flies pl.; fly

**schloß** 1. u. 3. Pers. Sg. Prät. v. **schließen**

**Schloß** das; Schlosses, Schlösser a) lock; (Vorhänge~) padlock; **hinter ~ und Riegel** (ugs.) behind bars; b) (Verschluß) clasp; c) (Wohngebäude) castle; (Palast) palace; (Herrschaftshaus) mansion

**Schlosser** der; ~s, ~: metalworker; (Maschinen~) fitter; (für Schlösser) locksmith; (Auto~) mechanic

**Schlot** der; ~[e]s, ~e od. **Schlöte** chimney[-stack]; (eines Schiffes) funnel

**schlottern** itr. V. a) shake; b) ⟨clothes⟩ hang loose

**Schlucht** die; ~, ~en ravine

**schluchzen** itr. V. sob

**Schluck** der; ~[e]s, ~e od. **Schlücke** swallow; mouthful; (großer ~) gulp; (kleiner ~) sip; **Schluck·auf** der; ~s

hiccups pl.; **Schlückchen** das; ~s, ~: sip; **schlucken** 1. tr. V. swallow; etw. hastig ~: gulp sth. down; 2. itr. V. swallow; **Schlucker** der; ~s, ~: **armer ~** (ugs.) poor devil or (Brit. coll.) blighter

**schluderig** s. schludrig; **schludern** itr. V. (ugs.) work sloppily; **schludrig** (ugs.) 1. Adj. a) slipshod ⟨work, examination⟩; botched ⟨job⟩; slapdash ⟨person, work⟩; b) (schlampig [aussehend]) scruffy; 2. adv. a) in a slipshod or slapdash way; b) (schlampig) scruffily

**schlug** 1. u. 3. Pers. Sg. Prät. v. **schlagen**

**Schlummer** der; ~s (geh.) slumber (poet./rhet.); **schlummern** itr. V. (geh.) slumber (poet./rhet.)

**Schlund** der; ~[e]s, **Schlünde** [back of the] throat; pharynx (Anat.)

**schlüpfen** itr. V.; mit sein slip; [aus dem Ei] ~: ⟨chick⟩ hatch out

**Schlüpfer** der; ~s, ~ (für Damen) knickers pl. (Brit.); panties pl.; (für Herren) [under]pants pl. or trunks pl.

**schlüpfrig** Adj. a) slippery; b) (anstößig) lewd

**schlurfen** itr. V.; mit sein shuffle

**schlürfen** 1. tr. V. slurp [up] (coll.); 2. itr. V. slurp (coll.)

**Schluß** der; Schlusses, Schlüsse a) end; (eines Vortrags o. ä.) conclusion; (eines Buchs, Schauspiels usw.) ending; **am** od. **zum ~**: at the end; (schließlich) in the end; b) (Folgerung) conclusion

**Schlüssel** der; ~s, ~: key

**Schlüssel-:** ~**bein** das collar-bone; clavicle (Anat.); ~**blume** die cowslip; (Primel) primula; ~**bund** der od. das bunch of keys; ~**loch** das keyhole

**schlüssig** 1. Adj. a) conclusive ⟨proof, evidence⟩; convincing, logical ⟨argument, conclusion⟩; b) **sich** (Dat.) ~ **werden** make up one's mind; 2. adv. conclusively

**Schluß-:** ~**licht** das; Pl. ~**lichter** tail- or rear-light; ~**strich** der [bottom] line; ~**verkauf** der [end-of-season] sale[s pl.]

**schmächtig** Adj. slight

**schmackhaft** Adj. tasty

**schmal** ~er od. schmäler, ~st... od. schmälst... Adj. narrow; slim, slender ⟨hips, hands, figure, etc.⟩; thin ⟨lips, face, nose, etc.⟩; **schmälern** tr. V. diminish; restrict ⟨rights⟩

**¹Schmalz** das; ~es dripping; (Schweine~) lard; **²Schmalz** der; ~es *(abwertend)* schmaltz *(coll.);* **Schmalz·brot** das slice of bread and dripping; **schmalzig** *(abwertend)* 1. *Adj.* schmaltzy *(coll.);* 2. *adv.* with slushy sentimentality

**schmarotzen** *itr. V. (fig.)* sponge; free-load *(sl.)*

**Schmarren** der; ~s, ~ *(österr., auch südd.)* pancake broken up with a fork *after frying*

**schmatzen** *itr. V.* smack one's lips; *(geräuschvoll essen)* eat noisily

**Schmaus** der; ~es, Schmäuse *(veralt., scherzh.)* [good] spread *(coll.)*

**schmecken** 1. *itr. V.* taste (**nach** of); |**gut**| ~: taste good; **schmeckt es** [**dir**]? are you enjoying it *or* your meal?; 2. *tr. V.* taste; *(kosten)* sample

**schmeicheln** *itr. V.* jmdm. ~: flatter sb.; **Schmeichler** der; ~s, ~: flatterer

**schmeißen** *(ugs.)* 1. *unr. tr. V.* chuck *(coll.);* sling *(coll.); (schleudern)* fling; hurl; 2. *unr. refl. V.* throw oneself; *(mit Wucht)* hurl oneself; 3. *unr. itr. V.* **mit etw.** [**nach jmdm.**] ~: chuck sth. [at sb.] *(coll.)*

**Schmeiß·fliege** die blowfly; *(blaue ~)* bluebottle

**schmelzen** 1. *unr. itr. V.; mit sein* melt; *(fig.)* ⟨doubts, apprehension, etc.⟩ dissolve, fade away; 2. *unr. tr. V.* melt; smelt ⟨ore⟩; render ⟨fat⟩; **Schmelz·käse** der processed cheese

**Schmerz** der; ~es, ~en a) *(physisch)* pain; *(dumpf u. anhaltend)* ache; **wo haben Sie ~en?** where does it hurt?; ~**en haben** be in pain; b) *(psychisch)* pain; *(Kummer)* grief; **schmerz-empfindlich** *Adj.* sensitive to pain *pred.;* **schmerzen** 1. *tr. V.* jmdn. ~: hurt sb.; *(jmdm. Kummer bereiten)* grieve sb.; cause sb. sorrow; 2. *itr. V.* hurt; **schmerzhaft** *Adj.* painful; **schmerzlich** 1. *Adj.* painful; distressing; 2. *adv.* painfully

**schmerz-, Schmerz-:** ~**los** 1. *Adj.* painless; 2. *adv.* painlessly; ~**stillend** *Adj.* pain-killing; ~**tablette** die pain-killing tablet

**Schmetterling** der; ~s, ~e butterfly

**schmettern** 1. *tr. V.* a) hurl (**an** + *Akk.* at, **gegen** against); b) *(laut spielen, singen usw.)* blare out ⟨march, music⟩; ⟨person⟩ sing lustily ⟨song⟩; c) *(Tennis usw.)* smash ⟨ball⟩; 2. *itr. V.* ⟨trumpet, music, etc.⟩ blare out

**Schmied** der; ~|e|s, ~e blacksmith; **Schmiede** die; ~, ~**n** smithy; forge; **schmieden** *tr. V. (auch fig.)* forge

**schmiegen** 1. *refl. V.* snuggle, nestle (**in** + *Akk.* in); **sich an jmdn.** ~: snuggle [close] up to sb.; 2. *tr. V.* press (**an** + *Akk.* against)

**schmieren** 1. *tr. V.* a) lubricate; b) *(streichen)* spread ⟨butter, jam, etc.⟩ (**auf** + *Akk.* on); **Brote** ~: spread slices of bread; 2. *itr. V.* a) ⟨oil, grease⟩ lubricate; b) *(ugs: unsauber schreiben)* ⟨person⟩ scrawl, scribble; ⟨pen, ink⟩ smudge, make smudges; **schmierig** *Adj.* greasy; **Schmier·seife** die soft soap

**schmilzt** 2. u. 3. Pers. Sg. Präsens v. schmelzen

**Schminke** die; ~, ~n make-up; **schminken** 1. *tr. V.* make up ⟨face, eyes⟩; 2. *refl. V.* make oneself up

**Schmirgel·papier** das emery-paper; *(Sandpapier)* sandpaper

**schmiß** 1. u. 3. Pers. Sg. Prät. v. schmeißen

**Schmöker** der; ~s, ~ *(ugs.)* lightweight adventure story/romance; **schmökern** *(ugs.)* 1. *itr. V.* bury oneself in a book; 2. *tr. V.* bury oneself in ⟨book⟩

**schmollen** *itr. V.* sulk; **Schmoll-mund** der pouting mouth

**schmolz** 1. u. 3. Pers. Sg. Prät. v. schmelzen

**Schmor·braten** der braised beef; **schmoren** 1. *tr. V.* braise; 2. *itr. V.* a) braise; b) *(ugs.: schwitzen)* swelter

**schmuck** *Adj.* attractive

**Schmuck** der; ~|e|s a) *(~stücke)* jewelry; jewellery *(esp. Brit.);* b) *s.* ~**stück**; c) *(Zierde)* decoration

**schmücken** *tr. V.* decorate; embellish ⟨writings, speech⟩

**schmuck-, Schmuck-:** ~**kästchen** das, ~**kasten** der jewelry *or (esp. Brit.)* jewellery box; ~**los** *Adj.* plain; bare ⟨room⟩; ~**stück** das piece of jewelry *or (esp. Brit.)* jewellery

**schmuddelig** *Adj. (ugs.)* grubby; mucky *(coll.); (schmutzig u. unordentlich)* messy; grotty *(Brit. sl.)*

**Schmuggel** der; ~s smuggling *no art.;* **schmuggeln** *tr., itr. V.* smuggle (**in** + *Akk.* into; **aus** out of); **Schmuggler** der; ~s, ~: smuggler

**schmunzeln** *itr. V.* smile to oneself

**schmusen** *itr. V. (ugs.)* cuddle; ⟨couple⟩ kiss and cuddle

**Schmutz** der; ~es dirt; *(Schlamm)* mud; **schmutzen** *itr. V.* get dirty; **schmutzig** *Adj.* dirty

**Schnabel** der; ~s, Schnäbel **a)** beak; **b)** *(ugs.: Mund)* gob *(sl.)*

**Schnake** die; ~, ~n **a)** daddy-long-legs; **b)** *(bes. südd.: Stechmücke)* mosquito

**Schnalle** die; ~, ~n *(Gürtel~)* buckle; **schnallen** *tr. V.* **a)** *(mit einer Schnalle festziehen)* buckle *(shoe, belt)*; fasten *(strap)*; **b)** *(mit Riemen/Gurten befestigen)* strap *(auf + Akk.* on to)

**schnalzen** *itr. V.* |mit der Zunge/den Fingern| ~: click one's tongue/snap one's fingers

**schnappen 1.** *itr. V.* **nach** jmdm./etw. ~ *(animal)* snap at sb./sth.; **nach Luft** ~: gasp for breath; **2.** *tr. V. (dog, bird, etc.)* snatch; [sich *(Dat.)*] jmdn./etw. ~ *(ugs.)* *(person)* grab sb./sth.; *(mit raschem Zugriff)* snatch sb./sth.; **Schnapp·schuß** der snapshot

**Schnaps** der; ~es, Schnäpse **a)** spirit; *(Klarer)* schnapps; **b)** *o. Pl. (Spirituosen)* spirits *pl.*

**schnarchen** *itr. V.* snore

**schnattern** *itr. V.* **a)** *(goose etc.)* cackle, gaggle; **b)** *(ugs.: eifrig schwatzen)* jabber [away]; chatter

**schnauben** *itr. V.* snort (vor with)

**schnaufen** *itr. V.* puff (vor with)

**Schnauze** die; ~, ~n **a)** *(von Tieren)* muzzle; *(der Maus usw.)* snout; *(Maul)* mouth; **b)** *(derb: Mund)* gob *(sl.)*; |halt die| ~! shut your trap! *(sl.)*; **schnauzen** *tr., itr. V. (ugs.)* bark; *(ärgerlich)* snap; snarl

**Schnecke** die snail; *(Nackt~)* slug; **Schnecken·haus** das snail-shell

**Schnee** der; ~s snow

**Schnee-:** ~**ball** der snowball; ~**besen** der whisk; ~**flocke** die snowflake; ~**gestöber** das snow flurry; ~**glöckchen** das snowdrop; ~**kette** die snow-chain; ~**matsch** der slush; ~**pflug** der snow-plough; ~**sturm** der snowstorm

**Schneewittchen (das)** Snow White

**Schneide** die; ~, ~n [cutting] edge; **schneiden 1.** *unr. itr. V.* cut (in + Akk. into); **2.** *unr. tr. V.* **a)** cut; *(in Scheiben)* slice *(bread, sausage, etc.)*; *(klein ~)* cut up, chop *(wood, vegetables)*; *(stutzen)* prune *(tree, bush)*; trim *(beard)*; cut, mow *(grass)*; **sich** *(Dat.)* die Haare ~ lassen have one's hair cut; **b)** eine Kurve ~: cut a corner

**Schneider** der; ~s, ~: tailor; *(Da-*

*men~)* dressmaker; **Schneiderei** die; ~, ~en tailor's shop; *(Damen~)* dressmaker's shop; **Schneiderin** die; ~, ~nen *s.* **Schneider**; **schneidern** *tr. V.* make; make, tailor *(suit)*

**Schneide·zahn** der incisor

**schneien 1.** *itr., tr. V. (unpers.)* snow; **es schneit** it is snowing; **2.** *itr. V.; mit sein (fig.)* rain down; fall like snow

**Schneise** die; ~, ~n *(Wald~)* aisle; *(als Feuerschutz)* firebreak

**schnell 1.** *Adj.* quick *(journey, decision, service, etc.)*; fast *(car, skis, road, track, etc.)*; quick, swift *(progress, movement, blow, action)*; **2.** *adv.* quickly; *(drive, move, etc.)* fast, quickly; *(spread)* quickly, rapidly; *(bald)* soon *(sold, past, etc.)*; **mach** ~! *(ugs.)* move it! *(coll.)*; **schnellen** *itr. V.; mit sein* shoot (aus + Dat. out of; in + Akk. into); **Schnelligkeit** die; ~, ~en speed; **Schnell·imbiß** der snack-bar; **schnellstens** *Adv.* as quickly as possible

**Schnell-:** ~**straße** die expressway; ~**zug** der express [train]

**Schnepfe** die; ~, ~n snipe

**schneuzen 1.** *tr. V.* sich *(Dat.)*/einem Kind die Nase ~: blow one's/a child's nose; **2.** *refl. V.* blow one's nose

**schnippeln** *(ugs.)* **1.** *itr. V.* snip [away] (an + Dat. at); **2.** *tr. V.* shred *(vegetables)*; chop *(beans etc.)* [finely]

**schnippen 1.** *itr. V.* snap one's fingers (nach at); **2.** *tr. V.* flick (von off, from)

**schnippisch 1.** *Adj.* pert *(reply, tone, etc.)*; **2.** *adv.* pertly

**Schnipsel** der od. das; ~s, ~: scrap; *(Papier~, Stoff~)* snippet; shred

**schnipseln** *s.* schnippeln

**schnitt** *1. u. 3. Pers. Sg. Prät. v.* schneiden

**Schnitt** der; ~[e]s, ~e **a)** cut; **b)** *(das Mähen) (von Gras)* mowing; *(von Getreide)* harvest

**Schnitt-:** ~**blume** die cut flower; ~**bohne** die French bean

**Schnitte** die; ~, ~n slice; **eine ~** [Brot] a slice of bread; **schnittig 1.** *Adj.* stylish, smart *(suit, appearance, etc.)*; *(sportlich)* racy *(car, yacht, etc.)*; **2.** *adv.* stylishly; *(sportlich)* racily

**Schnitt-:** ~**lauch** der chives *pl.*; ~**wunde** die cut; *(lang u. tief)* gash

**Schnitzel** das; ~s, ~ **a)** *(Fleisch)* [veal/pork] escalope; **b)** *(von Papier)* scrap; *(von Holz)* shaving; **schnitzeln** *tr. V.*

**chop up** ⟨*vegetables*⟩ [into small pieces]; shred ⟨*cabbage*⟩; **schnịtzen** *tr., itr. V.* carve

**schnọdderig** *(ugs.)* 1. *Adj.* brash; 2. *adv.* brashly

**schnöde** *(geh.)* 1. *Adj.* a) *(verachtenswert)* contemptible; b) *(gemein)* contemptuous, scornful ⟨*glance, reply, etc.*⟩. 2. *adv. (gemein)* contemptuously; ⟨*exploit, misuse*⟩ flagrantly

**Schnọ̈rkel** der; ~s, ~: scroll; *(der Handschrift, in der Rede)* flourish

**schnọrren** *tr., itr. V. (ugs.)* scrounge *(coll.)* (bei, von + *Dat.* off); **Schnọrrer** der; ~s, ~ *(ugs.)* scrounger *(coll.)*

**schnüffeln** *itr. V.* a) sniff; b) *(ugs.: spionieren)* snoop [about] *(coll.)*; **Schnüffler** der; ~s, ~ *(ugs.)* Nosey Parker; *(Spion)* snooper *(coll.)*

**schnupfen** 1. *tr. V.* sniff; **Tabak** ~: take snuff; 2. *itr. V.* take snuff; **Schnupfen** der; ~s, ~: [head] cold; **Schnupf·tabak** der snuff

**schnuppe: das/er ist mir ~/mir völlig ~** *(ugs.)* I don't care/I couldn't care less about it/him *(coll.)*

**schnuppern** *itr. V.* sniff; **an etw.** *(Dat.)* ~: sniff sth.

**Schnur** die; ~, **Schnüre** a) *(Bindfaden)* piece of string; *(Kordel)* piece of cord; b) *(ugs.: Kabel)* flex *(Brit.)*; lead; cord *(Amer.)*; **schnüren** *tr. V.* tie ⟨*bundle, string, etc.*⟩; tie, lace up ⟨*shoe, corset, etc.*⟩

**Schnurr·bart** der moustache; **schnurren** *itr. V.* ⟨*cat*⟩ purr; ⟨*machine*⟩ hum

**Schnür-:** ~**schuh** der lace-up shoe; ~**senkel** der; ~s, ~ *(bes. nordd.)* [shoe-]lace; *(für Stiefel)* bootlace

**schob** *1. u. 3. Pers. Prät. v.* schieben

**Schọck** der; ~[e]s, ~s shock; **schọkkieren** *tr. V.* shock; **über etw.** *(Akk.)* schockiert sein be shocked at sth.

**Schöffe** der; ~n, ~n lay judge *(acting together with another lay judge and a professional judge)*; **Schöffen·gericht** das *court presided over by a professional judge and two lay judges*

**Schokolade** die; ~, ~n a) chocolate; b) *(Getränk)* [drinking] chocolate

**Schokolade[n]-:** ~**eis** das chocolate ice-cream; ~**guß** der chocolate icing; ~**pudding** der chocolate blancmange; ~**torte** die chocolate cake *or* gateau

**schọll** *1. u. 3. Pers. Sg. Prät. v.* schallen

**Schọlle** die; ~, ~n a) *(Erd~)* clod [of

earth]; b) *(Eis~)* [ice-]floe; c) *(Fisch)* plaice

**schọn** 1. *Adv.* a) *(bereits) (oft nicht übersetzt)* already; *(in Fragen)* yet; **wie lange bist du ~ hier?** how long have you been here?; b) *(fast gleichzeitig)* there and then; c) *(jetzt)* ~ |mal| now; *(inzwischen)* meanwhile; d) *(selbst, sogar)* even; *(nur)* only; e) *(ohne Ergänzung, ohne weiteren Zusatz)* on its own; |allein| ~ **der Gedanke daran** the mere thought of it; ~ **deshalb** for this reason alone; f) *(wohl)* really; **Lust hätte ich ~, aber ...**: I'd certainly like to, but ...; 2. *Partikel* a) *(ugs. ungeduldig: endlich)* **nun komm ~!** come on!; hurry up!; b) *(beruhigend: bestimmt)* all right; c) *(durchaus)* **das ist ~ möglich** that is quite possible

**schön** 1. *Adj.* a) beautiful; handsome ⟨*youth, man*⟩; b) *(angenehm)* pleasant, nice ⟨*day, holiday, dream, relaxation, etc.*⟩; fine ⟨*weather*⟩; *(nett)* nice; **das war eine ~e Zeit** those were wonderful days; c) *(gut)* good; d) *(in Höflichkeitsformeln)* ~e **Grüße** best wishes; **recht ~en Dank für ...**: thank you very much for ...; e) ~! *(ugs.: einverstanden)* OK *(coll.)*; all right; f) *(iron.: leer)* ~e **Worte** fine[-sounding] words; *(schmeichlerisch)* honeyed words; g) *(ugs.: beträchtlich)* handsome, *(coll.)* tidy ⟨*sum, fortune, profit*⟩; considerable ⟨*quantity, distance*⟩; pretty good ⟨*pension*⟩; h) *(iron.: unerfreulich)* nice *(coll. iron.)*; **das sind ja ~e Aussichten!** this is a fine look-out *sing. (iron.)*; 2. *adv.* a) beautifully; b) *(angenehm, erfreulich)* nicely; ~ **warm/weich/langsam** nice and warm/soft/slow; c) *(gut)* well; d) *(in Höflichkeitsformeln)* **bitte** ~, **können Sie mir sagen, ...**: excuse me, could you tell me ...; e) *(iron.)* **wie es so ~ heißt, wie man so ~ sagt** as they say; f) *(ugs.: beträchtlich)* really; *(vor einem Adjektiv)* pretty; **ganz ~ arbeiten müssen** have to work jolly hard *(Brit. coll.)*; 3. *Partikel (ugs.)* **bleib ~ liegen!** lie there and be good

**schonen** 1. *tr. V.* treat ⟨*clothes, books, furniture, etc.*⟩ with care; *(schützen)* protect ⟨*hands, furniture*⟩; *(nicht strapazieren)* spare ⟨*voice, eyes, etc.*⟩; conserve ⟨*strength*⟩; 2. *refl. V.* take things easy

**Schönheit** die; ~, ~en beauty

**Schönheits-:** ~**chirurgie** die cosmetic surgery *no art.*; ~**pflege** die beauty care *no art.*

**Schon·kost** die light food

**schön|machen** *(ugs.)* **1.** *tr. V.* smarten ⟨*person, thing*⟩ up; make ⟨*person, thing*⟩ look nice; **2.** *refl. V.* smarten oneself up

**schonungs|los 1.** *Adj.* unsparing, ruthless ⟨*criticism etc.*⟩; blunt ⟨*frankness*⟩; **2.** *adv.* unsparingly; ⟨*say*⟩ without mincing one's words

**Schopf** der; ~|e|s, Schöpfe shock of hair

**schöpfen** *tr. V.* **a)** scoop [up] ⟨*water, liquid*⟩; *(mit einer Kelle)* ladle ⟨*soup*⟩; **b)** *(geh.: einatmen)* draw, take ⟨*breath*⟩

**Schöpfer** der; ~s, ~: creator; *(Gott)* Creator; **schöpferisch 1.** *Adj.* creative; **2.** *adv.* creatively

**Schöpf-:** ~**kelle** die, ~**löffel** der ladle

**Schöpfung** die; ~, ~en *(geh.)* creation; **die** ~ *(die Welt)* Creation

**Schoppen** der; ~s, ~: [quarter-litre/half-litre] glass of wine/beer

**schor** *1. u. 3. Pers. Sg. Prät. v.* **scheren**

**Schorf** der; ~|e|s, ~e scab

**Schorn·stein** der chimney; *(Lokomotiv~, Schiffs~)* funnel; **Schornstein·feger** der; ~s, ~: chimney-sweep

**schoß** *1. u. 3. Pers. Sg. Prät. v.* **schießen**

**Schoß** der; ~es, Schöße lap

**Schote** die; ~, ~n pod

**Schotte** der; ~n, ~n Scot; Scotsman; **die** ~**n** the Scots; the Scottish; **Schotten·rock** der tartan skirt; *(Kilt)* kilt; **Schottin** die; ~, ~nen Scot; Scotswoman; **schottisch** *Adj.* Scottish; ~**er Whisky** Scotch whisky; **Schottland (das)**; ~s Scotland

**schräg 1.** *Adj.* diagonal ⟨*line, beam, cut, etc.*⟩; sloping ⟨*surface, roof, wall, side, etc.*⟩; slanting, slanted ⟨*writing, eyes, etc.*⟩; tilted ⟨*position of the head etc., axis*⟩; **2.** *adv.* at an angle; *(diagonal)* diagonally; **Schräge** die; ~, ~n **a)** *(schräge Fläche)* sloping surface; **b)** *(Neigung)* slope

**schrak** *1. u. 3. Pers. Sg. Prät. v.* **schrecken**

**Schramme** die; ~, ~n scratch; **schrammen** *tr. V.* scratch

**Schrank** der; ~|e|s, Schränke cupboard; closet *(Amer.)*; *(Glas~; kleiner Wand~)* cabinet; *(Kleider~)* wardrobe; *(Bücher~)* bookcase; **Schränkchen das**; ~s, ~: cabinet

**Schranke** die; ~, ~n **a)** *(auch fig.)* barrier; **b)** *(fig.: Grenze)* limit

**Schraube** die; ~, ~n bolt; *(Holz~, Blech~)* screw; **schrauben** *tr. V.* **a)** *s.* **Schraube:** bolt/screw **(an, auf +** **Akk.** on to); **b)** *(drehen)* screw ⟨*nut, hook, light-bulb, etc.*⟩ **(auf +** **Akk.** on to; **in +** **Akk.** into)

**Schrauben-:** ~**schlüssel** der spanner; ~**zieher** der; ~s, ~: screwdriver

**Schraub·verschluß** der screw-top

**Schreber·garten** der ≈ allotment *(cultivated primarily as a garden)*

**Schreck** der; ~|e|s, ~e fright; scare; *(Schock)* shock; **jmdm. einen** ~ **einjagen** give sb. a fright; **schrecken** *regelm. (auch unr.) itr. V.* start [up]; **aus dem Schlaf** ~: awake with a start; start from one's sleep; **Schrecken** der; ~s, ~: fright; scare; *(Entsetzen)* horror; *(große Angst)* terror; **jmdm. einen** ~ **einjagen** give sb. a fright; **schreckhaft** *Adj.* easily scared; **schrecklich 1.** *Adj.* terrible; **2.** *adv.* terribly

**Schrei** der; ~|e|s, ~e cry; *(lauter Ruf)* shout; *(durchdringend)* yell; *(gellend)* scream; *(kreischend)* shriek

**Schreib·block** der; *Pl.* ~**blocks** od. ~**blöcke** writing-pad

**schreiben 1.** *unr. itr. V.* write; *(mit der Schreibmaschine)* type; **an einem Roman usw.** ~: be writing a novel *etc.*; **jmdm.** od. **an jmdn.** ~: write to sb.; **2.** *unr. tr. V.* **a)** write; *(mit der Schreibmaschine)* type; **wie schreibt man dieses Wort?** how is this word spelt?; **3.** *unr. refl. V.* be spelt; **Schreiben das**; ~s, ~ **a)** *o. Pl.* writing *no def. art.*; **b)** *(Brief)* letter; **Schreiber** der; ~s, ~: writer; *(Verfasser)* author; **Schreiberin** die; ~, ~en writer; *(Verfasserin)* authoress

**Schreib-:** ~**maschine** die typewriter; ~**maschinen·papier** das typing paper; ~**papier** das writing-paper; ~**tisch** der desk

**Schreibung** die; ~, ~en spelling

**Schreib-:** ~**waren** *Pl.* stationery *sing.*; ~**waren·geschäft** das stationer's

**schreien** *unr. itr. V.* ⟨*person*⟩ cry [out]; *(laut rufen/sprechen)* shout; *(durchdringend)* yell; *(gellend)* scream; ⟨*baby*⟩ yell, bawl; **zum Schreien sein** *(ugs.)* be a scream *(sl.)*

**Schreiner** der; ~s, ~ *(bes. südd.)* s. **Tischler**

**schreiten** *unr. itr. V.*; *mit sein (geh.)* walk; *(mit großen Schritten)* stride

**schrickst** *2. Pers. Sg. Präsens v.*

schrecken; **schrickt** 3. *Pers. Sg. Präsens v.* schrecken

schrie *1. u. 3. Pers. Sg. Prät. v.* schreien

schrieb *1. u. 3. Pers. Sg. Prät. v.* schreiben; **Schrieb** der; ~|e|s, ~e *(ugs.)* missive *(coll.)*

**Schrift** die; ~, ~en a) *(System)* script; *(Alphabet)* alphabet; b) *(Hand~)* [hand]writing; c) *(Werk)* work; **schriftlich** 1. *Adj.* written; 2. *adv.* in writing

**Schrift-:** ~steller der; ~s, ~: writer; ~stück das [official] document; ~wechsel der correspondence

**schrill** 1. *Adj.* shrill; 2. *adv.* shrilly; **schrillen** *itr. V.* shrill; sound shrilly

**schritt** *1. u. 3. Pers. Sg. Prät. v.* schreiten; **Schritt** der; ~|e|s, ~e a) step; einen ~ machen *od.* tun take a step; b) *Pl. (Geräusch)* footsteps; c) *(Entfernung)* pace; d) *(Gleich~)* aus dem ~ kommen get out of step; e) *o. Pl. (Gangart)* walk; **seinen ~ verlangsamen/beschleunigen** slow/quicken one's pace; [mit jmdm./etw.] ~ halten *(auch fig.)* keep up *or* keep pace [with sb./sth.]; f) *(~geschwindigkeit)* walking pace; „~ fahren" 'dead slow'; g) *(fig.: Maßnahme)* step; measure; **Schritt·geschwindigkeit die** walking pace

**schroff** 1. *Adj.* a) precipitous ⟨rock etc.⟩; b) *(plötzlich)* sudden ⟨transition, change⟩; *(kraß)* stark ⟨contrast⟩; c) *(barsch)* curt ⟨refusal, manner⟩; brusque ⟨manner, behaviour, tone⟩; 2. *adv.* a) ⟨rise, drop⟩ sheer; ⟨fall away⟩ precipitously; b) *(plötzlich, unvermittelt)* suddenly; c) *(barsch)* curtly; ⟨interrupt⟩ abruptly; ⟨treat⟩ brusquely

**schröpfen** *tr. V. (ugs.)* fleece

**Schrot** der *od.* das; ~|e|s, ~e a) coarse meal; *(aus Getreide)* whole meal *(Brit.)*; whole grain; b) *(Munition)* shot; **schroten** *tr. V.* grind ⟨grain etc.⟩ [coarsely]; crush ⟨malt⟩ [coarsely]

**Schrot-:** ~flinte die shotgun; ~kugel die pellet

**Schrott** der; ~|e|s, ~e a) scrap [-metal]; **ein Auto zu ~ fahren** *(ugs.)* write a car off; b) *o. Pl. (salopp fig.)* rubbish; **schrott·reif** *Adj.* ready for the scrap-heap *postpos.*

**schrubben** *tr. (auch itr.) V.* scrub; **Schrubber** der; ~s, ~: [long-handled] scrubbing-brush

**Schrulle** die; ~, ~n cranky idea; *(Marotte)* quirk

**schrumpelig** *Adj. (ugs.)* wrinkly; **schrumpeln** *itr. V.; mit sein (ugs.)* ⟨skin⟩ go wrinkled; ⟨apple etc.⟩ shrivel

**schrumpfen** *itr. V.; mit sein* shrink; ⟨metal, rock⟩ contract; ⟨apple etc.⟩ shrivel; ⟨skin⟩ go wrinkled; *(abnehmen)* decrease; ⟨supplies, capital, hopes⟩ dwindle

**Schub** der; ~|e|s, Schübe a) *(Physik: ~kraft)* thrust; b) *(Med.: Phase)* phase; stage; c) *(Gruppe, Anzahl)* batch

**Schuber** der; ~s, ~: slip-case

**Schub-:** ~karre die, ~karren der wheelbarrow; ~lade die drawer

**Schubs** der; ~es, ~e *(ugs.)* shove; **schubsen** *tr. (auch itr.) V. (ugs.)* push; shove

**schüchtern** 1. *Adj.* a) shy ⟨person, smile, etc.⟩; shy, timid ⟨voice, knock, etc.⟩; b) *(fig.: zaghaft)* tentative, cautious ⟨attempt, beginnings, etc.⟩; 2. *adv.* shyly; ⟨knock, ask, etc.⟩ timidly; **Schüchternheit die; ~:** shyness

**Schuft** der; ~|e|s, ~e scoundrel

**schuften** *(ugs.) itr. V.* slave away

**Schuh** der; ~|e|s, ~e shoe; *(hoher ~, Stiefel)* boot; **jmdm. etw. in die ~e schieben** *(fig. ugs.)* pin the blame for sth. on sb.

**Schuh-:** ~creme die shoe-polish; ~größe die shoe size; **welche ~größe hast du?** what size shoe[s] do you take?; ~macher der; ~s, ~: shoemaker; ~sohle die sole [of a/one's shoe]

**Schul-:** ~abschluß der schoolleaving qualification; ~buch das school-book; ~bus der school bus

**schuld** *s.* Schuld b; **Schuld** die; ~, ~en a) *o. Pl.* guilt; **er ist sich *(Dat.)* keiner ~ bewußt** he is not conscious of having done any wrong; b) *o. Pl. (Verantwortlichkeit)* blame; **es ist [nicht] seine ~:** it is [not] his fault; [an etw. *(Dat.)*] **schuld haben** *od.* **sein** be to blame [for sth.]; c) *(Verpflichtung zur Rückzahlung)* debt; ~en haben have debts of 5,000 marks, owe 5,000 marks; **schuld·bewußt** 1. *Adj.* guilty ⟨look, face, etc.⟩; 2. *adv.* guiltily; **schulden** *tr. V.* owe; **was schulde ich Ihnen?** how much do I owe you?; **Schuld·gefühl das** feeling of guilt; **schuldig** *Adj.* a) guilty; **der [an dem Unfall] ~e Autofahrer** the driver to blame [for the accident]; b) **jmdm. etw. ~ sein/bleiben** owe sb. sth.; c) *(gebührend)* due; proper; **Schuldige**

**der/die**; *adj. Dekl.* guilty person; *(im Strafprozeß)* guilty party; **schuld·los** *Adj.* innocent (**an** + *Dat.* of); **Schuld·spruch** der verdict of guilty

**Schule** die; ~, ~n a) school; **zur** *od.* **die ~ gehen, die ~ besuchen** go to school; **auf** *od.* **in der ~:** at school; **schulen** *tr. V.* train; **Schüler** der; ~s, ~: pupil; *(Schuljunge)* schoolboy; **Schülerin** die; ~, ~nen pupil; *(Schulmädchen)* schoolgirl

**schul-, Schul-:** ~**ferien** *Pl.* school holidays *or (Amer.)* vacation *sing.*; ~**frei** *Adj.* ⟨*day*⟩ off school; ~**hof** der school yard; ~**jahr** das a) school year; b) *(Klasse)* year; ~**junge** der schoolboy; ~**kind** das schoolchild; ~**klasse** die [school] class; ~**mädchen** das schoolgirl; ~**ranzen** der [school] satchel; ~**tag** der school day; ~**tasche** die school-bag; *(Ranzen)* [school] satchel

**Schulter** die; ~, ~n shoulder; **jmdm. auf die ~ klopfen** pat sb. on the shoulder *or (fig.)* back; **Schulterblatt** das *(Anat.)* shoulder-blade; **schultern** *tr. V.* shoulder; **das Gewehr ~:** shoulder arms

**Schul-:** ~**weg** der way to school; ~**zeit** die school-days *pl.*

**schummerig** *Adj.* dim ⟨*light etc.*⟩; dimly lit ⟨*room etc.*⟩

**Schund** der; ~[e]s trash

**Schuppe** die; ~, ~n a) scale; b) *Pl.* *(auf dem Kopf)* dandruff *sing.*; *(auf der Haut)* flaking skin *sing.*; **schuppen** 1. *tr. V.* scale ⟨*fish*⟩; 2. *refl. V.* ⟨*skin*⟩ flake; ⟨*person*⟩ have flaking skin

**Schuppen** der; ~s, ~ a) shed; b) *(ugs.: Lokal)* joint *(sl.)*

**schüren** *tr. V.* a) poke ⟨*fire*⟩; b) *(fig.)* stir up ⟨*hatred, envy, etc.*⟩

**schürfen** 1. *itr. V.* scrape; 2. *tr. V.* **sich** *(Dat.)* **das Knie** *usw.* ~: graze one's knee *etc.*; b) *(Bergbau)* mine ⟨*ore etc.*⟩ open-cast *or (Amer.)* opencut; **Schürf·wunde** die graze; abrasion

**Schurke** der; ~n, ~n rogue

**Schur·wolle** die new wool

**Schürze** die; ~, ~n apron; *(Frauen~, Latz~)* pinafore

**Schuß** der; Schusses, Schüsse a) shot (**auf** + *Akk.* at); **weit** *od.* **weitab vom ~** *(fig. ugs.)* well away from the action; b) *(Menge Munition/Schießpulver)* round; **drei ~ Munition** three rounds of ammunition; c) *(~wunde)* gunshot

wound; d) *(kleine Menge)* dash; e) *(Drogenjargon)* shot; fix *(sl.)*; f) *(Skisport)* schuss; ~ **fahren** schuss; g) *(ugs.)* **etw. in ~ bringen/halten** get sth. into/keep sth. in [good] shape

**Schüssel** die; ~, ~n bowl; *(flacher)* dish

**schusselig** *(ugs.)* 1. *Adj.* scatterbrained; 2. *adv.* in a scatter-brained way

**Schuß-:** ~**linie** die line of fire; **in die/ jmds. ~linie geraten** *od.* **kommen** *(auch fig.)* come under fire/come under fire from sb.; ~**verletzung** die gunshot wound; ~**waffe** die weapon *(firing a projectile)*; *(Gewehr usw.)* firearm

**Schuster** der; ~s, ~ *(ugs.)* shoemaker; *(Flick~)* shoe-repairer

**Schutt** der; ~[e]s rubble; „~ **abladen verboten"** 'no tipping'; 'no dumping'

**Schüttel·frost** der [violent] shivering fit

**schütteln** 1. *tr. V.* a) shake; **den Kopf [über etw.** *(Akk.)*] ~: shake one's head [over sth.]; **jmdm. die Hand ~:** shake sb.'s hand; shake sb. by the hand; b) *(unpers.)* **es schüttelte ihn [vor Kälte]** he was shaking [with *or* from cold]; 2. *refl. V.* shake oneself/itself; 3. *itr. V.* **mit dem Kopf ~:** shake one's head

**schütten** 1. *tr. V.* pour ⟨*liquid, flour, etc.*⟩; *(unabsichtlich)* spill ⟨*liquid, flour, etc.*⟩; tip ⟨*rubbish, coal, etc.*⟩; 2. *itr. V.* *(unpers.)* *(ugs.: regnen)* pour [down]

**schütter** *Adj.* sparse; thin

**Schutz** der; ~es protection (**vor** + *Dat.*, **gegen** against); *(Zuflucht)* refuge

**schutz-, Schutz-:** ~**bedürftig** *Adj.* in need of protection *postpos.*; ~**blech** das mudguard; ~**brief** der *(Kfz-W.)* travel insurance; *(Dokument)* travel insurance certificate

**Schütze** der; ~n, ~n a) marksman; b) *(Fußball usw.: Tor~)* scorer; c) *(Milit.: einfacher Soldat)* private; d) *(Astrol.)* Sagittarius

**schützen** 1. *tr. V.* protect (**vor** + *Dat.* from, **gegen** against); safeguard ⟨*interest, property, etc.*⟩ (**vor** + *Dat.* from); **gesetzlich geschützt** registered [as a trade-mark]; 2. *itr. V.* provide *or* give protection (**vor** + *Dat.* from, **gegen** against); *(vor Wind, Regen)* give shelter (**vor** + *Dat.* from)

**Schützen·fest** das *shooting competition with fair*

**Schutz·engel** der guardian angel

**Schützen-:** ~**graben** der trench; ~**panzer** der armoured personnel carrier; ~**verein** der rifle club

**Schutz-:** ~**helm** der helmet; *(bei Motorradfahrern usw.)* crash-helmet; *(bei Bauarbeitern usw.)* safety helmet; ~**hütte** die **a)** *(Unterstand)* shelter; **b)** *(Berghütte)* mountain hut; ~**impfung** die vaccination

**Schützling** der; ~s, ~e protégé; *(Anvertrauter)* charge

**schutz-, Schutz-:** ~**los** Adj. defenceless; ~**mann** der; Pl. ~**männer** od. ~**leute** *(ugs. veralt.)* [police] constable; copper *(Brit. coll.)*; ~**patron** der patron saint; ~**suchend** Adj. seeking protection *postpos.*; ~**umschlag** der dust-jacket

**schwabbelig** Adj. flabby ⟨*stomach, person, etc.*⟩; wobbly ⟨*jelly etc.*⟩; **schwabbeln** itr. V. *(ugs.)* wobble

**Schwabe** der; ~n, ~n Swabian; **Schwaben (das)** ~s Swabia; **Schwäbin** die; ~, ~**nen** Swabian; **schwäbisch** Adj. Swabian

**schwach; schwächer, schwächst...** 1. Adj. **a)** weak; weak, delicate ⟨*child, woman*⟩; frail ⟨*invalid, old person*⟩; low-powered ⟨*engine, bulb, amplifier, etc.*⟩; weak, poor ⟨*eyesight, memory, etc.*⟩; poor ⟨*hearing*⟩; delicate ⟨*health, constitution*⟩; ~ **werden** grow weak; *(fig.: schwanken)* weaken; *(fig.: nachgeben)* give in; **b)** *(nicht gut)* poor ⟨*pupil, player, performance, result, etc.*⟩; weak ⟨*argument, opponent, play, film, etc.*⟩; **c)** *(gering, niedrig)* poor, low ⟨*attendance etc.*⟩; slight ⟨*effect, resistance, gradient, etc.*⟩; light ⟨*wind, rain, current*⟩; faint ⟨*voice, pressure, hope, smile, smell*⟩; weak, faint ⟨*pulse*⟩; faint, dim ⟨*light*⟩; pale ⟨*colour*⟩; **d)** *(wenig konzentriert)* weak ⟨*solution, coffee, poison, etc.*⟩; **e)** *(Sprachw.)* weak; 2. adv. **a)** weakly; **b)** *(nicht gut)* poorly; **c)** *(in geringem Maße)* poorly ⟨*attended, developed*⟩; slightly ⟨*poisonous, sweetened, inclined*⟩; ⟨*rain*⟩ slightly; ⟨*remember, glow, smile*⟩ faintly; **d)** *(Sprachw.)* ~ **gebeugt** weak; **Schwäche die;** ~, ~**n** weakness; **eine** ~ **für jmdn./etw. haben** have a soft spot for sb./a weakness for sth.; **Schwäche·anfall** der sudden feeling of faintness; **schwächen** tr. V. weaken; **schwächlich** Adj. weakly ⟨*person*⟩; frail ⟨*old person, constitution*⟩; **Schwächling** der; ~s, ~e weakling

**schwach-, Schwach-:** ~**sinn** der; o. Pl. **a)** *(Med.)* mental deficiency; **b)** *(ugs.)* [idiotic *(coll.)*] rubbish; ~**sinnig** 1. Adj. **a)** *(Med.)* mentally deficient; **b)** *(ugs.)* idiotic *(coll.)*, nonsensical ⟨*measure, policy, etc.*⟩; rubbishy ⟨*film etc.*⟩; 2. adv. *(ugs.)* idiotically *(coll.)*; stupidly

**schwafeln** *(ugs.)* 1. itr. V. rabbit on *(Brit. sl.)*, waffle **(von** about); 2. tr. V. blether ⟨*nonsense*⟩

**Schwager** der; ~s, Schwäger brother-in-law; **Schwägerin** die; ~, ~**nen** sister-in-law

**Schwalbe** die; ~, ~**n** swallow

**Schwall** der; ~[e]s, ~e torrent

**schwamm** 1. u. 3. Pers. Sg. Prät. v. **schwimmen**

**Schwamm** der; ~[e]s, Schwämme **a)** sponge; ~ **drüber!** *(ugs.)* [let's] forget it; **b)** *(südd., österr.: Pilz)* mushroom; **Schwammerl** das; ~s, ~[n] *(bayr., österr.)* mushroom; **schwammig** 1. Adj. **a)** spongy; **b)** *(aufgedunsen)* flabby, bloated ⟨*face, body, etc.*⟩; 2. adv. *(unpräzise)* vaguely

**Schwan** der; ~[e]s, Schwäne swan

**schwand** 1. u. 3. Pers. Sg. Prät. v. **schwinden**

**schwang** 1. u. 3. Pers. Sg. Prät. v. **schwingen**

**schwanger** Adj. pregnant **(von** by); **Schwangere** die; adj. Dekl. expectant mother; pregnant woman; **schwängern** tr. V. make ⟨*woman*⟩ pregnant; **Schwangerschaft** die; ~, ~**en** pregnancy

**Schwank** der; ~[e]s, Schwänke comic tale; *(auf der Bühne)* farce

**schwanken** itr. V.; mit Richtungsangabe mit sein **a)** sway; ⟨*boat*⟩ rock; *(heftiger)* roll; ⟨*ground, floor*⟩ shake; **b)** *(fig.: unbeständig sein)* ⟨*prices, temperature, etc.*⟩ fluctuate; ⟨*number, usage, etc.*⟩ vary; **c)** *(fig.: unentschieden sein)* waver; *(zögern)* hesitate

**Schwanz** der; ~es, Schwänze **a)** tail; **b)** *(salopp: Penis)* prick *(coarse)*; cock *(coarse)*

**schwänzeln** itr. V. wag its tail/their tails

**schwänzen** tr., itr. V. *(ugs.)* skip, cut ⟨*lesson etc.*⟩; [**die Schule**] ~: play truant or *(Amer.)* hookey

**schwappen** itr. V. slosh

**Schwarm** der; ~[e]s, Schwärme **a)** swarm; **b)** *(fam.: Angebetete[r])* idol; heart-throb; **schwärmen** itr. V. **a)** *mit Richtungsangabe mit sein* swarm;

**b)** *(begeistert sein)* **für jmdn./etw. ~:** be mad about *or* really keen on sb./ sth.; **von etw. ~:** go into raptures about sth.; **schwärmerisch 1.** *Adj.* rapturous; **2.** *adv.* rapturously

**Schwarte die; ~, ~n a)** rind; **b)** *(ugs.: dickes Buch)* tome

**schwarz; schwärzer, schwärzest... 1.** *Adj.* **a)** black; Black *(person)*; filthy[-black] *(hands, finger-nails, etc.)*; **mir wurde ~ vor den Augen** everything went black; **der ~e Erdteil** *od.* **Kontinent** the Dark Continent; **das Schwarze Meer** the Black Sea; **ins Schwarze treffen** *(fig.)* hit the nail on the head; *(illegal)* illicit *(deal, exchange, etc.)*; **der ~e Markt** the black market; **2.** *adv. (illegal)* illegally; **Schwarz das; ~[es], ~:** black

**Schwarz·brot das** black bread

**Schwarze der/die;** *adj. Dekl.* Black; **schwärzen** *tr. V.* blacken

**schwarz-, Schwarz-: ~|fahren** *unr. itr. V.; mit sein* dodge paying the fare; **~fahrer der** fare-dodger; **~haarig** *Adj.* black-haired; **~handel der** black market **(mit in)**; *(Tätigkeit)* black marketeering **(mit in)**; **~markt der** black market; **~|sehen** *unr. itr. V.* **a)** *(pessimistisch sein)* look on the black side; be pessimistic **(für** about); **b)** *(schwarz fernsehen)* watch television without a licence; **~seher der a)** *(ugs.)* pessimist; **b)** *(jmd, der schwarz fernsieht)* [television] licence dodger; **~wald der; ~[e]s** Black Forest; **schwarz·weiß** *Adj.* black and white; **Schwarzweiß·foto das** black and white photo; **Schwarz-wurzel die** black salsify

**schwatzen,** *(bes. südd.)* **schwätzen 1.** *itr. V.* chat; *(über belanglose Dinge)* chatter; natter *(coll.)*; **2.** *tr. V.* say; talk *(nonsense, rubbish)*; **Schwätzer der; ~s, ~:** chatterbox; *(klatschhafter Mensch)* gossip; **schwatzhaft** *Adj.* talkative; *(klatschhaft)* gossipy

**Schwebe die: in der ~ sein/bleiben** *(fig.)* be/remain in the balance

**Schwebe-: ~bahn die** cableway; **~balken der** *(Turnen)* [balance] beam

**schweben** *itr. V.* **a)** *(bird, balloon, etc.)* hover; *(cloud, balloon, mist)* hang; **in Gefahr ~** *(fig.)* be in danger; **b)** *mit sein (durch die Luft)* float

**Schwede der; ~n, ~n** Swede; **Schweden (das); ~s** Sweden; **Schwedin die; ~, ~nen** Swede; **schwedisch** *Adj.* Swedish

**Schwefel der; ~s** sulphur

**Schweif der; ~[e]s, ~e** tail; **schweifen** *itr. V.; mit sein (geh.; auch fig.)* wander

**Schweige·geld das** hush money

**schweigen** *unr. itr. V.* remain *or* stay silent; say nothing; **ganz zu ~ von ...:** not to mention ...; **Schweigen das; ~s** silence; **schweigsam** *Adj.* silent; quiet

**Schwein das; ~[e]s, ~e a)** pig; **b)** *o. Pl. (Fleisch)* pork; **c)** *(salopp: gemeiner Mensch)* swine; *(Schmutzfink)* mucky devil *(coll.)*; mucky pig *(coll.)*; **d)** *(salopp: Mensch)* **ein armes ~:** a poor devil; **kein ~ war da** there wasn't a bloody *(Brit. sl.)* or *(coll.)* damn soul there; **e)** *(ugs.: Glück)* **[großes] ~ haben** have a [big] stroke of luck; *(davonkommen)* get away with it *(coll.)*

**Schweine-: ~braten der** roast pork *no indef. art.;* **~fleisch das** pork; **~kotelett das** *(Kochk.)* pork chop

**Schweinerei die; ~, ~en** *(ugs.)* **a)** *(Schmutz)* mess; **b)** *(Gemeinheit)* mean *or* dirty trick

**Schweine-: ~schnitzel das** escalope of pork; **~stall der** *(auch fig.)* pigsty; pigpen *(Amer.)*

**schweinisch** *(ugs.)* *Adj.* **a)** *(schmutzig)* filthy; **b)** *(unanständig)* dirty; smutty

**Schweins·leder das** pigskin

**Schweiß der; ~es** sweat; **mir brach der ~ aus** I broke out in a sweat

**Schweiß·brenner der** welding torch; **schweißen** *tr., itr. V.* weld; **Schweißer der; ~s, ~:** welder

**Schweiß-: ~fuß der** sweaty foot; **~perle die** bead of sweat

**Schweiz die; ~:** Switzerland *no art.;* **Schweizer der; ~s, ~:** Swiss; **schweizer·deutsch** *Adj.* Swiss German; **Schweizerin die; ~, ~nen** Swiss; **schweizerisch** *Adj.* Swiss

**schwelen** *(auch fig.)* smoulder

**schwelgen** *itr. V.* feast

**Schwelle die; ~, ~n a)** threshold; **b)** *(Eisenbahn~)* sleeper *(Brit.)*; [cross-] tie *(Amer.)*

**schwellen** *unr. itr. V.; mit sein* swell; *(limb, face, cheek, etc.)* swell [up]; **Schwellung die; ~, ~en** swelling

**Schwemme die; ~, ~n** glut **(an +** *Dat.* of)

**Schwengel der; ~s, ~ a)** *(Glocken~)* clapper; **b)** *(Pumpen~)* handle

**schwenken 1.** *tr. V.* **a)** swing; wave *(flag, handkerchief)*; **b)** *(spülen)* rinse;

**2.** *itr. V.; mit sein* ⟨*marching column*⟩ swing, wheel; ⟨*camera*⟩ pan; ⟨*path, road, car*⟩ swing

**schwer 1.** *Adj.* **a)** heavy; 2 Kilo ~ **sein** weigh two kilos; **b)** *(mühevoll)* heavy ⟨*work*⟩; hard, tough ⟨*job*⟩; hard ⟨*day*⟩; difficult ⟨*birth*⟩; es ~/nicht ~ **haben** have it hard/easy; **c)** *(schlimm)* severe ⟨*shock, disappointment, strain, storm*⟩; serious, grave ⟨*wrong, injustice, error, illness, blow, reservation*⟩; serious ⟨*accident, injury*⟩; heavy ⟨*punishment, strain, loss, blow*⟩; **2.** *adv.* **a)** heavily ⟨*built, laden, armed*⟩; ~ **tragen** be carrying sth. heavy [with difficulty]; **b)** ⟨*work*⟩ hard; ⟨*breathe*⟩ heavily; ~ **hören** be hard of hearing; **c)** *(schwierig)* with difficulty; **d)** *(sehr)* seriously ⟨*injured*⟩; greatly, deeply ⟨*disappointed*⟩; ⟨*punish*⟩ severely, heavily; ~ **verunglücken** have a serious accident

**Schwer-:** ~**arbeiter** der worker engaged in heavy physical work; ~**behinderte** der/die severely handicapped person; *(körperlich auch)* severely disabled person; die ~**behinderten** the severely handicapped/disabled; ~**beschädigte** der/die; *adj. Dekl.* severely disabled person

**Schwere** die; ~ **a)** weight; **b)** *(Schwerkraft)* gravity; **c)** *s.* **schwer 1c**: severity; seriousness; gravity; heaviness; **schwere·los** *Adj.* weightless; **Schwerelosigkeit** die; ~: weightlessness

**schwer-, Schwer-:** ~|**fallen** *unr. itr. V.; mit sein* jmdm. fällt etw. ~: sb. finds sth. difficult; ~**fällig 1.** *Adj.* *(auch fig.)* ponderous; cumbersome ⟨*bureaucracy, procedure*⟩; **2.** *adv.* ponderously; ~**gewicht** das **a)** *(Sport)* heavyweight; **b)** *o. Pl. (Schwerpunkt)* main focus; ~**hörig** *Adj.* hard of hearing *pred.*; ~**industrie** die heavy industry; ~**kraft** die; *o. Pl.* gravity; ~**krank** *Adj.; präd. getrennt geschrieben* seriously ill

**schwerlich** *Adv.* hardly

**schwer-, Schwer-:** ~|**machen** *tr. V.* jmdm./sich etw. ~**machen** make sth. difficult for sb./oneself; ~**metall** das heavy metal; ~**mütig 1.** *Adj.* melancholic; **2.** *adv.* melancholically; ~|**nehmen** *unr. tr. V.* take ⟨*sth.*⟩ seriously; ~**punkt** der centre of gravity; *(fig.)* main focus; *(Hauptgewicht)* main stress

**Schwert** das; ~|e|s, ~er sword; **Schwert·lilie** die iris

**schwer-, Schwer-:** ~|**tun** *unr. refl. V. (ugs.)* sich mit od. bei etw. ~**tun** *(ugs.)* have trouble with sth.; ~**verbrecher** der serious offender; ~**verdaulich** *Adj.; präd. getrennt geschrieben (auch fig.)* hard to digest *pred.*; ~**verletzt** *Adj.; präd. getrennt geschrieben* seriously injured; ~**wiegend** *Adj.* serious; momentous ⟨*decision*⟩

**Schwester** die; ~, ~n **a)** sister; **b)** *(Kranken~)* nurse; **schwesterlich 1.** *Adj.* sisterly; **2.** *adv.* ~ **handeln** act in a sisterly way

**schwieg** *1. u. 3. Pers. Prät. v.* **schweigen**

**Schwieger-:** ~**eltern** *Pl.* parents-in-law; ~**mutter** die mother-in-law; ~**sohn** der son-in-law; ~**tochter** die daughter-in-law; ~**vater** der father-in-law

**Schwiele** die; ~, ~n callus; ~n an den Händen horny hands

**schwierig** *Adj.* difficult; **Schwierigkeit** die; ~, ~en difficulty

**Schwimm-:** ~**bad** das swimming-baths *pl. (Brit.)*; swimming-pool; ~**becken** das swimming-pool

**schwimmen 1.** *unr. itr. V.* **a)** *meist mit sein* swim; **b)** *meist mit sein (treiben, nicht untergehen)* float; **c)** *(ugs.: unsicher sein)* be all at sea; ins Schwimmen geraten start to flounder; **2.** *unr. tr. V.; auch mit sein* swim; **Schwimmen** das; ~: swimming *no art.*; **Schwimmer** der; ~s, ~ **a)** swimmer; **b)** *(Technik)* float

**Schwimm-:** ~**flosse** die flipper; ~**lehrer** der swimming instructor; ~**weste** die life-jacket

**Schwindel** der; ~s **a)** dizziness; giddiness; **b)** *(Betrug)* swindle; *(Lüge)* lie; **schwindel·frei** *Adj.* ~ **sein** have a head for heights; **schwindelig** *s.* **schwindlig**; **schwindeln** *itr. V.* **a)** *(unpers.)* mich od. mir schwindelt I feel dizzy *or* giddy; **b)** *(lügen)* tell fibs

**schwinden** *unr. itr. V.; mit sein* fade; ⟨*supplies, money*⟩ run out; ⟨*effect*⟩ wear off; ⟨*fear, mistrust*⟩ lessen; ⟨*powers, influence*⟩ wane

**Schwindler** der; ~s, ~ *(Lügner)* liar; *(Betrüger)* swindler; *(Hochstapler)* con man *(coll.)*

**schwindlig** *Adj.* dizzy; giddy; jmdm. wird es ~: sb. gets dizzy *or* giddy

**schwingen 1.** *unr. itr. V.* **a)** *mit sein* swing; **b)** *(vibrieren)* vibrate; **2.** *unr. tr. V.* swing; wave ⟨*flag, wand*⟩; brandish ⟨*sword, axe, etc.*⟩; **3.** *unr. refl. V.* **sich aufs Pferd/Fahrrad ~**: leap on to one's horse/bicycle; **Schwingung die; ~, ~en a)** swinging; *(Vibration)* vibration; **b)** *(Physik)* oscillation

**Schwips** der; ~es, ~e *(ugs.)* **einen ~ haben** be tipsy

**schwirren** *itr. V. mit sein* ⟨*arrow, bullet, etc.*⟩ whiz; ⟨*bird*⟩ whirr; ⟨*insect*⟩ buzz

**schwitzen** *itr. V. (auch fig.)* sweat

**schwor** *1. u. 3. Pers. Sg. Prät. v.* **schwören; schwören 1.** *unr. tr., itr. V.* swear ⟨*fidelity, friendship*⟩; swear, take ⟨*oath*⟩; **2.** *unr. itr. V.* swear an/the oath

**schwul** *Adj. (ugs.)* gay *(coll.)*

**schwül** *Adj.* sultry; close

**Schwule** der; *adj. Dekl. (ugs.)* gay *(coll.); (abwertend)* queer *(sl.)*

**Schwüle** die; ~: sultriness

**schwülstig 1.** *Adj.* bombastic; pompous; over-ornate ⟨*art, architecture*⟩; **2.** *adv.* bombastically; pompously

**Schwund** der; ~[e]s decrease, drop *(Gen.* in); *(an Interesse)* waning; falling off

**Schwung** der; ~[e]s, Schwünge **a)** *(Bewegung)* swing; **b)** *(Linie)* sweep; **c)** *o. Pl. (Geschwindigkeit)* momentum; **~ holen** build *or* get up momentum; **d)** *o. Pl. (Antrieb)* drive; energy; **e)** *o. Pl. (mitreißende Wirkung)* sparkle; **schwung·haft** *Adj.* thriving; brisk, flourishing ⟨*trade, business*⟩; **schwung·voll a)** lively; **b)** *(kraftvoll)* vigorous; sweeping ⟨*movement, gesture*⟩; bold ⟨*handwriting, line, stroke*⟩; **2.** *adv.* spiritedly; *(kraftvoll)* with great vigour

**Schwur** der; ~[e]s, Schwüre **a)** *(Gelöbnis)* vow; **b)** *(Eid)* oath; **Schwur·gericht** das *court with a jury*

**sechs** *Kardinalz.* six; **Sechs** die; ~, ~en six

**sechs-, Sechs-:** ~**eck** das hexagon; ~**eckig** *Adj.* hexagonal; ~**fach** *Vervielfältigungsz.* sixfold; ~**hundert** *Kardinalz.* six hundred; ~**mal** *Adv.* six times

**sechst...** *Ordinalz.* sixth

**sechs·tausend** *Kardinalz.* six thousand

**sechstel** *Bruchz.* sixth; **Sechstel** das, *schweiz. meist der*; ~s, ~: sixth; **sechstens** *Adv.* sixthly; **sechzehn** *Kardinalz.* sixteen; **sechzig** *Kardinalz.* sixty; **sechzigst...** *Ordinalz.* sixtieth

**SED** [ɛs|e:'de:] die; ~: *Abk. (ehem. DDR)* Sozialistische Einheitspartei Deutschlands Socialist Unity Party of Germany

**¹See** der; ~s, ~n lake; **²See** die; ~: the sea; **an die ~ fahren** go to the seaside; **auf hoher ~**: on the high seas

**See-:** ~**bad** das seaside health resort; ~**fahrt** die *o. Pl.* seafaring *no art.;* sea travel *no art.;* ~**gang** der; *o. Pl.* leichter/starker **od. hoher od.** schwerer ~**gang** light/heavy *or* rough sea; ~**hund** der [common] seal; *(Pelz)* seal[skin]; ~**igel** der sea-urchin; ~**krank** *Adj.* seasick; ~**krankheit** die; *o. Pl.* seasickness; ~**lachs** der pollack

**Seele** die; ~, ~n soul; *(Psyche)* mind; **seelen·ruhig 1.** *Adj.* calm; **2.** *adv.* calmly; **seelisch 1.** *Adj.* psychological ⟨*cause, damage, tension*⟩; mental ⟨*equilibrium, breakdown, illness, health*⟩; **2.** *adv.* ~ **bedingt sein** have psychological causes; ~ **krank** mentally ill; **Seel·sorge** die; *o. Pl.* pastoral care; **Seelsorger** der; ~s, ~: pastoral worker; *(Geistlicher)* pastor

**See-:** ~**macht** die sea power; ~**mann** der; *Pl.* ~leute seaman; sailor; ~**meile** die nautical mile; ~**not** die; *o. Pl.* distress [at sea]; **in ~ geraten** get into difficulties *pl.;* ~**pferd[chen]** das sea-horse; ~**räuber** der pirate; ~**reise** die voyage; *(Kreuzfahrt)* cruise; ~**rose** die waterlily; ~**stern** der starfish; ~**tüchtig** *Adj.* seaworthy; ~**zunge** die sole

**Segel** das; ~s, ~: sail

**Segel-:** ~**boot** das sailing-boat; ~**flieger** der glider pilot; ~**flugzeug** das glider

**segeln** *itr. V.; mit sein* sail

**Segel-:** ~**schiff** das sailing ship; ~**tuch** das sailcloth

**Segen** der; ~s, ~: blessing; *(Gebet in der Messe)* benediction

**Segler** der; ~s, ~: yachtsman

**segnen** *tr. V.* bless

**sehen 1.** *unr. itr. V.* **a)** see; **schlecht/gut ~**: have bad/good eyesight; **mal ~, wir wollen od. werden ~** *(ugs.)* we'll see; **siehste!** *(ugs.)* there, you see!; **siehst mal** *(hin~)* look **(auf** + *Akk.* at); **sieh mal od.** **doch! look!; siehe da!** lo and behold!; **2.** *unr. tr. V.* **a)** *(auch fig.)* see; **jmdn./etw. [nicht] zu ~ bekommen** [not] get to see sb./sth.; **ich habe ihn kommen [ge]~**: I saw him coming; **b)** *(an~)* watch ⟨*television programme*⟩;

**sehens·wert** *Adj.* worth seeing *postpos.;* **Sehens·würdigkeit die;** ~, ~en sight; **Seher der;** ~s, ~: seer; prophet; **Seh·fehler der** sight defect

**Sehne die;** ~, ~n a) tendon; b) *(Bogen~)* string

**sehnen** *refl. V.* sich nach jmdm./etw. ~: long *or* yearn for sb./sth.

**sehnig** *Adj.* a) stringy ⟨meat⟩; b) *(kräftig)* sinewy ⟨figure, legs, etc.⟩

**sehnlichst** 1. *Adj.* das ist mein ~es Verlangen/mein ~er Wunsch that's what I long for most/that's my dearest wish; 2. *adv.* etw. ~ herbeiwünschen look forward longingly to sth.; **Sehn·sucht die** longing; ~ nach jmdm. haben long to see sb.; **sehn·süchtig** *Adj.* longing *attrib.*, yearning *attrib.* ⟨desire, look, gaze, etc.⟩

**sehr** *Adv.* a) mit *Adj.* u. *Adv.* very; ~ viel a great deal; jmdm. ~ gern haben like sb. a lot *(coll.)* or a great deal; b) mit *Verben* very much; greatly; danke ~! thank you *or* thanks [very much]; bitte ~, Ihr Steak! here's your steak, sir/madam

**Seh·test der** eye test

**sei** *1. u. 3. Pers. Sg. Präsens Konjunktiv u. Imperativ Sg. v.* **sein**

**seicht** 1. *Adj. (auch fig.)* shallow; 2. *adv. (fig.)* shallowly

**seid** *2. Pers. Pl. Präsens u. Imperativ Pl. v.* **sein**

**Seide die;** ~, ~n silk

**Seidel das;** ~s, ~: beer-mug

**seiden** *Adj.; nicht präd.* silk; **Seiden·papier das** tissue paper; **seidig** 1. *Adj.* silky; 2. *adv.* silkily

**Seife die;** ~, ~n soap

**Seifen-:** ~blase die soap bubble; ~schale die soap-dish; ~schaum der; *o. Pl.* lather

**Seil das;** ~s, ~e rope; *(Draht~)* cable

**Seil-:** ~bahn die cableway; ~tänzer der tightrope-walker; ~winde die cable winch

**¹sein** 1. *unr. itr. V.* be; *(existieren)* be; exist; *(sich ereignen)* be; happen; wie dem auch sei be that as it may; er ist Schwede/Lehrer he is Swedish *or* a Swede/a teacher; bist du es? is that you?; mir ist kalt/besser I am *or* feel cold/better; mir ist schlecht I feel sick; drei und vier ist *od.* (ugs.) sind sieben three and four is *or* makes seven; es ist drei Uhr/Mai/Winter it is three o'clock/May/winter; er ist aus Berlin he is *or* comes from Berlin; was

darf es ~? *(im Geschäft)* what can I get you?; es war einmal ein Prinz once upon a time there was a prince; 2. *mod. V.* (*in der Funktion von* können/müssen + *Passiv*) es ist niemand zu sehen there's no one to be seen; das war zu erwarten that was to be expected; die Schmerzen sind kaum zu ertragen the pain is hardly bearable; die Richtlinien sind strengstens zu beachten the guidelines are to be strictly followed; 3. *Hilfsverb* a) *(zur Bildung des Perfekts usw. im Aktiv)* have; er ist gestorben he has died; b) *(zur Bildung des Perfekts usw. im Passiv und des Zustandspassivs)* be; wir sind gerettet worden/wir waren gerettet we were saved

**²sein** *Possessivpron. (einer männlichen Person)* his; *(einer weiblichen Person)* her; *(einer Sache, eines Tiers)* its; *(nach man)* one's; his *(Amer.)*

**seiner** *(geh.) Gen. von* er: sich ~ erbarmen have pity on him; ~ gedenken remember him

**seiner-:** ~seits *Adv.* for his part; *(von ihm)* on his part; ~zeit *Adv.* at that time

**seines·gleichen** *indekl. Pron.* his own kind

**seinet·wegen** *Adv. s.* meinetwegen: because of him; for his sake; about him; as far as he is concerned

**Seismo·graph der;** ~en, ~en seismograph

**seit** 1. *Präp. mit Dat. (Zeitpunkt)* since; *(Zeitspanne)* for; ich bin ~ zwei Wochen hier I've been here [for] two weeks; 2. *Konj.* since; ~ du hier wohnst since you have been living here; **seit·dem** 1. *Adv.* since then; 2. *Konj. s.* seit 2

**Seite die;** ~, ~n a) side; zur *od.* auf die ~ gehen move aside *or* to one side; ~ an ~: side by side; jmdm. zur ~ stehen stand by sb.; von allen ~n *(auch fig.)* from all sides; nach allen ~n in all directions; *(fig.)* on all sides; b) *(Buch~, Zeitungs~)* page

**Seiten-:** ~ansicht die side view; ~hieb der *(fig.)* side-swipe (auf + *Akk.* at); ~ruder das *(Flugw.)* rudder

**seitens** *Präp. mit Gen. (Papierdt.)* on the part of

**Seiten-:** ~sprung der infidelity; ~straße die side-street; ~wind der; *o. Pl.* side wind; cross-wind; ~zahl die a) page number; b) *(Anzahl der Seiten)* number of pages

**seit·her** *Adv.* since then

**seitlich** 1. *Adj.* at the side *(postpos.)*; 2. *adv. (an der Seite)* at the side; *(von der Seite)* from the side; *(nach der Seite)* to the side; **seit·wärts** *Adv.* sideways

**Sekretär** der; ~s, ~e a) secretary; b) *(Schreibschrank)* bureau *(Brit.)*; **Sekretariat** das; ~|e|s, ~e [secretary's/secretaries'] office; **Sekretärin** die; ~, ~nen secretary

**Sekt** der; ~|e|s, ~e high-quality sparkling wine; ≈ champagne

**Sekte** die; ~, ~n sect

**sekundär** 1. *Adj.* secondary; 2. *adv.* secondarily; **Sekunde** die; ~, ~n a) *(auch Math., Musik)* second; b) *(ugs.: Augenblick)* second; moment; **Sekunden·zeiger** der second hand

**selb...** *Demonstrativpron.* same; **selber** *indekl. Demonstrativpron.* s. **selbst** 1; **selbst** 1. *indekl. Demonstrativpron.* myself / yourself / himself / herself / itself / ourselves / yourselves / themselves; **von** ~: automatically; 2. *Adv.* even

**Selbst·achtung** die self-respect

**selb·ständig** 1. *Adj.* independent; self-employed *(business man, tradesman, etc.)*; **sich** ~ **machen** set up on one's own; 2. *adv.* independently; ~ **denken** think for oneself; **Selbständigkeit** die; ~: independence

**selbst-, Selbst-:** ~**auslöser** der *(Fot.)* delayed-action shutter release; ~**bedienung** die self-service *no art.*; ~**befriedigung** die masturbation *no art.*; ~**beherrschung** die self-control *no art.*; ~**bewußt** 1. *Adj.* self-confident; 2. *adv.* self-confidently; ~**bewußtsein** das self-confidence *no art.*; ~**erkenntnis** die; *o. Pl.* self-knowledge *no art.*; ~**gefällig** 1. *Adj.* self-satisfied; smug; 2. *adv.* smugly; ~**gefälligkeit** die; *o. Pl.* self-satisfaction; smugness; ~**gemacht** *Adj.* home-made; ~**gespräch** das conversation with oneself; ~**los** 1. *Adj.* selfless; 2. *adv.* selflessly; unselfishly; ~**mord** der suicide *no art.*; ~**mörder** der suicide; ~**sicher** 1. *Adj.* self-confident; 2. *adv.* in a self-confident manner; ~**süchtig** 1. *Adj.* selfish; 2. *adv.* selfishly; ~**tätig** 1. *Adj.* automatic; 2. *adv.* automatically; ~**verständlich** 1. *Adj.* natural; **etw. für** ~**verständlich halten** regard sth. as a matter of course; *(für gegeben hinnehmen)* take sth. for granted; 2. *adv.*

naturally; of course; ~**vertrauen** das self-confidence; ~**verwaltung** die self-government *no art.*; ~**zweck** der; *o. Pl.* end in itself

**selig** 1. *Adj.* a) *(Rel.)* blessed; b) *(tot)* late [lamented]; c) *(glücklich)* blissful *(idleness, slumber, etc.)*; blissfully happy *(person)*; 2. *adv.* blissfully; **Seligkeit** die; ~, ~en bliss *no pl.*; [blissful] happiness *no pl.*

**Sellerie** der; ~s, ~|s| *od.* die; ~, ~: celeriac; *(Stangen~)* celery

**selten** 1. *Adj.* rare; infrequent *(visit, visitor)*; 2. *adv.* a) rarely; b) *(sehr)* exceptionally; uncommonly; **Seltenheit** die; ~, ~en rarity; **Seltenheits·wert** der; ~|es| rarity value

**Selters·wasser** das seltzer [water]

**seltsam** 1. *Adj.* strange; odd; 2. *adv.* strangely

**Semester** das; ~s, ~: semester

**Semikolon** das; ~s, ~s semicolon

**Seminar** das; ~s, ~e a) seminar (über + *Akk.* on); b) *(Institut)* department

**Semmel** die; ~, ~n *(bes. österr., bayr., ostmd.)* [bread] roll; **Semmel·knödel** der *(bayr., österr.)* bread dumpling

**Senat** der; ~|e|s, ~e senate; **Senator** der; ~s, ~en

¹**senden** *unr. (auch regelm.) tr. V. (geh.)* send

²**senden** *regelm. (schweiz. unr.) tr., itr. V.* broadcast *(programme, play, etc.)*; transmit *(signals, Morse, etc.)*; **Sender** der; ~s, ~: [broadcasting] station; *(Anlage)* transmitter

**Sende-:** ~**reihe** die series [of programmes]; ~**schluß** der the close-down

**Sendung** die; ~, ~en a) consignment; b) *(Rundf., Ferns.)* programme

**Senf** der; ~|e|s, ~e mustard

**senior** *indekl. Adj.; nach Personennamen* senior; **Senior** der; ~s, ~en a) *(Kaufmannsspr.)* senior partner; b) *(Sport)* senior [player]; c) *(Rentner)* senior citizen; **Senioren·heim** das home for the elderly

**Senke** die; ~, ~n hollow; **senken** 1. *tr. V.* lower; 2. *refl. V. (curtain, barrier, etc.)* fall, come down; *(ground, building, road)* subside, sink; *(water-level)* fall, sink

**senk-, Senk-:** ~**fuß** der flat foot; ~**recht** 1. *Adj.* vertical; ~ **zu etw.** perpendicular to sth.; 2. *adv.* vertically; ~**rechte** die vertical; *(Geom.: Gerade)* perpendicular

**Sensation** die; ~, ~en sensation;

**sensationell** 1. *Adj.* sensational; 2. *adv.* sensationally

**Sense die**; ~, ~n scythe

**sensibel** 1. *Adj.* sensitive; 2. *adv.* sensitively; **Sensibilität die**; ~: sensitivity

**sentimental** 1. *Adj.* sentimental; 2. *adv.* sentimentally; **Sentimentalität die**; ~, ~en sentimentality

**separat** 1. *Adj.* separate; self-contained *(flat etc.)*; 2. *adv.* separately

**September der**; ~|s|, ~: September

**Serbe der**; ~n, ~n Serb; Serbian; **Serbien (das)**; ~s Serbia; **serbisch** *Adj.* Serbian

**Serenade die**; ~, ~n serenade

**Serie die**; ~, ~n series; **serien·mäßig** 1. *Adj.* standard *(product, model, etc.)*; 2. *adv.* **a)** ~ ~ gefertigt *od.* gebaut produced in series; **b)** *(nicht als Sonderausstattung) (fitted, supplied, etc.)* as standard

**seriös** *Adj.* respectable *(person, hotel, etc.)*; trustworthy *(firm, partner, etc.)*; serious *(offer, applicant, artist, etc.)*

**Serpentine die**; ~, ~n hairpin bend

**Serum das**; ~s, Seren serum

**¹Service** [zɛr'viːs] **das**; ~, ~: [dinner *etc.*] service; **²Service** ['zøːɐ̯vɪs] **der**; ~, ~s ['zøːɐ̯vɪsɪs] *(Bedienung, Kundendienst)* service; **servieren** *tr. V.* serve; **Serviererin die**; ~, ~nen waitress; **Serviette** [zɛr'vi̯ɛtə] **die**; ~, ~n napkin; serviette *(Brit.)*

**Servo·lenkung die** power [-assisted] steering *no indef. art.*

**Sesam der**; ~s sesame seeds *pl.*

**Sessel der**; ~s, ~ a) armchair; **b)** *(österr.: Stuhl)* chair; **Sessel·lift der** chair-lift

**seßhaft** *Adj.* settled; ~ werden settle down

**Set das** *od.* **der**; ~|s|, ~s a) set, combination **(aus of)**; **b)** *(Deckchen)* table- *or* place-mat

**setzen** 1. *refl. V.* **a)** sit [down]; **setzen Sie sich** sit down; take a seat; **sich aufs Sofa** *usw.* ~: sit on the sofa *etc.*; **b)** *(coffee, froth, etc.)* settle; *(sediment)* sink to the bottom; 2. *tr. V.* **a)** put; **b)** *(einpflanzen)* plant *(tomatoes, potatoes, etc.)*; **c)** *(aufziehen)* hoist *(flag etc.)*; set *(sails, navigation lights)*; **d)** *(Druckw.)* set *(manuscript etc.)*; 3. *itr. V.* **a)** meist mit sein *(springen)* leap, jump; **b)** über einen Fluß ~ *(mit einer Fähre o.ä.)* cross a river; **c)** *(beim Wetten)* bet; **auf ein Pferd/auf Rot** ~:

back a horse/put one's money on red; **Setzer der**; ~s, ~, **Setzerin die**; ~, ~nen *(Druckw.)* [type]setter; **Setzling der**; ~s, ~e seedling

**Seuche die**; ~, ~n epidemic

**seufzen** *itr., tr. V.* sigh; **Seufzer der**; ~s, ~: sigh

**Sex der**; ~|es| sex *no art.;* **Sexualität die**; ~: sexuality *no art.;* **sexuell** 1. *Adj.* sexual; 2. *adv.* sexually

**sezieren** *tr. V.* dissect *(corpse)*

**sfr., *(schweiz. nur:)* sFr.** *Abk.* Schweizer Franken

**Shampoo** [ʃam'puː], **Shampoon** [ʃam'poːn] **das**; ~s, ~s shampoo

**Sherry** ['ʃɛrɪ] **der**; ~s, ~s sherry

**Show** [ʃoʊ] **die**; ~, ~s show

**siamesisch** *Adj.* Siamese; **Siam·katze die** Siamese cat

**Sibirien (das)**; ~s Siberia

**sich** *Reflexivpron. der 3. Pers. Sg. und Pl. Akk. und Dat.* **a)** himself/herself/ itself/themselves; *(auf man bezogen)* oneself; *(auf das Anredepronomen Sie bezogen)* yourself/yourselves; ~ freuen/wundern/schämen/täuschen be pleased/surprised/ashamed/mistaken; ~ sorgen worry; **b)** *(reziprok)* one another, each other

**Sichel die**; ~, ~n sickle

**sicher** 1. *Adj.* **a)** safe *(road, procedure, etc.)*; secure *(job, investment, etc.)*; **b)** reliable *(evidence, source)*; certain *(proof)*; reliable, sure *(judgment, taste, etc.)*; **c)** *(selbstbewußt)* [self-] assured *(person, manner)*; **d)** *(gewiß)* certain; sure; 2. *adv.* **a)** safely; **b)** *(zuverlässig)* reliably; ~ |Auto| fahren be a safe driver; **c)** *(selbstbewußt)* [self-] confidently; 3. *Adv.* certainly; **sicher|gehen** *unr. itr. V.; mit sein* play safe; **Sicherheit die**; ~, ~en a) *o. Pl.* safety; *(der Öffentlichkeit)* security; **jmdn./etw. in ~ [vor etw. *(Dat.)*]** bringen save *or* rescue sb./sth. [from sth.]; **b)** *o. Pl. (Gewißheit)* certainty; **c)** *(Wirtsch.: Bürgschaft)* security

**sicherheits-, Sicherheits-:** ~abstand der *(Verkehrsw.)* safe distance between vehicles; ~gurt der seatbelt; ~halber *Adv.* to be on the safe side; ~nadel die safety-pin; ~schloß das safety lock

**sicherlich** *Adv.* certainly; **sichern** *tr. V.* make *(door etc.)* secure; *(garantieren)* safeguard *(rights, peace)*; *(schützen)* protect *(rights etc.)*; **sich *(Dat.)* etw.** ~: secure sth.; **sicher|stellen** *tr. V.* **a)** impound *(goods, vehicle)*; **b)**

guarantee ⟨*supply, freedom, etc.*⟩; **Si-cherung die; ~, ~en a)** *o. Pl.* safe-guarding; *(das Schützen)* protection; **b)** *(Elektrot.)* fuse; **c)** *(techn. Vorrich-tung)* safety-catch

**Sicht die; ~:** view **(auf** + *Akk.,* **in** + *Akk.* of); **gute** *od.* **klare/schlechte ~:** good/poor visibility; **sichtbar 1.** *Adj.* visible; *(fig.)* apparent ⟨*reason*⟩; **2.** *adv.* visibly; **sichten** *tr. V.* sight; **sichtlich 1.** *Adj.* obvious; evident; **2.** *adv.* obviously; evidently; visibly ⟨*im-pressed*⟩

**Sicht-:** **~verhältnisse** *Pl.* visibility *sing.;* **~vermerk** der visa; **~weite die** visibility *no art.;* **außer/in ~weite sein** be out of/in sight

**sickern** *itr. V.; mit sein* seep; *(spärlich fließen)* trickle

**sie 1.** *Personalpron.; 3. Pers. Sg. Nom. Fem.* she; *(betont)* her; *(bei Dingen, Tieren)* it; s. auch **¹ihr; ihrer a.; 2.** *Personalpron.; 3. Pers. Pl. Nom.* they; *(be-tont)* them; *s. auch* **ihnen; ihrer b; 3.** *Akk. von* **sie 1** her; *(bei Dingen, Tieren)* it; **4.** *Akk. von* **sie 2 a** them

**Sie** *Personalpron.; 3. Pers. Pl. Nom. u. Akk; Anrede an eine od. mehrere Perso-nen* you; *s. auch* **Ihnen; Ihrer**

**Sieb das; ~[e]s, ~e** sieve; *(für Tee)* strainer; **¹sieben** *tr. V.* **a)** sieve ⟨*flour etc.*⟩; riddle ⟨*sand, gravel, etc.*⟩; **b)** *(auswählen)* screen ⟨*candidates*⟩

**²sieben** *Kardinalz.* seven; **Sieben die; ~, ~en** seven

**sieben-, Sieben-:** **~fach** *Vervielfäl-tigungsz.* sevenfold; **~mal** *Adj.* seven times; **~sachen** *Pl.* *(ugs.)* **meine/dei-ne** *usw.* **~sachen** my/your *etc.* belong-ings *or (coll.)* bits and pieces

**siebt...** *Ordinalz.* seventh; **siebtel** *Bruchz.* seventh; **Siebtel das,** *schweiz. meist* der; **~s, ~:** seventh; **siebtens** *Adv.* seventhly; **sieb-zehn** *Kardinalz.* seventeen; **siebzig** *Kardinalz.* seventy; **siebzigst...** *Or-dinalz.* seventieth

**siedeln** *itr. V.* settle

**sieden** *unr. od. regelm. itr. V.* boil; **Siede·punkt der** *(auch fig.)* boiling-point

**Siedler der; ~s, ~:** settler; **Siedlung die; ~, ~en a)** *(Wohngebiet)* [housing] estate; **b)** *(Niederlassung)* settlement

**Sieg der; ~[e]s, ~e** victory, *(bes. Sport)* win (**über** + *Akk.* over)

**Siegel das; ~s, ~:** seal; *(von Behör-den)* stamp

**siegen** *itr. V.* win; **über jmdn. ~:** gain

---

*or* win a victory over sb.; *(bes. Sport)* win against sb.; beat sb.; **Sieger der; ~s, ~:** winner; *(Mannschaft)* winners *pl.; (einer Schlacht)* victor; **Sieger-ehrung die** presentation ceremony; awards ceremony; **sieges·sicher 1.** *Adj.* confident of victory *pred.;* **2.** *adv.* confident of victory; **sieg-reich** *Adj.* victorious; winning ⟨*team*⟩; successful ⟨*campaign*⟩

**sieh, siehe** *Imperativ Sg. v.* **sehen; siehst** *2. Pers. Sg. Präsens v.* **sehen; sieht** *3. Pers. Sg. Präsens v.* **sehen**

**Signal das; ~s, ~e** signal; **signali-sieren** *tr. V.* indicate ⟨*danger, change, etc.*⟩

**Signatur die; ~, ~en a)** initials *pl.; (Kürzel)* abbreviated signature; *(des Künstlers)* autograph; **b)** *(Unter-schrift)* signature; **c)** *(in einer Biblio-thek)* shelf-mark; **signieren** *tr. V.* sign; autograph ⟨*one's own work*⟩

**Silbe die; ~, ~n** syllable

**Silber das; ~s a)** silver; **b)** *(silbernes Gerät)* silver[ware]; **Silber·medail-le die** silver medal; **silbern 1.** *Adj.* silver; silvery ⟨*moonlight, shade, gleam, etc.*⟩; **2.** *adv.* ⟨*shine, shimmer, etc.*⟩ with a silvery lustre; **Silber·pa-pier das** silver paper

**Silhouette** [zi'lŭɛtə] **die; ~, ~n** sil-houette

**Silo der** *od.* **das; ~s, ~s** silo

**Silvester der** *od.* **das; ~s, ~:** New Year's Eve

**Simbabwe (das); ~s** Zimbabwe

**simpel 1.** *Adj.* **a)** simple ⟨*question, task*⟩; **b)** *(beschränkt)* simple-minded ⟨*person*⟩; simple ⟨*mind*⟩; **2.** *adv.* **a)** simply; **b)** *(beschränkt)* in a simple-minded manner; **Simpel der; ~s, ~** *(bes. südd. ugs.)* simpleton; fool

**Sims der** *od.* **das; ~es, ~e** ledge; sill; *(Kamin~)* mantelpiece

**Simulant der; ~en, ~en** malingerer; **simulieren 1.** *tr. V.* feign, sham ⟨*ill-ness, emotion, etc.*⟩; simulate ⟨*situ-ation, condition, etc.*⟩; **2.** *itr. V.* feign illness

**simultan 1.** *Adj.* simultaneous; **2.** *adv.* simultaneously

**sind** *1. u. 3. Pers. Pl. Präsens v.* **¹sein**

**Sinfonie die; ~, ~n** symphony; **Sin-fonie·orchester das** symphony or-chestra

**singen** *unr. tr., itr. V.* sing

**Singular der; ~s** singular

**Sing·vogel der** songbird

**sinken** *unr. itr. V.; mit sein* **a)** ⟨*ship,*

*sun*⟩ sink, go down; ⟨*plane, balloon*⟩ descend, go down; **b)** *(nieder~)* fall; **c)** *(niedriger werden)* ⟨*temperature, level*⟩ fall, drop; **d)** *(an Wert verlieren; nachlassen; abnehmen)* fall, go down
**Sinn** der; ~|e|s, ~e **a)** sense; **b)** *Pl. (geh.: Bewußtsein)* senses; mind *sing.*; **nicht bei ~en sein** be out of one's senses *or* mind; **c)** *o. Pl. (Gefühl, Verständnis)* feeling; **d)** *o. Pl. (~gehalt, Bedeutung)* meaning; **e)** *(Ziel u. Zweck)* point; **Sinn·bild** das symbol
**Sinnes-:** **~organ** das sense-organ; sensory organ; **~täuschung** die trick of the senses
**sinn·gemäß** 1. *Adj.* eine ~e Übersetzung a translation which conveys the general sense; 2. *adv.* etw. ~ übersetzen/wiedergeben translate the general sense of sth./give the gist of sth.; **sinnlich** *Adj.* sensory ⟨*impression, perception, stimulus*⟩; sensual ⟨*love, mouth*⟩; sensuous ⟨*pleasure, passion*⟩; **Sinnlichkeit** die; ~: sensuality; **sinn·los** 1. *Adj.* **a)** senseless; **b)** *(zwecklos)* pointless; 2. *adv.* **a)** senselessly; **b)** *(zwecklos)* pointlessly; **Sinnlosigkeit** die; ~ **a)** senselessness; **b)** *(Zwecklosigkeit)* pointlessness; **sinn·voll** 1. *Adj.* **a)** *(vernünftig)* sensible; **b)** *(einen Sinn ergebend)* meaningful; 2. *adv.* **a)** *(vernünftig)* sensibly; **b)** *(einen Sinn ergebend)* meaningfully
**Sint·flut** die Flood; Deluge; **sintflut·artig** 1. *Adj.* torrential; 2. *adv.* in torrents
**Sippe** die; ~, ~n **a)** *(Völkerk.)* sib; **b)** *(ugs.: Verwandtschaft)* clan; **Sippschaft** die; ~, ~en *(ugs.)* s. Sippe b
**Sirene** die; ~, ~n siren
**Sirup** der; ~s, ~e syrup
**Sitte** die; ~, ~n **a)** *(Brauch)* custom; tradition; **b)** *(moralische Norm)* common decency; **c)** *Pl. (Benehmen)* manners; **sittlich** 1. *Adj.* moral; 2. *adv.* morally; **Sittlichkeit** die; *o. Pl.* morality
**Sittlichkeits-:** **~verbrechen** das sexual crime; **~verbrecher** der sex offender
**Situation** die; ~, ~en situation
**Sitz** der; ~es, ~e **a)** seat; **b)** *(Verwaltungs~)* headquarters *sing. or pl.;* **c)** *(von Kleidungsstücken)* fit
**sitzen** *unr. itr. V.; südd., österr., schweiz. mit sein* **a)** sit; **b)** *(sein)* be; **c)** *([gut] passen)* fit
**sitzen-:** **~|bleiben** *unr. itr. V. (ugs.)*

**a)** *(nicht versetzt werden)* stay down [a year]; **b)** *(unverheiratet bleiben)* be left on the shelf; **c)** **auf etw.** *(Dat.)* **~bleiben** *(für etw. keinen Käufer finden)* be left *or (coll.)* stuck with sth.; **~|lassen** *unr. tr. V. (ugs.)* **a)** *(nicht heiraten)* jilt; **b)** *(im Stich lassen)* leave in the lurch; **c)** etw. **nicht auf sich** *(Dat.)* **~lassen** not take sth.
**Sitzplatz** der seat; **Sitzung** die; ~, ~en meeting; *(Parlaments~)* sitting; session; **Sitzungs·saal** der conference hall
**Skala** die; ~, Skalen scale
**Skalp** der; ~s, ~e scalp
**Skalpell** das; ~s, ~e scalpel
**skalpieren** *tr. V.* scalp
**Skandal** der; ~s, ~e scandal; **skandalös** *Adj.* scandalous
**Skandinavien (das)**; ~s Scandinavia; **Skandinavier** der; ~s, ~: Scandinavian; **skandinavisch** *Adj.* Scandinavian
**Skat** der; ~|e|s, ~e *od.* ~s skat
**Skelett** das; ~|e|s, ~e skeleton
**Skepsis** die; ~: scepticism; **skeptisch** 1. *Adj.* sceptical; 2. *adv.* sceptically
**Ski** [ʃiː] der; ~s, ~er *od.* ~: ski; ~ **laufen** *od.* **fahren** ski
**Ski-:** **~läufer** der skier; **~lehrer** der ski-instructor; **~lift** der ski-lift; **~springen** das; ~s ski-jumping *no art.*
**Skizze** die; ~, ~n sketch; **Skizzen·block** der sketch-pad; **skizzieren** *tr. V.* sketch
**Sklave** der; ~n, ~n slave; **Sklaven·händler** der slave-trader; **Sklaverei** die; ~: slavery *no art.;* **Sklavin** die; ~, ~nen slave; **sklavisch** 1. *Adj.* slavish; 2. *adv.* slavishly
**Skonto** der *od.* das; ~s, ~s *(Kaufmannsspr.)* [cash] discount
**Skorbut** der; ~|e|s scurvy *no art.*
**Skorpion** der; ~s, ~e scorpion
**Skrupel** der; ~s, ~: scruple; **skrupel·los** 1. *Adj.* unscrupulous; 2. *adv.* unscrupulously; **Skrupellosigkeit** die; ~: unscrupulousness
**Skulptur** die; ~, ~en sculpture
**Slalom** der; ~s, ~s slalom
**Slawe** der; ~n, ~n Slav; **slawisch** *Adj.* Slav|ic|; Slavonic
**Slip** der; ~s, ~s briefs *pl.*
**Slowake** der; ~n, ~n Slovak; **Slowakei** die; ~: Slovakia *no art.*
**Smaragd** der; ~|e|s, ~e emerald

**Smoking** der; ~s, ~s dinner-jacket *or (Amer.)* tuxedo and dark trousers

**so** 1. *Adv.* **a)** *(auf diese Weise; in, von dieser Art)* like this/that; this/that way; **weiter so!** carry on in the same way!; **b)** *(dermaßen, überaus)* so; **c)** *(genauso)* as; **so gut ich konnte** as best I could; **d)** *(ugs.: solch)* such; **so ein Idiot!** what an idiot!; **so einer/eine/eins** one like that; **e)** *betont (eine Zäsur ausdrückend)* right; OK *(coll.);* **g)** *(ugs.: schätzungsweise)* about; **2.** *Konj.* **so daß ...** *(damit)* so that ...; *(und deshalb)* and so ...; **3.** *Partikel* **a)** *ugs.:* **ach, das hab' ich nur so gesagt** oh, I didn't mean anything by that; **b)** *(in Aufforderungssätzen verstärkend)* **so komm doch** come on now

**So.** *Abk.* Sonntag Sun.

**s. o.** *Abk.* siehe oben

**sobald** *Konj.* as soon as

**Socke** die; ~, ~n sock

**Sockel** der; ~s, ~ **a)** *(einer Säule, Statue)* plinth; **b)** *(unterer Teil eines Hauses, Schrankes)* base

**Soda·wasser** das; *Pl.* Sodawässer soda; soda-water

**Sod·brennen** das; ~s heartburn

**so·eben** *Adv.* just

**Sofa** das; ~s, ~s sofa; settee

**so·fern** *Konj.* provided [that]

**soff** *1. u. 3. Pers. Sg. Prät. v.* saufen

**so·fort** *Adv.* immediately; at once; **sofortig** *Adj. (unmittelbar)* immediate

**sog** *1. u. 3. Pers. Sg. Prät. v.* saugen; **Sog** der; ~[e]s, ~e suction; *(bei Schiffen)* wake; *(bei Fahr-, Flugzeugen)* slip-stream; *(von Wasser, auch fig.)* current

**so·gar** *Adv.* even

**so·genannt** *Adj.* so-called

**so·gleich** *Adv.* immediately; at once

**Sohle** die; ~, ~n **a)** *(Schuh~)* sole; *(Einlege~)* insole; **b)** *(Fuß~)* sole [of the foot]

**Sohn** der; ~es, Söhne son

**Soja-:** ~bohne die soy[a] bean; ~soße die soy[a] sauce

**so·lang[e]** *Konj.* so *or* as long as

**Solarium** das; ~s, Solarien solarium

**solch** *Demonstrativpron.* **a)** *attr.* such; **das macht ~en Spaß!** it's so much fun!; **b)** *alleinstehend* **~e wie die** people like that

**Sold** der; ~[e]s, ~e [military] pay

**Soldat** der; ~en, ~en soldier; **Soldaten·friedhof** der military *or* war cemetery; **Soldatin** die; ~, ~nen [female *or* woman] soldier; **soldatisch** 1. *Adj.* military ⟨discipline, expression, etc.⟩; soldierly ⟨figure, virtue⟩; **2.** *adv.* in a military manner

**Söldner** der; ~s, ~: mercenary

**solidarisch** 1. *Adj.* **~es Verhalten** zeigen show one's solidarity; **2.** *adv.* **~ handeln/sich ~ verhalten** act in/show solidarity; **solidarisieren** *refl. V.* show [one's] solidarity; **Solidarität** die; ~: solidarity

**solide** 1. *Adj.* **a)** solid; sturdy ⟨shoes, material⟩; [good-]quality ⟨goods⟩; **b)** *(gut fundiert)* sound ⟨work, education, knowledge⟩; solid ⟨firm⟩; **c)** *(anständig)* respectable ⟨person, life, profession⟩; **2.** *adv.* **a)** solidly ⟨built⟩; sturdily ⟨made⟩; **b)** *(gut fundiert)* soundly ⟨educated, constructed⟩; **c)** *(anständig)* ⟨live⟩ respectably, steadily

**Solist** der; ~en, ~en soloist

**Soll** das; ~[s], ~[s] **a)** *(Bankw.)* debit; **b)** *(Arbeits~)* quota; **sein ~ erfüllen** *od.* **erreichen** achieve one's target

**sollen** 1. *unr. Modalverb;* **2.** *Part.* **~ a)** *(bei Aufforderung, Anweisung, Auftrag)* **was soll ich als nächstes tun?** what should I do next?; [sagen Sie ihm,] **er soll hereinkommen** tell him to come in; **b)** *(bei Wunsch, Absicht, Vorhaben)* **das sollte ein Witz sein** that was meant to be a joke; **was soll denn das heißen?** what is that supposed to mean?; **c)** *(bei Ratlosigkeit)* **was soll ich nur machen?** what am I to do?; **d)** *(Notwendigkeit ausdrückend)* **man soll so etwas nicht unterschätzen** it shouldn't be taken so lightly; **e)** *häufig im Konjunktiv II (Erwartung, Wünschenswertes ausdrückend)* **du solltest dich schämen** you ought to be ashamed of yourself; **das hättest du besser nicht tun ~:** it would have been better if you hadn't done that; **f)** *(jmdm. beschieden sein)* **er sollte seine Heimat nicht wiedersehen** he was never to see his homeland again; **g)** *im Konjunktiv II (eine Möglichkeit ausdrückend)* **wenn du ihn sehen solltest, sage ihm bitte ...:** if you should see him, please tell him ...; **h)** *im Präsens (sich für die Wahrheit nicht verbürgend)* **das Restaurant soll sehr teuer sein** the restaurant is supposed *or* said to be very expensive; **i)** *im Konjunktiv II (Zweifel ausdrückend)* **sollte das sein Ernst sein?** is he really being serious?; **j)** *(können)* **mir soll es gleich sein** it's all the same to me; **2.** *tr., itr.*

*V.* **was soll das?** what's the idea?; **was soll ich dort?** what would I do there?

**Solo** das; ~s, ~s *od.* **Soli** solo

**so·mit** [auch: '--] *Adv.* consequently; therefore

**Sommer** der; ~s, ~: summer

**Sommer·ferien** *Pl.* summer holidays; **sommerlich** 1. *Adj.* summer; summery ⟨*warmth, weather*⟩; summer's *attrib.* ⟨*day, evening*⟩; 2. *adv.* **es war ~ warm** it was as warm as summer

**sommer-, Sommer-:** ~**reifen** der standard tyre; ~**schluß·verkauf** der summer sale/sales; ~**sprosse** die freckle; ~**sprossig** *Adj.* freckled; ~**zeit** die *(Uhrzeit)* summer time

**Sonate** die; ~, ~n *(Musik)* sonata

**Sonde** die; ~, ~n probe; *(zur Ernährung)* tube

**Sonder·angebot** das special offer; **sonderbar** 1. *Adj.* strange; odd; 2. *adv.* strangely; oddly; **Sonder·fall** der special case

**sonder·gleichen** *Adv., nachgestellt* **eine Frechheit/Unverschämtheit ~:** the height of cheek/impudence

**sonderlich** *Adv.* particularly; **Sonderling** der; ~s, ~e strange *or* odd person; **Sonder·müll** der hazardous waste

¹**sondern** *tr. V. (geh.)* separate (**von** from)

²**sondern** *Konj.* but; **nicht nur ..., ~** |**auch**| ...: not only ... but also ...

**Sonder-:** ~**schule** die special school; ~**zug** der special train

**sondieren** *tr. V.* sound out

**Sonett** das; ~|e|s, ~e sonnet

**Sonn·abend** der *(bes. nordd.)* Saturday; **sonn·abends** *Adv.* on Saturday[s]

**Sonne** die; ~, ~n sun; *(Licht der ~)* sun[light]; **sonnen** *refl. V.* sun oneself

**sonnen-, Sonnen-:** ~**aufgang** der sunrise; ~**baden** *itr. V.* sunbathe; ~**blume** die sunflower; ~**brand** der sunburn *no indef. art.;* ~**brille** die sun-glasses *pl.;* ~**energie** die solar energy; ~**finsternis** die solar eclipse; ~**hut** der sun-hat; ~**licht** das sunlight; ~**öl** das sun-oil; ~**schein** der *o. Pl.* sunshine; ~**schirm** der sunshade; ~**stich** der sunstroke *no indef. art.;* ~**strahl** der ray of sun[shine]; ~**uhr** die sundial; ~**untergang** der sunset

**sonnig** *Adj.* sunny

**Sonn·tag** der Sunday; **sonn·täg-** **lich** 1. *Adj.* Sunday *attrib.;* 2. *adv.* ~ **gekleidet** dressed in one's Sunday best; **sonntags** *Adv.* on Sunday[s]

**sonst** *Adv.* **a)** der ~ **so freundliche Mann ...:** the man, who is/was usually so friendly, ...; **alles war wie ~:** everything was [the same] as usual; ~ **noch was?** *(ugs., auch iron.)* anything else?; **wer/was/wie/wo |denn| ~?** who/what/ how/where else?; **b)** *(andernfalls)* otherwise; or; **sonstig...** *Adj.; nicht präd.* other; further

**sonst-:** ~**was** *Indefinitpron. (ugs.)* anything else; ~**wer** *Indefinitpron. (ugs.)* somebody else; *(fragend, verneinend)* anybody else; ~**wo** *Adv. (ugs.)* somewhere else; *(fragend, verneinend)* anywhere else

**so·oft** *Konj.* whenever

**Sopran** der; ~s, ~e *(Musik)* soprano *(im Chor)* sopranos *pl.;* **Sopranistin** die; ~, ~nen soprano

**Sorge** die; ~, ~n worry; **keine ~!** don't [you] worry!; **sorgen** 1. *refl. V.* worry (**um** about); 2. *itr. V.* **für jmdn./ etw. ~:** take care of sb./sth.

**sorgen-, Sorgen-:** ~**frei** 1. *Adj.* carefree; 2. *adv.* ~**frei leben** live in a carefree manner; ~**kind** das *(auch fig.)* problem child; ~**voll** 1. *Adj.* worried; 2. *adv.* worriedly

**Sorg·falt** die; ~: care; **sorg·fältig** 1. *Adj.* careful; 2. *adv.* carefully

**sorg·los** 1. *Adj.* **a)** *(ohne Sorgfalt)* careless; **b)** *(unbekümmert)* carefree; 2. *adv.* ~ **mit etw. umgehen** treat sth. carelessly; **Sorglosigkeit** die; ~ **a)** *(Mangel an Sorgfalt)* carelessness; **b)** *(Unbekümmertheit)* carefreeness; **sorgsam** 1. *Adj.* careful; 2. *adv.* carefully

**Sorte** die; ~, ~n **a)** sort; type; kind; **b)** *Pl. (Devisen)* foreign currency *sing.*

**sortieren** *tr. V.* sort [out] ⟨*pictures, letters, washing, etc.*⟩; grade ⟨*goods etc.*⟩

**Sortiment** das; ~|e|s, ~e range (**an** + *Dat.* of)

**so·sehr** *Konj.* however much

**Soße** die; ~, ~n sauce; *(Braten~)* gravy; sauce; *(Salat~)* dressing

**sott** *1. u. 3. Pers. Sg. Prät. v.* **sieden**

**Souffleur** [zu'fløːɐ̯] der; ~s, ~e, **Souffleuse** [zu'fløːzə] die; ~, ~n prompter; **soufflieren** [zu'fliːrən] *tr. V.* prompt

**Souvenir** [suvə'niːɐ̯] das; ~s, ~s souvenir

**souverän** [zuvə'rɛːn] *Adj.* sovereign; **Souveränität** die; ~: sovereignty

**so·viel 1.** *Konj.* as *or* so far as; **2.** *Indefinitpron.* ~ **wie** *od.* **als** as much as; **halb/doppelt** ~: half/twice as much

**so·weit 1.** *Konj.* **a)** as *or* so far as; **b)** *(in dem Maße, wie)* [in] so far as; **2.** *Adv.* by and large; *(bis jetzt)* up to now; ~ **sein** *(ugs.)* be ready

**so·wenig** *Indefinitpron.* ~ **wie** *od.* **als möglich** as little as possible

**so·wie** *Konj.* **a)** *(und)* as well as; **b)** *(sobald)* as soon as

**so·wie·so** *Adv.* anyway

**sowjetisch** *Adj.* Soviet

**Sowjet·union die** *(1922–1991)* Soviet Union

**so·wohl** *Konj.* ~ ... **als** *od.* **wie [auch]** ...: both ... and ...; ... as well as ...

**sozial 1.** *Adj.* social; **2.** *adv.* socially

**sozial-, Sozial-:** ~**abgaben** *Pl.* social welfare contributions; ~**arbeiter der** social worker; ~**demokrat der** Social Democrat; ~**demokratisch** *Adj.* social democratic; ~**hilfe die** social welfare

**Sozialismus der;** ~: socialism *no art.;* **Sozialist der;** ~**en,** ~**en, Sozialistin die;** ~, ~**nen** socialist; **sozialistisch 1.** *Adj.* socialist; **2.** ~ **regierte Länder** countries with socialist governments

**Sozial-:** ~**politik die** social policy; ~**produkt das** *(Wirtsch.)* national product; ~**staat der** welfare state

**Soziologe der;** ~**n,** ~**n** sociologist; **Soziologie die;** ~: sociology; **soziologisch 1.** *Adj.* sociological; **2.** *adv.* sociologically

**Sozius der;** ~, ~**se a)** *Pl. auch:* **Sozii** *(Wirtsch.: Teilhaber)* partner; **b)** *(beim Motorrad)* pillion

**so·zu·sagen** *Adv.* as it were

**Spachtel der;** ~**s,** ~ *od.* **die;** ~, ~**n** putty-knife; *(zum Malen)* palette-knife; **spachteln** *tr. V.* **a)** stop, fill ⟨*hole, crack, etc.*⟩; smooth over ⟨*wall, panel, surface, etc.*⟩; **b)** *(ugs.: essen)* put away *(coll.)* ⟨*food, meal*⟩

**Spagat der** *od.* **das;** ~**[e]s,** ~**e** splits *pl.*

**Spaghetti** *Pl.* spaghetti *sing.*

**spähen** *itr. V.* peer; *(durch ein Loch, eine Ritze usw.)* peep; **Späher der;** ~**s,** ~ *(Milit.)* scout; *(Posten)* look-out; *(Spitzel)* informer

**Spalier das;** ~**s,** ~**e a)** trellis; **b)** *(Ehren~)* guard of honour; ~ **stehen** line the route; ⟨*soldiers*⟩ form a guard of honour

**Spalt der;** ~**[e]s,** ~**e** opening; *(im Fels)* fissure; crevice; *(zwischen Vorhängen)* chink; gap; *(langer Riß)* crack; **Spalte die;** ~, ~**n a)** crack; *(Fels~)* crevice **b)** *(Druckw.)* column; **spalten** *unr. (auch regelm.) tr., refl. V.* split

**Span der;** ~**[e]s, Späne** *(Hobel~)* shaving

**Span·ferkel das** sucking pig

**Spange die;** ~, ~**n** clasp; *(Haar~)* hair-slide *(Brit.);* barrette *(Amer.);* *(Arm~)* bracelet; bangle

**Spaniel** ['ʃpaːni̯əl] **der;** ~**s,** ~**s** spaniel

**Spanien** ['ʃpaːni̯ən] **(das);** ~**s** Spain; **Spanier der;** ~**s,** ~: Spaniard; **spanisch** *Adj.* Spanish

**Span·korb der** chip basket; chip

**spann** *1. u. 3. P. Sing. Prät. v.* **spinnen**

**spannen 1.** *tr. V.* **a)** tighten ⟨*violin string, violin bow, etc.*⟩; draw ⟨*bow*⟩; tension ⟨*spring, tennis net, drumhead, saw-blade*⟩; stretch ⟨*fabric, shoe, etc.*⟩; draw *or* pull ⟨*line*⟩ tight *or* taut; flex ⟨*muscle*⟩; cock ⟨*gun, camera shutter*⟩; **b)** *(befestigen)* put up ⟨*washing-line*⟩; stretch ⟨*net, wire, tarpaulin, etc.*⟩ (**über** + *Akk.* over); **c)** *(schirren)* harness (**vor, an** + *Akk.* to); **2.** *refl. V.* **a)** become *or* go taut; ⟨*muscles*⟩ tense; **b)** *(geh.: sich wölben)* **sich über etw.** *(Akk.)* ~: span sth.; **3.** *itr. V.* ⟨*clothing*⟩ be [too] tight; ⟨*skin*⟩ be taut; **spannend 1.** *Adj.* exciting; *(stärker)* thrilling; **2.** *adv.* excitingly; *(stärker)* thrillingly; **Spannung die;** ~, ~**en a)** *o. Pl.* excitement; *(Neugier)* suspense; **b)** *o. Pl. (eines Romans, Films usw.)* suspense; **c)** *(Zwistigkeit, Nervosität)* tension; **d)** *(Elektrot.)* voltage

**Spann·weite die** [wing-]span

**Spar·buch das** savings book

**sparen 1.** *tr. V.* save; **2.** *itr. V.* **a)** save; **für** *od.* **auf etw.** *(Akk.)* ~: save up for sth.; **b)** *(sparsam wirtschaften)* economize (**mit** on); **an etw.** *(Dat.)* ~: be sparing with sth.; *(beim Einkauf)* economize on sth.; **Sparer der;** ~**s,** ~: saver

**Spargel der;** ~**s,** ~, *schweiz. auch* **die;** ~, ~**n** asparagus *no pl., no indef. art.*

**Spar-:** ~**groschen der** *(ugs.)* nest-egg; savings *pl.;* ~**kasse die** savings bank; ~**konto das** savings *or* deposit account

**spärlich 1.** *Adj.* sparse ⟨*vegetation, beard, growth*⟩; thin ⟨*hair, applause*⟩; scanty ⟨*left-overs, knowledge, news, evidence, clothing*⟩; poor ⟨*lighting*⟩; **2.** *adv.* sparsely, thinly ⟨*populated, covered*⟩; poorly ⟨*lit, attended*⟩; scantily ⟨*dressed*⟩

**sparsam 1.** *Adj.* thrifty ⟨*person*⟩; *(wirtschaftlich)* economical; **mit etw. ~ sein** be economical with sth.; **2.** *adv.* **~ mit der Butter/dem Papier umgehen** use butter/paper sparingly; economize on butter/paper; **Sparsamkeit die; ~:** thrift[iness]; *(Wirtschaftlichkeit)* economicalness

**Sparte die; ~, ~n a)** *(Teilbereich)* area; *(eines Geschäfts)* line [of business]; **b)** *(Rubrik)* section

**Spaß der; ~es, Späße a)** *o. Pl. (Vergnügen)* fun; **~ an etw.** *(Dat.)* **haben** enjoy sth.; **[jmdm.] ~ machen** be fun [for sb.]; **viel ~!** have a good time!; **b)** *(Scherz)* joke; *(Streich)* prank; **er macht nur ~:** he's only joking; **~ beiseite!** joking aside; **~ muß sein!** there's no harm in a joke; **~ verstehen** be able to take a joke; **im** *od.* **zum** *od.* **aus ~:** as a joke; for fun; **spaßen** *itr. V.* **a)** *(Spaß machen)* joke; **b) er läßt nicht mit sich ~:** he won't stand for any nonsense; **mit ihm/damit ist nicht zu ~:** he/it is not to be trifled with; **spaßes·halber** *Adv.* for the fun of it; for fun; **spaßig** *Adj.* funny; comical; amusing

**spät 1.** *Adj.* late; **wie ~ ist es?** what time is it?; **2.** *adv.* late; **~ am Abend** late in the evening

**Spaten der; ~s, ~:** spade

**später 1.** *Adj.* **a)** later ⟨*years, generations, etc.*⟩; **b)** *(zukünftig)* future ⟨*owner, wife, etc.*⟩; **2.** *Adv.* later; **spätestens** *Adv.* at the latest

**Spatz der; ~en, ~en a)** sparrow; **b)** *(fam.: Liebling)* pet

**Spätzle** *Pl.* spaetzle; *kind of noodles*

**spazieren** *itr. V.; mit sein* stroll

**spazieren-: ~|fahren 1.** *unr. itr. V.; mit sein* go for a ride; **2.** *tr. V.* **ein Kind |im Kinderwagen| ~fahren** take a baby for a walk [in a pram]; **~|gehen** *unr. itr. V.; mit sein* go for a walk

**Spazier-: ~gang der** walk; **~gänger der; ~s, ~:** person out for a walk

**SPD** [ɛspeː'deː] *die; ~* = *Abk.* **Sozialdemokratische Partei Deutschlands** SPD

**Specht der; ~|e|s, ~e** woodpecker

**Speck der; ~|e|s, ~e a)** bacon fat; *(Schinken~)* bacon; **b)** *(ugs. scherzh.: Fettpolster)* fat; flab *(sl.);* **speckig** *Adj.* greasy

**Spediteur** [ʃpediˈtøːɐ̯] *der; ~s, ~e* carrier; haulage contractor; *(Möbel~)* furniture-remover

**Speer der; ~|e|s, ~e a)** spear; **b)** *(Sportgerät)* javelin

**Speichel der; ~s** saliva

**Speicher der; ~s, ~ a)** storehouse; *(Lagerhaus)* warehouse; **b)** *(südd.: Dachboden)* loft; **c)** *(Elektronik)* memory; **speichern** *tr. V.* store

**speien** *(geh.) unr. tr., itr. V.* spit

**Speise die; ~, ~n a)** *(Gericht)* dish; **b)** *o. Pl. (geh.: Nahrung)* food

**Speise-: ~gaststätte die** restaurant; **~kammer die** larder; **~karte die** menu; **~lokal das** restaurant

**speisen** *(geh.)* **1.** *itr. V.* eat; *(dinieren)* dine; **2.** *tr. V.* eat; *(dinieren)* dine on

**Speise-: ~saal der** dining-hall; *(im Hotel, in einer Villa usw.)* dining-room; **~wagen der** restaurant car *(Brit.);* **~zettel der** menu

**Spektakel der; ~s, ~** *(ugs.) (Lärm)* row *(coll.);* rumpus *(coll.);* **spektakulär 1.** *Adj.* spectacular; **2.** *adv.* spectacularly

**Spekulation die; ~, ~en** speculation; **spekulieren** *itr. V.* **a)** *(ugs.)* **darauf ~, etw. tun zu können** count on being able to do sth.; **b)** *(Wirtsch.)* speculate **(mit in)**

**Spelunke die; ~, ~n** *(ugs. abwertend)* dive *(coll.)*

**Spelze die; ~, ~n** *(des Getreidekorns)* husk

**Spende die; ~, ~n** donation; contribution; **spenden** *tr., itr. V.* **a)** donate; give; **b)** *(fig. geh.)* give ⟨*light*⟩; afford, give ⟨*shade*⟩; give off ⟨*heat*⟩; **Spender der; ~s, ~, Spenderin die; ~, ~nen** donor; donator; **spendieren** *tr. V.* *(ugs.)* get, buy ⟨*drink, meal, etc.*⟩; stand ⟨*round*⟩

**Spengler der; ~s, ~** *(südd., österr., schweiz.) s.* **Klempner**

**Sperling der; ~s, ~e** sparrow

**Sperma das; ~s, Spermen** sperm; semen

**sperr·angel·weit** *Adv. (ugs.)* **~ offen** *od.* **geöffnet** wide open

**Sperre die; ~, ~n a)** barrier; *(Straßen~)* road-block; *(Milit.)* obstacle; **b)** *(fig.)* ban; *(Handels~)* embargo; *(Import~, Export~)* blockade; *(Nachrichten~)* [news] black-out; **sperren 1.** *tr. V.* **a)** close; close off ⟨*area*⟩; block ⟨*entrance, access, etc.*⟩; lock ⟨*mechanism etc.*⟩; **b)** cut off ⟨*water, gas, electricity, etc.*⟩; **c)** *(Bankw.)* stop ⟨*cheque, overdraft facility*⟩; freeze ⟨*bank account*⟩; **d)** *(ein~)* **ein Tier/ jmdn. in etw.** *(Akk.)* **~:** shut an animal/sb. in sth.; **e)** *(Sport: von der Teilnahme ausschließen)* ban; **f)** *(Druckw.: spationieren)* print ⟨*word,* *text*⟩ with the letters spaced; **2.** *refl. V.* **sich** |**gegen etw.**| ~: balk [at sth.]; **Sperr·holz** das plywood; **sperrig** *Adj.* unwieldy

**Sperr-:** ~**müll** der bulky refuse *(for which there is a separate collection service);* ~**sitz** der *(im Kino)* seat in the back stalls; *(im Zirkus)* front seat; *(im Theater)* seat in the front stalls; ~**stunde** die closing time

**Spesen** *Pl.* expenses; **auf** ~: on expenses

**Spezi** der; ~**s**, ~|**s**| *(südd., österr., schweiz. ugs.)* [bosom] pal *(coll.)*; chum *(coll.)*

**spezialisieren** *refl. V.* specialize **(auf + Akk.** in); **Spezialist** der; ~**en**, ~**en** specialist; **Spezialität** die; ~, ~**en** speciality; **speziell 1.** *Adj.* special; specific ⟨*question, problem, etc.*⟩; **2.** *Adv.* especially; *(eigens)* specially; **spezifisch 1.** *Adj.* specific; characteristic ⟨*smell, style*⟩; **2.** *adv.* specifically

**spicken** *tr. V.* lard

**spie** *1. u. 3. Pers. Sg. Prät. v.* **speien**

**Spiegel** der; ~**s**, ~ **a)** mirror; **b)** *(Wasser~, fig.: Konzentration)* level

**spiegel-, Spiegel-:** ~**bild** das reflection; ~**blank** *Adj.* shining; ~**ei** das fried egg; ~**glatt** *Adj.* like glass *postpos.;* as smooth as glass *postpos.*

**spiegeln 1.** *itr. V.* **a)** *(glänzen)* shine; gleam; **b)** *(als Spiegel wirken)* reflect the light; **2.** *tr. V.* reflect; mirror; **3.** *refl. V.* be mirrored *or* reflected

**Spiegel·reflex·kamera** die reflex camera

**Spiel** das; ~|**e**|**s**, ~**e a)** play; **b)** *(Glücks~; Gesellschafts~)* game; *(Wett~)* game; match; **auf dem** ~ **stehen** be at stake; **etw. aufs** ~ **setzen** put sth. at stake; risk sth.; **Spiel·bank** die; *Pl.* ...**banken** casino; **spielen 1.** *itr. V.* **a)** play; **auf der Gitarre** ~: play the guitar; **um Geld** ~: play for money; **b)** *(als Schauspieler)* act; perform; **c) der Roman/Film spielt im 17. Jahrhundert/in Berlin** the novel/film is set in the 17th century/in Berlin; **d)** *(fig.)* **das Blau spielt ins Violette** the blue is tinged with purple; **2.** *tr. V.* **a)** play; **Cowboy** ~: play at being a cowboy; **Geige** *usw.* ~: play the violin *etc.*; **b)** *(aufführen, vorführen)* put on ⟨*play*⟩; show ⟨*film*⟩; perform ⟨*piece of music*⟩; play ⟨*record*⟩; **den Beleidigten/Unschuldigen** ~ *(fig.)* act offended/play the innocent; **spielend**

*Adv.* easily; **Spieler** der; ~**s**, ~: player; *(Glücks~)* gambler; **Spielerei** die; ~, ~**en a)** *o. Pl.* playing *no art.;* *(im Glücksspiel)* gambling *no art.;* **b) eine** ~ **mit Worten/Zahlen** playing [around] with words/numbers; **Spielerin** die; ~, ~**nen** *s.* Spieler

**Spiel-:** ~**feld** das field; pitch *(Brit.);* *(Tennis, Squash, Volleyball usw.)* court; ~**film** der feature film; ~**kamerad** der playmate; ~**karte** die playing-card; ~**plan** der programme; ~**platz** der playground; ~**raum** der room to move *(fig.);* scope; latitude; ~**sachen** *Pl.* toys; ~**verderber** der; ~**s**, ~: spoil-sport; ~**waren** *Pl.* toys; ~**zeug** das **a)** toy; *(fig.)* toy; plaything; **b)** *o. Pl.* *(~sachen, ~waren)* toys *pl.*

**Spieß** der; ~**es**, ~**e a)** *(Waffe)* spear; **den** ~ **umdrehen** *od.* **umkehren** *(ugs.)* turn the tables; **b)** *(Brat~)* spit; **c)** *(Fleisch~)* kebab; **d)** *(Soldatenspr.)* [company] sergeant-major

**Spießer** der; ~**s**, ~ *(abwertend)* [petit] bourgeois; **spießig** *(abwertend)* **1.** *Adj.* [petit] bourgeois; **2.** *adv.* ⟨*think, behave, etc.*⟩ in a [petit] bourgeois way

**Spinat** der; ~|**e**|**s**, ~**e** spinach

**Spind** der *od.* das; ~|**e**|**s**, ~**e** locker

**Spindel** die; ~, ~**n** spindle

**Spinne** die; ~, ~**n** spider; **spinnen 1.** *unr. tr. V.* **a)** spin *(fig.);* plot ⟨*intrigue*⟩; think up ⟨*idea*⟩; hatch ⟨*plot*⟩; **2.** *unr. itr. V.* **a)** spin; **b)** *(ugs.: verrückt sein)* be crazy *or (sl.)* nuts; **Spinnen·netz** das spider's web; **Spinner** der; ~**s**, ~ **a)** *(Beruf)* spinner; **b)** *(ugs. abwertend)* nut-case *(sl.);* idiot; **Spinnerei** die; ~, ~**en** spinning mill; **Spinnerin** die; ~, ~**nen** *s.* Spinner

**Spinn-:** ~**rad** das spinning-wheel; ~**webe** die; ~, ~**n** cobweb

**Spion** der; ~**s**, ~**e a)** spy; **b)** *(Guckloch)* spyhole; **Spionage** [ʃpio'na:ʒə] die; ~: spying; espionage; **spionieren** *itr. V.* spy; **Spionin** die; ~, ~**nen** spy

**Spirale** die; ~, ~**n** spiral

**Spiral·feder** die coil spring

**Spirituose** die; ~, ~**n** spirit *usu. in pl.*

**Spiritus** der; ~, ~**se** spirit; ethyl alcohol

**Spiritus·kocher** der spirit stove

**Spital** das; ~**s**, **Spitäler** *(bes. österr., schweiz.)* hospital

**spitz 1.** *Adj.* **a)** pointed; sharp ⟨*pencil, needle, stone, etc.*⟩; fine ⟨*pen nib*⟩; *(Geom.)* acute ⟨*angle*⟩; **b)** *(schrill)* shrill

⟨*cry etc.*⟩; **c)** *(boshaft)* cutting ⟨*remark etc.*⟩; **2.** *adv.* **a)** ~ **zulaufen** taper to a point; ~ **zulaufend** pointed; **b)** *(boshaft)* cuttingly

**Spitz** der; ~es, ~e spitz

**spitz-, Spitz-: ~bart** der goatee; **~bube** der *(scherzh.: Schlingel)* rascal; **~bübisch 1.** *Adj.* mischievous; **2.** *adv.* mischievously

**spitze** *indekl. Adj. (ugs.) s.* **klasse; Spitze** die; ~, ~n **a)** point; *(Pfeil~, Horn~ usw.)* tip; **b)** *(Turm~, Baum~, Mast~ usw.)* top; *(eines Berges)* summit; **c)** *(Zigarren~, Haar~, Zweig~)* end; *(Schuh~)* toe; *(Finger~, Nasen~)* tip; **d)** *(vorderes Ende)* front; **an der** ~ **liegen** *(Sport)* be in the lead *or* in front; **e)** *(führende Position)* top; **f)** *(einer Firma, Organisation usw.)* head; *(einer Hierarchie)* top; *(leitende Gruppe)* management; **g)** *(Höchstwert)* maximum; peak; **h)** |**absolute/einsame**| ~ **sein** *(ugs.)* be [absolutely] great *(coll.)*; **i)** *(fig.: Angriff)* dig **(gegen** at); **j)** *(Textilwesen)* lace

**Spitzel** der; ~s, ~: informer

**spitzen** *tr. V.* sharpen ⟨*pencil*⟩; purse ⟨*lips, mouth*⟩; prick up ⟨*ears*⟩

**Spitzen-: ~erzeugnis das** top-quality product; **~klasse** die top class; **~qualität** die top quality; **~sportler** top sportsman

**spitz-, Spitz-: ~findig** *Adj.* hairsplitting; **~hacke** die pick; **~|kriegen** *tr. V. (ugs.)* tumble to *(coll.)*; **~name** der nickname

**Spleen** [ʃpliːn] der; ~s, ~e *od.* ~s strange habit; eccentricity

**Splitt** der; ~|e|s, ~e [stone] chippings *pl.; (zum Streuen)* grit

**Splitter** der; ~s, ~: splinter; *(Granat~, Bomben~)* splinter; **splittern** *itr. V.* **a)** *(Splitter bilden)* splinter; **b)** *mit sein (in Splitter zerbrechen)* ⟨*glass, windscreen, etc.*⟩ shatter; **splitternackt** *Adj. (ugs.)* stark naked; starkers *pred. (Brit. sl.);* **Splitter··partei** die splinter party

**sponsern** *tr. V.* sponsor; **Sponsor** der; ~s, ~en sponsor

**spontan 1.** *Adj.* spontaneous; **2.** *adv.* spontaneously

**sporadisch 1.** *Adj.* sporadic; **2.** *adv.* sporadically

**Spore** die; ~, ~n spore

**Sporn** der; ~|e|s, Sporen *(des Reiters)* spur; **einem Pferd die Sporen geben** spur a horse

**Sport** der; ~|e|s **a)** sport; *(als Unter-*richtsfach*)* sport; PE; ~ **treiben** do sport; **b)** *(Hobby, Zeitvertreib)* hobby; pastime

**Sport-: ~fest das** sports festival; *(einer Schule)* sports day; **~flugzeug** das sports plane; **~geist** der; *o. Pl.* sportsmanship; **~journalist** der sports journalist; **~kleidung** die sportswear

**Sportler** der; ~s, ~: sportsman; **Sportlerin** die; ~, ~nen sportswoman; **sportlich 1.** *Adj.* **a)** sporting *attrib.;* **b)** *(fair)* sportsmanlike; sporting; **c)** *(fig.: flott, rasant)* sporty ⟨*car, driving, etc.*⟩; **d)** *(zu sportlicher Leistung fähig)* sporty, athletic ⟨*person*⟩; **e)** *(jugendlich wirkend)* sporty, smart but casual ⟨*clothes*⟩; smart but practical ⟨*hair-style*⟩; **2.** *adv.* **a)** as far as sport is concerned; **b)** *(fair)* sportingly; **c)** *(fig.: flott, rasant)* in a sporty manner

**Sport-: ~platz** der sports field; *(einer Schule)* playing field/fields *pl.;* **~schuh** der sports shoe; **~stadion** das [sports] stadium; **~verein** der sports club; **~wagen** der **a)** *(Auto)* sports car; **b)** *(Kinderwagen)* pushchair *(Brit.);* stroller *(Amer.)*

**Spott** der; ~|e|s mockery; *(höhnischer)* ridicule; derision; **spott·billig** *Adj., adv. (ugs.)* dirt cheap; **spötteln** *itr. V.* mock [gently]; poke *or* make [gentle] fun; **spotten** *itr. V.* **a)** mock; poke *or* make fun; *(höhnischer)* ridicule; be derisive; **b)** **einer Sache** *(Gen.)* ~: be contemptuous of *or* scorn sth.; **Spötter** der; ~s, ~: mocker; **spöttisch 1.** *Adj.* mocking; *(höhnischer)* derisive; **2.** *adv.* mockingly; **Spott·preis** der *(ugs.)* ridiculously low price

**sprach 1. u. 3. Pers. Sg. Prät. v. sprechen; Sprache** die; ~, ~n **a)** language; **in englischer** ~: in English; **b)** *(Sprechweise)* way of speaking; speech; *(Stil)* style; **c)** **etw. zur** ~ **bringen** bring sth. up; raise sth.; **heraus mit der** ~**!** come on, out with it!; **Sprachen·schule** die language school

**Sprach-: ~fehler** der speech impediment *or* defect; **~führer** der phrasebook; **~kenntnisse** *Pl.* knowledge *sing.* of a language/languages; **~kurs** der language course

**sprachlich 1.** *Adj.* linguistic; **2.** *adv.* linguistically

**sprach-, Sprach-: ~los** *Adj. (über-*

*rascht)* speechless; **~rohr das** *(Repräsentant)* spokesman; *(Propagandist)* mouthpiece; **~unterricht der** language teaching

**sprang** *1. u. 3. Pers. Sg. Prät. v. springen*

**Spray** [ʃpreː] **das** *od.* **der;** ~s, ~s spray; **Spray·dose die** aerosol [can]; **sprayen** *tr., itr. V.* spray

**Sprech-:** **~anlage die** intercom *(coll.);* **~chor der** chorus

**sprechen** 1. *unr. itr. V.* speak (über + Akk. about; von about, of); *(sich unterhalten, sich besprechen auch)* talk (über + Akk., von about); *⟨parrot etc.⟩* talk; **deutsch/flüsternd** ~: speak German/in a whisper; **für/gegen etw.** ~: speak in favour of/against sth.; **mit jmdm.** ~: speak or talk with or to sb.; **mit wem spreche ich?** who is speaking please?; 2. *unr. tr. V.* **a)** speak *⟨language, dialect⟩;* say *⟨word, sentence⟩;* „**Hier spricht man Deutsch**" 'German spoken'; **b)** *(rezitieren)* say, recite *⟨poem, text⟩;* say *⟨prayer⟩;* **c) jmdn.** ~: speak to sb.; **d)** *(aus~)* pronounce *⟨name, word, etc.⟩;* **Sprecher der;** ~s, ~ **a)** spokesman; **b)** *(Ansager)* announcer; *(Nachrichten~)* newscaster; news-reader; **c)** *(Kommentator, Erzähler)* narrator

**sprech-, Sprech-:** **~funk·gerät das** radio-telephone; *(Walkie-talkie)* walkie-talkie; **~stunde die** consultation hours *pl.; (eines Arztes)* surgery; **~stunden·hilfe die** *(eines Arztes)* receptionist; *(eines Zahnarztes)* assistant; **~zimmer das** consulting-room

**spreizen** *tr. V.* spread *⟨fingers, toes, etc.⟩;* **die Beine** ~: spread one's legs apart; open one's legs

**Spreiz·fuß der** *(Med.)* spread foot

**sprengen** *tr. V.* **a)** blow up; blast *⟨rock⟩;* **etw. in die Luft** ~: blow sth. up; **b)** *(gewaltsam öffnen, aufbrechen)* force [open] *⟨door⟩;* force *⟨lock⟩;* burst, break *⟨bonds, chains⟩;* *(fig.)* break up *⟨meeting, demonstration⟩;* **c)** *(be~)* water *⟨flower-bed, lawn⟩;* sprinkle *⟨street, washing⟩* with water; *(verspritzen)* sprinkle; *(mit dem Schlauch)* spray

**Sprenkel der;** ~s, ~: spot; dot; speckle; **sprenkeln** *tr. V.* sprinkle spots of *⟨colour⟩;* sprinkle *⟨water⟩*

**Spreu die;** ~: chaff

**sprich** *Imperativ Sg. v.* **sprechen;** **sprichst** *2. Pers. Sg. Präsens v.* **sprechen;** **spricht** *3. Pers. Sg. Präsens v.*

**sprechen;** **Sprich·wort das;** *Pl.* **Sprichwörter** proverb

**sprießen** *unr. itr. V.; mit sein ⟨leaf, bud⟩* shoot, sprout; *⟨seedlings⟩* come or spring up; *⟨beard⟩* sprout

**Spring·brunnen der** fountain; **springen** 1. *unr. itr. V.* **a)** *mit sein (auch Sport)* jump; *(mit Schwung)* leap; spring; jump; *⟨frog, flea⟩* hop, jump; *(sich in Sprüngen fortbewegen)* bound; **b)** *mit sein (fig.)⟨pointer, milometer, etc.⟩* jump (auf + Akk. to); *⟨traffic-lights⟩* change (auf + Akk. to); *⟨spark⟩* leap; *⟨ball⟩* bounce; **c)** *mit sein ⟨string, glass, porcelain, etc.⟩* break; *(Risse, Sprünge bekommen)* crack; 2. *unr. tr. V.; auch mit sein (Sport)* perform *⟨somersault, twist dive, etc.⟩*

**Springer der;** ~s, ~ **a)** *(Sport)* jumper; **b)** *(Schachfigur)* knight

**spring·lebendig** *Adj.* extremely lively; full of beans *pred. (coll.)*

**Spring·reiten das** show-jumping *no art.*

**sprinten** *itr. (auch tr.) V.; mit sein* sprint; **Sprinter der;** ~s, ~, **Sprinterin die;** ~, ~nen *(Sport)* sprinter

**Sprit der;** ~[e]s, ~e **a)** *(ugs.: Treibstoff)* gas *(Amer. coll.);* juice *(sl.);* petrol *(Brit.);* **b)** *(ugs.: Schnaps)* shorts *pl.*

**Spritze die;** ~, ~n **a)** syringe; **b)** *(Injektion)* injection; **c)** *(Feuer~)* hose; *(Löschfahrzeug)* fire engine

**spritzen** 1. *tr. V.* **a)** *(versprühen)* spray; *(ver~)* splash; *(in Form eines Strahls)* spray, squirt *⟨water, foam, etc.⟩;* pipe *⟨cream etc.⟩;* **b)** *(be~, besprühen)* water *⟨lawn, tennis-court⟩;* water, spray *⟨street, yard⟩;* spray *⟨plants, crops, etc.⟩;* *(mit Lack)* spray *⟨car etc.⟩;* **jmdn. naß** ~: splash sb.; *(mit Wasserpistole, Schlauch)* spray sb.; **c)** *(injizieren)* inject *⟨drug etc.⟩;* *(ugs.: einer Injektion unterziehen)* **jmdn./sich** ~: give sb. an injection/inject oneself; 2. *itr. V.; mit Richtungsangabe mit sein ⟨hot fat⟩* spit *⟨mud etc.⟩* spatter, splash; *⟨blood, water⟩* spurt; **Spritzer der;** ~s, ~ *(kleiner Tropfen)* splash; *(von Farbe)* splash; spot; **spritzig** 1. *Adj.* **a)** sparkling *⟨wine⟩;* tangy *⟨fragrance, perfume⟩;* **b)** lively *⟨show, music, article⟩;* sparkling *⟨performance⟩;* racy *⟨style⟩;* nippy *(coll.);* zippy *⟨car, engine⟩;* agile *⟨person⟩;* 2. *adv.* sparklingly *⟨produced, performed, etc.⟩;* racily *⟨written⟩;* **Spritz·tour die** *(ugs.)* spin

**spröd, spröde** *Adj.* **a)** brittle ⟨*glass, plastic, etc.*⟩; dry ⟨*hair, lips, etc.*⟩; *(rissig)* chapped ⟨*lips, skin*⟩; *(rauh)* rough ⟨*skin*⟩; **b)** *(fig.: abweisend)* aloof ⟨*person, manner, nature*⟩

**sproß** *1. u. 3. Pers. Sg. Prät. v.* **sprießen**; **Sproß** der; **Sprosses, Sprosse** *(Bot.)* shoot

**Sprosse** die; ~, ~n **a)** *(auch fig.)* rung; **b)** *(eines Fensters)* glazing bar

**Sprößling** der; ~s, ~e *(ugs. scherzh.)* offspring; **seine** ~e his offspring *pl.*

**Sprotte** die; ~, ~n sprat

**Spruch** der; ~|e|s, **Sprüche** *(Wahl~)* motto; *(Sinn~)* maxim; *(Aus~)* saying; aphorism; *(Zitat)* quotation; **spruch·reif** *Adj.* **das ist noch nicht** ~: that's not definite, so people mustn't start talking about it yet

**Sprudel** der; ~s, ~ **a)** sparkling mineral water; **b)** *(österr.)* fizzy drink; **sprudeln** *itr. V.; mit sein* bubble; ⟨*lemonade, champagne, etc.*⟩ fizz, effervesce; **Sprudel·wasser** das; *Pl.* -wässer sparkling mineral water

**Sprüh·dose** die aerosol [can]; **sprühen 1.** *tr. V.* spray; **2.** *itr. V.; mit Richtungsangabe mit sein* ⟨*sparks, spray*⟩ fly; *(fig.)* ⟨*eyes*⟩ sparkle (**vor** + *Dat.* with); ⟨*intellect, wit*⟩ sparkle

**Sprüh·regen** der drizzle; fine rain

**Sprung** der; ~|e|s, **Sprünge a)** *(auch Sport)* jump; *(schwungvoll)* leap; *(Satz)* bound; *(fig.)* leap; **keine großen Sprünge machen können** *(fig. ugs.)* not be able to afford many luxuries; **auf dem ~|e| sein** *(fig. ugs.)* be in a rush; **b)** *(ugs.: kurze Entfernung)* stone's throw; **c)** *(Riß)* crack

**Sprung·brett** das *(auch fig.)* springboard; **sprunghaft 1.** *Adj.* **a)** erratic ⟨*person, character, manner*⟩; disjointed ⟨*conversation, thoughts*⟩; **b)** *(unvermittelt)* sudden; **c)** *(ruckartig)* rapid ⟨*change*⟩; sharp ⟨*increase*⟩; **2.** *adv.; s.* **1 b-c:** disjointedly; suddenly; rapidly; sharply

**Spucke** die; ~: spit; **spucken 1.** *itr. V.* spit; **in die Hände** ~ *(fig.: an die Arbeit gehen)* go to work with a will; **2.** *tr. V.* spit; cough up ⟨*blood, phlegm*⟩

**Spuk** der; ~|e|s, ~e [ghostly *or* supernatural] manifestation; **spuken** *itr. V.; unpers.* **hier/in dem Haus spukt es** this place/the house is haunted

**Spule** die; ~, ~n spool *(für Tonband, Film)* spool; reel

**Spüle** die; ~, ~n sink unit; *(Becken)* sink

**spulen** *tr., itr. V.* spool; *(am Tonbandgerät)* wind

**spülen 1.** *tr. V.* **a)** rinse; bathe ⟨*wound*⟩; **b)** *(landsch.: abwaschen)* wash up ⟨*dishes, glasses, etc.*⟩; **Geschirr** ~: wash up; **2.** *itr. V.* **a)** *(beim WC)* flush [the toilet]; **b)** *(den Mund ausspülen)* rinse out [one's mouth]; **c)** *(landsch.) s.* **abwaschen 2**

**Spül-:** ~**maschine** die dishwasher; ~**mittel** das washing-up liquid

**Spur** die; ~, ~en **a)** *(Abdruck im Boden)* track; *(Folge von Abdrücken)* tracks *pl.;* **eine heiße** ~ *(fig.)* a hot trail; **jmdm./einer Sache auf der** ~ **sein** be on to the track *or* trail of sb./sth.; **b)** *(Anzeichen)* trace; *(eines Verbrechens)* clue (*Gen.* to); **c)** *(sehr kleine Menge; auch fig.)* trace; **d)** *(Verkehrsw.: Fahr~)* lane; **die** ~ **wechseln** change lanes

**spürbar 1.** *Adj.* noticeable; distinct, perceptible ⟨*improvement*⟩; evident ⟨*relief, embarrassment*⟩; **2.** *adv.* noticeably; perceptibly; *(sichtlich)* clearly ⟨*relieved, on edge*⟩; **spüren** *tr. V.* feel; *(instinktiv)* sense

**spur·los 1.** *Adj.* total, complete ⟨*disappearance*⟩; **2.** *adv.* ⟨*disappear*⟩ completely *or* without trace

**Spür·sinn** der; *o. Pl. (feiner Instinkt)* intuition

**Spurt** der; ~|e|s, ~s *od.* ~e spurt; **spurten** *itr. V.* **a)** *mit Richtungsangabe mit sein* spurt; **b)** *mit sein (ugs.: schnell laufen)* sprint

**sputen** *refl. V. (veralt.)* make haste

**St.** *Abk.* **a) Sankt** St.; **b) Stück**

**Staat** der; ~|e|s, ~en state; **staatlich 1.** *Adj.* state *attrib.;* ⟨*power, unity, etc.*⟩ of the state; state-owned ⟨*factory etc.*⟩; **2.** *adv.* by the state; ~ **anerkannt/geprüft** state-approved/-certified

**staats-, Staats-:** ~**angehörige** der/die national; ~**angehörigkeit** die nationality; ~**anwalt** der public prosecutor; ~**bürger** der citizen; **er ist deutscher** ~**bürger** he is a German citizen *or* national; ~**bürgerlich** *Adj.* civil ⟨*rights*⟩; civic ⟨*duties, loyalty*⟩; ⟨*education, attitude*⟩ as a citizen; ~**bürgerschaft** die *s.* ~**angehörigkeit**; ~**grenze** die state frontier *or* border; ~**mann** der; *Pl.* -männer statesman; ~**oberhaupt** das head of state; ~**präsident** der [state] president

**Stab** der; ~|e|s, **Stäbe a)** rod; *(länger)*

pole; *(eines Käfigs, Gitters, Geländers)*
bar; **b)** *(Milit.)* staff; **c)** *(Team)* team
**stabil 1.** *Adj.* sturdy ⟨*chair, cupboard*⟩;
robust, sound ⟨*health*⟩; stable ⟨*prices,*
*government, economy, etc.*⟩; **2.** *adv.* ~
**gebaut** solidly built; **stabilisieren 1.**
*tr. V.* stabilize; **2.** *refl. V.* **a)** stabilize;
**b)** ⟨*health, circulation, etc.*⟩ become
stronger
**Stab·lampe** die torch *(Brit.)*; flashlight *(Amer.)*
**Stabs·arzt** der *(Milit.)* medical officer, MO *(with the rank of captain)*
**stach** *1. u. 3. Pers. Sg. Prät. v.* **stechen**
**Stachel** der; ~s, ~n **a)** spine; *(Dorn)*
thorn; **b)** *(Gift~)* sting; **c)** *(spitzes Me-*
*tallstück)* spike; *(an ~draht)* barb
**Stachel-:** ~**beere** die gooseberry;
~**draht** der barbed wire
**stachelig** *Adj.* prickly
**Stadion** das; ~s, **Stadien** stadium
**Stadium** das; ~s, **Stadien** stage
**Stadt** die; ~, **Städte a)** town; *(Groß~)*
city; **die** ~ **Basel** the city of Basel; **in**
**die** ~ **gehen** go into town; go downtown *(Amer.)*; **b)** *(Verwaltung)* town
council; *(in der Großstadt)* city council; city hall *no art. (Amer.)*
**Stadt-:** ~**bahn** die urban railway;
~**bummel** der *(ugs.)* **einen** ~**bummel**
**machen** take a stroll through the
town/city centre
**Städter** der; ~s, ~, **Städterin** die; ~,
~**nen a)** town-dweller; *(Großstädter,*
*-städterin)* city-dweller; **b)** *(Stadt-*
*mensch)* townie *(coll.)*
**Stadt-:** ~**führer** der town/city guidebook; ~**gespräch** das: ~**gespräch**
**sein** be the talk of the town
**städtisch 1.** *Adj.* **a)** *(kommunal)* municipal; **b)** *(urban)* urban ⟨*life, way of*
*life, etc.*⟩; **2.** *adv. (kommunal)* muni-
cipally
**Stadt-:** ~**mauer** die town/city wall;
~**mitte** die town centre; *(einer Groß-*
*stadt)* city centre; downtown area
*(Amer.)*; ~**park** der municipal park;
~**plan** der [town/city] street plan *or*
map; ~**rand** der outskirts *pl.* of the
town/city; **am** ~: on the outskirts of
the town/city; ~**rundfahrt** die sightseeing tour round a/the city;
~**teil** der district; part [of a/the town];
~**tor** das town/city gate; ~**viertel**
das district
**Staffel** die; ~, ~n **a)** *(Sport: Mann-*
*schaft)* relay team; **b)** *(Sport: ~lauf)*
relay race; **c)** *(Luftwaffe: Einheit)*
flight; **d)** *(Eskorte)* escort formation

**Staffelei** die; ~, ~en easel
**stahl** *1. u. 3. Pers. Sg. Prät. v.* **stehlen**
**Stahl** der; ~[e]s, **Stähle** *od.* ~**e** steel
**Stahl-:** ~**beton** der reinforced concrete; ~**blech** das sheet steel
**stählern** *Adj.; nicht präd.* steel
**stak** *1. u. 3. Pers. Sg. Prät. v.* **stecken**
**Stall** der; ~[e]s, **Ställe** *(Pferde~,*
*Renn~)* stable; *(Kuh~)* cowshed;
*(Hühner~)* [chicken-]coop; *(Schwei-*
*ne~)* [pig]sty; *(für Kaninchen, Klein-*
*tiere)* hutch; *(für Schafe)* pen; **Stal-**
**lung** die; ~, ~en *(Pferdestall)* stable;
*(Kuhstall)* cow-shed; *(Schweinestall)*
[pig]sty
**Stamm** der; ~[e]s, **Stämme a)**
*(Baum~)* trunk; **b)** *(Volks~)* tribe;
**Stamm·baum** der family tree; *(ei-*
*nes Tieres)* pedigree
**stammeln** *tr., itr. V.* stammer
**stammen** *itr. V.* come (aus, von
from); *(datieren)* date (aus, von from)
**Stamm-:** ~**gast** der *(im Lokal/Hotel)*
regular customer/visitor; regular
*(coll.)*; ~**tisch** der **a)** *(Tisch)* regulars'
table *(coll.)*; **b)** *(~tischrunde)* group of
regulars *(coll.)*; **c)** *(Treffen)* get-
together with the regulars *(coll.)*
**stampfen 1.** *itr. V.* **a)** *(laut auftreten)*
stamp; **b)** *mit sein (sich fortbewegen)*
tramp; *(mit schweren Schritten)*
trudge; **2.** *tr. V.* **a)** mit den Füßen den
**Rhythmus** ~: tap the rhythm with
one's feet; **b)** *(fest~)* compress; **c)**
*(zerkleinern)* mash ⟨*potatoes*⟩
**stand** *1. u. 3. Pers. Sg. Prät. v.* **stehen**
**Stand** der; ~[e]s, **Stände a)** *o. Pl. (das*
*Stehen)* standing position; [bei jmdm.
*od.* gegen jmdm.] einen schweren ~ **ha-**
**ben** *(fig.)* have a tough time [of it]
[with sb.]; **b)** *(~ort)* position; **c)** *(Ver-*
*kaufs~; Box für ein Pferd)* stall; *(Mes-*
*se~, Informations~)* stand; *(Zei-*
*tungs~)* [newspaper] kiosk; **d)** *o. Pl.*
*(erreichte Stufe; Zustand)* state; **etw.**
**auf den neu[e]sten** ~ **bringen** bring sth.
up to date; **e)** *(des Wassers, Flusses)*
level; *(des Thermometers, Zählers, Ba-*
*rometers)* reading; *(der Kasse, Finan-*
*zen)* state; *(eines Himmelskörpers)* position; **f)** *o. Pl. (Familien~)* status; **g)**
*(Gesellschaftsschicht)* class; *(Berufs~)*
trade; *(Ärzte, Rechtsanwälte)* [profes-
sional] group
**Standard** der; ~s, ~s standard
**Ständchen** das; ~s, ~: serenade;
**jmdm. ein** ~ **bringen** serenade sb.
**Ständer** der; ~s, ~: stand; *(Kleider~)*
coat-stand; *(Wäsche~)* clothes-horse

**stạndes-, Stạndes-:** ~**amt** das registry office; ~**amtlich 1.** *Adj.; nicht präd.* registry office ⟨*wedding, document*⟩; **2.** *adv.* ~**amtlich heiraten** get married in a registry office; ~**beamte** der registrar

**stạnd-, Stạnd-:** ~**fest** *Adj.* steady; stable; strong ⟨*stalk, stem*⟩; ~**haft 1.** *Adj.* steadfast; **2.** *adv.* steadfastly; ~**haftigkeit die;** ~: steadfastness; ~**|halten** *unr. itr. V.* stand firm; **einer Sache** *(Dat.)* ~**halten** withstand sth.

**stạndig 1.** *Adj.* constant ⟨*noise, worry, pressure, etc.*⟩; permanent ⟨*residence, correspondent, staff, member, etc.*⟩; standing ⟨*committee*⟩; regular ⟨*income*⟩; **2.** *adv.* constantly

**Stạnd-:** ~**licht** das *(Kfz-W.)* sidelights *pl.;* ~**ort der;** *Pl.* ~**orte a)** position; *(eines Betriebes o. ä.)* location; site; **b)** *(Milit.: Garnison)* garrison; base; ~**punkt der** *(fig.)* point of view; viewpoint; **auf dem** ~**punkt stehen, daß ...:** take the view that ...; ~**spur die** *(Verkehrsw.)* hard shoulder; ~**uhr die** grandfather clock

**Stạnge die;** ~, ~**n** pole; *(aus Metall)* bar; *(dünner)* rod; *(Kleider*~*)* rail; *(Vogel*~*)* perch; **ein Anzug von der** ~ *(ugs.)* an off-the-peg-suit

**Stạngen-:** ~**brot** das French bread; ~**spargel** der asparagus spears *pl.*

**stạnk** *1. u. 3. Pers. Sg. Prät. v.* stinken

**Stạpel der;** ~**s,** ~: pile; **ein** ~ **Holz** a pile *or* stack of wood; **stạpeln 1.** *tr. V.* pile up; stack; **2.** *refl. V.* pile up

**stạpfen** *itr. V.; mit sein* tramp

¹**Stạr der;** ~|e|**s,** ~**e** *od. (schweiz.)* ~**en** *(Vogel)* starling

²**Stạr der;** ~**s,** ~**s** *(berühmte Persönlichkeit)* star

³**Stạr der;** ~|e|**s** *(Med.)* **grauer** ~: cataract; **grüner** ~: glaucoma

**stạrb** *1. u. 3. Pers. Sg. Prät. v.* sterben

**stạrk;** stärker, stärkst... **1.** *Adj.* **a)** strong; potent ⟨*drink, medicine, etc.*⟩; powerful ⟨*engine, lens, voice, etc.*⟩; *(ausgezeichnet)* excellent; *s. auch* Stück c; **b)** *(dick)* thick; stout ⟨*rope, string*⟩; *(verhüll.: korpulent)* well-built *(euphem.);* **c)** *(zahlenmäßig groß, umfangreich)* sizeable, large; big ⟨*demand*⟩; **eine 100 Mann** ~**e Truppe** a 100-strong unit; **d)** *(heftig, intensiv)* heavy; severe ⟨*frost, pain*⟩; strong ⟨*impression, current, resistance, dislike*⟩; grave ⟨*doubt, reservations*⟩; great ⟨*exaggeration, interest*⟩; loud ⟨*applause*⟩; **e)** *(Jugendspr.: großartig)* great *(coll.);*

fantastic *(coll.);* **2.** *adv.* **a)** *(sehr, überaus, intensiv)* *(mit Adj.)* very; heavily ⟨*indebted, stressed*⟩; greatly ⟨*increased, reduced, enlarged*⟩; strongly ⟨*emphasized, characterized*⟩; badly ⟨*damaged, worn, affected*⟩; *(mit Verb);* heavily; *(exaggerate, impress)* greatly; ⟨*enlarge, reduce, increase*⟩ considerably; ⟨*support, oppose, suspect*⟩ strongly; ⟨*remind*⟩ very much; ~ **erkältet sein** have a heavy *or* bad cold; **b)** *(Jugendspr.: großartig)* fantastically *(coll.);* **Stạrk·bier** das strong beer; **Stärke die;** ~, ~**n a)** *o. Pl.* strength; *(eines Motors)* power; *(einer Glühbirne)* wattage; **b)** *(Dicke)* thickness; *(Technik)* gauge; **c)** *o. Pl. (zahlenmäßige Größe)* strength; **d)** *(besondere Fähigkeit, Vorteil)* strength; **jmds.** ~/**nicht jmds.** ~ **sein** be sb.'s forte/not be sb.'s strong point; **e)** *(Intensität)* strength; *(von Sturm, Schmerzen, Abneigung)* intensity; *(von Frost)* severity; *(von Lärm, Verkehr)* volume; **f)** *(organischer Stoff)* starch; **stärken 1.** *tr. V.* **a)** strengthen; boost ⟨*power, prestige*⟩; ⟨*drink, food, etc.*⟩ fortify ⟨*person*⟩; **b)** *(steif machen)* starch ⟨*washing etc.*⟩; **2.** *refl. V.* refresh oneself; **Stärkung die;** ~, ~**en a)** *o. Pl.* strengthening; **b)** *(Erfrischung)* refreshment

**stạrr 1.** *Adj.* **a)** rigid; *(steif)* stiff **(vor +** *Dat.* with); fixed ⟨*expression, smile, stare*⟩; **b)** *(nicht abwandelbar)* inflexible, rigid ⟨*law, rule, principle*⟩; **c)** *(unnachgiebig)* inflexible ⟨*person, attitude, etc.*⟩; **2.** *adv.* rigidly; *(steif)* stiffly

**stạrren** *itr. V.* **a)** stare **(in +** *Akk.* into, **auf, an, gegen +** *Akk.* at); **jmdm. ins Gesicht** ~: stare sb. in the face; **b) vor/ von Schmutz** ~: be filthy

**Stạrr·sinn der;** *o. Pl.* pig-headedness

**stạrr·sinnig** *Adj.* pig-headed

**Stạrt der;** ~|e|**s,** ~**s** start; *(eines Flugzeugs)* take-off; *(einer Rakete)* launch; **Stạrt·bahn die** [take-off] runway; **stạrt·bereit** *Adj.* ready to start *postpos.;* ⟨*aircraft*⟩ ready for take-off; **stạrten 1.** *itr. V.; mit sein* **a)** start; ⟨*aircraft*⟩ take off; ⟨*rocket*⟩ blast off, be launched; **b)** *(den Motor anlassen)* start the engine; **2.** *tr. V.* start; launch ⟨*rocket, satellite, attack*⟩; start [up] ⟨*engine, machine, car*⟩

**Station die;** ~, ~**en a)** station; **b)** *(Haltestelle)* stop; **c)** *(Zwischen*~, *Aufenthalt)* stopover; ~ **machen** stop over *or*

off; **d)** *(Kranken~)* ward; **stationär**
**1.** *Adj. (Med.)* ⟨*treatment*⟩ in hospital,
as an in-patient; **2.** *adv. (Med.)* in hospital; **jmdn. ~ behandeln** treat sb. as
an in-patient; **stationieren** *tr. V.*
station ⟨*troops*⟩; deploy ⟨*weapons,
bombers, etc.*⟩
**Stations-:** **~arzt** der ward doctor;
**~schwester** die ward sister; **~taste**
die *(Rundf.)* preset [tuning] button;
preset
**Statistik** die; **~:** statistics *sing., no
art.*
**statt 1.** *Präp. mit Gen.* instead of; **~**
**dessen** instead [of this]; **2.** *Konj.: s.* **an-
statt**
**statt-:** **~|finden** *unr. itr. V.* take
place; ⟨*process, development*⟩ occur;
**~haft** *Adj.* permissible
**stattlich 1. a)** well-built; imposing
⟨*figure, stature, building, etc.*⟩; fine
⟨*farm, estate*⟩; impressive ⟨*trousseau,
collection*⟩; **b)** *(beträchtlich)* considerable; **2.** *adv.* impressively
**Statue** die; **~, ~n** statue
**Statur** die; **~, ~en** build
**Status** der; **~, ~** ['ʃta:tu:s] status
**Statut** das; **~|e|s, ~en** statute
**Stau** der; **~|e|s, ~s** *od.* **~e a)** build-up;
**b)** *(von Fahrzeugen)* tailback *(Brit.)*;
backup *(Amer.)*
**Staub** der; **~|e|s** dust; **~ wischen** dust;
**~ saugen** vacuum *or (Brit. coll.)*
hoover; **sich aus dem ~|e| machen** *(fig.
ugs.)* make oneself scarce *(coll.)*;
**stauben** *itr. V.* cause dust; **staubig**
*Adj.* dusty
**staub-, Staub-:** **~saugen** *itr., tr. V.*
vacuum, *(Brit. coll.)* hoover; **~sau-
ger** der vacuum cleaner; Hoover
*(Brit. P)*; **~tuch** das; *Pl.* **~tücher**
duster
**Staude** die; **~, ~n** *(Bot.)* herbaceous
perennial
**stauen 1.** *tr. V.* dam [up] ⟨*stream,
river*⟩; staunch ⟨*blood*⟩; **2.** *refl. V.* ⟨*water, blood, etc.*⟩ accumulate, build up;
⟨*people*⟩ form a crowd; ⟨*traffic*⟩ form a
tailback/tailbacks *(Brit.) or (Amer.)*
backup/backups
**staunen** *itr. V.* be amazed *or* as-
tonished **(über +** *Akk.* at); *(beein-
druckt sein)* marvel **(über +** *Akk.* at);
**~d** with *or* in amazement; **Staunen**
das; **~s** amazement **(über +** *Akk.* at);
*(Bewunderung)* wonderment
**Stauung** die; **~, ~en a)** *(eines Bachs,
Flusses)* damming; *(des Blutes, Wassers)* stemming the flow; *(das Sich-*

*stauen)* build-up; **b)** *(Verkehrsstau)*
tailback *(Brit.);* backup *(Amer.);* jam
**Std.** *Abk.* Stunde hr.
**stechen 1.** *unr. itr. V.* **a)** prick; ⟨*wasp,
bee*⟩ sting; ⟨*mosquito*⟩ bite; **b)** *(hin-
ein~)* mit etw. in etw. *(Akk.)* ~: stick
*or* jab sth. into sth.; **2.** *unr. tr. V. (mit
dem Messer, Schwert)* stab; *(mit der
Nadel, mit einem Dorn usw.)* prick;
⟨*bee, wasp*⟩ sting; ⟨*mosquito*⟩ bite; **sich**
**in den Finger ~:** prick one's finger
**Stech-:** **~mücke** die mosquito; gnat;
**~uhr** die time clock
**Steck-:** **~brief** der description [of
a/the wanted person]; *(Plakat)*
'wanted' poster; **~dose** die socket;
power point
**stecken 1.** *tr. V.* **a)** put; **b)** *(mit Na-
deln)* pin ⟨*hem, lining, etc.*⟩; pin [on]
⟨*badge*⟩; pin up ⟨*hair*⟩; **2.** *itr. V.* be; **wo**
**steckt meine Brille?** *(ugs.)* where have
my glasses got to *or* gone?; **hinter etw.**
*(Dat.)* ~ *(fig. ugs.)* be behind sth.
**stecken-, Stecken-:** **~|bleiben**
*unr. itr. V.; mit sein* get stuck; **~|las-
sen** *unr. tr. V.* leave; **~pferd** das **a)**
*(Spielzeug)* hobby-horse; **b)** *(Liebha-
berei)* hobby
**Stecker** der; **~s, ~:** plug; **Steck·na-
del** die pin
**Steg** der; **~|e|s, ~e** *(Brücke)* [narrow]
bridge; *(Laufbrett)* gangplank;
*(Boots~)* landing-stage
**Steg·reif** der: **aus dem ~:** impromptu
**stehen** *unr. itr. V.; südd., österr.,
schweiz. mit sein* **a)** stand; **b)** *(sich befinden)* be; ⟨*upright object, building*⟩
stand; **c)** *(einen bestimmten Stand haben)* **auf etw.** *(Dat.)* ~ ⟨*needle, hand*⟩
point to sth.; **das Barometer steht tief/
auf Regen** the barometer is reading
low/indicating rain; **das Spiel/es steht**
**1 : 1** *(Sport)* the score is one all; **die Sache steht gut/schlecht** things are going
well/badly; **d)** *(einen bestimmten
Kurs, Wert haben)* ⟨*currency*⟩ stand
**(bei** at); **wie steht das Pfund?** what is
the rate for the pound?; **e)** *(nicht in
Bewegung sein)* be stationary; ⟨*machine etc.*⟩ be at a standstill; **meine Uhr**
**steht** my watch has stopped; **f)** *(geschrieben, gedruckt sein)* be; **in der
Zeitung steht, daß ...:** it says in the
paper that ...; **g)** *(Sprachw.: gebraucht
werden)* ⟨*subjunctive etc.*⟩ occur; be
found; **h) jmdm. |gut| ~** ⟨*dress etc.*⟩ suit
sb. [well]
**stehen:** **~|bleiben** *unr. itr. V.; mit
sein* **a)** stop; ⟨*traffic*⟩ come to a stand-

still; **b)** *(stehengelassen werden)* stay; be left; *(zurückgelassen werden)* be left behind; *(der Zerstörung entgehen)* ⟨*building*⟩ be left standing; ~|**lassen** *unr. tr. V.* **a)** leave; **b)** *(vergessen)* leave [behind]

**Steh·lampe** die standard lamp *(Brit.)*; floor lamp *(Amer.)*

**stehlen** *unr. tr., itr. V.* steal; *s. auch* **gestohlen 2**

**Steh·platz** der *(im Theater usw.)* standing place; *(im Bus)* space to stand

**Steiermark** die; ~: Styria *no art.*

**steif 1.** *Adj.* stiff; *(förmlich)* stiff; formal; **2.** *adv.* stiffly

**steigen 1.** *unr. itr. V.; mit sein* **a)** climb; ⟨*mist, smoke, sun*⟩ rise; ⟨*balloon*⟩ climb, rise; **auf die Leiter** ~: get on to the ladder; **in den/aus dem Bus/ Zug** ~: board *or* get on/get off *or* out of the bus/train; **b)** *(ansteigen, zunehmen)* rise; ⟨*price, salary, output*⟩ increase, rise; ⟨*debts, tension*⟩ increase, mount; ⟨*chances*⟩ improve; **2.** *unr. tr. V.; mit sein* climb ⟨*stairs, steps*⟩; **Steiger** der; ~s, ~ *(Bergbau)* overman

**steigern 1.** *tr. V.* **a)** increase ⟨*speed, value, sales, consumption, etc.*⟩ (**auf** + *Akk.* to); step up ⟨*demands, production, etc.*⟩; raise ⟨*standards, requirements*⟩; *(verstärken)* intensify ⟨*fear, tension*⟩; heighten ⟨*effect*⟩; **b)** *(Sprachw.)* compare ⟨*adjective*⟩; **2.** *refl. V.* ⟨*confusion, speed, profit, etc.*⟩ increase; ⟨*pain, excitement, tension, etc.*⟩ become more intense; ⟨*costs*⟩ escalate; ⟨*effect*⟩ be heightened; **Steigerung** die; ~, ~**en a)** increase *(Gen.* in); *(Verstärkung)* intensification; *(einer Wirkung)* heightening; *(Verbesserung)* improvement *(Gen.* in); *(bes. Sport: Leistungs~)* improvement [in performance]; **b)** *(Sprachw.)* comparison

**Steigung** die; ~, ~**en** gradient

**steil 1.** *Adj.* steep; meteoric ⟨*career*⟩; rapid ⟨*rise*⟩; **2.** *adv.* steeply; **Steil·hang** der steep escarpment

**Stein** der; ~[e]s, ~e stone; *(Fels)* rock; *(Bau~)* [stone]block; **mir fällt ein** ~ **vom Herzen** that's a weight off my mind; **Stein·bock** der **a)** ibex; **b)** *(Astrol.)* Capricorn; the Goat; **steinern** *Adj.* stone; **Stein·gut** das earthenware; **stein·hart** *Adj.* rock-hard; **steinig** *Adj.* stony

**Stein-:** ~**kohle** die [hard] coal;

~**metz** der; ~**en**, ~**en** stonemason; ~**obst** das stone-fruit; ~**pilz** der cep; ~**schlag** der rock fall; „**Achtung ~schlag**" 'beware falling rocks'; ~**zeit** die Stone Age; *(fig.)* stone age

**Steiß·bein** das *(Anat.)* coccyx

**Stelle** die; ~, ~**n a)** place; **an jmds.** ~ **treten** take sb.'s place; **ich an deiner** ~ **...:** ... if I were you; **an achter** ~ **liegen** be in eighth place; **die erste** ~ **hinter** *od.* **nach dem Komma** *(Math.)* the first decimal place; **an** ~ (+ *Gen.*) instead of; **auf der** ~: immediately; **b)** *(begrenzter Bereich)* patch; *(am Körper)* spot; **c)** *(Passage)* passage; *(Punkt im Ablauf einer Rede usw.)* point; **d)** *(Arbeits~)* job; post; **eine freie** ~: a vacancy; **e)** *(Dienst~)* office; *(Behörde)* authority; **stellen 1.** *tr. V.* **a)** put; *(mit Sorgfalt)* place; *(aufrecht hin~)* stand; **b)** *(ein~)* set ⟨*points, clock, scales*⟩; **den Wecker auf 6 Uhr** ~: set the alarm for 6 o'clock; **die Heizung höher/niedriger** ~: turn the heating up/down; **c)** *(bereit~)* provide; **d) jmdn. besser** ~: ⟨*firm*⟩ improve sb.'s pay; **gut/schlecht/besser gestellt** comfortably/badly/better off; **e)** *verblaßt* put ⟨*question*⟩; set ⟨*task, topic, condition*⟩; make ⟨*application, demand, request*⟩; **jmdm. eine Frage** ~: ask sb. a question; **2.** *refl. V.* **a)** place oneself; **sich auf die Zehenspitzen** ~: stand on tiptoe; **b) sich schlafend/taub/tot** *usw.* ~: feign sleep/ deafness/death *etc.;* pretend to be asleep/deaf/dead *etc.*

**stellen-, Stellen-:** ~**angebot** das offer of a job; *(Inserat)* job advertisement; „**~angebote**" 'situations vacant'; ~**gesuch** das 'situation wanted' advertisement; ~**weise** *Adv.* in places

**Stellung** die; ~, ~**en** position; **zu etw.** ~ **nehmen** express one's opinion on sth.; **Stellungnahme** die; ~, ~**n** opinion; *(kurze Äußerung)* statement; **Stell·vertreter** der deputy

**Stelze** die; ~, ~**n** stilt; **stelzen** *itr. V.; mit sein* strut; stalk

**stemmen 1.** *tr. V.* **a)** *(hoch~)* lift [above one's head]; **b)** *(drücken)* brace ⟨*feet, knees*⟩ (**gegen** against); **2.** *refl. V.* **sich gegen etw.** ~: brace oneself against sth.

**Stempel** der; ~**s**, ~: stamp; *(Post~)* postmark; **stempeln** *tr. V.* stamp ⟨*passport, form*⟩; postmark ⟨*letter*⟩; cancel ⟨*postage stamp*⟩

**Stengel** der; ~s, ~: stem; stalk
**steno-, Steno-:** ~**gramm** das shorthand text; ~**graph** der; ~en, ~en stenographer; ~**graphie** die; ~, ~n stenography *no art.;* shorthand *no art.;* ~**graphieren** *itr. V.* do shorthand; ~**typistin** die shorthand typist
**Stepp·decke** die quilt
**Steppe** die; ~, ~n steppe
**steppen** *tr. (auch itr.) V.* backstitch
**sterben** *unr. itr. V.; mit sein* die; **im Sterben liegen** lie dying; **sterbens·krank** *Adj.* mortally ill; **sterblich** *Adj.* mortal
**stereo** *Adv.* in stereo; **Stereo** das; ~s stereo; **Stereo·anlage** die stereo [system]
**steril** *Adj.* sterile
**Sterling** ['stɛːlɪŋ]: **Pfund** ~: pound/pounds sterling
**Stern** der; ~[e]s, ~e star; **Sternchen** das; ~s, ~ *(Druckw.)* asterisk; **Stern·schnuppe** die; ~, ~n shooting star
**Stethoskop** [ʃteto'skoːp] das; ~s, ~e *(Med.)* stethoscope
**¹Steuer** das; ~s, ~: [steering-]wheel; *(von Schiffen)* helm; **²Steuer** die; ~, ~n tax
**steuer-, Steuer-:** ~**berater** der tax consultant *or* adviser; ~**bord** das *od. österr.* der; *o. Pl. (Seew., Flugw.)* starboard; ~**erklärung** die tax return; ~**frei** *Adj.* tax-free; ~**mann** der; *Pl.* ~leute *od.* ~männer *(Rudersport)* cox
**steuern** 1. *tr. V. (fahren)* steer; *(fliegen)* pilot, fly ⟨*aircraft*⟩; fly ⟨*course*⟩; 2. *itr. V.* **a)** be at the wheel; *(auf dem Schiff)* be at the helm; **b)** *mit sein (Kurs nehmen, ugs.: sich hinbewegen; auch fig.)* head; **Steuerung** die; ~, ~en **a)** *(System)* controls *pl.;* **b)** *o. Pl. s.* steuern 1: steering; piloting; flying
**Steward** ['stjuːɐt] der; ~s, ~s steward; **Stewardeß** ['stjuːɐdɛs] die; ~, Stewardessen stewardess
**stich** *Imper. Sg. v.* stechen
**Stich** der; ~[e]s, ~e **a)** *(mit einer Waffe)* stab; **b)** *(Dornen~, Nadel~)* prick; *(von Wespe, Biene usw.)* sting; *(Mücken~ usw.)* bite; **c)** *(~wunde)* stab wound; **d)** *(beim Nähen)* stitch; **e)** *(Schmerz)* stabbing *or* shooting pain; **f)** *(Kartenspiel)* trick; **g)** jmdn./etw. im ~ lassen leave sb. in the lurch/abandon sth.; **sticheln** *itr. V.* make snide remarks *(coll.)* ⟨*gegen* about⟩
**stich-, Stich-:** ~**flamme** die tongue of flame; ~**haltig** *Adj.* sound ⟨*argu-*

*ment, reason*⟩; valid ⟨*assertion, reply*⟩; conclusive ⟨*evidence*⟩; ~**probe** die [random] sample; *(bei Kontrollen)* spot check
**stichst** *2. Pers. Sg. Präsens v.* stechen; **sticht** *3. Pers. Sg. Präsens v.* stechen
**Stich-:** ~**tag** der set date; deadline; ~**wunde** die stab wound
**sticken** 1. *itr. V.* do embroidery; 2. *tr. V.* embroider; **Stickerei** die; ~, ~en embroidery *no pl.; (gestickte Arbeit)* piece of embroidery; **Stick·garn** das embroidery thread
**stickig** *Adj.* stuffy; stale ⟨*air*⟩; **Stick·stoff** der nitrogen
**Stief-** step ⟨*brother, child, mother, etc.*⟩
**Stiefel** der; ~s, ~ boot
**Stief·mütterchen** das *(Bot.)* pansy; **stief·mütterlich** 1. *Adj.* poor, shabby ⟨*treatment*⟩; 2. *adv.* ~ behandeln treat ⟨*person*⟩ poorly *or* shabbily; neglect ⟨*pet, flowers, doll, problem*⟩
**stieg** *1. u. 3. Pers. Sg. Prät. v.* steigen
**Stieglitz** der; ~es, ~e goldfinch
**stiehl** *Imp. Sg. v.* stehlen; **stiehlst** *2. Pers. Sg. Präsens v.* stehlen; **stiehlt** *3. Pers. Sg. Präsens v.* stehlen
**Stiel** der; ~[e]s, ~e *(Griff)* handle; *(Besen~)* [broom-]stick; *(für Süßigkeiten)* stick; *(bei Gläsern)* stem; *(bei Blumen)* stem; *(an Obst usw.)* stalk
**Stier** der; ~[e]s, ~e bull
**stieren** *itr. V.* stare [vacantly] (**auf** + *Akk.* at)
**Stier·kampf** der bullfight
**stieß** *1. u. 3. Pers. Sg. Prät. v.* stoßen
**Stift** der; ~[e]s, ~e **a)** *(aus Metall)* pin; *(aus Holz)* peg; **b)** *(Blei~)* pencil; *(Mal~)* crayon; *(Schreib~)* pen
**stiften** *tr. V.* **a)** found, establish ⟨*monastery, hospital, etc.*⟩; endow ⟨*prize, scholarship*⟩; *(als Spende)* donate, give (**für** to); **b)** *(herbeiführen)* cause, create ⟨*unrest, confusion, strife, etc.*⟩; bring about ⟨*peace, order, etc.*⟩; arrange ⟨*marriage*⟩; **Stifter** der; ~s, ~: founder; *(Spender)* donor
**Stift·zahn** der *(Zahnmed.)* post crown
**Stil** der; ~[e]s, ~e style; **stilistisch** 1. *Adj.* stylistic; 2. *adv.* stylistically
**still** 1. *Adj.* quiet; *(ohne Geräusche)* silent; still; *(reglos)* still; *(wortlos)* silent; *(heimlich)* secret; **der Stille Ozean** the Pacific [Ocean]; 2. *adv.* quietly; *(geräuschlos)* silently; *(wortlos)* in silence; **Stille** die; ~: quiet; *(Geräuschlosigkeit)* silence; stillness; **stillegen** *tr. V.* close *or* shut down;

close ⟨railway line⟩; **stillen 1.** tr. V. **a)**
**ein Kind** ~: breast-feed a baby; **b)** (be-friedigen) satisfy; quench ⟨thirst⟩; **c)**
(eindämmen) stop ⟨bleeding, tears, pain⟩; **2.** itr. V. breast-feed
**still-, Still-:** ~|**halten** unr. itr. V.
keep or stay still; ~|**legen** s. stille-gen; ~**schweigen** das silence;
~**schweigen bewahren** maintain
silence; keep silent; ~**schweigend**
**1.** Adj. silent; (ohne Abmachung) tacit
⟨assumption, agreement⟩; **2.** adv. in
silence; (ohne Abmachung) tacitly;
~|**sitzen** unr. itr. V. sit still; ~**stand**
der; o. Pl. standstill; ~|**stehen** unr.
itr. V. **a)** ⟨factory, machine⟩ stand idle;
⟨traffic⟩ be at a standstill; ⟨heart etc.⟩
stop; **b)** (Milit.) stand to attention
**Stimm·bruch** der: **er ist im** ~: his
voice is breaking; **Stimme** die; ~, ~n
**a)** voice; **b)** (bei Wahlen) vote
**stimmen 1.** itr. V. **a)** be right or cor-rect; **stimmt es, daß ...?** is it true
that ...?; **b)** (seine Stimme geben) vote;
**mit Ja** ~: vote yes or in favour; **2.** tr.
V. **a)** (in eine Stimmung versetzen)
make; **b)** (Musik) tune ⟨instrument⟩
**Stimm-:** ~**enthaltung** die absten-tion; ~**recht** das right to vote
**Stimmung** die; ~, ~en **a)** mood; **b)**
(Atmosphäre) atmosphere
**Stink·bombe** die stink-bomb; **stin-ken** unr. itr. V. stink (**nach** of); **stin-kig** Adj. (salopp abwertend) stinking;
smelly
**stirb** Imp. Sg. v. **sterben**; **stirbst**
**2.** Pers. Sg. Präsens v. **sterben**; **stirbt**
**3.** Pers. Sg. Präsens v. **sterben**
**Stirn** die; ~, ~en forehead; brow
**stöbern** itr. V. (ugs.) rummage
**stochern** itr. V. poke
**¹Stock** der; ~[e]s, Stöcke **a)** stick; (Zei-ge~) pointer; stick; (Takt~) baton;
(Ski~) pole; stick; **b)** (Pflanze) (Ro-sen~) [rose-]bush; (Reb~) vine;
**²Stock** der; ~[e]s, ~ (Etage) floor;
storey; **in welchem** ~? on which
floor?; **stock·dunkel** Adj. (ugs.)
pitch-dark; **stocken** itr. V. **a)** ⟨traf-fic⟩ be held up; ⟨conversation, produc-tion⟩ stop; ⟨business⟩ slacken; ⟨jour-ney⟩ be interrupted; **b)** (innehalten)
falter; **stock·finster** Adj. (ugs.)
pitch-dark
**-stöckig** -storey attr.; -storeyed
**Stockung** die; ~, ~en hold-up (Gen.
in); **Stockwerk** das floor; storey
**Stoff** der; ~[e]s, ~e **a)** material; fabric;
**b)** (Materie) substance; **c)** o. Pl. (Phi-

los.) matter; **d)** (Thema) subject[-mat-ter]; (Gesprächsthema) topic; **Stoff-wechsel** der; o. Pl. metabolism
**stöhnen** itr. V. moan; (vor Schmerz)
groan
**Stola** die; ~, Stolen shawl; (Pelz~)
stole
**Stollen** der; ~s, ~ **a)** (Kuchen) Stol-len; **b)** (Bergbau) gallery; **c)** (bei Sport-schuhen) stud
**stolpern** itr. V.; mit sein stumble; trip
**stolz 1.** Adj. proud (**auf** + Akk. of);
**eine** ~**e Summe** (ugs.) a tidy sum; **2.**
adv. proudly; **Stolz** der; ~es pride
(**auf** + Akk. in); **stolzieren** itr. V.;
mit sein strut
**stop** Interj. stop; (Verkehrsw.) halt
**stopfen** tr. V. **a)** darn; **b)** (hineintun)
stuff; **c)** (füllen) stuff ⟨cushion, quilt,
etc.⟩; fill ⟨pipe⟩; plug, stop [up] ⟨hole,
leak⟩
**Stopf-:** ~**garn** das darning-cotton;
~**nadel** die darning-needle
**Stopp** der; ~s, ~s stop; (Einstellung)
freeze (Gen. on)
**Stoppel** die; ~, ~n stubble no pl.;
**stoppelig** Adj. stubbly
**stoppen** tr., itr. V. stop
**Stopp-:** ~**licht** das; Pl. ~er stop-light; ~**schild** das stop sign; ~**uhr**
die stop-watch
**Stöpsel** der; ~s, ~ plug
**Stör** der; ~s, ~e sturgeon
**Storch** der; ~[e]s, Störche stork
**stören 1.** tr. V. **a)** disturb; disrupt
⟨court proceedings, lecture, church ser-vice, etc.⟩; interfere with ⟨transmitter,
reception⟩; **b)** (mißfallen) bother; **2.**
itr. V. **a)** disturb; **b)** (Unruhe stiften)
make or cause trouble; **3.** refl. V. **sich**
**an jmdm./etw.** ~: take exception to
sb./sth.; **Störenfried** der; ~[e]s, ~e
trouble-maker
**störrisch 1.** Adj. stubborn; **2.** adv.
stubbornly
**Störung** die; ~, ~en **a)** disturbance;
(einer Gerichtsverhandlung, Vorlesung,
eines Gottesdienstes usw.) disruption;
**bitte entschuldigen Sie die** ~, **aber ...:**
I'm sorry to bother you, but ...; **b) eine**
**technische** ~: a technical fault
**Stoß** der; ~es, Stöße **a)** (mit der Faust)
punch; (mit dem Fuß) kick; (mit dem
Kopf, den Hörnern) butt; (mit dem Ell-bogen) dig; **b)** (mit einer Waffe) (Stich)
thrust; (Schlag) blow; **c)** (beim
Schwimmen, Rudern) stroke; **d)** (Sta-pel) pile; stack; **stoßen 1.** unr. tr. V.
**a)** auch itr. (mit der Faust) punch; (mit

*dem Fuß)* kick; *(mit dem Kopf, den Hörnern)* butt; *(mit dem Ellbogen)* dig; **b)** *(hineintreiben)* plunge, thrust ⟨*dagger, knife*⟩; push ⟨*stick, pole*⟩; **c)** *(schleudern)* push; **die Kugel ~:** put the shot; **2.** *unr. itr. V.* **a)** *mit sein (auftreffen)* bump (gegen into); **mit dem Kopf gegen etw. ~:** bump one's head on sth.; **b)** *mit sein (fig.)* **auf etw.** *(Akk.)* ~ *(etw. entdecken)* come upon sth.; **auf Ablehnung** ~ *(abgelehnt werden)* meet with disapproval; **c)** *(grenzen)* **an etw.** *(Akk.)* ~ ⟨*room, property, etc.*⟩ be [right] next to sth.; **3.** *unr. refl. V.* bump or knock oneself; **sich an etw.** *(Dat.)* ~ *(fig.)* object to sth.

**Stoß-:** **~seufzer** der heartfelt groan; **~stange** die bumper

**stößt** *3. Pers. Sg. Präsens v.* stoßen; **stoß·weise** *Adv.* **a)** spasmodically; **b)** *(in Stapeln)* by the pile; in piles

**Stotterer** der; ~s, ~: stutterer; **stottern** **1.** *itr. V.* stutter; **2.** *tr. V.* stutter [out]

**Str.** *Abk.* Straße St./Rd.

**stracks** *Adv.* **a)** *(direkt)* straight; **b)** *(sofort)* straight away

**straf·bar** *Adj.* punishable; **Strafe** die; ~, ~n punishment; *(Rechtsspr.)* penalty; *(Freiheits~)* sentence; *(Geld~)* fine; **strafen** *tr. V.* punish

**straff** **1.** *Adj.* **a)** tight, taut ⟨*rope, lines, etc.*⟩; firm ⟨*breasts, skin*⟩; **b)** *(energisch)* tight ⟨*organization, planning, etc.*⟩; strict ⟨*discipline, leadership, etc.*⟩; **2.** *adv.* **a)** |zu| ~ **sitzen** ⟨*clothes*⟩ be [too] tight; **b)** *(energisch)* tightly, strictly

**straf·fällig** *Adj.* ~ **werden** commit a criminal offence

**straffen** *tr. V.* **a)** tighten; firm ⟨*skin*⟩; **b)** *(fig.)* tighten up ⟨*text, procedure, organization, etc.*⟩

**straf-, Straf-:** **~frei** *Adj.* ~frei ausgehen go unpunished; **~gefangene** der/die prisoner; **~gesetz·buch** das penal code

**sträflich** **1.** *Adj.* criminal; **2.** *adv.* criminally; **Sträfling** der; ~s, ~e prisoner

**straf-, Straf-:** **~los** *Adj.* unpunished; **~tat** die criminal offence; **~täter** der offender; **~zettel** der *(ugs.)* [parking-, speeding-, *etc.*] ticket

**Strahl** der; ~|e|s, ~en *(auch Phys., Math., fig.)* ray; *(von Scheinwerfern, Taschenlampen)* beam; *(von Flüssigkeit)* jet; **strahlen** *itr. V.* **a)** shine; **bei ~dem Wetter/Sonnenschein** in glori-

ous sunny weather/in glorious sunshine; **~d weiß** sparkling white; **b)** *(glänzen)* sparkle; **c)** *(lächeln)* beam (vor + *Dat.* with); **Strahler** der; ~s, ~ **a)** radiator; **b)** *(Heiz~)* radiant heater; **Strahlung** die; ~, ~en radiation

**Strähne** die; ~, ~n strand; **eine graue ~:** a grey streak; **strähnig** **1.** *Adj.* straggly ⟨*hair*⟩; **2.** *adv.* in strands

**stramm** **1.** *Adj.* **a)** *(straff)* tight, taut ⟨*rope, line, etc.*⟩; tight ⟨*clothes*⟩; **b)** *(kräftig)* strapping ⟨*girl, boy*⟩; sturdy ⟨*legs, body*⟩; **c)** *(gerade)* upright, erect ⟨*posture, etc.*⟩; **2.** *adv.* **a)** *(straff)* tightly; **b)** *(kräftig)* sturdily ⟨*built*⟩

**strampeln** *itr. V.* ⟨*baby*⟩ kick [his/her feet]

**Strand** der; ~|e|s, Strände beach; **am ~:** on the beach; **Strand·bad** das bathing beach *(on river, lake)*; **stranden** *itr. V.;* **mit sein** ⟨*ship*⟩ run aground; **Strand·korb** der basket chair

**Strang** der; ~|e|s, Stränge rope

**Strapaze** die; ~, ~n strain *no pl.*; **strapazieren** *tr. V.* be a strain on ⟨*person, nerves*⟩; **strapazier·fähig** *Adj.* hard-wearing ⟨*clothes, shoes*⟩; durable ⟨*material*⟩

**Straße** die; ~, ~n *(in Ortschaften)* street; road; *(außerhalb)* road

**Straßen-:** **~bahn** die tram *(Brit.);* streetcar *(Amer.);* **~ecke** die street corner; **~feger** der *(bes. nordd.)* road-sweeper; **~graben** der ditch [at the side of the road]; **~karte** die road-map; **~sperre** die road-block

**sträuben** **1.** *tr. V.* ruffle [up] ⟨*feathers*⟩; bristle ⟨*fur, hair*⟩; **2.** *refl. V.* ⟨*hair, fur*⟩ bristle, stand on end; ⟨*feathers*⟩ become ruffled; **b)** *(sich widersetzen)* resist

**Strauch** der; ~|e|s, Sträucher shrub; **straucheln** *itr. V.;* **mit sein** *(geh.)* stumble

¹**Strauß** der; ~es, Sträuße bunch of flowers; bouquet [of flowers]

²**Strauß** der; ~es, ~e *(Vogel)* ostrich **Sträußchen** das; ~s, ~: posy

**streben** *itr. V.* **a)** *mit sein* make one's way briskly; **b)** *(trachten)* strive (**nach** for); **Streber** der; ~s; ~ *(abwertend)* pushy person *(coll.);* *(in der Schule)* swot *(Brit. sl.);* grind *(Amer. sl.);* **strebsam** *Adj.* ambitious and industrious

**Strecke** die; ~, ~n distance; *(Abschnitt, Route)* route; *(Eisenbahn~|*

line; **strecken 1.** *tr. V. (gerade machen)* stretch ⟨*arms, legs*⟩; *(dehnen)* stretch [out] ⟨*arms, legs, etc.*⟩; **den Kopf aus dem Fenster** ~: stick one's head out of the window *(coll.);* **2.** *refl. V.* stretch out; **strecken·weise** *Adv.* in places; *(fig.: zeitweise)* at times

**Streich** der; ~|e|s, ~e trick; prank; jmdm. einen ~ spielen play a trick on sb.; **streicheln** *tr. V.* stroke; **streichen 1.** *unr. tr. V.* a) stroke; b) *(an~)* paint; „frisch gestrichen" 'wet paint'; c) *(auftragen)* spread ⟨*butter, jam, ointment, etc.*⟩; *(be~)* ein Brötchen mit Butter/mit Honig ~: butter a roll/spread honey on a roll; d) *(aus~, tilgen)* delete; cancel ⟨*train, flight*⟩; **2.** *unr. itr. V.* a) stroke; jmdm. über den Kopf ~: stroke sb.'s head; b) *(an~)* paint

**Streich-:** ~holz das match; ~instrument das string[ed] instrument; ~käse der cheese spread; ~wurst die [soft] sausage for spreading; ≈ meat spread

**Streife** die; ~, ~n a) *(Personen)* patrol; b) *(Streifengang)* patrol; **streifen 1.** *tr. V.* a) *(leicht berühren)* touch; ⟨*shot*⟩ graze; b) *(kurz behandeln)* touch [up]on ⟨*problem, subject, etc.*⟩; c) den Ring vom Finger ~: slip the ring off one's finger; die Ärmel nach oben ~: pull/push up one's sleeves; **2.** *itr. V.* mit sein roam; **Streifen** der; ~s, ~ a) stripe; b) *(Stück, Abschnitt)* strip; **Streifen·wagen** der patrol car; **streifig** *Adj.* streaky

**Streik** der; ~|e|s, ~s strike; **Streik·brecher** der strike-breaker; blackleg *(derog.);* **streiken** *itr. V.* a) strike; be on strike; *(in den Streik treten)* come out *or* go on strike; strike; b) *(ugs.: nicht mitmachen)* go on strike; c) *(ugs.: nicht funktionieren)* pack up *(coll.);* **Streikende** der/die; *adj. Dekl.* striker; **Streik·posten** der picket

**Streit** der; ~|e|s, ~e *(Zank)* quarrel; *(Auseinandersetzung)* dispute; argument; **streiten** *unr. itr., refl. V.* quarrel; argue; *(sich zanken)* quarrel; **Streiterei** die; ~, ~en arguing *no pl., no indef. art.; (Gezänk)* quarrelling *no pl.;* **Streitigkeit** die; ~, ~en *meist Pl.* a) quarrel; argument; b) *(Streitfall)* dispute

**streng 1.** *Adj.* a) strict; severe ⟨*punish-*

*ment*⟩; stringent, strict ⟨*rule, regulation, etc.*⟩; stringent ⟨*measure*⟩; rigorous ⟨*examination, check, test, etc.*⟩; stern ⟨*reprimand, look*⟩; absolute ⟨*discretion*⟩; complete ⟨*rest*⟩; b) *(schmucklos, herb)* austere, severe ⟨*cut, collar, style, etc.*⟩; severe ⟨*face, features, hairstyle, etc.*⟩; c) *(durchdringend)* pungent, sharp ⟨*taste, smell*⟩; d) *(rauh)* severe ⟨*winter*⟩; sharp, severe ⟨*frost*⟩; **2.** *adv.* ⟨*mark, judge, etc.*⟩ strictly, severely; ⟨*punish*⟩ severely; ⟨*look, reprimand*⟩ sternly; ⟨*smell*⟩ strongly; **Strenge** die; ~ a) *s.* streng a: strictness; severity; stringency; rigour; sternness; b) *(von [Gesichts]zügen)* severity; c) *(von Geruch, Geschmack)* pungency; sharpness; d) *s.* streng d: severity; sharpness; **strengstens** *Adv.* [most] strictly

**Streß** der; Stresses stress

**Streu** die; ~, ~en straw; **streuen** *tr. V.* a) *(ausstreuen)* spread ⟨*manure, sand, grit*⟩; sprinkle ⟨*salt, herbs, etc.*⟩; strew, scatter ⟨*flowers*⟩; b) *auch itr.* die Straßen [mit Sand/Salz] ~: grit/salt the roads

**streunen** *itr. V.; meist mit sein* wander *or* roam about *or* around; ~de Katzen/Hunde stray cats/dogs

**Streusel·kuchen** der streusel cake

**strich** *1. u. 3. Pers. Sg. Prät. v.* streichen

**Strich** der; ~|e|s, ~e *(Linie)* line; *(Gedanken~)* dash; *(Schräg~)* diagonal; *(Binde~, Trennungs~)* hyphen; auf den ~ gehen *(salopp)* walk the streets; **stricheln** *tr. V.* a) sketch in [with short lines]; b) *(schraffieren)* hatch

**Strich-:** ~junge der *(salopp)* [young] male prostitute; ~mädchen das *(salopp)* street-walker; hooker *(Amer. sl.);* ~punkt der semicolon

**Strick** der; ~|e|s, ~e cord; *(Seil)* rope; **stricken** *tr., itr. V.* knit

**Strick-:** ~jacke die cardigan; ~nadel die knitting-needle; ~zeug das knitting

**striegeln** *tr. V.* groom ⟨*horse*⟩

**strikt 1.** *Adj.* strict; **2.** *adv.* strictly

**Strippe** die; ~, ~n *(ugs.)* string; an der ~ hängen *(fig.)* be on the phone *(coll.); (dauernd)* hog the phone *(coll.)*

**Stripperin** die; ~, ~nen *(ugs.)* stripper

**stritt** *1. u. 3. Pers. Sg. Prät. v.* streiten; **strittig** *Adj.* contentious ⟨*point, problem*⟩; disputed ⟨*territory*⟩; ⟨*question*⟩ in dispute, at issue

**Stroh** das; ~|e|s straw

**Stroh-:** ~**blume** die a) *(Immortelle)* immortelle; b) *(Korbblütler)* strawflower; ~**halm** der straw; ~**witwe** die *(ugs. scherzh.)* grass widow; ~**witwer** der *(ugs. scherzh.)* grass widower

**Strolch** der; ~|e|s, ~e *(fam. scherzh.: Junge)* rascal

**Strom** der; ~|e|s, Ströme river; *(fig.)* stream; *(Strömung; Elektrizität)* current; *(~versorgung)* electricity; **unter** ~ **stehen** be live

**strom-:** ~**abwärts** *Adv.* downstream; ~**auf[wärts]** *Adv.* upstream

**strömen** *itr. V.; mit* sein stream; **Strömung** die; ~, ~en current; *(Met.)* airstream; *(fig.)* trend

**Strophe** die; ~, ~n verse; *(einer Ode)* strophe

**strotzen** *itr. V.* von *od.* vor etw. *(Dat.)* ~: be full of sth.; **von** *od.* **vor Gesundheit** ~: be bursting with health

**strubbelig** *Adj.* tousled

**Strudel** der; ~s, ~ a) whirlpool; b) *(bes. südd., österr.: Gebäck)* strudel

**Strumpf** der; ~|e|s, Strümpfe stocking; *(Socke, Knie~)* sock

**Strumpf-:** ~**band das** garter; *(Straps)* suspender *(Brit.)*; garter *(Amer.)*; ~**hose die** tights *pl. (Brit.)*; pantyhose *(esp. Amer.)*

**Strunk** der; ~|e|s, Strünke stem; stalk; *(Baum~)* stump

**struppig** *Adj.* shaggy; tangled, tousled ⟨*hair*⟩

**Stube** die; ~, ~n a) *(veralt.: Wohnraum)* [living-]room; parlour *(dated)*; b) *Milit.)* [barrack-]room; **Stubenfliege die** [common] house-fly

**Stück** das; ~|e|s, ~e a) piece; *(kleines)* bit; *(Teil, Abschnitt)* part; **ein** ~ **Kuchen** a piece *or* slice of cake; **ein** ~ **Zucker/Seife** a lump of sugar/ a piece *or* bar of soap; **im** *od.* **am** ~: unsliced ⟨*sausage, cheese, etc.*⟩; b) *(Einzel~)* item; *(Exemplar)* specimen; **ich nehme 5** ~: I'll take five [of them]; **30 Pfennig das** ~: thirty pfennigs each; ~ **für** ~: piece by piece; *(eins nach dem andern)* one by one; **das ist [ja] ein starkes** ~ *(ugs.)* that's a bit much; **ein faules/freches** ~ *(salopp)* a lazy/cheeky thing *or* devil; c) *(Bühnen~)* play; *(Musik~)* piece; **Stückchen das** ~s, ~: [little] piece; bit; **stückeln** *tr. V.* put together ⟨*sleeve, curtain*⟩ with patches

**Student** der; ~en, ~en, **Studentin die**; ~, ~nen a) student; b) *(österr.: Schüler)* [secondary-school] pupil; **Studie** ['ʃtuːdiə] die; ~, ~n study

**Studien-:** ~**aufenthalt** der study visit (in + *Dat.* to); ~**freund** der university/college friend; ~**reise** die study trip

**studieren** *tr., itr. V.* study; **Studierende** der/die; *adj. Dekl.* student; **Studio das**; ~s, ~s studio; **Studium das**; ~s, Studien study; *(Studiengang)* course of study

**Stufe** die; ~, ~n a) step; *(einer Treppe)* stair; „**Vorsicht,** ~!" 'mind the step'; b) *(Raketen~, Geol., fig.: Stadium)* stage; *(Niveau)* level; *(Steigerungs~, Grad)* degree; *(Rang)* grade

**Stuhl** der; ~|e|s, Stühle chair

**Stuhl-:** ~**gang** der; *o. Pl.* bowel movement[s]; *(Kot)* stool; ~**lehne die** *(Rückenlehne)* chair-back; *(Armlehne)* chair-arm

**stülpen** *tr. V.* etw. auf *od.* über etw. *(Akk.)* ~: pull/put sth. on to *or* over sth.

**stumm** *Adj.* dumb ⟨*person*⟩; *(schweigsam)* silent; *(wortlos)* wordless; mute ⟨*glance, gesture*⟩; **Stumme der/die;** *adj. Dekl.* mute; **die** ~**n** the dumb

**Stummel** der; ~s, ~: stump; *(Bleistift~)* stub; *(Zigaretten~/Zigarren~)* [cigarette-/cigar-]butt

**Stümper** der; ~s, ~: botcher; bungler; **stümperhaft 1.** *Adj.* incompetent; botched ⟨*job*⟩; *(laienhaft)* amateurish ⟨*attempt, drawing*⟩; **2.** *adv.* incompetently; *(laienhaft)* amateurishly; **stümpern** *itr. V.* work incompetently; *(pfuschen)* bungle

**stumpf** *Adj.* a) blunt ⟨*pin, needle, knife, etc.*⟩; b) *(glanzlos, matt)* dull ⟨*paint, hair, metal, colour, etc.*⟩; **Stumpf** der; ~|e|s, Stümpfe stump

**Stumpf·sinn** der; *o. Pl.* a) apathy; b) *(Monotonie)* monotony; tedium; **stumpf·sinnig 1.** *Adj.* a) apathetic; vacant ⟨*look*⟩; b) *(monoton)* tedious; souldestroying ⟨*job, work*⟩; **2.** *adv.* a) apathetically; ⟨*stare*⟩ vacantly; b) *(monoton)* tediously

**Stunde** die; ~, ~n hour; *(Unterrichts~)* lesson; **eine** ~ **Aufenthalt/ Pause** an hour's stop/break; a stop/ break of an hour

**stünde** *1. u. 3. Pers. Sg. Konjunktiv II v.* stehen

**stunden** *tr. V.* jmdm. einen Betrag usw. ~: allow sb. to defer payment of a sum *etc.*

**stunden-, Stunden-:** ~**kilometer** der kilometre per hour; k.p.h.; ~**lang 1.** *Adj.* lasting hours *postpos.;* **2.** *adv.*

for hours; **~lohn der** hourly wage; **~plan der** timetable; **~zeiger der** hour-hand

**-stündig** *adj.* -hour; **-stündlich** *adj.* -hourly; **zwei-/halb~**: two-hourly/ half-hourly; *adv.* every two hours/ half an hour; **stündlich** *Adj.*, *adv.* hourly

**Stups der**; **~es, ~e** *(ugs.)* push; shove; *(leicht)* nudge; **stupsen** *tr. V. (ugs.)* push; shove; *(leicht)* nudge; **Stups·nase die** snub nose

**stur** *(ugs.)* **1.** *Adj.* **a)** obstinate; dogged ⟨*insistence*⟩; *(phlegmatisch)* dour; **b)** *(unbeirrbar)* dogged; persistent; **c)** *(stumpfsinnig)* tedious; **2.** *adv.* **a)** obstinately; **b)** *(unbeirrbar)* doggedly; **c)** *(stumpfsinnig)* tediously; ⟨*learn, copy*⟩ mechanically

**stürbe** *1. u. 3. Pers. Sg. Konjunktiv II v.* **sterben**

**Sturheit die**; **~** *(ugs.)* **a)** obstinacy; *(phlegmatisches Wesen)* dourness; **b)** *(Stumpfsinnigkeit)* deadly monotony

**Sturm der**; **~[e]s, Stürme a)** storm; *(heftiger Wind)* gale; **b)** *(Milit.)* assault **(auf + Akk.** on); **~ klingeln** ring the [door]bell like mad; **stürmen 1.** *itr. V.* **a)** *unpers.* es stürmt [heftig] it's blowing a gale; **b)** *mit sein (rennen)* rush; *(verärgert)* storm; **2.** *tr. V. (Milit.)* storm ⟨*town, position, etc.*⟩; *(fig.)* besiege ⟨*booking-office, shop, etc.*⟩; **Stürmer der: ~s, ~** *(Sport)* striker; forward; **stürmisch 1.** *Adj.* **a)** stormy; *(fig.)* tempestuous, turbulent; **b)** *(ungestüm)* tumultuous ⟨*applause, welcome, reception*⟩; wild ⟨*enthusiasm*⟩; passionate ⟨*lover, embrace, temperament*⟩; vehement ⟨*protest*⟩; **2.** *adv.* ⟨*protest*⟩ vehemently; ⟨*embrace*⟩ impetuously, passionately; ⟨*demand*⟩ clamorously; ⟨*applaud*⟩ wildly

**Sturz der; -es, Stürze a)** fall; *(Unfall)* accident; **b)** *(fig.: von Preis, Temperatur usw.)* [sharp] fall, drop *(Gen.* in); **c)** *(Verlust des Amtes, der Macht)* fall; *(Absetzung)* overthrow; *(Amtsenthebung)* removal from office; **stürzen 1.** *itr. V.; mit sein* **a)** fall; *(fig.)* ⟨*temperature, exchange rate, etc.*⟩ drop [sharply]; ⟨*prices*⟩ tumble; ⟨*government*⟩ fall, collapse; **b)** *(laufen)* rush; dash; **c)** *(fließen)* stream; pour; **2.** *refl. V.* **sich auf jmdn./etw. ~** *(auch fig.)* pounce on sb./sth.; **sich in etw. (Akk.) ~**: throw oneself into sth.; **3.** *tr. V.* **a)** throw; *(mit Wucht)* hurl; **b)** *(umdrehen)* upturn ⟨*mould*⟩; turn out ⟨*pudding, cake, etc.*⟩; **c)** *(des Amtes entheben)* oust ⟨*person*⟩ [from office]; *(gewaltsam)* overthrow ⟨*leader, government*⟩; **Sturz·helm der** crash-helmet

**Stute die; ~, ~n** mare

**Stütze die; ~, ~n** *(auch fig.)* support

**¹stutzen** *itr. V.* stop short

**²stutzen** *tr. V.* trim; dock ⟨*tail*⟩; clip ⟨*ear, hedge, wing*⟩; prune ⟨*tree, bush*⟩

**stützen 1.** *tr. V.* support; *(mit Pfosten o. ä.)* prop up; *(aufstützen)* rest ⟨*head, hands, arms, etc.*⟩; **2.** *refl. V.* **sich auf jmdn./etw. ~**: lean *or* support oneself on sb./sth.

**stutzig** *Adj.* **~ werden** begin to wonder; **jmdn. ~ machen** make sb. wonder

**s.u.** *Abk.* **siehe unten** see below

**Subjekt das; ~[e]s, ~e a)** subject; **b)** *(abwertend: Mensch)* creature; **subjektiv 1.** *Adj.* subjective; **2.** *adv.* subjectively; **Subjektivität die; ~**: subjectivity

**Substantiv das; ~s, ~e** *(Sprachw.)* noun; **Substanz die; ~, ~en a)** *(auch fig.)* substance; **b)** *(Grundbestand)* **die ~**: the reserves *pl.*

**sub·tropisch** *Adj.* subtropical

**Suche die; ~, ~n** search (**nach** for); **auf der ~ [nach jmdm./etw.] sein** be looking/*(intensiver)* searching [for sb./ sth.]; **suchen 1.** *tr. V.* **a)** look for; *(intensiver)* search for; „**Leerzimmer gesucht**" 'unfurnished room wanted'; **b)** *(bedacht sein auf, sich wünschen)* seek ⟨*protection, advice, company, warmth, etc.*⟩; look for ⟨*adventure*⟩; **2.** *itr. V.* search; **nach jmdm./etw. ~**: look/ search for sb./sth.

**Sucht die; ~, Süchte** *od.* **~en a)** addiction (**nach** to); **[bei jmdm.] zur ~ werden** *(auch fig.)* become addictive [in sb.'s case]; **b)** *Pl.* **Süchte** *(übermäßiges Verlangen)* craving (**nach** for); **süchtig** *Adj.* **a)** addicted; **b)** *(fig.)* **nach etw. ~ sein** be obsessed with sth.

**Süd** *o. Art.; o. Pl. (bes. Seemannsspr., Met.) s.* **Süden**

**Süd-: ~afrika (das)** South Africa; **~amerika (das)** South America

**Sudan (das); ~s** *od.* **der; ~s** Sudan

**Süden der; ~s** south; **der ~**: the South; **Süd·frucht die** tropical [or sub-tropical] fruit; **Südländer der; ~s, ~**: Southern European; **südländisch** *Adj.* Southern [European]; Latin ⟨*temperament*⟩; **~ aussehen** have Latin looks; **südlich 1.** *Adj.* **a)** southern; **b)** *(nach, von Süden)* southerly; **c)** *(aus dem Süden)* Southern; **2.** *adv.*

southwards; **3.** *Präp. mit Gen.* [to the] south of

**süd-, Süd-**: ~**pol** der South Pole; ~**see** die; ~: die ~: the South Seas *pl.;* ~**see·insel** die South Sea island; ~**tirol (das)** South Tirol ~**wärts** *Adv.* southwards; ~**wind** der south *or* southerly wind

**Sues·kanal** ['zuːɛs-] der; ~s Suez Canal

**Sühne** die; ~, ~n *(geh.)* atonement; expiation; **sühnen** *tr., itr. V.* |**für**| etw. ~: atone for *or* pay the penalty for sth.

**Sultanine** die; ~, ~n sultana

**Sülze** die; ~, ~n **a)** diced meat/fish in aspic; *(vom Schweinskopf)* brawn; **b)** *(Aspik)* aspic

**Summe** die; ~, ~n sum

**summen 1.** *itr. V.* hum; *(lauter, heller)* buzz; **2.** *tr. V.* hum ⟨*tune, song, etc.*⟩

**summieren** *refl. V.* add up (**auf** + *Akk.* to)

**Sumpf** der; ~|e|s, **Sümpfe** marsh; *(bes. in den Tropen)* swamp; **sumpfig** *Adj.* marshy

**Sund** der; ~|e|s, ~e *(Geogr.)* sound

**Sünde** die; ~, ~n sin; *(fig.)* misdeed; transgression; **Sünden·bock** der *(ugs.)* scapegoat; **Sünder** der; ~s, ~, **Sünderin** die; ~, ~nen sinner; **sündigen** *itr. V.* sin

**Super** das; ~s, ~: four star *(Brit.)*; premium *(Amer.)*; **super-** ultra-⟨*long, high, fast, modern, masculine, etc.*⟩; **Super-** super-⟨*hero, figure, car, group, etc.*⟩; terrific *(coll.)*, tremendous *(coll.)* ⟨*success, offer, chance, idea, etc.*⟩; **Superlativ** ['zuːpɐlatiːf] der; ~s, ~e *(Sprachw.)* superlative; **Super·markt** der supermarket

**Suppe** die; ~; ~n soup; **Suppen·löffel** der soup-spoon

**Surf·brett** ['sɔːf-] das surf-board; **surfen** ['sɔːfn̩] *itr. V.* surf; **Surfer** ['sɔːfɐ] der; ~s, ~: surfer

**surren** *itr. V.* **a)** *(summen)* hum; ⟨*camera, fan*⟩ whirr; **b)** *mit sein (schwirren)* whirr

**suspekt 1.** *Adj.* suspicious; jmdm. ~ sein arouse sb.'s suspicions; **2.** *adv.* suspiciously

**süß 1.** *Adj.* sweet; **2.** *adv.* sweetly; **süßen** *tr. V.* sweeten; **Süßigkeit** die; ~, ~en sweet *(Brit.)*; candy *(Amer.)*; ~en sweets *(Brit.)*; candy *sing. (Amer.)*; *(als Ware)* confectionery *sing.*; **süßlich 1.** *Adj.* **a)** [slightly] sweet; on the sweet side *pred.*; **b)** *(sen-*

*timental)* sickly mawkish; **2.** *adv.* ⟨*write, paint*⟩ mawkishly

**süß-, Süß-**: ~**most** der unfermented fruit juice; ~**sauer 1.** *Adj.* sweet-and-sour; *(fig.)* wry ⟨*smile, face*⟩; **2.** *adv.* **a)** etw. ~**sauer** zubereiten give sth. a sweet-and-sour flavour; **b)** *(fig.)* ⟨*smile*⟩ wryly; ~**speise** die sweet; dessert; ~**stoff** der sweetener; ~**wasser** das; *Pl.* ~**wasser** fresh water

**svw.** *Abk.* soviel wie

**Symbol** das; ~s, ~e symbol; **symbolisch 1.** *Adj.* symbolic; **2.** *adv.* symbolically

**Sympathie** [zʏmpa'tiː] die; ~, ~n sympathy (**für** with); **sympathisch 1.** *Adj.* congenial, likeable ⟨*person, manner*⟩; appealing ⟨*voice, appearance, material*⟩; **2.** *adv.* in an appealing way; *(angenehm)* agreeably

**Symphonie** *usw.* s. **Sinfonie** *usw.*

**Synagoge** die; ~, ~n synagogue

**Syrer** der; ~s, ~, **Syrerin** die; ~, ~nen Syrian; **Syrien** ['zyːriən] **(das)** ~s Syria; **syrisch** *Adj.* Syrian

**System** das; ~, ~e system; **systematisch 1.** *Adj.* systematic; **2.** *adv.* systematically

**Szene** ['stseːnə] die; ~, ~n *(auch fig.)* scene

# T

**t, T** [teː] das; ~, ~: t, T

**t** *Abk.* Tonne t

**Tab.** *Abk.* Tabelle

**Tabak** ['ta(ː)bak] der; ~s, ~e tobacco; **Tabaks·pfeife** die [tobacco-]pipe

**Tabelle** die; ~, ~n table

**Tabernakel** das *od.* der; ~s, ~: tabernacle

**Tablett** das; ~|e|s, ~s *od.* ~e tray; **Tablette** die; ~, ~n tablet

**tabu** *Adj.* taboo; **Tabu** das; ~s, ~s taboo

**Tacho** der; ~s, ~s *(ugs.)* speedo *(coll.)*; **Tacho·meter** der *od.* das speedometer

**Tadel** der; ~s, ~ **a)** censure; **b)** *(im*

*Klassenbuch)* black mark; **ta̲del·los** **1.** *Adj.* impeccable; immaculate ⟨*hair, clothing, suit, etc.*⟩; perfect ⟨*condition, teeth, pronunciation, German, etc.*⟩; **2.** *adv.* ⟨*dress*⟩ impeccably; ⟨*fit, speak, etc.*⟩ perfectly; ⟨*live, behave, etc.*⟩ irreproachably; **ta̲deln** *tr. V.* jmdn. [für *od.* wegen etw.] ~: rebuke sb. [for sth.]
**Ta̲fel die;** ~, ~**n a)** *(Schiefer~)* slate; *(Wand~)* blackboard; **b)** *(plattenförmiges Stück)* slab; **eine ~ Schokolade** a bar of chocolate; **c)** *(Gedenk~)* plaque; **d)** *(geh.: festlicher Tisch)* table; **Tä̲felchen das;** ~s, ~: *s.* Tafel **b:** [small] slab; [small] bar; **ta̲feln** *itr. V. (geh.)* feast; **tä̲feln** *tr. V.* panel
**Ta̲fel-:** ~**spitz der** *(österr.)* boiled fillet of beef; ~**wasser das;** *Pl.* ~wässer [bottled] mineral water; ~**wein der** table wine
**Ta̲ft der;** ~|e|s, ~e taffeta
**Ta̲g der;** ~|e|s, ~e day; **am** ~|e| during the day[time]; **guten** ~! hello; *(bei Vorstellung)* how do you do?; **an diesem** ~: on this day; **dreimal am** ~: three times a day; **am folgenden** ~: the next day; **eines** ~**es** one day; some day; **ta̲g·a̲us** *Adv.* ~, **tagein** day in, day out; day after day; **Ta̲ge·buch das** diary; **ta̲g·ei̲n** *Adv. s.* tagaus; **ta̲ge·lang 1.** *Adj.* lasting for days *postpos.;* **nach** ~**em Regen** after days of rain; **2.** *adv.* for days [on end]; **ta̲gen** *itr. V.* meet; **das Gericht/Parlament tagt** the court/parliament is in session
**Ta̲ges-:** ~**karte die a)** *(Gastron.)* menu of the day; **b)** *(Fahr-, Eintrittskarte)* day ticket; ~**kasse die a)** box-office *(open during the day);* **b)** *(~einnahme)* day's takings *pl.;* ~**licht das;** *o. Pl.* daylight; ~**zeit die** time of day; ~**zeitung die** daily newspaper
**-tä̲gig a)** *(... Tage alt)* ein sechstägiges Küken a six-day-old chick; **b)** *(... Tage dauernd)* nach dreitägiger Vorbereitung after three days' preparation; **tä̲glich 1.** *Adj.* daily; **2.** *adv.* every day; **zweimal** ~: twice a day; ~ **drei Tabletten einnehmen** take three tablets daily; **ta̲gs** *Adv.* **a)** by day; in the daytime; **b)** ~ **zuvor/davor** the day before; ~ **darauf** the next *or* following day; the day after; **ta̲gs·über** *Adv.* during the day; **ta̲g·tä̲glich 1.** *Adj.* day-to-day; daily; **2.** *adv.* every single day; **Ta̲gung die;** ~, ~en conference
**Tai̲fun der;** ~s, ~e typhoon
**Tai̲lle** ['taljə] **die;** ~, ~n waist
**Tai̲wan (das);** ~s Taiwan

**Ta̲kt der;** ~|e|s, ~e **a)** *(Musik)* time; *(Einheit)* bar; measure *(Amer.);* **aus dem ~ kommen** lose the beat; **b)** *o. Pl. (rhythmischer Bewegungsablauf)* rhythm; **c)** *o. Pl. (Feingefühl)* tact
**Ta̲ktik die;** ~, ~en: |eine| ~: tactics *pl.;* **ta̲ktisch 1.** *Adj.* tactical; **2.** *adv.* tactically
**ta̲kt-:** ~**los 1.** *Adj.* tactless; **2.** *adv.* tactlessly; ~**voll 1.** *Adj.* tactful; **2.** *adv.* tactfully
**Ta̲l das;** ~|e|s, Täler valley
**Tale̲nt das;** ~|e|s, ~e talent (zu, für for); *(Mensch)* talented person
**Ta̲lg der;** ~|e|s, ~e suet; *(zur Herstellung von Seife, Kerzen usw.)* tallow
**Ta̲lisman der;** ~s, ~e talisman
**Tampo̲n der;** ~s, ~s tampon
**Tamta̲m das;** ~s *(ugs. abwertend)* |großes| ~: [a big] fuss
**Ta̲ng der;** ~|e|s, ~e seaweed
**Tange̲nte die;** ~, ~n *(Math.)* tangent
**Ta̲nk der;** ~s, ~s tank; **ta̲nken** *tr., itr. V.* fill up; **Öl ~:** fill up with oil
**Ta̲nk-:** ~**säule die** petrol-pump *(Brit.);* gasoline pump *(Amer.);* ~**stelle die** petrol station *(Brit.);* gas station *(Amer.);* ~**wart der;** ~s, ~e petrol-pump attendant *(Brit.)*
**Ta̲nne die;** ~, ~n fir[-tree]
**Ta̲nnen-:** ~**baum der** *(ugs.)* fir-tree; *(Weihnachtsbaum)* Christmas tree; ~**grün das;** *o. Pl.* fir sprigs *pl.;* ~**zweig der** fir branch
**Tansa̲nia** [tan'za:nia̲] **(das);** ~s Tanzania
**Ta̲nte die;** ~, ~n **a)** aunt; **b)** *(Kinderspr.: Frau)* lady; **c)** *(ugs.: Frau)* woman
**Ta̲nz der;** ~es, Tänze dance
**Ta̲nz-:** ~**abend der** evening dance; ~**bar die** night-spot *(coll.)* with dancing; ~**café das** coffee-house with dancing
**ta̲nzen** *itr., tr. V.* dance; **Tä̲nzer der;** ~s, ~, **Tä̲nzerin die;** ~, ~nen dancer; *(Ballett~)* ballet-dancer
**Ta̲nz-:** ~**fläche die** dance-floor; ~**lokal das** café/restaurant with dancing; ~**orchester das** dance band; ~**stunde die a)** *(~kurs)* dancing-class; **b)** *(einzelne Stunde)* dancing lesson
**Tape̲te die;** ~, ~n wallpaper; **tape̲zieren** *tr. V.* [wall]paper
**ta̲pfer 1.** *Adj.* brave; **2.** *adv.* bravely; **Ta̲pferkeit die;** ~: courage; bravery
**ta̲ppen** *itr. V.* **a)** *mit sein* patter; **b)** *(tastend greifen)* grope **(nach** for); **Ta̲ps**

der; ~es, ~e *(ugs. abwertend)* clumsy oaf

**Tarif der**; ~s, ~e charge; *(Post~, Wasser~)* rate; *(Verkehrs~)* fares *pl.; (Zoll~)* tariff; *(Lohn~)* [wage] rate; *(Gehalts~)* [salary] scale

**tarnen 1.** *tr., itr. V.* camouflage; **2.** *refl. V.* camouflage oneself

**Tasche die**; ~, ~n bag; *(in Kleidung, Rucksack usw.)* pocket; **jmdm. auf der ~ liegen** *(fig. ugs.)* live off sb.

**Taschen-:** ~**buch** das paperback; ~**lampe** die [pocket] torch *(Brit.)* or *(Amer.)* flashlight; ~**messer** das penknife; ~**rechner** der pocket calculator; ~**tuch** das; *Pl.* ~**tücher** handkerchief; ~**uhr** die pocket-watch

**Tasse die**; ~, ~n cup

**Taste die**; ~, ~n a) *(eines Musikinstruments, einer Schreibmaschine)* key; b) *(Fuß~)* pedal [key]; c) *(am Telefon, Radio, Fernsehgerät, Taschenrechner usw.)* button; **tasten 1.** *itr. V. (fühlend suchen)* grope, feel **(nach** for); **2.** *refl. V. (sich tastend bewegen)* grope or feel one's way; **Tasten·telefon** das push-button telephone

**tat** *1. u. 3. Pers. Sg. Prät. v.* tun; **Tat die**; ~, ~en act; *(das Tun)* action; **eine gute ~:** a good deed; **in der ~** *(verstärkend)* actually; *(zustimmend)* indeed

**Tatar** das; ~|s| steak tartare

**Täter der**; ~s, ~, **Täterin die**; ~, ~nen culprit; **tätig** *Adj.* a) ~ **sein** work; b) *(rührig, aktiv)* active; **tätigen** *tr. V. (Kaufmannsspr., Papierdt.)* transact ⟨*business, deal, etc.*⟩; **Tätigkeit die**; ~, ~en activity; *(Arbeit)* job; **Tatkraft** die energy; drive; **tat·kräftig 1.** *Adj.* energetic ⟨*person*⟩; **2.** *adv.* energetically

**tätowieren** *tr. V.* tattoo; **Tätowierung** die; ~, ~en tattoo

**Tat·sache** die fact; **tatsächlich 1.** *Adj.* actual; real; **2.** *adv.* actually; really

**tätscheln** *tr. V.* pat

**Tatze die**; ~, ~n paw

**¹Tau** der; ~|e|s dew

**²Tau** das; ~|e|s, ~e *(Seil)* rope

**taub** *Adj.* a) deaf; b) *(wie abgestorben)* numb; c) *(leer, unbefruchtet usw.)* empty ⟨*nut*⟩; dead ⟨*rock*⟩

**¹Taube die**; ~, ~n pigeon; *(Turtel~; auch Politik fig.)* dove

**²Taube der/die**; *adj. Dekl.* deaf person; deaf man/woman; **die ~n** the deaf; **Taubheit die**; ~: deafness; **taub·stumm** *Adj.* deaf and dumb;

**Taub·stumme der/die**; *adj. Dekl.* deaf mute

**tauchen 1.** *itr. V.* a) *auch mit sein* dive **(nach** for); b) *mit sein (ein~)* dive; *(auf~)* rise; emerge; **2.** *tr. V.* a) *(ein~)* dip; b) *(unter~)* duck; **Taucher der**; ~s, ~, **Taucherin die**; ~, ~nen diver; *(mit Flossen und Atemgerät)* skindiver; **Tauch·sieder der**; ~s, ~: portable immersion heater

**tauen 1.** *itr. V.* a) *unpers.* **es taut** it's thawing; b) *mit sein (schmelzen)* melt; **2.** *tr. V.* melt; thaw

**Taufe die**; ~, ~n *(christl. Rel.)* a) o. *Pl. (Sakrament)* baptism; b) *(Zeremonie)* christening; baptism; **taufen** *tr. V.* a) baptize; b) *(einen Namen geben)* christen

**taugen** *itr. V.* nichts/nicht viel/etwas ~: be no/not much/some good or use; **tauglich** *Adj.* [nicht] ~: [un]suitable; *(für Militärdienst)* fit [for service]

**Taumel der**; ~s a) [feeling of] dizziness; b) *(Rausch)* frenzy; fever; **taumelig** *Adj.* dizzy; giddy; **taumeln** *itr. V.* a) *auch mit sein (wanken)* reel, sway *(vor + Dat.* with); b) *mit sein (sich ~d bewegen)* stagger

**Tausch der**; ~|e|s, ~e exchange; **ein guter/schlechter ~:** a good/bad deal; **tauschen 1.** *tr. V.* exchange **(gegen** for); **sie tauschten die Plätze** they changed places; **2.** *itr. V.* **mit jmdm. ~** *(fig.)* change places with sb.

**täuschen 1.** *tr. V.* deceive; **wenn mich nicht alles täuscht** unless I'm completely mistaken; **2.** *itr. V.* be deceptive; **3.** *refl. V.* be wrong or mistaken **(in + Dat.** about); **täuschend 1.** *Adj.* remarkable, striking ⟨*similarity, imitation*⟩; **2.** *adv.* remarkably; **Täuschung die**; ~, ~en deception; *(Selbst~)* delusion

**tausend** *Kardinalz.* a) a or one thousand; b) *(ugs.: sehr viele)* thousands of; ~ **Dank/Küsse** a thousand thanks/kisses; **Tausend** das; ~s, ~e *od.* ~ a) *nicht in Verbindung mit Kardinalzahlen; Pl.:* ~ thousand; b) *Pl. (eine unbestimmte große Zahl)* thousands; **tausend·ein[s]** *Kardinalz.* a or one thousand and one; **Tausender der**; ~s, ~ *(ugs.) (Tausendmarkschein usw.)* thousand-mark-/-dollar *etc.* note; *(Betrag)* thousand marks/dollars *etc.*; **tausenderlei** *Gattungsz.; indekl. (ugs.)* a thousand and one different ⟨*answers, kinds, etc.*⟩; **tausend·mal** *Adv.* a thousand times; **Tausend-**

**mark·schein** der thousand-mark note; **tausendst...** *Ordinalz.* thousandth; *s. auch* **acht...**; **tausendstel** *Bruchz.* thousandth; **Tausendstel** das (*schweiz. meist* der); ~s, ~: thousandth

**Tau·wetter** das thaw

**Taxi** das; ~s, ~s taxi; **Taxi·fahrer** der taxi-driver

**Tb, Tbc** [te:'be:, te:be:'tse:] die; ~ *Abk.* **Tuberkulose** TB

**Technik** die; ~, ~en **a)** *o. Pl.* technology; (*Studienfach*) engineering *no art.*; **b)** *o. Pl.* (*technische Ausrüstung*) equipment; **c)** (*Arbeitsweise, Verfahren*) technique; **Techniker** der; ~s, ~, **Technikerin** die; ~, ~nen technical expert; **technisch** ['tɛçnɪʃ] **1.** *Adj.* technical; technological ‹*progress, age*›; **2.** *adv.* technically; technologically ‹*advanced*›; **Technologie** die; ~, ~n technology

**TEE** [te:|e:'|e:] der; ~|s|, ~|s| *Abk.* **Trans-Europ-Express** TEE

**Tee** der; ~s, ~s tea

**Tee-:** ~**beutel** der tea-bag; ~**kanne** die teapot; ~**löffel** der teaspoon; ~**sieb** das tea-strainer; ~**tasse** die teacup

**Teich** der; ~|e|s, ~e pond

**Teig** der; ~|e|s, ~e dough; (*Kuchen~, Biskuit~*) pastry; (*Pfannkuchen~, Waffel~*) batter; **Teig·waren** *Pl.* pasta *sing.*

**Teil a)** der; ~|e|s, ~e part; **fünfter** ~: fifth; **b)** der *od.* das; ~|e|s, ~e (*Anteil, Beitrag*) share; **c)** der; ~|e|s, ~e (*beteiligte Person[en]; Rechtsw.: Partei*) party; **d)** das; ~|e|s, ~e (*Einzel~*) part; **teil·bar** *Adj.* divisible (**durch** by); **Teilchen** das; ~s, ~ **a)** (*kleines Stück*) [small] part; **b)** (*Partikel*) particle; **teilen 1.** *tr. V.* **a)** divide (**durch** by); **b)** (*auf~; teilhaben [lassen] an*) share (**unter** + *Dat.* among); **2.** *refl. V.* sich (*Dat.*) etw. |mit jmdm.| ~: share sth. [with sb.]; **teil|haben** *unr. itr. V.* share (**an** + *Dat.* in); **Teil·kaskoversicherung** die *insurance giving limited cover*

**Teilnahme** die; ~, ~n **a)** participation (**an** + *Dat.* in); ~ **an einem Kurs** attendance at a course; **b)** (*Interesse*) interest (**an** + *Dat.* in); **c)** (*geh.: Mitgefühl*) sympathy; **teilnahms·los** *Adj.* indifferent; **Teilnahmslosigkeit** die indifference; **teilnahms·voll 1.** *Adj.* compassionate; **2.** *adv.* compassionately; **teil|nehmen** *unr. itr. V.*

[an etw. (*Dat.*)] ~: take part [in sth.]; |an einem Lehrgang| ~: attend [a course]; **Teilnehmer** der; ~s, ~ **a)** participant (*Gen.,* **an** + *Dat.* in); (*bei Wettbewerb auch*) competitor, contestant (**an** + *Dat.* in); **b)** (*Fernspr.*) subscriber

**teils** *Adv.* partly; **Teilung** die; ~, ~en division; **teil·weise 1.** *Adv.* partly; **2.** *adj.* partial; **Teilzeit·arbeit** die part-time work *no indef. art.*

**Teint** [tɛ̃:] der; ~s, ~s complexion

**Telefon** ['te:lefo:n, *auch* tele'fo:n] das; ~s, ~e telephone; phone (*coll.*); **ans** ~ **gehen** answer the [tele]phone

**Telefon-:** ~**anruf** der [tele]phone call; ~**anschluß** der telephone; line; ~**apparat** der telephone

**Telefonat** das; ~|e|s, ~e telephone call

**Telefon-:** ~**buch** das [tele]phone book *or* directory; ~**gespräch** das telephone conversation

**telefonieren** *itr. V.* make a [tele]phone call; **mit jmdm.** ~: talk to sb. [on the telephone]; **telefonisch 1.** *Adj.* telephone; **2.** *adv.* by telephone; **Telefonist** der; ~en, ~en, **Telefonistin** die; ~, ~nen telephonist; (*in einer Firma*) switchboard operator

**Telefon-:** ~**nummer** die [tele]phone number; ~**verzeichnis** das telephone list; ~**zelle** die [tele]phonebooth *or* (*Brit.*) -box; call-box (*Brit.*)

**Telegraf** der; ~en, ~en telegraph; **Telegrafie** die; ~: telegraphy *no art.*; **telegrafieren** *itr., tr. V.* telegraph; **telegrafisch 1.** *Adj.* telegraphic; **2.** *adv.* by telegraph *or* telegram

**Telegramm** das telegram

**Tele·objektiv** das (*Fot.*) telephoto lens

**Teller** der; ~s, ~: plate

**Temperament** das; ~|e|s, ~e **a)** (*Wesensart*) temperament; **b)** *o. Pl.* (*Schwung*) **eine Frau mit** ~: a woman with spirit; **das** ~ **geht oft mit mir durch** I often lose my temper; **temperament·voll** *Adj.* spirited ‹*person, speech, dance, etc.*›

**Temperatur** die; ~, ~en temperature

**Temperatur-:** ~**anstieg** der rise in temperature; ~**rückgang** der drop *or* fall in temperature

**Tempo** das; ~s, ~s *od.* **Tempi a)** *Pl.* ~s speed; **b)** (*Musik*) tempo; time

**Tempus** das; ~, **Tempora** (*Sprachw.*) tense

**Tendenz die**; ~, ~**en** trend; **ten-dieren** *itr. V.* tend (**zu** towards)
**Teneriffa (das)**; ~**s** Tenerife
**Tennis das**; ~: tennis *no art.*
**Tennis-**: ~**ball der** tennis-ball; ~**platz der** tennis-court; ~**schläger der** tennis-racket; ~**spieler der** tennis-player
**Tenor der**; ~**s**, **Tenöre**, *(österr. auch:)* ~**e** *(Musik)* tenor; *(im Chor)* tenors *pl.*; tenor voices *pl.*
**Teppich der**; ~**s**, ~**e** carpet; *(kleiner)* rug; **Teppich·boden der** fitted carpet
**Termin der**; ~**s**, ~**e** date; *(Anmeldung)* appointment; *(Verabredung)* engagement; *(Rechtsw.)* hearing; **Terminal** ['tø:ɐminəl] **das**; ~**s**, ~**s** terminal; **Termin·kalender der** appointments book
**Terpentin das**, *(österr. meist:)* **der**; ~**s a)** *(Harz)* turpentine; **b)** *(ugs.: Terpentinöl)* turps *sing. (coll.)*; **Terpentin-öl das** oil of turpentine
**Terrain** [tɛ'rɛ̃:] **das**; ~**s**, ~**s** terrain
**Terrasse die**; ~, ~**n** terrace
**Terrier** ['tɛriɐ] **der**; ~**s**, ~: terrier
**Terrine die**; ~, ~**n** tureen
**Territorium das**; ~**s**, **Territorien** territory
**Terror der**; ~**s** terrorism *no art.*; **terrorisieren** *tr. V.* **a)** terrorize; **b)** *(ugs.: belästigen)* pester; **Terrorist der**; ~**en**, ~**en** terrorist
**Terz die**; ~, ~**en** *(Musik)* third
**Test der**; ~[**e**]**s**, ~**s** *od.* ~**e** test
**Testament das**; ~[**e**]**s**, ~**e a)** will; **b)** *(christl. Rel.)* Testament
**testen** *tr. V.* test (**auf** + *Akk.* for)
**teuer 1.** *Adj.* expensive; dear *usu. pred.*; **wie ~ war das?** how much did that cost?; **2.** *adv.* expensively; dearly; **etw. ~ kaufen/verkaufen** pay a great deal for sth./sell sth. at a high price; **Teuerung die**; ~, ~**en** rise in prices
**Teufel der**; ~**s**, ~: devil; **teuflisch 1.** *Adj.* **a)** devilish, fiendish ⟨*plan, trick, etc.*⟩; diabolical ⟨*laughter, pleasure, etc.*⟩; **b)** *(ugs.: groß, intensiv)* terrible *(coll.)*; dreadful *(coll.)*; **2.** *adv.* **a)** diabolically; **b)** *(ugs.)* terribly *(coll.)*
**Text der**; ~[**e**]**s**, ~**e** text; *(Wortlaut)* wording; *(eines Theaterstücks)* script; *(einer Oper)* libretto; *(eines Liedes, Chansons usw.)* words *pl.*; *(eines Schlagers)* words *pl.*; lyrics *pl.*; *(zu einer Abbildung)* caption; **texten** *tr. V.* write ⟨*song, advertisement, etc.*⟩

**Textilien** *Pl.* **a)** textiles; **b)** *(Fertigwaren)* textile goods
**Thailand (das)**; ~**s** Thailand
**Theater das**; ~**s**, ~ **a)** theatre; **ins ~ gehen** go to the theatre; **im ~**: at the theatre; ~ **spielen** act; *(fig.)* play-act; pretend; **b)** *o. Pl. (fig. ugs.)* fuss
**Theater-**: ~**abonnement das** theatre subscription [ticket]; ~**stück das** [stage] play
**Theke die**; ~, ~**n a)** *(Schanktisch)* bar; **b)** *(Ladentisch)* counter
**Thema das**; ~**s**, **Themen** subject; topic; *(einer Abhandlung)* subject; theme; *(Leitgedanke)* theme
**Themse die**; ~: Thames
**Theologe der**; ~**n**, ~**n** theologian; **Theologie die**; ~, ~**n** theology *no art.*; **theologisch 1.** *Adj.* theological; **2.** *adv.* theologically
**Theorie die**; ~, ~**n** theory
**Therapeut der**; ~**en**, ~**en**, **Therapeutin die**; ~, ~**nen** therapist; therapeutist; **therapeutisch 1.** *Adj.* therapeutic; **2.** *adv.* therapeutically
**Therapie die**; ~, ~**n** therapy (**gegen** for)
**Thermo·meter das** *(österr. u. schweiz. der od. das)* thermometer; **Thermos·flasche** ⓦ **die** Thermos flask (P); vacuum flask; **Thermostat der**; ~[**e**]**s** *od.* ~**en**, ~**e** *od.* ~**en** thermostat
**Thron der**; ~[**e**]**s**, ~**e** throne
**Thun·fisch der** tuna
**Thüringen (das)**; ~**s** Thuringia; **Thüringer Wald der** Thuringian Forest
**Thymian der**; ~**s**, ~**e** thyme
**ticken** *itr. V.* tick
**tief 1.** *Adj. (auch fig.)* deep; *(niedrig)* low; low ⟨*neckline, bow*⟩; deep; intense ⟨*pain, suffering*⟩; **2.** *adv.* deep; *(niedrig)* low; *(intensiv)* deeply; ⟨*stoop, bow*⟩ low; ⟨*breathe, inhale*⟩ deeply; **Tief das**; ~**s**, ~**s** *(Met.)* low
**tief-, Tief-**: ~**bewegt** *Adj. (präd. getrennt geschrieben)* deeply moved; ~**blau** *Adj.* deep blue; ~**druck der**; *o. Pl. (Met.)* low pressure
**Tiefe die**; ~, ~**n** depth; **in die ~ stürzen** plunge into the depths
**tief-, Tief-**: ~**garage die** underground car park; ~**greifend; tiefer greifend, am tiefsten greifend** *od.* **tiefstgreifend 1.** *Adj.* profound; profound, deep ⟨*crisis*⟩; far-reaching ⟨*improvement*⟩; **2.** *adv.* profoundly; ~**gründig** *Adj.* profound; ~**kühlen** *tr. V.* [deep-]freeze

**Tief·kühl-:** ~**fach das** freezer [compartment]; ~**kost die** frozen food
**tief-, Tief-:** ~**punkt der** low [point]; ~**see die** *(Geogr.)* deep sea; ~**sinnig** 1. *Adj.* profound; 2. *adv.* profoundly
**Tiegel der;** ~**s,** ~ *(zum Kochen)* pan; *(Schmelz~)* crucible; *(Behälter)* pot
**Tier das;** ~|e|s, ~e animal
**Tier-:** ~**arzt der** veterinary surgeon; vet; ~**garten der** zoo; zoological garden; ~**heim das** animal home
**tierisch** 1. *Adj.* a) animal *attrib.;* savage ⟨*cruelty, crime*⟩; b) *(ugs.: unerträglich groß)* terrible *(coll.);* ~**er Ernst** deadly seriousness; 2. *adv.* a) ⟨*roar*⟩ like an animal; savagely ⟨*cruel*⟩; b) *(ugs.: unerträglich)* terribly *(coll.)*
**tier-, Tier-:** ~**kreis der;** *o. Pl.* *(Astron., Astrol.)* zodiac; ~**kreis·zeichen das** *(Astron., Astrol.)* sign of the zodiac; ~**lieb** *Adj.* animal-loving *attrib.;* fond of animals *postpos.;* ~**park der** zoo; ~**pfleger der** animal-keeper; ~**quälerei** [---'-'-] die cruelty to animals; ~**reich das;** *o. Pl.* animal kingdom
**Tiger der;** ~**s,** ~: tiger
**tilgen** *tr. V.* a) *(geh.)* delete ⟨*word, letter, error*⟩; erase ⟨*record, endorsement*⟩; *(fig.)* wipe out ⟨*shame, guilt, traces*⟩; b) *(Wirtsch., Bankw.)* repay; pay off
**Tilsiter der;** ~**s,** ~: Tilsit [cheese]
**Tinte die;** ~, ~**n** ink; **in der** ~ **sitzen** *(ugs.)* be in the soup *(coll.);* **Tinten·fisch der** cuttlefish; *(Krake)* octopus
**Tip der;** ~**s,** ~**s** a) *(ugs.)* tip; b) *(bei Toto, Lotto usw.)* [row of] numbers; **tippen** 1. *itr. V.* a) **an/gegen etw.** *(Akk.)* ~: tap sth.; b) *(ugs.: maschineschreiben)* type; c) *(wetten)* do the pools/lottery *etc.;* **im Lotto** ~: do the lottery; 2. *tr. V.* a) tap; b) *(ugs.: mit der Maschine schreiben)* type; c) *(setzen auf)* choose; **sechs Richtige** ~: make six correct selections
**tipp·topp** *(ugs.)* 1. *Adj. (tadellos)* immaculate; *(erstklassig)* tip-top; 2. *adv.* immaculately
**Tirol (das);** ~**s** [the] Tyrol; **Tiroler der;** ~**s,** ~, **Tirolerin die;** ~, ~**nen** Tyrolese; Tyrolean
**Tisch der;** ~|e|s, ~e table; **reinen** ~ **machen** *(ugs.)* sort things out
**Tisch-:** ~**dame die** dinner partner; ~**decke die** table-cloth; ~**gebet das** grace; ~**herr der** dinner partner; ~**lampe die** table-lamp

**Tischler der;** ~**s,** ~: joiner; *(bes. Kunst~)* cabinet-maker; **Tischlerei die;** ~, ~**en** a) *(Werkstatt)* joiner's/cabinet-maker's [workshop]; b) *o. Pl. (Handwerk)* joinery/cabinet-making
**Tisch-:** ~**nachbar der** person next to one [at table]; ~**platte die** table-top; ~**tennis das** table tennis; ~**tuch das;** *Pl.* ~**tücher** table-cloth; ~**wäsche die** table-linen; ~**wein der** table wine; ~**zeit die** lunch-time
**Titel der;** ~**s,** ~ a) title; b) *(ugs.: Musikstück, Song usw.)* number
**Titel-:** ~**bild das** cover picture; ~**blatt das** title-page; ~**rolle die** title-role; ~**seite die** a) *(einer Zeitung, Zeitschrift)* [front] cover; b) *(eines Buchs)* title-page
**titulieren** *tr. V.* call
**tja** [tja(:)] *Interj.* [yes] well; *(Resignation ausdrückend)* oh, well
**Toast** [to:st] **der;** ~|e|s, ~e *od.* ~**s** toast; **Toast·brot das;** *o. Pl.* [sliced white] bread for toasting; **toasten** *tr. V.* toast; **Toaster der;** ~**s,** ~: toaster
**toben** *itr. V.* a) go wild (**vor** + *Dat.* with); *(fig.)* ⟨*storm, sea, battle*⟩ rage; b) *(tollen)* romp *or* charge about; c) **mit sein** *(laufen)* charge
**Tochter die;** ~, **Töchter** daughter
**Tod der;** ~|e|s, ~e death; **eines natürlichen/gewaltsamen** ~**es sterben** die a natural/violent death; **jmdn. zum** ~**e verurteilen** sentence sb. to death; **tod·ernst** 1. *Adj.* deadly serious; 2. *adv.* deadly seriously
**Todes-:** ~**anzeige die** a) *(in einer Zeitung)* death notice; b) *(Karte)* card announcing a person's death; ~**fall der** death; *(in der Familie)* bereavement; ~**nachricht die** news of his/her/their *etc.* death; ~**opfer das** death; fatality; ~**strafe die** death penalty; ~**ursache die** cause of death; ~**urteil das** death sentence
**Tod·feind der** deadly enemy; **todkrank** *Adj.* critically ill; **tödlich** 1. *Adj.* a) fatal ⟨*accident, illness, outcome, etc.*⟩; lethal, deadly ⟨*poison, bite, shot, trap, etc.*⟩; lethal ⟨*dose*⟩; b) *(sehr groß, ausgeprägt)* deadly ⟨*hatred, seriousness, certainty, boredom*⟩; 2. *adv.* a) fatally; b) *(sehr)* terribly *(coll.)*
**tod-, Tod-:** ~**müde** *Adj.* dead tired; ~**sicher** *(ugs.)* 1. *Adj.* sure-fire *(coll.);* 2. *adv.* for certain *or* sure; ~**sünde die** *(auch fig.)* deadly *or* mortal sin; ~**unglücklich** *Adj. (ugs.)* extremely *or* desperately unhappy

**Toilette** [tǫa'lɛtə] **die**; ~, ~n toilet
**Toiletten·papier das** toilet paper
**toi, toi, toi** ['tɔy 'tɔy 'tɔy] *Interj.* good luck!; *(unberufen!)* touch wood!
**Tokio** (das); ~s Tokyo
**toler**ạ**nt** 1. *Adj.* tolerant (gegen of); 2. *adv.* tolerantly; **Toler**ạ**nz die**; ~: tolerance; **toler**ịe**ren** *tr. V.* tolerate
**toll** 1. *Adj.* a) *(ugs.) (großartig)* great *(coll.)*; fantastic *(coll.)*; *(erstaunlich)* amazing; *(heftig, groß)* enormous ‹*respect*›; terrific *(coll.)* ‹*noise, storm*›; b) *(wild)* wild; 2. *adv.* a) *(ugs.: großartig)* terrifically well *(coll.)*; b) *(ugs.: heftig)* ‹*rain, snow*› like billy-o *(coll.)*; c) *(wild)* **bei dem Fest ging es ~ zu** it was a wild party; **toll**en *itr. V.* a) romp about; b) *mit sein* romp
**toll-, Toll-**: ~**kühn** 1. *Adj.* daredevil *attrib.*; daring; 2. *adv.* daringly; ~**wut die** rabies *sing.*; ~**wütig** *Adj.* rabid
**Tolpatsch der**; ~|e|s, ~e *(ugs.)* clumsy *or* awkward creature; **tolpatschig** *(ugs.)* 1. *Adj.* clumsy; awkward; 2. *adv.* clumsily; awkwardly
**Tölpel der**; ~s, ~: fool; **tölpelhaft** 1. *Adj.* foolish; 2. *adv.* foolishly
**Tom**ạ**te die**; ~, ~n tomato; **Tom**ạ**ten·mark das** tomato purée
**Tombola die**; ~, ~s raffle
**¹Ton der**; ~|e|s, ~e clay
**²Ton der**; ~|e|s, **Töne** a) *(auch Physik, Musik; beim Telefon)* tone; *(Klang)* note; b) *(Ferns. usw., ~ wiedergabe)* sound; c) *(ugs.: Äußerung)* word; d) *(Farb~)* shade; e) *(Akzent)* stress
**ton-, Ton-**: ~**angebend** *Adj.* predominant; ~**art die** a) *(Musik)* key; b) *(fig.)* tone; ~**band das**; *Pl.* ~**bänder** tape
**Ton·band·gerät das** tape recorder
**tön**en 1. *itr. V. (geh.)* sound; ‹*bell*› sound, ring; *(schallen, widerhallen)* resound; 2. *tr. V. (färben)* tint
**Ton·fall der** tone; *(Intonation)* intonation
**Tonne die**; ~, ~n a) *(Behälter)* drum; *(Müll~)* bin; *(Regen~)* water-butt; b) *(Gewicht)* tonne; **tonnen·weise** *Adv., adj.* by the ton
**Tönung die**; ~, ~en tint; shade
**Topf der**; ~es, **Töpfe** a) pot; *(Braten~, Schmor~)* casserole; *(Stielkasserolle)* saucepan; b) *(zur Aufbewahrung)* pot; c) *(Krug)* jug; d) *(Nacht~)* chamber pot; *(für Kinder)* potty *(Brit. coll.)*; e) *(Blumen~)* [flower]pot; **Topf·blume die** [flowering] pot plant

**Töpfchen das**; ~s, ~: potty *(Brit. coll.)*; **Töpfer der**; ~s, ~: potter; **Töpfer**ei **die**; ~, ~**en** a) *o. Pl. (Handwerk)* pottery *no art.*; b) *(Werkstatt)* pottery; potter's workshop; c) *(Erzeugnis)* piece of pottery; ~**en** pottery *sing.*
**Topf-**: ~**lappen der** oven cloth; ~**pflanze die** pot plant
**Tor das**; ~|e|s, ~e a) gate; *(einer Garage, Scheune)* door; *(fig.)* gateway; b) *(Ballspiele)* goal; c) *(Ski)* gate
**Torf der**; ~|e|s, ~e peat
**Torheit die**; ~, ~**en** *(geh.)* a) *o. Pl.* foolishness; b) *(Handlung)* foolish act
**Tor·hüter der** *(Ballspiele)* goalkeeper
**töricht** *(geh.)* 1. *Adj.* foolish; 2. *adv.* foolishly
**torkeln** *itr. V.; mit sein* stagger
**Tor·mann der**; *Pl.* ~**männer** *od.* ~**leute** *(Ballspiele)* goalkeeper
**Tornister** [tɔr'nɪstɐ] **der**; ~s, ~: knapsack; *(Schulranzen)* satchel
**torped**ịe**ren** *tr. V. (Milit., fig.)* torpedo; **Torpedo der**; ~s, ~s torpedo
**Törtchen das**; ~s, ~: tartlet; **Torte die**; ~, ~n *(Creme~, Sahne~)* gateau; *(Obst~)* [fruit] flan
**Torten-**: ~**boden der** flan case; *(ohne Rand)* flan base; ~**guß der** glaze; ~**heber der** cake-slice
**Tortur die**; ~, ~**en** a) ordeal; b) *(veralt.: Folter)* torture
**Tor-**: ~**wart der**; ~|e|s, ~e *(Ballspiele)* goalkeeper; ~**weg der** gateway
**tosen** *itr. V.* roar; ‹*storm*› rage
**tot** *Adj.* dead; ~ **umfallen** drop dead
**total** 1. *Adj.* total; 2. *adv.* totally; **totalit**ä**r** *(Politik)* 1. *Adj.* totalitarian; 2. *adv.* in a totalitarian way; ‹*organized, run*› along totalitarian lines; **Total·schaden der** *(Versicherungsw.)* **an beiden Fahrzeugen entstand ~**: both vehicles were a write-off
**tot|ärgern** *refl. V. (ugs.)* get livid *(coll.)*; **Tote der/die**; *adj. Dekl.* dead person; **die ~n** the dead; **töten** *tr., itr. V.* kill; deaden ‹*nerve etc.*›
**toten-, Toten-**: ~**blaß, ~bleich** *Adj.* deathly pale; ~**gräber der** grave-digger; ~**kopf der** a) skull; b) *(als Symbol)* death's head; *(mit gekreuzten Knochen)* skull and crossbones; ~**schädel der** skull; ~**still** *Adj.* deathly quiet; ~**stille die** deathly silence; ~**wache die** vigil by the body
**tot-, Tot-**: ~|**fahren** *unr. tr. V.* [run over and] kill; ~**geboren** *Adj.* (präd.

*getrennt geschrieben)* stillborn; **~geburt die** still birth; **~|lachen** *refl. V. (ugs.)* kill oneself laughing; **zum Totlachen sein** be killing *(coll.)*
**Toto das** *od.* **der;** ~s, ~s **a)** *(Pferde~)* tote *(sl.)*; **im ~:** on the tote; **b)** *(Fußball~)* [football] pools *pl.*; **|im|** ~ **spielen** do the pools; **Toto·schein der** pools coupon/*(sl.)* tote ticket
**tot-, Tot-:** ~|**schießen** *unr. tr. V. (ugs.)* jmdn. ~**schießen** shoot sb. dead; **~schlag der** *(Rechtsw.)* manslaughter *no indef. art.;* ~|**schlagen** *unr. tr. V.* beat to death; ~|**stellen** *refl. V.* pretend to be dead; play dead; ~|**treten** *unr. tr. V.* trample *(person)* to death; step on and kill *(insect)*
**Tötung die;** ~, ~en killing; **fahrlässige** ~ *(Rechtsspr.)* manslaughter by culpable negligence
**Toupet** [tu'pe:] **das;** ~s, ~s toupee; **toupieren** [tu'pi:rən] *tr. V.* backcomb
**Tour** [tu:ɐ̯] **die;** ~, ~en tour **(durch** of); *(kürzere Fahrt, Ausflug)* trip; *(mit dem Auto)* drive; *(mit dem Fahrrad)* ride; *(feste Strecke)* route; **in einer** ~ *(ugs.)* the whole time; **Tourismus** [tu'rɪsmʊs] **der;** ~: tourism *no art.;* **Tourist der;** ~en, ~en tourist; **Touristenklasse die** tourist class; **Touristin die;** ~, ~nen tourist
**Tournee** [tʊr'ne:] **die;** ~, ~s *od.* ~n [tʊr'ne:ən] **tour; auf** ~ **sein/gehen** be/go on tour
**Trab der;** ~|e|s trot; **im** ~: at a trot; **im** ~ **reiten** trot; **traben** *itr. V.; mit sein (auch ugs.: laufen)* trot
**Tracht die;** ~, ~en **a)** *(Volks~)* national costume; *(Berufs~)* uniform; **b) eine** ~ **Prügel** a thrashing; *(als Strafe)* a hiding
**trachten** *itr. V. (geh.)* strive **(nach** for, after)
**Tradition die;** ~, ~en tradition; **traditionell** 1. *Adj.* traditional; 2. *adv.* traditionally
**traf** *1. u. 3. Pers. Sg. Prät. v.* **treffen**
**träfe** *1. u. 3. Pers. Sg. Konjunktiv II v.* **treffen**
**Trafik die;** ~, ~en *(österr.)* tobacconist's [shop]
**Trag·bahre die** stretcher; **tragbar** *Adj.* **a)** portable; **b)** wearable *(clothes)*; **c)** *(finanziell)* supportable *(cost, debt, etc.)*; **d)** *(erträglich)* bearable; tolerable
**träge** 1. *Adj.* **a)** sluggish; 2. *adv.* sluggishly

**tragen** 1. *unr. tr. V.* **a)** carry; **b)** *(bringen)* take; **c)** *(ertragen)* bear *(fate, destiny)*; bear, endure *(suffering)*; **d)** *(halten)* hold; **einen/den linken Arm in der Schlinge** ~: have one's arm/one's left arm in a sling; **e)** *(von unten stützen)* support; **f)** *(belastbar sein durch)* be able to carry *or* take *(weight)*; **g)** *(übernehmen, aufkommen für)* bear, carry *(costs etc.)*; take *(blame, responsibility, consequences)*; **h)** *(am Körper)* wear *(clothes, wig, glasses, jewellery, etc.)*; have *(false teeth, beard, etc.)*; **j)** *(hervorbringen)* *(tree)* bear *(fruit)*; *(field)* produce *(crops)*; 2. *unr. itr. V.* **a)** carry; **b)** *(am Körper)* **man trägt |wieder| kurz/lang** short/long skirts are in fashion [again]; **c) der Baum trägt gut** the tree produces a good crop; **tragend** *Adj. (Stabilität gebend)* load-bearing; supporting *(wall, column, function, etc.)*
**Träger der;** ~s, ~ **a)** porter; **b)** *(Zeitungs~)* paper boy/girl; delivery boy/girl; **c)** *(Bauw.)* girder; [supporting] beam; **d)** *(an Kleidung)* strap; *(Hosen~)* braces *pl.*; **e)** *(Inhaber)* *(eines Amts)* holder; *(eines Namens, Titels)* bearer; *(eines Preises)* winner; **Trägerin die;** ~, ~nen *s.* **Träger a, b, e**
**Trage·tasche die** carrier-bag
**Trag-:** ~**fähigkeit die** load-bearing capacity; ~**fläche die** wing; ~**flügel·boot das** hydrofoil
**Trägheit die;** ~, ~en sluggishness
**Tragik die;** ~: tragedy; **tragi·komisch** 1. *Adj.* tragicomic; 2. *adv.* tragicomically; **tragisch** 1. *Adj.* tragic; **das ist nicht |so|** ~ *(ugs.)* it's not the end of the world *(coll.)*; 2. *adv.* tragically; **Tragödie die;** ~, ~n tragedy
**Trag·weite die;** *o. Pl.* consequences *pl.*
**Trainer** ['trɛ:nɐ] **der;** ~s, ~: coach; trainer; *(einer Fußballmannschaft)* manager; **trainieren** 1. *tr. V.* **a)** train; coach *(swimmer, tennis-player)*; manage *(football team)*; exercise *(muscles etc.)*; **b)** *(üben, einüben)* practise *(exercise, jump, etc.)*; **Fußball** ~: do football training; 2. *itr. V.* train; **Training** ['trɛ:nɪŋ] **das;** ~s, ~s training *no indef. art.*
**Trainings-:** ~**anzug der** track suit; ~**hose die** track-suit bottoms *pl.*
**Trakt der;** ~|e|s, ~e section; *(Flügel)* wing; **Traktor der;** ~s, ~en tractor

**trällern** *itr., tr. V.* warble
**trampeln** 1. *itr. V.* **a)** |mit den Füßen| ~: stamp one's feet; **b)** *mit sein (treten)* trample (**auf** + *Akk.* on); **2.** *tr. V.* trample; **Trampel·pfad** der [beaten] path
**trampen** ['trɛmpn̩] *itr. V. mit sein* hitch-hike
**Tramway** ['tramve] die; ~, ~s *(österr.)* tram *(Brit.);* streetcar *(Amer.)*
**Tran** der; ~|e|s train-oil
**tranchieren** [trãˈʃiːrən] *tr. V.* carve
**Träne** die; ~, ~n tear; ~n lachen laugh till one cries; **tränen** *itr. V.* ⟨eyes⟩ water
**tranig** *Adj. (ugs. abwertend: langsam)* sluggish; slow
**trank** *1. u. 3. Pers. Sg. Prät. v.* trinken; **Tränke** die; ~, ~n watering-place; **tränken** *tr. V.* **a)** water; **b)** *(sich vollsaugen lassen)* soak
**Transfer** der; ~s, ~s *(bes. Wirtsch., Sport)* transfer
**Trans·formator** der; ~s, ~en transformer
**Transistor** der; ~s, ~en transistor
**Transit** [tranˈziːt, *auch:* ˈtranzit] **das;** ~s, ~s transit visa; **transitiv** *(Sprachw.)* 1. *Adj.* transitive; 2. *adv.* transitively; **Transit·verkehr** der transit traffic
**transparent** *Adj.* transparent; *(Licht durchlassend)* translucent; **Transparent das;** ~|e|s, ~e *(Spruchband)* banner; *(Bild)* transparency; **Transparenz** die; ~ transparency
**Transport** der; ~|e|s, ~e **a)** transportation; **b)** *(beförderte Lebewesen od. Sachen) (mit dem Zug)* train-load; *(mit mehreren Fahrzeugen)* convoy; *(Fracht)* consignment; **transportabel** *Adj.* transportable; *(tragbar)* portable; **Transporteur** [...ˈtøːɐ̯] der; ~s, ~e carrier; **transport·fähig** *Adj.* moveable; **transportieren** *tr. V.* transport ⟨goods, people⟩; move ⟨patient⟩; **Transport·kosten** *Pl.* carriage *sing.;* transport costs
**Transvestit** der; ~en, ~en transvestite
**Trapez das;** ~es, ~e **a)** *(Geom.)* trapezium *(Brit.);* trapezoid *(Amer.);* **b)** *(im Zirkus o. ä.)* trapeze
**trappeln** *itr. V.; mit sein* patter [along]; ⟨feet⟩ patter; ⟨hoofs⟩ go clip-clop
**Trara das;** ~s *(ugs.)* razzmatazz *(coll.)*
**trat** *1. u. 3. Pers. Sg. Prät. v.* treten
**Tratsch** der; ~|e|s *(ugs.)* gossip; tittle-

tattle; **tratschen** *itr. V. (ugs.)* gossip; *(schwatzen)* chatter
**Traube** die; ~, ~n **a)** *(Beeren)* bunch; *(von Johannisbeeren o. ä.)* cluster; **b)** *(Wein~)* grape; **c)** *(Menschenmenge)* bunch; cluster
**trauen** 1. *itr. V.* jmdm./einer Sache ~: trust sb./sth.; **2.** *refl. V.* dare; **3.** *tr. V. (verheiraten)* ⟨vicar, registrar, etc.⟩ marry
**Trauer** die; ~ **a)** grief (über + *Akk.* over); *(um einen Toten)* mourning (um + *Akk.* for); **b)** *(~zeit)* [period of] mourning; **c)** ~ ~ tragen be in mourning
**Trauer-:** ~**fall** der bereavement; ~**feier** die memorial ceremony; *(beim Begräbnis)* funeral ceremony; ~**karte** die [pre-printed] card of condolence; ~**kleidung** die mourning clothes *pl.*
**trauern** *itr. V.* mourn; um jmdn. ~: mourn for sb.
**Trauer-:** ~**spiel** das tragedy; *(fig. ugs.)* deplorable business; ~**weide** die weeping willow
**träufeln** *tr. V.* [let] trickle (in + *Akk.* into); drip ⟨ear-drops etc.⟩
**Traum** der; ~|e|s, Träume ['trɔymə] dream; **träumen** 1. *itr. V.* dream (von of, about); *(unaufmerksam sein)* [day-] dream; **2.** *tr. V.* dream; **Träumer** der; ~s, ~, **Träumerin** die; ~, ~nen dreamer; **träumerisch** 1. *Adj.* dreamy; **2.** *adv.* dreamily; **traumhaft** *(ugs.)* 1. *Adj.* marvellous; fabulous *(coll.);* 2. *adv.* fabulously *(coll.)*
**traurig** 1. *Adj.* **a)** sad; unhappy ⟨childhood, youth⟩; painful ⟨duty⟩; **b)** *(kümmerlich)* sorry ⟨state etc.⟩; miserable ⟨result⟩; **2.** *adv.* sadly; **Traurigkeit** die; ~: sadness; sorrow
**Trau-:** ~**ring** der wedding-ring; ~**schein** der marriage certificate
**Trauung** die; ~, ~en wedding [ceremony]; **Trau·zeuge** der witness *(at wedding ceremony)*
**Trecker** der; ~s, ~: tractor
**Treff** der; ~s, ~s *(ugs.)* rendezvous; *(Ort)* meeting-place; **treffen** 1. *unr. tr. V.* **a)** hit; ⟨punch, blow, object⟩ strike; **ihn trifft keine Schuld** he is in no way to blame; **b)** *(erschüttern)* affect [deeply]; *(verletzen)* hurt; **c)** *(begegnen)* meet; **d)** *(vorfinden)* come upon, find ⟨anomalies etc.⟩; **es gut/ schlecht ~:** be *or* strike lucky/be unlucky; **e)** *(als Funktionsverb)* make ⟨arrangements, choice, preparations, de-

cision, etc.⟩; **2.** unr. itr. V. **a)** ⟨person, shot, etc.⟩ hit the target; **nicht** ~: miss [the target]; **b)** mit sein auf etw. (Akk.) ~: come upon sth.; **auf Widerstand/ Ablehnung/Schwierigkeiten** ~: meet with resistance/rejection/difficulties; **3.** unr. refl. V. **a)** sich mit jmdm. ~: meet sb.; **b)** unpers. es trifft sich gut/ schlecht it is convenient/inconvenient; **Treffen** das; ~s, ~: meeting; **treffend 1.** Adj. apt; **2.** adv. aptly; **Treffer** der; ~s, ~ **a)** (Milit., Boxen, Fechten usw.) hit; (Schlag) blow; (Ballspiele) goal; **b)** (Gewinn) win; (Los) winner; **trefflich** (geh.) **1.** Adj. excellent; splendid ⟨person⟩; **2.** adv. excellently; splendidly

**treff-, Treff-:** ~**punkt** der meetingplace; ~**sicher 1.** Adj. accurate ⟨language, mode of expression⟩; unerring ⟨judgement⟩; **2.** adv. accurately; ~**sicherheit** die; o. Pl. accuracy

**Treib·eis** das drift-ice

**treiben 1.** unr. tr. V. **a)** drive; **b)** (sich beschäftigen mit) go in for ⟨farming, cattle-breeding, etc.⟩; study ⟨French etc.⟩; carry on, pursue ⟨studies, trade, craft⟩; **viel Sport** ~: do a lot of sport; **es wüst/übel/toll** ~ (ugs.) lead a dissolute/bad life/live it up; **2.** unr. itr. V. meist, mit Richtungsangabe nur, mit sein drift; **Treiben** das; ~s **a)** (Durcheinander) bustle; **b)** (Tun) activities pl.; doings pl.

**Treib-:** ~**haus** das hothouse; ~**hauseffekt** der greenhouse effect; ~**stoff** der fuel

**Trenchcoat** ['trɛntʃkoʊt] der; ~[s], ~s trench coat

**Trend** der; ~s, ~s trend (**zu** + Dat. towards); (Mode) vogue

**trennen 1.** tr. V. **a)** separate (**von** from); sever ⟨head, arm⟩; **b)** (auf~) unpick ⟨dress, seam⟩; **c)** (teilen) divide ⟨word, parts of a room etc., fig.: people⟩; **2.** refl. V. **a)** (voneinander weggehen) part [company]; **b)** (eine Partnerschaft auflösen) ⟨couple, partners⟩ split up; **c)** sich von etw. ~: part with sth.; **Trennung** die; ~, ~en (von Menschen) separation (**von** from); (von Gegenständen) parting; (von Wörtern) division

**trepp-** ~**ab** Adv. down the stairs; ~**auf** Adv. up the stairs

**Treppe** die; ~, ~n staircase; [flight sing. of] stairs pl.; (im Freien, auf der Bühne) [flight sing. of] steps pl.

**Treppen-:** ~**absatz** der half-landing;

~**geländer** das banisters pl.; ~**haus** das stair-well; ~**stufe** die stair; (im Freien) step

**Tresen** der; ~s, ~ (bes. nordd.) bar; (Ladentisch) counter

**Tresor** der; ~s, ~e safe

**Tret·boot** das pedalo; **treten 1.** unr. itr. V. **a)** mit sein step (**in** + Akk. into, **auf** + Akk. on to); **b)** (seinen Fuß setzen) auf etw. (Akk.) ~ tread on sth.; **c)** (ausschlagen) kick; **2.** unr. tr. V. **a)** (Tritt versetzen) kick ⟨person, ball, etc.⟩; **b)** (trampeln) trample ⟨path⟩; **c)** (mit dem Fuß niederdrücken) step on ⟨brake, pedal⟩; operate ⟨bellows, clutch⟩

**treu 1.** Adj. faithful; loyal; faithful ⟨husband, wife⟩; loyal ⟨ally, subject⟩; **jmdm.** ~ **sein** be true to sb.; sich selbst (Dat.)/seinem Glauben ~ **bleiben** be true to oneself/one's faith; **2.** adv. faithfully; loyally; **Treue** die; ~ **a)** loyalty; (von [Ehe]partnern) fidelity; **b)** (Genauigkeit) accuracy

**treu-, Treu-:** ~**hand[anstalt]** die o. Pl. (Wirtschaft) German privatization agency; ~**herzig 1.** Adj. ingenuous; (naiv) naïve; (unschuldig) innocent; **2.** adv. ingenuously; (naiv) naïvely; (unschuldig) innocently; ~**los 1.** Adj. disloyal, faithless ⟨friend, person⟩; unfaithful ⟨husband, wife, lover⟩; **2.** adv. faithlessly

**Tribunal** das; ~s, ~e tribunal; **Tribüne** die; ~, ~n [grand]stand

**Trichter** der; ~s, ~ funnel

**Trick** der; ~s, ~s trick; (fig.: List) ploy

**trieb** 1. u. 3. Pers. Sg. Prät. v. treiben; **Trieb** der; ~[e]s, ~e **a)** (innerer Antrieb) impulse; (Drang) urge; (Verlangen) [compulsive] desire; **b)** (Sproß) shoot

**trieb-, Trieb-:** ~**feder** die mainspring; (fig.) driving or motivating force; ~**haft 1.** Adj. compulsive; carnal ⟨sensuality⟩; **2.** adv. compulsively; ~**wagen** der (Eisenb.) railcar

**triefen** unr. od. regelm. itr. V. **a)** mit sein (fließen) (in Tropfen) drip; (in kleinen Rinnsalen) trickle; **b)** (naß sein) be dripping wet; ⟨nose⟩ run

**triff** Imperativ Sg. v. treffen; **trifft** 3. Pers. Sg. Präsens v. treffen

**triftig** Adj. good ⟨reason, excuse⟩; valid, convincing ⟨motive, argument⟩

**¹Trikot** [tri'ko] der od. das; ~s, ~s (Stoff) cotton jersey; **²Trikot** das; ~s, ~ (ärmellos) singlet; (eines Tänzers) leotard; (eines Fußballspielers) shirt

**Triller** der; ~s, ~: trill; **trillern 1.** itr. V. trill; **2.** tr. V. warble ⟨song⟩; **Triller·pfeife** die police/referee's whistle

**Trimm-dich-Pfad** der keep-fit trail; **trimmen** tr. V. (durch Sport) get ⟨person⟩ into shape

**trinken 1.** unr. itr. V. drink; **auf jmdn./etw.** ~: drink to sb./sth.; **2.** unr. tr. V. drink; **einen Kaffee/ein Bier** ~: have a coffee/beer; **Trinker** der; ~s, ~: alcoholic; **Trinkerei** die; ~, ~en drinking no art.

**Trink-:** ~**geld** das tip; ~**wasser** das; Pl. ~**wässer** drinking-water; „**kein** ~**wasser**" 'not for drinking'

**Trio** das; ~s, ~s (Musik, fig.) trio

**trippeln** itr. V.; mit sein trip; ⟨child⟩ patter

**trist** Adj. dreary; dismal

**tritt** Imperativ Sg. u. 3. Pers. Sg. Präsens v. treten; **Tritt** der; ~[e]s, ~e (Schritt; Trittbrett) step; (Fuß~) kick; **Tritt·brett** das step

**Triumph** der; ~[e]s, ~e triumph; **triumphieren** itr. V. a) exult; b) (siegen) be triumphant; triumph (lit. or fig.) (über + Akk. over)

**trivial 1.** Adj. a) (platt) banal; trite; (unbedeutend) trivial; b) (alltäglich) humdrum ⟨life, career⟩; **2.** adv. (platt) banally; ⟨say etc.⟩ tritely

**trocken 1.** Adj. (auch fig.) dry; **2.** adv. drily; **Trocken·haube** die [hood-type] hair-drier; **Trockenheit** die; ~, ~en a) o. Pl. dryness; b) (Dürreperiode) drought

**trocken-, Trocken-:** ~|**legen** tr. V. a) ein Baby ~**legen** change a baby's nappies (Brit.) or (Amer.) diapers; b) (entwässern) drain ⟨marsh, pond, etc.⟩; ~**milch** die dried milk; ~|**reiben** unr. tr. V. rub ⟨hair, child, etc.⟩ dry; wipe ⟨crockery, window, etc.⟩ dry

**trocknen 1.** itr. V.; meist mit sein dry; **2.** tr. V. dry

**Troddel** die; ~, ~n tassel

**Trödel** der; ~s (ugs.) junk; (für den Flohmarkt) jumble; **trödeln** itr. V. a) (ugs.) dawdle (mit over); b) mit sein (ugs.: schlendern) saunter; **Trödler** der; ~s, ~ (ugs.) junk-dealer

**troff** 1. u. 3. Pers. Sg. Prät. v. triefen

**trog** 1. u. 3. Pers. Sg. Prät. v. trügen

**Trog** der; ~[e]s, Tröge trough

**trollen** (ugs.) refl. V. push off (coll.)

**Trommel** die; ~, ~n drum; **trommeln 1.** itr. V. a) beat the drum; (als Beruf, Hobby usw.) play the drums; b)

([auf etw.] schlagen, auftreffen) drum (auf + Akk. on, an + Akk. against); **Trommel·wirbel** der drum-roll; **Trommler** der; ~s, ~drummer

**Trompete** die; ~, ~n trumpet; **trompeten 1.** itr. V. play the trumpet; (fig.) ⟨elephant⟩ trumpet; **2.** tr. V. play ⟨piece⟩ on the trumpet; **Trompeter** der; ~s, ~trumpeter

**Tropen** Pl. tropics; **Tropen-** tropical; **Tropen·helm** der sun-helmet

**Tropf** der; ~[e]s, ~e (Med.) drip; **Tröpfchen** das; ~s, ~: droplet; (kleine Menge) drop; **tröpfeln 1.** itr. V. a) mit sein drip (auf + Akk. on to, aus, von from); b) unpers. (ugs.: leicht regnen) es tröpfelt it's spitting [with rain]; **2.** tr. V. let ⟨sth.⟩ drip (in + Akk. into, auf + Akk. on to); **tropfen 1.** itr. V.; mit Richtungsangabe mit sein drip; ⟨tears⟩ fall; unpers. es tropft [vom Dach usw.] water is dripping from the roof etc.; **2.** tr. V. let ⟨sth.⟩ drip (in + Akk. into, auf + Akk. on to); **Tropfen** der; ~s, ~ drop; ein guter/edler ~: a good/fine vintage; **Tropf·stein·höhle** die limestone cave with stalactites and/or stalagmites

**Trophäe** die; ~, ~n (hist., Jagd, Sport) trophy

**tropisch** Adj. tropical

**Troß** der; Trosses, Trosse a) (Milit.) baggage train; b) (Gefolge) retinue; (fig.: Zug) procession [of hangers-on]

**Trost** der; ~[e]s consolation; (bes. geistlich) comfort; **nicht [ganz od. recht] bei** ~ **sein** (ugs.) be out of one's mind; **trösten 1.** tr. V. comfort, console (mit with); **2.** refl. V. console oneself; **tröstlich** Adj. comforting; **trost·los** Adj. a) hopeless; (verzweifelt) in despair postpos.; b) (deprimierend, öde) miserable; dreary; hopeless ⟨situation⟩; **Trost·preis** der consolation prize

**Trott** der; ~[e]s, ~e trot; (fig.) routine

**Trottel** der; ~s, ~ (ugs.) fool; **trottelig** (ugs.) **1.** Adj. doddery; **2.** adv. in a feeble-minded way

**trotten** itr. V.; mit sein trot [along]

**trotz** Präp. mit Gen., seltener mit Dat. in spite of; despite; **Trotz** der; ~es defiance; **trotz·dem** [auch: '-'-] Adv. nevertheless; **trotzen** itr. V. a) (geh.: widerstehen) jmdm./einer Sache ~ (auch fig.) defy sb./sth.; b) (trotzig sein) be contrary; **trotzig 1.** Adj. defiant; (widerspenstig) contrary; difficult ⟨child⟩; **2.** adv. defiantly

**trüb[e]** 1. *Adj.* **a)** *(nicht klar)* murky ⟨*stream, water*⟩; cloudy ⟨*liquid, wine, juice*⟩; *(schlammig)* muddy ⟨*puddle*⟩; *(schmutzig)* dirty ⟨*glass, windowpane*⟩; dull ⟨*eyes*⟩; **b)** *(nicht hell)* dim ⟨*light*⟩; dull, dismal ⟨*day, weather*⟩; grey, overcast ⟨*sky*⟩; 2. *adv.* ⟨*shine, light*⟩ dimly

**Trubel** der; ~s [hustle and] bustle

**trüben** 1. *tr. V.* **a)** make ⟨*liquid*⟩ cloudy; cloud ⟨*liquid*⟩; **b)** *(beeinträchtigen)* dampen ⟨*mood*⟩; mar ⟨*relationship*⟩; cloud ⟨*judgement*⟩; 2. *refl. V.* ⟨*liquid*⟩ become cloudy; ⟨*eyes*⟩ become dull; ⟨*sky*⟩ darken; **Trübsal** die; ~, ~e *(geh.)* **a)** *(Leiden)* affliction; **b)** *o. Pl. (Kummer)* grief; ~ **blasen** *(ugs.)* mope (wegen over, about)

**trüb-, Trüb-:** ~**selig** 1. *Adj.* **a)** *(öde)* dreary, depressing ⟨*place, area, colour*⟩; **b)** *(traurig)* gloomy; 2. *adv. (traurig)* gloomily; ~**sinn** der; *o. Pl.* melancholy; ~**sinnig** 1. *Adj.* melancholy; 2. *adv.* gloomily

**Trübung** die; ~, ~en **a)** clouding; *(des Auges)* dimming; **b)** *(Beeinträchtigung)* deterioration; *(der Stimmung)* dampening

**trudeln** *itr. V. mit sein* roll

**Trüffel** die; ~, ~n truffle

**trug** *1. u. 3. Pers. Prät. v.* **tragen; trüge** *1. u. 3. Pers. Sg. Konjunktiv II v.* **tragen**

**trügen** 1. *unr. tr. V.* deceive; 2. *unr. itr. V.* be deceptive; ⟨*feeling, deception*⟩ be a delusion; **trügerisch** 1. *Adj.* deceptive; false ⟨*hope, sign, etc.*⟩; treacherous ⟨*ice*⟩; 2. *adv.* deceptively

**Truhe** die; ~, ~n chest

**Trümmer** *Pl. (eines Gebäudes)* rubble *sing.; (Ruinen)* ruins; *(eines Flugzeugs usw.)* wreckage *sing.; (kleinere Teile)* debris *sing.;* **Trümmer·haufen** der pile *or* heap of rubble

**Trumpf** der; ~[e]s, Trümpfe *(auch fig.)* trump [card]; *(Farbe)* trumps *pl.;* ~ **sein** *(fig.: Mode sein)* be the in thing; **trumpfen** *itr. V.* play a trump

**Trunk** der; ~[e]s, Trünke *(geh.) (Getränk)* drink; beverage *(formal);* **Trunkenheit** die; ~: drunkenness; ~ **am Steuer** drunken driving; **Trunk·sucht** die; *o. Pl.* alcoholism *no art.*

**Trupp** der; ~s, ~s troop; *(von Arbeitern, Gefangenen)* gang; *(von Soldaten, Polizisten)* squad; **Truppe** die; ~, ~n **a)** *(Einheit der Streitkräfte)* unit; **b)** *Pl. (Soldaten)* troops; **c)** *o. Pl. (Streit-*

*kräfte)* [armed] forces *pl.; (Heer)* army; **d)** *(Gruppe von Schauspielern, Artisten)* troupe; *(von Sportlern)* squad

**Trut·hahn** der turkey [cock]

**tschau** *Interj. (ugs.)* ciao *(coll.)*

**Tscheche** der; ~n, ~n Czech; **tschechisch** *Adj.* Czech; **Tschechoslowakei** die; ~: Czechoslovakia *no art.;* **tschechoslowakisch** *Adj.* Czechoslovak[ian]

**tschüs** *Interj. (ugs.)* bye *(coll.)*

**Tsd.** *Abk.* Tausend

**T-Shirt** ['tiːʃɔːt] das; ~s, ~s T-shirt

**Tube** die; ~, ~n tube

**Tuberkulose** die; ~, ~n *(Med.)* tuberculosis *no art.*

**Tuch** das; ~[e]s, Tücher *od.* ~e **a)** *Pl.* Tücher cloth; *(Kopf~, Hals~)* scarf; **b)** *Pl.* ~e *(Gewebe)* cloth

**tüchtig** 1. *Adj.* **a)** efficient; *(fähig)* capable, competent (in + *Dat.* at); **b)** *(ugs.: beträchtlich)* sizeable ⟨*piece, portion*⟩; big ⟨*gulp*⟩; hearty ⟨*eater, appetite*⟩; 2. *adv.* **a)** efficiently; *(fähig)* competently; **b)** *(ugs.: sehr)* really ⟨*cold, warm*⟩; ⟨*snow, rain*⟩ good and proper *(coll.); ⟨eat⟩* heartily; **Tüchtigkeit** die; ~: efficiency; *(Fähigkeit)* ability; competence; *(Fleiß)* industry

**Tücke** die; ~, ~n **a)** *o. Pl. (Hinterhältigkeit)* deceit[fulness]; *(List)* guile; **b)** *meist Pl. ([verborgene] Gefahr/Schwierigkeit)* [hidden] danger/difficulty

**tuckern** *itr. V.; mit Richtungsangabe mit sein* chug

**tückisch** 1. *Adj.* **a)** *(hinterhältig)* wily; *(betrügerisch)* deceitful; **b)** *(gefährlich)* treacherous ⟨*bend, slope, spot*⟩; 2. *adv.* craftily

**tüfteln** *itr. V. (ugs.)* fiddle (an + *Dat.* with); do finicky work (an + *Dat.* on); *(geistig)* rack one's brains (an + *Dat.* over)

**Tugend** die; ~, ~en virtue; **tugendhaft** 1. *Adj.* virtuous; 2. *adv.* virtuously

**Tüll** der; ~s, ~e tulle

**Tülle** die; ~, ~n *(bes. nordd.)* spout

**Tulpe** die; ~, ~n tulip

**tummeln** *refl. V.* romp [about]; **Tummel·platz** der *(auch fig.)* playground

**Tumor** der; ~s, ~en *(Med.)* tumour

**Tümpel** der; ~s, ~: pond

**Tumult** der; ~[e]s, ~e tumult; commotion; *(Protest)* uproar

**tun** 1. *unr. tr. V.* **a)** do; **so etwas tut man nicht** that is just not done; **[etwas] mit etw./jmdm. zu ~ haben** be concerned with sth./have dealings with sb.; **b)** *als Funktionsverb* make ⟨*remark, catch, etc.*⟩; take ⟨*step, jump*⟩; do ⟨*deed*⟩; **c)** *(bewirken)* work, perform ⟨*miracle*⟩; **d)** *(an~)* jmdm. etw. ~: do sth. to sb.; **e)** es ~ *(ugs.: genügen)* be good enough; **f)** *(ugs.: irgendwohin bringen)* put; **2.** *unr. itr. V.* **a)** *(ugs.: funktionieren)* work; **b)** **freundlich/geheimnisvoll** ~: pretend to be *or* *(coll.)* act friendly/ act mysteriously; **3.** *unr. refl. V.; unpers.* **es hat sich einiges getan** quite a bit has happened

**Tünche** die; ~, ~n distemper; wash; |weißel ~: whitewash; **tünchen** *tr. (auch itr.)* V. distemper; **weiß** ~: whitewash

**Tunell** das; ~s, ~s *(südd., österr., schweiz.)* s. **Tunnel**

**Tunesien** [tu'ne:ziən] **(das)**; ~s Tunisia; **tunesisch** *Adj.* Tunisian

**Tunke** die; ~, ~n *(bes. ostmd.)* sauce; *(Bratensoße)* gravy; **tunken** *tr. V. (bes. ostmd.)* dip

**Tunnel** der; ~s, ~ *od.* ~s tunnel

**tupfen** *tr. V.* **a)** dab; **b)** *(mit Tupfen versehen)* dot; **Tupfen** der; ~s, ~: dot; *(größer)* spot; **Tupfer** der; ~s, ~ *(Med.)* swab

**Tür** die; ~, ~en door; *(Garten~)* gate; **an die ~ gehen** *(öffnen)* [go and] answer the door; **vor die ~ gehen** go outside

**Turban** der; ~s, ~e turban

**Turbine** die; ~, ~n turbine

**turbulent 1.** *Adj. (auch fachspr.)* turbulent; **2.** *adv. (auch fachspr.)* turbulently

**Tür·griff** der door-handle

**Türke** der; ~n, ~n Turk; **Türkei** die; ~: Turkey *no art.*

**türkis** *indekl. Adj.* turquoise; **Türkis** der; ~es, ~e turquoise

**türkisch** *Adj.* Turkish

**Tür·klinke** die door-handle

**Turm** der; ~|els, **Türme a)** tower; *(spitzer Kirch~)* spire; steeple; **b)** *(Schach)* rook; **c)** *(Sprung~)* diving-platform; **Türmchen** das; ~s, ~: turret; **¹türmen 1.** *tr. V. (stapeln)* stack up; *(häufen)* pile up; **2.** *refl. V.* be piled up; ⟨*clouds*⟩ gather

**²türmen** *itr. V.; mit sein (salopp)* scarper *(Brit. sl.)*

**Turm·falke** der kestrel

**turnen 1.** *itr. V.* do gymnastics; *(Schulw.)* do gym; **2.** *tr. V.* do, perform ⟨*exercise, routine*⟩; **Turnen** das; ~s gymnastics *sing., no art.; (Schulw.)*

gym *no art.; PE no art.;* **Turner** der; ~s, ~, **Turnerin** die; ~, ~nen gymnast

**Turn-:** **~halle** die gymnasium; **~hemd** das [gym] singlet; **~hose** die gym shorts *pl.*

**Turnier** das; ~s, ~e *(auch hist.)* tournament; *(Reit~)* show; *(Tanz~)* competition

**Turn·schuh** der gym shoe

**Turnus** der; ~, ~se regular cycle

**Turn·verein** der gymnastics club

**Tusch** der; ~|els, ~e fanfare

**Tusche** die; ~, ~n Indian *(Brit.)* or *(Amer.)* India ink

**tuscheln** *itr., tr. V.* whisper

**Tüte** die; ~, ~n bag

**tuten** *itr. V.* hoot; ⟨*siren, [fog-]horn*⟩ sound

**Typ** der; ~s, ~en **a)** type; **b)** *Gen. auch* ~en *(ugs.: Mann)* bloke *(Brit. sl.);* **Type** die; ~, ~n *(Druck~, Schreibmaschinen~)* type

**Typhus** der; ~ typhoid [fever]

**typisch 1.** *Adj.* typical *(für of);* **2.** *adv.* typically

**Tyrann** der; ~en, ~en *(auch fig.)* tyrant; **Tyrannei** die; ~, ~en *(auch fig.)* tyranny; **tyrannisch 1.** *Adj.* tyrannical; **2.** *adv.* tyrannically; **tyrannisieren** *tr. V.* tyrannize

# U

**u, U** [u:] das; ~, ~: u, U

**ü, Ü** [y:] das; ~, ~: u umlaut

**u.** *Abk.* und

**u. a.** *Abk.* unter anderem

**U-Bahn** die underground *(Brit.);* subway *(Amer.); (bes. in London)* tube; **U-Bahn-Station** die underground station *(Brit.);* subway station *(Amer.); (bes. in London)* tube station

**übel** *Adj.* **a)** foul, nasty ⟨*smell, weather*⟩; bad, nasty ⟨*headache, cold, taste*⟩; nasty ⟨*consequences, situation*⟩; sorry ⟨*state, affair*⟩; foul, *(coll.)* filthy ⟨*mood*⟩; **nicht ~** *(ugs.)* not bad at all; **b)** *(unwohl)* jmdm. **ist/wird** ~: sb. feels sick; **c)** *(verwerflich)* bad;

wicked; nasty, dirty ⟨trick⟩. **Übel** das; ~s, ~ evil; **Übelkeit** die; ~, ~en nausea

**übel|nehmen** unr. tr. V. jmdm. etw. ~: hold sth. against sb.; etw. ~: take offence at sth.; **Übel·täter** der wrongdoer

**üben** tr. V. **a)** (auch itr.) practise; rehearse ⟨scene, play⟩; practise on ⟨musical instrument⟩; **b)** (trainieren, schulen) exercise ⟨fingers⟩; train ⟨memory⟩

**über 1.** Präp. mit Dat. **a)** (Lage, Standort) over; above; (in einer Rangfolge) above; ~ jmdm. wohnen live above sb.; zehn Grad ~ Null ten degrees above zero; sie trug eine Jacke ~ dem Kleid she wore a jacket over her dress; **b)** (während) during; ~ dem Lesen/der Arbeit einschlafen fall asleep over one's book/magazine etc./over one's work; **2.** Präp. mit Akk. **a)** (Richtung) over; (quer hinüber) across; ~ Ulm nach Stuttgart via Ulm to Stuttgart; **b)** (während) over; (für die Dauer von) for; **c)** (betreffend) about; ~ etw. reden/schreiben talk/write about sth.; ein Scheck/eine Rechnung ~ 1000 Mark a cheque/bill for 1,000 marks; **d)** Kinder ~ 10 Jahre children over ten [years of age]; **3.** Adv. **a)** (mehr als) over; **b)** ~ und ~: all over

**über·all** [od. --'-] Adv. **a)** everywhere; **b)** (bei jeder Gelegenheit) always

**über·anstrengen** tr. V. overtax ⟨person, energy⟩; strain ⟨eyes, nerves, heart⟩; sich ~: over-exert oneself

**über·arbeiten 1.** tr. V. rework; revise ⟨text, edition⟩; **2.** refl. V. overwork

**über·aus** Adv. (geh.) extremely

**über·backen** unr. tr. V. etw. mit Käse usw. ~: top sth. with cheese etc. and brown it lightly [under the grill/in a hot oven]

**überbelichten**[1] tr. V. (Fot.) overexpose

**über·bieten** unr. tr. V. **a)** outbid (um by); **b)** (übertreffen) surpass; outdo ⟨rival⟩; break ⟨record⟩ (um by); exceed ⟨target⟩ (um by)

**Über·blick** der **a)** view; einen guten ~ über etw. (Akk.) haben have a good view over sth.; **b)** (Abriß) survey; s) o. Pl. (Einblick) overall view; **über·blicken** tr. V. s. übersehen a, b

**über·bringen** unr. tr. V. deliver; convey ⟨greetings, congratulations⟩

---

[1] ich überbelichte, überbelichtet, überzubelichten

**über·brücken** tr. V. bridge ⟨gap, gulf⟩; reconcile ⟨difference⟩; **Überbrückung** die; ~, ~en (fig.) bridging; (von Gegensätzen) reconciliation

**überdacht** Adj. covered ⟨terrace, station platform, etc.⟩

**über·dauern** tr. V. survive ⟨war, separation, hardship⟩

**über·dies** Adv. moreover

**Über·druck** der; Pl. ~drücke excess pressure

**Überdruß** der; Überdrusses surfeit (an + Dat. of); **überdrüssig** Adj. jmds./einer Sache ~ sein/werden be/grow tired of sb./sth.

**über·eilen** tr. V. rush; **übereilt** overhasty

**über·einander** Adv. **a)** one on top of the other; **b)** ⟨talk etc.⟩ about each other

**übereinander-:** ~|legen tr. V. Holzscheite usw. ~legen lay pieces of wood etc. one on top of the other; ~|schlagen unr. tr. V. die Arme/Beine ~schlagen fold one's arms/cross one's legs

**überein|kommen** unr. itr. V.; mit sein agree; come to an agreement; **Überein·kommen** das; ~s, ~, **Übereinkunft** die; ~, Übereinkünfte agreement

**überein|stimmen** itr. V. **a)** (einer Meinung sein) agree (in + Dat. on); **b)** (sich gleichen) ⟨colours, styles⟩ match; ⟨figures, statements, reports, results⟩ tally, agree; ⟨views, opinions⟩ coincide; **Überein·stimmung** die **a)** agreement (in + Dat. on; Gen. between)

**über·empfindlich 1.** Adj. oversensitive (gegen to); (Med.) hypersensitive (gegen to). **2.** adv. oversensitively; (Med.) hypersensitively

[1]**über|fahren 1.** unr. tr. V. jmdn. ~: ferry or take sb. over; **2.** unr. itr. V.; mit sein cross over; [2]**über·fahren** unr. tr. V. **a)** run over; **b)** (hinwegfahren über) cross; go over ⟨crossroads⟩; **Über·fahrt** die crossing (über + Akk. of)

**Über·fall** der attack (auf + Akk. on); (aus dem Hinterhalt) ambush (auf + Akk. on); (mit vorgehaltener Waffe) hold-up; (auf eine Bank o.ä.) raid (auf + Akk. on); **über·fallen** unr. tr. V. **a)** attack; raid ⟨bank, enemy position, village, etc.⟩; (hinterrücks) ambush; (mit vorgehaltener Waffe) hold up; b) *(überkommen)* ⟨*tiredness, home-sickness, fear*⟩ come over; **über·fäl-lig** *Adj.* overdue

**über·fliegen** *unr. tr. V.* **a)** fly over; overfly *(formal);* **b)** *(flüchtig lesen)* skim [through]

**über·flügeln** *tr. V.* outshine; outstrip

**Über·fluß der;** *o. Pl.* abundance (**an** + *Dat.* of); *(Wohlstand)* affluence; **über·flüssig** *Adj.* superfluous; un-necessary ⟨*purchase, words, work*⟩

**über·fluten** *tr. V. (auch fig.)* flood

**über·fordern** *tr. V.* jmdn. |mit etw.| ~: overtax sb. [with sth.]; ask *or* demand too much of sb. [with sth.]

**¹über|führen** *tr. V.* transfer; **²über-führen** *tr. V.* **a)** *s.* **¹überführen; b)** jmdn. |eines Verbrechens| ~: find sb. guilty [of a crime]; convict sb. [of a crime]; **Über·führung die a)** trans-fer; **b)** *(eines Verdächtigen)* convic-tion; **c)** *(Brücke)* bridge; *(Hochstraße)* overpass; *(Fußgänger~)* [foot-]bridge

**über·füllt** *Adj.* crammed full (**von** with); *(mit Menschen)* overcrowded (**von** with); over-subscribed ⟨*course*⟩

**Über·gabe die a)** handing over (**an** + *Akk.* to); *(von Macht)* handing over; **b)** *(Auslieferung an den Gegner)* sur-render (**an** + *Akk.* to)

**Über·gang der a)** crossing; **b)** *(Stelle zum Überqueren)* crossing; *(Bahn~)* level crossing *(Brit.);* grade crossing *(Amer.);* *(Grenz~)* crossing-point; **c)** *(Wechsel, Überleitung)* transition (**zu, auf** + *Akk.* to)

**über·geben 1.** *unr. tr. V.* **a)** hand over; pass ⟨*baton*⟩; **b)** *(übereignen)* transfer, make over (*Dat.* to); **c)** *(aus-liefern)* surrender *(Dat.,* **an** + *Akk.* to); **d) eine Straße dem Verkehr ~:** open a road to traffic; **2.** *unr. refl. V. (sich erbrechen)* vomit

**¹über|gehen** *unr. itr. V.; mit sein* **a)** pass; **b) zu etw.** ~: go over to sth.; **c) in etw.** *(Akk.)* ~ *(zu etw. werden)* turn into sth.

**²über·gehen** *unr. tr. V.* **a)** *(nicht be-achten)* ignore; **b)** *(auslassen, über-springen)* skip [over]; **c)** *(nicht berück-sichtigen)* pass over

**über·geordnet** *Adj.* higher ⟨*court, authority, position*⟩; greater ⟨*signific-ance*⟩; superordinate ⟨*concept*⟩

**Über·gewicht das a)** excess weight; *(von Person)* overweight; **b)** *(fig.)* predominance

**über·glücklich** *Adj.* blissfully happy; *(hoch erfreut)* overjoyed

**über|greifen** *unr. itr. V.* **auf etw.** *(Akk.)* ~: spread to sth.

**Über·griff der** *(unrechtmäßiger Ein-griff)* encroachment (**auf** + *Akk.* on); infringement (**auf** + *Akk.* of); *(An-griff)* attack (**auf** + *Akk.* on)

**Über·größe die** outsize

**überhand|nehmen** *unr. itr. V.* get out of hand; ⟨*attacks, muggings, etc.*⟩ increase alarmingly; ⟨*weeds*⟩ run riot

**über|hängen** *tr. V.* **sich** *(Dat.)* **eine Jacke ~:** put a jacket round one's shoulders; **sich** *(Dat.)* **das Gewehr/die Tasche ~:** hang the rifle/bag over one's shoulder

**über·häufen** *tr. V.* jmdn. mit etw. ~: heap *or* shower sth. on sb.

**überhaupt** *Adv.* **a)** in general; **b)** ~ **nicht** not at all; ~ **keine Zeit haben** have no time at all; ~ **nichts** nothing at all

**überheblich 1.** *Adj.* arrogant; super-cilious ⟨*grin*⟩; **2.** *adv.* arrogantly; ⟨*grin*⟩ superciliously

**Überheblichkeit die;** ~: arrogance

**über·holen 1.** *tr. V.* **a)** overtake *(esp. Brit.);* pass *(esp. Amer.);* **b)** *(übertref-fen)* outstrip; **c)** *(wieder instand set-zen)* overhaul; **2.** *itr. V.* overtake *(esp. Brit.);* pass *(esp. Amer.);* **Überhol-spur die** overtaking lane *(esp. Brit.);* pass lane *(esp. Amer.);* **überholt** *Adj. (veraltet)* outdated; **Überholung die;** ~, ~**en** overhaul

**Überhol·verbot das** prohibition of overtaking

**über·hören** *tr. V.* not hear

**über·irdisch 1.** *Adj.* celestial; heavenly; *(übernatürlich)* supernat-ural; **2.** *adv.* celestially; *(übernatür-lich)* supernaturally

**über|kochen** *itr. V.; mit sein (auch fig. ugs.)* boil over

**über·kommen** *unr. tr. V.* **Mitleid/ Ekel/Furcht überkam mich** I was over-come by pity/revulsion/fear

**über·laden** *unr. tr. V. (auch fig.)* over-load

**über·lassen** *unr. tr. V.* **a)** jmdm. etw. ~: let sb. have sth.; **b) sich** *(Dat.)* **selbst ~ sein** be left to one's own de-vices; **c) etw. jmdm.** ~ *(etw. jmdn. ent-scheiden/tun lassen)* leave sth. to sb.

**über·lasten** *tr. V.* overload; overtax ⟨*person*⟩; *(mit Arbeit)* overwork ⟨*per-son*⟩

**Über·lauf der** overflow; **¹über|lau-fen** *unr. itr. V.; mit sein* **a)** overflow; **b)** *(auf die gegnerische Seite überwech-*

seln) defect; ⟨partisan⟩ go over to the other side; **²über·laufen** unr. tr. V. seize; **ein Frösteln/Schauer überlief mich, es überlief mich [eis]kalt** a cold shiver ran down my spine; **³über·laufen** Adj. overcrowded; **Überläufer der** (auch fig.) defector

**über·leben** tr. V. survive; **Über·lebende der/die**; adj. Dekl. survivor

**¹über|legen** tr. V. jmdm. etw. ~: put sth. over sb.; **²über·legen 1.** tr. V. consider; think about; **es sich anders ~**: change one's mind; **2.** itr. V. think;

**³überlegen 1.** Adj. **a)** superior; clear, convincing ⟨win, victory⟩; **jmdm. ~ sein** be superior to sb. (an + Dat. in); **b)** (herablassend) supercilious; **2.** adv. **a)** in a superior manner; ⟨play⟩ much the better; ⟨win, argue⟩ convincingly; **b)** (herablassend) superciliously; **Überlegenheit die**; ~ superiority; **überlegt 1.** Adj. carefully considered; **2.** adv. in a carefully considered way; **Überlegung die**; ~, ~en **a)** o. Pl. thought; **b)** (Gedanke) idea; ~en (Gedankengang) thoughts

**über·liefern** tr. V. hand down; **Über·lieferung die** tradition

**überlisten** tr. V. outwit

**überm** Präp. + Art. = über dem

**Über·macht die**; o. Pl. superior strength; (zahlenmäßig) superior numbers pl.

**über·mannen** tr. V. overcome

**Über·maß das**; o. Pl. excessive amount, excess (an + Dat. of); **über·mäßig 1.** Adj. excessive; **2.** adv. excessively

**über·menschlich** Adj. superhuman

**über·mitteln** tr. V. send; (als Mittler weitergeben) pass on, convey ⟨greetings, regards, etc.⟩

**über·morgen** Adv. the day after tomorrow

**Übermüdung die**; ~: overtiredness

**Über·mut der** high spirits pl.; **übermütig 1.** Adj. high-spirited; **2.** adv. high-spiritedly

**über·nächst...** Adj. **im ~en Jahr, ~es Jahr** the year after next; **am ~en Tag** two days later

**über·nachten** itr. V. stay overnight; **übernächtigt** Adj. ⟨person⟩ tired or worn out [through lack of sleep]; tired ⟨face, look, etc.⟩; **Übernachtung die**; ~, ~en overnight stay; **~ und Frühstück** bed and breakfast

**Übernahme die**; ~ (von Waren, einer Sendung) taking delivery no art.; (ei-

ner Idee usw.) adoption, taking over no indef. art.; (der Macht, einer Praxis usw.) take over

**über·natürlich** Adj. supernatural

**über·nehmen 1.** unr. tr. V. take delivery of ⟨goods, consignment⟩; take over ⟨power, practice, business, etc.⟩; take on ⟨job, position, etc.⟩; undertake to pay ⟨costs⟩; **b)** (sich zu eigen machen) adopt ⟨ideas, methods, subject, etc.⟩ (von from); borrow ⟨word, phrase⟩ (von from); **2.** unr. refl. V. overdo things or it; **sich mit etw. ~**: take on too much with sth.

**über·prüfen** tr. V. check (auf + Akk. for); review ⟨issue, situation, results⟩; **Über·prüfung die a)** o. Pl. checking no indef. art. (auf + Akk. for); **b)** (Kontrolle) check; (einer Lage, Frage usw.) review

**über·queren** tr. V. cross

**über·ragen** tr. V. **a)** jmdn./etw. ~: tower above sb./sth.; **b)** (fig.) **jmdn. an etw.** (Dat.) ~: be head and shoulders above sb. in sth.; **überragend 1.** Adj. outstanding; **2.** adv. outstandingly

**überraschen** tr. V. surprise; **Überraschung die**; ~, ~en surprise

**über·reden** tr. V. persuade

**über·reichen** tr. V. [jmdm.] etw. ~: present sth. [to sb.]

**über·rumpeln** tr. V. jmdn. ~: take sb. by surprise

**über·runden** tr. V. **a)** (Sport) lap; **b)** (übertreffen) outstrip

**übers** Präp. + Art. = über das

**Überschall-**: **~flugzeug das** supersonic aircraft; **~geschwindigkeit die** supersonic speed

**über·schätzen** tr. V. overestimate; overrate ⟨artist, talent, etc.⟩

**überschaubar** Adj. **eine ~e Menge/Zahl** a manageable quantity/number

**Über·schlag der a)** rough calculation or estimate; **b)** (Turnen) handspring; **c)** s. Looping; **¹über|schlagen 1.** unr. tr. V. **die Beine ~**: cross one's legs; **2.** unr. itr. V.; mit sein ⟨wave⟩ break; **²über·schlagen 1.** unr. tr. V. **a)** skip ⟨chapter, page, etc.⟩; **b)** (ungefähr berechnen) calculate or estimate roughly; **2.** unr. refl. V. go head over heels; ⟨car⟩ turn over

**über|schnappen** itr. V.; mit sein (ugs.) go crazy

**über·schneiden** unr. refl. V. cross, intersect; (fig.) overlap

**über·schreiben** unr. tr. V. **a)** entitle;

head ⟨*chapter, section*⟩; **b)** etw. jmdm. *od.* **auf** jmdn. ~: transfer sth. to sb.
**über·schreiten** *unr. itr. V.* cross; *(fig.)* exceed
**Über·schrift die** heading; *(in einer Zeitung)* headline; *(Titel)* title
**Über·schuß der** surplus **(an** + *Dat.* of); **überschüssig** *Adj.* surplus
**über·schütten** *tr. V.* cover
**Überschwang der;** ~|e|s exuberance
**über·schwemmen** *tr. V. (auch fig.)* flood; **Überschwemmung die;** ~, ~en flood; *(das Überschwemmen)* flooding *no pl.*
**über·schwenglich 1.** *Adj.* effusive ⟨*words etc.*⟩; wild ⟨*joy, enthusiasm*⟩; **2.** *adv.* effusively
**Über·see** *o. Art.* **aus** *od.* **von** ~: from overseas; **in/nach** ~: overseas
**über·sehen** *unr. tr. V.* **a)** look out over; **b)** *(abschätzen)* assess ⟨*damage, situation, consequences, etc.*⟩; **c)** *(nicht sehen)* overlook; miss; miss ⟨*turning, signpost*⟩; **d)** *(ignorieren)* ignore
**über·senden** *unr. (auch regelm.) tr. V.* send
¹**über|setzen 1.** *tr. V.* ferry over; **2.** *itr. V.; auch mit sein* cross [over]; ²**über·setzen** *tr., itr. V. (auch fig.)* translate; **Über·setzer der, Übersetzerin die;** ~, ~nen translator; **Übersetzung die;** ~, ~en translation
**Über·sicht die** **a)** *o. Pl.* overall view, overview **(über** + *Akk.* of); **b)** *(Darstellung)* survey; *(Tabelle)* summary; **über·sichtlich 1.** *Adj.* clear; ⟨*crossroads*⟩ which allows a clear view; **2.** *adv.* clearly
¹**über|siedeln,** ²**über·siedeln** *itr. V.; mit sein* move **(nach** to)
**über·spielen** *tr. V.* **a)** *(hinweggehen über)* cover up; smooth over ⟨*difficult situation*⟩; **b)** *(aufnehmen)* |**auf ein Tonband|** ~: transfer ⟨*record*⟩ to tape; put ⟨*record*⟩ on tape
**über·spitzen** *tr. V.* etw. ~: push *or* carry sth. too far
**über·springen** *unr. tr. V.* **a)** jump ⟨*obstacle*⟩; **b)** *(auslassen)* miss out
¹**über|stehen** *unr. itr. V.; südd., österr., schweiz. mit sein* jut out
²**über·stehen** *unr. tr. V.* come through ⟨*danger, war, operation*⟩; get over ⟨*illness*⟩
**über·steigen** *unr. tr. V.* **a)** climb over; **b)** *(fig.)* exceed
**über·stimmen** *tr. V.* outvote
**Über·stunde die:** ~n machen do overtime

**über·stürzen 1.** *tr. V.* rush; **2.** *refl. V.* rush; *(rasch aufeinanderfolgen)* ⟨*events, news, etc.*⟩ come thick and fast; **überstürzt 1.** *Adj.* hurried ⟨*escape, departure*⟩; over-hasty ⟨*decision*⟩; **2.** *adv.* ⟨*decide, act*⟩ over-hastily; ⟨*depart*⟩ hurriedly
**übertölpeln** *tr. V.* dupe; con *(coll.)*
**über·tönen** *tr. V.* drown out
**Übertrag der;** ~|e|s, Überträge *(bes. Buchf.)* carry-over; **über·tragbar** *Adj.* transferable **(auf** + *Akk.* to); *(auf etw. anderes anwendbar)* applicable **(auf** + *Akk.* to); *(übersetzbar)* translatable; *(ansteckend)* infectious ⟨*disease*⟩; **über·tragen** *unr. tr. V.* **a)** transfer **(auf** + *Akk.* to); transmit ⟨*power, torque, etc.*⟩ **(auf** + *Akk.* to); communicate ⟨*disease, illness*⟩ **(auf** + *Akk.* to); carry over ⟨*subtotal*⟩; *(auf etw. anderes anwenden)* apply **(auf** + *Akk.* to); *(übersetzen)* translate; **b)** *(senden)* broadcast ⟨*concert, event, match, etc.*⟩; *(im Fernsehen)* televise; **c)** *(geben)* jmdm. Aufgaben/Pflichten usw. ~: hand over tasks/duties *etc.* to sb.; *(anvertrauen)* entrust sb. with tasks/duties *etc.*; **Übertragung die;** ~, ~en **a)** *s.* übertragen **a:** transference; transmission; communication; carrying over; application; translation; **b)** *(das Senden)* broadcasting; *(Sendung)* broadcast; *(im Fernsehen)* televising/television broadcast
**über·treffen** *unr. tr. V.* **a)** surpass, outdo **(an** + *Dat.* in); break ⟨*record*⟩; **b)** *(übersteigen)* exceed
**über·treiben** *unr. tr. V.* **a)** *auch itr.* exaggerate; **b)** *(zu weit treiben)* overdo; **Übertreibung die;** ~, ~en exaggeration
¹**über|treten** *unr. itr. V.; mit sein* change sides; **zum Katholizismus/Islam** ~: convert to Catholicism/Islam; ²**über·treten** *unr. tr. V.* contravene ⟨*law*⟩; violate ⟨*regulation, prohibition*⟩; **Übertretung die;** ~, ~en **a)** *s.* ²**übertreten:** contravention; violation; **b)** *(Vergehen)* misdemeanour
**übertrieben** *Adj.* **1.** exaggerated; *(übermäßig)* excessive ⟨*care, thrift, etc.*⟩; **2.** *adv.* excessively
**Über·tritt der** change of allegiance, switch **(zu** to); *(Rel.)* conversion **(zu** to)
**über·trumpfen** *tr. V.* outdo
**über·vor·teilen** *tr. V.* cheat
**über·wachen** *tr. V.* keep under sur-

veillance ⟨*suspect, agent, area, etc.*⟩; supervise ⟨*factory, workers, process*⟩; control ⟨*traffic*⟩; monitor ⟨*progress, production process, experiment, patient*⟩; **Überwạchung** die; ~, ~en *s.* **überwachen**: surveillance; supervision; controlling; monitoring

**überwạ̈ltigen** *tr. V.* a) overpower; b) *(fig.)* ⟨*sleep, emotion, fear, etc.*⟩ overcome; ⟨*sight, impressions, beauty, etc.*⟩ overwhelm; **überwạ̈ltigend 1.** *Adj.* overwhelming ⟨*sight, impression, victory, majority, etc.*⟩; overpowering ⟨*smell*⟩; stunning ⟨*beauty*⟩; **2.** *adv.* stunningly ⟨*beautiful*⟩

**über·weisen** *unr. tr. V.* a) transfer ⟨*money*⟩ (**an, auf** + *Akk.* to); b) refer ⟨*patient*⟩ (**an** + *Akk.* to); **Überweisung** die a) *o. Pl.* transfer (**an, auf** + *Akk.* to); b) *(Summe)* remittance (**an** + *Akk.* to); c) *(eines Patienten)* referral (**an** + *Akk.* to)

**überwiegend 1.** [*auch* --'--] *Adj.* overwhelming; **2.** *adv.* mainly

**über·winden 1.** *unr. tr. V.* overcome; get past ⟨*stage*⟩; **2.** *unr. refl. V.* overcome one's reluctance; **sich** [**dazu**] ~, **etw. zu tun** bring oneself to do sth.; **Über·windung** die a) *s.* überwinden **1**: overcoming; getting past; b) *(das Sichüberwinden)* **es war eine große ~ für ihn** it cost him a great effort

**Über·zahl** die; *o. Pl.* majority; **über·zählig** *Adj.* surplus

**überzeugen 1.** *tr. V.* convince; **2.** *itr. V.* be convincing; **überzeugend 1.** *Adj.* convincing; **2.** *adv.* convincingly; **überzeugt** *Adj.* convinced; **Über·zeugung** die *(feste Meinung)* conviction

**¹über|ziehen** *unr. tr. V.* pull on; **²über·ziehen** *unr. tr. V.* a) **etw. mit etw. ~:** cover sth. with sth.; b) overdraw ⟨*account*⟩ (**um** by); **Überzug** der a) *(Beschichtung)* coating; b) *(Bezug)* cover

**üblich** *Adj.* usual; *(normal)* normal; *(gebräuchlich)* customary

**U-Boot** das submarine; sub *(coll.)*

**übrig** *Adj.* remaining *attrib.*; *(ander...)* other; **alle ~en Gäste ...:** all the other guests ...; **im ~en** besides; **es ist etwas ~:** there is some left; **übrig|bleiben** *unr. itr. V.*; *mit sein* be left; ⟨*food, drink*⟩ be left over; **übrigens** *Adv.* by the way; **übrig|lassen** *unr. tr. V.* leave; leave ⟨*food, drink*⟩ over

**Übung** die; ~, ~en a) exercise; b) *o. Pl.* *(das Üben, Geübtsein)* practice

**UdSSR** [u:de:|ɛs|ɛs|'ɛr] *Abk.* die; ~ *(1922–1991)* **U**nion **d**er **S**ozialistischen **S**owjet**r**epubliken USSR

**Ụfer** das; ~s, ~: bank; *(des Meers)* shore

**UG** *Abk.* Untergeschoß

**Ugạnda** (das); ~s Uganda

**Ụhr** die; ~, ~en a) clock; *(Armband~, Taschen~)* watch; *(Wasser~, Gas~)* meter; *(an Meßinstrumenten)* dial; gauge; **auf die** *od.* **nach der ~ sehen** look at the time; **rund um die ~** *(ugs.)* round the clock; b) *o. Pl.* **acht ~:** eight o'clock; **wieviel ~ ist es?** what's the time?; **what time is it?**

**Ụhr-:** **~armband** das watch-strap; **~kette** die watch-chain; **~macher** der watchmaker/clockmaker; **~werk** das clock/watch mechanism; **~zeiger** der clock-/watch-hand; **~zeiger·sinn** der: **im/entgegen dem ~zeigersinn** clockwise/anticlockwise; **~zeit** die time; **jmdn. nach der ~zeit fragen** ask sb. the time

**Ụhu** der; ~s, ~s eagle owl

**Ukraine** die; ~: Ukraine; **Ukrainer** der; ~s, ~, **Ukrainerin** die; ~, ~nen Ukrainian

**UKW** [u:ka:'ve:] *o. Art.*; *Abk.* Ultrakurzwelle VHF; **UKW-Sender** der VHF station; ≈ FM station

**Ụlk** der; ~s, ~e lark *(coll.)*; *(Streich)* trick; [practical] joke; **ụlkig** *(ugs.)* **1.** *Adj.* funny; **2.** *adv.* in a funny way

**Ụlme** die; ~, ~n elm

**Ultimạtum** das; ~s, Ultimạten ultimatum

**Ultra·kurz·welle** die ultra-short wave; *(Rundf.: Wellenbereich)* very high frequency; VHF

**Ultra·schall** der *(Physik, Med.)* ultrasound; **ultra·violett** *Adj.* ultraviolet

**ụm 1.** *Präp. mit Akk.* a) *(räumlich)* [a]round; **um die Ecke** round the corner; b) *(zeitlich) (genau)* at; *(etwa)* around [about]; c) **Tag um Tag/Stunde um Stunde** day after day/hour after hour; d) *(bei Maß- u. Mengenangaben)* by; **2.** *Adv.* around; about; **um** [**die**] **10 Mark/50 Personen** [**herum**] around *or* about ten marks/50 people; **3.** *Konj.* a) *(final)* **um ... zu** [in order] to; b) *(konsekutiv)* **er ist groß genug/ist noch zu klein, um ... zu ...:** he is big enough/is still too young to ...; c) **je ... um so the ..., the; um so besser/schlimmer!** all the better/worse!

**ụm|ändern** *tr. V.* change; revise ⟨*text, novel*⟩; alter ⟨*garment*⟩

**umạrmen** *tr. V.* embrace; *(an sich drücken)* hug; **Umạrmung die;** ~, ~en embrace; hug

**Ụm·bau der;** ~[e]s, ~ten *s.* umbauen: rebuilding; alteration; conversion; *(fig.)* reorganization; **ụm|bauen** *tr., auch itr. V.* rebuild; *(leicht ändern)* alter; *(zu etw. anderem)* convert (**zu** into); *(fig.)* reorganize ⟨*system, administration, etc.*⟩

**ụm|benennen** *unr. tr. V.* change the name of; rename

**ụm|biegen** 1. *unr. tr. V.* bend; 2. *unr. itr. V.; mit sein* turn

**ụm|binden** *unr. tr. V.* put on

**ụm|blättern** 1. *tr. V.* turn [over]; 2. *itr. V.* turn the page/pages

**ụm|blicken** *refl. V.* a) look around; b) *(zurückblicken)* [turn to] look back (**nach** at)

**ụm|bringen** *unr. tr. V.* kill

**Ụm·bruch der** a) radical change; *(Umwälzung)* upheaval; b) *o. Pl. (Druckw.)* make-up; *(Ergebnis)* page proofs *pl.*

**ụm|buchen** 1. *tr. V.* change (**auf** + *Akk.* to); 2. *itr. V.* change one's booking (**auf** + *Akk.* to)

**ụm|drehen** 1. *tr. V.* turn round; turn over ⟨*coin, hand, etc.*⟩; turn ⟨*key*⟩; 2. *refl. V.* turn round; *(den Kopf wenden)* turn one's head; 3. *itr. V.; auch mit sein (ugs.: umkehren)* turn back; *(ugs.: wenden)* turn round; **Um·drehung die;** *(eines Motors usw.)* revolution; rev *(coll.)*

**um·einạnder** *Adv.* sich ~ kümmern/sorgen take care of/worry about each other *or* one another

¹**ụm|fahren** *unr. tr. V.* knock down; ²**um·fạhren** *unr. tr. V.* go round; make a detour round ⟨*obstruction etc.*⟩; *(im Auto)* drive round; *(im Schiff)* sail round; *(auf einer Umgehungsstraße)* bypass ⟨*town, village, etc.*⟩

**ụm|fallen** *unr. itr. V.; mit sein* a) fall over; b) *(zusammenbrechen)* collapse; **tot** ~: fall down dead

**Ụm·fang der** a) circumference; *(eines Quadrats usw.)* perimeter; *(eines Baums, Menschen usw.)* girth; b) *(Größe)* size; c) *(Ausmaß)* extent; **ụm·fang·reich** *Adj.* extensive; substantial ⟨*book*⟩

**um·fạssen** *tr. V.* a) grasp; *(umarmen)* embrace; b) *(enthalten)* contain; *(einschließen)* include; span, cover ⟨*period*⟩; **umfạssend** 1. *Adj.* full ⟨re-

ply, information, survey, confession⟩; extensive, wide ⟨*knowledge, powers*⟩; 2. *adv.* ⟨*inform*⟩ fully

**ụm|formen** *tr. V.* reshape; revise ⟨*poem, novel*⟩; transform ⟨*person*⟩

**Ụm·frage die** survey; *(Politik)* opinion poll

**ụm|füllen** *tr. V.* etw. in etw. *(Akk.)* ~: transfer sth. into sth.

**Ụm·gang der;** *o. Pl.* a) *(gesellschaftlicher Verkehr)* contact; b) *(das Umgehen)* **den** ~ **mit Pferden lernen** learn how to handle horses; **ụmgänglich** *Adj.* affable; *(gesellig)* sociable

**Ụmgangs-:** ~**form die gute/schlechte/keine** ~**formen haben** have good/bad/no manners; ~**sprache die** colloquial language

**um·geben** *unr. tr. V.* a) surround; ⟨*hedge, fence, wall, etc.*⟩ enclose; b) **etw. mit etw.** ~: surround sth. with sth.; *(einfrieden)* enclose sth. with sth.; **Umgebung die;** ~, ~en surroundings *pl.; (Nachbarschaft)* neighbourhood; *(eines Ortes)* surrounding area

¹**ụm|gehen** *unr. itr. V.; mit sein* a) *(im Umlauf sein)* ⟨*list, rumour, etc.*⟩ go round, circulate; ⟨*illness, infection*⟩ go round; b) *(spuken)* **hier geht ein Gespenst um** this place is haunted; c) *(behandeln)* **mit jmdm. freundlich/liebevoll** *usw.* ~: treat sb. kindly/lovingly *etc.;* **er kann mit Geld nicht** ~: he can't handle money

²**um·gehen** *unr. tr. V.* a) go round; make a detour round; *(auf einer Umgehungsstraße)* bypass ⟨*town etc.*⟩; b) *(vermeiden)* avoid ⟨*question, issue*⟩; c) *(nicht befolgen)* circumvent ⟨*law, restriction, etc.*⟩; evade ⟨*obligation, duty*⟩; **ụmgehend** 1. *Adj.* immediate; 2. *adv.* immediately; **Umgehung die;** ~, ~en a) **durch** ~ **der Innenstadt** by bypassing *or* avoiding the town centre; b) s. ²umgehen c: circumvention; evasion; **Umgehungs·straße die** bypass

**ụmgekehrt** 1. *Adj.* inverse ⟨*ratio, proportion*⟩; reverse ⟨*order*⟩; opposite ⟨*sign*⟩; 2. *adv.* inversely ⟨*proportional*⟩

**ụm|graben** *unr. tr. V.* dig over

**Ụm·hang der** cape; **ụm|hängen** *tr. V.* a) etw. ~: hang sth. somewhere else; b) jmdm./sich einen Mantel/eine Decke ~: drape a coat/blanket round sb.'s/one's shoulders

**ụm|hauen** *unr. tr. V.* fell; *(fig.)* knock down

**um·her** *Adv.* around
**umher-:** s. **herum-**
**um|hören** *refl. V.* keep one's ears open; *(direkt fragen)* ask around
**um·jubeln** *tr. V.* cheer
**um|kehren** 1. *itr. V.; mit sein* turn back; 2. *tr. V.* turn upside down; turn over ⟨*sheet of paper*⟩; *(nach links drehen)* turn ⟨*garment etc.*⟩ inside out; *(nach rechts drehen)* turn ⟨*garment etc.*⟩ right side out
**um|kippen** 1. *itr. V.; mit sein* a) fall over; ⟨*boat*⟩ capsize, turn over; ⟨*vehicle*⟩ overturn; b) *(ugs.: ohnmächtig werden)* keel over; 2. *tr. V.* tip over; knock over ⟨*lamp, vase, glass, cup*⟩; capsize ⟨*boat*⟩; turn ⟨*boat*⟩ over; overturn ⟨*vehicle*⟩
**um|klappen** *tr. V.* fold down
**Umkleide·kabine die** changing-cubicle
**um|knicken** *itr. V.; mit sein* a) |mit dem Fuß| ~: go over on one's ankle; b) bend; ⟨*branch*⟩ bend and snap
**um|kommen** *unr. itr. V.; mit sein* die; *(bei einem Unglück, durch Gewalt)* get killed; die; ⟨*food*⟩ go off
**Um·kreis der** *o. Pl.* surrounding area; **im ~ von 5 km** within a radius of 5 km.; **um·kreisen** *tr. V.* circle; ⟨*spacecraft, satellite*⟩ orbit; ⟨*planet*⟩ revolve [a]round
**Um·lauf der** a) *(von Planeten)* revolution; b) *o. Pl. (Zirkulation)* circulation; **in** od. **im ~ sein** be circulating; ⟨*coin, banknote*⟩ be in circulation; **in ~ bringen** circulate; bring ⟨*coin, banknote*⟩ into circulation; **Umlaufbahn die** *(Astron., Raumf.)* orbit
**Um·laut der** *(Sprachw.)* umlaut
**um|legen** *tr. V.* a) *(um einen Körperteil)* put on; b) *(verlegen)* transfer ⟨*patient, telephone call*⟩; c) *(salopp: ermorden)* jmdn. ~: bump sb. off *(sl.)*
**um|leiten** divert; **Um·leitung die** diversion
**umliegend** *Adj.* surrounding ⟨*area*⟩; *(nahe)* nearby ⟨*building*⟩
**um|räumen** 1. *tr. V.* rearrange; 2. *itr. V.* rearrange things
**um|rechnen** *tr. V.* convert (**in** + *Akk.* into)
**¹um|reißen** *unr. tr. V.* pull ⟨*mast, tree*⟩ down; knock ⟨*person*⟩ down; ⟨*wind*⟩ tear ⟨*tent etc.*⟩ down
**²um·reißen** *unr. tr. V.* outline; summarize ⟨*subject, problem, situation*⟩
**um|rennen** *unr. tr. V.* [run into and] knock down

**um·ringen** *tr. V.* surround
**Um·riß der** *(auch fig.)* outline
**um|rühren** *tr. (auch itr.) V.* stir
**um|rüsten** *tr. V. (Technik)* convert (**auf** + *Akk.* to, **zu** into)
**ums** [ʊms] *Präp.* + *Art.* a) = **um das;** b) ~ **Leben kommen** lose one's life
**um|satteln** *itr. V. (ugs.)* change jobs; ⟨*student*⟩ change courses
**Um·satz der** turnover; *(Verkauf)* sales *pl.* (**an** + *Dat.* of); ~ **machen** *(ugs.)* make money
**um|säumen** *tr. V.* hem
**um|schalten** 1. *tr. V. (auch. fig.)* switch [over] (**auf** + *Akk.* to); move ⟨*lever*⟩; 2. *itr. V.* switch or change over (**auf** + *Akk.* to)
**Um·schlag der** a) cover; b) *(Brief~)* envelope; c) *(Schutz~)* jacket; *(einer Broschüre, eines Heftes)* cover; d) *(Med.: Wickel)* compress; *(warm)* poultice; **um|schlagen** 1. *unr. tr. V.* a) turn up ⟨*sleeve, collar, trousers*⟩; turn over ⟨*page*⟩; b) *(umladen, verladen)* turn round, trans-ship ⟨*goods*⟩; 2. *unr. itr. V.; mit sein* change (**in** + *Akk.* into); ⟨*wind*⟩ veer [round]
**¹um|schreiben** *unr. tr. V.* rewrite; **²um·schreiben** *unr. tr. V.* a) *(in Worte fassen)* describe; *(definieren)* define ⟨*meaning, sb.'s task, etc.*⟩; *(paraphrasieren)* paraphrase ⟨*word, expression*⟩; b) *(Sprachw.)* construct (**mit** with); **Um·schreibung die** description; *(Definition)* definition; *(Verhüllung)* circumlocution (**Gen.** for); **Um·schrift die** *(Sprachw.)* transcription
**um|schulen** 1. *tr. V. (beruflich)* retrain; 2. *itr. V.* retrain (**auf** + *Akk.* as)
**um|schütten** *tr. V.* a) pour [into another container]; decant ⟨*liquid*⟩; b) *(verschütten)* spill
**Um·schwung der** complete change; *(in der Politik usw.)* U-turn
**um|sehen** *unr. refl. V.* a) look; **sich im Zimmer ~:** look [a]round the room; b) *(zurücksehen)* look round or back
**umseitig** *Adj., adv.* overleaf
**um|setzen** *tr. V.* a) move; *(auf anderen Posten usw.)* move, transfer (**in** + *Akk.* to); *(umpflanzen)* transplant; *(in anderen Topf)* repot; b) *(verwirklichen)* implement ⟨*plan*⟩; translate ⟨*plan, intention, etc.*⟩ into action or reality; realize ⟨*ideas*⟩; c) *(Wirtsch.)* turn over, have a turnover of ⟨*x marks etc.*⟩; sell ⟨*shares, goods*⟩
**Um·sicht die** *o. Pl.* circumspection;

**um·sichtig 1.** *Adj.* circumspect; **2.** *adv.* circumspectly

**um|siedeln 1.** *tr. V.* resettle; **2.** *itr. V.; mit sein* move (**in** + *Akk.,* **nach** to)

**um·sonst** *Adv.* **a)** *(unentgeltlich)* free; for nothing; **b)** *(vergebens)* in vain

**Um·stand der a)** *(Gegebenheit)* circumstance; *(Tatsache)* fact; **unter Umständen** possibly; **b)** *(Aufwand)* business; **macht keine |großen| Umstände** please don't go to any bother

**umständlich 1.** *Adj.* involved, elaborate *(procedure, method, description, explanation, etc.)*; elaborate, laborious *(preparation, check, etc.)*; awkward, difficult *(journey, job)*; *(weitschweifig)* long-winded; *(Umstände machend)* awkward *(person)*; **2.** *adv.* in an involved *or* roundabout way; *(weitschweifig)* at great length

**Umstands·kleid das** maternity dress

**umstehend** *Adj.* standing round *postpos.*

**um|steigen** *unr. itr. V.* change (**in** + *Akk.* [on] to)

**¹um|stellen 1.** *tr. V.* **a)** rearrange, change round *(furniture, books, etc.)*; reorder *(words etc.)*; transpose *(two words)*; **b)** *(anders einstellen)* reset *(lever, switch, points, clock)*; **c)** *(ändern)* change *or* switch over (**auf** + *Akk.* to); **2.** *refl. V.* adjust (**auf** + *Akk.* to); **²um·stellen** *tr. V.* surround

**um|stimmen** *tr. V.* win *(person)* round

**um|stoßen** *unr. tr. V.* **a)** knock over; **b)** *(rückgängig machen)* change *(plan, decision)*; *(zunichte machen)* upset, wreck *(plan, theory)*

**umstritten** *Adj.* disputed; controversial *(book, author, policy, etc.)*

**Um·sturz der** coup; **um|stürzen 1.** *tr. V.* overturn; *(fig.)* topple, overthrow *(political system, government)*; **2.** *itr. V.* overturn; *(wall, building, chimney)* fall down; **umstürzlerisch** *Adj.* subversive

**Um·tausch der** exchange; **um|tauschen** *tr. V.* exchange *(goods, article)* (**gegen** for); change *(dollars, pounds, etc.)* (**in** + *Akk.* into)

**Um·trunk der** communal drink

**um|tun** *unr. refl. V. (ugs.)* look [a]round; **sich nach etw. ~:** be on the look-out for sth.

**um|wandeln** *tr. V.* convert *(substance, building, etc.)* (**in** + *Akk.* into); *(ändern)* change; alter

**Um·weg der** detour

**Um·welt die a)** environment; **b)** *(Menschen)* people *pl.* around sb.

**umwelt-, Umwelt-: ~bedingt** *Adj.* caused by the *or* one's environment *postpos.;* **~freundlich 1.** *Adj.* environment-friendly; **2.** *adv.* in an ecologically desirable way; **~schutz der** environmental protection *no art.;* **~schützer der** environmentalist; conservationist; **~verschmutzung die** pollution [of the environment]

**um|wenden** *regelm. (auch unr.) tr. V.* **a)** turn over *(page, joint, etc.)*; **b)** turn round *(vehicle, horse)*

**um|werfen** *unr. tr. V.* **a)** knock over; knock *(person)* down *or* over; *(fig. ugs.: aus der Fassung bringen)* bowl *(person)* over; stun *(person)*; **b)** *(fig. ugs.: umstoßen)* knock *(plan)* on the head *(coll.)*; **umwerfend** *(ugs.)* **1.** *Adj.* fantastic *(coll.)*; stunning *(coll.)*; **2.** *adv.* fantastically [well] *(coll.)*; brilliantly

**um·wickeln** *tr. V.* wrap; bind; *(mit einem Verband)* bandage

**Umzäunung die; ~, ~en** fence, fencing *(Gen.* round)

**um|ziehen 1.** *unr. itr. V.; mit sein* move (**an** + *Akk.,* **in** + *Akk.,* **nach** to); **2.** *unr. tr. V.* jmdn. **~:** change sb. *or* get sb. changed; **sich ~:** change *or* get changed

**um·zingeln** *tr. V.* surround; encircle

**Um·zug der a)** move; *(von Möbeln)* removal; **b)** *(Festzug)* procession

**UN** [uːˈɛn] *Pl.* UN *sing.*

**unabänderlich 1.** *Adj.* unalterable; irrevocable *(decision)*; **2.** *adv.* irrevocably

**unabhängig 1.** *Adj.* independent (**von** of); *(unbeeinflußt)* unaffected (**von** by); **2.** *adv.* independently (**von** of); **~ davon, ob .../was .../wo ...** *usw.* irrespective *or* regardless of whether .../what .../where ... *etc.;* **Unabhängigkeit die** independence

**unabkömmlich** *Adj.* indispensable; **sie ist im Moment ~:** she is otherwise engaged

**unablässig 1.** *Adj.* incessant; **2.** *adv.* incessantly

**unabsichtlich 1.** *Adj.* unintentional; **2.** *adv.* unintentionally

**unabwendbar** *Adj.* inevitable

**unachtsam 1.** *Adj.* **a)** inattentive; **b)** *(nicht sorgfältig)* careless; **2.** *adv. (ohne Sorgfalt)* carelessly; **Unachtsamkeit die; ~ a)** inattentiveness; **b)** *(mangelnde Sorgfalt)* carelessness

**unangebracht** *Adj.* inappropriate

**unangefochten** *Adj.* unchallenged; *(Rechtsw.)* uncontested ⟨*verdict, will, etc.*⟩

**unangenehm 1.** *Adj.* unpleasant (*Dat.* for); *(peinlich)* embarrassing ⟨*question, situation*⟩; **2.** *adv.* unpleasantly

**unannehmbar** *Adj.* unacceptable; **Unannehmlichkeit die** trouble

**unansehnlich** *Adj.* unprepossessing; plain ⟨*girl*⟩

**unanständig 1.** *Adj.* improper; *(anstößig)* indecent; dirty ⟨*joke*⟩; rude ⟨*word, song*⟩; **2.** *adv.* improperly; **Unanständigkeit die** impropriety; indecency; *(Obszönität)* obscenity

**unappetitlich 1.** *Adj.* unappetizing; *(fig.)* unsavoury ⟨*joke*⟩; disgusting ⟨*wash-basin, nails, etc.*⟩; **2.** *adv.* unappetizingly

**Unart die** bad habit; **unartig** *Adj.* naughty

**unästhetisch** *Adj.* unpleasant ⟨*sight etc.*⟩; ugly ⟨*building etc.*⟩

**unauffällig 1.** *Adj.* inconspicuous; unobtrusive ⟨*scar, defect, skill, behaviour, surveillance, etc.*⟩; discreet ⟨*signal, elegance*⟩; **2.** *adv.* inconspicuously; unobtrusively

**unaufgefordert** *Adv.* without being asked

**unaufhaltsam 1.** *Adj.* inexorable; **2.** *adv.* inexorably

**unaufmerksam** *Adj.* inattentive (**gegenüber** to); careless ⟨*driver*⟩

**unaufrichtig** *Adj.* insincere; **Unaufrichtigkeit die** insincerity

**unausbleiblich** *Adj.* inevitable

**unbändig 1.** *Adj.* **a)** boisterous; **b)** *(überaus groß/stark)* unbridled; **2.** *adv.* **a)** wildly; **b)** *(sehr, äußerst)* unrestrainedly; tremendously *(coll.)*

**unbarmherzig** *Adj.* merciless

**unbeabsichtigt 1.** *Adj.* unintentional; **2.** *adv.* unintentionally

**unbeachtet** *Adj.* unnoticed

**unbedenklich** *adv.* without second thoughts

**unbedeutend 1.** *Adj.* insignificant; minor ⟨*artist, poet*⟩; slight, minor ⟨*improvement, change, error*⟩; **2.** *adv.* slightly

**unbedingt 1.** *Adj.* absolute; **2.** *adv.* absolutely; **3.** *Adv.* (*auf jeden Fall*) whatever happens

**unbefangen** *Adj.* **a)** *(ungehemmt)* uninhibited; **b)** *(unvoreingenommen)* impartial

**unbefristet 1.** *Adj.* for an indefinite period *postpos.;* indefinite ⟨*strike*⟩; unlimited ⟨*visa*⟩; **2.** *adv.* for an indefinite period

**unbefugt 1.** *Adj.* unauthorized; **2.** *adv.* without authorization

**unbegreiflich** *Adj.* incomprehensible (*Dat., für* to); incredible ⟨*love, goodness, stupidity, carelessness, etc.*⟩

**unbegrenzt 1.** *Adj.* unlimited; **2.** *adv.* ⟨*stay, keep, etc.*⟩ indefinitely

**Unbehagen das** uneasiness, disquiet; *(Sorge)* concern (**an** + *Dat.* about); **unbehaglich 1.** *Adj.* uneasy ⟨*feeling, atmosphere*⟩; uncomfortable ⟨*thought, room*⟩; **2.** *adv.* uneasily

**unbeholfen 1.** *Adj.* clumsy; **2.** *adv.* clumsily

**unbekannt** *Adj.* **a)** unknown; *(nicht vertraut)* unfamiliar; unidentified ⟨*caller, donor*⟩; „**Empfänger ~**" 'not known at this address'; **b)** *(nicht vielen bekannt)* little known; obscure ⟨*poet, painter, etc.*⟩; **¹Unbekannte der/die**; *adj. Dekl.* unknown *or* unidentified man/woman; *(Fremde[r])* stranger; **²Unbekannte die**; *adj. Dekl. (Math.; auch fig.)* unknown

**unbekleidet** *Adj.* without any clothes on *postpos.;* bare ⟨*torso etc.*⟩; naked ⟨*corpse*⟩

**unbekümmert 1.** *Adj.* carefree; *(ohne Bedenken, lässig)* casual; **2.** *adv.* **a)** in a carefree way; **b)** *(ohne Bedenken)* without caring *or* worrying

**unbeleuchtet** *Adj.* unlit ⟨*street, corridor, etc.*⟩; ⟨*vehicle*⟩ without [any] lights

**unbeliebt** *Adj.* unpopular (**bei** with)

**unbemannt** *Adj.* unmanned

**unbemerkt** *Adj., adv.* unnoticed

**unbenutzt** *Adj.* unused

**unbequem 1.** *Adj.* **a)** uncomfortable; **b)** *(lästig)* awkward, embarrassing ⟨*question, opinion*⟩; troublesome ⟨*politician etc.*⟩; unpleasant ⟨*criticism, truth, etc.*⟩; **2.** *adv.* uncomfortably

**unberechenbar 1.** *Adj.* unpredictable; **2.** *adv.* unpredictably

**unberechtigt** *Adj.* **a)** *(ungerechtfertigt)* unjustified; **b)** *(unbefugt)* unauthorized

**unberührt** *Adj.* untouched; **sie ist noch ~:** she is still a virgin

**unbeschrankt** *Adj.* ⟨*crossing*⟩ without gates, with no gates

**unbeschreiblich 1.** *Adj.* indescribable; unimaginable ⟨*fear, beauty*⟩; ⟨*fear, beauty*⟩ beyond description; **2.**

*adv.* indescribably ⟨*beautiful*⟩; unbelievably ⟨*busy*⟩

**unbesorgt** *Adj.* unconcerned; **seien Sie ~**: don't [you] worry

**unbeständig** *Adj.* changeable ⟨*weather*⟩; fickle ⟨*lover etc.*⟩

**unbestimmt** 1. *Adj.* a) indefinite; indeterminate ⟨*age, number*⟩; *(ungewiß)* uncertain; b) *(ungenau)* vague; c) *(Sprachw.)* indefinite ⟨*article, pronoun*⟩; 2. *adv. (ungenau)* vaguely

**unbewacht** *Adj.* unsupervised; unattended ⟨*car-park*⟩

**unbewaffnet** *Adj.* unarmed

**unbeweglich** *Adj.* motionless; still ⟨*air, water*⟩; fixed ⟨*gaze, expression*⟩

**unbewußt** *Adj.* unconscious

**unbrauchbar** · *Adj.* unusable; *(untauglich)* useless ⟨*method, person*⟩

**und** *Konj.* and; *(folglich)* [and] so; **ich ~ tanzen?** what, me dance?; **sei so gut ~ mach das Fenster zu** be so good as to shut the window

**Undank** *der* ingratitude; **undankbar** *Adj.* ungrateful ⟨*person, behaviour*⟩

**undeutlich** 1. *Adj.* unclear; indistinct; *(ungenau)* vague ⟨*idea, memory, etc.*⟩; 2. *adv.* indistinctly; *(ungenau)* vaguely

**undicht** *Adj.* leaky; leaking; **~e Fenster** windows which do not fit tightly

**undurchführbar** *Adj.* impracticable

**undurchlässig** *Adj.* impermeable; *(wasserdicht)* watertight; waterproof; *(luftdicht)* airtight

**unehelich** *Adj.* illegitimate ⟨*child*⟩; unmarried ⟨*mother*⟩

**unehrlich** 1. *Adj.* dishonest; 2. *adv.* dishonestly; by dishonest means

**uneigennützig** *Adj.* unselfish

**uneinig** *Adj.* ⟨*party*⟩ divided by disagreement; [sich *(Dat.)*] **~ sein** disagree; **Uneinigkeit** *die* disagreement (**in** + *Dat.* on); **uneins** *Adj.; nicht attr.* **~ sein** be divided (**in** + *Dat.* on); ⟨*persons*⟩ be at variance *or* at cross purposes (**in** + *Dat.* over)

**unempfindlich** *Adj.* a) insensitive (**gegen** to); b) *(immun)* immune (**gegen** to, against); c) *(strapazierfähig)* hardwearing

**unendlich** 1. *Adj.* infinite; boundless; *(zeitlich)* endless; *(Math.)* infinite; 2. *adv.* infinitely ⟨*lovable, sad*⟩; immeasurably ⟨*happy*⟩; ⟨*happy*⟩ beyond measure

**unentbehrlich** *Adj.* indispensable (*Dat.*, **für** to)

**unentgeltlich** [*od.* '----] 1. *Adj.* free;

2. *adv.* free of charge; ⟨*work*⟩ for nothing, without pay

**unentschieden** 1. *Adj.* unsettled; undecided ⟨*question*⟩; *(Sport, Schach)* drawn; 2. *adv.* **~ spielen** draw

**unentwegt** [*od.* --'-] 1. *Adj.* a) *(beharrlich)* persistent ⟨*fighter, champion, efforts*⟩; b) *(unaufhörlich)* constant; incessant; 2. *adv.* a) *(beharrlich)* persistently; b) *(unaufhörlich)* constantly; incessantly

**unerbittlich** 1. *Adj. (auch fig.)* inexorable; unsparing ⟨*critic*⟩; relentless ⟨*battle, struggle*⟩; implacable ⟨*hate, enemy*⟩; 2. *adv. (auch fig.)* inexorably

**unerfahren** *Adj.* inexperienced

**unerfreulich** 1. *Adj.* unpleasant; bad ⟨*news*⟩; 2. *adv.* unpleasantly

**unerheblich** *Adj.* insignificant

**unerhört** 1. *Adj. (empörend)* outrageous; 2. *adv.* outrageously

**unerlaubt** 1. *Adj.* unauthorized; 2. *adv.* without authorization

**unermüdlich** 1. *Adj.* tireless, untiring (**bei, in** + *Dat.* in); 2. *adv.* tirelessly

**unerreichbar** *Adj.* inaccessible; *(fig.)* unattainable; **unerreicht** *Adj.* unequalled

**unerschöpflich** *Adj.* inexhaustible

**unersetzlich** *Adj.* irreplaceable

**unerträglich** [*od.* '----] *Adj.* unbearable; intolerable ⟨*situation, conditions, etc.*⟩

**unerwartet** 1. *Adj.* unexpected; **es kam für alle ~**: it came as a surprise to everybody; 2. *adv.* unexpectedly

**unerwünscht** *Adj.* unwanted; unwelcome ⟨*interruption, visit, visitor*⟩; undesirable ⟨*side-effects*⟩

**unfähig** *Adj.* a) **~ sein, etw. zu tun** *(ständig)* be incapable of doing sth.; *(momentan)* be unable to do sth.; b) *(inkompetent)* incompetent

**unfair** 1. *Adj.* unfair (**gegen** to); 2. *adv.* unfairly

**Un·fall** *der* accident

**Unfall-:** **~arzt** *der* casualty doctor; **~stelle** *die* scene of an/the accident; **~versicherung** *die* accident insurance

**unförmig** *Adj.* shapeless; huge ⟨*legs, hands, body*⟩; bulky, ungainly ⟨*shape, shoes, etc.*⟩

**unfrei** *Adj.* not free *pred.*; subject, dependent ⟨*people*⟩; ⟨*life*⟩ of bondage;

**unfreiwillig** 1. *Adj.* involuntary; *(erzwungen)* enforced ⟨*stay*⟩; *(nicht beabsichtigt)* unintended ⟨*publicity, joke, humour*⟩; 2. *adv.* involuntarily; without wanting to; *(unbeabsichtigt)* unintentionally

**unfreundlich** 1. *Adj.* unfriendly (**zu, gegen** to); unkind ⟨*words, remark*⟩; 2. *adv.* in an unfriendly way

**unfrisiert** *Adj.* ungroomed ⟨*hair*⟩

**unfruchtbar** *Adj.* infertile; *(fig.)* unproductive; **Unfruchtbarkeit die** infertility; *(fig.)* unproductiveness

**Unfug der;** ~|e|s **a)** [piece of] mischief; **grober** ~: public nuisance; **b)** *(Unsinn)* nonsense

**Ungar der;** ~n, ~n Hungarian; **ungarisch** *Adj.* Hungarian; **Ungarn (das)**; ~s Hungary

**ungeachtet** *Präp. mit Gen. (geh.)* notwithstanding; despite

**ungebildet** *Adj.* uneducated

**ungebräuchlich** *Adj.* uncommon; rare; rarely used ⟨*method, process*⟩

**ungedeckt** *Adj.* uncovered ⟨*cheque*⟩

**Ungeduld die** impatience; **ungeduldig** 1. *Adj.* impatient; 2. *adv.* impatiently

**ungeeignet** *Adj.* unsuitable; *(für eine Aufgabe)* unsuited (**für, zu** to, for)

**ungefähr** 1. *Adj.* approximate; rough ⟨*idea, outline*⟩; 2. *adv.* approximately; roughly

**ungefährlich** *Adj.* safe; harmless ⟨*animal, person, illness, etc.*⟩

**ungeheizt** *Adj.* unheated

**ungeheuer** 1. *Adj.* enormous; tremendous ⟨*strength, energy, effort, enthusiasm, fear, success, pressure, etc.*⟩; vast, immense ⟨*fortune, knowledge*⟩; *(schrecklich)* terrible *(coll.)*, terrific *(coll.)* ⟨*pain, rage*⟩; 2. *adv.* tremendously; terribly *(coll.)* ⟨*difficult, clever*⟩; **Ungeheuer das;** ~s, ~ *(auch fig.)* monster

**ungehindert** *Adj.* unimpeded

**ungehörig** 1. *Adj.* improper; *(frech)* impertinent; 2. *adv.* improperly; *(frech)* impertinently

**ungehorsam** *Adj.* disobedient (**gegenüber** to); **Ungehorsam der** disobedience (**gegenüber** to)

**ungekürzt** *Adj.* unabridged ⟨*edition, book*⟩; uncut ⟨*film, speech*⟩

**ungelegen** 1. *Adj.* **das kommt mir sehr** ~/**nicht** ~: that is very inconvenient or awkward/quite convenient for me; 2. *adv.* inconveniently

**ungelernt** *Adj.* unskilled

**ungemütlich** 1. *Adj.* uninviting; cheerless ⟨*room, flat*⟩; uncomfortable, unfriendly ⟨*atmosphere*⟩; 2. *adv.* uncomfortably ⟨*furnished*⟩

**ungenau** 1. *Adj.* inaccurate; imprecise, inexact ⟨*definition, formulation, etc.*⟩; *(undeutlich)* vague ⟨*memory, idea, impression*⟩; 2. *adv.* inaccurately; ⟨*define*⟩ imprecisely, inexactly; vaguely

**ungeniert** ['ʊnʒeniːɐ̯t] 1. *Adj.* free and easy; uninhibited; 2. *adv.* openly; ⟨*yawn*⟩ unconcernedly; ⟨*undress etc.*⟩ without any embarrassment

**ungenießbar** *Adj. (nicht eßbar)* inedible; *(nicht trinkbar)* undrinkable; *(fig. ugs.)* unbearable

**ungenügend** 1. *Adj.* inadequate; **die Note** „~"/**ein Ungenügend** *(Schulw.)* the/an 'unsatisfactory' [mark]; 2. *adv.* inadequately

**ungepflegt** *Adj.* neglected ⟨*garden, park, car, etc.*⟩; unkempt ⟨*person, appearance, hair*⟩; uncared-for ⟨*hands*⟩

**ungerade** *Adj.* odd ⟨*number*⟩

**ungerecht** 1. *Adj.* unjust, unfair (**gegen, zu, gegenüber** to); 2. *adv.* unjustly; unfairly; **Ungerechtigkeit die;** ~, ~en injustice

**ungern** *Adv.* reluctantly; **etw.** ~ **tun** not like or dislike doing sth.

**ungeschält** *Adj.* unpeeled ⟨*fruit*⟩

**ungeschickt** 1. *Adj.* clumsy; awkward; 2. *adv.* clumsily; awkwardly

**ungesetzlich** 1. *Adj.* unlawful; illegal; 2. *adv.* unlawfully; illegally

**ungestempelt** *Adj.* uncancelled ⟨*stamp*⟩

**ungestört** *Adj.* undisturbed; uninterrupted ⟨*development*⟩

**ungesund** *Adj. (auch fig.)* unhealthy

**Ungetüm das;** ~s, ~e monster

**ungewiß** *Adj.* uncertain; **über etw.** *(Akk.)* **im ungewissen sein** be uncertain or unsure about sth.; **Ungewißheit die** uncertainty

**ungewöhnlich** 1. *Adj.* **a)** unusual; **b)** *(sehr groß)* exceptional ⟨*strength, beauty, ability, etc.*⟩; outstanding ⟨*achievement, success*⟩; 2. *adv.* **a)** ⟨*behave*⟩ abnormally, strangely; **b)** *(enorm)* exceptionally

**ungewohnt** 1. *Adj.* unaccustomed; *(nicht vertraut)* unfamiliar ⟨*method, work, surroundings, etc.*⟩; 2. *adv.* unusually

**Ungeziefer das;** ~s vermin *pl.*

**ungezogen** 1. *Adj.* naughty; badly behaved; bad ⟨*behaviour*⟩; *(frech)* cheeky; 2. *adv.* naughtily; ⟨*behave*⟩ badly

**ungläubig** 1. *Adj.* **a)** disbelieving; **b)** *(Rel.)* unbelieving; 2. *adv.* in disbelief; **unglaublich 1.** *Adj.* incredible; **2.** *adv.* *(ugs.: äußerst)* incredibly *(coll.);* **unglaubwürdig** *Adj.* implausible; untrustworthy, unreliable ⟨*witness etc.*⟩

**ungleich 1.** *Adj.* unequal; odd, unmatching ⟨*socks, gloves, etc.*⟩*; (unähnlich)* dissimilar; **2.** *adv.* **a)** unequally; **b)** *(ungleichmäßig)* unevenly

**Unglück das;** ~|e|s, ~e **a)** *(Unfall)* accident; *(Flugzeug~, Zug~)* crash; accident; **b)** *o. Pl. (Not)* misfortune; *(Leid)* suffering; **c)** *(Pech)* bad luck; ~ **haben** be unlucky; **das bringt** ~: that's unlucky; **d)** *(Schicksalsschlag)* misfortune; **unglücklich 1.** *Adj.* **a)** unhappy; **b)** *(nicht vom Glück begünstigt)* unfortunate ⟨*person*⟩*; (bedauernswert, arm)* hapless ⟨*person, animal*⟩*;* **c)** *(ungünstig, ungeschickt)* unfortunate ⟨*moment, combination, meeting, etc.*⟩*;* unhappy ⟨*end, choice, solution*⟩*;* **2.** *adv.* **a)** unhappily; **b)** *(ungünstig)* unfortunately; *(ungeschickt)* unhappily, clumsily ⟨*translated, expressed*⟩*;* **unglücklicherweise** *Adv.* unfortunately; **Unglücks·fall der** accident

**ungültig** *Adj.* invalid; void *(esp. Law);* spoilt ⟨*vote, ballot-paper*⟩*;* disallowed ⟨*goal*⟩

**ungünstig 1.** *Adj.* **a)** unfavourable; unfortunate, bad ⟨*shape, layout*⟩*;* **b)** *(unpassend)* inconvenient ⟨*time*⟩*; (ungeeignet)* inappropriate, inconvenient ⟨*time, place*⟩*;* **2.** *adv.* **a)** unfavourably; badly ⟨*designed, laid out*⟩*;* **b)** *(unpassend)* inconveniently

**Unheil das** disaster; **unheilbar 1.** *Adj.* incurable; **2.** *adv.* incurably; **unheil·voll** *Adj.* disastrous; *(verhängnisvoll)* fateful

**unheimlich 1.** *Adj.* **a)** eerie; **b)** *(ugs.) (schrecklich)* terrible *(coll.)* ⟨*hunger, headache, etc.*⟩*;* terrific *(coll.)* ⟨*fun etc.*⟩*;* **2.** *adv.* **a)** eerily; **b)** *(ugs.: äußerst)* terribly *(coll.);* incredibly *(coll.)* ⟨*quick, long*⟩

**unhöflich 1.** *Adj.* impolite; **2.** *adv.* impolitely; **Unhöflichkeit die** impoliteness

**unhygienisch 1.** *Adj.* unhygienic; **2.** *adv.* unhygienically

**Uniform die;** ~, ~en uniform

**uninteressant** *Adj.* uninteresting; *(nicht von Belang)* of no interest *postpos.;* unimportant

**Union** [u'nĭo:n] **die;** ~, ~en union

**Universität die;** ~, ~en university

**Universum das;** ~s universe

**Unkenntnis die;** *o. Pl.* ignorance

**unklar** *Adj.* unclear; **sich** *(Dat.)* **über etw.** *(Akk.)* **im** ~**en sein** be unclear *or* unsure about sth.

**Unkosten** *Pl.* **a)** [extra] expense *sing.;* expenses; **b)** *(ugs.: Ausgaben)* costs; expenditure *sing.*

**Unkraut das** weeds *pl.*

**unleserlich 1.** *Adj.* illegible; **2.** *adv.* illegibly

**unmäßig 1.** *Adj.* immoderate; excessive; **2.** *adv.* excessively; ⟨*eat, drink*⟩ to excess

**Unmensch der** brute; **unmenschlich 1.** *Adj.* **a)** inhuman; brutal; appalling ⟨*conditions*⟩*;* **b)** *(entsetzlich)* appalling; **2.** *adv.* **a)** in an inhuman way; **b)** *(entsetzlich)* appallingly *(coll.)*

**unmißverständlich 1.** *Adj.* **a)** *(eindeutig)* unambiguous; **b)** *(offen, direkt)* blunt ⟨*answer, refusal*⟩*;* unequivocal ⟨*language*⟩*;* **2.** *adv.* **a)** *(eindeutig)* unambiguously; **b)** *(offen, direkt)* bluntly; unequivocally

**unmittelbar 1.** *Adj.* immediate; direct ⟨*contact, connection, influence, etc.*⟩*;* **2.** *adv.* immediately; directly

**unmöbliert** *Adj.* unfurnished

**unmodern 1.** *Adj.* old-fashioned; *(nicht modisch)* unfashionable; **2.** *adv.* in an old-fashioned way; *(nicht modisch)* unfashionably

**unmöglich 1.** *Adj.* impossible; *(ugs.: seltsam)* incredible; **2.** *adv. (ugs.) (behave)* impossibly; ⟨*dress*⟩ ridiculously; **3.** *Adv. (ugs.)* **ich/es** *usw.* **kann** ~ **...:** I/it *etc.* can't possibly ...

**unmoralisch 1.** *Adj.* immoral; **2.** *adv.* immorally

**unmündig** *Adj.* under-age

**unnatürlich 1.** *Adj.* unnatural; forced ⟨*laugh*⟩*;* **2.** *adv.* unnaturally; ⟨*laugh*⟩ in a forced way; ⟨*speak*⟩ affectedly

**unnötig 1.** *Adj.* unnecessary; **2.** *adv.* unnecessarily

**UNO** ['u:no] **die;** ~: UN

**unordentlich 1.** *Adj.* **a)** untidy; **b)** *(ungeregelt)* disorderly ⟨*life*⟩*;* **2.** *adv.* untidily; ⟨*tie, treat, etc.*⟩ carelessly; **Unordnung die** disorder; mess

**unparteiisch 1.** *Adj.* impartial; **2.** *adv.* impartially

**unpassend 1.** *Adj.* inappropriate; unsuitable ⟨*dress etc.*⟩*;* **2.** *adv.* inappropriately; unsuitably ⟨*dressed etc.*⟩

**unpersönlich 1.** *Adj.* impersonal; distant, aloof ⟨*person*⟩*;* **2.** *adv.* impersonally; ⟨*answer, write*⟩ in impersonal terms

**unpraktisch 1.** *Adj.* unpractical; **2.** *adv.* in an unpractical way

**unpünktlich 1.** *Adj.* unpunctual ⟨*person*⟩; late, unpunctual ⟨*payment*⟩; **2.** *adv.* late

**Unrecht** das; *o. Pl.* wrong; **zu ~:** wrongly; **unrecht haben** be wrong; **jmdm. unrecht tun** do sb. an injustice; **unrechtmäßig 1.** *Adj.* unlawful; **2.** *adv.* unlawfully

**unregelmäßig 1.** *Adj.* irregular; **2.** *adv.* irregularly

**unreif** *Adj.* a) unripe; b) *(nicht erwachsen)* immature

**Unruhe** die *(auch fig.)* unrest; *(Lärm)* noise; *(Unrast)* restlessness; *(Besorgnis)* anxiety; **unruhig 1.** *Adj.* a) restless; *(besorgt)* anxious; unsettled, troubled ⟨*time*⟩; b) *(laut)* noisy; c) *(ungleichmäßig)* uneven ⟨*breathing, pulse, etc.*⟩; fitful ⟨*sleep*⟩; disturbed ⟨*night*⟩; **2.** *adv.* a) restlessly; *(besorgt)* anxiously; b) *(ungleichmäßig)* unevenly; ⟨*sleep*⟩ fitfully

**uns 1.** a) *Akk. von* **wir** us; b) *Dat. von* **wir**; **gib es ~:** give it to us; **bei ~:** at our home *or (coll.)* place; **2.** *Reflexivpron. der 1. Pers. Pl.* a) *refl.* ourselves; b) *reziprok* one another

**unsachlich 1.** *Adj.* unobjective; **2.** *adv.* without objectivity

**unsauber 1.** *Adj.* a) dirty; b) *(nachlässig)* untidy; sloppy; **2.** *adv. (nachlässig)* untidily

**unschädlich** *Adj.* harmless

**unscharf** *Adj.* blurred ⟨*photo, picture*⟩

**unscheinbar** *Adj.* inconspicuous

**Unschuld** die; *o. Pl.* innocence; **unschuldig 1.** *Adj.* innocent; **2.** *adv.* innocently

**unselbständig** *Adj.* dependent [on other people]

**¹unser** *Possessivpron. der 1. Pers. Pl.* our; **das ist ~s** that is ours; **²unser** *Gen. von* **wir** *(geh.)* of us; **in ~ aller/ beider Interesse** in the interest of all/ both of us; **unser·einer, unser·eins** *Indefinitpron. (ugs.)* the likes of us *pl.;* our sort *(coll.)*; **unserer·seits** *Adv.* for our part; *(von uns)* on our part; **unser[e]s·gleichen** *indekl. Indefinitpron.* people *pl.* like us; **unsert·wegen** *Adv., s.* **meinetwegen:** because of us; for our sake; about us; as far as we are concerned

**unsicher 1.** *Adj.* uncertain; *(nicht selbstsicher)* insecure; **2.** *adv.* ⟨*walk, stand, etc.*⟩ unsteadily; *(nicht selbstsicher)* ⟨*smile, look*⟩ diffidently

**unsichtbar** *Adj.* invisible (**für** to)

**Unsinn** der nonsense; **~ machen** mess *or* fool about; **unsinnig** *Adj.* nonsensical ⟨*statement, talk, etc.*⟩; absurd, ridiculous ⟨*demand etc.*⟩

**Unsitte** die bad habit; **unsittlich 1.** *Adj.* indecent; **2.** *adv.* indecently

**unsr...** *s.* **¹unser**

**unsterblich** *Adj.* immortal

**unsympathisch** *Adj.* uncongenial, disagreeable ⟨*person*⟩; unpleasant ⟨*characteristic, nature, voice*⟩

**Untat** die misdeed; evil deed

**untauglich** *Adj.* unsuitable; *(für Militärdienst)* unfit [for service] *postpos.*

**unten** *Adv.* a) down; **hier/da ~:** down here/there; **von ~:** from below; b) *(in Gebäuden)* downstairs; **nach ~:** downstairs; c) *(am unteren Ende, zum unteren Ende hin)* at the bottom; **~ [links] auf der Seite/im Schrank** at the bottom [left] of the page/cupboard; d) *(an der Unterseite)* underneath; e) *(im Text)* below; **unten·genannt** *Adj.* undermentioned *(Brit.);* mentioned below *postpos.*

**unter 1.** *Präp. mit Dat. (Lage, Standort)* under; *(zwischen)* among[st]; **Mengen ~ 100 Stück** quantities of less than 100; **~ Angst/Tränen** in *or* out of fear/in tears; **2.** *Präp. mit Akk.* under; *(zwischen)* among[st]; **~ Null sinken** drop below zero; **3.** *Adv.* less than; **~ 30 |Jahre alt| sein** be under 30 [years of age]

**unter...** *Adj.* lower; bottom; *(ganz unten)* bottom; *(in der Rangfolge o. ä.)* lower

**Unter·arm** der forearm; **unterbe·lichten¹** *tr. V. (Fot.)* underexpose

**unter·bleiben** *unr. itr. V.; mit sein* **etw. unterbleibt** sth. does not occur *or* happen; **unter·brechen** *unr. tr. V.* interrupt; break ⟨*journey, silence*⟩; **Unter·brechung** die *s.* **unterbrechen:** interruption; break *(Gen.* in)

**unter|bringen** *unr. tr. V.* a) put; b) *(beherbergen)* put up; **Unterbringung** die; **~, ~en** accommodation *no indef. art.*

**unter·der·hand** *Adv.* on the quiet

**unter·dessen** *s.* **inzwischen; unterdrücken** *tr. V.* suppress; hold back ⟨*comment, question, answer, criticism, etc.*⟩; oppress ⟨*minority etc.*⟩; **Unterdrückung** die; **~, ~en a)** *(das Unter-*

---

¹ *ich unterbelichte, unterbelichtet, unterzubelichten*

*drücken)* suppression; **b)** *(das Unter-drücktwerden, -sein)* oppression

**unter·einander** *Adv.* **a)** *(räumlich)* one below the other; **b)** *(miteinander)* among[st] ourselves/themselves *etc.*

**unter·ernährt** *Adj.* undernourished; **Unter·ernährung** die malnutrition

**Unter·führung** die underpass; *(für Fußgänger)* subway *(Brit.)*; [pedestrian] underpass *(Amer.)*

**unter-, Unter-:** ~**gang** der **a)** *(Sonnen~, Mond~ usw.)* setting; **b)** *(von Schiffen)* sinking; **c)** *(das Zugrundegehen)* decline; ~|**gehen** *unr. itr. V.; mit sein* **a)** *⟨sun, star, etc.⟩* set; *⟨ship⟩* sink, go down; *⟨person⟩* drown, go under; **b)** *(zugrunde gehen)* come to an end; ~**geordnet** *Adj.* secondary *⟨role, importance, etc.⟩*; subordinate *⟨position, post, etc.⟩*; ~**gewicht** das; *o. Pl.* underweight; ~**grund** der *o. Pl. (bes. Politik)* underground

**Untergrund·bahn** die underground [railway] *(Brit.)*; subway *(Amer.)*

**unter-, Unter-:** ~|**haken** *tr. V. (ugs.)* jmdn. ~**haken** take sb.'s arm; ~**halb** **1.** *Adv.* below; ~**halb von** dem; **2.** *Präp. mit Gen.* below; ~**halt** der; *o. Pl.* **a)** living; **b)** *(~haltszahlung)* maintenance; **c)** *(Instandhaltung[skosten])* upkeep; ~**halten 1.** *unr. tr. V.* **a)** support; **b)** *(instand halten)* maintain *⟨building⟩*; **c)** *(betreiben)* run, keep *⟨car, hotel⟩*; **d)** *(pflegen)* maintain, keep up *⟨contact, correspondence⟩*; **e)** entertain *⟨guest, audience⟩*; **2.** *unr. refl. V.* **a)** talk; converse; **b)** *(sich vergnügen)* enjoy oneself; ~**haltsam** *Adj.* entertaining; ~**haltung** die **a)** *o. Pl. (Versorgung)* support; **b)** *o. Pl. (Instandhaltung)* maintenance; **c)** *(Gespräch)* conversation; **e)** *(Zeitvertreib)* entertainment; ~**händler** der *(bes. Politik)* negotiator; ~**hemd** das vest *(Brit.)*; undershirt *(Amer.)*; ~**hose** die *(Herren~)* briefs *pl.*; [under]pants *pl.*; *(Damen~)* panties; knickers *(Brit.)*; ~**irdisch 1.** *Adj.* underground; **2.** *adv.* underground; ~**kiefer** der lower jaw; ~|**kommen** *unr. itr. V.; mit sein* find suitable accommodation

**unter·kühlt** *Adj.* ~ **sein** be suffering from hypothermia *or* exposure

**Unter-:** ~**kunft** die; ~, ~**künfte** accommodation *no indef. art.*; lodging *no indef. art.*; ~**kunft und Frühstück** bed and breakfast; ~**kunft und Verpflegung** board and lodging; ~**lage** die **a)** *(Schreib~)* pad; *(für eine*

*Schreibmaschine usw.)* mat; **b)** *Pl.* documents; papers

**unter-:** ~**lassen** *unr. tr. V.* refrain from [doing]; ~**laufen** *unr. itr. V.; mit sein* occur; jmdm. **ist ein Fehler/Irrtum** ~: sb. made a mistake; ~**legen** *Adj.* inferior; jmdm. ~ **sein** be inferior to sb. **(an + Dat. in)**

**Unter·leib** der lower abdomen

**unter·liegen** *unr. itr. V.* **a)** *mit sein (besiegt werden)* lose; be beaten *or* defeated; **b)** *(unterworfen sein)* be subject to

**unterm** *Präp. + Art.* = **unter dem**

**unter·mauern** *tr. V. (mit Argumenten, Fakten absichern)* back up

**Unter-:** ~**miete** die subtenancy; sublease; ~**mieter** der subtenant; lodger

**untern** *(ugs.) Präp. + Art.* = **unter den**

**unter-, Unter-:** ~**nehmen** *unr. tr. V.* **a)** *(durchführen)* undertake; make; take *⟨steps⟩*; **b)** etwas ~**nehmen** do something; ~**nehmen das;** ~**nehmens, ~nehmen a)** *(Vorhaben)* enterprise; **b)** *(Firma)* concern; ~**nehmer** der; ~**nehmers, ~nehmer** employer; ~**nehmungs·lustig** *Adj.* active; **sie ist sehr** ~**nehmungslustig** she is always out doing things

**Unter·offizier** der **a)** non-commissioned officer; **b)** *(Dienstgrad)* corporal

**unter·ordnen 1.** *tr. V.* subordinate; **2.** *refl. V.* accept a subordinate role

**Unterredung** die; ~, ~**en** discussion

**Unterricht** der; ~|e|s, ~e instruction; *(Schul~)* teaching; *(Schulstunden)* classes *pl.*; **unterrichten 1.** *tr. V.* **a)** teach; **b)** *(informieren)* inform **(über + Akk.** of, about); **2.** *itr. V. (Unterricht geben)* teach; **3.** *refl. V. (sich informieren)* inform oneself **(über + Akk.** about); **Unterrichts·stunde** die lesson; period

**Unter·rock** der [half] slip

**unter|rühren** *tr. V.* stir in

**unters** *Präp. + Art.* = **unter das**

**unter·sagen** *tr. V.* forbid; prohibit

**Unter·satz** der *s.* Untersetzer

**unter-, Unter-:** ~**schätzen** *tr. V.* underestimate *⟨amount, effect, etc.⟩*; underrate *⟨talent, ability, etc.⟩*; ~**scheiden 1.** *unr. tr. V.* distinguish; **2.** *unr. refl. V.* differ **(durch** in, **von** from); ~**scheidung** die *(Vorgang)* differentiation; *(Resultat)* distinction

**Unter-:** ~**schenkel** der shank; lower leg; ~**schicht** die *(Soziol.)* lower class

**Unter·schied** der; ~[e]s, ~e difference; **unterschiedlich 1.** *Adj.* different; *(uneinheitlich)* variable; varying; **2.** *adv.* [sehr/ganz] ~: in [very/quite] different ways; **unterschieds·los 1.** *Adj.* uniform; equal ⟨*treatment*⟩; **2.** *adv.* ⟨*treat*⟩ equally; *(ohne Benachteiligung)* without discrimination

**unter·schlagen** *unr. tr. V.* embezzle ⟨*money, funds, etc.*⟩; *(unterdrücken)* intercept ⟨*letter*⟩; withhold ⟨*fact, news, information, etc.*⟩

**Unter·schlupf** der; ~[e]s, ~e shelter; *(Versteck)* hiding-place; hide-out; **unter|schlüpfen** *itr. V.; mit sein (ugs.)* hide out

**unter·schreiben** *unr. itr., tr. V.* sign; **Unter·schrift** die signature; *(Bild~)* caption

**Unter-:** ~see·boot das submarine; ~setzer der mat; *(für Gläser)* coaster **untersetzt** *Adj.* stocky

**Unter·stand** der *(Schutzbunker)* dugout; *(Unterschlupf)* shelter

**unter|stehen 1.** *unr. itr. V.* jmdm. ~: be subordinate *or* answerable to sb.; **2.** *unr. refl. V.* dare

¹**unter|stellen 1.** *tr. V. (zur Aufbewahrung)* keep; store ⟨*furniture*⟩; **2.** *refl. V.* take shelter

²**unter·stellen** *tr. V.* **a)** jmdm. eine Abteilung ~: put sb. in charge of a department; die Behörde ist dem Ministerium unterstellt the office is under the ministry; **b)** *(unterschieben)* jmdm. böse Absichten *usw.* ~: insinuate that sb.'s intentions *etc.* are bad; **Unterstellung** die *(falsche Behauptung)* insinuation

**unter·streichen** *unr. tr. V.* **a)** underline; **b)** *(hervorheben)* emphasize

**unter·stützen** *tr. V.* support; **Unter·stützung die a)** support; **b)** *(finanzielle Hilfe)* allowance; *(für Arbeitslose)* [unemployment] benefit *no art.*

**unter·suchen** *tr. V.* examine; *(überprüfen)* test (auf + *Akk.* for); *(aufzuklären suchen)* investigate; *(durchsuchen)* search (auf + *Akk.,* nach for); **Untersuchung die; ~, ~en a)** s. **untersuchen:** examination; test; investigation; search; **b)** *(wissenschaftliche Arbeit)* study; **Untersuchungshaft die** imprisonment *or* detention while awaiting trial

**Unter·tasse die** saucer

**unter|tauchen 1.** *itr. V.; mit sein* **a)**

*(im Wasser)* dive [under]; **b)** *(verschwinden)* disappear; **2.** *tr. V.* duck **Unter·teil** das *od.* der bottom part; **unter·teilen** *tr. V.* divide; *(gliedern)* subdivide

**unter·treiben** *unr. itr. V.* play things down

**Unter·wäsche die** underwear

**unterwegs** *Adv.* on the way; *(nicht zu Hause)* out [and about]

**unter·weisen** *unr. tr. V. (geh.)* instruct

**Unter·welt die;** ~: underworld

**unter·werfen 1.** *unr. tr. V.* **a)** subjugate ⟨*people, country*⟩; **b)** *(unterziehen)* subject (*Dat.* to); **2.** *unr. refl. V.* sich [jmdm./einer Sache] ~: submit [to sb./sth.]; **unterwürfig 1.** *Adj.* obsequious; **2.** *adv.* obsequiously

**unter·zeichnen** *tr. V.* sign

**unter·ziehen 1.** *unr. tr. V.* etw. einer Untersuchung/Überprüfung *(Dat.)* ~: examine/check sth.; **2.** *unr. refl. V.* sich einer Operation *(Dat.)* ~: undergo *or* have an operation

**untragbar** *Adj.* unbearable

**untreu** *Adj.* disloyal; *(in der Ehe, Liebe)* unfaithful; **Untreue die** disloyalty; *(in der Ehe, Liebe)* unfaithfulness

**untröstlich** *Adj.* inconsolable

**Untugend die** bad habit

**unüberlegt 1.** *Adj.* rash; **2.** *adv.* rashly

**unübersehbar 1.** *Adj.* **a)** *(offenkundig)* conspicuous; **b)** *(sehr groß)* enormous; **2.** *adv. (sehr)* extremely

**unübersichtlich 1.** *Adj.* unclear; confusing ⟨*arrangement*⟩; blind ⟨*bend*⟩; broken ⟨*country etc.*⟩; **2.** *adv.* unclearly; confusingly ⟨*arranged*⟩

**unübertrefflich 1.** *Adj.* superb; **2.** *adv.* superbly; **unübertroffen** *Adj.* unsurpassed

**unumgänglich** *Adj.* [absolutely] necessary

**unumwunden 1.** *Adj.* frank; **2.** *adv.* frankly; openly

**ununterbrochen 1.** *Adj.* incessant; **2.** *adv.* incessantly

**unveränderlich** *Adj.* unchangeable **unverantwortlich 1.** *Adj.* irresponsible; **2.** *adv.* irresponsibly

**unverbesserlich** *Adj.* incorrigible

**unverbindlich 1.** *Adj.* **a)** not binding *pred.;* without obligation *postpos;* **b)** *(reserviert)* non-committal ⟨*answer, words*⟩; impersonal ⟨*attitude, person*⟩; **2.** *adv.* ⟨*send, reserve*⟩ without obligation

**unverblümt 1.** *Adj.* blunt; **2.** *adv.* bluntly

**unverbraucht** *Adj.* untouched; unspent ⟨*energy*⟩; fresh ⟨*air*⟩

**unverdaut** *Adj.* undigested

**unverdorben** *Adj.* unspoilt

**unverfroren** *Adj.* insolent; impudent

**unvergänglich** *Adj.* immortal ⟨*fame*⟩; unchanging ⟨*beauty*⟩; abiding ⟨*recollection*⟩

**unvergeßlich** *Adj.* unforgettable

**unvergleichlich 1.** *Adj.* incomparable; **2.** *adv.* incomparably

**unverheiratet** *Adj.* unmarried

**unverhofft 1.** *Adj.* unexpected; **2.** *adv.* unexpectedly

**unverkäuflich** *Adj.* **diese Vase ist ~:** this vase is not for sale; *(nicht absetzbar)* unsaleable

**unvermeidlich** *Adj.* unavoidable; *(sich als Folge ergebend)* inevitable

**Unvermögen das** lack of ability

**unvermutet 1.** *Adj.* unexpected; **2.** *adv.* unexpectedly

**unvernünftig** *Adj.* stupid; foolish

**unverrichtet** *Adj.* **~er Dinge** without having achieved anything

**unverschämt 1.** *Adj.* **a)** impertinent ⟨*person, manner, words, etc.*⟩; barefaced ⟨*lie*⟩; **b)** *(ugs.: sehr groß)* outrageous ⟨*price, luck, etc.*⟩; **2.** *adv.* **a)** impertinently; ⟨*lie*⟩ barefacedly; blatantly; **Unverschämtheit die; ~, ~en** impertinence

**unversehens** *Adv.* suddenly

**unversehrt** *Adj.* unscathed; *(unbeschädigt)* undamaged

**unverständlich** *Adj.* incomprehensible; **Unverständnis das** lack of understanding

**unverträglich** *Adj.* **a)** quarrelsome; **b)** incompatible ⟨*blood groups, medicines, transplant tissue*⟩

**unverwechselbar** *Adj.* unmistakable; distinctive

**unverwüstlich** *Adj.* indestructible

**unverzeihlich** *Adj.* unforgivable

**unverzüglich 1.** *Adj.* prompt; **2.** *adv.* promptly

**unvollkommen 1.** *Adj.* **a)** imperfect; **b)** *(unvollständig)* incomplete; **2.** *adv.* **a)** imperfectly; **b)** *(unvollständig)* incompletely; **Unvollkommenheit die a)** imperfectness; **b)** *(Unvollständigkeit)* incompleteness

**unvollständig** *Adj.* incomplete; **Unvollständigkeit die** incompleteness

**unvorhergesehen** *Adj.* unforeseen; unexpected ⟨*visit*⟩

**unvorsichtig 1.** *Adj.* careless; *(unüberlegt)* rash; **2.** *adv.* carelessly; *(unüberlegt)* rashly

**unvorstellbar 1.** *Adj.* inconceivable; **2.** *adv.* unimaginably

**unvorteilhaft** *Adj.* **a)** unattractive ⟨*figure, appearance*⟩; **b)** *(ohne Vorteil)* unfavourable, poor ⟨*purchase, exchange*⟩; unprofitable ⟨*business*⟩

**Unwahrheit die a)** *o. Pl.* untruthfulness; **b)** *(Äußerung)* untruth; **unwahrscheinlich 1.** *Adj.* **a)** improbable; unlikely; **b)** *(ugs.: sehr viel)* incredible *(coll.)*; **2.** *adv. (ugs.: sehr)* incredibly *(coll.)*

**unweiblich** *Adj.* unfeminine

**unweigerlich 1.** *Adj.* inevitable; **2.** *adv.* inevitably

**Unwetter das** [thunder]storm

**unwichtig** *Adj.* unimportant

**unwiderruflich 1.** *Adj.* irrevocable; **2.** *adv.* irrevocably

**unwiderstehlich** *Adj.* irresistible

**Unwille[n] der;** *o. Pl.* displeasure

**unwillig 1.** *Adj.* indignant; *(widerwillig)* unwilling; **2.** *adv.* indignantly; *(widerwillig)* unwillingly

**unwillkürlich 1.** *Adj.* **a)** spontaneous ⟨*cry, sigh*⟩; instinctive ⟨*reaction, movement, etc.*⟩; **b)** *(Physiol.)* involuntary ⟨*movement etc.*⟩; **2.** *adv.* **a)** ⟨*shout etc.*⟩ spontaneously; ⟨*react, move, etc.*⟩ instinctively; **b)** *(Physiol.)* ⟨*move etc.*⟩ involuntarily

**unwirklich** *(geh.) Adj.* unreal

**unwirsch 1.** *Adj.* surly; ill-natured; **2.** *adv.* ill-naturedly

**unwirtschaftlich 1.** *Adj.* uneconomic ⟨*procedure etc.*⟩; *(nicht sparsam)* uneconomical ⟨*driving etc.*⟩; **2.** *adv.* ⟨*work, drive, etc.*⟩ uneconomically

**Unwissenheit die; ~:** ignorance; **unwissentlich 1.** *Adj.* unconscious; **2.** *adv.* unknowingly; unwittingly

**unwohl** *Adv.* unwell; **mir ist ~:** I don't feel well; **Unwohlsein das; ~s** indisposition

**unwürdig** *Adj.* **a)** undignified ⟨*person, behaviour*⟩; degrading ⟨*treatment*⟩; **b)** *(unangemessen)* unworthy

**unzählig** *Adj.* innumerable; countless

**Unze die; ~, ~n** ounce

**unzeitgemäß** *Adj.* anachronistic

**unzerbrechlich** *Adj.* unbreakable

**unzertrennlich** *Adj.* inseparable

**Unzucht die: ~ treiben** fornicate; **gewerbsmäßige ~:** prostitution; **unzüchtig 1.** *Adj.* obscene ⟨*letter, ges-*⟩

*ture*); **2.** *adv.* ⟨*touch, approach, etc.*⟩ indecently; ⟨*speak*⟩ obscenely

**ụnzufrieden** *Adj.* dissatisfied; *(stärker)* unhappy; **Ụnzufriedenheit die** dissatisfaction; *(stärker)* unhappiness

**ụnzugänglich** *Adj.* inaccessible ⟨*area, building, etc.*⟩; unapproachable ⟨*character, person, etc.*⟩

**ụnzulänglich** *(geh.)* **1.** *Adj.* insufficient; **2.** *adv.* insufficiently

**ụnzumutbar** *Adj.* unreasonable

**ụnzurechnungsfähig** *Adj.* not responsible for one's actions *pred.; (geistesgestört)* of unsound mind *postpos.*

**ụnzustellbar** *Adj.* *(Postw.)* „~": 'not known [at this address]'

**ụnzutreffend** *Adj.* inappropriate; *(falsch)* incorrect

**ụnzuverlässig** *Adj.* unreliable; **Ụnzuverlässigkeit die** unreliability

**ụnzweckmäßig** **1.** *Adj.* unsuitable; *(unpraktisch)* impractical; **2.** *adv.* unsuitably; *(unpraktisch)* impractically

**üppig 1.** *Adj.* lush ⟨*vegetation*⟩; thick ⟨*hair, beard*⟩; full ⟨*bosom, lips*⟩; voluptuous ⟨*figure, woman*⟩; *(fig.)* sumptuous, opulent ⟨*meal*⟩; **2.** *adv.* luxuriantly; *(fig.)* sumptuously

**Ur·abstimmung die** [*esp.* strike] ballot

**Ural der;** ~[s] Urals *pl.;* Ural Mountains *pl.*

**ur·alt** *Adj.* very old; ancient

**Uran das;** ~s uranium

**urbar** *Adj.* **ein Stück Land ~ machen** cultivate a piece of land

**Ur·einwohner der** native inhabitant; **Ur·enkel der** great-grandson; **Ur·groß·eltern** *Pl.* great-grandparents

**Ur·heber der;** ~s, ~ originator; initiator; *(bes. Rechtsspr.: Verfasser, Autor)* author

**urig** *Adj.* natural ⟨*person*⟩; real ⟨*beer*⟩; cosy ⟨*pub*⟩

**Urin der;** ~s, ~e *(Med.)* urine; **urinieren** *itr. V.* urinate

**Ur·kunde die;** ~, ~n document; *(Bescheinigung, Sieger~, Diplom~ usw.)* certificate

**Urlaub der;** ~[e]s, ~e holiday[s] *(Brit.);* vacation; *(bes. Milit.)* leave

**Urlaubs-:** ~**reise die** holiday [trip]; ~**zeit die** holiday period *or* season

**Urne die;** ~, ~n urn; *(Wahl~)* [ballot-]box

**Ur·sache die** cause

**Ur·sprung der** origin; **ur·sprünglich 1.** *Adj.* **a)** original ⟨*plan, price, form, material, etc.*⟩; **b)** *(natürlich)*

natural; **2.** *adv.* **a)** originally; **b)** *(natürlich)* naturally

**Ụrteil das;** ~s, ~e judgement; *(Strafe)* sentence; *(Gerichts~)* verdict; **urteilen** *itr. V.* form an opinion; judge; **über etw./jmdn.** ~: judge sth./sb.; **Ụrteils·vermögen das;** *o. Pl.* competence to judge

**Ụr·wald der** primeval forest; *(tropisch)* jungle

**USA** [u:|ɛs'|a:] *Pl.* USA

**usw.** *Abk.* und so weiter etc.

**Utensịl das;** ~s, ~ien [... iən] piece of equipment; ~**ien** equipment *sing.*

**Utopie die;** ~, ~n utopian dream; **utopisch** *Adj.* utopian

**UV** *Abk.* Ultraviolett UV

# V

**v, V** [vaʊ] **das;** ~, ~: v, V

**v.** *Abk.* von

**vage 1.** *Adj.* vague; **2.** *adv.* vaguely

**vakuum·verpackt** *Adj.* vacuum-packed

**Vanille** [va'nɪljə] **die;** ~: vanilla; **Vanille·zucker der** vanilla sugar

**variabel 1.** *Adj.* variable; **2.** *adv.* variably

**variieren** *tr., itr. V.* vary

**Vase** ['va:zə] **die;** ~, ~n vase

**Vater der;** ~s, Väter father; **Gott** ~: God the Father; **Vater·land das;** *Pl.* ~länder fatherland; **väterlich 1.** *Adj.* **a)** paternal ⟨*line, love, instincts, etc.*⟩; **b)** *(fürsorglich)* fatherly; **2.** *adv.* in a fatherly way; **väterlicherseits** *Adv.* on the/his/her *etc.* father's side; **Vaterschaft die;** ~, ~en fatherhood; **Vaterunser das;** ~s, ~: Lord's Prayer; **Vati der;** ~s, ~s *(fam.)* dad[dy] *(coll.)*

**Vatikan** [vati'ka:n] **der;** ~s Vatican

**v. Chr.** *Abk.* vor Christus BC

**Vegetarier** [vege'ta:riɐ] **der;** ~s, ~: vegetarian; **vegetarisch 1.** *Adj.* vegetarian; **2.** *adv.* **er ißt** *od.* **lebt** ~: he is a vegetarian; **Vegetation die;** ~, ~en vegetation *no indef. art.;* **vegetieren** *itr. V.* vegetate

**Veilchen** das; ~s, ~: violet
**Vene** ['ve:nə] die; ~, ~n vein
**Venedig** [ve'ne:dɪç] **(das); ~s** Venice
**Venezolaner** [venetso'la:nɐ] der; ~s, ~: Venezuelan; **venezolanisch** Adj. Venezuelan; **Venezuela (das); ~s** Venezuela
**Ventil** [vɛn'ti:l] das; ~s, ~e valve; **Ventilator** [vɛnti'la:tɔr] der; ~s, ~en ventilator
**Venus** ['ve:nʊs] die; ~: Venus no def. art.
**verabreden 1.** tr. V. arrange; **2.** refl. V. sich im Park/zum Tennis/für den folgenden Abend ~: arrange to meet in the park/for tennis/next evening; **Verabredung** die; ~, ~en a) arrangement; b) (verabredete Zusammenkunft) appointment; **eine ~ absagen** call off a meeting
**verabscheuen** tr. V. detest; loathe
**verabschieden 1.** tr. V. a) say goodbye to; b) (aus dem Dienst) retire ⟨general, civil servant, etc.⟩; **2.** refl. V. sich [von jmdm.] ~: say goodbye [to sb.]; **Verabschiedung** die; ~, ~en a) leave-taking; b) (aus dem Dienst) retirement
**verachten** tr. V. despise; **verächtlich 1.** Adj. a) contemptuous; b) (verachtenswürdig) contemptible; **2.** adv. contemptuously; **Verachtung** die; ~: contempt
**verallgemeinern** tr., itr. V. generalize; **Verallgemeinerung** die; ~, ~en generalization
**veralten** itr. V.; mit sein become obsolete
**Veranda** [ve'randa] die; ~, **Veranden** veranda; porch
**veränderlich** Adj. changeable; **verändern** tr., refl. V. change; **Veränderung** die change (Gen. in)
**verängstigen** tr. V. frighten; scare
**verankern** tr. V. fix ⟨tent, mast, pole, etc.⟩; (mit einem Anker) anchor
**veranlagen** tr.V. (Steuerw.) assess (mit at); **veranlagt** Adj. **künstlerisch/praktisch ~ sein** have an artistic bent/be practically minded; **Veranlagung** die; ~, ~en [pre]disposition
**veranlassen** tr. V. cause; induce; ~, **daß ...** see to it that ... **Veranlassung** die; ~, ~en reason
**veranschaulichen** tr. V. illustrate
**veranschlagen** tr. V. estimate (mit at)
**veranstalten** tr. V. organize; hold,

give ⟨party⟩; hold ⟨auction⟩; do ⟨survey⟩; **Veranstalter** der; ~s, ~ organizer; **Veranstaltung** die; ~, ~en **a)** (das Veranstalten) organizing; organization; **b)** (etw., was veranstaltet wird) event
**verantworten 1.** tr. V. etw. ~: take responsibility for sth.; **2.** refl. V. sich für etw. ~: answer for sth.; sich vor jmdm. ~: answer to sb.; **verantwortlich** Adj. responsible; **Verantwortung** die; ~, ~en responsibility (für for)
**verantwortungs-:** ~**bewußt** Adj. responsible; ~**los** Adj. irresponsible; ~**voll** Adj. responsible
**verarbeiten** tr. V. use; etw. zu etw. ~: make sth. into sth.; (geistig bewältigen) assimilate ⟨film, experience, impressions⟩
**verärgern** tr. V. annoy
**verarzten** tr. V. (ugs.) patch up (coll.) ⟨person⟩; fix (coll.) ⟨wound etc.⟩
**veräußern** tr. V. dispose of ⟨property⟩
**Verb** [vɛrp] das; ~s, ~en verb
**Verband** der a) (Binde) bandage; dressing; b) (von Vereinen, Clubs o. ä.) association
**Verband[s]-:** ~**kasten** der first-aid-box; ~**material** das dressing materials pl.
**Verband · zeug** das first-aid things pl.
**Verbannung** die; ~, ~en banishment
**verbergen** unr. tr. V. hide; conceal
**verbessern 1.** tr. V. a) improve; reform ⟨schooling, world⟩; b) (korrigieren) correct; **2.** refl. V. a) improve; b) ([beruflich] aufsteigen) better oneself; **Verbesserung** die a) improvement; b) (Korrektur) correction
**verbeugen** refl. V. bow (vor + Dat. to); **Verbeugung** die; ~, ~en bow
**verbieten** unr. tr. V. a) forbid; jmdm. etw. ~: forbid sb. sth.; ,,Betreten des Rasens/Rauchen verboten" 'keep off the grass'/'no smoking'; b) (für unzulässig erklären) ban
**verbinden 1.** unr. tr. V. a) (bandagieren) bandage; dress; b) (zubinden) bind; jmdm. die Augen ~: blindfold sb.; c) (zusammenfügen) join; d) (in Beziehung bringen) connect (durch by); link ⟨towns, lakes, etc.⟩ (durch by); e) (verknüpfen) combine ⟨abilities, qualities, etc.⟩; f) auch itr. (telefonisch) jmdn. [mit jmdm.] ~: put sb. through [to sb.]; **2.** unr. refl. V. a) (auch Chemie) combine (mit with); b) (sich zusammentun) join [together]; join

forces; **verbindlich 1.** *Adj.* **a)** friendly; **b)** *(bindend)* obligatory; compulsory; binding ⟨*agreement, decision, etc.*⟩; **2.** *adv.* **a)** *(freundlich)* in a friendly manner; **b)** ~ **zusagen** definitely agree; **jmdm. etw.** ~ **zusagen** make sb. a firm offer of sth.; **Verbindung die a)** *(das Verknüpfen)* linking; **b)** *(Zusammenhalt)* join; connection; **c)** *(verknüpfende Strecke)* link; **d)** *(durch Telefon, Funk, Verkehrs~)* connection **(nach** to); **e)** *(Kombination)* combination; **in** ~ **mit etw.** in conjunction with sth.; **f)** *(Kontakt)* contact; **sich mit jmdm. in** ~ **setzen** get in touch *or* contact with sb.; **g)** *(Zusammenhang)* connection

**verbissen 1.** *Adj.* dogged; doggedly determined; **2.** *adv.* doggedly

**verbitten** *unr. refl. V.* **sich** *(Dat.)* **etw.** ~: refuse to tolerate sth.

**verbittern** *tr. V.* embitter

**verblassen** *itr. V.; mit sein (auch fig. geh.)* fade

**Verbleib der;** ~|e|s *(geh.)* whereabouts *pl.;* **verbleiben** *unr. itr. V.; mit sein* remain; **wie seid ihr verblieben?** what did you arrange?

**Verblendung die;** ~, ~en blindness

**verblüffen** *tr. (auch itr.) V.* amaze; **verblüffend 1.** *Adj.* amazing; **2.** *adv.* amazingly

**verblühen** *itr. V.; mit sein (auch fig.)* fade

**verbluten** *itr. (auch refl.) V.; mit sein* bleed to death

**verbohrt** *Adj.* pigheaded

**verborgen** *Adj. (abgelegen)* secluded; *(nicht sichtbar)* hidden

**Verbot das;** ~|e|s, ~e ban *(Gen.,* **von** on); **Verbots·schild das;** *Pl.* ~schilder sign *(prohibiting sth.); (Verkehrsw.)* prohibitive sign

**Verbrauch der;** ~|e|s consumption; **(von, an** + *Dat.* of); **verbrauchen** *tr. V.* use; consume ⟨*food, drink*⟩; use up ⟨*provisions*⟩; spend ⟨*money*⟩; consume, use ⟨*fuel*⟩; *(fig.)* use up ⟨*strength, energy*⟩; **Verbraucher der;** ~s, ~: consumer

**Verbrechen das;** ~s, ~: crime **(an** + *Dat.,* **gegen** against); **Verbrecher der;** ~s, ~: criminal; **verbrecherisch** *Adj.* criminal

**verbreiten 1.** *tr. V.* spread; radiate ⟨*optimism, calm, etc.*⟩; **2.** *refl. V.* spread; **Verbreitung die;** ~, ~en **a)** *s.* **verbreiten 1:** spreading; radiation; **b)** *(Ausbreitung)* spread

**verbrennen 1.** *unr. itr. V.; mit sein* burn; **2.** *tr. V.* burn; cremate ⟨*dead person*⟩; *(fig.)* **den Mund** ~ *(fig.)* say too much; **Verbrennung die;** ~, ~en **a)** *s.* **verbrennen 2:** burning; cremation; **b)** *(Wunde)* burn

**verbringen** *unr. tr. V.* spend

**verbummeln** *tr. V. (ugs.)* **a)** waste ⟨*time*⟩; **b)** *(vergessen)* forget [all] about; clean forget; *(verlieren)* lose

**verbünden** *refl. V.* form an alliance; **Verbündete der/die;** *adj. Dekl.* ally

**verbüßen** *tr. V.* serve ⟨*sentence*⟩

**Verdacht der;** ~|e|s, ~e *od.* **Verdächte** suspicion; **verdächtig 1.** *Adj.* suspicious; **2.** *adv.* suspiciously; **Verdächtige der/die;** *adj. Dekl.* suspect; **verdächtigen** *tr. V.* suspect

**verdammen** *tr. V.* condemn; *(Rel.)* damn ⟨*sinner*⟩

**verdampfen 1.** *itr. V.; mit sein* evaporate; **2.** *tr. V.* evaporate

**verdanken** *tr. V.* **jmdm./einer Sache etw.** ~: owe sth. to sb./sth.

**verdarb** *1. u. 3. Pers. Sg. Prät. v.* **verderben**

**verdattert** *(ugs.) Adj.* flabbergasted; *(verwirrt)* dazed; stunned

**verdauen 1.** *tr. V. (auch fig.)* digest; **2.** *itr. V.* digest [one's food]; **verdaulich** *Adj.* digestible; **Verdauung die;** ~: digestion

**Verdeck das;** ~|e|s, ~e top; hood *(Brit.); (bei Kinderwagen)* hood; **verdecken** *tr. V.* hide; cover

**verderben 1.** *unr. itr. V.; mit sein* go bad *or* off, spoil; **2.** *unr. tr. V.* spoil; *(stärker)* ruin; spoil ⟨*appetite, enjoyment, fun, etc.*⟩; **3.** *unr. refl. V.* **sich** *(Dat.)* **den Magen/die Augen** ~: give oneself an upset stomach/ruin one's eyesight; **Verderben das;** ~s ruin; **verderblich** *Adj.* perishable ⟨*food*⟩; pernicious ⟨*influence, effect, etc.*⟩

**verdeutlichen** *tr. V.* **etw.** ~: make sth. clear; *(erklären)* explain sth.

**verdichten** *refl. V.* ⟨*fog, smoke*⟩ thicken, become thicker; *(fig.)* ⟨*suspicion, rumour*⟩ grow; ⟨*feeling*⟩ intensify

**verdienen 1.** *tr. V.* **a)** earn; **b)** *(wert sein)* deserve; **2.** *itr. V.* **beide Eheleute** ~: husband and wife are both earning; **Verdiener der;** ~s, ~: wage-earner; **¹Verdienst der** income; earnings *pl.;* **²Verdienst das;** ~|e|s, ~e merit

**verdienst·voll 1.** *Adj.* commendable; ⟨*person*⟩ of outstanding merit; **2.** *adv.* commendably; **verdient** *Adj.*

⟨*person*⟩ of outstanding merit; **sich um etw. ~ machen** render outstanding services to sth.

**verdoppeln 1.** *tr. V.* double; *(fig.)* double, redouble ⟨*efforts etc.*⟩; **2.** *refl. V.* double

**verdorben** *2. Part. v.* **verderben**

**verdorren** *itr. V.; mit sein* wither [and die]; ⟨*meadow*⟩ scorch

**verdrängen** *tr. V.* **a)** drive out ⟨*inhabitants*⟩; *(fig.: ersetzen)* displace; **b)** *(Psych.)* repress; *(bewußt)* suppress

**verdrehen** *tr. V.* **a)** twist ⟨*joint*⟩; roll ⟨*eyes*⟩; **b)** *(ugs. abwertend: entstellen)* twist ⟨*words, facts, etc.*⟩

**verdrießen** *unr. tr. V. (geh.)* irritate; annoy; **verdrießlich 1.** *Adj.* morose; **2.** *adv.* morosely; **verdroß** *1. u. 3. Pers. Sg. Prät. v.* **verdrießen; verdrossen 1.** *Adj. (mißmutig)* morose; *(mißmutig und lustlos)* sullen; **2.** *adv. (mißmutig)* morosely; *(mißmutig und lustlos)* sullenly; **Verdruß der; Verdrusses, Verdrusse** annoyance

**verdunkeln** *tr. V.* darken; *(vollständig)* black out ⟨*room, house, etc.*⟩

**Verdunk[e]lung die; ~, ~en** darkening; *(vollständig)* black-out

**verdünnen** *tr. V.* dilute

**verdunsten** *itr. V.; mit sein* evaporate; **Verdunstung die; ~:** evaporation

**verdursten** *itr. V.; mit sein* die of thirst

**verdutzt** *Adj.* taken aback *pred.;* nonplussed; *(verwirrt)* baffled

**verehren** *tr. V.* **a)** venerate; **b)** *(geh.: bewundern)* admire; *(ehrerbietig lieben)* worship; **Verehrer der; ~s, ~, Verehrerin die; ~, ~en** admirer; **Verehrung die; o. Pl.** **a)** veneration; **b)** *(Bewunderung)* admiration

**vereidigen** *tr. V.* swear in; **Vereidigung die; ~, ~en** swearing in

**Verein der; ~s, ~e** organization; *(der Kunstfreunde usw.)* association; society; *(Sport~)* club; **vereinbar** *Adj.; nicht attr.* compatible; **vereinbaren** *tr. V.* agree; arrange ⟨*meeting etc.*⟩; **Vereinbarung die; ~, ~en** **a)** agreeing; *(eines Termins usw.)* arranging; **b)** *(Abmachung)* agreement

**vereinfachen** *tr. V.* simplify

**vereinheitlichen** *tr. V.* standardize

**vereinigen** *tr., refl. V.* unite; *(in der Wirtschaft)* merge; **vereinigt** *Adj.* united; **Vereinigung die** **a)** organization; **b)** *(das Vereinigen)* uniting; *(von Unternehmen)* merging

**vereinzelt 1.** *Adj.; nicht präd.* occasional; **2.** *adv. (zeitlich)* occasionally; *(örtlich)* here and there

**vereisen** *itr. V.; mit sein* freeze *or* ice over; ⟨*wing*⟩ ice up; ⟨*lock*⟩ freeze up

**vereiteln** *tr. V.* thwart

**vereitern** *itr. V.; mit sein* go septic

**verenden** *itr. V.; mit sein* perish; die

**verengen** *refl. V.* narrow; ⟨*pupils*⟩ contract

**vererben** *tr. V.* leave, bequeath ⟨*property*⟩ *(Dat.,* **an** + *Akk.* to)

**Vererbung die; ~, ~en** heredity *no art.*

**verfahren 1.** *unr. refl. V.* lose one's way; **2.** *unr. itr. V.; mit sein* proceed; **Verfahren das; ~s, ~** **a)** procedure; *(Technik)* process; *(Methode)* method; **b)** *(Rechtsw.)* proceedings *pl.*

**Verfall der; o. Pl.** **a)** decay; *(fig.: der Preise, einer Währung)* collapse; **b)** *(Auflösung)* decline; **verfallen** *unr. itr. V.; mit sein* **a)** *(baufällig werden)* fall into disrepair; **b)** *(körperlich)* ⟨*strength*⟩ decline; **c)** *(untergehen)* ⟨*empire*⟩ decline; ⟨*morals, morale*⟩ deteriorate; **d)** *(ungültig werden)* expire

**verfassen** *tr. V.* write; draw up ⟨*resolution*⟩; **Verfasser der; ~s, ~, Verfasserin die; ~, ~nen** writer; *(eines Buchs, Artikels usw.)* author; writer; **Verfassung die** **a)** *(Politik)* constitution; **b)** *o. Pl. (Zustand)* state [of health/mind]; **in guter/schlechter ~ sein** be in good/poor shape

**verfaulen** *itr. V.; mit sein* rot

**verfehlen** *tr. V.* miss; **Verfehlung die; ~, ~en** misdemeanour; *(Rel.: Sünde)* transgression

**verfeinden** *refl. V.* **sich ~ mit** make an enemy of

**verfeinern** *tr. V.* improve; refine ⟨*method, procedure*⟩

**verfertigen** *tr. V.* produce

**verfilmen** *tr. V.* film; make a film of; **Verfilmung die; ~, ~en** **a)** *(das Verfilmen)* filming; **b)** *(Film)* film [version]

**verflixt** *(ugs.)* **1.** *Adj.* **a)** *(ärgerlich)* awkward, unpleasant ⟨*situation, business, etc.*⟩; **b)** *(verdammt)* blasted *(Brit.);* blessed; confounded; **~ [noch mal]!** [damn and] blast! *(Brit. coll.);* **c)** *nicht präd. (sehr groß)* **er hat ~es Glück gehabt** he was damned lucky *(coll.);* **2.** *adv. (sehr)* damned *(coll.)*

**verflossen** *Adj. (ugs.)* former

**verfluchen** *tr. V.* curse; **verflucht 1.**

*Adj. (salopp)* damned *(coll.);* bloody *(Brit. sl.);* ~ |noch mal|! damn [it]! *(coll.);* **2.** *adv. (sehr)* damned *(coll.)*
**verfolgen** *tr. V.* pursue; hunt, track ⟨*animal*⟩; *etw.* |strafrechtlich| ~: prosecute sth.; **Verfolgung die;** ~, ~en pursuit; *(eines Ziels, Plans usw.)* pursuance
**verfressen** *Adj. (salopp)* greedy
**verfügen 1.** *tr. V. (anordnen)* order; *(dekretieren)* decree; **2.** *itr. V.* über etw. *(Akk.)* |frei| ~ können be free to decide what to do with sth.; über etw. *(Akk.)* ~ *(etw. haben)* have sth. at one's disposal; **Verfügung die;** ~, ~en a) *(Anordnung)* order; *(Dekret)* decree; b) *o. Pl. (Disposition)* etw. zur ~ haben have sth. at one's disposal; jmdm. etw. zur ~ stellen put sth. at sb.'s disposal
**verführen** *tr. V.* a) *(verleiten)* tempt; b) *(sexuell)* seduce; **Verführer der** seducer; **verführerisch 1.** *Adj.* a) *(verlockend)* tempting; b) *(aufreizend)* seductive; **2.** *adv.* a) *(verlockend)* temptingly; b) *(aufreizend)* seductively; **Verführung die** a) temptation; b) *(sexuell)* seduction
**vergangen 1.** *Adj.* a) *(vorüber, vorbei)* bygone, former ⟨*times, years, etc.*⟩; b) *(letzt...)* last ⟨*year, week, etc.*⟩; **Vergangenheit die;** ~ a) past; b) *(Grammatik: Präteritum)* past tense; **vergänglich** *Adj.* transient; transitory; ephemeral; **Vergänglichkeit die;** ~: transience
**Vergaser der;** ~s, ~: carburettor
**vergaß** *1. u. 3. Pers. Sg. Prät. v.* vergessen
**vergeben** *unr. tr. V.* a) *auch itr. (geh.: verzeihen)* forgive; jmdm. etw. ~: forgive sb. [for] sth.; b) throw away ⟨*chance, goal, etc.*⟩; c) *(geben)* place ⟨*order*⟩ (an + *Akk.* with); award ⟨*grant, prize*⟩ (an + *Akk.* to); **vergebens 1.** *Adv.* in vain; vainly; **2.** *adj.* es war ~: it was of *or* to no avail; **vergeblich 1.** *Adj.* futile; vain, futile ⟨*attempt, efforts*⟩; **2.** *adv.* in vain; **Vergebung die;** ~, ~en *(geh.)* forgiveness
**vergehen** *unr. itr. V.;* mit sein ⟨*time*⟩ pass [by], go by; ⟨*pain*⟩ wear off, pass; ⟨*pleasure*⟩ fade; **Vergehen das;** ~s, ~: crime; *(Rechtsspr.)* offence
**vergelten** *unr. tr. V.* ~ repay
**vergessen 1.** *unr. tr. (auch itr.) V.* forget; **Vergessenheit die;** ~: oblivion; **vergeßlich** *Adj.* forgetful

**vergeuden** *tr. V.* waste; **Vergeudung die;** ~, ~en waste
**vergewaltigen** *tr. V.* rape; **Vergewaltigung die;** ~, ~en rape
**vergewissern** *refl. V.* make sure *(Gen.* of)
**vergießen** *unr. tr. V.* spill; **Tränen ~:** shed tears
**vergiften** *tr. V. (auch fig.)* poison; **Vergiftung die;** ~, ~en poisoning
**vergiß** *Imper. Sg. v.* vergessen; **vergiß·mein·nicht das;** ~|e|s, ~|e| forget-me-not; **vergißt** *2. u. 3. Pers. Sg. Präs. v.* vergessen
**Vergleich der;** ~|e|s, ~e a) comparison; b) *(Rechtsw.)* settlement; **vergleichbar** *Adj.* comparable; **vergleichen** *tr. V.* compare; **Vergleichs·form die** *(Sprachw.)* comparative/superlative form
**vergnügen** *refl. V.* enjoy oneself; have a good time; **Vergnügen das;** ~s, ~: pleasure; *(Spaß)* fun; viel ~! *(auch iron.)* have fun!; **vergnügt 1.** *Adj.* cheerful; **2.** *adv.* cheerfully; **Vergnügungs·viertel das** pleasure district
**vergolden** *tr. V.* gold-plate ⟨*jewellery etc.*⟩; *(mit Blattgold)* gild
**vergraben** *unr. tr. V.* bury
**vergrämt** *Adj.* care-worn
**vergreifen** *unr. refl. V.* sich an jmdm. ~: assault sb.; **vergriffen** *Adj.* out of print *pred.*
**vergrößern 1.** *tr. V.* a) *(erweitern)* extend ⟨*room, area, building, etc.*⟩; b) *(vermehren)* increase; c) *(größer reproduzieren)* enlarge ⟨*photograph etc.*⟩; **2.** *refl. V.* a) *(größer werden)* ⟨*firm, business, etc.*⟩ expand; b) *(zunehmen)* increase; **3.** *itr. V.* ⟨*lens etc.*⟩ magnify; **Vergrößerung die;** ~, ~en a) *s.* vergrößern 1, 2: extension; increase; enlargement; expansion; b) *(Foto)* enlargement; **Vergrößerungs·glas das** magnifying glass
**Vergünstigung die;** ~, ~en privilege
**vergüten** *tr. V.* a) *(erstatten)* jmdm. etw. ~: reimburse sb. for sth.; b) *(bes. Papierdt.: bezahlen)* remunerate, pay for ⟨*work, services*⟩; **Vergütung die;** ~, ~en a) *(Rückerstattung)* reimbursement; b) *(Geldsumme)* remuneration
**verhaften** *tr. V.* arrest; **Sie sind verhaftet** you are under arrest; **Verhaftung die;** ~, ~en arrest
**verhalten** *unr. refl. V.* a) behave; *(reagieren)* react; b) *(beschaffen sein)* be; **Verhalten das;** ~s behaviour

**Verhaltens·weise** die behaviour; **Verhältnis** das; ~ses, ~se a) ein ~ von drei zu eins a ratio of three to one; b) *(persönliche Beziehung)* relationship (zu with); mit jmdm. ein ~ haben *(ugs.)* have an affair with sb.; c) *Pl. (Umstände)* conditions; **verhältnis·mäßig** *Adv.* relatively; comparatively; **Verhältnis·wort** das; *Pl.* ~wörter *(Sprachw.)* preposition
**verhandeln 1.** *itr. V.* a) negotiate (über + *Akk.* about); b) *(strafrechtlich)* try a case; *(zivilrechtlich)* hear a case; 2. *tr. V.* a) etw. ~: negotiate over sth.; b) *(strafrechtlich)* try ⟨*case*⟩; *(zivilrechtlich)* hear ⟨*case*⟩; **Verhandlung** die a) ~en negotiations; b) *(strafrechtlich)* trial; *(zivilrechtlich)* hearing; die ~ gegen X the trial of X
**verhängen** *tr. V.* impose ⟨*fine, punishment*⟩ (über + *Akk.* on); declare ⟨*state of emergency, state of siege*⟩; *(Sport)* award, give ⟨*penalty etc.*⟩; **Verhängnis** das; ~ses, ~se undoing; **verhängnis·voll** *Adj.* disastrous
**verharmlosen** *tr. V.* play down
**verharren** *itr. V. (geh.)* remain
**verhärten 1.** *tr. V.* harden; make ⟨*person*⟩ hard; 2. *refl. V.* ⟨*tissue*⟩ become hardened
**verhaßt** *Adj.* hated; detested
**verhätscheln** *tr. V. (ugs.)* pamper
**verhauen** *(ugs.) unr. tr. V.* beat up; *(als Strafe)* beat
**verheben** *unr. refl. V.* do oneself an injury [while lifting sth.]
**verheeren** *tr. V.* devastate; lay waste [to]; **verheerend** *Adj.* a) devastating; b) *(ugs.: scheußlich)* ghastly *(coll.)*
**verhehlen** *tr. V. (geh.)* conceal (*Dat.* from)
**verheilen** *itr. V.; mit sein* ⟨*wound*⟩ heal [up]
**verheimlichen** *tr. V.* [jmdm.] etw. ~: keep sth. secret [from sb.]
**verheiraten** *refl. V.* get married; sich mit jmdm. ~: marry sb.; get married to sb.; **Verheiratete** der/die; *adj. Dekl.* married person; married man/woman; **Verheiratung** die; ~, ~en marriage
**verhelfen** *unr. itr. V.* jmdm./einer Sache zu etw. ~: help sb./sth. to get/achieve sth.
**verherrlichen** *tr. V.* glorify
**verheult** *Adj. (ugs.)* ⟨*eyes*⟩ red from crying; ⟨*face*⟩ puffy *or* swollen from crying
**verhexen** *tr. V. (auch fig.)* bewitch

**verhindern** *tr. V.* prevent; **Verhinderung** die; ~, ~en prevention
**verhöhnen** *tr. V.* mock
**Verhör** das; ~[e]s, ~e interrogation; questioning; *(bei Gericht)* examination; **verhören 1.** *tr. V.* interrogate; question; *(bei Gericht)* examine; 2. *refl. V.* mishear
**verhüllen** *tr. V.* cover; *(fig.)* disguise
**verhungern** *itr. V.; mit sein* die of starvation; starve [to death]
**verhüten** *tr. V.* prevent; **Verhütung** die; ~, ~en prevention; *(Empfängnis~)* contraception; **Verhütungs·mittel** das contraceptive
**verirren** *refl. V.* a) get lost; lose one's way; ⟨*animal*⟩ stray; b) *(irgendwohin gelangen)* stray (in, an + *Akk.* into)
**verjagen** *tr. V.* chase away
**verkalken** *itr. V.; mit sein* a) ⟨*tissue*⟩ calcify; ⟨*arteries*⟩ become hardened; b) *(ugs.: senil werden)* become senile
**Verkauf** der sale; **verkaufen** *tr. V. (auch fig.)* sell (*Dat.*, an + *Akk.* to); „zu ~" 'for sale'; **Verkäufer** der, **Verkäuferin** die a) seller; vendor *(formal)*; b) *(Berufsbez.)* sales *or* shop assistant; *(im Außendienst)* salesman/saleswoman; **verkäuflich** *Adj. (zum Verkauf geeignet)* saleable; *(zum Verkauf bestimmt)* for sale *postpos.*; **verkaufs·offen** *Adj.* der ~e Samstag Saturday on which the shops are open all day; **Verkaufs·preis** der retail price
**Verkehr** der; ~s a) traffic; b) *(Kontakt)* contact; communication; c) *(Geschlechts~)* intercourse; **verkehren** *itr. V.* a) auch mit sein *(fahren)* run; ⟨*aircraft*⟩ fly; b) *(in Kontakt stehen)* mit jmdm. ~: associate with sb.; c) *(zu Gast sein)* bei jmdm. ~: visit sb. regularly
**Verkehrs-:** ~ampel die traffic lights *pl.;* ~aufkommen das volume of traffic; ~hindernis das obstruction to traffic; ~knotenpunkt der [traffic] junction; ~kontrolle die traffic check; ~meldung die traffic announcement; ~mittel das means of transport; die öffentlichen ~mittel public transport *sing.;* ~schild das; *Pl.* ~schilder traffic sign; road sign; ~teilnehmer der road-user; ~unfall der road accident; ~zeichen das traffic sign; road sign
**verkehrt 1.** *Adj.* wrong; 2. *adv.* wrongly; alles ~ machen do everything wrong

**verkẹnnen** *unr. tr. V.* fail to recognize; misjudge ⟨*situation*⟩

**verklagen** *tr. V.* sue; take to court; **eine Firma auf Schadenersatz ~:** sue a company for damages

**verklẹben 1.** *itr. V.; mit sein* stick together; **2.** *tr. V. (zukleben)* seal up ⟨*hole*⟩*; (festkleben)* stick [down] ⟨*floorcovering etc.*⟩

**verklẹiden** *tr. V.* disguise; *(kostümieren)* dress up; **sich ~:** disguise oneself/dress [oneself] up; **Verklẹidung die a)** *o. Pl.* disguising; *(das Kostümieren)* dressing up; **b)** *(Kleidung)* disguise; *(bei einer Party)* fancy dress

**verklẹinern 1.** *tr. V.* **a)** make smaller; **b)** *(verringern)* reduce ⟨*size, number, etc.*⟩*;* **c)** *(kleiner reproduzieren)* reduce ⟨*photograph etc.*⟩*;* **2.** *refl. V.* become smaller; ⟨*number*⟩ decrease; **Verklẹinerungs·form die** *(Sprachw.)* diminutive form

**verknoten** *tr. V.* tie; knot

**verknüpfen** *tr. V.* **a)** *(knoten)* tie; knot; **b)** *(in Beziehung setzen)* link

**verkochen** *itr. V.; mit sein* boil away

**verkohlen** *itr. V.* char

**¹verkommen** *unr. itr. V.; mit sein* go to the dogs; *(moralisch, sittlich)* go to the bad; **²verkommen** *Adj.* depraved

**verköstigen** *tr. V.* feed; provide with meals

**verkrạften** *tr. V.* cope with

**verkrạmpfen** *refl. V.* ⟨*muscle*⟩ become cramped; ⟨*person*⟩ tense up; **Verkrạmpfung die; ~, ~en** tenseness; tension

**verkriechen** *unr. refl. V.* ⟨*animal*⟩ creep [away]; ⟨*person*⟩ hide [oneself away]

**verkrụmmt** *Adj.* bent ⟨*person*⟩*;* crooked ⟨*finger*⟩*;* curved ⟨*spine*⟩*;* **Verkrụmmung die** crookedness

**verkrụppeln** *tr. V.* cripple

**verkụmmern** *itr. V.; mit sein* ⟨*person, animal*⟩ go into a decline; ⟨*plant etc.*⟩ become stunted; ⟨*talent, emotional life, etc.*⟩ wither away

**verkụnden** *tr. V.* announce; pronounce ⟨*judgement*⟩*;* promulgate ⟨*law, decree*⟩*;* **verkụndigen** *tr. V. (geh.)* announce; proclaim; **Verkụndigung die** announcement; proclamation

**verkụrzen** *tr. V.* **a)** *(verringern)* reduce; *(abkürzen)* shorten; **b)** *(abbrechen)* cut short ⟨*stay, life*⟩*;* put an end to, end ⟨*suffering*⟩

**verladen** *unr. tr. V.* load

**Verlag der; ~|e|s, ~e** publishing house *or* firm; publisher's

**verlagern** *tr. V.* shift; *(an einen anderen Ort)* move; *(fig.)* transfer; shift ⟨*emphasis*⟩

**verlạngen** *tr. V.* demand; *(nötig haben)* ⟨*task etc.*⟩ require, call for ⟨*patience, knowledge, experience, skill, etc.*⟩*; (berechnen)* charge; *(sehen/sprechen wollen)* ask for; **du wirst am Telefon verlangt** you're wanted on the phone *(coll.);* **Verlạngen das; ~s, ~ a)** desire (nach for); **b) auf ~:** on request

**verlạngern** *tr. V.* extend; lengthen, make longer ⟨*skirt, sleeve, etc.*⟩*;* renew ⟨*passport, driving-licence, etc.*⟩*;* **Verlạngerung die; ~, ~en** *s.* verlängern: extension; lengthening; renewal

**verlạngsamen** *tr. V.* **das Tempo/seine Schritte ~:** reduce speed/slacken one's pace; slow down

**¹verlạssen 1.** *unr. refl. V.* rely, depend (auf + Akk. on); **2.** *unr. tr. V.* leave; **²verlạssen** *Adj.* deserted ⟨*street etc.*⟩*;* empty ⟨*house*⟩*; (öd)* desolate ⟨*region etc.*⟩

**verlạβlich 1.** *Adj.* reliable; **2.** *adv.* reliably

**Verlauf der; ~|e|s, Verläufe** course; **verlaufen 1.** *unr. itr. V.; mit sein* **a)** *(sich erstrecken)* run; **b)** *(ablaufen)* ⟨*test, rehearsal, etc.*⟩ go; ⟨*party etc.*⟩ go off; **2.** *unr. refl. V.* get lost; lose one's way; **Verlaufs·form die** *(Sprachw.)* progressive *or* continuous form

**verlautbaren** *tr. V.* announce [officially]; **verlauten** *itr. V.; mit sein* be reported; **wie verlautet** according to reports

**verleben** *tr. V.* spend; **verlebt** *Adj.* dissipated

**¹verlegen** *tr. V.* **a)** mislay; **b)** *(verschieben)* postpone (auf + Akk. until); *(vor~)* bring forward (auf + Akk. to); **einen Termin ~:** alter an appointment; **c)** *(verlagern)* move; transfer ⟨*patient*⟩*;* **d)** *(legen)* lay ⟨*cable, pipe, carpet, etc.*⟩*;* **²verlegen 1.** *Adj.* embarrassed; **2.** *adv.* in embarrassment; **Verlegenheit die; ~, ~en a)** *o. Pl. (Befangenheit)* embarrassment; **jmdn. in ~ bringen** embarrass sb.; **b)** *(Unannehmlichkeit)* embarrassing situation

**Verleger der; ~s, ~, Verlegerin die; ~, ~nen** publisher

**Verleih der; ~|e|s, ~e a)** *o. Pl.* hiring out; *(von Autos)* renting *or* hiring out;

**b)** *(Unternehmen)* hire firm; *(Film~)* distribution company; *(Video~)* video library; *(Auto~)* rental *or* hire firm; **verleihen** *unr. tr. V.* **a)** hire out; rent *or* hire out ⟨*car*⟩; *(umsonst)* lend [out]; **b)** *(überreichen)* award; confer ⟨*award, honour*⟩

**Verleihung die**; ~, ~**en a)** *s.* verleihen **a**: hiring out; renting out; lending [out]; **b)** *s.* verleihen **b**: awarding; conferring; *(Zeremonie)* award; conferment

**verleiten** *tr. V.* jmdn. dazu ~, etw. zu tun lead *or* induce sb. to do sth.

**verlernen** *tr. V.* forget

**verlesen 1.** *unr. tr. V.* read out; **2.** *unr. refl. V. (falsch lesen)* make a mistake/mistakes in reading

**verletzen** *tr. V.* **a)** injure; *(durch Schuß, Stich)* wound; **b)** *(kränken)* hurt ⟨*person, feelings*⟩; **c)** *(verstoßen gegen)* violate; infringe ⟨*regulation*⟩; break ⟨*agreement, law*⟩; **verletzlich** *Adj.* vulnerable; **Verletzte der/die**; *adj. Dekl.* casualty; *(durch Schuß, Stich)* wounded person; **Verletzung die**; ~, ~**en a)** *(Wunde)* injury; **b)** *(Kränkung)* hurting; **c)** *s.* verletzen **c**: violation; infringement; breaking

**verleugnen** *tr. V.* deny; disown ⟨*friend, relation*⟩

**verleumden** *tr. V.* slander; *(schriftlich)* libel; **Verleumdung die**; ~, ~**en** slander; *(in Schriftform)* libel

**verlieben** *refl. V.* fall in love (in + Akk. with); **Verliebte der/die**; *adj. Dekl.* lover

**verlieren** *unr. tr., itr. V.* lose; **Verlierer der**; ~s, ~: loser

**verloben** *refl. V.* get engaged; verlobt sein be engaged; **Verlobte der/die**; *adj. Dekl.* fiancé/fiancée

**verlockend** *Adj.* tempting; **Verlockung die** temptation

**verlogen** *Adj.* lying, mendacious ⟨*person*⟩; false ⟨*morality etc.*⟩

**verlor** *1. u. 3. Pers. Sg. Prät. v.* verlieren; **verloren** *2. Part. v.* verlieren; **verloren|gehen** *unr. itr. V.; mit sein* get lost

**verlosen** *tr. V.* raffle; **Verlosung die**; ~, ~**en** raffle; draw

**verlottern** *itr. V.; mit sein* ⟨*person*⟩ go to seed

**Verlust der**; ~[e]s, ~**e** loss (an + Dat. of)

**vermachen** *tr. V.* jmdm. etw. ~: leave *or* bequeath sth. to sb.; *(fig.: schenken, überlassen)* give sth. to sb.

**vermählen** *refl. V. (geh.)* sich [jmdm. od. mit jmdm.] ~: marry *or* wed [sb.]; **Vermählung die**; ~, ~**en** *(geh.)* **a)** marriage; **b)** *(Fest)* wedding ceremony

**vermehren 1.** *tr. V.* increase (um by); **2.** *refl. V.* **a)** increase; **b)** *(sich fortpflanzen)* reproduce; **Vermehrung die**; ~, ~**en a)** increase (Gen. in); **b)** *(Fortpflanzung)* reproduction

**vermeiden** *unr. tr. V.* avoid

**vermeintlich** *Adj.* supposed

**vermengen** *tr. V.* mix (miteinander together)

**Vermerk der**; ~[e]s, ~**e** note; *(amtlich)* remark; **vermerken** *tr. V.* make a note of; note [down]; *(in Akten, Wachbuch usw.)* record

**¹vermessen** *unr. tr. V.* measure; survey ⟨*land, site*⟩; **²vermessen** *Adj.* *(geh.)* presumptuous

**vermieten** *tr. (auch itr.) V.* rent [out], let [out] (an + Akk. to); hire [out] ⟨*boat, car, etc.*⟩; „Zimmer zu ~" 'room to let'; **Vermieter der** landlord; **Vermieterin die** landlady

**vermindern 1.** *tr. V.* reduce; decrease; reduce, lessen ⟨*danger, stress*⟩; lower ⟨*resistance*⟩; reduce ⟨*debt*⟩; **2.** *refl. V.* decrease; ⟨*resistance*⟩ diminish

**vermischen 1.** *tr. V.* mix (miteinander together); blend ⟨*teas, tobaccos, etc.*⟩; **2.** *refl. V.* mix; *(fig.)* mingle; ⟨*races, animals*⟩ interbreed; **Vermischung die** *s.* vermischen: mixing; blending; *(fig.)* mingling

**vermissen** *tr. V.* **a)** miss; **b)** *(nicht haben)* ich vermisse meinen Ausweis my identity card is missing; **Vermißte der/die**; *adj. Dekl.* missing person

**vermitteln 1.** *itr. V.* mediate, act as [a] mediator (in + Dat. in); **2.** *tr. V.* **a)** *(herbeiführen)* arrange; negotiate ⟨*transaction, cease-fire, compromise*⟩; **b)** *(besorgen)* jmdm. eine Stelle ~: find sb. a job; **c)** *(weitergeben)* impart ⟨*knowledge, insight, values, etc.*⟩; communicate ⟨*message, information, etc.*⟩; convey ⟨*feeling*⟩; pass on ⟨*experience*⟩; **Vermittler der**; ~s, ~ **a)** *(Mittler)* mediator; **b)** *s.* vermitteln **2c**: imparter; communicator; conveyer; **c)** *(von Berufs wegen)* agent; **Vermittlung die**; ~, ~**en a)** *(Schlichtung)* mediation; **b)** *s.* vermitteln **2a**: arrangement; negotiation; **c)** *s.* vermitteln **2c**: imparting; communicating; conveying; **d)** *(Telefonzentrale)* exchange; *(in einer Firma)* switchboard

**vermögen** *(geh.) unr. tr. V.* **etw. zu tun
~:** be able to do sth.; be capable of
doing sth.; **Vermögen das; ~s, ~ a)**
*o. Pl. (geh.: Fähigkeit)* ability; **b)** *(Besitz)* fortune; **er hat ~:** he has money;
**vermögend** *Adj.* wealthy; well-off;
**Vermögen[s]·steuer die** wealth
tax
**vermummen** *tr. V.* wrap up
[warmly]; *(verbergen)* disguise
**vermuten** *tr. V.* suspect; **das ist zu ~:**
that is what one would suppose *or* expect; we may assume that; **vermutlich 1.** *Adj.* probable; **2.** *Adv.* presumably; *(wahrscheinlich)* probably;
**Vermutung die; ~, ~en** supposition
**vernachlässigen** *tr. V.* neglect; *(unberücksichtigt lassen)* ignore; disregard; **Vernachlässigung die; ~, ~en**
neglect
**vernarben** *itr. V.; mit sein* [form a]
scar; heal *(lit. or fig.)*
**vernehmbar** *Adj. (geh.)* audible;
**vernehmen** *unr. tr. V.* **a)** *(geh.: hören, erfahren)* hear; **b)** *(verhören)*
question; **vernehmlich 1.** *Adj.*
[clearly] audible; **2.** *adv.* audibly;
**Vernehmung die; ~, ~en** questioning
**verneigen** *refl. V. (geh.)* bow **(vor** +
*Dat.* to, *(literary)* before)
**verneinen** *tr. (auch itr.) V.* **a)** say 'no'
to *(question)*; answer *(question)* in the
negative; **b)** *(Sprachw.)* negate; **Verneinung die; ~, ~en** *(Sprachw.)*
negation
**vernichten** *tr. V.* destroy; exterminate *(pests, vermin)*; **Vernichtung
die; ~, ~en** destruction; *(von Schädlingen)* extermination
**Vernunft die; ~:** reason; **vernünftig
1.** *Adj.* **a)** sensible; **b)** *(ugs.: ordentlich,
richtig)* decent; **2.** *adv.* **a)** sensibly; **b)**
*(ugs.: ordentlich, richtig)* *(talk, eat)*
properly; *(dress)* sensibly
**veröffentlichen** *tr. V.* publish; **Veröffentlichung die; ~, ~en** publication
**verordnen** *tr. V.* [jmdm. etw.] ~: prescribe [sth. for sb.]; **Verordnung die**
prescribing
**verpachten** *tr. V.* lease
**verpacken** *tr. V.* pack; wrap up
*(present, parcel)*; **Verpackung die a)**
*o.Pl.* packing; **b)** *(Umhüllung)* packaging *no pl.;* wrapping
**verpassen** *tr. V.* miss
**verpflanzen** *tr. V. (auch Med.)* transplant; graft *(skin)*

**verpflegen** *tr. V.* cater for; feed;
**Verpflegung die; ~, ~en a)** *o.Pl.*
catering *no indef. art.* *(Gen.* for); **b)**
*(Nahrung)* food; **Unterkunft und ~:**
board and lodging
**verpflichten 1.** *tr. V.* **a)** oblige; commit; *(festlegen, binden)* bind; **b)** *(einstellen, engagieren)* engage *(manager,
actor, etc.)*; **2.** *refl. V.* undertake;
promise; **sich vertraglich ~:** sign a
contract; **Verpflichtung die; ~, ~en
a)** obligation; commitment; **b)** *(Engagement)* engaging; engagement
**verprügeln** *tr. V.* beat up; *(zur Strafe)*
thrash
**Verputz der** plaster; *(auf Außenwänden)* rendering; **verputzen** *tr. V.*
plaster; render *(outside wall)*
**verquollen** *Adj.* swollen
**Verrat der; ~[e]s** betrayal **(an** + *Dat.*
of); **verraten** *unr. tr. V.* **a)** betray **(an**
+ *Akk.* to); **b)** *(ugs.: mitteilen)* **jmdm.
den Grund** *usw.* **~:** tell. sb. the reason
*etc.;* **c)** *(erkennen lassen)* show, betray
*(feelings, surprise, fear, etc.)*; show *(influence, talent)*; **Verräter der; ~s, ~:**
traitor; **Verräterin die; ~, ~en** traitress; **verräterisch** *Adj.* treacherous
*(plan, purpose, act, etc.)*
**verrechnen 1.** *tr. V.* include *(amount
etc.)*; *(gutschreiben)* credit *(cheque
etc.)* to another account; **2.** *refl. V.*
miscalculate; **Verrechnungsscheck der** crossed cheque
**verregnen** *itr. V.; mit sein* be spoilt *or*
ruined by rain
**verreiben** *unr. tr. V.* rub in
**verreisen** *itr. V.; mit sein* go away
**verrenken** *tr. V.* dislocate; **Verrenkung die; ~, ~en** dislocation
**verrichten** *tr. V.* perform
**verriegeln** *tr. V.* bolt
**verringern 1.** *tr. V.* reduce; **2.** *refl. V.*
decrease; **Verringerung die; ~:** reduction; decrease *(Gen.,* von in)
**verrosten** *itr. V.; mit sein* rust; **verrostet** rusty
**verrückt** *(ugs.)* **1.** *Adj.* **a)** mad; **~ werden** go mad *or* insane; **b)** *(überspannt,
ausgefallen)* crazy *(idea, fashion,
prank, day, etc.)*; **2.** *adv.* crazily; *(behave)* crazily *or* like a madman; *(dress
etc.)* in a mad *or* crazy way; **Verrückte der/die;** *adj. Dekl. (ugs.)*
madman/madwoman; lunatic
**verrühren** *tr. V.* stir together; mix
**verrutschen** *itr. V.* slip
**Vers der; ~es, ~e** verse
**versagen** *itr. V.* fail; *(machine, en-*

*gine*⟩ stop [working]; **menschliches Versagen** human error; **Versager der**; ~s, ~: failure
**versalzen** *unr. tr. V.* put too much salt in/on; *(fig. ugs.)* spoil
**versammeln** *tr., refl. V.* assemble; **Versammlung die a)** meeting; **b)** *(Gremium)* assembly
**versäumen** *tr. V.* **a)** *(verpassen)* miss; lose ⟨*time, sleep*⟩; **b)** *(vernachlässigen, unterlassen)* neglect ⟨*duty, task*⟩
**verschaffen** *tr. V.* jmdm. etw. ~: provide sb. with sth.; get sb. sth.; **sich** *(Dat.)* etw. ~: get hold of sth.; obtain sth.
**verschämt** [fɛɐʃɛːmt] **1.** *Adj.* bashful; **2.** *adv.* bashfully
**verschenken** *tr. V.* give away
**verscheuchen** *tr. V.* chase away
**verschicken** *tr. V. s.* **versenden**
**verschieben 1.** *unr. tr. V.* **a)** shift; move; **b)** *(aufschieben)* put off, postpone (**auf** + *Akk.* till); **2.** *unr. refl. V.* be postponed (**um** for); ⟨*start*⟩ be put back *or* delayed (**um** by); **Verschiebung die** postponement
**verschieden 1.** *Adj.* **a)** different (**von** from); **b)** *(vielfältig)* various; **die** ~**sten**...: all sorts of...; **die** ~**en**...: the various...; **c)** ~**es** various things *pl.*; **2.** *adv.* differently; **verschiedenartig 1.** *Adj.* different in kind *pred.*; *(mehr als zwei)* diverse; **2.** *adv.* diversely; **Verschiedenheit die**; ~, ~**en** difference; *(unter mehreren)* diversity; **verschiedentlich** *Adv.* on various occasions
**verschimmeln** *itr. V.*; mit sein go mouldy; **verschimmelt** mouldy
¹**verschlafen 1.** *unr. itr. (auch refl.)V.* oversleep; **2.** *unr. tr. V.* **a)** *(schlafend verbringen)* sleep through ⟨*morning, journey, etc.*⟩; **b)** *(versäumen)* not wake up in time for ⟨*appointment*⟩; not wake up in time to catch ⟨*train, bus*⟩; **c)** *(ugs.: vergessen)* forget about ⟨*appointment etc.*⟩; ²**verschlafen** *Adj.* half-asleep; *(fig.)* sleepy ⟨*town*⟩
**Verschlag der** shed
¹**verschlagen** *unr. tr. V.* **die Seite** ~: lose one's place *or* page; jmdm. die **Sprache** ~: leave sb. speechless; ²**verschlagen 1.** *Adj.* sly; shifty; **2.** *adv.* slyly; shiftily
**verschlechtern 1.** *tr. V.* make worse; **2.** *refl. V.* get worse; deteriorate; **Verschlechterung die**; ~, ~**en** worsening, deterioration (*Gen.* in)
**Verschleiß der**; ~**es**, ~**e a)** wear *no*

*indef. art.*; **b)** *(Verbrauch)* consumption (**an** + *Dat.* of); **verschleißen 1.** *unr. itr. V.*; mit sein wear out; **2.** *unr. tr. V.* wear out; *(fig.)* run down, ruin ⟨*one's nerves, one's health*⟩; use up ⟨*energy, ability, etc.*⟩
**verschleppen** *unr. tr. V.* **a)** carry off; take away ⟨*person*⟩; **b)** *(weiterverbreiten)* carry, spread ⟨*disease, bacteria, mud, etc.*⟩; **c)** *(verzögern)* delay; *(in die Länge ziehen)* draw out; let ⟨*illness*⟩ drag on [and get worse]
**verschleudern** *tr. V.* **a)** sell dirt cheap; *(mit Verlust)* sell at a loss; **b)** *(verschwenden)* squander
**verschließbar** *Adj.* closable; lockable ⟨*suitcase, drawer, etc.*⟩; |luftdicht| ~: sealable ⟨*container etc.*⟩; **verschließen** *unr. tr. V.* **a)** close; stop, *(mit einem Korken)* cork ⟨*bottle*⟩; **b)** *(abschließen)* lock; lock up ⟨*house etc.*⟩; **c)** *(wegschließen)* lock away (**in** + *Dat. od. Akk.* in)
**verschlimmern 1.** *tr. V.* make worse; **2.** *refl. V.* get worse; ⟨*position, conditions*⟩ deteriorate, worsen
**verschlingen** *unr. tr. V.* **a)** [inter]twine ⟨*threads etc.*⟩ (**zu** into); **b)** *(essen, fressen)* devour ⟨*food*⟩; *(fig.)* devour ⟨*novel, money, etc.*⟩
**verschlissen** *2. Part. v.* **verschleißen**
**verschlossen** *Adj. (wortkarg)* taciturn; *(zurückhaltend)* reserved
**verschlucken 1.** *tr. V.* swallow; **2.** *refl. V.* choke
**Verschluß der** *(am BH, an Schmuck usw.)* fastener; fastening; *(an Taschen, Schmuck)* clasp; *(an Schuhen, Gürteln)* buckle; *(am Schrank, Fenster, Koffer usw.)* catch; *(an Flaschen)* top; *(Stöpsel)* stopper
**verschmähen** *tr. V. (geh.)* spurn
**verschmerzen** *tr. V.* get over
**verschmieren** *tr. V.* smear ⟨*window etc.*⟩; *(beim Schreiben)* mess up ⟨*paper*⟩; scrawl all over ⟨*page*⟩; smudge ⟨*ink*⟩
**verschmitzt 1.** *Adj.* mischievous; **2.** *adv.* mischievously
**verschmutzen 1.** *itr. V.*; mit sein get dirty; ⟨*river etc.*⟩ become polluted; **2.** *tr. V.* dirty; soil; pollute ⟨*air, water, etc.*⟩; **Verschmutzung die**; ~, ~**en** *(der Umwelt)* pollution; *(von Stoffen, Teppichen usw.)* soiling
**verschnaufen** *itr. V. (auch refl.) V.* have *or* take a breather
**verschneit** *Adj.* snow-covered *attrib.*; covered with snow *postpos.*

**verschnörkelt** *Adj.* ornate

**verschnüren** *tr. V.* tie up

**verschollen** *Adj.* missing

**verschonen** *tr. V.* spare; **jmdn. mit etw. ~:** spare sb. sth.

**verschränken** *tr. V.* fold ⟨arms⟩; cross ⟨legs⟩; clasp ⟨hands⟩

**verschreiben** 1. *unr. tr. V. (Med.: verordnen)* prescribe; 2. *unr. refl. V.* **a)** make a slip of the pen; **b) sich einer Sache** *(Dat.)* ~: devote oneself to sth.; **verschreibungs·pflichtig** *Adj.* available only on prescription *postpos.*

**verschrie[e]n** *Adj.* notorious (**wegen** for)

**verschulden** 1. *tr. V.* be to blame for ⟨accident, death, etc.⟩; 2. *refl. V.* get into debt; **Verschulden das;** ~s guilt; **durch eigenes** ~: through one's own fault; **verschuldet** *Adj.* in debt *postpos.* **(bei** to); **hoch** ~: deeply in debt

**verschütten** *tr. V.* **a)** spill; **b)** *(begraben)* bury ⟨person⟩ [alive]

**verschwägert** *Adj.* related by marriage *postpos.*

**verschweigen** *unr. tr. V.* conceal *(Dat.* from)

**verschwenden** *tr. V.* waste (**an** + *Akk.* on); **Verschwender der;** ~s, ~ *(von Geld)* spendthrift; *(von Dingen)* wasteful person; **verschwenderisch** 1. *Adj.* wasteful ⟨person⟩; ⟨life⟩ of extravagance; 2. *adv.* wastefully; **Verschwendung die;** ~, ~en wastefulness; extravagance

**verschwiegen** *Adj.* discreet; *(still, einsam)* secluded; **Verschwiegenheit die;** ~: secrecy; *(Diskretion)* discretion

**verschwimmen** *unr. itr. V.; mit sein* blur

**verschwinden** *unr. itr. V.; mit sein* disappear; vanish; **verschwinde [hier]!** off with you!; go away!; hop it! *(sl.);* **ich muß mal** ~ *(ugs. verhüll.)* I have to pay a visit *(coll.)* or *(Brit. coll.)* spend a penny

**verschwommen** 1. *Adj.* blurred ⟨photograph, vision⟩; blurred, hazy ⟨outline⟩; vague, woolly ⟨idea, concept, formulation, etc.⟩; 2. *adv.* vaguely; ⟨remember⟩ hazily

**versehen** 1. *unr. tr. V.* **a)** *(ausstatten)* provide; equip ⟨car, factory, machine, etc.⟩; **b)** *(ausüben, besorgen)* perform ⟨duty etc.⟩; 2. *unr. refl. V.* make a slip; slip up; **Versehen das;** ~s, ~: over-

sight; slip; **aus** ~: by mistake; inadvertently; **versehentlich** 1. *Adv.* by mistake; inadvertently; 2. *adj.; nicht präd.* inadvertent

**Versehrte der/die;** *adj. Dekl.* disabled person; **die ~n** the disabled

**versenden** *unr. tr. V. (auch regelm.) tr. V.* send ⟨letter, parcel⟩; send out ⟨invitations⟩; dispatch ⟨goods⟩

**versetzen** 1. *tr. V.* **a)** move; transfer, move ⟨employee⟩; *(in die nächsthöhere Klasse)* move ⟨pupil⟩ up, *(Amer.)* promote ⟨pupil⟩ **(in** + *Akk.* to); *(umpflanzen)* transplant, move ⟨plant⟩; *(fig.)* transport **(in** + *Akk.* to); **b)** *(nicht geradlinig anordnen)* stagger; **c)** *(verpfänden)* pawn; **d)** *(verkaufen)* sell; **e)** *(ugs.: vergeblich warten lassen)* stand ⟨person⟩ up *(coll.);* **f)** *(vermischen)* mix; **g)** *(erwidern)* retort; **h) etw. in Bewegung/Tätigkeit** ~: set sth. in motion/operation; **jmdn. in die Lage** ~, **etw. zu tun** put sb. in a position to do sth.; **jmdm. einen Stoß/Fußtritt/ Schlag** *usw.* ~: give sb. a push/kick/ deal sb. a blow *etc.;* 2. *refl. V.* **sich in jmds. Lage** *(Akk.)* ~: put oneself in sb.'s position or place; **Versetzung die;** ~, ~en *(eines Schülers)* moving up, *(Amer.)* promotion **(in** + *Akk.* to); *(eines Angestellten)* transfer

**verseuchen** *tr. V. (auch fig.)* contaminate; **radioaktiv** ~: contaminate with radioactivity

**versichern** *tr. V.* **a)** assert ⟨sth.⟩; **b)** *(vertraglich schützen)* insure **(bei** with); **Versicherte der/die;** *adj. Dekl.* insured [person]; **Versicherung die a)** *(Beteuerung)* assurance; **b)** *(Schutz durch Vertrag)* insurance; *(Vertrag)* insurance [policy] **(über** + *Akk.* for); *(Gesellschaft)* insurance [company]

**Versicherungs-:** ~**beitrag der** insurance premium; ~**gesellschaft die** insurance company; ~**police die** insurance policy

**versickern** *itr. V.; mit sein* ⟨river etc.⟩ drain *or* seep away

**versiegeln** *tr. V.* seal

**versiegen** *itr. V.; mit sein (geh.)* dry up; run dry

**versinken** *unr. itr. V.; mit sein* sink; **im Schlamm** ~: sink into the mud

**versöhnen** 1. *refl. V.* **sich [miteinander]** ~: become reconciled; **sich mit jmdm.** ~: make it up with sb.; 2. *tr. V.* reconcile; **Versöhnung die;** ~, ~en reconciliation

**versọnnen** 1. *Adj.* dreamy; 2. *adv.*
dreamily

**versọrgen** *tr. V.* **a)** supply; **b)** *(unterhalten, ernähren)* provide for ⟨*chil-
dren, family*⟩; **c)** *(sorgen für)* look
after; **jmdn. ärztlich ~:** give sb. medical care; *(kurzzeitig)* give sb. medical
attention; **Versọrger der; ~s, ~,
Versọrgerin die; ~, ~nen** bread-
winner; **Versọrgung die; ~, ~en a)**
*o. Pl.* supply[ing]; **b)** *(Unterhaltung,
Ernährung)* support[ing]; **c)** *(Bedienung, Pflege)* care; **ärztliche ~:** medical care *or* treatment; *(kurzzeitig)*
medical attention

**Verspạnnung die** *(Med.: der Muskulatur)* tension

**verspäten** *refl. V.* be late; **verspätet**
*Adj.* late ⟨*arrival etc.*⟩; belated ⟨*greetings, thanks*⟩; **~ eintreffen** arrive late;
**Verspätung die; ~, ~en** lateness;
*(verspätetes Eintreffen)* late arrival;
**[fünf Minuten] ~ haben** be [five
minutes] late

**versperren** *tr. V.* block; obstruct
⟨*view*⟩

**verspielen** *tr. V.* gamble away; *(fig.)*
squander, throw away ⟨*opportunity,
chance*⟩; forfeit ⟨*right, credibility, etc*⟩;
**verspielt** 1. *Adj. (auch fig.)* playful;
fanciful, fantastic ⟨*form, design, etc.*⟩;
2. *adv.* playfully *(lit. or fig.)*; ⟨*dress,
designed*⟩ fancifully, fantastically

**verspọtten** *tr. V.* mock; ridicule

**versprẹchen** 1. *unr. tr. V.* promise;
**sich** *(Dat.)* **etw. von etw./jmdm. ~:**
hope for sth. *or* to get sth. from sth./
sb.; 2. *unr. refl. V.* make a slip/slips of
the tongue; **Versprẹchen das; ~s,
~, Versprẹchung die; ~, ~en**
promise

**versprühen** *tr. V.* spray

**verspüren** *tr. V.* feel

**Verstạnd der; ~[e]s** *(Fähigkeit zu denken)* reason *no art.*; *(Fähigkeit, Begrif-
fe zu bilden)* mind; *(Vernunft)* [com-
mon] sense *no art.*; **hast du denn den ~
verloren?** *(ugs.)* have you taken leave
of your senses?; **verständig** 1. *Adj.*
sensible; 2. *adv.* sensibly

**verständigen** 1. *tr. V.* notify, inform
**(von, über** + *Akk.* of); 2. *refl. V.* **a)**
make oneself understood; **sich mit
jmdm. ~:** communicate with sb.; **b)**
*(sich einigen)* **sich [mit jmdm.] über/auf
etw.** *(Akk.)* **~:** come to an understanding [with sb.] about *or.* on sth.; **Ver-
stạndigkeit die; ~:** understanding;
intelligence; **Verständigung die; ~,**

**~en a)** notification; **b)** *(das Sichver-
ständlichmachen)* communication *no
art.;* **c)** *(Einigung)* understanding;
**Verständigungs · schwierigkeit
die** difficulty of communication; **ver-
stạndlich** 1. *Adj.* **a)** comprehensible;
*(deutlich)* clear ⟨*pronunciation, presentation, etc.*⟩; **sich ~ machen** make
oneself understood; **jmdm. etw. ~ machen** make sth. clear to sb.; **b)** *(begreiflich, verzeihlich)* understandable; 2.
*adv.* comprehensibly; *(deutlich)*
⟨*speak, express oneself, present*⟩
clearly; **verstạndlicher · weise**
*Adv.* understandably; **Verstạnd-
lichkeit die; ~:** comprehensibility;
clarity; **Verstạndnis das; ~ses, ~se**
understanding; **ich habe volles ~ dafür, daß ...:** I fully understand that ...;
**für die Unannehmlichkeiten bitten wir
um [Ihr] ~:** we apologize for the inconvenience caused

**verstạndnis-:** **~los** 1. *Adj.* uncom-
prehending; 2. *adv.* uncomprehend-
ingly; **~voll** 1. *Adj.* understanding; 2.
*adv.* understandingly

**verstärken** 1. *tr. V.* **a)** strengthen; **b)**
*(zahlenmäßig)* reinforce ⟨*troops etc.*⟩
**(um** by); enlarge ⟨*orchestra, choir*⟩ **(um**
by); **c)** *(intensiver machen)* intensify,
increase ⟨*effort, contrast*⟩; strengthen,
increase ⟨*impression, suspicion*⟩; *(größer machen)* increase ⟨*pressure, voltage, effect, etc.*⟩; *(lauter machen)* amplify ⟨*signal, sound, guitar, etc.*⟩; 2. *refl.
V.* increase; **Verstärker der; ~s, ~:**
amplifier; **Verstärkung die; ~, ~en
a)** strengthening; **b)** *(zahlenmäßig)* re-
inforcement *(esp. Mil.);* **c)** *(Zunahme)*
increase *(Gen.* in); *(der Lautstärke)*
amplification; **d)** *(zusätzliche Person[en])* reinforcements *pl.*

**verstauben** *itr. V.; mit sein* get dusty;
gather dust *(lit. or fig.)*

**verstauchen** *tr. V.* sprain; **sich** *(Dat.)*
**den Fuß/die Hand ~:** sprain one's
ankle/wrist; **Verstauchung die; ~,
~en** sprain

**verstauen** *tr. V.* pack **(in** + *Dat. od.
Akk.* in[to]); *(bes. im Boot/Auto)* stow
**(in** + *Dat. od. Akk.* in)

**Verstẹck das; ~[e]s, ~e** hiding-place;
**~ spielen** play hide-and-seek; **ver-
stẹcken** 1. *tr. V.* hide **(vor** + *Dat.*
from); 2. *refl. V.* **sich [vor jmdm./etw.]
~:** hide [from sb./sth.]; **verstẹckt**
*Adj.* hidden; *(heimlich)* secret ⟨*malice,
activity, etc.*⟩; disguised ⟨*foul*⟩

**verstẹhen** 1. *unr. tr. V.* understand;

wie soll ich das ~? how am I to interpret that?; **jmdn./etw. falsch ~** : misunderstand sb./sth.; **2.** *unr. refl. V.* **sich mit jmdm. ~** : get on with sb.; **das versteht sich [von selbst]** that goes without saying

**versteigern** *tr. V.* auction; **etw. ~ lassen** put sth. up for auction; **Versteigerung die** auction

**verstellbar** *Adj.* adjustable; **verstellen 1.** *tr. V.* **a)** *(falsch plazieren)* misplace; **b)** *(anders einstellen)* adjust ⟨*seat etc.*⟩; alter [the adjustment of] ⟨*mirror etc.*⟩; reset ⟨*alarm clock, points, etc.*⟩; **c)** *(versperren)* block, obstruct; **d)** *(zur Täuschung verändern)* disguise ⟨*voice, handwriting*⟩; **2.** *refl. V.* pretend; **Verstellung die** pretence; *(der Stimme, Schrift)* disguising

**verstimmen** *tr. V.* put ⟨*person*⟩ in a bad mood; *(verärgern)* annoy; **verstimmt** *Adj.* **a)** *(Musik)* out of tune *pred.;* **b)** *(verärgert)* put out, peeved, disgruntled (**über** + *Akk.* by, about); **ein ~er Magen** an upset stomach; **Verstimmung die** bad mood

**verstohlen 1.** *Adj.* furtive; **2.** *adv.* furtively

**verstopfen 1.** *tr. V.* block; **verstopft sein** ⟨*pipe, drain, jet, nose, etc.*⟩ be blocked (**durch, von** with); **2.** *itr. V.; mit sein* become blocked; **Verstopfung die**; **~, ~en** *(Med.)* constipation

**verstorben** *Adj.* late; **Verstorbene der/die;** *adj. Dekl. (geh.)* deceased

**verstören** *tr. V.* distress; **verstört** *Adj.* distraught

**Verstoß der** violation (**gegen** of); **verstoßen 1.** *unr. tr. V.* disown; **2.** *unr. itr. V.* **gegen etw. ~** : infringe sth.

**verstreichen 1.** *unr. tr. V.* apply, put on ⟨*paint*⟩; spread ⟨*butter etc.*⟩; **2.** *unr. itr. V.; mit sein (geh.)* ⟨*time*⟩ pass [by]

**verstreuen** *tr. V.* scatter; put down ⟨*bird food, salt*⟩; *(versehentlich)* spill

**verstricken 1.** *tr. V.* **jmdn. in etw.** *(Akk.)* **~** : involve sb. in sth.; draw sb. into sth.; **2.** *refl. V.* **sich in etw.** *(Akk.)* **~** : become entangled *or* caught up in sth.

**verstümmeln** *tr. V.* mutilate; *(fig.)* garble ⟨*report*⟩; chop, mutilate ⟨*text*⟩

**verstummen** *itr. V.; mit sein (geh.)* fall silent; ⟨*music, noise, conversation*⟩ cease

**Versuch der;** **~[e]s, ~e** attempt; *(Experiment)* experiment (**an** + *Dat.* on); *(Probe)* test; **versuchen** *tr. V.* **a)** try; attempt; **b)** *(probieren)* try ⟨*cake etc.*⟩

**versündigen** *refl. V.* **sich an jmdm./ etw. ~** : sin against sb./sth.

**versüßen** *tr. V.* **jmdm./sich etw. ~** *(fig.)* make sth. more pleasant for sb./ oneself

**vertauschen** *tr. V.* exchange; switch; reverse ⟨*roles, poles*⟩; **etw. mit od. gegen etw. ~** : exchange sth. for sth.

**verteidigen** *tr. V.* defend; **Verteidiger der;** **~s, ~, Verteidigerin, die; ~, ~nen** *(auch Sport)* defender; *(Rechtsw.)* defence counsel; **Verteidigung die, ~, ~en** defence; **Verteidigungs·minister der** minister of defence

**verteilen** *tr. V.* distribute, hand out ⟨*leaflets, prizes, etc.*⟩ (**an** + *Akk.* to, **unter** + *Akk.* among); share [out], distribute ⟨*money, food*⟩ (**an** + *Akk.* to, **unter** + *Akk.* among); allocate ⟨*work*⟩; distribute ⟨*weight etc.*⟩ (**auf** + *Akk.* over); spread ⟨*cost*⟩ (**auf** + *Akk.* among); distribute, spread ⟨*butter, seed, dirt, etc.*⟩; **Verteilung die** distribution; *(der Rollen, der Arbeit)* allocation

**verteuern 1.** *tr. V.* make ⟨*goods*⟩ more expensive; **2.** *refl. V.* become more expensive

**verteufeln** *tr. V.* condemn; denigrate

**vertiefen 1.** *tr. V. (auch fig.)* deepen (**um** by); **2.** *refl. V.* **sich ~ in** (+ *Akk.*) bury oneself in ⟨*book, work, etc.*⟩; **in etw.** *(Akk.)* **vertieft sein** be engrossed in sth.; **Vertiefung die; ~, ~en** *(Mulde)* depression; hollow

**vertikal 1.** *Adj.* vertical; **2.** *adv.* vertically; **Vertikale die; ~; ~n** *s.* **Senkrechte**

**vertilgen** *tr. V.* **a)** *(vernichten)* exterminate ⟨*vermin*⟩; kill off ⟨*weeds*⟩; **b)** *(ugs.: verzehren)* devour, *(joc.)* demolish ⟨*food*⟩

**vertonen** *tr. V.* set ⟨*text, poem*⟩ to music; **Vertonung die; ~, ~en** setting

**Vertrag der; ~[e]s, Verträge** contract; *(zwischen Staaten)* treaty; **vertragen 1.** *unr. tr. V.* endure; tolerate *(esp. Med.);* *(aushalten, leiden können)* stand; bear; **ich vertrage keinen Kaffee** coffee disagrees with me; **2.** *unr. refl. V.* **sich mit jmdm. ~** : get on *or* along with sb.; *(passen)* **sich mit etw. ~** : go with sth.; **verträglich 1.** *Adj.* contractual; **2.** *adv.* contractually; by contract; **verträglich** *Adj.* **a)** digestible ⟨*food*⟩; **b)** *(umgänglich)* good-natured; easy to get on with *pred.*

**vertrauen** *itr. V.* jmdm./einer Sache ~: trust sb./sth.; **auf etw.** *(Akk.)* ~: [put one's] trust in sth.; **Vertrauen das**; ~s trust; confidence; jmdn. ins ~ ziehen take sb. into one's confidence; **vertrauen·erweckend** *Adj.* inspiring

**vertrauens-, Vertrauens-**: ~**bruch der** breach of trust; ~**person die** person in a position of trust; ~**sache die** matter *or* question of trust; ~**selig** *Adj.* all too trusting; ~**voll** 1. *Adj.* trusting *(relationship)*; *(collaboration, co-operation)* based on trust; *(zuversichtlich)* confident; 2. *adv.* trustingly; *(zuversichtlich)* confidently; ~**würdig** *Adj.* trustworthy

**vertraulich** 1. *Adj.* **a)** confidential; **b)** *(freundschaftlich, intim)* familiar *(manner, tone, etc.)*; intimate *(conversation)*; 2. *adv.* **a)** confidentially; **b)** *(freundschaftlich, intim)* in a familiar way; **Vertraulichkeit die**; ~, ~**en a)** *o. Pl.* confidentiality; **b)** *(vertrauliche Information)* confidence; **c)** *o. Pl. (distanzloses Verhalten)* familiarity; *(Intimität)* intimacy; **vertraut** *Adj.* **a)** close *(friend etc.)*; intimate *(circle, conversation, etc.)*; **b)** *(bekannt)* familiar; jmdn./sich mit etw. ~ **machen** familiarize sb./oneself with sth.; **Vertraute der/die**; *adj. Dekl.* close friend

**vertreiben** *unr. tr. V.* **a)** drive out (**aus** of); drive away *(animal, smoke, clouds)* (**aus** from); fight off *(tiredness, troubles)*; **b)** *(verkaufen)* sell

**vertreten** 1. *unr. tr. V.* **a)** stand in *or* deputize for *(colleague etc.)*; *(teacher)* cover for *(colleague)*; **b)** *(eintreten für, repräsentieren)* represent *(person, firm, interests, constituency, country, etc.)*; *(Rechtsw.)* act for *(person, prosecution, etc.)*; ~ **sein** be represented; **c)** *(einstehen für, verfechten)* support *(point of view, principle)*; hold *(opinion)*; advocate *(thesis etc.)*; 2. *unr. refl. V.* **sich** *(Dat.)* **die Füße** *od.* **Beine** ~ *(ugs.)* stretch one's legs; **Vertreter der**; ~**s**, ~ **a)** *(Stell~)* deputy; stand-in; **b)** *(Interessen~, Repräsentant)* representative; *(Handels~)* sales representative; commercial traveller; **c)** *(Verfechter, Anhänger)* supporter; advocate; **Vertretung die**; ~, ~**en** deputy; *(Delegierte[r])* representative; *(Delegation)* delegation; *(Handels~)* [sales] agency; **eine diplomatische** ~: a diplomatic mission

**Vertriebene der/die**; *adj. Dekl.* expellee [from his/her homeland]
**vertrocknen** *itr. V.; mit sein* dry up
**vertrödeln** *tr. V. (ugs. abwertend)* dawdle away, waste *(time)*
**vertrösten** *tr. V.* put *(person)* off (**auf** + *Akk.* until)
**vertun** 1. *unr. tr. V.* waste; 2. *unr. refl. V. (ugs.)* make a slip
**vertuschen** *tr. V.* hush up *(scandal etc.)*; keep *(truth etc.)* secret
**verübeln** *tr. V.* jmdm. **eine Äußerung** *usw.* ~: take sb.'s remark *etc.* amiss
**verüben** *tr. V.* commit *(crime etc.)*
**verunglücken** *itr. V.; mit sein* have an accident; *(car etc.)* be involved in an accident; **mit dem Auto/Flugzeug** ~: be in a car/an air accident *or* crash; **Verunglückte der/die**; *adj. Dekl.* accident victim; casualty
**verunreinigen** *tr. V.* pollute; contaminate *(water, milk, flour, oil)*
**verunsichern** *tr. V.* jmdn. ~: make sb. feel unsure *or* uncertain
**verunstalten** *tr. V.* disfigure
**verursachen** *tr. V.* cause
**verurteilen** *tr. V.* pass sentence on; sentence; *(fig.)* condemn *(behaviour, action)*; jmdn. **zum Tode** ~: sentence *or* condemn sb. to death; **Verurteilte der/die**; *adj. Dekl.* convicted man/woman; **Verurteilung die**; ~, ~**en** sentencing; *(fig.)* condemnation
**vervollkommnen** *tr. V.* perfect
**vervollständigen** *tr. V.* complete
**verwachsen** *Adj.* deformed
**verwählen** *refl. V.* misdial
**verwahren** 1. *tr. V.* keep [safe]; 2. *refl. V.* protest; **verwahrlosen** *itr. V.; mit sein* get in a bad state; *(house, building)* fall into disrepair; *(garden, hedge)* become overgrown; *(person)* let oneself go; **verwahrlost** neglected; overgrown *(hedge, garden)*; dilapidated *(house, building)*; unkempt *(person, appearance, etc.)*; *(in der Kleidung)* ragged *(person)*; **Verwahrlosung die**; ~: *(eines Gebäudes)* dilapidation; *(einer Person)* advancing decrepitude
**verwaisen** *itr. V.* be orphaned
**verwalten** *tr. V.* **a)** administer *(estate, property)*; run *(house)*; hold *(money)* in trust; **b)** *(leiten)* run, manage *(hotel, kindergarten, etc.)*; *(regieren)* administer *(area, colony, etc.)*; govern *(country)*; **Verwalter der**; ~**s**, ~, **Verwalterin die**; ~, ~**nen** administrator; *(eines Amts usw.)* manager; *(ei-*

*nes Nachlasses)* trustee; **Verwạltung die; ~, ~en a)** administration; *(eines Landes)* government; *(eines Amtes)* tenure; *(einer Aufgabe)* performance; **b)** *(Organ)* administration

**verwạndeln 1.** *tr. V.* convert **(in +** *Akk.,* **zu** into); *(völlig verändern)* transform **(in +** *Akk.,* **zu** into); **2.** *refl. V.* **sich in etw.** *(Akk.) od.* **zu etw. ~:** turn *or* change into sth.; *(bei chemischen Vorgängen usw.)* be converted into sth.; **Verwạndlung die; ~, ~en** conversion **(in +** *Akk.,* **zu** into); *(völlige Veränderung, das Sichverwandeln)* transformation **(in +** *Akk.,* **zu** into)

**verwạndt 2.** *Part. v.* verwenden

**verwạndt** *Adj.* related **(mit** to); *(fig.)* similar ⟨*views, ideas, forms*⟩; **Verwạndte der/die;** *adj. Dekl.* relative; relation; **Verwạndtschaft die; ~, ~en a)** relationship **(mit** to); *(fig.)* affinity; **b)** *o. Pl. (Verwandte)* relatives *pl.;* relations *pl.;* **die ganze ~:** all one's relatives; **verwạndtschaftlich** *Adj.* family ⟨*ties, relationships, etc.*⟩

**verwạrnen** *tr. V.* warn, caution **(wegen** for); **Verwạrnung die; ~, ~en** warning; caution

**verwẹchseln** *tr. V.* **a)** |miteinander| **~:** confuse ⟨*two things/people*⟩; **etw. mit etw./jmdn. mit jmdm. ~:** mistake sth. for sth./sb. for sb.; confuse sth. with sth./sb. with sb.; **b)** *(vertauschen)* mix up; **Verwẹchslung die; ~, ~en a)** [case of] confusion; **b)** *(Vertauschung)* mixing up; **eine ~:** a mix-up

**verwegen 1.** *Adj.* daring; *(auch fig.)* audacious; **2.** *adv. (auch fig.)* audaciously; **Verwegenheit die; ~:** daring; *(auch fig.)* audacity

**verwẹhren** *tr. V.* **jmdm. etw. ~:** refuse *or* deny sb. sth.

**Verwẹhung die; ~, ~en** [snow]drift

**verwẹigern** *tr. V.* refuse; **Verwẹigerung die; ~, ~en** refusal

**Verweis der; ~es, ~e a)** reference **(auf +** *Akk.* to); *(Quer~)* cross-reference; **b)** *(Tadel)* reprimand; **verwẹisen** *unr. tr. V.* **a) jmdn./einen Fall** *usw.* **an jmdn./etw. ~** *(auch Rechtsspr.)* refer sb./a case *etc.* to sb./sth.; **b)** *(wegschikken)* **jmdn. von der Schule/aus dem Saal ~:** expel sb. from the school/send sb. out of the room; **einen Spieler vom Platz ~:** send a player off [the field]; **c)** *auch itr. (hinweisen)* |jmdn.| **auf etw.** *(Akk.)* **~:** refer [sb.] to sth.

**verwẹlken** *itr. V.; mit sein* wilt

**verwẹndbar** *Adj.* usable; **Verwẹnd-**

**barkeit die; ~:** usability; **verwẹnden** *unr. od. regelm. tr. V.* **a)** use **(zu, für** for); **b)** *(aufwenden)* spend ⟨*time*⟩ **(auf +** *Akk.* on); **Verwẹndung die; ~, ~en** use

**verwẹrfen** *unr. tr. V.* reject; dismiss ⟨*thought*⟩; **verwẹrflich** *(geh.)* **1.** *Adj.* reprehensible; **2.** *adv.* reprehensibly

**verwẹrtbar** *Adj.* utilizable; usable; **verwẹrten** *tr. V.* utilize, use **(zu** for); make use of ⟨*suggestion, experience, knowledge, etc.*⟩

**verwẹsen** *itr. V.; mit sein* decompose; **Verwẹsung die; ~:** decomposition

**verwịckeln 1.** *refl. V.* get tangled up *or* entangled; **sich in etw.** *(Akk. od. Dat.)* **~:** get caught [up] in sth.; **2.** *tr. V.* involve; **Verwịcklung die; ~, ~en** complication

**verwịldern** *itr. V.* ⟨*garden*⟩ become overgrown; ⟨*domestic animal*⟩ return to the wild

**verwịrklichen 1.** *tr. V.* realize ⟨*dream*⟩; realize, put into practice ⟨*plan, proposal, idea, etc.*⟩; carry out ⟨*project, intention*⟩; **2.** *refl. V.* ⟨*hope, dream*⟩ be realized; **Verwịrklichung die; ~, ~en** realization; *(eines Wunsches, einer Hoffnung)* fulfilment

**verwịrren** *tr. (auch itr.) V.* confuse; verwirrt confused; ~**d** bewildering; **Verwịrrung die; ~, ~en** confusion

**verwịschen** *tr. V.* smudge ⟨*signature, writing, etc.*⟩; smear ⟨*paint*⟩; *(fig.)* cover up ⟨*tracks*⟩

**verwịtwet** *Adj.* widowed

**verwöhnen** *tr. V.* spoil; **verwöhnt** *Adj.* spoilt; *(anspruchsvoll)* discriminating; ⟨*taste, palate*⟩ of a gourmet

**verwọrren** *Adj.* confused, muddled ⟨*ideas, situation, etc.*⟩

**verwụnden** *tr. V.* wound; injure; **Verwụndete der/die;** *adj. Dekl.* casualty; **die ~n** the wounded; **Verwụndung die; ~, ~en** wound

**verwụnschen** *tr. V.* curse

**verwụsten** *tr. V.* devastate; **Verwụstung die; ~, ~en** devastation

**verzählen** *refl. V.* miscount

**verzaubern** *tr. V.* cast a spell on; bewitch; *(fig.)* enchant; **jmdn. in etw.** *(Akk.)* **~:** transform sb. into sth.

**Verzehr der; ~[e]s** consumption; **verzehren** *tr. V.* consume

**Verzeichnis das; ~ses, ~se** list; *(Register)* index

**verzeihen** *unr. tr., itr. V.* forgive; *(entschuldigen)* excuse ⟨*behaviour, re-*

*mark, etc.*⟩; ~ **Sie** |**bitte**|**, können Sie mir sagen ...?** excuse me, could you tell me ...?; **Verzeihung die;** ~: forgiveness; ~**!** sorry!; **jmdn. um ~ bitten** apologize to sb.

**verzerren** 1. *tr. V.* **a)** contort ⟨*face etc.*⟩ (**zu** into); **b)** *(akustisch, optisch)* distort ⟨*sound, image*⟩; **etw. verzerrt darstellen** *(fig.)* present a distorted account *or* picture of sth.

**Verzicht der;** ~|e|s, ~e **a)** renunciation (**auf** + *Akk.* of); **b)** *(auf Reichtum, ein Amt usw.)* relinquishment (**auf** + *Akk.* of); **verzichten** *itr. V.* do without; ~ **auf** (+ *Akk.*) do without; *(sich enthalten)* refrain from; *(aufgeben)* give up ⟨*share, smoking, job, etc.*⟩; renounce ⟨*inheritance*⟩; relinquish ⟨*right, privilege*⟩; *(opfern)* sacrifice ⟨*holiday, salary*⟩

¹**verziehen** 2. *Part. v.* **verzeihen**

²**verziehen** 1. *unr. tr. V.* **a)** screw up ⟨*face, mouth, etc.*⟩; **b)** *(schlecht erziehen)* spoil; 2. *unr. refl. V.* **a)** *(aus der Form geraten)* go out of shape; ⟨*wood*⟩ warp; **b)** *(wegziehen)* ⟨*clouds, storm*⟩ move away, pass over; ⟨*fog, mist*⟩ disperse; **c)** *(ugs.: weggehen)* take oneself off; 3. *unr. itr. V.; mit sein* move [away]; „**Empfänger** |**unbekannt**| **verzogen**" 'no longer at this address'

**verzieren** *tr. V.* decorate; **Verzierung die;** ~, ~**en** decoration

**verzögern** 1. *tr. V.* **a)** delay (**um** by); **b)** *(verlangsamen)* slow down; 2. *refl. V.* be delayed (**um** by); **Verzögerung die;** ~, ~**en** delay (*Gen.* in); *(Verlangsamung)* slowing down

**Verzug der;** ~|e|s delay; **im ~ sein/in ~ kommen** be/fall behind

**verzweifeln** *itr. V.; mit sein* despair; **über etw./jmdn.** ~: despair at sth./of sb.; **verzweifelt** 1. *Adj.* despairing ⟨*person*⟩; desperate ⟨*situation, attempt, effort, struggle, etc*⟩; ~ **sein** be in despair; 2. *adv.* desperately; **Verzweiflung die;** ~ despair

**verzweigen** *refl. V.* branch [out]

**Veteran** [vete'ra:n] **der;** ~**en**, ~**en** *(auch fig.)* veteran

**Vetter der;** ~**s**, ~**n** cousin

**vgl.** *Abk.* vergleiche cf.

**v. H.** *Abk.* vom Hundert per cent

**via** ['vi:a] *Präp.* via

**Viadukt** [vịa'dʊkt] **das** *od.* **der;** ~|e|s, ~**e** viaduct

**vibrieren** [vi'bri:rən] *itr. V.* vibrate

**video-, Video-** ['vi:deo-]: video; **Video das;** ~**s**, ~**s** *(ugs.)* video

**Vieh das;** ~|e|s **a)** *(Nutztiere)* livestock *sing. or pl.*; **b)** *(Rind~)* cattle *pl.*; **Vieh·zucht die;** *o. Pl.* [live]stock/cattle breeding *no art.*

**viel** 1. *Indefinitpron. u. unbest. Zahlw.* **a)** *Sg.* a great deal of; a lot of *(coll.)*; **wie/nicht/zu** ~: how/not/too much; ~|e**s**| *(vielerlei)* much; **der** ~**e Regen** all the rain; **um** ~**es jünger** a great deal younger; **b)** *Pl.* many; **gleich** ~|e| the same number of; **die** ~**en Menschen** all the people; 2. *Adv.* **a)** *(oft, lange)* a great deal; a lot *(coll.)*; **b)** *(wesentlich)* much; a great deal; a lot *(coll.)*; ~ **zu klein** much too small; **vielerlei** in dekl. unbest. Gattungsz. **a)** *attr.* many different; all kinds *or* sorts of; **b)** *subst.* all kinds of things

**viel-, Viel-:** ~**fach** 1. *Adj.* a multiple; **die** ~**fache Menge** many times the amount; **b)** *(vielfältig)* many kinds of; 2. *adv.* many times; ~**falt die;** ~: diversity; ~**fältig** 1. *Adj.* many and diverse; 2. *adv.* in many different ways

**vielleicht** *Adv.* perhaps; maybe

**viel-:** ~**mals** *Adv.* **ich bitte** ~**mals um Entschuldigung** I'm very sorry; **danke** ~**mals** thank you very much; ~**mehr** [*od.* '-'-] *Konj. u. Adv.* rather; ~**sagend** 1. *Adj.* meaningful; 2. *adv.* meaningfully; ~**seitig** *Adj.* versatile ⟨*person*⟩; ~**versprechend** 1. *Adj.* [very] promising; 2. *adv.* [very] promisingly

**vier** *Kardinalz.* four; **Vier die;** ~, ~**en** four; **eine** ~ **schreiben/bekommen** *(Schulw.)* get a D

**vier-, Vier-:** *(s. auch* **acht-, Acht-)** ~**beiner der;** ~**s**, ~ *(ugs.)* four-legged friend; ~**beinig** *Adj.* four-legged ~**eck das** quadrilateral; *(Rechteck)* rectangle; *(Quadrat)* square; ~**eckig** *Adj.* quadrilateral; *(rechteckig)* rectangular; ~**fach** *Vervielfältigungszeichen* fourfold; quadruple; ~**fache das** *adj. Dekl.* **um das** ~**fache:** fourfold by four times the amount; ~**hundert** *Kardinalz.* four hundred

**Vierling der;** ~**s**, ~**e** quadruplet

**vier-, Vier-:** ~**mal** *Adv.* four times ~**spurig** *Adj.* four-lane ⟨*road, motorway*⟩; ~**spurig sein** have four lanes ~**stellig** *Adj.* four-figure *attrib.* ~**sterne·hotel** [-'----] **das** four-star hotel

**viert...** *Ordinalz.* fourth; **vier·tausend** *Kardinalz.* four thousand **viertel** ['fɪrtl] *Bruchz.* quarter; **ein** ~

**Pfund** a quarter of a pound; **Viertel** ['fɪrtl] **das** (*schweiz. meist* **der**); ~s, ~ **a)** quarter; ~ **vor/nach eins** [a] quarter to/ past one; **drei ~:** three-quarters; **b)** (*Stadtteil*) quarter; district

**viertel-, Viertel-:** ~**finale das** (*Sport*) quarter-final; ~**jahr das** three months *pl.*; ~**jährlich 1.** *Adj.* quarterly; **2.** *adv.* quarterly; ~**liter der** quarter of a litre; ~**note die** (*Musik*) crotchet (*Brit.*); quarter note (*Amer.*); ~**pfund das** quarter [of a] pound; ~**stunde die** quarter of an hour; ~**stündig** *Adj.* quarter-of-an-hour; ~**stündlich 1.** *Adj.* every quarter of an hour *postpos.*; **2.** *adv.* every quarter of an hour

**viertens** *Adv.* fourthly; **viertürig** *Adj.* four-door *attrib.*; ~ **sein** have four doors

**Vierwaldstätter See,** (*schweiz.:*) **Vierwaldstättersee der** Lake Lucerne

**vier-** ['fɪr-]: ~**zehn** *Kardinalz.* fourteen; ~**zehn·tägig** *Adj.* two-week; ~**zehn·täglich 1.** *Adj.* fortnightly; **2.** *adv.* fortnightly

**vierzig** ['fɪrtsɪç] *Kardinalz.* forty; *s. auch* **achtzig; vierzigst ...** *Ordinalz.* fortieth; *s. auch* **acht ...**

**Vikar der;** ~s, ~e **a)** (*kath. Kirche*) locum tenens; **b)** (*ev. Kirche*) ≈ [trainee] curate

**Villa** ['vɪla] **die;** ~, **Villen** villa; **Villen·viertel das** exclusive residential district

**violett** [vi̯o'lɛt] purple; violet; **Violett das;** ~s, ~e *od. ugs.* ~s purple; violet; (*im Spektrum*) violet

**Violine** [vi̯o'liːnə] **die;** ~, ~**n** (*Musik*) violin

**Viper** ['viːpɐ] **die;** ~, ~**n** viper; adder

**Viren** *s.* **Virus**

**Virtuose** [vɪr'tu̯oːzə] **der;** ~**n**, ~**n** virtuoso; **Virtuosität die;** ~: virtuosity

**Virus** ['viːrʊs] **das;** ~, **Viren** virus

**Visa** *s.* **Visum; Visen** *s.* **Visum**

**Visier** [vi'ziːɐ] **das;** ~s, ~e (*am Helm*) visor; (*an der Waffe*) backsight

**Vision** [vi'zi̯oːn] **die;** ~, ~**en** vision

**Visite** [vi'ziːtə] **die;** ~, ~**n** round; ~ **machen** do one's round; **Visiten·karte die** visiting-card

**Visum** ['viːzʊm] **das;** ~s, **Visa** *od.* **Visen** visa

**Vitamin** [vita'miːn] **das;** ~s, ~e vitamin

**vitamin-, Vitamin-:** ~**arm** *Adj.* low in vitamins *postpos.*; ~**mangel der;**

*o. Pl.* vitamin deficiency; ~**reich** *Adj.* rich in vitamins *postpos.*

**Vitrine** [vi'triːnə] **die;** ~, ~**n** display case; (*Möbel*) display cabinet

**Vize-** vice-

**Vogel der;** ~s, **Vögel** bird; **einen ~ haben** (*salopp*) be off one's rocker (*sl.*)

**Vogel-:** ~**käfig der** birdcage; ~**nest das** bird's nest; ~**perspektive die** bird's eye view; ~**scheuche die;** ~, ~**n** scarecrow

**Vokabel** [vo'kaːbl] **die;** ~, ~**n** word; ~**n** vocabulary *sing.*

**Vokal** [vo'kaːl] **der;** ~s, ~e (*Sprachw.*) vowel

**Volk das;** ~[e]s, **Völker** people

**volks-, Volks-:** ~**abstimmung die** plebiscite; ~**eigen** *Adj.* (*ehem. DDR*) publicly *or* nationally owned; ~**entscheid der** (*Politik*) referendum; ~**fest das** public festival; (*Jahrmarkt*) fair; ~**hochschule die** adult education centre; ~**kunde die** folklore; ~**lied das** folk-song; ~**musik die** folk-music; ~**polizei die;** *o. Pl.* (*ehem. DDR*) People's Police; ~**republik die** People's Republic; ~**stamm der** tribe; ~**tanz der** folkdance; ~**tracht die** traditional costume; (*eines Landes*) national costume

**volkstümlich 1.** *Adj.* popular; **2.** *adv.* ~ **schreiben** write in terms readily comprehensible to the layman; **Volks·wirtschaft die** national economy; (*Fach*) economics *sing., no art.*; **volks·wirtschaftlich 1.** *Adj.* economic; **2.** *adv.* economically

**voll 1.** *Adj.* full; ample ⟨*bosom*⟩; (*salopp:* betrunken) plastered (*sl.*); ~ **von** *od.* **mit etw. sein** be full of sth.; **jmdn. nicht für ~ nehmen** not take sb. seriously; **2.** *adv.* fully; ~ **und ganz** completely; **voll·auf** ['--'] *Adv.* completely; **vollaufen** *unr. itr. V., trennbar* fill up; **etw. ~ lassen** fill sth. [up]

**voll-, Voll-:** ~**automatisch 1.** *Adj.* fully automatic; **2.** *adv.* fully automatically; ~**bad das** bath; ~**bart der** full beard; ~**bringen** [-'--] *unr. tr. V.* (*geh.*) accomplish; achieve

**voll·enden** *tr. V.* complete; **vollendet 1.** *Adj.* accomplished ⟨*performance*⟩; perfect ⟨*gentleman, host, manners, reproduction*⟩; **2.** *adv.* ⟨*play*⟩ in an accomplished manner; **vollends** *Adv.* completely; **Voll·endung die** completion; **voller** *indekl. Adj.* full of; ~ **Flecken** covered with stains

**Volley·ball** ['vɔlibal] **der** volleyball
**voll-, Voll-:** ~**führen** [-'--] *tr. V.* perform; ~|**füllen** *tr. V.* fill up; ~**gas das**; *o. Pl.* ~**gas geben** put one's foot down; **mit** ~**gas** at full throttle; ~|**gießen** *unr. tr. V.* fill [up]
**völlig 1.** *Adj.* complete; total; **2.** *adv.* completely; totally; **du hast** ~ **recht** you are absolutely right
**voll-, Voll-:** ~**jährig** *Adj.* of age *pred.*; ~**jährig werden** come of age; ~**jährigkeit die**; ~: majority *no art.*; ~**kasko·versicherung die** fully comprehensive insurance
**voll·kommen 1.** *Adj.* **a)** [-'-- *od.* '---] *(vollendet)* perfect; **b)** ['---] *(vollständig)* complete; total; **2.** ['---] *adv.* completely; totally
**voll-, Voll-:** ~**korn·brot das** wholemeal *(Brit.)* or *(Amer.)* wholewheat bread; ~|**laufen** *s.* vollaufen; ~|**machen** *tr. V.* fill up; [sich *(Dat.)*] **die Hosen/Windeln** ~**machen** *(ugs.)* mess one's pants/nappy; ~**macht die; ~, ~en a)** authority; **b)** *(Urkunde)* power of attorney; ~**milch die** full-cream milk; ~**milch·schokolade die** full-cream milk chocolate; ~**mond der**; *o. Pl.* full moon; ~**pension die**; *meist o. Art.*; *o. Pl.* full board *no art.*; ~**ständig 1.** *Adj.* complete; full ⟨*text, address, etc.*⟩; **2.** *adv.* completely; ⟨*list*⟩ in full; ~**ständigkeit die; ~:** completeness; ~**strecken** [-'--] *tr. V.* enforce ⟨*penalty, fine, law*⟩; carry out ⟨*sentence*⟩ (**an** + *Dat.* on); ~|**tanken** *tr. (auch itr.) V.* fill up; **bitte** ~**tanken** fill it up, please; ~**treffer der** direct hit; **ein** ~**treffer sein** *(fig.)* hit the bull's eye; ~**zählig** *Adj.* complete
**voll·ziehen** *unr. tr. V.* carry out (**an** + *Dat.* on); execute, carry out ⟨*order*⟩; perform ⟨*sacrifice, ceremony, sexual intercourse*⟩; **Voll·zug der** *s.* **vollziehen:** carrying out; execution; performance
**Volt** [vɔlt] **das**; ~ *od.* ~|**e|s,** ~: *(Physik, Elektrot.)* volt
**Volumen** [vo'luːmən] **das**; ~s, ~: volume
**vom** *Präp.* + *Art.* **a)** = **von dem; b)** *(räumlich)* from the; **links/rechts** ~ **Eingang** to the left/right of the entrance; ~ **Stuhl aufspringen** jump up out of one's chair; **c)** *(zeitlich)* ~ **Morgen bis zum Abend** from morning till night; ~ **ersten Januar an** [as] from the first of January; **d)** *(zur Angabe der Ursache)* **das kommt** ~ **Rauchen/Alko-**

hol that comes from smoking/drinking alcohol; **jmdn.** ~ **Sehen kennen** know sb. by sight; **von** *Präp. mit Dat.* **a)** *(räumlich)* from; **nördlich/südlich** ~ **Mannheim** to the north/south of Mannheim; **rechts/links** ~ **mir** on my right/left; ~ **hier an** *od. (ugs.)* **ab** from here on[ward]; ~ **Mannheim aus** from Mannheim; **b)** *(zeitlich)* from; ~**jetzt an** *od. (ugs.)* **ab** from now on; ~ **heute/morgen an** [as] from today/tomorrow; starting today/tomorrow; **in der Nacht** ~ **Freitag auf** *od.* **zu Samstag** during Friday night; **das Brot ist** ~ **gestern** it's yesterday's bread; **c)** *(anstelle eines Genitivs)* of; **acht** ~ **hundert/zehn** eight out of a hundred/ten; **d)** *(zur Angabe des Urhebers, der Ursache, beim Passiv)* by; **der Roman ist** ~ **Fontane** the novel is by Fontane; **müde** ~ **der Arbeit sein** be tired from work[ing]; **sie hat ein Kind** ~ **ihm** she has a child by him; **e)** *(zur Angabe von Eigenschaften)* of; **eine Fahrt** ~ **drei Stunden** a three-hour drive; **von·einander** *Adv.* from each other *or* one another; **vonstatten** *Adv.* ~ **gehen** proceed
**vor 1.** *Präp. mit Dat.* **a)** *(räumlich)* in front of; *(weiter vorn)* ahead of; in front of; *(nicht ganz so weit wie)* before; *(außerhalb)* outside; **kurz** ~ **der Abzweigung** just before the turn-off; ~ **der Stadt** outside the town; **etw.** ~ **sich haben** *(fig.)* have sth. before one; **das liegt noch** ~ **mir** *(fig.)* I still have that to come *or* have that ahead of me; **b)** *(zeitlich)* before; **es ist fünf [Minuten]** ~ **sieben** it is five [minutes] to seven; **c)** *(bei Reihenfolge, Rangordnung)* before; **knapp** ~ **jmdm. siegen** win just ahead *or* in front of sb.; **d)** *(auf Grund von)* with; ~ **Freude strahlen** beam with joy; ~ **Hunger/Durst umkommen** *(ugs.)* die of hunger/thirst; **e)** ~ **fünf Minuten/10 Jahren/Wochen** *usw.* five minutes/ten years/weeks ago; **heute** ~ **einer Woche** a week ago today; **2.** *Präp. mit Akk.* in front of; ~ **sich hin** to oneself
**Vor·abend der** evening before; *(fig.)* eve
**vor·an** *Adv.* forward[s] ahead; first
**voran-:** ~|**gehen** *unr. itr. V.; mit sein* **a)** go first; **b)** *(Fortschritte machen)* make progress; ~|**kommen** *unr. itr. V.; mit sein* **a)** make headway; **b)** *(Fortschritte machen)* make progress
**Vor·arbeiter der** foreman
**vor·aus 1.** [-'-] *Präp. mit Dat., nachge-*

*stellt* in front; **jmdm./seiner Zeit ~ sein** *(fig.)* be ahead of sb./one's time; **2.** *Adv.* **im ~** ['--] in advance

**voraus-, Vor<u>au</u>s-**: **~|gehen** *unr. itr. V.; mit sein* **a)** go [on] ahead; **b)** *(zeitlich)* **einem Ereignis ~gehen** precede an event; **~sage die** *s.* **Vorhersage; ~|sagen** *tr. V.* predict; **~|sehen** *unr. tr. V.* foresee; **~|setzen** *tr. V.* **a)** *(als gegeben ansehen)* assume; **~gesetzt, [daß]** ...: provided [that] ...; **b)** *(erfordern)* require ⟨*skill, experience, etc.*⟩; presuppose ⟨*good organization, planning, etc.*⟩; **~setzung die; ~, ~en a)** *(Annahme)* assumption; *(Prämisse)* premiss; **b)** *(Vorbedingung)* prerequisite; **unter der ~setzung, daß** ...: on condition *or* on the pre-condition that ...; **~sichtlich 1.** *Adj.* anticipated; **2.** *adv.* probably

**V<u>o</u>r·bau der;** *Pl.* **~ten** porch

**Vorbehalt der; ~[e]s, ~e** reservation; **unter dem ~, daß** ...: with the reservation that ...; **vor|behalten** *unr. tr. V.* **sich** *(Dat.)* **etw. ~**: reserve oneself sth.; „Änderungen ~" 'subject to alterations'

**vor·b<u>ei</u> Adv. a)** *(räumlich)* past; by; **an etw.** *(Dat.)* **~**: past sth.; **b)** *(zeitlich)* past; over; *(beendet)* finished; over; **es ist acht Uhr ~** *(ugs.)* it is past *or* gone eight o'clock

**vorb<u>ei</u>-**: **~|fahren 1.** *unr. itr. V.; mit sein* **a)** drive/ride past; pass; **an jmdm. ~fahren** drive/ride past *or* pass sb.; **b)** *(ugs.: einen kurzen Besuch machen)* **[bei jmdm./der Post] ~fahren** drop in *(coll.)* [at sb.'s/at the post office]; **~|gehen** *unr. itr. V.; mit sein* **a)** pass; go past; **an jmdm. ~gehen** pass *or* go past sb./sth.; **der Schuß ist ~gegangen** the shot missed; **b)** *(ugs.: einen kurzen Besuch machen)* **[bei jmdm./der Post] ~gehen** drop in *(coll.)* [at sb.'s/at the post office]; **c)** *(vergehen)* pass; **~|kommen** *unr. itr. V.; mit sein* pass; **an etw.** *(Dat.)* **~kommen** pass sth.; **~|reden** *itr. V.* **an etw.** *(Dat.)* **~reden** talk round sth. without getting to the point; **aneinander ~reden** talk at cross purposes; **~|schießen** *unr. itr. V.* miss

**vor|bereiten** *tr. V.* prepare; **jmdn./sich auf** *od.* **für etw. ~**: prepare sb./oneself for sth.; **Vor·bereitung die; ~, ~en** preparation; **~en [für etw.] treffen** make preparations for sth.

**vor|bestellen** *tr. V.* order in advance; **Vor·bestellung die** advance order

**vor·bestraft** *Adj.* with a previous conviction/previous convictions *postpos., not pred.*

**vor|beugen 1.** *tr. V.* bend ⟨*head, upper body*⟩ forward; **sich ~**: lean forward; **2.** *itr. V.* **einer Sache** *(Dat.)* *od.* **gegen etw. ~**: prevent sth.; **Vor·beugung die** prevention **(gegen** of); **zur ~**: as a preventive

**Vor·bild das** model; **jmdm. ein gutes ~ sein** be a good example to sb.; **vor·bildlich 1.** *Adj.* exemplary; **2.** *adv.* in an exemplary way

**vor|bringen** *unr. tr. V.* say; **eine Forderung/ein Anliegen ~**: make a demand/express a desire; **Argumente ~**: present arguments

**vor·christlich** *Adj.* pre-Christian

**vor|datieren** *tr. V.* postdate

**vorder...** *Adj.* front; **der Vordere Orient** the Middle East

**Vorder-**: **~grund der** foreground; **im ~grund stehen** *(fig.)* be prominent *or* to the fore; **~mann der;** *Pl.* **~männer** person in front; **jmdn. auf ~mann bringen** *(ugs.)* lick sb. into shape

**vor|drängen** *refl. V.* push [one's way] forward *or* to the front; *(fig.)* push oneself forward

**vor|dringen** *unr. itr. V.; mit sein* push forward; advance

**vor·dringlich 1.** *Adj.* **a)** priority *attrib.* ⟨*treatment*⟩; **b)** *(dringlich)* urgent; **2.** *adv.* **a)** as a matter of priority; **b)** *(dringlich)* as a matter of urgency

**Vor·druck der;** *Pl.* **V<u>o</u>rdrucke** form

**vor·eilig 1.** *Adj.* rash; **2.** *adv.* rashly

**vor·ein<u>a</u>nder** *Adv.* **a)** one in front of the other; **b)** *(einer dem anderen gegenüber)* opposite each other; face to face; **c) Angst ~ haben** be afraid of each other

**vor·eingenommen** *Adj.* prejudiced; biased; **für/gegen jmdn. ~ sein** be prejudiced in sb.'s favour/against sb.

**vorenthalten[1]** *unr. tr. V.* **jmdm. etw. ~**: withhold sth. from sb.

**vor·erst** [*od.* '-'-] *Adv.* for the present

**Vorfahr der; ~en, ~en** forefather; **vor|fahren** *unr. itr. V.; mit sein* **a)** *(ankommen)* drive/ride up; **b)** *(weiter nach vorn fahren)* ⟨*person*⟩ drive *or* move forward; ⟨*car*⟩ move forward; **c)** *(vorausfahren)* drive *or* go on ahead; **Vor·fahrt die;** *o. Pl.* right of way; „~ beachten/gewähren" 'give way'

---

[1] *ich enthalte vor (od. seltener: vorenthalte), vorenthalten, vorzuenthalten*

**Vorfahrt[s]-:** ~**schild** das right-of-way sign; ~**straße** die main road

**Vor·fall** der incident; occurrence; **vor|fallen** *unr. itr. V.; mit sein* a) *(sich ereignen)* happen; occur; b) *(nach vorn fallen)* fall forward

**vor|finden** *unr. tr. V.* find

**Vor·freude** die anticipation

**vor|führen** *tr. V.* show ⟨*film, slides, etc.*⟩; present ⟨*circus act, programme*⟩; perform ⟨*play, trick, routine*⟩; *(demonstrieren)* demonstrate; **jmdn. dem Richter** ~: bring sb. before the judge; **Vor·führung** die show; *(eines Theaterstücks)* performance

**Vor·gang** der occurrence; *(Amtsspr.)* file; **Vorgänger** der; ~**s**, ~, **Vorgängerin** die; ~, ~**nen** predecessor

**Vor·garten** der front garden

**vor|geben** *unr. tr. V.* pretend

**Vor·gebirge** das promontory

**vor·gefaßt** *Adj.* preconceived

**vor|gehen** *unr. itr. V.; mit sein* a) *(ugs.: nach vorn gehen)* go forward; b) *(vorausgehen)* go on ahead; **jmdn.** ~ **lassen** let sb. go first; c) ⟨*clock*⟩ be fast; d) *(einschreiten)* **gegen jmdn./etw.** ~: take action against sb./sth.; e) *(verfahren)* proceed; f) *(sich abspielen)* happen; go on; g) *(Vorrang haben)* have priority; come first

**Vor·geschmack** der; *o. Pl.* foretaste

**Vor·gesetzte** der/die; *adj. Dekl.* superior

**vor·gestern** *Adv.* the day before yesterday

**vor|greifen** *unr. itr. V.* **jmdn.** ~: anticipate sb. *or* jump in ahead of sb.

**vor|haben** *unr. tr. V.* intend; *(geplant haben)* plan; **Vor·haben** das; ~**s**, ~: plan; *(Projekt)* project

**Vor·halle** die entrance hall; *(eines Theaters, Hotels)* foyer

**vor|halten** *unr. tr. V.* a) hold up; **mit vorgehaltener Schußwaffe** at gunpoint; b) *(zum Vorwurf machen)* **jmdm. etw.** ~: reproach sb. for sth.; **Vorhaltungen** *Pl.* **jmdm. [wegen etw.]** ~ **machen** reproach sb. [for sth.]

**vorhanden** *Adj.* existing; *(verfügbar)* available; ~ **sein** exist *or* be in existence/be available

**Vor·hang** der *(auch Theater)* curtain; **Vorhänge·schloß** das padlock

**Vor·haut** die foreskin

**vor·her** [*od.* -'-] *Adv.* beforehand; *(davor)* before; **vorher|gehen** *unr. itr. V.; mit sein* **in den** ~**den Wochen** in the preceding weeks

**Vor·herrschaft** die supremacy; **vorherrschen** *itr. V.* predominate

**vorher-, Vorher-:** ~**sage** die prediction; *(des Wetters)* forecast; ~|**sagen** *tr. V.* predict; forecast ⟨*weather*⟩; ~|**sehen** *unr. tr. V. s.* voraussehen

**vor·hin** [*od.* -'-] *Adv.* a short time *or* while ago

**vorig...** *Adj.* last

**Vor·jahr** das previous year; **vor·jährig** *Adj.* of the previous year

**Vor·kämpfer** der pioneer

**Vorkehrungen** *Pl.* precautions

**Vor·kenntnis** die background knowledge

**vor|kommen** *unr. itr. V.; mit sein* a) *(sich ereignen)* happen; b) *(vorhanden sein)* occur; c) *(erscheinen)* seem; **das Lied kommt mir bekannt vor** I seem to know the song; **Vorkommnis** das; ~**ses**, ~**se** incident; occurrence

**vor|laden** *unr. tr. V.* summon; **Vorladung** die summons

**Vor·lage** die a) *o. Pl.; s.* vorlegen: presentation; showing; production; submission; tabling; b) *(Entwurf)* draft; c) *(Muster)* pattern; *(Modell)* model

**Vor·läufer** der precursor; forerunner; **vor·läufig** 1. *Adj.* temporary; provisional; interim ⟨*order, agreement*⟩; 2. *adv.* for the time being

**vor·laut** 1. *Adj.* forward; 2. *adv.* forwardly

**vor|legen** *tr. V.* present; show; produce ⟨*certificate, identity card, etc.*⟩; show ⟨*sample*⟩; submit ⟨*evidence*⟩; table ⟨*parliamentary bill*⟩

**vor|lesen** *unr. tr., itr. V.* read aloud *or* out; read ⟨*story, poem, etc.*⟩ aloud; **jmdm. [etw.]** ~: read [sth.] to sb.; **Vor·lesung** die lecture; *(~sreihe)* series *or* course of lectures

**vor·letzt...** *Adj.* last but one; penultimate ⟨*page, episode, etc.*⟩

**Vor·liebe** die preference; **vorlieb|nehmen** *unr. itr. V.* **mit jmdm./ etw.** ~: put up with sb./sth.; *(sich begnügen)* make do with sb./sth.

**vor|liegen** *unr. itr. V.* **jmdm.** ~: be with sb.; **die Ergebnisse liegen uns noch nicht vor** we do not have the results yet; **im** ~**den Fall** in the present case

**vorm** *Präp. + Art.* a) = **vor dem**; b) *(räumlich)* in front of the; c) *(zeitlich, bei Reihenfolge)* before the

**vor|machen** *tr. V.* *(ugs.)* **jmdm. etw.** ~: show sb. sth.; *(vortäuschen)* kid *(coll.)* *or* fool sb.

**vormalig** *Adj.* former; **vormals** *Adv.* formerly

**Vor·marsch** der *(auch fig.)* advance

**vor|merken** *tr. V.* make a note of; **ich habe Sie für den Kurs vorgemerkt** I've put you down for the course

**vor·mittag** *Adv.* **heute/morgen/Freitag ~:** this/tomorrow/Friday morning; **Vor·mittag** der morning; **vormittags** *Adv.* in the morning

**Vor·mund** der; *Pl.* **Vormunde** *od.* **Vormünder** guardian

**vorn[e]** *Adv.* at the front; **nach ~:** to the front; **von ~:** from the front; **noch einmal von ~ anfangen** start afresh; **von ~ bis hinten** *(ugs.)* from beginning to end

**vornehm** 1. *Adj. (nobel; adelig)* noble; *(kultiviert)* distinguished; *(elegant)* exclusive *(district, hotel, restaurant, resort)*; elegant *(villa, clothes)*; 2. *adv.* nobly; *(elegant)* elegantly

**vor|nehmen** *unr. refl. V.* **sich** *(Dat.)* **etw. ~:** plan sth.; **sich** *(Dat.)* **~, mit dem Rauchen aufzuhören** resolve to give up smoking

**vorn-:** ~**herein** *in* **von ~herein** from the outset; ~**über** *Adv.* forwards

**Vor·ort** der suburb

**Vor·rang** der; *o. Pl.* **a)** priority (vor + *Dat.* over); **b)** *(bes. österr.: Vorfahrt)* right of way

**Vor·rat** der supply, stock (**an** + *Dat.* of); **vorrätig** *Adj.* in stock *postpos.*

**Vor·recht** das privilege

**Vor·richtung** die device

**vor|rücken** 1. *tr. V.* move forward; advance *(chess piece)*; 2. *itr. V.; mit sein* move forward; **auf den 5. Platz ~:** move up to fifth place

**Vor·ruhestand** der early retirement

**vors** *Präp.* + *Art.* = **vor das**

**vor|sagen** *tr. V.* **a)** *auch itr.* jmdm. [**die Antwort**] **~:** tell sb. the answer; *(flüsternd)* whisper the answer to sb.; **b)** *(aufsagen)* recite

**Vor·saison** die start of the season; early [part of the] season

**Vor·satz** der intention; **vorsätzlich** 1. *Adj.* intentional; wilful *(murder, arson, etc.)*; 2. *adv.* intentionally

**Vor·schau** die preview

**Vor·schein** der: **zum ~ kommen** appear; *(entdeckt werden)* come to light

**vor|schieben** *unr. tr. V.* **a)** push *(bolt)* across; **b)** *(nach vorn schieben)* push forward

**vor|schießen** *unr. tr. V.* jmdm. **Geld ~:** advance sb. money

**Vorschlag** der suggestion; proposal; **vor|schlagen** *unr. tr. V.* jmdm. etw. **~:** suggest *or* propose sth. [to sb.]

**vor·schreiben** *unr. tr. V.* stipulate, set *(conditions)*; lay down *(rules)*; prescribe *(dose)*; **Vor·schrift** die instruction; order; *(gesetzliche od. amtliche Bestimmung)* regulation; **vorschrifts·mäßig** 1. *Adj.* correct; proper; 2. *adv.* correctly; properly

**Vor·schuß** der advance

**vor|sehen** 1. *unr. tr. V.* **a)** plan; etw. **für/als etw. ~:** intend sth. for/as sth.; **b)** *(law, plan, contract, etc.)* provide for; 2. *unr. refl. V.* **sich** [**vor** jmdm./etw.] **~:** be careful [of sb./sth.]

**vor|setzen** *tr. V.* jmdm. etw. **~:** serve sb. sth.; *(fig.)* serve *or* dish sb. up sth.

**Vor·sicht** die; *o. Pl.* care; *(bei Risiko, Gefahr)* caution; care; **zur ~:** as a precaution; **~! be careful!**; „**~, Stufe!**" 'mind the step!'; **vorsichtig** 1. *Adj.* careful; *(bei Risiko, Gefahr)* cautious; **sei ~! be careful!; take care!**; 2. *adv.* carefully; with care; **vorsichts·halber** *Adv.* as a precaution; to be on the safe side; **Vorsichts·maßnahme** die precautionary measure; precaution

**Vor·silbe** die [monosyllabic] prefix

**vor|singen** *unr. tr. V.* jmdm.] etw. **~:** sing sth. [to sb.]

**Vor·sitz** der chairmanship; **Vorsitzende** der/die; *adj. Dekl.* chair[person]; *(bes. Mann)* chairman; *(Frau auch)* chairwoman

**Vor·sorge** die; *o. Pl.* precautions *pl.*; *(für den Todesfall, Krankheit, Alter)* provisions *pl.*; **vor|sorgen** *itr. V.* **für etw. ~:** make provisions for sth.; provide for sth.; **Vorsorge·untersuchung** die *(Med.)* medical check-up; **vorsorglich** *adv.* as a precaution

**Vor·spann** der *(Film, Ferns.)* opening credits *pl.*

**Vor·speise** die starter; hors d'œuvre

**Vor·spiel** das *(Theater)* prologue; *(Musik)* prelude; **vor|spielen** *tr. V.* **a)** play *(piece of music)* (*Dat.* to, for); act out, perform *(scene)* (*Dat.* for, in front of) **b)** *(vorspiegeln)* jmdm. etw. **~:** feign sth. to sb.

**vor|sprechen** 1. *unr. tr. V.* **a)** *(zum Nachsprechen)* jmdm. etw. **~:** pronounce *or* say sth. first for sb.; **b)** *(zur Prüfung)* recite; 2. *unr. itr. V.* audition

**Vor·sprung** der lead (vor + *Dat.* over)

**Vor·stadt** die suburb

**Vor·stand** der *(einer Firma)* board [of directors]; *(eines Vereins, einer Gesellschaft)* executive committee; *(einer Partei)* executive

**vor|stehen** *unr. itr. V.* a) project, jut out; ⟨*teeth, chin*⟩ stick out; **~de Zähne** buck-teeth; projecting teeth; b) *(geh.: leiten)* **einer Institution ~:** be the head of an institution

**vor|stellen** 1. *tr. V.* **jmdn./sich jmdm. ~:** introduce sb./oneself to sb.; *(bei Bewerbung)* **sich ~:** come/go for [an] interview; **die Uhr |um eine Stunde| ~:** put the clock forward [one hour]; 2. *refl. V.* **sich** *(Dat.)* **etw. ~:** imagine sth.; **Vor·stellung die** a) *(Begriff)* idea; b) *o. Pl. (Phantasie)* imagination; c) *(Aufführung)* performance; *(im Kino)* showing

**Vor·stoß** der advance; **vor|stoßen** *unr. itr. V.; mit sein* advance; push forward

**Vor·strafe die** previous conviction

**vor|strecken** *tr. V.* stretch ⟨*arm, hand*⟩ out; advance ⟨*money, sum*⟩

**Vor·tag** der day before

**vor|täuschen** *tr. V.* feign; simulate ⟨*reality etc.*⟩; fake ⟨*crime*⟩

**Vor·teil** [*od.* 'fɔrtail] der advantage; **vorteilhaft** 1. *Adj.* advantageous; 2. *adv.* advantageously

**Vortrag der;** ~|e|s, **Vorträge** talk; *(wissenschaftlich)* lecture; **einen ~ halten** give a talk/lecture; **vor|tragen** *unr. tr. V.* a) sing ⟨*song*⟩; perform, play ⟨*piece of music*⟩; recite ⟨*poem*⟩; b) *(darlegen)* present ⟨*case, matter, request, demands*⟩; lodge, make ⟨*complaint*⟩; express ⟨*wish, desire*⟩

**vor·trefflich** 1. *Adj.* excellent; 2. *adv.* excellently

**vorüber** *Adv.* over; *(räumlich)* past; **vorüber|gehen** *unr. itr. V.; mit sein* a) go *or* walk past; pass by; **an jmdm./ etw. ~:** go past sb./sth.; pass sb./sth.; *(achtlos)* pass sb./sth. by; b) *(vergehen)* pass; ⟨*pain*⟩ go; **vorübergehend** 1. *Adj.* temporary; passing ⟨*interest, infatuation*⟩; brief ⟨*illness, stay*⟩; 2. *adv.* temporarily; *(für kurze Zeit)* for a short time; briefly

**Vor·urteil das** bias; *(voreilige Schlußfolgerung)* prejudice

**Vor·vergangenheit die** *(Sprachw.)* pluperfect

**Vor·verkauf** der advance sale of tickets

**vor|verlegen** *tr. V. (zeitlich)* bring forward *(auf + Akk.* to; *um by)*

**Vorwahl die, Vorwähl·nummer die** *(Fernspr.)* dialling code

**Vorwand** der; ~|e|s, **Vorwände** pretext; *(Ausrede)* excuse

**vor·wärts** *Adv.* forwards; *(weiter)* onwards; **vorwärts|kommen** *unr. itr. V.; mit sein* make progress; *(im Beruf, Leben)* get on; get ahead

**vor·weg** *Adv.* beforehand; **vor·weg|nehmen** *unr. tr. V.* anticipate

**vor|weisen** *unr. tr. V.* produce

**vor|werfen** *unr. tr. V.* **jmdm. etw. ~:** reproach sb. with sth.; *(beschuldigen)* accuse sb. of sth.

**vor·wiegend** *Adv.* mainly

**vor·witzig** *Adj.* bumptious; pert ⟨*child*⟩

**Vor·wort das;** *Pl.* ~e foreword

**Vor·wurf** der reproach; *(Beschuldigung)* accusation; **vorwurfs·voll** 1. *Adj.* reproachful; 2. *adv.* reproachfully

**Vor·zeichen das** a) *(Omen)* omen; b) *(Math.)* [algebraic] sign

**vor|zeigen** *tr. V.* produce; show

**Vor·zeit die** prehistory; **vorzeitig** 1. *Adj.* premature; early ⟨*retirement*⟩; 2. *adv.* prematurely

**vor|ziehen** *unr. tr. V.* prefer

**Vor·zimmer das** outer office

**Vor·zug der** a) *o. Pl.* preference (gegenüber over); b) *(gute Eigenschaft)* good quality; merit; **vorzüglich** 1. *Adj.* excellent; first-rate; 2. *adv.* excellently

**vulgär** 1. *Adj.* vulgar; 2. *adv.* in a vulgar way

**Vulkan** [vʊlˈkaːn] der; ~s, ~e volcano; **vulkanisch** *Adj.* volcanic; **vulkanisieren** *tr. V.* vulcanize

**v. u. Z.** *Abk.* vor unserer Zeit|rechnung| BC

# W

**w, W** [veː] das; ~s, ~: w, W

**W** *Abk.* a) West, Westen W.; b) Watt W.

**Waage die;** ~, ~n [pair *sing.* of] scales *pl.;* **waage·recht** 1. *Adj.* horizontal;

**2.** *adv.* horizontally; **Waage·rechte** die horizontal; **Waag·schale** die scale pan
**Wabe** die; ~, ~n honeycomb
**wach 1.** *Adj.* awake; **2.** *adv.* alertly; attentively; **Wache** die; ~, ~n **a)** *(Militt.)* guard *or* sentry duty; *(Seew.)* watch [duty]; **b)** *(Wächter, Milit.)* guard; *(Seew.)* watch; **c)** *(Polizei~)* police station; **wachen** *itr. V. (geh.)* be awake; **bei** jmdm. ~: stay up at sb.'s bedside; sit up with sb.; **Wachhund** der guard-dog
**Wacholder** der; ~s, ~: juniper
**Wach·posten** der *(Milit.)* guard
**Wachs** das; ~es, ~e wax
**wachsam** *Adj.* watchful; vigilant
**¹wachsen** *unr. itr. V.; mit sein* grow
**²wachsen** *tr. V.* wax
**Wachs-:** ~figur die waxwork; ~figuren·kabinett das waxworks *sing. or pl.;* waxworks museum
**wächst** *2. u. 3. Pers. Sg. Präsens v.* wachsen; **Wachstum** das; ~s growth
**Wachtel** die; ~, ~n quail
**Wächter** der; ~s, ~: guard; *(Nacht~, Turm~)* watchman; *(Park~)* [park-] keeper; **Wach[t]·turm** der the watchtower
**wackelig** *Adj.* **a)** wobbly ⟨chair, table, etc.⟩; loose ⟨tooth⟩; **b)** *(ugs.: kraftlos, schwach)* frail; **Wackel·kontakt** der *(Elektrot.)* loose connection; **wackeln** *itr. V.* wobble; ⟨tooth etc.⟩ be loose; ⟨house, window, etc.⟩ shake; **mit dem Kopf/den Ohren** ~: waggle one's head/ears
**wacker** *(veralt.)* **1.** *Adj.* upright; **2.** *adv.* valiantly; **sich** ~ **halten** put up a good show
**Wade** die; ~, ~n *(Anat.)* calf; **Waden·krampf** der cramp in one's calf
**Waffe** die; ~, ~n weapon
**Waffel** die; ~, ~n waffle; *(dünne ~, Eis~)* wafer; *(Eistüte)* cone
**Waffen-:** ~gewalt die; *o. Pl.* **mit** ~gewalt by force of arms; ~handel der arms trade; ~händler der arms dealer; ~schein der firearms licence; ~stillstand der armistice
**Wage·mut** der daring; **wage·mutig** *Adj.* daring; **wagen 1.** *tr. V.* risk; [es] ~, etw. **zu tun** dare to do sth.; **2.** *refl. V.* **sich irgendwohin/nicht irgendwohin** ~: venture somewhere/not dare to go somewhere
**Wagen** der; ~s, ~: *(PKW)* car; *(Pferde~)* cart; *(Eisenbahn~) (Personen~)* coach; *(Güter~)* truck; *(Straßen*

*bahn~)* car; *(Kinder~, Puppen~)* pram *(Brit.);* baby carriage *(Amer.); (Sport~)* push-chair *(Brit.);* stroller *(Amer.);* **Wagen·heber** der jack; **Waggon** [va'gon, *südd., österr.:* va'go:n] der; ~s, ~s, *südd., österr.:* ~s, ~e wagon; truck *(Brit.);* car *(Amer.)*
**waghalsig 1.** *Adj.* daring; *(leichtsinnig)* reckless; **2.** *adv.* daringly; ⟨*speculate*⟩ riskily; *(leichtsinnig)* recklessly; **Wagnis** das; ~ses, ~se daring exploit *or* feat; *(Risiko)* risk
**Wahl** die; ~, ~en **a)** *o. Pl.* choice; **eine/ seine** ~ **treffen** make a/one's choice; **b)** *(in ein Gremium, Amt usw.)* election; **geheime** ~: secret ballot; **wahl·berechtigt** *Adj.* eligible *or* entitled to vote *postpos.;* **Wahl·beteiligung** die turn-out; **wählen 1.** *tr. V.* **a)** choose; *(aus~)* select; **b)** *(Fernspr.)* dial ⟨number⟩; **c)** *(durch Stimmabgabe)* elect; **d)** *(stimmen für)* vote for ⟨party, candidate⟩; **2.** *itr. V.* **a)** choose; **b)** *(Fernspr.)* dial; **c)** *(stimmen)* vote; **Wähler** der; ~s, ~: voter; **Wahl·ergebnis** das election result; **Wählerin** die; ~, ~nen voter; **wählerisch** *Adj.* choosy; particular (**in** + *Dat.* about)
**wahl-, Wahl-:** ~gang der ballot; ~geheimnis das secrecy of the ballot; ~kabine die polling-booth; ~kampf der election campaign; ~kreis der constituency; ~lokal das polling-station; ~los **1.** *Adj.* indiscriminate; **2.** *adv.* indiscriminately; ~recht das *o.Pl.* right to vote
**Wähl·scheibe** die *(Fernspr.)* dial
**Wahl-:** ~sieg der election victory; ~spruch der motto; ~urne die ballot-box
**Wahn** der; ~[e]s mania delusion; **Wahn·sinn** der; *o. Pl.* **a)** insanity; madness; **b)** *(ugs.: Unvernunft)* madness; lunacy; **wahnsinnig 1.** *Adj.* **a)** *(geistesgestört)* insane; mad; **b)** *(ugs.: ganz unvernünftig)* mad; crazy; **c)** *(ugs.: groß, heftig, intensiv)* terrific *(coll.)* ⟨effort, speed, etc.⟩; terrible *(coll.)* ⟨fright, job, pain⟩; **2.** *adv. (ugs.)* incredibly *(coll.);* terribly *(coll.)*
**wahr** *Adj.* **a)** true; **nicht** ~? *translation depends on preceding verb-form;* **du hast Hunger, nicht** ~? you're hungry, aren't you?; **nicht** ~, **er weiß es doch?** he does know, doesn't he?; **b)** *(wirklich)* real ⟨reason, motive, feelings, joy, etc.⟩; actual ⟨culprit⟩; *(echt)* true, real ⟨friend, friendship, love, art⟩

**wahren** *tr. V. (geh.)* preserve ⟨*balance, equality, neutrality, etc.*⟩; maintain ⟨*authority, right*⟩; *(verteidigen)* defend
**währen** *itr. V. (geh.)* last; **während** 1. *Konj.* a) *(zeitlich)* while; b) *(adversativ)* whereas; 2. *Präp. mit Gen.* during; *(über einen Zeitraum von)* for
**wahr|haben** *unr. tr. V. in etw. nicht ~ wollen* not want to admit sth.; **wahrhaft** *(geh.)* 1. *Adj.* true; 2. *adv.* truly; **wahrhaftig** 1. *Adj. (geh.)* truthful ⟨*person*⟩; 2. *adv.* really; genuinely; **Wahrheit** die; ~, ~en truth; **wahrheits·getreu** 1. *Adj.* truthful; faithful ⟨*account*⟩; 2. *adv.* truthfully; ⟨*portray*⟩ faithfully
**wahr|nehmen** *unr. tr. V.* a) *(mit den Sinnen erfassen)* perceive; *(spüren)* feel; detect ⟨*sound, smell*⟩; *(bemerken)* notice; *(erkennen, ausmachen)* make out; b) *(nutzen)* take advantage of ⟨*opportunity*⟩; exploit ⟨*advantage*⟩; exercise ⟨*right*⟩; c) *(vertreten)* look after ⟨*sb.'s interests, affairs*⟩; d) *(erfüllen, ausführen)* carry out, perform ⟨*function, task, duty*⟩; fulfil ⟨*responsibility*⟩; **Wahrnehmung** die; ~, ~en a) perception; *(eines Sachverhalts)* awareness; *(eines Geruchs, eines Tons)* detection; b) *(Nutzung) (eines Rechts)* exercise; *(einer Gelegenheit, eines Vorteils)* exploitation; c) *(Vertretung)* representation; d) *(einer Funktion, Aufgabe, Pflicht)* performance; execution; *(einer Verantwortung)* fulfilment
**wahr·sagen** 1. *itr. V.* tell fortunes; 2. *tr. V.* predict, foretell ⟨*future*⟩; **Wahrsager** der; ~s, ~, **Wahrsagerin** die; ~, ~nen fortune-teller
**wahrscheinlich** 1. *Adj.* probable; likely; 2. *adv.* probably; **Wahrscheinlichkeit** die; ~, ~en probability; likelihood
**Währung** die; ~, ~en currency; **Währungs·reform** die currency reform
**Wahr·zeichen** das symbol; *(einer Stadt, einer Landschaft)* [most famous] landmark
**Waise** die; ~, ~n orphan; **Waisen·haus** das orphanage
**Wal** der; ~[e]s, ~e whale
**Wald** der; ~[e]s, Wälder wood; *(größer)* forest; **Wald·brand** der forest fire; **Wäldchen** das copse; **Waldmeister** der; *o. pl. (Bot.)* woodruff
**Waliser** der; ~s, ~: Welshman; **Waliserin** die; ~, ~nen Welshwoman; **walisisch** *Adj.* Welsh

**Wall** der; ~[e]s, Wälle earthwork; embankment; rampart *(esp. Mil.)*
**Wall-:** ~**fahrer** der pilgrim; ~**fahrt** die pilgrimage
**Wal·nuß** die walnut
**Wal·roß** das; *Pl.* -rosse walrus
**walten** *itr. V. (geh.) ⟨good sense, good spirit⟩* prevail; ⟨*peace, silence, harmony, etc.*⟩ reign
**Walze** die; ~, ~n roller; *(Straßen~)* [road-]roller; *(Schreib~)* platen; **walzen** *tr. V.* roll ⟨*field, road, steel, etc.*⟩; **wälzen** 1. *tr. V.* roll; heave ⟨*heavy object*⟩; *(fig.)* shove ⟨*blame, responsibility*⟩ *(auf + Akk.* on); etw. in Mehl usw. ~ *(Kochk.)* toss sth. in flour *etc.*; **Probleme** ~ *(fig. ugs.)* mull over problems; 2. *refl. V.* roll; *(auf der Stelle)* roll about or around; *(im Krampf, vor Schmerzen)* writhe around; **Walzer** der; ~s, ~: waltz
**wand** *1. u. 3. Pers. Sg. Prät. v.* winden
**Wand** die; ~, Wände wall; *(Trenn~)* partition; *(bewegliche Trenn~)* screen; *(eines Behälters, Schiffs)* side
**Wandel** der; ~s change; **wandeln** *refl., tr. V.* change *(in + Akk.* into)
**Wanderer** der; ~s, ~: rambler; hiker; **Wander·karte** die rambler's [path] map; **wandern** *itr. V.; mit sein* a) hike; ramble; b) *(ugs.: gehen; fig.)* wander *(lit. or fig.)*; c) *(ziehen, reisen)* travel; *(ziellos)* roam; ⟨*exhibition, circus, theatre*⟩ tour, travel; ⟨*animal, people, tribe*⟩ migrate
**Wanderung** die; ~, ~en a) hike; walking tour; **eine ~ machen** go on a hike/tour/trek; b) *(Zool., Soziol.)* migration
**Wander·weg** der footpath *(constructed for ramblers)*
**Wandlung** die; ~, ~en change; *(grundlegend)* transformation
**Wand-:** ~**malerei** die *(Bild)* mural; ~**schrank** der wall cupboard or *(Amer.)* closet
**wandte** *1. u. 3. Pers. Prät. v.* wenden
**Wange** die; ~, ~n *(geh.)* cheek
**wankelmütig** *Adj. (geh.)* vacillating; **wanken** *itr. V.* a) sway; ⟨*person*⟩ totter; *(unter einer Last)* stagger; b) *mit sein (unsicher gehen)* stagger; totter
**wann** *Adv.* when; **seit ~ wohnst du dort?** how long have you been living there?
**Wanne** die; ~, ~n bath[tub]
**Wanze** die; ~, ~n bug *(coll.)*
**Wappen** das; ~s, ~: coat of arms
**war** *1. u. 3. Pers. Sg. Prät. v.* sein

**warb** *1. u. 3. Pers. Sg. Prät. v.* **werben**

**ward** *(geh.) 1. u. 3. Pers. Sg. Prät. v.* **werden**

**Ware** die; ~, ~n a) ~[n] goods *pl.;* b) *(einzelne* ~) article; commodity *(Econ., fig.); (Erzeugnis)* product

**Waren-:** ~**haus** das department store; ~**lager** das *(einer Fabrik o.ä.)* stores *pl.; (eines Geschäftes)* stockroom; *(größer)* warehouse; ~**muster** das, ~**probe** die sample; ~**zeichen** das trade mark

**warf** *1. u. 3. Pers. Sg. Prät. v.* **werfen**

**warm; wärmer, wärmst ...** 1. *Adj. (auch fig.)* warm; hot *⟨meal, food, bath, spring⟩;* das Essen ~ **machen** heat up the food; „~" *(auf Wasserhahn)* 'hot'; keen, lively *⟨interest⟩;* 2. *adv.* warmly; ~ **essen/duschen** have a hot meal/shower; **Wärme** die; ~: warmth; *(Hitze; auch Physik)* heat; **wärmen** 1. *tr. V.* warm; *(aufwärmen)* warm up *⟨food, drink⟩;* 2. *itr. V.* be warm; *(warm halten)* keep one warm; **Wärm·flasche** die hot-water bottle

**Warm·wasser-:** ~**bereiter** der; ~s, ~: water-heater; ~**heizung** die hot-water heating

**Warn-:** ~**blinkanlage** die *(Kfz-W.)* hazard warning lights *pl.;* ~**dreieck** das *(Kfz-W.)* hazard warning triangle

**warnen** *tr. (auch itr.) V.* warn (vor + Dat. of, about); jmdn. [davor] ~, etw. zu tun warn sb. against doing sth.

**Warn-:** ~**schild** das warning sign; ~**schuß** der warning shot; ~**signal** das warning signal; ~**streik** der token strike

**Warnung** die; ~, ~en warning (vor + Dat. of, about)

**Warschau (das);** ~s Warsaw

**Warte-:** ~**halle** die waiting room; *(Flugw.)* departure lounge; ~**liste** die waiting list

**warten** 1. *itr. V.* wait (auf + Akk. for); 2. *tr. V.* service *⟨car etc.⟩*

**Wärter** der; ~s, ~: attendant; *(Tier~, Zoo~, Leuchtturm~)* keeper; *(Kranken~)* orderly; *(Gefängnis~)* warder

**Warte-:** ~**saal** der waiting-room; ~**zimmer** das waiting-room

**Wartung** die; ~, ~en service; *(das Warten)* servicing; *(Instandhaltung)* maintenance

**warum** *Adv.* why

**Warze** die; ~, ~n wart; *(Brust~)* nipple

**was** 1. *Interrogativpron. Nom. u. Akk. u. (nach Präp.) Dat. Neutr.;* ~ kostet das? what *or* how much does that cost?; ach ~! *(ugs.)* oh, come on!; ~ für ein .../~ für ...: what sort *or* kind of ...; 2. *Relativpron. Nom. u. Akk. u. (nach Präp.) Dat. Neutr.;* [das,] ~: what; **alles,** ~ ...: everything *or* all that ...; **vieles/nichts/etwas,** ~ ...: much/nothing/something that ...; ~ **mich betrifft,** [so] ...: as far as I'm concerned, ...; 3. *Indefinitpron. Nom. u. Akk. u. (nach Präp.) Dat. Neutr. (ugs.)* s. etwas; 4. *Adv. (ugs.) (warum, wozu)* why; what ... for

**Wasch-:** ~**anlage** die car-wash; ~**automat** der washing-machine; ~**becken** das wash-basin

**Wäsche** die; ~, ~n a) *o. Pl. (zu waschende Textilien)* washing; *(für die Wäscherei)* laundry; b) *o. Pl. (Unter~)* underwear; c) *(das Waschen)* washing no pl.; *(einmalig)* wash; **in der** ~ **sein** be in the wash; **wasch·echt** *Adj.* a) colour-fast *⟨textile, clothes⟩;* fast *⟨colour⟩;* b) *(fig.)* genuine

**Wäsche-:** ~**klammer** die clothespeg *(Brit.);* clothes-pin *(Amer.);* ~**korb** der laundry-basket; ~**leine** die clothes-line

**waschen** 1. *unr. tr. V.* wash; sich ~: wash [oneself]; have a wash; **Wäsche** ~: do the/some washing; 2. *unr. itr. V.* do the washing; **Wäscherei** die; ~, ~en laundry

**Wäsche-:** ~**schleuder** die spindrier; ~**trockner** der a) *(Maschine)* tumble-drier; b) *(Gestell)* clothes-airer

**Wasch-:** ~**gelegenheit** die washing facilities *pl.;* ~**küche** die laundryroom; ~**lappen** der [face] flannel; washcloth *(Amer.);* ~**maschine** die washing-machine; ~**mittel** das detergent; ~**pulver** das washing-powder; ~**straße** die [automatic] car-wash

**wäscht** *3. Pers. Sg. Präsens v.* **waschen**

**Wasser** das; ~s, ~/Wässer a) *o. Pl.* water; b) *(Mineral~, Tafel~)* mineral water; *(Heil~)* water; c) *o. Pl. (Gewässer)* ein fließendes/stehendes ~: a moving/stagnant stretch of water; d) *o. Pl. (Urin)* water; urine; ~ **lassen** pass water

**wasser-, Wasser-:** ~**ball** der a) beach-ball; b) *o. Pl. (Spiel)* water polo; ~**dicht** *Adj.* waterproof *⟨clothing, watch, etc.⟩;* watertight *⟨container, seal, etc.⟩;* ~**fall** der waterfall; ~**farbe** die water-colour; ~**hahn** der water-tap; faucet *(Amer.)*

**wässerig** *s.* **wäßrig**

**Wasser-**: **~kessel** der kettle; **~lei-tung** die water-pipe; *(Hauptleitung)* water-main

**wassern** *itr. V.; mit sein* land [on the water]; **wässern** *tr. V.* soak; *(Phot.)* wash ⟨*negative, print*⟩

**wasser-, Wasser-**: **~pflanze die** aquatic plant; **~rohr das** water-pipe; **~schlauch der** [water-]hose; **~schutz·polizei die** river/lake police; **¹~ski der** water-ski; **~ fahren** water-ski; **²~ski das**; **~s** water-skiing *no art.*; **~spiegel der a)** *(Oberfläche)* surface [of the water]; **b)** *(Niveau)* water-level; **~sport der** water-sport *no art.*; **~spülung die** flush

**Wasser·stoff der**; *o. Pl.* hydrogen; **Wasser·stoff·bombe die** hydrogen bomb

**Wasser-**: **~strahl der** jet of water; **~straße die** waterway; **~tempera-tur die** water-temperature; **~tiefe die** depth of the water; **~tropfen der** drop of water; **~turm der** water-tower; **~werfer der** water-cannon; **~werk das** waterworks *sing.*; **~zei-chen das** watermark

**wäßrig** *Adj.* watery

**waten** *itr. V.; mit sein* wade

**watscheln** *itr. V.; mit sein* waddle

**¹Watt das**; **~|e|s, ~en** mud-flats *pl.*

**²Watt das**; **~s, ~** *(Technik, Physik)* watt

**Watte die**; **~, ~n** cotton wool; **Wat-te·bausch der** wad of cotton wool

**Watten·meer das** tidal shallows *pl.*

**wattiert** *Adj.* quilted; padded ⟨*shoul-der etc., envelope*⟩

**WC** [ve:'tse:] *das*; **~|s|, ~|s|** toilet; WC

**weben** *tr., itr. V.* weave; **Weber der**; **~s, ~**: weaver; **Web·stuhl der** loom

**Wechsel der**; **~s, ~ a)** *(das Auswech-seln)* change; *(Geld~)* exchange; **b)** *(Aufeinanderfolge)* alternation; **im ~**: alternately; *(bei mehr als zwei)* in rota-tion; **c)** *(das Überwechseln)* move; *(Sport)* transfer; **d)** *(Bankw.)* bill of exchange (**über** + *Akk.* for)

**wechsel-, Wechsel-**: **~geld das**; *o. Pl.* change; **~haft** *Adj.* changeable; **~jahre** *Pl.* change of life *sing.*; menopause *sing.*; **~kurs der** ex-change rate

**wechseln 1.** *tr. V.* **a)** change; **das Hemd ~**: change one's shirt; **die Woh-nung ~**: move home; **b)** *(|aus|tau-schen)* exchange ⟨*letters, glances, etc.*⟩; **c)** *(um~)* change ⟨*money, note, etc.*⟩ (**in** + *Akk.* into); **2.** *itr. V.* change

**wechsel-, Wechsel-**: **~seitig 1.** *Adj.* mutual; **2.** *adv.* mutually; **~strom der** *(Elektrot.)* alternating current; **~stube die** bureau de change; **~wirkung die** interaction

**wecken** *tr. V.* jmdn. [aus dem Schlaf] ~: wake sb. [up]; *(fig.: hervorrufen)* arouse ⟨*interest, curiosity, anger*⟩; **Wecker der**; **~s, ~** alarm clock

**wedeln** *itr. V.* ⟨*tail*⟩ wag; [mit dem Schwanz] ~ ⟨*dog*⟩ wag its tail

**weder** *Konj.* ~ **A noch B** neither A nor B

**weg** *Adv.* away; *(verschwunden, ~ge-gangen)* gone; **er ist schon seit einer Stunde ~**: he left an hour ago; **weit ~**: far away; a long way away

**Weg der**; **~|e|s, ~e a)** *(Fuß~)* path; *(Feld~)* track; **b)** *(Zugang)* way; *(Pas-sage, Durchgang)* passage; **sich** *(Dat.)* **einen ~ durch etw. bahnen** clear a path *or* way through sth.; **c)** *(Route, Verbin-dung)* way; route; **d)** *(Strecke, Entfer-nung)* distance; *(Gang)* walk; *(Reise)* journey; **auf dem kürzesten ~**: by the shortest route; **auf halbem ~|e|** *(auch fig.)* half-way; **sich auf den ~ machen** set off; **etw. in die ~e leiten** get sth. under way; **e)** *(ugs.: Besorgung)* er-rand; **f)** *(Methode)* way; *(Mittel)* means

**weg-**: **~|bleiben** *unr. itr. V.; mit sein* *(nicht kommen)* stay away; *(nicht nach Hause kommen)* stay out; **~|bringen** *unr. tr. V.* take away; *(zur Reparatur, Wartung usw.)* take in

**wegen** *Präp. mit Gen.* **a)** because of; ~ **Umbau|s| geschlossen** closed for al-terations; **b)** *(um ... willen)* for the sake of; ~ **der Kinder/** *(ugs.)* **dir** for the chil-dren's/your sake; **c)** *(bezüglich)* about; regarding

**weg-**: **~|fahren 1.** *unr. itr. V.; mit sein* **a)** leave; *(im Auto)* drive off; *(losfah-ren)* set off; **b)** *(irgendwohin fahren)* go away; **2.** *unr. tr. V.* drive away; *(mit dem Handwagen usw.)* take away; **~|fallen** *unr. itr. V.; mit sein* be dis-continued; *(nicht mehr zutreffen)* no longer apply; **~|fliegen** *unr. itr. V.; mit sein* fly away; *(~geblasen werden)* fly off; **~|gehen** *unr. itr. V.* **a)** leave; *(ugs.: ausgehen)* go out; *(ugs.: ~zie-hen)* move away; **b)** *(verschwinden)* ⟨*spot, fog, etc.*⟩ go away; **c)** *(sich entfer-nen lassen)* ⟨*stain*⟩ come out; **~|jagen** *tr. V.* chase away; **~|kommen** *unr. itr. V.; mit sein* **a)** get away; **b)** *(abhan-den kommen)* go missing; **c)** **gut/**

**schlecht** *usw.* [bei etw.] ~**kommen**
*(ugs.)* come off well/badly *etc.* [in
sth.]; ~|**kriegen** *tr. V.* get rid of ⟨*cold,*
*pain, etc.*⟩; get rid of ⟨*stain*⟩;
~|**lassen** *unr. tr. V.* a) jmdn. ~**lassen**
let sb. go; *(ausgehen lassen)* let sb. go
out; b) *(auslassen)* leave out; omit;
~|**laufen** *unr. itr. V.; mit sein* run
away (von, vor + *Dat.* from); ~|**le-**
**gen** *tr. V.* put aside; *(an seinen Platz*
*legen)* put away; ~|**nehmen** *unr. tr.*
*V.* a) take away; move ⟨*head, arm*⟩; b)
jmdm. etw. ~**nehmen** take sth. away
from sb.; ~|**schicken** *tr. V.* a) send
off ⟨*letter, parcel*⟩; b) send ⟨*person*⟩
away; ~|**schmeißen** *unr. tr. V. (ugs.)*
chuck away *(coll.)*; ~|**schütten** *tr. V.*
pour away; ~|**sehen** *unr. itr. V.* look
away; ~|**stellen** *tr. V.* put away; *(bei-*
*seite stellen)* put aside; ~|**stoßen** *unr.*
*tr. V.* push *or* shove away; ~|**tragen**
*unr. tr. V.* carry away
**Wegweiser** der; ~s, ~ signpost
**weg-**: ~|**werfen** *unr. tr. V. (auch fig.)*
throw away; ~**werfend** *Adj.* dis-
missive ⟨*gesture, remark*⟩; ~|**wi-**
**schen** *tr. V.* wipe away; ~|**ziehen** 1.
*unr. tr. V.* pull away; draw back ⟨*cur-*
*tain*⟩; pull off ⟨*blanket*⟩; 2. *unr. itr. V.;*
*mit sein* a) *(umziehen)* move away; b)
*(wandern)* ⟨*animals, nomads, etc.*⟩
leave [on their migration]
**weh** *(ugs.)* 1. *Adj.* sore; 2. *adv.* ~ tun
hurt; mir tut der Magen/Kopf ~: my
stomach/head is aching *or* hurts;
**jmdm./sich** ~ **tun** hurt sb./oneself;
**Wehe** die; ~, ~n: ~n haben have
contractions; **in den ~n liegen** be in labour
**wehen** *itr. V.* a) *(blasen)* blow; b) *(flat-*
*tern)* flutter
**weh-, Weh-**: ~|**leidig** *(abwertend)* 1.
*Adj. (überempfindlich)* soft; *(weiner-*
*lich)* whining *attrib.*; 2. *adv.* self-
pityingly; *(weinerlich)* whiningly;
~**mut** die; ~ *(geh.)* wistful nostalgia;
~**mütig** *Adj.* wistfully nostalgic
¹**Wehr** die; ~, ~en sich [gegen jmdn./
etw.] zur ~ setzen make a stand
[against sb./sth.]; resist [sb./sth.];
²**Wehr** das; ~[e]s, ~e weir
**Wehr·dienst** der; o. Pl. military service *no art.;* seinen ~ **ableisten** do
one's military service
**Wehr·dienst-**: ~**verweigerer** der;
~s, ~: conscientious objector; ~**ver-**
**weigerung** die conscientious objection
**wehren** *refl. V.* defend oneself

**wehr-, Wehr-**: ~**los** *Adj.* defenceless; ~**pflicht** die; *o. Pl.* military service; **die allgemeine ~pflicht** compulsory military service; ~**pflichtig**
*Adj.* liable for military service *postpos.*
**Weib** das; ~[e]s, ~er a) *(veralt., ugs.)*
woman; female *(derog.)*; **Weibchen**
das; ~s, ~ female; **weiblich** 1. *Adj.*
a) female; b) *(für die Frau typisch;*
*Sprachw.)* feminine; 2. *adv.* femin-
inely
**weich** 1. *Adj. (auch fig.)* soft; ein ~es
Ei a soft-boiled egg; 2. *adv.* softly
¹**Weiche** die; ~, ~n *(Flanke)* flank
²**Weiche** die; ~, ~n points *pl. (Brit.);*
switch *(Amer.)*
**weichen** *unr. itr. V.; mit sein* move;
vor jmdm./einer Sache ~: give way to
sb./sth.
**weich·gekocht** *Adj. (präd. getrennt*
*geschrieben)* soft-boiled ⟨*egg*⟩;
**weichlich** 1. *Adj.* soft; *(ohne innere*
*Festigkeit)* weak; 2. *adv.* softly
¹**Weide** die; ~, ~n willow
²**Weide** die; ~, ~n pasture; **weiden**
*itr., tr. V.* graze
**Weiden·kätzchen** das willow catkin
**weigern** *refl. V.* refuse; **Weigerung**
die; ~, ~en refusal
**Weih·bischof** der *(kath. Kirche)* suf-
fragan bishop; **Weihe** die; ~, ~n
*(Rel.)* consecration; *(kath. Kirche:*
*Priester~, Bischofs~)* ordination;
**weihen** *tr. V.* a) *(Rel.)* consecrate;
*(zueignen)* dedicate *(Dat.* to); b) *(kath.*
*Kirche: ordinieren)* ordain
**Weiher** der; ~s, ~: [small] pond
**Weihnachten** das; ~, ~: Christmas;
frohe *od.* fröhliche *od.* gesegnete ~!
Merry *or* Happy Christmas!;
**weihnachtlich** *Adj.* Christmassy
**Weihnachts-**: ~**baum** der Christmas tree; ~**feiertag** der: der erste/
zweite ~**feiertag** Christmas Day/Box-
ing Day; ~**fest** das Christmas; ~**ge-**
**schenk** das Christmas present *or*
gift; ~**lied** das Christmas carol;
~**mann** der; *Pl.* ~**männer** Father
Christmas; Santa Claus; ~**markt** der
Christmas fair; ~**zeit** die Christmas
time
**Weih-**: ~**rauch** der incense; ~**was-**
**ser** das *(kath. Kirche)* holy water
**weil** *Konj.* because
**Weile** die; ~: while; **weilen** *itr. V.*
*(geh.) (ver~)* stay; *(sein)* be
**Wein** der; ~[e]s, ~e wine
**Wein-**: ~**berg** der vineyard; ~**brand**
der brandy

**weinen** *itr. V.* cry (über + *Akk.* over, about); *(aus Trauer, Kummer)* cry, weep (um for); **weinerlich** 1. *Adj.* tearful; weepy; 2. *adv.* tearfully

**wein-, Wein-:** ~**essig** der wine vinegar; ~**flasche** winebottle; ~**glas** das wineglass; ~**handlung die** winemerchant's; ~**karte die** wine-list; ~**lokal** das wine bar; ~**probe die** wine-tasting [session]; ~**rot** *Adj.* wine-red; ~**stube die** wine bar; ~**traube die** grape

**weise** 1. *Adj.* wise; 2. *adv.* wisely

**Weise die;** ~, ~**n a)** *(Art, Verfahren)* way; **b)** *(Melodie)* tune; melody

**weisen** 1. *unr. tr. V.* *(geh.: zeigen)* show; **jmdn. aus dem Zimmer** ~: send sb. out of the room; 2. *unr. itr. V.* *(irgendwohin zeigen)* point

**Weisheit die;** ~, ~**en a)** *o. Pl.* wisdom; **b)** *(Erkenntnis)* wise insight; *(Spruch)* wise saying; **Weisheits·zahn der** wisdom tooth; **weis|machen** *tr. V.* *(ugs.)* **das kannst du mir nicht** ~! you can't expect me to swallow that!

¹**weiß** *1. u. 3. Pers. Sg. Präsens v.* **wissen**

²**weiß** *Adj.* white; **Weiß das;** ~|e|s, ~: white

**weis·sagen** *tr. V.* prophesy; **Weissagung die;** ~, ~**en** prophecy

**Weiß-:** ~**bier** das weiss beer; ~**brot** das white bread; ~**dorn** der hawthorn

**Weiße der/die;** *adj. Dekl.* white; white man/woman; **weißen** *tr. V.* paint white; *(tünchen)* whitewash

**weiß-, Weiß-:** ~**gold** das white gold; ~**herbst** der ≈ rosé wine; ~**kohl** der, *(bes. südd., österr.)* ~**kraut** das white cabbage

**weißlich** *Adj.* whitish

**weißt** *2. Pers. Sg. Präsens v.* **wissen**

**Weiß-:** ~**wein** der white wine; ~**wurst die** veal sausage

**Weisung die;** ~, ~**en** *(geh., sonst Amtsspr.)* instruction; *(Direktive)* directive

**weit** 1. *Adj.* wide; long ⟨way⟩; **jmdm. zu** ~ **sein** ⟨clothes⟩ be too loose on sb.; 2. *adv.* **a)** *(räumlich ausgedehnt)* ~ **geöffnet** wide open; ~ **und breit war niemand zu sehen** there was no one to be seen anywhere; **b)** *(lang)* far; ~**er** further; farther; **am** ~**esten** [the] furthest *or* farthest; ~ |**entfernt** *od.* weg| **wohnen** live a long way away *or* off; live far away; **von** ~**em** from a distance; **das geht zu** ~ *(fig.)* that is going too

far; **c)** *(zeitlich entfernt)* ~ **nach Mitternacht** well past midnight; **d)** *(in der Entwicklung)* far; **Weit·blick der;** *o. Pl.* far-sightedness; **Weite die;** ~, ~**n a)** *(räumliche Ausdehnung)* expanse; **b)** *(bes. Sport: Entfernung)* distance; **c)** *(eines Kleidungsstückes)* width; **weiten** 1. *tr. V.* widen; 2. *refl. V.* widen; ⟨pupil⟩ dilate; **weiter** *Adv.* **a)** *s.* **weit** 2; **b)** **und so** ~: and so on; **c)** *(~hin, anschließend)* then; **d)** *(außerdem, sonst)* ~ **nichts** nothing more *or* else; **weiter...** *Adj.* further; **bis auf** ~**es** for the time being; *s. auch* **ohne**

**weiter-, Weiter-:** ~|**bringen** *unr. V.* **die Diskussion brachte uns nicht** ~: the discussion did not get us any further [forward]; ~|**erzählen** *tr. V.* **a)** continue telling; *itr.* **erzähl weiter!** do carry *or* go on; **b)** *(~sagen)* pass on; ~|**fahren** *unr. itr. V.;* **mit sein** continue [on one's way]; *(~ reisen)* travel on; ~|**führen** *tr., itr. V.* continue; ~|**geben** *unr. V.* pass on; ~|**gehen** *unr. itr. V.; mit sein* go on; **bitte** ~**gehen!** please move along *or* keep moving!; ~**hin** *Adv.* **a)** *(immer noch)* still; **b)** *(künftig)* in future; **c)** *(außerdem)* in addition; ~|**kommen** *unr. itr. V.; mit sein* **a)** get further; **b)** *(Fortschritte machen)* make progress; **im Beruf** ~**kommen** get on in one's career; ~|**machen** *(ugs.) itr. V.* carry on; go on; ~|**reichen** *tr. V.* pass on; ~|**sagen** *tr. V.* pass on; ~|**sehen** *unr. itr. V.* see; ~|**verarbeiten** *tr. V.* process; ~**verarbeitung die** processing

**weit-, Weit-:** ~**gehend** 1. *Adj.* extensive, wide, sweeping ⟨powers⟩; farreaching ⟨support, concessions, etc.⟩; wide ⟨support, agreement, etc.⟩; general ⟨renunciation⟩; 2. *adv.* to a large *or* great extent; ~**gereist** *Adj.* widely travelled; ~**hin** *Adv.* for miles around; ~**läufig** 1. *Adj.* **a)** *(ausgedehnt)* extensive; *(geräumig)* spacious; **b)** *(entfernt)* distant; 2. *adv.* **a)** *(ausgedehnt)* spaciously; **b)** *(entfernt)* distantly; ~**räumig** 1. *Adj.* spacious ⟨room, area, etc.⟩; wide ⟨gap, space⟩; 2. *adv.* spaciously; ~**reichend** 1. *Adj.* *(fig.)* far-reaching ⟨importance, consequences⟩; sweeping ⟨changes, powers⟩; extensive ⟨relations, influence⟩; 2. *adv.* extensively; ~**sichtig** *Adj.* long-sighted; ~**sichtigkeit die;** ~ long-sightedness; ~**sprung der** *(Sport)* long jump *(Brit.)*; broad jump *(Amer.)*; ~**verbreitet** *Adj.* widespread; common; common ⟨plant, animal⟩; **~winkel·objektiv** das wide-angle lens

**Weizen** der; ~s wheat

**welch** 1. Interrogativpron. (bei Wahl aus einer unbegrenzten Menge) what; (bei Wahl aus einer begrenzten Menge) (adj.) which; (subst.) which one; 2. Relativpron. (bei Menschen) who; (bei Sachen) which; 3. Indefinitpron. some; (in Fragen) any

**welk** Adj. withered ⟨skin, hands, etc.⟩; wilted ⟨leaves, flower⟩; limp ⟨lettuce⟩; **welken** itr. V.; mit sein ⟨plant, flower⟩ wilt

**Well·blech** das corrugated iron; **Welle** die; ~, ~n a) (auch fig.) wave; (Rundf.: ~nlänge) wavelength; b) (Technik) shaft

**wellen-, Wellen-:** ~**bad** das artificial wave pool; ~**brecher** der breakwater; ~**gang** der; o. Pl. swell; bei starkem ~gang in heavy seas; ~**länge** die wavelength; ~**sittich** der budgerigar

**Well·fleisch** das boiled belly pork; **wellig** Adj. wavy ⟨hair⟩; undulating ⟨scenery, hills, etc.⟩; uneven ⟨surface, track, etc.⟩; **Well·pappe** die corrugated cardboard

**Welt** die; ~, ~en a) o. Pl. world; **auf der** ~: in the world; **die Alte/Neue** ~: the Old/New World; **die dritte/vierte** ~ the Third/Fourth World; **auf die od. zur** ~ **kommen** be born; **alle** ~ (fig. ugs.) the whole world; everybody; b) (~all) universe

**welt-, Welt-:** ~**all** das universe; ~**anschauung** die world-view; ~**ausstellung** die world fair; ~**berühmt** Adj. world-famous

**Welten·bummler** der; ~s, ~globetrotter

**welt-, Welt-:** ~**fremd** 1. Adj. unworldly; 2. adv. unrealistically; ~**frieden** der world peace; ~**karte** die map of the world; ~**krieg** der world war; **der erste/zweite** ~**krieg** the First/Second World War

**weltlich** Adj. a) worldly; b) (nicht geistlich) secular

**welt-, Welt-:** ~**literatur** die world literature no art.; ~**macht** die world power; ~**markt** der (Wirtsch.) world market; ~**meister** der world champion; ~**meisterschaft** die world championship; ~**raum** der space no art.; ~**reise** die world tour; ~**rekord** der world record; ~**stadt** die cosmo-

politan city; ~**weit** 1. Adj. worldwide; 2. adv. throughout the world; ~**wirtschaft** die world economy

**wem** Dat. von wer 1. Interrogativpron. to whom; who ... to; **mit/von/zu** ~: with/from/to whom; who ... with/from/to; 2. Relativpron. the person to whom ...; the person who ... to; 3. Indefinitpron. (ugs.: jemandem) to somebody or someone; (fragend od. verneint) to anybody or anyone

**wen** Akk. von wer 1. Interrogativpron. whom; who (coll.); **an/für** ~: to/for whom ...; who ... to/for; 2. Relativpron. the person whom; 3. Indefinitpron. (ugs.: jemanden) somebody; someone; (fragend od. verneint) anybody; anyone

**Wende** die; ~, ~n change (zu for); **Wende·kreis** der a) (Geogr.) tropic; b) (Kfz-W.) turning circle; **Wendel·treppe** die spiral staircase; **¹wenden** 1. tr., auch itr. V. (auf die andere Seite) turn [over]; (in die entgegengesetzte Richtung) turn [round]; **bitte** ~! please turn over; 2. itr. V. turn [round]; 3. refl. V. **sich zum Besseren/Schlechteren** ~: take a turn for the better/worse; **²wenden** 1. unr. (auch regelm.) tr. V. turn; 2. unr. (auch regelm.) refl. V. a) ⟨person⟩ turn; b) (sich richten) **sich an jmdn. [um Rat]** ~: turn to sb. [for advice]; **wendig** 1. Adj. a) agile; manœuvrable ⟨vehicle, boat, etc.⟩; b) (gewandt) astute; 2. adv. a) (beweglich) agilely; b) (gewandt) astutely; **Wendung** die; ~, ~en a) (Änderung der Richtung) turn; b) (Veränderung) change

**wenig** 1. Indefinitpron. u. unbest. Zahlw. a) Sing. little; **das ist** ~: that isn't much; **zu** ~ **Zeit/Geld haben** not have enough time/money; **ein Exemplar/50 Mark zu** ~: one copy too few/50 marks too little; b) Pl. a few; **mit** ~**en Worten** in a few words; 2. Adv. little; ~ **mehr** not much more; **weniger** 1. Komp. von wenig; Indefinitpron. u. unbest. Zahlw. (+ Sg.) less; (+ Pl.) fewer; **immer** ~: less and less; 2. Komp. von wenig; Adv. less; **das ist** ~ **angenehm/erfreulich/schön** that is not very pleasant/pleasing/nice; s. auch mehr 1; 3. Konj. less; **fünf** ~ **drei** five, take away three; **wenigst...** 1. Sup. von wenig; Indefinitpron. u. unbest. Zahlw. least; **am** ~**en** least; 2. Sup. von wenig; **am** ~**en** the least; **wenigstens** Adv. at least

**wenn** *Konj.* **a)** *(konditional)* if; **außer
~:** unless; **~ es nicht anders geht** if
there's no other way; **b)** *(temporal)*
when; **jedesmal,** *od.* **immer, ~:** whenever; **c)** *(konzessiv)* **wenn ... auch** even
though; **d)** *(in Wunschsätzen)* if only
**wer** *Nom. Mask. u. Fem.; s. auch
(Gen.)* **wessen** *(Dat.)* **wem;** *(Akk.)* **wen
1.** *Interrogativpron.* who; **~ von ...:**
which of; **2.** *Relativpron.* the person
who; *(jeder, der)* anyone *or* anybody
who; **3.** *Indefinitpron.* *(ugs.: jemand)*
someone; *(in Fragen, Konditionalsät-
zen)* anyone; anybody
**Werbe-:** **~agentur die** advertising
agency; **~fernsehen das** television
commercials *pl.;* **~funk der** radio
commercials *pl.*
**werben 1.** *unr. itr. V.* advertise; **für
etw. ~:** advertise sth.; **2.** *unr. tr. V.* attract ⟨*readers, customers, etc.*⟩; recruit
⟨*soldiers, members, etc.*⟩; **Werbung
die; ~:** advertising; **für etw. ~ machen**
advertise sth.
**Werde·gang der** career; **werden 1.**
*unr. itr. V.; mit sein* become; get; **älter
~:** get *or* grow old[er]; **wahnsinnig** *od.*
verrückt ~: go mad; **das muß anders
~:** things have to change; **wach ~:**
wake up; **rot ~:** go *or* turn red; **Arzt/
Professor ~:** become a doctor/pro-
fessor; **zu etw. ~:** become sth.; **es wird
[höchste] Zeit** it is [high] time; **es wird
10 Uhr** it is nearly 10 o'clock; **es wird
Herbst** autumn is coming; **sind die Fo-
tos [etwas] geworden?** *(ugs.)* have the
photos turned out [well]?; **2.** *Hilfsverb; 2. Part.* **worden a)** *(zur Bildung
des Futurs)* **wir ~ uns um ihn kümmern**
we will take care of him; **es wird gleich
regnen** it is going to rain any minute;
**es wird um die 80 Mark kosten** *(ich ver-
mute, es kostet um die 80 Mark)* it will
cost around 80 marks; **b)** *(zur Bildung
des Passivs)* **du wirst gerufen** you are
being called; **er wurde gebeten** he was
asked
**werfen 1.** *unr. tr. V.* throw; drop
⟨*bombs*⟩; **2.** *unr. itr. V.* **a)** throw; **mit
etw. ~:** throw sth.; **b)** *(Junge kriegen)*
give birth; ⟨*dog, cat*⟩ litter; **3.** *unr. refl.
V.* throw oneself; **sich vor einen Zug
~:** throw oneself under a train
**Werft die; ~, ~en** shipyard
**Werk das; ~[e]s, ~e a)** work; **b)** *(Betrieb, Fabrik)* factory; works *sing. or
pl.;* **ab ~:** ex works
**Werk·bank die;** *Pl.* **~bänke** work-
bench

**Werk[s]-:** **~angehörige der/die**
factory *or* works employee; **~arzt der**
factory *or* works doctor
**werk-, Werk-:** **~statt die;** **~statt,
~stätten** workshop; *(Kfz-W.)* garage;
**~stoff der** material; **~tag der** working day; workday; **~tags** *Adv.* on
weekdays; **~tätig** *Adj.* working;
**~tätige der/die;** *adj. Dekl.* worker;
**~zeug das;** *Pl.* **~zeuge** *(auch fig.)* tool
**Werkzeug·kasten der** tool-box
**Wermut der; ~[e]s, ~s a)** *(Pflanze)*
wormwood; **b)** *(Wein)* vermouth
**wert** *Adj.* *(geh.)* esteemed; *(als Anrede)* my dear ...; **etw./nichts ~ sein** be
worth sth./be worthless; **Wert der;
~[e]s, ~e** value; **im ~[e] von ...:**
worth ...; **~ auf etw.** *(Akk.)* **legen** set
great store by *or* on sth.; **wert·be-
ständig** *Adj.* of lasting value *postpos.*; **werten** *tr., itr. V.* judge; assess
**wert-, Wert-:** **~gegenstand der**
valuable object; **~gegenstände** valuables; **~los** *Adj.* worthless; valueless;
**~papier das** *(Wirtsch.)* security;
**~sache die** valuable item; **~sachen**
valuables; **~sendung die** *(Postw.)*
registered item
**Wertung die; ~, ~en** judgement;
**wert·voll** *Adj.* valuable; *(moralisch)*
estimable
**Wesen das; ~s** nature; **wesentlich
1.** *Adj.* fundamental (**für** to); **im ~en**
essentially; **2.** *adv.* *(erheblich)* considerably; much
**wes·halb** *Adv. s.* **warum**
**Wespe die; ~, ~n** wasp
**wessen** *Interrogativpron.* **a)** *Gen. von*
**wer** whose; **b)** *Gen. von* **was: ~ wird er
beschuldigt?** what is he accused of?
**Wessi der; ~s, ~s** *(salopp)* West German
**West** *o. Art.; o. Pl. (bes. Seemannsspr.,
Met.) s.* **Westen;** **west·deutsch**
*Adj.* Western German; *(hist.: auf die
alte BRD bezogen)* West German;
**West·deutschland (das)** Western
Germany; *(hist.: alte BRD)* West Germany
**Weste die; ~, ~n** waistcoat *(Brit.);*
vest *(Amer.)*
**Westen der; ~s** west; **der ~:** the
West; **Western der; ~[s], ~:** west-
ern; **West·europa (das)** Western
Europe; **Westfalen (das); ~s** West-
phalia; **westfälisch** *Adj.* Westphal-
ian; **West·indien (das)** the West
Indies *pl.;* **westlich 1.** *Adj.* **a)** west-
ern; **b)** *(nach Westen)* westerly; **c)** *(aus*

*dem Westen)* Western; **2.** *adv.* west-
wards; **3.** *Präp. mit Gen.* [to the] west
of; **wẹst·wärts** *Adv.* [to the] west;
**Wẹst·wind** der west[erly] wind
**wes·wẹgen** *Adv. s.* **warum**
**Wẹtt·bewerb** der; ~[e]s, ~e **a)** competition; **b)** *o. Pl. (Wirtsch.)* competition *no indef. art.;* **Wẹtte** die; ~, ~n
bet; eine ~ [mit jmdm.] abschließen
make a bet [with sb.]; mit jmdm. um
die ~ laufen race sb.; **wẹtt·eifern**
*itr. V.* mit jmdm. [um etw.] ~: compete
with sb. [for sth.]; **wẹtten** *itr. V.* bet;
mit jmdm. ~: have a bet with sb.; mit
jmdm. um etw. ~: bet sb. sth.

**Wẹtter** das; ~s weather
**Wẹtter-:** ~**aussichten** *Pl.* weather
outlook *sing.;* ~**bericht** der weather
report; *(Vorhersage)* weather forecast;
~**karte** die weather-chart; weather-
map; ~**lage** die weather situation;
~**vorhersage** die weather forecast;
~**warte** die weather station
**wẹtt-, Wẹtt-:** ~**kampf** der competi-
tion; ~**lauf** der race; ~|**machen** *tr.
V.* make up for (durch with); ~**rennen** das race; ~**rüsten** das; ~s arms
race; ~**streit** der contest
**wẹtzen** *tr. V.* sharpen; whet
**WEZ** *Abk.* **Westeuropäische Zeit** GMT
**Whiskey** ['vɪski] der; ~s ~s whiskey;
**Whisky** ['vɪski] der; ~s, ~s whisky
**wịch** *1. u. 3. Pers. Sg. Prät. v.* **weichen**
**wịchtig** *Adj.* important; **Wịchtig-
keit** die; ~ importance
**Wịcke** die; ~, ~n vetch; *(im Garten)*
sweet pea
**Wịckel** der; ~s, ~: compress;
**wịckeln** *tr. V.* wind; *(ein~)* wrap (**in**
+ *Akk.* in); *(aus~)* unwrap (**aus** +
*Dat.* from); *(ab~)* unwind (**von** from);
**ein Kind** ~: change a baby's nappy
**Wịdder** der; ~s, ~: **a)** ram; **b)** *(Astrol.)*
Aries
**wịder** *Präp. mit Akk. (geh.)* against
**wider-:** ~**fahren** *unr. itr. V.; mit sein
(geh.)* etw. ~**fährt** jmdm. sth. happens
to sb.; ~|**legen** *tr. V.* etw. ~**legen** re-
fute sth.; jmdn. ~**legen** prove sb.
wrong
**widerlich 1.** *Adj.* revolting; repulsive
⟨*person, behaviour, etc.*⟩; awful
⟨*headache etc.*⟩; **2.** *adv.* revoltingly;
⟨*behave*⟩ in a repugnant *or* repulsive
manner; awfully ⟨*cold, sweet, etc.*⟩
**wịder-, Wịder-:** ~**rede** die: keine
~**rede!** don't argue!; ~**ruf** der retrac-
tion; [bis] auf ~**ruf** until revoked;
~**rufen** [--'--] *unr. tr., auch itr. V.* re-

tract ⟨*statement, claim, confession,
etc.*⟩; ~**setzen** [--'--] *refl. V.* sich
jmdm./einer Sache ~**setzen** oppose
sb./sth.; ~**spenstig 1.** *Adj.* unruly;
stubborn ⟨*horse, mule, etc.*⟩; **2.** *adv.*
wilfully; ~|**spiegeln,** ~**spiegeln**
[--'--] **1.** *tr. V. mirror; (fig.)* reflect; **2.**
*refl. V.* be mirrored; *(fig.)* be reflected; ~**sprechen** [--'--] *unr. itr. V.*
contradict; ~**spruch** der **a)** *o. Pl. (Widerrede, Protest)* opposition; protest;
**b)** *(etw. Unvereinbares)* contradiction;
~**sprüchlich** *Adj.* contradictory
⟨*news, statements, etc.*⟩; inconsistent
⟨*behaviour, attitude, etc.*⟩
**Wịder·stand** der **a)** resistance (**gegen**
to); **b)** *(Hindernis)* opposition
**widerstands-:** ~**fähig** *Adj.* robust;
resistant ⟨*material etc.*⟩; hardy ⟨*animal, plant*⟩; ~**los** *Adj., adv.* without
resistance *postpos.*
**wịder-:** ~**stehen** [--'--] *unr. itr. V.* **a)**
*(nicht nachgeben)* [jmdm./einer Sache]
~**stehen** resist [sb./sth.]; **b)** *(standhalten)* jmdm./einer Sache ~**stehen** with-
stand sb./sth.; ~**streben** [--'--] *itr. V.*
etw. ~**strebt** jmdm. sb. dislikes *or* detests sth.; ~**wärtig 1.** *Adj.* revolting;
repugnant ⟨*smell, taste, etc.*⟩; offensive ⟨*person, behaviour, etc.*⟩; **2.** *adv.*
⟨*behave etc.*⟩ in an offensive manner;
~**wille** der aversion (**gegen** to); ~**willig** *adv.* reluctantly; unwillingly
**wịdmen 1.** *tr. V.* **a)** dedicate; **b)** *(verwenden für/auf)* devote; **2.** *refl. V.* sich
jmdm./einer Sache ~: attend to sb./
sth.; *(ausschließlich)* devote oneself to
sb./sth.; **Wịdmung** die; ~, ~en dedication (**an** + *Akk.* to)
**widrig** *Adj.* unfavourable; adverse
**wie 1.** *Interrogativadv.* how; ~ [bitte]?
[I beg your] pardon?; ~ spät ist es?
what time is it?; **2.** *Relativadv.* ~ er es
tut the way *or* manner in which he
does it; **3.** *Konj.* **a)** *Vergleichspartikel*
as; [so] ... ~ ...: as ... as ...; ich fühlte
mich ~ ...: I felt as if I were ...; „N" ~
„Nordpol" N for November; **b)** *(zum
Beispiel)* like; such as; **c)** *(und, sowie)*
as well as; both
**wieder** *Adv.* again; alles ist ~ beim al-
ten everything is back as it was before; ich bin gleich ~ da I'll be right
back *(coll.)*
**wieder-, Wieder-:** ~|**bekommen**
*unr. tr. V.* get back; ~|**beleben** *tr. V.*
revive, resuscitate ⟨*person*⟩; ~**bele-
bungs·versuch** der attempt at re-
suscitation; ~|**erkennen** *unr. tr. V.*

recognize; ~|**finden** *unr. tr. V.* find again; ~**gabe die** *(Bericht)* report; *(Übersetzung)* rendering; *(Reproduktion)* reproduction; ~|**geben** *unr. tr. V.* **a)** *(zurückgeben)* give back; **b)** *(berichten)* report; *(wiederholen)* repeat

**wieder·gut|machen** *tr. V.* make good; put right; **den Schaden** ~ *(bezahlen)* pay for the damage

**wieder|haben** *untr. tr. V. (auch fig.)* have back

**wieder-:** ~**her|stellen** *tr. V.* **a)** re-establish ⟨*contact, peace*⟩; **b)** *(reparieren)* restore ⟨*building*⟩; ~**holen 1.** *tr. V.* repeat; *(repetieren)* revise ⟨*lesson, vocabulary, etc.*⟩; **2.** *refl. V.* **a)** *(wieder dasselbe sagen)* repeat oneself; **b)** *(erneut geschehen)* happen again; **c)** *(wiederkehren)* be repeated; recur

**wieder|holen** *tr. V.* fetch *or* get back

**wiederholt 1.** *Adj.* repeated; **2.** *adv.* repeatedly; **Wiederholung die;** ~, ~**en** repetition; *(eines Fußballspiels usw.)* replay; *(einer Sendung)* repeat; *(einer Aufführung)* repeat performance; *(von Lernstoff)* revision

**Wieder·hören das: |auf|** ~! goodbye! *(at end of telephone call)*

**wieder-, Wieder-:** ~**kehr die;** ~ *(geh.)* return; ~|**kehren** *itr. V.; mit sein (geh.)* return; ~|**kommen** *unr. itr. V.; mit sein* **a)** *(zurückkommen)* return; come back; **b)** *(noch einmal kommen)* come back *or* again; **c)** *(sich noch einmal ereignen)* ⟨*opportunity, past*⟩ come again; ~|**kriegen** *tr. V. (ugs.)* get back; ~**schauen das: |auf|** ~**schauen!** *(südd., österr.)* goodbye!; ~|**sehen** *unr. tr. V.* see again; ~**sehen das;** ~s, ~: reunion; **|auf|** ~**sehen!** goodbye!; ~**um** *Adv.* **a)** *(erneut)* again; **b)** *(andererseits)* on the other hand; ~**wahl die** re-election; ~|**wählen** *tr. V.* re-elect

**Wiege die;** ~, ~**n** *(auch fig.)* cradle

¹**wiegen** *unr. itr., tr. V.* weigh;

²**wiegen** *tr. V.* rock; shake ⟨*head*⟩

**Wiegen·lied das** lullaby; cradle-song

**wiehern** *itr. V.* whinny; *(lauter)* neigh

**Wien (das);** ~s Vienna; ¹**Wiener der;** ~s, ~: Viennese; ²**Wiener** *Adj.* Viennese; *s. auch* Würstchen; **Wienerin die;** ~, ~**nen** Viennese; **wienerisch** *Adj.* Viennese

**wies** *1. u. 3. Pers. Sg. Prät. v.* weisen

**Wiese die;** ~, ~**n** meadow; *(Rasen)* lawn

**wie·so** *Interrogativadv.* why

**wie·viel** *[od.* '--*] Interrogativpron.*

*(+ Sg.)* how much; *(+ Pl.)* how many; ~ **Uhr ist es?** what time is it?

**wie·viel·mal** *[od.* -'--*] Interrogativadv.* how many times

**wievielt...** *[od.* '--*] Interrogativadj.* **der ~e Band?** which number volume?; **der Wievielte ist heute?** what is the date today?

**wie·weit** *Interrogativadv.* to what extent; how far

**wild 1.** *Adj. (auch fig.)* wild; *(wütend)* furious ⟨*cursing, shouting, etc.*⟩; ~**es Parken** illegal parking; ~**er Streik** wildcat strike; ~ **auf etw./jmdn. sein** *(ugs.)* be mad *or* crazy about sth./sb. *(coll.)*; ~ **werden** get furious; **jmdn.** ~ **machen** infuriate sb.; **2.** *adv.* **a)** wildly; **wie** ~ *(ugs.)* like mad *(coll.)*; **b)** *(ordnungswidrig)* illegally; **Wild das;** ~|e|s **a)** *(Tiere, Fleisch)* game; **b)** *(einzelnes Tier)* [wild] animal; **Wild·bret** [~brɛt] **das;**~s *(geh.)* game; **Wilde der/die;** *adj. Dekl.* savage; **Wilderer der;** ~s, ~: poacher; **wild·fremd** *Adj.* completely strange; ~**e Leute** complete strangers; **Wildheit die;** ~: wildness; **Wild·leder das** suede; **Wildnis die;** ~, ~**se** wilderness

**Wild-:** ~**schwein das** wild boar; ~**wechsel der** *o. Pl.* game crossing; ~**west·film der** western

**will** [vɪl] *1. u. 3. Pers. Sg. Präsens v.* wollen

**Wille der;** ~**ns** will; *(Wunsch)* wish

**willen** *Präp. mit Gen.* **um jmds./einer Sache** ~: for sb.'s/sth.'s sake; **Willen der;** ~s *s.* Wille; **willen·los 1.** *Adj.* will-less; **2.** *adv.* will-lessly; **willens** *Adj.* ~ **sein, etw. zu tun** *(geh.)* be willing to do sth.; **willens·stark** *Adj.* strong-willed; **willentlich 1.** *Adj.* deliberate; **2.** *adv.* deliberately; on purpose; **willig 1.** *Adj.* willing; **2.** *adv.* willingly

**will·kommen** *Adj.* welcome; **jmdn.** ~ **heißen** welcome sb.

**Will·kür die;** ~: arbitrary use of power; *(Handlung o. ä.)* arbitrariness; **willkürlich 1.** *Adj.* arbitrary; *(vom Willen gesteuert)* voluntary ⟨*muscle, movement, etc.*⟩; **2.** *adv.* arbitrarily; *(vom Willen gesteuert)* voluntarily

**wimmeln** *itr. V.* **von Fehlern** ~: be teeming with mistakes

**wimmern** *itr. V.* whimper

**Wimpel der;** ~s, ~: pennant

**Wimper die;** ~, ~**n** [eye]lash

**Wind der;** ~|e|s, ~e wind; **Wind-beutel der** cream puff

**Winde** die; ~, ~n winch
**Windel** die; ~, ~n nappy *(Brit.);* diaper *(Amer.);* **Windel·höschen** das nappy pants *pl.*
**winden** 1. *unr. tr. V. (geh.)* make ⟨*wreath, garland*⟩; etw. **um** etw. ~: wind sth. around sth.; 2. *unr. refl. V.* ⟨*plant, tendrils*⟩ wind (**um** around); ⟨*snake*⟩ coil [itself], wind itself (**um** around); **sich vor Schmerzen~**: writhe in pain
**Windes·eile** die: **in** ~: in next to no time; **Wind·hund** der greyhound; **windig** *Adj.* windy
**Wind-:** ~**mühle** die windmill; ~**pocken** *Pl.* chicken-pox *sing.;* ~**schutz·scheibe** die windscreen *(Brit.);* windshield *(Amer.);* ~**stärke** die: ~**stärke 7/9** *usw.* wind force 7/9 *etc.;* ~**still** *Adj.* windless; still; ~**stoß** der gust of wind; ~**surfing** das windsurfing *no art.*
**Windung** die; ~, ~en a) bend; b) *(spiralförmiger Verlauf)* spiral; *(einer Spule o. ä.)* winding
**Wink** der; ~[e]s, ~e sign; *(Hinweis)* hint; *(Ratschlag)* tip; hint
**Winkel** der; ~s, ~ a) *(Math.)* angle; **toter** ~: blind spot; b) *(Ecke; auch fig.)* corner; **winkelig** *Adj.* twisty ⟨*streets*⟩
**winken** 1. *itr. V.* a) wave; **mit etw.** ~: wave sth.; b) *(auffordern heranzukommen)* jmdm. ~: beckon sb. over; **einem Taxi** ~: hail a taxi; 2. *tr. V.* beckon; **jmdn. zu sich** ~: beckon sb. over [to one]
**winklig** *Adj. s.* winkelig
**winseln** *itr. V.* ⟨*dog*⟩ whimper
**Winter** der; ~s, ~: winter; **Winteranfang** der beginning of winter; **winterlich** 1. *Adj.* wintry; winter *attrib.* ⟨*clothing, break*⟩; 2. *adv.* ~ **kalt** cold and wintry
**Winter-:** ~**reifen** der winter tyre; ~**schlußverkauf** der winter sale[s *pl.*]; ~**sport** der winter sports *pl.;* ~**zeit** die; *o. Pl.* winter-time
**Winzer** der; ~s, ~winegrower
**winzig** 1. *Adj.* tiny; 2. *adv.* ~ **klein** tiny; minute
**Wipfel** der; ~s, ~: tree-top
**Wippe** die; ~, ~n see-saw; **wippen** *itr. V.* bob up and down; *(hin und her)* bob about; *(auf einer Wippe)* see-saw
**wir** *Personalpron.;* 1. *Pers. Pl. Nom.* we; *s. auch (Gen.)* unser; *(Dat.)* uns; *(Akk.)* uns
**wirb** *Imperativ Sg. v.* werben

**Wirbel** der; ~s, ~ a) *(kreisende Bewegung) (im Wasser)* whirlpool; *(in der Luft)* whirlwind; *(kleiner)* eddy; *(von Rauch, beim Tanz)* whirl; b) *(Trubel)* hurly-burly; c) *(Aufsehen)* fuss; d) *(Anat.)* vertebra; **wirbeln** 1. *itr. V.* **mit sein** whirl; ⟨*water, snowflakes*⟩ swirl; 2. *tr. V.* swirl ⟨*leaves, dust*⟩; whirl ⟨*dancer*⟩
**Wirbel-:** ~**säule** die spinal column; ~**sturm** der cyclone
**wirbt** 3. *Pers. Sg. Präsens v.* werben
**wird** 3. *Pers. Sg. Präsens v.* werden
**wirf** *Imperativ Sg. v.* werfen; **wirft** 3. *Pers. Sg. Präsens v.* werfen
**wirken** *itr. V.* a) *(eine Wirkung haben)* have an effect; **gegen etw.** ~: be effective against sth.; b) *(erscheinen)* seem; appear
**wirklich** 1. *Adj.* real; 2. *Adv.* really; **Wirklichkeit** die; ~, ~en reality
**wirksam** 1. *Adj.* effective; 2. *adv.* effectively; **Wirksamkeit** die; ~: effectiveness; **Wirk·stoff** der active agent; **Wirkung** die; ~, ~en effect (**auf** + *Akk.* on); **mit** ~ **vom 1. Juli** *(Amtsspr.)* with effect from 1 July
**wirkungs-:** ~**los** 1. *Adj.* ineffective; 2. *adv.* ineffectively; ~**voll** 1. *Adj.* effective; 2. *adv.* effectively
**wirr** *Adj. (unordentlich)* tousled ⟨*hair, beard*⟩; tangled ⟨*ropes, roots*⟩; *(unklar, verwirrt)* confused; **Wirren** *Pl.* turmoil *sing.;* **Wirrwarr** der; ~s chaos; *(von Stimmen)* clamour
**Wirsing** der; ~s, **Wirsingkohl** der savoy [cabbage]
**Wirt** der; ~[e]s, ~e landlord; **Wirtin** die; ~, ~nen landlady
**Wirtschaft** die; ~, ~en a) economy; *(Geschäftsleben)* commerce and industry; b) *(Gast~)* public house; pub *(Brit. coll.);* bar *(Amer.);* c) *(Haushalt)* household; d) *o. Pl. (ugs. abwertend: Unordnung)* mess; shambles *sing.;* **wirtschaften** *itr. V.* **mit dem Geld gut** ~: manage one's money well; **mit Verlust/Gewinn** ~: run at a loss/ profit; **wirtschaftlich** 1. *Adj.* a) economic; b) *(finanziell)* financial; c) *(sparsam, rentabel)* economical; 2. *adv.; s. Adj.:* economically; financially; **Wirtschaftlichkeit** die; ~: economic viability
**Wirtschafts-:** ~**hilfe** die economic aid *no indef. art.;* ~**krise** die economic crisis; ~**minister** der minister for economic affairs; ~**politik** die economic policy

**Wirts:** ~**haus** das pub *(Brit. coll.);* ~**leute** *Pl.* landlord and landlady

**Wisch** der; ~|e|s, ~e *(salopp)* piece *or* bit of paper; **wischen** *itr., tr. V.* wipe; **Staub** ~: do the dusting; dust

**wispern** *itr., tr. V.* whisper

**wiß-, Wiß-:** ~**begier, ~begierde die;** *o. Pl.* thirst for knowledge; ~**begierig** *Adj.* eager for knowledge; ⟨*child*⟩ eager to learn

**wissen 1.** *unr. tr. V.* know; **von jmdm./ etw. nichts |mehr| ~ wollen** want to have nothing [more] to do with sb./ sth.; **2.** *unr. itr. V.* **von etw./um etw. ~:** know about sth.; **Wissen das;** ~s knowledge; **meines/unseres ~s** to my/ our knowledge; **Wissenschaft die;** ~, ~**en** science; **Wissenschaftler der;** ~s ~, **Wissenschaftlerin die;** ~, ~**nen** academic; *(Natur~)* scientist; **wissenschaftlich 1.** *Adj.* scholarly; *(natur~)* scientific; **2.** *adv.* in a scholarly manner; *(natur~)* scientifically; **wissens wert** *Adj.* ~ **sein** be worth knowing; **wissentlich 1.** *Adj.* deliberate; **2.** *adv.* knowingly; deliberately

**wittern 1.** *itr. V.* sniff the air; **2.** *tr. V.* get wind of; *(fig.: ahnen)* sense; **Witterung die;** ~, ~**en a)** *(Wetter)* weather *no indef. art;* **b)** *(Jägerspr.)* *(Geruchssinn)* sense of smell; *(Geruch)* scent

**Witwe die;** ~, ~**n** widow; ~ **werden** be widowed; **Witwer der;** ~s, ~: widower

**Witz der;** ~es, ~e joke

**Witz-:** ~**blatt** das humorous magazine; ~**bold der;** ~es, ~e joker

**witzig 1.** *Adj.* funny; **2.** *adv.* amusingly; **witz·los** *Adj.* **a)** dull; **b)** *(ugs.: sinnlos)* pointless

**wo 1.** *Adv.* where; **2.** *Konj.* **a)** *(da, weil)* seeing that; **b)** *(obwohl)* although; when; **wo·anders** *Adv.* somewhere else; **wo·bei** *Adv.* **a)** *(interrogativ)* ~ **hast du sie ertappt?** what did you catch her doing?; **b)** *(relativisch)* **er gab sechs Schüsse ab, ~ einer der Täter getötet wurde** he fired six shots – one of the criminals was killed

**Woche die;** ~, ~**n** week; **in dieser/der nächsten/der letzten ~:** this/next/last week; **heute in/vor einer ~:** a week today/a week ago today

**wochen-, Wochen-:** ~**bett** das: **im ~bett liegen** be lying in; ~**ende das** weekend; ~**lang 1.** *Adj.* lasting weeks *postpos;* **2.** *adv.* for weeks [on end];

~**tag der** weekday *(including Saturday);* ~**tags** *Adv.* on weekdays [and Saturdays]

**wöchentlich** *Adj., adv.* weekly; **Wochen·zeitung die** weekly newspaper; -**wöchig a)** *(... Wochen alt)* ... -week-old; **b)** *(... Wochen dauernd)* ... week's/weeks'; ...-week; **Wöchnerin die;** ~, ~**nen** woman who has just given birth

**Wodka der;** ~s, ~s vodka

**wo·durch** *Adv.* **a)** *(interrogativ)* how; **b)** *(relativisch)* as a result of which; **wo·für** *Adv.* **a)** *(interrogativ)* for what; **b)** *(relativisch)* for which

**wog** *1. u. 3. Pers. Sg. Prät. v.* **wiegen**

**Woge die;** ~, ~**n** wave

**wo·gegen 1.** *Adv.* **a)** *(interrogativ)* against what; what ... against; **b)** *(relativisch)* against which; which ... against; **2.** *Konj.* whereas

**wogen** *itr. V. (geh.)* ⟨*sea*⟩ surge; *(fig.)* ⟨*corn*⟩ wave

**wo·her** *Adv.* **a)** *(interrogativ)* where ... from; ~ **weißt du das?** how do you know that?; **b)** *(relativisch)* where ... from; **wo·hin** *Adv.* **a)** *(interrogativ)* where [... to]; **b)** *(relativisch)* where; **wo·hingegen** *Konj.* whereas

**wohl 1.** *Adv.* **a)** well; **jmdm. ist nicht ~, jmd. fühlt sich nicht ~:** sb. does not feel well; **b)** *(behaglich)* at ease; happy; **leb ~!/leben Sie ~!** farewell!; **c)** *(durchaus)* well; **d)** *(ungefähr)* about; **2.** *Partikel* probably; ~ **kaum** hardly; **Wohl das;** ~|e|s welfare; **auf jmds. ~ trinken** drink sb.'s health; **zum ~!** cheers!

**wohl-, Wohl-:** ~**auf** [-'-] *Adj.(geh.)* ~**auf sein** be well; ~**befinden das** well-being; ~**behagen das** sense of well-being; ~**behalten** *Adj.* safe and well ⟨*person*⟩; undamaged ⟨*thing*⟩; ~**fahrts·staat der** welfare state; ~**gefallen das** pleasure; ~**gemerkt** *Adv.* please note; ~**habend** *Adj.* prosperous

**wohlig 1.** *Adj.* pleasant; agreeable; **2.** *adv.* ⟨*sigh, purr, etc.*⟩ with pleasure

**wohl, Wohl-:** ~**klang der** *(geh.)* melodious sound; ~**schmeckend** *Adj.* *(geh.)* delicious; ~**stand der;** *o. Pl.* prosperity; ~**stands·gesellschaft die** *o. Pl.* affluent society; ~**tat die a)** *(gute Tat)* good deed; *(Gefallen)* favour; **b)** *o. Pl. (Genuß)* blissful relief; ~**tätig** *Adj.* charitable; ~**tuend** *Adj.* agreeable; ~|**tun** *unr. itr. V.* **etw. tut jmdm. ~:** sth. does sb. good; ~**ver-**

**dient** *Adj.* well-earned; **~weislich** *Adv.* deliberately; **~wollen das; ~s** goodwill; **~wollend 1.** *Adj.* benevolent; favourable ⟨*judgement, opinion*⟩; **2.** *adv.* benevolently; ⟨*judge, consider*⟩ favourably

**Wohn·anhänger** der caravan; trailer *(Amer.);* **wohnen** *itr. V.* live; *(kurzfristig)* stay

**wohn-, Wohn-: ~gemeinschaft** die group sharing a flat *(Brit.)* or *(Amer.)* apartment/house; **~haft** *Adj.* resident **(in** + *Dat.* in); **~heim** das *(für Alte, Behinderte)* home; *(für Obdachlose, Lehrlinge)* hostel; *(für Studenten)* hall of residence

**wohnlich** *Adj.* homely

**Wohn-: ~mobil** das; **~s, ~e** motor home; **~ort** der; *Pl.* **~e** place of residence; **~sitz** der place of residence; **ohne festen ~sitz** of no fixed abode

**Wohnung** die; **~, ~en a)** flat *(Brit.);* apartment *(Amer.);* **b)** o. Pl. *(Unterkunft)* lodging

**Wohn-: ~verhältnisse** *Pl.* living conditions; **~wagen** der caravan; trailer *(Amer.);* **~zimmer** das livingroom

**wölben 1.** *tr. V.* curve; vault, arch ⟨*roof, ceiling*⟩; **2.** *refl. V.* curve; ⟨*bridge, ceiling*⟩ arch; **Wölbung** die; **~, ~en** curve; *(einer Decke)* arch; vault

**Wolf** der; **~|e|s, Wölfe** wolf

**Wolke** die; **~, ~n** cloud

**wolken-, Wolken-: ~bruch** der; *Pl.* **~brüche** cloudburst; **~bruch·artig** *Adj.* torrential; **~kratzer** der skyscraper; **~los** *Adj.* cloudless

**wolkig** *Adj.* cloudy

**Wolle** die; **~, ~n** wool; **¹wollen** *Adj.* woollen

**²wollen 1.** *unr. Modalverb;* **2.** *Part.* **~** etw. tun ~ *(den Wunsch haben, etw. zu tun)* want to do sth.; *(die Absicht haben, etw. zu tun)* be going to do sth.; **die Wunde will nicht heilen** the wound [just] won't heal; **2.** *unr. itr. V.* **du mußt nur ~, dann ...** you only have to want to enough, then ... **ganz wie du willst** just as you like; *(ugs.)* **ich will nach Hause** I want to go home; **zu wem ~ Sie?** whom do you want to see?; **3.** *unr. tr. V.* want; **das habe ich nicht gewollt** I never meant that to happen

**wo·mit** *Adv.* **a)** *(interrogativ)* ~ schreibst du? what do you write with?; **b)** *(relativisch)* **~ du schreibst**

which *or* that you write with; *(more formal)* with which you write; **wo·möglich** *Adv.* possibly; **wo·nach** *Adv.* **a)** *(interrogativ)* after what; what ... after; **~ suchst du?** what are you looking for?; **b)** *(relativisch)* after which; which ... after

**Wonne** die; **~, ~n** *(geh.)* bliss *no pl.;* ecstasy; *(etw., was Freude macht)* joy; **wonnig** *Adj.* sweet

**woran** *Adv.* **a)** *(interrogativ)* ~ **denkst du?** what are you thinking of?; **b)** *(relativisch)* **nichts, ~ man sich anlehnen könnte** nothing one could lean against; **worauf a)** *(interrogativ)* ~ **wartest du?** what are you waiting for?; **b)** *(relativisch)* **etwas, ~ man sich verlassen kann** something one can rely on; **c)** *(relativisch: woraufhin)* whereupon

**woraus** *Adv.* **a)** *(interrogativ)* ~ **schließt du das?** what do you infer that from?; **b)** *(relativisch)* **es gab nichts, ~ wir den Wein hätten trinken können** there was nothing for us to drink the wine out of

**worden** 2. *Part. v.* werden 2

**worin** *Adv.* **a)** *(interrogativ)* in what; what ... in; **b)** *(relativisch)* in which; which ... in

**Wort** das; **~|e|s, Wörter/~e a)** *Pl.* Wörter, *(auch:)* **~e** word; **~ für ~:** word for word; **DM 1 000 (in ~en: tausend)** DM 1,000 (in words: one thousand); **b)** *Pl.* **~e** *(Äußerung)* word; **mir fehlen die ~e** I'm lost for words; **Dr. Meyer hat das ~:** it's Dr Meyer's turn to speak; **c)** *Pl.* **~e** *(Spruch)* saying; *(Zitat)* quotation; **d)** *Pl.* **~e** *(geh.: Text)* words *pl.;* **in ~ und Bild** in words and pictures; **e)** *Pl.* **~e** *(Versprechen)* word; |sein| **~ halten** keep one's word; **wort·brüchig** *Adj.* **~ werden** break one's word; **Wörter·buch** das dictionary

**wort-, Wort-: ~getreu** *Adj.* word-for-word; **~karg 1.** *Adj.* taciturn ⟨*person*⟩; **2.** *adv.* taciturnly; **~laut** der wording; **im |vollen| ~laut** verbatim

**wörtlich 1.** *Adj.* **a)** word-for-word; **b)** *(der eigentlichen Bedeutung entsprechend)* literal; **2.** *adv.: s. Adj.:* word for word; literally

**wort-, Wort-: ~los 1.** *Adj.* silent; wordless; **2.** *adv.* without saying a word; **~spiel** das play on words; pun; **~wechsel** der exchange of words; **~wörtlich** *Adj.* word-forword

**worüber** *Adv.* **a)** *(interrogativ)* over what ...; what ... over; **b)** *(relativisch)* over which; which ... over; **worum** *Adv.* **a)** *(interrogativ)* around what; what ... around; **b)** *(relativisch)* around which; which ... around; **worunter** *Adv.* **a)** *(interrogativ)* under what; what ... under; **b)** *(relativisch)* under which; which ... under; **wo·von** *Adv.* **a)** *(interrogativ)* from where; where ... from; **b)** *(relativisch)* from which; which ... from; **wo·vor** *Adv.* **a)** *(interrogativ)* in front of what; what ... in front of; **b)** *(relativisch)* in front of which; which ... in front of; **wo·zu** *Adv.* **a)** *(interrogativ)* to what; what ... to; *(wofür)* what ... for; **b)** *(relativisch)* ~ du dich auch entschließt whatever you decide on
**Wrack** das; ~|e|s, ~s od. ~e wreck
**wrang** *1. und 3. Pers. Sg. Prät. v.* wringen; **wringen** *unr. tr. V. (bes. nordd.)* wring
**Wucher** der; ~s profiteering; *(beim Verleihen von Geld)* usury; **wuchern** *itr. V.* **a)** *auch mit* sein ⟨*plants, weeds, etc.*⟩ proliferate, run wild; **b)** *(Wucher treiben)* |mit etw.| ~: profiteer [on sth.]; *(beim Verleihen von Geld)* lend [sth.] at extortionate interest rates; **Wucherung** die; ~, ~en growth
**wuchs** *1. u. 3. Pers. Sg. Prät. v.* wachsen; **Wuchs** der; ~es *(Gestalt)* stature
**Wucht** die; ~ force; *(von Schlägen)* power; weight; **wuchtig** *1. Adj.* **a)** *(voller Wucht)* powerful; mighty; **b)** *(schwer, massig)* massive; **2.** *adv.* powerfully
**wühlen** *1. itr. V.* **a)** dig; *(mit der Schnauze, dem Schnabel)* root (**nach** for); ⟨*mole*⟩ tunnel, burrow; **b)** *(ugs.: suchen)* rummage [around] (**nach** for); **2.** *tr. V.* burrow; tunnel out ⟨*burrow*⟩
**wulstig** *Adj.* bulging
**wund** *Adj.* sore; **Wunde** die; ~, ~n wound
**wunder** *Adv. (ugs.)* er denkt, er sei ~ wer he thinks he's really something; **Wunder** das; ~s, ~ **a)** miracle; ~ wirken *(fig. ugs.)* work wonders; ein/kein ~ sein *(ugs.)* be a/no wonder; **b)** *(etw. Erstaunliches)* wonder; **wunderbar** *1. Adj.* **a)** miraculous; **b)** *(sehr schön, herrlich)* wonderful; marvellous; **2.** *adv. (sehr schön, herrlich)* wonderfully; marvellously; **b)** *(ugs.: sehr)* wonderfully
**Wunder-:** ~**kerze** die sparkler; ~**kind** das child prodigy

**wunderlich** *1. Adj.* strange; odd; **2.** *adv.* strangely; oddly; **wundern** *1. tr. V.* surprise; **mich wundert** od. **es wundert mich, daß** ...: I'm surprised that ...; **2.** *refl. V.* sich über jmdn./etw. ~: be surprised at sb./sth.
**wunder-:** ~**schön** *1. Adj.* simply beautiful; *(herrlich)* simply wonderful; **2.** *adv.* quite beautifully; ~**voll** *1. Adj.* wonderful; **2.** *adv.* wonderfully
**wund||liegen** *unr. refl. V.* get bedsores (**an** + *Dat.* on); **Wund·starr·krampf** der *(Med.)* tetanus
**Wunsch** der; ~|e|s, Wünsche wish (**nach** to have); *(Sehnen)* desire (**nach** for); haben Sie |sonst| noch einen ~? will there be anything else?; **auf jmds.** ~: at sb.'s wish; **mit den besten/herzlichsten Wünschen** with best/warmest wishes; **wünschen** *tr. V.* **a)** sich *(Dat.)* etw. ~: want sth.; *(im stillen)* wish for sth.; **b)** *(in formelhaften Wünschen)* wish; jmdm. alles Gute/frohe Ostern ~: wish sb. all the best/a happy Easter; **c)** *auch itr. V. (begehren)* want; was ~ Sie?, Sie ~? *(im Lokal)* what would you like?; *(in einem Geschäft)* can I help you?
**Wunsch-:** ~**kind** das wanted child; ~**konzert** das request concert; *(im Rundfunk)* request programme; ~**zettel** der *(zum Geburtstag o. ä.)* list of presents one would like
**wurde** *1. u. 3. Pers. Sg. Prät. v.* werden; **würde** *1. u. 3. Pers. Sg. Konjunktiv II v.* werden
**Würde** die; ~ dignity; **würde·los** *1. Adj.* undignified; *(schimpflich)* disgraceful; **2.** *adv.* in an undignified way; *(schimpflich)* disgracefully; **Würden·träger** der dignitary; **würde·voll** *1. Adj.* dignified; **2.** *adv.* with dignity; **würdig** *1. Adj.* **a)** dignified; **b)** *(wert)* worthy; **2.** *adv.* **a)** with dignity; **b)** *(angemessen)* worthily; **würdigen** *tr. V.* **a)** *(anerkennen, beachten)* recognize; *(schätzen)* appreciate; *(lobend hervorheben)* acknowledge; **b)** *(für wert halten)* jmdn. keines Blickes/keiner Antwort ~: not deign to look at/answer sb.
**Wurf** der; ~|e|s, Würfe **a)** throw; *(beim Kegeln)* bowl; **b)** *o. Pl. (das Werfen)* throwing/pitching/bowling; **c)** *(Zool.)* litter
**Würfel** der; ~s, ~ cube; *(Spiel~)* dice; die *(formal)*; **Würfel·becher** der dice-cup; **würfeln** *1. itr. V.* throw the dice; **um etw.** ~: play dice for sth.; **2.**

*tr. V.* **a)** throw; **b)** *(in Würfel schneiden)* dice
**Würfel-**: **~spiel** das dice; *(Brettspiel)* dice game; **~zucker** der; *o. Pl.* cube sugar
**würgen 1.** *tr. V.* strangle; throttle; **2.** *itr. V. (Brechreiz haben)* retch
**Wurm der**; **~|e|s**, Würmer worm; *(Made)* maggot; **wurmig** *Adj.*, **wurmstichig** *Adj.* worm-eaten; *(madig)* maggoty
**Wurst die**; **~**, Würste sausage; **es geht um die ~** *(fig. ugs.)* the crunch has come; **jmdm. ist jmd./etw. ~** *(ugs.)* sb. doesn't care about sb./sth.; **Würstchen das**; **~s**, **~ a)** [small] sausage; **Frankfurter/Wiener ~**: frankfurter/wienerwurst; **b)** *(fig. ugs.)* nobody; *(hilfloser Mensch)* poor soul; **Würstchen·bude** die sausage-stand
**Würze die**; **~**, **~n** spice; seasoning
**Wurzel die**; **~**, **~n** *(auch fig.)* root; **wurzeln** *itr. V.* take root
**würzen** *tr. V.* season; **würzig** *Adj.* tasty; full-flavoured ⟨*beer, wine*⟩; aromatic ⟨*fragrance*⟩; tangy ⟨*air*⟩
**wusch** *1. u. 3. Pers. Sg. Prät. v.* **waschen**
**wußte** *1. und 3. Pers. Sg. Prät. v.* **wissen**; **wüßte** *1. und 3. Pers. Sg. Konjunktiv II v.* **wissen**
**wüst 1.** *Adj.* **a)** *(öde)* desolate; **b)** *(unordentlich)* chaotic; **c)** *(ungezügelt)* wild; *(unanständig)* rude; **2.** *adv.* **a)** *(unordentlich)* chaotically; **b)** *(ungezügelt)* wildly
**Wüste die**; **~**, **~n** desert
**Wut die**; **~**: rage; fury; **wüten** *itr. V. (auch fig.)* rage; *(zerstören)* wreak havoc; **wütend 1.** *Adj.* furious; angry ⟨*voice, mob*⟩; **2.** *adv.* furiously; in a fury

# X

**'x, X** [ɪks] **das**; **~**, **~**: x, X
**²x** *unbest. Zahlwort (ugs.)* umpteen *(coll.)*
**x-Achse die** *(Math.)* x-axis
**X-Beine** *Pl.* knock-knees

**x-beliebig** *Adj. (ugs.)* **irgendein ~er/irgendeine ~e/irgendein ~es** any old *(coll. attrib.)*; **jeder ~e Ort** any old place *(coll.)*
**x-fach 1.** *Vervielfältigungsz.* **die ~e Menge** *(Math.)* x times the amount; *(ugs.)* umpteen times the amount *(coll.)*; **2.** *adv. (ugs.)* **~ erprobt sein** ⟨*tested etc.*⟩ umpteen times *(coll.)*; **x-mal** *Adv. (ugs.)* umpteen times *(coll.)*
**x-t...** *Ordinalz. (ugs.)* umpteenth *(coll.)*

# Y

**y, Y** [ˈʏpsilon] **das**; **~**, **~**: y, Y
**y-Achse die** *(Math.)* y-axis
**Yacht** *s.* **Jacht**
**Yoga** *s.* **Joga**
**Ypsilon das**; **~|s|**, **~s** y, Y; *(im griechischen Alphabet)* upsilon

# Z

**z, Z** [tsɛt] **das**; **~**, **~**: z, Z
**Zacke die**; **~**, **~n** point; peak; *(einer Säge, eines Kamms)* tooth; *(einer Gabel, Harke)* prong; **Zacken der**; **~s**, **~** *s.* **Zacke**
**zaghaft 1.** *Adj.* timid; *(zögernd)* hesitant; **2.** *adv.* timidly; *(zögernd)* hesitantly; **Zaghaftigkeit die**; **~**: timidity; *(Zögern)* hesitancy
**zäh 1.** *Adj.* **a)** tough; heavy ⟨*dough, soil*⟩; *(dickflüssig)* glutinous; viscous ⟨*oil*⟩; **b)** *(widerstandsfähig)* tough ⟨*person*⟩; **c)** *(beharrlich)* tenacious; tough ⟨*negotiations*⟩; dogged ⟨*resistance*⟩; **2.** *adv. (beharrlich)* tenaciously; ⟨*resist*⟩ doggedly; **Zähigkeit die**; **~ a)** *(Widerstandsfähigkeit)* toughness; **b)** *(Be-*

*harrlichkeit)* tenacity; **mit** ~: tenaciously

**Zahl** die; ~, ~en number; *(Ziffer)* numeral; *(Zahlenangabe, Geldmenge)* figure; **in den roten/schwarzen** ~en in the red/black; **zahlbar** *Adj. (Kaufmannsspr.)* payable; **zahlen 1.** *tr. V.* pay **(an + Akk.** to); **2.** *itr. V.* pay; ~ **bitte!** *(im Lokal)* [can I/we have] the bill, please!; **zählen 1.** *itr. V.* **a)** count; **zu einer Gruppe** *usw.* ~: be one of *or* belong to a group *etc.;* **b) auf jmdn./etw.** ~: count on sb./sth.; **2.** *tr. V.* count; **jmdn. zu seinen Freunden** ~: count sb. among one's friends

**zahl-, Zahl-:** ~**karte** die *(Postw.)* paying-in slip; ~**los** *Adj.* countless; ~**reich** *Adj.* numerous

**Zahlung** die; ~, ~en payment; **Zählung** die; ~, ~en counting; **eine** ~: a count; **Zahlungs·mittel** das means of payment; **Zahl·wort** das; *Pl.* ~wörter *(Sprachw.)* numeral

**zahm 1.** *Adj.* tame; **2.** *adv.* tamely; **zähmen** *tr. V. (auch fig.)* tame

**Zahn** der; ~[e]s, Zähne tooth; *(Raubtier~)* fang; *(an einer Briefmarke usw.)* serration

**Zahn-:** ~**arzt** der dentist; *(mit chirurgischer Ausbildung)* dental surgeon; ~**bürste** die toothbrush

**zahnen** *itr. V. ⟨baby⟩* be teething

**zahn-, Zahn-:** ~**fleisch** das gum; *(als Ganzes)* gums *pl.;* ~**los** *Adj.* toothless; ~**lücke** die gap in one's teeth; ~**pasta** die; ~, ~pasten toothpaste; ~**prothese** die dentures *pl.;* [set *sing.* of] false teeth *pl.;* ~**schmerzen** *Pl.* toothache *sing.;* ~**stocher** der; ~s, ~: toothpick; ~**weh** das; *o. Pl. (ugs.)* toothache

**Zange** die; ~, ~n **a)** *(Werkzeug)* pliers *pl.; (Eiswürfel~, Zucker~)* tongs *pl.; (Geburts~)* forceps *pl.; (Kneif~)* pincers *pl.;* **eine** ~: a pair of pliers/tongs/forceps/pincers; **b)** *(bei Tieren)* pincer

**Zank** der; ~[e]s squabble; row; **zanken** *refl. (auch itr.)* V. squabble, bicker **(um** *od.* **über** + *Akk.* over); **zänkisch** *Adj.* quarrelsome

**Zäpfchen** das; ~s, ~ suppository; **zapfen** *tr. V.* tap, draw *⟨beer, wine⟩;* **Zapfen** der; ~s, ~ **a)** *(Bot.)* cone; **b)** *(Stöpsel)* bung; **Zapf·säule** die petrol-pump *(Brit.);* gasoline pump *(Amer.)*

**zappeln** *itr. V.* wriggle; *⟨child⟩* fidget

**Zar** der; ~en, ~en *(hist.)* Tsar; **Zarin** die; ~, ~nen *(hist.)* Tsarina

**zart 1.** *Adj. (auch fig.)* delicate; soft *⟨skin⟩;* tender *⟨bud, shoot; meat, vegetables⟩;* fine *⟨biscuits⟩;* gentle *⟨kiss, touch⟩;* soft *⟨pastel colours⟩;* **2.** *adv. (empfindlich)* delicately; *⟨kiss, touch⟩* gently; **zärtlich 1.** *Adj.* tender; **2.** *adv.* tenderly; **Zärtlichkeit** die; ~, ~en **a)** *o. Pl. (Zuneigung)* tenderness; affection; **b)** *meist Pl. (Liebkosung)* caress

**Zauber** der; ~s, ~ **a)** *(auch fig.)* magic; *(Bann)* [magic] spell; **b)** *o. Pl. (ugs. abwertend: Aufheben)* fuss; **Zauberei** die; ~, ~en **a)** *o. Pl. (das Zaubern)* magic; **b)** *(Zaubertrick)* magic trick; **Zauberer** der; ~s, ~: magician; **zauber·haft 1.** *Adj.* enchanting; **2.** *adv.* enchantingly; **Zauberin** die; ~, ~nen **a)** sorceress; **b)** *(Zauberkünstlerin)* conjurer; **Zauber·künstler** der conjurer; magician; **zaubern 1.** *itr. V.* **a)** do magic; **b)** *(Zaubertricks ausführen)* do conjuring tricks; **2.** *tr. V. (auch fig.)* conjure

**zaudern** *itr. V. (geh.)* delay

**Zaum** der; ~[e]s, Zäume bridle; **zäumen** *tr. V.* bridle; **Zaum·zeug** das bridle

**Zaun** der; ~[e]s, Zäune fence; **Zaun·könig** der wren

**z. B.** *Abk.* zum Beispiel e.g.

**ZDF** [tsɛtdeːˈʔɛf] das; ~ *Abk.* Zweites Deutsches Fernsehen Second German Television Channel

**Zebra** das; ~s, ~s zebra; **Zebra·streifen** der zebra crossing *(Brit.);* pedestrian crossing

**Zeche** die; ~, ~n **a)** *(Rechnung)* bill *(Brit.);* check *(Amer.);* **b)** *(Bergwerk)* pit; mine; **zechen** *itr. V. (veralt., scherzh.)* tipple

**Zeh** der; ~s, ~en, **Zehe** die; ~, ~n **a)** toe; **b)** *(Knoblauch~)* clove; **Zehen·spitze** die: **auf** ~n on tiptoe

**zehn** *Kardinalz.* ten; **Zehn** die; ~, ~en ten; **Zehner** der; ~s, ~ **a)** *(ugs.: Geldschein, Münze)* ten; **b)** *(ugs.: Autobus)* number ten; **c)** *(Math.)* ten; **zehn·fach** *Vervielfältigungsz.* tenfold; **Zehnfache** das; *adj. Dekl.* das ~: ten times as much

**zehn-, Zehn-:** ~**kampf** der *(Sport)* decathlon; ~**mal** *Adv.* ten times; ~**mark·schein** der ten-mark note; ~**pfennig·[brief]marke** die ten-pfennig stamp; ~**pfennig·stück** das ten-pfennig piece

**zehnt...** *Ordinalz.* tenth; **zehntausend** *Kardinalz.* ten thousand;

**zehntel** *Bruchz.* tenth; **Zehntel das** (*schweiz. meist* der); **~s, ~:** tenth; **zehntens** *Adv.* tenthly

**zehren** *itr. V.* **von etw. ~:** live on *or* off sth.

**Zeichen** das; **~s, ~** sign; *(Markierung)* mark; *(Chemie, Math., auf Landkarten usw.)* symbol; **jmdm. ein ~ geben** signal to sb.

**Zeichen-:** **~setzung** die punctuation; **~sprache** die sign language

**zeichnen** 1. *tr. V.* draw; *(fig.)* portray ⟨*character*⟩; 2. *itr. V.* draw; **Zeichner** der; **~s, ~, Zeichnerin** die; **~, ~nen** graphic artist; *(Technik)* draughtsman/-woman; **Zeichnung** die; **~, ~en** drawing

**Zeige·finger** der index finger; forefinger; **zeigen** 1. *itr. V.* point; 2. *tr. V.* show; 3. *refl. V.* a) *(sich sehen lassen)* appear; b) *(sich erweisen)* prove to be; **es wird sich ~, ...:** time will tell ...; **Zeiger** der; **~s, ~:** pointer; *(Uhr~)* hand

**Zeile** die; **~, ~n** line; *(Reihe)* row

**zeit** *Präp. mit Gen.* **~ meines usw./unseres usw.** **Lebens** all my *etc.* life/our *etc.* lives; **Zeit** die; **~, ~en** a) *o. Pl.* time *no art.*; **mit der ~:** with *or* in time; *(allmählich)* gradually; b) *(~punkt)* time; **zur ~:** at the moment; c) *(~abschnitt, Lebensabschnitt)* time; period; *(Geschichtsabschnitt)* age; period; d) *(Sprachw.)* tense

**zeit-, Zeit-:** **~alter** das age; era; **~gemäß** *Adj.* *(modern)* up-to-date; *(aktuell)* topical ⟨*theme*⟩; contemporary ⟨*views*⟩; ; **~genosse** der, **~genossin** die contemporary; **~genössisch** *Adj.* contemporary; **~geschehen** das: **das |aktuelle| ~geschehen** current events *pl.*

**zeitig** *Adj., adv.* early

**Zeit·lang** die: **eine ~:** for a while; **zeit·lebens** *Adv.* all one's life; **zeitlich** 1. *Adj.* ⟨*length, interval*⟩ in time; chronological ⟨*order, sequence*⟩; 2. *adv.* with regard to time

**zeit-, Zeit-:** **~los** 1. *Adj.* timeless; classic ⟨*fashion, shape*⟩; 2. *adv.* timelessly; **~lupe** die; *o. Pl.* slow motion; **~punkt** der moment; **~raubend** *Adj.* time-consuming; **~raum** der period; **~schrift** die magazine; *(bes. wissenschaftlich)* journal; periodical; **~spanne** die period

**Zeitung** die; **~, ~en** [news]paper; **Zeitungs·notiz** die newspaper item

**zeit-, ~Zeit-:** **~verschwendung**

die waste of time; **~vertreib** der; **~|e|s, ~e** pastime; **zum ~vertreib** to pass the time; **~weilig** 1. *Adj.* temporary; 2. *adv.* temporarily; **~weise** *Adv. (gelegentlich)* occasionally; *(von Zeit zu Zeit)* from time to time; **~wort** das; *Pl.* **~wörter** *(Sprachw.)* verb

**Zelle** die; **~, ~n** cell

**Zelluloid** [tsɛluˈlɔyt] das; **~|e|s** celluloid

**Zelt** das; **~|e|s, ~e** tent; *(Fest~)* marquee; *(Zirkus~)* big top; **zelten** *itr. V.* camp

**Zelt-:** **~lager** das camp; **~plane** die tarpaulin

**Zement** der; **~|e|s, ~e** cement

**Zensur** die; **~, ~en** mark; grade *(Amer.)*

**Zenti-** [tsɛnti-]: **~meter** der, *auch:* das centimetre; **~meter·maß** das [centimetre] measuring-tape

**Zentner** der; **~s, ~** a) metric hundredweight; b) *(österr., schweiz.) s.* **Doppelzentner**

**zentral** 1. *Adj.* central; 2. *adv.* centrally; **Zentrale** die; **~, ~n** a) *(zentrale Stelle)* head *or* central office; *(der Polizei, einer Partei)* headquarters *sing. or pl.*; *(Funk~)* control centre; b) *(Telefon~)* [telephone] exchange; *(eines Hotels, einer Firma o. ä.)* switchboard; **Zentral·heizung** die central heating

**Zentren** *s.* **Zentrum**

**Zentrifugal·kraft** die *(Physik)* centrifugal force; **Zentrifuge** die; **~, ~n** centrifuge

**Zentrum** das; **~s, Zentren** centre; **im ~:** at the centre; *(im Stadt~)* in the town/city centre

**Zeppelin** der; **~s, ~e** Zeppelin

**Zepter** das, *auch:* der; **~s, ~:** sceptre

**zerbeißen** *unr. tr. V.* bite in two

**zerbersten** *unr. itr. V.; mit sein* burst apart

**zerbrechen** 1. *unr. itr. V.; mit sein* break [into pieces]; smash [to pieces]; ⟨*glass*⟩ shatter; *(fig.)* ⟨*marriage, relationship*⟩ break up; 2. *unr. tr. V.* break; smash, shatter ⟨*dishes, glass*⟩; **zerbrechlich** *Adj.* fragile; *(fig.)* frail

**zerbröckeln** 1. *itr. V.; mit sein* crumble away; 2. *tr. V.* break into small pieces

**zerdrücken** *tr. V.* mash

**Zeremonie** die; **~, ~n** ceremony; *(fig.)* ritual; **Zeremoniell** das; **~s, ~e** ceremonial

**zerfallen** *unr. itr. V.; mit sein* a) *(auch*

*fig.)* disintegrate (**in** + *Akk.*, **zu** into); ⟨*building*⟩ fall into ruin, decay; ⟨*corpse*⟩ decompose, decay

**zerfetzen** *tr. V.* rip *or* tear to pieces; *(fig.)* tear apart ⟨*body, limb*⟩

**zerfleischen** *tr. V.* tear ⟨*person, animal*⟩ limb from limb

**zerfressen** *unr. tr. V.* **a)** eat away; ⟨*moth etc.*⟩ eat holes in; **b)** *(zersetzen)* corrode ⟨*metal*⟩; eat away ⟨*bone*⟩

**zergehen** *unr. itr. V.; mit sein* melt; *(in Wasser, im Mund)* ⟨*tablet etc.*⟩ dissolve

**zerhacken** *tr. V.* chop up (**zu** into)

**zerhauen** *unr. tr. V.* chop up

**zerkleinern** *tr. V.* chop up *(zermahlen)* crush ⟨*rock etc.*⟩

**zerknautschen** *tr. V. (ugs.)* crumple

**zerknirscht 1.** *Adj.* remorseful; **2.** *adv.* remorsefully

**zerknittern** *tr. V.* crease; crumple

**zerknüllen** *tr. V.* crumple up [into a ball]

**zerkratzen** *tr. V.* scratch

**zerkrümeln** *tr. V.* crumble up

**zerlegen** *tr. V.* **a)** dismantle; take to pieces; **b)** *(zerschneiden)* cut up ⟨*animal, meat*⟩; carve ⟨*joint*⟩

**zerplatzen** *itr. V.; mit sein* burst

**Zerr·bild das** distorted image

**zerreiben** *unr. tr. V.* crush

**zerreißen 1.** *unr. tr. V.* **a)** tear up; *(in kleine Stücke)* tear to pieces; break ⟨*thread*⟩; **b)** *(beschädigen)* tear ⟨*stocking, trousers, etc.*⟩ (**an** + *Dat.* on); **2.** *unr. itr. V.; mit sein* ⟨*thread, string, rope*⟩ break; ⟨*paper, cloth, etc.*⟩ tear

**zerren 1.** *tr. V.* **a)** drag; **b)** sich *(Dat.)* einen Muskel/eine Sehne ~: pull a muscle/tendon; **2.** *itr. V.* **an etw.** *(Dat.)* ~: tug *or* pull at sth.; **Zerrung die;** ~, ~en pulled muscle/tendon

**zerrütten** *tr. V.* ruin; shatter ⟨*nerves*⟩

**zerschellen** *itr. V.; mit sein* be dashed *or* smashed to pieces

**zerschlagen 1.** *unr. tr. V.* smash ⟨*plate, windscreen, etc.*⟩; smash up ⟨*furniture*⟩; *(fig.)* smash ⟨*spy ring etc.*⟩; **2.** *unr. refl. V.* ⟨*plan, deal*⟩ fall through

**zerschneiden** *unr. tr. V.* cut; *(in Stükke)* cut up; *(in zwei Teile)* cut in two

**zersetzen** *tr. V.* corrode ⟨*metal*⟩; decompose ⟨*organism*⟩

**zersplittern** *itr. V.; mit sein* ⟨*wood, bone*⟩ splinter; ⟨*glass*⟩ shatter

**zerspringen** *unr. itr. V.; mit sein* shatter; *(Sprünge bekommen)* crack

**zerstäuben** *tr. V.* spray

**zerstören** *tr. V.* destroy; ⟨*hooligan*⟩ smash up, vandalize; *(fig.)* ruin ⟨*health, life*⟩; **Zerstörung die** *s.* **zerstören:** destruction; smashing up; vandalization; *(fig.)* ruin[ation]

**zerstreuen 1.** *tr. V.* scatter; disperse ⟨*crowd*⟩; **jmdn./sich ~** *(ablenken)* take sb.'s/one's mind off things; **2.** *refl. V.* disperse; *(schneller)* scatter; **zerstreut 1.** *Adj.* distracted; *(vergeßlich)* absent-minded; **2.** *adv.* absent-mindedly; **Zerstreuung die;** ~, ~en *(Ablenkung)* diversion

**zerstückeln** *tr. V.* break ⟨*sth.*⟩ up into small pieces; *(zerschneiden)* cut *or* chop ⟨*sth.*⟩ up into small pieces; dismember ⟨*corpse*⟩

**zerteilen** *tr. V.* divide into pieces; *(zerschneiden)* cut into pieces; cut up

**Zertifikat das;** ~[e]s, ~e certificate

**zertrampeln** *tr. V.* trample all over ⟨*flower-bed etc.*⟩; trample ⟨*child etc.*⟩ underfoot

**zertreten** *unr. tr. V.* stamp on; stamp out ⟨*cigarette, match*⟩

**zertrümmern** *tr. V.* smash; smash, shatter ⟨*glass*⟩; smash up ⟨*furniture*⟩; wreck ⟨*car, boat*⟩; reduce ⟨*building*⟩ to ruins

**Zerwürfnis das;** ~ses, ~se *(geh.)* quarrel; dispute; *(Bruch)* rift

**zerzausen** *tr. V.* ruffle; **zerzaust aussehen** look dishevelled

**zetern** *itr. V.* scold [shrilly]; *(sich beklagen)* moan (**über** + *Akk.* about)

**Zettel der;** ~s, ~: slip *or* piece of paper; *(mit einigen Zeilen)* note; *(Bekanntmachung)* notice; *(Formular)* form; *(Kassen~)* receipt; *(Hand~)* leaflet

**Zeug das;** ~[e]s, ~e **a)** *o. Pl. (ugs.)* stuff; **dummes ~:** nonsense; rubbish; **b)** *(Kleidung)* things *pl.*; **Zeuge der;** ~n, ~n witness

**zeugen** *tr. V.* procreate; ⟨*man*⟩ father ⟨*child*⟩

**Zeugen·aussage die** testimony; **Zeugin die;** ~, ~nen witness; **Zeugnis das;** ~ses, ~se **a)** *(Schulw.)* report; **b)** *(Arbeits~)* reference; testimonial; **c)** *(Gutachten)* certificate

**Zeugung die;** ~, ~en procreation; *(eines Kindes)* fathering; **zeugungsfähig** *Adj.* fertile

**z. Hd.** *Abk.* zu Händen attn.

**Zickzack der;** ~[e]s, ~e zigzag

**Ziege die;** ~, ~n goat; *(Schimpfwort: Frau)* cow *(sl. derog.)*

**Ziegel** der; ~s, ~ brick; *(Dach~)* tile; **Ziegel·stein** der brick

**Ziegen-**: ~**bock** der he- *or* billy-goat; ~**käse** der goat's cheese

**ziehen** 1. *unr. tr. V.* **a)** pull; *(sanfter)* draw; *(zerren)* tug; *(schleppen)* drag; **etw. nach sich ~** *(fig.)* result in sth.; entail sth.; **b)** *(heraus~)* extract ⟨*tooth*⟩; take out, remove ⟨*stitches*⟩; draw ⟨*cord, sword, pistol*⟩; **den Hut ~**: raise one's hat; **die |Quadrat|wurzel ~** *(Math.)* extract the square root; **c)** *(dehnen)* stretch ⟨*elastic etc.*⟩; stretch out ⟨*sheets etc.*⟩; **d)** *(Gesichtspartien bewegen)* make ⟨*face, grimace*⟩; **e)** *(bei Brettspielen)* move ⟨*chess-man etc.*⟩; **f)** *(zeichnen)* draw ⟨*line etc.*⟩; **g)** *(anlegen)* dig ⟨*trench*⟩; build ⟨*wall*⟩; erect ⟨*fence*⟩; put up ⟨*washing-line*⟩; run, lay ⟨*cable, wires*⟩; draw ⟨*frontier*⟩; **h)** *(auf~)* grow ⟨*plants, flowers*⟩; breed ⟨*animals*⟩; 2. *unr. itr. V.* **a)** *(reißen)* pull; **an etw.** *(Dat.)* ~: pull on sth.; **b)** *(funktionieren)* ⟨*stove, pipe, chimney*⟩ draw; **c)** *mit sein (um~)* move (**nach, in +** *Akk.* to); **d)** *mit sein (gehen)* go; *(marschieren)* march; *(umherstreifen)* roam; *(weggehen)* go away; leave; ⟨*fog, clouds*⟩ drift; **e)** *(saugen)* draw; **an einer Zigarette/Pfeife ~**: draw on a cigarette/pipe; **f)** ⟨*tea, coffee*⟩ draw; **g)** *(Kochk.)* simmer; **h)** *unpers.* **es zieht** there's a draught; 3. *unr. refl. V.* ⟨*road*⟩ run, stretch; ⟨*frontier*⟩ run; **Zieh·harmonika** die piano accordion; **Ziehung** die; ~, ~en draw

**Ziel** das; ~|e|s, ~e **a)** destination; **b)** *(Sport)* finish; *(~linie)* finishing-line; *(Pferderennen)* finishing-post; **c)** *(~scheibe; auch Milit.)* target; **d)** *(Zweck)* aim; goal; **sein ~ erreichen** achieve one's objective *or* aim; **ziel·bewußt** 1. *Adj.* determined; 2. *adv.* determinedly; **zielen** *itr. V.* aim (**auf +** *Akk.*, at); *(fig.)* **auf jmdn./etw.** ~ ⟨*reproach, efforts, etc.*⟩ be aimed at sb./sth.

**ziel-, Ziel-**: ~**los** 1. *Adj.* aimless; 2. *adv.* aimlessly; ~**scheibe** die *(auch fig.)* target *(Gen.* for); ~**strebig** 1. *Adj.* **a)** purposeful; **b)** *(energisch)* single-minded ⟨*person*⟩; 2. *adv.* **a)** purposefully; **b)** *(energisch)* single-mindedly

**ziemlich** 1. *Adj. (ugs.)* fair, sizeable ⟨*quantity, number*⟩; 2. *adv.* **a)** quite; fairly; **b)** *(ugs.: fast)* pretty well

**Zierde** die; ~, ~n *(auch fig.)* ornament; **zieren** *refl. V.* be coy; **zierlich**

1. *Adj.* dainty; petite, dainty ⟨*woman, figure*⟩; 2. *adv.* daintily

**Ziffer** die; ~, ~n numeral; *(in einer mehrstelligen Zahl)* digit; figure; **Ziffer·blatt** das dial; face

**-zig, zig** *unbest. Zahlwort (ugs.)* umpteen *(coll.)*

**Zigarette** die; ~, ~n cigarette; **Zigarillo** der *od.* das; ~, ~s cigarillo; small cigar; **Zigarre** die; ~, ~n cigar

**Zigeuner** der; ~s, ~, **Zigeunerin** die; ~, ~nen gypsy

**zig·mal** *Adv. (ugs.)* umpteen times *(coll.)*; **zig·tausend** *unbest. Zahlwort (ugs.)* umpteen thousand *(coll.)*

**Zimmer** das; ~s, ~: room; **Zimmermädchen** das chambermaid

**zimmern** *tr. V.* make ⟨*shelves etc.*⟩; **Zimmer·suche** die room-hunt

**zimperlich** 1. *Adj.* timid; *(leicht angeekelt)* squeamish; *(prüde)* prissy; 2. *adv.*: *s. Adj.*: timidly; squeamishly; prissily

**Zimt** der; ~|e|s, ~e cinnamon

**Zink** das; ~|e|s zinc

**Zinke** die; ~, ~n prong; *(eines Kammes)* tooth

**Zinn** das; ~|e|s tin; *(Gegenstände)* pewter[ware]

**Zins** der; ~es, ~en interest; **Zinses·zins** der compound interest

**zins·los** 1. *Adj.* interest-free; 2. *adv.* free of interest; **Zins·satz** der interest rate

**Zipfel** der; ~s, ~ *(einer Decke, eines Tisch-, Handtuchs usw.)* corner; *(Wurst~, eines Halstuchs)* [tail-]end; **Zipfel·mütze** die [long-]pointed cap

**zirka** *Adv.* about; approximately

**Zirkulation** die; ~, ~en circulation; **zirkulieren** *itr. V.; auch mit sein* circulate

**Zirkus** der; ~, ~se **a)** circus; **b)** *(ugs.)* o. Pl. *(Trubel)* hustle and bustle; *(Krach)* to-do

**zirpen** *itr. V.* chirp

**zischeln** *tr. V.* whisper angrily

**zischen** *itr. V.* **a)** hiss; ⟨*hot fat*⟩ sizzle; **b)** *mit sein* hiss

**Zitat** das; ~|e|s, ~e quotation (*aus* from)

**zitieren** *tr., itr. V.* **a)** quote; *(Rechtsspr.)* cite; **b)** *(rufen)* summon

**Zitronat** das; ~|e|s candied lemon-peel; **Zitrone** die; ~, ~n lemon

**Zitronen-**: ~**limonade** die lemonade; ~**presse** die lemon-squeezer; ~**saft** der lemon-juice

**Zitrus·frucht** die citrus fruit

**zittern** *itr. V.* tremble (**vor** + *Dat.* with); *(vor Kälte)* shiver; *(beben)* ⟨*walls, windows*⟩ shake; **vor jmdm./ etw.** ~: be terrified of sb./sth.; **zittrig** *Adj.* shaky; doddery ⟨*old man*⟩

**Zitze** die; ~, ~n teat

**zivil** 1. *Adj.* **a)** civilian; non-military ⟨*purposes*⟩; civil ⟨*aviation, marriage, law, defence*⟩; **b)** *(annehmbar)* decent; 2. *adv. (annehmbar)* decently; **Zivil** das; ~s civilian clothes *pl.;* **Zivil · bevölkerung** die civilian population; **Zivilisation** [tsiviliza'tsio:n] die; ~, ~en civilization; **zivilisieren** *tr. V.* civilize; **zivilisiert** 1. *Adj.* civilized; 2. *adv.* in a civilized way; **Zivilist** der; ~en, ~en civilian; **Zivil · kleidung** die civilian clothes *pl.*

**Zofe** die; ~, ~n *(hist.)* lady's maid

**zog** *1. u. 3. Pers. Sg. Prät. v.* **ziehen**

**zögern** *itr. V.* hesitate; **ohne zu** ~: without hesitation

**Zoll** der; ~⟨e⟩s, Zölle **a)** [customs] duty; **b)** *o. Pl. (Behörde)* customs *pl.*

**zoll-, Zoll-:** ~**amt** das customs house *or* office; ~**beamte** der customs officer; ~**frei** 1. *Adj.* duty-free; free of duty *pred.;* 2. *adv.* free of duty; ~**kontrolle** die customs examination *or* check; ~**stock** der folding rule

**Zone** die; ~, ~n zone

**Zoo** der; ~s, ~s zoo; **Zoologe** der; ~n, ~n zoologist; **Zoologie** die; ~: zoology *no art.;* **zoologisch** *Adj.* zoological; ~**er Garten** zoological gardens *pl.*

**Zoom** das; ~s, ~s *(Film, Fot.: Objektiv)* zoom; **Zoom · objektiv** das *(Film, Fot.)* zoom lens

**Zopf** der; ~⟨e⟩s, Zöpfe plait; *(am Hinterkopf)* pigtail

**Zorn** der; ~⟨e⟩s anger; *(stärker)* wrath; fury; **zornig** 1. *Adj.* furious; 2. *adv.* furiously

**Zote** die; ~, ~n dirty joke; **zotig** 1. *Adj.* smutty; dirty ⟨*joke*⟩; 2. *adv.* smuttily

**zottig** *Adj.* shaggy

**zu** 1. *Präp. mit Dat.* **a)** *(Richtung)* to; **zu ... hin** towards ...; **b)** *(zusammen mit)* with; **zu dem Käse gab es Wein** there was wine with the cheese; **c)** *(Lage)* at; **zu beiden Seiten** on both sides; **d)** *(zeitlich)* at; **zu Weihnachten** at Christmas; **e)** *(Art u. Weise)* **zu meiner Zufriedenheit/Überraschung** to my satisfaction/surprise; *(bei Mengenangaben o. ä)* **zu Dutzenden/zweien** by the dozen/in twos; **f)** *(ein Zahlen-*

*verhältnis ausdrückend)* **ein Verhältnis von 3 zu 1** a ratio of 3 to 1; **g)** *(einen Preis zuordnend)* at; for; **h)** *(Zweck)* for; **i)** *(Ziel, Ergebnis)* into; **zu etw. werden** turn into sth.; **j)** *(über)* about; on; **sich zu etw. äußern** comment on sth.; **k)** *(gegenüber)* **freundlich/häßlich zu jmdm. sein** be friendly/nasty to sb.; *s. auch* **zum; zur;** 2. *Adv.* **a)** *(allzu)* too; **zu sehr** too much; **b)** *nachgestellt (Richtung)* towards; 3. *Konj.* **a)** *(mit Infinitiv)* to; **was gibt's da zu lachen?** what is there to laugh about?; **b)** *(mit 1. Part.)* **die zu erledigende Post** the letters *pl.* to be dealt with

**Zubehör** das; ~⟨e⟩s, ~e *od. schweiz.* ~**den** accessories *pl.;* *(eines Staubsaugers, Mixers o. ä.)* attachments *pl.;* *(Ausstattung)* equipment

**zu|bereiten** *tr. V.* prepare ⟨*meal etc.*⟩; make up ⟨*medicine, ointment*⟩; *(kochen)* cook ⟨*fish, meat, etc.*⟩

**zu|billigen** *tr. V.* **jmdm. etw.** ~: grant *or* allow sb. sth.

**zu|binden** *unr. tr. V.* tie [up]

**zu|blinzeln** *itr. V.* **jmdm.** ~: wink at sb.

**zu|bringen** *unr. tr. V.* spend; **Zubringer** der; ~s, ~ **a)** *(Straße)* access road; **b)** *(Verkehrsmittel)* shuttle

**Zucht** die; ~, ~en **a)** breeding; *(von Pflanzen)* cultivation; **ein Pferd aus deutscher** ~: a German-bred horse; **b)** *o. Pl. (geh.: Disziplin)* discipline; **züchten** *tr. V. (auch fig.)* breed; cultivate ⟨*plants*⟩; culture ⟨*bacteria, pearls*⟩; **Züchter** der; ~s, ~, **Züchterin** die; ~, ~nen breeder; *(von Pflanzen)* grower [of new varieties]; **Züchtung** die; ~, ~en **a)** breeding; *(von Pflanzen)* cultivation; **b)** *(Zuchtergebnis)* strain

**zucken** *itr. V.;* **mit Richtungsangabe mit sein** twitch ⟨*body, arm, leg, etc.*⟩ jerk; *(vor Schreck)* start; ⟨*flames*⟩ flicker; **mit den Achseln/Schultern** ~: shrug one's shoulders; **zücken** *tr. V.* draw ⟨*sword, dagger, knife*⟩

**Zucker** der; ~s, ~ **a)** sugar; **b)** *o. Pl. (ugs.: ~krankheit)* diabetes; ~ **haben** be a diabetic

**zucker-, Zucker-:** ~**dose** die sugar bowl; ~**hut** der sugar loaf; ~**krank** *Adj.* diabetic

**zuckern** *tr. V.* sugar

**Zuckung** die; ~, ~en twitch

**zu|decken** *tr. V.* cover up; cover [over] ⟨*well, ditch*⟩; **jmdn./sich** ~: tuck sb./oneself up

**zu̱|drehen** *tr. V.* **a)** *(abdrehen)* turn off; **b)** *(zuwenden)* **jmdm. den Rücken ~:** turn one's back on sb.

**zu̱·dringlich 1.** *Adj.* pushy *(coll.)*, pushing ⟨*person, manner*⟩; *(sexuell)* importunate ⟨*person, manner*⟩; prying ⟨*glance*⟩; **2.** *adv.* importunately; **Zu̱dringlichkeit die; ~, ~en a)** *o. Pl.* pushiness *(coll.); (in sexueller Hinsicht)* importunate manner; **b)** *(Handlung)* **~en** insistent advances *or* attentions

**zu̱|drücken** *tr. V.* press shut; push ⟨*door*⟩ shut; **jmdm. die Kehle ~:** choke *or* throttle sb.

**zu·eina̱nder** *Adv.* to one another

**zu·e̱rst** *Adv.* **a)** first; **b)** *(anfangs)* at first; to start with; **c)** *(erstmals)* first

**Zu̱·fahrt die a)** *o. Pl.* access [for vehicles]; **b)** *(Straße, Weg)* access road; *(zum Haus)* driveway; **Zu̱fahrts·straße die** access road

**Zu̱·fall der** chance; *(zufälliges Zusammentreffen von Ereignissen)* coincidence; **durch ~:** by chance; **zu̱|fallen** *unr. itr. V.; mit sein* **a)** ⟨*door etc.*⟩ slam shut; ⟨*eyes*⟩ close; **b)** *(zukommen)* **jmdm. ~** ⟨*task*⟩ fall to sb.; ⟨*prize, inheritance*⟩ go to sb.; **zu̱·fällig 1.** *Adj.* accidental; chance *attrib.* ⟨*meeting, acquaintance*⟩; random ⟨*selection*⟩; **2.** *adv.* by chance; **wissen Sie ~, wie spät es ist?** *(ugs.)* do you by any chance know the time?; **Zu̱fallstreffer der** fluke

**zu̱|fassen** *itr. V.* make a snatch *or* grab

**zu̱|fliegen** *unr. itr. V.; mit sein (ugs.)* ⟨*door, window, etc.*⟩ slam shut

**Zu̱·flucht die** refuge (**vor** + *Dat.* from); *(vor Unwetter o. ä.)* shelter (**vor** + *Dat.* from); **Zu̱fluchts·ort der** place of refuge; sanctuary

**Zu̱·fluß der a)** *o. Pl. (das Zufließen)* inflow; supply; *(fig.)* influx; **b)** *(Gewässer)* feeder stream/river

**zu̱|flüstern** *tr. V.* **jmdm. etw. ~:** whisper sth. to sb.

**zu·fo̱lge** *Präp. mit Dat.; nachgestellt* according to

**zu·fri̱eden 1.** *Adj.* contented; *(befriedigt)* satisfied; **mit etw. ~ sein** be satisfied with sth.; **2.** *adv.* contentedly; **zufri̱eden|geben** *unr. refl. V.* be satisfied; **Zufri̱edenheit die; ~:** contentment; *(Befriedigung)* satisfaction; **zufri̱eden|stellen** *tr. V.* satisfy; **zufri̱edenstellend 1.** *Adj.* satisfactory; **2.** *adv.* satisfactorily

**zu̱|frieren** *unr. itr. V.; mit sein* freeze over

**zu̱|fügen** *tr. V.* **jmdm. etw. ~:** inflict sth. on sb.; **jmdm. Schaden/[ein] Unrecht ~:** do sb. harm/an injustice

**Zufu̱hr die; ~:** supply; *(Material)* supplies *pl.;* **zu̱|führen 1.** *itr. V.* **auf etw.** *(Akk.)* **~:** lead towards sth.; **2.** *tr. V.* **a)** *(zuleiten)* **einer Sache** *(Dat.)* **etw. ~:** supply sth. to sth.; **b)** *(bringen)* **einer Partei Mitglieder ~:** bring new members to a party

**Zu̱g der; ~[e]s, Zü̱ge a)** *(Bahn)* train; **b)** *(Kolonne)* column; *(Umzug)* procession; *(Demonstrations~)* march; **c)** *(das Ziehen)* pull; traction *(Phys.);* **d)** *(Vorrichtung)* pull; **e)** *(Wanderung)* migration; **f)** *(beim Brettspiel)* move; **g)** *(Schluck)* swig *(coll.);* mouthful; *(großer Schluck)* gulp; **das Glas auf einen** *od.* **in einem ~ leeren** empty the glass at one go; **h)** *(beim Rauchen)* pull; drag *(coll.);* **i)** *(Atem~)* breath; **j)** *o. Pl. (Zugluft; beim Ofen)* draught; **k)** *(Gesichts~)* feature; *(Wesens~)* characteristic; trait

**Zu̱·gabe die a)** *(Geschenk)* [free] gift; **b)** *(im Konzert, Theater)* encore

**Zu̱·gang der a)** *(Weg, auch fig.)* access; *(Eingang)* entrance; **b)** *o. Pl. (das Hinzukommen) (von Personen)* intake; *(von Patienten)* admission; *(Zuwachs)* increase (**von** in); **zu·ga̱nge: ~ sein** *(ugs.)* be busy *or* occupied; **zugä̱nglich** *Adj.* **a)** accessible; *(geöffnet)* open; **b)** *(zur Verfügung stehend)* available *(Dat.,* **für** to); *(verständlich)* accessible *(Dat.,* **für** to); **c)** *(aufgeschlossen)* approachable ⟨*person*⟩

**zu̱·geben** *unr. tr. V.* admit; admit to ⟨*deed, crime*⟩

**zu·ge̱gen** *Adj.* **~ sein** be present

**zu̱|gehen** *unr. itr. V.; mit sein* **a) auf jmdn./etw. ~:** approach sb./sth.; **b) jmdm. ~** *(zugeschickt werden)* be sent to sb.; **c)** *(ugs.: sich schließen)* close; shut; **die Tür geht nicht zu** the door will not shut

**Zü̱gel der; ~s, ~:** rein; **zü̱gel·los** *(fig.)* **1.** *Adj.* unrestrained; unbridled ⟨*rage, passion*⟩; **2.** *adv.* without restraint; **zü̱geln** *tr. V.* rein [in] ⟨*horse*⟩; *(fig.)* curb, restrain ⟨*desire etc.*⟩

**zu̱|gesellen** *refl. V.* **sich jmdm./einer Sache ~:** join sb./sth.

**Zu̱·geständnis das** concession; **zu̱·gestehen** *unr. tr. V.* admit; concede

**zu·ge̱tan** *Adj.* **jmdm. [herzlich] ~ sein** *(geh.)* be [very] attached to sb.

**zugig** *Adj.* draughty, *(im Freien)* windy *⟨corner etc.⟩*

**zügig 1.** *Adj.* speedy; rapid; **2.** *adv.* speedily; rapidly

**zu·gleich** *Adv.* at the same time

**Zug·luft** die; *o. Pl.* draught

**zu|greifen** *unr. itr. V.* **a)** take hold; **b)** *(sich bedienen)* help oneself; **c)** *(fleißig arbeiten)* |hart *od.* kräftig| ~: [really] knuckle down to it; **Zu·griff** der *(Zugang)* access (**auf** + *Akk.* to)

**zu·grunde** *Adv.* **a)** ~ gehen *(sterben)* die (**an** + *Dat.* of); *(zerstört werden)* be destroyed (**an** + *Dat.* by); ~ richten destroy; *(finanziell)* ruin *⟨company, person⟩*; **b)** etw. einer Sache *(Dat.)* ~ legen base sth. on sth.; etw. liegt einer Sache ~: sth. is based on sth.

**zu|gucken** *itr. V.* *(ugs.)* s. zusehen

**zu·gunsten 1.** *Präp. mit Gen.* in favour of; **2.** *Adv.* ~ von in favour of

**zu·gute** *Adv.* jmdm. seine Unerfahrenheit *usw.* ~ halten *(geh.)* make allowances for sb.'s inexperience *etc.*; sich *(Dat.)* etwas/viel auf etw. *(Akk.)* ~ tun *od.* halten *(geh.)* be proud/very proud of sth.; jmdm./einer Sache ~ kommen stand sb./sth. in good stead

**zu|haben** *unr. itr. V.* *(ugs.)* *⟨shop, office⟩* be shut *or* closed

**zu|halten** *unr. tr. V.* hold closed; *(nicht öffnen)* keep closed

**zu|hängen** *tr. V.* cover *⟨window, cage⟩*

**zu|hauen** *(ugs.)* **1.** *unr. itr. V.* bang *or* slam *⟨door, window⟩* shut; **2.** *unr. itr. V.* hit *or* strike out

**Zu·hause** das; ~s home

**zu|hören** *itr. V.* jmdm./einer Sache ~: listen to sb./sth.; **Zu·hörer** der, **Zu·hörerin** die listener

**zu|kleben** *tr. V.* seal *⟨letter, envelope⟩*

**zu|knallen** *(ugs.)* **1.** *tr. V.* slam; **2.** *itr. V.; mit sein* slam

**zu|knöpfen** *tr. V.* button up

**zu|kommen** *itr. V.; mit sein* auf jmdn. ~: approach sb.

**Zukunft** die; ~: future

**Zulage** die extra pay *no indef. art.*; additional allowance *no indef. art.*

**zu|lassen** *unr. tr. V.* **a)** allow; permit; **b)** *(teilnehmen lassen)* admit; **c)** *(mit einer Lizenz usw. versehen)* jmdn. als Arzt ~: register sb. as a doctor; **d)** *(Kfz-W.)* register *⟨vehicle⟩*; **e)** *(geschlossen lassen)* leave closed *or* shut *⟨door, window, etc.⟩*; **zu·lässig** *Adj.* permissible; admissible *⟨appeal⟩*; **Zulassung** die; ~, ~en registration

**Zu·lauf** der *o. Pl.* ~ haben *⟨shop, restaurant, etc.⟩* enjoy a large clientele; *⟨doctor, lawyer⟩* have a large practice; **zu|laufen** *unr. itr. V.; mit sein* **a)** auf jmdn./etw. ~ *(auch fig.)* run towards sb./sth.; **b)** jmdm. ~ *⟨cat, dog, etc.⟩* adopt sb. as a new owner

**zu|legen** *refl. V.* sich *(Dat.)* etw. ~: get oneself sth.

**zu·letzt** *Adv.* **a)** last [of all]; **b)** *(als letzter/letzte/letztes)* last; **c)** *(fig.: am wenigsten)* least of all; **d)** *(schließlich, am Ende)* in the end; bis ~: [right up] to *or* until the end

**zum** *Präp. + Art.* **a)** = zu dem; **b)** *(räumlich: Richtung)* to the; **c)** *(räumlich: Lage)* etw. ~ Fenster hinauswerfen throw sth. out of the window; **d)** *(Hinzufügung)* Milch ~ Tee nehmen take milk with [one's] tea **e)** *(zeitlich)* at the; spätestens ~ 15. April by 15 April at the latest; **f)** *(Zweck)* ~ Spaß/ Vergnügen for fun/pleasure; **g)** *(Folge)* ~ Ärger seines Vaters to the annoyance of his father

**zu|machen** *tr. V.* close; fasten, do up *⟨dress⟩*; seal *⟨envelope, letter⟩*; turn off *⟨tap⟩*; put the top on *⟨bottle⟩*; *(stillegen)* close *or* shut down *⟨factory, mine, etc.⟩*

**zu·mal 1.** *Adv.* especially; particularly; **2.** *Konj.* especially *or* particularly since

**zumindest** *Adv.* at least

**zu·mute** *Adj.* jmdm. ist unbehaglich *usw.* ~: sb. feels uncomfortable *etc.*; mir war nicht danach ~: I didn't feel like it *or* in the mood

**zu|muten** *tr. V.* jmdm. etw. ~ *(abverlangen)* expect *or* ask sth. of sb.; *(antun)* expect sb. to put up with sth.; **Zumutung** die; ~, ~en unreasonable demand; eine ~ sein be unreasonable

**zu·nächst** *Adv.* **a)** *(als erstes)* first; *(anfangs)* at first; **b)** *(im Moment, vorläufig)* for the moment

**Zunahme** die; ~, ~n increase *(Gen., an* + *Dat.* in)

**Zu·name** der surname; last name

**zünden 1.** *tr. V.* ignite *⟨gas, fuel, etc.⟩*; detonate *⟨bomb, explosive device, etc.⟩*; let off *⟨fireworks⟩*; fire *⟨rocket⟩*; **2.** *itr. V.* *⟨rocket, engine⟩* fire; *⟨lighter, match⟩* light; *⟨gas, fuel, explosive⟩* ignite

**Zünd-:** ~holz das *(bes. südd., österr.)* match; ~schlüssel der *(Kfz-W.)* ignition key

**Zündung** die; ~, ~en **a)** s. zünden 1:

ignition; detonation; letting off; firing; b) *(Kfz-W.: Anlage)* ignition

**zu|nehmen** *unr. itr. V.* a) increase (**an** + *Dat.* in); ⟨*moon*⟩ wax; b) *(schwerer werden)* put on *or* gain weight

**Zu · neigung die;** ~, ~en affection

**Zunge die;** ~, ~n tongue; [jmdm.] die ~ herausstrecken put one's tongue out [at sb.]

**zu · nichte** *Adj.* etw. ~ machen ruin sth.

**zu · oberst** *Adv.* [right] on [the] top

**zupfen 1.** *itr. V.* an etw. *(Dat.)* ~: pluck *or* pull at sth.; **2.** *tr. V.* a) etw. aus/von usw. etw. ~: pull sth. out of/ from *etc.* sth.; b) *(auszupfen)* pull out; pluck ⟨*eyebrows*⟩; c) pluck ⟨*string, guitar, tune*⟩; d) jmdn. am Ärmel ~: pull *or* tug [at] sb.'s sleeve

**zur** *Präp.* + *Art.* a) = zu der; b) *(räumlich, fig.: Richtung)* to the; ~ Schule/ Arbeit gehen go to school/work; c) *(räumlich: Lage)* ~ Tür hereinkommen come [in] through the door; d) *(Zusammengehörigkeit,        Hinzufügung)* with; e) *(zeitlich)* at the; ~ Zeit at the moment; at present; f) *(Zweck)* ~ Entschuldigung by way of [an] excuse; g) *(Folge)* ~ vollen Zufriedenheit to the complete satisfaction

**zurechnungs · fähig** *Adj.* sound of mind *pred.*

**zurecht-:** ~|**finden** *unr. refl. V.* find one's way [around]; ~|**kommen** *unr. itr. V.; mit sein* get on (mit with); ~|**legen** *tr. V.* lay out [ready]; jmdm. etw. ~legen lay sth. out ready for sb.; ~|**machen** *tr. V. (ugs.)* a) *(vorbereiten)* get ready; b) *(herrichten)* do up; c) jmdn./sich ~: get sb. ready/get [oneself] ready; *(schminken)* make sb. up/put on one's make-up; ~|**weisen** *unr. tr. V.* rebuke; reprimand ⟨*pupil, subordinate, etc.*⟩

**zu|reden** *itr. V.* jmdm. ~: persuade sb.; *(ermutigen)* encourage sb.

**Zürich (das);** ~s Zurich

**zu · rück** *Adv.* back; *(weiter hinten)* behind; einen Schritt ~: a step backwards; ~! get *or* go back!

**zurück-, Zurück-:** ~|**behalten** *unr. tr. V.* a) keep [back]; retain; b) be left with ⟨*scar, heart defect, etc.*⟩; ~|**bekommen** *unr. tr. V.* get back; Sie bekommen 10 Mark ~: you get 10 marks change; ~|**bleiben** *unr. itr. V.; mit sein* a) remain; b) *(nicht mithalten)* lag behind; *(fig.)* fall behind; c) *(bleiben)* remain; ~|**erstatten** *tr. V.* refund;

jmdm. etw. ~erstatten refund sth. to sb.; ~|**fahren** *unr. itr. V.; mit sein* a) go back; return; b) *(nach hinten fahren)* go back[wards]; ~|**fallen** *unr. itr. V.; mit sein* a) *(in Rückstand geraten)* fall behind; b) *(auf einen niedrigeren Rang)* drop (auf + *Akk.* to); c) an jmdn. ~fallen ⟨*property*⟩ revert to sb.; d) auf jmdn. ~fallen ⟨*actions, behaviour*⟩ reflect [up]on sb.; ~|**fliegen** *unr. itr. V.; mit sein* fly back; ~|**führen** *tr. V.* etw. auf etw. *(Akk.)* ~führen attribute sth. to sth.; ~|**geben** *unr. tr. V.* give back; return; take back ⟨*defective goods*⟩; ~|**gehen** *unr. itr. V.; mit sein* a) go back; return; b) *(nach hinten)* go back; c) *(verschwinden)* disappear; ⟨*swelling, inflammation*⟩ go down; ⟨*pain*⟩ subside; d) *(sich verringern)* decrease; ⟨*fever*⟩ abate; ⟨*flood*⟩ subside; ⟨*business*⟩ fall off; e) *(zurückgeschickt werden)* be returned *or* sent back; ~|**greifen** *unr. itr. V.* auf jmdn./etw. ~greifen fall back on sb./sth.; ~|**halten 1.** *unr. tr. V.* a) jmdn. ~halten hold sb. back; *(von etw. abhalten)* stop sb.; b) *(am Vordringen hindern)* keep back ⟨*crowd, mob, etc.*⟩; c) *(behalten)* withhold ⟨*news, letter, etc.*⟩; d) *(nicht austreten lassen)* hold back ⟨*tears etc.*⟩; **2.** *unr. refl. V.* restrain *or* control oneself; sich in einer Diskussion ~halten keep in the background in a discussion; ~|**haltend 1.** *Adj.* a) reserved; b) ⟨*kühl, reserviert*⟩ cool, restrained ⟨*reception, response*⟩; c) *(Wirtsch.: schwach)* slack ⟨*demand*⟩; **2.** *adv.* ⟨*behave*⟩ with reserve *or* restraint; ⟨*kühl, reserviert*⟩ coolly; ~|**haltung die;** *o. Pl.* reserve; ⟨Kühle, Reserviertheit⟩ coolness; *(Wirtsch.)* caution; ~|**kehren** *itr. V.; mit sein* return; come back; ~|**kommen** *unr. itr. V.; mit sein* come back; return; *(zurückgelangen)* get back; ~kommen auf (+ *Akk.*) come back to ⟨*subject, question, point, etc.*⟩; ~|**kriegen** *tr. V. s.* ~bekommen; ~|**lassen** *unr. tr. V.* leave; ~|**legen** *tr. V.* a) put back; b) *(reservieren)* put aside, keep (*Dat.*, für for); c) *(sparen)* put away; d) *(hinter sich bringen)* cover ⟨*distance*⟩; ~|**lehnen** *refl. V.* lean back; ~|**nehmen** *unr. tr. V. (auch fig. widerrufen)* take back; ~|**rufen** *unr. tr. V.* a) call back; recall ⟨*ambassador*⟩; b) auch *itr. (telefonisch)* call *or* (*Brit.*) ring back; ~|**schicken** *tr. V.* send back ~|**schrecken** *regelm., veralt. unr. itr.*

*V.; mit sein* vor etw. *(Dat.)* ~**schrecken** *(fig.)* shrink from sth.; **er schreckt vor nichts ~:** he will stop at nothing; ~|**senden** *unr. od. regelm. tr. V. (geh.) s.* ~**schicken;** ~|**treten** *unr. itr. V.; mit sein* step back; *(von einem Amt)* resign; step down; *(government)* resign; *(von einem Vertrag usw.)* withdraw **(von** from); back out **(von** of); *(fig.: in den Hintergrund treten)* become less important; ~|**weisen** *unr. tr. V.* reject ⟨*proposal, question, demand, application, etc.*⟩; turn down, refuse ⟨*offer, request, help, etc.*⟩; turn away ⟨*petitioner, unwelcome guest*⟩; repudiate ⟨*accusation, claim, etc.*⟩; ~|**werfen** *unr. tr. V.* throw back; reflect ⟨*light, sound*⟩; repulse ⟨*enemy*⟩; *(fig.: in einer Entwicklung)* set back; ~|**zahlen** *tr. V.* pay back; ~|**ziehen 1.** *unr. tr. V.* **a)** pull back; draw back ⟨*bolt, curtains, one's hand, etc.*⟩; **b)** *(abziehen, zurückbeordern)* withdraw ⟨*troops*⟩; recall ⟨*ambassador*⟩; **c)** *(rückgängig machen)* withdraw; cancel ⟨*order, instruction*⟩; **2.** *unr. refl. V.* withdraw

**Zu·ruf** der shout; **zu|rufen** *unr. tr. V.* **jmdm. etw. ~:** shout sth. to sb.

**Zu·sage** die **a)** *(auf eine Einladung hin)* acceptance; *(auf eine Stellenbewerbung hin)* offer; **b)** *(Versprechen)* promise; undertaking; **zu|sagen 1.** *itr. V.* **a)** accept; **b)** jmdm. ~ *(gefallen)* appeal to sb.; **2.** *tr. V.* promise

**zusammen** *Adv.* together

**zusammen-, Zusammen-:** ~|**arbeiten** *itr. V.* co-operate; ~|**binden** *unr. tr. V.* tie together; ~|**brechen** *unr. itr. V.; mit sein* collapse; *(fig.)(order, communications, system, telephone network)* break down; ⟨*traffic*⟩ come to a standstill; ~**bruch** der collapse; *(fig., auch psychisch, nervlich)* breakdown; ~|**drücken** *tr. V.* press together; ~|**fahren** *unr. itr. V.; mit sein (~zucken)* start; jump; ~|**fallen** *unr. itr. V.; mit sein* **a)** collapse; **b)** |zeitlich| ~**fallen** coincide; ~|**fassen** *tr. V.* summarize; ~**fassung** die summary; ~|**fegen** *tr. V. (bes. nordd.)* sweep together; ~|**fließen** *unr. itr. V.; mit sein* ⟨*rivers, streams*⟩ flow into each other; ~**fluß** der confluence; ~|**fügen** *tr. V.* fit together; ~|**führen** *tr. V.* bring together; ~|**gehören** *itr. V.* belong together; ~**gehörig** *Adj.* [closely] related *or* connected ⟨*subjects, problems, etc.*⟩; matching *attrib.*

⟨*pieces of tea service, cutlery, etc.*⟩; ~**gehörigkeit** die; ~**:** **ein starkes Gefühl der** ~**gehörigkeit** a strong sense of belonging together; ~**hang** der connection; *(einer Geschichte, Rede)* coherence; *(Kontext)* context; ~|**hängen** *unr. itr. V.* **a)** be joined [together]; **b)** mit etw. ~**hängen** *(fig.)* be related to sth.; *(durch etw. [mit] verursacht sein)* be the result of sth.; ~|**laufen** *tr. V. (bes. südd.) s.* ~**fegen;** ~**klappbar** *Adj.* folding; ~|**klappen** *tr. V.* fold up; ~|**kommen** *unr. itr. V.; mit sein* **a)** meet; **mit jmdm.** ~**kommen** meet sb.; **b)** *(zueinanderkommen; auch fig.)* get together; *(gleichzeitig auftreten)* occur *or* happen together; ~**kunft** die; ~, ~**künfte** meeting; ~|**laufen** *unr. itr. V.; mit sein* **a)** ⟨*people, crowd*⟩ gather, congregate; **b)** ⟨*rivers, streams*⟩ flow into each other, join up; ~|**leben** *itr. V.* live together; ~**leben** das; *o. Pl.* living together *no art.;* ~|**legen 1.** *tr. V.* **a)** put *or* gather together; **b)** *(zusammenfalten)* fold [up]; **c)** *(miteinander verbinden)* amalgamate, merge ⟨*classes, departments, etc.*⟩; combine ⟨*events*⟩; **d)** put ⟨*patients, guests, etc.*⟩ together [in the same room]; **2.** *itr. V.* club together; ~|**nehmen 1.** *unr. tr. V.* **a)** summon up ⟨*courage, strength, understanding*⟩; **2.** *unr. refl. V.* get *or* take a grip on oneself; **nimm dich ~!** pull yourself together!; ~|**passen** *itr. V.* go together; ⟨*persons*⟩ be suited to each other; ~**prall** der; ~|e|s, ~e collision; ~|**prallen** *itr. V.; mit sein* collide (**mit** with); ~|**sein** *unr. itr. V.; mit sein; Zusschr. nur im Inf. u. Part.* **a)** be together; **b)** *(zusammenleben)* be *or* live together; ~|**setzen 1.** *tr. V.* put together; **2.** *refl. V.* **a) sich aus etw.** ~**setzen** be made up *or* composed of sth.; **b)** *(sich zueinander setzen)* sit together; *(zu einem Gespräch)* get together; ~|**stehen** *unr. itr. V.* stand together; ~|**stellen** *tr. V.* put together; draw up ⟨*list*⟩; ~**stoß** der collision; *(fig.)* clash (**mit** with); ~|**stoßen** *unr. itr. V.; mit sein* collide (**mit** with); ~|**treffen** *unr. itr. V.; mit sein* meet; **mit jmdm.** ~**treffen** meet sb.; *(zeitlich)* coincide; ~|**zählen** *tr. V.* add up; ~|**zucken** *itr. V.; mit sein* start; jump

**Zu·satz** der addition; *(Zugesetztes, Additiv)* additive; **zusätzlich 1.** *Adj.* additional; **2.** *adv.* in addition

**zu|schauen** *itr. V. (südd., österr., schweiz.)* s. **zusehen; Zu·schauer** der, **Zu·schauerin** die; ~, ~nen spectator; *(im Theater, Kino)* member of the audience; *(an einer Unfallstelle)* onlooker; *(Fernseh~)* viewer; **die ~:** *(im Theater, Kino)* the audience *sing.*

**zu|schicken** *tr. V.* send

**zu|schieben** *unr. tr. V.* **a)** push ⟨*drawer, door*⟩ shut; **b)** *(fig.)* **jmdm. die Schuld ~:** lay the blame on sb.

**Zu·schlag** der **a)** additional *or* extra charge; *(für Nacht-, Feiertagsarbeit usw.)* additional *or* extra payment; **b)** *(Eisenb.)* supplement ticket; **zu|schlagen** **1.** *unr. tr. V.* bang *or* slam ⟨*door, window, etc.*⟩ shut; close ⟨*book*⟩; *(heftig)* slam ⟨*book*⟩ shut; **2.** *unr. itr. V.* **a)** *mit sein ⟨door, trap⟩* slam *or* bang shut; **b)** *(einen Schlag führen)* throw a blow/blows; *(losschlagen)* hit *or* strike out; *(fig.)* ⟨*army, police, murderer*⟩ strike

**zu|schließen** **1.** *unr. tr. V.* lock; **2.** *unr. itr. V.* lock up

**zu|schnüren** *tr. V.* tie up

**zu|schrauben** *tr. V.* screw the lid *or* top on ⟨*jar, flask*⟩; screw ⟨*lid, top*⟩ on

**Zu·schrift** die letter; *(auf eine Anzeige)* reply

**Zu·schuß** der contribution (zu towards)

**zu|sehen** *unr. itr. V.* **a)** watch; **jmdm. [beim Arbeiten** *usw.*] **~:** watch sb. [working *etc.*]; **b)** *(dafür sorgen)* make sure; see to it

**zu|senden** *unr. od. regelm. tr. V.:* s. **zuschicken; Zu·sendung** die sending

**zu|spitzen** *refl. V.* become aggravated

**zu|sprechen** **1.** *unr. tr. V.* **a) er sprach ihr Trost/Mut zu** his words gave her comfort/courage; **b) jmdm. ein Erbe** *usw.* **~:** award sb. an inheritance *etc.*; **2.** *unr. itr. V.* **jmdm. ermutigend/tröstend** *usw.* **~:** speak encouragingly/comfortingly to sb.

**Zu·stand** der **a)** condition; *(bes. abwertend)* state; **b)** *(Stand der Dinge)* state of affairs; **zu·stande** *Adv.* **etw. ~ bringen** [manage to] bring about sth.; **~ kommen** come into being; *(geschehen)* take place; **zu·ständig** *Adj.* appropriate relevant ⟨*authority, office, etc.*⟩; **[für etw.] ~ sein** *(verantwortlich)* be responsible [for sth.]

**zu|stehen** *unr. itr. V.* **etw. steht jmdm. zu** sb. is entitled to sth.

**zu|steigen** *unr. itr. V.; mit sein* get on;

**ist noch jemand zugestiegen?** *(im Bus)* ≈ any more fares, please?; *(im Zug)* ≈ tickets, please!

**zu|stellen** *tr. V.* deliver ⟨*letter, parcel, etc.*⟩

**zu|stimmen** *itr. V.* agree; **jmdm. [in einem Punkt]** **~:** agree with sb. [on a point]; **einer Sache** *(Dat.)* **~:** agree to sth.; **Zu·stimmung** die *(Billigung)* approval (zu of); *(Einverständnis)* agreement (zu to, with)

**zu|stoßen** *unr. itr. V.; mit sein* **jmdm. ~:** happen to sb.

**Zu·tat** die ingredient

**zu·teil** *Adv.* **jmdm./einer Sache ~ werden** *(geh.)* be granted to sb./sth.; **zu|teilen** *tr. V.* **jmdm. jmdn./etw. ~:** allot *or* assign sb./sth. to sb.; **jmdm. seine Portion ~:** mete out his/her share to sb.

**zu|tragen** *unr. refl. V. (geh.)* occur; **zuträglich** *Adj.* healthy ⟨*climate*⟩; **jmdm./einer Sache ~ sein** be good for sb./sth.; be beneficial to sb./sth.

**zu|trauen** *tr. V.* **jmdm. etw. ~:** believe sb. [is] capable of [doing] sth.; **sich** *(Dat.)* **etw. ~:** think one can do *or* is capable of doing sth.; **Zutrauen** das; ~s confidence, trust (zu in); **zutraulich** **1.** *Adj.* trusting; **2.** *adv.* trustingly; **Zutraulichkeit** die; ~: trust[fulness]

**zu|treffen** *unr. itr. V.* **a)** be correct; **b) auf** *od.* **für jmdn./etw. ~:** apply to sb./sth.; **zutreffend** **1.** *Adj.* **a)** correct; **b)** *(geltend)* applicable; relevant; **2.** *adv.* correctly

**zu|trinken** *unr. itr. V.* **jmdm. ~:** raise one's glass and drink to sb.

**Zu·tritt** der entry; admittance; „**kein ~**", „**~ verboten**" 'no entry'; 'no admittance'; **~ [zu etw.] haben** have access [to sth.]

**zu·unterst** *Adv.* right at the bottom

**zuverlässig** **1.** *Adj.* reliable; *(verläßlich)* dependable ⟨*person*⟩; **2.** *adv.* reliably; **Zuverlässigkeit** die; ~: reliability; *(Verläßlichkeit)* dependability

**zuversichtlich** **1.** *Adj.* confident; **2.** *adv.* confidently

**zuviel** **1.** *indekl. Indefinitpron.* too much; *(ugs.: zu viele)* too many; **2.** *adv.* too much

**zu·vor** *Adv.* before

**zuvor|kommen** *unr. itr. V.; mit sein* **a) jmdm. ~:** beat sb. to it; **b) einer Sache** *(Dat.)* **~:** anticipate sth.; **zuvorkommend** **1.** *Adj.* obliging; *(höflich)* courteous; **2.** *adv.* obligingly; *(höf-lich)* courteously

**zu·weilen** *Adv. (geh.)* now and again

**zu|weisen** *unr. tr. V.* jmdm. etw. ~: allocate *or* allot sb. sth.

**zu|wenden** *unr. od. regelm. refl. V.* sich jmdm./einer Sache ~ *(auch fig.)* turn to sb./sth.

**zu·wenig 1.** *indekl. Indefinitpron.* too little; *(ugs.: zu wenige)* too few; **2.** *adv.* too little

**zuwider** *Adj.* jmdm. ~ sein be repugnant to sb.

**zu|winken** *itr. V.* jmdm./einander ~: wave to sb./one another

**zu|zahlen** *tr. V.* pay *(five marks etc.)* extra

**zu|ziehen 1.** *unr. tr. V.* pull *(door)* shut; draw *(curtain)*; do up *(zip)*; **2.** *unr. refl. V.* sich *(Dat.)* eine Krankheit ~: catch an illness; **3.** *unr. itr. V.; mit sein* move into the area

**zuzüglich** *Präp. mit Gen.* plus

**zwang** *1. u. 3. Pers. Sg. Prät. v.* **zwingen**; **Zwang** der; ~|e|s, Zwänge a) compulsion; b) *(unwiderstehlicher Drang)* irresistible urge; **zwängen 1.** *tr. V.* squeeze; **2.** *refl. V.* squeeze [oneself]; **zwanglos 1.** *Adj.* a) informal; casual *(behaviour)*; b) *(unregelmäßig)* haphazard *(arrangement)*; **2.** *adv.* a) informally; b) *(unregelmäßig)* haphazardly *(arranged)*; **Zwangs·lage** die predicament; **zwangs·läufig 1.** *Adj.* inevitable; **2.** *adv.* inevitably

**zwanzig** *Kardinalz.* twenty; *s. auch* achtzig; **zwanziger** *indekl. Adj.; nicht präd.* die ~ Jahre the twenties; **Zwanzig·mark·schein** der twenty-mark note; **zwanzigst ...** *Ordinalz.* twentieth

**zwar** *Adv.* a) admittedly; b) und ~: to be precise

**Zweck** der; ~|e|s, ~e purpose; *(Sinn)* point; es hat keinen ~: it's pointless; es hat keinen ~, das zu tun there is no point in doing that

**zweck-, Zweck-:** ~los *Adj.* pointless; ~mäßig **1.** *Adj.* appropriate; expedient *(behaviour, action)*; functional *(building, fittings, furniture)*; **2.** *adv.* appropriately *(arranged, clothed)*; *(act)* expediently; *(equip, furnish)* functionally; ~mäßigkeit die appropriateness; *(einer Handlung)* expediency; *(eines Gebäudes)* functionalism

**zwecks** *Präp. mit Gen. (Papierdt.)* for the purpose of

**zwei** *Kardinalz.* two; *s. auch* [1]acht; **Zwei** die; ~, ~en a) *(Zahl)* two; b) *(Schulnote)* B

**zwei-, Zwei-:** ~bettzimmer das twin-bedded room; ~deutig **1.** *Adj.* ambiguous; *(fig.: schlüpfrig)* suggestive *(remark, joke)*; **2.** *adv.* ambiguously; *(fig.)* suggestively; ~deutigkeit die; ~, ~en ambiguity; *(fig.)* suggestiveness; ~dimensional **1.** *Adj.* two-dimensional; **2.** *adv.* two-dimensionally; ~einhalb *Bruchz.* two and a half

**zweierlei** *Gattungsz.; indekl.* a) *attr.* two sorts *or* kinds of; two different *(sizes, kinds, etc.)*; odd *(socks, gloves)*; b) *(alleinstehend)* two [different] things; **zwei·fach** *Vervielfältigungsz.* double; *(~mal)* twice; **Zwei·fache** das; *adj. Dekl.* das ~: twice as much

**Zweifel** der; ~s, ~: doubt (an + *Dat.* about); ohne ~: doubtless; etw. in ~ ziehen question sth.; **zweifelhaft** *Adj.* a) doubtful; b) *(fragwürdig)* dubious; *(suspekt)* suspicious; **zweifel·los** *Adv.* undoubtedly; **zweifeln** *itr. V.* doubt; an jmdm./etw. ~: doubt sb./sth.; have doubts about sb./sth.

**Zweig** der; ~|e|s, ~e [small] branch; *(meist ohne Blätter)* twig

**zwei-, Zwei-:** ~hundert *Kardinalz.* two hundred; ~mal *Adv.* twice; ~mark·stück das two-mark piece; ~pfennig·stück das two-pfennig piece; ~reiher der double-breasted suit/coat/jacket; ~schneidig *Adj.* double-edged; ~sprachig **1.** *Adj.* bilingual; *(sign)* in two languages; **2.** *adv.* bilingually; *(written)* in two languages; *(published)* in a bilingual edition; ~spurig *Adj.* a) two-lane *(road)*; b) two-track *(vehicle)*; c) two- *or* twin-track *(recording)*; ~stellig *Adj.* two-figure *attrib. (number, sum)*; ~stöckig *Adj.* two-storey *attrib.*; ~stöckig sein have two storeys

**zweit...** *Ordinalz.* second; **jeder** ~e every other one; *s. auch* erst...

**zwei·tägig** *Adj. (2 Tage alt)* two-day-old *attrib.; (2 Tage dauernd)* two-day *attrib.;* **zweit·ältest ...** *Adj.* second oldest; **zwei·tausend** *Kardinalz.* two thousand; **zweit·best...** *Adj.* second best

**zweite·mal** *Adv.* das ~: for the second time; **zweiten·mal** *Adv.* zum ~: for the second time; **beim** ~: the second time [round]; **zweitens** *Adv.*

secondly; in the second place; **Zwei-te[r]-Klasse-Abteil das** second-class compartment; **zweit·rangig** *Adj.* of secondary importance *post-pos.; (~klassig)* second-rate; **zwei-türig** *Adj.* two-door ⟨*car*⟩

**Zweit-:** ~**wagen der** second car; ~**wohnung die** second home

**Zwei·zimmerwohnung die** two-room flat *(Brit.)* or *(Amer.)* apartment

**Zwerg der;** ~|e|s, ~e dwarf; *(Garten~)* gnome

**Zwetsche die;** ~, ~n damson plum

**Zwieback der;** ~|e|s, ~e *od.* Zwiebäcke rusk; *(unzählbar)* rusks *pl.*

**Zwiebel die;** ~, ~n onion; *(Blumen~)* bulb

**zwie-, Zwie-:** ~**gespräch das** *(geh.)* dialogue; ~**spalt der;** ~|e|s, ~e *od.* ~**spälte** [inner] conflict; ~**spältig** *Adj.* conflicting ⟨*mood, feelings*⟩; discordant ⟨*impression*⟩; *(widersprüchlich)* contradictory ⟨*nature, attitude, person, etc.*⟩

**Zwilling der;** ~s, ~e twin

**Zwillings-:** ~**bruder der** twin brother; ~**paar das** pair of twins; ~**schwester die** twin sister

**zwingen 1.** *unr. tr. V.* force; jmdn. zu etw. ~, jmdn. |dazu| ~, etw. zu tun force *or* compel sb. to do sth.; **zwingend** *Adj.* compelling ⟨*reason, logic*⟩; conclusive ⟨*proof, argument*⟩; imperative ⟨*necessity*⟩

**zwinkern** *itr. V.* |mit den Augen| ~: blink; *(als Zeichen)* wink

**Zwirn der;** ~|e|s, ~e [strong] thread *or* yarn

**zwischen** *Präp. mit Dat./Akk.* between; *(mitten unter)* among[st]

**zwischen-, Zwischen-:** ~**durch** [-'-] *Adv.* **a)** *(zeitlich)* between times;

*(zwischen zwei Zeitpunkten)* in between; *(von Zeit zu Zeit)* from time to time; ~**fall der** incident; ~|**landen** *itr. V.; mit sein* in X ~**landen** land in X on the way; ~**mahlzeit die** snack [between meals]; ~**menschlich 1.** *Adj.* interpersonal ⟨*relations*⟩; ⟨*contacts*⟩ between people; **2.** *adv.* on a personal level; ~**raum der** space; gap; *(Lücke)* gap; ~**zeit die** interim

**Zwist der;** ~|e|s, ~e *(geh.)* strife *no indef. art.; (Fehde)* feud; dispute; **Zwistigkeit die;** ~, ~en *(geh.)* dispute

**zwitschern** *itr. (auch tr.) V.* chirp

**Zwitter der;** ~s, ~ *(Biol.)* hermaphrodite

**zwo** *Kardinalz. (ugs.; bes. zur Verdeutlichung)* two

**zwölf** *Kardinalz.* twelve; ~ Uhr mittags/nachts [twelve o'clock] midday/midnight; *s. auch* ¹**acht; zwölft...** *Ordinalz.* twelfth; *s. auch* **acht...;** **zwölftel** *Bruchz.* twelfth; *s. auch* **achtel; Zwölftel das** *(schweiz. meist der)* ~s, ~: twelfth

**zwo...** *Ordinalz. (ugs.; bes. bei Datumsangaben)* second; **zwotens** *Adv. (ugs.)* secondly

**Zylinder** [tsi'lɪndɐ] **der;** ~s, ~ **a)** cylinder; **b)** *(Hut)* top hat; **zylindrisch 1.** *Adj.* cylindrical; **2.** *adv.* cylindrically

**zynisch 1.** *Adj.* cynical; **2.** *adv.* cynically

**Zynismus der;** ~: cynicism

**Zypern (das);** ~s Cyprus; **Zyprer der;** ~s, ~, **Zyprerin die;** ~, ~nen Cypriot

**Zypresse die;** ~, ~n cypress

**Zypriot der;** ~en, ~en, **Zypriotin die;** ~, ~nen Cypriot; **zypriotisch, zyprisch** *Adj.* Cypriot

**Zyste die;** ~, ~n *(Med.)* cyst

# Englische unregelmäßige Verben

Ein Sternchen (*) weist darauf hin, daß die korrekte Form von der jeweiligen Bedeutung abhängt.

| Infinitive *Infinitiv* | Past Tense *Präteritum* | Past Participle 2. *Partizip* | Infinitive *Infinitiv* | Past Tense *Präteritum* | Past Participle 2. *Partizip* |
|---|---|---|---|---|---|
| arise | arose | arisen | flee | fled | fled |
| awake | awoke | awoken | fling | flung | flung |
| be | was *sing.*, were *pl.* | been | floodlight | floodlit | floodlit |
| | | | fly | flew | flown |
| bear | bore | borne | forbid | forbade, forbad | forbidden |
| beat | beat | beaten | | | |
| become | became | become | forecast | forecast, forecasted | forecast, forecasted |
| begin | began | begun | foretell | foretold | foretold |
| bend | bent | bent | forget | forgot | forgotten |
| bet | bet, betted | bet, betted | forgive | forgave | forgiven |
| bid | *bade, bid | *bidden, bid | forsake | forsook | forsaken |
| bind | bound | bound | freeze | froze | frozen |
| bite | bit | bitten | get | got | got, (Amer.) gotten |
| bleed | bled | bled | | | |
| blow | blew | blown | give | gave | given |
| break | broke | broken | go | went | gone |
| breed | bred | bred | grind | ground | ground |
| bring | brought | brought | grow | grew | grown |
| broadcast | broadcast | broadcast | hang | *hung, hanged | *hung, hanged |
| build | built | built | | | |
| burn | burnt, burned | burnt, burned | have | had | had |
| burst | burst | burst | hear | heard | heard |
| bust | bust, busted | bust, busted | hew | hewed | hewn, hewed |
| buy | bought | bought | hide | hid | hidden |
| cast | cast | cast | hit | hit | hit |
| catch | caught | caught | hold | held | held |
| choose | chose | chosen | hurt | hurt | hurt |
| cling | clung | clung | keep | kept | kept |
| come | came | come | kneel | knelt, (esp. Amer.) kneeled | knelt, (esp. Amer.) kneeled |
| cost | *cost, costed | *cost, costed | | | |
| creep | crept | crept | know | knew | known |
| cut | cut | cut | lay | laid | laid |
| deal | dealt | dealt | lead | led | led |
| dig | dug | dug | lean | leaned, (Brit.) leant | leaned, (Brit.) leant |
| dive | dived, (Amer.) dove | dived | leap | leapt, leaped | leapt, leaped |
| do | did | done | learn | learnt, learned | learnt, learned |
| draw | drew | drawn | | | |
| dream | dreamt, dreamed | dreamt, dreamed | leave | left | left |
| | | | lend | lent | lent |
| drink | drank | drunk | let | let | let |
| drive | drove | driven | ²lie | lay | lain |
| dwell | dwelt | dwelt | light | lit, lighted | lit, lighted |
| eat | ate | eaten | lose | lost | lost |
| fall | fell | fallen | make | made | made |
| feed | fed | fed | mean | meant | meant |
| feel | felt | felt | meet | met | met |
| fight | fought | fought | | | |
| find | found | found | | | |

| Infinitive | Past Tense | Past Participle | Infinitive | Past Tense | Past Participle |
|---|---|---|---|---|---|
| *Infinitiv* | *Präteritum* | *2. Partizip* | *Infinitiv* | *Präteritum* | *2. Partizip* |
| mow | mowed | mown, mowed | spend | spent | spent |
| | | | spill | spilt, spilled | spilt, spilled |
| overhang | overhung | overhung | spin | spun | spun |
| pay | paid | paid | spit | spat, spit | spat, spit |
| prove | proved | proved, proven | split | split | split |
| | | | spoil | spoilt, spoiled | spoilt, spoiled |
| put | put | put | | | |
| quit | quitted, *(Amer.)* quit | quitted, *(Amer.)* quit | spread | spread | spread |
| | | | spring | sprang, *(Amer.)* sprung | sprung |
| read [ri:d] | read [red] | read [red] | | | |
| rid | rid | rid | | | |
| ride | rode | ridden | stand | stood | stood |
| ²ring | rang | rung | steal | stole | stolen |
| rise | rose | risen | stick | stuck | stuck |
| run | ran | run | sting | stung | stung |
| saw | sawed | sawn, sawed | stink | stank, stunk | stunk |
| say | said | said | strew | strewed | strewed, strewn |
| see | saw | seen | | | |
| seek | sought | sought | stride | strode | stridden |
| sell | sold | sold | strike | struck | struck |
| send | sent | sent | string | strung | strung |
| set | set | set | strive | strove | striven |
| sew | sewed | sewn, sewed | sublet | sublet | sublet |
| shake | shook | shaken | swear | swore | sworn |
| shear | sheared | shorn, sheared | sweep | swept | swept |
| | | | swell | swelled | swollen, swelled |
| shed | shed | shed | | | |
| shine | shone | shone | swim | swam | swum |
| shit | shitted, shit | shitted, shit | swing | swung | swung |
| shoe | shod | shod | take | took | taken |
| shoot | shot | shot | teach | taught | taught |
| show | showed | shown | tear | tore | torn |
| shrink | shrank | shrunk | tell | told | told |
| shut | shut | shut | think | thought | thought |
| sing | sang | sung | thrive | thrived, throve | thrived, thriven |
| sink | sank, sunk | sunk | | | |
| sit | sat | sat | throw | threw | thrown |
| slay | slew | slain | thrust | thrust | thrust |
| sleep | slept | slept | tread | trod | trodden, trod |
| slide | slid | slid | understand | understood | understood |
| sling | slung | slung | undo | undid | undone |
| slink | slunk | slunk | wake | woke | woken |
| slit | slit | slit | wear | wore | worn |
| smell | smelt, smelled | smelt, smelled | ¹weave | wove | woven |
| | | | weep | wept | wept |
| sow | sowed | sown, sowed | wet | wet, wetted | wet, wetted |
| speak | spoke | spoken | win | won | won |
| speed | *sped, speeded | *sped, speeded | ²wind [waɪnd] | wound [waʊnd] | wound [waʊnd] |
| | | | wring | wrung | wrung |
| spell | spelled, *(Brit.)* spelt | spelled, *(Brit.)* spelt | write | wrote | written |

# German irregular verbs

Irregular and partly irregular verbs are listed alphabetically by infinitive. 1st, 2nd, and 3rd person present and imperative forms are given after the infinitive, and preterite subjunctive forms after the preterite indicative, where they take an umlaut, change *e* to *i*, etc.

Verbs with a raised number in the German-English section of the Dictionary have the same number in this list.

Compound verbs (including verbs with prefixes) are only given if a) they do not take the same forms as the corresponding simple verb, e.g. *befehlen,* or b) there is no corresponding simple verb, e.g. *bewegen.*

An asterisk (*) indicates a verb which is also conjugated regularly.

| Infinitive<br>*Infinitiv* | Preterite<br>*Präteritum* | Past Participle<br>*2. Partizip* |
|---|---|---|
| abwägen | wog (wöge) ab | abgewogen |
| backen (du bäckst, er bäckt;<br>*auch:* du backst, er backt) | backte, *älter:* buk (büke) | gebacken |
| befehlen (du befiehlst,<br>er befiehlt; befiehl!) | befahl (beföhle, befähle) | befohlen |
| beginnen | begann (begänne,<br>*seltener:* begönne) | begonnen |
| beißen | biß | gebissen |
| bergen (du birgst, er birgt; birg!) | barg (bärge) | geborgen |
| bersten (du birst, er birst;<br>birst!) | barst (bärste) | geborsten |
| besinnen | besann (besänne) | besonnen |
| ²bewegen | bewog (bewöge) | bewogen |
| biegen | bog (böge) | gebogen |
| bieten | bot (böte) | geboten |
| binden | band (bände) | gebunden |
| bitten | bat (bäte) | gebeten |
| blasen (du bläst, er bläst) | blies | geblasen |
| bleiben | blieb | geblieben |
| bleichen* | blich | geblichen |
| braten (du brätst, er brät) | briet | gebraten |
| brechen (du brichst, er bricht;<br>brich!) | brach (bräche) | gebrochen |
| brennen | brannte (brennte) | gebrannt |
| bringen | brachte (brächte) | gebracht |
| denken | dachte (dächte) | gedacht |
| dreschen (du drischst, er drischt;<br>drisch!) | drosch (drösche) | gedroschen |
| dringen | drang (dränge) | gedrungen |
| dürfen (ich darf, du darfst, er darf) | durfte (dürfte) | gedurft |
| empfehlen (du empfiehlst,<br>er empfiehlt, empfiehl!) | empfahl (empföhle,<br>*seltener:* empfähle) | empfohlen |
| erklimmen | erklomm (erklömme) | erklommen |
| erlöschen (du erlischst, er erlischt;<br>erlisch!) | erlosch (erlösche) | erloschen |
| erschallen* | erscholl (erschölle) | erschollen |
| ¹,³erschrecken (du erschrickst,<br>er erschrickt; erschrick!) | erschrak (erschräke) | erschrocken |
| erwägen | erwog (erwöge) | erwogen |

| Infinitive *Infinitiv* | Preterite *Präteritum* | Past Participle *2. Partizip* |
|---|---|---|
| essen (du ißt, er ißt; iß!) | aß (äße) | gegessen |
| fahren (du fährst, er fährt) | fuhr (führe) | gefahren |
| fallen (du fällst, er fällt) | fiel | gefallen |
| fangen (du fängst, er fängt) | fing | gefangen |
| fechten (du fichtst, er ficht; ficht!) | focht (föchte) | gefochten |
| finden | fand (fände) | gefunden |
| flechten (du flichtst, er flicht; flicht!) | flocht (flöchte) | geflochten |
| fliegen | flog (flöge) | geflogen |
| fliehen | floh (flöhe) | geflohen |
| fließen | floß (flösse) | geflossen |
| fressen (du frißt, er frißt; friß!) | fraß (fräße) | gefressen |
| frieren | fror (fröre) | gefroren |
| gären* | gor (göre) | gegoren |
| gebären (*geh.:* du gebierst, sie gebiert; gebier!) | gebar (gebäre) | geboren |
| geben (du gibst, er gibt; gib!) | gab (gäbe) | gegeben |
| gedeihen | gedieh | gediehen |
| gehen | ging | gegangen |
| gelingen | gelang (gelänge) | gelungen |
| gelten (du giltst, er gilt; gilt!) | galt (gölte, gälte) | gegolten |
| genesen | genas (genäse) | genesen |
| genießen | genoß (genösse) | genossen |
| geschehen (es geschieht) | geschah (geschähe) | geschehen |
| gewinnen | gewann (gewönne, gewänne) | gewonnen |
| gießen | goß (gösse) | gegossen |
| gleichen | glich | geglichen |
| gleiten | glitt | geglitten |
| glimmen | glomm (glömme) | geglommen |
| graben (du gräbst, er gräbt) | grub (grübe) | gegraben |
| greifen | griff | gegriffen |
| haben (du hast, er hat) | hatte (hätte) | gehabt |
| halten (du hältst, er hält) | hielt | gehalten |
| [1]hängen | hing | gehangen |
| hauen | haute, *geh.:* hieb | gehauen |
| heben | hob (höbe) | gehoben |
| heißen | hieß | geheißen |
| helfen (du hilfst, er hilft; hilf!) | half (hülfe, *selten:* hälfe) | geholfen |
| kennen | kannte (kennte) | gekannt |
| klingen | klang (klänge) | geklungen |
| kneifen | kniff | gekniffen |
| kommen | kam (käme) | gekommen |
| können (ich kann, du kannst, er kann) | konnte (könnte) | gekonnt |
| kriechen | kroch (kröche) | gekrochen |
| [1,2]laden (du lädst, er lädt) | lud (lüde) | geladen |
| lassen (du läßt, er läßt) | ließ | gelassen |
| laufen (du läufst, er läuft) | lief | gelaufen |
| leiden | litt | gelitten |
| leihen | lieh | geliehen |
| [1,2]lesen (du liest, er liest; lies!) | las (läse) | gelesen |
| liegen | lag (läge) | gelegen |
| lügen | log (löge) | gelogen |
| mahlen | mahlte | gemahlen |
| meiden | mied | gemieden |

| Infinitive<br>*Infinitiv* | Preterite<br>*Präteritum* | Past Participle<br>*2. Partizip* |
| --- | --- | --- |
| melken* (du milkst, er milkt;<br>  milk!; du melkst, er melkt;<br>  melke!) | molk (mölke) | gemolken |
| messen (du mißt, er mißt; miß!) | maß (mäße) | gemessen |
| mißlingen | mißlang (mißlänge) | mißlungen |
| mögen (ich mag, du magst, er mag) | mochte (möchte) | gemocht |
| müssen (ich muß, du mußt, er muß) | mußte (müßte) | gemußt |
| nehmen (du nimmst, er nimmt;<br>  nimm!) | nahm (nähme) | genommen |
| nennen | nannte (nennte) | genannt |
| pfeifen | pfiff | gepfiffen |
| preisen | pries | gepriesen |
| quellen (du quillst, er quillt; quill!) | quoll (quölle) | gequollen |
| raten (du rätst, er rät) | riet | geraten |
| reiben | rieb | gerieben |
| reißen | riß | gerissen |
| reiten | ritt | geritten |
| rennen | rannte (rennte) | gerannt |
| riechen | roch (röche) | gerochen |
| ringen | rang (ränge) | gerungen |
| rinnen | rann (ränne, *seltener:* rönne) | geronnen |
| rufen | rief | gerufen |
| salzen* | salzte | gesalzen |
| saufen (du säufst, er säuft) | soff (söffe) | gesoffen |
| saugen* | sog (söge) | gesogen |
| schaffen* | schuf (schüfe) | geschaffen |
| schallen* | scholl (schölle) | geschallt |
| scheiden | schied | geschieden |
| scheinen | schien | geschienen |
| scheißen | schiß | geschissen |
| schelten (du schiltst, er schilt;<br>  schilt!) | schalt (schölte) | gescholten |
| ¹scheren | schor (schöre) | geschoren |
| schieben | schob (schöbe) | geschoben |
| schießen | schoß (schösse) | geschossen |
| schinden | schindete | geschunden |
| schlafen (du schläfst, er schläft) | schlief | geschlafen |
| schlagen (du schlägst, er schlägt) | schlug (schlüge) | geschlagen |
| schleichen | schlich | geschlichen |
| ¹schleifen | schliff | geschliffen |
| schließen | schloß (schlösse) | geschlossen |
| schlingen | schlang (schlänge) | geschlungen |
| schmeißen | schmiß | geschmissen |
| schmelzen (du schmilzt,<br>  er schmilzt; schmilz!) | schmolz | geschmolzen |
| schneiden | schnitt | geschnitten |
| schrecken* (du schrickst,<br>  er schrickt; schrick!) | schrak (schräke) | geschreckt |
| schreiben | schrieb | geschrieben |
| schreien | schrie | geschrie[e]n |
| schreiten | schritt | geschritten |
| schweigen | schwieg | geschwiegen |
| schwellen (du schwillst,<br>  er schwillt; schwill!) | schwoll (schwölle) | geschwollen |
| schwimmen | schwamm (schwömme,<br>  *seltener:* schwämme) | geschwommen |

| Infinitive *Infinitiv* | Preterite *Präteritum* | Past Participle *2. Partizip* |
|---|---|---|
| schwinden | schwand (schwände) | geschwunden |
| schwingen | schwang (schwänge) | geschwungen |
| schwören | schwor (schwüre) | geschworen |
| sehen (du siehst, er sieht; sieh[e]!) | sah (sähe) | gesehen |
| sein (ich bin, du bist, er ist, wir sind, ihr seid, sie sind; sei!) | war (wäre) | gewesen |
| senden* | sandte (sendete) | gesandt |
| sieden* | sott (sötte) | gesotten |
| singen | sang (sänge) | gesungen |
| sinken | sank (sänke) | gesunken |
| sitzen | saß (säße) | gesessen |
| sollen (ich soll, du sollst, er soll) | sollte | gesollt |
| spalten* | spaltete | gespalten |
| speien | spie | gespie[e]n |
| spinnen | spann (spönne, spänne) | gesponnen |
| sprechen (du sprichst, er spricht; sprich!) | sprach (spräche) | gesprochen |
| sprießen | sproß (sprösse) | gesprossen |
| springen | sprang | gesprungen |
| stechen (du stichst, er sticht; stich!) | stach (stäche) | gestochen |
| stehen | stand (stünde, *auch:* stände) | gestanden |
| stehlen (du stiehlst, er stiehlt; stiehl!) | stahl (stähle, *seltener:* stöhle) | gestohlen |
| steigen | stieg | gestiegen |
| sterben (du stirbst, er stirbt; stirb!) | starb (stürbe) | gestorben |
| stinken | stank (stänke) | gestunken |
| stoßen (du stößt, er stößt) | stieß | gestoßen |
| streichen | strich | gestrichen |
| streiten | stritt | gestritten |
| tragen (du trägst, er trägt) | trug (trüge) | getragen |
| treffen (du triffst; er trifft; triff!) | traf (träfe) | getroffen |
| treiben | trieb | getrieben |
| treten (du trittst, er tritt; tritt!) | trat (träte) | getreten |
| triefen* | troff (tröffe) | getroffen |
| trinken | trank (tränke) | getrunken |
| trügen | trog (tröge) | getrogen |
| tun | tat (täte) | getan |
| verderben (du verdirbst, er verdirbt; verdirb!) | verdarb (verdürbe) | verdorben |
| verdrießen | verdroß (verdrösse) | verdrossen |
| vergessen (du vergißt, er vergißt, vergiß!) | vergaß (vergäße) | vergessen |
| verlieren | verlor (verlöre) | verloren |
| verschleißen* | verschliß | verschlissen |
| verzeihen | verzieh | verziehen |
| ¹wachsen (du wächst, er wächst) | wuchs (wüchse) | gewachsen |
| waschen (du wäschst, er wäscht) | wusch (wüsche) | gewaschen |
| weichen | wich | gewichen |
| weisen | wies | gewiesen |
| ²wenden* | wandte (wendete) | gewandt |
| werben (du wirbst, er wirbt; wirb!) | warb (würbe) | geworben |
| werden (du wirst, er wird; werde!) | wurde, *dichter.:* ward (würde) | geworden; *als Hilfsv.:* worden |
| werfen (du wirfst, er wirft; wirf!) | warf (würfe) | geworfen |
| ¹wiegen | wog (wöge) | gewogen |

| Infinitive<br>*Infinitiv* | Preterite<br>*Präteritum* | Past Participle<br>*2. Partizip* |
|---|---|---|
| winden | wand (wände) | gewunden |
| wissen (ich weiß, du weißt, er weiß) | wußte (wüßte) | gewußt |
| wollen (ich will, du willst, er will) | wollte | gewollt |
| wringen | wrang (wränge) | gewrungen |
| ziehen | zog (zöge) | gezogen |
| zwingen | zwang (zwänge) | gezwungen |

# Weights and Measures / Maße und Gewichte

## Weight / Gewichte

| 1,000 milligrams (mg)<br>*1 000 Milligramm (mg)* | = 1 gram (g)<br>= *1 Gramm (g)* | = 15.43 grains |
|---|---|---|
| 1,000 grams<br>*1 000 Gramm* | = 1 kilogram (kg)<br>= *1 Kilogramm (kg)* | = 2.205 pounds |
| 1,000 kilograms<br>*1 000 Kilogramm* | = 1 tonne (t)<br>= *1 Tonne (t)* | = 19.684 hun-<br>dredweight |

|  | 1 grain (gr.) | = 0.065 g |
|---|---|---|
| 437$\frac{1}{2}$ grains | = 1 ounce (oz.) | = 28.35 g |
| 16 ounces | = 1 pound (lb.) | = 0.454 kg |
| 14 pounds | = 1 stone (st.) | = 6.35 kg |
| 112 pounds | = 1 hundredweight | = 50.8 kg |
| 20 hundredweight | = 1 ton (t.) | = 1,016.05 kg |

## Length / Längenmaße

| 10 millimetres (mm)<br>*10 Millimeter (mm)* | = 1 centimetre (cm)<br>= *1 Zentimeter (cm)* | = 0.394 inch |
|---|---|---|
| 100 centimetres<br>*100 Zentimeter* | = 1 metre (m)<br>= *1 Meter (m)* | = 39.4 inches /<br>1.094 yards |
| 1,000 metres<br>*1 000 Meter* | = 1 kilometre (km)<br>= *1 Kilometer (km)* | = 0.6214 mile $\approx$<br>$\frac{5}{8}$ mile |

|  | 1 inch (in.) | = 25.4 mm |
|---|---|---|
| 12 inches | = 1 foot (ft.) | = 30.48 cm |
| 3 feet | = 1 yard (yd.) | = 0.914 m |
| 220 yards | = 1 furlong | = 201.17 m |
| 8 furlongs | = 1 mile (m.) | = 1.609 km |
| 1,760 yards | = 1 mile | = 1.609 km |

## Square measure / Flächenmaße

| | | |
|---|---|---|
| 100 square metres (sq. m) | = 1 are | = 0.025 acre |
| *100 Quadratmeter (m²)* | *= 1 Ar (a)* | |
| 100 ares | = 1 hectare (ha) | = 2.471 acres |
| *100 Ar* | *= 1 Hektar (ha)* | |
| 100 hectares | = 1 square kilometre (sq. km) | = 0.386 square miles |
| *100 Hektar* | *= 1 Quadratkilometer (km²)* | |
| | 1 square inch | = 6.452 cm² |
| 144 square inches | = 1 square foot | = 929.03 cm² |
| 9 square feet | = 1 square yard | = 0.836 m² |
| 4,840 square yards | = 1 acre | = 0.405 ha |
| 640 acres | = 1 square mile | = 2.59 k² / 259 ha |

## Cubic measure / Raummaße

| | | |
|---|---|---|
| 1 cubic centimetre (cc) | | = 0.06 cubic inches |
| *1 Kubikzentimeter (cm³)* | | |
| 1,000,000 cubic centimetres | = 1 cubic metre (cu. m) | = 35.714 cubic feet / 1.307 cubic yards |
| *1 000 000 Kubikzentimeter* | *= 1 Kubikmeter (m³)* | |
| | 1 cubic inch | = 16.4 cm³ |
| 1,728 cubic inches | = 1 cubic foot | = 0.028 m³ |
| 27 cubic feet | = 1 cubic yard | = 0.764 m³ |

## Capacity / Hohlmaße

| | | |
|---|---|---|
| 10 millilitres (ml) | = 1 centilitre (cl) | |
| *10 Milliliter (ml)* | *= 1 Zentiliter (cl)* | |
| 100 centilitres | = 1 litre (l) | = 1.76 pints (2.1 US pints) / 0.22 gallons (0.264 US gallons) |
| *100 Zentiliter* | *= 1 Liter (l)* | |
| 4 gills | = 1 pint (pt.) (1.201 US pints) | = 0.568 l |
| 2 pints | = 1 quart (qt.) (1.201 US quarts) | = 1.136 l |
| 4 quarts | = 1 gallon (gal.) (1.201 US gallons) | = 4.546 l |

# Revisions to German spelling /
# die neue Regelung der Rechtschreibung

In July 1996, after much debate, wide-ranging changes to the spelling of German were agreed and ratified by the governments of Germany, Austria, and Switzerland. The following list, whilst not all-encompassing, details those changes which may be of interest to the user of this dictionary. It is worth noting that although these reforms are valid immediately, they will not be expected to be reflected in all written texts until 2005. Until that date, both old and new spellings will be acceptable.

The following list contains words which are not included in the A–Z text of this dictionary. Nonetheless, it is the editors' view that the learner of German will gain a better overview of the systematic changes involved by studying a more comprehensive list of words affected by the reforms.

| alt | neu |
| --- | --- |
| **A** | |
| [gestern, heute, morgen] abend | [gestern, heute, morgen] Abend |
| aberhundert | *auch:* Aberhundert |
| Aberhunderte | *auch:* aberhunderte |
| abertausend | *auch:* Abertausend |
| Abertausende | *auch:* abertausende |
| Abfluß | Abfluss |
| abgeblaßt | abgeblasst |
| Abguß | Abguss |
| Ablaß | Ablass |
| Abriß | Abriss |
| Abschluß | Abschluss |
| Abschuß | Abschuss |
| absein | ab sein |
| Abszeß | Abszess |
| abwärtsgehen | abwärts gehen |
| in acht nehmen | in Acht nehmen |
| außer acht lassen | außer Acht lassen |
| 8achser | 8-Achser |
| der/die achte, den/die ich sehe | der/die Achte, den/die ich sehe |

| alt | neu |
|---|---|
| jeder/jede achte kommt mit | jeder/jede Achte kommt mit |
| achtgeben | Acht geben |
| achthaben | Acht haben |
| 8jährig | 8-jährig |
| der/die 8jährige | der/die 8-Jährige |
| 8mal | 8-mal |
| achtmillionenmal | acht Millionen Mal |
| 8tonner | 8-Tonner |
| achtunggebietend | Achtung gebietend |
| über Achtzig | über achtzig |
| Mitte [der] Achtzig | Mitte [der] achtzig |
| in die Achtzig kommen | in die achtzig kommen |
| die achtziger Jahre | *auch:* die Achtzigerjahre* |
| die Achtzigerjahre | *auch:* die achtziger Jahre |
| ackerbautreibende Völker | Ackerbau treibende Völker |
| Action-painting | Actionpainting |
| | *auch:* Action-Painting |
| ade sagen | *auch:* Ade sagen* |
| Aderlaß | Aderlass |
| Adhäsionsverschluß | Adhäsionsverschluss |
| Adreßbuch | Adressbuch |
| afro-amerikanisch | afroamerikanisch |
| afro-asiatisch | afroasiatisch |
| Afro-Look | Afrolook |
| After-shave | Aftershave |
| ich habe ähnliches erlebt | ich habe Ähnliches erlebt |
| und/oder ähnliches (u. ä./o. ä.) | und/oder Ähnliches (u. Ä./o. Ä.) |
| Alkoholmißbrauch | Alkoholmissbrauch |
| alleinerziehend | allein erziehend |
| alleinseligmachend | allein selig machend |
| alleinstehend | allein stehend |
| es ist das allerbeste, daß ... | es ist das Allerbeste, dass ... |
| im allgemeinen | im Allgemeinen |
| allgemeingültig | allgemein gültig |
| allgemeinverständlich | allgemein verständlich |
| allzubald | allzu bald |

| alt | neu |
| --- | --- |
| allzufrüh | allzu früh |
| allzugern | allzu gern |
| allzulange | allzu lange |
| allzuoft | allzu oft |
| allzusehr | allzu sehr |
| allzuviel | allzu viel |
| allzuweit | allzu weit |
| Alma mater | Alma Mater |
| Alpdruck | *auch:* Albdruck |
| Alptraum | *auch:* Albtraum |
| als daß | als dass |
| aus alt mach neu | aus Alt mach Neu |
| für alt und jung | für Alt und Jung |
| er ist immer der alte geblieben | er ist immer der Alte geblieben |
| alles beim alten lassen | alles beim Alten lassen |
| Alter ego | Alter Ego |
| altwienerisch | alt-wienerisch |
| Amboß | Amboss |
| Anbiß | Anbiss |
| andersdenkend | anders denkend |
| andersgeartet | anders geartet |
| anderslautend | anders lautend |
| aneinanderfügen | aneinander fügen |
| aneinandergeraten | aneinander geraten |
| aneinandergrenzen | aneinander grenzen |
| aneinanderlegen | aneinander legen |
| aneinanderreihen | aneinander reihen |
| angepaßt | angepasst |
| Angepaßtheit | Angepasstheit |
| Anglo-Amerikaner | Angloamerikaner |
| jmdm. angst machen | jmdm. Angst machen |
| anheimfallen | anheim fallen |
| anheimstellen | anheim stellen |
| Anlaß | Anlass |
| anläßlich | anlässlich |
| Anriß | Anriss |

| alt | neu |
|---|---|
| Anschiß | Anschiss |
| Anschluß | Anschluss |
| ansein | an sein |
| der Archimedische Punkt | der archimedische Punkt |
| im argen liegen | im Argen liegen |
| bei arm und reich | bei Arm und Reich |
| Armee-Einheit | *auch:* Armeeeinheit |
| Aschantinuß | Aschantinuss |
| As | Ass |
| aufeinanderbeißen | aufeinander beißen |
| aufeinanderfolgen | aufeinander folgen |
| aufeinandertreffen | aufeinander treffen |
| aufgepaßt! | aufgepasst! |
| aufgerauht | aufgeraut |
| Aufguß | Aufguss |
| Auflösungsprozeß | Auflösungsprozess |
| aufrauhen | aufrauen |
| Aufriß | Aufriss |
| Aufschluß | Aufschluss |
| aufschlußreich | aufschlussreich |
| ein aufsehenerregendes Ereignis | ein Aufsehen erregendes Ereignis |
| aufsein | auf sein |
| auf seiten | aufseiten |
| | *auch:* auf Seiten |
| der aufsichtführende Lehrer | der Aufsicht führende Lehrer |
| aufwärtsgehen | aufwärts gehen |
| aufwendig | *auch:* aufwändig |
| auseinanderbiegen | auseinander biegen |
| auseinanderfallen | auseinander fallen |
| auseinandergehen | auseinander gehen |
| auseinanderhalten | auseinander halten |
| auseinanderleben | auseinander leben |
| auseinanderreißen | auseinander reißen |
| auseinandersetzen | auseinander setzen |
| Ausfluß | Ausfluss |
| Ausguß | Ausguss |

| alt | neu |
|---|---|
| Ausschluß | Ausschluss |
| Ausschuß | Ausschuss |
| aussein | aus sein |
| aufs äußerste gespannt | *auch:* aufs Äußerste gespannt |
| außerstande | *auch:* außer Stande |

**B**

| alt | neu |
|---|---|
| Bajonettverschluß | Bajonettverschluss |
| Ballettänzerin | Balletttänzerin |
| | *auch:* Ballett-Tänzerin |
| Ballokal | Balllokal |
| | *auch:* Ball-Lokal |
| Bänderriß | Bänderriss |
| jmdm. [angst und] bange machen | jmdm. [Angst und] Bange machen |
| bankrott gehen | Bankrott gehen |
| Baroneß | Baroness |
| baselstädtisch | basel-städtisch |
| baß erstaunt | bass erstaunt |
| Baß | Bass |
| Baßgeige | Bassgeige |
| Baßsänger | Basssänger |
| | *auch:* Bass-Sänger |
| Baukostenzuschuß | Baukostenzuschuss |
| beeinflußbar | beeinflussbar |
| Beeinflußbarkeit | Beeinflussbarkeit |
| beeinflußt | beeinflusst |
| befaßt | befasst |
| Begrüßungskuß | Begrüßungskuss |
| behende | behände |
| Behendigkeit | Behändigkeit |
| beieinanderhaben | beieinander haben |
| beieinandersein | beieinander sein |
| beieinandersitzen | beieinander sitzen |
| beieinanderstehen | beieinander stehen |
| beifallheischend | Beifall heischend |
| beisammensein | beisammen sein |

| alt | neu |
|-----|-----|
| Beischluß | Beischluss |
| belemmert | belämmert |
| jeder beliebige | jeder Beliebige |
| Beschiß | Beschiss |
| Beschluß | Beschluss |
| beschlußfähig | beschlussfähig |
| Beschlußfassung | Beschlussfassung |
| Beschuß | Beschuss |
| ich will im besonderen erwähnen ... | ich will im Besonderen erwähnen ... |
| bessergehen | besser gehen |
| es ist das beste, wenn ... | es ist das Beste, wenn ... |
| aufs beste geregelt sein | *auch:* aufs Beste geregelt sein |
| zum besten geben | zum Besten geben |
| zum besten haben/halten | zum Besten haben/halten |
| das erste beste | das erste Beste |
| bestehenbleiben | bestehen bleiben |
| Bestelliste | Bestellliste |
| | *auch:* Bestell-Liste |
| bestgehaßt | bestgehasst |
| bestußt | bestusst |
| Betelnuß | Betelnuss |
| um ein beträchtliches höher | um ein Beträchtliches höher |
| in betreff | in Betreff |
| betreßt | betresst |
| Bettuch *[zu: Bett]* | Betttuch |
| | *auch:* Bett-Tuch |
| bevorschußt | bevorschusst |
| bewußt | bewusst |
| bewußtlos | bewusstlos |
| Bewußtlosigkeit | Bewusstlosigkeit |
| Bewußtsein | Bewusstsein |
| in bezug auf | in Bezug auf |
| bezuschußt | bezuschusst |
| Bibliographie | *auch:* Bibliografie |
| Bierfaß | Bierfass |

| alt | neu |
|-----|-----|
| die Bismarckschen Sozialgesetze | die bismarckschen Sozialgesetze |
| | *auch:* die Bismarck'schen |
| | Sozialgesetze |
| Biß | Biss |
| bißchen | bisschen |
| du sollst bitte sagen | *auch:* du sollst Bitte sagen* |
| es ist bitter kalt | es ist bitterkalt |
| Bittag | Bitttag |
| | *auch:* Bitt-Tag |
| Blackout | *auch:* Black-out* |
| blankpoliert | blank poliert |
| blaß | blass |
| Bläßhuhn/Bleßhuhn | Blässhuhn/Blesshuhn |
| bläßlich | blässlich |
| blaßrosa | blassrosa |
| Blattschuß | Blattschuss |
| der blaue Planet *[die Erde]* | der Blaue Planet |
| blaugestreift | blau gestreift |
| bläulichgrün | bläulich grün |
| bleibenlassen | bleiben lassen |
| blendendweiß | blendend weiß |
| blondgefärbt | blond gefärbt |
| Bluterguß | Bluterguss |
| Bonbonniere | *auch:* Bonboniere |
| Börsentip | Börsentipp |
| im bösen wie im guten | im Bösen wie im Guten |
| Boß | Boss |
| Bouclé | *auch:* Buklee |
| braungebrannt | braun gebrannt |
| bräunlichgelb | bräunlich gelb |
| des langen und breiten | des Langen und Breiten |
| breitgefächert | breit gefächert |
| Brennessel | Brennnessel |
| | *auch:* Brenn-Nessel |
| Bruderkuß | Bruderkuss |
| Brummbaß | Brummbass |

| alt | neu |
|---|---|
| brütendheiß | brütend heiß |
| buntgefiedert | bunt gefiedert |
| buntschillernd | bunt schillernd |
| Büroschluß | Büroschluss |
| Butterfaß | Butterfass |

**C**

| alt | neu |
|---|---|
| Cashewnuß | Cashewnuss |
| Centre Court | Centrecourt |
| | *auch:* Centre-Court |
| Chansonnier | *auch:* Chansonier |
| Choreographie | *auch:* Choreografie |
| Cleverneß | Cleverness |
| Comeback | *auch:* Come-back* |
| Common sense | Commonsense |
| | *auch:* Common Sense |
| Corned beef | Cornedbeef |
| | *auch:* Corned Beef |
| Corpus delicti | Corpus Delicti |
| Countdown | *auch:* Count-down* |

**D**

| alt | neu |
|---|---|
| dabeisein | dabei sein |
| Dachgeschoß | Dachgeschoss *[in Österreich weiterhin mit ß]* |
| dahinterklemmen | dahinter klemmen |
| dahinterkommen | dahinter kommen |
| Dampfschiffahrt | Dampfschifffahrt |
| Danaidenfaß | Danaidenfass |
| darauffolgend | darauf folgend |
| Darmverschluß | Darmverschluss |
| darüberstehen | darüber stehen |
| dasein | da sein |
| daß | dass |
| daß-Satz | dass-Satz |
| | *auch:* Dasssatz |

| alt | neu |
|---|---|
| datenverarbeitend | Daten verarbeitend |
| Dein *[in Briefen]* | dein |
| mein und dein verwechseln | Mein und Dein verwechseln |
| die Deinen | *auch:* die deinen |
| die Deinigen | *auch:* die deinigen |
| Dekolleté | *auch:* Dekolletee |
| Delikateßgurke | Delikatessgurke |
| Delikateßsenf | Delikatesssenf |
| | *auch:* Delikatess-Senf |
| Delphin | *auch:* Delfin |
| Denkprozeß | Denkprozess |
| wir haben derartiges nicht bemerkt | wir haben Derartiges nicht bemerkt |
| dessenungeachtet | dessen ungeachtet |
| des weiteren | des Weiteren |
| auf deutsch | auf Deutsch |
| deutschsprechend | Deutsch sprechend |
| das d'Hondtsche System | das d'hondtsche System |
| | *auch:* das d'Hondt'sche System |
| diät leben | Diät leben |
| Dich *[in Briefen]* | dich |
| dichtbehaart | dicht behaart |
| dichtgedrängt | dicht gedrängt |
| Differential | *auch:* Differenzial* |
| Diktaphon | *auch:* Diktafon |
| Dir *[in Briefen]* | dir |
| Doppelpaß | Doppelpass |
| dortbleiben | dort bleiben |
| dortzulande | *auch:* dort zu Lande |
| draufsein | drauf sein |
| Dreß | Dress |
| etwas aufs dringendste fordern | *auch:* etwas aufs Dringendste fordern |
| drinsein | drin sein |
| jeder dritte, der mitwollte | jeder Dritte, der mitwollte |
| zum dritten | zum Dritten |

| alt | neu |
|-----|-----|
| die dritte Welt | die Dritte Welt |
| drückendheiß | drückend heiß |
| Du *[in Briefen]* | du |
| auf du und du stehen | auf Du und Du stehen |
| im dunkeln tappen | im Dunkeln tappen |
| im dunkeln bleiben | im Dunkeln bleiben |
| dünnbesiedelt | dünn besiedelt |
| Dünnschiß | Dünnschiss |
| durcheinanderbringen | durcheinander bringen |
| durcheinandergeraten | durcheinander geraten |
| durcheinanderlaufen | durcheinander laufen |
| Durchfluß | Durchfluss |
| Durchlaß | Durchlass |
| durchnumerieren | durchnummerieren |
| Durchschuß | Durchschuss |
| durchsein | durch sein |
| dußlig | dusslig |
| Dußligkeit | Dussligkeit |
| Dutzende Reklamationen | *auch:* dutzende Reklamationen |
| Dutzende von Reklamationen | *auch:* dutzende von Reklamationen |

**E**

| alt | neu |
|-----|-----|
| ebensogut | ebenso gut |
| ebensosehr | ebenso sehr |
| ebensoviel | ebenso viel |
| ebensowenig | ebenso wenig |
| an Eides Statt | an Eides statt |
| sein eigen nennen | sein Eigen nennen |
| sich zu eigen machen | sich zu Eigen machen |
| einbleuen | einbläuen |
| aufs eindringlichste warnen | *auch:* aufs Eindringlichste warnen |
| das einfachste ist, wenn ... | das Einfachste ist, wenn ... |
| Einfluß | Einfluss |
| einflußreich | einflussreich |

| alt | neu |
|-----|-----|
| aufs eingehendste untersuchen | *auch:* aufs Eingehendste untersuchen |
| einiggehen | einig gehen |
| Einlaß | Einlass |
| einläßlich | einlässlich |
| Einriß | Einriss |
| Einschluß | Einschluss |
| Einschuß | Einschuss |
| Einschußstelle | Einschussstelle |
| | *auch:* Einschuss-Stelle |
| Einsendeschluß | Einsendeschluss |
| einwärtsgebogen | einwärts gebogen |
| der/die/das einzelne kann ... | der/die/das Einzelne kann ... |
| jeder einzelne von uns | jeder Einzelne von uns |
| bis ins einzelne geregelt | bis ins Einzelne geregelt |
| ins einzelne gehend | ins Einzelne gehend |
| einzelnstehend | einzeln stehend |
| der/die/das einzige wäre ... | der/die/das Einzige wäre ... |
| kein einziger war gekommen | kein Einziger war gekommen |
| er als einziger/sie als einzige hatte ... | er als Einziger/sie als Einzige hatte ... |
| das einzigartige ist, daß ... | das Einzigartige ist, dass ... |
| Eisenguß | Eisenguss |
| die eisenverarbeitende Industrie | die Eisen verarbeitende Industrie |
| eisigkalt | eisig kalt |
| eislaufen | Eis laufen |
| Eisschnellauf | Eisschnelllauf |
| Eisschnelläufer | Eisschnellläufer |
| energiebewußt | energiebewusst |
| aufs engste verflochten | *auch:* aufs Engste verflochten |
| engbefreundet | eng befreundet |
| engbedruckt | eng bedruckt |
| Engpaß | Engpass |
| nicht im entferntesten beabsichtigen | *auch:* nicht im Entferntesten beabsichtigen |

| alt | neu |
|---|---|
| auf das entschiedenste zurückweisen | *auch:* auf das Entschiedenste zurückweisen |
| Entschluß | Entschluss |
| ein Entweder-Oder gibt es hier nicht | ein Entweder-oder gibt es hier nicht |
| Entwicklungsprozeß | Entwicklungsprozess |
| erblaßt | erblasst |
| Erdgeschoß | Erdgeschoss *[in Österreich weiterhin mit ß]* |
| Erdnuß | Erdnuss |
| die erdölexportierenden Länder | die Erdöl exportierenden Länder |
| erfaßbar | erfassbar |
| erfaßt | erfasst |
| Erguß | Erguss |
| erholungsuchende Großstädter | Erholung suchende Großstädter |
| Erlaß | Erlass |
| ermeßbar | ermessbar |
| ernstgemeint | ernst gemeint |
| ernstzunehmend | ernst zu nehmend |
| erpreßbar | erpressbar |
| nicht den erstbesten nehmen | nicht den Erstbesten nehmen |
| der erste, der gekommen ist | der Erste, der gekommen ist |
| das reicht fürs erste | das reicht fürs Erste |
| zum ersten, zum zweiten, zum dritten | zum Ersten, zum Zweiten, zum Dritten |
| die Erste Hilfe | die erste Hilfe |
| das erstemal | das erste Mal |
| zum erstenmal | zum ersten Mal |
| Erstkläßler | Erstklässler |
| die Erstplazierten | die Erstplatzierten |
| eßbar | essbar |
| Eßbesteck | Essbesteck |
| Eßecke | Essecke |
| essentiell | *auch:* essenziell* |
| Eßlöffel | Esslöffel |
| eßlöffelweise | esslöffelweise |

| alt | neu |
|-----|-----|
| Eßtisch | Esstisch |
| etlichemal | etliche Mal |
| Euch *[in Briefen]* | euch |
| Euer *[in Briefen]* | euer |
| die Euren | *auch:* die euren |
| die Eurigen | *auch:* die eurigen |
| Existentialismus | *auch:* Existenzialismus* |
| existentialistisch | *auch:* existenzialistisch* |
| existentiell | *auch:* existenziell* |
| Exportüberschuß | Exportüberschuss |
| Exposé | *auch:* Exposee |
| expreß | express |
| Expreßreinigung | Expressreinigung |
| Expreßzug | Expresszug |
| Exzeß | Exzess |

**F**

| alt | neu |
|-----|-----|
| Fabrikationsprozeß | Fabrikationsprozess |
| fahrenlassen | fahren lassen |
| Fairneß | Fairness |
| Fair play | Fairplay |
|  | *auch:* Fair Play |
| fallenlassen | fallen lassen |
| Fallinie | Falllinie |
|  | *auch:* Fall-Linie |
| Fallout | *auch:* Fall-out* |
| Familienanschluß | Familienanschluss |
| Fangschuß | Fangschuss |
| Faß | Fass |
| faßbar | fassbar |
| Faßbier | Fassbier |
| Fäßchen | Fässchen |
| faßlich | fasslich |
| du faßt | du fasst |
| Fast food | Fastfood |
|  | *auch:* Fast Food |

813

| alt | neu |
|---|---|
| Faxanschluß | Faxanschluss |
| Feedback | *auch:* Feed-back* |
| Fehlpaß | Fehlpass |
| Fehlschuß | Fehlschuss |
| jmdm. feind sein | jmdm. Feind sein |
| feingemahlen | fein gemahlen |
| fernliegen | fern liegen |
| fertigbringen | fertig bringen |
| fertigstellen | fertig stellen |
| Fertigungsprozeß | Fertigungsprozess |
| festangestellt | fest angestellt |
| festumrissen | fest umrissen |
| festverwurzelt | fest verwurzelt |
| fettgedruckt | fett gedruckt |
| feuerspeiende Drachen | Feuer speiende Drachen |
| die fischverarbeitende Industrie | die Fisch verarbeitende Industrie |
| Fitneß | Fitness |
| Flachschuß | Flachschuss |
| fleischfressende Pflanzen | Fleisch fressende Pflanzen |
| Flohbiß | Flohbiss |
| das Bier floß in Strömen | das Bier floss in Strömen |
| flötengehen | flöten gehen |
| Fluß | Fluss |
| flußabwärts | flussabwärts |
| flußaufwärts | flussaufwärts |
| Flußbett | Flussbett |
| Flüßchen | Flüsschen |
| Flußdiagramm | Flussdiagramm |
| flüssigmachen | flüssig machen |
| Flußsand | Flusssand |
| | *auch:* Fluss-Sand |
| Flußschiffahrt | Flussschifffahrt |
| | *auch:* Fluss-Schifffahrt |
| Flußspat | Flussspat |
| | *auch:* Fluss-Spat |
| die Haare fönen | die Haare föhnen |

| alt | neu |
|-----|-----|
| folgendes ist zu beachten | Folgendes ist zu beachten |
| wie im folgenden erläutert | wie im Folgenden erläutert |
| Fraktionsausschuß | Fraktionsausschuss |
| Fraktionsbeschluß | Fraktionsbeschluss |
| Free climbing | Freeclimbing |
| | *auch:* Free Climbing |
| Free Jazz | *auch:* Freejazz |
| Freßgier | Fressgier |
| Freßpaket | Fresspaket |
| Freßsack | Fresssack |
| | *auch:* Fress-Sack |
| Friedensschluß | Friedensschluss |
| frischgebacken | frisch gebacken |
| fritieren | frittieren |
| frohgelaunt | froh gelaunt |
| frühverstorben | früh verstorben |
| Full-time-Job | Fulltimejob |
| | *auch:* Full-Time-Job |
| Fünfpaß | Fünfpass |
| funkensprühend | Funken sprühend |
| Funkmeßtechnik | Funkmesstechnik |
| fürbaß | fürbass |
| fürliebnehmen | fürlieb nehmen |
| Fußballänderspiel | Fußballländerspiel |
| | *auch:* Fußball-Länderspiel |

**G**

| alt | neu |
|-----|-----|
| Gangsterboß | Gangsterboss |
| im ganzen gesehen | im Ganzen gesehen |
| im großen und ganzen | im Großen und Ganzen |
| Gärungsprozeß | Gärungsprozess |
| Gäßchen | Gässchen |
| gefangenhalten | gefangen halten |
| gefangennehmen | gefangen nehmen |
| gefaßt | gefasst |
| gefirnißt | gefirnisst |

| alt | neu |
|---|---|
| es ist das gegebene, schnell zu handeln | es ist das Gegebene, schnell zu handeln |
| gegeneinanderprallen | gegeneinander prallen |
| gegeneinanderstoßen | gegeneinander stoßen |
| von allen gehaßt | von allen gehasst |
| geheimhalten | geheim halten |
| gehenlassen | gehen lassen |
| Gelaß | Gelass |
| gutgelaunt | gut gelaunt |
| gelblichgrün | gelblich grün |
| Gemse | Gämse |
| wir haben gemußt | wir haben gemusst |
| die Wunde hat genäßt | die Wunde hat genässt |
| aufs genaueste festgelegt | *auch:* aufs Genaueste festgelegt |
| genaugenommen | genau genommen |
| genausogut | genauso gut |
| genausowenig | genauso wenig |
| Generalbaß | Generalbass |
| sie genoß den Sonnenschein | sie genoss den Sonnenschein |
| Genuß | Genuss |
| genüßlich | genüsslich |
| Genußmittel | Genussmittel |
| genußsüchtig | genusssüchtig |
| Geographie | *auch:* Geografie |
| es hat gut gepaßt | es hat gut gepasst |
| wir haben gepraßt | wir haben geprasst |
| frisch gepreßter Saft | frisch gepresster Saft |
| geradehalten | gerade halten |
| geradesitzen | gerade sitzen |
| geradestellen | gerade stellen |
| Gerichtsbeschluß | Gerichtsbeschluss |
| um ein geringes weniger | um ein Geringes weniger |
| es geht ihn nicht das geringste an | es geht ihn nicht das Geringste an |
| nicht im geringsten stören | nicht im Geringsten stören |
| geringachten | gering achten |
| geringschätzen | gering schätzen |

| alt | neu |
|-----|-----|
| Geruchsverschluß | Geruchsverschluss |
| Geschäftsschluß | Geschäftsschluss |
| er wurde geschaßt | er wurde geschasst |
| Geschichtsbewußtsein | Geschichtsbewusstsein |
| Geschirreiniger | Geschirrreiniger |
| | *auch:* Geschirr-Reiniger |
| Geschoß | Geschoss *[in Österreich* |
| | *weiterhin mit ß]* |
| gestern abend/morgen/nacht | gestern Abend/Morgen/Nacht |
| alle waren gestreßt | alle waren gestresst |
| getrenntlebend | getrennt lebend |
| Gewinnnummer | Gewinnnummer |
| | *auch:* Gewinn-Nummer |
| gewiß | gewiss |
| Gewissensbiß | Gewissensbiss |
| Gewißheit | Gewissheit |
| gewißlich | gewisslich |
| ich habe es gewußt | ich habe es gewusst |
| Ginkgo | *auch:* Ginko |
| Glacéhandschuh | *auch:* Glaceehandschuh |
| glänzendschwarz | glänzend schwarz |
| glattgehen | glatt gehen |
| glatthobeln | glatt hobeln |
| glattschleifen | glatt schleifen |
| glattstreichen | glatt streichen |
| das gleiche tun | das Gleiche tun |
| aufs gleiche hinauskommen | aufs Gleiche hinauskommen |
| gleich und gleich gesellt sich gern | Geich und Gleich gesellt sich gern |
| gleichlautend | gleich lautend |
| Gleisanschluß | Gleisanschluss |
| Glimmstengel | Glimmstängel |
| glühendheiß | glühend heiß |
| Gnadenerlaß | Gnadenerlass |
| die Goetheschen Dramen | die goetheschen Dramen |
| | *auch:* die Goethe'schen Dramen |
| Graphit | *auch:* Grafit |

| alt | neu |
|-----|-----|
| Graphologie | *auch:* Grafologie |
| gräßlich | grässlich |
| graugestreift | grau gestreift |
| grellbeleuchtet | grell beleuchtet |
| Grenzfluß | Grenzfluss |
| Greuel | Gräuel |
| greulich | gräulich |
| griffest | grifffest |
| jmdn. aufs gröbste beleidigen | *auch:* jmdn. aufs Gröbste beleidigen |
| grobgemahlen | grob gemahlen |
| ein Programm für groß und klein | ein Programm für Groß und Klein |
| im großen und ganzen | im Großen und Ganzen |
| das größte wäre, wenn ... | das Größte wäre, wenn ... |
| Großschiffahrtsweg | Großschifffahrtsweg |
| groß schreiben *[mit großem Anfangsbuchstaben]* | großschreiben |
| grünlichgelb | grünlich gelb |
| Guß | Guss |
| Gußeisen | Gusseisen |
| gußeisern | gusseisern |
| guten Tag sagen | *auch:* Guten Tag sagen* |
| es im guten versuchen | es im Guten versuchen |
| gutaussehend | gut aussehend |
| gutbezahlt | gut bezahlt |
| gutgehen | gut gehen |
| gutgehend | gut gehend |
| gutgelaunt | gut gelaunt |
| gutgemeint | gut gemeint |
| guttun | gut tun |
| gutunterrichtet | gut unterrichtet |

## H

| | |
|-----|-----|
| haftenbleiben | haften bleiben |
| haltmachen | Halt machen |
| Hämorrhoide | *auch:* Hämorride |

818

| alt | neu |
|---|---|
| händchenhaltend | Händchen haltend |
| handeltreibend | Handel treibend |
| Handkuß | Handkuss |
| Handout | *auch:* Hand-out* |
| hängenbleiben | hängen bleiben |
| hängenlassen | hängen lassen |
| Happy-End | Happyend |
| | *auch:* Happy End |
| Haraß | Harass |
| Hard cover | Hardcover |
| | *auch:* Hard Cover |
| Hard-cover-Einband | Hardcovereinband |
| | *auch:* Hard-Cover-Einband |
| hartgekocht | hart gekocht |
| Haselnuß | Haselnuss |
| Haselnußstrauch | Haselnussstrauch |
| | *auch:* Haselnuss-Strauch |
| Haß | Hass |
| haßerfüllt | hasserfüllt |
| häßlich | hässlich |
| Häßlichkeit | Hässlichkeit |
| Haßliebe | Hassliebe |
| du haßt | du hasst |
| Hauptschulabschluß | Hauptschulabschluss |
| nach Hause | *in Österreich und der Schweiz* |
| | *auch:* nachhause |
| zu Hause | *in Österreich und der Schweiz* |
| | *auch:* zuhause |
| haushalten | *auch:* Haus halten |
| Haushaltsausschuß | Haushaltsausschuss |
| Hawaii-Insel | *auch:* Hawaiiinsel |
| heiligsprechen | heilig sprechen |
| Heilungsprozeß | Heilungsprozess |
| heimlichtun | heimlich tun |
| heißbegehrt | heiß begehrt |
| heißgeliebt | heiß geliebt |

819

| alt | neu |
|-----|-----|
| heißumkämpft | heiß umkämpft |
| helleuchtend | hell leuchtend |
| hellicht | helllicht |
| hellila | helllila |
| hellodernd | hell lodernd |
| heransein | heran sein |
| heraussein | heraus sein |
| herbstlichgelb | herbstlich gelb |
| Heringsfaß | Heringsfass |
| hersein | her sein |
| herumsein | herum sein |
| heruntersein | herunter sein |
| Herzas | Herzass |
| jmdn. auf das herzlichste begrüßen | *auch:* jmdn. auf das Herzlichste begrüßen |
| heute abend/mittag/nacht | heute Abend/Mittag/Nacht |
| Hexenschuß | Hexenschuss |
| hierbleiben | hier bleiben |
| hierlassen | hier lassen |
| hiersein | hier sein |
| hierzulande | *auch:* hier zu Lande |
| High-Fidelity | Highfidelity |
| | *auch:* High Fidelity |
| High-Society | Highsociety |
| | *auch:* High Society |
| hilfesuchend | Hilfe suchend |
| hinaussein | hinaus sein |
| es wurde etwas hineingeheimnißt | es wurde etwas hineingeheimnisst |
| hinsein | hin sein |
| hintereinanderfahren | hintereinander fahren |
| hintereinandergehen | hintereinander gehen |
| hintereinanderschalten | hintereinander schalten |
| hinterhersein | hinterher sein |
| hinübersein | hinüber sein |
| er hißt die Flagge | er hisst die Flagge |

| alt | neu |
|-----|-----|
| Hochgenuß | Hochgenuss |
| Hochschulabschluß | Hochschulabschluss |
| aufs höchste erfreut sein | *auch:* aufs Höchste erfreut sein |
| hofhalten | Hof halten |
| die Hohe Schule | die hohe Schule |
| hohnlachen | *auch:* Hohn lachen |
| das holzverarbeitende Gewerbe | das Holz verarbeitende Gewerbe |
| Hosteß | Hostess |
| Hot dog | Hotdog |
| | *auch:* Hot Dog |
| ein paar hundert | *auch:* ein paar Hundert |
| viele Hunderte | *auch:* viele hunderte |
| Hunderte von Zuschauern | *auch:* hunderte von Zuschauern |
| Hungers sterben | hungers sterben |
| hurra schreien | *auch:* Hurra schreien* |

**I**

| alt | neu |
|-----|-----|
| auch Ihr seid herzlich eingeladen *[in Briefen]* | auch ihr seid herzlich eingeladen |
| im allgemeinen | im Allgemeinen |
| im besonderen | im Besonderen |
| Imbiß | Imbiss |
| Imbißstand | Imbissstand |
| | *auch:* Imbiss-Stand |
| im einzelnen | im Einzelnen |
| im nachhinein | im Nachhinein |
| Impfpaß | Impfpass |
| imstande | *auch:* im Stande |
| im übrigen | im Übrigen |
| im voraus | im Voraus |
| im vorhinein | im Vorhinein |
| in betreff | in Betreff |
| in bezug auf | in Bezug auf |
| Indizes | *auch:* Indices |
| Indizienprozeß | Indizienprozess |

| alt | neu |
|-----|-----|
| ineinanderfließen | ineinander fließen |
| ineinandergreifen | ineinander greifen |
| inessentiell | *auch:* inessenziell* |
| Informationsfluß | Informationsfluss |
| in Frage stellen | *auch:* infrage stellen |
| in Frage kommen | *auch:* infrage kommen |
| innesein | inne sein |
| insektenfressende Pflanzen | Insekten fressende Pflanzen |
| instand halten | *auch:* in Stand halten |
| instand setzen | *auch:* in Stand setzen |
| I-Punkt | i-Punkt |
| irgend etwas | irgendetwas |
| irgend jemand | irgendjemand |
| I-Tüpfelchen | i-Tüpfelchen |

## J

| alt | neu |
|-----|-----|
| ja sagen | *auch:* Ja sagen* |
| Jagdschloß | Jagdschloss |
| Jäheit | Jähheit |
| Jahresabschluß | Jahresabschluss |
| 2jährig, 3jährig, 4jährig ... | 2-jährig, 3-jährig, 4-jährig ... |
| ein 2jähriger, 3jähriger, 4jähriger kann das noch nicht verstehen | ein 2-Jähriger, 3-Jähriger, 4-Jähriger kann das noch nicht verstehen |
| Jaß | Jass |
| du jaßt | du jasst |
| Jauchefaß | Jauchefass |
| jedesmal | jedes Mal |
| Job-sharing | Jobsharing |
| Joghurt | *auch:* Jogurt |
| Joint-venture | Jointventure |
|  | *auch:* Joint Venture |
| Judaskuß | Judaskuss |
| Julierpaß | Julierpass |
| Jumbo-Jet | Jumbojet |
| für jung und alt | für Jung und Alt |

822

## K

| alt | neu |
|-----|-----|
| Kabelanschluß | Kabelanschluss |
| Kabinettsbeschluß | Kabinettsbeschluss |
| Kaffee-Ernte | *auch:* Kaffeeernte |
| Kaffee-Ersatz | *auch:* Kaffeeersatz |
| Kalligraphie | *auch:* Kalligrafie |
| kalorienbewußt | kalorienbewusst |
| kaltlächelnd | kalt lächelnd |
| Kameraverschluß | Kameraverschluss |
| Kammacher | Kammmacher |
| | *auch:* Kamm-Macher |
| Kämmaschine | Kämmmaschine |
| | *auch:* Kämm-Maschine |
| Kammuschel | Kammmuschel |
| | *auch:* Kamm-Muschel |
| Känguruh | Känguru |
| Kanonenschuß | Kanonenschuss |
| Kapselriß | Kapselriss |
| Karamel | Karamell |
| karamelisieren | karamellisieren |
| 2karäter, 3karäter, 4karäter ... | 2-Karäter, 3-Karäter, 4-Karäter ... |
| 2karätig, 3karätig, 4karätig ... | 2-karätig, 3-karätig, 4-karätig ... |
| Karoas | Karoass |
| Kartographie | *auch:* Kartografie |
| Kaßler | Kassler |
| Katarrh | *auch:* Katarr |
| kegelschieben | Kegel schieben |
| Kellergeschoß | Kellergeschoss *[in Österreich weiterhin mit ß]* |
| kennenlernen | kennen lernen |
| Kennummer | Kennnummer |
| | *auch:* Kenn-Nummer |
| die Keplerschen Gesetze | die keplerschen Gesetze |
| | *auch:* die Kepler'schen Gesetze |
| keß | kess |
| Keßheit | Kessheit |

| alt | neu |
| --- | --- |
| Ketchup | *auch:* Ketschup* |
| Kickdown | *auch:* Kick-down* |
| Kick-off | *auch:* Kickoff |
| an Kindes Statt | an Kindes statt |
| Kindesmißhandlung | Kindesmisshandlung |
| Kißchen | Kisschen |
| sich über etwas im klaren sein | sich über etwas im Klaren sein |
| klardenkend | klar denkend |
| klarsehen | klar sehen |
| klarwerden | klar werden |
| Klassenbewußtsein | Klassenbewusstsein |
| Klassenhaß | Klassenhass |
| klatschnaß | klatschnass |
| Klausenpaß | Klausenpass |
| klebenbleiben | kleben bleiben |
| Klee-Einsaat | *auch:* Kleeeinsaat |
| Klee-Ernte | *auch:* Kleeernte |
| bis ins kleinste geregelt | bis ins Kleinste geregelt |
| ein Staat im kleinen | ein Staat im Kleinen |
| ein Programm für groß und klein | ein Programm für Groß und Klein |
| kleingedruckt | klein gedruckt |
| kleinschneiden | klein schneiden |
| klein schreiben *[mit kleinem Anfangsbuchstaben]* | kleinschreiben |
| Klemmappe | Klemmmappe *auch:* Klemm-Mappe |
| Klettverschluß | Klettverschluss |
| klitschnaß | klitschnass |
| es wäre das klügste, wenn ... | es wäre das Klügste, wenn ... |
| knapphalten | knapp halten |
| Knockout | *auch:* Knock-out* |
| kochendheiß | kochend heiß |
| kohleführende Flöze | Kohle führende Flöze |
| Kolanuß | Kolanuss |
| Kollektivbewußtsein | Kollektivbewusstsein |
| Kolophonium | *auch:* Kolofonium |

| alt | neu |
| --- | --- |
| Koloß | Koloss |
| Kombinationsschloß | Kombinationsschloss |
| Kommiß | Kommiss |
| Kommißbrot | Kommissbrot |
| Kommißstiefel | Kommissstiefel |
| | *auch:* Kommiss-Stiefel |
| Kommuniqué | *auch:* Kommunikee |
| Kompaß | Kompass |
| kompreß | kompress |
| Kompromiß | Kompromiss |
| kompromißbereit | kompromissbereit |
| kompromißlos | kompromisslos |
| Kompromißlösung | Kompromisslösung |
| Komteß | Komtess |
| Konferenzbeschluß | Konferenzbeschluss |
| Kongreß | Kongress |
| Kongreßhalle | Kongresshalle |
| Kongreßsaal | Kongresssaal |
| | *auch:* Kongress-Saal |
| Kongreßstadt | Kongressstadt |
| | *auch:* Kongress-Stadt |
| Königsschloß | Königsschloss |
| Kontrabaß | Kontrabass |
| Kontrollampe | Kontrolllampe |
| | *auch:* Kontroll-Lampe |
| Kontrolliste | Kontrollliste |
| | *auch:* Kontroll-Liste |
| Kopfnuß | Kopfnuss |
| Kopfschuß | Kopfschuss |
| kopfstehen | Kopf stehen |
| Koppelschloß | Koppelschloss |
| krank schreiben | krankschreiben |
| kraß | krass |
| Kraßheit | Krassheit |
| krebserregende Substanzen | Krebs erregende Substanzen |
| Kreiselkompaß | Kreiselkompass |

| alt | neu |
|---|---|
| Kreppapier | Krepppapier |
| | *auch:* Krepp-Papier |
| Kreuzas | Kreuzass |
| die kriegführenden Parteien | die Krieg führenden Parteien |
| Kriminalprozeß | Kriminalprozess |
| Kristallüster | Kristalllüster |
| | *auch:* Kristall-Lüster |
| kroß | kross |
| krummnehmen | krumm nehmen |
| KSZE-Schlußakte | KSZE-Schlussakte |
| Kunststoffolie | Kunststofffolie |
| | *auch:* Kunststoff-Folie |
| Küraß | Kürass |
| den kürzeren ziehen | den Kürzeren ziehen |
| kürzertreten | kürzer treten |
| kurzgebraten | kurz gebraten |
| kurzhalten | kurz halten |
| Kurzpaß | Kurzpass |
| Kurzschluß | Kurzschluss |
| kurztreten | kurz treten |
| Kuß | Kuss |
| Küßchen | Küsschen |
| kußecht | kussecht |
| Kußhand | Kusshand |
| du/er/sie küßt | du/er/sie küsst |
| Küstenschiffahrt | Küstenschifffahrt |
| Kwaß | Kwass |

| alt | neu |
|---|---|
| **L** | |
| Ladenschluß | Ladenschluss |
| die La-Fontaineschen Fabeln | die la-fontaineschen Fabeln |
| | *auch:* die la-Fontaine'schen Fabeln |
| Lamé | *auch:* Lamee |
| Lamellenverschluß | Lamellenverschluss |

826

| alt | neu |
|---|---|
| etwas des langen und breiten erklären | etwas des Langen und Breiten erklären |
| langgestreckt | lang gestreckt |
| länglichrund | länglich rund |
| langstengelig | langstängelig |
| langziehen | lang ziehen |
| Lapsus linguae | Lapsus Linguae |
| läßlich | lässlich |
| du läßt | du lässt |
| zu Lasten | *auch:* zulasten |
| Lattenschuß | Lattenschuss |
| laubtragende Bäume | Laub tragende Bäume |
| auf dem laufenden sein | auf dem Laufenden sein |
| laufenlassen | laufen lassen |
| Laufpaß | Laufpass |
| Layout | *auch:* Lay-out* |
| Lebensgenuß | Lebensgenuss |
| Leberabszeß | Leberabszess |
| die lederverarbeitende Industrie | die Leder verarbeitende Industrie |
| leerstehend | leer stehend |
| leichenblaß | leichenblass |
| es ist mir ein leichtes, das zu tun | es ist mir ein Leichtes, das zu tun |
| leichtentzündlich | leicht entzündlich |
| leichtfallen | leicht fallen |
| leichtmachen | leicht machen |
| leichtnehmen | leicht nehmen |
| leichtverderblich | leicht verderblich |
| leichtverständlich | leicht verständlich |
| jmdm. leid tun | jmdm. Leid tun |
| Lenkradschloß | Lenkradschloss |
| Lernprozeß | Lernprozess |
| der letzte, der gekommen ist | der Letzte, der gekommen ist |
| als letzter fertig sein | als Letzter fertig sein |
| das letzte, was sie tun würde | das Letzte, was sie tun würde |
| bis ins letzte geklärt | bis ins Letzte geklärt |
| letzteres trifft zu | Letzteres trifft zu |

| alt | neu |
|-----|-----|
| zum letztenmal | zum letzten Mal |
| leuchtendblau | leuchtend blau |
| Lichtmeß | Lichtmess |
| es wäre uns das liebste, wenn ... | es wäre uns das Liebste, wenn ... |
| liebenlernen | lieben lernen |
| liebgewinnen | lieb gewinnen |
| liebhaben | lieb haben |
| liegenbleiben | liegen bleiben |
| liegenlassen | liegen lassen |
| Live-Mitschnitt | *auch:* Livemitschnitt |
| Lizentiat | *auch:* Lizenziat* |
| Lorbaß | Lorbass |
| Löß | *auch:* Löss *[bei Aussprache mit kurzem ö]* |
| Lößboden | *auch:* Lössboden *[bei Aussprache mit kurzem ö]* |
| Lößschicht | *auch:* Lössschicht oder Löss-Schicht *[bei Aussprache mit kurzem ö]* |
| Lötschenpaß | Lötschenpass |
| Love-Story | *auch:* Lovestory |
| Luftschiffahrt | Luftschifffahrt |
| Luftschloß | Luftschloss |

**M**

| | |
|-----|-----|
| Magistratsbeschluß | Magistratsbeschluss |
| 2mal, 3mal, 4mal ... | 2-mal, 3-mal, 4-mal ... |
| Malaise | *auch:* Maläse |
| Marschkompaß | Marschkompass |
| maschineschreiben | Maschine schreiben |
| maßhalten | Maß halten |
| Matrizes | *auch:* Matrices |
| Maulkorberlaß | Maulkorberlass |
| Megaphon | *auch:* Megafon |
| Mehrheitsbeschluß | Mehrheitsbeschluss |
| Meldeschluß | Meldeschluss |

| alt | neu |
|---|---|
| Meniskusriß | Meniskusriss |
| wir haben das menschenmögliche getan | wir haben das Menschenmögliche getan |
| Mesner | *auch:* Messner |
| Meßband | Messband |
| meßbar | messbar |
| Meßbecher | Messbecher |
| Meßbuch | Messbuch |
| Meßdaten | Messdaten |
| Meßdiener | Messdiener |
| Meßfühler | Messfühler |
| Meßgewand | Messgewand |
| Meßinstrument | Messinstrument |
| Meßopfer | Messopfer |
| Meßstab | Messstab |
| | *auch:* Mess-Stab |
| Meßtischblatt | Messtischblatt |
| Metallguß | Metallguss |
| Metallegierung | Metalllegierung |
| | *auch:* Metall-Legierung |
| die metallverarbeitende Industrie | die Metall verarbeitende Industrie |
| Midlife-crisis | Midlifecrisis |
| | *auch:* Midlife-Crisis |
| Milchgebiß | Milchgebiss |
| millionenmal | Millionen Mal |
| Milzriß | Milzriss |
| nicht im mindesten | nicht im Mindesten |
| mißachten | missachten |
| Mißbildung | Missbildung |
| mißbilligen | missbilligen |
| Mißbrauch | Missbrauch |
| Mißerfolg | Misserfolg |
| Mißernte | Missernte |
| mißfallen | missfallen |
| Mißfallenskundgebung | Missfallenskundgebung |
| Mißgeburt | Missgeburt |

829

| alt | neu |
|---|---|
| Mißgeschick | Missgeschick |
| mißglücken | missglücken |
| Mißgunst | Missgunst |
| mißgünstig | missgünstig |
| Mißklang | Missklang |
| Mißkredit | Misskredit |
| mißlich | misslich |
| mißlingen | misslingen |
| mißmutig | missmutig |
| mißraten | missraten |
| Mißstand | Missstand |
| Mißtrauen | Misstrauen |
| mißtrauisch | misstrauisch |
| Mißverständnis | Missverständnis |
| Mißwirtschaft | Misswirtschaft |
| mit Hilfe | *auch:* mithilfe |
| [gestern, heute, morgen] mittag | [gestern, heute, morgen] Mittag |
| Mixed Pickles | *auch:* Mixedpickles* |
| modebewußt | modebewusst |
| wir sprachen über alles mögliche | wir sprachen über alles Mögliche |
| sein möglichstes tun | sein Möglichstes tun |
| 3monatig, 4monatig, 5monatig ... | 3-monatig, 4-monatig, 5-monatig ... |
| 3monatlich, 4monatlich, 5monatlich ... | 3-monatlich, 4-monatlich, 5-monatlich ... |
| Monographie | *auch:* Monografie |
| Mop | Mopp |
| Mordprozeß | Mordprozess |
| morgen abend, mittag, nacht | morgen Abend, Mittag, Nacht |
| [gestern, heute] morgen | [gestern, heute] Morgen |
| Moto-Cross | *auch:* Motocross |
| Mückenschiß | Mückenschiss |
| Mulläppchen | Mullläppchen |
| | *auch:* Mull-Läppchen |
| Multiple-choice-Verfahren | Multiplechoiceverfahren |
| | *auch:* Multiple-Choice-Verfahren |

| alt | neu |
|---|---|
| Muskatnuß | Muskatnuss |
| Muskelriß | Muskelriss |
| ich muß | ich muss |
| du mußt | du musst |
| ich müßte | ich müsste |
| du müßtest | du müsstest |
| Mußheirat | Mussheirat |
| müßiggehen | müßig gehen |
| Musterprozeß | Musterprozess |
| Myrrhe | *auch:* Myrre |

**N**

| alt | neu |
|---|---|
| nachfolgendes gilt auch ... | Nachfolgendes gilt auch ... |
| nach Hause | *in Österreich und der Schweiz auch:* nachhause |
| im nachhinein | im Nachhinein |
| Nachlaß | Nachlass |
| Nachlaßverwalter | Nachlassverwalter |
| [gestern, heute, morgen] nachmittag | [gestern, heute, morgen] Nachmittag |
| Nachschuß | Nachschuss |
| der nächste, bitte! | der Nächste, bitte! |
| als nächstes wollen wir ... | als Nächstes wollen wir ... |
| im nachstehenden heißt es ... | im Nachstehenden heißt es ... |
| [gestern, heute, morgen] nacht | [gestern, heute, morgen] Nacht |
| nahebringen | nahe bringen |
| nahelegen | nahe legen |
| naheliegen | nahe liegen |
| naheliegend | nahe liegend |
| etwas des näheren erläutern | etwas des Näheren erläutern |
| näherliegen | näher liegen |
| nahestehen | nahe stehen |
| nahestehend | nahe stehend |
| Narziß | Narziss |
| Narzißmus | Narzissmus |
| narzißtisch | narzisstisch |

| alt | neu |
|-----|-----|
| naß | nass |
| naßforsch | nassforsch |
| naßgeschwitzt | nass geschwitzt |
| naßkalt | nasskalt |
| Naßrasur | Nassrasur |
| Naßschnee | Nassschnee |
| | *auch:* Nass-Schnee |
| | |
| nationalbewußt | nationalbewusst |
| Nationaldreß | Nationaldress |
| Nebelschlußleuchte | Nebelschlussleuchte |
| Nebenanschluß | Nebenanschluss |
| nebeneinandersitzen | nebeneinander sitzen |
| nebeneinanderstehen | nebeneinander stehen |
| nebeneinanderstellen | nebeneinander stellen |
| Nebenfluß | Nebenfluss |
| im nebenstehenden wird gezeigt ... | im Nebenstehenden wird gezeigt ... |
| Necessaire | *auch:* Nessessär |
| Negligé | *auch:* Negligee |
| nein sagen | *auch:* Nein sagen* |
| Netzanschluß | Netzanschluss |
| es aufs neue versuchen | es aufs Neue versuchen |
| auf ein neues! | auf ein Neues! |
| neueröffnet | neu eröffnet |
| New Yorker | *auch:* New-Yorker |
| nichtrostend | *auch:* nicht rostend |
| Nichtseßhafte | Nichtsesshafte |
| nichtssagend | nichts sagend |
| No-future-Generation | No-Future-Generation |
| die notleidende Bevölkerung | die Not leidende Bevölkerung |
| in Null Komma nichts | in null Komma nichts |
| das Thermometer steht auf Null | das Thermometer steht auf null |
| Nullage | Nulllage |
| | *auch:* Null-Lage |
| Nulleiter | Nullleiter |
| | *auch:* Null-Leiter |

832

| alt | neu |
|-----|-----|
| Nullösung | Nulllösung |
| | *auch:* Null-Lösung |
| numerieren | nummerieren |
| Numerierung | Nummerierung |
| Nuß | Nuss |
| Nüßchen | Nüsschen |
| Nußknacker | Nussknacker |
| Nußschale | Nussschale |
| | *auch:* Nuss-Schale |
| Nußschinken | Nussschinken |
| | *auch:* Nuss-Schinken |
| Nußschokolade | Nussschokolade |
| | *auch:* Nuss-Schokolade |
| Nußstrudel | Nussstrudel |
| | *auch:* Nuss-Strudel |
| Nußtorte | Nusstorte |

**O**

| | |
|-----|-----|
| O-beinig | *auch:* o-beinig |
| obenerwähnt | oben erwähnt |
| obenstehend | oben stehend |
| Obergeschoß | Obergeschoss *[in Österreich weiterhin mit ß]* |
| offenbleiben | offen bleiben |
| offenlassen | offen lassen |
| offenstehen | offen stehen |
| O-förmig | *auch:* o-förmig |
| des öfteren | des Öfteren |
| Ölmeßstab | Ölmessstab |
| Ordonnanz | *auch:* Ordonanz |
| Orthographie | *auch:* Orthografie |

**P**

| | |
|-----|-----|
| Panther | *auch:* Panter |
| die papierverarbeitende Industrie | die Papier verarbeitende Industrie |
| Pappmaché | *auch:* Pappmaschee |

| alt | neu |
|-----|-----|
| parallellaufend | parallel laufend |
| parallelschalten | parallel schalten |
| Paranuß | Paranuss |
| Parlamentsbeschluß | Parlamentsbeschluss |
| Parnaß | Parnass |
| Parteikongreß | Parteikongress |
| Parteitagsbeschluß | Parteitagsbeschluss |
| Paß | Pass |
| Paßbild | Passbild |
| passé | *auch:* passee |
| Paßform | Passform |
| Paßgang | Passgang |
| paßgerecht | passgerecht |
| Paßkontrolle | Passkontrolle |
| Paßstelle | Passstelle |
| | *auch:* Pass-Stelle |
| Paßstraße | Passstraße |
| | *auch:* Pass-Straße |
| Paßwort | Passwort |
| Patentverschluß | Patentverschluss |
| patschnaß | patschnass |
| Perkussionsschloß | Perkussionsschloss |
| Personenschiffahrt | Personenschifffahrt |
| Petitionsausschuß | Petitionsausschuss |
| Pfeffernuß | Pfeffernuss |
| Pferdegebiß | Pferdegebiss |
| pflichtbewußt | pflichtbewusst |
| Pflichtbewußtsein | Pflichtbewusstsein |
| Pfostenschuß | Pfostenschuss |
| Pikas | Pikass |
| Pimpernuß | Pimpernuss |
| er pißt | er pisst |
| Pistolenschuß | Pistolenschuss |
| pitschnaß | pitschnass |
| Platitüde | Plattitüde |
| | *auch:* Platitude |

| alt | neu |
|---|---|
| Playback | *auch:* Play-back* |
| plazieren | platzieren |
| pleite gehen | Pleite gehen |
| polyphon | *auch:* polyfon |
| Pornographie | *auch:* Pornografie |
| Portemonnaie | *auch:* Portmonee |
| Potemkinsche Dörfer | potemkinsche Dörfer |
| | *auch:* Potemkin'sche Dörfer |
| potentiell | *auch:* potenziell* |
| potthäßlich | potthässlich |
| Poussierstengel | Poussierstängel |
| präferentiell | *auch:* präferenziell* |
| er praßt | er prasst |
| preisbewußt | preisbewusst |
| Preisnachlaß | Preisnachlass |
| Preßform | Pressform |
| Preßluftbohrer | Pressluftbohrer |
| Preßsack | Presssack |
| | *auch:* Press-Sack |
| Preßschlag | Pressschlag |
| | *auch:* Press-Schlag |
| Preßspan | Pressspan |
| | *auch:* Press-Span |
| du preßt | du presst |
| Preßwehe | Presswehe |
| Prinzeßbohne | Prinzessbohne |
| privatversichert | privat versichert |
| probefahren | Probe fahren |
| Problembewußtsein | Problembewusstsein |
| Produktionsprozeß | Produktionsprozess |
| Profeß | Profess |
| Programmusik | Programmmusik |
| | *auch:* Programm-Musik |
| Progreß | Progress |
| Prozeß | Prozess |
| Prozeßkosten | Prozesskosten |

| alt | neu |
|-----|-----|
| Prozeßbevollmächtigte | Prozessbevollmächtigte |
| prozeßführend | prozessführend |
| Prozeßkosten | Prozesskosten |
| Prozeßrechner | Prozessrechner |
| pudelnaß | pudelnass |
| Pulverfaß | Pulverfass |
| pußlig | pusslig |

**Q**

| alt | neu |
|-----|-----|
| Quadrophonie | *auch:* Quadrofonie |
| qualitätsbewußt | qualitätsbewusst |
| Quartalsabschluß | Quartalsabschluss |
| Quellfluß | Quellfluss |
| Quentchen | Quäntchen |
| Querpaß | Querpass |
| Quickstep | Quickstepp |

**R**

| alt | neu |
|-----|-----|
| radfahren | Rad fahren |
| Radikalenerlaß | Radikalenerlass |
| radschlagen | Rad schlagen |
| Rammaschine | Rammmaschine |
| | *auch:* Ramm-Maschine |
| zu Rande kommen | *auch:* zurande kommen |
| Rassenhaß | Rassenhass |
| ich raßle mit den Ketten | ich rassle mit den Ketten |
| zu Rate ziehen | *auch:* zurate ziehen |
| Räterußland | Räterussland |
| Ratsbeschluß | Ratsbeschluss |
| Ratschluß | Ratschluss |
| Rauchfaß | Rauchfass |
| rauh | rau |
| rauhbeinig | raubeinig |
| Rauhfasertapete | Raufasertapete |
| Rauhfrost | Raufrost |
| Rauhhaardackel | Rauhaardackel |

| alt | neu |
|-----|-----|
| Rauhnächte | Raunächte |
| Rauhputz | Rauputz |
| Rauhreif | Raureif |
| Rausschmiß | Rausschmiss |
| recht haben | Recht haben |
| recht behalten | Recht behalten |
| recht bekommen | Recht bekommen |
| jmdm. recht geben | jmdm. Recht geben |
| Rechtens sein | rechtens sein |
| Rechtsbewußtsein | Rechtsbewusstsein |
| Redaktionsschluß | Redaktionsschluss |
| Regenguß | Regenguss |
| regennaß | regennass |
| Regreß | Regress |
| Regreßanspruch | Regressanspruch |
| Regreßpflicht | Regresspflicht |
| regreßpflichtig | regresspflichtig |
| reichgeschmückt | reich geschmückt |
| reichverziert | reich verziert |
| Reifungsprozeß | Reifungsprozess |
| Reisepaß | Reisepass |
| Reißverschluß | Reißverschluss |
| Reißverschlußsystem | Reißverschlusssystem |
|  | auch: Reißverschluss-System |
|  |  |
| Reschenpaß | Reschenpass |
| Rettungsschuß | Rettungsschuss |
| Rezeß | Rezess |
| Rhein-Main-Donau- | Rhein-Main-Donau- |
| Großschiffahrtsweg | Großschifffahrtsweg |
| das ist genau das richtige | das ist genau das Richtige |
| für mich | für mich |
| mit etwas richtigliegen | mit etwas richtig liegen |
| richtigstellen | richtig stellen |
| Riß | Riss |
| rißfest | rissfest |
| Roheit | Rohheit |

| alt | neu |
|---|---|
| Rolladen | Rollladen |
| | *auch:* Roll-Laden |
| Rommé | *auch:* Rommee |
| rosigweiß | rosig weiß |
| Roß | Ross |
| Roßbreiten | Rossbreiten |
| Roßhaarmatratze | Rosshaarmatratze |
| Roßkastanie | Rosskastanie |
| Roßkur | Rosskur |
| Rößl | Rössl |
| Roßtäuscherei | Rosstäuscherei |
| der rote Planet *[Mars]* | der Rote Planet |
| rotgestreift | rot gestreift |
| rotglühend | rot glühend |
| rötlichbraun | rötlich braun |
| die Rubensschen Gemälde | die rubensschen Gemälde |
| | *auch:* die Rubens'schen |
| | Gemälde |
| Rückfluß | Rückfluss |
| Rückpaß | Rückpass |
| Rückschluß | Rückschluss |
| rückwärtsgewandt | rückwärts gewandt |
| Ruhegenuß | Ruhegenuss |
| ruhenlassen | ruhen lassen |
| ruhigstellen | ruhig stellen |
| Runderlaß | Runderlass |
| Rußland | Russland |

**S**

| | |
|---|---|
| Säbelraßler | Säbelrassler |
| Saisonnier | *auch:* Saisonier |
| Saisonschluß | Saisonschluss |
| Salutschuß | Salutschuss |
| Salzfaß | Salzfass |
| Samenerguß | Samenerguss |
| Sammelanschluß | Sammelanschluss |

| alt | neu |
|---|---|
| Sankt Gallener | *auch:* Sankt-Gallener |
| sanktgallisch | sankt-gallisch |
| Sanmarinese | San-Marinese |
| sanmarinesisch | san-marinesisch |
| sauberhalten | sauber halten |
| saubermachen | sauber machen |
| sausenlassen | sausen lassen |
| Saxophon | *auch:* Saxofon |
| sein Schäfchen ins trockene bringen | sein Schäfchen ins Trockene bringen |
| Schalenguß | Schalenguss |
| Schallehre | Schalllehre<br>*auch:* Schall-Lehre |
| Schalloch | Schallloch<br>*auch:* Schall-Loch |
| Schalterschluß | Schalterschluss |
| etwas auf das schärfste verurteilen | *auch:* etwas auf das Schärfste verurteilen |
| er schaßte ihn | er schasste ihn |
| ein schattenspendender Baum | ein Schatten spendender Baum |
| schätzenlernen | schätzen lernen |
| Schauprozeß | Schauprozess |
| Scheidungsprozeß | Scheidungsprozess |
| schießenlassen | schießen lassen |
| Schiffahrt | Schifffahrt<br>*auch:* Schiff-Fahrt |
| Schippenas | Schippenass |
| Schiß | Schiss |
| Schlachtroß | Schlachtross |
| Schlagfluß | Schlagfluss |
| Schlammasse | Schlammmasse<br>*auch:* Schlamm-Masse |
| schlechtgehen | schlecht gehen |
| schlechtgelaunt | schlecht gelaunt |
| das schlimmste ist, daß ... | das Schlimmste ist, dass ... |

| alt | neu |
|---|---|
| sie haben ihn auf das schlimmste getäuscht | *auch:* sie haben ihn auf das Schlimmste getäuscht |
| er schliß Federn | er schliss Federn |
| Schlitzverschluß | Schlitzverschluss |
| Schloß | Schloss |
| Schlößchen | Schlösschen |
| Schloßherr | Schlossherr |
| Schloßpark | Schlosspark |
| Schluß | Schluss |
| Schlußbemerkung | Schlussbemerkung |
| schlußendlich | schlussendlich |
| schlußfolgern | schlussfolgern |
| Schlußfolgerung | Schlussfolgerung |
| Schlußlicht | Schlusslicht |
| Schlußpfiff | Schlusspfiff |
| Schlußpunkt | Schlusspunkt |
| Schlußsatz | Schlusssatz |
| | *auch:* Schluss-Satz |
| Schlußspurt | Schlussspurt |
| | *auch:* Schluss-Spurt |
| Schlußstrich | Schlussstrich |
| | *auch:* Schluss-Strich |
| Schlußverkauf | Schlussverkauf |
| Schlußwort | Schlusswort |
| Schmerfluß | Schmerfluss |
| sie schmiß mit Steinen | sie schmiss mit Steinen |
| Schmiß | Schmiss |
| Schmuckblattelegramm | Schmuckblatttelegramm |
| | *auch:* Schmuckblatt-Telegramm |
| schmutziggrau | schmutzig grau |
| Schnappschloß | Schnappschloss |
| Schnappschuß | Schnappschuss |
| Schnee-Eifel | *auch:* Schneeeifel |
| Schnee-Eule | *auch:* Schneeeule |
| Schneewächte | Schneewechte |
| Schnellimbiß | Schnellimbiss |

| alt | neu |
|---|---|
| Schnelläufer | Schnellläufer |
|  | *auch:* Schnell-Läufer |
| schnellebig | schnelllebig |
| Schnellebigkeit | Schnelllebigkeit |
| Schnellschuß | Schnellschuss |
| Schnepper | *auch:* Schnäpper |
| schneppern | *auch:* schnäppern |
| schneuzen | schnäuzen |
| Schokoladenguß | Schokoladenguss |
| aufs schönste übereinstimmen | *auch:* aufs Schönste |
|  | übereinstimmen |
| er schoß | er schoss |
| Schoß *[einer Pflanze]* | Schoss |
| schräglaufend | schräg laufend |
| Schraubverschluß | Schraubverschluss |
| schreckensblaß | schreckensblass |
| Schreckschußpistole | Schreckschusspistole |
| Schrittempo | Schritttempo |
|  | *auch:* Schritt-Tempo |
| Schrotschuß | Schrotschuss |
| Schulabschluß | Schulabschluss |
| an etwas schuld haben | an etwas Schuld haben |
| sich etwas zuschulden kommen | *auch:* sich etwas zu Schulden |
| lassen | kommen lassen |
| schuldbewußt | schuldbewusst |
| Schuldenerlaß | Schuldenerlass |
| Schulschluß | Schulschluss |
| Schulstreß | Schulstress |
| Schulterschluß | Schulterschluss |
| Schuß | Schuss |
| schußbereit | schussbereit |
| schußfest | schussfest |
| schußlig | schusslig |
| Schußlinie | Schusslinie |
| Schußschwäche | Schussschwäche |
|  | *auch:* Schuss-Schwäche |

| alt | neu |
| --- | --- |
| Schußwaffe | Schusswaffe |
| Schußwechsel | Schusswechsel |
| schwachbetont | schwach betont |
| schwachbevölkert | schwach bevölkert |
| aus schwarz weiß machen | aus Schwarz Weiß machen |
| Schwarze Magie | schwarze Magie |
| schwarzgefärbt | schwarz gefärbt |
| schwarzrotgolden | *auch:* schwarz-rot-golden |
| schwerfallen | schwer fallen |
| schwernehmen | schwer nehmen |
| schwertun | schwer tun |
| schwerverständlich | schwer verständlich |
| Schwimmeister | Schwimmmeister |
|  | *auch:* Schwimm-Meister |
| Science-fiction | Sciencefiction |
|  | *auch:* Science-Fiction |
| Sechspaß | Sechspass |
| See-Elefant | *auch:* Seeelefant |
| jedem das Seine | *auch:* jedem das seine |
| das Seine beitragen | *auch:* das seine beitragen |
| die Seinen | *auch:* die seinen |
| die Seinigen | *auch:* die seinigen |
| seinlassen | sein lassen |
| Seismograph | *auch:* Seismograf |
| auf seiten | aufseiten |
|  | *auch:* auf Seiten |
| von seiten | vonseiten |
|  | *auch:* von Seiten |
| selbständig | *auch:* selbstständig |
| Selbständigkeit | *auch:* Selbstständigkeit |
| selbstbewußt | selbstbewusst |
| Selbstbewußtsein | Selbstbewusstsein |
| selbsternannt | selbst ernannt |
| selbstgebacken | selbst gebacken |
| selbstgemacht | selbst gemacht |
| selbstgestrickt | selbst gestrickt |

| alt | neu |
|---|---|
| Selbstschuß | Selbstschuss |
| selbstverdient | selbst verdient |
| seligpreisen | selig preisen |
| seligsprechen | selig sprechen |
| Senatsbeschluß | Senatsbeschluss |
| Sendeschluß | Sendeschluss |
| Sendungsbewußtsein | Sendungsbewusstsein |
| Sensationsprozeß | Sensationsprozess |
| Séparée | *auch:* Separee |
| sequentiell | *auch:* sequenziell* |
| seßhaft | sesshaft |
| Seßhaftigkeit | Sesshaftigkeit |
| S-förmig | *auch:* s-förmig |
| die Shakespeareschen Sonette | die shakespeareschen Sonette |
| | *auch:* die Shakespeare'schen Sonette |
| Short story | Shortstory |
| | *auch:* Short Story |
| Showbusineß | Showbusiness |
| Showdown | *auch:* Show-down* |
| Shrimp | *auch:* Schrimp |
| auf Nummer Sicher gehen | *auch:* auf Nummer sicher gehen |
| das sicherste ist, wenn ... | das Sicherste ist, wenn ... |
| Sicherheitsschloß | Sicherheitsschloss |
| Sicherheitsverschluß | Sicherheitsverschluss |
| siedendheiß | siedend heiß |
| siegesbewußt | siegesbewusst |
| siegesgewiß | siegesgewiss |
| Simplonpaß | Simplonpass |
| die Singende Säge | die singende Säge |
| Siphonverschluß | Siphonverschluss |
| sitzenbleiben | sitzen bleiben |
| sitzenlassen | sitzen lassen |
| Skipaß | Skipass |
| Small talk | Smalltalk |
| | *auch:* Small Talk |

| alt | neu |
|-----|-----|
| so daß | sodass |
| | *auch:* so dass |
| Sommerschlußverkauf | Sommerschlussverkauf |
| alles sonstige besprechen wir | alles Sonstige besprechen wir |
|   morgen |   morgen |
| Soufflé | *auch:* Soufflee |
| soviel du willst | so viel du willst |
| soviel wie | so viel wie |
| noch einmal soviel | noch einmal so viel |
| es ist soweit | es ist so weit |
| soweit wie möglich | so weit wie möglich |
| ich kann das sowenig wie du | ich kann das so wenig wie du |
| Sowjetrußland | Sowjetrussland |
| hier gilt kein Sowohl-Als-auch | hier gilt kein Sowohl-als-auch |
| Spaghetti | *auch:* Spagetti |
| Spantenriß | Spantenriss |
| spazierenfahren | spazieren fahren |
| spazierengehen | spazieren gehen |
| Speichelfluß | Speichelfluss |
| Sperrad | Sperrrad |
| | *auch:* Sperr-Rad |
| Sperriegel | Sperrriegel |
| | *auch:* Sperr-Riegel |
| Spliß | Spliss |
| du splißt | du splisst |
| eine sporenbildende Pflanze | eine Sporen bildende Pflanze |
| Sportdreß | Sportdress |
| Sprenggeschoß | Sprenggeschoss *[in Österreich* |
| |   *weiterhin mit ß]* |
| Spritzguß | Spritzguss |
| es sproß neues Grün | es spross neues Grün |
| Sproß | Spross |
| Sproßachse | Sprossachse |
| Sprößchen | Sprösschen |
| Sprößling | Sprössling |
| staatenbildende Insekten | Staaten bildende Insekten |

| alt | neu |
|---|---|
| Stahlroß | Stahlross |
| Stallaterne | Stalllaterne |
| | *auch:* Stall-Laterne |
| Stammutter | Stammmutter |
| | *auch:* Stamm-Mutter |
| standesbewußt | standesbewusst |
| Standesbewußtsein | Standesbewusstsein |
| Startschuß | Startschuss |
| steckenbleiben | stecken bleiben |
| steckenlassen | stecken lassen |
| Steckschloß | Steckschloss |
| Steckschuß | Steckschuss |
| stehenbleiben | stehen bleiben |
| stehenlassen | stehen lassen |
| Stehimbiß | Stehimbiss |
| Steilpaß | Steilpass |
| Stemmeißel | Stemmmeißel |
| | *auch:* Stemm-Meißel |
| Stendelwurz | Ständelwurz |
| Stengel | Stängel |
| Step | Stepp |
| Steptanz | Stepptanz |
| Stereophonie | *auch:* Stereofonie |
| Steuererlaß | Steuererlass |
| Steuermeßbetrag | Steuermessbetrag |
| Stewardeß | Stewardess |
| stiftengehen | stiften gehen |
| etwas im stillen vorbereiten | etwas im Stillen vorbereiten |
| Stilleben | Stillleben |
| | *auch:* Still-Leben |
| stillegen | stilllegen |
| Stillegung | Stilllegung |
| Stoffarbe | Stofffarbe |
| | *auch:* Stoff-Farbe |
| Stoffetzen | Stofffetzen |
| | *auch:* Stoff-Fetzen |

845

| alt | neu |
|-----|-----|
| Stofffülle | Stofffülle |
| | *auch:* Stoff-Fülle |
| Stop | Stopp |
| Straferlaß | Straferlass |
| Strafprozeß | Strafprozess |
| Strafprozeßordnung | Strafprozessordnung |
| Straß | Strass |
| Streifschuß | Streifschuss |
| Streitroß | Streitross |
| strenggenommen | streng genommen |
| strengnehmen | streng nehmen |
| aufs strengste unterschieden | *auch:* aufs Strengste |
| | unterschieden |
| Streß | Stress |
| der Lärm streßt | der Lärm stresst |
| Streßsituation | Stresssituation |
| | *auch:* Stress-Situation |
| 2stündig, 3stündig, 4stündig ... | 2-stündig, 3-stündig, 4-stündig ... |
| 2stündlich, 3stündlich, | 2-stündlich, 3-stündlich, |
| 4stündlich ... | 4-stündlich ... |
| Stuß | Stuss |
| substantiell | *auch:* substanziell* |
| Sustenpaß | Sustenpass |
| **T** | |
| Tablettenmißbrauch | Tablettenmissbrauch |
| tabula rasa machen | Tabula rasa machen |
| zutage treten | *auch:* zu Tage treten |
| 2tägig, 3tägig, 4tägig ... | 2-tägig, 3-tägig, 4-tägig ... |
| Tankschloß | Tankschloss |
| Tarifabschluß | Tarifabschluss |
| Täßchen | Tässchen |
| ein paar tausend | *auch:* ein paar Tausend |
| Tausende von Zuschauern | *auch:* tausende von Zuschauern |
| T-bone-Steak | T-Bone-Steak |
| Tee-Ei | *auch:* Teeei |

| alt | neu |
|---|---|
| Tee-Ernte | *auch:* Teeernte |
| Teerfaß | Teerfass |
| Telephon | Telefon |
| Telephonanschluß | Telefonanschluss |
| Thunfisch | *auch:* Tunfisch |
| Tie-Break | *auch:* Tiebreak |
| aufs tiefste gekränkt | *auch:* aufs Tiefste gekränkt |
| tiefbewegt | tief bewegt |
| tiefempfunden | tief empfunden |
| tiefverschneit | tief verschneit |
| Tintenfaß | Tintenfass |
| Tip | Tipp |
| todblaß | todblass |
| Todesschuß | Todesschuss |
| Tolpatsch | Tollpatsch |
| tolpatschig | tollpatschig |
| Tomatenketchup | *auch:* Tomatenketschup |
| Topographie | *auch:* Topografie |
| Torschlußpanik | Torschlusspanik |
| Torschuß | Torschuss |
| totenblaß | totenblass |
| totgeboren | tot geboren |
| traditionsbewußt | traditionsbewusst |
| Tränenfluß | Tränenfluss |
| tränennaß | tränennass |
| Traß | Trass |
| Trekking | *auch:* Trecking |
| treuergeben | treu ergeben |
| triefnaß | triefnass |
| auf dem trockenen sitzen | auf dem Trockenen sitzen |
| sein Schäfchen ins trockene bringen | sein Schäfchen ins Trockene bringen |
| tropfnaß | tropfnass |
| Troß | Tross |
| im trüben fischen | im Trüben fischen |
| Truchseß | Truchsess |

| alt | neu |
|---|---|
| Trugschluß | Trugschluss |
| Trumpfas | Trumpfass |
| Tuffelsen | Tufffelsen |
| | *auch:* Tuff-Felsen |
| Türschloß | Türschloss |

## U

| alt | neu |
|---|---|
| übelgelaunt | übel gelaunt |
| übelnehmen | übel nehmen |
| übelriechend | übel riechend |
| Überbiß | Überbiss |
| Überdruß | Überdruss |
| übereinanderlegen | übereinander legen |
| übereinanderliegen | übereinander liegen |
| übereinanderwerfen | übereinander werfen |
| Überfluß | Überfluss |
| Überflußgesellschaft | Überflussgesellschaft |
| Überguß | Überguss |
| überhandnehmen | überhand nehmen |
| übermorgen abend, nachmittag | übermorgen Abend, Nachmittag |
| Überschuß | Überschuss |
| überschwenglich | überschwänglich |
| überwächtet | überwechtet |
| ein übriges tun | ein Übriges tun |
| im übrigen wissen wir doch alle … | im Übrigen wissen wir doch alle … |
| alles übrige später | alles Übrige später |
| die übrigen kommen nach | die Übrigen kommen nach |
| übrigbehalten | übrig behalten |
| übrigbleiben | übrig bleiben |
| übriglassen | übrig lassen |
| U-förmig | *auch:* u-förmig |
| Ultima ratio | Ultima Ratio |
| Umdenkprozeß | Umdenkprozess |
| die Liste umfaßt alles Wichtige | die Liste umfasst alles Wichtige |
| Umriß | Umriss |
| Umrißzeichnung | Umrisszeichnung |

| alt | neu |
|-----|-----|
| Umschichtungsprozeß | Umschichtungsprozess |
| Umschluß | Umschluss |
| umsein | um sein |
| um so [mehr, größer, weniger ...] | umso [mehr, größer, weniger ...] |
| Umstellungsprozeß | Umstellungsprozess |
| Umwandlungsprozeß | Umwandlungsprozess |
| Umwelteinfluß | Umwelteinfluss |
| sich ins unabsehbare ausweiten | sich ins Unabsehbare ausweiten |
| unangepaßt | unangepasst |
| Unangepaßtheit | Unangepasstheit |
| unbeeinflußbar | unbeeinflussbar |
| unbeeinflußt | unbeeinflusst |
| Anzeige gegen Unbekannt | Anzeige gegen unbekannt |
| unbewußt | unbewusst |
| und ähnliches (u. ä.) | und Ähnliches (u. Ä.) |
| unendlichemal | unendliche Mal |
| unerläßlich | unerlässlich |
| unermeßlich | unermesslich |
| Unfaireß | Unfairness |
| unfaßbar | unfassbar |
| unfaßlich | unfasslich |
| ungewiß | ungewiss |
| Ungewißheit | Ungewissheit |
| unigefärbt | uni gefärbt |
| im unklaren bleiben | im Unklaren bleiben |
| im unklaren lassen | im Unklaren lassen |
| unmißverständlich | unmissverständlich |
| unpäßlich | unpässlich |
| Unpäßlichkeit | Unpässlichkeit |
| unplaziert | unplatziert |
| unrecht haben | Unrecht haben |
| unrecht behalten | Unrecht behalten |
| unrecht bekommen | Unrecht bekommen |
| Unrechtsbewußtsein | Unrechtsbewusstsein |
| unselbständig | *auch:* unselbstständig |
| Unselbständigkeit | *auch:* Unselbstständigkeit |

| alt | neu |
|-----|-----|
| die Unseren | *auch:* die unseren |
| die Unsrigen | *auch:* die unsrigen |
| untenerwähnt | unten erwähnt |
| untenstehend | unten stehend |
| unterbewußt | unterbewusst |
| Unterbewußtsein | Unterbewusstsein |
| unterderhand | unter der Hand |
| untereinanderstehen | untereinander stehen |
| Untergeschoß | Untergeschoss *[in Österreich weiterhin mit ß]* |
| ohne Unterlaß | ohne Unterlass |
| Untersuchungsausschuß | Untersuchungsausschuss |
| unvergeßlich | unvergesslich |
| unverläßlich | unerlässlich |
| unzähligemal | unzählige Mal |

## V

| alt | neu |
|-----|-----|
| va banque spielen | *auch:* Vabanque spielen |
| Varieté | *auch:* Varietee |
| veranlaßt | veranlasst |
| verantwortungsbewußt | verantwortungsbewusst |
| Verantwortungsbewußtsein | Verantwortungsbewusstsein |
| Verbiß | Verbiss |
| verblaßt | verblasst |
| verbleuen | verbläuen |
| im verborgenen blühen | im Verborgenen blühen |
| das verdroß uns | das verdross uns |
| Verdruß | Verdruss |
| du verfaßt | du verfasst |
| vergeßlich | vergesslich |
| Vergeßlichkeit | Vergesslichkeit |
| Vergißmeinnicht | Vergissmeinnicht |
| du vergißt | du vergisst |
| verhaßt | verhasst |
| auf jmdn. ist Verlaß | auf jmdn. ist Verlass |
| verläßlich | verlässlich |

| alt | neu |
|---|---|
| Verläßlichkeit | Verlässlichkeit |
| verlorengehen | verloren gehen |
| vermißt | vermisst |
| Vermißtenanzeige | Vermisstenanzeige |
| er hat den Zug verpaßt | er hat den Zug verpasst |
| das Geld wurde verpraßt | das Geld wurde verprasst |
| Verriß | Verriss |
| verschiedenes war noch unklar | Verschiedenes war noch unklar |
| verschiedenemal | verschiedene Mal |
| Verschiß | Verschiss |
| Verschluß | Verschluss |
| Verschlußkappe | Verschlusskappe |
| Verschlußsache | Verschlusssache |
| | *auch:* Verschluss-Sache |
| verselbständigen | *auch:* verselbstständigen |
| Versorgungsengpaß | Versorgungsengpass |
| Vertragsabschluß | Vertragsabschluss |
| Vertragsschluß | Vertragsschluss |
| V-förmig | *auch:* v-förmig |
| Vibraphon | *auch:* Vibrafon |
| viel zuviel | viel zu viel |
| viel zuwenig | viel zu wenig |
| vielbefahren | viel befahren |
| vielgelesen | viel gelesen |
| Vierpaß | Vierpass |
| aus dem vollen schöpfen | aus dem Vollen schöpfen |
| voneinandergehen | voneinander gehen |
| von seiten | vonseiten |
| | *auch:* von Seiten |
| vorangehendes gilt auch ... | Vorangehendes gilt auch ... |
| im vorangehenden heißt es ... | im Vorangehenden heißt es ... |
| im voraus | im Voraus |
| vorgefaßt | vorgefasst |
| vorgestern abend, mittag, morgen | vorgestern Abend, Mittag, Morgen |
| Vorhängeschloß | Vorhängeschloss |

| alt | neu |
|---|---|
| vorhergehendes gilt auch ... | Vorhergehendes gilt auch ... |
| im vorhergehenden heißt es ... | im Vorhergehenden heißt es ... |
| im vorhinein | im Vorhinein |
| das vorige gilt auch ... | das Vorige gilt auch ... |
| im vorigen heißt es ... | im Vorigen heißt es ... |
| Vorlegeschloß | Vorlegeschloss |
| vorliebnehmen | vorlieb nehmen |
| [gestern, heute, morgen] | [gestern, heute, morgen] |
|   vormittag |   Vormittag |
| Vorschlußrunde | Vorschlussrunde |
| Vorschuß | Vorschuss |
| Vorschußlorbeeren | Vorschusslorbeeren |
| vorstehendes gilt auch ... | Vorstehendes gilt auch ... |
| im vorstehenden heißt es ... | im Vorstehenden heißt es ... |
| vorwärtsgehen | vorwärts gehen |
| vorwärtskommen | vorwärts kommen |

**W**

| alt | neu |
|---|---|
| ein wachestehender Soldat | ein Wache stehender Soldat |
| Wachsabguß | Wachsabguss |
| Wächte | Wechte |
| Waggon | *auch:* Wagon |
| Wahlausschuß | Wahlausschuss |
| Walkie-talkie | Walkie-Talkie |
| Walnuß | Walnuss |
| Walroß | Walross |
| Wandlungsprozeß | Wandlungsprozess |
| Warnschuß | Warnschuss |
| Wasserschloß | Wasserschloss |
| wäßrig | wässrig |
| Wehrpaß | Wehrpass |
| weichgekocht | weich gekocht |
| Weinfaß | Weinfass |
| aus schwarz weiß machen | aus Schwarz Weiß machen |
| weißgekleidet | weiß gekleidet |
| Weißrußland | Weißrussland |

852

| alt | neu |
|---|---|
| des weiteren wurde gesagt ... | des Weiteren wurde gesagt ... |
| weitgereist | weit gereist |
| weitreichend | weit reichend |
| weitverbreitet | weit verbreitet |
| Werkstattage | Werkstatttage |
| | *auch:* Werkstatt-Tage |
| Werkstofforschung | Werkstoffforschung |
| | *auch:* Werkstoff-Forschung |
| es besteht im wesentlichen aus ... | es besteht im Wesentlichen aus ... |
| Wetteufel | Wettteufel |
| | *auch:* Wett-Teufel |
| Wetturnen | Wettturnen |
| | *auch:* Wett-Turnen |
| widereinanderstoßen | widereinander stoßen |
| wieviel | wie viel |
| Winterschlußverkauf | Winterschlussverkauf |
| Wißbegierde | Wissbegierde |
| wißbegierig | wissbegierig |
| ihr wißt | ihr wisst |
| du wußtest | du wusstest |
| wir wüßten gern ... | wir wüssten gern ... |
| Witterungseinfluß | Witterungseinfluss |
| Wollappen | Wolllappen |
| | *auch:* Woll-Lappen |
| Wollaus | Wolllaus |
| | *auch:* Woll-Laus |
| als ob er wunder was getan hätte | als ob er Wunder was getan hätte |
| sich wundliegen | sich wund liegen |
| Wurfgeschoß | Wurfgeschoss *[in Österreich weiterhin mit ß]* |

**X, Y**

| | |
|---|---|
| X-beinig | *auch:* x-beinig |
| X-förmig | *auch:* x-förmig |
| zum x-tenmal | zum x-ten Mal |

## Z

| alt | neu |
|---|---|
| Zäheit | Zähheit |
| Zahlenschloß | Zahlenschloss |
| Zäpfchen-R | *auch:* Zäpfchen-r |
| Zaubernuß | Zaubernuss |
| Zechenstillegung | Zechenstilllegung |
| Zeilengußmaschine | Zeilengussmaschine |
| 2zeilig, 3zeilig, 4zeilig ... | 2-zeilig, 3-zeilig, 4-zeilig ... |
| eine Zeitlang | eine Zeit lang |
| zur Zeit *[derzeit]* | zurzeit |
| Zellehre | Zelllehre |
| | *auch:* Zell-Lehre |
| Zellstoffabrik | Zellstofffabrik |
| | *auch:* Zellstoff-Fabrik |
| Zersetzungsprozeß | Zersetzungsprozess |
| zielbewußt | zielbewusst |
| Zierat | Zierrat |
| zigtausend | *auch:* Zigtausend |
| Zigtausende | *auch:* zigtausende |
| Zippverschluß | Zippverschluss |
| Zirkelschluß | Zirkelschluss |
| Zivilprozeß | Zivilprozess |
| Zivilprozeßordnung | Zivilprozessordnung |
| Zoo-Orchester | *auch:* Zooorchester |
| sich zu eigen machen | sich zu Eigen machen |
| zueinanderfinden | zueinander finden |
| Zufluß | Zufluss |
| sich zufriedengeben | sich zufrieden geben |
| zufriedenlassen | zufrieden lassen |
| zufriedenstellen | zufrieden stellen |
| zugrunde gehen | *auch:* zu Grunde gehen |
| zugrunde legen | *auch:* zu Grunde legen |
| zugrunde liegen | *auch:* zu Grunde liegen |
| zugrundeliegend | zugrunde liegend |
| | *auch:* zu Grunde liegend |
| zugrunde richten | *auch:* zu Grunde richten |

| alt | neu |
| --- | --- |
| zugunsten | *auch:* zu Gunsten |
| zu Hause | *in Österreich und der Schweiz* |
| | *auch:* zuhause |
| bei uns zulande | bei uns zu Lande |
| zulasten | *auch:* zu Lasten |
| jmdm. etwas zuleide tun | *auch:* jmdm. etwas zu Leide tun |
| zumute sein | *auch:* zu Mute sein |
| Zündschloß | Zündschloss |
| Zungenkuß | Zungenkuss |
| Zungen-R | *auch:* Zungen-r |
| sich etwas zunutze machen | *auch:* sich etwas zu Nutze machen |
| jmdm. zupaß kommen | jmdm. zupass kommen |
| zugepreßt | zugepresst |
| zu Rande kommen | *auch:* zurande kommen |
| jmdn. zu Rate ziehen | *auch:* jmdn. zurate ziehen |
| sie hat zurückgemußt | sie hat zurückgemusst |
| zur Zeit *[derzeit]* | zurzeit |
| Zusammenfluß | Zusammenfluss |
| zusammengefaßt | zusammengefasst |
| zusammengepaßt | zusammengepasst |
| zusammengepreßt | zusammengepresst |
| Zusammenschluß | Zusammenschluss |
| zusammensein | zusammen sein |
| zuschanden werden | *auch:* zu Schanden werden |
| sich etwas zuschulden kommen lassen | *auch:* sich etwas zu Schulden kommen lassen |
| Zuschuß | Zuschuss |
| Zuschußbetrieb | Zuschussbetrieb |
| zusein | zu sein |
| zustande bringen | *auch:* zu Stande bringen |
| zustande kommen | *auch:* zu Stande kommen |
| zutage fördern | *auch:* zu Tage fördern |
| zutage treten | *auch:* zu Tage treten |
| zuungunsten | *auch:* zu Ungunsten |
| zuviel | zu viel |
| zuwege bringen | *auch:* zu Wege bringen |

| alt | neu |
|-----|-----|
| zuwenig | zu wenig |
| die zwanziger Jahre | *auch:* die Zwanzigerjahre* |
| die Zwanzigerjahre | *auch:* die zwanziger Jahre |
| das Zweite Gesicht | das zweite Gesicht |
| er hat wie kein zweiter gearbeitet | er hat wie kein Zweiter gearbeitet |
| jeder zweite war krank | jeder Zweite war krank |
| Zweitkläßler | Zweitklässler |
| Zwischengeschoß | Zwischengeschoss *[in Österreich weiterhin mit ß]* |